Edited by
John Gunn
Pamela J Taylor

forensic Psychiatry

clinical, legal and ethical issues

Second Edition

CRC Press
Taylor & Francis Group
Boca Raton London New York

CRC Press is an imprint of the
Taylor & Francis Group, an **informa** business

CRC Press
Taylor & Francis Group
6000 Broken Sound Parkway NW, Suite 300
Boca Raton, FL 33487-2742

© 2014 by Taylor & Francis Group, LLC
CRC Press is an imprint of Taylor & Francis Group, an Informa business

No claim to original U.S. Government works

Printed on acid-free paper
Version Date: 20131004

International Standard Book Number-13: 978-0-340-80628-9 (Pack - Book and Online)

Visit the Taylor & Francis Web site at
http://www.taylorandfrancis.com

and the CRC Press Web site at
http://www.crcpress.com

Printed and bound in Great Britain by CPI Group (UK) Ltd, Croydon, CR0 4YY

Contents

Contents

List of Contributors

Tim Amos, MA(Oxon), MSc, MB, BS, MRCPsych, DPMSA
Senior lecturer in forensic psychiatry at the University of Bristol, consultant forensic psychiatrist at Fromeside, the medium secure unit in Bristol. Previously Tim worked on the National Confidential Inquiry into Suicide and Homicide by People with Mental Illness. Now involved in research studying homicide and violence linked to mental illness, suicide and self-harm; risk assessment and management; and the evidence in various areas of clinical practice in forensic mental health. He has written a number of papers and book chapters.
Main contributor to chapter 11

Sarah Anderson, MSc., MPhysPhil
Development officer for the charity Revolving Doors Agency which aims to improve systems and services for adults with poor mental health and multiple needs who are in contact with the criminal justice system. Sarah has an MSc in criminal justice policy from the London School of Economics, where she was awarded the Titmuss Prize. She also has an MPhysPhil in physics and philosophy from the University of Oxford. She previously worked as a prison resettlement worker for the charity St Giles Trust and has been awarded a Churchill Fellowship to explore approaches to complex needs in Australia.
Contributor to chapter 25

Sue Bailey, OBE PRCPsych
President, Royal College of Psychiatrists, professor of adolescent forensic mental health at the University of Central Lancashire. Consultant, adolescent forensic psychiatrist Greater Manchester West NHS Foundation Trust. Sue's research and clinical practice have centred on evidence based service delivery to young offenders, developing age appropriate needs, risk assessments and innovative treatment interventions. She has worked with governments to shape child centred effective policies to prevent antisocial behaviour in children by working with families and multi-agency teams.
Main contributor to chapter 19

Roger Bloor, MD, M.PsyMed, FRCPsych, DipMedEd
A former RAF psychiatrist, Roger returned to the NHS in 1984 as a consultant with special responsibility for drugs and alcohol. He was medical director of an NHS trust and senior lecturer in addiction psychiatry at Keele University Medical School until he retired in 2009. His research has been in a variety of addiction-related topics and he is co-author of several chapters in textbooks on addiction. Roger is currently a teaching fellow at Keele and a part time consultant in addiction psychiatry with North Staffordshire Combined Healthcare NHS Trust.
Co-author of the illicit drug section, chapter 18

Frederick Browne, BSc(Hons), MB, BCh, BAO, FRCPsych
Consultant forensic psychiatrist Belfast, member of the departmental steering group that is forming new mental health and capacity legislation for Northern Ireland. Fred was one time chair of the Royal College of Psychiatrists in Northern Ireland and the All-Ireland Institute of Psychiatry. He has taken a lead role in the development of forensic mental health services in Northern Ireland, including establishing prison multidisciplinary teams, a police station liaison scheme, and the Shannon Clinic medium secure unit. Fred was a major contributor to the Bamford Review of mental health and learning disability services in Northern Ireland, and chaired the Forensic Services Committee and Forensic Legal Issues Subcommittee.
Contributor to Chapters 4, 24 and 25 on legislation and forensic services in Northern Ireland.

Peter F. Buckley, FRCPsych, MD
Professor and chairman in the Department of Psychiatry at the Medical College of Georgia from 2000 and now dean of the Medical College. Peter qualified at University College Dublin but joined the faculty at Case Western Reserve University, School of Medicine, Cleveland in 1992. Peter is a distinguished fellow of the American Psychiatric Association. He has published 340 original publications and is senior author of a postgraduate textbook of psychiatry. He has also authored or edited twelve other psychiatric books. He is editor of the journal *Clinical Schizophrenia & Related Psychoses and was the Journal of Dual Diagnosis*. His research focuses on the neurobiology and treatment of schizophrenia.
Lead author pharmacotherapy sections, chapter 23

Jenifer Clarke, RMN, MSc

Deputy Head for Mental Health and Vulnerable Groups/ Nursing Officer for Mental Health and Learning Disability Services for the Welsh Government. Jenifer has worked as a consultant nurse in both the public and independent sectors and within acute, community, forensic/ prison settings and specialist Personality Disorder Services. She completed her post graduate diploma in forensic psychotherapy and MSc in institutional and community care at the Portman/ Tavistock Clinic London. Jenifer has developed a 'Secure Model of Nursing Care' which integrates a psychodynamic understanding into nursing practice and co-edited *Therapeutic Relationships with Offenders* with Anne Aiyegbusi.
Co-author of the nursing sections, chapter 23.

Julian Corner, BA, PhD

Chief executive of the Lankelly Chase Foundation, and formerly chief executive of the Revolving Doors Agency, Julian twice worked as a civil servant, mainly in the Home Office but also in the Department for Education and Employment and the Social Exclusion Unit (SEU). While at the SEU he led its report on reducing re-offending by ex-prisoners which led to the creation of the National Reducing Re-Offending Strategy. He is a trustee of Clinks, the membership body for voluntary organisations that work with offenders and their families.
Author voluntary sector section, chapter 25.

Jackie Craissati, DClinPsy

Consultant clinical and forensic psychologist, clinical director at the Bracton Centre, Oxleas NHS Foundation Trust and project lead for a number of related community projects run in partnership with probation and third sector agencies. Jackie's special interest is the assessment and treatment of sexual and violent personality disordered offenders. She has published widely in this area and is the author of 'Managing High Risk Sex Offenders in the Community' and 'Managing Personality Disordered Offenders in the Community'.
Author specialist community services section, chapter 24

Ilana Crome, MA, MPhil, MB, ChB, MD, FRCPsych

Professor of addiction psychiatry at Keele University and St George's Hospital, Stafford, Ilana is a past chairman of the Faculty of Substance Misuse (Royal College of Psychiatrists), past president of the Alcohol and Drugs Section of the European Psychiatric Association and a past member of the Advisory Council on the Misuse of Drugs. She chaired 'Our invisible addicts' report (*RCPsych* 2011). Her clinical Interests include adolescents and older people and the enhancement of training in substance misuse in health professionals. Her research includes mental and physical comorbidity, smoking cessation trials, decision making in substance misusers, suicide and substance misuse, pregnant drug users, and addiction across the life course.
Lead author illicit drugs section, chapter 18

Rajan Darjee BSc(Hons), MBChB, MRCPsych, MPhil

Consultant forensic psychiatrist, The Orchard Clinic, Edinburgh, lead clinician for multi-agency public protection arrangements and sexual offending in the NHS Scotland Forensic Mental Health Services Managed Care Network, Rajan's clinical interests also include the multi-agency management of the personality disordered in the community, and the risk assessment and management of serious violent and sexual offenders. He is accredited by the Scottish Risk Management Authority to assess risk in serious violent and sexual offenders being considered for indeterminate sentencing. His research interests include mental health legislation, schizophrenia, risk assessment and the psychiatric characteristics of sex offenders.
Lead author Scottish section, chapter 4

Felicity de Zulueta, BSc, MA(Cantab), MBChB, FRCPsych, FRCP

Emeritus consultant psychiatrist in psychotherapy at the South London and Maudsley NHS Trust and honorary senior lecurer in traumatic studies at Kings College London. Felicity developed and headed the Traumatic Stress Service in Maudsley Hospital which specialises in the treatment of people suffering from complex post traumatic stress disorder(PTSD) including borderline personality and dissociative disorders. She has published papers on bilingualism and PTSD from an attachment perspective and is the author of *From Pain to Violence: The Traumatic Roots of Destructiveness*.
Author, attachment disorder sections, chapter 28

Roderick Lawrence Denyer QC called Inner Temple 1970 (bencher 1996)

Senior judge, Bristol Civil Justice Centre. Roderick was lecturer in law at the University of Bristol 1971–1973 after which he practiced as a barrister at the common law Bar until 2002, taking silk in 1990 and becoming a recorder

of the Crown Court until 2002, and a circuit judge (Wales & Chester Circuit) from 2002–2011 He was a member of the Criminal Procedure Rules Committee from its inception until September 2011. He has published regularly in the *Criminal Law Review*, is author of *Case Management in the Crown Court* (Hart 2008) and was consultant editor of *Blackstone's Guide to the Criminal Procedure Rules 2005*.
Judicial contribution to chapter 2

Mairead Dolan, MB, BAO, BCh (Hons), FRCPsych, FRANZCP, MSc, PhD

Professor of forensic psychiatry and neuroscience at Monash University, Australia, Mairead held a Wellcome Trust training fellowship at Manchester University between 1993 and 1996 obtaining a PhD on serotonergic function in personality disordered offenders. From 1996–2008 she was consultant forensic psychiatrist at the Bolton, Salford & Trafford Mental Health Trust. In 2008 Mairead moved to Melbourne where she has two main programmes of research: the neurobiology of antisocial behaviour and personality disorder and risk assessment. In 2005 the Brain & Behavior Research Foundation granted her a NARSAD award to study violent patients with schizophrenia. Mairead has published widely including contributing to and co-editing Bailey and Dolan (2004) and Soothill, Rogers & Dolan (2008).
Co-author, biochemical sections, chapter 12

Enda Dooley, MB, MRCPsych, HDip

Consultant psychiatrist, Tribunals Division, Mental Health Commission overseeing involuntary admissions to mental health units from 2009. Enda is a graduate of University College Dublin and trained first in Dublin then in forensic psychiatry at the Maudsley Hospital / Institute of Psychiatry, London. He was a consultant forensic psychiatrist at Broadmoor Hospital (1989–1990), then director of Prison Health Care, Irish Prison Service (1990–2009) with responsibility for the overall structural organisation of all health care services provided to prisoners within the State, with responsibility for operational policy and professional guidance relating to providing medical, psychiatric, and associated services.
Commentary on Irish services, chapter 25

Conor Duggan, BSc, PhD, MD, FRCPsych

Professor of forensic mental health at the University of Nottingham and an honorary consultant psychiatrist at Arnold Lodge, Regional Secure Unit in Leicester where he shares responsibility for a 22-bed in-patient unit that treats men with personality disorder and a history of serious offending. Conor's research interests are treatment efficacy in personality disordered offenders, their long-term course and the neuropsychological basis of psychopathy. He was editor of the *Journal of Forensic Psychiatry and Psychology* until 2011 and has chaired a NICE Guideline Committee on the treatment of antisocial personality disorder.
Co-author, chapter 16, with special contribution to the treatment sections

Emma Dunn, BSc

Research and development worker for the NHS, Wales. Emma spent ten years studying and working at Cardiff University, undertaking research in both mood disorders and forensic psychiatry. Her interests included delusions, social interaction and violence, and mental state change in prisoners.
Co-author, chapter 5

Sharif El-Leithy, BA (Hons), DClinPsych

Senior clinical psychologist, Traumatic Stress Service, Springfield University Hospital, Tooting, London, offering specialist psychological treatment to people with PTSD, including members of the military and victims of torture. Sharif qualified as a clinical psychologist from Canterbury Christ Church University in 2001. He is a BABCP-accredited cognitive therapist, and has acted as an expert witness on PTSD. Sharif has been involved in developing psychological aspects of local planning for disasters. He was also involved in the screen-and-treat programme that followed the 2005 London bombings, as well as in setting up a similar programme within local maxillofacial surgery services.
Co-author, chapter 28, with special contribution on the cognitive behavioural treatment sections

Sue E. Estroff, PhD

Professor in the Department of Social Medicine, School of Medicine, and in the departments of anthropology and psychiatry, University of North Carolina. Sue's research includes socio-cultural approaches to psychosis and other psychiatric

disorders and reconsidering the association of violence and psychiatric disorders. She is co-editor of *The Social Medicine Reader*, her publications include *'No Other Way to Go' 'Whose Story Is It Anyway: The Influence of Social Networks and Social Support on Violence by Persons with Serious Mental Illness'; 'Risk Reconsidered: Recognizing and Responding To Early Psychosis'; and 'From Stigma to Discrimination'.*
Co-author, chapter 14

Tim Exworthy, MB, BS, LLM, FRCPsych, DFP

Clinical director and consultant forensic psychiatrist at St Andrew's Hospital, Northampton, Tim has been a consultant in high-, medium- and low-security hospitals and, since 2006, has been chairman of the Special Committee on Human Rights at the Royal College of Psychiatrists. He has also been the medical member on three independent inquiries following homicides committed by people who had had contact with the mental health services. Tim is a visiting senior lecturer in forensic psychiatry at the Institute of Psychiatry, London. His academic interests include topics at the interface of psychiatry, law and human rights.
Contribution, enquiries after homicide, chapter 3

David P. Farrington, OBE, MA, PhD, Hon ScD, FBA, FMedSci

Professor of psychological criminology at the Institute of Criminology, Cambridge University, and adjunct professor of psychiatry at Western Psychiatric Institute and Clinic, University of Pittsburgh. David's major research interest is in developmental criminology, and he is director of the Cambridge Study in Delinquent Development, which is a prospective longitudinal survey of over 400 London males from age 8 to age 48. In addition to 550 published journal articles and book chapters on criminological and psychological topics, he has published over 80 books, monographs and government publications.
Author, chapter 7

Seena Fazel, BSc (Hons), MBChB, MD, FPCPsych

Clinical senior lecturer in forensic psychiatry at the University of Oxford and an honorary consultant forensic psychiatrist, Seena's research interests include the epidemiology of mental illness and violence, and the mental health of prisoners. Recent publications include a review of the health of prisoners (*Lancet*, 2011), a meta-analysis of studies examining the risk of violence in schizophrenia (*PLoS Medicine*, 2009), and an epidemiological study of bipolar disorder and violent crime (*Archives of General Psychiatry*, 2010).
Author, chapter 21

Adrian Feeney, MB, BS, BSc, LLM, FRCPsych

Consultant forensic psychiatrist, Ravenswood House Medium Secure Unit, Winchester and Winchester Prison, Adrian's interests include the relationship between substance misuse and offending, prison psychiatry and mental health law.
Co-author, alcohol section, chapter 18

Alan R. Felthous, MD

Professor and director of forensic psychiatry, Department of Neurology and Psychiatry, Saint Louis University School of Medicine and professor emeritus, Southern Illinois University, Alan has written numerous journal articles and book chapters on topics in legal and forensic psychiatry. He is author of the book *The Psychotherapist Duty to Warn or Protect*, senior editor of *Behavioral Sciences and the Law* and co-editor of *The International Handbook of Psychopathic Disorders and the Law*. He is secretary of the Association of Directors of Forensic Psychiatry Fellowship Programs.
Co-author, 5 with particular contribution of the USA sections

Phil Fennell, BA (Law) Kent, MPhil (Kent), PhD (Wales)

Professor of law at Cardiff University Law School, Phil is author of *Treatment Without Consent: Law, Psychiatry and the Treatment of Mentally Disordered People Without Consent Since 1845* (2006). He served on the Mental Health Act Commission from 1983 to 1989. In 2004–2005 Phil was specialist legal adviser to the Joint Parliamentary Scrutiny Committee on the Draft Mental Health Bill 2004, and in 2006–2007 to the Joint Committee on Human Rights on the Mental Health Bill 2006. His latest book is *Mental Health: Law and Practice*, 2nd Edition (2011). He co-edited (with Professor Larry Gostin and others) and wrote ten chapters for *Principles of Mental Health Law and Policy* (2010).
Co-author on mental health law, chapter 3

Pierre Gagné, MD, FRCPC

Associate professor in psychiatry in the Faculty of Medicine at the University of Sherbrooke, head of forensic services at the Sherbrooke University Hospital and director of the Forensic Psychiatric Clinic of the University of Sherbrooke, Pierre received his medical degree from Laval University, Quebec, and certification as a psychiatrist from the Royal College of Physicians of Canada. He has been a pioneer in the development of forensic psychiatry in the province of Quebec, contributing to the establishment of three forensic centres. He is author and co-author of publications on suicide, homicides in families, sexual offenders and on psychiatric services for mentally ill offenders.
Co-author, 5 with particular contribution of the Canadian sections

Harvey Gordon, BSc, MB ChB, FRCPsych

Past consultant forensic psychiatrist at Broadmoor Hospital, the Bethlem Royal and Maudsley Hospital and Littlemore Hospital, past honorary leisurer Institute of Psychiatry and honorary senior lecturer University of Oxford. Past academic secretary of the faculty of forensic psychiatry at the Royal College of Psychiatrists and past secretary of the section of forensic psychiatry of the European Psychiatric Association. Harvey has published on the treatment of paraphilias, on psychiatric aspects of terrorism, and on the history of forensic psychiatry. He has collaborated with colleagues from Europe, Russia, Israel, and the Palestinian Authority in teaching forensic psychiatry. A book on Broadmoor Hospital has been published.
Contributor, chapters 10 & 11 (motoring)

Nicola Gray, BSc, MSc, PhD, CPsychol, AFBPsS

Honorary professor at Swansea University and director of the Welsh Applied Risk Research Network (WARRN), Nicola received her PhD from the Institute of Psychiatry for her work on the neuropsychology of schizophrenia. She completed her MSc in clinical psychology before taking up a joint position at Caswell Clinic and Cardiff University. She is now head of psychology for Pastoral Cymru and has helped to set up a new specialist personality disorder service (Ty Catrin). Her research interests are in risk assessment and management, personality disorder, sexual offending and neuropsychology. She regularly trains professionals in these areas (e.g., HCR-20, PCL-R).
Co-author, chapter 22, with special contribution on risk assessment tools.

Don Grubin, MD, FRCPsych

Professor of forensic psychiatry at Newcastle University and consultant forensic psychiatrist in the Northumberland, Tyne & Wear NHS Foundation Trust; board member, Scottish Risk Management Authority; member of the Ministry of Justice Correctional Services Accreditation Panel Board; member of the England and Wales Independent Safeguarding Authority, Don trained at the Institute of Psychiatry, and the Maudsley and Broadmoor Hospitals. He moved to Newcastle in 1994, and was promoted to the chair of forensic psychiatry in 1997. His special interest is the assessment, treatment and management of sexual offenders and he is psychiatric adviser to the England and Wales National Offender Management Service sex offender treatment programmes.
Main author and editor chapter 10

John Gunn, CBE, MD, FRCPsych, FMedSci

Member of the Parole Board for England & Wales, emeritus professor of forensic psychiatry, Institute of Psychiatry, KCL; past chairman of the Royal College of Psychiatrists' Faculty of Forensic Psychiatry; founder member of the European Ghent Group, Member of the Royal Commission on Criminal Justice 1991–1993. One time adviser to several overseas governments, John's research interests and books include violence, prison psychiatry (especially Grendon) and epidemiology. He is a founding editor of *CBMH*. His clinical work embraced treatment in secure hospitals, the treatment of personality disorders and homelessness. He developed a specialist unit for teaching forensic psychiatry.
Co-editor of book – see chapter headings for details

Robert Hale, MRCS, LRCP, FRCPsych

General psychiatrist and a psychoanalyst, Rob has worked at the Portman Clinic for over 30 years where his area of clinical interest was the treatment of paedophilia. During this time he worked in the Tavistock Clinic where he established the Mednet service for doctors in need of psychological and psychiatric help. In both, the transgression of boundaries, whether personal or professional, is a central element. For the past 15 years he has provided weekly institutional consultation and professional supervision to four medium secure hospitals and one high secure hospital.
Contributor, chapter 27 with special contribution on psychodynamic issues

Timothy Harding, MD

Emeritus professor and former director of the University Institute of Forensic Medicine at the University of Geneva. Tim founded the multifaculty programme on Humanitarian Action (now the CERAH). He has also worked for the World Health Organisation, the International Council of Jurists, the Council of Europe and as a visiting professor at the Universities of Kobe and Osaka. His fields of interest have been the assessment of dangerousness, comparative health legislation, prison medicine and visits to places of detention with the CPT. Recently he participated in an Amnesty International study on the death penalty in Japan.
Co-author, chapter 5, editor for Forensic Psychiatry outside of the UK and Ireland.

Felicity Hawksley, BA, Social Sciences Professional Certificate In Management (Open University), Introductory Certificate (Association of Project Managers)

Civil servant in the Ministry of Justice, previously HM Treasury and the Home Office, Felicity has been involved in a diverse range of policy posts ranging from parole, victims of crime, approved premises and offender housing to religious cults and betting. She currently works as part of a programme to specify the outcomes for commissioning services for offenders, victims and the courts.
Author of sections on support in law and through Home Office and Ministry of Justice services, chapter 28

Andrew Hider, MA (Oxon), PPP, DClinPsy

Consultant clinical psychologist at Ty Catrin Low Secure Personality Disorder Unit in Cardiff (Pastoral Cymru Ltd) where he is developing with colleagues a structured treatment programme for problems related to personality disorder. Andrew has worked in both community and forensic settings; his main clinical interest is in the psychological treatment of severe psychopathology, where symptoms of psychosis, personality disorder and neuropsychological impairment overlap. Through involvement with the Wales Applied Risk Research Network (Warrn), he has helped develop a standardised risk assessment training model now used across the NHS in Wales
Co-author, chapter 16, main author of the personality disorder assessments sections

Michael Howlett LLM, FRSA

Director of the Zito Trust until its closure in 2009. Michael Howlett read law at Cambridge University and became a teacher until 1990 when he joined Peper Harow in Surrey as a member of the therapeutic staff working with severely disturbed adolescents and young offenders. In 1993 he joined the Special Hospitals Service Authority in London, the Authority responsible for the management of Ashworth, Broadmoor and Rampton high security hospitals for mentally disordered offenders. In 1994 he set up the Zito Trust with Jayne Zito to lobby for reforms to mental health policy for the severely mentally ill.
Co-author, chapter 28, with contribution on independent sector services for victims and survivors.

David James, MA, FRCPsych

Consultant forensic psychiatrist in London. David is clinical lead at the Fixated Threat Assessment Centre in London (www.fixatedthreatassessmentcentre.com). His most recent research work has been in the area of stalking, threats and harassment, and his publications in this field have concerned particularly the threat posed towards politicians and the prominent by such behaviours.
Co-author, section on the assessment and management of threats, chapter 21

Philip Joseph BSc, Barrister at Law, FRCPsych

Consultant forensic psychiatrist, Mental Health Centre, St Charles Hospital, London. Phillip trained at University College Hospital and the Maudsley Hospital, and has held research and consultant posts at the Maudsley and St Mary's Hospital since 1989. He has retained a longstanding interest in the homeless mentally ill. He was deputy coroner for Southwark Coroner's Court 1988–1996, examiner for the Diploma of Forensic Psychiatry at Kings College London, forensic member of the editorial advisory board *International Review of Psychiatry*. He is a recognised teacher in forensic psychiatry in the University of London, and represents the Royal College of Psychiatrists and University of London on consultant appointments in forensic psychiatry.
Author of section on the coroner' court, chapter 2

Sean Kaliski, BA, MB, ChB, Mmed, PhD, FCPsych (SA)

Associate professor in the Department of Psychiatry and Mental Health, University of Cape Town, and Principal Specialist for the Forensic Mental Health Services for the Western Cape, South Africa. Sean is also a member of the SWANZDSA-

JCS international research collaboration in forensic psychiatry and editor of the textbook *Psycholegal Assessment in South Africa* (2006).
Co-author, chapter 5, with particular contribution of the South African section.

Harry Kennedy, BSc, MD, FRCPI, FRCPsych

Consultant forensic psychiatrist and executive clinical director, National Forensic Mental Health Service, Central Mental Hospital, Dundrum, Dublin; clinical professor of forensic psychiatry, Trinity College Dublin; formerly consultant North London Forensic Service and Royal Free Hospital; trained in University College Dublin, Hammersmith Hospital and Maudsley / Institute of Psychiatry. Harry's research includes work on the epidemiology of suicide, homicide and violence; anger and mental illness; mental capacity; structured professional judgment and benchmarking admission and discharge criteria in forensic mental health services; international human rights law and mental disabilities.
Co-author Irish section, chapter 4, commentary on specialist Irish services, chapter 24

Michael Kopelman, PhD, FBPsS, FRCPsych, FMedSci

Professor of neuropsychiatry, King's College London, Michael runs the Neuropsychiatry and Memory Disorders Clinic at St Thomas's Hospital. He has been co-editor/co-author of *The Handbook of Memory Disorders*, Baddeley et al., *Lishman's Organic Psychiatry*, and *Forensic Neuropsychology in Practice*, Young et al. He is past-president of the British Neuropsychological Society, and currently president of the International Neuropsychiatric Association and the British Academy of Forensic Sciences. He has been an expert witness in cases involving memory disorders (neurological or psychogenic), neuropsychiatric disorders (including automatisms and frontal lobe cases), false confessions, civil liberties, death row, and extradition.
Author of amnesia section, chapter 12

Peter Kramp, DrMed

Consultant forensic psychiatry, head of the Clinic of Forensic Psychiatry in Copenhagen 1982–2011. From 1982, a member of the Danish Medico-Legal Council; from 1992, vice-president and head of the Section of Forensic Psychiatry; 1989–2011 chairman, Section of Forensic Psychiatry, Danish Psychiatric Association, and member of the Ghent group. His main research areas have been epidemiological studies of forensic patients, diagnoses, criminality and analyses of the reason for the growing number of forensic patients.
Co-author, chapter 5, with particular contribution of the Danish section

Veena Kumari, PhD

Professor of experimental psychology in the Department of Psychology, Institute of Psychiatry, London. Veena obtained a PhD in psychology from Banaras Hindu University, India and then moved to the Institute of Psychiatry, London. She was a Beit Memorial Research Fellow from October 1999 to September 2002, a Wellcome Senior Research Fellow in basic biomedical science from October 2002 to May 2009. Her research interests include neurobiological correlates of violence in psychosis and personality disorders, personality and brain functioning, and the neural predictors and correlates of pharmacological and psychological therapies in psychosis and forensic populations.
Co-author chapter 12, lead author for the imaging section

Annette Lankshear, PhD (York), MA (York), BSc (Edinburgh), RN

Director of research and reader in health policy in Cardiff University School of Nursing and Midwifery. Annette's research interests include multidisciplinary and inter-agency work in mental health, and whilst at the University of York she managed a trial of enhanced care for people newly diagnosed with depression. Her current portfolio of work focuses on patient safety and health improvement. She has undertaken a number of studies to assess the effectiveness of government strategies to reduce clinical risk and is currently engaged in an evaluation of the Health Foundation's Safer Patient Network.
Co-author, sections on the probation service, chapter 25

Ian Lankshear, MA (Edinburgh), MBA (Bradford), CQSW (Manchester)

Criminal justice consultant and a trustee for local community safety and development charities, chief executive of South Wales Probation Board/Trust 2005–2009. Ian spent 38 years (20 as a senior manager) in the probation service, in London, Greater Manchester, North and West Yorkshire as well as South Wales. His experience includes prison-, hostel-, court- and community-based practice. He has also had responsibility as a policy and strategic leader for training and staff development in services to the criminal courts and in partnership with mental health services. He is currently engaged in international development programmes with the Ministry of Justice.

Co-author, sections on the probation service, chapter 25

Heather Law, BA

Research programme coordinator Greater Manchester West NHS Foundation Trust. Heather coordinates a research programme exploring recovery from psychosis. This work will be submitted for a PhD degree. Previously, she was part of the team commissioned by the Department of Health and Youth Justice Board to develop a comprehensive health screening and assessment tool and a model care pathway for young people in the criminal justice system. She has also worked as an assistant psychologist within forensic youth services. Heather has publications on female sexual abuse, immigration and trauma in prison.

Co-author, Juvenile offenders chapter 19

Penny Letts, OBE, BSc, CQSW, DASS

Member of the Administrative Justice and Tribunals Council. Penny is a policy consultant and trainer specialising in mental health and capacity law. She is editor of the *Elder Law Journal* (Jordans), a contributor to Court of Protection Practice 2011 (Jordans, 2011) and Assessment of Mental Capacity (Law Society, 2010). She was specialist adviser to the Parliamentary Select Committee on the Draft Mental Incapacity Bill and prepared a major part of the Mental Capacity Act Code of Practice. Penny was formerly Law Society Policy Adviser on Mental Health and Disability and a Mental Health Act Commissioner.

Lead author on mental capacity, chapter 3

Per Lindqvist, MD, PhD

Associate professor at the Division of Forensic Psychiatry, Department of Clinical Neuroscience, Karolinska Institute, Stockholm, Sweden. Immediate past president and presently international secretary of the Swedish Association of Forensic Psychiatrists. Per is a specialist in child and adolescent psychiatry and in forensic psychiatry.

Co-author, chapter 5, with particular contribution of the Swedish section

William Lindsay, PhD, FBPS, FIASSID

He is Consultant Psychologist and Head of Research for Castlebeck Care. He was previously Head of Psychology (LD) in NHS Tayside and a Consultant Psychologist with the State Hospital, Scotland. He is Professor of Learning Disabilities and Forensic Psychology at the University of Abertay, Dundee and Visiting Professor at Bangor University. He is currently conducting research on the assessment of offenders and on cognitive therapy. He has published over 200 research articles and book chapters as well as 4 books including two volumes on sex offenders with intellectual and developmental disabilities.

Co-author of chapter 13 Offenders with intellectual disabilities

Ronnie Mackay, BA (Law), CNAA, MPhil (Leicester), Barrister, Fulbright Scholar

Professor of criminal policy and mental health at Leicester De Montfort Law School, De Montfort University. Ronnie has written about and researched mentally abnormal offenders for many years, and is the author of *Mental Condition Defences in the Criminal Law* together with numerous other scholarly publications. He was a member of the Parole Board of England and Wales 1995 to 2001, and consultant to the Law Commission for England and Wales for whom he has conducted empirical studies on unfitness to plead, the insanity defence, diminished responsibility, provocation and infanticide.

Co-author, section on the trial, chapter 2

Tony Maden, MD, FRCPsych

Professor of forensic psychiatry, Imperial College London. Tony is a forensic psychiatrist with a particular interest in violence risk assessment and the treatment of personality disorder. He trained at the Maudsley Hospital and the Institute of Psychiatry and was an honorary consultant and clinical director of forensic services at the Maudsley. Since 1999 he has been professor of forensic psychiatry at Imperial College London and was clinical director of the Dangerous and Severe Personality Disorder (DSPD) Directorate at Broadmoor Hospital. His book *Treating Violence* was published in 2007 and he also co-authored *Essential Mental Health Law* in 2010.

Main author of the section Dangerous and Severe Personality Disorder (DSPD) in chapter 16

Gill McGauley, MB, BS, MD, FRCPsych, PG Cert (HE)

Consultant and reader in forensic psychotherapy. Gill works at Broadmoor Hospital where she established the first forensic psychotherapy service in a high secure hospital, and academically at St George's, University of London. She has developed national and international training and educational initiatives in forensic psychotherapy as chairman of the National Reference Group for Training and Education in Forensic Psychotherapy. Gill is co-editor of *Forensic Mental Health: Concepts, Systems and Practice*. Her research interests include the application of Attachment Theory and the development of psychological therapies for personality-disordered forensic patients. In 2009 she was awarded a national teaching fellowship by the Higher Education Academy.
Lead author of the psychodynamic psychotherapy sections, chapter 23

Mary McMurran, PhD, FBPsS

Professor in the University of Nottingham's Institute of Mental Health. Mary has worked as a clinical and forensic psychologist in HM Prison Service and the National Health Service. Her research interests are (1) social problem solving theories of and therapies for personality disorders, (2) the assessment and treatment of alcohol-related aggression and violence, and (3) understanding and enhancing readiness to engage in therapy. She has written over 100 academic articles and book chapters on these topics. She is a fellow of the British Psychological Society, and recipient of the BPS Division of Forensic Psychology's lifetime achievement award in 2005.
Lead author of the alcohol section, of the addictions chapter 18

Gillian Mezey, MBBS, FRCPsych

Reader and consultant in forensic psychiatry at St George's, University of London. Gill has published extensively on the effects of domestic and sexual abuse, including male rape, psychological trauma and violence against women. She was the principal Investigator on two Medical Research Council funded studies looking at the prevalence and effects of domestic violence during pregnancy. She chaired two Royal College of Psychiatrists' working groups, which produced guidelines on working with victims of sexual and domestic violence. She was the expert advisor to the Department of Health's Victims of Violence and Abuse Prevention Programme (VVAPP).
Contributor chapter 28 on epidemiology of PTSD and some of the specific subtypes.

David Middleton, BA (Hons), CSSM, DipSW, CQSW

Independent consultant and visiting professor of community and criminal Justice at De Montfort University. During a 30-year career in probation, David specialised in sex offender treatment and risk management. At the Home Office he was responsible for all community-based sex offender treatment programmes in England and Wales. He also wrote the first accredited treatment programme for Internet sexual offenders. He was the UK representative on the Council of Europe Committee of Experts on the treatment of sexual offending and a member of the G8 Experts Group providing advice on Internet sex offender policy.
Contributor to chapter 10 particularly for internet offending

Terrie E. Moffitt, MA, PhD, FMedSci

Knut Schmidt Nielsen Professor of psychology and neuroscience, Duke University, North Carolina, USA. Professor of social behaviour and development, Institute of Psychiatry, London, Terrie studies how genetic and environmental risks work together to shape the developmental course of abnormal human behaviours. Her particular interest is in antisocial and criminal behaviour, but she also studies depression, psychosis and substance abuse. She is associate director of the Dunedin Longitudinal Study, which follows from birth 1,000 people born in 1972 in New Zealand. She also directs the Environmental-Risk Longitudinal Twin Study, which follows from birth 1,100 British families with twins born in 1994–1995. Website: www.moffittcaspi.com
Co-author, chapter 8, with special contributions on twin and adoption studies

Damian Mohan, FRCPsych

Consultant forensic psychiatrist, Central Mental Hospital in Dundrum, Dublin and the National Forensic Mental Health Service in Ireland. Lecturer in forensic psychiatry at Trinity College Dublin. Previously, lecturer in forensic psychiatry at University of Southampton and consultant forensic psychiatrist at Broadmoor Hospital. Damian's interests include mental health law, prison psychiatry in reach services and psychiatric aspects of employment litigation.
Co-author Irish section, Legal arrangements, chapter 4

John Monahan, PhD

Professor of psychology and of psychiatry and neurobehavioral sciences at the University of Virginia, where John, a psychologist, holds the Shannon Distinguished Professorship in Law. He was the founding president of the American Psychological Association's Division of Psychology and Law. John is the author or editor of 17 books and has written over 200 articles and chapters. He has been elected to membership in the Institute of Medicine of the U.S. National Academy of Sciences.

Lead author for the COVR section, chapter 22

Estelle Moore, BSc Hons, MSc, PhD, CPsychol, CSci, AFBPsS

Psychologist, both clinical and forensic and lead for the Centralised Groupwork Service, Newbury Therapy Unit, at Broadmoor Hospital. Estelle has 20 years of experience in promoting evidence-based clinical interventions in services for those with enduring mental health needs, the last 15 in high security focusing on the delivery and evaluation of therapeutic interventions for those who present with a history of serious offending behaviour. Estelle's longstanding research interest is in the working alliance formed with forensic service recipients within a range of therapeutic modalities, and the role this plays in their recovery.

Co-author, chapter 16, lead authorship on the clinical assessment and engagement sections; co-author chapter 23, lead authorship for the cognitive behavioural sections.

Paul Edward Mullen, MBBS, MPhil, DSc, FRCPsych, FRANZCP

Professor emeritus in forensic psychiatry at Monash University, Melbourne and ex- clinical director, Victorian Institute of Forensic Mental Health, previously professor of psychological medicine at the University of Otago (1982–1992). Paul's book on stalking won the APA Guttmacher prize in 2001. He has published over 190 articles, co-authored 4 books and contributed over 40 chapters. His research interests include the relationship between mental disorder and criminal behaviour, the long-term impact of childhood sexual abuse, jealousy, threats and threateners, litigious and chronic complainers and the Guantanamo Bay detention centre. He is a member of the Fixated Research Group in London, which conducts research into the stalking of public figures.

Author of the disorders of passion chapter 15 and 1st edition author for deception and dissociation, chapter 17

Leigh Anthony Neal, MD, FRCPsych, MRCGP

Consultant psychiatrist to a veterans NHS psychiatric clinic in Gloucester. Leigh qualified in 1981 and was a psychiatrist in the RAF until 2002, leaving as a wing commander and head of the tri-service inpatient psychiatric unit. In 2003 he was appointed a senior lecturer at Kings College Academic Centre for Military Mental Health. He has an ongoing academic interest in combat psychiatry and pain syndromes.

Contributor to chapter 4 on military law

Norbert Nedopil, DrMed

Head of the Department of Forensic Psychiatry, University of Munich, previously head of the Department of Forensic Psychiatry, University of Würzburg. Norbert began his career by specialising in psychopharmacology, schizophrenia and sleep research, but switched to forensic psychiatry in 1984.His special interests are the quality of psychiatric assessments, the causes of human aggression, the treatment of mentally disordered offenders, the prediction of recidivism in mentally ill offenders and psychiatric ethical and legal questions pertaining to psychiatry. Norbert has been awarded the Becceria Gold Medal from the Criminological Society of the German-speaking countries and the Alzheimer Kraepelin Medal. He is the author or editor of 7 books and more than 200 scientific papers.

Co-author of the international comparative law and services chapter 5, with particular contribution of the German sections

Elena Carmen Nichita, MD

Forensic psychiatrist currently employed at the State University of New York (SUNY) in Syracuse. After graduating from her forensic psychiatry fellowship from the University of South Carolina, Columbia, she was an assistant professor at Medical College of Georgia in Augusta. Her main interests are clinical work with individuals who have mental illness and encounters with the law, as well as teaching residents, fellows and students who are training in the field of psychiatry and forensic psychiatry. Her publications are related to violence and mental illness, antisocial personality disorder, and civil legal issues in psychiatry.

Co-author of the pharmacotherapy sections of the principles of treatment chapter 23.

Gregory O'Brien, MA, MD (Aberdeen), FRCPsych, FRCPCH

Senior psychiatrist, disability services, Queensland, Australia, associate professor of the University of Queensland and emeritus professor of developmental psychiatry at Northumbria University. Gregory is a certified specialist in learning disabilities, child and adolescent psychiatry and forensic psychiatry. He has served as a consultant to UNICEF and to the European Parliament. He has held office as associate dean of the Royal College of Psychiatrists, president of the Penrose Society, chairman of the MacKeith Meetings Committee, chairman of the Faculty of Learning Disability of the Royal College of Psychiatrists, scientific director of the Castang Foundation and associate medical director of Northumberland Tyne and Wear NHS Trust.
Co-author of the intellectual disability chapter 13.

James R P Ogloff, BA, MA, JD, Ph.D., FAPS

Foundation professor of clinical forensic psychology and director of the Centre for Forensic Behavioural Science at Monash University and Forensicare. Jim is trained as a lawyer and a psychologist. He is a leading researcher and forensic psychologist, having published several books and more than 220 publications. He has served as president/chair of the Australian and New Zealand Association of Psychiatry, Psychology and Law; the College of Forensic Psychologists of the APS; the Canadian Psychological Association; and the American Psychology–Law Society. Jim is the recipient of the 2012 Donald Andrews Career Contribution Award from the Canadian Psychological Association.
Co-author of the international comparative law and services chapter 5, with particular contribution of the Australian sections.

Jill Peay, BSc, PhD, Barrister at Law

Professor in the Department of Law at the London School of Economics and Political Science. Jill has interests in both civil and criminal mental health law, and in the treatment of offenders. She is the author of *Mental Health and Crime* (2011), and *Decisions and Dilemmas: Working with Mental Health Law* (2003).
Contributed to the chapter on "Other Crime", Chapter 11.

Hanna Putkonen, MD PhD

Associate professor and senior medical officer, Hanna is a forensic psychiatrist from Helsinki, Finland. She is currently working in the National Institute for Health and Welfare as a senior medical officer in the Forensic Psychiatric Department. She has previously worked with forensic psychiatric patients in the state mental hospital of Vanha Vaasa and in the Helsinki University Central Hospital. Her principal research themes have been female-perpetrated violence and filicide. She has also worked in other national and international research groups studying e.g. seclusion and restraint.
Main contributor to chapter 20 Women as offenders

David Reiss, MA, MB, BChir, MPhil, DFP, FRCPsych

Consultant forensic psychiatrist and director of forensic psychiatry education for West London Mental Health NHS Trust, and an honorary clinical senior lecturer at Imperial College London. David was formerly director of the Home Office Teaching Unit and clinical lecturer in victimology/forensic psychiatry at the Institute of Psychiatry, King's College London. His research examines the interface between clinical forensic psychiatry and public policy. His clinical and educational work focuses on enabling the multidisciplinary team to gain an enhanced understanding of patients, thereby improving care and reducing risk. He has recently co-edited a book designed to support the care of patients with complex disorders in the community.
Co-author of the victims and survivors chapter 28, including lead author on aspects of inquiries after homicide, workplace bullying and EMDR.

Anne Ridley, BSc, PhD, CPsychol, FHEA

Principal lecturer at London South Bank University. Anne's research interests include suggestibility and eyewitness testimony in adults and children. She is currently editing a book on suggestibility in testimony for Wiley's Psychology of Crime, Policing and Law. She teaches on London South Bank University's MSc in investigative forensic psychology as well as undergraduate courses, and was awarded a National Teaching Fellowship by the Higher Education Academy in 2008.
Contributed the section on suggestibility to chapter 6

Keith J B Rix, BMedBiol, MPhil, LLM, MD, CBiol, MSB, FEWI, FRCPsych

Consultant forensic psychiatrist at The Grange, Cleckheaton, and at Cygnet Hospital Wyke, Bradford; a visiting consultant psychiatrist at HM Prison, Leeds and a part-time lecturer at De Montfort Law School, Leicester. Keith's forensic experience began in London in the 1960s when he lived in hostels with ex-offenders and assessed prisoners for admission to after-care hostels. He qualified in medicine in Aberdeen and trained in psychiatry in Edinburgh and Manchester.

He started the Leeds Magistrates' Courts Mental Health Assessment and Diversion Scheme and the city's forensic psychiatry service. He has thirty years experience as an expert witness.
Co-author of chapter on court reports chapter 6.

Paul Rogers, RMN, PG Cert ENB 650 (CBT), PG Dip (CBT), MSc (Econ), PhD, MRCPsych (Hon)

Professor of forensic mental health, University of Glamorgan. One-time staff nurse at St Andrew's Hospital and charge nurse at Caswell Clinic. Trained in cognitive behavioural therapy at the Institute of Psychiatry, then as a clinical nurse specialist at Caswell Clinic. For his PhD Paul studied the association between command hallucinations and violence. An MRC Fellowship led to a study of suicidal thinking in prisoners. He was appointed professor in 2004, now developing a BSc in violence reduction. Paul has also worked as an external consultant to Broadmoor Hospital.
Co-author of the principles of treatment chapter 5, with particular contribution on the nursing sections.

Jane Senior, BA (Hons), MA, PhD, RM

Research fellow at the Offender Health Research Network, University of Manchester. Jane qualified as a mental health nurse in 1990 and has worked in a variety of acute, secure, community and prison settings. Her PhD studies examined ways of improving prison mental health care service configurations. Her main research and clinical interests centre on improving prison-based mental healthcare, suicide and self-harm management and the diversion of people with mental health problems away from the criminal justice system.
Co-author of the treatment in non-health services chapter 24, and lead authorship on some of the prison sections.

Nigel Shackleford, MA Cantab

As a career UK Home Office civil servant, Nigel transferred to C3 Division, dealing with mentally disordered offender policy, in 1993, and worked for the Home Office on the review of the 1983 Mental Health Act from its inception in 1998 to the implementation of the 2007 Act. Nigel's determination to protect the old policy of diversion for mentally disordered people who offend won him few friends outside forensic psychiatry, but the policy survived in law, popularity notwithstanding.
Contributions on legal administration to chapters 3 & 4

Jennifer Shaw, MB, ChB, MSc, PhD, FRCPsych

Professor of forensic psychiatry, research group lead and head of the School of Psychiatry. Associate medical director and director of research and development for Lancashire Care NHS Foundation Trust. Consultant forensic psychiatrist for Guild Lodge Medium Secure Unit in Preston, assistant director for the National Confidential Inquiry into Suicide and Homicide by People with Mental Illness, academic lead for the Offender Health Research Network. Collaborative papers by Jenny have been featured in *The Lancet, the BMJ,* and *Archives of General Psychiatry*. Research grants have been secured from the National Patient Safety Agency, the Department of Health and the National Institute of Health Research.
Lead author on the National Confidential Inquiry into Suicide and Homicide sections of the victims and survivors chapter (28) and on some of the prison sections in the treatment in non-health services chapter 24.

Jonathan Shepherd, CBE, MSc, PhD, FRCS, FMedSci

Professor of oral and maxillofacial surgery, and director, Violence Research Group, Cardiff University. Jonathan's PhD focused on violence risk factors and health impacts. He won the 2008 Stockholm Criminology Prize for his research and its application to violence prevention. Since the mid 1990s and utilising longitudinal data from the Cambridge Study of Delinquent Development he has led a series of investigations of links among offending, victimisation, illness and injury. He is a fellow of the Academy of Medical Sciences and an honorary fellow of the Royal College of Psychiatrists.
Lead author of the victim-centred measures of crime and the public health and safety sections in the victims and survivors' chapter 28

Jeremy Skipworth, MB, ChB, MMedSci (Hons), PhD, FRANZCP

Consultant forensic psychiatrist practicing in New Zealand as clinical director of the Auckland Regional Forensic Psychiatry Services (also known as the Mason Clinic). Member of the New Zealand National Parole Board. Jeremy did his undergraduate studies in Auckland, and completed his PhD through Otago University.
Co-author of the international comparative law and services chapter 5, with particular contribution of the New Zealand sections

Robert Snowden, PhD (Cantab)

Professor in the School of Psychology at Cardiff University. Robert was educated at York University and Cambridge University and worked as a post-doctoral fellow at MIT (USA) before moving to Cardiff. He has published widely in the domains of visual perception, visual attention, and forensic psychology.
Co-author of the risk assessment chapter 21, with special contribution on risk assessment tools.

Nicola Swinson, MBChB, BSc(Hons), MRCPsych

Consultant forensic psychiatrist at Guild Lodge, Lancashire Care NHS Foundation Trust and an honorary clinical research fellow at the National Confidential Inquiry into Suicide and Homicide by People with Mental Illness, University of Manchester. Nicola qualified from the University of Glasgow in 1999, and trained in psychiatry at the Maudsley Hospital, London. She then completed her training in forensic psychiatry in the North West of England. She is currently studying for a PhD in personality disorder in perpetrators of homicide.

Co-author author of the National Confidential Inquiry into Suicide and Homicide sections in the victims and survivors chapter 28.

John L Taylor, BSc (Hons), MPhil, DPsychol, CPsychol, CSci, AFBPsS

Professor of clinical psychology at Northumbria University and consultant clinical psychologist and psychological services, professional lead with Northumberland, Tyne & Wear NHS Foundation Trust, UK. Since qualifying as a clinical psychologist from Edinburgh University, John has worked in intellectual disability and forensic services in a range of settings in the UK (high, medium and low secure services, prisons and community services). He has published work on the assessment and treatment of offending and mental health problems associated with intellectual disabilities in a range of research journals, professional publications and books.

Lead author of the intellectual disability chapter 10.

Pamela J Taylor, MBBS, MRCP, FRCPsych, FMedSci

Professor of forensic psychiatry, School of Medicine, Cardiff University, consultant forensic psychiatrist ABMU and Cardiff & Vale Health Boards and forensic psychiatry advisor to the CMO for Wales. Pamela leads the Offender Health Research Network-Cymru (OHRN-C) and is a member of the scientific council of the Dutch Expertise Center for Forensic Psychiatry. Her main research themes include communication about delusions and violence and meeting the needs of the socially excluded. Pamela is lead editor of *Criminal Behaviour and Mental Health* and international editor of *Behavioral Sciences and the Law*. Her previous books include *Violence in Society, Couples in Care and Custody (co-edited),* and *Personality Disorder and Serious Offending* (with Newrith & Meux).

Co-editor of book – see chapter headings for details

Lindsay Thomson, MB, ChB, FRCPsych, MPhil, MD

Professor in forensic psychiatry at the University of Edinburgh and medical director of the State Hospitals Board for Scotland and the Forensic Mental Health Services Managed Care Network. Lindsay's research interests include outcomes in mentally disordered offenders, risk assessment and management of harm to others, the impact of legislative change, and service design for mentally disordered offenders. She has established the School of Forensic Mental Health under the auspices of the Forensic Network in collaboration with the Universities of Edinburgh, Glasgow Caledonian and Stirling. She is the co-author of *Mental Health and Scots Law in Practice* (2012).

Contributed to Scottish section chapter 4. Co-author of the international comparative law and services chapter (5), with particular contribution of the Scottish sections; author of the Scottish service commentaries in the health services and non-health services chapters 23 & 24.

Marianne van den Bree, MSc, PhD

Reader in the Department of Psychological Medicine at Cardiff University. Marianne studied experimental psychology at the Vrije Universiteit in Amsterdam, the Netherlands, followed by a PhD in human genetics at the Medical College of Virginia USA. Her interest in the study of substance abuse was triggered while working as a researcher at The National Institute on Drug Abuse, National Institutes of Health, in Maryland, USA. Her research has focused on genetic and environmental influences on the developmental pathways of substance use/abuse and other mental health–related traits, using epidemiological, twin study and molecular genetic research approaches.

Lead author of the genetics chapter 8.

Birgit Völlm, DFP, MRCPsych, MD, PhD

Clinical associate professor and consultant forensic psychiatrist at the University of Nottingham and in the Dangerous Severe Personality Disorder Unit at Rampton High Secure Hospital. Birgit's research interests are the neurobiology of personality disorders and social cognition, treatment of personality disorders and comparative mental health legislation. She has published several imaging and experimental pharmacological studies of antisocial groups. She has co-authored *Cochrane reviews* on psychological and pharmacological interventions for borderline, antisocial, Cluster A and C personality disorders.

Lead author of the biochemical sections of the brain structure and functions chapter 9.

Julian Walker, DClinPsy, PhD, CPsychol, AFBPsS

Consultant forensic clinical psychologist at Fromeside Medium Secure Unit, R&D director for AWP NHS Trust and honorary research fellow at the University of Bristol. After 9 years at the Institute of Psychiatry, Maudsley Hospital and HMP Brixton, Julian moved to Fromeside in 2003. He currently works in a service for high risk offenders with personality disorder. His PhD in violence led to a cognitive model of violence and the Maudsley Violence Questionnaire. His research interests and publications relate to violence, personality disorder and the psychological processes involved in aggression. *Co-editor and co-author of chapter 9, co-author of chapters 11 & 22.*

Lisa Jane Warren, MPsychClin, PhD, MAPS

Clinical and forensic psychologist who practices in the field of stalking and threat management. Research fellow within the Centre for Forensic Behavioural Science at Monash University, Melbourne, Australia. Lisa's primary research interest is the examination of explicit threats and their correlates with physical violence. She was the foundation manager of the Problem Behaviour Program, an Australian forensic mental health clinic where psychologists and psychiatrists specialise in particular forms of criminal conduct such as stalking, threatening and fire setting. She was also the foundation coordinator of the forensic psychology programme at the Monash University Clinical Psychology Centre. *Co-author, section on the assessment and management of threats, chapter 22.*

Nigel Williams

Senior lecturer in molecular genetics at the MRC Centre in Neuropsychiatric Genetics and Genomics, Cardiff University. Nigel's primary research interests focus on the molecular genetic analysis of common neuropsychiatric and neurological disorders, including schizophrenia, attention deficit hyperactivity disorder and Parkinson's disease. *Co-author of the genetics chapter 9 and lead author of the section on the molecular genetic studies of schizophrenia.*

Kazuo Yoshikawa, MD, PhD, DFP

Director of the Shuai Sugamo Clinic which has outpatient services for mentally disordered offender and addiction patients in Tokyo. Kazuo has a diploma in forensic psychiatry from the London University, where he was awarded the Essay Prize. He also has a PhD in psychiatry from the Tokyo Medical Dental University. He previously worked as a director of the Department of Forensic Psychiatry for the National Centre of Neurology and Psychiatry in Tokyo, and worked with governments to establish forensic mental health service system in Japan. He is a member of the international research project SWANZJACS. *Co-author of the international comparative law and services chapter 5, with particular contribution of the Japanese sections*

Jayne Zito, BSc

Founder of the Zito Trust to raise awareness of the problems with the implementation of community care policy, Jayne studied fine art and art therapy and became a manager in mental health services in Hertfordshire. In 1992 her husband Jonathan was stabbed and killed at a tube station. Jayne terminated her studies in social work to successfully lobby for an inquiry into the care of the patient who killed her husband. The report was published in 1994 (Ritchie et al.). The Zito Trust closed in 2009, and Jayne has trained as a counsellor and is a non-executive member of the Devon and Cornwall Police Authority. *Co-author of the sections on independent sector and voluntary organisations in the chapter on victims and survivors 28.*

Acknowledgements

It is, as ever, impossible to express sufficient gratitude to everyone who has helped us in some way with this book. Our generous and gracious authors are only the most visible. So many people, from so many walks of life have contributed – some have stimulated us with as little as a passing comment, many have helped with much, much more. Although in forensic psychiatry we are profoundly concerned with public safety, still our patients and offenders who may need help from mental health services have to be at the centre of everything, and we thank all those among them who, knowingly or not, have inspired us to think and work harder towards collating what we know more effectively and clarifying the areas where there is still so much to be done.

After that, our gratitude spills out in no particular order – as the weeks have passed, different people would seem to top the list, and it is frustrating that we are not going to be able to name them all. First equal, though, we must thank our long suffering publishing teams and our readers – and simultaneously apologise for the length of time it has taken us to produce the completed book. It was our original publisher – Butterworth Heinemann – that set us off with the plea that we update the first edition 'it won't take long, most of it is already there and it simply needs modification to bring it up-to-date'. We resisted at first, so it is hard to say exactly when the process started, but we probably began serious work on the second edition about 10 years ago. Our book has, therefore, now taken a year or two longer to produce the *King James's Bible*! Much of the slow pace was occasioned, to our frustration, by the inordinate delay in the ever promised new mental health legislation for England & Wales, caught in a battle between law and order minded politicians and the so-called *Alliance* – of many clinical and legal professionals, criminal justice and social agencies, third sector organisations and a wide range of patients, other service users, including survivors of criminal attacks, and their families or carers. Chapter 3 explains.

There have, however, been other reasons, too, for the apparent tardiness. One important one is the low status given to textbook writing by universities, where it seems most shocking, and many other relevant employers. This problem was not present 20 years ago, but now potential authors are often instructed by universities to stop wasting time on textbooks and write research grant applications instead. One or two potential authors, therefore, felt they had to decline project-textbook, but most of those invited did contribute and our gratitude is all the greater for the fact that they all worked long and hard out of their regular working days to provide the text. We had countless midnight email conversations over tricky points, and are less amazed that delivery dates fell behind than that any were achieved at all. The most important characteristics that this edition has in common with the first edition are that we have tried to recruit experts of the highest calibre and then work through an iterative process so that we could both truly understand what each had to convey and present a coherent thread through sometimes different, sometimes frankly conflicting, approaches in this complex field. We have felt both privileged and, briefly, wise as we completed hard debated chapters. We hope that some of this excitement remains for readers.

The good-news part of the length of time we have all taken over the text is that so much has changed and moved forward, so, in a good way, our Butterworth Heinemann friends were proved wrong. There are very few places in the textbook where we were able simply to do a little gentle updating. Almost all parts of the chapters with more-or-less original titles have been completely rewritten, and there are now richly informative chapters which were unthinkable given the state of knowledge in the field 20 years ago. The genetic influences chapter is probably the most technically difficult of these, but represents enormous strides in understanding mechanisms even if it will be a while before this work will progress to testable models for intervention. Developments in the measurement of disorders of brain structure and function have similarly meant that an area that formed a small part of one chapter in the first edition now has a full chapter in the second. It is, however, widespread development in service and treatment provisions that has brought the work on intellectual disability to a similar level. Other reasons for completely new chapters are less happy – older people are beginning to swell criminal statistics and need specific attention. More terribly, there have been such errors, dysfunctions or frank abuses of position by professionals expected to work towards the health and safety of all with whom they come into contact that we thought it important to consider how we can recognise difficulties at an earlier stage and, as far as possible, avoid breaching professional standards ourselves. These ventures have all added to the production time. Nevertheless, we remember with gratitude all the work our first edition authors did, because without that pioneering effort we would have had nothing at all to build on. Some of those authors are still clearly with us.

Acknowledgements

Traces of the rest who could no longer write, for a whole range of reasons, not least that a few have sadly died, remain in the text and we have tried to acknowledge them all, chapter by chapter. All first edition authors are listed in small type in the heading for each relevant chapter; we remain in their debt.

The publishing world seems to be in a constant state of turmoil. Since this project began we have been working with Butterworth Heinemann, Edward Arnold, Hodder, and now Taylor & Francis. Our longest spell was with Hodder and we are particularly grateful for the help and encouragement given by first Philip Norman, and then Caroline Makepeace of that company. They were ably assisted by Clare Patterson, then Joanna Silman. We mourned the fact that Susan Devlin, who had nurtured us through the first edition, had long since moved on, but then Philip and Caroline kept us going. Caroline went with the book to join Taylor & Francis, and we are delighted that she will share its final emergence with us. She also brought in further essential help. Carolyn Holleyman was our copyeditor. Sarah Binns was the indefatigable, wise and wonderfully sensitive reader of the first proofs. Mimi Williams has steered us through all the final proof entries to an accurate rendition of the finally agreed text, and a real book. Sybil Ihrig compiled the index. A complication of the digital age is that rarely do these people, working on such vital technical tasks, meet one another, or us, and the work is accomplished 'online' and in various countries. All of them have coped cheerfully with this cyber world, although we know that from time to time our pedantry and slowness have created frustrations. We thank them so much.

Back in our offices, two psychology undergraduates – Emma Smith and Katie Sambrooks – worked tirelessly checking references. Secretarial help is a scarce resource, so that has put a heavy burden on those who have worked with us. In Cardiff University's School of Medicine, Katarina Dienerova became a founder member of the team, helping with the initial structuring and mailings to prospective authors; Ceri Allen has subsequently helped with chapter manuscripts and references and Sue Cody added to our sense of security in the final versions of text with her proofreading skills. In the allied clinical services, at the Caswell clinic, Karina Sansom has been an unfailing support. They have all been essential to the task.

At a time when books are so little value in terms of university ratings, we are very grateful to the support we have had from the Institute of Psychological Medicine and Clinical Neurosciences in the School of Medicine of Cardiff University, and particularly Professor Michael Owen as head of department. He might be surprised to hear that his approach to the science of the genetics of mental disorder was an inspiration, but it has been. We are constantly inspired by other colleagues, too, in all parts of this country and others, as will be evident from the geographical spread of our authorship, but in clinical practice, influences are necessarily closer. Closest of all have been Tegwyn Williams, Emma Clarke, Jan Hillier, Gaynor Jones, Mark Janas, Sian Koppel, and Roger Thomas, our continuing professional development (CPD) peer group. One of us is more in evidence than the other, but we have both learned a lot from you all, and only ask that this book may count for a few CPD points! Our psychology colleagues, led by Ruth Bagshaw, our social work colleagues, led variously by Heather Edwards and Ray Elliott, our nursing colleagues, for most of the time led by Mike Sullivan, and our occupational therapy colleagues, again for most of the time, led by Sian Dolling have all, contributed in this way, too, while the Wales Strategic Review of Secure Mental Health Services came just at the right time for enhancing our knowledge and thinking about this area, under Ted Unsworth's tirelessly diplomatic and wise leadership.

We return to our authors. They have laboured hard for very little reward other than joining in the project they must have believed in at some level. Presumably, like us, they think that education is still of prime importance and good practice depends upon accurate and detailed knowledge. On this occasion we were even privileged to have among our company the president of the Royal College of Psychiatrists. We give special emphasis to child development and its management in this book as it is the key to good forensic psychiatry and Professor Sue Bailey had written an important piece for *A Handbook of Forensic Mental Health* which she was willing to use as the basis of our chapter on child and adolescent forensic psychiatry. We are therefore extremely grateful also to her co-author, Bill Kerslake, and especially to Keith Soothill as lead editor of that handbook and Willan, the publishers, for permission to transcribe portions of that text and a diagram into our chapter 19. In that chapter we have also copied a diagram from Professor John Muncie's book *Youth Crime, third edition* with John Muncie's kind permission. We have also copied a large section from Helen Marshall's translation of the paper by Robert Gaupp called 'The scientific significance of the case of Ernst Wagner' from Hirsch and Shepherd's *Themes and Variations in European Psychiatry*, with the kind permission of Professor Stephen Hirsch.

Finally we acknowledge the care and compassion for mentally disordered offenders which can be shown by the criminal justice system. Knowing that mental health workers are not alone in wanting to contribute to the relief of suffering and a simultaneous prevention of crime keeps us going when so many difficulties, such as small and reducing resources and rejecting attitudes, might otherwise drive us to give up. A judge's remarks made when sentencing a young perpetrator of a very serious crime illustrate this and are worth placing on long-term record:

> *I can only hope, by the time that you are considered for release, that some of the people who should be responsible for your care in the community take their responsibility and do so. I say that because I remain concerned that your mental illness causes you to be a serious risk to the public and also because, as with anyone else, you deserve to have the best care and treatment you can possibly expect while co-operating with those authorities. Therefore, I hope that whoever formulates your release, will bear those concepts in mind, understanding that it may be, as a result of the number of times you have come before the court and the pattern that you have established, that you need more care and more supervision than had originally been envisaged."* Nadine Radford QC (with permission).

Pamela Taylor and John Gunn

Preface

This textbook is intended to be of practical assistance in the assessment, management and treatment of offenders with mental disorder and other victims. It is not a comprehensive encyclopaedia, and is certainly not the last word on our subject, but it does try to draw extensively on the growing body of knowledge which is relevant and available. Inevitably it is biased. First, it has a medical bias, because we are doctors, and so are many of our authors. Other professionals have contributed substantially, and we are very attached to a multidisciplinary perspective, but it would be disingenuous and unfair to other disciplines to pretend that the prevailing view in this book is anything other than a medical one. The second bias affects parts of the book more than others. An essential component of forensic psychiatry is the engagement between psychiatry and the law. Criminal and mental health law, areas of legal practice which most concern us, to some extent the culture which underpins these areas, and the services which relate to them are country bound. Many of the authors are from the United Kingdom, and so the emphasis in the legal and service chapters is on the situation in England and Wales, with commentaries from other parts of the UK. UK legislation and common law practices have influenced many other systems around the world, and, notwithstanding the major differences in court practice, UK legislation has more recently been increasingly subject to wider European principles, particularly with respect to human and legal rights. Nevertheless, although we have tried to draw out alternative practices wherever relevant, all through the text, and have a substantial international comparative chapter, it has to be acknowledged that, rather than offering sufficient expositions of work in any other country we can only achieve with certainty one important purpose here – that of reminding us all that there are many ways of legislating and providing services, and no single 'right way' of proceeding. The more theoretical and disorder based chapters, by contrast, draw fully on international literature.

In addition to theory and evidence, we, and many of our clinically trained authors, draw on our experience to try and make at least some links, as we would in clinical practice, between the evidence base from groups as reported in the literature and the evidence base from the individual in front of us at the time of an assessment or in treatment. This, however, means some other biases – according to our range of expertise. Most of the text is intended for forensic clinicians who work with adults. It is essential that we consider child and adolescent psychiatry, and we do so, but this inevitably means that the 'super specialty' of forensic child and adolescent psychiatry is much less thoroughly covered. It is unfortunate that, to some extent, this coincidentally reflects the current position in the UK; specialist forensic child and adolescent hospital facilities are seriously underprovided. This is also true for forensic psychotherapy – another 'super specialty', of great importance to maintaining the effectiveness of treating clinicians in this field as to treating the offender-patients; in this case the specialist services tend to be geographically limited. We touch, too, on vital overlaps with other recognised specialties – the psychiatry of intellectual disability and of old age – and expert areas such as the treatment of substance misuse disorders.

We have a complete chapter on victims. We see them as at the heart of forensic psychiatry. The prevention of harm to others is one important aim of forensic psychiatry. Victims not only have their own set of medico-legal problems, but some of them turn their fears and their anger back on to society in antisocial reactions. Some adults have a complete personality change as a result of trauma. Victimization during childhood often seriously affects the development of the growing personality. Most offender-patients are themselves victims in one way or another.

Although we acknowledge the medical bias in the text, it is not written exclusively for medical practitioners. We aim to provide information which will also be helpful to nurses, psychologists, social workers, probation officers, lawyers, politicians and police officers, among others. This is a tall order, but we believe that, for example, it is useful for a probation officer to have ready access to a medical perspective. We urge our students and trainees to read into other disciplines. We hope that members of other disciplines will urge their students to read this book. We hope, too, that professionals who are dealing with a healthier population than we usually do will find some assistance from a closer understanding of the extent of the psychopathology, its development and management among many offenders. Other aspirations are that forensic psychiatry will begin to contribute to the prevention of disease and to the prevention of a part of the spectrum of antisocial behaviour. This could not be, however, without effective communication throughout psychiatry, with other clinical disciplines and with other relevant agencies, promoting mutual understanding and cooperation. Effective multidisciplinary and multi-agency work emerges from the advantage of real differences between the disciplines only when their members understand each other's strengths and limitations, and are confident in this knowledge and in comfortable, accurate and regular communication.

A comment is needed on one or two matters of style. First, author attributions: it has been impossible to acknowledge everybody who has contributed ideas and inspiration to this book. We have tried, however, to attribute correctly and fairly everyone who has written something original for the book. Some people have done much more than others and all have been subject to editing, mainly to try and minimise repetition in a lengthy volume, but also to achieve consensus where possible. A consensus approach was harder with some chapters than others, but where more extensive negotiation was needed to agree the script, we think we finished with much better chapters than ever we would have had if left to write the material ourselves and without challenge; we ourselves have been learning throughout the process. The attributions at the heads of the chapters are intended to reflect this. Most contributors are listed in alphabetical order at the beginning of each chapter to which they contributed, but within the chapters we have tried to avoid demarcations. We also introduce the authors in alphabetical order at the front of the book, and here provide a clearer indication of their contribution. This second edition of the text is largely new, and some of the chapters did not exist at all in the first edition, but we remain grateful to all the first edition authors who paved the way with us for this volume. Many were brave enough to write with us again, some are long since retired and some no longer with us at all. We have also listed all of them at the front of each chapter to which they originally contributed.

Our referencing is based on the Harvard system. We have included (we hope) a complete list at the end of the book giving full journal titles and publishers' names where appropriate. Readers should also be able to use this list as an author/article index. 'Cases cited' are referred to in the text by an identifying name. This name may have no meaning or significance beyond this textbook, but it will lead to the alphabetical list of legal references, which can also be used as an index. Where appropriate some of the references are given as World Wide Web addresses. We are conscious of the ephemeral nature of such references but some materials, for example, some government documents, are published only in this format. In any case we urge readers to use search engines (e.g. Google) and Wikipedia – to amplify their studies. Both have limitations, and Wikipedia acknowledges some inaccuracies. Both are useful for initiating searches for knowledge, but students and other surfers must not assume that if information cannot be retrieved by computer it does not exist! Some journals are now archiving all their old material for computer access but they are in the minority. We have included many important references which still require a visit to library shelves.

This edition has the advantage that it is published on paper and electronically. The electronic version includes links which should give direct access to the Web by clicking on them. We say 'should' because web pages are ephemeral – here today, gone tomorrow. UK government departments, for example, almost pride themselves on constantly changing their web sites. As we wrote the book links disappeared, web pages changed. All we can say is that the links given worked the last time we checked them. If a link is now missing or 'broken', a conventional search will usually find a more recent address or a message that the page has been deleted.

Abbreviations have been obsessionally listed and defined. This is partly to help non-medical readers but, as acronyms have multiplied, we found we needed them ourselves. Sometimes we have been quite conflicted about the use of abbreviations. An example is the use of PD for personality disorder. It is so much shorter to write this, but we have a sense that this is an abbreviation which may serve as a dehumanising device, and it reinforces reification (see Introduction page 8), so we have used this abbreviation sparingly. Otherwise we have tended to follow standard practice of spelling out a word or phrase in full on its first use in the text, and then using its abbreviation.

Our references give a reasonably comprehensive entrance into the factual and academic literature pertinent to forensic psychiatry. They omit, however, that wider literature which should be read for other insights: plays, novels, poetry and opera. There would be so much to include here – everything from Shakespeare's *Othello*, to Pushkin's *Queen of Spades*, from Ibsen's *Hedda Gabler* to Fowles's *The Collector*. Murray Cox, for many years a consultant psychotherapist at Broadmoor hospital and an honorary research fellow of the Shakespeare Institute at the University of Birmingham, never tired of using Shakespeare to illuminate inner processing of ideas and feelings – on the part of patients and observers, including therapists (Cox and Theilgaard, 1994). Furthermore, he was instrumental in getting leading national theatrical companies to perform Shakespeare for the patients (Cox, 1992), after which the actors joined groups with patients and staff to discuss something as difficult as their responses to *King Lear*. Gordon et al. (2007) considered the legacy of this work to that date.

In the preface to our first edition we included an extract from the remarkable early nineteenth century English poem *Peter Grimes* by George Crabbe (e.g. Opie and Opie, 1983).

He fished by water and he filched by land; ...

But no success could please his cruel soul,

He wished for one to trouble and control,

He wanted some obedient boy to stand

And bear the blow of his outrageous hand,

And hoped to find in some propitious hour

A feeling creature subject to his power ...

Some few in town observed in Peter's trap

A boy, with jacket blue and woollen cap; ...

Pinned, beaten, cold, pinched, threatened and abused –

His efforts punished and his food refused – ...

The savage master grinned in horrid glee ...

For three sad years the boy his tortures bore,

And then his pains and trials were no more ...

Another boy with equal ease was found,

The money granted and the victim bound

And what his fate? – One night it chanced he fell

From the boat's mast and perished in her well,

Then came a boy, of manners soft and mild – ...

His liquor failed and Peter's wrath arose –

No more is known – the rest we must suppose, ...

The mayor himself with tone severe replied –

'Henceforth with thee shall never boy abide,' ...

The sailors' wives would stop him in the street,

And say, 'Now, Peter, thou'st no boy to beat' ...

He growled an oath, and in an angry tone

Cursed the whole place and wished to be alone ...

Cold nervous tremblings shook his sturdy frame,

And strange disease – he couldn't say the name,

Wild were his dreams, and oft he rose in fright,

Furious he grew, and up the country ran,

And there they seized him – a distempered man.

Him we received, and to a parish-bed,

Followed and cursed, the groaning man was led ...

The priest attending, found he spoke at times

As one alluding to his fears and crimes; ...

'But, gazing on the spirits, there was I.

They bade me leap to death, but I was loath to die:

And every day, as sure as day arose,

Would these three spirits meet me ere the close'...

...– but here he ceased and gazed

on all around, affrightened and amazed; ...

Then dropped exhausted and appeared at rest ...

Then with an inward, broken voice he cried,

'again they come' and muttered as he died.

Thus is set out the career of one who might now be imprisoned, so that psychiatrists can declare that he has 'no formal mental illness' and is quite unsuitable for the parish bed. Clearly, this was based on an astute real life observation; a man who had an abnormal relationship with his father, became a young delinquent, found a way of acquiring young boys and sadistically controlling and then killing them and, when reviled, became increasingly isolated, then psychotic, ending his life in an institution. This story is so powerful that it has also been dramatized in operatic form, under the same title, by Benjamin Britten and the librettist Montagu Slater.

Here we also want to draw attention to the remarkable American author Herman Melville, perhaps best known for *Moby Dick* published in 1851; Melville also wrote some remarkable novellas which illustrate truths which are not always immediately noticed in patients. Perhaps the most obvious of these short stories is *Bartleby, the Scrivener*. Bartleby is a clerk who works for a Manhattan lawyer who is engaged to do nothing but copy manuscripts. This suits Bartleby perfectly and all is well until he is asked to deviate a little and do some proofreading. He simply replies 'I would prefer not to' and it is soon apparent that his limitation leads to conflict within others; the narrator, his employer, clearly has some sympathy for the man, but eventually finds him intolerable. Finally, the pressure to be flexible leads to the vulnerable Bartleby's psychological collapse. He ends up doing nothing and sleeping rough, finally dying of starvation. The story is a great stimulus to psychological discussion as to his condition.

Melville also has another psychological novella up his sleeve, this time concerned with a range of complex emotions present on a British warship in the Napoleonic Wars. *Billy Budd* is a Christ-like character who is stigmatised by his stammer which can lead to outbursts of rage. The story also deals with homosexual jealousy and bullying by a cruel Master at Arms of limited ability. Billy, unable to defend himself verbally, has a fit of rage and kills the Master at Arms, who has wrongly accused him. The apparently fair-minded captain is tormented by his conflict between his humanity and his duty to naval law. As with the Crabbe poem, Benjamin Britten picked up the power of this story and brilliantly portrayed it in an opera of the same name. A 2010 production of the opera at Glyndebourne was reviewed in *The Independent* by Anna Picard in the following terms:

Pressed into service on HMS Indomitable, blithely ignorant of the mutinous associations of the name of his former ship, The Rights o' Man, Billy Budd doesn't know how old he is. Abandoned at birth, he is a motherless child – cousin to Peter Grimes's workhouse prentices. ......What is Billy's defect? His stammer? His innocence? Why is Claggart set on his destruction? .... (Michael) Grandage's handsome, disciplined, period staging returns to the interior moral tragedy of Herman Melville's novella, eschewing the "sexual discharge gone evil" that librettist E M Forster believed to be the core of Claggart's ...... malevolence. De-sexing his sadism puts the focus on institutional brutality: the floggings, the press gang, the tension of a mass of men adrift in a vessel with no purpose but to attack an enemy few of them will ever see....... my angry contempt....was for the Captain, Vere. He exemplified Edmund Burke's statement: The only thing necessary for the triumph of evil is for good men to do nothing.

These books and operas seem particularly relevant for forensic psychiatry. When studying textbooks and Acts of Parliament has induced lethargy and boredom, trainee and specialist alike could do worse than immerse him or herself in Britten's operas, Melville's stories and other such works.

John Gunn

Pamela J. Taylor

References

Cox M. (1992) *Shakespeare comes to Broadmoor*. Jessica Kingsley: London.

Cox M and Theilgaard A (1994) *Shakespeare as prompter*. Jessica Kingsley: London.

Gordon H, Rylance M, and Rowell G (2007) Psychotherapy, religion and drama: Murray Cox and his legacy for offender patients. *Criminal Behaviour and Mental Health* 17: 8–14.

Melville, H (1924) *Billy Budd, Sailor*, as Volume XIII of the Standard Edition of *Melville's Complete Works* ed. by Raymond Weaver, Constable & Co, London.

Melville, H (1851) *Moby Dick*: The Whale Richard Bentley: London.

Melville, H (1853) *Bartleby, the Scrivner, a Story of Wall Street, Putnam's Magazine*, New York.

Opie I and Opie P (1983) *The Oxford Book of Narrative Verse*, Oxford University Press: Oxford.

Picard A (2010) Michael Grandage's handsome production of Britten's brutal classic is as good as opera can get. *The Independent*, Sunday May 30.

Legislation*

Australia
Mental Health Services Act 1974 (Queensland) (**134**)
New South Wales Mental Health Act 1983 (**134**)
Crimes (Mental Impairment and Fitness to Be Tried) Act 1997 (Victoria) (**130**)

Canada
Criminal Law Amendment Act 1977 (**116**)

Denmark
Enforcement of Sentences Act 2000 (**140**)
Mental Health Act (1989, revised 1999 & 2007) (**135**)
Tribunals Courts and Enforcement Act 2007 (**69**)

European legislation
European Convention on Human Rights and Fundamental Freedoms 1950 (**20, 57, 80, 87, 99, 104, 106, 107, 133, 660, appendix 1**)
Human Rights Act 1998 (**57**)

New Zealand
Children, Young Persons and their Families Act 1989
Mental Health (Compulsory Assessment and Treatment) Act 1992 (**479**)
Intellectual Disability (Community Care and Rehabilitation) Act 2003 (**134**)

Republic of Ireland
Mental Health Act 2001 (**106, 107, 108, 110**)
Criminal Law (Insanity) Act 2006 (**107, 108, 109, 110**)

South Africa
Criminal Procedure Act 1977 (**127, 130, 131**)
Criminal Matters Amendment Act 1998 (**127**)
Mental Health Care Act 2002 (**128**)

UK
Act to Prevent the Murthering of Bastard Children 1624 (**28, 237**)
Bill of Rights 1688 (**290**)
Shoplifting Act 1699 (**290**)
Gin Act 1736 (**441**)
Act for Preserving the Health of Prisoners in Gaol 1774 (**626**)
Act for the Safe Custody of Insane Persons Charged with Offences 1800 (**589**)
Lunatics Act 1800 (**24, 620**)
Irish Lunatics Asylums Act 1845 (**86, 616**)
Lunacy Act 1845 (**86**)
Juvenile Offenders Act 1847 (**500**)
Judicature Act 1873 (**19**)
Lunacy Regulation (Ireland) Act 1873 (**106**)
Habitual Drunkards Act 1879 (**442**)
Summary Jurisdiction Act 1879 (**474**)
Inebriates Act 1898 (**442**)
Probation of Offenders Act 1907 (**35**)
Children Act 1908 (**474, 479**)
Crime Prevention Act 1908 (**474**)
Marriage of Lunatics Act 1911 (**106**)
National Insurance Act 1911 (**431**)
Workmen's Compensation Act 1908 (**431**)
Infanticide Act 1922 (**28, 510**)
Mental Treatment Act 1930 (**57, 87**)
Children and Young Persons Act 1933 (**479**)
Infanticide Act 1938 (**28, 29, 103, 163, 510**)
Infanticide Act (Northern Ireland) 1939 (**103**)
Crown Proceedings Act 1947 (**104**)
Children Act 1948 (**475**)
Criminal Justice Act 1948 (**475, 588**)
Mental Health Act (Northern Ireland) 1948 (**87**)
Air Force Act 1955 (**103**)
Army Act 1955 (**103**)
Homicide Act 1957 (**26, 29, 30, 31, 33, 96, 163, 637**)
Naval Discipline Act 1957 (**103**)
Mental Health Act 1959 (**58–61, 67–69, 87, 442**)
Mental Health (Scotland) Act 1960 (**87, 90**)
Criminal Justice Act 1961 (**479**)
Mental Health Act (Northern Ireland) 1961 (**87**)
Children and Young Persons Act 1963 (**475**)
Criminal Justice (Insane Persons) (Jersey) Law 1964 (**105**)
Criminal Procedure (Insanity) Act 1964 (**24, 72**)
Police Act 1964 (**620**)
Criminal Justice Act (Northern Ireland) 1966 (**102, 103**)
Abortion Act 1967 (**622**)
Police Act 1996 (**620**)
Criminal Justice Act 1967 (**41**)
Children and Young Persons (Northern Ireland) Act 1968 (**481**)
Medicines Act 1968 (**453**)
Theft Act 1968 (**19, 21, 270**)
Children and Young Persons Act 1969 (**475–479**)
Mental Health (Jersey) Law 1969 (**106**)
Misuse of Drugs Act 1971 (**449–453**)

---

*This list itemises the legislation referred to in the text. It is in chronological order within the jurisdictions shown to illustrate the way in which law has grown in forensic psychiatry.

Naval Discipline Act 1971 (**103**)

Bail Act 1976 (**23**)

Race Relations Act 1976 (**635**)

Theft Act 1978 (**19, 270**)

Armed Forces Act 1981 (**104**)

Criminal Attempts Act 1981 (**476**)

Criminal Justice Act 1982 (**476**)

Mental Health Act 1983 (**13, 19, 38, 52, chapter 3, 87, 90, 96, 101, 102, 106, 315, 414, 416, 442, 590, 600, 632, 698, 708, 709**)

Mental Health Act 1983 (amended) (**19, 23–27, 37, 38, 40, 48, chapter 3, 87, 159, 164, 165, 261, 314, 477, 482, 491, 551, 594, 620, 623**)

Child Abduction Act 1984 (**504**)

Mental Health (Scotland) Act 1984 (**87, 90, 101**)

Police and Criminal Evidence Act 1984 (PACE) (**125, 160, 331, 620, 621**)

Prosecution of Offences Act 1985 (**49**)

Sporting Events (Control of Alcohol etc.) 1985 (**441**)

Legal Aid (Scotland) Act 1986 (**89**)

Mental Health (Northern Ireland) Order 1986 (**102, 103**)

Crown Proceedings (Armed Forces) Act 1987 (**104**)

Access to Medical Reports Act 1988 (**665**)

Road Traffic Act 1988 (**441**)

Children Act 1989 (**68, 465, 479, 481**)

Police and Criminal Evidence (Northern Ireland) Order 1989 (**655**)

Computer Misuse Act 1990 (**620**)

Criminal Justice Act 1991 (**158, 477**)

Criminal Procedure (Insanity and Unfitness to Plead) Act 1991 (**25**)

Criminal Justice and Public Order Act 1994 (**477**)

Police and Magistrates' Courts Act 1994 (**620**)

Criminal Procedure (Scotland) Act 1995 (**94–99, 612**)

Criminal Justice (Northern Ireland) Order 1996 (**102**)

Police Act 1996 (**620**)

Crime (Sentences) Act 1997 (**46, 48, 65**)

Police Act 1997 (**620**)

Sex Offenders Act 1997 (**41, 99, 645**)

Crime and Disorder Act 1998 (**44, 478, 479, 703**)

Data Protection Act 1998 (**622, 662, 665**)

Human Rights Act 1998 (**20, 57, 63, 104, 591, 660, 662**)

Human Rights Act 1998 (Commencement No. 2) Order 2000 (**660**)

Youth Justice and Criminal Evidence Act 1999 (**159, 160, 478**)

Adults with Incapacity (Scotland) Act 2000 (**89, 91, 93, 315**)

Criminal Justice and Courts Services Act 2000 (**41, 619**)

Human Rights (Jersey) Law 2000 (**105**)

Powers of Criminal Courts (Sentencing) Act 2000 (**44, 47, 479**)

Anti-terrorism, Crime and Security Act 2001 (**637**)

Criminal Justice and Police Act 2001 (**441**)

Mental Health Act (Scotland) 2001

The Misuse of Drugs Regulations 2001 (**453**)

Criminal Justice Act 2003 (**36, 40–48, 115, 145, 452, 453, 479, 588, 606, 619, 636–644**)

Criminal Justice (Scotland) Act 2003 (**88, 96, 99, 115, 548, 651**)

Mental Health (Care and Treatment) (Scotland) Act 2003 (**88–97, 106, 612, 615, 652, 667**)

Sexual Offences Act 2003 (**41, 49, 99, 243, 248, 714**)

Children Act 2004 (**479, 480**)

Domestic Violence, Crime and Victims Act 2004 (**24, 25, 27, 68, 645, 663, 709–711**)

Management of Offenders etc. (Scotland) Act 2005 (**100, 654**)

Mental Capacity Act 2005 (**56–67, 77–85, 166, 315**)

Serious Organised Crime and Police Act 2005 (**621**)

Armed Forces Act 2006 (**103**)

Fraud Act 2006 (**270**)

Police and Justice Act 2006 (**620**)

Offender Management Act 2007 (**638, 639**)

Mental Health Act 2007 (**chapter 3, 106, 314, 383, 401, 709**)

Tribunals, Courts and Enforcement Act 2007 (**69**)

Criminal Justice and Immigration Act 2008 (**40, 41**)

Coroners and Justice Act 2009 (**29, 31, 36, 55, 163**)

Criminal Justice and Licensing (Scotland) Act 2010 (**87, 94–96**)

Statutory instruments (UK)

Community Legal Service (Financial) Regulations 2000 (as amended) (**69**)

First-Tier Tribunal (Health Education and Social Care Chamber) Rules 2008 (SI 2008 No 2699) (for England) (**70**)

Mental Health Review Tribunal for Wales Rules 2008 (SI 2008 No 2705) (**70**)

HM Government Circular (UK)

Home Office Circular (1995) No.12 (**23**)

USA

Lanterman–Petris–Short Act (California) 1969 (**122**)

Revised Statutes, South Dakota, Criminal Code 27A-1-1 1987 (**121**)

Jacob Wetterling Crimes against Children and Sexually Violent Offender Registration Act 1994, Public Law 103-322 1994 (**146, 645**)

List of Abbreviations

5-HIAA	5-hydroxy-indole acetic acid
5-HT	5-hydroxytryptamine/serotonin
5-HTT	5HT transporter
A	adnenine, one of the four nitrogenous bases in the repeating units (nucleotides) in a strand of DNA
A&E	Accident and Emergency departments (UK)
a^2	relative contribution of additive genetic influences on a phenotype
AA	Alcoholics Anonymous
AAFS	American Academy of Forensic Sciences
AAI	Adult Attachment Interview
AAPL	American Academy of Psychiatry and the Law
ABA	applied behavioural analysis
ABS	Australian Bureau of Statistics
AC	approved clinician
ACC	Association of County Councils
ACCT	Assessment, Care in Custody and Teamwork system (prisons in England and Wales)
ACE	Assessment of clinical expertise
ACE	Assessment Case Management and Evaluation System (Gibbs, 1999; Raynor et al., 2000)
ACGME	Accreditation Council for Graduate Medical Education
ACMD	Advisory Council on the Misuse of Drugs (UK)
ACPO	Association of Chief Police Officers
ACSeSS	Admission Criteria of Secure Services Schedule
ACT	acceptance and commitment therapy
ACT	Assertive Community Treatment
ADH	alcohol dehydrogenase
ADHD	attention deficit hyperactivity disorder
ADSS	Association of Directors of Social Services
A + E	accident and emergency
ÆSOP study	Aetiology and Ethnicity in Schizophrenia and other Psychosis study (Europe)
AIAQ	Anger, Irritability, and Aggression Questionnaire
AIDS	acquired immunodeficiency syndrome
AIP	adaptive information processing
AKA	also known as
ALDH	aldehyde dehydrogenase
ALI	American Law Institute
AMA	American Medical Association
AMHP	approved mental health professional
AMP	approved medical practitioner – training and special experience in the diagnosis and treatment of mental disorder
AP	antisocial potential
APA	American Psychiatric Association
ASB	antisocial behaviour
ASBO	antisocial behaviour order
ASP	affected sibling pairs
ASPD	antisocial personality disorder
ASRO	addressing substance related offending
ASSET	Young Offender Assessment Profile

ASW	approved social worker
ATD	acute tryptophan depletion
AUC	area-under-the-curve, a statistical measure of receiver operator characteristics (ROC)
AUDIT	Alcohol Use Disorders Identification Test (Saunders et al., 1993)
BAP	British Association of Psychopharmacology
BC	Before Christ
BCS	British Crime Survey
BDH	Buss–Durkee Hostility Inventory
BDNF	brain-derived neurotrophic factor
BIS	Barrett Impulsivity Scale
BMA	British Medical Association
BME	black and/or minority ethnic status
BMJ	*British Medical Journal*, renamed *BMJ*
BNF	British National Formulary (http://BNF.org)
BPD	borderline personality disorder
BPRS	Brief Psychiatric Rating Scale (Overall and Gorham, 1962)
BVS	Brøset Violence Checklist (Almvik and Woods, 1998)
BWS	battered woman syndrome
c	*circa* (Latin) = around or approximately
C	cytosine, one of the four nitrogenous bases in the repeating units (nucleotides) in a strand of DNA
CALM	Controlling Anger and Learning to Manage it, a CBT based treatment programme
CAMHS	child and adolescent mental health services
CARAT	Counselling Assessment Referral Advice and Throughcare service (for substance misusers in prison)
CARAT	Counselling, Assessment, Referral and Advice
CART	classification and regression trees
CASC	clinical assessment of skills and competencies (a tool)
CASK	caregiver associated serial killings
CAST	Creative and Supportive Trust (a voluntary organization)
CaStANET	Cardiff Study of All Wales and North West of England Twins
CAST-MR	Competence Assessment to Stand Trial – Mental Retardation (Everington and Luckasson, 1992)
CAT	cognitive analytical therapy (Ryle, 1993)
CAT	computerized axial tomography
CATIE	Clinical Antipsychotic Trials of Intervention Effectiveness (US National Institute of Mental Health funded trials of antipsychotic medication)
CBD	case based discussion
CBNT	cognitive behaviour nursing therapy
CBT	cognitive behaviour therapy
CCJS	Centre for Crime and Justice Studies
CCT	client-centred therapy
CCT	completed certificate of training
CCTV	closed circuit television
CDRP	Crime and Disorder Reduction Partnership
CDVP	Thames Valley Community Domestic Violence Programme
CEMACH	the Confidential Enquiry into Maternal and Child Health
CESDI	Confidential Enquiry into Stillbirths and Deaths in Infancy
CGI-I	Clinical Global Impression Rating of Improvement
CHAID	Chi-squared automatic iteration detector, a statistical technique used in developing the COVR (*qv*)

CHIRRP	Canadian Hospitals Injury Reporting and Prevention Programme
CI	confidence interval, representing the generally accepted confidence limits in relation to an odds ratio
CIRCLE	Chart of Interpersonal Relations in Closed Living Environments
CISH	(National) Confidential Inquiry into Suicide and Homicide by People with Mental Illness (England and Wales)
CIS-R	Clinical Interview Schedule-Revised
CISS	Christo Inventory for Substance-misuse Services (Christo, 2000)
CJITs	Criminal Justice Integrated Teams
CJS	Criminal Justice System
CJ(s)A	Criminal Justice (Scotland) Act 2003
CL(I)A	Criminal Law (Insanity) Act
CM(T)	contingency management (therapy)
CNS	central nervous system
CNV	copy number variants
COMT	catechol-O-methyl transferase
CONI	Care of Next Infant scheme
COVR	The Classification of Violence Risk ©, (Monahan et al., 2005a)
CP	case presentation
CPA	Care Programme Approach (Department of Health, 1990b, 1995, 1999b)
CPD	continuing professional development
CPN	Community Psychiatric Nurse
CPR	Child Protection Register
CPR	Civil Procedure Rules
CPRS	Comprehensive Psychopathological Rating Scale (Åsberg et al., 1978)
CPS	Crown Prosecution Service
CP(s)A	Criminal Procedure (Scotland) Act (1995)
CPT	cognitive processing therapy (CPT)
CPT	Committee for the Prevention of Torture, Inhuman and Degrading Treatment or Punishment (Council of Europe)
CQC	Care Quality Commission
CRF	corticotrophin-releasing factor/hormone
CRS	Civil Registration System (Denmark)
CS	conditioned stimuli (see also US, unconditioned stimuli)
CSCP	Cognitive Self Change Programme
CSF/csf	cerebrospinal fluid
CT	cognitive therapy
CT	computerized tomography
CTO	Compulsory Treatment Order
CUDIT	Cannabis Use Disorders Identification Test (Adamson and Sellman, 2003)
CWSU	Cardiff Women's Safety Unit
DARE	Database of Abstracts of Reviews of Effects, a database of systematic reviews not confined to randomized controlled trials
DASA	Dynamic Appraisal of Situational Aggression (Ogloff and Daffern, 2006)
DAT	Drug Action Team
DBT	dialectical behaviour therapy
DC	District of Columbia
Dept.	department
DESNOS	Disorders of Extreme Stress Not Otherwise Specified
DFSA	drug-facilitated sexual assault
DH	Department of Health (England)

DHSS	Department of Health and Social Security (England)
DHSSPS	Department of Health, Social Services and Public Safety (Northern Ireland)
DIP	Drug Interventions Programme
DMP	Designated Medical Practitioner
DNA	deoxyribonucleic acid, which contains the genetic instructions for the development of living organisms
DoH	Department of Health (England)
DoJ	Department of Justice (Northern Ireland)
DOL	deprivation of liberty
doli incapa	incapable of crime (Latin)
DOM	Director of Offender Management
DPCR	Danish Psychiatric Central Register
DPP	Detention for Public Protection
DRROs	Drug Rehabilitation Requirement Orders (Criminal Justice Act 2003)
DSM	*Diagnostic and Statistical Manual*, the US based disease classification system, often referred to with a number as a suffix to indicate the edition (e.g. *DSM-II*, *DSM-III*, *DSM-III-R*, *DSM-IV*)
DSM-III-R	*Diagnostic and Statistical Manual*, 3rd edition revised.
DSM-IV	*Diagnostic and Statistical Manual* (of Mental Disorders), 4th edition (American Psychiatric Association, 1994)
DSM-IV TR	*Diagnostic and Statistical Manual* (of Mental Disorders) 4th edition revised
DSM-V	*Diagnostic and Statistical Manual of Mental Disorders,* 5th edition
DSPD	dangerous and severe personality disorder
DT	delirium tremens
DTI	diffusion tensor imaging
DTTOs	Drug Testing and Treatment Orders (Crime and Disorder Act 1998)
DUDIT	Drug Use Disorders Identification Test (Berman et al., 2005)
DVCV Act 2004	Domestic Violence, Crime and Victims Act 2004
DVLA	Driver and Vehicle Licensing Agency (UK)
DZ	dizygotic, twins developed from two different eggs
E	environment
e^2	Relative contribution of non-shared environmental influences on a phenotype
ECA	Epidemiologic Catchment Area study (USA)
ECF	Executive Cognitive Function
ECHR	European Convention on Human Rights or European Court of Human Rights according to context
ECS	The Exceptional Case Study, a US based study of assassins or people who threaten
ECT	electroconvulsive therapy
Ed./ed.	editor/edited
EE	expressed emotion
EEG	electroencephalogram, recording of the electrical traces of brain activity
e.g.	*exempli gratia*, Latin: = for example
EMCDDA	European Monitoring Centre for Drugs and Drug Addiction
EMDR	Eye Movement Desensitization and Reprocessing
EMG	electromyography, recording of the electrical traces of skeletal muscle activity
EPA	Enduring Power of Attorney
EPQ	Eysenck Personality Questionnaire (Eysenck and Eysenck, 1975)
EPS	extrapyramidal signs
ER	emergency room
ERASOR	Estimate of Risk of Adolescent Sexual Offense Recidivism
et al.	and others (Latin)
ETS	Enhanced Thinking Skills (Clark, 2000)

EU	European Union
f	feminine/female
FACTS	Forensic Adolescent Consultation and Treatment Service
FDA	Federal Drugs Agency, the body in the USA which approves drugs for prescription in medical practice.
ff	and the following pages
FGA	first generation antipsychotic medication, also referred to as 'typical' or 'conventional' antipsychotics/neuroleptics (see Chapter 23)
FII	factitious and induced illness (Munchausen syndrome by proxy)
FIP	family intervention project
FIPTS	Forensic Intensive Psychological Treatment Service (S. London)
FIRS	Fire Interest Rating Scale
FME	forensic medical examiner (formally police surgeon)
FMH/fmh	forensic mental health
fMRI	functional magnetic resonance imaging
FOTRES	Forensic Operationalized Therapy/Risk Evaluation System (Urbaniok, 2009)
FSAS	Fire-Setting Assessment Schedule (Murphy and Clare, 1996)
FTAC	Fixated Threat Assessment Centre, a UK based unit for assessment and management of people who threaten, mainly public figures
FTD	frontotemporal dementia
g	gene
G	guanine, one of the four nitrogenous bases in the repeating units (nucleotides) in a strand of DNA
G/g	gram
GABA	gamma aminobutyric acid
GAF	Global Assessment of Functioning Scale
GAM-anon	Gamblers Anonymous
GHB	gamma-hydroxy butyric acid
GHQ12	General Health Questionnaire 12 (Goldberg, 1992)
GMC	General Medical Council
GnRH	gonadotropin-releasing hormone
GP	General Practitioner (primary care physician; family doctor) (UK)
GPI	general paralysis of the insane (a neuro-psychiatric complication of syphilis)
GSS	Gudjonsson Suggestibility Scales (Gudjonsson, 1997)
GWA	genome wide analysis
GWAS	genome wide association studies
HAC	Health Advisory Committee for the Prison Service
HCR-20	The Historical Clinical and Risk Management Scale
HIA syndrome	hyperactivity-impulsivity-attention deficit syndrome (Loeber, 1988)
HIPP	Health in Prisons Project (World Health Organization)
HIV	Human Immunodeficiency Virus
HIV/AIDS	acquired immunodeficiency syndrome, a disease of the human immune system
HM	Her Majesty's
HMAG	Her Majesty's Attorney General
HMCS	Her Majesty's Court Service
HMIC	Her Majesty's Inspectorate of Constabulary
HMIP	Her Majesty's Inspectorate of Prisons
HONOS	Health of the Nation Outcome Scale for Secure Services
HPA	hypothalamo-pituitary-adrenocortical (hormonal regulatory system)
HPRT	hypoxanthine guanine phosphoribosyl transferase
HRP	Healthy Relationships Programme

i.e.	*id est* Latin = that is to say
IAS	Institute of Alcohol Studies
ibid	*ibidem* Latin = same as above
ICAP theory	Integrated Cognitive Antisocial Potential theory (Farrington, 2005b)
ICD	International Classification of Diseases (World Health Organization)
ICD-10	International Classification of (Behavioural and Mental) Disorders, 10th edn (WHO, 1992)
ICT	Iterative Classification Tree, the outcome of iteration analyses as produced in development of the COVR (*qv*)
ICVS	International Crime Victims Survey
ID	intellectual disability
IDAP	Integrated Domestic Abuse Programme
IDTS	Integrated Drug Treatment System
IED	Intermittent Explosive Disorder
IIP	Interpersonal Problems (Horowitz et al., 1988)
IM	intramuscular
IMB	Independent Monitoring Board (formally, Board of Visitors, Northern Ireland)
IMCA	Independent Mental Capacity Advocate
IMHA	Independent Mental Health Advocate
IPCC	Independent Police Complaints Commission
IPDE	International Personality Disorder Examination (Loranger, 1999)
IPP	indeterminate sentence for public protection
IPT	Imaginal Provocation Test (Novaco, 1975; Taylor et al., 2004)
IPV	intimate partner violence
IQ	intelligence quotient
IRA	Irish Republican Army
IRS	Integrated Resettlement Support
ISTD	Institute for the Study and Treatment of Delinquency
IV	intravenous
JG	John Gunn
JP	Justice of the Peace
J SOAP	Juvenile Sex Offender Assessment Protocol
KJV	The King James version of the Bible
LD	linkage disequilibrium
LMV	Life Minus Violence programme
LOD	log of the odds that two gene loci are linked
LPA	Lasting Power of Attorney
LSD	lysergic acid diethylamide
LSR-I	Level of Service Inventory-Revised (Andrews and Bonta, 1995)
m	million
m	masculine/male
M	Morgan, 100 centiMorgans (cM), a measure of the distance between loci on a gene
MacCAT-T	MacArthur Competence Assessment Tool for Treatment (Grisso et al., 1997)
MACT	manual assisted cognitive (behavioural) therapy
MADS	Maudsley Assessment of Delusions Schedule (Taylor et al., 1994)
MAO	monoamine oxidase inhibitor, neurotransmitter (in two forms)
MAO-A	monoamine oxidase-A, a neurotransmitter
MAO-B	monoamine oxidase-B, a neurotransmitter
MAOI	monoamine oxidase inhibitors (a class of antidepressant drug)
MAO-LPR	monoamine oxidase linked polymorphic region
MAP	Maudsley Addiction Profile (Marsden et al., 1998)
MAPPA	multi-agency public protection arrangements

MAPPP	Multi-agency Public Protection Panel
MASRAM	Multi-Agency Sex Offender Risk Assessment and Management Arrangements (Northern Ireland)
MATCH (Project)	Matching Alcohol Treatments to Client Heterogeneity (a multi-site clinical trial based in Connecticut, USA)
MBT	mentalization based therapy (Bateman and Fonagy, 2006)
MCA	Mental Capacity Act 2005
MCMI-III	Millon Clinical Multiaxial Inventory, 3rd edition (Millon, 1994)
MCN	managed clinical network
mCPP	meta-chlorophenylpiperazine
MDO	mentally disordered offender
MDT	mode deactivation therapy
Met	methionine, one of the 20 essential proteinogenic amino acids in the genetic code
mg	milligram
MH/mh	mental health
MHA	Mental Health Act
MHA 1959	Mental Health Act 1959 (England and Wales)
MHA 1983	Mental Health Act 1983 (England and Wales)
MHA 2001	Mental Health Act 2001 (Ireland)
MH (C+T)(s)A	Mental Health (Care and Treatment) (Scotland) Act (2003)
MHA 2007	Mental Health Act 2007 (England and Wales)
MHAC	Mental Health Act Commission
MHC	major histocompatibility complex
MHO	Mental Health Officer
MHRB	Mental Health Review Board
MHRT	Mental Health Review Tribunal
MHT	Mental Health Tribunal, First Tier Tribunal (Mental Health)
MHTR	Mental Health Treatment Requirement, condition attached to a community sentence for offenders with mental disorder under the Criminal Justice Act 2003, England and Wales
MHU	Mental Health Unit
MI	motivational interviewing
MI5	Military Intelligence (Section 5) (mainly UK)
MI6	Military Intelligence (Section 6) Secret Intelligence Service (Worldwide)
mini-ACE	mini Assessment of clinical encounter
mini-PAT	mini peer assessment tool
ml	millilitre
MMPI	Minnesota Multiphasic Personality Inventory
MMPI/MMPI-II-PD	Minnesota Multiphasic Personality Inventory/MMPI-II-Personality Disorder Scales (Morey et al., 1985)
MOAS	Modified Overt Aggression Scale (Sorgi et al., 1991); the original OAS was devised by Yudovsky et al. (1986)
MoD	Ministry of Defence
MoJ	Ministry of Justice
MP	Member of Parliament
MPA	medroxyprogesterone acetate
MPhil	Master of Philosophy (research degree)
MRI	magnetic resonance imaging
mRNA	messenger RNA
MRS	magnetic resonance spectroscopy
MSU	medium security unit
MWC	Mental Welfare Commission for Scotland

MZ	monozygotic (twins developed from the same egg)
N or n	number in sample
NA	Narcotics Anonymous (international)
NAA	N-acetyl aspartate
NACRO	National Association for the Care and Rehabilitation of Offenders – a voluntary organization
NAS	Novaco Anger Scale (Novaco, 2003)
NCCMH	National Collaborating Centre for Mental Health (part of NICE)
NCEPOD	the National Confidential Enquiry into Patient Outcome and Death
NCG	National Commissioning Group
NCI	National Confidential Inquiry into Suicide and Homicide (www.medicine.manchester.ac.uk/ psychiatry/research/suicide/prevention/nci)
NCISH	National Confidential Inquiry into Suicide and Homicide (UK)
NCR	National Crime Register (Denmark)
NCRS	National Crime Recording Standards
NCVO	National Council for Voluntary Organizations (England)
NCVS	National Crime Victimization Survey (USA)
NDPB	non-departmental public body
NEMESIS	Netherlands Mental Health Survey and Incidence Study
NESARC	National Epidemiologic Survey on Alcohol and Related Conditions (USA)
NGRI	not guilty by reason of insanity
NHS	National Health Service (UK)
NHSE	National Health Service Executive
NI	Northern Ireland
NICE	National Institute for Clinical Excellence (England)
NIDA	National Institute on Drug Abuse (USA)
NIMHE	National Institute for Mental Health in England
NIPS	Northern Ireland Prison Service
NMC	Nursing and Midwifery Council
NOMS	National Offender Management Service
NPIA	National Police Improvement Agency
NPSA	National Patient Safety Agency
NPY	neuropeptide y
NSF	National Service Framework
NSPCC	National Society for the Prevention of Cruelty to Children
NTA	National Treatment Agency for Substance Misuse (an NHS organization for England only)
NTORS	National Treatment Outcome Research Study (UK)
NZ	New Zealand
OAS	overt aggression scale
OAS-M	Overt Aggression Scale-Modified
OAS-R	Overt Aggressive Symptom-Revised
OASyS	offender assessment system
OBP	offending behaviour programmes
OCD	obsessive-compulsive disorder
OCJR	Office for Criminal Justice Reform
OGRS	Offender Group Reconviction Scale
OHPA	Office of the Health Professions Adjudicator
OLR	order for lifelong restriction (Scotland)
OM	offender manager (probation officer working directly with a convicted offender) (England and Wales)
ONS	Office for National Statistics
op cit	*opus citatum* (the work cited) (Latin)

OPCAT	operational protocol on the convention against torture
OPD	operational psychodynamic diagnostics (Cierpka et al., 2007; OPD Task Force, 2008)
OR	odds ratio, a statistical term indicating likelihood
OSAPs	offender substance abuse programmes
p.	page or plural according to context (see also pp.)
PACE	Police and Criminal Evidence Act 1984
PACS	Profile of Anger Coping Skills (Willner et al., 2005)
PACT	Prisoners Advice and Aftercare Trust
PAI	The Personality Assessment Inventory (Morey, 1991)
PALS	Patient Advice and Liaison Service
para.	paragraph
PAS	Personality Assessment Schedule (Tyrer, 2000)
PAS-R	Personality Assessment Schedule, rapid version (Tyrer and Cicchetti, 2000)
P-ASRO	Prisons – Addressing Substance Related Offending Programme
PBNI	Probation Board for Northern Ireland
PCL-R	Psychopathy Checklist – Revised (Hare, 1991); factor 1 affective, factor 2 lifestyle
PCL-SV	Psychopathy Checklist, Screening Version
PCSOT	post-conviction sex offender testing
PCT	primary care trust
PD	personality disorder
PDP	potentially dangerous persons (Northern Ireland)
PDQ4+	Personality Disorder Questionnaire 4+ (Hyler, 1994)
PE	prolonged exposure (CBT)
PERI	Psychiatric Epidemiology Research Interview (Dohrenwend et al., 1986)
per se	in itself (Latin)
PFT	positron emission tomography (see also SPET)
PhD	Doctor of Philosophy (higher research degree)
PI	Provocation Inventory (Novaco, 2003)
PICLS	prison mental health in-reach and court liaison service (Ireland)
PICU	psychiatric intensive care unit.
PIPE	psychologically informed planned environment
PITO	Police Information Technology Organization
PLOS	*Public History of Science* – open access journal
PMETB	Postgraduate Medical Education and Training Board
PMMT	prison-based methadone maintenance treatment
PMRS	prison medical record system
PNBI	Probation Board for Northern Ireland
PORT	the schizophrenia Patient Outcomes Research Team, a US based review group (e.g. (Dixon et al., 2009)
pp.	pages
PPANI	Public Protection Arrangements (Northern Ireland)
PPG	penile plethysmograph
PPI	Psychopathic Personality Inventory
P-ASRO	Prison – Addressing Substance Related Offending
PsyD	Doctor of Psychology (degree)
PTA	post-traumatic amnesia
PTSD	post-traumatic stress disorder
QACSO	questionnaire on attitudes consistent with sex offences (Broxholme and Lindsay, 2003; Lindsay et al., 2007)
QT_c	The interval between the Q and the T in an electrocardiogram crudely corrected for the speed of the heart

qv	*quod vide* (Latin) = see text elsewhere in chapter
r or R	Pearson's product moment correlation coefficient
R&R	Reasoning and Rehabilitation (Porporino and Fabiano, 2000)
RAO	Risk Assessment Order (Scotland)
RAP	resettlement and aftercare provision
RAPT	Rehabilitation of Addicted Prisoners Trust
RATED	Risk assessment tools evaluation directory
RC	responsible clinician (a technical term for the person in legal charge of the case of a detained person under mental health legislation in England and Wales; this person may be a psychiatrist, but may be any other qualified clinician who has had the necessary training)
RCT	randomized controlled trial
REBT	rational emotive behaviour therapy
RECON	Relationship and context based
REM	sleep: rapid eye movement sleep
RMA	Risk Management Authority (Scotland)
RMO	responsible medical officer (a technical term with similar meaning to RC (qv) but referring only to a psychiatrist with special training; in current use in Scotland, used in England and Wales before the Mental Health Act 2007)
rMZ/rDZ	resemblance rates between mono- and di-zygotic twins
RNA	ribonucleic acid, similar to DNA, but with some structural and functional differences. Has a role, and some influence on gene expression
rnhs	representative national household survey (US)
ROC	receiver operating curve
ROC	receiver operator characteristics, a signal frequency measure, commonly applied to evaluation of risk assessment
RP	relapse prevention
RQIA	Regulation and Quality Improvement Authority (Northern Ireland)
R R	relative risk
RSVP	Risk for Sexual Violence Protocol
s.	section of an act
SA	*Staphylococcus aureus*
SAP	Standardized Assessment of Personality (Pilgrim and Mann, 1990; Pilgrim et al., 1993)
SARN	Structured Assessment of Risk and Need
SCAN	Schedule for Clinical Assessment in Neuropsychiatry (WHO, 1992b)
SCH	secure children's home
sch.	schedule (usually of an act of Parliament)
SCID	Structured Clinical Interview for DSM-IV Axis I and II disorders
SCID-II	Structured Clinical Interview for DSM-IV Axis II disorders (First et al., 1997)
SCL	symptom check list (usually with 90 items)
SCT	supervised community treatment
sd	standard deviation
SDAs	service discipline acts
SDPs	Short Duration Programmes
SEP	supportive expressive therapy
SES	socioeconomic status
SFT	Schema focused therapy (Young 1994; Young et al., 2000)
SGA	second generation antipsychotic, also referred to as atypical antipsychotics/neuroleptics (see Chapter 23)
SHAPS	Special Hospitals Assessment of Personality and Socialization (Blackburn, 1986),
SIDS	Sudden Infant Death Syndrome ('Cot Death')
SMI	severe mental illness

SMS	short message service (on a telephone)
SNAP	security needs assessment profile
SNP	single nucleotide polymorphism
SOAD	second opinion appointed doctor
SOGS	South Oaks Gambling Screen
SONAR	Sex Offender Needs Assessment Rating
SOTP	Sex Offender Treatment Programme
SOVA	Safeguarding of Vulnerable Adults – voluntary organisation
SPECT	Single Photon Emission Tomography
SPET	Single Positron Emission Tomography
SPQ	Schizotypal Personality Questionnaire (Raine, 1993)
SRA	Structured Risk Assessment
SRB	suicide related behaviours
ss.	sections
SSKAT	Socio-Sexual Knowledge and Attitudes Test (Wish et al., 1980)
SSRIs	selective serotonin reuptake inhibitors (a class of antidepressants, international)
STAI	State-Trait Anxiety Inventory
STAIR-MPE	Skills training in affective and interpersonal regulation plus modified prolonged exposure
Staph aureus	*Staphylococcus aureus*
STAXI	Spielberger State-Trait Anger Expression Inventory (Spielberger, 1996)
STC	secure training centre
STEPPS	Systems training for emotional predictability and problem solving
SUD	substance use disorder
SUDS	Subjective Units of Disturbance Scale (Wolpe, 1982)
SUIDS	Sudden Unexpected Infant Death Syndrome ('Cot Death')
SVP	sexually violent predator
SVR-20	Sexual Violence Risk – 20 scale
T	thymine, one of the four nitrogenous bases in the repeating units (nucleotides) in a strand of DNA
TAU	treatment as usual
TBI	traumatic brain injury
TBS (Terbeschikkingstelling)	(Dutch – available to the government)
TC	therapeutic community
TCO (sometimes written T/C-O)	threat control override symptoms (of psychosis)
TF-CBT	trauma focused CBT
TFCT	trauma-focused cognitive therapy
ToM	Theory of Mind
TPH	tryptophan hydroxylase
TSO	The Stationery Office (UK Government Printer)
TTD	transfer for treatment direction s136 MH (C + T)(s) Act 2003
UK	United Kingdom of Great Britain and Northern Ireland
UKATT	United Kingdom Alcohol Treatment Trial
UKCC	United Kingdom Central Council for Nursing, Midwifery and Health Visiting
UKDPC	United Kingdom Drugs Policy Commission (UK)
UN	United Nations
us	unconditioned stimuli
USA/US	United States of America
val	valine, one of the essential proteinogenic amino acids in the genetic code
VCU	Victim Contact Unit (run by Probation Boards in England and Wales)

VIM	violence inhibition mechanism
ViSOR	Violence and Sexual Offenders Register
viz	*videlicet* (*videre licet*), Latin = that is, namely, or to wit
VLO	Victim liaison officer (probation officer with special training in work with victims of crime (England and Wales)
VOC	Validity of Cognition Scale (Shapiro, 1989)
VRAG	Violence Risk Appraisal Guide (Quinsey et al., 1998)
VRP	Violence Risk Program (Gordon and Wong, 2000; Wong et al., 2007, 2007)
VSO	voluntary sector organization
WAIS	Wechsler Adult Intelligence Test (Wechsler, 1999)
WARS	Ward Anger Rating Scale (Novaco, 1994)
WE	Wernicke's encephalopathy
WFSBP	World Federation of Societies of Biological Psychiatry
WHO	World Health Organization
WMA	World Medical Association
YJB	Youth Justice Board
YOI	Young Offenders' Institution
YOT	Youth Offending Team

1

Introduction

John Gunn and Pamela J Taylor

Forensic psychiatry is the prevention, amelioration and treatment of victimization which is associated with mental disease. (Gunn and Taylor 1993)

FORENSIC PSYCHIATRY

Forensic psychiatry is often regarded simply as that part of psychiatry which deals with patients and problems at the interface of the legal and psychiatric systems. Several definitions of it exist, partly reflecting its complexity. The definitions have a common core, but each highlights some special aspect of the work. The Royal College of Psychiatrists (2010) emphasizes *working with others* to assess, manage and treat people with mental disorders associated with offending and dangerous behaviour, and that recognition as a specialist in forensic psychiatry follows from specialist training which builds on more general psychiatric training. The American Academy of Psychiatry and the Law (AAPL) (2005) says:

Forensic Psychiatry is a subspecialty of psychiatry in which scientific and clinical expertise is applied in legal contexts involving civil, criminal, correctional, regulatory or legislative matters, and in specialized clinical consultations in areas such as risk assessment or employment.

For us, forensic psychiatry is more than that. We recognize all these features, but we see it as essential to include thinking about victims of crime, abuse, neglect and deprivation. This is partly because we envisage a duty to help them for their own sake, and partly because this, in turn, is at the core of prevention of harm or its repetition against others and, indeed, against self. So often there is ambivalence as to who will sustain the most physical harm – the aggressor or his/her target, but always there are waves of other people affected – lovers, children and other family as well as the great mass of the wider public who must pay in some way for the disruption.

Now nothing mattered: going or not going to Vozdvizhenskoe, getting or not getting a divorce from her husband...The only thing that mattered was punishing him. When she poured out her usual dose of opium, and thought that she had only to drink off the whole bottle to die, it seemed to her so simple and easy that she began musing with enjoyment on how he

would suffer, and repent and love her memory when it would be too late.

Finally, Anna Karenina's punitive drive was more violent and bloody, under a train:

...exactly at the moment when the midpoint between the wheels drew level with her, she threw away the red bag, and drawing her head back into her shoulders, fell on her hands under the car, and with a light movement, as though she would rise immediately, dropped on her knees. And at the instant she was terror-stricken at what she was doing. 'Where am I? What am I doing? What for?' She tried to get up, to throw herself back; but something huge and merciless struck her on the head and dragged her down on her back (Tolstoy, 1873–7).

In this book we include a substantial chapter on the problems of victims and how they may be helped to survive and recover. In the first edition, we offered the definition of forensic psychiatry with which we open this chapter, which seemed to us to be fundamental, which we hoped would lead to more and better therapeutics in this field and which we think may now be regarded as more central than ever to the field. We set out some of the reasons for that below, and expand further on the position in chapter 28. A European definition of forensic psychiatry incorporates this broad approach (Nedopil et al., 2012); forensic psychiatry is

- a specialty of medicine, based on a detailed knowledge of relevant legal issues, criminal and civil justice systems;
- its purpose is the care and treatment of mentally disordered offenders and others requiring similar services, including risk assessment and management, and the prevention of future victimization.

Although this definition does not explicitly refer to medico-legal work, it is presumed within the construct of management. The emphases are on service, on breadth of knowledge and on prevention; the reference to medicine is to capture the concept of a holistic approach with a recognized ethic.

Soon after the current models of forensic mental health service delivery started developing in the UK, one of us proposed a list of seven core skills for forensic psychiatry, as supplements to general psychiatry and basic knowledge of the other recognized psychiatric specialities (Gunn, 1986). We regard research mindedness for all and actual research for some, together with training skills and a capacity for acknowledging an indefinite need to continue learning as additional background necessities. The seven specialist skills proposed were:

- the assessment of behavioural abnormalities;
- the writing of reports for courts and lawyers;
- the giving of evidence in court;
- understanding and using security as a means of treatment;
- the treatment of chronic disorders, especially those which exhibit behavioural problems, including severe psychoses and personality disorders;
- a knowledge of mental health law;
- skill in the psychological treatments (particularly dynamic and supportive psychotherapies) of behaviour disorders.

Subsequently, the Royal College of Psychiatrists (2010), in setting specialty standards for the General Medical Council and for training purposes, has adopted a competency based approach, which, essentially, builds on these (table 1.1, below).

A VICTIM-CENTRED APPROACH

Most patients who come to forensic psychiatrists are victims of one sort or another. Many have often suffered multiple victimizations, from childhood through into adult life. Early deleterious childhood experiences include poverty, social deprivation, inconsistent discipline, violence and/or sexual abuse, and, once a pattern becomes established, affected individuals often continue to suffer victimization through adult life too. Both our contextual chapters – on the psychosocial milieu and on genetics – as well as the more clinically oriented chapters are pervaded by such issues. One of the great markers of progress since our first edition has been evidence for what was then a largely presumed interaction between harsh psychosocial experience and individual characteristics. Much information about links between early trauma and crime comes from retrospective surveys, but Widom (1989) paved the way towards a more strongly based acceptance of the links with her prospective study of children who had suffered verified abuse, later also showing their vulnerability

Table 1.1   Requirements for competency in formulation at general and specialist levels of training. (Extracted from Royal College of Psychiatrists, 2010b)

The task	Assessment methods	GMP domains
Formulation *at the general level*		
Knowledge		
Describe the various biological, psychological and social factors involved in the predisposition to, the onset of and the maintenance of common psychiatric disorders that affect adult patients	CBD*, CP, CASC	1
Skills		
Integrate information from multiple sources to formulate the case into which relevant predisposing, precipitating and protective factors are highlighted	CBD, CP, CASC	1
Attitudes demonstrated through behaviours		
Provide explanation to the patient and the family which enables a constructive working relationship	ACE, mini-ACE, CBD, CASC	1
Formulation *at the forensic psychiatry level*		
Knowledge		
Understand the balance between the primary duty of care to patients and protecting public safety and take proper account of this in professional decision-making	ACE, CBD, CP supervisor's report	1
Understands the philosophy of retribution, incapacitation, deterrence		
Skills		
Ability to collate and integrate information from clinical, risk and legal evaluation into a detailed formulation	CBD, CP, supervisor's report	1
Ability to develop a psychodynamic formulation		
Attitudes demonstrated through behaviours		
Recognizing the contribution of multi-disciplinary team members and other agencies in assessing patients, incorporating patient perspective	CBD, CP, supervisor's report, mini-PAT	1

*Abbreviations:
ACE: assessment of clinical expertise
CASC: clinical assessment of skills and competencies tool
CBD: case based discussion
CP: case presentation
mini-ACE: mini assessment of clinical encounter
mini-PAT: mini-peer assessment tool
GMP domain: good medical practice domain; for the list of seven seen main text.

to developing mental health problems, including substance misuse, and to completing suicide (Widom and Maxwell, 2001). Nevertheless, risk implies that such progression is not inevitable; Caspi et al. (2002) demonstrated the protective effect of the X-linked gene which encodes monoamine oxidase A (MAOA) in a New Zealand birth cohort study, and were thus able to include prospective or contemporaneous evidence of abuse. In a study with an independent sample, Fergusson et al. (2011), albeit with retrospective victim data collection, confirmed that the combination of experience of abuse in childhood and having low-activity MAOA was significantly associated with later offending and violence, even after controlling for potentially confounding factors such as low socioeconomic status or family dysfunction. None of this is to imply, however, that simple gene–environment interactions provide sufficient explanations for the range of pathways into and out of mental disorder and offending. There is evidence that mental disorder, albeit mainly later mental disorder, is in itself a vulnerability factor for becoming a victim (e.g. Chapple et al., 2004; Teplin et al., 2005; Walsh et al., 2003; and see chapter 14).

Our concept of a victim-centred approach is heavily weighted towards amelioration of symptoms for the victim, restoration of healthy social function, and towards prevention of tertiary problems such as crime. Apart from the possibility of preventing individuals moving from victim to perpetrator status, this last means learning from victims and survivors of crime and building the resultant knowledge into public health models (see also chapter 28). Particularly outside the UK, forensic psychiatrists and psychologists put a lot of emphasis on their work in civil law suits for compensation following accidents. This too is important work, and we do not wish to underplay its value in providing some victims with compensation, particularly when criminal proceedings will not occur and the only recourse against the perpetrators of the harm lies in making them pay financially. Nevertheless, we suggest that while such work may be necessary, it is not sufficient for the victims. Nor is it only victims of crime who have needs beyond financial compensation. When, in the late 1980s, we set up a clinic for the victims of transport disasters such as the sinking of the *Herald of Free Enterprise*, and soldier victims who had been blown up in Northern Ireland, we were concerned and surprised by the number of them who went on to commit violent acts themselves. Almost none of them had ever done such a thing before, and yet one or two attracted substantial prison sentences after being convicted of such offences (see Dooley and Gunn, 1995; Duggan and Gunn, 1995 for a psychological analysis of the sample).

For victims of crime there are also structures by which they may influence the justice process and, perhaps, engage with the criminal justice system in enhancing their own safety. In England and Wales, for example, victims of crime have rights in law to submit statements to the sentencing court and then, when a person has been sentenced to prison or directed to hospital after conviction, to have knowledge about review and release dates and to change conditions of release, for example by requesting an exclusion zone for the offender's movements (see also chapter 28). They are able, for example, to make submissions to the Parole Board and/or to Review Tribunals. Possibly bringing some peace of mind about safety, such processes also offer the victim a chance to feel more in control again of his or her life. These sound ideas and requirements, however, require both adequate financial resources and skilled people to support the victim through the process. In some states of the USA, the expenditure is on supporting a perception that victims of serious crime want or need a more punitive approach; some murderers are executed there, and the relatives of the murdered person may watch the perpetrator being killed. There is, in fact no evidence that such processes help victims in any way, while Prejean (1993) offers anecdotal evidence to the contrary. Once the surviving relatives have had their hate object taken away, then a possibly key coping strategy has been removed, and still neither the state nor any other party provides them with any practical or psychological help for recovery. Not all, but many such people need both the latter, to overcome the psychic trauma of being a victim. The Royal College of Psychiatrists motto, 'there is no health without mental health' is particularly apt in this context.

CONTEXT

'The trouble is he's crazy, the trouble is he drinks' (The Jets, *West Side Story*, Sondheim and Bernstein, 1957). The mix of truth and cynicism attributed to the 'JDs', as they call themselves, in the musical *West Side Story* draws attention to the difficulties facing professionals in psychiatry, social services and the criminal justice system, and indeed facing the clientele themselves. It is worth catching the whole song, which follows the mocking youths' perceptions of how each party to the criminal justice, psychiatric and social process washes its hands of them in turn (www.westsidestory.com/site/level2/lyrics/krupke.html). It is not only 'juvenile delinquents' who truly have wide ranging needs, while barely recognizing them in any real sense and evoking ambivalence in those who have to try and meet those needs, but also people with the complex mix of mental disorder, particularly personality disorder, and offending.

Our focus in this text is on disorders of mental health and their relevance in the criminal justice system, but, in order to provide an adequate service, forensic psychiatrists need a much wider knowledge of medicine than psychiatry alone, and an acquaintance with a wide range of other fields beyond even those often referred to as 'allied professional' fields, such as psychology, nursing and social work. Colleagues from each of these professions have helped us to write this book. In the wider group of relevant subjects we would include law, criminology, ethics and philosophy.

Starting from a medical perspective, many disorders of physical health are more prevalent among offenders and in turn have implications for how offenders are managed. The most obvious lies in the reason for the old prison medical service in the UK – control of infections (see also chapter 25) – and it remains true that infections are more common among prisoners than in the general population. This is just one of the many reasons why some public health knowledge and skills, and links to public health physicians are all of value. More is known about the health of prisoners than other offender groups, with the sobering recognition that, worldwide, mortality (all causes) is higher, age for age, among prisoners than in the general population (Fazel and Baillergeon, 2011). It is arguable too that, where people are detained in institutions, there is some onus on the detaining authorities to safeguard or even improve the health of their detainees. This may be, paradoxically, particularly hard to achieve in specialist forensic mental health services, where drug treatments which are specific for the psychoses, and often helpful in ameliorating some of the distress and behavioural disturbance associated with the kind of personality disorders suffered by people admitted to such services, have the potential for precipitating serious metabolic disorders. The public health skills which we have just flagged as important for individuals, are also of central importance in preventing victimization and crime (see chapter 28).

Psychiatrists have developed specialties within psychiatry, some of which are fully recognized in the UK as requiring defined and scrutinized specialist training and some which are called subspecialties, requiring particular knowledge and skills, but which are treated less formally in terms of the way in which people acquire those skills. Most are highly relevant to forensic psychiatry. The 'recognized specialities' are general adult psychiatry, forensic psychiatry, child and adolescent psychiatry, psychotherapy, the psychiatry of learning disability and old age psychiatry, while the subspecialties are addictions psychiatry, liaison psychiatry and rehabilitation psychiatry. Without a firm foundation in general adult psychiatry training, there could be no forensic psychiatry. An understanding of developmental processes is so important that a good grounding in child and adolescent psychiatric training is invaluable, but the needs of young people differ sufficiently from the needs of adults that a 'superspecialty' of child and adolescent forensic psychiatry has grown up, coupling higher/advanced training in forensic psychiatry with higher training in child and adolescent psychiatry, lengthening the process by about 12 months to accommodate the extra knowledge and skill development required. Forensic psychotherapy has developed in a similar way, linking recognized training in forensic psychiatry with recognized training in psychotherapy. Forensic learning disability psychiatry is emerging too.

Criminology

British forensic psychiatry has roots, not just in law and in medicine but also in criminology. For some people in continental Europe, Lombroso (1876) is the founder of criminology, with theories of atavism and degeneracy. A prison medical officer, Charles Goring (1913), went to good deal of trouble, using a large sample of British prisoners, to refute Lombroso's ideas. Modern British criminology emerged in the 1930s (Garland, 1988), with the founding of the Association for the Scientific Treatment of Criminals in 1931, before becoming the Institute for the Scientific Treatment of Delinquency (ISTD) in 1932. This led to a 'psychopathic clinic' the following year. In 1937 this became the Portman Clinic, which is still a specialist outpatient psychotherapy unit for people with antisocial behaviour, and especially for men who commit sex offences.

The ISTD separated into two parts in 1951, forming the Institute for the Study and Treatment of Delinquency and the Scientific Group for the Discussion of Delinquency. The latter became the British Society of Criminology in 1961. In its early years the British Society of Criminology looked to psychiatrists to play a prominent part in its affairs, but this slowly changed as criminologists began to question the importance of psychoanalytic theory and as psychiatrists became less interested in psychodynamics and more interested in organic and pharmacological problems. The ISTD had a further metamorphosis in 1999 becoming the Centre for Crime and Justice Studies (CCJS; www.crimeandjustice.org.uk).

Psychiatry and criminology may have grown apart in some respects, but a knowledge of the science of studying patterns in criminal behaviour and the impact of any interventions on these remains important to clinicians as well as criminal justice agencies. Criminologists, often with a grounding in psychology, have pioneered longitudinal, prospective studies of birth cohorts or cohorts of schoolchildren so that a more coherent, evidence based view of pathways into crime has become possible. In chapter 7 David Farrington writes principally about the cohort to which he has devoted his research career, but also references a range of other such studies which have been conducted worldwide. With the added value of genotyping, many of the studies referred to in the genetics chapter follow a similar model. It is mainly to criminologists and social scientists that we turn for evidence of the impact of the various methods of punishment employed by the courts – do they deter? Do they reduce recidivism? Does imprisonment have any harmful impact on prisoners? Psychiatrists are not at the centre of determining such policies, but if they are to work in such institutions as prisons, and have the potential for influencing practice there, they need to be aware of the outputs from both the Home

Office Research Unit (www.homeoffice.gov.uk) and the Ministry of Justice (www.justice.gov.uk) for the UK and from similar governmental bodies in other countries. Inspectorate reports for prison and probation, and occasional relevant reports from the National Audit Office (www.nao.org.uk) can also be useful. The medical profession has a central role in same debates. Since our last issue, for example, Donohue and Levitt (2001) found evidence in the USA of falling crime rates roughly 18 years after abortion was legalized. Other researchers have argued that their statistics were flawed (e.g. Foote and Goetz, 2008), while the position in England and Wales is that a crude link was found using recorded crime data from 1983 through 2001, which did not hold up after allowances were made for other key variables (Di Tella et al., 2008). Nonetheless, these authors consider that the issue is worthy of reflection given the likelihood that wanted children in stable homes are less likely to get caught up in offending than unwanted children placed in care.

Psychological input to criminal justice services is nowadays much more prominently from psychologists than psychiatrists. They have largely driven the development of formal risk assessment tools for the individual and intervention programmes mainly for groups. The group programmes aim to change the thinking of offenders as a stepping stone to them reducing or giving up their criminal behaviours. They have especially focused on sex offending, violence and illicit drug use. We explore examples of such programmes both in the respective behaviour and disorder chapters and also in chapter 25 on services in the criminal justice system. This is essential and welcome work, filling a gap where psychiatrists have largely abandoned people with mental and behavioural disorders, and it has been subject to research evaluation, but with results that remain open to interpretation and debate (Ho and Ross, 2012; Mann et al., 2012; Hickey, 2012). The programmes might be more effective if less rigid and more supported within a multidisciplinary clinical framework. Of perhaps more concern, however, is that such programmes are now being brought across from prison and probation where many people have no mental disorder or personality disorder, to hospitals where the commonest mental disorders are in the schizophrenia spectrum. They may well prove helpful for some, but need fresh evaluation which takes account of the even greater complexity of presentations among people who are hospitalized after offending. It is vital that psychiatrists play a full part in such evaluations.

Economics

Forensic mental health services are expensive, how can such costs be justified? This is a pertinent question at a time of economic stress in many developed countries which have such services, but also one which general psychiatrists in the UK have been asking ever since the surge in development of medium security units specifically and forensic psychiatry, in particular, in the decades since the Butler report (Home Office, DHSS, 1975). At the time of the first edition of this text, in 1993, there were just over 1,700 high security hospital beds, many of them provided in substandard facilities, and just over 650 specialist medium security hospital beds. By 2007, although the distribution of beds had shifted away from high to medium security, still the overall number of specialist secure beds available at any one time had about doubled (Rutherford and Duggan, 2007), not counting newer categories of 'low security', which may or may not have forensic psychiatric specialists involved. Scotland and Northern Ireland have developed medium security hospital services for the first time. It is arguable that such secure hospital service development is merely paralleling the rise in the prison population, in which rates of mental disorder are high; it is also arguable that neither health nor criminal justice services are using community provisions enough, and that their efforts directed at diversion of people with mental health problems should be increased (Bradley, 2009; see also chapter 25). A great deal depends on measured outcomes, which should include safety of the patient and public alike, but will include other measures too.

Bennett (2008), from the Centre for Crime and Justice, argues that there has been a shift, at least in the criminal justice system, from the optimism about the rehabilitative potential of criminals to conservative and defensive policies because of the enhanced importance given to the concept of dangerousness by the public and politicians alike, and this is costing society both in immediate financial terms as prison numbers escalate but also in 'moral impoverishment'. The National Audit Office (2010) confirms the poor return for investment with respect to short-term prison sentences. It may be that some of this sort of thinking has pervaded health service developments too, although in forensic psychiatric services, admission is reserved for people who really cannot be managed elsewhere and length of stay in an institution is rarely short. Difficulties in understanding real costs in this field lie in the extent of the ramifications of the effect of violent crime. As Cohen (1994) showed, they cross government departmental boundaries, affecting not only the criminal justice system in court and sentencing costs, and healthcare systems in managing the effects of the violence, but also social care systems in providing for loss of earnings and potential, perhaps if a parent is killed, taking on the cost of rearing the children and so forth. If, say, a secure unit bed really could reduce such costs, then it might seem cheap at the price in the absence of intergovernmental department competition for funds. In a US study of what the public actually wants (Cohen et al., 2006) a nationally representative sample of people were asked to trade off crime prevention and control policies and tax rebates. There was overwhelming support for increased spending on youth prevention, drug treatment for non-violent offenders and the police, and respondents would not request a tax rebate if this is how their money were spent. They would not, however, endorse new money for building more prisons. They were not asked about secure hospitals, but perhaps they would fit within the treatment and prevention modes that seemed to be favoured.

Philosophy

Evil

Evil is doing things that hurt people when you know they wouldn't want you to do them.

This was said by a behaviourally disordered patient of limited intelligence, but he has captured a useful perception of evil – and one of the commonest – intent to hurt when, in essence, you know it is wrong.

Textbooks of psychiatry do not usually mention the subject of evil; that is interesting in itself considering that it is such a widespread human concept. We do not believe that a textbook of forensic psychiatry can escape entirely from touching on this topic. In the trial of the co-called 'Yorkshire Ripper', a central feature was the question of whether the defendant was mad or bad (*Coonan 1 and 2*). An *Observer* correspondent (Read, 24 May 1981) wrote:

If one believes in the Devil, not as an abstract idea, but as a real being with the power of Satan in the Book of Job to 'roam about the earth' then it is possible to postulate demonic possession of a murderer like Sutcliffe ... It seemed plausible that some other being had entered into him – not the spirit of God as he claimed, but some demon with an ironic sense of humour ... If this was true then the contentions of both prosecution and defence would have been right. Peter Sutcliffe might have been both evil and mad.

This debate between madness and evil permeates much of forensic psychiatry; we do not always recognize it, but practitioners should be aware of it. In this context, the word is for the language of the layman and the politician, or perhaps prison governors. The governor of Strangeways prison blamed the 1990 prison riot on the work of the devil! Serious contemplation about evil or 'wickedness' is generally seen as the purview of religious leaders or philosophers, although reviewers have questioned whether even they remained interested. Midgley (1984), a philosopher, found her book on *Wickedness* greeted with the following observation from *The Spectator* (printed on the fly leaf of her book):

This topic raises so many problems that social scientists have lately tended to sweep it right under the carpet, reducing wrong-doing to mental illness, social conditioning, or a figment of the punitive imagination, while philosophers have concealed it behind a decent veil of general scepticism.

Note the '*reducing* of wrong-doing to mental illness' (our italics). Midgley herself concluded that evil is actually a negative, a void – the absence of good:

Evil, in spite of its magnificent pretentions, turns out to be mostly a vacuum.

This has some resonance with Arendt's (1963) concept of 'the banality of evil', a term coined in her description of Eichmann, a Nazi war criminal who was allegedly of low intelligence but otherwise found by several experts who examined him to have no mental abnormality; she suggested that his life was so empty that he may have preferred to be executed than live as a nobody. We cannot say whether this was an appropriate interpretation of the facts or not; the essential point is that there is a school of thought that views evil not as the domain of monsters and psychopaths, but of ordinary people and voids which have to be filled, perhaps by brutal and destructive ideologies which appear to them to be strong and decisive and/or to link them to other humans or powers. The experiments testing the extent to which 'ordinary people' are prepared to engage in damaging acts against others in order to keep in with authority (Milgram, 1974) or the group milieu (Zimbardo, 2007) perhaps provide some support for this. The idea of a 'normal' person being responsible for monstrous behaviour is so disturbing that it has provoked academic arguments against the position, but it is behind many of the difficulties faced by forensic psychiatry and psychology – and indeed general psychiatry and clinical psychology. There remains an expectation that we must find that monstrous behaviour is mad, or, if not that, then a construct such as 'psychopathic' will do. Notwithstanding Spence's (2008a) thought-provoking editorial 'Can pharmacology help enhance human morality?', we think that it is generally important to avoid amalgamating the language of morality with the language of medicine and science. It probably does more to further stigmatization of people with various mental disorders, but we nevertheless share Gilligan's (1996) concern to understand monstrous – or in his terms violent – behaviour in psychological terms:

But even the most apparently 'insane' violence has a rational meaning to the person who commits it...
And even the most apparently rational, self-interested, selfish or 'evil' violence is caused by motives that are utterly irrational and ultimately self-destructive...
Violent behaviour, whether it is 'bad' or 'mad', is psychologically meaningful.

We return, then, to the construction of evil as an absence of goodness – ordinary or not this seems to us to side-step the question, because it leaves the problem of understanding goodness. Midgley argued against the view of evil as an outside agency:

It seems necessary to locate some of its sources in the unevenness of (the) original equipment (i.e. our bodies and minds).

She commended Freud's notion of a destructive force within us, a death wish (Freud, 1920), but also noted that it is an idea akin to demonic possession. She highlighted Darwin's profound view that any animal whatever, endowed with well-marked social instincts, would inevitably acquire a moral sense or conscience as soon as its intellectual powers had become as well, or as nearly as well developed, as in man (Darwin, 1883), but she went on almost to equate evil with Fromm's concept of necrophilia: 'the attraction to what is dead, decaying, lifeless and purely mechanical' (Fromm, 1973). Fromm himself (1964), a psychoanalyst, had earlier chosen the term 'malignant narcissism' for what he regarded as the most severe form of pathology accounting for destructiveness and cruelty, a concept taken up as well by Kernberg (1975) and Scott Peck (1983), also medical analysts, and eventually taken over by the concept of psychopathy (Cleckley, 1976; Hare, 1980). So, psychiatrists and psychologists have perhaps been complicit in linking psychopathology and evil. This debate is furthered in much more detail than we can accommodate here in an issue of the journal *Philosophy, Psychiatry and Psychology*, with Ward (2002) and Mullen (2002) among the contributors. One other important problem, however, to which we will return in the context of concepts of mental disorder, is the tendency to regard evil as 'a thing'. This error of reification risks returning to ideas of evil as a 'force' or a 'possession', to which Hampshire (1989) comes close:

The notion of evil is the idea of a force, or forces, which are not merely contrary to all that is more praiseworthy and admirable and desirable in human life, but a force which is actively working against all that is praiseworthy and admirable.

On the one hand this is not far from the witch manias and other strange ideas that affected whole populations in the sixteenth and seventeenth centuries (Mackay, 1869), and on the other hand almost suggests a solution in quantum mechanics; this hardly seems likely!

There is no escaping, however, that forensic psychiatrists have to work in a context in which a moral perspective on behaviour exists. It may be that different views can legitimately coexist. This is sometimes difficult to accept, partly because if each view leads to action, then one view must prevail, as usually only one action can be taken at a time. This type of conflict can be particularly evident in court. To return to the Yorkshire Ripper trial, the moral argument that his behaviour was wicked led inevitably to his condemnation and imprisonment, whilst the view that he suffered from a disease led to hospital care (albeit indefinite secure hospital care) and an attempt to treat and change him. For some offences, courts are perhaps more likely to be able to take a little bit of the moral view and a little bit of the medical view. The depressed shoplifter, for example, may be found guilty, given a moral lecture and then handed over to doctors for treatment.

Society construes individuals as having moral responsibility, guilt, blame in terms of their goodness, and badness. Admittedly, in court, 'insanity' and other forms of mental ill health, concepts borrowed from a different language, are allowed as partial or complete 'excuses', but the very word excuse indicates that this too is done on moral grounds. Responsibility, then, a topic of much interest to lawyers and one on which they frequently consult the psychiatrist, is actually a question of morality. This is why we advocate that when debates about responsibility occur in court, those debates should be conducted by lawyers and laymen alone; the physician is likely to talk at cross-purposes and, in any case, is no expert in morality, even if the excuse which is being imputed is one of mental disorder. All the doctor can do is to give an objective medical view, suggest a medical remedy when appropriate and see whether the moral arguments will accommodate such positions in the case at issue (see Gunn, 1991 for further discussion).

We have emphasized the different perspectives of medicine and the law because we are doctors. In dealing with offenders who do not have a mental disorder, or whose mental disorder is largely irrelevant to their offending, many of the same principles apply to sociological constructs and social work interventions that may be advanced. The greatest potential for medico-legal conflict in the criminal court perhaps lies between the moral and the pragmatic – punishment or excuse on the one hand, and the pragmatics of working towards real prevention of harm on the other.

MEDICAL LANGUAGE

Medical Terminology

Words, phrases and terms which are of great importance in psychiatry and psychology are largely concerned with the way that people think, feel and act. Important clinical or legal decisions may hang on a particular term. Indeed, particular terms are chosen to have particular effects. In Britain, for example, it is not rare to find that a person may be labelled as suffering from, say, 'schizophrenia' until s/he is arrested for an offence or series of offences, whereupon the diagnosis changes to, say, 'personality disorder' (Taylor and Gunn, 2008). One reason for this is that most people accept that schizophrenia is a medical problem and merits health service care and treatment, whereas, unfortunately, there is less consensus about the best approach for people with personality disorder. It is easier to argue that such disorders are untreatable, and so no business of clinicians; perhaps non-medical social support, or maybe imprisonment, would serve instead.

Doctors, including psychiatrists, develop many technical terms and they give technical (largely private) meanings to words in the vernacular. Lawyers do the same, sometimes using the same words as the psychiatrists, but with different meaning. Yet the vernacular is important. Medicine, psychiatry, psychology and the law are rooted in it, and such disciplines are invented by the needs of ordinary people. Psychiatrists did not invent mental disorder. Mental disorder is a common experience, and psychiatrists and allied professional clinicians were invented to treat it. In the *Shorter Oxford Dictionary* there are definitions for most of the contentious words of psychiatry, examples including:

Illness: Badness, unpleasantness. Bad or unhealthy *conditions* of the body. Disease, ailment, sickness.

Disease: An absence of ease. A condition of the body or some part or organ of the body in which its functions are disturbed or deranged. A morbid *condition* of the mind or disposition. An ailment.

Disorder: An absence or undoing of order. Confusion. Irregularity. Disturbance. Commotion. Disturbance of mind. An ailment. Disease.

Disturb: To agitate and destroy. To agitate mentally, discompose the peace of mind. To trouble, perplex.

Although occasional reference to 'mental disturbance' may be made by people keen to avoid either disease or disorder concepts, reference to someone as 'psychologically disturbed' is close to playground or street slang. If the word disturbance has any meaning in clinical practice, it is as an indication of grounds for concern before much detailed understanding has become possible. We will not dwell on this word further.

Several points emerge from this list. First, the vernacular terms are almost interchangeable, secondly they appear to place equal weight on body and mind and, thirdly, several of the definitions include moral aspects; this is especially true for 'illness'.

Does all this matter when psychiatry can develop its own technical language? It does, because psychiatrists have to communicate with laymen. If a distraught family brings a suffering relative who is no longer coping with everyday life to a clinic, it is confusing, even hostile, to tell them to take him/her away again because s/he is not 'ill'. It is confusing because they probably would not have brought their loved one to the clinic unless they had come to the considered view that s/he is ill, and it is hostile because it means that the plea for help is being rejected. It might even be regarded as a betrayal of professional obligations if a distressed person volunteers himself for treatment and the assessing doctor makes no arrangement to help. These are illustrations of a political aspect of terminology. There is an underlying, perhaps ill-formed policy in the doctor's mind about how s/he will or will not deal with some kinds of case. This policy is then expressed in apparently technical language which either prevents arguments or shifts them on to obscure ground. It is important to recognize this tendency, because of the way in which psychiatrists make diagnoses. Usually, they decide on the diagnosis in the first few minutes of an interview, and spend the rest of the interview confirming this impression (Kendell, 1973).

It soon became clear in the construction of this book that terminological differences were just as prominent amongst our small group of similarly trained authors as anywhere else. In fact, even before getting to the nomenclature of disease, we found differences in what to call the person needing our services – patient, client or service user? In these terms, we think that there is a distinction to be made between a person for whom the only task is assessment and the person who is in treatment. The former may even have commissioned the report, and there is a case for referring to such a person as a client. The person who is in treatment has a very different kind of relationship with service providers and, it is arguable, different expectations and rights, so the term patient seems to us to be more appropriate. Everyone is a service user in some way, so that seems over-general to be useful. A concern that we have, which we believe to be shared by those professionals who are uncomfortable with the word 'patient' is that there is, again, a risk that such terms serve to distance and dehumanize, so although we have used the terms client and patient these ways throughout the text, more often than not, we hang on to the words 'person who' and the slightly cumbersome 's/he' and 'his/her' rather than 'they' to keep sight constantly that all those who we work for are, first, people like us.

In a textbook it is important to have some consistency in the use of language, and to have definitions or explanations which the reader can understand, if only to disagree. We have not entirely achieved this, we doubt whether a multi-author book ever could, so next we shall set out how we have struggled ourselves with a few other common words and ideas used in psychiatry.

Reification

In preparation for that we have a preliminary semantic consideration. Science and medicine are concerned not just with tangible objects but also with ideas. Ideas are essential and powerful for progress. They are human cognitive constructions which enable us to think and converse, they may lead to actions but they do not live outside our brains and minds, they are not real in the sense that a piece of furniture is real. The furniture may have begun as an abstract idea in somebody's head but the object generated by that idea is tangible.

All illnesses are abstract concepts. Pneumonia, for example, is not a thing. The *Pneumococcus* organism is a thing, but the term 'pneumonia' is an idea, a way of describing its effect on an afflicted person. The terminology helps us to understand something of the individual's problems, and how they might be helped, by reference to a body of technical knowledge, but the illness does not have substance and visibility like Mrs Brown, who suffers it, or the organisms that have invaded her.

Most of the time this philosophical issue is unimportant but it can, on occasion, lead to significant error if strong ideas are dealt with as though they were real things.

Mental illness

Mental illness is a term which is so widely used and so little agreed upon that we have kept its use in this textbook to a minimum. As with 'psychopathic disorder', its use even within the framework of mental health legislation is largely over. Illness is an evaluative term. It is something undesirable which happens to animals, but a term mainly reserved for human beings. There the consensus ends. It is not even clear whether physical illness and mental illness are both subcategories of the same broad category (Fulford, 1989), but that is how we shall regard them here. Having problems recognized as illness is the key to accessing important provisions and actions, yet illness remains undefined and is largely what the admitting/treating psychiatrist says it is. For Szasz (1962), it is a 'myth':

Psychiatrists are not concerned with mental illnesses and their treatments. In actual practice they deal with personal, social, and ethical problems in living... Human behaviour is fundamentally moral behaviour.

We largely reject this view of mental illness. As we have just described, we accept that human behaviour may be viewed in moral terms but that this does not, as Szasz believes, invalidate a medical view of human behaviour. The two views may run in parallel. Another potential source of confusion about the term 'illness' lies in the idea that illness is not merely a state or 'condition', but creates a social role (Parsons, 1951). Someone who is 'ill' is excused duties, and is treated differently from the healthy person, although, in turn that person has a new and specific duty – to engage in activities to get well. Problems may arise if medical examinations and tests are negative and the status of illness is removed. Occasionally, the reverse may occur and others will say 'you are ill' and, despite protests from the sufferer, normal social responsibilities may be removed and the new role instated instead. It is this social aspect of the term 'illness' with its removal of ordinary duties and responsibilities and the substitution of new ones – including that of submission to medical care – which makes the term so central to psychiatry, and so objectionable to some – including Szasz. S/he who has a mental disorder may, in some circumstances, be forced into the sick role under the powers of mental health legislation. For these complex social reasons we have tried to minimize the use

of the term 'mental illness' in this book and use the term 'disease' or the less explicit, but more widespread term 'disorder'.

Before leaving concepts of illness though, the strange expression 'formal mental illness' which has crept into modern British psychiatry requires comment. It is difficult enough to determine what is meant by a mental illness let alone a 'formal' one. What could this be? One possibility is that the term derives from misguided use of the word 'formal'. In psychiatry the term 'formal thought disorder' may be applied to refer to a disorder of the form of thoughts. Are clinicians trying to say that there is a disorder in the form of health? Scadding (1990) advanced a more likely explanation. He referred to a study of the use of psychiatric terms in general practice (Jenkins et al., 1988) and said (of general practitioners):

Faced with a patient in whom mood changes accompanied by various social and economic stresses and recognized physical diseases, they preferred to describe the situation in informal terms, rather than commit themselves to a formal diagnosis which would imply that the changed mood should be regarded as due to a postulated 'mental disorder'.

Perhaps the psychiatrists who say their patients have 'no formal mental illness' are indicating, like the general practitioners, that they recognize the features of mental disease, but are not prepared to make a diagnosis. Given the context in which this jargon arises, it may further mean that the doctor is not prepared to offer the social status of illness, is not prepared to allow any medical excuses for the patient's behaviour, and is not prepared to provide or recommend treatment. In other words, s/he would be using the jargon as a political statement. It seems to us that the correct response to the assessment of 'no formal mental illness' should be: but does s/he have medical problems at all? If so, what medical problems *does* s/he have? If not, please state that plainly. If s/he does have a medical problem, is there any medical intervention that would help? If so, are you in a position to offer it? If not, where and how can it be accessed?

Disease and disorder

Boorse (1975, 1976) argued that disease is a value-free term and that illness is a subcategory of it with value attached. Thus, most of us live with minor disease (e.g. haemorrhoids), but only severe diseases make us ill. Diseases can be identified objectively, he said, but illnesses are subjective and have social consequences. Disease is a term that is not very commonly used in psychiatry. Although psychiatrists regularly refer to the *International Classification of Diseases*, they then refer to the individual diseases as 'disorders' or 'diagnoses'. The fourth edition of the *American Diagnostic and Statistical Manual* (*DSM-IV*) does not apply the term disease to any purely psychiatric condition; its favoured term is 'disorder', which is defined as:

A clinically significant behavioral or psychological syndrome or pattern that occurs in an individual and that is associated with present distress... or disability... or with a significantly increased risk of suffering, death, pain, disability, or an important loss of freedom... Whatever its original cause, it must currently be considered a manifestation of a behavioral, psychological, or biological dysfunction in the individual. Neither deviant behavior (e.g. political, religious, or sexual) nor conflicts that are primarily between the individual and society are mental disorders unless the deviance or conflict is a symptom of the dysfunction in the individual. (American Psychiatric Association, 1994)

The American manual stresses that diagnostic lists are classifications of mental disorders, not of people; the diagnosis does not define the person. Thus, potentially stigmatizing terms such as 'schizophrenic' or 'alcoholic' should be avoided. Where there is a disorder, it is much better to say 'a person with schizophrenia' or 'a person with alcohol dependency'. This important point is too often disregarded, yet it is central to any therapeutic endeavour. Psychiatry is not alone in objectifying people with health problems in this disparaging and inaccurate way, but it may have more serious consequences. Rogers (1961), whose work included extensive experience with problem and delinquent children and adolescents, noted:

If, in my encounter with him, I am dealing with him as an immature child, an ignorant student, a neurotic personality, or a psychopath, each of these concepts of mine limits what he can be in the relationship.

In a brief, but masterly, review of the disease concept in psychiatry, Clare (1986) pointed out that two views of disease have existed since ancient Greek times. Hippocrates saw disease as a cluster of signs and symptoms occurring together – so frequently as to constitute a recognizable and typical picture. This syndromic perspective does not deal with aetiology, and is similar to the operational approach of the international and American diagnostic manuals. Plato, by contrast, envisaged diseases as separate entities, as having an existence of their own separate from the people afflicted by them, and thus a recognizable cause and natural course. Clare concluded:

Psychiatry lacks an accepted nomenclature or list of approved terms for describing and recording clinical observations. It also lacks a reliable system of classification. Nevertheless, the broad consensus within psychiatry at the present time is that the advantages of the disease approach, the diagnostic exercise, and the present rudimentary classification systems outweigh the disadvantages and that the early results of attempts to improve the situation are encouraging.

One function of the disease concept in medicine is to avoid the political use of terminology. Can we escape from it? Not entirely, and, indeed, the American DSM system has come under particular criticism in this respect. Mayes and Horwitz (2005) argue that *DSM-III* was strongly influenced not only by professional politics, but also by government and health insurers, valuing this approach to demonstrate the effectiveness of what they were doing. In addition, they suggest, the multiplicity of diagnoses generated was principally advantageous to if not driven by pharmaceutical companies. In 1952, *DSM-I* included just 106 diagnoses; by 1987, *DSM-III-R* included 292 diagnostic categories, a growth which Mayes and Horwitz do not believe was reflective of a growth in relevant science. Now, we await *DSM-V*, which is trailed as being more open to incorporating scientific advances and as having:

the potential for adding dimensional criteria to disorders, the option of separating impairment and diagnostic assessments, [the means to meet] the need to address the carious expressions of an illness across developmental stages of an entire lifespan, and the need to address differences in mental disorder expression as conditioned by gender and cultural characteristics (Regier et al., 2009).

For us, Wing (1978) offered one of the best expositions on how to be more scientific about diagnosis:

Putting forward a diagnosis is like putting forward a theory. It can be tested. Is it useful or not?... The first requirement of a disease theory is the recognition of a cluster of undesirable traits or characteristics that tend to occur together... The second essential element in any disease theory is the hypothesis that the cluster of traits is 'symptomatic' of some underlying biological disturbance.

Scadding (1990) emphasized the biological disadvantage of disease, and so defined it as the sum of the abnormal phenomena displayed by a group of living organisms in association with a specified common characteristic, or set of characteristics, by which they differ from the norm for their species in such a way as to place them at such disadvantage (Scadding, 1967). He argued that if the criterion of biological disadvantage applies, then 'there should be no doubt about the propriety of medical intervention'. He recognized that short-term distress, such as follows most bereavements, may be biologically adaptive, but this would not rule out medical assistance if the bereaved person wanted it and it would offer him/her some advantage. He also recognized a grey area where doctors will disagree about the degree of biological disadvantage. Here, his good advice can be taken straight into the heart of forensic psychiatry for he pointed out that it matters not whether a patient's symptoms are conceived of as part of a disease or merely as a response to social circumstances, the symptoms still merit medical attention. Of course, all this becomes much more complicated when *compulsory* treatment has to be considered.

As a psychologist, Ausubel (1961) took a slightly different perspective again. He made no distinction between 'illness' and 'disease', but he firmly tackled the Szasz (1962) view, which was just emerging at that time, that only physical lesions constitute disease. Rather, he noted the subjectivity of all disease assessments, whether physical or mental. He accepted Szasz's view that neurotic and personality disorders may be in some way regarded as expressions of problems in living, but suggested that it is nevertheless possible to construe a syndrome in these social terms and simultaneously construe it in medical terms also. Manifestations of impaired functioning, adaptive compensation, and defensive over-reaction also occur in physical disease.

Psychopathic disorder and psychopathy

We have tried, wherever possible, to avoid using the term 'psychopathic disorder' or, worse, 'psychopath'. Originally the term meant mental disease in general, but it has gradually become corrupted to a pejorative and stigmatizing term which is used quite widely by lay people and professionals alike as a means of rejection. No diagnostic system uses such terms, and with the shift in UK mental health legislation to having a single broad legal category of mental disorder there will soon be no justification even in legal terms for continuing with these words. Patients who were once labelled in this way can always be described in other ways which are more positive and may lead to progress. There remains a case for using the term 'psychopathy', providing that it is used in its very specific sense. The origins of the concept lie in Cleckley's (1976) attempt to medicalize various forms of unusual behaviour in his book *The Mask of Sanity* (first published in 1941). Through a series of detailed case histories, he wanted to draw attention to what he considered to be *forme fruste* of psychosis which lurked under a cover of normality. Hare derived an assessment device based on the Cleckley criteria, the Psychopathy Checklist-Revised (PCL-R; Hare, 1991; for quick reference, see http://en.wikipedia.org/wiki/Hare_Psychopathy_Checklist). The most defining criterion is, essentially, an affective disconnection not unlike that seen in some people with schizophrenia, which seems to limit the capacity of sufferers to perceive fear and distress in others; the more behavioural dimension really only provides for a systematic way of rating repeated antisocial behaviours. We discuss the concept of psychopathy in greater detail in chapter 16, but here we want simply to stress that it is a product of scores on a scale, and the literature is inconsistent in use of defining cut-off scores. Our preference is to refer more precisely to psychopathy checklist scores in *research literature* and higher scorers and lower scorers in clinical dialogue. Originally designed as a dimensional instrument, there are international differences in an accepted cut-off indicative of 'pathology'.

Insight

Lewis (1934) complained that little had been written about insight as part of a psychiatric problem. He defined complete insight as 'a correct attitude towards a morbid change in oneself', but went on to point out that it is very difficult to define what is meant by a 'correct attitude', and that, in these terms, insight may be as limited among those with physical disease as among those with mental disease. He also disliked the neurotic/psychotic dichotomy with the implication that loss of insight is necessarily confined to patients with psychosis, and he showed distaste for those who ask whether something is 'not really psychotic' or 'only neurotic', arguing:

> It is I think correct to say that gross disorders of insight are often found in neuroses... The obsessional's attitude towards his illness or to any special symptoms is vastly different from that of his wife, or his friend, or his doctor... As for the hysteric – who would suppose that a girl with dermatitis artefacta has a healthy or normal attitude towards her symptom?

Lewis (1934) also recognized that the clinician should be aware that acquisition of insight is far from straightforward as an indicator of outcome for a particular patient. Limited insight into illness, he thought, might be an advantage in some cases, because it may lead the patient to repudiate the disease. For patients in forensic mental health services, there is an added complexity – acquisition of accurate insight into their position may be psychologically unbearable. If, for example, in the most extreme form of his psychotic state a man kills something he truly believes to be a source of evil which is destroying the person he loves most, his mother, but in fact kills her, he is himself protected from the enormity of his act by his certainty in his 'saviour' role; insight brings him to a position in which not only must he grieve the loss of the person he was trying to save, but that he was, in reality, the only agent of her death.

In the second edition of the *Oxford Textbook of Psychiatry*, Gelder and colleagues (1989), having defined insight for those with mental disease as 'awareness of one's own mental condition', stressed that it is rarely simply absent or present but rather its presence is matter of degree. They suggested that the concept be unpacked into four components:

1. Is the patient aware of the phenomena noticed by others?
2. If so, does s/he recognize that these phenomena are abnormal?
3. If so, does s/he consider that they are caused by mental illness?
4. If so, does s/he think s/he needs treatment?

In a review David (1990) carried this idea forward and developed an assessment schedule for what he regarded as the three dimensions of insight:

1. awareness of illness;
2. the capacity to relabel psychiatric experiences as abnormal; and
3. treatment compliance.

The measurement of insight is a fundamental part of the Maudsley Assessment of Delusions Schedule (MADS; Taylor et al., 1994). This extends the range of enquiry not only to a patient's self-selected most important delusion, in which such independent variables as the patient's capacity to express his/her belief to others is rated, but also to the patient's possibly related antisocial action(s) when these occur. Separate enquiry is made about his/her understanding of the moral, legal, risk engendering and provocative implications of his/her act. In the evaluation of the schedule with actively psychotic patients these items did not co-vary.

Why should it be so important to separate out the components of insight? While Lewis's (1934) vision of a continuum between full insight and no insight is useful, the elemental approach recognizes that components of insight may be differentially impaired. One patient may adhere perfectly to his or her treatment régime and yet insist that s/he has no illness, disease or disorder – whatever we want to call it, while another may accept s/he has, say, schizophrenia and may even feel a bit better with medication, but still insist that this is not going to make any difference to the effect of the machines that are destroying her/his brain.

This leads us to a further problem that judgment about whether a patient has insight is subjective, and will depend not only on the skill of the clinician but perhaps also on the clinician's own attitudes and beliefs. To compound the difficulty further, discrepancy in ratings between patient and observer and even two observers does not necessarily mean that any one of them is wrong, but rather that each has only a partial picture. This dilemma is just one of the many reasons why the multidisciplinary team is so important to forensic mental health practice – first it brings the chance of recognizing that there are different perceptions of the individual's state, and also provides for testable clinical hypotheses which will help reconcile them.

Sometimes discrepancies in perception of symptoms or actions reflect complex interactions; sometimes they do lead to realization that in some aspect of their condition, a patient may be dissembling. One of us, for example, had a patient with schizophrenia whose delusions remitted with depot medication, but he continued to be agitated. Whilst denying this, he drank heavily and claimed that each drink had been the last, just a few hours before getting drunk again. He claimed that he was fit for work, or that he was studying, yet he spent most of his day doing nothing,

or drinking, in spite of prompts by nurses. The patient charmed casual observers, who agreed with him that he had 'recovered' and no longer required treatment, but consistent observations and objective measures of his alcohol levels helped him as well as the staff looking after him to recognize his poor insight in this respect. By contrast, in a study of delusions, it was observed that rather weak correlations between patient accounts of beliefs and action on them and relative-informant accounts given independently to researchers did not invalidate the beliefs (Wessley et al., 1993). For those patients who were talking about their beliefs, accounts were similar, but many patients were very reticent in this respect, and while aggressive actions were consistently reported and observed, when a patient's actions were avoidant or subtle, these were often not noticed. They could, however, be elicited by a trained clinical researcher. One patient, for example, had taken to wearing a green tie, which was a deliberate act of immense personal significance in the context of his delusion, but it was an act that had gone unobserved and had not been placed in a clinical context.

There is one particular question which relates to insight among offenders and offender patients which needs research, but gets no such attention and that is remorse. Some still expect prisoners and offender patients to show remorse for their offence before discharge can be agreed. It remains unclear, however, whether remorse can be measured with reliability and validity, and, to the best of our knowledge, there are no data confirming that people who do have this doubtfully measurable capacity have better outcomes with respect to reoffending than those who do not. Nevertheless, we think that if this is treated as a question about accurate insight, effort to establish such capacity is likely to be helpful. A useful starting point is to ask to what extent the patient understands the effect of his/her offence on other people – those directly involved and society as a whole. It is not enough to ask the patient about his/her guilt feelings, although this is a useful component of the process as patients carrying a substantial burden of guilt may themselves be vulnerable. Exploration with the patient of steps that, with hindsight, s/he could have taken to prevent the harm s/he did, and how s/he might be able to apply such knowledge in the future is also a useful strategy. Application of our victim-centred approach in practice may provide further evidence of a patient's progress in this respect. A first step is to engage the patient in an exercise about talking with his or her actual victim 'X' in respect of interpersonal violence. The patient is asked to think about what s/he did to X and then talk about it to the assessor/therapist as if the assessor were X (or, where X was killed, then a specified close relative or partner of X). The assessor must then consider the quality as well as the content of the patient's account.

A majority of patients in secure mental health services have harmed someone from their immediate social circle.

Once the treating clinician is satisfied that the patient can cope appropriately with the 'as if' interaction about what s/he did, it may be appropriate to support some replication of the interaction with the actual victims in a few cases. Certainly there will be a task to reconcile perceptions of how relationships may be as the patient moves on. Through misplaced good intentions, or perhaps fear, relatives and friends may be responsible for compounding failures to develop insight. Some are scared of aggressive repercussions if, for example, they tell the patient that s/he will never again live in the family or marital home. Some feel that the patient has already had to cope with so much that is bad that they do not want to remove hope that such a desired option remains available, but they are nevertheless clear to staff that they will not countenance the patient living at home again. Such patients have little chance to gain accurate perceptions of their new social circumstances, and thus begin to plan in an insightful and practical way. It is very rare that direct work with stranger victims occurs, but there are tasks to be done on recognition that such survivors may or do not want the patient to return to the community in which the offence occurred, and that they have rights in that respect.

Treatability

Since the passage of the Mental Health Act 2007, the vexed question of 'treatability' of some kinds of mental disease has become less contentious as certain requirements of the basic legislation – the Mental Health Act 1983 – have been removed. Nevertheless, debates about whether a person may be untreatable continue. There is a case for genuine concern on at least two grounds – first the position of the patient and second the near constant state of shortage of services.

From a patient perspective, it is important that any treatment under any circumstances is theoretically sound and/or evidenced-based; if coercion is to be used in delivering that treatment it is arguable that the evidence for its effectiveness should be particularly strong. Nevertheless, treatability should not be confused with curability. Many diseases are incurable, but they can usually be treated with great benefit to the patient. Specific treatments may be effective, but only partially so, or only so for a finite period of time. In addition, the patients may be treated with nursing, palliatives, support and environmental adjustment. Accepting a role more limited than that of 'curer' is difficult for some doctors, who may have been given inappropriate notions of medical omnipotence at medical school. Yet most of medical practice is concerned with the treatment of incurable problems.

From a service perspective, demand for beds exceeds their availability, so it seems to make sense to screen out people for whom treatment outcome may be less assured, certainly if poor response means that their hospital stay becomes very prolonged. Unfortunately, treatability, which, in effect, has become a political and gatekeeping concept, seems to have been adopted by all services, including those where coercion and inpatient stay is not an issue, and applied especially to people with personality disorder. This, in turn, partly explains why development in the field of treatment for personality disorders has been so slow. Since the first edition of this book there has been a remarkable government attempt to address this problem by the provision of a few, notionally experimental services for people with personality disorder. The story of service for 'dangerous people with severe personality disorder' is taken up in chapter 16. Here, we simply emphasize the important Department of Health initiative that services for people with personality disorder need to be part of mainstream health provision – *Personality Disorder, No Longer a Diagnosis of Exclusion* (National Institute for Mental Health, 2003).

Many doctors remain reluctant to offer patients with personality disorders the same judicious mixture of informal and compulsory care that they are willing to offer patients with other mental disorders. While this may be related to the uncertainty about whether personality disorder really constitutes a medical condition – 'a disease' – with related questions about its moral eligibility for treatment, reluctance may equally follow from an understanding that one of the key characteristics of people within the cluster of personality disorders which includes borderline and anti-social personality disorder is established recidivism. Given the populist view that nothing predicts reoffending as well as previous offending, fear of the responsibilities entailed in attempting to help thus supervenes. It is a sad fact that if such a patient commits a serious offence after leaving psychiatric care, then it often seems that the psychiatrist and psychiatric services are as likely to be condemned in the national media as the offender him/herself. It is perhaps unsurprising that some psychiatrists will try to avoid 'guilt by association'.

Psychiatrists are not alone in this; however, psychologists have promulgated the more quasi-scientific approach of determining treatability by a PCL-R score. Originally used in this context as an aid to selection for treatment in prison programmes, we have concerns about the possibility that a prisoner may be deprived of access to prison-based cognitive treatment programmes solely on grounds of his (and it is here usually a man) PCL-R score. This is not least because in some systems, such as those in England and Wales, he must show that he has completed such programmes and changed to be eligible for release. The transfer of the principle to the very different context of a hospital setting without further detailed research, however, seems much more worrying. First it is important to establish whether high PCL-R scores do indicate a high risk of failure to engage in treatment, and second, if this is so, research is required into why it is.

The Psychiatrist and the Law

In his short story *Billy Budd, sailor,* Herman Melville (1924) asks:

> Who in the rainbow can draw the line where the violet tint ends and the orange tint begins? Distinctly we see the difference of the colors, but where exactly does the one first blendingly enter into the other? So with sanity and insanity. In pronounced cases there is no question about them. But in some supposed cases, in various degrees supposedly less pronounced, to draw the exact line of demarcation few will undertake, though for a fee becoming considerate some professional experts will. There is nothing nameable, but that some men will, or undertake to, do it for pay.

The detection of the shades of pathology, the boundaries between diseases, between normality and mental disease and the contribution of mental diseases to socially proscribed acts is part of the art of forensic psychiatry. In any country where forensic clinicians are more than trained court experts, they are getting paid for much more than trying to answer unanswerable legal questions. Nevertheless, we would all be wise to see the risk of becoming a hired hack within the expert role.

It is inevitable that large sections of this book cover matters which are specifically medico-legal. One or two points are thus worth emphasizing. It is extremely important, in spite of the evident overlap of interests, for psychiatrists to avoid playing amateur lawyers and *vice versa*. It is vital for psychiatrists to recognize and listen to sound legal advice. This is a central skill in forensic psychiatry. There is much legal advice, only a proportion of which is sound. How can the sound be distinguished from the unsound? Sound legal advice will usually come from someone who is well read or experienced in the field concerned. Lawyers, like doctors, specialize. Sound legal advice will usually follow a coherent pattern of argument and make sense in a broader context; it will only rarely be dogmatic and/or partisan. Unsound legal advice is more likely to come from enthusiasts and zealots; it will frequently be dogmatic and difficult to follow to a logical conclusion. Another key route to successful medico-legal relationships is that when doctors are asked to provide reports, they ensure that they have complete clarity about the questions their evidence must deal with and that they do not go beyond those questions.

A major factor in barriers to effective medico-legal practice lies in fundamental differences in thinking styles between clinicians and lawyers. Aubert's (1963a) six points are helpful here:

1. Law tends to favour simple dichotomies: guilty/not guilty, insane/not insane, while clinicians work with probabilities and with disease continua.
2. Thus, lawyers tend to apply only one or two simple concepts of probability, such as 'beyond reasonable doubt' or 'on the balance of probabilities', whereas clinicians generally see more variation.
3. Lawyers test the fit between an event or person and a formula with rather narrowly defined circumstances. In the event of fit, specified consequences follow. An example might be in relation to the diminished responsibility defence. In England and Wales, this is of interest in law exclusively in respect of a murder charge in which case the diminution refers specifically to the individual's cognitions and/or capacity for self-control; clinicians would reflect on a wider range of impairments and set them in their context, in practice applying the idea to a much wider range of behaviours.
4. Courts rely mainly on the past to decide on the future, imposing punishment according to the nature and context of the index offence, perhaps taking previous offending into account. Clinicians certainly do this, drawing on family history, personal psychiatric history including treatment responsiveness and evidence for previously harmful behaviour patterns, but they also consider the future in terms of what treatment and/or service framework will be available.
5. In common law countries, such as England and Wales, lawyers deal in specifics, including case precedents, in determining outcome for complex cases, while clinicians are more influenced by group research data.
6. The Court decides what happened in disputed incidents according to legal rules of causal relationships, which cannot be falsified, only overruled. Clinicians/scientists, at their best, are concerned only with scientifically demonstrable or falsifiable causes.

On the whole, British law is very supportive of good professional practice. The doctor who works well within the limits of medical ethics, who puts patients before personal interests, and who practises to the best of his/her ability and within recognized practice guidelines where available, will rarely, if ever, be in conflict with the law. The first prerequisite for lawful practice, therefore, is good medicine. The law intrudes into medical practice in only a limited number of ways. Specific laws dealing with medical problems are enacted by Parliament, and should always be available for reference. Some sections of the British mental health acts are appended to this book. Patients may sue doctors after a poor outcome to a course of treatment. Here the best defence lies in high professional standards, tested with an informed peer or peer group. In psychiatry, because of the psychiatrists' special powers of detention, there is a complex set of laws, regulations and institutions to deal with these powers. Knowledge of the local arrangements is as essential to the practice of psychiatry as is knowledge of the pharmacopoeia. Any psychiatrist should therefore see this knowledge, or access to it, as part of good professional practice.

Beyond a basic knowledge of the legal framework of psychiatry and good practice, the best way of avoiding legal difficulties is to engage in frequent peer review. This may be done through informal consultations, formal one-to-one consultations, seminars and medical audit. One useful model is practised in the medium security hospital unit in Wales where one of us works. Each clinical team will call a peer review conference for each patient as a routine within the first year of admission, as discharge is being considered and on an *ad hoc* basis whenever else the team considers that it would be useful to do so. The peer review is regarded as quorate if there is at least one representative from each clinical discipline present at the meeting in addition to the presenting clinical team representatives. Observations from the clinicians from outside the patient's team are regarded as purely advisory, as the patient's team retains full responsibility for that patient, but the debate is often influential.

Court work

Court work may have a significant impact on the work of a psychiatrist, especially a forensic psychiatrist. Such work can be mystifying, intimidating, time-consuming and frustrating. Guidance is given in subsequent chapters about techniques for avoiding these negative factors. As a preliminary to those chapters, it is worth reiterating that court work should never, for the psychiatrist, become an end in itself. It should always be possible to explain easily and openly why a particular piece of court work is of benefit to a patient or to patients as a group. Court work should be strictly limited and, if the benefits are not obvious, avoided unless legal demands require it. Court work should always be justifiable in terms of efficiency, that is the time invested should be in proportion to the benefits obtained.

In court, no quarter should be given to the view that 'our side must win'. Doctors are likely, as we outlined, to have quite different considerations from the lawyers with whom they work. A doctor should take an objective view of the issues before him or her, and only be as partisan as medical ethics require. In law, the doctor, like any other expert, is supposed to have 'no other desire than to assist the court' (*Nowell*). That implies that everything, including all clinical duties, should be suspended for this high purpose. In practice, it can be taken to indicate that the doctor is expected to give a wholly truthful and balanced view, not dependent on which 'side' employed him or her, but professional judgments will have to be made in each case as to how far the court's desires should interfere with medical standards. In England this doctrine has been taken to the point where it seems perfectly proper for a doctor to provide the court with information which the employing solicitor would prefer to suppress (*Edgel*).

A book by Janet Malcolm (2011), *Iphigenia in Forest Hills*, describes a New York murder trial. It should be compulsory reading for all lawyers working in the adversarial system and it would be useful reading for anyone who attends such

a court as an expert witness. It is the story of a young couple who disagreed about child rearing methods in respect of their only daughter. They separated pending divorce, but the husband was murdered by an unseen man at a routine custody handover meeting of the child to her mother. The mother was accused of hiring an assassin to kill her husband. The trial is described in considerable detail and is not comfortable reading. Even though it is possible for a British reader to say with a modicum of accuracy, 'Oh that's America, it's not like that here', the author lays bare the mechanisms of a criminal trial in the adversarial system and shows how easy it is for evidence to be distorted, misrepresented, and misunderstood. The author also points to the doubts that may arise in respect of 'factual' scientific evidence. She documents the huge influence, indeed power, that a single judge, with all his or her personal prejudices, may have on a trial. As the trial was in America the author was able to interview some of the jurors after the case was over and thus illustrate something that remains a mystery in the UK, the arguments which are used within the jury room to convict or otherwise. No one can read this book and feel comfortable that justice is bound to be done in our well-established system. The forensic psychiatrist who agonizes about the accuracy of risk assessments can take a crumb of comfort from realizing that other parts of the criminal justice system probably do not do any better. The judge in the case, Judge Robert Hanophy, of Caroline Beale fame,[1] saw himself as having a matter of fact approach; 'somebody's life was taken, somebody's arrested, they're indicted, they're tried and they're convicted. That's all this is'. Janet Malcolm, however, sets the trial in context by describing as much about the family involved as she can and showing, as any psychiatrist will know, that there is likely to be a great deal more to a story than emerges in court and that, here, the whole narrative was full of ambiguity.

Perhaps the most disturbing chapter in Malcolm's book is the last one, which should be read by all child psychiatrists and social workers. It describes the New York legal guardian system whereby a lawyer is appointed to protect the best interests of the child. Such lawyers may decide what they think is the child's best interests without reference to family opinions or to the child's opinion. They may not even meet the child who is presumably regarded as totally unable to think for him/herself on account of his/her legal infancy. The author may be going too far in

---

[1] Caroline Beale was a 30-year-old British woman who was arrested in September 1994 at JFK airport in New York with the body of her dead baby under her shirt. She was charged with murder, but after a great deal of legal wrangling and expert evidence both pathological and psychiatric she pleaded guilty to manslaughter and was released to an English probation service for psychiatric treatment. Caroline's father called the New York system of justice mediaeval. This infuriated Judge Hanophy who, in turn, was very critical of the English legal system citing the Irish miscarriages of justice (see Campbell, 1997).

inferring that the domestic homicidal tragedy described was triggered by an eccentric decision of the child's guardian in law to remove this little girl from her mother and give her to her father against the wishes of both parents and the child, but Malcolm does thus highlight the need for skilled multidisciplinary discussions before such a decision is taken, and the potential dangers of lawyers, inexpert in everything but the law, having complete control of such matters. Again it is easy to say that this could only happen in America but anyone who has experience of British family court matters knows that some individuals are much more powerful in the process than others and that full consultation is not invariably undertaken.

ACHIEVING THE KNOWLEDGE AND SKILLS

In the UK, the professions have generally been seen as responsible for developing, directing and scrutinizing their training, although the years since our first edition have seen some substantial changes. Regulation of training was changed, trainers and trainees had to accommodate to the European working directive and professional bodies reached out to other professions and service users to develop new approaches to training and new ways of working. A main effect of the European working directive, reducing weekly working hours to 48, meant that there had to be a rapid expansion of undergraduate training and of consultant posts, and postgraduate trainees and trainers alike have found it difficult, at times, to accommodate (Temple, 2010). Forensic psychiatric trainees and trainers have had to adjust, like everyone else, and the resultant competency-based curriculum was developed by the Royal College of Psychiatrists (2010b), with its specialist faculties working in conjunction with the curriculum committee, which included lay members. Competencies are organized within a framework of seven 'good medical practice domains', with acknowledgement that there is much overlap between them:

1. Medical expert.
2. Communicator.
3. Collaborator.
4. Manager.
5. Health advocate.
6. Scholar.
7. Professional.

The process is one of following basic medical training with postgraduate foundation training, then core psychiatry training, finally building to advanced training in forensic psychiatry. Clinical service providers work in conjunction with Deanery Schools of Psychiatry to support training and to complete workplace evaluations of emerging competencies. Successful progress through this system leads to specialist certification, whereupon the new specialist has a responsibility to establish him- or herself in a continuing professional development (CPD) cycle. This is supported by membership of a CPD peer group and annual reporting to the Royal College of Psychiatrists of continuing training achievements, which should follow from a specified job plan and peer agreed objectives.

Table 1.1 gives an indication of what competency-based training looks like, and how forensic psychiatry is built on to general adult psychiatry. It takes one core task (diagnostic formulation) within the good medical practice domain of being a medical expert, first in general terms and then for the specialist forensic psychiatrist. The table has to be read on the assumption that the basic skill, once gained is retained and developed and the specialist skills added. Even within this one skill, it can be seen that the specialist will be expected to be able to draw on a considerable range of the medical and non-medical knowledge and skills background which we have introduced.

The Ghent Group

Citizens of the European Union who have a medical qualification are entitled to practise their specialty in all countries of the Union provided that they have a completed certificate of training (CCT) in their specialty from their home country. Presumably this works easily for some specialties, maybe anaesthetics and pathology, but in psychiatry training differs between countries, and only three countries have specialist certification in forensic psychiatry – the UK, Germany, and Sweden. Furthermore psychiatry is a discipline that is dependent on highly sophisticated language skills; among the British, few are fluent in anything but English. This means that the freedom to practise in other countries is somewhat theoretical, nevertheless, it is important to prepare for working internationally within Europe.

In order to work towards the European objective of cross-border practice a few forensic psychiatrists from a number of European countries met together in Ghent in 2004 to discuss this matter (Gunn and Nedopil, 2005). An annual meeting of trained forensic psychiatrists and, whenever possible, trainee forensic psychiatrists has followed, each in a different European city. Differences in practice, in training, recruitment, national laws and their history, and specialist facilities have all been discussed, and fostered more detailed reflection on training within member countries (e.g. Goethals and van Lier, 2009). One important objective was to find an agreed framework and indeed definition for forensic psychiatry. This was achieved in Copenhagen in 2006, and was given near the opening of this chapter.

One innovation which has proved popular has been a training summer school held at Kloster Irsee in Bavaria, bringing together the Universities of Munich and Cardiff and strong support from the forensic psychiatry group in Denmark. This achieves the goal, not always attained with the more routine meetings, of linking young and inexperienced practitioners with more experienced ones, and has been found to be a useful educational week for all, regardless of experience level or country.

The Ghent group welcomes new members and has a web site for interested readers.

FURTHER ENQUIRY

One of the main purposes of this book is to stimulate further enquiry. Knowledge has increased extensively since our first edition, so most of the text is completely fresh, and very little simply updated. Particular areas of growth have also meant that tantalizing possibilities have presented in the form of taking ever more sophisticated scientific medical evidence into court. Perhaps foremost in this area is neuroimaging. It may have a place in end-of-life decisions (Skene et al., 2009) and arguments have been advanced for its use in civil cases – perhaps as an aid to determining truth of a claim – and against its use in the criminal courts (Sinnoth-Armstrong et al., 2008). The legal evidential standard of 'beyond reasonable doubt' in UK courts is relevant here. Attempts have been made to rely on imaging as evidence of incapacity (USA, Appelbaum, 2009) or guilty mind (India, Giridharadas, 2010), but the weight of argument remains against using such evidence in this context (Reagu and Taylor, 2012). We are reassured that there is some evidence that jurors would be appropriately cautious with it (Schweitzer and Saks, 2011). Advice to exercise caution in expressing evidence which can so easily be made to appear unequivocally scientific by the injudicious expert is pervasive, extending from the Royal Statistical Society (2002; see also chapter 22, risk and chapter 26, ethics) to the diagnostic classification systems. ICD-10 notes that its standard version (WHO, 1992) is intended for general clinical, educational and service use, with a second version (WHO, 1993) for research, but makes no reference to its use in court; DSM-IV is explicit about the risks of its being misused or misunderstood if used for 'forensic purposes' and counsels against its use for legal purposes of establishing mental disorder, disability, disease or defect (American Psychiatric Association, 1994a).

The possibilities of obtaining information, and keeping up-to-date, have extended enormously since our first edition was published. Now, students and practitioners in the UK are able to access the vast wealth of material which is available on the Internet. Dependency on the local university library is no longer absolute, and in any event may be remotely accessed. Librarians are now helpful not only in assisting with acquiring references, but also in advising on search techniques and other technological advances. We expect readers to use this text as a starting point for further reading and research. Where we can, we have generally provided web references, which were accessible at 31 December 2011. We have found that relevant UK governmental websites are quite difficult to navigate, because when articles or research reports are archived, they are given a new electronic reference and inserting key words into their search engines often only produces tracts of irrelevant material. Nevertheless, they provide a wealth of information, some of it only available electronically, and most relevant documents may be downloaded without charge. Google is a good back up, and will often yield the elusive reference when other searches fail. We have not eschewed Wikipedia, although this website warns that its material should be checked. It should be, but we have found it to be very useful and a reliable starting point for further searching. This book itself and its internet references are available on-line to purchasers.

2

Criminal and civil law for the psychiatrist in England and Wales

John Gunn,

with additional material from

Philip Joseph

RD Mackay

with a view from the bench by

Judge Rod Denyer QC

1st edition authors: **Oliver Briscoe, David Carson, Don Grubin, John Gunn, Paul Mullen, Peter Noble, Stephen Stanley** and **Pamela J Taylor**

Laws are not invented. They grow out of circumstances.
(Azarias)

COMMON LAW AND CIVIL OR ROMAN LAW

Legal systems arise from diverse local customs, and become formalized as a society's development requires uniformity and predictability in the control of crime, the regulation of interpersonal relations, and the ordering of commercial transactions. The two most influential legal systems are civil law and systems derived from it, and English common law with its developments overseas. Countries in continental Europe have legal systems derived from Roman law, now called civil law. The lasting influence of the British Empire can be seen in the many of the countries of the Commonwealth, and in North America, which are common law countries. Of course there are other legal traditions which have influenced many countries, for example the soviet system of law, and sharia law in Moslem countries. The Christian canon law, developed both by the church and in the medieval universities, enriched the development of the English common law, particularly in the importance to be attached to the individual conscience in the determination of criminal responsibility and to the pledge in contracts. Mercantile law flowed into the common law in the seventeenth century with the growth of trade. The term civil law is confusing in Britain as part of British common law is called civil law to distinguish it from criminal law, and thus civil law in Britain has a different meaning.

Perhaps the most fundamental difference between civil (Roman) law and common law is in the way that common law developed by legal precedent and is established by the courts, whereas in civil law countries this is thought to be somewhat primitive, as all law in that tradition is formulated by the legislature and handed to the courts in the form of statutes and codes. It is very puzzling to someone brought up in a civil law country to learn that in England and Wales, for example, murder is a common law offence and has no statutory basis.

Some call the two main systems of criminal law procedure in the Western World the inquisitional system and the adversarial system. In essence the inquisitorial system conducts an enquiry into an alleged crime, a judge supervises that enquiry and s/he, alone or with others (judges or jury), make a finding. In the adversarial (or accusatorial) system the state prosecutes a case against an alleged criminal in front of a judge or jury and the accused answers the case as best as he or she can by refuting evidence, producing alibis and so forth. When both sides have fully aired their respective cases the court (judge or jury) decides who has the better argument according to agreed standards of proof such as 'beyond reasonable doubt' or 'on the balance of probabilities'. Inevitably this is an oversimplification and it should be noted that the two systems are influencing each other and drawing closer together. For example, the UK undertakes many enquiries which are inquisitorial in nature such as, for example, mental health review tribunals and Parole Board hearings. Continental European countries usually allow some degree of argument from prosecution and defence in court. In North America some jurisdictions that have been heavily influenced by French culture, e.g. Quebec in Canada and Louisiana in the USA, have retained some elements of the Napoleonic Code (this is humorously exaggerated in the play *A Street Car Named Desire* by Tennessee Williams).

A strength of the common law is its roots in the country's history and social customs. It became an integral and growing part of society, adapted by the judges as they saw the need. This natural indigenous strength enabled it to withstand the otherwise probable introduction of civil law at the time of the Renaissance. Civil law has the attraction of a logically coherent system. The contrast was drawn by the celebrated American judge, Justice Holmes, who said, 'The life of the (common) law is experience and not logic.' Thus, the common law grew by adaptation and response to actual circumstances and situations, instead of starting with a general theoretical formulation of legal principles which would then be applied to particular cases as in civil law (see Pollock and Maitland, 1968 for further reading).

This chapter, indeed this book, is almost exclusively concerned with common law. It would be impossible to have it any other way for each country has its own legal system and generalizations of 'common law' and 'civil law' don't really give much guidance to the system that might be found in any particular country. For example the laws of France and those of Germany, two very large continental countries both claiming to practice civil law, are remarkably different from one another and together they are different from most other civil law countries. A useful and most informative book 'written for amateurs, not professionals' is by Merryman and Pérez-Perdomo (2007) and should be consulted by any British forensic psychiatrist abroad.

In England the post conquest Norman seignorial courts gradually gave way to the unifying effect of a common law administered by the royal judges riding out on circuit from Westminster to hold assizes in major towns and, by the end of the thirteenth century, the supremacy of the King's courts was established. To ease the burden upon the royal judges of administering the criminal law nationwide, the forerunners of present-day magistrates were appointed by 1328. The King's Bench was one of the principal central courts set up at that time. The exercise of the early common law depended upon a limited number of particular writs issued by the King's Chancery and only certain wrongs were recognized as capable of being redressed. The embryonic centralized or common law was developed by the royal judges adapting customs and such principles as they knew. They were held to be the repository of the law and would declare what it was when confronted by a particular set of circumstances. Thus, we can see the origins of the present concept of precedent where an established principle decided in a specific case is applicable in subsequent cases, although superior courts can overrule a precedent.

The early writs were not sufficiently flexible for a developing society, and pleas for justice, where no writ was available, began to be made to the King. The Court of Chancery was established as the pleas addressed to the King were passed to the Lord Chancellor who tended to decide according to what he thought was equitable instead of following strict common law principles hammered out by the King's judges. So the common law grew by the experience of innumerable cases, leavened by the individualistic remedies of the Chancery. As more cases were heard in the Chancery courts, it too began to develop rules and principles as precise as those of common law. That system came to be known as equity. For many years the common law and equity developed side by side, practised in different courts by different judges. In 1873 the Judicature Act fused these two systems so that courts today employ both blended together. A contemporary example would be the legal mortgage and the equitable mortgage, both capable of being held in respect of the same property, but subject to different rules (see Walker, 1980 for definitions).

In England the adversarial system of justice is employed. When a criminal case is heard in the Crown Court the parties to the case are the accused or defendant, and the Crown or prosecution. The legal representatives of both sides present their view of the facts, examine and cross examine witnesses, and make closing speeches to the jury. The judge sums up, and instructs the jury upon the law. The jury are the judges of fact, they consider the evidence, bring in a verdict, and the judge passes sentence. Only some cases are officially reported, but those that are add to the ever-growing body of reported decisions which influence the results in future cases on identical or similar relevant facts. There are many sets of printed reports. The *All England Law Reports* are an example. Databases, such as *Lexis,* are now recording all the decisions of the High Court and above.

The doctrine of precedent is very important to the practice of law in England. Judgments are said to be binding or persuasive. Thus a judgment in the Court of Appeal on a particular set of facts will bind judges in the Crown Court in a case on conceptually similar facts. A judgment in the Supreme Court will bind the Court of Appeal. A judgment in the Crown Court will be only of persuasive authority if a similar case is heard in the Crown Court.

In modern English law, statute (i.e. acts of Parliament) plays an increasingly important part. Sometimes statutes are used to codify parts of the law, where perhaps a myriad of individual case decisions have become what Cromwell called an 'ungodly jumble', and have made the law uncertain. The Theft Acts 1968 and 1978 are examples of codifying statutes. Sometimes, like the Mental Health Act 1983 (amended) statutes arise purely from Parliamentary concern and debate. Statutes are often framed in general terms, and precise definition may not be given. Thus the term mental disorder in the Mental Health Act 1983 (amended) is not defined. If a particular case required the term to be defined, this would be a question of law for a judge in the particular circumstances of the case. Another example might be the meaning of 'treatment' in a particular statute.

Thus the common law in its broadest sense is a cycle of accumulating case decisions which may require clarification by statute, itself to be interpreted by further case law. How the cases concentrate and what statutes are required depend upon the issues in contemporary society, its philosophy, its politics, ethics, and its concept of rights. Since Britain joined the European Economic Community, the European Court has erected a further tier of binding authority above the Supreme Court. Common law is, obviously, an older system of law than modern statute law. It is gradually being codified by parliamentary statutes, but it should not be thought that in situations where little or no statute law has been enacted there is no law. Usually there is well-developed common law. A case in point is the law of battery. This is the infliction of unlawful personal violence by one person on another. Violence in this sense includes all degrees of personal contact (e.g. touching) without consent or other lawful authority. Clearly, this is of great importance in medicine, for much that is done by a doctor could be called battery unless it is with the consent of the patient. Hence the importance of the law of consent and an individual's capacity to give consent (see chapter 4). Many other circumstances are covered by the common law. It is not possible to deal extensively with the common law authorities or cases in this book. Professionals in doubt about the legal position in a particular case should consult legal textbooks and, on occasions, legal advisers. However, and this is most important, they should not allow ignorance of the law, or absence of advice, to prevent them from acting in the patient's best interests. If a matter is urgent, then good medical care should be offered without looking backwards to law. The commonest suit that patients bring against clinicians is one of negligence, but the law of negligence emphasizes both contemporary standards of professional practice and what level of competence was to be reasonably expected. Acting in good faith with proper professional skill on behalf of the patient is usually a sound defence when negligence is alleged, particularly in an emergency. Indeed, inaction may itself be unlawful in some situations because, if the law construed that someone has a duty to take a particular action, then failure to take that action may give rise to a criminal charge or to a civil liability.

EUROPEAN COURTS

In addition to national courts Europe has two influential international courts. The European Court of Justice (mentioned above) is in Luxembourg and deals with all matters relating to the laws and regulations of the European Union, disputes between member states and the European Union and matters of that kind. So far it has had little to say about psychiatric practice. However, the European Court of Human Rights in Strasbourg, established as part of the European Convention on Human Rights of 1950, has had a profound effect on both mental health law and prison law throughout Europe including the United Kingdom (see Council of Europe).

The *Convention for the Protection of Human Rights and Fundamental Freedoms* (usually known as the *European Convention on Human Rights*) is a remarkable achievement. It is a treaty between the 47 member states of the Council of Europe. The states maintain their sovereignty but commit themselves through conventions and co-operate on the basis of common values and common decisions. The Convention was adopted in 1950 and became operational in 1953. It created the European Court of Human Rights which sits in Strasbourg. The Court supervises compliance with the European Convention on Human Rights and thus functions as the highest European court for human rights. It is to this court that Europeans can bring cases if they believe that a member country has violated their rights. It has 59 articles and 13 protocols. It is the section on rights and freedoms, articles 2 to 18, especially article 5, which is of most interest to the forensic psychiatrist. An abbreviated version of the Convention is given in appendix 1.

The Human Rights Act 1998 brought the Convention rights into UK domestic legislation. The impact of the Convention and particularly article 5 is seen at its most marked in the various mental health acts of the UK and the Republic of Ireland.

COURT STRUCTURE, ENGLAND AND WALES

Figure 2.1 shows the overriding importance of the new Supreme Court and also the lines of appeal, but not all courts are included, e.g. coroners' courts are omitted and there is no mention of the Parole Board which functions as a court. Tribunals are included but they now are part of a separate tribunal service. For this text coroners' courts will be included in this chapter and mental health review tribunals in chapter 3.

CRIMINAL LAW IN ENGLAND AND WALES

It is a long-standing principle of English common law that to be guilty of a crime and subject to the full rigours of the appropriate punishment two elements should be proved (except in cases of strict liability, such as careless driving). First, it has to be shown that an illegal act or omission has occurred and been carried out by an identified person (*actus reus*). Further, it has to be shown that the act or omission caused the offending consequences. Second, it has to be shown that the person had the state of mind (*mens rea*) proscribed in relation to that crime. There is plenty of room for debate on both of these issues in many cases; resolution of these is one important function of criminal courts. The second or 'mental' element is the one with the greater potential for debate.

If this sounds somewhat arcane, a simple hypothetical example may illustrate both the importance and the difficulty of making decisions about these concepts. Let us suppose that two people are coming, side-by-side, down a long stone staircase. One of them falls, crashes to the bottom,

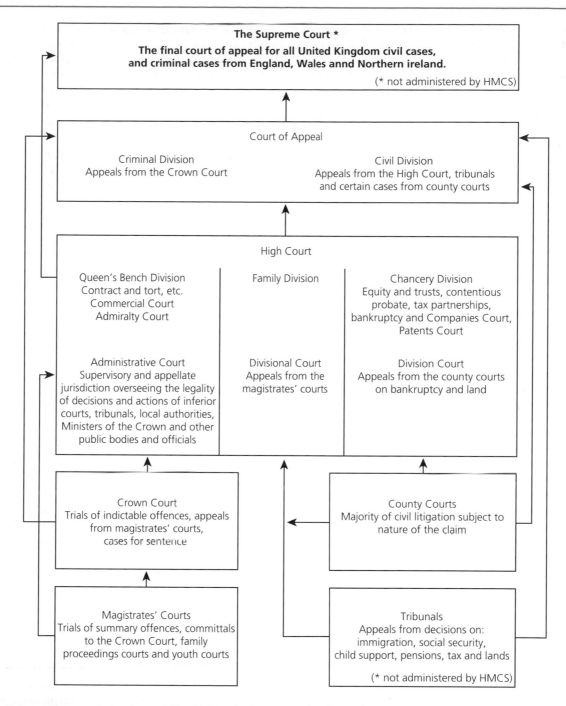

Figure 2.1 The court structure of Her Majesty's Courts Service (HMCS) in England and Wales. Reproduced from the HMCS website: www.hmcourts-service.gov.uk/aboutus/structure/index.htm

suffers a head injury and dies. Did the survivor touch the deceased? Was the touch a push or a trip? If it was a push or a trip was it deliberate or an accident? If it was deliberate what was the intention? The answers to these questions determine whether the incident was an accident or a crime, and if a crime, the seriousness of the crime.

In the real case of *White*, Mr. White put poison in his mother's drink in order to kill her; she drank some of the poison and died, but from a heart attack; thus no *actus reus* of murder took place and Mr. White was convicted of attempted murder instead.

In the law, *mens rea* means the mental state or quality of behaviour (such as 'recklessly') required for the offence under consideration, and it is expressly stated or implied in the definition of the particular offence. For example, in the Theft Act 1968, theft is defined in section 1 as dishonestly appropriating property belonging to another with the intention of permanently depriving the other of it. Thus the *mens rea* for the offence of theft requires both dishonesty and an intention permanently to deprive the victim of the property. In other offences expressions such as 'knowingly' and 'maliciously' describe the required *mens rea*. Clearly 'mental state' is used here in a very restricted sense; it is concerned largely with the cognitive aspects of a person's mental state and not with the emotional aspects. *Mens rea* may include intentionality, recklessness, 'guilty knowledge' (i.e. knowing that one is doing wrong), competence and responsibility. Such concepts are abstract ideas, antedate psychiatry, and are *not* subservient to medical ideas.

The concept of responsibility, for example, is fundamental to our view of man as a free, intentional being. Every society, every culture uses it. It is the basis of every criminal code and system of punishment. We understand that some people (e.g. the young, the mentally abnormal) are less responsible than others, and we sometimes excuse people of responsibility altogether. Lawyers use a list of excuses which includes mistake, accident, provocation (to a charge of murder), duress and insanity (Hart, 1968). Psychiatrists are sometimes called upon to give evidence in support of these excuses. As we shall see below, they should, on the whole, resist the temptation except in very special circumstances or in the case of insanity. They should note too that they are called upon to give *evidence* rather than take the decision, even though courts press hard on occasions for medical opinions about these non-medical matters. The rules concerning expert testimony limit such witnesses to their expertise and psychiatrists should, in particular, avoid being drawn into discussions of moral or legal responsibility.

In considering the way a legal system handles these matters, it is as well to remember that 'the law' is neither logical nor consistent, nor does it satisfy everyone's notion of justice. It is human, pragmatic, and has developed by piecemeal legislation, by precedent and by tradition (see Ormerod, 2008 for a good account). In England, it is so pragmatic that it has produced the apparent paradox that all but a tiny handful of mentally abnormal people are found guilty of their antisocial/illegal acts even if they were clearly mentally abnormal at the time of the act, and matters of responsibility and culpability are dealt with as mitigation of sentence. This is probably true even in other legal systems which use the insanity defence more often.

For convenience, the criminal process including the court hearing will be divided into three phases: pretrial, trial, and sentence. These three phases can be detected in every criminal hearing even if they are very brief or amalgamated. Table 2.1 indicates the issues to be considered in each phase.

Magistrates' Courts

No matter how grave, all crime has its first hearing in the magistrates courts, where basic issues are addressed, such as whether there is sufficient evidence against the accused

Table 2.1   Criminal hearing

Pretrial	Trial	Sentence
Prosecution	Automatism	Psychiatric mitigation
Fitness to plead	Insanity	
	Infanticide	
	Diminished responsibility	

to constitute a 'case to answer' in a higher court, and whether s/he should be granted bail.

Over 95% of cases are finalized in the magistrates' courts, almost 92,000 cases are sent or committed to the Crown Court for trial, and a further 20,000 cases committed to the Crown Court for sentence.

In magistrates' courts, approximately 7% of defendants plead not guilty; in the Crown Court, approximately 33% plead not guilty. Details of the history, composition and procedure of these courts may be found in various texts such as Walker (1985), White (1991) and Skyrme (1983). Such courts try offences occurring within their own catchment area or local criminal justice areas, of which there are some 254 in England and Wales. The maximum penalty which may be imposed is 6 months' imprisonment for a single offence (and 1 year for two offences), in addition to fines, the upper limit of which is £5,000 (2007). The magistrates' court may also order the defendant to pay compensation of up to £5,000. Apart from about 300 district judges and deputy district judges who are legally qualified, paid for the work, and who sit alone, the function of judge (in sentencing) and jury (in deciding issues of innocence and guilt) is performed by two or three justices of the peace, who are unpaid lay members of the public who have had some training. The linchpin in the magistrates' court is the legal advisor to the justices, who advises on points of law and procedure. The courts are of 'summary' jurisdiction, in which brevity is of the essence. Over 90% of cases are dealt with without a request for psychiatric opinion or intervention. Even so, magistrates' courts pass the bulk of the hospital orders which are made each year (these data are from the Crown Prosecution Service annual report 2006/7); more up to date data can be obtained from www.cps.gov.uk/Publications/reports/

Mental Health Courts

It is noticeable that mental health courts do not appear in figure 2.1. They are new, experimental and may not last. They are adjunctive to magistrates' courts.

Most authorities now recognize that large numbers of mentally disordered people are caught up with the criminal justice system. Since the 1990s Britain has developed criminal justice liaison and diversion services which operate as an interface between mental health services and criminal justice agencies to ensure that offenders with mental health problems are diverted into treatment. Rutherford (2010) estimates that there are

150 such schemes in England and Wales. The schemes however do not in any way meet the demand for such services. Rutherford lists some of the reasons why this might be so: for example there are no national guidelines; they are poorly funded; they rely on inadequately trained staff; they do not seek to influence the decision of the court; they do not have assertive interventions.

In the United States a different system also known as mental health courts has developed. Two mental health court pilot projects were established in England in 2009. They are not running parallel to the general court system (as in the USA) but are integrated into magistrates' courts. The two pilot schemes were established in Brighton and in Stratford (east London). These schemes also do not meet with universal approval. Bradley (2009) questioned the value of such courts in his report 'the majority (of benefits) could be met by effective liaison and delivery services which would eventually be available to all courts.' Such optimism is hardly justified by the results of the first 10+ years of the criminal justice liaison and diversion services. In reality if either type of service is to succeed, a great deal will depend on the level of both psychiatric interest and resources which support them, above all psychiatrists and psychiatric nurses will need to be specifically trained.

The existence of two slightly different services working towards the common goal of diverting mentally disordered people from the criminal justice system provides an ideal comparative research opportunity. Who is betting on that opportunity being taken?

Pretrial

For illustration let us take a mentally abnormal man who has been violent. The police are called and the criminal process begins. As soon as the facts are clear and a defendant is arrested, the police officer in charge of the case has decisions to make about *mens rea* and/or mitigation (although s/he does not call them that); s/he has to decide whether a prosecution should proceed at all. If the patient is already having psychiatric treatment, s/he may ask the doctor and/or hospital to deal with the matter as a medical one. S/he is told that 'provided sufficient evidence exists, the decision whether to charge must be guided by what is in the public interest. The existence of mental disorder should never be the only factor considered and the police must not feel inhibited from charging where other factors indicate prosecution is necessary in the public interest.' It is essential to take account of the circumstances and gravity of the offence and what is known of the person's previous contacts with the criminal justice system and psychiatric and social care services (Home Office Circular 1995, No. 12). If a hospital or doctor declines to take the patient or the police officer believes that to fail to prosecute would be against the public interest s/he will report the case to the Crown Prosecution Service. Once again, the question of going forward will be

debated and here, too, it is possible for psychiatric advice to be sought and, if appropriate, for the case to be diverted from the penal system to the healthcare system.

Another option available to the police officer, if the arrest was made in a public place, is to move the offender directly into a mental hospital under the police powers (s.136) within the Mental Health Act 1983 (amended). This can be done irrespective of whether the offender is already a patient or not. If the offensive behaviour was in a public place and the police officer thinks that the individual is 'suffering from mental disorder and to be in immediate need of care or control' in the patient's own interests or for the protection of others, the constable should take the patient to 'a place of safety', which can be a hospital, to await a medical examination. The detention is for a maximum of 72 hours and the hospital has to agree to take the patient (it may refuse). The 'place of safety' may also be a police cell, but no one believes that this is an appropriate place to care for an acutely disturbed patient and the Code of Practice (Department of Health, 2008) sees it as a place of last resort. The Code emphasizes that:

The purpose of removing a person to a place of safety in these circumstances is only to enable the person to be examined by a doctor and interviewed by an AMHP (approved mental health professional), so that the necessary arrangements can be made for the person's care and treatment. It is not a substitute for an application for detention under the Act, even if it is thought that the person will need to be detained in hospital only for a short time. It is also not intended to substitute for or affect the use of other police powers (para. 10.14).

Prosecution decisions are not necessarily affected by this process, although admission to hospital may make prosecution less likely and hospital rejection may make it more likely. Phillips and Brown (1998), in their study of 4,250 people detained at ten police stations in England and Wales, in 1993/4 found that, 'Those whom the police treated as mentally disordered were much less likely than average to be charged: this was the outcome in just 44% of cases.' Robertson et al. (1996) reported a similar pattern in their research: 'The below average charge rate for mentally disordered detainees partly reflects the fact that a third had been detained under the Mental Health Act and not for an offence. However, those arrested for offences were also less likely than average to be charged.'

If it is decided to prosecute the offender, then s/he will have to appear in a magistrates' court. Here s/he will be remanded on bail or in custody according to the rules of the Bail Act 1976. The bail decision will be influenced by medical opinion about suitability for treatment and availability of treatment facilities. The court may also wish to remand the offender to hospital, either as a voluntary patient, or under the powers of the Mental Health Act 1983 (amended). As the criminal process moves on, the magistrates' court will have to decide whether there is a case to answer (the ancient grand jury function) and, if so, whether it should be tried in a lower court or moved up to the Crown Court. The rules which are applied are complicated but, briefly there are three categories of seriousness: the most serious or indictable which have to go to the higher court, the least serious or non-indictable which are always tried in a magistrates' court (summary trial), and a large middle group which is triable either way, and in which any of the parties – prosecution, defence, or court – can opt for trial by jury in the Crown Court.

Fitness to plead

If someone is so mentally disordered that it is thought unfair to proceed with his or her trial, then the trial can be postponed, often indefinitely. Magistrates may postpone or adjourn the case to await a more favourable time; if they adjourn the proceedings *sine die* (i.e. postpone the case without a date for a further hearing), this is tantamount to excusing the accused from a trial. The other options available to them are either to promote the case to the Crown Court, so that the question of fitness to plead can be properly tested, or to proceed with the trial in order to hear the facts against the accused and consider a hospital order without recording a conviction (see below). If a remanded prisoner is suffering from 'mental illness or severe mental impairment', it is also possible to transfer him or her to hospital under section 48 of the Mental Health Act 1983 (amended).

The concept of being unfit to plead emerged from the rituals of the medieval court of law where a trial had to begin with the taking of the plea. If an individual was mute and did not enter a plea, the court had to decide whether this was through malice or by visitation of God. By the nineteenth century, the court also made a further determination of whether the accused could conduct a 'defence with discretion' (*Dyson*). An individual who was unfit to plead was said to be insane on arraignment and, subsequent to the Lunatics Act 1800, held at Her Majesty's Pleasure, usually in an asylum.

The criteria by which an individual is determined to be unfit to plead evolved through nineteenth-century case law, mainly in relation to cases of deaf mutes who were unable to communicate; the most important case was that of *Pritchard*. In essence, an individual is unfit to plead if s/he is not able to make a proper defence. Fitness has been interpreted as:

> being able to plead with understanding to the indictment; being able to comprehend the details of evidence; being able to follow court proceedings; knowing that a juror can be challenged; being able to instruct legal advisers.

Clearly, these criteria are concerned with intellectual performance. This is one illustration of the difference between the legal category of insanity and the medical concept of mental illness, showing how much weight is put on understanding or cognition in the former. Although the Criminal Procedure (Insanity) Act 1964 codified the process whereby a person is found unfit to plead (known in it as 'disability in bar of trial') and integrated it into modern legal practice, it remained silent on the factors that actually render an accused unfit to plead. The criteria, therefore, remain those relating to nineteenth-century legal concepts of insanity.

The question of fitness to plead can be raised by the defence, the prosecution or the judge. Although the judge can delay consideration of the question until after the prosecution has presented its case to ensure that there is, in fact, a case to answer, in practice, the issue is usually raised and decided pretrial. Since the passing of the Domestic Violence, Crime and Victims Act 2004 the issue of fitness to plead is decided by the court without a jury. This involves evidence and testimony by a psychiatrist directed towards the criteria listed above, as the 1964 Act was amended by the Criminal Procedure (Insanity and Unfitness to Plead) Act 1991 to ensure that a finding of unfitness to plead cannot be made except on the evidence of two registered medical practitioners, at least one of whom is duly approved by the Secretary of State under the Mental Health Act.

The number of individuals found unfit to plead had been declining steadily since the late 1940s (Walker, 1968). Between 1980 and 1992 there were on average about 20 cases a year in England and Wales (Grubin, 1991a). Individuals who were then found unfit to plead, including those who are mentally impaired or deaf, were sent to 'such hospital as may be specified by the Secretary of State'. The bed had to be made available within 2 months. Little was known about the fate of those who had been found unfit to plead before 1976, but the course of all individuals found unfit to plead between 1976 and 1988 has been documented (Grubin, 1991a,b,c). Most had been sent to local, catchment area hospitals, although about 30% had been sent to high security special hospitals. Once in hospital, the patient was treated as though detained on a hospital order with restrictions on discharge, and came under the jurisdiction of the Mental Health Act 1983, amended 2007. Thus, it was possible for an individual found unfit to plead to be held in hospital for the remainder of his or her life without ever having been tried. Because of this risk of unlimited detention, it was often said that the issue of fitness to plead was only raised in cases where the charges were serious. In fact, however, only about one-quarter of cases between 1976 and 1988 involved charges of a severe nature; about one-third were related to cases of only mild severity, the most infamous of which involved Glen Pearson, accused of stealing £5 and three light bulbs from a neighbour's house (the case is described by Emmins, 1986).

Thus the arrangements for this group of mentally disordered people were very unsatisfactory. Only a few cases found unfit to plead were returned for their day in court after their mental health had improved. However, for those subject to restrictions, the Secretary of State could also discharge the patient from restrictions instead of remitting him or her for trial. In addition, because the patient was detained under the Mental Health Act (amended), discharge via a mental health review tribunal was also possible. Patients who did not recover were subject to long-term compulsory hospitalization. Of those found unfit to plead between 1976 and 1988, almost a quarter remained in hospital in 1990. Most were, in fact, quite unwell and needed to be in hospital in view of their mental health. However, because they were held on the grounds of being unfit to plead, some of them were cases who would not otherwise have attracted a restriction order.

Following repeated criticism the law relating to both fitness to plead and insanity was amended in the Criminal Procedure (Insanity and Unfitness to Plead) Act 1991. This law made two important reforms. In the case against an individual likely to be found unfit to plead, it requires a trial of the facts to be held to determine whether s/he has committed the act or omission in question. In effect this means that the prosecution must prove that the accused has committed the *actus reus* which forms the basis of the charge. If they cannot do so the accused will be acquitted. So it is only in those cases where the prosecution can satisfy a jury as to this requirement that the accused will be the subject of any further disposal by the court. Further, although the House of Lords in the case of *Antoine* confirmed that the trial of the facts does not include proof of the *mens rea* but only the *actus reus*, nevertheless the accused in such proceedings may be able to use certain defences. For example, if the accused is charged with assault but there is clear evidence that s/he was acting in self-defence then s/he ought to be able to use such a defence.

The 1991 Act also introduced flexible disposals for findings of unfitness to plead and verdicts of not guilty by reason of insanity, removing the inevitability of a hospital order with indefinite restrictions on discharge. This meant that a range of disposal options became available to the court. Subsequently, the Domestic Violence, Crime and Victims Act 2004 refined the disposal options. There are three available disposals. As before an individual may be admitted to hospital with or without restrictions, but any hospital order must now comply with all the required conditions for the making of such an order under the Mental Health Act 1983 (amended), and the court will determine which hospital the patient will go to. This important change was in order to protect those who are unfit to plead but not mentally disordered, such as the deaf mute, from possible hospitalization. A second option is for the court to use a community disposal, e.g. a supervision order under the 2004 Act which specifically includes those who are physically as well as mentally disordered; a medical treatment requirement can be added if appropriate. The court may also order an absolute discharge. In the light of this disposal flexibility the number of findings of unfitness to plead has risen (see Mackay et al., 2007a).

One way of avoiding or illuminating these weighty matters in the case of an individual who meets the required criteria is for the court to remand the patient to hospital under s.36 Mental Health Act 1983 (amended). If the patient improves quickly, then the trial may proceed, if not, then there is more information available. Another way (see below) is to make a hospital order without recording a conviction.

Amnesia

From time to time, a good deal of attention has been given to the question of memory and fitness to plead. It is sometimes argued that if someone has a loss of memory for the time during which s/he is alleged to have committed an offence, then s/he cannot properly defend him- or herself and so should be regarded as unfit to plead. All common law jurisdictions have ruled that amnesia does not affect fitness to plead. They could hardly rule otherwise if the courts are to continue to function. The most notable case concerning this issue was that of *Podola*.

Mr Podola was charged with the murder of a policeman by shooting. He submitted that he was unfit to plead because of amnesia for the events. He was found fit to plead and subsequently convicted. On appeal, the principle that the defence should only have to prove the unfitness on the balance of probabilities was clearly enunciated, and the jury's verdict that the hysterical amnesia from which Mr Podola was alleged to have suffered was insufficient to amount to a disability in relation to the trial was confirmed. His counsel had submitted that he could not 'comprehend' the details of the evidence. The Appeal Court judges ruled that, nevertheless, he was of sufficient intellect to comprehend the course of the trial proceedings and that was what mattered. Further, a previous Scottish case had ruled that loss of memory on the part of a defendant did not render his trial unfair because he could tell the jury that he had no recollection of events. The Court of Appeal concurred and agreed that the jury should take the loss of memory into account, but of itself this should not render an accused unfit to plead.

Between one-half and one-third (O'Connell, 1960; Taylor and Kopelman, 1984; Kopelman, 1987) of people charged with serious offences, especially homicide, have some degree of amnesia for their offence and cannot adequately recall what happened at the time. Few questions about this issue will be asked of the psychiatrist in the pretrial phase in England.

The clinical aspects of amnesia are dealt with in chapter 12.

The Trial

The three main issues for psychiatrists in the trial are automatism, insanity, and diminished responsibility. It is only in homicide that English law allows degrees of responsibility according to degrees of mental health. In all other cases a defendant is found responsible or not responsible and findings of non-responsibility on psychiatric grounds are extremely unusual. The special verdict, like all serious convictions until the nineteenth century, carries a mandatory sentence, (meaning no judicial discretion), if the jury believes there is malice aforethought. In other words it is a common law offence which has survived into the twenty-first century with a minimum of codification by statute. The reasons for this are political and historical. Until the abolition of the death penalty in Britain in 1965 the mandatory sentence was execution. Execution is always popular with the tabloid press and it was a struggle for abolitionist MPs to get the sentence repealed. They did so, in part, by agreeing to keep the verdict of murder different from all other verdicts by giving it the mandatory sentence of life imprisonment. The reality is however that homicide, like all other serious offences, comes in different shades of intent and malice. The calculated killing of someone for their money is different from a drunken fight in which someone dies and different again from a mercy killing. During the time of capital punishment all three such cases would probably have been sentenced to death although mitigation was often exercised by the Secretary of State. The Homicide Act 1957 was introduced to circumvent this nonsensical position to some extent by allowing special mitigation for mental disorder and for provocation. This did not solve the problem entirely and several attempts have been made to persuade various governments to remove the mandatory sentence for murder as allowing judicial discretion which would enable the judge to give a sentence appropriate to all the circumstances of the case. Politicians however are adamant that murder must remain different.

Automatism

Automatism is difficult enough to define in medical terms. It is even harder in legal terms. A good discussion of the legal principles involved is to be found in Ashworth (2006). Automatic behaviour is involuntary behaviour and most likely unconscious behaviour. English courts have divided automatism into non-insane (sane) automatism and insane automatism. A successful defence of automatism will always lead to a finding of not guilty, however the distinction between sane automatism and insane automatism means that the latter is subject to the McNaughton[1] Rules (see below) and thus disposals available to the court are as for insanity. The basis for the distinction is whether or not the automatism was caused by 'a disease of the mind'. As Ormerod (2008) reminds us 'whether a cause is a disease of the mind is a question of law' i.e. not medicine or psychiatry. Any 'internal factor', mental or physical, is, in law, a disease of the mind, so automatism caused by cerebral tumour or arteriosclerosis, epilepsy (see below), or diabetes arises from a disease of the mind. Convulsions, muscle spasms, acts following concussion, anaesthesia, medication or hypnosis are external causes

[1] Also spelt M'Naughten.

and if successfully proved lead to a verdict of not guilty. As time has passed courts have tended to put more types of automatic and/or unconscious behaviour into the insane category, largely on the pragmatic ground that behaviour which is otherwise criminal and is likely to recur is better regarded as insanity. For example, sleepwalking at one time could be said to lead to sane automatism but since 1991 (*Burgess*) it has been regarded as insane automatism.

Two matters of medical importance concern self-induced intoxication which cannot *per se* give rise to a defence of automatism, but is complicated and dealt with under insanity below. The second matter is epilepsy which illustrates how legal thinking in this area has developed. At one time epileptic automatism was a fairly certain non-insane excuse. Bratty killed a girl by strangulation with one of her stockings. He said that a 'blackness' came over him and that he did not know what he was doing. He was said to suffer from psychomotor epilepsy. At the trial, the defences of insanity and automatism were both raised, but the trial judge refused to allow the defence of automatism. The jury found Bratty guilty of murder. On appeal, the conviction and the refusal to allow the defence of automatism were upheld in the House of Lords. Lord Denning said:

> It seems to me that any mental disorder which has manifested itself in violence and is prone to recur is a disease of the mind. At any rate, it is the sort of disease for which a person should be detained in hospital rather than be given an unqualified acquittal.

Thus was the concept of insanity enlarged and that of sane automatism diminished. A further step on the road was the case *of Sullivan,* also finally decided in the House of Lords. Mr. Sullivan was described as a man of 'blameless reputation' who suffered from epilepsy and had been treated for several years as an outpatient. When he was visiting a neighbour, he probably had a seizure and attacked an elderly man who was talking to him. The elderly man had to be treated in hospital, and Mr. Sullivan was charged with causing grievous bodily harm. His defence was automatism and evidence was given that he was almost certainly in an epileptic state at the time of the assault. Nevertheless, the judge ruled that the defence was really one of not guilty by reason of insanity. The defendant changed his plea to guilty and was given 3 years on probation with a condition of treatment. Lord Diplock dismissed an appeal against conviction on the grounds that epilepsy is properly described as a 'disease of the mind'. This meant that epilepsy is to be regarded as insanity in the legal sense. It has also been decided that hyperglycaemia may be regarded as a disease of the mind (*Hennessy*) if caused by failure to take insulin for diabetes. (The position in respect of hypoglycaemia is less clear; see for example *Watmore*.)

The Sullivan case sparked off letters to the medical journals and a symposium to discuss it all (see Fenwick and Fenwick, 1985). What had happened was the pragmatic reaffirmation that people who do violent things will be subject to legal controls whatever semantic contortions have to be endured. Mr. Sullivan was found guilty, and the mitigating factors in his case were taken into account at the sentencing stage. He received a sensible disposal and was not punished for his automatic behaviour. The effect of all this on the patient has been described:

PS, like Rogozhin (Dostoevsky's character in The Idiot*), never contradicted his clever counsel, although he clearly found his eloquence beyond his comprehension....We told him that the judge was prepared to consider him not guilty by reason of insanity 'But I'm not insane,' said PS. We advised him, because of the consequences of this, to plead guilty. 'But I'm not guilty,' said PS. Even the eloquent counsel paused, then PS spoke again: 'But you're three intelligent, educated people – I'll do whatever you say' (Taylor, 1985).*

Things improved with the passage of the Domestic Violence, Crime and Victims Act 2004. Now unless the accused is suffering from a 'mental disorder' within the meaning of the Mental Health Act 1983 (amended) which warrants treatment in a psychiatric hospital s/he cannot be sent to hospital. This means that if the only reason for the automatism (as in the Sullivan case) is found to be epilepsy, then only a non-custodial disposal would be available. No longer then would Mr. Sullivan be 'forced' to change his plea to one of guilty. However he would still carry the stigma of being labelled 'insane' which is a disincentive to using such a plea (see MacKay and Reuben [2007] for a discussion).

As the door closed on epilepsy and sleep-walking being non-insane automata in England and Wales, it is still left open for concussion and drug-induced states of altered consciousness. Two mental hospital nurses were charged with causing actual bodily harm to a patient by assaulting him. One of them had diabetes and he said that, before the assault, he had taken his insulin, but had eaten too little and had no recollection of the incident. His medical evidence supported hypoglycaemia at the material time. The trial judge (J Bridge) ruled that the proper defence would be insanity, whereupon the defendant pleaded guilty. His appeal was, however, allowed on grounds that a disease of the mind within the meaning of the McNaughton Rules is a malfunction caused by disease as opposed to a transitory external agent (such as insulin). The Court concluded:

In our judgment the fundamental concept is of a malfunctioning of the mind caused by disease. A malfunctioning of the mind of transitory effect caused by the application to the body of some external factor such as violence, drugs, including antibiotics, alcohol, and hypnotic influences, cannot fairly be said to be due to disease. Such malfunctioning, unlike that caused by a defect of reason from disease of the mind, will not always relieve an accused from criminal responsibility. A self-induced incapacity will not excuse, see Lipman, *nor will one which could I have*

been reasonably foreseen as a result of either doing, or omitting to do something, as, for example, taking alcohol against medical advice after using prescribed drugs, or failing to have regular meals while taking insulin (Quick).

Although the very rare problem of violence associated with epilepsy has been firmly put in the insanity category, this case opens the possibility (no more than that) that an epileptic seizure caused by an external agent, for example a flickering light, could still successfully plead sane automatism (see Mackay and Reuben, 2007).

Insanity

A prominent myth concerning forensic psychiatry is that questions of insanity in the trial are an important part of the job. In reality, very few cases of insanity come to the courts each year in England and Wales and the average forensic psychiatrist can expect to deal with only one or two in a professional lifetime.

Hospital orders without a conviction

There is a special mechanism in the lower or magistrates' court for dealing with mentally disordered offenders. Quite simply, the magistrates press on with the case if it is within their jurisdiction, hearing the evidence for and against conviction. If they are persuaded that the accused carried out the act as charged, they can then take psychiatric evidence about him or her. If a recommendation is forthcoming that the defendant should go to hospital rather than prison, and hospital order papers are signed, they can then accept that option and simultaneously decide, under section 37(3) of the MHA 1983 (amended) not to record a conviction. This neat device ensures a proper hearing, but allows a psychiatric disposal without the stigma of what would be a criminal conviction in the tradition that the mentally ill should be excused the behavioural consequences of their illness (insanity). The disposal is not used very often; most such offenders are convicted and then given a psychiatric disposal. Perhaps it should be used more often. It should always be considered as a possibility by the examining psychiatrist and discussed with the patient's lawyer when the patient is to be recommended for a hospital order in the lower court. It is also helpful in cases where the accused is charged with a relatively trivial offence, but seems unfit to plead.

The special verdict

In England and Wales, legal insanity is a valid defence to any charge which can be tried in the Crown Court.[2] The Criminal Procedure (Insanity and Unfitness to Plead) Act 1991, as with unfitness to plead, brought in flexible disposal following an insanity verdict, giving the court a range of disposal options. The tests of insanity used in the trial

---

[2] It is also available in a magistrates' court where there is no special verdict so may in an appropriate case give rise to an unqualified acquittal, see *Singh*.

focused on knowing and understanding. The tests are the 1843 McNaughton Rules (see West and Walk, 1977). The Rules state:

> *Every man is presumed to be sane, until the contrary be proved, and that to establish a defence on the ground of insanity it must be clearly proved that at the time of committing the act the accused party was labouring under such a defect of reason, from disease of the mind, as not to know the nature and quality of the act he was doing, or if he did know it, that he did not know that what he was doing was wrong.*

In essence this has two limbs. The first, which is the 'nature and quality' limb, has been interpreted to require that the accused because of a disease of the mind 'did not know what he was doing' (*Sullivan*). The second, the 'wrongness limb', is limited to those who, again because of a disease of the mind, did not know that what they were doing was legally wrong (Johnson, 2007; EWCA Crim, 1978). Both limbs are so narrow and limited in their application that they will rarely be applicable to those who are mentally ill, irrespective of the severity of the illness.

A lesser-known rule says:

> *If the accused labours under a partial delusion only, and is not in other respects insane, he should be considered in the same situation as to responsibility as if the facts with respect to which the delusion exists were real.*

This latter rule relates to the defence of mistake, and is difficult for psychiatrists to understand because of the difficulty of knowing what is meant here by a partial delusion and, in practice, is rarely employed. A partial delusion is probably not simply an overvalued idea, but is more likely a monosymptomatic delusion. The rule seems to be saying that if, for example, the man accused held a single delusional belief that his ear surgeon had implanted a transmitting device in his head and the device was interfering with his brain or giving out messages, then an assault (let us say on the surgeon) should be judged by the jury as if that were really true.

Clearly, the McNaughton Rules are strict rules. However, much as with unfitness to plead, the introduction of flexibility of disposal has resulted in an increase in the use of the insanity defence (see Mackay et al., 2007b).

Most jurisdictions using these rules have found them unsatisfactory and tried various devices to circumvent them. For example in the USA there is the Durham Rule, the American Law Institute Rule, and there is even a verdict of guilty but mentally ill in some states. This last piece of legislation has been highly contentious because it is argued that an insane person cannot be guilty (see Blunt and Stock, 1985, and Weiner, 1985, for discussions). However, very few mentally abnormal offenders in any jurisdiction are protected against conviction by their mental status at the time of the offence. The special verdict was of much greater importance in Britain when the mandatory sentence for murder was capital punishment and there was no diminished responsibility law. Arguments about the McNaughton Rules became arguments about life and death.

Diminished responsibility

Infanticide

Special legislation concerning women who kill their children originated in an 'Act to Prevent the Murthering of Bastard Children' of 1624, which decreed that if an unmarried woman concealed a birth and the child was subsequently found dead, she was presumed to have killed it unless she could prove that the child was born dead. The Act was aimed as much at discouraging immorality as against the killing of children, and the penalty was death. In the seventeenth and eighteenth centuries most infanticide charges were under this statute; three-quarters of the accused were spinsters (Beattie, 1986). By the mid-eighteenth century attitudes began to change and both judges and juries became reluctant to convict. An Act of 1803 changed the onus of proof, and infanticides were then treated like other kinds of murder. Concealment of birth became a separate offence in 1828 (Smith, 1981). The last woman executed for killing her child was Rebecca Smith in 1849; she had used poison (suggesting premeditation) and was suspected of poisoning several other children (Walker, 1968). Since the mid-nineteenth century the death penalty has invariably been commuted, and by 1864–65, when the first Royal Commission on Capital Punishment heard evidence, most witnesses were in favour of exculpatory legislation on infanticide. After a series of unsuccessful bills the first Infanticide Act was passed in 1922. It was restricted to the killing of 'newly-born' children, but uncertainties of interpretation led to the enactment of the Infanticide Act 1938 which extended the age limit to 12 months.

The Act provides that if a woman kills her child under the age of 12 months in circumstances which would otherwise amount to murder, but at the time 'the balance of her mind was disturbed by reason of her not having fully recovered from the effect of giving birth to the child or by reason of the effect of lactation consequent upon the birth of the child', she will be convicted of infanticide, an offence punishable as if she had been guilty of manslaughter. In practice, it is dealt with leniently and the defence is falling into disuse. In 1971 there were 18 cases; between 1997/8 and 2007/8 there were 20 cases, 5 in 2000/1 but only 3 between 2001/2 and 2007/8. This gives an annual average of 6.8 women convicted of infanticide in the last third of the twentieth century and one in the first 8 years of the twenty-first century. Although the majority since 1997 were put on probation three were sentenced to terms of imprisonment of 4 years or under (Povey et al., 2009).

About half the women convicted of infanticide kill new-born children in the context of unwanted, concealed pregnancies, and about half are battering mothers. Social and psychological stresses are more relevant than mental illness (d'Orban, 1979), although puerperal psychosis must not be forgotten as a potentially lethal illness (see chapter 20).

Infanticide can be charged in the first instance, but often the initial charge is murder, and infanticide is either replaced as the charge or is pleaded as a defence to the murder charge. Once evidence has been adduced to raise the defence, the burden of disproving it rests on the Crown; in this respect it differs from the defences of insanity or diminished responsibility, where the burden of proof is on the defence using the balance of probabilities standard. Further differences are that infanticide does not require proof that the killing resulted from the abnormal mental state, merely that, at the time, the mother's 'balance of mind' was disturbed. The jury does not have to weigh the question of responsibility. The degree of abnormality implied by the disturbance of 'balance of mind' is, in practice, much less than that required to substantiate 'abnormality of mind' in the diminished responsibility defence (d'Orban, 1979).

Despite some anomalies, the Infanticide Act 1938 continues to serve a useful purpose. One anomaly is that it only applies to the killing of the last born child although the mother's other children may also become victims. Another anomaly, the lack of provision for an offence of attempted infanticide, has been remedied by the Criminal Attempts Act 1981, so that a woman whose baby victim survives can now be charged with attempted infanticide rather than attempted murder (Wilkins, 1985). Third, the Court of Appeal has decided in *Gore* that infanticide is not restricted to cases where the offence would only have amounted to murder in the sense that it must be proved that the accused intended to kill or cause grievous bodily harm at the time of the killing. Rather, infanticide is wider and may be used where the accused is charged with manslaughter. This makes infanticide a wider offence/defence than was originally thought and will protect those women who, whilst mentally disturbed as a result of childbirth, kill their children under the age of 12 months but do so by neglect rather than intentionally. In short, such women will not be required to acknowledge that they murdered their children before they can benefit from a charge of infanticide.

Scotland, like some civil law countries, has used diminished responsibility since the nineteenth century (Walker, 1968). England embraced the concept for the same reason that it had embraced infanticide: growing abhorrence of the death penalty. Both these concepts allow a killer to be convicted of a serious offence, one carrying life imprisonment if appropriate, but they give discretion to the judge and avoid any mandatory sentence death until 1969 (1965 in effect) and now life imprisonment. There is considerable confusion about the future of this concept in England with the enactment of the Coroners and Justice Act 2009 in November 2009 (see below). It abolishes the provocation defence and significantly changes the diminished responsibility legislation. It is worth noting something of the existing diminished responsibility legislation and its history to set this change in context.

Section 2 of the Homicide Act 1957 stated:

S.2 Persons suffering from diminished responsibility

1. *Where a person kills or is a party to the killing of another, he shall not be convicted of murder if he was suffering from such abnormality of mind (whether arising from a condition of arrested or retarded development of mind or any inherent causes or induced by disease or injury) as substantially impaired his mental responsibility for his acts and omissions in doing or being a party to the killing.*

2. *On a charge of murder, it shall be for the defence to prove that the person charged is by virtue of this section not liable to be convicted of murder.*

3. *A person who but for this section would be liable, whether as principal or as accessory, to be convicted of murder shall be liable instead to be convicted of manslaughter.*

4. *The fact that one party to a killing is by virtue of this section not liable to be convicted of murder shall not affect the question whether the killing amounted to murder in the case of any other party to it.*

Provocation

Where on a charge of murder there is evidence on which the jury can find that the person charged was provoked (whether by things done or by things said or by both together) to lose his self-control, the question whether the provocation was enough to make a reasonable man do as he did shall be left to be determined by the jury; and in determining that question the jury shall take into account everything both done and said according to the effect which, in their opinion, it would have on a reasonable man.

It was not long before this curious Parliamentary wording was subject to a deal of legal wrangling. In *Byrne* a judge's direction was overturned by the Court of Appeal and Lord Chief Justice Parker ensured that, from 1960 onwards, the concept of abnormality of mind used in the statute could be interpreted very widely. He ruled:

Abnormality of mind... means a state of mind so different from that of ordinary human beings that the reasonable man would term it abnormal. It appears to us to be wide enough to cover the mind's activities in all its aspects, not only the perception of physical acts and matters and the ability to form a rational judgment whether an act is right or wrong, but also the ability to exercise willpower to control physical acts in accordance with that rational judgment.

This remarkable judgment made legal history. It introduced the long-disputed concept of the irresistible impulse into the law on homicide and allowed all forms of mental disorder – handicap, neurosis, personality disorder – to be considered for the verdict. Byrne himself was an unintelligent, personality-disordered individual.

Presumably the intention was to allow the most disordered people to be excused as insane, other middle ground cases to be liable to conviction of manslaughter, leaving only the mentally normal to the full rigours of a conviction for murder. Presumably too, the Lord Chief Justice would have expected the proportion of people excused from murder on psychiatric grounds to increase, but this did not happen.

The defence can only raise the question of diminished responsibility on medical grounds, and it has to be demonstrated on the balance of probabilities. Sometimes, the prosecution and defence agree that there is such a probability. If so, they can then put their agreement to the trial judge; if s/he accepts the position and the facts are clear, there is no trial, the accused is convicted of manslaughter and the sentencing can begin. If either the prosecution or the judge disputes the defence submission, then the matter is argued out in the usual way in front of a jury who make the final decision.

Griew (1988) and others have argued that the wording of the Homicide Act is extremely odd and makes for legal difficulties. As a result:

Psychiatrists, rather more than lawyers, have agonized over the statutory expression, have looked unavailingly to the lawyers for enlightenment, and have contributed to the inconsistency in the use of the section by the differences in their own reading of it... There can be little doubt that the fate of some people charged with murder since 1957 has turned on the qualities of robustness and sophistication shown by those professionally involved in their cases.

Yet something more fundamental than this is happening. When Griew was writing in 1988 approximately 16 or 17% of murder charges were being reduced to manslaughter by reason of diminished responsibility. Since that time the picture has completely changed and at the beginning of the twenty-first century the rate of such decisions has dropped to 2 or 3% (figures calculated from Povey et al., 2009). This must be due to changing social pressures and illustrates that legal decisions are subject to those pressures just like all other behaviour. It is difficult to know what factors have brought about this fairly dramatic change, but impressions from the courtroom would suggest that prosecution policies have changed so that many fewer 'diminished' cases are dealt with by agreements between the prosecution and the defence and many more are subject to trial and the opinion of the jury. Standing in the court room, it often seems that juries are reluctant to grant any mitigation from mental disorder; indeed they sometimes seem to regard mental disorder as an aggravating factor. In addition to these legal issues it seems also that psychiatrists are less and less willing to acknowledge the role which mental disorder plays in many serious crimes. This may be due in part to swimming with the tide of increasing toughness and incarceration for interpersonal offences and it may also be affected by resource issues. A diminished responsibility verdict may imply to the judge, for example, that hospital admission would be more appropriate than imprisonment and, as the stock of long-term security beds falls, such admissions are less and less palatable to psychiatrists.

These trends are much longer term than they appear on superficial examination and they are almost certainly rooted in British government policy, in spite of frequent declarations that diversion of the mentally disordered to prison is a government objective. Dell (1984) showed that, between 1964 and 1979, in spite of an increasing number of homicides in England and Wales, and in spite of the fact that at that time the proportion of men who had their conviction reduced to manslaughter by reason of diminished responsibility remained fairly constant at 20%. The number of such convicted men going to hospital had not changed (about 24 per annum) but the number of such men going to prison increased sharply (12 men in 1964, 48 in 1979). Dell suggested possible reasons for this increasing proportion being sent to prison and concluded that the main factor was a decreasing readiness of psychiatrists and prison doctors to recommend hospital places. In turn, this reluctance was based on a tightening up of the criteria for admission to special hospitals. The Department of Health had tightened the criteria for admission to high security hospitals with the hope that regional health authorities would provide a bed instead. In practice, reporting doctors increasingly failed to recommend this option and more and more men went to prison.

The myth that high security hospitals are not really needed and that they can be supplanted (largely if not completely) by a scattering of medium security units across the country is driven by a fine idealism, but omits to take into account important and practical considerations such as the extra cost of managing long-term patients this way, the hostility to serious offenders which exists within many mental health trusts, and the important domestic needs of long-term patients which are often not adequately met in medium security units. The idealism is driven by the notion that most if not all psychiatric care can be managed 'in the community'. Serious offenders who have significant mental disorders cannot be admitted to the community; they require long-term hospital care. Caution has been urged about the consequences of running down the high security hospital population (see for example Abbott, 2002; Coid and Kahtan, 2000; and Gunn and Maden, 1998) but it has largely fallen on deaf political ears. The special or high security hospital population in England peaked at 2,522 patients in 1956 and has been falling steadily since that time; by 1987 it was 1,724 and 10 years after the turn of the century it is approximately 400. It is no wonder that the trend towards imprisoning mentally disordered serious offenders has continued and now is virtually changing the law with the marked reduction in the proportion of homicide offenders who are able to take advantage of the Homicide Act 1957. Of course this should not occur; each case should be considered on its merits and the consequences of doing that should put pressure on the government to change its policies and services. Reality is different however, and although the actors in the pageant are not aware of colluding with a paradoxical government policy, that is what they do.

It is generally agreed that homicide legislation in England and Wales is unsatisfactory. The Law Commission (2006) produced a proposal to modify the common law offence, as has been done in many of the United States, so that homicide could be prosecuted in different degrees thus producing first-degree murder and second-degree murder with only first-degree murder continuing to carry the mandatory sentence. They said:

The law governing homicide in England and Wales is a rickety structure set upon shaky foundations. Some of its rules have remained unaltered since the seventeenth century, even though it has long been acknowledged that they are in dire need of reform. This state of affairs should not continue. The sentencing guidelines that Parliament has recently issued for murder cases presuppose that murder has a rational structure that properly reflects degrees of fault and provides appropriate defences. Unfortunately, the law does not have, and never has had, such a structure... We will recommend that, for the first time, the general law of homicide be rationalized through legislation. Offences and defences specific to murder must take their place within a readily comprehensible and fair legal structure. This structure must be set out with clarity, in a way that will promote certainty and in a way that non-lawyers can understand and accept.

However, the Law Commission shied away from shooting the elephant in the room. The mandatory sentence bedevils all legal discussion about murder because it removes all discretion about punishment and disposal from the court. The Homicide Act 1957 is an attempt to acknowledge the varying degrees of culpability of homicide. This Act and its successor would not be necessary if the mandatory sentence were removed. The judge who tried the case could impose the penalty appropriate to the facts of the crime. The mystical significance of the mandatory sentence is lost on most people who have grown up in Europe in which capital punishment is outlawed by protocol 13 of the Council of Europe. To shrink the elephant somewhat the Law Commission

recommended that England and Wales should follow the American system of having two degrees of murder in addition to manslaughter.

HM government responded to the 'Murder Report' as they called it with a consultation document (Ministry of Justice, Home Office 2007) which was issued during the summer holiday season of 2007. The document made it clear that the crime of murder was not to be considered. They said:

The Murder Report recommends wholesale reform of the law in this area and, specifically: a new offence structure for homicide, including new offences of first degree and second degree murder, as well as manslaughter; reforms to the partial defences of provocation and diminished responsibility; reforms to the law on duress and complicity in relation to homicide; and improved procedures for dealing with infanticide... In taking forward this (report), the Government is proceeding on a step-by-step basis, looking first at the recommendations which relate to: the partial defences of provocation and diminished responsibility; complicity in relation to homicide; and infanticide. The Law Commission's recommendations in these areas are predicated on their proposed new offence structure, but this paper considers them in the context of the existing structure (italics added). The wider recommendations in the Law Commission's report may be considered at a later stage of the review.

This is perverse, as the partial defence proposals have to be seen in the context of the new proposals for murder.

HM government went on to set out their own proposals:

To abolish the existing partial defence of provocation and replace it with two new partial defences of:

- *killing in response to a fear of serious violence;* and
- (to apply only in exceptional circumstances) *killing in response to words and conduct which caused the defendant to have a justifiable sense of being seriously wronged.*

There were 73 responses representing the 54 million people of England and Wales. The end result is the Coroners and Justice Act 2009. For diminished responsibility the Act has produced the following amendments to section 2. The first clause has now been divided into three subclauses with their own subdivisions. The reader should be warned that our consultation with lawyers who study this particular field has produced no simple answers as to the meaning of the new wording which will obviously give rise to many courtroom disputes and Court of Appeal judgments. The only advice that can be given in a textbook is to watch out for the date of implementation, take the best legal advice available to you after that date and follow the judgments which will arise. The other clauses of section 2 remain the same. However, and this may be the real meat of the changes, section 3, the defence of provocation has been abolished.

S.2 Persons suffering from diminished responsibility

1. A person ('D') who kills or is a party to the killing of another is not to be convicted of murder if D was suffering from an abnormality of mental functioning which – (a) arose from a recognized medical condition; (b) substantially impaired D's ability to do one or more of the things mentioned in subsection (1A); and (c) provides an explanation for D's acts and omissions in doing or being a party to the killing.

> *1A. Those things are – (a) to understand the nature of D's conduct; (b) to form a rational judgment; (c) to exercise self-control.*
>
> *1B. For the purposes of subsection (1c), an abnormality of mental functioning provides an explanation for D's conduct if it causes, or is a significant contributory factor in causing, D to carry out that conduct.'*

Will this improve the situation? It is impossible to say especially as the new wording for diminished responsibility in the 2009 act is difficult to understand but in the face of the continuing mandatory sentence it is unlikely. Some further thoughts on the use of the new law in court are given on p.168.

Disputed facts and mental disorder

A small but important point to note about a murder trial is the peculiar difficulty in which a defendant finds him- or herself if s/he both disputes the facts of the alleged killing and is also mentally disordered. In the case of any other charge up to and including attempted murder, the matter is straightforward; the defendant simply pleads not guilty using whatever evidence is available to him or her (e.g. an alibi). If that defence does not succeed, then at the sentencing stage psychiatric evidence can be adduced in mitigation. If, however, the victim dies and the charge is murder, the same defendant would be in a much more difficult situation. There is no mitigation possible against the life sentence for murder. Any psychiatric evidence would have to be adduced in the trial to either insanity or diminished responsibility, and this would have to be done at the same time as trying to convince the jury that the wrong person had been charged anyway. A difficult task indeed – the psychiatric case is almost bound to reduce the credibility of the factual one and the jury may become muddled as to their task.

Alcohol and drugs

Intoxicating substances require a special section because they raise legal and philosophical issues which are quite different from other issues dealt with in the trial.

Self-induced intoxication is generally no defence to a criminal charge. Traditionally, it has been regarded as an aggravating factor rather than an excuse. Thus Aristotle (BC 330) in book 3 of the Nichomachean Ethics stated that penalties were doubled if the offender was drunk. He also formulated the modern concept of recklessness: the drunken man is punished even if he did not know what he was doing because he is responsible for getting himself drunk. Coke in the seventeenth century, and Blackstone, in the eighteenth, both regarded drunkenness as an exacerbating the offence (Whitlock, 1963; Walker, 1968). However, during the nineteenth century these rigid views were modified to allow for the partial exculpation of the intoxicated offender in the case of serious crimes which would otherwise attract harsh penalties (Fingarette and Hasse, 1979). There are now two circumstances in which drugs or alcohol may be relevant to criminal responsibility: first, if intoxication is of such a degree that the accused does not have the necessary intent to commit the offence; second, if it gives rise to a mental disorder. In some cases either of these arguments could, at least in theory, lead to a defence under the McNaughton Rules.

Intoxication and intent

The difficulty is that intoxication is a temporary form of brain damage which is, for the most part, self-induced. The basic principle is that anyone who intoxicates him- or herself should understand and take responsibility for all the consequences. Intoxication should not be available as an excuse; it is easy to see that if intoxication could be a defence against serious crime anyone planning such a crime with care could take the precaution of being drunk while committing it. On the other hand courts have found it difficult to rule out intoxication as a defence in all cases. A system to cope with this complexity has been developed in England and Wales which is confusing (note also that this does not necessarily apply to other common law countries). The psychiatrist does not need to know all this esoteric law and should lean heavily on experienced legal opinion. Ormerod (2008) gives a good account and what follows is a sketchy version of that authority.

A distinction has been developed between crimes that require a mental element of 'specific intent' and those that require only 'basic intent'. The objective is to allow some intoxicated offenders to be convicted of offences that carry less serious penalties. Crimes of specific intent are those in which the intention (*mens rea*) can be negated by intoxication; examples are murder, wounding with intent to cause grievous bodily harm, robbery, theft, handling stolen goods, burglary and criminal damage. Other crimes such as manslaughter, rape, sexual assault, malicious wounding and grievous bodily harm require only 'basic intent' which cannot be negated by intoxication. The point of this artificial distinction is that intoxication may be a defence to crimes of 'specific intent' if it can be shown that the accused was so intoxicated that s/he could not form the intent required for the offence. The accused may still be convicted of a lesser offence for which only 'basic intent' is required. For example, a killer may have been too drunk to form the intent to commit murder, but that would not matter if s/he was reckless, because recklessness is sufficient to constitute the *mens rea* of manslaughter.

This doctrine was formulated by Lord Birkenhead in the case of *Beard*, who had suffocated a girl while raping her. Things however have become complicated, particularly by *Majewski* which went to the House of Lords, which could not decide unanimously the basis for the distinction between crimes of specific intent and basic intent. Further complications were added by *Heard* but the listing approach to the two forms of intent remains a reasonable starting point. Even so the law does seem confusing and illogical, for example it is possible for a drunken shoplifter to be acquitted of theft but to be convicted of assaulting the arresting store detective. The Butler Committee (Home Office, DHSS, 1975) suggested the creation of a new offence of 'dangerous intoxication' to deal with this problem, but this idea has never been taken up.

Although the law originally developed in relation to alcohol intoxication, drugs are treated in a similar fashion. Lipman killed a girl while under the influence of LSD; he thought he was struggling with snakes and asphyxiated her by stuffing a sheet down her throat. He was acquitted of murder, as he lacked the required specific intent, but was convicted of manslaughter as he was deemed to have been reckless and thus had basic intent or *mens rea*.

Alcohol, drugs and mental disorder

1. **The insanity defence (special verdict).** If alcohol or drugs give rise to psychotic illness (for example delirium tremens or amphetamine psychosis) the McNaughton Rules, in theory, may be applicable, although, in practice, the insanity defence is now rarely used. In *Davies,* a man was charged with wounding with intent to murder during an attack of delirium tremens. Stephen J drew a clear distinction between simple intoxication and disease caused by alcohol:

   Drunkenness is one thing and the diseases to which drunkenness lead are different things: and if a man by drunkenness brings on a state of disease which causes such a degree of madness, even for a time, which would have relieved him of responsibility if it had been caused in any other way, then he would not be criminally responsible.

2. **Diminished responsibility.** Under section 2 of the Homicide Act 1957, an 'abnormality of mind' must arise from one of the causes specified in the Act; those of possible relevance to drugs and alcohol are disease, injury or inherent causes. An abnormality of mind arising from intoxication is no defence (*Fenton*).

It is doubtful whether alcohol or drug dependence alone without any psychiatric complications or additional factors would qualify as a disease causing 'abnormality of mind'. The essence of the legal disease concept of dependence is

the assumption that the conduct of the addict is involuntary, and this cannot be accepted as a general proposition (Fingarette and Hasse, 1979). In *Tandy*, it was explicitly stated that the very first drink of the day would have to be completely involuntary – a tough test indeed.

The question of alcohol dependence as an 'inherent cause' was discussed in *Fenton* where the defence argued that:

Part of the appellant's mental make up is.... an inability to resist the temptation to drink, and accordingly when he succumbs to this temptation he must be regarded as succumbing to an abnormality of mind due to inherent causes.

Dismissing the appeal, the court nevertheless left the door open, stating that:

A case may arise where the defendant proves such a craving for drink or drugs as to produce in itself an abnormality of mind within the meaning of section 2 (of the Homicide Act).

In *Di Duca* the defendant who was convicted of murder in the furtherance of theft had pleaded an abnormality of mind arising from injury by alcohol, as he had been drinking beforehand. Dismissing the appeal, the Court found that whether or not alcohol caused 'injury', in Di Duca's case, there was no evidence that it had led to 'abnormality of mind'. This leaves open the possibility that demonstrable evidence of 'injury' by alcohol, if sufficiently severe, could substantiate diminished responsibility. Cortical atrophy on a CT scan combined with psychological deficits (Ron, 1977, 1983) would seem consistent with the concept of injury from the toxic effects of alcohol.

'Pathological intoxication' was once considered to be a specific disease and therefore available as a defence within section 2 of the Homicide Act 1957. In a review Coid (1979) argued that pathological intoxication is an ill-defined diagnostic category and that 'pathological drunkenness' should be omitted from the International Classification of Diseases. It should not be used as a defence. States of supposed pathological intoxication may be attributable to alcohol-induced hypoglycaemia or organic brain damage.

Alcoholic amnesia is a common clinical problem, but the issue of diminished responsibility is unlikely to arise unless there is some abnormality additional to intoxication and subsequent amnesia. If the amnesia is accepted as genuine, the problem is to decide whether the accused was able to form intent at the material time (Glatt, 1982). The same consideration applies to other drugs which may cause amnesia, particularly benzodiazepines (Subhan, 1984).

In most cases where diminished responsibility becomes an issue, drugs or alcohol interact with other factors such as depression, personality disorder or organic brain damage. Although it is an artificial exercise, for legal purposes the effects of intoxication have to be discounted. In order to establish diminished responsibility the associated condition (such as depression) must in itself be of sufficient severity to constitute an 'abnormality of mind'. Thus in *Fenton*, five psychiatrists agreed that the accused had a personality disorder, that he suffered from reactive depression and that he was disinhibited and possibly confused by drink. The jury were directed to convict him of murder if they were satisfied that the combined effect of the factors other than alcohol was insufficient to substantially impair responsibility, and this direction was upheld on appeal. The ruling was confirmed by *Gittens*. A man suffering from depression who took drink and prescribed drugs was taunted by his wife about the paternity of their sons; he clubbed her to death and then raped and strangled his stepdaughter. Three doctors said he had diminished responsibility due to depression, while a fourth said his abnormality of mind was brought on by drink and drugs and was not due to illness. The jury were invited to decide the substantial cause of his behaviour, and they convicted him of murder. On appeal it was held that the judge's direction was improper: the jury must be instructed to disregard the effects of drugs or alcohol and then to consider whether the other matters which fall within section 2 amounted to an abnormality of mind which would substantially impair his responsibility; a verdict of manslaughter was substituted.

The decision in *Gittens* was upheld in *Hendry* and also approved by the House of Lords in *Deitschmann* where Lord Hutton remarked: '*a brain damaged person who is intoxicated and who commits a killing is not in the same position as a person who is intoxicated, but not brain-damaged, and who commits a killing*'.

The defence of involuntary intoxication is applicable both to cases where a person's drink is laced without his knowledge, and to intoxication by drugs prescribed in the course of medical treatment. If successful, the defence of involuntary intoxication results in acquittal but, in practice, it is extremely rare. d'Orban (1989) reported the case of a man who developed a severe psychotic illness from dexamethasone administered for a maxillary operation. Suffering from messianic delusions, he attacked his fiancée believing that he had to kill her to save the world. He was charged with her attempted murder, but was acquitted on the grounds of involuntary intoxication. The Court made no distinction in this case between drug intoxication and a drug-induced mental illness.

Since then, courts have distinguished unforeseen intoxication or unexpected side-effects produced by 'therapeutic drugs' from intoxication caused by alcohol or 'dangerous drugs' (*Bailey*; *Hardie*). In the case of therapeutic drugs, the defendant may be considered reckless if he appreciates that the drug 'may lead to aggressive, unpredictable, and uncontrollable conduct, yet deliberately runs the risk or otherwise disregards it' (*Bailey*). Therapeutic drugs do not necessarily refer to those prescribed for the patient; they may include, for example, diazepam taken in good faith from another person's medicine cabinet (*Hardie*). The distinction between the two classes of drug is not entirely clear, but dangerous drugs seem, in law, to be those that are commonly known to cause aggressive or unpredictable behaviour (*Bailey*).

Law in this area is long overdue for reform. In 2009 the Law Commission produced a report suggesting reform with this press statement:

> *The present rules governing the extent to which the offender's intoxicated state may be relied on to avoid liability are inadequate. Our recommendations would remove the unsatisfactory distinction between basic intent and specific intent and provide a definitive list of states of mind to which self-induced intoxication is relevant.*

In 2012 the Lord Chancellor told Parliament that 'The Government is not minded to implement the Commission's recommendations' (Ministry of Justice 2012, para. 50).

Other 'mental' excuses

So far in the trial phase we have been concerned with automatism, insanity (which may be used for any charge), infanticide and diminished responsibility (which are specific to a murder charge). What about lesser degrees of mental abnormality that do not amount to insanity in respect of other charges? We have noted the way in which magistrates either disregard such questions altogether and simply convict an otherwise acknowledged offender or send him or her to hospital without conviction. In the Crown Court the second option does not apply and mentally ill offenders, not charged with murder, are simply found guilty, even if their illness is severe.

Theoretically, there is no reason to prevent psychiatric evidence being called to support the other 'excuses' (as Hart [1968] calls them) i.e. mistake, accident, provocation, and duress. For example, it could be argued in the case of a man who stabs his wife that he was not McNaughton insane but, nevertheless, was so depressed and as a result so absent-minded that, during an argument with his victim, he did not realize he was wielding a knife and hence the stabbing was accidental. Such a defence is highly unlikely to succeed and in the Crown Court the judge is likely to rule that all psychiatric matters should be dealt with under the McNaughton Rules, i.e. as insanity *v* sanity, and so these defences are rare in English courts and seem to be confined to property offences such as shoplifting (theft). In *Clarke*, the defendant pleaded not guilty to stealing from a shop on the grounds that she was absent-minded as a result of a depressive illness. The assistant recorder directed that her defence was actually the insanity defence and the McNaughton Rules applied, so she changed her plea to guilty. However, the Court of Appeal said the judge was wrong in his interpretation and the conviction was quashed; absent-mindedness did not amount to insanity.

So, psychiatric evidence in the trial is virtually limited to insanity, infanticide or diminished responsibility, or automatism; *Chard* indicates why. Peter Chard was convicted of murder; he had been examined by a prison doctor who pronounced 'mental illness, substantially diminished responsibility, the McNaughton Rules, subnormality and psychopathic disorder, do not appear to me to be relevant to the issue,' but the doctor went on to add, 'what does seem clear to me in the light of this man's personality was there was no intent or *mens rea* on his part to commit murder at any time that evening.' Defence counsel believed that opinion should have been admitted at the trial, even although he could find no precedent for so doing. Roskill LJ was not surprised that no precedent could be found:

It seems to this Court that his submission, if accepted, would involve the Court admitting medical evidence in other cases not where there was an issue, for example, of insanity or diminished responsibility, but where the sole issue which the jury had to consider, as happens in scores of different kinds of cases, was the question of intent.

Concurring, Lane LJ said:

One purpose of jury trials is to bring into the jury box a body of men and women who are able to judge ordinary day-to-day questions by their own standards. … where, as in the present case, they are dealing with someone who by concession was on the medical evidence entirely normal, it seems to this Court abundantly plain... that it is not permissible to call a witness, whatever his personal experience, merely to tell the jury how he thinks an accused man's mind – assumedly a normal mind – operated at the time of the alleged crime with reference to the crucial question of what the man's intention was (Chard).

The Sentence

The length and complexity of the discussion of the role of psychiatry in the trial phase of a hearing does not signify especial importance. It is more a reflection of the detailed complexity which legal philosophy leads to and which can be so disconcerting to the medical practitioner. In practice, it is in the sentencing phase where the psychiatrist is most needed, can do most good, and is most comfortable, for the philosophical issues are simpler, the legal jargon is minimal, the adversarial process is over and a genuine clinical discussion can be held. One word of warning at the outset may, nevertheless, be appropriate. At the sentencing stage, a great deal of power and authority is, on occasions, loaned to the psychiatrist who should realize that this may be happening. It is not part of a doctor's function to recommend that people are punished, e.g. recommendations for imprisonment, or for particular lengths of imprisonment should always be eschewed. Punishments may be inevitable, but those recommendations will come from elsewhere and the doctor's role is the provision of a realistic and practical disposal. Realistic mitigation means the provision of explanation and meaning to the crime being considered; it means sensible offers of treatment and disposal. Both rejection and/or condemnation on the one hand and wildly overoptimistic proposals on the other are bad practice, as is any encouragement of the belief that the offender will get adequate treatment in prison.

Sentencing theory

Before the question of psychiatric disposal is examined, it is as well to note briefly some of the principles of sentencing to which the judge will attend. Textbooks of sentencing theory and practice have emerged in Britain (see for example Thomas, 2008; Easton and Piper, 2008). The psychiatrist does not need to be an expert in this field, but it is important for him or her to understand what is happening in this crucial phase of the hearing, as it is the phase in which psychiatry and the law have the greatest impact on each other.

Thomas (1979) reminds us that in legal terms discretionary sentencing practice is a modern development beginning in the latter half of the nineteenth century. Originally, the common law allowed the sentencer no discretion in cases of felony other than recommendations of royal clemency and/or transportation to the colonies for the many capital offences then extant. By 1840, however, the number of capital offences was considerably reduced and, later, transportation gave way to penal servitude. In the twentieth century Parliament began to give to courts powers to deal with offenders as individuals. Perhaps the most notable milestone in this respect is the Probation of Offenders Act 1907 which gave courts the power to make probation orders in any case they chose except where the penalty was fixed by law. In Thomas's view the effect of the British legal history of sentencing has been to create two distinct systems of sentencing, reflecting different penal objectives and governed by different principles. The sentencer may choose either a sentence to reflect culpability, or may subject the offender to an appropriate measure of supervision, treatment or confinement.

Underlying the first type of sentencing, which is usually done in the name of general deterrence, is the tariff. This 'represents a complex of penal theories – general deterrence, denunciation, occasionally expiation,' with an overriding principle of proportionality between the offence and the sentence (Thomas, 1979). This means that the sentence is chosen more by reference to the offence than to the offender.

Individualization, on the other hand, looks primarily to the offender; however the offence is always taken into account. Individualizing measures are more likely for five grades of offenders: those under 21, those in need of psychiatric treatment, recidivists who have reached a critical point in their life, persistent recidivists, and offenders who are thought to be a continuing danger to the public. The court will generally rely heavily on psychiatric advice in respect of those requiring psychiatric treatment provided such people are clearly identified, the nature of their problem is explained comprehensively, and a practical plan of management is outlined which is compatible with the judge's view of public safety.

Sentencing was however completely changed by the Criminal Justice Act 2003. It is probably best to let the Act speak for itself through its explanatory notes:

> The Act aims to provide a sentencing framework which is clearer and more flexible than the current one. The purposes of sentencing of adults are identified in statute for the first time, as punishment, crime reduction, reform and rehabilitation, public protection and reparation. The principles of sentencing are set out, including that any previous convictions, where they are recent and relevant, should be regarded as an aggravating factor which will increase the severity of the sentence. A new Sentencing Guidelines Council will be established. Sentences will be reformed, so that the various kinds of community order for adults will be replaced by a single community order with a range of possible requirements; custodial sentences of less than 12 months will be replaced by a new sentence (described in the Halliday report: Home Office, 2001, as 'custody plus'), which will always involve a period of at least 26 weeks post-release supervision in the community; and sentences over 12 months will be served in full, half in custody, half in the community, with supervision extended to the end of the sentence rather than the ¾ point as now. Serious violent and sexual offenders will be given new sentences which will ensure that they are kept in prison or under supervision for longer periods than currently. At the other end of the custodial scale, several 'intermediate' sanctions will be introduced. These include intermittent custody and a reformed suspended sentence in which offenders have to complete a range of requirements imposed by the court. The intention is for the court to be able to provide each offender with a sentence that best meets the need of the particular case, at any level of seriousness, and for sentences to be more effectively managed by the correctional services who will need to work together closely in delivering the new sentences.

This appears to be a mixture of legislative directives and hoped for greater individualization. It is also part of the Labour government 'risk' agenda, as discussed in chapter 3, and puts a heavy emphasis on 'dangerousness'. The Court of Appeal was the authority on sentencing guidelines until the Sentencing Guidelines Council was set up by this Act.

However, it didn't last long. The aim of the Sentencing Guidelines Council had been to issue *sentencing guidelines* to courts to improve consistency in sentencing. The Council was an independent body which took over responsibility for developing sentencing guidelines from the Court of Appeal and the Magistrates' Association. It was chaired by the Lord Chief Justice. It received advice from the Sentencing Advisory Panel, which produced draft guidelines which were published for consultation. All the publications of the Council and the Panel can be accessed at www.sentencing-guidelines.gov.uk

All this has been overtaken by the Coroners and Justice Act 2009. Following recommendations from the Gage Committee (Sentencing Commission Working Group, 2008) the Act amalgamated the Sentencing Guidelines Council with the Sentencing Advisory Panel to form the Sentencing Council for England and Wales. The new Council has four main areas of responsibility: (a) devising sentencing guidelines, and monitoring their use and impact; (b) assessing the impact of sentencing practice and non-sentencing related factors; (c) when requested, assessing the impact of policy and legislation proposals; and (d) promoting awareness of sentencing matters. Functions (b) and (c) are additional to the functions given to the old Sentencing Guidelines Council. The Council is expected to produce and maintain a 'robust' set of guidelines for the criminal courts dealing with criminal cases. When deciding a sentence courts 'must' follow the guidelines 'unless it would be contrary to the interests of justice to do so.' Although the Council undertakes widespread consultation, the final decision on the content of a guideline is that of the Council which is an independent body.

The Council has 14 members. Its President is the Lord Chief Justice who is entitled to attend meetings. There are eight other judicial members, one of these chairs the Council and there are six non-judicial members.

There are four types of sentence available to the courts in respect of adults: discharges, fines, community punishments, and imprisonment. All offences have a maximum penalty set out in law and a limited number of crimes have a minimum sentence. These, for adults, are:

- Life imprisonment for murder.
- Indefinite imprisonment for public protection for a second serious sexual or violent offence (there is a list of qualifying offences), (this replaces the old automatic life sentence). (This has been repealed; see below.)
- 7 years imprisonment for third-time trafficking in class A drugs.
- 3 years imprisonment for third-time domestic burglary.
- 5 years imprisonment for possession or distribution of prohibited weapons or ammunition.

Discharges

A court can make an order to discharge an offender who has been found guilty. There are two types of discharge: (1) absolute discharge in which no further action is taken, since either the offence was very minor, or the court considers that the experience has been enough of a deterrent. (2) conditional discharge in which the offender is released and no further action is taken unless they commit a further offence within a period decided by the court (no more than

3 years). Discharges, conditional or absolute, can be used, on the recommendation of a mental health professional, when a mentally disordered individual needs the opportunity to undertake psychiatric treatment, either inpatient or outpatient, is willing to have such treatment but, in the circumstances of the case, a community order with a condition of medical treatment would be inappropriate (perhaps too severe). An example in this category is the first-time shoplifter who is depressed. The discharge is usually a conditional discharge which is made on condition that the offender does not reoffend within a specified period of time, usually 1 year.

Community orders

Previous community sentences for adults have been replaced by a single generic community order with a range of possible requirements. Judges are able to choose different elements to make up a bespoke community order. The elements which may be included are: compulsory (unpaid) work; participation in any specified activities; programmes aimed at changing offending behaviour; prohibition from certain activities; curfew; exclusion from certain areas; residence requirement; mental health treatment (with consent of the offender); drug treatment and testing (with consent of the offender); alcohol treatment (with consent of the offender); supervision; attendance. Some of these are useful for psychiatric patients.

Supervision

The offender may be required to attend appointments with an offender manager from the Probation Service. The subject of the supervision and the frequency of contact will be specified in the sentence plan. The offender manager can also delegate supervision to another person.

Programme requirement

A court can impose a programme requirement for the offender to attend a group or individual programme. These are usually accredited programmes run by the probation service designed to address the offender's criminal behaviour in the five categories of general offending, violence, sex offending, substance misuse and domestic violence.

Residence requirement

The court can instruct the offender to reside at a place specified, an approved hostel, and a private address or in the case of a mental health treatment order (below) a hospital or a care home.

Mental health treatment requirement (MHTR)

With the offender's consent, the court may direct the offender during a period or periods specified in the order, to treatment by or under the direction of a registered medical practitioner (usually a psychiatrist) or a chartered psychologist (or both). When deciding upon this requirement, the judge must be satisfied that:

- on the evidence of a registered medical practitioner, the mental condition of the offender is such that it requires treatment, but does not need the intervention of a hospital or guardianship order;
- arrangements can be made for the treatment needed; and
- the requirement is suitable for the offender.
- the treatment may be as an outpatient or as an inpatient in an independent hospital or care home within the meaning of the Care Standards Act 2000 or a hospital within the meaning of the Mental Health Act 1983 (amended), but not a high security hospital. The nature of the treatment is not to be otherwise specified in the order.

The offender has to remember that serious challenges to the authority of the supervisors may be dealt with as a breach of the order and lead the offender back to court. Leaving hospital against medical advice, or failing to attend an outpatient clinic, are examples of matters which may be regarded as a breach of the order. As far as treatment is concerned, however, no breach may be implied simply on the ground that the probationer has refused to undergo any particular treatment. The provisions of the Mental Health Act 1983 (amended) would be needed to enforce any particular treatment.

The Centre for Mental Health found that at least 40% of offenders on community orders are thought to have a diagnosable mental health problem (Khanom et al., 2009), but there has been very little uptake of the MHTR since its introduction in 2005. Only 686 orders commenced in the year to the 30 June 2008, and a total of 221,700 other requirements issued with community orders. This compares with 12,347 requirements for drug rehabilitation and 3,846 for alcohol treatment. The CMH team found that probation officers, defence solicitors, and psychiatrists were not fully familiar with the use of the MHTR, some were not aware of it at all, many felt that the court should not get involved in mental health issues! Many others felt that the MHTR was not suitable for people with personality disorder, depression, or anxiety. The research team found that the biggest barrier to the creation of an MHTR was the need for a psychiatric report and some of these, when obtained, did not deal with the possibility of treatment from local mental health services. Court diversion and liaison teams rarely played an active role in the operation of the MHTR. Courts seemed happier with the drug rehabilitation requirement because they were more familiar with it and because the process of making and managing such a requirement is clearer. The team recommended that primary care trusts should commission services to enable the courts to issue MHTRS and the National Offender Management Service should provide detailed information for probation officers. Liaison between courts, probation and health services is obviously important if services are to be implemented.

Drug rehabilitation requirement

A drug rehabilitation requirement provides fast access to a drug treatment programme. Offenders agree their treatment plan with the probation and treatment services. The plan will set out the level of treatment and testing and what is required at each stage of the order. This type of sentence is for problem drug users aged over 16 who commit crime to fund their drug habit and show a willingness to co-operate with treatment. The requirement lasts for between 6 months and 3 years. Treatment is carried out either as an inpatient or outpatient and includes regular drug testing and court reviews. Failure to stick to the treatment plan will mean a return to court for breach of the order.

Alcohol treatment requirement

As with other drugs the alcohol treatment requirement provides access to a tailored treatment programme with the aim of reducing drink dependency. Again the requirement can last between 6 months and 3 years.

Hospital orders

Hospital orders are available to both the Crown Court and magistrates' courts (including youth courts) for individuals who have been convicted of an offence for which they could suffer imprisonment, provided two doctors (one of whom is approved under s.12 of the Mental Health Act 1983 [amended]) are prepared to sign forms stating that the offender suffers from mental disorder.

This gives very wide powers to commit offenders to hospital, including offenders with personality disorders and mental impairment, provided (and it is a very big proviso) that a hospital is willing to accept them. The practical effect is to hand the offender over to medical care which is almost identical to the care provided for civilly committed people under s.3 of the Mental Health Act 1983 (amended). However, unlike patients on treatment orders, those on hospital orders cannot apply to the Mental Health Tribunal for discharge within the first 6 months, and relatives never gain any powers of discharge. The powers given to magistrates to impose a hospital order without recording a conviction have already been mentioned (p.28).

The issue of finding a bed is crucial, especially as available NHS resources decline. If, after an order is made, the hospital changes its mind, then the order lapses 28 days after it was imposed. This does not prevent a new order being made. If the patient is not transferred within 21 days, the Ministry of Justice may try to bring pressure on the hospital concerned. The **interim hospital order** (under s.38) is an arrangement whereby, if the court is in a position to make a hospital order, it can arrange for a trial period first. The arrangement is for 12 weeks in the first instance, renewable for further periods of 4 weeks (28 days) by the court (on the advice of the responsible clinician) up to a maximum of 12 months. Some of the conditions are slightly different to a full hospital order. One of the doctors signing the forms has

to work at the receiving hospital. The patient is not entirely handed over to the hospital; his/her final sentence is yet to be determined so if, during the period of the order, s/he runs away, s/he can be brought back to court. The grounds for making the interim order are slightly less rigorous in that the doctors only have to state that there is 'reason to suppose' that a hospital order is appropriate rather than it 'is' appropriate. An important difference between interim and full hospital orders is that patients on interim orders do not have the right to apply to the hospital managers or to the Mental Health Tribunal at all. Magistrates' courts do not have the power to impose an interim hospital order without recording a conviction. The point of all this is that if there is any doubt about the suitability of a particular patient for a hospital order, then a trial period can be undertaken before (or instead of) a full commitment. It was perhaps primarily intended to test the treatability of those with mental impairment or psychopathic disorder (Mental Health Act 1983), but it is little used in this way.

Another way of carrying out a trial period of treatment before the hospital order decision is finally made is for the Crown Court to remand the offender to hospital (under s.36 MHA 1983 (amended)) for treatment. Magistrates' courts cannot make an order under s.36; it can only be done for patients suffering from mental illness or severe mental impairment, and is only possible for periods of 28 days at a time and 12 weeks in all.

Restriction orders

The effect of a restriction order is to give the powers of leave, transfer and discharge, which are normally held by the responsible clinician, to the Justice Secretary. Such orders are made after a hospital order has been made (they are not available for civilly committed cases) or in respect of transferred prisoners. They are made under s.41 of the Mental Health Act 1983 (amended) only when – *it appears to the court, having regard to the nature of the offence, the antecedents of the offender and the risk of his committing further offences if set at large, that it is necessary for the protection of the public from serious harm.*

One of the reporting (form filling) doctors in respect of the hospital order has to give oral evidence in court before the order can be made, and the order can only be made in the Crown Court. If magistrates believe that a restriction order might be appropriate, they have to promote the case to the Crown Court.

In his/her oral evidence, the doctor will be asked for his/her views on the appropriateness of a restriction order. They will have to think about questions of dangerousness bearing in mind that the restriction order provides, compulsory aftercare with both medical and social work supervision. Whatever the doctor thinks, however, the judge has the last word (once the hospital order is in place) and will impose a restriction order if s/he believes that the criteria have been fulfilled and the public need to be protected.

It should be noted that a restriction order may be imposed when the current offence, perhaps a burglary or a petty theft, would not seem to warrant it, because other factors such as the antecedents of the offender and the content of any medical reports are taken into account. All patients with a restriction order have an opportunity to appeal to the Mental Health Tribunal chaired by a judge.

Guardianship orders

A court may impose a guardianship order instead of a hospital order in suitable cases. Such orders are, however, rare. The usual effect of such an order is to hand over the care of the offender to the local authority, thus giving a social worker limited powers over the patient. It is also possible for someone else to become the guardian. The patients who are most likely to benefit are those who are mentally handicapped or socially impaired. Like a community order, there may be a stipulation about where the patient is to reside; unlike a community order, however, the patient's consent is not required before the order is imposed. One problem with the order is that little can be done if the patient refuses to co-operate, but some patients respond to the knowledge that there is a formal order imposed upon them. Other patients co-operate completely and are relieved to have a social worker advise them on most of the important decisions in their life. The conditions of the order give to the guardian (1) the power to decide where the patient is to reside; (2) the power to require the patient to attend for medical treatment, occupation, education, or training; (3) the power to require access to the patient by a doctor, social worker, or other specified person. Such guardianship orders are underused, partly because local authorities are reluctant to supervise them, and partly because psychiatrists do not have much experience with them.

Prison sentences

For the most serious offences a court may impose a prison sentence. The length of sentence imposed by the court will be limited by the maximum penalty for that crime. Such a custodial sentence can only be imposed if: (a) the offence is so serious that neither a fine alone nor a community sentence can be justified for the offence; or (b) the offender refuses to comply with the requirements of a community order; or (c) the offender is convicted of a specified sexual or violent offence and the court finds that the offender poses a risk of harm to the public.

The sentence imposed by the court represents the maximum amount of time that the offender will remain in custody. Prisoners serving sentences of less than 4 years are released at the halfway point of their sentence. Those who receive a sentence of 4 years or more may apply to the Parole Board for release at the half-way point of the sentence. If the Parole Board does not recommend release, then the offender will be automatically released at the two-thirds point of the sentence.

For those offenders assessed as 'dangerous' and serving indeterminate sentences for public protection release arrangements are different. These sentences ensure that dangerous sexual and violent offenders are subject to assessment by the Parole Board and are not released from prison until and unless their level of risk to the public is assessed by the Parole Board as manageable in the community. If the risk is not reduced to a safe level, they may never be released.

Fixed-term sentences

Many mentally abnormal people are sentenced to fixed-term imprisonment. This may be because their disorder has not been recognized, or it has been ignored, or because no one offered the court a sensible alternative disposal. When a psychiatrist has no offer to make, s/he can sometimes assist a patient by indicating any damage which could occur to the individual if sent to prison. A patient with severe epilepsy, for example, lived on a knife-edge of fit control; previous prison sentences had produced either paranoid psychotic states or status epilepticus, or both. He persisted in being a lorry thief. The court was told of the dangers to his health of imprisonment, but no suitable hospital accommodation could be found, and he was sentenced to 3 years' imprisonment. He died in prison in unrecognized status epilepticus.

A potential trap for the unwary psychiatrist lies in making statements about the length of treatment required in prison should an offender receive it. Some judges will base a sentencing decision on such statements. Psychiatric resources are very scarce in prison and courts have no control over activities within a prison. They have, for example, no power to send a man to a particular prison, such as Grendon. A court can make recommendations about these matters, but that is all. Further, it is no part of the medical role to recommend punishment. Sometimes, the use of custody has to be advised to hold a patient until treatment can be arranged, but this is different from recommending imprisonment itself.

Under the Legal Aid, Sentencing and Punishment of Offenders Act 2012, the judge may decide to extend a fixed-term sentence beyond the need for punishment in order to provide some extra public protection. S/he can do this if the offender is convicted of two specified offences (see below), life imprisonment or custody for life is either not available or not justified, the judge considers that the offender is dangerous and the offence requires a custodial sentence of at least 4 years.

Indeterminate sentences

Indeterminate sentences available to the Crown Court include, for adults: *life sentences*, both *mandatory* and *discretionary*, and *indeterminate sentences for public protection between 2005 and 2012*. Indeterminate sentences for public protection (IPPs) replaced the automatic life sentence for persistent violent offenders and extended sentence to protect people from dangerous offenders. IPP sentences were imposed where the offender would be required to serve at least 2 years in custody or (in the cases of offenders under the age of 18) where the offender has a previous conviction for one of a specified list of very serious offences. Imprisonment for life is the maximum sentence for those over 21 convicted of some serious offences, e.g. manslaughter, attempted murder, rape, armed robbery, arson etc.

Young people who commit very serious offences are dealt with under sections 90/91 of the Powers of Criminal Courts (Sentencing) Act 2000. If the conviction is for murder, the young person is sentenced under s.90 to **Detention during Her Majesty's pleasure**, which is a mandatory sentence for a child who was aged 10 or over but under 18 at the time of the offence. As with life imprisonment the court will set a minimum term (the tariff) to be spent in custody, after which the young person can apply to the Parole Board for release. Once released, the young person will be subject to a supervisory licence for the rest of their life. **Custody for life** is the mandatory sentence for a person aged 18 or over but under 21 at the time of the offence who is convicted of murder and sentenced while under 21, this sentence may also be imposed where a person aged 18 or over but under 21 at the time of the offence is convicted of any other offence for which a discretionary life sentence may be passed on an adult. **Detention for life** is the maximum sentence for a child aged 10 or over but under 18, who is convicted of offences other than murder for which a discretionary life sentence may be passed on a person over 21. Youth court sentences for less serious offences by young people are dealt with below.

The terminology makes it clear that unlike a determinate sentence a release date cannot be calculated for a prisoner with an indefinite or indeterminate sentence, indeed the prisoner has no right to release and a few will remain in prison all the rest of their life. Each prisoner must serve a minimum period in prison custody to meet the needs of retribution and deterrence. This punitive period is decided by the trial judge and is known as the 'tariff'. After serving the tariff period an indeterminate sentence prisoner will be reviewed by the Parole Board, which needs to be satisfied that the prisoner now poses a risk of harm to the public which is acceptable. The release of indeterminate sentence prisoners is entirely a matter for the Parole Board (see below).

The **indeterminate sentence of imprisonment for public protection (IPP)** original statute produced a surge in the prison population but was modified by section 47 and schedule 8 of the Criminal Justice and Immigration Act 2008 so that IPP sentences were only imposed where

the offender would otherwise be required to serve at least 2 years in custody.

All indeterminate sentence prisoners are released on a licence and are supervised by the Probation Service. The release licence contains a number of standard conditions that the released prisoner must adhere to. On the recommendation of the Parole Board the licence may also contain additional conditions that are specific to the individual prisoner such as the requirement to undertake further offending behaviour work in the community or conditions to exclude the individual from certain places in order to protect the victim or victim's family.

Two differences from lifer prisoners exist for IPP prisoners after release. The licence for a lifer remains in force until they die and they may be recalled to prison at any time if it is considered necessary to protect the public. Released IPP prisoners, however, can apply to the Parole Board to have their licence cancelled after 10 years (and if unsuccessful at yearly intervals thereafter). At the time of sentencing someone convicted of murder may be given a whole life tariff by the sentencing judge; this cannot be done in respect of other indeterminate prisoners. Although a whole life order applies only in mandatory lifer cases, it is open to a trial judge in non-murder cases to decline to set a minimum period of imprisonment which has the same effect. In either case the prisoner can appeal. It is also possible, in theory at least, for a prisoner serving an IPP sentence to remain in custody for the rest of his or her natural life because the Parole Board does not find the risk the prisoner poses to the public to be acceptable in the community.

The new regime of sentencing dangerous offenders and the IPP in particular have brought very significant changes to the way in which a group of offenders, who are of particular interest to forensic psychiatrists, are managed. The new regime has brought problems for the judiciary, for the prisons, for psychiatry and for the offenders themselves. The sharp rise in the prison population as a consequence, coupled with the totally inadequate provision for the management of the new indeterminate sentences brought embarrassment to the government that introduced the measures, hence the revision in the Criminal Justice and Immigration Act 2008 and the Legal Aid and Punishment of Offenders Act 2012. The new provisions about dangerous offenders do not change the rules governing the making of hospital orders and restriction orders pursuant to sections 37 and 41 of the Mental Health Act 1983 (amended).

Rutherford and his colleagues (2008) discovered that by July 2008 there were 4,619 prisoners serving IPP sentences but just 31 had been released. They found that nearly one in five had previously received psychiatric treatment, and one in ten continued to receive treatment in prison and one in five was still on psychotropic medication. One in twenty of them had previously been a patient in a secure hospital unit. Using the standard NOMS Offender Assessment System (OASyS) the IPP prisoners were shown to be needier people than either lifer prisoners or fixed term prisoners, needier for such basic requirements as accommodation and employment as well as medical treatment, they were prone to alcohol abuse and had poor emotional well being. Further nearly seven in ten of the IPP prisoners were assessed as requiring a clinical assessment for personality disorder compared to four in ten of lifer prisoners and three in ten of the general prison population.

IPP prisoners find it difficult to live alongside prisoners on determinate sentences who know when they are getting out of prison. The IPP prisoners complained that the indeterminacy was removing their sense of hope and it was damaging their relationships with families and friends. It was particularly demoralizing for them when they reached their tariff date, and they expected to be released, only to be told by the Parole Board that they had more psychological work to complete, work that often they could not complete, either because it was not available to them or because of their mental health problems.

The Rutherford report suggested that mental health legislation should be used in preference to criminal justice legislation for these dangerous prisoners. This of course implies that NHS commissioners should pay more attention to the provision of specialist services for dangerous people. It also means that most released IPP prisoners should be referred automatically to a community mental health team and secure hospitals should be prepared to receive more transfers of IPP prisoners.

The new measures are extremely unpopular with the judiciary, mainly because of the prescriptive nature of the legislation which removes, in their view, a great deal of judicial discretion. To address this important question, which of course interacts with the health issues identified by Rutherford et al. (2008), a judicial view has been included in this chapter.

Additional controls for sex offenders

The Sex Offenders Act 1997 introduced a system of notification to the police for convicted sex offenders. This was reinforced by the provisions of the Criminal Justice and Courts Services Act 2000 which introduced other child protection measures and the matter was consolidated by the Sexual Offences Act 2003.

Under the 2003 Act a convicted sex offender has to notify the police of his or her whereabouts; any changes of address and travel have to be notified. This system which enables the police to monitor the activities and movements of some sex offenders (the ones they are most worried about) is often called a sex offenders' register, but the onus of notification is on the offender with criminal penalties for failure to do so. The notification periods vary according to the seriousness of the sexual offence as measured by the severity of the sentence given. Anyone who is given a sentence of 2½ years or more, or an indefinite sentence, or is admitted to hospital under a restriction order for a sexual offence is subject to an indefinite notification period. If the period of imprisonment is between 6 and 30 months, the notification period is 10 years. For sentences of less than 6 months or admission to hospital without a restriction order, the notification period is 7 years. Other lesser sentences attract notification periods of 2 or 5 years. Finite notification periods are halved if the person is under 18 when convicted or cautioned.

Parole Board

The Parole Board of England and Wales functions as a court and is an essential part of the judicial system. It is of increasing importance as the number of indeterminate prisoners gets larger, as it, and it alone, determines the length of time an indeterminate prisoner spends in prison. Technically it is an executive non-departmental public body (NDPB) appointed by the Justice Secretary, but its position in the court system is under discussion; it is likely to become part of the tribunal service and have a few more powers. It has powers to discharge prisoners who have reached a certain point in their sentence (see below), and to advise the Justice Secretary about prisoners suitable for open conditions. It was originally established by the Criminal Justice Act 1967 and has been significantly modified by the Criminal Justice Acts of 1996, and 2003 and the Criminal Justice and Immigration Act 2008. This history means that it sometimes seen as a part of the civil service, but those days are in the past. The Board has a brief to protect the public and to contribute to the rehabilitation of prisoners. Although the Board is funded by the Ministry of Justice it is not an agent of the Crown and it has unfettered power of discharge, and the Secretary of State cannot discharge prisoners who have been refused release by the Board.

Members of the Board, including its chairman and its chief executive, are appointed by the Justice Secretary using the Commissioner for Public Appointments. Members are judges, both serving and retired, psychiatrists, psychologists, probation officers, criminologists, and other 'independent' members who represent the laity. The chairman and the vice-chairman are senior lawyers (although this is not a fixed requirement); the chief executive and three other members of the Board are full-time, all the rest being part-time except serving judges who are expected to fit 15 days parole work per year into their judicial workload. The expectations for psychiatrists and psychologists are 20 to 35 days a year. Following the increased workload created by the Criminal Justice Act 2003, the Board is increasing its membership to about 200 people. There is also a secretariat of between 50 and 60 people, divided into five teams.

The Board mainly deals with two classes of prisoners who have committed a violent or sexual assault:

1. *Those serving indeterminate sentences* Indeterminate sentences include life sentences (mandatory life, discretionary life and automatic life sentence prisoners and Her Majesty's Pleasure detainees) and indeterminate sentences for public protection (IPPs). The Parole Board considers whether prisoners are safe to release into the community once they have completed their tariff (the minimum time they must spend in prison) and also whether the Secretary of State was justified in recalling them to prison for a breach of their life licence conditions and, separately, whether they are safe to re-release following recall.

2. *Those serving determinate sentences of two kinds*
   a) Discretionary conditional release prisoners serving more than 4 years whose offence was committed before 4 April 2005.
   b) Prisoners given extended sentences for public protection for offences committed on or after 4 April 2005.

As with indeterminate prisoners the Board considers whether these prisoners are safe to release into the community once they have completed their tariff and review those recalled for a breach of their parole licence conditions.

The details of the law and practice of the Board are given in Arnott and Creighton (2010) which also includes the rules as agreed by the Secretary of State in Parliament. In essence oral hearings involve a three person panel, chaired by a judge or a specially trained independent member of the Board. The hearings use a relatively informal inquisitorial approach, the matter being enquired into is the risk which the prisoner poses to other people if s/he is released.

The risk to be assessed is the likelihood of the prisoner 'committing serious offences'. This has been the clarified and somewhat narrowed by the Court of Appeal as a test of the risk of harm to the life or limb of another person (see *Bradley*). It is attempted by using a thorough but straightforward technique. The first step is to identify all the factors associated with the violent or sexual behaviour in the prisoner's convictions. The list is often quite long and may include alcohol, other drugs, impulsiveness, deviant sexual drives, aggressiveness and anger, distorted thinking, jealousy, mental disorder and social isolation. Many other factors turn up in individual cases and the list tends to grow as the prisoner is better understood and is observed by prison staff. The second step is to seek evidence of change in all the factors that have been listed. The evidence presented to the Board is a mixture of staff reports, particularly key staff such as the offender supervisor and the offender manager (probation officer), specialized reports from, for example, a forensic psychologist, and very occasionally a clinical psychologist or a forensic

psychiatrist, and reports from courses that the offender may have undertaken such as Enhanced Thinking Skills, a sex offender treatment programme, CALM (Controlling Anger and Learning to Manage), RAPT (Rehabilitation of Addicted Prisoners Trust), Cognitive Self Change and many others (see chapter 25). Psychologists may have used risk assessment instruments such as the Offender Group Reconviction Scale (OGRS) (see Howard et al., 2009) and/or HCR 20 (Webster et al., 1997; see also chapter 22). Oral evidence is taken from the prisoner and from staff who know him/her well and who are responsible for his/her welfare and progress. The final step is to evaluate all this information on an individualized basis. The starting point is the so-called 'static risk', i.e. the number and severity of the previous convictions, together with static risk scales such as OGRS. This may be quite influential in the final decision but the skill is in judging the amount of change that has taken place during the prisoner's sentence. This may include motivation, time spent on offender work, external evidence, such as success or otherwise in work activities, especially work external to the prison, and success or otherwise on town visits and home leaves. As this suggests, testing out is an important part of the assessment and in most cases the release decision is staged by recommending transfer to open conditions where the prisoner takes a lot of responsibility for him/herself and can demonstrate, or otherwise, trustworthiness.

There are two major difficulties with this system, the first is that the final release decision is all or nothing. The prisoner is handed over to the probation service. If things go wrong and/or the risk assessment of the releasing panel of the Board was incorrect, the offender manager can recall the prisoner, but this is heavy handed and in many ways a counterproductive procedure, quite unlike the flexibility which is available for moving patients between an outpatient clinic and an inpatient service in the NHS.

Inevitably the procedures and practice of the Board owe something to its history, which is set out in Arnott and Creighton, especially in Sir Duncan Nichol's foreword to the first edition of that book (Arnott and Creighton, 2006). Nichol explains that the oral hearings only began in 1992 and the concept of fairness which that brought was enhanced by the increasingly transparent approach from that time. A good deal of academic debate about the pros and cons of the Parole Board, its practice, decisions, and effectiveness has been generated. An excellent starting point for this literature is Padfield (2007). In that volume Thornton gives an overview of the functions of the Board, and particularly the impact of the European Court of Human Rights on its decisions. The complex Parole Board rules can be found on its website www.paroleboard.gov.uk.

When an oral hearing is due the prison holding the potential parolee will prepare a dossier of reports, some dating back to the trial, others concerned with coursework the prisoner has undertaken, perhaps a psychology report, reports from the offender supervisor in prison, the personal officer, the offender manager (probation officer) and other relevant people. This is sent to the Parole Board and an experienced member who has undertaken special training will review the dossier, check that the appropriate documents for the hearing are present, identify witnesses who should attend the hearing, note whether a psychiatrist or psychologist should be on the panel, and estimate the time that the hearing will take. This is the intensive case management which has significantly reduced the number of deferred hearings.

The oral hearing takes the form of an informal tribunal or court. The prisoner attends and usually has a legal representative (solicitor or counsel); the Secretary of State may send a written opinion on the case, or if it is considered to be of special importance a public protection advocate or even a barrister who will argue the Secretary of State's position (which is usually for the prisoner to remain in custody). Questioning of witnesses is formalized to the extent that each witness is heard separately and questioned by each side and by the panel. The prisoner is usually a key witness in his or her own case. Decisions are usually unanimous, but occasionally are taken on a majority basis. The chairman drafts a letter to the prisoner, the so-called 'reasons' letter, according to a template setting out the decision of the panel, the evidence considered by the panel, an analysis of the prisoner's offending, a description of the factors which are thought to increase and decrease the prisoner's risk of re-offending and causing harm, evidence of change during the sentence, the panel's assessment of current risks, the risk management plan which was presented by the offender manager, the conclusion and if release is being directed the licence conditions which must apply. This draft is then agreed by the panel before being sent out to the prisoner and all the relevant parties by the secretariat.

A prisoner's case should be reviewed by the Board at least every 2 years. A prisoner can request a hearing to be deferred, and some do, to complete a course or to get more evidence.

In 2008–09 28,596 cases were considered. As in previous years 15% of prisoners receiving an oral hearing were released. A total of 89 prisoners on life licence were recalled during the year; this is 5.4% of the 1,646 prisoners with life licences under active supervision in the community. If the recall is for a serious offence, perhaps a quarter of that number, then the case would be referred to the Board's review committee to analyse the case, and write to the original panel in confidence telling them the outcome of that analysis. The review committee includes experienced criminal justice personnel who are not on the Parole Board.

The frustration for a mental health professional in this process is the limited powers of the Board. The Board is told that suggestions about moves within the prison estate other than to open conditions and suggestions about the sentence plan are not welcome. However it is plain common sense that a detailed analysis of a case in the presence of three parole experts, one or more of whom may have expertise in psychiatry or psychology, may produce useful ideas to assist with the prisoner's progress and as such should not be kept under wraps. Prison officials are not obliged to take any notice of Parole Board suggestions, however, many prison staff say that they're very grateful for the outside views which the Board may bring.

The Justice Secretary can overrule the recommendation for open conditions; some ministers do this more often than others. Many of the prisoners require psychiatric help, often this is not recognized either by the prisoner or by the prison and probation staff. Even if it is, getting a psychiatric assessment is difficult, and treatment next to impossible. Resources and attitudes have improved in recent years, but there is still a shortage of resources and considerable antipathy to offender patients, especially ones who have committed terrible crimes. 'Untreatable personality disorder' is code for 'don't expect me to help this person', or maybe 'I have no psychotherapeutic skills and don't know how to treat him/her', or occasionally 'I would take him/her if I had a bed, but I don't'. It would help individual prisoners and also the process of getting more resources if professionals were more candid in acknowledging mental disorder and the real reasons for failing to assist.

A Parole Board hearing thus gives an opportunity to review a case in the presence of relevant people, so that discussions about diagnosis and treatment options can take place. The reasons letter can draw attention to medical issues and problems which might otherwise be overlooked. Parole Board membership should be seen as an important post for a forensic psychiatrist at some stage in his or her career. The educational aspects of the work are particularly important both for the psychiatrist member and for the rest of the Board; the role, function and skills of psychiatry are still widely misunderstood. It is still too easy for non-psychiatrists to believe that psychiatry is both stigmatizing and ineffective and thus best avoided!

Young Offenders

Young offenders, in law, are people under the age of 18 years. A child under the age of 10 years in England, Wales and Northern Ireland is deemed not to have criminal responsibility. The age of criminal responsibility varies widely between countries, from 6 years in some states of the USA to 18 years in Belgium. The European average is about 12 years.

The Youth Justice Board for England and Wales (YJB) is an executive non-departmental public body. It was set up under the Crime and Disorder Act 1998 to monitor the performance and operation of the entire youth justice system. Its statutory duties include commissioning and purchasing places in the juvenile secure estate (young offender institutions, secure training centres and local authority secure children's homes) for young people sentenced or remanded to custody. Young people from the age of 10–18 years who commit offences are the responsibility of the Youth Justice Board. The primary aim of the Board is to prevent offending by children and young people. This is an enormous task as the peak age of offending is 14 years. (See also chapter 19.)

Youth Offending Teams (YOTs) were set up by the Crime and Disorder Act 1998. There is a YOT in every local authority in England and Wales. They are made up of representatives from the police, probation service, social services, health, education, drugs and alcohol misuse and housing officers. Each YOT is managed by a YOT manager who is responsible for co-ordinating the work of the youth justice services. YOTs supervise young people who have been ordered by the court to serve sentences in the community or in the secure estate. They also arrange for appropriate adults to advise young people, who have been arrested, at the police station. Education and supervision are key functions of a YOT; they may employ, for example, educational psychologists. As with adults mental health issues are prominent in young offenders, but psychiatric input into their work is the exception rather than the rule (see chapter 19 and Harrington and Bailey, 2005).

Sentences for young offenders

A wide range of sentences are available to the youth justice system, and custody is a last resort. When young people first get into trouble for committing minor offences or for antisocial behaviour, they can be dealt with outside the courts. For antisocial behaviour, the police and local authority can use precourt orders such as antisocial behaviour orders (ASBOs) or child safety orders. For first or second time minor offences the police can use reprimands and final warnings. When a young person is charged with an offence they will appear before a youth court (the Crown Court in very serious cases). The young offender may receive the following sentences:

- Discharge, absolute or conditional.
- Referral order, given to all young offenders (aged 10–17) pleading guilty to a first offence unless it is very serious or very trivial, the offender is referred to a youth offender panel of two local volunteers who consider the best course of action.
- A fine.
- Compensation order, paid to the victim (may be combined with another sentence).
- Reparation order, for example repairing damage caused to property.
- Action plan order, for up to 3 months for supervision, counselling, training, etc.
- Curfew order, requiring the offender to remain in a specified place for set periods of time (2 and12 hours a day) for up to 6 months for those 16 years of age and

above (3 months if under 16 years of age), may use tagging, (may be combined with another sentence).
- Attendance centre order, supervision by police on Saturdays.
- Supervision order for 6 months to 3 years, details tailored to offender by YOT and court, may include residence and or curfew or an ISSP.
- Intensive supervision and surveillance package (ISSP) for up to 6 months as an alternative to custody, the first 3 months may require up to 25 hours supervision per week.
- Community rehabilitation order, for 16 to 17 year olds, this is like a supervision order for older adolescents and is supervised by a YOT or by probation and can include an ISSP.
- Community punishment order, for 16 to 17 year olds, this is usually unpaid work under supervision.
- Community punishment and rehabilitation order for, 16 to 17 year olds, a combination order.
- Drug treatment and testing order.
- Detention and training order for 12 to 17 year olds with a history of previous offending, if the offence would be punishable with imprisonment for an adult; it lasts between 4 months and 2 years, the first half of the sentence is served in custody and the second half in the community under the supervision of a YOT when it may include an ISSP.
- The Crown Court dealing with the most serious offences uses section 90/91 of the Powers of Criminal Courts (Sentencing) Act 2000; if the conviction is for murder, the young person is sentenced to 'Her Majesty's Pleasure' under s.90, if the conviction is for an offence for which an adult could receive at least 14 years in custody, the young person may be sentenced for any length of custody up to the adult maximum for the same offence, which may be life. The young person will be released automatically at the halfway point of the sentence and selected cases could be released up to a maximum of 135 days early on the home detention curfew scheme. Once released, the young person will be subject to a supervisory licence until their sentence expires, if the sentence is 12 months or more; or a notice of supervision for a minimum of 3 months, if the sentence is less than 12 months.

Secure accommodation

There are three types of secure accommodation in which a young person can be placed.

Secure Training Centres (STCs)

STCs are purpose-built centres for young offenders up to the age of 17. They are run by private operators under Home Office contracts. There are four STCs in England. They have a minimum of three staff members to eight trainees.

The regimes in STCs are education-focused. Trainees are provided with formal education 25 hours a week, 50 weeks of the year and all services are provided on-site, including all education and training, primary health care, dentistry, social work and mental health services.

Local Authority Secure Children's Homes

Local Authority Secure Children's Homes are run by local authority social services departments, overseen by the Department of Health and the Department for Education and Skills. They provide secure accommodation for children and adolescents who have been through the criminal justice system. They should have a high staff ratio and are generally small facilities, ranging from six to 40 beds and are usually used to accommodate offenders aged 12 to 14 years, although some who are assessed as vulnerable can stay until they are 16.

At the time of writing there were 15 such homes providing 509 beds covering most of England and Wales, however provision is inadequate, for example London has only one such home (Orchard Lodge in Croydon).

Young Offender Institutions (YOIs)

Young offender institutions (YOIs) are prisons for young people and are run by the Prison Service. They accommodate 15 to 21 year olds. The Youth Justice Board is only responsible for those under 18 years of age. The male YOIs can house up to 360 youngsters in wings of 30–60 and should have 3–6 prison officers on each wing. Some are stand alone prisons; others are simply a separate wing in an adult establishment.

Sentencing Dangerous Offenders: A View from the Bench

There are a number of offences which carry a potential maximum sentence of life imprisonment. Obvious examples are attempted murder, wounding with intent to do grievous bodily harm, rape and robbery. All have in common a generally accepted view that they could properly be described as grave offences. However, a life sentence as opposed to a lengthy determinate sentence was only to be imposed if the offence itself was a serious example of the crime in question and there were good reasons for believing that the offender might remain a serious danger to the public for a period which could not reliably be estimated at the time of sentencing. The reasons which might found such a belief often, but not necessarily, related to the mental condition of the offender as well as the facts of the particular offence. As a general proposition, life sentences were not to be passed where a lengthy determinate sentence could properly be regarded as providing sufficient protection for the public. Subject to these criteria, a judge had a genuine discretion as to whether to impose a life sentence and, generally, such sentences were only imposed in bad cases.

The first significant attempt to fetter judicial discretion in this area came with section 109 of the Powers of Criminal Courts (Sentencing) Act 2000. Unless there were exceptional circumstances that section *required* a judge to pass a life sentence where the defendant was convicted of a serious offence such as robbery whilst in possession of a firearm and that defendant had a previous conviction for a serious offence such as for example wounding with intent to do grievous bodily harm.

The Criminal Justice Act 2003 introduced an even more prescriptive regime in respect of offences committed after 4 April 2005.

Specified offences

The first concept that has to be grappled with is that of the 'specified offence'. These offences fall into two categories, namely specified violent offences and specified sexual offences. By section 224(3) of the Act, a specified violent offence means an offence specified in part 1 of schedule 15 and a specified sexual offence means an offence specified in part 2 of schedule 15. Part 1 sets out some 65 specified violent offences. Apart from obvious crimes such as manslaughter and wounding with intent the schedule also includes matters such as unlawful wounding, affray, death by dangerous driving and harassment. Part 2 sets out some 88 specified sexual offences. Again they range from obviously serious matters such as rape and assault by penetration to behaviours such as exposure and voyeurism and sex with an adult relative who consents to penetration.

Specified serious offences

Having mastered the concept of the specified offence, we next have to consider the specified 'serious' offence. By section 224(2) a specified serious offence is one which is capable of being punishable in respect of persons aged 18 or over with imprisonment for life (regardless of the new provisions) or a determinate sentence of 10 years or more. In other words, any specified violent or sexual offence which carries a potential maximum of life imprisonment or a prison sentence of 10 years or more is a specified serious offence.

Sentencing régime for those over the age of 18 years[3]

Section 225 of the Criminal Justice Act 2003 applies when any person aged 18 years or more is convicted of a serious offence and 'the court is of the opinion that there is a significant risk to members of the public of serious harm occasioned by the commission by him of further specified offences'. We shall consider the 'significant risk' provision later. By section 225(2), where the offence is one which is capable of attracting a life sentence (apart from the provisions that we are considering) and 'the court considers that the seriousness of the offence, or the offence and one or more offences associated with it, is such as to justify the imposition of a sentence of imprisonment for life' the court must impose a sentence of life imprisonment. By section 225(3), where the case does not fall within subsection (2) the court must impose a sentence of imprisonment for public protection. By section 225(4), a sentence of imprisonment for public protection is a sentence of imprisonment for an indeterminate period. The crucial point to note is that a life sentence can only be imposed where the

---

[3] This was written before IPP sentences were abolished.

seriousness of the offence/associated offences justifies life. In all other cases, it is imprisonment for public protection whether or not the particular offence carries with it a theoretical maximum of life imprisonment. The practical differences between life imprisonment on the one hand and imprisonment for public protection on the other are not great. The only difference is that pursuant to section 31A of the Crime (Sentences) Act 1997, the Parole Board may order the Secretary of State, 10 years after the prisoner's release from custody, to say that the prisoner shall no longer be on licence. If no such direction is given a person released from such a sentence remains on licence for life.

When should it be life?

It would seem that even now a life sentence should only be imposed where such a sentence would have been passed under the pre-2003 regime – see *Lang* at paragraph 8, *Samuel* at paragraph 21 and *Folkes* at paragraph 14. Unless those pre-2003 criteria are satisfied, it should be public protection not life.

The extended sentence

Schedule 15 of the Criminal Justice Act 2003 sets out a large number of offences many of which carry a maximum sentence of less than 10 years imprisonment. Obvious examples are unlawful wounding, assault occasioning actual bodily harm and affray. These are catered for in the new regime by the extended sentence. By section 227, when the relevant significant risk is present in respect of an individual convicted of a specified but not serious offence, 'the court must impose on the offender an extended sentence of imprisonment.' This is a sentence of imprisonment the total length of which is equal to (a) the appropriate custodial term and (b) a further period (called the 'extension period') for which the offender is to be subject to a licence which is of such length as the court considers necessary for the purpose of public protection. The section further provides that the 'appropriate custodial term' must be at least 12 months' imprisonment and that the extension period must not exceed 5 years in the case of a violent offence or 8 years in the case of a sexual offence. Section 247 of the Act also deals with extended sentences. By subsection (2), as soon as the prisoner has served one half of the appropriate custodial term and the Parole Board has directed his/her release under this section, it is the duty of the Secretary of State to release him/her on licence. By subsection (3) the Parole Board may not direct the prisoner's release 'unless it is satisfied that it is no longer necessary for the protection of the public that the prisoner should be confined.' However, once the custodial term has been served in full, the prisoner must be released – see section 247(4).

Assume therefore a custodial term of 2 years and an extension period of 4 years. If the Parole Board has not directed his release, the prisoner serves 2 years in prison. He is then on licence for a period of 4 years. If he commits a further offence or otherwise acts in breach of his licence conditions, he is liable to be recalled to prison and may be kept there until the expiry of the licence period.

In *S*, the Court of Appeal came to the tentative conclusion that in the case of a prisoner released part way through the custodial period of his sentence there could effectively be two licence periods, namely the ordinary period to which all prisoners are subject that is until the end of the custodial period, and then the extension period which only started at the end of the notional custodial period. In our example therefore, if the prisoner were released after 12 months, he would be on normal licence for the remaining 12 months of the custodial term, then the extended licence of 4 years would kick in.

Dangerousness

Whether it be life, public protection or an extended sentence, the dangerousness criterion has to be considered. It will be remembered that before imposing any of these sentences, the court has to be 'of the opinion that there is a significant risk to members of the public of serious harm occasioned by the commission by him of further specified offences.' Accordingly, there are two matters that have to be considered, namely (1) is there a risk of the defendant committing further specified offences and (2) would such further offending cause a significant risk of serious harm to members of the public? It might be thought that an assessment of these matters could properly be left to the discretion of the sentencing judge. However, section 229 introduced a highly prescriptive regime particularly in the case of those with previous convictions for a specified offence.

Section 229(1) provides as follows:

1. This section applies where:
   a) a person has been convicted of a specified offence and
   b) it falls to a court to assess … whether there is a significant risk to members of the public of serious harm occasioned by the commission by him of further such offences.

Section 229(2) deals with those who have not previously been convicted of a specified offence. Its provisions are somewhat anodyne. In making the assessment the court must (a) take into account all such information that is available to it about the nature and circumstances of the offence, (b) may take into account any information which is before it about any pattern of behaviour of which the offence forms a part, and (c) may take into account any information about the offender which is before it. I observe in passing that it might be thought that any sentencing exercise would involve considerations like this!

The more interesting and difficult provision is that arising under section 229(3). This applies to those who have been previously convicted of a specified offence. In such a case 'the court must assume that there is such a risk' unless 'the court considers that it would be unreasonable to conclude that there is such a risk.' In making the judgment that it would be unreasonable to conclude that there is such a risk, the court must take into account (a) all such information as is available to it about the nature and circumstances of each of the offences; (b) where appropriate, any information which is before it about any pattern of behaviour of which any of the offences form part; and (c) any information about the offender which is before it.

As a matter of commonsense, if a defendant has previous convictions for violence or sexual offending there is clearly a risk that s/he will commit further such specified offences and indeed that such future offences might be serious specified offences. In other words, the first of the risk factors namely further offending can relatively easily be satisfied. It is the second limb which causes the difficulty namely predicting that such further offending 'poses a significant risk to members of the public of serious harm.'

Section 224(3) provides that 'serious harm' means 'death or serious personal injury whether physical or psychological.'

In *Lang*, which is the leading case on the whole subject, Rose LJ said at paragraph 17(i) that 'the risk identified must be significant. This is a higher threshold than mere possibility of occurrence and in our view can be taken to mean (as in the concise Oxford dictionary) noteworthy, of considerable amount … or importance.' So, some risk is not enough: It has to be significant. The serious harm that might ensue has to be serious within the meaning of 224(3).

Accepting that reported cases on sentencing are very much dependent upon their own facts, it is illustrative to look at how robbery offences have been dealt with under the new provisions. In *Lang* itself, Rose LJ said at paragraph 17(iii) 'if the foreseen specified offence is serious, there will clearly be some cases, though by no means all, in which there may be significant risk of serious harm. For example, robbery is a serious offence. But, it can be committed in a wide variety of ways many of which do not give rise to a significant risk of serious harm. Sentencers must therefore guard against assuming there is a significant risk of serious harm merely because the foreseen specified offence is serious.' In *Lang*, the appellant had several previous convictions for robbery: The current robbery involved threatening the victim with a knife. The court held that a sentence of imprisonment for public protection (though not a life sentence) was appropriate.

In *McGrady*, the offence was robbery of the bag snatch type albeit that there had been a bit of a struggle. The appellant had previous convictions for specified violent offences. The Court of Appeal took the view that although there was clearly a risk of future offending, those offences did not carry with them the risk of serious harm. Accordingly an indeterminate sentence was not justified. This should be compared with *Bryan and Bryan*. In that case, two brothers carried out a betting shop robbery involving the use of actual violence. Both defendants had previous convictions for specified offences including robbery. The Court of Appeal had no difficulty in upholding a sentence of imprisonment for public protection. There was a clear risk of serious harm if anyone resisted their threats of violence – they were obviously prepared to use violence. Reference should also be made to *Sharrock* and *Thomas*. Lastly, it was said in *Johnson and Others* that 'it did not automatically follow from the absence of actual harm caused by the offender to date, that the risk that he would cause serious harm in the future was negligible.' It might be that serious harm had been avoided to date simply because the victim or victims had not chosen to resist. If the hypothetical future victim did resist was there a risk that the offender would use violence and cause serious harm?

I have already set out the matters that the court must consider pursuant to 229(3) in deciding whether there was significant future risk or whether it would be unreasonable to make that assumption. In practical terms, as was said in *Lang* at paragraph 17(iii), 'a presentence report should usually be obtained before any sentence is passed which is based on significant risk of serious harm. In a small number of cases where the circumstances of the current offence or the history of the offender suggest mental abnormality on his part, a medical report may be necessary before risk can properly be assessed.' But, it should be remembered, as the Court of Appeal said in *Betteridge*, that a trial judge is entitled to form his or her own view about future risk without hearing expert evidence on the point and is not bound to accept the assessment made in the pre-sentence report.

Young offenders

For legal purposes, a young offender is a person under the age of 18 years at the date of conviction (not sentence) – see *Robson*. Sections 226 and 228 are applicable here. Section 226 provides a regime for detention for life or detention for public protection for such offenders. There is one important difference between the regime for the under 18s compared with the 18+ group. By section 226(2) if the court decides that it is not a case requiring detention for life, it should only impose a sentence for public protection if 'the court considers that an extended sentence under section 228 would not be adequate for the purpose of protecting the public.' In other words, once detention for life is ruled out, the court should only consider detention for public protection after it has considered (and rejected) the extended sentence regime. Whichever option is being considered, the assessment of 'dangerousness' pursuant to section 229 is less prescriptive than in the case of an 18+ even where he has a previous conviction for a specified offence. The court is not bound to make the rebuttable presumption of dangerousness which it has to in the case of those aged 18 years or more when section 229(3) bites. Even in the context of the extended sentence, it is worth remembering what Rose LJ said in *Lang* at paragraph 17(vi) namely 'it is still necessary, when sentencing young offenders, to bear in mind that, within a shorter time than adults, they may change and develop. This and their level of maturity may be highly pertinent when assessing what their future conduct may be and whether it may give rise to significant risk of serious harm.'

Tariff

We turn now to a provision which mystifies the public and the press. Section 82A of the Powers of Criminal Courts (Sentencing) Act 2000 applies to most discretionary life sentences and to all sentences of imprisonment for public protection. When passing such a sentence, the judge has to specify the minimum term that must be served before the prisoner is eligible to apply for parole (note – 'eligible to apply' not 'entitled to be given'). In specifying the minimum term the court is obliged to give credit for the period of time that the prisoner has served on remand – see section 240 of the Criminal Justice Act 2003. In addition, the sentencer has to consider Section 244 of that Act. That provides that in respect of a fixed term prisoner, the Secretary of State must release him on licence once he has served half his sentence. If a person is sentenced to a determinate term of 12 years, he is automatically released after 6 years. Now it is necessary to factor in section 144 of the Act. The sentencer must take into account, if it be the case, that the defendant has pleaded guilty. By section 172, the sentencer has to take account of guidelines issued by the Sentencing Guidelines Council and they have indicated that a person who indicates an intention to plead guilty at the earliest available opportunity is entitled to a discount of one-third from his sentence. Accordingly, we end up with a sentencing process as follows:

a) the allegation is rape of a young child
b) the sentence is one of imprisonment for public protection but

c) the judge has to spell out the appropriate custodial term which means –

   i. deciding what the term would have been had the defendant pleaded not guilty but had been convicted by a jury, say 18 years but

   ii. the defendant has pleaded guilty at the first available opportunity therefore one reduces the sentence to 12 years but

   iii. if it were a determinate 12-year sentence the defendant would automatically be released after 6 years plus any time spent on remand so

   iv. the appropriate custodial term before the defendant is eligible to apply for parole is 6 years less the time spent on remand.

As to eligibility for parole, this is governed by sections 28 and 34 of the Crime (Sentences) Act 1997. By section 34 'life prisoner' and 'life sentence' include those subject to imprisonment for public protection pursuant to section 225 of the 2003 Act. Section 28 provides that as soon as a life prisoner has served the relevant part of his sentence, he must be released by the Secretary of State when the Parole Board is satisfied 'that it is no longer necessary for the protection of the public that the prisoner should be confined.' In other words release is in the hands of the parole board.

AGENCIES OF THE LAW

The police

The police take the first policy decisions in administering the criminal law, and exercise considerable discretion in investigating and initiating the prosecution process in criminal cases. The police are responsible for the decision to charge a suspect in simple and straightforward cases. In all other cases, the decision to charge lies with the Crown Prosecution Service, and the police must obtain advice on the appropriate charges before the suspect is charged. The police are so closely connected with forensic psychiatry services that they feature in more than one chapter (see chapter 25). Here we are concerned with their diversion activities to avoid offenders, especially mentally disordered ones (where appropriate), having unnecessary court appearances and imprisonment.

Police have a range of measures they can use instead of the courts to deal with low-level crimes. For adults, these include simple cautions, conditional cautions, cannabis warnings, penalty notices for disorder and fixed penalty notices for driving offences. For youths aged 10 to 17, there are no cautions but reprimands and final warnings instead; penalty notices for disorder can be given to those aged 16–17 as well.

The conditional caution was introduced by the Criminal Justice Act 2003 as a disposal available for adults who are willing to admit their guilt and want to prevent the offence recurring. The authority of the Crown Prosecution Service is required before a conditional caution can be given. A prosecution may occur if any of the conditions attached to the caution are breached. Conditions must be rehabilitative or reparative. Rehabilitative conditions could include attendance at drug or alcohol misuse programme, or other services aimed at interventions tackling other problems, such as gambling or debt management. Reparative conditions could include apologies, physical repairs and financial recompense to an individual or to a charity.

The police may decide to divert a mentally disordered offender from the criminal justice system altogether by taking the person to a place of safety, under section 136 Mental Health Act 1983 (amended), so that the person can be assessed and receive appropriate treatment. Too little is known about police activity in relation to the mentally disordered in their caring capacity. Most of the studies carried out refer to London in the twentieth century (Fahy and Dunn, 1987; Fahy et al., 1987; Pipe et al., 1991; Turner et al., 1992; Simmons and Hoar, 2001; see also chapter 25). Clearly, in an era of deinstitutionalisation and community care for psychiatric patients, the role of the police is important.

The Royal College of Psychiatrists report (2011) on the use of s.136 recommends that police stations should only be used as the place of safety on an exceptional basis. This point has been endorsed by the Code of Practice to the MHA 1983 (amended) (Department of Health, 2008). The report acknowledges that this will mean there should be sufficient places of safety in psychiatric facilities to meet local needs, and these should have dedicated staffing on a 24-hour basis to ensure continuous patient care and allow the police to leave promptly after a handover even when the patient is agitated. Once an individual has been taken to a 'place of safety', s/he must be assessed by an approved clinician and by an approved mental health practitioner (AMHP). A new arrangement brought by the 2007 Mental Health Act is that a patient may be taken from one place of safety to another within the 72-hour period of the order. In spite of these admonitions most patients are still taken to police stations (11,000 in 2008; Bather et al., 2008)

When the police decide to take no action, the possibility of prosecution ends forthwith unless the victim decides to bring a private prosecution. However, Community Legal Service Funding is unlikely to be available to finance a private prosecution, which makes a private prosecution expensive as well as legally complex. The police have considerable discretion in investigating criminal offences and initiating the prosecution process; chief constables, for example, have discretion in how their force should in general be allocated to fulfil the various functions of the police; in individual cases, in the face of undoubted evidence, there is discretion as to whether a prosecution should be brought. The widespread use of cautioning has led to a lot of criticism. On 11 June 2007, the BBC News website reported that 'Almost 8,000 sex offenders have been cautioned across England in the past five years, rather than being charged.' This apparently included 230 cases of rape. The Association of Chief

Police Officers answered in some detail pointing out that such sex offenders can be put on the sex offenders register, victims' views are taken into account, and rape includes statutory rape amongst youngsters.

Multi-Agency Public Protection Arrangements

Multi-agency public protection arrangements (MAPPA) support the assessment and management of the most serious sexual and violent offenders. They were introduced in 2001 and bring together the police, probation and prison services into the MAPPA responsible authority. Other agencies are under a duty to co-operate with the responsible authority, including social care, health, housing and education services.

Just to confuse the uninitiated there are three categories of offenders dealt with by the multi-agency arrangements at three levels which do not correspond to the categories. The offenders are categorized as: (1) registered sex offenders (around 30,000 offenders in 2004/05); (2) violent or other sex offenders (around 12,600 offenders in 2004/05); and (3) other offenders (around 3,000 offenders in 2004/05). The offenders are managed at three different levels determined by seriousness and the perceived management requirements which are orthogonal to the categories.

Level One: involves normal single agency management. Offenders managed at this level will have been assessed as presenting a low or medium risk of serious harm to others. In 2004/05 just more than 71% of MAPPA offenders were managed at this level.

Level Two: local inter-risk agency management e.g. police and probation; most offenders assessed as high or very high risk of harm are managed at this level, about 25% of MAPPA offenders in 2004/05.

Level Three: known as multi-agency public protection panels (or MAPPPs); these are appropriate for those offenders who pose the highest risk of causing serious harm, or whose management is so problematic that multi-agency co-operation and oversight at a senior level is required. MAPPPs have the authority to commit exceptional resources in some cases. Problematic management may be about risk to the offender for example from vigilantes, or door stepping by the press. In 2004/05 just more than 3% of MAPPA offenders were managed at this level.

(The data quoted here are from the MoJ website: http://www.justice.gov.uk/statistics/prisons-and-probation/mappa/)

Sharing of information is highlighted by the MoJ website as follows: 'MAPPA promotes information sharing between all the agencies, resulting in more effective supervision and better public protection.' For example, police will share information with offender managers that they have gathered about an offender's behaviour from surveillance or intelligence gathering and local authorities will help find offenders suitable accommodation where they can be effectively managed. It is very important that victims' needs are represented in MAPPA, with the result that additional measures can be put into place to manage the risks posed to known victims. It is for these reasons that the Faculty of Forensic Psychiatrists in the Royal College of Psychiatrists has strongly recommended that the health representative sitting on a MAPPA panel should be a consultant psychiatrist, preferably a consultant forensic psychiatrist; other individuals may not have the ethical background or the authority to examine in detail the ethical issues which are posed by this policy. (See chapters 25 and 26 for more commentary on confidentiality.)

National Policing Improvement Agency

The National Policing Improvement Agency (NPIA) is a UK wide police resource for the storing and rapid transfer of information. It embraces automatic car number plate recognition, a fingerprint database, a list of those who have applied for firearms certificates, the Police National Computer and a dangerous persons database (Violence and Sexual Offenders Register (ViSOR), see below).

ViSOR

To quote the NPIA website:

ViSOR is designed to facilitate the work of the multi-agency public protection arrangements (MAPPA) by assisting co-operative working between the three responsible authorities (police, probation and prison services) in their joint management of individuals posing a risk of serious harm. The system is very secure – rated at CONFIDENTIAL level in the Government Protective Marking Scheme – to ensure that details of both offenders and those contributing intelligence to the system are kept safe. It is used by specially-trained and security-cleared public protection professionals.

The register includes those required to notify the police under the Sexual Offences Act 2003 (see above), those jailed for more than 12 months for violent offences, and unconvicted people thought to be at risk of offending.

The Crown Prosecution Service

The Crown Prosecution Service is the principal prosecuting authority for England and Wales. It was established under the Prosecution of Offences Act 1985 in order to prosecute cases investigated by the police. It deploys the power of the State to put people on trial, acting on behalf of the Crown.

The Crown Prosecution Service is headed by the Director of Public Prosecutions, England and Wales are divided into areas, each headed by a Chief Crown Prosecutor. All members of the Service are civil servants. In all but simple and straightforward cases, Crown Prosecutors are responsible for deciding whether a person should be charged with a criminal offence, and if so, what that offence should be. These decisions are made in accordance with the Code for Crown Prosecutors (February 2010) and the Director's Guidance on Charging (September 2008).

Non-Crown prosecutions constitute one-fifth to one-quarter of all cases coming before the criminal courts, mostly involving relatively minor matters, the vast majority in the magistrates' courts (Samuels, 1986). About one-quarter of crime is thus prosecuted 'privately'. The agencies bringing these prosecutions are diverse and include, for example, local authorities (food and drugs, or false trade descriptions) and the Royal Society for the Prevention of Cruelty to Animals. They retain the power to conduct the prosecution in court, but they vary widely in practice. Some, for example, appear to be quick to prosecute (e.g. the Department of Social Security in social security fraud); yet others see prosecution as a very last resort (e.g. the Health and Safety at Work Inspectorate). Such a diversity of practice raises important questions of public interest and social justice. For example, tax frauds are often not prosecuted; thefts from shops frequently are. In the overwhelming majority of tax contraventions, prosecution is seen as the ultimate sanction and used infrequently (Samuels, 1986).

CIVIL LAW

Non-criminal or civil law disputes in England and Wales

Civil law is the term used here for the law dealing with disputes between individuals or organizations (as opposed to criminal law in which the dispute is between an individual and the state, i.e. the Queen (*Regina*) in the UK and some parts of the British Commonwealth); it relies heavily upon common law. The civil law system used in most parts of the world is quite different.

Non-criminal disputes may concern a contract, a will, or property for example. The civil law equivalent of a crime is a tort. A tort is a civil wrong or breach of a duty to another person which creates a liability if a fault can be demonstrated. Much of the work of the civil court is concerned with providing compensation for personal injury and property damage caused by negligence. Personal injury nowadays does include psychiatric injury.

Civil courts are different from criminal courts. They still use an adversarial system of collecting evidence but they usually do not use a jury, the decision-making being undertaken by a lone judge. The standard of proof is different in a civil court. Whereas in a criminal court guilt has to be the proved by the prosecution 'beyond a reasonable doubt,' liability in a civil court simply has to be proved 'on the balance of probabilities.'

Compensation

There are three ways in which compensation can be awarded by the legal system for wrongs done to an individual.

1. The first is within the criminal system. An English criminal court may, after a finding of guilt, make a *compensation order* to direct the offender to pay monies to his or her victim and this will be in addition to any other penalties imposed. This can be compensation for personal injury or loss, but it cannot be for losses associated with motor vehicles nor for losses arising from the death of a victim. The offender's means have to be taken into account. If damages are awarded in a civil action, the level given has to take into account the sum already awarded under a compensation order.

2. A Criminal Injuries Compensation Board was set up in 1964. It has subsequently been substantially modified and superseded by the *Criminal Injuries Compensation Authority* which covers the whole of the United Kingdom and is based in Glasgow. A *Criminal Injuries Compensation Scheme* was established in 2008 (http://www.justice.gov.uk/downloads/victims-and-witnesses/cic-a/how-to-apply/cica-guide.pdf) under the Criminal Injuries Compensation Act 2005. The scheme is mainly (although not exclusively) concerned with violent injury and claims may be made for both physical and psychiatric injury. The rules which cover awards reflect the common-law precedents which have been set in the civil courts and are discussed below. The claimant does not have to show that an offender has been convicted of a crime which injured them. No awards are given for injuries from motor accidents unless the vehicle was used as a weapon. Awards of up to £500,000 may be given according to the Authority's tariff. Although this scheme technically relates to the criminal justice system its standards of proof and evidence are those used in the civil system.

3. Lawsuits for damages to compensate financially for both physical and psychiatric injury may be pursued in the civil court.

Psychiatric injury ('nervous shock')

In the nineteenth century there was no question of compensation for psychiatric injury. 'In February 1888, the Judicial Committee of the Privy Council, in the case of *Victorian Railways* decided that the plaintiff was not entitled to recover damages for nervous shock caused by the defendant's negligence, in the absence of proof of actual impact, even though serious physical injuries resulted from the shock.' The House of Lords said 'damages arising from mere sudden terror unaccompanied by actual physical injury, but occasioning a nervous or mental shock, cannot ... be considered a consequence which ... would flow from... negligence' (*Victorian Railways*).

Readers interested in the depressing history of the psychiatric consequences of frequent rail accidents in the nineteenth century (*railway spine*) should read Cohen and Quinter (1996).

The first chink in this heavy armour defending against psychological matters came at the very beginning of the twentieth century. In *Dulieu* in 1901 Ms. Dulieu, a pregnant barmaid, suffered shock followed by the premature birth of her child when runaway horses and a cart crashed into the pub where she was working. There was no impact causing physical injury, but she was in fear of her own safety and it was on this basis that her claim succeeded.

Since 1974 in the USA (*Prince*) and 1982 in the UK (*McLoughlin*) it has been possible for someone suffering psychological injury following trauma to receive compensation even when they were not directly threatened with death or injury themselves. In the USA, following the Buffalo Creek disaster, it was held that:

> *all survivors – even those who were outside the valley at the time of disaster – could collect for mental injury if we could convince the jury that the coal company's conduct was reckless (i.e. more than merely negligent), and that this reckless conduct caused the survivors' mental suffering.* (Stern, 1976)

Psychic impairment was the American term coined for these injuries. In the UK we stick with the quaint old-fashioned term of *nervous shock* which whilst being picturesque does not really do justice to the medical conditions involved.

Nervous shock was defined in *McLoughlin* by Lord Bridge.

> *The common law gives no damages for the emotional distress which any normal person experiences when someone he loves is killed or injured. Anxiety and depression are normal human emotions. Yet an anxiety neurosis or a reactive depression may be recognizable psychiatric illnesses, with or without psychosomatic symptoms. So the first hurdle which a plaintiff claiming damages of the kind in question must surmount is to establish that he is suffering, not merely grief, distress, or other normal emotion, but a positive psychiatric illness.*

Lord Bridge said that there are three criteria for nervous shock in English law:

1. *The plaintiff must be suffering from a 'positive psychiatric illness.'*
2. *A chain of causation between the negligent act and the psychiatric illness must be clearly established.*
3. *The chain of causation was 'reasonably foreseeable' by the reasonable man.*

The term 'positive psychiatric illness' embraces the whole range of morbid emotional responses as well as the neurotic and psychotic disorders in the standard diagnostic classifications. The important and difficult matter is to say whether the emotional response is 'normal' or 'abnormal', e.g. grief or depression. An important clinical point is that almost any mental illness may be caused by trauma. A great deal of attention is usually given to the anxiety state which is defined as being caused by trauma, post-traumatic stress disorder (PTSD), but it should always be remembered that other illnesses can occur alongside PTSD or instead of it (see Law Commission, 1998 for a discussion). Illnesses such as depression, alcoholism, personality change and sometimes psychosis (Morrison et al., 2003) can all occur (interestingly, like many medical observers the Law Commission does not mention psychosis in its discussion).

A further major medico-legal difficulty is the language of the law which can be at variance with the vernacular or other technical uses of language such as medical uses. A case in point here is 'cause'. A useful discussion of the use of this word and its derivatives such as 'causation' can be found in the Wikipedia encyclopaedia under the headings of 'proximate cause' and 'causation in English law'. To quote this website:

> *In the law, a proximate cause is an event sufficiently related to a legally recognizable injury to be held the cause of that injury. There are two types of causation in the law, cause-in-fact and proximate (or legal) cause. Cause-in-fact is determined by the 'but-for' test: but for the action, the result would not have happened. For example, but for running the red light, the collision would not have occurred. For an act to cause a harm both tests must be met; proximate cause is a legal limitation on cause-in-fact.*

And:

> *The basic test for establishing causation is the 'but-for' test in which the defendant will be liable only if the claimant's damage would not have occurred 'but for' his negligence. Alternatively, the defendant will not be liable if the damage would, or could on the balance of probabilities, have occurred anyway, regardless of his or her negligence (see* South Australia*).*

See also Elliot and Quinn (2005). J Devlin in *Lamb* said that:

> *duty, remoteness and causation – are all devices by which the courts limit the range of liability for negligence... All these devices are useful in their way. But ultimately it is a question of policy for the judges to decide.*

This seems to indicate that the court's main task is to do justice as between the parties which requires a weighing evaluative process, rather than a clear-cut rule of law, a view which seems to be held very strongly by the judiciary and which may be the basis on which Parliament refused to endorse the recommendations of the Law Commission for statutory changes in this area (see below).

In *Meah* the claimant suffered head injuries and brain damage as a result of the defendant's negligent driving, which led to a personality disorder. Four years later, he sexually assaulted and raped three women and was sentenced to life imprisonment. The illegal nature of his conduct was not raised at the civil trial, and the claimant was held entitled to damages of £61,000 to compensate him for being imprisoned following his conviction. In separate proceedings, the three women assaulted obtained a judgment for compensation from the imprisoned rapist, so he sought indemnification from the negligent driver and his insurers for the amounts he had been ordered to pay. This was not a claim for his own personal injuries nor direct financial loss, but indirect loss. The three women could not have sued the driver directly because they were not foreseeable victims and so no duty of care was owed to them. The question was whether a person convicted of a crime was entitled to be indemnified against the consequences of that crime. J Woolf dismissed the action on two grounds. First, the damages were too remote to be recoverable and, if such actions were to be allowed, it would leave insurers open to indefinite liability for an indefinite duration. Second, as a matter of policy, claimants should not have a right to be indemnified against the consequences of their crimes.

In *Clunis* the claimant had been discharged from hospital where he had been detained under s.3 Mental Health Act 1983. He was to receive aftercare services in the community under s.117 Mental Health Act 1983, but his mental condition deteriorated and, two months later, he fatally stabbed a stranger at a London Underground station. He pleaded guilty to manslaughter on the ground of diminished responsibility and was ordered to be detained in a secure hospital. Subsequently, he brought an action against his local health authority for negligence. The health authority applied to strike out the claim as disclosing no cause of action on two grounds. First, that the claim arose out of the health authority's statutory obligations under s.117 Mental Health Act 1983 and those obligations did not give rise to a common law duty of care. Second, that the claim was based on the plaintiff's own criminal act. In the Court of Appeal, the health authority's appeal was allowed on both grounds.

As the psychological consequences of trauma become increasingly recognized and understood so the law, which finds scientific concepts difficult to embrace, ties itself in knots trying to dispense justice without reference to the science involved. Major accidents, such as the Zeebrugge disaster already mentioned, tend to set the scene. In March 1987, moments after leaving the Belgian port of Zeebrugge, the passenger ferry *Herald of Free Enterprise* carrying 459 passengers capsized killing 193 people. Many of the survivors suffered injuries and 70 were referred to the Maudsley Hospital seeking help with post-traumatic stress disorder and asking for help in recovering damages for nervous shock. In all over 400 compensation claims were made for survivors and relatives. Later the same year in the King's Cross station fire, 31 people died and more than 60 received injuries ranging from severe burns to smoke inhalation; many of these also sought help with PTSD and claims for nervous shock. The following year 35 people were killed

in the Clapham Junction rail disaster and 500 people were injured; this too produced many psychological injuries and legal claims. Just two years later in August 1989 the *Marchioness* Thames pleasure boat, carrying 131 people at a birthday party, sank after being run down by the dredger *Bowbelle;* 51 drowned and again many, both survivors and relatives, sought psychiatric or psychological help. Immediately preceding the river Thames disaster in April 1989 came the notorious Hillsborough disaster in which 96 Liverpool football fans were crushed to death when the police allowed far too many spectators into a particular fenced enclosure. The police were severely criticized in the subsequent Taylor reports (Taylor, 1989, 1990).

The clustering of these major incidents in so few years gave rise to a good deal of legal interest and activity in respect of the compensation claims which were made in the context of a more psychologically sophisticated society.

It was the aftermath of the Hillsborough disaster which developed the law dealing with claims for psychiatric injury ('nervous shock'). There are several good sources which can be consulted, for example Elliott and Quinn (2005) and Slapper and Kelly (2006). The Law Commission (1998) report *Liability for Psychiatric Illness* also gives a very clear account of the problems posed by the Hillsborough disaster and gives a very thorough analysis of the legal decisions. As an aside it should be noted that, apart from omitting hysteria and psychosis as responses to trauma, the report gives a textbook analysis of the psychiatry of 'nervous shock'.

It also noted that:

While most of the officers were held entitled to recover damages, nearly all of the relatives of the dead and injured failed in their claims. The apparent injustice of this position has been acknowledged by judges, newspapers, MPs and legal commentators.[4]

What happened was that the Chief Constable admitted liability towards those physically harmed. Sixteen relatives and friends, some of whom saw the event on television also made claims; 10 of them succeeded initially. The Chief Constable appealed in a test case (*Alcock*) and all 16 cases were rejected. The House of Lords decided that while it was clear that deaths and injuries in traumatic accidents commonly cause suffering that went well beyond the immediate victims, it was generally the policy of the common law not to compensate third parties (Elliott and Quinn 2005).

It was ruled, among other things, that parents and others who watched the Hillsborough disaster on television could not claim because television pictures are not normally equated with actual sight or hearing at an event or its aftermath. Clearly, this is a way of limiting claims against commercial organizations and their insurers. According to Elliott and Quinn (2005) *Alcock* confirmed that the claimants must

---

[4] Much is being done to remedy this following the publication of the report of the Hillsborough Independent Panel in 2012.

prove that their psychiatric damage amounts to a recognized psychiatric illness and that the psychiatric damage must have been caused by the claimants suffering a 'sudden and unexpected shock' caused by a 'horrifying event'. This rules out chronic stress and bereavement. *Alcock* further makes it clear that relatives are the people most likely to succeed in an action for psychiatric damage as a secondary victim, but the dividing line between those who are close enough to be considered for damages and disinterested observers is not easy to draw. For example does a recent boy/girl relationship count, or will the couple need to be engaged to be able to claim damages for nervous shock if one of them dies or is injured?

The public outrage about this particularly mean decision came when police officers on duty during the tragedy, suing their employer, were awarded damages (*Frost*) as a result of carrying out their professional duties at the scene.

It was in this climate that the Law Commission undertook a widespread consultation exercise and published its Report 249 in March 1998.

The Report concluded:

> that in some respects, and most notably in the decision of the House of Lords in Alcock v Chief Constable of South Yorkshire Police, 5 the common law has taken a wrong turn. Legislation can cure the defects in the common law at a stroke and with certainty.

It recommended:

> there should be legislation laying down that a plaintiff, who suffers a reasonably foreseeable recognisable psychiatric illness as a result of the death, injury or imperilment of a person with whom he or she has a close tie of love and affection, should be entitled to recover damages from the negligent defendant in respect of that illness, regardless of the plaintiff's closeness (in time and space) to the accident or its aftermath or the means by which the plaintiff learns of it.

See http://lawcommission.justice.gov.uk/docs/lc249_liability_for_psychiatric_illness.pdf

In any event Parliament rejected the idea of a new bill preferring to leave the whole matter to the common law and thus to the Court of Appeal and the House of Lords.

The Law Commission report was followed, however, by a further test case, again initiated by the Chief Constable against the decisions which had been made against him in *Frost*. The police officers concerned had been dealing with dead and injured fans. They claimed that they were not secondary victims and therefore not subject to the *Alcock* restrictions. Their claims succeeded on appeal but only to the extent that it is those who are in danger of physical injury, or thought themselves to be so, who could be viewed as primary victims. Rescuers were not to be considered as a special category of secondary victims either, which ruled out those officers who were simply rescuers and who had no pre-existing close relationships with the primary victims.

As this is the common law, the position continues to change, e.g. in 2002 in *North Glamorgan* it was decided, on appeal, that a 'horrifying event' need not be a single event or sudden. A mother had to watch her baby son die over a period of 36 hours when his acute hepatitis was not diagnosed and irreparable brain damage followed so that a life support machine had to be switched off. The Court of Appeal ruled that the plaintiff was not the primary victim, but could nevertheless succeed in her claim for damages for psychiatric injury as in this case the single shock could be considered to be composed of a number of shocks experienced over a period of time. In the same year a claim by secondary victims (husband and son) succeeded following a negligent mastectomy (*Froggatt*). Mrs Froggatt was wrongly diagnosed as suffering from invasive carcinoma of the breast and underwent a mastectomy. Shortly afterwards she was told that there had been a mistake and the lump had been benign. She was awarded damages for her physical injury and psychiatric injury. Her husband said that he had sustained a sudden shock when he saw her undressed for the first time after the mastectomy and as a result had developed an adjustment disorder. Her son overheard a telephone conversation in which Mrs Froggatt had discussed the fact that she had cancer and was likely to die. The son developed post-traumatic stress disorder. All the claims were allowed as they were thought to lie within the criteria set down for secondary victims in *Alcock* (http://www.psychiatryforlawyers.com). It is therefore important that legal opinion on recent developments is always sought at an early stage.

A clinical point to remember is that procedural considerations are important in compensation cases because cases that go to court can become protracted, wearisome, highly expensive and traumatic. Rehearsal of the traumatic events, especially under cross-examination, can produce flashbacks and an exacerbation of the underlying illness. Out of court settlements are ideal if the parties are willing to enter negotiations. A simple measure which can ease negotiations and be therapeutic in its own right is a straightforward and fulsome apology. Some of the victims of the *Herald of Free Enterprise* disaster said that an apology was all they wanted. They didn't get one in spite of their successful claims for damages, so the inner rage, especially concerning the accusations in the hearing that they were exaggerating their difficulties, continued its destructive course.

THE CORONER'S COURT

The office of the Coroner dates from the Norman invasion of Britain. By the twelfth century each county in England and Wales had appointed a coroner to protect the rights of the Crown. All violent and unexplained deaths were investigated, and where a guilty individual was identified, revenue was collected through fines and confiscation of goods.

Although the power of the coroner's court has waned in modern times, it continues to conduct its proceedings on an inquisitorial rather than adversarial basis, reflecting its Norman origins. For detailed information on coroners' courts, readers are directed to the following textbooks (Matthews, 2004; Christian et al., 2002).

The modern system of the Coroner's court stems from the recommendations of the Brodrick Report (Home Office, 1971) and is supposed to be a failsafe procedure, which provides that the registration of every death shall be subject to scrutiny and investigation for possible unlawful involvement. Since 1837 the law has required the registration of the death of every person, and registration cannot be effected without two stringent conditions being fulfilled. First there must be a valid certificate giving the cause of death and, second, the cause of death must be 'natural'. If the death is shown to be violent or 'unnatural', the coroner is required by law to conduct an inquest. In England and Wales there are approximately 550,000 deaths per year, 70% result in cremation and 30% result in burial. 200,000 deaths are reported to the coroner each year, 120,000 require a post-mortem and 20,000 require inquests.

An inquest is an impartial inquiry, conducted by a coroner on behalf of the Crown, for the purpose of establishing the truth concerning the events leading to and the ultimate cause of the death of an individual. Certain particulars are required by law to be registered concerning the death, namely the identification of the deceased person, the date and place where death occurred and how it occurred. There are no opposing parties, no provision of legal aid except in exceptional circumstances, and no enforceable judgment or order can be made.

At the inquest a coroner always has the discretion to summon a jury but has a statutory duty to summon one in prescribed situations, for example where a death occurred in custody or on a railway. Whilst not a statutory requirement following deaths in other institutions, for example, psychiatric hospital, a coroner may conclude that a jury is required in the public interest. Every inquest must be opened, adjourned and closed in a formal manner. Sometimes the coroner has a statutory duty to adjourn where, for example, a person may be involved in criminal proceedings connected with the death, and this will take precedence.

The procedure at an inquest is under the control of the coroner. The coroner must examine on oath any person having relevant evidence to give concerning a death. Any person who has a 'proper interest' in the circumstances in which an unnatural death has occurred is entitled to attend in person or be represented at the inquest and question witnesses. Interested parties can ask questions of the witnesses with the permission of the coroner, but may not address the court on the facts.

In announcing his or her verdict the coroner is strictly limited by the coroner's rules. S/he does not produce any legally enforceable judgment or order, and no finding of negligence, blame, culpability or guilt will be recorded. S/he no longer has a duty to commit for trial persons to be charged with murder, manslaughter or infanticide but must instead adjourn the case and send particulars to the Crown Prosecution Service. The verdict at the inquest is not subject to appeal but it may be questioned in the Divisional Court by way of judicial review on grounds such as fraud, error of law, bias, excessive jurisdiction or insufficiency of evidence. Whilst the standard of proof in a coroner's court is on a balance of probabilities, in those cases where the verdict is 'suicide', it has been established in the High Court that this verdict should only be made on the clearest and most unequivocal evidence, and that the stricter standard of 'beyond reasonable doubt' should be applied.

Following a number of major inquiries, the whole coroner's system has been overhauled. Disquiet was first publicly expressed at the Brodrick Committee (Home Office, 1971) that homicide might pass undetected through the existing certification system. This view had been put forward by Dr John Havard, later Secretary of the British Medical Association, who had expressed his concerns in his book *The Detection of Secret Homicide* (Havard, 1960). However the Brodrick Committee concluded that the risk of secret homicide had been much exaggerated. The systems of death and cremation certification remained virtually unchanged, and an opportunity to overhaul the system was lost.

The status quo could not be preserved, however, following the conviction of Dr Harold Shipman at Preston Crown Court on 31 January 2000 of the murder of 15 of his patients. The following day it was announced that an inquiry would be held to establish what changes to current systems should take place in order to safeguard patients in the future. It was held publicly and chaired by Dame Janet Smith (2002–5). Six reports were subsequently published between July 2002 and January 2005. She concluded that Dr Shipman killed 215 patients, and that the present systems of death and cremation certification had failed to detect any of those unlawful killings.

In her third report 'Death Certification and the Investigation of Deaths by Coroners' published 14 July 2003, Dame Janet Smith proposed radical changes to the current system. Her inquiry overlapped with a review chaired by Mr Tom Luce (Home Office, 2003b). The Luce review drew conclusions broadly in line with those of the Shipman Inquiry with the result that the momentum for change became irresistible and the Government had to respond. Dame Janet Smith urged the Secretary of State for Home Affairs not to allow the work of the Shipman Inquiry to meet the same fate as the Brodrick Report, and subsequently a Home Office position paper entitled 'Reforming the Coroner and Death Certification Service' was published in March 2004 and presented to Parliament (Home Office, 2004c).

The paper argued that certifying death should involve more rigorous procedures. A new two-stage death certification process would be introduced in the hope that the concealed homicide of patients by doctors would be detected. Under the new system a death would be verified by a doctor, a paramedic or senior nurse who would then complete a verification form. The doctor who had last treated the person would then issue a Certificate of the Medical Cause of Death. After that a new Medical Examiner, appointed to each coroner's area, would seek relevant factual information to confirm the cause of death and authorize burial or cremation without having to refer the death to the Coroner. Thus it would no longer be possible for an individual doctor to sign a death certificate without further scrutiny within the system. In addition, it was proposed to reduce the number of coroners from 127, who are currently full or part-time, to between 40 and 60 full-time coroners, all legally qualified.

It was anticipated that the reforms would take approximately 3 years to implement fully. During that period a National Coroners' service would be set up under a Chief Coroner with a medical adviser. Coroners would be given additional powers allowing them to seize medical documents as part of their investigation.

However when the Coroners' and Justice Act 2009 finally received Royal Assent on 12 November 2009, some 5 years later, the fear of Dame Janet Smith that the Shipman Inquiry would meet the same fate as the Brodrick Report seems to have been partially realized. Although described as the first major reform to the coroner system for over 100 years, the radical measures she urged have, as yet, not been fully implemented. There will, as promised, be a new post of Chief Coroner to lead the coroner service, with powers to intervene in cases in specified circumstances, including presiding over an appeals process designed specifically for the coroner system. There will be a senior coroner for each coroner area, previously known as coroner districts, with the appointment of area coroners and assistant coroners in place of existing deputy coroners and assistant deputy coroners. Although the names have been changed, the functions remain broadly the same.

In response to Dame Janet Smith's concerns, the notification of deaths to the coroner is more rigorous, with the appointment of medical examiners with leadership from a new National Medical Examiner, allowing the independent scrutiny and confirmation of medical certificates relating to the cause of death. Medical examiners will be attached to the local Primary Care Trust and will provide advice, but will not be accountable, to the coroner. The medical examiner will scrutinize and confirm the cause of all deaths that are not investigated by the coroner. Authorization of those deaths by the medical examiner will replace the current cremation forms and provide a single system for cremations and burials. However during the consultation phase as the Bill passed through Parliament, concerns were raised that the new scrutiny process should not cause significant delays to funerals and that medical examiners should maintain the necessary degree of independence from the NHS and other public authorities.

In the decade following the apprehension of Dr Shipman, political concern about the activities of homicidal doctors has been replaced by the threat posed by terrorists and the state's counter terrorism measures. An attempt was made to introduce inquests, hidden from public scrutiny, into the Coroners and Justice Act 2009 thereby reviving the plan for so called 'secret inquests' which had been originally considered in the Counter Terrorism Act 2008, but was subsequently dropped. There followed vociferous objection from various groups, such as Liberty and the charity Inquest, fearing that this measure would extinguish the ancient right of every citizen to a coroner's inquest in open court in the event of an unexplained death. It was feared that secret inquests would be used to protect agents of the state from damaging revelations about their conduct. Examples where secret inquests might have been held are the shooting of Jean Charles de Menezes in July 2005 in the mistaken belief that he was a terrorist, the deaths of soldiers in Iraq or Afghanistan from 'friendly fire' and the excess deaths resulting from serious deficiencies at Mid Staffordshire Trust (Delamonthe, 2010). Although concessions were made at the final hour and secret inquests seemingly abandoned, there does remain the provision in the Act for inquests to be suspended and substituted with inquiries under the Inquiries Act 2005 (Inquest Law Reports editorial, 2009). This will result in a few highly sensitive cases, as suggested above, where families and their lawyers will be prevented from accessing key evidence, they will be excluded from the process and there will be no jury. This sits uneasily with the government's claim that the Act would establish more effective, transparent and responsive justice for victims, bereaved families and the wider public.

3
Mental health and capacity laws including their administering bodies

Edited by
John Gunn

Written by
Phil Fennell
John Gunn
Penny Letts

Additional material from
Tim Exworthy
Nigel Shackleford
(Ministry of Justice)

1st edition authors: **Ann Barker, Oliver Briscoe, David Carson, Paul d'Orbán, Don Grubin, John Gunn, John Hamilton, Paul Mullen, Stephen Stanley and Pamela J Taylor**

Note: British law gets more complex and confusing by the week; this includes mental health law, hence the constant advice here and elsewhere to check legal textbooks, the acts themselves and the relevant codes of practice. This chapter is mainly concerned with four acts: the pre-2007 Mental Health Act 1983, the Mental Capacity Act 2005, the Mental Health Act 2007 (which amended the other two acts), and the amended Mental Health Act 1983.

PREAMBLE

Mental health law is concerned with the management of people who are afflicted with poor mental health. The origins of modern mental health law are to be found in the nineteenth-century lunacy acts, the first of which for England and Wales was passed in 1845. The word lunacy implies periodic or psychical madness which was once thought to be related to the phases of the moon. The lunacy acts needed to be read in conjunction with the county asylum acts and the poor law for the legislation was concerned with locking away mentally disordered people who were considered to be dangerous to themselves or others, or simply to be nuisances and unproductive. The legislation being considered here is a long way from that but it is still concerned with restraints, sometimes institutional restraints, used for the management of mentally disordered people. The great lunatic asylums were virtual prisons. They have gone but many mentally disordered people still find their way into institutions including modern prisons.

Mental disorder is destructive both to personality and to normal social life. It's a curious fact that as modern medicine has advanced a good deal of attention is paid to physical hygiene, but mental hygiene is largely ignored. For example most restrictions on the sale of alcohol have been removed and the price has fallen, so that a pleasurable but highly poisonous toxin is as cheap to buy as bottled water; large scale gambling is encouraged; investment in the care of marginalized children is very low; and education pays little attention to mental health issues. There are many psychiatric casualties. The new community-based system of psychiatric treatment, which has not produced many miraculous breakthroughs, is in no position to counter large-scale social changes, and is not resourced in terms of people or revenue to deal with all these casualties. Perhaps therefore it is no surprise that newspapers and ultimately politicians believe that community care has failed, not that politics has failed, nor that the prevention of psychiatric disorders is a low priority, but psychiatry has failed. It follows as winter follows autumn that parliamentarians want new laws. That's what members of Parliament do; they pass new laws and many of them. New laws are almost always regarded as 'a good thing' and indeed they can, on occasion, bring considerable benefits but new laws do not change attitudes, the fundamentals.

This chapter will focus on two large-scale legal changes that have occurred in England and Wales since the publication of the first edition of this text, the Mental Capacity Act 2005, and the Mental Health Act 2007. The Mental Capacity Act 2005 had a reasonably straightforward passage through a Parliament dominated by a large government majority, but a replacement for the Mental Health Act 1983 gave the Labour government very serious difficulties. Following a lengthy debate over nine years during which the two mental health bills of 2002 and 2004 which would have provided comprehensive new statutes were withdrawn, the government finally steered through Parliament the Mental Health Act 2007, an amendment Act. Some of the Government's policy goals remained intact: the broadening of the definition of mental disorder; the removal of all 'exclusions' except those in relation to alcohol or drugs; and the removal of the so-called 'treatability test'. However the government's desire to break the link between necessity for detention in hospital and treatment without informed consent was not realized; community treatment orders (CTOs) were introduced but capable or competent patients cannot be treated without their consent in the community, even in an emergency, they have to be detained in hospital for such treatment.

The Parliamentary process during those 9 years does to some extent reflect the conflict between public perceptions and medical reality. It also reflects a basic tension in society about the role of psychiatry. All medicine has a strong public health role, dealing with infectious diseases for example, but no other branch is regarded as part of the public order system.

HUMAN RIGHTS LEGISLATION

Mental health legislation, like all European legislation, is subject to the European Convention on Human Rights. In Lord Falconer's preface to the third edition of the Guide to the Human Rights Act 1998 (Falconer, 2006) he says;

In recent years human rights have been unfairly blamed for a range of ills in society. They have been blamed for encouraging a compensation culture. They have been blamed for forcing the release of dangerous prisoners to rape and kill again. They have been blamed for tying the hands of Government in dealing with the terrorist threat.' The guide tells us: 'The 1950 European Convention on Human Rights (ECHR) is a binding international agreement that the UK helped draft and has sought to comply with for over half a century. The Convention enshrines fundamental civil and political rights.'

The convention can be found on the Internet as a Council of Europe document (www.echr.coe.int/nr/rdonlyres/d5cc24a7-dc13-4318-b457-5c9014916d7a/0/englishanglais.pdf). It deals with a wide range of topics including the right to life, the right not to be tortured or to be subject to inhuman or degrading treatment, protection against slavery and forced labour, the right to physical integrity and, the one provision which specifically mentions persons of unsound mind, the right to liberty and security. The text of the Convention is given in appendix 1.

This clinical text does not have room to deal with the detailed legal issues raised by these two pieces of legislation (the European Convention on Human Rights and the Human Rights Act 1998) and the detailed court judgments which have followed. Most of the material is available on the internet and there are a number of scholarly texts which should be consulted by anyone in doubt about the laws involved. We recommend four books: Fennell (2011), Barber et al. (2009), Bowen (2007) and Jones (2009). There are others but most libraries keep copies of these remarkably informative tomes.

HISTORICAL BACKGROUND

During the nineteenth century, local authorities built large and somewhat forbidding institutions for mentally disordered people, generally known as lunatic asylums, and patients were committed to these asylums against their wishes and were dependent on the progress of their health plus the goodwill of the medical staff for release at some future date. Henry Maudsley, a pioneer forensic psychiatrist in London, was among those who were horrified by this arrangement. He regarded mental disorder as having a physical basis and believed that psychiatric patients should be treated in much the same way as patients with other physical disorders. He did not just believe these things but gave £30,000 of his personal fortune (made largely in the courts as an expert witness) to London to build a hospital for the mentally disordered that would include outpatient care and beds which could be used for voluntary patients. The gift was dependent on the understanding that no compulsory patients should be admitted to this new institution. The hospital was called the Maudsley Hospital after its benefactor. When one of us (JG) joined the staff there in 1963, the hospital was still unwilling to admit compulsory patients because of the terms of the Maudsley legacy. This produced an interesting but somewhat distorted practice of psychiatry, even though the hospital quickly became perhaps the most famous psychiatric teaching hospital in the world. Eventually, social pressures meant that this policy had to be abandoned and these days it is difficult to find a patient in the Maudsley Hospital who is not under compulsory detention.

It may well have been the example of Henry Maudsley that stirred Parliament to set up the Royal Commission in 1924 which reported in 1926, and led to the Mental Treatment Act 1930. This Act was probably the most significant in liberalizing mental healthcare in Britain in that it required local authorities to set up outpatient services for mentally disordered people and it also allowed such people to be short-term patients and most importantly, voluntary patients so that they could leave the hospital any time they wished. The Second World War produced an upheaval in thinking about public services and very significant changes were made to all medical care by the Labour government of 1946–52. A further Royal Commission on the law relating to mental illness and mental deficiency began its work in 1954 and reported in 1957 (often known as the Percy Commission as it was chaired by Lord Percy). This commission recommended new principles of mental health treatment:

'as far as possible the mentally disordered should be treated using the same informal relationships as occur in every other branch of medicine.'

They were echoing the views of Henry Maudsley and his hospital. The Commission recognized that detention brings stigma and tremendous disadvantage. Previous detention procedures had been in the hands of lawyers and magistrates; doctors were able to make recommendations but a somewhat cumbersome legal process had to be followed. The Percy Commission recommended that courts should no longer have anything to do with civil detention and lawyers should simply be involved in the process of reviewing a patient's detention through a mental health review tribunal system. The Mental Health Act 1959 which followed this report put the principle of informality right at the top (s.5) of the new statute.

The 1959 Act worked well and was generally regarded as a pioneering Act which other countries were keen to take note of. However by the early 1980s people began to regard it as out of date and in particular insufficiently liberal in its operation. An amendment act which created the Mental Health Act 1983 introduced new patient safeguards such as reviews by tribunals, the removal of the assumption that compulsory detention could mean compulsory treatment without further opinion, and special safeguards against the compulsory use of electroconvulsive therapy and psychosurgery. The new Act also worked well, but by the mid-1990s there was a general feeling that it was too oriented towards hospital care, not taking sufficient account of the large-scale shift from hospital care to community care. There were also some medical voices complaining that when a psychiatric patient killed someone (and such tragedies have always occurred on an infrequent basis) then no matter what the circumstances the consultant psychiatrist looking after the patient was in fact responsible for homicide.

Between 1954 and 2004, total number of inpatient beds in psychiatric hospitals fell from a peak of 154,000 to 32,400 (Warner, 2005). During the same period the general population in England and Wales increased from 45 million to over 53 million. This meant a large number of people with severe

mental illness being looked after in the community. At the same time compulsory admissions were steadily increasing from less than 20,000 per year in the 1960s and 1970s to over 30,000 in 2010–2011. In 2010–2011 there were 30,092 admissions under powers of detention in the Mental Health Act 1983 (2.2% down from the previous year). On 31 March 2011 there were 16,647 people detained in hospital, and 4291 in Community Treatment Orders (National Health Service Information Centre, 2011a). In 2010/11, two in every five people who spent time in hospital during the year had experienced detention. There was an 8.2% increase in people for whom this detention was via the criminal justice system (National Health Service Information Centre, 2011b, p.8). It used to be that 90% of all psychiatric hospital admissions were informal – now the figure is just over 60%.

In December 1992 Christopher Clunis, who had a history of schizophrenia, stabbed and killed Jonathan Zito while he waited on a London Underground platform. In the same month Ben Silcott, who also had a history of mental health problems, climbed into the lions' enclosure at London Zoo and was mauled but survived. These two events, close in time and representing respectively the risk to others and the risk to self of persons suffering from mental illnesses, added to the perception of the general public that such people were ill-served by the system of care in the community.

In July 1998 Mr Frank Dobson, Secretary of State for Health, announced

'I am setting up a review of the Mental Health Act 1983. The aim of this review will be to ensure that mental health legislation supports the safe and effective delivery of modern patterns of clinical and social care for people with a mental disorder, and to ensure that we achieve a proper balance between individual rights and the requirements of the safety of both the individual and the wider community.' (http://hansard.millbanksystems.com/written_answers/1998/jul/29/mental-health-act-1983).

This review was to be chaired by Professor Genevra Richardson. It is difficult to believe that the 'failure' which Frank Dobson kept referring to (see below) related to a close analysis of data, it is more likely that it related to a close analysis of newsprint, which had focused on two particularly horrifying homicides. The Zito/Clunis case has already been mentioned. The second was Michael Stone who was convicted of killing Megan Russell and her mother; the victims were out walking on a common. It was said that Michael Stone had a personality disorder and was refused admission to a psychiatric hospital. In fact he had not been refused admission (Francis et al., 2006).

In December 1998 Mr Dobson (1998) expanded on his reasons thus:

We must bring the law on mental health up to date. That law was formulated at a time when most mentally ill patients were treated in hospitals, so it now reflects the

practices of a bygone age and must be modernized to cope with the problems of today. At present, some people who would once have been left locked up in a hospital are fine living in the community; others are only safe providing they take their medication. However, some of those can become a danger to themselves and others refuse to comply with the treatment they need. That cannot be allowed to go on, which is why I have set up a review of the law on mental health. We need a law that works in a crisis, not one that fails in a crisis. Similarly, there is a small group of people with an untreatable psychiatric disorder, which makes them dangerous. At present, neither law nor practice is geared to cope with them. They cannot be taken into a mental hospital if they will not respond to treatment, and they cannot be put in prison unless they have committed an offence. If they are sent to prison, they can be a danger upon their release. Therefore, the Home Secretary and I are considering proposals to create a new form of renewable detention for people with a severe personality disorder who are considered to pose a grave risk to the public. That raises all sorts of ethical and practical problems, but we are convinced that the safety of the public must be the prime concern. People whose mental illness poses a threat to others constitute a very small minority, but we must be able to deal with them. Their illness is often an even bigger threat to them, and our new system should be better both for them and for the public.

In the debate that followed Mr Dobson re-emphasized some of his points:

The Victorians may have built great lunatic asylums so that people were out of sight and out of mind; under the previous Government, people were turned out of hospital and off the books, but we can no longer tolerate that sort of thing. We must ensure that people are properly looked after.'

Thus began one of the most prolonged legislative struggles in British Parliamentary history. The purpose of the proposal was plain and in response to a public perception that dangerous mentally ill people were walking the streets and committing murder when they should be locked up and/or treated compulsorily, and that they were committing random homicides. The perception was wrong; the proportion of homicides attributable to the mentally disordered was coming down even though there had been a rise in the overall number of homicides (Taylor and Gunn, 1999). Several members of Parliament in the debate argued that the policy of community care had not been a failure and where it could be shown to be deficient this was usually due to a lack of resources. The myth that personality disordered individuals could not be admitted to hospital was also wrong; however ministers were understandably impressed by the refusal of many psychiatrists to admit such patients under the pretext that they were 'untreatable'. As a result the threat of compelling hospitals and

doctors to admit such patients was contained within the ministerial statement.

In the event, the Richardson Committee (Department of Health, 1999a) did not take their main cues from this or subsequent ministerial statements and produced instead a legalistic solution which would have overturned one of the principles of the Percy Commission and put lawyers in the driving seat for all matters of compulsion in clinical psychiatry. They also placed emphasis on notions of mental capacity rather than mental status and diagnosis as the central issue to be determined when compulsory care was being considered. The Committee attached great importance to the inclusion of principles at the front of any new act. They regarded the principle of non-discrimination on grounds of mental health as central to the provision of treatment and care to those suffering from mental disorder. The Committee also recommended that the legislation should state as one of its main purposes the recognition and enhancement of patient autonomy. They wanted a principle included that would ensure that care, treatment and support would be provided in the least invasive and the least restrictive manner compatible with the delivery of safe and effective care. They did, however, want to reinforce the Percy principle of preferring informal and consensual care and they wanted to include reciprocity, participation, quality and respect for diversity, as well as the recognition of carers and the provision of information to patients.

None of these proposals was to have much impact on the consultation process that was to follow, largely, presumably, because they did not fit very well with the public protection agenda set out by Mr Dobson. A white paper in 2000 was followed by a draft bill in 2002. From the outset it was clear that the Department of Health was working closely with the Home Office in preparing this legislation and many believed that compulsory mental healthcare had been virtually handed over to the Home Office. So widespread was the opposition to the public order ethos of the proposals that a number of organizations joined together to oppose them and they formed the Mental Health Alliance. This alliance encompasses all the major stakeholders outside the government, including service user organizations, carer groups, the major mental health charities, the Royal Colleges of Psychiatrists and Nursing, the British Psychological Society, the trade union Unison, the British Association of Social Workers, the Law Society, the British Medical Association and organizations representing children in mental healthcare. In broad terms, the Mental Health Alliance agenda was to seek restoration of the Richardson Committee proposals, which have largely been taken up in Scotland by the Millan Committee (Scottish Executive, 2001). After some 2,000 largely negative responses to the published bill were received it was dropped and reintroduced in 2004 in a revised form. It too became subject to strong criticism by the Joint Pre-Parliamentary Scrutiny Committee. At first the government expressed determination to proceed with the 2004 bill but later dropped it and introduced instead a very different bill which became the Mental Health Act 2007, an amending act modifying the Mental Health Act 1983.

Curiously, most of the parties who had been involved in this protracted process felt vindicated by the final compromise solution, indeed the Zito Trust which had been set up in response to the tragic killing of Jonathan Zito was closed down after the enactment of the 2007 Act claiming that the objectives which they had campaigned for had been achieved. Their 'successes' included the closure of the much used and abused loophole of allowing patients with 'untreatable personality disorder' to escape mental health controls and the introduction of community treatment orders.

Undoubtedly better arrangements for people with personality disorder have been introduced, not primarily by the new Act, but by new services and the beginnings of a change of attitude within the psychiatric profession. In 2003 The Department of Health issued new Policy Guidance on the development of personality disorder services entitled *Personality Disorder: No Longer a Diagnosis of Exclusion* (National Institute for Mental Health in England, 2003) (www.dh.gov.uk/en/Publicationsandstatistics/Publications/PublicationsPolicyAndGuidance/DH_4009546). The law in respect of personality disorder remains much the same as it has since 1959 even though it is widely perceived to have changed because the so-called treatability criterion has been replaced by an appropriate treatment test. Both these tests are subject to psychiatric opinion and the availability of inpatient services; however mental health tribunals may be significantly influenced by the new wording and more ready to accept that people with personality disorder are sometimes appropriately detained in hospital.

MENTAL CAPACITY

Mental capacity was hardly mentioned in psychiatric books in the twentieth century; now it is everywhere and causing some confusion. It is a legal term and it is difficult to define; yet the underlying concept is fundamental and universal in human thinking. Like so many legal ideas it can be useful but it is abstract and to some extent a product of fashion. Does it differ from mental capability? What is autonomy? Does it differ from mental responsibility? Does it differ from competence? If so, why and how? We all understand that paternalism, i.e. the taking over of responsibilities on behalf of others, is appropriate and indeed necessary on occasions. We understand that children are not in a position to take full adult responsibilities because they are not capable of doing so. We understand that debilitating brain diseases such as dementia interfere with an adult's capacity to take appropriate decisions. We all understand that some mental disorders reduce an individual's capacity for making good decisions in their own best interests. Paternalistic legislation gives others the authority to intervene in all these cases in an attempt to ensure that the best interests of the individual concerned are protected.

In the past special legislation has been developed to ensure that mentally disordered individuals are protected from some of the worst consequences of their illness. Until effective treatment was available such measures were not only paternalistic, they were oppressive. However in England and Wales the Mental Health Act 1959 and its successor the Mental Health Act 1983 made great strides in putting an emphasis on providing the least restrictive paternalistic care with a number of safeguards to ensure that oppression was minimized. The patients who did not receive such consideration were those whose mental incapacities were much more related to physical disorders than mental ones, such as patients with dementia, brain damage, and in coma. They had to rely on clinical judgment guided by what came to be known as the *Bolam* test, and on the Court of Protection. The law for these patients has been clarified and the Mental Capacity Act 2005 introduced.

So Britain now has two types of legislation dealing with matters of mental capacity and capability in addition to matters of responsibility and 'fitness'. For England and Wales we have the Mental Health Act 1983 as amended, and the Mental Capacity Act 2005 (MCA, 2005). The first of these Acts deals with mental and psychiatric disorders and the second with both mental and physical disorders but they overlap and interact as we shall see below.

The Richardson Committee (Department of Health, 1999a) proposed that the new mental health legislation should include tests of mental capacity. However they also acknowledged that tests of risk (to self and others) would be of central importance in any mental health legislation. The Government did not accept this idea enthusiastically and in their consultation or green paper (Department of Health, 1999b), they suggested keeping a non-capacity based approach as in previous Acts based on the presence of a serious mental disorder which requires care and treatment in specialist services. After consultation the Government chose the second option which they regarded as not involving complex arguments about capacity but clearly focused on 'risk'. This annoyed many psychiatrists who argued that it made the Mental Health Act a law and order act and discriminated against mental disorders. Szmukler and Holloway (1998) went so far as to call mental health legislation 'a harmful anachronism' saying that it reinforces discriminatory stereotypes and arguing that the new legislation should be based on mental capacity tests to provide 'a rational approach'. The problem is that both sides are mistaken in this argument. Deciding to act paternalistically necessarily involves judgments concerning the patient's mental capacity. Furthermore the reason for acting paternalistically relates to risk. If a patient with mental disorder, or any other disorder, poses absolutely no risk to himself or to others then there is no reason for insisting upon a course of treatment. The other matter which has caused some dismay is that the 'best interests' for the patient are spelled out in the new mental capacity legislation but not in the amended Mental Health Act. It may have been better to have spelled this out, but medicine itself is based on the ideology of providing for the best interests of patients and new legislation won't change anything very much in that respect. In the context of harm to others it is worth remembering that it is not in the interests of any patient to break the law and damage others.

The problem for clinicians using either the capacity test spelled out in the Mental Capacity Act or in the mental state assessment required for compulsory admission under the Mental Health Act is that the process is highly subjective, subject to fluctuations and very few measuring aids or tests are available. The assessment therefore has to be made clinically. In the USA Grisso et al. (1997) have developed the MacArthur Competence Assessment Tool for Treatment (MacCAT-T) which is a clinical tool to assess the patient's capacity to make treatment decisions. It takes about 15 to 20 minutes to administer, but some patients won't co-operate with the test. The authors counsel that the patient's overall clinical condition in the context of the treatment situation remains an all important factor in determining mental capacity. It should also be noted that the legal framework in the United States is different with different safeguards.

MENTAL HEALTH ACT 1983 AMENDED BY THE MENTAL HEALTH ACT 2007

As the Mental Health Act 2007 is an amendment Act, the main mental health legislation in England and Wales remains the Mental Health Act 1983. The practitioner will find this dual legislation confusing. The Department of Health has provided an amended version of the Mental Health Act 1983 which is reproduced as an appendix in order to help comprehension. It has been edited and shortened for this book. Needless to say this appendix should not be used as a legal authority.

This brief outline for forensic psychiatrists is by no means comprehensive. The Code of Practice 2008, which is published by the Department of Health and for Wales by the Welsh Assembly Government is available online and can also be bought in paper form; every psychiatrist should have a copy. The four textbooks mentioned above (Fennell, Bowen, Barber et al. and Jones), should also be consulted.

The Welsh Assembly Government has also introduced a *measure* to extend the group of qualifying patients under the Act entitled to support from an independent mental health advocate (IMHA) (see below and http://www.wales.gov.uk/topics/health/nhswales/healthservice/mentalhealthservices/measure/?lang=en).

Informal Admission

The Mental Health Acts passed in 1959 and 1983 were based on the principle that, wherever possible, patients should be admitted to hospital on an informal basis and powers of compulsion should be used as a last resort. Approximately 250,000 admissions to psychiatric hospitals take place, in England and Wales, every year. Over 90% of these admissions are informal (Bartlett and Sandland, 2007). In spite of all the controversy concerning the Mental Health Act 2007, this principle has survived and section 131 of the Mental Health Act 1983 (amended) remains, stating that nothing in the Act

shall be construed as preventing a patient who requires treatment for mental disorder from being admitted to any hospital or registered establishment in pursuance of arrangements made in that behalf and without any application, order or direction rendering him liable to be detained under this Act.

Informal patients are free to leave hospital at any time unless a holding power under section 5 is invoked.

The Bournewood Gap

Under the Mental Heath Act 1959 and the unamended Mental Health Act 1983 it was accepted practice that patients who lack capacity and did not resist admission to hospital should be admitted informally without using powers of detention. It was only if the incapacitated person persistently and purposefully attempted to leave hospital, or refused to go there in the first place, that powers of detention were used. The legality of this approach was not questioned until the case of HL who since childhood had lived in Bournewood hospital. His care had been transferred to paid carers with whom he resided as part of the family, and who had been looking after him for over 3 years under an adult fostering scheme. On one day each week he attended a day-care centre to enable his carers to have a break. His mental state deteriorated and he was taken to the accident and emergency unit at Bournewood hospital and admitted as an emergency. He was admitted informally as he did not resist. His carers were told not to visit and they didn't see him for 4 months. Eventually the carers challenged this situation and the Court of Appeal ruled that his detention was unlawful, so the hospital admitted him under the Mental Health Act 1983. HL was subsequently discharged by a mental health review tribunal. The Court of Appeal decision meant that hundreds of other patients in similar circumstances were also potentially detained unlawfully. Possibly as a result the House of Lords allowed an appeal from the hospital saying that HL had not really been 'detained' before the Mental Heath Act was used, or if he had been it was necessary and therefore justified (*Bournewood*). HL's carers disagreed and brought a case before the European Court of Human Rights which ruled that HL's deprivation of liberty had not been 'in accordance with a procedure prescribed by law' and was therefore contrary to article 5 (1) (*HL v UK*) (see Bowen, 2007 for a good account of the case). This gave the government a problem and the solution devised in the MHA 2007 is to say that there are two groups of patients who can be admitted informally, those who are capable and consenting to admission, and those who, although they lack the capacity to consent to admission or treatment, are not resisting hospitalization in circumstances where the level of control to be exercised over residence, movement, and treatment is insufficient in degree and intensity to amount to a deprivation of liberty. The Mental Health Act 2007 amended the Mental Capacity Act 2005 to introduce new safeguards for people lacking capacity to consent who are being cared for in conditions that amount to a deprivation of their liberty, and new procedures for the deprivation of liberty to be authorized.

The Mental Health Act Code of Practice (DoH, 2008a) (4.10) says that where a patient presents a 'clear danger to self or others' compulsory admission should be considered even though the patient has expressed willingness to be admitted voluntarily, so detention may be justified even when the patient has capacity and is consenting, if without detention there will be danger to self or others, and the patient's history or current behaviour suggests that consent will be withdrawn.

The Code also says (4.14) that 'the fact that patients cannot consent to treatment they need, or to be admitted to hospital, does not automatically mean that the Act must be used. It may be possible to rely instead on the provisions of the Mental Capacity Act 2005 to provide treatment in the best interests of patients who are aged 16 or over and who lack capacity to consent to treatment.'

Definition of Mental Disorder

The Mental Health Act 1983 (amended) now has one broad definition of mental disorder: 'any disorder or disability of the mind' used for all types of psychiatric detention whether as an offender or a non-offender patient. Thus any patient, whether suffering from a serious mental disorder, a personality disorder, learning disability, or even a minor neurosis is liable for detention under the Act if s/he is deemed to warrant hospital admission in the interests of his or her own health or safety or with a view to protecting other people if there is appropriate treatment available. This is a very wide provision. The terms mental impairment and psychopathic disorder disappear from the amended Act and are consigned to legal history. Further, patients with learning disability shall not be considered as suffering from mental disorder, unless they also manifest abnormally aggressive or seriously irresponsible conduct. A person with a learning disability who does not exhibit such conduct may be detained for assessment under s.2 or s.4, may be removed to a place of safety under s.135 or s.136 or prevented from leaving hospital under s.5 of the Act.

This wide definition is almost certainly an attempt by the Government to avoid arguments about whether such patients are treatable or not. In practice this change will make very little difference because in *Reid* the House of Lords held that the term 'treatable' was wide enough to include treatment which alleviates or prevents deterioration in the symptoms of the disorder, not the disorder itself. Jones (2009) opines that the interpretation in the case law of the treatability test was so broad that 'it is difficult to imagine the circumstances that would cause a patient to fail it'. This is as it should be, and it was probably the practice of psychiatrists using the old treatability clause as a means of rejecting difficult patients that was one of the key factors in the Government bringing forward a new act. We might note in passing the irony of a clause inserted into the previous acts to prevent psychiatrists admitting too many patients ending up as a means of psychiatrists rejecting patients. The change in the law may however be irrelevant because the power of admission still remains with the hospital and is still determined by attitudes rather than statutes. As attitudes change, as resources improve, more patients may be admitted.

Who Can Admit?

Although it was and remains possible for an application for detention or guardianship to come from the patient's nearest relative, under the pre-2007 Mental Health Act 1983 it would normally have come from a specially trained approved social worker, whose role was to ensure that the necessary treatment could not be provided without detention, to see that the admission was carried out correctly, medical recommendations were obtained and the patient was safely conveyed to the hospital. The Mental Health Act 2007 widens this power to approved mental health professionals who need not be a social worker, and could be a nurse, a psychologist, or occupational therapist, with appropriately recognized training. The Act still requires an application for non-emergency admissions to be supported by two medical recommendations, to the effect that the patient is suffering from mental disorder of nature or degree requiring detention in the interests of his health or safety or for the protection of others. One of the recommending doctors must be approved under s.12 of the Mental Health Act 1983 (amended) as having special experience in the diagnosis or treatment of mental disorder.

The Responsible Clinician (RC)

Until the Mental Health Act 2007 amendments came into force the person in charge of decisions about treatment without consent and prolongation of detention was the responsible medical officer (RMO) who had to be a doctor. The RMO has been replaced by the responsible clinician who may be a doctor but could also be a nurse, a psychologist, an occupational therapist, or a social worker, provided they have undergone special training.

The Approved Clinician (AC)

An approved clinician may be a doctor or other mental health professional who has had specialized training. Some previously exclusively medical roles now fall to approved clinicians; they may, for example, be required to lead a multidisciplinary team.

Nearest Relative

The identity of the nearest relative is determined according to a statutory list, beginning with husband or wife, father or mother, son or daughter. The Mental Health Act 2007 widens that list to recognize civil partners and opposite or same sex couples living together but the rights of the nearest relative remain essentially unchanged. The Act does however introduce the possibility for the patient to seek displacement of an unsuitable nearest relative. This is necessitated by successful challenges in the European Court of Human Rights and in the English courts under the Human Rights Act 1998 (see Fennell, 2011).

Independent Mental Health Advocates (IMHAs)

A new s.130A of the Mental Health Act 1983 (amended) places new duties upon the Secretary of State (or Welsh Assembly) to provide advocacy services for most detained patients, guardianship patients and patients subject to community treatment orders. Advocacy must include help in obtaining information about understanding the provisions of the Act which subject her/him to compulsion, any conditions or restrictions, what medical treatment is being given or is proposed and why, and the authority under which the medication is given. Advocacy must also include help in obtaining information about the patient's rights. Advocates will only have access to patient records, however, where a capable patient gives consent, or, in the case of an incapable patient, where access would not conflict with the decision of the Court of Protection, and the person holding the records agrees that the records are relevant to the matter at issue and access is 'appropriate'.

Admission Criteria

The admission criteria are essentially unchanged (i.e. suffering from mental disorder, necessary for health and safety and protection of others, treatment being available) save for the removal of the old subcategories of mental disorder and the replacement of the so-called treatability test with the test of availability of appropriate treatment.

Medical treatment for mental disorder is redefined in s.145. It includes nursing, psychological intervention, specialist mental health habilitation, rehabilitation and care. Psychological interventions are expressly mentioned for the first time. These include psychotherapy and other interactive treatments requiring cooperation from the patient. Treatment must have the purpose of alleviating or preventing 'a worsening of the disorder or one or more of its symptoms or manifestations.' The patient's refusal to accept treatment can no longer be an obstacle to detention, as long as treatment is available.

The general definition of mental disorder means the welcome disappearance of the stigmatizing term psychopathic disorder from British mental health legislation. It preserves and extends the possibility to detain people with a personality disorder, who are believed to pose a risk to self or others. If violent conduct is a manifestation of their disorder, appropriate treatment of that manifestation might include nursing supervision, as well as psychological interventions such as anger management or cognitive behaviour therapy.

Exclusions

The pre-2007 Mental Health Act 1983 contained various 'exclusions whereby a person might not be treated as suffering from a mental disorder by reason only of promiscuity or other immoral conduct, sexual deviancy or dependence on alcohol or drugs.' All these exclusions have been removed except dependence on alcohol or drugs. It should be noted that the exclusion refers to dependence; extreme intoxication is not prevented from being a mental disorder by this provision. The Code of Practice emphasizes that other mental disorders relating to the use of outlawed drugs are not excluded and these include withdrawal states with delirium or associated psychotic disorder, organic mental disorders associated with the prolonged abuse of drugs or alcohol and severe acute intoxication (drunkenness). This is illogical, but since when have laws been logical? It is important to remember that dependence on alcohol or drugs is not a reason to exclude the possibility of detention of a person who also suffers from another mental disorder such as depression or a psychotic illness in addition to their addiction.

The removal of all exclusions except drug and alcohol dependence means that patients with paedophilia (even if that is the only disorder) can still be detained under the Act (as they could before under the psychopathic disorder provision).

Availability of Appropriate Treatment

The treatability test has been removed and replaced by a requirement that before a detention order is made, appropriate treatment is available regardless of whether the patient accesses it or not. This, together with the virtual absence of exclusion criteria for compulsory admission means there are few reasons for clinicians not to use compulsory powers under the Act but, to reiterate, attitudes will still hold sway.

Place of Safety

Section 136 of the Mental Health Act 1983 empowers a police officer who finds a person in a public place who appears to be mentally disordered and to require care and control to take that person to a place of safety entirely on his/her own initiative. Such a detention can last up to 72 hours during which time a doctor is called to make an assessment as to whether grounds for detention are met, and, where appropriate, arrangements should be made for transfer to a hospital. A place of safety can be police station, a care home, a hospital or any other suitable place. The Mental Health Act 2007 amendments enable a person who has been removed in one place of safety to be transferred to another within the 72-hour period.

Offender-Patients

Part 3 of the Mental Health Act 1983 provides a framework of powers to transfer mentally disordered people to hospital during a criminal court hearing with or without restrictions, to remand to hospital for reports or treatment, and to transfer mentally disordered prisoners from prison to hospital. The new broad definition of mental disorder applies to all these powers as does replacing the treatability test with the test that appropriate treatment is available. Section 37 enables offenders with mental disorder to be sent to hospital for 6 months renewable. Section 41 provides that a Crown Court judge who considers it necessary to protect the public from serious harm may impose restrictions on discharge. The harm need not be physical. It could be psychological. It must however, be serious (see *Birch*). These restrictions will automatically be without limit of time and prevent the patient being granted leave of absence or discharge from hospital without the permission of the Ministry of Justice, or, in the case of discharge, the Mental Health Tribunal.

Assessment of mentally disordered offenders

The Code of Practice 2008 says that 'people subject to criminal proceedings have the same rights to psychiatric assessment and treatment as other citizens. Any person who is in police or prison custody, or who is before the courts charged with a criminal offence, and who is in need of medical treatment for mental disorder should be considered for admission to hospital.' This is an exposition of the general British policy that mentally disordered people should, whenever possible, be detained in hospitals rather than prisons, a policy breached more often than it is kept, but a policy for mental health professionals to aspire to.

Compulsory treatment of mental disorder is not really possible in prison except (a) under common law in an emergency where treatment is immediately necessary and proportionate for the protection of others; or (b) where the affected person or prisoner lacks mental capacity and treatment is necessary in her or his best interests and restraint is necessary to prevent harm to the patient, when treatment can be given using restraint if necessary and is proportionate under sections 5 and 6 of the Mental Capacity Act 2005.

Remands to hospital

Under the Mental Health Act 1983 there are three remand powers for mentally disordered offenders. (1) The power to remand an accused person for reports on his/her mental condition under section 35; (2) the power to remand for psychiatric treatment under section 36; (3) the power to impose an interim hospital order under section 38.

Remands for a psychiatric report, s.35

An accused person may be remanded to hospital for a report when the court has reason to suspect that the accused is suffering from mental disorder and it would be impracticable for a report to be obtained were s/he to be remanded on bail. The report should contain a statement of whether the patient is suffering from a mental disorder, identifying its relevance to the alleged offence. Reports may be prepared not just by doctors but also by approved clinicians who can be nurses, psychologists, social workers, or occupational therapists. A person remanded for reports is not subject to the consent to treatment provisions of part 4 of the Act and therefore retains the common law right to refuse treatment but the Mental Capacity Act 2005 introduces the possibility that the person could be given treatment without consent under its sections 5 or 6 using the 'best interests' doctrine. The Code of Practice has also suggested that remand patients may be detained under part 2 if treatment without consent is necessary.

Remands for treatment, s.36

A remand for treatment may be used to provide treatment before trial and hence potentially avoid an accused person being found unfit to plead (see p.25). Such an order may only be made by the Crown Court on the evidence of two doctors, but under the amended Act it is available for all forms of mental disorder. A person accused of murder cannot be remanded for treatment because the sentence is fixed by law at life imprisonment.

The hospital order s.37

A hospital order may be made by magistrates or by the Crown Court if the person is convicted of an offence punishable with imprisonment, except in the case of murder. A magistrates' court can make a hospital order without recording a conviction, see also p.28.

A hospital order detains a convicted mentally disordered person in hospital for treatment rather than sending him/her to prison. It may be imposed without restrictions in which case the patient's responsible clinician may discharge the patient on the clinician's own initiative and as the detention can be renewed in the same way as under section 3, i.e. 6 months in the first instance, then renewable for a further 6 months, then every 12 months.

The effect of a hospital order is similar to that of admission for treatment as a non-offender under section 3. Detention is renewed under section 20, the patient has the right to appeal for discharge to a mental health tribunal and treatment for mental disorder is subject to part 4 of the Mental Health Act 1983 (amended). The most important differences are that a hospital order patient cannot be discharged by his or her nearest relative, and the patient does not have a right to apply to the tribunal within the first 6 months of detention.

Interim hospital orders, s.38

Either the Crown Court or a magistrate's court may make an interim hospital order on the evidence of two doctors. An interim order is made initially for 12 weeks and may be reviewed at 28-day intervals thereafter up to a maximum of 12 months. This is available for patients with any form of mental disorder.

Restriction order, s.41

When a hospital order has been made, the Crown Court may make a restriction order on grounds of dangerousness if necessary to protect the public from serious harm, and if one of the two doctors supporting the hospital order has given oral evidence. If such an order is imposed this will be without limit of time and the patient may not be discharged by the responsible clinician, so the renewing arrangements mentioned above don't apply. Only the Secretary of State for Justice or the Mental Health Tribunal may direct discharge (see below). A magistrates' court has no power to make a restriction order but may commit offenders over 14 years of age to the Crown Court for such an order to be made. The restriction order is to protect the public from serious harm. The patient cannot be granted leave of absence, transferred, or discharged by the responsible clinician, or the hospital managers without the consent of the Secretary of State for Justice.

The patient detained in this way has the right to apply to a mental health tribunal to seek discharge, but not within the first 6 months of detention. Absolute discharges are rare and most patients who are under restrictions who are discharged from hospital either by the Secretary of State or a tribunal have conditions attached to their discharge arrangements such as where they may live, which clinic they will attend, etc. The conditional discharge option is seen as an effective means of risk management. It's a bit like a parole licence but any recall needed is usually initiated by a clinician rather than by a probation officer. The Tribunal has no power to order transfer or leave.

Transfer to hospital of sentenced prisoners, s.47 and s.49

Section 47 allows for the transfer of a sentenced prisoner to hospital by the Secretary of State's direction which, if the patient is still in hospital at the end of the sentence, results in the patient being treated as if detained under a hospital order without restrictions. Section 49 allows the Secretary of State to attach a restriction direction identical to the one which can be imposed after a hospital order. By far the majority of transfers are subject to restrictions.

Hospital limitation directions, s.45A, the hybrid order

Section 45A was introduced into the Mental Health Act 1983 by the Crime (Sentences) Act 1997. This provides that a mentally disordered offender may be given a sentence of imprisonment coupled with an immediate direction to hospital. Initially confined to people with personality disorder, the Mental Health Act 2007 extends this to people with any disorder or disability of mind. To make a hospital direction the court must have written or oral evidence from two doctors stating that the offender is suffering from mental disorder, that it is appropriate for him or her to be detained in a hospital for medical treatment and that appropriate medical treatment is available. The effect of this order is that although hospitalized the offender has the legal status of a prisoner rather than a patient, so that if he or she is successfully treated before the expiry of the prison sentence he or she can be returned to prison to serve the remainder of that sentence. It has hardly been used since it was introduced. A sentence which mixes treatment and punishment is a compromise which makes neither legal nor clinical sense.

Care in the Community

Under the Mental Health Act 1983 (amended) there are four compulsory powers over patients in the community. The restriction order has been mentioned above, there are also guardianship orders under sections 7 or 37, extended leave under section 17, and supervised community treatment often known as a community treatment order.

Care programme approach (CPA)

All psychiatric patients whether or not they have been detained are entitled to be dealt with under the care programme approach. The care programme approach requires a risk assessment, a needs assessment, a written care plan which will be regularly reviewed and a key worker (or care co-ordinator). Under guidance issued by the Department of Health patients should be managed with the care programme approach if a mental disorder is assessed as posing a potential risk to their own safety or to other people (Department of Health, 2008b).

Aftercare section 117

Section 117 of the Mental Health Act 1983 (amended) places a duty jointly on primary care trusts and social service authorities to provide after-care services for patients who have been detained in hospital. The duty applies when the patient ceases to be detained and leaves hospital.

Leave section 17

Under section 17 the responsible clinician may grant either indefinite leave or leave for a specified period to non-restricted patients. Where it appears to the responsible clinician to be necessary in the interests of the patient's health or safety or for the protection of others, the patient may be recalled from leave by giving notice in writing. Hitherto psychiatrists have preferred to use section 17 leave instead of guardianship. It is intended that this type of leave will be reduced and supplanted by the community treatment order under section 17A (below). Current case law holds that the patient's liability to detention may be renewed repeatedly while s/he continues to live in the community, so long as the patient needs some treatment in hospital, not necessarily as an inpatient. A limitation on the use of s.17 is that before sending a patient on extended leave for 7 days or more, the responsible clinician must consider whether the patient should be placed on a community treatment order.

Guardianship S.7 and S.37

Guardianship applications in respect of non-offender patients are made under section 7. As with civil detention orders, either the nearest relative or an approved mental health professional may apply. Two medical recommendations are necessary. The guardian has three powers: to require the patient to live at a specified place, to require the patient to attend for medical treatment, education, training or work, to require access to the patient at his or her home. The courts also have the power to make a guardianship order under section 37 as an alternative disposal for offender patients. About 450 new receptions into guardianship are made each year but little use is made of guardianship orders by the courts, fewer than 30 cases per year.

Community Treatment Orders S.17A

The role of section 17 leave (above) will be reduced under the amendments introduced by the Mental Health Act 2007. It will be supplemented by the community treatment order (CTO) under section 17A of the Mental Health Act 1983 (amended). To reinforce that point a responsible clinician considering granting leave, under section 17, for more than 7 days must first consider whether the patient should be dealt with under section 17A instead.

To effect a community treatment order the responsible clinician must certify in writing that the patient is suffering from mental disorder which makes it appropriate for him or her to receive treatment, the treatment is necessary for his or her health or safety or for the protection others, such treatment can be provided in the community, but subject to the clinician being able to exercise the power to recall the patient to hospital, and appropriate treatment is available. A second certificate from an approved mental health professional, agreeing with the responsible clinician's opinion is also required. A list of specific conditions will need to be made for each patient, such as where s/he lives and which clinic to attend.

This new order has attracted quite a lot of criticism. Some are concerned that it is not in keeping with the spirit of European human rights legislation (see Fennell, 2011), and there is no power to seek review before the Mental Health Tribunal about the need for specified conditions, although the basis of the order in itself can be challenged via the Tribunal. In spite of the criticisms the order is used a great deal but insufficient resources are available for this unexpected popularity. When interviewed on the radio a Minister of Health was driven to arguing that health trusts should only make the number of community treatment orders which they can afford, thus implying that more patients will stay in hospital for longer, a curious economic argument. Within the last 2 months of the community treatment order the responsible clinician must re-examine the patient and consult other professionals about continuation of the order which may be for a further 6 months at the first renewal and for 12 months in the case of second or subsequent renewals.

Community treatment order patients, who lack capacity, may be treated without their consent in an emergency or with the consent of someone with authority to consent on his or her behalf under the Mental Capacity Act. If the patient is capable and refuses treatment in the community the treatment may only be given by recalling the patient to hospital.

Both patients on leave under section 17 and those restrained by a community treatment order may be recalled to hospital by the responsible clinician if s/he believes that further treatment in hospital is required, or safety issues are raised by the patient's continuance in the community, and in the case of a CTO if one of the conditions is breached. If a CTO patient is recalled, the hospital managers have power to detain the patient for 72 hours from the time the patient is re-admitted to hospital. During that time, an assessment must be made as to whether the CTO should be revoked with the effect that the patient is detained in hospital under the original section, which was suspended while the patient was on the CTO. If the CTO is not revoked the patient must be released back on to CTO, within 72 hours.

Safeguards

Hospital managers

Hospital managers are the detaining authority for patients who are not subject to Ministry of Justice restrictions. Applications for admission are addressed to the hospital managers; managers receive a report from the responsible clinician which renews detention. Managers have the power to direct discharge, and they have duties to give information to patients about their rights under the Act. The Mental Health Act 2007 also introduced a duty on hospital managers to ensure that an age appropriate environment is provided for patients under the age of 18 years.

Tribunals (Mental Health)

Mental health review tribunals were established in 1959 with the task of reviewing the continued need for detention of a patient with powers to discharge. They are dealt with separately below.

Consent to Treatment (part IV of the Mental Health Act 1983 (amended))

In most circumstances, attempts to enforce any form of physical treatment on a patient without his or her explicit consent could result in a civil suit alleging battery. The nature of mental disorder, however, means that a number of patients will not be able to understand the nature of their illness or the implications of treatment, that is, they are thought not to be able to give valid consent to treatment. Further, they may refuse treatment as a result of their illness e.g. as a result of pathological thinking. Part IV of the Act, entitled 'Consent to Treatment', regulates treatment for mental disorder and allows certain treatments to be given without consent to detained patients subject to second opinion safeguards. The key to the formal consent procedures is the second opinion appointed doctor (SOAD), who has been appointed by the Care Quality Commission.

Section 57 treatments require consent and a second opinion. Such treatments include psychosurgery and hormone implants to reduce male sex drive. A certificate from a panel of three people appointed by the Care Quality Commission is required stating that the patient is capable of giving consent **and** has consented. The medical member of the panel must certify that that it is appropriate for the treatment to be given. These procedures apply whether or not the patient is detained. Capacity to consent to treatment means that the patient understands the nature, purpose and likely effects (good and bad) of the treatment.

Section 58 treatments which require consent or a second opinion include psychotropic medication after 3 months of treatment (the first 3 months of pharmacological treatment can be given without consent and without a certificate). At the 3-month point either the patient must

consent or a written statement from a second opinion appointed doctor must certify that the treatment ought to be given and it is appropriate. Before issuing a certificate the second opinion appointed doctor must consult two other professionals (not doctors) concerned with the patient's treatment. It doesn't matter whether the patient is capable of giving consent or not. The Court of Appeal has held that fairness requires the second opinion appointed doctor to give reasons in writing for his or her opinion when certifying that the detained patient should be given medication against his or her will, and that these reasons should be disclosed to the patient unless the second opinion appointed doctor or the responsible doctor considers that such disclosure would be likely to cause serious harm to the physical or mental health of the patient or others.

Electroconvulsive therapy (ECT) may not be given if a capable patient has refused it. ECT may, however, be given subject to a second opinion when a patient lacks capacity, if it is appropriate to give the treatment, and giving it does not conflict with a valid advance decision refusing it, or with a decision of a health and personal welfare attorney or a deputy acting within their powers under the Mental Capacity Act 2005.

Section 62 enables the administration of ECT or medicines for mental disorder without consent or a second opinion in urgent circumstances where immediately necessary to save life or to prevent serious deterioration in the patient's condition, but it is vital that a detailed note of the emergency and patient's condition, including the patient's mental capacity or capability is made.

In the community s.64A

'Relevant treatment' (s.64A Mental Health Act 1983 (amended)) can also be given to a community patient (on a community treatment order) who has not been recalled to hospital (a) if there is valid consent from the patient or someone authorized under the Mental Capacity Act 2005 to make decisions on the patient's behalf; or (b) if the patient lacks capacity and force is not necessary to secure compliance and a certificate from the second opinion appointed doctor has been signed; or (c) if there is consent from a health and personal welfare attorney or a deputy acting within their powers under the Mental Capacity Act 2005; or (d) in an emergency, where the patient lacks capacity to consent using force if necessary. If force is necessary to secure compliance in an emergency the force must be a proportionate response.

In an emergency any treatment can be given which is immediately necessary to save the patient's life or is immediately necessary to prevent a serious deterioration, or to alleviate serious suffering or is immediately necessary to prevent the patient from behaving violently or dangerously to him or herself or to others. Details of emergency treatment given under s.62 (see above) and the reasons for it must be recorded fully.

In summary, the Mental Health Act 2007 puts a new emphasis on a patient's community obligations. S/he is to accept medication and to behave in accordance with conditions. If s/he does not comply s/he may be recalled to hospital. Emergency treatment for mental disorder may be given without consent in the community using reasonable force if necessary, where the patient lacks capacity or is an incompetent minor. Non-emergency treatment may be given if the patient is capable and consents. Treatment may be given if there is reason to believe the patient is refusing it so long as force is not necessary.

If a patient in the community is capable of refusing treatment, force may only be used to give the treatment if the patient is recalled to hospital and the treatment is authorized under s.62A.

Victims' Rights

Under the Domestic Violence, Crime and Victims Act 2004 a victim of a sexual or violent offence has a right to make representations, if the offender is subject to restriction order, about whether the patient should be subject to any conditions in the event of a conditional discharge from hospital. The Mental Health Act 2007 extended this right to victims of sexual or violent offences where the offender is sentenced to a hospital order without restrictions.

Principles and Codes of Practice

The Parliamentary Joint Committee on the draft Mental Health Bill 2004 recommended that principles should appear on the face of the Act. However the government disagreed and the principles for the Act do not appear anywhere within the Act but are in the Code of Practice instead. Section 118 of the Mental Health Act 2007 says that the code of practice shall include principles and that in those principles 11 matters are to be addressed. These are, respect for patients' past and present wishes and feelings, respect for diversity, minimizing restrictions on liberty, involvement of patients in planning, developing and delivering care and treatment appropriate to them, avoidance of unlawful discrimination, effectiveness of treatment, views of carers and other interested parties, patient wellbeing and safety, public safety, the efficient use of resources, and the equitable distribution of services. England and Wales have separate codes of practice.

Children

A child, for mental health purposes, is defined as anyone under 18 years old. Children may be admitted under the Mental Health Act 1983 informally with their own consent, with parental consent, using the compulsory powers of parts 2 or 3 of the Mental Health Act 1983 (amended), or under the Children Act 1989. Guardianship may not be used if the patient is under 16. A child of 16 or 17 may not be admitted by parental consent if the child objects, so detention under the 1983 Act will be necessary. A new section 131A of the Mental Health Act 1983 (amended) places a limited duty on hospital managers to ensure that the hospital environment of the child patient is 'suitable having regard to his or her age (subject to his or her needs)' and to carry out this duty managers must consult 'a person who appears to them to have knowledge or experience of cases involving patients who have not attained the age of 18 years'. At least one of the two doctors or the approved mental health professional involved in any mental health assessment of a child should be a clinician specializing in child and adolescent mental health. Before a child patient can have electroconvulsive therapy (ECT) s/he must give consent and a second opinion appointed doctor must certify that the patient is capable of understanding the nature, purpose and effects of the treatment, has consented, and that the treatment is appropriate.

Dangerous and Severe Personality Disorder (DSPD)

As a footnote to the description of the Mental Health Act it is necessary to mention DSPD. It is a term invented by English politicians. It has neither clinical nor legal meaning. It first arose in a green paper published in 1999 (Home Office, Department of Health, 1999; you won't find this on the internet it has been removed!) when it was floated as a possible legal device for getting psychiatrists to identify individuals with personality disorder and bring them into hospital, compulsorily, without a conviction and before they had committed serious violence. The idea was abandoned in the face of an incredulous storm of protest from professionals in the field especially civil liberties lawyers and psychiatrists.

The idea behind the proposal was to find a way to institutionalize people who were considered to be dangerous. The politicians seemed unaware that in Britain there had been legislation permitting the compulsory admission of people with personality disorder to hospital since 1959. If they were aware of this legislation they were complaining that it was under-used. This was correct because psychiatrists were and are very reluctant to treat patients with personality disorder in any circumstance, let alone under compulsion.

Mullen (1999) summed up the situation beautifully:

There is a crying need for mental health services for severely personality disordered individuals. Such services would decrease the morbidity and staggering mortality associated with these conditions. In the process they would contribute to community safety. The British government's proposals largely ignore this central issue of developing appropriate treatment services in favour of creating a system for locking up men and women who frighten officials. On first reading this document created both disappointment and foreboding. On more careful consideration it became clear that the contradictions were so glaring, the deceptions so open and palpable, and the agenda so obvious, that these proposals can surely not have any chance of influencing reality.

He was right, the proposals were abandoned; they did however leave some legacies. The first was a proposal for the development of units in various parts of the National Health Service, dedicated to the treatment of personality disorder. Second, four so-called DSPD units were developed in high security, two in hospitals and two in prisons. These are no longer to be funded, nor is the DSPD name to endure. The principle that the personality-disordered offender population is a shared responsibility of HOMS and the NHS will be reinforced, and service delivery based on a 'whole systems pathyway' approachch across the two services, with emphasis on both criminal justice and health serices on 'psychologically informed planned environments' (PIPES; Joseph and Benefield, 2012) see also chapter 16.

Tribunal (Mental Health)

The Tribunal (Mental Health) is the most important means that dctaincd patients in England have of appealing against their compulsory detention. Wales has a separate Mental Health Review Tribunal.

Constitution and administration

Mental health review tribunals were established by the Mental Health Act 1959 with the task of reviewing the continued need for detention of a patient and they were empowered to direct discharge. Since the Implementation of the Tribunals Courts and Enforcement Act 2007 mental health review tribunals in England have been absorbed into the Health Education and Social Care Chamber of the First Tier Tribunal. Officially they are called the First-tier Tribunal (Mental Health) (see http://www.tribunals.gov.uk/Tribunals/Firsttier/firsttier.htm). They are likely to be known as the Mental Health Tribunal: the term we will use in this book. There is a separate Mental Health Tribunal for Wales, which is administered and based in Cardiff. Appeals and judicial review of tribunal decisions are dealt with by an Upper Tribunal. This appeal system applies to Wales as well as to England.

The Tribunal's task is to determine whether at the time of the hearing, the criteria justifying detention continue to be met. There is a good deal of case law following judicial reviews and references to the European Court of Human Rights in Strasbourg (see Fennell, 2011), which has modified the work of tribunals and indeed the role and function of clinicians. Originally mental health review tribunals operated under a reverse of the common law presumption that it is for those carrying out the detention to justify it. This meant that patients seeking discharge had to establish a negative, the absence of mental disorder, but this has been changed by the European Court of Human Rights and now the Tribunal must find positive evidence that the patient is suffering from mental disorder before they can continue the detention.

Representation and legal aid

Detained patients are entitled to legal aid for tribunal representation under the Community Legal Service (Financial) Regulations 2000 and this is regardless of means because the liberty of the subject is engaged. The Law Society maintains a panel of solicitors who are recognized as having the expertise necessary to provide such representation. Hospital managers and social workers assist patients in finding a solicitor. A solicitor may obtain the services of a psychiatrist to prepare an independent psychiatric report. Such experts are entitled to interview the patient in private and to see his or her hospital case notes.

Applications and reference

All patients detained for more than 72 hours (other than those on orders for remand to hospital for assessment or treatment, interim hospital orders or the first 6 months of a hospital order) may apply for a tribunal hearing within certain periods of eligibility. Only one application may be made in each eligibility period. If a patient does not make use of his/her opportunity to apply within a certain period, his/her case should be automatically referred to the Tribunal by the hospital managers or, if s/he is a restricted patient, by the Secretary of State. The initial 6-month period beyond which a detained patient must have a tribunal hearing is calculated from the first day of detention. There is also a duty to refer a patient to the Tribunal if 3 years have elapsed since the Tribunal last considered the case. A child under the age of 16 must have his or her case heard at least annually. The Secretary of State for Health or the Justice Secretary can refer to the Tribunal at any time the case of any unrestricted or restricted patient even when the patient is not eligible to apply him or herself. A patient may withdraw an application with the consent of the Tribunal, in which case s/he does not lose the eligibility to apply again within the same eligibility period.

For non-offender patients, the nearest relative may make an application to the Tribunal if the responsible clinician has issued a certificate barring the nearest relative from discharging the patient from hospital. Other than in these circumstances, nearest relatives cannot make applications to the Tribunal for discharge of patients detained under assessment orders or treatment orders. (Strictly, the Tribunal discharges the detention order but as, in practice, this generally means discharging the patient, we often refer below to discharge of the patient.) For patients on hospital orders without restrictions, the nearest relative can apply as often as the patient. Nearest relatives cannot apply to the Tribunal in respect of patients on restriction orders.

Procedure and hearings

Following receipt of an application, the Tribunal obtains from the hospital authority a statement including a medical report from the responsible clinician, who often represents the detaining authority at the hearing. The report will include the patient's medical history and a full report on the patient's mental condition. An up-to-date social circumstances report is also required from the detaining authority, and in the case of a detained patient a nursing report. In Wales a social circumstances report need only be provided if practicable, and a nursing report is not required by the rules. In the case of restricted patients, the Secretary of State for Justice must provide a further statement giving his/her view on the patient's suitability for discharge.

Prior to the hearing, the medical member of the Tribunal examines the patient and may interview others to assist him/her in forming an opinion as to the patient's mental condition. Social workers and nursing staff may be called to give evidence, and the Tribunal has the power to subpoena witnesses. The hearings usually take place at the hospital where the patient is detained.

Hearings may be in private or in public. The procedure at hearings in England is governed by the First-Tier Tribunal (Health Education and Social Care Chamber) Rules 2008 (SI 2008 No 2699), and in Wales by the Mental Health Review Tribunal for Wales Rules 2008 (SI 2008 No 2705). The detaining authority and the Secretary of State for Justice can ask for any part of their statement not to be disclosed to the patient. A new test of non-disclosure has been introduced in the rules for both England and Wales. The presumption is in favour of disclosure unless the Tribunal is satisfied that such disclosure would be likely to cause that person or some other person serious harm; and (b) having regard to the interests of justice, that it is proportionate to give such a direction. In England the Tribunal has discretion to order non-disclosure if the tests are met (rule 14). The 'Tribunal may give a direction prohibiting the disclosure of a document or information to a person if: (a) the Tribunal is satisfied that such disclosure would be likely to cause that person or some other person serious harm; and (b) the Tribunal is satisfied, having regard to the interests of justice, that it is proportionate to give such a direction.' The Mental Health Review Tribunal for Wales has a *duty* to direct non-disclosure (rule 17). The same test of serious harm and proportionality is used, but the Tribunal must direct non-disclosure if it is satisfied that the tests are met. The document to be withheld must be kept separate so that the Tribunal may decide whether to direct non-disclosure, and reasons have to be given by the responsible authority. The Tribunal must then consider if disclosure would have the adverse effect claimed and, if satisfied that it would, must record in writing its decision not to disclose. The Tribunal must also conduct proceedings so as to avoid undermining the effect of a direction to withhold information. The Tribunal may adjourn the hearing to obtain additional information relevant to the issues before them, but not in order to review the patient's progress at a later date.

Unrestricted patients

The Tribunal must discharge a patient detained on an assessment order, if it is not satisfied that s/he is then suffering from a mental disorder of a nature or degree which warrants his or her detention in hospital for assessment for at least a limited period, or if not satisfied that the detention is necessary in the interests of his or her health or safety or for the protection of others.

For any other unrestricted patient, the Tribunal must discharge him or her if it is not satisfied that s/he is then suffering from mental disorder, as defined in the Act, of a nature or degree which makes detention in hospital appropriate, or if not satisfied that his or her detention is necessary in the interests of his/her health or safety or for the protection of others. In the case of a patient on a transfer direction who still has time to serve on a prison sentence, the tribunal may only state whether the patient would be entitled to discharge, and the decision to discharge or to remit to prison resides with the Parole Board. On an application by the nearest relative for non-offender patients, the tribunal must discharge the patient if it is not satisfied that the patient, if released, would be likely to act in a manner dangerous to him/herself or others. The Tribunal also must discharge a patient from guardianship if it is satisfied that s/he is not suffering from mental disorder as defined in the Act, or if it is considered that it is not necessary in the interests of the welfare of the patient or for the protection of others that s/he should remain under guardianship.

Besides these obligations on the Tribunal, it has discretion to discharge unrestricted order even in cases where the criteria given above are not met. In so doing, it must consider the risk that the patient if discharged will cease to accept treatment or take medication.

For unrestricted patients, the Tribunal may also recommend that s/he be granted leave of absence, be transferred to another hospital or be placed under guardianship if it believes that the patient should not be immediately discharged, but that such action would be appropriate with a view to facilitating his or her discharge at a future date. If such recommendations are not put into action, the Tribunal may further consider the patient's case. Tribunals may also direct that a patient be discharged at a future date, thus leaving time for adequate after-care arrangements to be made.

Restricted patients

Restricted patients are dealt with by a special tribunal chaired by a judge, or a recorder who is a QC. The discretionary powers given to the Tribunal in respect of unrestricted patients do not apply to those subject to restriction orders.

In such cases the Tribunal may only discharge when it is satisfied that the relevant statutory criteria are met. Section 73 (1) requires the Tribunal to direct *absolute discharge* of the patient if they are not satisfied that s/he is then suffering from mental disorder, or not satisfied that it is necessary for the health and safety of the patient or the protection of others that s/he should receive treatment or that appropriate medical treatment is available. This is one place where the new appropriate treatment rule will be helpful. In the past patients suffering from a personality disorder could be deemed 'untreatable' by one or more of the psychiatrists involved in the hearing and if the Tribunal was impressed by their approach it would have to grant an absolute discharge. This can be inhumane and illogical. It will probably be more difficult in the future to tip a patient who 'only' has a personality disorder out of hospital.

Section 72 (2) requires the Tribunal to direct *conditional discharge* where it is satisfied that the patient needs to be subject to recall but is not satisfied that the patient has mental disorder of the requisite nature or degree for continued detention. In such a case the patient must abide by any conditions laid down by the Tribunal or subsequently imposed by the Secretary of State for Justice. A patient who is conditionally discharged may be recalled to hospital by the Secretary of State, who may also vary any condition which has been imposed. The Tribunal can also defer a conditional discharge by making an order for discharge which is to take effect at a specific date in the future. Deferred conditional discharges can be very unsatisfactory because they may create an impasse when the Tribunal suggests conditions which are not or cannot be met by the relevant authorities.

Patients who have been transferred from prison and who are subject to a restriction direction cannot be discharged by the Tribunal. The Tribunal may, however, inform the Secretary of State for Justice of its opinion that the patient could, if not subject to a prison sentence, be conditionally or absolutely discharged and may recommend that, if the patient cannot be discharged, s/he should continue to be detained in hospital rather than be returned to prison. Following receipt of the Tribunal's recommendation, the Secretary of State for Justice may agree that the patient be discharged and thus allow the Tribunal to discharge the prisoner, or s/he may return the prisoner to prison, or s/he can allow him or her to remain in hospital. The Secretary of State will usually refer the case to the Parole Board for advice or discharge.

Research

Tribunals are one of the few courts or bodies overseeing and administering the law which have been subjected to any form of systematic research or scrutiny.

Peay (1989) undertook a descriptive study of the workings of review tribunals focusing primarily on patients detained in special hospitals. She interviewed patients in a special hospital and also talked to their RMOs and to the judicial members of the tribunal relating to that special hospital. She observed tribunals in different settings, and looked at the tribunal files in two regional offices. Although she had a number of harsh things to say about the tribunal system, she also conceded that:

from many perspectives the tribunals could be assessed to be working reasonably well. Decision-making is approached judiciously, decisions to release may be characterized by the care, indeed caution, with which they are made. Full consideration is usually given to therapeutic considerations. Patients as the consumers of the system, by and large, do not express dissatisfaction.

Peay made a number of recommendations including improved training for tribunal members, especially the 'lay' members, and the urgent provision of real alternatives to compulsory hospital care, concluding that 'legal safeguards are only likely to be effective in the context of adequate resource provisions' for 'decisions to discharge are resource-, and reality-oriented, not rule-, and law-oriented'.

In 1994 Blumenthal and Wessely calculated the cost of each mental health review tribunal as approximately £2000 at 1993 prices. It is extremely unlikely that in the interim tribunals have become cheaper, so it would be reasonable to multiply £2,000 by whatever inflation factor is appropriate for the year in which you are reading this. Taylor et al. (1999) calculated that in 1992 the bill for tribunals in the special (high security) hospitals for a year would have been in excess of £1.5 million. Of the 623 people who had 661 tribunals only 43 (7%) received a form of discharge. Four of those had still not left 4 years later. The authors endorsed the Peay recommendation that improved training should be given to tribunal members and they added that psychiatrists and social workers would benefit from specific training in risk assessment. Taylor et al. call for an audit of tribunal decisions and their effects. They also suggested that tribunals should have the power to direct transfer to lower security. Later research (Perkins, 2003) carried out for the Policy Studies Institute identified significant differences between the tribunals studied and such was the degree of variation that the book raised questions as to whether tribunals were in fact working properly.

All the studies on tribunals have identified flaws and called for better training of tribunal members. Training has improved since 2003 and is now subject to oversight by the Judicial Studies Board. Whether training can ever resolve the philosophical differences between the legal and clinical worlds which tribunals have to operate within is too big a topic to embark upon here but clinical studies of outcome are urgently needed as well as legal studies.

The changes to the tribunal arrangements and rules will render the book by Eldergill (1997) less useful than hitherto but it remains a remarkably comprehensive textbook, including a lot of psychiatry, nevertheless.

The Ministry of Justice

In England and Wales, the Ministry of Justice, under the Lord Chancellor (Secretary of State for Justice), manages the prison service centrally; it coordinates and funds the probation services of England and Wales. It has special responsibilities in relation to the care and control of dangerous convicted offenders, including mentally abnormal offenders, and of those who have been charged with serious offences, but are so mentally ill that they are considered to be either unfit to plead or not guilty by reason of insanity. The Ministry also has the responsibility to provide the law courts, and the judiciary, including the Parole Board. Within the prisons, there are many mentally abnormal people. These are the responsibility of the Prison Health Service which is run by the Department of Health under the prison service in-reach programme.

Mental Health Unit

The Mental Health Unit (MHU) of the Ministry of Justice has delegated powers to perform the Lord Chancellor's functions in respect of (1) mentally abnormal offenders who have been convicted and sent to hospital by courts under a hospital order with a restriction order; (2) those who are found unfit to plead and (3) those who have been found to be not guilty by reason of insanity, and who receive a hospital order with restrictions under the Criminal Procedure (Insanity) Act 1964 amended by the Criminal Procedure (Insanity and Unfitness to Plead) Act 1991. The last two groups are small in number. Patients with restriction orders may be sent to any psychiatric hospital, but a high proportion of them are admitted to secure hospitals. Control of the patient's movements and discharge may be exercised only with the consent of the Secretary of State for Justice. In practice, the powers are administered by officials of the Mental Health Unit. The civil servants in the MHU maintain a dossier on each restricted patient. This contains information about the original offence (the index offence), a full criminal history, copies of all official correspondence, and copies of medical, psychological and social work reports. At regular intervals, the hospital consultants have to send reports to the Ministry of Justice about the progress of their patients.

Discharge decisions are almost never initiated by Ministry of Justice officials. However, the Mental Health Unit is concerned that responsible clinicians (RCs) should make proposals for discharge to the Ministry wherever practicable, and not rely on applications to the Mental Health Tribunal. The responsible clinician must consult the Mental Health Unit about leave, transfer and or discharge arrangements.

If the responsible clinician wishes to send a patient on escorted or unescorted leave, or to prepare his or her discharge, the proposal will need to be made to the Ministry of Justice. The Mental Health Unit provides guidance, including a checklist of points to be included in any proposal, but the civil servants who are involved in the decision may request further information from the responsible clinician. Informal telephone and other oral communications between the Mental Health Unit and the responsible clinician are extremely useful in effective patient management. One of the best ways of informing Ministry of Justice officials about the care and progress of a particular patient and his/her readiness for an onward move is to invite the caseworker involved to a case conference.

Questions in the checklist include the motivation for the index offence, evidence of persistent and/or preoccupying fantasies about violent, sexually abnormal or fire-raising behaviour, the response to medication (if any), the patient's ability/willingness to co-operate with medication, impulsivity, explosive behaviour, frustration tolerance, insight into the disorder, and the role of alcohol and drugs in the patient's life and/or offending.

When the caseworker has all the information needed to make an informed risk assessment, he or she will respond to the responsible clinician, either authorizing the proposal or explaining what factors appear to need further work before the proposal can be authorized. The Mental Health Unit has time targets for responding to applications for authority, but the target is measured from the date all necessary information is received, and not from an initial incomplete approach. A further application can be made later, as soon as the responsible clinician (RC) is satisfied there is evidence of further adjustment to the patient's condition and/or circumstances. The patient is entitled, under the Mental Health Act 1983, to apply to the Mental Health Tribunal for discharge. Patients under a restriction order can be absolutely or conditionally discharged, by one of the special Tribunal panels chaired by a judge. The Justice Secretary makes a statement to the Tribunal of his or her reasons for not having discharged the applicant under his/her own powers, but s/he has no veto over the Tribunal's power of discharge.

The Mental Health Unit also has responsibility for transferring prisoners to hospital under section 47 of the Mental Health Act 1983 (amended) and making a restriction direction under section 49. The Unit also oversees the prisoner's management in hospital. However, transferred prisoners' situations are slightly different as they are primarily subject to a sentence of imprisonment. Indeterminate (life and imprisonment for public protection) sentence prisoners may be given periods of rehabilitative leave with the consent of the Ministry of Justice if they are still in hospital after they have served their tariff period. Determinate sentence prisoners who reach their release date in hospital may remain there at the discretion of their RC. The Justice Secretary loses control over their movement at the time at which they would have been released from prison. All prisoners may be returned to prison during their sentence if the RC recommends to the Secretary of State that they no longer require treatment in hospital. Prisoners serving an indeterminate sentence may also be rehabilitated directly from hospital if this is thought desirable on mental health grounds, but decisions on their discharge are the preserve of the Parole Board.

Supervision of conditionally discharged restricted patients

When a patient on a restricted hospital order is conditionally discharged from hospital, he or she will be subject usually to a combination of social work and medical supervision. Guidance notes on the arrangements for social and psychiatric supervisions are issued by the Ministry of Justice and can be found on the Ministry of Justice website at http://www.justice.gov.uk/downloads/offenders/mentally-disordered-offenders/guidance-for-clinical-supervisors-0909.pdf

Social supervision is usually provided by an approved social worker and guidance for them can also be found on the Ministry of Justice website http://www.justice.gov.uk/downloads/offenders/mentally-disordered-offenders/guidance-for-social-supervisors-0909.pdf

Social supervision has several components. It involves monitoring the mental state of the patient and reporting any changes, rehabilitation, giving advice to a patient who is considering any change of circumstances, and regular reporting to the Ministry of Justice on the progress of supervision, so that the Ministry can form a view as to the appropriateness of continued community care, the patient's readiness for absolute discharge or the need for recall to hospital. The monitor role, the duty to report deterioration both to the MOJ and the RC, has to take priority. Jarvis's *Probation Officers' Manual* (Weston, 1987) states that the responsibilities of the supervising officer are:

1. *to provide support and guidance to the patient;*
2. *to provide an early warning of any relapse in the patient's mental condition or deterioration in behaviour, giving rise to danger to himself/herself or others.*

The hope is that by close social supervision, including home visits and appropriate medical treatment in the community a relapse will be avoided.

This description emphasizes the helping relationship, the resettlement of the patient into the community being the main objective, with after-care supervision the method available to achieve it, and recall being a sanction available should it fail to do so. Recall may be necessary to prevent harm to the patient or to others on occasions but, clearly, recall in those circumstances is also good clinical practice. Furthermore, recall does not have to be for a prolonged period.

Psychiatrists should be aware of the importance of working closely with the social supervisor, seeing the patient frequently, monitoring medication carefully and providing regular reports to the MHU. Untoward or unexpected developments can be reported immediately by phone. The MHU caseworker will always provide a contact number.

The Care Quality Commission (CQC)

The Mental Health Act Commission (MHAC) was established in 1983 as a special health authority and was responsible to the Secretary of State for Health, but it functioned as an independent body with a chairman and 91 other part-time members from the fields of medicine, nursing, law, social work and psychology together with lay members and academics. Its duty was to oversee the use of compulsory powers under the Mental Heath Act (the scrutiny of admission documents has always been and remains the province of hospital managers and the jurisdiction to discharge is with the MHT). The Mental Health Act Commission had the duty of investigating the handling of complaints made by or on behalf of detained patients. It reported biennially to Parliament. Commissioners visited hospitals regularly and interviewed detained patients.

The Commission's functions have been taken over by the Care Quality Commission in England and by the Health Service Inspectorate Wales in Wales.

Second opinions

An important function of the Commission concerns the requirement under the Mental Health Act 1983 (amended) for consultant psychiatrists to obtain a concurring second opinion from a doctor appointed by the Commission before administering either medication for more than 3 months or electroconvulsive therapy (ECT) at any time to a patient who is incapable of consent or who refuses consent to treatment. In its first biennial report (Mental Health Act Commission, 1985) the Mental Health Act Commission said that the great majority of doctors have adopted this system without complaint and with increasing ease. It said there has been a high measure of agreement between appointed doctors and consultants, probably over 90%. There have, however, been some difficulties: there is no formal appeal mechanism for consultants against the refusal of an appointed doctor to provide an authorizing certificate; coherently written treatment plans supporting the proposal for treatment are sometimes lacking; and there has been difficulty in the availability of qualified professionals whom the appointed doctor is required to consult before issuing a certificate.

There is also some confusion about the legal responsibilities following the refusal of the appointed second opinion doctor to allow a plan of treatment to proceed. The legal responsibility for the patient's care remains with the RC. However, it seems unlikely that the appointed second opinion doctor can escape legal liabilities for his or her own quite powerful actions, for when giving a second opinion, s/he is acting as an independent medical practitioner, but this has never been tested in law.

The lack of possibility of appeal against a refusal to permit a plan of treatment causes great consternation sometimes. It is best dealt with by reviewing the case in the light of the remarks of the second opinion, reviewing the clinical arguments and, if it is thought appropriate, making a new request to the Commission for a further second opinion; it is bound to provide such an opinion and it may instruct a different doctor, although it does not have to do so.

Reports on detention

The Commission receives reports from RCs, where treatment has been given in the above circumstances, at the time when the detained patient's detention is renewed or at the time of the statutory annual report by the RC concerning a patient subject to a restriction order. The Commission may also request a report from the RC on the patient's treatment and condition at any time.

Visits and complaints

The Commission has a duty to visit and interview detained patients in hospital. It also has a duty to investigate a detained patient's complaints when the patient considers these have not been satisfactorily dealt with by the hospital managers.

Biennial reports

The Commission has the duty to publish a report every two years which must be laid before Parliament. These reports deal with matters such as: factors affecting black and ethnic minority groups; further development of multidisciplinary teamwork; consent to treatment of long-stay informal patients, and the mentally disordered in prison; overcrowding; delays in transferring patients from one hospital to another; escorted leave for restricted patients; provision for difficult offender patients, patients with learning difficulties; and the investigation of complaints.

Inquiries after Homicide

The Clunis and Silcott cases of 1992 have already been mentioned (p. 61). Following these, the English Department of Health set up an internal review, which reported in August 1993 (Department of Health, 1993). Its remit was to examine whether the existing legal powers were being using effectively or whether new legislation was required. Among the Review's recommendations was the promise of guidance on the key considerations ... *when considering the discharge and aftercare of potentially violent or dangerous patients.'* The guidelines (Department of Health, 1994) emphasized that risk was the prime consideration when making discharge decisions and, thereafter, the Care Programme Approach (CPA) was to provide the framework within which the continuing care of mentally ill people could be organized. Under the heading of 'If things go wrong' the guidelines highlighted the need to learn lessons for the future, adding that *'in cases of homicide it will always be necessary to hold an inquiry which is independent of the providers involved'* (paragraph 34). The guidelines were subsequently amended so that an investigation 'should' be commissioned 'when a homicide has been committed by a person who is or has been under the care ... of specialist mental health services in the six months prior to the event' (Department of Health, 2005a). Such investigations should employ a process such as root cause analysis, which aims to uncover the fundamental cause of the error or failure. However, even this method of inquiry is not without its own difficulties (Munro, 2004a,b)

In addition to individually commissioned inquiries the National Confidential Inquiry into suicide and homicide by people with mental illness uses an epidemiological approach to collect data that are aggregated in occasional reports (National Confidential Inquiry 1999, 2001, 2006) (see also chapter 28).

Much criticism is levelled against inquiries after homicides. In part, the criticisms arise because of the many purposes the inquiries are expected to serve. In general terms 'an inquiry (is) a retrospective examination of events or circumstances surrounding a service failure or problem, specially established to find out what happened, understand why, and learn from the experiences of those involved' (Walshe and Higgins, 2002). Article 2, European Convention on Human Rights (right to life), places procedural requirements on the State following such events to conduct an 'effective investigation or scrutiny which enables the facts to become known to the public and in particular to the relatives of any victim (*McCann*). However, the need to understand why events progressed to their fatal outcome takes the inquiry process beyond a fact finding exercise' and the 'construction of a coherent narrative' (Goldberg, 2005). This brings in judgments concerning professionals' decision-making in managing the case under scrutiny. Article 2 requires an 'effective official investigation' 'to ensure the accountability (of State agents or bodies) for deaths occurring under their responsibility'. The same obligations demand the involvement of 'the next of kin to the extent necessary to safeguard his or her legitimate interests' (*Edwards*). Thus the purposes of inquiries can be seen to involve learning, accountability and discipline and public catharsis (Eastman, 1996; Reder and Duncan, 1996; Department of Health, 2000) (see also chapter 28).

Procedure of Inquiries

Department of Health guidance (1994, 2005) sets out the various elements for consideration when setting up the investigation. Independence from the health authority and the services under examination is an essential requirement. Panels of inquiry almost invariably have a lawyer as chairman, together with a psychiatrist and then a senior member of social services, the nursing profession or health service management depending on the areas of potential concern under investigation.

Inquiries are established by the responsible health authority after the criminal proceedings against the perpetrator have been concluded. The terms of reference are drawn up by the health authority and typically require the panel to examine the care and treatment afforded to the patient from a given point up to the homicide. The standard of care delivered is examined against statute, national guidance and professional requirements and the level of care is assessed against the patient's health and social care needs.

Inquiries have been criticized for having no common terms of reference or prescribed rules of procedure, for holding private hearings, not allowing cross-examination of the evidence and there being no right of appeal to challenge the findings of the panel (Eastman, 1996; Department of Health, 2000 at para 4.50). Panels should meet with representatives of the family of the victim(s) and, ideally, with the family of the perpetrator early in the process to ensure their concerns are given due emphasis.

Access to the patient's medical and social services records requires consent from the patient and does not usually present an issue. In the Stone Inquiry (Francis et al., 2006) consent for release of medical records was forthcoming but the extent of disclosure from those records in the published report was challenged in court. Although Michael Stone accepted publication of some of the report he challenged publication of the full report as a violation of his right to privacy (Article 8) and, also as a matter of wider public interest, that a person should be able to discuss sensitive information with professionals and fully co-operate with an inquiry without being deterred by the risk of subsequent disclosure. The claim failed, in part, because the professionals involved, the wider professions and 'the public can legitimately expect to know the full reasons' for any criticisms made (*Stone*).

Key personnel involved in the patient's care are invited to provide oral evidence as well as submit written witness statements to the inquiry. Live witnesses can also elect to be accompanied to the hearings by a legal representative or a colleague for support but not advocacy. Any professionals criticized in the report from the inquiry should be served with a 'Salmon' letter,[1] setting out the areas of criticism of their individual performance at the earliest opportunity. This affords them an opportunity to respond if necessary to misinterpretation of evidence or to offer further evidence if they believe they have been unfairly criticized, before final publication.

---

[1] The Salmon Commission (Royal Commission on Tribunals of Inquiry 1996) set out new principles of fairness for the conduct of inquiries. These should be read by all *potential* witnesses at the outset of the enquiry.

Criticisms of inquiries

The inquiry process itself is the subject of various criticisms. An inevitable difficulty is the likelihood of 'hindsight bias': 'the tendency for individuals with outcome knowledge to claim that they would have estimated a probability of occurrence for the reported outcome that is higher than they would have estimated in foresight' (Hawkins and Hastie, 1990). Acknowledging this difficulty does not eliminate it and, if anything, the inquiry process, with its access to vast amounts of material through exhaustive collection of records and interviewing witnesses, makes the outcome seem more likely. Some of this material may not have been available to the clinical team treating the patient (Szmukler, 2000) when decisions have to be made in real time. In addition, inquiry panels may also distort their perception of past events through counterfactual thinking (Reiss, 2001).

It is also said that single case studies in 'organizational failure' (Walshe and Higgins, 2002) are not suited to making wide ranging recommendations, such as changes to mental health law (Buchanan, 1999). However, while a detailed study of a clinician's 'worst ever case' may be a poor basis for recommending changes to the wider service, by virtue of the longitudinal perspective taken by inquiries it is possible to form a judgment as to whether or not a mental health professional's general standard of care does match up to the requirements found in national or local guidance. Moreover, increasingly inquiries no longer restrict themselves to examining the performance of individuals but broaden their focus to scrutinize the systems within which individuals have to operate (Scotland et al., 1998; Weereratne et al., 2003).

Muijen (1997) has noted that the concept of accountability is poorly served by inquiries. The inquiry report on Christopher Clunis summarized his care and treatment as being 'a catalogue of failure and missed opportunity' (Ritchie et al., 1994). It commented that problems were cumulative and there was no single person to blame or point of failure, notwithstanding individual comments on the actions of certain professionals in the body of the report. By contrast the Luke Warm Luke inquiry report (Scotland et al., 1998) made extensive criticisms of services and individuals although it was the consultant who was singled out for particular censure, even though he had made attempts to see the patient during the final crisis the day before the homicide. The 'atmosphere of blame and unlimited sense of liability' for a patient's actions engendered by inquiry reports is linked to falling morale within the profession (Bristow, 2001) and defensive clinical practice. There is also the possibility that the publicity attached to the process of inquiry reporting heightens the public's concern about the risk of violence from mentally ill people in general, although the degree of media coverage is a function of the comparative rarity of a mentally ill person committing a homicide.

Findings and recommendations from inquiries

Common findings from inquiry reports include organizational isolation, poor team working or inadequate leadership, system or process failures, poor communication, disempowered staff or patients, and relatives' concerns being ignored. Risk assessment and management issues have also been prominent. Findings have included a failure to act assertively, including the timely use of the powers of the Mental Health Act, to prevent further deterioration in the patient's mental health (Blom-Cooper et al., 1995); ignoring a past history of violence, missed opportunities to prosecute, minimizing or overlooking continuing physical aggression (Ritchie et al., 1994); or the progressive loss of detail of earlier convictions for violence (Blom-Cooper et al., 1996).

Reports have also criticized mental health services for not implementing the Mental Health Act properly. For example, the relative success of guardianship in providing a period of stability in a patient's community living was not attempted again (Blom-Cooper et al., 1995). The same report also discussed the difficulty in deciding the correct threshold for formal admissions of deteriorating patients and observed the legal requirements for leave of absence from hospital of detained patients were not adhered to. A more recent inquiry criticized the failure of both the mental health service and the Home Office (now Ministry of Justice) to monitor satisfactorily a conditionally discharged restricted patient in the community (Robinson et al., 2006) (see also chapter 28).

Overview

Inquiries are criticized for producing reports with recommendations that repeat those found in earlier reports but research has demonstrated there are five categories of recommendations common to most inquiries. These are communication; technical; attempted foresight (to forestall potential future problems); personnel issues; and authority (attempts to improve safety through new rules, regulations or laws) (Department of Health, 2000; at p.66 citing Toft and Reynolds, 1997). Attempts have been made to draw together the accumulated recommendations of inquiry reports in an effort to generate themes for changes to services (Sheppard, 1995, 1996; Petch and Bradley, 1997).

While acknowledging that not all violence can be eliminated, Maden's structured case review study (2006) nonetheless called for greater use of structured clinical risk assessments to guide the management of patients with a history of violence and for more attention to be paid to alcohol and drug issues as well as to the concerns of carers. Better use of the care programme approach framework allied with crisis intervention plans has also been advocated as a way of preventing homicides (National Confidential Inquiry, 2006).

The findings and recommendations of some inquiries have been used as vehicles of change in a national context.

The terms of reference of at least one inquiry (Francis et al., 2006) included an invitation to report 'on the adequacy of mental health law, national guidance and local policies and practices in the context of the care, supervision and services provided in respect of Michael Stone'. The murders of a mother and her 6-year-old daughter together with a very serious assault on the surviving daughter which prompted that inquiry ensured it had a high media profile. Although the report's publication was delayed for several years while the convictions were unsuccessfully challenged. However, the politicians reacted swiftly; changes to policy, mental health law and services were advocated, and in some cases implemented, to address the perceived deficiencies relating to the care and management of personality disordered people. The later publication of the report did not supply the expected support for these suppositions, declaring: 'This is emphatically not a case of a man with a dangerous personality disorder being generally ignored by agencies or left at large without supervision' (p.5).

The National Confidential Inquiry (2006) has estimated that in 24% of homicides better compliance with medication after discharge from hospital would have lowered the risk posed by the patient. Improved medication compliance is the most frequently cited factor to make homicides less likely. Maden (2006) argued for compulsory community treatment as a practical way of managing risk more effectively. It has been estimated that eight homicides a year occur following non-compliance with medication or community follow-up (National Confidential Inquiry, 2006). The Government's response has been the introduction of supervised community treatment, through amendment to the Mental Health Act (p.69). This is promoted as a way to 'ensure' patients remain compliant with the prescribed medication (Department of Health, 2007). Supervised community treatment will effectively replace supervised discharge orders which themselves were incorporated into mental health legislation after the Department of Health's internal review (1993) following the killing of Jonathan Zito in 1992.

Although homicide inquiries are no longer mandatory and in any case they often reach similar conclusions in each case, some commentators question the value in persisting with a system of investigation which seems to add little to our understanding of why such incidents had taken place and how they can be prevented in the future (Muijen, 1997; Szmukler, 2000). Instead clinical governance audits are advocated, or an extension of the National Confidential Inquiry which aggregates data and can then make evidence-based recommendations to change practice or policy. This ignores the significant pressure which is applied by the public when a patient kills someone. What should be feasible is a switch to a root cause analysis which aims to examine system and other fundamental failures instead of concentrating on the apparent failings of individuals involved on the day in question (National Patient Safety Agency, 2009).

It is also worth noting that the World Health Organization launched the WHO Patient Safety Programme in 2004 which aims to coordinate, disseminate and accelerate improvements in patient safety worldwide (http://www.who.int/patientsafety/en/index.html).

MENTAL CAPACITY ACT 2005 (MCA)

The Mental Capacity Act 2005, implemented during 2007, creates a comprehensive statutory framework setting out when and how decisions can be made on behalf of people aged 16 and over who may lack capacity to make specific decisions for themselves. It also clarifies what actions can be taken by others involved in the care or medical treatment of people lacking capacity to consent to those actions. In addition, the Mental Capacity Act extends the arrangements available for adults who currently have capacity and want to make preparations for a time when they may lack capacity to make certain decisions in the future This part of the chapter describes the key elements of the new jurisdiction and explains the concepts it is based on, looking in particular at the implications for psychiatrists. The new 'deprivation of liberty' safeguards are also described.

The New Jurisdiction

The Mental Capacity Act sets out an integrated jurisdiction for the making of personal welfare decisions, healthcare decisions and financial decisions on behalf of people without the capacity to make such decisions for themselves. It also includes provisions to ensure that people are given all appropriate help and support to enable them to make their own decisions or to maximize their participation in decision-making. The Act starts with a statement of principles to underlie the provisions of the Act and govern how it is used in practice.

The statutory framework is based on two fundamental concepts: lack of capacity and best interests. For those who lack capacity to make specific decisions, the Act provides a range of processes, extending from informal arrangements, to decision-making requiring formal powers and ultimately to court decisions, governing the circumstances in which necessary decisions can be taken on their behalf and in their best interests.

The Code of Practice

The Mental Capacity Act is accompanied by a statutory Code of Practice (Department of Constitutional Affairs, 2007) providing guidance to anyone using the Act's provisions, including anyone involved in caring for or working with people who may lack capacity to make particular decisions.

The Act imposes a duty on certain people to 'have regard to' any relevant guidance in the Code of Practice when acting in relation to a person lacking capacity, s.42(4).

The specified people are those acting in one or more of the following ways (as described later):

- as an attorney acting under a lasting power of attorney;
- as a deputy appointed by the Court of Protection;
- as a person carrying out research under the Act;
- as an independent mental capacity advocate;
- anyone involved in using the new Deprivation of Liberty procedures;
- as a representative appointed for someone being deprived of their liberty;
- in a professional capacity;
- for remuneration.

The statutory duty to have regard to the Code therefore applies to those exercising formal powers or duties under the Act, and to professionals (including lawyers, health and social care professionals) and others acting for remuneration (such as paid carers). There is no duty to 'comply' with the Code – it should be viewed as guidance rather than instruction. However, the specified people must be able to demonstrate that they are familiar with the Code, and if they have not followed relevant guidance contained in it, they will be expected to give cogent reasons why they have departed from it (see *Munjaz*).

The Act also confirms that a provision of the Code, or a failure to comply with the guidance set out in the Code, can be taken into account by a court or tribunal where it appears relevant to a question arising in any criminal or civil proceedings s.42(5). There is no liability for breach of the Code itself, but compliance or non-compliance may be a factor in deciding the issue of liability for breach of some other statutory or common law duty. This may apply to anyone using the Act's provisions, since they are obliged to act in accordance with the principles of the Act and in the best interests of a person lacking capacity, as described below.

The Statutory Principles

Section 1 of the Mental Capacity Act sets out five statutory principles to reinforce the underlying values of the Act and to govern how it is to be interpreted and implemented:

1. *A presumption of capacity* – 'A person must be assumed to have capacity unless it is established that he lacks capacity.'
2. *The right for individuals to be supported to make their own decisions* – 'A person is not to be treated as unable to make a decision unless all practicable steps to help him to do so have been taken without success.'
3. *The right to make unwise decisions* – 'A person is not to be treated as unable to make a decision merely because he makes an unwise decision.'
4. *Best interests* – 'An act done, or decision made, under this Act for or on behalf of a person who lacks capacity must be done, or made, in his best interests.'

5. *Less restrictive intervention* – 'Before the act is done, or the decision is made, regard must be had to whether the purpose for which it is needed can be as effectively achieved in a way that is less restrictive of the person's rights and freedom of action' – so long as that is in their best interests.

These principles confirm that the Act is intended to be enabling and supportive of people lacking capacity, not restrictive or controlling of their lives (Code of Practice, p.19). The aim is to protect people who lack capacity to make particular decisions, but also to maximize their decision-making abilities, or their ability to participate in decision-making, as far as they are able to do so. Anyone using the Mental Capacity Act's powers or provisions must act in accordance with the statutory principles.

The Act's starting point is to enshrine in statute the existing presumption at common law that an adult has full legal capacity unless it is shown that s/he does not. All practicable steps must be taken to help the person make the decision in question. Chapter 3 of the Code of Practice gives detailed guidance on a range of practicable steps which may assist in maximizing a person's decision-making capacity. The Act then goes on to define what it means to lack capacity to make a decision and how to determine whether a particular decision or action is in the best interests of a person lacking capacity to make the decision in question.

Lack of Capacity

The Act adopts the common law notion that capacity is a functional concept, requiring capacity to be assessed in relation to each particular decision at the time the decision needs to be made, and not the person's ability to make decisions generally. This means that individuals should not be labelled 'incapable' simply on the basis that they have been diagnosed with a particular condition, or because of any preconceived ideas or assumptions about their abilities due, for example, to their age, appearance or behaviour (s.2(3)), or because they have been deemed to lack capacity in some other area. Rather it must be shown that they lack capacity for each specific decision at the time that decision needs to be made. Individuals retain the legal right to make those decisions for which they continue to have capacity.

Section 2(1) of the Act sets out the definition of a person who lacks capacity:

'For the purposes of this Act, a person lacks capacity in relation to a matter if at the material time he is unable to make a decision for himself in relation to the matter because of an impairment of, or a disturbance in the functioning of, the mind or brain.'

Capacity is therefore decision-specific and time-specific and the inability to make the decision in question must be because of 'an impairment of, or a disturbance in the functioning of, the mind or brain'. The impairment or disturbance may be permanent or temporary (s.2(2)) and the matter is decided on the balance of probabilities (s.2(4)).

The definition imposes a two-stage test in order to decide whether a person lacks capacity to make a decision. It must be established that:

- there is an impairment of, or disturbance in the functioning of, the person's mind or brain, and
- the impairment or disturbance is sufficient to render the person incapable of making that particular decision at the relevant time.

Section 3 sets out the test for assessing whether a person is unable to make a decision for him/herself. A person is unable to make a decision if s/he is unable to:

a. understand the information relevant to the decision;
b. retain that information;
c. use or weigh that information as part of the process of making the decision; or
d. communicate his/her decision (whether by talking, using sign language or any other means).

Information relevant to the decision will include the particular nature of the decision in question, the purpose for which it is needed, the likely consequences of deciding one way or another or of making no decision at all (s.3(4)). Every effort must be made to provide the information in a way the individual can understand, using the means of communication that is most appropriate for the person's circumstances (s.3(2)). The ability to retain information for a short period only should not automatically disqualify the person from making the decision (s.3(2)) – it will depend on what is necessary for the decision in question. The ability to use or weigh the information relevant to the decision as part of the process of making the decision has already been considered extensively by the court (see for example *Re MB*).

The final criterion – that the person is unable to communicate the decision by any possible means – is likely to affect a minority of people (such as those with so-called 'locked in syndrome') where it is impossible to tell whether the person is capable of making a decision or not. Strenuous efforts must first be made to assist and facilitate communication before any finding of incapacity is made. It is likely in cases of this sort that professionals with specialist skills in verbal and non-verbal communication will be required to assist in the assessment.

Under the Act, many different people may be required to make decisions or act on behalf of someone who lacks capacity to make specific decisions for themselves, whether as family members, carers, health and social care professionals or those with formal decision-making powers. In any particular situation, the person proposing to make the decision or take action (referred to in the Code as the decision-maker (see paragraphs 4.38–4.43 and 5.8–5.12)) is responsible for assessing the person's capacity to make the decision in question. For most decisions, the Act merely requires the decision-maker to take 'reasonable steps' to establish a lack of capacity – formal processes are rarely required except in cases of doubt or in relation to complex or major decisions, where a professional opinion (for example, from a psychiatrist or psychologist) may be helpful. The Code of Practice (para. 4.45) suggests possible steps that may be regarded as 'reasonable'; it also sets out situations where a professional opinion may be required, paras. 4.51–4.54. However, it would be inappropriate and unfeasible for professional experts to be routinely called upon in situations when assessments using the test of capacity set out in the Act can be carried out by other decision-makers.

Best Interests

Where someone lacks capacity to make a particular decision, the Act establishes 'best interests' as the criterion for any action taken or decision made on that person's behalf. In view of the wide range of decisions and actions covered by the Act and the varied circumstances of the people affected by its provisions, the concept of best interests is not defined in the Act. Instead, section 4 sets out a 'checklist' of common factors which must be considered in determining what is in a person's best interests, which can be summarized as follows:

- *Equal consideration and non-discrimination* – The person determining best interests must not make assumptions about someone's best interests merely on the basis of the person's age or appearance, condition or aspect of his/her behaviour.
- *All relevant circumstances* – Try to identify all the issues and circumstances relating to the decision in question which are most relevant to the person who lacks capacity to make that decision.
- *Regaining capacity* – Consider whether the person is likely to regain capacity (e.g. after receiving medical treatment). If so, can the decision wait until then?
- *Permitting and encouraging participation* – Do whatever is reasonably practicable to permit and encourage the person to participate, or to improve his/her ability to participate, as fully as possible in any act done or any decision affecting the person.
- *The person's wishes, feelings, beliefs and values* – Try to find out the views of the person lacking capacity, including:
  - The person's past and present wishes and feelings – both his/her current views and whether the person has expressed any relevant views in the past, either verbally, in writing or through behaviour or habits.
  - Any beliefs and values (e.g. religious, cultural, moral or political) that would be likely to influence the decision in question.
  - Any other factors the person would be likely to consider if able to do so.

- *The views of other people* – Consult other people, if it is practicable and appropriate to do so, for their views about the person's best interests and to see if they have any information about the person's wishes, feelings, beliefs or values, but be aware of the person's right to confidentiality – not everyone needs to know everything. In particular, try to consult:
  - Anyone previously named by the person as someone to be consulted on the decision in question or matters of a similar kind.
  - Anyone engaged in caring for the person, or close relatives, friends or others who take an interest in the person's welfare.
  - Any lasting power of attorney made by the person.
  - Any deputy appointed by the Court of Protection to make decisions for the person, or
  - For decisions about serious medical treatment or a change of residence and where there is no one who fits into any of the above categories, an independent mental capacity advocate (see below).
- Life-sustaining treatment – Where the decision concerns the provision or withdrawal of life-sustaining treatment (defined in the Act as being treatment which a person providing healthcare regards as necessary to sustain life (s.4(10)), the person determining whether the treatment is in the best interests of someone who lacks capacity to consent must not be motivated by a desire to bring about the individual's death (s.4(5)).

Not all the factors in the best interests 'checklist' will be relevant to all types of decisions or actions, but they must still be considered if only to be disregarded as irrelevant to that particular situation. Any option which is less restrictive of the person's rights or freedom of action must also be considered, so long it is in the person's best interests.

Acts in Connection with Care or Treatment

Previously, legislation had been silent about what actions could lawfully be taken by carers in looking after the day-to-day personal or healthcare needs of people who lack capacity to consent to those actions. Equally, doctors, dentists and other healthcare professionals were hesitant about carrying out examinations, treatment or nursing care on patients unable to consent to those medical procedures. In the absence of any clear statutory provision, it was left to the courts to establish the common law 'principle of necessity', setting out the circumstances in which actions and decisions could lawfully be taken on behalf of adults who lack capacity (*Re F*).

The courts confirmed that where the principle of necessity applied, i.e. that it was necessary to act to safeguard the wellbeing of a person lacking capacity to consent, and the action taken was reasonable and in the person's best interests, that action which would otherwise amount to a civil wrong, or even a crime (e.g. of battery or assault) would in fact be lawful. The principle of necessity is *not* equivalent to having consent but may constitute a defence if an action is subsequently challenged.

The common law 'principle of necessity' is not widely understood, however, and it was felt necessary to clarify the confused state of the law governing such actions (Law Commission, 1995). To achieve this aim, section 5 of the Mental Capacity Act makes provision to allow carers (both informal and paid carers) and health and social care professionals to carry out certain acts in connection with the personal care, healthcare or treatment of a person lacking capacity. These provisions give legal backing, in the form of protection from liability, for actions which are essential for the personal welfare or health of people lacking capacity to consent to having things done to or for them. Such actions can be performed as if the person concerned had capacity and had given consent (s.5(2)). There is no need to obtain any formal powers or authority to act.

The Act also makes clear that anyone acting unreasonably, negligently or not in the person's best interests could forfeit that protection. Before taking action, the person doing the act must take reasonable steps to establish that the person lacks capacity in relation to the matter in question. The principles of the Act must be complied with and the person taking action must reasonably believe that what they are doing is in the person's best interests.

As a general rule, any act that is intended to restrain a person lacking capacity will not attract protection from liability (s.6(1)). Any carer or professional using restraint (s.6(4)) could be liable for their actions. However, the practicalities of caring for and providing protection for people who are unable to protect themselves are also recognized. The Act therefore permits the use of some form of restraint or physical intervention in limited circumstances, where two conditions are satisfied (s.6(2)):

- The person using it must reasonably believe that restraint is necessary in order to prevent harm to the person lacking capacity; and
- The restraint used must be a proportionate response, both to the likelihood and the seriousness of that harm.

In such circumstances, only the minimum necessary force or intervention may be used and for the shortest possible duration.

Deprivation of liberty

As originally drafted, section 6(5) expressly confirmed that someone carrying out an act under section 5 will do more than 'merely restrain' a person lacking capacity if s/he deprives that person of liberty within the meaning of article 5(1) of the European Convention on Human Rights.

Therefore the defence against liability provided by section 5 is not available to anyone whose actions result in a deprivation of liberty of a person lacking capacity. The Code of Practice provides some guidance on acts that may be seen as depriving a person of their liberty (paras. 6.49–6.53).

The Mental Health Act 2007 amended the Mental Capacity Act to introduce new procedural safeguards (described below) for people who lack capacity to make relevant decisions who need to be deprived of their liberty in their best interests, other than under the Mental Health Act 1983. These new provisions confirm that specific authorization is required to deprive someone of their liberty and that section 5 alone cannot be relied on in such cases.

The Lord Chancellor produced in 2008 a supplement to the Mental Capacity Act code of practice entitled *Deprivation of Liberty Safeguards* (http://legislation.gov.uk/uksi/2008/1858/contents/made; see also p.82).

Interface with Mental Health Act 1983 (amended)

Section 5 applies to care or treatment for both physical and mental conditions. It can therefore provide a legal basis for the treatment of people with serious mental disorders, whether or not they could instead be treated under the Mental Health Act 1983 (amended). The question may arise, therefore, as to which legal framework should be used to provide care or treatment for mental disorders for people who lack capacity to consent to that care or treatment.

The Code of Practice describes some possible circumstances which might indicate the need for assessment for admission to hospital under the Mental Health Act rather than relying on the Mental Capacity Act, where:

- it is not possible to give the person the care or treatment they need without carrying out an action that might deprive them of their liberty;
- the person needs treatment that cannot be given under the Mental Capacity Act (for example, because the person has made a valid and applicable advance decision to refuse all or part of that treatment);
- the person may need to be restrained in a way that is not allowed under the Mental Capacity Act;
- it is not possible to assess or treat the person safely or effectively without treatment being compulsory (perhaps because the person is expected to regain capacity, but might then refuse to give consent);
- the person lacks capacity to decide on some elements of the treatment but has capacity to refuse a vital part of it – and they have done so; or
- there is some other reason why the person may not get the treatment they need, and they or someone else might suffer harm as a result. (Code of Practice, para. 13.12.)

The provisions of the Mental Capacity Act do not apply to any treatment that is regulated by Part IV of the

Mental Health Act (MCA 2005, s.28). In other words, the consent to treatment provisions and safeguards in Part IV will 'trump' the Mental Capacity Act's provisions in relation to treatment for mental disorder of patients liable to be detained under the Mental Health Act. The Mental Capacity Act section 5 will therefore not provide protection from liability for treatment for mental disorder given to a person lacking capacity who is detained under the Mental Health Act 1983. Nor can attorneys and deputies consent to, or refuse, such treatment on a patient's behalf.

Nevertheless, section 5 will be relevant to treatment for mental disorder of patients:

- who have been admitted to hospital in an emergency (Mental Health Act s.4(4a));
- temporarily detained in hospital pending a decision on whether to make an application for their substantive detention (Mental Health Act s.5);
- remanded by a court to hospital for a report on their medical condition (Mental Health Act s.35);
- detained in a place of safety (Mental Health Act 1983 s.37(4), s.135 or s.136);
- subject to guardianship, or who have been conditionally discharged (and not recalled to hospital).

Part IV of the Mental Health Act does not apply to such patients. Therefore, any treatment for mental disorder provided for them may attract protection from liability offered by section 5, so long as the Mental Capacity Act's principles have been complied with and the treatment is in the patient's best interests. Similarly, section 5 also applies in relation to the care or treatment for any physical condition of patients who lack capacity to consent, whether or not they are detained.

'Bournewood' safeguards

In the case of *HL v UK,* also known as the Bournewood case, the European Court of Human Rights held that a procedure prescribed by law must be followed where a person with mental disorder is cared for or given treatment in conditions which amount to a deprivation of their liberty. Section 50 and schedules 7 and 8 of the Mental Health Act 2007 introduce amendments to the Mental Capacity Act 2005 setting out such procedures to authorize the lawful deprivation of liberty of a person with a mental disorder who lacks capacity to consent, if that is in the person's best interests. The new sections 4A and 4B inserted into the Mental Capacity Act 2005, which came into force in April 2009, permit someone to be deprived of their liberty under the 2005 Act in one of three situations:

1. where the deprivation is authorized by the Court of Protection by making a personal welfare order under s 16(2a); or

2. where the deprivation is authorized in accordance with the procedures set out in Schedule A1 (known as the Deprivation of Liberty (DOL) procedures);
3. where deprivation of liberty is necessary in order to give life-sustaining treatment or to carry out a vital act to prevent serious deterioration in the person's condition while a decision about any relevant matter is sought from the court.

The above provisions are not available for people who are or should be detained under Mental Health Act powers, except for (3) in cases where urgent treatment is required while a decision is sought from the court.

The deprivation of liberty procedures

Schedule A1 sets out procedures for the managing authority of a hospital or care home to obtain authorization to deprive someone of their liberty for the purpose of giving care or treatment in their best interests. Two mechanisms are available – 'standard authorization' or 'urgent authorization'.

Standard authorization

The authorization procedure will usually begin with a request by the managing authority (generally the managers of a hospital or care home where the person is, or may be, deprived of their liberty) to the supervisory body (usually the primary care trust[2] (England) or local health board (Wales) for a person in hospital, or the local authority for someone in a care home). A managing authority must request a standard authorization when it appears likely that, either currently or within the next 28 days, a person in their care is accommodated in circumstances amounting to a deprivation of liberty (MCA 2005, Schedule A1, para. 24). A request must also be made if there is, or is to be, a change in the place of detention. The supervisory body will then arrange for assessments to be carried out to determine whether the following six qualifying requirements are met:

- The age requirement – The person must be aged 18 or over.
- The mental health requirement – The person must be suffering from mental disorder within the meaning of the Mental Health Act 1983 (amended) which is 'any disorder or disability of mind', including for these purposes, a learning disability, whether or not associated with abnormally aggressive or seriously irresponsible conduct.
- The mental capacity requirement – The person must lack capacity to decide whether or not they should be accommodated in the hospital or care home for the purpose of being given the care or treatment

---

[2] When primary care trusts are abolished local authorities will be the supervisory body for both hospitals and care homes.

concerned. This must be in accordance with ss.1–3 of the Mental Capacity Act 2005.

- The best interests requirement – It must be in the person's best interests to be a detained resident and the deprivation of liberty must be necessary to prevent harm to the person and must be a proportionate response to the likelihood and seriousness of that harm. The assessor must consult the managing authority and take into account the views of anyone named by the person, anyone engaged in caring for the person or interested in their welfare, any donee[3] of a lasting power of attorney (LPA) granted by the person or deputy appointed by the court. If the person does not have anyone to speak for them who is not paid to provide care, an independent mental capacity advocate (IMCA) must be appointed to support and represent them during the assessment process (see below).

- The eligibility requirement – A person is ineligible if already subject, or could be subject, to Mental Health Act powers in one of the following ways:
  - being detained in hospital under the Mental Health Act or meeting the criteria for detention and objecting to being detained in the hospital or to some or all of the treatment (i.e. in those circumstances the Mental Health Act powers should be used if the person is to be detained);
  - on leave of absence or subject to guardianship, a community treatment order or conditional discharge and subject to a measure which would be inconsistent with an authorization if granted; or on leave of absence or subject to a community treatment order or conditional discharge and the authorization if granted would be for deprivation of liberty in a hospital for the purpose of treatment for mental disorder (see Schedule 1A to the Mental Capacity Act 2005);

- The no refusals requirement – There must be no valid and applicable advance decision made previously by the detained person refusing the treatment in question (see below), nor a valid refusal by a deputy or donee of a lasting power of attorney within the scope of their authority.

It is the responsibility of the supervisory body to appoint appropriate assessors. Regulations (SI 2008 No 1858) specify who can carry out assessments, the professional skills, training and competences required and the timeframe within which the assessments must be completed. The mental health and best interests assessments must be carried out by different assessors. All assessors must be independent from decisions about providing or commissioning care for the person concerned. Anyone carrying

out assessments (other than the age assessment) must have undergone specific training.

If all the qualifying requirements are met, the supervisory body must grant a standard authorization and:

- set the period of the authorization of up to 1 year, but no longer than the maximum period identified in the best interests assessment;
- issue the authorization in writing, stating the period for which it is valid, the purpose for which it is given and the reason why each qualifying requirement is met;
- If appropriate, attach conditions;
- appoint someone to act as the person's representative during the term of the authorization (SI 2008 No 1315);
- provide a copy of the authorization to the managing authority, the person being deprived of their liberty and their representative, any independent mental capacity advocate who has been involved and any other interested person consulted by the best interests assessor.

While a standard authorization is in place, the managing authority must:

- ensure that any conditions are complied with;
- take all practicable steps to ensure that the detained resident understands the effect of the authorization, their right to request a review and their right of appeal to the Court of Protection;
- give the same information to the person's representative; and
- keep the person's case under consideration and request a review if there is a change in the person's circumstances.

The detained person or their representative may also request a review at any time. A review is carried out by the supervisory body and may lead to the authorization being terminated, a change in the recorded reasons or a change in the conditions attached to the authorization. The Department of Health has produced a useful leaflet on deprivation of liberty safeguards in England (http://www.dh.gov.uk/prod_consum_dh/groups/dh_digitalassets/@dh/@en/documents/digitalasset/dh_080717.pdf).

Urgent authorization

Urgent authorizations may be given by the managing authority of a care home or hospital to allow a deprivation of liberty for up to seven days whilst a standard authorization is being obtained. The managing authority must believe that the deprivation of liberty is urgently required and the qualifying requirements appear to be met. The urgent authorization must be recorded in writing setting out the reasons for giving it. An urgent authorization may be extended for up to a further 7 days by the supervisory body if there are exceptional reasons why it has not been possible to decide on a request for

---

[3] A donee is an appointed attorney (see also p.86).

standard authorization and it is essential that the detention continues.

Review by the Court of Protection

A person who has been deprived of his or her liberty or his or her representative may apply to the Court of Protection for a review of the lawfulness of the deprivation of liberty. The court may make an order terminating or varying the authorization, or requiring the supervisory body (or in the case of an urgent authorization, the managing authority) to do so.

Lasting Powers of Attorney

One of the main ways in which the Mental Capacity Act 2005 allows people (aged 18 and over) to plan for future incapacity is to make a lasting power of attorney, appointing their chosen representative(s) to make decisions on their behalf when they no longer have capacity to make their own decisions. The lasting power of attorney scheme replaces enduring powers of attorney (EPAs), although enduring powers of attorney made before the Mental Capacity Act came into effect will continue to be valid for as long as they are needed. It also extends the areas in which donors can authorize others to make decisions on their behalf. In addition to property and financial affairs, donors can appoint attorneys (called 'donees' in the Act) to make decisions concerning their personal welfare, including healthcare and consent to medical treatment, when they may lack capacity to do so for themselves. Different attorneys may be appointed to take different types of decisions. Healthcare professionals therefore need to be familiar with lasting powers of attorney and the powers delegated to attorneys to make healthcare decisions on the donor's behalf.

There are two statutory forms for making a lasting power of attorney – one for property and affairs and one for personal welfare decisions. Each form must include a certificate signed by an independent person, confirming that the donor understands what is involved in making a lasting power of attorney and has not been put under any undue pressure to do so.

A lasting power of attorney must be registered with the Public Guardian before it can be used. A property and affairs lasting power of attorney can be used, with the donor's consent, while s/he still has capacity to make financial decisions. However, a personal welfare lasting power of attorney can only be used when the donor lacks capacity to make the decision in question. Attorneys must comply with the Act's principles and must always act or make decisions in the best interests of the donor. Chapter 7 of the Code of Practice sets out duties and responsibilities of attorneys acting under a lasting power of attorney.

Court of Protection

Section 45 of the Mental Capacity Act establishes a specialized court, known as the Court of Protection, with a jurisdiction covering all areas of decision-making for adults who lack capacity. The court has wide powers (ss.15–23) to make declarations or decisions on behalf of people lacking, or alleged to lack, capacity or, in cases where on-going decision-making may be required, to appoint a 'deputy' with authority to make such decisions. Therefore, if an adult lacks capacity to make specific decisions and has not previously made a lasting power of attorney appointing an attorney to make such decisions, the Court of Protection may be involved in the handling of property or finances; in making complex health or welfare decisions; in dealing with cases where a person lacking capacity to consent may be deprived of their liberty; or in settling disputes which cannot be resolved in any other way.

The new Court of Protection is a superior court of record able to establish precedent and build up a body of case law and expertise in all matters affecting people who lack capacity. It has the same powers, rights, privileges and authority as the High Court.

Proceedings relating to a 16 or 17 year old who lacks capacity could, potentially, be heard either in the Family Division of the High Court or in the Court of Protection. The Act allows for transfer of proceedings from the Court of Protection to the family courts, and vice versa. The choice of court will depend on what is appropriate in the particular circumstances of the case.

Deputies

Where the court believes that there is a need for on-going decision-making powers for a person lacking capacity to make welfare and/or financial decisions, it may appoint a deputy to make such decisions on the person's behalf. The court must first be satisfied that the matter before it cannot be resolved by a less restrictive approach, by making a single order or decision, and that the appointment of a deputy is in the person's best interests. The Act also requires that the powers conferred on a deputy should be as limited in scope and duration as is reasonably practicable in the circumstances. The order of appointment will specify the particular decisions or actions the deputy is authorized to take, the powers available to him/her and the duration of the appointment.

The choice of who to appoint as deputy is a decision for the court to make in the best interests of the person lacking capacity, and those applying will need to demonstrate why an appointment is necessary. Chapter 8 of the Code of Practice sets out the duties and responsibilities of deputies.

Advance Decisions to Refuse Treatment

Case law relating to advance decisions to refuse treatment (also known as advance directives or living wills) has confirmed that so long as the person was competent at the time the decision was made, and the decision is unambiguous and applicable in the particular circumstances, an advance refusal of treatment is as valid as a contemporaneous decision (*Re C*, *Re T* and *HE*). The Mental Capacity Act gives statutory recognition to this right.

For the purposes of the Act, an advance decision is a decision made by a person aged 18 or over, who has capacity to do so, refusing specified medical treatment, intending it to take effect at a future time when s/he lacks capacity to give or refuse consent to that treatment. No particular format is required, except that an advance decision refusing life-sustaining treatment must be in writing and be witnessed, and must include a clear statement that it is to apply 'even if life is at risk' (ss.25(5–6)). Section 62 makes it clear that an advance decision cannot be used to give effect to an unlawful act, such as euthanasia or assisted suicide or any intervention with the express aim of ending life.

The Act includes important statutory safeguards concerning the making and implementation of advance decisions to refuse treatment. In order for the refusal to be legally effective at the time when it is proposed to carry out or continue treatment, there must be proof that an advance decision exists and that it is both *valid* and *applicable* to the proposed treatment. Section 25 sets out events or circumstances that would make an advance decision invalid or not applicable. Validity is lost if the person has subsequently withdrawn the advance decision while still capable, has subsequently made a lasting power of attorney giving an attorney authority to make the decision in question, or if the person has since acted inconsistently with the advance decision. An advance decision is not applicable if any of the specified circumstances are absent or if new circumstances have arisen (such as the development of new treatments or changes in personal circumstances) which were not anticipated by the person when making the advance decision and which might have affected the decision.

Advance decisions regarding treatment for mental disorder

Where a patient is liable to be detained under the Mental Health Act 1983 (amended), the contents of any advance decision refusing treatment for mental disorder may be overridden by the compulsory treatment provisions of Part IV of that Act. However, if the person is being treated informally for a mental disorder, an advance decision refusing specific types of treatment for that disorder should be respected in the same way as any other advance decision, so long as it is valid and applicable to the treatment in question.

Similarly, an advance decision to refuse treatment for a physical condition, as opposed to a mental disorder, may still be effective regardless of whether the patient was liable to be detained or compulsorily treated under the Mental Health Act 1983 (amended).

Independent Mental Capacity Advocate Service

For the first time, the Mental Capacity Act provides a statutory right to advocacy services for particularly vulnerable people who lack capacity to make certain serious decisions. These are people who have no supportive family or friends or anyone else who can be consulted about their best interests, other than people engaged in their care or treatment in a professional or paid capacity. The Independent Mental Capacity Advocate (IMCA) service has been established to provide support for such people where potentially life-changing decisions are being contemplated.

The particular local authority or NHS body involved in the decision is responsible for ensuring that an independent mental capacity advocate is instructed for anyone who qualifies for the service (ss.37–39). An independent mental capacity advocate *must* be appointed to support and represent people lacking capacity who have no one else to support them where:

- a decision is needed concerning the provision, withholding or withdrawal of serious medical treatment;
- an NHS body or local authority is proposing to move a person into long-term care in a hospital (for more than 28 days) or a care home (for more than 8 weeks); or
- a long-term move to a different hospital or care home is proposed.

Serious medical treatment is defined in Regulations (SI 2006 No 1832) as the provision, withholding or withdrawal of treatment in circumstances where:

- if a single treatment is proposed, there is a fine balance between the likely benefits and the burdens to the patient and the risks involved; or
- a decision between a choice of treatments is finely balanced; or
- the proposed treatment is likely to have serious consequences for the patient.

The duty to appoint an independent mental capacity advocate does not apply if the decision is urgent or where the proposed treatment is given under Part IV of the Mental Health Act 1983 (amended).

The independent mental capacity advocate scheme has also been expanded to allow local authorities and NHS bodies a discretionary power to instruct an independent mental capacity advocate for a person lacking capacity in relation to two further types of decisions (SI 2006 No 2883)

An independent mental capacity advocate *may* be instructed:

- where a care review is being carried out to review the arrangements made for the person's accommodation (as part of a care plan or otherwise) and there are no family or friends who it would be appropriate to consult;
- in adult safeguarding procedures, where the person lacking capacity is either the victim or the alleged abuser. In adult protection cases (and no other cases) access to independent mental capacity advocates is not restricted to people who have no family or friends to support them.

Independent mental capacity advocates have a right to interview the person in private and examine any relevant health or social care records. Their role is to support and represent the person in the decision-making process, using all possible means to ascertain the person's past and present wishes, feelings, beliefs and values which may be relevant to the decision in question, consulting with relevant professionals and carers, investigating all the circumstances relevant to the decision (including obtaining a second opinion where relevant), and checking that the decision-maker is acting in accordance with the Mental Capacity Act's principles and requirements. The independent mental capacity advocate must prepare a report which the decision-maker must take into account. In the event of disagreement or dispute about the person's best interests, independent mental capacity advocates have the right to challenge the decision taken, for example by using the relevant local complaints procedure or in serious cases, by seeking permission to refer the matter to the Court of Protection.

The Mental Health Act 2007 has amended the Mental Capacity Act to introduce a further role for independent mental capacity advocates where a person is, or is to be, deprived of their liberty under the deprivation of liberty safeguards (as described above). Independent mental capacity advocates must be appointed where there is no one else available to act as the person's representative (Sch A1, Part 10). Independent mental capacity advocates will have additional functions to represent and support the person in relation to the procedures for reviewing or appealing against the deprivation of liberty.

Research

As a matter of general principle under the common law, medical research involving any invasion of bodily integrity could not lawfully be carried out with an adult lacking capacity to consent, unless the medical treatment being given as part of the research was in the person's best interests. There are two avenues whereby some research may be carried out with people who lack capacity to consent to their participation. The first is research that involves the clinical trials of medicines under the Medicines for Human Use (Clinical Trials) Regulations 2004. The second is the framework provided under sections 30–34 of the Mental Capacity Act, which applies to 'intrusive research', defined as research that can normally only lawfully take place if the participant concerned, having the capacity to consent, has consented to his/her participation in that research.

Intrusive research may lawfully be carried out with a person lacking capacity to consent, provided the research project is approved by an 'appropriate body' (i.e. an ethics committee) and the research is carried out in accordance with other conditions specified in the Act, which relate to consultation with someone involved in the care of the person lacking capacity and respecting the objections of the person lacking capacity during the course of the research.

The appropriate body can only approve a research project if the following requirements are met:

- the research is connected with an 'impairing condition' affecting the person lacking capacity or the treatment of that condition;
- there are reasonable grounds for believing that research only involving people who have capacity to consent to it will not be as effective;
- the research:
  - has a potential benefit to the person lacking capacity that is not disproportionate to the burden of participating in the research; **or**
  - the research is intended to provide knowledge of the causes or treatment of, or of the care of persons with, the same or similar condition as the person lacking capacity (in which case, the risk to the individual must be negligible and any interference with their freedom of action or privacy limited);
- reasonable arrangements are in place to ensure that the necessary consultation with carers or other consultees will take place and other safeguards implemented.

The Act imposes additional safeguards to ensure that individuals are withdrawn from research if there is any indication that they object or wish to be withdrawn. In any event, the person's interests must be assumed to outweigh those of science and society.

4
Legal arrangements in the rest of the British Isles and Islands[1]

Edited by
John Gunn

Written by
Fred Browne
Rajan Darjee
John Gunn
Harry Kennedy
R D Mackay
Damian Mohan

Leigh Neal
Lindsay Thomson

Additional material from
Nigel Shackleford
(Ministry of Justice)

1st edition authors: **Ann Barker, Fred Browne, Derek Chiswick, Enda Dooley, John Gunn, John Hamilton and Stephen Stanley**

PREAMBLE

The bias of this book is towards the law, the services, and the practices of England and Wales. We aim wherever possible, however, to broaden the picture and to embrace general principles, whilst accepting that we cannot, in one text, deal with the detail of other systems. In this chapter we complement the emphasis on relevant law for England and Wales by mentioning in varying degrees of detail similar laws in some of the other jurisdictions of the British Isles. We cannot deal with them all but it is important to note the wide variations.

To set these other systems in context it is worth noting that throughout the nineteenth century both Great Britain and Ireland were dominated by the Westminster parliament in London. Separation of mental health services began in the nineteenth century, but is now more marked. When Haslam published his treatises on insanity in 1817 psychiatry as a therapeutic enterprise hardly existed, the mentally abnormal were subject to ignominy, social rejection, and strict legal controls (Haslam, 1817a,b). Under the 1845 Lunacy Act no patient was to be

discharged from a licensed house or hospital if the medical superintendent or attendant objected on the grounds that the patient was dangerous or unfit to be at large. The first hint of legal divergence within the mental health system was perhaps the Criminal Lunatics (Ireland) Act of 1838, followed by the Criminal Lunatic Asylum (Ireland) Act 1845 'for the establishment of a central asylum for insane persons charged with offences in Ireland' which led to the building of the Central Mental Hospital in Dublin (Dundrum), the first forensic psychiatry hospital in the British Isles. Scotland began to diverge in 1857 with the Lunacy and Asylums Act, Scotland. The nineteenth-century lunacy laws, modified occasionally, held sway throughout the first quarter of the twentieth century in all of the United Kingdom as it was then.

Historically Irish law is complex, but from the seventeenth to the twentieth centuries it was dominated by English law. In 1920, Ireland was partitioned, and the Irish Free State, later the Republic of Ireland, was formed in 1922. The new Irish government, not surprisingly,

[1] The term British Isles has no political or legal significance. It is a geographical term referring to an archipelago of approximately 6,000 islands off the northwest coast of Europe. The Isles include two sovereign states the United Kingdom and the Republic of Ireland. The British Islands are those islands (not all in the British Isles e.g. the Channel Isles) which relate politically to the United Kingdom.

didn't give mental health law much priority and the old lunacy acts have been the basis of Irish mental health law until the twenty-first century. Northern Ireland, from 1922 a separate jurisdiction, has shadowed changes in English law more closely (for a useful overview see Dickson, 2001).

In England and Wales the influence of the Maudsley Hospital, with its insistence on outpatient treatment and voluntary admission, was felt in the report of the Macmillan Royal Commission of 1926, which in turn led to the Mental Treatment Act 1930. This substantially amended the old lunacy acts and the old mental deficiency acts introducing the principles of voluntary treatment and care at home as well as abolishing the terms 'lunacy' and 'asylum'. Northern Ireland introduced these principles in its act of 1948. Mental health law in the United Kingdom was further revolutionized by the publication of the Percy Royal Commission report in 1957. It was followed by the Mental Health Act (1959), the Mental Health (Scotland) Act (1960) and the Mental Health Act (Northern Ireland) (1961). These three statutes were closely related and repealed all the old lunacy laws and mental deficiency laws, replacing them instead with a complex system of mental health law which was built on a premise of informality for the treatment of mental abnormality; compulsion is to be a very last resort and, except in Scotland, courts were removed from involvement in compulsory care. These principles were further built on by the amending Acts of 1983, 1984, and 1986.

The incoming Labour government of 1997 decided it wanted a 'root and branch' reform of mental heath law. After 9 years of struggle it didn't get one, but it did amend the 1983 Act in 2007, producing much more risk averse legislation than practitioners and patients wanted (see chapter 3 for details). The new government had also granted devolution to Scotland and Wales so that whilst the Westminster Parliament was grappling with the Mental Health Alliance, Scotland was able to get on and enact legislation.

SCOTLAND

Despite being united with England and Wales since 1707, Scotland has retained its own legal system. Devolution in 1999 re-established the Scottish Parliament with authority to make statutes in relation to devolved issues (e.g. criminal justice and mental health legislation). Scots law has developed differently from English law, is less codified and more dependent on case law. As in England and Wales the European Convention on Human Rights has been incorporated into domestic law in Scotland. For an introduction to the Scottish legal system see McManus (2005). Before describing mental health legislation and arrangements for mentally disordered offenders, an introduction to the general legal framework may be useful.

General Criminal Matters

The procurator fiscal service, under the authority of the Lord Advocate, is responsible for investigating crime. In practice the police do this and gather evidence, reporting to the procurator fiscal. There are eight police forces in Scotland, each headed by a chief constable. The expanded role of the police in supervising and monitoring offenders in the community is a relatively recent development.

Apart from very rare cases where private prosecutions are pursued, the Lord Advocate and his deputy, the Solicitor General, are responsible for the prosecution of crime. In serious cases much of this work is delegated to advocates-depute who, along with a staff of civil servants, constitute the Crown Office in Edinburgh. The Crown Office has responsibility for criminal justice policy and the operation of the criminal justice system. The Lord Advocate and Solicitor General are members of the Scottish Government. The Procurator Fiscal Service is the local agent of the Crown Office, spread through Scotland on a regional basis mirroring the six sheriffdoms. Procurators fiscal initiate all prosecutions, with serious cases being referred to the Crown Office. Procurators fiscal pursue prosecutions in less serious cases.

More minor (summary cases) are heard in a district or a sheriff court without a jury. More serious cases (solemn cases prosecuted on indictment) are heard in a sheriff court by a sheriff sitting with a jury or in the High Court by a judge and jury. An accused must be brought to trial within a year in solemn cases. If remanded in custody (either prison or hospital) then the trial must happen within 40 days in summary cases or 140 days in solemn cases. Scotland has one of the shortest average periods in custody pending trial in the world. Much of the criminal law is not set out in statute and relies on common law. The maximum sentence for any common law violation is life imprisonment, but different levels of court have specific maximum sentencing powers.

Appeals against conviction and sentence under summary procedure are made to the High Court of Criminal Appeal in Edinburgh, which may also hear an appeal by the prosecution on a point of law. Under solemn procedure, appeals are made to at least three judges sitting at the High Court of Criminal Appeal. Unlike civil cases, there is no appeal from the criminal courts of Scotland to the Supreme Court of the United Kingdom.

The age of criminal responsibility was 8 years, until the Criminal Justice and Licensing (Scotland) Act 2010 raised it to 12. There are no juvenile courts, and prosecution of children under 16 is rare, only taking place on the instruction of the Lord Advocate. Since 1971 children who, for whatever reason (including child protection, child welfare, offending behaviour), may be in need of compulsory measures of care are referred to three lay people (children's hearing) drawn from a list (the children's panel) which each local authority must establish.

Community sentences (probation and community service orders) and periods in the community on parole following release from prison are supervised by criminal justice social workers employed by local authorities. There is no 'probation service' in Scotland. Criminal justice social workers prepare pre-sentence social enquiry reports. The Scottish Prison Service is responsible for providing prisons and young offenders' institutions. There are 15 prisons in Scotland, including one for women and one for young offenders. There are two private prisons. Short-term prisoners (serving less than 4 years) are released automatically after serving half their sentence. Long-term determinate sentence prisoners may be considered for parole at the half-way point, but are automatically released after serving two-thirds of their sentence. Release of prisoners on parole licence is at the discretion of the Justice Minister of the Scottish Government, but can only occur with the agreement of the Parole Board for Scotland. For long-term determinate sentence prisoners the Parole Board considers the case based on a dossier of reports. Life-sentenced prisoners may be referred to the Parole Board after serving a punishment part imposed at sentencing. Release is then dependent on the risk posed to the public as determined by a tribunal of Parole Board members with a legally qualified chair. The Parole Board also considers the need to recall to custody offenders who have breached their licence conditions and, subject to the statutory test, may direct their re-release. In the case of some serious violent and sexual offenders an extended sentence may be imposed, extending the period of supervision and monitoring, with potential for recall to prison, beyond the end of any determinate sentence.

General Civil Matters

Scotland is divided into six sheriffdoms, each presided over by a sheriff principal, and each divided into sheriff court districts. These are the same sheriff courts that deal with criminal cases as described above. Most civil litigation is dealt with in the sheriff court, e.g. debt, contract, damages, actions concerning the use of property, divorce and the custody of children. Appeals against the decision of a sheriff are to a sheriff principal, and thereafter to the Court of Session, and ultimately to the Supreme Court of the United Kingdom since 2009 (previously to the House of Lords). Sheriffs also have responsibility for conducting formal inquiries into fatal accidents and sudden deaths; they do so without a jury. The office of Her Majesty's Coroner does not exist in Scotland.

The Court of Session sits at Parliament House in Edinburgh and consists of the Lord President, the Lord Justice-Clerk and judges appointed by the Queen on the recommendation of the First Minister after being recommended by the Judicial Appointments Board. Decisions are made by judges sitting singly, but are subject to review by a plurality of judges. The Court of Session is divided into an Inner House, which functions as a court of appeal, and an Outer House, which is a court of first instance.

Statutory Bodies

The **Mental Welfare Commission for Scotland** is the principal body charged with protecting the interests of people with mental disorder and ensuring mental health legislation is used properly. The Commission's role is to: promote best practice; provide advice; report on issues regarding the welfare of people with mental disorder; highlight individual cases involving unlawful detention, deficiency of care, neglect, or damage or loss of property; using a formal inquiry to investigate a case if necessary (e.g. in some cases where homicide is committed by psychiatric patients); visit patients subject to mental health and incapacity legislation and inspect hospitals and other premises where patients reside; publish reports (including annual reports and outcomes of investigations).

The **Mental Health Tribunal for Scotland** was established under the Mental Health (Care and Treatment) (Scotland) Act 2003, replacing the sheriff courts as the legal forum making decisions about the compulsory treatment of individuals with mental disorder. Tribunals, with a legal chairman, a medical member and a general member, consider appeals, review compulsory orders and make long-term civil orders (see below). A shrieval panel, chaired by a sheriff, considers cases involving restricted patients. The decision of the Tribunal may be appealed to the local sheriff principal, and his/her decision may be appealed to the Court of Session. As with civil appeals generally, the ultimate court of appeal is the UK Supreme Court.

The **Mental Health Division at the Scottish Government** has a dedicated staff to deal with restricted patients on behalf of Scottish ministers. A forensic psychiatrist is seconded on a full time basis to provide advice to Scottish ministers in such cases. Scottish ministers are responsible for deciding about transfer between hospitals and leave for restricted patients. Conditional discharge, absolute discharge or rescinding a restriction order may only be authorized by the Tribunal. Scottish ministers must refer a case to the Tribunal if the patient's psychiatrist recommends any of these changes, and may make legal representations at the Tribunal regarding decisions on these matters. Scottish ministers may appeal against decisions of the Tribunal in relation to restricted patients. With restricted patients appeals are directly to the Court of Session.

The **Risk Management Authority (RMA)** was established by the Criminal Justice (Scotland) Act 2003, and although it is independent from the Scottish Government, it is accountable to Scottish ministers, via the Scottish

Government Criminal Justice Directorate. The MacLean Committee (Scottish Executive, 2000), which reviewed the assessment, sentencing and management of serious violent and sexual offenders, recommended the establishment of the Risk Management Authority, primarily to oversee new arrangements for the assessment and management of high risk offenders. This is the operational role of the Risk Management Authority sitting within a wider remit in relation to policy, research and education of relevance to assessing and managing risk in violent and sexual offenders. The Risk Management Authority has a chief executive, a board (whose members come from psychology, psychiatry, social work, law and prison service backgrounds), and a number of development and administrative staff. It has responsibility for accrediting risk assessors (who may prepare risk assessment reports where courts are considering imposing an indeterminate sentence on a violent or sexual offender), issuing standards and guidance for these assessors (Risk Management Authority, 2006), approving risk management plans (where one of these indeterminate sentences – an Order for Lifelong Restriction (OLR) – is imposed; Risk Management Authority, 2007a), and issuing standards and guidelines for these plans. The Risk Management Authority has also produced a risk assessment tools evaluation directory ('RATED'; Risk Management Authority, 2007b), has reviewed the assessment and management of the risk posed by restricted patients in Scotland (Risk Management Authority, 2007c), and has recently been involved in developing risk assessment and management approaches for violent and sexual offenders managed by criminal justice agencies.

The Adults with Incapacity (Scotland) Act 2000 created the **Office of the Public Guardian** with specific functions relating to incapable adults' financial and property affairs. These include: supervision of individuals authorized to act on behalf of an incapable adult; maintaining registers of all documents relating to powers and orders made in relation to incapable adults; investigating complaints or any circumstances where there is risk relating to the property or financial affairs of an incapable adult; providing advice for individuals authorized to act on behalf of an incapable adult; and consulting the Mental Welfare Commission and any local authority where there is a common interest.

The Regulation of Care (Scotland) Act 2001 established a system of care regulation in Scotland. The **Scottish Commission for the Regulation of Care** is required by that Act to regulate certain care services, including private hospitals and nursing homes. There is currently one private sector secure hospital in Scotland. The Commission registers and inspects services against a set of national care standards and produces inspection reports. The same role in relation to NHS psychiatric hospitals, including secure hospitals, is performed by the Mental Welfare Commission (MWC) for Scotland.

Legal aid is the responsibility of the Scottish Legal Aid Board established under the Legal Aid (Scotland) Act 1986; it includes advice, assistance and representation in criminal and civil court proceedings. Individuals subject to compulsory measures under mental health legislation who are legally aided may be legally represented at Tribunals.

Mental Health Legislation

Scottish mental health law reform began with the Millan Report (Scottish Executive, 2001a) which identified several principles of mental healthcare.

- *Non-discrimination* – people with mental disorder should retain the same rights and entitlements as those with other needs.
- *Equality* – all powers must be exercised without any direct or indirect discrimination on the grounds of physical disability, age, gender, sexual orientation, language, religion or national or ethnic or social origin.
- *Respect for diversity* – service users should receive care, treatment and support in a manner that accords respect for their individual qualities, abilities and diverse backgrounds and takes into account their age, gender, sexual orientation ethnic group, social, cultural and religious background.
- *Reciprocity* – where society imposes an obligation on an individual to comply with a programme of treatment and care, it should impose a parallel obligation on the health and social care authorities to provide safe and appropriate services, including ongoing care following discharge from compulsion.
- *Informal care* – wherever possible, care, treatment and support should be provided to people with mental disorder without the use of compulsory powers.
- *Participation* – patients should be fully involved, to the extent permitted by their individual capacity, in all aspects of their assessment, care, treatment and support. Account should be taken of both past and present wishes, so far as they can be ascertained.
- *Respect for carers* – those who provide care to service users on an informal basis should receive respect for their role and experience, receive appropriate information and advice, and have their views and needs taken into account.
- *Least restrictive alternative* – patients should be provided with any necessary care, treatment and support both in the least invasive manner and in the least restrictive manner and environment compatible with the delivery of safe and effective care, taking account where appropriate of the safety of others.

This report was followed by the Mental Health (Care and Treatment) (Scotland) Act 2003 which governs the compulsory treatment of people with mental disorder.

This Act superseded the Mental Health (Scotland) Act 1984, and its roots lie in that act. Key changes were the introduction of statutory guiding principles, compulsory measures in the community, an impaired decision-making ability criterion and the Mental Health Tribunal as legal forum. The philosophy behind the new legislation has been welcomed widely, but we wait to see whether there are improvements in patient care. The new Act imposes a higher bureaucratic burden and there are concerns about resource implications (Darjee and Crichton, 2004). A comprehensive three volume Code of Practice (Scottish Executive, 2005a) guides practitioners through a statute that is barely understandable due to poor use of English. For detailed information see Thomson (2005), Patrick (2006) and Franks and Cobb (2006).

Principles

Sections 1 and 2 of the 2003 Act set out some of the principles to guide its application: taking into account the patient's past and present wishes and the views of relevant others; allowing the patient to participate as fully as possible; providing maximum benefit to the patient; not discriminating against the patient; providing appropriate services; taking into account the needs and circumstances of carers; using the least restrictive measures; and, if the patient is a child, best securing their welfare.

Mental disorder

Mental disorder is defined as mental illness, personality disorder or learning disability however caused or manifested. It is not further defined. There is a mistaken assumption that Scottish legislation has not allowed detention of individuals with personality disorder. A legal category allowing the detention of such persons has existed since 1913 and an innominate category identical to 'psychopathic disorder' in England and Wales was in the Mental Health (Scotland) Acts of 1960 and 1984 (Darjee and Crichton, 2003). Psychiatrists in Scotland have been reluctant to detain individuals with personality disorder and there are few patients with primary personality disorder detained in secure hospitals compared with England.

The following are excluded as sole bases for evidence of mental disorder: sexual orientation, sexual deviancy, transexualism or transvestism; dependence on or use of alcohol or drugs; behaviour that causes, or is likely to cause harassment, alarm or distress to others; acting as no prudent person would. It is important that this is not interpreted to mean that compulsion cannot be used for mentally ill people who are acting 'imprudently' or causing 'alarm'.

Criteria for compulsion

A number of criteria must be met before compulsory measures are applied (table 4.1). The 'treatability' test applies to all categories of mental disorder, and is analogous to the same test for psychopathic disorder and mental impairment under the unamended Mental Health Act 1983 and the Mental Health (Scotland) Act 1984. The leading case on the interpretation of this test is *Reid* where the House of Lords confirmed its broad interpretation (Darjee et al., 1999). The 'decision-making ability' test represents the introduction of a capacity test into mental health legislation, which is innovative. But if case law on capacity in medical settings is anything to go by courts are likely to be flexible in its interpretation. Case law on the 'decision-making ability' test will be required to clarify its interpretation. It clearly relates to the capacity to make decisions about psychiatric treatment but sets a lower threshold than 'incapacity'. The 'risk' test sets a relatively low threshold and clearly goes beyond just risk of violence to self or others.

Table 4.1   Criteria for making a compulsory order under the Mental Health (Care and Treatment) (Scotland) Act 2003

The following criteria are set out under section 57 (3) of the Mental Health (Care and Treatment) (Scotland) Act 2003. They all have to be met for a compulsory treatment order to be made. For other orders see table 4.2; the application of these criteria may vary.
(a) that the patient has a mental disorder;
(b) that medical treatment which would be likely to –
(i) prevent the mental disorder worsening; or
(ii) alleviate any of the symptoms, or effects, of the disorder, is available for the patient;
(c) that if the patient were not provided with such medical treatment there would be a significant risk –
(i) to the health, safety or welfare of the patient; or
(ii) to the safety of any other person;
(d) that because of the mental disorder the patient's ability to make decisions about the provision of such medical treatment is significantly impaired; and
(e) that the making of a compulsory treatment order is necessary.

Compulsory measures

Short-term detention (up to 28 days) is the preferred route to detention in hospital where the person needs to be detained in hospital soon. Emergency detention (up to 72 hours) may be applied if there is insufficient time to follow short-term detention procedures. A longer-term compulsory treatment order (CTO), lasting up to 6 months initially, may be applied either in hospital or the community; it can only be made after an application to the Mental Health Tribunal for Scotland. The criteria for, and the effects of, these orders, and other orders that may be applied by nurses and the police, are set out in table 4.2.

'Suspension of detention' procedures allow patients to leave hospital for periods. Other compulsory measures (for example a condition that a patient resides at a specific address in the community) may also be suspended. Patients who abscond may be taken into custody and returned. If a patient subject to a community treatment order is not compliant then s/he may be detained in hospital. Specific procedures have to be followed when transferring patients between hospitals. If a patient or named person opposes a transfer an appeal may be made to the Tribunal.

Treatment

Medical treatment is defined widely to include nursing care, psychological interventions, habilitation and rehabilitation as well as physical treatments. For some physical treatments there are specific safeguards. Medication for mental disorder may be given for 2 months, then the patient has to consent in writing or if s/he is unwilling or incapable a second opinion is required from a designated medical practitioner (DMP; a doctor with the necessary qualifications and experience who is on a list maintained by the Mental Welfare Commission). Patients under compulsion in the community may not be given medication using physical force, but if they refuse treatment they may be taken to a hospital or clinic and given medication. Electroconvulsive therapy (ECT) may only be given if a patient can and does consent, or if incapable of consenting, with the authorization of a designated medical practitioner. ECT may not be given, even in an emergency, to a patient with capacity who refuses. Treatment that is urgently necessary may be authorized by the responsible medical officer (RMO) without consent or a second opinion; this may be used for giving ECT to severely ill and at risk patients lacking capacity while awaiting a second opinion, or for giving medication to acutely disturbed patients.

Neurosurgery for mental disorder may only be carried out with an independent opinion from a designated medical practitioner that the treatment will be beneficial; and opinions from two lay people appointed by the Mental Welfare Commission that the person has capacity and consents, or if they do not have capacity, that they do not object. If the person is incapable but not objecting, the treatment must be authorized by the Court of Session. This procedure applies to all patients whether they are subject to compulsion or not.

Appeals and other safeguards

The Mental Health Tribunal hears appeals against compulsory orders; they may cancel or vary the terms of orders (for example changing a hospital based order to a community based one). Where a patient is detained in the State Hospital, they may make a determination that a patient is being held in conditions of excessive security and direct the responsible health board to find an appropriate placement. The Mental Welfare Commission for Scotland may discharge patients from orders or refer cases for consideration by the Tribunal.

The patient may nominate a named person who must receive certain information, must be consulted about the patient's treatment and can appeal against any compulsory order. If the patient does not make a nomination then the named person is their primary carer or nearest relative. A patient may make an advance statement. When a person carries out duties under the Act they must 'have regard to the wishes specified in the advance statement'. They may only act against these if this is justified and recorded. Every person with mental disorder has a right of access to independent advocacy, and it is the duty of the local authority and health board to ensure its availability.

Voluntary patients may appeal to the Tribunal against unlawful detention. The patient, the patient's named person, a mental health officer (MHO), the Commission, any guardian, any welfare attorney or a person having an interest in the welfare of the patient may apply. This safeguard may protect patients from *de facto* detention where they stay in hospital under the threat of detention and voluntary patients who are incapable of consenting to admission to hospital.

Incapacity Legislation

The Adults with Incapacity (Scotland) Act 2000 governs welfare, financial and medical treatment of incapable adults. Before this Act, Scots law in this area was confusing and archaic (Crichton, 2000). Traditionally, a distinction has been drawn between decisions involving financial matters and those pertaining to personal welfare. This distinction is retained in the 2000 Act. For a more detailed examination of this area see Crichton (2005) and Ward (2003).

Table 4.2   Civil compulsory orders under the Mental Health (Care and Treatment) (Scotland) Act 2003

Legal measure	Purpose	Evidence	Psychiatric conditions	Powers	Duration	Renewal	Revocation or variation
Emergency detention s.36 MH(CT)S 2003	Emergency detention	Medical certificate Consent of MHO****	Mentally impaired Hospital needed urgently Risk to self or others	Immediate detention in hospital Emergency treatment	Up to 72 hours	Nil	By AMP**
Short-term detention s.44 MH(CT)S 2003	Emergency and/or short-term detention	Medical certificate from AMP Consent of MHO	Mentally impaired Mental disorder Risk to self or others	Detention in hospital Medical treatment (16***)	Up to 28 days	Apply for CTO ss.47,68	By RMO* or MWC***** or MHT******
Compulsory treatment order (CTO*******) s.57 MH(CT)S 2003	Longer term compulsory treatment	Application to MHT by MHC; measures to specified. 3 medical reports AMP, GP, MHO	Mentally impaired Mental disorder Treatment available Risk to self or others	**Either** detention in hospital and medical treatment (part 16) **Or** medical treatment (part 16) in community at specified address plus outpatient attendance	Up to 6 months and then annual	RMO and MHO or RMO and MHT	By RMO or MWC or MHT
Place of safety order s.297 MH(CT)S 2003	Removal from a public place	Police officer suspects mental disorder and risk		Removal to a place of safety – usually hospital	Up to 24 hours	Nil	Nil
Removal order s. 293 MH(CT)S 2003	Removal from a private residence	Application to sheriff (or JP in emergency) by MHO	Mental disorder 16+ years Risk to self Insufficient care	Removal to a place of safety – usually hospital	Up to 7 days	Nil	Nil
Nurses order s.299 MH(CT)S 2003	Emergency detention of informal patient	Opinion of registered mental nurse	Risk to self or others Medical examination needed	Immediate detention in hospital	Up to 2 hours	Nil	Nil

*RMO, Responsible Medical Officer.

**AMP, Approved Medical Practitioner – this is a doctor with the required qualifications, experience and training who has special experience in the diagnosis and treatment of mental disorder.

***Part 16 medical treatment is defined as treatment for mental disorder and includes nursing; care; psychological intervention; habilitation and rehabilitation including education, training in work, social and independent living skills. Special provisions exist for neurosurgery, ECT, medication and urgent medical treatment.

****MHO, Mental Health Officer.

*****MWC, Mental Welfare Commission.

******MHT, Mental Health Tribunal.

*******CTO, Community Treatment Order.

Principles and definition of incapacity

The following principles must be followed in relation to any intervention in the affairs of an incapable adult: beneficence, minimum intervention, consideration of the present and past wishes of the adult, consultation with relevant others, and encouraging the adult to exercise residual capacity.

Incapable is defined as meaning incapable of acting or making decisions or communicating decisions or understanding decisions or retaining the memory of decisions, as mentioned in any provision of the Act:

by reason of mental disorder or of inability to communicate because of physical disability; a person shall not fall within this definition by reason only of a lack or deficiency in the faculty of communication if that lack or deficiency can be made good by human or mechanical aid (whether of an interpretative nature or otherwise).

There must be an assessment of the effect of any condition on decision-making ability. A functional approach to this assessment, based on that set out in *Re C*, is suggested in the Code of Practice.

Supervising bodies

The 2000 Act established the Office of the Public Guardian whose functions include monitoring, supervising and recording areas of the Act relating to property and financial matters. The Mental Welfare Commission for Scotland's protective functions incorporate all adults with incapacity subject to an intervention or guardianship order relating to personal welfare. The Commission has a statutory duty to provide advice to individuals authorized to make welfare decisions for incapable adults.

Powers of attorney

A person may anticipate becoming incapable by granting a power of attorney over financial affairs or a welfare attorney with authority over personal welfare decisions, commencing on the grantor's incapacity. The powers of the attorney may be revoked by order of the Sheriff or end automatically with the appointment of a financial or welfare guardian. If the adult recovers capacity they may revoke the power of attorney.

Management of funds

Individuals may obtain authority to access funds to meet an incapable adult's living expenses. The office of the Public Guardian has the authority to allow the intromission of funds for a period of 3 years. Part 4 of the 2000 Act allows for the management of residents' funds in nursing homes and for patients in hospital. Health Boards (for NHS hospitals) and the Care Commission (which regulates care services for nursing homes and independent hospitals) supervise this part of the Act.

Medical treatment

Section 47 of the 2000 Act grants a medical practitioner a general authority to treat, where an adult is incapable in relation to a decision about medical treatment. Medical treatment is defined broadly as 'any procedure or treatment designed to safeguard or promote physical or mental health'. Certificates issued under section 47 are valid for 1 year and are renewable. The general authority to treat does not apply when there is a proxy authorized under the Act to make welfare decisions. In such circumstances the doctor must seek consent from the proxy if this would be reasonable and practicable. If the proxy and the medical practitioner disagree then the Mental Welfare Commission appoints a nominated medical practitioner with expertise in the relevant specialty. Decisions may be appealed to the Court of Session. The general authority to treat does not apply to treatment for mental disorder where a person is subject to compulsory treatment under the Mental Health (Care and Treatment) (Scotland) Act 2003. Nor does it apply to sterilization (where there is no serious disease of the reproductive organs), surgical implantation of hormones for the purpose of reducing sex drive, drug treatment for the purpose of reducing sex drive, electroconvulsive therapy for mental disorder, abortion or any medical treatment considered likely to lead to sterilization as an unavoidable result. Special safeguards apply to such treatments.

The justification of life-saving treatment under the common law of necessity is preserved. The doctor must be satisfied that treatment was immediately necessary to preserve life or prevent a serious deterioration and that the necessary procedures could not be followed due to the urgency of the situation. Unfortunately there is very little case law to guide the medical practitioner. Legally it appears that necessity is an aspect of coercion, 'the coercion of circumstance' (MacCall Smith and Sheldon, 1997). Necessity appears limited to situations where there is 'an immediate danger of death or great bodily harm'.

The general authority to treat does not extend to the use of force or detention unless immediately necessary (and then only for as long as is necessary) or detention in hospital for treatment of mental disorder against an adult's will. The Act, therefore, identifies that incapable adults who do not show dissent and are admitted to psychiatric hospital should be treated pursuant to part 5 of the Act.

Research

Section 51 of the Act allows research involving incapable adults if such research cannot be carried out with capable adults and is to obtain knowledge of the causes, diagnosis, treatment and care of the adult's incapacity. Such research is conditional on requirements including: it is likely to reveal real and direct benefit to the adult or to others with similar conditions; the adult does not indicate unwillingness to participate; the research entails no, or only a minimal, foreseeable risk to the adult; the research imposes no more than minimal discomfort on the adult; consent has been obtained from any guardian or welfare attorney or, where there is no such proxy, from the adult's nearest relative.

Intervention and guardianship orders

Sheriff courts may grant intervention and guardianship orders. Intervention orders allow for single decisions on either financial or personal welfare matters. Guardianship orders grant powers to a guardian in relation to financial matters, welfare matters or both areas. The guardian's powers are similar to those of an attorney. They are intended to provide a proxy where continuous management of a person's finances or personal welfare is required. For either an intervention or guardianship order two medical reports are required, one of which must be from a psychiatrist. The second will normally be the patient's general practitioner. Where an order is sought in relation to welfare matters, a third report is required by a social worker. In financial cases, a third report should be submitted by a person with sufficient knowledge to report on the appropriateness of the order sought and the suitability of the nominee. Guardians must keep records of how they exercise their powers and have a duty of care to the incapable adult. Financial guardians must keep an inventory of assets and keep the adult's financial affairs under review.

Criminal Procedures for Mentally Disordered Offenders

In Scotland mentally disordered offenders are dealt with under the Criminal Procedure (Scotland) Act 1995, amended by later legislation. In this respect Scottish law differs from that in England and Wales, but the effects are similar.

As in England and Wales a number of procedures are available at various stages of the criminal justice process to allow for the assessment and/or treatment of a mentally disordered offender in hospital or the community. A range of procedures are available after an individual has been convicted which allow for a mental health disposal rather than a penal one. Therefore a mentally disordered offender does not have to be found insane (either acquitted on the ground of insanity or found unfit to plead) to receive a mental health disposal. The range of mental health disposals available following conviction is almost identical to the disposals available following a finding of insanity. A small proportion of mental health disposals result from a finding of insanity. Between 1992 and 2005, of 1319 mentally disordered offenders placed on hospital orders in Scotland only 133 (9%) had been found insane. Nevertheless this is a much greater proportion than in England and Wales, a difference between the two jurisdictions which has been noted for a number of decades (Chiswick, 1978, 1990).

Psychiatric defences

The law relating to psychiatric defences (fitness to plead and criminal responsibility) has been overhauled by the Criminal Justice and Licensing (Scotland) Act 2010, which has yet to be implemented at the time of writing. These changes followed a review by the Scottish Law Commission (2004). The criteria for insanity in bar of trial, insanity at the time of the offence and diminished responsibility were previously set out in case law. Now there are new statutory criteria for 'unfitness for trial', 'criminal responsibility of mentally disordered persons' and diminished responsibility. The term 'insanity' finally has no place in the language of law and mental disorder in Scotland. To give an understanding of the development of the law in this area in Scotland, the following sections will incorporate information on the law prior to the 2010 Act. For a more detailed description of the development of psychiatric defences in Scotland see Darjee (2005a) and Christie (2001).

Unfitness for trial

Insanity in bar of trial was the legal term used for unfitness to plead in Scotland. The use of the term insanity in this context had the unfortunate consequence of causing confusion for both lawyers and psychiatrists in differentiating fitness to plead from insanity at the time of the offence (Chiswick, 1990). The leading case was *Wilson*:

> *a mental alienation of some kind which prevents the accused giving the instruction which a sane man would give for his defence or from following the evidence as a sane man would follow it and instructing his counsel as the case goes, along any point that arises.*

Similar criteria were set out in *Stewart*:

> *The question for [the trial judge] was whether the appellant, by reason of his material handicap, would be unable to instruct his legal representatives as to his defence or to follow what went on at his trial. Without such ability he could not receive a fair trial.*

A requirement of a previous judgment (*Brown*) that the accused be able to tell the truth and remember events accurately was overturned. The test excluded amnesia for the circumstances of the alleged offence in itself (*Russell*), inability to give instruction due to physical defects, such as deaf mutism, was probably excluded.

The new statutory criteria, following the Criminal Justice and Licensing (Scotland) Act 2010, are set out under the newly inserted section 53F in the amended Criminal Procedure (Scotland) Act 1995:

1. A person is unfit for trial if it is established on the balance of probabilities that the person is incapable, by reason of a mental or physical condition, of participating effectively in a trial.
2. In determining whether a person is unfit for trial the court is to have regard to:

a) the ability of the person to –
  i. understand the nature of the charge;
  ii. understand the requirement to tender a plea to the charge and the effect of such a plea;
  iii. understand the purpose of, and follow the course of, the trial;
  iv. understand the evidence that may be given against the person;
  v. instruct and otherwise communicate with the person's legal representative; and
b) any other factor which the court considers relevant.

3. The court is not to find that a person is unfit for trial by reason only of the person being unable to recall whether the event which forms the basis of the charge occurred in the manner described in the charge.

Until 1995 a finding of insanity in bar of trial led to automatic indefinite detention in hospital. Now following such a finding the court holds an examination of facts to determine if the accused did the act charged. Only if the facts are found may the person be given a mental health disposal. There is a range of disposals available depending on clinical needs and the risk posed: a compulsion order, a compulsion order with a restriction order, an interim compulsion order, a guardianship or intervention order, a supervision and treatment order, or discharge with no order. The supervision and treatment order is similar to treatment as a condition of probation, but does not have the backing of criminal sanctions for non-compliance.

Criminal responsibility of mentally disordered persons

Kidd was generally accepted and used as the basis of the insanity defence in Scotland:

... in order to excuse a person from responsibility on the grounds of insanity, there must have been an alienation of reason in relation to the act committed. There must have been some mental defect ... by which his reason was overpowered, and he was thereby rendered incapable of exerting his reason to control his conduct and reactions. If his reason was alienated in relation to the act committed, he was not responsible for the act, even although otherwise he may have been apparently quite rational.

This definition had its origins in Hume's writings from the late eighteenth century:

An absolute alienation of reason ... such a disease as deprives the patient of the knowledge of the true aspect and position of things about him, hinders him from distinguishing friend from foe, and gives him up to the impulse of his own distempered fancy (Hume, 1844).

The Scottish insanity defence therefore had cognitive and volitional prongs, and has a wider scope than the McNaughton Rules. Self-induced intoxication was excluded (*Brennan*).

The new statutory criteria, following the Criminal Justice and Licensing (Scotland) Act 2010, are set out under the newly inserted section 51A in the amended Criminal Procedure (Scotland) Act 1995:

1. A person is not criminally responsible for conduct constituting an offence, and is to be acquitted of the offence, if the person was at the time of the conduct unable by reason of mental disorder to appreciate the nature or wrongfulness of the conduct.
2. But a person does not lack criminal responsibility for such conduct if the mental disorder in question consists only of a personality disorder which is characterized solely or principally by abnormally aggressive or seriously irresponsible conduct.
3. The defence set out in subsection (1) is a special defence.
4. The special defence may be stated only by the person charged with the offence and it is for that person to establish it on the balance of probabilities.
5. In this section, 'conduct' includes acts and omissions.

As mental disorder takes its definition form the Mental Health (Care and Treatment) (Scotland) Act 2003, any mental illness, learning disability or personality disorder (except that defined under subsection (2)) may form the basis for an acquittal, as long as the disorder renders the person unable to appreciate the nature or wrongfulness of their conduct. This newly defined defence, unlike the previous common law one, is purely 'cognitive' and does not appear to have a 'volitional' aspect, although the term 'appreciate' appears to give wider scope than other cognitive terms such as 'know' or 'understand'.

Where a person is acquitted in this way they are subject to the same range of disposals as where a person is found unfit for trial with the facts found (see above).

Automatism

Despite historical cases where automatism was not regarded as a form of insanity, the concept of sane automatism was rejected in *Cunningham* in 1963. However *Ross* and *Sorley* have since established sane automatism as a recognized legal concept in Scotland. The finding of sane automatism is limited to cases where the automatic behaviour is not self-induced and where the factor leading to the automatic behaviour is not due to a 'continuing disorder of the mind or body which might lead to the recurrence of the disturbance of ... mental faculties'. In *Sorley* the conditions required for a defence of sane automatism were set out: first, that the automatic behaviour was caused by an external factor that was not self-induced; second, this factor was not foreseeable; and third, this factor caused a total alienation of reason leading to complete loss of self-control. The current legal position in Scotland is therefore essentially similar to that in England and Wales (see chapter 2).

Diminished responsibility

The British version of diminished responsibility was invented in Scotland (Crichton et al., 2004). In the seventeenth century it first occurred to Sir George Mackenzie (1678) to moderate the punishment of those who were not 'absolutely furious'. In capital cases courts would recommend royal mercy following a murder conviction in such cases. In *Dingwall* in 1867 Lord Deas went a step further in suggesting to the jury that they might bring a verdict of culpable homicide by taking into consideration the mental condition of the accused. Until 2001 the leading case was *Savage* from 1923 and there was a narrow interpretation of diminished responsibility in Scotland compared to the concept exported to England under the Homicide Act 1957. This narrow interpretation was set aside in *Galbraith*, with the Court of Criminal Appeal re-defining diminished responsibility and widening its scope:

> the accused was suffering from an abnormality of mind which substantially impaired the ability of the accused, as compared with a normal person, to determine or control his acts.

'Psychopathic personality disorder' (*Carraher*) and voluntary intoxication (*Brennan*) were excluded from the defence. What 'psychopathic personality disorder' meant in the 1940s is unclear (Darjee and Crichton, 2003).

The new statutory criteria, following the Criminal Justice and Licensing (Scotland) Act 2010, are set out under the newly inserted section 51B in the amended Criminal Procedure (Scotland) Act 1995.

1. A person who would otherwise be convicted of murder is instead to be convicted of culpable homicide on grounds of diminished responsibility if the person's ability to determine or control conduct for which the person would otherwise be convicted of murder was, at the time of the conduct, substantially impaired by reason of abnormality of mind.
2. For the avoidance of doubt, the reference in subsection (1) to abnormality of mind includes mental disorder.
3. The fact that a person was under the influence of alcohol, drugs or any other substance at the time of the conduct in question does not of itself –
   a) constitute abnormality of mind for the purposes of subsection (1), or
   b) prevent such abnormality from being established for those purposes.
4. It is for the person charged with murder to establish, on the balance of probabilities, that the condition set out in subsection (1) is satisfied.
5. In this section, 'conduct' includes acts and omissions.'

All mental disorders, as defined in the Mental Health (Care and Treatment) (Scotland) Act 2003, are included as conditions that may be considered abnormalities of mind, and so personality disorders, including 'psychopathy', may form the basis of a diminished responsibility plea. The crux will be whether such conditions will be seen as substantially impairing a person's ability to determine or control their conduct. Personality disorders have not played any real role in consideration of culpability in murder cases in Scotland. This is about to change.

As in England and Wales diminished responsibility in murder cases avoids the inflexibility of the mandatory life sentence for murder allowing the court to apply a range of penal and mental health disposals. Unlike England and Wales, there is no legally recognized offence of infanticide. In such cases it is usual for the Crown to charge the woman with culpable homicide.

Procedures allowing for diversion to mental health services

Court disposals are set out in the Criminal Procedure (Scotland) Act 1995, as amended by the Mental Health (Care and Treatment) Scotland Act 2003 and the Criminal Justice (Scotland) Act 2003. The disposals available are similar to those set out under sections 35 to 49 of the Mental Health Act 1983 for England and Wales (table 4.3). The criteria for the application of these disposals are similar to those that apply to civil powers (table 4.1). An important difference is that the impaired decision-making ability criterion does not apply to criminal procedure. So whether an individual retains or recovers capacity in relation to making decisions about psychiatric treatment is irrelevant to the application and renewal of these powers.

Many mentally disordered offenders are diverted from prosecution at an early stage. The police have the power to take a mentally disordered person to a place of safety (table 4.2). Where offences are minor and psychiatric care is required then charges are usually dropped and voluntary treatment or compulsory treatment under civil measures arranged. Where a person is prosecuted then they may be remanded in hospital for assessment or treatment, instead of being remanded on bail or in prison, under an assessment order or a treatment order. Most mentally disordered offenders who eventually receive a hospital disposal are initially detained in hospital under one of these orders.

The procedure followed after a person is found insane in bar of trial or insane at the time of an offence is set out above. If a mentally disordered offender is convicted, as happens in most cases, then prior to a final disposal being made remand in hospital under an assessment order or treatment order can occur, particularly where a period of remand in hospital did not occur prior to conviction. In cases where a compulsion order and restriction order is being considered then courts should first impose an interim compulsion order to allow clarification regarding diagnosis, treatment needs and risk assessment.

The compulsion order operates in a very similar way to a compulsory treatment order under civil procedure. Where there is an ongoing risk of serious harm then a restriction

Table 4.3 The Criminal Procedure (Scotland) Act 1995 as amended by the Mental Health (Care and Treatment) (Scotland) Act 2003: Legislation for Mentally Disordered Offenders

Legal measure	Purpose	Evidence	Psychiatric factors	Powers	Duration	Duties	Revocation or variation
Assessment Order s.52 B-J CP(S)A 1995	Assessment in hospital prior to trial or sentencing. From court or prison	Written or oral from one registered doctor	Mental disorder Risk Detention in hospital necessary to determine if treatment order criteria met. Assessment could not be undertaken if patient not in hospital. Bed available in 7 days	Detention in hospital (not treatment). Restricted patient status	28 days (7 day extension)	RMO* court report. Social circumstances report	RMO applies to court
Treatment Order s.52 K-S CP(S)A 1995	Treatment in hospital pretrial and pre-sentencing. From court or prison	Written or oral from two registered doctor (one AMP**)	Mental disorder Treatability Risk Bed available in 7 days. Can be applied for directly or after an assessment order.	Detention in hospital and treatment (part 16***). Restricted patient status	Remand period	RMO court report	RMO applies to court
Pre-sentence Inquiry into Mental of Physical condition s.200 CP(S)A 1995	To assess mental or physical condition	Written or oral from one registered doctor	Convicted of an offence punishable by imprisonment. Needs inquiry into mental or physical condition. If hospital proposed – suffering from a mental disorder – suitable hospital placement available. N.B. Overlap with S52 B-J/K-S	To remand a convicted person in custody in prison or hospital. or on bail for assessment of mental or physical condition	3 weeks (extension for 3 weeks)	Medical/psychiatric report prepared in hospital, community or prison	RMO applies to court
Interim Compulsion Order s.53 CP(S)A 1995	Inpatient assessment	Written or oral from two doctors (1 AMP)	Mental disorder treatability Risk Bed available in 7 days. Likely compulsion and restriction orders or hospital direction. N.B. Not just relevant to State Hospital	Detention and treatment in hospital (part 16)	3–12 months (12 weekly renewal)	RMO report Social Circumstances Report	No procedure/ write to court
Compulsion Order s.57A CP(S)A 1995	Treatment in hospital or community	Written or oral from two doctors (one AMP)	Mental disorder Treatability Risk Hospital – bed available in 7 days. Convicted of an offence punishable by imprisonment	Part 16 treatment, attendance, access, residence requirements	6 months (renewable for 6 months and yearly thereafter)	Care plan	RMO, Mental Welfare Commission, Tribunal
Restriction Order s.59 CP(S)A 1995	Control of high risk patients. Combined with inpatient compulsion order	Oral evidence of one medical practitioner	Serious offence Antecedents of individual Risk of further offences as a result of mental disorder if set at large	Detention in hospital. Leave and transfer – Scottish Ministers	Without limit of time	RMO (annual) report Scottish Ministers duty to review	Tribunal

(Continued)

Table 4.3 (Continued)

Legal measure	Purpose	Evidence	Psychiatric factors	Powers	Duration	Duties	Revocation or variation
Hospital Direction s.59A CP(S)A 1995	Combines hospital detention and prison sentence	Oral or written from two doctors (one AMP). Doctors can recommend a hospital direction	As compulsion order. Link between mental disorder, offence +/– risk is weak	Detention in hospital. Leave and transfer – Scottish Ministers	Length of prison sentence/ Compulsory treatment order can follow	RMO (annual) reports. Scottish Ministers duty to review	Scottish Ministers and Tribunal Earliest date of liberation Parole
Probation Order s.230 CP(S)A 1995	Medical or psychological treatments of a mental condition	Oral or written by one doctor or a chartered psychologist	Mental disorder – needs treatment compulsory treatment order or compulsion order not required patient and criminal justice social worker agree	Attendance for specified treatment	6 months to 3 years	Liaison with CJSW. Social Enquiry Report	Agreement of supervising officer. Inform court. Non-compliance: notification to court
Intervention and Guardianship Orders s.60B CP(S)A 1995 s.58(1A) CP(S)A 1995	Personal welfare decisions or management (not financial)	Two medical reports (one AMP), MHO**** or Chief Social Work Officer report	Found insane/offence punishable by imprisonment Mental disorder Compulsion order not required Personal welfare issues	Intervention Order authorises single decisions. Guardianship Order provides continuous management	One decision 3 years to indefinite	Guardian must keep record of decisions	Guardian Sheriff
Urgent Detention of an Acquitted Person s.134 MH(C&T)(S)A 2003/s.60C CP(S)A 1995	For medical assessment re emergency or for medical assessment	Two medical recommendations for mental health disposal	Mental disorder Treatability Risk Not convicted Not practicable to secure immediate examination	Detention in a place of safety	6 hours	Medical examination	
Transfer for Treatment Direction (TTD) s.136 MH(C&T)(S)A 2003	Treatment in hospital of sentenced prisoners	Two medical reports (one AMP) to Scottish Ministers	Mental disorder Treatability Risk TTD necessary Bed available in 7 days	To transfer and treat in hospital, via a place of safety if necessary. Restricted patient status	Length of prison sentence	RMO (annual report)	Scottish Ministers or Tribunal Earliest date of liberation Parole

*RMO, Responsible Medical Officer.
**AMP, Approved Medical Practitioner – this is a doctor with the required qualifications, experience and training who has special experience in the diagnosis and treatment of mental disorder.
***Part 16 medical treatment is defined as treatment for mental disorder and includes nursing; care; psychological intervention; habilitation and rehabilitation including education, training in work, social and independent living skills. Special provisions exist for neurosurgery, ECT, medication and urgent medical treatment.
****MHO, Mental Health Officer.
CJSW, Criminal Justice Social Worker (equivalent of probation officer in other jurisdictions).

order may be added to a compulsion order. A restriction order has no time limit and operates in a similar manner to the hospital order with restriction order in England and Wales. Scottish ministers have to give permission for such patients to leave hospital or to be transferred between hospitals. Only a branch of the Mental Health Tribunal chaired by a sheriff (a 'shrieval panel') can grant absolute or conditional discharge. Conditionally discharged patients are subject to ongoing scrutiny by Scottish ministers, who may order recall to hospital if conditions are breached or there is an escalation in the risk posed. Guidance on the management of restricted patients is issued by the Scottish Executive (2005b). Where a restricted patient continues to have a mental disorder and there appears to be a risk of serious harm to others all other issues are irrelevant in considering continued detention; the person must remain detained in hospital. This measure was introduced under the Mental Health (Public Safety and Appeals) (Scotland) Act 1999 following the *Ruddle* case, a homicide offender who gained his absolute discharge from the State Hospital on appeal. It remains in place under the 2003 Act and has not been found to breach the European Convention on Human Rights (Darjee and Crichton, 2005). All restricted patients must be managed using a robust case management system (the care programme approach; CPA) and are subject to review under multi-agency public protection arrangements (MAPPA) where issues of risk to the public in the community arise (see below).

The hospital direction allows a court to impose a prison sentence and direct a person to hospital for treatment. This hybrid order applies to all categories of mental disorder. It can only be used where cases are prosecuted on indictment and, unlike any other psychiatric disposal, can be imposed along with a life sentence where there is a conviction for murder. It is used rarely but is seen as a useful disposal where serious offences have been committed, but either treatment may not adequately address the risk of further serious offending or there is little relationship between the index offence and mental disorder (Darjee et al., 2000, 2002).

If a sentenced prisoner requires treatment in hospital then transfer can be arranged under a transfer for treatment direction. All patients detained under this direction are treated as restricted patients. If a patient remains in hospital when their prison sentence ends then they may be detained under civil measures if they meet the legal criteria.

For a more detailed description of legislation for mentally disordered offenders see Darjee (2005b).

Sex offender legislation

The Cosgrove Committee (Scottish Executive, 2001b) reviewed the management of sex offenders in Scotland and has set the framework for the management of sex offenders in the community in Scotland. The Sex Offenders Act 1997 introduced mandatory notification arrangements for sex offenders in the UK, including Scotland. This has been superseded by the Sexual Offences Act 2003. The notification requirements for sex offenders in Scotland are very similar to those in England. Depending on the sentence imposed, when a convicted sex offender is placed in the community, there will be a period of time when that individual must make personal details, including where they live, known to the police. These notification requirements apply to mentally disordered sex offenders who receive a mental health disposal.

There is no publicly available register, although the small number of high risk offenders who fail to register as required may be named publicly. There is a range of civil orders that may be imposed on sex offenders to place restrictions on them in the community. These are very similar to orders available in England: Sexual Offences Prevention Order, Foreign Travel Order and Risk of Sexual Harm Order. A breach of one of these civil orders may lead to criminal sanctions including imprisonment.

Sentencing of 'dangerous' offenders: The order for lifelong restriction (OLR)

In Scotland, as in several other jurisdictions, there has been concern about serious offenders who are considered to pose a continuing risk. The MacLean Committee (Scottish Executive, 2000) reviewed this area and its recommendations were enacted under part 1 of the Criminal Justice (Scotland) Act 2003, amending the Criminal Procedure (Scotland) Act 1995 Act. This introduced provisions for the assessment and sentencing of high-risk offenders.

If a person is convicted of a sexual offence, a violent offence, an offence which endangers life, or an offence the nature or circumstances of which indicate a propensity to commit such offences, and it appears that the 'risk criteria' (see below) may be met, then the court may make a risk assessment order remanding the person in prison for a risk assessment report to be prepared. If the offender meets criteria for detention under mental health legislation, then the court may instead make an interim compulsion order (see above) during which a risk assessment report must be prepared. The risk assessment report, whether the person is assessed in prison or hospital, must be submitted by an individual accredited by the Risk Management Authority, and the assessment must follow the guidance issued by the Risk Management Authority. The purpose of the preparation of the risk assessment report is to assist the court in determining whether the 'risk criteria' (under section 210E Criminal Procedure (Scotland) Act 1995 as amended by the Criminal Justice (Scotland) Act 2003) are met:

... the nature of, or the circumstances of the commission of, the offence of which the convicted person has been found guilty either in themselves or as part of a pattern of behaviour are such as to demonstrate that there is a likelihood that he, if at liberty, will seriously endanger the

lives, or physical or psychological well-being, of members of the public at large.

If the court is satisfied that these criteria are met, then the court will make an order for lifelong restriction, which is an indeterminate prison sentence. If the court is satisfied regarding the section 210E criteria in the case of a convicted offender who suffers from mental disorder, then the disposal will be either a compulsion order with a restriction order or a hospital direction with an order for lifelong restriction. Where an order for lifelong restriction is imposed a tariff is set, and after this period of imprisonment has been served release will depend on the assessed risk to public safety and the manageability of that risk, as determined by the Parole Board who will impose licence conditions if the offender is released. Non-compliance with licence conditions or concerns about an escalation in the risk posed may lead to recall to custody.

In the 4 years since the introduction of this procedure in June 2006, over 60 offenders were placed on risk assessment orders, 46 of whom had had an order for lifelong restriction imposed by June 2010. In these cases tariffs have ranged from 1 to 20 years. Many cases have been sexual offenders and fewer have been violent offenders. The number of orders for lifelong restrictions imposed in Scotland is in marked contrast to the greater use of the equivalent sentence in England and Wales (the imprisonment for public protection sentence – see chapter 2) which has been applied in over 7,000 cases in its first 5 years. In England and Wales there is no standardized assessment process in such cases and sentencing guidelines for judges are rigid.

To become an accredited risk assessor an individual must meet a number of criteria in the following areas: standing and character; qualifications and experience; and commitment to maintaining and improving professional standards. S/he must also demonstrate competence in the following: knowledge and understanding, evidence collection and analysis, report formulation and presentation, communication and liaison, planning and organization. S/he must submit examples of risk assessments conducted to demonstrate his or her competence. Assessors are subject to re-accreditation after a year and then 3-yearly. At the time of writing (June 2010) there were 15 accredited assessors in Scotland, two psychiatrists and 13 psychologists.

The risk assessment involves a prolonged and thorough assessment which takes a minimum of 3 months. Standards and guidance from the Risk Management Authority set out the process to be followed and the format of the report to be submitted. The assessment is a structured clinical formulation based assessment informed by, but not dominated by, the use of appropriate assessment instruments. The Risk Management Authority has reviewed and approved a range of risk assessment instruments for this purpose, but

none are prescribed. There must be a minimum of 6 hours over three interviews spent with the offender, a thorough review of all relevant documents and consideration of information from all agencies that have been involved (e.g. police, prison, courts, social work and health service). The law requires that the assessor states whether the offender poses a low, medium or high risk of serious physical and/ or psychological harm. Guidance defines these in terms of a number of domains including factors indicating risk of serious harm, protective factors, contextual factors and manageability of risk.

The offender may commission their own risk assessment. This does not have to be carried out by an accredited assessor, but should follow the same process and structure, and the defence assessor should have access to the same information as the court appointed assessor. If the defence decides to challenge the court appointed assessor's report then oral evidence may be heard, and the defence and prosecution may both lead witnesses of relevance to the risk assessment.

If an offender is made the subject of an order for lifelong restriction, then a risk management plan, in accordance with Risk Management Authority guidance must be prepared by the agency managing the offender (in most cases the prison service) within 9 months. This must be reviewed annually and has to be approved by the Risk Management Authority.

It should be noted that this is a health oriented approach to public protection and contrasts sharply with the statutory/judicial approach being used in England and Wales (see chapter 2).

Multi-agency public protection arrangements

Multi-agency public protection arrangements (MAPPA) were introduced in Scotland in April 2007 for all sex offenders subject to statutory supervision. These arrangements will be extended later to cover violent offenders under statutory supervision and other offenders causing concern in the community. All restricted patients, whether sexual or violent offenders, have been subject to multi-agency public protection arrangements since April 2008. The statutory basis for multi-agency public protection arrangements is the Management of Offenders etc. (Scotland) Act 2005. The arrangements operate in a very similar way to similar arrangements that have been in place in England for longer. There are three MAPPA levels depending on the current assessment of the risk of serious harm posed by the offender and the complexity of risk management. The cases posing greater concern are reviewed regularly to ensure that there is robust multi-agency risk management.

The health service has a duty to co-operate with these arrangements and this may involve sharing information with other agencies where appropriate. The main agencies involved in managing MAPPA cases in Scotland are the police and criminal justice social workers. But for patients on restriction orders mental health services have a lead role within MAPPA, and unlike England and Wales the health service is a statutory 'responsible authority' in such cases. These patients must be managed using the care programme approach, which until 2008 was not mandatory in Scotland. MAPPA provides oversight of the management of risk in these cases.

The health service has several roles to play in multi-agency public protection arrangements: sharing of relevant information with other agencies, within the framework of laws and professional codes on patient confidentiality, to help with the assessment and management of risk; ensuring that where there is a risk to patients or staff in health settings appropriate measures are taken; working with other agencies to manage the risk posed by mentally disordered offenders; providing clinical input to help with the assessment and management of violent and sexual offenders with disorders that may not lead to diversion to mental healthcare settings, such as personality disorders and paraphilias. It is crucial that the NHS engages in multi-agency public protection arrangements and that there are appropriate managerial and clinical links with the other agencies involved in the arrangements.

Comment

During the eight long years in which the Westminster Parliament struggled with the new mental health act for England and Wales, the Scottish Parliament raced ahead with its legislation. Many in England and Wales were envious and believed that the Scots have produced much better legislation mainly because the Scottish legislation purported to include important principles from the Millan committee which preceded it whereas the proposed legislation for England and Wales rejected the principles set out in the Richardson Committee. One of us wrote a critique of the new Scottish legislation under the heading 'A Step Forward or a Step into the Dark?' (Thomson, 2005b,c) pointing out that there was concern that some of the principles, especially on reciprocity, spelt out in the Millan Report were diluted. The bureaucratic emphasis wrought by the new law has already been mentioned and it has tortuous language in places. The concern is that the new Tribunal may set social worker again psychiatrist and it is to be regretted that the World Health Organization principle that people have the right to be free from illness has been omitted.

However the new legislation has been well received, in particular its underlying principles. Since the 2003 Act came into force, fewer people have been given compulsory treatment than under the previous 1984 Act. The Mental Welfare Commission thinks this is because of tighter grounds for compulsion and because the procedure for admission is more demanding and needs greater expertise. More expert assessment should mean that compulsory

treatment is applied only when absolutely necessary. Inevitably, legal and bureaucratic challenges have arisen. Initially the Mental Health Tribunal for Scotland took a very adversarial and legalistic line in its proceedings but later there was a move towards pragmatism and understanding of clinical issues whilst considering the legal tests. Some parts of the new Act have been revolutionary, for example appeals against excessive security have contributed greatly to the redesign of the forensic estate in Scotland.

NORTHERN IRELAND

Mental Health Legislation

At the time of writing the mental health legislation in Northern Ireland is the Mental Health (Northern Ireland) Order 1986 ('The Order'). The Order is a wide-ranging piece of legislation that is similar in many respects to the Mental Health Act 1983 of England and Wales and the Mental Health Act 1984 of Scotland. For further details, the reader is referred to the Order itself at http://www.legislation.gov.uk/nisi/1986/595 and to the accompanying Guide and the Code of Practice which were published by the Department of Health and Social Services (Northern Ireland) (as it then was). The Order has been amended over the years, for example to take account of changes in the structure of the health and social services, and new provisions have been introduced by the Criminal Justice (Northern Ireland) Order 1996 in relation to insanity and unfitness to be tried. Account should also be taken of guidance that was published in 2010 by the Department of Health, Social Services and Public Safety (DHSSPS) on risk assessment and management in mental health and learning disability services.

Part I of the Order defines mental disorder, mental illness, mental handicap, severe mental handicap and severe mental impairment. It is the first piece of legislation in the United Kingdom to define mental illness:

A state of mind which affects a person's thinking, perceiving, emotion or judgment to the extent that he requires care or medical treatment in his own interests or the interests of other persons.

The Order defines severe mental handicap as:

A state of arrested or incomplete development of mind which includes severe impairment of intelligence and social functioning.

Severe mental impairment is defined as:

A state of arrested or incomplete development of mind which includes severe impairment of intelligence and social functioning and is associated with abnormally aggressive or seriously irresponsible conduct on the part of the person concerned.

Patients detained in hospital for treatment must suffer from mental illness or severe mental impairment and patients received into guardianship must suffer from mental illness or severe mental handicap.

The Order provides no definition of psychopathic disorder and indeed article 3(2) states: *No person shall be treated under this Order as suffering from mental disorder, or from any form of mental disorder by reason only of personality disorder...* However individuals who suffer from personality disorder in addition to either mental illness or severe mental impairment may be detained for treatment provided all the necessary criteria are fulfilled.

Article 4(2) of the Order states that:

An application for assessment may be made in respect of a patient on the grounds that:

a) *he is suffering from mental disorder of a nature or degree which warrants his detention in a hospital for assessment (or for assessment followed by medical treatment); and*

b) *failure to so detain him would create a substantial likelihood of serious physical harm to himself or to other persons.*

To fulfil this latter criterion at article 4(2) (b) there must be evidence:

that the patient has inflicted, or threatened or attempted to inflict serious physical harm to himself; or that the patient's judgment is so affected that he is, or would soon be, unable to protect himself against serious physical harm and that reasonable provision for this protection is not available in the community, or that the patient has behaved violently towards other persons or that the patient has so behaved himself that other persons were placed in reasonable fear of serious physical harm to themselves.

The Order contains unified procedures for admission to hospital for assessment, rather than having separate procedures for admission for assessment in cases of emergency as are contained in section 4 of the Mental Health Act 1983 of England and Wales. The medical recommendation for admission to hospital is made by the patient's general practitioner or another registered medical practitioner and supported by an application for admission which is completed either by the nearest relative or an approved social worker. The patient is initially detained in hospital for a period of up to 7 days. S/he must be seen within the first 48 hours of admission by the responsible medical officer or another doctor approved under part II of the Order (in practice, a consultant psychiatrist), and by the same doctor or a doctor of similar standing before admission for assessment can be extended for a further period of up to 7 days. Article 10 of the Order allows this initial period of admission for assessment to be disregarded for many purposes, for example when giving information about the patient's health to an employer.

If, approaching the end of 14 days' admission for assessment, the patient satisfies the criteria for further detention, s/he can be detained for treatment for a period of up to 6 months in the first instance with further extensions potentially available thereafter. Throughout the processes of admission for assessment and detention for treatment, there is a range of safeguards for patients. The Order contains provisions on consent to treatment that are similar to those in the Mental Health Act 1983 of England and Wales. The Order also contains provisions for a Mental Health Review Tribunal. The functions of the previous Mental Health Commission have been transferred to the Regulation and Quality Improvement Authority (RQIA).

For patients concerned in criminal proceedings or under sentence, the Order provides a range of remands to hospital, hospital and guardianship orders and restriction orders that are similar to those contained in the Mental Health Act (1983) of England and Wales. There is currently no provision in Northern Ireland that combines a hospital order with a sentence of imprisonment. There are a few differences in procedure between the Order and the 1983 Act, for example in Northern Ireland before a court order is made the approved psychiatrist must give *oral* evidence to the court, and the relevant Trust must be given an opportunity to make representation to the court.

The care programme approach used in other parts of the United Kingdom does not apply to Northern Ireland. Guidance has been issued by the Department of Health Social Services and Public Safety (2010) on risk assessment and management in mental health and learning disability services. This provides risk assessment and management tools, sets standards for audit and promotes learning from adverse incidents.

Psychiatric Defences in Northern Ireland

The Criminal Justice Act (Northern Ireland) 1966 defines the psychiatric defence of insanity and states that a defendant who is found to have been at the time of the alleged offence 'an insane person within the meaning of the Act' shall not be convicted. 'Insane person' means a person who suffers from mental abnormality which prevents him or her

from appreciating what he is doing; or from appreciating that what he is doing is either wrong or contrary to law; or from controlling his own conduct.'

'Mental abnormality' is defined as

an abnormality of mind which arises from a condition of arrested or retarded development of mind or any inherent causes or is induced by disease or injury.

The use of the word 'prevent' would appear to indicate a high threshold for the defence of insanity.

Article 50 of the Mental Health Order contains procedures in relation to the finding of insanity and the powers available to the court to make a hospital order together with a restriction order. This article has been amended by Articles 50 and 51 of the Criminal Justice (Northern Ireland) Order 1996 which specify details of the medical evidence required by the court and broaden the range of powers available to the court to include a hospital order, a guardianship order, a supervision and treatment order and an order for absolute discharge.

The Mental Health Order and the Criminal Justice Order also contain provisions in relation to defendants who are found unfit to be tried and article 51 of the Criminal Justice Order introduces the same powers as are available to the court where persons are found not guilty by reason of insanity.

In cases of homicide the Criminal Justice (NI) Act 1966 defines the defence of 'impaired mental responsibility':

Where a party charged with murder has killed or was party to the killing of another, and it appears to the jury that he was suffering from mental abnormality which substantially impaired his mental responsibility for his acts and omissions in doing or being a party to the killing, the jury shall find him not guilty of murder but shall find him guilty (whether as principal or accessory) of manslaughter.

Infanticide

The Infanticide Act (Northern Ireland) 1939 defines the offence of infanticide in an identical manner to the Infanticide Act 1938 of England and Wales.

Future Directions for Mental Health Legislation in Northern Ireland

The Bamford Review of Mental Health and Learning Disability was established in 2002 to carry out an independent review of the effectiveness of current policy and service provision and of the Mental Health Order. The Review conducted its work through 10 expert working committees, including a Forensic Services Committee and a Legal Issues Committee and it concluded its work in 2007. It recommended a single, comprehensive legislative framework that encompassed the reform of mental health legislation and the introduction of capacity legislation in Northern Ireland to be founded upon explicit principles. It further recommended that persons who are subject to the criminal justice system should have access to assessment, treatment and care which is equivalent to that available to all other people. Legislation must provide appropriate public and individual protection to the community against persons whose decision-making capacity is impaired and who present a risk to others. On the other hand, legislation must not discriminate unjustifiably against persons who suffer from a mental health problem or learning disability. Further

information about the Review, including the reports of the committees and subcommittees, is available at http://www.dhsspsni.gov.uk/bamford_consultation_document.pdf.

MILITARY LAW IN THE UNITED KINGDOM

The disciplinary powers of the armed services are contained in a distinct legal code known as military law. All servicemen, members of their families, and civilians employed by the forces outside of the United Kingdom are subject to military law.

Military law reflects civilian UK law as much as possible but it enforces higher standards of behaviour, which are distinctive to the armed forces, such as obeying lawful commands to ensure operational efficiency. Military law also enables personnel deployed overseas to be dealt with in a language they understand and by a system, which is now fully compliant with the European Convention on Human Rights.

The Royal Navy, the Army and the Royal Air Force have operated for many years within separate statutory frameworks of discipline. The respective bases for these systems are the Army Act 1955, the Air Force Act 1955 and the Naval Discipline Act 1957. Collectively they are known as the Service Discipline Acts (SDAs). The Service Discipline Acts are concerned largely, but not exclusively, with discipline. Since 1955 the Army and Air Force Acts (and, since 1971, the Naval Discipline Act) have been subject to renewal by primary legislation every 5 years. This requirement for Parliamentary agreement for their continuation has its origins in the Bill of Rights 1688, which provides that the raising of a standing army is against the law unless Parliament consents to it. Since the 1950s the 5-yearly Bills have been used primarily to make necessary and desirable amendments to the Service Discipline Acts, often to reflect changes in the civilian criminal law of England and Wales.

The main purpose of the Armed Forces Act 2006 is to replace the three separate systems of service law with a single, harmonized system governing all members of the armed forces. This has become necessary because the three services are increasingly working together on joint overseas operations.

Most contraventions of civil law by service personnel may be dealt with by the military authorities under military law and there are, in addition, a range of particular offences which are peculiar to military law. In the United Kingdom, the offences which affect the person or property of a civilian are normally dealt with by a civil court, but offences which involve only service personnel or property are normally dealt with by the military authorities. The offences of murder, manslaughter, treason-felony, rape or war crimes may not be dealt with under military law in the United Kingdom. In the majority of overseas countries, where British forces are based, the jurisdiction of these civil powers are waived in favour of the military authorities in keeping with standing agreements or treaties. Offences of a minor nature committed by junior ranking servicemen may be dealt with by commanding officers who have limited powers of summary jurisdiction. More serious cases will be tried by court martial and, in some instances, a judge advocate general will sit with the court to advise on legal matters. The same rules of evidence apply as in the criminal courts of England.

Punishment is considered to be one of the means available for the maintenance of discipline. In awarding a sentence, courts martial will always take into account the level of sentence a particular offence might have attracted in a civilian court. The award of a custodial sentence, which would be undertaken in a civil prison, necessarily entails dismissal from the service. Detention, on the other hand, is intended to provide a means of reform in rehabilitating an offender prior to returning to military service and is carried out in the Military Corrective Training Centre.

The findings and sentences of courts martial are no longer subject to reviews by higher military authorities. The court martial is now a compliant court within the meaning of the European Convention of Human Rights and those convicted have a right of appeal to the Courts Martial Appeal Court which is composed of judges of the civil Court of Appeal.

Until recently the death penalty was still available for five military wartime offences: serious misconduct in action; communicating with the enemy; aiding the enemy or furnishing supplies; obstructing operations; or giving false air signals and mutiny. The last execution under military law was in 1942. With the passage of the Human Rights Act in November 1998, the United Kingdom introduced an amendment that removed the death penalty as a possible punishment for military offences under the Armed Forces Acts.

Prior to May 1987 service personnel were prevented from pursuing claims for compensation from the Ministry of Defence by section 10 of the Crown Proceedings Act 1947. Section 10 was repealed by the Crown Proceedings (Armed Forces) Act 1987. Since the change in the law, which was not made retrospective, service personnel who suffer loss or injury as a result of negligence by the Ministry of Defence have been entitled to make common law claims for compensation. The landmark judgment *Multiple Claimants* sets out the parameters for future claims for negligence against the Ministry of Defence in cases of psychiatric injury.

The Ministry of Defence has not been able to avoid the issues relating to the application of civilian social, employment and health and safety legislation to service personnel. Issues that have been addressed include the minimum wage, pregnancy, parental rights, bullying,

harassment and discrimination on the grounds of age, race, gender and sexual orientation. Until 1999 homosexual acts were still an offence under military law. In September 1999 the European Court of Human Rights in Strasbourg delivered its judgments in the cases brought by four ex-service personnel who had been discharged because of their homosexuality. The Court found that in each case there had been a violation of the right to respect for private and family life accorded by Article 8 of the European Convention of Human Rights. In response to this judgment, in January 2000, a Code of Social Conduct was introduced by the Ministry of Defence across all three services. The Code has established a framework governing the attitude and approach to personal relationships of members of the Armed Forces, regardless of rank, sex, or sexual orientation, and set out the principles according to which the acceptability of individuals' social conduct should be judged.

Mental Health Legislation

The last remaining armed services hospital in the UK, with an inpatient mental health unit, closed in 2003. Since 2003, inpatient mental health services for most service personnel in the UK and overseas have been subcontracted to the NHS and independent sector.

Limited powers to detain and treat patients in overseas service hospitals are provided in the Armed Forces Act 1981, section 13. These powers are enacted by the signing of a 'detention in hospital order' by an authorized officer, usually the individual's commanding officer, on the recommendation of one registered medical practitioner for a 5-day order, or of two registered medical practitioners, one of whom must have special experience in psychiatry, for a 28-day order. No longer form of treatment order is available under military law, but the available powers do provide for the removal of a patient to the UK, if this should be considered necessary, with provision that, on return to the UK, such a detained patient must become an informal patient within 24 hours, or be detained in a NHS hospital under UK mental health legislation.

The Armed Forces Act 1981, section 14, also provides for the temporary removal to a place of safety of children of persons subject to military law overseas who are considered to be at risk. The Armed Forces Act 1986 set up the formal legal framework for the transfer of a child back to care in the UK when this was the recommendation of an executive case conference.

Psychiatric Advice in the Armed Services

The three services retain a number of multidisciplinary, community, psychiatric teams based at operational military units across the UK and overseas. These comprise a mixture of uniformed and civilian psychiatrists, psychologists, community psychiatric nurses and social workers. Uniformed psychiatrists and community psychiatric nurses are deployed on overseas military operations. The armed services also have honorary civilian consultant advisers in psychiatry. The Kings Centre for Military Health Research, at Kings College London, launched in 2004, collaborates with the Ministry of Defence to research mental health in the armed forces.

There are regulations, which outline a procedure whereby commanding officers, in consultation with the unit medical officer, may arrange for an accused to be examined by a service psychiatrist. The only situation in which psychiatric examination is mandatory is that of a serviceman remanded for trial by court martial overseas on a charge of murder, although reports are frequently requested in other situations. The service psychiatrist acts in an impartial way, providing a forensic opinion available to both prosecution and defence.

ISLE OF MAN

The Isle of Man (also known as Mann) is a self-governing British Crown dependency, located in the Irish Sea. The head of state is Queen Elizabeth II, who holds the title of Lord of Mann. The Lord of Mann is represented by a lieutenant governor. The island's foreign relations and defence are the responsibility of the UK Government.

Isle of Man mental health law is based on English mental health law. The Mental Health Law 1998 has been amended by further acts in 2002 and 2006. In 2010 mental health services were incorporated in a new Department of Social Care which is separate from the Department of Health.

CHANNEL ISLANDS

Guernsey and Jersey

The Channel Islands fall into two separate self-governing bailiwicks of Guernsey and Jersey. Both are British crown dependencies, but neither is part of the United Kingdom. They have been part of the Duchy of Normandy since the tenth century and Queen Elizabeth II is often referred to by her title of 'Duke of Normandy'. The Channel Islands are not represented in the United Kingdom Parliament and each island has its own primary legislature, known as the States of Guernsey and the States of Jersey, with Chief Pleas in Sark and the States of Alderney. Laws passed by the States are given Royal Sanction by the Queen in Council, to which the islands' governments are responsible. The Ministry of Justice provides the main channel of communication between the UK government and the three crown dependencies.

A bailiwick is a territory administered by a bailiff. The bailiff in each bailiwick is the civil head,

presiding officer of the States, and also head of the judiciary. The Bailiff is President of the States, in which role s/he determines procedure, and acts very much as does the Speaker of Parliament in the United Kingdom. In the event of the Bailiff's absence, there is a Deputy Bailiff who acts as President of the States. The bailiwicks have been administered separately from each other since the late thirteenth century. The two bailiwicks of Guernsey and Jersey have no common laws, no common elections, and no common representative body. The legal courts are separate and separate courts of appeal have been in place since 1961. Both appeal courts, staffed by QCs or retired judges from the UK, sit several times each year and hear appeals from their respective Royal Courts in both civil and criminal matters; final appeals go to the Judicial Committee of the Privy Council which bases its decisions on the laws of the relevant bailiwick.

Guernsey and Jersey have no laws in common and each has a different test for unfitness to plead and a different defence of insanity. Here, by way of illustration, is a brief discussion of the tests for unfitness to plead and insanity and the outlines of Jersey mental health law.

Unfitness to plead and insanity

Before 2000, neither unfitness to plead nor the defence of insanity had been litigated in Jersey. The latter was the first to be the subject of judicial scrutiny in *Prior*. In that case, the Bailiff Sir Philip Bailhache, ruled that the McNaughton Rules did not form part of the law of Jersey.[1] Instead the judge adopted a new test stating:

I should therefore adopt a definition of 'insanity' which is consistent with the evidence given to the Royal Commissioners in 1846, compliant with Convention rights under the Human Rights (Jersey) Law 2000, and appropriate to the state of medical knowledge in the twenty-first century. Counsel for the defence laid out a number of options for me in the course of her submissions. I prefer, and I respectfully adopt, a definition suggested by Professor R.D. Mackay. I therefore hold that a person is insane within the meaning of Article 2 of the Criminal Justice (Insane Persons (Jersey), Law 1964 if, at the time of the commission of the offence, his unsoundness of mind affected his criminal behaviour to such a substantial degree that the jury consider that he ought not to be found criminally responsible (paras 30–31).

In *Simao* at para. 23 the Jersey Court of Appeal stated that the *Prior* test remained '*the appropriate test for insanity in Jersey*'. However, this is not the case in Guernsey, where in

---

[1] See R. Mackay 'The Insanity Defence – Recent Developments in Jersey and Guernsey' [2003] Jersey and Guernsey Law Review 185–195; R.D. Mackay and C.A Gearty 'On Being Insane in Jersey – the case of *A-G v Jason Prior*' [2001] Criminal Law Review 560.

the case of *Derek Lee Harvey* (3 August 2001 unreported) the Bailiff of Guernsey ruled that the McNaughton Rules continued to apply in that jurisdiction.

As far as unfitness to plead is concerned, once again the Bailiff of Jersey made new law. He did so in the case of *O'Driscoll*. As he had done in *Prior* he ruled that the test for unfitness to plead laid down in England, namely that in *Pritchard*, should not be adopted but instead a new test should be formulated which would be (a) consonant with the idea of effective participation in the criminal process found in the European Convention on Human Rights; (b) conscious of the developments in medical science since the English test was adopted; and (c) appropriate to the social needs of Jersey. This new test is as follows:

> *An accused person is so insane as to be unfit to plead to the accusation, or unable to understand the nature of the trial if, as a result of unsoundness of mind or inability to communicate, he or she lacks the capacity to participate effectively in the proceedings.*

In determining this issue, the [Court] shall have regard to the ability of the accused:

a. to understand the nature of the proceedings so as to instruct his lawyer and to make a proper defence;
b. to understand the substance of the evidence;
c. to give evidence on his own behalf; and
d. to make rational decisions in relation to his participation in the proceedings (including whether or not to plead guilty), which reflect true and informed choices on his part (para. 29).

Paragraph (d) above departs from the narrow approach in *Pritchard* and introduces, as was advocated by Mackay in *O'Driscoll* (at para. 25), the notion of 'decisional competence'.[2] With regard to Guernsey, it seems likely that the Pritchard test applies in that jurisdiction.

Jersey Mental Health Law

Mental Health Law is described at http://www.jerseylaw.je/ law/display.aspx?url=lawsinforce%5Chtm%5CLawFiles%5C 2004%2FL-08-2004.html.

Under the Mental Health (Jersey) Law 1969 there are three Articles providing for the detention of a patient:

Article 10 – Under which a person can be detained for up to 72 hours.
Article 6 – For up to 28 days.
Article 7 – For up to 1 year.

The consultant decides as to when a person should be discharged. If a person absconds, the police will be called to have them returned to hospital.

---

[2] See R.D. Mackay 'On Being Insane in Jersey Part Three – the case of *Attorney General v. Neil Liam O'Driscoll*' [2003] Criminal Law Review 291.

A person can be discharged prior to expiration of their detention order; again the consultant's decision.

The person detained under Article 7 has a right of appeal to the Mental Health Review Tribunal. The burden of proof rests with the Health and Social Services Department who will attempt to convince the tribunal that a patient must continue to be detained.

REPUBLIC OF IRELAND

Recent Developments in Irish Mental Health Law

The evolution of mental health law in Ireland (the Republic of Ireland) has diverged from its roots which were in UK law until the early twentieth century. Irish legislation is now derived from the written constitution, Irish case law and case law from the European Court of Human Rights. Despite this divergence from the UK, the rulings of the Strasbourg court provide a continuing force for convergence between the European jurisdictions. The consolidated case law of the European Court of Human Rights in Strasbourg (Council of Europe, Committee of Ministers (1983) and (2004), is evident in the language of recent mental health acts in all the jurisdictions of the UK as well as Ireland.

In Ireland, legislation tends to be brief, lacking in operational detail and dependent on the interpretations of the High Court and Supreme Court. The Mental Health Act 2001 contains just 75 sections and the Criminal Law (Insanity) Act 2006 has a further 26. By way of comparison, the 1983 Mental Health Act for England and Wales contains 149 sections with extensive further schedules, regulations and tribunal rules, a further 59 sections in the Mental Health Act 2007 and numerous further schedules and amendments. The Mental Health (Care and Treatment) (Scotland) Act 2003 runs to 333 sections.

As yet the Irish jurisdiction has no legislation dealing with mental incapacity other than an 1873 Lunacy Regulation (Ireland) Act and some other pieces such as the Marriage of Lunatics Act 1911. The higher courts have been busy with interpretative case work since the Mental Health Act 2001 commenced in 2006 and this is likely to continue for some time. A keen debate between legal theorists can be observed in the recent judgments of the High Court in Ireland, with some judges following the Supreme Court guidance regarding previous legislation (*Phillip Clarke, Gooden*) that mental health legislation is intended to be paternalistic and should be interpreted in this 'purposive' way (e.g. *T O'D*) while others take a stricter view of legal procedure (*WQ, AM*).

Irish insanity law had been the subject of criticism by both the public and the judiciary for many years. The main criticisms were the narrow definition of insanity and the absence of an appeal process. These factors meant that Irish insanity law was incompatible with the European Convention for the Protection of Human Rights and Fundamental Freedoms. At the beginning of the twenty-first century there were major reforms within both civil mental health law and criminal insanity law. The provisions of the Mental Health Act 2001 for patients detained under civil law came into effect in November 2006. The Criminal Law (Insanity) Act 2006 came in to effect in June 2006. This latter Act brings about important changes in how the issues of fitness to plead, insanity and diminished responsibility are dealt with (table 4.4).

Definitions of Mental Illness

Under the new Criminal Law (Insanity) Act 2006 'Mental Disorder' includes mental illness, mental disability, dementia or any disease of the mind but does not include intoxication. This is a broader definition than that contained in the civil mental health act. In the Mental Health Act 2001, 'Mental Disorder' means mental illness, severe dementia or significant intellectual disability. The MHA 2001 specifically excludes personality disorder and addiction to drugs or intoxicants and social deviance.

Assessment and Treatment

The Criminal Law (Insanity) Act 2006 defines a place of treatment as a 'Designated Centre'. Presently, the Central Mental Hospital is the sole designated centre in the Republic of Ireland. In the Government's policy document 'A Vision for Change' (Department of Health and Children, 2006), it is planned to have four designated centres distributed geographically throughout the country. Under the Mental Health Act 2001 a place of treatment is known as an 'approved centre'. Local psychiatric hospitals are in effect 'approved centres' under Mental Health Act 2001. All designated centres must be approved centres and both are overseen by the Mental Health Commission.

Fitness to Plead

Under the new law a judge sitting alone, rather than a jury, will make the determination of unfitness to plead. The issue of fitness is determined by the court of trial to which the person would have been sent forward if s/he were fit to

be tried. The judge is not required to hear evidence from a consultant psychiatrist or other registered medical practitioner, though it is assumed that such evidence will be heard as it is a requirement in the event of an appeal.

If the judge determines the accused is unfit to be tried, then s/he can adjourn the proceedings and can use a 14-day inpatient assessment order 4(6) in a designated centre to determine which is the better of the following disposal options:

1. commit the accused to a specified designated centre under section 4(3) if suffering from mental disorder within meaning of Mental Health Act 2001 and in need of inpatient care; or
2. order outpatient treatment in a designated centre.

The majority of severely mentally ill people before the courts do not require treatment in a designated centre which has heightened conditions of security, but do require treatment in a local approved centre. At present the only designated centre is the Central Mental Hospital. This makes the outpatient treatment disposal option impracticable for courts sitting outside Dublin.

A possible solution to this dilemma is to use a disposal option available under civil legislation. Gardai (police) are empowered to initiate applications under section 12 and section 9 of the Mental Health Act 2001.

An addition to the new Criminal Law (Insanity) Act 2006 is the provision whereby if an accused person is found unfit to plead, an application may be made for trial of the facts.

Not Guilty by Reason of Insanity

For a verdict of 'not guilty by reason of insanity' the McNaughton Rules still apply with the addition of an 'irresistible impulse' limb. The accused must have been suffering at the time from a mental disorder (CL(I)A2006 definition). The mental disorder must have been such that the accused person ought not to be held responsible for the act alleged by reason of the fact that he or she did not know the nature and quality of the act or did not know the act was wrong or was unable to refrain from committing the act *Doyle*.

Following the verdict of not guilty by reason of insanity there is a period of hospital inpatient assessment. The judge commits the person to a designated centre for 14

Table 4.4   Comparison of MHA 2001 and Criminal Law (Insanity) Act 2006 in Ireland

	MHA 2001	CL(I) Act 2006
Definition of mental disorder	Specifically excluded personality disorder and social deviance	Does not specifically exclude personality disorder and social deviance
Centres for treatment	Approved centres	Designated centres
Review boards	Independent of Executive, appointed by Mental Health Commission	Not independent, chosen by Minister for Justice, who has the power also to dismiss
Pathways to care	Spouse, relative, GP	Courts

days to assess whether they come within the definition of mental disorder within the Mental Health Act 2001. The court may extend this period of committal, but not beyond 6 months. The doctor then reports back on whether or not the accused meets the criteria for mental disorder as defined within Mental Health Act 2001. Only if then coming within the more stringent definition of mental disorder in the Mental Health Act 2001 can the court make an order committing the person to a designated centre.

Mental Health Review Boards

The Mental Health (Criminal Law) Review Board was established under the Act of 2006 to review both the welfare and safety of the person detained under the Act and the public interest. The Court is obliged to make the records of its proceedings available to the Board.

Detention is reviewed at intervals of not more than 6 months. The Review Board is chaired by a lawyer of 10 years' experience or a judge or former judge of the Circuit Court, High Court or Supreme Court.

Diminished Responsibility

The introduction of diminished responsibility is a significant development in Irish insanity legislation. If a jury finds that the person accused of murder did the act alleged and was at the time suffering from a mental disorder as defined in section 1 CL(I)Act 2006 and the mental disorder was not such as to justify finding him or her not guilty by reason of insanity but was such as to diminish substantially his or her responsibility for the act, then the defendant is found guilty of manslaughter on grounds of diminished responsibility. There is no therapeutic disposal option available to the Court, only punitive sentencing.

Criminal Law (Insanity) Act 2006: Potential Anomalies

The most controversial case in Irish Insanity Law is that of John Gallagher who successfully pleaded he was insane when he killed Anne Gillespie and her mother in 1988. A few months later he claimed he had recovered his sanity and started a campaign for his release. Under the new law it is possible to envisage something similar happening again. Having two definitions of mental disorder is the main contributing factor to this potential anomaly. The Criminal Law (Insanity) Act 2006 and the Mental Health Act 2001 are compared and contrasted in table 4.4. It is highly probable that some future defendants will be found 'insane' under the Criminal Law (Insanity) Act 2006 but not mentally disordered within the meaning of the Mental Health Act 2001 thus, instead of amending the Gallagher hiatus, CL(I)A2006 has institutionally widened the anomaly.

Inclusion of diminished responsibility alongside third limb insanity has lowered the threshold for those seeking an insanity verdict. Further, no guidance has been given to the courts on who may raise the issue of insanity.

Another matter giving rise to some controversy is the direct relationship between the Mental Health Review Boards and the Executive. The Mental Health Review Boards are appointed by and paid for directly by the Minister of Justice. Some believe this may be in breach of the United Nations Principles for the protection of persons with mental illness.

The Mental Health Act (2001)

Principles

In making a decision under the Act concerning the care or treatment of a person or a decision to make an admission order in relation to a person, the best interests of the person shall be the principle consideration with due regard being given to the interests of other persons who may be at risk of serious harm if the decision is not made. The person shall so far as is reasonably possible be notified of the proposal and be entitled to make representations before deciding the matter and due regard shall be given to the need to respect the right of the person to dignity, bodily integrity, privacy and autonomy.

Approved centres

The Act of 2001 established a Mental Health Commission with responsibility for maintaining a register of approved centres – hospitals or other inpatient facilities for the care and treatment of persons suffering from mental illness or mental disorder. All centres for such purposes must be approved and registered, and a person suffering from a mental disorder shall not be detained in any place other than an approved centre. The latter point means that any designated centre under the Criminal Law (Insanity) Act 2006 must also be an approved centre.

Mental disorder

The definition of mental disorder in the Mental Health Act 2001 is grounded in Council of Europe, Committee of Ministers (1983). Compared to definitions in other jurisdictions it is convoluted. It is carried over at various points into the Criminal Law (Insanity) Act 2006 which includes a broad definition unique to that Act and at times requires in addition the narrower definition in the Act of 2001:

s.3 *In this Act* 'mental disorder' *means mental illness, severe dementia or significant intellectual disability where – (a) because of the illness, disability or dementia, there is a serious likelihood of the person concerned causing immediate and serious harm to himself or herself or to other persons, or (b) (i) because of the severity of the illness, disability or dementia, the judgment of the person concerned is so impaired that failure to admit the person to an approved centre would be likely to lead to a serious deterioration in his or her condition or would prevent the administration of appropriate treatment that could be given only by such admission, and (ii) the reception, detention and treatment of the person concerned in an approved centre would be likely to benefit or alleviate the condition of that person to a material extent.*

'mental illness' means a state of mind of a person which affects the person's thinking, perceiving, emotion or judgment and which seriously impairs the mental function of the person to the extent that he or she requires care or medical treatment in his or her own interest or in the interest of other persons; 'severe dementia' means a deterioration of the brain of a person which significantly impairs the intellectual function of the person thereby affecting thought, comprehension and memory and which includes severe psychiatric or behavioural symptoms such as physical aggression; 'significant intellectual disability' means a state of arrested or incomplete development of mind of a person which includes significant impairment of intelligence and social functioning and abnormally aggressive or seriously irresponsible conduct on the part of the person.

These definitions are further qualified later in the Act, in keeping with Council of Europe Committee of Ministers (2004):

s.8 (1) A person may be involuntarily admitted to an approved centre pursuant to an application under section 9 or 12 and detained there on the grounds that he or she is suffering from a mental disorder. (2) Nothing in subsection (1) shall be construed as authorizing the involuntary admission of a person to an approved centre by reason only of the fact that the person – (a) is suffering from a personality disorder; (b) is socially deviant; or (c) is addicted to drugs or intoxicants.

In a useful ruling (*MR*), J. O'Neill has clarified that 'serious likelihood' should mean 'a high level of probability, less than the criminal standard of beyond reasonable doubt, but more than the civil standard of the balance of probabilities. 'Immediate' means a propensity or tendency towards harm to self or others that is present to the same standard of proof and is unpredictable as to when it might occur. 'Harm' includes physical and mental harm. 'Serious harm' depends on whether the harm is to the person themselves or to others. Clearly the infliction of any physical injury on another could only be regarded as 'serious' harm, whereas the infliction of a minor physical injury on the person him or herself could be regarded as not serious. However for self-harm, only serious actual physical harm to the person concerned should be regarded as serious harm.

The definition of mental disorder in this Act is used as a pre-condition for some but not all treatment orders under the Criminal Law (Insanity) Act 2006. There is a need for consolidation of these Acts which could usefully begin with a 'nested' definition of mental disorder (Kennedy, 2008).

Admission orders and legal process

The legal process is that a member of the family, or a member of the police force, or any other person with certain exclusions, may make an application in writing to a registered medical practitioner who must then see the person concerned within 24 hours and if satisfied that the person concerned is suffering from a mental disorder, sends a recommendation to the clinical director of an approved centre who arranges for a consultant psychiatrist on the staff of an approved centre to carry out an assessment. If the consultant psychiatrist is satisfied that a mental disorder is present, he or she makes an admission order. The first admission order is for 21 days and must be reviewed by the Mental Health Tribunal appointed by the Mental Health Commission. Prior to the Tribunal hearing an independent consultant psychiatrist examines the patient and reports to the Tribunal. Each renewal order is independent of the previous order and each is reviewed by the Mental Health Tribunal.

Transfer of civilly detained patients from an approved centre to a central mental hospital

An application for admission to a central mental hospital cannot be made from the community. A central mental hospital is an approved centre under the Mental Health Act and protections inherent in the Mental Health Act apply, for example concerning consent to treatments. Once a patient has been admitted to an approved centre under the Mental Health Act the clinical director of the approved centre may apply for a transfer to the central mental hospital on the grounds that it would be for the benefit of the patient or that it is necessary for the purpose of obtaining special treatment. The transfer must be approved by the Mental Health Tribunal sitting within 14 days, which must consider whether it is in the best interest of the health of the patient concerned. The transfer may not take place until the expiration of the time for the bringing of an appeal to the circuit court or if such an appeal is brought, the determination or withdrawal thereof. It follows that urgent transfer to a central mental hospital is not available for patients detained in approved centres unless they are charged with some offence and can then be dealt with under the Criminal Law (Insanity) Act 2006. In spite of this, about a fifth of the patients at a central mental hospital are detained under the Mental Health Act.

Court diversion In Ireland

The Criminal Law (Insanity) Act 2006 includes a power to transfer remanded or sentenced prisoners to the Central

Mental Hospital, and a further power to transfer those found unfit to stand trial or not guilty by reason of insanity. However these are disproportionate and unnecessary measures for the great majority of those before the courts charged with minor offences who have major mental illnesses. The Mental Health Act 2001 includes a power for members of the Garda Siochana (police) to initiate an application for admission to an approved centre, and they have a common law discretion to arrange for voluntary assessments and treatment.

In practice however about 3% of those committed to remand prisons in Ireland have a severe mental disorder (Curtin et al., 2009) and a systematic screening and diversion service has been established for remand prisoners (O'Neill, 2006) which relies on the use of the civil Mental Health Act rather than the Criminal Law (Insanity) Act, to ensure that those charged with minor offences are speedily diverted to the least restrictive mental healthcare and treatment appropriate to their needs and the public interest.

CONCLUDING COMMENTS

Taken together, chapters 3 and 4 provide an overview of mental health law, capacity law, and medico-legal processes relating to these in five jurisdictions in one corner of Europe. They have in common historical roots in British law but legal practices are now diverging. It may well be heuristic to consider why this should be so. A useful and fundamental question may be to query whether or not the practical consequences in the jurisdictions described are markedly different one from another or whether in spite of apparent legal and process differences the experience for defendants, patients, and relatives is much the same in each. If there are differences what has generated those differences? Is it simply the different laws and structures, or do other factors such as resources provided, training, and background economic factors play an equal or even more significant role? To answer these questions properly would take complicated research and even then certainty would be difficult to come by. The discerning student should at least bear in mind that the system s/he works in may not be overwhelmingly important and that while day-to-day practical knowledge of that system is crucial to satisfy rules and regulations there may also be other ways of approaching the same problem. Finally it is worth noting, always, that for the psychiatrist the local rules and regulations should be stepping-stones to a satisfactory medical outcome.

5
Forensic psychiatry and its interfaces outside the UK and Ireland

Edited by
Pamela J Taylor

Written by
Emma Dunn
Alan R Felthous
Pierre Gagné
Tim Harding
Sean Kaliski
Peter Kramp
Per Lindqvist
Norbert Nedopil
James R P Ogloff
Jeremy Skipworth
Pamela J Taylor
Lindsay Thomson
Kazuo Yoshikawa

1st edition authors: **Hans Adserballe, Wolfgang Berner, Petko Dontschev, Tim Harding, Stephen J Hucker, Assen Jablensky, Bruce Westmore and Robert M Wettstein**

Other nations of different habits are not enemies: they are godsends. Men require of their neighbours something sufficiently akin to be understood, something sufficiently different to provoke attention, and something great enough to command admiration. We must not expect, however, all the virtues. (Alfred North Whitehead, Science in the Modern World, 1925)

In most countries, forensic psychiatry has its origins in providing psychiatric reports for the courts. Some countries have a tradition of providing specialist treatment facilities too. The extent to which offenders are treated within specialist forensic mental health (FMH) services, generic mental health services or in the criminal justice system (CJS) settings varies between them. As the main tasks differ, so also the nature and extent of specialist training varies between jurisdictions. The extent to which forensic psychiatry has formal recognition as a clinical specialty differs too. For Europeans, freedom of movement and employment between the now 27 European Union (EU) countries has focused attention on trying to agree a definition of forensic psychiatry and even to harmonize training. The definition agreed in an informal group of forensic psychiatrists from Northern Europe, Spain and Portugal is:

Forensic psychiatry is a specialty of medicine based on a detailed knowledge of relevant legal issues, criminal and civil justice systems and the relationship between mental disorder, antisocial behaviour and offending. Its purpose is the care and treatment of mentally disordered offenders and others requiring similar services, including risk assessment and management and the prevention of further victimization. (http://www.ghentgroup.eu)

This definition, with its emphasis on the medical ethic as well as the more specialist aspects of the field, may well be applicable elsewhere too, at least where there is an emphasis on service provision.

In offering the following comparisons, we emphasize that our goals are limited. We have tried to draw out principles of practice which we share in the application of psychiatry to offenders with mental disorder. Our clinical work has much in common despite linguistic, cultural, and legal differences, as well as contrasts in its fiscal and ethical climate. Across national boundaries, forensic mental health services are truly multidisciplinary. It is important to retain this fact in reading this chapter, as most of us, the authors, are psychiatrists, and so we tend towards a mainly psychiatric perspective. There are also less happy things that we share internationally, for example failure to meet fully the needs of some groups, including many people with personality disorder. Our discussion of legal and procedural differences is just illustrative; there are other legal systems, such as Sharia law, which we do not have the expertise to consider. Even with these differences, though, there is common ground in that people who practise at the clinical and legal interface must have a good working knowledge of the law affecting their patients/clients as well as clinical skills.

THE SCOPE AND LIMITS OF THE COMPARATIVE APPROACH

Comparison is a powerful tool in medicine. Concepts of health and disease are founded on observations of similarities and differences between physical and/or mental states in different people. A disease, for example, is defined on the one hand by the sum of those of its characteristics which are similar in all its presentations and on the other by the sum of the differences which demarcate it both from health and from other abnormal states. Comparison between groups of individuals forms the basis of epidemiological and clinical trials. Comparisons of diseases across national, geographical and cultural boundaries have resulted in recognition of real differences in prevalence and outcome, but also that discrepancies in attribution and measurement can confuse the picture.

Comparative studies have contributed particularly to recognizing difficulties in international work on disorders of mental health. Kendell et al. (1971) demonstrated the extent to which even diagnosis of the psychoses varied within and between countries prior to the introduction of structured interviews and explicit diagnostic criteria. Various structured mental state examination systems have followed, and diagnostic and classification systems continue to be refined, but in learned articles (e.g. Kendell and Jablensky, 2003) and in the preamble to the diagnostic manuals themselves (American Psychiatric Association (APA), 1994; World Health Organization (WHO), 1992), cautions are expressed about the lack of specificity of most of the currently accepted categories. Many advocate what would be, essentially, an extension of the comparative approach, by moving to dimensional systems. Both these manuals emphasize that they are dealing in agreed descriptions and guidelines, which generally carry no theoretical

implications. Furthermore, the American *Diagnostic and Statistical Manual* (*DSM-IV*) explicitly raises concerns about its use in the Court, and specifies:

> *When such categories, criteria and textual descriptions are employed for forensic purposes, there are significant risks that diagnostic information will be misused or misunderstood ... In determining whether an individual meets a specified legal standard (e.g. for competence, criminal responsibility or disability) additional information is usually required'* (APA, 1994, p. xxiii).

The 2000 update to this version (*DSM-IV-TR*™) makes a similar point (APA, 2000). There is almost an implication that 'forensic terms' may be more precise. For sure they are fundamentally different from disease measures, but, if anything, comparison here poses even more of a challenge, since legal definitions and practices are, by definition, culture bound.

THE SCOPE AND LIMITS OF THIS CHAPTER

This chapter provides a comparative framework, with descriptions of law and forensic psychiatric practice mainly from nine countries which form part of a research group: five have a common legal heritage based on common law and largely adversarial legal systems: Australia, Canada, Wales (and England), and New Zealand, three are in the Roman law tradition of continental Europe, where the Napoleonic code provided a model of criminal law and the courts follow an inquisitorial system: Denmark, Japan, and Sweden, and two – South Africa and Scotland – have an amalgam of Roman and common law. We have also incorporated a short description of the development of forensic psychiatry in Germany, a country which has one of the longest traditions of delivering forensic mental health services, and also a comprehensive training scheme for forensic psychiatrists. Japan has closely followed the German model in its legal developments in the field, although its service models may have more in common with those in England and Wales. We also have commentary from the USA, in which there are some inter-state variations, but where the most widely used legal framework is founded in common law. There, differences from the other main contributors to this chapter lie more in the philosophy and delivery of forensic psychiatry *per se*. In the USA, forensic psychiatrists tend to confine their contributions to the courts, and, indeed, express concern about mixing court work, treatment and service development. The USA and Japan retain the death penalty for specified crimes. This poses a special burden on forensic psychiatrists and other clinicians if asked to provide reports for the court in a capital case.

No example of developing countries has been included here, although, with high levels of immigration from other parts of Africa and short life expectancy rates outside the Western Cape Province, South Africa has some qualities in common with developing countries. Japan enacted law to enable the genesis of forensic mental health services as recently as 2003, whereas the other countries have a longer forensic mental health service history. In earlier comparative studies of forensic psychiatric examinations (Soothill et al., 1983), dangerousness assessments (Montandon and Harding, 1984) and involuntary hospitalization (Soothill et al., 1981) the then developing countries of Egypt, Thailand, Brazil and Swaziland were included. In few developing countries has there been any legislative innovation concerning psychiatry (exceptions being Senegal, and Trinidad and Tobago). In most, resources are too limited to permit significant service development in such a specialized field. Indeed, the pressing need for development of MH care for common conditions in the community (WHO Expert Committee on Mental Health, 1975) would seem to argue against promoting forensic psychiatry as a distinct entity in the early developmental stages of MH service provision.

It is now recognized that there are, nevertheless, many mentally disordered persons in the prisons of developing countries, and that they may be subject to particularly harsh régimes, including long-term solitary confinement, and/or physical restraint, in the absence of any effective treatment. Collomb (1979), though, has warned forcefully of the dangers of scientific imperialism in psychiatry, and against the imposition of values and judgments from one culture to another. The transplantation of the custodial mental hospital during the colonial period tended to result in prison-like hospital facilities (Collomb, 1972). Mental health legislation provides a fine example of the tenacity of inappropriately alien models, with many developing countries retaining laws imposed by colonial powers long after the occupiers had left.

Even between industrialized countries, there are striking differences between the conceptual and institutional bases of forensic psychiatry, as was shown clearly in the different points of view expressed by representatives from European countries more or less at the beginning of the current phase of development (WHO, 1977), and again in a more recent survey just before the expansion of the European Community (Salize and Dressing, 2005a,b). A key issue for the multidisciplinary group convened for the WHO meeting was the extent to which forensic psychiatrists should be limited to the role of assisting the courts. Through most of Europe, and non-European countries other than the USA participating in this chapter, an active therapeutic role is generally taken in prisons, hospitals, special units and the community, but there is little standardization in training for the tasks. A group of European psychiatrists holds informal meetings to consider common ground in training needs and provision (Gunn and Nedopil, 2005; http://www.ghentgroup. eu), and there are training links between European countries and elsewhere. Japan, for example, has strong links with both Germany and the UK; the UK and other Commonwealth countries retain constructive training dialogue.

At the end of this chapter, we describe four cases of people involved in criminal proceedings with an account of

how each case would be dealt with in each of the countries in our comparative survey and the USA, giving the reader an opportunity to see how the legal provisions, court procedures and forensic services, described below, function in practice.

NATIONAL, SUBNATIONAL AND SUPRANATIONAL LEGAL STRUCTURES

The social and political structure of a country influences its laws. Variations in political structure can introduce complexities in comparative descriptions in that for some countries legislation is enacted entirely at a national level, while for others there are both state or provincial and national or federal laws.

Europe has a further legal complexity. The European Convention of Human Rights guarantees certain fundamental rights for citizens of the member states of the Council of Europe, including procedural guarantees for all individuals deprived of their liberty, and freedom from torture and inhuman or degrading treatment. For offenders with mental disorder, these 'human rights' are crucial, as there are real risks of their violation. The Convention, dating from 1950, originally applied to a handful of Western European democracies and to Turkey. Since 1991, however, it has been ratified by almost all the former Soviet bloc countries, and now covers 47 states, including all EU countries, the Russian Federation, Ukraine and the other countries of Eastern Europe, as well as the Caucasus region, with a combined population of more than 800 million. Many member states have enacted the provisions of the Convention into national legislation, and many have revised, or are in the process of revising, criminal justice and mental health law, in part to ensure that it is compliant with international human rights law. The originality of the European Convention is that it provides for a supranational, independent court, the European Court of Human Rights, to which individuals who believe that their rights have been infringed at national level can appeal. Many prisoners and patients in forensic mental health institutions have made applications to the Court and, in a growing number of cases, the Court has handed down judgments finding that States have indeed violated such rights. The Court may award pecuniary compensation, but, more importantly, the State concerned must take steps to prevent further similar violations. Moreover, the Court's findings are binding on all other State parties to the Convention. There is now a substantial body of 'European human rights case law' of direct relevance to forensic psychiatry, which thus applies in nearly 50 countries (Lewis, 2002; Niveau and Marten, 2007; Fennell, 2008).

In the early days of this system in Europe, several important judgments of the European Court of Human Rights directly affected psychiatric patients (Harding, 1989a). *Winterwerp* concerned a civilly committed patient in Holland. The Court's decision provided important procedural safeguards, notably the requirement that decisions concerning involuntary hospitalization must be confirmed rapidly and subject to regular review by an independent tribunal. The Court subsequently extended its jurisprudence to the appeals procedures for mentally disordered offenders subject to hospital orders or other security measures (*see Luberti; also X*) and to prisoners sentenced to 'life imprisonment' on the grounds of their dangerousness (*Thynne*). The latter case concerned men convicted of very violent sexual crimes.

In more recent decisions, the Court has turned its attention to core issues in the treatment of mentally ill persons within the criminal justice system. Lack of adequate psychiatric treatment is considered to be a form of 'inhuman treatment' and therefore a violation of article 3 of the Convention. Mark Keenan, a young man with a known history of mental disorder, took his own life while in disciplinary segregation. The lack of psychiatric assessment and ineffective monitoring were considered as 'not compatible with the standard of treatment required in respect of a mentally ill person'. This failure in care therefore constituted 'inhuman treatment' (*Keenan*). In a similar, tragic case, *Renolde*, of a young, mentally retarded man who hanged himself while in a punishment cell, the Court found that there had been violations of both Articles 2 ('the right to life') and 3. In its judgment, the Court emphasized that:

> *the assessment of whether the treatment or punishment concerned is incompatible with the standards of article 3 has, in the case of mentally ill persons, to take into consideration their vulnerability and, in some cases, their inability to complain coherently or at all about how they are being affected by any particular treatment*

The 45-day punishment in solitary confinement of such a vulnerable person was found to constitute inhuman and degrading treatment and punishment. In another case, however, despite the fact that a mentally ill prisoner's 'condition made him more vulnerable than the average detainee and that his detention may have exacerbated to a certain extent his feelings of distress, anguish and fear' and that he was kept in custody 'despite a psychiatric opinion that continuing detention could jeopardize his life because of a likelihood of attempted suicide', there had been no violation of article 3 because the prison medical service had nevertheless provided adequate psychiatric supervision and treatment (*Kudla*).

Perhaps the case with the widest repercussions for the psychiatric treatment of prisoners with psychiatric disorders is *Rivière*, where the 2006 judgment broke new ground in treatment standards. M. Rivière was sentenced to life imprisonment in 1982. While serving his sentence, he developed a serious, chronic mental disorder. The Court considered that, despite the fact that he was seen once a month by a psychiatrist and once a week by a nurse, his psychiatric care was inadequate. The Court was particularly concerned about the impossibility under current French law of transfer to a psychiatric hospital or unit during exacerbations of his illness.

Finally, the *Soering* case is of relevance beyond Europe, where the death penalty has been abolished. In 1989, the Court held that the extradition of a German national from the UK to the USA, where he faced charges which could have resulted in the death penalty, would be 'inhuman and degrading' because of the effects of prolonged detention on 'death row'.

CONTROVERSIAL ISSUES AND SHIFTS IN PUBLIC AND PROFESSIONAL OPINIONS

Social and political climate influences responses to antisocial behaviour, the extent to which it is criminalized, the extent to which 'excuses' may be accepted and levels of punitiveness or constraint which citizens will demand or tolerate. Forensic clinicians who give evidence in court, provide services or assist in parole decisions may themselves become objects of public controversy.

In the European Community, and, indeed, in most developed countries, capital punishment is illegal – so Europe's forensic clinicians are spared requests to assess competency for execution. This is not so in the USA, Japan, and some other countries. European law takes account of this – *Soering* has already been mentioned. In some states of the USA, the State will attempt to establish, through its own psychiatric testimony, that the defendant is likely to repeat his/her antisocial behaviour in the future unless executed (Dix, 1984). Serious articles are still published about how to assess competency for execution according to what the authors call 'professional standards' (Zapf *et al.*, 2003) despite, at least for the medical profession, ethical codes, such as the Declaration of Geneva; international bodies such as the World Psychiatric Association (1989) and professional bodies, such as the American Medical Association (see American Psychiatric Association, 1989a) unequivocally state, respectively, that:

> *the participation of psychiatrists in any such action [execution] is a violation of professional ethics' and 'a physician should not be a participant in a legally authorized execution.*

Assessment for competence to be executed is participation in the execution.

The task of the forensic psychiatrist becomes intolerable when asked to behave in a way which is legal, but unethical. In the USA, people under death sentence tend to spend many years on death row. This is hardly conducive to mental health, although many were unwell on arrival. From a clinician's perspective, when treatment can improve the wellbeing of a sick individual, then there is a moral obligation to treat, but if consequent improvement in mental health were to render the individual competent for execution, is that not participation in the execution process? Many states either have now or are seeking a moratorium on carrying out the death penalty. Some vulnerable groups have been exempted, including people with mental retardation (*Atkins*), but even the latter is not straightforward (French, 2005). French reminds us of other ways too in which the law and psychiatry have previously mixed uneasily, for example in eugenic sterilization practices in the early twentieth century (Sofair and Kadjian, 2000; see also chapter 26).

In other countries, current controversies seem less dramatic, but nevertheless illustrate similar underlying conflicts between individual rights and collective security as well as between therapeutic, welfare-based reactions to antisocial behaviour and punitive, 'just deserts' values. We seem to have common ground in not yet having found a satisfactory resolution of the role of forensic psychiatrists in assessing, managing and treating people who have a personality disorder. We also struggle to provide adequate services for people with mental state abnormalities which do not quite reach the threshold for a categorical diagnosis, but who are regarded as dangerous. In such cases, it is not uncommon for forensic psychiatrists to contribute to risk assessment but offer little or nothing in the way of treatment.

In Sweden, in 2002, a parliamentary committee recommended new legislation for offender-patients, with the proposed re-introduction of the concept of lack of responsibility as one main change, and indeterminate sentencing for dangerous offenders with personality disorder as another. The latter would 'guard against' sentences which could otherwise be perceived as too short. In Sweden today, such people may be directed into forensic psychiatric care, as compulsive disorders or personality disorders may be construed as 'severe mental disorder'. The new Bill of 2012 does not, in fact, include indeterminate detention as standard for people with personality disorder but indeterminate incarceration may be an option in exceptional cases (for example 'special patients' in New Zealand.

UK countries have actually implemented laws to extend eligibility for indefinite detention of some offenders through the criminal justice process. In Scotland, the Criminal Justice (Scotland) Act 2003 introduced the Order for Life-long Restriction (OLR) (see also chapter 4), which may be imposed by the High Court following conviction for a serious violent or sexual offence and if a specialist risk assessment (under a Risk Assessment Order) shows that the serious offending is part of a pattern of behaviour likely to endanger the public were the convicted offender to be at liberty. The Act was implemented in 2006, and just five orders were imposed over the next 2 years. For England and Wales, the Criminal Justice Act 2003 introduced Indefinite Public Protection sentences (IPPs) (see also chapter 2). Three years after its implementation (July 2008), there were

4800 IPP prisoners in England and Wales; only 33 of them had ever been released, in spite of some having short tariffs (Rutherford et al., 2008). The UK government forecast was for more than 12,000 IPP prisoners by 2014, but further legislation will stop this (see chapter 2). One of the requirements before such prisoners can be considered for parole is that they must have completed relevant 'treatment programmes' in prison, but the system is, as yet, unable to cope. Two such prisoners, *Walker* and *James* were successful in obtaining a ruling in the High Court, upheld in the Court of Appeal, that:

> *The Secretary of State for Justice acted unlawfully in failing to provide courses which would allow prisoners serving indeterminate sentences for public protection to show the Parole Board by the expiry of their minimum terms that it was no longer necessary to confine them.*

This aside, after the tariff for the offence has been served, psychiatrists and psychologists will be expected to provide evidence on risk to the public which will affect parole decisions. In a population which is already overburdened with mental disorder, it has been shown that about twice as many IPP prisoners are mentally ill as the general prison population (Rutherford et al., 2008).

A similarly rapidly rising prison muster placed New Zealand fifth among OECD (Organization for Economic Co-operation and Development) countries in 2007 for prisoners per capita population, with a higher rate than the UK, Canada and Australia. Worse still, the numbers are heavily biased toward the indigenous Maori population, who comprise 50% of prisoners but only 16% of the population. A major Government initiative is now seeking to reduce prisoner numbers by providing effective interventions to reduce recidivism. These include improved identification of people with mental illness and/or drug or alcohol dependency, and provision of treatment for them while in custody. Timely access to secure inpatient forensic mental health facilities is under increasing pressure as the rate of prison population increase far exceeds forensic mental health service development.

In Denmark, a strong treatment philosophy heavily influenced the penal code from 1930, partly in the appointment of psychiatrists, psychologists, other clinicians and teachers in prisons. This treatment-oriented approach was at its height in the early 1950s, but then swung back. Penal code reform followed in 1973/1975, with particular regard to sanctions that could be imposed on 'psychopaths' and other non-psychotic but mentally abnormal offenders. They would receive ordinary sentences, but a sanction of unlimited duration – a 'security detention' – could be imposed (penal code, section 70). During the 1990s, however, this 'nothing works' attitude towards non-psychotic offenders was increasingly replaced by one of 'something works for some people'. Minor changes in the penal code or its regulations followed. In cases of non-violent sexual crimes, for example, the offender might be given a suspended sentence on condition of attending a sex offender programme, or psychiatric treatment more generally, or drunken drivers might have a prison sentence suspended on condition of treatment for their alcohol abuse. Furthermore, the Danish Department of Prisons and Probation started to develop treatment programmes for youths, drug and alcohol abusing inmates, inmates with violent behaviour and other specific groups. There is also an increasing array of social disposals for offenders aged 14–17 (14 is the age of criminal responsibility in Denmark).

While Canada has enjoyed a progressive approach to incarceration, offender rehabilitation, and parole, the more recent Conservative government has begun to impose a populist, get-tough-on-crime approach, despite empirical evidence of falling crime rates and stable incarceration rates over many years. Since 1947, the Canadian Criminal Code has had provisions to imprison habitual offenders and criminal sexual psychopaths indefinitely. A government perspective that this did not adequately protect the public led to the Criminal Law Amendment Act 1977 which provides the legal framework for current rules on dangerous offenders. In 1997, a further addition authorized the monitoring of long-term offenders for up to 10 years after return to the community. The number of people designated as dangerous offenders has increased sharply (from an average of 8 per year 1978–1987 to 22 per year 1995–2004). Most of the accused whom the crown prosecutors seek to have declared dangerous have been convicted of a sexual offence. The largest single group of dangerous offenders (49%), and most long-term offenders (61%), have victimized children. As part of this process, a court must order an expert assessment, conducted by a psychiatrist and/ or psychologist. The resultant report(s) will then be used in evidence. The obligation to have the offender assessed by two psychiatrists, one for the crown and one for the defence, was replaced in the 1997 Act by a requirement for assessment by 'a person who can perform an assessment'. In most provinces this would still be a psychiatrist. Risk assessment tools, most of them devised by Canadian psychologists or criminologists, are routinely included in such assessments, notwithstanding some limitations on applying group statistics to an individual (see also chapter 21). Many forensic psychiatrists in Canada have raised the ethical issue of contributing to a process that culminates in indeterminate detention in prison without the assurance of psychiatric treatment or periodic psychiatric assessment.

The issue of compulsory treatment is an additional controversy in Canada, as reflected by the differences in the ten provincial mental health acts. Some Canadian jurisdictions do not permit an involuntary patient, regardless of capacity, to refuse psychiatric treatment considered necessary by clinicians, while others, such as Quebec, will not allow their forcible treatment if deemed to have capacity. In a recent decision by the Supreme Court of Canada, *Starson*, it was established that no treatment may be enforced without proof of lack of capacity to make a treatment decision; in other words, the patient's right to autonomy must prevail over any notion of his/her best interest.

Following the movement in the USA to detain sexual offenders in prison beyond expiry of their sentences, four Australian States have enacted post-sentence criminal detention legislation (Calkins-Mercado and Ogloff, 2007). Victoria has enacted a law that provides for the post-sentence supervision of sexual offenders for up to 15 years (Wood and Ogloff, 2006). Unlike the USA, however, these post-sentence detention and supervision provisions have been embedded in criminal legislation. Away from the criminal justice system mental health legislative provisions for involuntary commitment and treatment in Australia, like Canada, generally intertwine notions of need for involuntary care with mental incapacity. While advances have been made in forensic mental health service development in most jurisdictions, legislative and human rights protections still lag behind.

The existence of controversies in so many countries – we have just given a few examples – suggests that the relationship between psychiatry and the criminal justice system will always be, and perhaps always should be, uncomfortable. Societies, which have slowly and grudgingly accepted the reality of the suffering of people with serious mental disordered, remain highly ambivalent towards mentally disordered offenders. Forensic psychiatrists should be sensitive to these issues, and not only in their own countries. They should be prepared to intervene actively in public debate and political decision-making. If they do not, they risk finding themselves expected to do assessments and/ or deliver treatments under impossible conditions, possibly against their professional ethics.

FORENSIC MENTAL HEALTH (FMH) SERVICES AND INTERVENTIONS UNDER CRIMINAL AND CIVIL LAW: GERMANY AND THE USA

Forensic mental health services are still developing even in countries where they were established some years ago. This, together with the fact that they are usually reliant on government funding, often in the face of intense public and media interest, is behind the need for FMH clinicians to have basic political skills. In Germany, like the UK, the development of forensic psychiatric services has a long history.

Germany

Forensic psychiatry existed in Germany before 1825, when the first textbook on forensic psychiatry appeared. The first German language psychiatric journal, appearing in 1848, included forensic psychiatry in its title. At first, different criminal codes existed in the different states; it was not until 1871 that the first penal law for all of Germany was passed. Its *Paragraph 51* defined the 'imputability' (lack of responsibility) of a perpetrator and limited it to 'unconsciousness' and 'disorders of mind', which excluded determination of free will. The law was changed in 1933, when provisions for diminished 'putability' as well as for preventive detention for those considered dangerous were included in the law. The latter provision was tragically misused until 1945. Law reforms started in the 1950s, finally coming into effect in 1975. The relevant terms of the new paragraphs 20 and 21 of the reformed penal law are 'inculpability' and 'diminished culpability'; the spectrum of disorders to be considered under this paragraph was broadened. Four terms were included as preconditions for considering the application of those paragraphs: 'serious mental disorder', 'profound disturbance of consciousness' (a term which would equate to 'automatism' in some jurisdictions), 'feeble mindedness' and 'other serious mental abnormalities'. The latter term includes serious personality disorders, severe paraphilias and other not specifically classified disorders.

Preventive detention for mentally ill offenders as well as for dangerous serial offenders was still possible, but the intention was that it should be used rarely, as explained in the accompanying commentaries on the law reform. Indeed, the number of hospitalizations of mentally ill offenders decreased from 4,413 in 1965 to 2,454 in 1989, then stayed at approximately the same level until 1997, when 3188 patients were under hospital orders made in the criminal courts. Following a trend in most western countries, preventive detention of serious offenders became an issue in German legislation from 1998. Since then, nine new laws have been passed, reducing the restrictions on putting offenders under preventive detention and tightening the requirements for release. All decisions according to the new laws require risk assessments by forensic psychiatrists. These new laws led to an increase in numbers of forensic inpatients to 6,287 in 2008, but in 2011 almost all of these new laws were declared unconstitutional by the Federal Constitutional Court, which demanded complete reform of this legislation and its application by May 2013. Uniquely in Europe, Germany also has provisions for preventive detention and treatment for offenders suffering from addiction disorders (paragraph 64 of the penal law) and 2,656 inpatients were treated under this provision in 2008.

According to the German Constitution, only a judge can deprive an individual of his/her liberty, so committal into and release from a forensic institution have to be decided by judges and not by panels or boards, as in some British or US jurisdictions. The forensic psychiatrist is just an adviser in Germany, which has an inquisitorial structure in penal law, distinctive in the active part played by the judge, who him/herself searches for the facts, listens to witnesses and experts, examines documents, and orders the taking of evidence. The forensic psychiatric expert is appointed by the judge for each single case. The advice that the judge seeks during a criminal trial almost always focuses on culpability and risk, requiring answers to a rather rigid sequence of questions:

1. Is there a clinical diagnosis to be established for the offender?
2. If so, does the disorder fall within the criteria of the penal law?
3. If so, did the disorder abolish the insight of the offender into the wrongfulness of his/her criminal act?
4. If that is not the case, did the disorder abolish or severely diminish his/her capability to act through lack of insight?
5. If the answer to questions 3 or 4 is yes, will the offender pose a risk of future offences because of his/her disorder?
6. If the answer to questions 3 or 4 is no, and the offender has committed more than one serious crime, will the offender be more likely than not to commit another serious crime?

The answers to questions 1, 2, 5 and 6 are regarded as empirically based, falling into the domain of the psychiatrist, while the answers to questions 3 and 4 are regarded as of a more general nature and must be answered by the judge, taking the empirical knowledge of the forensic psychiatrist into account. Thus, as in England and Wales, the decision on lack of culpability or diminished culpability rests with the judge, and an insanity or diminished responsibility verdict is for the court, only taking account of the expert evidence.

United States of America

Forensic psychiatry developed in the context of evolving medical and psychological sciences, health and MH services and, of course, the law. FMH practice is shaped by the legal framework in which it functions. In principle, from the inception of the fledgling US government, spawned from England, the power of the law was not to be vested in an autocratic or even centralized governing body, but in the people themselves. Those powers the US government would exercise were broadly delineated in the US Constitution, all other governmental powers remained with individual states, originally 13. It took 9 years for all the states to accept the Constitution and, therefore, the federal government. The main concern was over how much power should rest with federal government. Not until the first ten amendments, also known as the Bill of Rights, that specified limitations on federal authority and established autonomy rights for individual citizens, did all the states ratify the Constitution (Morris, 2007). It was adopted in 1789. Some of these as well as later amendments were tools in making MH services available and curbing abuse.

Designed to prevent emergence of an autocracy or oligarchy, the Constitution presciently divided and balanced power between the three branches of government: the legislative branch (Congress) enacts laws;

the executive branch (the President) administers and enforces them; and the judiciary branch (the courts) interprets and settles conflicts about them (Morris, 2007). Each state has this three parallel branch system. All powers not assigned to the federal government, including much of the criminal and civil justice systems and MH and public forensic systems, remained with the states. The highest judicial authority is the US Supreme Court. When the Supreme Court interprets state laws as needing to conform to one or more of the amendments, this can shape rules for administering justice and MH services throughout the land.

Both civil and criminal procedures in the USA are adversarial. It is assumed that each party to a legal conflict should have an opportunity to present its facts and logic, as the truth is most accurately and fairly reached only when both sides have had their say. Both private and public legal services are available. In criminal trials the prosecutor is a government official. Usually the defendant's counsel is a public defender in felony cases (Goldstein, 2007; *Gideon*), but some defendants retain private legal representation. Defence counsel must advance the defendant's defence against the charge and ensure that his/her procedural rights are protected.

Early in the eighteenth century, years before the American Revolution, Dr Thomas Bond visited the Bethlem Hospital in England. He was impressed by the care provided there, and thus hatched his idea for a similar hospital in the colony of Pennsylvania (Deutsch, 1949, p.17); also advocated by Benjamin Franklin, the Pennsylvania Hospital opened in Philadelphia in 1752 as America's first mental hospital (Daine, 1976; Prosono, 2003). Dorothea Dix spearheaded an impassioned crusade to improve the housing and care of the mentally ill in the first half of the nineteenth century. Her effective persuasion resulted in the development of numerous state hospitals (Zilboorg, 1941 (1967)), and, by 1844, a number of private asylums had also opened (Prosono, 2003).

The first formal national professional association of physicians who concerned themselves with mental disorders was the Association of Medical Superintendents of American Institutions for the Insane. This forerunner of first the American Medical-Psychological Association (1892) and then the American Psychiatric Association (1921) (Barton, 1987), founded the *American Journal of Insanity* (forerunner of today's *American Journal of Psychiatry*) in 1844 and endeavoured to educate community physicians about legal issues in treating people with mental illness (Prosono, 2003). One early superintendent and private practitioner, Isaac Ray (1962), wrote *A Treatise on the Medical Jurisprudence of Insanity* in 1838, described by Walker (1968) as 'one of the most influential books' on insanity. Ray criticized English tests of insanity, arguing that emotional impairment caused by mental illness, as well as cognitive distortion, may affect behaviour.

The American Academy of Forensic Sciences (AAFS) was founded in 1948. Disciplines in this organization were psychiatry, pathology, toxicology, anthropology, and engineering. Each professional section (e.g. forensic psychiatry) furthered its own professional, scientific and educational interests, but also participated in collaborative educational programmes with fellow sections. Today the AAFS is the largest organization of forensic sciences in North America. The psychiatry and behavioural sciences section includes PhD and PsyD forensic psychologists. New sections of AAFS are formed according to need (e.g. forensic DNA testing).

Fifteen forensic psychiatrists met during the 1968 APA meeting with the idea of forming an organization dedicated to the education of forensic psychiatrists and promotion of the field, leading to the foundation of the American Academy of Psychiatry and the Law (AAPL) in 1969. AAPL has become the largest organization for forensic psychiatrists in the USA. AAPL sponsors annual educational meetings, a quarterly journal (*Journal of the American Academy of Psychiatry and Law*), a newsletter, and practice guidelines.

As forensic psychiatry grew and matured after the mid-twentieth century, MH services, therapeutic innovations, the criminal justice system and criminal and mental health law were transforming too. Modern psychopharmacology improved outcome for individuals with serious mental illness, and most became candidates for community treatment. Incompetent defendants could be restored to competence, and proceed to trial. Even insanity acquitees, who had committed horrific crimes, could gain symptom control and release from confinement. As treatment and improvement became realities, state hospital populations, having peaked in the 1950s, began to fall in the 1970s and 1980s, but, as in so many other countries, state legislatures saw only cost savings in closing such hospitals. Criteria for involuntary hospital commitment shifted from *parens patriae* to a more police power approach. Rights to autonomy for the mentally ill became of increasing concern. Courts became activists in promoting better treatment and care and protecting individual autonomy. Community mental health centres then received greater government support and became vibrant, productive enterprises. Many people with mental illness functioned better as a result. Others did not fare so well: they drifted to living on the streets, confinement in jails and prisons, and worse.

Capacity in the court and before coming to trial in the USA

As in many other countries, a defendant's right not to be tried for a criminal offence while incompetent for this purpose is a fundamental principle in the USA. Received through its English common law heritage, decisions of the US Supreme Court have moulded the legal concepts and practices. The moral and legal importance of competence determination is found in its four purposes: (1) to safeguard the accuracy of criminal adjudications; (2) to preserve the dignity and integrity of the legal procedures; (3) to support a fair trial; and (4) to ensure that a defendant who is found guilty knows why he will be punished (Ennis and Hansen, 1976). American jurisprudence places special emphasis on fairness.

The early standard for such competence had two prongs: the cognitive – the ability to understand court proceedings – and the functional prong – the ability to act (rationally) in one's own defence, that is to assist in one's defence or to consult with one's attorney. Historically, despite the right to legal representation guaranteed by the Sixth Amendment of the US Constitution, defendants in state trials, even of serious offences, could not count on having legal representation. The right to legal representation was finally guaranteed by the US Supreme Court for felony defendants in state courts (*Gideon*). A defendant who is cognitively or functionally incompetent to stand trial, or both, cannot be tried until restoration of competence.

The most widely known test of competence to stand trial is that adopted by the US Supreme Court in *Dusky*: does the defendant have 'sufficient present ability to consult with his lawyer with a reasonable degree of rational understanding and whether he has a rational as well as factual understanding of the proceedings against him?' (p.402). Thus, the defendant need not be absolutely bereft of cognitive or functional capacities to be found incompetent.

Using parameters set by the US Supreme Court, each state enacts its own criminal procedure law, including that on competence to stand trial. Judicial law established by the US Supreme Court serves to make the determination available in all states, and to curb potential abuses of its application. The defence, prosecution or judge can raise the issue of competence. In *Pate*, the Supreme Court held that, where circumstances cause doubt about the defendant's competence, the Due Process Clause of the Fourteenth Amendment of the US Constitution requires a hearing on the issue. In *Drope*, the Supreme Court advised consideration of three factors in whether to consider competency: (1) A history of irrational behaviours; (2) comportment during trial; and (3) medical opinion. Mere allegation of incompetence is insufficient; but the evidence need not be substantial to warrant a hearing.

A defendant is presumed to be competent unless and until the court rules otherwise. The burden of proof of incompetence is on the defence *(Medina)*. In general, three levels of certainty are available for proof at trial: by preponderance of the evidence/balance of probabilities (over 50% certain), clear and convincing evidence (about 75%) and beyond a reasonable doubt (about 90–95%). The Supreme Court established a balance of probabilities standard of proof for incompetence to stand trial (*Cooper*).

Supreme Court decisions have made competence determinations more accessible and incompetence more uniformly provable. They have also served to correct specific abuses of excess. The dehospitalization movement resulted in growing numbers of people with mental disorder living in the community. Some, although not dangerous and so not subject to the increasingly stringent civil commitment criteria, were nonetheless a social nuisance. Courts could sequester such individuals by finding them incompetent or sending them to a secure hospital for competency assessment (Stone, 1976). If competence was not restorable, then the person might be detained for life. In 1972, the US Supreme Court held that due process must limit the period of such confinement. In this event, 'the State must either institute the customary civil commitment proceedings or release the defendant' (*Jackson*).

The next abuse illustrates why it is so important for American forensic psychiatrists and psychologists to become familiar with landmark cases and their own professional ethical codes. It used to be the practice in Texas for a competence evaluation in capital cases to be ordered by the court, on recommendation by the prosecution, *before defence counsel had been assigned*. The psychiatrist would represent the evaluation to the defendant as one intended to address competence to stand trial, but if the defendant were then be found competent, based on that examination, the same psychiatrist would then testify in the sentencing hearing in support of imposition of the death sentence – to the surprise of the defendant and defence counsel. In 1981, the Supreme Court held that, if evidence based on a forensic psychiatric examination is to be used in the determination of the death penalty, the defendant must be informed of this possibility before the examination (*Estelle*); the defendant can then consult with counsel and/or refuse the examination. This decision could be regarded as an issue specific to a jurisdiction with the death penalty, but it led to forensic clinicians refusing to conduct competence evaluations before assignment of defence counsel in *all* criminal cases.

The jurisprudence concerning involuntary medication to restore competence is an important matter both for forensic psychiatry and the legal regulation of psychiatry. A defendant has a constitutional right not to be tried for a criminal offence while incompetent, but, after having been restored to competence, and in consultation with counsel, s/he may decide that the defence is best presented if not in a medicated state in the courtroom. Then a conflict may arise about involuntarily medication, in order for the trial to proceed in keeping with due process. In 1992, the Supreme Court held that involuntary antipsychotic medication, without demonstrated 'overriding justification', violated due process and the defendant's right to a fair trial (*Riggins*).

If a defendant, having been found incompetent to stand trial, refuses medication recommended for his/her mental disorder and restoration of competence, litigation of the case is blocked. Apart from the Riggins exception, an incompetent defendant cannot be tried. If, in addition to having been adjudicated incompetent, the medication-refusing defendant satisfies jurisdictional criteria for involuntary medication (e.g. imminent danger to self or others due to the mental illness), then, through proper procedures, s/he can be medicated involuntarily by court order and restored to competence, but these criteria may not be fulfilled. In 2003, the US Supreme Court provided Constitutional parameters for involuntary medication in such circumstances. It is permitted if the medication, 'is medically appropriate, is substantially unlikely to have side effects that may undermine the fairness of the trial, and, taking account of less intrusive alternatives, is necessary significantly to further important governmental trial related interests (*Sell*).'

Criminal adjudicative competencies, which may extend beyond the court itself, including competence to confess, to waive Miranda rights, such as the right to an attorney and to remain silent, to plead guilty, to waive representation by legal counsel, to waive a jury trial, to waive appeals, to waive extradition, to be sentenced, to face revocation of probation or parole and to be executed (Miller, 2003a). Other competencies are rarely raised (Perlin, 1996). Much of the law on such competencies has been created by the courts. The US Supreme Court sets thresholds and standards that apply nationwide.

With respect to confession, it is important that the accused was not subjected to coercion and that the confession was therefore constitutionally voluntary, not whether mental disturbance *per se* might have influenced the confession (*Connelly*). States may, however, enact more protective law (Miller, 2003a). The focus of competency then shifts from competence to confess to 'competence to waive Miranda rights'. This is a matter that the Supreme Court has addressed for juveniles, but not mentally disordered adults. Evaluation of a juvenile for competence to waive Miranda rights must include the circumstances of the interrogation, the juvenile's age, education, background, experience, and intelligence. Specifically, the juvenile should have the capacity to understand the warnings given to him, the nature of his Fifth Amendment rights prohibiting coerced self-incrimination and the consequences of waiving them (*Fare*).

The US jurisprudence on competence to plead guilty, competence to waive counsel, and competence to represent oneself illustrates a dynamic tension between the view that all such competencies should follow a single 'competence to proceed' standard and a contrary view that such standards should correspond to specific abilities that will be needed. A defendant who opts to plead guilty will forfeit his privilege against self-incrimination, right to a jury trial and right to confront witnesses. By pleading guilty, s/he is admitting actual guilt and consenting to the judge's adjudication of guilt and sentencing (American Bar Association,

1968; Miller, 2003a). In *Godinez*, the Supreme Court adopted the unifying approach. The *Dusky* standard for competence to stand trial is constitutionally sufficient for competence to plead guilty, but states are not prohibited from enacting higher standards. The act of pleading guilty must be 'knowing and voluntary', a separate determination made by the court; this judgment is not of a mental capacity and therefore does not warrant psychiatric or psychological assessment (*Godinez*).

Similarly, competence to waive counsel is a decisional capacity for which the *Dusky* standard for competence to stand trial is constitutionally sufficient, and must also be voluntary and knowing (*Godinez*). In some cases, the waiver is followed by a guilty plea, so the same standard for the two decisions is logical, but, in others, the defendant who has waived counsel will have to defend himself in court, a task that is far more demanding of psychological function (American Psychiatric Association, 1989a and American Academy of Psychiatry and the Law, 2002; Felthous, 1979; Felthous, 1994; Perlin, 1996). In 2008, the Supreme Court held that the Constitution does not prohibit a state from finding a defendant to be competent to stand trial, but at the same time incompetent to represent himself (*Edwards*). For now it is left to states and lower courts, including the trial courts themselves, to establish the standards (Felthous and Flynn, 2009), but with *Dusky* as the minimum standard.

Psychiatric defences in the USA

In the USA, crimes are defined in terms of the act *and* state of mind, and both must be proved beyond a reasonable doubt before conviction or sentence. A defendant may plead guilty without anything having to be proven in court; when accepted, the plea establishes agreement on both the physical and mental elements of the crime. Mental state is defined in law differently for different crimes, and even somewhat differently for the same ones across state jurisdictions – the definitions influenced by public policy, science and public opinion. A core element of the *mens rea* for most crimes is intent. A defendant who did not intend to do what s/he did should not be held morally or legally responsible for that act, insofar as the act is considered a criminal offence. Even the *mens rea* of 'recklessness', which does not require intent to cause the wrong, requires the offender to have taken the risks consciously, after foreseeing the possibility of harm (Garner, 1999, p.1,277). More ambiguous exceptions to the remarkably consistent requirement of intent are lesser offences requiring only 'criminal negligence'; this concept is borderline between civil negligence in tort law and criminal intent or recklessness.

Intent is so integral to the crime itself that US courts do not allow psychiatric or psychological testimony on whether the defendant had the requisite intent. Affirmative defences, that can negate *mens rea*, are diminished actuality, duress, alibi, coercion, automatism, self-defence, intoxication and insanity. An affirmative defence is one in which 'a defendant's assertion raising new facts and arguments that, if true, will defeat the ... prosecution's claim, even if all allegations in the complaint are true' (Garner, 1999, p.430). A partial defence pertains to either 'part of the action or toward mitigation' of punishment (*ibid*), and includes extreme emotional disturbance, passion, provocation, and imperfect self-defence (Nair and Weinstock, 2007). The California Supreme Court defined the latter: '... when the trier of fact finds that a defendant killed another person because the defendant *actually* but unreasonably believed he was in imminent danger of death or great bodily injury, the defendant is deemed to have acted without malice and thus can be convicted of no crime greater than voluntary manslaughter' (Miller, 2003b; *Laffoon*).

Though rarely used, the insanity defence is far better known to mental health professionals and the general public than diminished capacity; only about a third of states have a diminished capacity defence (Slovenko, 1995) wherein a defendant can offer evidence that s/he lacked the mental capacity to have formed the requisite intent specific to the crime. As elsewhere, if the prosecution is unable to prove specific intent beyond reasonable doubt, the defendant may still be convicted of a lesser included crime, e.g. second degree instead of first degree murder. US federal law, and about half of the states, permit evidence of mental disorder to negate *mens rea* (Nair and Weinstock, 2007). Most jurisdictions restrict such testimony more than for the insanity defence. Given inter-state differences, forensic psychologists and psychiatrists must familiarize themselves with relevant law in the state where they practise (Felthous et al., 2001; Miller, 2003b).

Like competence to stand trial, the insanity defence in the USA derived from English common law. Early in the nineteenth century, well before *McNaughton*, parallel versions of right–wrong or good–evil tests were used by courts in both England and the USA (Greenberg and Felthous, 2007); (for an account of the *McNaughton* rules of 1843, see p.29). In the USA, although the Supreme Court was instrumental in establishing a standard for competence to stand trial, it left states free to craft their own insanity tests. With rare exceptions, they adopted a version of the *McNaughton* test during the first half of the twentieth century, although several added a so-called 'irresistible impulse' alternative where loss of behavioural control was more pronounced than the cognitive impairment. The US Court of Appeals for the District of Columbia in 1954 replaced the *McNaughton* test with the 'product test':

> *An accused is not criminally responsible if his unlawful act was the product of mental disease or defect. (Durham, pp.874–875)*

In 1972, this Court replaced the USA's most liberal insanity test with the test developed by the American Law Institute:

> *A person is not responsible for criminal conduct if at the time of such conduct as a result of mental disease or defect he lacks substantial capacity to appreciate the criminality (wrongfulness) of his conduct or to conform his conduct to the requirements of the law.*

As used in this model test, the terms 'mental disease or defect' do not include an abnormality manifested only by repeated or otherwise antisocial conduct (American Law Institute (ALI) Model Penal Code, 1962).

This American Law Institute test was a model, not itself law, but most states and federal court districts adopted it. It contains both cognitive and 'irresistible impulse' elements. More liberal than the 'not knowing' test of McNaughton, the cognitive prong is satisfied if the defendant 'lacks substantial capacity to appreciate the criminality (wrongfulness) of his conduct.' The earlier product test in the District of Columbia (DC) ambiguously allowed antisocial personality disorder to qualify here, but the 'second paragraph' of the ALI test attempts to eliminate this ambiguity and to exclude antisocial personality disorder (Felthous, 2010).

Even before John Hinkley's attempt to assassinate President Reagan, insanity jurisprudence in the USA was becoming more conservative. With his unpopular insanity acquittal under the DC's ALI test, US insanity laws took a hard right turn. Several jurisdictions dropped the volitional prong, while leaving a cognitive test of insanity in place; others, having modified or replaced the more liberal first paragraph of the Institute test, left the second exclusionary one in place. The intention was to limit use of the insanity defence (Felthous, 2004; Greenberg and Felthous, 2007). Further, by 1983, 15 states adopted the alternative plea option commonly known as the 'guilty but mentally ill' plea and verdict (McGinley and Pasewark, 1989). The three standard criteria for being found guilty but mentally ill are: (1) commission of the criminal act; (2) mental illness at the time of the act; and (3) absence of criteria sufficient for insanity. In practice, a defendant found guilty but mentally ill is given the same prison sentence that s/he would receive if s/he had just been found guilty; any need for mental health services is provided in prison, essentially at the same level as in a mental hospital (Greenberg and Felthous, 2007).

Today most states have a McNaughton/modified McNaughton test for insanity; most of the rest have an ALI/modified ALI, but some have a test that resembles neither (e.g. Revised Statutes, South Dakota Criminal Code 27A-1-1, 1987). Five states no longer have an insanity defence: Montana, Idaho, Utah, Kansas and Maryland. The first four left a *mens rea* defence in place (Greenberg and Felthous, 2007), but the Maryland state supreme court simply abolished its insanity defence (*Pouncy*). Although the legislature for Nevada abolished that state's insanity defence in 1995, the Nevada Supreme Court found that abolition was unconstitutional (*Finger*), abolition was upheld by the state supreme courts in Idaho (*Searcy*) and Montana (*Korell*). Insanity laws for all 50 states and federal jurisdictions are listed in the *Practice Guidelines on the Insanity Defense of the American Academy of Psychiatry and the Law* (2002).

Civil commitment in the USA

The first mental hospital in the USA, the Pennsylvania Hospital of Philadelphia, first admitted patients in 1756 (Mora, 1975). Early in the nineteenth century, small private mental hospitals were built (e.g. McLean Hospital in Massachusetts, Bloomingdale Asylum in New York City, the Hartford Retreat in Connecticut; Mora, 1967). A patient in McLean Hospital, Josiah Oakes, protested his involuntary hospitalization in court in 1845 (Matter of Josiah Oakes, 1845). The court held that the US Constitution does not permit involuntary hospitalization without procedural safeguards. Both protective and therapeutic purposes are required to justify involuntary hospitalization (Brakel *et al.*, 1985).

The USA owes a debt of gratitude to a retired school teacher, Dorothea Dix, whose energy, passion and indefatigability moved her to crusade for the benefit of society's mentally ill 'pariahs' (Zilboorg, 1941 (1967)). This led to the development of state mental hospitals intended to provide refuge and care for the mentally ill, but as Slovenko (1973, p.202) observed, small hospitals that offered humane treatment gave way, after the civil war, to large custodial facilities. Commitment criteria were vague, inconsistent and procedural safeguards were lacking (Habermeyer et al., 2007; Schwartz et al., 2003). Mrs Packard, a victim of these circumstances and Illinois' sexist commitment law at the time, was committed on petition of her husband. A husband could then lawfully commit his wife 'without the evidence of insanity or distraction required in other cases' (Slovenko, 1973, p.202). After her release, 3 years later, she successfully campaigned for procedural rights within commitment laws, for example the right to a court hearing was brought into commitment laws.

Parens patriae governmental power permitted lax criteria and procedures for involuntary hospitalization until the mid-twentieth century. Custodial care was justified on what medical and legal authorities thought was 'best' for a person with mental disorder, entry into a state hospital was procedurally simple, but exit not so. In the 1950s, the nationwide inpatient census peaked at around 560,000, with many mentally ill people remaining hospitalized for decades. With de-institutionalization, supported by modern pharmacotherapy, numbers of people in long-stay hospital beds fell substantially, state hospitals closed, and government support was directed into community mental health centres. Patient autonomy had to be considered alongside treatment, care and protection needs. In addition, attempts by both state governments and healthcare businesses to control the costs of mental healthcare contributed to the trend towards limiting involuntary hospitalization to manifestly dangerous mentally ill individuals (Habermeyer et al., 2007). With requirements for both mental illness and dangerousness, government relied on *parens patriae* and police power to justify coerced hospitalization (Gutheil and Appelbaum, 2000).

The US Supreme Court, by applying specific amendments of the US Constitution, established threshold hospitalization procedures, requirements and limitations; all state mental health law must comply, but state legislation can fine tune the procedures. Some Supreme Court cases that shaped national civil commitment procedures touch on, or directly involve, criminal issues. In 1966, for example, the Supreme Court found no basis for distinguishing hospital commitment of a prisoner at the end of his/her prison term from any other civil commitment (*Baxtrom*); fewer procedural safeguards for an ex-prisoner would violate the Due Process Clause of the Fourteenth Amendment. In the same year, the highest court for the District of Columbia, the nation's capital, applied the concept of 'least restrictive alternative' (*Lake;* Hoge et al., 1989). At least in that district, an individual could not be involuntarily hospitalized if her/his treatment needs could be equally satisfied under a less restrictive arrangement. This principle has been adopted to some degree in many other jurisdictions.

California led the country in enacting sweeping mental health legislative reforms to limit application and duration of civil commitment and protect individual autonomy (Lanterman-Petris-Short Act, 1969). This Act required presence of mental illness and overt dangerousness, or disability so grave that the individual would be at risk of physical harm if not hospitalized. The law limited periods of involuntary confinement and required periodic court review. In the event of grave disability, a conservator must be appointed to protect the individual's interests (Brakel et al., 1985; Schwartz et al., 2003). Other states have followed with similar codes. The most radical change in jurisdictional law to protect individual autonomy, though, came from the Wisconsin federal district court in 1972 (*Lessard*). Procedural safeguards approached those for criminal prosecution, with the standard of 'beyond reasonable doubt'. This standard can be aspired to, at vast increase in costs of civil commitment procedures, but is probably not achievable, given limitations on risk prediction. To the extent that dangerousness is based upon past, often recent acts, the commitment becomes a response to a behaviour, like criminal prosecution. No other court or state legislature has developed such extreme law, though elements of *Lessard* have been adopted in other jurisdictions.

The *Lessard* case involved civil commitment for restoration of competence to stand trial. Although this is a criminal matter, in 1972, the Supreme Court articulated the general principle that the length of *any* involuntary hospitalization should correspond to a legal purpose (*Jackson*). Three years later, the High Court held that 'a State cannot constitutionally confine *without more* a non-dangerous individual who is capable of surviving safely in freedom by himself or with the help of willing and responsible family members or friends' (*O'Connor*, p.2,494) (emphasis added). The Court has never established an *unambiguous* right to treatment for civilly committed individuals, and lower courts have interpreted 'without more' as 'without further justification' instead of 'without treatment' (Hicks, 2003).

The standard of proof for civil commitment must be at least 'clear and convincing evidence' (*Addington*, 1979), higher than for many other civil law issues: 'preponderance of the evidence'. The criminal law standard 'beyond reasonable doubt' is too high to be constitutionally required, but states may enact a higher, but not lower, standard than clear and convincing evidence.

Children may be civilly committed without the full panoply of procedural rights that are mandatory for commitment of adults (*Parham*).

Until 1990, an individual's voluntary decision to sign him/herself into an MH facility, without legal action taken for or against him/her, was honoured. In *Zinermon*, in a situation not unlike the *Bournewood* in the UK, the Court found that voluntary hospitalization of a person who is not competent to consent to hospital admission is an unconstitutional deprivation of that person's liberty. Paradoxically, the person's autonomy rights are better protected under civil commitment, than if his/her incompetent decision is accepted. Thereafter, screening for competence to consent to admission has been prudent practice.

Most state mental health codes provide for two types of voluntary hospital admission and two types of involuntary hospitalization (Schwartz et al., 2003). Informal admission is accomplished when the individual voluntarily and orally agrees to come into the hospital. Once admitted, if the person requests discharge, this is granted without delay. The more common practice of formal voluntary admission requires that the person give written consent for admission, in which case, if s/he requests discharge, but immediate discharge is not recommended by the psychiatrist, that person can be held for a period, usually, of 3 to 5 days, to allow further clinical risk assessment, and determination of whether criteria exist for involuntary hospitalization.

The two types of involuntary mental hospitalization are emergency detention and civil commitment. The legal criteria for emergency detention typically include presence of mental illness, imminent risk of serious harm to self or others unless hospitalized and unwillingness to consent to admission. Designed to address emergent conditions, emergency certification must be completed by a licensed physician or other qualified professional, and reviewed by an appropriate court; in many jurisdictions a probable cause hearing is required soon after emergency admission (Schwartz et al., 2003). Civil commitment, though, requires a court hearing, and may initially be for up to 90 days. Criteria are similar to those for emergency commitment, but may include 'substantial' rather than imminent risk

of harm to self or others. Also, a common alternative to the dangerousness criteria is 'grave disability' (inability to take care of him/herself outside hospital because of mental illness). The civilly committed individual may be released as soon as the criteria are no longer met, or may change his/her status at any time by signing the consent form for 'formal voluntary' hospitalization. If detention is required beyond the statutorily limited period, another court hearing is required.

Except in a few states (e.g. Utah), civil commitment does not disturb the individual's right to refuse psychotropic medication. In order to treat seriously disturbed individuals, clinicians must use reason and persuasion, although there are procedures, in some states within the hospital in others through court, which may allow for compulsory medication or ECT if the individual needs it but persists in refusing it. In addition to the civil detention criteria, a risk–benefit analysis must produce reason to assume that the individual's condition will improve as a result of the proposed treatment.

By changing mental health codes and providing community treatment, the USA has substantially reduced the use of extended inpatient hospitalization over the last half century, but, over the same period, the number of people with mental illness in jails and prisons has increased substantially. Public policy concerns must be directed towards increasing services there as well as enhancing continuity of correctional services with community mental health centres, general hospitals and mental hospitals; reduction in criminal incarcerations would be an outcome measure.

Civil commitment of sexual offenders in the USA

Sexual offenders in the USA have traditionally been managed under criminal law. Once found guilty of a sex offence, a person would be sentenced to a prison term determined by statute. In the late 1930s, the view that sexually offending behaviour was caused by psychological or medical deviation led to the hope that treatment or rehabilitation programmes could be corrective. Laws were enacted in most states that allowed for indeterminate sentences, but both psychiatrists and lawmakers became disenchanted with them. Psychiatrists found the laws ineffective in achieving their stated goals and lawyers were concerned about restriction of autonomy. Most states with sexual psychopathy laws repealed them between 1975 and 1985 (Tucker and Brakel, 2003). Illinois retained its 'sexually dangerous person' commitment law, and the US Supreme Court held this to be constitutional (*Allen*).

After the law reverted to a more uniformly retributive position, a new problem emerged. Offenders could be imprisoned for terms commensurate with the seriousness of their offences, but then had to be released. Some committed further serious sexual offences. In 1990, the state of Washington was the first to enact a 'sexually violent predator' law, designed to provide treatment and/or rehabilitation for such offenders under civil detention. At least 15 other states followed suit by 2000 (Tucker and Brakel, 2003). Typically, four criteria must be satisfied for court adjudication and civil commitment as a sexually violent predator. It must be proven beyond a reasonable doubt that s/he: (1) was charged/convicted of one or more sexually violent offences; (2) has a mental abnormality; (3) evidences a probability of committing future predatory sexual violence; and (4) that there is a causal link between risk of recurrence and the mental abnormality exists.

In constitutional challenges, the US Supreme Court has supported sexually violent predator laws. The Washington statute did not violate the double jeopardy (not being tried for the same offence twice) or *ex post facto* (not being subject to a law that was enacted after the incident offence was committed) clauses of the US Constitution. Sexually violent predator commitment was a civil, not criminal procedure, and therefore not punitive. The right of the individual to remain silent in criminal proceedings did not, therefore, apply (*Young*). The Kansas law was similarly held to be constitutional when challenged. A subsequent constitutional challenge to the Kansas law was dealt with by the Supreme Court. In 2002, the High Court clarified that an individual need not have 'total or complete lack of control' of sexually offending behaviour, but 'there must be proof of serious difficulty in controlling behaviour' (*Crane*, p.1). Thus it can be argued that a person with a sexual paraphilia who struggles ineffectively to control sexually offending behaviour would better qualify as a sexually violent predator than as a psychopathic offender with impairment of behavioural control.

Civil commitment for other conditions

Several conditions that are neither mental illness nor sexual offending may qualify for special commitment laws, including alcohol/drug abuse/addiction, mental retardation/developmental disability, and dementia. The federal government and several states allow for the civil commitment of individuals whose substance use disorder is accompanied by dangerousness to self or others, or grave disability (Kermani and Castaneda, 1996). The statute, or appropriate court, may require existence of a specialized programme before ordering such commitment, even if the person presents a substantial danger as a result of the disorder (e.g. see Beckson et al., 2003).

Institutions and programmes in the USA

In the USA county and city jails (the latter more-or-less equivalent to English remand prisons) are intended for detention of defendants awaiting trial, including those who need competency, insanity or other pre-trial evaluations; for some, community assessment may be possible. A magistrate or judge sets the amount of money needed to ensure the defendant's presence at trial (Bassiouni, 1974); the defendant who pays his/her bail, or a specified percentage of it, may be permitted to await trial in the community and be assessed there. Some states, however, require that the defendant be evaluated for criminal competence in hospital; in most this remains common practice (Miller, 2003a). This is especially likely when the defendant is unwilling or unable to co-operate with forensic interviews (Miller, 2003a).

The evaluating psychiatrist may be an 'impartial' expert, appointed by the court. Resultant reports are then submitted to and paid for by the court; confidentiality limited to one attorney or the other is not expected. Alternatively, the expert may be retained by the defence counsel or the prosecutor. Confidentiality begins with the referring attorney but ceases once the report is introduced into evidence. The retaining attorney is responsible for paying the expert. In hybrid models, the expert may be appointed and retained by the court, yet the report sent only to the attorney requesting the evaluation. The military uses an insanity commission wherein three evaluators prepare and sign a single report. Several large metropolitan areas have court clinics to provide routine evaluations and, occasionally, treatment (Barboriak, 2003).

Most defendants with serious mental illness who are evaluated while in jail and found incompetent to stand trial, or not guilty by reason of insanity, must remain in jail until such finding, whereupon they are remanded for hospital treatment. Thus, jails often have to provide psychiatric care for months. Only in rare and extreme cases, where the defendant meets civil commitment criteria and refuses treatment in the jail, may civil commitment to a designated hospital be possible. Large jails have an infirmary with a limited number of cells that must be reserved for people who are acutely suicidal or who need intensive treatment. State prisons have their own maximum security hospitals but, in jails and prisons, most inmates with mental disorder are treated as 'outpatients', that is, by mental health professionals while remaining on general location in the prison.

Most defendants who are found incompetent to stand trial are remanded to a state forensic security hospital for treatment and restoration of competence, although jurisdictional law may allow some defendants whose conduct is reliable, and who present no concern of dangerousness, to be treated for restoration of competence as outpatients (Miller, 2003a). Insanity acquittees are similarly court ordered to receive inpatient treatment in a state forensic security hospital, which is typically within the state mental health system; in some states it belongs to the correctional system. The federal government and the US military have their own forensic security hospitals. Where security is of less concern, and jurisdictional law and practices allow, some incompetent defendants or insanity acquittees are treated as civil patients.

Sex offender programmes in the USA

Four basic programme models exist for the treatment of sexual offenders:

1. for convicted and imprisoned sexual offenders who volunteer to participate;
2. for offenders designated as 'sexually dangerous persons', who, committed for treatment and rehabilitation, thereby avoid conviction and imprisonment; such treatment programmes, located in prison facilities, are rare;
3. for 'sexually violent predators' (SVP), who have been charged or convicted of specified sexual crimes *and* have a mental abnormality rendering them likely to reoffend in a similar way; most have served their prison sentence and would otherwise be eligible for release; instead, they are civilly committed to a specialized SVP programme, typically in a state correctional system unit;
4. for treating paraphilias as outpatients; either for unconvicted people who voluntarily pursue treatment or released prisoners who have been in one of the above residential programmes. The most common treatment approach in residential settings is cognitive-behavioural (e.g. Wood et al., 2000), although anti-androgenic pharmacotherapy can be a useful adjunct, especially for outpatient treatment (Rösler and Witztum, 2000); funding can, unfortunately, be prohibitive, and the most limiting step. Other treatment approaches include olfactory aversion, masturbatory satiation, aversive behavioural rehearsal, victim empathy, improvement in social skills (Able and Osborn, 2003) and psychodynamic psychotherapy (Wood et al., 2000). The effectiveness of such programmes is considered in chapter 10.

FORENSIC PSYCHIATRIC SERVICES AND INTERVENTIONS UNDER CRIMINAL AND CIVIL LAW: THE NINE NATIONS (SWANZDSAJCS[1]) STUDY

Questions of Capacity to Stand Trial in the Nine Nations Study

Competency to stand trial is the most widely recognized pre-trial forensic psychiatric issue, although other specific pre-trial criminal competencies are important too, including competency to provide a confession, waive rights to counsel, or plead guilty. Defendants are rarely found incompetent in the latter areas, but safeguards in police interviews before charge and/or trial have been built into law or practice in most countries. If the case comes to trial, and the police cannot demonstrate that they have followed the rules, the case may fall. Miscarriages of justice have

followed from failures in this phase of the criminal process, and such cases have sometimes led to new safeguards. The Police and Criminal Evidence (PACE) Act 1984 in England and Wales is one example (see also chapters 2, 25). Similarly, new law was enacted in Denmark with the overturn of a rape conviction of a mentally retarded man once DNA evidence linking the crime to another man became available (*Meddelelse*).

In Canada, the Charter of Rights sets out the obligations of the police towards arrested persons. They must inform the person that s/he is under arrest, of her/his rights to remain silent and to consult with an attorney. Police officers cannot abuse their authority in order to obtain a confession. In Québec, police cannot be indifferent to the health or safety of anyone in their custody, but there is no obligation on arresting officers to report evidence of a suspect's mental disorder or deficiency. It is, however, common practice throughout Canada for them to do so and even to recommend psychiatric examination.

In Australia, as in Canada, the police have the responsibility of ensuring that arrested persons can read and comprehend their legal rights. In some states, independent third parties are available to observe police interviews when the police have identified a person as having questionable capacity. In Victoria, for example, volunteers with the Office of the Public Advocate are available if police consider anyone they want to interview may have impaired capacity.

The principle that, if charged with a criminal offence, the accused should have sufficient mental capacity to be able to understand and plead to the charge and instruct a lawyer accordingly is widely accepted, but the extent of its formal testing in court, criteria for fitness and the process for testing them vary between jurisdictions. Mainland European countries and others influenced by Roman law (e.g. Japan) do not test fitness to plead, but do ensure legal representation for the accused. Countries in the common law tradition tend to have relevant laws, recently reformed in many, but to use them little.

Sweden and Denmark

In Sweden and Denmark all accused persons will appear before the Court, and be tried as if fit to plead, regardless of mental state; counsel for the defence is supposed to safeguard the interests of the accused in all circumstances. Psychiatric evidence is not regarded as relevant in court unless and until the case reaches the sentencing phase. Clinicians in both countries have concerns about this, and occasionally the issue has generated media debate in Denmark, but there has been no indication that governments in either country will change the law.

Australia

The concept of unfitness to plead or to stand trial exists in Australia, but, as criminal laws are state-based, the

---

[1] SWANZDSAJCS links Sweden, Wales, Australia, New Zealand, Denmark, South Africa, Japan, Canada and Scotland. See figure 5.1.

1. Sweden

History of social democratic welfare system
High standard of living and life expectancy
Healthcare, childcare and education basically free
Strong national quest for equality
Low population density – large inland areas of forests and mountains
Three major urban centres
Stockholm, Gothenberg and Malmö.

Development of legislation and forensic services driven by:

Public safety
Equality
Public opinion following high profile cases
Increasing availability of illicit drugs
Decreased bed availability in psychiatry
Increased incidence of patients with comorbidities, especially where diagnosis relates to substance abuse.

2. Wales

Devolved health and education systems under Welsh Assembly control
Legal system and law enforcement shared with England
Healthcare, childcare and education all free
Strong quest for nationality (bilingualism; Welsh and English)
Low population density – large inland mountainous areas
Major urban belt in the south: Swansea, Cardiff, Newport
Heavy industry (coal and steel) declined; farming declining. Highest male suicide rate in UK around Swansea

Development of legislation and forensic services driven by:

Same issues as in Sweden; alcohol a problem

3. Australia

Constitutional monarchy retaining the British monarch as head of state.
Mental health and criminal law is devolved to the six states and two territories.
Public/private healthcare model and a strong and almost complete deinstitutionalization process characterizes mental health.
Increasing rates of incarceration with high levels of incarceration of indigenous Australians.
Australia's English common law heritage has resulted in legislative schemes in the past decade that have abolished automatic detention of those found not guilty of offences on account of mental impairment.

4. New Zealand

Independent nation, although British monarch retained as Head of State.
Majority of population live in the geographically smaller North Island.
Economy traditionally reliant on agriculture, now diversifying.
Comprehensive free healthcare system and free education.
Bilingualism (English and Maori).

Development of legislation and forensic services driven by:

1988 enquiry (the Mason Report: see p.143) – provided a template for development of forensic services – supported by government.

5. Denmark

Scandinavian welfare country similar to Sweden.
A peninsula and many islands, incl. Greenland and Faroe Is. (both self-governing overseas territories).
Strong flexible economy, well-educated labour force, stable currency.

Development of legislation and forensic services driven by:

'Law and order' reforms
Decreased availability of beds in general psychiatry, and increasing number of individuals identified as 'forensic patients'.

6. South Africa

Nine varied provinces – each with own legislature
Courts, prisons and criminal justice independent of provincial control
Diverse economy; very high unemployment, mismatch of labour skills
30% in private healthcare (60% of health spend)
Public healthcare requires fee based on earnings

Development of legislation and forensic services driven by:

Human rights and equality of justice
Forensic mental health system
'resinstitutionalization by stealth' national government funded.

7. Japan

Technology industries – strong work ethic
Efficient criminal justice system – police, courts, prisons and citizens work closely; low rate of imprisonment
High rate psychiatric hospitalization; 85%+ use private healthcare, partly funded by National Insurance, partly paid at point of use
Forensic mental health services publicly funded
Most education through state system

Development of legislation and forensic services driven by:

High profile cases.

8. Canada

Ten provinces; Yukon, North West Territories and Nunavit each have their own legislature. Although one criminal code applies to all, the administration of criminal justice, as well as of prisons for sentences of less than 2 years, are under provincial jurisdiction.
Healthcare (hospital and community) is provided free in all parts of Canada

Development of legislation and forensic services has been driven by:

Rulings by the Supreme Court of Canada which have followed from high profile cases and the law and order philosophies of the ruling political parties.

9. Scotland

Devolved government with full legislative powers
Healthcare, free childcare and education (incl. tertiary)
Four main urban areas 30% population – Glasgow, Edinburgh, Aberdeen and Dundee
Economy diversifying following losses in trad. industries (shipbuilding and fishing); 100,000 jobs lost 1998–2002

Development of legislation and forensic services driven by:

High profile cases and research findings; the Forensic Mental Health Services Managed Care Network, established in 2003.

Figure 5.1   The nine countries in the SWANZDSAJCS Study.

substantive law and legal procedures vary between the states. Generally, though, the legal test for unfitness follows from English common law, and includes the principles of: understanding the nature and severity of the charges, understanding and being able to follow the legal process, and being able to instruct counsel. Consequences of a finding of unfitness differ too. In Queensland, for example, a jury finding of unfitness to plead in cases of indictable offences leads to admission to the Security Patients' Hospital, as a restricted patient. Further decisions are always passed by the Patient Review Tribunal (see also below). In New South Wales, provision exists to ensure that persons found unfit for trial will not be detained longer than they would have been if they had been found guilty of the offence with which they were charged and had been sentenced to an appropriate term of imprisonment. The Mental Health Review Tribunal determines if the person is likely to be fit to plead within 12 months. If not, a special trial by jury is held. If the person is found guilty of the offence, a 'limiting term' is fixed, beyond which the offender may not be detained in prison or hospital. A similar situation pertains in Victoria and Tasmania, and in Victoria, if fitness cannot be restored, a special hearing may be held to try the facts. If it is found that the evidence would not support a conviction, the person is released from custody, though may be detained involuntarily under mental health law if it would otherwise apply. If the evidence would sustain a conviction, then custodial or non-custodial detention is determined by the court. In South Australia and Western Austria, a finding of unfitness results in indefinite hospitalization in a secure institution, with the possibility of trial in the event of sufficient recovery.

New Zealand

In New Zealand, a defendant is unfit to stand trial if any form of mental impairment renders him/her unable to conduct his/her defence or instruct counsel to do so. Following 2003 legislation, the court must be satisfied of the defendant's involvement in the offence *prior to* a finding of unfitness. Disposition options since then have included diversion through stand alone legislation into services for the intellectually disabled. An unfit defendant facing serious charges will usually be detained as a 'special patient' if mentally ill, or a 'special care recipient' if s/he has intellectual disability, until either sufficient recovery to return to court for trial or, in the case of permanent disability, for a period of time equal to half the maximum term of imprisonment time they could have received if convicted (10 years for an offence punishable by life imprisonment). If a special patient/care recipient order is not considered necessary, civil detention is an option. In addition, notwithstanding ongoing unfitness, if either order is no longer considered necessary, reclassification to civil status by the Minister of Health and Attorney-General is possible.

South Africa

Section 79 of the Criminal Procedure Act 1977, as amended by the Criminal Matters Amendment Act 1998, provides for the referral of a defendant for psychiatric or psychological assessment. The Act distinguishes between non-violent and seriously violent offences. For the former, enquiry into the mental capacity of the accused may be conducted by the medical superintendent of the psychiatric hospital, or his/her nominated psychiatrist. For cases involving serious violence, the court must appoint a panel, consisting of the state employed psychiatrist, a psychiatrist not in the full-time service of the state, a psychiatrist for the accused, and a clinical psychologist 'where the court so directs'; the accused is usually admitted under warrant to a state (usually forensic) psychiatric hospital for up to 30 days' observation.

The Director of Public Prosecutions must supply the following information:

- whether the accused is being assessed for fitness to stand trial or criminal capacity (or both);
- at whose request, or on whose initiative the referral was made;
- the nature of the charge against the accused;
- the stage of the proceedings at which the referral took place;
- statements that the accused may have made before or during the court proceedings that are relevant to the enquiry;
- the purport of the evidence that has been presented that may be relevant to the enquiry;
- any information that the prosecutor may have concerning the social background and family composition of the accused, names and addresses of near relatives; and
- any other information that, in the prosecutor's opinion, may be relevant in the evaluation of the mental capacity of the accused.

The terms 'mental illness', 'mental disorder' and 'mental defect' are used liberally in legislation, but nowhere are they precisely defined. Further, although the court may order an enquiry under the Criminal Procedure Act 1977 (s.77) at any stage in a trial '[if] it appears ... that the accused is by reason of mental illness or mental defect not capable of understanding the proceedings so as to make a proper defence', neither the courts nor legislature have clarified criteria or thresholds for unfitness; decisions tend to follow the assessor's subjective opinion.

If an accused is 'not fit to stand trial' due to mental illness (or 'defect') the report to the court must recommend appropriate treatment. The court then has to decide whether the weight of evidence indicates that the accused committed the alleged act; if probably not, or the offence did not involve serious violence, civil procedures may be followed. When the offence did involve serious violence, the accused must be admitted to a forensic psychiatry facility as a state patient under the Mental Healthcare Act 2002 (s.41). This allows the court to direct indefinite detention for treatment in a forensic psychiatric unit. At this stage, the court may also consider capacity at the time of the alleged offence (see also below).

Japan

Japan had its first written criminal code in 1742 – the 'Kujikata osadame gaki', founded in the privileged class system of the Samurai. During the Meiji period of 1868–1912, with its extensive interchange between European and Asian countries, the Japanese government sought to update its legislative systems, and turned initially to France for guidance. Professor Boassonade de Fontarabie, from the University of Paris, was invited to Japan for the purpose. He drew up a criminal code for Japan in 1880, said to be a direct translation of the Napoleonic Code. Japanese criminal law was, however, amended under the influence of German criminal law in 1907. The legal system, consequently, still has much in common with that of most mainland European countries. With respect to fitness to plead, a public prosecutor would not prosecute a person with mental disorder even if s/he were alleged to have committed a serious criminal offence, because of the risk of acquittal in such cases. On suspicion of a mental disorder, a psychiatric report is generally requested before trial. Anyone charged with an offence who is thought to have a mental disorder would be entitled to a court-appointed or privately hired lawyer.

Canada

Criteria for unfitness to stand trial are enshrined in the Canadian Criminal Code. The criteria are familiar to any country which applies the concept: inability on account of mental disorder to understand the nature or object of the proceedings, to understand the possible consequences of the proceedings, or to communicate with counsel. An assessment order for fitness may be made at any stage of proceedings, specifying by whom, where and for how long the examination will be made; the presumption is against detention for the duration of the assessment. A medical report must then be submitted to the Court. No order for treatment may be made during the period unless the report concludes that the accused is unfit but medical treatment would be likely to render him/her fit to stand trial within 60 days. In that event, medical treatment other than psychosurgery or electroconvulsive therapy (ECT) may be enforced, regardless of the capacity of the accused with respect to treatment decisions.

A 2004 decision by the Canadian Supreme Court (*Demers*) has led to a legislative change for an accused person considered permanently unfit. If that person is not deemed to present a significant threat to the public, a Court, either on the recommendation of the Review Board or of its own accord, may conduct an inquiry to determine whether to discontinue the case. A person found unfit may not be detained in a psychiatric facility only on those grounds.

Psychiatric Defences and Measures in Criminal Proceedings in the SWANZDSAJCS Countries

All legal systems exercise some limits on the nature of proceedings following a criminal charge, as all carry some concept that, with the exception of a few offences of absolute liability, two conditions must be satisfied for a criminal conviction to be sustained – evidence that a criminal act was committed by the person under charge *and* that s/he had a 'guilty mind'. Children, for example, are exculpated by their age, although countries vary in the specified age of criminal responsibility (e.g. 8 years in Scotland, 10 in Wales, New Zealand and Australia; 12 in Canada; 14 in Denmark, Western Cape/South Africa and Japan, 15 in Sweden; states in the USA are inconsistent, some failing to specify a minimum age (Cipriani, 2009).

There are also various circumstances which may justify reducing or even 'excusing' an offence. Provocation is an example of the former, and might be applicable to any alleged perpetrator. Since ancient times, there has been some concept that a person with, say, a psychotic illness may be incapable of controlling his/her thinking and/or actions, and so excused. A more recent approach is that which regards the mentally disordered person as guilty, but less so than a healthy person committing the same act. Neither exculpation nor allowance of reduced responsibility is commonly used in any of the jurisdictions considered; where it is used, it is often to avoid the mandatory sentence associated with certain convictions, for example the life sentence required after a murder conviction in England and Wales. In a few countries without mandatory sentencing, such as Denmark and Sweden, such concepts do not apply in the trial, but they are considered in sentencing. In neither country would a person found to have had a 'serious mental disorder' at the time of the offence be considered punishable; s/he would inevitably be sent into the healthcare system. Most cases are of people with psychosis. Other diagnoses do not exclude a healthcare disposal, but mental retardation is not usually treated as a mental disorder for these purposes. Nevertheless, an alternative to imprisonment would be usual; where behavioural disturbance is prominent, for example, reclassification as personality disorder is an option. Just as for input during the trial elsewhere, it is for the psychiatrist to give evidence on mental disorder, but for the court to decide on its relevance to legal outcome.

When mentally abnormal offenders benefit from one or other form of exculpatory 'generosity', societal ambivalence towards them is, nevertheless, reflected by imposition of security measures. An order for health service disposal may mean loss of liberty for at least as long, sometimes longer than a prison sentence for an equivalent offence. If the alleged offence is serious, then it is likely that the order will be 'without limit of time'. This need not mean that the individual will be detained indefinitely, but s/he must demonstrate that s/he is no longer dangerous before the order may be lifted. Resolution of tensions between excusing and constraining varies between our countries.

In jurisdictions in the Roman law tradition, the term 'responsibility' is a unified concept covering the capacity to understand the unlawful nature of an act and the capacity for behavioural control ('démence' in article 64 of the French Penal Code). If either or both of these capacities is absent, the accused is not considered guilty and is not subject to punishment.

In countries which lean to a common law system, these capacities tend to be split, with 'insanity' referring to, essentially, cognitive deficits, applying to any offence other than one of absolute liability, and leading to a not-guilty finding. The application of defences founded in lesser degrees of acknowledged impairment are more variable between countries, with differences in the range of offences to which such defences may be applied, the extent to which they encapsulate merely a lesser degree of impairment and the extent to which they incorporate also volitional defects. In two states of Australia (Queensland, New South Wales), for example, the term 'diminished responsibility' has limited application, as in England and Wales, as a special defence in murder cases; if the defence is successful, the conviction is reduced to manslaughter, but in Japan, a diminished responsibility defence may be available for any offence.

Psychiatric defences available and their consequences will now be taken in more detail for each of the countries under consideration here (except Wales and Scotland, see chapters 2 and 3 respectively).

Sweden

Although the concept of 'responsibility' at the time of an offence does not exist in Swedish law, if mental disorder is suspected, a forensic psychiatric assessment is requested to assist the court with disposal. Should the forensic psychiatrist conclude that the defendant suffered 'a *severe* (allvarlig) mental disorder' at the time of the offence and at the time of the trial, and the court agrees, the person will be ordered into forensic psychiatric treatment. The report may also be used in mitigation, with a possible reduction in sentence on evidence of psychiatric disorder, not amounting to '*severe* mental disorder'.

An order into forensic psychiatric treatment may be imposed, with or without further court proceedings, on grounds of mental disorder when the court, assisted by forensic psychiatric expertise, finds that there is a future risk of serious violence. In such instances, which comprise 80% of all cases ordered into forensic psychiatric treatment,

the period of hospitalization is decided according to both clinical factors and risk of re-offending. Leave or discharge is considered 6-monthly by a civil court, with advice from the responsible clinician. There is no question of tariff in these circumstances.

There are two kinds of forensic psychiatric reports, both strictly regulated by the National Board of Forensic Medicine. One is short, based on a screening assessment by one certified psychiatrist; the other is a full assessment by a multidisciplinary forensic mental health team. The conclusions of the latter may be challenged by any of the parties. In this event, the court will have the report scrutinized by a national expert committee of the Swedish Board of Health and Welfare. Decisions in a lower court, including the issue of disposal, may be overruled by regional higher courts or, in special cases, by the national Supreme Court.

Australia

Criminal responsibility legislation varies for each state and territory, but all rely on a McNaughton-based test to determine whether, as a result of 'mental impairment' (mental illness or intellectual impairment), the accused knew the nature and quality of the act or that the act was wrong at the time of the offence. Queensland has added the possibility of a volitional element within the McNaughton standard (deprived of capacity to control his/her action). In all jurisdictions, the law allows for those found not guilty on account of mental impairment to be detained in custody or supervised in the community. In most states, there are too few hospital beds to accommodate the number of people found not guilty on account of mental impairment, so, although frowned on by courts and clinicians, many such people are held in prison. There has been a legislative trend, though, to require that those found not guilty on account of mental impairment be detained in a secure hospital (e.g. Victoria).

The criteria for diminished responsibility, as used in Queensland and New South Wales, are explicitly broad:

when a person who unlawfully kills another, which would normally constitute murder, is at the time of doing the act or making the omission which causes death in such a state of abnormality of mind as substantially to impair his capacity to understand what he is doing, or his capacity to control his actions, or his capacity to know that he ought not to do the act or make the omission, he is guilty of manslaughter only.

In all states except for Queensland, determination of criminal responsibility is for the district/county or supreme courts. The innovation in Queensland's legislation resides in the function of the Mental Health Tribunal in criminal matters. This consists of a Judge of the Supreme Court who is advised by two psychiatrists (the latter not a constituent part of the tribunal). It is divorced from the atmosphere of a criminal court and unique in mental health legislation. When there is reasonable cause to believe that a person alleged to have committed an indictable office is mentally ill, or was at the time of the alleged offence, the matter of the person's mental condition may be referred to the Mental Health Tribunal. Additional Mental Health Tribunal functions include determining fitness to plead and to be tried, and hearing appeals from the Patient Review Tribunal.

Regardless of the findings of the Mental Health Tribunal, a person may elect to go to trial, or appeal to the Court of Criminal Appeals. Cases which, once dealt with by the Mental Health Tribunal, do not go to trial are referred to the Patient Review Tribunal for determination of certain management issues (e.g. placement). The Patient Review Tribunal consists of three to five members (including a medical practitioner and mental health professional). The Patient Review Tribunal has jurisdiction over criminal matters as well as civil commitment.

Legislative changes were made in Victoria in 1997 – The Crimes (Mental Impairment and Fitness to be Tried) Act, 1997 – which significantly overhauled criminal responsibility law and procedure. While the legal test is still based on *McNaughton*, the second element of the test has been broadened by the language s/he 'did not know that the conduct was wrong (that is, he or she could not reason with a moderate degree of sense and composure about whether the conduct, as perceived by reasonable people, was wrong)' (s.20).

Of more importance, though, the automatic indeterminate custodial disposition which formally occurred with the 'governor's pleasure' provisions was abandoned. This means that patients have a good chance of being discharged, when in the past they would have languished in prison. In a few non-fatal cases, judges have ordered noncustodial supervision orders. Other states are beginning legislative changes following similar principles.

New Zealand

In New Zealand, too, *mens rea* must be proven in all but strict and absolute liability offences. In the event of serious mental illness, the insanity defence is likely to be advanced. Infanticide (but not diminished responsibility) is available as a partial defence to murder.

New Zealand retains an essentially cognitive variant of McNaughton's Rules:

No person shall be convicted of an offence by reason of an act done or omitted by him when labouring under natural imbecility or disease of the mind to such an extent as to render him incapable (a) of understanding the nature and quality of the act or omission; or (b) of knowing that the act or omission was morally wrong, having regard to the commonly accepted standards of right and wrong.

Following a finding of insanity by a judge or jury, disposition options include special patient status, a civil mental health committal order, or an order for release. The least restrictive order necessary is preferred. An equivalent suite of disposal options for those with intellectual disability has been available since stand alone legislation for them in 2003. 'Special patients' are initially detained in secure forensic hospitals, and 'special care recipients' go to equivalent intellectual disability services. Special patient/special care orders are indefinite. A period of safe community living is generally required before reclassification is considered, during which time readmission to hospital is not uncommon. Research indicates that inpatient care averages 6 years for those charged with murder, and, overall, re-offending is uncommon (6% re-offend violently up to 2 years after discharge to the community; Skipworth et al., 2006). Graduated leave and release may be allowed according to clinical risk perception, but leave for longer than a week must be approved by the Minister of Health, as must reclassification from special status (this contrasts with England and Wales, where it is the Ministry of Justice that holds the discharge of restricted patients function). Civilly committed patients may be reclassified at the discretion of their treating clinician, just as all other civilly committed patients. Appeal to the Mental Health Review Tribunal is possible for both special and civilly committed patients, but the judgment on special patients is not binding on the Minister of Health.

If an offender is convicted, the court may, instead of passing sentence, substitute a civil committal order, using MH or intellectual disability legislation. Within either, the court also has the option of a hybrid special patient order, sentencing to both a prison term and compulsory treatment. In this, the sentence runs during hospitalization, but the offender may be returned to prison in the event of recovery before sentence completion; if in hospital on the completion of tariff, their status then reverts to civil commitment.

Denmark

The situation with respect to psychiatric defences is very similar to that in Sweden. Major differences arise at the point of disposal from Court for those who need hospitalization. In Denmark, such offenders with major mental disorder are generally managed in mainstream MH services.

South Africa

Enquiry into the criminal capacity of an accused person may be conducted at any stage of a court case, even between conviction and sentencing. If the accused is found to be so mentally disordered that he was not criminally responsible, the conviction may be set aside and a finding of 'not guilty by reason of insanity' substituted. The Criminal Procedure Act 1977 (as amended in 1998) describes incapacity *per se* in almost the same terms as other jurisdictions (s.78(1)); criminal responsibility is assumed, the accused must raise the issue and the burden of proof rests with him/her. Although not explicit in the legislation, the Courts differentiate between *pathological incapacity* and *non-pathological incapacity*.

The defence of *pathological incapacity* rests on a finding that the accused suffers from an inherent mental disorder or defect. It is presumed that the disorder exists independently of the offence, although influencing it; this is taken to mean that the other circumstances of the offence were not as important as the mental disorder. Pathological incapacity is confirmed by a psychiatric diagnosis; it is presumed that the causative disorder is amenable to medical intervention, and that risk of recidivism remains high while symptoms persist. Successful use of this defence may thus result in a verdict of 'not guilty by reason of insanity', but still leave the accused indefinitely detained, albeit for psychiatric treatment. If the disorder merely impaired the ability to act in accordance with an appreciation of wrongfulness, or with reduced control over actions, the court may consider substituting *diminished responsibility* for *pathological incapacity*. Diminished responsibility is the more commonly used in SA courts; relevant factors include intense provocation, naïve intoxication, cultural beliefs, PTSD, and depression.

Non-pathological incapacity

Since 1981 (*Chretian*) the courts have accepted that there may be instances when an accused lacks criminal capacity, even though s/he was not suffering from mental illness or defect at the time. The term 'non-pathological incapacity' was coined by Joubert in *Laubscher* for criminal incapacity due to circumstances supposedly external to the accused, such as intoxication, provocation or emotional stress. This carries the assumption, unfounded, that there will be no recurrence of the behaviour, so the successful use of this defence results in acquittal. As pathological states are not invoked, psychiatric diagnoses are seldom offered. The courts have, thus, generally relied on experts using quaint terms, such as 'emotional storm', 'emotional collapse', or 'total disintegration of the ego' to describe the relevant states. This defence is almost exclusively confined to murder cases. Typically the individual would have endured increasing degrees of stress over a period, usually in interpersonal conflict in which s/he was subjected to humiliation or abuse. It would be argued that an intensely distressing precipitant ('trigger'), like emotional rejection, caused a climax which was followed by automatic behaviour, and culminated in the offence. After this 'automatism', there should be evidence that the perpetrator responded with bewilderment or horror, and did not try to escape from the scene. Rather, s/he should have attempted to get help for the victim and/or called the police. S/he should have amnesia for the offence, but not for preceding and subsequent events, including the 'trigger'. As in England and Wales, courts differentiate between an 'insane automatism' due to inherent brain disease, and 'sane (non-insane) automatism' due to external factors such as drugs or head

injury. This distinction does not make medical sense and has consistently baffled clinicians, nevertheless, non-pathological incapacity is, in essence, a sane/non-insane automatism defence, emphatically affirmed in *Eadie*. Ironically the Courts have accepted that expert testimony may not actually be necessary, but generally require it.

The dangerous offender

In post-apartheid South Africa, the courts have adopted more liberal sentencing, and prisons have prematurely released many habitually violent offenders on parole. The country has a precipitously high violent crime rate. In 1993, legislation was introduced to remove 'psychopathy' as a certifiable mental disorder. Simultaneously, the Criminal Procedure Act 1977 was amended to include provisions that, if an accused, after conviction '... represents a danger to the physical or mental wellbeing of other persons, and that the community should be protected against him, (the court may) declare him a dangerous criminal' (ss.286A, 286B). This finding can only be reached after a psychiatric examination over a 30-day observation period. The court may then sentence him/her to indefinite imprisonment, but sets a date for return to court for reconsideration of sentence. No guidelines for the courts have been issued on which defendants ought to be referred or the standard of the psychiatric evaluation. The requirement that the accused be a 'danger ... to the mental wellbeing of others' is worrying. Not only is it unclear as to who these 'others' might be, but the term 'mental wellbeing' is vague. A narrow definition was intended, but no threshold has been given.

The intention is to provide a means for dealing with violent 'psychopaths', who will no longer be diverted to MH services, but to allow for the possibility that they may improve, and become less likely to be dangerous. The examining psychiatrist, however, is not required to recommend any intervention, so the expectations that a high risk offender will improve, and that this improvement can be assessed are puzzling. Even though the court sets a review date, it is unlikely that meaningful psychiatric re-assessment would be possible, as the long-term prisoner will not have had a chance to prove his non-dangerousness in the community. Institutional performance, in prison or closed psychiatric hospital, is not necessarily indicative of future community behaviour.

Japan

Japanese criminal law, unchanged in this respect since 1907, also provides safeguards for the person with mental disorder at the time of a criminal act. Two levels of impaired responsibility are recognized, not specified in the criminal law itself, but defined in case precedent in 1931 (*Dai-sin-in*):

- shinshin sôshitsu – lost mind – in which, because of his/ her mental disorder, the individual is considered to lack capacity to distinguish between right and wrong and/or to act in accordance with that knowledge (sekinin mu nôryoku); such an individual is not punished;

- shinshin kôjaku – feeble mind – in which, because of his/her mental disorder, these abilities are not absent but are remarkably diminished; for such an individual (gentei sekinin nôryoku) sentence would be mitigated. This is almost identical to diminished responsibility in England and Wales, except that it may be applied to any crime.

This legislation meant that prosecution was abandoned for over 90% of crimes committed in Japan by people with mental disorder; until 2005, this included serious crimes such as homicide. Several cases, in particular one of a man with mental disorder who killed several children in a school, radically changed public opinion. Although he was executed, in 2003, the Japanese government passed a new law 'concerning the medical treatment and observation of people who commit serious harm to others under the condition of lost mind and the like' (Yoshikawa and Taylor, 2003). This law was implemented in 2005. It may be applied only to serious crimes; all other cases must be dealt with under civil mental health law.

Under the 2003 Act, on receipt of a claim from the prosecutor's office that the accused person may lack capacity, the Court must refer the case to a tribunal composed of a judge, psychiatrist and psychiatric social worker. They may order inpatient or outpatient treatment under forensic MH law if the three elements of disease, treatability and risk management/prevention can be met. Specifically, the tribunal must be satisfied that the person:

- is suffering from a mental disorder which caused the state of lost/feeble mind at the time of the index offence (disease element), *and that*
- treatment under the law is necessary for improving this mental disorder or for preventing its deterioration *and* that this mental disorder is treatable at the current standard of mental health services (treatability element), *and that*
- without treatment under the law the person is at such risk of doing a similar act that they could not be rehabilitated into society (risk management/prevention element).

In the event of such an order, dangerous people would be sent to a specialist forensic secure unit and the less dangerous to a specialist outpatient clinic. As forensic mental health services are only just developing, however, many dangerous people must still be treated within general adult psychiatry services. There is also a problem that will be familiar elsewhere – that, in the face of difficult patients and scarce resources, some psychiatrists are ready to manipulate the concept of 'treatability'. There is, too, a lack of 'step-down' services and community outreach, exacerbating a problem of prolonged bed occupancy in many units.

Canada

In Canada, there is a presumption of criminal responsibility, but prosecution or defence may raise the question of mental disorder sufficient to impair it. The burden of establishing this is then on the party that raises it, according to the familiar 'cognitive' tests. Several specific conditions have been considered as mental disorder for this purpose by the Canadian Supreme Court, including dissociative state, delirium tremens, and any psychosis. Indeed, any mental disorder may lead to acquittal providing it impaired appreciation of the act or of its wrongness; others successfully used include somnambulism (*Parks*), panic reactions, and the 'battered women syndrome' (*Lavallée*). Self-induced intoxication, though, cannot be used as a defence to assault or other threat to the bodily integrity of another person.

When a verdict of *not criminally responsible on account of mental disorder* is given by the Court, a disposition hearing may be held without delay if the Court decides that it has the required elements to do so, otherwise it falls to the Review Board. This Board has a maximum of 90 days after such a verdict to make a decision about disposal, which must be the least restrictive after consideration of public protection, the mental state of the accused and his/her related needs to facilitate his/her reintegration into society. Options are: absolute discharge, conditional discharge, or hospital detention, subject to conditions fixed by the Court or Review Board. The Canadian Supreme Court has taken the position that a person who does not pose a significant threat to the safety of the public, meaning a real risk of physical or psychological harm to members of the public, must be granted an absolute discharge (*Winko*).

As a consequence of changes in the criminal code, Canada has seen a substantial increase in the number of people found not criminally responsible on account of a mental disorder. This defence was previously limited to the most serious crimes, but it is now presented by defence attorneys who have no reason to fear an indefinite psychiatric detention for their clients.

Civil Commitment in the Nine Nations Study

Civil commitment standards are nearly always based on the presence of mental disorder of a nature or degree which warrants detention in hospital together with protection of the health and/or safety of the patient and/or of others. Detention may be for assessment, for treatment or both. 'Need for treatment' is based on paternalism (Chodoff, 1983), and is typically associated with a welfare model of state intervention. A phase of increasing emphasis on dangerousness as a criterion, even for civil commitment (Harding and Curren, 1979), while reducing paternalism, may have encouraged a public view of people with major mental disorder as necessarily dangerous

(Phelan and Link, 1998). The conceptualization of commitment as a form of deprivation of liberty, rather than a treatment intervention, corresponds to the provisions of the European Convention of Human Rights which defines exceptions to the right of liberty as including 'the lawful detention of ... persons of unsound mind, alcoholics or drug addicts or vagrants' (article 5.1e), although substance misuse disorders alone are not regarded as grounds for detention under European mental health laws. If commitment is seen as a form of detention, albeit requiring procedural guarantees of due process before an independent court (article 5.4), then what Stromberg and Stone (1983) have called the 'cruel paradox' of psychiatric detention without treatment becomes possible for the committed patient who is considered competent to refuse treatment. Fortunately, for EU countries, the jurisprudence of the European Court of Human Rights has gone some way towards establishing a treatment model as implicitly necessary within psychiatric commitment. Thus, in member states of the EU, detention must take place in a hospital or an establishment conceived for the mentally ill and conditions must conform to therapeutic standards. Another important principle, established in *Winterwerp*, was the right to regular review. Over 100 psychiatric cases concerning civil commitment have been the subject of published decisions of the European Commission of Human Rights and the European Court (Harding, 1989a, and see above). An increasingly frequent aspect of modern legislation is the requirement that attempts to provide treatment in the community have been exhausted; this tendency is associated with interest in community treatment orders as an alternative form of involuntary intervention, thus avoiding custodial treatment.

Perhaps more important than the difference between 'need for treatment' and 'dangerousness' standards are the broadness or precision of their criteria as constraints on professional discretion. Segal (1989) demonstrated, in a comparative study between England and Wales, Italy and the USA, that more loosely defined 'need for treatment' criteria, as opposed to more narrowly defined 'dangerousness' standards, were associated with different hospitalized patient profiles. Beigel et al. (1984), however, in a decision-making exercise, were unable to demonstrate that a narrow definition of dangerousness led to more restrictive patient selection.

A note on international standards

Professional organizations, including the World Psychiatric Organization, have been increasingly active in the field of forensic psychiatry, but the UN system, including the WHO, has given it scant attention. In the 2001 *World Health Report*, in well over 100 pages devoted to mental health, less than half a page was devoted to mentally disordered offenders.

The UN attempt at standard setting was also disappointing. The *Draft Body of Principles, Guidelines and Guarantees for the Mentally Ill* considered by the UN Sub-Commission on Prevention of Discrimination and Protection of Minorities on the initiative of its special rapporteur (Erica Daes), is regarded as impractical, over legalistic and badly drafted. Substantial revision of these principles was proposed by the WHO in 1988, and incorporated in new draft guidelines (the Palley report: UN Economic and Social Council, 1988), but, in the final stages before adoption by the UN General Assembly, several governments, notably Japan and the USA, intervened to render some of the safeguards ineffective. The modified guidelines were adopted by the UN General Assembly in December 1991. The principles are not regarded as constituting 'international human rights law' and are essentially unenforceable. Gendrea (1997) considers that they remove human rights safeguards of mental patients rather than reinforcing them.

Once again, it is within the member states of the Council of Europe where some effective norms have been established. Reference has already been made to case law from the European Court of Human Rights. Furthermore the Council's Committee of Ministers has adopted a number of relevant recommendations, such as Recommendation R(83), in 1983, concerning civil commitment and R(98)7 concerning 'ethical and organizational aspects of healthcare in prison'. The most innovative source of standards for forensic services comes from the Council of Europe's Committee for the Prevention of Torture, Inhuman and Degrading Treatment or Punishment (CPT) (Harding, 1989b). The CPT has substantial powers to inspect places of detention including specialized forensic hospitals, prisons and police stations. Norms concerning the use of physical restraint were set out following a CPT visit to forensic mental health centres in Germany in 2005, and reviewed at intervals since (http://www.coe.int; http://www.cpt.coe.int). In some cases, CPT findings have reinforced decisions by the European Court of Human Rights. Thus, in the same year as the *Rivière* judgment, a report of a visit to France was highly critical of standards of care for prisoners needing mental healthcare, in particular the practice of placing acutely mentally ill prisoners nude in a bare cell while awaiting transfer to a hospital.

Sweden

Current Swedish mental health legislation dates from 1992. Dangerousness criteria remain implicit rather than explicit, but lack of insight is expressly added to the criteria of severe mental disorder and need for hospital treatment. Two new amendments came into effect in 2008. Both appear to restrict access to psychiatric hospital beds for criminal and civil patients alike, but in practice are unlikely to make much difference:

1. A person convicted of a criminal offence may be sentenced to prison even if suffering from a severe mental disorder at the time of the crime, if that crime was serious (attracting a minimum of 4 years imprisonment) *and* if s/he was not completely mentally deteriorated at the time of the crime *and* that there is little or no need for treatment at the time of trial.

2. The responsible psychiatrist may apply to the civil court for involuntary community psychiatric treatment for civil as well as forensic patients.

Australia

Each state and territory in Australia has separate mental health legislation. While the civil provisions do vary, they are generally more similar than the criminal ones. Each jurisdiction provides for the involuntary hospitalization and treatment of people with mental illnesses that could lead to compromise of their own or others' safety, self-neglect or deterioration in mental state.

Since the 1980s there has been a growth in coerced outpatient treatment, or 'outpatient commitment'. Thousands of such outpatient orders are now made annually in Victoria. In an emergency, provisions variously allow police to force entry into premises where there are reasonable grounds for believing that there is a mentally ill person putting him/herself or others at risk, and to require a medical examination. This may result in involuntarily hospitalization, but even in an emergency, a community order may be considered. Discharge may be by the psychiatrist or the Mental Health Board.

Queensland legislation (Mental Health Services Act 1974) defines three forms of involuntary admission. *Medical admission* provides for a complex interaction between medical examination by at least two independent doctors, one a psychiatrist, an 'authorized person' (mental health professional or patient's relative) and the Patient Review Tribunal. Patients may then appeal against their detention to the Patient Review Tribunal at any stage of their regulated admission. Two much simpler forms of admission are available for emergencies. One requires a warrant to be issued by a justice of the peace (JP), who must be satisfied that a psychiatric emergency exists and that the interests of the person or the safety of others is at issue. The warrant is acted on by the police, a medical practitioner or a 'designated authorized person' to hospitalize the patient. Secondly, in situations of imminent danger for the person or others, the police may conduct the patient to hospital without a warrant. The New South Wales Mental Health Act 1983, by contrast, is characterized by an emphasis on patients' 'right to treatment', on community-based services and on stringent standards of proof for establishing the presence of mental illness and criteria for dangerous behaviour.

New Zealand

The introduction of the Mental Health (Compulsory Assessment and Treatment) Act 1992 saw a range of changes including:

- a new definition of mental disorder;
- a move from a custodial to an assessment and treatment approach;
- the introduction of concepts of community care;
- philosophies of treatment in the least restrictive environment;
- a greater emphasis on patients' rights;
- strengthening processes of appeal and review of the legitimacy of detention and/or treatment; and
- formal recognition of the importance of cultural factors in diagnosis and treatment.

Mental disorder is now defined as an abnormal state of mind (whether continuous or intermittent), characterized by delusions, or disorders of mood or perception or volition or cognition, of such a degree that it (a) poses a serious danger to the health or safety of that person or of others; or (b) seriously diminishes the capacity of that person to take care of him/herself. This definition is much more restrictive than in the previous Act, and excludes 'criminal delinquents', the intellectually disabled and substance abusers. The Intellectual Disability (Community Care and Rehabilitation) Act 2003 closed the resultant gaps for people with intellectual disability.

An application for assessment under the Act can be initiated by any person, and leads to a medical evaluation. Where two medical practitioners certify that there are reasonable grounds to suspect mental disorder, a patient may be detained for assessment for up to 5 days, renewable for up to 14 more days. If further extension is required, an application to the court is made for a compulsory treatment order, which may incorporate further assessment.

Perhaps the most significant change in 1992 was the still controversial introduction of community treatment orders, which now account for approximately 80% of compulsory treatment orders in New Zealand. In 2006, at any given time, about 58 persons per 100,000 population were detained under a compulsory community treatment order and now account for about two-thirds of everyone under compulsory treatment; 22 per 100,000 were under a compulsory inpatient treatment order, of whom 6 per 100,000 were on leave.

The 1992 Act acknowledged, for the first time, that many patients are capable of making decisions about their treatment. Treatment without consent is allowed during initial assessment, or the first month of a compulsory treatment order, but, thereafter, it must be deemed to be in the interests of the patient. The increase in emphasis on patients' rights was also marked by the introduction of much greater opportunities to challenge the legitimacy of detention expeditiously at all stages of the committal process, either through the Family or District Court prior to a compulsory treatment order being made, or by the MHRT thereafter. District inspectors of mental health were retained to investigate complaints of breaches of patients' rights. They are lawyers functioning as ombudsmen for the Act.

Denmark

The legal basis for civil involuntary hospitalization is the MHA 1989, revised in 1999, and again in 2007. The fundamental criteria for detention have changed little since 1938. Essentially the patient must have a psychotic illness which cannot be treated any other way, and meet 'need for treatment criteria' or 'dangerousness' (to self or others) criteria; people with a condition 'similar to a psychosis' might also be eligible. Such conditions might include depression with suicidal ideas but without overtly psychotic symptoms, or paranoia short of psychosis but with accompanying disorder of affect and threats made to self or others in this context. Each year, about 10% of admissions are compulsory. The changes in legislation have mainly been to incorporate specific directions for clinical acts while the person is under detention, ranging from enforced medication to compulsory baths for people with seriously compromised hygiene through illness related self-neglect. A community treatment measure, with very restrictive criteria, was finally introduced in Denmark in 2010, after years of debate.

An important principle for civil patients in Denmark is that they should spend no longer in hospital than their voluntary peers. There are a number of channels for challenging orders through bodies which are independent of the detaining hospital. The first appeal is to a regional body; if the decision is against release, the patient may take his/her case to an appeal court. Decisions against other kinds of coercion may be appealed through the National Board of Patients' Complaints of the Danish Public Health Authorities.

South Africa

The Mental Healthcare Act (MHCA) 2002 stipulates that all 'mental healthcare users' are entitled to treatment in the least restrictive environment, but neither these environments nor the admission criteria are well defined.

Healthcare in South Africa is organized in three concentric rings: the outer primary, inner secondary and the innermost tertiary care systems. Everyone must initially be assessed at the primary level before referral to any higher level. General practitioners, community healthcare centres and district hospitals have to assess and admit mentally ill individuals for a 72-hour assessment, and thereafter either to discharge home, or refer to a psychiatric hospital.

A person who suffers/is alleged to suffer from mental illness can only be received or detained at a healthcare facility in accordance with the MHCA 2002. The Act provides for three categories of admission: voluntary, assisted (patient not opposing admission) or involuntary (compulsory).

Admission procedures for assisted patients (referred to as a 'third party voluntary procedure') are less formal than those for involuntary admission. Application for assisted admission may be made only by the spouse, next of kin, partner, associate, parent or guardian of a mental healthcare user, except in the following cases, when a healthcare provider may apply:

1. The user is below the age of 18 years on the date of the application, the application must be made by the parent/guardian of the user unless that parent/guardian is unwilling, incapable or not available; or

2. The spouse/partner, next of kin, associate, of the adult user is unwilling, incapable or not available to make such an application.

The Act provides the power to commit a mentally ill person to a health facility if:

a. an application in writing is made to the head of the health establishment concerned to obtain the necessary services;

b. at the time of making the application, there is reasonable belief that the MH care user has a mental illness of such a nature that:

   i) s/he is likely to inflict serious harm to her/himself or others; or

   ii) care, treatment and rehabilitation of the user is necessary for the protection of her/his financial interests or reputation; and

   iii) at the time of the application the user is incapable of making an informed decision on the need for care, treatment and rehabilitation services and/ or unwilling to receive them as needed.

Japan

The Mental Health and Welfare Law 1988, revised in 1999, regulates voluntary admissions and civil detention. The latter is usually for the medical care and protection of the individual, but, until the 1980s, there were serious concerns about the abuse of this law, as over 70% of hospital admissions for mental disorder were involuntary, and most hospitals then were in the private sector. Only one medical opinion, generally from the hospital superintendent, was required for detention, together with agreement by the person's nearest relative or guardian; rights of appeal were minimal. The responsibilities of the nearest relative or guardian were considerable. They encompassed ensuring co-operation with a doctor so that an appropriate medical examination could be properly carried out, following the instructions of that doctor, further ensuring that the patient received medical care and that s/he was supervised so as not to injure him/herself or others or act with impropriety. The resultant burden on relatives could include compensation in the event of tragedy; for example, one patient's father was ordered to pay 100 million yen when his mentally ill son killed another person. The 1999 reform of this law eased the burden on relatives, but there is still high dependence on involuntary admission. In 2005, 36% of patients in mental hospitals were there under civil detention.

Canada

There is much consistency in provincial mental health legislation on civil detention, with variation being mainly in the duration of detention periods. In the initial involuntary admission process, power lies with physicians, the judiciary playing their role through review of applications and appeals. In most provinces, the legislation provides for initial short-term confinement (usually 24–72 hours) for assessment. If the formal criteria for admission are satisfied, admission certificates can be completed to authorize continued involuntary hospitalization, provincial variation on this being between 2 weeks and a year. In all jurisdictions, the police may apprehend mentally disturbed persons without a warrant, although there are some provincial differences in the scope of this power and the conditions attached to it.

Criteria for civil detention hold as common ground that there be evidence of a mental disorder, but there is provincial variation in specificity of definition. Some provinces use specific diagnostic categories, others favour symptom descriptions. 'Dangerousness', the second criterion, is prominent in most of the provincial MHAs, although its meaning varies from reference to 'safety' of the patient or others to a very narrow definition.

Most provinces have established a special review board to which civil patients can apply for review of their detention. These boards usually have three to five members including a lawyer, a lay person and a psychiatrist independent of the detaining facility. In some provinces, review applications are brought before a provincial court rather than a review board; in others it can be either. Most provinces require the patient or his/her representative to take the initiative in requesting review, but Saskatchewan, Ontario and Quebec provide for automatic reviews. In all provinces, the patient must give written consent for release of information from his clinical records to designated third parties; the patient's right to see his/her own record varies between the provinces.

In cases where a patient is incapable or refuses to consent to treatment, authorization may be given by an appointed guardian or a court, the mechanism for this varying between provinces. In Newfoundland and Saskatchewan, the treating physician authorizes the treatment, while in British Columbia, it must be the director of the psychiatric facility. In New Brunswick, a quasi-judicial tribunal must be convened, but in Quebec only a Court may authorize involuntary psychiatric treatment, and only in cases where a patient is seen as incompetent to give or refuse consent. In Ontario, Prince Edward Island, Alberta and Manitoba a substitute decision-maker may be appointed.

Forensic Mental Health (FMH) Services and Institutions

The increasing diversity of units and institutions in the grey area between prisons and general psychiatric hospitals provides a kind of professional identity for forensic psychiatrists. Single hospital unit developments occurred in a number of countries in the nineteenth and early twentieth centuries, but national service networks tend to be a feature of the late twentieth and early twenty-first centuries. Only a few countries, such as Denmark, eschew altogether specialist FMH unit developments, either continuing to integrate offender patients needing hospitalization within generic MH service provision or providing specialist prison units. France provides a network of hospital units within prisons (Balier, 1988). Countries with a network of specialist secure health services have embraced a model of providing appropriate specific treatments within a healthcare philosophy but in a physically secure building with highly developed procedural and relational security measures. In general, those with later specialist service developments have, so far, resisted the high security hospital provision which still exists in the UK. A key research question is the extent to which such resistance is successful, or whether it leaves more of the most seriously distressed and dangerous people with mental disorders in the penal system than would be true in places which do have a high security option.

Specialist FMH services tend to be under cycles of review. This is partly because, whether or not they are in hospitals, they rely heavily on closed institutions and are thus always vulnerable to the pathologies of institutional life (see also chapters 23, 24). Other reasons are that they tend to be expensive relative to other mental health provision and to be commissioned differently, making free movement between specialist and generic MH services more difficult than it should be. Another factor which affects integration of offender patients within mainstream services is the widespread trend to reduce general psychiatric bed numbers. While welcoming support for the principle of preference for community care wherever possible, some are beginning to question whether general psychiatric bed closure programmes may have gone too far. In Denmark, for example, with comprehensive community mental heath and social services, the number of forensic patients was around 300 in 1980, but by 2007 had increased to around 2,000, about 70% of them suffering from schizophrenia. Although there is less service separation of forensic and general psychiatric patients there than in some countries, this change has made even politicians question whether there is a greater than anticipated need for long-term psychiatric beds.

Sweden's FMH service provision has been reviewed (Värd och stöd till psykiskt störda lagöverträdare [The National Psychiatric Services Cordination], 2006; Psykiatrin och lagen-trångsvård, straffansvar och samhällsskydd [Psychiatry and the law – compulsion, responsibility and public protection] SOU 2012:17; http://riksdagan.se/en). There, most offenders with mental illness who need incarceration are already in a hospital. The main recommendations of the new reports (into general as well as forensic psychiatry provision) are to strengthen forensic psychiatry while seeking ways of improving forensic and general psychiatry links, and, in turn, links with social services. The crucial point is to ensure treatment and rehabilitation rather than long, passive incarceration periods. At present most forensic mental health resource goes into inpatient services; only a little goes into prison or short-term aftercare; almost nothing goes to prevention or continued support. In future, the proportion of the budget spent on inpatients may be reduced, and uplift given to 'step-down' services, prevention and longer term support, perhaps mainly through consultation–liaison services to both health and criminal justice system facilities.

This textbook is about forensic psychiatry, so it is inevitable that psychiatry receives a good deal of emphasis. Forensic mental health services could not function, however, without specialist expertise in all the other relevant disciplines, good communication between them and effective team work. Each other clinical discipline providing forensic mental health services is similarly beginning also to define its role in a way which distinguishes it from that of their generic peers, and to develop training accordingly. For psychologists, for example, there are, in most countries, at least two routes into work in the field: those who, in health service units, tend to have trained first as clinical psychologists, and then added specialist training and those who work primarily in prisons and pursue a more specific and less clinically oriented training.

Forensic psychology, including clinical forensic psychology, has developed since about 1980. Practices, training requirements, and roles vary considerably across countries. In the USA and Canada, for example, it has been 40 years since the scientist-practitioner model of doctoral training in psychology has been the norm. This required completion of a 4-year undergraduate degree in psychology, followed by a 2-year masters' degree and a further 3-year doctorate before an internship. Post-doctoral fellowships in forensic psychology have become more common, combining coursework, clinical training, and empirical research. Perhaps as a result of the extensive training and empirical advances made by psychologists, in the USA they regularly conduct fitness (competency) and insanity assessments. Similarly in Canada, psychologists' roles have expanded,

and it is not unusual for psychologists to be clinical directors of forensic or general MH services.

Within correctional services, psychologists also have increasingly prominent roles. This is partly because it has become ever more difficult to attract psychiatrists to work there. Not long ago, in many countries, psychiatrists were directly employed in the health team in prisons, but more often now their contact with prisoners and staff is limited to seeing a parade of prisoners referred for assessment and/or treatment.

Provision of reports for the Court remains central to forensic mental health service work everywhere. Court clinics have been established in cities in the USA. In Canada, Ministers of Health in each province have designated facilities for the custodial assessment or treatment of accused persons in accordance with the dispositions of the criminal code. These facilities, dealing with outpatients as well as inpatients, are generally university affiliated, and thus also provide teaching and research. In major cities, there is a trend towards opening Mental Health Courts to specialize in work with people with mental disorders who have been charged with criminal offences. Sweden, Denmark and Finland have a national government body which appoints psychiatrists, and/or specially designated inpatient teams, for formal 4-week mental health assessments for the courts. In the Netherlands, staff at the Pieter Baan Centre perform about 200 7-week long multidisciplinary assessments each year (Beyaert, 1980). In countries without specialist pre-trial units, forensic psychiatrists and psychologists, and to a lesser extent other clinicians, carry out pretrial assessments in settings which include remand prisons, psychiatric hospitals or outpatient clinics.

Other variations in specialist FMH include ways in which it is sanctioned, funded, commissioned and monitored. In some countries, such as Japan, special laws had to be enacted to allow for such development nationally. In others, there is a requirement in other health legislation for governments to provide for the services. Funding for each patient/client in each country comes from the public purse, but the way in which that money is spent varies between being wholly in the public sector or in a mixed economy of public and private/independent providers. In some countries the money comes entirely from national health budgets and in some partly from criminal justice system budgets. Some services are commissioned nationally, some regionally, but the relatively low contribution from local commissioners in most places has tended to feed tensions between generic and forensic service providers, and this has slowed patient movement. Depending partly on other service capacity, countries vary in the extent to which specialist community FMH services are provided, or to which services are integrated but, in general, most patients revert to generic services for their community management and treatment.

Interesting variations come about when highly specialized services are provided, for example the clinics for stalkers in the Victorian Institute of Forensic Mental Health in

Victoria, Australia, specialist units for people with 'dangerous and severe personality disorder' in England and Wales (see chapters 15, 22), the TBS (Terbeschikkingstelling) units in the Netherlands (Greeven, 2002), Herstedvester prison in Denmark (see below), or a sexual offenders' clinic in Ottawa, Canada and the Canadian Correctional Services out-patient clinic for long-term offenders with paraphilias in Montreal.

Any substantial institution and/or service which includes constraint as a core element of its business has the potential for ethical compromise. Safeguards against this include the extent to which standards for the service are explicit, how they were set, and the nature, quality and frequency of monitoring exercises according to those standards. Appropriate standards are generally achieved through joint government and professional input. A basic aim is that units/services are compliant with general national/jurisdictional health policies and evidenced based treatment guidance and have a clear role within the service framework. More specific service standards are added. Generally, each unit has its own internal audit and peer review systems, but, in addition, there are wholly independent systems, with designated powers sanctioned in law for considering individual cases and for inspecting the institutional standards. Professional bodies also take a role in such matters.

Things may still go wrong, and there are commonly systems for responding to that too. In the UK there is a government fondness for independent, often public inquiries – whether the problem was primarily one of a failing institution or an individual case failure. For all European countries there are always additional layers of inspection. The Committee for the Prevention of Torture (see also p.137), for example, may visit any hospital or prison and provide a report for the country's government, confidentially in the first instance, but made public if any documented abuses are not dealt with. New Zealand is a signatory to the operational protocol on the convention against torture (OPCAT), and the New Zealand government has appointed an ombudsman to carry out these functions.

In Canada, funding for court ordered psychiatric assessment and all medical/psychiatric treatment for offenders comes from provincial MH departments and FMH services are part of the wider mental healthcare system, so facilities are regularly visited by the Canadian Council on Hospital Accreditation. It establishes the standards. Juveniles are admitted to special facilities, with separate standards. In cases of major problems, rare in Canadian forensic mental health facilities, internal inquiries have generally been held to be sufficient, although complaints about the régime at Pentanguishene in 1982 led to an independent inquiry set up by the Ontario Provincial Government (see also chapter 24). In the event of self-inflicted death or homicide, a coroner's investigation or inquest is mandatory. Denmark has a system for setting up an independent inquiry in the event of any serious crime (not just homicide) committed by a person who had been in contact with mental health services.

Sweden

The organization of forensic mental health services in Sweden is split into two separate and independent systems; assessments for courts fall under the National Board of Forensic Medicine, while care and treatment are provided by 20 standard regional healthcare providers. There are no private forensic psychiatric facilities in Sweden, although there are many nursing homes, often in rural areas, for long-term care of any psychiatric patient on leave from hospital, including forensic patients.

There are five regional forensic psychiatric hospitals, referred to in Sweden as 'high security units', although none would qualify as such in the UK. The Swedish National Board of Health and Welfare has issued a new security classification; according to this, while none of these hospitals is rated overall as providing the highest level of hospital security, one or two of them have a few high security beds. Offender patients can also be referred to local low secure forensic psychiatric units. Low-risk patients are likely to be managed in generic psychiatric units. In a 2005 survey, 40% of the forensic patient population was in one of the then four regional forensic hospitals, 50% in local forensic units and 10% in generic psychiatric units.

Staff, treatment and institutions in the Swedish forensic mental health services are monitored by Sweden's National Board of Health and Welfare, just like all other MH service providers. Serious adverse incidents, including suicides or suspected patient mistreatment, must be reported to this Board for further investigation.

The duration of forensic psychiatric inpatient stay varies considerably. The 2005 survey by the National Board of Health and Social Welfare reported just three people who had been hospitalized for more than 40 years, and nine for more than 30 years, but, overall, there was a marked increase in the time spent in hospital compared to an identical survey of 1995. This is similar to a finding with English high security hospital patients (Jamieson and Taylor, 2005). There is otherwise little research on this, but, clinicians in Sweden generally consider that it is harder for patients to be discharged from hospital than it used to be. Many can spend years there after violence such as common assault, especially if the onset of their offending was when they were young and associated with substance misuse. By contrast, people convicted of serious offences, such as homicide, are sometimes discharged into the community after a relatively short period of time. This has led to a proposal for 'hybrid orders', whereby the punitive element of sentencing is not removed, and mentally disordered serious offenders who recover quickly must return to prison to fulfil justice requirements.

A promising development in 2008 for quality assurance of forensic psychiatric treatment is the establishment of a national quality register, run by the professions but funded by government. Most Swedish forensic psychiatric service providers will contribute to this data base. It will then be possible to compare a range of clinical variables and outcomes between services.

Australia

Australian forensic mental health services are publicly funded, and governed by each of the states and territories; all states have them. They are normally state-based and within the health service. While the general legal principles governing patients are similar, the service models and organization vary considerably across the country. In a population four times that of Scotland, Australia has half as many forensic beds! In Western Australia, with almost 1.5 million inhabitants, in an area almost half as large as continental USA, there are only 30 forensic psychiatric beds. Thus, it is very unusual for prisoners with mental illness to be treated in hospital; if they are, they are shunted back to prison almost as soon as they stabilize, and often before. Simply stated, mentally ill offenders do not figure prominently among the social fabric of Australian society.

The extent to which standards of care are in place or regulated is variable. Some services, including the Victorian Institute of Forensic Mental Health, have secure hospitals which are accredited by the general hospital accreditation system. Other services are neither accredited nor monitored in this way. The patient and prisoner mix varies, generally men outnumber women by 10 to 1, indigenous people are over-represented by at least 10-fold, and the populations are marked by increasing racial and cultural diversity as the Australian cultural mix changes.

While the description of services in Australia veers toward the negative, many exciting and innovative advances are being made. At the time of writing *every* state and territory is at least planning for additional hospital beds, some (NSW and Tasmania) have recently opened new hospitals. Innovative programmes, such as the Problem Behaviour Programme, operated by the Victorian Institute of Forensic Mental Health, provide assessment and treatment for a range of offenders and potential offenders with specific problems (e.g. sexual offending, stalking, threatening, arson). Self-referrals are accepted, and voluntary treatment thus offered (Warren et al., 2005). The restructuring of FMH services in New South Wales also shows great promise. After years of strong academic research and the development of clinical expertise, evidence based services are emerging.

New Zealand

The Mason Report (Mason et al., 1988) was the driving force for development of modern forensic mental health services in New Zealand. It followed a series of homicides by people with a mental disorder, and its proposed template for the development of FMH services has been supported by successive governments. Subsequent tragedies have ensured maintenance of public and government focus on the needs of such patients.

Forensic mental health services in New Zealand aim to provide assessment, treatment and rehabilitation for people charged with or convicted of a criminal offence who have or may have a mental illness and for people whose potential danger to themselves and/or others is such that adult mental health services cannot manage them safely. A continuum of care is provided in all regions, through prisons, secure hospitals and limited parallel community services, but the basic philosophy is that most such patients will return to general adult MH services after discharge from specialist FMH inpatient care.

The government funds District Health Boards to provide health services to meet the needs of the population, including FMH needs, the latter provided on a regional basis. Virtually all FMH service providers are government agencies, but there is one non-governmental provider. General mental health sector standards apply, and FMH services are audited against these on a 3-year cycle. More frequent inspections are undertaken by District Inspectors, who are lawyers acting as ombudsmen for the Mental Health Act. They investigate breaches of rights.

Approximately 220 forensic beds are funded for the country's population of just over 4 million; there are 400 general psychiatry beds. Half of the forensic patients stay less than 12 months in hospital, with most of the rest staying 1–5 years, and only 5% more than 6 years. Half of the forensic caseload is resident in the community. Most suffer from schizophrenia or similar psychosis; median age is mid-30s for both men and women, but the range is from teens to old age. A 2005 survey revealed that 10% of patients were undergoing pre-trial assessments, 8% were unfit to stand trial, 13% were on post-conviction treatment orders, 27% were insanity acquittees, and 7% were prison transfers; the remaining third were on civil orders. A naturalistic study of outcome suggests that those selected for treatment in these specialist services generally do well (Simpson et al., 2006).

Denmark

People who have been ordered to hospital from the courts are managed among general psychiatric patients at a level of security commensurate with their needs. All places are funded by and in the public sector. As psychotic offenders are deemed to be not punishable under Danish law, then, in theory, all are transferred to the health service. In practice, due to pressure on hospital beds, there are always a few people with psychosis among remanded prisoners; for a few more, psychosis emerges or is recognized only during sentence. The law allows for transfer to hospital at any of these stages.

Treatment of offenders with non-psychotic mental disorders is more likely than not to occur within the criminal justice system. The prison and probation services are under Ministry of Justice funding and control. There are five closed prisons with a capacity of about 1,000 places, nine open prisons with around 1,550 places, and 38 remand prisons with 1,700 places between them. Most of the latter have 15–45 beds, with just one, serving greater Copenhagen, having a capacity of about 400. Occupancy is generally at about 95% capacity. There are also probation offices and a staff training centre. There are no maximum security institutions. The prison and probation services also run two institutions for asylum-seekers and eight halfway houses (200 places). Neither asylum-seeker camps nor halfway houses are discussed further.

In Denmark, prisoners must have access to the same quality of medical care and treatment as other citizens. Practice has followed this principle for years, but it is now enshrined in legislation – Enforcement of Sentences Act 2000. If they need specialist treatment, they are referred to the Danish Health Service or to private practitioners, as appropriate. When they need hospitalization, this is always to an ordinary hospital, if necessary accompanied by prison officers.

Sex offenders

In 1997, Denmark launched a nationwide sex offender treatment programme. NHS psychiatric services and the Department of Prisons and Probation collaborate in its provision. Offenders convicted of non-violent sexual crimes who are motivated for treatment might receive a suspended sentence with a condition of specialist treatment within a sex offender programme. This treatment takes place at one of three psychiatric facilities, each based in a university department. The clinics offer counselling, cognitive therapy, psychoanalytically oriented psychotherapy or group therapy, together with psychopharmacological treatment, according to individual need. Each offender is also supervised by a probation officer, who, in conjunction with the local social authority, is responsible for providing social support and help.

Offenders convicted of more serious sexual crimes receive prison sentences, but their sentence starts with a short stay in a special unit at the Herstedvester institution (see below), to examine motivation for treatment, and, where necessary, engagement in motivational work. Treatment-motivated offenders may then serve their sentence in open prisons, where they receive specialist treatment. Only the most dangerous sex offenders stay in Herstedvester, but they too are offered treatment.

Research into the effectiveness of the programmes was built into them from the outset. Preliminary results show that neither sexual crime recidivism rates nor type of reoffending differs between treated and untreated groups (an English summary is available at www.kriminalforsorgen. dk). Based on these results, some referral and treatment procedures have been modified, for example there is now greater emphasis on treatment of alcohol abuse within the programme. The research continues, but, as recidivism may occur after many years, definitive results will not be available in the short term.

The Herstedvester Institution

Herstedvester Institution opened in 1936 as a specialist prison for offenders with personality disorder. It operates under exactly the same regulations as other prisons, and is not regarded as a hospital, but it is well-staffed and treatment-oriented. The staff/inmate ratio of 2:1 is much higher than in other Danish prisons. At any one time it holds about 130 prisoners, nearly all lifers or men under preventive detention; about 12% of all inmates in closed prisons are in Herstedvester. Treatment staff consists of five psychiatrists and seven psychologists, so each wing has a psychiatrist/psychologist attached; there are also psychiatric nurses and social workers. A full time general practitioner not only treats the inmates' physical illnesses, but also manages the libido suppressing medications which are prescribed for some of the sex offenders. The chief psychiatrist is part of the prison's management structure.

As far as possible, Herstedvester is run as a therapeutic community (see also chapters 16 and 23); all staff participate in some way in the treatment. Prison officers and clinical staff openly share information, as each may separately acquire material valuable to the therapeutic process. This means that time and effort must be spent explaining the régime to the prisoners on entry. They receive written and verbal explanations of the treatment and its setting. This approach has been approved by the Council of Europe's Commissioner for Human Rights. Each inmate is reviewed at the daily community meeting.

Offenders serving sentences for serious sexual crimes form a special subgroup at Herstedvester; the institution has a long history of experience with them. Surgical castration was once used, but now – in the most serious cases – hormonal suppression is achieved with anti-libidinal drugs, generally cyproterone acetate 300 mg depot injection intramuscularly 2-weekly and leuprorelin 11.25 mg depot injection subcutaneously 3-monthly. The anti-libidinal drugs can only be initiated with the offender's oral *and* written consent, and such prescription is always combined with an offer of psychotherapy. A naturalistic trial has shown that anti-libidinals are effective compared with no treatment (http://www.kriminalforsorgen.dk). Sex-offenders treated with anti-libidinals had significantly fewer relapses into sexual crime; those lapses that did occur were later than expected and less serious. The formal links between Herstedvester and the three national university clinics means that a sex offender can continue supervised treatment after release.

South Africa

Specialized forensic mental health facilities exist in only five of the nine provinces. Gauteng has two units, and the Western Cape has one unit between two hospitals. In the Western Cape, court assessments are conducted in specialist security of an appropriate level at Valkenberg Hospital; admission is for up to 30 days, and the assessment multidisciplinary. There is one maximum security ward, one medium security one and two low security wards. Lenteguer Hospital has four low security wards and a step-down facility for this group. Patients tend to move between wards at the two sites, and those under assessment in low or medium security may live in the community, supervised by their families or other agencies. Some have jobs or are studying, but large numbers have poor social circumstances and are thus seldom granted leave outside the hospital. Community leave is decided by the multidisciplinary team. The authorities are notified using a standard form, in which the period of leave, names and contact details of supervisors and the conditions of the leave are provided. Any breach of leave conditions results in return to the hospital by the police.

Very few patients achieve discharge, which can only be granted by a judge-in-chambers following applications accompanied by reports from a treating psychiatrist, psychologist, social worker or other mental health practitioner. Discharge is usually conditional for a period (usually 2–5 years), the restrictions automatically expiring if rehabilitation continues without problems.

Forensic psychiatry is not recognized as a specialty in South Africa. A proposal for a diploma in forensic psychiatry has been submitted to the College of Psychiatry; this will be used to convince the Health Professions Council of South Africa (the equivalent of the UK General Medical Council) to register forensic psychiatry formally as a specialty. It is already part of most general psychiatry training rotations. There is a 2-year MPhil in Forensic Mental Health at the University of Cape Town.

Japan

Until the 2003 Act concerning medical treatment and observation for people who commit serious harm to others, any interventions for offenders with mental disorder were provided by psychiatrists going into prisons, where conditions for people with mental disorder are poor, or by psychiatrists in general services for people who had been diverted from the criminal justice system on grounds of their mental disorder. Since the Act, the provision of specialist forensic mental health services has become possible. The aim is to have one small forensic unit of 15–34 beds in each of the 47 prefectures; so far, ten units have been established. The new units are modelled on the UK's medium security hospital units, with a high nurse: patient ratio (e.g. in Tokyo, 47:34, compared with 6:34 in a general psychiatric unit). The government has decided that the appropriate length of admission will be 18 months. While this may seem reassuring for patients, and in terms of preventing the units

from silting up, it hardly seems realistic to clinicians used to patients with medication resistant schizophrenia who form the main complement of the admissions. It remains to be seen how far the government will enforce its time limit by, for example, requiring psychiatrists to declare patients untreatable if their mental disorder has not responded to treatment within this time, and the extent to which further difficulties may ensue because step-down and outpatient provision for such cases is scarce.

Canada

Forensic mental health services exist in all provinces, operating in close collaboration with the justice department and correctional services. Most centres located in cities are part of wider hospital services; a few have maximum security, like Montreal's Philippe Pinel Institute. Other secure hospitals include the Nova Scotia hospital in Halifax and the Forensic Psychiatric Institute in Vancouver. Unique to Canada are the regional psychiatric centres that are part of the Correctional Service of Canada. The centre in Saskatoon, Saskatchewan, is an accredited hospital, operated by the correctional service, which also serves as the provincial secure hospital.

Provision of psychiatric services to convicted prisoners is complicated, as different organizations are responsible for them, according to sentence length. Sentences of 2 years or more are served in federal prisons, and shorter sentences in provincial prisons. Mentally ill inmates may be transferred to forensic units, but with better health services now available in prisons, and greater availability of consultants, mentally ill offenders tend to remain in prison during their sentence. Exceptions arise as prisons do not allow for involuntary treatment, and need for it would usually result in transfer to hospital. Within federal penitentiaries, there is a more clearly identifiable assessment and treatment pathway, often linked with university clinics. In 2002, the correctional service opened a clinic for long-term sex offenders in Montreal, so that, once their sentence had been served, the men may continue treatment and rehabilitation under expert supervision. This programme is run in collaboration with the University of Sherbrooke, and also provides training for psychiatry residents.

SPECIALIST RECOGNITION IN EUROPE AND SWANZDSAJCS COUNTRIES

Within Europe, forensic psychiatry is formally recognized as a specialty only in the UK, Ireland, Sweden and Germany, but most countries in the old European Union, and some in the new, provide specialist training, albeit to a varying degree in terms of range of topics and time allocated. All require a general professional training in psychiatry before embarking on forensic specialty work, and some, such as

Sweden, require prior specialist certification in general adult psychiatry, which in itself requires at least 5 years' training. The length of specialist training, and its details then vary. In Sweden, for example, the length is set at about 2 years, with specifications to have produced a minimum of 40 court reports in that time and have spent at least a year in a specialist treatment setting. Denmark is moving towards formal recognition of forensic psychiatry as a specialty; at present, the Danish Psychiatric Association arranges four 3-day courses to teach the theory, supplemented with specialized meetings and seminars within Denmark and annual study tours to the UK.

In Germany, over the last few years, emphasis has been laid on quality assurance of forensic psychiatry. The establishment of competency through training was regarded as the first step in that direction. In 1968, the first university department of forensic psychiatry was opened; by 1983 there were five, offering independent and sometimes contradictory training programmes. Today eight universities have special forensic psychiatry institutes. In 1990, interdisciplinary training for interns was developed and, by 1997, forensic psychiatry was being treated as a separate specialty, with certification by the German Psychiatric Association (DGPPN). This meant a structured training programme and regulations for Certification. In 2003, The German Medical Association (Deutscher Ärztetag) also agreed to recognize forensic psychiatry as a specialty of psychiatry. These developments led to improvement in quality of specialist reports for the courts, but barely reached the attention of the judges who employed the experts. In order to improve that situation, in 2005, a task force of prominent judges and forensic psychiatrists at the highest court of appeals in Germany (Bundesgerichtshof) published minimal requirements for the psychiatric assessment of culpability. Encouraged by the good reception these received, in 2006, the group published minimal requirements for risk assessments (Boetticher et al., 2005, 2006). Both publications improved acceptance of quality assurance measures by courts.

In Australia and New Zealand, the Royal Australian and New Zealand College of Psychiatrists oversees the specialist training of psychiatrists. A number of services are recognized as providing specialist training in forensic psychiatry both for general professional trainees (registrars/residents) and higher trainees. Given the dearth of training places, and the variability of available opportunities, there are few uniform standards. A number of formal postgraduate training courses exist for psychiatrists and psychiatry trainees, as well as for other forensic mental health professionals.

As noted earlier, there have been major advances in the training of clinical and forensic psychologists since the 1980s. Canada, the USA, Australia, New Zealand, and many European countries have accredited masters and doctoral courses. Most countries have specialist boards or colleges to set standards and scrutinize the training, e.g. the American Psychological Association in the USA or the Canadian Psychological Association in Canada.

Postgraduate training in psychology has followed two general models, or combinations thereof, with research degrees in addition. In many European countries, Australia and New Zealand, those with a major research interest complete PhDs, but clinical and applied trainees generally do a research component in a master's or doctoral degree. The first model of clinical/applied training is the clinical–forensic psychology model. In these courses, graduate students commence with training in clinical psychology and then specialize in forensic psychology. The second type of courses focus more exclusively on forensic psychology and the exposure to basic clinical training (psychopathology, psychological assessment, therapy and intervention) varies. In addition to the clinical/applied training models, there is a distinction between clinical/applied training and experimental training. The latter is particularly for people who are interested in non-clinical forensic psychology, such as eyewitness testimony or jury research.

Japan, at an early stage of its specialist forensic mental health service development, is only just beginning to develop specialist clinical training within the country. Several leading clinicians, from psychology and nursing as well as psychiatry, have completed overseas courses of various lengths and depths, and a few have had extended experience in overseas clinical services. In Canada, many universities have set up fellowship programmes in forensic psychiatry. The Canadian Psychiatric Association and Royal College of Physicians are working together to obtain special recognition for people who have completed such training, a 2-year programme of knowledge and skills acquisition in university programmes and approved clinical placements.

US Forensic Psychiatry Expert Recognition and Training

Two organizations of critical importance to the development of the specialty of forensic psychiatry in the USA were the American Academy of Forensic Sciences (AAFS) and the American Academy of Psychiatry and the Law (AAPL) (see also p.117–8). AAFS leaders in forensic psychiatry, including Maier Tuchler and Lowell Sterling, promoted the concept of developing a certifying body in forensic psychiatry in the 1950s (Prosono, 2003). With financial support from the Legal Enforcement Assistance Administration, AAFS and AAPL established the American Board of Forensic Psychiatry. This developed and administered a comprehensive two part examination aimed at certifying competence in forensic psychiatry. The written exam included both multiple choice and essay questions; after passing this, candidates underwent an oral examination which included questions about an observed, videotaped forensic interview, questions on three submitted reports, and a more general topic based viva.

In 1982, the AAFS and AAPL again collaborated on a report: *Standards for Fellowship Programs in Forensic Psychiatry*. The Accreditation Council on Fellowships in Forensic Psychiatry was created in 1988 as the first body to accredit fellowships in forensic psychiatry, ensuring standardization of curricula and programme quality (Reeves et al., 2007). Once the American Board of Medical Specialists recognized the subspecialty of forensic psychiatry, the American Board of Psychiatry and Neurology began to certify psychiatrists in it and the Accreditation Council for Graduate Medical Education (ACGME) began accrediting the programmes; the earlier bodies were disbanded in the 1990s (Prosono, 2003). Meanwhile, the Association of Directors of Forensic Psychiatry Fellowships, a Council of AAPL, continued to promote quality in the fellowship programmes and, for example, develop 'core competencies', that must be demonstrably mastered (Reeves et al., 2007).

The USA has 44 ACGME approved forensic psychiatry fellowship programmes (subspecialty residency programmes), with 106 fellowship positions in the 2004–2005 academic year (Reeves et al., 2007). Most such fellowships last a minimum of 12 months. The curriculum must be structured, written, and with clearly stated goals, objectives, including core competencies, and methods for assessing the fellow's progress and achievement of the core competencies. Clinical assignments must include treating individuals within the criminal justice system, consultation to general psychiatric services on issues of the legal regulation of psychiatry, and performing civil and criminal forensic evaluations for individuals with a diversity of demographic or mental disorder variables and legal circumstances (Reeves et al., 2007). The didactic component must include topics in civil law, criminal law, services structures and writing specialist reports. Participation in forensic conferences and research or writing is also expected (Reeves et al., 2007; Reeves and Rosner, 2003).

Completion of a fellowship in forensic psychiatry and prior certification in psychiatry by the American Board of Psychiatry and Neurology are prerequisites for forensic psychiatry certification. Such certification is valid for 10 years (Reeves and Rosner, 2003), when follow-up examinations are needed to maintain certification. Both initial and re-certification examinations are now multiple choice and computer administered.

AAPL continues to provide leadership, excellent learning opportunities and diverse resources in promoting foundational and continuing education, and high ethical and quality standards. Through its Journal and Newsletter, AAPL also makes landmark legal cases in mental health law available as well as ensuring its ethical and clinical practice guidelines receive the widest audience. Philip Resnick directs the ever popular, outstanding review course in conjunction with AAPL meetings. The annual meetings of the American Academy of Forensic Sciences are also valuable for continuing education and professional development, especially for its links with other disciplines.

RESEARCH IN FORENSIC PSYCHIATRY, PSYCHOLOGY AND ALLIED PROFESSIONS

Forensic mental health research is hard to sustain, although the number of specialist journals and the rate relative to generalists at which people from the forensic mental health field publish in mainstream journals suggests that there is a healthy academic core. Even in countries such as Japan, where development of forensic mental health services is so recent, there is a small but productive research establishment (e.g. Dussich et al., 2001; Yoshikawa et al., 2007). The most important challenge for such researchers is the dearth of funding, especially non-governmental funding. There is no charitable foundation specifically associated with FMH work, and those of us who have attempted to secure funding from more generally oriented bodies have a sense that few want to be associated with mentally ill offenders.

It is essential that research is constantly renewed, not only for the most obvious reason – that progress for most of the people who use forensic mental health services is dependent on new knowledge – but also to ensure that the quality of teaching and training is constantly sustained and improved. In addition, the best trainees will only be attracted to the field if it is clearly in a process of development and includes successful clinical academics and basic scientists as well as people with special clinical and managerial skills.

In a number of European countries, academic forensic psychiatrists have considered both the barriers to research in the field, and strategies for overcoming them (Taylor et al., 2009). In Canada, clinical research in the field is funded by government and universities. Academics work in collaboration with clinicians, and clinical trainees are encouraged to do research. Clinical research in most countries is generally not well funded, but smaller specialities are most affected by shortage of funds. These tend to be allocated on standard measures of previous success, such as peer reviewed papers in high impact journals and previous success with funding; by definition specialist journals in small specialties, with their small circulation, cannot have the impact of more general journals with their large readerships. In some countries, such as England and Wales, the difficulty of identifying specialist funding was recognized for a while through a small but ring-fenced research budget held by the government's Department of Health. The fact that that has now been removed might be taken as an encouraging sign that forensic mental health research is seen to have developed to a point to be sustainable under ordinary competitive conditions, but, in fact, it is more reflective of government adoption of a perceived US strategy to focus funding on a small number of centres and topics. When especially reliant on government funds, however, such a field is also vulnerable to being corralled into researching those aspects of the work which government regards as most important rather than necessarily being scientifically or clinically driven. Some have even expressed concern about the ethics of research funding which may be politically driven.

Creative networking seems to be the best way forward. In a speciality where most senior academic posts are as likely as specific research projects to be funded through the health service budget, senior academics can otherwise be isolated. Networking can not only create useful associations between clinical and non-clinical researchers in all disciplines, who can boost the range of skills necessary for effective research in this complex field, but also make links between clinical centres. Only with multi-centre research is it likely that sample sizes can be generated which are sufficient to test most hypotheses or clinical interventions, given the fairly small size of most specialist units and the generally slow turnover of the residents. In many countries there is now some support for generating national networks, and we are working together to collaborate in research internationally, in spite of, or even because of, the differences between us in details of law and service development.

In the USA, with a few exceptions, research is not regarded as a strong suit of forensic psychiatrists, yet the need is great. Fellows are encouraged by AAPL and AAFS to pursue research; each organization offers an annual prize to a fellow who submits an outstanding research paper, and AAPL offers a 'young investigator award'. AAFS has an endowment fund for research in the forensic sciences generally. AAPL recently developed its Institute for Education and Research, intended to spur and support research as well as educational projects through funds provided by tax-exempt donations. AAPL members are encouraged to submit research proposals. AAPL, especially through its research committee, organizes research methodology courses focused on forensic issues, and how special barriers to research in the field can be negotiated (Trestman, 2007). Ash (2003) has provided a concise website guide for forensic psychiatry and psychology researchers.

ILLUSTRATIVE CASES

In order to strengthen the comparative framework of this chapter, we have considered four offenders with mental disorder from the Nine Nation Study described in brief vignettes. For each country, the most likely sequence of events in criminal procedure and management of these cases is presented in table 5.1.

Case 1

A 28-year-old single man, with a long criminal record and previous prison sentences, a history of intermittent opiate abuse and dependence over 10 years, in whom the ICD-10 criteria for dissocial personality disorder (ASPD)are amply met, charged with robbery with violence, an offence committed while under the influence of alcohol.

Case 2

A 30-year-old married woman with three children, with no previous convictions, has drowned her 1-month-old son while in a state corresponding to a major depressive episode with psychotic (mood congruent) features in the context of a bipolar affective disorder (ICD-10 criteria).

Case 3

A 35-year-old divorced man suffering from schizophrenia, paranoid type, chronic course with acute exacerbations (DSM-III-R criteria), who had previously knifed his father 'because he (the father) was transformed into a rat'. On numerous occasions punched strangers in public places while under the influence of delusional beliefs and recently fatally wounded a stranger in the street while a voice was telling him he would be 'walled alive unless he killed a man'. His violent behaviour has always been associated with active psychotic symptoms. Treatment including neuroleptics is usually effective in producing remission, but the man is non-compliant in treatment programmes.

Case 4

A 30-year-old married man who is arrested for the first time admits a series of sexual offences against children involving threats, orogenital contacts and buggery. According to DSM-III-R criteria he has paedophilia and personality disorder (dependent type), but no other psychiatric disorder. He appears motivated to undertake treatment for his sexual deviation.

In brief, table 5.1 shows that practice has more in common than not between countries in responding to the two psychotic offenders. Differences in court relate almost entirely to the absence of incapacity rulings in Sweden or Denmark; in all cases it is considered that these individuals would be placed in hospital, with differences arising only through the different philosophies of provision – in specialist forensic hospitals (most), in mainstream psychiatric hospitals (Denmark) or prison based psychiatric wings (the USA, some Canadian provinces and Australia).

Differences in response to the robber with alcoholism are almost entirely reflected in length of custodial penalty. The sex offender raised most variation in terms of presentation of psychiatric or psychological reports before trial, although no one envisaged this man being placed anywhere

Table 5.1 Most likely input at various stages in the criminal justice process from (forensic) psychiatry or other mental health professionals: responses to illustrative cases

		Sweden	(England and) Wales	Victoria (Au)	New Zealand	Denmark	Western Cape (SA)	Japan	Quebec (Ca)	Scotland	USA
Case 1: male, 28 years, offending history, previous prison sentences, 10-year history opiate abuse, ASPD – robbery with violence under influence of alcohol											
Pre-trial	Psych report	No	No	No	No	No	Yes[1]	No	No	No	No
	Psych remand	No	No	No	No	No	Yes[1]	No	No	No	No
Trial	Psych evidence	No	No	No	No	No	No	No	No	No	Note[2]
	Verdict	CR	CR	CR	CR	CR	CR	CR	CR	CR	CR
Post-trial	Disposal	P	P	P	P	P	P	P	P	P	P
	Duration	2–3 yrs	IPP[3]	1–3 yrs	7–10 yrs	2–3 yrs	7–10 yrs	5 yrs	2–3 yrs	15 yrs	5–20 yrs
	Management	NR	NR	NR+SA+VR	NR	NR+SA+VR	NR	NR	NR	NR+SA	NR
Case 2: female, 30 years, three children, no offence history, bipolar affective disorder – drowned son 4 weeks post-partum during depressive psychosis											
Pre-trial	Psych report	Yes	Yes	Yes	Yes	Yes	Yes	Yes	Yes	Yes	Yes
	Psych remand	Yes	Yes	Maybe[4]	Yes	Yes	Yes	Yes	Yes	Yes	Yes
Trial	Psych evidence	Yes	Yes	Yes	Yes	Yes	Yes	Yes	Yes	Yes	Yes
	Verdict	CR	DR	NGRI	NGRI	CR	NGRI	NGRI	DR	DR	NGRI[5]
Post-trial	Disposal	SH	SH	SH	SH	H[6a]	SH	SH	?	SH	SH/prison[6b]
	Post-discharge	CD	CD	CD	CD	CD	CD	CD	CD	CD	CD
Case 3: male, 35 years, history serious violence driven by delusions, paranoid SZ, poor treatment compliance – fatal wounding during psychosis											
Pre-trial	Psych report	Yes	Yes	Yes	Yes	Yes	Yes	Yes	Yes	Yes	Yes
	Psych remand	Yes	Yes	Maybe[4]	Yes	Yes	Yes	Yes	Yes	Yes	Yes
Trial	Psych evidence	Yes	Yes	Yes	Yes	Yes	Yes	Yes	Yes	Yes	Yes
	Verdict	CR	DR	NGRI	NGRI	CR	NGRI	NGRI	NGRI	NGRI	NGRI/ GBMI[7]
Post-trial	Disposal	SH	SH	SH	SH	H[6a]	SH	SH	SH	SH	SH/prison[6b]
	Post-discharge	CD	CD	CD	CD	CD	CD	CD	CD	CD	CD
Case 4: male, 30 years, paedophilia+dependent PD, no other mental disorder – on first arrest admits multiple sex offences against children, motivated for treatment											
Pre-trial	Psych report	Yes	Yes	No	Yes	Yes	Yes	No	Yes	Yes	No
	Psych remand	No	No	No	No	No	Yes	No	No	No	No
Trial	Psych evidence	Yes	No	No	Yes	Yes	Yes	No	Yes	No	No
	Verdict	CR	CR	CR	CR	CR	CR	CR	CR	CR	CR
Post-trial	Disposal	P	P (SW)	P	P	P	P	P	P	P (SW)	P
	Duration	2–5 yrs	IPP[3]	2–5 yrs	8–10 yrs	2–5 yrs	1–3 yrs	3–20 yrs	2–5 yrs	10–15 yrs	5–10 yrs
	Management	SOTP	SOTP[8]	SOTP	SOTP	SOTP	NR	SOTP	SOTP	SOTP	SOTP[8]

Abbreviations

CD, Supervision and/or compliance a condition of discharge; CR, criminally responsible (if found guilty on facts of offence); DR, diminished responsibility/equivalent e.g. manslaughter; GP, general psychiatric service; IPP, indefinite public protection sentence (see note 2); NGRI, not guilty by reason of insanity/not criminally responsible; NR, normal regime; P, prison; P (SW), prison, special wing for prisoner's own protection; SA, substance abuse treatment; SH, secure/forensic hospital facility; SOTP, sex offender treatment programme; VR, violence reduction treatment e.g. anger management, cognitive skills.

Notes:

1. Defendants in cases such as this in South Africa often attempt to raise a psychiatric defence, making remand in hospital for reports likely.

2. In the USA, depending on jurisdictional law, if intoxication is sufficiently severe, it could be argued that intoxication abolished one or more mental elements of the crime, allowing for conviction of a lesser offence than the most serious charged; if voluntary intoxication resulted in an unusual psychotic state, in some states, e.g. Texas, this may qualify for 'temporary insanity', which does not lead to an insanity acquittal or finding of diminished responsibility, but may allow for a less severe sentence.

3. For England and Wales, the Criminal Justice Act 2003 introduced indefinite public protection sentences (IPPs), more or less equivalent to a life sentence. A tariff date would also be given with such sentences, indicating the earliest possible opportunity to apply for parole. 2012 legislation returns likelihood of fixed term sentences in most cases.

4. Any admission would only be for involuntary clinical assessment and urgent treatment during the pre-trial period.

5. NGRI is only possible where psychotic symptom content was directly related to the killing; if they only added to general distress and despair, the cognitive element of the McNaughton test would not be satisfied; states with the ALI insanity test (see p.125) may allow for a successful insanity defence under its volitional prong.

6a. In Denmark, would be admitted to a general psychiatric ward – whether open or closed would depend on severity of illness, not offence; 6b. in the USA, hospitalization – forensic or general – only after NGRI verdict, otherwise treatment in prison.

7. The presence of driving psychotic symptoms may be insufficient for NGRI unless the man knew what he was doing was morally wrong; a 'guilty but mentally ill' option is possible in some states.

8. In England and Wales, and in some US states, the law may require registration on a sex offender register before release.

Parts of this table were published previously in the *International Journal of Forensic Mental Health* (2009).

except prison. Again, there was considerable variation in estimates of likely sentence length, although this may only reflect the fact that none of us has judicial training or experience. Only in South Africa was it considered unlikely that a sex offender treatment programme would be offered, although it should be said that in some countries, including Wales/England, programmes are sufficiently under-resourced that they are not always available in a timely way. Some countries, notably the UK and the USA, have introduced sex offender registers (see also chapter 10), and case 4 would undoubtedly be a candidate. In this respect, the USA goes furthest, in that not only did the US Congress enact law in 1994 that required states to develop registers with the addresses of convicted sexual offenders (Jacob Wetterling Crimes Against Children and Sexually Violent Offender Registration Act 1994), but, in 1996, the Wetterling Act was amended to allow states to notify the public of the names and addresses of sexual offenders. This may assist the public in its own protection, but it can also result in job loss, property damage, threats and other negative consequences for the offender (Levenson et al., 2007).

CONCLUSIONS

This chapter shows that forensic psychiatry is about fundamental issues in the relationship between society and the individual and not simply about interpreting mental health laws and criminal codes. Ideal legislation does not exist and international models of detailed provisions are probably undesirable. Some 'bottom-line' guarantees of human rights are useful, as in the European Convention. Forensic psychiatrists should seek a dialogue not only with lawyers and the judiciary, but also with politicians and the general public on underlying issues such as risk management and the degree of acceptable danger in the community. Psychiatrists have to accept that some issues are subject to irrational swings in public opinion, for example the move towards more punitive responses for sex offenders. The USA illustrates the major ethical problems that the forensic psychiatrist faces in relation to the death penalty.

Abuses of psychiatry in a few countries have illustrated how badly things can go wrong in the relationship between the state and psychiatrists. This shows that professional autonomy from the state is essential. Nevertheless, legal supervision of non-voluntary forms of intervention must be accepted by the profession. We have shown that societies generally accept that certain antisocial behaviours which are the direct consequence of clearly defined serious mental illness can be dealt with by psychiatric treatment rather than by penal sanctions. Deciding how wide the definition of mental disorder should be, and how diverse the institutional treatment setting should be, depends upon the generosity implicit in any medical treatment model, medical attitudes, medical knowledge and social attitudes about unacceptable behaviour.

The comparative approach shows that we have much common ground, and also much to learn from each other. It reminds us that we may be divided by legal systems, that what constitutes crime may differ to an extent across national boundaries, and that crime (reoffending) as an outcome measure will be considerably influenced by regional demographics. As seems appropriate for a clinical specialty, our strongest points of agreement are on clinical status and clinical outcomes.

FURTHER READING

For this chapter, we have chosen to supplement the references by suggesting key texts which refer to law and practice for mentally disordered offenders in the countries discussed. This is not, therefore, a comprehensive list of forensic texts, but a selection of material, mainly in English, which will allow the interested reader some greater insight into what happens outside the UK.

Canada

Bloom H and Schneider RD (2006) *Mental Disorders and the Law: A Primer for Legal and Mental Health Professionals*. Toronto: Irwin Law.

Gray SE, Shone MA, Liddle PF (2000) *Canadian Mental Health Law and Policy*. Toronto: Butterworth.

Schneider RD, Bloom H, and Heerema M (2007) *Mental Health Courts: Decriminalizing the Mentally Ill*. Toronto: Irwin Law.

Denmark

Lansted LB, Garde P and Greve V (2003) *Criminal Law, Denmark*. Denmark: DJØF Publishing.

Germany

Nedopil N (2007) *Forensische Psychiatrie*, 3rd Edn. Stuttgart: Thieme (in German).

Europe

Bertrand D and Niveau G (2006) *Médicine Santé et Prison*. Chêne-Bourg: Editions Medicine et Hygiene (in French).

Salize HJ and Dressing H (eds) (2005b) *Placement and Treatment of Mentally Disordered Offenders: Legislation and Practice in the [old] European Union*. Lengerich: Pabst Science Publishers.

New Zealand

Brookbanks W and Simpson S (eds) (2007) *Psychiatry and the Law*. Wellington: LexisNexis NZ Limited.

Scotland

McManus JJ and Thomson LDG (2005) *Mental Health and Scots Law in Practice*. Edinburgh: Green and Sons.

South Africa

Kaliski SZ (2006) *A Guide to Psycholegal Assessment in South Africa*. Cape Town: Oxford.

Sweden

Grann M and Holmberg G (1999) Follow up of Forensic Psychiatric Legislation and Clinical Practice in Sweden 1988 to 1995. *International Journal of Law and Psychiatry* **22**: 125–131.

Kullgren G, Grann M, and Holmberg G (1997) The Swedish forensic concept of severe mental disorder as related to personality disorders. *International Journal of Law and Psychiatry* **19**: 191–200.

USA

Felthous A and Sass H (eds) (2007) *International Handbook on Psychopathic Disorders and the Law*. Chichester: Wiley-Blackwell.

Felthous AR, Kröber HL, Sass H (2001) Forensic Evaluations for Civil and Criminal Competencies and Criminal Responsibility in German and Anglo-American Legal Systems. In F Henn, N Sartorius, H Helnchen and H Lauter (eds) *Contemporary Psychiatry: Vol. 1 Foundations in Psychiatry*. Berlin: Springer-Verlag, 285–302.

Rosner R (ed.) (2003) *Principles and Practice of Forensic Psychiatry*, 2nd edn. London: Arnold.

6

Psychiatric reports for legal purposes in England and Wales

Edited by
John Gunn

Written by
John Gunn

Anne Ridley

Keith Rix

1st edition authors: **David Carson, Nigel Eastman, Adrian Grounds, Gisli Gudjonsson and John Gunn**

The courts have been assisted by medical experts since at least as early 1345 when surgeons were summoned to court to opine on the freshness of a wound (Rix, 2006a) and the courts have admitted psychiatric evidence since at least the eighteenth century when Dr John Monro, the Physician Superintendent of Bethlem Royal Hospital, gave evidence at the trial of Lord Ferrers who had shot his former steward in a fit of temper and pleaded insanity (Ferrers) (Walker, 1968).

THE FORUM OF THE COURT: BACKGROUND ISSUES

Forensic psychiatry is, among other things, a meeting place between law and psychiatry; but they do not always meet as friends or supportive acquaintances (Fennell, 1986; Rix, 2006b). Lawyers, particularly in the UK, tend to be legal positivists (*jus positivum*) and pragmatists. They are positivists in that they take law and justice as given. The law is there in the statutes and precedent reports. That is where they research, not in the behaviour of the police, judges or other law enforcers. Scientists also use rules, 'laws', but these are 'natural' laws which they discover as opposed to those devised by human beings in statute or precedence. Lawyers see facts existing independently of observation. There may be problems in establishing what happened, but, for lawyers, those problems are in the witness and not in the process of observing and witnessing. The law is forced into pragmatism because courts are places where conflicts are resolved, guilt is determined, and punishment or restitution is awarded. There has to be a decision at the end of the case.

Witnesses before UK courts are witnesses to facts, professional witnesses or expert witnesses. The psychiatrist who witnesses one patient attack another may be called as a witness to fact. His/her record of the mental state of the assailant at the time of the attack may make him/her a professional witness. A psychiatrist's analysis of the assailant's reasons for his or her actions is expert opinion evidence. Expert evidence is an exception to the rule that witnesses may only give evidence of facts within their own experience (Rix, 1999a). So evidence, for lawyers, is either fact or opinion. Lawyers also use this distinction in their cross-examination techniques. Witnesses stating facts are perceived as being more certain; witnesses expressing opinions can, much more easily, be made to change their evidence (Evans, 1983; Napley, 1983). This either fact or opinion distinction seems false. Witnesses in courts must use words. In doing so, they must form an opinion about which words are the most appropriate to describe the 'facts'. There are even opinions about the meanings of particular words. Sometimes, judges will declare that a word or phrase has its ordinary or natural meaning as used by ordinary English language users, but who are such people? Judges have gone on to declare what ordinary people mean by such terms as 'mental illness' (*W.v.L.*), ignoring psychiatrists' skills.

Psychiatrists, however, are usually aware that their knowledge of patients, generally and individually, is dependent upon interpretation, upon understanding cultural and other differences, upon the nature and quality of the relationships they have with their patients, and upon empathy with certain experiences.

Reasoning Differences

Aubert (1963a) outlined six ways in which legal thought differs from social scientific thought, differences which also apply to psychiatric modes of thought which are essentially interpretative.

1. Lawyers tend to dichotomize; you are guilty or not guilty, depressed or not depressed, it was reasonable or unreasonable, one or the other.

2. Lawyers try to match events and words. The object is to fit an event or person into a formula, for example a defendant into the diminished responsibility defence. For lawyers, the issue is not the totality or essence of the event or a person's problems, but whether enough facts match a verbal formula, because that justifies a particular response. Raitt and Zeedyk (2000), using the example of a woman who eventually kills her abusive and violent partner, are critical of this 'decontextualization':

> By giving attention to some elements of the context but not others, the description of the circumstances facing the woman is selectively altered – so much so that an entirely different context from the one which the woman herself experienced is constructed...With the basis for her fear excised from the story, the woman's action comes to look like revenge or murder rather than self-defence. The "story" of an event must make sense, and by limiting the features which can be included in the narrative an alternative one is created. The meaning of the act becomes that which the law permits it to have, not the meaning it held for the person committing it.

In contrast, good psychiatrists respond to the whole person and not just the parts that fit into a disorder.

3. Although courts make decisions for the future, for example concerning punishments, they mainly decide upon the past. What a defendant did justifies and explains the legal decision taken as to his or her future. For psychiatrists the decision for the future needs to take account of what is and will be available.

4. Psychiatrists aim to be able to make increasingly general statements that will encompass more people, more situations, more treatments. This will not always be possible, but it is an implicit objective. They wish to encompass as much as possible within a statement. The difference between legal and psychiatric thought is that for the lawyer there is no such generalizing objective, arguing that a client's problems arising from being a black council tenant, a man, a woman, an employee, or whatever, are of no legal relevance in themselves, however powerful an identifying feature may be as a historical, sociological or political explanation.

5. Law is not probabilistic in a scientific sense. Certainly, concepts of probability are used in court; generally the prosecution must prove the defendant guilty beyond reasonable doubt and, in civil cases, the claimant must prove his or her case on a balance of probabilities. Percentages are sometimes used to explain these concepts, but are otherwise rarely used. There is controversy over adopting probability theories

(Eggleston, 1983; Tapper, 2007; Hodgkinson, 1990). Psychiatrists will use probability theory and tests much more readily, for example in assessing the likelihood of a drug reaction.

6. Law is not causal. Certainly, it decides what happened in disputed incidents, but it does so according to legal rules of causal relationships. For example, someone will only be treated as having caused something by omission if he or she had a special relationship with, or duty of care to, the victim (Hart and Honoré, 1983). Psychiatrists are not restricted in their recognition of causes, they are concerned with scientifically demonstrable or falsifiable causes. Legal rules of causation cannot be falsified, only overruled.

Point 6 reflects to some extent the dilemma facing the psychiatrist in a risk assessment. Risks are more properly assigned to populations or groups than to individuals but decisions have to be applied to individuals.

As neuroscience develops so it is expected to throw increasing light on the causes of, say, violent behaviour and sexual abnormalities. Will this science help the courts? It doesn't help much at all at the moment and probably will not do so in the foreseeable future (Reagu and Taylor, 2012). The conflict will always be about certainty which is difficult to arrive at in science and the dichotomous decisions which have to be made in a court. An excellent article setting out these arguments *in extenso* is Eastman and Campbell (2006) which identifies the mismatch between questions that the courts need to answer and those that neuroscience is capable of answering. Science with its probabilities, and its uncertainties, will always be welcome in the courts as, like them, it strives for truth, but the 'ultimate decisions' of responsibility and guilt will always be taken by lay men (jurors and magistrates) and lawyers.

Value Differences

Lawyers and psychiatrists are likely to hold different values. For example, lawyers will emphasize free will more than determinism (Rix, 2006b). This is reinforced by the content of the law and court procedures. It is difficult, for example, to be unfit to plead. Likewise, the McNaughton Rules do not help the person who only has an inability to control his or her behaviour.

Lawyers are more likely to value explicit and certain outcomes. Imprisonment for a fixed or recommended time will often be seen as better than detention in a hospital for an indeterminate period. Explicitness and predictability are highly valued by lawyers. Freedom from interference, for example the right to die 'with your rights on' is valued. Lawyers value the right to make decisions for oneself and, indeed, would see that as a major constituent of individuality (Gostin, 1983). Psychiatrists are more likely to interpret the experience of their patients, their personal or social distress, and justify intervention to reduce pain because the experience is the primary issue rather than ascribed rights.

Arguing Differences

Lawyers frequently reify. They create explanatory concepts and then treat them as if they really exist. The effect is seductive. Concepts of rights, of the rule of law, of property and personality have an appeal for us. Often these are based upon a natural law theory that argues that these concepts exist and adhere to us simply because of our human or social nature. In reality these are man-made abstract concepts. As shorthand descriptions of values they are unobjectionable, but the risk is that they become more. Many people prefer the rule of law, to rule by people, without appreciating that the former is only the latter by very successful people. Social values, opinions or standards are reified so that differences and plurality are minimized. The process also exaggerates the effects of a lawyer's tendency to classify. When a defendant is found guilty by a court, all the decisions taken in consequence of that decision will ignore the controversy. There is no reduction in sentence, for example, for uncertainty about conviction or evidence that was, or could not be, admitted.

A favourite way of arguing for lawyers is to declare. The emphasis is upon persuasion and rhetoric (Perelman, 1963). H.L.A. Hart, when Professor of Jurisprudence at Oxford University, wrote:

Legal reasoning characteristically depends on precedent and analogy, and makes an appeal less to universal logical principles than to certain basic assumptions peculiar to the lawyer... (Hart, 1963).

Extensive appeal is made to commonsense; whether it is common or makes sense is rarely investigated. Frequent use is made of 'reasonable', 'sensible', 'fair' and similar words, so that a declaration, by lawyer or judge, that something is 'reasonable' tends to be accepted both for itself and by disarming others who do not wish to be regarded as unreasonable.

Campbell (1974) argued that these distinctive features of lawyers' reasoning and arguing are the product of court work being the paradigm form of legal work and reasoning. They flow from the practical requirements of obtaining decisions in courts. Particularly in the adversarial system of the common law world, judges have to choose from the two (or more) versions put before them. They have to deal with the particular case and cannot refuse to decide. Every decision needs to be justified. By being able to choose and state the facts found, the judge is able to minimize any controversy there may have been and which might otherwise continue.

Common Ground

It may well be then that the needs of the courts, rather than the law itself, are the principal source of the difficulties between lawyers and psychiatrists. More than most specialties in medicine, psychiatry is dependent upon interpretation and opinion. Kenny (1983) suggested that psychiatry, as represented in the courts, appears unscientific because of the difficulty of distinguishing fact and value. Chiswick (1985) described how, in preparing reports for particular sides in the court process, psychiatrists may be breaching their ethical duties to their patient. Courts, unfortunately, provide a seductive forum for publicity and intellectual sparring; a 'heady atmosphere' is Chiswick's phrase.

Courts are not, however, and need not be, the focus and determinant of the relationships between psychiatry and law. The cases which attract attention and give concern to psychiatrists and/or lawyers are relatively few and atypical. Much commoner than the aggressive cross-examination will be the letter or report, by a psychiatrist or general practitioner, for which the court will be grateful. The medical report will often provide the court with an easy solution to its dilemma. Here there will be few problems. Perhaps we should be more concerned about the potential for collusion in the 'easy' cases.

The potential for a co-operative relationship has been marred by this preoccupation with courts as the locus of interaction and with the psychiatrist's role in legal contexts only as an expert witness. Stone (1982) has vigorously condemned legal interventions in psychiatry, but his strictures relate to a few court decisions and legislative inventions. His concern is at the grand level of the few court cases that excite controversy and the impact of new legislation.

Rose (1986) argued that the differences between law and psychiatry have been exaggerated. Like Moore (1984) he argued that they hold a similar theory of human nature. Rose noted that the antagonism is most acute in courts, but he did not see that as an explanation. He demonstrated that both law and psychiatry are inherently interpretative and subjective. He believed that the criticism of psychiatry for not being objective is misguided, for

all clinical medicine involves the application of socially, historically and culturally variable norms of health and sickness to particular cases.

Diagnosis involves much more than checking the patient's symptoms against a checklist.

We believe that the conflicts between lawyers and psychiatrists are diminishing. Perhaps both can concede the limits of their roles and claims to knowledge. Lawyers could become more genuine advocates looking to the broader social, political and civil interests of their clients, instead of only providing solutions where a problem fits a legal category, for example they might concede that their clients' best interests are as important as their clients' instructions. This would not produce a cosy consensus, but could continue to challenge psychiatry, for example in the use of diagnostic statements about people with problems in ordinary living. The more that lawyers and psychiatrists work together the sooner mutual under-standing will increase. An example of this can already be seen in the way in which the Parole Board, with its heavy emphasis on judicial decisions, includes a good deal of clinical discussion about progress in prison and risk assessment at least in part because of the contribution of psychiatrists and psychologists.

As far as the court is concerned the pretrial conference is a good forum for ironing out differences in approach and the psychiatrist should see it as a professional obligation to attend these conferences. Psychiatrists could issue self-denying ordinances. For example, they could collectively announce that they will refuse to give evidence on whether their patient's 'mental responsibility for his act', within the diminished responsibility defence, was 'substantially impaired' on the basis that such a judgment involves moral rather than psychiatric concepts and should be left to non-experts (juries or lawyers). They could give some practical reality to team work by encouraging other professions to give evidence. Psychiatry, on occasions, seeks legitimacy through involvement with courts, but courts also need a legitimacy and objectivity through association with being scientific.

Reports: Preliminary Matters

When asked to provide a psychiatric report, the first question the psychiatrist has to address is whether it is appropriate to take the case. In particular, is it within the scope of his or her expertise? Both the Civil Procedure Rules (http://www.justice.gov.uk/civil/procrules_fin/) and the Criminal Procedure Rules (http://www.justice.gov.uk/criminal/procrules_fin/rulesmenu.htm) that govern the admission of expert evidence in civil and criminal proceedings in England and Wales identify the overriding duty of the expert as being to help the court on matters 'within his expertise'. For example, does it truly concern a psychiatric matter, and, if so, might it require more specialist psychiatric expertise (for example neuropsychiatry)? Apart from technical qualifications, practical questions should also be considered, such as whether the catchment area psychiatrist would be a better choice if outpatient care or hospital admission could ultimately be required.

If it is appropriate to take the referral, it is important next to consider the type of *role* expected. Is the request (as in the majority of cases) for an expert opinion in the form of a report which is going to be available to the court, or is the request one which will result only in 'advice to counsel' (or solicitors), in which case the involvement is not independent, except in the obvious respect that a medical opinion will always be a responsible profes-sional one. In making this distinction, it is important to note that, in many cases, it is common for psychiatrists called to give oral evidence in criminal or civil cases to adopt both roles, consecutively, so that an 'independent expert opinion' is given to the court through a report and in the witness box, but the psychiatrist also gives 'advice to counsel' regarding psychiatric matters in the hear-ing, for example in relation to the evidence of another expert. Some psychiatrists eschew such an 'adviser' role and see it as inconsistent with the role of independent expert to the court; however, most accept it as necessary and ethically valid so long as clear demarcation between essentially different roles is maintained. The distinction between 'advice' and a 'report' is important because the Civil Procedure Rules and the Criminal Procedure Rules only apply to expert evidence that is prepared for the pur-pose of the court proceedings and, although the expert is 'immune from suit', in the sense of being sued for damages in relation to an opinion for, or evidence given in, court proceedings, no such immunity applies to advice given before proceedings are commenced, to advice which the parties do not intend to adduce in litigation or only to comment on a single joint expert's report and so the expert is advised to have indemnity insurance to cover opinion given in the form of such advice.

Next, it is essential to be clear about the *issues* that are to be addressed and, in particular, to distinguish clearly between legal and medical issues. The *Protocol for the Instruction of Experts to Give Evidence in Civil Claims* (Civil Justice Council 2005) ('the Protocol') states that: 'Experts who do not receive clear instructions should request clari-fication and may indicate that they are not prepared to act unless and until such clear instructions are received' (para. 8.2). Clarification of this will facilitate relevant thought as well as ensure that medical role boundaries are maintained, and that opinion and advice are restricted to medical issues (as they relate to particular legal questions).

It is important to be aware of the potential for in-built bias which can arise where the request derives from one side or the other (that is, not from the court itself). Such bias can occur simply by virtue of the particular issues and questions raised in the referral, since other potentially rel-evant questions may be omitted. In these circumstances the psychiatrist must decide whether to respond in the report only to those questions asked (as most do), or whether to anticipate other issues where they are sufficiently obvious. As experts are open to criticism by the courts for dealing with issues they have not been asked to address, it is advis-able in the first instance to write to the instructing party identifying these other issues and explaining why they ought to be addressed. It may be helpful to include in the report something to the effect: 'Unless I have indicated otherwise, these are the only matters I have been asked to address. The absence of an opinion on a particular issue does not mean that I have no opinion on the issue. It means only that I have not been asked to address the issue.'

Special Ethical Considerations

While keeping strictly within the core of medical ethics there are differences between ordinary clinical psychiatric practice and preparing psychiatric court reports. The expectations which are an integral part of a normal clinical interview may be modified. The subject of the report is therefore, not necessarily a 'patient' (unless s/he happens to have been the psychiatrist's patient beforehand), but also a lawyer's 'client'. This means that issues of confidentiality will be different from the simple doctor/patient ones. Some regard these differences as 'ethical' differences whereas, with care, it is perfectly possible to resist any major breach of ethical practice when working within a legal framework, indeed experienced lawyers, especially the judiciary do not expect a doctor to depart from his or her basic medical morality.

The more general 'ethical' matters which arise repeatedly in legal psychiatric practice mostly derive from the relationship and boundaries between law and psychiatry. Psychiatrists differ in how they interpret and operate their role boundary and they must make their own decisions. It must be noted however that the understandable expectation that the courts will correctly define the boundary is not always borne out. Judges can rule wrongly in regard to such specific matters as psychiatric evidence. They may, for example, order a psychiatrist to express an opinion about the responsibility or otherwise (i.e. the guilt or otherwise) for a defendant's actions, a matter which is clearly moral, not psychiatric. In the majority of cases which occur in lower courts, it is usually up to the psychiatrist to be boundary vigilant.

An important issue that has arisen in debates with American colleagues is whether a psychiatrist remains medical even when giving evidence to lawyers or courts i.e. does he or she adhere to basic medical ethics in all circumstances? The generally accepted European position is that doctors remain bound by the culture and rules of their profession even when in court although at no time should they behave illegally. It is difficult to be a doctor one minute and a 'forensicist' the next. Everybody in court, judge, jury, counsel and other witnesses, understands this. If medical bias is suspected in an opinion no one objects provided the facts are not distorted. The decision-makers, judge or jury, will hear all the evidence and understand the doctor's position. Doctors are 'experts' in court precisely because they are doctors; they are neither decision-makers, nor amateur lawyers.

The position of both being expert witness and the patient's own psychiatrist is more difficult. It is acceptable in England and Wales, but EU countries are divided on this issue (Taylor et al., 2012).

The Forums in England and Wales

A psychiatrist may be asked to provide reports for any legal forum. The main ones which may call on a psychiatrist, in England and Wales, are shown in box 6.1. They can range in location from the formal setting of the Royal Courts of Justice to the informal surroundings of the lounge bar of a country public house where an Agricultural Land Tribunal may convene (Rix et al., 1997).

Different forums use different procedures and rules of evidence. This may affect the presentation of psychiatric information and the range of recommendations that may be available. In England and Wales reports prepared for civil and criminal proceedings have to comply with the Civil Procedure Rules and the Criminal Procedure Rules respectively, there are additional requirements for reports prepared at the request of the police or Crown Prosecution Service in criminal cases. The Family Division has issued guidance for experts preparing reports in family cases and recent cases have added further requirements (Rix, 2008a,b). This guidance is regularly updated. The psychiatrist is not expected to remember all these complexities but s/he should be aware that such complexities exist, and the various documents can be readily consulted on the internet. It is particularly important that a psychiatrist does not assume the role of amateur lawyer and does consult closely with their legal team throughout.

Box 6.1 Courts relevant to psychiatry

Criminal Courts

Supreme Court
Court of Appeal (Criminal Division)
Crown Court (including the Central Criminal Court)
Magistrates' courts, including youth courts

Civil Courts

Supreme Court
Court of Appeal (Civil Division)
High Court, including
  Queen's Bench Division
  Chancery Division
  Family Division
Court of Protection
County courts

Tribunal Service

Upper Tier Tribunal (for appeals from England and Wales)
Mental Health Review Tribunal for Wales
First-tier Tribunal (Mental Health) (part of the Health, Education and Social Care Chamber) for England

Special Courts

Coroners' Courts
Parole Board
Information about HM Courts including some High Court listings can be found on the internet: http://www.hmcourts-service.gov.uk, go to 'information about...'

It must be emphasized that the preparation of such reports should always be founded upon ordinary good psychiatric practice, uninfluenced by the legal setting. The practice of providing psychiatric reports for courts involves presenting a full but relevant history, making ordinary diagnoses and prognoses with comments about treatment and its availability, presented in a way which acknowledges the court's needs and complies with the appropriate rules and guidance. It is worth remembering, however, that courts often turn to psychiatrists for help in understanding the central character (usually the defendant) in the case. A full and historic description of the individual's background, upbringing, and psychological problems may provide meaning to an otherwise senseless crime or dispute. Psychiatry is in large part biography.

CONSTRUCTING A REPORT

Case preparation

Providing a psychiatric report does not begin with interviewing the subject. Preparatory work is necessary and this is emphasized in major cases by the awareness that what is done (or not done) may be explored in cross-examination. Similar standards of investigation should apply to minor cases, even though such public exposure is less likely.

First of all, it is necessary to ensure that the instructions from the referring source are adequate and make clear what issues the lawyers wish addressed. If the instructions do not ask clear questions, then clarification can be requested before going further. It is unwise to respond to a request that says merely 'please provide a psychiatric report' without a phone call to the lawyer. On the other hand, the lawyer may be seeking guidance about a puzzling case. S/he may be unaware of treatment which is available for a client. S/he may be unaware of all the pros and cons of pursuing a psychiatric approach so preliminary discussion will help to clarify and inform.

It may be helpful to list the legal and medical issues which appear to be the crux of the case. It is also important to ensure that all relevant documents concerning the case are available. In a criminal case these will be the charge sheet or indictment, prosecution case summary, witness statements, record of interview, social enquiry reports, previous convictions, previous or current psychiatric reports, and post-mortem or other pathology reports. In a civil case, such as a personal injury case, the documents are likely to include the pleadings (such as the particulars of claim, defence, schedule of special damages and witness statements), medical records and other expert reports. In a family case the Court is likely to have agreed to the expert seeing various documents filed with the court, such as the application for a care order, statements of various parties, such as the applicant local authority, the parents, social workers and other professionals, a chronology of the case and other expert reports. Disclosure in a family case is different because the permission of the court is required before any document can be disclosed to an expert.

Interviewing the Subject

Practical matters

1. *Location:* this may be in an outpatient or another consulting room (for example in a criminal case where the defendant is on bail); in prison (for example in a criminal case); in a police cell or in hospital (if remanded by the court or transferred from custody) or even in a lawyer's office or the subject's home (but chaperone issues may arise). It is important to determine that adequate assessment can be made in the place and conditions available.
2. *Time:* allow sufficient time before the hearing or the deadline for the report for further investigations to be conducted should they prove necessary. Also, allow sufficient time for each interview, especially bearing in mind prison restrictions on hours, which are usually strictly maintained. Several interviews are better than one, and may be essential in a difficult case, although resources will frequently only permit one.

Ethical matters

It is important to ensure that both doctor and the interviewee have correct perceptions and expectations. The difference from the normal professional role of the psychiatrist should be explained to the interviewee. The matter of confidentiality most obviously reflects the distinction between the report situation and an ordinary doctor/patient relationship. This arises because third parties are automatically involved, and because a single piece of information may have both psychiatric and legal significance. Hence a doctor may be obliged for medical reasons to include information which has direct legal impact, perhaps even on the verdict. Even if the information is of legal relevance only (and therefore is not included in a report), there is no right of privilege over such information and, if the psychiatrist were giving oral evidence, the court could insist on its disclosure (even though this is extremely rare). As a result, it is good practice to explain clearly the nature of the professional interaction and its purpose, including that of preparing a report for defence lawyers or the court. The use of a written consent form (Rix, 2008b; http://www.drkeithrix.co.uk) is becoming more common and can assist if subsequently an interviewee complains, for example, that something was not explained or that s/he did know the purpose of the consultation.

The setting of the interview may have coercive significance and the psychiatrist should be aware of this. Where access to general practice, previous psychiatric or other hospital records is needed, specific patient consent should be gained (if s/he is competent). This can be covered in the consent form. Explicit discussion of the offence charged in a criminal case is dealt with below, but here we note that, if the defendant denies the alleged offence or is inconsistent, the psychiatrist must decide whether questioning is really necessary for psychiatric assessment. In general, it is probably good practice to err on the side of exclusion of legally relevant material in a disputed verdict case. However, where the mental state and the supposed criminal act are intimately linked, this advice may be hard to follow. In any case, it is important to get the accused person's view on why s/he has been charged with the offence.

Clinical interview

Once the purpose and context of the interview have been explained, the interview proceeds like any other assessment interview, although the relevant clinico-legal issues will affect the weight given to various aspects of the interview.

It is probably sensible not to discuss the offence or the cause of action (i.e. the accident or allegedly negligent treatment) right at the beginning of the interview, but time must be allowed for the interviewee to give his/her version of events, and explanations, for example, for an alleged offence or his/her reactions to an accident or alleged childhood sexual abuse. Pain, repression, and embarrassment may all interfere with this, so a high degree of sensitivity and tact is needed.

Questioning about family history, personal history and social history should be weighted according to their relevance to diagnosis, prognosis and the legal issues. Too much time spent on mundane irrelevances may squeeze out crucial questions. The previous medical history and previous psychiatric history will always be of importance, and the psychosexual history may be emphasized where a sexual offence is concerned or where sexual dysfunction is being attributed to an accident. There should always be enquiries about substance misuse.

In a criminal case it is usually helpful to get the interviewee to describe recent psychiatric symptoms (both pre- and post-arrest) and this may then lead into a discussion of the mental state at the time of offence. Reference to the offence should concentrate on psychiatric aspects, with particular reference (where possible) to the mental mechanisms as well as mental state at the time, as well as possible mental mechanisms. Eliciting and recording the current mental state is, of course, important, not only in pointing to the possible mental state at the time of the offence, but in determining disposal recommendations.

In a civil case where a claimant is alleging injuries resulting from an accident or alleged medical negligence it is important to distinguish between the medical, specifically the psychiatric, history prior to the cause of action and the medical history subsequent to the cause of action.

This assists the reader in seeing to what extent, if at all, the symptoms of which the interviewee complains can be attributed to the litigated event.

At the end, it may be helpful to reorganize the clinical information in terms of the important legal issues concerning, in a criminal case, verdict and disposal, or in a civil case, diagnosis (condition) and treatment given and to review what further information and/or investigations may be necessary.

Further Investigations

It is good practice to gain further information about an interviewee from relatives or friends (provided that the interviewee and his/her relatives and friends give permission) and from the various documents provided or obtained. Obtaining previous medical and psychiatric records will be important (subject to consent), including the prison hospital case records ('inmate medical record') in the case of a defendant on remand in custody. If it is important to refer to family members in a report, this should be in broad terms, to preserve as much of their confidentiality as possible (e.g. 'there is a family history of schizophrenia').

Further specific clinical investigations most commonly involve psychometry. This may be in the form of intelligence tests, tests of memory, and tests aimed at eliciting generalized or focal neuropsychological deficits. Occasionally, in criminal cases the issues of suggestibility and compliance arise. All these matters require specialist psychological assessment, and the lawyers should be so advised. It is not appropriate for psychiatrists to play at being amateur psychologists. Where indicated, physical and neurological investigations may be arranged, but no attempt should be made to stray very far into the fields of general medicine and neurology, and a separate opinion should also be advised for these fields.

Other Psychiatric Experts

In a criminal case when an opinion has been formed it may be sensible to contact other experts who have also seen the patient. It is courteous to inform the instructing solicitor before this is done and essential to do so if instructed by the defence because the defendant's solicitors will need to decide first whether or not their expert's report is going to be disclosed to the prosecution. In general, such contact is to be encouraged, since it ensures that any differences of opinion are not based on different data bases, and it also often focuses any differences of opinion in advance of the hearing. In court it is useful to reduce the differences between apparently competing experts by explaining to the court how much is agreed upon and why there are differences on specific points. There is now a power to order the experts to 'discuss the expert issues in the proceedings; and ... prepare a statement for the court of the matters on which they agree and disagree, giving their reasons' (Criminal Procedure Rules, 33.5 (1)) (see Reports: Preliminary Matters). In minor cases, it is uncommon for more than one psychiatrist to be involved. There are similar provisions for experts' discussions in civil and family cases.

The Structure of the Written Report

Psychiatrists vary greatly in how they prefer to present information in reports. One suggested broad framework and a few guidelines are given below. For further reading on reports, see Grounds (2000); Carson (1990a) and Rix (1999b). For examples of a model criminal report, on Daniel McNaughton and a model civil report, and on Charles Dickens see http://www.drkeithrix.co.uk. A few general points in regard to court reports are in order.

1. A court report is not a 'formulation' or 'case presentation'; rather, it is the presentation of psychiatric information for a non-psychiatric purpose.

2. Clarity is crucial so the report should be arranged in short sentences and paragraphs.

3. Conciseness and pursuit of legal relevance should be the aims.

4. Technical terms and abbreviations should be avoided wherever possible; if it is considered appropriate to include them, then definitions and explanations must also be offered; these can be within the text if brief, as a footnote or in the form of a glossary.

5. Only opinions that can be sustained under cross-examination should be included in a report; always indicate the source of the facts. In a civil case, except for objective findings on mental state examination (facts within the knowledge of the author of the report), the opinion may depend almost entirely on what the interviewee has reported (assumed facts). It will be for the parties to agree, or for the court to decide, the facts in the case, so it is important that the structure of the report allows the reader to distinguish between 'facts', 'assumed facts' and 'opinion'.

6. The interviewee will probably see the report, so avoid giving personal information of which s/he is unaware (for example, adoptive status or illegitimacy).

7. The report is about the interviewee so avoid disclosing privileged information about others other than with their permission.

8. Write with conscious reference to the limits of the psychiatric role.

9. Remember that others might use the report during subsequent hospital treatment or sentence but for this reason it may be wise to indicate that the report ought not to be used for any purpose other than that for which it was requisitioned and should not be disclosed outside the proceedings without appropriate permission.

10. Once a report has been presented in court, it ceases to be a confidential document. Some confidentiality can be preserved in some cases by asking a judge or magistrate to avoid reading aloud sensitive parts of the report. They will usually respect the request. However, even if a report is not presented in court, confidentiality cannot be guaranteed once it leaves the hands of the writer.

11. Avoid value laden statements.

12. Be specific and avoid general terms.

13. Give reasons for conclusions. This is a requirement of the Civil Procedure Rules, the Criminal Procedure Rules and the Family Division 'where there is a range of opinion'.

14. Exclude psychiatric information not relevant to the court's purposes.

A report should be as long, and no longer, than is necessary for its legal purpose. As a result, the forum will, to some extent, influence the report. In criminal cases magistrates and district judges have little time to read reports, often doing so in front of the defendant, and will welcome brevity. Judges in the Crown Court and the High Court will have time to deliberate on reports and, in more major cases, issues are often not only weightier, but more complex medico-legally. As a further general rule, it is probably wise to include only limited background information, being selective on the basis that it supports and makes more comprehensible the legally definitive aspects of the report.

The problem of hearsay and assumed facts

Psychiatrists frequently rely upon information provided by others, that is 'hearsay' from a legal point of view, and information from the interviewee which may or may not be true, i.e. assumed facts. No problem usually arises except where such information might be given in oral evidence. Judges generally do not require separate 'proof' of such information (by requiring informants to give evidence in court) but if any of the facts are disputed the court may have to decide the facts. The psychiatrist should be aware of the distinction between quoting statements of informants as explanatory and justificatory of a psychiatric opinion as opposed to being evidence of the factual truth of those statements (which the jury might rely upon). It is specifically important to avoid re-statement, even in the written report, of allegations by others (or other legally relevant hearsay). It is good practice to indicate the source of information: 'From his mother I learned that...' or 'The police file indicates...', or to indicate sources generally by subheadings e.g. 'family history (from the patient)'. It is also helpful to separate the information from different sources, e.g. 'medical history as given by the defendant/claimant', 'medical history as set out in the medical records'. It is worth noting too that it may be inadvisable to say: 'The claimant/defendant claims...', or worse, 'the defendant denies', as this could indicate that the writer does not believe his informant, which may not be the case at all. The requirement under the Criminal Procedure Rules and the Civil Procedure Rules to 'make clear which of the facts stated in the report are within the expert's own knowledge' makes it particularly important to allow the reader to see which facts are within the expert's own knowledge (which may not be more than the mental state examination findings) and which facts or assumed facts come from other sources and what those sources are.

Introduction

The report should begin by identifying the author of the report and giving a brief description of his/her qualifications so that their qualification for preparing the report is clear. As it may be necessary for the court to judge whether or not the expert has the experience, expertise and training appropriate to the case, this section should refer to a more detailed account of the expert's qualifications, training and experience that can be included as an appendix to the report. This is not an ego trip. The details given should be commensurate with the nature and complexity of the case and it may be sufficient merely to state academic and professional qualifications but where more highly specialized expertise is required the expert should include sufficient details to show that s/he is qualified to provide the evidence required so there is no place for false modesty. This and other useful advice, including a model declaration of impartiality, can be found on the Academy of Experts website http://www.academy-experts.org/cprbits.htm which is updated regularly. The procedural rules published by the Ministry of Justice (both criminal and civil) (see Reports: Preliminary Matters) are also worth keeping an eye on, especially part 33 of the criminal rules which refers to expert witnesses. The rules are regularly updated.

Although, in civil cases at least, those instructing the expert should have established that there is no potential conflict of interest, the next section should be a statement either to the effect that the expert is not aware of any actual or potential conflict of interest or, if such might be identified, for example if the subject of the report was, or still is, under the care of the expert, as occurs in some criminal cases, the expert should indicate whether or not s/he regards this as affecting his/her ability to provide an independent opinion. A conflict of interest does not automatically disqualify an expert because the test is the independence of the opinion (*Toth*).

The next section of the report is a summary of the case, setting out the assumed or given factual background to the case as it is understood by the psychiatrist at the point s/he has been instructed. This is so that the reader of the report is able to see the issues the psychiatrist

has to address and the opinion reached in context. More importantly and critically, in order to comply with the Civil Procedure Rules and the Criminal Procedure Rules it is the place to include the 'statement setting out the substance of all facts and instructions given to the expert which are material to the opinions expressed in the report or upon which those opinions are based' (Civil Procedure Rules Practice Direction 2.2 (3)); Criminal Procedure Rules Part 33.3(c)). Very often this can be based on the letter of instruction. This section serves two purposes: it orientates the reader and it ensures compliance with the required standards.

This summary of the case leads naturally to the next section which concerns the issues to be addressed. The properly instructed expert should be able to list and set these out clearly. They determine the format and the content of the rest of the report. They enable the reader to focus on the content of the report with the issues in mind. This section is also the place to comply with the requirement that an expert should make it clear when a question or issue falls outside his/her expertise (Civil Procedure Rules, Practice Direction 1.5 (a)).

The description of the enquiry

Following these introductory sections there should be a section setting out the expert's methods. This makes it clear how the expert has gone about dealing with the issues s/he has been asked to address, e.g. a consultation with the subject of the report, interviews with informants, consideration of materials provided or obtained, tests. It is essential to list exactly the sources of information (including clinical interviews and tests) on which the opinion is based. This should include reference to the documents and other materials seen and particular informants interviewed, as well as past medical and psychiatric notes read. Except in rare cases where the only documents or materials fall into a single category, such as the general practice records, it is good and accepted practice to refer the reader to an appendix in which the documents and materials studied are listed. Where, ideally, access to other information would have been helpful, note its non-availability. A full list of documents, within reason, has the advantage of avoiding subsequent unnecessary correspondence or questions in court as to whether or not the expert has seen a particular document.

The facts on which the opinion is based

The factual section of the report contains all of the information used to form an opinion(s): facts which the writer has been asked to assume; facts which the writer has observed (e.g. mental state examination, tests); and opinions of others upon which the writer relies in forming his or her own opinion. It is likely to comprise background history, medical history, information concerning the matter that is the subject of the proceedings (e.g. alleged offence, accident), mental state examination and any tests administered.

Background history. Since most family, personal and social history is not usually of direct legal relevance, it may be helpful to use a composite heading which lays a simple backcloth for the court, perhaps highlighting matters that may be of explanatory help in regard to the opinion and recommendations to be made in the report. If it is absolutely essential to make reference to the disorders or the behaviour of identifiable others then their permission should be sought wherever possible.

Psychosexual history. The psychosexual history may be appropriately incorporated into the background history in many cases, but if it is of direct and major relevance to the court (for example, in the case of an alleged sexual offence or historic child abuse) a separate heading is probably helpful.

Substance abuse. There should always be enquiries about alcohol and other drugs which influence mental activity and, where relevant, appropriate information should be included in the report.

Previous medical history. Only information relevant to the ultimate opinion and recommendations need be included under the previous medical history.

Previous psychiatric history. The previous psychiatric history will be of major importance, and some detail should be offered of previous episodes of mental disorder, treatment and outcome, including on what legal basis (formal or informal) treatment occurred. Technical terms should be avoided as far as possible or clearly explained (in footnotes or an appendix in the form of a glossary) so that the court can use the information correctly.

Alleged offence(s). Where it is appropriate to refer to the alleged offence, it is wise to apply the general rule of restricting reference to the defendant's account solely to those aspects which help to define his or her concurrent mental state or to those which are psychiatrically relevant in some other way. For example, where a defendant retells the story of his or her killing of a victim in terms that are delusional or hallucinatory it may be necessary to quote him or her verbatim (whilst not necessarily implying his or her 'confession' is valid).

To reiterate, the alleged offence should not be referred to in a pretrial case where the defendant denies committing it, unless there is some overriding reason to make such reference (e.g. the description of the mental state would be seriously incomplete without it).

Mental state examination. A thorough mental state examination is required in every case, but in the report it should be described as far as possible in simple terms. It is not always necessary to use all of the conventional subheadings in the text. Often positive and significant negative findings will suffice. Full notes should, however, be retained.

Opinion

An opinion should be written in terms of answers to the issues identified in the introduction. Each question or issue should be individually stated, followed by an answer that states the psychiatric opinion and then relates it to the particular legal question. There should only be such repetition of fact as is necessary for the exposition of the opinion. There used to be a common law rule that witnesses, both expert and lay, were not allowed to give evidence on an ultimate issue (i.e. an issue to be determined by the court). This rule was often breached and is now regarded as defunct simply because the judge or jury decides which opinion and which part of an opinion to accept and juries can be clearly told this. (See Tapper, 2007; chapter XI.) For example, the opinion of a psychiatrist or psychologist about the truthfulness of a witness may be 'interesting' but the jury (in a jury case) will be instructed that it is for them to decide that issue.

Opinions should always be expressed with reference to any measure of doubt there may be and if appropriate the standard of proof, i.e. on a balance of probability (the civil standard) or beyond reasonable doubt (the criminal standard). Firm conclusions are required and if unable to give an opinion without qualification, the qualification should be stated. Likewise, if there is insufficient information to reach an opinion, this should be made clear.

If introduced by 'In my opinion', it is clear that the possibility of other views is accepted but for all reports in criminal, civil and family proceedings, where there is a range of opinion on the matters dealt with in the report, the expert must summarize the range of opinion and give reasons for his or her own opinion. The sources and qualifications of those who hold a contrary opinion should be given. This section should set out any material facts or matters that detract from the writer's opinion and any points that should fairly be made against the writer's opinions. The latest guidance from the Family Division states that the use of a balance sheet approach to the factors that support or undermine an opinion can be of great assistance to the court.

Where the opinion concerns questions relevant to the verdict in a criminal case, there may be a request to deal with possible links between a mental disorder and the criminal act. Although the link is sometimes apparently obvious, it is wise to acknowledge that perceived connections are often little more than hypotheses. In some cases, it is better to restrict opinion to coincidental description of the mental state and the alleged crime, without explicitly presuming. If an opinion is based on a hypothesis, especially if it is controversial, this should be highlighted. In general, description is more reliable and robust than explanation. On the other hand, the court does want an opinion not just a reiteration of facts, and a report that is hedged with too much doubt may be completely disregarded. Thus a balance has to be struck which acknowledges uncertainty, but which also gives an authoritative view. Whatever style the opinion is written in, it should always include somewhere a clear medical statement about the patient's condition. If a mental disorder is discovered, then this should be stated and labelled medically. If several are discovered, they should all be listed. Equally, if requested to do so, the report should also refer to prognosis and give some indication of what treatment is required. In doing this it should be remembered that courts are not particularly interested in the classification games played by psychiatrists, for example in compensation work the term 'positive psychiatric illness' can embrace the whole range of morbid emotional responses as well as the specific neurotic and psychotic disorders. The doctor must attempt to determine the existence of *any* psychiatric disorder. The court is more concerned with the existence of disorder in itself, its attribution, and its consequences than with niceties of diagnosis and classification. Diagnostic terms should be used simply and conventionally, but it is unnecessary to follow slavishly definitions from textbooks and glossaries such as the latest *DSM* or *ICD*. *DSM IV* explicitly notes that it should not be used in this way: (American Psychiatric Association, 1994). These medical views can be used to answer or illuminate the legal questions posed. As indicated previously, in answering the legal questions care should be taken to avoid straying beyond medicine into law or morals.

Where other types of expert have seen the defendant, especially psychologists, it is important to encourage submission of a separate report to the court, although a summary of that report may be included in the psychiatric report. If the expert has employed another person, such as a psychologist or junior doctor, to carry out any examination, measurement or test, this person has to be identified along with their qualifications, relevant experience and accreditation, the expert has to indicate whether or not s/he supervised the person and s/he has to summarize the findings on which s/he relies.

Recommendations

Recommendations in criminal cases are usually concerned with disposal, and are dealt with below in 'Issues at the Sentencing Stage'. Clarity of argument is vital, with clear reasons given for any suggested disposal. Recommendations should be restricted to those that relate to psychiatric care. No patient should be recommended for a punitive disposal such as imprisonment, even by implication, though it is appropriate to spell out the consequences of imprisonment as courts must consider its effects under the Criminal Justice Act 1991.

Summary of conclusions

In criminal and civil cases it is a requirement that there should be a summary of the conclusions.

Declarations and statements of truth

Reports in criminal, civil and family cases all require some sort of declaration of compliance with the court's requirements and there are prescribed forms for the statements of truth that have to be included in reports (see Rix 1999b; Rix 2000a,b; Rix 2008b and the model forms of expert report produced by the Academy of Experts and the Expert Witness Institute).

Signature

The report should be signed. Doctors in junior and training posts should indicate somewhere, preferably in this section, the name of the consultant who is ultimately responsible for the case and for supervising their preparation of the report.

Appendices

The usual appendices are: curriculum vitae (including those of any persons who have assisted); documents and materials studied; glossary of medical or technical terms; published material to which reference has been made (with copies including the preceding and succeeding pages sufficient for the extract to be read in context) with details of the qualifications of the author(s).

THE USE OF REPORTS IN CRIMINAL PROCEEDINGS

In England and Wales all criminal cases minor or serious begin in a magistrates' court. The vast majority of cases remain, and can only be dealt with, in a magistrates' court, the rest progress to the Crown Court where it sits locally or to the Central Criminal Court in London (the 'Old Bailey').

Legal issues, and therefore psychiatric matters which potentially relate to those issues, can be categorized most simply according to legal 'stages'.

Pretrial Stage

At the initial magistrates' court hearing, if the case is not dealt with immediately, the defendant will be remanded, either in custody or on bail (and, therefore, at restricted liberty), to a further hearing. Such remands can be repeated until such time as the case is either dealt with by a magistrates' court or, alternatively, is transferred to the Crown Court. At the defendant's appearance for trial (either at a magistrates' court or the Crown Court) the immediate issue (although usually not formally addressed) is that of the defendant's 'fitness to plead' (see chapter 2, Fitness to Plead). A defendant may be referred by the court for a psychiatric report through one of a number of mechanisms during the pretrial stage. These reports will address issues specific to the pretrial stage itself, but may also commonly consider trial and disposal issues since, in the majority of minor cases, the psychiatric report does not influence the verdict, but only the disposal. The mechanisms of referral are as follows:

1. A magistrates' court or the Crown Court may remand a defendant to hospital for a report under section 35 of the Mental Health Act 1983 (amended). This allows assessment, but in itself does not provide for compulsory treatment of the defendant, although this may be justified on common law grounds, in an emergency, and there is no bar to addition of a hospital treatment order under section 3 of the Mental Health Act. Such a remand order can be made in favour of any type of psychiatric hospital or ward (secure, locked or open) and the defendant then becomes a patient detained under the MHA 1983 (amended).

2. The Crown Court may remand to hospital for treatment under section 36 of the MHA 1983 (amended).

3. The court may remand the defendant on bail, but with a condition that he or she resides in a particular hospital ward. This may also be a route, therefore, to achieving a 'remand psychiatric report'; however, the defendant is not a patient detained under the MHA 1983 (amended).

4. If the court does not consider it necessary for the defendant to be either in custody or an inpatient, then it can remand on bail with ordinary conditions of residence (for example, at home or in a bail hostel) and require at the same time that an outpatient psychiatric assessment and report be carried out.

5. The court may remand the defendant in custody and, at the same time, request that a psychiatric report be provided. The ways in which courts obtain psychiatric reports vary. The court can ask directly, for example by a request to the prison in the case of a defendant remanded in custody, or it can do so through either the probation service or the defence solicitors, who would then make the referral to the psychiatrist.

6. If the court has not requested a psychiatric report, then such a report may be provided in any event via two other routes:

    a) Whilst on remand, either in custody or bail, defence solicitors (or the probation service) may independently request an opinion. It is the duty of the defence solicitors to do so if they suspect the defendant may be mentally disordered.

    b) Whilst on remand in custody, a prison doctor (for example the prison's visiting general practitioner) may consider that the defendant suffers from a mental disorder and s/he may, therefore, offer a 'voluntary report' to the court. This happens much less often since the Prison Medical Service gave way to National Health Service 'in reach'.

Any report prepared at the pretrial stage should address the issue of fitness to plead (see chapter 2), although unfitness is a rarity in practice, and the issues addressed by most remand reports are concerned with trial or sentence issues.

Trial Stage

Psychology and psychiatry

In a British criminal trial there are only a few issues which require psychiatric evidence. Insanity can be raised in any trial. Diminished responsibility may be pleaded in a murder trial. A mother may be charged with infanticide if she kills her baby before his/her first birthday (see p.29). These matters are dealt with below. In a magistrates' court psychiatric evidence may be admitted in order to achieve a hospital order without conviction

These psychiatric matters are not particularly common given the very large number of cases passing through the criminal courts. In serious cases in the Crown Court the evidence itself may be disputed. A number of very high profile convictions in England and Wales have been found to be flawed because of the quality of the evidence submitted by the Crown Prosecution Service. Evidence in court can be witness statements where individuals tell of their experiences and what they have seen or heard. It can also encompass scientific tests for specific chemicals, bloodstains, DNA material, etc. The presentation of any of this evidence is subject to human error and on occasion deliberate distortion or fabrication. The pressure on the police force to get a conviction is very high indeed in a high-profile case. In an adversarial system each piece of prosecution evidence should be tested fully by the defence. As far as witness statements are concerned, which are frequently relied on as main evidence, new psychological investigations have been devised to test the likely validity of these statements (Gudjonsson, 2007). Gisli Gudjonsson has devised psychological tests which examine the competence and reliability of a witness, whether a confession is likely to be false, and whether a witness is suggestible to psychological pressure. The tests applied are technical and they are applied by specially trained psychologists. Other practitioners, such as psychiatrists, should not attempt these tests without the specialist training needed.

Readers who are interested in the reasons for the development of this work, the recommendations of the Royal Commission, and the basic scientific work should read the appropriate books and reports e.g. Gudjonsson (2003a); Gudjonsson (2003b); Royal Commission on Criminal Justice (1993).

Vulnerable witnesses and suspects

Thus the ability of victims and witnesses to cope with the stressful environment of examination and cross-examination is important. This situation has been improved by the Youth Justice and Criminal Evidence Act 1999.

Witnesses are likely to be vulnerable by virtue of factors such as their age, sex, intellectual capacity or mental health status. Communication difficulties including an inability to deal with the vocabulary and style of questioning in court may well be present, particularly in the case of children and adults or children with intellectual disabilities. An important provision of the Youth Justice and Criminal Evidence Act 1999 is the introduction of 'special measures'. One of these was the use of videotaped evidence-in-chief and live-link or screens for courtroom appearances and this is widely available to help vulnerable witnesses. Another was to provide direct assistance to children and adults with communication difficulties. After considerable delay, the Office for Criminal Justice Reform piloted the use of intermediaries in court. Intermediaries are typically specially trained speech and language therapists or teachers. Ideally they are involved with the witness from prior to the evidence gathering interview through to the trial stage. The intermediary provides a report on the communication needs of the witness for use by the police, barristers and judges. The intermediary also accompanies the witness during the trial and assists the witness if required. The pilot study was considered successful enough for the scheme to be rolled out across England and Wales (see also Plotnikoff and Woolfson, 2007).

Mental health professionals writing reports or giving evidence on the competence of witnesses may now find themselves liaising with intermediaries. Furthermore, the outcome of assessing competence should take into account the availability of intermediaries, particularly if communication difficulties are pivotal to the competence assessment. Although intermediaries were introduced to support victims and witnesses, the question of whether they should also be made available in the case of suspects with communication difficulties is likely to become an issue.

The reliability of evidence

The ultimate determination of the reliability of evidence is a matter for the jury. It has two components. The first component is the person's ability to report observed events or experiences accurately and completely. This is the cognitive side to reliability and is dependent upon the person's intellectual and memory functioning, and general susceptibility to suggestive influences, in addition to the factors which influence the acquisition, retention and retrieval of information.

The second component is the willingness to tell the truth, or to cooperate with the assessment. Here, the expert is beginning to trespass into the area reserved for the jury, so in Britain experts don't usually give evidence on general psychological factors which are likely to affect the reliability of evidence given by the ordinary member of the public. Psychological evidence regarding eyewitness testimony has to be very circumspect. It normally has to be demonstrated that the defendant, victim, or witness, possesses some abnormal characteristics which makes

him/her especially vulnerable to giving erroneous testimony. There are two kinds of circumstances where mental health professionals are likely to be asked to give expert evidence on reliability issues in criminal trials. First, they may be asked to give an opinion on the likely reliability of evidence of mentally handicapped witnesses or victims. Second, they may be asked to act as expert witnesses in cases where people have retracted self-incriminating confessions made to the police during interrogation (see also section on provocation below).

In court, the competence and reliability of a witness are dealt with as separate matters. Competence is a matter for the judge; reliability is a matter for the jury. In Gudjonsson and Gunn (1982), a woman suffering with intellectual impairment alleged that she had been raped. The prosecution challenged both her competence and reliability as a witness. She was asked to undergo a combined psychiatric and psychological examination. In the absence of the jury, expert evidence was given about her ability to understand the truth, her concept of God, and her understanding of contempt of court. The judge also asked her questions on these points and satisfied himself that she was sufficiently competent to be a witness. In front of the jury, further expert evidence, mainly psychological, testified to her suggestibility, in particular whether she was thought to claim perceptions that had no objective basis, and whether she could be easily persuaded to give expected or suggested answers to questions. Special tests were devised for this.

False confessions

Defendants may retract confessions they had previously made to the police and where the principal evidence against them is their own confession. How many of these retracted confessions are actually false confessions is not known. However, a sufficiently large number of false confession cases have been documented in the literature to warrant the attention of mental health professionals (Gudjonsson and MacKeith, 1988).

With the introduction of the Police and Criminal Evidence Act 1984 (PACE), the two specific elements to the exclusionary rule of confession statements are 'oppression' and 'reliability'. The Codes of Practice of PACE <police.homeoffice.gov.uk/operational-policing/powers-pace-codes/pace-code-intro> contain provisions relating to the interviewing of mentally disordered or otherwise mentally vulnerable persons (Ventress et al., 2008). Incidental breaches of the Codes will support arguments as to unreliability under section 76(2) b. The relevance and admissibility of a confession are matters of law and are dealt with by the judge, whereas the question of weight is a matter for the jury. The expert witness may give evidence twice, once during a 'trial within a trial' (where the judge decides on the admissibility of the self-incriminating statements) and, subsequently, during the trial proper, and in front of the jury, if the judge allows the statements in evidence.

Kassin and Wrightsman (1985) have suggested three psychological types of false confession:

1. *The voluntary confession*, where the confession is made in the absence of any form of external pressure or elicitation.
2. *The coerced-compliant confession*, where defendants falsely confess for some instrumental gain (e.g. in order to get out of the police station) whilst under police pressure, knowing full well that they did not commit the crime they have confessed to.
3. *The coerced-internalized confession*, where defendants become subtly persuaded during police questioning that they committed the crime of which they are accused. The coerced-compliant confession is most commonly reported in the literature.

Retracted confessions involve varied and complicated phenomena. Persistent personality characteristics such as phobic symptoms, memory problems, intellectual deficits, suggestibility and compliance are often relevant, in addition to the mental state of the defendant at the time of questioning (Gudjonsson and MacKeith, 1988). Further issues to be considered include the interrogation technique used by the police, the length of time kept in custody and interrogated, the degree of access to a solicitor, family and friends, and the amount of sleep and food taken.

It is important to note that contrary to intuition it is not psychologically vulnerable suspects who are particularly likely to confess. Suspects were more likely to confess if they reported having consumed an illicit (non-prescribed) drug in the previous 24-hour period and less likely to confess when interviewed in the presence of a legal adviser or if they had had experience of prison or custodial remand. Younger suspects were also more likely to confess (Pearse et al., 1998).

Memory (recall), suggestibility and compliance

Of particular relevance for both witnesses and suspects is recall of events, and in particular the role of *interrogative suggestibility* defined as 'the extent to which, within a closed social interaction, people come to accept messages communicated during formal questioning, as the result of which their subsequent behavioural response is affected' (Gudjonsson and Clark, 1986). For a suspect, the worst effect of suggestibility is a false confession to a crime leading to conviction. In witnesses, suggestibility as a result of leading or misleading questioning techniques or exposure to incorrect information can potentially lead or contribute to miscarriages of justice.

Interrogative suggestibility can be measured using the Gudjonsson Suggestibility Scales (GSS) developed as a forensic tool in cases involving retracted confessions (GSS 1, GSS 2, Manual – Gudjonsson, 2007). The scales measure an individual's responses to leading questions and negative feedback (styled 'yield' and 'shift' when scoring) as well as

logical memory and confabulations. Studies of validity and reliability are reported as good, although proper administration of the test is important (for a full review of the properties of the scale see Gudjonsson, 2007). However, White and Wilner (2005) found that participants with intellectual disability were significantly less suggestible following a *real* witnessed event compared to their score on the GSS, raising the possibility that the GSS may be too rigorous a test. Further research on this point is needed before any firm conclusions can be reached. According to Gudjonsson (2003b) the GSS 2 is more appropriate than the GSS 1 for children and adults with intellectual disabilities because it has a simpler stimulus story, and alternative versions of the GSS specifically for children have also been developed: the GSS Short (Henry and Gudjonsson, 2006) and a video version (Scullin and Ceci, 2001).

Other personality and behavioural factors, of particular relevance in this context and in relation to suggestibility in witnesses and suspects, include anxiety, compliance and acquiescence (see below), intelligence and memory itself. (For a full review of these and other individual differences in adults' suggestibility and memory see Eisen et al., 2002.)

The effect of anxiety on memory and suggestibility is a concern because of the stress caused by being a witness, victim or suspect in court. Studies by Gudjonsson using the Spielberger State-Trait Anxiety Inventory (STAI, Spielberger et al., 1983) have shown that state anxiety is more reliably related to suggestibility than trait anxiety, as would be expected given that state anxiety is situation bound whereas trait anxiety is relatively stable (Gudjonsson, 1988a). However in experimental studies in which misleading information was incidentally introduced and suggestibility was later measured during a memory test, state anxiety was associated with lower suggestibility whether state anxiety was manipulated or measured using the STAI. This was observed in both adults and children (Ridley et al., 2002; Ridley and Clifford, 2004, 2006). It therefore appears that using anxiety measures to assess likely witness performance should be undertaken with caution given these inconsistent findings. Associations between anxiety and eyewitness memory generally are variable and no firm conclusions can be drawn. Although, in a meta-analysis of 27 studies which investigated the effect of stress on eyewitness identification and a further 36 studies looking at memory for details of a crime, Deffenbacher et al. (2004) concluded that stress has a negative impact on memory for both kinds of detail. (Although see Christianson (1992) and Heuer and Reisberg (2007) for alternative perspectives.) The studies cited in this paragraph were not carried out among people with mental health problems or intellectual disabilities, but there is no reason to assume that the effects would be any less in these groups than in healthy populations.

Compliance differs from suggestibility in that there is no private acceptance of the misleading information. It

161

can be measured using the Gudjonsson Compliance Scale (Gudjonsson, 1989, 2007. See Gudjonsson (2003b) for a review of its reliability and validity, which tends to be less robust than the GSS.) Correlations were observed between suggestibility and compliance (Gudjonsson, 1990). This has been supported by experimental studies which have shown that compliance manipulated by discussing an event with a fellow participant who has witnessed a similar event which differed in an essential detail substantially increases levels of suggestibility relative to controls (Gabbert et al., 2007). Acquiescence is the tendency to answer all questions positively. Weak but significant correlations have been found between suggestibility and acquiescence (Gudjonsson, 1986), but null findings were observed in a later study (Gudjonsson, 1990).

Intelligence and memory have both been found to be negatively related to suggestibility at average or below-average levels of intelligence. The effect disappeared at higher levels of intelligence (Gudjonsson, 1988a). In contrast, Tata (1983) did not observe any relationship between the GSS and intellectual disabilities.

Factors associated with the interview itself are also important when reaching a conclusion about the reliability of a confession or a witness's memory. As already noted factors such as interrogation technique, length of interrogation, sleep deprivation and the presence of legal and/or family support should be taken into account. Similarly, witness memory may be affected by time delay, poor visibility and the stress of witnessing a violent offence.

Anecdotal evidence from police officers suggests that due to the measures imposed by PACE, the number of confessions obtained at interview is low. If this is indeed the case, then miscarriages of justice due to false confessions should become fewer and the need for mental health professionals to assess associated appeals should reduce. Any mental health professional required to review false confession cases is referred to Gudjonsson (2003a,b), which contains a comprehensive guide to the various types of false confession (voluntary, internalized and coerced) and the factors associated with them.

Children

A recent research development has investigated the effect of cross-examination on the testimony of children. While even quite young children can be highly accurate when age-appropriate techniques are used at the evidence gathering stage, the leading and/or oppressive questioning typically used during cross-examination has been found to result in their frequently changing their original testimony (Zajac et al., 2003). Experimental studies have shown that this is often from correct to incorrect (Zajac and Hayne, 2003, 2006; Bettenay, 2010). See Zajac (2009) for a review.

Bettenay (2010) investigated this in an experimental study among both children with intellectual disability and typically developing children. On most measures those with intellectual disability did not perform any worse than their age-matched peers. Furthermore, it was found that state anxiety measured after cross-examination was related to the number of changed responses children made, which may indicate awareness of, and distress caused by, 'giving in' to repeated pressure to change responses.

Intent

To recap from chapter 2, to be guilty of an offence (except in cases of absolute liability, usually quite minor offences) a defendant must be shown to have committed the *actus reus* ('guilty act') whilst having, *mens rea* (the relevant 'guilty mind').

Intention is not a psychiatric concept; however, the capacity to form any particular intention may be related to medical or psychiatric disorder. Some crimes are designated as requiring 'specific intent', and it may be possible, therefore, to argue in a psychiatric report and in court that a particular medical or psychiatric disorder removed the relevant capacity (see for example, Rix and Clarkson, 1994). But, to give an opinion as to the fact and nature of (legal) intent is to speak to the 'ultimate issue' that the jury must address so care must be exercised. Hence, it may be appropriate to describe in detail a defendant's mental state at the time of the *actus*, as it can sometimes be reconstructed retrospectively, and to do so in such a fashion that the court can, if it so wishes, draw an inference as to the nature of the defendant's (legal) intent. Any report or oral evidence should fall short of an opinion on the intention. Some psychiatrists appear to take a different stance on this issue and to be prepared to address the fact or quality of the intention itself. Such a view fails to distinguish between the description of the quality of the mental state and the quality of intention. Even courts themselves will, on occasions, fail to draw the relevant distinction clearly, but the psychiatrist should, at the very least, be aware of it and of the way in which it relates to the proper demarcation of role boundaries.

Psychiatric defences

The substantive law relating to psychiatric defences is dealt with in chapter 2, and this section will consider only matters which concern the application of such defences in the practice of writing opinions and giving oral evidence.

The importance of understanding and being limited by different role boundaries is nowhere better illustrated than in giving opinions in regard to various psychiatric defences.

Insanity

The defence of insanity is little used in practice today (see chapter 2 for more details). In writing a report which addresses insanity, it is important to understand the relatively narrow criteria which are implied by the definition and, in particular, to appreciate its essentially 'cognitive' basis; that is, it is a defence to do with 'knowing' rather than 'feeling'. It is likely to be restricted to abnormal mental states where there is serious cognitive impairment and cases where delusions cause a defect of reasoning.

Diminished responsibility

The defence of manslaughter on the grounds of diminished responsibility, to a charge of murder, in England and Wales has almost entirely replaced, in usage, that of insanity under the McNaughton Rules. As discussed in chapter 2, however, the Homicide Act 1957 which allows the plea of diminished responsibility has been substantially amended by the Coroners and Justice Act 2009. What this will mean in practice is not at all clear at the time of writing. For example will changing 'abnormality of mind' to 'abnormality of mental functioning' produce different results in court? Certainly some of the fundamental principles for the psychiatrist will still apply.

The replacement of 'mental responsibility for acts or omissions' with the 'ability' of the defendant to understand his or her own conduct, form a rational judgment or exercise self-control (Coroners and Justice Act, 2009) means that psychiatrists are now unlikely to have to worry about role boundaries and being asked to address a moral rather than psychiatric question. Although sometimes the question will be difficult to answer, psychiatrists are likely to feel more comfortable assisting the court in deciding if the abnormality of mental functioning caused, or made a significant contribution, to the defendant's conduct in carrying out, or being a party to, the killing.

Where the psychiatric diagnosis, as it can be reconstructed at the time of the *actus*, is a psychotic one, there will often be little difficulty in offering an opinion as regards the effect of the disorder on judgment. In cases of personality disorder, there will be greater difficulty and this is reflected in differing general professional approaches adopted by psychiatrists.

A further problem arises in relation to transiently abnormal mental states. Where a defendant has an episode of acute mental disturbance which is not related to intoxication the court has to decide whether there is an 'abnormality of mental functioning' within the meaning of the Homicide Act 1957. Fortunately, all that psychiatry is has to do is to set out the medical facts, as the jury determine the ultimate and moral issue of the level of responsibility with guidance from the judge.

To the extent that any change has occurred in the defendant's mental state between the time of the *actus* and any psychiatric assessment, there will always be a need to reconstruct the defendant's mental state as it most likely was at the relevant time. This will be based partly on what the defendant recalls of the period, upon evidence from witness statements and records of interview, inference from previous observations of the defendant as they emerge from his/her previous psychiatric history and, where available, evidence from the defendant's family and friends. Such reconstruction is always open to criticism, as it relies partly on the defendant's own recollection. Courts have, on occasion, chosen to cast doubt on the skill of psychiatrists in determining whether alleged abnormal mental phenomena at the time of the *actus* have been validly elicited from the defendant. Corroborative evidence is, therefore, of great importance.

Infanticide

Infanticide is another partial defence to a charge of murder which, if successful, effectively reduces the offence to one of manslaughter. It is also an alternative to manslaughter. It differs from 'diminished responsibility' in that it can be charged from the outset and so it can avoid a woman being charged with the murder of her own child. It is defined by s.1 of the Infanticide Act 1938 (as amended by s.57 of the CJA 2009). It is thereby limited to a woman who is charged with, or would otherwise be convicted of, the murder or manslaughter of her child under the age of 12 months. It is not a defence open to a man, to a woman who kills another woman's child or where the child is 12 months or older. It applies where the woman has caused her child's death by any wilful act or omission. In order for the defence to be accepted, or to be successful, 'at the time of the act or omission', there has to be evidence that: '...the balance of her mind was disturbed by reason of her not having fully recovered from the effect of giving birth to the child or by reason of the effect of lactation consequent upon the birth of the child...' The 'lactation' limb is now redundant given the lack of any evidence that lactation causes mental abnormality. On a strict interpretation of the law, the reference to 'giving birth to the child' means that if a mother kills her newborn baby and her 11-month-old child, when her balance of mind is disturbed by reason of giving birth to the newborn baby, she will not have a defence of infanticide to the killing of the 11-month-old child if she had by then recovered from giving birth to the older child.

The offence predates the defence of 'diminished responsibility' by half a century but, even though it serves a similar purpose, it has survived. This is partly because it can be charged as an offence at the outset. It is partly because, even though it is of more limited application, analysis of the successful cases suggests that it is an easier defence than 'diminished responsibility'. It is probably also because in 'diminished responsibility' the burden of proof is on the defence, whereas if the defence of infanticide is raised to a charge of murder the prosecution carries the more difficult burden of proving beyond reasonable doubt that it is not infanticide.

The difficulty for the psychiatrist is that disturbance of the balance of the mind is not a psychiatric concept and, whereas case law has defined 'abnormality of mind', there is no such definition of disturbance of the balance of the mind. Furthermore, as Mackay (1995) has pointed out, in the cases he reviewed, there was little analysis or discussion by the psychiatrists of this criterion. The nearest definition is in *Sainsbury* where the appeal court judges used the phrase 'left the balance of your mind disturbed so as to prevent rational judgment and decision.'

The cases reported by Mackay in 1993 in a report to the New South Wales Law Commission http://www.lawlink. nsw.gov.au/lrc.nsf/pages/DP31CHP5 and the case reports of d'Orbán (1979) and Bluglass (1990) assist as to the practical application of the law by the courts. Some of the cases analysed by Mackay were of women with fairly obvious mental disorders such as 'puerperal depressive illness', 'clinical depression' and a manic–depressive psychosis that manifested in command hallucinations, but his series also included a case of 'severe hysterical dissociation' and one in which the only abnormality was 'emotional disturbances'. This is consistent with that fact that half of the women in the series reported by d'Orbán were not suffering from any identifiable mental disorder. Bluglass reported similar cases: a woman in whom no persisting psychiatric disorder was found other than her distressed state after the homicide; a woman who was depressed and distressed but showed 'no underlying disorder'; and a woman who gave birth to a baby with Downs syndrome and in which case nothing more abnormal is reported than her shock, inability to accept the appearance of the baby and her sense of hopelessness about its future. The cases reported by Mackay and Bluglass therefore confirm the impression of d'Orbán that for infanticide 'the degree of abnormality is much less than that required to substantiate "abnormality of mind" amounting to substantially diminished responsibility.'

In the case of a woman who has allegedly killed her own child aged less than 12 months the psychiatrist should set out, if it be so: (1) how the woman's mental state has changed since childbirth, whether or not the changes could be regarded as amounting to an 'abnormality of mind' or recognizable mental disorder; (2) indicate how this amounts to a disturbance of the balance of mind, if possible showing how it has affected rational judgment and decision-making; and (3) explain, if possible, how this mental state can be attributed to the effects of childbirth. It is not necessary to identify a mental disorder within the meaning of s.1 of the Act, albeit that this is now a broad definition, or show that the woman has an 'abnormality of mind'.

Although the maximum sentence for infanticide is life imprisonment, in 59 cases between 1979 and 1988 there were no custodial sentences and all disposals were by way of probation, supervision and hospital orders (*Sainsbury*), so reports in such cases are likely to need to give careful consideration to issues related to sentencing.

Sentencing

In the great majority of cases, a psychiatric report will have its legal impact not on the verdict, but rather on disposal. Most cases do not involve homicide or some other charge where a psychiatric defence is likely to be pleaded. Hence recommendations about disposal are often the nub of a report, particularly so far as the court is concerned.

A court may use any psychiatric report either specifically in relation to recommendations for some form of medical disposal or more generally in sentence mitigation.

Psychiatric reports in mitigation

Although the law allows in various ways for the negating of *mens rea* on the basis of psychiatric disorder, in practice most mentally disordered defendants who have committed the *actus reus* are found guilty of the offence, even where there may have been a direct relationship between the disorder and the *actus*. It might be thought, following the responsibility argument, that the psychiatric disorder would mitigate punishment to some extent.

Medical disposal

Any medical recommendation must be practical and within the court's power. To this end, it is essential to hold discussions with any other people who would be involved in the recommended disposal. If a hospital order or an interim hospital order is to be recommended and the relevant bed is under a different psychiatrist, then this should be discussed with that psychiatrist. If possible, the latter should have assessed the defendant by the time of the hearing, and agreed to provide a bed, since no order can be made without a statement of bed availability. Where a recommendation of placement in a special hospital is being made, this will require the support of the admissions panel of the special hospital concerned. Similarly, if a community sentence is recommended, it will be necessary to gain the relevant probation officer's agreement that community rehabilitation is appropriate.

In the past some psychiatrists have argued that for a medical disposal to be appropriate, especially a hospital order, there must have been a connection between the mental disorder and the *actus*. This is not necessary, the Mental Health Act 1983 (amended) makes the position crystal clear, the offender has to be suffering from any disorder or disability of mind such that it is appropriate for him/her to be detained in hospital for medical treatment, that treatment is available, and the court must agree that it is the best method of dealing with the offender.

If a hospital order is recommended, either the report must be accompanied by the relevant form duly completed or, alternatively, the 'recommendations' section of the report must include one of the forms of words required by the relevant section of the Act to justify detention in hospital. Additionally, there must, of course, be a further medical opinion, and it is wise to ensure this is available to the court simultaneously.

Reviews of detention

Psychiatrists provide reports for the Mental Health Tribunal and the Parole Board in relation to detention, either in their capacity as responsible clinician in the case of a hospital patient or as a psychiatrist acting independently or instructed by the patient or his/her legal representative.

When reports are prepared at the request of the patient's legal representative, the lawyer will decide whether or not to use the report. In addition, it is improper for the psychiatrist to disclose the report to anyone else without the consent of the legal representative. However, the High Court has held that a doctor's duty of confidence to a patient detained in a secure hospital for reasons of public safety could be subordinate to a public duty of disclosure, if the doctor considered such disclosure necessary to ensure that the tribunal were fully informed about the patient's condition (*Egdell*).

It should be noted that the Mental Health Tribunal and the Parole Board do not use the adversarial system of the trial. The process is inquisitorial, an investigation, and the rules of evidence and procedure are informal and controlled by the chairman.

A report to a the Mental Health Tribunal should be based not only upon recent interviewing of the patient and clinical staff caring for him or her, but also upon a detailed review of the previous psychiatric history and records. Its conclusion should be addressed to the key issues which concern the tribunal and which relate to its powers. Hence, it may be appropriate for the 'opinion' to express a well argued view as to the current presence or absence of mental disorder, as defined in the relevant section of the MHA 1983 (amended). It should go on explicitly to express the question of the, again current, need to be in hospital either for the health or safety of the patient or for the protection of others. It is important to note that under the amended Mental Health Act 1983 the burden of proof has shifted from the applicant to the responsible authority so that the Tribunal is under a duty to discharge if it is not satisfied that the applicant is suffering from a mental disorder of a nature or degree justifying detention. Any 'recommendations' should be written in the knowledge that, for example, where there is no current mental disorder in terms of the Act, the Tribunal must discharge the order, however dangerous the patient is to self or others. The recommendation may not favour immediate discharge, and it may be appropriate to recommend deferred discharge in order to allow necessary arrangements to be made. It may also be useful to make a recommendation even though the tribunal has no power to implement it, for example a move to a less secure hospital setting, whilst still detained in hospital

under the Act, because the Tribunal can include such a suggestion in its report, even though the suggestion does not carry the force of law. If they were to do so Tribunals would have much greater impact (Taylor et al., 1999).

Reports to the Parole Board should similarly review the prisoner's progress, any treatment received, and the need for further treatment. The main issue for the Board is the question of public safety: would it be safe to continue this man or woman's detention in open conditions, would it be safe to release the prisoner to the community? Does s/he pose a life and limb risk to one or more other persons? These risk issues can only be assessed in a context of full documentation including a full mental health assessment, and a considered appraisal of the release plan if that is being proposed. If the prisoner requires psychiatric treatment before onward movement then that treatment should be specified with suggestions about its implementation, bearing in mind that prison staff are often unfamiliar with the range and the complexities of psychiatric care. Prisons welcome practical suggestions about treatment, especially when they are accompanied by an offer of an NHS bed, even for a short period.

CIVIL MATTERS

Civil courts differ from criminal ones both in the 'sides' to the dispute and the 'level' of required proof. The level of proof is not one of 'beyond reasonable doubt', but of 'on the balance of probabilities'.

There is a variety of types of proceedings in which a psychiatrist may become involved. Some involve psychiatric patients, or persons putatively suffering from mental disorder (for example, in relation to various types of civil capacity); others concern alleged 'psychological damage' (in negligence actions); another group involves not patients but doctors, where the instructed psychiatrist gives an opinion on the quality of psychiatric care offered to a patient by another psychiatrist (again in negligence actions). The psychiatrist will most usually write a psychiatric report for the court, but might in some cases simply write advice to counsel (or solicitors) after reading the papers relating to the case.

The Civil Justice Council has a very clear protocol available on its website: http://www.justice.gov.uk/courts/procedure-rules/civil/protocol/prot_pic. This should be consulted when undertaking civil work. An abbreviated version is given in this book for convenience in appendix 3.

Civil Capacity (see also chapter 3)

The law applies an 'action specific' concept of competence. Hence, a person may be competent to marry or to make a contract, yet be lacking testamentary capacity. Similarly, a person may even be competent to manage his/her affairs (currently) and yet not possess legal testamentary capacity. Thus, capacity is specific to the decision to be made. box

6.2 identifies a number of commonly encountered capacity issues. It is not an exhaustive list.

Fitness (or capacity or competence) to plead and stand trial is governed by the 'Pritchard criteria' (see chapter 2). The criteria for testamentary capacity derive from the *Banks* case. Capacity to litigate in a civil case was determined for a long time by the unreported first instance case of *White v Fell* (Rix, 1999c) which was eventually recognized in the still leading case of *Masterman-Lister*. A number of cases have involved capacity to consent to treatment and most importantly *Re T* in which the expert witness (Eastman), proposed, and the court adopted, a three stage test for capacity to consent.

Much case law has now been superseded by statute law in the form of the Mental Capacity Act 2005 (see chapter 3). As statute law its provisions are now of potential relevance to all cases where the issue is one of capacity. The four stage test in s.3 clearly has its origins in 'the Eastman test' in *Re T*.

The Mental Capacity Act has confirmed that the test for capacity is a 'functional' test and not a 'state' or 'outcome' test. A person with schizophrenia ('state') may or may not be fit to plead and stand trial because the issue is, for example, whether or not they can give valid instructions ('function'). A person with dementia ('state') may retain testamentary capacity if s/he can carry out the functions derived from *Banks*. Section 1 of the Mental Capacity Act 2005 states that someone should not be deemed incapable merely because they make an unwise decision, but outcomes 'can often cast a flood light on capacity' (Kennedy LJ in *Masterman-Lister*).

The role of a psychiatrist in capacity cases is to use psychiatric skill to obtain and analyse evidence in relation to the legal criteria which apply to the particular capacity at issue. Can the defendant with dementia in a criminal case understand the evidence to be given in his/her case? Can the claimant with brain damage in a personal injury case understand what it means to compromise his or her

claim? Does the person with schizophrenia understand the risks of declining amputation of his/her gangrenous foot? Although there is no such thing as 'general mental capacity' in law, the psychiatrist can and should take into account 'capacity at other times and in other contexts' (LJ Kennedy in *Masterman-Lister*).

Psychiatric assessment in such cases may call for a different approach to usual psychiatric assessment (Rix, 2006c). Details of previous psychiatric history and background history are relevant but only to the extent that they assist in determining capacity at the relevant time. The report should concentrate on the mental state and the ways in which aspects of mental functioning, such as, for example, attention, concentration, memory, thinking, delusions, intelligence, affect decision-making.

As an example, testamentary capacity requires that the person is able to know the extent of his/her estate and those who might have a call upon it, so as to be able to decide how to distribute that estate. In this example, it is often the case that the issue arises only after the subject has died, and so medical evidence must rely on past knowledge of the testator (concurrent with the making of the will) or (less reliably) reconstruction of his/her capacity from documentary and other evidence, such as the statements of friends and relatives. When fitness to plead is an issue, for example, in a charge of fraud involving complex financial dealings, a defendant's ability to explain the charges to the psychiatrist may be powerful evidence of the defendant's ability to understand the charge and the evidence to be given in his/her case. In a civil personal injury case, a claimant's inability to explain who his/her case is against and why s/he should be entitled to damages may be evidence that s/he lacks litigation capacity and needs to have a 'litigation friend' appointed to act for him/her. A capacity assessment involves a painstaking analysis of all witness statements, documentary exhibits and medical records. The psychiatrist also needs to be alert to unexpected evidence. The defendant who has presented to the psychiatrist on examination with a gross impairment of short-term memory but is overheard outside court pointing out and naming his/her psychiatrist may not have such a severe deficit of short-term memory.

Considerable adaptability may be needed in adjusting the assessment according to the nature of the case. Where there is an issue of cognitive impairment an extended cognitive examination may be required and in some cases a neuropsychological assessment may be advisable. It may take not just hours but days and the use of specialized techniques to assess the decision-making processes of someone in a near-persistent vegetative state from whom it is proposed to withdraw life-sustaining treatment (Coughlan et al., 2005).

As in any case in which the psychiatrist advises the courts or the parties in a dispute, history, mental state examination, appropriate and valid tests and careful consideration of

---

Box 6.2 Capacity issues (based on Rix, 2006c)

Make a gift
Enter into a contract
Make and execute a will or a codicil to a will
Marry
Defend a divorce
Consent to a sexual relationship (s.30(1) of the sexual offences act 2003)
Grant a power of attorney
Consent to medical treatment
Make an advance decision/directive
Plead and stand trial in a criminal court
Bring or defend an action in a civil court
Manage and administer property and affairs

all documentary evidence are necessary. The opinion as to capacity must be expressed in such a way that the reasons for the opinion can be seen to arise clearly from psychiatric and/or medical phenomena observed and, ultimately, from the impairment of, or disturbance in the functioning of, the mind or brain. There must be consideration of the seriousness of the decision because the more serious the decision the greater the level of capacity that is required (*Re T*).

Damages for Psychiatric Injury (compensation)

Psychiatrists are sometimes called upon to give evidence as to psychological sequelae of some event of legal significance. The law relating to 'nervous shock' is dealt with chapter 2.

Here it is important to note that the psychiatric report should be detailed and include, where possible, evidence from third parties, preferably an informant interviewed by the psychiatrist, but failing this evidence from witness statements of partner, family and friends. Basically, it should have a structure akin to the structure outlined for criminal cases above, but with a different emphasis. In particular, the reader should be able to see from the report the mental health of the claimant before the accident (or, say, the allegedly negligent medical care), the mental health immediately after the accident or alleged negligence and the mental health at the time of the examination. It should outline the claimant's life history, personality development and previous psychiatric history. The report should give the claimant's version of the accident or incident, but only to the extent necessary to convey the experience or trauma, and their subsequent history. A detailed mental state examination should be made, preferably on more than one occasion and documented fully. Every effort should be made to obtain previous psychiatric information, including other contemporary opinions, and consideration of the complete general practice records is usually essential.

The opinion should include an argued view as to whether the incident has caused psychiatric injury. If the opinion is that it did, then a diagnosis or diagnoses should be listed with evidence in the report. For each diagnosis there should follow a view on prognosis, especially in relation to capacity for employment and any loss of employment prospects. This is essential as the quantum of damages will partly turn on the projected duration of the disorder(s) and the amount of special damages will be determined by employment prospects. Diagnoses should be reasonably standard, and may include post-traumatic stress disorder, pathological grief and substance abuse.

A further opinion should also be given about 'loss of amenity'. This is a description of the dysfunctions resulting from the psychiatric disorders and is sometimes also termed the 'condition' of the claimant. It should refer to ability to cope with life in general and work in particular,

and the effects on marital, family and other relationships and on social life. Often an opinion will be requested on the issue of causation. This is because the law allows the claimant only to recover damages for pain and suffering caused by the accident and in complicated cases, such as those where there is a pre-existing psychiatric disorder or where there have been adverse events and circumstances unrelated to the accident, the court may require the effects of the accident to be separated from other potential causes of psychiatric disorder. The report should set out the treatment that has been carried out and include any recommendations for treatment along with a consideration of the prognosis if this treatment is undertaken. The prognosis section, so as to assist the court on the matter of provisional damages, should also deal with the likelihood, in percentage terms, of any delayed or serious long-term effects of the accident or alleged negligence.

The list of headings for the body of the report could be as follows:

- **Family history** – in broad general terms.
- **Personal history** – from birth to accident including sexual and marital history.
- **Personality.**
- **Previous medical and psychiatric history** – up to the accident.
- **The accident/alleged negligence** – a detailed account of what the claimant experienced.
- **Immediate aftermath** – an account of the patient's life and health for, say, 1 month after the accident; this should include any impulsive or self-destructive behaviour, substance abuse (including tobacco), and deterioration of personal relationships.
- **Subsequent progress** – bringing the story up to the date of examination.
- **Examination** – a *detailed* mental state evaluation.
- **Opinion** – *all* psychiatric diagnoses, their severity, prognosis and relationship to the accident plus an account of any loss of amenity; the relationships between psychiatric disease and physical disease (e.g. anxiety leading to excess smoking leading to a physical threat) should also be mentioned; causation is a key matter and a clear opinion, arguing from the data available, should be given including reservations and uncertainties.

Psychiatric Negligence Actions

Psychiatrists are sometimes called to give advice to solicitors and counsel or opinions in court concerning the quality of professional care offered to a patient by another psychiatrist. The court will not be concerned with a standard of whether the advising psychiatrist would have treated the patient in a similar fashion, but rather with 'whether the treatment fell within a range of competent treatment such as could be expected from a clinician of that particular grade and level of experience'. Hence, the advising psychiatrist should refrain from giving an opinion in the vein of 'I would not have treated the patient in that way'. The report will have to be constructed according to the issues involved, but it should include where possible an examination of the patient, an examination of the relevant medical records, and a discussion of the treatment in the context of the appropriate literature. Two sorts of report are often needed and at different stages in the litigation: 'liability (breach of duty and causation)' and 'condition and prognosis'. In order for the instructing solicitors to decide whether or not to proceed with, or defend, a claim they need a 'liability (breach of duty and causation)' report that addresses the issue of the standard of care having regard to the legal tests established in *Bolam* and *Bolitho* and whether or not any breaches have been causative of damage. It is clear, therefore, that this type of report is sometimes better undertaken by an expert in the field in question, since the predominant skill required is knowledge of particular medical techniques rather than the art of writing reports. Forensic psychiatrists, however, are sometimes instructed because of their familiarity with medico-legal matters. In order to quantify the damages in what may be a successful claim, or one that has to be compromised, the instructing solicitors need a 'condition and prognosis' report as to the current condition and prognosis of the claimant and what the prognosis would have been but for the allegedly negligent psychiatric care.

Appearance as a Witness

Most of the discussion in this chapter concerns the preparation of written reports. With careful planning and consultation, the majority of medico-legal work can be conducted on a written basis. It is imperative that it should; the limited psychiatric resource available to any given community must be husbanded very carefully. Most psychiatrists will have to appear in court on occasions, e.g. in England and Wales a court cannot send a patient to hospital with a restriction order unless *oral* evidence has been given by a psychiatrist.

Standing in a witness box, even with the cloak of 'expert' about one's shoulders, is a daunting business. It is especially difficult when there is cross-examination. An appearance in the sentencing stage of a criminal hearing, so that a judge can inform him/herself better before s/he decides on a sentence, usually amounts to a congenial three-way conversation between the expert, the defence counsel and the judge. An appearance on behalf of a patient claiming damages from a wealthy industrialist following an accident is quite a different matter. Large sums of money may be at stake, and the company will employ an experienced counsel to discredit, as far as possible, the medical evidence given on behalf of the claimant, so the cross-examination can be hostile and full of traps for the unwary. In a criminal trial, which is highly publicized, the Crown counsel may wish to discredit the

psychiatrist appearing for the defence as part of his/her strategy to obtain a conviction, or the most serious conviction possible.

When psychiatrists go into the witness box, they should be well prepared. Gee and Mason (1990) give good practical advice written from the perspective of experienced medical witnesses. Carson (1990b) gives lots of wrinkles from a lawyer's perspective.

Grounds (2000) also has some useful advice:

Before going to court it is generally helpful to discuss the case and the psychiatric evidence with experienced colleagues. It is important to be well briefed in advance by the legal representatives who have requested the court attendance, so that the expert witness knows in advance what questions or aspects of their written report are likely to be the focus of questioning, and what kind of cross-examination from the opposing side may be anticipated...

The adversarial process can put pressures on expert witnesses particularly when being cross-examined, efforts may be made to discredit or cast doubt on the expert's evidence. Not uncommonly this is done by putting to the expert a series of propositions and questions which commence with statements the expert witness can agree with, but which will lead to conclusions that the cross-examining counsel wishes to demonstrate. It is important not to feel intimidated or that one is in a contest... in giving oral evidence the psychiatric expert should seek always to ensure that answers are clear, and that they accurately and succinctly convey his or her views.

EXAMPLES OF OTHER DOCUMENTS WHICH MAY BE CONSULTED

- Para 67 of *Good Medical Practice*, published by the General Medical Council http://www.gmc-uk.org/guidance/good_medical_practice/how_gmp_applies_to_you.asp
- *Medical Expert Witnesses*: Guidance from the Academy of Medical Royal Colleges 2005 www.aomrc.org.uk/publications/statements/doc_view/214-medical.expert-witnesses.html
- *Court Work (CR147)* from the Royal College of Psychiatrists http://www.rcpsych.ac.uk/publications/collegereports/cr/cr147.aspx
- A virtual seminar on being an expert psychiatric witness, including the history of giving expert witness, new civil procedure rules and some of the business issues which need to be addressed can be obtained from *Advances in Psychiatric Treatment*, which is published by The Royal College of Psychiatrists and is available on the College website http://www.rcpsych.ac.uk/publications/journals/advancesinfo.aspx

The relevant reference papers are Rix (1999a,b; 2000a,b; 2008a,b). The firmest advice that can be given to the putative expert witness here is – know your case; understand the background concepts you are going to use; make sure that you have included and identified as such in your report all of the points that could be used to undermine your opinion; discuss your evidence with the lawyer calling you; be confident in the witness box; and use plenty of eye contact with lawyers, judge and jury. If your evidence is discredited, do not take it to heart, courts are arenas, theatres, which pursue a legal purpose which is often unrelated to psychiatry.

7
The psychosocial milieu of the offender

Edited by | Written by
Pamela J Taylor | **David P Farrington**

INTRODUCTION

Offending is part of a wider range of antisocial behaviour that may arise in childhood and persist into adulthood. There seems to be continuity over time, since the antisocial child tends to become the antisocial teenager and then the antisocial adult, just as the antisocial adult then tends to produce another antisocial child. The main focus of this chapter, however, is on types of behaviour classified as criminal offences, rather than on the wider range of anti- or a social behaviours which would constitute conduct disorder or antisocial personality disorder. Furthermore, the types of offences of most interest here are those which dominate the official criminal statistics, principally theft, burglary, robbery, violence, vandalism and drug abuse rather than the more specialized offences such as white collar crime or sex crime. Most of the work cited is from the United Kingdom (UK) and the United States (USA), with some reference to other similar Western democracies, principally Canada, Australia, New Zealand and the Scandinavian countries. The chapter also emphasizes offending by boys or men, since most criminological research has been conducted with them, and since they are more likely to commit serious predatory and violent offences than girls or women.

It is plausible to suggest that criminal behaviour results from the interaction between a person, with some criminal potential or antisocial tendency, and the environment, which provides criminal opportunities. Given the same environment, some people will be more likely to commit offences than others, and conversely the same person will be more likely to commit offences in some environments than in others. Criminological research typically concentrates on either the development of criminal persons or the occurrence of criminal events, but rarely on both. The focus in this chapter is primarily on offenders rather than offences. An advantage of studying offenders is that they tend to be versatile rather than specialized. The typical offender who commits violence, vandalism or drug abuse is likely also to commit theft or burglary. For example, in the Cambridge Study (described later) 86% of violent offenders had convictions for non-violent offences (Farrington,

1991). Also, violent and non-violent but equally frequent offenders were very similar in their childhood and adolescent features in the Cambridge Study, in the Oregon Youth Study (Capaldi and Patterson, 1996) and in the Philadelphia Collaborative Perinatal project (Piquero, 2000). In studying offenders, it is unnecessary to develop a different theory for each different type of offence. In contrast, in trying to explain why offences occur, the situations are so diverse and specific to particular crimes that it may be necessary to have different explanations for each type of offence.

In an attempt to identify possible causes of offending, this chapter reviews risk factors that influence the development of criminal careers. Fortunately or unfortunately, literally thousands of variables differentiate significantly between convicted offenders and non-offenders and/or correlate significantly with reports of offending behaviour by young people. Here, it is possible only to review briefly some of the most important risk factors for offending: individual difference factors such as high impulsivity and low intelligence (see also chapter 8), family influences, such as poor child-rearing and criminal parents, and social influences, including socioeconomic deprivation, peer relationships, school, community and situational factors.

Within a single chapter, it is impossible to review everything that is known about the psychosocial milieu of the offender, so I will be very selective, choosing only the more important and replicable findings obtained in some of the projects with the strongest methodology, namely prospective longitudinal follow-up studies of large community samples. Such projects are defined here according to their possession of as many as possible of the following criteria:

a. a large sample size of at least several hundred;
b. chosen as representative of the community;
c. having repeated personal interviews;
d. using a large number of different types of variables measured from different data sources (which makes it possible to study the effect of one independently of others, or interactive effects);
e. including self-reported and official measures of offending (replicated results probably providing

Table 7.1   Twenty prospective longitudinal surveys of offending

Elliott, Huizinga (National Youth Survey, US)	Nationally representative US sample of 1,725 adolescents aged 11–17 in 1976. Interviewed in five successive years (1977–81) and subsequently at 3-year intervals up to 1993, and in 2002–03. Focus on self-reported delinquency, but arrest records collected (Elliott, 1994).
Eron, Huesmann (Columbia County Study, US)	All 876 third-grade children (aged 8) in Columbia County in New York State first assessed in 1960. Focus on aggressive behaviour. Interviewed 10, 22 and 40 years later. Criminal records searched up to age 48 (Eron et al., 1991).
Farrington, West (Cambridge Study in Delinquent Development, UK)	411 boys aged 8–9 in 1961–62; all of that age in six London (UK) schools. Boys interviewed nine times up to age 48. Information also from parents, teachers, and peers. Boys and all biological relatives searched in criminal records up to 2004 (Farrington, 2003b).
Fergusson, Horwood (Christchurch Health and Development Study, New Zealand)	All 1,265 children born in Christchurch in mid-1977. Studied at birth, 4 months, 1 year, annually to age 16, and at ages 18, 21 and 25. Data collected in parental interviews, self-reports, psychometric tests, teacher reports and official records (Fergusson et al., 1994).
Hawkins, Catalano (Seattle Social Development Project, US)	808 grade 5 students (age 10) in 18 elementary schools in Seattle in 1985. Also intervention study. Followed up annually to age 16 and then every 2–3 years at least to age 33, with interviews and criminal records (Hawkins et al., 2003).
Huizinga, Esbensen (Denver Youth Survey, US)	1,528 children aged 7, 9, 11, 13 or 15 in high-risk neighbourhoods of Denver, Colorado, in 1988. Children and parents assessed at yearly intervals up to1998. Youngest two cohorts assessed in 2002. Focus on self-reported delinquency; criminal record data collected up to 1992 (Huizinga et al., 2003).
Janson, Wikström (Project Metropolitan, Sweden)	All 15,117 children born in Stockholm in 1953, and living there in 1963. Tested in schools in 1966. Subsample of mothers interviewed in 1968. Followed up in police records to 1983 (Wikström, 1990).
Kolvin, Miller (Newcastle Thousand Family Study, UK)	1,142 children born in Newcastle-upon-Tyne in mid-1947. Studied between birth and age 5 and followed up to age 15. Criminal records searched at age 33, and subsamples interviewed (Kolvin et al., 1990).
LeBlanc (Montreal Two-Samples Longitudinal Studies Canada)	Representative sample of 3,070 French-speaking Montreal adolescents. Completed self-report questionnaires in 1974 at age 12–16 and again in 1976. Followed in criminal records to age 40. Males interviewed at ages 30 and 40 (LeBlanc and Frechette, 1989).
Loeber, Stouthamer-Loeber, Farrington (Pittsburgh Youth Study, US)	1,517 boys in first, fourth, or seventh grades of Pittsburgh public schools in 1987–88 (ages 7, 10, 13). Information from boys, parents, and teachers every 6 months for 3 years, and then every year up to age 19 (youngest) and 25 (oldest). Focus on delinquency, substance use, and mental health problems (Loeber et al., 2003).
Magnusson, Stattin, Klinteberg (Orebro Project, Sweden)	1,027 children age 10 (all those in third grade) in Orebro in 1965. School follow-up data between ages 13 and 15. Questionnaire and record data up to age 43–45 (Klinteberg et al., 1993).
McCord (Cambridge-Somerville Youth Study, US)	650 boys (average age 10) nominated as difficult or average by Cambridge-Somerville (Boston) public schools in 1937–39. Randomly assigned to treated or control groups. Treated group visited by counsellors for an average of 5 years, and all followed up in 1975–80 by interviews, mail questionnaires and criminal records (McCord, 1991).
Moffitt, Caspi (Dunedin Multidisciplinary Health and Development Study, New Zealand)	1,037 children born in 1972–73 in Dunedin and first assessed at age 3. Assessed every 2–3 years on health, psychological, education and family factors up to age 32. Self-reported delinquency measured from age 13. Convictions collected up to age 32 (Moffitt et al., 2001).
Patterson, Dishion, Capaldi (Oregon Youth Study, US)	206 fourth grade boys (age 10) in Eugene/Springfield (Oregon) in 1983–85. Assessed at yearly intervals, with data from boys, parents, teachers, and peers, at least to age 30. Followed up in criminal records at least to age 30 (Capaldi and Patterson, 1996).
Pulkkinen (Jyvaskyla Longitudinal Study of Personality and Social Development, Finland)	369 children aged 8–9 in Jyvaskyla in 1968. Peer, teacher, and self-ratings collected. Followed up five times to age 42 with interviews and questionnaires and in criminal records (Pulkkinen and Pitkanen, 1993).
Thornberry, Lizotte, Krohn (Rochester Youth Development Study, US)	1,000 seventh and eighth graders (age 13–14) in Rochester (New York State) public schools, first assessed in 1988, disproportionally sampled from high-crime neighbourhoods. Followed up initially every 6 months, then every year, then at intervals to age 32. Self-reports and criminal records collected (Thornberry et al., 2003).

(Continued)

Table 7.1 *(Continued)*

Tremblay (Montreal Longitudinal-Experimental Study, Canada)	1,037 French-speaking kindergarten boys (age 6) from poor areas of Montreal assessed by teachers in 1984. Disruptive boys randomly allocated to treatment (parent training plus skills training) or control groups. All boys followed up each year from age 10 to age 26, including self-reported delinquency and aggression (Tremblay et al., 2003).
Wadsworth, Douglas (National Survey of Health and Development, UK)	5,362 children selected from all legitimate single births in England, Scotland, and Wales during one week of March 1946. Followed in criminal records to age 21. Mainly medical and school data collected, but samples were interviewed at ages 26, 36, 43 and 50 (Wadsworth, 1991).
Werner, Smith (Kauai Longitudinal Study, US)	698 children born in 1955 in Kauai (Hawaii) assessed at birth and ages 2, 10, 18, 30 and 40. Criminal records up to age 40. Focus on resilience (Werner and Smith, 2001).
Wolfgang, Figlio, Thornberry, Tracy (Philadelphia Birth Cohort Studies, US)	(1) 9,945 boys born in Philadelphia in 1945 and living there at least from 10–17. Sample interviewed at age 26 and followed up in police records to age 30 (Wolfgang et al., 1987). (2) 27,160 children born in Philadelphia in 1958 and living there at least from 10–17. Followed up in police records to age 26 (Tracy and Kempf-Leonard, 1996).

information about real offending rather than reflecting measurement bias);

f. a prospective and longitudinal research design;

g. spanning at least 5 years, making it possible to establish causal order, to study the strength of effects at different ages, and to control better for extraneous variables by investigating changes within individuals (see Farrington, 1988).

Very few projects fulfil all or nearly all of these criteria. A summary of the most important is given in table 7.1. My main reference point, however, is the Cambridge Study in Delinquent Development, which is a prospective longitudinal survey of over 400 London males from age 8 to age 48 (Farrington et al., 2006). Fortunately, results obtained in British longitudinal surveys of delinquency are highly concordant with those obtained in comparable surveys in North America, the Scandinavian countries and New Zealand and, indeed, with results obtained in British cross-sectional surveys. A systematic comparison of the Cambridge and Pittsburgh studies, for example, showed numerous replicable predictors of offending over time and place, including impulsivity, attention problems, low school attainment, poor parental supervision, parental conflict, an antisocial parent, a young mother, large family size, low family income, and coming from a broken family (Farrington and Loeber, 1999).

MEASUREMENT AND EPIDEMIOLOGY

Offending is commonly measured using official records of arrests or convictions or self-reports. The advantages and disadvantages of official records and self-reports are to some extent complementary. In general, official records identify the worst offenders and the worst offences, while self-reports include more of the 'normal range' of delinquent activity. The worst offenders may be missing from samples interviewed in self-report studies (Cernkovich et al., 1985). Self-reports have the advantage of including undetected offences, but the disadvantages of concealment and forgetting. By generally accepted psychometric criteria of validity, self-reports are valid (Junger-Tas and Marshall, 1999a). Self-reported delinquency predicted later convictions in the Cambridge Study (Farrington, 1989). In the Pittsburgh Youth Study, the seriousness of self-reported delinquency predicted later court referrals (Farrington et al., 1996b), but predictive validity was enhanced by combining self-report, parent and teacher information about offending.

The key issue is whether the same results are obtained with both methods. If, for example, official records and self-reports both show a link between parental supervision and delinquency, it is likely that this supervision is truly related to delinquent behaviour rather than reflecting any biases in measurement. Generally, the worst offenders (taking account of frequency and seriousness) identified by self-reports are the same as those identified from official records (Huizinga and Elliott, 1986). The predictors and correlates of official and self-reported delinquency are very similar (Farrington, 1992a).

THE NATURAL HISTORY OF OFFENDING

Even when measured by convictions, the cumulative prevalence of offending is substantial. In the Cambridge Study, by the age of 40 years, 40% of males had been convicted of at least one criminal offence (Farrington et al., 1998). According to national figures for England and Wales (Prime et al., 2001), 33% of males and 9% of females born in 1953 were convicted up to age 45 for a 'standard list' offence (i.e. a more serious offence, excluding, for example, traffic infractions and drunkenness). The prevalence of offending rises to a peak in the late teenage years (15–19), and then declines (Farrington, 1986a).

The prevalence of offending, according to self-reports, is even higher. In the large-scale Denver, Rochester and Pittsburgh longitudinal studies, the annual prevalence of 'street crimes' (e.g. serious theft, robbery, aggravated assault; burglary was also included here) increased from less than 15% at age 11 to almost 50% at age 17 (Huizinga et al., 1993). Similarly, in the US National Youth Survey, the annual prevalence of self-reported violence increased to a peak of 28% among 17-year-old males and 12% among 15- to 17-year-old females (Elliott, 1994).

Criminal career research using official records of delinquency generally shows a peak age of onset of offending between 13 and 16. In the Cambridge Study, the peak age of onset was 14, with 5% first convicted at that age (Farrington, 1992b). The onset curves up to age 25 of working-class males in London and Stockholm were quite similar (Farrington and Wikström, 1994). Among Montreal delinquents LeBlanc and Frechette (1989) discovered that the onset of shoplifting and vandalism tended to occur before adolescence (average onset 11), burglary and motor vehicle theft in adolescence (average onset 14–15), and sex offences and drug trafficking in the later teenage years (average onset 17–19).

In the Cambridge Study, the males first convicted at the earliest ages (10–13) tended to become the most persistent offenders, committing an average of nine offences leading to convictions in an average criminal career lasting 13 years up to age 50 (Farrington et al., 2006). Similarly, Farrington and Wikström (1994), using official records in Stockholm, and LeBlanc and Frechette (1989) in Montreal, using both self-reports and official records, showed that the duration of criminal careers decreased with increasing age of onset.

Generally, there is significant continuity between offending in one age range and offending in another. In the Cambridge Study, nearly three-quarters (73%) of those convicted between ages 10–16 (juveniles) were reconvicted between ages 17–24, in comparison with only 16% of those not convicted as juveniles (Farrington, 1992b). Proportions for those reconvicted at age 25–32 were 45% and 8% respectively. Furthermore, for 10 specified offences, the significant continuity between offending in one age range and in a later age range held equally well for self-reports and for official convictions (Farrington, 1989).

Other studies show similar continuity in offending. For example, in Sweden, Stattin and Magnusson (1991) reported that nearly 70% of males registered for crime before age 15 were registered again between ages 15 and 20, and nearly 60% were registered between ages 21 and 29. The number of juvenile offences is an effective predictor of the number of adult offences (Wolfgang et al., 1987). In both London and Stockholm, there is considerable continuity in offending between the ages of 10 and 25 (Farrington and Wikström, 1994).

Continuity means that there is relative stability in the ordering of people on some measure of antisocial behaviour over time, but this is a statement of probability, and thus not incompatible with the assertion that the prevalence of offending varies with age or that many antisocial children become conforming adults. Between-individual stability in antisocial ordering is perfectly compatible with within-individual change in behaviour over time (Farrington, 1990a). People may, for example, graduate from cruelty to animals at age 6 to shoplifting at age 10, burglary at age 15, robbery at age 20, and eventually spouse assault and child abuse later in life. Also, they may desist. While some offenders are 'early-onset-life-course-persistent', others are 'adolescence-limited' (Moffitt, 1993; Moffitt et al., 2001).

Another important and consistent finding is that chronic offenders, a small fraction of the offending population, commit a large proportion of all crimes (Farrington and West, 1993). There is a great deal of criminological research on other criminal career features such as desistance, duration of careers, escalation and de-escalation, but no space to review this here (see Farrington, 1997; Piquero et al., 2007). Rather, the importance of individual difference factors such as hyperactivity, impulsivity, low intelligence and low attainment will be reviewed. Family factors such as poor child-rearing, teenage motherhood and child abuse, parental conflict, family disruption and large family size as well as parental criminality will be discussed, followed by social factors such as socioeconomic deprivation and peer, school, community and situational influences. A developmental theory of offending will then be presented, and, finally, effective prevention programmes.

FACTORS ASSOCIATED WITH DELINQUENCY AND OFFENDING

Individual Factors

Hyperactivity and impulsivity

Hyperactivity and impulsivity are among the most important personality or individual difference factors that predict later offending (Pratt et al., 2002; see also chapter 8). Hyperactivity is usually apparent before age 5, and often before age 2. It tends to persist into adolescence, but may continue into adult life. It is associated with restlessness, impulsivity and a short attention span, and for that reason Loeber (1988) has coined the term 'hyperactivity-impulsivity-attention deficit' or HIA syndrome, similar to attention deficit hyperactivity disorder (ADHD), a clinical syndrome. People with HIA or ADHD may also have poor ability to defer gratification and a short future time perspective.

Many investigators have reported a link between HIA and offending. In the Swedish Orebro longitudinal survey, for example, Klinteberg et al. (1993) found that hyperactivity rated by teachers at age 13 predicted violent offending up to age 26. The highest rate of violence was among males with both motor restlessness and concentration difficulties. The most extensive research on different measures of impulsivity was carried out by White et al. (1994) in the Pittsburgh Youth Study. This showed that cognitive or verbal impulsivity (e.g. acting without thinking, unable to defer gratification) was more strongly related to delinquency than was behavioural impulsivity (e.g. clumsiness in psychomotor tests).

In the Cambridge Study, a combined measure of HIA deficit was developed at age 8–10. It significantly and independently predicted later juvenile convictions (Farrington et al., 1990). Similar constructs to hyperactivity, such as sensation seeking, have also been related to delinquency. In the Cambridge Study, the extent to which a boy was daring or took risks at age 8–10, as well as his restlessness and poor concentration, significantly predicted his convictions and high self-reported offending. Daring was consistently one of the strongest independent predictors of offending (Farrington, 1992a).

Low intelligence and attainment

Intelligence can be measured very early in life, when scores at the lower end of the normal range constitute an important predictor of offending. In a prospective longitudinal survey of about 120 Stockholm males, Stattin and Klackenberg-Larsson (1993) found that frequent offenders (4+ offences) had an average IQ of 88 at age 3 compared with an average 3-year-old IQ of 101 among the non-offenders. All of these results held after controlling for social class. In the Perry preschool project, there was a similar finding, with lower IQ at age 4 predicting arrests up to age 27 (Schweinhart et al., 1993).

In the Cambridge Study, boys scoring 90 or less on a non-verbal IQ test (Raven's Progressive Matrices) at age 8–10 were twice as likely to sustain later convictions as their higher scoring peers (Farrington, 1992a). It was difficult, however, to disentangle low intelligence and low school attainment. Low non-verbal intelligence was highly correlated with low verbal intelligence (vocabulary, word comprehension, verbal reasoning) and with low school attainment, and all of these measures predicted juvenile convictions to much the same extent, a consistent finding in longitudinal studies. In addition to their poor school performance, delinquents tended to leave school at the earliest possible age (which was then 15) and to take no school examinations. Lower non-verbal intelligence predicted self-reported juvenile offending to almost exactly the same degree as juvenile convictions (Farrington, 1992a), suggesting that the link between lower intelligence and delinquency was not caused by the less intelligent boys having a greater probability of being caught. Also, measures of intelligence and attainment predicted measures of offending independently of other variables such as family income and family size. Other studies have found that delinquents often do better on non-verbal performance tests, such as object assembly and block design, than on verbal tests (Moffitt and Silva, 1988).

School failure may be the mediating factor between low IQ and delinquency. Another plausible explanation may rest in the ability to manipulate abstract concepts. Children who are poor at this tend also to do badly in IQ tests and in school attainment, and they also tend to commit offences, mainly because of their poor ability to foresee the consequences of their offending and to appreciate the feelings of victims (Raine et al., 2005).

Family Factors

Child-rearing

Many different types of child-rearing methods predict offending. The most important dimensions of child-rearing are supervision or monitoring of children, discipline or parental reinforcement, warmth or coldness of emotional relationships, and parental involvement with children. Parental supervision refers to the degree of monitoring by parents of the child's activities, and their degree of vigilance. Of all these child-rearing methods, poor parental supervision is usually the strongest and most replicable predictor of offending (Smith and Stern, 1997). Many studies show that parents who do not know where their children are when they are out, and parents who let their children roam the streets unsupervised from an early age, tend to have delinquent children. In McCord's (1979) classic Cambridge–Somerville study in Boston, for example, poor parental supervision in childhood was the best family predictor of both violent and property crimes up to age 45.

Parental discipline refers to how parents react to a child's behaviour. Harsh or punitive discipline, involving physical punishment, predicts offending. In their follow-up study of nearly 700 Nottingham children, John and Elizabeth Newson (1989) found that physical punishment at ages 7 and 11 predicted later convictions; 40% of offenders had been smacked or beaten at age 11, compared with 14% of non-offenders. Erratic or inconsistent discipline also predicts delinquency. This can involve either erratic discipline by one parent, sometimes turning a blind eye to bad behaviour and sometimes punishing it severely, or inconsistency between two parents, with one parent being tolerant or indulgent and the other being harshly punitive.

Cold, rejecting parents tend to have delinquent children, as McCord (1979) found in the Cambridge–Somerville study. More recently, she concluded that parental warmth could act as a protective factor against the effects of physical punishment (McCord, 1997). Whereas she found that 51% of boys with cold physically punishing mothers sustained a criminal conviction, only 21% of boys with warm physically punishing mothers were convicted, similar to the 23% of boys with warm non-punitive mothers. The father's warmth was also a protective factor against physical punishment by him.

Most explanations of the link between child-rearing methods and delinquency focus on attachment or social learning theories. Attachment theory was inspired by the work of Bowlby (1951; and see chapter 28). Children who are not emotionally attached to warm, loving and law-abiding parents tend to become offenders. Social learning theories suggest that children's behaviour depends on parental rewards and punishments and on the models of behaviour that parents represent (Patterson, 1995). Children will tend to become offenders if parents do not respond consistently and contingently to their antisocial behaviour and if parents themselves behave in an antisocial manner.

Teenage mothers and child abuse

At least in Western industrialized countries, early childbearing, or teenage pregnancy, predicts many undesirable outcomes for the children, including low school attainment, antisocial school behaviour, substance use and early sexual intercourse. The children of teenage mothers are also more likely to become offenders. Morash and Rucker (1989), for example, analysed results from four surveys in the USA and UK (including the Cambridge Study) and found that being a teenage mother was associated with being in a low income family, being on welfare support and the biological father of the child being absent, that teenage mothers used poor child-rearing methods, and that their children were characterized by low school attainment and delinquency. If the biological father had stayed, this mitigated many of these adverse factors and generally seemed to have a protective effect. In the Cambridge Study, convicted youths were more likely to have had teenage mothers with large numbers of children (Nagin et al., 1997). In the Newcastle Thousand-Family study, mothers who married as teenagers (a factor strongly related to teenage childbearing) were twice as likely as others to have sons who became offenders by age 32 (Kolvin et al., 1990).

There is considerable evidence that abused children are more likely than others to become aggressive or violent, as Maxfield and Widom (1996) found in a prospective study of over 900 abused children in Indianapolis. Children who were physically abused up to age 11 were significantly more likely to become violent offenders in the next 15 years than those who were not abused. In the Cambridge–Somerville study in Boston, McCord (1983) found that about half of the abused or neglected boys were convicted for serious crimes, became alcoholics or mentally ill, or died before age 35. In the Rochester Youth Development Study, experience of maltreatment under the age of 12 (physical, sexual or emotional abuse or neglect) predicted later self-reported and official offending (Smith and Thornberry, 1995), findings which held up after controlling for gender, race, socioeconomic status and family structure.

Parental conflict and disrupted families

Many studies show that broken homes or family disruption predict offending. In the Newcastle Thousand-Family Study, Kolvin et al. (1988) found that divorce or separation during the first 5 years of a boy's life doubled his risk of later convictions up to age 32. Similarly, in the Dunedin birth cohort study, children who were exposed to parental discord and many changes of the primary caretaker tended to become antisocial and delinquent (Henry et al., 1996). This same study also showed that single parent families disproportionally tended to have convicted sons; 28% of violent offenders were from single parent families, compared with 17% of non-violent offenders and 9% of unconvicted boys.

The importance of the cause of the broken home was demonstrated by Wadsworth (1979) in the UK National Survey of Health and Development. Boys from homes broken by divorce or separation had an increased likelihood of being convicted or officially cautioned up to age 21, in comparison with those from homes broken by death or from unbroken homes. Homes broken while the boy was under age 5 especially predicted offending, while homes broken while the boy was between ages 11 and 15 were not particularly criminogenic. Remarriage (which happened more often after divorce or separation than after death) was also associated with an increased risk of offending. The meta-analysis by Wells and Rankin (1991) also indicates that broken homes are more strongly related to delinquency when they are caused by parental separation or divorce rather than by death.

Most studies of broken homes have focused on the loss of the father rather than the mother, simply because the loss of the father is much more common. McCord (1982) in Boston carried out an interesting study of the relationship between homes broken by loss of the natural father and later serious offending of the children. She found that the prevalence of offending was high for boys reared in broken homes without affectionate mothers (62%) and for those reared in united homes characterized by parental conflict (52%), irrespective of whether they had affectionate mothers. The prevalence of offending was low for those reared in united homes without conflict (26%) and – importantly – equally low for boys from broken homes with affectionate mothers (22%). These results suggest that it is not so much the broken home which is criminogenic as the parental conflict which often causes it, and that having a loving mother may be a protective factor.

In the Cambridge Study, both permanent and temporary separations from a biological parent before age 10 (usually from the father) predicted convictions and self-reported delinquency, providing that they were not caused by death or hospitalization (Farrington, 1992a), although homes broken at an early age (under 5) were not unusually criminogenic (West and Farrington, 1973). Separation before age 10 predicted both juvenile and adult convictions (Farrington, 1992c), and it predicted adult convictions independently of other factors such as low family income or poor school attainment. It was also an important predictor of adult social dysfunction more generally (Farrington, 1993a).

Explanations of the relationship between disrupted families and delinquency fall into three major classes. Trauma theories suggest that the loss of a parent has a damaging effect on a child, most commonly because of the disruption of attachment. Life course theories focus on separation as a sequence of stressful experiences, and on the effects of multiple stressors such as parental conflict, parental loss, reduced economic circumstances, changes in parent figures and poor child-rearing methods. Selection theories argue that disrupted families produce delinquent children because of pre-existing differences from other families in risk factors such as parental conflict, criminal or antisocial parents, low family income or poor child-rearing methods.

Hypotheses derived from the three theories were tested in the Cambridge Study (Juby and Farrington, 2001). While boys from broken homes (permanently disrupted families) were more delinquent than boys from intact homes, they were not more delinquent than boys from intact high conflict families. Overall, the most important factor was the post-disruption trajectory. Boys who remained with their mother after the separation had the same delinquency rate as boys from intact low conflict families. Boys who stayed with their father, with relatives or with others (e.g. foster parents) had high delinquency rates. Such living arrangements were more unstable, while other research has shown that frequent changes of parent figures predict offending (Henry et al., 1996). It was concluded that the results favoured life course theories rather than trauma or selection theories.

Criminal parents

Robins et al. (1975) showed that criminal, antisocial and alcoholic parents tend to have delinquent sons. Robins followed up over 200 males in St. Louis. She found that parents who had been arrested by the police tended to have children who were arrested, and that the juvenile records of the parents and children were similar in rates and types of offences. McCord (1977) also reported that convicted fathers tended to have convicted sons. She found that 29% of fathers convicted of violent offences had sons convicted of such offences, compared with 12% of other fathers.

In the Cambridge Study, the concentration of offending in a small number of families was remarkable (Farrington et al., 1996a). Less than 6% of the families were responsible for half of the criminal convictions of all members (fathers, mothers, sons, and daughters) of all 400 families. Having a convicted mother, father, brother or sister significantly predicted a boy's own convictions. As many as 63% of boys with a convicted parent were themselves convicted before the age of 40. Furthermore, having a convicted parent and/or one or more delinquent siblings predicted self-reported as well as official offending. In this respect same-sex links were stronger than opposite-sex associations, while having an older criminal sibling was a stronger predictor than having a younger criminal sibling. Intergenerational continuity in offending was established.

It is not entirely clear why criminal parents tend to have delinquent children. In the Cambridge Study, there was no evidence that criminal parents encouraged their children to commit crimes or taught them criminal techniques. On the contrary, criminal parents were highly critical of their children's offending; for example, 89% of convicted men at age 32 disagreed with the statement that 'I would not mind if my son/daughter committed a criminal offence'. Also, it was extremely rare for a parent and a child to be convicted for an offence committed together. An important link in the chain between criminal parents and delinquent sons seemed to be poor parental supervision (West and Farrington, 1977).

There are several other possible explanations, not mutually exclusive, as to why offending tends to be concentrated in certain families and transmitted from one generation to the next. First, there may be intergenerational continuities in exposure to multiple risk factors. Each successive generation, for example, may be entrapped in poverty, disrupted families, single and/or teenage parenting, and living in the most deprived neighbourhoods. Secondly, the effect of a criminal parent on a child's offending may be mediated by environmental mechanisms such as poor parental supervision. Thirdly, the effect of a criminal parent on a child's offending may be mediated through genetic mechanisms (see chapter 8). Fourthly, criminal parents may have delinquent children because of police and/or court bias against criminal families, who tend to be known to other official agencies too. In the Cambridge Study this was not the only explanation for the link between criminal fathers and delinquent sons, because boys with criminal fathers had higher self-reported delinquency scores and higher teacher and peer ratings of bad behaviour as well as more criminal convictions (West and Farrington, 1977).

Large family size

Large family size is a relatively strong and highly replicable predictor of offending (Ellis, 1988). It was similarly important in the Cambridge and Pittsburgh studies, even though families were, on average, smaller in Pittsburgh in the 1990s than in London in the 1960s (Farrington and Loeber, 1999). In the Cambridge Study, if a boy had four or more siblings by his 10th birthday, this doubled his risk of being convicted as a juvenile, and large family size predicted self-reported offending as well as convictions (Farrington, 1992a). In a logistic regression analysis, it was the most important independent predictor out of all the age 8–10 variables of convictions up to age 32 (Farrington, 1993a).

In the National Survey of Health and Development, Wadsworth (1979) found that the percentage of boys who were convicted increased from 9% for families containing one child to 24% for families containing four or more children. Newson et al. (1993), in their Nottingham study, also concluded that large family size was one of the most important predictors of offending. A similar link between family size and antisocial behaviour was reported by Kolvin et al. (1990) in their follow-up of Newcastle children from birth to age 33.

Various explanations have been advanced for this family size effect. First, as the number of children in a family increases, the amount of parental attention that can be given to each child decreases. Secondly, in these circumstances, the household tends to become overcrowded, possibly leading to increases in frustration, irritation and conflict. Findings from the Cambridge Study lend some support to this in that large family size did not predict delinquency for boys living in the least crowded conditions (West and Farrington, 1973). Brownfield and Sorenson (1994) reviewed several further explanations, including parental features (e.g. criminality, teenage parenting), parenting style (e.g. poor supervision) and economic deprivation or family stress. Another possibility is that birth order is important; large families include more later-born children, who tend to be more delinquent. Based on an analysis of self-reported delinquency in a Seattle survey, they concluded that the most plausible intervening causal mechanism was exposure to delinquent siblings. In the Cambridge Study, co-offending with brothers was surprisingly common; about 20% of boys who had brothers close to them in age were convicted for a crime committed with their brother (Reiss and Farrington, 1991).

Social Factors

Socioeconomic deprivation

The voluminous literature on the relationship between socioeconomic status (SES) and offending is characterized by inconsistencies and contradictions, and some reviewers (e.g. Thornberry and Farnworth, 1982) have concluded that there is no relationship between socioeconomic status and either self-reported or official offending. British studies have reported more consistent links between low social class and offending. In the UK National Survey of Health and Development, Wadsworth (1979) found that the prevalence of official criminal convictions among young men varied considerably according to the occupational prestige and educational background of their parents, from 3% in the highest category to 19% in the lowest. It has been suggested that low socioeconomic status families tend to produce delinquent children because their child-rearing tends to be poor (Larzelere and Patterson, 1990).

Numerous indicators of socioeconomic status were measured in the Cambridge Study, both for the boy's family of origin and for the boy himself as an adult, including occupational prestige, family income, housing, and employment instability. Most of the measures of occupational prestige (based on the Registrar General's scale) were not significantly related to offending. Low socioeconomic status of the family when the boy was aged 8–10 significantly predicted his later self-reports of offending but not his official criminal record. Low family income and poor housing were more consistent predictors of both official and self-reported, juvenile and adult, offending (Farrington, 1992a,b).

It was interesting that the peak age of offending, at 17–18, coincided with the peak age of affluence for many convicted males. In the Cambridge Study, convicted males tended to come from low income families at age 8 and later tended to have low incomes themselves at age 32. However, at age 18, they were relatively well paid in comparison with non-delinquents (West and Farrington, 1977). Whereas convicted delinquents might be working as unskilled labourers on building sites and getting the full adult wage for this job, non-delinquents tended to be in poorly-paid jobs, but with prospects, such as bank clerks, or they might still be students. These results already show that the link between income and offending is quite complex, but unemployment was a factor too. Between ages 15 and 18, the study boys were convicted at a higher rate when they were unemployed than when they were employed, suggesting that unemployment may cause crime, and conversely that employment may lead to desistance from offending (Farrington et al., 1986). Since crimes involving material gain (e.g. theft, burglary, robbery) especially increased during periods of unemployment, it seems likely that financial need is an important link in the causal chain between unemployment and crime.

Peer influences

Having delinquent friends is an important predictor of later offending. Battin et al. (1998) showed that peer delinquency and gang membership predicted self-reported violence in the Seattle Social Development Project. Delinquent acts tend to be committed in small groups, usually of two or three people, rather than alone. Large gangs are comparatively unusual. In the Cambridge Study, the probability of committing offences with others decreased steadily with age. Before age 17, boys tended to commit their crimes with other boys similar in age and living close by. After age 17, co-offending became less common (Reiss and Farrington, 1991).

The major problem of interpretation is whether young people are more likely to commit offences while they are in groups than while they are alone, or whether the high prevalence of co-offending merely reflects the fact that, whenever young people go out, they tend to go out in groups. Do peers tend to encourage and facilitate offending, or is it just that most kinds of activities out of the home (both delinquent and non-delinquent) tend to be committed in groups? Another possibility is that the commission of offences encourages association with other delinquents, perhaps because 'birds of a feather flock together' or because of the other more stigmatizing and isolating effects of court appearances and institutionalization. Thornberry et al. (1994) in the Rochester Youth Development Study concluded that there were reciprocal effects, with delinquent peers causing delinquency and delinquency causing association with delinquent peers.

177

In the Pittsburgh Youth Study, the relationship between peer delinquency and a boy's offending was studied both between individuals (e.g. comparing peer delinquency and offending between boy X and boy Y at a particular age, then aggregating these correlations over all ages) and within individuals (e.g. comparing peer delinquency and offending of boy X at different ages, then aggregating these correlations over all individuals). Peer delinquency most strongly correlated with offending in between-individual correlations, but did not predict within-individual offending (Farrington et al., 2002). In contrast, poor parental supervision, low parental reinforcement, and low involvement of the boy in family activities predicted offending both between and within individuals. We concluded that these three family variables were the most likely to be causes, while having delinquent peers was most likely to be an indicator of the boy's it.

Associating with delinquent friends at age 14, however, was an important independent predictor of convictions at the young adult ages in the Cambridge Study (Farrington, 1986b). Also, the recidivists at age 19 who ceased offending differed from those who persisted, in that the desisters were more likely to have stopped going round in a group of male friends. Furthermore, spontaneous comments by the youths indicated that withdrawal from the delinquent peer group was an important influence on ceasing to offend (West and Farrington, 1977). While associating with delinquent friends may not cause offending, it may be a key factor in maintaining it.

School influences

The prevalence of delinquency among students varies significantly between different secondary schools, as Power et al. (1967) showed many years ago in London. Characteristics of high delinquency-rate schools are well known (Graham, 1988). For example, such schools have high levels of distrust between teachers and students, low commitment to school by students, and unclear and inconsistently enforced rules. What is much less clear is how much of the variation between schools should be attributed to differences in school organization, climate and practices, and how much to differences in the composition of the student body.

In the Cambridge Study, attending a high delinquency-rate school at age 11 significantly predicted later offending (Farrington, 1992a). The effects of secondary schools on delinquency were investigated by following boys from their primary schools to their secondary schools (Farrington, 1972). The best primary school predictor of juvenile delinquency was the rating of the boy's troublesomeness at age 8–10 by peers and teachers, showing the continuity in antisocial behaviour. The secondary schools differed significantly in their official delinquency rates, from 21 court appearances per 100 boys per year at one extreme to just 0.3 per 100 boys per year at the other. Going to a high

delinquency-rate secondary school was a significant predictor of later convictions. It was, however, very noticeable that the most troublesome boys tended to go to the high delinquency-rate schools, while the least troublesome boys tended to go to the low delinquency-rate schools. Most of the variation between schools in their delinquency rates could be explained by differences in their intakes of troublesome boys, with the secondary schools themselves having only a very small effect.

The best known study of school effects on delinquency was also carried out in London, by Rutter et al. (1979). They studied 12 comprehensive schools, and again found big differences in official delinquency rates between them. High delinquency-rate schools tended to have high truancy rates, low ability pupils, and low social class parents, but the differences between the schools in delinquency rates could not be entirely explained by parental social class or pupils' intake abilities (age 11). Therefore, there must have been a school effect, or perhaps an effect of other, unmeasured factors. Rutter and his colleagues found that the main school factors that were associated with delinquency were a high amount of punishment and a low amount of praise given by teachers in class, but establishing cause or consequences was more difficult. Nevertheless, they argued that an academic emphasis, good classroom management, the careful use of praise and punishment, and student participation were important features of successful schools.

Community influences

Offending rates vary systematically with area of residence. For example, the classic studies by Shaw and McKay (1969) in Chicago and other American cities showed that juvenile delinquency rates (based on where offenders lived) were highest in inner city areas characterized by physical deterioration, neighbourhood disorganization, and high residential mobility. A large proportion of all offenders came from a small proportion of areas, which tended to be the most deprived. Furthermore, these relatively high delinquency rates persisted over time, despite the effect of successive waves of immigration and emigration of different national and ethnic groups in different areas.

Living in a deprived neighbourhood, whether based on parent ratings or on census measures of poverty, unemployment or being in a female-headed household, significantly predicts official and self-reported offending (Farrington, 1998). It is difficult, however, to establish how much the areas themselves influence antisocial behaviour and how much it is only that antisocial people tend to live in deprived areas, for example because of their poverty or public housing allocation policies. Sampson et al. (1997) argued that a low degree of 'collective efficacy' of a neighbourhood, that is poor informal social controls, caused high crime rates.

One key question is why crime rates of communities change over time. Answering this requires longitudinal research in which both communities and individuals are followed up. The best way of establishing the impact of the environment is to follow people who move from one area to another. For example, in the Cambridge Study, moving out of London led to a significant decrease in convictions and self-reported offending (Osborn, 1980). This decrease may have occurred because moving out led to a breaking up of co-offending groups, or because there were fewer opportunities for crime outside London.

Situational influences

It might be argued that all the risk factors reviewed so far in this chapter – individual, family, socioeconomic, peer, school and community – essentially influence the development of a long-term individual potential for offending. Another set of influences – more immediate situational factors – may explain how potential for offending is actualized at any given time. Situational factors may be specific to particular types of crimes: robberies as opposed to rapes, or even street robberies as opposed to bank robberies.

The most popular theory of offending events is a rational choice theory suggesting that they occur in response to specific opportunities, when their expected benefits, such as stolen property or peer approval, outweigh their expected costs, such as legal punishment or parental disapproval. Clarke and Cornish (1985), for example, suggested that residential burglary depended on such influencing factors as whether a house was occupied, whether it looked affluent, whether there were bushes to hide behind, whether there were nosy neighbours, whether the house had a burglar alarm and whether it contained a dog. A related theory is the 'routine activities' idea of Cohen and Felson (1979). They suggested that, for a predatory crime to occur, the minimum requirement was the convergence in time and place of a motivated offender and a suitable target in the absence of a capable guardian. They argued that predatory crime rates were influenced by routine activities that satisfied basic needs such as food and shelter. Changes in routine activities, they suggest, lead to changing opportunities for crime; for example, as more women go out to work, so more homes are left unattended during the day.

Crime analysis is a form of research in the UK which begins with a detailed analysis of patterns and circumstances of crimes. This then informs development and implementation of crime reduction strategies, which are then evaluated. Barker et al. (1999), for example, found that most street robberies in London occurred in predominantly ethnic minority areas, and most offenders were 16- to 19-year-old Afro-Caribbean males. The victims were mostly Caucasian females, alone, and on foot. Most offences occurred at night, near the victim's home. The main motive for robbery was to get money, and the main factor in choosing victims was whether they appeared wealthy. In other examples, in Sweden, Wikström (1985) found that violence preceded by situational arguments typically occurs in streets or restaurants, while violence preceded by relationship arguments typically occurs in homes. In England, stranger assaults typically occur in streets, bars, or discotheques, non-stranger assaults typically occur at home or work, and robberies typically occur in the street or on public transport. Most violence occurs during weekend nights, around pubs and clubs, and involves young men who have been drinking (Allen et al., 2003). Shepherd (2007; see also chapter 28) has developed a prevention strategy based on such work. More research on situational influences on offending needs to be incorporated in prospective longitudinal studies, in order to link up the developmental and situational perspectives.

EXPLAINING THE DEVELOPMENT OF OFFENDING

Developmental and life-course criminology is concerned with the natural history and development of offending, risk and protective factors, and the effects of life events on the course of offending (Farrington, 2003a). This is a difficult field because most risk factors tend to coincide and are inter-related. Adolescents living in physically deteriorated and socially disorganized neighbourhoods, for example, also tend to come disproportionately from families with poor parental supervision and erratic parental discipline and tend also to have high impulsivity and low intelligence. The concentration and co-occurrence of these kinds of adversities makes it difficult to establish their independent, interactive and/or sequential influences on offending and antisocial behaviour. Hence, any theory of the development of offending is inevitably speculative in the present state of knowledge.

A first step is to establish which factors predict offending independently of other factors. In the Cambridge Study, it was generally true that each of six categories of variables – impulsivity, intelligence or attainment, poor parenting, criminal family, socioeconomic deprivation, child antisocial behaviour – predicted offending independently of each other category (Farrington, 1990b). Independent predictors of convictions between ages 10 and 20 included high daring, low school attainment, poor parental child rearing, a convicted parent, poor housing and troublesomeness (Farrington and Hawkins, 1991). Any theory needs to give priority to explaining these results.

Figure 7.1 shows the key elements of my theory, which was primarily designed to explain offending by boys and men from lower socioeconomic groups. I have called it the Integrated Cognitive Antisocial Potential (ICAP) theory (Farrington, 2005b). It brings together ideas from many other theories, including strain, control, learning, labelling and rational choice approaches (see Agnew, 2002). Its key construct is antisocial potential (AP), and it assumes that the translation from antisocial potential to antisocial behaviour depends on thinking and decision-making processes that take account of opportunities and victims. Figure 7.1 is deliberately simplified in order to show the key elements of the ICAP theory on one page. It does not, for example, show how processes operate differently for onset compared with desistance or at different ages.

Enduring between-individual differences in antisocial potential are distinguished from short-term within-individual variations in antisocial potential. Enduring antisocial potential depends on impulsiveness, on strain, modelling and socialization processes, and on life events, while short-term variations in antisocial potential depend on motivating and situational factors. The long-term component of antisocial potential may be ordered on a continuum from low to high. Its distribution in the population at any age is highly skewed; relatively few people have high levels of antisocial potential, and people who do are more likely to commit many different types of antisocial acts, including those which would constitute offences. Hence, offending and ASB are versatile not specialized. The relative ordering of people on enduring antisocial potential tends to be consistent over time, but its absolute level varies with age, peaking in the teenage years, because of changes

within individuals in the factors that influence it, such as the increasing importance of peers and decreasing importance of parents between childhood and adolescence.

Hypotheses about how risk factors influence this longer-term antisocial potential are represented by the concept labels in the boxes. Following strain theory, the main energizing factors that lead to high long-term antisocial potential are desires for material goods, status among intimates, excitement and sexual satisfaction. These motives, however, only lead to high antisocial potential if antisocial methods of satisfying them are habitually chosen. Antisocial methods tend to be chosen by people who find it difficult to satisfy their needs legitimately, such as people with low income, unemployed people, and those who fail at school. The methods chosen also depend on physical capabilities and behavioural skills; for example, a 5-year-old would have difficulty in stealing a car. For simplicity, energizing and directing processes and capabilities are shown in one box in figure 7.1.

Long-term antisocial potential also depends on attachment and socialization processes. It will be low if parents consistently and contingently reward good behaviour and

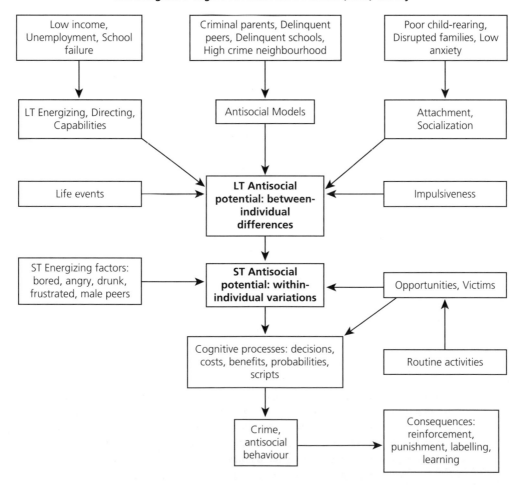

The Integrated Cognitive Antisocial Potential (ICAP) Theory

Figure 7.1   The Integrated Cognitive Antisocial Potential (ICAP) Theory. LT, long-term; ST, short-term

punish bad behaviour, but avoid harsh physical punishment. Children with low anxiety will be less well socialized, because they care less about parental punishment. Antisocial potential will also be high if children are not attached to prosocial parents, for whatever reason. Either coldness on the part of the parents or family disruption may impair attachment and socialization processes.

Exposure to and influence of antisocial models, such as criminal parents, delinquent siblings, and delinquent peers, for example in high crime schools and neighbourhoods, provide an additional set of risk factors for high antisocial potential.

The final two boxes relating to long-term antisocial potential highlight both the more intrinsic factor of impulsiveness, which will include a tendency to act without thinking about the consequences, and the external factor of life events. The latter have the potential to influence antisocial potential in either direction, with a likely decrease in antisocial potential for men after they marry or move out of high crime areas, or an increase in antisocial potential after separation from a partner.

Given an individual with high, average or low enduring antisocial potential, the short-term antisocial potential determines whether, how and when the enduring potential will be realised as antisocial behaviour. According to the ICAP theory, levels of short-term antisocial potential are also influenced by energizing and environmental factors, but different ones. Energizing factors for short-term antisocial potential include being bored, angry, drunk, or frustrated, or being encouraged by male peers. Environmental factors include the availability of victims and opportunities, and the individual's routine activities may affect these considerably.

The commission of a crime depends on cognitive processes, including consideration of the subjective benefits, costs and probabilities of the different outcomes and stored behavioural repertoires or scripts, as well as social factors such as likely disapproval by parents or female partners, and encouragement or reinforcement from peers. In general, people tend to make decisions that seem rational to them, on the basis of a benefit–cost assessment. Those with low levels of enduring antisocial potential, however, will generally not commit offences even when, on the basis of subjective benefit and low risk of detection, it appears rational to do so. If, however, short-term antisocial potential levels are significantly raised in some way, for example by anger or drunkenness, even people with low enduring antisocial potential may commit an offence, sometimes even when it is not rational for them to do so.

The consequences of offending may, as a result of a learning process, lead to changes in long-term antisocial potential and in future cognitive decision-making processes. This is especially likely if the consequences are clearly positively reinforcing, such as obtaining material gain or peer approval, or clearly negatively reinforcing, for example receiving legal sanctions or parental disapproval.

Also, if the consequences involve labelling or stigmatizing the offender, this may make it more difficult for him or her to achieve his or her aims legally, and hence may lead to an increase in antisocial potential. The ICAP is, in fact, a dynamic model, but the plethora of arrows required to illustrate this fully risks making the diagram confusing.

For more detailed accounts of this theory, see Farrington (2003a, 2005b) and for extended reviews of other developmental and life-course theories, see Farrington (2005a).

IMPLICATIONS FOR PREVENTION

The main benefit of any theory of the origins of unwanted behaviours is its potential for generating strategies for prevention. In this section, I will summarize briefly some of the most effective programmes for preventing delinquency and antisocial behaviour, for which effectiveness has been demonstrated in high quality research. My focus is especially on programmes evaluated in randomized experiments with large enough samples for adequate power (Farrington and Welsh, 2006).

The basic idea of developmental or risk-focused prevention is very simple: having identified the key risk factors for offending, then prevention techniques are designed to counteract them. There is often a related attempt to enhance prevention strategies through enhancing detected protective factors. Risk-focused prevention links explanation and prevention, links fundamental and applied research, and links scholars, policy makers, and practitioners. The book *Saving Children From a Life of Crime: Early Risk Factors and Effective Interventions* (Farrington and Welsh, 2007) contains a detailed exposition of this approach. Risk-focused prevention is easy to understand and to communicate, and it is readily accepted by policy makers, practitioners, and the general public. Risk factor informed interventions are based on empirical research rather than on more speculative theory, avoiding questions about which risk factors have causal effects.

Family-Based Prevention

If poor parental supervision and inconsistent discipline are causes of delinquency, it is plausible that family-based prevention should succeed in reducing offending. The behavioural parent management training developed by Patterson (1982) in Oregon is one of the most influential approaches. His careful observations of parent–child interaction showed that parents of antisocial children failed to tell their children how they were expected to behave, and/or failed to do so consistently, failed to monitor their behaviour to ensure that it was desirable, and failed to enforce rules promptly and unambiguously with appropriate rewards and penalties. Such parents also used more punishment, such as scolding, shouting or threatening, used it inconsistently and/or failed to make it contingent on the child's behaviour. Accordingly, Patterson's intervention involved linking antecedents, behaviours and consequences. He attempted to train parents in effective child rearing methods: noticing what their child is doing, monitoring the child's behaviour over long periods, setting clear rules, making rewards and punishments consistent and contingent on the child's behaviour, and negotiating disagreements so that conflicts and crises did not escalate.

Patterson's parent training was shown to be effective in reducing child stealing and antisocial behaviour over short periods in small-scale studies (Dishion et al., 1992; Patterson et al., 1992). The treatment worked best, however, with children aged 3–10 and less well with adolescents. Also, there were problems in achieving co-operation from the families experiencing the worst problems. In particular, single mothers on welfare were experiencing so many different stresses that they found it difficult to use consistent and contingent child-rearing methods. This indicates the importance of appropriate packages of assistance for the most needy, so that appropriate practical help is available to enable parents to engage in more therapeutic work to bring about stable change in children's behaviour.

Home Visiting Programmes

In the most famous intensive home visiting programme by Olds et al. (1986), in Elmira, New York State, 400 mothers were randomly allocated to receive either home visits from nurses during pregnancy, or to receive visits both during pregnancy and during the first 2 years of the child's life, or to a control group who received no visits at all. Each visit lasted about one and a quarter hours, and the mothers were visited on average every 2 weeks. The home visitors provided a general parent education programme, giving advice about prenatal and postnatal care of the child, about infant development, and about the importance of proper nutrition and avoiding smoking and drinking during pregnancy.

The results of this experiment showed that the postnatal home visits reduced the likelihood of recorded child physical abuse and neglect during the first 2 years of life, especially by poor unmarried teenage mothers; 4% of visited compared with 19% of non-visited mothers of this type were guilty of child abuse or neglect. In a 15-year follow-up, the main focus was on low socioeconomic status, unmarried mothers. Among these mothers, those who received prenatal and postnatal home visits had fewer arrests than those who received prenatal visits or no visits (Olds et al., 1997). Also, children of these mothers who received prenatal and/or postnatal home visits had fewer than half as many arrests as children of mothers who received no visits (Olds et al., 1998). According to Aos et al. (2001), $3 were saved for every $1 expended on high-risk mothers in this programme.

Parent Management Training

One of the most famous parent training programmes was developed by Webster-Stratton (1998) in Seattle. She evaluated its success by randomly allocating 426 children aged 4, most with single mothers on welfare, either to an experimental group which received parent training or to a control group which did not. The experimental mothers met in groups every week for 8 or 9 weeks, watched videotapes demonstrating parenting skills, and then took part in focused group discussions. The topics included how to play with your child, helping your child learn, using praise and encouragement to bring out the best in your child, effective setting of limits, handling misbehaviour, how to teach your child to solve problems, and how to give and get support. Observations in the home showed that the experimental children behaved better than the control children.

Webster-Stratton and Hammond (1997) also evaluated the effectiveness of parent training and child skills training with about 100 Seattle children, average age 5, referred to a clinic because of conduct problems. The children and their parents were randomly allocated to receive either (a) parent training; (b) child skills training; (c) both parent and child training; or (d) to a control group. The skills training aimed to foster prosocial behaviour and interpersonal skills using video modelling, while the parent training involved weekly meetings between parents and therapists for 22–24 weeks. Parent reports and home observations showed that children in all three experimental conditions had fewer behaviour problems than control children, immediately and during the following year. There was little difference between the three experimental conditions, although the combined parent and child training condition produced the most significant improvements in child behaviour during the year of follow-up. A finding that combined parent and child interventions are more effective than either one alone has been replicated more than once.

Scott et al. (2001) evaluated the Webster-Stratton parent training programme in London and Chichester. Parents of about 140 mainly poor, disadvantaged children aged 3–8 who were referred for antisocial behaviour were randomly assigned to receive training or to be in a control group. The parent training programme, based on videotapes, covered praise and rewards, setting limits, and handling misbehaviour. Follow-up parent interviews and observations showed that the antisocial behaviour of the experimental children decreased significantly compared to that of the controls. Furthermore, after the intervention, experimental parents gave their children more praise to encourage desirable behaviour, and used more effective commands to obtain compliance.

Sanders et al. (2000) in Brisbane, Australia, developed the Triple-P Parenting programme. This programme can either be delivered to the whole community in primary prevention using the mass media or can be used in secondary prevention with high-risk or clinic samples. Sanders evaluated the success of Triple-P for high-risk children aged 3 by randomly allocating their parents either to receive Triple-P or to be in a control group. The Triple-P programme involves teaching parents 17 child management strategies including talking with children, giving physical affection, praising, giving attention, setting a good example, setting rules, giving clear instructions, and using appropriate penalties for misbehaviour ('time-out', or sending the child to his or her room). The evaluation showed that the Triple-P programme was successful in reducing children's antisocial behaviour. A review of parent training programmes by Piquero et al. (2009) concluded that they were effective.

Pre-School Programmes

The most famous pre-school intellectual enrichment programme is the Perry project carried out in Ypsilanti (Michigan) by Schweinhart and Weikart (1980). This was essentially a 'Head Start' programme for disadvantaged African American children. A total of 123 children aged 3–4 were allocated, more or less randomly, to experimental or control groups. The experimental children attended a daily pre-school programme, backed up by weekly home visits, usually lasting two years. The aim of the 'plan–do–review' programme was to provide intellectual stimulation, to increase thinking and reasoning abilities, and to increase later school achievement.

This programme had long-term benefits. Berrueta-Clement et al. (1984) showed that, at age 19, the experimental group was more likely to be employed, more likely to have graduated from high school, more likely to have received college or vocational training, and less likely to have been arrested. By age 27, the experimental group had accumulated only half as many arrests on average as the controls (Schweinhart et al., 1993). Also, they had significantly higher earnings and were more likely to be home-owners. More of the experimental women were married, and fewer of their children were born to them while unmarried.

The most recent follow-up of this programme, with the participants aged 40, found that there appeared to be a continuing effect of the intervention on the lives of the participants (Schweinhart et al., 2005). Compared with the controls, those who received the programme had significantly fewer life-time arrests for violent crimes (32% vs. 48%), property crimes (36% vs. 56%), or drug crimes (14% vs. 34%), and they were significantly less likely to be arrested five or more times (36% vs. 55%). Improvements were also recorded in many other important life course outcomes. Compared with controls, the programme group reported significantly higher levels of schooling (77% vs. 60% graduating from high school), better employment records (76% vs. 62%), and higher annual incomes.

Several economic analyses show that the financial benefits of this programme outweighed its costs. The Perry project's own calculation (Barnett, 1993) included crime and non-crime benefits, intangible costs to victims, and even included projected benefits beyond age 27. This generated a famous benefit-to-cost ratio of 7 to 1. Most of the benefits (65%) were derived from savings to crime victims. The most recent cost–benefit analysis at age 40 found that the programme produced $17 in benefits per $1 of cost.

School Programmes

The Montreal longitudinal-experimental study combined child skills training and parent training. Tremblay et al. (1995) identified disruptive, aggressive or hyperactive boys at age 6, and randomly allocated over 300 of them to experimental or control conditions. Between ages 7 and 9, the experimental group received training designed to foster social skills and self-control. Coaching, peer modelling, role playing and reinforcement contingencies were used in small group sessions on such topics as 'how to help', 'what to do when you are angry' and 'how to react to teasing'. In addition, their parents were trained using the parent management training techniques developed by Patterson (1982).

This prevention programme was successful. By age 12, the experimental boys reported less burglary and theft, less drunkenness, and less involvement in fights than the controls. Also, the experimental boys had higher school achievement. At every age from 10 to 15, the experimental boys had lower self-reported delinquency scores than the control boys. Differences in antisocial behaviour between experimental and control boys increased as the follow-up progressed. A later follow-up showed that fewer experimental boys had a criminal record by age 24 (Boisjoli et al., 2007).

One of the most important school-based prevention experiments was carried out in Seattle by Hawkins et al. (1991). They implemented a multiple component programme combining parent training, teacher training and child skills training. About 500 first-grade children (aged 6) in 21 classes in eight schools were randomly assigned to experimental or control classes. The children in the experimental classes received special treatment at home and school which was designed to increase their attachment to their parents and their bonding to the school. Also, they were trained in interpersonal cognitive problem-solving. Their parents were trained to notice and reinforce socially desirable behaviour in a programme called 'catch them being good'. Their teachers were trained in classroom management, for example to provide clear instructions and expectations to children, to reward them for participation in desired behaviour, and to teach them prosocial methods of problem solving.

This programme had long-term benefits. By the sixth grade (age 12), experimental boys were less likely to have initiated delinquency, while experimental girls were less likely to have initiated drug use (O'Donnell et al., 1995). In a later follow-up, Hawkins et al. (1999) found that, at age 18, those who received the intervention from grades 1–6 reported less violence, less alcohol abuse and fewer sexual partners than the late intervention group (grades 5–6 only) or the control group. According to Aos et al. (2001), over $4 were saved for every $1 spent on this programme.

183

Anti-Bullying Programmes

School bullying is a risk factor for offending (Farrington, 1993b). Several school-based programmes have been effective in reducing bullying, the best known in Norway (Olweus, 1994). The general principles of the programme were: to create an environment characterized by adult warmth, interest in children, and involvement with children; to use authoritative child-rearing, including warmth, firm guidance, and close supervision, since authoritarian child-rearing is related to child bullying (Baldry and Farrington, 1998); to set firm limits on what is unacceptable bullying; to consistently apply non-physical sanctions for rule violations; to improve monitoring and surveillance of child behaviour, especially in the playground; and to decrease opportunities and rewards for bullying.

The Olweus programme aimed to increase awareness and knowledge among teachers, parents and children about bullying and to dispel myths about it. A 30-page booklet was distributed to all schools in Norway, describing knowledge about bullying and steps schools and teachers could take to reduce it. A 25-minute video about bullying was also made available to schools. Simultaneously, the schools distributed a four-page folder containing information and advice about bullying to all parents. In addition, anonymous self-report questionnaires about bullying were completed by all children.

Each school received feedback information from the questionnaire, about the prevalence of bullies and victims, in a specially arranged school conference day. Teachers were encouraged accordingly to develop explicit rules about bullying, for example do not bully, tell someone when bullying happens, try to help victims, try to include children who are being left out, and to discuss bullying in class, using the video and role-playing exercises. In addition, teachers were encouraged to improve monitoring and supervision of children, especially in the playground.

The effects of this anti-bullying programme were evaluated in 42 schools in one town, Bergen. Olweus measured the prevalence of bullying before and after the programme using self-report questionnaires completed by the children. Since all schools received the programme, there were no control schools, but children of a specified age before the programme was implemented were compared with children in the same age band in the same schools afterwards. Overall, bullying rates were halved.

A similar programme was implemented in 23 Sheffield schools by Smith and Sharp (1994). The core programme involved establishing a 'whole-school' anti-bullying policy, raising awareness of bullying and clearly defining roles and responsibilities of teachers and students, so that everyone knew what bullying was and what they should do about it. In addition, there were optional interventions tailored to particular schools: curriculum work, such as reading books or watching videos; direct work with students, such as assertiveness training for those who were bullied; and playground work, including training of lunch-time supervisors. This programme was successful in reducing bullying by 15% in primary schools, but only by 5% in secondary schools. A systematic review of anti-bullying programmes by Ttofi and Farrington (2009) showed that they were generally successful, reducing bullying by about 20%.

CONCLUSIONS

A great deal has been learned since the late 1980s, particularly from longitudinal surveys, about risk factors for offending and other types of antisocial behaviour. Offenders differ significantly from non-offenders in many respects, including impulsivity, intelligence, family background and socioeconomic deprivation. These differences are present before, during and after criminal careers. While the precise causal chains that link these factors with antisocial behaviour, and the ways in which these factors have independent, interactive or sequential effects, are not known, individuals at risk can be identified with reasonable accuracy.

Prevention programmes should be based on identified risk factors for offending, including protective factors. The continuity of antisocial behaviour from childhood to adulthood suggests that prevention efforts should be implemented early in life. Because of the link between offending and numerous other social problems, any measure that succeeds in reducing offending will have benefits that go far beyond this. Any measure that reduces offending will probably also reduce alcohol abuse, drunk driving, drug abuse, sexual promiscuity, family violence, truancy, school failure, unemployment, parental disharmony and divorce. Problem children tend to grow up into problem adults; problem adults tend to produce more problem children. Continued efforts are urgently needed to advance knowledge about offending and antisocial behaviour and to tackle the roots of crime.

High quality evaluation research shows that prevention programmes may be effective in reducing delinquency and antisocial behaviour and that in many cases the financial benefits of these programmes outweigh their financial costs. Early, smaller scale studies, however, tended to find better results than the larger studies (e.g. Conduct Problems Research Group, 1999a,b; LeMarquand et al., 2001). Harrington and Bailey (2004) explored some of the reasons for this, albeit in relation to the prevention of personality disorder rather than offending *per se*. These include the reduction of enthusiasm or programme integrity as initial interventions are rolled out on a larger scale and extended to less carefully selected groups. The best programmes include general parent education in the context of home visiting, parent management training, pre-school intellectual enrichment programmes, child skills training, and anti-bullying programmes. Notwithstanding concerns about stigmatization, programmes should be focused on those particularly in need rather than being scaled down for more general application.

In order to advance knowledge about development and risk factors for offending, new multiple-cohort longitudinal studies are needed in all countries. Also, the time is ripe to mount a large-scale evidence-based integrated national strategy for the reduction of crime and associated social problems, including rigorous evaluation requirements, in all countries. This should implement effective programmes to tackle risk factors and strengthen protective factors. Primary prevention has been effective in improving health, and it could be equally effective in reducing delinquency and antisocial behaviour in all countries.

8

Genetic influences on antisocial behaviour, problem substance use and schizophrenia: evidence from quantitative genetic and molecular genetic studies

Edited by
Pamela J Taylor

Written by
Marianne BM van den Bree

Nigel Williams

Terrie E Moffitt

INTRODUCTION

The concept of development into a criminal career carries with it some inevitable connotation of a mingling of factors which are variously intrinsic and extrinsic to the person. The previous chapter, while mainly concentrating on psychological and social environmental factors which may predispose to a criminal career, or protect against it, introduced some preliminary consideration of relevant individual differences which may in part be founded in genetics – such as impulsivity and intelligence. This chapter considers the genetic contribution in more detail. The first part provides a basic introduction to concepts and an overview of research methods in the fields of most relevance to forensic psychiatry. These include quantitative genetic studies, which can help disentangle the extent to which personal traits are influenced by genes rather than environmental factors, and molecular genetic studies aimed at finding the particular genes involved in those disorders which have been most consistently linked with offending – antisocial personality traits, problem substance use and schizophrenia. The second part of the chapter provides a summary of quantitative genetic and molecular genetic findings in these areas. Genetic factors relevant among people with intellectual disabilities who may get caught up with the criminal justice system, and in particular some specific relevant genetic syndromes are covered in the chapter on offenders with intellectual disabilities (chapter 10).

BASIC GENETICS
Genes and Proteins

Located in the nucleus of all living cells are chromosomes. These contain deoxyribonucleic acid (DNA), the molecular structure of which is an anti-parallel double helix composed of two DNA molecules (strands). Each strand is a linear rearrangement of repeating units called nucleotides, which are composed of one sugar, one phosphate, and one of four nitrogenous bases: adenine (A), guanine (G), cytosine (C) or thymine (T). The linear order of bases along the sugar phosphate backbone is termed the DNA sequence. The two DNA strands are held together by weak hydrogen bonds between the bases (base pairs); because of their particular steric properties A always pairs with T and G always pairs with C. Consequently, the sequence of bases in one strand will always be complementary to the other strand. This allows a mechanism for DNA replication, whereby the two DNA strands of each chromosome can be unwound, with each DNA strand directing the synthesis of a complementary DNA strand to generate two daughter DNA duplexes, each of which is identical to the parent molecule.

Genetic information is encoded in the DNA sequence; however, its expression follows a principle that has become known as the 'central dogma' of molecular genetics: DNA encodes ribonucleic acid (RNA), which, in turn, specifies the synthesis of protein. The first step of this process is termed *transcription* and results in the linear DNA sequence being copied to give a complementary single stranded linear sequence of nucleotides in RNA. The RNA molecules which specify polypeptides are known as messenger RNA (mRNA). These are transported from the nucleus to the site of protein synthesis, the cytoplasm. Then, at RNA–protein complexes called ribosomes, the mRNA is decoded in groups of three nucleotides (codons) to give a linear sequence of amino acids which form the polypeptide product. This process is termed *translation*. The structure and, ultimately, the specific functional properties of each protein product are largely dictated by its specific sequence of amino acids.

Individuals inherit one copy of a chromosome from each parent, the paired copies being termed *homologous chromosomes*. Each individual has 22 pairs of autosomal chromosomes, and one pair of sex chromosomes (X and Y) that determine sex: females carry two X chromosomes while males carry one X and one Y chromosome. Broadly speaking, genes have a complex linear organization of specific coding and non-coding segments (*exons* and *introns*) together with more ambiguous regions that precisely regulate expression at the locus. A genetic *locus* (position) on a specific homologous chromosome is termed an *allele*, with the pair of alleles being known as the *genotype*.

Assortment and Segregation

In the late nineteenth century, based on his work on pea plants, the Moravian monk Mendel (1866) developed two laws of genetic inheritance that remain crucial to understanding molecular genetics. His law of *independent segregation* states that pairs of alleles separate (or *segregate*) during gamete formation and unite randomly at fertilization, so that each allele has an equal probability of ending up in a gamete. His second law, of *independent assortment*, states that two loci that lie on different chromosomes will segregate independently. Meiotic cell division provides the molecular mechanisms.

Cell Division and Genetic Variation between Individuals

There are two kinds of cell division: mitosis and meiosis. Mitosis is the most common form, in which a parent cell duplicates its complete genetic material (DNA replication) before cell division, resulting in daughter cells that are genetically identical. Meiosis is a form of cell division that produces sperm and egg cells. It involves two successive cell divisions, but only one round of DNA replication. Detailed description of meiotic cell division is beyond the scope of this chapter, but there are features of meiosis which are crucial to studies of genetic inheritance. First, in a process known as 'crossing over', there is physical breakage of the double helix followed by *recombination*, which results in exchange of segments of DNA between homologous chromosomes. Following this, at the first meiotic cell division, each pair of homologous chromosomes separate and assort themselves independently so

that each daughter cell contains random combinations of each maternally and paternally derived set. Finally, a second meiotic division yields four daughter gametes, which are said to be *haploid* as they only have one representative of each chromosome pair. The full genetic complement is restored at fertilization, with the union of sperm and egg. The coupling of independent assortment and recombination ensures that the number of genetically different gametes that can be produced by a single individual is almost unlimited, resulting in considerable genetic variation between individuals, even family members.

Inheritance of Complex Traits

When an accurate prediction can be made that a genetic trait is segregating in a family or population in a Mendelian manner it is possible to estimate the risk of its transmission within that family or, if the allele frequencies are known, its prevalence rate in a population. Molecular geneticists have been highly successful in identifying genes causing Mendelian (monogenic) disorders. Most disorders, however, have complex origins and disentangling their genetic origins is much more complicated.

Most, if not all psychiatric diseases result from the combined action of a number of different genes, each of which, in itself, may have small impact, but rather non-additive effects with the others (gene–gene interaction or epistasis) and with the environment (gene–environment interaction (*G×E*); gene–environment correlation (*rGE*) also occurs, whereby co-occurrence of genes and environmental factors confers risk of psychopathology, as may pleiotropy, in which a gene has effects on multiple phenotypes (Schork and Schork, 1998; van den Bree and Owen, 2003). Elucidation of the origins of complex traits therefore poses a scientific challenge, requiring large samples and sophisticated statistical designs.

GENETIC STUDY METHODS

There are two main ways to study the genetic basis of complex disorders. Quantitative genetic studies are based on relating similarity of outward presentation – phenotypic similarity – to degree of genetic relatedness, thus using family, adoptee, or twin studies. Molecular genetic studies are based on relating presence/absence or degree of affected status with variation in genomic DNA, in linkage, association, or genome-wide association studies. Both approaches have contributed to improved understanding of the causes of psychiatric disease.

Quantitative Genetic Studies

Family studies

Family studies may contribute to determining the extent to which traits run in families. Each parent and his/her child(ren) share, on average, 50% of their genes, as do full siblings, while second and third degree relatives share, on average, 25% and 12.5%, respectively (Falconer, 1965). These estimates refer to additive genetic influences, and not dominance or epistatic genetic variation, accounting for most of the resemblance between family members (Falconer, 1965). Higher rates of a disorder in the family members of an affected individual may indicate that genetic influences play a role, although family members also share environmental factors, particularly when they live together. Shared environmental influences, some described in the previous chapter, may be particularly important with respect to antisocial behaviour. Without adoption or twin studies, it is not possible from family studies to estimate separately the impact of genetic and environmental influences on a phenotype.

Adoption studies

Adoption studies are based on the premise that adoptees share their genes but not their environment with their biological relatives and their environment but not their genes with their adoptive families, thus making it possible to establish the significance of each influence separately. There are two main types of adoption studies (Kringlen, 1991). The adoptees' method compares the adopted-away offspring of biological parents affected with a condition with control adoptees whose biological parents were unaffected. The adoptees' relatives' method compares the biological and adoptive relatives of affected adoptees with those of non-affected control adoptees. In both designs, a higher prevalence of the disorder amongst adoptees with affected biological relatives suggests that genetic factors play a role. A higher prevalence of disorder in adoptees with affected adoptive parents than those with non-affected adoptive parents suggests that environmental factors play a role. Such studies require cases and controls to be matched on relevant covariates, such as age, sex, socioeconomic status of the adoptive family and time spent with the biological mother (Ingraham and Kety, 2000).

Adoption studies, however, have a number of specific limitations which must be kept in mind when drawing inferences from them (see also Moffitt, 2005a). First, 'selective placement' is likely to occur. Due to screening of prospective adoptive parents, it is unlikely that environmental conditions for adoptees, as a group, are randomly distributed. This may introduce underestimates of shared environmental factors and overestimates of genetic ones (Miles and Carey, 1997; Stoolmiller, 1999). In some cases, adoption agencies actively try to maximize similarity between biological and adoptive families, to increase the adoptee's chances of fitting in with their new family. Greater than chance resemblance between adoptive parent and adoptee may occur, and may result in overestimation of genetic influences, where selective placement variables correlate with features under study (Clerget-Darpoux et al., 1986). A second area of difficulty is

that biological parents who offer their children for adoption may not be representative of the general population, but, rather, more likely to have alcohol problems or criminal records (Bohman, 1996); further, rates of maternal stress, drug abuse and/or poor care during pregnancy may be higher for young unmarried mothers. A third confounder is that adoptees have not necessarily been separated from their parents at birth, and so notional separation of genetic and environmental factors is, accordingly, contaminated.

A fourth major limitation is that adoption studies rely on comparisons of people at times when, phenotypically, they are not strictly comparable, and thus often use measurement tools that are not best suited for all parties. Behavioural phenotypes are more likely than not to vary with age, so use of the same measure for parents and children could be misleading, but interpretation of different, more age appropriate measures even more challenging. In this respect, twin studies, measuring the phenotype at the same age, in the same historical cohort, using the same instrument have a considerable advantage. The extent of this effect in adoption studies is apparent in that, although genetic relatedness in pairs of first degree relatives is always 50%, reported parent–child correlations are almost always lower than sibling correlations. Finally, child adoption rates have fallen since the 1970s, making it more difficult to conduct such studies. In contrast, with advances in IVF technology, the number of twins and other multiple births has been rising.

Twin studies

Identical, or monozygotic (MZ), twins are the result of a zygote dividing early in its development, while non-identical or dizygotic (DZ) twins develop from two different eggs that have been fertilized at the same time. MZ twins, therefore, are genetically identical while DZ twins share, on average, 50% of their genes, just like other first-degree relatives; 'on average' means that it is theoretically possible (although highly unlikely) for a DZ twin pair to be completely genetically identical or completely different, but taking all possibilities that arise during meiosis into account, in a large sample of twins, a rate of genetic sharing of 50% can be assumed. A comparison of resemblance rates of MZ and DZ twin pairs makes it possible to obtain estimates of the relative contributions of genetic and environmental influences on a phenotype. MZ twins share twice the genetic complement of DZ twins, so an estimate of genetic influences can be obtained by doubling the difference in resemblance rates between MZ and DZ twins. If resemblance is measured in terms of correlation coefficients, the formula would be: $2*(rMZ - rDZ)$. MZ correlations that are approximately twice those of DZ twins are indicative of additive genetic influences (denoted by a^2).

Two types of environmental influences can be distinguished in twin studies: *shared environmental influences*, denoted as c^2, which increase resemblance amongst family members (see basic family studies, above) and *non-shared environmental influences* (or e^2), which are not shared by family members and therefore decrease their resemblance. Shared environmental influences will increase the resemblance of DZ twins relative to those of MZ twins. An estimate of shared environmental influences can be obtained by taking twice the correlation between DZ twins and deducting the MZ correlation (2rDZ – rMZ). DZ correlations greater than half those of MZ correlations thus suggest the presence of shared environmental influences. Finally, non-shared environmental influences can be estimated by the formula 1 – rMZ, because they are the only influences that can make MZ twins dissimilar. When interpreting results of twin studies, measurement error tends to make twins less alike (and is included in e^2). It is generally assumed that the impact of measurement error on e^2 can be reduced by using multiple data sources, for example acquiring information on adolescent conduct problems from self-report, parental *and* teacher reports (Moffitt, 2005a). When raters are in full agreement on phenotype, rater-specific measurement error can be eliminated. Twin study methods are described in more detail in Neale and Cardon (1992).

Assumptions about the environment, however, constitute the first of a series of limitations which must be taken into account when interpreting twin studies. The '*equal environments assumption*' requires that MZ and DZ twins are equally exposed to environmental factors of importance for the trait under study, but if MZ twins, are treated more similarly than DZ twins, this assumption is violated (Kendler et al., 1994; Kendler et al., 1993); because MZ twins look identical, and spend more time together when growing up, this tends to occur (Kendler and Gardner, 1998). This would result in greater MZ than DZ environmental similarity, but MZ similarities would probably have been estimated as entirely due to genetic influences. Having said this, in practice, the problem has not been found to play an important role in twin resemblance in psychiatric disorders, including problem substance use (Kendler et al., 1994).

A second assumption in twin studies is of random parental mating. If, however, *assortative mating* occurs, that is non-random pairing of mates based on their phenotypes, this can bias heritability estimates. To the extent that assortative mating results in increased sharing of genes in genetically unrelated spouses, this will increase the genetic resemblance of DZ twins, but not MZ twins, whose gene sharing is already 100%. In addition, assortative mating will also lead to correlated spousal environments, thus increasing the environmental similarity between parents and children. As a result of these processes, heritability estimates will be biased downward and shared environmental influences inflated (Neale and Cardon, 1992). Extensions of the traditional twin design, incorporating parental data, allow for modelling assortative mating and cultural transmission (Eaves et al., 1978; Neale and Cardon, 1992), but this is an area where adoption studies have a clear advantage (Heath et al., 1985).

Assortative mating seems to be a particularly important issue for studies of mental and behavioural disorders. Evidence for correlations between spouses have been reported for antisocial behaviour (Galbaud du Fort et al., 2002; Krueger et al., 1998) and problem substance use (Stallings et al., 1997; Hopfer et al., 2003; Clegg et al., 2005). The situation may be a bit more complicated with respect to schizophrenia, with little evidence of assortative mating between people with the disorder *per se* (Ingraham and Chan, 1996), but some evidence of it in respect to schizophrenia-related symptoms (Parnas, 1985). In addition, there is a trail of evidence suggestive of a shared inherited characteristic which links violence and schizophrenia. In a US sample, Heston (1966) found a higher rate of both schizophrenia and violence in the fostered away children of mothers with schizophrenia. Moffitt (1984) made a similar finding among the adopted away children of Danish mothers, but noted also the higher than expected rate of violence among the fathers, suggesting assortative mating. Brennan et al. (1996), however, studied another series of US adopted away offspring, this time showing a higher rate of schizophrenia in the children of violent fathers, regardless of socioeconomic state, age at adoption, mother's or father's mental illness generally or schizophrenia specifically, or knowledge of criminal background, so there is more to resolve in this story.

A third area of difficulty is that twins may differ from siblings who are not twins in areas other than their genetic complements. It is well established, for example, that twins have lower birth weight than single babies, mostly attributable to shorter gestation (Buckler and Green, 2004; Jacquemyn et al., 2003), although MZ twins may also differ from DZ twins in prenatal factors affecting intrauterine growth. MZ twins sharing the same chorion (about two-thirds), for example, have significantly lower birth weights than dichorionic MZ twins (Ramos-Arroyo et al., 1988), possibly due to suffering increased fetal competition for nutrients. These intrauterine differences would tend to make MZ twins less alike, giving rise to downward biased heritability estimates (Rutter, 2002). To the extent that any differences between twins and non-twins are correlated with a trait studied using a twin design, it cannot, therefore, be assumed that the results may be generalized. Studies of specific mental and behavioural traits, however, have suggested that prenatal differences between twins and non-twins tend to be negligible (van den Oord et al., 1995; Andrew et al., 2001; Kendler, 1982; Kendler et al., 1995).

Our fourth point is that twin studies assume that genetic variation is predominantly additive in nature, but the components of the variation which are non-additive make DZ twins less alike than MZ twins. DZ twins, for example, have just 25% of their dominant genes in common, compared with 100% for MZ twins (Falconer, 1965), which could lead to overestimation of heritability and underestimation of shared environmental estimates, if present but not incorporated in the statistical model testing associations. Then, too, it is difficult to estimate epistasis reliably in humans, unless only a small number of loci are involved (epistasis occurs when the effects of one gene are modified by one or more others). Presence of non-additive genetic variation may account for discrepancy in results between twin and adoption studies, as siblings share more interactive variation than parents and offspring (Eaves et al., 1998).

Finally, twin studies have relatively low power to detect shared compared with non-shared environmental influences and with genetic influences. Therefore, considerably larger sample sizes are required to detect significant influences of the estimated shared environment than the other two latent factors (Martin et al., 1978). Many published twin studies report the 'best-fitting model'; that is the model from which non-significant parameters have been deleted. For studies in which the influences of the shared environment are small and the sample size is modest, this means these estimates will be equated to zero, even when confidence intervals around them indicate that their effect size could be small to moderate (Moffitt, 2005a). This may result in underestimation of environment role.

What heritability is and is not

Twin studies frequently report how heritable a trait is (the *heritability estimate* or h^2). This is obtained by expressing the influences of all genetic factors relative to the total phenotypic variation (i.e. genetic, plus shared and non-shared environmental factors) and can therefore range from 0 (no genetic influence) to 1 (completely genetically influenced). *Broad-sense heritability* refers to the relative contribution to the total phenotypic variation of both additive genetic and dominant genetic influences, while the more commonly used *narrow-sense heritability* refers to the relative contribution of additive genetic influences only.

The concept of heritability estimate has previously been misrepresented on occasion, so it is important to consider what it is *not* (see also Moffitt, 2005a). First, it is a population-based statistic, and therefore has no predictive value for an individual. Heritability estimates may differ in different populations under different environmental circumstances, possibly concealing important heterogeneity in genetic effects within subgroups, such as males versus females or children versus adults (Slutske, 2001). For this reason, cross-sectional twin studies, based on one measurement only, may not necessarily apply to earlier or later observations. Longitudinal twin studies, based on multiple measurements in the same sample are informative, because they allow measurement of the extent to which continuity in behaviour may be attributed to the same genetic or environmental influences over time.

A second issue is that a high heritability estimate does not mean that genes involved in a trait will be found easily. This is illustrated by the fairly slow progress, until the first decade of the twenty-first century, in molecular genetic studies searching for genes involved in the highly heritable condition

of schizophrenia (see below). One explanation of this is that high heritability can be the result of the additive or interactive effects of many genes of small effects, which are more difficult to find than single genes of large effect. Nonetheless, high heritability is an indication for pursuing molecular genetic research in any condition (Martin et al., 1997).

A third potential misinterpretation with heritability estimates is that evidence of genetic influence for a trait implies immutability or resistance to intervention. This is not the case: the mean height of the population in Western countries, for example, increased through the twentieth century during a time when individual height variation attributable to genes remained the same. A fourth point is that, while evidence of genetic influence implies that physical biological processes are involved in the aetiology of traits, it does not mean that change is necessarily only through this route. A genetic liability to alcoholism, for example, will not be manifest in the absence of alcohol consumption. In addition, adoption studies have repeatedly illustrated that an adoptive environment facilitating stable attachment can counter a genetic liability to antisocial behaviour (Cadoret et al., 1995a; Mednick et al., 1984). Finally, evidence of high heritability does not imply that the role of non-genetic factors is trivial. Rather, the heritability coefficient indexes not only the direct effects of genes, but also the effects of interplay between genes and environments (Rutter and Silberg, 2002; Purcell, 2002). In fact, it has been suggested (Kendler, 2001) that heritability of many behavioural traits may be lower in restrictive environments than in permissive ones, with greater opportunities to live up to one's genetic potential. There is evidence for gene–environment interplay for all three sets of behaviours at the heart of this chapter: antisocial traits, problem substance use and schizophrenia. Where such interactions exist, the effect of an environmental risk may be larger than previously reported among those of vulnerable genotype.

Recent advances in twin studies

Prior to the 1980s, researchers were mainly concerned with whether a trait was influenced by genetic factors, reporting percentages of MZ compared with DZ twins who were concordant for a disorder, or testing for association between adoptees' and biological parents' diagnoses (Moffitt, 2005b). Developments in statistics allowed for evaluation of more complex models. Quantitative model-fitting approaches, based on solving series of structural equations which specified the relationships between observed phenotypes and both genetic and environmental factors, became standard practice (Neale and Cardon, 1992; Plomin et al., 2005). Such approaches allow a systematic comparison of models which variously specify genetic influences only, genetic and shared environmental influences and shared environmental influences only, thereby also reducing subjectivity in decision-making (van den Bree and Owen, 2003). Research questions also evolved, with more recent examples including whether:

- sex, age and cohort differences affect genetic and environmental contributions to traits;
- genetic and environmental contributions change with increasing disease severity;
- deviance is a distinct category from 'normal' behaviour or, rather, one extreme of a continuum;
- comorbidity is attributable to genetic or environmental factors shared in common between traits, and to what extent.

In studying conduct problems and drug use, for example, the last question is answered by correlating one twin's symptoms of conduct problems with the other twin's drug use. Where such cross-twin cross-trait correlations are approximately twice as high in MZ versus DZ twins this suggests that genetic influences play a role in the co-occurrence of the traits, while DZ cross-twin cross-trait correlations greater than half those of the MZ twins suggest shared environmental factors also play a role in the comorbidity.

Twin studies are known for their estimation of latent (genetic and environmental) factors, but some more recent studies have included a measured environmental risk factor (Purcell and Koenen, 2005), although it is also possible to include a measured genetic factor. One method that may help elucidate non-shared environmental influences on the co-occurrence of traits, while taking genetic influences into account, is the MZ twin differences method. This is based on correlating phenotypic difference scores in MZ twins (Pike et al., 1996; Caspi et al., 2004); because MZ twins reared together are perfectly correlated for genetic and shared family environmental factors, any correlation in their differences on two traits must be due to non-shared environmental influences.

Another extension in methodologies lies in time-series analysis-based twin models, developed to analyse genetic and environmental influences on longitudinal data (Neale and Cardon, 1992). Extensions of the classic twin pair design have also been developed, to include the twins' parents in the model (Eaves et al., 1978), or their offspring (Nance and Corey, 1976). This means that issues like assortative mating, cultural transmission and/or maternal effects can be dealt with, thus further refining estimation of genetic and environmental contributions to behavioural traits.

Gene–environment interplay

The importance of gene–environment interplay on complex traits has gained increasing recognition (Moffitt et al., 2005). As noted above, two different types of processes can be distinguished: gene–environment interaction ($G{\times}E$) and gene–environment correlation (rGE). In statistical terms, the former is a situation in which the impact on a trait of changing one explanatory variable depends on the value of the other. Thus, $G{\times}E$ occurs when the effect on health of exposure to an environmental 'pathogen' is conditional on a person's genotype, or, conversely,

when environmental experience moderates gene effects on health. Gene–environment correlation, by contrast, refers to the co-occurrence of genes and environments conferring risk for psychopathology. An example of passive rGE is when a child's behaviour and the environment his/her parents provide are correlated because they have the same origins in the parents' genotype. Such processes can result in associations between the family environment and young people's antisocial behaviour, which are really an artefact of a third variable causing both: genetic factors in the parents. Active rGE, on the other hand, refers to a person's behaviour and environment being correlated because they have the same origins in his/her own genotype; the person's genetically influenced behaviour leads them to '(1) create; (2) seek; or (3) otherwise end up in environments that match their genotypes' (Rutter and Silberg, 2002).

In twin studies, if the presence of gene–environment interplay has not been incorporated into the statistical model, its variation will be estimated as part of either genetic or environmental influences, depending on the type of interplay (Purcell, 2002), and, in such circumstances, lead to biased results, variously over- or underestimating the genetic role. $G{\times}E$ can be quantified more accurately in twin studies by obtaining information on the relevant environmental factor, separating MZ and DZ twins into groups concordant for exposure, discordant for exposure or concordant for non-exposure, and subsequently testing whether there are differences in the magnitude of genetic influences on the trait under study in these different situations (Neale and Cardon, 1992; Ottman, 1994). The problem here, however, is that such tests are characterized by low statistical power (Eaves et al., 1977), although some have offered at least partial solutions (Purcell and Koenen, 2005; Heath et al., 2002).

In adoption studies, because genetic factors (shared with biological parents) and shared environmental factors (shared with adoptive parents) are more neatly separated, the study of gene–environment interplay is less complicated than in twin studies. If, for example, adoptees with affected biological *and* affected adoptive parents are at considerable greater risk of a disorder compared to the combined risk found for adoptees with only affected biological parents *or* only affected adoptive parents, this points to gene–environment interaction. The biological parent is different from the parent who provides the rearing environment, so interpretation is not complicated by passive rGE (Turkheimer et al., 2003). Paradoxically, however, this probably results in an underestimate of the influence of $G{\times}E$ on outcomes such as antisocial behaviour. In real life situations, genetically vulnerable children are not necessarily removed from a potentially damaging home to a potentially protective one, even though the second home is different and has been screened for its overtly abusive or neglectful potential. For this reason, adoption studies of $G{\times}E$ should, ideally, be complemented with twin studies.

The study of gene–environment interaction entails substantial methodological challenges. It requires measured environments that are truly free of genetic influence, some means of separating each from the other, and enough statistical power for a sensitive test of interaction (Rutter and Silberg, 2002). Under close scrutiny, many seeming environmental factors are under the influence of genes. A family's socioeconomic status, for example, is likely to be influenced by parental personality, intelligence, persistence, and motivation, or, perhaps, depression or substance abuse, each of which is partially heritable. Similarly, relationships between parents and offspring are influenced by genes that impact on behavioural and other factors (Shelton et al., 2008). Evidence is starting to accumulate on the importance of interactive mechanisms in psychiatric traits, from both quantitative and molecular genetic studies. It is crucial to allow for this in research, as studies which neglect the co-occurrence of relevant genetic and environmental risks will have only limited relevance for prevention. By contrast, findings from studies of genetic and environmental risk coincidence may be more easily applied to development of practical interventions (for more detail on gene–environment interplay principles, see Moffitt et al., 2005; Moffitt, 2005a,b).

Molecular Genetic Studies

Adoption and twin studies yield information about the relative contributions of genes and environment to antisocial behaviour, problem substance use and schizophrenia, but molecular genetic studies are needed to elucidate their genetic architecture. This, however, is no easy task because not only are most manifestations of these phenotypes likely to be a product of interactions between multiple genetic and environmental factors, but also the operational definitions and/or diagnoses of these conditions, however reliably derived, incorporate considerable phenotypic heterogeneity. Genetic mapping studies, with the aim to identify each susceptibility gene from approximately 22,000 others in the human genome, are conducted in this difficult clinical context. The two main types of molecular genetic approaches are: linkage mapping and association analysis.

Linkage mapping

Mendel's law of independent assortment, which states that two loci which lie on different chromosomes will be expected to segregate independently during meiosis (Strachan and Read, 1999), means that there is a 50% probability of a pair of alleles being inherited together. As noted, during meiosis, a recombination event occurs when two chromosomes meet at a chiasma (crossover) and then separate, resulting in exchange of segments to one side of the chiasma. As chiasmata may occur with approximately equal frequency at any point on a chromosome, it follows

that the probability of a pair of alleles from two loci lying on the same chromosome (syntenic) being inherited together will also be 0.5. The closer together two loci lie on the same chromosome, however, the more likely they are to segregate non-randomly, as only a chiasma located in the space between them will create recombinants. Linkage occurs when two syntenic markers recombine during meiosis at under the expected rate of 50%, representing a deviation from this Mendelian law. The occurrence of linkage is assessed using a statistical measure, the *recombination fraction (theta/θ)*, defined as the probability that there is an odd number of crossovers along the chromosomal segment between the loci (Strachan and Read, 1999). This recombination fraction can range from close to zero, indicating tight linkage, to 0.5, indicating independent assortment. The further apart two loci lie on a chromosome, the more likely it becomes that a crossover will separate them, so it follows that the recombination fraction is related to the genetic distance between two loci. The genetic distance between two loci is the number of recombination events per meiosis that occur in the section of DNA in between the two loci, and is measured in Morgans (M) or centiMorgans (cM; 100 cM = 1M). In these terms, if a population of 100 meioses are examined, and only one recombination event found to have occurred between two loci A and B, these loci would be 1 cM apart.

Genetic linkage analysis is an approach used to identify broad genomic regions likely to harbour susceptibility loci (Botstein and Risch, 2003), that is positions on a chromosome where a gene is located. In its simplest form, such investigation involves calculating the genetic distance between the disease locus and genetic markers. A genetic marker can be any gene or DNA sequence associated with a specific chromosome, but must be polymorphic (two or more variants with a population frequency >1%) so that its variation can be studied in relation to a specific trait. In practice, in linkage analyses, polymorphic genetic markers are typed in pedigrees with multiple affected family members and analysed for co-segregation with the disease phenotype. Ideally, this takes the form of a genome-wide linkage analysis using several hundred markers evenly distributed throughout the genome. Regions containing markers that co-segregate with disease more often than expected by chance are said to be linked and, if the linkage is real, will contain a susceptibility gene for the disorder under investigation. Evidence for linkage is expressed in terms of a *lod score*, which is the logarithm (base 10) of the odds that two loci are linked, divided by the likelihood of no recombination (Elston, 1998). Traditionally, a lod score of three or more is considered to be significant, corresponding to a p-value of 10^{-4}. A range of *lod scores* is typically obtained for different recombination fractions, with the value of $θ$ associated with the maximum positive *lod score* taken as the best estimate of the distance between gene and marker. Linkage analysis is a positional approach, which aims to identify disease-related genetic variation solely based on its location in the genome; it is not necessary to have an *ad hoc* hypothesis about the reason why this variant may be involved in the condition.

Parametric linkage analysis has been applied with considerable success in studies of Mendelian disorders, which have a single major disease locus with rare, highly penetrant alleles. Here, a number of genetic parameters for the disease under study can be specified, including a precise genetic model detailing the mode of inheritance, gene frequencies, penetrance rate (frequency with which the disease phenotype manifests itself in the presence of the analysed gene) and phenocopy rate (the frequency with which the disease phenotype occurs in the absence of the analysed gene). Psychiatric disorders, however, do not have these straightforward characteristics of Mendelian disorders, and, as a result, it is much more difficult to define their genetic model. Parametric linkage analysis is therefore performed using large numbers of multiply affected pedigrees under several estimated genetic models. This remains a powerful gene mapping approach even in these circumstances, but the potential is considerable for both false positive results due to multiple testing and false negative results under the wrong genetic parameters. Successful linkage analysis in psychiatric disorders depends on overcoming the challenge posed by genetic and phenotypic heterogeneity.

One approach to dealing with heterogeneity in this context is to restrict analysis to multiply affected pedigrees that segregate the disease in a classical Mendelian manner. This is largely based on the assumption that, although heterogeneity exists, such pedigrees will segregate genes of major effect, which linkage analysis will have sufficient power to detect. This approach has had its successes, most notably in familial Alzheimer's disease studies (Campion et al., 1999), but pedigrees segregating rare Mendelian forms of common psychiatric phenotypes are extremely difficult to ascertain, and may not exist for most complex disorders. Another way of reducing heterogeneity, of both genetic and environmental factors, is to use population isolates. These are populations that have become geographically and/or culturally isolated over many generations (Arcos-Burgos et al., 2002). Either way, because of the difficulty in ascertaining such pedigrees, some researchers have used a non-parametric form of linkage analysis called allele sharing, to identify marker alleles that are shared more often than is expected by chance by affected individuals within pedigrees. They do not require prior specification of a genetic model, and, on this basis, they may be considered more robust than parametric linkage methods for complex disorders. In psychiatric disorders, it is possible to limit analysis to large numbers of narrowly defined small nuclear pedigrees, and allele sharing analysis is particularly suitable for mapping genes in such circumstances. The method requires large sample sizes for adequate power in

the analysis (more than 600 affected sibling pairs (ASP)), but, for a common disease, this is not difficult to achieve. Psychiatric genetic linkage studies are, nevertheless, often difficult to interpret; studies providing compelling evidence for linkage are rare and failures to replicate proposed linkages are common, but this is typical for disorders involving the combined action of several genes of small effect.

Association analysis

Association analysis is also referred to as linkage disequilibrium mapping. Allelic association or linkage disequilibrium is defined as the deviation in populations from the random occurrence of alleles in a haplotype. Markers are said to be in linkage disequilibrium (LD) when they are so close that they have not been separated by recombination over successive generations.

Association studies have a number of practical advantages over linkage studies: they do not require multiply affected families; the analysis requires no prior definition of the disease model; they require smaller sample sizes for sufficient power to detect common genetic variants that contribute only modestly to disease (e.g. a sample of 700 well-matched cases and controls should have sufficient power to detect an allele contributing only 10% of a disease in a population, compared to the over 5,000 ASPs that would be required to detect a significant linkage). The case–control design is the most common form of association study. It can be a powerful way of identifying relatively common risk alleles of small effect, but if case and control samples are from different populations, it may be misleading because allelic association may arise only because one allele is more common in one population then the other, but unrelated to disease status. Statistical methods exist that identify and/or correct for this problem, termed population stratification (Cardon and Palmer, 2003). Family based association studies offer an alternative approach which is resistant to stratification problems (Zhao, 2000), although sufficiently large samples may be difficult to obtain. In general, family based approaches measure the probability of transmission of alleles from parents to affected offspring, where there is evidence of linkage if disease alleles are transmitted significantly more than 50% of the time to the affected offspring.

Direct association analysis

Association analysis is particularly powerful when testing a marker which is either the disease locus itself or is highly correlated with it, due to high linkage disequilibrium. Markers are said to be in linkage disequilibrium when they are so close that they have not been separated by recombination over successive generations. In this context, there is an advantage to studying unrelated patients within a single population who segregate the same disease susceptibility allele, because they would be expected to share much shorter chromosomal segments at the disease locus than affected relatives within a family. The reason for this is that their common ancestors are separated by many more genetic recombination events.

A gene is selected as a candidate for association analysis either due to its physical location within a region previously identified by linkage analysis and/or because its proposed function is relevant to a particular functional hypothesis; such genes are known as candidate genes. For most if not all complex traits, and certainly for the mental and behavioural disorders discussed in this chapter, it is difficult to select plausible candidate genes based on strong biological hypotheses, because the underlying pathogenic mechanisms are still poorly understood (van den Bree and Owen, 2003). This situation renders the *a priori* odds of a significant finding low (O'Donovan and Owen, 1999). In the absence of plausible hypotheses, attention has tended to focus on a limited number of genes involved in neuro transmitter systems implicated by the action of drug treatments (Jones and Craddock, 2001). Activity in the nervous system depends on electrical impulses travelling along nerves until they reach the gap, or synapse, between them. Crudely, transmission across the synapse occurs with release of chemicals by the presynaptic nerve ending and their effect on the postsynaptic receptors. Thus, for problem substance use and schizophrenia, most studies have focused on the pre- and postsynaptic receptors and the chemical transporters between them, and the same is largely true for antisocial behaviour. This situation is rapidly changing, however, with recent advances in molecular genetic studies.

Indirect association analysis

Association analysis can be made more efficient by exploiting the population's linkage disequilibrium at a region of interest, making it the method of choice for refining a region on the chromosome originally identified by linkage analysis. Linkage disequilibrium is not equally distributed across the genome. Instead, a large proportion of the genome falls into segments of strong linkage disequilibrium within which there are a limited number of haplotypes. A haplotype is a combination of alleles of closely linked loci on a chromosome that tend to be inherited together (Gabriel et al., 2002). It is possible to select a small number of informative single nucleotide polymorphisms (SNPs) which, when analysed, either individually or as haplotypes, will 'tag' a high proportion of the genetic variation (Johnson et al., 2001). Indirect linkage disequilibrium association mapping, therefore, typically requires a dense set of informative markers spanning the region of interest to be genotyped in a subset which is representative of the population being studied (typically 100 chromosomes). From this first stage analysis, a set of informative SNPs that 'tag' the full set are selected and then genotyped in the entire sample. Whilst such an approach does not test directly for a disease variant, the 'tag' SNPs will be likely to be highly correlated, either individually or as haplotypes, with such a variant.

Genome-wide association studies

Genome-wide association (GWA) studies (also referred to as whole genome association studies) were not feasible before the twenty-first century, because of the prohibitively large number of genotypes required. They have become possible because millions of human DNA sequence variations have now been catalogued and new technologies developed which allow the rapid and accurate assaying of these variants.

GWA studies represent a large-scale version of linkage disequilibrium mapping in which variation in common SNPs (by convention, varying on at least 5% of chromosomes) is systematically searched amongst individuals and examined for possible association with disease status (Psychiatric GWAS Consoritum Coordinating Committee, 2009; Corvin et al., 2010). DNA from large samples of individuals is typed using genome-wide marker panels, which can read millions of DNA sequences. GWA studies have been conducted with cases and controls or cases and their parents. Typically, associations are found between a disease and a number of SNPs, most of which will not be causally linked to the disease, but rather reside in the vicinity of the disease-causing gene. Identification of the disease-causing gene(s) requires subsequent in-depth sequencing approaches, during which the sequence of nucleotides is determined for a chromosomal region. Although genome-wide sequencing studies are currently cost-prohibitive, it is anticipated that, with the advance of technology, this will become another powerful tool for elucidating the genetic architecture of complex traits.

According to the common-variant/common-disease model (Lander, 1996), most risk alleles underlying complex health-related traits are common, not rare; and a relatively small number of these common variants contribute moderately to complex diseases. On the other hand, according to the common disease/many rare variants hypothesis (Pritchard, 2001), disease is caused by multiple variants of strong effect, each of which is found in only a few people. Variants may be rare because they are new (only a few generations old) and have therefore not undergone long periods of selection against them (negative selection), or because they are sufficiently deleterious to reduce the evolutionary fitness in the individuals who carry them (Schork et al., 2009).

GWA studies have the advantage over linkage strategies of increased power for detecting relatively common alleles and more refined localization of signals to smaller chromosomal regions; linkage strategies are better suited to detect effects of rare alleles that are present in only a small proportion of affected individuals and their families. At present, GWA approaches will miss most associations with rare

SNPs (allele frequency 0.1–3%) (Frazer et al., 2009) which are more likely to be detected by resequencing of relevant regions in hundreds or thousands of individuals.

It has recently been proposed that many associations with common variants may, in fact, be indirect, a phenomenon known as 'synthetic association' (Dickson et al., 2010). This means that, among people with a common variant associated with a disease, only a proportion may also have the rare variant which actually causes the disease. Synthetic associations make it seem as if many people share a genetic sequence conferring a small risk of disease when, in fact, some of those individuals have a rare variant making a much greater contribution to disease risk.

To date, hundreds of GWA studies have been performed, associations have been identified between genetic variants for many different diseases and some of the findings are leading to new biological insights (Cichon et al., 2009; Schork et al., 2009). In general, however, the disease-related loci that have been identified account for small increments in risk, and explain small amounts of the genetic variance of a trait; furthermore, elucidation of the functional link between associated variants and phenotypic traits remains elusive (Frazer et al., 2009). A complicating issue is that GWA studies are conducted without an underlying hypothesis, and so prone to false-positive results because of the very large number of statistical tests performed (Hunter and Kraft, 2007). Replication of any findings is, therefore, essential, in independent samples. One reason for failure to have done so to date could be where genetic vulnerability only becomes manifest in the presence of environmental risk factors. Increasingly, large-scale studies including both genome-wide genetic information and detailed high-quality environmental measures are becoming available, so these mechanisms may be explored further. Finally, marker panels used in current GWA studies only include SNPs. There is increasing awareness that other genetic variants, such as copy number variants (CNVs), are important in disease, but these issues cannot be explored with current GWA approaches. An example lies in 22q11 deletion syndrome (22q11DS), which is caused by a deletion of a segment of one of a person's two chromosomes 22; this leads to hemizygosity (presence of only one copy) of approximately 40 genes. Although this syndrome is rare (c.1:4,000 live births), it represents the strongest known risk factor for development of psychosis in adulthood (Murphy et al., 1999).

New Advances

Mechanisms of genetic coding for proteins are still poorly understood, and their implications for susceptibility to disease unclear. New technologies should change this: mRNA or gene expression profiling techniques, for example, allow monitoring of the expression levels of thousands of genes simultaneously in relation to disease status, by comparing expression profiles in affected versus non-affected individuals; also the effects of a specific pharmacological treatment may be evaluated by comparing treated versus non-treated cells or tissues. One area of particular interest in this context is how substance-induced changes in gene expression lead to alterations in brain structure and function, and, in turn, how these are associated with subsequent behaviour.

Integrating quantitative and molecular genetic studies

Kendler (2005) presents several examples of important questions that molecular genetic studies alone cannot answer, and argues convincingly that progress in psychiatric genetics would benefit most.

THE GENETICS OF ANTISOCIAL BEHAVIOUR, PROBLEM SUBSTANCE USE AND SCHIZOPHRENIA

Antisocial Behaviour

Antisocial behaviour is a term covering a wide variety of personal traits, and studies in this area have used many different phenotypic definitions. Thus, we are generally driven to use a broad definition: those behaviours that violate the rights and safety of others. Reference is also, however, made to studies which deal with more specific problem behaviours, including externalizing behaviour, oppositional and disruptive behaviour, conduct problems, delinquency, aggression, violence, dishonourable discharge from the army, conflict and bullying, as well as criminal involvement. One potential limitation of several of the studies we report is that certain patterns of substance misuse, generally alcohol misuse, have been included as antisocial behaviour. While much of lay society would endorse that, it may complicate attempts to draw conclusions about antisocial traits which are not alcohol-related.

Quantitative genetic studies of antisocial behaviour

A consistent finding is that crime does run in families (Farrington et al., 2001; Rowe and Farrington, 1997; and chapter 7). In general, fewer than 6% of families account for more than 50% of the criminal offending in their community. Quantitative genetic studies of antisocial behaviour have been conducted in a number of western nations since the 1930s, in a wide range of age groups (19 months to 70 years). A 1997 meta-analysis of 24 studies showed that genetic factors may explain up to 50% of the variation in aggression (Miles and Carey, 1997), while a later one (Rhee and Waldman, 2002), with additional studies estimated that additive genetic influences explain 32% of the variation in antisocial behaviour more broadly, with another 9% contributed by dominant genetic factors, yielding a slightly lower broad heritability estimate of 41%. Shared and non-shared environmental influences contributed 16% and 43%, respectively. There were no significant differences in the magnitude of genetic and environmental influences between males and females.

A more recent review by one of us (Moffitt, 2005a), of 60 different samples, has provided over 100 heritability estimates from twin and adoption studies. Such estimates tend to fall into the lower or higher ranges when studies have small sample sizes or specific sampling properties, as in very wide age ranges or very young children, or specific measures, such as observational measures or retrospective report of childhood symptoms by adults. When focusing on large, population-based twin studies, using sophisticated quantitative modelling approaches, heritability estimates are generally consistent at around 50%, even with studies having been conducted as far afield as Australia, the Netherlands, Norway, Sweden, the UK and the USA. Estimates of shared environmental influences were much more variable between studies, with 20% considered to be a reasonable guide. The remaining 20–30% of the variation was attributable to non-shared environmental influences. No evidence was found for significant gender differences in genetic and environmental influences on antisocial behaviour.

Although the results of these reviews are broadly in line with each other, the magnitude of both genetic and environmental estimates may vary with sample characteristics. Miles and Carey (1997) reported that genetic influences tended to be higher and shared environmental influences lower in older samples. On the other hand, Rhee and Waldman (2002) reported that both genetic and shared environmental influences were smaller in older samples. It is possible that such discrepancies are due to age, but reporting source may be a confounder, with studies in children tending to rely on parental reports, studies with adolescents on self-report and studies with adults commonly based on official crime records. Miles and Carey, for example, found self-report measures of antisocial behaviour to result in higher heritability and lower shared environmental estimates than parental reports. In addition, different concepts of antisocial behaviour may also yield different estimates of genetic and environmental influences. Rhee and Waldman (2002), for example, reported that diagnosis of aggression and antisocial behaviour yielded broad heritability estimates of around 45%, while higher heritability estimates were found with respect to officially recorded criminality. Other studies have indicated that aggressive antisocial behaviour may be more strongly genetically influenced than non-aggressive antisocial behaviour, and that antisocial behaviour combined with high levels of callous-unemotional traits in children may be under greater genetic influence than antisocial behaviour with low levels of callous-unemotional traits (Eley et al. 1999; Viding et al., 2005).

Using a developmental approach, a distinction has been proposed between two types of antisocial behaviour: life-course persistent and adolescence-limited antisocial behaviour (Moffitt, 1993). The latter is common, even near normal, thought to be more founded in social influences than genetics, flaring up in adolescence but falling away again in young adulthood. Life-course persistent antisocial behaviour, by contrast, begins in childhood, is rare and pathological, and is thought to have its origins in neuro-developmental processes, being more strongly influenced by genetic factors (Moffitt, 2003a, 2005a).

Studies have also indicated that pervasiveness of anti-social behaviour may play a role. In the Cardiff Study of All Wales and North West of England Twins (CaStΛNET), we found that heritability estimates for self-reported conduct problems were lower than for parent and teacher reports (Scourfield et al., 2004). Nevertheless, a common underlying vulnerability phenotype of pervasive conduct problems, created by combining data from all three informants, was found to be entirely explained by genetic influences. Other studies have similarly found that antisocial behaviour that is pervasive across settings is more heritable than situation specific antisocial behaviour (Arseneault et al., 2003). An important question, then, is to what extent stability in antisocial behaviour over time can be attributed to genetic rather than environmental factors. Longitudinal twin studies have indicated that stability in aggressive behaviour in childhood and adolescence is largely explained by genetic influences, while both genetic and shared environmental factors play a role for non-aggressive antisocial behaviour (van Beijsterveldt et al., 2003; Eley et al., 2003). The *Vietnam Area Twin Register study* (Lyons et al., 1995) found that genetic influences explained 7% of the variation in juvenile delinquency but 43% in adult antisocial behaviour, although the same set of genetic and environmental factors accounted for both. This suggests that the greater genetic influence in adulthood was due to an increase in magnitude of effect, rather than the expression of new sets of genes.

Another of the more recent twin studies which includes measured environmental risk factors is the *Virginia Twin Study of Adolescent Behavioural Development*, which used the extended twin-family design approach to assess whether aspects of home environment increase risk of antisocial behaviour (Meyer et al., 2000). Information was obtained on antisocial conduct problems for adolescent twins and their parents and on parenting behaviour. No effect was found for marital discord, but family adaptability, which was modelled to operate as an effect that was shared by twins, was found to account for 3.5% of the phenotypic variance in adolescents' conduct problems. In the longitudinal *Dunedin Multidisciplinary Health and Development Study (the Dunedin Study)*, twin analyses including a putative environmental risk factor have indicated that living in a deprived neighbourhood explains 5% of the shared environmental variation in 2-year-olds' behaviour problems (Caspi et al., 2000). Another study using this approach emphasized domestic violence, finding that it explained 13.5% of the shared environmental variance in outcome for children in terms of simultaneous development of externalizing and internalizing problems (Jaffee et al., 2002).

There is a caveat about twin studies including a measured environmental risk factor that is shared between twin pairs: inference of environmental causation is compromised if parent and child share genes that simultaneously influence both the measure of environment and the measure of child antisocial behaviour.

Twin studies have also included measures of the environment that are specific for each twin, like personal abuse, rather than one measure, like marital discord or many neighbourhood factors, which applies to both twins. Examining the effects of physical maltreatment on young children, Jaffee et al. (2004) found that it plays a causal role in the development of their antisocial behaviour. A similar analytical approach using twin-specific measures of risk was taken in the *Minnesota Twin Family Study* (Burt et al., 2003), of 11-year-old twin pairs. Models revealed that measured parent–child conflict, as a specific environmental measure, accounted for 12% of the variance in the externalizing syndrome of oppositional, conduct, and attention-deficit-hyperactivity disorders. This measured variable accounted for 23% of the estimated shared environmental variation.

Finally, using the MZ twin differences design, Caspi et al. (2004) found that differences in the antisocial behaviour of MZ twins could be predicted statistically by differences in maternal expressed emotion, possibly indicating an environmental effect of the relationship between mother and child on behavioural problems.

Molecular genetic studies of antisocial behaviour

There is a dearth of molecular genetic studies of antisocial behaviour. Methods of those that have been published have tended to lag behind those in studies with, say, schizophrenia. Furthermore, genetic studies of antisocial behaviour have frequently been based on small, often convenience samples, and often in relation to surrogate behaviours, such as antisocial alcoholism or violent suicide. In contrast to other conditions in psychiatry, there are few, if any, large consortium efforts to elucidate genetic contributions to a well-defined phenotype.

There have been several genome-wide studies of antisocial behaviour. In one such, Ehlers et al. (2008) evaluated a panel of 791 micro-satellite polymorphisms typed in a rather small sample of 251 American Indians from 41 families. They reported six locations with a log of the odds (LOD) score of 2.0 or above on chromosome 13 for antisocial

personality disorder (ASPD) alone and on chromosomes 1, 3, 4, 14, 17 and 20 for ASPD/conduct disorder. Stallings et al. (2005) conducted a search for quantitative trait loci (QTL) that might influence antisocial drug dependence. QTL are loci associated with variation in phenotypes that have been assessed on a continuous scale, rather than as a category. Stallings, sample consisted of 249 adolescent and young adult sibling pairs from 191 families, ascertained through adolescents in treatment for substance abuse and/or delinquency. They found LOD scores for conduct disorder symptoms in excess of 1 on chromosomes 9 and 17. The region on chromosome 9 was also found to be suggestive of linkage to substance dependence vulnerability. Dick et al. (2004) did a genome-wide linkage analysis, here with adults taking part in the *Collaborative Study on the Genetics of Alcoholism* (COGA), and reported a history of earlier conduct problems. They reported LOD scores ≥1.50 on chromosomes 2, 3, 12, and 19 for conduct disorder as a diagnosis and 1 and 19 for symptoms of conduct disorder. Kendler et al.'s (2006) genome-wide linkage analysis in the *Irish Affected Sib Pair Study* yielded evidence suggestive of linkage to conduct disorder on chromosome 1 and 14. When comparing their results with those of the Dick group, Kendler et al. suggested that chromosomal regions 1q and 2p might be good starting points for further efforts to localize susceptibility genes for conduct disorder. A later study (Dick et al., 2010) was of genome-wide association with retrospectively reported conduct disorder symptoms, in samples of cases with alcohol dependency and controls, found four markers that met criteria for genome-wide significance (two of them on chromosome 4p in the gene *C1QTNF7* (C1q and tumour necrosis factor-related protein 7)) and six additional SNPs yielded converging evidence of association.

It is clear from these results that there is, so far, a lack of consistency in findings in genome-wide studies. Consistent with their methods, conducted without an *a priori* theory about the biological mechanisms involved in antisocial behaviour, they must be regarded as screening studies. We emphasize, therefore, that we are only at the beginning of understanding the complex mechanisms involved in antisocial behaviour. Progress usually takes place by studying one specific aspect of a trait in detail until it is understood and then adding in other factors to take the next step in building towards the full picture of a complex behaviour. We take the view that identification of a gene (or genes) both necessary and sufficient for the development of antisocial behaviour is unlikely. Rather, we expect this process to result from accumulating mostly small effects of a variety of risk factors, including individual genes, specific environmental risk factors and their interactions. We would also expect that the specific combinations and relative importance of genetic and environmental risk factors to differ according to different forms of antisocial behaviour.

Other published accounts of genetic studies into antisocial behaviour have tended to focus on candidate genes, particularly genes involved in specific neurotransmission systems, and mainly 5-hydroxytryptamine (5-HT) or serotonergic neurotransmission. It is beyond the scope of this chapter to present an exhaustive account of the candidate gene findings for antisocial behaviour, addiction and schizophrenia, so we have opted to present the more consistent positive findings, without presenting the relevant references for contradictory findings. When reading these sections, therefore, it is important to keep in mind that this area of study has been notorious for findings which have not been replicated.

According to convention, throughout the remainder of this chapter, we will refer to a gene name in *italics*.

Serotonergic neurotransmission

The serotonergic system has been implicated in a variety of traits, including impulsivity, addictive behaviour, suicide, mood regulation, sexual activity, appetite and eating disorder as well as cognition, sensory processing and motor activity. Studies in rodents, non-human primates and humans have suggested that serotonergic systems play a role in aggression and antisocial behaviour (Lesch and Merschdorf, 2000; Nelson and Chiavegatto, 2001; also see chapter 12). It has been hypothesized that aggression arises as a consequence of faulty regulation in brain regions that are associated with emotion controls, including the prefrontal cortex, which receives major serotonergic projections (Davidson et al., 2000).

In rhesus monkeys, levels of cerebrospinal fluid (CSF) concentrations of the 5-HT metabolite 5-hydroxyindoleacetic acid (5-HIAA) have been found to be associated with aggression and reduced social competency (Higley et al., 1996). In the rat, stimulation of a restricted area of the hypothalamus can elicit unprovoked violent attacks, which can be inhibited by serotonergic drugs affecting serotonin type 1 (5-HT1) receptors (Kruk, 1991). This seemed, therefore, a promising area for study in humans, among whom impulsivity and high aggression have been associated with reduced brain 5-HT turnover in a wide variety of samples, including aggressive psychiatric patients, impulsive violent offenders, impulsive arsonists and suicide victims (Virkkunen et al., 1995; Mitsis et al., 2000; Davidson et al., 2000; Lesch and Merschdorf, 2000). Longitudinal studies have shown that low CSF 5-HIAA levels can predict aggression for up to 2–3 years in boys with disruptive behaviour disorders (Kruesi et al., 1990). Examining the steps in serotonin biosynthesis is also instructive. The first step is catalysed by the rate-limiting enzyme tryptophan hydroxylase (TPH). TPH depletion has been shown to be associated with an increase in rate of aggressive responses in healthy males. Alcohol, in conjunction with tryptophan, has an additive effect on aggression (Dougherty et al., 1999).

Genes involved in serotonergic neurotransmission which have been studied in relation to antisocial behaviour include serotonin receptor genes *5-HT1B* and *5-HT3B* as well as the serotonin transporter gene (*SERT* or *SLC6A4*) and *TPH1* and *monoamine oxidase A* (*MAOA*).

Serotonin receptor genes *5-HT1B* (on chromosome 6) and *5-HT3B* (on chromosome 11) have both been associated with antisocial alcoholism (Lappalainen et al., 1998; Ducci et al., 2009).

SERT (on chromosome 17) contains a specific polymorphism (5HTTLPR) consisting of a 20–23 imperfect repeat sequences, with two major allelic variants: the short (S, low-expressing variant) involves 14 copies, and the long (L, high-expressing variant) involves 16 copies. Sakai et al. (2006) and Fowler et al. (2009) found associations between this S-allele and aggressive behaviour and 'psychopathy', respectively.

In humans, two different tryptophan hydroxylase (TPH) genes exist (*TPH1* and *TPH2*), which are located on chromosomes 11 and 12, respectively. A polymorphism of *TPH1* has been associated with aggression and anger-related traits and a history of suicide attempts as well as low levels of CSF 5-HIAA (New et al., 1998; Virkkunen et al., 1995; Goodman et al., 2004; Hennig et al., 2005). Any association studies of genes involved in serotonergic neurotransmission and psychiatric traits are complicated by the fact that neurotransmitter systems interact. Variations in other systems may contribute to some of the contradictory findings in genetic studies of antisocial behaviour.

Monoamine oxidase (MAO)

Monoamine oxidase (MAO) exists in A and B forms. The genes for both types are located on the X chromosome, and the proteins for both types are present in the brain. MAOA is a mitochondrial enzyme that oxidizes serotonin as well as the neurotransmitters dopamine and noradrenaline/norepinephrine. MAOA has been implicated in conditions and behaviours such as depression, anxiety, aggression, alcoholism, autism, suicide related behaviours and impulsiveness.

A large Dutch family study, in which eight males were affected by a syndrome of borderline mental retardation and antisocial behaviour (including impulsive aggression, arson, attempted rape, fighting and exhibitionism), has provided evidence of a deficiency in MAOA enzymatic activity (Brunner et al., 1993). In the affected males, a point mutation was identified in the eighth exon of the MAOA structural gene, which changes a glutamine to a termination codon. This mutation truncates the amino acid sequence, rendering the MAOA enzyme inactive. This can lead to decreased concentrations of 5-hydroxyindole-3-acetic acid (5-HIAA) in CSF. No other families, however, have so far been found in which the association between this mutation and antisocial behaviour has been reported.

More recently, a 30 bp repetitive sequence polymorphism in the promoter of *MAOA* was discovered, which appears to regulate its activity. It has been termed MAOA-linked polymorphic region, or MAO-LPR. MAO-LPR has been studied in relation to antisocial traits (Williams et al., 2009), conduct problems and conduct disorder in girls (Lawson et al., 2003; Prom-Wormley et al., 2009), aggression, and impulsivity (Eisenberger et al., 2007; Manuck et al., 2000); gang membership and using a weapon in a fight for males (Beaver et al., 2010) and 'psychopathy' in youngsters with attention deficit hyperactivity disorder (ADHD) (Fowler et al., 2009). Sjöberg et al. (2008) have reported that *MAOA* genotype and CSF testosterone may interact to predict antisocial behaviours.

Some studies have suggested that the relationship between *MAOA* activity and antisocial behaviour may be mediated by emotional processing deficits. Williams et al. (2009), for example, have suggested that low *MAOA* activity may increase susceptibility to antisocial traits through alterations to the neural systems for processing threat-related emotion, while Eisenberger et al. (2007) have presented evidence that the relationship between MAOA and aggression *can* be explained by a heightened sensitivity to negative socio-emotional experiences like social rejection. An imaging study (Meyer-Lindenberg et al., 2006) has found that during emotional arousal, but not under neutral conditions, individuals with low *MAOA* activity alleles show greater reactivity in the amygdala and lower activity in the regulatory prefrontal areas, suggesting that *MAOA* may mediate differences in the limbic circuitry for emotion regulation and cognitive control of antisocial behaviour.

Catechol-O-methyl transferase (COMT)

Genes may also underpin antisocial behaviour through *COMT*, which plays a role in the metabolism of the catecholamine neurotransmitter group, which includes dopamine, noradrenaline and adrenaline. The *COMT* gene, which resides on chromosome 22, has been associated with a variety of phenotypic states, including prefrontal (higher executive) cognitive function, mood disorder, schizophrenia and obsessive compulsive disorder.

COMT enzyme activity is associated with a functional polymorphism due to a DNA nucleotide transition (G to A) at codon 158, which results in substitution of the essential amino acid methionine (met) for valine (val). The 'met' allele is associated with 3-4 times lower *COMT* activity, in turn related to better performance on the prefrontal cortex tasks of executive function and working memory (Anderson et al., 1999), but higher levels of anxiety and greater sensitivity to pain and stress. It is frequently referred to as the low-activity allele. The substituted allele – the 'val' or high-activity allele – may be associated with an advantage in processing aversive stimuli, and has been associated with antisocial behaviour. The 'val' and 'met' alleles have also been referred to respectively as the warrior and the worrier alleles and it has been suggested that, under stressful circumstances, when there is increased dopamine release in the brain, 'val' carriers may have improved dopaminergic transmission and better performance, while 'met' carriers have less efficient neurotransmission and worse performance (Stein et al., 2006).

Several studies in a number of different samples have reported that children with ADHD who are homozygous for the 'val' allele have an increased risk of antisocial behaviour. Thapar et al. (2005) have reported that the 'val'–'val' genotype in children with ADHD is associated with early onset antisocial behaviour. This finding was replicated by Caspi et al. (2008), who reported that these children exhibited early onset pervasive and persistent antisocial behaviour and were convicted of a disproportionate share of crimes as adults. Langley et al. (2010) replicated this association between the 'val' allele and extreme antisocial behaviour, in the presence of ADHD, suggesting also that this association may in part be explained by impaired social understanding. It is noteworthy that these findings differ from those with respect to antisocial behaviour in the context of schizophrenia, when it is the 'met' allele of the *COMT* gene which is associated with internally and externally directed antisocial behaviour (Strous et al., 1997; Strous et al., 2003).

Gene–environment interplay and antisocial behaviour

Adoption studies in Sweden in the 1980s were influential in contributing to confirmation that genetic risk factors combine with environmental ones to put individuals at particularly increased risk for development of antisocial behaviour (Bohman, 1996). It was found that 40% of male adoptees in the *Stockholm Adoption Study* who had both genetic and environmental risk factors present for criminality or alcoholism acquired a criminal record. This was close to 14 times the rate among male adoptees with neither risk factor (3%); presence of only environmental risk factors was associated with a 7% rate of criminality, while presence of only genetic risk factors increased risk to 12%.

Studies of adoptees from Iowa and Missouri have indicated that they were most likely to display antisocial behaviour if they had biological mothers with antisocial personality problems or alcoholism (Cadoret et al., 1983). Adoption studies have, furthermore, provided some evidence that gene–environment correlation may contribute to the development of antisocial behaviour (Ge et al., 1996; O'Connor et al., 1998). The O'Connor group's longitudinal study, for example, reported that adoptees at higher genetic risk for antisocial behaviour (i.e. those with antisocial biological parents) were more likely to receive negative parenting from their adoptive parents than adoptees without genetic risk for antisocial behaviour, providing evidence of evocative *rGE*. Another adoption study found that adoptees with greater genetic risk for antisocial behaviour were more likely to receive harsh discipline from their adoptive parents in homes where there was social adversity (Riggins-Caspers et al., 2003), suggesting, as might be expected, that the gene–environment relationships are, indeed, complex. In further studies of the effect of physical maltreatment on risk for conduct problems it was also found that the adverse consequences are significantly stronger among children at high genetic risk than among children at low genetic risk (Jaffee et al., 2005). In this study the experience of maltreatment was associated with an increase of 24% in the probability of diagnosable conduct disorder among children at high genetic risk, but an increase of only 2% among children at low genetic risk.

In our UK twin studies, we found that genetic influences contributed to hostility in the mother–child relationship. Furthermore, these genetic influences were correlated with those impacting on the youngster's conduct problems and cigarette use (Shelton et al., 2008). This suggests that genetic influences on problem behaviour can also adversely affect family environment. It is plausible that this can, in turn, lead to a worsening of problem behaviour, although this needs to be explored in longitudinal twin studies.

Studies based on genotypic information from participants in epidemiological or clinical samples have provided further evidence for gene–environment interplay in antisocial behaviour. A landmark paper from the *Dunedin Study* showed that genotypes can moderate the sensitivity of children to environmental insults (Caspi et al., 2002). Specifically, it was found that the (*MAOA-LPR*) polymorphism moderated the effect of experiences of childhood maltreatment. Maltreated boys with a genotype conferring low levels of *MAOA* expression were more likely to develop antisocial behaviour later in life. Among boys having the combination of the low-activity allele and severe maltreatment, 85% developed some form of antisocial outcome. They represented only 12% of the male birth cohort, but accounted for 44% of the violent convictions within it; they offended at a higher rate, on average, than other violent offenders in the cohort. It has been well recognized since Widom's important prospective study of children who had suffered verified abuse that progression to mental health difficulties, suicidal behaviour and/or offending against others is not invariable (Widom, 1989; Widom and Maxfield, 2001). The data from the *Dunedin Birth Cohort* provide some explanation for this.

These findings have been replicated and extended by findings from several other studies (Foley et al., 2004; Haberstick et al., 2005; Nilsson et al., 2006; Huang et al., 2004; Kim-Cohen et al., 2006; Frazzetto et al., 2007; McDermott et al., 2009; Weder et al., 2009). Kim-Cohen et al. (2006), after a meta-analysis of relevant studies, concluded that *MAOA* does influence vulnerability to environmental stress. Vanyukov et al. (2007) also reported evidence of gene–environment interaction, where the strength of association between parenting index and conduct and ADHD depended on the *MAOA–LPR* genotype. Unlike earlier findings, however, the parenting–risk relationships were observed for the high rather than low-activity genotypes. Ducci et al. (2008) have reported evidence of G×E with *MAOA* in women, where the *MAOA* low-activity allele was associated with alcoholism, particularly antisocial alcoholism, but only in women who had been sexually abused. Finally, Thapar et al. (2005) reported that early onset antisocial behaviour in a high-risk sample of children with ADHD is influenced by the adverse effects of prenatal risk, indexed by low birth weight, as well as *COMT* genotype, while, furthermore, youngsters with low birth weight as well as the 'val'-'val' genotype were most likely to display early onset antisocial behaviour.

Problem Use of Alcohol and Other Drugs

Substance dependency may involve a variety of pharmacological agents administered in different ways and for different purposes, but clinical symptoms consistently include tolerance, physiological dependence, loss of control over intake, preoccupation with substances, and continued use despite problems (see also chapter 18). Addictive substances are thought to activate and dysregulate a common brain reward circuit 'the reward pathway' (see below). Studies with animals as well as humans have indicated that the tolerance, dependence, dysphoria, and sensitization occurring with chronic substance use are associated with stable changes in the brain, including changes in gene expression, protein products, neurogenesis and synaptogenesis (Nestler, 2001; Kreek et al., 2005a,b). It is likely that variation in these changes accounts for some of the individual differences in response to repeated substance use. Although it is still a commonly held notion that alcohol and drug addiction are the result of 'lack of willpower', it is increasingly recognized that they are chronic relapsing disorders that, like other chronic diseases such as diabetes and asthma, benefit from physical and psychological interventions and require long-term relapse prevention (e.g. Koob et al., 2004; O'Brien, 2003; see also chapter 18). Social and health costs to the individual and society are high (Rice et al., 1990). There is a particularly strong association with antisocial behaviour (van den Bree et al., 1998a,b). The following discussion will cover advances in the genetics of hazardous alcohol and drug use generally, but with particular focus on their antisocial use.

Quantitative genetic studies of problem substance use

US based estimates of alcohol and drug dependence rates in the general population are between 8–14% and 3.5–7.5% (Kessler et al., 1994; Regier et al., 1990), but much higher amongst individuals with ASPD, when it is 70% for any alcohol diagnosis and 30–40% for any drug diagnosis (Lewis et al., 1983). While rates vary between countries, and over time, this relationship with ASPD is robust (see also chapter 18). A family history of alcohol or drug addiction is a potent risk factor for the development of drug disorders (Merikangas et al., 1998; Bierut et al., 1998). Siblings of alcohol dependent probands have higher rates not only of alcoholism but also of illicit drug addiction compared with siblings or controls. There is also evidence, however, for substance-specificity as siblings of marijuana dependent, probands have elevated risk of developing marijuana dependence while siblings of cocaine dependent probands have an increased risk of developing cocaine dependence. Despite familial clustering, most children of substance dependent parents do not develop problem use themselves (Goodwin, 1979; Cotton, 1979), underlining the complexity of the routes into addiction.

Alcohol

Most quantitative genetic studies of problem substance use have focused on alcoholism. A meta-analysis of twin and adoption studies reported that genetic influences explained 39–60% of the variation in alcoholism while shared environmental influences accounted for less (0–30%; Heath, 1995). There has generally been consistency in findings across studies, despite a wide range of assessment criteria, and no evidence for gender differences. A later meta-analysis of 50 family, twin and adoption studies of problem drinking and alcohol dependence (Walters, 2002) found a genetic influence of 20–26% after combining studies, but, here, gender and severity of abuse were found to be significant moderators; heritability in males with severe alcohol dependence was 30–36%. Evidence that genetic influences are lower among women has also been found in some later studies (Prescott et al., 2005), although not all (Whitfield et al., 2004; Heath et al., 1997). Pioneering studies on extent of use were conducted by Heath and co-workers in the 1990s (Heath et al., 1991a,b), who analysed abstinence and amount of alcohol consumption using the *Australian National Health and Medical Research Council Twin Register*. The results suggested that abstinence from alcohol was strongly influenced by shared environmental factors, with no evidence of genetic influences, while frequency and quantity of alcohol consumption were influenced by genetic factors. Some of us recently replicated these findings in the UK CaStANET sample; in adolescent twins, genetic factors were found to be stronger and shared environmental influences smaller for progression of alcohol use than for initiation (Fowler et al., 2007a), compatible with biological mechanisms being strong in maintenance of heavier substance use (van den Bree, 2005). In a further twist in the story, Whitfield et al. (2004), in a longitudinal twin study, found an important contribution of genetic influences to the consistency in alcohol intake over time; they also found overlap in genes influencing alcohol use and dependence. About 25% of the variation in alcohol dependence was attributable to genes that also affect

alcohol use, but a third due to genes not shared with use but unique to dependence.

Consistency in heritability estimates over time is in agreement with twin studies of alcoholism that have demonstrated consistency across different cohorts in findings on genetic influence, even when *per capita* alcohol consumption increases with economic changes (Heath, 1995; Kendler et al., 1997). The latter also reported that genetic factors accounted for 54% of the variation in alcohol abuse in men, with shared environmental influences accounting for another 14%. Similar findings have also been reported for other substances (Kendler et al., 2005), suggesting that changes in availability of substances have no major effects on estimated genetic influences.

Almost all adoption studies provide evidence of genetic influences, but there is less agreement on the extent of environmental influences. In the *Danish Adoption Study* (Goodwin et al., 1974), sons of alcoholic parents who had been given up for adoption in infancy were compared with their brothers who had been raised by their biological parents. Rates of alcoholism were high in both groups, 25% among adopted sons and 17% among sons remaining with their biological parents, suggesting that genetic factors may be more important than environmental ones. In the *Stockholm Adoption Study*, it was found that alcoholism in adoptees was correlated with alcoholism in their biological parents, presenting further evidence for genetic influences (Bohman, 1996; Cloninger et al., 1981; Cloninger et al., 1988). No such association was found with the adoptive parents, but rates of alcohol problems in the adoptive parents (as assessed from Temperance Board registration) were low.

Reports from the *Iowa Adoption Study* differed (Cadoret et al., 1985; Cadoret et al., 1987); they found associations between alcohol-related problems in adoptees and both biological and adoptive parents, suggesting both genetic and environmental influences.

Quantitative genetic studies have also provided evidence for different subtypes of alcoholism, with different genetic and environmental loadings. The *Stockholm Adoption Studies* (Cloninger et al., 1981; Cloninger et al., 1988) distinguished two types:

Cloninger Type 1, or milieu-limited alcoholism: characterized by relatively mild misuse, onset in adulthood, minimal criminality and a stronger influence of environmental factors (especially adoptive homes with low socioeconomic status).

Cloninger Type 2: alcoholism, generally with teenage onset, more heavy use, confined to males with co-occurring antisocial behaviour, and more heritable.

A study in which we assessed heritability estimates for several different classification systems for alcoholism in a male twin sample has subsequently indicated that type 2 alcoholism, which includes binge drinking and antisocial behaviour, is one of the more genetically influenced sub-types (h^2=0.54) (van den Bree et al., 1998). For Type 1 alcoholism, we found a heritability estimate of h^2=0.40.

The *Stockholm Adoption Study* also suggested that any genetic influences on criminal behaviour may be through different pathways, according to the nature of the crime. Bohman (1996) confirmed an association between alcoholism and repeated violent offences, whereas non-alcoholic criminals tended to commit a small number of petty property offences. The petty, non-alcoholic criminals tended to have biological parents with similar criminal histories but no alcoholism, while for the violent, alcoholic offenders risk of crime was correlated with the severity of their alcohol problems, but not with criminality in either biological or adoptive parents.

Illicit drugs

The small number of adoption studies into other problem drug use also indicates heterogeneity and that both genetic and environmental influences play a role (Boutros and Bowers, 1996; Cadoret et al., 1995b). In a sample of male and female adoptees, two genetic mechanisms were identified. Alcohol problems in the biological family of adoptees were found to contribute to risk for other drug abuse, while antisocial problems in biological relatives constituted a second, independent genetic risk factor, suggesting at least two genetic pathways to drug abuse. Environmental factors of divorce and psychiatric disturbances in the adoptive family were also associated with increased drug use. These results were replicated in a different sample of male adoptees only (Cadoret et al., 1995b). In a study exclusively of female adoptees, the second path, but not the first, was replicated, suggesting possible gender differences here (Cadoret et al., 1996).

The number of twin studies into illicit drug involvement is increasing. An excellent review of several large twin studies of use of alcohol, illicit drugs and/or other addictive agents showed that heritabilities may vary with drug, but are generally moderate to high, ranging from 0.39 (for hallucinogens) to 0.72 (for cocaine) (Goldman et al., 2005). The drug variability lies within its addictive properties; the most addictive substances (opiates and cocaine) were amongst the most heritable, while the less addictive substances, such as the hallucinogens, have a corresponding lower heritability. In our study of adult twin probands, who had been recruited through alcohol and drug treatment programmes, and their co-twins, we established heritability estimates for experimentation with a number of illicit drugs (sedatives, opioids, cocaine, stimulants and cannabis) on the one hand and *DSM* diagnoses relating to these same drugs on the other (van den Bree et al., 1998). We found greater variability in heritability estimates for experimentation with each of the individual drugs than for abuse and/or dependence on each drug. Combining information on all drugs into a single measure of 'any drug experimentation' or 'any drug

abuse and/or dependence', we found a higher heritability for the latter measure as well as a smaller influence of shared environmental factors; heritability estimates for any abuse and/or dependence were 0.79 for males and 0.47 for females, compared with 0.16 for males and 0.23 for females for any experimentation, providing further evidence that problem use is more strongly influenced by genetic mechanisms than experimentation. Shared environmental influences were small for 'any abuse and/or dependence' (0.09 for males, 0.04 for females, respectively), compared to 'any experimental use' (0.61 for males, 0.69 for females). These findings are in line with those of other twin studies of illicit drug involvement in adults (Kendler, 2001), as well as our own studies of marijuana use in adolescent twins (Fowler et al., 2007).

Studies in males of the population-based *Virginia Twin Sample* have reported similar heritabilities for any illicit drug use (0.27) and problem use (0.74 for abuse; 0.65 for dependence) (Kendler et al., 2000). For females in the *Virginia Twin Sample*, only cannabis and cocaine use were examined, providing heritabilities of use of around 0.40 for both substances, and, again, stronger genetic influences for heavier use (0.70–0.80), with no evidence for shared environmental influences. Studies in male twins of the *Vietnam Era Twin Register Study* have yielded somewhat lower heritability estimates and greater shared environmental influences, reporting that abuse of marijuana, stimulants, sedatives, opiates and psychedelics is influenced by genetic factors (from 30% to 50%) as well as shared environmental factors (between 13% and 29%) (Tsuang et al., 1996; Tsuang et al., 1998).

Studies which examine males and females separately include the population-based *Virginia Twin Sample* work by Kendler et al. (2000), who found that heritability was similar by sex, although a more restricted range of substances was examined among the women (males: 0.27 any/problem illicit drug use, 0.74 abuse, 0.65 for dependence; females: cannabis use 0.40, heavy use 0.70, cocaine use 0.40, heavy use 0.80), with no evidence for shared environmental influences. Studies with adolescents have, however, suggested stronger genetic influences in males than females (Hopfer et al., 2003; McGue et al., 2001; Miles et al., 2002), as did work with a treatment-based sample of adult twins (van den Bree et al., 1998), but female sample sizes have tended to be smaller. One population-based sample of young adult twins found that genetic factors were more important contributors to cannabis dependence in men than women (Lynskey et al., 2002). These authors suggested that drug dependent females may have a greater degree of genetic or shared environmental risk factors than drug dependent males. Age at investigation has to be taken into account in interpreting results of twin analyses in this area (Hopfer et al., 2003; Koopmans and Boomsa, 1996; Rose et al., 2001). Genetic influences appear stronger the older the sample, suggesting the possibility that some genetic influences have delayed effects.

Comorbid problem use of different substances is common, raising the question whether the same genetic and shared environmental influences may increase risk of use/abuse of multiple substances.

In the *Vietnam Era Twin Study*, Tsuang et al. (1998) found that, in males, marijuana abuse, more than abuse of other drugs, was influenced by shared environmental factors, and that each category of drug, except psychedelics, also had unique genetic influences, not shared with other drug categories, with heroin misuse most genetically influenced. Kendler et al. (2003a) also conducted a study in male twins and found that the genetic and shared environmental effects on risk for use and misuse of illicit drugs were largely or entirely non-specific, while a common genetic factor had a strong influence on all drugs. Environmental experiences unique to the person largely determined whether predisposed individuals used or misused one class of psychoactive substance or another. Using a discordant co-twin design, Lynskey et al. (2003) reported that individuals who used cannabis by age 17 years had 2–3 times the risk of going on to other drug use – whether alcohol or illicit drugs – than their co-twin who did not use cannabis before age 17 years, suggestive of unique environmental influence. Karkowski et al. (2000), using the Kendler registry, found that females appeared similar to males in this respect. An extension of this work included both licit and illicit drug dependence (cannabis, cocaine, alcohol, caffeine, and nicotine) by both sexes (Kendler et al., 2007). Findings indicated there are two genetic factors – one predisposing largely to licit drug dependence and one to illicit drug dependence; evidence was for quite large specific genetic influences on both nicotine and caffeine dependence.

Studies in adolescent twins have also provided evidence of a common predisposition to use of different substances, but in contrast to studies in adults, this factor may be most influenced by shared environment (Han et al., 1999).

Taken together, these results suggest that genetic factors play an important role in the abuse of or dependence on a range of drugs, while shared environmental factors may be more important in co-occurrence of the use of different substances in adolescents. There is also, however, evidence that the associations between early drug use and later use and abuse/dependence cannot be entirely explained by genetic or shared environmental factors, but that unique environmental experiences are important too.

Comorbidity of antisocial behaviour and substance use/abuse

The extensive comorbidity between antisocial behaviour and substance addiction has raised questions about possible shared genetic influences (van den Bree et al., 1998). The Stockholm adoption studies (Bohman, 1996; Cloninger et al., 1981, 1988) were among the first to present evidence of a subtype of severe problem substance use comorbid with ASPD (Type 2 alcoholism), supported by later studies. In one of the two pathways to drug abuse described by the Cadoret group (Boutros and Bowers, 1996; Cadoret et al., 1995b), antisocial behaviour in biological relatives was found to be an important factor. Indeed, in a later adoption study, they showed that risk for problem drug use in adoptees was elevated when at least one biological parent had both ASPD and problem substance use (Langbehn et al., 2003). These adoptees were at increased risk not only compared to adoptees with no biological risk, but also adoptees with either a biological background for substance problems only or antisocial personality only, suggesting the combination of antisocial and substance problems may be particularly genetically influenced.

In adolescent twins, some of us have found that conduct problems and marijuana use share genetic influences, while environmental influences tend to be more specific to these problems individually (Miles et al., 2002). In another multivariate study of adolescent twins, in whom conduct problems, ADHD, substance experimentation and novelty seeking were assessed, a common underlying factor with a heritability of 0.84 was found, but no evidence at all of shared environmental influences on this factor (Young et al., 2000), suggesting these adolescent problem behaviours may co-occur mainly because of a common underlying genetic risk. There was some evidence, however, of shared environmental effects on the relationship between conduct disorder and substance experimentation specifically. Other adolescent twin studies, such as the *Minnesota Twin Study*, have similarly suggested that, like antisocial behaviour, problem substance misuse is best construed as a form of externalized problem behaviour, and that transmission of such behaviours in families occurs as a general vulnerability rather than being disorder specific, again highly heritable (0.80; Hicks et al., 2004). This conclusion built on their earlier, similar work with multivariate twin models, which had also shown a single highly heritable externalising factor (0.81), with no effect from shared environmental factors (Krueger et al., 2002). In addition, however, some phenotype-specific influences were present, that is, there was evidence for a shared environmental factor specific to conduct problems and a genetic factor specific for the personality trait of disinhibition. In adults, twin studies of antisocial behaviour and problem alcohol use have produced similar results. Slutske et al. (1998) reported that over 70% of the association between retrospectively reported childhood conduct disorder and a history of alcohol dependence was accounted for by genetic factors, the rest being due to non-shared environmental factors. Fu et al. (2002), using the *Vietnam Era Twin Registry*, reported that the genetic effects on ASPD were also a major risk factor for other psychiatric traits, accounting for 50% of the total genetic variance in risk for alcohol dependence, 58% for marijuana dependence and 38% for major depression. They also found that the genetic correlations between major depression and both alcohol dependence and marijuana dependence were largely explained by genetic effects on ASPD, although some effects specific to major depression and alcohol dependence remained.

Kendler et al. (2003b) fitted twin models to psychiatric syndromes in both externalizing (e.g. ASPD) and internalizing behavioural domains (e.g. anxiety, depression). They reported evidence of two genetic factors, with no gender differences: one loaded more strongly on to externalizing disorders and the second on to the internalizing disorders. There were, however, also substantial disorder-specific genetic risk factors for alcohol and drug dependence. Shared environmental factors were most pronounced for conduct disorder and adult antisocial behaviour. They concluded that lifetime comorbidity of common substance use and psychiatric disorders, whether externalizing or internalizing, is mainly under the influence of genetic risk factors.

In contrast, many studies of adolescents suggest that associations between substance use and externalizing problems during adolescence are largely attributable to shared environmental influences (Rose et al., 2004; Knopik et al., 2009). Researchers using the *Minnesota Twin Family Study* have conducted longitudinal analyses to elucidate the relationships between problem behaviour in youth and externalizing psychopathology in adulthood. McGue et al. (2006) assessed relationships between an early problem behaviour factor (use of alcohol, tobacco, and illicit drugs; sexual intercourse; and police contact before age 15) and an adulthood 'disinhibitory psychopathology' factor (antisocial behaviour, nicotine dependence, and abuse and dependence on alcohol and drugs at age 20). They confirmed earlier reports that early adolescent problem behaviour is weakly heritable (c. 20%), with a greater influence of shared environmental factors, but that 'disinhibitory psychopathology' in adulthood was strongly heritable (c. 75%). Furthermore, the phenotypic correlation between early adolescent problem behaviour and later disinhibitory psychopathology was strong (approximately 0.60), accounted for primarily by genetic factors common to the two domains.

Molecular genetic studies of problem substance use

In spite of strong indications of genetic influences on problem substance use, molecular genetic studies have been almost as slow to take off as in the area of antisocial behaviour, perhaps partly because of a continued preference by public and professionals alike for taking a moral perspective over endorsing a disease model. The research picture is now, however, changing, with growth in number of studies and evidence of replicated findings, some of which appear to be specific to the antisocial problem user subgroup.

For alcohol dependence and related phenotypes, such as alcohol severity or withdrawal, linkage findings have been reported for regions on chromosomes 1, 2, 3, 4, 6, 7, 11, 12, 15 and 16 (see reviews, van den Bree, 2005; Ducci and Goldman, 2008; Gelernter and Kranzler, 2009). Candidate genes close to some of these regions include a γ-aminobutyric acid receptor (GABA$_A$) gene cluster and genes for alcohol dehydrogenase (ADH), on chromosome 4p and 4q respectively, and, on chromosome 11, the dopamine D4 receptor (DRD4) and tyrosine hydroxylase (TH). In a recent GWA study in males with early-onset alcoholism, with follow-up genotyping in an independent sample, Treutlein et al. (2009) found evidence for associations with regions on chromosome 4 (in which *alcohol dehydrogenase 1C (ADH1C)* is located), as well as chromosome 2. The *peroxisomal trans-2-enoyl-CoA reductase (PECR)* gene resides in the latter region, which seems to be a key enzyme of fatty acid metabolism.

There is some overlap with potential candidates with respect to illicit drug abuse or dependence. One study of drug abusers reported 41 potential candidates, including regions on chromosomes 3, 4 (where the ADH locus resides), 10, 11 (where the *Brain-Derived Neurotrophic Factor (BDNF)* locus resides), 12 and X (Uhl et al., 2001). *BDNF* plays an important role in nervous system development and function, by helping to support the survival of existing neurons, and encourage the growth and differentiation of new neurons and synapses.

A number of studies have related to a specific drug. A study on cocaine dependence, and other involvement with cocaine, has reported evidence for linkage on chromosomes 9, 12 and 18 and suggestive linkage on chromosome 10 and 3 (Gelernter et al., 2005), while a genome-wide linkage study of opioid dependence identified a region on chromosome 14q in a region encompassing the *neurexin 3 gene (NRXN3)* (Lachman et al., 2007). Nielsen et al. (2008) conducted a GWA study of heroin addiction followed by further analyses with a combination of the three most significant variants. One genotype pattern of these unlinked alleles was associated with development of heroin addiction while another combination of these same genotypes was found to protect from developing heroin addiction. Findings also pointed to involvement of the *opioid receptor μ1 (OPRM1)* locus (see below) in heroin addiction.

Drgon et al. (2010) conducted a GWA study to identify chromosomal regions and genes which, when taken together, might confer vulnerability to substance dependence. They identified a number of chromosomal regions containing genes related to 'cell adhesion', which they described as 'processes whereby neurons recognize and respond to features of their environments that are important in establishing and maintaining proper connections' (Uhl, Drgon et al. 2008), as well as genes that are likely to be readily targeted and modulated by pharmacotherapeutic drugs.

Li et al. (2008) trawled widely in a quest for relevant single genes and chromosomal areas implicated in substance misuse. They collected 2,343 items of evidence on this from peer-reviewed publications of single-gene strategies, microarray, proteomics, or genetic studies and identified 1500 human addiction-related genes, as well as 18 statistically significant enriched molecular pathways. Five of these were found to be common to many addictive drugs, possibly contributing to their rewarding and addictive properties. They postulated a molecular network for drug addiction, including the neurotransmitters glutamate and dopamine, and a number of secondary messengers, signal pathways and factors associated with gene expression and secretion.

Candidate gene studies

The genes that have received most attention in molecular genetic studies of alcohol and drug addiction to date are those involved in substance metabolism and the reward pathway.

Genes involved in substance metabolism

The enzymes alcohol dehydrogenase (ADH) and aldehyde dehydrogenase (ALDH) are responsible for the oxidative metabolism of alcohol/ethanol. ADH metabolizes ethanol to acetaldehyde, a toxic substance, which is converted to acetate by ALDH. These enzymes are encoded by the genes *alcohol dehydrogenase1B* (*ADH1B*) and *aldehyde dehydrogenase2* (*ALDH2*) (Enoch, 2003). Following alcohol consumption, individuals with higher activity of *ADH1B* (associated with increased synthesis of acetaldehyde) or lower activity of *ALDH2* (associated with decreased rates of conversion of acetaldehyde to acetate) will be particularly prone to the unpleasant side effects of acetaldehyde, including facial flushing, nausea and dysphoria. This reaction serves to protect against development of alcoholism (Murayama et al., 1998). Functional loci in *ADH1B* and *ALDH2* have been associated with alcohol dependence (Luczak et al., 2006), but the prevalence of specific variants depends on the population. A non-functional *ALDH2* variant is confined to certain Asian populations, while an *ADH1B* variant is common in African Americans, but rare in people of European ancestry. Thus, the relationship with risk of alcoholism will differ in different ethnic groups.

In addition, genes coding for cytochrome P450 enzymes have been studied in relation to addiction. The function of these enzymes is to catalyse the oxidation of toxins. The genes coding for the cytochrome p450 enzyme 2E1 and enzyme 2D6 have been associated with risk of alcohol and opioid dependence, respectively. Individuals with two non-functional alleles at the latter gene are poor at metabolizing oral opiates, which may be protective against opioid addiction (Tyndale et al., 1997).

Genes involved in the reward pathway

The rewarding properties of drugs of addiction are thought to result from neuropharmacological actions on a common brain reward circuit (Leshner and Koob, 1999). This reward circuitry is essential to survival of the species by reinforcing behaviours such as eating, sexual intercourse, exercise, social

interaction, and procedural and emotional learning and memory (Nestler, 2005), but it can be hijacked by substances with addictive properties and become dysfunctional. The pathway involves the mesolimbic dopamine system, which conveys signals from the ventral tegmentum area in the midbrain to the nucleus accumbens in the striatal region and glutamatergic inputs on the striatum coming from the amygdala, the hippocampus and the frontal cortex (Chao and Nestler, 2004). Additional neurotransmitter systems interact at various points along the mesolimbic dopaminergic pathway, thereby modulating its activity, including the gamma aminobutyric acid (GABA), opioid, serotonergic, and noradrenergic systems (Kreek et al., 2002a,b). Although the initial targets and actions vary for each specific substance, they share many features after addiction has occurred.

Molecular genetic evidence is currently most strong for genes influencing dopamine, serotonin, and GABA neurotransmission as well as the MAO, COMT opioid, cannabinoid systems, and stress hormones, each of which will be briefly detailed in turn.

Specific gene involvement

Dopaminergic neurotransmission

Polymorphisms in the dopamine D2 receptor gene (*DRD2*, chromosome 11) have been associated with alcoholism and addiction to various illicit drugs (Kreek et al., 2005a; Ho et al., 2010). Gelernter and Kranzler (2009), however, have suggested these accounts may be explained by linkage disequilibrium with adjacent alleles, which may directly affect risk.

A repeat polymorphism in the dopamine D4 receptor gene (*DRD4*, chromosome 11) has been associated with novelty seeking (Ebstein et al., 1996), as well as with alcohol craving, alcoholism and illicit drug addiction (Kreek et al., 2004; Ho et al., 2010).

Associations have also been reported between the dopamine transporter gene (*DAT*, or *SLC6A3*, chromosome 5) and alcoholism, as well as cocaine dependence, and cocaine- and amphetamine-induced psychosis (Kreek et al., 2005b; Ho et al., 2010). A haplotype of two polymorphisms at the *dopamine β-hydroxylase* gene (*DBH*, chromosome 9), which is involved in the biotransformation of dopamine into norepinephrine, has been associated with cocaine-induced paranoia (Kreek et al., 2004).

Serotonergic neurotransmission

Studies in animals and humans have suggested that changes in central serotonin neurotransmission affect alcohol intake (LeMarquand et al., 1994a,b). Reduced central serotonin neurotransmission may be specifically associated with type 2 or antisocial subtypes of alcoholism (Hill et al., 1999).

A polymorphism at *5-HT1B* has been associated with alcoholism and antisocial alcoholism, as has a polymorphism in the TH gene, while a *serotonin receptor 2A* (*5-HT2A*) polymorphism has been implicated in impulsivity and in alcohol intake (Kreek et al., 2004). *SERT* has also been related to different aspects of alcoholism as well as heroin addiction (Kreek et al., 2004; Kreek et al., 2005a; Ho et al., 2010).

TPH1 and *TPH2* have also been implicated in alcohol as well as heroin dependence (Ho et al. 2010).

Gamma aminobutyric acid (GABA) neurotransmission

GABA is the primary inhibitory neurotransmitter in the central nervous system. $GABA_A$ receptor-mediated chloride currents into neurons are facilitated by a number of drugs, including ethanol, benzodiazepines and barbiturates. $GABA_A$ *receptor* genes α1 (*GABRA1*, chromosome 5), α2 (*GABRA2*, chromosome 4), α6 (*GABRA6*, chromosome 5), β1 (*GABBR1*, chromosome 4), β2 (*GABBR2*, chromosome 9) and γ2 (*GABRG2*, chromosome 5) have all been associated with sensitivity to alcohol, alcoholism and/or antisocial alcoholism (Kreek et al., 2004; Ducci and Goldman, 2008; Gelernter and Kranzler, 2009; Ho et al., 2010).

Monoamine oxidase (MAO)

Type 2 alcoholism may be associated with low platelet MAO activity (Virkkunen et al., 1993; Knorring et al., 1985) and polymorphisms in *MAOA* have been associated with alcoholism, early onset alcoholism/abuse and antisocial alcoholism (Kreek et al., 2004).

Catechol-O-methyl transferase (COMT)

The 'val'/'met' polymorphism has been implicated in alcohol intake, type 1 alcoholism, early onset alcoholism, and drug addiction (Kreek et al., 2004; Ho et al., 2010). There has been some inconsistency, however, on which allele is associated with increased risk of addiction. Ducci and Goldman (2008), have suggested this may be explained by the co-occurrence of other psychopathology in the samples under study, where an association with the 'val' (or warrior) allele is more likely to be seen among people who score high on externalizing behaviour scales, such as polysubstance abusers (Vandenbergh et al., 1997), while an association with the 'met' (or worrier) allele may be found particularly in addicted populations with high frequencies of internalizing disorders, such as late-onset alcoholics and social drinkers (Tiihonen et al., 1999; Kauhanen et al., 2000). In a review, however, Tammimaki and Mannisto (2010) concluded that, although there are reports indicating a positive association with *COMT* polymorphisms and addiction, most studies have failed to detect such a link.

Opioidergic and cannabinoid neurotransmission

The opioidergic system is involved in many neuroendocrine functions, including stress responses and possibly affective, cognitive and eating disorders. Medications currently used for opiate addiction have their effect by acting directly on opioid receptors (Kreek et al., 2002b), while naltrexone, which is a μ and κ opioid receptor antagonist, is used in the treatment of alcoholism. A genetic explanation is quite well evidenced; polymorphisms in the μ1 (*OPRM1*, chromosome 6), κ1 (*OPRK1*, chromosome 8) and σ1 (*OPRD1*, chromosome 1) opioid receptors have been implicated in alcoholism and/or drug addiction (Ho et al., 2010), while *OPRM1* has also been reported to be related to variation in response to naltrexone in alcoholism (Kranzler et al., 1998; Oslin et al., 2003; Anton et al., 2008; Oroszi et al., 2009; Ho et al., 2010).

The *cannabinoid receptor1* gene (*CNR1*, chromosome 6) has also been associated with alcohol and other drug addiction, together with symptoms of delirium in alcohol withdrawal (Comings et al., 1997; Schmidt et al., 2002; Zhang et al., 2004; Zuo et al., 2007; Proudnikov et al., 2010).

Interpretation of the findings in this group, however, may be complicated by epistasis. Lopez-Moreno et al. (2010) have provided evidence that endogenous cannabinoid and opioid systems interact, and stress the importance of taking variation in *CNR1* into account when examining associations between addiction phenotypes and *OPRM1,* and *vice versa.*

Stress hormones

Neuropeptide Y (*NPY*) is involved in anxiety, reward, appetite and energy balance. The *NPY Pro7* allele (chromosome 7) has been implicated in alcohol intake, alcohol dependence and type 1 and type 2 alcoholism.

Gene–environment interplay and problem substance use

Gene–environment interplay is inevitably important in understanding addiction. After all, individuals who are at genetic risk would never develop problem substance use in societies where addictive substances are not available. In addition, in societies where certain substances, such as alcohol, are readily available, most users do not become dependent. Gene–environment interactions have not, however, so far been studied extensively in relation to human addictions, although there has been some improvement in this situation. Much of the basic understanding comes from animal models.

Studies with animals have indicated not only that stressors have an effect on substance use, withdrawal and relapse but also that some individuals may be genetically more vulnerable to these influences than others. In mice lacking a receptor involved in the corticotropin-releasing system, which mediates endocrine and behavioural responses to stress, exposure to social or physical stress leads to progressively increasing alcohol intake (Sillaber et al., 2002). The effects of repeated stress on drinking alcohol were found to persist throughout life. In animals, too, it has been shown that social stress associated with aggressive confrontations has persistent effects on cocaine self-administration, possibly by dysregulation of dopaminergic pathways in the brain (Miczek et al., 2004). In monkeys, major early life stress, such as removal from mother, has been found to increase risk of drinking to intoxication as well as impulsivity and aggression, but particularly so in individuals with low-expressing serotonin transporter genotypes (Barr et al., 2004).

For humans, we have already indicated the value of differentiating Cloninger type 1 and type 2 alcoholism, with the relative insensitivity to early environmental factors of the latter combination of externalizing behaviours (Cloninger et al., 1981; Sigvardsson et al., 1996). Type 1, the more pure form of alcoholism, is more complex, with more gene–environment interaction. According to adoption studies, environmental adversity such as conflict or psychopathology in the adoptive family, may add to the risk of alcoholism particularly for individuals with a genetic predisposition to it (Cutrona et al., 1994).

An early report of gene–environment interaction came from a twin study by Heath et al. (1989), who found that the genetic influence on alcohol consumption was greater in unmarried than married women. Legrand et al. (1999), also in a twin study, examined genetic factors – parental substance use disorder – and environmental risk exposure – engagement with peers likely either to encourage or discourage substance use. Parental and environmental factors at age 11 independently predicted earlier (by age 14) and more substance use; in addition, however, good environmental qualities, such as positive peer pressure, were protective even in the presence of family risk. Carrying both parental and environmental risk factors had more than a simple additive effect on substance use. Evidence for gene–environment correlations in adolescent alcohol use comes from our own UK work with twins (Fowler et al., 2007b). We found a genetic influence on whether adolescents have alcohol using friends, as well as overlap between these genes and the ones influencing adolescents' own alcohol use.

In addition to behavioural genetic studies, there are a number of molecular genetic studies in which gene–environment interaction has been evaluated. As explained earlier, lower activity of *ALDH2* can protect against alcoholism in Asian populations, but Higuchi et al. (1994) have observed an increasing number of heterozygotes amongst alcoholic patients, a finding they attributed to changes in sociocultural factors, in particular increased social pressure on Japanese men to drink after work.

Several studies have focused on interactions between vulnerability-increasing genotypes and stressful/adverse life experiences. Madrid et al. (2001), for example, reported that stress may mediate the association between the *DRD2* and alcoholism, while Enoch et al. (2010) reported that substance dependence may be influenced by interactions between childhood trauma and *GABRA2* variation. Other accounts include findings of interactions between: the *MAOA-LPR 3-repeat* allele, quality of family relations and maltreatment in the development of alcohol dependence (Nilsson et al., 2006); the *MAOA-LPR 3-repeat* allele and childhood sexual abuse with later antisocial alcoholism (but not alcoholism in general) (Ducci et al., 2008); and

CRHR1 and negative life events and heavy alcohol use in adolescents (Blomeyer et al., 2008).

The *5HTTLPR S*-allele has been reported to interact with various measures of adversity, such as low maternal care, poor family relationships, maltreatment and negative life events, to increase risk of alcohol or drug misuse (Nilsson et al., 2005; Covault et al., 2007; Kaufman et al., 2007; Gerra et al., 2010), but such findings have not invariably been replicated, and there is some contrary evidence. Laucht et al. (2009), for example, found that individuals homozygous for the higher expression L allele reported more hazardous drinking, when exposed to high psychosocial adversity.

In interpreting these findings, it is important to keep in mind that most are based on small sample sizes, and that many may represent false positives (Flint and Munafo, 2008). Thus, replication is essential. In addition, candidate genes tend to be selected because they have yielded positive findings in linkage or GWA studies, but in samples where there is very low exposure to the relevant environmental risk factor, the most relevant genes are unlikely to emerge.

Genetics of Schizophrenia

Schizophrenia is a psychiatric disease, or perhaps cluster of diseases, characterized by distortions of thinking and perception together with inappropriate or blunted affect in a state of clear consciousness (World Health Organization, 1992). It often runs a chronic and, not uncommonly, deteriorating course. Cognitive and/or behavioural signs may be present in early childhood, but the more typical features tend to become established in adolescence or early adulthood. There is consensus that schizophrenia is, at least in part, neurodevelopmental (Weinberger, 1995). At the structural level, there are reductions in neuropil and neuronal size that are widespread but not uniform, with temporal lobe structures, notably the hippocampus, particularly affected (Harrison 1999; see also chapter 12). These changes, in turn, probably result from alterations in synaptic, dendritic and axonal organization (Harrison 1999). At the functional level, accumulating evidence also implicates altered glutamate neurotransmission in addition to 'classical' hyperdopaminergic explanations (Moghaddam, 2003). A number of risk factors have been identified in epidemiological studies (Murray et al., 2003), but, in many instances, the direction of causation is unclear. Most risk factors do not suggest particular pathological mechanisms, and in all cases the relative risks are small compared with those conferred by close genetic relatedness to a person who has already manifest the disease.

Epidemiological studies since 1990 have consistently shown a small but significant association between schizophrenia and violence; there are also data which link it with crime more generally (see chapter 14). In 1993, Bina Coid and colleagues reported on possibly common heritable factor/factors. They studied the lifetime psychiatric and criminal histories of 280 twin probands with a diagnosis of major functional psychosis, recruited in England 1948–88 (*The Maudsley Twin Series*), and of their 210 co-twins, a third of whom had similar diagnoses. Among 220 complete twin pairs, significantly more probands (25.7%) than co-twins (14.0%) had been convicted; men with schizophrenia were significantly more likely to have been so than those with affective psychosis. The authors concluded that the results did not support 'a substantial independent genetic basis for criminal behaviour' among people with psychosis. They also found a significant temporal correlation between onset of illness and onset of offending, with first offending post-dating the first psychiatric contact in nearly two-thirds of cases, echoed in the small number of specifically violent offenders (Taylor and Hodgins, 1994). This study is now 30 years old. Subsequent work has suggested that there are two main patterns in the association between schizophrenia and violence (see also chapter 14). In the first, a person has generally been unremarkable until the onset of the illness, and a direct relationship between the illness and the violence is likely. Coid's twin study had probably mainly captured people of this kind. In the second group, there is strong evidence of conduct and/or major emotional disorders in childhood, co-terminous with personality disorder as an adult, together with a developing schizophreniform psychosis. People in this group are particularly likely also to abuse substances, and the violence is less likely to be directly related to psychotic symptoms. The question arises as to whether, for them, the genetic and environmental factors underpinning crime/violence and disease relationships are best considered within the antisocial behaviour and substance misuse framework and only the 'pure' psychotic disorder groups within the schizophrenia framework.

As a separate issue, Boutros and Bowers (1996) reviewed the role of substance abuse, including psychostimulants, hallucinogens, cannabis, and possibly industrial inhalants, in increasing the risk of psychosis, taken up again more recently, especially with respect to cannabis (reviews: Arseneault et al., 2004; Moore et al., 2007), with high potency cannabis shown to put people especially at risk (Di Forti et al., 2009). A recent study has reported that a functional polymorphism in the *COMT* gene may moderate the effect of adolescent-onset cannabis use on adult psychosis (Caspi et al., 2005). The results indicated that carriers of the 'val' allele (who have higher enzymatic activity and a greater breakdown rate of dopamine in synapses) may have an increased risk compared to those with the 'met' allele.

Quantitative genetic studies of schizophrenia

Family, twin and adoption studies all provide evidence that the risk of developing schizophrenia has a large genetic contribution. Family studies have indicated that offspring of a schizophrenic parent have an increased risk of schizophrenia as well as schizophrenia spectrum disorders (Gottesman, 1991; Erlenmeyer-Kimling et al., 1997). Sullivan et al. (2003) found that heritability estimates were over 50% in 10 of 12 previously published twin studies, with evidence of shared environmental influences showing in seven. Meta-analysis of these studies yielded a heritability estimate of 81%, and a significant but much smaller shared environmental influence (11%). Cardno et al. (1999), with the *Maudsley Twin Series*, found that heritability was over 80% for schizoaffective disorder and affective psychosis as well. A large study of Finnish twins found no evidence of gender-specific differences in magnitudes of genetic influences (Cannon et al., 1998). Adoption studies, using both the adoptees' study method and the adoptees' relatives method, have provided further support for high heritability of schizophrenia and schizoaffective disorder (Kringlen, 1991, for a review; Tienari et al., 2000; Ingraham and Kety, 2000). The latter study also reported rates of latent schizophrenia to be higher in the biological relatives of adoptees with schizophrenia (10.8%) than those without (1.7%), support for Bleuler's (1911) original hypothesis that relatives of patients with schizophrenia would have an increased risk of similar but less severe illness.

Molecular genetic studies of schizophrenia

Results of linkage studies with schizophrenia were not initially compelling. Attempts to replicate them failed. Gradually, with reporting of 20 genome-wide linkage studies and increase in sample sizes and power, several strong and well-established regions have emerged as linked to schizophrenia (reviewed in O'Donovan et al., 2003). Association analysis has become the main method for elucidating the situation further; most studies have focused on specific candidate genes. Such genes are defined either by their physical location within a region previously identified by linkage analysis – positional candidates – and/or because the function of their protein product fits into a proposed model explaining the physiology of schizophrenia – hypothesis-driven candidates. While a number of candidate gene association studies have yielded positive evidence for association with schizophrenia (Chumakov et al., 2002; Shifman et al., 2002; Chowdari et al., 2002; Straub et al., 2002), almost all of them have yielded ambiguous results. In general, this is because most of them have modest sample sizes and, thus, limited statistical power, so later independent studies do not replicate earlier findings (Alaerts et al., 2009). In addition, candidate gene selection is generally hampered by our general ignorance of the biological underpinnings of schizophrenia. For genetic studies, this means that there are thousands of potential candidate genes for schizophrenia, and so the prior odds of one being a true susceptibility locus are low.

In the late 2000s, a number of developments have allowed genome-wide association studies (GWAS) to become routine. The several GWAS published have each followed a slightly different design, and each is thus differently powered for detection of the susceptibility genes. First, Sullivan et al. (2008) analysed a total of 650,000 SNPs in a sample of 738 cases and 733 controls. This study was underpowered for detecting risk alleles of small effect, so its failure to identify any markers that met criteria for genome-wide significance did little more than confirm that schizophrenia risk alleles are likely to impart a very small risk to carriers. Next, O'Donovan et al. (2008) dealt with some of these limitations by analysing data from over 16,000 people, obtaining strong evidence for an association ($p = 1.61 \times 10^{-7}$) which implicated 'zinc finger protein 804a' (*ZNF804A*) on chromosome 2 as a susceptibility gene for schizophrenia.

The Molecular Genetics of Schizophrenia Consortium has performed GWAS on 2681 cases and 2653 controls of European descent and also 1286 cases and 973 controls of African American origin. No SNPs exceeded their threshold for genome-wide significance (Shi et al., 2009). With a slightly larger sample of 3322 cases and 3587 controls from Europe, however, the International Schizophrenia Consortium was more successful with such methodology, identifying evidence of significant association at two independent loci: the *myosin XVIIIB* (*MYO18B*) gene ($p = 3.4 \times 10^{-7}$) on chromosome 22 and the major histocompatibility complex (MHC) region on chromosome 6 (Purcell et al., 2009). At about the same time, though, despite using a large sample (1,500, 2,663 cases and 13,498 controls from Europe), the *SGENE-plus Consortium* initially failed to identify any markers that exceeded their threshold of genome-wide significance (Stefansson et al., 2009). In a larger sample, including an additional 4,000 cases and 15,555 controls, and analysing the top 1,500 SNPs, the group was able to identify genome-wide evidence for association at the *neurogranin* (*NGRN*) locus on chromosome 11 ($p = 5.0 \times 10^{-7}$), and again at the MHC locus. The strongest evidence from GWAS, however, was obtained from bringing all three studies together into a larger sample still: 12,945 European cases and 34,591 European controls. Then, significant evidence emerged for association with schizophrenia at the MHC locus ($p = 1.4 \times 10^{-12}$), *NGRN* ($p = 2.4 \times 10^{-9}$), and, in addition, at the *transcription factor 4* (*TCF4*) locus on chromosome 18 ($p = 4.1 \times 10^{-9}$) (Stefansson et al., 2009). These findings provide an unprecedented insight into the molecular pathogenesis of schizophrenia. In particular the MHC findings are consistent with there being an immune component to risk of schizophrenia, while the associations at *NRGN* and *TCF4* indicate the importance of molecular pathways involved in brain development, memory and cognition.

Since 2000, molecular studies have revealed that our genomes carry many segments that are susceptible to deletion, duplication or complex rearrangements (Redon et al., 2006). Collectively, these segments are called copy number variants (CNVs) and can encompass none, one or even a large number of contiguous genes. Analysis of schizophrenia cohorts has yielded strong evidence that some CNVs can increase risk of developing schizophrenia. Individuals who carry a small interstitial deletion at chromosome 22q11 have an approximately 20–30-fold increase

in risk of psychosis, especially schizophrenia (Murphy et al., 1999; Papolos et al., 1996; Pulver et al., 1994; Shprintzen et al., 1992). Similarly, a balanced reciprocal translocation between the long arms of chromosomes 1 and 11 has been shown to co-segregate with schizophrenia and other psychiatric disorders in a single Scottish family (Blackwood et al., 2001). The breakpoint site on chromosome 1 physically disrupts a gene which, because of its unknown function, was named 'disrupted in schizophrenia 1' (*DISC1*) (Millar et al., 2000). While the pathogenic mechanisms in this family remain unknown, subsequent molecular studies have implicated the *DISC1* protein as well as its binding partners in mechanisms important in brain development (Fatemi et al., 2008; Pickard et al., 2007).

More recently, the application of techniques that allow the detection of CNVs at a higher resolution has revealed further evidence that some rare CNVs increase risk of developing schizophrenia. First, two independent studies identified deletions intersecting the *neurexin 1* gene (*NRXN1*), located at chromosome 2p16.3, in schizophrenia cases (Walsh et al., 2008; Kirov et al., 2008). These findings were particularly intriguing as the NRXN1 protein plays a vital role in GABAergic and glutamatergic synaptic differentiation (Craig and Kang, 2007), making it an excellent candidate for schizophrenia. These were followed by the simultaneous publication of two more studies, both of which identified CNVs at 22q11.21, 1q21.1 and 15q13.3 to be significantly associated with schizophrenia (Stefansson et al., 2008; the International Schizophrenia Consortium, 2000). In addition, one study identified significant enrichment of CNVs at 15q11.22 (Stefansson et al., 2008). All of these regions harbour a large number of contiguous genes; however, while not reported as part of the main findings, both of these studies also identified a predominance of rare deletions at the *NRXN1* locus in people with schizophrenia (Kirov et al., 2009). In addition, by carefully collating several large datasets, two studies have now demonstrated that people with schizophrenia carry a highly significant excess of CNVs at both chromosomes 16p13 ($p = 0.0001$) and 16p11 ($p = 4.8 \times 10^{-7}$) (Ingason et al., 2011; McCarthy et al., 2009).

The evidence just described is intriguing, but it is important to note that these genes should be considered risk factors for schizophrenia and not highly penetrant Mendelian mutations. In addition, it is typically seen that the CNVs showing association with schizophrenia also confer risk for other psychiatric diseases, indicating that they do not conform to classic nosological disease boundaries (Cook and Scherer, 2008).

So, together, the positive association data in three genetic locations and the fact that all studies have reported more significant results from haplotypic analysis than from single marker analysis suggest that the true causative variants directly increasing susceptibility to schizophrenia, or psychosis more generally, have not yet been found (Williams et al., 2004, 2006; Stefansson et al., 2002). In addition, the high number of different associated haplo-types that have been reported, especially at *DTNBP1* and *NRG1*, indicates either substantial heterogeneity in linkage disequilibrium structure in different populations or the presence of multiple risk alleles, perhaps both.

Gene–environment interplay and schizophrenia

Several non-genetic risk factors have been established for schizophrenia through epidemiological studies, including prenatal infection and social stresses, both in childhood and adulthood. It has been hypothesized that such risk factors interact with susceptibility genes in the development and course of the illness (Howes et al., 2004; Rapoport et al., 2005). The longitudinal *Finnish Adoptive Family Study of Schizophrenia* has produced evidence of gene–environment interaction for schizophrenia spectrum disorders. Adoptees considered to be at genetic risk for schizophrenia, because of a diagnosis of schizophrenia spectrum disorder in their birth mother, were found to be more sensitive to the presence of adverse rearing patterns in their adoptive home than adoptees without such risk; these patterns included criticism, conflict, constriction and boundary problems (Tienari et al., 2004). One study suggested that family communication difficulties might leave individuals exceptionally prone to formal thought disorder (Wahlberg et al., 1997), but later work indicated that when deviant communication by the adoptive parents interacts with genetic risk, subsequent mental ill health is not limited to schizophrenia spectrum disorder (Wahlberg et al., 2004).

Specific Genetic Disorders and Risk for Antisocial Behaviour and Schizophrenia

The study of patients with known genetic abnormalities and behavioural deviance may guide genetic studies when antisocial behaviour is apparently associated with a specific disorder which does not invariably carry that association. Of particular interest in relation to schizophrenia, although so far not linked to aggression, despite deletion of the *COMT* gene on chromosome 22, is *22q11DS*. This complex condition is characterised by multiple tissue and organ abnormalities, resulting in cardiac and cognitive deficits, increased risk of a range of psychiatric and behavioural problems in childhood and of schizophrenia and bipolar disorder in adulthood (Murphy et al., 1999). This has helped focus study in the q11 region of chromosome 22 in people with primary schizophrenia. Prader–Willi syndrome is another in which affected individuals have intellectual disabilities and propensity for psychosis, here caused by deletions on chromosome 15 (for more detail, see chapter 13). Lesch–Nyhan syndrome (e.g. Nyhan, 1976; Palmour, 1983; see also chapter 13) results in extreme aggression towards self and others, and has been a focus for researchers seeking to improve understanding of genetic mechanisms underpinning aggression and violence.

CONCLUSIONS

There has been considerable progress in understanding traits that are associated with increased risk of antisocial behaviour, but with each new step forward comes increased realization of how complex the developmental pathways are and how much is still unknown. Quantitative genetic studies almost invariably agree that genetic factors play a role in antisocial behaviour, problem drug use (including alcohol) and schizophrenia, and molecular genetic studies have started to yield some convergent results suggesting loci of particular interest on the chromosomes.

For each condition discussed in this chapter, there is evidence that genetic influences are important, with the highest heritability estimates reported for schizophrenia. The extent to which the most promising candidate genes influence specific aspects of behaviours is not, however, known. It is possible that heritability estimates capture influences of genes on personality traits, such as irritability, willingness to try new experiences, shyness, and/or capacity to conform socially, perhaps mediated by how the brain processes information, such as interpretation of perceptual input – as in the jumping to conclusions paradigm in development of delusions (see chapter 14) or failures to learn from experience in respect of harmful antisocial behaviours (see chapter 16). For problem substance use, substance-specific biological mechanisms will also play a role, including those affecting variability in ability to metabolize drugs, and the reinforcing effects of substances.

It remains true that a substantial amount of behavioural variation is environmental, and quantitative genetic studies in part serve to confirm this. For antisocial behaviour and problem substance use, environmental aspects include qualities in the family, neighbourhood, peers and school (see also chapter 7), while for schizophrenia reported risk factors include stressors, such as infections during pregnancy and/or delivery complications as well as family stressors in some cases. Gene–environment interplay, however, also has a role, with increased genetic risk only manifest in the face of particular environmental stressors and/or increasing the chances that vulnerable individuals receive or create the additionally risk laden environmental. The development of antisocial behaviour and associated traits may be best represented as an accumulation of genetic and environmental risk factors, whereby their combined effects are considerably stronger than each individual effect (van den Bree and Pickworth, 2005). Several developmental pathways into antisocial behaviour are likely, alone or in relation to illness and/or personality disorder and/or substance misuse. Increasing recognition and understanding of these pathways will clarify optimal intervention points, to minimize secondary damage and maximize effective and efficient use of resources.

9
Violence

Edited and written by
John Gunn
Julian Walker

1st edition authors: **Ron Blackburn, John Gunn and Pamela J Taylor**

Editorial note

Violence is such a common phenomenon but such an important part of forensic psychiatry that it is an aspect of almost every part of this book. Each disorder chapter has been chosen because, from overt brain disorder through psychosis and personality disorder to misuse of alcohol or other drugs, these conditions have some form of special relationship with violence. It is useful, therefore, for all forensic practitioners to have a core understanding of antisocial violence itself as well as being able to place it in a context of mental disorder. What, if any, are the distinctions between psychotic and non-psychotic violence? When, if ever, does antisocial violence itself indicate pathology beyond the violent acts? Even the most apparently abnormal of psychopathology, as in psychosis, is generally viewed as being on a continuum between healthy experience and serious illness, so distinctions between 'healthy but antisocial' violence and 'disorder driven or related' violence are not always clear and we haven't entirely succeeded in separating them. This chapter, for example, includes a number of illustrations of violence which are best regarded as psychotic (even by those who are very parsimonious in the use of this term). They are here for convenience and to emphasize the way in which different types of pathology merge. We are not convinced that the strict categorical divisions of pathology which are sometimes used in psychiatry are helpful in clinical practice.

Both glamorizing and demonizing violence help us avoid having to understand the violent mind. We should enter the violent person's subjective world, not just in order to be able to offer treatment, but also to anticipate the nature of the risks they embody both to themselves and to society. To explain is not to exculpate, but understanding is the first step in the prevention of violence. The answer to the riddle of how individuals can lose restraint over their propensity to injure others must lie in what is ordinary rather than extraordinary: normal human development (Fonagy, 2003).

THEORETICAL BACKGROUND

Violence is a universal phenomenon, an integral part of any social system. Social activity does not exist without it. For human beings it is a very wide term which embraces everything from boxing matches to baby battering, armed robbery and war. Nevertheless, serious violence is a very unusual activity, whilst lesser forms of aggression are occurring continually. In most societies rigorous attempts are made to control levels of violence, and legal distinctions are made between sanctioned and unsanctioned violence.

The reasons that violence exists and persists in social systems are complicated. Even so, those who work with offenders are advised to have some understanding of the universality of violence in social mammals, the functions it performs, and the ideas which have been generated to explain these phenomena. For more detailed understanding, therefore, the reader is referred to other sources (Daniels et al., 1970; Gunn, 1973; Kutash et al., 1978; Hays et al., 1981; Klama, 1988; Gunn, 1991b).

Most definitions of violence refer to physical violence, i.e. the 'contact' form of violent behaviour (e.g. 'actual bodily harm') compared to 'non-contact' forms of violent behaviour such as 'threats to kill'. It is recognized, however, that there is a continuum of violent behaviour which includes verbal behaviour, through direct physical violence, to extreme forms of violence which may be indirectly caused by an aggressor (e.g. an act of war perpetrated by one state upon another). Therefore, it cannot be simply argued that all violence is criminal or maladaptive. The law recognizes 'reasonable force' or 'self-defence' as exceptional circumstances in which the aggressor should not be convicted for such an act even if it does involve some use of violence. Furthermore, there are situations in which violence can be seen as an acceptable, understandable and legitimate response to certain situations, for example police use of control and restraint techniques in controlling crime. A thoroughly researched taxonomy of violence is presented by Parrott and Giancola (2007) who separate direct from indirect aggression and violence to objects and people; they note that the target should also be motivated to avoid harm (excluding such activities as consensual sado-masochism).

The term 'aggression' although often used interchangeably with the term 'violence' is defined by Howells and Hollin (1989) as 'the intention to hurt or gain advantage over other people, without necessarily involving physical injury'; thus aggression can refer to a broader range of behaviour that may also include violence. Theories of aggression vary in the extent to which they emphasize unlearned or learned components, affective or cognitive processes, and internal or external determinants. They therefore differ in how they address three critical questions:

1. How does aggression originate?
2. How is it provoked or instigated?
3. How is it maintained and regulated?

Biological Perspectives

Ethnological studies of lower vertebrates led Lorenz (1966) to propose that there is a universal instinct of aggression which functions to ensure population control, selection of the strongest animals for reproduction, brood defence, and social organization. Instinct relates to a spontaneously generated energy source in the nervous system which discharges through fixed action patterns in response to specific releasing stimuli. Lorenz saw parallels between human militaristic displays or competitive sports and aggressive activities in geese and other animals. The theory postulated that human behaviour is governed by a constant need to discharge aggressive energy. There is, however, no evidence to support this hydraulic model of a reservoir of energy, even in lower animals, and Lorenz has been criticized for anthropomorphic extrapolation and his neglect of the role of learning.

Phylogenetic continuity of anatomical structure and behaviour was also assumed by Moyer (1981), who drew on studies of the effects of electrical brain stimulation and surgical lesions in animals and in patients with organic pathology. He suggested that there are organized neural circuits in the brain which are sensitized by hormones and blood constituents, and which when fired in the presence of a relevant target, produce integrated attacking behaviour. Human learning can influence the selection of targets and the inhibition of behaviour, but feelings of hostility will be experienced, whether or not aggressive behaviour occurs.

A recent study by Wood and Liossi (2006) of the neuropsychological and neurobehavioural correlates of aggression following traumatic brain injury suggested that in a prospective cohort study where 134 brain injured individuals showing aggression were compared with 153 similarly brain injured individuals who were not aggressive, there were significant differences. Those showing aggression had impairments in verbal memory, visuo-perceptual skills and executive-attention functioning – it was tentatively

suggested that impairment in these areas was associated with aggression following traumatic brain injury. A review of 17 neuroimaging studies by Bufkin and Luttrell (2005) suggested that 'the areas associated with aggressive and/or violent behavioural histories, particularly impulsive acts, are located in the prefrontal cortex and the medial temporal regions'. Functionally, these areas are associated with the regulation of negative emotion and led Bufkin and Luttrell to recommend that neurophysiological knowledge and assessment is integrated into the work of criminologists and psychologists working to reduce offending (particularly violence). Brower and Price's (2001) review of frontal lobe dysfunction and violence suggested that although no particular frontal network dysfunction could predict violent crime, there was an association between significant frontal lobe dysfunction and aggressive dyscontrol.

Psychodynamic Perspectives

There is no single psychodynamic theory of aggression, but again an aggressive instinct or drive is commonly assumed. The main interest has been in how the aggressive drive is accommodated within the hypothesized psychic structures, and how it comes to be channelled and controlled in the course of individual development.

In his earlier writings, Freud saw aggression as a reaction to frustration and pain. He later introduced the notion of a death instinct (Thanatos), a tendency to self-destruction which is diverted by the self-preserving libidinal instinct (Eros) to the external world (Freud, 1920). Some psychoanalysts accept an instinct of aggression, but reject the notion of a death instinct. Others see aggression as reactive, but attribute extreme violence to the eruption of destructively motivated energy. Manifestations of aggressive instinct are said to include the rage reaction to frustration, which mobilizes the organism for combat, but aggressive drive is also subject to the same developmental vicissitudes as the libido. It is, therefore, thought to be manifest in biting (oral sadism) or faeces retention (anal sadism). The theory also suggests that through fixation these reactions may be transformed into hostile character traits. Instinctual discharge is thought then to occur through fantasy or overt aggression and is also occasioned by rivalry with siblings or parents, which may have counterparts in later life.

Ego psychologists have elaborated on the transformation of aggressive energy. Hartmann et al. (1949) proposed that the destructive aims of aggression become modified by displacement or sublimation, and through neutralization, constructive energy is supplied to the ego, enabling it to fulfil self-assertive and adaptive functions. Superego development is thought to permit the internalization of aggressive energy in the form of guilt, but the theory suggests that instinctual energy is nevertheless still generated and may conflict with the demands of the libido, the superego, or reality, so that continuous sublimation or neutralization is necessary for healthy functioning.

Neo-Freudian psychoanalysts criticize the instinct concept, and argue for sociocultural origins of aggression. Fromm (1973) distinguished defensive or benign aggression, a biologically programmed reaction to threat, from destructive or malignant aggression, which is a specifically human phenomenon arising when socioeconomic conditions prevent the fulfilment of existential needs for interpersonal ties or personal effectiveness. Fromm saw malignant aggression in cruelty, torture, or disproportionate revenge, and believed it typifies sadistic characters who need to control others. He suggested that it is not derived from benign aggression, and is distinct from instrumental aggression.

The shortcomings of a hydraulic concept of instinct have already been noted, and the proposal that non-aggressive behaviours, such as constructive self-assertion, are manifestations of transformed destructive energy allows virtually any activity to be construed as aggressive. For this and other reasons the intuitive view of aggression has largely withered outside psychodynamic theory, although psychodynamic perspectives do emphasize early learning of aggressive solutions to conflict and processes of regulation which have parallels in other theories.

Perhaps one of the most popular models of violence in clinical settings was proposed by Gilligan (1996). He proposed that violence was a response to (unjustified) humiliation by individuals who lack a healthy sense of self-esteem and pride. This vulnerability (related to past abuse or neglect) leaves individuals more sensitive to verbal attacks by others. Violence results when the individual becomes enraged, lacks a non-violent alternative and is uninhibited by feelings of guilt or empathy. Gilligan's (1996) book *Violence: Reflections on our Deadliest Epidemic* provides a theoretically clear and clinically useful description of his model and clinical work with violent men in the North American prison system.

Learning Perspectives

While accepting the possibility of some archaic connections between threatening events and motor responses, learning theorists see aggression as acquired and maintained by rewarding or reinforcing contingencies. Theoretical attention focuses on how particular classes of antecedent and consequent events promote aggression.

Dollard et al. (1939) drew on early Freudian theory in formulating the frustration–aggression hypothesis, and asserted that aggression is a consequence of frustration in the form of thwarting of goal-directed activity. Frustration thus instigates a motive to injure the source of frustration, its intensity depending on the value of the blocked goal and the degree of frustration. The theory suggests that aggression is a function of prior reinforcement or punishment. If

punishment is anticipated, the response is inhibited unless displaced to an alternative target.

Although influential, the original theory has not been widely accepted since frustration instigates responses other than aggression, and aggression is equally provoked by insult or attack, threats to self-esteem or pain (Berkowitz, 1989). Anger can increase attempts to injure, and that injury is sometimes a positive reinforcer for further aggression. Frustration, however, only leads to anger when it is perceived as unjustified. Other workers have shown that aggression is negatively reinforced by the termination of an aversive state, and question the notion of a specific aggressive drive (Patterson, 1979). Tension produced by frustration or other aversive events can be reduced by direct aggression, but also by non-aggressive behaviour which removes aversion. This casts doubts on the psychodynamic notion that aggression can be reduced by catharsis, e.g. the 'purging' of aggressive tension by means of substitute aggressive expression. Instrumental aggression, on the other hand, is positively reinforced by the attainment of rewards such as material goods, status, or approval. In these terms, persistent aggression may be not only the result of positive or negative reinforcement for aggressive behaviour, but also the failure to learn non-aggressive ways of coping with aversive events or obtaining desired rewards.

Although the anticipation of punishment is considered to be the major inhibitor of aggression in both psychodynamic and learning theories, its effects are variable (Baron, 1983). Actual punishment is frustrating, and unless incapacitating, may increase angry aggression. It also constitutes counter aggression and provides a model for aggression. Threatened punishment has been found to deter angry aggression of low intensity and instrumental aggression motivated by modest gains. It is less likely to reduce aggression motivated by strong positive reinforcers, or by intense anger, which impairs consideration of future consequences.

Social Cognitive Perspectives

Learning theories evolved from studies of conditioning processes in animals. Some theorists question whether these processes apply in any simple way to human aggression, and stress complex cognitive mediation as the source of aggression. The effects of frustration and punishment, for example, depend on whether the recipient perceives them as justified. This clearly entails normative judgments and cognitive appraisals about the intent of a frustrater. Similarly, physiological arousal energizes aggressive behaviour, but only when it is attributed to frustration or provocation. When people are provoked to anger, further arousal from extraneous sources, such as noise or heat, may be 'misinterpreted' and intensify aggression (Zillmann, 1979).

A comprehensive cognitive theory of aggression is the social learning theory of Bandura (1983). He saw reinforcing contingencies as providing information about the effects of behaviour, but held that such information is most readily acquired through observational learning or modelling. Aggression originates in modelling and reinforcement, through which people develop expectations about the likely outcomes of different behaviours in meeting their goals. These, however, include consequences for the self, and behaviour is adjusted to meet personal and social standards through the self-regulatory process of self-reward and punishment. Standards may, nevertheless, be overridden or neutralized by cognitive distortions such as blaming or dehumanizing the victim.

Bandura, like most workers, rejected the notion of a specific aggressive drive, and proposed that both aversive experiences and positive incentives produce a general increase in emotional arousal. This motivates whatever relevant responses are strongest in the behavioural repertoire. In coping with aversive experiences, aggression is only one of several possible strategies, which might include avoidance or constructive problem-solving, depending on the individual's skills.

Zillman (1979) suggested a similar model which emphasized the interaction of arousal and cognitive guidance of aggression. Social events influence behaviour through the causal attributions people assign to them, but also through moral evaluations of behaviour, including one's own, relative to social norms. Thus the attribution to another of an intentional infliction of aversion will result in compensatory retaliation to a level dictated by social norms of equity, due account being taken of personal rewards and costs. Aggression then, in this theory, is to a degree rational, but the cognitive control of aggression is determined by the level of physiological arousal. At high or low levels, cognitive guidance is minimized, and aggression is likely to be impulsive and under immediate situational control.

Social cognitive approaches are consistent with recent proposals that human emotional behaviour has significant cultural components and serves social functions of communication (Averill, 1983). While not wholly incompatible with biological or psychodynamic perspectives, such a view dictates an analysis of human aggression in terms of its meaning for the individual and the social context in which it occurs.

A group of scientists interested in animal behaviour, anthropology, and human development (Klama, 1988) argued that aggression is not a thing or a class of things that can be located somewhere in the brain, neither is it a core of impulses overlaid by cultural modifiers and restraints. They drew heavily on the ideas in game theory and particularly Axelrod's theory of the evolution of co-operation (Axelrod, 1984) which incorporated an analysis of the prisoner's dilemma. The essence of the argument is that individuals (not species) evolve in an environment of dilemmas, conflicts, and pay-offs, such that the costs and benefits of any particular strategy or tactic by an individual are complex. Some circumstances give advantages if an individual is very nasty to his or her fellows and other circumstances give advantages to being very nice.

The prisoner's dilemma is the theoretical problem faced by two prisoners, arrested and separated, who have committed a series of crimes together. There may be advantage for each in saying nothing, and going to prison for a short period or, alternatively, there may be advantage in grassing (defecting) on their colleague in return for a let-off. Everything depends on what the other one does. The usual analysis is that it is better to defect, because that produces the best overall risk–benefit profile whatever the other prisoner does. Axelrod said that if the game is played more than once by the same two people, then the best profile is produced by saying nothing and thus co-operating with the other prisoner. This is because each knows that the other can either follow suit and co-operate next time round, or retaliate next time, and it is better to avoid retaliation. Axelrod suggested, therefore, that an individual playing the game this way can help him or herself (and his/her opponent) best by not being envious, not being the first to defect, reciprocating both co-operation and defection, and not being too clever.

Dominance and helplessness

Powerlessness, the search for control, subjective feelings of weakness and helplessness, distorted perceptions of power, are all factors found in human aggression. One of us in previous publications (Gunn, 1973, 1991b) has proposed a social dominance theory of violence suggesting that violence tends to occur when there is an imbalance of power within a social system or between individuals. This idea gives rise to ideas for reducing levels of violence and could enable further ideas of intervention for treatment to be generated and tested.

On the face of it, the discussion of the iterated prisoner's dilemma, and the distribution of power is all concerned with rational activity, thus apparently leaving out irrational, motiveless violence. However, it is even possible to attribute these rational ideas to psychotic individuals to some extent. Equally, irrationality is a judgment passed by one observer on another. Once a patient's sense of helplessness, his/her terror of being attacked by neighbours, rays, gas, or whatever, and other aspects of his/her inner world have been understood, then aggressive behaviour from them also becomes understandable.

Those ideas lead to a consideration of the cognitive component of aggressive behaviors.

Cognitive Behavioural Theories

The cognitive behavioural literature takes violence as a conscious behavioural choice based on problematic ideas and erroneous belief systems rather than attempting to understand the problem as a clinical disorder (Bush, 1995; Ross et al., 1986). Clinical approaches to violence have tended to focus on the attributes of violent individuals who engage in angry or hostile aggression rather than instrumental aggression (Howells and Hollin, 1989) with particular emphasis in the last 30 years on anger management as the best available approach with growing empirical evidence (Beck and Fernandez, 1998). Anger as a risk factor for violence has been researched and presented by Novaco (1994, 1997).

Novaco and Welsh (1989) propose that:

while anger is neither necessary nor sufficient for aggression to occur, it is nonetheless a central activator of both individual and collective violence and is significantly involved in a range of mental health disturbance (p.39).

They go on to propose that poor anger control and regulation is an important risk factor in relation to harming others. Anger is described elsewhere by Novaco (1986) as a negatively toned emotion, which is experienced by normal individuals and only constitutes a clinically significant problem if the outcomes are destructive to others or to the individual's own health (Chesney and Rosenman, 1985). There are now recognized ways of treating the problem through anger management training (Williams and Barlow, 1998).

Despite the importance of anger as a risk in relation to violence it has generally not been seen as a psychiatric issue. Where fear, sadness and other 'normal' emotions have a range of psychiatric disorders associated with them, equivalence is lacking for anger. This may be because anger is rather more difficult to assess safely or because it causes extreme discomfort for both patient and assessor, but it is nevertheless interesting that it is underemphasized in psychiatry. Perhaps it is more the preserve of psychologists, particularly those working within the prison system given that anger management is a common treatment for violent offenders (Hollin and Palmer, 2006). However, there are concerns over how anger relates to violence, and whether it is relevant or deserves its current status (Walker and Bright, 2009a; Mills and Croner, 2003; Loza and Loza-Fanous, 1999).

Other cognitive approaches to violence have looked at the role of social problem solving (McMurran and McGuire, 2005) or the inhibiting effect on aggression of pro-social emotions (e.g. guilt/remorse) and attitudes. The finding that even young children can begin to behave aggressively with associated positive feelings rather than negative ones (such as guilt or anxiety) suggests an early and perhaps reinforcing pathway for aggressive antisocial behaviour which shows some consistency with findings from the developmental literature on antisocial behaviour (Moffit, 1993). Problems in emotion attributions (particularly guilt) and associated problems with inhibiting violent behaviour have been suggested by Blair et al. (1995). The 'Violence Inhibition Mechanism Model' is based on animal studies of submissive behaviour and associated decreases in aggression by an attacker (see Blair, 2001). Morrison and Gilbert (2001) found extremely high levels of internalized shame and sensitivity to humiliation in some people with antisocial personality traits coupled with a tendency to assume dominance in response. A further study by Gilbert and

Miles (2000) suggested that externalizing or blaming others mitigated the effect of shame. Therefore, it is possible that what underpins aggression even in extreme violence-prone individuals is the absence or disabling of a violence inhibition mechanism (associated with guilt and empathy) which may be triggered by shame and humiliation.

Perhaps it is partly *shame* that drives people to carry out violent instructions given by others. Certainly much non-pathological violence (e.g. warfare and state violence by police and prison officers) is carried out obediently in a dominance hierarchy. The famous Milgram experiment that apparently caused non-violent citizens to electrocute subjects under their control demonstrated this very clearly (Milgram, 1963, 1974).

Based on a systematic review of the literature, Walker and Bright (2009a,b) have proposed a cognitive formulation of violence which has as a central component low and unstable self-esteem – covered by false inflated self-esteem which appears as the characteristic arrogance of some violent offenders. The rules and beliefs underpinning the use of violence as a way of solving difficult or threatening social situations is seen as the result of lacking other ways of boosting self-esteem when in humiliating or potentially humiliating situations. This 'macho' approach of using aggression to put people down or put them in their place is extremely reinforcing, and so regardless of the consequences, Walker and Bright argue that fighting will always seem to be the best or 'least worst' option – certainly better than walking away from or backing down in a confrontation. The model deals mainly with reactive rather than sadistic or sexual violence where the use of power is different and more closely entwined with perversion. The authors propose a cognitive approach to treatment that emphasizes work on self-esteem and on formulating the individual pattern of violence with the patient in intricate detail to aid understanding and choice in potentially violent situations.

An important additional dimension, as far as human beings are concerned, which must be added to these perspectives of violence and aggression, is the dimension of self-destructiveness. Human beings are not the only animals that destroy themselves but, presumably because of the great cognitive component of all human behaviour, they are more likely to destroy themselves in a planned way. Self-destruction and destruction of others seems to be closely linked in human thinking and behaviour, therefore self-destruction has to be kept in mind as an important and special human factor when matters of violence are considered. These ideas are closely aligned to those concerning dominance in the previous section.

Developmental Perspectives and Attachment Theory

The idea that violence is unlearned rather than learned has been proposed by Fonagy (2003) who cites the first 'peak' of physically aggressive behaviour at 2 years of age. This view is supported by evidence from longitudinal cohort studies (Tremblay et al., 2004; Nagin and Tremblay, 2001). These suggest that not only do children generally decrease levels of physical aggression from 2 years of age to pre-school age, but also that distinct groups fell into ostensibly non-aggressive, moderately aggressive, or who show high levels of and increasing physical aggression at this early life stage. The behaviour of this higher risk group shows a tendency to carry through school age years to the second peak of physical aggression in late teenage years.

Physical aggression in school age children has been associated with various factors including psychological factors such as personality traits and social problem solving (e.g. Bennett et al., 2005) or peer and family influences (e.g. Nagin and Tremblay, 2001). Pre-school aggression has also been related to family factors, in particular maternal factors (Tremblay et al., 2004), and to childhood abuse (Dodge et al., 1997). The central mechanism for the effect of parenting on later aggressive behaviour is suggested by Fonagy (2003) to be deficits in the attachment relationship(s) of the child, which results in a poor ability to 'mentalize' (the capacity to understand other's subjective experience). Conversely, an increasing capacity to mentalize helps children to empathize, to work with rather than against others to get their needs met, and to begin to see violence as a taboo rather than a response to problems and conflicts.

De Zulueta's (2006) contention about the origins of aggression and violence is based in attachment theory (Bowlby, 1988) which is a set of psychobiologically driven behaviours, partially mediated by the opioid system, which developmentally allow an individual to relate securely to his or her care givers and develop future secure and healthy attachments with others based on these early childhood relational models for attachment. Satisfactory attachments then are important for the development of our relationships and for the quality of our relatedness to others. De Zulueta (2006) comments that:

any disruption of this essential developmental process leads to serious long-term effects both at a psychological and physiological level (p.179),

including detachment from others, lack of attunement and empathy, poor emotional understanding, labelling and wellbeing and inability to contain (own and other's) emotions. De Zulueta concluded that:

the insecurely attached infant, who has been emotionally deprived or abused, has little self-confidence and tends to relate to others with hostility (p.179).

In the absence of normal attachment processes, the child fails to develop nurturing and empathy skills which help to resolve conflicts and relate to others as adults. The result is the experience of increased anxiety in interpersonal situations and a reliance on aggression as a way of dealing with conflict.

Visual media and violence

Does watching violent films and television or playing violent video games make us more likely to commit violent acts in reality? We know that visual media can only ever be one of many influences which shape our behaviour, but it is probably easier to understand their educational impact than some of the more complex and perhaps painful influences outlined above. People are also aware that manufacturers and politicians will pay money to have their products and ideas advertised – presumably, therefore, those manufacturers and politicians have evidence that they can alter the viewer's behaviour? To maintain perspective, it has to be remembered that violence is not a new phenomenon that has appeared since the advent of the cinema and television. The twentieth century may have been the most violent in recorded history but most of the appalling violence occurred before the visual media became ubiquitous. It is unlikely that an angry hostile attitude to women in a violent rapist will have been gleaned from cop movies; it is more likely it was learned from adverse early experiences, from modelling on powerful adult figures actually in the household, and a range of internal psychological problems.

What of the research? There are mountains of reports, e.g. the US Surgeon General's report (US Public Health Service, 1972), a Home Office report (Brody, 1977), an overview from New York (Liebert and Sprafkin, 1988), and a review taking a much broader perspective of the influence of television on children (Gunter and McAleer, 1990). Most studies focus on children and young people. Rothenberg (1975) pointed out that, on leaving school, the average American child will have watched 15,000 hours of television, but received only 11,000 hours of formal classroom instruction. S/he will have witnessed some 18,000 murders and countless examples of lesser violence. Rothenberg reviewed 50 studies involving 10,000 children and adolescents from 'every conceivable background', and argued that the evidence was consistently supportive of the view that viewing violence produces increased aggressive behaviour in young people. The Eisenhower Commission (National Commission on the Causes and Prevention of Violence, 1969) was only slightly more modest in its conclusions:

We do not suggest that television is a principal cause of violence in society. We do suggest that it is a contributing factor.

Brody (1977) examined the four basic hypotheses about the generation of social violence from screen violence, by imitation, by arousal of aggressive feelings, by emotional reactions, by the debasement of social and moral values. He concluded that young children do imitate novel actions, including aggressive ones, boys imitate aggression more than girls, but all this has to be seen in an emotional context which may outweigh all other factors.

The research has been subjected to much technical criticism. As for arousal of aggressive feelings, laboratory experiments have repeatedly shown that college students are more ready to administer powerful electric shocks to strangers after they have seen violent films, but there is little evidence that these data can be generalized to ordinary social circumstances. The idea that emotional responsiveness can be blunted by repeated exposure to violence seems to be supported by the fact that people are less upset the second time they see a violent film than they were the first time, but there is also evidence that this is highly situationally specific with little or no generalization. The debasement of moral values is the most serious charge against violent films and video-games. Whilst there is evidence that a specific film may change specific ideas, just as educational films are intended to, there are very few data on whether this generalizes very far. It is hardly surprising that Brody concluded:

It can be stated quite simply that social research has not been able unambiguously to offer any firm reassurance that the mass media in general, and films and television in particular, either exercise a socially harmful effect, or that they do not.

This debate could run for ever as no one can do the definitive experiment. What is needed is a prosperous, westernized town that has all aspects of modern life except television. Its violence levels would have to be measured accurately and then the town provided with television for a few years. Violence levels would again have to be measured. Finally, the television sets would need to be taken away (just imagine!) and the violence levels measured again. The nearest we can come to this experiment is the study by Hennigam et al. (1982) which compared crime rates in American cities with and without television between 1949 and 1952. The introduction of television did not increase violent crime, but it was associated with an increase in larceny! Could this have been due to an increased awareness of relative poverty on the part of some people?

Liebert and Sprafkin (1988) suggested that television violence can provide instruction in antisocial and aggressive behaviour, which will sometimes lead to direct copying or disinhibition of such behaviours. These effects do not invariably occur, however, and depend upon the characteristics of the viewers and the situation. Nevertheless, the value shaping and cultivation effects of television violence appear to be very widespread, suggesting that television violence can work in subtle and insidious ways to adversely influence youth and society.

A broadly based review of the impact of television on children (Gunter and McAleer, 1997) has challenged the whole concept of television as a monster. These authors pointed out that it is the possible negative effects of television which receive all the publicity. There may be many beneficial effects which are less often discussed. They reviewed the known facts about British children's television viewing, and asked, 'Why do children watch television?',

finding a range of reasons from boredom to arousal and the amount of attention they are prepared to give a programme is related to whether it means much to them. Perhaps similar results would appear if the study were repeated with video games.

Browne and Hamilton-Giachritis (2005) reviewed the influence of violent media on children and adolescents. They noted some evidence of short-term effects on arousal, thoughts and emotions which increased the likelihood of aggressive of fearful behaviour in younger children with boys being more likely to become aggressive than girls. Inevitably long-term effects have not been fully demonstrated, although they believe that the work of Johnson et al. (2002) and Huesmann et al. (2003) does show a small, significant effect which may be a public-health concern. They therefore go on to propose a series of recommendations for parents, professionals, media producers and policy makers including such things as public education and greater controls over visual materials for people in secure institutions.

VIOLENCE AS A HEALTH ISSUE

In 2002 the World Health Organization published a report on violence and health (Krug et al., 2002). Violence is described as

a universal scourge that tears at the fabric of communities and threatens the life, health and happiness of us all.

Each year more than 1.6 million people worldwide lose their lives to violence, many more are injured and suffer from a range of physical, sexual, reproductive, and mental health problems. Violence is among the leading causes of death for people aged 15 to 44 years worldwide, accounting for about 14% of deaths among males and 7% of deaths among females. Being a public health document it puts a lot of emphasis on the prevention of violence discussing everything from individual approaches including education, social development, and treatment relationship approaches, including training in parenting mentoring and family therapy programmes. It advocates community-based efforts such as extracurricular activities for young people, training for police and other professionals, specific programmes for schools, workplaces, refugee camps and care institutions. There are even nine recommendations for action. Forensic psychiatry, however, doesn't get a mention in the document, even though antisocial behaviour is a major target. The health aspects of domestic violence are strongly endorsed by the Department of Health resource manual *Domestic Violence* (Henwood, 2000), yet this manual hardly mentions the perpetrator, or psychiatry, let alone forensic psychiatry.

This textbook is highlighting violence and its prevention as a major public health task for forensic psychiatry. The definition of forensic psychiatry given in the introduction embraces this concept. Psychiatry cannot work alone in this task, the problem is too enormous and too complex, however nor can it be omitted. It has already embraced the task of reducing suicide rates and this work is not discussed in this text. However it is not difficult to see that the approach which has had some success in suicide reduction in the United Kingdom may have lessons for the reduction of harm to others. Clearly the approach must be multidisciplinary and scientific but the skills of psychiatry are required in what may be the biggest health challenge of the twenty-first century.

Domestic Violence

Relationship strife is common and may spill over into violence, sometimes severe violence up to and including homicide; it may also involve sadism and torture in some cases. Men are physically stronger than women; men are more likely to be extrapunitive, women intropunitive. Historically, women have had few legal protections in marriage. In Britain until 1878, wives were regarded as part of a man's property and could be forcibly detained in the man's home.

The feminist perspective on domestic violence raised the profile of the issue and probably contributed to the fact that domestic violence went from being studied very little, to being studied a great deal from the 1970s onwards. Rates of voilence can be evaluated looking at criminal statistics (which show generally lower rates than surveys), looking at surveys of victims, and looking at surveys of 'perpetrators'. Depending on which approach is taken, the results can seem rather different.

The generally accepted view is that men are responsible for the majority of violence and crime generally in society (at the time of writing, of the 83,000 people in prison, fewer than 5,000 are women). Furthermore, the majority of violence in the home is thought to be perpetrated by men and this is supported by the British Crime Survey suggesting that women are twice as likely to report domestic violence as men; however, the use of survey methodology may be affected by reporting rates (men are less likely to report victimization). Also the rate of perpetration is not necessarily the same as the rate of injury, and it is these factors that some well respected researchers have begun to question in reviewing the rates of violence by sex (Moffitt et al., 2001; see also chapter 20). Dutton and Nicholls (2005), Archer (2002) and Straus (2009) have argued more for 'gender symmetry' than patriarchy in relation to domestic violence. Dutton and Nicholls (2005) suggest that the process for measuring violence is important, and that the ratio of male to female violence varies according to the method used. For example, they found that crime surveys and police call data reveal male to female violence ratios of 7:1–13:1 and 9:1 respectively, but that 'family conflict' studies reveal ratios of 1:1. In their review, they summarize as follows:

Feminist core beliefs about domestic violence include the following: that most men are violent, that women's violence is in self-defense, that male violence escalates,

and that women are by far, the most injured. The data reviewed above reveal something very different; that both genders use violence, women use it against non-violent men, more violence de-escalates than escalates, and both groups are injured, with women somewhat more likely to experience negative outcomes. (p.705).

They go on to review the evidence for a number of factors involving the continuation of the male-violent female-victim paradigm and suggest that not only do males under-report victimization, but that when asked about behaviour towards spouses (rather than victimization), both sexes report a similar amount of violence. When they compared male callers' reports to a domestic victim call line, the findings were remarkably similar to the original studies of women in refuges that began in the 1970s and have been seen as the standard way to gather data on domestic violence ever since (Dutton and Nicholls, 2005). John Archer's meta-analytic review (2002) of 48 studies indicated that:

Women were more likely than men to throw something at the other, slap, kick, bite, or punch, and hit with an object. Men were more likely than women to beat up, and to choke or strangle. Differences ranged from very small to medium. Samples selected for marital problems showed large effects in the male (perpetration) direction, and student samples showed effects more in the female (perpetration) direction than community samples. Effect sizes derived from partners' reports (of victimization) were more in the male direction than those derived from self-reports (of perpetration), but the overall pattern of results was similar (p.313).

It is important to note that although the combined sample size was large in this meta-analysis, the effect sizes were relatively small indicating more similarity than difference between male and female domestic violence. The finding that women are more likely to suffer injury may be explained by physical size and strength (Felson, 1996); however, size and strength became irrelevant when knives or guns were involved. Nevertheless, as quoted above, in England and Wales, in the domestic setting more women are hurt by men than vice versa.

Carney, Buttell and Dutton (2007), concluded that female perpetrators of domestic violence showed similar profiles to male perpetrators such as motives and risk factors (substance abuse, previous violence and personality disturbance). In fact, many of the factors associated with domestic violence are the same as those associated with violence generally. Richardson and Hammock (2007) argue that violence has to be understood in its social and cultural context and that role may be a more important factor than sex in understanding violence. This is consistent with Walker and Gudjonsson's (2006) finding that 'machismo' (tendency to resolve difficult social situations using aggression) was related to violence in both male and female adolescents from the general population.

Violence in same-sex relationships has been relatively unstudied in the research literature, even though there is a considerable amount published on the topic (mainly in books). A prominent case of homicide and violence within a male homosexual relationship involved the American serial killer Jeffrey Dahmer who famously killed male partners and could have been stopped sooner than he was had emergency calls not been dismissed as 'a boyfriend thing'. Potoczniak et al. (2003) suggested that one of Dahmer's victims (a 14-year-old boy) should have been protected under child protection laws, and would have been better protected had he been female because of domestic violence laws (which excluded specific reference to same-sex relationships). Turrell (2000) provides a descriptive analysis of a large sample (*n*=499) of gay men and women and bisexual and transsexual people. Her findings suggest that violence in same-sex relationships occurs at similar or even greater rates than in heterosexual relationships:

> *Physical violence was reported in 9% of current and 32% of past relationships. One per cent of participants had experienced forced sex in their current relationship. Nine per cent reported this experience in past relationships. Emotional abuse was reported by 83% of the participants. Women reported higher frequencies than men for physical abuse, coercion, shame, threats, and use of children for control. Across types of abuse, ethnic differences emerged regarding physical abuse and coercion (Turrell, p.281).*

The additional difficulties faced by same-sex couples include an even greater array of myths and preconceptions about the pattern of domestic abuse than those encountered by heterosexual couples (including the role of stereotyping and the view that men are not likely to be victimized).

Protection for victims of domestic violence would be better undertaken through preventative means, but this is rarely possible and most interventions are reactive to prevent further repeat victimization (most victims will have suffered multiple attacks before reporting or seeking help); strategies include refuges and support services, but also criminal justice interventions such as imprisonment, restraining orders and psychological treatment. Most treatment for perpetrators of domestic violence takes place in groups in the community (often as part of a community sentence). In their review of the literature on treatment, Sartin et al. (2006) conclude that:

> *Despite lingering disagreement about the effectiveness of domestic violence treatment, it appears that domestic violence treatment results in some positive changes in batterers who complete. Moreover, batterers who complete domestic violence treatment are less likely to subsequently recidivate and have fewer re-assaults when they do recidivate than those who drop out of treatment. However, given the lack of true control groups,*

> *it is difficult to determine the extent to which batterer treatment is actually responsible for the lower recidivism rates (p.438).*

Thus the home while often harmonious can be the scene of much serious violence. This has probably always been the case. The pathology of nineteenth century homes (e.g. alcoholism, delusional disorder, morbid jealousy) is fictionalized in, for example, *The Tenant of Wildfell Hall* (Bronte, 1848), *The Woman in White* (Collins, 1859–60), and *He Knew He Was Right* (Trollope, 1869a). For an historical perspective the reader is referred to May (1978). In an Irish study Bradley et al. (2002) surveyed 1871 women attending general practices. Of the 1,692 women who had ever had a sexual relationship, 651 (39%) had experienced violent behaviour by a partner. Only 78 of the 651 (12%) women reported that their doctor had asked about domestic violence even though 298 of them (46%) had been injured, of those only 60 (20%) said that their doctor had asked about domestic violence.

The British Crime Survey (BCS) noted that questionnaires provide disclosure rates that are five times higher than in face-to-face interviews. Nicholas et al. (2007) reported that:

> *just over a third of the estimated 2,471,000 violent incidents recorded by the BCS in 2006/07 were incidents of stranger violence, and a further third were incidents of acquaintance violence. Sixteen per cent of violent incidents were incidents of domestic violence (p.61).*

So despite being a high frequency problem, domestic violence is under-reported and the victims are often caught in a cycle of repeat victimization. In the BCS:

> *domestic violence had the highest rate of repeat victimization, with 42% of victims being victimized more than once. Repeat victimization accounts for 70% of all incidents of domestic violence as measured by the BCS. Almost one in four (23%) were victimized three or more times (op cit).*

Stanko conducted a one-day audit, on 28 September 2000, in England of all calls to the police services relating to domestic violence. She found that just under 3% of all calls to police were for assistance relating to domestic violence. Extrapolating, the police were receiving over 13,000 calls a day or 570,000 calls each year of domestic violence in the UK. This is equivalent to a call from the public nearly every minute. In England two forces were able to supply details about the incidents; 81% related to female victims being attacked by males, 8% of male victims being attacked by females, 4% were female victims being attacked by females, and 7% were male victims being attacked by males. Stanko described how she used the media to publicize the audit, and this in turn produced 'massive attention' and the debate continued for about 2 weeks. She recommends using the media to highlight social and criminal problems.

An important study by Gilchrist et al. (2003) in England suggested that men convicted of a domestic violence crime were about 35 years old, unemployed, with many previous convictions including for violence. A large minority had mental health problems, the commonest being fresh and that they also suffered from anger, stress and anxiety states; half of them were alcohol abusers and a fifth abused other substances. The authors attempted to classify the kind of men receiving convictions for domestic violence offences using psychometric tests and decided that the majority exhibited to a greater or lesser degree antisocial and narcissistic traits. One group, which they called, borderline/emotionally dependent were different, having interpersonal dependence, high levels of anger, symptoms of depression and anxiety, and low self-esteem. They tended to blame others for their circumstances and were likely to have experienced physical and sexual abuse in childhood.

Browne and Herbert (1997) prefer the term 'family violence' to 'domestic violence'. In a sense, domestic violence is simply violence occurring within the home, but family violence is more complicated and can be seen impacting beyond the immediate family and perpetuating through generations. Browne and Herbert noted that there are a number of different forms of abuse within families, often relating to power, including violence by adults to children or spouses, violence by children to siblings or parents, and violence by adults and children to elders. In particular, they highlight the importance of anger in active abuse, but also remind the reader of other forms of abuse including neglect, psychological abuse and sexual abuse in addition to violence.

Rees and Rivett (2005) reinforce this point that 'not all abusers are the same' and argue that programmes for domestic violence perpetrators need to be varied. The National Society for the Prevention of Cruelty to Children (NSPCC) established in Cardiff a group programme for perpetrators which takes both volunteers and referrals from courts. It is based on an educational model developed in the United States at Duluth (University of Minnesota) by Pence and Paymar (1993). Cardiff also has the Cardiff Women's Safety Unit (CWSU) to which women can be referred by courts and police. A detailed report of the unit has been published by Cardiff University (Robinson, 2003 and http://www.cardiff.ac.uk/socsi/resources/robinson-wsu-sec-eva.pdf). The CWSU was referred 1150 women and their 1482 children between December 2001 and January 2003. Most of the clients were white females, under 40 years old, with children and receiving benefits. Their partners tended to be white males of the same age, employed, with previous domestic violence. The typical CWSU client had experienced about 6 years of physical abuse from her current partner. On average she had experienced more than five violent acts from her current partner, and more than seven violent acts from a partner in her lifetime. This violence had left the women with many injuries (e.g. bruised faces, arms and legs, split lips and black eyes) as well as negative mental health (e.g.

about 4 in 10 were currently experiencing depression and/or anxiety). Partners with drug problems inflicted significantly more violence. A quarter of the women reported that they had been sexually abused by their current partners. The services offered by the CWSU were locks, panic alarms, safety advice (for both women and children), advocacy, counselling, a survivors' forum, referral to other agencies, group work for children. Client perceptions of CWSU service were overwhelmingly positive.

Rivett and Kelly (2006) tell us that after decades in which resources and policy incentives on protecting women and children from domestic violence, policy makers have woken up to the need to treat the men who perpetrate this violence. They also remind us that one out of every four women had experienced physical abuse from their male partners during their lifetime and that perhaps 750,000 children in the UK witnessed domestic violence every year (Department of Health, 2002c). As practitioners, Rivett and Kelly lament that the management of perpetrators of domestic violence is compartmentalized away from other services, particularly mental health services in the UK. We believe that intimate partner/family/domestic violence should be a central concern of forensic psychiatry: forensic psychiatry is a preventive discipline as well as a therapeutic discipline.

Domestic violence should nevertheless mainly be a matter for primary care. It is identified all too rarely, often because it is not considered (Thompson et al., 2000). Psychiatrists are rarely consulted and yet psychiatric issues may be playing a big role in the problem, in brief the three a's and the two d's: anxiety, anger, alcohol, depression and drugs. There are services and interventions available to help with all these problems. By the time the matter has reached the courts or becomes apparent during a prison sentence the probation and the forensic psychology services find themselves in leading roles.

The probation and prison services run two or three cognitive behaviour treatment groups for well-motivated domestic violence offenders. These include the Integrated Domestic Abuse Programme (IDAP), the Healthy Relationships Programme (HRP) and the Thames Valley Community Domestic Violence Programme (CDVP). The programmes are for men aged 17 years and over convicted of offences of domestic violence who exhibit an imminent risk of further domestic violence. The men must demonstrate some motivation to change and possess some recognition of the unacceptability of their behaviour. The programmes are unsuitable for offenders with severe mental illness, low risk offenders and those with learning difficulties. Perpetrators are systematically encouraged to understand the link between beliefs, feelings, intents, and actions. The development of understanding and self knowledge is accompanied by instruction on the use of non-violent strategies. Groups are usually between four and 12 men. The sessions include discussions, role play, video clips and written exercises. The rub for some men is that sessions in many of the programmes are recorded on video for audit and staff training purposes.

The IDAP is available mainly in the community, but also in open prisons and in full custody. It is a rolling programme of nine modules consisting of 3×2 hourly sessions in each. Offenders can start the programme at the beginning of any module except the sexual respect module. It teaches non-controlling behaviour strategies, and victim empathy. The Thames Valley (CDVP) programme is only available in the community and is has up to 28×2 hourly group sessions.

Women's Safety Workers is a voluntary organization which collaborates with the National Probation Service offering support, advice and information to the victims and partners of men undertaking the IDAP and CDVP programmes. All 42 probation areas of England and Wales deliver either CDVP or IDAP courses.

The Healthy Relationships Programme is only available in custody. It is also run by the prison service and probation service. According to Spread (part of the European Daphne programme under the umbrella of SURT[1] (http://www.surt.org/spread/docs/spread_docs/United_Kingdom.pdf), the programme has six modules and lasts about 24 weeks. There are two types of HRP, the moderate and the high intensity programmes. The moderate intensity programme runs over a 2-month period and is designed for those men assessed as having a moderate risk/moderate need, who have been violent in their intimate relationships. The high intensity programme runs over a 5-month period and is designed for high risk/high need offenders, who have been violent in their intimate relationships. The programme is 68 sessions long and has at least 10 individual sessions. There are no similar programmes for women.

There is, as yet, no information about the efficacy of these programmes. As the Ministry of Justice(National Offender Management Service) puts it (http://www.swmprobation.gov.uk/wp-content/uploads/2010/06/What-works-Domestic-violence.pdf) 'research has not yet clearly indicated which interventions for domestic violence are most effective in reducing reoffending'; it should add 'if any' into that sentence. An American review (Babcock et al., 2004) of 22 studies suggests, however, that there is little to differentiate the cognitive behavioural approach and the Duluth model,[2] both reduce recidivism by 5 to 15%. Both courses do have high face validity and give purpose and meaning to time in prison. Inevitably they emphasize male aggression and do not deal very extensively with female provocation and aggression. An important review of the

---

[1] A European women's foundation which is concerned with domestic violence.

[2] The Duluth model originated in Duluth in Minnesota in USA on the basis of a power systems theory of the domestic environment, with a strong feminist agenda using the concept of patriarchy. It is not used extensively outside of the USA because it treats men as 'the problem' rather than examining all aspects of the relationship.

various treatment approaches to the perpetrators of domestic violence (Rivett, 2006) ends with a plea 'it is time that mental health practitioners, especially those with forensic skills, engage with domestic violence services and contribute their clinical and research skills.'

Violence to Children

Withhold not correction from a child: for if thou strike him with the rod, he shall not die. Thou shalt beat him with the rod, and deliver his soul from hell (Proverbs 23:13–14 bible).

Cruelty and violence to children seem to be as inherent a part of human nature as does tender nurturing. Reading a little social history about almost any period can be a disturbing experience when the treatment of children is under scrutiny. 'Discipline' has almost invariably been violent. Even in twenty-first century Britain it is legal to assault children in ways which are illegal if the victim is an adult. Things have improved; however, in Britain, children are no longer driven to early deaths by being expected to work long hours in appalling conditions. Dotheboys Hall in *Nicholas Nickleby* is history thanks in part to the journalistic skills of Charles Dickens (see Dickens, 1995). Maltreatment of children in institutions has continued, however. A particularly horrific example was treatment meted out at the Bryn Estyn Home in Wrexham (Waterhouse, 2000).

These horrors set the background for the individual cases of cruelty and violence which the psychiatrist may encounter. It is of interest that the term 'battered child syndrome' has disappeared from the lexicon. It was coined in 1962 for a purpose by an American paediatrician, Henry Kempe. It is difficult to grasp now that until that time there was significant social denial about the physical abuse of children in the domestic environment. In Kempe's seminal paper (1971) he said:

I coined the term' The Battered Child Syndrome', in 1962, despite its provocative and anger-producing nature. I had for the preceding 10 years talked about child abuse, non-accidental, or inflicted injury, but few paid attention. ... When I was a houseman 25 years ago I saw many bashed babies and I was taught that abusive parents were either drunk fathers or inadequate mothers, all from the lower social classes. It was only when Dr. Silver and I, between 1956 and 1960, saw a great number of parents who did not fit this stereotype that we began to reach out for a better explanation.

It is worthwhile pondering whether we have actually found a better explanation. Perhaps the most startling of Kempe's comments is:

The resistance of physicians to the diagnosis of the battered child syndrome, particularly in its mild form, is overwhelming. Physicians will go to enormous lengths to deny a possibility of physical abuse of a child by his parents. Rare bleeding disorders, osteogenesis imperfecta tarda, obscure endocrine disease, 'spontaneous' subdural haematoma, malabsorption syndrome are invoked. All are an attempt to deny the fact that failure to thrive or injuries could be due to pathological mothering.

Reading the story of Baby P (see below) makes some of us wonder whether we have entirely overcome this resistance. Is the zealous prosecution of some mothers who lose children in puzzling circumstances (see chapter 26) a reaction to this resistance?

In 2008/2009, the age group most at risk of homicide in England and Wales was children under 1 year old, at 27 per million population, with males in this group being the most vulnerable at a rate of 36 per million population (Smith et al., 2010). Older than this and the rate of child killing varies between 1 and 6 per million until the age of 16 when the death rate for young males jumps to 35 per million, although it remains at 6 per million for girls. Most of the under 16s were killed by parents or someone they knew; eight were thought to have been killed by strangers.

At one time vulnerable children could be listed on a child protection register, but In *Working Together to Safeguard Children* (2006) the Government announced that the maintenance of a separate child protection register would be replaced by the Integrated Children's System and, more specifically, through the existence of a child protection plan. This policy has been updated by a revised *Working Together to Safeguard Children* in 2010 (https://www.education.gov.uk/publications/standard/publicationdetail/page1/DCSF-00305-2010).

The NSPCC reported 50,552 children on a child protection register in March 2011; this is a rise from 34,623 in 2009 (+43%), most of the rise being accounted for by a 53% rise in England. In England, 1,870 (44%) were in the category of neglect, 4,500 physical abuse, 2,300 sexual abuse and 12,100 emotional abuse, this last category is the one growing fastest, although physical abuse has also increased over the 5 years (www.nspcc.org.uk/inform/research/statistics/child_protection_register_statistics_wda48723.html). It should be borne in mind that these figures represent cases that are known about, and the true rate of violence to children may be far higher than these figures suggest. For example seven out of 10 children are hit by their parents (Bennett, 2006), and it may be that a lot of child abuse and neglect still goes undetected.

A questionnaire survey in the USA (Gil, 1969) suggested that perhaps 3% of families cause deliberate injury to children in that country. In a British study of 134 children under the age of 5, located from hospitals and various social agencies in a 2-year period in Birmingham and suffering from non-accidental injury, it was found that nearly half had serious injuries and 21 (16%) died (Smith and Hanson, 1974). The children were equally divided between the sexes. The injuries reported in all surveys embrace every conceivable type of injury and torture, from internal damage, to head injuries, broken bones, burns, starvation and wasting, and poisoning. Beatings with hands, fists, belts, sticks, bars, burnings and scaldings, are all quite common. Parental explanations for the injuries vary but are often vague; 'fell on his head', 'bruises easily', 'fell down the stairs', 'sat on the radiator' are the general pattern. In the Birmingham study the 'battered' children were younger than other children brought to hospital because of injuries. Over one-third of the children had an intracranial haemorrhage (usually subdural); one-fifth had serious burns or scalds. One-third of the dead children had been battered before. Neurological sequelae that required long-term rehabilitation developed in 15% of cases. Other findings were that, regardless of head injury, language retardation occurred in the 'battered' sample.

For some time the case of Victoria Climbié in 2000 was frequently cited as the worst case of child abuse and systemic failure to protect a child at risk in modern Britain. She died of multiple organ failure with 128 separate injuries, following a year of abuse by her guardians who had brought her to England for education with the agreement of her parents who lived in the Ivory Coast. The Inquiry by Lord Laming made over 100 recommendations on the safeguarding of children from abuse (House of Commons Health Committee, 2003). The 2004 Children Act was a direct result of this case, so was the Every Child Matters Agenda (https://www.education.gov.uk/publications/eOrdering/Download/CM5860.pdf) which followed it and the appointment of the first Children's Commissioner in 2005. The systemic failures in Victoria Climbié's case were multiple, given that she (and her mistreatment) was known to several social services, housing, police and health services. The Children Act 2004 was designed to take a more global or holistic approach to the welfare and wellbeing of children, not just to protect them from harm as in the 1989 Children Act. The 2004 Act makes mention of children's physical and mental health and emotional wellbeing; protection from harm and neglect; education, training and recreation; the contribution made by them to society; and social and economic wellbeing.

If you are somewhat cynical about the 'modern Britain' bureaucratic response to every problem then what happened in a few short years will have confirmed your worst fears and dashed your spirits. The 'Every Child Matters Agenda' produced no fewer than five different government reports, and the original overarching report was signed by 13 smiling ministers. There were lots of other reports as well and complex almost incomprehensible flowcharts; the whole exercise implying that tragedies such as that suffered by Victoria Climbié were a thing of the past. On 23 August 2007 Peter Connelly (Baby P) died aged 17 months of horrific injuries and total neglect. He had more than 50 injuries and over an 8-month period he was repeatedly seen by Haringey Children's services and NHS health professionals. Haringey was exactly the same borough that Victoria Climbié lived in; he was 'looked after' by the same social services department as Victoria Climbié. The timeline published in the online version of the *Guardian* (http://www.guardian.co.uk/society/2008/nov/11/baby-p-death) gives a graphic account of the horror this child had to bear and the incredibly incompetent responses to his needs which were made by the professionals involved in his case, social workers, health visitors, police officers, administrators and doctors. Once again Lord Laming was called upon to write a report. The first report resulted in 14 recommendations from the House of Commons Select Committee on Health; the second one, called a progress report (Laming, 2009), added another 58 recommendations. Laming's anger showed through when he said:

> The... recommendations, are aimed at making sure that good practice becomes standard practice in every service. This includes recommendations on improving the inspection of safeguarding services and the quality of Serious Case Reviews as well as recommendations on improving the help and support children receive when they are at risk of harm. The utility of the policy and legislation has been pressed on me by contributors throughout this report. In such circumstances it is hard to resist the urge to respond by saying to each of the key services, if that is so 'NOW JUST DO IT!'

His criticisms were aimed at social services departments which he said suffered from 'low staff morale, poor supervision, high caseloads, under-resourcing and inadequate training'.

Child protection work was felt to be a 'Cinderella service' and social workers were losing confidence because of an 'over-emphasis on process and targets'. He singled out computer systems for recording information about vulnerable children, saying they were 'hampering progress' because professional practice and judgment were being compromised by an 'over-complicated, lengthy and tick-box assessment and recording system'. All professionals might reflect on these comments which seem pertinent to all areas of healthcare and social work at the present time.

Yet early diagnosis is critically important as Baby P's story illustrates. Predictions are of course impossible and as Laming reminds us ticking boxes in the hope that they constitute a risk assessment doesn't get us very far. Browne and Herbert (1997), psychologists who have extensively studied this area, warn of the potential for screening checklists to yield false positive and negative rates. Nevertheless, they list 12 items identified at birth (in descending order of importance) that they found to be associated with later abuse in the first 5 years of life, and which should draw attention to a family which will probably need support and certainly merit close observation:

1. History of family violence.
2. Parent indifferent, intolerant or over-anxious towards the child.
3. Single or separated parent.
4. Socioeconomic problems such as unemployment.
5. History of mental illness, drug or alcohol addiction.
6. Parent abused or neglected as a child.
7. Infant premature, low birth weight.
8. Infant separated from mother for more than 24 hours post-delivery.
9. Mother less than 21 years old at time of birth.
10. Step-parent or cohabitee present.
11. Less than 18 months between birth of children.
12. Infant mentally or physically handicapped.

Browne and Herbert (1997) also note that a third of families in their prospective study ($n=106$) that went on to abuse were identified as 'low risk' using the above checklist at the time of birth.

In an ideal world, child protection services would be preventative rather than reactive, and certainly the aim of social services is to prevent re-occurrence of abuse and to avert abuse in families with serious problems. The reality is that services will struggle to provide an effective reactive service let alone institute large interventions for parents across the board to prevent the occurrence of child abuse. Thus the screening approach with all of its limitations is an attempt to focus limited resources to those who may need it. In fact this more socio-demographic approach can only work if suitable interventions are available, and when a family is seen as 'high-risk' on a screening assessment, a more in depth, individualized and multidisciplinary evaluation is provided. Browne (1995) suggests six important aspects to that assessment of high-risk parent–child relationships and the child's need for protection:

1. The evaluation of the caretaker's knowledge and attitudes to parenting the child.
2. Parental perceptions of the child's behaviour and the child's perceptions of the parent.
3. Parental emotions and responses to stress.
4. The style of parent–child interaction and behaviour.
5. The quality of child to parent attachment
6. The quality of parenting.

Browne and Herbert (1997) go on to explain the research behind these items and the approaches to intervention. They suggest that resolving some of these problems in high-risk families is the key to preventing child abuse or the recurrence of child abuse.

Kevin Browne has also reviewed eight European assessment tools to identify families at risk of child abuse (http://www.dji.de/bibs/Expertise_Browne.pdf). He concluded as follows:

> None of the assessment instruments reported over 90% sensitivity except Brockington et al. (2001) whose primary focus was actually maternal bonding on a small clinical sample. Therefore, it is inappropriate to use any of the assessments to assess the 'risk' of child

maltreatment. Nevertheless, with a reasonable level of accuracy, they can be used as an assessment of need in families. Prioritising families for more intensive support may in turn prevent child maltreatment as the 'sensitivity' shows that the majority of maltreating parents are in the high need (or priority) group.

This is an important statement which is worth hanging on to in almost any so-called risk assessment exercise.

Forensic psychiatrists are rarely front line workers in dealing with the family in any case of child abuse whether by neglect, violence, or sex. They should, however, be familiar with current social policy. This however is easier said than done. For England and Wales the best website at the time of writing (and they change frequently) is probably http://www.webarchive.nationalarchives.gov.uk/20100202100434/dcsf.gov.uk/everychildmatters/strategy/. This uses opaque language and plenty of jargon. There are letters to everybody and the main point seems to be the establishment of family intervention projects (FIPs) right across England and Wales. FIPs are explained in another document entitled *Family Intervention Projects and Safeguarding* which gives 'model protocols for practice', beginning as follows:

Family Intervention Projects (FIPs) provide intensive support to vulnerable families. Utilizing multi-agency, whole-family support plans alongside assertive working methods FIPs help families avoid negative sanctions they may be facing and help families to address their problems in a way that sustains positive change across social, environmental and economic areas.

Nowhere is there a hint of the clinical skills required.

The Royal College of Psychiatrists has a pamphlet for the general public (http://www.rcpsych.ac.uk/expertadvice/youthinfo/parentscarers/parenting/childabuseandneglect.aspx) which lists a few signs which may indicate bullying and/or abuse:

- watchful, cautious or wary of adults;
- unable to play and be spontaneous;
- aggressive or abusive;
- bullying other children or being bullied themselves;
- unable to concentrate, underachieving at school and avoiding activities that involve removal of clothes, e.g. sports;
- having temper tantrums and behaving thoughtlessly;
- lying, stealing, truanting from school and getting into trouble with the police;
- finding it difficult to trust other people and make friends.

If child abuse is suspected, more than one opinion on the case should be sought urgently. Paediatric, general practice, orthopaedic, child psychiatry and social work opinions may all be relevant. If, on consultation, there seems to be a serious likelihood of child abuse, then the local authority social services department must be informed immediately. The responsibility to protect a child from harm is the personal responsibility of every member of staff working within the health service, and the obligations are clearly set out in the Children Acts 1989 and 2004 (see also chapter 19). Initially contact with Social Services should be verbal, but should be followed up immediately with written information. Although difficult in practice, any written report should be restricted to factual information rather than opinion. If this is not possible, then fact and opinion should be clearly delineated. Social workers from that department should then consult with those who know the case and consider some preventive action. This may be advice to the parents, the provision of day care, a play group, a child minder, attendance at a family centre, advice about voluntary fostering and the like. In very urgent and serious cases, compulsory action may be considered, such as an emergency protection order.

Longer term

In the longer term, a care order or a supervision order may be provided by the courts for the child, and this may mean placement away from the parental home.

Every area of the country has to have child protection plans for all the children in the area who have been abused or who are at risk of abuse. Five categories of abuse are considered for plans: neglect, physical abuse (e.g. violence, poisoning), sexual abuse, emotional abuse, grave concern (e.g. other children in the family have been abused).

Twice-yearly case conferences are at the heart of the protection scheme; they should allow for a frank multi-professional discussion about the child's progress, and will include a social worker, teacher, the family doctor, a liaison police officer, and other significant professionals. This should include psychiatric advisers, both to the child and the parents. If a psychiatrist treating a parent is not invited to the conference, s/he should make every effort to remain as informed about the conferences as possible and should be prepared to swap sensitive information with the team (with the patient's knowledge of course). Parents are rarely invited to these conferences, but they could be and perhaps should be more often.

It would be helpful in all child abuse cases, if the parents or abusers were referred for psychiatric examination. The needs of distressed adults are frequently overlooked when children have been hurt. It is right that the needs of children should be put first, but abusing parents are usually in severe psychological distress themselves. A psychiatric referral is not only humanitarian, it may also be a source of extra useful information which will help make better predictions and management plans for the child. In an ideal world, *each* member of a family in which abuse is occurring should have a personal counsellor. This may be a social worker, a nurse, or a psychiatrist, but should be someone who puts the interests of that individual high on the agenda of concern. Resources will limit the implementation of this ideal, but it should be approached as far as possible. This is not to neglect the needs of the child who will have suffered considerably, who will be a candidate to become a violent adult, and who should be referred for psychiatric and/or psychological treatment in his/her own right.

The details of the management of each individual child abuser will depend on a full psychiatric (including social and psychological) assessment. Diagnosis, family dynamics, personality characteristics should all be investigated in some detail so that a clear understanding of the processes of aggression can be obtained, shared and discussed with other professionals concerned with the case particularly the social services department. Removal of one or more individuals from the family may be necessary (this should only be the child as a last resort), family discussions may be fruitful, practical assistance with access to a nursery or play group, and medication to effect symptom relief in depressed, anxious, or psychotic parents may be needed. Counselling to reduce drinking is occasionally helpful; above all support for the frightened abusing parents must be forthcoming, especially if they are to be prosecuted.

Sometimes the parental problem can be identified as one of the severer forms of psychosis or personality disorder, in which case admission to hospital may be necessary for that person. Whenever possible, contacts between members of the family should be maintained during such hospitalization. Feelings of guilt and rejection in the various parties, particularly the children, can thus be reduced.

In England and Wales, the prosecution of abusing parents is a matter for the Crown Prosecution Service (CPS). This service is provided with evidence by the police. All cases of serious abuse will be reported to the police. The police and the CPS will decide whether the evidence is strong enough for prosecution and whether prosecution would be in the public interest. Following a successful prosecution, the courts will decide on the disposal of an abusing adult. The majority of seriously abusing parents will be given prison sentences, possibly life or an IPP. This seems to signify that the courts regard these people as 'normal' but wicked. This is of course nonsense, but it does divert the therapeutic responsibilities from the NHS to the prisons. This is happening in many areas. It has the advantage of being cheap and appeasing public opinion, but inevitably means a second rate service; prisons are not hospitals and are not well equipped to deliver therapeutic activities. Indeed, apart from specially designed therapeutic communities, such as Grendon prison, prison activities are anti-therapeutic. The pros and cons of so-called 'convergence' are well argued in the Sainsbury document (Rutherford, 2010).

Prison Treatment

The day-to-day reality in prison is that almost no psychiatry or psychotherapy is offered. It is still very difficult in Britain for trained psychiatrists to conduct treatment in prison, and almost impossible to link any prison treatment with the family or with long-term community care. A lengthy prison sentence is almost bound to break up the family if it has not been broken by the prosecution itself, and child abusers in prison are vulnerable to savage attacks from other prisoners. The best that a prisoner can hope for is his/her inclusion on various prison courses that provide cognitive group programmes which are run by the forensic psychology service within the prisons. A prisoner may be offered the healthy relationships programme mentioned above, but will probably begin with a course on enhanced thinking skills (ETS) and move on to a violence reduction programme such as CALM (Controlling Anger and Learning to Manage it) (http://www.myexistenz.com/Probation3/CALM.html). Heavy drinking and drug abuse are often an integral part of severe violence. For these the prison service offers access to RapT (a voluntary body – The Rehabilitation for Addicted Prisoners' Trust) and P-ASRO (Prisons Addressing Substance Related Offending – see below).

It is not part of the psychiatrist's job to advise or recommend punishment such as imprisonment. If it is thought advisable for a family to separate, there are other ways of achieving this. If treatment in security is required, or it is clear that the court will not accept treatment unless it begins in security, then a hospital order is the correct recommendation. It may be that the hospital system would be overwhelmed if this advice were followed in every case, but that is a political matter concerning resources, and should be kept separate from the consideration of an individual case (see also chapter 25).

Enhanced thinking skills (ETS): According to McDougall et al. (2009), who undertook a randomized controlled trial, ETS is a 20-session programme designed to provide training in impulse control, flexible thinking, taking the viewpoint of others, values and moral reasoning, general reasoning and inter-personal problem solving. The courses are run by two course tutors, with a maximum of ten people in each group. Sessions involve exercises and assignments, using role play and discussion. The sessions are interactive. Generally sessions last 2 hours and are run between three and five times a week, over a time period of 4 to 6 weeks. Using the Eysenck impulsivity scale (Eysenck and Eysenck, 1978) the researchers showed that the programme is effective at a statistically significant level in reducing self-report of impulsivity. 'Completion of the ETS course also had a statistically significant impact in a positive direction on a number of secondary measures. These were locus of control (i.e. the extent to which offenders think that they are responsible for their own problem behaviour or whether they perceive it to be externally controlled), general attitudes to offending, and cognitive indolence (i.e. an indication of lack of attention to consequences, and short-cut problem solving), which are also targeted in the programme.'

CALM: Controlling Anger and Learning to Manage it is a cognitive behavioural programme aimed at prisoners for whom problems in managing their emotions are components in current or previous offending. Prisoners who have a psychotic illness, those with no literacy skills and those who use aggression solely to achieve a purpose (e.g. robbery, control) are excluded. There are six modules with a total of 26 sessions (www.prisonmentalhealth. org/downloads/other_info/10-1_offending_behaviour_ programmes.pdf).

The six core subjects are run over 24 sessions (each lasting 2 hours) at a rate of 2–3 sessions per week. Throughout the programme personal assignments are set to provide participants an opportunity to consolidate learning and to try out skills as they are introduced. One regular assignment involves self-monitoring of arousal, cognitions and behaviours throughout the programme duration. Others include problem solving without anger (jealousy, anxiety, etc), and challenging irrational thinking. The programme is not suitable for those who use premeditated violence, e.g. with weapons.

Factitious and Induced Illness (Munchausen Syndrome by Proxy)

Factitious and induced illness (FII) is the revised name of the previous Munchausen syndrome by proxy (MSBP). This new name is a great help, as it describes the problem and avoids questions about the colourful Baron Munchausen, an eighteenth century mercenary, who has nothing to do with medicine or disease, imported into psychiatry in a romantic moment by Richard Asher (1951) to describe patients who made up illness stories about themselves in order to attract medical attention. The term Munchausen syndrome by proxy was coined in the USA by Money and Werlwas (1976) in a case of induced dwarfism in a child by starving and beating the child. The following year Meadow (1977) used it in Britain to describe two mothers who consistently produced false stories and fabricated evidence in order to attract hospital attention to their children. He called it 'the hinterland of child abuse'. As more information about the syndrome has become available it has become clear that such behaviour is a strange but very real threat to the few children who are unfortunate enough to be in the hands of very needy parents to attract medical help to their families in this way. Many of the children trapped in this situation are permanently damaged and between 8 and 10% of them die of their injuries.

Such a strange disorder has attracted a great deal of controversy, partly because it is difficult to believe, partly because we instinctively rise up against the idea that in some cases mothering can be bad for a child and partly because of clinical misjudgments in an extremely sensitive situation. Meadow's misjudgment of parents who he believed were damaging children finally, as we shall see later (Chapter 26), proved to be his undoing or perhaps more accurately the undoing of some unfortunate mothers who lost their children by way of sudden death in infancy and went to prison to compound their misery.

The disorder is very difficult to diagnose accurately and misdiagnosis can lead either to further harm to a child or to harm to a parent. The children can present with a variety of baffling symptoms which have to be investigated by skilled and sensitive paediatricians. The presentation can be almost anything as the harm can be induced by partial suffocation, minor injuries, poisons of various kinds, or even fictitious seizures. In her review of the disorder Rosenberg (1987) lists 69 symptoms and signs that had been reported up to that date varying from abdominal pain to weight loss, including ataxia, haematemesis, and acute renal failure.

Meadow (1995) defined Munchausen syndrome by proxy in terms of what it is not. In his view the essence of the syndrome is that the parent is seeking a sick role for herself. He described eight other types of unhelpful and even dangerous mothering which failed to meet this criterion. In other words he wanted to incorporate the concept of motivation into the syndrome. This may be a guide to some of the psychopathology, but it is a poor definitional criterion. It is almost impossible to get inside the head of somebody else to determine the motivation for their behaviour. There are a number of definitions available but the one given by Rosenberg (1987) following a literature review may well be the most apt:

1. illness in a child which is simulated (faked) and/or produced by who is in loco parentis; and

2. presentation of the child for medical assessment and care, usually resulting in multiple medical procedures; and

3. denial of knowledge by the perpetrator as to the aetiology of the child's illness; and

4. acute symptoms and signs of the child abate when the child is separated from the perpetrator.

The review found 117 cases had been reported: 46% were boys; 45% were girls. There were 67 cases with no information about the child's age at the time of diagnosis. The age range was 1 month to 252 months. Of the 117 children, 10 died (9% mortality). Of the 107 survivors, at least 8% had long-term morbidity, including necessity for multiple oesophageal surgeries and impairment of gastrointestinal function, serious psychiatric problems, destructive joint changes and a limp, and mental retardation with cerebral palsy and cortical blindness. Several had multiple abdominal surgeries for laparotomy, colectomy, or ileostomy, predisposing to future medical problems.

All the children died at the hands of their mothers (one was an adoptive mother, and in one case there was question of paternal collusion). Four of these mothers had at least some nursing training (two were qualified), and one mother was a social worker. There was distinct evidence of Munchausen syndrome in two mothers, and the same two mothers became suicidal after their children's deaths. No mother admitted to homicide. One mother was convicted of murder. In 20% of the death cases the parents had been confronted with the diagnosis of MSBP and the children had been sent home to them, subsequently to die.

Psychiatric or psychological assessment of the mother was described in detail in only a very few cases but it is of interest that loneliness and isolation seemed to be prominent.

All the perpetrators in this series were women, usually mothers. In one case a husband colluded and in the original case described by Money and Werlwas both parents were implicated, hence the title of the paper *Folie à deux*.[3] Meadow (1998) wrote a paper on male perpetrators noting, 'I did not encounter a male perpetrator in the first 10 years of dealing with these families. However, in the last 10 years I have been involved with 15 cases involving male perpetrators.' Nevertheless the syndrome is particularly associated with females and mothering.

The psychopathology behind these extraordinary attacks on children is difficult to unravel and generalizations may be misplaced. Bools et al. (1994) looked at the lifetime psychiatric histories of 47 mothers, 34 had a history of a factitious or a somatoform disorder, 26 a history of self-harm, 10 had a history of alcohol or drug misuse, 9 had a criminal history unrelated to child abuse. This study may give an important clue to unconscious psychopathology for it links self-inflicted injury, in some cases, to injury to a child. This would be understandable if the mother, say, experienced, at some level, the child as part of herself. Gray and Bentovim (1996) studied 37 families and found that all the mothers had suffered at least one of the following: privation, child abuse, psychiatric illness, or significant loss (e.g. bereavement). In addition nearly half of the parents had serious marital problems. They hypothesized that the illness induction was initiated by the parents perceiving the child to be ill and using this focus of illness as a way of solving major personal or marital or family difficulties. These authors did not use diagnostic labels, but noted that in some cases the parents held their beliefs about the child's health with delusional intensity. Adshead and Bluglass (2005) undertook a semi-structured interview assessing attachment representations in 67 mothers who had induced illness in their children. They rated 12 of others as secure in terms of their own childhood attachment but for the rest there was evidence of unresolved trauma or loss reactions (40 cases) and/or 18 gave unusually disorganized and incoherent accounts of attachment relationships (18 cases) in their own childhoods.

Treatment is difficult; denial intrudes and obstructs. Hospitalization of the child is essential for full evaluation. This helps to separate the child from the abuser and in some cases that separation may be needed on a long-term basis or permanently. If the abuse of the child is clinically proved, then confrontation is necessary. It is important that the whole team is certain that child abuse is occurring; wrongful accusation is disastrous for all, including the medical team concerned. Schreier and Libow (1993) recommend that this is done in a family group to assess family complicity and support for mother and child. Confrontation must be followed immediately by psychological support for the abuser who may decompensate and perhaps become suicidal. The child's siblings must also be assessed and protected, perhaps by removal. Clearly this must all be done in tandem with the relevant social services.

As Schreier and Libow (1993) say there are few encouraging data available on successful therapeutic work with perpetrators of factitious and induced illnesses in children.

While there is not much literature to guide us, our theories of the dynamics of this disorder and social context … suggest that it would be useful in therapy for these patients to explore their early as well as current feelings of neglect and how their relationships with medical staff may enact those earlier relationship issues. Exploration of relationships with significant figures in their childhoods as well as current adult relationships, especially spouses, is likely to reveal patterns of experienced abandonment and deprivation. In reality, most of these mothers appear to have little support or attention from their partners, who themselves would likely benefit from psychotherapy.

Violence to the Elderly

As with babies, older individuals who make constant demands for attention and succour will stretch the patience of others, particularly those who have a vulnerable, brittle personality. If the dynamics between the younger individual and the elderly person include complex power struggles, then violence may ensue. As with children and women, the physically weak individual will fare badly.

A particularly vulnerable group of old people are those who suffer from dementia. They are both demanding and intensely frustrating; they can be aggressive and they provide few rewards, as they no longer respond with smiles or gratitude. In surveys of caregivers (Pillemer and Suitor, 1992) 20% reported a fear that they may become violent to the patient they are caring for and 6% actually engaged in violence; this figure was higher at 12% in another similar study (Coyne et al., 1993). Risk is increased when caregivers lack understanding of the illness or of aggression, where patients themselves are hostile or aggressive and where there is a premorbid family history/cycle of violence.

---

[3] French=madness shared between two people.

Perhaps the most notable thing about so-called 'granny bashing' is the way in which it is tolerated. Whilst the public conscience about other forms of domestic violence has to some extent been awakened by increased knowledge, minimal action has followed the identification of violence to the elderly (Marsden, 1978).

The extent of the problem has been captured for the UK by the Study of Abuse and Neglect of Older People, carried out by the National Centre for Social Research and King's College London (O'Keeffe, M, Hills, A et al., 2007). It was commissioned by Comic Relief and the Department of Health. Over 2100 people aged 66 and over, living in private households (including sheltered accommodation), took part in the survey. Overall, 2.6%, or about 1 in 40 of people aged 66 and over living in private households reported that they had experienced mistreatment involving a family member, close friend or care worker in a 1-year period. This is probably an underestimate but it means that at least 227,000 elderly people are being mistreated each year. The authors suggest that maybe only 3% of these cases come to the notice of the authorities. Prevalence rates for the individual types of mistreatment were: neglect (1.1%), financial (0.7%), psychological (0.4%), physical (0.4%) and sexual (0.2%). Six per cent of the misused reported two different types of mistreatment. Thus the rates of actual reported violence are fairly low, although the figures mean that over 30,000 pensioners are physically abused each year in the UK. The rate for physical violence went up to 0.8% if the subjects were asked about all mistreatment since the age of 65 years. The authors say that these figures are comparable to other western countries. When trying to tease out the risk factors for mistreatment only one stood out consistently across all types of mistreatment: depression. Whether this is cause or effect could not be discerned in the survey, but it emphasizes the need for psychiatric services to the elderly.

The survey had little to say about perpetrators, but a previous US study (Brownell et al., 2000) looked at them in New York City. They studied 404 abusers and found that over half were men, the average age was 45 years, and 64% lived with the victim. Physical abuse was reported in 28% of cases.

The majority of abusers were unemployed (64%). Overall, 17% of abusers had been in prison, 3% were incarcerated at the time of the study and 5% were on probation. Just over one-third of them were adult children (39%); 22% were non-relatives; 8% were partners or spouses and 15% relatives other than child or spouse/partner; 161 (74%) were identified as mentally disordered. Of the 161 cases, 82 (51%) were substance (including alcohol) abusers. The next largest category of impairment was mental illness, with 42 or 26% of abusers identified as mentally ill. The two smallest categories were mental illness from chemical addiction (27 or 17%) and dementia (10 or 6%). This is yet another demonstration of the significant relationship between brain dysfunction (drugs, alcohol or illness) and violence of almost any kind.

Alcohol, Substance Misuse and Violence

Nestor (2002) noted that *substance abuse disorders represent by far the strongest correlates of violence among all mental disorders.* When rates of violence and impact of psychiatric disorders are compared, the rate of violence for individuals with substance abuse disorders is 12–16 times higher than the rate for those without, which compares to a rate five times higher in those with major mental illness such as schizophrenia (Swanson et al., 1990). For young psychiatric patients discharged into the community, the rate of violence is doubled by the presence of a substance abuse disorder (Steadman et al., 1998).

Not only is general offending more prevalent in young offenders who are heavy drinkers (Fergusson et al., 1996a), but as alcohol intake increases, so does violent offending (Norström, 1998). It is no surprise therefore that surveys of offenders show that offenders generally (and particularly those aged 16–24) tend to drink more heavily than non-offenders and that rates of 'hazardous' levels of drinking in prisons run to 60% of the male population and 40% of the female prison population (McMurran 2003). McMurran went on to list a variety of mechanisms that may explain the relationship between excess alcohol consumption and crime:

Alcohol may cause crime directly (e.g. disinhibition, cognitive impairment); alcohol and crime may be linked through a shared third factor (e.g. personality, social disadvantage); they may be in a conjunctive relationship, connected by social and contextual factors (e.g. being in a pub with other drinkers); crime may lead to drinking (e.g. having the money, to assuage guilt); or the relationship may be spurious (e.g. lying about drinking to mitigate crime).

For further discussion of the relationship between alcohol abuse and violence, see chapter 18. Here, finally, it should be noted that while alcohol is a risk factor for violence, not all who have such problems become violent.

A Swedish study (Lindelius and Salum, 1975) showed that alcoholic patients of all sorts are largely non-violent. Violence was related to social deterioration such as homelessness. The association between alcoholism and homicide is also discussed in Chapter 14.

Boles and Miotto (2003) reviewed the drug misuse literature but report relatively few sources of data. They concluded that stimulants or drugs which disinhibit the user may play a more direct causative role in violence, but that violence may also be committed in the broader context of drug culture through 'sales and marketing' disputes, rivalries and 'turf wars'. Furthermore, crimes such as theft and burglary may be committed to finance drug addiction. Clearly the relationship between alcohol and violence is a complex one and affected by a number of other factors including anger and coping strategies.

In prisons of England and Wales the importance of intoxicants is acknowledged. There are very few resources available to tackle the problem adequately although every prison does have a CARAT team and in some prisons specific drugs and alcohol treatments are offered such as the RAPt programme and P-ASRO. See also chapter 25 for more information.

CARAT (Counselling Assessment Referral Advice and Throughcare) is a drug service that is available in every prison in the UK. Prisoners can be assessed by a CARAT team, given advice about drug misuse and referred to appropriate drug services. CARAT workers may also offer counselling and group work to prisoners who want to stop misusing drugs. The common drugs dealt with by CARAT are heroin, crack cocaine and cannabis. One of the anomalies of the service is that it doesn't deal with the commonest and most dangerous drug consumed by offenders, viz alcohol. It only deals with illegal substances.

RAPt: the Rehabilitation for Addicted Prisoners Trust (www.rapt.org.uk) works to help people with drug and alcohol dependence, both in prison and in the community through support, advice, counselling, and group work. It also works with the families and carers of substance misusers. The RAPt treatment is a rolling, abstinence-based programme adapted from the 12-step Alcoholics Anonymous (AA) programme. It lasts 16 to 20 weeks, often on a prison wing in which a drug-free environment is enforced. The treatment involves groups, peer evaluations, community meetings and activities and written work. There are also lectures, workshops and one-to-one counselling. Up to half of the counsellors are themselves in recovery from addiction.

The Trust also provides CARAT services (see above).

P-ASRO: Prisons – Addressing Substance Related Offending is a cognitive behavioural group work programme designed to address drug dependence and related offending (http://www.edp.org.uk/Criminal-Justice-Services). The programme targets offenders who are dependent on one or more drug, or a combination of drugs and alcohol. The programme is usually divided into four sections, made up of 20 sessions run over a 5–6 week period. Sessions can be run at a minimum of three or a maximum of four times per week. Section 1 is devoted to motivation to change; confrontation is avoided and the relationship between substance use and crime is explored. Offenders are asked to set goals for change. Section 2 attempts to enhance self-awareness and encourages participants to monitor their thoughts of using drugs, and generate incentives for maintaining change. Section 3 aims to prevent relapse by preparing participants to meet and deal with high-risk situations for substance use. These sessions attend to both internal and external risk factors, including cravings, mood changes and interpersonal problems. The last section, Section 4, is concerned with lifestyle modification encouraging the individual to substitute new activities for criminogenic ones.

CRIMES OF VIOLENCE

Crimes are socially determined phenomena, defined as such by manmade laws and are therefore, by definition, closely linked to culture. Criminal patterns will differ from time to time and place to place. It is sometimes thought that we live in a violent age, and perhaps that is true compared with the 1920s and 1930s, but is it true compared with previous centuries? When Anthony Trollope (1869) was writing *Phineas Phinn* he described London's after-dark street violence in horrifying terms. At the time, it was usual for personal protectors (e.g. truncheons) to be carried by men walking out at night anywhere in a large city and for women to stay indoors. In the eighteenth century, travel between towns was highly risky because of highway robbers. In the Glencoe massacre of 1692 (Prebble, 1966) 'only' 78 people died, because of the valley's low population, but the atrocity was an act of genocide which must rank alongside many of recent times in ferocity.

Home Office figures show that levels of violence in England and Wales are steadily falling (see table 9.1). The 2008/2009 figure for homicide is the lowest since 1989.

Table 9.1   Levels of violence in England and Wales, 2002/2009

	Homicide (includes murder, manslaughter and infanticide)	Attempted murder	Intentional destruction of viable unborn child	Causing death by dangerous driving or by careless driving when under the influence of drink or drugs	More serious wounding or other act endangering life
2002/03	1,047	822	2	414	18,016
2003/04	904	888	8	445	19,528
2004/05	868	740	4	441	19,612
2005/06	764	920	5	432	18,825
2006/07	758	633	5	459	17,276
2007/08	774	621	4	419	15,121
2008/09	662	576	8	427	. . .

Compiled from http://www.rds.homeoffice.gov.uk/rds/pdfs09/recorded-crime-2002-2009rev.xls

Homicide

The term 'homicide' covers the offences of murder ('intentional' killing), homicide ('accidental' or 'unintentional' killing) and infanticide (intentional killing of a child by his/her mother – usually associated with a psychiatric condition – within the first 12 months of life). The homicide rate in England and Wales has varied between one per 100,000 population in 1901 (approximately) and 1.6 per 100,000 in 2001 and was around 1.4 per 100,000 in 2009. There was a marked decline in the homicide rate during the first half of the twentieth century, dropping to around 0.5 per 100,000 in 1961. The actual numbers of homicides were lowest in 1906 (263) according to a remarkable Home Office website which traces the prevalence of crime in England and Wales from 1898 until 2001 when the counting rules for crime changed (www.homeoffice.gov.uk/rds/pdfs07/recorded-crime-1898-2002.xls).

Homicide figures, perversely, always omit causing death by dangerous or drunken driving. These motoring figures fluctuate between 31 in 1956 when they make their first appearance until their peak of 769 in 1973, since then they have dropped, reaching their lowest at 189 in 1983, rising again to 419 in 1990 and falling to 335 in 2001. Clearly if these figures were to be added to the other types of homicide then the recent rates would be well above 2 per 100,000. The recorded homicide rate of approximately 1.4 per 100,000 is on a par with the European average (Tavares and Thomas, 2009). Most countries in Europe including the United Kingdom have seen falls in the homicide rate during the first part of the twenty-first century and compare favourably with the United States homicide rate of 5.6 per 100,000 population (Flatley et al., 2010).

In the year 2008/2009 there were 651 deaths recorded as homicide by the police in England and Wales. The risk of being a victim of homicide was 12 per million population, although much higher in babies less than 1 year old (27 per million population). As with previous years the most common method of killing was with a sharp implement (39%), men were more likely to be victims (71%), half of their assailants being strangers; female victims were more likely to be killed by someone they knew (76%) and of these (69%) were killed by a partner or ex-partner. Shooting accounted for 6% of homicides in 2008/2009; a figure which is reducing year by year.

The proportionate contribution of people with mental disorder to national homicide figures has fallen as overall figures for homicide have risen (Taylor and Gunn, 1999). Although it is generally accepted that this proportionate contribution depends on the homicide base rate (the low rate of mentally disordered offenders remains constant), this assumption has been challenged (Lange et al., 2009) (see chapter 14 for a discussion).

It is artificial to divide violence up into categories such as we have in this text; the categories merge and overlap.

The subheadings used are merely for convenience and partly because they are currently in common usage. A separate category for homicide is used because, when a victim actually dies, then different attitudes, different criteria, even different laws come into effect. Murder is said to be 'a crime apart'. Manslaughter runs it close. Further, it might be noted that homicide is more likely to be reported to the police than any other crime.

In the subsequent discussion, however, it should be borne in mind that in biological terms homicide is simply at one end of a spectrum of violence, and the distinction between homicide and a lesser form of violence may simply be chance, the health, age and strength of the victim, the angle of a blow, the efficacy and proximity of the medical services and so on. The points made in respect of homicide may be also appropriate for other types of dangerous violence which could have ended fatally.

A significant number of violent people are mentally disordered. It is important to note that this is NOT to say that a significant number of mentally disordered people are violent, they are not. However it is very appropriate for forensic psychiatry services to focus on the minority of mentally disordered people who are violent; in this group the phenomena may well be linked.

The interest from the psychiatric point of view is to know how many of these cases are related to mental disorder. This would require a psychiatric examination of each case and reliable figures to be collected. The only national statistics that are collected relate to court decisions concerning diminished responsibility and insanity. As we have seen in chapter 11 such figures are more related to legal fashions and psychiatric attitudes than they are to pathological phenomena. A complete survey of London male prisoners remanded in custody charged with murder in the early 1980s showed that about 1 in 10 of them suffered from psychosis (mainly schizophrenia) (Taylor and Gunn, 1984). This figure has stood the test of time, but of course it does not give information about non-psychotic disorders. Unfortunately there is a tendency for psychiatrists and other professionals to emphasize psychotic phenomena implying that these are the only important and/or remediable characteristics of defendants charged with crimes.

A population-based study carried out in Sweden (where systematic psychiatric data are collected) showed the wide variety of pathology present in those convicted of homicide or attempted homicide between 1988 and 2001 (see table 9.2). A total of 2005 offenders (166, 8.3% women) ranging in age from 15 to 90 years were studied (Fazel and Gramm, 2004). Over 90% of them had a diagnosable mental disorder. Besides the 9% with schizophrenia which so often is used as the key in the door to services, there are people with affective disorders, substance abuse, organic disorders, mental retardation, etc., all of whom would benefit from treatment. The exact numbers are not

Table 9.2 Study carried out on probation data in Sweden: Fazel and Grann (2004)

Diagnosis	No. of offenders	Percentage with diagnosis
Psychoses		
Schizophrenia	179	8.9
Bipolar affective disorder	50	2.5
Other psychoses	131	6.5
Drug-induced psychoses	29	1.4
Organic psychoses	20	1.0
All psychoses	409	20.4
Personality disorders		
Cluster A	24	1.2
Cluster B	71	3.5
Cluster C	16	0.8
Not otherwise specified	116	5.8
Principal diagnosis	227	11.3
Substance use disorder		
Principal diagnosis	394	19.7
Non-psychotic depressive disorders	47	2.3
Anxiety disorders	28	1.4
PTSD	10	0.5
Adjustment disorders	56	2.8
Child and adolescent disorders	42	2.1
Mental retardation	13	0.6
Other axis one diagnosis	238	11.9
No diagnosis	161	8.0

critical; it is the large pool of psychiatric need which is so arresting. It is legitimate to extrapolate this need into the much bigger population of people committing sublethal violence.

For the UK similar figures are available from the national confidential inquiry into suicide and homicide (http://www.medicine.manchester.ac.uk.cmhr/centreforsuicideprevention/nci). Shaw et al. (1999) looked at 718 homicides reported to the enquiry between April 1996 and November 1997. At least 220 had a lifetime history of mental disorder and 71 had symptoms of mental disorder at the time of the homicide; 102 had been in contact with mental health services at some previous time; 58 in the year immediately before the killing. The authors concluded that

'There are substantial rates of mental disorder in people convicted of homicide. Most do not have severe mental illness or a history of contact with mental health services.'

Other key messages were that mental health services need to prevent loss of contact with patients and that the clinical management of patients with both mental illness and substance misuse needs to be improved.

Parricide

A murder of a parent by his or her child is rare, approximately five mothers and five fathers in England and Wales each year (unpublished Home Office figures).

Given the immense system of taboos (both genetic and social) that a person has to overcome to kill a parent, one would expect that the killer would be very psychotic or suffer from some other serious psychopathology or be severely provoked. It is probably safe to say that the 'mentally normal' prisoner one of us met who was serving a life sentence for killing his mother, allegedly simply to steal some petty cash, has not been properly investigated. There are surprisingly few studies of parricide which is one extreme aspect of domestic violence.

Hillbrand et al. (1999) reviewed the literature attempting to separate matricide from patricide, male killers from female killers, and adolescents from adults. They concluded that the literature supports both child abuse and mental illness as explanatory models of parricide, sufferers of abuse being particularly likely to kill an abusing father, but they note that whilst the incidence of child abuse is common, it is still rare for an abused child to kill his/her parent. They also note that in the USA middle-class white people make up the bulk of youthful as well as adult parricide.

Bourget et al. (2007) studied domestic homicide in Quebec, Canada, between 1990 and 2005. There were 720 victims including 64 parricides; 52 were committed by sons, four by daughters; nine cases of double parricide were found and the remainder were 27 mothers and 37 fathers. In eight cases the perpetrator attempted or committed suicide following the killing; most (36/56) were mentally ill, the commonest diagnosis being schizophrenia or other psychosis; some were seriously depressed; four were intoxicated. Only two matricidal men and two patricidal men were not given an axis one diagnosis. In this study, unlike some others, patricide occurred more frequently than matricide. Most cases occurred without warning or knowledge that anything was wrong with the killer. In a few cases, however, the eventual victim predicted his/her own demise but his/her concerns were not taken seriously.

An earlier study (d'Orban and O'Connor, 1989) is particularly important because it focuses on women who kill their parents. The authors collected as complete a sample as possible from south-east England and found 14 matricides and three patricides; six of the women suffered from schizophrenia, five had psychotic depression, three had personality disorders and one was alcoholic; two of the patricides had no psychiatric disorder but were severely provoked by their violent father. The parricide was directly related to psychotic symptoms in 10 subjects. Five of the women with schizophrenia had persecutory delusional ideas (in three cases of being poisoned). One killing was an extended suicide, with the primary suicidal desire 'not to leave the mother behind'. A sexual element was involved in three cases. A woman aged 26 with antisocial personality disorder claimed that her father had had an incestuous relationship with her since the age of 18. She stabbed him as he approached her when he was drunk. The authors noted that some features of matricide by daughters are similar to those shown by matricidal sons. Characteristically (they say) female matricide occurs when women in midlife live alone with an elderly domineering mother in marked social isolation. The mother–daughter relationship was characterized by mutual hostility, interdependence and the killing was often carried out with extreme violence. Three of the subjects suffered from hypochondriacal delusions, which embraced the mother as well as themselves, and two of these committed multiple killings.

Heide (1994) reviewed adolescent parricide as a separate phenomenon, looking first at the types of maltreatment a child may suffer including physical abuse, sexual abuse, verbal abuse and psychological abuse (for example putting a child's pet to death in front of the child). She reviewed 10 studies of adolescent parricide and found that these forms of child maltreatment were common to all. She then personally studied seven young people, all white, aged 12 to 17 years; six of these were boys. The results from the 11 studies were amalgamated. Between them they killed six fathers, three mothers, and one brother. As this was America they all used firearms. Child physical abuse and spouse abuse were each identified in eight of the studies. In the cases of patricide severe spouse abuse frequently coexisted with and often preceded child physical abuse. Physical neglect was evident in five of the 11 studies. Emotional incest (when a parent aligns with a child and relates to that child as though the child were the spouse) was also identified in eight of the studies.

Parricide is thus an extreme version of domestic violence and always involves serious psychopathology, such as psychosis, abusive relationships and heavy drinking. The victim is frequently part of the psychopathology, may be incorporated in delusions, may be an abuser, certainly a provocation even if only a delusional one. The psychopathology needs to be fully assessed and appropriate treatment offered, whether that is to be in prison, in hospital, or in the community. In cases which fall short of a complete homicide urgent action is required to begin treatment and protect potential victims. Wherever possible a psychiatric disposal should be offered to the court involved in the case.

Below we deal with a few distinctive categories of homicide.

Homicide followed by suicide

Practitioners should never forget that suicide is a form of homicide and the two can be linked. There may be intense ambivalence between the two in psychotic states. One of the subjects in the 1984 homicide remand study (Taylor and Gunn, 1984) was suffering from schizophrenia. He first jumped in front of a bus at the behest of hallucinated suicidal instructions, but the driver swerved and braked and the man was not killed. A few hundred yards down the down the road he grabbed a passer-by and threw her under a bus; she was killed. Cases like this give some support for the Freudian theory of the interchangeability of self-directed and other-directed aggression (Freud, 1917). Some individuals with a high level of aggression may turn the aggression against others or against themselves according to circumstances (e.g. the deserted husband who went looking for his wife and her lover in order to kill them both but who, when he could not find them, returned home and gassed himself and his children).

Killers who kill themselves are more likely to be responsible for several killings at the one time (e.g. the whole family, Gibson, 1975). In Wolfgang's (1958a,b) study in Philadelphia, of 621 killers identified between 1948 and 1952, 24 (4%) committed suicide, 22 of these were men, 10 of whom had killed their wives; in all, 18 of the killers killed someone in their own family and in only three cases were the killer and the victim of the same sex. West (1965) studied 148 murder/suicide incidents in London and the Home Counties. There were considerable differences between these killers and those who survived:

The most striking distinguishing features of murder-suicides were the large numbers of women offenders and child victims, the very small numbers of offenders with previous convictions, and the total absence of the young thug who kills in the furtherance of theft or robbery.

From an analysis of the files of the dead individuals, it was estimated that insane killers were outnumbered by sane ones, the majority killing their relatives and then themselves under the pressure of collapsing physical health or impending disaster. Many of the incidents could thus have been extended suicides in individuals who have a strong feeling for and close identification with their families perhaps in the context of depression. In Norway a study of murder–suicides from 1990–2007 found that 90% of the perpetrators were men and 80% of the victims were females. Most of the killings were in the context of intimate relationships, usually with firearms. One in four Norwegians who kills a near acquaintance goes on to commit suicide (Galta et al., 2010).

A 5-year report of the confidential inquiry into the mental health aspects of homicide and suicide in England and Wales (National Confidential Inquiry, 2006) was notified of 2,670 homicide convictions in Wales during the 5 years April 1999 to December 2003. They were also notified of 109 unconvicted homicide suspects who died by suicide. As with the Norwegian cases these were predominantly male (97 cases) and had a median age of 42 years. Eighty-five of the victims were female. Females were more likely to kill a male (eight cases) and males were more likely to kill a female (81 cases). Females were also more likely than males to kill their son or daughter. Of the 109 cases, nine had previous contacts with psychiatric services, six had contact with services in the 12 months before the offence, five men and one woman, they were all community patients with a variety of diagnoses.

Liem et al. (2009) studied homicide–suicide in the Netherlands between 1992 and 2006; they found 103 such events took place involving 135 deaths, i.e. about seven per year or 4% of all homicides. They also found the usual 9 to 1 male to female ratio among the perpetrators The youngest perpetrator was 16 years old, and the oldest was aged 85, the mean age of the perpetrators being 44. When this small group of homicides was compared with the 3,203 homicides that were not followed by suicide, it was found that they were nearly twice as likely to have occurred at home; to involve multiple victims including children under the age of 12 years (one-third of the sample); two-thirds of the victims were female as opposed to less than one-third in other homicides; and the victims were younger with a mean age of 28 years. The perpetrators were on average 10 years older than the mean age of other homicide perpetrators.

Various attempts have been made to classify homicide-suicide (Marzuk et al., 1992; Harper and Voight, 2007; Liem et al., 2009) but the cases are few in number, the people involved are dead, and the motivations vary from psychoses, particularly depressive psychoses, to jealous rage (if I can't have you, nobody can), to revenge, to deteriorating physical health, to terrorism, to rampant killing sprees, all of which makes generalization and classification difficult if not pointless.

The best analysis of the problem is the book by Liem, based on her doctoral thesis. She suggests that there are two broad groups of homicide–suicide, one based primarily on suicidal motives, e.g. extended suicides in which the secondary victim is taken along, the other is primarily homicidal in nature. Either way (with some spectacular exceptions, e.g. terrorist suicide bombings) the majority of homicide–suicides occur within families. Liem divides these homicide–suicides into *uxoricides*, both amorous jealousy and suicide pacts (usually the result of declining health, *child homicide–suicide*, *parent homicide–suicide* and *sibling homicide–suicide*. In jealous uxoricide male perpetrators may kill themselves; female perpetrators don't as a rule; those who do kill themselves are older than those that don't and frequently suffer from mental illness, especially depression and paranoid states. Women are commonly represented among the child homicide–suicide perpetrators; again depression with or without psychotic features is present in many of the perpetrators. Suicide following the killing of a parent or a sibling is much less common than in the killing of a partner or child. Perhaps identification is less intense or complete in these cases.

The important clinical point is that the build up to these events is frequently a suicidal one. Risk assessments and management plans for suicide should always bear in mind the possibility of extension to others.

Extrafamilial homicide–suicides are the least common and the most publicized and feared. Fox and Levin (2012) have catalogued multiple killings in the Western world. Some of these killers go on to kill themselves, or in the case of the suicide bomber carry out the homicides and the suicide simultaneously. Any of these acts may be extended suicides.

Children who kill

Murder by a child is an infrequent crime, only two or three cases each year in Britain. The variety of child killings is as wide as the variety of adult killings, except that the places and events of childhood colour the incidents. Wilson (1973), a journalist, identified and described 57 incidents of homicide involving children under the age of 16 years, between 1743 and 1972. Forty-eight of the incidents, involving 75 children (12 girls and 63 boys) were British, but they are by no means a complete set of cases as Wilson relied upon newspaper reports, and apparently such things were not reported between 1865 and 1920!

Wilson made an attempt to categorize the 57 incidents into overlapping categories; this gives some idea of the motives and circumstances. Five girls and one boy each killed a baby in their charge, 10 incidents were drownings, five children killed more than one victim, two were cases of patricide, one of matricide, two killed their grandfathers and three their brothers. There were 16 incidents related to sex, 17 to theft, and eight occurred in fights or brawls, six took place in schools or children's homes, and at least 15 of the children were likely to have been mentally disturbed. One boy (Wm Allnutt), aged 12, poisoned his grandfather with arsenic. Graham Young escaped inclusion because his first childhood conviction was only administering poisons, but by the time he was 9 years old, he was collecting dangerous chemicals, studying black magic and Nazism. Hitler was already an obsession, and he wore a swastika (Holden, 1974).

It is not possible from the material which Wilson was able to collect to glean much about the mental states of these children. Of the 15 described as mentally abnormal, several were subnormal in intelligence and in no case was there convincing evidence of delusions or hallucinations. In a number of cases, not only those where issues of psychiatric abnormality were raised at the trial, there is a suggestion of the early stages of either a schizophrenic illness, or a sadistic personality, or sexual sadism. There were, for example, several strangulations of girls during or after intercourse, and one case in which a 15-year-old boy killed twice. There was a 16-year-old girl who gleefully planned, with her companion, to murder her mother and make it look like an accident; in her diary she wrote:

Next time I write in the diary Mother will be dead. How odd, yet how pleasing! ... I felt very excited and the night-before-Christmassy last night.

She told the psychiatrist she had set out to break all of the Ten Commandments and had succeeded.

A famous case involved two boys aged 11 years who abducted and killed the 2-year-old boy Jamie Bulger after luring him away from his mother in a shopping centre in Liverpool. This high profile crime caused great concern amongst the British public and a campaign to keep the perpetrators in prison for longer than their original sentence (10 years). The then Home Secretary Michael Howard increased their tariff to 15 years in 1995, but this was later overturned by the Court of Appeal in 1997; the High Court and the European Court of Human Rights have since ruled that politicians can no longer decide on the tariff of life sentence prisoners, this has to be done by the judiciary (Wolff and McCall Smith, 2000). In many European countries the perpetrators would have been considered to be under the age of criminal responsibility.

Fixations and assassinations

Assassination has come to mean the killing of a prominent individual, often a political leader or head of state by a stranger or by a political opponent. It is usually carried out in public and in some ways can be regarded as at the opposite end of the homicide spectrum to domestic violence. Not surprisingly, it is of special interest in the United States of America, a country which has seen 10 presidential assassination attempts, four of them successful, two others wounding the President, and the shootings of such prominent politicians as Martin Luther King, Robert Kennedy and George Wallace. Nevertheless, assassinations occur throughout the world, e.g. President Allende of Chile, President Sadat of Egypt, and are often the basis of a *coup d'etat*. Even in Britain, assassinations and attempts occur. Perhaps the most famous of all is Daniel McNaughton's attempt on Robert Peel. Queen Victoria was shot at three times and in the late 1970s and early 1980s, Lord Mountbatten was killed by the Irish Republican Army (IRA); Queen Elizabeth II had blanks fired at her; and the British Prime Minister, Margaret Thatcher, was bombed by the IRA when she was staying in a hotel and escaped death by inches.

A description of a series of assassins is given by Taylor and Weis (1970) who briefly review nine presidential assassins from Lawrence to Oswald. They pointed out that they were all smaller than average in stature; all except Booth were unknowns; five were born outside the USA; eight of them were unmarried at the time of the attack; and for seven of them there had been a striking socioeconomic deterioration during the year leading up to the attack. Taylor and Weis regarded seven of the nine presidential assassins as mentally disordered. Ideas of persecution and/or grandeur were discovered in most of the individuals. McNaughton believed that the Tory party was plotting

against him and, more recently, Hinckley's belief that a film star was in love with him may have fuelled his attempt on Ronald Reagan's life. Frank paranoid psychoses, especially schizophrenia, seem not uncommon.

On an anecdotal level it is worth remembering that paranoid individuals with highly deprived backgrounds, constant failure, very low self-esteem, who are low down in a sibship, have sexual identity problems, no friendships, and who may have contemplated suicide can turn their anger outwards and on occasions direct it towards a prominent figure on whom they project their failings. Heads of state, royal families, and the like play a prominent part in many people's fantasy life, so it is not surprising that famous people become the focus of pathological fantasies too. Indeed they can become the object of a 'fixation'. This word has now come into the psychiatric lexicon to indicate an obsessive preoccupation, which is usually paranoid, and usually directed towards one or more individuals who are thought to be persecutory in some way.

The best systematic study of the problem is by James et al. (2007). This is detailed in chapter 21. The authors note:

> in the mentally disordered cases, many of whom were actively psychotic, some of the attacks might have been prevented. This would have required greater awareness of the link between delusional preoccupations with public figures and subsequent attacks. The vast majority of those with delusions centering on public figures and supposed governmental malfeasance never act on their beliefs. A few do. The important fact is that, whether or not they ever attack, all of these people are deluded and in need of treatment. As a group, many suffer severe disruptions to their lives as a result of their delusional preoccupations. They are all in need of treatment.

James has gone on to establish a Fixated Threat Assessment Centre in London (James et al., 2010).

If the patient requires psychiatric services, inpatient or outpatient, they are referred to the appropriate catchment area service. In 70 cases, there was direct engagement with the relevant community mental health team and in 46 direct liaison with the general practitioner. In 15 cases, there was liaison with regional forensic psychiatry services. In four cases, there was contact with psychiatric services in other countries. Eventually 57 were admitted to hospital, 26 received care from mental health services in the community and four received care from their general practitioner.

The authors noted that levels of symptomatology and associated distress in the case series included examples of psychotic illness which were among the most severe that the authors have encountered in clinical practice. They pointed out that a proportion of cases admitted to hospital supports previous observations that attention to inappropriate contacts with public figures is a useful tool for identifying the severely ill who have fallen through the care net

(James et al., 2009) and that participation by psychiatrists in threat assessment fulfils an important public health function (Mullen et al., 2009). It is of course impossible to know whether the work of the centre saved any lives or injuries. It is entirely possible that it has done so, however, and probably prevented morbidity and mortality among patients referred.

One of the startling findings of the study is that 81% of the cases had previously received psychiatric care and 57% had previously been admitted to psychiatric hospital on a compulsory basis; 54 cases were known to have defaulted from community care packages. The authors ask themselves why there should have been such a high fall-out rate and note that the characteristics of the fixated are often such as to make them unwelcome as patients. They are by definition without insight, frequently paranoid and nearly always resistant to psychiatric intervention and follow-up; querulant cases are in addition markedly litigious. A proportion of cases were suffering from delusional disorders or schizophrenic illnesses which were suficiently encapsulated to allow individuals to function efiectively in many aspects of day-to-day living. In other words, they did not exhibit the gross behavioural disturbances that oblige mental health services to provide care.

Mullen et al. (2009) also said that it may also be the case that the significance of inappropriate communications and approaches to prominent people is insufficiently appreciated by treating teams, who may erroneously regard such behaviours as innocuous or quaint. In many ways the study suggests that for severe mental illness matters are much the same as they were in the mid-twentieth century when London established observation centres to which the police could bring patients on an emergency basis. The important point is that it seems that these people are not readily seen as ill; even if they are seen as potential perpetrators of violence, there is a high risk that this will be seen as non-psychotic violence and opportunities for prevention missed.

Terrorists

Terrorism is closer to warfare and group violence than to individual violence. The definition of terrorism is itself a matter of dispute, and is partly a moral or value judgment about the validity of the terrorist's cause. Thus Nelson Mandela was imprisoned for many years for terrorism prior to eventually becoming the democratically elected President of South Africa. Terrorism is sometimes grouped with organized crime, because some of the underlying structures of organization may be similar, but the objectives may be different. Certainly some of the most widely reported and extreme violence in recent years has been seen as either terrorism (the 9/11 2001 attacks on the Twin Towers in New York, USA) or as responses to terrorism (the invasion of Afghanistan and Iraq by US forces and their allies in the 'War on Terror'). Much published work on terrorism is journalistic rather than academic in style, but interesting overviews are provided by Levi (2007) and Wolf and Frankel (2007).

For mental health staff, involvement is likely to be concerned with assessing the mental state of a suspect or interviewee, or perhaps of evaluating the impact of detention on mental state. Such issues are difficult to evaluate objectively without reference to political, moral and ethical issues. Our advice would be as far as possible not to deviate from standard procedures even in unusual situations, to take sufficient time and advice to think things through thoroughly and to attempt to bear in mind the complex and even competing demands of working with both patients and perpetrators (see McGuire, 1997 for a succinct discussion of these psychological issues in forensic settings). As in all difficult clinical situations second opinions are invaluable. Grounds (2004) discusses the involvement of forensic psychiatrists in political controversy, in particular terrorism, and other narrative reviews of terrorism and mental health, psychology and psychiatry are also available (Palmer, 2007; Wolf and Frankel, 2007; Reid, 2003). The Royal College of Psychiatrists (2005) has provided a position statement (see also chapter 25).

Multiple homicides

Amok, autogenic massacres and shooting sprees

Terminology in this area is unsatisfactory. Amok is usually regarded as a culture bound dissociative state. It is defined in *DSM IV* (American Psychiatric Association, 1994) thus:

A dissociative episode characterized by a period of brooding followed by an outburst of violent, aggressive, or homicidal behavior directed at people and objects. The episode tends to be precipitated by a perceived slight or insult and seems to be prevalent only among males. The episode is often accompanied by persecutory ideas, automatism, amnesia, exhaustion, and a return to premorbid state following the episode. Some instances of amok may occur during a brief psychotic episode or constitute the onset or an exacerbation of a chronic psychotic process. The original reports that used this term were from Malaysia. A similar behavior pattern is found in Laos, Philippines, Polynesia (cafardor cathard), Papua New Guinea, and Puerto Rico (maldepeled), and among the Navajo (iich'ad).

This implies the syndrome is irrelevant for western medicine, yet this description is almost perfect for the western phenomenon known as a 'shooting spree', which is not in DSM and not usually regarded as a dissociative state and may well be carried out in a psychotic state. If 'shooting spree' is Googled, it produces about 743,000 results, nevertheless shooting sprees are mercifully rare, for example three in the UK between 1987 and 2010. One of the best documented cases of multiple homicide is also one of the

MAD TEACHER KILLS 15 AND WOUNDS 16

Murders His Family, Fires Houses, and Holds Whole Village at Bay

BERLIN. Sept. 5 – Mülhausen in Swabian Würtemberg was the scene in the early hours this morning of a terrible outbreak by an insane teacher named Wagner, who, after setting fire to the village and murdering his wife and four children, killed ten villagers and dangerously wounded nine. Seven other persons are suffering from injuries more or less grave in consequence of the deadly fusillade which the maniac poured from a pair of army revolvers, until he was overcome and nearly beaten to death.

The streets of Mülhausen are described in to-night's telegrams as resembling a battlefield. Wagner, who regularly performed his school duties up to a few days ago, and whom nobody suspected of madness, yesterday mailed the following letter to a Stuttgart newspaper: 'To my people: I want the Devil, for I want to make martyrs of everything and everybody within range of my pistol; but I know that is not always possible. After I have accomplished my purpose, I want to be a martyr, too. For years I have always gone to bed with a dagger and a revolver, though I cannot really say anything very bad about myself.' At about 1:30 o'clock this morning the residents of Mühlhausen were alarmed by the outbreak of fires in four different parts of the village. Men women and children tumbled out of bed to save their lives and property. The first to reach the street observed a man with a black mask or flimsy veil over his face attempting to push his way through the crowd and jostling aside all who attempted to block his progress.

Two men standing at a window, who called to him to ask what the trouble was; received an answer in the form of shots, which instantly killed them. The crowd, which numbered nearly a hundred, tried to seize the assassin, whom they suspected to be a bandit; but he held them back with a revolver in each hand, and presently opened fire upon all within range. Eighteen fell, six of them shot dead. Two of the wounded have since died. Five of the victims were middle-aged men, and one an 11-year-old girl.

Terrified by the arrival of scores of other villagers, the murderer took refuge in a barn, where in frenzy he shot down an ox with his one remaining bullet. Before he could reload from the reserve in his belt, which was found to contain 250 cartridges, his infuriated pursuers succeeded in overpowering him with spades, pitchforks, and scythes. Only then did they discover to their horror that the madman was their respected village schoolteacher.

One of his assailants swung an axe, and in the struggle Wagner's right hand was cut off. The police interfered in time to prevent the mob from putting Wagner to death on the spot, and he was shackled and conveyed to a hospital more dead than alive.

As soon as Wagner's identity had been established his home was searched. His wife was found on the floor with her throat cut, while his four children, two boys and two girls, lay dead in their beds with bullets through their heads. Wagner evidently killed them yesterday, several hours before starting out to attack the village.

The murderer is 40 years old and has hitherto been regarded as normal in every respect. He had only recently returned from a holiday visit to his wife's parents.

Swathed in bandages and manacled, Wagner was led before an examining Magistrate late this afternoon. He was quite self-possessed and showed no signs of remorse.

When asked how he came to carry out such a fiendish plan he nonchalantly replied: 'Oh, I had been preparing it for a long time.'

Reminded that his wife and all his children were among his victims, he only grinned and shrugged his shoulders. http://www.query.nytimes.com/mem/archive-freepdf?res=9C07E1DC113CE633A25755C0A96F9C946296D6CF

---

oldest and now least studied. Ernst Wagner killed his wife and four children and nine other people in September 1913. A contemporary account from the *New York Times*, September 6, 1913 gives the details:

Wagner was looked after in Winnental asylum, and studied by both Ernst Kretschmer and Robert Gaupp.

A good description of the case is given in Wikipedia (http://www.en.wikipedia.org/wiki/Ernst_August_Wagner), but it was Gaupp (1914) who studied Wagner in great detail who gave the best descriptions of the assassin's history and psychopathology. From his study of Wagner, Gaupp gave a lucid description of paranoia, dominating, but encapsulated from the rest of, the personality. He distinguished it from dementia praecox (schizophrenia) and put paid to the notion that it has to be accompanied by cognitive deterioration. Wagner never wavered in his beliefs about his persecutors, remained angry that he had failed to kill himself and that he was refused an execution, but continued to write reasonable poetry and plays. Here are some extracts from Gaupp's paper translated by Helen Marshall reprinted in Hirsch and Shepherd's *Themes and Variations in European Psychiatry*.

The evening before he killed his whole family he was his usual friendly polite self chatting with a teacher's wife and her daughter, also a teacher, commenting on the lovely warm September evenings and asking his young colleague about a certain textbook on physical education. From his writings we know that four years earlier he had already worked out his plan of murder and arson down to the last detail, with a degree of care and deliberation that could not have been more precise. These few facts make it clear that Wagner's mental illness must have been of a special kind, far removed from the commonly accepted picture of a mentally sick man ... On the day of the crime Wagner was, from a psychiatric point of view, no different from what he had been throughout the previous four years. On 4 and 5 September there were no acute symptoms whatsoever ... He is an educated, intelligent man, with a fanatical love of truth, a reliable memory and a good capacity for self-analysis, able to delve deeply into his thoughts and feelings ... According to his own account, he killed his family out of compassion and he set fire to Muhlhausen out of revenge: he wanted to destroy the men of the village because they were his deadly enemies, and he wanted to end his life of torture. There seemed to be no reason for his hatred, because in fact he had no enemies in Muhlhausen; on the contrary, he was remembered by many there as a former teacher and as the son-in-law of a respected citizen. No one knew of the indecent behaviour which he said in his letters that he had been guilty of, and no one understood the vague hints which he gave after the murders; his mother-in-law said they were unbelievable ... In Wagner ... hereditary taints converge significantly: from his father he gets his inflated self-esteem, his discontent, his tendency to drink too much; and from his mother comes his gloomy outlook on life, his proneness to ideas of persecution, his bitter critical attitude and his sexual appetite. He shares his maternal uncle's fondness for Biblical language as well as his self-reproach for masturbation. Wagner himself attributes his weaknesses to his father's influence. He believes that his family stock was diseased and that it should be destroyed. Disease and weakness are to him the 'greatest burdens' ... His outstanding ability gained him a free place in the teachers' training school, first in Nürtingen and later in Esslingen. At that time he is described by several of his fellow students as a lively, somewhat self-conscious boy, interested particularly in literature, with a growing tendency to destructive criticism and to a dark pessimism. At the age of 17 he inscribed in a friend's album the following saying of Holderlin: 'It is best never to be born at all but, if you exist, better hasten to your end.' ... At the age of 18 Wagner began to practise masturbation spontaneously ... This event heralded a new, calamitous period in his life. Foolish popular writings on the subject filled him with anxiety and he ran to the doctor to tell him of his suffering. His doctor reassured him and pointed out that there was no need to entertain scruples or have a bad conscience since 90% of young boys and girls behaved in the same way. But this comfort was of no avail. Wagner's self-torment continued: he would look at himself in the mirror, convinced of his poor appearance; he was certain that others could also see his secret sins in his appearance ... From the numerous reports which were collected by the court in 1913 about his earlier behaviour, he emerges as a self-conscious, pleasant man, usually quiet, interested in literature and philosophy and given to critical remarks. Even at that time people were struck by his fanatical love of truth. The need to conceal his masturbation caused him much suffering: the habit seemed to him irreconcilable with his pride and his high opinion of himself ... In 1901 he was appointed assistant teacher at Muhlhausen-an-der-Enz, still unable to control his masturbation. It was soon after he took up this appointment that the events took place which were to set his whole life on a disastrous course. On the way home from the local inn, his sexual appetite aroused by drink, he committed several acts of indecency with animals. How often this happened, or with what kind of animals, we still do not know. No one knew anything at all about these lapses until he himself betrayed the secret in the farewell letters he wrote on the day of the murders ... Wagner entered a state of unspeakable excitement. What angered him most of all was the way in which they all, even the peasant boys, seemed to speak about his guilt, not with anger or grave reproach, but with jeers, mockery, and contempt directed at him, the teacher, the one educated man in the village, who thus became an object of general scorn and entertainment. And he was defenceless, for if he turned on those who mocked him, his crime would be known and he would lose not only respect, but his job, his very bread. At examinations he carried a loaded revolver in his pocket, so that he could shoot himself at any moment, should the police come for him. At his wedding he even carried two revolvers. His relationship with the innkeeper's daughter freed him from abnormal sexual activities, but soon had other consequences which became known. He undertook to marry the girl and was transferred to Radelstetten, a rough, lonely village in the hills ... His wife bore him four children. This made it more difficult for him to carry out his plan: he came to the conclusion that if he were going to kill himself he must also kill his family, since he believed that the children might carry within them the germ of equally bad or even worse sexual anomalies. During his first four or five years in Radelstetten he did not develop further delusions of reference, but he retained his delusion of persecution by the men of Mühlhausen. Whenever he went there he could tell by their bearing, gestures, and words that he was still an object of scorn and mockery. He therefore avoided his wife's home village. In 1908 his delusions of reference expanded to cover Radelstetten and the neighbouring villages: he believed that he was despised there too, his friends and colleagues making remarks which showed that they knew about his abnormal practices ... Part 1 of his autobiography shows that by October, 1909, this plan had already taken shape, in the exact form in which it was to be implemented in September, 1913. He got hold of powerful pistols and a revolver, practised shooting with them, and made a trial trip to Mühlhausen in order to perfect his plans by studying the site for his destructive enterprise. Again and again, however, he shrank from killing his family and for years the deed remained undone. His impotent rage was discharged in his poetry and in his autobiography. As he felt the persecution in Radelstetten grow more tormenting, he asked for a transfer and in May, 1912, he was moved to a city school in the suburbs of Stuttgart. But the same torments recurred in his new abode where he soon came to believe that his bestial misdemeanours were common knowledge, attracting scorn and contempt. And so his resolution at last ripened into action. The farewell letters also testify clearly to the care with which this action had been prepared ...

Wagner's case proves unequivocally that psychiatrists have been mistaken in their theory that fixed paranoid delusions can occur only when there is a certain degree of mental defect (Schwachsinn). Wagner was always an able, gifted man and today, after entertaining delusional beliefs for twelve years, he is still an intelligent person whose judgment in matters outside his delusion is shrewd and accurate: he shows no trace at all of mental debility. It is true that his grandiose literary ideas are absurd, and that he regards bestiality as a graver crime than planned multiple murder, although in regard to other crimes his judgment is reasonable ... But in recognizing their (delusions') importance we must not neglect Wagner's own statements: he himself considered that the years of torture, the 'ocean of his suffering', the unceasing persecution, formed a psychological force which increased his inflated self-esteem and heightened his passionate, grandiose ideas. (For example, the following statement: 'However paradoxical it may seem, even my pride and my vanity are increased rather than diminished by this,' i.e., by the suffering of his abnormal sexual life which weighed upon him.)

Gaupp used the case to give a lucid description of paranoia, dominating, but encapsulated from the rest of the personality. He distinguished paranoia from dementia praecox (schizophrenia).

This case is highlighted because it is a classic, the suicidal assailant survived and his psychopathology has been set out by Gaupp in detail in several publications. Most of these have not been translated into English but the papers in Hirsch and Shepherd (1974) are useful English sources. The events were clearly related to an intense psychosis. Wagner was apparently well integrated into his family and into his work as a schoolteacher. He was an obsessional, methodical man, but it is clear that those who knew him had no idea about his preoccupations and his plans.

A more modern well-documented case is Charles Whitman, a student at the University of Texas, who consulted a psychiatrist about his loss of temper control and his thoughts of shooting people. Later, he stabbed his wife and his mother to death, then climbed a 300 foot university tower carrying a variety of firearms and shot 44 people, killing 14, before being shot himself (Macdonald, 1968). At post-mortem a glioblastoma was found in the right temporal occipital white matter (http://www.alt.cimedia.com/statesman/specialreports/whitman/findings.pdf). The Governor's task force declined to make a psychiatric

diagnosis but said 'the highly malignant brain tumour could have contributed to his inability to control his emotions and actions'. Michael Ryan shot 16 people in Hungerford, Berkshire, England in 1987. In 1996 Thomas Hamilton walked into the gymnasium of the Dunblane primary school in Scotland shooting indiscriminately, and killed 15 children and a teacher. He then killed himself. Lord Cullen, in his enquiry, concluded that 'Thomas Hamilton was not mentally ill but had a paranoid personality with a desire to control others in which his firearms were the focus of his fantasies. The violence which he used would not have been predictable. His previous conduct showed indications of paedophilia' (Cullen, 1996). In 2010 in Cumbria, England, Derrick Bird, killed 12 people and injured 11 others with a shotgun and a rifle before shooting himself dead.

All these events and many others, particularly some school shootings in the US, spark enquiries which are readily available on the Internet. Scientific enquiry is very limited. A review was published by Meloy et al. (2004). The best systematic study available is by Mullen (2004).

The phenomenon, which Mullen (2004) calls 'autogenic massacre', although remaining very rare, has become much commoner in the second half of the twentieth century. It is probably best regarded as a particularly pernicious form of extended suicide. Very few perpetrators survive to give the kind of information that helps us to understand the phenomenon, and those who do are either inept at self-destruction or ambivalent about it. A number of cases have, however, survived in Australia; perhaps the most notorious of these is Martin Bryant who killed 35 people and injured many others in 1996. His case has been described by Sale (2008) but unfortunately, unlike Ernst Wagner, he has not cooperated with detailed mental state examinations. Mullen (*op. cit.*) has described five survivors who he has personally examined. His paper should be read by all who are interested in this topic as the best systematic live study of such assassins. He extracts 19 characteristics of such perpetrators which occurred commonly: maleness, age under 40 years, social isolation, a marginal work record, being bullied as a child, fascinated with weapons, a collector of guns, no previous history of antisocial behaviour or violence, no previous contact with mental health services, no threats or indications of a massacre, no significant substance abuse, a rigid obsessive personality, suspiciousness, maybe persecutory ideas which can be of delusional intensity, a tendency to resentment with intrusive ruminations about humiliation and injury, daydreaming particularly about murderous heroism, narcissistic and grandiose traits including feelings of entitlement, a planned large-scale murder and suicide and imitation of previous publicized massacres.

Mullen emphasizes that the cases reported were not normal men: 'they had personality problems and were, to put it mildly, deeply troubled people. Almost all were overly sensitive, self-referential, and suspicious. At the time of the killings one case probably suffered from major depression and two had apparent disorder, which in one probably amounted to a delusional disorder.'

The problem of prior identification and possible prevention has of course not advanced at all since 1913. The cases reported emphasize just how unlikely it is that such tragedies can ever be averted entirely; a normal presentation and secretiveness seem to be a common part of the syndrome.

Serial killers

Another type of multiple murder, in which repeated killings take place over a longish period (weeks, months or years), can be called serial murder. It is probably better viewed as the extreme end of the violence spectrum. In other words, the factors which lead individuals to kill may on occasion lead a particular individual to kill repeatedly. Serial murderers will sometimes be mentally healthy (e.g. terrorists), sometimes psychotic, sometimes sadistic, and sometimes necrophilic. It is difficult to specify why in some cases one killing leads to another. Clearly, the motive for killing has to be something other than a sudden impulse or a rage attack. It would seem reasonable to speculate that in some cases there is pleasurable reinforcement of a murderous drive by an actual killing, in other cases the problem to be solved by a killing (e.g. the elimination of persecution) is not solved so the search for peace goes on. The late twentieth century fascination for such killers produced a crop of books and films (e.g. Ellis, 1991; *Silence of the Lambs*, and *Henry, Portrait of a Serial Killer*) and even computer games (e.g. *Manhunt*).

These cases are rare and generalizations about motives are not really possible. Some writers, however, like us to use the term 'addictive behaviour' for some of them (e.g. Gresswell and Hollin 1997) on the basis that what they call 'addiction variables' can be demonstrated in such cases. The six addiction variables they describe are:

1. salience – the issue dominates the individual's thinking;
2. conflict – usually internal;
3. tolerance – i.e. dose escalation;
4. withdrawal symptoms in the absence of the behaviour;
5. relief – obtained by carrying out the addictive behaviour;
6. relapse.

Relapse is not pertinent for an identified serial killer but Gresswell and Hollin argue that all the other features can be found in selected cases, such as the well described case of Dennis Nilsen. He killed at least 15 men between 1978 and 1983. Nilsen was a lonely homosexual who picked up casual sexual partners from bars. He would persuade lonely young men to stay the weekend for sex and to keep him company. Nilsen also had necrophilic fantasies and would make himself up to look like a corpse so that he could masturbate to his cadaverous image in the mirror. Eventually he combined these needs and killed a young

man to stop him from going away and to provide him with necrophilic sexual pleasure. Once he had crossed this threshold he felt different: 'a murderer' and bad, and repeated the cycle knowing that his victims were unlikely to be missed. However, to describe his subsequent killings as related to an addiction does not add much meaning for us. The case is better understood by reading the narrative supplied by Gresswell and Hollin and by Brian Masters (1985) who wrote Nilsen's biography. Harold Shipman (see below) could also be described as an addictive killer, but with similar caveats.

The behaviour may fit some of the criteria for an obsessive compulsive disorder; i.e. compulsive urge, the rituals, and an element of collecting, but again this doesn't add much meaning to an individual case.

Norris (1988), a clinical psychologist who has interviewed some 260 serial killers, has tried to draw some generalizations which should stimulate useful discussion. Unfortunately although Norris has a PhD in psychology and has set up the International Committee of Neuroscientists to Study Episodic Aggression, his book has no index and no references! It is basically a political tract trying to convince general readers and politicians that serial killing is a special disease. If this sounds somewhat off the wall, it isn't entirely and the book is worth reading. Part of the Norris argument is that serial killing is on the increase, especially in the United States, and it constitutes a serious public health problem. He is also arguing, although not in so many words, that the premise which courts and sometimes even health professionals use that serial killers have normal brain function is unlikely to be true. He is much more interested in physical brain dysfunction than psychological brain dysfunction and finds significant neurological abnormalities in many of the cases he has studied. The book has an old-fashioned air with its emphasis on epileptic and dreamlike states accompanying the killings. He proposes that more resources be allocated to study the individuals who are captured and to devise a programme for identifying them earlier and treating them. He points to the severe levels of childhood physical abuse suffered by some of the well-known American killers (Bianchi, Manson, Lucas for example) and suggests a crisis intervention programme designed to protect all children from abuse and if a nurse or physician recognizes a child with extraordinary levels of violence or homicidal aggression the child should be seen as an individual suffering from an illness, thoroughly investigated, and treated. Whether or not this would reduce the number of individuals who go on to be serial killers, such a proposal makes good sense in its own right and would have positive effects in all kinds of cases. The problem is in the politics, getting others to accept the therapeutic rather than a punitive approach in circumstances which may well seem counterintuitive to the general population. As an interesting aside Norris also wants the early nineteenth century legal definition of insanity to be updated to include severely disordered individuals such as serial killers; his targets are certainly ambitious!

Perhaps 90% of all serial killers are male. This means that approximately 10% of these rare criminals are women. Frei et al. (2006) reviewed the literature and found almost no academic studies. They quote the Holmes and Holmes (1998) classification i.e.

- visionary (or psychotic);
- comfort (e.g. material gain);
- hedonistic;
- power seeking; and
- disciple (acting under the influence of another – Myra Hindley and Rosemary West are examples).

An earlier classification by Kelleher and Kelleher (1998) talked of team killers who kill in conjunction with others, black widows (named after the poisonous female spider) who kill spouses, partners, and other family members, angels of death who murder people in their care, revenge killing, killing for profit, insane killing, and sexual predation.

The phenomenon is not recent; the famous Mary Ann Cotton of Durham was probably the most prolific female serial killer in English history (Whitehead, 2000); she poisoned (using arsenic) an estimated 21 people. She was hanged in 1873. These crimes were probably exceeded in number by the notorious Bella Gunness, a Norwegian woman who emigrated to Chicago in the USA (see Wikipedia for an account and newspaper references). After a settled but boring married life fires began in 1896 and children started to die with 'colitis'. When her husband died unexpectedly she remarried but the second husband had a serious accident. After this she employed labourers to work on a farm and a number of them disappeared. In 1908 the farmhouse was completely destroyed by fire which was thought to be arson. In the wreckage searchers found the remains of three children and a headless adult female. The skull was never found and a farm labourer was charged with the arson. The coroner believed that the female body was that of Bella Gunness, but the labourers said that she had set the fire and then caught a train to Indiana. She was never seen again. It is believed she killed over 40 people, mainly by poisoning. At the time of writing the most recent alleged female serial killer was Irina Gaidamachuk, a 39-year-old Russian mother of two who confessed to 17 murders by smashing in their heads http://www.thesundaytimes.co.uk/sto/news/world_news/Europe/article329368.ece.

CASK (clinicide)

According to Whittle and Ritchie (2000) a British forensic toxicologist (Forrest) has coined the term 'caregiver associated serial killings' (CASK) to describe the unnatural deaths of multiple patients in the course of clinical treatment. Angels of death might be a more elegant description!

Kaplan (2007) uses the term 'clinicide' to refer to murders by doctors. These crimes are clearly special forms of serial killing. Dr Harold Frederick Shipman has been described as the most prolific serial killer in modern history. He killed many of his patients during his work as a GP in Greater Manchester, at least 215 (probably 250) people using large doses of diamorphine by injection. The killings went undetected for many years, and at his trial he was convicted of 15 specimen charges. He was convicted in 2000 and sentenced to 15 consecutive life sentences; he subsequently killed himself in Wakefield Prison in 2004. The most obvious point to make here is that opportunity is an important factor in premeditated homicide. Healthcare professionals have unprecedented access to vulnerable people and to potent toxins and other ways of extinguishing life. See chapter 27 for a fuller discussion.

Other violence

The number of violent crimes in England and Wales rose steadily from 1981 to 1995 and thereafter the number fell steadily until in 2009 it was half the 1995 level (see Roe et al., 2010 for details). The British Crime Survey (BCS) estimates that there were 2,114,000 violent incidents against adults in England and Wales in 2008/2009. Just over half (52%) of all violent incidents reported to the BCS resulted in injury to the victim. Weapons were used in about one in five (21%) violent crimes and this figure has been stable over the past decade. Knives were used in 7% of violent incidents, glasses or bottles in 5%, hitting implements in 4% and firearms in 1%. Men, particularly young men, were at greater risk of victimization for overall violence, although women were more likely to experience domestic violence.

Based on the 2008/2009 BCS self-completion module on intimate violence, approximately 3% of women aged 16 to 59 and less than 1% of men (of the same age) had experienced a sexual assault (including attempts) in the previous 12 months. The majority of these are accounted for by less serious sexual assaults. Less than 1% of both women and men reported having experienced a serious sexual assault. There were 51,488 sexual offences recorded by the police in 2008/2009, 4% less than in the previous year and the lowest figure since the introduction of the National Crime Recording Standard (NCRS), but the sensitivity of reporting sexual offences has almost certainly resulted in underreporting of these offences.

Serious violent crime, although occurring at a lower frequency than say theft or motoring offences, tends to cost more in victim and financial terms. Dubourg and Hamed (2005) have provided an index of crimes and calculated relative costs (based on prices in 2003) of different types of crime. Clearly homicide represents the highest cost crime, but the top five crimes in terms of cost are violent (table 9.3).

Table 9.3 Estimates by crime type of total cost per crime/victim cost per crime. (From Dubourg and Hamed, 2005)

Crime type	Total cost	Victim cost
Homicide	£1,460,000	£1,310,000
Sexual offences	£31,400	£27,200
Serious wounding	£26,000	£10,300
Robbery	£7,280	£4,160
Other wounding	£5,990	£3,660
Theft of vehicle	£4,140	£3,020
Burglary in a dwelling	£3,270	£1,720
Common assault	£1,440	£1,060
Criminal damage	£866	£690
Theft from vehicle	£858	£641
Theft – not vehicle	£634	£299

Stanko et al. (1998) estimated that the cost of domestic violence for 1 year in a single borough of London ran to £5m. This included costs by police, civil justice, housing refuge and health service costs. Violence has far reaching impacts not only in financial terms but also in the psychological and physical costs to the victims and perpetrators.

As we will now see most of these crimes pose health problems for both the perpetrator and the victims or survivors. The criminal categories are revisited in the next section as health issues.

Assessment

The beginning of this chapter stressed the ordinariness, even the healthiness of violent behaviour. The remainder of the chapter has shown, however, how difficult it is to draw lines between 'normal' and 'abnormal' violence. Further, it should now be clear that there is a legitimate limited medical interest even in 'normal' violent behaviour. The psychiatrist will often be asked to elucidate the cause or causes behind an act of violence and to prevent it happening again. S/he may be asked to do this partly because s/he is seen as a special kind of priest, a shaman who brings understanding and reduces anxiety, but more importantly because there is an increasing realization that medical factors do play a part in many violent interactions.

A violent individual may manifest distress or abnormality in his/her mental state. This can vary from understandable feelings of hate and rage right through to pathological paranoia and other delusional ideas. Some violence is based on chronic feelings of inferiority, inadequacy, and insecurity, marked abnormalities of mental state which are frequently missed, or dismissed as 'normal', because they are common. Rage and anger are increasingly understood as separate affects with their own treatments. Sometimes violent individuals will be acting in a style to

which they have been trained. Individuals who are unacceptably violent have often learnt to respond to stress and difficulty in a violent fashion through modelling of parental or other influential examples.

A great deal of ordinary social life, the hierarchy in which we work or live, the success and satisfaction we obtain from life depends upon subtle aggression. Yet sophisticated, successful non-violent aggression is difficult to learn and depends upon optimal biological function. Individuals with poor skills and/or psychological dysfunctions may resort more readily to extreme forms of aggression in a desperate attempt to win some status or satisfaction. Optimal biological function implies an intact brain, and individuals with minor brain damage who are deficient in specific skills may resort to violence more frequently than other people because they are deficient in skills and because, for organic reasons, they are more prone to experience unpleasant ideas and affect, e.g. rage and paranoia. A similar pattern can be produced in some individuals with intact brains by intoxicating substances, such as alcohol. Thus the exact form which violence may take, and its seriousness, will depend upon a complex interaction of a range of factors, such as the health, especially the mental health, of the violent individual, his/her repertoire of learned behaviours, the social context, levels and type of intoxication and such environmental matters as the availability of a weapon.

It is clear, therefore, that when a psychiatrist is asked to examine the background to a violent event, s/he has to try and construct the interaction which led up to it, by conducting something akin to a root cause analysis, looking at developmental, social, organic, intoxicating and psychological circumstances. If s/he can construct a coherent explanation for the event, s/he then should try to evaluate which factors, if any, can be modified or treated. It may have been an explosive incident that is unlikely to recur, but it may be that drunkenness, a sense of inferiority, brain damage, anger or depression, will require medical attention; it may be that a psychosis will be uncovered; it may be that the family dynamics are inducing the pathological aggression. In each case, it is reasonable to offer medical and/or social assistance. Anybody who asks for help with violence should always receive some help – that help will usually need to be multidisciplinary in nature, and it will usually need to be long term as well. Those who are sent for help with violence problems, against their own inclinations, pose more complex questions which are dealt with in other parts of this book.

When assessment of violence is mentioned, this usually refers to risk assessment, practised in a variety of ways in different areas of psychiatry (and discussed in more detail in chapter 22. A more comprehensive and psychological approach to the assessment of violent behaviour (part of which may include risk assessment) has been argued for elsewhere (Walker and Bright, 2009a,b). Any in-depth analysis of behaviour needs to take into account a variety of factors including the frequency, severity and outcome of the behaviour for the individual and victim(s). We suggest that attention is paid not only to mental state factors, but also personality traits, neuropsychological functioning and environmental factors which are all too easily overlooked. Objective information such as the individual's criminal record and depositions from the index offence are essential, as is a face-to-face assessment with the individual asking about the violent behaviour itself along with the thoughts, emotions and environmental triggers that went with it. For a fuller description see Walker and Bright (2009a,b).

Howells (1998) lists the following variables to include in functional analyses of aggression and violence:

1. Frequency, intensity, duration and form of aggression.
2. Environmental triggers (including background stressors).
3. Cognitive antecedents (including biases in appraisal of events, dysfunctional schemata, underlying beliefs and values supporting aggression).
4. Affective antecedents (emotions preceding aggressive acts, e.g. anger or fear).
5. Physiological antecedents.
6. Coping and problem-solving skills.
7. Personality dispositions (e.g. anger-proneness, impulsivity, psychopathy, general criminality, over-control, under-control).
8. Mental disorder variables (mood, brain impairment, delusions, hallucinations, personality disorders).
9. Consequences/functions of aggressive acts (for perpetrator and others, short term and long term; including emotional consequences such as remorse and peer group or institutional reinforcement).
10. Buffer factors (good relationships, family support, achievement in some area).
11. Opportunity factors (weapons, victim availability, restrictions).
12. Disinhibitors (alcohol, drugs).

The following additional variables also need emphasis:

13. Social skills and communication deficits.
14. Cognitive distortions (e.g. minimizing violence, victim blame, machismo).
15. Ability to co-operate with treatment, and response to previous treatment.
16. Cultural and environmental issues (e.g. cultural expectations, environmental factors such as overcrowding).
17. Association with criminal behaviour (other criminal behaviour present, or violence as a method for other crime – e.g. robbery, rape).

Intervention

Most violent offenders will never see a psychiatrist, but some will find themselves being assessed for a variety of reasons. Those charged with homicide tend to be assessed, particularly where there is a not guilty plea and any question over mental illness or fitness to plead. Some violent offenders are referred in prison or by probation, usually because they are recognized as being 'not normal' violent offenders by colleagues in these settings. Multi-agency public protection panels comprising police, probation, housing, health and other agencies, have begun referring high risk offenders in the community for psychiatric assessments (usually to the local forensic psychiatric service often attached to a medium secure unit). What is offered as part of an assessment will vary from a basic consultation to the offer of therapy if available. Increasingly, services are being asked to complete risk assessments on unusual individuals and to offer help with risk management in the community. The emphasis has moved from health, police and probation working separately to much closer multi-agency working with the prison and probation services joining together to become the National Offender Management Service. Such collaborative working is beneficial for vulnerable patients whose risk is high, but can also lead to ethical dilemmas around the role of the doctor in terms of confidentiality and protection of the public.

Medication is not often used as a first line treatment for violence, and perhaps this is appropriate. However, with inpatients violence is often a reason for an urgent pharmacological review or even the use of sedation. Hodgins and Muller-Isberner (2000) provide a useful review of studies indicating that fluoxetine has been used in a number of studies to successfully reduce anger, aggression and violence in 'personality disordered' patients. One study was a double blind placebo controlled trial with 40 patients (Coccaro and Kavoussi, 1997) in which fluoxetine significantly reduced irritability and aggression.

In the UK prison system where rates of personality disorder are typically several times the rate in the community (Singleton et al., 1998a), group therapy is the most widely used intervention for violence and other offending. Accredited prison programmes such as Enhanced Thinking Skills (ETS), the Cognitive Self Change Programme (CSCP) and the Controlling Anger and Learning to Manage it programme (CALM) are all primarily cognitive behavioural therapy based and often include a large didactic component as well as skills based learning (see Hollin and Palmer, 2006 or Towl, 2003 for reviews of psychological treatments in prisons). The evidence for the effectiveness on prison inmates is equivocal, particularly for the main 'hard' outcome of reoffending (e.g. Falshaw et al., 2004). These groups are now being used with mentally disordered offenders. It is likely to be many years before we have evidence of the effectiveness of such treatments for such unusual individuals on their criminal outcomes.

10
Disordered and offensive sexual behaviour

Edited by
Don Grubin

Written by
Jackie Craissati
Harvey Gordon
Don Grubin
John Gunn
David Middleton

1st edition authors: **Don Grubin, Gisli Gudjonsson, John Gunn and Donald J West**

Sex offending accounts for a small proportion of crime – in England and Wales, it represents just 1% of criminal offences reported to the police in a typical year (Nicholas et al., 2007). And though much sex crime goes unreported, the British Crime Survey (a large scale, nationally representative, interview-based household survey of adults over the age of 16) also describes low rates, with about 3% of women and 1% of men reporting that they were the victim of a sexual assault in the previous year, mostly of a 'less serious' nature (Coleman et al., 2007). Why then does sex offending occupy such a prominent position in the public perception of crime?

There are probably three main reasons for this:

1. A large proportion of the victims of sex crime are children, although accurate estimates of how many are difficult to come by. The British Crime Survey includes only adults, but community surveys in general tend to generate wide ranges in the numbers of individuals who report having been sexually abused as children. North American studies in the 1980s, for example, described historical rates of child abuse ranging from 6–60% of adult females and 3–30% of adult males (Peters et al., 1986). The most likely reasons for these wide variations in prevalence rates included the way in which information is collected, differing definitions of sexual abuse, and variations in base populations and refusal rates. A notable feature of these surveys, however, is the low rate of disclosure: in a review of surveys that had been carried out in 21 countries, for example, Finkelhor (1994) found that in general only about one half of the victims said that they had disclosed their experiences of abuse to anyone.

2. Victim impact. Although not easy to quantify, a useful attempt to do so can be found in a provisional 'weighted

crime index' developed by the Home Office to provide an estimate of the cost of crime that includes both economic (for example, costs to the criminal justice system and loss of income for victims), and intangible costs related to the physical and psychological impact on victims (Nicholas et al., 2007). Excluding homicide, which is by far the most 'expensive' crime, sex offences were the top of all non-lethal crime (table 10.1).

3. The high emotion generated by sex crime, and by sexual behaviour generally, accompanied as it is by strong moral beliefs, religious teaching, and the mixed messages given by the media.

Much sex crime takes place in the home, and for both adults and children involves perpetrators known to the victim. Of the sex crimes reported in the British Crime Survey, 89% of female and 83% of male victims said they knew the perpetrator, while about 50% of female victims described the offender as a partner or former partner (Nicholas et al., 2007) – is a further indication of the special nature of sex crime. For a more in depth review of the nature of sex offending against children, see Grubin (1998).

This special nature of sex offending, however, should not disguise an apparent drop in its incidence. Although a statistical increase in sex crime in England and Wales followed the introduction of the Sexual Offences Act 2003. This Act that brought about wholesale changes in the law in respect of sex offences in Britain – for example, widening the definition of rape to include oral penetration, creating specific offences in respect of children under 13, 16, and 18, defining the meaning of consent, and creating offences designed to protect individuals with mental disorders or who are being looked after in care settings). Nevertheless there has been an 8% reduction in total sex offences since the implementation of the Act in 2004.

Table 10.1 Estimated total cost of crime for the top five crimes excluding homicide considered by Nicholas et al. (2007) (at 2003 values)

	Total cost (£)	Victim cost (£)
Sex offences	31,400	27,200
Serious wounding	26,000	10,300
Robbery	7,280	4,160
Other wounding	5,990	3,660
Vehicle theft	4,140	3,020

Moreover, Finkelhor and his colleagues have described a 40% decline in child sex abuse cases recorded by child protection service agencies in the United States since their peak in 1992; this decline appears to be genuine rather than a reporting artefact or due to differing practices in these agencies (Jones et al., 2001; Finkelhor and Jones, 2004). A decline in the 1990s was also apparent in the UK (Grubin, 1998).

The reasons for this apparent decline in child sex abuse and sex offending generally are not clear, although one might speculate it relates to one or more of heightened awareness of the problem, the success of intervention and prevention strategies, legislation, and societal and cultural changes (Finkelhor and Jones, 2004). It may be, however, that the 1970s and 1980s saw a temporary increase in sex offending that has now reverted to the mean. In support of this, Feldman et al. (1991) compared child sex abuse rates in a number of North American studies published in the 1980s with those reported in the major study of sexual behaviour in American females carried out by Kinsey and colleagues in the 1940s (Kinsey et al., 1948, 1953). They found that in spite of increased reporting, overall prevalence rates of child sexual abuse appeared to be similar in the 1980s to those described by Kinsey 40 years earlier.

Overall, the vulnerable nature of the victims of sex crime, the effects it has on them, the fact that it is typically committed by individuals known and trusted by the victim, its tendency to remain hidden, and the emotions generated by it mean that the perpetrators of sex crime are often portrayed as being different from other criminals. Indeed, there was a time when sex offending and mental disorder were strongly linked (Bancroft, 1991), with the work of doctors like Krafft-Ebbing (1885), Freud (1905), and Ellis (1931) all emphasizing the psychopathology of sexually problematic behaviour. Times have changed, however, and many psychiatrists are now reluctant to become involved in the assessment and treatment of sex offenders. Any review of the forensic psychiatric aspects of sex offending, therefore, must first clarify the role of forensic psychiatry in respect of sex offending.

SEX OFFENDING, SEXUAL DEVIANCE AND PARAPHILIA

The concepts of sex offending, sexual deviance and paraphilia are sometimes used interchangeably, but they are distinct entities. Distinguishing between them is necessary if the relationship between forensic psychiatry and problematic sexual behaviour is to be properly understood.

Sex Offending

Sex offences are specific, defined behaviours that are proscribed by a society because of the harm they cause its citizens, or because of their impact on public order. What constitutes an offence varies over time, place, and culture, and can change virtually overnight with the passage or repeal of individual pieces of legislation. Sex offences themselves represent a wide range of behaviours, and are motivated by a variety of factors, typically a combination of social, physiological and psychological variables.

Social variables relate to cultural understandings and expressions of sexual behaviour. In relation to rape, Sanday (1981), for instance, in a review of the anthropological literature, claimed that societies where rape is most common are characterized by male authority and power. In support of this, Baron et al. (1988) compared rape rates in the 50 American states with a range of indicators of cultural support for violence in those states (as well as with a number of other variables). A strong correlation was found between the rape rate for the state and what was referred to as 'legitimate violence' – that is, the extent to which violence is condoned in the state, measured creatively by factors such as the circulation of violent magazines, the number of hunting licences issued, the acceptance of corporal punishment in schools, and responses on a survey in respect of situations where it is thought appropriate to use violence. In respect of sex crime against children, the sexualization of children in advertising (so-called 'corporate paedophilia') is an example of putative social pressures that influence offending (Rush and La Nauze, 2006), albeit a clear link between this and sex crime is yet to be demonstrated.

Many different physiological theories for sex offending have been put forward, such as that it is a function of male cerebral organization (Flor-Henry, 1987), brain injury (Blanchard et al., 2002), excess testosterone (Rada, 1981), and neurotransmitter abnormalities (Kafka, 2003a). Only occasionally, however, can a relationship be made between sex offending behaviour and an overtly physical cause. This is not to say that biological considerations do not contribute to problematic sexual behaviour, or that they cannot be a useful target for treatment, only that it is unlikely that sex offending can be understood primarily through the actions of brain systems, hormones and neurotransmitters. At a higher level, it has been argued that at least some sex offences can be explained by evolutionary pressures (Thornhill and Palmer, 2000), an interesting theory that can be demonstrated in some species but has yet to be proven in humans.

Psychological explanations for sex offending are also not in short supply. Prominent have been learning theories (from both conditioning and experiential type perspectives), and theories based on cognitive functioning and attachment (Beech and Ward, 2004; Thornton, 2002; Ward et al., 2006), but psychoanalytic constructs related to infantile desires and experiences have of course also been put forward (Rosen, 1996). Of heuristic value, and proving particularly useful in the context of developing treatment strategies, it remains the case that sex offending is almost certainly too heterogeneous to be explained by any one of these theoretical models.

Although systemic reviews of the aetiology of sex offending have not been carried out, a good review of the various theories to explain sexual offending behaviours, including attempts to integrate them into a single theory (Ward and Beech, 2008), can be found in Laws and O'Donohue (2008a). What is clear, however, is that while some who commit sex offences may be mentally disordered, most are not, and sexual offenders are dealt with primarily through criminal justice rather than mental health systems. Because of this, there is no direct role for psychiatrists to play in respect to most sex offenders, and many psychiatrists are concerned that if they are drawn into sex offender management they risk becoming agents of social control, carrying out the bidding of law makers and politicians, rather than acting in the best interests of their patients. This, however, is not inevitable; indeed, it is a tension that permeates virtually all of forensic psychiatry.

Sexual Deviation

Sexual deviance refers to sexual behaviours that contravene the norms of society, and may or may not amount to sex offending. It involves regular, rather than one-off or occasional, interests or behaviours. What is recognized as deviant depends on the shared norms of a culture (Bancroft, 1989), although it may reflect a general perception of what *should* be 'normal' or 'proper' rather than what people actually do in private. Like sex offending, concepts of sexual deviance also vary greatly over time and between societies (Grubin, 1992). Attitudes towards homosexuality, and the continuing uncertainty in the minds of some about whether homosexual practices should be considered deviant or not, are a good example of the fluidity inherent in the concept of sexual deviance. Another illustration can be found in the history of medical attitudes to masturbation (Hare, 1962).

Although sometimes defined in statistical terms, there are many subcultures in which 'sexually deviant' behaviour is the norm, ranging from fetishism to sado-masochism (Gosselin and Wilson, 1980). In some cases sexual deviation may relate directly to sex offending, as when sexual arousal to children leads to the sexual assault of a child; in most cases it does not. Similarly, few of those who engage in 'sexually deviant' practices ever come to the attention of the medical profession, and as such the true incidence of such behaviour is unknown, although some indication can be obtained from consideration of the popularity of specialist pornographic literature pre-internet (Dietz and Evans, 1982) or the proliferation of pornographic sites on the world wide web (Thornburgh and Lin, 2002). Regardless, as Bancroft (1989) has pointed out, social rather than medical (and one could add legal) criteria determine what is considered to be deviant. In other words, sexual deviance is a moral rather than a legal or psychiatric construct, and as with sexual offending there is typically no reason for a psychiatrist to become involved.

Paraphilia

Paraphilia is a diagnostic term used in the *DSM-IV* (American Psychiatric Association, 2000) for sexual behaviours that are considered to amount to mental disorder; in the *ICD-10* (World Health Organization, 1993), the phrase 'disorders of sexual preference' is favoured. Both classification systems require symptoms or behaviours to be persistent or recurrent, and for them to cause distress to the individual or to interfere with the individual's personal functioning; the impact of the behaviour on others is not part of the definition. Recognition of disorders of sexual preference as a psychiatric disorder in their own right is a relatively recent phenomenon, with the first two editions of the *DSM*, for example, categorizing them under 'personality disorder'.

The two manuals include a number of specific types of 'abnormal' sexual preferences under the rubric of mental disorder (six in *ICD-10* and 8 in *DSM-IV*), but each also contains a ragbag category of 'other' unusual preferences on the basis that, as stated in the *ICD-10* (World Health Organization, 1993), '*Erotic practices are too diverse and many too rare or idiosyncratic to justify a separate term for each*'. Even Fedoroff (2009), who lists over 100 different types of unconventional sexual practice in a review of the paraphilias (including taphophilia – arousal to being buried alive, pygmalionism – arousal to statues, and formicophilia – arousal to insects), still feels it necessary to leave room for the category 'paraphilia not otherwise specified'.

This tremendous diversity in what can stimulate sexual arousal raises the question of whether it is sensible to define specific manifestations of sexually deviant behaviour as mental disorders at all. What is of note, however, is that it is not the direction of the drive *per se* that causes problems, but its intensity, dominance or the ability to control it, together with the impact this has on the individual concerned, perhaps leading to relationship difficulties, or contributing to breaking the law. In this respect, a number of authors have observed that 'non-deviant' but hypersexual behaviour can also be the cause of marked distress or dysfunction (Coleman, 1991; Kafka, 2003b), and have suggested that a new category of 'paraphilia related disorder' should be created. While an interesting suggestion, it might be more sensible to reconsider altogether when abnormal sexual behaviour becomes a mental disorder, focusing less on the direction of the drive and more on the factors referred to above, thereby delineating more finely the distinction between sexual deviance and mental abnormality. This would certainly make the conditions more relevant to the forensic psychiatrist, and meet the valid criticism of authors like Laws and O'Donohue (2008b), who comment that it is not at all clear how decisions are made regarding which paraphilic behaviours qualify as 'a dysfunction in the individual', and which do not.

It may be therefore helpful to consider sexual deviance as a dimensional rather than a categorical phenomenon. Christie-Brown (1983) suggested that sexual behaviour varies along five dimensions: the sexual identity of the individual, the object choice or direction of preference, the rate of arousability, the level of arousal, and the frequency of sexual activity. Thus, it is not the case that one is either homosexual or heterosexual, for instance, or attracted to children or to adults; depending on circumstances, an individual's position on each of the five dimensions may vary.

As with the aetiology of sex offending, explanations for the causes of abnormalities in sex drive are diverse and unproven. A good review of various theories can be found in Fedoroff (2009), who refers to four main explanatory perspectives to account for the development of abnormal, or 'unconventional', sexual behaviour:

- Disease, implying a pathophysiological basis, whether due to a physiological imbalance caused by masturbation as suggested by Krafft-Ebbing (1895), or more modern notions of disturbances in brain development.
- Behavioural, whereby it arises from learned associations combined with behavioural reinforcement, suggesting that given a specific set of reinforced experiences, any individual could develop abnormal sexual preferences.
- Dimensional, in which 'abnormal' interests represent statistical extremes of normal sexual behaviour (Kinsey et al., 1948; Kinsey et al., 1953; Christie-Brown, 1983).
- Life-story, characterized by a search for the 'meaning' behind behaviour (for example, linking transvestism in a male to having been dressed as girl when young), typified by psychoanalytic type interpretations.

An attempt to integrate these approaches was made by Money (see, for example, Money and Lamacz (1989), cited in Fedoroff, 2009), who argued that all children have the potential to develop a full range of sexual interests, but the specific ones they eventually express are determined by learning that takes place during critical periods of development. This theory gains some support from experimental findings that in males, brain organization is 'sculpted' into a relatively permanent adult state at two different stages of development, one in the perinatal period, the other during adolescence around puberty, both of which are strongly influenced by testosterone; animal experiments suggest that social experience also has an impact at least during the second, pubertal phase (Sisk and Zehr, 2005; Sisk, 2006).

Although multiple paraphilias were once believed to be unusual, there is an increasing amount of evidence to show that so-called crossover in sexual interest, at least among sex offenders, is more common than previously thought. Abel and colleagues in an often quoted series of publications (Abel et al., 1987; Abel et al., 1988; Abel and Rouleau, 1990) reported that when elaborate steps are taken to ensure confidentiality, sex offenders (as well as sexually deviant individuals who have not been convicted of any crime) describe a wide range and high frequency of sexually deviant behaviour. At the time these findings were criticized on a number of grounds, including for the way in which the study sample was recruited and the manner in which behaviours were tabulated (Marshall et al., 1991). The increasing use of polygraphy as a means of clarifying sexual history in sex offenders has supported the results reported by Abel and his colleagues, with crossover rates ranging from 30% to 70% in respect of offences against both children and adults, and between 20% and 40% in respect of those who offend against both females and males (summarized in Heil and Simons, 2008).

Given the weakness of current classifications of paraphilias, the numerous unconventional sexual arousal patterns that have been described (and the many more undoubtedly waiting to be catalogued), and the lack of specificity in the expression of these patterns, there is little to be gained by a detailed description of the individual paraphilias listed in the *DSM* and *ICD*. The interested reader can refer to comprehensive accounts found in Laws and O'Donohue (2008a). It is in the area of 'sexual disorder', whether related to sex drive or sexual functioning, that forensic psychiatry can have a role to play, a theme that will be returned to later in this chapter.

Male Sexual Offences

The sexual *behaviours* that are of special interest to forensic psychiatry are indecent exposure, obscene telephone calls, voyeurism, bestiality, necrophilia, rape, incest, sex with children and collecting pictures of children engaged in sexual activities. All of these are illegal; all of these may be based on paraphilias, but many are not in individual cases. Some may be related to other disorders, for example personality problems and/or mental illness.

Indecent exposure (exhibitionism)

'Indecent exposure of the male person with intent to insult a female' is the statutory definition of the offence colloquially known as 'flashing'. In clinical terms, it is the urge to expose the genitals, usually before strangers, in a public place. It is one of the most common of heterosexual offences but, judging from the large number of 'one time only' offenders, it is a form of behaviour that is not necessarily indicative of a persistent tendency. Sometimes, however, literally hundreds of such incidents occur before an offender is finally reported and apprehended, and some men are reconvicted repeatedly over the best part of a lifetime, seemingly incapable of resisting the temptation, in spite of the most damaging social consequences to themselves. Exhibitionism is a form of sexual disturbance that, despite its superficially innocuous nature, can be extremely persistent and disruptive. A small minority of exhibitionists escalate their offending and in the course of time commit sexual assaults, but this seems to be the exception. Mohr et al. (1964) reported that, in a Toronto study, the reconviction rate for first offenders was 19%, 57% for those with a previous sexual offence, and 71% for those with previous sexual and non-sexual offences. In a follow-up study, those who received treatment did not differ in terms of reconviction rates from those who did not receive treatment.

As with other types of deviant sex offender, clinical examination reveals contrasting personality types. The most common finding is a tendency to shyness, timidity and inhibition, with little confidence in courtship or sexual performance. Many contract marriages in which they feel unhappily dominated and frustrated by their wives. Incidents of exposing sometimes follow sexual failures or marital disputes. These men often struggle against what is tantamount to an addiction, experience considerable shame, and may even feel relieved when caught. Other offenders are less inhibited, being aggressive, impulsive and antisocial in their ordinary life and often prone to alcohol abuse and non-sexual crime. Some are homosexual in orientation, some are misogynists.

If the victims appear shocked, or at any rate impressed, this provides a feeling of sexual power and control, albeit at a safe distance, and compensates for feelings of inadequacy in real life (Rooth, 1971). One reason why these offences need to be taken seriously is that the victims chosen are often pubescent or prepubescent girls. Some of the offenders have clear paedophile tendencies (Rooth, 1973). Whilst Gebhard et al. (1965) found that the majority of exhibitionists do not resort to violence, 10% attempt or contemplate rape.

Obscene telephone calls (scatologia)

During an exhibitionist encounter, a man may make obscene remarks to his victim. An extension of this behaviour is telephoning women and engaging them in erotic, obscene, and sometimes frightening conversations. Orgasm with or without concurrent masturbation may occur during the phone call. Such calls are mainly of nuisance value, but they can cause considerable distress and alarm; indeed threats are often part of the communication, partly because they are erotic in themselves, partly because they hold the attention of the female victim which is essential for the caller's orgasm. Such offenders are rarely caught. When they are, they usually have a number of other deviant sexual behaviours as well, such as exhibitionism, writing obscene letters, voyeurism, and sometimes assaultative urges. Almost all such lewd callers are men, they may find normal sexual relationships difficult, and they may have been sexually abused as children.

Voyeurism

Peepers or peeping toms are adult males who obtain some sexual satisfaction by secretly watching women undress, urinate, or have sexual intercourse. It is an extension of normal behaviour in that most males use visual material as part of their erotic stimulus, and it is quite close to watching strip-tease. Sometimes the offender may suddenly draw attention to himself by, say, tapping on a window or by making a telephone call, to frighten the woman and enhance his own excitement. The activity is frequently accompanied by masturbation to orgasm. Gebhard et al. (1965) noted that peepers rarely spied on relatives, but sought strangers for preference. Only a very few of them were married. One or two cases were men who had also raped or exhibited themselves. So whilst the disorder is largely of nuisance value, the peeping Tom who gets so excited that he goes on to rape or even kill (e.g. *Byrne*) has been described.

Necrophilia

The term necrophilia is usually reserved for what might be called a corpse fetish, sexual arousal obtained from seeing, touching, and copulating with dead bodies, usually very recently dead bodies. It is much commoner in males and is usually an attraction to female bodies, although homosexual necrophilia does occur (Bartholomew et al., 1978, and the Nilsen case – Masters, 1985) and a female necrophiliac has been described (Rosman and Resnick, 1989).

Unlike some paraphilias, this deviation, if acted on at all, is difficult to keep secret. It is possible for such a person to work in a mortuary and obtain private access to bodies; others would have to intrude in some way such as tomb robbing. Some documented cases such as Nilsen and Christie provided themselves with dead bodies by murder. It is likely that a number of sadistic killers are also partly necrophiliac and that the culmination of the sadistic thrill is intercourse with the now lifeless, motionless, totally submissive body. Some argue that sexual deviation is always symptomatic of some other disturbance. This must surely be the case with necrophilia, and individuals usually show a range of personality difficulties that include obsessional traits, narcissism, sadism and a preoccupation with destruction. Most have poor reality testing and a few are frankly psychotic.

The disorder is rare, of no known specific aetiology and can be treated in the context of a broad approach to the patient's personality. No recommendations for specific treatments are in the literature apart from a case study using behavioural treatment for a man with necrophiliac fantasies (Lazarus, 1968).

Bestiality (zoophilia)

In law a form of buggery, bestiality is a person of either sex having sexual intercourse with an individual of another species either *per anum* or *per vaginum*. Sexual activity with non-human mammals is probably quite common. It is largely undetected – the victims not being able to complain.

Rape and other sexual violence towards women

The seventeenth-century common law concept of rape in England and Wales was 'intercourse without consent by force, fear or fraud'. The Sexual Offences Act 2003 of England and Wales tightens and clarifies this to some extent and defines the types of criminal sexual assault a person can commit, e.g.

> *Rape (1) A person (A) commits an offence if – (a) he intentionally penetrates the vagina, anus or mouth of another person (B) with his penis; (b) B does not consent to the penetration; and (c) A does not reasonably believe that B consents. (2) Whether a belief is reasonable is to be determined having regard to all the circumstances, including any steps A has taken to ascertain whether B consents.*

There is also assault *by penetration, sexual assault and causing a person to engage in sexual activity without consent.*

These first four offences are against adults, there are others against children, from whom consent is not possible. The Act is available on line (http://ww.opsi.gov.uk/Acts/acts2003).

Recorded sexual crimes against women have risen during the decade 1997–2007, but it is unclear whether the increase represents an actual rise in the amount of sexual violence that is occurring in the community, or whether it instead reflects a greater willingness of women to report offences to the police.

Rape is an offence which involves both sex and violence. There is a tendency amongst people writing about rape, however, to emphasize the primacy of one or the other of these elements. Some argue that rape is a fundamentally sexual act, in which aggression is used to achieve a sexual aim, while others claim that rape is in essence an act of violence expressed in a sexualized way. Indeed, Groth has downplayed the importance of sex altogether, calling rape a pseudosexual act in which power or anger, not sex,

are the driving forces (Groth and Birnbaum, 1979). This view has found widespread support with feminist authors, many of whom argue, in addition, that more important in the aetiology of rape than either sexual or psychological factors *per se* are the cultural norms which determine the relative roles of men and women in society.

General statements about the nature of rape, however, should be viewed with caution. Rape is a crime which can result from a range of complex behaviours, and rapists form a heterogeneous group of individuals in whom social, cultural and psychological factors combine in a variety of ways. The search for unique attributes by which rapists can be categorized has included attitudes, hormones, pornography use, and sexual arousal patterns to name but a few (see Quinsey, 1984, for a review), but the most that can be said is that some factors are important for some rapists; none separates rapists as a group from the general male population once variables such as age or social class are taken into account.

Most studies of rapists have described young men of lower social class background and limited educational attainment; ethnic minorities, particularly black men, are heavily overrepresented. The majority already have past criminal records: up to a quarter have past convictions for offences of violence, and up to a third have convictions for past sex offences. Rapists do not seem to differ significantly from other prisoners, however, either in terms of background or general attitudes (Gebhard et al., 1965; Amir, 1971; Dietz, 1978; Lloyd and Walmsley, 1989; Grubin and Gunn, 1990). These studies, of course, are necessarily biased by the selection processes of the criminal justice system, and it is difficult to know to what extent they are an accurate reflection of men who rape. They are, however, probably representative of the more serious end of the offence spectrum. It is also of interest that a British study which compared men convicted of rape in 1961 with those acquitted found few differences between them in terms of their past or future offending behaviour (Soothill et al., 1980).

Among young men actually charged with rape, those who are generally delinquent are prominent. Analysis of criminal records alone suffices to identify a substantial proportion with convictions for non-sexual crime and many with at least one previous or subsequent conviction for personal violence Gibbens et al., 1977). These offenders are not unusual in their sexual aims and interests. They may choose victims under 16 but, as many are themselves still teenagers, this does not indicate true paedophilia. Like other delinquent youths, they are generally undersocialized, tending to resort to physical aggression or antisocial acts at slight provocation, especially after drinking. They are likely to be poorly educated, ill-informed about sexual relationships and identified with crudely macho ideas. Many convince themselves that the girl was 'asking for it' or that she 'led me on'. Sometimes they seek assurance from the victim, who may be willing to agree to anything to get away, that she enjoyed the experience. Indeed, some offenders are caught through making an appointment to meet the victim again. These young men are unlikely to view themselves as being in need of psychiatry, but educative programmes, social skills training, group discussion and even confrontational sessions with women who have been victimized are less resisted and more relevant.

Existing classification schemes for rapists, as for sex offenders generally, tend to be anecdotal and based on intuition and interpretation of motive rather than empirically derived and tested. Terms such as amoral delinquent, explosive assaulter, sadistic, impulsive and antisocial have a long history of use in describing types of rapist, but there has been little attempt to test their reliability or validity (see Knight and Prentky, 1989, for a review).

Another approach to classification has been taken in a large English study of imprisoned rapists. In this study, simple, single variables relating to either the offence or the offender were found to offer some help in distinguishing types of rapist (Grubin and Gunn, 1990). Serial rapists, for instance, were characterized by the large amount of sexually disturbed behaviour found in their histories when compared with men who had raped only once, while sexual murderers were notable for their social isolation and reserved, overcontrolled personalities. Group rapists, on the other hand, seemed to be driven more by peer interaction than by issues relating to either sexuality or aggression.

Rapes are looked upon as 'understandable' crimes, so the offenders are not perceived as abnormal or suitable for referral to a psychiatrist. Yet rapists include many disordered people and even a few with psychosis. Like any other act of violence, rape can be instrumental, expressive or a combination of both. It can be instrumental simply in the satisfaction of sexual urges, but it can also be an extreme example of the assertion of the macho stance of male power over women. It can be expressive of uncontrolled emotions other than sexual passion, notably anger, hostility or contempt towards a particular victim or towards women at large. For the sadist, the use of violence is a means of obtaining sexual arousal. Like other violent offenders, some rapists are undercontrolled characters who give way to impulses, whether erotic or aggressive, at slight provocation. A minority are overcontrolled, ordinarily shy and inhibited with the opposite sex, whose offences appear completely unexpected and out of character.

As with other forms of criminal behaviour, the incidence of rape is much influenced by social circumstance and cultural factors. For example, incidents frequently follow on from social drinking and are commoner at weekends when socializing peaks. For whatever reason, fantasies of rape are very prevalent among normal men who have never been found guilty of any offence (Malamuth, 1981). Gratuitous brutality is especially likely to occur during gang rapes when young men seek to impress each other with their toughness (Katz and Mazur, 1979). Societies with restrictive attitudes to premarital sex, where males are dominant and women economically and psychologically subservient, are said to have more rapes than more 'liberal' societies (Sanday, 1981).

The treatment of rapists should follow the same principles as those used in the treatment of other sex offenders: contributory factors to offending should be identified, and then addressed in a therapeutic context. It is important, however, that goals other than a simple reduction in recidivism are chosen. Two long-term follow-up studies of convicted rapists, one of 12 years, the other of 22 years, found that about 15% were convicted of further sexual offences, and about a quarter of further offences of violence (Soothill et al., 1976; Gibbens et al., 1977). Of particular interest was the finding that sexual re-offending continued throughout the follow-up period.

Many rapists also have some of the personality traits and histories of neglectful, disorderly or violent upbringings commonly associated with a diagnosis of dissocial personality disorder. Their conflicts become dangerous to others because of their propensity for expressing frustration in physical violence. A few rapists are manifestly psychotic (Smith and Taylor, 1999). Delusions of bewitchment, grandiose notions of ridding the world of immoral women or psychotic ideas of vengeance against the whole female sex have been found to underlie the otherwise inexplicable behaviour of some multiple sex murderers.

Rape of males

Some American research has suggested that male victims of sexual assault are more likely to be physically injured than female rape victims, and are more likely to be victims of multiple assailants (Groth and Burgess, 1980; Kaufman et al., 1980). Contrary to popular prejudice, the perpetrators of male rape are not all homosexual (Groth and Birnbaum, 1979). They include a number of heterosexuals, particularly in institutions, who sexually assault men they perceive to be homosexual or sexually deviant. These attacks appear to be an extension of 'gay bashing' and, as in female rape, can be an expression of anger and an attempt to humiliate the victim (Groth et al., 1977). The rapist uses these assaults to defend against his own inadequate sexuality, and to assert his dominance over the victim. The most disordered rapists appear to be gender blind and attack both men and women (Sagarin, 1976).

Incest and child sexual abuse

Sexual abuse of children has been proscribed throughout history (Rousseau, 2007; Davis, 2008) but not with the same stridency and panic that occurs now. Paedophilia was hardly mentioned as an issue in early textbooks of forensic psychiatry. The most important pre-modern academic forensic psychiatrist, Norwood East (1936), mentions it not at all in his early textbook *Medical Aspects of Crime*, but 8 years later he wrote a chapter on sexual offenders

(East, 1944), which was a study of 894 men and 88 women convicted of sexual offences during 1938. The biggest category for men was defilement of girls under 16 years 210 (23.5%). The next was bigamy – 195 men (21%) and 81 women (92%); 199 men (22%) were convicted of either indecency with males or 'unnatural offences' (mainly buggery). Five years later still, Norwood East (1949) was using the term 'paedophilia' but it was not of central importance in his chapter on sexual offenders. In the 1960s and 1970s, 'incest' was a prominent criminological preoccupation. During the 1980s, the number of cases recorded by the police in England and Wales ranged from 241 to 516 per year, accounting for 1–2% of all recorded sex offences. In 1991 they were down to 157 and by 2004 they fell to 43, but in 2006 they were back to 153. This does not reflect a real change in behaviour. Most of the cases were children being sexually abused by adults and these are more commonly recorded now as sexual activity with an underage child. The changing numbers may however show two things. Attitudes about sexual activity with underage children have hardened and much child sexual abuse occurs in families and is not about assaults on complete strangers. Consenting incest between consanguineous adults is unusual because of taboos rather than laws; Napoleon legalized it in France 200 years ago, but the taboo continues. Community surveys inevitably uncover a large number of individuals who report that they were sexually victimized when children (Kinsey et al., 1953; Baker and Duncan, 1985; La Fontaine, 1987; Mullen et al., 1988). Most studies have concentrated on female victims, but there is now an awareness of sexual victimization of male children by mothers and older siblings (Finkelhor, 1984; O'Connor, 1987). Some argue that incest is primarily a symptom of family pathology, distinct from paedophilia, and thus see the incest offender as representing little danger to the community at large. One American study, however, reported that nearly half of self-reported father or stepfather incest offenders had also abused children outside the family, and 18% had raped adult women (Abel et al., 1988). It is also known that some men target and subsequently marry or cohabit with single mothers in order to gain access to their children.

Whilst physical coercion is frequently involved in the more serious forms of child sexual molestation, physical injury occurs in only a small proportion of cases. By no means all adults who seek sexual gratification from children are paedophiles in the sense of being erotically aroused only by children. The so-called 'regressed' paedophiles are individuals who have been married or have had adult sexual relationships, but in the face of difficulties in or loss of their relationships, they turn to children as the best and most readily available substitute. A regressive pattern appears more commonly in heterosexual than homosexual males. Some men indulge with children because their sexual or social inadequacies have blocked adult relationships. They may approach children of either sex, sometimes choosing boys simply because boys are less chaperoned and more amenable. For treatment purposes, it is necessary to distinguish these patterns from that of the lifelong fixated paedophiles with no interest in and perhaps a positive aversion to partners of mature age.

Paedophilia

Paedophilia, a technical and medical term, has entered common parlance but with an intense stigma attached and much inaccuracy. It is defined in the *International Classification of Diseases* (*ICD*) as '*A sexual preference for children, boys or girls or both, usually of prepubertal or early pubertal age.*' Note that it is classified as a disease. Child sexual abuse is not a disease, it is a crime; the two things have erroneously become synonymous in common parlance. Paedophilia is a preference; child sexual abuse may derive from acting on a preference, it may derive from other social and family pressures, it may be, for example, more related to social inadequacy, or phobia of adults, than to real preference. Therapists will need a clear understanding of the origins of the behaviour.

It is important in the treatment of paedophilia for those managing the patients to realize that they did not choose their sexual preferences any more than anybody chooses their sexual preferences. The disease model of paedophilia does not fit the concept very well, but it does emphasize the involuntary nature of the condition and the need to search for its origins, both internal and external.

An important book, *Innocence Betrayed* (Silverman and Wilson, 2002), begins thus:

> *The paedophile is the bogeyman of our age. The very word itself has become a conduit for fear and public loathing, often beyond all moderation. Indeed, despite the fact that the overwhelming majority of paedophiles are male, commentators reach easily for parallels with a reviled figure from a bygone age – the witch. While we haven't yet reinvented the ducking stool or trial by water, we have found a pretty effective twenty-first century equivalent in trial by newspaper. And, after being named and shamed, the 'guilty' are hounded from the community by a mob baying for blood.*

Note that even here the offender in question is a 'paedophile', not 'a man suffering from paedophilia', thus not really a human being but a terrifying monster.

Internet sex offending

Practitioners working in the field of assessment and treatment of sexual offenders will be aware of the increase in the volume of convictions for offences related to possession, making and distributing indecent images of children. In the 5 years between 1999 and 2004 there was an almost 500% increase in convictions of this sort in England and Wales, from 238 to 1162 (Home Office Offending and Criminal

Justice Group, internal data). This trend is also apparent in North America (Taylor and Quayle, 2006; Quayle, 2008).

In June 2004 BT, a leading UK telecommunications company, launched an operation to block customer access to sites containing indecent images of children listed by the Internet Watch Foundation. At the time BT was blocking 10,000 hits a day; by February 2006, 18 months later, the number of attempted daily hits to these sites had risen to 35,000 (BBC online, 2006). Since BT is estimated to provide internet service for approximately one-third of the UK domestic market, and as there is no reason to suppose that its customers have a disproportionate interest in viewing these images compared with those of other Internet Service Providers, it is likely that the total volume of attempts to log on to sites hosting indecent images of children is over 100,000 per day.

Crossover from viewing images to contact offences

Viewing indecent images of children is known to be used as an aid to generate sexual fantasy, which is then reinforced through masturbation (Eldridge, 2000). It has been suggested that the repeated use of these images normalizes the fantasy, and can disinhibit the user, who becomes familiar with, and bored by, the pornography (Sullivan and Beech, 2004). A combination of disinhibition, increased risk taking, cognitive distortions regarding the impact of offending, and the need to seek more intense experiences gives rise to the possibility of an escalation in behaviour, with the individual seeking opportunities for 'real-life experiences' and hands-on abuse (not forgetting that many images of child pornography are in fact images of actual abuse).

The evidence for such escalation, however, is weak, and does not support the view that crossover offending is inevitable, or even that it occurs in the majority of cases. Wolak et al. (2005), for example, examined a sample of 1,713 arrests for possession of child pornography in the United States over a 12-month period from 2000 to 2001. They found that 17% of cases involved both possession of child pornography and evidence of contact sexual abuse of children, but most of these 'dual offenders' were detected in investigations that began as allegations of child sexual victimization – in other words, it would appear that in the course of investigating child contact offence allegations the police *also* found collections of pornography. While this may indicate that many contact offenders use pornography, it does not provide evidence that offenders who possess these images are also child contact offenders, or that they progressed from viewing images to physical offending.

Seto and Eke (2005) looked at the criminal records of 201 adult males listed on the Ontario Sex Offender Registry who had ever been convicted of possession, distribution or production of child pornography as defined by Canadian law, in order to identify potential predictors of later offences. They found that child pornography offenders

with prior or concurrent contact sexual offences were the most likely to have more than one conviction, both general and sexual, but that those with child pornography offences only were rarely reconvicted. In as yet unpublished work they followed-up 198 offenders from the original sample for 3.6 years, during which 6.6% of the men committed a new contact sexual offence (all of whom had previous contact sex offences), and 7.1% another child pornography offence. The most consistent predictor of new offences was violent offence history, whether non-sexual or sexual. The sample, however, had a high proportion of men with prior offences generally – 57% had one or more previous convictions, 24% had previous contact sexual offences, 17% had previous non-contact sexual offences, and 15% had previous child pornography offences. This, together with the small sample size, may have led to a bias in the reported results.

Although there is little evidence to show that collectors of indecent images of children go on to commit contact sex offences against children, there is emerging evidence of psychological and sexual arousal similarities between them and men who do commit such offences. For example Seto et al. (2006) report on a sample of 685 male patients referred for assessment of sexual interests and behaviour, including 100 child pornography users. The latter group showed greater sexual arousal to children (measured by phallometric assessment) than to adults. Overall, child pornography offenders had nearly three times greater odds of showing phallometric arousal to children then did men who had committed contact sex offences against children.

Middleton et al. (2006) compared a sample of 213 offenders convicted of sexualized behaviour associated with internet use with 191 sex offenders convicted of contact offences against children. The groups were similar in many ways, with the largest clusters for both characterized by intimacy deficits and problems with emotional regulation. It was suggested, however, that intimacy deficits were more characteristic of the Internet users, while emotional dysregulation was more a feature of the contact offenders.

Middleton et al. (2006) also noted, however, that the internet offender sample had larger numbers of offenders both with low scores on all their psychometric measures, and with elevated scores, demonstrating that the term 'internet offender' covers a large range of behaviours and offender types, indicating that they represent a heterogeneous subgroup of sex offenders.

In assessing internet offenders it may be useful to look for evidence of intimacy deficits, especially difficulty in entering age-appropriate relationships, perhaps coupled with a socially isolated predisposition. Alternatively, the individual may appear able to make and sustain intimate relationships, but be unable to gain support within the relationship for dealing with emotional stressors. In addition, evidence of high emotional identification with children may indicate that sex is used as a coping strategy, with the internet serving to relieve stress or providing a means to seek pseudo-intimacy.

Viewing indecent images of children can be used to stimulate, develop and fuel sexual fantasy. Frequent use may be linked to sexual preoccupation and attitudes that normalize deviant behaviour with potential victims. Undoubtedly some sex offenders will use pornography to increase arousal prior to an offence, but the evidence to date does not suggest a substantial generic risk of escalation from internet to 'hands-on' sex offending.

SEX OFFENDING BY FEMALES AND ADOLESCENTS

Female Sex Offenders

The limited literature on female sex offenders is reviewed in Grubin (1998) and Logan (2008). Both sex offending and sexual deviance, however, are markedly less common in women; less than 1% of those convicted of sex offences are women, and it is estimated that sexual deviance is about a tenth as common in women as in men (Fedoroff et al., 1999). It is difficult to be sure of the actual extent of the problem, however, as in western societies women are permitted greater freedom than men in their physical interactions with children, and hence are better able to disguise abusive behaviour; similarly, when they engage in non-offending but unconventional sexual behaviour this is often portrayed as being at the behest of men. Furthermore, overt sexual activity between an adult female and a boy may not be conceptualized by the child as 'sexual abuse' even if he is emotionally unprepared for it and psychologically destabilized as a result (Finkelhor et al., 1990; Johnson and Shrier, 1987).

A large proportion of female sex offenders commit their offences together with men, often but not always coerced by them; most of those who have studied female sex offenders (most of whom have offended against children), however, also describe a smaller group whose offending is driven by anger, emotional loneliness, or deviant sexual arousal in a manner similar to men (Saradjian and Hanks, 1996; Nathan and Ward, 2002). Sex of victim tends to reflect the sexual orientation of the woman in the case of older children, but victim gender is less relevant where the children are very young. Like male offenders, women may also 'groom' children both to obtain compliance and to prevent disclosure; they may carry out similar sexual behaviours (using their fingers or objects instead of a penis); and they may offend over an extended period of time. Although psychotic illnesses are unusual, mood and anxiety disorders, as well as PTSD, are relatively common in female sex offenders (Logan, 2008).

While it is important not to deny the reality of sexual abuse perpetrated by females, nor to minimize the impact it has on victims, from both a criminal and a health perspective it is dwarfed by the problem of sex crime carried out by men.

Adolescent Sex Offenders

Some estimate that adolescent males are responsible for between 33% and 40% in both North America and the UK (Oates, 2007). Sexually deviant behaviour in adolescents cannot be assumed to be innocent sexual learning and exploration without further consideration (Becker et al., 1986); for example, about 15% of arrests for forcible rape in the United States in the 1990s were of youths under 18 years of age (Ryan et al., 1996).

Richardson et al. (1997) reported on a group of 100 male adolescent offenders (aged 11–18) in England, differentiating them according to victim age as well as by relationship between offender and victim. They described four groups: a 'Child Group' who abused a victim 4 or more years younger then themselves, an 'Incest Group' who abused siblings, a 'Peer Group' who abused similar or older aged victims, and a 'Mixed Group'. Victims from the 'Child Group' tended to be younger neighbourhood children, members of their extended families, or other residents in foster or children's homes, and were often male. Antisocial behaviour in general was common across all the groups, but greatest amongst those who offended against peers or older victims, and least so in the incest offenders. The backgrounds of those who offended against victims of a similar age or older were found to have much in common with adult rapists. In general, adolescent sex offenders appear to be as heterogeneous as their adult counterparts, and the types of behaviour they carry out are not dissimilar.

Although a large proportion of adult sex offenders report that their deviant interests began in adolescence (Abel et al., 1987), most adolescent sex offenders do not re-offend, with rates under 10% typically found (Worling and Curwen, 2000; Gretton et al., 2001). The incidence of subsequent offending not of a sexual nature, however, is much higher.

PSYCHIATRIC QUESTIONS

Medical Models

So-called medical models of sex offending have been criticized on the grounds that most sexual offenders are not mentally ill, and deviant sexual behaviour does not fit neatly into the concept of 'mental disorder'. In addition, there is sometimes a belief held by doctors and others who work with sex offenders that a medical approach to sex offending lessens the responsibility of the offenders for their behaviour, and therefore should be avoided (Grubin and Mason, 1997; Grubin, 2008a). The reluctance of many psychiatrists to become involved in the treatment of sex offenders, however, is unfortunate – not only can a medically based perspective contribute to a better understanding of sex offending behaviour; it also offers potentially powerful adjuncts to treatment.

The problems in using *DSM* or *ICD* concepts of paraphilia in formulating medical diagnoses of sexual disorder have been outlined above. Their focus tends to be on describing behaviour rather than psychopathology, and as such the distinction between deviant behaviour and mental disorder can be blurred. It is possible, however, to develop formulations based on psychopathology, modelled on other, better defined disorders.

Psychiatric Morbidity

Psychiatric diagnoses are a complicating factor in trying to understand the basis of sex offending behaviour as high levels of psychiatric morbidity are often found in sex offender populations. For example, Kafka (2003a) described a number of studies reporting high levels of psychiatric disorder amongst sex offenders, with depression and dysthymia particularly common in child abusers, but these tended to take place in mental health contexts; Kafka and Hennen (2000) also point to an apparently high incidence of attention deficit hyperactivity disorder (ADHD) in the childhood histories of sex offenders, a condition rarely considered when assessing sex offenders in the UK. Sahota and Chesterman (1998), in a review of sex offending in the context of mental illness, identified a number of studies which reported an incidence of mental illness in up to 10% of sex offenders.

The small number of studies that have looked at psychiatric morbidity in non-selected samples also report high rates of psychiatric morbidity (Långström et al., 2004), but whether this differs significantly from non-sex offenders is unclear, making it difficult to determine the extent to which mental disorder is associated with sex offending as opposed to offending more generally. Fazel et al. (2007a,b) addressed this issue in a study that looked at mental health data for all sexual offenders convicted over a 13-year period in Sweden, comparing psychiatric morbidity with rates found in the general population and also with offenders who had been convicted of homicide or attempted homicide. Compared with the general population, all categories of psychiatric illness were increased in sex offenders, especially diagnoses related to substance abuse, but even psychotic illnesses were markedly higher, with a prevalence of just over 4%, although the strength of associations decreased when adjusted for socioeconomic variables. However, the prevalence of mental disorder in sex offenders was lower than in homicide offenders for nearly all diagnostic categories.

Obsessive compulsive disorder spectrum (OCD spectrum)

Because sexual fantasy can have an obsessive quality to it with the associated behaviour appearing to be compulsive in nature, it has been suggested that in some cases paraphilias should be included within the OCD spectrum (Hollender et al., 1996; Bradford, 2001). The finding that selective serotonin reuptake inhibitors, an effective treatment for OCD, can reduce the intensity and frequency of sexual fantasies suggests the possibility of shared brain networks and a common causal role for the neurotransmitter serotonin.

Addictions and disorders of impulse control

Some paraphilias appear to share many characteristics with the addictions, including features such as tolerance, craving, narrowing of interests and even withdrawal phenomena. The term 'sexual addictions' has been used to describe such cases, with a link made in particular to pathological gambling. Screening and diagnostic instruments have been developed towards this end, although none is well validated (Carnes, 1991; Kafka, 1997). It has been suggested that because the addictions, disorders of impulse control, and conditions such as eating disorder have many factors in common that they, together with some sexual disorders, form part of the same psychiatric spectrum (Hollander and Allen, 2006).

Affective disorder

As noted above, mood clearly has an impact on libido and sexual behaviour, some claim that mood disorders and sexual psychopathology are in fact linked through common neurological substrates, particularly via serotonergic pathways and the hypothalamic–pituitary axis (Kafka, 2003a).

None of these constructs is a perfect fit, and they raise questions of whether the sexually deviant behaviours under consideration are the result of ego dystonic compulsions, ego syntonic repetitive activities, or a failure to control impulses. Approaching the paraphilias in this manner, however, emphasizes the need to describe properly the sets of symptoms and behaviours involved, and the importance of elucidating the natural histories of the conditions.

RISK ASSESSMENT

One theme of this book (see chapter 22) is that risk assessment should always be viewed as the beginning of a management process, so when making the necessary risk assessment of a sex offender, that assessment must include a formulation that sets out a scheme for risk management. Thus the assessment should be more than simply a determination of how dangerous a sex offender might be – it should also inform an identification of treatment needs and the development of supervision plans.

Most individuals with 'unconventional' sexual arousal patterns, even when amounting to a paraphilia, do not commit sexual offences. Conversely, the majority of sex offenders are not diagnosed with paraphilias, nor is it even the case that abnormal arousal is usually demonstrated in them. Virtually any type of unconventional drive, however, can lead to offending. What determines whether or not offending occurs relates less to the nature of the drive itself (even men with preferential arousal to children can find legal ways to express this), and more to the association between drive and other characteristics of the individual, such as his/her attitudes and beliefs, ability to regulate his/her emotions, life management skills, and the presence of personality disorder (Hanson and Bussiere, 1998; Hanson and Morton-Bourgon, 2005). Other factors such as opportunity may also play a part.

Sexual Arousal

Although sex offending is usually about more than sex, it should not be forgotten that sex is one of its inherent components. Assessment of sexual interest and arousal is therefore important. In theory, the most accurate way to do so would be through self report, but unfortunately self report is often highly unreliable. The extent to which sexual arousal to specific stimuli can be demonstrated with special tests is also problematic. The penile plethysmograph (PPG), for example, which directly measures penile responses to sexual cues in pictures or audiotapes, can provide clear evidence of arousal, but it has a high false negative rate (Kalmus and Beech, 2005). Techniques based on viewing time have also been developed, but so far appear to work best in respect of arousal to children (especially boys), and less well in respect of other types of deviant arousal; false negatives are also common here (Abel et al., 1998; Letourneau, 2002; Glasgow et al., 2003; Laws and Gress, 2004). Virtual reality protocols with which to evaluate sexual preferences are in their infancy, but have the potential to make laboratory investigations less artificial (Renaud et al., 2002). The best use of the PPG is as an aid to treatment, the results can be discussed with the patient and used to inform psychotherapy in its different forms. It is also helpful in getting a patient beyond the stage of denial.

Demonstration of sexual arousal, however, while of interest, provides no information on the extent to which an individual has acted on that arousal, if at all. More useful in this respect is polygraphy, which can elicit disclosures regarding both behaviour and masturbation to deviant fantasies (Grubin et al., 2004; Ben-Shakhar, 2008; Grubin, 2008), although tests that do not result in disclosure can be difficult to interpret. Sex history disclosure polygraph tests are a routine component of many sex offender treatment programmes in the United States.

The Meaning of Risk

When assessing a sex offender, at least five different types of risk need to be considered (Grubin, 2006):

- likelihood of re-offending;
- imminence of re-offending;
- frequency of re-offending;
- consequences of a re-offence;
- escalation of offending.

Although these different aspects of risk seem clear, it is easy to slip between them unawares. Assessing each requires a different approach, with the use of differing tools and techniques. It also must be recognized that variables relating to the risk of *re-offending* are not necessarily the same as those that relate to *offending* in the first place – much of what we know about in this respect comes from studies of men who already have a conviction for a sex offence, and one must be cautious in generalizing to individuals whose fantasies or behaviours may cause concern, but who have not actually committed an offence.

To best appreciate the components of sex offender risk assessment, consider how a general practitioner might go about assessing the risk of myocardial infarction in one of his patients. A man aged 20 with a strong family history of heart disease and myocardial infarction will be considered to have a high *long-term* risk of suffering from a myocardial infarction himself, based on his family history. This long-term risk is static and unchanging. Once recognized, however, attention can be paid to factors that might influence his risk, such as raised blood pressure or high blood cholesterol levels (which in the end may turn out to be the underlying mediators of his risk). These are relatively stable characteristics, and though treatment can have an impact on them, they tend to return to baseline when treatment stops. There is then another set of factors that will have a more immediate impact on his risk of myocardial infarction, such as smoking and stress. These influences fluctuate over short periods of time, and can be modified reasonably quickly. The patient's *current* risk will depend on the interaction between the long-term, stable and acute factors that apply to him (figure 10.1).

Risk assessment of sex offenders can be thought of in a similar manner (figure 10.2). In this case, *static* risk factors are based on historical characteristics such as past convictions, offence type, and age, and provide an estimate of *long-term* risk. This is relatively inert and changes only passively, individuals get older, and may commit more and different types of offences. These static factors typically comprise the components of actuarial risk assessment tools, which are the most accurate means of determining long-term risk (Hanson and Morton-Bourgon, 2007). Examples are Risk Matrix 2000 (Thornton et al., 2003; Grubin, 2008b), which is used widely in the UK, and Static-99 (Hanson and Thornton, 2000; Barbaree et al., 2001), the most commonly used actuarial measure of sex offender risk in North America. Most of the actuarial tools in use perform to similar levels of predictive accuracy (not surprising given that the basic variables are similar between them), typically in the 'moderate' range. Reviews of sex offender risk assessment instruments can be found in Doren (2002) and Grubin (2004).

For those with an interest in actuarial type instruments that can be used with adolescents, the Juvenile Sex Offender Assessment Protocol (J-SOAP) (Righthand et al., 2005) and the Estimate of Risk of Adolescent Sexual Offense

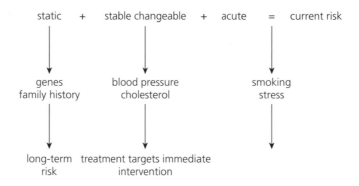

Figure 10.1 Risk assessment in myocardial infarction (see text).

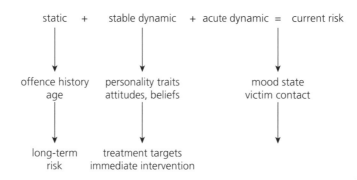

Figure 10.2 Risk assessment in offenders with examples of risk factors.

Recidivism (ERASOR; Worling, 2004) appear to be of benefit in contributing to the assessment of risk in adolescent sex offenders, although research in relation to them is limited.

Other risk factors, generally referred to as stable dynamic risk factors (Hanson and Harris, 2001), relate to features such as an offender's attitudes and beliefs, his ability to form relationships, and his capacity to 'regulate' himself in respect of sexual and more general behaviour (meta-analytic reviews of relevant characteristics can be found in Hanson and Bussiere, 1998; Hanson and Morton-Bourgon, 2005). These features represent the psychological underpinning of offending, and represent targets for treatment. They are best assessed clinically (for example, Thornton, 2002) and through psychometric evaluation (Beech et al., 2002); structured clinical judgment instruments, such as the Sexual Violence Risk – 20 scale (SVR-20; Boer et al., 1997) and the Risk for Sexual Violence Protocol (RSVP; Hart et al., 2003) provide a helpful means by which to assess stable dynamic risk factors in a systematic manner.

In England and Wales, HM Prison Service uses a dynamic risk assessment protocol called the Structured Assessment of Risk and Need (SARN) as part of its national sex offender treatment programme. SARN formulates risk based on a consideration of four domains: sexual interests; distorted attitudes; emotional regulation and social functioning; and self-management. No attempt has been made to measure its association with re-conviction, but a similar

scale called Structured Risk Assessment (SRA) has been used in this way (Thornton, 2002; Knight and Thornton, 2007). In respect of SRA, it was found that the domains on their own had good predictive accuracy, but in addition when used together with actuarial measures the predictive accuracy of both was improved.

More rapidly changing, *acute dynamic* risk factors include such things as mood state, intoxication, and activities that bring an offender into contact with potential victims (Grubin, 2006). In addition to self-report, useful information in respect of these acute factors can be obtained from informants, as well as through techniques such as polygraphy, which is described below.

Hanson and Harris (2001) developed a comprehensive assessment that integrated long-term, stable and acute risk in a scale called the Sex Offender Needs Assessment Rating (SONAR). SONAR was evaluated in a large prospective study in Canada and the United States, and was found to improve upon actuarial assessment used on its own (Hanson et al., 2007). Modifications were made based on this trial, from which two scales emerged:

- Stable 2007, which is composed of five factors: significant social influences, intimacy deficits, general self-regulation, sexual self-regulation, and co-operation with supervision.
- Acute 2007, which is composed of seven factors: victim access, hostility, sexual preoccupation, and rejection

of supervision, emotional collapse, collapse of social supports, and substance abuse.

Although one must be cautious about simply accepting the results of a single study, it appears that these tools can be used reliably, and assist both in the identification of treatment targets and the detection of increases in immediate risk.

Before leaving the topic of assessment, it is worth noting the difficulty that arises from use of the term 'predictive accuracy'. Although helpful when evaluating the efficacy of risk assessment instruments in a research study, prediction is not what is taking place in a clinical setting; assessment is not prediction. An insurance company, for example, does not conclude that its risk assessment was wrong because a young, inexperienced driver who it assessed as 'high-risk' did not have an accident. Risk assessments seek to make *relative* judgments of risk by categorizing individuals as 'low', 'medium', 'high', and so on, but they are not intended to make predications about any specific individual. Knowing that an individual is in a high-risk group, however, will influence the way in which he/she is managed. This difference between research studies of assessment tools where prediction is the key outcome measure, and clinical applications where the tools are used to establish baseline levels of long-term risk, is often ignored, particularly in critiques of actuarial approaches (e.g. Hart et al., 2007) (but see also chapter 22).

Polygraphy

In the United States polygraph testing is used widely in the treatment and supervision of sex offenders, where it is referred to as post-conviction sex offender testing (PCSOT) (English et al., 2000; McGrath, Cumming and Burchard, 2003). Although polygraphy is not yet used in the UK, there have been two trials in probation settings in England (Grubin et al., 2004; Grubin, 2008), and legislation was passed in England in 2007 enabling a national trial of mandatory testing by the probation service.

PCSOT has two main aims: to enhance treatment and to improve supervision. In terms of the former, it is argued that polygraphy provides more complete and more accurate information about an offender's history, sexual interests and offence behaviour, enabling treatment needs to be better identified and targeted; in respect of supervision, PCSOT is used to assist in monitoring behaviour, with supporters arguing that it both acts as a deterrent to reoffending and aids in the detection of reoffending when it occurs (Grubin, 2008). Proponents of PCSOT emphasize that its value comes from the disclosures it facilitates, rather than the passing or failing of a test *per se*, with which polygraphy is more typically associated. Offenders themselves have reported PCSOT to be helpful (Grubin and Madsen, 2005; Kokish et al., 2005).

PCSOT also has its critics. Some of their criticism arises from concerns relating to polygraphy generally, for instance regarding its validity (although a definitive review by the National Research Council (2003) concluded that the accuracy rate of polygraphy is in the region of 80–90%), its utility in some of the criminal, security and employment settings in which it is relied upon, and the ethics of its use (British Psychological Society, 2004; Fiedler et al., 2002; Grubin and Madsen, 2005; National Research Council, 2003). More particular to PCSOT, objections have been raised regarding the validity of the specific test methods employed (Ben-Shakhar, 2008; Cross and Saxe, 2001), and the potential for inappropriate and coercive applications (British Psychological Society, 2004). A fuller discussion of these issues can be found in Grubin (2008).

SEX OFFENDER TREATMENT

The History of Sex Offender Treatment and the Current Context

Most reviews of the state of sex offender treatment prior to the 1970s summarize the literature in one or two rather dismissive sentences (Marshall, 1999), referring to the dominance of psychoanalytic models during this period. There was little specialization, interventions involved either individual or group psychodynamic therapy, and there was an absence of evaluative research, save for the publication of individual case studies. There appears to have been a culture in which treatment was provided with little or no reference to the legal framework within which offending occurred, and ideas were discussed in the literature in relation to the role of victims and non-offending partners that would today appear to collude with the sex offender's propensity to avoid taking responsibility for his/her behaviour.

Since then there have been significant changes in the approach to treatment (reviewed by Mann, 2004). Initially, therapeutic interventions based on behavioural techniques focused on modifying sexual fantasy together with social skills training. In the 1980s there was a shift to incorporate work on the cognitive factors that supported offending behaviour (referred to as cognitive distortions), and a new focus on relapse prevention techniques taken from the addiction literature. The 1990s were characterized by theoretical developments that made use of attachment theory, with treatment expanded to include work on loneliness and intimacy deficits. Similar to the development of cognitive behavioural work in the mental health field generally, attention was increasingly placed on the role of the schema (core dysfunctional beliefs) that underpinned behaviour, particularly in respect of higher risk and more psychologically disturbed sex offenders. There has since been greater acknowledgement of process issues and the importance of therapist characteristics, which have been linked with greater attitudinal change and improved outcome. Over this time there has been a shift in emphasis from a challenging stance and focus on avoidance goals, to a more collaborative, strength-based approach.

Currently in England and Wales, accredited treatment programmes for convicted sex offenders have been introduced in both the prison and probation services. These programmes are based on a cognitive behavioural model and target dynamic risk factors, as referred to earlier in this chapter. In the prisons there are a number of programme types: a core programme that aims to reduce denial and minimization, promote an understanding of victim impact, and develop preliminary strategies to avoid reoffending; an extended programme for those with greater treatment needs, which focuses on schemas and the interpersonal skills deficits found in many offenders; a Healthy Sexual Functioning programme that targets high-risk, high deviancy sex offenders, incorporating behavioural modification within a broader package focusing on relationships and sexuality; a rolling programme that allows for a more individualized approach in lower risk offenders; and a booster programme that re-visits work completed in previous programmes and emphasizes relapse prevention skills in anticipation of rehabilitation into the community. In all, treatment may involve between 50 and 300 hours of therapy.

In the community, there are three accredited programmes run by the probation service. They vary in terms of their delivery, but all are largely similar in content and resemble the prison core programme.

Does Treatment Work?

Furby et al. (1989), in one of the first reviews of sex offender treatment, concluded that treatment had little impact on re-offending, although what was particularly notable about their findings was the lack of good quality studies. Hall (1995) subsequently analysed 12 studies published since 1989, and reported a small treatment effect, with 19% of treated offenders committing further sex offences compared with 27% of those in comparison conditions. He noted that the strongest effects were found in studies where base rates of recidivism were high and follow-up periods of over 5 years were used; cognitive behavioural and hormonal treatments were significantly more effective than behavioural treatments, but not different from each other.

Alexander (1999) reviewed 79 sexual offender treatment outcome studies encompassing 10,988 subjects and covering the period from 1943 to 1996. She found that overall 14% of treated child molesters re-offended compared with 26% of untreated child molesters. Relapse prevention using a cognitive behavioural model appeared to be the most effective type of intervention, with a reoffending rate of 8% compared with a rate of 18% for other psychological interventions, and 14% for unspecified treatment modalities. There were also interesting

differences in victim gender and incest non incest type offending, with treatment effects found in respect of child molesters with male victims and incest offenders, but none in the case of child molesters with female victims.

Hanson et al. (2002), in a review of 43 studies involving over 9000 offenders, confirmed a small positive treatment effect overall for current treatments, with a re-conviction rate of 12% in treated sex offenders compared with 17% in those who were untreated, over an at-risk period of nearly 4 years, although they cautioned that more and better quality research was needed. Sexual recidivism was significantly greater for those who dropped out of treatment, but not where treatment was refused in the first place. Again, cognitive behavioural treatment was associated with greater reductions in sexual recidivism, with a rate 10% in those who were treated compared to 17% in comparison groups.

A still larger meta-analysis was carried out by Lösel and Schmucker (2005), who reviewed 69 studies published in five languages, involving over 20,000 offenders. They found that recidivism was 6% less in treated samples, with what they referred to as organic treatments (that is, castration or medication) having a greater effect than psychological therapies. In terms of psychological treatment, cognitive behavioural approaches were the most efficacious, with an odds ratio of 1.45. Psychodynamic psychotherapy did not appear to have any impact on re-offending rates. But, while pharmacological treatments had a greater impact on recidivism than did psychological treatments on their own, the authors noted that pharmacological studies typically also included a cognitive behavioural component, and that this had an independent treatment effect.

The meta-analyses suggest that treated offenders have recidivism rates 6 to 8% lower than untreated offenders, amounting to about a 30% reduction from baseline. The type of meta-analyses referred to above have been criticized on the grounds that many of the included studies were open to bias. Indeed, Rice and Harris (2003) claimed that if only studies meeting rigorous criteria are included, that positive treatment effects disappear, a finding also reported by others (Brooks-Gordon et al., 2006).

What emerges from the meta-analyses is the dearth of randomized control trials of sex offender treatment. Such studies are difficult to carry out, given the numbers needed to treat, the long-term follow-up required, and issues associated with randomizing potentially high-risk individuals to a 'no-treatment' condition. However, there has been one large scale randomized control trial involving adult sex offenders – the Sex Offender Treatment and Evaluation Project (SOTEP) that was run in California (Marques et al., 2005). This study evaluated inpatient cognitive behavioural treatment based on relapse prevention principles, the effect an recidivism of comparing treated offenders in two untreated prison control groups (one consisting of men who volunteered for treatment but were randomized to the non-treatment group, the other comprising men who refused treatment). No significant differences were found between the three groups in their rates of sexual or violent reoffending over an 8-year follow-up period, regardless of whether rapists or child molesters were considered. However, it was argued that offenders who met the programme's treatment targets did have lower re-offence rates than those who did not. Non-completion of treatment was also found to be an important factor in re-offending.

The relevance of 'benefiting from treatment' was also observed in an English study, where psychometric measures administered both pre- and post-treatment were used to determine treatment efficacy in sex offenders who had taken part in community programmes in the early 1990s (Beech et al., 2001). At 6 years follow-up, the overall sexual reconviction rate was 15%, but only 10% of those judged to have 'benefited from treatment' based on psychometric outcome were re-convicted, compared to 23% of those had not 'responded' to treatment.

The Main Treatment Models

The thrust of treatment approaches from the criminal justice perspective emphasizes the need to consider 'risk–needs–responsivity' principles in designing intervention programmes (Andrew and Bonta, 2006):

- Risk: treatment should be provided to those at highest risk of recidivism (otherwise it is difficult to demonstrate a treatment effect).
- Needs: treatment should target the offender's criminogenic needs, incorporating as wide a range of factors as possible.
- Responsivity: interventions should be sensitive to the offender's individual abilities and capabilities.

The criminal justice perspective pays little or no attention to issues such psychological distress which, for mental health services, are often a legitimate focus of treatment in their own right.

As referred to above, a range of treatment models have been applied to sex offenders (see Craissati, 1998, for a full review of the various models; behavioural treatments that focus specifically on deviant sexual arousal are described in Maletzky, 1991). The dominant mode of treatment at present is cognitive behavioural therapy.

Cognitive behavioural therapy (CBT)

CBT incorporates elements of both cognitive and behavioural theories that have been developed since the 1970s. More recently, concepts from schema therapy have been included within this rubric. This is an integrative approach, with roots in psychoanalytic thinking, in which emphasis is placed on core beliefs, affective responses, and early life experiences.

In relation to sex offenders, the CBT/schema model is based on the premise that schemas are stable cognitive patterns that develop in early life, and are shaped by events and relationships. These schemas give rise to underlying assumptions, or conditional beliefs, which trigger automatic thoughts, often reflecting persistent cognitive distortions, resulting in habitual patterns of action. Recidivist sex offenders would be expected to hold deviant schema associating with their offending, and which contribute to it. These schema can also be conceptualized as implicit theories held by offenders, such as that 'women are dangerous', 'women are sex objects', or 'the male sex drive is uncontrollable', which are implicated in 'pathways' to offending found in rapists (Polaschek and Gannon, 2004), or 'children are sexual objects', 'the world is dangerous', and 'the world is uncontrollable' found in the offending pathways of child molesters (Ward and Keenan, 1999).

There are six main components to most sex offender CBT treatment programmes (Beckett et al., 1994):

- *denial and minimization* are targeted, as breaking down denial is considered to be an important prerequisite for change and the assumption of responsibility;
- *victim empathy* is developed with the aim of strengthening the motivation to engage in treatment and not to re-offend;
- *justifications and cognitive distortions* are elicited and challenged to stop the offender giving himself 'permission' to offend;
- *lifestyle and personality* issues related to self-esteem, fear of adult intimacy and inappropriate assertiveness are addressed with the aim of improving the way in which the offender functions in society;
- *deviant sexual fantasies* are targeted to help the perpetrator control deviant arousal, although actual modification of deviant fantasies is usually beyond the scope of most programmes;
- *relapse prevention* plans assist offenders to recognize risky situations, feelings, moods, and thoughts, and to develop strategies to prevent re-offending.

At the centre of many treatment programmes sits the sexual assault cycle (also variably known as the offence cycle, offence chain, or decision chain). This is a functional analysis of offending which, at the very least, draws together specific criminogenic factors, offence triggers, and high-risk cognitions, feelings and behaviours in order to develop personalized relapse prevention plans that emphasize self management skills.

Psychoanalytic psychotherapies

Psychoanalysis seeks to provide an aetiological account of perversion and violence, including rape and child molestation (although more has been written about the latter). Perversion, in this sense, is used specifically to denote sexualization of the aggressive instinct, and is characterized by repetitive fixed behaviour – a sexual act which is insistent and gratifying. Three main themes can be found in the analytical literature (Rosen, 1996): perversions such as paedophilia that occur in the context of avoidance of anxiety-laden heterosexuality; the identification of important non-sexual components in deviant sexual behaviour, such as coping and mastery, in which fantasy or behaviour is rewarding because it induces a sense of control, competence or dominance; and, in the case of the paedophile, involvement with children that occurs in the context of an idealization of the characteristics of childhood. Elements of neediness and hostility are said to be found in all sexual offences, albeit masked at times.

Psychoanalytic interventions are usually intensive and of long duration. They often require high levels of motivation and a degree of psychological health in the patient, neither of which are always found in sex offenders. The process of therapy is different from cognitive behavioural approaches in that particular attention is paid to unconscious and partially conscious mental states, which are explored as they appear in the therapist–patient interaction. Addressing how the offender thinks, feels and acts through the vehicle of the therapeutic relationship is believed to provide the offender with a cognitive and emotional understanding of himself and his interpersonal relationships, leading to change. The main role for psychodynamic therapy in this field is in supporting and supervising other staff and therapists (see chapter 23).

Systemic approaches and family reunification

Family systems therapists aim to extend issues that involve the individual into a family and social context. Observation of the family is based on the premise that a system (or family) can be defined as an organized arrangement of elements consisting of a network of interdependent coordinated parts which function as a unit. The presenting symptom – usually child molestation, but also rape – is considered in terms of its importance in stabilizing the family unit, and the degree to which it is in turn maintained by family dysfunction. In relation to abuse within families as well as to the offending of children, Bentovim (1996) gives an account of the terms used to describe family patterns, such as affective life, boundaries, alliances, adaptability, stability, and competence.

Both Bentovim (1996) and Furniss (1991) discuss families in which child sexual abuse has occurred in two broad typologies: conflict-avoiding and conflict-regulating. Conflict-avoiding families are described as being highly enmeshed with intense over-involvement between father and daughter, and a more distant and hostile relationship between mother and daughter; conflict between the parents is avoided because of fear that it would result in family destruction and breakdown, with sexual abuse often emerging out of long-standing sexual failure in the marriage. Conflict-regulating families are more likely to present with chaos and poor care, and with weak boundaries between both generations and individuals; violence and punitiveness often arise in communication patterns, and marital conflict may be openly visible. Child molestation provides an outlet for aggression by the father, reducing marital conflict that could lead to family break up. Collusion between the parents increases the father's dependence on his wife, who tolerates the abuse as it keeps him emotionally bound to the family.

There is sometimes professional discomfort in systemic models that, by attempting to explain abuse, seem to allow for responsibility for it to be spread across family members, colluding with an offender's minimization of, and justifications for, his abusive behaviour. Nevertheless, family therapy approaches are crucial when exploring the relationship of the non-offending parent to the children in the family (Calder, 2001; Craissati, 2004), and also when considering the possible reunification of a family, where a shared understanding of offence cycles and relapse prevention plans are necessary.

Medication

Although sex offender treatment typically takes the form of psychological interventions, it should not be forgotten that at its root lies the pressure exerted by sexual drive. Sex drive, sexual arousal, and sexual behaviour are mediated by biological mechanisms, and because of this can be influenced by pharmacological interventions, which offer a useful adjunct to psychological treatment in appropriate cases (see Grubin, 2008a for a review and Thibault et al., 2010).

The male sex drive is dependent on testosterone, although the main actions of this hormone in respect of sexual function relate to spontaneous sexual interest and behaviour – sexual performance itself, including the ability to have erections and to engage in sexual intercourse, may still be preserved to some extent even in the absence of testosterone (Bancroft, 1989). Variations in testosterone levels do not have an immediate effect on sexual functioning – changes in blood concentrations take weeks to manifest themselves (Bancroft, 2005). When testosterone levels are experimentally raised in men from normal baseline concentrations, gradual changes in sexual arousal and mood (typically an increase in irritability) are sometimes but not always observed. It is only when plasma concentrations of testosterone fall below a very low threshold (or perhaps rise above a very high one) that overt changes in function and behaviour are observed.

While testosterone is a necessary component of normal sexual function, it does not act in isolation. Other hormones and neurotransmitters also influence sex drive, with dopamine and serotonin being especially relevant. Dopamine is involved in a number of drive related behaviours (eating, sleeping, as well as sex), with dopamine pathways tending to be facilitative in nature. In respect of sexual arousal, dopamine appears to act synergistically with testosterone: testosterone increases dopamine activity in the limbic region of the brain, while dopamine in turn appears to enhance the effects of testosterone (Hull et al., 2004). Serotonin (or 5-HT), on the other hand, tends to have effects that oppose those of dopamine; in terms of appetitive behaviours, it acts primarily in an inhibitory manner (Hull et al., 2004). Drugs that increase serotonin levels, such as the selective serotonin reuptake inhibitors (SSRIs), therefore, often have a negative impact on various aspects of sexual functioning, for example, loss of libido, erectile dysfunction, and impaired ejaculation.

Through our understanding of the detail of how dopamine, serotonin and testosterone interact to modulate sex drive, each provides a target for pharmacological manipulation. Two main pharmacological strategies have been employed in the treatment of sex offenders: one seeks to reduce the activity of testosterone directly through the use of anti-androgen medication, the other aims to increase and enhance the influences of serotonin. In theory, drugs that reduce or block the activity of dopamine in the limbic region of the brain, such as the major tranquillizers prescribed in schizophrenia (well known for their side-effects of impotence and loss of libido, although this may be at least partly caused by a rise in prolactin levels) could also be of benefit. The response to them is in general too unpredictable to recommend their routine use in the treatment of problematic sexual behaviour.

Anti-androgens

Anti-androgens reduce testosterone activity in a variety of ways, including interference with testosterone synthesis, blocking its access to receptors in its target cells, and increasing its breakdown and removal from the body. In the 1940s, oestrogens were first prescribed for sex offenders, and were reported to reduce substantially their levels of sexual interest and masturbatory activity. However, nausea, serious cardiovascular complications, and feminization limited their use (Prentky, 1997). They were superseded in the 1960s by two anti-androgens, cyproterone acetate in Europe and Canada, and medroxyprogesterone (MPA) in the United States (and to a lesser extent in Canada). Both these drugs reduce testosterone concentration and activity to pre-pubertal levels, but doses can be titrated so that sexual arousal is lessened but not eliminated. Side-effects, however, are a problem, particularly breast growth, the risk of ischaemic heart disease, endocrine abnormalities, and various other symptoms associated with the female menopause, such as hot flushes; liver and endocrine function need to be routinely monitored.

A number of studies involving the use of these agents have been carried out (for reviews, see Ortmann, 1980; Prentky, 1997; Saleh and Berlin, 2003; Grubin, 2008a). They typically describe reductions in sexual interest, fantasy and behaviour, as well as low recidivism rates, usually under 5%. However, most involve small numbers of subjects, they often fail to take into account those who drop out of treatment, and they are reliant on self-report measures of sexual activity. Double-blind randomized controlled trials are rare, although one such study involving cyproterone acetate and placebo demonstrated a close association between medication and decreased sexual interest (Bradford and Pawlak, 1993).

More recently GnRH (gonadotropin-releasing hormone) agonists, which are used in the treatment of testosterone sensitive prostate cancer, have been prescribed as anti-androgens in sex offenders. They act at the level of the hypothalamus, draining it of gonadotropin releasing hormone (which controls the release of luteinizing hormone, which in turn is necessary for testosterone production in the testes), and have been increasingly prescribed. These drugs, which include leuprolide, tryptorelin, and goserelin, appear to have a more potent impact on testosterone levels and on sexual arousal and activity than the traditional anti-libidinals, possibly because of their action on GnRH neurons that project to brain areas beyond the pituitary, in particular the amygdala (Rösler and Wiztum, 2000). A review of the small literature on the use of these drugs with sex offenders described very low reoffending rates, with apparently improved outcomes in subjects who had previously been prescribed medroxyprogesterone acetate (MPA) or cyproterone acetate (Briken et al., 2003). Again, however, sample sizes are small, comparison groups are absent, and outcome is highly dependent on self-report. Nevertheless, GnRH agonists appear to be associated with fewer side-effects than the traditional anti-libidinals, although osteoporosis is particularly problematic; because they are given by long acting injection, compliance is less of an issue than it is with oral cyproterone acetate (in the UK, depot versions of cyproterone are available only on a named patient basis). They are, however, much more expensive than either MPA or cyproterone.

Selective serotonin reuptake inhibitors

Because of the relationship between serotonin and sexual functioning, and because of the resemblance between the sexual ruminations, intrusive fantasies and apparently compulsive sexual behaviours found in some sex offenders and obsessive compulsive disorders (OCD) in which selective serotonin reuptake inhibitor (SSRI) medication can be effective, SSRIs were introduced for the treatment of paraphilias (Kafka and Prentky, 1994). Since the early 1990s, there have been over 200 case published reports and open studies of SSRIs and problematic sexual behaviour, with most reporting success in reducing the frequency and intensity of sexual fantasy, urges and arousal (Kafka, 2003a). Fluoxetine, sertraline and fluvoxamine are the SSRIs most commonly prescribed, and though in theory there should be little difference between them in terms of efficacy, Kafka (1994) found that men who did not respond to sertraline improved when switched to fluoxetine.

The main effect of the SSRIs is to reduce the intensity and frequency of sexual fantasies, and to lessen the force of sexual urges. They are associated with a much milder side-effect profile than the anti-androgens, although gastrointestinal symptoms such as nausea and change in bowel habit are relatively common. They do not have the primary anti-libidinal effects of the anti-androgens, and they seem most effective when sexual rumination, or sexually compulsive behaviour, are the main concern.

As with the anti-libidinals, the evidence concerning the use of SSRIs in paraphilias is supportive, but not robust. Most trials involve small numbers of patients and short follow-up periods, and there is a heavy reliance on self-report with a lack of double-blind controlled studies.

Overall, clinical trials indicate that medication is effective in reducing risk in sex offenders (Lösel and Schmucker, 2005; Thiboult et al., 2010). From a clinical perspective, when medication is successful it often appears to be dramatically so, with offenders reporting great benefit from no longer being preoccupied by sexual thoughts or dominated by their sexual drives. It can also allow them to participate in psychological treatment programmes where previously they may have been too distracted to take part.

Under Section 57 of the Mental Health Act 1983 (amended), hormone implants for the reduction of sexual drive require that a patient is capable of giving valid consent to the procedure and is consenting that the treatment is approved by an appointed doctor and two other non-medical personnel. In 1988 a sex offender prescribed the GnRH agonist goserelin with his consent was nonetheless refused a certificate under Section 57. This was challenged in the High Court, where it was decided that goserelin was neither a hormone nor an implant, and thus it, and by extension the other anti-libidinals currently in use, are not covered by this section of the Act. Fennell (1988) summarizes the various legal issues involved in this case.

Before leaving this review of medication, it is worth considering briefly a physical intervention that is sometimes advocated for sex offenders – orchidectomy, or physical castration. In the early part of the twentieth century a number of European countries, including Denmark, Sweden, Norway, the Netherlands, Switzerland and Germany passed legislation to enable the castration of high-risk sex offenders. Although in practice many of those castrated were neither prolific offenders nor were their offences severe (many of those castrated, for example, were learning disabled or mentally ill, and their offences appear to have included crimes such as homosexuality and indecent exposure), recidivism rates of under 5% over long follow-up periods have been reported (Heim and Hursch, 1979; Ortmann, 1980; Sturup, 1968a,b; Weinberger et al., 2005).

Castration, however, is associated with a significant side-effect profile, including osteoporosis, cardiovascular disease, gynaecomastia, redistribution of body fat, loss of muscle tone, and 'menopausal' symptoms like hot flushes. It is also mutilating, and it can easily transmute into punishment rather than treatment. It is now mainly of historical interest, but prisoners or patients will on occasions request surgical castration (Alexander, 1993), and the forensic psychiatric practitioner needs be prepared to respond in an informed manner. In British mental health legislation there is no mention of surgical castration in the treatment of sex offenders, and were it to be employed there are currently no legal safeguards in place to prevent its misuse (Bingley, 1993).

When medication is used in the treatment of sex offenders it is frequently referred to as 'chemical castration'. This fails to distinguish between the different types of drugs that are prescribed, not all of which act directly through testosterone. Unlike castration, even with anti-libidinals medication dose can be titrated and stopped if necessary; side-effects are more easily managed. Because the negative connotations of the term 'chemical castration' in itself may deter offenders from considering a potentially effective treatment, the term 'castration' should probably be kept in reserve for the surgical procedure.

Managing Denial

Denial in sex offenders is widely prevalent, with total denial described in up to a third of all sex offenders (Kennedy and Grubin, 1992; Marshall, 1994). It is important to distinguish between complete denial for an offence, and denial which represents a justification for, or minimization of, offending behaviour in terms of victim impact or personal responsibility (Salter, 1988). Absolute denial is observed more commonly in offenders against adult women rather than child molesters, and is often associated with feelings of shame, a wish to protect family members, or a need to maintain a strong self image in relation to a criminal peer group.

The relationship between denial and risk is unclear. Although meta-analyses do not suggest a direct link (Hanson and Bussiere, 1998), two recent studies have reported an association, one in respect of low-risk and incest offenders (Nunes et al., 2007), the other in a subgroup of high-risk offenders when a continuous measure of minimization was used (Langton et al., 2008). Regardless of whether or not denial is predictive of re-offending, however, it can prevent offenders from benefiting from treatment, and indeed it can exclude them from treatment programmes altogether.

There are two types of psychological intervention typically employed in respect of absolute denial:

1. Motivational interviewing models have been applied to sex offenders in a manner similar to their use in the addictions (Miller, 1995). It is important to recognize that many of the methods recommended reflect standard, albeit high quality, therapeutic skills which

many experienced practitioners will deploy intuitively, for example the use of open questions and reflective listening. Nevertheless, the skills required are often underestimated. Throughout, the interviewer aims to elicit and reinforce self-motivating statements which approach some recognition that there is a problem or that express concern, as well as any intention to change (Beckett et al., 1994; Tierney and McCabe, 2002).

2. There is limited evidence for the benefits of brief structured group interventions, particularly in respect of child molesters. Such approaches tend to include elements of victim empathy, cognitive restructuring, education about sex offender therapy and a discussion of the possible consequences of continued denial.

In addition, it is possible to focus on criminogenic issues other than the offence, such as self-esteem, relationships, coping strategies and relapse prevention, without requiring the offender to admit the offence (Marshall et al., 2001).

Treatment in Special Groups

Mentally ill offenders

Although only a minority of sex offenders suffer from mental illness, they comprise a large proportion of secure hospital populations. Sahota and Chesterman (1998) and Smith and Taylor (1999, 2000) highlight the need for careful appraisal of the role of symptoms in offending behaviour, evaluated against known risk factors associated with sex offending generally. For example, a sex assault may arise directly from delusional beliefs or hallucinations, or it may relate to less specific features of an illness, such as heightened arousal and irritability, or confused thought processes. However, the assault may be largely unrelated to mental illness, but instead be a function of underlying personality problems or sexually deviant interests.

Determining the temporal relationship between offending and illness can be difficult, and often requires retrospective evaluation involving information from informants as well as the patient himself. Craissati and Hodes (1992), in a study of 11 mentally ill sex offenders, found no evidence of mental illness within the prosecution evidence, including the transcript of the police interview, even though the majority of the sample were found to be floridly psychotic when assessed shortly afterwards in prison. It seemed likely that three of the offences were committed in relation to hallucinations and delusional beliefs, while many of the others took place in the context of deteriorating social behaviour and self-care, heightened feelings of anxiety or depression, and a degree of sexual preoccupation in a prodromal phase of the illness.

In terms of specific interventions for sex offenders with severe mental illness, the initial consideration is to treat psychotic symptomatology with anti-psychotic medication. For some patients, insight into their illness and compliance with medication may form the primary relapse prevention strategy. More usually, treatment involves a combination of medication, psychological and social therapies which address a range of pro-offending attitudes, social competencies and personality factors, in addition to the symptoms of the illness.

The relationship between depressive illness and sex offending is not well researched, largely because the prevalence of such patients appears to be small. However, some depressed individuals may suffer from persistent and distressing ruminations, and present with anxieties regarding recurring thoughts or impulses to sexually offend; this may or may not be associated with 'approach' behaviours such as following women. Similarly, deviant ruminations already present in a sex offender may worsen in the context of depressive illness. In such cases, anti-depressant medication should be considered before embarking on cognitive behavioural treatment approaches, with SSRIs being an obvious choice.

The potential relationship between personality disorder and sex offending is perhaps self-evident insofar as many of the dynamic risk factors associated with sexual recidivism are likely to be present in those with personality disorder. Managing personality disordered offenders in treatment programmes, however, can be challenging. Whilst sex offenders with antisocial personality disorder may resist attempts to engage them in treatment, sex offenders with borderline features may seek treatment in a chaotic manner, characterized by intense distress and a raised propensity to self harm. Craissati and Beech (2001) found that evidence of emotional and behavioural disturbance in childhood, as well as trauma and contact with mental health services as an adult (excluding those with diagnoses of mental illness) predicted both missed treatment sessions and attrition from treatment in a community sex offender programme. Similar findings have been reported by others (Chaffin, 1992). Given the established link between treatment attrition and recidivism, there may need to be a much greater degree of structure and support underpinning treatment programmes for personality disordered sex offenders, including psychiatric back-up.

Men who score highly on the Psychopathy Checklist (PCL-R, Hare, 2003) have been thought to perform poorly in therapeutic programmes. They frequently drop out of treatment, and recidivate quicker following release; in addition, sexual recidivism had been found to be strongly predicted by a combination of high PCL-R score and physiological evidence of deviant sexual arousal (Rice and Harris, 1997). However, the methodological problems with these studies have been noted by D'Silva et al. (2004), who point out the need for a control group and to take account of treatment non-completion. In a review of data from 10 studies relating to four treatment programmes, Doren and Yates (2008) found no evidence to indicate that sex offender treatment lowered *serious* recidivism for men with high PCL-R scores to the levels of other sex offenders, but re-offence rates varied, and some of the high scorers did in fact have similar sexual recidivism rates to low scorers following treatment. They concluded that while high-scoring sex offenders maintain a heightened degree of serious recidivism risk even after participation in sex offender treatment, treatment may be effective for some, and they were reluctant to conclude that, as a general statement, high scorers on the PCL-R scale do not benefit from sex offender treatment.

Learning Disability

Determining the relationship between learning disability and a sexual offence can be complex. The choice of a child victim may reflect the emotional immaturity of the offender, who feels threatened by, or unable to access peer relationships; the offender may have difficulty conceptualizing the nature of consent, or lack the ability to establish whether consent has been given; there may simply be a skills deficit, in so far as the offender may be ignorant about sexual matters and the necessary skills involved in establishing sexual relationships. Furthermore, a diagnosis of learning disability is often associated with other mental disorders, with a prevalence three to four times greater than in the general population (World Health Organization, 1992). However, it may also be the case that sexual offending is related to personality factors or deviant sexual interest separate from the cognitive impairment itself.

As with research into sex offender treatment generally, studies of treatment outcome in learning disabled sex offenders is characterized by the absence of control groups, very small sample sizes, and multi-modal therapeutic approaches that complicate evaluation (Courtney and Rose, 2004). Interventions range from educational group treatment and social–sexual skills interventions, to adaptations of treatment approaches developed for mainstream populations in which concepts are simplified and much greater use is made of visual imagery (Lambrick and Glaser, 2004). While little can as yet be drawn from outcome studies, the evidence suggests that pro-offending attitudes can be modified, and that greater treatment length is associated with increased attitude change and a reduction in recidivism (Courtney and Rose, 2004).

Adolescents

Whilst a range of variables have been associated with juvenile offending in general – maltreatment in childhood, early onset of aggressive behaviour, family instability, substance misuse – the evidence for factors specific to sex offending has been inconsistent (Righthand and Welch, 2001). Much of the research on incarcerated (and therefore higher risk)

juvenile sex offenders suggests that their offending is but one expression of antisocial, violent behaviour (Jacobs et al., 1997).

The evidence base for adolescent sex offender treatment programmes is described in a review for the US Department of Justice carried out by Righthand and Welch (2001). They argue that consideration needs to be given to the developmental tasks of the adolescent stage of life, a period of fluidity and transition. Specifically, extreme caution needs to be taken before considering emerging deviant sexual interests and fantasies as a major risk factor in this group. The goals of adolescent programmes should include a focus on gaining control over sexually abusive behaviours, and increasing pro-social interactions with peers. Treatment content includes addressing issues of denial and distortion, sex education, social skills, as well as decreasing deviant arousal and relapse prevention, the latter emphasizing external controls.

Unlike adult sex offenders, denial in adolescents is likely to be strongly influenced by family attitudes. Where possible, family work should be undertaken to reduce denial by providing information and education, through carers groups and family therapy (Stevenson et al., 1990). Additional treatment components incorporate the resolution of family dysfunction, enhancing a positive sexual identity, promoting dating skills, and positive school attachments. Specialist treatment developments have included the use of vicarious sensitization – exposure to audiotaped crime scenarios designed to stimulate arousal, followed by a video portraying the negative consequences of sexually abusive behaviour – which appears to reduce deviant arousal in adolescents who are sexually aroused by prepubescent children (Weinrott, et al., 1997).

Although there is a lack of empirical support for the superior efficacy of groups, this remains the preferred mode of intervention. Practitioners have warned against a confrontational, offence-focused approach with adolescents, given that they may be more susceptible to suggestion, and may feel pressurized to falsely 'confess' to offending behaviours. There is limited evidence to suggest that comprehensive treatment models which include group, individual and family work may reduce sexual recidivism (Borduin et al., 1990), but the evidence base is thin. As yet, it is not clear whether residential or community treatment is more efficacious, or whether treatment is more successful in a specialist or non-specialist setting. It is likely that a greater range and intensity of treatment, rather than setting, is most important to outcome.

Given that a significant number of adolescent sex offenders present with a range of delinquent behaviours, programmes which are not sex offence specific, but which address antisocial behaviours more generally, may be effective. Meta-analytic reviews (Lipsey and Wilson, 1998) have demonstrated the effectiveness of cognitive behavioural interventions, and those which focus on interpersonal skills and use behavioural programmes, for juvenile delinquents.

Women

Few structured treatment programmes for female sex offenders are described in the literature, and inevitably much of the therapeutic work has taken place on an individual basis. In England and Wales, group work for women, mainly in prison, is in its infancy. In many ways, treatment goals are viewed as similar to those for male offenders: reducing pro-offending attitudes, addressing intimacy deficits, and developing relapse prevention skills. Some programmes view victimization experiences as an important secondary treatment target, while others emphasize the need to engage women as victims in their own right, often in individual therapy (Saradjian and Hanks, 1996) before addressing their personal responsibility for offending. There are, of course, risks inherent in both approaches: offence-focused work may ignore profound individual difficulties which interfere with an offender's capacity to make use of therapy, but attention to personal trauma may encourage the therapist to collude with the defensive stance of a woman who wishes to distance herself from facing up to her offending behaviour. Saradjian and Hanks (1996), however, argue that addressing an offender's life history and trauma is the most effective way of effectively engaging her in meaningful therapeutic work and overcoming denial.

Atkinson (2000) suggests that female sex offenders may have different treatment needs according to their 'typology'. For example, women who offend under the influence of a male partner may respond reasonably quickly to offence focused work, with the development of self-confidence and social skills, although they may also require help in understanding dependency difficulties and achieving independence from abusive partners. Sexually deviant offenders (referred to as 'predisposed'), however, may be more difficult to treat because of the extent of their psychological disturbance, and attention will need to be paid in the first instance to their deviant sexual fantasies, and subsequently to the repercussions of their abuse. There would appear to be considerable benefits to a programme which has multiple components.

TREATMENT OR CONTROL

In the case of any offender who poses a risk to others, there is an inevitable dual objective of treatment and of protection of the public. Reference to public safety, however, raises particularly difficult issues for forensic practitioners: are they treating a patient, or are they acting as agents of social control whose primary responsibility is to society rather than the patient in their care? Although the issue comes most to the fore when medication is under consideration, given its potential for side-effects, all treatment can cause harm. Most would agree that patients should consent to treatment, informed of its risks and benefits, but to what extent is this consent affected when the alternative is detention in custody? Of course, there is no obvious reason why an offender should not be able to weigh-up the pros and cons of imprisonment as opposed to community supervision with treatment (including pharmacological treatment), but once treatment becomes a condition, it ceases to be provided on purely medical grounds, and there may be unrealistic expectations of its efficacy.

In general, it probably makes most sense for treatment to be viewed as part of a wider package of care and supervision, and that no decisions should be taken dependent wholly on whether or not the offender complies. Penalties, then, would not be for default, but for returning to the types of behaviour that the treatment is intended to reduce. In this context, the treatment provider does not assume primary responsibility for public safety, but nonetheless contributes to it by assisting the offender to address those factors which make him/her more likely to re-offend; treatment protocols can therefore be based on clinical need rather than on offender risk.

Public Hostility

A special factor in the management of sex offenders is the high degree of stigma attached to the behaviour which in turn leads to serious and sometimes violent public hostility. Newspapers run campaigns to name and shame individual offenders. Summer 2000 saw an estate in Portsmouth called Paulsgrove stage a mini riot and campaign against an ex-prisoner and convicted sex offender who had moved into the estate. This somewhat hysterical response to the problem of rehabilitating sex offenders is in part based on the public image that 'paedophiles' are strangers, probably of a different race and may be of a different species! Attempts to inform the public better with the reality that most sex offenders offend against people they know and this includes child sex offenders are not likely to be very successful in the face of overwhelming stigma and fear. (See Silverman and Wilson, 2002 for a discussion.) In reality there are complex and comprehensive means employed in Britain to identify and control convicted sex offenders.

Treatment has to include a workable rehabilitation programme which can ensure that any risks of re-offending are reduced to a minimum and at the same time offer the ex-offender a reasonable chance of normalization. This can be very difficult especially when a man (it's usually a man) is rejected by his family and needs to find single accommodation in a new area. He is particularly likely to be perceived as the stranger paedophile. Specialized hostels, religious orders and sympathetic members of the public can be enlisted to some extent on occasions. A new development for Britain which has been available in Canada since the 1980s is Circles of Support. These are trained and supervised volunteers who agree to work in a group to help an individual sex offender who is without other types of social support and who is well motivated to give up his illegal activities. The arrangements have to be entirely voluntary on both sides and cannot be made a licence condition for someone who is leaving prison. Little research has yet been done on their effectiveness but the humanitarian benefits are obvious. A website describes the arrangements which are being developed in Britain: http://www.circles-uk.org.uk.

Treatment Checklist

1. When resources are limited, concentrate them on high-risk rather than low-risk offenders, as treatment impact will be greater with this group.
2. Remember that denial is a normal human response, and has not been shown to be related to treatment outcome.
3. Victim empathy has not been shown to be associated with risk of re-offending (Hanson and Morton-Bourgon, 2004), although it is difficult to measure; lack of empathy, however, may limit engagement with treatment.
4. A common weakness in assessment is a failure to take enough notice of sexual preoccupations.
5. Treatment is long term (as, for example, is treatment for diabetes). Continuing professional support beyond the treatment programme is important in the prevention of reoffending.
6. Medication, in particular SSRIs and anti-androgens, can be of great benefit for some offenders.
7. Psychodynamic treatment may have its place in selected cases and psychodynamic support for members of staff is important.

Postscript

The play *Future Me* by Stephen Brown (2007) gives a sensitive rendition of many of the problems created by paedophile abuse and is well worth seeing, or failing that, reading.

11

The majority of crime: theft, motoring and criminal damage (including arson)

Edited by
John Gunn

Written by
Tim Amos

Harvey Gordon

John Gunn

Jill Peay

Julian Walker

1st edition authors (*for 'Ninety-five Percent of Crime'*): **Ann Barker, David Forshaw, Gisli Gudjonsson, John Gunn and Robert Sharrock**

No punishment has ever possessed enough power of deterrence to prevent the commission of crimes. On the contrary, whatever the punishment, once a specific crime has appeared for the first time, its reappearance is more likely than its initial emergence could ever have been (Hannah Arendt).

INTRODUCTION

The focus of contemporary forensic psychiatry tends to be on crimes against the person, in particular violent and sexual crimes. This reflects the caseload of forensic psychiatrists in medium secure settings where a substantial proportion of inpatients are admitted because of violent or sexual crimes or acts. A survey of almost 3500 admissions to seven regional secure units reported that 60% were admitted either having been convicted of violent crimes or because of non-criminal violent behaviour, with a further 10% admitted after sexual crimes or behaviour (Coid et al., 2001a,b). The corresponding figures for special hospitals were similar with 62% of those admitted, over a 10-year period, having committed a violent offence and 8% a sexual offence (Jamieson et al., 2000). Yet of approximately 5.5 million crimes recorded by the police in England and Wales each year, only 20% are crimes of violence, less than 1% are sexual crimes, and an even smaller proportion involve murder or manslaughter (i.e.

homicide = 0.01%; see table 11.1 and figure 11.1). Two conclusions may be drawn from these gross statistics: first, offenders who have committed crimes of a violent or sexual nature are in the minority of the offending population generally; second, that they feature disproportionately, but unremarkably, in confined populations including secure hospitals.

Crime is heterogeneous and ubiquitous, embracing everything from parking on a double yellow line and exceeding the duty free allowance to rape and murder. Given that the majority of referrals to forensic psychiatric services are for crimes against the person, is it reasonable to conclude that the vast majority of crime has little to do with psychiatric disorder? Even though there may be few special reasons to link, say, property offending such as theft with psychiatric disorder, there will be some individuals who are stealing in association with, or as a result of, a range of psychiatric disorders, from personality disorders to confusional states, from depression to alcoholism. It is easy for these individuals, who may be very needy, to get lost or to be ignored.

Crime is in large part a social and political construct. It is multifaceted, it is defined by fashion, and by consensus which changes (note for example laws on suicide and homosexuality), and ultimately by lawmakers. Comparisons between one place and another, one time and another, can be very misleading. Crime of any kind may be one way in which mental disorder is manifest. It is not just sexual and violent crimes that may be symptomatic of mental disorder. Much mental disorder will go unnoticed if the psychiatrist is not cognizant of the phenomena of crime in general. There is a further complication. Is the persistent offender against social mores, who is not overtly mentally ill, simply a 'criminal' that society and medicine should reject or is s/he a disordered person who cannot (rather than will not) conform?

Table 11.1 Crime figures for 2006/2007 according to Police Recorded Crime figures and the British Crime Survey

Crime	Police Recorded Crime figures[1]	British Crime Survey figures
Criminal damage (excluding arson)	1,142,000	2,731,000
Arson	43,000	N/A
Burglary (non-domestic)	330,000	N/A
Burglary (domestic)	292,000	733,000
Drug	194,000	5,000,000[2]
Fraud	200,000	N/A
Robbery	101,000	311,000
Theft (vehicle related)	765,000	1,731,000
Theft (non-vehicle related)	1,181,000	3,369,000
Sexual	58,000	1,081,000[3]
Violence	1,046,000	2,420,000
Other	76,000	N/A
Total	5,428,000	N/A

[1]To nearest 1000.

[2]Estimate based on the BCS finding that 10.5% of 16 to 59 year olds had taken an illicit substance during the previous year (population of England and Wales 54,046,224).

[3]Estimate based on the BCS finding that 3% of women and 1% of men reported being victims of sexual assault during the previous year.

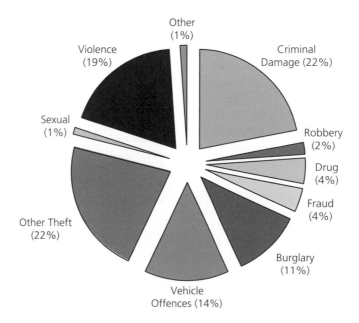

Figure 11.1 Types of criminal offences as a proportion of total offending figures based on police recorded crime in England and Wales (2006/2007).

RECORDING OF CRIME[1]

Criminal statistics are notoriously difficult to interpret (Maguire, 2007). Police recorded crime statistics are only a very partial representation of crimes committed. Much criminal activity goes unrecognized; if recognized by the victim it may not be reported, and if reported it is not invariably recorded. Concurrent publication of data from the British Crime Survey, which is based on annual reports of victimization amongst representative samples of householders (see Walker et al., 2006), helps to illustrate the persistent gulf between crimes perpetrated and crimes recorded, but even the British Crime Survey is a partial account.

The absolute number of recorded crimes in England and Wales has increased since 1988 (3.7 million in 1988 to 5.2 million offences in 2006/2007), but the factors influencing the increase in this figure are not simple. Not only will these have been influenced by variations in crime detection and recording habits by the police but crime counting and recording systems have changed. In 1998 new categories of offence were included and racially aggravated offences were separately recorded, the crime total was thus artificially increased. In 2002/2003 British Transport Police data were included. Some tables showing crimes trends have a break in the statistics in the year 1998–99 as this was the year when the 'counting rules' changed, leading to a significant increase in the numbers of crimes the police were obliged to report. Before 1998 if the police did not believe a victim they need not record a crime. From 1998 the police had to take at face value what victim said for recording purposes.

There are several ways of adding up the number of crimes committed each year. The most commonly quoted figures are those recorded by the police, who provide data for England and Wales (http://www.homeoffice.gov.uk/science-research/research-statistics/crime/crime-statistics/police-recorded-crime/). The British Crime Survey data, also available online on the same Home Office website provide the most reliable indicator of victimization and of trends in crime over time, whilst giving some insight into victims' experiences and perceptions of crime. Since 2003 there has also been the Offending, Crime and Justice Survey (Budd et al., 2005), a national longitudinal self-report survey for England and Wales, which has resulted in a whole series of specialist publications providing valuable data which are offender rather than offence focused. Self-report studies not only document the extent of minor offending, including drug use, shoplifting and antisocial behaviour generally, but also illustrate the inherent unreliability of re-conviction statistics as a measure of offending: quite simply, most such offending goes unpunished.

The third point about the recording of crime is that certain types of crime are not included in police recorded

figures – many driving offences are not notifiable (i.e. the police do not need to inform the Home Office about them) – such offences are dealt with in magistrates courts; parking offences are not even dealt with at magistrates courts being largely dealt with through fixed penalty notices. In 2006 there were 12.7 million motoring offences in England and Wales, 8.3 million were parking tickets, nearly 2 million were speeding offences and just over 1 million related to licence or insurance offences (Fiti et al., 2008). Revenue and customs offences are also dealt with separately.

In this chapter we refer to police recorded crime and the British Crime Survey figures for England and Wales which have figures available online.

Criminal Statistics

This section shows some trends in England and Wales over a period of 30 years. The crime rates recorded by the Police and the British Crime Survey statistics are shown in table 11.1. British Crime Survey figures are consistently 2–3 times the rate of police recorded crime.

This makes theft the highest volume crime by a substantial margin: taken together with criminal damage these offences account for nearly half of all crime recorded by the police.

Vehicle crimes, theft, burglary and fraud account for just over half of all crime, with criminal damage (including arson) accounting for almost a quarter. This chapter covers the 80% of crime, according to police records, that is not officially classified as violent or sexual in nature.

Offenders and criminal continuity

Figures from the Home Office have shown that of those born in 1953, 33% of men and 9% of women will have had a conviction for a standard list (serious) offence by their 46th birthday; 8% of the men will have had four or more convictions by this time (Prime et al., 2001)

The peak age of offending is also different for men and women with the peak age for offending being about 17 for boys and 15 for girls (see figure 11.2). The peak age for males has been increasing over the years (which may reflect the increasing school leaving age).

Crime extends throughout the life span, with continuities in antisocial behaviour being noted from childhood onwards in some individuals. Moffit (1993) has proposed that there are two main groups of individuals; there is a small group who engage in antisocial behaviour of one sort or another at every life stage, and a larger group who are antisocial only during adolescence and early adulthood.

The peak age for offending in England and Wales is 17 years for males and 15 years for females (Ministry of Justice, 2010). This peak age has fallen during the first decade of the 21st century.

---

[1] NB: Crime statistics, hitherto published by the Home Office in England and Wales, are now (from April 2012) published by the Office for National Statistics. The data in this chapter came from the old system.

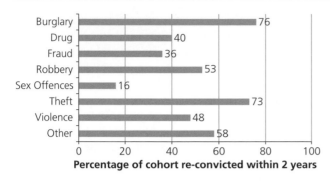

Figure 11.2 2-year re-conviction data by offence type (2002 cohort; from Cuppleditch and Evans, 2005).

Figure 11.2 gives an indication of the relative re-conviction rates for different crimes by all offenders from the first quarter of 2000 following release from prison or from the commencement of a community penalty who were followed up for a 2-year period (i.e. to 2002). We emphasize that the re-conviction rate is accordingly a measure of successful prosecution; these figures are an underestimate of the actual amount of crime committed. Necessarily, some crimes are more difficult to detect than others and the figures reflect this bias. Having considered these caveats, the figures do suggest that burglary and theft are the two crimes with the highest rates for re-conviction, with the overall re-conviction rate being in excess of 50%, i.e. those convicted of an offence were more likely than not to be re-convicted within 2 years of community exposure.

Figure 11.2 indicates what the individual was re-convicted of rather than their original index offence; this may have been different or similar to the re-conviction, although the literature suggests that offenders are remarkably heterogenous in their offending patterns. According to Cuppleditch and Evans (2005) factors associated with a higher rate of re-conviction included previous custody, high offending density (more offences in a short period), a higher number of previous offences and particular index offences (theft, burglary, motoring). Older offenders were less likely to re-offend than younger offenders.

ACQUISITIVE OFFENDING

Property crime includes all those crimes where:

individuals, households or corporate bodies are deprived of their property by illegal means (or where there is intent to do so) or where their property is damaged. These include burglaries, thefts and handling stolen goods, criminal damage and fraud (including identity fraud)' (Nicholas et al., 2007, p.74).

Acquisitive offending as an overall category includes vehicle theft, aggravated vehicle taking, theft from a vehicle and vehicle interference (i.e. where there is deprivation of property or the intent to do so). Car crime and driving offences

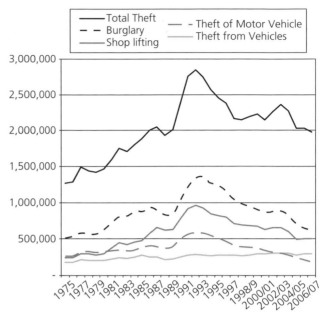

Figure 11.3 30-year trend for burglary and theft in England and Wales.

are dealt with below, but as figure 11.3 illustrates, car related theft comprises a significant proportion of the total theft figure (this may be partly influenced by the fact that most people have car insurance and hence reporting obligations). Shoplifting comprises a further significant proportion of total theft figures, but theft also includes theft from the person and other 'theft and handling' offences. Burglary offences are not included under theft and comprise a separate category of offences, burglary being defined as entering a dwelling or other building as a trespasser with intent to steal or commit grievous bodily harm or rape, or commit unlawful damage; where the offender is armed with a weapon, firearm or explosive the offence is classified as 'aggravated'.

Robbery, comprising 2% of all crime, is

an offence in which force or the threat of force is used either during or immediately prior to a theft or attempted theft. It covers a wide variety of different incidents including bank robbery, mobile phone robbery and street mugging, regardless of the amount of money or property stolen. If there is no use or threat of force, an offence of theft from the person is recorded (Nicholas et al., 2007, p.59).

Twenty-three per cent of crime in 2006/2007 was classified as theft (excluding theft of or from a vehicle), making it the highest recorded crime single category. The trend suggested by figure 11.3 is downward in recent years.

Theft

Theft, or larceny, in Britain was once limited in common law to the taking of a tangible object from the possession of another without their consent. Numerous reform and consolidation acts in the nineteenth century improved and clarified the law, but the Theft Act 1968, followed by the Theft Act 1978 and Fraud Act 2006, completely recast the criminal law of property into its present form giving new definitions of different types of theft. The two main provisions of the 1968 Act are theft and obtaining property by deception where:

> A person is guilty of theft if he dishonestly appropriates property belonging to another with the intention of permanently depriving the other of it and 'thief' and 'steal' shall be constructed accordingly.

Dishonesty and deception are almost universal human phenomena. Hartshorne and May (1928) produced a remarkable series of studies showing that it is difficult to find a child who does not cheat, lie, or steal in some circumstances (although there *were* a few such children). The type of deception employed varied greatly between individuals and between circumstances and about 15% of children took the opportunity to steal when presented with it. The authors concluded:

> 'No one is honest or dishonest by "nature". Where conflict arises between a child and his environment, deception is a natural mode of adjustment, having in itself no "moral" significance.'

Children who are dishonest frequently or persistently are of special interest to child psychiatrists. Stealing is used, in *DSM-III-R* (American Psychiatric Association, 1987), as a defining sign of 'conduct disorder' with 'repeated serious thievery' contributing towards subclassifying the conduct disorder as 'severe'. Wolff (1985) suggests that stealing is the commonest antisocial behaviour in childhood and occurs in about 5% of primary school children.

Rich (1956) proposed a classification of childhood stealing. He identified *marauding* offences carried out by three or more boys which are unplanned or only semi-planned; *proving* offences which are attempts to prove toughness and/or manhood and include breaking and entering, as well as stealing to show off, and taking and driving away; *comforting* offences, either stealing from parents or impulsive pilfering; *secondary* offences, planned with a clear objective in view; and *other offences* for everything else.

It is curious that psychiatrists dealing with adults pay much less attention to these behavioural abnormalities. Most people undertake some stealing during their lifetime, but many only steal when the opportunity presents itself fairly blatantly (e.g. taking items from work), and when detection is highly unlikely. It may be heuristic therefore to develop the Rich classification into one for adults as follows.

- *Needy stealing* is theft which takes place in the context of poverty and/or deprivation and is largely instrumental (i.e. rationally purposeful).
- *Normal stealing* is opportunistic and/or a way of making money, e.g. pilfering from shops and offices, professional crime such as white collar crime and robbery.
- *Status stealing* is a theft akin to childhood proving offences, but related to adult fantasies of power and wealth.
- *Delinquent stealing* is theft occurring in the context of a more generalized delinquent way of life.
- *Attention-seeking stealing* is theft with the primary purpose seeming to be to identify the thief as a person with problems; by definition the stealing is carried out in a manner which will ensure capture. A malign subcategory of this type is self-destructive stealing in which the attention drawn is harmful; for example, a policeman suffering from post-traumatic stress disorder carried out a series of shop break-ins taking nothing of value or use until he was caught, dismissed, disgraced and imprisoned.
- *Compulsive stealing* is repeated theft, often of unwanted articles which is experienced by the thief as a symptom, an urge which it is difficult to control. It is sometimes called kleptomania. A subcategory of this type may be the morbid greed in Medlicott (1968) which included women with eating disorders. Some steal large quantities of food to eat and then later vomit. Crisp et al. (1980) suggested that stealing of food, usually from shops, occurs in at least 14% of patients with anorexia nervosa. They said that it usually occurs in those who are chronically ill and who couple overeating with vomiting and purging. Another subcategory may be fetish stealing in which men with masturbatory fantasies involving female clothing (usually underwear) also seem to need to obtain the fetish object by theft, although on occasions the reasons may be more mundane, e.g. a ballgown fetishist who could not afford the dresses.
- *Symbolic stealing* is akin to comfort stealing. The object stolen is usually representing something important that has been, or is about to be, lost. It may occur when an individual is grieving from the departure of a loved one, or the impending departure of a loved one. It may also occur when the individual's own life seems to be in jeopardy; illness related to cancer is a common theme in the patient's mind. Other forms of depressive stealing may also occur, but most are explicable in terms of loss, confusion or attention-seeking.
- *Psychotic stealing* is theft which can only be accounted for in terms of delusional ideas or hallucinatory instructions.
- *Absentminded or confused stealing* is not really theft at all, because the unsanctioned appropriation is erroneous in some way and related to cognitive deficits, which maybe as a result of stress, or mental illness, or other (organic) brain dysfunction.

It is clear that these categories are rough and ready and are not mutually exclusive. For example, a patient with chronic schizophrenia may steal because his/her voices tell him to, s/he may also steal because s/he is hungry, and s/he may even steal in order to draw attention to his/her plight and get into a prison or a hospital (Belfrage, 1994). A particular act of stealing may embrace more than one of these motives. The first three types are less likely to lead to a psychiatric referral, and account for most of the acquisitive offences dealt with by the criminal justice system.

Shoplifting

Shoplifting, which is simply a very common form of theft, is no longer regarded as psychiatrically important. At one time it was considered to be a central concern for the forensic psychiatrist and some ran special clinics for shoplifters.

The term has a long legal history, the Shoplifting Act 1699 made the theft of 5 shillings or more from a shop a capital felony! Mrs Leigh-Perrot, aunt of Jane Austen, was charged with stealing a card of white lace from a haberdasher's shop in Bath in 1799. She was remanded in custody for 8 months and brought before the Assizes in Taunton. If found guilty, she could have been hanged, or transported, or branded. The evidence against her was overwhelming, but she was acquitted, although somewhat poorer (James, 1976).

Shoplifting has probably lost its significance for two reasons. Modern shops present a very good opportunity for stealing, indeed the shopkeeper's philosophy is to thrust temptation at the shopper, hoping s/he will take attractive items and then pay for them. Shopkeepers build the inevitable losses from theft into their business. One Canadian study has suggested that if shoplifting could be eliminated, prices could decline by 20% (Bradford and Balmaceda, 1983). Surveys which have followed shoppers at random have suggested that one in 12 shoppers in New York City, one in 23 in Boston, one in 13 in Philadelphia, and one in 18 in Dublin are shoplifters. Buckle and Farrington (1984) conducted an observation study on a small department store in England and they found that between 1 and 2% of customers entering a store took goods without paying for them. Self-report surveys indicate that up to 700,000 people in the UK admit to shoplifting.

Shoplifters, do, however, show all the types of theft given in the list above. Numerically thieves who are psychotic are a very small proportion of the total and as the emphasis in forensic psychiatry has narrowed for some practitioners to a 'psychosis only' specialty the other interesting neurotic disorders which may manifest themselves in shoplifting are largely ignored. However, schizophrenia, serious depression, mania, alcoholism, drug addiction may all present as a shoplifting charge. Shoplifting may also follow brain damage. There are the simple classic cases of patients with dementia being confused and forgetful.

One arguably important explanation for shoplifting is absent-mindedness. Reason and Lucas (1984) postulated that little lapses of memory or episodes of absent-mindedness are common events, especially in shops. In a questionnaire survey of 150 people not involved in shoplifting, 85% admitted they had on occasions forgotten why they had gone into a shop, 72% had left goods behind they had paid for, 67% had on occasion failed to wait for their change, 40% had bought something they did not want, 31% had started to push the wrong trolley round a supermarket, and 18% had left the shop without paying for something and had to go back. The authors also analysed 166 letters received by the Portia Trust, protesting their innocence of shoplifting charges: 53% of the protestors blamed the theft on absent-mindedness or confusion, 69% mentioned being distracted or preoccupied, 23% of the protestors were receiving medical help, and 50% were in the midst of negative life events such as separation, divorce, illness or bereavement. All correspondents wrote of the great distress they experienced; several mentioned suicidal ideas, drink problems, loss of weight, and subsequent accidents.

The term compulsive shoplifting overlaps with the term kleptomania, which is defined in *ICD-10* as 'a recurrent failure to resist impulses to steal objects not needed for personal use or their monetary value'; the definition in *DSM-IV* (American Psychiatric Association, 1994) is almost identical. The condition is associated with a build-up of tension immediately before the commission of the act and then a feeling of relief afterwards. It is not known what proportion of all arrested shoplifters fulfil the criteria of the condition, but probably fewer than 5% do so. A study of shoplifters (Gudjonsson, 1987) pointed to the importance of low self-esteem and general dissatisfaction with life in the development of compulsive shoplifting. It was considered that these factors provide a starting point for a chain of developments where feelings of anger, frustration and lack of self-fulfilment become temporarily relieved through shoplifting activity. A behavioural model of compulsive shoplifting (Gudjonsson, 1987) included the basic premise that a distinction must be drawn between the motivation behind the initial shoplifting and the development of its compulsive features. Shoplifting becomes 'compulsive' because it provides some vulnerable individuals with psychological fulfilment and relief which are highly reinforcing. Compulsive shoplifting and obsessive compulsive problems (e.g. checking and washing compulsions) may to some extent overlap (Gudjonsson, 1988), but there is no evidence that compulsive shoplifting is an obsessive compulsive disorder *per se*. It is better construed as a specific type of behaviour which is perceived by the shoplifter at the time as comprising 'an irresistible impulse'. It involves initial arousal enhancement, which momentarily relieves frustration and depressive mood, and sudden reduction in anxiety afterwards, which provides a temporary sense of wellbeing. It is probably the combination of the two stages, rather than each acting in isolation, which is reinforcing for the compulsive shoplifter.

Mood elevation and anxiety relief may be particularly rein-forcing for individuals with a depressive disposition. However, it is evident that only a small proportion of all depressives who shoplift become compulsive shoplifters.

CRIMINAL DAMAGE

Criminal damage as a general category represented 22% of crime in 2006/2007 (figure 11.4). Within this category are included: criminal damage to a dwelling; criminal dam-age to a building other than a dwelling; criminal damage to a vehicle; 'other' criminal damage (e.g. threat or possession with intent to commit criminal damage). All of these crimes are separately recorded if 'racially aggravated'; this carries an additional penalty. Arson is also included under criminal damage and is described in more detail in the next section.

The trend in the late 1990s of increasing amounts of criminal damage has stabilized since 2003/2004. According to officially recorded crime by the police, there were over 1 million recorded offences of criminal damage in 2006/07. The figure for the same category of offences from the British Crime Survey was 2,731,000 – over twice the officially recorded figure. From the British Crime Survey it is esti-mated that 8 in 100 households experience some form of criminal damage each year. Criminal damage is widespread and much of it is not reported to the police and even the British Crime Survey figures are likely to underestimate it. The problem of criminal damage is not new and has always been seen as a facet of the behaviour of young people. An Egyptian priest writing 4000 years ago expressed a view that is still heard today 'Vandalism is rife, and crime of all types is rampant among our young people (Madison, 1970).

Given the widespread nature of criminal damage, there is little research on its links to individual disorders. The

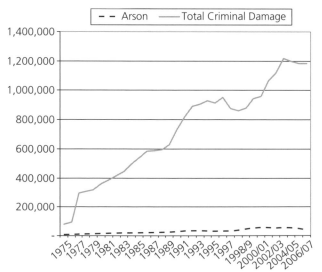

Figure 11.4   30-year trend for arson and criminal damage in England and Wales. (See http://www.justice.gov.uk/government/uploads/system/uploads/attachment_data/file/6940/207751 1.pdf)

WHO's *ICD-10* classification does list 'severe destructiveness to property' within the list of behaviours on which a diagno-sis of childhood conduct disorders can be made, but this is one of many behaviours and the emphasis is on 'an enduring pattern of behaviour' amounting to 'major violations of age-appropriate expectations' rather than casual vandalism. In studies of adults that consider associations between mental disorders and offending behaviour criminal damage is rarely cited as a separate category and is often placed in the 'other' category. This is in contrast with arson which, despite its comparative rarity, is often considered separately.

ARSON

Arson is a serious and dangerous crime, it can be a form of violence, it can certainly endanger life. In criminal terms it is just one category of criminal damage, but it is dealt with here separately as it is often a matter of psychiatric impor-tance. It is also given special attention by governments. In 1999 (April 20) the UK government issued a press release stating that an average of two homes an hour were torched by arsonists in the UK and that the number of arson attacks had more than doubled since 1989 (BBC, 1999). They sug-gested that 65 deaths and 2000 injuries are attributable every year to arson and that fires cost an estimated £55 million in insurance. Their accompanying fact sheet said that each day three schools suffer arson attacks, 130 cars are deliberately set alight every day, car arson having risen 250% in the previous decade, and that an estimated 20% of known arsonists suffer from mental health problems.

As a result of these findings HM Government set up an Arson Prevention Bureau which issued reports and advice on controlling arson. Local authorities, who run fire services in Britain, and also develop their own strategies. This makes the lower profile in psychiatry somewhat puz-zling. The outside observer to psychiatry could be forgiven for thinking that the main interest in the specialty with fire-setting is a rare disease called pyromania. Yet even the official estimates suggest that 20% of deliberate fire-setters have significant mental health problems.

The press release was in 1999. Subsequent figures show some improvements although the seriousness and dan-gerousness remain. In 2006 4,26,200 fires were attended by the fire service in the UK, the majority being outdoor fires which include car fires, 55,800 (13%) being in dwellings. The figures given focused mainly on so-called 'primary' or serious fires i.e. uncontrolled burning and/or involving casualties or rescues. Accidental primary fires numbered 87,300 in 2006, 3% less than the previous year. Deliberate primary fires decreased by 9% from the previous year to 72,600. In 2006 there were 491 fire related deaths in the UK, a drop from 1096 in 1979. The majority of fire-related deaths occurred in dwelling fires; the highest fire fatality rates were for people aged 80+, for males, and in Scotland. The fall in deliberate fire-setting is mainly attributable to in the number of cars set on fire which peaked in 2002 at 80,205 falling to 42,093 in 2006. The explanation for this drop in vehicle fires is related in part to abandoned vehicle removal schemes and to increases in the price of scrap metal which have increased the value of end of life vehicles.

Psychiatric Aspects

Medical interest in the subject of fire-raising goes back to the nineteenth century and continental writers in particular, e.g. Marc, Planer, Meckel (see Lewis and Yarnell, 1951). Several of the nineteenth-century authors apparently thought that fire-raising was especially a problem among retarded servant girls. They had no data but they may even have been right about an association between intellectual disability and fire-setting. Meckel described 'impulsive incendiarisme' in 1820 (see Lacey and Evans, 1986)

Probably the most comprehensive survey of arson ever undertaken is that by Lewis and Yarnell (1951). They studied 2,000 files from the National Board of Fire Underwriters in the USA, eliminated those cases with very sketchy data and thus examined 1145 cases of males 16 years or older, 220 younger males, 201 adult female fire-setters and 18 young girls. Of the total (1584), 100 were interviewed. From this material Lewis and Yarnell developed a classification of fire-setters which has been the basis of many subsequent classifications (e.g. Scott, 1978; Prins et al., 1985). They had four basic groups:

1. Profiteers.
2. Accidental fire-setters.
3. Occasional fire-setters.
4. Habitual fire-setters.

They divided the motives for fire-setting into six categories:

1. Reactions to society.
2. Vengeance against an employer.
3. Simple revenge.
4. Jealous rage.
5. An opportunity for heroism.
6. Perverted sexual pleasure.

Interest in fire is almost universal in childhood, starting at about 2–3 years of age, with a high level of understanding of its dangerousness by the age of 8 (Kafry, 1980). Among children in particular, there is a need for a clear definition of what constitutes abnormal behaviour, since with fire, experiment may rapidly turn into disaster and firelighting by children may range from simply playing with matches or fires to malicious fire-setting (Kosky and Silburn, 1984).

Personal Characteristics and Background

Those detected committing arson tend to be young although a paper by Soothill et al. (2004) concludes that the age of those convicted of arson has been rising since the 1960s and the average is now 24 years old. This may reflect a low arrest and/or conviction rate for young people. Whilst most criminal acts are commoner in youth than in adult life, there is some basis to the belief that this is especially true of fire-setting. For example in England and Wales in 1979 (Home Office, 1980), there were 52 people under the age of 17 brought to trial for arson out of a total of 732 children and young persons tried for serious offences. In statistical terms, this means that 7% of young persons brought to trial for serious offences were charged with arson compared with an arson charge rate for all ages brought to trial in Crown courts of only 1.7%.

Fire-setting is associated with psychosis (Anwar et al., 2011) and possibly with femaleness. Coid et al. (2000) found that of patients admitted to secure psychiatric hospitals in England and Wales proportionately more women than men were charged with or convicted of arson and they were more likely to have a history of fire-setting. Anwar et al. found that patients with psychoses have a significantly increased risk of being convicted of arson.

Intellectual Disability, Alcohol and Mental Illness

It is commonly believed that there is an association between arson and intellectual disability. There are however few data to support this notion. It is probable that among children it is poor school performance rather than a lack of intelligence that is significant. In a study off 153 adult Yorkshire arsonists referred for pre-trial psychiatric reports (Rix, 1994) the referrals were mainly men and young men, 10% had intellectual disability and a further 13% had a history of special schooling for educational or learning difficulties.

There has been a long-known association of arson with alcohol (Koson and Dvoskin, 1982; Tether and Harrison, 1986); the tendency is as great among females as among males (Harmon et al., 1985). Kammerer et al. (1967) noted that arson can be associated with any of the states seen in alcohol abuse: acute intoxication, chronic alcoholism, hallucinosis and dementia.

Drinking is common among those who die by fire in their own homes; a survey of victims in Glasgow found that 25% had blood levels over 150 mg/100 mL at the time of death, a level which at the least would severely inhibit their chances of escaping (Anderson et al., 1981).

Arsonists on the whole are probably not psychotic; only about 2 per 100 convicted arsonists receive a hospital order each year in England and Wales and, of those arrested for arson, about 10% are mentally ill (Molnar et al., 1984). Nevertheless a Swedish population study has shown that, among convicted arsonists, men are 20 times and women are 40 times more likely to have schizophrenia than the general population (Anwar et al., 2011; see also chapter 14.

A factor of concern (Koson and Dvoskin, 1982; Molnar et al., 1984) is the failure of psychiatric services to deliver healthcare to mentally disordered arsonists who 'had been involved with the agencies just prior to their act of fire-setting and either were rejected or lost to follow-up' (Koson and Dvoskin, 1982).

Prognosis

Soothill and Pope (1973) conducted a 20-year follow-up of the 67 people convicted of arson in 1951 on whom they could get complete information (15 could not be traced). Only three men were re-convicted of arson by the end of 1971, 32 (48%) were not re-convicted of a serious offence at all. All three of the re-offenders seemed to be solitary offenders with problems of social adjustment. The first was a recidivist thief who set fire to a haystack. Some years later he set a few fires in huts on a building site and was sent to hospital on a hospital order as suffering from schizophrenia. The second set fire to stacks of straw as a farm worker. The prison doctor described him as a 'pyromaniac' and one who got a 'deep feeling of satisfaction' when he lit fires. He was re-convicted some years later for three further cases of arson. The third man was also convicted of setting fire to a haystack, later fires included firing a Dutch barn and setting fire to a house. He had lots of shoplifting convictions as well and was a homeless vagrant who had spent time in a mental hospital.

Group fire-setters are thought to show less severe psychopathology, and to have a better prognosis for recidivism (Molnar et al., 1984).

Classification

Doley (2003a) has reviewed some of the attempts to classify arson and pointed out that for most of the time the classifications focus on motive but some focus on behaviour. She particularly notes the Federal Bureau of Investigation typology (Douglas et al., 1992) describing arsonists as either 'organized' or 'disorganized'. She concludes that 'to date, no one system has been developed that adequately represents the range and depth of five setting behaviour and characteristics'. This is a truism which probably can be applied to attempts at classifying any kind of behaviour. Our proposed classification has been found useful in the medico-legal setting, giving clues to the kind of management which an individual fire-setter requires.

Profitable arson

The destruction of one's own property in order to claim, for example, the insurance money, or to be rehoused, is a well-established type of fraudulent activity and one which fire departments and insurers look out for. Under the heading of profitable arson, we can also place the arson which is designed to destroy evidence of other crimes, perhaps a murdered body, perhaps evidence of theft, or accounts books which reveal a fraud. We might also place in this category the 'protection gang fire', i.e. the fire set by a gang of extortionists when the owner of a property does not pay the dues demanded from them.

Political arson

Perhaps the best-known political arsonist is Guy Fawkes, and the tradition of Catholic v. Protestant political arson still exists in Northern Ireland. Political bombing can also be included here; bombing is a closely related activity to fire-setting and it does often cause serious fire. Urban rioting may lead to fires, some accidental, some set by petrol bombs, others set by other means. Very little of this activity has direct relevance for psychiatry, although an assessment may be helpful because some apparently political motives are delusional.

Revenge fire-setting

Lewis and Yarnell (1951) divided their revenge category into the subcategories of revenge against society in general (the child who doesn't like school, so burns it down, the rioter who hates the police, so s/he fires the police station), revenge against employers (the disgruntled, sacked employee who burns down the bosses' premises), and jealous revenge usually in a sexual context. A good deal of revenge fire-setting can be 'understood' if the individual's feelings and perceptions of his/her world are understood. Perhaps some of the easiest cases for courts to comprehend are the cases of sexual jealousy; so a man who set fire to his girlfriend's wardrobe with her treasured collection of clothes because she had jilted him received the relatively light sentence of 2 years' imprisonment, even though the house was occupied at the time of the fire and was badly damaged. However, to regard fire-setting as a 'normal' consequence of jealousy would be mistaken indeed, and whenever possible much greater elaboration of the fire-setter's psychopathology is desirable. For example, a woman was referred for assessment after setting fire to the curtains in her own home, thus causing a lot of damage. This was in response to her husband having an affair with another woman and threatening to leave her. The reason for the fire became a little clearer when their mutual feelings about the house were revealed; he cherished it, she didn't. It was further revealed that their only child was asleep in bed upstairs at the time of the fire, was seriously endangered and had to be rescued by the husband. Tentative exploration of the woman's feelings suggested that either she was identifying the child with the husband, and was thus murdering him vicariously or, more likely, was putting him through a primitive ordeal, in that he had to rescue his beloved child to prove himself worthy of her. The revenge fire-setter is probably best regarded as a special type of violent individual. Sometimes the vengeful fire-setter chooses fire as his/her weapon for its instrumental or convenience value and has no other attachment to fire itself. A patient who exhibited rage attacks when insulted or emotionally hurt illustrates the point. He was a married man with a good work record and an ability to make and keep friends. He suffered from some inferiority feelings which he covered with a macho style of life and heavy drinking. On several occasions when he had been drunk, he reacted to insults by highly excessive violence, e.g. when drunk in the street one night he responded to verbal abuse from an upstairs window by climbing a drainpipe, forcing his way into the startled abuser's window and beating him up savagely. One day in his favourite pub, in front of his friends, he was called a 'queer' by a newcomer. He immediately challenged the man, fought him, but lost. He then went back to his car, pulled out a spare can of petrol, spread some on the pub floor, threw a match into it, ran out and locked the door.

Hero fire-setters

Fire has a fundamental fascination for most people – there is drama and excitement in a building on fire, the fire engines themselves create a thrill, and quite a lot of people have fantasies about rescuing or being rescued from a fire. Some people, usually men, take a special interest in fires, collect pieces of fire fighting equipment, log the activities of the fire brigade, join the fire brigade, or volunteer as fire officer at work. Much of this is healthy sublimation but, for some people, such things do not sufficiently satisfy the need for fiery excitement and they, therefore, set extra fires to increase their own involvement. A prisoner had been commended for bravery in fires no less than five times. He was a fire officer at his factory, and it took the firm a long time to work out that, since his appointment, the prevalence of fires had increased sharply and that he was always the first on the scene, saving lives and putting out the fire. He was eventually convicted of over 20 episodes of arson, and that was probably an underestimate. Fire chiefs and factory safety officers need to be constantly on the lookout for excessive zeal in members of their staff. Fire investigators should always take note of individuals who turn up to help the brigade especially if this happens more than once. Lewis and Yarnell (1951) found 51 cases of volunteer firemen who set fires.

Fire-bugs

Fire-bugs are individuals who derive intense satisfaction or relief from setting fires. A good description is given by Scott (1978):

> He suffers from periods of mounting tension, becoming increasingly restless and edgy, and then suddenly his actions are out of control having been triggered off, for example by a quarrel at home or dismissal from work. The fire-bug has learnt that starting a blaze releases tension and so may begin a fire-setting spree. Some fire-bugs may find only one blaze sufficient to discharge tension while others start many fires within a short period. The fires are usually unplanned and lit in hallways, staircases, and passages where the general public have access … the fire-bug is … likely to thrust a match into a brimming dustbin and rush away to start others elsewhere in the neighbourhood, creating chaos and confusion. After such acts he may return home feeling calm.

The fire-bug can be particularly dangerous for s/he may resort to arson under stresses of all sorts. It is tempting to link the fire-setting in these patients to their only too evident sexual problems, but they almost invariably have personality disorders with a galaxy of difficulties, especially interpersonal problems.

This group of fire-setters is the closest to the journalistic category of pyromania which persists in the literature, mainly because it has found its way into the *American Diagnostic and Statistical Manual* as a form of impulse disorder. It also owes its origins to Freud's theory expressed in *Civilization and Its Discontents* that impulses to set fires are related to sexual impulses:

> It is as if primitive man had had the impulse when he came into contact with fire, to gratify an infantile pleasure in respect of it and put it out with a stream of urine. The legends that we possess leave no doubt that flames shooting upwards like tongues were originally felt to have a phallic sense. Putting out fire by urinating… therefore represents a sexual act with a man, an enjoyment of masculine potency in homosexual rivalry… It is remarkable how regularly analytic findings testify to the close connection between the ideas of ambition, fire and urethral eroticism (Freud, 1929).

Individuals who set fires for sexual excitement are very rare. In a survey of patients in a security hospital which specializes in personality disordered people Rice and Harris (1991) found only six such men in 243 fire-setters they studied. An excellent review of this 'diagnosis' has been given by Doley (2003b).

Psychotic and organic fire-setters

In the selected Lewis and Yarnell (1951) sample of fire-setters, by far the largest diagnostic category of mental disorder was schizophrenia. The only other prominent group was senile psychosis among the women. Other diagnoses also represented were alcoholic psychosis, epilepsy, encephalitis, depression and GPI. Another series of arsonists came from Poland (Fleszar-Szumigajowa, 1969); in this study, 311 referred cases of arson were examined at the Institute of Psychoneurology in Pruszkow over the 10-year period 1953–62. The Polish clinic found similar causes to the American study, the top five categories being: schizophrenia, mental deficiency, personality disorder, alcoholism and organic psychoses. The Polish paper also analysed motives. Revenge and hatred were the commonest motivations, and were particularly associated with personality disorders. The 'hero' fire-setters were uncommon as were fire-bugs and erotic fire-setters. Some of the fires were accidental (especially among the patients with schizophrenia). A few were suicide attempts and others in response to persecutory ideas.

Suicide by fire

Self-immolation by fire as a sign of total detachment from the world before the attainment of Nirvana has long been a part of the tradition of Buddhist monks. Suicide by fire has also been a part of some cultural traditions in the East (in the form of suttee) for centuries and has been noted in Israel (Modan et al., 1970) and in Cuba (Davis, 1962). Suicide by fire became prominent in France following the widely publicized self-immolations of Buddhist monks in Saigon in 1963 as political protests against the Diem government, and later the self-immolation of Jan Palach as a political protest against the Russian invasion of Czechoslovakia in 1969 (Bourgeois, 1969). A similar 'epidemic' in Britain was carefully recorded by Ashton and Donnan (1981), following a political or quasi-religious suicide which was highly publicized. In the USA, Andreasen and Noyes's (1975) study in a burns unit had indicated suicidal intentions in 2% of patients with a very wide range of psychopathology, none of whom had any political motivation. It is probable that this method of suicide is too little suspected. Death by fire is a known hazard in an institution. It may be difficult to know whether, say, a schizophrenic patient who dies in a self-induced fire was responding to suicidal ideas or has accidentally suffered from outwardly directed aggression such as the burning of a hated object. Some patients may try to scare the staff by setting a fire which then overwhelms them. Topp (1973) described such an incident in an English borstal when three lads barricaded themselves in their cell as part of a more general protest against conditions. When their protest produced no immediate results, they threatened to set a fire and later did so. As the door was barricaded, it took staff some minutes to smash it down during which time all three were so badly burnt that they all subsequently died.

By contrast, a resident of a young offender institution set a fire in his cell and barricaded himself inside it. He was, however, rescued, resuscitated and sent to hospital, where he longed to thank the prison officers who saved him.

Child fire-setters

In her important study of 60 children attending the Bellevue Hospital in New York, Yarnell (1940) divided her cases into children aged 6–8 years and older adolescents. The little children were usually referred for other antisocial behaviour such as stealing and truancy, most of the fires they set were at home and the fire-setting was coupled with intense anxiety, including anxiety about the fire. Their fantasies included aggression, anxiety and self-punishment and often a desire to burn a member of the family who either withheld love or became a serious rival for parental love. Most of the fires were easily controlled. All the children showed some evidence of sexual conflicts, but enuresis was infrequent and was not specifically associated with the fire-setting. Adolescents showed a number of similarities, but enjoyed their fire-setting much more, often doing it away from home, sometimes in pairs, deriving excitement from the flames and the fire engines. Most of these features were confirmed by Vandersall and Wiener (1970). They drew attention to the ineffective role played by the fathers of the 20 children in their sample. In 10 cases the father was totally absent. The mothers were found wanting in being distant, rejecting or overprotective. These authors also confirmed the relative unimportance and non-specificity of enuresis as a symptom in fire-setting children. Unlike Yarnell they could not find any material which was directly suggestive of sexual conflicts. Their most demonstrable difficulty seemed more centred about issues of aggression and impulse control. A sense of exclusion, inadequacy and loneliness was conveyed by many of the boys, originating from a real or perceived unfulfilled needs and low self-esteem.

Management and Treatment

As with all psychiatric patients, good management of fire-setters is dependent upon an accurate diagnosis and formulation. It is not enough just to categorize a particular fire-setter, although that is a good start. It is also important to understand as far as possible why a particular individual chose fire as a weapon and to know something of his/her fantasy life. Following that, treatment is along straightforward lines.

A problem is that hospitals, just like all other institutions, are very afraid of arsonists. It is hardly surprising that an old people's home will wish to rid itself of, say, a confused old lady who keeps lighting fires in her waste paper bin. Even though the diagnosis of her brain syndrome may be clear, a hospital will not relish her admission either, because she will require constant supervision and will create continuous anxiety about the safety of other patients. Such a patient should definitely not be admitted unless adequate supervision can be provided. On the other hand, it is the responsibility of public hospitals to make provision for the problems that actually present rather than the ones staff hope will present and any district psychiatric service should be able to care for such a patient.

Many more problems will be presented by the intelligent fire-bug who schemes to get opportunities to set fires and who is highly secretive in his/her activities. Most ordinary psychiatric hospitals decline to admit such patients and most of them go instead to prison. It should be possible for a regional security unit to nurse such an individual, at least on a short to medium-term basis, although a few of these patients are often best managed, particularly on a long-term basis, in high security hospitals. In a security setting, the nurses will ensure that they know the whereabouts of the patient at all times, and they will ensure s/he has no access to fire-setting materials such as matches unless they are used under supervision. Within such a restrictive context, it will be important to try and give the patient as much pleasure as possible and to offer appropriate treatments, such as behavioural treatment, psychotherapy and anxiolytic drugs (see also chapter 24).

Outside hospital, the treatments available to the fire-bug are extremely limited. Sometimes adjustment of mood or level of anxiety by antidepressant or tranquillizing drugs is helpful. This may be especially true for the patient who is setting fires to relieve tension. Behavioural treatments may also be worth a try, although it must be noted that, as yet, there are no studies reporting successful outcome. One of us has tried such techniques as flooding in imagination, flooding in reality (48 hours stoking a bonfire), relaxation, stimulus avoidance in occasional patients, all without much success. Psychotherapy is traditionally the treatment of choice for the fire-bug; the sessions are likely to be rich in fantasy material, including sexual feelings if the patient is of average intelligence or above. Some patients who are of limited intelligence may find it difficult to be other than concrete. There are no data suggesting that psychotherapy is effective in controlling the urges to set fires, even though it seems likely that other elements of personality disturbance may improve. It may be that, occasionally, where there is clear evidence that the fire-raising is erotic, a male patient may benefit from an anti-androgen such as cyproterone acetate. Experience gives no cause for great optimism. One of us treated a fire-bug who had a considerable number of personality problems, including marked interpersonal difficulties, severe mood swings, both high and low, and sexual difficulties. His fire-setting seemed to have an erotic component as he always used fire in his sexual fantasies. A long period of psychotherapy brought little or no benefit, mood stabilizing drugs, including lithium, did not help either and so eventually he was offered anti-libidinol injections. These he accepted with some benefit, his libido fell to zero, thus simplifying his life and producing a marked reduction in tension. However his urges to set fires were unaffected and he had to be sent to a special hospital for long-term treatment.

The most satisfying group of arsonists to treat are probably those in which the fire-setting is secondary to a fluctuating disorder, e.g. depression or schizophrenia. The treatment in these cases is the treatment of the underlying condition plus the special management during the acute stage and the careful observation during follow-up which the fire-setting propensity deserves. Special attention should also be given in psychotherapy to the dynamics and other factors leading to fire as a choice of weapon or means of expression.

MOTORING OFFENCES

Since motor vehicles are largely an innovation of the twentieth century, little exists in common law to regulate their use. There is, however, in most countries a good deal of legislation that governs road traffic and related offences such as speeding, driving without a licence or without being insured, and careless driving, although even standard legal texts eschew a consideration of the plethora of such offences (e.g. Ormerod, 2005). The vast majority of motoring offences in England and Wales are dealt with by magistrates' courts and a fixed penalty scheme. Penalties are usually of a relatively minor nature.

It should be noted, however, that death and injury on the roads constitute major sources of mortality and morbidity. Many more people lose their lives on the roads of Great Britain than die as a result of a homicide e.g. in 2004/2005, 3,201 people were killed on the roads of Great Britain, and 973 people lost their lives as a result of homicide (839 in England and Wales and 134 in Scotland). Whilst the deliberate use of a car to injure or kill may constitute a charge of murder or manslaughter, deaths on the road associated with bad driving will usually attract charges of specific motoring offences with lesser sentences. Whilst the offender may not have had any intent to harm or kill, the injured or dead victim's family may well feel traumatized not only by the 'accident' but also at times by an apparent leniency by the courts (Corbett, 2003).

Psychiatric patients who have been hospitalized for suicidal behaviour have a considerably raised risk of both accident involvement and road traffic offences (Crancer and Quiring, 1969), with a disproportionate number of drinking and driving and reckless driving offences. Psychiatric inpatients in general have higher accident rates compared to the general population (Waller, 1965). This may, in part, reflect prescribed medication and the use of illegal drugs (Barbone et al., 1998). Phillips (1977) found a substantially raised fatality rate on Californian highways after well-publicized suicide stories, possibly reflecting, he suggested, the imitative nature of some suicidal behaviour.

In the UK, the Driving and Vehicle Licensing Authority (www.dft.gov.uk/dvla/medical/ataglance.aspx) issues guidance on medical aspects of driving which is updated every 6 months. In general the guidelines indicate that patients should stop driving during the acute stages of any illness. Once the illness has stabilized, driving may often recommence; the clinical judgments about individual patients are subtle and complex but the rules on confidentiality are clear:

> *When a patient has a condition which makes driving unsafe and the patient is either unable to appreciate this, or refuses to cease driving, GMC guidelines advise breaking confidentiality and informing DVLA.*

A good textbook on this complex area of clinical medicine which may be just as critical for public safety as a parole decision is Carter (2006). Psychiatrists with any concerns regarding a patient's ability to drive safely may find it helpful to discuss the relevant issues with a doctor employed by the DVLA.

A robust evidence base for DVLA guidance does not exist. Driving behaviour is complex and human error may occur through unintended actions as well as deliberate violation of traffic law (Reason et al., 1990). Patients with schizophrenic illness have shown no conclusive excess of road traffic accidents but this may be due to such patients driving less frequently (Armstrong and Whitlock, 1980; Silverstone, 1988). Where psychotic symptoms are active, especially when paranoid elements are present, risk is probably high and drivers should be advised to stop driving until they are stabilized on appropriate medication (Harris, 2000). Risk is probably raised where the content of delusions or hallucinations incorporate other road users. As a mental state evaluation is not undertaken routinely on drivers involved in road crashes, it is possible that some may be suffering from psychotic states, see Whitlock (1990). In the case of bipolar affective disorders, hypomanic patients may drive rapidly and recklessly (Cremona, 1986) whilst depressed patients with psychomotor retardation may show impaired concentration (Cremona, 1986) and increased suicidality whilst driving. (Silverstone, 1988). Various studies have shown an increased motor vehicle accident rate for drivers with dementia (Kolowski and Rossiter, 2000), borderline cognitive impairment (Marottoli et al., 1994) or neurological impairment (McKenna, 1998). An antisocial lifestyle may comprise behaviours including violent and non-violent offences, substance abuse, sexual promiscuity and reckless driving (Carter, 2003). Personality disorder of antisocial type has long been known to be associated with bad driving; younger males being the most aggressive on the roads (Tillman and Hobbs, 1949; Aberg and Rimmo, 1998; Moffatt, 2002). Road rage has been found to be associated with higher levels of aggression as well as a history of substance abuse and abnormal personality traits (Fong et al., 2001). Road traffic accident rates may also be elevated in people affected by adverse life events such as recent separation or divorce (McMurray, 1970).

The theft of a motor vehicle or property from it is common (Corbett, 2003). Drivers of stolen cars have a higher likelihood of involvement in a car crash (Knowles, 2003). The theft of cars is often the precursor to a criminal career, beginning usually in adolescence but occasionally as early as age 10 years (Corbett, 2003). Driving without a valid driving licence is also associated with other forms of traffic offending and raised crash risk (de Young et al., 1997). Patients under psychiatric care should be asked whether or not they have a valid driving licence, without which they are not properly insured or driving legally. A recent form of atypical car crime is the misuse of disabled parking permits, applications for which require a doctor's

recommendation (Webster, 2006). More serious crime may also be facilitated by motor vehicles, such as burglary, rape, child abduction, drive-by-shooting and car bombing (Gordon, 2004).

Intoxicants

Alcohol abuse is a major factor in road traffic accidents (Bierness, 1993; Del Rio et al., 2001) and early age of onset of drunk driving has been found to be associated with mental illness and violent criminality (Rasanen et al., 1999). In 2006, about 17% of all deaths on the road in Great Britain (540 out of 3172) involved drivers who were over the legal alcohol limit. The legal limit in the British Isles is 0.08% of alcohol in the bloodstream, the highest tolerated level in the European Union (although the Irish Republic may reduce it to the commoner 0.05%). One in 50 fatal crashes has drug impairment as a contributory factor. Almost 6% of drivers who die have traces of medicinal drugs that may have affected their driving (Brake, 2006).

In road traffic accidents involving fatal casualties, the 1990s in Britain saw an increase in multiple drug abuse. Driving under the influence of cannabis increases the risk of involvement in a crash (Tunbridge et al., 2001), and so does driving while using amphetamines and cocaine (Laumon et al., 2005). Users of medically prescribed drugs such as anxiolytics and hypnotics are also at heightened risk of road traffic accidents (Barbone et al., 1998). It is important to note that Section 4 of the Road Traffic Act 1988 does not differentiate between illicit drugs and prescribed medication. So, any person who is driving whilst unfit due to any drug is liable to prosecution.

Suicide

Some deaths on the road perceived as accidents may in fact be concealed suicides. A range of studies into driver suicides have shown varying suicide rates (MacDonald, 1964; Selzer and Payne, 1962; Tabachnick et al., 1966; Schmidt et al., 1977; Tsuang et al., 1985; Jenkins and Sainsbury, 1980; Isherwood et al., 1982). A Finnish study estimated that 5.9% of driver deaths were suicide (Ohberg et al., 1997). Only some driver suicides have a history of suicidal ideation, indicating that many may be impulsive acts in response to acute distress rather than well-established suicide. Textbooks on suicide have tended to focus on car exhaust gas as a means of suicide rather than the act of driving as such (Cantor, 2000).

Certain methods of suicide create a risk of harm not only to the person him/herself, but also concurrently to others who may be in the immediate vicinity. Such methods may include suicide by arson, jumping from a height or self-destruction by means of transportation such as aircraft (Gordon et al., 2004) or motor vehicle. In Ohberg et al.'s study (1997), the death occurred of a person other than the driver in almost 4% of the road crashes, but that driver suicides frequently involved young men driving alone, the 'accident' being frequently a head-on collision with another vehicle of much heavier weight, the suicide victim often having experienced stressful life-events and suffered from a mental disorder including alcohol abuse. In other occasional cases a clearly psychotic driver may kill him/herself and others, and from time to time patients have been admitted to secure hospitals after such offences. Some have argued that sizable numbers of deaths on the road caused by dangerous driving are really instances of homicide, the main difference being the impersonal context of road crashes as compared to instances of lethal interpersonal violence (see Brookman, 2005). Indeed forensic psychiatric research into dangerous behaviour on the roads is deficient, taking account of how many people are killed by motor vehicles on a daily basis, many victims being children. This is not to deny the role played by incautious pedestrians in some cases, including those who are intoxicated.

In Court

A mentally disordered defendant charged with any of these motoring offences may, according to the circumstances, make use of a number of legal defences. In a rare instance where a charge of murder is at issue, a plea of manslaughter with diminished responsibility may be appropriate where the defendant is suffering from a mental disorder which substantially impaired his/her mental responsibility for the act. Occasional cases are heard involving the defendant claiming s/he was physically unconscious at the time of a road crash and that at the time s/he did not know what s/he was doing and was not therefore engaging in voluntary conduct (McCutcheon, 1998). Depending on the cause of the unconsciousness this may lead to either acquittal on grounds of automatism, or a verdict of 'insane automatism' which would involve psychiatrists in advising the court about (non-penal) disposal. Sleep-related vehicle accidents may not be uncommon (Horne and Reyner, 1995). Instances of drivers falling asleep at the wheel, suffering from an epileptic fit or hypoglycaemia induced by diabetes or theoretical possibilities of the driver being hit by a stone thrown up from the road or being stung by a swarm of bees have been cited as examples in which an accident may occur at a time when a driver became unconscious. Nonetheless a reasonable driver would be expected to stop driving in the event of anticipating impairment in driving ability (this is the doctrine of prior fault).

OVERVIEW

There is ongoing debate about the relationship between mental disorder and crime. One viewpoint holds that 'most psychiatric disorders are only very occasionally associated with criminality' (Prins, 1990; Peay, 2011) which concurs with earlier opinions that, whilst 'sociopathy, alcoholism and drug dependency' were associated with criminality, other psychiatric disorders such as schizophrenia and manic-depressive disease were 'not seen more frequently in criminals than in the general population' (Guze et al., 1969).

This is patently incorrect, as the bulk of this textbook demonstrates. Studies have indicated that at least one-third of prisoners in England and Wales have a significant mental illness (Gunn et al., 1991; Lader et al., 2000; O'Brien et al., 2001). In the USA, Torrey (1995) has called prisons the 'new mental hospitals'.

The majority of studies and publications on mental disorder and crime focus on violent offending rather than non-violent offending (Peay, 2007). The material reported in this chapter, however, shows that even where common criminal activities are concerned, such as theft and motoring offences, there is a substratum of mental disorder that should be identified and treated.

A number of studies have shown that a significant proportion of those in receipt of mental health services have had contact with the criminal justice system and many of these have convictions. A study in the early 1980s found that 38% of young adult psychiatric patients (between the ages of 18 and 35) had been arrested (Holcomb and Ahr, 1988). More recently Theriot and Segal (2005) discovered that almost half (45%) of a group of new attenders to outpatients had at least one contact with the criminal justice system with over a third (36%) having at least one criminal conviction, with theft being the commonest offence closely followed by assault- and drug-related convictions. Almost one-quarter (24%) of a sample of 6,624 people with serious mental illness were arrested in a 10-year period; the majority (62%) was for non-violent crime (Cuellar et al., 2007).

The link between mental disorder and crime may be partly sociological as people with mental disorder are more likely to come from lower socioeconomic circumstances; characteristics shared with the majority of convicted offenders (McFarland et al., 1989). Determining the exact nature of these associations and any causality is difficult. People with mental disorder may be more likely to be: caught whilst offending; arrested; remanded; have a court disposal with mental health associations; and be noticed in prison. Prison may precipitate an episode of illness, especially in those with pre-existing mental disorder. Mental disorder, including drug dependency, may predispose individuals to offending behaviour.

The police are usually the first statutory figures called when a crime has been committed. Police officers are therefore often in a position of triaging and gatekeeping offenders who appear to have mental health problems; such a role has led to the police being described as 'street-corner psychiatrists' (Teplin and Pruett, 1992) or 'frontline mental health workers' (Green, 1997) who provide 'psychiatric first aid' (Bittner, 1967). This role has enlarged over the years due to an increased emphasis on care in the community. One review in the early 1990s concluded that 'between one third and one half of psychiatric patients have been arrested at some point' (Schellenberg et al., 1992). A more recent review found that studies in the 1950s and early 1960s indicated there was a lower rate of arrest for individuals with mental illness but, since 1965, studies have shown a trend toward higher arrest rates (Patch and Arrigo, 1999). The authors cite research which suggests three possible reasons for the change: higher numbers of formerly hospitalized patients in the community due to deinstitutionalization; higher numbers of persons with previous arrests being hospitalized; and law enforcement agencies using the criminal justice apparatus in order to remove people from the community in cases where the mental health system will not act. This last point is emphasized by the view that, unlike mental health services, the criminal justice system has become the 'system that can't say no' (Borzecki and Wormith, 1985).

Robertson (1988) suggested that people with mental disorder were more vulnerable to being detected and arrested; and furthermore were at least twice as likely to report themselves to the police – 23% of those with mental disorder did so as opposed to 11% of general offenders. Earlier reviews had come to the conclusion that patients discharged from psychiatric hospitals did have higher arrest rates than non-patients and this was largely due to a disproportionate number of patients having prior police records (Rabkin, 1979); with many of these individuals being poor, young, unmarried, unskilled minority men (Cohen, 1980). Lurigio (2000) pointed to the compartmentalizing of mental health services as another factor which had fostered the criminalization of the mentally ill. The bulk of psychiatric services treat 'pure' patients, either mentally ill or developmentally disabled or with alcohol or drug dependency. Most of those with mental disorders in the criminal justice system have a number of problems, including dual diagnosis or comorbidity, and thus are unable to access mental health services because they do not meet the criteria imposed by those services (Abram and Teplin, 1991).

The nature in the offence may be a factor into which system, criminal justice or mental health, the offender is sent. Research evidence from the 1960s pointed to crimes against property tending to be handled by penal institutions whereas crimes against the person were frequently referred to the mental health system (Giovannoni and Gurel, 1967). Three decades later this emphasis was reversed and violent behaviour was the factor most strongly associated with entry into the criminal justice system (Robertson et al., 1996).

The emphasis in most of the literature examining the association between mental disorder and crime considers mental illness as predisposing towards crime. But there is an increasing body of literature that those with mental health problems are more likely to be the victims of crime. Many studies have focused on violent crime (Hiroeh et al.,

2001) and even those studies which have not have found that, whilst the rate of non-violent victimization (22%) was similar to that in the general population (21%), the rate of violent criminal victimization was more than double that in the general population (8% v. 3%) (Hiday et al., 1999). (See chapters 14 and 28 for more detailed discussion.)

Specific Disorders

This chapter attempts to highlight that the majority of crime which is dismissed as irrelevant to psychiatry may hide many mentally disordered individuals who are exhibiting their problem through antisocial behaviour. Here are a few of the disorders that may present in this way.

Psychotic disorders

Much of the offending by individuals with schizophrenia (and other psychosis) is trivial and often relates to poor social skills. Such offending has been labelled 'social dropout criminality' (Belfrage, 1994). In one Swedish study of 893 individuals with psychosis, predominately schizophrenia, the most frequent crime was theft with assaults being no more common than criminal damage or shoplifting and fraud being rare (Belfrage, 1998). Furthermore the type of crime often reflected a narrow band of offending so many shoplifters stole food and threats were usually directed against relatives or neighbours. A German study had similar results with theft being more common than physical assaults (Soyka et al., 2004). Some studies have found little violent offending amongst those with schizophrenia. One American study, of 461 psychiatric patients, found that, in a 10-year period, no individual with a diagnosis of schizophrenia was arrested for a violent crime (Durbin et al., 1977).

Much of the academic literature on schizophrenia and crime however reflects the public perception and concentrates on violent behaviour. There is therefore a large literature that provides evidence of an association between schizophrenia and violent offending. There are far fewer studies on schizophrenia and non-violent crime. The studies which have been published do support an association between schizophrenia and non-violent offending, although the increase in offending is modest and may often be mediated by coexisting substance misuse (Wallace et al., 1998). Some studies show that the increase is predominately for violent offending with either the increase for non-violent crime being significantly less (Modestin and Ammann, 1996) or very little (Tiihonen et al., 1997). There may be differences between the sexes, with some studies showing an increase in all offence categories for women with schizophrenia but not for men with schizophrenia (Lindqvist and Allebeck, 1990; Wessely, 1998). Whilst for some individuals a diagnosis of schizophrenia is a risk factor for offending; for others it is a protective factor. Manifestly, the nature of the disorder and the balance between positive and negative symptomatology can increase or decrease the opportunities for and likelihood of offending (Swanson et al., 2006a).

Evidence that those with more chronic psychosis offend in only a minor way comes from a UK study of three cohorts of long-term patients, that is those who had been in hospital for at least 1 year, although the 278 individuals in the three cohorts had an average length of stay of over 15 years in hospital (Dayson, 1993). Twelve patients had been involved with the police informally, mainly because they required help getting home. Only nine individuals were involved in crime as perpetrators with non-violent crime more common than violence. Three people became victims; two were assaulted by youths in the street. One suggestion is that it is deterioration in personality and social functioning that usually leads to the more minor offending.

There have been major concerns that deinstitutionalization and the emphasis on care in the community have had a major impact on those with mental disorder and increased the proportion of offending linked to those with severe mental illness, especially schizophrenia (Torrey, 1995). One Australian study found that there has been an increase in the rate of criminal conviction for those with schizophrenia over a 20-year period; however this increase was matched by a similar increase in convictions among the community controls and moreover the relative risk of offending in those with schizophrenia actually decreased from 3.5 in 1975 to 3.0 in 1985 (Mullen et al., 2000). The tragedy is, however, that when people with mental illness can no larger cope in the community, they are banished to jails and prisons rather than being admitted to hospital (Torrey, 1995).

One of the most important factors that increases the risk of those with severe mental disorder offending is substance misuse. The added diagnosis of a substance use disorder increases the risk of behaviour which results in dealings with the criminal justice system. The vast majority (83%) of one group of 203 individuals in specialized dual diagnosis treatment had contact with the legal system in a 3-year period, with nearly half (44%) being arrested on at least one occasion (Clark et al., 1999). The most common reasons for actual arrests were theft, including shoplifting, substance abuse related charges and disorderly conduct with assaults being less frequent than the aforementioned. An English study reported that 74% of individuals with dual diagnosis had committed an offence whilst only 34% of those with psychosis alone had done so (Scott et al., 1998). Other studies have had the same findings that dual diagnosis patients were more likely to report a lifetime history of offending than patients with psychosis only (Wright et al., 2002).

There is very little information on specific psychotic symptoms and non-violent offending. Occasionally, fraud may be associated with grandiose delusions. Individuals, especially with manic type symptoms, may believe that they are very wealthy and may spend excessively on expensive objects they cannot afford. Within the criminal justice process, delusions or ideas of guilt and unworthiness may lead to false confessions.

Neurotic disorders

Most of the research literature on mental disorder and crime concentrates on mental disorder and violence; similarly most of the literature on non-violent crimes concentrates on severe mental illness. There is therefore relatively little evidence about the association between non-psychotic mental illness and offending. Part of the reason for this is the difficulty in making a clear diagnosis in cases which are sometimes seen on the continuum of normal behaviour, especially by the courts. Furthermore one common thesis is that most, if not all, of the relationship between the less severe forms of depression, and other minor mental illness, and law breaking can be explained by common antecedents, such as socioeconomic status, stressful life events, and adolescent problems 'which shape social relationships and identities, which together influence the likelihood of both early adult crime and depression' (de Coster and Heimer, 2001). Neurotic disorders are the most common type of mental disorders and are therefore the most likely group of disorders to be present in those who offend, regardless of any association between the disorder and the actual offending behaviour.

One study, on individuals with depression, reported that a higher rate of offending was found in those with minor depression compared to matched controls from the population and that property crimes were more common in those with minor depression (Modestin et al., 1997). There were however diagnostic difficulties with many individuals also being given the additional diagnosis of personality disorder which may be more directly linked to the criminal behaviour than the depression.

There can also be something of a feedback loop with the crime itself or more usually the legal process, especially prison, leading to depression and self-destructive acts.

Eating disorders

Many clinicians may be aware of the relationship between stealing (in particular shoplifting) and eating disorders. A review by Baum and Goldner (1995) however notes that few controlled studies have been undertaken and so conclusions are reliant on observational studies, often with small sample sizes. They found 13 studies ranging from 25 to 312 participants, some with comparison groups. Despite a relative lack of data on prevalence of stealing in the general population (most thieves and shoplifters don't get caught) they concluded that there was a relationship between bulimic symptoms and stealing. They also discovered that 'non-bulimic anorexic patients appear to have a lower prevalence of stealing behaviour than one would expect in the general population.' The main problem with the studies used in the review was the lack of a psychiatric control group, leading to uncertainty about whether the relationship with stealing is due to the severity of psychiatric symptoms generally or the more specific symptoms of bulimia.

Baum and Goldner (1995), on the basis of their review, proposed a number of aetiological relationships between eating disorders and stealing. These include results of the effects of starvation or medication; affective symptoms including affective spectrum disorder, dissociation or tension reduction; personality disorder (i.e. as the root of both the stealing and eating disorder); psychodynamic pathways (e.g. self-punishment); and finally pseudopubertal impulsivity and sociocultural influences. These mechanisms are tentative suggestions rather than confirmed or elaborated aetiology and an in depth clinical assessment of the relationship between stealing and psychiatric morbidity would always be recommended in practice.

In terms of treatment, Baum and Goldner (1995) refer to various case studies demonstrating use of medication, group and individual psychotherapy, but note that the optimal judicial approach to psychiatric patients caught stealing has yet to be defined.

Personality disorders

The WHO's *ICD-10* classification defines 'dissocial personality disorder' by characteristic symptoms such as: 'gross and persistent attitude of irresponsibility and disregard for social norms, rules and obligations'; 'very low tolerance to frustration and a low threshold for discharge of aggression, including violence'; and 'incapacity to experience guilt and to profit from experience, particularly punishment'. These are characteristics often found in offenders. It is therefore easy to understand that the rates of such a disorder (if such it is) might be higher in those who offend than those who do not. Other personality disorders, especially the emotionally unstable and paranoid types, also have features which may lead to offending. A systematic review of 62 surveys of mental disorder in prisoners concluded that 65% of male prisoners had a personality disorder, with 47% having an antisocial (dissocial) personality disorder (Fazel and Danesh, 2002). For women, the figures were 42% with any personality disorder; 21% with antisocial personality disorder and 25% with borderline personality disorder. chapter 16 has further details.

Substance misuse disorders

The above sections on the mental illnesses have already indicated the major role of alcohol and drugs in offending behaviour. The addition of a diagnosis of substance misuse increases the rate of offending behaviour in those with a primary diagnosis of a mental illness, especially psychotic disorders. However substance misuse by itself is implicated in much criminal behaviour. Cookson (1992) concludes from a survey of over 600 young offenders that 'habitual drunkenness was associated with self-reports of all types of delinquency'.

Surveys of offenders showing that offenders generally (and particularly those aged 16–24) tend to drink more heavily than non-offenders and that rates of 'hazardous' levels of drinking in prisoners run to 60% of the male and 40% of the female prison population (McMurran, 2003). A minimum of one in five people arrested by police test positive for alcohol.

According to the Institute of Alcohol Studies (IAS) (2007), who also quoted an all-party group of members of parliament being advised by the British Medical Association, alcohol is a factor in: 60–70% of homicides, 75% of stabbings, 70% of beatings, and 50% of fights and domestic assaults. An interesting approach to the association between alcohol and crime, taken by the British Crime Survey, is to ask victims whether their assailant was under the influence of alcohol or not. In 2008, 47% of victims answered yes to this question, and 43% answered no. This finding has remained remarkably consistent since at least 1995. Stranger victims report a much higher rate of intoxication (62%) than other victims, and 38% of domestic violence was reported as related to alcohol (Walker et al., 2009). The IAS fact sheet is a valuable source of information (http://www.ias.org.uk/resources/factsheets/crime.pdf).

For other drugs, the category of the drug and the nature of its use result in major differences. There is little evidence that rates of criminal behaviour are much higher in cannabis users (except possession) whilst 80% of opiate users have at least one conviction. Data from the UK indicate that over a third of male prisoners have used cannabis (Maden et al., 1992) and in a study of a local prison in Wales, Plant and Taylor (2012) found that 80% of prisoners reported using this drug.

There are a number of ways in which alcohol and drugs contribute to criminal behaviour: acute intoxication leads to impaired judgment; intoxication reduces inhibitions; alcohol is toxic to the brain; various forms of theft are used to finance an individual's use of illegal substances; intoxication and the time taken up by the habit reduce employment opportunities; inhibitions against antisocial behaviour are reduced. Chapter 18 has further details.

12

Disorders of brain structure and function and crime

Edited by
Pamela J Taylor

Written by
John Gunn

Michael D Kopelman

Veena Kumari

Pamela J Taylor

Birgit Völlm

Mairead Dolan

1st edition authors: **Paul d'Orbán, John Gunn, Anthony Holland, Michael D Kopelman, Graham Robertson and Pamela J Taylor**

EXPECTATIONS AND ADVANCES: CONCEPTUALIZATION AND MEASUREMENT OF BRAIN STRUCTURE

Psychiatry and psychology have proved difficult enough fields with their emphasis on gathering and documenting subjective data about alien and distressing experiences. The skilled clinician has learned to collate the content of reported symptoms with the manner in which they are reported, a few other directly observable behaviours and the reports of other, more consistently present witnesses, such as family members, before making a diagnosis. This will allow predictions about the course of the distress and disorder and about interventions likely to change that course for the better. The psychiatric diagnostic process has, however, remained largely subjective, and vulnerable to political misuse, both at the rather grand level of an occasional national government allegedly highjacking the system to deal with dissidents and at the less well-recognized and more common level of using diagnosis to exclude individuals from services (Taylor and Gunn, 2008). Exclusion is made easier by the fact that so many of the people who present with the greatest distress, the greatest risk of harm to themselves and others and the greatest challenge to treatment have a complex mix of disorders. A long nurtured dream has been that in psychiatry, as in the rest of medicine, diagnostic tests would one day become available and practice more scientific. There have been many false dawns, from 'pink spots' in urine, through the rather non-specific dexamethasone suppression test, to a variety of electroencephalogram (EEG) and X-ray techniques which, when measures were averaged, were able to indicate some significant differences between groups of people with and without disorders, but proved disappointing for detection of disorder in individuals or mapping progress or progression.

The art of defining disorder and linking it to behaviour has been at its most stretched in understanding criminal behaviours. That has not held experts back from giving evidence in court, nor courts from asking for that evidence. Some of it is of the highest possible quality, but, wisely, the court reserves judgment on such matters to itself, and, in common law countries, in disputed cases, to the collection of lay people who make up the jury. This is unlikely to change in the near future, but an important collection of articles published by *The Royal Society*, signposted by Zeki and Goodenough (2004) would have us believe that we are on the verge of a new dawn, when the developments both in technology and philosophical thinking about mind-brain convergence will mean that the results of brain examinations specifically will become prime tools for the law to determine the operation of free will and capacity, motive and truth telling. According to their introduction to a special themed issue of *Behavioral Sciences and the Law* on 'international perspectives on brain imaging and the law', Felthous and Sass (2008) think not. Even if the technology were to become as definitive as hoped, its use in practice will be limited by costs. Older evidence from the USA on the likely extent of organic brain damage in capital cases (Lewis et al., 1986, 1988) shows that much of this was never presented at original hearings and executions followed in some cases. More recent evidence from the USA confirms the continuing financial limits on justice (Bach, 2009), a growing problem in the UK too. Even in a perfectly funded system, however, Felthous and Sass draw on the wisdom of Tancredi and Brodie (2007) in their conclusion:

In the end, perhaps we should never rely on a single test, however impressive or technologically sophisticated, to impute a causal connection between something as complex as a single criminal behavior...

This chapter inevitably touches on some of these issues, but it remains an essentially clinical effort to explore the extent to which it may be possible to have a better understanding of how, in general, brain structure and function mediate relationships between psychiatric disorders and antisocial behaviours, with a particular focus on those major disorders which are more commonly associated with violence.

EPILEPSY IN RELATION TO OFFENDING

The Nature and Classification of Epilepsy

The diagnosis of epilepsy depends upon clinical judgment. Rarely, a patient's EEG may be recorded during the course of a seizure, and the diagnosis made on electrical grounds, but this is generally only possible when seizures are frequent, or 24-hour monitoring available. The EEG between seizures may be normal. Even an abnormal EEG between seizures, showing spike phenomena, does not, however, prove that the seizures are, in fact, epileptic.

Although the cause of epilepsy is often unknown, or 'idiopathic', many causes are recognized. It may follow brain injury, perhaps at birth or due to congenital malformations, during febrile convulsions in infancy, or, at any age, due to head injury, infections of the brain and meninges, cerebrovascular disease, cerebral tumours, degenerative disorders, drugs (such as alcohol) or toxins (e.g. in uraemia). Some of these precipitating disorders are themselves associated with social conditions such as poverty, poor maternal care or drunkenness and such variables may, in part, explain the varying prevalence rates found in different communities. In their review of the socioeconomic correlates of epilepsy, Whitman et al. (1980) conclude that 'poor people have more epilepsy'.

The International Bureau for Epilepsy (Fisher et al., 2005) defines epilepsy as:

a disorder of the brain characterized by an enduring predisposition to generate epileptic seizures and by the neurobiologic, cognitive, psychological, and social consequences of this condition. The definition of epilepsy requires the occurrence of at least one epileptic seizure.

A pragmatic definition of a seizure, which has stood the test of time, is:

an intermittent, stereotyped disturbance of behaviour, emotion, motor function or sensation which, on clinical grounds, is judged to be the result of pathological cortical neuronal discharge (Gunn, 1977).

The many types of epilepsy can be classified in a variety of ways. A consensus system, developed in 1970 by the International League Against Epilepsy (Lishman, 1998), is set out below.

Varieties of epilepsy

1. *Generalized epilepsies*:
   a primary generalized epilepsy (petit mal, grand mal);
   b secondary generalized epilepsy.
2. *Focal epilepsies ('partial' or 'local' epilepsies)*:
   a with elementary (simple) symptomatology (e.g. motor Jacksonian epilepsy);
   b with complex symptomatology (mostly temporal lobe in origin, e.g. with cognitive or affective symptomatology, psychomotor attacks, psychosensory, attacks).
3. *Unclassifiable and mixed forms.*

The phenomena of epilepsy may be divided into three phases: pre-ictal, ictal and post-ictal. Pre-ictal prodromes may include affective changes and irritability, and be experienced by the patient as a warning that a seizure is coming on; they may last up to 24 hours. An aura is the initial focal onset of the attack and may be a sensation or a movement lasting from a few seconds to a minute or two, thus giving some patients an opportunity to protect themselves slightly from the forthcoming loss of consciousness.

Almost any form of motor activity can occur during the seizure, or ictus, itself. The classic tonic–clonic movements in an unconscious patient, with or without tongue biting and loss of bladder control, are common, but not invariable. Lishman (1998) describes the full range of ictal phenomena. Psycho-motor seizures are perhaps the most important form of epilepsy in relation to offending. These may entirely replace tonic–clonic seizures, or accompany them. Consciousness may be completely or only partially lost; there may be automatic behaviour, confusion, wandering, strange or repetitive speech, affective changes such as panic, terror, anger or ecstasy, visual and/or auditory hallucinations, and delusions, especially of the paranoid kind.

After seizures, further confusional states, which may resemble psychomotor seizures, may also be experienced. It is sometimes difficult to determine when the seizure stopped and the post-seizure phase began.

Epilepsy, Violence, Personality and Popular Fears

The history of the relationship between epilepsy and crime, with an apparent need to create a new category of disorder when supporting physical evidence fails, has some resemblances to the more modern English story of dangerous and severe personality disorder (DSPD) (chapter 16). Temkin (1945) wrote of the received wisdom on epilepsy *per se* during the first half of the twentieth century, observing:

Epilepsy has always been treated with reverence, respect or fear.

Lombroso went so far as to suggest that, although not all epileptics are criminals, most criminals are epileptics. According to him, there are three types of criminal, the epileptic criminal, the insane criminal, and the born criminal, but all three stem from an 'epileptoid base' (Ferrero, 1911).

Gradually the implied association between unacceptable, undesirable behaviour, and epilepsy evolved into the notion of a special epileptic personality. Sjöbring called this 'ixophrenia' and, as recently as 1973, said that people with epilepsy become torpid and circumstantial, 'sticky', tense and 'suffer from explosive outbursts of rage, anxiety and so on.' By the 1970s, however, these historic concepts had largely been replaced by a new one: 'the episodic dyscontrol syndrome'. In 1999, Gordon wrote:

episodic dyscontrol syndrome may affect both children and adults. Those who treat children with neurological disorders are likely to see patients referred for investigation of outbursts of aggressive behaviour, especially if episodes are possibly of an epileptic nature... The syndrome consists of recurrent attacks of uncontrollable rage, usually with minimal provocation and often out of character.

Episodic dyscontrol may seem like a gift to the forensic psychiatrist, but, it is a rarely used diagnosis, which does not appear in either of the two main standard disease classification systems. Both, however, retain a concept of habit and impulse disorders/impulse control disorders. *ICD 10* modestly notes this simply as a category of behavioural disorder that will not fit anywhere else, and includes a concept of 'intermittent explosive disorder' within the 'other category' of that vague cluster (World Health Organisation, 1992). *DSM-IV* gives intermittent explosive disorder its own category, but acknowledges it as 'apparently rare' and a diagnosis of exclusion, when other physical explanations have been ruled out (American Psychiatric Association, 1994).

The best current summary suggests that there are five possible associations between epilepsy and violence: (1) violent automatism; (2) prodromal irritability; (3) post-ictal confusion; (4) lower socioeconomic status and (5) brain damage (Nedopil, personal communication). This is precisely what one of us found in a 1970s survey of prisoners with epilepsy (Gunn, 1977). Nedopil (2007) also stresses the rarity of a direct relationship between epilepsy and violent acts.

In the past, special laws have been enacted to restrain people with epilepsy. In 1939, for example, a law was enacted in North Carolina, USA, to limit marriage by people with epilepsy. Anti-marriage laws had been drawn up in Sweden as early as 1757, and many states in the USA still have such laws on their statute books, even though they no longer operate them. Gallup poll data from the UK indicates that attitudes towards epilepsy are improving, but even in 1979, 12% of a sample interviewed in a Gallup survey thought that people with epilepsy should not be employed like others and

5% said they would object to their children associating with children who had seizures (Gunn, 1981, 1991c). In a time of full employment, Pond and Bidwell (1960) found that 40% of people with epilepsy in their survey had at some time had serious difficulties finding employment. Kate Collins et al. (2007) compared attitudes to people with epilepsy in 1981 with attitudes in 2006. They found that, apart from physicians, who improved their attitudes over the quarter of a century studied, other people, including medical students, did not; overall, about a quarter of those studied considered violence and epilepsy to be associated. Krauss et al. (2000) found that about a third of media stories in the English language contained gross errors about epilepsy; seizures were described with demonic images in 6% of stories and disease used to encompass the person described as 'epileptic' in 45% of stories. Most celebrities with recurring seizures denied having 'epilepsy'. Jacoby et al. (1996, 2005) discussed the impact of the continuing stigma on people with epilepsy, recommending more education about this disorder.

Epilepsy and psychological damage

Stigma is not the only burden to be carried by a person with epilepsy. As Taylor (1969a) pointed out:

Every fit reinforces the view of witnesses that the epileptic cannot be relied upon to participate fully in society, since he is liable, at any time, to go out of control.

The damage to self-esteem of someone who has to suffer such feelings must be considerable and may itself contribute to the excess number of psychiatric complications suffered by the patient with epilepsy.

Toone (2000) reported that affective illnesses and schizophrenia have both been shown to have a higher prevalence among people with epilepsy than those without. It is, however, the post-ictal psychoses that may be more likely to have some forensic significance, and these are dealt with below. Irritability is classically associated with brain damage and brain damage is an aetiological factor in a high proportion of epilepsies; irritability can also accompany other mood changes. Some authors regard explosive, immature aggressiveness as especially characteristic of patients with temporal lobe epilepsy, occurring as a prominent feature in about one-third of patients who present for temporal lobectomy (Falconer and Taylor, 1970). Falconer (1973) reported a marked reduction in aggressiveness in such patients after the operation. An increase in frustration tolerance and a diminution in irritability are said to be related to improved fit control, but there are no properly controlled epidemiological studies to determine whether these apparent associations between irritability and epilepsy are valid or in excess of what would be expected in any population suffering from a chronic debilitating disorder.

There does, however, seem to be clear evidence that people with epilepsy are more prone to suicide than people without. As far back as 1941, Prudhomme estimated an incidence twice that of the general population, and five times greater when the figures were corrected for age. Henriksen et al. (1970) found the suicide rate to be about three times that in the general population, but more modern estimates suggest that it may be up to 10 times the general population rate (e.g. Jones et al., 2003).

Prevalence of Epilepsy in the General Population

In view of the subjectivity of diagnosis, estimates of the prevalence of epilepsy will be contentious, and are probably changing. A study of the prevalence of epilepsy in Rochester, Minnesota, between 1940 and 1980 suggested that the prevalence of epilepsy rose from 2.7 to 6.8 per 1,000 population between these years. European authors have placed the population figure at about 5 per 1,000 (Gunn, 1977; Lishman, 1998) when surveys in the USA have suggested a slightly higher prevalence (Hauser and Kurland, 1975; Whitman et al., 1980). Total population figures, however, mask important variations, for example that epilepsy is commoner in younger than in older people. A survey of a population of about a quarter of a million people in Bradford, England, in the 1990s suggested that the prevalence of epilepsy is 7.3 per thousand population (Wright et al., 2000).

Prevalence of Epilepsy in Offender Populations

An important study in Illinois prisons (Whitman et al., 1984) found a prevalence of epilepsy of 24 per 1,000 prisoners, four times the rate among the 20- to 29-year-old men in the Rochester, Minnesota study (see above). Head injury was the probable cause among 45% of these prisoners with epilepsy, a much higher percentage than that reported in general populations.

An earlier, English, national study of prisoners (Gunn, 1977) found the prevalence of epilepsy to be 7.2 per 1,000 in 1966. This was only a small excess prevalence over that in the general population of the time, and could not be accounted for by the relatively youthful age structure of the prisoners. Although there was evidence that this figure was an underestimate, as an undiagnosed group was found among the control sample supposedly without epilepsy, it is unlikely that any adjusted prevalence figure would have been commensurate with that of the Minnesota study. A later prison survey of England and Wales (Gunn et al., 1991) confirmed the earlier English figure.

The excess prevalence of epilepsy among prisoners, the clinical impression of increased irritability in some people with epilepsy, and the frightening idea that people with epilepsy may do dangerous things when they are unconscious all lead to the expectation that there will be an excess incidence or prevalence of violent criminal activity in a population of epileptic patients with epilepsy, but there is no evidence for this. Gudmundsson (1966) studied the complete adult population with epilepsy in Iceland and found that 8.3% had a police record, three times the general population rate there. This is an important finding as a complete national survey of a relatively stable population, but many of the offences were of drunkenness or breaches of customs and price control regulations. Juul-Jensen (1964) studied a Danish population with epilepsy and found the prevalence of any crime was 9.5% among the men and 1.9% among the women, figures similar to those among the general population. An earlier Swedish report (Alström, 1950) found that patients with epilepsy attending a neurological clinic had a similar prevalence of criminality to the general population after allowing for geographical area, social class and age.

Ictal and post-ictal violence

In spite of the different rates between the England and Wales and the USA prison studies, they came to a similar conclusion with respect to violent or sexual offending: control prisoners and those with epilepsy had similar rates of such offences. The England and Wales survey looked carefully for any cases of ictal violence. Automatic action of any kind in association with a fit is rare (10% of cases), but acts of violence in this context are exceptionally so (Knox, 1968). No prisoner in the England and Wales survey (Gunn, 1977) met criteria for having been violent during the seizure itself. Only 10 men reported seizures within 12 hours of the offence; four said they had had one just before it, five just after, and one man claimed both. Very little direct relationship between the crimes committed and the men's epilepsy could be detected (Gunn and Fenton, 1971). This is in line with other work. Macdonald (1969), in the USA, found only two crimes committed as a result of an epileptic seizure in a series of 1,000 cases, while according to Delgardo-Escueta et al. (2002) only 15 cases in the whole of the USA had cited epilepsy as a defence in law against violent or disorderly conduct between 1889 and 2001. Treiman and Delgardo-Escueta (1983) reviewed the world medical literature between 1872 and 1981 and found only 29 cases in which violent events were reported to be directly due to a seizure. This included the two cases from Broadmoor, one of England's high security hospitals, mentioned below (Gunn and Fenton, 1971). In his comprehensive review of the relationship between epilepsy and violence, Treiman (1986) concluded that violence by people with epilepsy is probably due to associated brain lesions or to adverse social factors rather than to the epilepsy directly.

A survey of patients with epilepsy in the English high security hospitals was conducted to amplify the England and Wales prison data (Gunn, 1977). Here, among people selected as in need of hospital treatment, only three were found to have had a definite epileptic seizure within the 24-hour period around the offence. Of these, two men probably did commit dangerous offences in a state of altered consciousness. The first was a 32-year-old man who had developed convulsions at the age of 18. Two and a half years later, he had a generalized seizure early in the morning, while getting ready for work. On apparent recovery, 20 minutes later, his speech was slurred and his eyes seemed 'vacant'. He attacked an elderly man who lived in the house, striking him with a spade and kicking him. The victim died from the resultant severe head injuries; the man then attacked his girlfriend and the victim's wife, smashed some panes of glass, and cycled away aimlessly with blood on his arms. Some way down the road he fell off his cycle and, on admission to hospital, was mentally confused and amnesic for all events following the seizure. In the second case, the man had a fit after an evening spent pigeon shooting. The following morning, still in a state of confusion, he rose early, took his shotgun into the street and brandished it about, firing it occasionally. These do appear to be cases of post-ictal violence.

It seems, then, that 'automatic' criminal behaviour in relation to an epileptic fit is very rare. Aggressive behaviour during a post-ictal confusional state is only slightly less so. Lishman (1998) neatly summarizes the criteria for suspecting that a criminal act may be the result of epilepsy or post ictal confusion:

- there must be unequivocal evidence of epilepsy, though not necessarily a previous history of automatic behaviour;
- the crime will have been sudden with an absence of obvious motive, and no evidence of planning or premeditation;
- the crime will appear senseless and, typically, there will have been little or no attempt at concealment or escape;
- the abnormal behaviour will usually have been of short duration, lasting minutes rather than hours, and never entirely appropriate to the circumstances;
- witnesses may have noticed impairment of awareness, for example inappropriate actions or gestures, stereotypic movements, unresponsiveness or irrelevant replies to questions, aimless wanderings or a dazed and vacant expression on the part of the person concerned;
- amnesia for the act is the rule, but there should be no continuing anterograde amnesia for events following the resumption of conscious awareness.

This guidance is very good for ictal violence but it does not cover post-ictal violence. One of us (Gunn, 1978) reported a case which did not fit these guidelines. The man concerned had no known history of epilepsy and had killed his wife with a hammer before fleeing their home. He was convicted of manslaughter and sentenced to life imprisonment. His EEG was strongly suggestive of epilepsy, and, in prison, he subsequently showed evidence of this disorder. As time went by, it became clear that he had killed his wife in a post-ictal confusional state during which he developed paranoid delusions. Mendez (1998)

has also described a man who experienced an overwhelming sense of threat during his post-ictal phase. He would focus on anybody nearby as the source of the threat and sometimes felt impelled to attack a person. Several times he had been charged with aggravated assault.

Ictal and post-ictal sex offences

There is no evidence that sex offending is commoner among people with epilepsy than among others. There are reports that sexual disturbance is associated with temporal lobe epilepsy, but the commonest disturbance is hyposexuality. Taylor (1969b) found poor sexual adjustment in two-thirds of 100 consecutive cases referred for temporal lobectomy, the commonest problem being lack of sexual drive. Hypersexuality appears to be rare. Transvestism has been reported, as have unusual forms of fetishism (see Lishman, 1998). The sample of 158 male prisoners with epilepsy (England and Wales) included 14 who had been convicted of sexual offences (Gunn, 1977), constituting a rate no different from the control men. The offences were wide ranging – indecency, living off immoral earnings, bigamy and exhibitionism to incest and, in the case of three men, rape. Epilepsy was not thought to be of direct relevance in any case.

Nature of the relationship between imprisonment and epilepsy

There is so little association between epilepsy and crime that any co-occurrence cannot explain the probable excess of epilepsy among prisoners. Any relationship between epilepsy and imprisonment is complex, with at least seven possible explanations.

- People with epilepsy have always been more likely than the general population to be placed in institutions of some kind.
- The widespread belief that people with epilepsy are liable to behave in an antisocial way has largely been discredited, but attitudes linger.
- Brain damage or dysfunction may provide a common cause for epilepsy and behaviour disorder. Child abuse is a potential common ground here. Kempe et al. (1962), for example, reported on 302 children who had been attacked by their parents. Of these, 33 had died but 85 had suffered permanent brain injury. An example of adult acquired brain damage preceding epilepsy and behaviour disorder emerged in the English and Welsh prisoner study. At the age of 29, a man sustained a severe skull fracture and meningitis in a motor-cycle accident. At that time, he was happily married and had a good work record having enjoyed an apparently normal childhood in a well-integrated home. After the accident he was left with right-sided weakness, some disorientation and fits. He was discharged home from

hospital, but his marriage disintegrated and he lost his job. He became an unemployed drifter, living rough or in hostels. In the 10 years following his accident, he acquired 15 convictions for theft.

- Low self-esteem in the person with epilepsy, related to social rejection, may be a precursor of antisocial behaviour. In a survey of children, Graham and Rutter (1968) concluded:

  The widespread community prejudice against epilepsy was probably an adverse factor in the epileptic child's development and it may have been one reason for the high rate of (psychiatric) disorder in the epilepsy group.

- Epilepsy carries an increased risk of mental disorder, particularly schizophrenia-like psychoses, affective psychoses and suicidal behaviour. These psychiatric problems can, on occasion, lead to antisocial behaviour, especially petty theft and property damage offences.

- Poor environments may cause both epilepsy and antisocial behaviour. A number of studies have shown an association between maternal care and quality of childhood environment, and the likelihood of developing fits (e.g. Miller et al., 1960). Modelling, learning by imitation, is a powerful force in determining behaviour and attitudes. It does not seem unreasonable to suppose that an uncaring or even brutal home environment during childhood will increase the likelihood not only of physical brain damage but also of learning to cope with the adult world in a brutal uncaring fashion.

- Behaviour disorders may lead to accidents which produce brain injuries. One prisoner in the English study came from a disturbed background, his parents continually rowing. They finally separated when he was 9 years old, and 3 years later he was convicted for stealing a lorry and sent for special schooling. Thereafter, he was frequently in trouble. At 17, shortly after joining the army, he crashed one of their vehicles and sustained a head injury. Following this accident, he developed typical tonic–clonic seizures.

The Treatment of Offender Patients with Epilepsy

This is not a textbook of neurology, nor do we encourage psychiatrists to treat epilepsy without neurological advice. There is a place, however, for a few psychiatrists to undertake specialist work in this area as offender patients tend to be unpopular with other professionals. A specialist clinic, providing the personal resources for long-term tolerance and the skills to manage the combination of medico-legal issues and complex psychosocial problems, can be of great value.

Treatment of epilepsy in any circumstances is much more than providing medication to obtain seizure control, but the range of needs is likely to be especially high in an offender group. In spite of this, as it is a common condition, most people with epilepsy are managed by general practitioners. The Royal College of General Practitioners has issued detailed and helpful guidance (Stokes et al., 2004). People with epilepsy frequently present with a wide range of problems, including mood disturbance, low self-esteem, suicidal ideas, irritability, a poor work record, difficulty in personal relationships, accommodation problems and a history of frequent injuries, all of which require attention. The basis of treatment is the establishment of a trusting long-term relationship between patient and doctor, who can make links with others for specialist support. General support and the boosting of self-esteem are the first requirements. It is also important to explore the patient's fantasy life, discover what s/he really feels is happening to him/her during a seizure and provide as much reality orientation as is feasible. Within this context, adherence to taking anti-convulsant drugs is likely to be much greater than it might otherwise be. In other words, there is a significant role for psychiatry in the treatment of epilepsy.

Drugs for seizure control have to be given on an empirical and pragmatic basis. Every effort should be made to keep the régime simple and to control the seizures with one type of drug only. Although this may prove to be a counsel of perfection, it is nevertheless important that if monotherapy with the first choice drug has failed, monotherapy with a second should be tried before adding drugs. A further complication may be an additional need for psychotropic medication. When drug régimes have to be changed, this must proceed slowly and with caution. As a last resort, more than one medication will have to be used. All anti-convulsant drugs have their pros and cons, and a useful discussion is to be found in Lishman (1998, pp.299–306).

The more disturbed and non-compliant the patient, the more important it is to avoid seriously toxic drugs if possible. Carbamazepine and sodium valproate have toxic side-effects, but are probably less dangerous than some of the other drugs; carbamazepine may eventually be replaced by oxcarbazepine. Phenytoin is an effective anti-convulsant, but highly toxic to the cerebellum and is best reserved for otherwise intractable cases. Various barbiturates, including phenobarbitone and primidone, may occasionally be useful, but induce drowsiness and depression and are dangerous in overdose, so they have largely fallen into disuse. Benzodiazepines are very good anti-convulsants and are safe drugs, but highly addictive. They are the drugs of choice in status epilepticus, prolonged, uncontrolled fitting. Intravenous lorazepam is probably the drug of choice in hospital, but in the absence of resuscitation facilities, as may occur in a prison, other methods, such as a rectal solution of diazepam may have to be considered. Status epilepticus is a medical emergency; failure to respond to intravenous anti-convulsant means that intensive care and anaesthetization may be indicated.

Diazepam is best avoided as a regular anti-convulsant medication because tolerance to it develops very quickly; clonazepam and clobazam are probably better in this regard. Gabapentin is useful as an add-on treatment for partial seizures. Vigabatrin, introduced in 1989, is useful for the control of complex partial seizures. Lamotrigine may help patients with partial or generalized seizures, and has the advantage that it may be taken as a single daily dose. Anti-convulsant pharmacology has advanced slowly but steadily, as illustrated by a good recent review (Glauser et al., 2006).

Anti-convulsant blood levels should always be regularly monitored. The correct dose for a particular patient is the minimum dose that will prevent seizures, or at least reduce fit frequency to an acceptable level without producing serious unwanted effects. This has to be discussed with the patient. It is wrong to prescribe exclusively according to the serum reports from the laboratory, but such reports do give some indication of compliance, upward or downward trends, and when toxic levels are reached. Liver function tests, blood counts and serum folate should also be checked at fairly frequent intervals.

Medication should be supported with counselling on matters including self-protection and lifestyle. On rare occasions, it may be necessary to break medical confidentiality and tell an employer of the patient's condition. This would be imperative, for example, if a patient were training to be a bus or train driver and refused to disclose his/her seizures him/herself. In the UK, driving may be permitted if the patient has been fit free for 1 year or, if attacks occur only in sleep for 3 years without a waking attack, however s/he is never allowed to drive a heavy goods or passenger vehicle (Driver and Vehicle Licensing Agency (DVLA), 2010). Updated reports are required every 6 months. Where disclosure is necessary, every effort must be made to persuade the patient to be a partner in that. Breach of confidentiality is often disastrous for the therapeutic alliance, but the doctor has a duty to safeguard the patient and public in such circumstances.

Suicidal ideas and behaviour are common among people with epilepsy. Self-destructive behaviour may be manifest in direct or indirect ways (e.g. recklessness) and the patient will need careful support. Alcohol may also be a special problem, as some people with epilepsy try using it as an anti-convulsant (with a modicum of success), but more often it increases seizure frequency; furthermore, seizures may be induced by alcohol withdrawal.

One special problem for the person who has a criminal record as well as epilepsy is accommodation. There have been some improvements in this area but the double stigma may still make placement, for example in a hostel, extremely difficult. There are still only one or two specialized centres for people with epilepsy and, on occasion, these centres will admit patients with a history of antisocial behaviour. Hostels for this group of patients are needed for two kinds of situation: for those leaving prison where the Parole Board has insisted on a period of supervised hostel accommodation and those who, for a variety of reasons, find independent living difficult. A specialized hostel for ex-prisoners with epilepsy was established in South London (Gunn, 1977; Channon, 1982; Gunn, 1991b) and proved to be of considerable value. As attitudes to epilepsy improved, there were fewer referrals on this account, but more for people with intellectual disability. The hostel no longer functions in this way.

Management of Prisoners with Epilepsy

The general principles of treatment are identical within and outside institutions. Prisoners may need extra psychological support because of the severe stigmatization they may suffer from other prisoners. The prisoner should be asked for details of any previous treatment, and every effort should be made by clinical staff in the prison to contact the prisoner's immediately previous GP or specialist to check the nature and dose of any medication. As far as possible, the medication should be maintained as outside prison. Epilepsy is a potentially fatal condition, and it has been known for prisoners to die through failure to follow these simple rules. Although prisoners may require slightly less medication, perhaps because of improved regularity of dose and the absence of alcohol, there is a risk that the stress of imprisonment might increase fit frequency, so it is important to continue monitoring through clinical observation and blood levels of medication or its metabolites. If in doubt, expert advice should always be sought. On discharge, if not already doing so, such prisoners should always be offered the opportunity of attending a specialist clinic, including psychiatric help. Unless the prisoner explicitly objects, an appointment should be made for him/her, with clear directions on how to get there. An adequate supply of medication must be provided to cover him/her until the next GP or clinic appointment.

SLEEP DISORDERS

Sleep disorders, according to both major systems for classifying diseases (*DSM* and *ICD*) are broadly of four types – those secondary to organic brain dysfunction such as narcolepsy or the Kleine–Levin syndrome, those intrinsic to major mental disorders such as schizophrenia or depression, dyssomnias, in which the main disturbance is in the amount, quality or timing of sleep, and the parasomnias, in which abnormal events sometimes occur during sleep. Sleep disorders of organic origin are rare. The Kleine–Levin syndrome is particularly rare, but of interest here because it affects young men and behaviour disorders may accompany the core features of excessive sleepiness and, often, over-eating. Its cause is unknown, and the evidence base for treatment slight (Oliveira et al., 2009).

People who become patients in psychiatric services commonly have sleep problems, most of which are attributable to their primary mental disorder, sometimes compounded by histories of substance misuse. It may be that, in the interests of parsimony in diagnosis, dyssomnias are not often enough recognized; often the late sleeper/late riser poses a real challenge to nursing management, not readily helped by conventional medication and routine sleep hygiene practices. At worst, patients show complete sleep reversal. The focus of most interest for specialist forensic mental health clinicians, however, lies in the parasomnias, because, occasionally, it is alleged that a serious crime has taken place during sleep. This brings the attendant implication that the individual is not responsible for his or her act and therefore not culpable so that, if the relevance of the sleep disorder can be established in relation to a criminal charge, the person might be acquitted and walk free from the court. In England and Wales, courts have made a distinction between insane and 'none-insane' automatism since *Kemp*. Sleepwalking, a parasomnia, was, then, included alongside concussion, involuntary intoxication and insulin-induced hypoglycaemia as a non-insane automatism. Changes followed; in *Quick*, a distinction was introduced between external and internal factors causing the abnormality of mind. Since then, abnormalities due to external factors have been regarded as non-insane automatisms, whereas those due to internal factors are regarded in law as insane automatisms due to 'disease of the mind'. In March 1991, the English Court of Appeal ruled that sleepwalking was 'an abnormality or disorder, albeit transitory, due to an internal factor' and that it should, therefore, be regarded as an insane automatism (*Burgess*). There remains the possibility, however, that an external factor, such as change in medication, might be sufficient to be accepted as an 'external trigger'. Elsewhere, legal responses vary within and between jurisdictions. Cartwright (2004), for example, described two similar cases for which she gave evidence to the Court as a sleep expert. In neither case was the fact of the homicide disputed. In one case, under Canadian law, the man was acquitted as having been suffering a non-insane automatism, while the other, under US law, was convicted of first degree murder. She sets out clearly how both cases nevertheless fitted well with the criteria proposed by Bonkalo (1974), with EEG evidence of exceptional frequency of arousals from early non-REM (non-rapid eye movement) sleep. In brief, Bonkalo's criteria are: an established history of sleep disorder, but absence of history of violence; timing (soon after sleep onset, following a period of goal directed behaviour that was initially non-violent); affection for the victim and absence of motivation for the attack; cognitive features (confusion after the attack, amnesia for it, no

attempt to conceal it); presence of some potential trigger factors like stress and/or a period of poor sleep; and absence of others, like taking alcohol or illicit substances.

Many reports of violence in sleep predate the modern understanding of the physiology of sleep disorders. Walker (1968) provided an historical account of cases, the first recorded in the literature probably having been a homicide during a night terror (Yellowlees, 1878). Howard and d'Orban (1987) reviewed the medical and legal literature and, on the basis of this and two of their own cases, distinguished four groups. The first three of these – violence associated with confusion on sudden awakening (sleep drunkenness), violence associated with sleep-walking and violence associated with night terrors – would now generally be grouped together as disorders of arousal, but we will retain the full breakdown here. Each arousal disorder does present slightly differently from another in clinical practice, and more than one disorder of arousal may present in the same individual (Kales et al., 1980). Pressman (2007) conducted a more recent historical review of the legal and medical literature. The prevalence of such sleep arousal disorders is not completely known, but estimates vary from 2% (Ohayon et al., 1997) to 4% among adults (Hublin et al., 1997), although the Hublin group suggest that fewer than 1/10 of these would experience a weekly occurrence. Nevertheless, these figures indicate that such disorders are quite common, and thought to be even more so among children. In children, however, the disorders very rarely cause any risk to the child or to others. Most concern is vested in those disorders which persist into adulthood, or arise while an adult.

Disorders of Arousal from Sleep

1. Violence associated with confusion on sudden awakening (sleep drunkenness)

This was first described in European literature as *l'ivresse du sommeil* or *Schlaftrunkenheit* (Gudden, 1905; Broughton, 1968). It is characterized by confusion, disorientation and misinterpretation of reality on sudden arousal from deep (stage 3 or 4) slow wave sleep. The sufferer may perform complex actions, generally without leaving the bed, including apparently defending him/herself against attack. The individual is profoundly cognitively impaired in such attacks, and has no subsequent recall for them. Omitting the cases described by Schmidt (1943), in Germany, Pressman identified 10 cases in legal and medical literature in which murder, attempted murder or assault had occurred and details were available of the attack. In all these cases there appeared to be an external trigger – touching in six cases and in four cases a noise, with the victim being close by.

Although it appears to have been accepted that these sleep disorders are independent of psychiatric disorders, there is some evidence that in both men (Lindberg et al., 2003) and women (Lindberg et al., 2006) with personality disorder there is an increased amount of slow wave sleep. Theoretically, this would create increased time at risk for disorders of sleep arousal, but it has not yet been shown that personality disorders are associated with a higher rate of them.

2. Violence associated with sleep-walking

Complex, co-ordinated actions resulting in destruction of surrounding objects, self-injury or injury to others may occur while sleep-walking or after a night terror and have the same pathophysiology as confusional arousal. In such cases, the victim is commonly a spouse (Hopwood and Snell, 1933; Gibbens, 1983; Tarsh, 1986), although in Pressman's (2007) series of 10, just half had attacked a wife, girlfriend or lover. There was little evidence of immediate 'provocation' in these cases; where behaviour had been directly observed, some seemed incompatible with profound cognitive impairment. One man, for example, was not seen repeatedly stabbing his wife, but he was observed some 45 minutes later leaving the scene, fetching a pair of gloves, moving his wife and then holding her head underwater in a pool. Most people in this series were convicted of the crime as charged.

3. Violence associated with night terrors

This has been recognized at least since Simon Fraser's case, described by Yellowlees (1878). Fraser had a history of sleepwalking. He killed his baby son by throwing him against a wall, afterwards reporting a vivid image of a wild beast attacking the child, experiencing himself as defending that child. The jury acquitted him, and he was released after giving an undertaking to sleep alone in future. Night terrors differ from bad dreams, or nightmares, both physiologically and in presentation. As disorders of sleep arousal, night terrors are associated with waking from slow wave sleep, while nightmares occur during REM sleep. A night terror presents simply as a highly arousing image; if the individual is observed, he is plainly terrified. A nightmare is generally a sequence of images. Pressman (2007) identified 11 cases of criminal acts under night terror in the international literature; in three the legal outcome was unknown, but all the rest were acquitted (in one case after appeal).

There may be some overlap between these groups, as night terrors and sleep-walking both arise in slow wave sleep and the two conditions often coexist in the same individual (Kales et al., 1980).

Rapid Eye Movement (REM) Sleep Behaviour Disorder

In normal REM sleep there is paralysis of all skeletal muscles, but in the 1980s, Schenck and colleagues described a disorder of REM sleep in which there is an absence of this expected paralysis, verifiable by simultaneous EEG and EMG recording, and which may be associated with violence (Schenck et al., 1986, 1987; Schenck and Mahowald, 2005). It is often associated with other neurological abnormalities, and tends to occur mainly in older men (90%) (Schenck et al., 1993). It is particularly striking that people who have this problem show no evidence of violence when awake (Fantini et al., 2005). Oudiette and colleagues (2009) have shown that elaborate behaviours other than violence may also occur during sleep.

Earlier literature was mainly about violence and its risk in the event of one of these sleep disorders, but two groups of researchers have focused on atypical sexual behaviour (Guilleminault et al., 2002; Schenck et al., 2007). Guilleminault et al. described ten men and one woman with such difficulties, and were struck that, in spite of the similarity of the clinical presentations, the actual sleep disorders were various, including partial complex seizures, disordered breathing, disorders of arousal from slow wave sleep and disorders of REM sleep. In all but two of the cases, the behaviour was injurious – to the 'perpetrator' as well as the bed partner – but the couples were slow to seek help, the only two cases to be seen at the onset of the problem being those two which involved police intervention. Schenck et al. (2007) conducted a systematic literature review, first noting that none of the Kinsey reports (e.g. Reinisch, 1990) nor the Hite report (1981) covered this area at all. An internet survey (Trajanovic et al., 2006) was reported as attracting 219 respondents, two-thirds of whom were men, and 92% of whom reported multiple episodes of atypical sexual behaviours in sleep, in two-thirds of cases involving the bed partner, and commonly following stress (52%) or fatigue (41%) Alcohol or other drugs were implicated, but more rarely. Schenck and colleagues went on to identify 31 published cases of parasomnias and seven of epilepsy with abnormal sleep related sexual behaviours. They drew on their review to propose a classification encompassing the four categories of parasomnias with abnormal sexual behaviours, sleep related seizures with sexual features, sleep disorders with abnormal behaviours during wakefulness and/or the sleeping-waking transition, and a final group of miscellaneous conditions which could not be fitted into the other three, like cataplexic orgasm in narcolepsy. The abnormal sexual functions observed or reported were commonly confined to exceptional arousal, painful erections, agitation or masturbation, but included complex behaviours and assaults. Four-fifths of the cases were men, mean age 32, but with an onset of the disorders, on average, in their late 20s for men, teens for the women, and duration of problems for a mean of 8 years for the men and 13 for the women.

Assessing Sleep Disorders for Clinical and Legal Purposes

There is consistency in recommendations for a full clinical history from the sufferer, and the bed partner if there is one, as well as physiological measures of sleep and muscular activity, with audiovisual recording, under laboratory conditions to establish the presence, or not, of a sleep disorder. As might be expected in an area in which, as Pressman (2007) points out, proximity to the disordered sleeper may be a factor in precipitating the violence, there is guidance too on safety in the sleep laboratory (Hobby, 2006). There is little reason for history taking to differ between the legal and clinical situations, as it is just as important to understand the behaviour patterns clinically, but it has received most attention in the legal context, where the court has to decide on responsibility for complex behaviours. The Schenck group's guidance (Bornemann et al., 2006) has similarities to Bonkalo's (1974) proposals, but also some differences. Bournemann and colleagues suggest that once having established a *bona fide* sleep disorder the following points are also helpful:

- the onset – generally at least an hour after falling asleep, often with attempts to waken; may be potentiated by alcohol ingestion or sleep deprivation;
- the action – duration generally brief, onset abrupt, and apparently senseless;
- the victim – known or unknown to the sufferer, just happened to be present; may have precipitated arousal;
- level of consciousness – impaired during the action;
- after the action – perplexity, horror where there has been violence, partial or full amnesia.

From a medico-legal point of view, however, Bournemann and colleagues insist that there can be no absolute certainty possible, even with laboratory evidence of sleepwalking, that any given behavioural episode was necessarily the result of sleepwalking. This is reflected in the variability of court verdicts with respect to apparently similar cases already noted.

Management and Treatment of Sleep Disorders

Again, there is consensus in the literature already cited that most sleep disorders are treatable. While specific treatment will depend on the nature of the disorder, the first priority when there has been any report of violence or sexually damaging behaviour is to re-establish safety. In *Fraser,* back in the nineteenth century, an undertaking was required by the court that he would, thereafter, sleep alone; this would probably happen now too. At the least, any potential weapons must be removed from the sleeping environment. It may be advisable that the individual sleeps on the ground floor, with extraneous noise or other intrusions kept to a minimum, possibly with alarms on doors or windows, but certainly with any sleeping partner well aware of potential risks, in particular of waking the sufferer. Potentially exacerbating conditions, such as stress, fatigue or alcohol use, should be removed where possible, and reduced where not. Attention to breathing, and airway maintenance may

be useful; positive airways pressure has been reported as helpful on a single case basis. If seizure disorders have been ruled out, which will require anti-convulsants, clonazepam seems to be the medication of choice whether the disorder lies in slow wave or REM sleep, but psychotherapy, and such techniques as relaxation or even hypnosis have been recommended.

Sleep disorders remain a small but important area of interest for forensic psychiatry. Guidance on their assessment and management seems sensible and has been fairly consistent over time. Knowledge is growing, but, perhaps inevitably as sleep and seriously harmful behaviour are so rarely linked, most of that knowledge is derived from individual cases or quite small case series, so there remains considerable scope for modesty and caution in treating people, or providing reports for the courts, in this field.

AMNESIA AND OFFENDING

When defendants claim amnesia for their alleged crimes, psychiatrists or psychologists may be asked to assess the relevance of this amnesia. Details of the legal issues are covered in chapter 2, but there is a dearth of studies investigating this intriguing form of forgetfulness. More fully reviewed elsewhere (Kopelman, 1987), this situation contrasts with the study of eyewitness testimony, which has re-emerged in the past three decades as a popular topic for scientific enquiry (e.g. Loftus, 1979; Heaton-Armstrong et al., 2006).

Prevalence and Characteristic Features of Amnesia for Offences

Amnesia has been reported most commonly following homicide. Table 12.1 summarizes the rates of amnesia obtained in the principal studies of people convicted of homicide. Between 25% and 45% of such offenders claim amnesia for the killing, but the figures are somewhat higher if partial memory loss is accepted. Bradford and Smith (1979), for example, found that 60% of their cases reported amnesia if 'hazy' memory were included, while Tanay (1969) reported that 70% of his cases were in a 'dissociative state … (involving) … spotty memory'. In addition, in a sample of 88 homicide offenders, psychotic at the time of the offence (Nielssen et al., 2007), the rate of amnesia for the lethal assault was 34% (Neilssen, personal communication).

Pyszora et al. (2003) located the files of 207 of the 233 people sentenced to life imprisonment in England and Wales in 1994, 85% of whom had an index conviction of homicide. Only 3% of the people convicted of rape, arson, acquisitive offences, kidnap or sexual assault reported amnesia for the offence compared with 31.4% of those convicted of murder or manslaughter. Amnesia for the offence was also more common when the victim had been either related to or a partner of the defendant and/or female. There was a trend for it to be more likely when the offender

Table 12.1 Relationship between amnesia for offending and type of offence (Kopelman, 1987)

Study	n (%) in crime category within amnesic groups			
	Fatal violence	Other violence	Non-violent crime	Total n
Hopwood & Snell, 1933, UK high security hospital	90 (90%)	8 (8%)	2 (2%)	100
Lynch & Bradford, 1980, Canada forensic psychiatry service	5 (23%)	13 (63%)	4 (14%)	22
Taylor & Kopelman, 1984, UK remand prisoners	9 (47%)	10 (53%)	0	19

Table 12.2 Relationship between amnesia for offending and type of offence

	Study		
	Hopwood and Snell (1933) Max. security hospital (UK)	Lynch and Bradford (1980) Forensic Psychiatry service (Canada)	Taylor and Kopelman (1984) Remand prison (UK)
Crime	Number and (percentage) of amnesic patients		
Homicide/att. homicide	90 (90%)	5 (23%)	9 (47%)
Other violence	8 (8%)	13 (63%)	10 (53%)
Non-violent crime	2 (2%)	4 (14%)	0 (0%)
Total	100 (100%)	22 (100%)	19 (100%)

Reproduced with permission from Kopelman (1987).

was intoxicated with alcohol, and it was significantly more so when the offender had a history of alcoholic 'blackouts' (alcohol-induced amnesic gaps at other times) than when not. Pyszora and colleagues (in preparation) further examined follow-up data 3 years after conviction. One-third of those who had had amnesia for the offence reported a complete return of memory, 26% a partial return, and 41% no return of memory. Those who recovered memories had had a longer initial amnesic gap and a significantly higher rate of previous alcoholic blackouts, suggesting that partially recovered memories from a period of 'blackout' may be one mechanism resulting in the return of memory. These findings are somewhat similar to those in an earlier follow-up study by Hopwood and Snell (1933) of 100 amnesic offenders in Broadmoor (high security) hospital. They considered 78 to have 'genuine' amnesia, of whom 38% recovered their memories during hospitalization, but amnesia persisted in the remaining 62%. In this study, those who recovered memory of the offence usually did so within 6 months of the crime (range 3 days to 3 years).

Amnesia is also reported after other types of crime. Table 12.2 summarizes results from three studies which reported types of crime associated with amnesia. It appears that violent crime is particularly associated with amnesia, although the definitive prevalence study, examining amnesia rates following a range of offending behaviours, whether or not they come to court, has never been done.

The three studies included in table 12.2 were carried out in very different settings (a secure hospital in Britain, a Canadian forensic psychiatry service, and a British remand prison), yet the association with violent crime was evident in all of them. It has to be emphasized, however, that all three samples were small.

Despite the substantial agreement about the prevalence of amnesia in homicide, and its particular association with violent crime, there is considerable disagreement over the characteristic features of such amnesic episodes (Kopelman, 1987). O'Connell (1960), for example, reported that they are often transitory, whereas Leitch (1948) described a man in whom such amnesia had lasted 'several years', and Bradford and Smith (1979) stated that it was 'permanent' in all their cases. Findings on the duration of the amnesic gap also differed. Leitch (1948) maintained that it 'might cover the whole life of the individual', whereas Bradford and Smith (1979) found that it had lasted less than 24 hours in all their cases, and was less than half an hour in the majority (60%). Pyszora et al. (2012) found it to be from under one minute to several hours. In the latter study, the longer gaps, with greater likelihood of at least partial resolution over time, were more likely in cases of 'alcoholic blackout'.

Principal Factors Associated with Amnesia for Crime

The factors most commonly associated with claims of amnesia are:

1. violence, particularly homicide;
2. extreme emotional arousal;
3. alcohol abuse and intoxication;
4. depressed mood.

(See also Taylor and Kopelman, 1984; Kopelman, 1987, 2002a,b.)

These factors are discussed below.

1. Violence

As already described, amnesia has been reported most commonly in relation to homicide, but it also occurs in a range of other violent crimes. This association with violence may be secondary to the extreme emotional arousal and/or alcohol abuse commonly involved in such offences, and it is intriguing that studies of the victims and eyewitnesses of offences have also revealed that impaired recall is related to the violence of the crime (e.g. Kuehn, 1974; Clifford and Scott, 1978; Yuille and Cutshall, 1986). Mechanic et al. (1998), Bourget and Bradford (1995) and Kaszniak et al. (1988) described amnesic gaps in victims of rape.

2. Extreme emotional arousal

Extreme emotional arousal is important in so-called 'crimes of passion' – homicide cases in which the offence is unpremeditated and unplanned (Hopwood and Snell, 1933; O'Connell, 1960; Bradford and Smith, 1979; Taylor and Kopelman, 1984; Pyszora et al., 2003). In these cases, the victim is usually closely related to the offender. In one series, for example, the victim was a lover, wife, close friend or family member in 88% of the cases (Taylor and Kopelman, 1984). Pyszora et al. (in preparation) found that evidence of peri-traumatic dissociation is common in such cases. There is often an accompanying diagnosis of depression, and occasionally a diagnosis of schizophrenia.

3. Alcohol abuse and intoxication

Various studies have shown that a history of chronic alcohol abuse and/or acute intoxication at the time of the offence is common in people who report amnesia for their offence (see table 12.3). Other drug abuse has also been implicated, although without specifying the types of drugs involved (Bradford and Smith, 1979; Lynch and Bradford, 1980; Petursson and Gudjonsson, 1981; Parwatikar et al., 1985; Pyszora et al., 2003). When homicide is committed during intoxication, the victim seems less likely to be related to the offender than when extreme emotional arousal occurs in the absence of alcohol abuse (Taylor and Kopelman, 1984). Pyszora et al. (2012) showed that dissociative mechanisms may exacerbate the effects of alcohol in producing amnesia and, if so, a past history of alcoholic blackouts, unrelated to an offence, is common.

Goodwin et al. (1969) described three types of memory loss for significant episodes in people hospitalized for alcohol abuse (see also Kopelman, 1987).

i. *State dependent* effects. The affected person cannot remember events or facts when sober; they are easily recalled as soon as s/he is intoxicated again (e.g. where money is hidden).

ii. *Fragmentary blackouts*. The person becomes aware of his/her memory loss on being told of an event later. There are 'islets' of preserved memory, and the amnesia tends to recover partially through time by a shrinking of the amnesic gap, similar to that which occurs in head injury.

iii. *En bloc blackouts*. The person becomes abruptly aware of a memory gap (e.g. on waking up), and s/he describes a sense of 'lost time'. The amnesic gap has a definite starting point, islets of preserved memory are rare, and the memories are very seldom recovered.

Table 12.3 Relationship between alcohol and amnesia for crime: proportions of amnesic and non-amnesic cases with problem drinking

Study	Amnesic cases	Non-amnesic cases
(a) Chronic abuse		
Hopwood and Snell, 1933	38%	N/A[1]
Lynch and Bradford, 1980	72%	N/A[1]
Taylor and Kopelman, 1984	42%	10%
Parwatikar et al., 1985	71%	58%
Pyszora et al., 2003	46%	29%
(b) Intoxicated at time of offence		
O'Connell, 1960	30%	13%
Bradford and Smith, 1979	30%	10%
Taylor and Kopelman, 1984	42%	20%
Parwatikar et al., 1985	87%	42%
Pyszora et al., 2003	61%	43%

[1]N/A: figures not available, no comparison group.

Mild or moderate degrees of persistent memory impairment are sometimes found on standard (anterograde) tests in people claiming amnesia for an offence when alcohol abuse is implicated (Kopelman, 1987). The degree of impairment is consistent with that found in other (non-criminal) alcoholics, and it may be accompanied by a mild or moderate degree of cortical atrophy demonstrable on computerized tomography (CT) or magnetic resonance imaging (MRI) of the brain.

4. Depressed mood

Hopwood and Snell (1933) reported that amnesia occurred 'with some frequency' in states of depression; the precise figure was not given. Using the Minnesota Multiphasic Personality Inventory (MMPI), Parwatikar et al. (1985) reported that 'amnesic' killers showed significantly raised scores on the depression scale in comparison with 'confessed' killers. Two of us (Taylor and Kopelman, 1984) found no overall difference between amnesic and non-amnesic offenders in the rate or type of *ICD-9* psychiatric diagnosis, apart from a raised prevalence of alcohol abuse, but evidence of depressed mood was much more commonly present in the amnesic cases as rated at semi-structured interview (The Comprehensive Psychiatric Rating Scale, Asberg et al., 1978) or on a self-rating scale (The Beck Inventory for Depression, Beck et al., 1961). There was usually evidence that the depressed mood had been present for weeks or months preceding the offence. This association of amnesia with depressed mood in the absence of a clinical diagnosis of depression is consistent with similar findings obtained in studies of fugue states (Kanzer, 1939; Stengel, 1941; Berrington et al., 1956). In the middle-aged and elderly, an association between depression and shoplifting has been described (Gibbens et al., 1971), and people with this combination occasionally claim amnesia for their offences.

Other Psychiatric Disorders and Amnesia for Offending

Psychosis

In the pretrial prisoner study already referred to (Taylor and Kopelman, 1984), a small group of men with schizophrenia was identified who had damaged property during floridly psychotic episodes and who, while not denying the acts, presented accounts of what had happened which were at complete variance with what others had observed. Their trivial acts of aggression and paramnesic accounts could be given little meaning except in terms of their psychoses. Perhaps the phenomena were best described as delusional memories. An additional man was excluded from the study who, out of the blue, presented to police with a convincing confession to a homicide, was held on remand for nearly 2 years while the crime was investigated, but no evidence was ever found to link him with this or any other homicide and, finally, he was freed, unconvicted.

Hysterical personality traits

O'Connell (1960) suggested that claims of amnesia were associated with a hysterical personality, while Parwatikar et al. (1985) reported that amnesic killers showed significantly raised scores on the hysteria and hypochondriasis scales of the MMPI, relative to confessed killers. Gudjonsson et al. (1999) found that high scores and measures of over-controlled hostility and over-control were *not* associated with amnesia. Pyszora et al. (in preparation) found a strong association with evidence of dissociation around the time of the alleged offence, but failed to find any association with a repressive coping style, evidence of post-traumatic stress disorder for the offence, or high shame scores.

A fugue state is a syndrome involving a transient loss of memory and of sense of personal identity accompanied by a period of wandering. A fugue only very exceptionally accounts for amnesia for crime (Schacter, 1986; Kopelman, 1987), but an offence may very occasionally precipitate a fugue (Wilson et al., 1950; Berrington et al., 1956; Kopelman et al., 1994). Instances have occasionally been reported in which the assessment of a fugue is made particularly difficult by the accused having a possible motivation for using such a state as a defence in law.

Brain disorder and amnesia

Although rare, organic brain disorder is an important concomitant of amnesia for crime (Kopelman, 1987). Hopwood and Snell (1933) reported that 20% of their cases had a history of head injury, 12% of previous amnesia, and 9% of epilepsy. In contrast, other studies have failed to find an increased frequency of neurological disorder or EEG abnormalities among amnesic offenders, relative to non-amnesic offenders. O'Connell (1960) attributed one of his 20 amnesic cases to epilepsy and one to hypoglycaemia, but failed to find any organic disorder in the remainder. Bradford and Smith (1979) found no association between amnesia and head injury or EEG abnormalities in their series. In an English pretrial prisoner study (Taylor and Kopelman, 1984), no differences between amnesic and non-amnesic groups were found in terms of a past history of head injury or other neurological disorder. In all these series, however, the amnesic samples were small and the base rates for a medical disorder would have been low. Taken together, they do perhaps indicate that a brain or metabolic disorder may be rare determinants of amnesia for an offence. A full medical and physical assessment remains very important in such cases when providing evidence for the criminal courts because, although amnesia *per se* does not affect the subject's fitness to plead or issues of responsibility in England and Wales, these issues become pertinent when the question of an 'automatism' is raised. For present purposes, an automatism may be defined as 'an abrupt change in behaviour in the absence of conscious awareness or memory formation, associated with certain specific clinical disorders, such as epilepsy, parasomnias, or hypoglycaemia' (Kopelman, 2009; Christianson et al., 2006).

Epilepsy

As already noted, crime can only very rarely be attributed to epileptic automatisms or post-ictal confusion. When this does occur there is always bilateral involvement of the limbic structures involved in memory formation, including the amygdaloid–hippocampal complex and the mesial diencephalon (Fenton, 1972). Hence, amnesia for the period of automatic behaviour is always present and usually complete (Knox, 1968; Fenwick, 1990).

Parasomnias

Somnambulism and REM sleep behaviour disorder are grounds for automatism, and there is typically amnesia for any attack which has occurred during a sleep disorder.

Hypoglycaemia

Any person with diabetes, alcohol intoxication, the 'dumping' syndrome or insulinoma, or abusing insulin may suffer hypoglycaemia. Insulin abuse has been implicated in a number of serious offences, including violent crime against children and the so-called Munchausen syndrome by proxy (Scarlett et al., 1977; Lancet, 1978; see also chapters 9 and 20). When hypoglycaemia results from administration of an external agent such as insulin, unless the administration was deliberate, the case for a 'non-insane' automatism may be argued and, if successful, result in acquittal.

Head injury

When head injury is associated with amnesia for an offence, there is a brief period of retrograde amnesia, which may shrink through time, a longer period of post-traumatic amnesia (PTA), and there may be islets of preserved memory within the amnesic gap (Kopelman, 2002a). Occasionally, there is a particularly vivid memory for images or sounds occurring immediately before the injury, on regaining consciousness, or during a lucid interval before the onset of PTA (Russell and Nathan, 1946). The length of PTA is assumed to reflect the extent of diffuse brain pathology, resulting from rotational forces, and it is predictive of eventual psychiatric, social and cognitive outcome (Lishman, 1968; Brooks, 1984; Fleminger, 2009).

Other brain disorders

Other disorders which produce a discrete or transient episode of memory loss, such as toxic or post-ECT confusional states, transient ischaemic episodes, or the transient global amnesia syndrome are very unlikely to be associated with crime (Kopelman, 1987). This is also true of severe states of chronic amnesia, although occasional instances do occur in cases of mental retardation or dementia (e.g. Brooks et al., 1987), and one of us (MK) has personally been involved in the successful appeal against conviction of a man who was amnesic for his alleged offence because of an alcoholic Korsakoff syndrome.

Authentic Amnesia or Deliberate Malingering?

Many lay observers consider that the amnesia claimed by offenders is a deliberate strategy to try to avoid the legal consequences of their offence. Schacter (1986), for example, declared that 'many claims of amnesia after crimes are simulated,' as did Christianson and Merckelbach (2004; see also Christianson et al., 2006). On the other hand, Hopwood and Snell (1933) conducted a retrospective review of follow-up information in the case notes of 100 high security hospital patients who, at the time of their trials, had claimed amnesia for their offences and concluded that 78% of the amnesias had been 'genuine', 14% had been 'feigned', and 8% were 'doubtful'. In Pyszora et al.'s (2003) follow-up, at 3 years, five (2.4%) of the amnesic offenders were suspected of having feigned their memory loss, and four cases (1.9%) admitted having originally feigned their amnesia. There are a number of reasons for supposing that many cases of amnesia are indeed authentic. The issue may be less clear-cut, however, and perhaps less critical, than it sometimes appears (Kopelman, 1987, 2002b)

First, many amnesic cases have been described in the literature, who have either reported their own crime or have failed to take measures to avoid their capture

(Hopwood and Snell, 1933; Leitch, 1948; Gudjonsson and MacKeith, 1988; Taylor and Kopelman, 1984; Gudjonsson and Taylor, 1985). This makes an account of amnesia as simulation to avoid punishment seem less plausible.

Secondly, factors which have been associated with amnesia in offenders are similar to those which have been implicated in cases of impaired recall by the victims or eyewitnesses of crime, including violent crime, extreme emotional arousal and alcohol intoxication (see e.g. Kuehn, 1974; Clifford and Scott, 1978; Yuille and Cutshall, 1986; Deffenbacher, 1988, Mechanic et al., 1998).

Thirdly, there may not be any distinct demarcation between 'conscious' malingering and 'unconscious' hysteria. O'Connell (1960) favoured the view that the difference between them was a matter of degree rather than kind, and he provided examples of what he called the 'passive disregard' towards their crime, which was evident in the remarks of both amnesic and non-amnesic offenders. One non-amnesic offender, for example, described letting the memory 'drift into the background... like putting something into... a safe and locking it away'. By comparison, people reporting amnesia for the offence described having 'buried everything about [the] case' and feeling that recall was prevented because the memory gets 'all jumbled up again'. Qualitatively similar remarks are sometimes made by patients coming out of a fugue episode, when no offence occurred.

Fourthly, we reiterate that, in England and Wales, amnesia *per se* does not constitute a barrier to trial or a defence (see chapter 2); other problems, perhaps underpinning the amnesia, would have to be identified to support any grounds for automatism or unfitness to plead. Consistent with this, two of us (Taylor and Kopelman, 1984) found that there were no significant differences between amnesic and non-amnesic prisoners in terms of fitness to plead, the types of plea made, or the reasons offered for those pleas, even though not being able to remember an alleged offence may make conducting a defence and instructing one's lawyer more difficult.

Assessment of amnesia and its causes

A detailed interview is essential, with particular attention to the pattern and extent of the amnesic gap, and, if possible, noting how this changes through time. It is particularly important to obtain corroborative evidence about the affected person's behaviour at the time of and after the offence – from all available sources, including the legal documentation, the results of social and probation enquiries, and any available family member or other informant. Any previous episode of amnesia or of an associated condition such as head injury, epilepsy, or other neurological disorder must be noted. Evidence of alcohol or drug abuse should be sought and, if there is any suspicion of current memory impairment, this will require detailed specific neuropsychological and neuropsychiatric investigation.

Various specific techniques have been proposed for differentiating between authentic and feigned amnesia following an alleged crime, to supplement the clinical examination (see Kopelman, 1987; Christianson et al., 2006). Some of these tests, however, such as the *Symptom Validity Test* or the *Structured Inventory of Malingered Symptomatology* (see Christianson and Merckelbach, 2004) have limited applicability for assessing what may be a very brief amnesia occurring in familiar surroundings but in extreme circumstances.

Aside from deliberate simulation, various mechanisms have been proposed to account for amnesia for crime, including repression, dissociation, a failure of initial encoding, an encoding–retrieval interaction, and state-dependent retrieval problems (Kopelman 1987, 2002a,b). The various theories can be grouped into those which place emphasis on the failure of memory at the time of initial encoding, which may be particularly true of those cases in which alcohol is implicated, and those which place emphasis on a failure of memory retrieval, which is possibly more true in cases such as unpremeditated homicide, which take place in a state of extreme emotional arousal. In the present state of knowledge, any theory about the nature of amnesia for crime is bound to be somewhat speculative, and it seems unlikely that any one explanation will cover all cases. As discussed above, Pyszora et al. (2003, 2012) have provided evidence for the importance of dissociative mechanisms or alcoholic blackouts in many cases. The apparent similarity between the factors which produce impaired recall by the victims, eyewitnesses and perpetrators of crime alike is intriguing and should perhaps direct further investigation in the topic.

Summary of Issues in Amnesia for Offending

Amnesia for a homicide is a common claim – 25–45% of cases – but it may also follow other types of violent crime and, occasionally, non-violent crimes. It is particularly associated with states of extreme emotional arousal, alcohol intoxication and depressed mood, and occasionally with episodes of florid psychosis. Overt brain disorder is rarely implicated, but it is essential to identify any medical factor, such as epilepsy, head injury or hypoglycaemia, because of their potential medico-legal importance. In the absence of any claim of automatism, the presence of amnesia carries no legal implications in England and Wales, so the differentiation between 'authentic' and 'feigned' amnesia is not pertinent to determination of responsibility at trial. It is sometimes debated in court with regard to the light this may shed on the defendant's truthfulness in other matters; whether it should be when there is no foolproof test of the differentiation is doubtful. Many people who are amnesic for their offence have either reported the crime themselves or made no attempt to conceal it, which argues against the view that they are simulating in order to avoid punishment. There is evidence for the importance of dissociative mechanisms and alcoholic blackouts, rather than repression or post-traumatic stress disorder being factors underlying such amnesias, but detailed, longitudinal studies are required for further elucidation.

BRAIN IMAGING STUDIES AS A ROUTE TO UNDERSTANDING VIOLENT AND CRIMINAL BEHAVIOUR

The main focus of this section is on observations emerging from structural and functional imaging studies of individuals with schizophrenia and/or personality disorder and/or high scores on the Psychopathy Check List-Revised (PCL-R, Hare, 2003), as these are the psychiatric and psychological difficulties which have been most consistently linked with elevated rates of violence (see chapters 14 and 16); in fact, among people who commit the most serious kind of violence, many are comorbid for psychosis and personality disorder. Where possible, the type of violence will be clarified, specifically the 'reactive' versus the 'instrumental' type (Blair, 2001), or the 'affective' versus the 'predatory' type (Raine et al., 1998a), or the symptom related type, generally delusionally driven (Taylor, 1985b; Taylor et al., 1998). Reactive (or affective) violence is expressed in response to a real or perceived threat or provocation or frustration. The instrumental (or predatory) type, on the other hand, is generally unprovoked, goal-directed, and calculating. Offenders whose violent acts fall mainly under the 'reactive' type are commonly characterized by traits of impulsivity, anger and negative affect, whereas those who mainly, but not necessarily exclusively, engage in violent acts of instrumental type are more likely to be characterized by traits of fearlessness and low anxiety (Patrick, 2006; Herba et al., 2006). For people with psychosis, when the violence is driven by delusions, it is rarely yet entirely clear how that is mediated in these terms, and it may be that both mechanisms apply. Delusions which make people very frightened or anxious are more likely to be associated with violence than those which do not (Buchanan et al., 1993), so violence in such circumstances may well be reactive. Other mechanisms, however, also seem to operate. Delusions are not immutable, and may be elaborated or the intensity of belief changed in response to hypothetical challenge, although little is known about real life social interactions about delusions, or delusional development once established (Taylor, 2006). The person's affective responsiveness may be impaired by such illnesses as schizophrenia, but in some mono-delusional states, the affected individual may consider him or herself to be 'on a mission'. In these last circumstances, it may be appropriate to regard any violence as instrumental.

Violent and Antisocial Behaviour as a Result of Brain Damage

Localized brain injuries provided some of the earliest indicators of which brain structures are particularly involved in modulating aggression. In the mid-nineteenth century, for example, in a rail-road accident, one of the workers, Phineas Gage, had an iron bar driven through the orbitofrontal part of his brain, just over his left eye (Harlow, 1848). Before the accident he had been considered a well-behaved man but, after it, he was socially inappropriate, unrealistic and impulsive despite maintaining apparently normal levels of cognitive functioning (Damasio et al., 1994). Since this case, evidence has mounted that damage to the orbitofrontal region is linked to reduced inhibition and an increased predisposition towards inappropriate violent behaviour, most likely due to misinterpretation of social stimuli and impaired decision-making (Damasio, 1995; Bechara et al., 1997, 1999, 2000; for reviews see Schoenbaum et al., 2006 and Wallis, 2007). In a more recent case, Blair and Cippolotti (2000) also reported damage to the orbitofrontal cortex resulting in violent behaviour as well as impaired facial emotion recognition in a previously non-aggressive individual. Such damage in itself is likely to be linked to violence, but, in addition, the orbitofrontal cortex receives direct input from the thalamus, amygdala, ventral tegmentum and olfactory brain regions and sends output to the amygdala, hippocampus, hypothalamus, cingulate cortex and remaining frontal lobe areas (Weiger and Bear, 1988).

Damage to the prefrontal cortex, made up of the anterior frontal lobes, has also been implicated in violence. Anderson and colleagues (1999) found normal basic cognitive abilities but impaired social behaviour, insensitivity to future consequences of decisions, defective autonomic responses to punishment contingencies, and failure to respond to behavioural interventions in two patients who had suffered early damage to the ventromedial/lateral area of the prefrontal cortex specifically. One patient had been run over by a vehicle at age 15 months and the other had undergone resection of a right frontal tumour at age 3 months. Their actions and their defective social and moral reasoning resembled those of high scorers on the PCL-R. Severely impaired decision-making and inappropriate social behaviour have also been observed in patients with adult-onset prefrontal cortex damage, although retaining factual knowledge of social conventions and moral rules (for a review, see Grafman, 1995).

It is now recognized that the prefrontal cortex is involved in planning, organizing and forming strategy and integrating working memory and attention in order to form, collectively, the higher executive cognitive functions (Miller and Cohen, 2001). Its ventrolateral part is considered specific for the processes governing impulse control and behavioural inhibition (Sakagami et al., 2006; Sakagami

and Pan, 2007). The prefrontal cortex also has strong connections to the limbic regions and, together with the limbic system, forms a complex circuit that has been implicated in various aspects of emotion, affective style and emotion regulation (Phillips et al., 2003). Dysfunctions within this circuit are considered to constitute the neural substrates of violence (Davidson et al., 2000).

Measurements of brain abnormalities as correlates of violent and antisocial behaviour

Computerized tomography (CT) studies

A number of earlier studies used computerized tomography (CT), also known as computerized axial tomography (CAT), to compare groups of sexual offenders with non-violent, non-sexually offending, control individuals. This technique employs multiple radiographic images through slices of the brain, providing a moderately non-intrusive technique for creating images of its structures. About half of these studies showed temporal lobe reduction in sex offenders, especially if violent (for a review see Bassarath, 2001).

Other such studies focused on structural anomalies in relation to violence and/or aggression. Tonkonogy (1991) investigated a group of 14 violent patients and found a local lesion in the anterior–inferior temporal lobes of five of them. He speculated that the loss of amygdaloid nuclei or adjacent neural structures, along with the kindling of the remaining limbic regions, contributes to violence. Wong and colleagues (1994) carried out a retrospective records study of all brain investigations done for clinical reasons with 372 male high security hospital psychiatric patients; 77 had had CT scans, of which 27 (35%) were abnormal. Ratings on the Gunn–Robertson scale (Gunn and Robertson, 1976), allowing for frequency and seriousness of violence, placed their sample in three groups of high, medium and low pre-admission violence. Over half of the 22 men with CT scans in the most violent group had abnormal scans, compared with 30% in the moderate group and a fifth (3/15) in the least violent group. Where damage was localized, it was generally to the temporal lobe (9, 41% in the high group; 3, 7.5% in the moderate group; 1, 6.4% in the least violent group). This is likely to be an underestimate of problems, given that Chesterman and colleagues (1994) failed to detect brain abnormalities on the CT of 10 male patients in the same hospital, but six of these were found to have atrophy in the mesial temporal lobe when investigated using magnetic resonance imaging (MRI) (see table 12.4). Finally, a CT study by Herzberg and Fenwick (1988) detected no differences between 14 aggressive and 17 non-aggressive patients with temporal lobe epilepsy.

Overall, CT studies reveal a weak association between temporal lobe abnormalities and violence, and show little else. Clinical experience in forensic mental health units is that they are generally reported as normal. CT scans are susceptible to bone artefacts and limited to a two dimensional space. This imaging modality is clearly not sensitive enough, even as a research tool, to detect anomalies that are likely to be present in the temporal or other regions of the brain among people with a history of violence.

Magnetic resonance imaging (MRI) studies

The main observations from MRI studies with people who have been violent are summarized in table 12.4. Apart from Chesterman et al. (1994); Wong et al. (1997a); Aigner et al. (2000); Barkataki et al. (2006) and Hoptman et al. (2006), their focus is on men with antisocial personality disorder

Table 12.4 Summary of main magnetic resonance imaging (MRI) investigations in violent/antisocial samples

Study	Sample and diagnoses	Main observations
Chesterman et al. (1994)	10 male high security hospital psychiatric inpatients (6 with schizophrenia, 4 personality disorder)	6 of 10 patients had mesial temporal lobe atrophy.
Wong et al. (1997a)	39 high security hospital men with schizophrenia, of whom 20 with history of repeated violent offending 19 with one serious violent offence	Asymmetrical gyral patterns at the temporo-parietal region present in most recidivist violent offenders and absent in the single violent offenders. Non-specific white matter changes present in both groups.
Aigner et al. (2000)	82 mentally ill but not psychotic male offenders (50 sex offenders), divided into low and high violent group	The scans were coded according to presence or absence of brain abnormality. 49% of the sample had MRI abnormalities. A significantly higher percentage of patients in the high violent group (65.5%) showed MRI abnormalities than in the low violent group (16.6%). No significant difference in MRI abnormality rate between sex offender and non-sex offender groups.
Raine et al. (2000)	21 men with ASPD 21 men without ASPD matched for comorbid psychiatric disorders, including schizophrenia, anxiety, depression and other PD 26 men with substance dependence disorders but not ASPD 34 healthy men with none of these disorders	Serious violent crimes were four times more likely in the ASPD group. Arrests were almost five times more likely than among healthy men and just under twice as likely as among substance misusing men. ASPD men showed an 11.0% reduction in prefrontal grey matter compared with healthy men, 13.9% reduction compared with substance-dependent men and 11.0% reduction compared with psychiatric controls.
Laakso et al. (2001)	18 habitually violent male offenders with ASPD and type 2 alcoholism	Strong negative correlations, up to −0.79, found between PCL-R scores and volume of the posterior half of the hippocampi, bilaterally.
Laakso et al. (2002)	24 non-psychotic, violent men with ASPD and type 2 alcoholism 33 healthy male controls	Significantly smaller dorsolateral, orbitofrontal, and medial frontal volumes on the left in ASPD men, but difference became non-significant after controlling for differences in education and duration of alcoholism.
Dolan et al. (2002)	18 impulsive-aggressive male patients with personality disorder 19 healthy male controls	20% reduction in temporal lobe volumes in PD group compared to healthy men. No significant difference in frontal lobe volume, but impairments in executive function.
Raine et al. (2003)	15 ASPD men, PCL-R score mean 30 (sd = 5) 25 healthy men, PCL-R score mean 11 (sd = 3)	The ASPD group showed a 22.6% increase in estimated callosal white matter volume, 6.9% increase in callosal length, 15.3% reduction in callosal thickness, and increased functional inter-hemispheric connectivity compared with the healthy men.
Raine et al. (2004)	16 'unsuccessful male psychopaths' (male offenders) 12 'successful male psychopaths' (unconvicted men with high PCL-R scores) 23 healthy male controls	'Unsuccessful psychopaths' had an exaggerated anterior hippocampal asymmetry (right v. left) relative both to 'successful psychopaths' and healthy controls.
Yang et al. (2005)	16 'unsuccessful male psychopaths' 13 'successful male psychopaths' 23 healthy male controls	'Unsuccessful psychopaths' (higher total and subfactor scores), but not 'successful psychopaths', had a 22.3% reduction in prefrontal grey matter volume compared with controls.

(Continued)

Table 12.4 (*Continued*)

Study	Sample and diagnoses	Main observations
Barkataki et al. (2006)	13 men with ASPD and serious violence history 13 men with schizophrenia and serious violence history 15 men with schizophrenia, no violence history, 15 healthy non-violent men	The ASPD group, relative to the healthy group, had reductions in whole brain and temporal lobe volumes as well as increases in putamen volume. Both schizophrenia groups, regardless of violence history, had increased lateral ventricle volume; the violent schizophrenia group had further abnormalities, including reduced whole brain and hippocampal volumes and increased putamen size.
Hoptman et al. (2006)	49 patients with schizophrenia assessed on measures of aggression (43 men, 6 women)	Larger caudate nucleus volumes were associated with aggressive behaviour ratings. This association was independent of effects due to age, alcohol use or substance use disorders.
de Oliveira-Souza et al. (2008)	15 ASPD patients (8 men, 7 women) with PCL: SV scores of 18 or above 15 healthy controls (8 men, 7 women)	The patient group, relative to the control group, had grey matter reductions in the frontopolar, orbitofrontal and anterior temporal cortices, superior temporal sulcus and the insula. The degree of structural abnormalities was associated with the interpersonal/affective dimension of psychopathy.
Müller et al. (2008)	17 men with PCL-R score >28 (mean=33.3, sd=4.06) 17 men with PCL-R score <10	The high-score PCL-R group, relative to the control group, had grey matter reductions in frontal and temporal brain regions, most strongly in the right superior temporal gyrus.
Tiihonen et al. (2008)	26 persistently violent men with ASPD and substance dependence, PCL-R score ≥ 21 25 control non-violent men	The violent group, relative to the control group, had markedly larger white matter volumes, bilaterally, in the occipital and parietal lobes, and in the left cerebellum, and larger grey matter volume in right cerebellum. Within the violent group no association between volumes of these areas and PCL-R scores, substance abuse, psychotropic medication, or global IQ scores. The violent group also showed grey matter reductions bilaterally in the postcentral gyri, frontopolar cortex, and orbitofrontal cortex. Offenders with high PCL-R scores showed the strongest reductions in these areas.
Yang et al. (2009)	27 individuals with mean PCL-R score 27.96 (range 23–40), 32 controls, mean PCL-R score 10.56 (range 5–14)	High PCL-R scorers showed significant bilateral reductions (left, 17.1%; right, 18.9%) in the amygdala compared with controls. Significant correlations between reduced amygdala volumes and increased PCL-R scores, with strongest correlations for the affective and interpersonal facets of 'psychopathy'.

ASPD, Antisocial personality disorder; MRI, Magnetic resonance imaging.

(ASPD) and/or 'psychopathy'. The Chesterman et al. study included men with ASPD as well as schizophrenia, but it was small, and its main aim was to test for congruence between findings according to different measures of brain structure and function among people with major mental disorder who were also seriously violent. Wong et al. and Aigner et al. focused exclusively on men with mental illness, in the former case schizophrenia or schizo-affective disorder but in the latter only non-psychotic illnesses. Only Barkataki and colleagues had psychosis and personality disordered groups.

Raine and colleagues (2000) compared prefrontal grey and white matter volumes in men with ASPD, who had higher violence and arrest rates than the other groups, with those in healthy men, men with lifetime diagnoses of substance abuse but no ASPD, and men with axis I disorders (see table 12.4). Prefrontal grey matter volumes were significantly reduced in the ASPD group relative to all other groups. They suggested that this prefrontal deficit is an underlying factor in reduced arousal, lack of conscience and the cognitive impairments that are typically associated with ASPD. Dolan and colleagues (2002), however, found no difference in the frontal lobe volumes of impulsive-aggressive men with personality disorder relative to healthy controls, although smaller temporal lobes were reported in the former. In an earlier study, Laakso and colleagues (2001) tested for relationships between PCL-R scores and brain measures within a sample of men with ASPD and type 2 alcoholism, and found that posterior hippocampal volumes were smaller, the higher the psychopathy score. Their later study, however, emphasizes the importance of a control group in such studies (Laakso et al., 2002). In a slightly expanded sample they found that such differences disappeared when they controlled for education and duration of alcoholism. Raine and associates (2003) focused on corpus callosum abnormalities. They found that men with ASPD and high PCL-R scores had a number of differences from healthy control men, with increased callosal volume and length, but decreased thickness reflected in increased interhemispheric connectivity. They considered these abnormalities to reflect atypical neurodevelopment. More recent studies (de Oliveira-Souza et al., 2008; Müller et al., 2008; Tiihonen et al., 2008; Yang et al., 2009) have shown lower grey matter volumes in the frontal, temporal and limbic regions in individuals with high PCL-R scores. One of these studies (Müller et al., 2008) also found larger grey matter volumes in posterior brain areas which, according to the researchers, may reflect atypical neurodevelopmental processes that cause early-onset persistent antisocial behaviour.

Raine and colleagues (2004) compared structural MRI findings between 'unsuccessful male psychopaths' (men convicted of offences) with their 'successful psychopathic' peers and healthy men. The results are somewhat difficult to interpret, as there were no main effects. After a series of analyses to examine and compare parts of the hippocampus separately, however, they concluded that the 'unsuccessful psychopaths' had significant hippocampal asymmetry compared with the other two groups – a slight decrease in left anterior hippocampal volume and a slight corresponding increase on the right. They considered this effect to reflect an underlying neurodevelopmental abnormality that disrupts hippocampal–prefrontal circuitry, and causes affect dysregulation, poor fear conditioning and insensitivity to environmental cues signalling danger and capture. Yang et al. (2005) studied these men further, but found the cerebral differences to rest in markedly reduced prefrontal grey matter volume in the 'unsuccessful psychopath' group compared with controls. These cerebral deficits were associated with subfactor PCL-R scores (arrogant/deceptive, affective, and impulsive/unstable) as well as total score.

A study from our group (Barkataki et al., 2006) observed reductions in whole brain and temporal lobe volumes as well as increases in putamen volume in men with ASPD and a history of violence, relative to healthy controls. Men with schizophrenia with and without a history of violence showed increased lateral ventricle volume, but further abnormalities including reduced whole brain and hippocampal volumes and increased putamen volume characterized the men with schizophrenia and a violence history. While a number of previous investigations have associated fronto-temporal abnormalities with violence and ASPD or psychopathy, this study, for the first time, linked putamen enlargement to violence history, regardless of diagnosis. We believe this abnormality to be related to impulsivity and poor behavioural control in the violent groups, given the established role of the putamen in inhibitory circuits and mechanisms (Garavan et al., 2002). Another group (Hoptman et al., 2006) has recently reported a significant association between increased caudate volume and higher ratings of aggression in a sample of 47 treatment-resistant patients with schizophrenia or schizoaffective disorder. They had a different view, however, of reasons for this. They considered the iatrogenic effects of long-term treatment with typical antipsychotics or a direct effect of the schizophrenic processes on the caudate.

Structural imaging studies published so far thus most consistently implicate frontal and/or temporal/hippocampal volume reductions in violent men, although abnormalities of the corpus callosum and basal ganglia have also been detected. Mechanisms whereby these reductions come about remain speculative, with some researchers considering them to represent developmental abnormalities and other discovering that their findings are confounded by substance misuse. These possibilities need not be mutually exclusive. Sample sizes are small and tend to be highly selected, whether from security hospitals, correctional samples or special work projects. Women are much less likely than men to be convicted of serious violence, and it is notable that all the work so far has been done with men, except for the study by de Oliveira-Souza et al. (2008). Nothing at all is known about the female brain in the context of violence, with or without mental disorder.

Diffusion tensor imaging

Diffusion tensor imaging (DTI) is offering greater insights into the human brain than that afforded by traditional MRI studies. The mean diffusivity and fractional anisotropy measures provided by this technique yield information about the underlying tissue properties of grey and white matter. In addition, three-dimensional fibre tractography based on DTI allows the study of connections between neurons in the human brain. This technique, however, is yet to be applied to examine causes and correlates of violent behaviour. One relevant DTI study, by Hoptman and colleagues (2002), confirmed that impulsivity and aggression were related to inferior frontal dysfunction in 14 male patients with schizophrenia. The patients showed altered white matter infrastructure and impaired connectivity between the frontal lobes and other cerebral structures. A more recent study (Craig et al., 2009) showed reduced fractional anisotropy in the uncinate fasciculus of nine men with high PCL-R scores (mean 28.4, range 25–34) compared with nine age- and IQ-matched controls with low scores on the PCL-SV.

Magnetic resonance spectroscopy

Magnetic resonance spectroscopy (MRS) is another newer, complex neuro-imaging technique, allowing reliable and reproducible quantification of brain neurochemistry. In the only relevant study so far, Critchley et al. (2000) first examined concentrations and ratios of N-acetyl aspartate (NAA), creatine phosphocreatine and choline-related compounds in the prefrontal cortex of 10 violent inpatients and eight controls, and then these ratios in the amygdalo–hippocampal complex of 13 violent inpatients with mild mental retardation and 14 non-violent inpatient or staff controls from the same hospital. The violent patients had lower prefrontal concentrations of NAA and creatine phosphocreatine and a lower ratio of NAA/creatine phosphocreatine in the amygdala and hippocampus compared with the controls, covarying for age and IQ. Critchley et al. further observed a strong correlation ($r=-0.72$) between frequency of observed violence to others and (lower) frontal lobe NAA concentration. These observations are consistent with most previous structural imaging evidence in showing that integrity of the prefrontal and medial temporal lobes may be compromised in violent groups. Both their regional specificity and generalizability to others, including people with personality disorder or schizophrenia, remain to be confirmed.

Positron emission tomography and single photon emission tomography studies

Positron emission tomography (PET) relies on a radioactive tracer. A scanner detects radioactivity as positron emitters build up in different parts of the brain/body. Single photon emission tomography (SPET) is similar in principle, but the photon emitters are from isotopes with a larger half-life, and so more practical. Single photon emission computed tomography (SPECT) allows the creation of a three-dimensional image. Both SPET and SPECT studies have confirmed abnormalities in the prefrontal cortex of seriously violent and/or antisocial people with personality disorders, and extend research into functional analysis. Prefrontal cortex dysfunction probably predisposes to criminal behaviour through impairments in fear conditioning, stress responsivity, arousal regulation, planning and impulse control (Brower and Price, 2001). Prefrontal cortex dysfunction is, however, not the only functional abnormality found, as shown in table 12.5. Raine et al. (1994) found lower glucose metabolism in lateral and medial areas of the prefrontal cortex in people charged with murder than in controls, but no differences between the groups in the posterior frontal, temporal or parietal lobes, although their offender sample was heterogeneous. Other studies have revealed temporal lobe hypoperfusion and dysfunction in association with violent and antisocial behaviour, mainly in the context of Alzheimer's disease or dementia (Hirono et al., 2000; Lancôt et al., 2004).

Raine et al. (1998a) raise important possibilities in suggesting that (a) excessive subcortical activity may predispose people to aggressive impulses and (b) predatory, but not affective, 'murderers' may have sufficiently good prefrontal cortex functioning to control these aggressive impulses. They also consider that brain abnormalities may be a stronger predictor of psychopathy in people with little or no history of psychosocial adversity (Raine et al., 1998b).

Functional magnetic resonance imaging studies

With the advent of functional magnetic resonance imaging (fMRI), researchers began to probe in greater detail

Table 12.5   Summary of main positron emission tomography (PET) and single photon emission computed tomography (SPECT) investigations of violent and antisocial samples

Study	Sample and diagnoses	Main observations
Volkow and Tancredi PET (1987)	4 psychiatric patients with a history of repetitive purposeless violent behaviour	Metabolic abnormalities in the left temporal lobe (all cases). Frontal dysfunction in two cases.
Goyer et al. PET (1994)	12 men; 5 women with personality disorder (6 antisocial, 6 borderline, 2 dependent and 3 narcissistic) 43 controls	Within the patient group there was a significant negative correlation between life-long aggressive impulse difficulties and regional cerebral metabolic rates of glucose in the frontal cortex.
Raine et al. PET (1994)	20 male and 2 female mentally ill offenders accused of murder 22 age- and sex-matched controls	Significantly lower glucose metabolism in the lateral and medial prefrontal cortex (PFC) in offenders relative to controls while performing a continuous performance task. No group differences in posterior frontal, temporal, or parietal glucose metabolism.
Volkow et al. PET (1995)	8 male psychiatric patients with a history of repetitive violence 8 healthy male controls	Lower relative metabolic values in the prefrontal and medial temporal lobe in 7 of 8 patients relative to controls.
Amen et al. SPECT (1996)	40 violent adolescents and adults (30 males, 10 females) (physical attack on another person or property) 40 psychiatric patient controls with no reported aggressive behaviour	The violent group showed significantly different activity from the control group in several brain areas, including reduced activity in the PFC, increased activity in the anteromedial areas of the frontal lobes, increased activity in the left-sided basial ganglia and/or limbic system relative to the whole brain, and focal abnormalities in the left temporal lobe.
Intrator et al. SPECT (1997)	8 males with PCL-R scores of 25 and above 9 male substance abusers (PCL-R 17 or below) 9 healthy male controls, PCL-R unspecified	High scorers on the PCL-R showed greater relative activation in fronto-temporal, medial frontal and contiguous subcortical regions during the processing of emotional words than low PCL-R scorers and controls.

Table 12.5   (*Continued*)

Study	Sample and diagnoses	Main observations
Raine et al. PET (1997)	41 people charged with murder (39 men, 2 women), pleading NGRI 41 age- and sex-matched controls	Murder charge cases showed reduced glucose metabolism in the prefrontal, superior parietal gyrus, left angular gyrus, and the corpus callosum compared with controls during the continuous performance task and abnormal asymmetries of activity (left < right) in the amygdala, thalamus, and medial temporal lobe.
Wong et al. PET (1997b)	31 male schizophrenia patients (17 with multiple violent offences and 14 with one previous offence) 6 healthy, non-violent controls	Reduced glucose uptake in left and right anterior inferior temporal regions in single serious offence cases, but only left anterior inferior temporal region in recidivist cases.
Seidenwurm et al. PET (1997)	6 men and 1 woman with histories of extreme violence 9 non-violent controls (all women)	Lower temporal lobe metabolism in the violent group relative to the non-violent group. Medial temporal lobe metabolism was 39% lower than that in the occipital cortex in the violent group but only 27% lower in non-violent group.
Raine et al. PET (1998a)	15 affective (impulsive) 'murderers' 6 'predatory murderers' 41 controls	Affective (impulsive) murderers had lower prefrontal activity and higher subcortical activity than controls. 'Predatory murderers' had activity levels similar to controls, but had greater subcortical activity.
Raine et al. PET (1998b)	As in Raine et al. (1997) 41 people charged with murder (39 men, 2 women) pleading NGRI 41 age- and sex-matched controls	Those charged with murder *without* a history of psychosocial deprivation had significantly lower prefrontal glucose metabolism than those with psychosocial deprivation and than controls.
Soderstrom et al. SPECT (2000)	21 non-psychotic impulsive-type violent offenders (20 men, 1 woman) 11 controls (8 men, 3 women)	Violent offenders, with or without medication or history of substance abuse or head trauma, had reduced regional cerebral blood flow in the temporal and frontal regions relative to controls. Unexpectedly, there was also increased regional cerebral blood flow in the parietal association cortices in the violent group.
Söderström et al. SPECT (2002)	32 violent offenders (29 men, 3 women) (not included in Söderström et al., 2000) 11 controls (8 men, 3 women)	Offenders showed hypoperfusions of the right hippocampus and angular gyrus compared to controls. Significant negative correlations occurred between interpersonal facets of the PCL-R and frontal and temporal perfusion.
Nakano et al. SPECT (2006)	22 patients (14 men, 6 women) with fronto-temporal dementia (FTD) 76 healthy controls (37 men, 39 women)	FTD patients, relative to controls, had reduced regional cerebral blood flow in widespread frontal cortical areas. Antisocial behavioural symptoms were associated with reduced regional cerebral blood flow in the orbitofrontal cortex.

into dysfunction of the areas implicated by earlier studies, mainly the prefrontal cortex and the limbic regions and, perhaps more importantly, to examine impaired functional connectivity between these regions as causes and correlates of violence. The findings of relevant studies published so far are shown in table 12.6. Most of them have focused on emotion processing and fear conditioning deficits in samples with ASPD and/or high PCL-R scores, many motivated, at least in part, by the 'violence inhibition mechanism' (VIM) hypothesis proposed by Blair (1995). According to this hypothesis, in a parallel with submission displays in animals, display of distress by a person who is being attacked is thought to play a central role in limiting aggressive behaviour by the attacker. During normal development, individuals can mentalize – create internal images referenced from personal experience – and empathize with the role of the one in distress. Blair (1995) argues that '...

representations formed through role taking will become, through classical conditioning, trigger stimuli for VIM.' The further hypothesis is that there is disruption to this system among people with high PCL-R scores, such that distress of a victim does not trigger the VIM (Blair, 2001).

Schneider et al. (2000) used an aversive conditioning paradigm to compare men with ASPD and high PCL-R scores with healthy male controls. During fMRI, the researchers presented them with two unconditioned stimuli (US) (US–: neutral room air, and US+: smell of rotten yeast) and two conditioned stimuli (CS) (CS–/+: both neutral faces). Both groups rated the CS paired with the US+ negatively as indicated by subjective ratings of the emotional valence attributed to the neutral faces. The CS paired with the US– maintained its neutral rating. Their fMRI examinations were of the amygdala, hippocampus, thalamus, cingulate gyrus, orbitofrontal cortex, dorsolateral prefrontal cortex, and

303

Table 12.6 Summary of main functional magnetic resonance imaging (fMRI) investigations of violent and antisocial samples

Study	Sample and diagnoses	Main observations
Schneider et al. (2000)	12 male patients with ASPD 12 healthy male controls	ASPD group showed signal increases, relative to controls, who showed signal decreases, in the amygdala and dorsolateral prefrontal cortex (PFC) during the acquisition phase of an aversive conditioning paradigm.
Kiehl et al. (2001)	8 criminal men, PCL-R score 32.8 (sd 2.9) 8 criminal men, PCL-R score 16.6 (sd 6) 8 healthy male controls	High PCL-R scorers showed significantly less activity in the amygdala/hippocampal formation, ventral striatum, and anterior and posterior cingulate, but more activity in the frontotemporal cortex compared to low PCL-R scoring criminals and controls during an affective memory task.
Veit et al. (2002)	4 men with mean PCL-R score 25.30 (sd 7.04); 3 of these met DSM-IV criteria for ASPD 4 men with social phobia 6 healthy male controls	The healthy group showed differential activation in the limbic–prefrontal circuit (orbitofrontal cortex, insula, anterior cingulate, and amygdala) during the differential aversive delay conditioning with neutral faces as conditioned stimuli and painful pressure as unconditioned stimuli. High PCL-R scoring men displayed brief amygdala, but no further brain activity.
Kiehl et al. (2004)	8 criminal male PCL-R score 32.8 (sd 2.9) 8 healthy male controls	High PCL-R scoring men showed poorer behavioural processing of abstract words, and a failure to show appropriate neural differentiation between abstract and concrete stimuli in the right anterior temporal gyrus and surrounding cortex.
Muller et al. (2003)	6 men, PCL-R score 30 6 healthy male controls, PCL-R <10	High PCL-R scoring men showed increased activity to negative pictures in the right-sided prefrontal regions and amygdale and reduced right-sided activity in the subgenual cingulate and the temporal gyrus.
Gordon et al. (2004)	6 male college students with high Psychopathic Personality Inventory (PPI) scores 6 male college students with low PPI scores	The low PPI scoring group showed more activity in the inferior frontal cortex, right amygdala and the medial frontal cortex than the high scoring group during a recognition task that required paying attention to valence of the stimuli, and the opposite in the right dorsolateral prefrontal cortex and the visual cortex.
Birbaumer et al. (2005)	10 men with PCL-R scores above 25 10 healthy male controls	The healthy controls showed enhanced differential activation in the limbic–prefrontal circuit (amygdala, orbitofrontal cortex, insula, and anterior cingulate) during the acquisition of fear and successful verbal and autonomic conditioning, and also conditioned skin conductance and emotional valence ratings; the high PCL-R scorers did not, despite normal contingency and arousal ratings.
Völlm et al. (2004)	8 men with personality disorder (borderline or antisocial) 8 healthy male controls	During a response inhibition task, the healthy men activated mainly the prefrontal cortex, specifically the right dorsolateral cortex and left orbitofrontal cortex; personality disordered men showed a more bilateral pattern of activation across medial, superior and inferior frontal gyri, extending to the anterior cingulate.
Deeley et al. (2006)	6 men with mean PCL-R score 29.33 (range 25–36) 9 healthy non-violent men	The high PCL-R group, relative to the control group, showed less activation in fusiform and extrastriate cortices when processing fearful and happy (relative to neutral) facial emotions. Additionally, the control group showed increased activation but the high PCL-R group decreased activation in the fusiform gyrus when processing fearful (relative to neutral) faces.
Kumari et al. (2006)	10 men with ASPD and serious violence history 13 men with schizophrenia and serious violence history 12 non-violent schizophrenic men 13 healthy non-violent men	Violent schizophrenic men had bilateral frontal and precuneus activation deficits compared to the healthy men, and right inferior parietal deficits compared to non-violent schizophrenia men during a working memory task. Bilateral frontal and especially right inferior parietal activity was inversely associated with violence ratings in all men with schizophrenia. ASPD patients showed activation deficits in the left frontal gyrus, anterior cingulate and precuneus compared with healthy controls.
Joyal et al. (2007)	12 violent men with schizophrenia 12 violent men with schizophrenia and comorbid ASPD and substance use disorder (SUD) 12 non-violent healthy men	Reduced orbitofrontal activation in the schizophrenia +ASPD+SUD group, compared to the two other groups, during the execution of a go/no go task. In addition, higher activation of frontal motor, premotor and anterior cingulate regions in the schizophrenia +ASPD+SUD group than in the schizophrenia-only group.
Barkataki et al. (2008)	14 men with ASPD and serious violence history 12 men with schizophrenia and serious violence history 12 non-violent schizophrenic men 14 healthy non-violent men	Both violent groups, relative to the control group, showed reduced thalamic activity in association with modulation of inhibition by task demands during a Go/No Go task. In addition, the violent schizophrenia group showed reduced caudate activity during the inhibitory inhibition.

Table 12.6   (*Continued*)

Study	Sample and diagnoses	Main observations
Dolan and Fullam (2009)	24 violent men with schizophrenia categorized as high/low scorers relative to the median PCL-SV score of 12.5 (12 men below and 12 men above the median)	Patients with higher PCL-R scores, relative to those with lower PCL-R scores, had reduced amygdala activation during exposure to fearful faces.
Hoptman et al. (2010)	25 patients with schizophrenia or schizoaffective disorder (22 men, 3 women) 21 healthy controls (16 men, 5 women)	The patient group, relative to the control group, showed significant reductions in functional connectivity between the amygdala and ventral prefrontal region. In patients, lower amygdala–ventral prefrontal functional connectivity was associated with higher levels of self-rated aggression (also found for life history of aggression and total arrests).
Kumari et al. (2009)	13 men with ASPD and serious violence history 13 men with schizophrenia and serious violence history 13 non-violent schizophrenic men 14 healthy non-violent men	Violent men with schizophrenia showed exaggerated, whereas violent ASPD patients showed attenuated, thalamic–striatal activity during the latter part of threat-of-shock periods. Violent men with schizophrenia also had the highest, and ASPD men the lowest, level of shock anticipation and fear during the threat-of-shock periods, with intermediate ratings by non-violent schizophrenia and healthy groups.

the occipital cortex. They found more brain activity in the amygdala and the dorsolateral prefrontal cortex during the acquisition phase in the ASPD group, relative to the healthy group. These effects were interpreted as reflecting the additional effort required by the men with ASPD and high PCL-R scores to perform the aversive conditioning task.

Veit and colleagues (2002) also examined aversive conditioning and found evidence of hypo-activity in fronto-limbic regions during emotional learning in men with a mean score of just over 25 on the PCL-R. These men also failed to show skin conductance responses when anticipating the aversive stimuli, consistent with much previous research (Hare, 1998). This also fits with the somatic marker hypothesis (Damasio, 1996), according to which increases in skin conductance would provide feedback that is essential and necessary for emotional responding. More recently, Birbaumer and colleagues (2005) observed activation deficits in the prefrontal–limbic circuit during fear and successful verbal and autonomic conditioning paradigms in men with mean PCL-R scores just below 25, but emotional detachment subscale scores of at least 10.5. They similarly failed to show conditioned skin conductance and emotional valence ratings despite normal contingency and arousal ratings. They suggest that dissociation of emotional and cognitive processing may be the neural basis of failures by male offenders with higher PCL-R scores generally, and emotional detachment specifically, to anticipate aversive events.

Two studies by Kiehl and colleagues (2001, 2004) compared eight male prisoners with PCL-R mean scores of 32.8 (standard deviation [sd] 2.9), with eight who had mean scores of 16.6 (sd 6.0) and eight healthy controls, using lexical decision tasks. In the first study, they examined bilateral amygdala, anterior superior temporal gyrus, left parahippocampal gyrus, anterior and posterior cingulate, ventral striatum, and left inferior frontal gyrus activity. They observed significantly less activity during an affective memory task in the amygdala/hippocampal formation, ventral striatum, and anterior and posterior cingulate, but more activity in the fronto-temporal cortex in convicted men with high PCL-R scores compared with their low-scoring peers and controls. They concluded that the brain systems associated with attentional processing of affective stimuli at the limbic and paralimbic level must be abnormal in high PCL-R scoring men, even though, in this study, they did not show impaired performance. In fact, there was a trend for them to show better recognition of affectively laden than neutral words (Kiehl et al., 2004), they found poorer processing of abstract words in the same men with high PCL-R scores relative to healthy controls, accompanied by a failure to show appropriate neural differentiation between abstract and concrete stimuli in the right anterior temporal gyrus and surrounding cortex. A different research group (Gordon et al., 2004) examined brain activity in groups of male college students with low and high scores on the Psychopathic Personality Inventory (PPI) (Lilienfeld and Andrews, 1996) – so their results are not strictly comparable in terms of participant choice or measure. Nevertheless, during a recognition task that required the participants to pay attention to either the affect or the identity of target stimuli, and using a region of interest approach, they observed significantly more activity in the low relative to the high scoring PPI group in the inferior frontal cortex, right amygdala and the medial frontal cortex. The high scoring group elicited more activity than the low scoring group in the right dorsolateral prefrontal cortex and the visual cortex. In a study by Völlm et al. (2004), using a Go/No Go task requiring response inhibition, a much more extended pattern of frontal activity was seen among men with ASPD or borderline personality disorder (BPD) during the task than in the healthy control group. This may reflect the greater effort required by patients to inhibit a prepotent motor response.

Contradictory findings, however, have been published by Müller et al. (2003), who reported increased right-sided prefrontal and amygdala activity and reduced right-sided subgenual cingulate and temporal gyrus activity when six men with PCL-R scores of over 30 were shown pictures of negative emotions and compared with six men who had scores of under 10. This study, while getting good separation on PCL-R scores, investigated brain activation by contrasting positive and negative pictures rather than negative with neutral pictures in the control condition. The findings are thus difficult to interpret.

Deeley et al. (2006) demonstrated decreased visual cortical responses to fearful faces (relative to neutral faces) in their high PCL-R scoring group, compared to the control group. More recent studies have examined relationships between brain activation patterns and levels of 'psychopathic traits' in the general population (i.e. within the normal range) assessed with instruments such as the PPI. Findings suggest a negative association between the level of PPI scores and activation of the medial prefrontal cortex in response to pictures depicting moral violations among 10 women (Harenski et al., 2009) and in the brain circuitry implicated in deception and related processes, such as behavioural restraint, and social cognition among 24 men (Fullam et al., 2009).

A number of studies have focused on fMRI abnormalities in men with schizophrenia and a history of serious violence. The first of these (Kumari et al., 2006) suggests that bilateral frontal and right inferior parietal dysfunctions are related to a history of violence in schizophrenia, contrasting with dysfunctions of the anterior cingulate among men with ASPD and similar violence histories. Abnormalities of the thalamus, hippocampus and sensorimotor cortex were the common ground in both disorders when associated with violence. Barkataki et al. (2006) examined cognitive deficits in the same sample. Using a Go/No Go task, another research group, Joyal et al. (2007), found reduced orbitofrontal activation in men with schizophrenia and comorbid ASPD and substance use disorder compared with violent men with schizophrenia alone and non-violent healthy men. In addition, there was higher activation in the frontal motor, premotor and anterior cingulate regions in the comorbid schizophrenia groups than the schizophrenia alone group. We also used a variant of the Go/No Go task, finding reduced activation of both the caudate and thalamus in violent men with schizophrenia, but of the thalamus only in violent ASPD men (Barkataki et al., 2008). Dolan and Fullam (2010) demonstrated blunted amygdala responses during exposure to fearful faces in violent men with schizophrenia and high PCL-R scores compared with violent men with schizophrenia but a low PCL-R scores. Hoptman et al. (2010), using resting state fMRI, observed an association between reduced functional connectivity between the amygdala and ventral prefrontal cortex and aggression in patients with schizophrenia. Finally, stronger aversive conditioning was found in men with schizophrenia

and a history of violence than in men with ASPD and a similar violence history, with non-violent men, with or without schizophrenia, falling into an intermediate aversive conditioning range (Kumari et al., 2009). This study also showed opposite patterns of alternations in thalamic–striatal activity in violent men with schizophrenia (enhanced activity) and ASPD individuals (reduced activity) when exposed to threat cues over a sustained period, underscoring the need for differential strategies to manage threat processing (and violent behaviour) in these two disorders.

Overall, the application of fMRI to study violence and criminality has allowed researchers to generate and test specific hypotheses regarding the neural basis of violence and criminality, and results so far appear promising. Of particular note is the consistency in findings of fronto-limbic/paralimbic deficits in association with high PCL-R scores, despite the fact that most of these studies employed somewhat different activation paradigms, had small sample sizes, and that areas such the amygdala and the orbitofrontal cortex are particularly difficult to image.

Conclusions from Imaging Studies

Collectively, imaging studies confirm structural and functional deficits in multiple brain systems among men who are violent and/or criminal. The prefrontal cortex is the most obvious and consistently implicated, as are the limbic and paralimbic systems. Recent imaging studies implicate a number of additional areas such as the thalamus, sensorimotor and parietal regions. A factor here is that these areas had received considerably less attention in earlier studies, and selective imaging, albeit to some extent theory driven, may still be limiting findings. Our own findings suggest that the underlying neural pathology of violence and antisocial behaviour may be somewhat different in schizophrenia and ASPD. Even within the ASPD population, men who get low scores on the psychopathy checklist – perhaps impulsive reactive offenders – may be characterized by a different pattern of brain deficits from that in those with high scores – perhaps the more predatory. All these findings, however, are based on studies with very small numbers of people, who are not invariably offenders. There is undoubtedly more to be learned.

SEROTONERGIC FUNCTION IN AGGRESSIVE AND IMPULSIVE BEHAVIOUR: RESEARCH FINDINGS AND TREATMENT IMPLICATIONS

Both animal and human studies point to the involvement of multiple neurotransmitters in the modulation of aggressive behaviour (for a general review, see Nelson and Trainer, 2007). The most intensely studied neurotransmitter system with regard to impulsivity and aggression is serotonin, chemically known as 5-hydroxytryptamine (5-HT). A substantial number of reports have indicated that central nervous system (CNS) 5-HT function may be altered in suicidal and aggressive/impulsive behaviour. An inverse relationship between 5-HT levels and aggression and/or impulsivity has been shown across a broad range of people, using various behavioural and neurochemical measures. It constitutes one of the most consistent findings in biological psychiatry.

Early evidence of a role for 5-HT in aggression came from animal studies. For example, in rats, lesions to the serotonergic system have been shown to cause highly aggressive behaviour (Grant, 1973). Rats with such lesions were also ineffective in suppressing behaviour which might lead to negative outcomes (punishment) in behavioural tasks (Gray, 1982). In humans, measurement of serotonergic function has been more restricted because of the invasive nature of some of the techniques for doing so. Approaches to the study of 5-HT function in humans are described below, followed by a review of the evidence on 5-HT dysfunction in impulsive and aggressive behaviour, and an appraisal of imaging studies which have specifically and significantly contributed to understanding of how 5-HT may exert its modulatory role. This section concludes with illustrative evidence for effective treatments using serotonergic drugs.

Measuring Serotonergic Function in Humans

Serotonin/5-HT is synthesized from L-tryptophan, an essential amino acid, and degraded to 5-hydroxy-indole acetic acid (5-HIAA) by the enzyme monoamine oxidase-A (MAO-A). Serotonin-containing cell bodies are located in brain nuclei in the midbrain and in the brainstem. From here, serotonergic neurons project widely to other regions of the brain. After being released from the presynaptic cell into the synaptic cleft, serotonin exerts its effects through a number of different postsynaptic receptor subtypes, or is transported back into the presynaptic cell via the 5-HT transporter (5-HTT) (Arbuthnott, 1998).

5-HT may now be studied in humans in life as well as after death. Post-mortem brain studies are plagued by the rapid alteration in neurotransmitter levels that follows death (Oquendo and Mann, 2000). In vivo studies include measures of peripheral and central serotonergic activity (Cocarro and Kavoussi, 1996). Peripheral measures are minimally invasive but may not accurately reflect central 5-HT activity. 5-HT receptor structure, however, is similar in platelets to that in neurons, so platelets provide a suitable model for studying serotonergic binding sites in living people (Callaway et al., 2005). Other peripheral measures include blood levels of tryptophan and serotonin while central 5-HT function has been evaluated in life by measuring concentrations of the serotonin metabolite 5-HIAA in cerebrospinal fluid (CSF) (Cocarro et al., 1997a).

Neuroendocrine challenge studies with selected pharmacological agents allow assessment of responsivity of specific neurotransmitter systems. Fenfluramine, for example, releases 5-HT and blocks its presynaptic reuptake, thereby indirectly stimulating postsynaptic 5-HT receptors. This challenge results in an increased release of the hormones prolactin and cortisol due to receptor stimulation in the limbic–hypothalamic system, which can be seen as a window of overall neurotransmitter function in the brain (Cherek and Lane, 1999). Changes in plasma levels of these hormones can easily be measured in the blood, but these techniques are somewhat limited due to the non-selective nature of some of the stimulant agents employed and their inability to differentiate between pre- and postsynaptic 5-HT function and to localize dysfunction to specific brain parts.

Serotonin levels can also be manipulated using a tryptophan free diet, resulting in decreased 5-HT synthesis (acute tryptophan depletion; ATD) (Reilly et al., 1997). Pharmacological challenge studies and ATD have the advantage that they allow manipulation of serotonin levels and subsequent observation of changes in state measures with performance on neuropsychological tests. More recently brain imaging methods have been employed to measure 5-HT receptor density as well as changes in brain activations during specific tasks following pharmacological 5-HT challenges (see below).

Studies of Peripheral Serotonergic Function

Greenberg and Coleman (1976) provided the first evidence for an inverse relationship between whole blood 5-HT and hyperactivity and/or aggression in a sample of patients with intellectual disabilities. Similar correlations have been described in patients with episodic behavioural problems (Brown et al., 1989), juvenile delinquents (Golubchik et al., 2009) and children of alcoholic parents (Twitchell et al., 1998). By contrast, others have found higher blood serotonin levels to be associated with hyperactivity (Cook et al., 1995), ratings of behavioural disturbance in adolescent offenders (Pliszka et al., 1988; Unis et al., 1997) or aggression scores in depressed patients with comorbid personality disorder (PD) (Mann et al., 1992). Moffitt et al. (1998) studied whole blood 5-HT in New Zealand's Dunedin birth cohort, and reported that higher 5-HT levels were related to violence in men but not women. These results are difficult to interpret, as the relationship between blood and brain serotonin levels is unclear, but they appear to be inversely related (e.g. Mann et al., 1992). It has been postulated that variations in 5-HT transport from plasma into platelets or neurons may account for this. Zhou et al. (2006) studied blood 5-HT levels in violent Chinese men. Consistent with previous research, they reported increased plasma 5-HT levels compared to the healthy control sample, but these levels did not correlate with personality traits or performance on an aggression paradigm. The authors suggested that raised 5-HT levels might represent a compensatory rather than a causal mechanism in violent individuals.

Paroxetine and imipramine are selective serotonin reuptake inhibitors (SSRIs) and antidepressants. Reduced numbers of paroxetine and imipramine binding sites (i.e. binding to the 5-HTT) on platelets, and significant inverse correlations between binding sites and measures of aggression and impulsivity, have been described in children with conduct disorder and ADHD (Stoff et al., 1987; Oades et al., 2002; Stadler et al., 2004), outpatients with episodic aggression (Brown et al., 1989), adolescents with schizophrenia (Modai et al., 1989), patients with personality disorder and a history of self-mutilation (Simeon et al., 1992) and various samples of patients with mixed personality disorders (Cocarro et al., 1995, 1996a,b, 1997a,b). These studies have been almost exclusively conducted with boys or men. There is only one study reported of a sample of women with borderline personality disorder (BPD) (Ng et al., 2005); reduced platelet paroxetine binding was found but 5-HT function did not correlate with self-reported impulsivity.

Contrary to the relationship between measures of aggression or impulsivity and presynaptic 5-HT binding sites, most authors have reported an opposite relationship with postsynaptic 5-HT$_{2A}$ receptor binding. This observation was first made by Marazziti and Conti (1991) in aggressive psychiatric patients. In patients with mixed PD diagnoses, Cocarro et al. (1997b) reported a correlation between the density of 5-HT$_{2A}$ platelet binding sites and self-reported aggression. The authors suggested that this might reflect genetically driven adaptation of postsynaptic receptors associated with low presynaptic 5-HT function.

Cerebrospinal Fluid (CSF) Studies

CSF studies are invasive, and have not survived into the twenty-first century. Older literature on CSF studies indicated a robust inverse relationship between CSF 5-HIAA levels and measures of aggression, whether scores on aggression scales or actual physical violence. Åsberg et al. (1976) were first to report lower levels of CSF 5-HIAA in depressed patients who made violent suicide attempts compared to those who did not. Among army recruits with personality disorder, an inverse correlation between CSF 5-HIAA levels and lifetime history of pathological 'aggression' (according to the Brown–Goodwin Scale) was observed by Brown et al. (1979). Negative correlations between 5-HIAA CSF and 'aggression' have also been described in people with alcoholism while abstinent (Limson et al., 1991), in boys with behavioural disturbances (Kruesi et al., 1992) and in various offender samples (Linnoila et al., 1983; Lidberg et al., 1985; Virkkunen et al., 1987, 1989, 1994).

Brown and Goodwin (1984) originated the suggestion that low 5-HIAA might be a trait rather than state

indicator of aggression, after observing that 5-HIAA CSF levels correlated negatively with the psychopathic deviance subscale of the MMPI, irritability scores and history of childhood antisocial aggression in army recruits with BPD. Confirmation that impulsivity or irritability may be the key correlates of 5-HT have also come from a series of studies examining less pathological aspects of disinihibited and/or impulsive behaviour. These reported negative correlations between CSF 5-HIAA and psychoticism (i.e. non-conformity, hostility) but not extraversion on the Eysenck Personality Questionnaire in non-depressed patients, suicide attempters, and healthy volunteers (Schalling et al., 1984; Traskman-Bendz et al., 1986). Among people who had attempted suicide and healthy men, low CSF 5-HIAA levels were associated with high scores on avoidance, impulsiveness and low socialization scores, but not aggression (Åsberg et al., 1987). Variations on this theme include inverse correlations between CSF 5-HIAA and 'the urge to act out hostility' (Roy et al., 1988).

Taken together this evidence suggests a particular role for 5-HT in aggression driven by impulsivity or lack of inhibition in non-offender samples, although not all findings are consistent with this (e.g. Cocarro, 1992; Gardner et al., 1990; Simeon et al., 1992; Cocarro et al., 1997c). Observations in offender samples have shown that CSF 5-HIAA concentrations differentiate impulsive offenders from those committing premeditated crimes and recidivists from non-recidivists (Virkkunen et al., 1989, 1996), but the direction of association varies. A *positive* correlation between 5-HIAA levels and inhibition of aggression was described by Virkkunen et al. (1994) while Soderstrom et al. (2003) found that low 5-HIAA CSF levels predicted psychopathy scores in violent offenders.

Pharmacological Challenge Studies

Early studies with depressed patients with a history of suicide attempts (Meltzer et al., 1984) as well as with aggressive, impulsive substance abusers who had ASPD (Fishbein et al., 1992), showed increased 5-HT responses to pharmacological 5-HT challenges. Later studies, however, have consistently produced evidence for under-responsivity of the serotonergic system in both depressed and impulsive-aggressive individuals.

Blunted prolactin response in personality disorder samples was first described in men with BPD (Cocarro et al., 1989); group differences between patients with BPD and patients with other personality disorders as well as healthy controls were accounted for by ratings of impulsivity but not affective symptoms. A number of studies have replicated findings of an inverse relationship between 5-HT responsiveness and dimensional rather than categorical ratings of aggression, impulsivity, assaultiveness, irritability and history of suicide attempts in groups of patients with BPD or mixed personality disorders (Brown et al., 1979, 1989; Cocarro, 1992; Siever et al., 1993; Cocarro et al., 1995; Cocarro et al., 1996a; Cocarro et al., 1997a; Soloff et al., 2003; New et al., 2004). Only two of the studies (Soloff et al., 2003; New et al., 2004) included both men and women; reduced 5-HT response was observed in men only. O'Keane et al. (1992) confirmed these observations among incarcerated men with antisocial personality disorder. Reduced serotonergic responsiveness to a fenfluramine challenge has also been described in criminals with a history of conduct disorder (Cherek and Lane, 1999) and impulsive offenders with personality disorder in a high security hospital setting (Dolan et al., 2001). Two studies (Manuck et al., 1998), in non-patient samples have shown negative correlations between prolactin response and life-time history of aggression and self-reported impulsivity.

Meta-chlorophenylpiperazine (mCPP) acts as releasing agent and reuptake inhibitor at most serotoninergic receptors. Studies using it as a pharmacological challenge have largely confirmed observations from fenfluramine challenge studies with people who have BPD (Hollander et al., 1994; Rinne et al., 2000). Moss et al. (1990) found blunted 5-HT sensitivity in a sample with ASPD and comorbid substance abuse disorders. A general pattern of inverse correlation between prolactin responses and Buss–Durkee hostility inventory assaultiveness subscale scores was found in all participants, including the healthy controls. A negative relationship between prolactin response and the irritability subscale was also found in two mCPP studies in patients with mixed personality disorders (Cocarro et al., 1991, 1997b).

In order to characterize further the relationship between serotonergic response and psychopathology, Cocarro et al. (1996b) divided their sample of 20 patients with personality disorder into 'blunters' and 'non-blunters' to a fenfluramine challenge. Negative correlations with 5-HT function were observed in both groups, but differed in detail. Prolactin values correlated best with assault scores in blunters but with indirect and verbal aggression in non-blunters, suggesting that reduced 5-HT may be associated specifically with assaultive behaviour. This fits with previous observations by Cocarro et al. (1989) of a strong relationship between 5-HT function and physical/motor but not ideational aspects of assaultiveness and impulsivity, tending to support a behavioural inhibition model of 5-HT function in aggressive behaviour. This is broadly in line with findings by Dolan and Anderson (2003) showing that 5-HT function, assessed by fenfluramine challenge, correlated negatively with the impulsive–antisocial component of the PCL-SV but not its arrogant/deceitful factor.

Acute Tryptophan Depletion (ATD) Studies

5-HT manipulation through ATD provides a further way of assessing links between 5-HT activity and aggression or impulsivity. The literature just reviewed leads to a prediction that ATD would cause an increase in aggressive/impulsive responding, but results have been inconsistent.

Smith et al. (1986) used the Buss paradigm to evaluate the effect of ATD created through dietary depletion in normal men. In this paradigm participants have to deliver electric shocks in response to a stimulus tone to a partner who, unknown to them, does not exist. Although reduced central 5-HT metabolism was achieved, this did not alter levels of aggressiveness. In an adapted design using higher levels of provocation, however, an inverse relationship between tryptophan levels and aggressive responding was found (Pihl et al., 1995). Cleare and Bond (1995) also demonstrated increased subjective feelings of aggression during a competitive task in normal people. This effect was only observed, however, in those with higher self-reported aggression ratings. Although these findings suggest that lowering 5-HT levels may not predispose normal individuals to aggressive overreactions to environmental stimuli, it is possible that 5-HT may modulate aggression in people with significant psychopathology or high base rates of aggression. In line with this suggestion, Bjork et al. (2000) found that ATD produced a marked increase in ratings of aggression during provocation among people with high but not low trait aggression. This differential effect of ATD has also been found in healthy individuals using other paradigms (e.g. Dougherty et al., 1999). The few other published reports on use of ATD in clinical samples, however, have found no such effects in them, for example Salomon et al. (1994) who studied people with intermittent explosive disorder (IED) and McCloskey et al. (2009).

As serotonin appears to be related primarily to the impulsive type of aggression, through inhibition of impulsive responding, it might be more fruitful to study the effects of serotonergic manipulation on impulsivity tasks rather than aggression. LeMarquand et al. (1999a,b) thus studied sons of alcoholic fathers and found increased error rates on a behavioural inhibition impulsivity task but no difference in aggressive responding after ATD. Walderhaug et al. (2002) described increased impulsiveness on a continuous performance task after ATD among healthy controls. One research group, however, found improved performance (Crean et al., 2002). Most studies did not detect any effect of ATD on impulsivity tasks, such as continuous performance tasks, stop tasks (Cools et al., 2005; Clark et al., 2005) or Go/No-Go tasks (LeMarquand et al., 1999; Rubia et al., 2005).

Other healthy volunteer studies have described how 5-HT affects learning. It has been shown that lowering 5-HT impairs the ability to respond appropriately to rewarding or punishing stimuli, thereby altering the individual's capacity to adapt behaviour according to feedback (Rogers et al., 1999; Cools et al., 2005). This is an exciting new line of work, but it has not yet been done with samples selected for their aggression or impulsiveness.

Brain Imaging Studies and 5-HT

While there is consistent evidence for a role of 5-HT in impulsive aggression, how it exerts this is not yet understood. More specifically, it is not known how 5-HT modulates brain activity and which 5-HT receptor types may be involved.

Neuroimaging studies allow the localization of such effects *in vivo*. PET studies have been used to identify the distribution of 5-HT receptors in humans. Conflicting findings have been reported on the relationship between aggression and receptor density. Parsey et al. (2002) found a negative correlation between 5-HT$_{1A}$ binding sites and life-time aggression in healthy men. Rabiner et al. (2002), however, again only with men, found no associations, while Witte et al. (2009) reported a positive relationship between prefrontal 5-HT$_{1A}$ binding sites and aggression scores in a mixed sex sample. Differences in sample composition and aggression measures are likely to have contributed to these differences in findings. Frankle et al. (2005), investigating serotonin transporter distribution, found significantly reduced serotonin transporter availability in the anterior cingulate in individuals with impulsive aggression compared with healthy controls. 5-HT$_{1A}$ receptor binding in prefrontal structures has been shown to be lower too in violent people than in healthy controls (Meyer et al., 2008).

PET has also been used to investigate regional metabolic activity in response to serontonergic stimulation. New et al. (2002) compared the effect of an mCPP challenge in 13 impulsive aggressive participants and 13 healthy controls, and found decreased brain activations in the orbitofrontal cortex and anterior cingulate, regions known to be involved in inhibition of impulsive aggression. In a separate study, the New group found that a course of fluoxetine had a normalizing effect on prefrontal cortex metabolism in people with impulsive aggressive behaviour, and that these changes correlated with clinical improvement (New et al., 2004).

Brain activations associated with neuropsychological tasks after serontonergic manipulation have been studied using fMRI. Anderson et al. (2002) showed enhanced activations in the lateral orbitofrontal cortex in healthy controls in a behavioural inhibition task after an mCPP challenge. Other studies with normal volunteers also suggested enhanced activations in prefrontal areas during a Go/No-Go task after citalopram (Del Ben et al., 2005) and mirtazapine (Völlm et al., 2006) challenge. This is consistent with the fMRI demonstration by Rubia et al. (2005) of reduced right orbital prefrontal activation during a Go/No Go task after tryptophan depletion. These findings suggest a possible interaction between serotonergic function and task specific brain activations, but the application of these methods to patient groups is still in its infancy. One recent study by Völlm et al. (2010) used fMRI to study men with ASPD, using behavioural inhibition and reward paradigms following mCPP challenge. Serotonergic modulation of reward pathways was impaired during the Go/No Go task

in the ASPD group. Improving serotonergic function might, thus, be useful for people with ASPD.

Treatment Implications of Serotonergic Research

The inverse relationship between measures of 5-HT function and indices of impulsivity and aggression raises the possibility that drugs which enhance serontonergic activity may be effective in reducing impulsive aggressive behaviour. Experimental studies in non-clinical samples have provided some support for this suggestion. Knutson et al. (1998) reported reduced hostility and increased social co-operation in healthy volunteers after a 4-week trial of fluoxetine. Among men with a history of criminal behaviour, Cherek and Lane (2001) showed that a single fenfluramine challenge significantly reduced impulsive responses during a reward choice paradigm. More recently, Kamarck et al. (2009), in a randomized controlled trial of citalopram in a large sample of healthy men and women, found that it reduced their anger, hostility and aggression. A meta-analysis of animal studies investigating the effect of serotonergic agents on aggression (Carrillo et al., 2009) concluded that increasing 5-HT levels had an inhibitory effect on aggression. To date, though, there have been few well-conducted trials of serotonergic drugs with patients with impulsive aggressive behaviour. The National Institute for Clinical Excellence (NICE) in England offers no support for such interventions for BPD or ASPD (National Collaborating Centre for Mental Health 2009a,b).

Table 12.7 provides an overview of such treatment trials with patients with personality disorder for whom ratings of impulsivity or aggression are included; sample sizes of the first few shown are too small for statistical analysis.

A consistent picture is beginning to emerge which holds some promise for treatment, despite the limitations of the studies listed, which include small sample sizes, high drop out rates and short trial duration of trials. SSRIs appear to be effective in the treatment of anger, impulsivity and aggression, an effect which seems to be independent of reduced depression or other psychopathological improvements. This emerging picture is corroborated by studies with people with a wide range of Axis I disorders, and no personality disorder, who tend to show improvement on anger and aggression ratings after SSRI treatment. Primary disorders have included depression (Fava et al., 2000); repeated suicidal behaviour (Verkes et al., 1998); dysthymia (Hellerstein et al., 1993); panic disorder (Neuger et al., 2002); pervasive developmental disorder (Couturier and Nicholson, 2002); head injury (Kant et al., 1998); bipolar depression (Mammen et al., 2004); PTSD (Davidson et al., 2004); intellectual disability (Janowsky et al., 2005); and post-stroke depression (Choi-Kwon et al., 2006). Rubey et al. (1996) reported improvements in anger ratings, regardless of primary diagnosis, in a small adult patient sample.

Table 12.7   SSRI treatment studies in personality disordered and impulsive–aggressive patients

Author, year	Drug, dose	Trial type	Duration of trial	Participants	Measures aggression or impulsivity	Outcome
Cocarro et al., 1990	Fluoxetine, titrated to 60 mg	Open trial	6 weeks	2 BPD, 1 ASPD	Overt Aggression Scale (OAS) Self-rated global aggression (from Hopkins Symptom Checklist-90)	Reduction in all OAS and self-ratings from week 1.
Cornelius et al., 1990	Fluoxetine 20–40 mg	Open trial	8 weeks	5 inpatients	Impulsivity sub-scale Buss–Durkee Hostility Inventory (BDHI) Hostility Subscale of the Symptom Checklist SCL-90	Large decrease in impulsivity. No overall change in hostility on BDHI; change on SCL-90.
Heller, 1994	Sertraline, up to 200 mg (six patients) or fluoxetine, 20–40 mg (four patients)	Open trial	Not stated	10 outpatients with BPD	Questionnaire ratings of mood swings, chronic anger, emptiness/boredom, emotional pain	Improvement with both drugs on both measures; fluoxetine superior due to better tolerability.
Kavoussi et al., 1994	Sertraline, flexible dosing	Open trial	8 weeks	11 with any personality disorder	Overt Aggression Scale (OAS)	Significant decrease of irritability and overt aggression from week 4 onwards, maintained at week 8.
Salzmann et al., 1995	Fluoxetine, up to 60 mg	RCT[1]	12 weeks	27 outpatients with BPD; 22 completed – 13 treatment, 9 controls	Profile of Mood States (POMS) McLean Hospital Overt Aggression Symptom checklist-revised (OAS-R)	Significant improvement in anger in treated group.
Silva et al., 1997	Fluoxetine, 20–60 mg	Open trial	7 weeks	46 patients with BPD	Clinical Impulsivity Scale	Significant improvements in clinical measures and Impulsivity Scale scores from week 1 of treatment, continued until week 7.
Cocarro and Kavoussi, 1997	Fluoxetine, 20–60 mg	RCT	12 weeks	40 outpatients with personality disorder and history of impulsive aggression (27 treatment, 13 placebo)	Anger, Irritability, and Aggression Questionnaire (AIAQ) Overt Aggression Scale-Modified (OAS-M)	Sustained reduction in irritability and overt aggression on OAS-M and CGI but no improvement in depression.
Rinne et al., 2002	Fluvoxamine, mean 166 mg	RCT	Cross-over trial: 6 weeks + 6 weeks placebo, or the opposite, then 12 weeks open follow up	38 women with BPD, all outpatients; 20 treatment 18 controls	Subscales mood swings, anger and impulsivity of the Borderline Personality Disorder Severity Index	Improvement on rapid mood swings but not impulsivity and anger.
Reist et al., 2003	Citalopram, mean dose 45.5 mg	Open trial	8 weeks	20 individuals with cluster B personality disorders or intermittent explosive disorder from general population	Barratt Impulsivity Scale (BIS) Buss Durkee Hostility Inventory Overt Aggression Scale (OAS-M)	Improvement on all scales except BIS motor impulsivity, BDHI assault, negativism and suspicion.
Simpson et al., 2004	Fluoxetine, 40 mg/placebo (all receiving DBT[2])	RCT	12 weeks	20 women with BPD: 9 fluoxetine 11 placebo	State Trait Anger Expression Inventory (STAXI) Overt Aggression Scale (OAS)	No advantages for fluoxetine

(Continued)

311

Table 12.7   *(Continued)*

Author, year	Drug, dose	Trial type	Duration of trial	Participants	Measures aggression or impulsivity	Outcome
Zanarini, 2004	3 groups: olanzapine fluoxetine olanzapine + fluoxetine	RCT	8 weeks	45 women with BPD; 14 fluoxetine 16 olanzapine 15 both	Overt Aggression Scale (OAS)	Improvement in all three drug groups for chronic dysphoria and impulsive aggression; olanzapine and combination superior to fluoxetine alone.

[1]Randomized controlled trial.
[2]Dialectical Behavioural Therapy.

Reductions in overt aggression have also been observed in child and adolescent outpatients in a trial of citalopram (Armenteros and Lewis, 2006). It is of note, however, that two trials involving women found SSRIs had no such effects (Rinne et al., 2002; Simpson et al., 2004). This is consistent with our earlier observations that the relationship between serontonergic dysfunction and impulsive or aggressive behaviour is less well established in women than in men.

Several authors have suggested SSRIs as first line intervention for symptom-specific treatment of impulsive-aggressive symptoms, notwithstanding the modest evidence (e.g. Soloff, 1998). This strategy was adopted in the practice guidelines of the American Psychiatric Association (2001) on BPD, but more recent Cochrane reviews (Lieb et al., 2010; Bateman, 2012) have concluded that these recommendations can no longer be supported; there is better evidence for other pharmacological agents, such as mood stabilizers or atypical antipsychotics, at least for BPD (see also chapter 16). More well-conducted randomized controlled trials are needed. In particular, treatment studies of hospitalized offenders are lacking. It remains to be seen whether SSRI treatment will be effective in those with higher baseline levels of impulsive aggression.

Serotonergic Function: Conclusions

The literature shows robust evidence for an inverse relationship between serotonin levels and both aggression and impulsivity. These relationships have been observed in a wide range of samples, providing support for the suggestion that the role of 5-HT/serotonin is not restricted to people with pathologies, but mechanisms are not fully understood. One suggestion has been that serotonergic dysfunction leads to a decreased ability to inhibit behaviour as well as impairing capacity to suppress behaviours through learning of their adverse effects, including punishment. Cocarro and Kavoussi (1996) proposed that:

the threshold to act aggressively, given the proper environmental circumstances, is modulated by overall 5-HT system function. The lower the functional status of the 5-HT system, the more likely the individual is to respond to similar degrees of threat, frustration, or aversive circumstances with an aggressive outburst.

This proposal is consistent with findings that serotonin plays a particular role in the impulsive type of aggression, and probably affects actions more than hostile or aggressive thoughts or feelings.

Nevertheless, more research is needed, especially with women and with people whose aggression is instrumental and planned. The little work done so far with these groups suggests that they may have different serotonergic system relationships with their aggression. Future research should also further investigate possible interactions between neurotransmitter systems. Brain imaging studies using carefully designed behavioural paradigms may illuminate this, and also possibly more focal deficits. Genotyping, to identify genetic markers of serontonergic function, would provide another promising approach. Finally, the evidence for treatment of patients with impulsive-aggressive behaviour using SSRIs is merely promising; more large scale RCTs are needed, in well defined samples, to translate findings about serotoninergic dysfunction in impulsive aggression into clinically relevant outputs.

IMPLICATIONS OF CURRENT KNOWLEDGE OF BRAIN STRUCTURE AND FUNCTION FOR FORENSIC MENTAL HEALTH PRACTICE AND RESEARCH

Studies of brain structure and function continue to provide evidence that abnormal behaviour in any of its cognitive, emotional or direct action elements has some physical foundation in the brain. In a growing field, we have focused on the literature which has the most direct relevance to offenders and offender-patients, but much of the more general literature is important in its focus on symptoms of potential relevance to offending. When asked in court, for example, it maybe useful to say that such an individual with, say, psychotic symptoms, has evidence of organic brain structural damage or dysfunction that is more consistent with that found among others with such symptoms than among healthy people. Shergill's group have shown structural brain changes among people with hallucinations (e.g. O'Daly et al., 2007) and the Bentall–Blackwood group have shown functional abnormalities among people with delusions (e.g. Blackwood et al., 2004). Lui and colleagues (2009) have found early associations between psychotic symptoms and brain structure, particularly reduction of grey matter in the temporal lobe, before antipsychotic medication is established, with evidence, in addition, of changed functional connectivity. The order of association is not clear, although others (Wexler et al., 2009) have found that brain connective tissue (white matter) loss appears to be associated with cognitive impairment while the grey matter loss was common to groups with psychotic symptoms without cognitive impairment. Rasetti et al. (2009), after examining healthy siblings and healthy unrelated controls as well as people with schizophrenia, found that the neuropathology, here amygdala dysfunction, was characteristic only of the patient group, so concluded that this dysfunction at least was a feature of illness rather than inherent difficulties. With increasingly thoughtful and inventive protocols, however, a sense persists that there is still a long way to go before we can be much more definite than invoking prefrontal, temporal and limbic system damage or dysfunction to account for most behavioural anomalies – perhaps a bit more or less of one or the other in some conditions than others, but still quite a general picture of what is going on.

Spence has investigated truth telling of a more direct kind (Spence et al., 2008b) using an fMRI protocol with the hypothesis that, focusing on the ventro-lateral prefrontal cortex and the anterior cingulate gyrus, response time would be longer and activation greater when endorsing false rather than true statements. Applying this to a woman with alleged Munchausen syndrome by proxy, when, as requested, she endorsed the accusations of others and not when she gave her own story, they argue:

while we have not 'proven' that this subject is innocent, we demonstrated that her behavioural and functional anatomical parameters behave as if she were.

Spence (2008) further advocated caution in reliance on neuro-imaging for detecting lies, having reviewed 16 imaging studies in this field. Greater activation of the prefrontal lobes, as with most deviance, is associated with lying compared with telling the truth, but sample sizes are generally small, there is much variation between the findings and the investigators have never replicated their own findings. To all this, one might add, the samples are all apparently of healthy people, many of them students and most, although not all, men. Then, too, would the findings necessarily generalize to offender samples, so often struggling with a range of psycho- and neuropathology?

So, we return to our theme of relying mainly on studies of brain structure and function to inform clinical work and further research to improve understanding of the mechanisms that link mental disorder and crime. They may inform treatment on the one hand and perhaps enhance techniques for determining recovery and safety on the other. Where a treatment is truly effective, being able to show that it has fundamentally changed structure or function in the brain would be a substantial advance. An exciting study in this regard, given the link between passivity delusions and serious violence (chapter 14), was one from Spence and colleagues (1997), which used a joystick protocol with men with schizophrenia during PET scanning. Hyperactivation of parietal and cingulate cortices was confined to those men who had passivity delusions, and not seen in the others; it was no longer evident 4–6 weeks later *in those men whose passivity delusions had recovered*. The study is however, tantalizing. Where are the replications? How much can really be inferred from just seven men with passivity delusions, six schizophrenic peers without such delusions and six healthy men? There has been little longitudinal study in this field to date, but surely that is the way forward.

13
Offenders with intellectual disabilities

Edited by
Pamela J Taylor

Written by
William R Lindsay
Gregory O'Brien
John L Taylor

CLINICAL AND LEGISLATIVE DEFINITIONS

The term 'intellectual disability' (ID) is gaining international currency. Its use corresponds with the terms 'learning disability', commonly used in health and social services in the UK, and 'mental retardation' in North America and in the international (*ICD-10*, World Health Organization (WHO) 1992) and US (*DSM-IV*, American Psychiatric Association, 1994) diagnostic and classification manuals. Although people with intellectual disability do not constitute a homogeneous population, *ICD-10* and *DSM-IV* include three core criteria for what they call mental retardation, and we will refer to as intellectual disability:

- significant impairment of intellectual functioning;
- significant associated impairment of adaptive or social functioning; and
- age of onset within the developmental period before adulthood.

All three criteria must be present for a diagnosis of intellectual disability.

Impairment of intellectual function

Impairment of intellectual function, particularly in a forensic context, should be assessed using an individually administered, reliable and valid, standardized test, such as the third edition of the Wechsler Adult Intelligence Scale (WAIS-III; Wechsler, 1999). Using such a test, based on normal distribution of general intelligence, a 'significant' impairment of intellectual functioning is conventionally understood to be a score of more than two standard deviations below the population mean. According to this approach, an IQ score of less than 70 is indicative of intellectual disability. Intelligence scores on such a measure are used as the basis for distinguishing between levels of severity.

Adaptive functioning

Adaptive functioning is a broad concept referring to an individual's ability to cope with the day-to-day demands of his/her environment. Thus, an assessment of adaptive function must take into account a person's age, environment and cultural expectations.

Age of onset criterion

The 'age of onset' criterion, according to general international consensus, means below the age of 18 years (American Psychiatric Association, 1994; British Psychological Society, 2000), although *ICD-10* does not specify a criterion age.

Legislative terms

Mental health legislation in England and Wales, Scotland, and Northern Ireland may apply to people with intellectual disability as well as to people with mental illness or personality disorder, and this is generally true in most countries around the world. The extent to which mental impairment or intellectual disability is explicit in the legislation varies between countries, and indeed also over time. In the Mental Health Act (MHA) 1983, for example, which covers only England and Wales, the term *mental disorder* included the explicit and defined categories of 'mental impairment' and 'severe mental impairment'. The Mental Health Act 2007, however, removes such sub-categorization and replaces 'mental impairment' with 'learning disability', while retaining the intent that such disorder may render a person liable to detention, as, for example, set out in the Code of Practice for England (Department of Health, 2008). As is often the case, however, legal concepts are not co-terminous with clinical concepts. The Mental Health Act 2007 legal concept of *learning disability* requires

abnormally aggressive or seriously irresponsible conduct on the part of the person concerned...

to be coupled with

> ...*a state of arrested or incomplete development of mind ... which includes significant impairment of intelligence and social functioning*

and this distinction is retained in the guidance in the English Code of Practice. The Code recommends specialist assessment. (See chapter 3 of this book and chapter 34 of the English Code of Practice for further details.)

The Adults with Incapacity (Scotland) Act 2000 and the UK Mental Capacity Act (2005) have clarified the role of mental capacity in the responsibility of an individual for his/her own actions. Having intellectual disability and/or another form of mental or cognitive impairment does not automatically absolve an individual from responsibility for his/her actions. The assumption must be made that adults have capacity unless there is evidence to the contrary. The approach to be taken in assessing an individual's capacity for decision-making is described in detail in the legislation and the accompanying secondary legislation, codes of practice and policy guidance.

PEOPLE WITH INTELLECTUAL DISABILITY DETAINED IN SECURE HEALTH SERVICE FACILITIES IN THE UK

In March 2006, in England and Wales, a total of 14,625 patients were resident in NHS or independent hospitals under a section of the MHA 1983 (The Information Centre, 2009). Of this total, 1098 (7.5%) were detained under the categories of mental impairment/severe mental impairment. Of the 12,132 patients detained in NHS facilities, 5.6% (684) were categorized as having mental or severe mental impairment, whereas the corresponding percentage in independent hospitals was 16.6% (414) of the total 2,493 patients detained there. During 2005–2006, a total of 25,740 people were admitted to NHS facilities (including high security hospitals) under the MHA 1983 (The Information Centre, 2009). Most of these detentions (8,435) were under civil sections of the Act, less than 1% were in the mental impairment/severe mental impairment categories. Of the 1304 detentions under court disposal or prison transfer orders during this period, over 4% were categorized as mental impairment/severe mental impairment.

The proportion of people in the general population with IQ scores under 70 is approximately 2.5% (assuming a normal distribution), so almost double the expected number of people with impaired intellectual function are compulsorily detained in NHS facilities under the Mental Health Act 1983; in the independent hospital sector the figure is as high as one in six detained patients. More recent NHS admissions under civil sections of the 1983 Act are in the anticipated range, but admissions under criminal sections remain somewhat higher than expected (The Information Centre, 2009).

CRIME AND PEOPLE WITH INTELLECTUAL DISABILITIES

In the late nineteenth and early twentieth centuries, criminal behaviour and intellectual disability were firmly linked in the ideology of the menace of the feeble-minded (Trent, 1994). In 1889, Kerlin (reviewed by Trent, 1994, p.87) suggested that vice was not the work of the devil, but the result of physical infirmity and an inability to perceive moral sense both of which were inherited and non-remediable. Kerlin's views directly challenged the optimism of earlier authorities that viewed people with intellectual disability as full of potential and remediable by suitable education. These more pessimistic views became dominant for the next 50 years. Terman (1911), an author of one of the earliest IQ tests, wrote:

> *there is no investigator who denies the fearful role of mental deficiency in the production of vice, crime and delinquency... not all criminals are feeble-minded but all feeble-minded are at least potential criminals (p.11).*

Goddard (1922), author of *The Criminal Imbecile*, concluded:

> *the results of the most careful studies indicate that somewhere in the neighborhood of 50 per cent of all criminals are feeble minded (p.106).*

Despite the long alleged association between delinquency and impaired intellectual functions, it is clear neither whether people with intellectual disability commit more crime than those without (Lindsay et al., 2004) nor whether those who do offend have any distinctive patterns in terms of the nature or frequency of their offending (Holland, 2004). This lack of clarity is due in large part to methodological problems in prevalence studies in this area (Sturmey et al., 2004). Inclusion criteria used in prevalence studies vary and are often unclear. This can affect prevalence rates, particularly if individuals with IQ scores in the 'borderline intelligence' range (70–85) are included. Differences in measurement also mean that studies are not strictly comparable, for example whether intellectual disability is assessed through formal IQ tests, educational history or both. Further, sampling bias and filtering effects result from the nature of the base population – whether this was a true community sample, a prison sample or a hospital sample (Holland et al., 2002). Even within highly selected samples, estimates vary. A Scottish prison survey of the early 1990s, for example, suggested that less than 0.5% of prisoners had intellectual disability, while poor literacy and low educational attainment were also problems (Davidson et al., 1995). Using the Quick test (Ammons and Ammons, 1962), the 1997 Office of National Statistics survey of prisoners in England and Wales found that 5% of male and 9% of female sentenced prisoners together with 11% of remand prisoners, regardless of gender, scored in the lowest band (25 or below), probably indicating intellectual impairment (Singleton et al., 1998). Loucks (2007), in the most recent review of the literature, also acknowledged methodological problems, but estimated that 20–30% of prisoners have intellectual difficulties sufficient to impair their ability to benefit from services in prison, including offender treatment programmes.

There is a dearth of good quality studies of other kinds too, for example comparing the prevalence of offending in whole populations of people with intellectual disability with that in populations without (Sturmey et al., 2004) or of comparative recidivism rates for offenders with and without intellectual disability. Recidivism rates for offenders with intellectual disability have generally been reported as high. In their study of 250 detained male intellectual disability patients in the UK, Gibbens and Robertson (1983) reported a re-conviction rate of 68%, while Lund (1990) found a re-offending rate of 72% in a follow-up of Danish offenders with intellectual disability who had been detained on statutory orders. He also found a doubling of sex offending incidents when he compared sentencing in 1983 to that of 1973. He suggested that this rise may have been a result of a policy of de-institutionalization whereby people with intellectual disability are no longer indefinitely detained in hospitals, but he did not set this finding in the context of any change in overall sex offending rates over the same period. He thought that, given de-institutionalization, those with higher propensities towards offending would be preferentially discharged, as perhaps also appearing more able; in fact, they would also be more likely to be arrested at the scene of any incident and possibly less able to defend themselves.

Linhorst et al. (2003) reported that, among 252 offenders with developmental disabilities who completed a case management community programme, just 25% were re-arrested within 6 months of case closure, while 43% of those who dropped out of the programme were re-arrested during the same period. These figures are similar to those for large samples of general offenders studied over the same period, albeit in the USA; Langan and Levin (2002) found that among 300,000 prisoners of all kinds, 30% were re-arrested within 6 months of release, while the re-arrest rate for 79,000 general offenders on probation was 43% (Langan and Cunniff, 1992).

The historical scaremongering concerning the association between low IQ and offending was influential in setting up large institutions for people with intellectual disability, although there were also compassionate arguments for this institutional policy, such as the notion that people with intellectual disability required separate, supportive cultures in order to live fulfilling lives. It was not until after 1970 that the institutionalization philosophy changed in the UK, and people with intellectual disability were (re)integrated in community settings. In Europe and Australasia, implementation of deinstitutionalization policies has resulted in substantial changes in all aspects of service organization and delivery in this field. These changes have been particularly evident in both the design and location of services for offenders with intellectual disability, which work for those with uncomplicated intellectual disability, although there

are now fewer options for their diversion from criminal justice proceedings (Sturmey et al., 2004). This issue is reflected in reports from the UK Prison Reform Trust, as part of its *No One Knows* initiative to highlight the predicament of prisoners with intellectual disability and of those with less severe learning difficulties (Jones and Talbot, 2010; O'Brien, 2008b). Loucks (2007) reports on studies that have indicated that people with intellectual disability may account for up to 7% of prisoners while those with lesser or specific learning difficulties may account for up to 32%. In another report by the Prison Reform Trust (Jacobson, 2008), recommendations were made for diversion of those individuals with intellectual disability away from the criminal justice system to alternative provision. The Bradley Report (Bradley, 2009) emphasizes that the needs of people with intellectual and developmental disabilities in the criminal justice system require collaborative planning and person-centred care by a range of agencies.

Although it would appear that service development for offenders with intellectual disability has been consistent with the development of all intellectual disability services, entry into secure services often involves people being sent by service commissioners to out-of-area facilities, whether NHS or independent sector hospitals, with a resultant drain on the resources of local services (Crossland et al., 2005), and potential further exclusion of the clientele from their local community. In turn, this can lead to a lack of alternative pathway development, local staff failing to develop knowledge and skills for helping these people, and geographical variability in the type and quality of provision available (Sturmey et al., 2004). It has been suggested that the resources currently invested in out-of-area secure services would be better directed towards developing local community-based support services (National Development Team, 2007). Another concern about specialist secure hospital development is that it means that institutions for people with intellectual disability are being re-established, perhaps on a smaller scale, and specifically for people with offending or challenging behaviour, but nevertheless re-institutionalization is taking place.

THEORIES OF OFFENDING APPLIED TO PEOPLE WITH INTELLECTUAL DISABILITIES

It is possible that low IQ itself may be a vulnerability factor for offending, but the evidence is complex. There is a body of literature supporting a relationship between low IQ and higher rates of offending (e.g. Hirschi and Hindelang, 1977; Goodman et al., 1995) and there have been a number of studies linking the combination of socioeconomic deprivation, antisocial influences and lower IQ to a higher rate of delinquency. West and Farrington (1973) reported that only 9% of multiple offenders had measured IQ scores of 100 or greater while 28% of recidivist delinquents scored below 90. Farrington (1995), reviewing a number of large scale studies on the development of criminal careers, found that measures at 8–10 years old which are significant predictors of adult criminality are troublesome behaviour, an unco-operative family, poor housing, poor parental behaviour and low IQ.

There is much less evidence, however, concerning the relationship between delinquency and IQ scores around or greater than two standard deviations below the mean (i.e. IQ ≤70). McCord and McCord (1959) evaluated an early intervention with 650 underprivileged boys in Massachusetts. The Cambridge–Somerville Youth Study was set up 'to prevent delinquency and to develop stable elements in the characters of children' (*ibid*, p.2). The boys were divided into 325 matched pairs and assigned to treatment and control conditions. There was a relationship between IQ and rates of conviction in that, for the treatment group, 44% of those in the IQ band 81–90 had a conviction while 26% of those with an IQ above 110 had a conviction. The 10% of individuals in the lowest IQ group (less than 80), however, had a conviction rate of 35%, that is, lower than that recorded in the IQ band 81–90, but there was a twist. The highest percentage going to penal institutions (19%) was in the lowest IQ band, and none from the highest was sentenced to imprisonment. The results were similar in the control group. Maughan et al. (1996) also found that the rate of adult crime among boys who had significant reading difficulties (an indication of developmental and intellectual disability) was lower than the rate of adult crime in the general population comparison group. This finding held true independently of psychopathology and/or measured social abilities. This suggests that the relationship between intelligence and delinquency is not simple and linear when considering individuals 1.5 or more standard deviations below the mean.

The work of Farrington (1995, 2000) and others – including the work of Patterson and his colleagues on the relationships between family interactions and social learning (e.g. Snyder and Patterson, 1995) – established the strong links between social and environmental factors and the development of criminality. Based on the results of their longitudinal research, Huesmann et al. (1987) suggested that, in early childhood, those with lower intellectual abilities are prone to developing aggressive behaviour because of difficulties in learning more complex non-aggressive, pro-social interpersonal skills. Aggressive behaviour, in turn, may result in failure to develop intellectually, due to its isolating and alienating effects that minimize opportunities for effective education. Novaco and Taylor (2004) found evidence that this dual-process social learning model has applicability for people with intellectual disability and significant offending histories.

The ability to identify with the values of society – or lack of it – has long been a core concept in sociological theories of criminality. Control theory (Hirschi, 1969) is focused on the learning of criminal behaviours through positive reinforcement in association with criminal sub-cultures and family influences as well as the development of self-control through appropriate social learning from positive role models. Hirschi (1969) wrote that the success of social learning was dependent on four factors: attachment, commitment, involvement, and belief, using the terms in his own specific ways. 'Attachment' referred to the extent to which the individual identified with the expectations and values of others within society, such as parents and teachers. 'Commitment' invokes a rational element in criminality; individuals make subjective evaluations about the loss they will experience following arrest and conviction. 'Involvement' deals with the balance between engagement in ordinary activities, such as work, education and other occupational activities, and opportunity to consider delinquency; the less that individuals are involved with the day-to-day activities of society the more likely they are to engage in criminal activity. He considered 'belief' as the extent to which individuals accept the laws of society as being reasonable mores to which they would conform. There is a wealth of evidence supporting this hypothesis, leading to recommendations that community engagement and quality of life should be central treatment components in programmes for offenders with intellectual disability (Lindsay and Taylor, 2005). Measures to promote pro-social influences and community integration must be coupled with more specific interventions for offending behaviours such as fire-setting, assault or sexual offending. The evidence base thus informs clinical work with offenders with intellectual disability.

OFFENDERS WITH INTELLECTUAL DISABILITIES AND ADDITIONAL DIAGNOSES

People with intellectual disability have a high prevalence of psychiatric disorders, including mental illness (Reid, 1972), other pervasive developmental disorders and/or neuropsychiatric disorders related to the cause of their brain damage (Gillberg et al., 1986).

Intellectual Disability and Mental Illness

The prevalence of mental illness, including the psychoses and the neuroses, among adults with intellectual disability is estimated to be in the region of 20% (Cooper et al., 2007; Taylor et al., 2004a). If challenging/problem behaviour is included as a diagnostic category, the reported prevalence jumps to around 40% (e.g. Cooper et al., 2007). Evidence that psychiatric disorders are common among offenders with intellectual disability comes from both inpatient (e.g. Day, 1997; Novaco and Taylor, 2004) and community studies (e.g. Lindsay et al., 2002). Findings may, however, be a function of these studies having been carried out in clinical settings. What is clear is that psychiatric disorder is common in this population and carries major implications for treatment and management.

Treating people with mental illness in the context of intellectual disability

Drug treatment for mental illness in offenders with intellectual disability follows the same principles as in all psychiatric practice, but framed according to their needs arising from their developmental disabilities. First, and most importantly, there are three key principles:

1. start low;
2. go slow; and
3. avoid polypharmacy.

The notion of 'start low' is intended to reflect the fact that doses of most psychotropic medications in adults with intellectual disability should be started at around half the usual adult dose (O'Brien, 2002a). This is necessary partly to avoid common major side-effects such as movement disorders, sedation, and other dose-related problems, all of which are more likely to appear in this group. Secondly, the suggestion to 'go slow' refers to incremental tapering of dosage. It is recommended that dose is altered over a period of about twice the time usual in mainstream psychiatric practice. This is both to avoid side-effects and to monitor very carefully changes in clinical response, which can take longer to appear in this population than among people with illness alone. Finally, avoidance of polypharmacy is a reflection of the fact that, while several drugs are often required in this population, numbers should be kept to a minimum. Adverse drug interactions are more likely among people for whom metabolic disorders are common.

It is important to consider the timing of drug use. Very often, when first admitted into services, people are in a state of distress and intra-psychic disorganization, partly due to mental illness and partly to a range of other factors. Prompt treatment can then be very helpful in preparing the way for structured offence-related interventions, described later in this chapter. An essential step in engaging the patient in a treatment milieu which enables other interventions to proceed lies in helping him/her to become more psychologically organized. In addition, in the course of offence-related treatments, it is common for problems of anxiety and mood problems to worsen. Indeed, in the face of the emotions engendered in such therapy psychotic symptoms and may re-emerge and will also need careful prescription and management.

For further reading about management of mental illness, and in particular the drug treatment of mental illness in the context of intellectual disability, see O'Brien (2002a), and for further notes on the management of pervasive developmental disorders in this context of younger offenders with intellectual disability see O'Brien and Bell (2004).

Intellectual Disability and Pervasive Developmental Disorders

Pervasive developmental disorders, especially autism, are common among adults with intellectual disability. The best evidence at present is that autism is no more common among offenders with intellectual disability than people with intellectual disability who do not offend (O'Brien, 2002b). The management of those adults with intellectual disability and autism in offender services, however, can be particularly daunting, as the interaction of autism with offending is complex. Autism may result in offending through obsessional fixations but, more often, through mutual misunderstandings between the person with autism and others, and resultant mismatch in their behaviours; sometimes the two mechanisms act together. Also common is the propensity of people with autism to panic, and to have sudden aggressive outbursts in this context.

Treating offenders with pervasive developmental disorders in the context of intellectual disability

These matters are relevant to the management of people on the autism spectrum who have offended. First, drug treatment can be helpful. This is particularly so for those individuals who experience anxiety and are likely to panic or become aggressive. They often respond well to low dose antipsychotic therapy, such as risperidone. Selective serotonin reuptake inhibitors (SSRIs) may also be helpful in this context. Either medication may be helpful for those individuals on the autism spectrum whose offending is driven by obsessional fixations.

Individuals with autism are likely to find the experience of inpatient treatment or offence-related interventions anxiety provoking, and symptom worsening is common at times during such treatment. Consequently, in addition to optimizing inter-personal functioning and psychological organization at the start of a course of treatment, through drug therapy, it is important to monitor the progress closely throughout, in order to detect early any need for modifying medication or adding support over the course of the programme.

Intellectual Disability in People with Epilepsy and Other Neuropsychiatric Disorders

As intellectual disability from childhood is generally explained by very early brain damage, developmental disorders or a combination of the two, a range of neuropsychiatric disorders is common among adults with intellectual disability, epilepsy among them (Tyrer et al., 2006). As with mental illness in people with intellectual disability, the key is to provide optimal treatment as early as possible. This helps the individual to access their latent cognitive resources, facilitates engagement in other treatments, including psychological interventions, and prevents further damage. Perhaps contrary to popular belief, it is as uncommon in clinical forensic practice to encounter offending during epileptic fits or post-ictal confusion or fugues among people with intellectual disability as it is more generally (see also chapter 12). It is far more common find individuals who may be behaviourally disturbed and/or aggressive as part of irritability in the context of poor epilepsy control, highlighting the need for prompt and effective anti-convulsant therapy.

Intellectual Disability and Personality Disorders

Reported prevalence of personality disorders among offenders with intellectual disability has varied quite widely. In reviewing this literature, Lindsay (2007) made several recommendations for considering their nature in this group, including:

a. greater use of behavioural observation and informant information to make diagnostic classifications; and

b. greater awareness of cultural factors affecting the diagnosis for this group. People with intellectual disability have often lived more restricted lives than those in the mainstream population and consequently have less opportunity to experience a range of social and sexual relationships which, in turn, may have hindered personality development. This must be taken into account when making a diagnosis of personality disorder, as must the lower levels of occupational activity, and higher levels of necessary dependency. Other contextual factors too, such as higher levels of suggestibility, may affect responses to questionnaire assessments.

In a large multi-centre study, Lindsay et al. (2006a) compared rates of personality disorder in offenders with intellectual disability in community, low/medium secure and high secure settings, using *DSM-IV* criteria (American Psychiatric Association, 1994). The reliability between independent raters was generally over 80%, and the assessment and diagnosis of personality disorder among people with intellectual disability appeared valid. The prevalence of personality disorder across the study population was 39%. Perhaps unsurprisingly, antisocial personality disorder (ASPD) was the most frequently diagnosed, and significantly more individuals receiving this diagnosis were in the high secure setting than in the other two settings. There were no diagnoses of dependent personality disorder, which might have been anticipated given the extent of the study group's developmental delay. When data for the three groups were combined, personality disorder was positively associated with risk of violence according to the Violence Risk Appraisal Guide (VRAG; Quinsey et al., 1998).

Evaluating data from the same study groups, Hogue et al. (2006) reported that ICD-10 personality disorder classifications (WHO, 1992) presented in a manner consistent with that reported by Lindsay et al. (2006a), with participants from high security settings having a higher rate of these diagnoses than participants from the other two settings. In addition, having an ICD-10 dissocial personality diagnosis was a significant predictor of level of security.

GENETIC DISORDERS, INTELLECTUAL DISABILITY AND OFFENDING: GENOTYPES AND BEHAVIOURAL PHENOTYPES

The links between specific genetic syndromes and offending behaviour are as complex as they are sometimes controversial. Although the process of drawing inferences from individual research studies as well as from their combination is dealt with at length in chapter 8, we deal with some of the issues here too. This is because there are some matters of particular importance to people with intellectual disability generally, and also there are some conditions in this field which are more specific than in the field of mental illness in the inherited component of the resultant difficulties, conditions such as fragile X or Prader–Willi syndrome (see below). Nevertheless, any proposition that inheritance of a specific genotype might result in an individual's carrying out a particular offence is fraught with difficulty. The history of eugenics renders it unpalatable, but, at a more practical level, the possible intervening variables are extensive. Notwithstanding the need for extreme caution to be observed in any proposal that a particular genotype might result in offending behaviour, recent research on *behavioural phenotypes* has gone to great lengths to clarify mechanisms of expression of the genotype. This may be of value to inform and pave the way for care and intervention. In this context, the useful concept of a *behavioural phenotype* may be defined as 'a characteristic pattern of social, linguistic, cognitive and motor observations which is consistently associated with a biological/genetic disorder' (O'Brien and Yule, 1995).

The observed phenotype of any one genetic condition varies from time to time and from person to person: there is nothing in this definition that suggests that the behavioural features of a genetic syndrome are inevitable, fixed, or irremediable. When considering the genetic basis of the behavioural phenotypes observed, and how these might contribute to offending behaviour, certain themes are apparent. These are:

1. the role of generalized intellectual disability;
2. the relationship between genotype severity and phenotype severity;
3. the different considerations which apply in respect of progressively deteriorating central nervous system syndromes and non-progressive conditions;

4. the mechanism of action of discrete genes, in certain common and/or familiar syndromes;
5. behavioural phenotype expression through gene–environment interactions.

The Mediating Role of Generalized Intellectual Disability

In considering the pathway from genotype to behavioural phenotype to offending behaviour, the first issue is whether the observed behaviour is mainly a reflection of the breadth and/or severity of intellectual disability which is typical of the genetic syndrome in question. Overall, there is a strong association between occurrence of disturbed behaviour and degree of intellectual disability (Gillberg and O'Brien, 2000). In the assessment of offending behaviour, the common occurrence of restless and over-active behaviour, often compounded by excitability and/or aggression, tends to be more problematic at lower than higher levels of tested IQ, the exception to this being at the very lowest end of the IQ spectrum. Here, many are so disabled that disturbed behaviour is not an issue, but rather apathetic and listless behaviour dominates the presentation. This tends not to apply to other behaviours figuring prominently in some of the more specific syndromes, such as the insatiable over-eating in Prader–Willi syndrome and the compulsive self-injury in Lesch Nyhan syndrome (see also O'Brien and Yule, 1995). In some genetic syndromes, certain behaviours present over the whole IQ range, as, for example, in Prader–Willi syndrome. Thus, while many of the behavioural anomalies which figure among the behavioural phenotypes of genetic syndromes mainly reflect low IQ, some have a more specific organic basis.

The implication of these observations is that in the assessment of any offending behaviour in the context of a genetic syndrome which has a putative behavioural phenotype, clinical assessment should include expert psychological testing of intellectual function.

The Relationship Between Genotype Severity and Phenotype Severity

Since the beginnings of genetic research, one fundamental tenet has been that more extreme variations in genotype are associated with more extreme variations in phenotype. Many of the whole chromosome replication syndromes, for example, feature very severe levels of intellectual disability, and, in some cases, also other phenotypic features such as life-threatening congenital cardiac abnormalities and other health problems. Mosaicism, where there is admixture of normal and abnormal cell lines, also impacts directly on phenotypic expression; there is a direct correlation between the degree of mosaicism and phenotypic expression. Thus, individuals who have a greater proportion of normal cell lines typically show milder variants of the phenotype, especially in terms of degree of intellectual disability. This has major implications for their behaviour. When it comes to recording and interpreting genetic findings with respect to offending behaviour, one important issue is to be clear whether the genetic finding displays such quantitative elements.

The Different Considerations in Respect of Progressively Deteriorating CNS Syndromes and Non-Progressive Conditions

Special consideration must be given to those conditions which feature progressively deteriorating CNS function, because the manifest behavioural phenotype in such syndromes changes over time, with implications for the occurrence of disturbed and/or offending behaviour. With loss of skills, and disorganized and often (early in course) disinhibited behaviour, the risk of aggressive offending behaviour may be increased. In non-deteriorating conditions, by contrast, improvement and development are the norm, through education and other influences aimed at optimizing self-organization and related skills.

The Mechanism of Action of Discrete Genes in Certain Common and/or Familiar Syndromes

When the action of a single gene has a strong effect, then these simple principles guiding the pathway from genotype to phenotype begin to unravel. In this case, the essential steps are as follows (O'Brien and Pearson, 2005):

- genes code for proteins, that is they provide a template for the production of a specific protein;
- proteins design, build and develop all body systems; they comprise the matrix against which other tissue constituents are taken up and laid down in the body, and proteins regulate this, in all body tissues;
- including the brain;
- which controls behaviour;
- so, any variation in a gene involved in any aspect of brain development or maturation may result in a behavioural phenotype.

Some insight into the nature of the mechanisms of expression of gene–behaviour associations can be gleaned from consideration of three of the most widely studied conditions, namely: fragile X syndrome, in which a micro-anatomical effect on neuronal dendritic arborization over the course of brain maturation is seen; Lesch–Nyhan syndrome, where the gross impact of an aberrant metabolite on the whole organism is manifest; Prader–Willi syndrome, in which a gender-specific imprinting effect on a psychosis gene is postulated (see also below).

Behavioural Phenotype Expression Through Gene–Environment Interactions

The behavioural expressions of these (primarily) CNS genes are not simple direct results of gene on behaviour. In the definition of behavioural phenotype, the pattern of behaviour, given a particular genotype, is *characteristic*, not *universal*, or *non-mutable*. All behaviour – especially offending behaviour – is to an extent contingent on the personal environment and the reactions of others, but environment is thought to have a more powerful role in some conditions (see also chapter 8).

There is now growing evidence, however, that demonstrates how reactions of parents and carers to behaviour in the developing individual has a shaping effect in even some of the most florid features of behavioural phenotypes. This has been shown elegantly in the context of research on an important behaviour which had previously been thought to be independent of personal or social environment – that is, the socially inappropriate laughter of children with Angelman syndrome (see below). Oliver et al. (2002) found evidence that, on the contrary, the laughter of these children is heavily dependent on reactions by others, especially the social reactions of their parents to their laughter in their early years. Such findings may indicate new directions for management and facilitating optimal development among affected individuals.

For each of these important conditions, we describe common considerations with regard to offending behaviour, in particular the implications of the behavioural phenotype for assessment of offending behaviour.

Angelman syndrome

This syndrome shares the same deletion on chromosome 15q (11–13) as Prader–Willi syndrome, but in Angelman syndrome this is maternally derived. The intellectual disability of affected individuals is usually in the severe to profound range. Lack of speech is characteristic. Facial features are usually characteristic, with a prominent jaw, wide mouth, with widely spaced teeth and thin upper lip, flat occiput, mid-facial hypoplasia and deep-set eyes. The behavioural features include general motor restlessness and overactivity, short attention span, ataxia, and, notably, a prominent pattern of episodic excessive and socially inappropriate laughter. This resulted in the now discredited eponym – 'happy puppet syndrome', which families and carers find unhelpful, and insulting.

Clinical note on assessment of offending behaviour in a person with Angelman syndrome

Behaviour may be misinterpreted as deliberately socially awkward, and may be regarded as offensive and threatening. Any allegation of offending behaviour – especially of interpersonal offending behaviour – on the part of an affected individual should include assessment of the cognitive and behavioural traits described above.

Fragile X syndrome

The gene underlying fragile X syndrome (*FMR-1*) is located on the distal arm of the X chromosome, Xq27.3, and is associated with a large expansion of a sequence of CGG (cytosine–guanine–guanine) trinucleotide repeats. This gene exerts its impact on brain development by regulating neuron dendritic arborization. In affected individuals, there is failure of inhibition of dendritic arborization, which results in too many inter-neuronal connections: effectively, a reduction of the pruning effect on cerebral structure, which is part of normal development over adolescence. Consequently, the brain of affected individuals is larger – around 10% heavier – than the normal young adult brain, but many of the connections detract from functional adaptation, rather then add to it.

There is a direct correlation between the length of the repeat CGG sequence, and the severity of phenotypic expression, in physical, intellectual and behavioural terms. Phenotypic expression of fragile X syndrome depends on the sex of the affected individual. Intellectual disability in males is typically mild to moderate, while females – having one normal X chromosome – generally show IQ in the low normal to borderline range. Affected boys show a combination of an atypical form of autism spectrum disorder, and an attention deficit hyperactivity disorder (ADHD)-type pattern of overactivity. Repetitive behaviour and social anxiety are prominent, but theory of mind test results are less impaired than in typical autism. As they develop, boys become less overactive, indeed, many are quite underactive and listless by adulthood, but the autistic-type features and social anxiety are more persistent among men (Turk, 1992; Hagerman, 2005). Girls and women generally have few autistic features, but some social anxiety.

Clinical note on assessment of offending behaviour in a person with fragile X

Most such people are not aggressive, nor are they likely to engage in offending behaviour. Nevertheless, as such syndromes go, fragile X, is common, and the condition's behavioural phenotype of social cognitive deficits, which feature ADHD, and autistic traits can result in an affected individual being involved in behaviour which may lead to allegations of offending. In assessment of any alleged offending behaviour here, the first issue will usually be to clarify whether either of the two common developmental disorders – ADHD or autism – is also present. If so, the task then is to explore the role of the disorder in the offending behaviour.

The behaviours of people with fragile X syndrome, in common with others who are on the autism spectrum, are also liable to provoke unfortunate or even bullying reactions on the part of others. This common problem is also relevant to the assessment of any allegations of offending, whether it is the alleged offender or the victim who is affected by fragile X syndrome. Careful analysis of the interpersonal actions and reactions is important to an understanding of what happened and to developing strategies for preventing repetition.

Lesch–Nyhan syndrome

Lesch–Nyhan syndrome occurs almost exclusively in males, caused by gene mutations on the X chromosome, resulting in an almost complete lack of activity of the enzyme hypoxanthine guanine phosphoribosyl transferase (HPRT). This enzyme normally plays a key role in the recycling of the purine bases, hypoxanthine and guanine. When it is inactive purines are not salvaged, but rather degraded, while, also, as a compensatory mechanism, increased synthesis of purines takes place (Deutsch et al., 2005). Uric acid is overproduced, leading to clinical features of gout, and, given the stage of development of the affected person, intellectual disability, spastic cerebral palsy, involuntary, choreoathetoid movements and aggressive behaviour, including self-mutilation, all exacerbated under stressful circumstances (Nyhan, 1976; Palmour, 1983). Self-mutilation is severe and compulsive, with unrestrained patients biting off digits and parts of their lips, even though they experience pain and scream while doing so. Aggression is also compulsive and sufferers have been heard apologizing while hurting others. The mechanisms behind the neurology of the condition are incompletely understood, but may include abnormalities of dopaminergic, GABAergic and glutamatergic neurotransmitter systems (Deutsch et al., 2005).

Clinical note on assessment of offending behaviour in a person with Lesch–Nyhan syndrome

The aggressive behaviour is profoundly distressing and potentially very damaging to both the affected individuals and anyone with whom they come into close contact. The behaviour is so obviously part of the syndrome, that it would be almost unheard of to prosecute a sufferer. The condition has, however, been of particular interest to those studying genetic mechanisms relevant to aggression.

Prader–Willi syndrome

In most cases, Prader–Willi syndrome is caused by a deletion on the paternal chromosome 15 (q11–13) (a deletion on the same chromosome of maternal origin results in Angelman syndrome, see above). intellectual disability is variable, from severe through to normal IQ range, but most affected individuals are in the mild intellectual disability range. Irrespective of IQ, all affected people show a pattern of insatiable over-eating of carbohydrates from mid-childhood onwards. If unchecked, the resultant obesity can be crippling and life-threatening. This is preceded in early life by difficulties establishing eating and, often, failure to thrive. With careful attention and strict supervision, weight management from childhood into late adulthood can be attained.

The behavioural and psychiatric features of the condition have been subject to close study. There is a well-documented distinctive pattern of self-injury, which takes the form of skin-picking (Boer and Clarke, 1999). Affected individuals often have mood problems, with anxiety and depression. Paranoid psychosis is common in Prader–Willi syndrome, compared with other individuals with a similar degree of intellectual disability. Genetic family pedigree studies have revealed that, where this psychosis presents in paternal deletion cases, it is merely a reflection of familial heredity. In those in whom there is maternal disomy of chromosome 15 only, however, not all individuals develop the psychosis, although most do, and this is independent of familial heredity (Boer et al., 2002).

Clinical note on assessment of offending behaviour in a person with Prader–Willi syndrome

In a condition in which insatiable over-eating occurs, allegations of offending behaviour related to obtaining food might be expected, or, in children, sweets or candy. In clinical experience, however, this is not common outside the home. The mood problems and psychosis which commonly present in the condition are, in some cases, important considerations in the assessment of offending behaviour of affected individuals.

There have been court cases after people with Prader–Willi syndrome have died in states of extreme obesity, and their carers have been called to account for how they have dealt with the known trait of over-eating. Such cases have not resulted in prosecution: it is accepted that limiting food intake in these individuals may be very challenging. It is likely, however, that such cases will continue to be tested in court – particularly as successful techniques of managing the over-eating of the condition become more widely available, and it might be suggested that extreme obesity in the syndrome is avoidable.

Tuberous sclerosis

Tuberous sclerosis is a complex autosomal dominant neurocutaneous multisystem condition, most often involving either chromosome 9q34.3 or 16p13.3. The typical presentation of the full-blown syndrome is of hamartias (a focal malformation of disorganized tissue types), hamartomas (benign tumours), true neoplasms, skin lesions, intellectual disability, behavioural abnormalities – especially autism, ADHD and disturbed sleep – and seizures. The clinical presentation of the condition is, however, extremely variable, from individuals who only have mild cutaneous lesions, and are often undiagnosed, through to those who have the most severe forms of the condition, depending upon the location and extent of the lesions, particularly in the brain and kidney. About half have intellectual disability. In most individuals the disorder is non-progressive, but for a minority, with brain and kidney involvement, progressive degeneration occurs.

Clinical note on assessment of offending behaviour in a person with tuberous sclerosis

Some people with tuberous sclerosis, especially young adults, can be very aggressive and disturbed in behaviour. The behaviour is more often restless and disorganized than deliberately violent. Autism and ADHD in the condition may be the correlates of alleged offending in some cases.

Williams syndrome

This syndrome is associated with a microdeletion on chromosome 7. The microdeletion accounts for disruption of the elastin gene, which contributes to the vascular and connective tissue pathology associated with the syndrome. Intellectual disability is usually in the moderate range. There is a characteristic 'elf-like' facies, with prominent cheeks, a wide and long philtrum (infra-nasal depression), flat nasal ridge, and heavy orbital ridges. There is a distinctive cognitive profile, with impaired visuo-spatial processing abilities, but relatively superior verbal abilities. The social behaviour of affected individuals features a superficial pattern of affable conversation, which has been referred to as 'cocktail party' syndrome, which tends to mean that the general abilities of affected individuals are over-estimated by others, especially on first meeting.

Clinical note on assessment of offending behaviour

The unusual social behaviour of the condition, coupled with its characteristic appearance, are so prominent that affected individuals are often referred to psychiatric services, usually in childhood (Howlin and Udwin, 2006), where one of the key concerns is sexual vulnerability on the part of young women. Their affable and misleadingly effective social behaviour may predispose to being victims of crime more generally. In the assessment of any alleged offence, a full cognitive and social assessment of the affected individual is crucial, in addition to the standard investigations of any such event.

Historical Lessons From Research Into Two Genetic Syndromes

The history of research into behavioural phenotypes provides lessons in the need for a cautious and careful approach, particularly in clinical diagnosis and assessment.

Early research findings in XYY syndrome concluded that affected individuals had an exceptionally aggressive and violent behavioural profile and were predisposed to criminal activities (Sandberg et al., 1961; Jacobs et al., 1965; Hook, 1973). These conclusions were based on findings in psychiatric and penal institutions, with inherent sample biases. Assumption of a direct relationship between the extra male chromosome and criminality oversimplifies the genotype–phenotype relationship. Theilgaard (1984), in a true community sample, found little difference in violence or anti-social behaviour between XYY, XXY and healthy control men; although the XXY men had more often been arrested, they had not more often been convicted. The XYY men reported more difficulties in childhood, including teasing or challenge by other children on account of their size. Ratcliffe (1999) concluded that there is a moderate, but important, increased incidence of antisocial behaviour in XYY, but this is by no means invariable, and is not a simple or inevitable effect of having an extra Y chromosome. Society's response to the large physical stature, intellectual disability, and tendency to impulsivity of affected individuals all operate as intermediary risk factors.

In fragile X syndrome, the early research indicated that the phenotypic expression resembled that of autism (reviewed in Gillberg and O'Brien, 2000). This resulted in the application of the term AFRAX syndrome (autism–fragile X), with the proposition that the fragile X (now known as FMR-1) gene might be an 'autism gene'. Subsequent research has revealed important differences between the fragile X syndrome behavioural phenotype and classical autism, or Kanner syndrome. While individuals with fragile X syndrome do have social and language difficulties which are on the broader autism spectrum, in other respects the phenotype is unique – with social anxiety being particularly prominent.

These syndromes highlight some of the important lessons of direct relevance to the consideration of offending behaviour among people with specific genetic syndromes. These include the need to consider:

- whether any claims for the genetic basis of behaviour are derived from skewed or biased samples;
- whether appropriate clinical assessment and measurement approaches have been employed;
- whether sufficient attention has been paid to the complex intervening social and interpersonal variables between any psychological traits which are linked to the syndrome in question, on the one hand, and manifest offending behaviour, on the other.

By these means, the clinician is well-placed to bring genetic syndromes of intellectual disability and their behavioural phenotypes into the assessment and understanding of offending behaviour, where relevant.

ALCOHOL AND SUBSTANCE MISUSE

In general, studies have found that people with intellectual disability are less likely to misuse alcohol or other drugs than the mainstream population (Stavrakaki, 2002). In a study of 329 people with intellectual disability, Rimmer et al. (1995) found that less than 5% of individuals used alcohol at all. Consistent with these findings, Sturmey et al. (2003) estimated that fewer than 5% of people with intellectual disability have a co-existing substance related disorder and that those individuals who do have such a disorder are likely to be in the mild or borderline ranges of intellectual disability, since these people are well able to access sources. Taggart et al. (2006) found that 67 individuals with intellectual disability in a UK region had significant substance related problems – this translates to an estimated 0.8% of the adult population with intellectual disability. This is likely to be an underestimate, however, as the study involved only people known to services. An important effect of de-institutionalization for people with intellectual disability is that they have thus become able to access alcohol and drugs like everyone else and, as availability of substances has increased, so for people with intellectual disability living in the community prevalence of substance misuse has increased somewhat in recent years (Annand and Stavrakaki, 2007).

Despite this relatively low prevalence, clinicians (e.g. Krishef and DiNitto, 1981) have suggested that, within this minority of substance misusers, patterns of misuse may differ from those in the general population. People with intellectual disability tend to be older at first use and have less physiological dependency but, when problems do arise, they are likely to be similar to those experienced by the general population including social, biomedical, occupational and family difficulties. Westermeyer et al. (1996) found that, although individuals with intellectual disability generally used less alcohol, the lower quantities nevertheless precipitated the typical problems associated with misuse amongst their intellectually average peers. A particular problem seems to be that when people with intellectual disability use alcohol, a far higher proportion – almost 50% – than in the general population also misuse other substances (McGillicuddy and Blane, 1999). McGillivary and Moore (2001) compared the rate of self-reported alcohol and substance use in 30 offenders with intellectual disability to a control group of 30 non-offenders with intellectual disability. The offender group reported greater use of both legal and illegal substances than the controls and many reported that they had been under the influence of alcohol or drugs at the time of committing their offences. Significant knowledge about substances was found in both groups, although the offenders had greater overall awareness about alcohol and drugs.

In their report on prisoners with intellectual disability in New South Wales, Australia, Hayes and McIlwain (1988) found that around 66% of offenders with intellectual disability were either alcohol abusers or were intoxicated at the time of the offence. In a further investigation, Hayes (1996) reported that of individuals with intellectual disability appearing before two rural courts in New South Wales, 90% had consumed some alcohol on the day of the alleged offence. A further study in Australia (Klimecki et al., 1994) reported that 45% of first offenders, 71% of second offenders, 67% of third offenders and 88% of fourth offenders had a history of substance abuse. Cockram et al. (1998) reported that two-thirds of a sample of 20 offenders with intellectual disability were identified by family members as misusing substances. In a larger scale study of 247 offenders with intellectual disability in Scotland, non-sexual offenders had a far higher rate of alcohol related crime than sexual offenders (Lindsay et al., 2006a). Overall, these findings, mainly from Australia, suggest that while alcohol abuse may be fairly unusual among people with intellectual disability overall, it is far more common among offenders with intellectual disability.

CARE PATHWAYS FOR OFFENDERS WITH INTELLECTUAL DISABILITIES

The care pathways of offenders with intellectual disability share, necessarily, many of the characteristics of the care pathways of all other offenders. Treatment and management strategies occur within a given legal and national policy context, and there is a limited range of options. There are, however, certain differences. These are, to some extent, a reflection of the nature of people with intellectual disability and their offending behaviour, but the care pathways mainly reflect societal attitudes towards them, as evidenced in the development of services and their underlying policies. The complex interplay of these factors may be drawn together in consideration of the typical steps to be considered in building a care pathway for an offender with intellectual disability.

Step One – The Offence, Including Context and Contributory Factors

Elsewhere in this chapter, we have described the characteristics of the offending behaviour of people with intellectual disability, and how this relates to their intellectual and cognitive function, educational attainment and social context. Their offending profile does, to some extent, set the scene for a care pathway that shares some of the characteristics of that for offenders with more average abilities, while having differences in emphasis. A real case for differences in care pathway is clearer for those with more severe intellectual disability, whose offending behaviour is also more divergent from that of the general population, and whose developmental characteristics are such that mainstream services are inappropriate to their needs (Holland, 1997).

Step Two – Recognition and Reporting

Although offending in the wider community by more able offenders with intellectual disability may leave them more susceptible to arrest, there is some evidence of under-reporting of their offending behaviour in residential settings. The reluctance of carers and/or statutory authorities to report to the police is most marked for those with more severe disabilities, where ability to form intent is genuinely more severely impaired. In one study, Lyall et al. (1995) investigated such reporting by staff in community residential services. They found that staff declared themselves to be unlikely to record and report even quite serious offending behaviour by their residents, including assaults resulting in serious injury. Such attitudes, which may be described as misplaced tolerance on their part, do not, in fact, serve the interests of their residents well, although they tend to be reinforced by the police and Crown Prosecution Service (CPS) alike. Among people who may already be struggling to understand social boundaries and mores, lack of action in this respect may be regarded by transgressors as endorsement of their behaviour, and has been identified as one important factor in the maintenance of ongoing offending behaviour among adult offenders with intellectual disability (O'Brien and Bell, 2004).

Step Three – Criminal Prosecution

A variety of prevalence studies, using various methodologies, indicate that people with intellectual disability may be over-represented among those seen at police stations, which findings are in line with the observations of the extent not only of offending behaviour among this population but also the likelihood that this will be immediately identified, as just outlined. The numbers of adults with intellectual disability who are known to services who are actually charged and convicted of offences, however, would appear to be low (see Holland et al., 2002 and Murphy and Mason, 1999 for reviews). Overall, the reluctance by care workers to record and report offending behaviour by people with intellectual disability is paralleled by similar reluctance on behalf of police and CPS to process such offences. Indeed, these reviewers report that, in a number of studies, staff stated that their disinclination to report any such offending was partly based on their expectation that no prosecution would ensue without a huge struggle on their part. It is important to engage the police and prosecution services, at the highest levels, in dialogue about such circumstances so that each can understand the difficulties and limitations of the other in ensuring that community safety extends to families, other care workers and clinical staff while continuing effort to enhance the management and safeguard the rights of those people with intellectual disability who do offend.

Step Four – Diversion From Custody

Diversion from custody for offenders with intellectual disability entails referral to an appropriate specialist team, offering expertise in assessment, formulation and treatment. Such assessment/formulation is best carried out as early as possible in the care pathway – and is often carried out prior to involvement of police and other statutory agencies, particularly in respect of offenders already known to services. Assessment does not necessarily result in automatic acceptance into specialist treatment programmes. In fact, careful assessment and formulation will typically result in a range of options, including:

No further action

This is where there is no indication of need for a clinical disposal – for example, in respect of an individual who has previously been through a programme of treatment, and that further intervention is not warranted.

Referral to mainstream (non-intellectual disability) forensic mental health services

Which is often indicated for intellectually higher functioning individuals, who are able to access and use such services.

Consideration of community/outpatient treatment and support by specialist intellectual disability services

To be successful, such services typically require the invocation of some statutory power, whether under criminal justice (e.g. probation) or mental health legislation (e.g. Lindsay et al., 2006). Many clinicians involved in such work prefer to operate such services within a clinical justice framework, because of the particular statutory agency involvement which that option entails (Holland et al., 2002), and the positive results from such community-based work (e.g. Lindsay et al., 2006b; Linhorst et al., 2003).

Consideration of admission to inpatient (secure) provision

Most developed countries have some kind of secure hospital/health service facility available for offenders with intellectual disability when their needs cannot be met within prison, generic (non-intellectual disability) forensic mental health services or specialist community intellectual disability services. In a minority of cases there is a need for a secure setting in order to contain a significant level of risk of harm to self or others. There is current concern that the pathways into and between services for this group of people are neither dependent on the nature of the offending behaviour nor on the clinical needs of the individuals concerned, but rather on the availability and accessibility of local health and social care services (O'Brien, 2004). Admission of a person into secure provision frequently entails a long period of time a long way from his/her usual home, cutting any useful ties and making discharge back to the community less likely.

At present, therefore, too many individuals remain in long-term secure care. As suggested earlier, the policies of de-institutionalization and community care which produced positive change in service provision for people with intellectual disability took little or no account of the subgroup who offend. In the UK at least, developments of hospital-based services, similar to those for people with mental illness, have been provided on an *ad hoc* basis rather than strategically planned for holistic care along a continuum of need. The institutional model has crept back, with inadequate complementary community services (Murphy et al., 1996). Although that is beginning to change, improvements remain patchy.

Looking Ahead

What should be the way forward? In the management of offenders with intellectual disability, it is important not to adopt a 'one-size-fits-all' approach. Services and systems working with these people must be responsive to their learning needs, to their styles and preferences and to those of the professionals operating the services if they are to achieve good outcomes. Also, while the delineation of discrete steps in the care pathway is helpful to frame thinking, in actual case work the separate steps are often not readily discernible. Nevertheless, it is important that clinicians and case managers retain a clear picture of the structure that lies behind this pathway, and the principles that should underpin it including: inclusiveness, equity, the evidence-base, rationality, accessibility, (cost) efficiency, accountability, and social responsibility. To support this approach, a recent UK Department of Health multi-centre systematic study has been undertaken to investigate the demographic, individual, offence and service characteristics of adults with intellectual disability referred to a range of service settings in order to examine and define the service pathways and determinants of their offending and antisocial behaviour (Carson et al., 2010; Lindsay et al., 2010; O'Brien et al., 2010; Wheeler et al., 2009).

ASSESSMENT AND TREATMENT OF ANGER AND AGGRESSION

Prevalence and impact

Studies of the prevalence of aggression, which includes more than infliction of actual physical violence, have been conducted in large samples of people with intellectual disability across three continents. They indicate aggression rates in community populations of 11–16% in centralized service provider surveys (Harris, 1993; Sigafoos et al., 1994) and direct carer interview studies (Hill and Bruininks, 1984; Smith et al., 1996). Aggression rates were consistently higher in institutional than in community settings – at between 35% and 40%. In a study involving detained offenders with intellectual disability, Novaco and Taylor (2004) found that 47% had been physically violent on at least one occasion following admission to the specialist forensic service. This finding was replicated by McMillan et al. (2004) in a study also involving offenders with intellectual disability detained in secure settings. Anger is rarely assessed routinely in intellectual disability services, but Law et al. (2000) found that more than 60% of people with intellectual disability referred to a community-based service for challenging or offending behaviours were found to have clinically significant anger.

Aggression carries high costs for services generally and staff specifically as well as potentially very serious consequences for individuals (e.g. Attwood and Joachim, 1994; Bromley and Emerson, 1995). In a study of aggression against staff working in an NHS intellectual disability service, Kiely and Pankhurst (1998) found that there were almost five times more incidents of patient violence than were recorded in the Trust's sister mental health service. Following aggressive incidents, staff reported feeling wary of the perpetrator, and less confident in their own abilities.

Assessment of anger among people with intellectual disability

Despite the importance of anger and aggression problems for people with intellectual disability, literature on reliable and valid measures of these phenomena in this population is sparse (Taylor, 2002). Studies by Benson and Ivins (1992) and Rose and West (1999) have indicated that a modified self-assessment measure of *anger reactivity* (the Anger Inventory) has some limited reliability and validity with people with intellectual disability. Oliver et al. (2007) reported that the Modified Overt Aggression Scale (MOAS; Sorgi et al., 1991), an informant-rated measure of the frequency and severity of aggression (verbal and physical against self, others and property), had high levels of inter-rater reliability when used with a small number of people with intellectual disability as part of a treatment outcome study.

Novaco and Taylor (2004) evaluated the reliability and validity of several specially modified anger assessment measures with detained male offenders with intellectual disability. The Novaco Anger Scale (NAS; Novaco, 2003), Spielberger State-Trait Anger Expression Inventory (STAXI; Spielberger, 1996), both self-report measures of *anger disposition*, and the Provocation Inventory (PI; Novaco, 2003), a self-report *anger reactivity* scale, along with the Ward Anger Rating Scale, an informant-rated *anger attribution* measure (*WARS*: Novaco, 1994) were evaluated. The modified anger self-report measures were found to have high internal consistency and less robust, but reasonable, test–retest stability. The STAXI and NAS showed substantial inter-correlation, evidence of concurrent validity for these instruments. Staff WARS ratings of patient anger were found to have high internal consistency and to correlate significantly with patient anger self-reports. Anger, self-reported by the patients, was significantly related to their record of assault behaviour in hospital. The NAS was found to be significantly predictive of whether the patient physically assaulted others following admission to hospital and of the total number of physical assaults.

Anger scales such as the NAS and PI are 'nomothetic', which means that they are best suited to detecting mean differences for groups of people with reference to normative data, rather than highlighting clinically significant changes for individuals. Taylor et al. (2004b) further developed the Imaginal Provocation Test (IPT; originally developed by Novaco, 1975) as an alternative 'idiographic' anger assessment procedure for people with intellectual disability. It is easy to administer, and taps key elements of the experience and expression of anger (emotional reaction, behavioural reactions, and anger control). The IPT indices (*anger reaction, behavioural reaction, anger composite* and *anger regulation*) had respectable internal reliabilities and concurrent validity. In a small controlled trial, the IPT anger reaction, behavioural reactions and anger composite indices were shown to be sensitive to clinical change following treatment for anger (Taylor et al., 2004b).

Willner et al. (2005) developed the Profile of Anger Coping Skills (PACS) to measure specific skills in managing angry situations among people with intellectual disability. Informants are asked to rate the person's use of eight anger management strategies in specific anger-provoking situations salient to that individual. The strategies assessed include use of relaxation skills, counting to 10, walking away calmly, requesting help, use of distraction activities, cognitive re-framing and being assertive. The PACS was found to have acceptable test–retest and inter-rater reliability coefficients and to be sensitive to change associated with an intervention to reduce anger. Following involvement in a community-based anger management group, informant ratings showed that participants' PACS scores were significantly improved compared with scores for those in a no-treatment control group. In the treatment group, coping skills had improved significantly in terms of cognitive re-framing, assertiveness, walking away calmly, and asking for help. These latter two areas of improvement were maintained at 6-months follow-up.

Treatment for anger disorders among people with intellectual disability

Taylor (2002) reviewed psychopharmacological treatment of aggression for people with intellectual disability, but found little reported empirical research. Reviews by Baumeister et al. (1998), Brylewski and Duggan (1999) and Matson et al. (2000) suggested that, due to methodological problems with this research, firm conclusions about the effectiveness of psychotropic medications in

the treatment of aggression in people with intellectual disability are impossible.

The most extensive literature concerning treatment of their aggression is in the applied behavioural analysis (ABA) field. Taylor and Novaco (2005) summarized this, describing several extensive reviews, and concluded that ABA-type behavioural interventions that are generally applied to low functioning individuals in institutional settings may not be as effective for the anger and aggression encountered among higher functioning but intellectually disabled offenders who display low frequency, but very serious aggression and violence, and live in relatively uncontrolled environments.

Treatment of anger and aggression using cognitive behavioural therapy (CBT) based interventions has now been extensively evaluated with children, adolescents, adults with mental illness and offenders (see Novaco and Taylor, 2006 for a review). Taylor (2002) and Taylor and Novaco (2005) have also reviewed numerous single case and case-series studies as well as uncontrolled group anger treatment studies of individual and group therapy for people with intellectual disability; these have generally indicated positive outcomes. Novaco's (1975) anger treatment approach that incorporates Meichenbaum's (1985) stress inoculation paradigm frequently provides the platform on which these modified interventions are based. More recently, a number of small treatment trials have shown the effectiveness of group CBT for anger over waiting-list/no-treatment control conditions with people with intellectual disability living in community settings (Lindsay et al., 2004; Rose et al., 2000; Willner et al., 2005; Willner et al., 2002). In the follow-up study by Lindsay et al. (2004), the numbers of physical assaults by treatment group participants and those in the waiting-list control condition were monitored for equivalent time periods following completion of treatment. It was found that significantly fewer participants in the treatment condition physically assaulted others compared to those in the control condition (14% versus 45% respectively).

There have also been a small number of studies of CBT for anger with offenders with intellectual disability that have yielded positive outcomes. Allan et al. (2001) and Lindsay et al. (2003) reported on group CBT for anger for a series of five women and six men with intellectual disability. The participants were living in community settings, however they had all been referred following violent assaults which had resulted in CJS involvement. In both studies, improvements which were reported for all participants at the end of treatment were also maintained at 15-months follow-up. Burns et al. (2003) evaluated a CBT-framed group anger management intervention for three offenders with intellectual disability residing in a specialist NHS medium secure unit. Using multiple assessment points to carry out time series analysis, the results were mixed in terms of self-reported anger and informant rated aggression measures. The authors suggest that the relatively short length of the unmodified intervention and unstable baseline measures contributed to the limited treatment effects observed.

Taylor et al. (2002, 2004c, 2005) evaluated individual CBT for anger among detained male patients with mild–borderline intellectual disability and violent, sexual and fire-setting histories in a series of concatenated waiting-list controlled studies. The 18-session treatment package includes a 6-session broadly psycho-educational and motivational preparatory phase, followed by a 12-session treatment phase based on individual formulation of each participant's anger problems and needs. The treatment phase follows the classical cognitive behavioural stages of cognitive preparation, skills acquisition, skills rehearsal and then practice in vivo. These studies showed significant improvements on self-reported measures of anger disposition, anger reactivity and behavioural reaction indices following intervention in the treatment groups compared with scores for the control groups. These differences were maintained for up to 4 months following treatment. Staff ratings of study participants' anger disposition did not reach statistical significance, but tended to converge with patient self-reports.

In summary, there are some indications that reliable and valid assessment measures are being developed for offenders with intellectual disability who are angry and/or aggressive. Limited but growing research evidence suggests that CBT based interventions may be effective for this population.

ASSESSMENT AND TREATMENT OF SEXUALLY AGGRESSIVE BEHAVIOUR AMONG PEOPLE WITH INTELLECTUAL DISABILITY

Assessment

The Socio-Sexual Knowledge and Attitudes Test (SSKAT; Wish et al., 1980) has been used widely to consider the role and relevance of sexual knowledge in sexual offending by a person with intellectual disability. Griffiths and Lunsky (2003) have comprehensively revised the SSKAT and shown that sexual offenders have superior knowledge to non-sexual offenders in a number of key areas.

Developments in sex offender treatment work have emphasized the centrality of cognitive processes in the planning, commission and post hoc justification of sexually offensive incidents by people with intellectual disability (Hudson et al., 1999). Broxholme and Lindsay (2003) and Lindsay et al. (2007) have developed the Questionnaire on Attitudes Consistent with Sex Offences (QACSO), an assessment of attitudes consistent with, or permissive of, sexual offending. This measure assesses attitudes towards rape, voyeurism, exhibitionism, dating abuse, stalking, homosexual assault and offences against children. The QACSO scales were shown to have good internal reliability (Cronbach alphas of around 0.8 in each case) and on each

of the scales, sex offenders scored significantly higher than other types of offenders, non-offenders or a group of non-offending normal men. The QACSO has also been shown to be sensitive to change over time (Lindsay et al., 1998; Rose et al., 2002). There is also some preliminary evidence that the QACSO *offences against children* scale may differentiate between offenders against children and offenders against adults, with the latter scoring significantly lower on this scale (Lindsay et al., 2007).

Treatment of intellectually disabled sex offenders

The evidence base for the treatment of inappropriate sexual behaviour in men with intellectual disability is reasonably extensive (Lindsay, 2002; Courtney and Rose, 2004). Until the late 1990s, behavioural management approaches remained the most common basis for psychological treatment of their sexual offending (Plaud et al., 2000). These authors noted that the purpose of a behavioural treatment programme is to improve behavioural competency in daily living skills, general interpersonal and educational skills as well as the more specialized skills related to pro-social sexual behaviour. Griffiths et al. (1989) developed a comprehensive behavioural management régime for sex offenders with intellectual disability. Their programme included modifying deviant sexual behaviour through education, training in social competencies, improving relationship skills, and relapse prevention through alerting support staff and training on issues related to responsibility. In a review of 30 cases, they reported no re-offending and described a number of successful case studies to illustrate their methods.

In their review, Plaud et al. (2000) also describe aversion therapy techniques and masturbatory retraining techniques in some detail. Although there are few reports on the use of these methods with offenders with intellectual disability, Lindsay (2004) successfully employed imagined aversive events to control deviant sexual arousal and routines.

A major recent development in the use of psychological treatment for sex offenders with intellectual disability has been the employment of cognitive and problem-solving techniques within therapy. Among mainstream offenders, Hanson et al. (2002) reported, in a meta-analytic study, that those treatments that used cognitive techniques showed greater reductions in recidivism rates than treatments using other techniques, including behavioural treatments. A central assumption in cognitive approaches is that sex offenders are likely to hold a number of cognitive distortions about sexual behaviour and its expression that, for them, provide justification for their sexual aggression. Cognitive distortions fall into a number of categories, but generally include: complete denial that an offence occurred, mitigation or even denial of responsibility, denial of harm to the victim, denial or mitigation of intent to offend, thoughts of entitlement, and mitigation through claims of altered mental states such as depression or intoxication.

Lindsay et al. (1998) reported a series of case studies of treatment of paedophiles, exhibitionists and stalkers with intellectual disability using cognitive behavioural interventions in which various forms of denial and mitigation of the offence were challenged over treatment periods of up to 3 years. Strategies for relapse prevention and the promotion of self-regulation were also components of the treatment. Across these studies, participants consistently reported positive changes in cognitions during treatment. Each of these reports provides examples of how cognitive distortions are elicited and challenged during treatment. This component of the intervention was evaluated directly using the QACSO (Lindsay et al., 2007). Reductions in the number of endorsements given to cognitive distortions were found following extended treatment periods. These treatment gains were maintained for at least 1 year following cessation of treatment. More importantly, more lengthy follow-up of some cases (4–7 years) showed that none had re-offended.

Rose et al. (2002) reported on a 16-week group treatment for five men with intellectual disability who had perpetrated sexual abuse. The group treatment included self-control procedures, consideration of the effect of the offences on their victims, emotional recognition and strategies for avoiding risky situations. Individuals were assessed using the QACSO, a measure of locus of control, an assessment of knowledge of sexually inappropriate behaviour, and a victim empathy scale. Significant differences from pre- to post-treatment were found only on the locus of control scale. It has to be acknowledged that the length of treatment was short in comparison to most sex offender treatment programmes (usually 12–18 months), nevertheless, participants had not re-offended at 1-year follow-up.

Unfortunately, treatment comparison studies fall well short of optimum experimental standards, and it is important to consider the results in the light of this. Lindsay and Smith (1998) compared seven individuals who had been in treatment for 2 or more years with a group of seven who had been in treatment for less than 1 year. The comparisons were serendipitous in that time in treatment reflected the length of their probation orders made by the court. There were no significant differences between the two groups in terms of severity or type of index offence. The 1-year treatment group showed significantly poorer progress and were more likely to re-offend than those treated for at least 2 years. This suggests that shorter treatment periods may be of limited value for such men.

Keeling et al. (2007) compared treatment outcomes for 11 'special needs' sexual offenders and matched mainstream controls. These were convenience samples, and the authors note the difficulties in ensuring the equivalence of treatment and assessments between the two groups. There were no assessed differences between the groups following treatment and no re-offending reported at 16 months follow-up for either. Lindsay et al. (2006b) compared 121 sex offenders with 105 other types of male offenders and 21 female offenders, all with intellectual disability. Re-offending rates were reported for up to 12 years after the index offence. There were no differences between the groups in IQ; the sex offender cohort tended to be older than the other two cohorts. The female offenders had higher rates of mental illness although about one-third of the men also had mental illness. The differences in re-offending rates between the three groups was highly significant with rates of 24% for male sex offenders, 19% for female offenders but 59% for other types of male offenders. Number of offences by recidivists following treatment was also reduced – to about a quarter to a third of those recorded before treatment, indicating a considerable amount of harm reduction as a result of interventions.

Based on the limited evidence available it is possible to conclude tentatively that psychologically informed and structured interventions appear likely to improve outcomes for sex offenders with intellectual disability, CBT to have a positive effect on offence-related attitudes and cognitions, and that longer periods of treatment will yield better outcomes that are maintained for longer.

FIRE-SETTING BEHAVIOUR AMONG PEOPLE WITH INTELLECTUAL DISABILITY

Prevalence of fire-setting with intellectual disability

It has been suggested that fire-setting is over-represented amongst offenders with intellectual disability (e.g. Day, 1993; Raesaenen et al., 1994) but, as with so many other areas with respect to intellectual disability, this research too is sparse and limited by methodological problems, and the prevalence may, in fact, be unremarkable. Irrespective of the scale of the problem, there is general agreement that that there are people with intellectual disability who have histories of fire-setting who need specialist assessment, treatment and management. In a hospital-wide study of male forensic inpatients with intellectual disability, Taylor et al. (2002b) found that 20% of them (26 of 129) had convictions for arson prior to admission.

Assessment of intellectually disabled fire-setters

Literature on clinical practice with fire-setters with intellectual disability is even more limited than prevalence research. Murphy and Clare (1996) interviewed 10 fire-setters with intellectual disability about their cognitions and feelings prior to and after setting fires, using a newly developed Fire-Setting Assessment Schedule (FSAS). Participants were also asked to rate their feelings in relation to a series of fire-related situations described in a new 14-item Fire Interest Rating Scale (FIRS) (Murphy and Clare, 1996). The construction of the FSAS was guided by the functional analytical approach to fire-setting proposed by Jackson et al. (1987), in which it is proposed that fire-setting is associated with a number of psychological functions, including the need for peer approval, need for excitement, need to alleviate or express sadness, mental illness, or a wish for retribution. Murphy and Clare (1996) found that their study participants identified antecedents to fire-setting with more reliability than they could the consequences. The most frequently endorsed antecedents were anger, followed by being ignored and then feelings of depression. The FSAS has proved to be clinically useful since its inception, but was little further investigated until Taylor et al. (2002) used it to assess the effectiveness of a treatment programme for 14 fire-setters with intellectual disability. Consistent with the results of the Murphy and Clare (1996) study, Taylor et al. (2002b) found that anger, being ignored and depression (in rank order) were the most frequently endorsed antecedents to and consequences of fire-setting in this group according to ratings on the FSAS.

Treatment of intellectually disabled fire-setters

Rice and Chaplin (1979) conducted a study of social skills training for two groups of five fire-setters in a high security psychiatric facility in North America. People in one of the groups were reported to have mild to borderline intellectual disability. After treatment, both groups improved significantly on a reliable observational rating scale of role-played assertive behaviour. At the time of reporting, eight of the 10 patients in this study had been discharged for around 12 months and none had been convicted or suspected of setting fires.

Clare et al. (1992) reported a case study of a man with mild intellectual disability who had been admitted to a secure hospital after two convictions for arson. He had a prior history of arson and making hoax calls to the fire service. On transfer to a specialist inpatient unit he received a comprehensive treatment package, which included social skills and assertiveness training, development of coping strategies, covert sensitization, and surgery for a significant facial disfigurement; significant clinical improvements were observed in targeted areas. Discharged to a community setting, this man had not engaged in any fire-related offending behaviour at 30 months follow-up.

Hall et al. (2005) described application of cognitive analytical therapy (CAT), an integrative model of short-term psychotherapy (Ryle, 1993), to arsonists with intellectual disability, with the aim of reformulating the origins of the distress and maladaptive coping strategies that had resulted in fire-setting behaviour. They also described the delivery of a 16-session group CBT approach for six male fire-setters with intellectual disability, detained in an NHS medium secure setting, to help them identify personal risk factors associated with their fire-setting and develop alternative coping strategies to reduce their risk of re-offending.

Two group follow-up sessions were held, the first 6 weeks after the original group and the second after 6 months. Unfortunately, although well designed, this work rests wholly on description and no outcome measures are given – just an indication that the men 'responded positively'.

Taylor et al. (2002b) reported a group study involving 14 men and women with intellectual disability and arson convictions who were assessed pre- and post-treatment on a number of fire-specific, anger, self-esteem and depression measures. The intervention comprised 40 CBT based group sessions over 4 months that involved work on offence cycles, education about the costs associated with setting fires, training of skills to enhance future coping with emotional problems associated with previous fire-setting behaviour, and work on personalized plans to prevent relapse. Following treatment, significant improvements were found in all areas assessed, except depression.

A case series of four detained men with intellectual disability and convictions for arson offences were evaluated before and after completion of the same intervention (Taylor et al., 2004d). The patients engaged well, and all showed high levels of motivation and commitment that were reflected in generally improved attitudes with regard to personal responsibility, victim issues and awareness of risk factors associated with their fire-setting behaviour.

The same methods were used in a further case series of six women with a similar range of problems (Taylor et al., 2006), again, the participants engaged well and all completed the programme. Their scores on measures related to fire-specific treatment targets generally improved following the intervention. All but one of the participants had been discharged to community placements at 2-year follow-up, and there had been no reports of participants setting any fires or engaging in fire risk-related behaviour.

There is, then, little more than pilot work to support therapeutic interventions for people with intellectual disability who set fires, but that work does seem to offer promise, based on CBT methods delivered in a group setting.

ASSESSMENT AND MANAGEMENT OF RISK OF OFFENDING AND/OR HARM TO OTHERS AMONG OFFENDERS WITH INTELLECTUAL DISABILITIES

Advances have been made in the general forensic research field in the development of measures designed to predict violence and sexual aggression amongst those with a history of offending (e.g. Banks et al., 2004; see also chapter 22). This work has now been extended to include offenders with intellectual disability. Quinsey et al. (2004) demonstrated that the Violence Risk Appraisal Guide (VRAG; Quinsey et al., 1998), an established actuarial risk measure in the general offender literature, has good predictive accuracy when used with intellectual disability offenders. Gray et al. (2007) conducted a more extensive investigation of the VRAG with 145 patients with intellectual disability and 996 mainstream patients, all discharged from hospital having been admitted with serious mental illness, intellectual disability or personality disorder – and having been convicted of a criminal offence or having exhibited behaviour that might have led to a conviction in different circumstances. They found that the VRAG predicted re-conviction rates in the intellectual disability sample with an effect size as large as that for the non-intellectual disability sample.

This important research on the assessment and management of risk in offenders with intellectual disability has continued in a study involving 212 people in a range of security settings: high, medium and low hospital security, and community forensic intellectual disability services (the 212 Multi-Centre Risk Study: Hogue et al., 2006). The most complex presentations, in particular those with comorbid personality disorder, were found in the more secure settings; more participants in the high security group had sustained both index and previous convictions for violence.

Lindsay et al. (2008) combined the total cohort of offenders with intellectual disability from the 212 Multi-Centre Risk Study to evaluate the predictive validity of a range of static and dynamic risk assessments. They found that the VRAG, the Short Dynamic Risk Scale (Quinsey, 2004), and the Emotional Problems Scale (Prout and Strohmer, 1991) showed significant areas under the curve (AUC), using receiver operator characteristics (ROC) analyses (for an explanation of these measures see chapter 22) in relation to the prediction of violent incidents. The Static-99 (Hanson and Thornton, 1999) also showed a significant AUC in relation to the prediction of sexual incidents. With the same study sample, Taylor et al. (2010) reviewed the psychometric properties and predictive validity of the HCR-20 (Webster et al., 1997 and chapter 22). Exploratory factor analysis found that the H Scale (historical items) constituted three factors (delinquency, interpersonal function and personality disorder) while the C (clinical items) and R (risk items) scales made up distinctly separate factors. Using ROC analyses, they found that all three scales were predictive of incidents recorded prospectively over a 12-month period, concluding that the HCR-20 is a robust instrument for guiding clinicians to reach clinically consistent and defensible decisions.

In an extension of the 212 Multi-Centre Risk Study, Morrissey and colleagues (Morrissey et al., 2005, 2007a,b) investigated the utility, discriminant and predictive validity of the Psychopathy Checklist–Revised (PCL-R: Hare, 2003). The results show that the PCL-R predicts both good response to treatment and positive moves from high to medium secure conditions, both within 2 years of assessment. The PCL-R did not, however, predict institutional violence at a better than chance level.

Overall, risk assessment research has demonstrated that several well established actuarial, dynamic and clinical instruments, some developed specifically for this group, have good reliability, discriminative validity and predictive validity with offenders with intellectual disability.

LEGAL AND ETHICAL CONSIDERATIONS IN WORKING WITH OFFENDERS WITH INTELLECTUAL DISABILITIES

Intellectual Disability and the Criminal Justice System

People with intellectual disability are vulnerable at each stage of the criminal justice process – pretrial, during any court hearing and on sentencing. Their disability may affect their capacity to understand their rights on arrest, to deal with police questioning/interrogation, and/or to provide valid statements or confessions. Then, if the case comes to court, their capacity to enter a plea, to understand court proceedings, and/or to instruct their counsel may be limited. On sentencing, particularly if this is to prison, their capacity to access and make use of the various educational, treatment and rehabilitative packages offered in the mainstream CJS may impede their progress, and even compromise their rights to fair treatment.

'Responsibility' and 'competency' or 'capacity' are key concepts in criminal justice systems around the world and are particularly pertinent to offenders with intellectual disability. In the pretrial phase, defendants with intellectual disability are exceptionally vulnerable to giving self-incriminatory statements or confessions. In fact, in England and Wales, the Confait case, which ultimately led to the Police and Criminal Evidence Act (PACE) 1984 through a route including a judicial enquiry (Fisher, 1977) and the Royal Commission on Criminal Procedure 1981, was of two 17 year olds and a man with intellectual disability, who had been 'prompted' into a false confession. PACE and its accompanying Codes of Practice have particular provisions for people with intellectual disability with regard to police questioning and confessional evidence (Sanders and Young, 2000). Before beginning an interview with a person with intellectual disability, or who appears to have intellectual disability, the presence of an 'appropriate adult' is required. An appropriate adult is distinct from a legal advisor, and is more likely to be a relative or guardian of the interviewee, or someone with experience of working with people with intellectual disability (e.g. social worker or community nurse) who is not employed by the police service.

The issue of suggestibility of accused persons with intellectual disability during police interviews has been well researched. Gudjonsson (1992) argued that people with intellectual disability were more susceptible to yielding to leading questions and shifting their answers under interrogation by the police and, as such, more liable to give false confessions. He developed the Gudjonsson Suggestibility Scales (GSS; Gudjonsson, 1997), which are used widely. Clare and Gudjonsson (1993) found that participants with intellectual disability confabulated more and were more acquiescent during interrogative interview while Everington and Fulero (1999) found that people with intellectual disability were more likely to alter their answers in response to negative feedback. Beail (2002), however, in a review of a number of studies involving the GSS, questioned whether artificial test situations were similar enough to real-life interrogation situations:

> ...because the results are based on an examination of semantic memory whereas police interviews are more concerned with episodic or autobiographical event memory. Also, experienced events usually involve multi-modal sensory input, resulting in a more elaborate trace in associative memory (p.135).

Beail concluded that the GSS may be limited in its applicability to criminal justice proceedings.

These concerns about competence to be interviewed are important because confessional evidence should be considered to be valid only if it is voluntary, knowing and intelligent (Baroff et al., 2004). People with intellectual disability can be particularly vulnerable to coercion, threats and promises of leniency, thus raising concerns about the 'voluntariness' of their confessions. Understanding of the concepts of the right to silence and other rights to protect oneself have rarely been tested with suspects who have intellectual disability, and yet such interviewees are probably more likely to answer questions in the manner and direction they believe they are expected to, the so-called *social desirability bias* (Baroff, 1996), or simply to want to please. A valid confession rests on the suspect's understanding that in waiving his or her rights s/he may be placing him- or herself in jeopardy. In the stressful and confusing context of arrest and interrogation it can be exceptionally difficult for suspects with intellectual disability to make a reasoned choice about information they will volunteer or withhold, or to grasp the implications of their responses to police questions (Baroff et al., 2004).

In assessing competency or fitness to stand trial and enter a plea, a defendant's abilities in the following areas should be considered: (a) understanding of the crime of which they are accused; (b) knowledge of the purpose of the trial and the roles of the principal players; and (c) ability to instruct one's counsel (Baroff et al., 2004). In the UK, assessment and management of a claim to be unfit to plead or stand trial follows the same path, regardless of the nature of the disorder (see chapter 2). There are a number of assessments which may be of particular value in assessing a defendant's understanding of court proceedings when s/he has intellectual disability, all from the USA. The Competence Assessment to Stand Trial–Mental Retardation (CAST-MR: Everington and Luckasson, 1992) assesses competence in three areas: basic legal concepts, skills to assist the defence counsel and understanding of court procedures. The CAST-MR was used by 45% of psychologists surveyed about practices used when evaluating competence to stand trial among juveniles (Ryba et al., 2003), but this and similar assessments have a number of limitations. These include the lack of an underlying conceptual structure, no standardized administration procedures, no criterion based scoring, and limited normative data (Otto et al., 1998).

In law, a criminal conviction generally requires proof beyond reasonable doubt of two elements – the act (*actus reus*) and the state of mind, or intent, necessary for this to have been a crime (*mens rea*). Historically, people with severe intellectual disability were considered incapable of forming such intent and thus not responsible for their actions (Fitch, 1992). Traditionally, in common law systems, judgment about responsibility for acts on the part of a person with intellectual disability was made in terms of his/her ability to distinguish right from wrong, but, in the US at least, courts are moving away from this dichotomous approach to 'moral understanding' in favour of case-by-case consideration (Baroff et al., 2004) (see also chapters 2 and 5).

Ethical Issues and Offenders with Intellectual Disability

As Sturmey and Gaubatz (2002) have indicated, issues concerning offenders in secure settings pose classic problems for professional ethics. People with intellectual disability may be particularly vulnerable to various forms of abuse involving the application of dangerous treatment and research interventions without due process. While some people with intellectual disability will be able to understand the elements necessary for consent to treatment, many cannot and even fewer are likely to be able to comprehend all the elements necessary for participation in clinical research (Arscott et al., 1998, 1999). The tension lies in the fact that it is crucially important also to avoid any situation where discriminatory decisions might exclude people with intellectual disability from potentially beneficial or benign treatment or from research because of erroneous assumptions about their capacity to give consent. A balance is needed (Sturmey et al., 2004).

Valid consent requires that people are provided with accurate information about the treatment or research intervention, that they have capacity to make a decision about it and that they understand the consequences of the decision and that their decision to participate is voluntary (Lord Chancellor's Department, 1999); It is possible to make information about treatment and research understandable and accessible to people with intellectual disability (Arscott et al., 1998, 1999); however, research is needed concerning functional assessments of the elements (comprehension, assimilation, recall and decision-making) required for capacity to give valid consent (Iacono and Murray, 2003).

These important considerations aside, the extent to which decision-making by offenders with intellectual disability can ever be totally voluntary and free of a degree of coercion is a matter that needs to be aired openly by practitioners in this field. This would encourage clarity for clinicians and researchers, ethics committees, and offenders themselves, in this difficult area. In most jurisdictions, treatment for offenders may be mandated by the courts. The need to punish offenders, to protect the public, and to rehabilitate creates a tension. In Europe, clinicians are fortunate that they do not have to struggle at all with giving evidence in capital cases, but even in the USA, in 2002, the Supreme Court outlawed the death penalty for people with mental retardation (*Atkins*). The decision acknowledged that such defendants face a greater risk of wrongful conviction and warrant special protection accordingly, although, as French (2005) describes, the ruling still allows the state to determine how such offenders are to be assessed and measured, and provision of appropriate services remains patchy. As a number of people have shown, including French (2005) and Sturmey et al. (2004), psychological assessment, treatment and research in the intellectual disability field have been subject to fashions and trends which have at times been far from benign, including enactment of sterilization laws (Sofair and Kaldjian, 2000). Now, in Europe, the USA and many other countries, there are legal protections against abuse in this respect.

Unproven treatments or interventions have the potential to do harm even when the intention is benign. Facilitated communication is an example of one such that was not just unhelpful and ineffective (Mostert, 2001), but resulted in the wrongful conviction of parents of sexual abuse of their children and separated their children from their families. It is important, therefore, that treatment and research with this vulnerable group are not simply well intended, but are supported by evidence of their effectiveness and offered to offenders with intellectual disability within a robust and transparent ethical consent framework.

CONCLUSIONS

The policy of de-institutionalization of services for people with intellectual disability has had an impact on offenders with intellectual disability, who are now more visible than before (Taylor and Lindsay, 2007). Larger numbers of people with intellectual disability who transgress society's mores are being dealt with through regular CJS channels, and the courts are sending more people with intellectual disability to forensic mental health programmes for offence-related interventions (Lindsay and Taylor, 2005). Services, research and practice for this offender group have grown apace since the early 1990s (Lindsay et al., 2004), but, as illustrated, even in the field of epidemiology the research has limitations. Most evidence for treatments and intervention comes from naturalistic studies or single case work. Beyond the need to develop the evidence base for treating offenders with intellectual disability, we anticipate that, in common with other health, criminal and human service areas, the most pressing future issue is understanding how to translate knowledge into practice and make a real difference to the lives and prospects of this subgroup of people with intellectual disability, improving their safety at home and in the wider community.

14

Psychosis, violence and crime

Edited by
Pamela J Taylor

Written by
Pamela J Taylor
Sue Estroff

1st edition authors: **Paul Mullen, Pamela J Taylor and Simon Wessely**

The personality of any normally constituted person must be capable of at least a certain flexibility, otherwise the machinery for doubt would be absent, and what is more irrefutable proof of madness than an inability to have doubt. No, no, to ensure sanity there must at least be the elements of internal disagreement ever present in a personality (Ustinov, 1977).

VULNERABLE TO VIOLENCE AND VULNERABLE TO BEING VIOLENT

The psychoses are intrusive and often chronic debilitating illnesses that profoundly alter the lives of those who have them. Among their most common symptoms are delusions, which allow little room for doubt. Among their many unfortunate consequences they leave sufferers very vulnerable to violence in all its directions. The risk of becoming a victim of violence is higher among people with schizophrenia and similar illnesses than among the general population, but risk engaging in destructive acts to self or harming others is also elevated.

Victimization is mainly dealt with in chapter 28. Here we provide only an illustrative summary of the consistent findings in this area. Among about 700 people attending psychiatric services in the UK (Walsh et al., 2003) and 962 in Australia (Chapple et al., 2004), it has been shown that 16–18% of people with psychosis become a victim of violence during the course of a year, with social exclusion factors, such as homelessness, substance misuse and more severe psychopathology increasing the risk of this happening. In the United States of America (USA), Teplin et al. (2005) drew from the 32,449 people participating in the nationwide USA Crime Victimization Survey to compare crime victimization among 483 men and 453 women with severe mental illness (SMI) and their peers without. The former were randomly selected, but stratified for ethnicity, from 16 mental health treatment agencies in Chicago. Over 25% of the people with severe mental illness had become the victim of a violent crime in the preceding 12 months, 11

times the rate in the comparison group. Teplin's group then reviewed all 31 US empirical studies since 1990 of violence among people with psychosis. Choe et al. (2008) found that, overall, 12–18% of all patients – resident in hospital or in the community – had been perpetrators of violence, but 35% had been victims of violence in the 6–18 months prior to the study. Just three of the studies had evaluated perpetration and victimization in the same sample. One found that, in an outpatient commitment sample over a short period (4 months), a higher proportion of the patients had been victimizers than victimized, but in the other two studies having become a victim of violence was far more prevalent than inflicting it (Brekke et al., 2001; Brunette and Drake, 1997).

Violence to self is another indicator of harmful distress which sometimes affects others as well as the sick person. Among people with schizophrenia and similar disorders, non-fatal self-directed violence occasionally takes on a specifically destructive form if body parts are involved in the delusional symptoms (e.g. Chand et al., 2010). More commonly than this, self-directed violence may be fatal; the risk of suicide by people with psychosis is higher than their risk of homicide. Data from the National Confidential Inquiry into Suicide and Homicide (NCISH) (see also chapter 28) are illustrative. For the period April 2000–December 2004 (NCISH, 2006), 6367 Inquiry cases of suicide, about 27% of the total suicides for the period, were defined by having had some contact with mental health services in the 12 months before death; 1,145 (19%) had schizophrenia or other delusional disorders and 2,821 (46%) depression or bipolar disorder. There were 2,670 homicide convictions and 14 cases of murder charges where the defendant was unfit to plead or not guilty by reason of insanity over a similar period (April 1999–December 2003); 141 (5%) of the homicides were by people with schizophrenia, 806 (30%) by people with any lifetime psychiatric diagnosis. In the public mind, the risk of a person with psychosis being violent to others is generally the source of greater concern than the other types of vulnerability to violence. Constant efforts are needed to inform the public better and, above all, to diminish fear about violence to strangers. This is, in fact, less common on the part of psychosis sufferers than within other diagnostic groups (Johnson and Taylor, 2003) or the wider public (e.g. NCISH, 2006). We are, however, writing for a text on forensic psychiatry, so the main focus of this chapter will be on violence perpetrated by people with schizophrenia or similar psychoses.

A great deal is known about a few individuals with psychosis who have killed another person, often driven to the deed by their illness. Worldwide, at least since 1800, the public and political imagination has been captured by spectacular cases. Not infrequently these tragic figures then inadvertently become the impetus for new mental health law, or mental health aspects of criminal law, often bearing the names of those who were killed, and for specialist secure forensic mental health services. *Post hoc*, efforts are made to insert the more pragmatic mix for science and humanity which is essential both for the specialist services to be successful and for established generic services to improve management of complex cases, and so prevent harm. Evidence for the effectiveness of most current strategies and services, however, remains slight, as does an evidence-based understanding of the nature of links between psychosis and violence.

Some Strengths and Limitations of the Literature

Much of the research has focused on the epidemiological question of whether violence is associated with psychosis more often than would be expected by chance. In the 1980s, evidence in this area was incomplete and inconclusive, and each of the three main claims – that violence was more, less, or as common among people with psychosis than without it – had some support (Taylor, 1982). A main limitation was that research followed a pattern of inquiring about violence in groups of people with psychosis who were in treatment or about psychosis in established criminal populations; there were no true community surveys (Monahan and Steadman, 1983). Since the 1990s, several good epidemiological studies have emerged. After a period of consistent findings and growing certainty about the elevated risk of violence among people with psychosis, however, ever larger more recent studies seem to be beginning to call this into question again. A major problem in this field is that political overtones seem inescapable, both in the commissioning of research and in its interpretation and application. From a clinical perspective, the size of the relationship between psychosis and violence matters primarily in terms of planning effective services with adequate capacity. From a civil and legal rights perspective, there has been much concern that an epidemiology which establishes a link between psychosis and violence may merely serve to stigmatize an already disparaged group, and put their civil liberties in peril. Where an association is found between the two, those who fear an increase in

discrimination invoke the contributions to violence of common comorbid conditions. One person's altruistic interpretation, however, can feed another's search for reasons for re-labelling and rejecting those seeking help from their services. Since the 1983 edition of this text there have been many publications on the numerical relationship between psychosis and violence, but it is less clear that there has been a commensurate increase in understanding how psychosis may predispose a person to being the recipient or perpetrator of violence or of how to decrease the number and seriousness of violent incidents through therapeutic intervention with the individual and his/her social environment.

Psychosis and Perpetration of Violence: Some Illustrative Cases and Their Consequences

In England, widely reported links between psychosis and infamous crimes which had implications for law and mental health or social services first became prominent in the nineteenth century. In 1800, Hadfield shot at King George III (Walker, 1968). Hadfield was put on trial for high treason, but his post-traumatic psychosis was recognized. Powerful arguments for compassion on the one hand and pragmatics on the other resulted in a finding of:

Not Guilty: he being under the influence of Insanity at the time the act was committed.

Since he was manifestly dangerous, legislation was hastily enacted and implemented retrospectively, thus allowing his detention in hospital. McNaughton's trial for murder in 1843 brought elaboration of the insanity rules, still referred to by his name. It also brought some of the best descriptions of links between psychosis and serious violence, as not only was his concurrent mental state described, but also witnesses who had known him long before the culminating homicide were cross-examined about the development of his delusions (West and Walk, 1977). This is not the place for a long list of notorious and/or influential English cases, but a leap forward to the latter part of the twentieth century will show their continuing power. On 17 December 1992, Christopher Clunis killed Jonathan Zito. The men did not know each other and the attack, in full public view, was unprovoked and, at least to onlookers, at random. Clunis had sought help. In the 4 years prior to the fatal attack he had seen 43 different psychiatrists (Ritchie et al., 1994), and it is hard to imagine that any one of them could have developed an in-depth understanding or therapeutic relationship with him. He was a man with a near classic social decline into schizophrenia, but he had difficulty in engaging in treatment, had given warnings of violence and sometimes used illicit drugs, so his diagnosis varied as he moved between services. On one occasion his condition was even described as 'manipulation for a bed'. Sadly, the landmark change was not that services became uniformly more receptive to such people. The Ritchie report, together with the charitable trust set up by Jonathan Zito's widow (see also chapter 28) was, however, instrumental in establishing the principles that every homicide by a person who had been in contact with psychiatric services before the homicide would be subject to an individual independent inquiry (Department of Health, 1994) and that there should be a National Confidential Inquiry into these homicides (see also this chapter below and chapter 28). It also influenced many of the changes in mental health legislation for England and Wales, finally enacted in 2007.

Other parts of the UK have had experience with similar individuals for whom psychosis, for a variety of reasons, was not much helped by services, and led to serious violence. The extent, however, to which understanding that mental health services could and should have a more effective role in preventing such tragedies is global, and transcends cultures and less porous national boundaries. Another man who had been trying to get help for his psychotic illness was Andrew Goldstein in New York. He had had a good deal of attention, and had accumulated over 3,500 pages of hospital psychiatric records by the time he committed a homicide, but he too was chaotic and often skipped appointments. Just days before the killing, a case worker sent him a note saying that if he had not called by a specified date, his case would be closed (Winerip, 1999). Three days before that deadline, he pushed a young woman, Kendra Webdale, to her death under a subway train. Later that year, the New York State Assembly and Senate passed The New York Mental Hygiene Law 1999 (MH Law 9.60), also known as 'Kendra's Law', and injected money into developing an 'Assisted Outpatient Treatment Program'. For adults still capable of living in the community but likely to be unsafe without supervision, this required attendance at a designated clinic, included a mandate for medication and, as necessary, periodic blood tests/urinalysis, individual or group therapy, day treatment, educational or vocational training, and supervision of living arrangements. Preliminary evaluation of the programme suggested that it had been effective in reducing violent and suicidal behaviour as well as rates of hospital admissions, so the law was renewed in 2005, but with a requirement for further evaluation. Subsequent research replicated these positive findings (Swartz et al., 2009, 2010), with the qualification that this New York programme is probably more comprehensive than other such programmes in the USA. Improvements in many aspects of the lives of the people in the programme were reported, including reduction in use of inpatient facilities and arrests, without those people feeling unduly stigmatized and without adverse effect on their use of other services.

In Japan, in June 2001, the by now familiar story of a young man with schizophrenia, well known to psychiatric services – 'institutionalized more often than he had been arrested' – and yet never quite connecting with those services came to a disastrous end. He ran amok in a school, and killed several schoolgirls. On arrest, he said:

Anything and everything has become unbearable. Time and time again I tried to kill myself but I could not do it. I wanted to be arrested and get the death sentence.

He was later executed, but the Prime Minister's immediate response was:

The imperfection of the law has become clear and certain changes to Japan's psychiatric system should be considered for mentally ill offenders.

In 2003, the Japanese parliament, the Diet, enacted the Law Concerning Medical Treatment and Observation for People Who Commit Serious Harm to Others Under the Condition of Lost Mind and the Like 2003, which, among other provisions, for the first time enabled the development of specialist forensic psychiatric services (Yoshikawa and Taylor, 2003; see also chapter 5).

The cases that drive service change tend to involve offences by men, and there are common claims that forensic mental health services have been particularly oriented towards men to the detriment of treating women. Among people with psychosis, as those without, recorded violence is more common among men than women, so more men present to services. As we shall see, however, proportionately more violence among women may be accounted for by psychosis than among men, but then, most research has necessarily been done with men. Our examination of the work on violence in relation to psychosis will, therefore, mainly reflect research with men only, or with men forming the majority of any sample. Where issues more specific to women can be examined, these are mainly covered in chapter 20.

PSYCHOSIS AND CRIME: THE EPIDEMIOLOGY

Relative Proportions of People with and without Psychosis Who are Violent

Even if single cases are powerful, it is scientifically inappropriate to draw from them the inference that there is more than chance or 'special circumstances' that link psychosis and violence. Swanson et al. (1990) may be regarded as the pioneers of an acceptable epidemiology of psychosis and violence, using US Epidemiologic Catchment Area (ECA) interview data from over 10,000 people who participated in a household survey. This study was, thus, of a general population based sample, albeit excluding some groups of particular interest in this context, such as homeless people. Just over 12% of the people with schizophrenia had reported being violent within the year prior to interview, compared with about 2% of the people without mental disorder. When schizophrenia alone was considered, there was just a four-fold elevation in rate of violence. Depression alone was associated with about twice the rate of violence of the general population. Having more than one diagnosis, however, had a substantial effect, with over 30% of the people with schizophrenia *and* substance misuse disorders being violent.

Interpretation of other studies requires the observation that while some are diagnostically precise, and some refer only to schizophrenia, others take a broader definition of psychosis, albeit noting that schizophrenia is the most common of the psychoses to be associated with violence. Still other studies take the concept of 'major mental disorder', which seems to more or less equate with psychosis. The picture for schizophrenia and schizophrenia-like psychoses is generally clearer than that for bipolar and/ or depressive psychosis. It may even be that mania *per se* is protective against violence, indeed some have argued that, providing that a person has a fixed belief in his or her omnipotence, then violence is unnecessary. Häfner and Böker (1973) found just one case of mania among their national study series of homicides in Germany 1955–64 and Schipkowensky (1968) found just four over the 40 years up to 1965 in Sofia, Bulgaria. Craig (1982) failed to find a single episode of violence among 20 consecutive admissions to hospital with mania, despite the high levels of anger and agitation among these people. The stories for bipolar disorder and depressive psychoses in these studies, however, differ from the much more recent study using Swedish health and criminal justice registers in Sweden (Fazel et al., 2010). Like other recent studies, there is no separate consideration of mania in this study, but rather 3,743 individuals with two or more discharge diagnoses of bipolar disorder were identified in the 32-year period 1973–2004 and compared with over 37,000 general population controls. There was a small elevation of risk among those with pure bipolar disorder, but people with bipolar disorder in combination with substance abuse disorders were about 6.5 times more likely to be violent.

Focus on schizophreniform psychoses suggests that the order of elevation in rate of violence by people suffering with one is something in excess of four times the general population rate. This is fairly consistent from Swanson through other well constructed association studies emerging through the 1990s, despite the fact that details of method differed. Five studies linked health and criminal records in Nordic birth cohorts (Hodgins, 1992; Hodgins et al., 1996; Tiihonen et al., 1997; Brennan et al., 2000; Ortman, 1981, available only in Danish). An Australian study linked health and criminal records through the electoral role in Australia (Wallace et al., 2004). The Dunedin birth cohort provides for a true community survey, relying on repeated interview and records searches in a longitudinal design with remarkable follow-up rates of over 90% (see chapter 2 of Moffitt et al., 2001). For estimates of the quantitative relationship between psychosis and violence, however, cross-sectional

analyses were applied. In this cohort, only three conditions independently affected violence rates at age 21: schizophrenia spectrum disorder, alcohol dependency and cannabis dependency, with a five-fold (criminal convictions) to sevenfold elevation in (self-reported) violence rates among those with schizophrenia spectrum disorder (Arseneault et al., 2000). No study is without its methodological problems, however. Here, although bias by subgroup exclusion was eliminated, difficulties lie in the sample characteristics. There were just six people in the subgroup with criminal convictions for violence at age 21, and only 13 in the violence self-report group. At age 26, the relationship between schizophrenia spectrum disorders and violence remained similar, but numbers in the groups of interest were still small (Arseneault et al., 2003).

Proportions of People Who Kill Who Have Psychosis

Another popular way of estimating the frequency of association between psychosis, generally schizophrenia, and violence has been to study homicide figures. Homicide is chosen for this purpose because it is a crime with a high clear-up rate, and so it is generally considered that studying national or regional criminal statistics in this regard will yield something very close to the real figures. It is, though, also an unusual and generally non-recidivist crime (see also chapter 19). Furthermore, like other violence, there has been consistent evidence over time that the contribution of people with mental disorder to homicide statistics will depend in part on the base rate for homicide (Schipkowensky, 1973; Coid, 1983; Reiss and Roth, 1993), which varies substantially internationally (e.g. Reiss and Roth, 1993). Large et al. (2009) have, however, posed a persuasive challenge to this assumption, based on a systematic review and meta-analysis of all published studies, which included diagnostic assessments, from developed countries, between 1960 and 2008. This does not, of course, demolish the argument that, untreated, schizophrenia or similar psychoses may impose some risk for violence. The figures which follow underscore that, but also suggest the importance of risk factors likely to be common to all homicides, and the obvious point that tackling these more general risk factors, including availability of weapons, alcohol and illicit drugs and social adversities may exert an influence on people with psychosis as much as people without.

The proportion of homicides attributed to people with psychosis across a wide range of countries is remarkably consistent, with the tiny population of Iceland being the only real outlier: Australia (New South Wales) 6.7% (Nielssen et al., 2007); Australia (Victoria) 7.1% (Wallace et al., 1998); Austria 5.4% (Schanda et al., 2004); Finland 5.7% (Laajasalo and Hakkanan, 2005, 2006); Germany 8.9% (Erb et al., 2001; Hafner and Boker, 1973); Iceland 28% (Petursson and

337

Gudjonsson, 1981); Singapore 8.2% (Koh et al., 2006); Sweden 8% (Lindqvist, 1989), 8.9% (Fazel and Grann, 2006); New Zealand 3.8% (Simpson et al., 2004); the UK 5–8% (NCISH, 2010); USA (Contra Costa County, California) 10% (Wilcox, 1985). There is also some consensus on trends over time, with indications of a reduction in the proportion of homicides committed by people with a mental disorder at least since the 1950s (Taylor and Gunn, 1999; Simpson et al., 2004). Some recent increase and restablilization is evident in England and Wales (NCISH, 2010); in Nordic countries, as in other Western countries, there has been an increase in overall homicide rates during the 1990s and 2000s, but with alcohol and other drug misuse rather than psychosis accounting for this rise (Gudjonsson and Petursson, 2007).

The Impact of People with Psychosis on Violence in the Population

Swanson and colleagues (1990) emphasized that their work was suggestive only of a higher relative risk of violence by people with psychosis. Among the more than 10 000 respondents in three of the four US cities participating in the ECA survey (Baltimore, Raleigh-Durham and Los Angeles) just 3% of the violence was accounted for by people with schizophrenia. Measuring the impact of psychosis in this way not only yields figures which are more helpful for public health initiatives, but makes allowance for possible differences in violent episodes per person and some other confounding factors. Wallace et al. (2004) showed the potential relevance of this in finding that people with schizophrenia were convicted of about twice as many offences over a lifetime as people without. Accordingly, there have been a number of studies of 'population attributable risk'. In the Wallace et al. (2004) study this was very similar (3.2%) to the Swanson figure. Fazel and Grann (2006) studied linked crime and health registers for people over the age of criminal responsibility (15) in Sweden for the 13-year period 1988–2000. The average population for the period was just over 7 million, and the number of people discharged from hospital with a diagnosis of psychosis just over 98,000. The population attributable risk for psychosis generally was 5.2% and for schizophrenia specifically 6.3%. In the UK, however, in a computer assisted interview household survey in the year 2000, Coid et al. (2006) found this risk to be just 1%, little different from the likely representation of psychosis in the community.

Longitudinal Risk Based Studies

Elbogen and Johnson (2009) have taken a welcome longitudinal perspective on the relationship between psychosis and other mental disorders. They used the US National Epidemiologic Survey on Alcohol and Related Conditions (NESARC) database to study this. The advantages of this database are that it is large – 34,653 participants – and

representative of the US general population. People were sampled from every state and from homeless or temporarily housed populations as well as people in stable homes, and longitudinal data were collected in two waves about three years apart (2001–2003 and 2004–2005). Only the institutionalized were excluded. The research question was about whether mental illness at the first wave of data collection predicted violence between the first and second interviews. It did, but only when associated with a history of violence and/or other antisocial behaviour, substance abuse, and/or certain demographics (sex, age, income) and contextual factors, which were stressors of various kinds.

The authors concluded that, because mental illness did not independently predict future violent behaviour, these findings challenge perceptions that mental illness is a leading cause of violence in the general population. This is persuasive research, as far as it goes with the longitudinal model, but the conclusions seem influenced as much by policy considerations and concerns about stigmatizing people with psychiatric disorders as with science. It is hard to think of anyone in this research field who has ever suggested that mental disorder is a leading cause of violence. The common claim since 1990 is that psychosis is a small but significant contributor – and, more to the point, a contributor that may be amenable to prevention or measurable decrease through appropriate treatment. Furthermore, this study neither considers directional relationships between substance misuse and psychosis nor impact of treatment. The UK based National Comorbidity Study of about 1.4 million people attending general practices 1993–98 (Frischer et al., 2004) suggested a greater vulnerability of people with psychosis going on to develop substance misuse disorders than the other way around. When the MacArthur study of mental disorder and violence group examined the relationship between psychotic symptoms and violence in terms of symptoms at time-1 predicting violence at time-2, without taking account of treatment of or change in those symptoms, they found no relationship between symptoms and violence (Appelbaum et al., 2000). Subsequently, however, they demonstrated symptom change over those periods (Appelbaum et al., 2004) and an overall relationship between specific psychotic symptoms and violence (Monahan et al., 2001). Interpretation of longitudinal data on people with psychosis, especially when they have been identified by their patient status, must take account of treatment and illness changes if it is to be useful.

Fazel et al. (2009a) examined hospital and criminal records data on just over 8000 patients with schizophrenia subsequent to their first recorded admission in the period and 80,000 general population controls in Sweden (1973–2006). After adjusting for demographics, these patients were about twice as likely as the controls to have had at least one violent conviction (13.2% : 5.3%). Substance abuse comorbidity, however, was a strong mediator; such patients were over four times more likely to have a violent conviction than their general population peers while those with schizophrenia alone had only a slightly increased odds ratio (1.2; CI 1.1–1.4). In an interesting additional analysis, it was found that when the people with schizophrenia were compared with their siblings who did not have the disorder, the substance misuse comorbidity effect was much less, suggesting that genetic or early environmental factors also had their part to play. This finding further underscores something with which practising forensic clinicians are already familiar, that substance misuse among people with psychosis must be assessed, and, where the misuse amounts to more than a simple palliation of symptoms, must be treated in its own right. More importantly, it is not, in most cases, an alternative explanation for violence by people with psychosis. Rather the inter-relationships between illness and other relevant factors must be seen as many and complicated.

The Epidemiology of Psychosis and Violence: Need for More Knowledge and Less Interpretation?

So, a small but significant relationship between psychosis and perpetration of violence has been consistently reported in a variety of studies since 1990. Fazel et al. (2009b) brought most of the studies just described together with a few additional ones in a systematic review; the additional studies were of relatively small geographical areas and/or patient samples defined by an episode of treatment so long as there was a general population comparison group. They conducted a meta-analysis despite the diverse range of methodologies, with different sampling techniques, different measures of psychosis and/or violence, different times scales for those measurements and procedural differences. Although they did some separate analyses according to gender, and separate homicide from other violence, they mixed cross-sectional and longitudinal work. They concluded nonetheless that there is about twice the risk of violence among people with 'pure' psychosis compared with the general population, but about eight times the risk if substance misuse is involved. This may be vital information, but the preferred emphasis on the substance misuse could mislead the unwary:

> *Most of the excess risk appears to be mediated by substance abuse comorbidity. The risk in these patients with comorbidity is similar to that for substance abuse without psychosis.*

Few of these studies were in a position to go one step further and cite comorbidity with personality disorder, in some cases since they often relied on measures of personality disorder for identifying the violence (e.g. Swanson et al., 1990). In practice, however, psychiatrists often do take this step and infer personality disorder from comorbid substance

abuse, and use it to exclude people from services, sometimes with disastrous consequences (e.g. Health Inspectorate Wales, 2008). Diagnosis of any kind is an approximate art, and the kind of research diagnoses used in these studies tend to be reliable operationalized descriptions of presentation rather than diagnoses in a conventional medical sense, with its implications of understanding causation, context and course (Taylor and Gunn, 2008). Could reliance on measurement of psychotic symptoms rather than focusing on diagnosis be more helpful?

Psychotic symptoms as a more useful or valid variable to test for relationship with violence?

The prevalence of psychotic symptoms is substantially higher than the prevalence of diagnosed or treated psychotic illness. This was suggested in Mackay's (1857) historical description of 'popular delusions and the madness of crowds', but there is now also systematic scientific evidence in support of this observation. In the Netherlands Mewal Health Survey and Incident (NEMESIS) study at least 17.5% of participants reported at least one psychotic symptom, in a population in which the prevalence of a *DSM-III-R* non-affective psychosis was 2.1% (van Os et al., 2000). This led to the idea of a symptomatic continuum between the general population and people diagnosed with psychosis, and that a more instructive route to treatment may lie in investigating factors which influence the modulation of psychotic symptoms – and their effects – rather than being centred on diagnosis (Verdoux and van Os, 2002). Other researchers, in other countries, have also found that the prevalence of psychotic symptoms exceeds expected rates of disorder. Mojtabai (2006), for example, in a US household survey, found that 5% of over 38,000 respondents described what he referred to as 'psychotic-like' symptoms, so named because the data had been collected by trained lay researchers rather than clinicians. In an Australian national household survey, Scott et al. (2006) found that, among over 10,500 respondents, 4.5% endorsed at least one delusional experience. In the UK National Comorbidity Survey 2,406 respondents completed two interviews, on average 18 months apart; 414 (10.9%) had at least one psychotic symptom at first interview and 128 (3.3%) had symptoms persistent between the two (Wiles et al., 2006). A cross-national study by Nuevo et al. (2012) included 256,445 people from the general population of 52 countries and found a 6% prevalence for hallucinations and 5–8% for delusions, with 12.5% having at least one psychotic symptom, albeit with much variation from country to country.

Link and Stueve (1994) were probably the first to recognize the role of symptoms *independently of diagnosis* in the generation of violence. They identified 367 patients in various stages of treatment and 286 never treated community controls, all from New York State. Everyone was interviewed using the Psychiatric Epidemiology Research

Interview (PERI; Dohrenwend et al., 1986) which, among a full range of symptoms, allows recording of three referred to as 'threat/control-override symptoms' (TCO symptoms). There has been some debate as to whether these constitute true psychotic symptoms, as the questions are: *'how often do you feel that ... your mind was dominated by forces beyond your control? ... thoughts were put into your head that were not your own? ... that there were people who wished to do you harm?'* They do seem, however, to reflect the kind of experience as many patients with psychosis would describe them. The violence measures were hitting someone in the last year and/or fighting and/or weapon use in the previous 2 years. There was a difference between patients and never treated controls on these violence measures, but the significance of this difference was reduced by entering the range of psychotic symptoms in a preliminary regression analysis. Several alternative statistical models were tested, but when TCO symptoms were treated separately from the other symptoms, and potentially relevant demographic variables were also allowed for, the TCO symptoms accounted for the violence, rendering the patient–non-patient status non-significant.

Swanson et al. (1996) applied measures of these symptoms to the ECA data, referred to above. They provided further endorsement of the potential importance of psychotic symptoms in the absence of illness in relation to occurrence of violence as participants with TCO symptoms were about five times as likely as those without to have been violent in the previous year, but here the independence of the symptom relationship from diagnosis or service use is less clear. Mojtabai's (2006) household survey, also already referred to, took up the psychotic symptom–violence question too. Attacks intending to hurt, violence to an intimate partner and arrest for aggravated assault were each about five times more likely among people who had reported psychotic symptoms, here not necessarily TCO symptoms.

On logical and empirical grounds, then, there is reason to explore further the role of symptoms, with or without diagnosis, in understanding the link between psychosis and violence.

Psychosis and Offending Other than Interpersonal Violence

Psychosis and sex offending

Many would regard sex offending as a form of violence but, as it may have somewhat different implications for treatment, separate mention seems useful. Sexual violence and offending has been neglected relative to research on violence in schizophrenia. Philips et al. (1999), in a small series of high security hospital patients, found that about 15% had been convicted of a sexual offence or had behaved in an antisocial sexual way. In almost all of these cases the sexually offensive behaviour had post-dated the onset of the illness and occurred in the context of psychotic symptoms. The men who showed such behaviours were distinguished from

those who did not mainly by having retained an unimpaired interest in sexual relationships while struggling with the emotional aspects of interpersonal relationships. Official statistics for men detained in hospitals under mental health legislation with restrictions on discharge at about the same period indicated that 10% had been convicted of a sexual offence (Home Office, 1997). Smith and Taylor (1999) examined a complete national (England and Wales) sample for the month of May 1997 and identified 84 male sex offenders with schizophrenia at that time. For most, antisocial sexual acts were only part of their offending repertoire. All but four of them had been psychotic at the time of the index offence, and about half had hallucinations or delusions directly relevant to the offending. Fazel et al. (2007a,b) conducted a much more substantial study, using Swedish national registers. They identified all 8,495 male sexual offenders on record for the 3 years 1988–2000 and compared them with a random sample of nearly 20,000 men in the general population. Twenty per cent of such crimes had been committed by men who were or had been hospitalized for psychiatric disorder. Men with psychosis were just over five times more likely to have a psychotic illness than the general population (OR: 5.2, 95% CI: 3.9–6.8; schizophrenia specifically OR: 4.8, 95% CI: 3.4–6.7). The temporal and causal pathways between sexual offense and psychiatric disorder deserve further scrutiny.

Psychosis and arson

It is now generally accepted that, in England and Wales at least, the largest group of women detained in secure hospitals according to offence – about 40% – is of women who have set fires or been convicted of arson (e.g. Coid et al., 2000; see also chapter 20). From Swedish national registers, Anwar et al. (2011) extracted all 1,340 men and 349 women who had been convicted of at least one offence of arson in the 13-year period 1988–2000, and compared them with a sample of over 40,000 of the general population over the age of criminal responsibility (age 15), randomly selected for sex and year. People with non-schizophrenic psychosis had a substantially elevated rate of arson, but those with schizophrenia were most at risk, with men over 20 times more likely and women nearly 40 times more likely to have had this illness if they had been convicted of arson (men: OR: 22.6, CI: 14.8–34.4; women 38.7, CI: 20.4–73.5).

Psychosis and other offending

People with schizophrenia or other chronic psychoses may be more likely to be convicted of all sorts of less serious crime than their healthy peers, although in this context, less serious crime such as property damage or vagrancy is much less studied. A factor in any such excess rates may be the greater likelihood of arrest without detection of people with psychosis (Robertson, 1988), but also there may be vulnerabilities through social marginalization of various kinds, including homelessness and poverty, and, for the increasing proportions who complicate their illness with alcohol or drug use, a need to finance this 'medication'. There is some evidence that, when committed by people with psychosis, this sort of crime is more likely than violent crime to follow from rational motives (Taylor, 1985b).

PATHWAYS INTO VIOLENCE THROUGH PSYCHOSIS: DISTINCTIVE OR COMMON TO MOST VIOLENT OFFENDERS?

Discovery of patterns in the individual and/or his/her environment prior to the onset of the illness or behaviour of concern is useful for establishing cause, course and identifying potential intervention points. This certainly applies to schizophrenia and similar disorders, and early treatment is increasingly seen as important such that, at best, resolution of prodromal states might prevent the development of the full blown illness (e.g. Mrazek and Haggarty, 1994) or, at worst, rigorous treatment of the illness *per se* could prevent cumulative damage. Insofar as offending behaviour among people with psychosis is consequent upon the illness, then this too might be prevented. The difficulty is that the prodromal phase of illness is often not distinctive, with depression, anxiety, stress and substance misuse among the features, and treatment with medication carries its own set of risks.

Although schizophrenia and similar psychoses are generally regarded as illnesses because, at least in full blown form, they emerge after a long period of relative normality, in many cases there is an argument to be made that the schizophrenias, like conduct and personality disorders, are also developmental disorders. Chapter 8 provides evidence of genetic influences in the emergence of schizophrenia as well as antisocial behaviour, and also substance abuse, the latter so often complicating either or both of the former conditions. Two important points emerge. The first is that we are only just beginning to learn about the particular genetic organization that may contribute to the psychoses, and even underpin overlap between it and these other conditions. Secondly, even in the presence of a genetic role in the condition or its associated disorders, a substantial amount of the variation in behaviour in these conditions must still be accounted for through environmental differences. Environmental candidates for which there is at least moderate evidence include epigenetic factors such as obstetric complications (e.g. Geddes et al., 1999), maternal use of alcohol and other drugs during pregnancy (e.g. Frank et al., 2001) and maternal infections during pregnancy (e.g. Adams et al., 1993). The literature has tended to emphasize externally observable physical differences (e.g. Lane et al., 1997) or delays in motor or cognitive development (e.g. Marenco and Weinberger, 2000) between people with schizophrenia and those without as evidence of the neurodevelopmental nature of the disorder, and this is the area where ever more evidence is called for (e.g. Yung and McGorry, 2007). Although some of the maternal factors cited may be indirect evidence of social disadvantage, in many cases this is an area of research where all too little is known. Early work, to an extent, captured the public imagination, but seemed to lay blame rather than provide explanations of potential therapeutic value, for example on parenting styles (e.g. Fromm-Reichmann, 1948; Bateson et al., 1956) or the family more generally (e.g. Laing and Esterson, 1964; Wynne et al., 1958). The more scientific 1960s work on expressed emotion was about emotional climate in families once the disorder was established (e.g. Brown et al., 1962, 1972; Leff and Vaughn, 1985). More recently, evidence has been accumulating that early experience of abuse and/or neglect is not only associated with psychosis, but also in the causal pathway (Read et al., 2005), but this group highlighted the relative poverty of work in the field. They noted that their systematic search of the literature identified just 23 articles about child abuse and schizophrenia – 0.05% of all the articles captured on schizophrenia overall, compared with 4.1% on the genetics of schizophrenia and 8% on brain damage or dysfunction and schizophrenia.

The environmental influences cited above may be taken as part of the ongoing debate about the social causes and contexts of mental illness. Kirkbride and Jones (2011) examined data in support of taking a primary prevention approach to schizophrenia. They argued that by taking an 'eco-epidemiological view' it is apparent that:

variation exists along a number of other fascinating domains, including migration and minority status, place of birth and upbringing, life events and social disadvantage, pre- and perinatal stressors (i.e. famine or viruses).

Similarly, in a recent re-analysis of the leading social cause hypotheses, Hudson (2005) concluded that:

the idea that the impact of SES (socioeconomic status) on mental illness is mediated by economic stress received the strongest support, with this model substantially fitting the data.

As these two perspectives coalesce, we find further impetus to take a developmental, socially situated view not just of causal pathways to psychosis, but of the environment in which symptoms are experienced and expressed.

This is not the place, however, for an extended review of pathways into the psychoses *per se* but rather to explore the pathway through psychosis to violence. Longitudinal, often birth cohort, studies have provided invaluable information on pathways into crime and violence (see chapter 7). Again, the underlying hope is that a map of critical developmental stages and of points of deviance from them could assist with early intervention and prevent accumulation of harm. One of the most often cited findings is of two principal pathways, albeit clearly evidenced only for men, of early-onset life-course persistent offending/violence and late-onset adolescent-limited offending/violence (Moffitt, 1993a; Moffitt et al., 2001). The first is likely to reflect an interaction between individual genetic and physical factors on the one hand and environmental factors on the other, while the second is much more environmentally dependent.

Given the prevalence of schizophrenia in the general population, it is hardly surprising that the birth and child-hood cohort studies which include repeated, multi-source based evaluations over time include too few people with schizophrenia, schizophrenia spectrum disorders or other psychoses to offer adequate information on pathways into violence for such groups. The Cambridge study, for example (see chapter 7), included no one with schizophrenia or similar psychoses, while in the Dunedin birth cohort of over 1000 individuals, there were just six at age 21 with a schizo-phrenia spectrum disorder and a conviction for a violent offence, and just 13 with the disorder and a self-reported history of violence (Arseneault et al., 2000). Nevertheless, the Dunedin study both at age 21 and at age 26 (Arseneault et al., 2003) hints at more than one route into violence for this group. A regression analysis showed that about one-third of the risk of the adult schizophreniform disorder violence could be accounted for by childhood psychotic symptoms, but childhood violence independently and together with these symptoms also accounted for a small but significant effect. This finding, however slight, pro-vides some prospective evidence for the idea that there may indeed be different pathways into psychosis related violence – one related chiefly to the illness and likely to be symptom driven and one embedded in comorbidity and historically more complex social relationships.

Larger, mainly Nordic country birth cohort studies, without the richness of data of these interview studies, can and do answer simpler questions about relative age of onset of psychosis and offending, while criminal justice and health service case register studies also contribute. Studies, albeit not always prospective studies, with a starting point of childhood abuse indicate that this also is worth investi-gation as an antecedent of both psychosis and antisocial behaviour and, probably, the combination. Studies which track psychotic symptoms over time, and their temporal relationship to violence are also developmental studies, but of a rather different kind, and will be dealt with separately.

Early Versus Late Onset of Offending Distinctions Among People with Psychosis

East (1936) was among the earlier researchers to draw attention to the older average age of people with major mental disorder who had killed compared either to con-victed killers without such disorder or people with psy-chosis who had not offended. During the 1960s and 1970s, when inpatient treatment was still more routinely used in

an episode of schizophrenia, several studies made similar observations with respect to people who had schizo-phrenia, suggesting that if people with such illnesses did offend, it might be a later complication of their illness, rather than the illness being more-or-less coincidental. Walker and McCabe (1973), for example, compared the records of three 1963/4 cohorts of people – those who were detained in hospital as offenders with mental dis-order, everyone found guilty of an indictable offence and everyone admitted to a mental hospital – and found the mentally disordered offenders were significantly older than the other two groups. Häfner and Böker (1973), with a 1955–1964 German national cohort of homicides, found that, although a person might kill during a first episode of schizophrenia or depression, this was very unusual and that people with schizophrenia were generally 10–15 years older than people without a mental disorder, and people with an affective psychosis even older still. Mowat (1966), in his study of morbid jealousy among high security hospi-tal patients, added the observation that some subgroups of homicidal offenders with psychosis might be older still – here suggesting that the older age of the morbid jealousy reflected the length of time needed for the delusions to develop to the point of driving violence. There is some suggestion from later research, however, that the age dif-ferential may have decreased since inpatient hospitaliza-tion has been less routine; in an English pretrial prisoner study the age difference between alleged offenders with and without psychosis was 3–4 years (Taylor and Gunn, 1984; Taylor, 1987).

Two different research approaches from Sweden hinted at two developmental paths. Historical data for a Stockholm county patient discharge cohort revealed two peaks of offending onset, more typical of men than women, and different from the offending pattern of the healthy comparison group (Lindqvist and Allebeck, 1990). A Swedish birth cohort study, for which hospital and criminal records were obtained, found a peak of onset of offending in the mid-teenage years and a second peak after age 21 for the men but a single later peak for the women (Hodgins, 1992). Wessely et al. (1994) found similar variation in male : female offending patterns when com-paring case register people with and without schizophre-nia who had had any contact with psychiatric services in South London. The possible clinical relevance of the two developmental pathways was suggested by an English high security hospital resident cohort in which two dis-tinct groups of people with psychosis were apparent: those who had been unremarkable until the onset of their illness, with an index offence almost invariably reported as having been driven by psychotic symptoms and those who had established conduct and/or emotional disorders in childhood, continuous with adult personality disorders, who had also developed an illness indistinguishable from schizophrenia. The index offence in the comorbid group was significantly less likely to have been driven by psychotic symptoms (Taylor et al., 1998).

For people with schizophrenia, therefore, concepts of early- and late-onset offending are promising. Although not formally tested, it appears that both the earlier and the later onset groups tend to be older at onset than their respective non-psychotic counterparts and desistance from offending tends to occur earlier than in any of the non-psychotic samples; this may be related to treatment. The other major area of pathway research here lies in attempts to establish whether the illness or the offending start first, or at least whether mental health service involvement precedes criminal justice service use as, even in prospective studies, it is much harder to date precisely the onset of particular behaviours, or the point at which they may be regarded as pathological.

In Finland, Laajasalo and Häkkänen (2005) studied a consecutive series of people with schizophrenia who had been charged after a homicide between 1983 and 2002. They observed little difference in index offence characteristics, but that, for some, the homicide was the only offence while others had sustained at least one criminal conviction before the onset of their illness; the latter group were significantly more likely to have had established behaviour problems in childhood. While these findings tended to support the two-pathway model, Fresán et al. (2004) studied a consecutive series of 75 outpatients with schizophrenia in Mexico, and found that worse premorbid adjustment through childhood and adolescence was characteristic of the violent group – so here the suggestion was of two developmental pathways into schizophrenia, but one main route into schizophrenia with violence. The latter sample, however, was small, and the violence confined to levels which were apparently manageable in the community.

Munkner et al. (2003a) used the Danish Psychiatric Central Register (DPCR), the National Crime Register (NCR) and the Civil Registration System (CRS) to identify all 4,619 live individuals in Denmark born on or after 1 November 1963 with a diagnosis of schizophrenia and who had attained the age of criminal responsibility; 41% had been convicted of any criminal offence, 17% of at least one violent offence. Men were more likely to have sustained convictions than women. Again, men and women differed in the temporal relationship between onset of offending and first presentation to health services with their psychotic illness; 71% of the men with a criminal record but only 37% of such women had established their criminal career before the onset of their illness. Of all violent offenders, 58% of the 700 men and 21% of the 81 women had sustained their first violent conviction before their first psychiatric contact. In a second study with the same cohort, however, it was apparent that those with schizophrenia who had been convicted of a criminal offence were older at first contact with services and first diagnosis of schizophrenia

than their non-offending peers (Munkner et al., 2003b). It is unclear whether there were distinct groups of early- and later-onset offenders among these people with schizophrenia, with the early-onset group following a more typically criminogenic pattern, or whether age at presentation and/or diagnosis was an artefact of antisocial behaviour distancing them from health services.

Gosden et al. (2005) also used Danish criminal justice (NCR) and health (DPCR and Danish National Cause of Death Register) registers to conduct a prospective study of the careers of 794 15–19-year-old males and 54 15–19-year-old females in a complete 1992 national cohort of people in contact with the Danish Probation and Prisons Service, followed up in 2001. From birth to index day (the start of the study), just over 3% of the cohort of 732 male and 48 female survivors with adequate records had been diagnosed with schizophrenia and 4.5% with any psychosis; 12 of the young men, but none of the young women, had been convicted of serious violent crimes, including homicide, and 382 of the young men and 15 of the young women of lesser violence; just 59 young men and seven young women had ever been admitted as psychiatric inpatients. Two variables were independently related to a diagnosis of schizophrenia/ psychosis – previous psychiatric admission and previous violence – offering yet further evidence for two subgroups of people whose psychosis is complicated by violence, and also that they tend to be treated differently from an early stage.

The extant research, therefore, despite limitations in method and varying findings, makes a strong case for continued pursuit of pathways to the co-occurrence of psychosis, psychotic symptoms, and violence. It is through these exploratory and descriptive studies that we will develop the next generation of more targeted and precise inquiry which, of necessity, will precede launching effective intervention trials.

First Episode of Illness Offending

Humphreys et al. (1992) were among the first to study violence, ascertained from multiple sources, including self-report, family or friend reports and records, in a consecutive series of 148 men and 105 women referred while in a first episode of schizophrenia; the study period was 1979–81 and the area was within a 35-mile radius of a hospital in the south of England. Most had not been violent at this stage, but a fifth of them had behaved in a way that was threatening to the lives of others. This did not, however, imply that the violence had necessarily preceded the illness. About half of the incidents occurred after the person had been ill for at least a year, and violence was more common the longer the person had been ill. Volavka et al. (1997) found a similar overall figure for violence during a first episode of schizophrenia, at a similar time (1978), when drawing on a sample of 570 men and 447 women from three developing and seven developed countries (including the UK); this overall figure of 20% violent in their first episode, however, obscured a three-fold difference between the developing (31.3%) and developed (10.5%) countries.

In a study of 280 psychotic twins and 210 healthy co-twins Coid et al. (1993) established that, not only did a higher proportion of the psychotic twins (21%) have a criminal record than their co-twins (11%), but also that there was a significant correlation between offending and onset of illness. Specific examination of the violent offenders showed that the violence clearly post-dated the onset of the illness in 12 of the 14 men and both women with schizophrenia who had been violent. One of the remaining men had been in prodromal phase of his illness and for one only did the offending clearly precede psychotic symptoms (Taylor and Hodgins, 1994).

Large and Nielssen (2011) conducted a systematic review of studies of violence during a first episode of schizophrenia. They identified nine studies (Dean et al., 2007; Foley et al., 2007; Harris et al., 2010; Humphreys et al., 1992; Milton et al., 2001; Spidel et al., 2010; Steinert et al., 1999; Verma et al., 2005; Volavka et al., 1997), with a total of 2,545 cases. From various meta-analyses, the pooled estimate of serious violence during the first episode from all the studies except Spidel was 16.6% (CI 12.9–21.3%). This occurrence of serious violence was associated with 'forensic history', duration of untreated illness and total symptom scores.

Childhood Trauma in the Pathway to Violence Through Psychosis

The way in which seriously adverse childhood experiences fit into the pathways through psychosis to violence is, as yet, unclear. Studies generally do not explicitly map them into such developmental models, but rather into the causes of psychotic symptoms or psychosis (e.g. Read et al., 2005) or the emergence of violence (e.g. Widom, 1989; Widom and Maxfield, 2001) separately. Work with people with schizophrenia in just one of the English high security hospitals suggested that early-childhood victim experiences clustered in the conduct disorder subgroup, but that was a small sample (*n* = 101), selected for perceived high threat to others (Heads et al., 1997).

A systematic review by Read et al. (2005) covered published articles between 1872 and 2004, locating 46 after expanding the diagnosis to the wider concept of psychosis. They found, overall, a strong association between reports of childhood abuse and schizophrenia, psychosis and psychotic symptoms, particularly delusions and hallucinations, with a suggestion of a 'dose–response' relationship – the more severe the abuse, the higher the chance of psychosis. In their 2007 'critical review', however, Morgan and Fisher (2007) argued that the Read group's conclusions might be misleading because of the diagnostic heterogeneity of the samples included in their review. Morgan and Fisher tried to focus on more diagnostically homogeneous studies. Although they found the evidence to be weaker, they considered the likelihood of a link between trauma and psychosis to be enhanced by some plausible explanatory links through the impact of stress on the dopaminergic system. We have subsequently found volumetric brain differences which may differentiate traumatized men with psychosis who have been violent from those who have not, the former suffering thalamic loss and the latter hippocampal and frontal lobe loss (Kumari et al., in press).

Subsequent to these reviews, Scott et al. (2007), with an Australian sample of 10,641 in the National Survey of Health and Wellbeing, effectively endorsed this view, albeit referring to people traumatized at any age. There was not only a relationship between number and type of events and endorsement of delusional experiences, but also, where a diagnosis of post-traumatic stress disorder (PTSD) had been made, there was almost four times the rate of reporting delusions among the traumatized than when they did not reach criteria for PTSD. Bebbington et al.'s (2004) study of 8580 adults in a household survey – the British National Survey of Psychiatric Morbidity – also suggested that type of abuse was relevant; people reporting having been sexually abused before the age of 16 were nearly four times more likely to have psychosis while people who had experienced violence were twice as likely to be psychotic.

As with all material in this field, however, it is perhaps better to consider the results as suggestive rather than conclusive. One substantial prospective study in Australia had diametrically opposite results, although later studies in the Netherlands, Germany and Britain have endorsed the association between childhood trauma and later psychosis. The Australian study was of people who had experienced verified abuse (Spataro et al., 2004). No relationship was found between childhood sexual abuse and psychosis, although there were some important biases in this study; the average age of the people who had suffered abuse, in the early 20s, was significantly lower than that of the comparison group, so 'time at risk' for schizophrenia was significantly different. This may not have been very important as Kelleher et al. (2008), in a small British study of 12 to 15 year olds, found an association between reports of abuse or bullying and psychotic symptoms even within this age group. Read and colleagues (2005), however, raised a further interesting point with respect to the Spataro study; although prospective studies of the effects of verified abuse are notionally methodologically among the most robust, many children never report their abuse, and so a 'verified group' may be unusual. Further, there may, after all, be little difference between prospectively documented and retrospectively reported maltreatment in this context (Scott et al., 2012). Janssen et al.'s (2004) style of prospective study in the Netherlands differed in that it relied on collection of self-reported childhood abuse in an adult general population sample of 4,045, but at a time when the participants were psychosis free. They were reassessed two years later. Depending on whether the psychosis measure was of diagnosis or symptoms, the rate of psychosis in the abused group was between 2.5 and 9 times that of those who had reported no abuse. Spauwen et al. (2006), in a longitudinal German study, reported on 2,524 people who were 14 to 24 years old at the time of first interview, and found an association between childhood trauma, including abuse, and psychotic symptoms, particularly when the trauma had been associated with intense fear. Fisher et al. (2009), using data from the Aetiology and Ethnicity in Schizophrenia and other Psychosis (ÆSOP) case (390) control (391) study found a relationship between childhood abuse and adult psychosis only in the women.

Childhood trauma is probably one of the many risk factors for adult psychosis, and probably one for violent behaviour also. Could there be an interaction between all three? The reality is that almost any unfortunate outcome in terms of illness or behaviour has been found to relate to childhood trauma or adversity (Green et al., 2010; McLaughlin et al., 2010; Kessler et al., 2010). A great deal more work needs to be done to clarify inter-relationships, and how they work. To what extent are violence and psychosis related in such circumstances only by the common antecedent of childhood trauma? To what extent might they be related through the mediation of substance misuse – the individual needing to 'block out' the memory of the experience, resorting to illicit drugs to do so, and thus inducing psychosis, or at least triggering it in the context of a propensity for it? Bebbington et al. (2011), on further work with the British National Survey of Psychiatric Morbidity, found that the association between sexual abuse before age 16 and later psychosis was mediated by anxiety and depression, but not by heavy cannabis use or revictimization in adulthood. The Janssen group's explanation was that distress caused by traumatic experiences may consolidate non-clinical psychotic experiences, leading to psychotic illness (Bak et al., 2005). Neither of these studies, however, went on to explore how violence perpetration might come into this. Finally, there is the possibility too that there may be a more or less direct relationship between childhood trauma and psychotic symptom formation. There are three major psychological theories about delusion formation (Bentall and Taylor, 2006) and here the more apt would rest in the idea that psychosis may arise out of an unconscious attempt to construct a model of construing the world that will improve self-esteem (Colby, 1977) or to attribute negative experiences to agents other than self (Zilger and Glick, 1988).

The ultimate question here, however, is about interactions between childhood trauma, psychosis and violence.

We have already made reference to the small-scale study of Heads et al. (1997) in the UK. Swanson et al. (2002), in the USA, found that, while early victimization in men with severe mental illness was directly associated with violence, for women factors both in mental state and environment current to the research evaluation mediated its effects. This is important, as it may indicate differing intervention opportunities, here between women and men. Participants were 280 women and 522 men with complete data on victimization, violent behaviour and clinical and environmental variables from a larger study of sexually transmitted diseases among people with severe mental disorder attending public health services. Victimization was determined by self-report. Two-thirds of the participants had a diagnosis of schizophrenia or schizo-affective illness, a further 17% bipolar disorder, and the rest 'major depression' or 'other serious mental disorders'. The work is particularly interesting, however, because, taking psychosis/severe mental disorder as the underlying problem, it identified a hierarchy of impact of victim experiences on violent outcomes:

- People who had been a victim of physical or sexual abuse before the age of 16, but not victimized as adults, were no more likely than those who did not report childhood victim experiences to be violent as adults.
- Those who reported no such childhood experience, but did report victimization as an adult were more likely to report violence as an adult.
- Those who had both childhood *and* adult victim experiences were the most likely to have been violent themselves.

The association of repeated victimization with later violence was significant for both women and men, although conferring greater risk on the men. Mediating factors for the women were more serious illness (more hospitalizations and more symptoms at evaluation) and recent homelessness. In the statistical models created here, substance misuse was not an independent influence. This may be because of its complex relationships with abuse experience and disorder. On the one hand it may be part of the risk taking behaviour of conduct/personality disorder, but on the other it may be a means of blocking out unpleasant experiences – victimization, psychosis or both.

PSYCHOSIS, COMORBID MENTAL DISORDERS AND VIOLENCE

When some researchers use the terminology of comorbidity, they go beyond clinical conditions to include violence and antisocial behaviour *per se* (e.g. McCord and Enslinger, 1997). Others take a narrower operational view that two or more conditions as defined in one of the disease classification systems must be present at the same time (Clarkin and Kendall, 1992). Here we take Feinstein's (1970) intermediate position: the presence of 'an additional clinical entity that has existed or that may occur during the clinical course of a patient who has the index disease under study'. Jaspers (1923) took the view that the concept of comorbidity arises out of the categorical approach to diagnosis. The *American Diagnostic and Statistical Manual* (*DSM-IV*) partly deals with this through the structural framework of multiaxial classification (American Psychiatric Association, 1994). Then, the term 'dual diagnosis' became popular through the 1990s, typically referring to the combination of a psychotic illness with a substance-misuse diagnosis. For forensic mental health practitioners, however, this rarely captures the multiplicity of clinical problems suffered by people who come to their services. Compton et al. (2005), in a study of nearly 2000 people in contact with general psychiatric services in the USA, amply illustrated the range of concurrent social disadvantage and dysfunction, including offending, presented by people with the combination of schizophrenia-spectrum and substance-misuse disorders, but even this does not capture the evidence of developmental disorder and antecedent disadvantage that is apparent for a substantial subgroup. Perhaps terminology such as 'triply troubled' (Lindqvist, 2007) or even 'multiply troubled' would better capture the complexity of presentations.

Psychosis, Personality Disorder and Violence

There is perhaps little distinction to be made between concepts of anomalies in developmental pathways and comorbidity of personality disorder with psychosis; indeed it is arguable that personality disorder should not be diagnosed without substantial verified evidence of conduct and emotional disorders through childhood, but there is now also a literature on personality measures made among adults with schizophrenia. At one time, it would have been anathema to make diagnoses of personality disorder *and* psychosis in the same person, as operational definitions required exclusion of psychosis before making a diagnosis of personality disorder (Hare and Cox, 1978). Then, too, it has been shown in longitudinal studies that schizotypal personality disorder so commonly progresses to schizophrenia, but not other illnesses, that those two conditions might even be regarded as varying presentations of essentially the same condition, whereas other personality disorders, such as borderline personality disorder, do not progress in this way (e.g. McGlashan, 1983).

Moran and colleagues (2003) interviewed 670 of the UK 700 psychosis cohort using the rapid version of the Personality Assessment Schedule (PAS-R) (Tyrer and Cicchetti, 2000): 186 of them (28%) had a comorbid personality disorder, and nearly twice as many in this group were violent (OR: 1.71, CI: 1.05–2.79). There was an independent association with substance misuse (OR: 1.85,

95% CI: 1.18–2.91). At first sight, the personality disorder rate may seem surprising in a general psychiatry cohort, when only 20% of English high security hospital residents had such comorbidity (Taylor et al., 1998). There are two possible explanations. First, the Moran group included schizoid personality disorder in their calculations, and secondly a lower proportion of their study patients had schizophrenia. Both the general and the high security hospital studies suggested that schizophrenia was less likely than other psychoses to be comorbid with personality disorder, although the Moran group found that this difference was not significant. Blackburn, by contrast, favouring dimensional measures of personality, found that personality disorder comorbidity was the rule rather than the exception among high security hospital residents with a primary psychosis diagnosis, and that they were similar to patients with primary personality disorder on a range of personality measures (e.g. Blackburn, 1974).

In Finland, Putkonen et al. (2004) interviewed people whom they described as constituting a nationally representative group of homicide offenders with a major mental illness, using the Structured Clinical Interview for *DSM-IV* Axis I and II disorders (SCID). They found that more than half of their sample of 90 had a personality disorder, and nearly three-quarters had a substance misuse diagnosis. In this series *all* of those with major mental illness and personality disorder also had a substance misuse disorder – triply troubled. Nestor et al. (2002), working in the USA with a smaller group of 26 hospitalized psychotic men who had killed another person, relied on the Psychopathy Checklist – Revised (PCL-R; Hare, 1991) as the measure of personality. They, like the UK researchers, found two distinct groups, but in this case one with low psychosis and high PCL-R ratings and the other with the converse. They also found evidence of distinct neuropsychological characteristics between the groups. In a review, Nestor (2002) went on to suggest four key dimensions of personality dysfunction in the context of people with psychosis who had been seriously violent: impulse control, affect regulation, narcissism, and paranoid cognitive personality.

Psychosis and the PCL-R

The PCL-R (Hare, 1991) has increasingly been used as a measure with offenders with schizophrenia, although the meaning of doing so is not entirely clear. Taking the two factor model, which Hare has favoured, there is no reason to suppose that the repeated antisocial behaviour factor would be confounded by diagnosis; it is difficult, however, to know how the affective impairment factor relates to the affective blunting and/or incongruity commonly seen as a part of schizophrenia. Be that as it may, Tengström et al. (2004) set out to clarify inter-relationships between such illness, PCL-R scares, substance misuse and offending among 202 male offenders with schizophrenia, with and without substance misuse disorders, and 78 men with a primary personality problem. Among the men with schizophrenia, those with high PCL-R scores (26+) committed more offences that those with scores below the cut-off; men with high PCL-R scores but no schizophrenia committed more offences than those with high scores and schizophrenia. A high PCL-R score was associated with similar rates of offending within disorder groups, regardless of the presence or absence of a substance misuse disorder. They concluded that traits yielding high PCL-R scores accounted for offending better than any associated substance misuse disorder, among men with psychosis and primary personality disorder alike.

Psychosis and Substance Misuse

Substance misuse, particularly of alcohol and/or a range of more stimulant illicit drugs, is undoubtedly a major contributor to violence by people without major mental illness, so it would be very surprising indeed if it were not a risk factor for violence among people with psychosis if they have access to such substances. Early studies, however, were suggestive of an inverse relationship between substance misuse and violence among people with schizophrenia, whether examining homicide (Häfner and Böker, 1973) other crime (Virkkunen, 1974), alleged crime (Taylor, 1993a,b) or simply general psychiatric patients admitted to hospital (Tardiff and Sweillam, 1980). Almost certainly two factors were operating here, the lower availability of substances, including alcohol, during these years and, during the earlier ones at least, the protective effect of long periods of institutionalization. From the 1990s, there appeared to be increasing acceptance that if people with psychosis had substance misuse problems, sometimes identified formally as a substance misuse disorder and sometimes not, then, as a group, they were at increased risk of violent behaviour. This seemed apparent, for example, in the USA-based ECA Survey, in which rates of violence among people with schizophrenia and substance misuse disorder were many times higher than rates among those with schizophrenia alone (Swanson et al., 1990). It was also true, however, that people with schizophrenia appeared to be more vulnerable to using substances. Regier et al. (1990), for example, showed that people with schizophrenia were about four times as likely to misuse substances and people with mania about six times as likely to do so as people without the disorders. Tiihonen and Swartz (2000) provide a good framework for understanding both the likely higher rate of substance misuse and its role in increasing the risk of violence among people with psychosis, suggesting that their hypotheses are not mutually exclusive:

- psychotic and other symptoms lead to self-medication;
- medication side-effects lead to self-medication with illicit substances;
- medication non-compliance leads to substance use;
- boredom and lack of structure lead to substance use;
- exposure to adverse social environments leads to substance use and aggressive behaviour;
- substance abuse exacerbates psychotic and other symptoms;
- substance abuse reduces impulse control;
- substance abuse is a proxy measure for personality disorder.

Mueser et al. (1998) reviewed evidence for various of these possibilities, suggesting that only the evidence for the self-medication model was weak.

More recent studies of the psychosis–substance misuse–violence links, with wide geographical spread but smaller and more selected patient groups, present a mixed picture. In the Czech Republic, for example, Vevera et al. (2005) did not find an elevated rate of violence among those with psychosis and substance misuse, while in Switzerland Modestin and Wuermle (2005) and in Turkey Erkiran et al. (2006) emphasized the increased probability of criminal behaviour among men with schizophrenia, with or without substance misuse. Larger community-based studies have shown that relationships between illness and substance misuse disorder may not be associated with all types of offending (Wallace et al., 2004), or may be affected by genetic or early environmental factors (Fazel et al., 2009a).

Why such discrepancies? There may be special methodological issues in identifying substance abuse, with offenders perhaps preferring to attribute their offending to alcohol or drugs than to mental illness. Preliminary examination of attribution of offending among 113 jail detainees in the USA, for example, suggested that neither substance misuse nor mental illness had a substantial effect on offending, but offences were more likely to have been attributed to substance abuse than mental illness (Junginger et al., 2006). This hints at an even greater problem, that 'substance abuse' or 'substance misuse' may refer to categorization based on diagnostic manual criteria, to scores on dimensional screening tools, occasionally to measures of substances or their metabolites in blood or urine, or to unqualified reports of use. Most of the more substantial studies use diagnostic criteria, so it is reasonable to think of comorbidity here, and this choice probably creates an underestimate of the risks posed by substances – among people with psychosis as well as those without. The other major issue is that use of substances by people with and without psychosis undoubtedly changes over time, with changing access, mores and fashions in use. Over 25 years of admissions (1975–1999) to the English high security hospitals, for example, problem drinking in the year prior to the index offence or act was strongly associated with illicit drug use over the same period, and the proportion of patients who had been consuming to problem levels showed a linear increase over time (McMahon et al., 2003). Problem drinking was defined as taking in excess of 21 units of alcohol per week during that period. The increase affected the women more than the men and cut across all diagnostic groups, however those with psychosis as the *sole* diagnosis were least affected.

Implications for Practice of Findings About Comorbidity and/ or Distinctive Pathways into Violence by People with Psychosis

There is, then, growing evidence, from a variety of research approaches, of at least two developmental pathways into offending by people with schizophrenia – one in which conduct disorder and antisocial behaviours are established early, probably before the onset of the psychosis, and the other in which the onset of the psychosis clearly precedes violent offending, sometimes by many years, and with the individual having appeared unremarkable until the onset of the illness. There may be a possible further variant, with antisocial behaviour and psychosis emerging more or less simultaneously. There is much more to be understood about how experience of major trauma and/or substance misuse fit into these pathways. The implications of the likely range from having psychosis alone to having a number of inter-related conditions means that no single strategy for prevention and management of violence among people with psychosis is likely to be effective (see also Volavka and Citrome, 2011). Refinement of definition of subgroups to allow for presence or absence of significant developmental problems, presence or absence of certain personality types or traits, and presence or absence of substance misuse is likely to be necessary for effective clinical practice and useful new research alike. In addition, it now seems that it is as important to be vigilant for the possibility of early or current experiences of sexual or physical abuse. This may need emphasizing, because Young et al. (2001) noted that asking about victim experience is not yet routine in clinical practice, and also that a diagnosis of schizophrenia is one of the factors that renders such inquiry particularly unlikely. Here the emphasis has been on pathways into violent behaviour, and the likely treatment needs that these may raise. In going on to explore how specific clinical characteristics may trigger violence, it is worth saying that even those people who, like McNaughton, seem to have been unremarkable before psychosis devastated their lives and its symptoms drove them to some terrible act, are likely to have complex needs. They, their families and their communities will be so changed by the combination of their illness and act that they too are likely to

need multi-faceted management and treatment plans in order to approach a recovery trajectory.

CLINICAL CHARACTERISTICS OF PSYCHOSIS ASSOCIATED WITH VIOLENCE

A number of psychotic symptoms have been implicated in acts of violence, especially delusions. Deficits in capacity for empathy and affective states, in particular anger, which may accompany or even be induced by the psychosis, have also been implicated. Difficulties arise in making sense of these findings, because, in a field where multiple and complicated inter-relationships between a plethora of factors might be expected to influence interpersonal violence, research tends to focus on simple, single links. So, questions are more likely to be about whether or not symptoms are associated with violence rather than the factors which might render a particular delusion or hallucination risky. Much of what follows in this chapter refers to psychotic symptoms in the context of a long-standing psychotic illness, but, as noted, there may well be a continuum between symptom presentation and full blown illness. Furthermore, the border between normality and pathology is sometimes hard to distinguish, for example between 'over-valued ideas' and full delusions, and such ideas/delusions may persist in apparent isolation from a diagnosis of schizophrenia or similar illness. Studies in the field often do not make absolute distinctions and, indeed, it may not matter in practice except insofar as monodelusional states (e.g. see *Behavioral Sciences and the Law*, issue 3, 2006) or disorders of passion (see chapter 12) lack the bizarre qualities of some schizophrenic states and may be more easily missed.

Psychotic Symptoms and Violence

Delusions and threat/control-override symptoms

Beliefs, by definition, require some sort of acceptance that a proposition is true in the absence of evidence for it. Most people have beliefs of some kind, whether religious, political or something else. This in itself is not pathological, but some beliefs have characteristics which are. A pathological belief is referred to as a delusion. Kräupl Taylor (1979) defined a 'psychotic delusion' as a belief based on an absolute conviction of the truth of a proposition that is idiosyncratic, incorrigible, ego-involved and often preoccupying. Reference to 'incorrigibility' is consistent throughout the literature, from Jaspers (1923) to Oltmanns (1988), and reiterated in the *DSM-IV* (American Psychiatric Association, 1994). In these terms, delusions are beliefs which are not just held without evidence, but rather in the face of contrary evidence, and are not amenable to change. This conceptualization is helpful in many circumstances, and perhaps particularly so when the beliefs are bizarre. It may, however, provide insufficient guidance for clinicians when beliefs centre on more ordinary social situations. Mullen and Maack (1985), for example, noted that in cases of morbid jealousy it is not uncommon for the partner who was believed to be unfaithful to end up with the postulated lover; people who have paranoid delusions about their neighbours may indeed have neighbours who have become antagonistic to them or even reported them to the police if they have been acting strangely or dangerously in this context, but some truth in the neighbours' hostility does not necessarily invalidate classification of the paranoid belief as a delusion. In such cases, indicators of the way in which the belief was formulated, or the way in which it is maintained may be more helpful than evidence of its truth or falsity *per se*. To complicate matters further, it has long been recognized that the apparently consistent view of a delusion as 'incorrigible' cannot be defended either. Beck's (1952) description of change in a delusion suffered by a man with schizophrenia in response to psychotherapy is generally taken as the first clinical step in recognizing this, followed by others adding evidence to support such a position (e.g. Sacks et al., 1974; Rudden et al., 1982) and the development of scales for measuring delusions along one or more dimensions (e.g. Hole et al., 1979; Kendler et al., 1983; Shapiro, 1961; Strauss 1969; Brett-Jones et al., 1987; Taylor et al., 1994; Peters et al., 1999). Delusions may fluctuate in another sense too – they are not necessarily experienced consistently throughout the whole period for which they are generally a problem. Myin-Germeys et al. (2001) developed an 'experience sampling method' to find out how much of the time people with delusions were aware of them and/or preoccupied with them. On average, people reported awareness of their delusions for about a third of their time, this period being characterized by more negative affect. Withdrawal from social and other 'distracting' activities increased the likelihood of delusional awareness. Bell et al. (2006) provide a useful review of the growing number of standardized rating schedules to facilitate reliable determination of a delusion.

A concept which is closely related to that of the delusion, but possibly not fully co-terminous with it, is of threat/control-override (TCO) symptoms. Link and Stueve (1994) highlighted this cluster as a strong correlate of violence. It is constituted by three symptoms, as rated on the Psychiatric Epidemiologic Research Interview (PERI; Dohrenwend et al., 1980):

- a feeling that one's mind is dominated by forces beyond one's control;
- a feeling that thoughts are being put into one's mind that are not one's own;
- a feeling that there are people who wish to do one harm.

Use of the word 'feeling' has raised doubts for some clinicians about whether these symptoms are truly the equivalent of, respectively, passivity delusions, thought insertion and persecutory delusions, but researchers generally treat them as if they are.

The most commonly researched question about delusions or TCO symptoms and violence has been about overall frequency of association. Although such studies consistently demonstrate an association, as symptoms and violent acts are measured during long periods of time which are not necessarily co-terminous, they can do little more than indicate to clinicians that this is an area of concern. A common choice is to test the relationship between any delusion and any violence reported as having occurred at any time over the 12 months prior to interview (e.g. Mojtabai, 2006; Swanson et al., 1996); some have adopted a generally similar strategy, but with some more serious violence included in analysis if it occurred up to 5 years previously (e.g. Link and Steuve, 1994). This is where the point about incorrigibility or changeability becomes important. This sort of difficulty is perhaps best illustrated by comparing publications on the matter from the MacArthur risk assessment study. The oft quoted evidence against a relationship between delusions and violence comes from the Appelbaum et al. (2000) report, which was, in fact, about the *predictive value* of delusions. In this early report, which included evaluations of mental state at baseline (time-1) and re-examination at 10-weekly intervals for up to a year, the MacArthur group had not yet made the all important intermediate test of whether delusions at time-1 predicted delusions at time-2 (or subsequently). In a later study Appelbaum et al. (2004) confirmed that one-third of the subgroup of patients with delusions at any measured interview no longer had them 10 weeks later, so there was indeed symptomatic change. Violent action was associated with persistence of delusions. Over the whole study period there was a small but significant relationship between both delusions and violence and hallucinations and violence (Monahan et al., 2001).

Individual case reports, such as those referred to above have long implicated delusions as drivers to violence, and some historical samples, unselected for violence, have also done so (Wilkins, 1993). In both criminological (Häfner and Böker, 1973) and clinical samples (Rofman et al., 1980) there were further indications of this likelihood, but systematic documentation of a quantitative association probably started with our UK prisoner studies, in which men who had been under pretrial remand in prison, mostly for 4 weeks or less, were asked about their mental state during interview and around the time of the alleged offence; they were also asked, specifically, how they explained their actions in relation to the index offence (Taylor, 1985b). It was found that almost all of those with psychosis had been symptomatic at the time of the offence, regardless of the type of offence (Taylor, 1985), but specific inquiry about motive for the offence revealed that only about 40% of the men actually *attributed* the offending behaviour to any psychotic symptom. Where a symptom was linked with offending, it was almost invariably a delusion, although not necessarily recognized by the man as such. Further examination of the data revealed that there was a significant relationship between acting on delusions and the more serious violence. Findings from a later, records based study of homicide offenders in Finland fitted well with these British data in that over 90% of these Finnish men and women had been symptomatic at the time of the offence, and, given the seriousness of the crime, a rather higher proportion of offences had been directly attributed to the psychotic symptoms (two-thirds) (Laajasalo and Häkkänen, 2006). That said, Laajasalo and Häkkänen did not find that 'excessive violence', meaning more than was necessary to kill, was more likely among the delusionally driven. Swanson et al. (2006a), drawing on a sample of over 1,400 people from across the USA, also reported that presence of psychotic symptoms was linked with more serious violence. Teasdale et al. (2006), using McArthur risk study data on men and women who were discharged general psychiatric patients in the USA, found a sex difference in that there was an association between delusions and violent acts for the men, but not the women, when experiencing threat delusions specifically.

With regard to TCO symptoms, a comparison of patients and never treated community controls in New York showed that TCO symptoms best differentiated people who had been violent and people who had not, regardless of patient status or demographic characteristics (Link and Stueve, 1994). So, with TCO symptoms, as with delusions, presence of the symptoms rather than having a diagnosis of psychosis and/or being in treatment seems to be the critical factor. Although, in this study, symptoms and various forms of violence were measured over different time periods, Swanson et al. (1996) subsequently tested the relationship between TCO symptoms and violence using US ECA data with reference to the year prior to interview and to whole lifetime, confirming a relationship over both periods. Link et al. (1998) replicated the finding of a relationship in an Israeli sample. Two smaller studies in European countries have added further support for the role of this cluster. In Norway, Bjørkly and Havik (2003) found that TCO symptoms were present close in time to a serious violent act; in Austria, Stompe et al. (2004) showed that TCO symptoms did not distinguish between offenders with psychosis and non-offender patients with psychosis, but did distinguish the seriously violent from other offenders. Hodgins et al. (2003) interrogated longitudinal data on 128 men discharged from psychiatric hospitals in four countries. Comorbid personality disorder was more likely in the subsequently violent group but, after controlling for personality disorder, 'severe positive symptoms' were more likely among the men who were violent on follow-up.

Rare, apparently dissenting studies may not be measuring true delusions and/or may not be primarily testing the relationship between delusions and violence. Skeem et al. (2006), for example, reported no evidence of association between TCO symptoms and violence in an emergency room cohort ($n = 132$) followed for 6 months, but the people were selected on a criterion of 'high risk' and the sample was diagnostically heterogeneous. Given that psychosis emerged as a protective factor against violence, it is likely that the case mix prevented adequate assessment of the question about TCO symptoms and violence.

So, there is consistent evidence of a general association between delusions and violence, and growing evidence that when such acts are attributed to abnormal beliefs, they are likely to be particularly serious. Delusions, however, are common in psychosis and many who suffer them are never violent, so the next question must be about whether it is possible to determine which are the more risky delusions and/or in which contexts they may be most likely to result in violence. Personality may be a mediating factor. When personality disorder is treated in terms only of current trials, it appears to be almost invariably present (e.g. Blackburn et al., 2003), and thus not especially useful in discriminating likely relevance of delusions. Confining attribution of personality disorder only to those with conduct or emotional disorders established in childhood does, however, discriminate. Those who are unremarkable before onset of their illness are more likely to have been driven to their offence by their delusions than those with comorbid personality disorder (Taylor et al., 1998). A comparison of such patients between Scotland on the one hand and England and Wales on the other confirmed that, while the prevalence of premorbid personality disorders may vary between communities, this inter-relationship with the impact of delusions is consistent (Taylor et al., 2008). Other possibilities lie in the characteristics of the delusions and in social interactions about them, the latter perhaps being of particular importance as violence in the context of psychotic illness seems to be exceptionally likely to be directed towards people in the family, or who are close socially (Johnston and Taylor, 2003; Nordström and Kullgren, 2003; Nordström et al., 2006).

Most of the standard mental state assessment schedules which inquire about psychotic symptoms, including those which are useful in measuring change, such as the Comprehensive or Brief Psychiatric Rating Scales (CPRS: Åsberg et al., 1978; BPRS: Overall and Gorham, 1962), allow rating of delusions by main content, such as persecutory, passivity or religious. In these terms in the pretrial prisoner study, the main distinguishing quality for the men driven to act violently on their delusions was passivity (Taylor, 1999). Paranoid delusions were more common, but occurred at a similar rate in both groups. The TCO cluster may be so powerful, when it occurs, because the passivity element endorses violent actions on the belief in being threatened.

The Maudsley Assessment of Delusions Schedule (MADS) (Taylor et al., 1994) was developed to describe other characteristics of delusions, particularly factors maintaining them, or their consequences. Thus, with the MADS, the patient-rated most important delusion is measured along nine dimensions: belief maintenance factors (e.g. seeking evidence for the belief, finding it, dealing with hypothetical contradiction), level of conviction, of preoccupation, of systematization, of its idiosyncrasy, affective impact of the belief, actions on it, including talking about it, withdrawal because of it and level of insight. In a series of 83 general hospital patients, some sort of action on the belief designated by the patient as the most important to him or her was common, and violent action in just one 28-day period had occurred in about one-quarter of the cases (Wessely et al., 1993).

Qualities associated with violent action on a delusion included first having acted on it in another, less threatening way – by seeking evidence for it, and, for some, having found evidence for it; secondly, being affectively distressed by the belief – especially frightened by it; and, thirdly, the nature of response to hypothetical challenge to the belief (Buchanan et al., 1993). Hypothetical challenge means that a proposition related to the belief is created by the interviewer who then asks the person with the belief whether, if the proposition were true, it would affect the belief. An example would be if a person believed that she had a transmitter implanted in her head by the aliens who were persecuting her, the interviewer might say that it might be possible to do a very sensitive X-ray of the area, and ask a skilled radiologist to read it. The interviewer would then ask: 'If this specialist could find no evidence of the device, would that change the position? Would you feel reassured?' In the series of general psychiatric patients under study, Buchanan et al. found that no one abandoned his/her belief in these circumstances but, while some ignored such challenge, others became even more convinced of the validity of their belief, or developed it further in some way. People in this latter group were more likely to have acted violently.

The MADS incorporates the gentlest way of posing potentially contradictory evidence to the responder's self-designated most important belief, but how, and under what range of circumstances do people routinely talk about their beliefs and/or their delusions? What sort of response do they get? To what extent is the affective response to the belief influenced by social context or interaction – perhaps a more direct or affectively laden challenge? To what extent is the propensity to modify a delusion rather than ignore challenge or potentially contradictory evidence intrinsic?

The MADS findings, then, suggested three possible pathways to violence in the context of delusions: first, a primary delusional effect – the person acts on a delusion because the belief is sufficient in itself; secondly, action may follow as a result of the affective distress, apparently caused by the delusion, but perhaps also because the social climate between the person with the delusion and his/her significant others is profoundly altered by the delusion and/or its attendant distress; thirdly, it may be that the social interaction modifies the belief over time, along a pathway which finally makes action imperative.

Perhaps the mechanism by which the belief has formed in the first place is critical here. There are parallels in the three main routes to belief formation that have been hypothesized. One explanation lies in 'logical' explanations for perceptual abnormalities (Maher 1974, 1988). Such abnormalities not only refer to hallucinations, but also impairments such as deafness (Thewisson et al., 2005) or hyperacute perceptions, such as enhanced or selective ability to recognize negative emotions in others (Davis and Gibson, 2000). With respect to impairments, there are even some data to show that healthy people may develop a paranoid state in the context of hypnotically induced deafness (Zimbardo et al., 1981). The Bentall group has consistently demonstrated selective attention to threat related input (e.g. Bentall and Kaney, 1989; Bentall et al., 1995). A second possibility is that delusions constitute a form of personal defence. Psychoanalysts have long held a view that paranoia emerges as a form of resolution of difficulties with self-esteem (e.g. Colby, 1977), while others have emphasized a so-called 'self-serving bias', which allows attribution of any good outcomes to self and all negative outcomes to others (Campbell and Sedikides, 1999). There is even some evidence from CBT-based studies that improvement in self-esteem may be associated with improvement of psychotic symptoms, albeit here delusions of grandeur and negative symptoms (Jones et al., 2010). The third is a cognitive route (Magaro, 1980) by which people with certain cognitive styles process information differently from the 'average person', in particular through 'jumping to conclusions' (e.g. Huq et al., 1988; Abroms et al., 1996). The possible routes to delusion formation are not necessarily mutually exclusive.

So, how might these various theories apply when violence is an issue? Carlin et al. (2005) found that offender patients with psychosis were more likely to make external attributions for negative events than those without psychotic symptoms, regardless of delusion type within the psychotic group. Hurn et al. (2002) showed how response to hypothetical challenge might differ according to mechanism in belief formation. Those psychotic patients who rejected hypothetical contradiction were more likely to have beliefs founded in hallucinatory experiences, beliefs which they rated more strongly as 'truthful'; patients who accepted the hypothetical challenge were more likely to report that their belief had affected their behaviour and interfered with their thoughts and their lives. Freeman et al. (2007) explored 'safety behaviours' in relation to paranoid delusions. Safety behaviours were first described in relation to anxiety (Salkovskis, 1991). They are most commonly avoidant, and have the risk of maintaining the pathology, because the person attributes their continued safety to their safety behaviours rather than, perhaps, a false perception or interpretation of the dangers. It was this that prompted Freeman and colleagues to ask about their relationship to delusions. All but four of 100 patients with paranoid delusions reported carrying out at least one safety behaviour in the month prior to interview. Here too the most common was avoidance, but 24 of the patients had been aggressive. Greater use of safety behaviours was associated with a higher level of distress about the delusions, and, in turn, with the greater likelihood of a history of violent acts against others and suicide attempts.

One of Junginger's (2006) main interests was in the constancy or variation of delusions over time, and another in whether, insofar as they do vary, their characteristics are consistent in different phases of illness. His brief review of previous studies showed how little work had been done in this field, with somewhat contradictory results. In his small series ($n = 54$) of delusional patients, 40 reported at least one episode of violence which had coincided with a delusion, 16 of them motivated by it. Eight patients had at least two episodes of delusionally motivated violence, separated in time, and on each occasion the violence had been motivated by a delusion with the same characteristics. Junginger proposed a simple method to aid prediction of delusion development, and thus, where this has been observed to underpin violence in a particular case, to aid assessment or risk of violence. He suggests characterizing delusions by gaining a detailed narrative of the experience and then applying questions to each element of it: Who? What? Where? When? How? Why? The following is how it might work if applied to Daniel McNaughton, from descriptions by his father and others:

> Father: [Daniel] said he wished me ... to put a stop to a persecution raised against him – it was some of the gentlemen connected with the conservative parties [who] in Glasgow [where]... I assured him there was no such persecution ... he shook his head, and said there certainly was a system of persecution [what] existing against him ...

> the interviews on the same subject were frequent for a year and a half – he told me ... he had left the city of Glasgow ... that he went to England to avoid them, and even to France, to escape from the persecution; that he had no sooner landed in France than he saw the spies following him there [the 'where' expanding and developing].

> Alexander Johnstone, MP: [McNaughton said] ... that he could get no rest, night nor day [when], on account of being watched ...

> Edward Thoms Monroe, MD: [McNaughton said] that they wanted to murder him [why they were following him] ...he had on one or two occasions found something pernicious in his food [how] ...the system destroying his health [how] (Old Bailey Proceedings, 2011, with analytic comments inserted).

Interpersonal communications about delusions and violence

The fact that McNaughton talked to other people about his most important delusion, of being the object of systematic persecution, and that other people responded in various ways, may well be typical of ordinary exchanges about such beliefs, but there are few empirical data. The first study using the MADS established that over 90% of people with at least one delusion, interviewed within a week of admission to a psychiatric unit, reported having spoken to someone in their social circle about that delusion in the previous 28 days (Taylor et al., 1994). If one enters a phrase like 'talking about delusions' into Google, then pages of entries appear with either relatives of people suffering from delusions asking how they should respond, or others – some relatives, some psychologists or other professional clinicians – offering advice, but, in fact, this advice is not based on systematic study. Langlands et al. (2008) consulted 45 'consumers', 60 carers and 52 clinicians from Australia, Canada, New Zealand, the UK and the USA about essential preliminaries – they called it 'first aid' – for helping people with psychosis. They sought consensus through the Delphi method. 'How to deal with delusions and hallucinations' and 'how to deal with communication difficulties' were among the nine categories of needs which were endorsed by more than 80% of the participants.

A systematic review of talking about delusions (Fadhli and Taylor, under submission), however, revealed that only the MADS study and one other (McCabe et al., 2002) have collected data on such communication in a structured way, and neither have data on outcome of *routine* exchange. The McCabe study recruited about half of patients attending two outpatient clinics in London and most of the psychiatrists treating them (39 in total) to participate in an observational study. They noticed that patients actively tried to talk about their psychotic symptoms, but each such interaction lasted for about 67 seconds, and occurred, on average, 1.4 times per interview (range 0–4), with the psychiatrists commonly 're-aligning' the focus of the session away from the symptom, by responding with another question, or laughing, or, if a relative or carer were present, speaking to that person instead. The MADS study, as noted above, showed that a 'set piece' research exchange about the patient-designated most important belief – the hypothetical challenge – could result in a change in the belief, in the direction of its intensification or elaboration.

In theory, there is a more substantial literature on the impact of communication about delusions in the more actively therapeutic context of cognitive behaviour therapy for people with psychosis. It is arguable, however, that such communication differs considerably from the range of everyday talking about beliefs which may occur as relatives or carers seek variously to reassure, or perhaps argue with the sufferer, because the impact of arguments from a loved one, whether warm and supportive or harassed, distressed and irritable, would be likely to have a different impact from interactions with someone who would be regarded as an essentially neutral figure by the patient. Even here, however, there is not much information. Jones et al. (2004; and see also below) conducted a systematic review of CBT for schizophrenia, with the express criterion that any treatment included must have amongst its aims the 'correction of misperceptions, irrational beliefs and reasoning biases.' Just two of the 19 trials identified met the analytical standards set by Jones and colleagues according to generally accepted criteria *and* measured delusions over time. One of them showed a slight advantage for CBT over 'standard treatment', which disappeared when allowance was made for missing ratings on the assumption that these reflected serious continuing illness (Drury et al., 2000) and the other described no effect at all (Durham et al., 2003). These studies do not, however, make reference to aggression or violence, except in some cases as an exclusion from trial criterion, and, indeed, none makes reference to side effects of any kind. An extended discussion of the extent to which these studies leave us in an uncertain position on how talking about delusions affects them or affects the behaviour of the sufferer is provided elsewhere (Taylor, 2006a). The few subsequent specifically therapeutic developments are discussed below, with one now having considered aggression.

Hallucinations and violence

Hallucinations may occur in any sensory modality. There is a small literature with data on gustatory and/or olfactory hallucinations in the context of delusions of being poisoned (Mawson, 1985; Mowat, 1966), but, in the context of the functional psychoses, most concern has been expended on auditory hallucinations, particularly command hallucinations. There is an expectation that if the commands are to do harm, then there is a risk that this will indeed follow. It may be partly for this reason that, taken together, research findings suggest that auditory hallucinations *per se* are not particularly associated with violence (e.g. Taylor, 1985b; Rogers et al., 1988). They may, however, add to risk of action on congruent delusions (Taylor et al., 1998). Further, the usual absence of violence may be an artifact of staff concern about the possible risk from command hallucinations and their implementation of effective management strategies. One study of the period (Hellerstein et al., 1987) identified 151 hallucinating patients among 789 consecutive hospital admissions and found no excess of violence in the hallucinating group. The people with hallucinations were, however, significantly more likely to have been secluded or under 1:1 staff assignments. Thus, staff interventions may

mask associations between hallucinations and violence in treated samples.

Rudrick (1999) and Barrowcliff and Haddock (2006) have reviewed the literature of various periods on command hallucinations. Barrowcliff and Haddock considered studies in three groups: those examining an association between command content and compliance in general psychiatric and community samples; those doing the same in offender patient samples; and the role of psychological factors in understanding the relationship between compliance and command. They identified 17 published studies of compliance with command hallucinations, of which three referred to harm to others (Rogers et al., 2002; Fox et al., 2004; Lee et al., 2004). Factors associated with a greater likelihood of action on hallucinations included beliefs about the hallucinations, such as the likely consequences of not complying, 'knowing' the identity of the voice, attitude to the voice(s), seriousness of the command, concurrent mood and more social factors like placement at the time – being in the community rather than in hospital may increase likelihood of compliance with violent commands – and self-perception of social rank (e.g. Fox et al., 2004). Monahan et al. (2001) found a weak relationship between hallucinations and violence over 1 year of follow-up of a mixed diagnosis sample of people discharged after a brief general psychiatric hospital admission.

Other psychotic symptoms and violence

None of the other 'positive symptoms' of a psychotic illness has been shown to be of any great relevance to actions (Hafner and Boker, 1973; Taylor, 1985b). There have been suggestions that negative symptoms are either neutral or protective, but much may depend on context here, as such difficulties often lead to 'encouragement' towards activities and in this context, negative symptoms have been associated with irritable violence (Nilssen et al., 1988). The only other phenomenon worth considering is 'motivelessness', which is not strictly a symptom but was at one time taken as almost pathognomonic of a psychotic killing. Generally, a motiveless crime is taken to be one in which there has been very definite action on the part of the offender, but it has not been possible to formulate any reason at all for it, at least up to the time of trial. It is a commonly expressed lay view that a 'senseless' crime must imply mental abnormality, although psychiatrists should always try to demonstrate disorder from evidence independent of the crime. Wilmanns (1940) described 18 killers who showed no clear evidence of psychosis at the time of their crime, but went on to develop schizophreniform psychoses in prison. Gillies (1965) noted, in a different series, that, although some went on to develop florid symptoms of psychosis, others merely remained affectless and withdrawn, much as at the time of the offence. It must remain in some doubt as to whether those in either series who went on to develop a florid psychosis had really been free from illness at the time of the offence. Lanzkron (1963) presented the view that no less than 27% of his series of homicide offenders had become psychotic after their offence. It would be compatible with current views on the impact of major trauma that psychiatric illness, including the psychoses, could be precipitated by such major life events as a killing, trial and imprisonment.

Häfner and Boker (1973) found that motive was unrecorded for less than 20% of the German mentally abnormal homicide series, and that this proportion was not peculiar to those with psychosis. It varied little between diagnostic groups. In our early pretrial prisoner study (Taylor, 1985b), there was a much lower proportion who could give no account of motives – 8% among the psychotic men and 7% in the non-psychotic group, the difference probably being accounted for by the fact that the latter study was interview based and allowed for a good deal of probing. A small number of the men were motiveless in a different sense. No positive motive could be recorded as their 'antisocial behaviour' almost amounted to a negative symptom of their illness, aimlessness possibly being a better word to describe the reason for what had happened. In this case, the offence was not violent.

Empathy, Psychosis and Violence

Derntl et al. (2009) have suggested a general deficit of all empathic abilities in people with schizophrenia compared with the general population. In a systematic review of empathy and offending, in which they identified 35 relevant studies, Joliffe and Farrington (2004) found a strong relationship between low cognitive empathy and offending, particularly violent offending, and a weak relationship between affective empathy and offending. The question then arises as to whether impaired empathy may be an important mediator of violence among people with schizophrenia or similar psychosis. In a systematic review of this (Bragado-Jimenez and Taylor, 2012), six eligible studies were identified, but sample selection, and empathy, illness and violence measures differed between the studies, as did procedures of study. Data were thus too heterogeneous for meta-analysis. It was more likely than not for a relationship to be found in the better controlled studies between perceptual or cognitive empathy and violence, but the literature was not consistent. Responsive empathy has not been studied in this context.

Anger, Psychosis and Violence

Anger is an emotion which affects people with and without psychosis alike, but there is evidence that it is more prevalent among people with psychosis than their healthy peers (e.g. Freeman et al., 2001; Green et al., 2006). Anger is neither necessary nor sufficient to explain all violence, nor is it inherently dysfunctional, but there is evidence that it has a significant association with violent acts (Anderson and Bushman, 2002).

It thus made logical sense for the MacArthur risk assessment group to include anger measurement among their research tools when studying a cohort of discharged psychiatric patients, and it was not surprising that they found an association (Monahan et al., 2001). Their group was, however, heterogeneous by diagnosis, so the next question is whether anger may be the critical link to violence among people with psychosis. In a systematic review of the literature on this more specific area of anger work, 13 studies were identified and, in all but one of them, mean anger scores were elevated among those who had been violent compared with those who had not (Reagu et al., 2013, in press). In order to make use of such findings clinically, however, as Novaco (e.g. 1994) has repeatedly emphasized, it is important to understand the context of the anger – is it driven by the internal state, as might be expected of paranoid states (e.g. Beck, 1999; Hareli and Weiner, 2002), or is it driven by tense exchanges and/or the potentially negative emotional climate that may surround a person who is chronically ill with a psychotic illness? There is much more to be learned, but it is not too soon to be asking clinical questions.

ENVIRONMENTAL FACTORS WHICH MAY BE RELEVANT TO VIOLENT OUTCOMES AMONG PEOPLE WITH FUNCTIONAL PSYCHOSIS

Environment with respect to people who have psychosis is generally taken to mean social environment, and this is where we will focus, but it is worth noting that factors beyond the personal may also be important. Schory et al. (2003) compared records of humidity, wind speed and low barometric pressure in one city in the USA (Louisville, Kentucky) with documentation of psychiatric emergency room visits, violence data from the city police department and suicide data from the county medical examiner. Diagnoses are not recorded, but acts of violence and emergency visits rose during periods of low barometric pressure.

The Family and Close Social Circle

When violence is perpetrated by people with psychosis, it is so often within the family that it is arguable that research to investigate family interactions and needs in this context should be the highest priority. The National Confidential Inquiry into Homicide for England and Wales confirms that people with a history of mental illness, of contact with psychiatric services or with symptoms at the time of the offence are less likely to kill strangers than those without (Shaw et al., 2004). In Sweden, Nordström et al. (2006) reported on all 48 homicide offenders between 1992 and 2000 who had schizophrenia and showed that those who had killed a family member were more likely to have been delusional and less likely to have been intoxicated or had a criminal career. Most were known to psychiatric services, although few of them were still in contact, and only two were taking medication. In an earlier study (Nordström and Kullgren, 2003), they had investigated all 207 men of 18 years of age and over who had committed at least one violent crime and presented for a first specialist forensic psychiatric evaluation between 1992 and 2000, with the main research question: do violent offenders with schizophrenia who attack family members differ from those with other victims? As in our English high security hospital study (Johnston and Taylor, 2003), injuries to family victims were more likely to have been serious or fatal than injuries to people outside the family. Beyond that, the Swedish results suggested that there had been a substantially greater family burden from the illness of those who had attacked family. This was echoed in a study in Austria (Stompe et al., 2006) which found that family burden with schizophrenia was twice as high among those with schizophrenia who had also offended as among those who had not. This was, however, complicated by the parents of some of the men also having had schizophrenia. In general, family burden from psychotic illness has received a little attention, and much of that focused solely on family members other than the person with psychosis. Cousins et al. (2002) have described a way of assessing this in people living with and/or caring for people with Parkinson's disease, which could be applied to help families of people with psychosis, but in addition, Greenberg (Greenberg et al., 1994; Chen and Greenberg, 2004) points out, we must also take into account positive contributions to families by people with psychosis in order to have an accurate view of household and family dynamics.

Earlier studies are also consistent on the vulnerability of relatives and household members, perhaps especially mothers (Estroff and Zimmer, 1994; Estroff et al., 1994, 1998; Steadman et al., 1998; Tardiff et al., 1997; Vaddadi et al., 1997). Violence is not contingent on proximity per se, so what possible explanations might there be? The sequencing of symptoms and any conflict is unclear, but three, possibly inter-related aspects of close relationships may be relevant: the roles in key relationships, emotional climate in them and the way in which they may influence symptom development. Roles within the family tend to be altered by chronic illness. Parents, particularly mothers, often find themselves taking over various aspects of life management, tasks which in other circumstances would not be regarded as appropriate for the age of their 'child'. This has been found to have an association with violent behaviour between the parties concerned (Estroff et al., 1994), fuelled in particular by the financial dependence of the person with psychosis, and a mutually hostile and threatening relationship between parent and adult child.

Emotional climate in relationships between people with schizophrenia and their families has been an area of interest since the 1960s (e.g. Brown et al., 1962; Leff and Vaughn, 1985). The term 'expressed emotion' (EE) was used to indicate qualities in emotional climate, with high EE reflecting tension, emotional over-involvement, critical remarks and even outright hostility on the part of the family member(s). Initially the main thrust of the research was in showing that not only was a person who had schizophrenia more likely to relapse when family members had high EE in relation to him/her but also that the high EE was the provocation (Brown et al., 1972). Subsequent studies have endorsed the position that high EE in this context carries at least twice the risk of relapse for the person with schizophrenia, and that about two-thirds of people returning to a high context after treatment would be expected to relapse (Butzlaff and Hooley, 1998; Stanhope and Solomon, 2007). A more multidirectional model of understanding the emergence of high expressed emotion and its consequences is now better recognized (e.g. Kavanagh, 1992), based on the stress and coping model of Lazarus and Folkman (1984). The finding that not only may high EE be apparent in certain family relationships but also in particular professional care staff–patient relationships (Moore and Kuipers, 1999) provides further evidence, if needed, that it is more useful to explore the interpersonal dynamic than to attribute attitudinal difficulties. The burden of care on the families of people with schizophrenia may be substantial, and probably the more so since the ever growing shift towards treating in the community any but the most acutely ill (Awad and Voruganti, 2008). Factors which increase the burden include the perception on the part of the relatives of the severity of symptoms and their ability to cope with them (e.g. Barrowclough and Parle, 1997), the mood of the person with psychosis (Boye et al., 2001) and perceived hostility (Estroff et al., 1994, 1998; Swanson et al., 1997). Relatives who are less well informed about the illness, and tend to attribute blame for its disruptive qualities to the person with the illness rather than the illness itself appear to be at higher risk for developing high expressed emotion (Chan, 2010; Kavanagh, 1992). It is less clear, however, how schizophrenia, family burden, high EE and violence relate – there has been too little enquiry. In a preliminary study, part of an ongoing, longitudinal study of people with schizophrenia and their relatives and professional carers, we encountered both patient and relative centred difficulties in recruiting relative participants. Among those relatives who did participate, half had high EE. Qualitative analysis of 5-minute speech samples, of uninterrupted talking about the relationship with the patient according to five written prompts (Magana et al., 1986), revealed that the core concern was about the identity of the person with schizophrenia (Rowntree et al., 2011). This polarized relatives with high EE who regarded the person as a patient and the delusions as distressing and salient, and those with low EE who viewed the individual as 'the person s/he had always been'. Where violence had occurred, it was, perhaps contrary to expectations, in the latter group.

Residential proximity creates opportunities for relatives to comment on delusions to the person who has them, or discuss them, but this has not been systematically studied (Fadhli and Taylor, under submission). We have already mentioned research showing that responsiveness to hypothetical challenge to a delusion may be associated with violence, but we can find no systematically collected information on how families deal with the symptoms with which their psychotic member suffers. There is, however, plenty of evidence in publicly accessible search engines that family members are sufficiently concerned about such matters to seek advice on how to respond to reported delusions and that there are people offering them apparently untested advice. Locating the pathways to and expression of violence within the families of people with psychosis complicates research and challenges simpler causal formulae. As we argued earlier with regard to 'unpacking' diagnosis into actual symptoms, it is necessary, in the same way, to increase the granularity with which we consider family processes, traditions, affective and cognitive traditions to illuminate the links between violence and psychosis.

The Clinical Environment

Some difficulties in the nature of dialogue between patients and their clinicians have already been noted (McCabe et al., 2002; Estroff 2004). Such difficulties in communication may contribute directly to violence. Omerov et al. (2004) compared staff and patient experiences of the same violent incidents in a hospital in Sweden, where staff were able to identify fewer than 50% of the provocations that the patients reported experiencing. One of the more consistent discrepancies in perception arose over medication. Secker et al. (2004) picked up this theme in a qualitative study undertaken in a south London hospital, in England. They considered the most striking theme to be lack of staff engagement with the patients, and a particular inability to look at the world through the eyes of the patients (see also Gilburt et al., 2008). In a partner study, Benson et al. (2003) found patients reluctant to talk with researchers, but striking congruence between one patient participator who had been violent and the staff in the discourse about two incidents, in particular in attributing blame. Bowers et al. (2006) tested the relationship between specific nurse training in prevention and management of violence in the inpatient setting, with rather discouraging results.

Elbogen et al. (2006), using the MacArthur study multi-site cohort of over 1,000 patients discharged into the community after a brief hospitalization, studied patient perceptions of their treatment need, adherence and effectiveness, and compared these self-ratings with community violence. Perceived treatment need was couched in negative statements, to which patients were asked to agree or disagree, such as: 'You think that going for help probably wouldn't do any good.' Adherence was a binary variable, derived in response to: 'In the past six months, were there times when you thought you should go to a doctor or clinic... but did not go?' Answers to four questions defined perception of treatment effectiveness: 'As a direct result of the services I received: (a) I deal more effectively with my daily problems; (b) I am better able to control my life; (c) I am getting along better with my family; (d) my symptoms are not bothering me very much.' Perceived treatment need, positive perceptions of treatment and treatment adherence were all associated with reduced odds of violence over the 6 months of outpatient care. Diagnostic differences did not affect perceived treatment need, but people with psychosis were more likely to perceive their treatment as effective and report treatment adherence than people in other diagnostic groups.

Day et al. (2005) completed a similar study in Wales and north-west England of 228 people who had been hospitalized with schizophrenia or schizo-affective disorder. Attitudes towards treatment and treatment adherence were predicted by insight, attitudes towards staff and the treatment experience. In particular, people with poor insight, with a poor relationship with the prescribing psychiatrist and who had experienced any coercion in their treatment were more likely to have a negative attitude to that treatment. Research conducted by and in collaboration with investigators with first hand experience of hospitalization provides a range of findings about the experience and outcomes of psychiatric inpatient treatment (Russo and Wallcraft, 2011). The first few hospitalizations may represent an exquisitely vulnerable time, during which enduring experiences of trauma or of authentic therapeutic alliance are formed. It is particularly important that people who might benefit from mental healthcare do not avoid it later due to the lingering effects of prior humiliation, violence, or coercion in treatment settings.

Zygmunt et al. (2002) reported a systematic review of the literature on strategies to improve treatment adherence. Studies of psycho-educational interventions with patients or their families were popular, but typically ineffective. Problem-solving or motivational techniques directed specifically at treatment adherence appear most likely to be successful in improving this. We would also suggest that more attention may be needed in the support and supervision of staff. Moore and Kuipers (1992) and Moore et al. (1992) did much of the early work on expressed emotion in staff relationships to patients, finding that, generally, where critical style was found, it was not typical of the staff concerned, but rather seemed responsive. Since then, there have been about 27 studies in this field, yielding mixed results both on prevalence of the difficulty and on its consequences (Berry et al., 2011). Some studies had small samples and did not attempt prevalence reporting, for example one study of 20 staff and 20 patients did not find high expressed emotion, but did note critical comments – mainly about enduring features which were seen as being 'within the patient's control'. One important factor in the differences may lie in length and intensity of relationships – there has to be close contact over at least 3–6 months before it would be expected that any such difficulties might emerge. Moore and colleagues have specifically studied staff–patient pairs in secure hospital settings (Moore et al., 2002), where 55/61 staff who participated had high expressed emotion in the specified relationship, which correlated exclusively with irritability, argumentativeness and violence on the part of the patients. The rate was much higher than for staff working with long-term patients in general services, where a quarter of staff showed high expressed emotion, but here the patient problems were 'difficult' and socially embarrassing behaviours', a finding endorsed in other studies. More information is needed about the impact of such difficulties, but it seems likely that when clinical staff recognize their emergence, they may use the recognition as a cue to distance themselves from the patient, and this may even be a factor in rejection from services; where not, then the main effect may be on quality and extent of patient benefit from treatment. It is arguable that enhanced recognition of developing expressed emotion could be used to clinical advantage.

The Wider Community

The main factors in the wider community which are likely to affect violence by people with psychosis are almost certainly similar to those which affect people without psychosis, or indeed mental disorder of any kind, and these are availability of alcohol and other drugs. We have already noted that there seems to have been an increase in the use of substances by people with psychosis over time in England and Wales at least, as licensing laws have relaxed, street drugs have become more readily available, and 'care in the community' has left many people with psychosis struggling to maintain symptom control and/or with little to distract or occupy them. Experiences which are more problematic for people with psychosis than their healthy peers are dealing with stigma and the higher rates of community victimization they experience (see opening paragraphs). They are also probably more vulnerable to a range of other significantly stressful life events which may have an impact on their propensity for violence (e.g. Silver and Teasdale, 2005). Becoming homeless is among these. Such problems are in part related to the tendency for people with psychosis and other major mental disorders to find themselves resettled in problem communities (Silver, 2000; Silver et al., 2002) and on social support for their finances, sometimes explicitly contingent on complying consistently with treatment; some are without supports of any kind. Swanson et al. (2002) studied factors associated with the 1-year prevalence of violence among 802 adults with psychosis or major

mood disorders attending public health services in four states of the USA and, indeed, found that apart from a past history of violent victimization, homelessness and violence in the surrounding community were the factors associated with higher rates of patient violence. The lack of accessible or affordable residential options in safe settings for people with psychosis may contribute to perpetuating their use and need of violence that may be context appropriate, but nonetheless detrimental clinically and socially. If absent from research consideration, these contextual influences on violence may be inaccurately attributed to symptoms or substances.

MANAGEMENT AND TREATMENT

Practically useful, high-quality research information about treatments specifically for people with psychosis who have been violent is difficult to obtain. The gold standard for treatment trials is always considered to be the randomized controlled trial (RCT), notwithstanding its undoubted limitations in tending to focus on average, consenting and co-operating men. People with psychosis who need forensic mental health services are rarely 'average', often having atypical presentations, combinations of disorders or medication resistant psychosis, they often go through periods when they are reluctant to take treatment, sometimes frankly refusing, and, although the majority are men, 10–20% are women, for whom the evidence base on medication is much less good (see also chapter 20). Some who have engaged in the most serious or repetitive violence may even be regarded as unique, and, perhaps for these few, treatment trials might best be created as individualized trials, with on–off–on design around treatment of their specific problems.

Cure et al. (2005), nevertheless, provided a tantalizing report of the range of randomized trials that they considered could be relevant to the provision of forensic mental health services. They searched 29 electronic databases of literature for the period 1955–2000, none of them, they observed, standing out as a definitive source of 'forensic studies'. Of approximately 22,000 studies identified, 409 were described as relevant to highly aggressive or aggressive people with psychosis, and were made available through the Cochrane Central Register of Controlled Trials. The authors offered further encouragement in describing the range of treatments evaluated, noting that a higher proportion of the studies than in other mental health fields had been pursued for at least 6 months and suggested that additional studies were still likely to be discovered or underway at the time of their searches. Nevertheless, they hardly stimulated much further interest in the work, by describing the quality of most of the studies as 'poor' according to the Jadad scale (Jadad et al., 1996).

The principles of treatment are considered in chapter 23, emphasizing the therapeutic context and the importance of establishing sound treatment engagement in order to sustain specific treatments. As far as possible, it is important first, to be working within an explicit, evidence-based multidisciplinary and interagency framework; secondly, to be ensuring that people are stabilized on medication which has maximum impact on all the features of psychosis – not just the positive symptoms – while inflicting the minimum unwanted effects; thirdly, to be making full use of relevant psychological interventions; and, fourthly, to be employing all relevant educational and occupational techniques to enhance the prospect of gaining healthy independence or, in some terminology, moving along the recovery pathway.

For people with psychosis, it will be important to make some specific efforts to improve or maintain physical health in the face of the combination of an illness which often imposes anergia on the sufferer and the medications which themselves have a tendency to promote weight gain and, in some cases, metabolic diseases such as diabetes. The specialist clinical models and medico-legal frameworks for enhancing continued treatment adherence with a health service lead, such as provisions within mental health legislation, are mainly covered in chapter 24, and those with a criminal justice system lead, such as community or suspended prison sentences with a mental health treatment requirement, are dealt with in chapter 25. Only some of the issues more specific to psychosis will be considered here, with the same caveat, as in the more general treatment chapter (23), that this is a field that is under more-or-less continuous update. We recommend here, and there, that, for both physical and psycho-social treatments, the reader keep checking sources such as the Cochrane Library of systematic literature reviews (www.thecochranelibrary.com), which deals exclusively with randomized controlled trials (RCTs), and the Database of Abstracts of Reviews of Effects (DARE) (www.crd.york.ac.uk/cms2web/), which goes beyond randomized controlled trials in its scope. The reader should also be aware that, from time to time, previously well-regarded and useful reviews, particularly Cochrane reviews, are removed from the site before new reviews are available, so it is worth saving reviews in areas of interest. In addition, in England, standard guidance in treatment, as far as possible based on such reviews, is available on the National Institute of Health and Clinical Excellence website: www.nice.org.uk. In fact, the increments of change are generally quite small and the principles of working remain solid. While specific treatment guidance ought to be very similar across national boundaries, there may be some differences with respect to medication, as there may be more or less caution about licensing certain products in different countries. Thus, where national guidelines are available these will be most useful. In the USA, for example, the American Psychiatric Association provides *Practice Guidelines* and occasional *Task Force Reports* (www.psych.org). Specifically

for schizophrenia, the Patient Outcomes Research Team (PORT) also provides regular updates for evidence based treatment recommendations (e.g. Dixon et al., 2009).

Medication

Medication for people who are acutely psychotic with a risk of being violent is dealt with in chapter 23. There is insufficient space for comprehensive coverage of the evidence on the range of new (second generation antipsychotic/SGA) and older (first generation antipsychotic/FGA) medications, singly and in combination, for treating schizophrenia or similar psychoses *per se*, but, as medication has long been recognized as such a fundamental component of the treatment of schizophrenia and similar psychoses, at least since the study of May (1968), it may be useful here to refer to one or two of the more recent reviews of this. First, it is useful to have a working knowledge of the range of antipsychotic medications available, and here again, to avoid repetition, we refer the reader to chapter 23 for a brief description of the subgroups within these main classes and of the main individual drugs.

Kane et al. (2003) conducted a consensus survey of expert opinion on medication for psychosis, which covered not only medication preferences but also aspects of prescribing practice. There was a high return rate (over 90%) on a very detailed questionnaire derived from literature review, which brought consensus on nearly 90% of the options offered for rating. Atypical antipsychotics were preferred. Three to six weeks on a particular drug was considered an adequate trial, but most would continue for four to ten weeks if there was at least a partial response. When switching between oral antipsychotics, cross-titration was considered to be the best strategy, while for a switch to depot medication, stress was placed on maintaining oral antipsychotic medication until therapeutic levels of the depot were attained. Emphasis was placed on the importance of monitoring physical health, particularly metabolic status and sexual health. Antipsychotic medications tend to impair sexual function, most noticeably among men, and may be a reason for discontinuing such medication, with or without the knowledge of the doctor (Baldwin and Mayers, 2003).

Notwithstanding the apparent confidence expressed by clinicians in the Kane study, evidence for an advantage of any particular antipsychotic medication in any particular circumstance is actually quite slight. Such misplaced confidence may reflect over-reliance on open studies which, Leucht and colleagues (2009) suggest, systematically favour second generation drugs. Lepping and colleagues (2011) showed, in a systematic review of 300 data sets, that findings of change in drug trials are generally measured in terms of increments on scales which are of limited clinical relevance. They are at pains to point out that this tends to be about differences between drugs, and that they are not arguing that, overall, drugs have negligible effects in clinical practice, but still they have one more message of caution about the nature of the evidence on which we must base our practice. In England, the NICE guidance reflects this (2009, and under regular review). After a general preamble about the context of care, rather than a formulaic approach, it recommends for people in a first episode of illness that 'the choice of drug should be made by the service user and healthcare professional together'. For non-responders, it recommends reviewing diagnosis, checking adherence to treatment at an adequate dose for an adequate period, interference by other drugs – including alcohol or illicit drugs, and whether adjunctive psychological treatments have a role and, where so, have been tried. The advice for a trial of at least two antipsychotic medications from two different classes before progressing to clozapine has been modified only slightly since Kane et al. (1988) defined medication refractoriness. NICE guidance suggests at least one of these medications should be from second generation/atypical group.

So, what evidence is there from trials? Davis et al. (2003) completed a systematic review with meta-analysis of clinical trials of antipsychotic mediation, covering 'grey' material as well as peer-reviewed publications during 1953–2002. They located 124 RCTs comparing the efficacy of conventional and atypical antipsychotics and 18 comparing antipsychotics within the atypical group. The effect sizes of clozapine, amisulpiride, risperidone, and olanzepine were significantly greater than those of conventional antipsychotics, but the other six atypicals investigated had no such advantage. In a series of reviews, Leucht and colleagues reflect that SGAs do not constitute a homogeneous class of drugs, and so, perhaps, a simple answer should not be expected. In 2003, they varied the question to cover relapse prevention and the systematic review to include RCTs comparing atypicals with placebo as well as with conventional antipsychotics, but covered a slightly shorter time period (1966–2002). They found 11 studies, including over 2,000 patients, comparing one or more drugs from the atypical and conventional groups. Rates of relapse and overall treatment failure were significantly lower among patients taking atypical antipsychotics, but the authors were not impressed with the effect size and were concerned about aspects of methodology in some studies. In 2008, Leucht et al. published a review and meta-analysis of 78 studies of comparisons of the second generation antipsychotic medications for schizophrenia, concluding that, although there was some evidence for an advantage for one or two over others, almost exclusively in relation to positive symptoms, for the individual patient, any small research based advantage for a particular medication must be weighed against large differences in side-effects and cost. By 2009, their review was of 150 double-blind, but mostly short-term studies with no fewer than 21,533 people. Just four of the SGAs had small to medium effect size advantage in terms of efficacy over FGAs, but the side-effect profile was not necessarily advantageous.

Delusional disorder is rarely considered separately from schizophrenia in medication trials, mainly because it is so much less common, perhaps affecting just 0.3% of the population. Smith and Buckley (2006) have reviewed the sparse evidence for effectiveness of medications used specifically in this situation.

Krakowski et al. (2006) explicitly found no advantage in psychotic symptom reduction for two second generation antipsychotics – clozapine and olanzapine – over haloperidol (an FGA) after completing a double-blind RCT with 110 patients, about 80% of whom were men who had schizophrenia or schizo-affective disorder. The Clinical Antipsychotic Trials of Intervention Effectiveness (CATIE) trial similarly failed to find much difference between the two broad groups of antipsychotics (Leibermann et al., 2005), but this study is controversial on the main grounds that it has insufficient power (Kraemer et al., 2009). A useful extended account of the main findings from the trial is to be found in a series of articles in *Psychiatric Services*, May 2008. Jones et al. (2006), in England, focused on 227 people with schizophrenia or similar psychosis who were already on medication, but considered to need a change because of response failure or side effects. The new prescription was randomized between conventional or atypical antipsychotic groups, but the treating clinician could choose within group. Blind assessments of outcome were made at intervals for just over 1 year. There was little difference in outcome between the two groups in symptomatic stability or change, or in quality of life. No clear preference for either drug group emerged from participant reports, and costs were similar. In 2001–2002, a group of us attempted to extend this trial into one of the high security hospitals in England. Ethical approval was obtained, but in spite of some extensive liaison work, no consultant psychiatrist referred a single patient for the trial, which was formally abandoned in 2004.

Most of the studies which have been included in systematic reviews and meta-analyses are of short-term treatment with antipsychotic medication. Tiihonen et al. (2006) reported a substantial Finnish national naturalistic study of longer-term outcome in relation to 10 antipsychotic medications commonly prescribed, from first and second generation groups. For an average of 3.6 years, they followed 2,230 people who had been consecutively hospitalized for schizophrenia or schizo-affective disorder at some time between January 1995 and December 2001. Perphenazine depot, olanzapine and clozapine were the three medications associated with lowest rehospitalization rates, while patient mortality was substantially raised among those who were not taking any antipsychotic medication.

Apart from medication type, questions have been raised about dose, frequency of medications, their combination and whether depot or oral forms are to be preferred.

359

1. *Dose*. In the UK, it is recommended that doses of antipsychotic medication should not exceed the ranges given in the British National Formulary (BNF), available online (http://BNF.org). This recommendation includes allowing for the possibility of additive effects of prescribing more than one antipsychotic and 'as necessary' medications. From time to time, there has been a vogue for high dose prescribing, particularly where violence may be an issue. The Royal College of Psychiatrists (2006), which keeps the situation under review, notes in its consensus statement that there is *no* evidence of any advantage for high dose medication, but some evidence of high risk, for example of cardiac arrhythmias leading to sudden death. In rare, individual cases, where there is no response to conventional doses of a range of medications, then the consensus statement acknowledges that it may be acceptable for a strictly observed trial of high dose medication on an individual case basis. The principle behind the clinically based observations of lack of effectiveness are that, essentially, relevant neuron receptor sites become saturated, and so continuing to raise levels of drugs with an effect on such sites would be pointless. At the other extreme, could low dose medication suffice once symptoms are under control and the issue is mainly one of preventing relapse? The answer, according to a meta-analysis of 13 studies with 1,395 participants between them, is that it depends on how low. 'Very low doses will not suffice, but there appears to be no disadvantage to low dose', although the authors argue that there are insufficient data for firm conclusions (Uchida et al., 2011).

2. *Frequency of administration of medication*. Could there be advantage in giving doses of medication more frequently, or, conversely with 'medication holidays'? Remington and Kapur (2010) discuss the evidence, finding a suggestion of advantage among stabilized patients of, say, alternate day prescription of oral antipsychotics. They recommend more research in this field.

3. *Combining antipsychotics*. Polypharmacy is common, with perhaps 30–40% of patients on more than one antipsychotic medication (Goff and Dixon, 2011). A systematic review and meta-analysis of 18 RCTs, with 1,229 participants, indicated an advantage for polypharmacy, both in terms of effectiveness and maintenance of treatment (Correll et al., 2009). This seems counterintuitive, and against all advice that, in general, treatment with a single drug is to be preferred. A more recent study (Essock et al., 2011) has, however, provided limited further endorsement for this. Treatment compliance and consistency was better maintained in the polypharmacy group, and the only disadvantage seemed to be a slightly greater weight gain in the latter, perhaps best accounted for by the specific drugs involved rather than the combination.

4. *Depot or oral maintenance treatment?* Here too, perhaps unexpectedly, it seems that there are no certainties. Haddad et al. (2009) built on a review of five Cochrane reviews by Adams et al. (2001), noted each of the Cochrane updatings and found one subsequent RCT, then went on to consider observational studies too. No newer data altered the conclusion from meta-analysis of RCT findings that there is no significant difference in efficacy or in relapse rates between oral and depot administration of FGA medications. The four prospective observational studies identified offered, between them, mixed results. Two found lower discontinuation rates for the depot groups while two found that outcome was no different or better with oral medication. The 11 mirror-image studies, however, in which each patient is observed for an equivalent period before and after a change in medication régime, suggested an advantage for long-acting medication in terms of number of hospital admissions and of inpatient days. In two retrospective observational studies identified, one showed an advantage in terms of lower readmission rate for long-acting medication and one did not, however the study which measured adverse effects found that patients receiving depot medications were more likely to need anticholinergic drugs. This last finding may constitute an important caution when trying to ensure that patients continue to receive an uninterrupted supply of medication. Ho et al. (2011) repeated neuroimaging of the brains of 211 patients over 7–14 years, such that the average number of scans available over time was three (range 2–5). They compared the four clinical measures of illness severity, length, quantity of psychotropic medication and alcohol or illicit drug use with brain volume on each occasion. In each case controlling for the other three variables, they found that alcohol and/or illicit drug use were not associated with volumetric changes, severity of illness had a small association with them, but length of illness and quantity of medication consumed had a relatively large and significant association with loss of both grey and white matter. Data are too few to make much comment on long-acting SGAs (Fleischhacker, 2009); risperidone has been available in this form for about 8 years, and is at least as safe as its oral counterpart. Use of olanzepine is less well studied, but risk of profound sedation (7/1,000 injections) means that the depot variant should only be given if the patient can be observed for at least 3 hours afterwards. Results of long-term trials of paliperidone palmitate are awaited.

Medication, some conclusions

There is little evidence for clinicians' conventional views on choosing medication which will suit most people in terms of symptom relief and maintenance of psychological improvements without major adverse effects. In some ways this is unsurprising, because of the nature of the research studies, RCTs in particular, which are designed with the knowledge that incremental *group* differences between treatments are likely to be quite small. In any case, as we note elsewhere, group data can only ever provide a basic guide in respect to an individual case. The fairly wide range of medications available, and styles of delivering them, coupled with the lack of clear cut group advantages means that the clinician really does have to be well informed about the nuances of both patient and treatment. In the everyday practice of psychiatry, the availability of adequate time per patient, duration of relationship with the patient, and the means to actual shared decision-making may be difficult to achieve, but a 'need to medicate' must not obscure the process of constructing the necessary working alliance between patient and physician. It is also important to consider that some patients will want to minimize medication, if not avoid it altogether, and that treatment should not hinge on medications alone, or even be the main intervention. Only if these contingencies are taken into account will the patient be sufficiently well informed and in a position to make a real choice of medication in partnership with the clinician whenever it is possible to do so. Real choice may well prove to be the best predictor of treatment adherence and a long term recovery process.

Psychological Treatments

Even after varying medication type and doses, ensuring compliance, and, where possible, having confirmation of blood levels of active components of the drug concerned, for some people the illness and violence will remain refractory. Since the 1990s, there has been increasing optimism that more psychological approaches to treatment may help, and cognitive behaviour therapy (CBT) has been particularly favoured for people with schizophrenia or similar psychosis (see also chapter 23). The literature on such psychological approaches is now quite substantial, and includes a number of RCTs as well as observational studies, which, as specific to schizophrenia, we will review briefly below. There are two limitations to the literature which are sufficiently general and sufficiently important for work with people who have both psychosis and a propensity for violence that we will introduce them here. The first is that trials of such treatment, unlike drug trials, have rarely if ever considered the possibility of adverse reactions to the treatment. Any treatment of any power may be expected to carry risks of unwanted as well as desired effects, so this is a serious omission. The second is an extension of the problem of medication trials, that evaluation tends to be done with people who have problems in the middle range – serious enough for there to be some prospect of change, but not so serious that they would be unable to comply or likely to break down in some sort of crisis during the research – and participants in such studies must consent, so

they tend to be the most pro-socially minded. For these various reasons not only is it unlikely that people with psychosis who also have difficulties with antisocial behaviours would be recruited to trials of psychological therapies, but a number of studies explicitly exclude them. A notable exception to the latter rule is the study by Haddock et al. (2009), which explicitly recruited people with psychosis who had violent histories (see also below).

Cognitive behavioural therapy (CBT) for schizophrenia

Jones et al. (2004) conducted a systematic review of randomized controlled trials of CBT for schizophrenia and other functional psychoses, providing they were not primary affective disorders. Their definition of treatment for these purposes was: a procedure that would enable the recipient to establish links between thoughts, feelings and actions, monitor behaviour, and develop alternative ways of coping, the core goal being 'correction of misperceptions, irrational beliefs and reasoning biases'. They identified 30 articles on 19 randomized controlled trials, which together included 2,154 people as participants, more or less equally divided between treatment and control groups. The collective evidence from these trials was of only modest impact, with the principal advantages in improving global mental state ratings in the medium term and possibly reducing the length of inpatient stay. None of the studies made any reference to violence during the course of the treatment programme, even though the CBT was generally lengthy – up to 2 years in duration. This is surprising, given the number of people and length of time involved and a general assumption based on the epidemiological studies described earlier that a conservative estimate would be of about 10% of the patients being violent. As noted, some studies are explicit about excluding people who had been violent or who were detained in hospital, but it seems unlikely that this alone could account for a wholly violence-free passage for over 2000 people. The importance of thinking about the possibility of violence in such circumstances arises from findings discussed in more detail above, especially that a key factor associated with violent action in the context of delusions was response to hypothetical challenge. People who accommodated the challenge and/or strengthened their belief were more likely to have acted violently in the 28 days under study than those who ignored it (Buchanan et al., 1993). Hypothetical challenge has much in common with methods of encouraging people to review their symptoms within the framework of CBT. Among some smaller, uncontrolled studies of treatment in which delusions appear to have been approached in this way, there are hints at further grounds for concern (e.g. Garety et al., 1994), although there are also anecdotal reports of CBT being applied successfully and safely among people with schizophrenia who are also serious offenders (e.g. Benn, 2002). Notwithstanding its still useful content, the Jones et al. (2004) review has now been withdrawn from the Cochrane website, pending update.

Zimmerman et al. (2005) conducted a systematic review of CBT for symptom change in schizophrenia, schizoaffective and delusional psychoses. They identified 15 trials (not all RCTs) in which, collectively, 515 people had had CBT and 486 were in comparison groups. Meta-analysis of 14 trials revealed an advantage for CBT in reducing symptoms, with a higher effect size in acute cases (0.57) compared with chronic cases (0.27). Improvement scores were generally, however, given in terms of overall ratings for positive psychotic symptoms, so it was not possible to tell which symptoms were most affected. Gaudiano's (2006) systematic review and meta-analysis identified only 12 studies, and questioned the *clinical* importance of statistically significant findings. The proportion of patients showing significant and reliable scale score change in at least one psychotic symptom was significantly higher in the CBT groups than in those receiving routine or alternative treatments, but clinically important changes did not distinguish the groups.

Wykes et al. (2008) tried to resolve any discrepancies between individual and review study findings with a particularly rigorous system of six separate meta-analyses, allowing for treatment and research method differences, with data extracted from 33 of 34 studies identified. They found an overall advantage for CBT on the researcher defined target problem, on positive symptoms, on negative symptoms, on 'functioning' and on mood but not on hopelessness, however when only blinded studies were considered the effect was small (0.243, 95% CI 0.017–0.428). With respect to positive symptoms of psychosis specifically they were able to enter 24 studies, with 1,450 participants between them, with a homogeneous treatment approach – CBT delivered individually. There was a mean effect size of nearly 0.4 (95% CI 0.243–0.556). As other reviews, however, they did not distinguish between positive symptoms in describing the impact, nor did they mention violence. Efforts to modify delusions specifically continue. Ross et al. (2011) offer the prospect of a way forward. They compared 34 people with delusions and 24 comparison participants, confirming that those with delusions were more inclined to 'jump to conclusions', here measured by the amount of information they requested before making a decision. A single session of training about neutral situations and the idea that it would be preferable not to reach decisions too quickly was found to have a short-term beneficial effect on such behaviour. This did not translate into any significant change in flexibility of thinking or less conviction in the delusion, but it could be argued that an absence of this further effect is hardly surprising after one session only. No behavioural correlates of those changes identified were reported.

Given the rate of comorbidities with psychosis when offending is also a problem, in addition to cognitive behaviourally based treatments more specifically for schizophrenia and similar psychoses, such approaches could be useful adjuncts in the treatment of comorbidities, particularly problems with substance misuse. A 2010 Cochrane review found 25 randomized controlled trials of various interventions, which had included nearly 2500 people, some of them offender patients. Drop out rates were high. No one psychological intervention, singly or in integrated combination (e.g. motivational interviewing with CBT within an overall care package) appeared to have a particular advantage in reducing substance use or improving mental state (Cleary et al., 2008; see also chapters 8, 23). In addition, there have been calls for application of cognitive behaviour therapy-based approaches specifically for offending for people with schizophrenia (e.g. Hodgins and Müller-Isberner, 2004). While we understand that trials of such interventions may have started, to date, we believe there are none reported in print. A comparison has been completed, however, between CBT and social activity therapy (SAT), the former aimed at reducing both psychotic symptoms with their accompanying distress and anger and the latter to help patients identify things they enjoy doing, and doing them (Haddock et al., 2009). Sixty-eight of 108 eligible patients, all with psychosis and a history of violence, completed at least 10 and up to 25 sessions of the therapies, and the follow-up period. Results suggested an advantage for the CBT but were quite complex. Delusions but not hallucinations improved during CBT but the improvement was not sustained, while anger was unaffected according to any measure. Groups were similar at the outset in terms of previously recorded aggressive incidents; CBT had an advantage during but not after treatment in terms of numbers of recorded new aggressive incidents, with verbal aggression principally accounting for this pattern; physical violence analysed separately did not differentiate the groups during treatment, but CBT had an advantage during follow-up both for numbers of people violent and number of incidents.

Other psychosocial treatments

This is not the place for an exhaustive examination of all possible psychosocial treatments relevant for people with schizophrenia. Some, such as social skills training, we would regard in some form as simply part of the overall context of (re)habilitation, whether or not the individual has offending as part of his/her cluster of problems. Cognitive remediation therapy for schizophrenia is a behavioural training based intervention that aims to improve cognitive processes (attention, memory, executive function, social cognition or metacognition) with the goals of durability and generalization. This reflects observations that impairments in cognition may affect longer term outcome, including social functions and patients' concerns about the impact such deficits may have on their everyday lives. Given the findings that men who have psychosis and are also violent may have more structural and functional brain difficulties than those who have psychosis and no problems with violence, and, in turn, than healthy controls (see chapter 12), one might expect particular benefit from such treatment for people with psychosis who become offenders. It hardly needs saying, but there have been no studies with psychotic offender groups. A number of systematic reviews have suggested a general advantage for social function with cognitive remediation, but this finding was not consistent with two major dissenters (Dixon et al., 2009; NICE, 2009). This may arise partially from the different ways in which the training is delivered and partly from research methodology. Wykes et al. (2011) completed a systematic review and meta-analysis of all evaluations with a specified allocation procedure in the context of all participants receiving 'standard care', then allowing for sampling and other potential methodological biases. They identified 40 studies with, collectively, 2,014 participants. They found that cognitive remediation had a small to medium effect on both cognition and function, which was durable, with best effects obtained when the interventions were delivered at a time when the patients were clinically reasonably well and stable, and as part of a rehabilitation package rather than in isolation. There was no reference at all to violence or offending.

Family interventions may also be potentially useful. As described above, for anyone with schizophrenia, social climate within the family may be affected by and affect the illness. Much family work has been around these issues, and evaluated in these terms. Pilling et al. (2002) and Pitschel-Walz et al. (2001) provide evidence from systematic review and meta-analysis that longer interventions – 6 months or more – are most likely to be helpful in reducing the risk of patient relapse and/or rehospitalization, while Cuijpers (1999) showed a reduction in family burden as a result of such work with families. Subsequent controlled studies (e.g. Mueser et al., 2001), have shown that psycho-educational programmes for families improve family relationships to the extent that not only do the patients enjoy a better outcome, but also the relatives rate their burden as less. Garety et al. (2008), however, found no effect of family intervention on symptoms or distress reduction in the patients, or on their duration of hospital stays or relapse rate. A Cochrane review of RCTs identified a total of 53 of family interventions; there were data from 2,981 people included in analysis of frequency of relapse, which was lower in the family intervention groups, and from 481 people in analysis of hospital (re)admission, which was also lower, and 696 people in analysis of medication compliance, which was better (Pharoah et al., 2010). We await studies, however, which are specific for families in which there has been violence on the part of the person with schizophrenia, within or outside the family.

Psychosocial resources provided in settings run by people with psychosis themselves are increasingly available, many with research and evaluation components; such peer contributions vary considerably, although are mostly focussed on individual work (e.g. Salzer et al., 2010). Peer provided care emphasizes shared experience, expertise in coping, and mutuality between the participants. It is beyond the scope of this chapter to review the wide variety of models of service user run interventions, but they will no doubt continue to spread, and deserve careful attention by researchers. These programmes tend to be less likely than professionally directed offerings to exclude people with histories of violence, yet they grapple with similar issues of staff, peer, and setting safety.

Summary on psychosocial treatments

There are growing numbers of controlled studies of various psychological treatments for schizophrenia and similar psychoses, generally on the principle that the psychological treatments will be additional to medication, but applying to people with acute as well as chronic illnesses. There have been several systematic reviews of studies evaluating cognitive behaviour therapy for schizophrenia, most concluding with an endorsement for it, although the effect size is not impressive. Where there is an effect, it often appears to be more general in terms of reducing, say, days spent in hospital rather than altering specific symptoms of the disorder and, where there is evidence for symptom reduction, it is often in the broad terms of 'positive symptoms'. An important issue is that studies vary both in the detail of the treatment given and of the methods of evaluation. Over time, systematic reviewers have attempted to take more and more of these issues into account. This is increasingly true for other psychosocial treatments too. Insofar as there is remaining doubt about the strength and consistency of the evidence for the value of such interventions it is more about which particular approach is more advantageous, delivered individually or in groups, or for how long, and in comparison with which other treatment than whether adding some form of psychosocial treatment to medication is beneficial. A caveat is that so little research, and only one controlled trial, has been completed specifically with people who have psychosis and are violent. The same sort of principle as put forward for medication would seem to be the best way forward – that choice of psychosocial intervention should, as far as possible, be taken in conjunction with the patient. Particularly for offender-patients, one might add that, as far as possible, such decisions should include relatives and others in the close social circle of the individual.

Models for a Treatment Framework

Complex problems call for complex solutions, and there is as much need for research that can define and evaluate the therapeutic framework for delivering specific treatments as for research into the individual treatments. Few such models are or will be unique to people with psychosis who offend; they are commonly designed for people with a range of mental disorders, and often a multiplicity of them. Nevertheless, as the individuals who have driven service change and the people who are most commonly treated within forensic mental health settings in many countries are people with schizophrenia or similar psychoses, so the frameworks for treatment delivery are often designed with this group principally in mind.

Tyrer and Simmonds (2003), in a systematic literature review, identified three UK trials of different models of care in general psychiatric services – early community intervention versus hospitalization, community-focused care versus standard care, and intensive versus standard case management – for people with severe mental illness or psychosis and comorbid personality disorder. Group allocation did not permit adequate analysis of the latter group, but the other two studies showed that, while outcome for the groups was similar in respect of hospital admissions, with an advantage for the community groups, both general social and offending outcomes were worse for the comorbid groups in the community treatment conditions. Assertive community treatment (ACT) originated in the USA, particularly for people who had had repeated hospitalizations and/or recent homelessness, and there is evidence that it is effective in stabilizing people with such problems to the extent of reducing recurrence of homelessness or hospitalization (e.g. Coldwell and Bender, 2007; Nelson et al., 2007). Replication of this approach, with high staff:patient ratio, high frequency of patient contact, the multidisciplinary team being available around the clock, seeing people in the community, working with their own social networks where they have them and actively seeking patients in the community in the event of their failure to contact staff as agreed, has not shown the same advantages in the UK (Fiander et al., 2003). The latter group argued that the model fidelity was good. Again, as with so many studies in this field, interpretation of the absence of significant differences from other approaches may better reflect that the treatment models are as good as each other rather than a failure of the newer approach under trial. Given that the people needing treatment services do not constitute a homogeneous group, availability of more than one treatment approach with an equivalent prospect of helping can only be an advantage. As the approach was applied to patient groups ever more similar to offender patients with psychosis, however, even in the USA, the results become more equivocal. With people who have substance misuse difficulties as well as psychosis, for example, Essock et al. (2006) found no advantage in terms of reducing misuse even for enhanced assertive community treatment, when some of the intensive input was by specialist addictions clinicians. Evaluation of assertive community treatment modified for offender patients similarly showed no advantage in terms of days in jail or hospital or in substance misuse (Chandler and Spicer, 2006; Lamberti et al., 2004).

Economou et al. (2005) described outcomes after an 'optimal treatment model', referring to integrated pharmacological and psychosocial treatments to cover the full range of need. In their small study of 50 people, just over a third had shown some form of aggressive behaviour at the outset, although actual physical violence was rare and no one had used a weapon. No serious violence emerged over 4 years, and aggression generally was reduced. El-Guebaly's (2004) overview of integrated treatment for those with a mix of psychosis and substance misuse problems took account of the fact that outcome studies had come from a range of different countries, and argued that integration must reflect, as necessary, issues specific to local culture and service provision. In the USA, the impact of 'managed care' was evaluated, and found to offer no improvement over more *ad hoc* arrangements (Dickey et al., 2003). Subsequently, a range of new measures has been introduced and evaluated, mainly with the aim of improving treatment compliance, for example the Mental Health (MH) Courts (Christy et al., 2005; Cosden et al., 2005). Steadman et al. (2011) compared 447 people who had been through the MH Courts with 600 conventionally treated people drawn from four counties – two in California, one in Minnesota and one in Indiana. They were equivalent on all measures on entry to the study, but the MH Court groups had fewer arrests or incarceration days in the following 18 months.

'Outpatient commitment', also known as 'mandated community treatment', similar to a community treatment order in the UK, has also received considerable attention in the USA (Erikson, 2005). Hiday (2003) provided a useful overview, and there have been a number of important subsequent studies. A substantial study of 8,752 new orders and 5,684 renewals were made in New York State under 'Kendra's law' (see also chapters 24 and 25) where the terminology is of 'assisted outpatient treatment' (AOT) (Swartz et al., 2009). The orders are for a group of high risk people who have either been in hospital or jail at least twice in the preceding 36 months and/or made acts and/or threats of harm to self or others. Being on an order made no difference to how they viewed mental health services, but advantages with respect to treatment engagement, use of medication, maintenance in the community and a reduction in arrest rates were not only observed during the orders but also sustained if the orders had been for more than 6 months.

Mandated community treatment of any kind, and perhaps innovative supplementary incentives to treatment compliance in particular, require ethical debate as well as evidence for effectiveness. Geller et al. (2006), for example, discussed the risk that, in the USA, mandated or 'assisted' outpatient treatment is simply 'deinstitutionalized coercion', but observe important differences between states, with some having competency base legislation in this respect (e.g. Massachusetts) while others have dangerousness focused statutes. Winick (2003) analysed the issues from a jurisprudential position (see also chapters 2, 3 and 5). Benefits for people with major mental disorder, including disability income and housing, are made dependent on their attendance for treatment. Swanson and colleagues (2006b) have shown, among over 1,000 people, that those with mental disorder and some evidence of violence perpetration, but also those with demographic characteristics that may just mark them out as unfortunate rather than necessarily at risk for violence, are disproportionately likely to be subject to such 'leverage'. Robbins et al. (2006) interviewed 200 outpatients, however, and found that the participants who had housing used as leverage were much *more* likely than those who had not to believe that housing leverage is effective in helping people to stay well.

A repeated concern expressed is that, even if there are risks of harm to and by people with major mental disorder, the prospect of coercion into treatment may be a deterrent against seeking help, and thus, indirectly, a danger in itself. Swartz et al. (2003) evaluated this proposition among 85 members of staff and 104 patients in one state in the USA. Among the staff, only 80% thought that coercive measures were more likely to make their patients with schizophrenia stay in treatment. Among the patients, there was considerable lifetime experience of some form of coercion (63%), and over 30% reported that fear of coerced treatment was a barrier to their seeking help. The barrier principally related, however, to compulsory inpatient treatment; coercion as an outpatient was not such a barrier, whereas threats, or what Swartz and colleagues more tactfully refer to as 'recent reminders or warnings' of coerced treatment were as bad as the experience of coerced treatment itself. Link et al. (2008) found somewhat differently among their study of people subject to Kendra's Law in New York. In particular, they reported:

self-reported coercion increases felt stigma (perceived devaluation–discrimination), erodes quality of life and through stigma leads to lower self-esteem.

Phelan et al. (2010) reported a modest improvement for people who were in outpatient commitment, but concluded that neither the absence of adverse effects nor the presence of such modest improvements supports the expansion of coerced outpatient treatment. Kisely et al.'s (2011) Cochrane Review of outpatient commitment found only two trials that met criteria, and concluded that the evidence did not establish the efficacy of coerced outpatient treatment. They noted:

in terms of numbers needed to treat, it would take 85 outpatient commitment orders to prevent one readmission, 27 to prevent one episode of homelessness and 238 to prevent one arrest.

Community treatment orders of various types continue to proliferate in US and EU countries, yet there are few data on which to judge their effectiveness in preventing or reducing violence associated with psychosis.

Criminal justice system models of management

Reports between 2002 and 2006 on jail diversion programmes and their effectiveness have come almost exclusively from the USA (Broner et al., 2004; Draine et al., 2005a; Steadman and Naples, 2005). The latter group studied over 1,600 participants in a number of states, focusing particularly on people with psychosis and co-occurring substance misuse disorders. Costs of the programmes were similar, but diversion reduced time spent in jail without compromising public safety. Draine et al. (2005a) compared a diversion programme with treatment in jail for a similar, but smaller and single, state (Pennsylvania) group. They highlighted likely differences in people referred to the services. Active psychotic symptoms increased the likelihood of diversion, while those treated within the in-jail services were more likely to have had a track record of being managed in some part of the criminal justice system. The take-up of services in a larger (baseline sample 2000), multi-site US study suggested a similar bias (Broner et al., 2004). Such issues will need consideration in all such studies. Police response is another issue that has been taken up, at the interface between the criminal justice system and people with major mental health problems (Sellars et al., 2005).

Community re-entry models have been considered from the perspective of people leaving jail (Draine et al., 2005b). Frustrated by the crude outcome measures in most studies of people with psychosis and other major mental disorders, relying almost wholly on mortality and re-offending, we conducted a grounded theory study to establish a testable theoretical model of the process of discharge from high security hospitals (Jamieson et al., 2006). A substantive theory emerged from open coding and constant comparative analysis of interviews with a range of professional people, inclusive of a lawyer and Home Office officials as well as a range of clinicians. The theory was of a continuum between pathological dependence and healthy independence, with the role of the various professionals being facilitation along the pathway towards healthy independence, and factors such as re-offending entering the model as terminators of independence. This could provide the basis for improvement in outcome measures of future studies of secure hospital care and treatment, and perhaps related treatment packages.

Summary of impact of models for treatment and management

While the specific treatment literature tends to focus on disease, and pay little regard to accompanying behaviour disorders, including violence, the study of complex treatment models, or frameworks within which specific treatments may be delivered, leans in the opposite direction. Work commonly includes people with psychosis but is not specific to them. The areas of initiative are too wide-ranging for simple conclusions, but treatment models that include an element of coercion or explicit incentive do appear to carry advantages in reducing violence or other antisocial behaviours not only by the person suffering from psychosis but also, as noted earlier, towards him or her.

CONCLUSIONS

Detail about the frequency with which homicide and other violence is associated with schizophrenia has been consolidated and developed, together with a good deal of new insight into how the symptoms of illness and/or comorbid conditions may variously explain, at least in part, how the violence comes about in this context. Specific treatments have occasionally been evaluated within a group of people who have psychosis and problems with violence, but, more often, inferences still have to be made from studies in which violence is either not mentioned or from which those people with psychosis who have been violent have been explicitly excluded. Complex treatment models, or frameworks for treatment, continue to emerge and be evaluated, here often including people with psychosis but not exclusive to them. Our tasks are to take our concepts further, make our measures better, include people who have been violent in more research samples, and to learn how to ask more pertinent, potentially useful questions. With both frameworks for treatment and specific treatments, even in group analysis it is hard to draw definitive conclusions about what works best. A more positive interpretation is that there is a good deal that works better than doing nothing, and clinical skills lie in working with individual offender-patients to identify the best combination of treatment framework, specific medication and psychosocial interventions that will be likely to work in that case, and then monitor each person's progress with a good researcher's rigor.

15

Pathologies of passion and related antisocial behaviours

Edited by
Pamela J Taylor

Written by
Paul Mullen

Pamela J Taylor

The pathologies of the passions of love, jealousy and entitlement may all form parts of major mental illness. When so, they are usually without any obvious external provocation, are accompanied by other features of that disorder, and follow a course closely linked to that of the underlying disorder. Sometimes, however, they are the sole feature of a person's disorder, generally emerge after some real provocation, although not necessarily one that would appear important to a casual observer, and in the context of some susceptibility in personality trait, a previous sensitizing experience, low mood or some combination of these; the course is dependent in part on the actual situation and the reactions of others. People with these pathologies of passion have in common associated convictions that one or more other people are abrogating their rights, which must be asserted. The preoccupations and pathologies often overlap; it is a short step for some from love to jealousy and sense of entitlement, although perhaps jealousy and certainly entitlement may arise in relation to other desires. These states are of particular importance to forensic psychiatry, because people who suffer with them tend at best to frighten others and at worst to harm them, and are almost invariably intrusive. Furthermore, these pathologies not uncommonly involve clinicians as the object of the passion, whether as 'love' object or obstacle to love and/or justice.

EROTOMANIAS AND MORBID INFATUATIONS

The emergence of stalking as a category of problem behaviour gave erotomania renewed prominence. Previously regarded as a rare syndrome, anti-stalking laws brought to light many previously unrecognized cases (Mullen et al., 2008).

Esquirol (1965, originally 1845) coined the term erotomania for the irrational sentimental attachment to someone who in reality has little or no relationship to the sufferer. In his view, the disorder represented 'an exaggeration to the extreme limit of the amorous passions' (p.339). Over generations, the concept changed. De Clerambault (1942) probably had the greatest influence on current formulations of this disorder. He shifted the emphasis to an exclusive focus on delusions that the object of the patient's disordered affections loves him/her and initiated the supposed relationship. De Clerambault's viewpoint is parroted in the international (ICD) and US (DSM) disease classificatory systems. This is a pity, as it conforms poorly with clinical reality, which is served better by the wider formulations which preceded his theorizing (Krafft-Ebing and Chaddock 1904, originally 1879; Kraepelin 1921, originally 1913).

Erotomanics, like all lovers, endow the loved one with those qualities that make them an object of delight. For the erotomanic, reality plays little part in constraining the process of endowing, so an idealized other can be constructed (Mullen, 2008a). The judgments of the erotomanic, again unconstrained by reality, create the certainty of mutuality, or mutuality to come, or even of the lover as infatuated pursuer. The erotomanic is secure in his/her constructed attachment so holding the delights of being in love uncontaminated by the uncertainties evoked by real relationships. The desires of the erotomanic are often for an ethereal love, abstracted from the challenges of the carnal, but not always so. Fantasy plays the major role in the world of erotomania. Exploration of the fantasies is important, as occasionally they can reveal unexpected and unpleasant possibilities.

Erotomania can be characterized as involving:

- *either* a conviction of being loved despite the supposed lover having done nothing to encourage or sustain that belief but, on the contrary, having either made clear their lack of interest or remained unaware of the claimed relationship;

- *or* an intense infatuation without necessarily any marked accompanying conviction that the affection is currently reciprocated;

- a propensity to reinterpret the words and actions of the object of their attentions to maintain the belief in their supposed romance;
- preoccupation with the supposed love which comes to form a central part of the subject's existence.

These three essential criteria are often accompanied by:

- a conviction that the claimed relationship will eventually be crowned by a permanent and loving union;
- repeated attempts to approach or communicate with the supposed lover.

Periods of intense infatuation may occur in normal individuals, particularly in adolescence, but fade when it is clear that no favourable response is to be expected from the beloved. The teenage 'crush' lacks the conviction of eventual fulfilment, even though fantasies of such fulfilment are common, and acts as a pleasurable embellishment of life rather than as a preoccupying and disruptive element. Teenage crushes are often social experiences which are shared with likeminded peers and pursued through groups and clubs. This is in stark contrast to the isolating nature of pathological infatuations (Mullen, 2008a).

Erotomanic preoccupations are probably more commonly secondary to a range of disorders, most frequently in the schizophrenia spectrum; monodelusional states may account for about a quarter of cases (Rudden et al., 1990) but this, like so many of the earlier studies, may be biased through drawing exclusively on treated patient samples. Such cases can often be accommodated under the heading of delusional disorder, or paranoid state. The problem with this is that though the preoccupation may dominate the life of the sufferer, it does not always have the phenomenological characteristics which establish the experience as delusionally based. In such 'primary' erotomanics there is usually a pre-existing vulnerability in the form of an oversensitive and self-referential individual, living a life bereft of intimacy and without close confidantes.

There is a traditional view that erotomania is more common among women, although it has always been recognized as occurring in men too (Taylor et al., 1983). Brüne (2001) confirmed a roughly 7:3 ratio, albeit only among the 246 cases published in the psychiatric literature between 1900 and 2000, with an obvious potential for bias in such a highly selected sample. His more interesting observations are about the extent to which, in this series, the different presentations between men and women reflect the sexual strategies theory of Buss and Schmitt (1993), covering differences in mating strategies between men and women in healthy populations. Most of his predictions were sustained by the data, including the older age of onset among the women and the greater likelihood that they would involve older, higher status men, retain a single love object and remain chaste. The difference between men and women in likely progression to 'forensically relevant behaviour' was

particularly striking – over half of the 76 men but under 5% of the 170 women.

For the forensic clinician, erotomania is chiefly of interest for its possible progression into pathological jealousy and/or stalking behaviours. Most accounts of stalking behaviours prior to the twentieth century concern intimacy seeking by erotomanic or infatuated pursuers rather than the more aggressive behaviours of the jealous and querulant rights seekers. The historical perspective is considered more fully below.

JEALOUSY

Jealousy deserves a privileged place in forensic mental health, firstly because of its close relationship to two of the commonest forms of serious criminal violence: domestic violence and the killing of sexual partners (Kingham and Gordon, 2004) and secondly, because of the way laws have traditionally tended to mitigate the severity of punishment accorded jealous men who have killed their partners, by appeals to justification, provocation and, most recently, diminished responsibility.

Jealousy has failed to find a place among the risk factors which comprise the myriad instruments, computer programs and lowly checklists which claim to be able to assign the probability of future violence to an individual (Mullen and Ogloff, 2009). Experience should, though, shout a warning whenever you confront a patient caught up in the passion of jealousy, particularly if he, or she, has a history of assault, or has made threats. Threats constitute another harbinger of violence usually omitted from the technology of violence prediction (but see chapter 22). Those who have killed or maimed in one relationship out of jealousy acquire a terrible propensity to repeat the performance in future relationships.

Given this potential importance of jealousy and its pathological extensions, it is perhaps surprising that it currently has a rather low profile in psychiatry in general and forensic mental health in particular. This was not always the case, for, in classical psychiatry, jealousy occupied a prominent position, perhaps never more so than when Karl Jaspers (1910) used jealousy both in his initial essay on the phenomenological method and to illustrate the division of mental pathologies into developments, reactions and processes. The decline in the profile of jealousy reflects many of the same qualities which gave it interest for classical psychiatry. Jealousy fits ill with today's attempts to fit psychopathology into the committee created boxes of the *DSM* and *ICD* systems of definition. Attempts to distribute the pathologies of jealousy across a range of today's sanctioned diagnostic categories as a symptom work only as long as jealousy which exists in, and only in, the pathological aspects of the jealousy itself, is ignored. Unfortunately for those therefore turned away by psychiatrists as 'not ill', it is exactly these types of pathological jealousy which so often manifest in propensities to violence. These include the intense jealousy which is evoked on the slightest of suspicion, the jealousy which totally preoccupies, the jealousy which generates extraordinary delusions of infidelity (calling that a delusional disorder is comforting but obviously circular), the jealousy of obsessive doubt, the jealousy of paralysing fear, and that of uncontrollable rage, and the absurd but potentially lethal jealousy sometimes found in people who are senile and/or have brain damage.

Normal Jealousy in the Modern World

Jealousy is a complex emotion generated by a perceived threat to a valued relationship (White and Mullen, 1989). The threat is usually, but not always, experienced as coming from a rival. Jealousy can and does emerge in close relationships which are not sexual (Hill and Davis, 2000). The valued relationship is, however, most frequently sexual and/or intimate and as this is where violence is most frequently evoked, such romantic jealousy will be the main focus here.

In everyday speech, jealousy and envy are occasionally conflated. Jealousy is about that which you believe you possess but fear you may lose. Envy is about that which you do not have but desire. Envy comes in two forms: one positive and one negative. Aristotle suggested that the positive is the desire is to become like, or acquire the properties, such as virtue, success or status of another, perhaps resulting in the action of emulation. The negative is destructive envy, in which the desire is to dispossess the other of the properties you believe make them superior. The critical distinction is that jealousy is about fighting the apprehended loss, and perhaps destroying the object of desire if it becomes truly unattainable, but envy is about seeking to gain what others possess and you desire.

Most adults have been in intimate relationships and most have experienced jealousy at some time and to some degree (Mullen and Martin, 1994). It is perhaps the commonplace nature of ordinary jealousy that makes it so difficult to recognize any shift towards pathology. It hardly takes the skills of a psychiatrist to recognize the madness in a firmly held belief that mutant rodents are circulating in the blood stream because of having eaten cheese contaminated by alien rays; the firmly held belief of a mildly unkempt and obese man about the infidelity of his attractive wife with one of their sleek and prosperous neighbours may hardly seem outlandish, but may nonetheless be a delusion. The jealousy of the normal population is primarily about the loved one, not the rival, and usually involves the following:

1. judgment that an intimate relationship in which you believe your partner owes you loyalty is threatened by a potential, or actual, relationship to another;

2. a state of arousal occasioned by such an intrusion which may involve fear and sadness at apprehended loss, anger at betrayal, pride at possessing a desired object, but, usually, above all, the distress of uncertainty;

3. a conflicting group of desires compounded in varying proportions of the desire to know, to deny, to expose, to repossess, the desire for revenge and, ultimately, the desire to resolve the jealousy either through reassurance that the suspicions were false, or acceptance of the infidelity with subsequent reconciliation, or separation;

4. fantasies which, even among the general population may involve vivid mental images of the partner in sexual congress with the actual or supposed rival, or of various revenge scenarios;

5. predispositions to behave in ways which serve one or more of the desire to know, to strike back, or to re-establish the lost or threatened intimacy – thus, actions follow, which may include spying, cross-questioning, checking, threatening, actual assault (almost always directed at the partner), making yourself more attractive or derogating the rival.

The problem for mental health professionals lies in deciding where the limits of normal jealousy end and the realm of the pathological begins. A simple and appealing solution such as 'jealousy which leads to violence is pathological' could leave clinics overwhelmed, given research which suggests some 15% of the population report being subjected to assault as a result of a partner's jealousy (Mullen and Martin, 1994). Jealousy motivated violence continues to be normalized as an unfortunate manifestation of love, which attracts far less condemnation than non-jealousy related aggression (Puente and Cohen, 2003). Equally, any attempt to distinguish on the basis of whether the feared infidelity is based on actual infidelity wilts before the knowledge that jealousy in both its pathological and its normal variants may either be in error or correct in its accusations (Odegard, 1968).

The behaviours commonly associated with jealousy in the general population can provide at least a signpost to pathology. In a questionnaire survey of over 350 community residents, representing a higher than 60% return rate on the questionnaires, everyone endorsed at least one jealousy item and 40% acknowledged having experienced jealousy without good cause (Mullen and Martin, 1994). Nearly 15% of men and 19% of women considered that their partner's jealousy had caused problems. When jealous, 30% of the participants admitted repeatedly cross-questioning their partner in an attempt to catch them out in a lie. Some 10% also described phoning to check the partner was where they said they were, turning up unexpectedly, and even searching their belongings for evidence. Today, checking the partner's mobile phone SMS data base and recent calls, plus careful examination of credit card records, would have to be added to the relatively common behaviours of the ordinary jealous individual. What was very uncommon, or never admitted, was opening mail, following, checking underclothes for signs of semen or other incriminating stains, or examining the partner's body for indicators of recent sexual activity. These are all behaviours frequently described in pathological jealousy.

Another area that may help at least suggest when jealousy is pathological lies in the nature of the fears evoked when infidelity is suspected. In the general population, jealousy is about a plausible rival and the commonest fear is loss of the partner, feared especially by men, followed by loss of attention and alienation of resources. Fear of loss of intimacy was more often cited by women, but loss of sexual exclusivity was not related to gender (Mullen and Martin, 1994). In pathological jealousy, fears of being shamed (made to look a fool), cheated, lied to and generally humiliated dominate, although fear of loss of the partner to another is usually also acknowledged. The egocentricity of pathological jealousy can be mimicked by the self-absorption of some personality types.

In the latter part of the twentieth century, at least in the West, it seems that adultery has become a sport indulged in by the majority of the population (Lawson, 1987). It is so common that both the statistically sophisticated and the cynical are likely to assume its existence, even in the absence of evidence. The ways in which people deal with actual sexual infidelity often determine whether relationships survive. Jealousy in such a social context is likely to be viewed as a problem with few positives, particularly as jealousy is just as likely to fix on the innocent as the guilty, and may well precipitate the unjustly suspected into the very behaviour of which they stand accused. Jealousy may still claim the virtue of being a cry of pain at disappointed hopes, but even that raises the question of the wisdom of investing hope in such a fragile quality as sexual constancy.

The History of Jealousy

The notion that emotions have histories, in the sense of having been experienced differently at different historical periods, is totally foreign to the view of emotions taken by orthodox psychology. Emotional tendencies are regarded as being part of inherited nature, perhaps modified by early attachment experiences. They are viewed as representing fixed responses to specific situational triggers, short-circuiting the slower reactions mediated by judgment. There is, however, plenty of evidence to support emotions such as anger, love and jealousy having been experienced differently with changing economic, social, and cultural realities (Singer, 1966, 1987; MacIntyre 1988; Stearns, 1989; Mullen, 1991).

Romantic jealousy is tied to the meaning of infidelity. In agrarian economies an individual's position in society is largely determined by his/her parentage. Being born to power or to servitude and your place in the social system depend primarily on who your father was, and who his father was before him. The hierarchy of such societies rests on ensuring female fidelity. Infidelity is a challenge to the social order, and jealousy serves the purposes of social stability. Jealousy may be experienced by the individual (man), usually as a challenge to the honour of his family and caste, but is also understood as a threat to the community. Agrarian societies tolerate, or even mandate, the violence of jealousy both as punishment and as a warning to others. Their laws reflect this reality (Northrop, 1960; Smith and Weisstub, 1983).

In mercantile societies, social castes and rigid hierarchies are undermined by the power of wealth and possessions. Though birth still constrains the individual's possibilities, the acquisition and loss of wealth may radically alter social relationships. In such societies, marriages for the powerful become less about ensuring blood lines and more about acquiring financial advantage. Infidelity for the wealthy represents a contractual breach, though for rich and poor it still encompasses a challenge to honour, but now embodied in personal rather than social status. Jealousy becomes individualized and, for the law, ceases to be relevant to social duty and takes on the guise of a personal provocation which can engender justified violence.

In industrial society, the further diffusion and obfuscation of the roots of power and influence almost remove infidelity from any role in determining social position. Jealousy ceases to be part of the public realm and becomes entirely a matter for the citizen's private life, in which neither society nor law have a legitimate interest. Jealousy is stripped of all social relevance and becomes a private and isolating experience whose utility becomes marginal at best. In late industrial society, jealousy has undergone a final stage of its inversion to become a piece of personal psychopathology, disruptive of the free market in goods, services and people, damaging to happiness, and destructive of good order. For the law, jealousy comes finally to rest as a potential mental disorder, perhaps mitigating behaviour, perhaps, in the event of a killing, indicating diminished criminal responsibility.

These neat divisions into social societal models, such as agrarian, mercantile, capitalist, or post-industrial, are idealized rather than entirely distinguishable historical epochs. Today's world contains societies in which elements of all such systems exist and in which the influences and ideas from earlier stages of economic development continue to resonate, even after a shift to a new phase. The most obvious mediating variable is religion. All the world's great religions developed against the background of agrarian, or even more basic nomadic, systems. Though some reinterpretation of the moral injunctions of such systems has occurred, in important ways they still reflect the reality of the societies in which they were generated. Thus, they embody powerful injunctions against infidelity, mandate the control, if not active repression, of female sexuality, and place great value on sexual continence in general.

The greater the influence of these religions in any modern society, the greater are the contradictions which afflict the responses to infidelity and the experiences of jealousy (Vandello and Cohen, 2003). Theology, ideology, and the impact of social and economic realities compete for the experience of jealousy, making each individual's jealousy a fascinating insight into our culture.

Pathological Extensions of Jealousy

Pathological jealousy, then, may be a psychological state, in and of itself, in which it forms the only, or the primary disturbance in the individual's mental state, and not only a symptom emerging out of a pre-existing condition such schizophrenia or chronic amphetamine abuse. The distinction is perhaps best illustrated by a comparison of two cases.

The first case illustrates something of the psychopathology of symptomatic jealousy – jealousy which has its origin in mental illness.

A man with a long history of intermittent obsessional symptoms related to fears of contamination began to develop anxieties about his wife's fidelity. These concerns would almost always intrude into his thinking at work in the form of a vivid mental image of his wife in the arms of another. He would resist these insights as absurd and developed a ritual of mental arithmetic both as distraction and as 'proof' of the falsity of the intrusive image; falsity that is if the calculation was completed correctly. Unfortunately the patient had high level mathematical skills and gradually escalated the complexity of the calculation to a point where either errors occurred, or he could not be sure whether he had obtained the right answer via a faulty process. His anxiety would build to the point when he felt compelled to rush home to reassure himself. His wife was exposed on an almost daily basis to her husband bursting in on her at home, in shops, and at friends' houses, tearful and apologetic for his absurd behaviour. The jealousy itself never rose above a suspicion, recognized as almost certainly false. There were no associated threats, violence or even intrusive enquiries. At no point was his partner exposed to worse than embarrassment. Yet the jealousy was clearly pathological; here, it formed the content of an obsessional disorder.

Selection of jealousy as the content of a delusional or other disorder of mental state is unlikely to be purely random. The jealousy probably represents aspects of the individual's life experience or personality vulnerabilities which predate the emergence of active symptoms. In another example of jealousy as a symptom of mental disorder, an elderly man with dementia developed delusions about the infidelity of his wife, bizarre because she was even more elderly and disabled than he was. A colleague who knew the family was able to describe the wife's colourful reputation when

younger, and the general opinion that the husband had been an angel to tolerate her flagrant infidelities.

Pathological jealousy which emerges as the sole or primary abnormality may be more difficult to separate with confidence from the more flamboyant manifestations of the extreme variates of jealousy which fall just within normal limits. Indicators that such jealousy has reached a pathological level include

1. The insatiable nature of the passion. A person with 'normal jealousy' generally finds resolution, be that through accepting reassurance, accepting infidelity has occurred and seeking separation or reconciliation, or even enacting specific elements of revenge or reparation. In the pathological state, nothing can satisfy the jealous desires. The revelations are never sufficient and some detail, some unacknowledged act or residual affection is always being sought. For the pathological, no evidence can be sufficiently weighty to establish innocence, separation is impossible, but the extent of the guilt remains forever in doubt. Pathological jealousy continues, even beyond the grave of the suspected partner. Those who have killed from jealousy rarely, in our experience, accept they may have been in error, nor cease searching their memories for further pointers to infidelity.

2. The pattern of behaviour evinced by the jealousy falls outside of that which is acceptable in the individual's cultural and social context.

3. The jealousy becomes totally preoccupying, disrupting normal function

4. The suspicions fall on an implausible rival, or a multiplicity of implausible rivals, who are often believed to consort with the partner under conditions, and within time spans, which are difficult to reconcile with the possible let alone the probable.

5. The jealousy has a course and evolution that is difficult to relate reasonably to the supposed provoking events and subsequent events, even taking the most generous view of the situation.

Jealousy and Domestic Violence

Domestic violence and spousal homicide emerge from a complex concatenation of influences in which sexual jealousy may be prominent, though of itself rarely sufficient (Buss, 2000; Jewkes, 2002). Jealousy is common, infidelity is common, but violence, though far too common, occurs in only a minority of such cases, and killing is an extreme rarity. Jealousy may well be the prime motivation for an act of violence but this still leaves an open question as to why this individual, on this particular occasion, resorted to force.

A community study of jealousy found that 15% of both men and women had, at some time, been subjected to physical violence at the hands of a jealous partner (Mullen and Martin, 1994). In a study carried out in Scotland, nearly half of 109 battered women interviewed identified the excessive possessiveness and sexual jealousy of their partner as the precipitant of violence (Dobash and Dobash, 1980). Two-thirds of the women at a refuge for battered women in the London area reported that their partner's excessive jealousy was the primary cause of the violence and that, in many cases, the partner's suspicions were entirely without foundation (Gayford, 1975, 1979). Studies from North America produced similar results. Hilberman and Manson (1977), for example, reported that extreme jealousy contributed to the violence in most of their group of 60 battered women, and Rounsaville (1978) noted similar findings with just over half of the battered women listing jealousy as the main problem and no less than 94% naming it as a frequent cause. In one of the few studies in which men were asked why they battered their partners, the men most frequently nominated anger at supposed infidelity (Brisson, 1983). Whitehurst (1971), reporting on 100 cases of spousal violence, noted that in nearly every case the husband appeared to be responding out of frustration at his inability to control his partner but that the overt justification, and accusation, was that the partner was sexually unfaithful. From such studies, jealousy would appear to be both a motive for domestic batterers and also an excuse, or rationalization, for the violence.

The statistics on violence and jealousy in the general community are grim, but evidence from samples of people who are pathologically jealous is worse. A UK study of all 138 psychiatric patients with pathological jealousy admitted to the Bethlem Royal and Maudsley hospitals over a 14-year period (1967–80), none referred from the criminal justice system and only six referred because of a violent incident, found that more than half had a history of having assaulted their partners and only 15% of the men and 27% of the women had neither threatened or enacted violence against partners (Mullen and Maack, 1985). In a later, US sample of 19 men and one woman, Silva et al. (1998) similarly found that most had harmed their spouse.

Jealousy has emerged as one of the more frequently identified motives for homicide in a number of studies (Gibbens, 1958; West, 1968; Wolfgang, 1958). Daly and colleagues (1982) concluded that male sexual jealousy is the commonest motive for killing in domestic disputes. Jealous homicides are usually perpetrated by men, with the usual victim being their female partner, although same sex homicidal jealousy is increasingly recognized as an important issue, and may be a particular concern in secure settings, where the sexes are segregated. Where domestic disputes generated by jealousy lead to women killing, it is claimed this is typically an act of self-defence to ward off the male partner's jealous rage (Daly and Wilson, 1988).

Assessment of the possibility that violence will occur in the context of jealousy is important, always. In the context of pathological jealousy rates of violence toward the partner are so high that there have to be very good – and clearly documented – reasons not to make the assumption that it will happen, and to devise a management strategy accordingly.

Careful and repeated questioning of the jealous individual and his/her partner is advisable. Specific enquiry should be made about:

- threats;
- damaging the partner's, or rival's, personal property;
- throwing objects;
- pushing, shoving or shaking;
- blows with hands, fists or feet;
- threatening with a (potential) weapon;
- throttling;
- the possession of firearms or other weapons;
- attacks with weapons;
- any other action which could have inflicted harm (e.g. driving at him/her with a vehicle or trying to produce an accident whilst partner was a passenger; poisoning).

The last point is important as, in this area, the improbable does occur. One elderly lady caught up in jealous suspicions about her husband of over 30 years was so dismissive of earlier enquires about violence it seemed silly to ask if she had ever tried to harm or even kill her husband by other means. In the event she happily described the unsuccessful attempts to kill him with rat poison in his meals.

When violence has occurred, the intent, the context and the nature of the damage inflicted must be noted. The level of the victim's fear is only a guide when it appears high in relation to acknowledged actions; it should not be taken as reassuring if it is apparently low, despite escalating aggression, indeed, in such cases it is arguable that the victim is exceptionally vulnerable, as s/he is unable to perceive the risks for her/himself. In most cases, violence is preceded by clear indicators of mounting danger. These may be ignored or downplayed by the partner who cannot believe they are at risk from their loved one. A prudent clinician should not make the same mistake.

The features in a jealous individual which increase concern about violence include:

- escalating conflict between the couple;
- threats;
- a history of violence in the domestic context in particular;
- fantasies of violent retribution or strong impulses to attack (however reassuring s/he is about never 'really doing it');
- depression, especially in the presence of suicidal preoccupations or behaviour;
- substance abuse;
- where the cultural and social background of the jealous individual is one which tends to condone resort to violence in the face of infidelity.

In general, jealous preoccupations tend to be more intense in younger people, who also resort more readily to violence. In pathological forms of jealousy, however, advancing years do little to ameliorate the risks of violence. Gender differences are largely in terms of the seriousness of the damage inflicted rather than the frequency of assaultive behaviours.

Apprehending violence is one thing, preventing its realization another. The option of admission to hospital, whether voluntarily or compulsorily, offers one protective route but, when pathological jealousy is not clearly secondary to a severe mental illness, this may be difficult. Both mental health review tribunals/boards, as well as fellow clinicians, on occasion, take a broad view of 'sanity', particularly in face of delusional disorders. This may result in a detained patient returning early to the community, untreated, but now with additional 'cause' for grievance, and thus more convinced than ever of the evil machinations of the partner. Negotiating separation with a couple embroiled in conflict over jealousy is usually difficult and frustrating, even at the limits of normality, but certainly when jealousy becomes pathological, it often reflects a relationship which, although conflicted, is also intensely involved. Partners in such a relationship are not easily separated; even with less over-involved couples there may be, despite clear warnings, little appreciation of the risks. It is helpful to consider also the needs and, perhaps the pathology of the victim-partner. Perhaps attraction to jealous men reflects a fear of being unlovable; the fact that these men do take a real interest in their partners and most particularly in what they do and how they spend their days may at first be very reassuring. By contrast, people who are less prone to jealousy show the more usual spectrum of concern for their partners – ranging from mild interest to polite indifference.

In those not labouring under frank delusions of infidelity it is sometimes possible to alter behaviour and de-escalate tensions simply by enumerating the risks and sharing one's anxieties about the future conduct. Where delusions are present, then medication for the jealous partner may help pave the way for psychosocial interventions to have some prospect of assisting the couple, and easing the torment of both. Separation, at least until the ideas/delusions are under some control, must always be considered, although it may be hard to enforce as the object of the jealous ideas may sometimes be as hard to persuade as the jealous. (For more on management, see Crow and Ridley, 1990; Dolan and Bishay, 1996; Kingham and Gordon, 2004; Pines, 1992; Mullen, 1995; de Silva, 2004; White and Mullen, 1989; chapter 22.)

STALKING

Stalking is a problem behaviour characterized by one person repeatedly imposing unwanted contacts and/or communications on another person in a manner which creates fear, or at least significant distress. The contacts can be in the form of approaches, following, loitering nearby, and keeping under observation. The communications are commonly by phone calls, SMS, letters, email, notes attached to property and graffiti. The imposed contacts and communications form the core of stalking behaviour, but there are a range of associated behaviours. These include threats, ordering or cancelling goods and services in the victim's name, unsolicited gifts, spreading unfounded rumours, vexatious complaints and legal actions, 'cyber-terrorism', and, ultimately, assault.

Stalking has only emerged as a significant social problem since the 1990s. Initially it claimed public attention with respect to celebrities, especially after the killing in 1989 of television star Rebecca Shaefer by her long-time stalker Richard Bardo. Later, stalking became more associated with domestic violence and the pursuit of ex-partners, but a more balanced view now prevails. The behaviour is recognized as occurring in a range of contexts and against a wide range of victims (Lowney and Best, 1995; Mullen et al., 2008).

History

Stalking is not a new behaviour. There are clear descriptions in novels, in psychiatric texts, in law reports, and even in autobiographies dating back centuries (Alcott, 1997; Esquirol, 1965 orig 1845; Kierkegaard, 1987 orig 1848). What made it emerge in the 1990s as a matter of public and forensic concern? One possibility is a decreasing tolerance of threatening or otherwise disruptive behaviours, another the increasing value placed on personal privacy, but the possibility that its newfound prominence reflects an increasing prevalence of the behaviour in today's society is worth considering; community studies suggest far higher lifetime rates are reported by younger cohorts (e.g. Budd and Martinson, 2000).

The commonest form of stalking has become that by a rejected ex-partner. Such stalking usually emerges in the context of the breakdown of a sexual relationship in which one partner, almost always the man, either refuses to accept that the relationship is at an end or embarks on a course of harassment to express his rage at rejection. The probability of such stalking is likely to increase as the frequency increases of people entering and, more importantly, exiting relationships. Stalking by a rejected male may also reflect the changed balance of power between men and women in the Western world where, in sexual relationships, female choice is beginning to replace female acceptance and subservience. In societies with high separation and divorce rates, the risk of one partner refusing to accept the end of the relationship gracefully is higher too, and this brings with it the possible resort to stalking.

Another currently common form of stalking involves men, usually lonely and unattached, pestering and following young women to whom they are strangers, in the hope of starting a relationship. Such behaviour may reflect a society in which less socially adept and prepossessing men are finding it more difficult to establish relationships, while being immersed in a culture which places a high value on visible indications of sexual relationships, or at least activity. It may also reflect increasing suspicion between neighbours in urban environments, where we live among strangers. Finally, those who stalk out of resentment for some perceived injustice or mistreatment may actually be becoming more frequent in societies which emphasize individual rights and promote unattainable expectations.

The Impact of Stalking

The central reason to take stalking behaviours seriously is the damage they can inflict, or presage, for the victim. Data are now available from studies both of selected samples and random community samples. Initially, studies focused on self-identified victims of stalking who sought help, joined stalking support organizations, or responded to adverts placed by researchers (e.g. Bjerregaard, 2000; Blaauw et al., 2002; Hall, 1998; Kamphuis and Emmelkamp, 2001; Pathé and Mullen, 1997). The studies report broadly similar results. A number of random community samples have not only determined the prevalence of stalking but investigated aspects of the impact on victims (e.g. Budd and Matttison, 2000; Dressing et al., 2005; Kuehner et al., 2007; Purcell et al., 2002, 2005). Though rates of overt anxiety, post-traumatic and depressive disorders are lower than in studies of clinic samples, the psychological and social impact of stalking is nevertheless considerable. Among a random sample of German women, for example over 40% acknowledged anxiety and sleep disturbance, over a third psychosomatic symptoms, and only slightly lower proportions acknowledged depression (28%) and/or panic attacks (12%) (Dressing et al., 2005). The impact of threats and violence more specifically is discussed below.

Stalking, then, if it persists for longer than a few weeks, will create psychological and social problems for the victim, which, in some cases, may be both long-lasting and disabling. In their systematic review and meta-analysis of 175 studies of stalking, Spitzberg and Cupach (2007) found eight main categories of effect:

1. *general disturbance*, in which they included PTSD;
2. *affective health*, referring to such problems as anxiety, anger and depression;
3. *social health*, covering relationship difficulties;
4. *cognitive health*, incorporating such states as confusion, suspiciousness, self-esteem or suicidal ideation; as with members of so many victim groups, their distress is often compounded by self-blame – for choosing such a partner in the first place, for not managing the separation more adroitly, for not recognizing the problem, for failing to deal appropriately with the unwelcome advances, and much, much more;
5. *physical health*, including appetite or sleep disturbance, but also addictions;
6. *behavioural disturbance* – victims often react to an ongoing sense of threat by decreasing social outings and work attendance, or changing residence and/or place of employment; the worst affected became virtual prisoners in their own homes, afraid to go out or answer the telephone or doorbell;
7. *resilience* – some victims report heightened appreciation of family networks or development of self-confidence through learning new skills, such as self-defence;
8. *resource impact*; in the USA, efforts have been made to estimate the costs from medical, psychiatric and/or social care needed, through time lost from work to the judicial system costs of pursuing the stalker. In the early part of the new millennium, the societal cost in these terms was estimated to be $342 million (Centers for Disease Control, 2003).

The impact of stalking on the stalker is rarely considered, but the stalker usually also pays a high price for what is generally a futile, time wasting, and resource consuming enterprise. Stalkers can disrupt their own lives to an almost similar degree as they disrupt the lives of their victims. Stalking can become an all encompassing preoccupation which puts the stalker at risk of alienating those social supports that s/he has, and eventually brings significant legal sanctions. In managing the stalker remembering that stalkers also suffer from their behaviour is important in reconciling one's role as agent of the community and agent of the patient.

The Epidemiology of Stalking

The answer to the question 'how common is stalking?' depends on how the behaviour is defined, the methods of ascertainment, and the population investigated. In practice what is counted is the victim recall of stalking, usually in terms both of lifetime experiences and of 1-year prevalence (period prevalence).

The earliest study confined itself to women stalked by men (Australian Bureau of Statistics (ABS), 1996). A lifetime rate of 15% for women was reported, with 2.4% having been stalked in the previous year. The ABS repeated this study a decade later using very similar methodology except, on this occasion, men were included. In this later study, 19% of women and 9.1% of men reported having ever been stalked (Australian Bureau of Statistics, 2005). The increase is partly explained by explicitly including same sex stalking in the second survey, which was not done in the first study. A first US study was on a larger scale and included a random community sample of men and women (US Department of Justice, 1997; Tjaden and Thoennes, 1998). Using a more restrictive definition, they reported lifetime rates of 8% for women and 2% for men. The British Crime Survey (BCS) first incorporated enquiries about having been the victim of stalking in 1998, when lifetime rates of 11.5% were found (women 16.1%, men 6.8%) with 2.8% stalked in the year prior to interview (Budd and Mattinson, 2000). Dressing and colleagues (2005) reported a similar lifetime rate of 11.6% with an annual rate of 1.6% in a random community sample in Mannheim, Germany.

The various studies generally agree about the sex distribution of victims (70–80% females) and perpetrators (80–85% males). The apparent numerical discrepancy here is accounted for by same sex stalking, which occurs in some 20% of cases, and more frequently involves male on male than female on female. There is more variation between studies in the frequency with which victims are pursued by ex-partners, strangers, or acquaintances. In the BCS, 29% of victims were pursued by former partners, 32% by acquaintances and 34% by strangers (Budd and Mattison, 2000). Studies are consistent in reporting higher lifetime rates of stalking among younger respondents. This could be an issue of recall or even willingness to construct experiences of harassment in terms of stalking. The discrepancy persists however even for those exposed to very lengthy (more than a year) and often distressing experiences of stalking, which suggests the probability that rates of stalking have increased since the 1990s.

The duration of stalking varies widely from a matter of days to years. A careful analysis of duration suggested there may be two separable types of stalking (Purcell et al., 2002, 2004). One group stalk for less than 2 weeks, with a modal duration of a couple of days; people in the other group who persist beyond 2 weeks have a modal duration of 12 months. The briefer episodes of often intense harassment are usually perpetrated by strangers (75%) who predominantly employ approaches and following. The longer episodes of stalking are usually by prior intimates and acquaintances (80%) and involve a range of unwanted communications and contacts. As might be expected, significant social and psychological damage is virtually confined to those victims pursued for longer than 2 weeks (Purcell et al., 2004).

Stalking Classifications and Typologies

A variety of stalking classifications have been advanced on the basis of the supposed underlying psychopathology, nature of the prior relationship or variety of stalking behaviours employed as well as mixing elements of the behaviour – for example motivation – together with psychopathology (Boon and Sheridan, 2001; Canter and Ioannou, 2004; Harmon et al., 1995; Mohandie et al., 2006; Sheridan and Boon, 2002; Wright et al., 1996; Zona et al., 1993, 1998). The typology employed here has obtained wide currency among clinicians (Mullen et al., 1999; Pinals, 2007). This has the following five characteristic patterns which, though not entirely mutually exclusive, do provide a basis for understanding and managing most cases.

1. *The Rejected Stalker.* In this case, stalking emerges in the context of the breakdown of a close relationship. The pursuit of the former intimate is initially motivated by the search for reconciliation, or exacting revenge for rejection, or a fluctuating mixture of both. The stalking may persist way beyond a time when reconciliation or revenge seem plausible motives, at least in part because

the stalking is sustained by the communications and enforced contacts becoming a substitute for the lost relationship, and a parody of past intimacy.

Rejected stalkers are usually men (80–90%). The lost relationship was usually sexual and intimate, though occasionally another family relationship, or close friendship. If these are broken unilaterally, they may engender such stalking. Rejected stalkers rarely have psychotic disorders, though personality traits of overdependence, narcissism, or obsessiveness are frequently encountered. The influence of jealousy and domestic violence in the relationship prior to separation and subsequent stalking remains uncertain, in part because several studies have conflated stalking-like behaviours during the time the partners are living together with such behaviours after separation. Though this approach is defensible it seems to ignore an essential element: that stalking is about imposing one's presence in situations where one has no legitimate right to be (Mullen et al., 2008).

2. *The Intimacy Seeking Stalker.* Here, the behaviour emerges in a context of loneliness, in which the stalker experiences him/herself) as bereft of love or companionship. The initial motivation is to establish a close relationship, usually romantic, though occasionally one of friendship, or maternal or child-like interdependence is the goal. The victim is usually a stranger or acquaintance selected from celebrities, public figures, or casual and professional contacts. Health professionals are favoured targets of such misplaced affections. The stalking is sustained despite the lack of response, or outright rejection, because the fantasy or delusion of a close relationship is so much better than no intimacy at all.

This is the only type of stalking in which women predominate. These stalkers have high rates of psychopathology, including pathologically erotomanic infatuations. This may be the most persistent of all types of stalking. Violence is uncommon but not unknown.

3. *Incompetent Suitors.* This type of stalking also comes out of loneliness, and sometimes also sexual frustration. The initial motive is to establish contact, usually with a stranger encountered in a public place, such as a shop or entertainment venue, in the hope this will lead to friendship and/or a sexual relationship. The approaches tend to be crude and insistent, and may evoke fear or revulsion. The stalker is blind, or indifferent, to the cool response and continues to pester even in the face of obvious distress. The lack of a positive response coupled with increasingly active resistance from the victim usually eventually makes it clear to the stalker that his/her efforts are fruitless, and they stop. Occasionally the more insensitive will persist for weeks, though most go away after a day or so. This type of stalking can be more persistent when some semblance of a relationship, however casual, preceded the unwanted approaches.

This type of stalker is socially incompetent, often as a result of intellectual or interpersonal defects, but occasionally just youth. The difference between the approaches of an overenthusiastic, gauche and inexperienced suitor and the stalking of the incompetent suitor is the indifference or blindness not just to the lack of interest on the part of the target figure, but also to their actual distress. This margin may be narrow, but it is important. Spitzberg and Cupach (2001) have described what they term 'obsessional relational intrusions'. These, they suggest, are found among young people attempting unsuccessfully to negotiate their way through society's courtship rituals. In unacceptable levels of courtship persistence, the would-be suitor ignores the signs of lack of interest in part because they misread the messages. This may be because they assume outdated cultural stereotypes, for example that apparent lack of interest is coquetry. The emphasis in their mode of acting is on reciprocity, and their targets may actually provide inadvertent encouragement, for example through misplaced politeness or because they initially felt flattered. Employing a similar model, Sinclair and Frieze (2000, 2005) studied a large cohort of students who had been either the subject, or object, of unrequited affections. They concluded that the stalking behaviours which may emerge in such situations depend on this mix of failures to read correctly the intentions and responses of the other party and blindness to the distress caused. On the edges of the normal range, most of the clinically incompetent stalkers have an extreme level of inappropriate intrusiveness and of indifference to the victim's responses. Unusual persistence, of longer duration than the typical brief episodes of stalking of this type may occur because of obsessional relational intrusions and/or prior acquaintanceship. Incompetent suitors often have personality vulnerabilities in the schizoid or antisocial spectrum, with Asperger's syndrome not infrequent.

4. *The Predatory Stalker* emerges in the context of sexual deviation, usually related to fantasies of rape and subjugation, but occasionally of child molestation. The initial motivation is related to the selection of a victim and the acquiring of information about that victim preparatory to launching an attack. The victim is selected on the basis of fit with the predator's desires and fantasies. The stalking is prolonged beyond the time necessary for selection, information acquiring and planning, to obtain gratification from the voyeurism, the rehearsing of the planned attack in fantasy while watching the victim, and the sense of power and control obtained from observing the victim, who remains unaware of the oncoming danger.

Predatory stalkers are men, often with histories of deviant sexual behaviour and/or prior sexual offending. Clinical encounter with a predatory stalker is more likely to be in the context of assessing sex offenders than from a referral specifically because of stalking. Serial rapists of the more organized type almost always have histories of predatory stalking, not infrequently with some victims of the stalking escaping the ultimate attack. The victims of a predatory stalker may be unaware of the unwanted attentions, but some will recount unease and events which led them to suspect they were being followed and kept under observation.

5. *The Resentful Stalker.* All the stalker types described so far are motivated by the desire to form, or reform, a relationship, however impoverished, one sided, and potentially destructive. Resentful stalkers are different. Their dramas are played out like all stalking, in a dyadic relationship, but their motivation is to damage the other and not to relate to him/her. It might seem that a person from this group might be equated with a vengeful ex-partner but, in practice, the latter, even if predominantly aiming to harm, has at least aspects of nostalgia for what was lost.

Resentful stalking emerges in the context of events which the stalker experiences as unjust, humiliating, and injurious. Such stalkers focus their animus either on someone who they blame for a perceived injury, or on a representative of the group they hold responsible. The initial motive is to strike back, often surreptitiously. The stalking is sustained because of the sense of power and control which comes from harassing the victim, and from a self righteous conviction they are fighting back against an oppressor. People from this group of stalkers often have sensitive and self-referential personalities, and/or fall into one of the paranoid spectrum disorders, though usually into well-organized types.

Stalking Among Juveniles

No reliable data exist on the frequency of stalking behaviours by juveniles but existing evidence points to it being substantial (Mullen et al., 2008). McCann (1998, 2000, 2001) was the first investigator to suggest that stalking by juveniles could be just as damaging to victims as that by adults, with threats and assaults being at least as frequent. Purcell and colleagues (2009) studied the records of some 300 juveniles appearing before the children's court following stalking behaviours. Most perpetrators were male (64%) and victims female (69%). The mean age of the stalkers was some 15 years, but that for victims several years older. Almost all of these young people stalked someone they knew (98%); ex-boyfriends/girlfriends made up a fifth of the victims but, unlike adults, same sex stalking was common (57%). Threats and assaults were surprisingly frequent (75% and 50% of cases respectively), though this may reflect the court based data set.

Juvenile stalker typology has much in common with its adult counterpart, but the commonest form among young people appears to be an extension of bullying, with the purpose of taking the tormenting beyond the school context into the victim's home and social life. The juvenile resentful stalker might be more accurately described as 'retaliatory', as, in the Purcell series, it usually involved a more direct and rapid response to a supposed insult or injury; this was the next most frequent (22%). Threats were common as were harassing phone calls and approaches but, like the adult equivalent, actual assault was infrequent. Among rejected stalkers (22%), the perpetrator was usually male and assault common (44%) and occasionally seriously injurious. A group not seen among adults was of youths who harassed multiple victims, often spanning schoolmates, neighbours and acquaintances and frequently targeting adults. These were an unhappy, angry and delinquent group of young people, often with histories of conduct disorder, and at war with their world (Mullen et al., 2008). Infatuated stalkers, seeking intimacy, were uncommon among youths.

The impact of being stalked can be just as serious among adolescent as adult victims. In fact, given its potential to disrupt social behaviour and academic performance at critical moments in development, its long-term effects may be more damaging. Stalking among juveniles needs more research, particularly research not starting from a premise that this is a normal developmental variant of no great significance for perpetrator or victim.

Stalking and The Law

Stalking has been criminalized in most Western jurisdictions. Stalking offences, however, present problems for the law. Usually each of the acts which make up the offence of stalking, such as phoning, sending letters or approaching with banal requests, are, in themselves, legal. Furthermore, the intentions of the stalker are often lawful – such as seeking reconciliation or attempting to establish a relationship – and the stalker often regards his/her activities as offering friendship or love or otherwise well intentioned. A critical element in the definition of the offence is the victim's statement as to how they were affected by the behaviour, but some of those who are stalked have an obvious mental disorder by the time the case comes to the attention of the law. Those who draft anti-stalking statutes often struggle to frame the offence in a manner which deals with what is a criminal offence, partly victim-defined, in which guilty intent may be absent, and which only becomes criminal by virtue of the repetition of lawful acts. The result can be a law which either creates multiple loopholes for the well-represented offender or, conversely, a breadth of coverage which places the harmlessly enthusiastic, or reasonably enquiring, at risk of prosecution. It is perhaps most important, if such laws are to provide the protection victims of stalking need, that they are understood and accepted by the police, who will generally be responsible for the first steps in applying them in practice.

Cyberstalking

Cyberstalking has attracted great public interest, but little systematic research. Definitions offered of this behaviour vary from the parsimonious: 'the use of information communication technologies to harass and intrude on others' to the all-inclusive, which incorporate mention of a range of sexual, aggressive, and even terrorist activities (Barak, 2005; Bocij and McFarlane, 2002, 2003; Ogilvie, 2000). Sheridan and Grant (2007) conducted a systematic examination of the differences between cyberstalking and other forms of stalking. They reported that most cases of cyberstalking formed one element among more familiar stalking behaviours rather than a distinct type of activity.

Cyberstalking behaviours include:

1. sending repeated, unwanted, and disturbing emails or SMSs;
2. ordering goods and services on a victim's behalf;
3. publicizing private information of a potentially damaging or embarrassing nature;
4. spreading false information;
5. information gathering online about the victim;
6. identity theft;
7. encouraging others to harass the victim;
8. attacks against the victim's computer and its data bases.

The prevalence of cyberstalking is hard to estimate, particularly as the various attempts have used widely discrepant definitions and ascertainment methods. One of the more informative approaches has been to study the frequency of receipt of repeated harassing emails; this experience has been reported by about 25% of stalking victims who had been drawn from US college samples (Alexy et al. 2005; Fisher et al., 2000; Spitzberg and Hoobler, 2002).

Stalking of Celebrities and Public Figures

The definition of stalking has to be modified when applying it to public figures. Superstars and the truly powerful are so well-screened by security services that they are often unaware of being stalked. The fear criterion has, therefore, to be transferred to the raising of significant concern for their protective services.

A high public profile attracts unwanted attentions. A Dutch study of public figures suggested a third had been stalked (Malsch et al., 2002). A study of television personalities in Germany reported even higher rates (Hoffmann and Sheridan, 2005). For those in elevated political or state positions, like the US President or the British Queen, stalkers are a constant problem (James et al., 2008; Mullen et al., 2009; Scalora et al., 2002a,b). Public figures attract the unwanted attentions of intimacy seekers and the resentful, but in addition they are a magnet for a mixed bag of publicity seekers, campaigners and the deluded. It is unsurprising that the famous and powerful can attract attention and become the focus of a wide range of emotions from admiration, through emulation, to envy, and detestation. Interest in, or even preoccupation with, a public figure only becomes problematic when it is either an all absorbing fixation and/or motivates damaging behaviours. These include:

1. intimacy and intimacy seeking, with the desire for or assertion of an amorous or advisory relationship;
2. unusually persistent petitioning, from belief in a cause or a highly personal grievance; this group is characterized by an intense sense of entitlement, which easily translates into resentment when hopes are disappointed; it overlaps with querulous complainants;
3. delusions about the right to the position or title occupied by their target, and a need to assert that ('pretenders');
4. a perception of the public figure as the cause or solution of their problems, in the first case already 'persecuted' and in the second, when disappointed in their hope of protection, shifting to a view of their one time saviour as the prime persecutor;
5. the chaotic, for whom the motivation is felt as intense, but remains unclear because of the disorganized and fluctuating nature of their mental state in general and their beliefs in particular.

Those who stalk and intrude on public figures are far more likely to have serious mental illnesses than those who plague more mundane targets. This may be because of the prominence of intimacy seekers, who have the highest rate of mental illness among the various types of stalking, or because fame and power attracts those with a range of grandiose, and persecutory, and identity delusions who would be unlikely to fixate on the less famous or powerful.

Some public figures attract literally hundreds of fixated people who make repeated attempts to communicate or establish contact. Threatening behaviour is not uncommon, but only a tiny minority will ever present a threat to the safety of anyone, except themselves. This is little comfort, however, without some way of identifying the dangerous few and managing their risk effectively. Considerable efforts have been made to distinguish those who pose a threat from the accompanying crowds of harmless nuisances (Dietz et al., 1991a,b; Fein and Vossekuil, 1995, 1998, 1999, 2003; Phillips, 2006; Meloy et al., 2008; Scalora et al., 2002a,b; see also chapter 22).

Stalking of Health Professionals

Health professionals in general, and mental health professionals in particular, are brought into daily contact with people who suffer distress and disorder, particularly the lonely, the angry, and the self-absorbed. Their stalkers, therefore, from this population, are usually intimacy seekers, occasionally seeking parental caring rather than

romance, or resentful stalkers, who believe they have been let down, mistreated, or humiliated by the professional and are pursuing retribution.

There are now a range of studies of the prevalence of stalking of mental health professionals (Galeazzi, et al., 2005; Gentile et al., 2002; McKenna et al., 2003; Purcell et al., 2005; Regehr and Glancy, 2011; Sandberg et al., 2002). Though the study methods varied, all reported high rates of stalking victimization. Purcell and colleagues (2005), in the methodologically most adequate study, reported that nearly 20% of clinical psychologists had been stalked by a patient. The highest rate was among those preparing reports for accident compensation or benefits, when they might have been acting for the agency rather than the person who became a stalker. The male preponderance among stalkers was about half that in general population samples (37%:63%). Resentful stalkers formed the largest group (42%) followed by intimacy seekers (19%). Most clinicians were pursued for months, using a range of stalking methods; a third were threatened and 10% assaulted. Perhaps equally troubling was that one-third of the stalkers made vexatious complaints to registration boards and health boards.

The Royal College of Psychiatrists has carried out a postal survey of its membership (Mullen et al., 2010; Whyte et al., 2008), using a conservative definition of stalking, involving extended pursuit and multiple intrusions. About 10% of responding psychiatrists reported having been stalked; with a broader definition, the level was over 20%, and one in three reported harassment. Most (71%) of the stalkers were patients, with the next largest category being relatives or friends of the patients; just 5% experienced stalking by partners/ex-partners and 5% by colleagues. In more than half the cases (58%) the stalking went on for more than a year, and most (65%) experienced significant anxiety or fear.

Minimising stalking behaviours against clinicians

Studies to date thus suggest that being stalked is a significant professional hazard. Falling victim to such behaviour is unrelated to experience or gender but mainly reflects the patients encountered. Avoiding being stalked can only be assured by not seeing patients. The impact may be minimised, however, in several ways.

1. *Early recognition of being stalked.* Some professionals seem to tolerate a range of inappropriate communications and contacts outside designated appointment times, for lengthy periods and without apparent concern, so stalking may be well established before even being recognised.
2. *Discussion of concerns with colleagues at the earliest moment.* This allows checking the perceptions of being stalked with that of more detached colleagues. Usually, but not always, it will confirm the behaviour is stalking;

colleagues, including receptionists and security staff, need to know about the stalking, first so they may assist, and secondly to protect themselves.

3. *Telling family and friends*. Again, they cannot help you or protect themselves if they don't know about the stalking.

4. *Transference of the care of the patient* to a colleague. It is important neither to abandon the patient nor to continue working personally with him or her in such circumstances, so transfer to a colleague, preferably at another clinic, is essential at the earliest opportunity. The patient must be informed personally of the transfer, ideally by the senior clinician, even if that clinician is the victim. A colleague may be present if the stalker is considered to pose a risk of violence, or even security personnel in extreme circumstances. In our experience a non-confrontational approach is best, at least initially, advising the patient that his/her communications and unscheduled contacts have created anxiety; the word 'stalking' should not be used with the patient, for a number of reasons, but especially because it is not therapeutic for the patient to see an anxious and frightened therapist. This is *not* the time for discussion, debate or argument about possible gaps between intention and reality ('you may not have intended to frighten Dr X but you have'), but for firm action and clear transfer to a new treatment situation. Any refusal to accept this on the part of the patient should be met with a courteous but unambiguous statement that continuing with the current arrangements is not an option. Then the patient must be informed that there can be no further attempt to communicate with or contact the professional concerned and that breaking that rule could lead to legal consequences.

We owe our colleagues who are stalked the assistance of accepting the referrals of such patients. It is a low-risk kindness as the stalker is unlikely to transfer the unwanted attention to the new clinician. In over 300 stalkers seen in the Melbourne service only one has gone on to stalk a clinician in the service.

5. *Break all direct contact with the stalker*. However reasonable and inoffensive any further approaches or queries from the patient may seem, the stalked clinician must cease all contact once the patient has been transferred to a colleague's care.

6. *Resort to civil or criminal law if the stalking persists*. Restraining orders and other civil orders to not deter most committed stalkers, but may stop the less dedicated. The protections of the criminal laws, if available and if properly administered, are the most effective.

7. *Meticulous record keeping*. Assume that the stalker will make an official complaint at some stage and there will be an enquiry.

8. *Retain evidence of all unwanted communications*. Retain tapes of phone calls and record the unwanted contacts, with names of potential witnesses where possible. If the case goes to court, such material is invaluable (see Pathé, 2002).

9. *Take sensible security measures*. Over-enthusiasm about security can add little in the way of safety but adds greatly to the victim's own fears.

Evaluating and Managing Risk in Stalking

Risk in stalking is usually considered only in terms of the chances of escalation to violence to the victim. There is indeed, as described, some risk of this, but the stalking victim faces other important risks too, especially those of significant psychological and social harms when stalking is persistent or recurrent.

The stalker also faces future hazards, which include continuance and/or escalation of their stalking until it undermines his/her social and psychological functioning and/or incurs criminal sanctions.

Initial and somewhat tentative approaches have been made to apply actuarial, structured clinical judgment, and classification and regression tree approaches to predicting violence by stalkers (Kropp et al., 2002; Meloy et al., 2001; Mullen et al., 2006; Rosenfeld and Lewis, 2005; see also chapter 22). None is entirely successful in the clinical situation. The approach we employ involves:

1. assigning stalkers and victims to high- or low-risk groups, applying broadly relevant risk factors such as prior relationship, presence of prior threats or violence, and whether the intensity of the stalking is increasing, decreasing or apparently stable;

2. monitoring, where possible, the level of fear produced in the victim; this may be a useful indicator of escalation, and is certainly not a factor to be dismissed;

3. identifying current risk factors and future hazards which are potentially remediable;

4. using the information derived from this process to inform management strategies.

The following is a list of empirically established and clinically identifiable risk factors for the main problems.

a. *Persistence or recurrence*: risk is associated with the stalker being female, either rejected or intimacy seeking in type, with a duration already exceeding 2 weeks, and multiple methods of intruding, particularly letters and unsolicited gifts (Hart et al. 1999; McEwan et al., 2007; Mohandie et al., 2006; Purcell et al., 2004).

b. *Psychological and social damage to the victim*: risk is increased by the stalker being male and the victim female, a prior intimate relationship between stalker and victim, a greater type and number of intrusions, threats and assault, victim withdrawal from social contact and work roles in response to the pursuit, and victim failure to seek help from the law, stalker support groups, or experienced therapists (Blaauw and Sheridan, 2002;

McEwan et al., 2007; Pathé and Mullen, 1997; Purcell et al., 2005).

c. *Assault*: risk is increased when stalker and victim are ex-intimates, the stalker is of predatory type, has marked personality pathology and/or abuses substances, has breached restraining and other court orders, threats to assault have been made, there is escalating intrusiveness, and victim response includes counter-threats and confrontation (Mohandie et al., 2006; Purcell et al., 2002; Rosenfeld and Harmon, 2002; Rosenfeld and Lewis, 2005).

Ideal management of stalking will provide treatment and risk reducing interventions for the stalker *and* support in various forms for the victim, usually through different clinical services or agencies. The victim needs practical advice, may need treatment for anxiety and depressive symptoms as they arise, and sometimes needs dissuading from self-destructive responses (Mullen et al., 2008; Pathé, 2002). A first step for the stalker lies in establishing a relationship which is sufficiently secure to allow the clinician to lead him or her to accept s/he is stalking and damaging both the victim and self. In this context, it becomes possible to establish treatments, as appropriate, for general factors which may be fuelling the stalking, including:

- treatment of any mental disorder;
- treatment of any substance misuse disorder;
- treatment for personality traits or social skills deficits;

as well as interventions more specifically directed at the stalking behaviours, including:

- forbidding/stopping contact between stalker and victim;
- reduction of denial of the damaging nature of the behaviour, perhaps supported by CBT;
- assisting the intimacy seeking stalker to relinquish false hopes of the relationship with the victim;
- focusing on the harm the behaviour is doing/will do to the stalker;
- enhancing victim empathy;
- encouraging alternative outlets to meet desires and needs, including education, sports or other club attendance.

Stalking: Summarizing Knowledge and Progress

Stalking is a problem behaviour which can result from a range of social, interpersonal, psychopathological and cultural influences. Its recognition is increasing and, thanks to new legal protections for victims, there is a real chance of reducing the damage stalking produces. Mental health professionals have a role in supporting and advising victims, for which task they need adequate knowledge about the nature of stalking. They also have a role in both assessing and managing stalkers to reduce the risks to the victim and the damage to the stalker themselves.

PERSISTENT COMPLAINANTS AND VEXATIOUS LITIGANTS

Morbid querulousness is a pattern of behaviour which is characterized by unusually persistent pursuit of a personal grievance, which becomes damaging to the person in pursuit and damaging and disruptive to the pursued, and to social structures such as courts or other agencies seeking to resolve the dispute. There are three broad types of querulous behaviour, which are not necessarily mutually exclusive: the laying of persistent complaints without recourse to the law; the persistent presentation of petitions, which generally includes harassment of people perceived to be powerful; and seeking redress through the courts. A wide variety of possibilities may form the focus of the grievance, but clinicians are probably most familiar with hypochondriacal claimants, who particularly direct their resentment against doctors who they believe have failed to cure them, or even harmed them, by giving the wrong treatment or withholding the correct one. In common with the other conditions considered in this chapter, the primary sufferer believes that s/he is entitled to something – here some goods or rights rather than love or intimacy, not having attained that entitlement; persistent complainers, petitioners or litigants then believe they must seek redress, which they pursue relentlessly. From time to time, failure to get the relief they seek boils over into violence against those perceived to be being obstructive.

Persistent Complainants

Many organizations, including health services, now encourage complaints, and have literature on systems for making them. Even so, a minority of complainants account for disproportionate use of the resources. In Australia, for example, various agencies of accountability estimated that less than 1% of complaints were from such persistent complainers, but they consumed up to 30% of resources (Lester et al., 2004). Very often their grievance seems to be about a small matter, and certainly not of the order that would justify a sustained campaign. A case–control study of 52 unusually persistent complainants found that the persistent complainers pursued their cases for longer and showed characteristic patterns in the complaint material. The latter included its form, which showed multiple methods of emphasis, numerous foot or marginal notes, irrelevant attachments of substantial length, and its content, which included rambling discourse, misuse of legal and technical terms, inappropriately ingratiating statements, ultimatums and threats (Lester et al., 2004). Persistent complainants differed most from controls, however, in seeking retribution not only against the person/people whom they believed had inflicted the initial hurt, but also people they believed had been obstructing their route to justice. While seeking to have individuals dismissed or prosecuted and/or institutions closed or subjected to punitive damage, they also differed in expecting public recognition for their crusading work.

Persistent Petitioners

Less studied than other groups, persistent petitioners tend to be rather similar to persistent complainants in terms of the voluminous and repeated written communications the make. They do sometimes progress to contacting the influential figures they believe will take up their cause and, although violence seems rare in this group, they have been responsible for many of the attacks on politicians in Western governments over the last 20 years (Mullen and Lester, 2006).

Vexatious Litigants

The main practical difference between persistent complainants and vexatious litigants is that the latter have extended their complaining into the courts. Rowlands (1988) reviewed the development of legal restraints in England. First applied under the Vexatious Actions Act 1896, the situation now is that the Attorney General may make application in the High Court, under section 42 of the Supreme Court Act 1981, prohibiting an individual from continuing or initiating legal actions. The names of such people are published in the *London Gazette*. This limitation is extremely rarely used; on average, only five or six orders per year are made. Most countries have some legal measure whereby continuing action may be prohibited (Freckleton, 1988), although how this affects the actual behaviours is less clear.

In many cases, there is an understandable grievance at the centre of the claims of the morbidly querulous, and it is only with time that those trying to assist them begin to suspect the presence of any pathology. Appropriate inquiry will elicit characteristic cognitive distortions:

- those who do not fully support their case are their enemies;
- lack of progress is the product of malevolent interference;
- any compromise is humiliating defeat;
- the grievance is the defining moment of their lives;
- because they are in the right, the outcomes they seek must be not only possible but necessary.

Like the complainants, they may have voluminous documentation of their case; they often represent themselves in court, and may find themselves under contempt charges from time to time as their passionate involvement in promoting their rights may bring them into direct conflict with the judge. As with the other conditions included here, there is advantage for all parties in early recognition of the nature of the problem, but this is difficult and, as the following case illustrates, unchecked, the querulant state is progressive and may end in violence.

John Brown was living alone when, at 65, he had a heart attack. He was admitted to hospital, high blood pressure diagnosed, and medication prescribed for this – a beta-blocker. He was apparently recovering, when he complained that he was having difficulty with his hearing. He attributed this to the medication. His hearing was examined. It was found that he did have some mild loss in one ear, but the ear, nose and throat specialist reassured him first that his hearing was more or less within normal limits for his age, secondly that there had been no previous reports of this medication affecting hearing, and thirdly that as the hearing loss only affected one ear, it was extremely unlikely that any medication could be implicated.

Mr Brown was not reassured. He asked for a second opinion, which yielded the same advice.

Mr Brown was again not reassured, particularly as he now thought that maybe his eyesight was less good than it had been. He wanted to see a neurologist. He did, and the same advice was forthcoming.

Mr Brown was still not reassured. He demanded, and got, further opinions, insisting that each new specialist should be wholly independent of the others.

Mr Brown was still not reassured, and so he acquired many records at a number of hospitals, which, initially, were not connected. Finally, his general practitioner refused further referrals. Mr Brown was offended and angry He complained to the body which oversaw the practice. This body found that Mr Brown had received appropriate care.

Mr Brown was still not reassured. He began to complain of professional protectionism and that all the healthcare organizations were in league with each other. He sought legal advice about redress in law. His first lawyer got legal aid for him to pursue his case, and helped him to collate his by now voluminous records. Mr Brown, however, felt that the case was proceeding too slowly, so he changed his lawyer. His second lawyer followed much the same pattern as the first, so Mr Brown changed his lawyer again and again. He began to realize that his failure to achieve redress for all his suffering was part of a wider professional protectionism, and started petitioning his local member of parliament to help him expose this travesty.

Mr. Brown got no relief from this either, and he threatened, then attacked his latest lawyer.

After the attack, he rushed away from the office. Given the extent of his documentation, and his own sense of being right, it was easy for the police to find him at home, but less easy for them to arrest him. He had booby trapped the front door with electrical wires and a long-bore shotgun trained at it, to be triggered by a pulley system if the door was opened. Fortunately his mechanical skills were poor, so no other person was hurt. When asked, he explained that he had set up the defences at home because it had come to him that the reason why his efforts to get his dues were still being foiled was that his neighbours had joined the others, and had been intercepting his mail to remove crucial documents.

Finally, Mr Brown was referred for the treatment he actually *needed, but in a secure psychiatric unit.*

There is little evidence to support a particular way forward for helping people like Mr Brown, partly because his state is unusual, and partly because of its nature – even if he would consent to participation in research, how many researchers would want to engage him in experimental treatment? If recognized earlier, then both the person with such problems and the healthcare and legal systems attempting to provide him with services would be likely to be helped by referring him to a team experienced in managing such situations; a single worker, however experienced, would be likely to be overwhelmed in time by such a case, even if such a patient would remain in a single 1:1 relationship. The patient will be to some extent reassured by being referred to a team with specialist knowledge and experience of the problem. The tasks of resolving what can be resolved, setting limits to further actions and offering sympathy and support may pave the way to more specific treatment attempts. Although efforts to treat have been reported as discouraging (e.g. Astrup, 1984; Winokur,

1977), there is a suggestion that pimozide might be helpful (Ungvari, 1993), and a view that, as the condition appears to be founded in cognitive distortion, cognitive behavioural therapy may help (Caduff, 1995). The age and sparseness of the literature is more reflective of treatment difficulties than useful guidance. In the Melbourne clinic, low-dose atypical antipsychotic medication together with support has been found to offer some relief, but progress is very slow.

CONCLUSIONS

These various disorders of passion and drive are difficult to diagnose early, because the ideas that drive them are on a continuum between health and pathology and the individual sufferer often has initial competence in engaging the sympathy of the person consulted, and yet there are so many advantages for the sufferer and the system in identifying them at the earliest possible stage. Once established, any of them may finally drive the sufferer to violence if the condition is not ameliorated and other methods of attaining the object – be it love, retribution or justice – are unsuccessful. A team with special interest in and experience of managing such difficulties has an advantage; persistence with care, which may include antipsychotic medication, may produce some real change, but there is very little research into therapeutic outcome to inform treatment strategies.

16
Personality disorders

Edited by
Pamela J Taylor

Written by
Conor Duggan
Andrew Hider
Tony Maden
Estelle Moore
Pamela J Taylor

1st edition authors: **Ron Blackburn, John Gunn, Jonathan Hill, David Mawson and Paul Mullen**

Doctors came to see her singly and in consultation, talked much in French, German, and Latin, blamed one another, and prescribed a great variety of medicines for all the diseases known to them, but the simple idea never occurred to any of them that they could not know the disease Natasha was suffering from, as no disease suffered by a live man can be known, for every living person has his own peculiarities and always has his own peculiar, personal, novel, complicated disease, unknown to medicine. (Leo Tolstoy, 'War and Peace')

CONCEPTS OF PERSONALITY DISORDER

The Legal and Political Context

The personality disorders may simultaneously be the most over-used and under-considered collection of diagnoses in the practice of psychiatry and psychology – forensic or otherwise. This is unfortunate, since the application of such a diagnosis exerts a powerful effect on whether the person attracting the label gains any access to treatment and, whether in hospital or custody, probably also on his/her liability to preventive detention in the event of a criminal act. At one extreme, the diagnosis may be misused as an excuse for doing nothing for a person who is suffering and asking for help, sometimes with disastrous consequences for others as well as the primary sufferer. Ms A, in fact suffering from schizophrenia, killed a fellow shopper who was a stranger to her:

Ms A's contact with mental health services … can be divided into two periods: 1992–1998, when she was given a diagnosis of schizophrenia and treated with antipsychotics and followed up by services. And in 2003–2005 when she was given a diagnosis of borderline personality disorder and not given continued treatment or followed up (Healthcare Inspectorate Wales, 2008; p.5, para 1.8).

At the other extreme, in England and Wales, it is arguable that seeming political determination to provide for indefinite secure hospital detention of a subset of people with personality disorder, regardless of their treatability, has now largely succeeded in the form of the Mental Health Act 2007, which applies a wide definition of mental disorder and, with respect to treatment, the criterion only that it should be available (see chapter 3). This, and the blossoming and waning of special 'dangerous and severe personality disorder' (DSPD) services, described further below, followed a single tragic case in England. Here, the facts finally revealed in a report completed in 2000 but not published until 2006 (Francis et al., 2006), hardly seemed to warrant such radical changes. Nevertheless, new and useful thought about personality disorder and treatment activity have emerged from the resultant stimulation and from the English Department of Health's attempts to destigmatise the disorder (National Institute for Mental Health in England, 2003; Duggan, 2011a,b).

Concepts and Diagnoses

The task of diagnosing personality disorder is complicated by the nosological confusion around the whole concept (Mann and Moran, 2000). Buchanan (2005) provided an introduction to problems in the use of categorical diagnosis of personality disorder as grounds for compulsory detention in hospital, together with a prescient warning for clinicians involved in the care and treatment of such patients in the current political climate:

When doctors practice in politically contentious fields, a robust nosology is one defence to the charge that their motives are political.

It is arguable that, masquerading as descriptive psychiatry, personality disorder diagnoses reflect the categorical absolutism of nineteenth century 'moral insanity' (Prichard, 1837; Maudsley, 1885). First steps seem to have been to observe and consolidate a distinction from illness – hence the concept of 'mania without delirium' coined by Pinel in his 1801 *Treatise on Insanity* (translated Davies, 1806). This was followed by recognition of developmental impairments, but in the absence of intellectual disability – in Prichard's terms 'moral insanity', a concept which persisted into the twentieth century:

> *a form of mental derangement in which the intellectual faculties [are uninjured], while the disorder is manifested principally or alone in the state of feelings, temper, or habits... The moral ... principles of the mind ... are depraved or perverted, the power of self-government is lost or greatly impaired... (Prichard, 1837).*

From the perspective of forensic mental health practice, there have been particular questions relating to the concept of agency and, by extension, culpability. Far from being of purely scholastic concern, as categorical diagnoses, personality disorders would seem to be amenable to the legal system's habit of shoehorning criminal behaviour into the categories of 'guilty' or 'not guilty'. The presence of a personality disorder, however, does not share the same relationship with behaviour as, say, the presence of a leg fracture shares a relationship with the ability to walk unaided. Personality disorders, it is arguable, are emergent from normality rather than distinct from it. They are existentially elusive, being significantly dependent on the context in which individuals live. They are interpersonal diagnoses in a way not comparable to other forms of psychiatric classification. Paraphrasing George Vaillant (1987), it is possible to imagine a human being alone on a desert island and suffering from depression, or panic disorder, or schizophrenia, but more difficult to imagine how it would be meaningful to ascribe to such a person a disorder of personality. Even the two main mental disorder classification systems – the *American Diagnostic and Statistical Manual* (*DSM*) and the *International Classification of Diseases* (*ICD*) which still tend to treat these, as other conditions, categorically, emphasize this interactive quality, the *ICD* also acknowledging a dimensional conceptualisation:

> *[personality disorders] comprise deeply ingrained and enduring behaviour patterns, manifesting themselves as inflexible responses to a broad range of personal and social situations. They represent either extreme or significant deviations from the way the average individual in a given culture perceives, thinks, feels and particularly relates to others... They are frequently, but not always, associated with various degrees of subjective distress and problems in social functioning and performance (World Health Organization (WHO), 1992a).*

ICD-10 (WHO, 1992), also makes the requirement that personality disorders, as developmental disorders, must have appeared in childhood or adolescence and persisted into adulthood – any such disorders which arise later must be regarded as conditions of personality change. *DSM-IV* (American Psychiatric Association [APA], 1994), in its multi-axial approach to classification, formally places personality disorders on a separate axis – axis II – not only from illnesses, which generally represent a clear break from health, but also such conditions as substance-related disorders, impulse control disorders and adjustment disorders. Insofar as such distinctions are helpful, this hardly seems an advance on Jaspers' (1923, translated by Hoenig and Hamilton, 1963) earlier, essentially multi-axial separation of organically based conditions (Group I), from the major psychoses (Group II), and from the personality disorders (Group III). In the latter he included 'isolated abnormal reactions that do not arise on the basis of illness, neuroses and neurotic syndromes and abnormal personalities and their development', while acknowledging that 'in Group III the classifications attempted by various investigators show the least agreement'.

Later academics have gone further than acknowledging the struggle for agreement. Kendell (2002), for example, concluded:

> *The historical reasons for regarding personality disorders as fundamentally different from illnesses are being undermined by both clinical and genetic evidence.*

Millon (1996) views axis I disorders as being, essentially, decompensated variants of axis II problems. Many current experts are resigned to the explanatory inadequacy of the atheoretical *DSM-IV*, and look forward to the inclusion of some kind of dimensional classification, allowing personality level dysfunction to be explained in terms of specific traits, such as impulsiveness, as well as in terms of categorical variables (Sperry, 2003). The actual proposals, however, are complex (Shedler et al., 2010 and below).

Such dilemmas are challenging for academics, but they pose serious practical problems for practising forensic clinicians:

> *When relating to the Criminal Justice System, forensic... views need to be expressed in understandable clear language, not theoretical 'psychobabble', the meaning of which is only understood by the initiated (Williams, 1997).*

This is hard when the initiated do not agree the *lingua franca*. The criminal justice system expects its experts to know what they are talking about, so a retreat to nihilism is neither acceptable nor necessary. The diagnostic and classification systems are themselves explicit about the need for caution and caveats in making reference to their guidance in court. *DSM-IV*, for example:

> *When the DSM-IV categories, criteria, and textual descriptions are employed for forensic purposes, there are significant risks that diagnostic*

information will be misused or misunderstood. ... In most situations, the clinical diagnosis of a DSM-IV mental disorder is not sufficient to establish the existence for legal purposes of a 'mental disorder'...

The pertinence of such caution becomes even more apparent when considering individual personality disorders. Both main classification systems go on to subdivide personality disorder into a number of smaller categories, reflecting the main areas of personal and social disruption. This has some face validity, but 'diagnosis' of an individual personality disorder tends to be less reliable than the more general attribution of 'personality disorder' (Bronsich, 1992; Bronsich and Mombour, 1994); even inter-rater reliability may be barely satisfactory (mean kappa 0.56, range 0.26–0.75, APA, 1980; mean kappa 0.41, range 0.00–0.49, Mellsop et al., 1982). Others, while acknowledging the limitations on reliability of diagnosis have also highlighted the problem of excessive focus on observable behaviour rather than core dysfunctions (e.g. Zimmerman, 1994). Then, too, according to Fleiss (1981) and Cicchetti (1994), although the names of personality disorders are similar between *ICD* and *DSM*, the concepts do not quite match. Furthermore, although it could be argued that the extent of so-called comorbidity between these single categories calls into question their validity as discrete entities (see also below), others have argued that important aspects of personality pathology are ignored within the standard classificatory frameworks, for example passive–aggressive or sadistic traits (Westen and Arkowitz-Westen, 1998; Clark, 2007; Clark et al., 1997). A partial response to 'comorbidity of personality disorders', while retaining a categorical approach, has been to consider them as belonging to clusters (Tyrer and Alexander, 1979; Cloninger, 1987). These are

- *Cluster A*, a withdrawn group, avoidant of social contact including paranoid and schizoid personality disorders (*DSM* adds the schizotypal);
- *Cluster B*, a risk-taking irresponsible group, which includes antisocial (*DSM*)/dissocial (*ICD*), borderline (*DSM*)/emotionally unstable (*ICD*) and histrionic personality disorders (*DSM* adds the narcissistic).
- *Cluster C*, an anxious, avoidant, sometimes rigid group includes the avoidant (*DSM*)/anxious (*ICD*), obsessive–compulsive (*DSM*)/anankastic (*ICD*) and dependent personality disorders.

Longitudinal, prospective studies provide limited endorsement for the validity of individual personality disorder types. Indeed, while borderline personality disorder (BPD) may be a relatively robust concept, some disorders, such as schizotypal, seem so closely to predict onset of illness that it may be better to consider them almost as a *forme fruste* of the illness (McGlashan, 1983).

An alternative approach is to consider personality disorders as statistical extremes on trait dimensions. Concepts of extraversion and neuroticism, and, to a lesser degree, psychoticism have been shown to be robust dimensional

measures (Eysenck and Eysenck, 1975; Weinryb et al., 1992), although others advocate an overlapping five factor model of personality: neuroticism–stability; extraversion–introversion; agreeableness–antagonism; conscientiousness–lack of self-discipline; openness to experience–rigidity (John, 1990; Costa and McCrae, 1992a; McCrae and Costa, 1996). Some would argue further, however, that the hallmark of disorder here is not necessarily extremes *per se*, but rather the inability to adapt adequately to the interpersonal environment (e.g. Leary, 1957; Blackburn 1998).

In work with offender patients, psychopathy has become a widely used concept (Hare, 1980, 2003), building on characteristics common to the people in Cleckley's (1976) clinical stories. Psychopathy in these terms overlaps, but is not precisely coterminous with, antisocial personality disorder (Hart and Hare, 1989). While Hare and his team initially evidenced a two-factor model (Hare et al., 1990), others have found a three-factor model better fits the picture (Cooke and Michie, 1997), and the Hare group has progressed to a '2 factor, 4 facet' model (Neumann et al., 2007). There is, however, agreement on the core factor being affective and empathic impairment. Impulsive behavioural style is also broadly agreed, with Cooke and Michie adding grandiose and deceitful style as the third factor, although it may be these aspects which show more variation across cultures (Cooke and Michie, 1999). The concept and measurement of psychopathy undoubtedly have some research evidence basis, but the Cleckley–Hare list of items making up PCL-R also reflects another important issue – the nature of the countertransference between the person with the presumed disorder and the raters. A person described as glib and superficially charming, with a grandiose sense of self-worth, given to pathological lying, lacking sincerity, remorse or guilt for, say, promiscuous sexual behaviour and many types of offence – to take just seven of the potentially 20 negative attributes – is unlikely to attract caring clinicians. Bowers (2002) studied nursing staff attitudes to working with people with personality disorder in a high security hospital. The characteristics of patients who they labelled, in confidence, as 'evil' or 'monstrous' were: their index offence had been serious violence against vulnerable victims; it had been planned in advance and often involved torture; they had not been abused as children; they showed no remorse and refused treatment, *but* they appeared to be nice people. Bowers went on to show that it was not impossible for staff to work effectively with such people, but that 'moral commitment' and '[therapeutic] beliefs about the disorder' were essential.

In clinical practice, the tendency towards categorical classification seems almost inescapable – even dimensional measures, such as that of psychopathy, tend to be used in a categorical way, so that, for example, the person 'has psychopathy', or not, as the case may be. According to Shedler et al. (2010), the 5th edition of the American *DSM* is proposing to try combining five clinical personality 'prototypes' – antisocial/psychopathic, avoidant, border-line, obsessive–compulsive and schizotypal – with six dimensions: (1) negative emotionality, which includes 'facets' of depression, anxiety, shame and guilt; (2) intro-version, including withdrawal from social interaction; (3) antagonism, including exaggerated sense of self-impor-tance; (4) disinhibition and impulsivity; (5) compulsivity, including perfectionism and rigidity; and (6) schizotypy, which includes odd perceptions and beliefs; Livesley (2012) correctly notes a sixth prototype, narcissistic. Shedler and Westen (2004a) have argued for more prototypes and they propose that dimensional measures should be confined to characteristics such as severity. In forensic mental health practice, we generally practise in this way already – using some simple shorthand category for brief communica-tions, but in any serious assessment incorporating dimen-sional approaches.

The *DSM-5* proposal has features in common with Livesley's (2007a) conceptualisation, but, as one comes to expect in this field, is not quite the same, and Livesley (2012) himself sets out proper concerns about the *DSM-5* proposal neither maintaining continuity with *DSM-IV* – the *DSM-5* prototypes carry the same names as *DSM-IV* classes but are different – nor becoming evidence based. *ICD-11* may do better. Duggan (2011b) highlights some of the differences more specific to antisocial personality disorder (ASPD). Livesley suggests three general features which underpin all personality disorder, with both social aetiological and treatment implications: (a) failure to develop attachment or intimacy in interpersonal relation-ships; (b) failure to behave pro-socially so that one can be part of a group; and (c) failure to achieve a coherent sense of self. He also subscribes to four higher order factors, con-stituting the secondary domains. Mulder and Joyce (1997) named them as the 'four As': the *antisocial* (the equivalent of cluster B), the *asthenic* (anxious dependent as in cluster C *and* those with emotional dysregulation as in borderline personality disorder), the *asocial* (those prone to social withdrawal as in cluster C *and* A) and the anankastic (people with obsessive–compulsive traits as in cluster C, although some would create an additional cluster, cluster D for them). Livesley simply uses slightly different termi-nology here, and regards these four factors, essentially phenotypes, as the core types which are explained by genetic and organic factors (Livesley et al., 1998; Livesley, 2007b), although he also identifies 30 primary traits which make up the main four (Livesley, 2005). This system, which may sound rather complicated in narrative, is summarised in table 16.1.

This domain-based conceptualisation of personality dis-order has a number of advantages for the clinician and for the prospective patient. Empirically derived, they are more likely to be valid than operational definitions drawn up by commit-tee. It allows for potentially greater accuracy in identifying the core problems by emphasizing interpersonal difficulties

Table 16.1 Secondary domains of personality disorder and their components (the Mulder and Joyce [1997] nomenclature is given in brackets). (After Livesley, 2007a)

Secondary domain	Primary trait
Dissocial behaviour (*Antisocial*)	Narcissism
	Exploitativeness
	Sadism
	Conduct problems
	Hostile-dominance
	Sensation seeking
	Impulsivity
	Suspiciousness
	Egocentrism
Emotional dysregulation (*Asthenic*)	Anxiousness
	Emotional reactivity
	Emotional intensity
	Pessimistic anhedonia
	Submissiveness
	Insecure attachment
	Social apprehensiveness
	Need for approval
	Cognitive dysregulation
	Oppositional
	Self-harming acts
	Self-harming ideas
Inhibitedness (*Asocial*)	Low affiliation
	Avoidant attachment
	Attachment need
	Inhibited sexuality
	Self-containment
	Inhibited emotional expression
	Lack of empathy
Compulsivity (*Anankastic*)	Orderliness
	Conscientiousness

over deviant acts and encourages flexibility in identifying disorders of personality through the two-level approach of first identifying – or not – the three general features and then screening for detail in the secondary domains.

PERSONALITY DISORDER ASSESSMENT TOOLS

Broadly, instruments used for the assessment of per-sonality and its disorders are founded in two principal approaches – the structured clinical interview – with the patient and/or with informants – and the self report questionnaire. In line with the conceptual approaches to personality disorder, the assessment instruments may be further characterised by whether they map on to the descriptive classifications of *DSM-IV-TR* or *ICD-10* or whether they are trait-based and dimensional. Here, we present a guide to some of the main assessment tools rather than a comprehensive overview; further informa-tion may be found in specialist books, such as Part 3 of Livesley's (2001) *Handbook of Personality Disorders*.

Among clinicians, however, these conventional tools are commonly seen as being of limited value in clinical practice; they perceive direct questions as being much less useful in assessing personality disorder than either listening to patient narratives about their lives and drawing inferences about repeating patterns and/or observing a patient's behaviour with him/her in the consulting room (Westen, 1997). Accordingly, Westen and others devised a further method of systematising assessment, which provides clinicians with 200 cards, each of which provides a statement such as 'living arrangements are chaotic and unstable' or 'tends to be passive and unassertive' which they have to sort according to their experience of the patient (Westen and Shedler, 1999; Shedler and Westen, 2004b; Westen and Muderrisoglu, 2006). The Operationalized Psychodynamic Diagnostic system (OPD Task Force, 2008), described more fully below, also emphasises the importance of being able to assess relational capacities and interactions.

Interview Schedules Yielding a Diagnostic Perspective on Personality Disorder

Diagnostically based interviews guide the clinician through a structured set of questions designed to gather information from the patient, relevant to his or her concordance with the categorical criteria of *DSM-IV-TR* and/or *ICD-10*. Such measures include the Structured Clinical Interview for *DSM-IV* Axis II Personality Disorder (SCID-II, First et al., 1997) and the International Personality Disorder Examination (IPDE, Loranger et al., 1995, 1999a). The latter was developed at the request of the WHO and the USA National Institute of Health to improve international reliability in diagnoses. Its items are distributed under six categories (work, self, interpersonal relationships, affects, reality testing and impulse control). It is designed to be rated by experienced clinicians trained in its use, and to take account of information about age of onset and duration of behaviour from informants as well as the individual under assessment. Both inter-rater (agreement between two raters at any one time) and test–retest reliability (the extent to which the measure yields the same results over time, given the same level of disorder) vary with personality disorder type, but for any specific personality disorder are acceptable (kappas: 0.7 and 0.63 respectively; Loranger et al., 1994, 1997). An important determinant of reliability lies in clinical experience and training, so, given the considerable impact that the results of such assessments may have on the present and future care of the person being assessed, it is arguable that these measures should only be used by appropriately trained clinicians, assiduously following the guidance in the manuals. When presenting evidence based on such measures in the court, clinicians should be prepared to set out their level of expertise for using any instrument cited and have a good knowledge of its reliability and validity.

The other important indicator of a test's usefulness is its validity – whether it measures that which it is purporting to measure. Broadly, personality disorder interviews show poor convergent validity (that is, it is not possible to say with confidence that the same person would receive the same diagnosis when assessed using different measures). A review of the literature in this area concludes that problems of validity present an overwhelming foil to the use of a truly scientific nosology in the area of personality disorder.

Until a revised conceptualization of personality disorders provides a firmer basis on which to develop convergent assessment instruments, personality disorder research will remain fragmentary because instrument-based findings will be the rule rather than the exception (Clark and Harrison, 2001).

Trait-Based Interviews of Pathological Personality

Loranger (1999b) observed that the switch from categories to dimensions improved reliability of his measure. UK based clinicians also use Tyrer's Personality Assessment Schedule (PAS, Tyrer, 2000), which yields scores on a number of pathological traits thought to be subordinate to the DSM-IV and ICD-10 criteria. Cluster analytic techniques are used to reduce 24 traits into five higher order personality styles or dimensions. A specific advantage of the PAS is its ability to yield not only trait-based and dimensional scores, but also to map such scores onto existing diagnostic criteria. Further, the PAS also provides a measure of severity as a function of the number of criteria the person meets.

The advantage of dimensional measures is that they are generally more anchored in theory about the aetiology of disorders of personality. This, coupled with their ability to delineate homogeneous trait structures, gives these measures greater utility in research, whether organically (e.g. see chapters 8 and 12) or behaviourally based (see also Gray et al., 2003). Nonetheless, clinicians should be aware that any attempt to isolate traits and measure them as if unpolluted by other psychological constructs is problematic. In the case of the PCL-R, for example, scores on the 'affective/interpersonal dimension' might, in some cases, be as well explained by schizophrenia as psychopathy *per se*.

Diagnostic Questionnaires for Personality Disorders

The widespread use of questionnaires, often in the context of legal situations such as Mental Health Review Tribunals, has tended to foster an acceptance of the reliability and validity of these instruments which outstrips the scientific data. This is unsurprising, given that they are easy to use and, in providing a quickly obtainable quantitative estimate of personality function or dysfunction, they seem to add objectivity to assessment reports. Well known examples include the Millon Clinical Multiaxial Inventory, 3rd Edition (MCMI-III™, Millon, 2009), the Minnesota Multiphasic Personality Inventory Personality Disorder Scales (MMPI-II-PD, Morey et al., 1985), the Personality Assessment Inventory (PAI, Morey, 1991) and the Personality Disorder Questionnaire 4+ (PDQ4+ Hyler, 1994; Hyler et al., 1990). Of these, the MCMI-III purports to assess both DSM-IV categories and also patients' overall personality profile based on Millon's own, evolutionary based, theory of general psychopathology. The MMPI-PD and PAI are confined to the assessment of the categorical descriptors of DSM-IV. The PDQ4+ is a useful screening tool among prisoners (Davidson et al., 2001).

Reliability indicators for these tests are, in the main, measures of internal consistency (i.e. the strength of correlation between different items designed to measure the same trait or category) rather than inter-rater or test–retest reliability (see Rogers, 2001 for an extended discussion of such psychometric properties). This may account for the extent to which test scores vary over time for the same person. In the case of personality variables, a high level of temporal stability should be expected, given the definition and theory of personality disorder as an enduring state.

In terms of validity, the self-report measures are as prone to the problems just described in relation to structured interviews and, indeed, have commonly been validated against them (e.g. Hyler et al., 1990). In general, however, self-report measures show, at best, modest convergent validity between each other (Livesley, 2001). Further, their discriminant validity tends to be poor, and they generate too many false positives (Zimmerman, 1994 provides useful reflections on these issues, and limitations of other approaches too). The limitations of self-report tests are perhaps unsurprising as, after all, they are essentially measures of 'meta-function', an individual's own appraisal of his/her personality. They must assume that individuals are accurate in their self-perception, a situation ameliorated somewhat by the presence of scales within the measures which purport to measure the extent to which respondents adopt a self-abasing or 'desirable'/'faking good' pattern of response. It is these 'validity indices' which seem to have specific relevance to forensic practice, in particular in the detection of symptom dissimulation. There is a small research literature around the use of the MCMI-III for this purpose (e.g. Schoenberg, 2003).

For the clinician, the most important thing to remember is that, while self-report measures have their place, they function best as screening instruments, and should not be used in isolation as diagnostic instruments. Nevertheless, they have an important role to play in the process of case formulation and, indeed, Millon has developed a 'personalized psychotherapy' based on appropriate clinical responses to psychological presentations as characterized by high scores on the various subscales of the MCMI-III (Millon and Grossman, 2007).

Trait-Based Non-Diagnostic Questionnaires About Personality

Experimental psychology has an extensive history of developing measures to quantify 'latent traits' – underlying psychological variables which are relatively fixed and which underpin behaviour, cognition and emotion, for example, the Eysenck Personality Questionnaire (EPQ, Eysenck and Eysenck, 1969, 1975). This yields three dimensions (extraversion, neuroticism and psychoticism), but, according to current consensus, there are five superordinate personality dimensions which act as a psychological substrate to all human trait like variables (McCrae and Costa, 1987). Assessments of these are most commonly used in *non-clinical* environments, such as in personnel recruitment, with the most commonly used measure being the NEO Five Factor Inventory (NEO FFI), the five factors being neuroticism, extraversion, openness to experience, agreeableness and conscientiousness; the revised version is the NEO PI-R (Costa and McCrae, 1992b), while dimensions on instruments such as the Omnibus Personality (OMNI) and Personality Disorder (OMNI-IV) inventories (Loranger, 2001) have been adapted for both non-clinical and clinical purposes. Such inventories may be more widely used in the future, particularly with the move towards *DSM-V* combining dimensional and categorical approaches (Widiger and Samuel, 2005).

Assessments of Specific Domains of Personality Pathology

A number of assessment tools follow the principles of structure or administration just described, but focus on specific domains of personality pathology, for example the PCL-R (Hare, 2003) or the Schizotypal Personality Questionnaire (SPQ, Raine, 1991). In forensic mental health settings, such tools are extensively used in offender assessment as an aid to delineating social function and making links between it and risk of further social breakdown, including offending. The standardised Special Hospitals Assessment of Personality and Socialisation battery (SHAPS, Blackburn, 1986), for instance, has been used to correlate particular aspects of personality pathology with re-offending risk (Craig et al., 2006), whereas the PCL-R has been used as a risk assessment in itself (see also chapter 22). The latter, in its short form, is even incorporated into the best known structured professional judgment approach to risk assessment – the 20-item Historical/Clinical Risk Assessment (HCR-20, Webster et al., 1997), although there is evidence that it adds little to the risk assessment function here (Douglas et al., 1999).

Beyond Self-Assessment of Personality

Klonsky et al. (2002), in a review of the literature examining concordance between self-report and informant report of personality disorder, found that concordance was highest in the case of those personality disorders with which people most commonly present to forensic psychiatrists – the cluster B disorders. Nevertheless, given the potential legal and clinical implications of a diagnosis of personality disorder, reliance on either a single clinical interview and/or a self-rating schedule would be indefensible. Milton (2000), reporting on the results of a postal survey into assessment practice in inpatient forensic psychiatric facilities in the UK, calls for the establishment of a common set of standardised personality assessment instruments to be used within them, so that diagnostic inconsistency may be minimised. While it would be difficult from a scientific perspective to endorse a particular package of specific instruments, it is surely a sound principle to have a package which incorporates within it a mix of self-report, interview data and external observations from a range of people who have been socially and/or clinically involved with the person over time.

Measures of personality pathology which rely on informant information include the Standardized Assessment of Personality (SAP) (Pilgrim and Mann, 1990; Pilgrim et al., 1993), the best known of these in the UK, drawing on an interview with a relative or close friend of the person being assessed. For offender-patients, the Chart of Interpersonal Relations in Closed Living Environments (CIRCLE) (Blackburn and Renwick, 1996) was developed for use in a hospital inpatient setting, and relies on staff perceptions of the patient. Both these instruments may be used to create *ICD/DSM* style classifications. The CIRCLE may also have a specific role in assisting assessment of risk of inpatient violence (Doyle and Dolan, 2006a,b), and has, on occasion, been used as a self-report measure (Milton et al., 2005).

Such assessments lead to a more detailed consideration of assessments of interpersonal function. Some are explicitly derived from the original interpersonal theories of Stack Sullivan (1953) and Leary (1957) and, in a more recent development, from psychoanalytic theory. They all yield a circumplex picture which allows clinicians to describe the overall interpersonal functioning of patients on more than one bipolar dimension (e.g. dominance–submissiveness), with structured narrative formulations also encouraged in the psychodynamic model. Of the former, the Inventory of Interpersonal Problems (IIP, Horowitz et al., 1988) may be particularly useful in treatment planning for improving social functioning. The CIRCLE has been widely used in this spirit with offender patients in the UK.

The Operational Psychodynamic Diagnostics system (OPD, OPD Task-Force, 2001, 2008) measures more than personality and its disorders, and is, again, used particularly as a treatment aid. Preliminary ratings can be made on the basis of a 1–2 hour guided interview along four psychodynamically relevant axes: axis I experience of illness and pre-requisites for treatment; axis II interpersonal relations; axis III inner conflicts; axis IV personality structure. A fifth axis maps on to *ICD/DSM*. Axis I allows for identification of personal and social network strengths as well as prioritising areas for treatment. The 2008 edition of the manual incorporates a specific module for offender-patients. The interpersonal axis is exceptionally useful in clinical practice, for helping staff identify countertransference issues which could interfere with good management or treatment, and to develop an effective language for communicating the four perspectives of patient experience: how the patient *habitually* experiences him/herself, how s/he *habitually* experiences others, how others, including the therapist, *habitually* experience the patient and how the others, including the therapist, *habitually* experience themselves when relating to the patient. The seven basic internal conflicts are harder to rate, as, almost by definition, an offender-patient has difficulty in internalising conflict, and so there is a risk of 'floor effects'. The seven are: dependence v. autonomy; submission v. control; desire for care v. autarchy; conflicts of self-value; guilt conflicts; oedipal sexual conflicts; identity conflicts. On the personality structure axis, four levels are recognised – from well to poorly integrated – on six categories: self-perception; self-regulation; defence; object perception; communication; and bonding. Reliability is good under research conditions and satisfactory under clinical conditions; criterion, construct, concordant and predictive validity have been found to be acceptable in several studies (Cierpka et al., 2007).

HOW COMMON ARE DISORDERS OF PERSONALITY?

Personality disorders are common in the general population. To our knowledge, there are three community-based epidemiological surveys of the prevalence of the full range of recognised personality disorders; the communities from which the samples were drawn differ, and the prevalence figures differ. In Norway, Torgersen et al. (2001) drew a random sample of 3,590 18–65 year olds from the National Register of Oslo. After attrition because of death, illness, refusal, language problems and one or two other smaller groups of reasons for non-inclusion, 2,053 people were interviewed, using the SCID (see above), leaving a sample slightly biased towards women, older people and outer city dwellers. A total of 13.4% had at least one personality disorder of any kind; the most common was avoidant personality disorder (5%), followed by paranoid personality disorder (2.4%). The other two studies were household surveys rather than true community samples, but substantial, and also used standardised interviews. In the USA, Samuels et al. (2002) used IPDE data on a subset of 742 individuals aged 34–94 from the Baltimore

Epidemiologic Catchment Area follow-up survey (Eaton et al., 1997). Sub-sampling reasons are not entirely clear, but the sex and ethnic distribution of the group included in the study was apparently similar to the parent cohort, although younger. Overall, 9% had any personality disorder, with the most common being antisocial personality disorder (4.1%), and the next avoidant (1.8%). This study had the advantage of informant interviews to supplement the primary participant interviews. For England, Wales and Scotland, Coid et al. (2006) drew from the British National Survey of Psychiatric Morbidity (Singleton et al., 2001) of 8,886 people aged 16–74 completing a computer assisted screening interview. The sample included in the personality disorder study was of 626 people who had completed a face to face interview, using the SCID-II, as well as the computer screening. Selection was complex, but transparent, and differences from the parent cohort were allowed for in analysis. Here, just 4.4% had any personality disorder; obsessive–compulsive personality disorder was the most common of the individual disorders (1.9%), with no other single personality disorder exceeding a prevalence of 1%.

Questions have been raised as to whether prevalence of personality disorder varies according to ethnic group. McGilloway et al. (2010) conducted a systematic literature review but found little information. As would be expected from the observations on the general state of the epidemiology, this is hardly surprising, but a potentially interesting possibility emerged – that 'black', but not Hispanic nor Asian groups, may be less likely to attract a personality disorder diagnosis than 'white' groups, mainly evident in UK studies, and mainly in those which rely on case note data. The Baltimore, Samuels et al. (2002) study samples, described above, despite a roughly 60:40 white:black distribution, did not allow for ethnicity in their calculations. Not quite 3% of the sample was non-white in the interview based Coid et al. (2006) study in the UK, and no difference in personality disorder distribution was found. The authors argue that the apparently lower prevalence of personality disorder among black groups in some studies may be due to reliance on case record analysis rather than structured interviews. They did not raise the more serious issue of the impact of immigration, either for its possible selection bias with respect to mental disorders or, of particular relevance to personality disorder diagnoses, the likelihood of being unable to obtain good informant histories. It would be interesting indeed if 'black' group membership were truly a protective factor against personality disorder.

The epidemiology of antisocial personality disorder has been more extensively studied, and ably reviewed by Moran (1999). His monograph shows how a range of factors influenced the community-based figures produced to that date, with higher figures for prevalence being found before the publication of *DSM-III* than after. Dohrenwend and Dohrenwend (1982) calculated a median prevalence

of 4.8%, but with a considerable range; Merikangas and Weissman (1986) put this between 0.5 and 9.4%. About half of the post *DSM-III* studies yielded a rate of under 1%, with the highest rate given as 3.7%. Moran then goes on to review prevalence figures in various treated populations, from general practitioner surveys, where the prevalence is higher, through general hospital settings, with a still higher prevalence, to specialist forensic hospitals and prisons with the highest prevalence figures.

CLINICAL ASSESSMENT AND ENGAGEMENT IN PRACTICE

The Process of Clinical Assessment of Personality Disorder

Underpinning the assessment process in clinical forensic practice is the principle that, using a combination of evidence based findings and practical experience, the scientist-practitioner is aiming to achieve the best fit between the needs of each individual who is referred and treatment. Interventions are necessarily multi-modal in the case of personality disorder (Taylor, 2006b), and thus the quality of the final package is dependent on the quality of the assessment phase of intervention. This requires description of the problems and their impacts, a formulation of what maintains or escalates them, and strategies for introducing change. The precise objectives of assessment will vary by setting and purpose, but the ultimate goal is to gather good enough information for a sound decision on readiness for treatment and prioritising its elements. As far as possible, the process should leave the individual under assessment feeling satisfied if not better for the exchange, whatever the outcome. In some circumstances, even simply helping such a person towards a sensitive understanding of his/her difficulties may be an important step forward. An emergency room psychiatric team in New York described how the provision of a framework for understanding chaotic interpersonal lives enhanced the readiness of outpatients with personality disorder to comply with suggested interventions (Sneed et al., 2003). Where treatment is likely to follow, the assessment process should facilitate preliminary engagement and preparation for interventions which will increase wellbeing and reduce risk.

As just described, clinical and/or informant interview, scrutiny of records and self-report measures are all components of assessment, and early stages of assessment may include overcoming the reluctance of the patient to participate in one or more elements of the process. Tyrer (2000a) has proposed the notion of severity of personality disorder as useful in forensic psychiatry, because it distinguishes between subgroups of people with disorders with different levels of impact on self and others, and complementary differences in needs. The concept of severity also links to issues around comorbidity, whether in terms of meeting criteria for more than one personality disorder or pathology in more than one trait, or in cases where the personality disorder is complicated by having other developmental conditions or illnesses as well. Outcome in personality disorder depends in part on severity: the more ingrained and pervasive maladaptive traits are, the worse the prognosis (Stone, 1993). Tyrer and Johnson (1996) delineate a procedure for reflecting levels of severity of disorder categories, including: no personality abnormality; sub-threshold; 'simple' personality disorder (one or more personality disorders, same cluster); complex personality disorder (two or more, different clusters), and 'severe' (two or more personality disorders from different clusters creating 'gross societal disturbance'). Tyrer's (2000b) criteria for gross societal disturbance are evidence of: (1) personality disturbance that has influenced a wider group than family and friends; (2) the creation of significant problems to at least 50 other individuals; and (3) threat created by the pattern of disturbance, typically through aggressive impulses, irresponsibility that puts others at risk, outbursts of anger and violence, and insensitivity to social norms.

Given that personality disorder is associated with relationship breakdown that ranges from less than optimal to abusive, highly toxic and overtly dangerous, it is not surprising that assessment of personality disorder, dependent as it is on the formation of some kind of interpersonal alliance or collaboration, poses particular challenges for clinicians undertaking this task. Clinical assessment is a two-way process, including how the (potential) patient experiences the assessor and how the assessor experiences the (potential) patient, and this is nested within the wider culture and ideology of the service. It is always helpful to document the stated reasons for the assessment, and to re-visit these at the point of summary, formulation and recommendation.

Extreme poverty in level of collaboration is rare, even in forensic clinical services (Moore and Gudjonsson, 2002), but occasionally the interpersonal difficulties even with a highly trained clinician may be so challenging that it is impossible to get clarity on the nature of the disorder. Factors which are associated with such difficulties include co-existing axis I disorder, or a history of previous assessments of interventions that were experienced as alienating and unhelpful. Probing questions or prompts to self-reflection may elicit hostility, evasion, sometimes departure, and/or failure to elaborate beyond 'don't know'. This may be anticipated and the order of the problem reduced to some extent if the clinician takes responsibility for transparently explaining the context for the assessment and its possible outcomes, and if time can be set aside to allow the interviewee to respond at his/her own pace. A preliminary assessment of this kind may take 3 to 4 hours of 1:1 work, before starting with informant interviews and other data-gathering. 'Collaborative assessment' (Ben-Porath, 2004), an interview process in which the patient is actively enlisted to participate, is likely to pay dividends in the direction of solidifying commitment to suggested treatments.

Structuring the Clinical Approach in Assessment Interviews for Personality Disorder

As recommended in the first edition of this book, assessment of personality disorder – and indeed other disorders too – in a forensic mental health context is more usefully concerned with symptoms and traits than with diagnostic categories. Schotte (2002) took up this theme when considering borderline personality disorder, regarding the classificatory system criteria as just the first tier of description. The second tier would then identify the relevant physical and psychological components, linking to a theoretical frame of reference and thus underpinning theoretically driven treatments. It is helpful to consider the symptom tier within five over-arching fields, all in the context of the interviewee's life history, including:

1. *Affect*: what are the dominant emotions? What is the level of arousal in relation to events as told?
2. *Cognition*: what thoughts/beliefs seem to be underpinning the actions described? What thinking styles are in evidence (e.g. justifications for offending)? What are the beliefs about the world, self and others, and what rules has the person generated (consciously or otherwise) to compensate for these enduring beliefs (schema)?
3. *Behavioural disorder*: what is the range and scope of problem/offending behaviours? What is the occupational history? Is impulsivity a problem? What seem to be the antecedents to significant events? What is the nature of the discrepancies between the interviewee's account of events and that of others? Who were witnesses, and what, if any, might be their biases?
4. *Interpersonal functioning*: to whom does/has the interviewee relate(d) and with what success? (See further below.) How does s/he view her/himself? How does s/he view others? What is her/his capacity to sustain relationships? What actions have been taken at times of relationship crisis in the past?
5. *Insight*: to what extent (if at all) does the interviewee recognise that there are problems, and to what or to whom are they attributed?

Motivation for change is another important issue for early assessment. It is not a static predictor of successful engagement, or indeed, in its initial absence, of unsuccessful engagement. Rather, it is best conceptualised as a potentially changeable state of readiness or eagerness to change (Sainsbury et al., 2004), which may be affected by other personal characteristics. Motivation to engage in interview (and subsequent treatment) is likely, for example, to be influenced by 'insight'. David (1990) describes three components to insight, including: acknowledgement/recognition of mental illness, treatment compliance and the readiness/ability to re-label unusual mental events as pathological. He generated his concepts through research with people who had schizophrenia, and they do not always map precisely onto personality disturbance as the latter is, almost by definition, 'egosyntonic' (perceived as compatible with the self-image) rather than 'dystonic', or alien to it. Often, patients experience the system and the staff as biased and malevolent, and locate problems 'in' others rather than in their encounters, which renders others as difficult to trust. Patients with personality disorder, therefore, tend not to share the view of (significant) others about how best to describe or categorise their experiences, or may be unable to conceptualise their problems due to cognitive constraints, such as emotional processing deficits (Blair and Frith, 2000). In these circumstances, the primary objective of the assessor must shift from assessment of the personality disorder *per se* to exploration of this process, and subsequent formulation of what is likely to create future impasses, together with possible strategies for resolving these.

The measurement of stage or readiness for change can be a useful proxy for treatability, particularly if resources are scarce (Kosky and Thorne, 2001). If patients with personality disorder are not in a position to commit to a course of treatment it is likely that problems will escalate if staff proceed regardless. Stone (2003) notes that, for people with personality disorder, the particular combination of opposition to internal change with unrelenting insistence on the need for 'external change' is typically fatal to any hopes for psychotherapeutic benefit.

In a clinical context, then, a basic aim of the diagnostic evaluation is to obtain valid information that leads to a constructive conceptual framework, or case formulation, in which interventions are understood, selected and implemented (Schotte, 2002). The impact of personality disorder will require further articulation through specific review of the interviewee's interpersonal relationships over a reasonable period of time (Van-Velzen and Emmelkamp, 1996). What is a reasonable period of time? Bateman and Fonagy (2006) recommend 5 years. With whom are the important past and current relationships? What are the connections between these and the problems the interviewee or others describe? It is important, for example, to note if suicide attempts are linked in time to relationship break-ups. In their practical guide to Mentalization Based Therapy (MBT), Bateman and Fonagy (2006) suggest that clinicians characterise the interviewees' relationships according to their form, the interpersonal processes they entail, any changes that are desired in the relationship, and the specific behaviours such changes may require. Underpinning the questions is the framework that 'normal' relationship representations are flexible, stable and balanced, distinguishing them from less healthy relationships which are 'centralised' or 'distributed' and less stable, distancing or self-focused and inflexible.

A number of diagnostic systems, particularly those with a history of influence within the dynamic–analytic tradition, such as the OPD described above, employ the notion of stable patterns in relationships. Research indicates that these are linked with (early) attachment experiences (Allen, 2001). Patients with borderline personality disorder are identified as insecure, preoccupied and fearful in their relationships (Gunderson, 1996). It is essential, and inevitable, that the attachment relationship is stimulated in treatment. When this occurs, the patient's mental capacities are likely to become subsumed by over-arousal, and a reduction in 'mentalisation' (see below) ensues. Thus, clinicians are alerted to repetition of identified patterns through their own encounters with the patient. The task at the assessment stage is to describe and document such patterns. The OPD system has refined a useful method for expressing such patterns in a formal but coherent way. The assessor is asked to rate '*time and again*':

(1) The patient experiences her/himself in such a way that s/he is......;
(2) The assessor experiences the patient in such a way that s/he is......;
(3) The patient experiences others in such a way that......;
(4) The assessor experiences him/herself in the relationship with the patient in such a way that......'.

Thirty options are available for the assessor to fill those gaps and frame the experience (e.g. 'much admiring and idealising', 'rejecting', 'self-justifying', 'cutting him/herself off').

Case Formulation

It could be argued that the most crucial component of the entire assessment process is the formulation of the problem(s) within a framework that makes sense to the patient and referrer (court, clinical team, outside agency). Lengthy psychiatric reports usually contain detailed description and may only include general recommendations during the early stages of alliance with the patient, because much has yet to unfold. Unless the information is clearly summarised, however, and integrated at the end of such a report, the potential value of the assessment may be undermined, particularly as a 'baseline' document underpinning a pathway of treatment.

Formulation constitutes the integration within a theoretical framework of information pertinent to the potential treatment of the problem. What factors (probably) gave rise to the disorder? What factors are currently maintaining it? – this is the opportunity to describe the adverse factors in the patient's social context. What factors seem to improve things for him/her? What factors exacerbate the problems? What among such factors could be changed;

how might this be evaluated, and to what extent might this be associated with a reduction in offending? It is at the formulation stage that the strengths of the individual, and the frequency and duration of previous periods of comparative wellbeing/less toxic inter-relationships may be highlighted as well as the difficulties. The former are likely to serve a protective function against deterioration and/or future offending, and may present obvious starting places for interventions that will be most tolerable for the patient.

The outline of what such an assessment should achieve is summarised in table 16.2. This could be extended to take a specific model of intervention into account. As a precursor to dialectical behaviour therapy (DBT), for example, the therapist might focus on examples of interpersonal effectiveness, skills deficits, and emotion dysregulation in more detail. For mentalisation based therapy (MBT), the emphasis would be on capacity for perceiving and interpreting behaviour as conjoined with intentional mental states (Bateman and Fonagy, 2006).

CAUSES AND EXPLANATIONS OF PERSONALITY DISORDERS

Introduction to Genetic and Developmental Factors

Our emphasis on the interpersonal and interactive in assessing personality applies as strongly to considerations of its development. The basic substrate of a person may be a collection of genes and genetically programmed physical structures but, before as well as after birth, the environment has an effect of varying degrees on whether, when and how physical characteristics present, and both primary and developing physical characteristics determine aspects of whether, when and how the environment has its impact. Development is a constant cycle

of 'recognition', response, adjustment, re-evaluation and re-adjustment. So long as an individual remains healthy, even though this process may slow, it continues. In general, development is simultaneously at its most active and most vulnerable during the earlier phases of life, and this is certainly true of personality. Even newborn infants have been shown to have distinctive temperamental traits (Thomas et al., 1963; Thomas et al., 1970). Qualities in parenting have an effect on infants, but the infant's traits also have an effect on how the parents – and others – respond (Thomas and Chess, 1984).

The difficulties outlined in conceptualising and diagnosing personality disorder also apply to efforts to understand how abnormal personalities emerge. The literature, which vacillates between categorical diagnoses and dimensional traits and, indeed, antisocial behaviour not amounting to personality disorder, has barely tackled the complexity of combining the approaches in aetiological studies, although Livesley has been prominent in trying to formulate a way to do so (Livesley et al., 1998; Livesley, 2005; Livesley, 2008). Most research which is relevant for forensic mental health clinicians, however, focuses on antisocial personality disorder (ASPD) specifically, or referring only to personality disorder more broadly, or to psychopathy, a construct defined by a threshold score on the PCL-R, but with the chosen cut-off varying in part according to whether studies are from Europe or the USA. These various labels do not necessarily reflect states which are co-terminous or even meaningful.

For an understanding of social and genetic influences, we refer readers to chapters 7 and 8, although both emphasise antisocial behaviour rather than antisocial personality disorder *per se*. As the antisocial behaviour to which they refer is a distinguishing feature of the people under study, the antisocial characteristics of these people were, by definition, different in nature, degree or both from those of the general population, but that does not

Table 16.2   Steps in forensic–clinical assessment of personality disorder

• Document reasons for referral
• Explain rationale and context for assessment
• Explain possible outcomes/implications of the findings
• Prepare from (medical) records: history of problems, their extent, range, duration
• List and date sources of information relating to historical events
• Diagnose axis I disorders (illnesses) where present
• Interview to describe impacts of axis II personality disorders according to: affect, cognition, actions, interpersonal functioning, insight, motivation (for treatment), readiness for change
• Interview to focus on relationship history: patterns in past and current relationships, describe attachments, significant events, critical periods
• Summarise and FORMULATE: history, personal background and antecedents (to offending), what motivates the person to behave pro/antisocially, with/without regard for others, what appears to have moderated these actions in the past; what could bring about desired change (i.e. positive increases in wellbeing and risk reduction)
• Recommend specific next steps/estimate a pathway of intervention
• Discuss the formulation with the patient and elicit feedback (which may lead to its revision)

necessarily mean they had antisocial personality disorder. The association between antisocial personality disorder and antisocial behaviour of a nature or degree that leads to imprisonment is very high (Singleton et al., 1998a), but not absolute. Thus, any numerical extrapolations from strength of relationship between genetic and environmental contribution to antisocial behaviour on to antisocial personality disorder must be made with caution, but the principles drawn out in these chapters are sound. When disorders run in families, explanations must be sought variously in heritability, in shared family environment, in interactions between these, and in events, like abuse, which may not be shared but which nevertheless commonly happen within the context of a dysfunctional environment. Even the impact of seriously traumatic events may be determined in part by a particular genetic heritance (Caspi et al., 2002). This study of the male participants in the Dunedin birth cohort showed that, at age 26, those having the X-linked gene for monoamine oxidase-A (MAO-A), conferring high levels of this neurotransmitter, were less likely to develop antisocial behaviour problems after abuse. Usually, where there are more directly heritable factors, these will be for traits, like impulsivity, which contribute substantially to the personality type or disorder and its impact rather than determining the disorder *per se*. Genetic influences may, however, have as great a role as the environment on key comorbidities, such as alcohol or drug dependency disorders. When considering complex disorders, it is unlikely that a single explanation will suffice either for the population with the disorder or individuals within it. The effect of neighbourhood environment must also be considered.

Physical Routes to Disorders of Personality

Neuropsychiatry

Evaluations of brain structure and function in people with personality disorder remain largely a matter for research. Personality *change* has been observed after cerebral insults of various kinds, including head injury, encephalitis and the dementias. As with other psychiatric conditions, experience with localising injuries has provided guidance on where to look for damage or dysfunction among people with primary personality disorder. The limbic system and frontal lobes are particularly implicated (see chapter 12), but the damage and/or dysfunction is usually subtle and not yet generally susceptible to identification on investigations routinely available to clinicians, such as skull X-ray, standard electroencephalogram or computerised tomography scan.

The clinical implications of such damage or dysfunction are that preliminary work to correct any deficits, as far as it is possible to do so, is likely to create a more advantageous position for other therapies, particularly psychological

therapies. Many people with personality disorder have, for example, subtle difficulties with language and communication, which are not immediately apparent in a structured interview or from their vocabulary. Some may be founded in such problems as theory of mind deficits, explored more fully below. Not only may these be of direct causative relevance, but, again, they may exert their effect through creating adverse responses from others and, eventually, a toxic social environment. They may hinder therapy if not recognised and either ameliorated or allowance made for them. Extensive damage or dysfunction is not necessarily a barrier to psychological treatments but, if present, will mean that the work may need to be structured differently, perhaps allowing for more than usual repetition, and will take longer.

Neurochemistry

Dysfunctions in the serotonergic, dopaminergic and noradrenergic neurotransmitter systems have each been implicated as underpinning aspects of personality disorder (Bhagwager and Cowan, 2006). The story is essentially one of reduction in plasma and/or cerebrospinal fluid (CSF) levels of the transmitters associated with impulsivity or aggression rather than personality disorder *per se*. The evidence is weak or mixed with respect to the noradrenergic or dopaminergic systems, but quite strong with respect to the serotonergic system (see chapter 12 for more detail). Again, however, there is little here that would help with routine assessment. Methods of measurement of such neurotransmitters tend to be intrusive – requiring at best blood samples, but ideally CSF samples – and are just not practical even for extended clinical evaluations. Their main value lies in their confirmation in principle that there is likely to be an organic substrate for personality disorder.

Psychological Routes to Development of Personality Disorder

Theory of mind and empathy

Theory of mind (ToM) refers to an ability to represent the mental states of others within one's own mind, and distinguish them from one's own mental state, allowing explanation and prediction of the behaviour of others (Leslie, 1987). It is, essentially, a two-stage, largely cognitive process, first of recognition of the separate mental situation of the other; and secondly, the processing of this information so that the other person's perspective can be taken accurately. It is thus related to role-taking (e.g. Chandler et al., 1974) and perspective taking (e.g. Selman, 1976), and underpins the concept of empathy: 'an affective response more appropriate to someone else's situation than one's own' (Hoffman, 1987). Accurate empathy relies on the two elements of theory of mind together with a capacity for emotional responsiveness (Feshbach, 1987). It has been postulated that such capacities are linked with inhibition of aggressive and/or antisocial behaviour (Eisenberg, 1986; Feshbach, 1987), moral development (Kohlberg, 1981; Turiel, 1983) and prosocial development (Underwood and Moore, 1982). It follows that impairments in one or more of the elements of theory of mind or emotional responsiveness might result in pathological aggression and/or antisocial behaviour.

Blair (2005, 2008; Blair et al., 2005) has been chiefly responsible for drawing out the complexities of the relationships between dysfunction with respect to theory of mind, other aspects of empathy, psychopathy as a particular type of personality difficulty and other disorders in which aspects of empathy are impaired. His choice to focus on people who are given high scores on the PCL-R is based on an idea, which he shares with many others, that the category of antisocial personality disorder, as defined in the main diagnostic classification systems, is founded in a social deviance model while the concept of psychopathy, which may or may not result in detected antisocial behaviour, indicates the primary personal developmental disorder. His research path started with work with children with autism. Such children have consistently been shown to have theory of mind impairments (e.g. Baron-Cohen et al., 1985), which cannot be explained by language difficulties (e.g. Leslie and Frith, 1988). They have also been shown to have difficulties with recognising emotions in others (e.g. Tantam et al., 1989) and, as in adults, there is some evidence of association between autistic spectrum disorders and violence (Scragg and Shah, 1994). Blair, however, found that children with autism and theory of mind impairments do respond to distress in others, finding it distressing (Blair, 1996) and arousing (Blair, 1999a). By contrast children with 'psychopathic tendencies' were found to have reduced electrodermal responses to distress in others, but not to sense of threat from them (Blair, 1999b).

While this work may be suggestive of a distinctive pattern of deficits in empathic development, it was done entirely with small numbers of children. A series of 25 adult men crossing the PCL-R cut off and resident in high security hospital had similar theory of mind function to healthy controls (Blair et al., 1996). In a later series, of 18 experimental men and 18 controls, such 'psychopathic' adults were shown to have impaired responses to distress cues, but not to threat cues (Blair et al., 1997). Few others have worked in this specific area, so the findings have to be regarded with caution, however further indirect support is provided through neuroimaging studies. Amygdala dysfunction has been particularly associated with psychopathy and with impaired abilities to recognise facial emotions in others, especially fear (Blair, 2008; Blair and Fowler, 2008). As Blair observes, however, theory of mind functions are not associated with the amygdala. He also observes that the ventro-medial prefrontal cortex is commonly compromised in the presence of high PCL-R scores, and theory of mind is associated with the medial frontal cortex (Fletcher et al., 1995). There is, then, the potential

here for understanding the cause of one important type of personality dysfunction, but a case has been made for further research rather than a definitive theory, or basis for treatment of people with personality disorder.

Maladaptive learning and personality disorder

Learning takes place as qualities in the environment are perceived and accommodated by the individual, resulting in a change in one or more of the three components of behaviour: thinking, feeling or action. Identification of what constitutes adaptive and maladaptive learning is, however, far from straightforward. Those behaviours which would be construed as maladaptive in a well ordered society may also be behaviours which, at some stage in the life of an individual who has been subject to extremes of deprivation or abuse, have constituted the only possible survival strategies. As a result, they can be extremely resistant to change.

The origins of learning theory rest first in the idea that behaviour can be learned or 'conditioned' by pairing almost any stimulus with a particular outcome. The classic Pavlovian experiment with dogs coupled the sound of a bell with the arrival of food, so the experimental dogs were, effectively, trained to salivate on the sound of the bell; eventually, they did so regardless of whether the food was provided (Pavlov, 1927; a translation of all his lectures and a bibliography is available at http://psychclassics.yorku.co.pavlov/). The concept of operant conditioning followed – that more complex behaviours are, essentially, shaped by a system of 'rewards' and 'punishments', such that any behaviour which changes an individual's inner experience relatively positively will tend to be reinforced and any which changes it negatively will tend to be extinguished (Thorndike, 1931; Skinner, 1974). Thus, enduring traits may arise as an individual learns that a particular behaviour or sequence of behaviours may relieve emotional pain, but, to the observer, initially including the therapist, the behaviours may seem unpredictable because the negative affect is a conditioned response to something associated with the original trigger. Thus, an abused child may become conditioned to associate a particular colour and/or smell with being beaten and, in turn, to respond to any contact with such a trigger with a particular pattern of behaviours which have at least reduced the pain of this. This might incorporate avoidance of authority figures – so never keeping outpatient appointments – and/or taking alcohol or other drugs 'to block things out' and/or being aggressive or frankly violent to anyone in the vicinity at such moments. To compound such difficulties, the learning of behavioural responses to situations through social modelling may be impaired (Bandura, 1969), especially in families and/or communities where there is a higher than average risk of abuse in any of its forms.

The idea that maladaptive learning makes at least a contribution to the development of disorders of personality is important because of the potential role it creates for identifying and extinguishing the maladaptive patterns and engaging the individual in learning new strategies to create and maintain a sense of inner security – even, perhaps, more effectively than with the old strategies. More pro-social behaviours, which can provide for the individual's prospects of establishing him/herself in a safer external environment, may also be developed. Almost by definition, however, if persistent adversity or abuse within the relatively consistent environment of family, school and local community have provided any of the triggers or reinforcers of habitual behavioural presentation, the usual environment of the individual is unlikely to be congenial or safe in a way which would be recognisable to most therapists, and there is a resultant risk that changes in behaviour which are advantageous outside the home community are risky within it. Therapies which yield such changes thus, in effect, have potentially serious side-effects. This sort of issue was, for example, thought to be a key explanation for the finding that young male offenders in the experimental treatment group in a US custodial setting who initially appeared to do significantly better than the controls in a standard custodial setting were apparently doing much less well at long-term follow-up; they had gained skills which were useful in the therapeutic community and while supported in the community, but less so when left to cope for themselves back home (McCord and Sanchez, 1982). Recognition of a need to take a whole systems approach is well established outside offender/offender-patient settings (Mikesell et al., 1995; Magnavita, 2000; McGoldrick and Gerson, 1985; Paris, 1996), and perhaps needs more emphasis within them.

Attachment theory

Bowlby (1944) was probably the first to propose a relationship between early disorders of attachment and crime, founded in his observations of the family life of young thieves attending a child guidance clinic. He went on to extensive observations of infants with their primary caretakers, most often their mothers. He postulated that attachment bonds were formed during the first year of life, healthy attachments serving to protect the vulnerable infant and safeguard its development and survival (Bowlby, 1969, 1973, 1980). Disruption of these bonds for any reason would leave the infant in a painful affective state which could predispose to later sustained psychopathology, in particular sustained difficulties in regulating affect. Ainsworth extended ethological study of children with their parents, drawing attention to the importance both of the main caregiver's capacities and patterns in the child's attachment behaviours to the development of secure bonding (e.g. Ainsworth and Wittig, 1969). Contributions to the attachment process thus come on the one hand from the main caregiver's capacity for internalization of the mental state of the child, and thus their sensitivity to emotional signals from the child and ability to respond appropriately, and on the other from the child's ability to seek their caregiver, communicate distress and be sufficiently reassured to resume exploratory play. Next steps were to apply infant models of attachment to adults (e.g. Main et al., 1985). This is dealt with more fully in chapter 28, albeit there in relation to post-traumatic stress disorder.

Evidence for a relationship between insecure attachments and personality disorder is partly inferred from observations of the conditions of separation, deprivation and abuse that underpin such pathological attachments being particularly evident in the early lives of people who develop those personality disorders which are so prominent in offender populations, including borderline personality disorder (Ogata et al., 1990; Brown and Anderson, 1991; McClellan et al., 1995) and antisocial personality disorder (Luntz and Widom, 1994). Although there is some more direct evidence of measured insecure attachment among people with personality disorder (Patrick et al., 1994; Fonagy et al., 1995; van Ijzendoorn and Bakermans-Kranenburg, 1997; Frodi et al., 2001), sample sizes tend to be small, and personality disorder groups to be proportionately more likely to show insecure attachments rather than there being any absolute relationship. Nevertheless, this conceptualisation of the pathway to personality disorder also provides for theoretical models of intervention. First, it paves the way – or should do so – for understanding how it is that people with personality disorder have such difficulty in committing themselves to treatment – in effect attaching themselves to therapists or services. Secondly, it suggests the importance of tackling emotional regulation in the short term, perhaps with medication, to facilitate improvements in reflective functions (Fonagy et al., 2002).

Trauma as a precursor to personality disorder

A distinction between the traumatic origins of personality disorder and an understanding of the emergence of the disorder as a form of chronic attachment disorder is to some extent an artificial one, since early trauma commonly has the effect of disrupting attachment. Insofar as adult experienced trauma is associated with chronic dysfunction in interpersonal relationships, the disorder classification systems, somewhat artificially, label the resultant disorder as a personality change rather than personality disorder. The importance of bearing this aetiological pathway in mind may lie less in the style of therapy to be offered as in recognition of the risk of re-traumatising patterns in the individual's life-course. These may affect treatment relationships as well as ordinary social ones, and increase the risk of avoidant behaviours, including avoidance of therapy. Thus, work will have to be expended on sustaining the therapeutic relationship as well as resolving the particular traumas which may have contributed to the shaping of the individual.

Comorbidity

This brief review of explanations of how personality disorder may emerge raises questions as to how far the disorders observed in clinical practice are correctly designated as personality disorders alone, and how far there are, in effect, multiple disorders to be dealt with – perhaps multiple disorders of personality, but also other specific developmental disorders, such as attention deficit hyperactivity disorder, other traumatic/attachment related disorders, such as post-traumatic stress disorder, and illnesses, to which perhaps, people with personality disorder may be disproportionately vulnerable. It has, for example, been shown that attention deficit hyperactivity disorder as a child is not only a risk factor for antisocial behaviour and alcohol abuse in adult life (Loeber et al., 2003; Langley et al., 2010) but also may persist into adult life and complicate the presentation of personality disorder and other conditions (Young et al., 2003; Young and Toone, 2000).

The term comorbidity was probably coined by Feinstein (1970) but, as a concept, has a longer history. It has always created philosophical, theoretical and practical difficulties, but has a certain practical value too, so the concept is retained. It indicates that two or more conditions may occur together, perhaps concurrently throughout their course, perhaps with one being more intermittent than the other. Jaspers (1923/1963) recognised the co-occurrence of different clinical phenomena, but considered that the principles of medical diagnosis meant that a single, primary disease entity should be diagnosed, with the remaining phenomena being regarded as secondary or accidental. Clarkin and Kendall (1992), by contrast, were comfortable with the notion that two or more diagnoses could co-occur, but took a strict view of comorbidity within the framework of disease classifications. Still others have extended the concept to include a range of behaviours beyond diagnosis, such as violence or antisocial behaviour (e.g. McCord and Enslinger, 1997; Slomkowski et al., 1997).

The diagnostic systems, if anything, confuse the picture further, in that a multi-axial classification system such as the American *DSM* system would seem to encourage recognition of comorbidities, perhaps artificially inflating their rate of occurrence; however, also in such systems, some categories of disorder are defined explicitly by the absence of others, thus perhaps artificially lowering their prevalence. The tensions relating to comorbidity are particularly strong with respect to personality disorder *per se*. Some clinical researchers are adamant that several personality disorders may co-occur (e.g. Pfohl et al., 1986; Coid, 1992), while others indicate the absurdity of this position, arguing that the high rates of co-occurrence simply indicate that the disorders are not independent of each other; Tyrer and Stein (1993) are among the latter, suggesting that their finding of a co-occurrence of 46% between borderline and histrionic personality disorders

was indicative that these conditions were not independent in the first place. Fyer et al. (1988) found that only 8% of their series of 180 cases of borderline personality disorder had 'pure' disorder, however, this was a treated sample, so may have been biased towards inclusion of more complex cases. It makes some sense to be as parsimonious as possible with such diagnoses, because variety in symptom presentation may only indicate different manifestations or phases of the same disorder. Furthermore, both main diagnostic classificatory systems offer an option for diagnosing mixed personality disorder, *ICD* (WHO, 1992a), explicitly with this name:

With features of several of the disorders in F60. – but without a predominant set of symptoms that would allow for a more specific diagnosis.

Apparent co-occurrence with a personality disorder of other developmental disorders also poses a theoretical challenge in that, like other personality disorders, they too may lack real independence from the main disorder of interest. Generalised or specific learning disabilities may, for example, appear to co-occur with personality disorder, but to what extent, when they do so, are all these developmental disorders, including the personality disorder, multiple manifestations of a single pathology? To what extent may one have a powerful causative effect in the emergence of another or others? Here, however, there is a practical advantage in recognising the multiple presentations, because of implications for treatment. One or more of the apparently co-occurring conditions may have to be treated effectively to enable the individual to engage in the more active requirements of treatment of the personality disorder *per se*.

Injury or illness, even in the presence of personality disorder, may at first sight seem to pose a sufficiently clear break in relative health that it seems obvious that they should be regarded as comorbid conditions, although this has not always been accepted (Hare and Cox, 1978). Now, both the multi-axial structure of the *DSM* system, which places personality disorder on a different axis from illnesses, impulse-control disorders and adjustment disorders and an explicit statement in ICD-10 (p.201) seem to endorse this:

If a personality disorder precedes or follows a time-limited or chronic psychiatric disorder, both should be diagnosed.

Even this is not, however, straightforward, as the transition between some disorders of personality and later onset of illness is so consistent that the recommendation is to regard them as manifestations of the same condition, for example schizotypal personality disorder and schizophrenia (McGlashan, 1983). Nevertheless, there are now several published studies in substantial general psychiatric samples (e.g. Moran et al., 2003), forensic psychiatric samples (e.g. Taylor et al., 1998; Blackburn et al., 2003; Putkonen et al., 2004) and among prisoners (e.g. Singleton et al., 1998a) which report findings of extensive personality disorder–illness comorbidity. These are all, however, cross-sectional studies, and the parallel courses of the disorders over time are not at all clear. Neither are the implications for treatment of personality disorder. There are many studies which illustrate the extent to which the presence of personality disorder may complicate the treatment of comorbid illnesses (e.g. Reich and Green, 1991; Alnaes and Torgersen, 1997), although Mulder (2002), in a systematic review of the treatment of major depression in the context of personality disorder, found a main problem that, even in such trials, people with personality disorder were less likely to receive adequate treatment for their depression. What, however, is the effect of comorbid illness on the treatment of personality disorder? One study in a high security hospital hints at a lower success rate (Reiss et al., 1996), but substantive studies are urgently needed in this area. The implications for the structure of treatment programmes are potentially substantial, not only in a hospital setting but also, given the high rates of comorbidity among prisoners presented in the Singleton et al. (1998) England and Wales national prisoner survey, within prisons.

TREATMENT OF PERSONALITY DISORDER

The Challenge of Providing Treatment for People With Personality Disorder

There is no difficulty in listing potential barriers to delivering treatment for offenders with personality disorder, but four are especially salient. First, the evidence base for the effectiveness of any currently recognised intervention is weak. While the nihilist might interpret this as 'nothing ought to be done', in practice it often has the opposite meaning, since the results of treatment trials generally reflect small effects from each treatment and/ or little difference between them in their impact, rather than an absence of effect or harmful impact. Thus, a more appropriate interpretation of the findings may be that any of a wide range of treatments may be tried, since, from dynamic psychotherapy on the one hand to antipsychotic medication on the other, the weakness of the evidence is on what works best for whom.

One reason why evaluation of treatments yields less information than the practitioner would like lies in the second major challenge – that there is disagreement on the purpose(s) of interventions for offenders with personality disorder. To put the dilemma in its crudest form – is the main aim to reduce the rate of re-offending or to improve psychological wellbeing, or both – perhaps achieving the former through the latter? Underpinning this confusion is a further question about the nature of the psychological improvement to be expected even if it accepted that this is

the main requirement. It is, after all, impossible to measure outcome adequately unless the desired outcome is clear. Setting aside for a moment the potential role for resolving comorbid conditions, which may be the critical factors in episodes of decompensation, ought the function of intervention for personality factors *per se* be to achieve the minimal sufficient adjustments needed for slightly improved social integration or should they be aimed at more radical personality change? Many who suffer with personality disorder are as likely as those who do not to equate their personality with their sense of self and being an independent human being, so they are understandably both offended and frightened by the idea that, in effect, they must be changed. Perhaps they would be reassured by the suggestion:

> *Psychotherapists do not aim to make radical changes in a patient's personality, but rather to smooth down the rough edges with fine sandpaper – to make the abrasive person more polite, the impulsive person more restrained, and so on (Stone viii, 2006a).*

A third major challenge lies in finding the optimal timing for interventions. It seems logical to postulate that interventions should be offered as early as possible, preferably as preventive measures for children and adolescents at risk of developing personality disorders. This makes sense, because traits and risk factors which are associated with personality disorder in an adult are, by definition, already evident in children and/or adolescents and they pose considerable risks to the health of the individual concerned, including accidental death and suicide (Robins and Rutter, 1990), as well as risks to others and substantial costs to society (Scott et al., 2001; Walsh, 2001). Furthermore, given the nature of the pathologically intrusive disorders of interpersonal function which are at the heart of personality disorder, it is arguable that the counter-transferences engendered over time, and perhaps other environmental influences, will serve to reinforce the pathological traits (Maughan and Rutter, 2001). Thus, the longer treatment is deferred, the harder it will be to get a good outcome. On the other hand, there is a view that, insofar as there are more organic explanations for the difficulties, interventions which have a fundamentally holding function may be sufficient to keep the individual safe while natural maturation processes take place (Stone, 1990).

A final problem for consideration here, although this is by no means an exhaustive list, is that even among the subgroup of people with personality disorder who become offenders, a very large number need help with personality disorder, but resources for providing this are scarce – both in terms of the cash needed to fund services and the expertise needed even when funds are available. Thus, many people languish in prison or in the community with substantial unmet need, surrounded by a largely untrained workforce that ought to offer some treatment, but cannot do so. The magnitude of the resultant task facing those trying to develop a sensible and sustainable policy is clear. The issue of resources also poses limits on what can be achieved through preventive programmes.

Faced with these challenges, there is a temptation to be disheartened. If, for instance, practitioners cannot agree on such fundamentals as the nature and categorisation of personality disorder, the novice might be tempted to abandon the field altogether and focus only on people with axis I conditions where the terrain appears more certain. Succumbing to this temptation is, we believe, a mistake as there is now sufficient agreement on essentials that sensible and informed plans can be developed for offenders with personality disorder, potentially saving lives and money. In fact, for a set of disorders in which there is inherent possibility of maturation over time, the prognosis in appropriately treated cases may be much better than that for people with the chronic deteriorating conditions which constitute the more severe forms of schizophrenia and other functional psychosis.

Prevention of Personality Disorder

Harrington and Bailey (2003, 2004a) summarised the different approaches to prevention of antisocial personality disorder and reviewed evidence of their effectiveness. Broadly, there are two main approaches to primary prevention, aimed at reducing the incidence of adult antisocial personality disorder – the application of 'universal', school-based programmes and selective prevention. The former is aimed at improving relevant aspects of the environment for everyone, and particularly targets aggressive behaviours, academic failure and low commitment to school. Thus, interventions include reduction in class size, improved organisation and oversight of classroom behaviour, behaviour management strategies and good citizenship skill promotion (Hawkins and Herrenkohl, 2003). Bullying has received specific attention, and effective programmes reduce this by at least 50% (e.g. Olweus, 1994). A criticism of this type of approach with respect to prevention of disorder is that, because it has to be relevant to everyone, it is too dilute to be of much use to those who are most at risk.

Selective prevention, however, requires identification of those children thought to be most at risk, which in itself requires resources, but also raises concerns in the minds of many workers about the risk of stigmatising children, and that the resultant sense of otherness and/or open acknowledgement of the difficulties of these children could add to their burden. Interventions here may be vulnerability focused – for some personal problem which may increase the risk of personality disorder, such as attention deficit hyperactivity disorder – or they may be situation focused – for alleviating aspects of the child's environment which would put him/her at increased risk of developing personality disorder. With respect to the latter, prevention and amelioration of the effects of child abuse are particularly important, through early health visitor attention (Olds et al., 1998) or other home visit programmes designed to improve parental safety skills and knowledge (MacMillan et al., 2009). The difficulties in sustaining such programmes are, however, considerable. Most people struggle to maintain beneficial health strategies which will prevent disease and other forms of harm at some notional time far in the future – hence the difficulties in establishing healthy eating or drinking programmes and preventing smoking (e.g. Connor and Norman, 1996). Mere knowledge of the issues is necessary, but insufficient, and outcomes influenced by factors such as perceived ability to influence one's own life and, in effect, capacity for delayed gratification. The concept of promoting the possible absence of some unwanted problem at some vague time in the future at the cost of denying oneself the more immediate and obvious rewards of a clearly pleasant or wanted experience is hard for any of us. Such problems are multiplied when the primary beneficiaries, almost by definition, lack motivation for prevention programmes. Further, in economically strained times, the community too must be motivated to maintain financial commitment to relevant programmes (Offord and Bennett, 2002).

The third major approach lies in, effectively, secondary prevention and actual treatment of the child or adolescent at risk, and/or his/her family.

Paving the Way to Effective Treatment of Personality Disorder

Recognising the needs of the staff

Clinicians justifiably complain about a disconnection between the careful assessment and diagnosis of personality disorder and deciding on the most appropriate treatment. Problems are as likely to lie with the staff as with the prospective patients. For staff, some difficulties arise in their reading of the literature on effectiveness of treatments, which we will explore more fully below, but there are likely to be even more fundamental difficulties in getting started. A qualitative evaluation of narratives on the concerns of psychiatrists in general about working with people who have a personality disorder revealed a core category of 'echoing the pathology', which indicated that the complex pathologies of these disorders tend to be reflected in the behaviours and attitudes of professionals (Jones, 2011). This was underpinned by five conceptual categories of 'failure to pin down the concept', 'disruption of role identity', 'projection of blame', 'absence of buy-in' and 'intra/

inter-professional turmoil'. The theory generated is that work with people with personality disorder is a process of working with this echo of pathology. The process entails movement along a continuum between simply echoing the pathology at one end, through recognition and management of this, to being able to use personal experience to help both the patient and colleagues. Factors likely to provide barriers to this process include perception of the wide array of treatments available, each needing its own set of skills, unfamiliarity with most of those skills and with the kind of intensively supportive team work which must accompany them. All of this may engender a sense of helplessness. Factors facilitating treatment include provision of appropriate training (Miller and Davenport, 1996; Krawitz, 2004; Commons Treloar and Lewis, 2008), supervision and reflective practice (Moore, 2012).

Setting boundaries

If there is something in this concept of working with 'echoes of pathology' – an echo in itself of psychoanalytic concepts of transference and countertransference – it follows that boundary recognition and setting are important steps in preparing for treatment. Boundaries may be physical – the most obvious being the physical structures inherent in secure hospitals or prisons – but they must also be psychological. Walls and locks are an aid, not a substitute for well-structured and maintained clinical teams, members of which meet regularly, communicate clearly, have explicit lines of responsibility, and keep their work under constant review. These teams need to be embedded in a supportive, wider management structure, in which, in turn, there is honesty about what may go wrong as well as achievements expected. As part of a process of enhancing service quality and keeping adverse events to a minimum, resources are necessary, but administrators can only provide these if they are adequately justified and if all parties are working in a climate in which good practice is at least as well marked as any poor practice, and there can be full and frank inquiry into the adverse events which will inevitably occur from time to time, however good the practice.

Promoting patient engagement during the assessment process through a collaborative approach

With expert support, in a treatment unit in which the patient can gain a sense of personal safety, offender-patients with personality disorder may be helped towards engagement with treatments designed to meet their needs (Sainsbury et al., 2004; Cordess, 2006). How might the foundation for such a climate be created? It must start early in the assessment process, so that, from the outset, the patient has an opportunity to feel like a partner in the decisions to be made about treatment. For offender-patients under compulsory hospital detention and/or a treatment contract under a community sentence, those aspects of management which relate to security may be non-negotiable, but with respect to treatment all the usual clinical principles of information sharing and real consent should apply. By definition, however, most people with personality disorder will have difficulties in forming a healthy therapeutic alliance. Common to several models of personality disorder is the expectation that acts of sabotage are likely to threaten the alliance and therefore continuity of the intervention (Bender, 2005). These issues are therefore taken up at the outset, using non-punitive interpretation and collaborative assignment of responsibility for preservation of the treatment with the patient, (Plakun, 1994). Derksen (1995), Millon (1999) and Bender (2005), amongst others, have provided summaries of characteristic ways of relating allied to each cluster (A, B and C) of personality disorders which have specific value in framing appropriate responses for effectively involving and retaining the patient in treatment. These are very broadly summarised in table 16.3, but we recommend that readers seek out the original texts for full context and further information.

Ben-Porath (2004) notes that the first five sessions with a prospective patient with personality disorder may hold particular significance, as an alliance is being established. It has been argued that factors such as the indifference and inexperience of some 'therapists' contributes

Table 16.3   Characteristics that complicate the process of engagement in forensic clinical assessment, according to personality types. (Sources: Derksen, 1995; Bender, 2005; Millon, 1999.)

Cluster A: Schizotypal, schizoid, paranoid personality disorders
Key issue: Profound impairments in interpersonal relationships
Strategies: Seek to establish trust, build alliances slowly over time, respect the need for distance
Cluster B: 'Dramatic': antisocial, borderline, histrionic, narcissistic personality disorders
Key issues: Limit pushing and impulsivity; emotion dysregulation; discontinuities in the sense of self; relationship breakdown; grandiosity
Strategies: Collaborate, contract, formulate, set limits, repair ruptures, manage countertransference
Cluster C: 'Anxious/fearful': avoidant, dependent, obsessive–compulsive personality disorders
Key issues: Emotional inhibition; aversion to interpersonal conflict
Strategies: Note instances of feeling guilty and internalisation of blame; empower to reduce over-compliance; monitor treatment objectives particularly in relation to the termination of contact

to treatment failures with offenders with psychopathy (Martens, 2004). In addition to the general clinical ethic of collaboration, the use of contracts, goal-setting and techniques of validation, including overt listening to and understanding the patient (Linehan, 1997), may assist with engagement. What have offender-patients themselves reported to be helpful? Detained patients with personality disorder in high security preferred a 'firm but fair' staff attitude (Ryan et al., 2002). In addition, clinicians have been asked to share the basic issues without jargon, ask relevant questions, and be flexible about time; this last refers to the tension between boundaried and containing practice and the experience of some in secure conditions that it is difficult to convey adequately the complexity of their histories within an hour on a once a week basis (Denborough, 1996).

In an interesting study with people with drug dependence histories in residential treatment under a criminal justice mandate, Sung et al. (2001) observed that incidents of rule violation were common. They added, however, that, aside from a minority who never engaged with treatment, the more minor episodes of non-compliance seemed not to pose serious obstacles to eventual recovery. Reports in the literature thus seem unanimous in highlighting two essentials for successful assessment of people with complex/ severe personality disorder:

- continuing attention to the potential need for repairing ruptures in the patient–doctor/therapist alliance, and an ability to do so, especially during early meetings (Plakun, 1994);
- flexibility of approach within clearly boundaried interchanges (Meux and Taylor, 2006). The therapeutic community model of treatment includes patient involvement from the outset, and staff structures that are sufficiently flexible to avoid unnecessarily hierarchical and authoritarian styles that can undermine engagement (Stern et al., 1986; Norton, 1992; Warren and Dolan, 1996).

Sharing the diagnosis of personality disorder with patients

Fears of somehow compromising the therapeutic alliance through mention of the 'label' of personality disorder to the patient appear in the clinical literature of the early 1990s (Davidson, 2000). Every patient is, however, entitled to know and understand his/her diagnosis. In England and Wales this is even now stipulated in the *Patient's Charter for Mental Health Services* (DOH, 1997a), perhaps reflecting the extent to which mutual denial of the condition may become a problem. The essential question becomes: how might the diagnosis of personality disorder be most constructively shared with the recipient? In a short paper on the benefits of feedback, Tyrer (1998) observed that, rather than diminishing collaboration, feedback typically

enhanced it, with patients spontaneously contributing to the process of the description of their problems.

As Schotte (2002) has suggested, descriptive diagnostic assessment of personality disorder, based on a biopsychosocial model, involves feedback to the patient in the clinical context. There is some small scale research evidence (D'Silva and Duggan, 2002) that patients with personality disorder in forensic settings remain less likely to 'know' their diagnosis than those with other mental health problems, and more likely to have undertaken their own search for this type of information by reading their clinical records. Building on the usefulness of a psycho-educational package, Banerjee and colleagues (2006) have demonstrated positive impacts on the therapeutic alliance following four sessions of information sharing in which the patterns associated with specific personality traits are articulated, and areas for change are identified by the patient. If this type of feedback and engagement were routinely applied, or even adapted as a groupwork package which incorporates a supportive function, talking about personality disorder would no longer be done in the patient's absence, and active inclusion would become a more richly embedded clinical practice. Such processes are used in the English high security hospitals (e.g. Perkins et al., 2007; Tennant and Howells, 2010; Willmot and Gordon, 2011),

Setting the goals of treatment

Cure is a false hope in many conditions in all fields of medicine. 'Cure', meaning complete resolution of the condition, is desirable, and may be achievable, but it is often an unrealistic goal. This is also true in respect of work with people who have a personality disorder but, also as in other fields in medicine, there are other acceptable alternative goals. These include improvement, holding without deterioration and even palliation, in the form of some relief of the maximum distress to self or others without real change. Until the Mental Health Act 2007, for England and Wales, most of the goals from this range were even explicit when considering compulsory detention for treatment.

The process of assessment just described allows for setting attainable goals for treatment with the patient, and for their prioritisation. At best, this leads to an explicit statement of a series of desired outcomes, such that the patient and the therapists all have clear markers for success, and thus can recognise progress when it is being made. The creation of stepwise goals is important – achieving change in personality, or even personality traits, is a large and complex task and, as an entirety, too hard for most people, including staff, to contemplate. Modest increments of change are more attainable, and markers of success along the way provide a framework which better engages the patient and therapist alike. At first, the increments of change must be small, so that they are fairly quickly achievable, and reinforce the idea for all parties that change is possible. Completion of a complex assessment process is in itself an indication of progress for many people. Everyone needs evidence of progress to stay motivated.

Structuring the programme with achievable goals which reward patient and staff alike

Completion of an extended assessment is in itself an achievement, which needs to be acknowledged by staff and patients alike. Next steps are commonly around treating comorbid illness, offering treatment or training in coping strategies for certain developmental and/or educational deficits and perhaps offering medication to reduce the impact of specific enduring traits. Patients for whom a particular trait, such as impulsivity, is a prominent part of presentation may not be able to engage in psychological therapies until they are able to get some relief from this through medication. Failure to cover this ground may limit capacity to engage. In this context, even comorbid psychosis, so long as it is well controlled, is not necessarily a bar to treatment of personality disorder. The sort of developmental issues which are critical here relate to speech and language. It is not uncommon for people with personality disorder to have language skills in the borderline impaired range, and yet most treatment opportunities depend on being competent enough for quite sophisticated psychotherapies; some of the language difficulties may be quite subtle, such as difficulties in understanding and dealing with irony or certain forms of humour, like satire; so, testing to ensure recognition of such difficulties and teaching relevant coping strategies may be vital.

Thereafter, a programme of therapeutic work may be mapped out according to need and developmental stage in recovery. In one comprehensive model for working with personality disorder in a high security hospital (Newrith et al., 2006) the post-stabilising programme of psychological work included structured, task oriented streams of group work and an unstructured more psychodynamic stream, each delivered in an acknowledged hierarchy, such that, with progress, patients 'graduated' from a lower level group to a higher level group. True psychodynamic/analytic therapy would invariably be the pinnacle of active psychological treatment with, as an inpatient, the task also of beginning to prepare for separation from the institution and away from perhaps the only healthy attachments many of the patients had so far achieved. The task oriented stream, largely based on a cognitive behavioural method of working, but including drama work as a means of accessing affect and empathic responses, included social, sexual and self and sensory awareness streams. The hierarchy of tasks within such streams was from social attitudes and skills, through anger management to assertiveness and social coping in the first, sexual knowledge, interpersonal relationships and then sexual relationships within those in the second, and self and sensory awareness, followed by family awareness

and finally victim empathy at the highest level of the third. A variant of this model is shown in figure 16.1. Setting out with a clear structure of this kind, while retaining the capacity for flexibility as the treatment is implemented, is the key to successful engagement and retention of the patient. An attentive therapist will see when this more-or-less sequential approach needs adjustment, and, for example, be able to help an individual work on self-integration (phase 3) while also working on relationships with others (phase 1).

Evidence for the Effectiveness of Treatments of Personality Disorders

Measurement of the effects of treatment on personality disorder is extremely difficult. The general principles for doing so are that the condition to be treated, the treatment itself and the increments of change which are indicative of success should all be clearly definable. As we have already discussed, while there is still some concern over the reliability of diagnosing individual personality disorders, uncertainty about the life course of personality disorders is even more substantial. Moran (1999, pp.43–50) purports to show the 'natural course' of antisocial personality disorder/psychopathy, but the studies he lists are, in fact, of people with whom health and criminal justice services have intervened a good deal, albeit perhaps not therapeutically. Others have followed people with borderline personality disorder for up to 27 years but, again, people identified by service use, and at least intermittently using services (e.g. Stone, 1990; Paris and Zweig-Frank, 2001; Zanarini et al., 2010). True natural course studies are, realistically, unlikely among people who are such heavy service users, and would probably be unethical. Interpretations of the outcomes of trials of treatment are, as for most conditions, further bedeviled by the fact that the most valued form of evaluation – the randomised controlled trial – is invariably completed with the most altruistic and co-operative people, often with disorder which is in the middle range of seriousness. Altruistic, co-operative people are, by definition, unusual among those with serious personality disorder, so it is arguable that results of such trials should be regarded with more than usual caution in this field. Measurement of change within treatment programmes, particularly when that is within a therapeutic institution of some kind, may be further confounded by the difficulty in these circumstances of knowing when change is sufficiently extensive and robust that it is generalisable to other environments or whether the measured changes better reflect the institution's capacity to find a good fit with the individual's needs. If the latter, this could mean that as long as s/he remains there, s/he functions optimally, but once back in his/her natural environment, the pathological traits and coping mechanisms will come to the fore again. That said, it would be unthinkable to discharge a person with psychotic illness from inpatient treatment without an adequate package of ongoing treatment

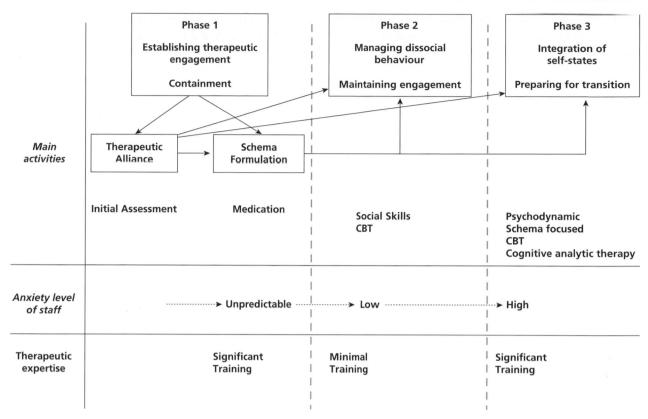

Figure 16.1   A stepped approach to the treatment of personality disorder.

and reviews. There is, however, a tendency not to structure transitional and discharge arrangements with the same rigour for people who have personality disorder. Small wonder, then, that from an early general overview of the evidence on treatment of personality disorder (Dolan and Coid, 1993) to more recent systematic reviews (see below), the overall answer to questions about the effectiveness of treatment for personality disorder is equivocal.

Drug treatments for personality disorders

Medication is commonly prescribed for people with personality disorder, at least at times. Early estimates were that from about half (Soloff, 1981) to more than three-quarters (Andrulonis et al., 1982) of people presenting for treatment would be prescribed something. There is no specific 'personality disorder drug', so an ever present question is whether any medication is really treating aspects of the personality disorder *per se* or, rather, helping with comorbid conditions which may have been the trigger to a period of decompensation, and, in the presence of personality disorder, may not always present in classical form. Perhaps this doesn't matter as long as the patient improves, and, in this context, if it can be said that any medication appears to be helpful, then it may at least not be contraindicated. In the UK, however, no drug has been licensed as a specific treatment for personality disorder, so drug use must still be regarded as experimental

except when treating comorbid conditions. This does not mean that drugs cannot be used, but rather that they should be used with caution and with particularly systematic monitoring of any positive and/or negative effects.

Stein (1993), in what is not styled as a systematic review, but appears to be so, examined the evidence for the effectiveness of the range of substances which had been studied in this context up to that date – treatment with low doses of neuroleptics, tricyclic antidepressants for people with borderline personality disorder, monoamine oxidase inhibitors (MAOIs), lithium, benzodiazepines, anticonvulsants, psychostimulants and even electroconvulsive treatment. He was positive about progress in the field, since he considered that both medications available and evidence on their effects had improved so much during the 1980s, albeit starting from a state of almost no knowledge at all of this particular aspect of treatment. Most of the evidence, however, appeared to relate to people with borderline personality disorder, and a range of methods of study had been applied, including simple observational accounts of naturalistic studies. He discussed the difficulties in completing trials with people who have such problems, not least because of difficulties, inherent to the disorders, with drug compliance and retaining people in trials, and because some drugs which appeared to confer benefit might be just too risky; an example of the latter would be the MAOIs, which for the patient's physical safety require abstinence from alcohol, and a good many other substances – legal and illegal. Nevertheless, even by 1983, several randomised controlled trials (RCTs) had been completed.

By 2006, then with the aid of 15 electronic databases, 35 RCTs of pharmacological treatments for personality disorder could be located (Duggan et al., 2008). The range of treatments tried showed little difference from the Stein study; atypical neuroleptics were added, electroconvulsive treatment not mentioned, and one experiment had been conducted each with a hypotensive agent (clonidine) and a dietary supplement (omega-3 fatty acids). The studies included are shown in table 16.4. Probably the most striking features are the small sample sizes in most studies and also the brevity of treatment in the majority. A few of the studies had targeted a particular behaviour, such as substance misuse or suicidal acts, but among people with personality

disorder; again, trials were most commonly with people who had borderline personality disorder. Multiple meta-analyses were performed with the data to take account of the nine classes of drugs trialed and the range of behavioural features measured. The latter were cognitive perceptual symptoms, affective dysregulation (including depression, anxiety, anger and hostility), impulsive behavioural dyscontrol, global functioning – this area including perhaps the most typical of personality disorder features in interpersonal symptoms/signs – physical function, and leaving the study early. Reduction of aggression in the context of anticonvulsant prescription and modulation of cognitive perceptual and other subjective mental state disturbance with anti-psychotic medication were the only two domains of significant success.

Lieb et al. (2010) set out to update the review specific to treatment of borderline personality disorder. They found

Table 16.4 Summary of completed randomised controlled trials of pharmacological treatments for people with personality disorder

Study	Sample	Drug tested	Usable outcomes[1]	Duration of trial	Authors' claims
* Arndt et al.,1992	29 men with ASPD among 59 substance misusers	Desimipramine v. placebo, both with standard methadone treatment	Days with psychological problems, opiate use, or medical problems	12 weeks[2]	Those with ASPD made few gains with desimipramine or placebo
* Battaglia et al., 1999	32 men 25 women repeated self-harm with PD	Low dose v. 'ultra-low' dose fluphenazine	Leaving the study early; suicidal behaviour	6 months	Marked reduction in self-harm in both groups
* Bogenschutz and Nurnberg, 2004	15 men, 25 women with BPD	Olanzapine v. placebo	Leaving the study early	12 weeks	Olanzapine superior on BPD measures on BPD-clinical global impressions scale
* Coccaro and Kavoussi, 1997	28 men 12 women, any PD with aggression and irritability	Fluoxetine v. placebo	Leaving early; side-effects; quality of life; mental state[3]; aggression/irritability	12 weeks	Sustained reduction in irritability and global rating of improvement with fluoxetine, regardless of depression, anxiety, or alcohol use
* de la Fuente and Lotstra, 1994	6 men 14 women BPD	Carbamazepine v. placebo	Leaving early; behavioural dyscontrol	32 days	Carbamazepine: no significant positive effects
Zanarini et al., 2011	119 men 322 women	2.5 mg olanzapine v. 5–10 mg olanzapine v. placebo	Mental state, self-harm, core BPD symptoms (Zanarini scale)	12 week trial + 12 week open label	Higher dose olanzapine superior on ZAN-BPD total score, but not depression nor self-harm; 2.5 mg superior on self-harm and identity disturbance only
Schulz et al., 2008	91 men 223 women with BPD	Flexible dose olanzapine v. placebo	Mental state, self-harm, core BPD symptoms (Zanarini scale)	12 week trial; 12 week open label extension	Olanzapine superior on aggression and irritability measures, but not core BPD measures
* Frankenburg and Zanarini, 2002	27 women with BPD	Divalproex sodium v. placebo	Leaving early, mental state, behaviour, side-effects	6 months	Divalproex superior in reducing anger and interpersonal sensitivity
* Goldberg et al., 1986	21 men 29 women with BPD and/or schizotypal PD	Thiothixine v. placebo	Leaving early	12 weeks	Significant thiothixene effect on psychotic, obsessive–compulsive and phobic anxiety symptoms, 'more than an antipsychotic effect'

Table 16.4 (Continued)

Study	Sample	Drug tested	Usable outcomes[1]	Duration of trial	Authors' claims
Hallahan et al., 2007	7 men 15 women	Omega-3 fatty acid v. placebo, both with standard psychiatric care	Depression, self-harm, impulsivity, aggression, daily stresses	12 weeks	Omega-3 fatty acids superior on depression, self-harm and daily stresses, not impulsivity or aggression
* Hollander et al., 2001	10 men 11 women BPD	Divalproex v. placebo	Leaving early; global state; mental state; behaviour	10 weeks	Divalproex superior to placebo for impulsive aggression, irritability and cluster BPD global rating
* Hollander et al., 2003[4]	91 (63% men)	Divalproex v. placebo	Leaving early; behaviour	12 weeks	Divalproex superior for impulsive aggression
* Joyce et al., 2003	40 men 43 women, 30 BPD, 53 other PD, all major depression	Fluoxetine v. nortryptyline	Leaving early; mental state	6 weeks + 6 months follow-up	Poor outcome for depressed patients with BPD on nortryptiline
* Koenigsberg et al., 2003	19 men 4 women with schizotypal PD	Low dose risperidone v. placebo	Leaving early, global state, mental state, schizotypal symptoms	9 weeks	Risperidone superior on PANNS negative and general scale by week 3 and positive symptoms scale by week 7
* Leal et al., 1994	11 men 8 women ASPD + cocaine abuse	Amantidine v. desimipramine v. placebo, all + standard care	Leaving early; money per week spent on cocaine	12 weeks	ASPD poor prognostic indicator; medication no advantage
* Leone, 1982	32 men 48 women with BPD	Loxapine succinate v. chlorpromazine	Symptom changes; leaving early; side-effects	6 weeks	Both drugs improved symptoms with loxapine being superior, side-effects occurred in a third
* Loew et al., 2006	56 women with BPD	Topiramate v. placebo	Leaving early, side-effects, mental state, quality of life	10 weeks	Significant advantage for topiramate on mental state and PD measures
* Montgomery et al., 1983	20 men 38 women with BPD and/or histrionic PD + self-harm	Mianserin v. placebo	Suicide attempts	6 months	No improvement; no significant difference between groups
* Nickel et al., 2006	9 men 43 women BPD	Aripripazole v. placebo	Mental state (SCL-90); self-injurious outcomes	8 weeks	Aripripazole superior on most mental state scores and state-trait anger but not self-harm
* Nickel et al. 2005	44 men with BPD	Topiramate v. placebo	Leaving early, mental state	8 weeks	Topiramate superior in treating anger in men with BPD
* Nickel et al., 2004	31 women with BPD	Topiramate v. placebo	Leaving early, mental state	8 weeks	Topiramate superior in treating anger in women with BPD
* Oosterbaan et al., 2001	48 men 34 women, 50% with avoidant PD, all with social phobias	Moclobemide v. CBT v. placebo	Leaving early, side-effects	15 weeks + 2 and 15 month follow-up	CBT superior (but for social phobia rather than PD)
Pascual et al., 2008	60 patients with BPD	Ziprasidone v. placebo	Clinical Global Impression Scale for BPD	12 weeks	No significant advantage for ziprasidone
* Philipsen et al. 2004a	9 women with BPD	Naloxone v. placebo	Dissociative symptoms 15 min before and after naloxone/placebo	Given twice in double blind cross-over design during 6–35 days	No significant advantage for naloxone, but the more BPD criteria the better the naloxone response
* Philipsen et al. 2004b	14 women with BPD	Clonidine 75 µg v. clonidine 150 µg	None	4–16 days	Acute inner tension, dissociation, suicide related behaviours reduced in both groups (within the hour)

(Continued)

Table 16.4 *(Continued)*

Study	Sample	Drug tested	Usable outcomes[1]	Duration of trial	Authors' claims
* Powell et al., 1995	65 men ASPD + alcohol dependence	Nortryptiline v. bromocriptine v. placebo	Leaving early; alcohol abstinence	6 months (post-detox)	Only significant advantage of active drugs was with nortryptiline in the ASPD group
* Rinne et al., 2002	38 women with BPD	Fluvoxamine v. placebo+	Leaving early, side-effects, mental state, behaviour	6 weeks double blind; 6 weeks single blind; 12 weeks follow-up	Fluvoxamine superior for sustained reduction in rapid mood shifts, but not impulsivity or aggression
* Salzman et al., 1995	8 men 14 women with BPD/BPD traits	Fluoxetine v. placebo	Mental state	12 weeks	Fluoxetrine superior in reducing anger
* Serban and Siegal, 1984	36 men 16 women BPD and/or schizotypal	Thiothixene v. haloperidol	Leaving early, side-effects	3 months	84% patients markedly improved at 3 months in both groups
* Simpson et al., 2004	20 women with BPD	Fluoxetine v. placebo, both + DBT	Leaving early; global state; mental state; impulsive aggression, suicide related behaviours, ER visits	12 weeks	No added benefit for fluoxetine
* Soler et al., 2005	8 men 52 women with BPD	Olanzapine v. placebo, both with adapted BPD	Leaving early, global state, mental state	12 weeks	Improvement in both groups; olanzapine superior for depression, anxiety and impulsive aggression
* Soloff et al., 1993	26 men 82 women with BPD	Haloperidol v. phenelzine	Leaving early, global state, mental state	5 weeks	Phenelzine superior for anger and hostility; no other drug advantages
* Soloff et al., 1989	22 men 68 women with BPD	Haloperidol v. amitryptiline v. placebo	Leaving early, global state, mental state, impulsivity	5 weeks	Haloperidol superior to placebo in depression, hostility, schizotypal symptoms, impulsivity global function; amitriptyline only superior for depression
Steiner et al., 2008	24 women with BPD	Olanzapine v. placebo, both with DBT	Standard measures or irritability, aggression, self-harm and depression	6 months	More rapid reduction of irritability with olanzapine; self-injury tended to decrease more with DBT alone
* Tritt et al., 2005	24 women with BPD	Lamotrigine v. placebo	Leaving early, mental state	8 weeks	Lamotrigine superior for all aspects of anger except internally directed anger
* Verkes et al., 1998	37 men 54 women, recent suicide attempt, 84 with PD	Paroxetine v. placebo	Leaving early	Up to 52 weeks	Paroxetine superior in reducing suicide related behaviours; not other behaviours/symptoms
* Zanarini and Frankenburg, 2001	28 women with BPD	Olanzapine v. placebo	Leaving early	6 weeks	Olanzapine superior in rate of improvement in all areas except depression
* Zanarini and Frankenburg, 2003	30 women with BPD	Omega-3 fatty acids v. placebo	Leaving early, mental state, behaviour	8 weeks	Omega-3 fatty acids superior in reducing aggression and depression
* Zanarini et al., 2004	45 women with BPD	Olanzapine (o) v. fluoxetine (f) v. o+f	Leaving early; side-effects	8 weeks	All three conditions effective, but fluoxetine alone least so

[1] Usable outcomes refers to all those outcomes measured systematically and reported sufficiently transparently to allow for meta-analysis;

[2] Times all refer to periods of active treatment; many studies explicitly added baseline periods;

[3] Reference to mental state as an outcome means that a systematic measure was used;

[4] A later publication (Hollander et al., 2005) is not included here, it overlapped with other Hollander studies. It analysed borderline personality disorder data separately, suggesting divalproex superior for impulsive aggression.

*Included in Duggan et al. (2008) meta-analyses.

ASPD, antisocial personality disorder; BPD, borderline personality disorder; DBT, dialectical behaviour therapy; ER, emergency room; PANNS, positive and negative symptoms of schizophrenia; PD, personality disorder; SCL-90, symptom checklist 90 items.

just four new trials, two of olanzapine (one of these a drug company trial of its own product), one an additional study of omega-3 fatty acids, and a study of ziprasidone. These have been added to table 16.4. There was really no update of conclusions possible, and the article drew somewhat acid observations from Kendall et al. (2010). It is hard to see why this update justified a major publication; what is needed is a simple system of notes to provide clinicians with periodic updates. For the USA, the American Psychiatric Association (APA) does this in the form of a 'guideline watch' (APA, 2005), which updates its position on the treatment of borderline personality disorder (APA, 2001). This is the only APA guidance on treatment of personality disorder. In England, the National Institute of Health and Clinical Excellence (NICE) guidelines on treatment of antisocial personality disorder and borderline personality disorder are more recent (NICE, 2009a,b), with their cautious recommendations that for antisocial personality disorder 'prescribers will use a drug's summary of product characteristics to inform their decisions for each person' and the slightly more specific, additional advice with respect to borderline personality disorder on use of drugs to manage crises, comorbid conditions and insomnia.

Time limited psychological treatments for offenders with personality disorder

> *A major consideration influencing the take-up of an effective treatment is the amount of effort and skill needed from care providers and the amount of technical back-up that they require (Marks, 1991).*

Brief, simple and effective treatments will have a much greater impact in the population overall than those that require a great deal of technical knowledge and expertise. Most treatment offered to offenders with personality disorder – if they are fortunate enough to be offered any at all – is likely to be of this brief type, although the national guidance for England on treatment both of antisocial personality disorder (NICE, 2009a) and borderline personality disorder (NICE, 2009b) both express caution about the need for a full and appropriate clinical framework whenever brief psychological treatments are given; such guidance draws on advice from an international collaboration of researchers from elsewhere in Europe, Canada, New Zealand and the USA (http://www.agreecollaboration.org). The idea, however, of time limited treatment for personality disorder may read like a contradiction in terms. After all, surely people with a personality disorder are, by definition, suffering from a long-term disturbance, so how could, say, 10–20 sessions of treatment be adequate? Could it even be harmful? Further, if people with a personality disorder are also offenders, they have not been found to be especially responsive to interventions of any type (Woody et al., 1985; Huband et al., 2007). It could be argued that forensic mental health services in particular, and prisons more generally,

are dealing with such complex presentations that similarly complex interventions are needed in response. Reconciling this tension between simple, brief interventions available to many versus complex interventions available only to the few is the leitmotif of current service provision.

There are, however, many types of brief psychological interventions. Given the current state of the evidence on effectiveness, how does one choose? Frank et al. (1991) and Wampold (2001), among others, have observed that many specific types of psychotherapeutic treatments achieve virtually the same effects, largely because of a common set of curative processes. While few disagree that this is true, many, nonetheless, feel uncomfortable with its implications. Does this emphasis on the non-specificity of any one treatment, not discredit that treatment's effectiveness? Glass (2001), for example, wrote:

> *There are those health policy analysts who argue that any therapy that uses non-specific diagnoses and non-specific treatments is somehow bogus witchcraft lacking indications of when to begin and when to end, and its application should be excluded from third-party coverage.*

Rachman and Wilson (1980), drawing on Alice in Wonderland and the Dodo Bird's verdict on the caucus race that 'everyone has won and all must have prizes', wrote trenchantly on results of clinical trials in the field, which usually arrive at the conclusion that there is little difference between the various psychological treatments:

> *If the indiscriminate distribution of prizes carried true conviction ... we end up with the same advice ... 'Regardless of the nature of your problem seek any form of psychotherapy.' This is absurd. We doubt even the strongest advocates of the Dodo Bird argument dispense this advice (p.167).*

How, then, does one reconcile the research evidence supporting importance of common factors on the one hand with the clinical reality that practitioners choose specific therapies for certain specific problems? This dilemma may be resolved at two levels. Frank and Frank (1991), who were among the first to develop the common factor position, deal with one of these levels:

> *[our] position is not that technique is irrelevant to outcome. Rather, as developed in the text, the success of all techniques depends on the patient's sense of alliance with the actual or symbolic healer. This position implies that ideally therapists should select for each patient the therapy that accords, or can be brought to accord, with the patient's personal characteristics and view of the problem. Also implied is that therapists should seek to learn as many approaches as they find congenial and convincing. Creating a good therapeutic match may involve both educating the patient about the therapist's conceptual scheme and, if necessary, modifying the scheme to take into account the concepts the patient brings to therapy.*

Given that the therapist's person is, in part, the therapeutic tool, a partial solution to this dilemma that differing psychological therapies may be equally effective is to accept that treatments are only likely to be effective when used by a practitioner who finds that therapy congenial, believes in it and practises it consistently. Hence, the choice of therapy has to fit the therapist as well as the patient for it to be effective. The wide range of psychological therapies available for personality disorder may appropriately reflect the wide range of practitioners in the field.

A further important issue along these lines, which is almost never considered in the research literature, is the fit not only between therapist and therapy, but also between therapist and patient. Early observations suggested that this was critical for people with schizophrenia – that therapists with certain personality styles did not or could not engage such patients and treat them successfully (Whitehorn and Betz, 1954, 1960). Similar work would be important to explore fit between personal style of the therapist and patients with the main types of personality disorder presenting for treatment.

A second possible solution to this dilemma over postulated lack of specificity of treatments is that, while a range of therapies may be applied, each will only work when there is a clear rationale for its use – both for those who deliver the treatment and for the patient making use of it. Most forensic psychiatrists will have limited opportunity for consistent, long-term, individual psychotherapeutic contact with their patients, indeed it may be inappropriate for the same person to have the overarching management responsibility in the case and be the therapist (see also chapters 23 and 26). Thus, forensic psychiatrists require an understanding of the strengths and weaknesses of the various approaches and the strengths of their colleagues in this particular respect, in order to be able to integrate this information into the decisions on therapy. Thus, specific psychological treatments may be provided as the mainstay of short-term intervention or, perhaps more commonly, as an element of a treatment package, as already described.

Another important argument for short-term treatment is that people with personality disorder struggle to complete treatment, although the data are largely restricted to those with borderline personality disorder. Figures as high as 60% early withdrawal rates have been reported in some trials (Waldinger and Gunderson, 1984; Gunderson et al., 1989), although a systematic review of 41 studies of treatment completion specifically relating to people with borderline personality disorder was more encouraging (Barnicot et al., 2011). For interventions of less than 12 months, they found that a random effects meta-analysis gave an overall completion rate of 75% (95% confidence interval (CI): 68–82%); it was barely different for longer interventions (71%, CI: 65–76%). Factors predicting dropout were low commitment to change, poor therapeutic relationship and high impulsivity; sociodemographics were not relevant. Another meta-analysis of non-completion for people with personality disorder more generally yielded slightly worse completion

rates, with patient characteristics and need together with some environmental factors influencing this (McMurran et al., 2010). The four studies that investigated the relationship between non-completion and treatment outcome showed adverse outcomes for non-completers. One even showed a higher rate of re-offending among those who disengaged than among those who were never offered treatment in the first place (McMurran and Theodosi, 2007). Hence, there is an ethical obligation to consider the risks of disengagement, and what can be done to minimise it.

Motivational interviewing (Rollnick et al., 2008) is one way of reducing the risk of dropout from treatment, psychoeducation (Livesley, 2001) is another, either way helping the patient into a position whereby s/he can make accurate observations about her/his own behaviour rather than this coming more directly from the therapist and carrying a sense of threat. Methods have also been developed specifically to encourage these observations and help co-operation over prioritising the individual's difficulties so that they seem less overwhelming (e.g. D'Silva and Duggan, 2002). Such interviewing styles also help to direct the therapist's attention as to where possible fault lines in the therapeutic alliance are likely to develop, so that these can be anticipated and worked through. Thus, for instance, the therapist might say to someone with a paranoid personality disorder: 'I realise that it is part of your personality to feel suspicious of strangers, and perhaps that they might wish to take advantage of you – so, you may from time to time feel like that about me too. This is something that we both need to be aware of, and we need to be able to work together on finding ways to increase your confidence in our working relationship so that your concerns don't get in the way of treatment.' Preventive measures are not invariably successful, however, so it is important, as well, to have strategies for dealing with therapeutic ruptures if they occur. Safran and Muran (2000) offer suggestions for identifying early 'rupture markers', which may include increased irritability or other change within or outside the sessions, or decreased involvement in homework, and note that they must immediately be actively explored in the here and now. This is often daunting for both patient and therapist, as the tendency for both is to ignore the rupture, so the therapeutic alliance needs constant monitoring. Confrontation and interpretation should be used sparingly at this stage, as these approaches provoke anxiety and are likely to be interpreted as attacks, increasing the risk of withdrawal. Such anxiety is better contained by helping the individual to observe and explore his/her own behaviour. Giving feedback to a patient with clinically significant narcissistic traits is particularly difficult; in one case, one of us (CD) found that no matter what was said, the patient interpreted it as a 'put down', and so became extremely angry and sullen for the rest of the day. He was helped by encouraging him to examine this recurrent pattern for himself. He then started to recognise his need for unequivocal admiration, and that no matter what was said, it would never be sufficient. He saw that other patients were also being provided with feedback at the same time, but he was envious of them, believing that they were seen as performing better than he. He began to move forward when he agreed that this was beginning to interfere with his capacity to work in therapy.

Collating the evidence for psychological treatments for personality disorder

A number of useful systematic reviews have been published of studies evaluating the main psychological treatments for personality disorder. These range from the more specific, for example randomised controlled trials of psychodynamic psychotherapy (Gerber et al., 2011), through comparing psychodynamic therapy with cognitive behavioural approaches but incorporating a range of trial designs (Leichsenring and Liebing, 2003), to those confining themselves to RCTs but covering a wider range of treatments. The latter include the psychodynamic therapies and their developments such as mentalization therapies, the cognitive behavioural therapies (CBT), and their developments, such as dialectical behaviour therapies (DBT), and schema-focused therapies (SFT), and practical, holding therapies

such as social skills training, psychoeducation and supportive therapies (Brazier et al., 2006; Duggan et al., 2007). The NICE guidelines on treatment of antisocial personality disorder (NICE, 2009a) and borderline personality disorder (NICE, 2009b) while the Brazier (2006) review incorporates evidence on cost as well as effectiveness. Leichsenring and Leibing (2003) came to an optimistic conclusion, that there was evidence for the effectiveness of both dynamic and cognitive therapies, but a larger overall effect size for the dynamic therapies. Other reviewers are more cautiously positive. Gerber et al. (2011) note the superiority of psychodynamic therapy to non-specific work or waiting list conditions, but equivalence with other therapies. Table 16.5 builds on and updates material from the Duggan et al. (2007) review of randomized controlled trials. Therapeutic communities will be dealt with separately, below.

The most striking thing about the randomised controlled trials summarised in table 16.5 is that there have been few evaluations of treatment for any personality disorder other than borderline personality disorder, and there is also a heavy bias towards women as patients. Most of the trials were of treatment in an outpatient setting. The table gives little flavour of the very wide range of outcome measures used, but it must be noted that, in many cases,

Table 16.5 Summary of completed randomised controlled trials of psychological treatments for people with personality disorder

Study	Sample	Therapy	Usable outcomes[1]	Duration of trial	Authors' conclusions
* Bateman and Fonagy, 1999; 2001	44 women with BPD	Psychoanalytically oriented partial hospitalisation v. general psych. care	Leaving early[2]; quality of life; psych. service use	18 months + 18 months follow-up	Psychoanalytically oriented treatment better on range of measures from 6 months, maintained through follow-up
Bateman and Fonagy, 2009	27 men 107 women with BPD; many with axis I comorbidity and add. PDs	Mentalization based treatment v. structured clinical management	Suicide/self-harm attempts, hospitalisations, length of hosp.	Up to 18 months	Improvement in both groups, more in the mentalisation group
Blum et al., 2008	21 men 103 women with BPD	Systems Training for Emotional Predictability and Problem Solving (STEPPS) +TAU[4] v. TAU	Zanarini BPD scale; depression, self-harm, impulsivity, crisis service use; global function	20 weeks + 12 months follow-up	Discontinuation rate high in both groups; advantage for STEPPS group on BPD and other measures except for self-harm or hospitalisations
* Brooner et al., 1998	35 men 8 women with opioid dependence and ASPD	Contingency management intervention v. methadone substitution	Leaving early; return to routine care	13 weeks	Both groups did well, n.s. difference between them
Clarkin et al., 2007	7 men 83 women with BPD	Transference focused psychotherapy v. DBT v. supportive therapy	Mental state, suicidality, impulsivity, aggression and violence	12 months	Improvements in all groups, most in transference based
* Colom et al., 2004	9 men 28 women with bipolar disorder and any PD	Psychoeducation v. unstructured intervention, both + medication	Global state	20 weeks; add. follow-up 6, 12, 18, 24 months	100% control group relapsed: 67% psychoeducation; latter longer to relapse

(Continued)

Table 16.5 (*Continued*)

Study	Sample	Therapy	Usable outcomes[1]	Duration of trial	Authors' conclusions
* Davidson et al., 2006	17 men 89 women with BPD	CBT + TAU[4] v. TAU	Self-harm, mental state, quality of life, service use, leaving early	12 months, add. follow-up 18 and 24 months	CBT group less likely to be hospitalised or use A&E; reduced no. of suicidal acts
Doering et al., 2010	104 women with BPD	Transference-focused psychotherapy v. treatment by community psychotherapists	Leaving early, self-harm; general mental state; personality organisation, global function	12 months	Transference-focused therapy superior on most measures (including specific PD)
* Emmelkamp et al., 2006	30 men 32 women with PD	CBT v. brief dynamic therapy v. waiting list	Behaviour avoidance scale; mental state; quality of life	6 months; follow-up at 12 months	At end of treatment and follow-up: CBT best; brief dynamic therapy equivalent to waiting list
* Evans et al., 1999	34 men and women (proportions not stated) cluster B PD	MACT (manual-assisted cognitive-behaviour therapy) v. TAU	Leaving early; global mental state; quality of life	6 months	MACT superior in reducing suicidal acts and depression
* Giesen-Bloo et al. 2006	6 men 80 women with BPD	Schema-focused v. transference focused therapies	Leaving early, mental state, behaviour	3 years	Both therapies significantly reduced BPD specific and general psychopathology
* Gratz and Gunderson, 2006	22 women with BPD	Emotional regulation groups v. TAU	Leaving early, mental state, behaviour	14 weeks	Emotional regulation groups advantage for self-harm, BPD specific and general psychopathology
* Kool et al., 2003	49 men 79 women with depression, 128 with PD	Short psychodynamic supportive therapy + antidepressants v. antidepressants	Mental state, global state	6 months	Combined therapy was more effective for depressed PD patients but not for depressed patients without PD
* Koons et al., 2001	28 women with BPD	DBT v. TAU	Service admissions; parasuicide, mental state, leaving early, no BPD criteria	6 months	Decrease in parasuicide, experienced anger and dissociation
* Linehan et al., 1991	63 women with BPD	DBT v. TAU	Parasuicide; early leaving	12 months + 12 months follow-up	Less parasuicide, more treatment engagement and fewer inpatient days with DBT
* Linehan et al. 1999	28 women with BPD	DBT v. TAU	Leaving early; death; substance use	12 months + 4 months follow-up	DBT group greater reductions in drug abuse in treatment year and at follow-up; in treatment longer; better global and social adjustment at follow-up than TAU group
* Linehan et al. 2002	23 women with BPD	DBT v. comprehensive validation therapy + 12 step	Leaving early; time spent in prison	12 months + 4 months follow-up	Both treatments effective; small differences between them
* Linehan et al. 2006	101 women with axis I and II disorders	DBT v. 'community treatment by experts'	Quality of life; behaviour; mental state	12 months + 12 months follow-up	DBT uniquely effective in reducing suicidal behaviours; not a general effect of psychotherapy
McMain et al., 2009	15 men 165 women with BPD and 2 + self-injuries in past 5 years	DBT v. general psychiatric management	Frequency and severity of self-harm	12 months	Both groups improved significantly on self-injury and other clinical measures
* Messina et al., 2003	34 men 14 women with ASPD and substance misuse	CBT v. contingency management (CM) v. CBT + CM, all with methadone maintenance (MM) v. MM alone	Substance use	16 weeks + up to 40 weeks follow-up	CM most effective

Table 16.5   (*Continued*)

Study	Sample	Therapy	Usable outcomes[1]	Duration of trial	Authors' conclusions
* Oosterbaan et al., 2001	48 men 34 women with social phobia, 50% avoidant PD	CBT v. moclobemide v. placebo	Leaving early; side-effects	15 weeks + up to 15 months follow-up	CBT superior (but for social phobia rather than PD)
* Springer et al., 1996	10 men 21 women with PD several types	DBT-based creative coping group v. wellness and lifestyles group	Mental state; behaviour	Not stated	Both groups improved, n.s. differences between them
* Stravynski et al. 1994	18 men 13 women with avoidant PD	Social skills training in the clinic v. training 'in vivo'	Leaving early	8 weeks; 6 months follow-up	Both groups showed benefits but the 'in vivo' training did not enhance the social skills training
* Svartberg et al., 2004	25 men 25 women with cluster C PDs	CBT v. short-term psychodynamic therapy	Mental state; quality of life	40 weeks; follow-up @ 12 and 24 months	Both groups improved; n.s. differences between them
* Turner, 2000	5 men 19 women with BPD	DBT v. client centred therapy (CCT)	Mental state, no. of new admissions; leaving early	12 months	DBT more improvement than the CCT group on most measures. Quality of therapeutic alliance accounted for significant variance for both treatments
* Tyrer et al., 2004	154 men 326 women with deliberate self-harm, 202 with PD	MACT v. TAU	Number with PD having at least one self-harm incident	Up to 7 treatments; follow-up @ 6 and 12 months	No difference in self-harm rates; MACT more expensive than TAU for patients with BPD, but less so with other PDs
* van den Bosch et al. 2005	58 women with BPD	DBT v. TAU	Parasuicidal and self-mutilation; substance use; behaviour scale scores	52 weeks; follow-up @ 78 weeks	Advantage for DBT in self-harm and impulsive behaviours and alcohol use, sustained @ 6 months; no difference for illicit drug use
* van den Bosch et al., 2002	64 women with BPD	DBT v. TAU	Leaving early; behaviour; substance use	12 months	BPD as Verheul et al. 2003; this article confirmed no effect on substance misuse
* Verheul et al., 2003	58 women with BPD	DBT v. TAU	Suicidal and self-mutilating behaviours; service engagement	12 months	DBT better retention rates and more reduction in self-harm than TAU
* Vinnars et al., 2005	49 men 107 women with PD	Manualised supportive expressive psychotherapy (SEP) v. psychodynamic psychotherapy (PsDP)	Global state; mental state	SEP 40 weeks; 21 sessions PsDP	Improvement in global function, reduced prevalence of PD both groups; SEP group fewer follow-up visits to community mental health teams
* Weinberg et al., 2006	30 women BPD	MACT + TAU v. TAU	Suicidal acts and behavioural scale	6-8 weeks, follow-up @ 8 months	Reduced frequency and severity of deliberate self-harm with MACT; no reduction in suicidal ideation
* Winston et al., 1994	33 men 48 women with PD	Brief adaptive psychotherapy v. short-term psychodynamic v. waiting list	Leaving early; mental state; social function	6 months; up to 4.5 years follow-up (mean 1.5 years)	Both treatment groups had significant advantage over waiting list group

[1]Usable outcomes refers to all those outcomes measured systematically and reported sufficiently transparently to allow for meta-analysis.

[2]Leaving early refers to leaving the therapy and/or the study before complete.

Abbreviations: as table 16.4 and add., additional; A&E, accident and emergency; psych, psychiatric; hosp., hospitalisation; n.s., not significant; TAU, treatment as usual.

any advantage found for a therapy was in reduction in self-harm rate or some specific symptom change rather than fundamental personality change. This is perhaps unsurprising as in under half the cases was treatment given for 12 months or more, but examination of briefer interventions does offer some help with our starting point – that brief therapies may be most desirable for reasons of access and economics. Comparison of one active treatment against another brought less clarity, which takes us back to our non-specificity discussion. It is reassuring, at least, that all trials of active treatment against placebo favoured the active treatment in some respect.

Therapeutic communities

The term 'therapeutic community' (TC) is generally attributed to Main (1946), however in initial concept it was rather similar to the Quaker reforms to mental health institutions introduced in the late eighteenth century, for example at the Retreat, York, in England. Much later, this interpretation of the idea was taken up by the anti-psychiatry movement to create 'alternative asylums', with flattened hierarchies within and between staff and residents and, often, commitment to a particular philosophical style. Two more specific approaches are relevant to treatment of personality disorder. The 'true therapeutic community' was originally a principally British development led by Maxwell Jones (Jones, 1968, 1982). It is a small, cohesive, 'democratic community' in which there is a clear distinction between staff and residents, although little hierarchical difference, and they work together at all times in a spirit of co-operation, jointly setting the rules and procedures for the community – and the sanctions if broken – and commonly sharing decisions about who should become residents. While therapeutic expertise may lie with the staff, the whole community is expected to take a part in the therapeutic process, and in supporting community members through crises. The Henderson hospital model is probably the best known example of a democratic therapeutic community in the UK (Whitely, 1980; Dolan, 1997). The 'concept based community' was originally founded in the USA, when a recovering alcoholic, Charles Dederich, set up *Synanon* in response to the perceived needs of addicts. In his hands, this form of community relied on membership for which people qualified through their abuse of drugs, and were sustained in conformity by aggressive confrontation; in the absence of professionals, and reliant on the charisma of its leader, this pioneer of the model lost its way, amid law suits about cruelty and coercion (Galanter, 1999). The principle of the concept based community, however, survived through more openness to external review, with the Phoenix House model (De Leon, 1973) perhaps best known for its incarnations in the UK. While the US route to introducing TC models for offenders through the correctional system

generally followed the conceptual TC route (e.g. Wexler, 1997), in the UK, even in prisons, the democratic TC has been the leading model (e.g. Gunn et al., 1978; Morris, 2004; Genders and Player, 2010).

Lees et al. (1999, 2004) conducted a systematic review of studies of the effectiveness of therapeutic communities for people with personality disorder, covering the literature from the inception of TCs up to 1997. The search located over 8,000 studies, but just 10 randomised controlled trials to that date, 10 cross-institutional, cross-treatment or comparative studies and 32 other studies using some sort of control; 41 of the total of 52 studies related to democratic TCs and 11 to concept-based TCs; 29 studies were amenable to meta-analysis. This indicated a positive effect, with an effect size of 2.5, which it has been suggested is what is required to indicate a clinically significant, but small outcome (Haddock et al., 1998). Another way of looking at their findings is to observe that four of the eight RCTs and 15 of the 21 other controlled studies favoured TCs. Restricting consideration to the RCTs, the US study of a secure democratic TC suggested that its graduates did about twice as well as those from a conventional setting (Auerbach, 1977; odds ratio (OR): 0.524, 95% confidence interval (CI) 0.28–0.98), but the British counterpart was equivocal (Cornish and Clarke, 1975); open, democratic TCs fared little better. Results were better for the concept based therapeutic communities. We cannot find a more up-to-date review of therapeutic communities. Most of the controlled studies of TCs are, therefore, quite old, and we are not aware of current trials in this field with people who explicitly have personality disorder. A later systematic review and meta-analysis of concept TCs (Smith et al., 2006), albeit here strictly for substance misuse rather than personality disorder, found results of RCTs to be equivocal overall, but observed that the two prison studies were positive in finding lower recidivism rates for the TC men for up to 12 months after release (Sacks et al., 2004; Wexler et al., 1999). This, however, leads to another word of caution. Long-term follow-up was for up to 10 years in a US prison-based TC study. Therapeutic community graduates had an early advantage compared with youths in an ordinary prison environment, but, after 10 years there was a cross-over, with the TC graduates faring worse (McCord and Sanchez, 1982). Speculation was that this could be explained by the development of new skills and ways of thinking in the TC having been outside the participants' own cultural context. There is a great deal more to learn about the place of therapeutic communities, but results of their evaluation to date are sufficiently promising that this should be attempted.

Managed Clinical Networks

Life events literature confirms that people commonly find major transitions in relationships or accommodation extremely difficult, with a higher chance of becoming psychologically distressed or ill at these times (Holmes and Rahe, 1967). It is arguable that most people who have attachment difficulties as a fundamental part of their personality disorders are going to find change exceptionally difficult, particularly if they have just made a healthy attachment in therapy, or to the therapeutic community. It is important, therefore, that treatment is not happening with one person in isolation, but a system, or network is in place to support the individual in all his or her areas of difficulty, and that it is particularly robust at times of transition. Furthermore, the importance of the network in supporting the therapist and other key workers is not to be underestimated.

Baker and Lorimer (2000) define a managed clinical network (MCN) as:

> a linked group of health professionals and organizations from primary, secondary, and tertiary care, working in a coordinated way that is not constrained by existing organizational or professional boundaries to ensure equitable provision of high quality, clinically effective care....The emphasis ... shifts from buildings and organizations towards services and patients.

The MCN has the following functions:

- monitoring and updating core standards of care;
- developing and updating skills and knowledge;
- audit and research;
- leadership and authority;
- coordinating and managing change.

MCNs are important for offenders with personality disorder for several reasons. First, personality disorder is an enduring condition, so it is important that provision is made seamlessly across the life span. Secondly, and this especially applies to offenders with personality disorder, many agencies are likely to be involved, fielding personnel with different philosophies and priorities. Thirdly, psychological therapies, the mainstay of treatment if available, are delivered by '...a range of sometimes rivalrous professionals – psychologists, psychiatrists, nurses – who are currently managed in different ways' (Holmes and Langmaack, 2002). Fourthly, there are few practitioners who have particular skills in this field, so it is difficult to build up a critical mass of them. Finally, assessment, management and treatment of personality disorder are still developing, so, not only is time needed to keep abreast of scientific advances and adapt service provision accordingly, but also it is an advantage to bring together people with different knowledge bases and skills.

A formal MCN builds on informal arrangements and professional relationships. It is fundamental that there should be defined areas of accountability between the individuals within the network and that boundaries are clearly defined. The idea has been promoted particularly strongly in Scotland, where the Scottish Office (1998c) has provided the following guidance on framework:

1. one person to be appointed with overall responsibility for each patient's network: a clinician, manager or other professional;
2. the purpose is to improve equality and convenience of access to care and its co-ordination; expected service improvements (and cost savings) are made explicit from the outset, and effectiveness of the MCN measured against these;
3. adherence to evidence-based treatments, and support for research wherever these are lacking; support for professional development;
4. audit is an integral part of the network;
5. each network makes an annual overview of its activities available to the public;
6. all members of the network, including the patients/service users, are involved in shaping it.

DANGEROUS AND SEVERE PERSONALITY DISORDER (DSPD): THE RISE AND FALL OF A CONCEPT

The term 'dangerous and severe personality disorder' (DSPD) is uniquely English, having been created by politicians and civil servants in 1999 to define a group of offenders who often fell uncomfortably between the criminal justice system on the one hand and forensic mental health services on the other. As perceived by the government, the problem was that mental health services wanted to deal only with psychotic or seriously mentally ill offenders – whilst growing public concern about sexual and violent recidivism had no regard for diagnostic niceties. This perception was thrust into the spotlight by the case of Michael Stone, who was convicted of killing a mother and daughter in an unprovoked attack in rural Kent, the second daughter making a miraculous recovery from potentially fatal injuries.

> Does the Home Secretary believe that further measures will be needed to deal with offenders who are deemed to be extremely violent because of mental illness or personality disorder, but whom psychiatrists diagnose as not likely to respond to treatment? Alan Beith, MP.

> Yes, I entirely agree with the Right Honourable gentleman that there must be changes in law and practice in that area. We are urgently considering the matter with my Right Honourable friends in the Department of Health ... the psychiatric profession ... 20 years ago adopted what I would call a common sense approach ... but these days go for a much narrower interpretation of the law. Jack Straw, MP (Hansard 26 October 2000).

These politicians had not seen, at that stage, the report of the independent inquiry into the killings:

> The Panel is of the firm view that the policy debate concerning the adequacy of the law, policy and guidance should take place in the context of the actual

facts of the case of Michael Stone, as opposed to the incomplete and in some cases inaccurate accounts that have appeared to date. (Francis, Higgins & Cassam, 2006; South East Coast Strategic HA, Kent County Council, Kent Probation Area commissioned independent report, 30 November 2000, published October 2006.)

The issues are, in fact, better illustrated by a series of killings by predatory paedophiles (Oliver and Smith, 1993). When some of them came to medical attention towards the end of prison sentences, there was general agreement on the presence of mental disorder and continuing risk, yet psychiatrists refused to detain them in hospital because they considered that the problems of these offenders were 'untreatable' in terms of the Mental Health Act 1983.

A fierce debate ensued. The government charged the profession with evading its responsibilities for dangerous and difficult patients, whilst the profession took the supposed moral high ground, arguing that doctors should not become jailers. There was and is a moral and philosophical argument, but there are also practical and economic dimensions. Mental health services operate at full capacity and, except for a handful of tertiary services such as the high security hospitals, generally have little or no expertise in treating personality disorder. So, the government took the initiative, not only by creating this new category of disorder, and proposing radical new services, but also providing funds for developments. The concept of DSPD was born, and 300 new beds were created, half in high security hospitals and half in prisons; later developments extended to medium secure hospitals and the community.

DSPD: An Operational Definition

The DSPD service was defined as being for offenders who met the following criteria:

1. *severe* personality disorder, severe meaning a score of 30+ on the PCL-R for men or 25 for women, or a score of 25+ and one or more personality disorders other than antisocial personality disorder, according to international classification of mental disorder, or two or more such personality disorders;
2. high risk of committing a further *serious* sexual or violent offence, this risk to be informed by standardised instruments at a cut-off indicating a greater than 50% risk over the time frame of the instrument. Serious, here, to be defined as likely to cause physical or psychological harm from which the victim was unlikely ever to recover fully;
3. a functional link between the personality disorder and the risk;
4. absence of major mental illness.

The problems with this definition arise from its non-clinical origins. It was intended that standardised measures of personality disorder and risk would allow precise identification of a population with so-called DSPD. It took hard lobbying by clinicians to force an acceptance that standard measures, particularly on risk, have been validated for groups, and translation from this to the individual is not straightforward. It is not possible to avoid a measure of clinical judgment as the final arbiter for admission to any treatment service, and, given a scarce and costly resource, hospital staff must also consider clinical treatment needs as well as diagnosis and risk.

DSPD services were implemented in 2003. Evaluation was built in to the pilot projects. Preliminary evaluation reports fuelled further debate, in 2007 a whole issue of the *British Journal of Psychiatry* (190:49) being allocated to this. It has become possible to identify strengths and weaknesses of the programme.

A Critique of DSPD

The term DSPD may be unique, but the problems it attempts to encompass are not, nor are methods of assessing and treating personality disorder. The origins of the programme can be traced to four major influences:

1. decreasing tolerance of the risks associated with crime and violence;
2. growth of standardised risk assessment and the PCL-R;
3. the Dutch TBS (Terbeschikkingstelling) system (van Marle, 2002; McInerny, 2000);
4. the development of cognitive behavioural programmes for sexual and violent offenders.

1. Decreasing tolerance of risk of crime

Over the last two or three decades, most developed countries have become less tolerant of the risks associated with sexual and violent offending, as reflected in changes to criminal justice legislation and sentencing. The reasons for these changes are complex. It is a mistake to see them as the whims of authoritarian governments; they owe far more to populist democracy, the growth of feminism, and increasing respect for the rights of children and of victims of crime. DSPD was also consistent with a strategy to combat social exclusion. Furthermore, knowledge has changed substantially since the 1980s, with greater and more widespread understanding of predatory paedophiles (D'Arcy and Gosling, 1998; Oliver and Smith, 1993) and of the lasting psychological harm done to many survivors of physical and sexual assault.

These social changes had their greatest impact on the criminal justice system, but mental health services could not expect to remain isolated from these evolving values and expectations. Indeed, over the same period there has been growing demand that professionals become more responsive to the needs and concerns of their clients or patients. In this context, psychiatrists' attempts to wash their hands of responsibility for offenders with personality disorder were anachronistic and doomed to failure. DSPD developments may have been the starting point of a new approach to people with personality disorder, but it has become just one small part of a process that includes policy and attitude change, as in the NIHME (2003) document *Personality Disorder: No Longer a Diagnosis of Exclusion*, the development of Multi-Agency Public Protection Panels/ Panel Arrangements (MAPPPS/MAPPAs), development and demise of a National Patient Safety Agency and an overarching determination to develop safer services.

2. Standardised risk assessment and the Psychopathy Checklist

We introduced this chapter with concerns about reliable and valid diagnosis of personality disorder; in particular, categorical diagnosis of antisocial personality disorder has been so confounded with criminality that it hardly discriminates between prisoners. In the USA, for example, one study found 90% of prisoners had the diagnosis (Guze, 1976), while in England and Wales the rate was so high that the Office of National Statistics researchers took the decision to exclude it from most calculations (Singleton et al., 1998a). This unsatisfactory situation changed to some extent with the concept of the psychopathy, and development of the Psychopathy Checklist – Revised (PCL-R; Hare, 2003). It is not perfect, and there is plenty of room for argument about the nature of psychopathy, but the PCL-R satisfied the first precondition for research by allowing measurement and discrimination between groups. Similar considerations apply to the management of risk; some of the claims for actuarial risk measures are overblown, and they are of limited use in individual risk prediction, but standardised measures have allowed systematic description and communication of risk, and lend themselves to population studies (see also chapter 22). It is fair to say that, without the improvements resulting from the use of standardised measures of personality disorder and risk, there could never have been a DSPD service. An early vision of DSPD services was that *all prisoners* would be measured on a battery of scales and those with the 'correct scores' would go to the new service. This approach oversimplifies the hazy boundaries between different types of deviance, and it risks repetition of old mistakes in medicalising criminality (Sim, 1990; Maden, 1993).

We have also explored another historical problem in the treatment of personality disorder – how to measure change. Clinicians accustomed to monitoring progress by the fading of symptoms such as hallucinations or delusions struggle with patients who often do not present with sustained descriptions of subjective complaints in this kind of way, and it is easy to lose sight of treatment goals. DSPD services were ahead of most UK forensic mental health services in exploring the use of structured dynamic measures to define goals and progress towards them. We do not yet know how well these proxy measures of change will correlate with behaviour in the community when patients move on. Any attempt to measure such correlations is fraught with methodological problems – not least, the fact that only patients who appear to do well on the proxy measure are likely to be exposed to the outside world.

One of the original concerns about the emphasis on the PCL-R and risk assessment tools in defining DSPD was that this would result in the locking away of 'people who have not done anything', but just happened to get a high score on an instrument about an abstract concept. This worry has proved unfounded. The main reason is that, for all the claims to statistical sophistication, violence risk assessment relies on the old adage that the past is the best guide to the future. The risk threshold set for entry to DSPD services ensures that people must have done something in order to get over the bar. In this context, strengths of the risk assessment tools recommended are that they rely largely on historical and verifiable fact and are transparent.

3. The Dutch TBS system

The Dutch TBS system has been managing violent and sexual offenders in institutions and in the community since 1928. Under TBS legislation, offenders convicted of a serious sexual or violent offence and judged to present a high risk of re-offending are sentenced by the criminal court to a TBS order. They serve a prison sentence appropriate to the offence and are transferred to a TBS facility for treatment at the end of that sentence. They remain within the TBS system indefinitely (subject to regular review by a tribunal), first in a secure institution and, when safe, as conditionally discharged, supervised patients in the community. Dutch courts rarely give a sentence of life imprisonment and the TBS order is in many ways a substitute.

Treatment within the TBS system is eclectic, but CBT is prominent, and there is also an emphasis on therapeutic community principles and on work; patients are expected to spend about half the week in paid employment. Anti-libidinal medication is widely used with sex offenders, and accounts for much of the medical input as most other treatments are delivered by psychologists or specially trained (non-medical) therapists.

The practical outcome of a TBS order – prison then indefinite detention in hospital – is the same as for many English prisoners transferred to hospital near the end of their sentence, but the Dutch system is more transparent. The future is spelled out at the time of sentencing; planning can begin early. The experience of staff in DSPD hospital units has been that they spend much time and energy mollifying patients who are understandably angry at being transferred to hospital just as they were expecting release to the community. The nature of DSPD means that the information to support detention on grounds of risk was available at the time of sentencing, so it is reasonable to ask why, if an indeterminate order is appropriate, it was not considered so by the sentencing judge.

The problem was often compounded by the Mental Health Act (MHA) 1983, worded so as to encourage patients in a belief that refusal to co-operate would lead to their being deemed untreatable and, therefore, not detainable. In fact mental health review tribunals rarely discharge patients on such grounds, and perhaps the removal of the language of 'treatability' by the MHA 2007 will help. By contrast, people in the TBS system are always given the simple message that movement through the system depends on progress in treatment, so, where possible, everything works much more quickly. Nevertheless, the TBS units also suffer from difficulties in discharging patients; after a minimum of 6 years of treatment, about 20% of patients are judged unlikely ever to be discharged and plans are made for indefinite detention, subject to rights of appeal and regular review, with priority given to quality of life. Hitherto, even high security hospitals in England have rarely had to contemplate indefinite stay for any patient, least of all those with personality disorder (Jamieson and Taylor, 2002). A threat was that the DSPD initiative might have made English hospital units more like the Dutch TBS units in this less appealing way. Sentencing within the 'indefinite public protection' (IPP) framework, however, went some way down this road, attracting a great deal of approprium as result (See chapter 2).

4. Cognitive behavioural programmes for sexual and violent offenders

DSPD may also be seen as a part of the backlash against the therapeutic nihilism that infected prisons in the 1970s and 1980s. The 'what works?' movement of the 1990s (McGuire, 1995) sought to counter this pessimism and led to a rapid growth in CBT based programmes for sexual and violent offenders. Canada can claim to be the birthplace of such offending behaviour programmes (OBPs), but they have now been developed in prisons in many countries, and some specialist mental health services are beginning to consider that versions of them might usefully be developed for patients too. Inevitably, some offenders benefit more than others from OBPs, and there have been research reports claiming that people with high scores on the PCL-R are likely to do worse than others in most respects: more likely to drop-out, to disrupt treatment or to re-offend after treatment. There have even been claims in this last respect that such programmes make high PCL-R scorers worse, although a systematic review of the literature found that of the 24 studies of this identified, only three were of appropriate design for the research question, and none met the reviewers' methodological standards (D'Silva et al., 2004). There may, in fact, be little case for the gloom about potential responsiveness.

Nevertheless, there is a problem with offending behaviour programmes which must be acknowledged. They are designed to reach the maximum number of offenders at minimum cost so are, by nature, 'one size fits all', with little attempt to tailor the intervention to individual pathology. One would not, therefore, expect outliers on any dimension to do well. Drop-outs are not of major concern so long as most people complete the course – indeed, drop-outs create a place for someone else when places on such courses are in high demand. High PCL-R scorers were, thus, often excluded from standard programmes, so some more specialist versions have been developed through the DSPD initiative, for example the Chromis programme (Wallace and Newman, 2004).

At present, only evidence relating to the generally available programmes, applied to less selected groups of offenders, is available, although there are no RCTs. Most of the published trials have relied on matching. Hanson et al. (2002) reviewed 43 studies that included at least a matched, untreated group, yielding a total of 9,454 sexual offenders (5,078 treated and 4,376 untreated). Meta-analysis showed treated v. untreated recidivism rates of 12.3% v. 16.8% for sexual offending and 27.9% v. 39.2% for all offending. For both groups of offenders, these differences are statistically significant; when analysis is restricted to interventions explicitly meeting current standards for OBPs, the differences are more substantial: 9.9% v. 17.4% for sexual recidivism, and 32% v. 51% for all recidivism. So, there is cautious optimism about such programmes, although Marshall and McGuire (2003) note we do not know 'with which types of offenders' treatment is most likely to be effective (p.654). It is likely, however, that impact will be least on predatory offenders or those with 'stranger' victims and perhaps those with high psychopathy scores – in other words, those for whom DSPD services were designed (Maden, 2007). Brooks-Gordon and Bilby (2006) echo the note of caution, albeit principally for sex offenders, and draw attention to the 'enormous political and institutional pressure to prove that treatment works'.

Despite this uncertainty, cognitively based programmes remain at the heart of OBPs for DSPD, not least because of the advantage that staff in a prison can be maximally involved in delivering such programmes; training, and support in delivering the programme, is far less costly than a full clinical training, for whatever clinical discipline. Then, too, explanations of behaviour couched in cognitive terms make sense to staff and offenders alike, and they help both to structure expectations and plan care pathways. Explicit procedures and aims facilitate evaluation. Even if more evidence is needed on effectiveness, they also provide for methods to achieve that. The Violence Reduction Programme (Wong et al., 2007) at Saskatoon's Regional Psychiatric Centre (RPC), a specialised unit of the Canadian correctional system, is an example of one of these programmes. Maden et al. (2004) contrasts it with the DSPD programme, for which it served as a model. There are two major differences: first, the Saskatoon unit is part of the prison system. All programme participants are serving prisoners who have volunteered and can be sent back to ordinary prisons if they are violent within the unit, or if treatment is not progressing; second, the Canadian correctional system includes a 'Supermax' prison (see also chapter 25) that, effectively, provides backup in dealing with the most disruptive or violent behaviour. By contrast, the English DSPD system is committed to providing two parallel and different services – the hospital stream and the prison stream. The challenge for the high secure hospitals is daunting; if there is too much emphasis on control and security the CBT will not work, yet too much reliance on self-control may lead to indiscipline and the disruption of therapy.

The Future: Beyond DSPD

The DSPD service was expensive, with a bed in a high secure hospital costing about £240,000 per annum. This is a huge sum when it is anticipated that standard cases will require between 3 and 5 years of treatment and many patients will be there for much longer, although compared to some innovative treatments in physical medicine, the figure may pale into insignificance. Whatever the ethical and scientific controversies about the service have been, to a large extent, economics have determined its future. Study of the economics of treating personality disorder more generally is becoming ever more sophisticated (e.g. Soeteman et al., 2010), and the full NICE guidelines on treatment of antisocial personality disorder and borderline personality disorder (NICE, 2009a,b) include financial information along these lines. The true cost of untreated personality disorder in serious offenders, including recidivist child sex offenders is, however, incalculable. Decommissioning of some of the DSPD pilot units will allow for funding of a 'personality disorder pathway', with access to psychologically informed planned environments (PIPES) in prisons and the community and extension of currently accredited programmes (Joseph and Benefield, 2012).

PERSONALITY DISORDER: SOME CONCLUSIONS

Personality disorder is a common problem – in one form or another far more common in the general population than schizophrenia – and yet its assessment and treatment has been peripheral in most general psychiatric services. Forensic mental health services are beginning to respond, and some have specialist personality disorder services, with naturalistic outcome data that are promising. Personality disorders are the cause of much misery for the primary sufferers and for their family and friends. They have serious consequences in the associated mortality rates from suicide and accident, which are much higher than in the general population; some personality disorders have a strong association with repeated offending, sometimes serious offending. The nature of disorders of personality is becoming clearer, but there is still much to learn to meet the substantial personal and population needs created by them. With such improvements in knowledge about genetic loading and environmental hazards that may contribute in various mixes to causing them, personality disorders may, with benefit, be conceptualised as developmental disorders. Improvements in assessments can and are being brought to bear on improving treatment, and there is growing, if far from good enough evidence that treatment, especially psychological treatments delivered within an appropriately multi-professional framework, can make a positive difference to health and social function. Borderline and antisocial personality disorders are not the most common in the general population, but they tend to be the ones most frequently seen in specialist forensic services, whether based in health or criminal justice services. Forensic mental health practitioners currently lead much of the good practice in working with people with such disorders. It is important that the skills and the willingness to treat people with personality disorder are disseminated more widely throughout mental health services if such people are to be held on a recovery trajectory and, where the disorders are linked with serious offending, they, their families and the wider community are to be made safer.

17
Deception, dissociation and malingering

Edited, written and revised by
John Gunn

Written by
John Gunn
David Mawson
Paul Mullen
Peter Noble

1st edition edited by **Paul Mullen**

I have done that – says my memory. I could not have done that – says my pride; [the] end remains inexorable. Eventually memory gives in. (Nietzche, 1886)

DECEPTIVE MENTAL MECHANISMS

Deception occupies a central and privileged place in forensic psychiatry. The founding fathers of the speciality, such as Haslam (1817a,b), Ray (1838) and East (1927), were all much concerned with the need to recognize fraudulent claims in the accused, the claimant and the conscripted serviceman, to potentially mitigating, compensable or exempting disorders. The touchstone of the expert's skill used to be in distinguishing between the genuine and the simulated. Although this particular question has lost much of its urgency, what remains central are issues surrounding those, all too human, tendencies to deny, to lie to others, and to lose oneself in self-deception.

The tendency to modify our experiences of current reality by how we think rather than by what we do, and to interpret and edit memories of the past in pursuit of present needs is universal. We try to escape the contingencies of reality by a variety of mechanisms, many wholly unconscious.

Substituting

Available alternatives are sometimes substituted for those objects of our desire which appear beyond reach. Pets may be substituted for people, especially children. The displacement of desire, or aggression, on to a more available, or vulnerable object, is common. In some claimants and litigants this mechanism can be at work. The bereaved, deprived of their loved one, may displace their energy from the pursuit of the lost love on to the pursuit of compensation. At first glance, their actions may appear venal and self-serving, but behind this appearance can lie a tragic attempt to restore an unbearable loss through pursuit of the substituted goal.

Daydreaming

Daydreaming is the way in which we turn away from the daunting task of wresting the desired from reality, or from the conflicts inherent in current obligations, into a world of fantasy and make-believe. In children, the world of private make-believe and public reality can merge and mix. In some adults, the dividing line between the internal world of fantasy and the shared external world of consensual reality remains wavering and uncertain. The French concept of mythomania, often treated as synonymous with pathological lying, captures this quality of being caught up in one's own fantasies and imaginery adventures.

Lying

Lying, or to use the minimally less pejorative and far broader term 'deception', is universal. Advertisers 'put a gloss' on their products, companies fail to disclose the whole story, politicians distort, sportsmen break rules when they think they will not be detected, and we all deceive on occasions to obtain advantage or avoid embarrassment. Lying may even be part of normal development and individuation (Ford et al., 1988). Hartshorne and May (1928) conducted a series of elegant experiments demonstrating the frequency of deceptive behaviour amongst youngsters. Most authors agree that lying involves the consciousness of falsity, the intent to deceive, and a preconceived goal or purpose. Normal prevarication is instrumental and, at least initially, the liar is aware of the deception. In practice, the intentional lie merges into self-deception and we move, all too easily, from knowingly fabricating into believing our own stories.

In pathological lying (*pseudologia fantastica*; see below), there is created a tissue of fantastic lies in which the deception is not merely about matters of fact, but aims to create a whole new identity. The lies, though they may begin as instrumental, in the sense of bringing pecuniary advantage or prestige, rapidly develop to a stage where they are disproportionate to any discernible end or personal gain. Commonplace lies deceive about matters of fact, the fabrications of the pathological liar deceive about who and what s/he is; they are about creating a new identity and recreating the world. Pseudologia fantastica is about lying, but it is also about fantasy run riot which involves self-deception as much as deceiving others.

Denial

Denial of current reality is one way of coping with the disturbing and the threatening. Denial differs from lying in that it is not an attempt to convince others, or oneself, of a different reality, but involves turning away from the unacceptable. Clearly, denial involves deception and self-deception, but lacks the intention to affirm a new and false reality. In practice, denial often slips into fabrication. Denial involves the claim that something did not occur or, if it did, the subject has no memory for the events.

Amnesia

Amnesia is an inability to remember or a denial of memory. Selective memory which leaves convenient blanks is a common enough indulgence, and is to be expected in those where forgetting may bring considerable advantage. The distinctions and overlaps between so-called psychogenic amnesia and organic memory disturbances are considered later in this chapter and in chapter 12.

Self-deception

Self-deception is a concept presenting profound theoretical ambiguities, but is none the less potentially of wide applicability in psychiatry. Many aspects of what we term unconscious, dissociative, hysterical, or even abnormal illness behaviour can, from a different perspective, be spoken of as types of self-deception.

The central paradox of self-deception was described by Fingarette (1969):

For as deceiver one is insincere, guilty: whereas if genuinely deceived, one is the innocent victim.

Is then the self-deceiver both perpetrator and sufferer? The psychiatrist's view of self-deception is often influenced by the Freudian vocabulary which articulates the phenomenon as one of helplessness in the grip of unconscious conflict, for the self-deceiver is spoken of as the victim of the compulsive force of the unconscious.

Self-deception is in part about how information is interpreted and what aspects are acknowledged but, more important, it is about self-presentation; it is about what we avow as our motivations and what we accept has been our behaviour. The simplest model of self-deception is of holding two incompatible beliefs, one of which is not noticed or acknowledged. Self-deception is not just persisting in beliefs in the face of contrary evidence, nor merely holding incompatible beliefs, for it implies an active engagement which strives to maintain ignorance. The characteristics of self-deception as viewed from the vantage point of an observer include:

1. activities which appear incompatible with the individual's previous claims or behaviour;
2. the refusal of the self-deceiver to give adequate (or at least acceptable) justifications for his or her activities;
3. a refusal to accept responsibility for activities and their consequences which appears to stem not from disregard of those responsibilities, but from an inability to recognize the transgressions;
4. an adherence to the deception which persists even when it becomes personally disadvantageous.

The latter two characteristics which speak of loss of self-control tend to soften, or even remove, the moral condemnation of the self-deceiver. What of the experience of self-deception for the self-deceiver? This is difficult to pin down. Totally successful self-deception would presumably be experienced as having a conviction or desire no different from any other. We assume that some discomfort and disequilibrium accompanies most self-deceptive engagements, which may be experienced as unease or a puzzlement at one's own apparently disproportionate vehemence.

Self-deception covers a wide range of human activity. It covers the exuberant, if shallow individuals, who commit themselves to a course of action in the enthusiasm of the moment, only to later disavow that commitment. It includes the envious, who undermine and damage those around them under the guise of friendship, apparently in ignorance of their own motives. It includes those who convince themselves of their own illness and disability. It includes most of us as we try and impose coherence and create a flattering tale out of our past and present activities.

Occasionally, it is possible to see self-deception emerging. A young man who had strangled his girlfriend was examined a matter of a few hours after the event. He gave, at that time, an account of the killing marked by great distress and genuine perplexity about how he came to commit such an act. A few days later he claimed to have only the vaguest memories of the event leading up to the killing and none for the act itself. A week or so later, a story began gradually to emerge as he 'remembered' what had really happened and the provocations which had occasioned the act. The following month, he gave a clear account of intolerable provocation which culminated in his loss of control and which 'must have led to the killing', although he said he could not recall committing the deed. Somewhere in that progression, self-deception must have played a part but, by the time this man went to trial, he seemed to honestly believe his own account of the events, and certainly he was filled with a genuine sense of grievance and injustice when his defence foundered.

Self-deception involves the editing and reorganization of memory to serve the needs of current imperatives. In fact, such restructuring of memory is to some degree a normal process which is going on constantly. The view of human memory as analogous to a massive filing system or the hard disk of a computer, which assuming you employ the correct access codes calls up exactly what was filed away, is increasingly coming under critical scrutiny. Memory is, at least in part, a functional and selective system which is constantly evolving and adapting to current needs (Rosenfield, 1988). In a mundane way, we all re-write our own histories so as to ease the disjunctions between our present attitudes and positions and our past actions and views. Self-deception is essential to righteousness, or any other form of pomposity. Equally, it plays a prominent role in creating and maintaining some of our patients' difficulties.

PATHOLOGICAL FALSIFICATION

Confabulation

Confabulation is the falsification of memory occurring in clear consciousness in association with an organically derived amnesia (Berlyne, 1972). On occasion, it is the fabricating of false statements by someone with impaired memory in order to cover his or her embarrassment at forgetting. It is typically encountered in amnesic disorders when the patients lack insight into their impairment and, therefore, would be incapable of constructing falsifications to cover a deficit which they were unaware existed. Bonhoeffer (1904) distinguished between 'momentary' confabulation, where the patient, when asked specifically about recent events, responds by recounting more distant unrelated memories and 'fantastic' confabulations which involved spontaneous creations, often grandiose or absurd. The fantastic, or spontaneous, confabulations tend to be associated with amnesias in which there is associated frontal lobe dysfunction, whereas the provoked, or momentary confabulations, are the result of an attempt to respond to specific enquiries in those with a defective memory. It is found in amnesic patients and, to a lesser extent, in normal subjects whose memory fails them for some reason (Kopelman, 1987a). It is not a form of intentional deception.

This chapter is concerned with a variety of conditions, disparate in many ways, but in which deception, both of others and the self, plays a part. The introduction was intended to emphasize the extent to which there is a continuum between the experiences and activities of us all and the disorders to be described. Deception is, however, a term redolent of judgment and rejection. Here the emphasis is on the recognition of distress and disorder, so that it can be treated, rather than identifying deceptions in order to confound or condemn them.

Lying

Lying, as has been noted, is a frequent, universal, human activity. It needs to be distinguished from confabulation which does not include any intent to deceive. Lying is so ubiquitous that it must have many different functions, for example in social parlance we distinguish between 'white' lies and other types such as 'barefaced'. White lies may be to assist someone else for example giving them reassurance or unwarranted praise. The lie that is most frowned upon is of course the lie to gain dishonest advantage or to escape from the consequences of one's actions. There is a large industry in the criminal justice world of trying to tell whether a witness or a potential perpetrator is telling the truth or not. This arises from the somewhat mistaken notion that the best witness to an event is the central participant who will be able to explain what they saw or did to other people. Many police officers see their central role in detective work as getting a guilty person to 'cough' or 'confess'. More sophisticated police officers and others involved in crime detection know that uncorroborated confessions are poor evidence. Yet the belief that somehow, in some way 'science' will enable the liar to be unmasked, dies very hard indeed. It is possible to find at least 10 ways of attempting to detect lies with various forms of technology. These include the polygraph, the fMRI scanner, the voice stress test, and others. Most of the techniques are trying to detect a rise in arousal and anxiety when the subject is being questioned or interviewed. This is based on the premise that all lying is accompanied by anxiety. Most of us can subjectively refute this notion and indeed the research results from the various instruments are disappointing if they are to be the centrepiece of, for example, a criminal investigation. None of the results from this type of technology are allowed in British courts.

An exception to the arousal theory is the attempt to detect lying by using the fMRI scanner. Initial research suggested that the act of lying produces more prefrontal cortex activity than telling the truth does. However some sophisticated transAtlantic collaborative research has found that subjects can beat the scanning test by simple distracting countermeasures, presumably to deflect their concentration, when they are lying (Ganis et al., 2011). The authors conclude that this renders the otherwise attractive lie detector as vulnerable in 'real world situations'. In fact the accuracy dropped from 100% to 33% if the subject applied countermeasures; a fairly stark warning to the overenthusiastic technological interrogator.

The basis of this work lies in experiments conducted by Spence and others (e.g. Spence et al., 2004; Spence 2005; Spence et al., 2008). These showed that deception is an executive task; it elicits greater activation of the prefrontal regions and also incurs a processing cost, manifest in longer response times.

A scholarly account of what lies are about and how to detect them is given by Vrij (2008) who goes on to discuss ways in which training can assist in the difficult task of detecting lies. At the end of his book he lists 24 studies giving an indication of how far training can help. By and large the studies show that observers are only about 50% accurate in detecting lies (i.e. not much better than guessing) but this can be improved by training sessions, in one remarkable example raising the detection rate from 54% to 69%. However he concludes:

> In this book I reported that several researchers have claimed to have developed techniques that discriminates between truths and lies with very high accuracy. My advice to them is to keep their feet firmly on the ground. In my view no tool is infallible.

Our view remains that would-be lie detectors, for example police officers, will be better employed in trying to get evidence by other means, even though no criminal investigation would be complete without talking to the alleged offender.

The dangers of using neuroscience results as evidence of crime are perhaps best shown in India. Angela Saini (2009), a web journalist wrote of the case of a woman tried for murder in June 2008. She headed the article 'The Brain Police: Judging Murder With an MRI'. However the article says that the accused had an 'EEG' brain scan.

> To Judge Shalini Phansalkar-Joshi, sentencing her last June to life in prison, Sharma's electro-encephalogram left no doubt: the brain scan revealed 'experiential knowledge' which proved that she had to be the killer. Her ex-fiancé Udit Bharati, a 24-year-old fellow student at Pune's Indian Institute of Modern Management, had been found dead after eating sweets laced with arsenic... As the judge saw it, the proof was in the science. Sharma had manifested an undeniable 'neuro experiential knowledge' of the crime – which the brain could acquire only through direct experience – when she had undergone a brain scan in Mumbai a year earlier... A tape played a voice reading a series of statements in Hindi, each detailing an aspect of the murder as the investigators understood it. Sharma said nothing as the EEG machine measured her brain activity. For a while, the statements elicited no detectable EEG response. Then she heard: 'I had an affair with Udit.' A section of her brain previously dormant registered a brightly coloured response on the EEG. More statements followed and the voice on the tape each time elicited similar EEG responses: 'I got arsenic from the shop.' 'I called Udit.' 'I gave him the sweets mixed with arsenic.'
>
> 'The sweets killed Udit.' Throughout the test, she did not say a word. She didn't have to. As each statement was read, the EEG machine measured the frequencies of the electrical signals from the surface of her scalp and fed them through a set of rainbow-coloured wires into the room next door. Here a computer, almost five feet tall, performed a set of calculations and spat out its conclusion in red letters on to its screen: 'Experiential knowledge'. This meant knowledge of planning the murder, of getting the sweets, of buying the arsenic and of calling Bharati and arranging the fatal meeting. Guilty. Evidence from the scan took up almost ten pages of the judge's ruling when a year later, on 12 June 2008, he jailed Sharma for life – making her the first person in the world reported to be convicted of murder based on evidence that included a brain scan. 'I am innocent and have not committed any crime,' she implored Phansalkar-Joshi... But science had spoken: and in the six months that followed, the same lab would provide evidence that convicted two more people of murder. Neuro-imaging as truth teller had come of age.

It is important that we do not get bemused by new technologies. No doubt they will find a niche, but let us hope that they do not become used extensively until they can be shown to produce valid evidence. That day is a long way off and in the meantime we should heed careful studies such as the one quoted above by Ganis et al.

Pseudologia fantastica (pathological lying)

A group of disorders have been reported which involve fantastic lies that are developed into complex systems of deception. The terms employed for this condition include pseudologia fantastica, mythomania and pathological liars (Delbrueck, 1891; Dupré, 1905, 1925; Healy and Healy, 1915; King and Ford, 1988; Myslobodsky, 1997). The following are the clinical characteristics:

1. Extensive and gross fabrications.
2. The content and extent of the lies are disproportionate to any discernible end or personal advantage.
3. The lies deceive not just about matters of fact, but attempt to create a new and false identity for the liar.
4. The subject appears to become caught up in his or her own fabrications which take on a life of their own in which the subject seems eventually to believe.
5. The lying is a central and persistent feature of the patient's life and the mythologism of a lifetime comes to supplant valid memories.

When pathological liars are enmeshed in their fabric of lies, the degree of self-deception may make it difficult to distinguish them from patients in the grip of a delusional system. Kraepelin (1896) included some patients with systematized delusions under pseudologia fantastica and Krafft Ebing (1886) used the term 'inventive paranoia' for both pathological liars and deluded subjects. Most writers, however, excluded deluded or otherwise psychotic subjects (e.g. Healy and Healy, 1915). Closely related conditions are Munchausen's syndrome (Asher, 1951) and feigned bereavement (Snowdon et al., 1978).

Two clinical examples may help illustrate this disorder:

A patient was brought to the outpatient department by his landlady who was concerned with his increasing depression which she feared might lead him to harm himself. She explained that he was now living in much reduced circumstances, having suffered major financial losses and the desertion of his erstwhile friends. It became clear that he had been living rent free for some considerable time, and the landlady was providing all his meals and a regular supply of pipe tobacco, to say nothing of comfort and support. The patient was a well-dressed man in his early 60s, who wore tinted spectacles and assumed an air of profound sadness. He was induced to give his history despite several claims that he did not want to go over the past. The personal history provided was of humble origins from which he escaped via a university scholarship. He claimed to have left university prematurely to join the government forces fighting in Spain. At the end of the Spanish civil war, he reported a brief period in Rhodesia before joining the British army during the Second World War. A distinguished army career was followed by a period working in the United Nations. The tale continued with a series of great successes followed by undeserved disasters until he reached his present homeless, lonely plight. The stories had plausibility and a wealth of detail. Suspicions as to their authenticity were raised by the remarkable similarity of some aspects of his account to the memoirs of such figures as Orwell and Wingate. Over subsequent months, it emerged that the patient had lived most of his life in London, he had never been in the army, far from being unmarried he had been married on a number of occasions and his reported childlessness ignored a number of offspring. Following the exposure of his identity, the patient disappeared, but was encountered some years later having created for himself a new persona and an equally dedicated supporter in the form of another middle-aged lady sponsoring the ageing and misunderstood artist. At a second encounter, he greeted his doctor with apparent pleasure and without a blush, or any visible unease, told of his new circumstances. He did not seem to be concerned about, or even aware of, the possibility that his new identity might be threatened. He believed in himself, or at least he evinced no insecurity.

The second case was admitted from prison where he was said to have become depressed and suicidal.

He was a small young man who, though in his early 20s, could have passed for 12 or 13 years of age. He gave an account of having been raped in prison with the connivance of a number of prison officers. He had made these allegations previously, and they had been extensively investigated without any basis having been found. He gave a history of having been seduced in his early teens by the mother of a school friend, and described a number of romantic adventures prior to his arrest on arson charges. Other aspects of his history included a graphic account of child abuse, remarkable academic and artistic success, cut short by circumstance, and a period of army service. This young man attempted to create by his stories an identity characterized by remarkable talents and charm, but a personal history replete with disadvantage and tragedy. Misunderstood, abused, cheated and victimized, nevertheless, he struggled to realize his potential. Different stories were given to different members of staff and even more dramatic discrepancies emerged between his self-presentation to other patients and that to the staff. During his time on the unit, his use of mimesis became obvious. He latched on to a patient and later a staff member whom he found admirable and began not only to talk like his new-found models, but tried to present himself in an identical manner. He even borrowed aspects of the personal histories of these two admired individuals, and presented them as his own.

Schneider (1959) regarded this group of patients as attention-seeking individuals who love to boast about themselves, and invent or act out fairy tales of self-aggrandizement. He noted that the true pathological liar begins as a story teller, but becomes so caught up in his/her fabrications that 'they forsake actuality and finish up on the stage of their own mind.' Kraupl-Taylor (1979) took a similar view describing the stories as hysterical confabulations. He believed that recent reminiscences are temporarily replaced by hallucinated reminiscences, which are true memories to the patient, at least for a time. Kraupl-Taylor emphasized the negative or disadvantageous aspects of this behaviour. Whilst the pathological liar has the gratification of an occasional audience that is impressed, this pleasure is short-lived, only to be followed by the humiliation of being treated as a liar. Such patients are soon generally disbelieved, and they may be teased mercilessly. Such behaviour does merge into more externally goal-oriented deception.

Pathological lying is usually encountered in forensic practice in those accused of fraud, swindling, making false accusations or false confessions (Powell et al., 1983; Sharrock and Cresswell, 1989). Once the counterfeit is exposed, the pathological liar will often give up his deceptions and readily confess, sometimes to offences in which he was not involved, thus beginning a new cycle of attention-seeking mythologies in the very act of acknowledging the previous deceptions. The frauds and swindles perpetrated by the pathological liar usually form part of an attempt to create a false identify. Such frauds are often flamboyant and have little in common with the furtive and carefully planned dishonesty of the more typical fraud. Pathological liars are closer to confidence tricksters, though unlike them, they do not take the money and run, but persist in the pretence long after exposure is inevitable. Their lies are rarely aimed at excusing or exculpating their offences, but more frequently, at attracting notice and inflating their importance.

After reviewing 72 published cases King and Ford (1988) suggested that the sex distribution of cases is approximately equal and the age of onset is usually adolescence. Forty per cent of the cases they reviewed had a history of some central nervous system abnormality, such as an abnormal EEG, a history of head trauma, or CNS infection. Twenty-five per cent of the men had epilepsy. Other notable problems were criminality, psychiatric hospitalization, suicide attempts and a family history of psychiatric illness. King and Ford suggest that when disease simulation (Munchhausen syndrome, about a quarter of the cases) or impersonation of another person occurs it is the pseudologia fantastica which is the primary disorder. King and Ford concluded their review by saying ' Further research in this clinical area, particularly of the neurophysiologic correlates, is sorely needed.' That remains the position; no further research on this topic has been conducted. An interesting further case has been published (Birch et al., 2006). The woman in this case showed an interesting extra feature in that she was able to get other people, intimates, to corroborate her fictional stories. This characteristic is rare but has been reported before (Healy and Healy, 1915; Wooton, 1996). It has also, apparently, been labelled by Helene Deutsch in a German paper as 'pseudologie à deux' or 'shared daydreams' (quoted in Birch et al., 2006).

Enoch and Ball (2001) sub-classified pathological lying into four types:

1. The professional impersonator who pretends to be a doctor, a priest, a lawyer.
2. The swindler who pretends to be wealthy and/or an important business man.
3. An outraged woman who alleges a fictitious sexual assault.
4. A false confessor who claims to have committed a serious crime.

To this list we would add the common fantasist, common because the condition occurs more frequently than the others and s/he tells a whole series of apparently pointless tall stories set in a context of ordinariness.

The common fantasist is not particularly dangerous, but the other types can produce serious consequences including bodily harm. Management is extremely difficult. Even when prosecuted the fantastic tales may not subside. The best that can be offered is support and detailed discussion in an attempt to provide some insight and help induce some self-control, but these efforts often fail.

Abnormal Illness Behaviour

Parsons (1951) regarded illness and health as socially institutionalized roles. A sick person's role is legitimated and allowed by its undesirability and the need to co-operate with others to get well. While in the sick role, normal obligations are suspended and responsibilities are reduced, but the role might not be granted unless adequate evidence of disease were available. Mechanic (1962) described 'illness behaviour' which referred to

the ways in which symptoms may be differentially perceived, evaluated and acted (or not acted) upon by different kinds of persons.

Later, Mechanic (1986) emphasized that in his view illness and illness experience are shaped by socio-cultural and socio-psychological factors, irrespective of their genetic, physiological and other biological bases. Away from the research laboratory illness is often used to achieve a variety of social and personal objectives, having little to do with biological systems or the pathogenesis of disease.

He went on to ask himself: Why do 50% of patients entering medical care have symptoms and complaints that do not fit the International Classification of Diseases? Why are rates of depression and the use of medication relatively high among women, whereas alcoholism, hard drug use and violence are particularly common among men? Why among the Chinese are affective expressions of depression uncommon, but somatic symptoms relatively frequent? Why are rates of suicide among young black people in the USA relatively low, but rates of homicide high? Rather than attempting answers to such questions, he urged us to look beyond individuals to their social environment. He pointed out that the nineteenth-century phenomenon of female hysteria has all but disappeared in the west, perhaps due to a change in social response to the characteristic symptoms. Illness behaviour is more than a psychological response among persons faced with a situation calling for assessment. It arises in response to troubling social situations, and may serve as an effective means of achieving release from social expectations, as an excuse for failure, or as a way of obtaining variety of privileges, including monetary compensation. A complaint of illness is one way in our society of obtaining reassurance and support.

Pilowski (1969) proposed 'abnormal illness behaviour' as a subcategory of illness behaviour for those patients who have physical symptoms for which no organic explanation can be found. This is a useful extension of the concept of illness behaviour, even though it is not clear why it should be confined to physical symptoms and organic disease. The forensic psychiatrist may be called to see a number of conditions which in some ways can be regarded as variants of malingering, but which can also be regarded as gross abnormalities of illness behaviour, abnormalities of such a degree that instead of eliciting support and sympathy, they produce rejection and anger on the part of doctors, which are sometimes coupled with frankly punitive responses.

DISSOCIATIVE DISORDERS

Dissociation

Dissociation is a commonly described mental mechanism. It implies separation and splitting. It often means that one part of the mind is paying no attention to another or is unaware of it. It can be induced by hypnosis. For example Charcot, the nineteenth-century 'king of hysteria', hypnotized one of his female patients (all his patients were female) and suggested to her that she was two people. Each side of her was to have a different boyfriend. She was introduced to these two men as she lay on a couch and she would allow each to caress his specified side of her body, but if his hand ventured to the other side she would angrily turn it away.

The idea of splitting and separation so that parts of an individual's body are dysfunctional and out of touch with other parts, and parts of the individual's mind, including their memory, are separated from other parts, lies underneath many of the topics discussed in this chapter. Psychogenic non-epileptic seizures can be, at least in part, understood in this way and are sometimes called dissociative seizures. A remarkable philosophical treatise has been written on the subject, not by psychiatrists but by a philosopher, Ian Hacking (1995) in a book entitled *Rewriting the Soul*. He draws together many different threads and implants the topic in its history. Dissociative phenomena have been observed from ancient times but the manifestation of these phenomena changes and so does the naming. For example Hacking suggests that the hysteria of Charcot which captivated the whole of France in the nineteenth century, turning his kind of neurology into a public spectacle didn't just disappear at the beginning of the twentieth century, as many people believe, but it changed into other forms. Hacking suggests that in the United States it became multiple personality disorder.

A full discussion about dissociative disorders does not belong in a textbook of forensic psychiatry and they will therefore be dealt with briefly. They are mentioned at all because of their relevance to simulation and malingering which may come to the attention of the forensic psychiatrist who undertakes medico-legal compensation work. They also have some relevance to the broader subject of dishonesty and require a textbook in their own right.

To set the subject in context it is worth briefly considering the history of hysteria, for hundreds of years an important disorder, particularly in women, which is now disappeared from the psychiatric lexicon, although it is almost certainly just transmuted into other disorders. The term hysteria obviously implies something to do with the uterus and it was originally thought to be a disorder which affected women exclusively and was caused by a wandering uterus. The term is still used colloquially to mean emotional excesses and loss of self-control probably related to panic. Charcot used to give his public demonstrations at the famous Paris hospital, Salpêtrière. He described the course of the illness in these terms:

A little girl about seven years old begins to cough and goes on coughing for two months without any known cause. An experienced physician recognizes at once that he has not to deal with a case of bronchitis but one of hysteria. Then the little girl is all at once affected with a stiff neck... Hysterical torticollis is made out. …. The child's leg becomes stiff and painful. This is hysteric contracture... Things go along pretty smoothly till menstruation. Then the child begins to get peculiar – to have curious ideas. She is alternately sad or cheerful to excess. Then, one day she utters a cry, falls to the ground, and presents all the symptoms of an attack of hystero-epilepsy. She begins to assume various postures, to speak of fantastic animals, to mention words which are neither suitable to her age nor to her position in society.[1]

Charcot unhooked hysteria from the uterus and from the demonic possession theories that also abounded. He described it as an inherited neurological disorder, neither madness nor malingering (Hustvedt, 2011). The patients may suffer from anaesthesia, hypersensitivity, anorexia, bulimia, constipation, diarrhoea, excessive urination, retention of urine, depressed intellectual functions, heightened intellectual functions, insomnia, attacks of sleep, and violent seizures, said Bournville, a disciple of Charcot's; in other words contrasting bodily symptoms which vary and fluctuate. Charcot himself described 'grand hysteria' characterized by episodic convulsions in four phases. First, the epileptoid phase of tonic and clonic seizures, preceded by an aura, just as in epilepsy. Second, grand movements or clownism simulated the contortions and acrobatics of circus performers. The third phase of 'passionate poses' was when the patient acted out emotional states such as terror, ecstasy, and amorous supplication, all ending in the final and fourth stage of delirium. This material comes from a remarkable book on Charcot, his life and work and the story of three of his patients by Asti Hustvedt (2011).

This history gives many clues to the disorders which at the beginning of the twenty-first century we call dissociative disorders. The twentieth century saw the disease of hysteria transmuted into other conditions such as shellshock which reinforced the notion that the symptoms

---

[1] This quote is taken from Hustvedt (2011) who is quoting Charcot's paper 'De l'influénce des lesions traumatiques sur le développement des phénomènes d'hystérie locale,' in *Progrès Médical*, May 4, 1878, cited in Goetz, Bonduelle, and Gelfand, *Charcot*, p.173.

arise from stress and trauma. By 2000 the nomenclature of these disorders was crystallized into perhaps six types of dissociation:

> *depersonalization disorder in which an individual feels detached from his or her surroundings and may feel outside of the body; psychogenic non-epilepetic seizures (see below); dissociative amnesia (see below); fugue (see below); dissociative identity disorder, sometimes known as multiple personality disorder (see below); and possession states.*

This list is not exhaustive of dissociative phenomena, symptoms change with time and place and often overlap, Stengel (1941) included, in his series of fugue cases, a case which could also be considered a case of multiple personality disorder. One of Burt's (1923) cases of pathological lying has subsequently appeared in the literature as illustrative of typical multiple personality (McKellar, 1979). It is the core of dissociation which is important to understand if treatment is to be provided.

Psychogenic Non-epileptic Seizures

In our first edition we had a section on 'pseudo-epileptic seizures'. Like other dissociative disorders the name has changed. At one time many neurologists and psychiatrists assumed that non-epileptic seizures were simulated or malingered. It is interesting that Charcot thought they were always genuine. Modern thinking has moved nearer to Charcot than was the case in the mid-twentieth century. Undoubtedly some non-epileptic seizures will be consciously simulated in order to gain something, perhaps attention, perhaps some compensation, perhaps a reason to be excused duties. However, the topic of non-epileptic seizures illustrates as clearly as any how difficult it is to discern underlying motive and distinguish it from distress and organic pathology which justifies medical intervention. Indeed it is possible to argue that even if the seizures are consciously contrived with an object in view, they are still an important flag-waving phenomenon which requires skilled intervention.

A good review of this topic is given by Benbadis (2005) in Wyllie's textbook on the treatment of epilepsy. Benbadis divides non-epilepetic seizures into three groups: somatoform disorders, factitious disorders and malingering. Somatoform disorders are physical symptoms caused by unconscious psychological factors. In turn somatoform disorders can be subdivided into conversion disorders and somatization disorders, but the nomenclature is now becoming esoteric and unhelpful. Similarly the distinction between factitious disorders and malingering is arcane and boils down to whether the patient is to be treated as such or rejected as a fraud. These distinctions are extremely difficult if not impossible to make clearly, and the only time that malingering can be considered a certainty is when clear evidence is available of some sort of conscious intervention to produce the fit. Even then mistakes are made. One of us has a vivid memory of a patient who used to fold his glasses away carefully, take out his hearing aid and lie on the floor before having his seizure. Many thought he was a fraud, but investigation showed that he was not having a non-epileptic seizure, but an epileptic one, and he was preparing himself for the seizure during a fairly long aura.

The diagnosis of epilepsy as opposed to a non-epileptic seizure is based on careful observation, especially of the electroencephalogram, which ought, if there is any doubt, to be a continuous recording over several hours and whilst ambulant.

The features of non-epileptic seizure include

1. attempted restraint of the convulsive movements leads to struggling, even combativeness;
2. absence of cyanosis;
3. normal pupil responses and corneal reflexes present;
4. pressure on the supraorbital arch causes head withdrawal;
5. the level of consciousness fluctuates during the seizure;
6. marked emotionality after the episode.

Such seizures can be preceded by auras involving somatic or visual symptoms and headache. Unlike true epilepsy, in which the onset is usually abrupt, the non-epileptic seizure may be gradual in onset. Such seizures rarely result in injuries either from falls or biting of the tongue. It should be remembered that epilepsy is more often misconstrued as a psychogenic seizure than the other way round. Fully deliberately simulated seizures are rare. All psychogenic seizures, even if they are considered to be factitious should be treated by attention to any underlying mood disturbance or other psychological problem, and fairly prolonged psychotherapy in order to unravel the driving force behind the seizures, whether that force is conscious or unconscious, so it may be faced and attended to psychotherapeutically or practically. Nevertheless it is well to remember that well-established, long-standing, non-epileptic seizures are difficult to treat and have a poor prognosis.

Dissociative or Psychogenic Amnesia

As we have seen in chapter 12, amnesia is a complex symptom. Distinguishing between genuine and feigned amnesia may be difficult. Those charged with homicide offences are particularly likely to claim amnesia (Taylor and Kopelman, 1984). However, Pyszora et al. (in preparation) in a 3-year follow-up study, suspected that 10% of a sample of men on remand in custody claimed amnesia for the alleged offence, a finding only elicited in those charged with offences of violence. Within the amnesic group, nearly half were charged with murder. Only five of 59 amnesic offenders were suspected of feigning; the others were thought to have this dissociative amnesia (see also chapter 12).

Lishman (1998) has suggested that the traditionally rigid distinction between psychogenic and organic memory disturbance may be an artificial one. Pathophysiology of some kind accompanies psychogenic amnesia, just as a psychological basis underlies the influence of emotion and motive in normal forgetting. Clinically, psychogenic amnesia is either global and dense or more circumscribed. Global amnesia may occur for long periods of life. The amnesia may cover emotionally important events or issues, such as a violent outburst. Normal ability to learn new facts, but severe problems or recall of past events hints at psychogenic amnesia. A total inability to retain new information, even briefly, also favours the psychogenic form.

The classic case of alleged malingered amnesia (*Podola*), is dealt with in chapter 2. We will never know whether it was malingered or not as he was executed. The case demonstrates that it is not critical to a murder trial that the defendant remembers what happened. Whether malingered or dissociative, forgetting is almost certainly a means of coping with appalling guilt and shame. The amnesia becomes a problem when somebody has been convicted of a killing and still cannot remember what happened and so is able to participate in psychotherapy in a limited way. The first aim of psychotherapy, and it may take a long time, is to get the person concerned to retrieve some memory of the events in question. This is a long supportive process requiring much patience and continuity of psychotherapist. One of the interesting issues which may occur in that process, if it is successful, is that the patient may say, after s/he has recovered their memory, that they were simply lying and were in fact able to remember all along. Another dissociative mechanism in action perhaps? Certainly it illustrates the vague borderland between unconscious repression of thoughts and dissimulation.

Multiple Personality Disorder

Multiple personality has been described as:

The presence in one patient of two or more personalities each of which is so well defined as to have a relatively coordinated, rich, unified, and stable mental life of its own. (Taylor and Martin, 1944).

These differing personality systems tend to lose communication with each other and amnesic barriers commonly divide and prevent integration between them (Hilgard, 1977).

Before the eighteenth century, cases which may attract the label multiple personality disorder now would probably have been regarded as possession states. Cases of dual or multiple personality were reported in the scientific literature from the late eighteenth century onward and, by the end of the nineteenth, they had become a popular theme for philosophers, psychiatrists and novelists (Ellenberger, 1970; McKellar, 1979). Robert Louis Stevenson's (1886)

Strange Case of Dr Jekyll and Mr Hyde is a celebrated literary example. Prince's (1906) account of the case of Christine Beauchamp and her three personalities and James's (1890) account of Ansel Bourne, led to considerable interest in the topic, particularly in America.

In the 1950s, multiple personalities re-emerged from the pages of old textbooks. A surge of reports, both in the popular and scientific literature, followed publication of Thigpen and Cleckley's (1957) case of Eve and her three faces. This is a fictionalized account of a real case and the woman concerned has written two books giving her own account of her illness (Sizemore, 1977 and 1989). The film was popular, and may have had a role in the large number of cases that subsequently appeared in the USA (Boor, 1982). The books written by the patient may give a clearer insight into what it feels like to be in this situation.

The central clinical feature is the existence within the individual of two or more distinct personalities. The recognition of this extraordinary state of affairs may be complicated by the primary personality being unable to provide any account of the *alter egos* which are hidden behind a barrier of amnesia. A number of diagnostic signs have been described to assist the clinician (Greaves, 1980). The patient may report time distortions or unexplained memory lapses for the period when the other personality is in residence. Accounts may be provided by independent observers of discrepant behaviour patterns and patients calling themselves by different names. Writings, drawings, or other artefacts by patients may be discovered which they have no memory of producing. Other features include headaches, deep sleeps, employing 'we' rather than 'I', and pseudo-hallucinations. The condition is said to begin in childhood or adolescence, often in the context of abuse, neglect, or trauma (Congdon and Abels, 1983). Histrionic personality disorder, other dissociative states, superior intellect and high hypnotizability, are all claimed to be associated with multiple personality disorder.

The origins of multiple personality have been hypothesized to lie in repeated dissociations. These patients are peculiarly prone to dissociative states in response to stress. They defend against fear, anxiety and depression by either denying that it is happening to them or escaping into the new personality (Ludwig et al., 1972; Spiegel, 1984). These repeated dissociations are said to produce a separate store of memories which ultimately lead to different chains of integrated memories with groups of specific behaviours that can be separated by impermeable barriers (Braun, 1984). William James put this more elegantly:

Alternating personality in its simplest phases seems based on lapse of memory... any man becomes, as we say, inconsistent with himself if he forgets his engagements, pledges, knowledge and habits, and it is merely a question of degree at which point we shall say that his personality is changed (James, 1890).

The authenticity of multiple personality as a clinical entity has been repeatedly questioned, although its advocates, such as Greaves (1980), considered its existence to be demonstrated beyond reasonable doubt. He claimed that its infrequency in some services reflects not rarity, but clinical oversight on the part of those who cannot, or will not recognize the condition. This presumably means everywhere outside of North America, with the possible exception of the Netherlands. British scepticism was outlined by Fahy (1988) in a review which plotted the rise of interest in the disorder in the twentieth century. He was critical of the vagueness of the diagnostic criteria which use the word 'personality'. All disorders which use the word 'personality' in their criteria are necessarily vague, as the concept of personality is complex, subjective, and very difficult to measure. He described the disorder as an hysterical symptom; this term was still fairly widespread in the 1980s and fitted with the Hacking view given above. Fahy was taken to task by a correspondent (Fleming 1989) who said that he believed the condition exists! A beautiful example of reification.

What is difficult when dealing with dissociations in any form is to understand what the symptoms/syndrome represent to the patient. It is probably a culture bound syndrome wrought out of the dissociative potential and suggestibility of distressed and confused people looking for a way out of their predicament. It is widely acknowledged that, in practice, the new personalities allow the patient to avoid the constraints, limitations and stresses of their normal life (Prince, 1906; Taylor and Martin, 1944; Ludwig et al., 1972; McKellar, 1979).

In the United States, where the syndrome is diagnosed more commonly, the potential significance of multiple personality for questions of responsibility and culpability was quickly recognized. It has been argued that multiple personality is equivalent to sleepwalking and sufferers should benefit from a similar defence. Presumably, three lines of defence could theoretically be argued; one would be that multiple personality disorder is a form of insanity, the other would be that the usual personality cannot take responsibility for the other personalities, i.e. the fictional Dr Jekyll could not be held responsible for the actions of the fictional Mr Hyde (Stevenson, 1886), and the third would be that like the sleepwalker the individual could be regarded as unconscious when in an altered state of personality.

Without a proper study being available it is difficult to know how often such defences are used in the United States and whether they are successful, although Abrams (1983) quotes a case from Ohio where a man accused of multiple rapes was found not guilty by reason of insanity because of his multiple personality disorder. The unconsciousness argument has been advanced by French and Schechmeister (1983). To reiterate, these observations made by others do not help very much with understanding what the patient experiences, and why.

A story, probably apocryphal, is told of an Old Bailey judge called upon to sentence a man whose defence claimed he suffered from multiple personality. The judge admitted to the sadness he felt that the model citizen and blameless character who stood before him should have to share his body with the villainous perpetrator of the offences and, moreover, would have to be confined together with this criminal in a prison cell for the period of the sentence which he was about to impose.

The lack of responsibility argument is akin to the arguments that were once put (but not now allowed) about the function of amnesia. If splitting or dissociation is a response to unpleasant realities, and a way of coping with stress, then it is perhaps an exaggeration of normal mental mechanisms. If it is believed to involve a separation of different elements in the subject's character and behaviour, these elements arise from the individual's responses to the real world. The different personalities may, perhaps, be regarded as different aspects of self, albeit compartmentalized, rather than different selves. The appeal of the Jekyll and Hyde story is surely, in part, that we all recognize the splits and incompatibilities in our desires, fantasies and even actions, and that most of us have done things which retrospectively, or even at the time, seemed foreign to our personalities and we can say, afterwards, 'that really wasn't me'. If the multiple personality is to be given the benefit of repudiating legal responsibility for forbidden actions, why not all criminals who can argue they acted out of character and were thus not themselves at the time?

Fugue States

Fugue literally means to take flight or escape, but its use in psychiatry is best confined to transitory abnormal behaviour characterized by aimless wandering with alteration of consciousness, often associated with subsequent amnesia (Stengel, 1941). Fugues are encountered as one of the signs of a wide variety of psychiatric disorders, though their manifestation probably depends on a predisposition to disturbances of consciousness and dissociation. A traumatic event may act as the precipitant of the actual fugue state. During the fugue the individual may be completely amnesic for their usual life and they may assume a new personality. The relationship between fugues, multiple personality disorder, and dissociative amnesia is fairly clear. Such states are a gift for novel writers, but perhaps one of the most famous fugues was the 11-day absence of Agatha Christie who never explained where she had been or why; she may have had amnesia. A fugue state is usually short-lived (hours to days), but can last months or longer. After recovery from a fugue, previous memories usually return intact, but there is complete amnesia for the fugue episode. Fugues are usually precipitated by a stressful episode, and upon recovery there may be amnesia for the original stressor.

Fugues may be encountered in forensic psychiatric practice in subjects who, following committing a criminal act, or in the context of imminent detection, suddenly wander off apparently in a state of disturbed consciousness. For example, a young man may disappear suddenly from work, only to turn up 5 days later in a state of total exhaustion and inanition wandering in the outskirts of a foreign city. When questioned, he claims no knowledge of the events of the previous days, or how he had managed to get there. Subsequently, it may emerge that an audit at his place of work revealed that he had been misappropriating funds. Another example might be a man of previous good character stabbing an acquaintance in an argument, wandering off into the freezing cold of a winter's night without a jacket or overcoat, to be found some hours later walking apparently aimlessly and in a perplexed and disoriented state and claiming total amnesia for the night's events. Occasionally, acts committed during a fugue state may lead to criminal charges.

As with all dissociative states, treatment, if considered necessary after a spontaneous recovery, should be supportive psychotherapy which aims to uncover, in a safe relationship, the stresses that have driven the behaviour.

Possession States

Possession states, which are a rare form of dissociative disorder in western societies, are characterized by claims to have been taken over by a spirit or some external power. They have to be distinguished from the passivity experiences and delusions of control found in the schizophrenias.

In cases where fugue or possession states are claimed to have been present at the time of a serious act of violence, the defence, in Britain, may raise the issue of non-insane automatism, but they are unlikely to succeed now that violent automatic behaviour has been designated as insane automatism.

Amok and windigo

Amok (or amuck) is a term that has been applied to any sudden outbursts of violence, but in psychiatry it has tended to be confined to a so-called culture bound reactive syndrome involving the peoples of the Malay archipelago (Linton, 1956; Yap, 1969; Carr and Tan, 1976). Amok in Malay has the meaning of rushing in a state of frenzy to the commission of indiscriminate murder (Oxford English Dictionary). There were reports from Java by early Dutch and British colonists of Malays running amok (Spores, 1988).

Amok was claimed originally to have three phases (Gimlette, 1901; Burton-Bradley, 1968; Westermeyer, 1982):

1. a prodrome characterized by social withdrawal and anxious brooding;
2. a sudden furious outburst in which a number of people are attacked at random; and

3. sudden termination of the attacks, sometimes in extended stuporous sleep, but always with subsequent amnesia for the events.

This description is probably, at least in part, overlain by mythology (see below).

A number of precipitants have been described, the most common involving some overwhelming blow to the individual's self-esteem and social prestige. Others include acute intoxication (Westermeyer, 1973); organic brain syndromes (Van Loon, 1927); social stress as in migration; and relationship difficulties such as jealousy (Carr and Tan, 1976). The Malay culture is said to place a strong emphasis for males on retaining social prestige and avoiding loss of face. A powerful interdiction exists towards suicide. The act of running amok (becoming a pengamok) in traditional Malay culture allowed a discredited or shamed male to bring about his own destruction, as the amok was often terminated by the killing of the pengamok or, if he survived, restoring his prestige. Amok was a recognized, if not sanctioned, social performance.

Windigo is a related syndrome described in the Ojibwa Indians of sub-Arctic North America. The males of this tribe spend the long winter months hunting alone in the frozen wastes. Their prestige depends on success, and failure brings shame (Friedman, 1982). The windigo is believed to be a giant phantom compounded of all those who have starved to death in the past (Meth, 1974). This phantom is believed to be capable of possessing a man and metamorphosing him into a murderous cannibalistic monster. The development of windigo is associated with failure in the hunt and especially famine. A prodrome of sleeplessness, depression and brooding is described, followed by an outburst of murderous activity in which the family as well as fellow members of the tribe are attacked and attempts made to consume their flesh (Landes, 1938). The state is terminated by the killing of the windigo or by his suicide. As with amok, this picture is at least in part mythological.

Analogies have been drawn between amok and the sudden outbursts of murderous violence directed at a number of victims which occur periodically in western societies (Teoh, 1972; Westermeyer, 1982). Superficial similarities certainly exist in that they both involve a public display of apparently motiveless violence, often terminated by the killing or suicide of the perpetrator. Both seem to have elements of contagion in that amok violence has been described as spreading epidemics through some Asian communities (Westermeyer, 1973) and spectacular mass killings can spawn copy-cat killings. The analogy, however, obscures more than it illuminates. Mass killers in western societies are a heterogeneous mixture including disgruntled teenagers, gun-obsessed inadequates, deluded psychotics and misguided fanatics. Those who live to tell of their outbursts are not reported to claim amnesia for the events. To describe a sudden outburst of violence as amok, in the technical rather than lay sense, evokes a spurious confidence that we have somehow understood the events. This could inhibit the proper exploration of the actual context and state of mind of the perpetrator.

From a treatment perspective it is essential to distinguish these dissociative states from systematized paranoia which frequently involves long-standing delusions, sexual thoughts, planning, and mass destruction, often including suicide. The case of Ernst Wagner (chapter 9) is the first and one of the best descriptions of this dangerous condition.

DECEPTION

This section deals with topics where the possibility of deception is frequently raised. Many of the patients discussed here are, however, not deceiving anyone.

Compensation Neurosis

It is probably wrong to include compensation neurosis under the general heading of deception as most of the people claiming compensation after an accident are deceiving neither themselves or anyone else, yet unfortunately compensation neurosis has become a pejorative term which has many pseudonyms, e.g. 'accident neurosis', 'greenback neurosis', 'profit neurosis', 'railway spine', and 'unconscious malingering'. Kennedy (1946) gave expression to such prejudice in the following aphorism:

> A compensation neurosis is a state of mind, borne out of fear, kept alive by avarice, stimulated by lawyers, and cured by a verdict.

The difficulty is that the emotional effects of an injury manifest themselves within a personal and social context. Least psychological damage occurs when injury can be accepted as part of a natural order. Feelings of anger and resentment exacerbate physical and psychiatric symptoms. Litigation is almost always protracted and involves repeated medical examination. The patient's attention is focused on his or her grievance and symptoms. Finally, in court, disability is financially rewarded and any recovery may reduce the level of compensation. This process exacerbates psychological symptoms and hampers recovery. The experience in New Zealand of a government-run accident compensation scheme has, however, amply demonstrated that merely removing the courts and the litigation process in no way reduces either the psychological problems or the temptation to exaggerate or fabricate compensatable injuries. In fact, it may increase these problems, as all injuries become potentially compensable irrespective of whose responsibility they may have been.

The problem is neatly illustrated by considering the effects of minor concussional head injury. Virtually every individual who leads an active life has sustained an injury causing a brief interruption of consciousness. Recovery is almost always prompt and complete, except where litigation is involved. Thus, if a man falls off his own ladder and bangs his head he recovers quickly, but if he falls off his employer's ladder and becomes involved in compensation, persistent disability may follow.

Lishman (1968) noted:

> Central to most descriptions are headaches and dizziness, but to these may be added abnormal fatiguability, insomnia, sensitivity to noise, irritability, and emotional instability. Anxiety and depression are often prominent. Difficulties with concentration and memory may feature strongly among the complaints, and some degree of overt intellectual impairment may on occasion be detected. With this mixture of quasi-organic and subjective symptoms, variously reported, it is scarcely surprising that the concept lacks clarity and that its aetiology has remained in doubt. Nevertheless, its ubiquity following even minor blows to the head, and the regularity with which it features among claims for compensation, have ensured that it persists as an important subject for medical interest and debate.

In his textbook Lishman (1998) pointed out:

> In some, probably rare, cases there will be entirely conscious simulation for gain, but in the great majority the compensation issue colours the picture in more subtle ways. Once the possibility of compensation is raised the patient finds himself in complex legal dealings; there are frustrations due to delays, anxieties due to conflicting advice and often capital outlay. In effect the injured person is invited to complain and, having done so, finds he has to complain repeatedly, over years to a number of specialists. Repeated questioning from lawyers and doctors not only focuses the patient's attention on early symptoms which perhaps were due to recede, but in addition reinforces the prospect of their continuance and worse to come.

Thus in the early days or weeks after injury the postconcussional syndrome is probably directly related to the cerebral trauma but, subsequently, it becomes overlain by psychological factors and in some cases deliberate exaggeration.

The literature on the recovery of psychological symptoms after settlement is confused. Miller (1961, 1966) followed-up an unrepresentative sample of 50 neurotic patients from a total of 200 head injury cases and found that 90% returned to the same or similar employment after their cases were settled. Kelly (1981) documented 100 'post-traumatic syndrome' patients, but traced only 43 after a follow-up period averaging 2.8 years. No patient was personally interviewed. Many patients had improved and returned to work by the time the case was settled, but of the 26 not working by settlement, 22 were still not working at follow-up, which led him to conclude that the 'cured by a verdict' jibe is not correct.

Perhaps the most comprehensive review is by Mendelson (1984). He looked at 18 follow-up studies of personal injury litigants. Of these only three studies, including the one by Miller, favoured the view that claimants improved within a fairly short time of the finalization of their claims. Six studies were discounted because of the small number of patients examined. Nine studies indicated that of patients who stopped work following a head injury, between 50 and 85% failed to return to work after a settlement. For patients with a low back injury, 35% were unemployed after a minimum of 3 years following settlement. Patients with neck injuries had persistent disability of a severe degree, namely, 12–60% of cases 5 years after the injury. Tarsh and Royston (1985) carried out a follow-up of 35 claimants who had an 'accident neurosis'. Patients were followed-up from 1 to 7 years after compensation was received. Few recovered and such recovery as did take place was unrelated to the time of compensation. Most cases still had continuing and often severe symptoms at follow-up, and about one-third of the group seemed certain to be always going to lead lives of invalidism, totally dependent on other family members.

Mendelson (2003) summarizes the situation well. He traces the beginnings of so-called compensation neurosis to the development of the railways in about 1830 which gave rise to a lot of higher speed transport accidents and to symptoms that had not been noticed very often before, and thence to the new diagnoses of 'railway spine' and 'nervous shock'. This latter term is still used within the legal world (see p.53). Mendelson also indicates that the introduction of workers' compensation legislation at the end of the nineteenth century led many to postulate that it was the financial gain which led to the prolongation of disability. This implied that compensation neurosis was a subtype of malingering. Mendelson described such explanations as 'inaccurate and simplistic'. He said:

> There are many factors that influence outcome following compensable injury... and a new paradigm is needed that takes into consideration these variables and provides a comprehensive explanatory model that, ultimately, may lead to effective interventions.

Beck (1829) wrote in a nineteenth-century law textbook that where illness might be feigned we have a

> double duty... to guard the interests of the public... and also those of the individual so that he be not unjustly condemned.

That advice may be nearly 200 years old, but it is a useful benchmark for the twenty-first century.

In considering an individual case it is useful to remember that 'recovery' and 'return to employment' are very different. Many complainants are manual workers in mid-life who have little motivation to return to the sort of poorly paid employment which would leave them little better off than when in receipt of state benefit. The boundary is blurred between what is genuine, what has a genuine basis, but is exaggerated, and what is gross malingering. Often one develops chronologically from the other. It may be that the immediate response to injury, be it physical or psychological, is almost always genuine and would have occurred in the absence of any compensation claimed. To reiterate the point made by Lishman above, the lengthy process of pursuing compensation hampers recovery and encourages exaggeration; sometimes naturally occurring recovery is not frankly admitted. As the litigation progresses over years, some suggestible individuals elaborate their symptoms; these cases tend to carry a poor prognosis. The plaintiff's account of the past is often distorted and pre-accident physical and psychological disabilities may be concealed. Careful examination of the full family practitioner case notes and correspondence is often revealing. Malingering can occur, but is difficult to detect on the basis of a single psychiatric examination. Sometimes enquiry agents' reports and videos indicate that allegedly disabled subjects are, in fact, working clandestinely and leading comparatively normal lives.

Management therefore requires a good deal of sensitive enquiry, a working relationship with the whole family (if there is one) and above all the application of pressure to the lawyers involved in the case to resolve the matter as quickly as possible. This is difficult because lawyers believe that their client has a right to the best possible financial settlement even if this means delay, and therefore delay in return to health. Once the settlement has been agreed rehabilitation may become difficult because an important purposeful activity will have been removed from the patient's life and new activities which can fill that vacuum need to be negotiated. The Miller view that patients get better as soon as the compensation is paid is not our clinical experience and many of the symptoms persist for many years as does the disability.

Malingering

Malingering is a highly pejorative term, linked not only with words such as lying and deceit, but also with scrounger, workshy, coward. It implies the wrongful acquisition of the privileged status of the ill, and it is further linked with dishonest acquisition of money. In times of war it has the special odium of seeking personal safety and comfort when others are making sacrifices to achieve highly desired group objectives. Such people may be branded as shirkers, funks and degenerates. Above all, pretending to be ill is regarded as 'shameful'. It is no wonder it is a vexed topic for medical professionals as they are expected to accurately point the finger at those who shall be deprived of the illness status, and their claims and who will thus fall to the very bottom of the social hierarchy. In times of war some alleged malingerers may be regarded as so heinous that they are executed.

The history of this problem has been briefly but well documented by Wessely (2003). He pointed out that the simulation of illness is as old as humankind. He suggested that it was the introduction of progressive social legislation in Germany between 1880 and 1890 and in Britain in 1908 with The Workmen's Compensation Act and the 1911 National Insurance Act, that made this simulation a medical problem. These acts were regarded by the medical profession as inducements to malinger and quite a number of doctors set themselves up as gatekeepers for the state against such temptations. Initially malingering was thought to be mainly a matter for physicians and surgeons, but the First World War added a very significant psychological dimension even though the psychiatric casualties of that war were considered to be suffering from 'nervous shock' which was also thought to be a physical disorder (damage to the nervous system by terrible noise and blast from the heavy guns). Wessely suggested that at the beginning of the twentieth century there was a perceived decline in the pre-war moral codes that had governed society. Malingering was considered to be a form of lying and medical man was best placed to detect it!

As we have seen, if it really is lying, then it is going to be mighty difficult to detect. Perhaps courts who claim to be able to detect liars are better placed to do this work than doctors. Sprince (2003) suggested that medical evidence about malingering is not particularly significant in a court of law. Where claims have been resisted in whole or in part by reference to malingering, courts have rarely reached a positive finding that an individual is or is not malingering and in appeal cases malingering rarely arises. Further where the claim has been lost, presumably because the claim is not considered to be genuine in all respects, it is rarely followed by a criminal prosecution for fraud.

For a comprehensive text on malingering and illness deception see Halligan et al. (2003).

Feigned mental illness

In the nineteenth century, there was considerable interest in identifying malingerers who simulated mental disorder. Beck (1829), in spite of his views quoted above, devoted considerable space in his text on medical jurisprudence to the recognition of feigned diseases and, in particular, offered no fewer than 12 strategies for unmasking those pretending madness. Tuke (1892) noted that simulators of insanity made errors in such matters as adding 3 and 4, or the number of shillings in a sovereign, or in identifying commonplace objects. He stated that the unskilled malingerer answers nothing right, constantly falling into absurdities quite foreign to true insanity. Maudsley (1867) also noted:

Imposters generally overact, thinking the lunatic widely different from a sane person... [he] pretends he cannot remember things such as what day follows another, or how many days there are in a week, that he cannot add the simplest figures... [he] answers stupidly where a real lunatic who was not an idiot would act cunningly and answer intelligently.

Chesterman has written two articles on psychiatric malingerer catching. Broughton and Chesterman (2001) described a man who assaulted a teenage boy and then feigned mental illness. He later confessed to malingering but doesn't seem to have done very well. The authors do stress however that the discovery that an individual has fabricated symptoms should not exclude him or her from further assessment and treatment, as such fabrication should be viewed as a form of abnormal illness behaviour in an often resourceless, inadequate and vulnerable individual. Chesterman et al. (2008) take twenty-first century British psychiatrists, especially authors of this textbook, to task for not giving enough attention to malingering. They believe that this is due to a false assumption that psychotic symptoms are faked in order to ward off real psychosis (Jung 1903). The paper is a useful review of the research in this field and suggests some tests which have all the drawbacks and low validity one might expect, in order to detect malingered psychosis. They go on to say:

It appears that the incidence of malingered psychosis may well have increased over recent years as a consequence of the closures of long-stay psychiatric institutions and the move towards care in the community. Many chronically mentally ill patients, who may have preferred the stable environment of the asylum, are now living in marginal circumstances in the community... Such individuals may therefore consciously exaggerate their symptoms in an effort to obtain shelter in the new generation of psychiatric hospitals... It has also been proposed that there has been a change in coping strategies among society's disenfranchized individuals, who now present with psychological rather than physical symptoms.

They also emphasize the importance of detecting malingering but don't say what this importance is, other than a possible miscarriage of justice in a homicide case in which a manslaughter verdict of diminished responsibility on grounds of mental disorder is preferred to a murder verdict. There is no research on the prevalence of such problems.

The question of what is malingering is claimed by some to be straightforward. An early authority, whose text on the subject was dedicated 'to my friend the British workman, to whom I owe so much' (Collie, 1917) cited Lord Justice Buckley. The judge defined a malingerer as 'one who is not ill and pretends that he is.' Collie also cited Bramwell who distinguished between 'malingering' (conscious, deliberate simulation of disease, or exaggeration of symptoms) and 'valetudinarianism', where the process is unconscious or subconscious. In a more recent study of feigning after brain or spinal injury, Miller and Cartlidge (1972) defined malingering as: 'all forms of fraud relating to matters of health.' This includes the stimulation of diseases or disability which are not present; the much commoner gross exaggeration of minor disability; and the conscious and deliberate attribution of a disability to an injury, or accident that did not in fact cause it, for personal advantage. In a lecture, a psychiatrist with a medico-legal compensation practice in Australia (Parker, 1988), claimed:

> A week will not go by without seeing at least two malingerers, and about the same number with gross conversion hysteria.

Nevertheless, he went on to warn, using the words of Asher (1958):

> The pride of a doctor who has caught a malingerer is akin to that of a fisherman who has landed an enormous fish; and his stories (like those of fishermen) may become somewhat exaggerated in the telling.

It could be that there is a special form of malingering, the feigning of psychotic illness. The following kind of argument may not be uncommon.

> The trouble is that as soon as the language of 'patient-treatment-disease' is used, it is hard to diagnose insanity in anyone who commits a really horrible act; for to be cured of mental disease is to be sane, and a sane man does not do such things; there is a merging of the language of medicine and the language of morality; if bad is sick, then sick is bad, and sane must be good. The more we treat someone as a patient, the more likely we are to give his sincerity the benefit of the doubt. We tend to ask 'What makes him behave like that' instead of 'is he telling the truth?' and 'could he behave differently if it was to his advantage?' (Mount, 1984).

It is certainly a robust statement of the antipsychiatry position. Yet medical practitioners can also have considerable scepticism about mental disorder in those charged with serious crimes. An anecdote from Ray (1838) illustrates just how far preconceptions about deception, malingering and moral responsibility will take even the experienced observer.

> Jean Gerard, a bold villain, murdered a woman at Lyons in 1829. Immediately after being arrested, he ceased to speak altogether and appeared to be in a state of fatuity. He laid nearly motionless in his bed, and when food was brought his attendants raised him up and it was given to him in that position. His hearing also seemed to be affected. The physicians who were directed to examine him concluded that if this was actually what it appeared to be, paralysis of the nerves of the tongue and ear, actual cautery applied to the soles of the feet would be a proper remedy. It being used, however, for several days without any success, it was agreed to apply it to the neck. For two days no effect was produced, but on the third, while preparations were making for its applications, Gerard evinced some signs of repugnance to it, and after some urging, he spoke, declaring his innocence of the crime of which he was charged. His simulation was thus exposed.

Whether or not this practice resolved the question of malingering, today it should surely be a matter for a professional licensing body.

To try to understand just how easy or difficult it is to simulate mental disorder, Anderson et al. (1959) carried out a study in Australia. Eighteen psychology students were asked to simulate mental disorder. Six were asked to imagine that they had committed murder and they were to feign insanity to escape the consequences. Twelve were asked to feign insanity for their own reasons. The subjects were then subjected to a standard psychiatric examination. None of the pictures presented resembled well-defined psychiatric disorders. Even the better performances lacked consistency and persistence. The commonest simulation was of depression, in two people accompanied by amnesia; three also simulated paranoid features. On cognitive testing, errors were produced, especially approximate answers. One tried to make out he was an epileptic, another tried to simulate feeble-mindedness. Unfortunately, the psychiatric examinations were not carried out blindly, so although the experimenters were not very impressed by their students' acting, it is difficult to know whether they could have actually been fooled.

Perhaps the most famous test of simulated psychosis is 'on being sane in insane places' (Rosenhan, 1973). Five male and three female volunteers, a psychology student, three psychologists, a paediatrician, a psychiatrist, a painter, and a housewife became pseudo-patients and gained 'secret admission' to 12 different hospitals. The pseudo-patients complained that they were hearing voices, they changed their names and occupations, but otherwise told the truth. The 'voices' were stopped immediately on admission. Each was diagnosed as having schizophrenia, but soon discharged as in remission (length of stay varied from 7–52 days). Other patients sometimes recognized the pseudo-patients as frauds. Rosenhan concluded, 'it is clear we cannot distinguish the sane from the insane in psychiatric hospitals.' A torrent of replies disagreed. The strongest criticism was perhaps by Spitzer (1975), who pointed out that it is not very surprising that psychiatrists do not diagnose pseudo-patients when they are not looking for them. He concluded himself, however, that the data actually supported the view that psychiatrists are good at distinguishing the sane from the insane.

None of this is much help if a psychiatrist is faced with a patient in a situation in which having a psychosis would be a distinct advantage. There is no simple answer and the principles of assessment and management will be the same as if simulation of physical disorder is suspected. As much information as possible should be collected from as many sources as possible, and a professional relationship should be built with the patient. In this way, the nature of the patient's problem will emerge (for the one thing that will be true, unless s/he is one of Rosenhan's research workers, is that s/he will have a problem).

Malingered psychiatric disorders are encountered both in situations where compensation is at issue and in those facing criminal charges. Malingered psychiatric disorders may occasionally be encountered in those seeking admission or transfer to a psychiatric hospital from prison. The malingerer sometimes believes s/he has to appear mad or idiotic in every sphere of function and thus presents such an exaggerated picture that suspicions are raised, even in the most trusting. This type of malingerer, who counterfeits a disorder too mad to be mad, often claims gross disorientation under the misapprehension that the mentally disordered suffer a global confusion. More subtle malingerers draw on their experience with mentally disordered individuals. They may claim to be hallucinated, in which case the hallucinations tend to be described as omnipresent, distressing and without the usual association with mood changes or delusional developments. Flamboyant claims about the content and extensive nature of hallucinations often contrast with the meagre and vague account provided of the form of the experience in terms of being experienced in objective space, having directional qualities. Malingered hallucinations may also take atypical forms as when a vision of a person is described which talks to the patient and may even enter into conversation. Occasionally, command hallucinations are offered as an explanation of offending. These should be treated with some scepticism when presented in the absence of other features of psychotic illness.

Command hallucinations have a particular appeal to the malingerer as they offer both evidence of mental disorder and at the same time incorporate a direct exculpatory element. Claims are made by offenders that they committed criminal acts because the voices told them to do so, and they were unable to resist the instruction. In fact violent acts secondary to command hallucinations are rare, even among people suffering from psychosis (see chapter 14). Occasionally, distressed and disturbed individuals will report command hallucinations to dramatize their suicidal or homicidal impulses.

Fabricated delusions are less common. Malingerers usually present a straightforward account of persecution or control which accounts conveniently for their acts or makes necessary their transfer. The accounts differ from actual delusional experiences both in providing an unusually clear storyline and paradoxically containing elements of the totally fantastic. One young man gave an account of being followed and persecuted by shadowy figures whom he claimed had arranged for him to be locked in a cell on board a ship which was about to be sunk. When questioned, he went to the prison window and pointed out at the surrounding sea, then abruptly fled under the table claiming the boat (prison) was sinking. Fabricated accounts, unlike true systematized delusions, rarely contain the typical mixture of self-referential material and laboured constructions placed on minor points

proving, to the patient's complete satisfaction, the delusional claims. Malingered delusions are often said to have emerged at a particular point, usually relatively recently, and to have, from the outset, their fully fledged content. In genuine delusions, it is usually possible to discern their gradual development from the initial intuition through an extended process as the patient uncovers the full extent of 'the truth'.

Language disorders are rarely, if ever, malingered. Manic states are difficult to imitate, but depressive syndromes relatively easy. Most of us have sufficient experience of despair and despondency to mimic depression. Where suicidal intent is claimed in the context of an account of depression which appears so atypical as to raise suspicions about malingering, it is probably wiser to give the benefit of the doubt to the individual until s/he can be observed carefully. In disorganized and disturbed personalities, so common in forensic psychiatry, instability of mood and markedly atypical depressive syndromes occur not infrequently, and they are all too often coupled with self-destructive behaviour.

Malingered mental disorders are often presented flamboyantly and insistently. Any questioning of the reported experiences is likely to be greeted by assurances that it is 'the truth', or with the accusation that you don't believe the patient. In genuine disorders, the abnormalities of mental state usually emerge gradually as the interview progresses. Some malingerers are suggestible and can be induced to add contradictory and absurd symptoms to their account, but more calculating malingerers will stick doggedly to their basic story.

To summarize, the detection of malingering is a difficult, but not entirely mysterious art. The longer the patient is studied, the more carefully the information is gathered and checked, the easier it becomes to detect malingering. The patient should be encouraged to talk freely rather than to answer formulaic questions. Malingering patients tend to have an air of exaggeration, a disproportionate bias in their symptoms, and their complaints do not fit with objective observations from others. They tend to tell lies and so their accounts differ from time to time. However, it also has to be remembered that differences between objective and subjective accounts may be due to many factors other than malingering. Inconsistencies between interviews may be entirely compatible with the memory failures of normal recall, and with clinical change as the disorder progresses. Exaggerated, overoptimistic, or even pessimistic accounts may be due to mood changes. Self-deception may replace conscious lying and dissimulation. There are no absolutes in the detection of malingering, but standard techniques of cross-checking, observation, repeated interviewing, together with the skill of an experienced interviewer who is alive to the possibility of malingering are the best that can be done. It is worth remembering that hostile questioning of distressed patients will probably increase rather than reduce error.

The growing neuroscience of perceptual and cognitive distortions explored by Myslobodsky (1997) and Halligan et al. (2003) is likely to enhance our understanding of just how blurred the boundaries between normality and abnormality may be.

Munchausen's syndrome

Munchausen's syndrome was described and named by Asher in 1951. Like the famous Baron whose tales were bowdlerized and published by Raspe (1786), the affected persons had travelled widely, and they related tales which were both dramatic and untruthful. Typically, such patients will be admitted to hospital with an acute, harrowing, but not entirely convincing history; their manner is evasive and truculent; and, on enquiry, it may be revealed that they have attended and deceived other hospitals, often discharging themselves against advice.

Most cases resemble organic emergencies and favour three main variants:

1. The acute abdomen type which is usually accompanied by a multiplicity of abdominal scars.
2. The haemorrhagic type, usually reporting haemoptosis, haematemesis, or haematuria.
3. The neurological type, with headache, odd fits, or loss of consciousness.

Asher's title for this group of patients now seems well-established. The patients tend to be emotionally labile, lonely, attention-seeking and establish little rapport. Multiple aliases and repeated admissions are central features and some cases also fulfil the criteria for pseudologica fantastica. Some are seeking narcotic drugs.

A sinister variant of the condition has been described as 'Munchausen syndrome by proxy' (Meadow, 1977, 1982, 1989; Black, 1981). This involves children whose mothers or caregivers invent stories of illness about their child and in some cases fabricate false physical signs. Older children may even be coached by the parent on how to deceive the doctor. Meadow (1989) describes the consequences for children who are falsely labelled as ill:

1. They receive needless investigations and treatment.
2. Real injury may be caused by the mother's action, for example by giving drugs to induce unconsciousness.
3. They are at risk from becoming chronic invalids or hospital addicts in their own right.

The parents' motivations have been considered to include a desire for the status and attention provided by being the mother of a sick child, the enjoyment of help from the various medical professionals, and as a way of resolving or avoiding marital conflicts.

Self-mutilators

A related, and to some extent overlapping group of patients are those who obtain medical attention, if not care, by repeated self-injury. There is usually no attempt at mimicking of genuine medical disorders, although occasionally bizarre skin lesions are induced which raise questions as to their origin. In one case, the patient injected air under the skin and persuaded one hospital to treat her for gas gangrene.

Ganser states

A strange mental state described by Ganser in 1898 was regarded in its day as a 'prison psychosis'. If it occurs at all nowadays it is extremely rare and is included here for completeness and historical interest and show how dissociative/malingered symptoms vary with time and place. The clinical features are

1. approximate answers;
2. clouding of consciousness with disorientation in time, place, and occasionally person;
3. vivid hallucinosis, both visual and auditory;
4. areas of analgesia and hyperalgesia with, on occasion, motor disturbances which were considered 'hysterical stigma';
5. complete and often sudden clearing of the disorder, leaving the patient with a total amnesia for the period of the disorder.

The description of the peculiar way of answering questions was the feature which intrigued subsequent investigators and guaranteed the survival of the putative syndrome (Auerbach, 1982). The phenomenon of approximate answers (*Vorbeireden* or *Vorbeigehen*) was described by Anderson and Mallinson in 1941 as

> *A false response of a patient to the examiner's question, where the answer, although wrong, is never far wrong and bears a definite and obvious relation to the question, indicating clearly that the question has been grasped.*

Anderson and Mallinson went on to make clear that this is not merely giving random responses. Among Ganser's examples was a prisoner who, when asked how many fingers he had, replied 11 and said a horse had three legs, but an elephant five. Counting, simple arithmetic, identifying letters of the alphabet and reading, are all reported to produce obvious errors and omissions. One of our cases, when shown a chessman and asked what it was, replied after several minutes of puzzled examination that it was a little statue whose function quite escaped him. This same man correctly identified a watch and could tell the time, but called a key a knife, and added a little pantomime of horrified withdrawal. One of Ganser's own cases identified a key as a revolver.

The possibility that the Ganser state is a manifestation of the conscious simulation of mental disorder is considered frequently in the literature, usually to be dismissed in favour of unconscious mechanisms, or the impact of major stress on somebody who already has a mental disorder. What Ganser added to previous descriptions of feigned mental disorder in prisoners was his personal assurance that 'it could not be doubted' that the prisoners being examined were not malingering, but 'truly sick'.

The Ganser state has almost disappeared, but before it goes entirely it might help to consider whether we think of it as malingering, pathological lying, or a dissociative disorder. Some of the patients we have seen labelled as 'Ganser' turned out later to be psychotic; all of them needed help.

Malingerophobia

We cannot leave the topics of malingering and feigned mental illness without reference to Pilowsky's (1985) paper on malingerophobia. It describes an important syndrome which every physician, and especially every psychiatrist, should know about. Pilowsky likened the medical altruistic impulse to body temperature which can under stress become too warm or too cold. He maintained that it is a contagious condition and is defined as

an irrational and maladaptive fear of being tricked into providing healthcare to individuals who masquerade as sick, but either have no illness at all, or have a much less severe one than they claim.

It is at its worst in large teaching hospitals, he said, and can easily be diagnosed by the general practitioner who telephones to seek admission for a patient. The condition then manifests itself in the form of a newly qualified intern treating the general practitioner as though he were a medical student presenting himself for a *viva*. The least subtle sign is when the body language and voice inflection asking the patient about symptoms gives the distinct impression that the assessing doctor believes the patient is a liar. The main complication of malingerophobia is that the patient is rejected and the patient's problems are undiagnosed. Doctors dealing with such patients become bored and impatient. The worst complication is the enquiry, sometimes by a coroner, when something goes wrong. The cure for this disorder is simple, says Pilowski, it is an increased readiness to take patients on, especially for treatment, coupled with a tolerance of occasional malingering. This will prevent the development of a fortress mentality and improve working conditions as well as treatment. Perhaps we can add to Pilowsky's remedies that much more attention should be paid to understanding and assessing the rich diversity of mental states that patients present, an approach which may well save a lot of time in the long run and certainly gets closer to the core task of being a medical practitioner.

18

Addictions and dependencies: their association with offending

Edited by
Pamela J Taylor

Written by
**Mary McMurran and
Adrian Feeney: Alcohol**

**Ilana Crome and
Roger Bloor: Other drug
abuse and offending**

**John Gunn and
Pamela J Taylor:
Gambling**

1st edition authors: **John Gunn, John Hamilton, Andrew Johns, Michael D Kopelman, Anthony Maden, John Strang and Pamela J Taylor**

Society remains ambivalent about use and abuse of mind altering substances and towards the people who use and abuse them. Even the professions seem to struggle with attitudes to the behavioural disorders associated with such substances in ways that perhaps reflect tensions between construing them as primary disorders of mental health or as moral lapses. It is not uncommon even for people with unequivocal psychotic illnesses to be rejected from psychiatric services on grounds that their disorder is substance-induced rather than illness. Terminology is also elusive. The two main diagnostic and statistical manuals (*ICD-10*, WHO, 1992a; *DSM-IV*, American Psychiatric Association, 2004) no longer use the terminology of addiction. The former deals with a variety of 'mental and behavioural disorders due to psychoactive substance use' in a simple descriptive way, while the latter takes the simpler label of 'substance-related disorders', but suggests a fundamental distinction between 'substance-induced disorders', subliminally justified by including toxic substances which are not abused as well as those that may be, and 'substance use disorders'. In the case of substance-induced disorders, the implicit blame falls on the substances. DSM criteria for substance abuse and dependency disorders make repeated use of the word 'failure'. For dependency,

The key issue ... is not the existence of the problem, but rather the individual's failure to abstain from using the substance despite having evidence of the difficulty it is causing (DSM-IV, p.179).

DSM-IV substance abuse amounts to repeated social failures in the context of using the drug (including alcohol, but not nicotine or caffeine) but with patterns falling short of dependency.

In the UK, the Academy of Medical Sciences (2008) has taken a lead in bringing a more scientific perspective. It has brought back the terminology of addiction, and made clear its multi-factorial origins. It acknowledges risk factors and protective factors, and that these lie in a range of personal, physical and experiential domains as well as in availability of the objects of addiction and attitudes in wider society and the media. The Academy further notes the similarities in presentation between addictions to chemical substances and to other repeated behaviours, particularly problem gambling (euphoria on winning, tolerance on repetition, compulsion, withdrawal and craving). It makes parallels between them in terms of similar areas of brain activation when winning and after administration of drugs of abuse (e.g. Reuter et al., 2005). We too extend this chapter to consideration of behavioural addictions, here exemplified by gambling, although in some cases, shoplifting, arson, and even interpersonal violence may fall within this spectrum. Such a broad construction means that addictions, dependencies or substance abuse in an individual are central issues for the health service, even though many may first present to criminal justice services. It also means that public health policies and legislative controls have a fundamental part to play in protecting both the individual and wider society. This chapter is mostly about clinical detection, legal issues, relationships between substance misuse and offending, management and treatment of the addictions. Consideration of genetic and other aetiological factors is mainly in chapter 8.

ALCOHOL

The World Health Organization (WHO, 2002a) placed alcohol consumption among the top 10 global risk factors in terms of the burden of disease caused. In the year 2000, 1.8 million deaths worldwide were attributable to alcohol consumption as well as 4% of the total global burden of disease, including an estimated 20–30% of each of the following: liver disease, oesophageal cancer, epilepsy, road traffic accidents and intentional injuries. Problem drinking presents a risk for mental ill health too, although mental disorders also increase the risk of alcohol-related problems (WHO, 2004a). Globally, alcohol is a major contributor to violence, including homicide, domestic violence and child abuse, and sexual violence (WHO, 2002b).

Perhaps in recognition of its part in this global crisis, the prime minister's strategy unit developed an 'Alcohol harm reduction strategy for England' (Cabinet Office, 2004). Similar strategies already existed for Scotland (Scottish Executive, 2002/7), Wales (Welsh Assembly Government, 2008b), and Northern Ireland (DHSSPS, 2000). All focus on combating alcohol-related crime and disorder through prevention, early intervention, and treatment, but specifically, too, endorse the development of offender treatments. In parallel with the Cabinet Office work, other bodies, as diverse as the Academy of Medical Sciences (2004), and the Prison Reform Trust (2004; http://www.prisonreformtrust.org.uk) and The Royal college of Physicians (2001) have also provided strategic reviews.

These documents were consistent in pointing out that over 8 million adults in the UK exceeded the safe weekly drinking limits, then 14 units for women and 21 units for men (a unit is 8 g/10 ml of alcohol). About half of all violent crimes each year are alcohol-related, amounting to 1.2 million in England and Wales alone, perhaps not surprising given the age range of the heaviest drinkers. The UK General Household Survey 2002 (Rickards et al., 2004) showed that these were among 16- to 24-year-old men, averaging 21.5 units per week. The trend, however, is for a slight decrease in consumption by young men but increasing consumption among 16- to 24-year-old women who, in 2002, had been averaging 14 units. A revision of national health service (NHS) policy now recommends a maximum intake of 2–3 units per day for women and 3–4 units for men, with at least two alcohol-free days per week, and its alcohol learning centre regularly produces guidance sheets for clinical staff and for patients, variously showing what a unit looks like and offering advice (http://www.alcohollearningcentre.org.uk).

Overall, in England and Wales alone, alcohol misuse costs around £20 bn per year in healthcare, crime-related costs, and loss of productivity in the workplace.

How Alcohol Exerts its Effects

Intoxication

The immediately observable effects of alcohol intoxication are impairments such as slurred speech, slowed mental and physical reaction times, and difficulty walking. They may be apparent even at small doses, are dose-dependent and are due to the depressant effects of alcohol caused by reduced excitatory actions of the neurotransmitter glutamate and increased inhibitory actions of gamma-aminobutyric acid (GABA) (National Institute on Alcohol Abuse and Alcoholism, 2000). In most cases, the impairments caused by intoxication are temporary, but intoxication can lead to death from respiratory failure, accidents associated with loss of consciousness (e.g. hypothermia; choking on vomit) or accidents associated with cognitive or motor impairment (e.g. road or machinery accidents).

Pathological intoxication (*mania à potu*) has generally been defined as sudden onset aggressive behaviour, atypical for the individual when sober and seen after a small quantity of alcohol, and which, in normal people, would not be associated with such behaviour. It may be associated with alcohol-induced amnesia for the events involved. Coid (1979), however, cast doubt over its authenticity, after reviewing the literature. Close scrutiny of any case commonly shows that the person has had more than a small drink of alcohol and has a history of violence.

In an uncontrolled study, Maletzky (1976) gave alcohol infusions to 22 people with histories suggestive of the condition. At high blood alcohol levels (mean: 195 mg/100 ml) 15 of them had unusual reactions. Nine became violent, four showed delusions and hallucinations, and a further two presented with mix of these problems. Maletzky concluded that reactions to alcohol were on a continuum and that there was no discrete entity of pathological intoxication. It is of note that high blood alcohol levels were required to precipitate the phenomena Maletzky observed. Nevertheless, pathological intoxication remains of interest to defence counsels as simple intoxication provides no legal excuse for actions.

Blackouts

Blackouts occur during drinking bouts. They are characterized by discrete amnesic periods of up to several hours, during which the individual is apparently able to carry out normal activities. In an influential study, 100 hospitalized alcohol-dependent patients were interviewed. Sixty-four reported blackouts which were of two very distinct types: (1) classic *en bloc*, with total memory loss; (2) fragmentary blackouts after which the sufferer may be able to recall, with prompting, some of the events which occurred during the blackout which were not initially remembered (Goodwin et al., 1969; see also chapter 12). Goodwin et al. (1970) also studied blackouts by giving 16–18 ounces of 86% proof alcohol to 10 alcohol-dependent men in controlled conditions. They were then presented with novel information and tested 2 minutes, 30 minutes and 24 hours later. All were able to recall the information at 2 minutes but five were unable to do so at 30 minutes and 24 hours. This suggests that blackouts are a result of an inability to transfer information from immediate recall to short-term memory rather than inattention or a process of forgetting. Sweeney (1990) argued that the high blood alcohol levels required for an alcoholic blackout may severely disrupt other brain functions, such as reasoning and planning, but Lishman (1998) observed that they are probably associated with a sharp rise and fall in blood alcohol rather than high levels *per se,* and they do not appear to be predictive of cortical atrophy (Ron, 1983). They may be relevant in court if ability to form intent is compromised. Fenwick (1990) asserted that they are examples of 'sane automatism' (see also chapter 2).

A Dutch study of drivers stopped by traffic police or involved in car accidents supports a sceptical view of a direct link between alcohol level and alleged blackout (van Oorsouw et al., 2004). Of the 100 people stopped, 14 told the traffic police that they had had an alcoholic blackout, but their blood alcohol levels were not significantly different (180 mg/100 mL) from those of the people who made no such claim (190 mg/100 mL). The main difference between the two groups was in whether or not they had had an accident. Twelve of the 14 (86%) claiming a blackout had caused an accident compared with 30 (35%) of the rest. Interpretation of this is difficult; could the high reporting rate of blackouts among those who had crashed reflect at some level avoidance of prosecution, or the lower reporting rates a reluctance to put their driving licence in jeopardy? Could alleged blackouts be related more to the trauma of the accident than the alcohol?

Dependence

The alcohol dependence syndrome, as described by Edwards and Gross (1976), remains a useful guide for recognition of need for intervention:

1. a narrowed drinking repertoire, characterized by a set routine of consumption in an effort to maintain blood alcohol levels and therefore avoid withdrawal symptoms;
2. increased salience of drinking, such stereotyped drinking is pursued to the exclusion of all other activities;
3. increased tolerance to alcohol, a manifestation of both increased metabolic capacity based upon hepatic enzyme induction and increased brain receptor tolerance;
4. withdrawal symptoms;
5. relief or avoidance of withdrawal symptoms by further drinking;
6. subjective awareness of the compulsion to drink;
7. reinstatement after abstinence, the phenomenon of rapidly returning to the previous stereotyped drinking pattern after a period of abstinence, for instance a period of imprisonment.

The alcohol dependence syndrome represents a change in the relationship between the individual and alcohol. Instead of using alcohol in the context of social cues, drinking becomes an end in itself and is self-perpetuating.

Withdrawal, fits and delirium tremens

If an alcohol-dependent person stops or reduces alcohol consumption s/he may trigger a withdrawal syndrome, generally 3–12 hours after the change. Alcoholic withdrawal is not infrequent among people detained after arrest, is possibly becoming more likely and may affect fitness to be interviewed. In a sample from the 1980s, at least 4% of pretrial male prisoners showed signs of withdrawal on reception into prison (Taylor and Gunn, 1984). In a 2007–2008 sample of newly remanded men at least 17% had alcohol withdrawal symptoms on reception, although over 40% had an Alcohol Use Disorders Identification Test (AUDIT; Saunders et al., 1993) score indicating dependency (Taylor et al., 2009), which was a higher proportion than the Office of National Statistics figure of 30% from the 1987 England and Wales prison survey (Singleton et al., 1999). Withdrawal in prison may also be precipitated by abrupt cessation of drinking 'hooch', brewed there from such diverse sources as rotten fruit or boot polish.

Withdrawal is characterized by autonomic hyperactivity, including tremor, insomnia, sweating, tachycardia, hypertension and anxiety (Raistrick, 2001). It may be accompanied by acute hallucinosis in clear consciousness; hallucinations may occur in any modality, but visual and tactile modes are especially common. Violent or criminal acts may be committed while blood alcohol levels are falling.

Withdrawal fits may occur 12–48 hours after cessation of drinking; 5–10% of alcohol-dependent individuals experience them. The fits are generalized, tonic–clonic bursts of activity and are therefore characterized by loss of consciousness followed by involuntary movements of the limbs and accompanied by an abnormal electroencephalogram (EEG). The EEG is, however, generally normal between such fits, indicating that they are a manifestation of the withdrawal rather than an independent epileptiform phenomenon. Having a withdrawal seizure is a risk factor for further seizures during subsequent withdrawal states, therefore a history of withdrawal seizures is an indication for detoxification to be undertaken as an inpatient.

Delirium tremens (DT) presents 3–4 days after abstinence (Victor and Adams, 1953). It has a mortality of up to 5 per cent; cause of death is typically cardiovascular collapse, hypothermia or intercurrent infection. It presents with vivid hallucinations, delusions, profound confusion, tremor, agitation, insomnia, and autonomic over-activity. Visual hallucinations may be Lilliputian (very small). The onset may be sudden, although often there is a prodromal phase, which went unnoticed. The patient may be gripped with terror, although this is not invariable. DT usually lasts up to 3 days, ending with a prolonged sleep. The patient wakes feeling better, if tired, although occasionally an amnesic syndrome is evident. Delirium tremens *may* provide for an insanity defence (see also chapter 2).

Best practice in managing withdrawal states is preventive – to identify people at high risk and provide them with planned detoxification (see below). Use of the AUDIT to supplement interview questions as part of screening on reception into custody may enhance identification of those at risk.

Wernicke/Korsakoff's syndrome

Wernicke's encephalopathy (WE) is an acute brain disorder caused by vitamin B_1 (thiamine) deficiency, commonly linked to alcohol dependence in combination with poor appetite, malnutrition, poor absorption, and impaired thiamine storage by the liver. This deficiency causes abnormalities in and around the third ventricle and the aqueduct of the brain. Such changes have been found at post-mortem in 12% of people who had been alcohol-dependent (Torvik et al., 1982) although they have also been found in 1.5% of people who had neither abused alcohol nor had neurological abnormalities in life (Thomson and Pratt, 1992). WE may be of sudden onset, and there may be memory problems even in the acute phase. Only 10% of patients present with the classic triad of opthalmoplegia/nystagmus, ataxia, and delirium, and there is a risk that the condition may be mistaken for drunkenness. A presumptive diagnosis should be made in anyone undergoing detoxification who develops any one of these signs, or hypotension or impaired consciousness (Cook, 2000). Failure to treat immediately with parenteral B-complex vitamins puts the person at risk of permanent brain damage or death. Victor et al. (1971), studying patients with Wernicke's encephalopathy, found that over 84% went on to develop Korsakoff's syndrome.

Korsakoff's syndrome is a similar, but more chronic state characterized by abnormalities of both anterograde and retrograde memory in the presence of apathy but otherwise relatively well-preserved intellectual function. At post-mortem, the cerebral pathology is virtually identical to that in Wernicke's encephalopathy (Malamud and Skillicorn, 1956). As Lishman (1998) observed, the pathological process following thiamine deficiency is the same, merely differing in speed of development.

Classically, the patient is able to register new information (e.g. to perform the digit span test) but is unable to retain new information for 5 minutes or more. Temporal sequencing of events is particularly impaired, and sufferers may make up stories to try to hide such deficits (confabulation); these are not invariably far-fetched. Confabulation is not unique to Korsakoff's syndrome. Prognosis is poor, but not invariably hopeless; 25% of people recover, one half show some improvement with time and the other quarter

show no change (Victor et al., 1971). Schacter (1986) was unable to find any recorded case of an amnesic syndrome being cited as a defence. One of us, however, has experience of unfitness to plead being found in the presence of Korsakoff's syndrome, since the defendant could neither remember the alleged assault nor could he follow a trial.

In view of the high risks attached to Wernicke's encephalopathy, prophylactic vitamin B_1 (thiamine) should be given to dependent drinkers, particularly during withdrawal. British Association of Psychopharmacology guidelines (Lingford-Hughes et al., 2004) recommend a 1-month course of 100–200 mg thiamine per day for healthy, low risk alcohol-dependent patients undergoing detoxification and those who are thought to be at high risk of developing Wernicke's encephalopathy. (Cook [2000] suggests that anyone meeting criteria for inpatient detoxification, for whatever reason), or already showing signs of Wernicke's encephalopathy, should be treated with parenteral B-vitamin complex for up to 5 days. Such parenteral administration, which includes vitamin C, has a small associated risk of anaphylaxis and must only be given where there is adequate medical support.

Alcoholic hallucinosis

Alcoholic hallucinosis is rare, characterized by auditory hallucinations, commonly derogatory comments, in clear/very slightly clouded consciousness which follows heavy drinking. It may generally be distinguished from schizophrenia, even though secondary delusions may follow. Glass (1989) provides a full account of its controversial history as a concept and a review of outcome. Treatment is absolute abstinence, although low dose antipsychotic medication may be helpful.

Alcohol and behaviour

Alcohol affects behaviour idiosyncratically: people respond differently from each other and, indeed, one person may react differently on separate drinking occasions. The factors explaining these individual differences will be explored with particular reference to aggression and violence.

It has been noted that 'alcoholic intoxication dissolves the super ego before it dissolves the power to act' and that drunken people do things which they would not do when sober (Merikangas, 2004). In laboratory studies, alcohol fuels aggression mainly in men who have personality traits of irritability or aggression (Chermack and Giancola, 1997; Godlaski and Giancola, 2009). The effect of alcohol on aggression is observed after provocation and is most evident at higher doses. Acute intoxication is more commonly associated with violence than is chronic, heavy drinking (Pillman et al., 2000). Throughout the UK, there is particular current concern over 'binge drinking' and disorderly conduct among young people, although there is no generally accepted definition of binge drinking. Commonly, it is taken to mean consumption of more than twice the recommended upper daily limit of alcohol in one sitting (over 8 units for men or 6 units for women). According to this measure, about one-third of people in their twenties binge on alcohol (Williamson et al., 2003a). Binge drinking is a strong predictor of violence, at least in young males (Richardson and Budd, 2003). Accepting that alcohol changes behaviour, it is instructive to identify the mechanisms that explain this.

- *Anxiety reduction.* At high doses and in settings which are highly provocative of anxiety, the anxiolytic effect of alcohol reduces the inhibitory effect of fear (Ito et al., 1996), without which aggression and social rule breaking are more likely.
- *Pain reduction.* Alcohol is an analgesic, and one common euphemism for drunkenness – 'feeling no pain' – has literal truth to it. Knowledge from experience of this may reduce fear of starting fights; the analgesic effect removes a reason for ceasing any fight (Cutter et al., 1979).
- *Increasing psychomotor activity.* At lower doses, alcohol increases psychomotor activity, which may increase the risk of instigating trouble or provoking others (Pihl et al., 2003; Pihl and Hoaken, 1997).
- *Disruption to executive cognitive functioning (ECF).* The concept of executive cognitive functioning has been defined by Giancola (2000, p.582) as '... a higher order cognitive construct involved in the planning, initiation, and regulation of goal-directed behaviour'. He presents a strong case for its disruption affecting alcohol-related aggression and violence. Alcohol disrupts regulation of goal-directed behaviour by reducing ability to attend to all the features of a situation, interfering with appraisal of information, reducing ability to see the situation from the perspective of others, diminishing the ability to consider the consequences of one's actions, and reducing availability of alternative responses in a situation. Disruption to any of these processes results in failures of behaviour control. The effects of alcohol will depend on sober-state function, that is how good one's executive cognitive functioning is to begin with. Its disruption may explain much impulsive or imprudent behaviour associated with alcohol intoxication, including risky sexual behaviour, disorderly conduct, and driving while drunk.
- *Outcome expectancies.* Alcohol may influence behaviour through outcome expectancies, which are cognitive representations of an 'if–then' relationship; here, they represent what has been learned about the effects of alcohol through instruction, observation, and experience. They are important in that they may predict future actions (Goldman et al., 1999). Male offenders expect alcohol to give them confidence in social situations (McMurran, 2007a). Some outcome expectancies are criminogenic: for instance 'if I drink, then I will be

violent' and 'if I drink I can take sexual risks' (McMurran and Bellfield, 1993). Recent research has, however, indicated that alcohol–aggression expectancy effects disappear after controlling of for an aggressive disposition; it is the conjunction of the psychopharmacological effects of alcohol with an aggressive disposition which really leads to aggression (Giancola, 2006).

- *Type of beverage.* Different drinks affect behaviour differently, for example violence is more likely with spirits than beer or wine (Gustafson, 1999). This may be accounted for by chemical differences between beverages (different congeners), by differing speed of alcohol ingestion and metabolism (drinks of different strengths lead to intoxication at different rates), the effects of social custom (e.g. 'aggression-producing drinks' are preferred by aggressive people), or expectation (e.g. a person's perception of drink type-specific behaviour links).
- *Context.* Alcohol and aggression co-occur in certain settings, typically city centre entertainment venues where young men gather and drink heavily, especially at weekends (Lang et al., 1995). It is also important that people tend to gather there to seek sexual partners, even to compete over them, thus increasing the volatility of the situation (Charles and Egan, 2005).
- *Excuses or facilitators.* Some people drink deliberately to 'loosen up' or give them courage to behave in ways they otherwise would not, thus making alcohol an excuse for antisocial behaviour, or blaming it after the act (Zhang et al., 2002).

Each of these aspects may play some role in any alcohol-related offence. Furthermore, the aggregation of factors should be understood within a cultural context, with differences in cultural (or subcultural) norms providing a behavioural baseline, regardless of intoxication. Factors that need to be taken into account in explaining alcohol-related crime are summarized in figure 18.1.

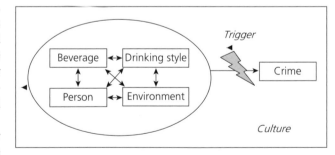

Figure 18.1 Factors implicated in explaining alcohol-related crime.

Alcohol and the Law

General

In the UK, alcohol is legally available but subject to controls. In his social history of drinking, Barr (1998) noted that

Britons have always been heavy drinkers, with documented references to exceptional levels of drunkenness as far back as the eighth century, and the heaviest drinking period in British history occurring in the eighteenth century. It was then that legislation to control alcohol began, and that Thomas Trotter completed his MD thesis describing habitual drunkenness as a 'disease of the mind' (Trotter, 1804/1985). According to Barr (1998), when William of Orange took the English throne in 1688, war was declared on France and trade sanctions reduced the availability of French brandy. This was accompanied by promotion of domestic manufacture of spirits to maximize state revenue. British-grown corn was distilled into gin, consumption of which increased from half a million gallons in 1688 to 19 million by 1742. Consequent social and medical problems eventually led to the Gin Acts. The first, in 1736, levied a heavy duty on gin so that most people could no longer afford it. In 2009, raising the price of alcohol was again suggested as a route to containing the public health threat. In 1736, however, increased duty perversely led to greater problems. Production was driven underground. Over the next 15 years, the Act was revised, lowering the duty but restricting availability. Consumption eventually fell. The principle of imposing a duty on the sale of alcohol and requiring producers and retailers to be licensed, at a cost, has been retained ever since, with a consequent tension between the health of the population and the health of the economy.

The most recent legislation for England and Wales is the Licensing Act 2003. It covers a range of 'licensable activities', including the sale and supply of alcohol, the provision of regulated entertainment, and the provision of late night refreshments. It brought relaxation of previous licensing laws, permitting citizens and visitors the 'opportunity to enjoy themselves with a drink or a meal at any time' (Home Office, 2000, p.5). As before, sale of alcohol was restricted to licensed premises, but with without nationally prescribed opening hours. Alcohol may be sold 24 hours a day, 7 days per week.

The legal age for purchasing and drinking alcohol in licensed premises is 18 years, although 16 and 17 year olds are permitted to drink it if less than spirit strength with meals served at table. Children under 16 may enter licensed premises only if accompanied by an adult; younger children may be excluded. Children of 5 years and over are allowed alcohol, but not on licensed premises. Children under 5 years old may be given alcohol only on medical order.

In conjunction with longer drinking hours, government goals for the Licensing Act 2003 included reduction in crime and disorder and improved domestic and public safety, the rationale being that the risk of intensive bouts of drinking in anticipation of closing time would be less likely. Anyone seeking a licence to sell alcohol must demonstrate a plan for minimizing the likelihood of crime, disorder, nuisance, or harm. The Act also provides for conditions for conducting an orderly house. It is an offence for the licensee or any employee to allow disorderly conduct on licensed premises, to sell alcohol to a person who is drunk, or to sell alcohol to underage drinkers. If such breaches occur, then the police have authority to take action to suspend or withdraw a license.

In addition, other laws exist to control disorderly or dangerous conduct relating to alcohol. Its consumption may be prohibited in certain public places, for example city centre streets, parks, special transport to sporting events, and at sporting events (Criminal Justice and Police Act 2001; Sporting Events (Control of Alcohol etc.) Act 1985). Driving a motor vehicle with more than 80 milligrams of alcohol per 100 millilitres of blood is an offence under the Road Traffic Act 1988.

Intoxication and the law

While intoxication may lead to criminal charges, such as 'drunk and disorderly', might it also constitute evidence for a defence against more serious crimes? Self-induced intoxication is generally no defence to a criminal charge, and, explicitly, may not be raised in respect of crimes of basic intent (*Majewski*). In England and Wales, however, it may, rarely, be raised as a defence or mitigation if it can be shown that the defendant was so intoxicated as to have been unable to form the *specific intent* necessary for the crime (*Beard*). Beard was extremely drunk and suffocated a young girl while raping her. It was ruled that he lacked the *mens rea* for murder and was convicted instead of manslaughter. A North American mock court room study showed that volunteer jurors there readily rejected the intoxication defence, and emphasized the personal responsibility of the defendant for his or her actions even when intoxicated (Golding and Bradshaw, 2005). This is formally recognized in Dutch law, where there is a concept of *culpa in causa*: an individual is responsible for his/her actions under the influence of alcohol because he is expected to know the effects of alcohol before s/he drinks. Scottish law similarly is less concerned with the ability to form intent than the actual harm caused.

Alcohol and defences when charged with a crime

Other alcohol-related defences can only be sustained where it can be shown that there is either cerebral damage secondary to the use of alcohol or if the drinking has become involuntary, e.g. *Tandy*. When an alcoholic mother appealed a conviction for the murder of her 11-year-old daughter, the court ruled that alcoholism could only qualify as a disease of the mind if the drinking were involuntary. This state would only be recognized if the first drink of the day were involuntary. It is, though, apparent that the 'first drink of the day' test is an arbitrary criterion with which to identify alcohol dependence.

Mental health legislation and alcohol

The earliest legislation enacted to control public drunkenness was the Habitual Drunkards Act 1879, which allowed for voluntary inpatient treatment at designated 'retreats' for up to 2 years. The Inebriates Act 1898 followed, allowing for the compulsory detention in a 'reformatory' for up to 3 years of any offender found to have been intoxicated with alcohol at the time of his/her offence. All such institutions had been closed by 1921.

As scientific acceptance grows that substance dependencies and misuse disorders, like mental illnesses, have their origins as much in genetics and/or physical brain damage as environmental factors, so mental health legislation has moved away from embracing these conditions as disorders which might lead to a requirement for detention in hospital or forms of coerced treatment. The Mental Health Act (MHA) 1959 did not specifically exclude alcohol dependence from its definition of mental disorder, although these grounds were seldom used; the MHA 1983 did if dependency on alcohol or drugs was the sole presenting condition. Under Section 1(3) this explicit exclusion has been retained in the MHA 2007 revision, notwithstanding the widening of the definition of mental disorder to include almost everything else (see also chapter 3).

Alcohol and Offending

Alcohol and violence

In 2007–2008, almost 5 million crimes were recorded by the police in England and Wales; 961,175 (19%) of them were crimes of non-sexual violence (Home Office, 2009). It is estimated that around half of violent incidents involve alcohol, with increased alcohol consumption associated with increased violence rates most marked in countries where binge drinking is a typical pattern (Room and Rossow, 2001). Homicide rates are associated with total alcohol sales, most strongly so in northern rather than southern European countries (Rossow, 2001).

Alcohol appears as a problem in all custodial settings. In a study of 622 men and women in police custody, Bennett (1998) identified 25% testing positive for alcohol, a likely underestimate since those who were unfit to be interviewed through drink or drugs or posing a threat of violence were not tested. Singleton et al. (1999) examined pre-imprisonment alcohol use with the AUDIT in a survey of prisoners in England and Wales. This 10-item screening tool includes items on quantity, frequency, dependency, and associated problems; scores range from 0–40, with 8 the accepted cut-off for hazardous drinking. The Singleton group found that 63% of sentenced men were hazardous drinkers, as were 58% of male remand prisoners, 36% of female remand prisoners and 39% of female sentenced prisoners. The hazardous drinkers were typically young (16–24), single and white, with men, but not women, being

held for violent offences. McMurran (2005) used the AUDIT with a much smaller sample of male prisoners, and found that those convicted of alcohol-related violence were the most extreme drinkers.

Findings from these cross-sectional studies are augmented by longitudinal studies. In a large New Zealand birth cohort ($n = 1,265$), for example, Fergusson et al. (1996) found that 15- to 21-year-old heavy drinkers, after controlling for shared risk factors such as socioeconomic status, education, and family background, were three times as likely to be violent as light drinkers. Similarly, Farrington (1995) found that heavy drinking at age 18 was predictive of violent crime in adulthood.

Alcohol and domestic violence

Alcohol is strongly associated with domestic violence (Leonard, 2001). Gilchrist and colleagues (2003) found that nearly half of 336 offenders on probation for domestic violence offences had a history of alcohol abuse; 73% had consumed alcohol just before the offence. Fals-Stewart's (2003) study of drinking and domestic violence showed that violence to partners was eight times more likely on drinking days than abstinent days, with the risk of *severe* violence 11 times higher on drinking days. Nevertheless, the role of drinking and intoxication in domestic violence remains controversial. Little is known about whether partner violence risk decreases after alcohol treatment (O'Farrell et al., 2003), and such treatment is unpopular. Many domestic violence treatments have emerged from a feminist perspective, where the root cause is seen as the man's desire to control his female partner (Corvo and Johnson, 2003). McMurran and Gilchrist (2008) argued that, while power and control may be fundamental to some domestic violence, interventions to reduce drinking are important for reducing risk of injury.

Alcohol and sexual offending

Several researchers have reported that between 30 and 50% of rapists had been drinking at the time of the offence (Maldonado et al., 1988; Martin, 2001; West and Wright, 1981), while others have shown that alcohol consumption by convicted rapists and child molesters is significantly higher than that of non-sexually violent offenders (Abracen et al., 2000). Sex offending theories place alcohol variously in the roles of overcoming internal inhibitions to offend (Finkelhor, 1984), interfering with self-regulation (Ward and Hudson, 1998), and impairing cognitive function (Seto and Barbaree, 1995). Emotional loneliness may be a common factor that explains both drinking and sexual offending (Abracen et al., 2000). Research testing these putative roles is scarce. Findings from laboratory research are equivocal, but there is evidence that alcohol may disinhibit sexual arousal (Seto and Barbaree, 1995), and some to suggest that rapists expect drinking to lead them to doing something sexually risky (McMurran and Bellfield, 1993).

Alcohol and acquisitive offending

Alcohol-related acquisitive crime has received far less attention than its drug-related counterpart. The 'economic necessity' argument, that 'addicts' are driven to purchase expensive drugs, is applied less to heavy drinkers, but drinking and associated activities (e.g. entrance to clubs, taxis) are expensive. Acquisitive offences may also be committed under the influence of alcohol, through impaired judgment, but this aspect too has rarely been investigated.

Bennett and Wright (1984) studied 121 offenders serving sentences for burglary, and found that over a third admitted committing their offence under the influence of alcohol. Bennett (1998) found that 26% of those arrested for burglary tested positive for alcohol, but only 2% of those who drank reported offending to get money to buy alcohol. Arrestees who tested positive for alcohol did, however, accrue over £4,000 *per annum* by illegal means. McMurran and Cusens (2005) found that, among 126 male prisoners in England and Wales, 11% of those convicted of violent acquisitive offences (e.g. robbery) said that their offending had been to support their alcohol habit, compared with 18% of those convicted of strictly property based offences (e.g. burglary). The former had significantly higher scores on the AUDIT than those with other motives.

Drunk driving

In the UK, about 15% of road deaths occur when the driver is over the legal alcohol limit (Department of Transport, 2012). There is evidence that the relative risk of involvement in a fatal vehicle crash increases steadily with increasing blood alcohol concentration, for both sexes and all ages, although the risk is disproportionately increased for young male drivers (Zadok et al., 2000).

Alcohol, Mental Disorder and Offending

While associations between schizophrenia, substance misuse in general, and offending have been extensively investigated, this is less true of the more specific relationship between alcohol dependence, schizophrenia and offending. In their England and Wales prison survey, Singleton et al. (1999) reported that severe alcohol problems were associated with mental ill health. Having an AUDIT score of 16 or more increased the odds of having a diagnosed personality disorder by 2.27, psychosis by 1.75, and neurosis by 1.53, as measured by the Schedules for Clinical Assessment in Neuropsychiatry (SCAN; WHO, 1992b).

In a study of 618 offenders in Canada, 26% of those with schizophrenia who abused alcohol were violent, but only 7% who had schizophrenia uncomplicated by alcohol abuse (Rice and Harris, 1995a). Among 1423 people convicted of homicide in a 12-year period in Finland, Eronen et al. (1996c) identified 93 with schizophrenia; those with uncomplicated schizophrenia had a homicide rate about seven times that of the general population, but men with schizophrenia and comorbid alcoholism were 17 times more likely to have killed.

Räsänen and colleagues (1998) did a prospective study of an unselected Finnish birth cohort ($n = 11,017$) over 26 years. Using national databases, they calculated the likelihood of offending and recidivism for people with schizophrenia with and without alcohol dependence. There were 51 men with schizophrenia in the sample, 11 of whom were dependent on or abusing alcohol. Seven of the 51 had committed a violent offence, four with alcohol problems and three without. The men with both schizophrenia and alcohol problems were 25 times more likely to have offended violently compared with increased odds among those with uncomplicated schizophrenia of only 3–4. None of the men with schizophrenia uncomplicated by alcohol problems had offended more than twice, while those with both problems had a 10-fold increase in such recidivism compared with the general population. The odds seem impressive, but they rest on just seven men who had been violent as well as having schizophrenia. Further, the extra elevation in rate of violence among people who abuse alcohol as well as having schizophrenia was not borne out by a US study with much larger numbers in the groups of interest (Tardiff and Sweillam, 1980); however, as a sample of patients admitted to a pair of US psychiatric hospitals during 1 year in the mid-1970s, the sample was highly selected – for treatment. There is no perfect study; population-based samples are doomed to tiny groups of core interest, but larger samples selected for the disorder, the violence or both may be subject to selection biases.

Another explanation for discrepancies may be real change over time. McMahon et al. (2003) analysed all admissions to England's high security hospitals between 1975 and 1999. During that time, there was a linear increase in the proportion of people admitted who had been drinking more than 21 units of alcohol per week in the year prior to their index offence. By diagnosis, the highest increase was in the psychosis with personality disorder group.

Alcohol, personality disorder and offending

Comorbidity between substance misuse disorders and personality disorders is common, with stronger associations between illicit drug use (rather than alcohol) and any personality disorder and between substance misuse generally and the cluster B types (e.g. antisocial personality disorder (ASPD), borderline personality disorder (BPD)) (Verheul et al., 1995). Among substance misusers, co-occurrence of ASPD is twice as common in men as women, and most

443

likely in those who use both alcohol and illicit drugs (Flynn et al., 1996), while severity of substance misuse is associated with multiple abnormal traits (Cecero et al., 1999). Mood disorders often further complicate the picture, being about three times more common among substance misusers with a personality disorder than those without (Kokkevi et al., 1998); they are also related to severity of the dependence (Cecero et al., 1999); alcohol misuse, alone or with illicit drugs, has also been associated with anxiety disorders (Flynn et al., 1996).

Rates of substance misuse and personality pathology comorbidity are so high that some are concerned that this conceptualization is tautologous (Rounsaville et al., 1998); however, even when substance-related symptoms are excluded from the criteria for personality disorder diagnoses, such comorbidity is only somewhat lowered (Rounsaville et al., 1998; Verheul et al., 1995). This suggests that personality disorder diagnoses are not simply surrogates for substance abuse, or vice versa. One way of unpicking the association with ASPD particularly is to separate its likely components, for example as in the anti-social behaviour and the affective coldness dimensions on the Psychopathy Checklist – Revised (PCL-R; Hare, 2003). In one study, those with a diagnosis of ASPD had a higher rate of alcohol problems, drug problems, and criminal activity than those with a high PCL-R score (Windle, 1999). Smith and Newman (1990), studying low security prisoners, showed that substance misuse was related to the PCL-R antisocial lifestyle dimension (Factor 2) rather than the affective dimension (Factor 1).

A comparison of alcohol-dependent, violent offenders with and without ASPD yielded two subgroups (Tikkanen et al., 2007). The smaller (20% of the sample) were high scorers on the PCL-R and demonstrated low harm avoidance but were responsible for fewer acts of impulsive violence; only half fulfilled diagnostic criteria for ASPD. The majority (80%) showed high harm avoidance but higher levels of impulsive behaviour, and were more likely to have ASPD or BPD. A study of offenders followed for an average of 8 years after discharge from a maximum security institution, either psychiatric hospital or prison, yielded similar findings. Overall, alcohol abuse was associated with violent recidivism, but high PCL-R scorers were the most likely to be violent recidivists and, in their case, alcohol abuse did not add to the accuracy of violence prediction (Rice and Harris, 1995a). If violent people who get high scores on the PCL-R are likely to be violent with or without taking alcohol, then treatment of alcohol misuse is unlikely to reduce their violence. After treatments to reduce violence, however, control of substance misuse remains important, not only on health grounds, but also so that unchecked abuse does not interfere with other treatment gains.

In a complete resident cohort of England's high security hospital patients, the prevalence of substance misuse disorders among those diagnosed with a personality disorder alone was found to be 14%, although rather higher in the psychosis–personality disorder comorbid group (Taylor et al., 1998); Corbett et al. (1998) gave a rather similar figure (18%) in another, with 4.5% being illicit drug dependent and 6.4% alcohol dependent. Coid et al. (1999), studying other secure settings, offered much higher figures; 53% of patients with personality disorder were judged as having a lifetime alcohol misuse diagnosis, and 47% were considered to have a lifetime drug misuse diagnosis. There are a number of possible reasons for such apparent discrepancies. Some studies, as the Taylor group, stick strictly to diagnostic concepts, whereas others depend more heavily on amounts of substance used. A more likely explanation for the substantial differences described here, however, lies in changing habits over time. Many of the high security hospital residents were last in the community when availability of substances was much lower, indeed observation of admission cohorts over time, confirms that rates of substance misuse in the year prior to admission were very significantly higher in the 1990s than the 1970s (McMahon et al., 2003).

Treatment gains are generally less in people who misuse substances and also have personality disorder than those without personality disorder, yet in both groups treatment does lead to reduced substance misuse and symptoms over time (Brooner et al., 1998; Cecero et al., 1999; Kokkevi et al., 1998; Linehan et al., 1999). Treatment for substance misuse may also have different effects according to personality type; it has been shown to reduce crime in those with ASPD, although not those with BPD (Hernandez-Avila et al., 2000). People with comorbid personality disorder, particularly ASPD, are more likely to drop out of treatment for substance abuse, but there is evidence that this may actually be related to comorbid depression rather than personality disorder (Kokkevi et al., 1998). Since treatment completion is important to a good outcome, it is crucial to assess for and treat depression in substance misusers, with or without personality disorders; withdrawal from substances may be a cause of low mood, but does not preclude depressive illness. People with ASPD often complete substance abuse treatment when that treatment is compulsory, in which case they too show good outcomes (Hernandez-Avila et al., 2000).

Alcohol, intellectual disability and offending

Reviews of alcohol use among people with intellectual disability suggest that their problematic drinking rates are low, but when they do use alcohol their risk of misuse is high (McGillicuddy et al., 1998). In many respects, alcohol misusers with intellectual disability are similar to their peers without it; most are men, living alone, more likely to smoke tobacco, use soft drugs, experience consequent work problems and get into trouble for offences such as public intoxication, disturbing the peace, assault, indecent exposure, breaking and entering, and driving whilst intoxicated (Krishef and DiNitto, 1981; McGillicuddy and Blane, 1999).

Treatment of Alcohol Problems

Voluntary versus compulsory treatment

Compulsory treatments for alcohol problems may be effective (Sullivan et al., 2008), although positive outcomes for compulsory treatment of offenders may only be evident in community settings (Parhar et al., 2008). Gregoire and Burke (2004) used a measure of 'readiness to change' to study motivation in a mixed group of substance misusers, 41% of whom were abusing alcohol. Their study suggested that treatment under a compulsory order was associated with increased motivation to change during treatment.

Detoxification

Once alcohol dependence has become established, the brain physically adapts to the presence of the depressant effects of alcohol. In consequence there are compensatory changes in brain chemistry, which lead to over-activity when alcohol is withdrawn. For those who are only mildly dependent, cessation of alcohol may be possible by gradual reduction of alcohol consumption. However, those drinking more than 15 units per day are likely to need some form of pharmacological support to control withdrawal symptoms. Detoxification is the process of substituting alcohol with a reducing course of medication to alleviate withdrawal symptoms and prevent the associated seizures.

Benzodiazepines have become the treatment of choice in detoxification, since they relieve withdrawal symptoms and have good anti-convulsant properties. A reducing course over 5 to 7 days is generally adequate. The two drugs most often used are chlordiazepoxide and diazepam, although the latter has a greater street value. These two drugs have long half-lives and, therefore, theoretically have less mood altering effects and less addictive potential than short-acting agents such as lorazepam. A typical starting dose of chlordiazepoxide is 20 mg three to four times a day, and of diazepam 15 mg four times per day. Doses may be doubled (with longer reducing courses) in adult *men* who are severely dependent (consuming over 40 units per day); such doses are not recommended for women or the elderly. Higher doses are also required for those with a history of dependence on both alcohol and benzodiazepines. Small does of lorazepam, with a shorter half-life, are preferable for people with established liver impairment, who should be inpatients due to their risk of fatal accumulation of benzodiazepines if their metabolism is compromised. Chlormethiazole had previously been a popular drug here, but it may cause fatal respiratory depression if taken with alcohol, and has a greater addiction potential if abused. It is important that the patient does not drink alcohol during the detoxification regime, but s/he sometimes does.

Outpatient detoxification is possible for people who are moderately dependent (Bennie, 1998). Daily collection of medication gives an opportunity to check for signs of withdrawal or alcohol consumption and to give encouragement and advice. Inpatient detoxification is indicated for those with a history of withdrawal fits, delirium tremens, early signs of encephalopathy, who lack social support and/or who are unlikely to remain abstinent during the detoxification. The same criteria may be used to identify those in prison who can be safely detoxified on normal location and those who need to be admitted to the healthcare/detox unit.

Adequate management of withdrawal should reduce the likelihood of withdrawal fits and delirium tremens (DT). If fits do occur, then diazepam should be given either by slow intravenous injection or *per rectum*. If DT becomes established then the patient should be nursed in a low stimulus environment and fluid balance closely monitored and supported as necessary. Oral rather than parenteral use of a shorter acting benzodiazepine, possibly with a neuroleptic, may be helpful. Attempts should be made to identify any contributory medical conditions such as head injury, hypoglycaemia, hepatic failure, gastro-intestinal bleeding, liver failure or infection, through full physical examination and regular checks of body temperature, blood glucose and electrolytes. If the patient becomes agitated then parenteral sedation (IV diazepam and/or IM haloperidol) may be indicated.

Pharmacological agents promoting abstinence

- *Disulfiram* (Antabuse) is the most established agent designed to promote sobriety. The two newer agents (acamprosate and naltrexone) have only been studied as adjuncts to psychosocial interventions. Comparison of outcome data between these drugs is difficult as the trials used different end points and outcome measures.

Disulfiram blocks the liver enzyme aldehyde dehydrogenase. After consumption of alcohol, blockade of this enzyme results in the accumulation of acetaldehyde. Resultant signs include: flushing, nausea, vomiting, headache, tachycardia and palpitations. After a large alcohol load the reaction can be severe, resulting in hypertension, circulatory collapse and death. The enzyme is effectively blocked after several days of disulfiram at a daily dose of 100–200 mg. The reaction is so aversive that disulfiram acts as a deterrent from further drinking, although it may also deter the individual from taking further disulfiram if s/he is determined to continue drinking. The drinker needs only one tablet in the morning to know that s/he is effectively protected for a day or so against lapses.

Disulfiram has been available for a considerable time, yet there are few controlled trials of its efficacy. There are data to show that it is associated with reduction in the number of drinking days and the amount of alcohol consumed but not an increase in abstinence (Garbutt et al., 1999; Hughes and Cook, 1997). Supervised consumption enhances its efficacy. In a naturalistic follow-up study comparing patients attending a disulfram clinic, those patients compelled to attend under a court order were significantly more likely to attend than those under voluntary arrangements (61%:18.2%) (Martin et al., 2004).

- *Acamprosate.* A number of meta-analyses have found acamprosate to be superior to placebo on a variety of abstinence-related outcomes (Lingford-Hughes et al., 2004), although its mode of action is still not clear. Verheul and colleagues (1999) hypothesize that it works by reducing craving for alcohol. It should be started as soon as possible after stopping alcohol for people who are aiming for abstinence, ideally in combination with psychosocial interventions. It has some gastro-intestinal side effects (diarrhoea and nausea).
- *Naltrexone* is an opioid antagonist, which is not licensed for marketing for the treatment of alcohol dependency, but it may be prescribed. Some drinkers report that it reduces the high they associate with alcohol, and this is why it may be prescribed (Ulm et al., 1995). Several meta-analyses have suggested that it is better than placebo on a number of outcomes but there are studies which have not found this. The British Association for Psychopharmacology guidance on the management of substance misuse gives a good summary of the evidence (Lingford-Hughes et al., 2004). There is some evidence that it reduces the risk of relapse to heavy drinking (Garbutt et al., 1999).

Psychosocial interventions for alcohol misuse

Cognitive behavioural treatments are particularly well suited to helping people gain control over drinking behaviours. The key components are motivation enhancement, behavioural self-control, cognitive coping skills, interpersonal skills, relapse prevention, and lifestyle change.

- *Motivation enhancement.* Motivating substance users to engage in treatment has long been acknowledged as the key to treatment effectiveness. Miller (1985) argued that motivation to change should be viewed as a dynamic state, and the task of therapy should be to alter both internal and external factors to increase the probability of the person actively engaging in the treatment process. Motivational interviewing (MI) is a strategic counselling technique which has been developed from this position (Miller and Rollnick, 2002). Its aims are to help the user to move from ambivalence to change towards taking action, based upon a spirit of collaboration between therapist and user, and drawing on his/her own capacity and resources for change. In Project MATCH, a four-session motivational enhancement therapy worked as well for most people as 12 sessions of either cognitive behaviour therapy (CBT) or a

12-step programme in reducing drinking (Project MATCH Research Group, 1997). A review of motivational interviewing interventions with offenders indicated that it can lead to improved retention in treatment, enhanced motivation to change, and behaviour changes (McMurran, 2009).

- *Behavioural self-control.* Like motivation to change, self-control is not a trait, but rather the likelihood of drinking in response to a range of physical, emotional, and psychological triggers that are associated with drinking. The task in therapy is to teach the user to identify the triggers for drinking, control urges to drink, and develop coping strategies. Behavioural self-control training has proved effective as a component of intervention for alcohol problems (see Miller, 1992), and is now core practice in many cognitive behavioural interventions.
- *Cognitive coping skills.* Cognitive coping includes micro-skills, such as positive self-talk and self-instruction (Meichenbaum, 1977). Positive self-statements are taught to assist people to cope with cravings (e.g. 'This feeling won't last'; 'I don't have to use') and avoid the goal violation effect ('A lapse does not have to become a relapse'). Self-instruction involves the construction and use of scripts to use as an internal commentary to support implementation of new coping skills. Alcohol outcome expectancies require both attention to moderate positive outcome expectancies, such as improving social confidence, and to diminish the strength of associated criminogenic beliefs, for example that sexually risky behaviour or violence will happen after drinking (McMurran and Bellfield, 1993; Quigley et al., 2002). Training in problem-solving skills is usually integrated into CBT to teach strategies for increasing independent functioning.
- *Interpersonal skills.* Peer pressure to drink may be tackled by teaching assertion and refusal skills, but must be augmented by helping people resist the desire to fit in with their drinking peers. The ability to make and sustain satisfying relationships is important for maintenance of treatment gains; interpersonal conflict is a potent risk relapse factor (Marlatt, 1996). Interpersonal skills which will generally benefit from attention include negotiation and conflict resolution.
- *Relapse prevention.* Marlatt and Gordon (1985) redefined relapse as a process, rather than an event. Marlatt (1996) identified several risk factors for relapse into drinking which require specific attention to increase the chances of maintenance of change. Relapse prevention (RP) teaches participants to identify and cope with high-risk situations, for example by avoiding or escaping from cues that trigger cravings or urges, and learning to cope with them if they happen. RP helps people limit the goal violation effect, which occurs when a minor lapse (e.g. one drink) turns into a full-blown relapse (e.g. the whole bottle). Relapse rehearsal enhances self-effectiveness

through developing the ability to imagine coping in a high risk situation. RP may also tackle broader issues, such as social support for change, stress management, lifestyle balance, and positive substitutes for the addictive behaviour. In a review of clinical trials, Carroll (1996) found RP to be more effective than no treatment for substance misuse, but not convincingly superior to other active interventions. There was evidence of a delayed effect, where RP reduced the severity of lapses when they did occur, and that RP was more effective with severely impaired substance users.

- *Lifestyle change.* Sustaining a non-substance using, non-criminal life may also require general changes in accommodation, work, leisure activities, social networks, and close relationships; promoting abandonment of the 'addict' or 'criminal' identity can promote commitment to a new lifestyle.

General versus specific programmes for alcohol misusers

Generic programmes that help people to reduce or stop drinking may be effective also in reducing crime. Programmes aimed at specific alcohol related offences may, however, be useful in some cases. Intoxicated aggression requires the integration of treatments for anger and aggression with those for alcohol abuse (Graham et al., 1998). Treatments for domestic violence also show a convergence of CBT with interventions focusing on drinking (Corvo and Johnson, 2003). A similar combined approach for drink-drivers has proven effective. A meta-analysis of 215 treatment programmes indicated an 8–9% reduction in recidivism for treated over untreated participants, with the most effective interventions combining education, psychological therapy, and supervision (Wells-Parker et al., 1995).

Therapeutic communities for alcohol misusers

The aim of therapeutic communities (TCs) is to foster a functional lifestyle through democratic process, in which residents confront and correct each other's maladaptive behaviour, offer each other support through the difficult change process, and sometimes reward improvement by offering those achieving change promotion within the community. A 'concept TC' is one specifically designed for people with substance use problems (Wexler, 1995). The abstinence-oriented, 12-step approach of Narcotics Anonymous (NA) and Alcoholics Anonymous (AA) has been widely adapted by professionals into concept TCs. TCs have also been adapted for correctional settings, where they have a good track record, (e.g. in the USA: Wexler and De Leon 1997; in the UK: Gunn et al., 1978, Malinowski, 2003, and Martin and Player, 2000; see also chapters 16 and 25).

Alcoholics Anonymous (AA)

AA is a worldwide self-help network based on a simple set of principles offering life-long support to the recovering alcohol-dependent drinker. Alcoholism is described as a disease 'like an allergy to alcohol'. Members are encouraged to avoid the first drink, as their condition can never be cured, only arrested by absolute sobriety.

The AA meeting is central. Meetings have a set format, which includes one or two testimonies from recovering alcoholics highlighting the problems associated with their former drinking life, the moment when they decided to seek sobriety and the positive contribution AA has had in supporting that sobriety. This leads to contributions from the floor, as those present identify with each speaker's experiences and encourage further sobriety. Meetings may be held in prisons and hospitals, secure or not, or the wider community. Meetings are open to those who are only recently abstinent and those who have not drunk for many years, and this mix is an important feature of AA, providing role models for newcomers and allowing those who have been abstinent for many years to revisit the AA principles (the 12 steps) in their role as mentors.

The first of the 12 steps is to 'admit that we are powerless over alcohol – that our lives had become unmanageable.' The second step is to recognize that there is a higher power that can restore sanity. This religious/spiritual component may be off-putting to an atheist, but many AA members do not interpret this in a religious way, while some see it as the power of the group itself. Vaillant (1995) concluded, after a long-term outcome study of alcohol dependency, that lasting improvement in an individual's life was associated with a commitment to change and at least one of the following: (1) a substitute for the dependency; (2) powerful resources of self-esteem and hope; or (3) a new stable relationship. AA may offer all these.

A 12-step approach has been shown to be as effective as the cognitive behavioural or motivation based approaches just described. Outcomes at 3-year follow-up were slightly better with the 12-step approach than the other two modes for those drinkers who lacked a non-drinking support network (Project MATCH, 1998). In a meta-analysis comparing AA attendance with other treatments and no treatment, however, AA was found to be associated with worse outcomes. It has been suggested that this is because some of those attending AA groups were obliged to do so and so biased the outcome data (Kownacki and Shadish, 1999).

Treatment in the context of comorbidity

The term 'dual diagnosis' is widespread, generally indicating co-occurrence of a psychotic illness and a substance use disorder, but it is rarely an accurate indicator of the multiplicity of disorders of health and behaviour that need attention. Nevertheless, the 'dual diagnosis' literature recognizes the importance of integrating a number of approaches in order to bring about useful change. It is acknowledged that a balance must be struck between empathy, unconditional regard and nurturance to develop motivation on the one hand, and discipline and structure to foster self-control on the other (Mueser et al., 2003). A national outcome survey of all 959 patients discharged from UK medium secure units in the 12 months after 1 April 1997 demonstrated both the extent of co-occurrence of alcohol problems and illness in an offender-patient population and the association between such problems and poorer outcomes (Scott et al., 2004). Patients were classified as having alcohol problems if there were records of excessive drinking. They were evident in 381 people (40%), with similar rates in men and women. During the 2-year follow-up period, there was a significant difference in re-conviction rates between those with alcohol problems and those without (49%:39% reconvicted).

For those with substance misuse diagnoses complicating mental illness, the latter often resolves with antipsychotic medication within a secure, drug-free environment. Ongoing risk is then closely linked to the likelihood of further substance abuse, but, since alcohol and illicit drugs are forbidden in secure settings, and rare commodities even if the cordon is occasionally breached, treatment of the substance problems may not be adequately prioritized. O'Grady (2001) argued for better integration of forensic, general psychiatry and substance misuse services to tackle this problem, although there is little evidence for the benefits of integrated treatment (Cleary et al., 2010).

The Royal College of Psychiatrists' Research Unit survey of the 28 medium secure units (MSUs) in England (excluding learning disability, personality and adolescent units) highlighted their inadequacies in tackling substance misuse:

- despite security measures, alcohol and drugs had been used in every English MSU during the 1-year survey period;
- of the drugs abused, cannabis and alcohol were thought to cause the greatest problems;
- few MSUs had comprehensive treatment services for substance misuse;
- few MSUs employed staff with specialist training in substance misuse;
- disagreement regarding the model of care: some units pursued and abstinence approach, others favoured controlled drinking (Durand et al., 2005).

In the period before a patient's discharge, controlled drinking or abstinence may be tested out during leave periods. Ideally, patients should begin to engage with community support at this stage, such as their future community psychiatric nurse (CPN), alcohol treatment services, or AA group, building towards seamless transfer of support on discharge. The receiving CPN should not only monitor

mental state and compliance with medication (possibly including disulfiram) but also alcohol-related work.

OTHER SUBSTANCE MISUSE

Misuse of psychoactive drugs other than alcohol is also a cause for concern worldwide. The World Health Organization (WHO), for example, has had an Expert Committee on Drug Dependence since 1949, which produces regular reports and has a mandatory task, under international treaties, to carry out medical and scientific evaluations of the abuse liability of dependence-producing drugs falling within the terms of the 1961 Single Convention on Narcotic Drugs and the 1971 Convention on Psychotropic Substances. It then makes recommendations to the United Nations (UN) Commission on Narcotic Drugs on the control measures, if any, that it considers appropriate.

Since the late 1990s there has been increasing interest in and awareness of drug problems in the UK, reflected in a raft of policy initiatives, including

- *Purchasing effective treatment and care for drug misusers* (Department of Health (DoH) 1997b);
- *Clinical guidelines on the management of drug misuse and dependence* (DoH, 1999c; DoH et al., 2007);
- *Substance misuse detainees in police custody* (3rd edn) (Association of Forensic Physicians and Royal College of Psychiatrists, 2006);
- *Safer services* (NCISH, 1999);
- *Safety First* (NCISH, 2001);
- *Avoidable deaths* (NCISH, 2006);
- *Tackling drugs to build a better Britain* (HM Government, 1998);
- *National drugs strategic statements* (HM Government, 2012; Home Office, 2012);
- *Recommendations* from the British Association of Psychopharmacology (Lingford-Hughes et al., 2004);
- *Drug misuse: Opioid detoxification* (National Institute for Health and Clinical Excellence (NICE), 2008a);
- *Psychosocial interventions in drug misuse* (NICE, 2007a).

Why Is Knowledge About Drug Misuse So Important to the Practising Forensic Clinician?

Drug misusers present in some form to all the major specialties in medical practice, perhaps especially accident and emergency units, general medical and surgical specialities (Fingerhood, 2000), but forensic, liaison, adolescent and old age psychiatry in hospital, community and criminal justice settings are increasingly contributing to their treatment. Even if the patient presents with a drug problem, this may not be his or her major problem; conversely, the presenting problem may not immediately be recognized as relating to drug misuse. People may present with abstinence syndromes, convulsions, acute disturbance (psychosis, panic, confusion, perceptual dysfunction), trauma, cancer, or cardiovascular conditions.

What Is a Drug?

In this chapter, the term 'drug' will be used to cover illicit substances, central nervous system depressants such as opiates and opioids (e.g. heroin, methadone), stimulants (e.g. cocaine, crack, amphetamine, ecstasy), and LSD, khat and magic mushrooms. It will also be used to describe street use and non-compliant use of prescription drugs such as benzodiazepines and non-compliance in use of over-the-counter preparations such as codeine-based products (e.g. cough medicines, decongestants).

Clinical experience and a growing literature base indicate that people may use a combination of licit and illicit substances, as well as prescribed and over-the-counter medications used both compliantly and non-compliantly. Patients may borrow and/or share drugs, may not report all medications, may use out-of-date drugs, may take foods and drugs that interact, and may store drugs inappropriately. This complexity, and so-called polypharmacy or polydrug misuse is a particular issue in older people who have physical or psychological comorbidity. 'Misuse' may be the result of lack of judgment, misconceptions about the drug(s), inability to purchase medications, inability to manage the combination of medications (perhaps due to memory problems) or patients may be intentionally using medications for purposes other than those intended. Unravelling all this is what makes this work challenging and stimulating!

Concepts of Harmful Use and Dependence

Criteria for the diagnosis of substance problems from both main current disease classification systems are outlined in tables 18.1 and 18.2 (*ICD-10*: WHO, 1992a; *DSM-IV*, 1994; APA, 1994). For the purposes of treatment and management it is helpful to distinguish non-dependent substance misuse from dependent use. In the UK, drugs are classified, according to perceived seriousness of consequences of taking them, under the Misuse of Drugs Act 1971; the government may change a drug's classification from time to time as new evidence about its properties emerges. The current classification according to this act is set out in table 18.3.

The inter-relationships between physical health, mental health, and drug misuse are well-documented. Apart from the direct effects of drugs on general health (see later), there are indirect effects such as dietary neglect, impoverishment, trauma, bereavement and loss. Malnutrition, for instance, may emanate from drug-induced anorexia, malabsorption and/or economic deprivation. Liver dysfunction, for example with HIV, hepatitis B or C, produces psychological as well as physical problems.

Psychiatric conditions such as anxiety, depression, post-traumatic stress disorder, drug-induced psychosis, schizophrenia, delirium, and dementia may lead to, be a consequence of, or coincide with drug misuse. Withdrawal from barbiturates and benzodiazepines leads to delirium, whereas head injuries and serious infections are associated with dementia. The differing mechanisms and types of relationship require careful history-taking and judicious interpretation. Depression, dementia, delirium and a heightened risk of suicide are probably the problems most commonly faced by clinicians. Some of these conditions are associated with chronic pain and sleep disorders, which may be the problems which made the patient seek relief from prescription and non-prescription medications in a non-compliant way. Since there are effective interventions for many psychiatric conditions, correct diagnosis and treatment have real benefits.

Table 18.1   Criteria for substance abuse (*DSM-IV*) and harmful use (*ICD-10*)

DSM-IV (American Psychiatric Association, 1994)	ICD-10 (World Health Organisation 1992a)
(A) A maladaptive pattern of substance use leading to clinically significant impairment or distress, as manifested by one (or more) of the following occurring within a 12-month period	A pattern of psychoactive substance use that is causing damage to health. The damage may be physical or mental
(1) Recurrent substance use resulting in a failure to fulfil major role obligations at work, school, or home	Actual damage should have been caused to the physical or mental health of the user
(2) Recurrent substance use in situations in which it is physically hazardous	Harmful patterns of use are often criticized by others and frequently associated with adverse social consequences
(3) Recurrent substance-related legal problems	
(4) Continued substance use despite having persistent or recurrent social or interpersonal problems caused or exacerbated by the effects of the substance	
(B) Symptoms have never met the criteria for Substance Dependence for this class of substance	Acute intoxication not in itself evidence. Should not be diagnosed if… another specific form of drug- or alcohol-related disorder is present

Table 18.2 Criteria for substance dependence (*DSM-IV*) and dependence syndrome (*ICD-10*)

DSM-IV (American Psychiatric Association, 1994)	ICD-10 (World Health Organisation 1992a)
A maladaptive pattern of substance use, leading to clinically significant impairment or distress, as manifested by three (or more) of the following, any time in the same 12-month period	A cluster of physiological, behavioural and cognitive phenomena. [...] A definite diagnosis should usually be made only if three or more of the following have been experienced or exhibited at some time during the previous year
(1) tolerance, as defined by *either* need for markedly increased amounts of substance to achieve intoxication or desired effect, *or* markedly diminished effect, with continued use of the same amount of the substance	(1) a strong desire or sense of compulsion to take the substance
(2) withdrawal, as evidenced by *either* of the following: the characteristic withdrawal syndrome for the substance, *or* the same (or closely related) substance is taken to relieve or avoid withdrawal symptoms	(2) difficulties in controlling substance-taking behaviour in terms of its onset, termination, or levels of use
(3) the substance is often taken in larger amounts over a longer period than was intended	(3) a physiological withdrawal state when substance use has ceased or been reduced, as evidenced by: the characteristic withdrawal syndrome for the substance or use of the same (or closely related) substance with the intention of relieving or avoiding withdrawal symptoms
(4) persistent desire or repeated unsuccessful efforts to cut down or control substance use	(4) evidence of tolerance, such that increased doses of the psychoactive substance are required in order to achieve effects originally produced by lower doses
(5) a great deal of time is spent in activities necessary to obtain the substance, use the substance, or recover from its effects	(5) progressive neglect of alternative pleasures or interests because of psychoactive substance use, increased amount of time necessary to obtain or take the substance or to recover from its effects
(6) important social, occupational, or recreational activities given up or reduced because of substance use	(6) persisting with substance use despite clear evidence of overly harmful consequences (physical or mental)
(7) the substance use is continued despite knowledge of having had a persistent or recurrent physical or psychological problem that is likely to have been caused or exacerbated by the substance	

Table 18.3 UK drug classification framework in 2011

Class	Example drugs[1]	Maximum penalty	
		Possession	Supply
Class A	Cocaine and crack cocaine ecstasy, heroin, LSD, methadone, methamphetamine, magic mushrooms, any Class B drug which is injected	Magistrates' court 6 months and £5,000 fine Crown Court 7 years, an unlimited fine or both	6 months and £5,000 fine Life, an unlimited fine or both
Class B	Amphetamine, barbiturates, codeine	Magistrates' court 3 months and £2,500 fine Crown Court 5 years, a fine or both	6 months and £5,000 fine 14 years, a fine or both
Class C	Cannabis[2], ketamine, anabolic steroids, minor tranquillizers	Magistrates' court 3 months and £500 fine Crown Court 2 years, a fine or both	3 months and £2,000 fine 14 years, a fine or both

[1]These are examples and reference should be made to amendments to the legislation, which are accessible online: http://www.legislation.gov.uk/all?title=drugs/
[2]Cannabis was in Class B under the Misuse of Drugs Act 1971; cultivation of the cannabis plant carries a maximum penalty of 6 months or fine of £5,000 in a magistrates' court; 14 years in prison or an unlimited fine or both in a Crown Court.

Epidemiology of Illicit Drug Use

The UK has among the highest levels of substance misuse in Europe and illicit substance misuse is a substantial problem. In post-millennium surveys carried out in England and Wales, about one-third of the population have admitted to illegal drug misuse in the year prior to rating. The British Crime Survey, a household interview study, found in 2006/7 that 35.5% of 16–59 year olds (11¼ million) had used one or more illicit drugs in their lifetime, 10% had used one or more illicit drugs in the year (¾ million) and 5.9% (2 million) in the month prior to interview (Murphy and Roe, 2007). Four and a half million (13.8%) reported use of Class A drugs at least once in their lifetime, 1 million (3.4%) in the previous year, and 500,000 (1.7%) in the previous month (Murphy and Roe, 2007). Cannabis was the most likely drug to have been taken, having been used by 8.2% of these 16–59 year olds, followed by cocaine (powder or crack), which was used by 2.6%. Class A drugs had been used by proportionately more people during the year prior to interview in 2006/7 than in 1998, but the proportion using any illicit drug in the previous year was lower in 2006/7 than in 1998.

Young people generally report higher levels of drug use than older people, but Class A drug use among young people has remained stable since 1998 and the reported use of any drug in the previous decade actually fell in the 16- to 24-year-old age group. Over the course of their lifetime, 2¾ million (44.7%) young people aged 16–24 had used an illicit drug, 1½ million (24%) had used an illicit drug in the previous year, and 1 million (14.3%) in the previous month. One million (16.3%) had used a Class A drug during their lifetime, 500,000 (8.1%) in the previous year and 250,000 (4.3%) in the previous month. Young women are one and a half to three times more likely to use substances than older women. International studies demonstrate that about 20–25% of women in younger age groups have used illicit drugs in the past year.

One of the problems in planning services for drug users is the considerable country and regional variation in drug use overall and in choice of specific drugs, so some local knowledge is essential. When comparing English Government Office Regions and Wales with each other, for example, according to the 2006/07 British Crime Survey, the South West (11.1%) and the North West (11.0%) had the highest levels of any drug use while the West Midlands (9.2%) and the Eastern region (9.1%) had the lowest levels. Class A drugs were nearly twice as likely to be used in the highest regions (North East: 4.1%; North West: 4.0%) as in Wales (2.5%) (Murphy and Roe, 2007).

Problem drug users are much more likely to be found within the criminal justice system than in the general population. A review commissioned by the UK Drugs Policy Commission (UKDPC) reported that:

- at least 1/8 arrestees (equivalent to about 125,000 people in England and Wales) are estimated to be problem heroin and/or crack users, compared with about 1/100 among the general population;
- of arrestees who used heroin and/or crack at least once a week, 81% said that they had committed an acquisitive crime in the previous 12 months, compared with 30% of other arrestees; of arrestees who had used heroin and/or crack at least once a week, 31% reported an average of at least one crime a day, compared with 3% of other arrestees;
- between one-third and one-half of all new receptions to prison are estimated to be problem drug users (about 45,000–65,000 prisoners in England and Wales);
- drug-related crime costs an estimated £13.5 billion in England and Wales alone (UKDPC, 2008).

In addition, illicit drugs as well as alcohol play a role in about 45% of homicides. One in six homicides is committed by a person with severe mental illness who was abusing substances (Shaw et al., 2006).

Mortality

Premature mortality is high among substance misusers (Ghodse et al., 1998; Lind et al., 1999); illicit drug misuse is responsible for approximately 3,000 deaths each year, although in numerical terms deaths from legally available substances are even higher (in England and Wales 120,000 deaths annually from smoking-related disorders and 40,000 from alcohol-related disorders). The mortality associated with alcohol and drugs is between nine and 16 times higher than in the general population and substance misuse is a very strong predictor of completed suicide (Marsden et al., 2000; NCISH, 2006, 2001, 1999; Weaver et al., 2003; Wilcox et al., 2004). In England and Wales, 33% of inpatient suicides have a history of alcohol misuse and 30% a history of drug misuse, while 41% of suicides in the community have a history of alcohol misuse and 28% a history of drug misuse (NCISH, 2001). The Confidential Enquiry into Maternal Deaths in the UK from 2002–2004 found that, when all deaths up to 1 year from delivery were taken into account, 8% were caused by substance misuse (Lewis, 2004).

Morbidity

Alcohol, drugs and nicotine affect all organs of the body and the interactions of substance misuse with health are multiple and complex. Effects may be very rapid or insidious, and by a direct pharmacological or physiological action or indirectly due to associated behaviours. As with alcohol, the acute effects of intoxication with illicit drugs, the impact of chronic use and the development of withdrawal and dependence may lead to an array of physical and psychological problems and social consequences. Dependence on some substances develops very rapidly, within weeks or months. These conditions may be related to high-risk behaviours such as injecting, needle sharing, unsafe sex and the use of substances to the point of intoxication. Psychological symptoms or signs, including hallucinations, mood change, impulsivity, aggression and disinhibition or psychiatric syndromes, such as anxiety, depression, psychotic illness, post-traumatic stress disorder, personality disorder or eating disorders are all among the risks of use. Self-harm may result, with eventual suicide.

These difficulties may lead to homelessness, unemployment, poverty and criminality, as well as disengagement from families, communities and services. Patients with comorbid conditions have poorer prognosis and place a heavy burden on services because of higher rates of relapse and re-hospitalization, serious infections such as hepatitis and HIV, and/or prostitution, violence, arrest and even imprisonment. All substance misuse, but perhaps especially multiple use, must be seen in the context of its social as well as its medical difficulties (Little et al., 2005; Okah et al., 2005; Velez et al., 2006).

Comorbidity is a term used to describe the co-occurrence of psychiatric disorder and substance misuse (Banerjee et al., 2002; Crome and Day, 2002; Day and Crome, 2002; Waller and Rumball, 2004). Chronic use or intoxication with depressant drugs, or withdrawal from stimulants produce symptoms similar to depression, while acute intoxication from stimulants and cannabis may mimic a schizophrenic illness. Withdrawal from depressant drugs may result in symptoms of anxiety, panic, and even confusional states. The difficulty for the clinician is, therefore, the extent to which the presentation is a simple drug effect and the extent to which there is an additional independent mental disorder. An association between drug use and psychiatric conditions has been consistently documented in substance misusing clinical populations, psychiatric populations, the general population, prisons, and among the homeless. Indeed, in the US Epidemiological Catchment Area (ECA) study, drug addiction was associated with a 53.1% lifetime rate of an additional mental disorder (Regier et al., 1990).

In any patient the following hypotheses for association between apparent mental illness and substance use should be considered:

- a primary psychiatric and/or physical illness may precipitate or lead to a substance problem;
- substance misuse may worsen or alter the course of a psychiatric and/or physical illness;
- intoxication and/or substance dependence may lead to psychological and physical symptoms;
- substance misuse and/or withdrawal may lead to psychiatric or physical symptoms or illnesses;
- it is no longer possible to tell which came first but each contributes to a cycle of deterioration.

Practitioners working with substance misusers need to be aware that substance misusers may have vascular, infectious, carcinogenic or traumatic conditions directly related to their misuse. Life-saving measures could be required. For these reasons, it is vital to establish whether recent substance use, including the types, quantities, route and the time course of use, may have a bearing on overt and covert physical and psychological symptoms. Even where the incidence of serious adverse effects is low, the unpredictability of these events makes the health consequences important.

In the UK, Weaver et al. (2003) examined mental illness and substance misuse presenting to community mental health teams and substance misuse services. Forty-four per cent of patients in community mental health teams reported substance misuse in the previous year, while 75% of drug service patients and 85% of alcohol service patients had suffered from a psychiatric disorder in the previous year. In England and Wales, one-third of suicides in the community have a history of alcohol and/or drug misuse (NCISH, 2001). A recent Canadian psychological autopsy study (Séguin et al., 2006) demonstrated that 90% of people who complete suicide suffer from comorbid mental disorders, mainly mood disorders and substance misuse.

In 1997 the Office for National Statistics (ONS) undertook a survey of psychiatric morbidity among 3,000 remand and sentenced prisoners aged 16–64 in England and Wales (Singleton et al., 1998; see chapter 25 for more detail). A high proportion, particularly of the men, had substance misuse disorders. Prisoners with antisocial personality disorder were over six times more likely than the others to report drug dependence in the year before coming to prison, though without a detailed chronology there may be a risk of over-diagnosing such comorbidity (Kaye et al., 1998).

In Greece, male drug users from community treatment services were compared with male prisoners registered as drug dependent in the previous 12 months (Kokkevi and Stefanis, 1995). Lifetime affective disorders (32%:20%, $p = 0.10$) and anxiety disorders (53%:14%) were more prevalent among drug users recruited from treatment services than among drug users in prison, while ASPD was more prevalent among prisoners (76%:61%), suggesting considered service selection biases.

Current UK legislation on Drugs

Most countries have legislation to limit the production, administration, use, supply, import and export of certain drugs. They differ considerably, but here discussion will be confined to UK law.

Misuse of Drugs Act 1971 and its amendments

This act, which evolved from a series of UK legislative interventions, is designed to control the use of certain drugs that are viewed as having medical applications. It has been the subject of many amendments since the original version in 1971, which can be found online: (http://www.ukcia.org/pollaw/lawlibrary/misuseofdrugsact1971.php).

It first classified drugs into three categories (A, B and C; see table 18.3) and defined the penalties for their production, supply and possession. A 2001 amendment to the Act created the offence of 'knowingly allowing premises' owned or managed by a person to be used for the unlicensed production, use or supply of any controlled drug. In England and Wales, cannabis and cannabis resin were reclassified from Class B to Class C from 2004, after the Criminal Justice Act 2003 amended the Misuse of Drugs Act 1971. This amendment also increased the maximum penalty for trafficking in Class C drugs, from 5 to 14 years. Cannabis is being considered by the UK government for reclassification back to Class B, despite advice to the contrary given by the Advisory Council on the Misuse of Drugs ((ACMD), 2008; Home Office, 2012).

The Misuse of Drugs Regulations 2001

These regulations cover the overlap between the Misuse of Drugs Act 1971 and instances where there are legitimate medical applications of controlled drugs. These regulations further classify drugs into schedules to reflect the degree of control over possession, use, prescribing and supply, summarized in table 18.4.

Medicines Act 1968

The manufacture, supply and prescription of medicinal drugs are also controlled by the Medicines Act, which has undergone many amendments since 1968. Such drugs are classified into prescription only drugs, pharmacy sales drugs and general sales drugs. There is a complex overlap with the regulations of the Misuse of Drugs Act, particularly with regard to the possession of some minor tranquillizers.

Some drugs, such as heroin and LSD, can only be prescribed by doctors who possess a specific licence. Other drugs, such as schedule 3 and schedule 4, part 1 benzodiazepine tranquillizers may be prescribed by any doctor, but it is now illegal to be in possession of these drugs if they are not prescribed. It is illegal to sell or supply any Class C drug to another person.

Mental health legislation

Throughout the UK, mental health legislation explicitly excludes compulsory detention in hospital on grounds solely of substance misuse or dependence. The expectation generally is that people must engage voluntarily in treatment. Community-based coercion into treatment or rehabilitation, incorporating regular drug testing, is confined to convicted offenders. In England and Wales they may receive a Drug Testing and Treatment Order (DTTO) under the Crime and Disorder Act 1998, or more likely now, a Drug Rehabilitation Requirement Order (DRRO) in conjunction with a community sentence or suspended prison sentence under the Criminal Justice Act 2003.

Drugs and Crime

The association between drug use and criminal behaviour varies in terms both of strength of association and of severity of the behaviour. A simple classification of crime categories and the strength of association with drug use has been constructed (Parker and Bottomley, 1966); it recognizes five patterns:

- Type A: Drug users who rarely commit crimes and offenders who rarely use drugs.
- Type B: Acquisitive criminal behaviour to fund drug use.
- Type C: Drug supply for financial gain.
- Type D: Criminal acts committed as a result of the psychotropic effect of drugs.
- Type E: Those with a previous criminal career who move to heavy drug use, which increases their criminal behaviour. Those drug users whose criminal behaviour moves to a level beyond funding their own use.

Table 18.4   Summary of Schedules of the Misuse of Drugs Regulations 2001

Schedule	Main drugs included	Restrictions
1	LSD, ecstasy, raw opium, psilocin, cannabis (herbal and resin)	Import, export, production, possession and supply only permitted under Home Office licence for medical or scientific research. Cannot be prescribed by doctors or dispensed by pharmacists.
2	Heroin, cocaine, methadone, morphine, amphetamine, dexamphetamine, pethidine and quinalbarbitone	May be prescribed and lawfully possessed when on prescription. Otherwise, supply, possession, import, export and production are offences except under Home Office licence. Particular controls on their prescription, storage and record keeping apply.
3	Barbiturates, temazepam, flunitrazepam, buprenorphine, pentazocine and diethylpropion	May be prescribed and lawfully possessed when on prescription. Otherwise, supply, possession, import, export and production are offences except under Home Office licence. Particular controls on their prescription and storage apply. Temazepam prescription requirements are less stringent than those for the other drugs in this Schedule.
4 Part 1	Benzodiazepines (except flunitrazepam and temazepam) and pemoline	May be prescribed and lawfully possessed when on prescription. Otherwise, supply, possession, import, export and production are offences except under Home Office licence.
4 Part 2	Anabolic steroids	May be lawfully possessed by anyone even without a prescription, provided they are in the form of a medical product.
5	Compound preparations such as cough mixtures which contain small amounts of controlled drugs such as morphine. Some may be sold over-the-counter	Authority needed for their production or supply but can be freely imported, exported or possessed (without a prescription).

An analysis of the association between crime patterns and drug use patterns using this model suggested that most people involved in crime are not drug users, or only use substances recreationally, and most of those involved in drug use are not involved in crime (Royal College of Psychiatrists, 2000).

An alternative empirical classification of the association, particularly taking causative mechanisms into account, has been proposed by Boles and Miotto (2003). In this system violence is seen as following from:

a. pharmacological consequences, such as intoxication or withdrawal, *or*

b. systemic issues, such as drug trade disputes, drug gang violence, violence to informants and violence related to collection of drug-related debts, *or*

c. economic factors related to the need to fund drug use through crime.

A more recent meta-analysis of 30 studies confirmed that there is an association between drug use and crime and provided a quantitative measure of the strength of the relationship and variation with type of drug used (Bennett et al., 2008): the odds of offending were greater for drug users than for non-drug users, but the odds were not the same for all drug types. Crack users carried the highest risk of offending, followed by heroin users, then other cocaine users. Recreational drug use was shown to carry a lower risk of offending, but within this group, cannabis users had the highest risk, followed by amphetamine users.

Interaction between drugs of abuse, mental illness and crime

At least since Swanson and colleagues (1990) examined mental illness and violence relationships in the US ECA data (see also chapter 14), it has been recognized that use of drugs and alcohol by people with a mental illness substantially increases their risk of violence. In the UK, Wheatley (1998) compared patients detained in specialist forensic psychiatric services with those in generic services and found that it was the higher prevalence of substance use by the former which distinguished them. This was confirmed by Penk et al. (2000), who showed that people diagnosed with schizophrenia and substance abuse disorders were more behaviourally dysfunctional (though more socially competent) than their non-substance misusing schizophrenic peers. Those with both diagnoses had a high prevalence of childhood trauma. Scott et al. (1998) investigated the relationship in more detail, but with a small sample, by interviewing 27 comorbid and 65 'pure' psychotic patients from medium security hospitals, and reviewing their records. They also interviewed staff working closely with them. Individuals with illness and substance misuse comorbidity were more likely to report any history of committing an offence or recent hostile behaviour and key workers were more likely to report recent aggression by those patients. A combination of illicit substance misuse and non-adherence to medication prescribed for the illness is particularly risky. In the USA, Swartz et al. (1998) found that violence is twice as likely among such patients as among those with either problem alone. Erkiran et al. (2006) showed that seriousness of violence as well as its frequency was higher among people comorbid for psychosis and substance misuse disorders than those with psychosis alone.

Drug misuse and acquisitive crimes

Property theft, car theft, shoplifting, fraud and defrauding social benefit schemes are among the commonest crimes associated with drug use in the UK. These crimes are most commonly committed to fund the purchase of drugs or to maintain basic living needs in the absence of any legal, paid employment.

Drug misuse and sexual crime

Sex-related crime in a drug use setting is most commonly involved with prostitution. Studies of pathways into prostitution have often given conflicting results. One study of 1142 female prisoners, for example, found that drug abuse did not explain their entry into prostitution (McClanahan et al., 1999), but Gossop et al. (1994) reached a different conclusion. They studied 51 women who were working as prostitutes and found that half of them had started this in order to pay for drugs. A more recent study supported the Gossop findings, and also showed that crime other than prostitution is little reported in this population. This may reflect the displacement of other criminal activity or that the sums of money obtained from prostitution (£112–132 per day, on average 2004/5) are adequate for the individual's drug use needs (Bloor et al., 2006).

The use of drugs to facilitate sexual assault (drug-facilitated sexual assault: DFSA) has no adequate definition, according to Hall and Moore (2008) in their review of the field. They propose a distinction between proactive (planned) DFSA and opportunistic DFSA. The more popular terminology of 'date rape drugs' refers in the main to the use of rohypnol, together with other drugs such as gamma-hydroxybutyric acid (GHB), which can easily be concealed in alcoholic drinks. Reviews of cases of 'date rape' using drugs such as rohypnol have indicated that, in many cases, the level of alcohol ingested was also considerable and that the involvement of rohypnol itself may not be as central as previously believed (Advisory Council on the Misuse of Drugs, 2007a).

Drugs and driving

Fitzpatrick et al. (2006), in Ireland, reviewed the prevalence of positive drug tests in drivers suspected of being intoxicated through alcohol or drug use; over 30% of drivers whose alcohol level was below the legal limit when tested were positive for one or more illicit drugs. Of those drivers whose alcohol level was above the legal limit, 14% were positive for one or more illicit drugs. Zero blood concentration limits for controlled substances whilst driving have been introduced in Sweden, but have not resulted in a reduction in the number of cases of driving under the influence of drugs (Jones, 2005).

Types of Drugs and Their Effects

The health risks posed by drug use include the toxicity of the drug itself, the route of use, blood-borne pathogens, contaminants, unknown purity, and quantity. Adverse effects for each of the most commonly used drugs are summarized below (Banerjee et al., 2002).

Heroin

Effects of intoxication

Diverted pharmaceutical opiates and opioids may be formulated for injection or oral use, or as suppositories. Tablets may be crushed and injected. Dependence can develop within weeks. Since tolerance also develops rapidly, but diminishes quickly after abstinence, relapse can lead to overdose and death. This is also the case for methadone. Heroin may be smoked, inhaled or heated on foil and the fumes inhaled. The short-term effects include a rapid onset of euphoria with a sensation of heavy extremities. The user will then experience alternating wakeful and drowsy states. Heroin is a central nervous system depressant and has effects on reaction times and ability to concentrate.

Health complications

Repeated use of heroin induces a state of dependency with a need for increased doses and increased frequency of use. The occurrence of withdrawal symptoms triggers further use to relieve these symptoms. Repeated injections result in collapsed veins, infection of the heart lining and valves and skin and muscle infections. Sharing of injection equipment also carries a high risk of blood-borne infections such as HIV and hepatitis C. Opiates and opioids depress coughing, breathing and heart rate, dilate blood vessels, reduce bowel activity and produce constipation. Overdose usually occurs when in combination with other drugs.

Offending

Hoaken and Stewart (2003), in a review of aggressive behaviour in heroin users, concluded that their high rates of aggression may be independent of their heroin use and more closely related to personality factors linked with that dependence.

Cannabis

Effects of intoxication

Cannabis is either smoked or eaten. Use is accompanied by distorted time perception, impaired coordination and difficulty in thinking. These effects on cognitive functions may persist for over 24 hours after use of cannabis.

Health complications

Cannabis has effects on physical health, with even higher rates of lung and heart disease, and cancers of the head and neck, among cannabis smokers than among nicotine cigarette smokers. Cannabis use may lead to depression, anxiety and paranoia. Panic attacks are a feature and there is controversy as to whether cannabis 'causes' an enduring schizophrenia-like psychosis or simply exacerbates it (Sewell et al., 2009; Tucker, 2009). Memory and learning are impaired.

Offending

Review of the evidence linking cannabis use with aggression has indicated that cannabis intoxication reduces the risk of violence, whereas withdrawal from cannabis may increase it (Hoaken and Stewart, 2003). Cannabis dependency was one of only three disorders of mental health independently linked to violence in the Dunedin birth cohort (Arsenault et al., 2000).

Psychostimulants – amphetamines and cocaine

Effects of intoxication

Most psychostimulants may be used orally, 'snorted' as a powder through the nose, or injected or smoked, producing an intense euphoric state, possibly accompanied by restless and agitation, rapid speech and increased wakefulness.

Health complications

Psychostimulants may precipitate anxiety states, confusion, convulsions and cardiovascular problems, and acute psychotic episodes are not uncommon. The sharing of injection equipment carries the same risks as for heroin use, but its risk is often underestimated in the stimulant using population. Use of stimulants may lead to exhaustion, depression, and weight loss. A paranoid and/or confusional state may also occur. Hypertension, cardiac arrhythmias, stroke, hepatic and renal damage and abscesses are the result of heavy use, especially if injecting. Violent and aggressive behaviour may ensue. Snorting of cocaine leads to nasal septal perforation and damage to the nasal passages.

Offending

Methamphetamine use is often cited as having a direct link with violent crime, but the relation between its use and violence is indirect and unclear (Tyner and Fremouw, 2008).

Benzodiazepines

Effects of intoxication

In the short term, users may experience tiredness, depressed respiration, dizziness, and unsteadiness.

Health complications

If combined with other depressants such as alcohol or opiates, overdose can be fatal. Dependence can develop on low doses and convulsions occur with withdrawal. Rebound symptoms such as insomnia, anxiety, and tension may occur.

Offending

The evidence regarding the effect of benzodiazepines use on offending behaviour is conflicting. A case-crossover study of the role of alcohol and drugs in triggering criminal violence (Haggard-Grann et al., 2006) showed that whilst alcohol is a strong trigger for criminal violence, the use of benzodiazepines in combination with the alcohol does not increase the risk. Other studies have suggested that in some individuals the use of benzodiazepines may trigger a paradoxical aggressive reaction, but that this is more related to individual personality factors rather than a pharmacological, dose-related effect (Bramness et al., 2006).

Polysubstance use

People commonly use more than one substance, but an Australian study reported that only the use of alcohol and inhalants appeared to have significant relationships with recidivism in young offenders (Putniņš, 2003).

Screening, Assessment and Diagnosis of Drug Misuse

A number of screening methods for illicit drug use are available (see box 18.1). These depend on the purpose, setting, nature of the target group and the technology and resources available for the screening programme. Screening and assessment are not the same thing. Screening is an initial, simple enquiry about indicators of health and social problems. Assessment is an ongoing, sometimes protracted, process (Crome et al., 2006).

Drug screening

Some biological indicators, such as blood, urine and saliva drug or drug metabolite levels, are more commonly used than others. Hair analysis, for example, enables detection of regular use of many drugs over periods of several months. A secure 'chain of custody' from initial collection is essential to ensure accurate sample attribution to a specified individual. There is variability between substances in duration of time for detection, from a few hours to 10 days or more (see table 18.5). It is important to ensure that appropriate, rigorously applied laboratory testing procedures are used, with appropriate cut-offs for interpreting results (Wolff et al., 1999a,b).

Examination of drug users

It is recommended that, as drug use is of such a high prevalence, all healthcare professionals should be able to identify and carry out a basic assessment of people who use drugs (NICE, 2008a), and that this should include examination of the user both as an aid to confirming drug use and identifying the physical complications of drug use, such as infections and abscesses.

Drug use assessment tools

Current guidance for England and Wales suggests that all drug users should have an assessment that includes the following (NICE, 2007b):

- medical, psychological, social and occupational needs;
- history of drug use;
- experience of previous treatment, if any;
- goals in relation to his or her drug use;
- treatment preferences.

A review of assessment data for the evaluation of drug misuse has been published (Effective Interventions Unit, 2002), which provides information on three commonly used assessment tools.

- The Maudsley Addiction Profile (MAP): A short assessment tool, which takes around 12 minutes to administer and covers four areas: substance use, health risk behaviour, physical and psychological health, and personal/social functioning (Marsden et al., 1998).
- The Christo Inventory for Substance-misuse Services (CISS): A 10-item questionnaire with a single score of

---

Box 18.1 Screening methods

Self-report questionnaire
Psychiatric history taking assessment
Semi-structured interview
Structured interview
Physical markers
    Urinalysis
    Blood tests
    Hair tests
    Fingernail clippings

Table 18.5 Period of time over which more commonly used substances are likely to remain detectable in the blood (Adapted from Banerjee et al., 2002)

Drug	Maximum range
Cocaine	12–72 hours
Amphetamines	2–4 days
Heroin	2–4 days
Codeine	2–4 days
Cannabis	30 days
Diazepam	30 days

0–20, covering areas such as physical and psychological health, drug use, HIV risk and criminal behaviour (Christo, 2000).

- The Rickter scale: A non-paper based self-assessment, allowing the user to identify treatment goals and can be used to develop treatment action plans (Hutchinson and Stead, see Northumbria University, 2012).

The National Treatment Agency (NTA) care planning practice guide (NTA, 2006a) provides a summary of the characteristics of a selection of tools that may be used for assessment and outcome measurement in a drug treatment setting (for a list, see box 18.2).

Based on the AUDIT (Saunders et al., 1993), a cannabis screening instrument has been developed (the Cannabis Use Disorders Identification Test (CUDIT) Adamson and Sellman, 2003). More recently, the Drug Use Disorders Identification Test (DUDIT) has been developed and piloted in criminal justice settings (Berman et al., 2005). There are also instruments for screening and assessing substance use in young people (Effective Interventions Unit, 2004). A brief six-item questionnaire by Knight et al. (2002) is also useful (see box 18.3).

People who are drug dependent may seek *urgent* professional help, asking for immediate treatment of withdrawal symptoms, often claiming to be unable to get to their usual treatment unit or that their prescribed supplies have been lost or stolen. In this situation, and regardless of manipulative threats that, if they are not given a prescription, they will have to resort to illegal activity, the governing principle is that nothing should be prescribed unless there are clear physical signs of the relevant abstinence syndrome. Rigid application of this rule is essential, otherwise hospital

Box 18.2 Drug use outcome measurement tools (NTA, 2006a)

Maudsley Addiction Profile (MAP)
Addiction Severity Index (ASI, European adaptation)
Opiate Treatment Index (OTI)
OTI modified for amphetamine users
Global Appraisal of Need (GAIN)
Leeds Dependence Questionnaire (LDQ)
Severity of Dependence Scale (SDS)
The Craving Questionnaires
Readiness to Change Questionnaire (RTQ) (Treatment Version)
Injecting Risk Questionnaire
Drug Taking Confidence Questionnaire (DTCQ)
Inventory of Drug-Taking Situations
Quality of Life Inventory (QOLI)
Beck Depression Inventory (BDI)
Beck Anxiety Inventory (BAI)
Hospital Anxiety and Depression Scale (HADS)
General Health Questionnaire (GHQ-28)

Box 18.3 The CRAFFT questionnaire (Knight et al., 2002)

1. Have you ever ridden in a **c**ar driven by someone (including yourself) who was 'high' or had been using alcohol or drugs?
2. Do you ever use alcohol or drugs to **r**elax, feel better about yourself, or fit in?
3. Do you ever use alcohol or drugs when you are by yourself, **a**lone?
4. Do you ever **f**orget things you did while using alcohol or drugs?
5. Do your family or **f**riends ever tell you that you should cut down on your drinking or drug use?
6. Have you ever gotten into **t**rouble while you were using alcohol or drugs?

For each positive response, score 1. A CRAFFT score of ≥2 identifies a substance problem, disorder, or dependence.

A&E departments or GP surgeries may be used as regular supplementary sources of supply. There is also a risk that casual non-dependent users will thus get pharmaceutically pure preparations of dependence-producing drugs, on which they may accidentally overdose. A careful history to establish that there is dependence is, therefore, always essential, as is a thorough physical examination to establish the nature and severity of any abstinence syndrome.

Treatment for Drug Misuse
Pharmacological treatment options

A detailed account of specific treatment régimes and the supporting evidence is beyond the scope of this chapter. A range of guidance is available, such as that produced by the British Association of Psychopharmacology (Lingford-Hughes et al., 2004), Department of Health (2007) and the National Institute of Clinical Excellence (NICE 2007a,b,c, 2008a). Much of this does not, however, deal with complex comorbid conditions such as those found in the criminal justice system.

A growing variety of pharmacological treatments are available (Lingford-Hughes et al., 2004), for stabilization, detoxification, reduction, maintenance and relapse prevention, in addition to treatment for psychiatric disorder or physical problems (Chandler and McCaul, 2003; Rayburn and Bogenschutz, 2004). Most of these treatments can be administered in the community, with close supervision, but patients may need to be admitted to hospital or to a rehabilitation unit. These decisions are clinically complex and depend on a range of factors, including degree of dependence, number of substances used, social stability and support network. The treatment must be individualized.

457

The benefits must, where possible, be weighed against the potential risks, which the patient must understand. It cannot be over-emphasized that pharmacological treatments must always be prescribed in full knowledge of the person's psychosocial situation, *and* with psychological support, which may include individual, group or family interventions. In summary, the most usual situations in which medication may be helpful are

- emergencies, e.g. overdose, fits, dehydration, hypothermia;
- detoxification and withdrawal syndromes, e.g. lofexidine, methadone, buprenorphine;
- substitution, e.g. methadone, buprenorphine;
- relapse prevention, e.g. naltrexone;
- comorbid substance problems;
- comorbid psychiatric disorders;
- comorbid physical disorders, e.g. HIV, hepatitis C, diabetes.

Summary of recommendations from the British Association of Psychopharmacology (BAP) guidelines

In the BAP guidelines, Lingford-Hughes et al. (2004) cite considerable evidence for the use of methadone, buprenorphine, and α2 agonists (clonidine, lofexidine) in managing withdrawal. Differences in choice of medication may depend on priorities such as duration of treatment, adverse effects (brachycardia and hypotension due to α2 adrenergic agonists) and withdrawal severity. The patient's clinical condition, degree of dependence, preference and practitioner experience will determine choice of drug.

Similarly, there is an established evidence base for methadone maintenance treatment and for buprenorphine. There is inadequate evidence for treatment with naltroxone or injectable opioids, or for using coercive methods.

For stimulant drugs, such as cocaine and amphetamine, the guidelines do *not* recommend the use of dopamine agonists, anti-depressants, or carbamazepine. Furthermore, there is no clear evidence to support substitute prescribing of dexamphetamines. In fact, 'psychosocial' interventions are considered the 'mainstay' of treatment, although the evidence is limited.

The guidelines also make recommendations for benzodiazepine dependence, whether the benzodiazepines have been prescribed or are illicit. In early or mild dependence, 'minimal' interventions, such as relaxation or general practitioner advice, are suggested. For more severe dependence, graded discontinuation is advised. For 'illicit' misusers, there is no evidence that continued prescribing is beneficial, except possibly in reducing illicit use.

Psychological interventions for drug misusers

Most treatments in this field are based on learning theory models, but there is also recognition that a holistic approach, including practical social interventions, is essential to improvement (Crome and Ghodse, 2007). Information-based approaches are useful in less complex situations. These might include education about harm minimization, immunization and vaccination.

In the addiction literature the term 'counselling' is used to incorporate brief or intensive interventions, in the form of supportive, directive or motivational approaches, delivered for the individual, family or group, and also social network behavioural therapy. Cognitive behavioural or person centred techniques are most commonly employed, but psychodynamic techniques also used. The aim of counselling may be to reduce the use of alcohol and drugs, their negative consequences, or related problems. Assessment should move seamlessly into engagement, support and therapy. The non-judgmental and empathic method of engaging the patients in challenging decisions and assumptions him/herself in motivational interviewing is important. Objectives may include

- problem solving: developing competence in dealing with a specified problem;
- acquisition of social skills: mastery of social and interpersonal skills by assertiveness or anger control;
- cognitive change: modification of irrational beliefs and maladaptive patterns of thought;
- behaviour change: modification of maladaptive behaviour;
- systemic change: introducing change into family systems.

The main treatment options, the choice of which depends on the nature and extent of the problem, will now be dealt with in a bit more depth.

1. *Non-directive counselling* comprises the following components: patient determination of content and direction of the counselling; exploration of inner conflict and emotions at the time; empathic reflection from the counsellor, while the counsellor desists from offering advice and feedback.
2. *A cognitive behavioural* approach assumes that the patient would like to change. Identification, then analysis of situations that cause drug use are central, so that these can be altered. Problem-solving techniques, self-monitoring, anger management, relapse prevention, assertiveness training and the acquisition of social skills and modification of irrational beliefs or patterns of thought or behaviour are used. Individual, group and family therapies used in the treatment of addiction are often based along cognitive behavioural lines.
3. *Social network behaviour therapy* considers the social environment as being important in the development, maintenance and resolution of substance problems. It maximizes positive social support, which is central to the process. The therapist offers advice and feedback and thereby facilitates change in the patient's social world. Behaviour is not interpreted and engagement

with significant others is the key to bringing about change and achieving goals.

4. *Family therapy* involves trying to understand and interpret family dynamics in order to change the psychopathology. Substance use is perceived as a symptom of family dysfunction and, therefore, altering the family dynamics will bring about change in the substance misuse. Family members are viewed as contributing to the problem. Behavioural and psychodynamic techniques may be used.

5. *Group therapies and 12-step programmes.* Participation in self-help groups is an important feature of many treatment programmes, in which participants receive support from recovering members who often go back over the negative consequences of substance misuse. The 12-step approach is one form of this. Central to the 12-step philosophy is the idea that recovery from addiction is possible only when the individual recognizes his/her problem and admits that s/he is unable to use substances in moderation. Alcoholics Anonymous (AA) and Narcotics Anonymous (NA) are examples of this; users have to abstain completely.

6. *Motivational interviewing.* The most influential and popular form of treatment currently has been motivational interviewing, a 'brief', 'minimal', 'non-judgmental' intervention, the aim of which is to build motivation for change and alter the decisional balance so that users themselves can direct the process of change (Rollnick et al., 2008). The focus is on the user's own concerns about, and choices regarding, future drug use. Motivational enhancement supports motivation for change through empathic feedback, advice and information. Significant people in the user's social group may have a treatment role, but not a major one; the individual's motivation is seen as central. The key characteristics are best described by the acronym FRAMES (Miller and Sanchez, 1993):

- personalized **f**eedback or assessment results detailing the target behaviour and associated effects and consequences on the individual;
- emphasizing the individual's personal **r**esponsibility for change;
- giving **a**dvice on how to change;
- providing a **m**enu of options for change;
- expressing **e**mpathy through behaviours conveying caring, understanding and warmth;
- emphasizing **s**elf-efficacy for change and instilling hope that change is not only possible, but also within reach.

There is growing evidence for the benefits and cost effectiveness of this type of intervention (Dunn et al., 2001; Project MATCH Research Group, 1998).

Treatment effectiveness among adult drug misusers

The first longitudinal, prospective, observational study on outcome in drug misusers in the UK, the National Treatment Outcome Research Study (NTORS), has been underway since 1995 (Gossop et al., 2003). In this study, 1,075 drug misusers are being followed-up through and beyond two types of residential services (inpatient and residential units) and two kinds of community services (methadone reduction and methadone maintenance). Their age range was 16–58. Half of them were responsible for caring for children. There was a history of treatment for psychiatric disorder in the 2 years prior to programme entry; in the 3 months prior to entry, 30% had had suicidal ideation. Over 27,000 acquisitive criminal offences were reported by people in the cohort, also during the 3 months prior to starting treatment (Stewart et al., 2000), with shoplifting the most common. Ten per cent of the sample was responsible for three-quarters of crimes committed. Higher frequency of illicit drug use was associated with higher levels of criminal behaviour. High-rate offenders were more likely to be regular users of heroin and were three times more likely to have used cocaine regularly.

There is an important difficulty with this study in that the specifics of the treatment modalities have not been described in detail, so, from the study reports, it would be difficult to replicate the complex mix of treatments and services delivered within each main group. Outcome measures, however, are strong and various. Opiates, amphetamines, cocaine, non-prescription benzodiazepines and alcohol levels have been assessed, as has the impact of treatment on psychological health, suicide, other mortality and crime. After 5 years, 62 people had died, alcohol use remained at a constantly high level, with 25% still drinking above safe limits; 80 people were long-term users of two or more illicit drugs. Nevertheless, there was significant progress. Also after 5 years, a third of users achieved abstinence in the community as did half of those in residential services. Although 20% of the study sample continued to use daily and 40% about once a week, this had reduced from 66% at intake in the residential services group and 80% in the community services group. Likewise, injecting reduced from 60% to 40%, criminal activity halved. This is encouraging, despite the limitations in study design noted above, suggesting that adults have a reasonable prospect of benefitting from current UK treatment programmes.

Despite the high rate of mental illness histories in the NTORS study, and advances in the effectiveness of pharmacological and psychological treatments for substance misuse (Lingford-Hughes et al., 2004; Project MATCH Research Group, 1998; UKATT Research Team, 2005a,b), it is not clear that more positive outcomes will generalize to comorbid cases (Cornelius et al., 2004; Haddock et al., 2003). Evaluations of combined treatments (pharmacological and psychological *or* two types of pharmacological treatments) have only just begun with people with substance misuse disorders and mental illness. Nunes and Levin (2004), in a systematic review and meta-analysis of treatment of people with standardized diagnoses of unipolar depression and alcohol or other drug dependence, found just 14 double-blind, randomized controlled trials (RCTs) of antidepressant medication with recorded effects on depression and substance use (8 alcohol, 4 opioids, 2 cocaine). There was a modest beneficial effect on the depression and, where effect sizes for depression were largest, on quantity of substance misuse, but rates of abstinence were low. Additional specific targeting of the substance misuse disorders was recommended. Even 'effective' treatments are not effective for all who seek help and not all who need help will seek it.

In the most comprehensive review to date, Tiet and Mausbach (2007) considered both psychological and pharmacological treatments for substance misuse associated with depression, anxiety, schizophrenia, bipolar disorder or other severe mental illness. Fifty-nine studies met standards for inclusion, of which 36 were RCTs. Although there was no clear evidence of superiority of any one intervention over the comparison treatment for either psychiatric disorder or substance misuse, and treatments had not been replicated, the review did demonstrate that effective treatments for psychiatric conditions tended to reduce psychiatric symptomatology and effective treatments for substance misuse tended to reduce substance use, even in the presence of comorbidity. The value of integrated treatment was not, however, substantiated.

Evidence in general is, therefore, scant, but data more specific to people in the criminal justice system (CJS) even more so; such people are rarely represented in treatment trials. Furthermore, treatments and services are not as accessible or available as is required, for these and other especially vulnerable groups. Some principles of treatment, however, are filtering through into the CJS. Both mental health and substance problems are likely to be chronic conditions, so treatment cannot be conceptualized or presented as a 'cure', but rather as support and care, which can improve some substance, health and psychosocial outcomes. Emphasis is on engagement of the service user, and, where possible, carers in the community rather than in an institutional setting, with continuity, responsiveness, and flexibility in care, and in attempting to integrate educational and employment options and accommodation needs as well as special relationships within the treatment framework.

Treatment Delivery Models for Drug Misusers in the Criminal Justice System (CJS) in England and Wales

In 2008, the UK Drugs Policy Commission (UKDPC) reported some startling statistics. The budget for adult drug interventions within the CJS in England and Wales was over £330 million in 2006/7. By January 2008, 3750 offenders a month were entering treatment through the Drug Interventions Programme (DIP), while 15,799 community

sentences with a drug treatment element were started in England in 2006/7. Investment in prison treatment increased tenfold, from £7 million in 1997/8 to £80 million in 2007/8. In the 12 years 1996–2007 there was an increase from 14,000 prisoners on maintenance or detoxification to 51,000 (UKDPC, 2008). The NTA has described a series of key elements which should be in place in criminal justice settings, as shown in box 18.4.

A Cochrane review of the effectiveness of community and prison based interventions to reduce offending behaviour in drug users concluded that the evidence from the 24 RCTs selected was equivocal (Perry et al., 2006). This was mainly due to the broad range of studies and lack of standardization in the outcome measures, although the authors did comment that the use of therapeutic communities combined with an aftercare programme showed 'promising results for the reduction of drug use and criminal activity in drug using offenders'. The evidence reviewed, though, generally excludes important populations, such as women and young offenders, who have not been participants in any major evaluations of intervention effectiveness.

A more recent review of the evidence for the effectiveness of a variety of interventions for the UKDPC (McSweeney et al., 2008) concluded that, whilst there is strong evidence that individual criminal behaviour can be modified by drug interventions, the evidence for the effectiveness of some interventions is not strong. The findings are summarized in table 18.6.

Community provisions for drug misusing offenders

The range of community-based CJS provisions for England and Wales was summarized in a review of the evidence supporting current drug-related interventions (UKDPC, 2008). Programmes listed include testing for drugs on arrest, mandatory assessment following a positive

> **Box 18.4** Key elements in treatment delivery for drug misusing offenders (NTA, 2006b)
>
> - Drug-misusing offenders should have quick access and entry into drug treatment.
> - They should be retained in continuous drug treatment for at least 3 months.
> - They should have the option of methadone maintenance (and not rely on detoxification alone).
> - Comprehensive care management techniques are needed to deal with an individual's multiple needs.
> - There needs to be close co-ordination between specialist and generic services across a range of interventions.

test, restrictions on bail (including compulsory drug treatment) following a positive test, and conditional cautioning by a police officer. Failure to comply may result in prosecution for the original offence. Legislative framework for community-based coerced treatments is under Drug Testing and Treatment Orders (DTTOs) or Drug Rehabilitation Requirement Orders (DRROs). There are a number of accredited treatment programmes that may be attached to community orders, including Offender Substance Abuse Programmes (OSAPs) and Addressing Substance Related Offending (ASRO).

The Drug Interventions Programme (DIP)

The Drug Interventions programme provides a framework for interaction between CJS workers, providers of drug treatment services and other related services to provide an individualized package of care for a drug user in the CJS. It is delivered through Criminal Justice Integrated Teams (CJITs) and is designed to provide a service from first point of contact with the CJS to discharge and beyond.

Safe and ethical management of drug users in police custody

The assessment and treatment of drug users in police custody poses particular management problems, as unrecognized withdrawal states or injuries masked by intoxication can result in death. Advice on this is available from a number of sources (Association of Forensic Physicians and Royal College of Psychiatrists, 2006; Royal Pharmaceutical Society of Great Britain, 2007). At present there is no national policy on best management, and management is subject to considerable regional variation. Newer models here involve community psychiatric nurse location at police stations to screen arrivals, triage and guide on safe management (see also chapter 25).

Substance abusers detained by the police may need to be transferred to hospital, sometimes to the A&E department, particularly if they are intoxicated or suffering drug-related injuries. Following treatment, a patient may be well enough to be discharged from hospital but may not be fit enough for detention in a police cell. The hospital doctor should take this into account when assessing the patient's fitness for discharge and, if necessary, recommend reassessment by the forensic physician at the police station (Crome and Ghodse, 2007).

The police may ask doctors for their opinion about the patient's fitness for interview. Before providing this, it must be established whether the patient is currently under the influence of drugs or alcohol, whether there is evidence of the abstinence syndrome or whether the detainee is fully aware of his/her surroundings and is able to understand potentially stressful questioning, cope with the interview and, if necessary, instruct a solicitor. The timing and duration of the interview will help to inform this advice, which is important because of questions about the admissibility of confessions obtained if the individual's mental state is impaired or s/he is in withdrawal and desperate for a 'fix'. If an individual is obviously intoxicated, it is customary to wait for the effects of the drug to wear off; however, the mental state may fluctuate markedly following hallucinogenic drugs, making it difficult to ascertain when the patient is fit for interview (Association of Forensic Physicians and Royal College of Psychiatrists, 2006).

An intimate search for drugs must be carried out at a hospital or other medical premises, by a registered medical

Table 18.6   Summary of evidence base for interventions for illicit drug misusing offenders (UKDPC, 2008)

Intervention	Reasonable evidence	Mixed evidence	No effectiveness evaluations
Drug courts	✓		
Community sentences	✓		
Prison-based therapeutic communities	✓		
Opioid detoxification and methadone maintenance	✓		
RAPt 12-step programme	✓		
CJIT		✓	
Restriction on bail		✓	
Drug testing in addition to a community order		✓	
Counselling Assessment Referral Advice and Throughcare (CARAT) interventions			✓
CBT based interventions			✓
Addressing Substance Related Offending order (ASRO)			✓
Conditional cautions			✓
Diversion from prosecution schemes			✓
Intervention orders			✓

practitioner or registered nurse, but responsibility for it lies with the forensic physician, not the hospital doctor.

Treatment for drug misusers in prisons

The poor general health of prisoners is often related to substance abuse, and has ramifications, both during imprisonment and after it. Tuberculosis and HIV may start or worsen whilst in prison, but there is also an opportunity to improve health generally, and coincidentally reduce the likelihood of re-offending and negative impact on public health (European Monitoring Centre for Drugs and Drug Addiction (EMCDDA), 2007).

Efficient management of drug problems in prisons is central to reducing drug-related harm there. The two main high-risk periods are just after reception and at discharge from prison. There is a correlation between drug withdrawal symptoms and suicide in the first week of custody (Shaw et al., 2004) and a seven- to nine-fold increase in overdose deaths in the weeks after release from prison (Bird and Hutchinson, 2003; Farrell and Marsden, 2008); some are accidental but there is also an increased risk of intent to die just after release (Pratt et al., 2006).

Interventions available range from simple prison-based detoxification, methadone maintenance and placement on drug-free prison wings through to more structured multi-method programmes, such as the Integrated Drug Treatment System (IDTS) and/or Counselling, Assessment, Referral, Advice and Throughcare (CARAT) service activities. Prison in-reach services have also been used to deliver a comprehensive mental healthcare package, including management of patients with co-existing addiction and mental illness. These services have, however, not been standardized and are described as variable and idiosyncratic in their delivery methods (Steel et al., 2007).

The Integrated Drug Treatment System (IDTS)

The IDTS is designed to expand the range of clinical interventions available within prisons, with a particular emphasis on improvement in prescribing substitute medications and provision of a range of psychosocial interventions. The aims of the IDTS are summarized in an overview produced by the NTA, one of the bodies responsible for the roll-out of the service across the UK (see box 18.5) (NTA, 2001–2008). The components of the IDTS have not yet been rigorously evaluated within a prison setting, but there is evidence for the effectiveness of some components in other settings.

Substitute prescribing is a well-recognized treatment for opiate dependence, supported by several studies, particularly in its impact on social outcomes such as reduced debt and crime (Seivewright and Iqbal, 2002). The effectiveness of prison-based methadone maintenance treatment (PMMT) has been reviewed by Stallwitz and Stöver (2007), who concluded that findings from other settings broadly

apply to PMMT. The key ideas are that methadone doses should be sufficiently high (>60 mg daily) and treatment duration of sufficient length (probably that of the prison sentence) to reduce drug use and injection in prisons as well as improving retention in treatment and reducing illegal drug use and criminal behaviour on release.

Counselling, Assessment, Referral, Advice and Throughcare (CARAT)

The CARAT service was set up in every prison in England and Wales in 1999. CARAT workers offer counselling and support to prisoners about drug misuse and act as link workers to other services, both in custody and on release from prison. A review of findings from the research database was published in 2005, which covered 2 years of the service from 2002 (May, 2005). This review concentrated on descriptions of the population engaged by CARAT rather than on outcomes, and showed that 40% of the prison population accessed the CARAT service during the study period.

Other prison-based services for drug users

Additional measures for prisoners who have drug problems include:

- drug-free wings and voluntary testing programmes;
- Short Duration Programmes (SDPs) (4 weeks) based on cognitive behavioural therapy;
- Prison-Addressing Substance Related Offending (P-ASRO) – a behaviour programme of low to medium intensity targeting offending behaviours connected with drug use;
- therapeutic communities providing treatment based on social learning.

Comprehensive treatment programmes

A number of initiatives have been funded within the UK to provide integrated care for those in the CJS who have drug-related problems. These initiatives focus on the concepts of throughcare and aftercare, the former describing arrangements for managing the continuity of care provided to a

---

Box 18.5 Aims of the Integrated Drug Treatment System (IDTS) in prisons (NTA, 2001–2008)

- Increasing the range of treatment options available to those in prison, notably substitute prescribing.
- Integrating clinical and psychological treatment in prison into one system that works to the standards of Models of Care and the Treatment Effectiveness Strategy, and according to one care plan.
- Integrating prison and community treatment to prevent damaging interruptions either on reception into custody or on release back home.

drug user from the point of arrest through sentencing and linking seamlessly with aftercare, this being the package of support planned for when the user reaches the end of a prison or community based treatment programme within sentence. These programmes often include basic drug treatment supplemented by support packages including housing, financial management, basic educational skills, family and relationship problem solving and employment skills development.

Medicinal support for relapse prevention

Naltrexone is an opioid antagonist without euphoric effects which blocks the effects of opiates. It can be provided prior to release for abstinent users as a support to psychosocial treatment. This is *only* recommended in association with psychosocial treatment; there is evidence that drop-out from treatment is associated with increased mortality (Minozzi et al., 2011).

The Evidence Base for Treatment of Drug Users

Evaluation of these programmes is beginning to suggest progress (UKDPC, 2008). One-third of new drug treatment episodes in England are referrals from the criminal justice system. Half of all offenders in contact with the DIP reduced offending, while only a quarter increased it. Successful completion of a DRRO or DTTO almost doubled between 2003 and 2008; re-conviction rates of completers are about half those of non-completers. Nevertheless, 1 in 200 injecting heroin users may still die from heroin overdose within 2 weeks of leaving prison.

Some Special Groups of Drug Misusers
Women who misuse drugs

There is great variability in the prevalence of substance misuse among women in different countries and regions of countries, and in different ethnic groups (Crome and Kumar, 2007). This may be explained in part by differences in definitions, in patterns and modes of use, in screening, assessment and diagnostic tools, the time window during which use is being measured (e.g. lifetime, previous year or previous month usage), and study settings, as well as in wider environmental influences such as availability, price, social acceptability, seizure and arrest policies. Regardless of the methods used to assess psychiatric disorder among opiate users, however, or stage of treatment, female opiate users meet criteria for psychiatric disorders and symptoms more frequently than do male users. In Ireland, for example, 48% of men and 75% of women in prison were found to be mentally ill, while 72% and 83% respectively reported lifetime experience of drug use (Hannon et al., 2000). Women who use drugs are more likely than men to say that they are using to alleviate psychological distress (Chatham et al., 1999).

Two large community studies in Europe have recently supported this. Both the Netherlands Mental Health Survey and Incidence Study (Bilj et al., 1998) and the UK Psychiatric Morbidity Study among adults living in private households (Singleton et al., 2003) showed that, while anxiety and mood disorders rates were higher among women, drug use and dependence were higher among men. In the Dutch study, substance use disorder was more likely to be comorbid with a mood disorder among the women than among the men (de Graaf et al., 2003).

Studies of people in treatment provide further evidence that women are more likely to have mental illness in conjunction with substance abuse. Among people newly entering treatment in NTORS in England, women were twice as likely as men to report anxiety (32%:17%), depression (30%:15%), paranoia (27%:17%) or psychoticism (33%:20%) in the previous 90 days (Marsden et al., 2000). In Germany, the 6-month prevalence of such psychiatric disorders was greater among female (46%) than male (31%) opiate users in regular contact with treatment services for 1 year (Krausz et al., 1998). Furthermore, female drug users met the criteria for significantly more diagnoses than their male peers. A Norwegian study examined gender differences in poly-substance users attending clinics (85% heroin users) compared with people dependent exclusively on alcohol. All groups had high rates of mental illness and/or personality disorders (93%), but the female poly-substance users differed significantly from all other groups due to their high levels of major depression, simple phobia and borderline personality disorder, while the male poly-substance abusers were distinguished by their higher rate of antisocial personality disorder (Landheim et al., 2003). A small Portuguese study found that 65% of 231 pregnant drug misusers in community treatment had other mental disorders (28.5% personality disorders, 22.5% neurotic/somatoform disorders, 10% schizophrenia) (Flores, 2002).

The one study with slightly different findings was of consecutive admissions to a clinical detoxification centre in the Netherlands (Hendriks, 1990). Whilst a significantly higher proportion of female (73%) than male (45%) opiate users met criteria for non-substance-related Axis I disorders, the men were 11 times more likely to have both an anxiety disorder *and* a depressive disorder, while women were only twice as likely to have the two.

Abuse histories, particularly sexual abuse histories tend to be more common among female than male drug misusers. A study by Gilchrist (2002) of female drug users attending a crisis centre, a drop in centre and a methadone clinic in Scotland (Glasgow), found that 71% had a lifetime experience of emotional abuse, 65% had been physically abused, and 20% had a history of sexual abuse. Brown et al. (1995), in an English sample, found that female drug users were more likely than male users to report lifetime physical abuse (30%:6%) or sexual abuse (25%:4%), this is echoed in the study by Grice et al. (1995) (60%:17%). Drug users who have experienced abuse have poorer psychological functioning and are significantly more likely to have anxiety disorders, suicide attempts, self-harming behaviours, and eating disorders (Grice et al., 1995; Jarvis and Copeland, 1997; Kang et al., 1999), as well as depression or PTSD (Plotzker et al., 2007).

In Europe, drug use is highly prevalent among female prostitutes (Bretteville-Jensen and Sutton, 1996; Church et al., 2001; Gossop et al., 1994). In the UK, it has been estimated that about 80% of women engaged in street prostitution are working there to finance a serious drug habit (Hester and Westmarland, 2004), with at least three-quarters of their income being spent on the drugs (May et al., 1999). These women commonly experience physical and sexual violence from their clients (Barnard 1993; el-Bassel et al., 1997; Gilchrist et al., 2001). A UK study found that 81% of street prostitutes reported physical violence from clients (Church et al., 2001). Despite these findings, and knowledge of the impact of abuse on psychiatric morbidity, the mental health of drug users involved in prostitution has not been widely examined. Female drug users are more likely to be involved in prostitution than male drug users (Chatham et al., 1999; Grella, 2003), but may well be supporting the habit of their male partners too. Indeed one of the barriers to treatment for such women may be the lack of provision for couples therapy in these circumstances (Smith and Marshall, 2007).

The difference in prevalence of drug use and psychiatric morbidity between female drug users with lifetime involvement ($n = 176$) and no involvement in prostitution ($n = 89$) was examined among female drug users recruited from three services in Glasgow (Gilchrist et al., 2005). Two-thirds of the prostitutes had experienced emotional abuse, 57% physical abuse and 33% sexual abuse during adulthood alone; 53% of them had attempted suicide in their lifetime and 72% had depressive symptoms at interview.

In a US study of 33 male and 97 female prostitutes, 68% of them met criteria for post-traumatic stress disorder (PTSD). The severity of PTSD was not only related to physical abuse in childhood but also to being raped in the course of work as a prostitute, the likelihood rising with number of rapes as an adult. Experience of physical assault while a prostitute did not have the same effect, nor was duration of involvement in prostitution a factor (Farley and Barkan, 1998). In Edinburgh, Scotland, Nelson (2001) showed the impact of childhood sexual abuse on the development of both addiction and mental health problems among female prostitutes.

Pregnancy and drug misuse

The American National Pregnancy Health Survey found that 5.5% of pregnant women were using at least one illicit drug (including non-medical use of prescribed medication)

(National Institute on Drug Abuse (NIDA), 1996). figures were similar (5.2%) in Australia according to a study using birth certificate report of substance misuse (Slutsker et al., 1993) and the Australian National Drug Strategy Household Survey (6%) of women who stated that they were or had been pregnant and/or breastfeeding in the previous 12 months (Australian Institute of Health and Welfare, 2004).

- *Opiates/opioids:* Reported prevalence of their use during pregnancy ranges from 1.6–8.5% (Bauer et al., 2002; Pichini et al., 2005). The Maternal Lifestyle Study in the USA, based on meconium analysis (Lester et al., 2001), found a prevalence of 2.3%, but a wide range (1.6–7.2%) according to self-report.
- *Cocaine:* Again, reported prevalence varies, from 0.3% (Buchi et al., 2003) to 9.5% (Lester et al., 2001). In the UK, cocaine exposure is probably less than 1.1% among pregnant women (Farkas et al., 1995; Sherwood et al., 1999; Williamson et al., 2003b). Based on maternal self-report and meconium analysis, one American study reported 9.5% exposure to cocaine (Lester et al., 2001), but the NIDA (1996) study found only 1.1%.
- *Cannabis:* Since cannabis was used by 16.6% of women aged 16–24 years and 5.9% of those aged 16–59 years during 1 year in the UK (2005; Roe and Mann, 2006), the potential impact on the fetus must be considered. Prevalence of use in UK urban communities is between 8.5% and 14.5% at 12 weeks gestation (Farkas et al., 1995; Sherwood et al., 1999). In the Glasgow perinatal sample, meconium analysis showed that 15% of mothers had used it in the second or third trimester (Williamson et al., 2003b). US figures are from 1.8% (Buchi et al., 2003), through 7.2% (Lester et al., 2001) to 15% (Williamson et al., 2003b). In Australia, 5% of those women who stated that they were pregnant and/or breastfeeding in the last 12 months had used cannabis (Australian Institute of Health and Welfare, 2004).

Substance misusers are poor candidates for pregnancy. They are frequently underweight, anaemic and socially disadvantaged. They are often poor attendees at antenatal clinics, and young users tend to present late in their pregnancies. Substance misuse also increases the risk for other conditions, for example sexually transmitted diseases, hepatitis B, hepatitis C, HIV and domestic violence. These associated problems can, in themselves, present a significant risk to the pregnant mother and her unborn child. Intravenous drug users have the extra increased risks of cellulitis, phlebitis, thrombosis, endocarditis, septicaemia, septic osteomyelitis and, importantly, difficult intravenous access (Crome and Ismail, 2010).

Substances may affect the growth and maturation of the fetus (Scher et al., 1998, 2000). The long-term developmental neurocognitive, physical and psychosocial effects resulting from in-utero exposure to opioids and other drugs are poorly understood, and difficult to study because of the complexities of the situation. It is increasingly common that substance misusers take a combination of different drugs at different times during pregnancy. Child and adolescent mental health services report that a parent's longstanding drug and/or alcohol misuse is a substantial risk factor for poor mental health in children (Mountenay, 1998) and, particularly with respect to alcohol, for offending in later life (Popova et al., 2011). Children may also be at high risk of maltreatment, emotional or physical neglect or abuse, family conflict, and inappropriate parental behaviour (Barlow, 1996; Famularo et al., 1992; Wasserman and Leventhal, 1993). Children may be exposed to, and involved in, drug-related activities and associated crimes (Hogan, 1998). They are more likely to display behavioural problems (Wilens et al., 1995), experience social isolation and stigma (Kumpfer and DeMarsh, 1986), misuse substances themselves when older (McIntosh et al., 2003), and/or develop problem drug use (Hoffman and Su, 1998).

Parents with chronic drug addiction spend considerable time and attention on accessing and using drugs, which reduces their emotional and actual availability for their children. Conflicting pressures may be especially acute in economically deprived, lone-parent households and where there is little support from relatives or neighbours (Rosenbaum, 1979). In the long term, children of substance misusing parents may have severe social difficulties, including strong reactions to change, isolation, difficulty in learning to have fun, and estrangement from family and peers (Barlow, 1996).

Despite this, substance misusers should not automatically be stereotyped as poor parents. Pregnancy may motivate individuals to modify their behaviours spontaneously or to be susceptible to advice for the health of the baby (McBride et al., 2003). Indeed, about two-thirds of American women who drank prior to conceiving, and up to 40% of those who smoked, stopped spontaneously during pregnancy (Durham et al., 1997). A telephone survey of pregnant women, also in the USA, yielded similar findings: 65.6% were drinking before pregnancy compared with 5.2% during pregnancy (Pirie et al., 2000). Hispanic ethnicity and younger age were significantly associated with spontaneous alcohol abstinence. The Australian Institute of Health and Welfare study (2004) showed that women who were pregnant either abstained from alcohol (38%) or drank less (59%); only 3% continued to drink at the same levels after becoming pregnant.

Since the prevalence of substance misuse among teenagers increased in the 10 years since the mid-1990s, this group is of great immediate and future concern (Crome et al., 2004). Many studies described above have noted the vulnerability of young and disadvantaged women who are increased risk of substance use and imprisonment as a result of activities associated with their use. They also risk premature death and the possibility of leaving bereaved children.

Drug-using parents and child protection

This is a complicated, emotional area (Ghodse, 2002). In England and Wales, the needs of the child are paramount (Children Act 1989), but every effort is made to consider the rights and needs of the parents too. A thorough assessment includes the ability of the parents (and perhaps the extended family) to provide shelter, food, safety and emotional security. The nature and extent of the substance misuse, its impact on the child, the social circumstances and wider support network have to be taken into consideration. The preference of most clinicians and allied professionals is to work together to retain the integrity of the family if at all feasible, by engaging them in treatment and support. The situation may be monitored regularly under the Child Protection Register. In some countries it is routine for children of addicts to be placed on a child protection register. Fear that this might happen is a strong force in pregnant women and mothers not seeking treatment early on, so it is necessary to encourage an atmosphere that appeals to their needs (Crome and Ghodse, 2007). Nevertheless, there are occasions when the child is considered to be at immediate risk and it is in his/her best interests to live away from his/her birth parents. An initial step is generally an Emergency Protection Order under Section 44 of the Children Act 1989, but permanent removal might follow. Psychiatric evidence may be requested by the Court in such circumstances. A promising intervention of intensive social work attendance has been trialed in Wales for families where child removal in such circumstances was imminent (Emlyn-Jones, 2007).

Physical treatment during pregnancy

- *Detoxification* from opiates/opioids should be avoided in the first trimester and carried out very cautiously in the third (Luty et al., 2003). The risks must be explained.
- *Substitution and maintenance:* Methadone is the mainstay of the management of opioid abuse in pregnancy. It has been used safely for many years, although this use is unlicensed in the UK. Methadone maintenance treatment decreases illicit opioid use, maternal mortality and morbidity, criminality, drug-seeking behaviour, prostitution, sexually transmitted diseases and incidence of obstetric complications. It increases foetal stability and ensures improved compliance with obstetric care (Burns et al., 2006). Since buprenorphine has become available, a number of small-scale studies have been undertaken (Fischer et al., 2006, 2000; Johnson et al., 2003; Jones et al., 2005; Lacroix et al., 2004). At this stage it is not clear whether there is any advantage over methadone. In the USA, it is an advantage that buprenorphine may be dispensed by prescription, rather than at federally certified methadone clinics (Nocon, 2006).
- *A comprehensive care plan:* Despite considerable progress in engaging and retaining pregnant substance

users in treatment, illicit use and its subsequent complications should not be downplayed (Tuten and Jones, 2003) and therefore, the use of contingency management as an adjunct has been described (Jones et al., 2001). Currently, 'good practice' must encompass prescribing within a comprehensive care plan.

- *Stimulants and cannabis:* As there is no evidence to suggest that substitution is effective and safe for stimulants, and there is no pharmacotherapy for cannabis, psychosocial support is fundamental.

Young people and drug misuse

Sixteen to 24 year olds form one-sixth of the population (in England and Wales, about 6.8 million people). Overall mortality of adolescent addicts is 16 times that of the general adolescent population. Adolescents become dependent much more quickly than do adults. The latest data from the NHS Information Centre on 11–15 year olds have demonstrated a fall in those who have tried drugs at least once, from 29% in 2001 to 25% in 2007, but 10% (300,000) were likely to have taken drugs in the past week (Fuller, 2008).

People aged 20–24 use approximately twice as many illicit drugs as 16–19 year olds (see table 18.7). In those who attend specialist services there is considerable comorbidity – about 75% have an additional psychiatric illness and many also suffer physical ill health.

Outcome research in young people shows that, while only a small minority will achieve and maintain abstinence at 1–4 years after treatment, about two-thirds reduce substance use and improve in other areas, for example in offending, education and employment as a result of improved confidence, self-esteem, academic attainment, mental health and family relationships (Chung and Maisto, 2006; Chung et al., 2004). Evidence for effective treatment is mainly from the USA, where there is emphasis on brief motivational work, cognitive behavioural therapy and multisystemic therapies (Dennis et al., 2004; Henggeler et al., 2006). Some of these packages have been tested specifically with young offenders. The involvement of the family may be necessary for consent for treatment, and is generally desirable for support, information and advice, and enhancing coping skills. In the UK, there is also emphasis on harm reduction, including needle exchange, prevention of drug-related deaths and treatment for physical illness and injury. There is little provision or evidence for residential treatment, but it may be needed for those with chronic, relapsing states.

NICE guidance for buprenorphine and methadone is aimed at those over the age of 18, but their opioid detoxification guidance covers those aged 16 and over, while that on community-based interventions in vulnerable disadvantaged young people is for under 25 year olds. There are very few studies on pharmacological treatments in adolescents,

Table 18.7 2007/08 Estimates of proportions of young people taking Class A drugs (Hoare and Flatley, 2008)

Class A Lifetime	16–19	9.3%
Class A Lifetime	20–24	22.3%
Class A Last year	16–19	5.4%
Class A Last year	20–24	10.4%
Class A Last month	16–19	2.9%
Class A Last month	20–24	5.5%

and most are from the USA. There are many unanswered questions around what the appropriate goals and outcomes are for adolescents, how services can best be integrated for them, and which specialist teams and agencies should lead and co-ordinate the pathways. There is recognition that the situation is dynamic for all parties. Offending is commonplace among the most severely affected young drug users, often in the context of parental substance misuse and/or mental illness, family conflict, school exclusion, mental illness in the young, self-harming, poor housing and social service involvement. For this reason, the Pathways into Problems report (ACMD, 2006) recommended that

...the NTA should continue to promote and monitor the development of accessible services for young people with serious tobacco, alcohol or drug-related problems, and to take active steps that these services are coordinated with other initiatives that engage with vulnerable young people.

Policy directions for younger drug users

A number of initiatives have a direct or indirect positive bearing on young people. For England, these include the establishment of national governmental bodies such as NICE and the NTA, which aim to improve outcomes through the collation of up-to-date evidence and consequently improved services.

The new drugs strategy (HM Government, 2012) focuses on families and communities. In the UK, a series of policy initiatives has evolved, including *Hidden Harm* (ACMD, 2003); *Hidden Harm: Three Years On* (ACMD, 2007b); *Every Child Matters* (HM Government, 2003); the National Service Framework for Children, Young People and Maternity Services (DoH and Department for Education and Skills, 2004); *Every Child Matters: Change for Children, Young People and Drugs* (HM Government, 2005); the updated *Working Together to Safeguard Children* (HM Government, 2013; with its updated and revised models of care for drug treatment (National Treatment Agency, 2006); *Pathways to Problems* and the implementation of its recommendations (ACMD, 2006) and the report of the most recent Confidential Inquiry into Maternal and Child Health (2007), *Saving Mothers' Lives.*

Greater involvement of users and carers is encouraged in this process. This is sometimes accompanied not only by an increasing focus on the regulation of clinical and professional issues and service and resource management, but also on research and publication governance. Some of this regulation impacts on the training and education methods, with a far greater weight now given to competencies than knowledge alone. There are university-accredited courses on addiction and mental health. These may be used as opportunities to enhance and develop the multiple skills that practitioners require when faced on a regular basis with patients with multiple problems. Comorbid populations are still seriously excluded in terms of availability and accessibility of services (NCISH, 2006; Hodges et al., 2006) and are generally excluded from NICE guidance (NICE 2007a,b,c, 2008a). Accessibility, social acceptability and the legal framework not only influence substance use but also treatment options. Differences across national and international boundaries must be considered when devising policy.

The main themes of these policies involve strong leadership to build bridges between child and adult health and social care and the CJS, through collaborative working by integrated multidisciplinary and multi-agency teams, training, and practical resources such as checklists, protocols, and briefings.

Older people and drug misuse

The number of older people is projected to increase, so that people over the age of 65 will comprise 23% of the population by 2020. Older people are at risk of substance misuse for many reasons, including the development of multiple chronic physical and psychiatric illnesses, for which they receive prescription medication. There is also the continuation of substance use into older age by users who began their substance use in the 1960s, the initiation of substance use in older age due to isolation, losses and/or illness, and the relapse into substance use of older people coping with disability, pain, anxiety and/or insomnia.

While there is some information on good practice and a limited evidence base for treatment of older substance misusers, raising awareness about the problems and potential solutions, it has not been the focus for training health and social care professionals, treatment providers and the policy establishment in the UK that it has been, for example, in the USA (Crome, 2005; Crome and Bloor, 2006a,b, 2007). Some evidence from studies with younger adults may, with caution, be extrapolated to older people. Appropriate help can only be offered if relatives and professionals can detect problems.

Illicit Drug Use and Offending: Conclusions

The 2008 UKDPC report called for a strengthening of the evidence base in this field, but also highlighted the need for comprehensive services, which will promote reintegration into society. Areas for improvement include: screening and assessments, with reviews and re-assessments; training and supervision for staff; simplification of funding, management and commissioning systems; and reorientation of treatment to a positive, problem-solving approach rather than a punitive one. This report explicitly encourages improvements in prison service standards, including adherence to clinical guidelines, performance management and clinical governance and a safe and seamless transition between prison and community services.

Some of the areas highlighted for research include independent evaluation of the DIP, conditional cautions, diversion from prosecution schemes and prison interventions. The need for comparative evaluation of DTTOs/DRROs and drug courts, and of the costs and benefits of community and prison services was noted. The report raises strikingly similar issues to those raised by Kastelic et al. (2008) in a practical guide to opioid substitution in custodial settings. Recurring themes include that:

> drugs and prisons have to be seen in the wider social context, that imprisonment should not mean more punishment than the deprivation of liberty; that prisons must be safe, secure and decent places (WHO Health in Prisons Project and Pompidou Group, 2001a).

It is vital to capitalise research, which has identified gaps in the evidence and so directs practice and policy (Copeland et al., 2007; Dolan et al., 2003; London et al., 2003; MacDonald et al., 2008; Melnick et al., 2001; Nace et al., 2007; Reuter and Stevens, 2007; Sullivan et al., 2008).

PATHOLOGICAL GAMBLING
Gambling as a Social Phenomenon

Gambling is ubiquitous in Western society, reaching the point in Britain where it merited a major investigation by a Royal Commission (1978) (Rothschild), then further review, in 2001, by a specially constituted gambling review body, which produced the Budd Report (Gambling Review Body, Department for Culture, Media and Sport, 2001). In the USA, gambling was reviewed by a congressionally mandated commission (Commission on the Review of the National Policy toward Gambling, 1976). KPMG (2000), a firm of advisors and accountants, gave the gambling industry an estimate that the total amount wagered in the UK in 1998 was over £41 billion, producing a profit for the industry of £867 million; the annual per capita spend, net of winnings, on all gambling activities was £100–£150, putting the UK among the high gambling nations of the world along with the USA, Australia, and New Zealand. The most profitable sectors were off-course bookmaking, gaming machines, and the National Lottery.

Gambling is, then, an important entertainment industry, but the constant attention from official bodies indicates that this is an entertainment industry which gives concern. Besides providing pleasure, jobs and revenue for the Exchequer, gambling also produces considerable misery for a large number of people. The USA Commission estimated that nearly 1% of the adult population of the USA were 'probable compulsive gamblers'. The more recent UK gambling review report estimated that there are 275,000–370,000 problem gamblers in the UK, a number that is likely to increase if their recommendations for decreasing the controls on gambling are implemented, as most have been. They drew immediate attention to the paucity of research into problem gambling, even though the Rothschild Commission's first recommendation was that a gambling research unit should be established. The Budd Report went on to note that it is not part of the standard school curriculum to advise children of the dangers of gambling, unlike the situation with regard to tobacco, drugs, alcohol and irresponsible sex. This is in spite of evidence that there is a higher incidence of problem gamblers among adolescents than among adults and that, in general, the younger a person starts gambling, the more likely s/he is to become a problem gambler. Budd further notes:

Gambling does not come with a health warning, and the incidence and nature of problem gambling, and the existence of facilities for problem gamblers, are not widely known.

Gambling Terminology

Some of the terminological confusion about gambling will already be apparent. Problem gambling is the term used in the Budd Report, but the US Commission wrote of compulsive gamblers. Orford (1985) prefers the term 'excessive appetite' as a conceptual means to understanding five forms of addiction – alcohol, drugs, food, gambling and sexuality. Add to this the general debate in psychiatry as to whether and when unwanted behaviours can be regarded as 'illness' or 'pathological' and we have a mini Tower of Babel.

To some extent, this confusion is a product of the difficulty in conceptualizing abnormal behaviours and, to some extent, an attitudinal statement about how we believe we should respond to individuals presenting themselves with behavioural difficulties. In 1968, for example, a spat broke out in the *British Medical Journal (BMJ)*, after an article in *The Times* reported that a thief appearing in court was referred to a psychiatrist and then a brain surgeon for a leucotomy to cure 'a compulsive urge to gamble'. A leader writer in the *BMJ* took umbrage about this terminology – although made no comment on the proposed treatment! The writer asked:

Where does social misdemeanour end and mental illness begin?

S/he suggested that

a compulsion in its strict psychiatric definition, is a repetitive act performed by a patient against his will, which he is unable to suppress.

S/he preferred the man to be called:

an excessive gambler

and said

the gambler's behaviour is a source of pleasure in which he indulges irrespective of cost; the compulsive's is a burden which makes him anxious and depressed.

According to the writer, the motivation of an excessive gambler is no different to that of the ordinary gambler

every man in the street can imagine himself in his place, which alone puts him outside the pale of psychiatry.

The author then returned to the mantra that

antisocial behaviour must not be confused with mental illness, and psychiatrists must beware of having forced on them the role of controlling misfits or regarding it as their function to normalize them, the abnormal and nonconforming.

Would this leader writer now eat his/her words in sight of the Academy of Medical Sciences (2008) review?

The article provoked a flurry of responses in the letter pages. Moran (1968) agreed that the term compulsive should not be used in the context of excessive gambling and urged the term 'pathological gambling' as an all-embracing term, which could include different types of excessive gambling which require assistance; he was the only correspondent to question the wisdom of leucotomy here. One of us (Gunn, 1968) drew attention to the inconsistency within the *BMJ*, which only 3 years before had published a leading article describing the plight of the pathological gambler in terms of personality deterioration.

In some ways the terminological argument is sterile, but it does lead to differences in response, which are very important to the individual concerned, and perhaps wider society too. Blaszczynski and McConaghy (1989) argue that a dimensional model of gambling may allow controlled gambling as a treatment goal, but disease model proponents argue that complete abstinence is the only acceptable aim. These tensions pervade addictions work. The only valid test of such a distinction is an empirical one, and this is not yet forthcoming.

Orford's review of the psychology of addictions (1985) may be the best available way of reconciling the different approaches and embracing a therapeutic approach. He acknowledged the important benefits of a disease model:

How else could... the wife of an excessive gambler, be persuaded that her husband's beastliness was attributable to his modifiable gambling rather than to his unmodifiable character, without recourse to some notion of sickness?

He also, however, pointed out that disease models can retard understanding in over-emphasizing the role of medicine and, in particular, physical features of the problem to the neglect of psychological mechanisms. Orford was at pains to identify similarities between a range of 'excessive appetitive' activities, including drinking and drug taking, postulating that some of their strongest determinants are social, both in terms of restraints and encouragements. In turn, these appetitive activities come to serve personal functions for different individuals, such as mood modification and tension reduction. All this, he suggested, is subject to lifelong social and psychological changes.

He imported the law of proportionate effect from operant learning theory into his model; this generates increasing attachment to the behaviour, such that it becomes automatic and functionally autonomous. An altered biological response can then occur, so that the individual experiences a feeling of less control, greater desire and craving. At this point the costs or harm from the behaviour may amplify an increasing attachment, for example by encouraging alterations of role and social group, and weakening relationships with sources of social control and restraint. He noted that supporting agencies have often taken a religious form and suggested that change in appetitive behaviour constitutes a kind of moral passage. He concluded that, besides these naturally occurring processes, expert treatment plays only a modest part in appetitive behaviour change but this is not to suggest it is ineffective. The common factors in individual treatment and self-help groups are engagement, the feeling of being listened to, involvement of family and the expectation of change. This means that professional and traditional religious moral agencies and ideas can co-exist.

Clinical Features of Pathological Gambling

According to Moran (1970), recognition of pathological gambling depends on four features:

1. concern on the part of the gambler and/or the family about the amount of gambling;
2. the presence of an overpowering urge to gamble so that the individual may be intermittently or continuously preoccupied with thoughts of gambling, usually associated with the subjective experience of tension relieved only by further gambling;
3. the subjective experience of an inability to control the amount of gambling;
4. economic and/or social and/or psychological and/or family disturbances which result from the gambling.

After reviewing 50 patients, Moran suggested five subtypes of pathological gambling.

1. Symptomatic gambling associated with mental illness, for example a depressive illness, giving rise to guilt feelings which are then expiated by gambling. It is sometimes difficult to distinguish depression causing the gambling from depression which is reactive to the gambling.

2. 'Psychopathic' gambling, as part of a generalized anti-social response to life, mixed with stealing and other criminal activities (not only related to gambling) and poor social adjustment in terms of work and personal relationships.
3. Neurotic gambling, as a response to stress such as a disturbed marriage. One partner in such a marriage may use the gambling as a means of punishing the other. Adolescent stress is another possible cause of gambling.
4. Impulsive gambling, characterized by loss of control which cannot readily be accounted for by illness, or the environment and is not part of an antisocial response to life. Sometimes it is controlled when the money runs out. It is usually feared by the gambler who is aware that s/he loses control to his/her own detriment, but it also brings relief from craving.
5. Subcultural or socially acceptable heavy gambling.

These clinical descriptions have stood the test of time and are probably the best available; however, modern practitioners seem uneasy unless they can invoke the official international or US classifications (*ICD* or *DSM*). The definition in *ICD-10* (WHO, 1992a) seems in part to be based on Moran's definition; the slight differences may detract somewhat from its clinical usefulness. *F63.0* asserts that

The disorder consists of frequent, repeated episodes of gambling which dominate the individual's life to the detriment of social, occupational, material, and family values and commitments.

Those who suffer from this disorder may put their jobs at risk, acquire large debts, and lie or break the law to obtain money or evade payment of debts. They describe an intense urge to gamble, which is difficult to control, together with preoccupation with ideas and images of the act of gambling and the circumstances that surround the act. These preoccupations and urges often increase at times when life is stressful.

This disorder is also called 'compulsive gambling' but this term is less appropriate because the behaviour is not compulsive in the technical sense, nor is the order related to obsessive-compulsive neurosis.

In the differential diagnosis, however, we are told that pathological gambling should be distinguished from (a) frequent gambling for excitement; (b) excessive gambling by manic patients; and (c) gambling by people with sociopathic personalities in which there is a wider persistent disturbance of social behaviour.

The American *DSM-IV* (APA, 1994) is only slightly different and includes the same differential diagnostic advice. None of this is of great significance provided the clinical understanding of the patient's problem is clear, although those undertaking research may want the aid to reliability provided by such operational definitions. Perhaps even better for such circumstances, in spite of some criticisms (see Orford et al., 2003), the *South Oaks Gambling Screen* (SOGS) (Lesieur and Blume, 1987) is widely used; it is a sensitive rather than specific clinical aid – over-predicting problem gambling.

The exclusion of mania-related behaviour from the diagnosis of pathological gambling in the official classifications could divert attention from an association between gambling and affective disorders, which has been consistently identified (e.g. Moran, 1970; Taber et al., 1987a,b). McCormick et al. (1984) reported that, in a group of 50 men, highly selected by virtue of their admission to an inpatient treatment unit for gamblers, 76% had a major depressive disorder, 38% hypomanic disorder and 8% manic disorder, while 36% had at least one important cross-addiction to alcohol or drugs. The men also showed a very high rate of suicidal behaviours, all but 10 having shown at least one in the year prior to admission; nearly half had shown at least moderately severe suicidal behaviour, for example having thought of a specific plan. Six men had made a lethal attempt. Linden et al. (1986), studying people attending Gamblers Anonymous meetings, found that over 70% of their sample had had a major depressive illness at some time in their lives. Findings of abnormalities on the dexamethazone suppression test (Ramirez, 1988) and in monoamine levels and peptides in the cerebrospinal fluid, plasma and urine of gamblers (Roy et al., 1988) have added weight to these associations.

A more recent review of the clinical features of pathological gambling emphasises DSM criteria for pathological gambling and draws attention to the similarities between gambling addiction and other forms of addiction, including the notion of withdrawal symptoms (Lesieur and Rosenthal, 1991). The losing phase or what gamblers call 'chasing' (trying to get money back that was lost gambling), to the extent that this becomes an obsession, is, however, unique to gambling. They also draw attention to the possibility of multiple addictions and to the misery and problems suffered by relatives, especially the wives of male gamblers, and their children. A wide range of criminal behaviour has been detected among such gamblers, from forgery and embezzlement to armed robbery and fencing stolen goods. The review includes some of the psychoanalytic literature, which begins with Freud's (1928) essay on Dostoevsky, a man who wrote not only perceptively about the problem from his own first hand experience but also often to a deadline in order to pay off his gambling debts (e.g. his 1867 novel, *The Gambler*).

According to Freud (and Dostoevsky), the gambler does not necessarily gamble for money, but for the gambling itself. In fact, Freud suggested that the gambler may gamble in order to lose. Losing is a form of self-punishment, to expiate guilt, what Freud called 'moral masochism'. Bergler (1958), building on the idea of the masochistic neurosis, postulated that the 'classical gambler' has never relinquished the omnipotent phase of childhood – but, with his alcoholic violent father could Dostoevsky ever have had an omnipotent childhood phase? Bergler wrote of 60 gamblers he treated by psychoanalysis; 25% gave up treatment after a 4–6 week trial period but he implied that the other 44 patients all gave up gambling. These apparently remarkable results need replication.

Management of Pathological Gamblers

The prognosis in many cases of excessive gambling is poor. There is ambivalence on the part of the gambler, social pressure to continue gambling, psychological dependence intermittently reinforced, and perhaps powerful unconscious destructive drives. Psychiatric and psychological treatments have limited success. Punishments, however, such as fines or imprisonment are also unlikely to yield positive change, and may even make the gambler worse. The pathological gambler is quite likely to try and win his/her fine on a racehorse! Prisons are ideal places in which to gamble, since boredom is excessive, everybody is short of money, tobacco, and other desirables, and important support systems such as employment, wife, family are removed, maybe permanently.

The efficacy of treatment for gamblers may be as much affected by the quality and extent of the service delivery as the treatment itself. Volberg and Steadman's (1988) telephone survey of the prevalence of pathological gambling in New York illustrated how one service delivery seemed to be failing. Thirty-six per cent of problem gamblers were women, but only 7% of those coming into one of the three treatment programmes in New York State were women; 43% of the surveyed gamblers were non-white, but 91% of treatment places were taken up by a white clientele; only half the expected group of young people presented for treatment. All the differences were significant. A disproportionate number of women, non-white people and young folk were thus failing to connect with services.

The importance of extended assessment

People who gamble excessively are difficult to assess briefly; a detailed knowledge of the person's background, current social environment and psychopathology before a management programme is necessary. Particular care should be taken not to miss depressive disorder or suicidal ideation. It is almost never possible to treat gamblers successfully without involving the spouse or close contacts, as the behaviour and the treatment will profoundly affect their life also. This is especially true in Moran's type (c) cases, where family stress may be the main pressure to gamble.

Building a supportive network for gamblers and their families

The two vital elements of management are support and counselling. The necessary qualities of support include accepting the individual without accepting his/her behaviour, making and keeping to a long-term commitment, refusing to reject the person when others do as the problem seems hopeless. In addition, where the gambler has retained family and friends, support should be extended, as far as possible, to them too, whether directly or through other professional or voluntary bodies. Counselling will include a discussion about the patient's behaviour and its consequences, may involve advice about restructuring his/her life, but is likely to follow a motivational approach (see above).

Specific treatments for pathological gambling

Toneatto and Ladouceur (2003) reviewed the literature on treatment for pathological gambling and point out the paucity of information about it, especially given its high prevalence (1–2% of the population). McConaghy et al. (1983) did a number of studies on imaginal desensitization. For this, the key to intervention is the instruction to relax in the presence of several imagined gambling-related episodes. In their hands, this proved to be superior in outcome to aversion therapy, using electric shocks. They also reported that imaginal desensitization was superior to imaginal relaxation, a similar treatment but one that does not instruct the individual to visualize gambling situations; instead the participants are asked to remain in the presence of visualized relaxing scenes. There were no group differences at follow-up, with 30% of both groups reporting abstinence or controlled gambling. McConaghy et al. (1991) reported on the long-term follow-up (an average of 5½ years) of 120 participants who were randomly assigned to five treatments. Again, in their estimation, imaginal desensitization proved to be superior to the other treatments but as Toneatto and Ladouceur (2003) point out, there are serious problems with the outcome variable of 'ceased' gambling; although 30% of the imaginal desensitization participants were said to have stopped gambling, 27% of the participants who received combined behavioural treatments also ceased.

Echeburua et al. (1996) compared three active treatments with a waiting list control group. Treatments consisted of individual exposure response prevention, group cognitive restructuring, and combined treatment. In exposure response prevention, participants are trained to manage money better, avoid gambling situations, and remain in the presence of high-risk gambling situations but resist gambling. The cognitive treatment challenges the 'illusion of control'; the combined treatment included both treatments. All three treatments were administered over 6 weeks, with a goal of abstinence. The 64 participants were all slot machine gamblers. Of interest is the finding that the control group, who received no specific treatment, showed considerable improvement at 6 months on most of the gambling variables, doing as well as the combined treatment group; the authors considered the individual work a cost-effective therapy.

Sylvain et al. (1997) compared the efficacy of CBT with a waiting list control group. There were 29 participants, most of whom were video poker players and racetrack gamblers. The treatment group did better than the controls. Ladouceur et al. (2001) conducted a randomized controlled trial of individual cognitive therapy with 66 slot machine and video gamblers. On measures of clinically significant change and end-stage functioning virtually all the treated sample and none of the waiting list controls improved, which was similar to their earlier study (Sylvain et al., 1997). There is, thus, some evidence for the efficacy of cognitive therapy for problem gamblers.

Several approaches to group work have been tried but, again, there have been very few evaluations. An interesting idea, in view of the prominent marital problems in some cases, was reported by Boyd and Bolen (1970) who treated husband and wife pairs; of nine pathological gamblers and their wives, one pair dropped out, leaving four pairs in each of two groups. All improved, five nearly stopped gambling, three actually stopped, all the marriages were reported as improved. These are promising results, but need replication.

Perhaps the most important form of group treatment for gamblers is that run by the gamblers themselves. As for alcoholism, a self-help group Gamblers Anonymous (http://www.gamblersanonymous.org.uk/) has gained a prominent place in treatment and should always be considered as one option a patient may take. A description of the California branch where it all began is given by Scodel (1964). Again following the lead of the sufferers from alcoholism, another self-help group has sprung up for spouses of gamblers – Gam-Anon (http://www.gamanon.org.uk/).

Although Toneatto and Ladouceur (2003) are generally critical of research to date, they conclude that the cognitive behavioural spectrum of treatments does have some empirical support as being superior to other forms of specific treatment, and give guidance on how methodological flaws can be eliminated from future research. Another review focuses on pharmacological treatments (Grant et al., 2003). Again, the first point is the disparity between the prevalence of pathological gambling and the attention paid to it in well-designed research. At the end of their review, Grant and colleagues conclude:

emerging data from short-term controlled clinical trials suggests that pathological gambling frequently responds to pharmacological intervention. Mounting evidence suggests that SSRIs represent an efficacious and well-tolerated short-term treatment for pathological gambling. Treatment of pathological gambling appears to require doses of SSRIs that are comparable to those used in the treatment of obsessive compulsive disorder and higher than those required for the treatment of major depressive disorder. Whether subgroups of pathological gambling (e.g. those with depression or strong urge symptoms) respond better or worse to SSRI treatment is not known at this time. Preliminary evidence also suggests that opioid antagonists are effective in the treatment of pathological gambling, especially for those who have strong urge symptoms.

Among the studies to have examined the use of selective serotonin reuptake inhibitors (SSRIs), Hollander et al. (2000) conducted a double-blind cross-over trial with pathological gamblers using fluvoxamine against placebo. Both groups improved rapidly within 1–2 weeks of medication and remained relatively stable thereafter. Studies with naltrexone have also been shown to benefit pathological gamblers, though it is not clear whether this is a specific effect or not. Grant et al. (2008), in a double-blind placebo-controlled trial showed that, although not dose related, people on naltrexone had significantly greater reduction in rating scale scores, gambling urges and actual gambling than those taking placebo.

LaPlante and colleagues (2008) have conducted the most recent systematic review on the stability of gambling behaviours over time. The results may go some way to explaining why treatment outcome studies seem so equivocal. Their focus was on longitudinal, prospective, empirical studies of 'disordered gambling'. Of 92 peer reviewed articles published up to October 2006, 13 met initial inclusion criteria, but four were excluded as treatment outcome studies and four for methodological reasons. One Dutch study (DeFuentes-Merillas et al., 2004), one Australian study (Abbott et al., 2004), and three US studies (Shaffer and Hall, 2002; Slutske et al., 2003; Winters et al., 2002) collectively followed 1289 people ranging from college freshmen to acknowledged problem gamblers over periods ranging between 2 and 16 years. Using these data, they tested three hypotheses. The first was that pathological gambling (reaching threshold on the measure, typically the Oaks Gambling Screen) is persistent; in fact, as a group, the pathological gamblers showed the least stable behaviour patterns in this respect. The second hypothesis was that more severe gambling problems are less likely to improve than less severe ones – evidence did not support this; the third test was that individuals with some gambling problems are more likely to progress to pathological gambling than those without – they were not.

In challenging received beliefs, LaPlante and colleagues perhaps open renewed hope for treatment in the field, but also underscore the importance of randomized controlled trials conducted over substantial periods to test the effectiveness of any given treatment. Perhaps too, their findings open routes to refining subgroups of people with different needs. Are the truly persistent more likely to show the brain differences outlined by Reuter et al. (2005)? Could this mean that treatment approaches for them would be more likely to need to incorporate of physical treatments as part of the package, whereas the psychosocial treatments alone may suffice for the others? Clearly these are among areas for future research.

19

Juvenile offenders and adolescent psychiatry

Written by
Susan Bailey,
John Gunn and
Heather Law

1st edition written by
Loraine Gelsthorpe and
Allison Morris

The Child is father of the Man (Wordsworth, 1802).

This textbook is primarily concerned with adult forensic psychiatry. As a result adolescent forensic psychiatry gets limited attention. Yet it really is true that 'the child is father of the man'. Wordsworth had a reasonably congenial and stable childhood, but most of the individuals who come into contact with the criminal justice system did not have such good fortune. It is not possible to understand the behaviour of an adult without understanding his/her childhood. Every forensic psychiatrist should have some experience of working with adolescents. For these reasons we have included this chapter on adolescent forensic psychiatry/delinquency. It should be read in conjunction with chapter 7, which is about psychosocial development, and chapter 8, which deals with some genetics questions. We also note a few legal provisions for juveniles in parts of the book. The adolescent population in the UK constitutes half of the child population with around 7.5 million young people in the transitional stage between childhood and adulthood (age 10–18) (Coleman and Schofield, 2005).

More than at any other time of life, adolescence is the stage of possibility and of the promises and worries that attend this possibility (Oyserman and Martois, 1990). The adolescent strives to find autonomy and independence, yet connection with others; rebellion and the development of identity (distinction from and continuity with others) are part of this process. The physical changes of puberty are generally seen as the starting point of adolescence. Adolescence ends with attainment of maturity. A range of social and cultural influences including the legal age of majority may influence the definition of maturity (Bailey, 2006).

In contrast to almost all other age groups, mortality rates did not fall during the second half of the twentieth century, the main causes of death being accidents and self-harm (Coleman and Schofield, 2005). Health needs are greater in this age band than in children in middle childhood (5–12 years) or young adults, and arise mainly out of chronic illness and mental health problems. The main concerns of young people are problems with skin, weight, appearance, emotions and sexual health including contraception.

Many of the patients who come to adult forensic psychiatry services are victims of various kinds of abuse, neglect, and deprivation in childhood. Adolescent forensic psychiatry is involved with intervening in these negative circumstances and thus giving some small hope of amelioration or prevention of future problems. A study of adolescent forensic psychiatry is the easiest way to understand the cycle of victimization which the whole discipline of forensic psychiatry is involved with.

The other understanding which child and adolescent forensic psychiatry brings is the interweaving of mental health and criminal justice issues. It is unusual to find an offender of any age who has no mental health problems and during adolescence it is possibly easier to understand how those mental health issues drive the aberrant behaviour which is so troublesome. Child and adolescent psychiatrists do not make great distinctions between mental disorder and behaviour disorder, indeed behaviour disorder is almost automatically regarded as a mental disorder. Were this simple understanding of the common relationship between these phenomena to be carried over into adult life services would look rather different to the ones we have and the management of behaviour disorders in adults would become easier. It is also important to note that the peak age for crime is in the juvenile years; it has gone up a little as the school leaving age has gone up.

We strongly recommend that any training course in forensic psychiatry includes elements of adolescent psychiatry, perhaps with postings to appropriate services, as well as a thorough reading about the psychology and psychiatry of adolescents. We recommend Bailey and Dolan (2004a) together with Rutter and Smith (1995) as British textbooks.

JUVENILE DELINQUENCY

At first glance it seems that for most of history there was no such thing as *juvenile* delinquency. Infractions against the law were dealt with in the same way whatever the age of the offender. Children were simply small people who needed to know their place and were required to keep society's rules or pay the same sort of penalty as an adult. Even so, some understanding of what we now call 'capacity' and some compassion may have been creeping into English thinking in the tenth century, for example King Aelhelstan in 924 rebuked his archbishop for the execution of a child for theft saying that it seemed to him cruel that so young man should be killed, and besides for so little. The Norman conquest put paid to developments of that kind and if we move forward to Tudor times we see stories of young boys (perhaps 12 years old), including a blind boy, being burned for heresy (see Sanders, 1970).

An interesting book on the history of juvenile delinquency from 1700 onwards is Horn (2010). It does, however, suffer from the deficiency that mental health issues, including psychiatry and psychology, do not get a mention. This perhaps illustrates a basic problem; most people, including health professionals, like to keep behavioural problems and human psychology and psychiatry in separate compartments. When behaviour disturbances arise they need professional services including psychiatry. This is not to diminish the role of fundamentals such as social engineering, social services and poverty relief but while these are always necessary they are not always sufficient on their own. It may also be a facet of the welfare v. justice argument that runs through criminology, especially in relation to juveniles. More recent history is dealt with in satisfying detail in the must read, must have, book on youth crime by John Muncie (2009).

In the nineteenth century, half of those convicted of crimes were under 21 and both adults and juveniles were still largely subject to the same laws and penalties. However reformers had noted the plight of poor children. Charles Dickens must have been one of the first; *Oliver Twist* and *Nicholas Nickleby* both appeared as serials in 1837 and 1839, in response to 'the great London waif crisis' (hundreds of orphans wandering the streets), but the London (later National) Society for the Prevention of Cruelty did not get going until 1884. In nineteenth-century England, however, the common law defined the age of criminal responsibility as 7 years. Juveniles between the ages of 7 and 14 were presumed incapable of committing crimes (*doli incapax*), but this presumption was usually rebutted by the mere commission of the offence. The reasoning was that the law sought not to reform offenders, but to punish them in order to expiate the crime and to deter potential offenders. Thus juveniles were executed, transported and imprisoned.

Gradually, the dangers of holding juveniles and adults together in the same institutions were recognized and separate facilities for juveniles were developed: initially houses of refuge and, later in the century, industrial and reformatory schools. Similar thinking led to modifications in (or attempts to modify) procedures which influenced the trials of juveniles. For example, in 1847, the Juvenile Offenders Act was passed which allowed thefts committed by persons under 14 to be heard by magistrates in petty sessions. This was amended in 1850 to those under the age of 16 and in 1879 there was a further major change. Under the Summary Jurisdiction Act 1879, juveniles under 16 could be tried summarily for nearly all indictable (serious) offences.

The turn from the nineteenth to the twentieth century produced significant changes in attitudes towards young offenders. The first specialized detention centre for young offenders was built at Borstal in Kent under the aegis of the Crime Prevention Act 1908. All the inmates were under 21 and the emphasis at the centre was on training. There was an indefinite period of training for between 1 and 3 years, the regime is based on strict discipline, hard work and drill. A survey in 1915 reported. reconviction rates as low as 27 to 35% (Muncie, 2009). This institution was copied in many parts of the country and the small village in Kent, which still has a prison, had the privilege of seeing its name in lowercase all over the country[1].

Chicago introduced a juvenile court in 1899. Some towns began to operate separate juvenile courts in England at the beginning of the twentieth century and these were established throughout England and Wales by the Children Act 1908. That Act set out for the first time the principle that juvenile offenders should be heard separately from adults in special sittings of the magistrates' court. In essence, however, the new juvenile courts functioned as criminal courts and the mode of trial was much the same as it was for adults. The prevailing idea was that the juvenile was a wrongdoer and that the procedures for dealing with adult offenders were appropriate in most respects for dealing with juveniles. In addition, although the courts were given a wide and flexible range of dispositions – for example, admonition, fines, whipping, committal to a reformatory or industrial school and probation – decisions were governed by such considerations as the seriousness of the offence and the interest of the public. On the other hand, there was some concern for the welfare of the child. Herbert Samuel, in introducing the bill, stated that one of its main principles was that juvenile offenders should receive at the hands of the law a treatment differentiated to suit their special needs.

The juvenile courts remained like this until 1933, when the Children and Young Persons Act was passed: its provisions

---

[1] In 1982 the institutions called borstals were renamed youth custody centres and then became part of a wider network of young offender institutions (YOIs). Gone is the training ethos; these places are now, as their name suggests, prisons for young people, sometimes just a wing in an adult prison.

included the appointment of magistrates with a special interest in juveniles, restrictions on reporting cases affecting juveniles in newspapers, the abolition of the terms 'conviction' and 'sentence' and the substitution of the terms 'finding of guilt' and 'order on such a finding', and the direction that magistrates should have regard to the welfare of the child. The reformatory and industrial schools were also merged into one type of institution – approved schools – and the age of criminal responsibility was raised to 8.

Two further changes were made in Britain in 1948. One of the concerns which had emerged from the Second World War years was the apparent increase in the number of juveniles who were from broken homes or who were illegitimate. Consequently, in 1948 the Government initiated an enquiry (the Curtis Committee) into the child care services to review means of providing substitute families for such juveniles (House of Commons, 1946). The Children Act 1948 which followed the recommendations of this committee enabled local authorities to take juveniles considered to be in need of care or protection into their care and to assume the powers and duties of their parents. That same year, however, the Criminal Justice Act 1948 increased the range of penalties available to magistrates for dealing with juvenile delinquents. It introduced detention centres and attendance centres as a substitute for whipping, which was abolished.

From the 1950s, juvenile crime was increasing and it was widely believed that there were categories of juveniles, with whom the juvenile justice system, particularly the approved schools, could not cope. These concerns about appropriate responses to juvenile offenders reflected concerns about the juvenile justice process itself. Thus, in 1956, the Home Office set up a committee, chaired by Viscount Ingleby, to inquire into the operation of juvenile courts and to make recommendations for their improvement. The committee was also invited to consider whether local authorities should be given new powers and duties to prevent or forestall the suffering of juveniles through neglect in their own homes. The committee made no radical proposals for change (Home Office, 1960) and the subsequent Children and Young Persons Act 1963 merely raised the age of criminal responsibility from 8 to 10 years. Section 1 of the Act emphasized the need for preventive work with juveniles and their families, but few resources were committed to this.

The Children and Young Persons Act 1969

Also in the early 1960s, the Labour Party began to rethink the role of the criminal law in relation to juveniles and, when it became the Government, it produced a series of white papers – *The Child, The Family and The Young Offender* (Home Office, 1965) and *Children in Trouble* (Home Office, 1968). Underlying the proposals was the belief that delinquency was often a normal part of growing up and that criminal proceedings were inappropriate where delinquency was trivial. The existing machinery of the law

was said to be reserved for working-class juveniles; middle-class juveniles were to be dealt with without the intervention of the juvenile courts (for example, through schools or the psychiatric services). Serious delinquency, on the other hand, was seen as evidence of the need for help and guidance. Criminal proceedings in such cases were said to be indefensible; what was needed was the application of the necessary treatment without the stigma of a criminal court appearance. In these cases, the causes of juvenile delinquency, like child neglect, were traced to family breakdown or incompetence. Delinquency was viewed as evidence of the lack of care, guidance and opportunities which good parents should provide. The juvenile who offended was assumed to have needs which could be diagnosed, treated and eventually cured. Protecting society from delinquency and helping the juvenile delinquent's development were seen as complementary objectives. As a consequence, it was proposed that the juvenile court should perform a new role – enabling juveniles to receive the help they required. The exact form and content of that help was to be left to those with specialist skills, such as social workers, and the order providing such help was to be of sufficient length to enable the juvenile to be properly treated. When circumstances changed, different treatments were to be tried.

These principles were embodied in the Children and Young Persons Act 1969. Although the formal composition and constitution of the juvenile courts were left virtually unchanged, their jurisdiction was radically altered. Juveniles under the age of 14 were not to be referred to the juvenile court solely on the ground that they had committed offences. Rather, where it could be established that such juveniles were not receiving the care, protection and guidance a good parent might reasonably be expected to give, it was proposed that 'care and protection' proceedings should be brought. Criminal proceedings were to be possible against juveniles aged 14–17 who had committed offences, but only after mandatory consultation had taken place between the police and social service department. The expectation was that these juveniles would also, in the main, be dealt with under care and protection proceedings. Integral to these proposals was the creation of an enlarged and significant role for local authority social workers. Magistrates were no longer to make detailed decisions about the kind of treatment appropriate for juveniles. Social workers, within the limits of the particular order, were to determine this. Thus approved school orders were to be replaced by care orders which allowed social workers to place juveniles wherever they felt appropriate, including leaving them at home. Attendance centres and detention centres were also to be replaced by a new form of treatment – intermediate treatment – and the form which this would take was also to be determined by the social services. It was envisaged both as a component in a supervision order (which was to replace the probation order) and as a pre-court preventive measure.

Thus the general aims of the Act were to reduce the number of juveniles appearing before the juvenile court – that is, to divert them wherever possible – and to make the commission of an offence no longer a sufficient ground for intervention – that is, to 'decriminalize' the court's jurisdiction. The juvenile court was to become a welfare providing agency, but it was also to become an agency of last resort: referral to the juvenile court was to take place only where a voluntary and informal agreement could not be reached between social workers, juveniles and their parents.

The 1969 decriminalization model never came to fruition. Ideological differences between the political parties caused key sections of the Act to remain unimplemented. Criminal proceedings for offenders under 14 years old were not prohibited, nor were they restricted in the case of offenders aged 14–17 years. Similarly, the minimum age qualification for a borstal sentence was not increased from 15 to 17, and detention centres and attendance centres were not phased out. Thus parts of the new system were introduced – care orders and supervision orders – but the old one continued.

Fines, attendance centre orders and custodial sentences were increasingly relied upon by magistrates for 14- to 16-year-old boys at the expense of middle-range, community-based alternatives, the precise operation of which was left in the hands of social workers. For example, in 1968, one in 800 of the 14- to 16-year-old boys referred to the juvenile court was sent to a detention centre or borstal. By 1979, the chances of that happening had substantially increased so that one in every 180 in this age group was given a custodial penalty. Only one-sixth of this increased use of custody could be explained on the basis of changes in juvenile crime (Department of Health and Social Security, 1981). About a third was attributable to the more frequent use of custodial sentences for theft and about a quarter to the more frequent use of custodial penalties for burglary. The DHSS report also showed that throughout the 1970s, those given custodial penalties had not necessarily experienced previously the full range of non-custodial options which the juvenile courts had available to them. This was particularly so for boys given detention centre orders. The opposite effect to that intended by the 1969 Act had occurred – sentencing had become more penal rather than more welfare-orientated – and, paradoxically, the Act was blamed for this. This rapid growth in the use of custodial penalties was accompanied by a parallel growth in the number of secure places within the child care system. Between the passing of the 1969 Act and the end of the 1970s, these increased from 60 to over 300.

The Re-Emergence of the Delinquent

Reports were published in the 1970s which criticized the 1969 Act, for example the Report of the House of Commons Expenditure Committee (1975). These culminated in the publication in 1980 of the white paper *Young Offenders* (Home Office, DHSS, 1980). It proposed giving the power to juvenile court magistrates to impose a residential care order on a juvenile offender already in the care of the local authority who was found guilty of a further imprisonable offence; to impose on offenders aged 15–16 a sentence of youth custody for a term of up to 12 months; to order a supervision order which would include a specific programme of activities; to impose community service orders on offenders aged 16 and to require parents to pay the fines imposed on their children. The white paper also proposed increasing the amount of financial recognizance which parents could be ordered to forfeit if they failed to exercise proper control over their child, and retained attendance and detention centres for male offenders aged 14–16. Basically, these proposals hit at the root of the social welfare philosophy underlying the 1969 Act. They represented a move back towards notions of punishment and individual and parental responsibility. They also represented a move away from executive (social worker) to judicial decision-making and from the belief in 'the child in need' to the juvenile criminal, what Tutt (1981) called the 'rediscovery of the delinquent'. Indeed, the white paper is noteworthy in that, throughout, it refers to juvenile and young adult offenders as young offenders. The recommendations of this white paper formed the basis of the Criminal Justice Act 1982. Details of the current sentencing powers of the juvenile court are discussed in detail below. In brief, the 1982 Act made available to justices three new powers of disposal: youth custody, care orders with care and control conditions and community service.

Youth courts look now much as juvenile courts did at their inception in 1908. Few such courts are in buildings separate from the magistrates' court, although changes in architecture, building materials and design have made courtrooms somewhat less austere than their Victorian counterparts. A panel of magistrates, drawn from the bench of each petty sessional division because of interest in juveniles, appointed to the youth court. Youth court sittings usually form only a part of the magistrates' wider duties. In the Inner London area there is a distinct youth court bench.

Ordinarily, three magistrates or a district judge sit in the youth court, at least one of whom must be a woman and one a man. It is not uncommon to find a preponderance of female magistrates on youth court panels. Similarly, younger magistrates are also encouraged to take on these responsibilities. Youth court magistrates can serve until they are 65 years of age, although they can continue to sit in the magistrates' court until their 70th birthday. While magistrates are lay people who are intended to represent the character of the local community, the selection process is such that they tend to be drawn disproportionately from the professional and higher social classes (Baldwin, 1976). Induction training is provided to all those appointed to the youth court, as are refresher courses for longer serving magistrates and special courses for chairmen. Such training includes summaries of the law, practice developments, sentencing exercises and recent policy initiatives from both central and local government. Contributions are usually made by justices' clerks, social workers, probation officers, police officers and, occasionally, academics.

Magistrates are assisted by the clerk to the court. The clerk, who is usually professionally trained in the law or undergoing such training, should have up-to-date information on the criminal law and on sentencing policy and practice. In addition to advising the magistrates on these matters, the clerk has a key role in ensuring the smooth administration of the court.

Integral to providing resources to the youth court are the probation service and local authority social services department. They both provide reports to the courts and supervise juveniles on behalf of the courts. With increasing frequency, lawyers are present in courts, even in non-contested cases. For the prosecution, a lawyer from the Crown Prosecution Service will appear and an increasing number of defendants are legally represented. Whereas, in 1969, only 3% of juveniles appearing in a juvenile court were represented with legal aid support, by 1988 the figure had reached 57% (Home Office, 1989). These figures do not include those cases in which representation has been privately financed and research suggests that, in some courts, over 70% of juvenile defendants are represented in delinquency cases (Parker et al., 1981).

Most juveniles appear in the youth court on a summons. Where the juvenile is charged with a more serious offence and has been bailed to attend the court, then the youth court will remand the juvenile, either on bail, to be looked after by the local authority or in custody. The youth court may also adjourn for reports after a finding of guilt. Where the youth court is dealing with a mentally ill juvenile, it may remand the youth to a mental hospital for assessment or treatment or may make an interim hospital order (sections 35, 36 and 38 of the MHA 1983/2007). All of these procedures operate in much the same way as for adults. Normally, where juveniles cannot be bailed to their own homes, remands are to local authority accommodation.

In exceptional circumstances juveniles can be and are detained in penal establishments. The Criminal Justice Act 1991 provides that a court may not remand a juvenile in custody unless 'the court is of the opinion that only remanding him to a remand centre or prison would be adequate to protect the public from serious harm from him'. Most juveniles who appear in the youth court admit the offence and the main role of magistrates is to deal with or sentence (as it would be called in the adult court) juvenile offenders. The powers of disposition are briefly summarized in chapter 2. There are special powers available for mentally ill juvenile offenders, namely hospital orders, guardianship orders and supervision orders with a condition of treatment by a specified medical practitioner. A hospital order authorizes the juvenile's treatment in a hospital. Where it appears to the juvenile court that the offence is so serious that there should be an order restricting the offender's discharge, the court can commit the juvenile to the Crown Court to be dealt with under the Mental Health Act 1983, section 43. A guardianship order which applies only to those who are 16 years or over allows the juvenile to remain as an out-patient. Both hospital and guardianship orders are rarely used for juveniles. A youth court may also, as with adults, make an order under the Mental Health Act 1983, section 37, without making a finding of guilt if, having heard all the evidence including medical evidence, it is satisfied that the offender committed the offence. Mental health legislation in England and Wales gives no special protection to juveniles. However, the formal detention in mental hospitals of patients who are juveniles is rare.

1994 Onwards

The Criminal Justice and Public Order Act 1994 marked the start of a more punitive approach to juvenile delinquency. It created a new custodial sentence, the secure training order for children aged from 12 to 14 years. The government also introduced secure training orders for young offenders. This act was followed in 4 years, after a change to a Labour government, by the Crime and Disorder Act 1998. Among other things it increased the maximum sentence of detention for a young person up to 24 months. It also introduced antisocial behaviour orders (ASBOs). These were introduced for people of all ages, but were mainly given to juveniles in order to prohibit the defendant from doing anything mentioned in the order for a minimum period of 2 years. Many youngsters regarded the acquisition of one of these orders as a badge of honour. The Liberal/Conservative Coalition government disapproved and announced the scrapping of them in July 2010. The Crime and Disorder Act 1998 abolished separate sentences for youth custody and replaced them with a generic detention and training order, which can be given two youths aged 15 to 17 years for any offence considered serious enough to warrant custody and the 12 to 14 year olds who are considered to be 'persistent offenders'. The orders are for between 4 and 24 months. Half of the order is served in the community under the supervision of a social worker, a probation officer, or a member of a youth offending team. A custodial sentence of detention (without the training component) is restricted to those aged 18 to 20 years. All this has meant that the number of young people in custody in England and Wales doubled between 1992 and 2002. As Muncie (2009) points out:

(C)hildren in custody are routinely drawn from some of the most disadvantaged families and neighbourhoods. They are already likely to have endured family discord and separations, ill health and physical and emotional

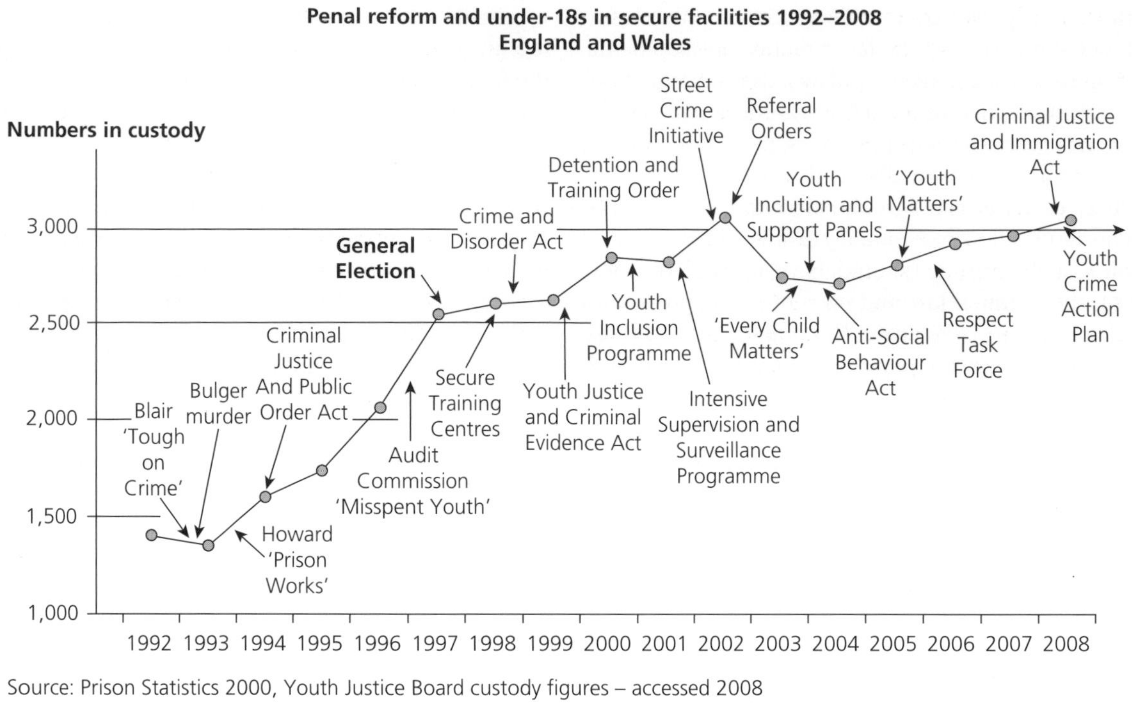

Penal reform and under-18s in secure facilities 1992–2008
England and Wales

Source: Prison Statistics 2000, Youth Justice Board custody figures – accessed 2008

Figure 19.1   Penal reform and under 18s in secure facilities 1992–2008. Reprinted from Muncie (2009, p.343).

abuse... Between 1990 and 2007, 30 children died while in penal custody... The juvenile (under-18) prison population rose from 1328 in June 1992 to 3012 in April 2008... Over this period there was a notable tendency to incarcerate the under-15s, ethnic minorities and young women. During the 1990s the average sentence length for 15- to 17-year-olds doubled... England and Wales now lock up young people at a rate that is five times more than in France, 10 times more than in Italy and 290 times more than in Norway, Sweden and Finland and often in conditions condemned by the Chief Inspector of prisons as 'utterly unsuitable'.

In 2000 the Department of Health youth treatment centres (therapeutic communities, St Charles and Glenthorne) were closed; 2008 was probably the peak of this phase as custody figures dropped to 2,000 in 2010 and some juvenile establishments were closed.

Figure 19.1, reproduced from Muncie's textbook, shows the political actions and philosophy in a timeline between 1992 and 2008 and the consequences in terms of incarceration of juveniles. It demonstrates how much juvenile criminal justice is subject to politics.

Is there any philosophy behind this? Three ideologies seem to have clashed since 1969. The Labour Party came to power in Britain with a clear welfare agenda for young people. It was introduced by David Owen in the Children and Young Persons Act 1969. The dominance of social workers over magistrates, introduction of care orders and intermediate treatment were to be the new deal for young

people. This philosophy was at variance with both the views of the Conservative Party and the tabloid press; it never really happened. The newspapers were for increased punitiveness, especially increased incarceration. The borstal experiment of treating young people quite differently from adults was deemed to have failed. The courts believed that their hands were tied and that quite serious offenders were escaping punishment altogether. For adults everybody in the criminal justice system talks of the tariff, i.e. the price that must be paid for a particular crime. The notion that tariffs should be applied to juveniles is very popular. Less popular is the restorative justice model. In this model crime is understood as harm to individuals rather than the breach of some abstract rule. There is less talk of guilt and innocence and more discussion about problem behaviour and harm. Victims are central to the decision-making. This means that negotiation and reconciliation are used instead of formulaic punishments. Advocates of the traditional justice model allow that some element of restorative justice may also be used. Gelsthorpe and Morris (2002) indicate that the punitive approach impinges adversely on the restorative justice model but believe that the Crime and Disorder Act 1998 and the Youth Justice and Criminal Evidence Act 1999 had aspirations to introduce elements of restorative justice. Victims are no longer marginalized in quite the way they were and offenders may be coerced into reparation. Gelsthorpe and Morris believe, however, that the main aims of restorative justice to promote accountability and provide victim satisfaction do not function properly.

They argue that the welfare agenda has been replaced (or perhaps we can say overwhelmed) by a moral agenda. They cite Australia and New Zealand as being in the forefront of the restorative justice movement, but are pessimistic about such a trend moving to the United Kingdom.

The best book on comparative youth justice is by Muncie and Goldson (2006). In their own piece in this anthology Muncie and Goldson call the developments which took place during the Labour government years 1997 to 2010 'the new correctionalism'. Such justice-based models of corrections emerged in numerous Western countries based on principles of proportionality. The Crime and Disorder Act 1998 was one landmark along the road and it abolished the very old principle of *doli incapax* which meant that 10 to 13 year olds had all their legal safeguards removed and as in ancient times were placed back on a level footing with adults as far as criminal responsibility is concerned. As noted above at the end of that period England and Wales were locking up more young people than any other country in Europe. This is in direct contravention of the UN Convention on the Rights of the Child which stipulates that children should be protected from custody whenever possible.

The acclaimed New Zealand system of youth justice is dealt with by Bradley et al. (2006) in the same book. It is thought by many to be a model because is based on the idea of restorative justice. In fact it is mainly based on the Children, Young Persons and their Families Act 1989 (NZ) which emphasizes that criminal proceedings should not be used if there are alternative means and should not be used for welfare purposes. In line with UN principles the Act says that young people should be kept in the community as far as possible. The restorative justice elements which have attracted a good deal of attention are an add-on. These authors think that the successes of the New Zealand system have been exaggerated and that it is difficult to show that this system is any better at preventing crime than any other.

Very Serious Offenders

Most jurisdictions have arrangements to transfer juveniles from, or waive the jurisdiction of, the juvenile system when dealing with very serious offences. In England and Wales, the Powers of Criminal Courts Act 2000 replaced section 53 of the Children and Young Persons Act 1933 for this purpose. Juveniles appearing before the Crown Court on serious charges can be made the subject of section 90–92 sentences whereby a 10 to 17 year old can be detained at the discretion of the Minister of Justice, for a period longer than 2 years, either in a local authority secure unit or in a prison service establishment. The number of juveniles detained in this way has increased: from 11 in 1970 to 177 in 1988 and to over 700 in 2002. In its original form, section 53 of the 1933 Act was limited to offences of murder,

manslaughter and wounding with intent to cause grievous bodily harm. The Criminal Justice Act 1961 extended the range of offences to include all those for which an adult convicted on indictment could be sentenced to imprisonment for 14 years or more. This meant robbery, arson, some sexual offences and burglary. The ambit was further extended by the Criminal Justice Act 2003 which increased sentencing powers for extended sentences and imprisonment for public protection for specified violent and sexual offences which captured 240 young people in 2005/2006 (Muncie, 2009).

Children Acts

Juvenile courts were established throughout England and Wales after the Children Act 1908 and the see-saw battle between a welfare and a moral or just deserts approach to delinquency which has continued since then has been outlined. The Children and Young Persons Act 1933 established that courts should have primary regard to the 'welfare of the child'. This has survived throughout, but the liberalism of the Children and Young Persons Act 1969 did not survive. The Children Act 1989 tidied up previous legislation, placed a great deal of emphasis on parental responsibility and gave new responsibilities to local authorities for identifying children in need and then taking such steps to reduce the need to bring criminal proceedings against juveniles. The Children Act 2004 followed the *Every Child Matters* Green Paper (HM Government, 2003) which in turn followed the Victoria Climbié inquiry report (Laming, 2003). It established the duty of every local authority to form children's trusts designed to integrate all services for all children including those in the justice system. The Act established the office of Children's Commissioner for England. The new post was introduced in order to give children and young people, and learning disabled people under 21, a voice at national level. The Commissioner is charged with promoting awareness of the views and interests of children. S/he will also be able to hold enquiries even at his or her own initiative into individual cases which have policy relevance. The Act also removed the defence of 'reasonable punishment' for a charge of actual bodily harm, one step along the road towards entirely protecting children from legalized assault. Some have seen the Act as a turn back towards a welfare agenda for managing juveniles who are troublesome. It should be noted that the Children Act 2004 was a direct response to the Victoria Climbié tragedy, yet Baby P died at the hands of his carers in the same London Borough in August 2007.

Youth Justice Board

The Youth Justice Board (YJB) for England and Wales is an executive public body (http://www.justice.gov.uk/about/yjbuk/en-gb/practitioners/). It was set up under the Crime and Disorder Act 1998 to monitor the performance and operation of the entire youth justice system. Its statutory duties include commissioning and purchasing places in the juvenile secure estate (young offender institutions, secure training centres and local authority secure children's homes) for young people sentenced or remanded to custody. It is concerned with the welfare of offenders under the age of 18 years. The primary aim of the Board is to prevent offending by children and young people! It commissions some 2,800 custodial places at any one time for young people under the age of 18 years in 12 Prison Service young offender institutions, 10 local authority secure children's home and 4 private-sector secure training centres (STCs).

The government proposed its abolition but after protests it was transferred to the Ministry of Justice. As part of the protest the chairman of the Board claimed that the Board had provided leadership to the youth justice system and overseen real progress, significantly reducing the numbers of first-time entrants to the youth justice system, reducing the frequency of re-offending and dramatically reducing the numbers of young people in custody – and at the same time making custody safer and more effective. 'Our achievements have led to fewer victims of crime and safer communities.' Yet the director of the Howard League for Penal Reform described the track record of the Board as 'pretty poor', accusing it of failing to protect children in custody, reduce the unnecessary use of custody or influence practitioner and public attitudes to children in the criminal justice system. She argued for raising the age of criminal responsibility to take children out to the criminal justice system altogether (http://www.howardleague.org/francescrookblog/the-age-of-criminal-responsiblity).

At the time of writing there were 157 youth offending teams in England and Wales. In 2008–2009 there were 127,197 young people aged 10–17 years who committed 244,583 offences resulting in a disposal, the three commonest were theft and handling (20%), violence against the person (19%) and criminal damage (13%). Boys aged 15–17 years were responsible for 58% of the offences. There was a reduction in custodial sentences given to 10–17 year olds from 7,096 in 2005/2006 to 6,720 in 2008/2009. The proportion of custodial sentences remained stable, accounting for 6% of all sentences given between 2005/2006 and 2008/2009. During 2008/2009 there were an average of 2,881 young people in custody at any one time, a slight decrease on the average number in 2007/2008 of 2,932. Young females in 2008/2009 accounted for around 10% (621 out of 6,720) of all custodial sentences. The commonest form of custodial sentence given to all young people is a detention and training order, accounting for 6,142 custodial sentences in 2008/2009, which combines a period of custody with a period of supervision in the community. During 2008/2009, young people were serving a custodial sentence for violence against the person (25%),

robbery (23%), breach of statutory orders (criminal) (13%) and domestic burglary (12%) (Youth Justice Board, 2010).

UK COMPARISONS

Wales

This book cannot cover all the jurisdictions of the British Isles, but it is worth mentioning here one or two general points. The developments in England and Wales usually run in parallel although Wales has its own Department of Health. The law, however, and the Ministry of Justice, cover both countries. This produces minor anomalies in policy. For example, part 1 of the Children Act, which established the Commissioner, extends to the whole of the United Kingdom. Part 2 of the Act is concerned only with England and part 3 only with Wales. Part 4 devolves to Wales functions previously exercised across England and Wales together. The provisions of part 5 on the whole apply to England and Wales together, although section 63 which deals with matters of tax applies to the whole of the UK.

Scotland

The English system of juvenile justice is an amalgam of welfare, justice, crime control and diversion and so it inevitably reflects the tensions inherent in these diverse approaches. What other alternatives are there? Some continue to look with favour towards Scotland (Association of County Councils, 1984; McCabe and Treitel, 1984; the Association of Directors of Social Services, 1985). Scotland managed to implement, at least in theory, a social welfare approach. An interesting question is how the Scots were able to achieve this, in 1971, given the considerable opposition to similar proposals in England and Wales. Indeed, the Scottish system may have been even more radical than the English, for it abolished the juvenile courts and replaced them with welfare tribunals staffed by lay people. Children's hearings, as these are called, are concerned only with disposition. There is a complete separation between the judicial and disposition functions. If the juvenile or parent denies the commission of the offence, the case is referred to the sheriff's court for the offence to be proved. If the defendants object to the decision made by the children's hearing on the appropriate disposition they can also appeal to the sheriff's court. In both these instances, the parents and the juvenile are entitled to legal aid. This is not available before a children's hearing. Key figures in the system are the reporters. It is their function to decide, on the basis of reports, whether the juvenile referred to them by the police, social worker or education department is 'in need of compulsory measures of care'. If the reporter believes that this is so, the juvenile is then referred to the children's hearing. The new system applies to juveniles under the age of 16, although where they enter the system before 16, they remain within it until the age of 18 unless the children's hearing terminates its jurisdiction. The children's hearing can discharge the referral or impose a supervision order – the latter may include residential conditions. The hearing has continuing jurisdiction; cases are reviewed annually. It has no power to fine, to send the juvenile to a detention centre or to remit him (or her) to the sheriff's court. It is important, however, to keep in mind that, strictly speaking, Scotland has a two-tier or bifurcated system: that is, some juvenile offenders are still dealt with in the sheriff's courts.

Northern Ireland

The current procedures for dealing with children in need are governed by the Children and Young Persons (Northern Ireland) Act 1968. The Northern Ireland Youth Justice Agency puts all young people who plead guilty, except for the most serious offences, through a Restorative Conference Order. About 70% of victims are directly involved in such conferences. The existing provisions for place of safety orders, care orders and so on thus correspond generally to those in operation in England and Wales prior to the Children Act 1989. However, as in the case of Scotland, Northern Ireland is proposing changes to some aspects of the law relating to children. Both private law relating to guardianship and custody of children, and illegitimacy, and public law, which governs in the main the child care responsibilities of the Department of Health and Social Services, and Health and Social Services Boards are under scrutiny and Northern Ireland hopes to introduce legislation which broadly corresponds with the Children Act 1989.

MENTAL HEALTH

Child and adolescent psychiatry lagged behind many of the changes described above. Paediatrics developed in the nineteenth century and the first children's hospital opened in Great Ormond Street in 1852; others followed elsewhere but these hospitals did not provide for mentally ill children. Maudsley (1867) was the first psychiatrist to acknowledge child psychiatry as such with his chapter 'The Insanity of Early Life' in his textbook. He included such fascinating diseases as monomania, choreic delirium, cataleptoid insanity and epileptic insanity, as well as mania and melancholia. He also included moral insanity with some remarkable examples such as the farmer's daughter who 'preferred raw vegetables', was persistently cruel to her sisters by pinching them when she could, took to eating her own faeces, swore like a fish wife and destroyed things. After doing something wrong she would explain, 'Well Mrs H I have done it... I know you will be angry, but I can't help it.' Among her habits was defaecating on to the carpet of the sitting room.

William Healy, an American physician, was employed in 1909 to direct the Juvenile Psychopathic Institute in Chicago and he was required to provide the court with assessments of troublesome repeat offenders (see http://www.faqs.org/childhood/Gr-Im/Healy-William-1869-1963.html). Healy

published his understanding of juvenile crime in 1915 as *The Individual Delinquent*, a masterly compendium which merits reading even 100 years on. Healy rejected unidimensional theories of causation, arguing instead for an eclectic approach. The task for the court and the clinic, he believed, was to determine the unique combination of factors that shaped each delinquent's individual personality. This profile could be deduced only through a thorough investigation of the delinquents and their families by a team of medical, psychological, and social work professionals; the process included efforts to elicit the child's 'own story'. His reputation was such that he was soon poached by Boston and with Augusta Bronner, a psychologist, established the first child guidance clinic at the Judge Baker clinic in Boston in 1917 (see Healy and Bronner, 1926).

In Britain, Mapother established a child clinic at the Maudsley Hospital in 1923. In 1925 a visit was made from London to look at the American child guidance clinics, Mrs Strachey, a London magistrate, returned to set up similar clinics in Britain and Cyril Burt, a psychologist, who had just published *The Young Delinquent* (1925) took some of the initiating steps (Wardle, 1991). Wardle gives an excellent account of the development of child psychiatry in Britain in the twentieth century. He entitled this paper 'The developments in Britain of services for child and adolescent psychiatry', but adolescents get scant attention compared with younger children. He does mention, in passing, the pioneering Warwick Asylum for juveniles opened in 1818. This was virtually an industrial school for delinquents and hardly counts as a mental health unit. The prominent part paid by the pioneers in child psychiatry at the Maudsley Hospital are given full credit by Wardle and indeed as Warren (1952) explained describing his new inpatient service at the Bethlem Royal Hospital a few delinquents were admitted, but

Such a child is apt to get at loggerheads with all the other patients, and care may need to be taken not to allow him also to be at enmity with the staff. He may regard himself as fit if unhappy; and, puzzled by admission to hospital, he may resent any attempt to explore his problems. An unusual degree of patience may have to be exercised over mischievous or aggressive qualities... confirmed delinquents have proved the toughest propositions to handle; they have only been equalled in other ways by those with severe obsessional neurosis.

This observation explains, perhaps, some of the reluctance of psychiatric services to get involved with this needy group.

Wardle does however put some emphasis on the multidisciplinary approach of the child guidance movement, particularly the development of the profession of psychiatric social work. The first psychiatric social worker (PSW) was appointed to the Manhattan State Hospital in 1906. It was Healy who encouraged the widespread use of social workers. At first they were mediators and links between the home and clinic, visiting schools and occasionally giving evidence in court. It was the Maudsley Hospital that introduced a specialized training course to give social workers therapeutic skills in the early 1950s. Psychoanalysts were early starters in the field of child psychotherapy. Freud (1909) analysed a 5-year-old boy; Melanie Klein published *The Psychoanalysis of Children* in 1932 (Isaacs, 1961); and Lowenfeld started an Institute of Child Psychology in 1933, but none of these pioneering workers ventured into the adolescent field.

What Wardle doesn't deal with is the long struggle between hospitals and schools (to simplify), or between the Ministry of Health and the Ministry of Education, or between psychiatrists and psychologists. Warren (1971) deals with this in some detail mainly as a plea for more manpower. His take on the struggle is that:

> *Perhaps more than any other specialty or subspecialty in medicine, child psychiatry has come to serve different administrative bodies that have claimed paternal responsibility for its care and wellbeing; at the same time, it has suffered varying degrees of maternal deprivation from shortages of staff and money.*

Colourful phrasing which still applies, to some extent, 40 years later. The psychiatry/psychology battle is tackled boldly by Thomas (1985). He sets out various therapeutic approaches that have been developed since the 1950s. He puts particular emphasis on the development of child guidance clinics which he regards as separate from both the medical model and the educational one believing that these clinics set up by educational psychologists legitimized a psychological approach. However he noted with some feeling the comment of an exponent of child guidance clinics, Olive Sampson, that child guidance is 'a dream that is dying' (Sampson, 1976). He identified the following approaches as all being appropriate to child guidance: individual therapy, environmental manipulation, remedial teaching, medication, family therapy and behaviour modification.

The elephant in the room is what Warren called the 'seriously disturbed adolescent', the one who needs security as well as treatment. He pointed to the deficiencies of the Underwood Report (Ministry of Education, 1955) which unrealistically believed that all disturbed children could be managed at home. He was happier with the London Boroughs Association (1967) report which recognized the important role of psychiatrists in the management of seriously disturbed adolescents, recommending that they be based in hospital services with a community role including children's homes, and with some emergency beds.

Mental Health Needs of Young People in the Youth Justice System

Mental health legislation in England and Wales gives no special protection to juveniles. Where the youth court is dealing with a mentally ill juvenile, it may remand the youth to a mental hospital for assessment or treatment or may make an interim hospital order (sections 3S, 36 and 38 of the Mental Health Act 1983). All of these procedures operate in much the same way as for adults, but the formal detention in mental hospitals of patients who are juveniles is rare. Generally, they are placed there by parents or guardians.

Standard 9 (the Child and Adolescent Mental Health Services (CAMHS) standard) of the *National Service Framework for Children, Young People and Maternity Services* (Department of Health, 2004) in England aspires to a comprehensive child and adolescent mental health service. A young person in contact with the criminal justice system, whether in custody or in the community, should have the same access to this comprehensive service as any other child or young person within the general population. Treatment options should not be affected by a young offender's status within the criminal justice system. This is consistent with the principles set out in *Every Child Matters: Change for Children*. The Change for Children Programme has the aim of improving outcomes for all children in the following five areas: being healthy, staying safe, enjoying and achieving, making a positive contribution, and achieving economic wellbeing, and narrowing the gap in outcomes between those who do well and those who do not. Aspirations are not necessarily the same as practical reality.

Mental disorders in adolescents

Delinquency research has resulted in the recognition of a large number of environmental and individual risk factors (Rutter et al., 1998). Research on psychiatric pathology as a risk factor for delinquency fell out of favour for some time (Vermeiren, 2003), but since 2000 some sound prevalence studies on psychiatric disorders in juvenile delinquents have been published (Dixon et al., 2004; Gosden et al., 2003; Lederman et al., 2004; McCabe et al., 2002; Ruchkin et al., 2003; Teplin et al., 2002; Vreugdenhil et al., 2004; Wasserman et al., 2002) and interest has been rekindled. These prevalence studies indicate that there are notable differences between rates of mental disorders in adolescent offenders compared to both adult offenders and the general adolescent population. For example, in a study of over 3000 adolescent and young adult offenders there were significantly higher rates of depression and developmental disorders when compared with adult offenders, and a higher prevalence of depression and attention-deficit or disruptive disorders when compared to general adolescent psychiatric inpatients (Fazel et al., 2008).

In their systematic review of 25 prevalence studies including a total of 16,750 incarcerated adolescents, Fazel et al. (2008) found that mental disorders are substantially more prevalent among adolescents in the juvenile justice system than in their age matched peers within the general population. Adolescents in custody were around 10 times more likely to suffer from psychoses and two to four times more likely to have attention-deficit disorder. Risk of conduct disorder was increased by between five and 20 times for adolescents in custody dependent on their sex, with girls showing the greatest increase in risk. Similarly, major depression was four to five times more common in girls in custody and twice as common in detained boys.

Although the research quoted consistently revealed high levels of psychiatric disorders among detained juveniles, rates varied widely by study, ranging from more than 50% to 100% (see also Atkins et al., 1999; Shelton, 2001; Vermeiren et al., 2002). Conduct disorders and substance use disorders carry the highest prevalence rates, but other mental disorders also present commonly in this population. With current research showing consistently high rates of some disorders, the debate is slowly shifting towards aspects of clinical relevance (for judicial handling and therapeutic intervention).

Grisso and Zimring (2004) have listed three principal reasons for concern regarding mental disorders in youthful offenders – the custodial treatment obligation, the assurance of due process and public safety, and the obligation to offer specific provisions). Too often, mental health treatment within the juvenile justice system is lacking for those in need. Domalanta et al. (2003) showed that only about 20% of depressed incarcerated youth and only 10% of adolescents with other disorders were receiving treatment. Fewer than half of incarcerated youth who required treatment because of substance use disorder received intervention (Johnson et al., 2004).

Limitations of current research

The variations of rates can be explained. First the type and nature of psychiatric interviews varied by study. Second, the moment of investigation and the period of diagnostic assessment also differed by study; some studies focused on youth shortly after detention (Teplin et al., 2002), whereas others investigated youth in the post-adjudication phase (Vreugdenhil et al., 2004; Wasserman et al., 2002). The moment of assessment is relevant because detention itself may influence the psychological condition (e.g. by exacerbating depressive symptoms) (Vermeiren et al., 2003). Third, enormous differences exist among studies on relevant socio-demographic and criminological characteristics, such as age, sex, ethnicity, family structure, socioeconomic status and the nature of criminal behaviour. Fourth, studies were conducted in different countries and, for those in the United States, in different states. Fifth, some studies investigated antisocial youths referred specifically for psychiatric assessment. Although this population provides evidence of the types of psychopathology typically present in the delinquent youths referred for clinical services, using this information to generalize to the whole delinquent population is unjustified. Sixth, because information from parents is largely unavailable, almost all current prevalence studies have relied uniquely on the youths themselves as informants. Although understandable given the difficulties in finding parents willing to be interviewed, this approach may hamper the reliability of findings. Despite most research indicating the level of agreement between multiple informants is low to moderate, it is often these differences in ratings which reveal the most about a child's presentation, for example across different settings or with different care providers (Collinshaw et al., 2009).

Research into practice

Studies with delinquents in the USA and Europe have been carried out using large samples across custody and community with clear definitions of mental disorders and better measures of adolescent psychopathology (Chitsabesan et al., 2006; Odgers et al., 2005; Kazdin, 2000; Kroll et al., 2002; Teplin et al., 2002; Vermeiren et al., 2003). Young offenders under 20 account for more than half of the violent crimes in the UK. Statistics on the onset of serious and violent delinquents show that about half of persistent juvenile offenders are active by 12 to 13 years old and prevalence peaks between 17 and 18 (Coleman and Schofield, 2005). This has major service implications for child and adolescent mental health and multi-agency child services. The real costs of children's needs not being met early are overall:

- the impact of their antisocial behaviour on society;
- their own vulnerability as they drift and/or are captured into juvenile justice systems, with marked communication problems, learning disability and/or mental disorder;
- the challenge of successful diversion from court when already in the juvenile justice system; and
- the provision of out- and in-reach services to young people in both secure youth justice facilities (those, for example, in the UK who are being dealt with in multi-agency youth offending teams) is key for specialist CAMHS services in keeping a clear focus on the overlapping but different tasks of meeting mental health need and assisting multi-agency teams in offence reduction interventions.

Forensic mental health assessment and treatment includes both those offenders who have mental disorder and those whose behaviour has led or could lead to offending. Thus the area of interest and the workload for forensic psychiatry is potentially enormous. Public health policy recognizes the government's obligation to attend to the basic health needs of prisoners and the importance of meeting the health and mental health needs of children, delivery is a different matter. Traditionally, child and adolescent mental health practitioners have continued to work as generalists. Within their specialism they may include offender work, not only in child care proceedings, but also direct medico-legal work where young children are the alleged perpetrators rather than the victims. Child psychiatrists need to be closely involved with developing specialist community and inpatient resources, including secure facilities for children and adolescents who may be

- mentally disordered offenders;
- sex offenders and abusers;
- severely suicidal and self-harming adolescents;
- very severely mentally ill adolescents;
- adolescents who need to begin psychiatric rehabilitation in secure circumstances;
- brain-injured adolescents or those with severe organic disorders.

Generic child and adolescent mental health services can be augmented by advice and training from a forensic child and mental health team (Bailey, 2005). The primary responsibility remains with the staff of local services and the specialist services are supportive and consultative. Services delivered directly to patients and their families by specialist forensic centres include specialist assessment and treatment for generic mental health services, as well as secure social care units, young offender institutions/correctional institutions and juvenile justice services in the community.

Clinical Screening and Assessment: a) In Non-Forensic Settings

In generic child and adolescent mental health services, checklists, rating scales, questionnaires and (semi)-structured interview schedules have been devised to improve the reliability of assessing a child's inner world, including, for example, suicidal thoughts, whereas parents and caregivers report more reliably about observable problems.

A youngster's abnormal behaviour can usually be recognized with sufficient accuracy for routine screening purposes by a brief symptom/behavioural checklist such as the Rutter A Scale (Rutter, 1967) or the Child Behaviour Checklist (Achenbach and Edelbrock, 1983). The Strengths and Difficulties Questionnaire (Goodman, 1997; Bourdon et al., 2005) is a newer instrument that has the merit of being shorter than the Child Behaviour Checklist. More specific instruments such as the Conners' Parent and Teacher Questionnaires (Conners, 1971) have shown particular value in identifying attention deficit hyperactivity disorder (ADHD) and evaluating the response to pharmacological treatment of children and young adolescents who have the disorder.

Diagnostic assessments may include a number of highly structured interviews, such as the Diagnostic Interview for Children and Adolescents (Herjanic and Reich, 1982) and the Diagnostic Interview Schedule for Children (Costello et al., 1985), and semi-structured instruments that require greater clinical interpretation and thus greater training to ensure validity. The most widely used semi-structured interview is the Schedule for Affective Disorder and Schizophrenia for School Age Children (Orvaschel et al., 1982). In addition, assessment of family relationships is important, as is the developmental history and, when specific dysfunction exists, neuropsychological tests. See Gowers (2004) for details.

Clinical Screening and Assessment: b) In Forensic Settings

In the forensic clinical field where written communication between various disciplines is common, a commonly understood language of reliable and valid diagnoses is important. In forensic settings, assessment of adolescents who have mental health problems is beset with obstacles. The fear of being sentenced on the basis of their own information can make adolescents reticent. They may perceive forensic experts as part of the court process rather than as professionals who might be able to provide help. Similarly, they may view professionals in the same way they view other adults (e.g. parents and teachers) with whom they have had difficulty in sustaining positive relationships. In any assessment, the interviewer needs to strike a balance between engagement and the need to elicit information. Another important aspect is the instability of adolescents' emotions from day to day, especially in the context of incarceration (Kroll et al., 2002) where emotional reactions may be seen as a real expression of fear and helplessness.

In the United States and Europe, recent studies of young offenders have used large samples across custody and community settings with clear definitions of mental disorders and reliable measures of adolescent psychopathology (Kroll et al., 2002; Kazdin, 2000; Harrington et al., 2005; Teplin et al., 2002; Vermeiren, 2003; Vreugdenhil et al., 2004). Developmental psychopathology (Garmezy and Rutter, 1983; Cicchetti, 1984) has enabled clinicians to understand better how mental disorders in adolescence emerge, evolve and change in a developmental context. Grisso and colleagues (2005) point to four conceptual aspects of mental disorders in the forensic adolescent population that should be taken into account when screening for and assessing disorders (and the subsequent trajectory of the disorders into adulthood, including links with violence, delinquency and early onset psychosis). The concepts are age relativity, discontinuity, comorbidity and demographic differences.

Needs assessment

Needs and risk assessment are two separate but intertwined processes. Assessment of danger to others and the need to address this problem is at the centre of legislative and policy decision-making. The attention of the public and media is focused on this area.

Risk assessment has a theory and methodology distinct from needs assessment. It combines statistical data with clinical information in a way that integrates historical variables, current personal variables with the contextual or environmental factors. Some of these clinical and contextual factors are potential areas of need. Therefore needs assessment may both inform and be a response to the risk assessment process (Bailey, 2002a; Bailey and Dolan, 2004b). The reciprocal process can be termed 'risk management' when accurate information about the risk assessment, combined with recurrent needs assessment, informs management strategy. Appropriate mental health screening tools and processes are central to this (Bailey and Tarbuck, 2006).

Two studies in the United Kingdom used the Salford Needs Assessment Schedule for Adolescents (Kroll et al., 1999). One study adopted a cross-sectional design investigating 301 young offenders, 151 in custody and 150 in the community, in six geographically representative areas across England and Wales. Each young person was interviewed to obtain demographic information and mental health and social needs. Participants were found to have high levels of need in a number of different areas, including mental health (31%), education/work (48%) and social relationships (36%), but these needs were often unmet because they were not recognized. One in five young offenders was identified as having intellectual disability (IQ < 70) (Chitsabesan et al., 2006).

Age relativity

Developmental psychopathologists delineate symptoms of disorder if young offenders deviate from the average behaviours for a particular developmental stage and, importantly, if they lead to psychosocial problems in the context of the developmental period (Cicchetti and Rogosch, 2002; Mash and Dozois, 2003). In juvenile justice, age is a critical factor in establishing criminal responsibility and in the appropriate placement of young persons who are deemed to require incarceration. These factors vary from jurisdiction to jurisdiction. For example, legal responsibility in the Netherlands starts at 12 years of age and in England and Wales at 10 years. This variety has implications for the design of instruments, applicability across countries and comparability of samples.

Discontinuity

Cicchetti and Rogosch (2002) used two concepts (and neologisms) to identify complex pathways in the development and remission of disorders during childhood and adolescence that they believe should be considered in every forensic assessment. *Equifinality* means that disorders of different origins can lead to the same outcomes e.g. adolescent depression which may have presented with different problems in childhood. *Multifinality* refers to clinical presentations with similar starting points leading to different disorders (Coll et al., 1984). Repeated assessments of young people are therefore essential.

Comorbidity

Dual diagnosis is commoner in delinquents than in the general population (Teplin et al., 2002; Harrington and Bailey, 2004) with some disorders such as conduct disorder, depression and substance misuse frequently co-occurring (Harrington et al., 2005).

Demographic differences

A complex range of factors influences the varying rates of mental disorders across communities and settings. Arrest patterns, for instance, vary from city to city, from neighbourhood to neighbourhood and from decade to decade. Mental disorder is more prevalent in children and adolescents who live in poverty (Bailey et al., 2004). Responses to different backgrounds need much more investigation.

Prevalence of mental disorders among juvenile offenders differs at the different stages of the juvenile justice system. Doreleijers (2005) found 30% of arrested adolescents had mental disorders as did, 65% of adolescents brought before the court, 70% of adolescents having an assessment on the request of the court and 90% of those who were sentenced to detention or forced treatment.

PATHWAYS OF CARE AND THE JUVENILE JUSTICE SYSTEM

Early identification of mental health needs may result in diversion from custody by using community services rather than adjudication and, thus, derive economic benefit from a non-custodial disposal. Nonetheless, a significant number of young persons progress to pretrial assessment.

Pre-adjudication dispositions should be informed by the best available screening and assessment processes. Specific tools may be used to derive markers of psychopathology and of ongoing risk to self and others.

For those detained in prison, a first-look screen must determine if urgent problems (such as suicidal intent or consequences of substance use) require immediate attention; a detailed diagnostic assessment of the young person may take a longer period of time and continue as the youngster moves from one institution to another. Later critical transitions, for which an additional screening may be useful, include re-entry into the community, assessment of readiness for re-entry, mental health planning for integrated continuing care post-detention as part of a multiagency re-entry strategy and, where necessary, community residential programmes monitoring emotion or reactions, especially where the young person is returning to stressful conditions such as a troublesome family.

Overarching Interventions With Juvenile Delinquents

A large number of different treatments have been used to try to reduce antisocial behaviour. These include psychotherapy, pharmacotherapy, school interventions, residential programmes and social treatments. Kazdin, in 1993, documented over 230 psychotherapies that were available, the great majority of which had not been systematically studied. Here we will be concerned with treatments with a testable scientific basis and which have been evaluated in randomized trials (Sukhodolsky and Ruchkin, 2006) and applied to populations of young offenders.

Meta-analyses of treatment approaches to juvenile delinquency have produced reasonably consistent findings (Andrews et al., 1990; Lipsey, 1995; Lipsey and Wilson, 1993; Losel, 1995). Lipsey (1995) considered nearly 400 group-comparison studies published since 1950. The main finding was that there was an overall reduction of 10% in re-offending rates in treatment groups as compared to untreated groups. As might be expected, there were considerable variations in the results of individual studies. The best results were obtained from cognitive behavioural, skills-orientated and multi-modal methods. The results from deterrent trials were particularly poor, though the numbers in these studies were relatively small. Specifically, treatment approaches that were participatory, collaborative and problem-solving were particularly likely to be beneficial. Family and parenting interventions also seem to reduce the risk of subsequent delinquency among older children and adolescents (Woolfenden et al., 2003).

McGuire and Priestley (1995) identified six principles for effective programmes. First, the intensity should match the extent of the risk posed by the offender. Second, there should be a focus on active collaboration, which is not too didactic or unstructured. Third, there should be close integration with the community from which the offender came. Fourth, there should be an emphasis on behavioural or cognitive approaches. Fifth, the programme should be delivered well and the staff should be trained adequately and monitored. Sixth, more attention should be paid to proximal causes of offending behaviour rather than distal causes. This means attending to peer groups, promoting family communication and enhancing self-management and problem-solving skills. There should not be a focus on early childhood or other distal causes of delinquency.

All of these reviews suggest that there are a number of promising targets for treatment programmes, which include antisocial thoughts, antisocial peer associations, promotion of family communication and affection, promotion of family supervision, identification of positive role models, improving problem-solving skills, reducing chemical dependencies, provision of adequate living conditions, and helping the young offender to identify high-risk situations for antisocial behaviours. Conversely, the systematic reviews have also suggested a number of approaches that are unlikely to be promising, such as improving self-esteem without reducing antisocial cognition. Similarly, it is unlikely that attention to emotional symptoms that are not clearly linked to criminal conduct will be of great benefit.

Oppositional Disorders, Conduct Disorder and Attention Deficit Hyperactivity Disorder (ADHD)

Fonagy (2003) reminds us that aggression and violence appear to be present from early childhood, and perhaps from birth. Substantially higher rates of physically aggressive behaviour are found in children and adolescents with attention deficit hyperactivity disorder (ADHD), with those who meet the criteria for ADHD and conduct disorder having substantially greater risks of delinquent acts in adolescence, harmful acts in later adolescence and continued violence and offending into adulthood (Fischer et al., 1993). Environmental factors and family adversity are known to contribute to various forms of psychopathology, and families of children with ADHD report higher rates of family conflict and more negative parent–child relationships (Barkley, 1998). Some research has questioned the direction of this relationship suggesting that parent–child hostility does not alter ADHD symptoms, but ADHD symptoms may negatively influence parent–child interactions (Lifford et al., 2008, reminiscent of the pioneering studies by Thomas, Chess and Birch, 1968).

Distorted or biased thought processes have over time been implicated in the development of violence (Beck, 1999). Psychological treatments aimed at reducing violent behaviour in adolescents and young adults have traditionally centred on violence as learned behaviour (McGuire and Priestly, 1995). In juvenile delinquents significant cognitive attributional bias has been shown in aggressive children and youths. They are more likely to perceive neutral acts by others as hostile, and more likely to believe conflicts can be satisfactorily resolved by aggression. In the social context, as the young individual becomes more disliked and rejected by peers, the opportunity for viewing the world this way increases (Dodge and Schwartz, 1997). By their late teens they can hold highly suspicious attitudes and be quick to perceive disrespect from others (Scott, 2004). The relationship between antisocial behaviour in adolescence and paranoid thinking has recently been reviewed (Bailey, 2007). In the social context of juvenile incarceration; being 'para' (paranoid) can become the shared norm in peer group interactions (Farrant, 2001).

Depression, Anxiety and PTSD in Childhood and Adolescence

As well as the recognized feelings of low mood in depression there is also some evidence of irritability, hostility and anger when depression occurs in adolescence. Irritability in adolescence leads to interpreting annoyances by others as direct threats, increasing the risk of defensive aggression (Dubicka and Harrington, 2004). Nowhere is this more apparent than in juvenile justice populations (Harrington et al., 2005; Kroll et al., 2002). It has resonance in the adult paranoid thinking literature (Bentall et al., 1994; Martin and Penn, 2001). A self-serving bias with a tendency to attribute good outcomes to the self and bad outcomes to external causes is usually regarded as a mechanism for maintaining self-esteem in the face of threats to the self when seen in ordinary people. Post-traumatic stress disorder (PTSD) is related to the conditioning of neurobiological fear responses underlying tendencies to react aggressively to protect the self when exposed to reminders of earlier trauma (Fletcher, 2003). For children who have experienced violence in war-torn countries and those who live in 'urban war zones', Garbarino (2001) set out an ecological framework to explain the process and conditions that transform the 'developmental challenge' of violence into developmental harm in some children – an accumulation of risk models for understanding how and when children suffer the most adverse consequences of exposure to community violence and go beyond their limits of resilience.

The combination of depression, anxiety and severe PTSD is being increasingly recognized in the child literature as being linked to a trajectory into adult antisocial personality disorder (Harrington and Bailey, 2004).

Autism Spectrum Disorders and Learning Disability

Autism spectrum disorders are being increasingly recognized in adolescent forensic populations. Their identification is critical to the understanding of violent offending. This is particularly so if an offence or assault is bizarre in nature or the degree or nature of aggression is unaccountable. O'Brien (1996) and Howlin (1997) proposed four reasons for offending and aggression in autistic persons:

- their social naivety may allow them to be led into criminal acts by others;
- aggression may arise from a disruption of routines;
- antisocial behaviour may stem from a lack of vunderstanding or misinterpretation of social cues;
- crimes may reflect obsessions, especially when these involved morbid fascination with violence – there are similarities with the intense and obsessional nature of fantasies described in some adult sadists (Bailey, 2002b).

Drawing on theory of mind paradigms, authors such as Craig et al. (2004) and Blackshaw et al. (2001) conclude that for adults

the paranoia observed in Asperger syndrome ...does not appear to stem from the same factors as seen in the paranoia observed in people with a diagnosis of schizophrenia (Blackshaw et al., 2001, p.158).

They postulate that the paranoia in the former has a different quality to that observed in the latter. Rather than stemming from a defensive strategy, it may stem from a confusion of not understanding the subtleties of social interaction and social rules.

Early Onset Psychosis

Non-psychotic behavioural disturbance occurs in about half of the cases of early onset schizophrenia and can last between one and seven years. It includes externalizing behaviours, attention deficit disorder and conduct disorder. This emphasizes the need for mental health assessments repeated over time to include a focus on changes in social function (often from an already chaotic baseline level) to a state including perceptual distortion, ideas of reference and delusional mood (James, 2004).

As in adult life (see chapter 14), most young people with schizophrenia are non-delinquent and non-violent. Nevertheless, there may be an increased risk of violence to others when they have active symptoms, especially when there is misuse of drugs or alcohol. The risk of violent acts is related to subjective feelings of tension, ideas of violence, delusional symptoms that incorporate named persons known to the individual, persecutory delusions, fear of imminent attack, feelings of sustained anger and fear, passivity experiences reducing the sense of self-control and command hallucinations. Protective factors include responding to and compliance with physical and psychosocial treatments, good social networks, a valued home environment, no interest in or knowledge of weapons as a means of violence, good insight into the psychiatric illness and any previous violent aggressive behaviour, and a fear of their own potential for violence. These features require particular attention but the best predictors of future violent offending in young people with mental disorder are the same as those in the general adolescent population. For example Clare et al. (2000) found in a retrospective study of 12 to 18 year olds admitted to adolescent units, one medium-secure and one regional, that violence was related to developmental and social factors rather than psychopathology, which included persecutory delusions present in most of the patients.

Traumatic Brain Injury

The relationship between damaged frontal lobes of the brain and disinhibited, sometimes aggressive, behaviour has been known for a century or more (see chapter 12). At one time nearly all aggressive behaviour was thought to be due to brain dysfunction; people with epilepsy were regarded as more likely to be violent that other people.

A survey of prisoners with epilepsy (Gunn, 1977) showed this to be a myth (see chapter 12). It was concluded that the association between imprisonment and epilepsy was probably an epiphenomenon in that the factors which led to brain injuries causing the epilepsy were the same or related factors which underlay the criminal behaviour. More recent studies have suggested that brain injuries taken as a whole are perhaps more related to violent and sexual crimes (Tyrer, 2007); perhaps this relates more to the frontal lobes than to the limbic system.

Traumatic brain injury (TBI) has been shown to be commoner in prisoners than in the general population (Blake et al., 1995; Fazel et al., 2009; Slaughter et al., 2003; Williams et al., 2010b). Williams noted that prisoners who suffer brain injuries in their early years are more likely to be sent to prison at a younger age and to serve more years in prison during their lifetime than other prisoners. He suggested that brain injury should be regarded as a marker of vulnerability in offender and potential offender populations. It could be that if adequate neurological and psychological treatment was given to young people with brain injury their criminality might be reduced, certainly it should be more readily identified by medical screening in offender populations than it is currently so that specialist rehabilitation can be offered to a somewhat disabled population that is frequently overlooked.

Williams et al. (2010a) studied 186 young male offenders aged 11 to 19 years. They completed self-reports on TBI, crime history, mental health and drug use. Traumatic brain injury with loss of consciousness was reported by 46% of the sample. Repeat injury was common, 32% reporting more than one loss of consciousness. The frequency of self-reported brain injury was associated with more convictions. Three or more self-reported such injuries were associated with greater violence in offences. The authors concluded that as brain injury may be associated with offending behaviour and worse mental health outcomes, neurorehabilitative interventions in affected adolescent offenders may be important for improving wellbeing and reducing re-offending.

Substance Misuse

The relationship between substance misuse, and more specifically cannabis use, and the development of schizophrenia and other psychoses has been well documented (Green et al., 2005; Semple et al., 2005), although recent research has implied either a common vulnerability or bi-directional relationship between the use of cannabis and psychosis (Ferdinand et al., 2005) rather than a direct link. In comparing psychiatric outcomes at age 26 with the use of cannabis during adolescence, Arseneault et al. (2002) added three new findings to the current evidence base. The authors found that cannabis use is associated with an increased risk of experiencing symptoms of schizophrenia. After controlling for those symptoms that precede the onset of cannabis use, the onset of cannabis use before the age of 16 increases the risk of such symptoms developing and this risk is specific to cannabis use. However, this study included a total sample of only 759 participants, 494 of which were controls who had 'never' or only 'once or twice' used cannabis. In a much larger cohort of 50,087, Zammit et al. (2002) concluded that cannabis use was associated with an increased risk of schizophrenia, suggesting a causal relationship. Most of this sample was aged between 18 and 20 years old and, with the added caveat that the participants were all army conscripts and possibly multiple drug users, the conclusions should be acknowledged with some caution. In a prospective cohort study of young people (2,437 participants aged 14 to 24 years) and cannabis use, Henquet et al. (2005) reported that cannabis use moderately increases the risk of psychotic symptoms in young people but has a much stronger effect in those with evidence of predisposition for psychosis.

In opposition to this view, Frischer et al. (2005) examined 1.4 million patients registered on the general practice research database and looked specifically at 3,969 individuals with substance misuse and psychiatric diagnosis. This study did not support the hypothesis that comorbidity between substance misuse and psychiatric illness is a result of substance misuse and found that only a small proportion of psychiatric illness could possibly be attributed to substance misuse.

GOVERNMENT POLICY FOR ENGLAND

Standard 8 of the English National Service Framework (NSF) (Department of Health, Department of Education and Skills (2004)) specifically states that young people with complex needs should have access to services that promote social inclusion. Standard 9 of the English NSF has established a responsibility for primary care trusts to ensure that local needs assessments identify young people in special circumstances, including young offender institutions (YOIs), and sets out expectations that services are in place to meet their needs. It also states that all young people from birth to their 18th birthday should have access to timely, integrated services.

Practitioners of all kinds working in the criminal justice system, particularly the court system, need to be able to identify young people have mental health problems. A good understanding of a young person's mental health problems and their influence on offending behaviour can inform the sentencing and placement process and help ensure that young people have access to the mental health services they require. A key area of concern for the Youth Justice Board and the courts is the length of time it can take for psychiatric reports to be provided to the courts.

Bradley (2009) was mainly concerned with adult mentally disordered offenders, but he made three recommendations for children and young people:

1. All staff in schools and primary healthcare, including GPs, should have mental health and learning disability awareness training in order to identify individuals (children and young people in particular) needing help and refer them to specialist services.

2. The membership of all youth offending teams must include a suitably qualified mental health worker who is responsible for making appropriate referrals to services.

3. The Government should undertake a review to examine the potential for early intervention and diversion for children and young people with mental health problems or learning disabilities who have offended or are at risk of offending, with the aim of bringing forward appropriate recommendations which are consistent with this wider review.

In 2009 the Department of Health published *Healthy Children, Safer Communities* – which was described as a strategy to promote the health and wellbeing of children and young people in contact with the youth justice system (http://www.dh.gov.uk/en/Publicationsandstatistics/Publications/PublicationsPolicyAndGuidance/DH_109771). It was a response to the recommendations specific to the youth justice system made within the Bradley review of people with mental health problems and learning disabilities in the criminal justice system. The document includes some important statistics. There were 5 million children in England aged 10 to 17. Of these: 138,692 committed an offence in 2007/2008, about 3,000 children and young people were in the secure estate at any one time and 7,000 children and young people were held in the secure estate during the course of a year. The majority of offences committed by young people (79%) were committed by boys, but the number of offences committed by girls had risen. The majority of children and young people in contact with the youth justice system were white; black children and young people were over-represented in the system overall, and they were particularly over-represented in custody. It is policy to try and reduce the number of youngsters locked up.

The health and wellbeing needs of children and young people tend to be particularly severe by the time they are at risk of receiving a community sentence, and even more so when they receive a custodial sentence. Over three-quarters of those in custody have a history of school exclusion and serious difficulties with literacy and numeracy. Over half of young people committing crimes have difficulties with speech, language and communication, problems with peer and family relationships and have been a victim of crime themselves – twice the rate for non-offenders. More than a third of those in custody have a diagnosed mental health disorder and the same proportion have experienced homelessness. Over a quarter of young men in custody and a third of young women in custody report a long-standing physical complaint; a similar number have a learning disability. A high proportion of children from black and minority ethnic groups, compared with others, have post-traumatic stress disorder and have experienced bereavement and loss through death and family breakdown.

Access to Child and Adolescent Mental Health Services (CAMHS)

Figure 19.2 depicts how child and adolescent mental health services inter-relate with youth justice services in a four-tier model.

Some health workers – and especially workers in youth offending teams – have developed close links and protocols with child and adolescent specialist services. Where there are child and adolescent mental health workers in youth offending teams, they could operate as virtual or direct members of local specialist child and adolescent mental health services, providing an outreach community service to the youth offending team while receiving clinical supervision from the child and adolescent mental health team. It is important that all health workers receive direct professional supervision from their host agency. In 2010 the majority of, but not all, youth offending teams had a health worker as part of the team, provided by local primary care trusts. Such a person is required to be provided under s.39 of the Crime and Disorder Act 1998. The Commission for Healthcare Audit and Inspection (2007) found that at that time 17% of youth offending teams did not have a health worker. What will happen when primary care trusts are abolished is not clear at the time of writing.

The Greater Manchester West NHS Trust pioneered a national forensic adolescent consultation and treatment service (FACTS) which works with young people who exhibit high risk offending behaviour and mental disorder. It is an assessment/outreach team with the facility to provide outpatient treatment. The service aims to provide multidisciplinary assessments of young people for child and adolescent psychiatrists, youth offending teams, social workers and forensic psychiatrists. Second opinions, and training may also be provided. Similar services have subsequently been developed in other parts of England.

Young Offenders with Health Needs in Custodial Settings

After April 2003, the Department of Health took on responsibility for funding health services within all prison service establishments in England and Wales. Primary care trusts that have a prison in their boundary took on the commissioning role for health services for their local unit. The Youth Justice Board, Department of Health and HM Prison

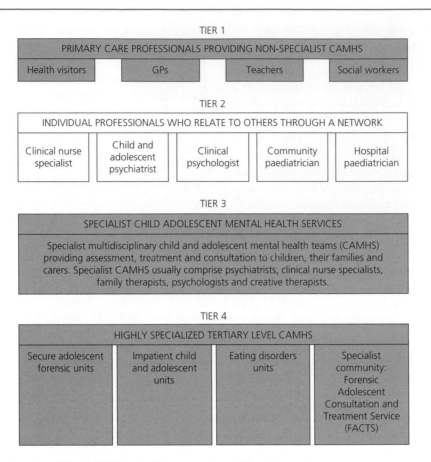

Figure 19.2 A tiered model of child and adolescent mental health services.

Service had a Joint Health Steering Group and Management Board in order to deliver a joint health and wellbeing development programme to improve access to health services for young people in the youth justice system. It is not clear at the time of writing what will happen after the Youth Justice Board and primary care trusts have been abolished.

Comprehensive Screening Tool

The Young Offender Assessment Profile (ASSET) is a structured assessment tool used by youth offending teams in England and Wales on young offenders who come into contact with the criminal justice system. It provides a systematic framework for documenting a young person's offences, circumstances and risks (http://www.justice.gov.uk/youth-justice/assessment/asset-young-offender-assessment-profile).

The information gathered from ASSET can be used to inform court reports and appropriate intervention programmes. The Youth Justice Board commissioned the University of Manchester and Salford NHS Trust to develop a child and adolescent mental health screening tool to be attached to the Youth Justice ASSET form. This manual may be found on http://www.justice.gov.uk/youth-justice/health/mental-health.

The website links to a short screening questionnaire interview for adolescents (SQUIFA), and to guide notes.

The longer screening interview for adolescents (SIFA) is a modified Salford Needs Assessment Schedule for Adolescents (SNASA) (Kroll et al., 1999).

Secure Accommodation

At the time of writing there were 2,491 secure beds within the criminal justice system, 1,993 beds for boys 18 years or under in young offender institutions (YOIs) and 41 such beds for girls. In addition there were 301 beds in secure training centres and 166 beds in secure children's homes. Secure training centres (STCs) are purpose-built centres for young offenders up to the age of 17 years. They are run by private operators under contracts and provide educative rehabilitation. There are four in England: Oakhill in Milton Keynes, Hassockfield in Consett, Rainsbrook in Rugby, and Medway in Rochester. Secure children's homes (SCHs) are run by local authority social services departments, overseen by the Department of Health and the Department for Education. They have a high ratio of staff to young people and are generally small facilities, ranging in size from 6 to 40 beds. They generally accommodate young offenders aged 12 to 14 years, girls up to the age of 16 years, and 15- to 16-year-old boys who are assessed as vulnerable.

Provision for young people with complex, severe or persistent mental disorders may include referral to the Secure

Forensic Mental Health Service for Young People which is an inpatient service commissioned by the NHS National Commissioning Group (NCG). There are 95 beds in seven units: 20 (male and female) at the Ardenleigh Unit, in Birmingham; 10 male beds in the Bill Yule Adolescent Unit at the Bethlem Royal Hospital in south London; 10 beds at the Gardener Unit in Manchester; 10 beds (male and female) for people with a learning disability in Malcolm Arnold House, Northampton; 25 beds (male, female and learning disability) at the Roycroft Unit, in Northumberland; 10 beds (male) at the Wells Unit, West London; and 20 beds (male and female) at Bluebird House, in Southampton.

Referral for one of these secure units can come from any psychiatrist, the NHS, or prison. The criteria for admission are set out in a useful government leaflet (http://www.specialisedservices.nhs.uk/library/23/Admission_Criteria_and_Process_Following_Referral_to_the_Secure_Forensic_Mental_Health_Service_for_Young_People.pdf) as follows:

The potential patient must be under 18 years of age and detainable under either part II or part III of the Mental Health Act 1983/2007 and EITHER present a risk to others of direct violence, sexually aggressive behaviour, or destructive and potentially life-threatening use of fire OR is in custodial care presenting a serious risk of suicide and/or severe self-harm AND serious consideration and testing of alternatives has already been tried without success. It is not necessary that the young person should be facing criminal charges for these behaviours.

At the time of writing there was no waiting list for the NHS secure units for young people. It would be important to carry out a national survey of need for such units, using the criteria set out by the National Commissioning Group (above) before concluding that 95 secure beds for young people is adequate.

Substance Misuse

According to the 2008/2009 British Crime Survey, around two in five young people (aged 16–24 years) (42.9%) have *ever* used illicit drugs; nearly one in four had used one or more illicit drugs in the *last year* (22.6%); and around one in eight in the *last month* (13.1%) (Hoare, 2009). Cannabis is the drug most likely to be used by young people; 18.7% used cannabis in the previous year. Young offenders are thought to be more likely to use drugs than other groups of young people and are hence more likely to suffer substance misuse-related problems. This was confirmed by the study *Substance Misuse and the Juvenile Secure Estate* (Galahad, 2004) which found that 90% of young offenders in custody had taken an illegal drug at some point in their life, 72% had used cannabis daily in the 12 months before their arrest, 74% drank alcohol more than once a week with the majority drinking more than six units each time, and 51% were polydrug users and used two or more substances more than once a week. The same study identified significant levels of dual diagnosis mental health needs and the use of substances to self-medicate, with 30% saying they had used a drug not to get high but to feel normal, and 38% had taken a drug to 'forget everything' or 'blot everything out'.

There are over 200 youth substance misuse worker posts across England and Wales and the Youth Justice Board works with the National Treatment Agency to try and improve access to services for young people supervised by youth offending teams in England. In 2005/2006, youth offending teams in England and Wales screened 79,027 young people for substance misuse; 15,414 required a further assessment and 12,874 received an intervention within 20 working days.

The Youth Justice Board commissioned Galahad SMS (a private research company) to survey the substance misuse problems in the youth secure estate. They made a long list of recommendations beginning with the need to improve substance misuse assessments. The research showed that 84% of the young people studied had problematic or potentially problematic levels of substance misuse while they were in the community, yet few could recall being offered interventions other than advice from a substance misuse worker. The researchers suggested the development of a standardized screening and assessment tool for substance abuse in young people, which should be used repeatedly. They pointed out that many young people under-report their substance misuse initially, but were later willing to engage with services.

The research also revealed evidence that many young people were not receiving the mental health services that they required, partly because they did not exhibit overt signs of psychological disorders, but many said that they used substances for reasons that relate to their emotional state, self-medication in effect. Thus not only should drug screening be repeated after admission to the secure service, but mental health screening should also be repeated.

Educational programmes were recommended to impart knowledge about harmful substances, but with a special focus on cannabis and alcohol, their effects and dangers. The research suggested that 16% of subjects said that they drank alcohol every day and 67% got drunk at least once a week. There was a marked shortfall between the number of long-term residents who wanted help and the number accessing such services.

It was also recommended that stress management courses or group psychotherapy should be provided given that many young people said that they used substances to relieve stress or to calm themselves down. A total of 23% of the young people studied for the research said that they had been involved in dealing or delivering drugs. The researchers urged that programmes should be developed to address this problem directly.

The researchers thought that regional centres should be developed to provide services for the small number of high level substance misusers in order to concentrate resources for this difficult group. They also recommended regional detoxification centres for similar reasons.

The researchers said that multidisciplinary conferences and workshops are needed for training and continuing professional development. In this context, self-harm and suicide awareness were particularly mentioned. Training should also cover areas such as cognitive behavioural approaches, solution-focused therapy, motivational enhancement therapy, and relapse prevention techniques. A particular emphasis was given to providing staff with a basic understanding of the emotional, cognitive and developmental differences between a child, an adolescent and an adult, because during the study, differences were observed in how young people were treated from unit to unit in the secure estate. In the secure children's home study site, researchers witnessed high levels of understanding of child and adolescent psychology, particularly in respect of conflict, challenging behaviour and aggression, but in the young offender institutions and secure training centres studied, levels of understanding of how to deal with young people and their frustrations were 'less well developed'. They noted however that the recommendations of the Warner report (Department of Health, 1992) have been introduced throughout the secure estate with the aim of changing the predominantly control-based culture of some establishments to a predominantly care-based culture. Plant and Taylor (2012) found that young male prisoners failed to recognize hazardous drinking and dependence. Adolescents were less likely than older men to experience withdrawal symptoms.

One of the handicaps in this field is the shortage of information on effective treatment. Three reviews are available. The first comes from the Health Development Agency (Canning et al., 2004) before it became the National Institute for Health and Clinical Excellence (NICE); the second (McGrath et al., 2006; http://www.nice.org.uk/niceMedia/docs/drug_use_prev_update_v9.pdf) takes the first one as its starting point. Both discover the paucity of evidence about interventions for substance misuse in young people. The 2006 document reviewed seven reviews; the data collected are quite substantial but they don't approach the standard of controlled trials and they are almost exclusively American. How far their findings can be applied to British populations is not at all clear as many of the target groups and individuals are native Americans. McGrath et al. conclude that not much has changed since the earlier review in 2004 and that research on the effectiveness of drug treatments is urgently required, especially in Britain for British youths. They emphasize that drug intervention programmes should, like all medical and psychological interventions, be informed by research evidence. Perhaps their most important conclusion from the data they reviewed is that a 'one size fits all' approach to substance misuse is unlikely to be very useful, a point also made by the Galahad study (above).

Intensive Resettlement and Aftercare Provision Schemes

The Youth Justice Board developed an aftercare scheme for those in custody called Integrated Resettlement Support (IRS). Fifty-nine youth offender teams (local authorities, in effect) have such an integrated support scheme that provides support to those young people leaving custody and on community sentences, who have been substance misusers. The teams provide support during the community element of a custodial detention and training order for up to 25 hours per week, and they can provide up to 6 months of further support following the end of the sentence. Many schemes are supported by the voluntary sector and recruit volunteer mentors for evenings and weekends to provide extended periods of aftercare; participation is voluntary. Early monitoring data are showing significantly lower reoffending, breach and return to custody rates among young people while on IRS than in those without such support.

Specialist Medico-Legal Assessment

In *T & V* the European Court of Human Rights stated that a child's age, level of maturity and intellectual and emotional capacities must be taken into account when s/he is charged with a criminal offence and that appropriate steps should be taken in order to promote his/her ability to understand and participate in the court proceedings. A responsibility therefore falls on the defence lawyer to be aware of the possibility that a young person may not be able to participate effectively in the trial process, particularly if s/he is under 14 years old or has learning problems or a history of absence from school (Ashford et al., 2006). In 1985, the Office of the High Commissioner for Human Rights, in reference to the age of criminal responsibility, stated that there is a close relationship between the notion of responsibility for delinquent or criminal behaviour and other social rights and responsibilities.

In discussing issues of fitness to plead and capacity to participate in legal proceedings, Ashford and Bailey (2004) said that all young defendants, regardless of the offences they are charged with, should be tried in youth courts with permission for adult sanctions for older youths if certain conditions are met. This should enable a mode of trial for young defendants to be subject to safeguards that can enhance understanding and participation. Assessment of cognitive and emotional capacities should occur before any decisions on venue and mode of trial take place.

One fundamental distinction in the criminal law is between conditions that negate criminal liability and those that might mitigate the punishment deserved under particular circumstances. Very young children and the profoundly mentally ill may lack the minimum capacity necessary to justify punishment at all. Those exhibiting less profound impairments of the same kind may qualify for a less than full level of punishment even though they may meet the minimum conditions for some punishment. Immaturity, like mental disorder, can serve both as an excuse and as mitigation in the determination of just punishment. Capacity is sometimes thought of as a generic skill that a person either has or lacks, but this is not so. To begin with, it is multifaceted, with four key elements as follows:

- the capacity to understand information relevant to the specific decision at issue (understanding);
- the capacity to appreciate one's situation when confronted with a specific legal decision (appreciation);
- the capacity to think rationally about alternative courses of action (reasoning);
- the capacity to express a choice among alternatives (choice).

Any evaluation of competence (Grisso, 1997) should include assessment of possibly relevant psychopathology, emotional understanding as well cognitive level, the child's experiences and appreciation of situations comparable to the one relevant to the crime and to the trial, and any particular features that may be pertinent in this individual and this set of circumstances. The general principles to be used in the assessment are broadly comparable to those employed in any clinical evaluation. Particular attention needs to be paid to developmental background, emotional and cognitive maturity, trauma exposure and substance misuse. The likely appropriate sources for obtaining clinical data relevant to assessment of a juvenile's competence to stand trial will include a variety of records, a range of interviews and other observations, and in some cases, specialized tests. Records of the child's school functioning, past clinical assessment, treatment history and previous legal involvements need to be obtained. In coming to an overall formulation, there should be a particular focus on how both developmental and psychopathological features may be relevant to the forensic issues.

The main focus is on the youth's ability to understand and cope with the legal process. This comes from three sources: direct questioning of the defendant, inferences from function in other areas and direct observation of the defendant's behaviour and interaction with others. It is useful to inquire about the youth's expectations for the potential consequences of the court involvement. Because the course of juvenile proceedings can vary so widely, with consequences ranging from the extremely aversive to extremely beneficial, rational understanding will necessarily involve a high degree of uncertainty. Potentially relevant problems include: inattention, depression, disorganization of thought processes that interfere with the ability to consider alternatives, hopelessness such that the decision is felt not to matter, delusion or other fixed beliefs that distort understanding of options (or their likely outcomes), maturity of judgment and the developmental challenges of adolescence.

In providing information to the court, written reports have the advantage of a standard format that helps the consultant to be sure that s/he has considered all the relevant questions; it also provides a familiar structure for readers. In essence, for the sake of consistency and clarity, competence reports need to cover the following areas:

- identifying information and referral questions;
- the description of the method of evaluation including sources and a notation of the confidentiality expectations;
- the provision of clinical and forensic data.

Ashford et al. (2006) itemize the issues that a clinical psychologist with experience of assessing adolescents should be asked to address. This includes the young person's understanding of the charges and the possible consequences of guilty and not guilty pleas, and their ability to make rational decisions relevant to the legal process, to remember relevant facts, to communicate in a coherent manner, to understand testimony in court and to behave appropriately in the courtroom. Grisso (2000) outlined a conceptual framework for psychiatric/psychological assessment of competence in young people that includes assessment of their understanding of the charges they face and the potential consequences, an understanding of the trial process, the young person's capacity to communicate with their lawyer in their defence and their general ability to participate in the courtroom proceedings.

In court, a child's ability to give an account of events may be impaired by a number of factors, including poor physical health on the day of the trial, overwhelming anxiety or anger about giving evidence, or intimidation by the physical surroundings of the court. From a psychological perspective, however, the basic evidential capacity of the child defendant will depend on two main components:

- the child's mental state – this needs to be stable, therefore any disturbance that interferes with the child's perception of the world and/or the ability to understand it will impair evidential capacity;
- the child's cognitive ability – a concept that includes memory, understanding and the ability to communicate. The last includes both verbal and non-verbal means, as well as the ability both to comprehend and to express thought. Any psychological assessment therefore has to be across a range of domains.

Discrepancies are particularly likely in the areas of educational achievement, adaptive skills and social and emotional development. A child's ability is often gauged on educational achievement and given as being equivalent to that of a certain age, e.g. a 15-year-old child might have the everyday living skills of a 7-year-old. A child who might be unable to cope with monetary change or public transport might well, however, have the emotional and social experiences of an older child and the drives of an adolescent.

When discussing developmental psychology and child development, it is important to bear in mind that none of these processes operates in a vacuum. The child's experiences of parenting (important in relation to physical and emotional development), the provision of appropriate role models (moral development and self-control depend heavily on appropriate modelling and social learning) and the learning environment (whether it fostered or hindered intellectual development) all have a vital role. For instance, during adolescence, as young people take on a wider and more social perspective and become integrated within a peer group, they will nevertheless tend to adopt social values and norms (i.e. ideas about 'right and wrong') that are very similar to those of their parents. Hence, despite any demonstrations of teenage rebellion (often short-lived), the majority of adolescents will tend to adopt parental mores, either law-abiding or delinquent.

It should be emphasized that clear-cut ages do not apply to the completion of physical, intellectual, emotional and social development. For most young people, given appropriate parenting, normal biological development and a structured, emotionally supportive and stimulating environment, the bulk of the development processes should be achieved by late teenage years and a considerable degree of intellectual maturation may have occurred by the age of 14.

It is, therefore, important that child and adolescent services are specially designed for young people. Such specific design will require long-term planning to enable the training and supervision of the staff in sufficient numbers (Williams, 2005).

Specialist training for practitioners

We have already emphasized the importance of adult forensic psychiatrists and psychologists having the opportunity to spend time within adolescent forensic services. They will learn something about the often unrecognized neurodevelopmental disorders in adult patients and the ongoing impact in adults of childhood maltreatment and abuse. The experience should also teach adult practitioners something of how the jurisdictions of juvenile justice, social care, education and child mental health come together to work with families when there are significant child safety issues. Both adult and child and adolescent practitioners need to understand the psychiatric morbidity in individuals within families and how they interact. Most importantly the adult practitioner will learn some of the differences in child, adolescent and adult medicolegal work, and the importance of not claiming expertise in the psychiatry and psychology of young people without proper training. Adolescents are not adults, but just a bit younger.

The transition of mentally disordered adolescents from child to adult general and or community mental health services will be improved by this increased understanding.

Adult antisocial behaviour, including sex offending and personality disorders all begin in childhood and adolescence; witnessing these problems at their beginnings may help with their later management.

There are now fully dual trained child and adolescent forensic psychiatrists; the opportunity to complete dual training should be encouraged. Such practitioners are able to provide specialized support to child and adolescent practitioners as their patients grow up and help to identify potentially high risk children who may need specialized interventions over a lengthy period.

SPECIAL CRIMES

Juvenile Homicide

Studies show that children and adolescents who murder share a constellation of psychological, cognitive, neuropsychiatric, educational and family system disturbance (Cornell et al., 1987; Myers et al., 1995; Myers and Scott, 1998). In the UK, young people who commit grave sadistic crimes including juvenile homicide are liable to periods of lengthy incarceration. Detention itself can provide time for further neurodevelopmental, cognitive and emotional growth. Irrespective of treatment models, the provisions of education, vocational training, consistent role models and continued family contact are of critical importance.

Youths who have been prosecuted for murder or manslaughter vary only slightly or not at all from other juvenile delinquents on points such as age, gender and ethnic background, and only to a limited extent on risk factors. Murder and manslaughter are more often committed alone, and, on average, the perpetrators start their criminal activities at a later age and are much less likely to have previous convictions than (other) minors taken into judicial youth institutions. At the same time, it is clear that the very small group of youths involved in murder and manslaughter is anything but homogeneous. There is great variety in terms of motives, victims and *modus operandi*. In simple terms each case stands on its own.

Sexually Abusive Behaviour

Sexually inappropriate behaviour in children and adolescents constitutes a substantial health and social problem (James and Neil, 1996). Most, but not all, abusers are male, often from disadvantaged backgrounds with a history of victimization, sexual and physical abuse (Skuse et al., 1998) and high rates of psychopathology (Dolan et al., 1996; Hummel et al., 2000). Of particular concern is a subgroup with mild learning disability whose treatment programmes have to be tailored to their level of development and cognitive ability. Young abusers come within the criminal justice system but also need a child protection framework. Most adult sexual abusers of children started their abuse when adolescents and yet neither ICD-10 nor DSM-IV has a diagnostic category for paedophilia in those under 16. Vizard and colleagues (1996) suggested the creation of a new disorder 'sexual arousal disorder of childhood' to help identify this vulnerable group who in turn place vulnerable others at risk. Långstörm and colleagues (2000) advocated the development of empirically based typologies for this offender group.

A structured, carefully planned multi-agency approach is required when working with sexually aggressive younger children and sexually abusive adolescents. The three stages to assessment of juvenile sexual offenders (Becker, 1998; O'Callaghan and Print, 1994; Vizard, 2006) are

1. Clarification and rapport building.
2. Mapping the abuse: the fantasies, strategies and behaviours.
3. The future, placement treatment and personal change.

The treatment process occurs in the context of

- the crisis of disclosure;
- family assessment;
- therapeutic work in a protective context for the victim; and
- reconstruction and reunification of the family.

The 'family' (Bentovim, 1998) in this context may include foster carers or long-term residential carers.

Treatment

The earliest possible interventions with young over-sexualized children, before their patterns of sexually aggressive behaviours become entrenched, are likely to be most effective. There is a dearth of longitudinal follow-up studies looking at treatment outcomes with this younger group of children.

New approaches to cognitive behaviour therapy (CBT) with sexually abusing youth have recently been described (Steen, 2005) and a more complex cognitive behaviour therapy intervention, known as mode deactivation therapy (MDT), has been suggested for disturbed, sexually abusive young people with reactive conduct disorders (Apsche and Ward Bailey, 2005). Mode deactivation therapy is a cognitive method which aims to understand an adolescent's core beliefs and aims to shift him/her from these in very small increments. Cognitive group work with sexually abusing children and young people is widely practised in the UK and the principles of this work are described by Print and O'Callaghan (1999).

Other treatment approaches will take into account the living context of the young person and the need for his or her carers to be provided with support and explanation of the treatment process in order to maximize positive results. When children and young people who sexually abuse are still living at home or in contact with their parents, family work is usually needed. Hackett et al. (2002) describe an approach to group work with parents of children with sexually abusive behaviour.

There are a small number of mid-adolescent, recidivist, delinquent, sexually abusive youths who are too dangerous to other children and young people to be treated (with any treatment modality) alongside other young people. Most of these young people have been through the court system or are currently facing charges. For these reasons, treatment of such young people needs to be undertaken within a closely supervised, intensive, community-based foster placement with specially trained foster carers who are experienced in dealing with young offenders, risk and dangerousness. This type of approach is known by various names such as multidimensional treatment foster care (Chamberlain and Reid, 1998) or forensic foster care (Yokely and Boettner, 2002). Early results from small-scale studies with this type of intervention are reasonably encouraging.

In summary, the components of effective treatment for children and young people who sexually abuse will include

- a well planned, child protection orientated, treatment context;
- positive interventions in the life of the young person and his or her family;
- an agreed inter-agency care plan; and
- offence-specific interventions, such as CBT, aimed at changing the distorted cognitions and self-justifications.

Treatment programmes which focus solely on the victimization of the young person are likely to be seriously counterproductive and to miss opportunities to challenge the young person on his or her offending behaviour. Interventions should occur at all possible levels simultaneously including individual work with the young person, family work (where relevant), support for foster carers or for professional care staff and consultation with the professional network.

Fire-Setting/Arson

Arson can have a devastating impact on the victim and the wider society. Juvenile arsonists are not a homogeneous group, but have a wide range of familial (Fineman, 1980), social (Patterson, 1982), developmental, interpersonal (Vreeland and Lowin, 1980), clinical and 'legal' needs. Kolko and Kazdin (1992) highlighted the importance of attraction to fire, heightened arousal, impulsivity and limited social competence. As with other forms of serious antisocial behaviours, no single standard treatment approach will be appropriate for all individuals (Repo and Virkunnen, 1997). In addition to the general assessment of antisocial behaviour the specific domains to be considered include

- history of playing with fire;
- history of hoax telephone calls;
- social context of fire-setting (whether alone or with peers);
- where the fires were set;

- previous threats/targets;
- type of fire, single/multiple seats of fire-setting;
- motivation (anger resolution, boredom, rejection, cry for help, thrill seeking, fire fighting, crime concealment, no motivation, curiosity and peer pressure).

For recidivistic fire setters, therapy may include

- psychotherapy to increase the understanding of the behaviour, including antecedents defining the problem behaviour, and establishing the behavioural reinforcers;
- skills training to promote adaptive coping mechanisms;
- understanding of environmental factors to manage or self-trigger solutions;
- counselling to reduce psychological distress;
- behavioural techniques to extinguish the behaviour;
- education to promote understanding of cause and effect; and
- supervision for the staff caring for the adolescent.

Early modelling experiences and early exposure to related phenomena militate against a good outcome.

ADOLESCENT GIRLS

Longitudinal data demonstrate that girlhood aggression contributes to a cascading set of negative outcomes as young women move into adolescence and adulthood. Young girls who engage in disruptive behaviour and fighting are at risk for

- being rejected by peers and adults;
- feeling alienated and unsupported;
- struggling academically;
- affiliating with other peers prone to deviant behaviour;
- becoming involved in more serious antisocial behaviours;
- choosing antisocial romantic partners;
- initiating and receiving partner violence;
- becoming adolescent mothers;
- having children with excess health problems;
- being less sensitive and responsive as parents.

Some are sufficiently antisocial and even violent, that they may be incarcerated. If they are also mothers, they may lose custody of their children. Opportunities for stable employment and relationships are much diminished.

Given the low base rates of girls engaging in physical aggression, early identification of girls at risk is important. High-risk groups include (i) those girls who are temperamentally overactive as toddlers and pre-schoolers, those who have early pubertal development, girls who report engaging in high levels of bullying as they enter puberty; this group are likely to be victims as well as perpetrators. (ii) Sexually abused girls – especially those abused by their biological fathers over a long period of time.

Interventions to reduce rates of aggression, relational aggression and violence in female children and adolescents should include

- pre-natal programmes for high-risk expectant mothers (i.e. young mothers and those themselves aggressive or disruptive as children);
- augmenting the parenting skills of at risk young mothers by teaching hygiene, childproofing of homes, good nutrition, meal planning and household management.

Given that these at-risk mothers are prone to maternal irritability and harsh parenting they are likely to perceive normal infant behaviour, such as a child being irritable during nappy changing, as an intentionally malevolent act on the part of the child. Therefore there is a need to help young mothers to respond optimally rather than negatively to their infants and toddlers. This may reduce the likelihood of these children themselves becoming aggressive and antisocial.

In middle childhood girls, episodes of physical aggression are often preceded by relational aggression. Interventions are needed to help these girls relate to others, manage strong emotions, understand the unfolding of their own aggression, understand how 'girl talk' ignites into hurtful indirect social aggression, and understand how relational aggression leads to physical violence towards peers, adults and romantic partners. Therapists need to be able to recognize when a girl's aggression is adaptive in the immediate situation as a means of social ascendancy or standing up to abuse.

CONCLUSIONS

The major challenge of altering the trajectories of persistent young offenders has to be met in the context of satisfying public demands for retribution, together with welfare and civil liberties considerations. In England and Wales, we lock up nearly 3,000 juveniles at any one time (at the time of writing). Therefore the treatment of delinquents in institutional settings has to meet the sometimes contradictory need to control them, to remove their liberty, to maintain good order and at the same time offer education and training. In England and Wales, the Crime and Disorder Act 1998 has mandated practitioners to bridge the gap between residential and community treatments and to involve families, using youth offending teams to meet this complex mix of needs, but the public demand to remove antisocial youths from the street has led to the implementation of antisocial behaviour orders including those for children with learning disabilities.

Since the 1980s there has been a gradual shift in opinion regarding the effectiveness of intervention with delinquents, from the 'nothing works' approach to a 'what works' approach. In practice, pressure from politicians and public will remain for quick-fix solutions to problems that span cultures, countries and generations. The most important childhood predictors of adolescent violence include troublesome behaviour, daring, hyperactivity, low IQ, low school attainment, antisocial parents, poor child rearing, harsh and erratic discipline, poor supervision, parental conflict, broken families, low family income and large family size (Losel and Bender, 2006) (see also chapter 7). Important policy implications are that home visiting programmes, parent training and skills training programmes singly and in combination should be implemented at an early stage to prevent adolescent high-risk behaviour and offending.

Provision of appropriately designed programmes can significantly reduce recidivism among persistent offenders. The mode and style of delivery is important: high-quality staff and staff training are required, together with a system for 'monitoring integrity'. Where comparisons are possible, effect sizes are higher for community-based rather than institution-based programmes. In prison settings, the strongest effects are obtained when programmes are integrated into the institutional régimes.

Our knowledge of the true prevalence rates of mental disorders in a young offending population is developing (Kazdin, 2000), so that mental health issues (Bailey, 2006) can be addressed with a good evidence base. Child and adolescent mental health practitioners have the skills to set the understanding of delinquency in a developmental context and treat those young offenders with mental disorders (Bailey, 2006). However, it is a contentious area, and likely to remain so.

20
Women as offenders

Edited by
Pamela J Taylor

Written by
Hanna Putkonen
Pamela J Taylor

1st edition authors: **Paul T d'Orbán, Anthony Maden and Pamela J Taylor**

WHY A CHAPTER ON WOMEN?

'Oh Lord, please don't let me be misunderstood.' (Bennie Benjamin, Gloria Caldwell and Sol Marcus, 1964).

A current notion in Western society is that women have achieved equality with men. Women are active in all areas of society, including work, sports and arts as well as the domestic environment. Many men, on the other hand, having traditionally been the out-of-home workers, are becoming more and more involved with family life. Feminism perhaps had its peak back in the 1960s; should we not leave it there? Could it marginalize women yet again to treat those who offend as different from men who offend?

Women and men still live different lives. Outside the professions, women often do not have parity with men in their pay; the highest positions in the work environment – including politics, company management, universities and medicine – are still held mostly by men while women still have greater responsibility at home. Throughout history, perpetration of crime has been male dominated, for which perhaps women should rejoice. In England and Wales, for example, about one in five of all arrests recorded by police in 2009 were of females, and only about 5% of prisoners are female. In the USA, women are still in the minority among criminals, but still, in 2010, about 25% of arrests were of women or girls (Federal Bureau of Investigation (FBI), 2010). In most prison systems worldwide (about 80%), female prisoners constitute between 2% and 9% of the total prison population. Within prison, however, the rate of adverse events such as punishment for disciplinary offences or suicide related behaviour is much higher among women (Ministry of Justice, 2010b).

Aside from the overall male predominance in criminal statistics, in England and Wales there are probably more similarities than differences between women and men in crime 'preferences'. Acquisitive offences account for the largest proportion of criminal proceedings against women and men alike, with the next most common broad group of offences being crimes of violence against the person for both (Ministry of Justice, 2010). Popular perspectives on the gender of victims of crime are not borne out by statistics. While women may have more fear of becoming a victim of crime, in reality they are much less likely to be so, with intimate or domestic violence being a possible exception to this rule (e.g. Flatley et al., 2010).

In his review of female crime in 1971, d'Orban commented that female criminality has received far less attention than its interest merits. This is perhaps inevitable given the relatively small numbers of women in the criminal justice system, although research into female offending has since grown, and continues to do so. For offenders with mental disorder, however, difficulties arise because of the small numbers in dedicated forensic mental health services, while in many trials of treatment for disorders of mental health, whether or not the participants were also offenders, women are often excluded. When the treatment is with medication, this is perhaps understandable; no pharmaceutical company wants to be responsible for damage to an unborn child, an ever present risk in women of child bearing years. Even when both sexes have participated in a trial, however, it is often hard to disentangle any female:male differences in the findings (Taylor and Bragado-Jimenez, 2009).

In order to ensure inclusion of the best possible evidence on women, mental disorder and crime, we conducted various systematic searches for relevant literature, including a PubMed search using common search words related to female criminality and mental disorder, read reviews and high quality published discussion papers from experts in the field, and accessed relevant national statistics in Finland, the UK and the USA. Our aim was to be as comprehensive as possible, but almost all the material found was from Western countries, and so the contents of this chapter are not necessarily generalizable to other cultures. Furthermore, an emphasis on Finland and Finnish studies and the UK and UK studies is likely, reflecting the authors' nationalities. This has advantages, however. Finland has had an excellent opportunity for epidemiological studies because of the high crime clearance rate, comprehensive registers and the established practice for most homicide offenders and many other more serious offenders having thorough forensic psychiatric examinations before trial. On a less happy note, Finland has the highest homicide rate in Western and Northern Europe. In England and Wales, although national forensic mental health databases are no longer so well developed, national crime reporting and conviction statistics are well established, together with a more health based National Confidential Inquiry into Suicide and Homicide (NCISH): (http://www.medicine.manchester.ac.uk/mentalhealth/research/suicide/prevention/nci).

A word of caution is necessary, however. In the discussion of general crime rates one should remember that laws may change over time and are not universal. Thus, what is regarded as criminal differs at different times and, of course, in different countries and jurisdictions. d'Orban (1971), for example, wrote that, apart from prostitution, there is no type of offence to be considered specifically female. It is now the case, however, that prostitution is not a crime in every country, and there are male prostitutes. Neonaticide is often regarded as a female crime but, although killing a newborn is more likely than not to be a woman's offence, it is not unique to women; infanticide is specifically defined in law as an offence of women in some countries, but, when killing within the first 12 months of life is considered, women contribute proportionately more than they do to other homicides but still they constitute a minority of perpetrators in some studies (Flynn et al., 2007). Discussion on psychiatric morbidity is complicated by the fact that diagnostics evolve in time and place.

WOMEN AND CRIME

Early theories on becoming criminal were largely developed from studying boys and men, as more of them were most visibly antisocial. Insofar as girls or women were criminal, it was assumed that they were more 'mad than bad'. Where studies had been done with girls or women, they were often also with single sex samples and the assumption that women were necessarily different. Occasionally, in the face of a particularly heinous crime by a woman, the will towards scientific understanding has seemed disproportionately threatened by almost a reversion to dehumanizing such women altogether as 'witches' or 'evil'. There is a long history of this. Although no sex or age group was immune, the witch finders' guide *Malleus Malficarum*, which had already run to 14 editions by 1520, mainly aided the entrapment of women, a pursuit which continued to a degree in various Western countries at least until the early nineteenth century. As Mackay (1869) notes:

So deeply rooted are some errors, that ages cannot remove them (p.190).

In the UK, Myra Hindley was effectively demonized in this way for her part in the so-called Moors Murders between 1963 and 1965, and an academic understanding of her role remains elusive. Other individual cases have fared slightly better and, while they help little in forming an overview of criminality among women, such accounts are worth reading for the light they throw both on the pathway into *and out of* the rare but extreme violence which even young girls may inflict (e.g. Sereny, 1972, 1998). Perhaps the most important study to date which offers more truly scientific balance was drawn from the Dunedin birth cohort (Moffitt et al., 2001). As a population based, multi-informant, prospective study, in which primary participants were about equally distributed by sex, it allowed, more-or-less for the first time, thorough testing of some of the more important claims about female:male differences in antisocial and criminal behaviour. Some accepted truths in rates of antisocial behaviour were confirmed, including the generally lower rate of offending and the generally lesser seriousness of female crime, but other findings were perhaps less expected. While the female participants had lower scores than their male peers on physical aggression and violence in every age band, an important exception lay in partner violence, where the violent behaviour of the then young women matched or even exceeded that of the young men. Rates of self-reported drug and alcohol offences in the mid-teens were almost the same.

In 1971, d'Orban reflected on eight different explanations for the female: male disparity in crime rates (1–8 below), which we use as a starting point, develop according to subsequent research findings and supplement with further perspectives from Widom (1978), Høigård (1990) and the Moffitt–Caspi group (e.g. Moffitt et al., 2001). Although, here, d'Orban and the other writers were often considering crime generally, the categories of explanation would as well assist with thinking about differences in violent crime more specifically. It may be assumed that the same broad theoretical models of the pathway to antisocial violence (discussed more extensively in chapter 9), such as attachment theory or social conditioning, apply to women as to men, although authors rarely make specific reference to women as a group separate from men. Attempts at adapting models so that they are more gender specific include reference to the 'battered woman syndrome' (e.g. Walker, 1989), psychoanalytic perspectives which have focused on female perversions and projective identification underlying psychological distress and anger (e.g. Welldon, 1991; Motz, 2001), and feminist adaptations of social conditioning theory.

Explanations for Female:Male Differences in Crime Rates and Patterns

1. The masked character of female crime

Early claims that women offend as much as men, but do so in a way that never reaches official statistics (Pollak, 1950) have been partially vindicated by the Moffitt et al. (2001) findings that violence at home is equally distributed between the sexes. By definition, however, hidden criminality is difficult to study. Other self-report studies also tend to show that the sex difference is sustained for antisocial behaviour more generally, for example in girls self-reporting less delinquency than boys (Honkatukia, 2011).

2. The effect of social upheaval and female emancipation

Social upheaval and social control may seem like polar opposites, but often co-exist. It has been argued that, when the protective effect of the family is weakened by family disruption, the incidence of female crime may increase (Pollak, 1950). An extension of this idea is that the traditional role of women in society tends to reduce their crime rate, but there is evidence against this. Leventhal (1977) found that criminal women were no feminists; on the contrary, relative to non-criminal controls, female criminals were against women's liberation. Widom (1978) found that female offenders adopted traditional attitudes toward women and their role in society. Steffensmeier (1980), however, found that economic marginalization of women is a factor in their criminality. While it is true that countries with rigid cultural and religious restraints on women also, in effect, restrict their opportunity to participate in crime, in more liberal cultures criminal women are mainly those who have dropped out from society, not those who have benefited from the freedom to be educated, work, vote and generally participate in society (e.g. Høigård, 1990). Høigård went on to develop an 'expulsion theory' on how women, independently of men, are divided into social classes, with those involved in crime having a problematic relationship of some kind with the labour market. She concluded that there is a connection between gender role and criminality, and that the censoring characteristics of the female role modify women's criminality. The female role, reflected in the specialized but transient position of many in the labour market, their specialized place in the family unit and the ideology behind this, is still a barrier to crime. Høigård predicted that women's criminality will continue to increase but will also remain at a considerably lower level than that of men.

3. Social controls

Regardless of 'emancipation', girls are likely to experience more family controls than are boys, partly because of fears of sexual vulnerability (e.g. Crockett et al., 1996). Furthermore, behaviours at the borderline with delinquency and sexual experimentation are more likely to be construed as merely 'adventurous' for boys but unacceptable for girls. Social controls may change over time, however, for the better as well as worse. In Finland, data show that between 1995 and 2004 people under 18, regardless of sex, had become less tolerant of crime and more punitive. Their more widespread self-reported conformity was reflected in lower rates of participation in property crimes and stabilization of the prevalence of violent and drug-related offences. Those who do offend, however, appear to do so more often, and within the offending group there are proportionately more girls than there used to be, although, as Høigård predicted, they remain in the minority (Kivivuori, 2002; Kivivuori and Salmi, 2005; Honkatukia, 2011).

4. Administrative aspects of crime and mental disorder

Women may be treated differently by the criminal justice system. One suggestion has been that they may receive more lenient treatment in the legislative processes than men. In the USA, a study of murder cases supported this chivalry/paternalism hypothesis (Franklin and Fearn, 2008). Certainly, for indictable offences in England and Wales recorded in 2009, women were about half as likely as men to be given an immediate custodial sentence (14%:27%), and they tend to serve shorter sentences whether in prison or in the community (Ministry of Justice, 2010b). This is more or less consistent with earlier findings (Hedderman and Hough, 1994) but, to be sure that there is any real leniency towards women here, the details of the index offence and antecedents would have to be studied more closely. With respect to the specific offence of killing one's own infant of 12 months or younger, a British study found that fathers received more severe sentences than mothers, and the authors speculated that sentencing might be related more to the sex of the perpetrator than to the violence of the offence (Marks and Kumar, 1993). Oberman (1996), however, commented on a polarization with respect to such women, along the lines already mentioned – as either crazy women who should be treated with lenience or as evil women who should be punished particularly harshly. A Swedish study with practising forensic psychiatric clinicians, psychology students and chief judges, using homicide case vignettes varying the gender of the perpetrator, found that the clinicians and students were more likely to assess the female perpetrators as needing a psychiatric disposal (Yourstone et al., 2008). The judges tended to make decisions according to their own sex – female judges were more likely to choose psychiatric disposal for the female offenders, but the male judges favoured the men in this respect.

Risk of offending may also be decreased by the fact that women access mental health services more often than men (Alha and Pirkola, 2006). This may be both because women themselves are more likely to seek help and because they are more likely to be seen as worthy of admission, or, even, safe to admit (Maden et al., 1994a,b).

5. Constitutional predisposition and stress

It has been proposed that girls have greater constitutional resistance against crime and only when extreme adverse psychological or environmental influences overwhelm this resistance do girls become delinquent (Otterström, 1946). It has long been recognized that the brains of male infants mature at a different rate from those of female infants, leaving young boys potentially more exposed to cerebral damage from infections (e.g. Taylor, 1969). In this context, it is perhaps not surprising that the main difference which Moffitt et al. (2001) found between the sexes in risk factors which might predispose to a criminal career was that the boys had higher rates than the girls of neurocognitive compromise, with hyperactivity and early emerging 'uncontrolled temperament'. The Moffitt–Caspi group do not make much mention of autistic traits, but, these too tend to be far less common among girls than boys. Such traits are also neurologically based, and at least in part may emerge from the same sort of cerebral compromise. Further, there may be some parallels between autistic traits and so-called psychopathic traits. Other studies of developmental trajectories of delinquent youths have shown more similarities than differences between the sexes (e.g. Miller et al., 2010; Odgers et al., 2008).

6. Genetic factors

Moffitt et al. (2001) demonstrated that an important difference between the sexes in evolution of antisocial behaviour was the extent to which they fitted her early-onset-life-course-persistent versus later-onset-adolescence-limited taxonomy (Moffitt, 1993). While it was possible to find girls who fitted the former pattern, the life-course-persistent type was almost exclusively confined to males in the Dunedin birth cohort. As this was the pattern most closely linked to neurocognitive abnormalities, aside from the possibility that girls are relatively protected from early cerebral insults, genetic differences may be hypothesized. Miller et al. (2010) also found that boys were more likely than girls to be on a chronically delinquent pathway, but they did find a small but discernible group of girls with early onset and persistent delinquency. There is still much to learn in this area, but there are suggestions of sex differences in genetic risk for antisocial behaviour (e.g. Eley et al., 1999) and for potentially related behaviours such as substance misuse (e.g. Miles et al., 2002) (see also chapter 16).

7. Physique

d'Orban (1971) noted that earlier studies suggested that delinquent girls were physically overdeveloped, taller and weightier than average, or more 'masculine', so we have included this category for completeness, but there is no up-to-date evidence to support this.

8. Physiological factors

An obvious difference between women and men lies in their hormonal balance. In the nineteenth century it was widely thought that menstruation was associated with female crime, particularly with shoplifting and violence (Pollak, 1950). There was a short vogue during the 1980s for using the premenstrual syndrome (PMS) as a criminal defence in courts, with some success in the UK and in Australia, but little in the USA (d'Orban 1983; Lewis, 1990; McSherry, 1994: Downs, 2002). Although it may be that the risks of behavioural disturbance are increased around this time in a woman's menstrual cycle, the main effect is probably in a subgroup of female offenders who are prone to psychological or behavioural disturbances at other times too. Thus, as McSherry argues, while it may be appropriate to ask for PMS to be taken into account at the time of sentencing – and it may indeed have some relevance for treatment – it is not helpful generally to build a picture of women as not responsible 'because of their raging hormones'. Downs (2002) noted a small subgroup of women who may actually develop psychotic symptoms premenstrually. For those who have a psychotic illness, it has been noted that psychotic symptom presentation varies over the course of the menstrual cycle (Hallonquist et al., 1993; Reicher-Rossler et al., 1994) and, separately, it has been noted that women are more vulnerable to psychotic breakdown when post-partum and after the menopause (Häfner et al., 1998, 2003). Treatment with oestrogen replacement, with or without progesterone supplements, has, however, proved disappointing (Chua et al., 2005).

The puerperium has been associated with psychosis, commonly manifesting with unusual psychotic symptoms, bizarre behaviour, and a labile clinical picture (Spinelli, 2004). In this context, violence against the mother's own baby may occur, although this is not common. When considering pregnancy associated mortality, however, homicide and suicide are important contributors (Palladino et al., 2011). In the UK, suicide is the leading cause of maternal death during or up to a year after pregnancy, with violent methods of suicide predominant and, it is argued, preventable (Oates, 2003). Reporting on figures from the 2001 Confidential Enquiry into Maternal Deaths 1997–1999, Oates noted that almost all of these women were known to psychiatric services, and nearly half in contact at the time of death. She also highlighted an apparently particularly high risk among professional women. This reached its apogee for the UK's Royal College of Psychiatrists when one of its members died with her baby after suicidal acts (North East London Strategic Health Authority, 2003). In this 1997–1999 cohort of mothers, there was no loss of infant or maternal life through suicidal acts when women with mental illness had been admitted to a mother and baby unit with their baby.

9. Social and demographic characteristics and childhood experiences

Criminal women are more likely than not to come from lower socioeconomic groups and from families with a high incidence of parental absenteeism and/or psychopathology. In a large, Finnish, prospective female birth cohort study, women whose father had been absent during childhood were over twice as likely to become criminal as those with a constant paternal presence; this was the strongest risk factor for criminality among them, although maternal smoking during pregnancy and being the first born were also important factors (Kemppainen et al., 2001). According to Dunedin birth cohort data, however, where it was possible to compare women who had sustained criminal convictions directly with their male peers, women do not differ from men in socio-demographic factors and childhood disadvantage of various kinds (Moffitt et al., 2001). Among homicide offenders specifically, another Finnish study found that women were significantly more likely than men to report having had experiences of violence in childhood and less likely than their male peers to have made a timely completion of primary education (Putkonen et al., 2011). Moreover, among female homicide offenders traumatic childhood experiences, especially the loss of a parent, were related to the interpersonal, affective and lifestyle features of psychopathy, whereas in males they were related only to antisocial features (Weizmann-Henelius et al., 2010a). An evaluation of the predictive validity of the Level of Service/Case Management Inventory (LS/CMI) found no sex differences in any of its eight domains individually, but that a total score reflective of criminogenic risk and need was more strongly predictive of recidivism among women than men (Andrews et al., 2011).

10. Psychiatric diagnosis

We have already alluded to a prevailing idea that if women commit crimes, they must be 'mad'. Widom (1978), however, cautioned against concluding that female offenders are more likely to have a mental disorder than their male peers. Figures for rates of psychiatric disorder among offenders generally are not readily available, but figures from various subgroups offer a complex message. According to a systematic review of studies of, collectively, nearly 23,000 prisoners, of whom about 19% were women, there is little evidence that mental disorder *per se* is more prevalent among female prisoners (Fazel and Danesh,

2002). Nevertheless, at least in England and Wales, women seem to fare less well than men during imprisonment, with about one in three women in prison harming themselves compared with fewer than one in ten men (Ministry of Justice, 2010b). This may mainly reflect the higher risk of non-lethal self-harm among women generally (e.g. Madge et al., 2011). Historically, women may have been less likely to have had substance misuse disorders (e.g. Butler et al., 2005), but there is evidence that, at least for more serious offenders with mental health disorders, women have nearly caught up with men (MacMahon et al., 2003; Häkkänen-Nyholm et al., 2009; Putkonen et al., 2011a).

Taking a perspective of population attributable risk, there is a suggestion that the burden of serious mental disorder may be particularly heavy for women. In Sweden, Fazel and Grann (2006) calculated the proportion of violence in the community that could be attributed to psychosis. It was almost equivalent for women and men between the ages of 15 and 24; at older ages, not much more than 5% of violent crime committed by men was by men with psychosis, but up to 20% of violent crime by women was by women with psychosis. In a later study, they found that moderation of the relationship by substance misuse comorbidity was more pronounced among women (Fazel et al., 2009). Data on homicide more specifically are only partly consistent but, here, risk ratios may be exaggerated by the fact that female perpetrated homicide is rare. Eronen et al. (1996a) and Schanda et al. (2004) found the population attributable risk to psychosis was similarly elevated for women, and disproportionately raised further for women with comorbid alcohol dependency (Eronen et al., 1996c). Another Finnish study, however, of people convicted of homicide between 1995 and 2004, found no such gender differences (Putkonen et al., 2011).

11. Personality

Widom (1978) distinguished several disordered personality traits from diagnoses of mental disorder and, in turn, the 'normal criminal'. She listed three personality types: 'primary psychopathy' – low in anxiety, high in aggression and impulsiveness; secondary, 'neurotic psychopathy' – high in aggression and impulsiveness, but also high in anxiety and depression; and 'overcontrolled', which she considered underpinned mechanisms in both female and male offending. More recently, researchers have struggled with the concept of 'psychopathy' in relation to women (see also below).

Some Offence Categories of Particular Interest with Respect to Women

An overview

Women are less likely than men to be convicted in almost every offence category; and that remains true, even though the conviction rate for women is rising and that for men falling in a number of countries. In the USA, in the 1990s, it was estimated that the number of female defendants convicted of felonies has grown at over twice the rate of increase in male defendants (Greenfeld and Snell, 1999). In 2009 women accounted for 25% of all *arrests* in the USA. The female and male arrest rate trends showed some differences in specific crimes between 1980 and 2009. By 2009 the female arrest rate for simple assault, for example, was nearly four times its 1980 level (an increase of 281%) and the increase among men was much lower (69%); a similar pattern was observed for aggravated assault arrests. Over the same period, female arrest rates for burglary remained fairly constant while those for men fell (by 61%) (Snyder, 2011). In Finland, between 1991 and 2010, women's share of all offences solved by the police had increased from approximately 13% to 19%; embezzlement and petty theft accounted for the largest single cluster of female crime (30%), while the proportion of women's offending attributable to violence has been rising, from about 5% in 1980 to about 17% in 2010 (Honkatukia, 2011). In 2006, women accounted for 13% of all convictions, including 13% of violent offences (Official Statistics of Finland, 2011). Also in Finland, women's share of homicide convictions increased from nearly 8% in the period 1977–1989 to nearly 11% in 1990–2008 (Putkonen, 2011a). Criminal statistics for England and Wales show that, in 2009, women accounted for about 15% of convictions for indictable offences, but confirmed that numbers of women dealt with in the criminal justice for the 5 years 2005–2009 had been rising while the numbers of men had been falling (Ministry of Justice, 2010b). Here, the top offence group for women (45%) as well as men (28%) was theft and handling stolen goods, with the other acquisitive offences of women being more commonly fraud, while men were more commonly convicted of burglary or robbery; the second most common offence for women was violence against the person (W: 13%, M: 16.5%).

Trend statistics suggest that girls are forming an increasing proportion of juvenile offenders. In the USA, in 1980, 20% of all juvenile arrests were of girls; by 2003, this percentage had increased to 29%. The female contribution to violent crime arrests increased from 10% to 18% and for property crime from 19% to 32% over the same period (Snyder and Sickmund, 2006). In Finland, a comparison of the years 1997 and 2010 showed that girls' share of all crimes known to the police increased from 15% to 22% (Honkatukia, 2011). Self-reported crime rates did not increase comparably, suggesting that the figures may best reflect an increase in control, reporting to the police, processing, and registering. We have already noted some possible differences in the treatment of women in the criminal justice system.

Prostitution

Prostitution has been labelled as 'the oldest profession', but, while it is a legal source of income in some countries, it remains a criminal offence in others and, in some, it is punishable by death. In Sweden a 1999 law prohibited *the purchase* of sexual services, thus shifting the burden of criminality on to the one who buys the sexual services (Ekberg, 2004). In this context the person who is bought is construed as a victim. Since the introduction of this law, street prostitution in Sweden has been halved (Ministry of Justice (Sweden), 2010). Norway has become the second country to legislate along these lines. In England and Wales, while activities such as loitering or soliciting for prostitution remain offences, the Crown Prosecution Service (CPS) issues regular guidance which emphasizes its close working relationship with the Association of Chief Officers of Police (ACPO) in a commitment to recognizing prostitution as a victim-centred crime (e.g. CPS, 2011). Women are so commonly implicated in prostitution *per se*, and in this context trafficked, exploited or abused, that the CPS treats the matter as sexual exploitation within its violence against women strategy. This encourages police to help the women make links to services to help them develop routes out of the activity and develop safer lifestyles while investigating and facilitating prosecution of those who exploit, traffic or otherwise abuse the women in these ways.

Prostitutes, whether female, male or transgendered, have increased mortality and morbidity rates and form a troubled group. In a study of female prison inmates, for example, a substantial relationship was found between Cluster A personality disorders and prostitution (Warren et al., 2002). The authors considered the inevitable conundrum – does psychiatric disorder leave individuals more vulnerable to sexual exploitation? Does sexual exploitation, not uncommonly also a feature of childhood for this group, open up vulnerability to disorder? Is there a common antecedent to the disorder and prostitution? Or, as with so much socially unacceptable behaviour, are people with mental disorder just much more likely to be caught at it? Then, too, there is a close relationship for many sex workers between the sale of their bodies and drug abuse (Byqvist, 1999). A complication for this group may be that even when women are offered help for their addiction and possible ways out of prostitution, their intimate partners are often also addicts, and they are not helped; the women are thus, essentially, forced to keep working in the sex industry for the sake of their partners (Smith and Marshall, 2007). Harcourt and Donovan's (2005) literature review on prostitution found that the reasons for sex work varied, but most had a strong economic basis. Street or other public place was the most widespread type of prostitution globally, though it was often regarded most undesirable because of the dangers of violence and other forms of hostility, and probably increased risk of sexually transmitted infections.

Sexual offending by women is rare, but not unknown (e.g. West et al., 2011; Wijkman, 2011; see also chapter 10 and sexual abuse of children, below).

Arson

Arson and criminal damage by fire are offences which follow from a wide range of motives, including the frankly commercial. At the turn of the nineteenth to twentieth centuries, arson was regarded as a crime of women – mainly young female servants (Barker, 1994; see also chapter 11). In reality, again, men predominate in criminal statistics for these offences; among inpatients in specialist secure psychiatric facilities, arson was the index offence for about 40% of the female residents and studies have consistently shown that these are the only offences which are significantly more common among the women than the men in such settings (e.g. in the UK: Taylor, 1997; Coid et al., 2000). An early study of women in a high security hospital showed that arson may well be under-reported among women, since, at that time, fewer than half of the women detained there after fire-setting had actually been charged with this offence (Tennant et al., 1971). Linaker (2000) sent a questionnaire to each psychiatrist in charge of the treatment of in- or outpatients over the age of 18 throughout Norway in 1995, asking about diagnosis, behaviour disorder and violence. Fifty-four women were identified who had been violent or dangerous, most of whom (44) had psychosis, their only significant difference from their 275 violent male peers being in their propensity for arson. Sometimes, in our experience, women also set fire to themselves, even when in hospital or prison. It is interesting to contemplate the motives attributed to arsonists by Lewis and Yarnell (1951), a classification that has been the basis of so many others (see also chapter 11): (1) reactions to society; (2) vengeance against an employer; (3) simple revenge; (4) jealous rage; (5) opportunity for heroism; (6) perverted sexual pleasure. Apart from jealous rage, which is occasionally relevant, the women we see do not fit with these types. Commonly they are women who, whether suffering from psychosis or not, have had prolonged experience of abuse, and there is a sense in which fire has a cleansing or purging role for them. Gannon (2010) has further highlighted how much more research is needed for this small group of offenders. She suggested prevalence of depression and psychosis and absence of sexual fetishism associated with the fire are some of the key features which differentiate female arsonists from their male counterparts. An American study of 407 people with a lifetime history of firesetting found that the women in the sample were significantly more likely than the men to have a lifetime diagnosis of alcohol misuse and/or antisocial personality disorder or schizoid personality disorder (Hoertel et al., 2011).

Child abduction

In England and Wales, the taking of a child without her/his legally designated parent's or guardian's consent may be dealt with as kidnapping, under common law. This may apply to a person who knows the child as much as to a stranger. In addition, law has been enacted to provide further protections, such as The Child Abduction Act 1984, which makes it a criminal offence for a 'person connected with the child' to take her/him out of the UK. Where the parents are unmarried, the mother generally has automatic parental rights, and the father only acquires legal parental status by court order or formal agreement with the mother. It should be noted, however, that each jurisdiction in the UK has its own legislation in this respect, so any order made in one UK jurisdiction must be registered in the others to have effect there.

This note on the legal situation highlights the fact that child abduction may be one (or more) of many things. Child abduction by a 'person connected to the child' is usually reflective of a broken parental relationship and care or custody disputes. It is not commonly a maternal offence because of the likely parental rights balance, but, as with most offences, women are occasionally perpetrators; a few such abductions end in tragedy because the deprived parent, probably as a result of mental disorder, would prefer to die with the child(ren) than have them live with the other parent. Child abduction, or attempted abduction by a stranger, is generally but not exclusively by men, sometimes for financial gain as in extortion/ransom demands or trafficking, sometimes for sexual abuse, these categories overlapping. The category of interest with respect to women is the tiny 'cared for' abduction group. In England and Wales in 2002–2003 there were 757 convictions for attempted or actual child abduction, with the overall average age of the abducted children being 10 (Newiss and Fairbrother, 2004). Although not specified in this document, the small group of 14 attempted abductions, often by impersonating a health or social services professional, best maps on to this little group of mainly female offenders.

The perspective of Beasley et al. (2009) cuts across legal niceties and placed child abductors into two groups. The first was made up of offenders (42%) who had abducted a child who was later found alive and the second of offenders (58%) who had abducted a child who was either found murdered or was still missing and presumed dead. Women had committed 31 (10%) of the offences in the first group and 10 (2%) of the offences in the second.

Women and violent offending

Non-lethal violent offending is much more common than homicide among both women and men, but it is not often studied among women. Most of the risk factors for violence are similar for women and men, and a recent study has shown that the aetiology of violent behaviour may not be as gender specific as previously presumed (Lewis, 2010). We have already referred to some differences between women and men when psychosis is implicated in violence (Taylor and Bragado-Jimenez, 2009; Fazel et al., 2009). Intoxicated violent female offenders, however, exhibit more of the characteristics previously found in violent men than do the non-intoxicated female offenders (Weizmann-Henelius et al., 2009). In other studies, the finding from the Dunedin birth cohort by Moffitt et al. (2001) that inter-partner violence seems to be at least as frequent among women as among men has been endorsed (Archer, 2000; Whitaker et al., 2007). Of particular importance here is a Finnish study with children, who reported that they had witnessed violence inflicted by the mother on the father in equal measure to that of father on mother (Ellonen et al., 2008). Equivalence of such violence may be especially true of younger groups, and their stated reasons for the violence tend to be similar (Fiebert and Gonzalez, 1997; Dutton and Nicholls, 2005). Among violent relationships, nearly half have been characterized as reciprocally violent (Whitaker and Nicholls, 2005). Women, however, seem more prepared to report partner violence. In Finnish victim studies, it has been found that 10% of such violence appears to have been reported to the police when a woman was the main victim but only 4% when a man was (Salmi et al., 2009).

Child abuse

Child abuse occurs worldwide, and may be sexual, violent or emotional (see chapters 9 and 10). Neglect and reckless behaviour in relation to a fetus or child is sometimes included too. Counterintuitive though it may be, women may directly abuse children; they may also fail to protect their children from an abusive partner.

Child sexual abuse

Women rarely become sex offenders, and this is the area of crime where the female:male ratio is at its lowest, but child sexual abuse by women does occasionally occur (see chapter 10). A more prominent and under-researched problem in this area is that some mothers fail to protect their children from sexual abuse, sometimes through passive collusion with the abusing man. Wijkman et al. (2010), in their classification of female sex offenders, referred to a 'passive mothers' group, who were the oldest of the four groups suggested (over 41 years) and the child victims most likely to fall between 7 and 11 years. In clinical practice, we have worked with predatory male paedophiles who have targeted vulnerable women because of their children, and some of those women have been unable to give up the financial security, rewards or sense of their own safety that this may apparently bring them. Patients talking about their own experience of child abuse may report as much

anger with their disbelieving or passive mother as with their actual abuser.

Violent child abuse and neglect

Children are probably as likely to be abused by women as men. It is hard to be sure, because child abuse is almost certainly under-reported, but some child self-report studies tend to support this position. In the USA, nearly two-fifths of child abuse victims have been found to have been maltreated by their mother alone, one-fifth by their father alone and 18% by both parents (National Child Abuse and Neglect Data System (NCANDS), 2009). In Finland there is no significant difference in violence inflicted on children by mothers and fathers, although the occurrence of disciplinary violence has significantly decreased since 1988 (Ellonen et al., 2013). In a self-report study, a quarter of 9th graders reported that their mother had shaken them by the hair and 18% that their father had; serious violence was, in fact, reported to have been perpetrated more often by the mothers than the fathers (Ellonen et al., 2013). Child abuse is rarely lethal, but it may be. In the USA, in 2009, the national fatality rate per 100,000 children in the population was 2.34, with the fatality rate having increased over the previous 5 years (NCANDS, 2009). More fatalities were caused by mothers alone (27%) than fathers alone (15%).

Factors which put a mother at risk for abusing her own child(ren) include having herself been a victim of childhood abuse, young maternal age, inadequate social support, poverty, low educational level, inter-partner violence, maternal stress, substance abuse, and depression; in addition, child related issues such as infant prematurity, delayed development or 'being demanding' may increase the chance of child harm (e.g. Windham et al., 2004; Wu et al., 2004; Taylor et al., 2009; Berlin et al., 2011; Hien et al., 2010).

A 2002 study of children identified as victims of abuse or neglect by US child protection services suggested that prevention of such behaviour by mothers would be enhanced by giving them relevant prenatal attention. The two factors with the highest adjusted relative risks (RR) of a child subsequently coming to harm were the mother's smoking during pregnancy (RR 2.8) and her having at least two children already (RR 2.7) (Wu et al., 2004). Wu and colleagues recommended that greater emphasis should be placed on exploring underlying stressful conditions for which smoking may be a marker and providing more information about and access to family planning options. Support for women with larger families, regardless, might also be indicated. Another study noted the relevance of intergenerational drug misuse, with mothers whose own parents had had alcohol- or drug-related problems being more likely to have polydrug problems themselves, in turn associated with poor parenting (Locke and Newcomb, 2004). A Japanese study suggested that, although negative or merely passive acceptance of the maternal role was related to neglectful parenting behaviour, it was also related to aggressive parenting (Sagami et al., 2004). The correlation between postnatal depression and neglectful or, especially, aggressive parenting behaviour was significant.

Depression has been more widely studied in relation to child abuse, but the picture is not simple. Community-resident mothers identified as being at risk for maltreating their child(ren) were studied during the first 3 years after the birth of their infants. Severe physical assault against the child was significantly associated with maternal depression and partner violence when the mother was also a perpetrator of that partner violence and not only the victim (Windham et al., 2004). Among drug-using mothers, the higher the mother's perception of her infant's demands, the greater was the likelihood of a physical assault on the child. In this high-risk sample, abuse was not associated with mother's age, education, race, parity, or household income level. These authors concluded that treatment of depression in new mothers is as important for the safety of their children as for the mothers' wellbeing. Taylor et al. (2009), by contrast, found that major maternal depression conferred essentially no independent risk for child maltreatment (except for spanking) after controlling for confounding factors such as inter-partner violence. They concluded that associations between types of violence are complex and that integration of assessment and management of inter-partner violence and child maltreatment is needed in order to prevent or minimize either. Further, Hien et al. (2010) found that depressed mothers did *not* differ from substance misusing mothers in their potential for child abuse and that deficits in ability to manage anger arousal and reactivity were significantly associated with abuse.

Factitious and induced illness (Munchausen syndrome by proxy) and sudden infant death

Undue parental concern over a child's health is not an offence, even though it may ultimately harm a child through unnecessary medical investigations. Induction of symptoms of illness in a child is a form of assault and, if detected, might be treated as such under criminal law. If caught at a stage when there has been no physical injury to the child, it is arguable that the parent needs professional clinical assessment and treatment rather than prosecution, but this is undoubtedly a potentially dangerous behaviour which requires some intervention of an appropriate kind. Harm arising from such circumstances may even extend to child deaths. In Rosenberg's (1987) series, 10 of the 117 children died. Davis et al. (1998) similarly confirmed high mortality as well as morbidity. The problem has already been considered in some detail in chapter 9, but, because it is almost exclusively a female problem and because of its importance as a risky and potentially criminal behaviour

on the part of a small group of women, we will also consider it briefly here. In their 2-year prospective series of 128 cases, McClure et al. (1996) found that 85% of the perpetrators were the mothers. Earlier studies (e.g. Rosenberg, 1987) described only female perpetrators.

Three forms of this type of factitious disorder have been considered: the 'help seekers', the 'active inducers' and the 'doctor addicts'. Bools (1996), in his review of so-called Munchausen by proxy syndrome, recommended a classification that takes account of the consequences of the abuse together with details of the perpetrator's behaviour and mental state, thus including

1. behavioural descriptive classification of the type of fabrication (verbal fabrication, falsification of specimens and charts, poisoning, smothering, other direct means, withholding nutrients and medicines);
2. the category of child abuse – determined by existing guidelines and procedures;
3. any psychiatric diagnosis applicable to the perpetrator.

Initially, the observed behaviour of the mother, or very occasionally both parents or some other carer, would be that of an exceptionally caring mother/person, unusually close to her child, over-involved and over-dependent (Bools 1996). Some mothers are surprisingly calm and trusting despite the seriousness of their child's condition; others are very critical. Stanton and Simpson (2001) reported a tragic case in which a mother clearly loved her baby, but nevertheless smothered her. Their observations about the tensions in the assessor's role are useful here, noting:

the difficult cognitive processes involved for a paediatrician to shift from being the parent's ally in attempting to alleviate a child's suffering, to suspecting the parent of being the agent responsible for the child's suffering.

Common, but not invariable, features of the women involved are unresolved traumatic experiences and/or unstable attachment relationships in their own childhood (Gray and Bentovim, 1996; Adshead and Bluglass, 2005). Bass and Jones (2011) studied the records of 28 mothers (mean age 31.3 years) who, between 1996 and 2009, had been referred for a detailed psychiatric assessment on suspicion of fabricating or inducing illness in their child. Over half of the mothers had involved the child in a web of deceit, but the reflection of their own childhood problems was clear for some; these had a history of feigning symptoms themselves when young, in order to avoid beatings. Reports of treatment outcomes to date have been little more encouraging than for the more classic forms of factitious disorders (Schreier and Libow, 1993), although the literature is hardly replete with evidence of treatment efforts here. Key issues are that it seems likely that some form of dissociation is involved; the woman (or others) are, by definition, not able to recognize their own distress or disorder and can only present this by these indirect means. Furthermore, where attachment disorders are at the heart of the problem, it is likely to be exceptionally difficult for a therapist to achieve engagement with the person as a patient, although not impossible (see also chapter 16 on treatment of personality disorder and chapter 28 on trauma and attachment disorders). Guidance for clinicians in this difficult area emphasizes thorough evaluation of all medical charts as well as the patients themselves and, above all, clear communication between all those professionals involved in the case (Stirling, 2007).

Women and homicide

Homicide has already been discussed in chapter 9. More details about its relationship to mental disorder are in the relevant disorder chapters. Here, the focus is on those subgroups of women among whom the risk of homicidal behaviour is very high and on gender differences in homicidal behaviour.

Women account for about one-tenth of the homicide convictions in many countries (e.g. USA: Federal Bureau of Investigation, 2011; Finland, Sweden and the Netherlands: Granath et al., 2011). In England and Wales, during the 10 years 1997–2006, women accounted for 589 of the 5857 recorded homicides in the period (National Confidential Inquiry into Suicide and Homicide, 2010), and this 10% contribution was more-or-less stable for the period. In Finland, however, the proportionate contribution of women to homicide convictions has been increasing – from 6% (1977–1989) to 11% (1990–2008) (Putkonen, 2011). The increase seems to arise from cases related to alcohol use (Putkonen, 2008). A subgroup seems to be emerging of female homicide offenders who resemble their male counterparts more and more, with their victims more likely to be strangers, or at least not intimates, the offender poorly adjusted within society and intoxicated (Putkonen et al., 2008; Weizmann-Henelius et al., 2009, 2012; Putkonen et al., 2011).

Women who kill have more often than not attacked someone close to them, particularly their partner and/or children. Other family killings, including the killing of a parent (Marleau et al., 2003; d'Orban and O'Connor, 1989), are unusual, as are stranger killings (Häkkänen-Nyholm et al., 2009). Outside Finland, studies in the latter part of the twentieth century portrayed female homicide as the result of interpersonal conflicts, with women commonly defending themselves (Husain et al., 1983; Jurik and Winn, 1990; Masle et al., 2000). In one Finnish pre-trial study of this period, nearly one-third of women who had killed reported during their pretrial assessment that they had previously suffered long-term violence at the hands of their victim (Putkonen et al., 2001a). By contrast, in a *post-trial* interview study of 39 women hospitalized or imprisoned in Finland, only four of them reported that their victim had been violent over a long period, or her relationship one of conflict (Weizmann-Henelius et al., 2003). Another Finnish study comparing female and male homicides during 1995–2004 showed that women reported self-defence (or accident) as the motive in 16% and men in 12% while a quarrel or jealousy was the motive for 37% of the women and 22% of the men (Häkkänen-Nyholm et al., 2009). Yet, in intimate partner homicides, women's defensive reactions following abuse differ from similar homicides perpetrated by men (Weizmann-Henelius, 2012).

Mental disorder seems to have a significantly greater impact on the risk of homicide by women than by men. Both antisocial personality disorder and substance misuse or dependency are among disorders which have been found to affect the risk of homicide disproportionately (Eronen et al., 1996b). Evidence with respect to psychosis has been more mixed with Eronen et al. (1996c) and Wallace et al. (1998) finding more or less identical odds ratios between women and men for risk of homicide with schizophrenia, while Schanda et al. (2004) and Hodgins (1992) found a higher risk of homicide for women with schizophrenia. Overall, it is likely that a higher proportion of homicidal behaviour among women can be attributed to psychosis than among men (Fazel and Grann, 2006).

Other issues which have been raised include the suggestion that, where mental disorder is a problem, its nature may influence the relationship to the victim in particular ways. In both Danish and Finnish studies, for example, it is unusual for women who kill a spouse to have a psychotic illness, but much more likely that a woman who kills a child has psychosis (Gottlieb et al., 1987; Putkonen et al., 2001a). Women are more like men, however, in the interaction between disorder and substance misuse; intoxication at the time of homicide appears to be more prevalent among women with personality disorder than those with psychosis (Spunt et al., 1996; Putkonen et al., 2001a).

It is extremely rare for a woman to become a serial killer, so there is little research on this. When it does occur, the motive is generally material and such women, unlike corresponding men, tend to know their victims, for example in a caring/treatment context, and their methods are usually covert; sadistic gratification hardly occurs (Frei et al., 2006). Mass murder, such as school or market place massacre, is an even more atypical event among women than men, although in a domestic setting, women may kill several children or the whole family. As far as we know only one case of a female workplace mass murderer has been reported (Katsavdakis et al., 2011). Here there was clear murder–suicide intent. The woman had a history of chronic paranoid psychosis. Women have been recruited as suicide bombers by terrorist groups; informal reports suggest that they are generally women who have been seriously traumatized by extensive and sudden family loss in the ongoing conflict, but, almost by definition, formal firsthand study cannot be done.

Filicide

The victims of female homicide perpetrators are so frequently their own children that we will consider filicide, the killing of a child by her/his parent, as a special category. Filicide has been reported in ancient cultures and, at times, has been socially accepted. At other times, in some cultures, the thought of a mother killing her child seems so terrible and so far against the traditional concept of maternal love that such mothers can only be termed crazy (Oberman, 2003) or 'evil'.

The estimated rate of child homicide per 100,000 inhabitants is 1.92 for girls and 2.93 for boys of 17 years or under (Pinheiro, 2006). These rates are considered likely to be underestimates, especially for infanticides and neonaticides, for various reasons, including classification difficulties and differences within and between reporting systems and the very nature of the deaths. These are, for example, often covert – a body may never be found in cases of neonaticide – or the cause of death cannot be proved beyond reasonable doubt (Putkonen et al., 2009a; Flynn et al., 2009). Children are at greatest risk of being killed on their first day, then during the first year of their life, and thereafter the risk decreases steadily (Bourget and Labelle, 1992; Marks and Kumar, 1996; Putkonen, 2009b). In the US series of Overpeck et al. (1998), half of the killings during the first year of life had occurred by the fourth month. The younger the child, the more probable it is that the perpetrator is the mother (Marks and Kumar, 1996; Bourget et al., 2007; Putkonen et al., 2009a). Overall, however, reported percentages of mothers and fathers killing their children vary across studies, partly because of methodological differences and partly perhaps because there are some real international differences. Some report a majority of female perpetrators (e.g. Putkonen et al., 2009b; Goetting, 1988; Resnick, 1969) and some put women in the minority (e.g. Dawson and Langan, 1994; Liem and Koenraadt, 2008; Somander and Rammer, 1991). Complete national figures for England and Wales suggest that, here, the female:male ratio is about 1:3 (Flynn et al., 2009). West et al. (2009) reviewed the international literature, so are probably in a position to provide the best estimate – which they concluded is 1:1.

Special features that differentiate maternal from paternal filicide include victim characteristics, method of killing and filicidal motive as well as perpetrator characteristics (Bourget and Gagné, 2005). Filicidal mothers are, on average, younger than filicidal fathers (Friedman et al., 2005a; Putkonen et al., 2010), but they differ little in their own history of troubled childhoods (Putkonen et al., 2011). Youth, little education and poor experience of childrearing tends to leave such parents without adequate personal resources for coping with stressors (e.g. McKee and Shea, 1998; Overpeck et al., 1998); potentially fatal stressors include additional children, and yet these mothers are often difficult to identify and help as they tend to have little prenatal care. More contemporary studies have also found that economic, educational and occupational difficulties with an impoverished primary support group linked with additional, more immediate stressors are important risk factors (Bourget et al., 2007; Krischer et al., 2007; Stanton and Simpson, 2002; Putkonen et al., 2011; Bourget et al., 2007; Friedman et al., 2005b; West et al., 2009). The violent disintegration of the family unit, which some have regarded as important (Mugavin, 2008), may, however, be less important for filicidal mothers than their male peers (Putkonen et al., 2011). This leads to speculation that the driving forces are more intrapersonal for women but interpersonal for men.

Filicidal mothers neglect, drown or poison their children, while fathers tend to use more overtly violent methods like shooting (Bourget et al., 2007; Putkonen et al., 2011). Such mothers are less likely than such fathers to report retaliation, rage, abuse or impulsivity among their motives (Bourget et al., 2007; Marks and Kumar, 1996; Stanton and Simpson, 2002; Putkonen et al., 2011) and comparatively rarely kill their partner in the context of filicide (Stanton and Simpson, 2002; Putkonen et al., 2011). Mothers are less likely than fathers to be intoxicated at the time of the killing (Bourget and Bradford, 1990; Bourget et al., 2007; Putkonen et al., 2011).

An association between filicide and parental psychiatric illness, especially psychotic depression, has often been reported (e.g. Stanton and Simpson, 2002; Bourget et al., 2007; Friedman and Resnick, 2011; Webb et al., 2007), although actual figures vary (Bourget et al., 2007; Vanamo et al., 2001). Bourget et al. (2007), in their review, concluded that up to 70% of filicidal mothers are depressed and/or psychotic, while, in a separate review, West et al. (2009) focused more on the fathers, finding that just 20% had psychosis, although about half were depressed. An Austrian–Finnish study of all filicides in these countries between 1995 and 2005 allowed for direct comparison between women and men. About 80% of all examined offenders had at least one psychiatric diagnosis (Putkonen et al., 2010), but the filicidal mothers were more likely than the fathers to have psychotic disorders (35%:13%) and less likely to have non-psychotic depression (18%:30%); the women were also more likely than the fathers to have been considered to be not criminally responsible for killing their children. Psychotic mothers seem apart from other filicidal mothers in that they have been reported as more likely to use weapons (Lewis et al., 1998), and to be more educated and less socially disadvantaged than their non-psychotic peers (Lewis and Bunce, 2003).

Alcohol abuse has also been cited as a problem for filicidal mothers (Friedman et al., 2005a), but one study which made direct comparisons of this by sex found that it was less frequently implicated than among fathers (Putkonen et al., 2010). Personality disorders, particularly borderline personality disorder but not psychopathy, have also been reported to have an association with filicide (Bourget et al.,

2007; Dolan et al., 2003; Putkonen et al., 2007a; Putknonen et al., 2009a).

Filicide, infanticide particularly, is more closely linked to suicide than are other forms of homicide (Lester, 1991; Putkonen et al. 2009a), although reported rates of association vary (Bourget et al., 2007; West et al., 2009). It seems, perhaps surprisingly, that fathers tend to have higher rates of filicide–suicide than do mothers (Friedman et al., 2005b). In the Austrian–Finnish study, almost 40% of the fathers committed suicide immediately after the filicide compared with just 15% of the mothers (Putkonen et al., 2010).

An important number of filicidal parents had sought professional help before their offence (Bourget et al., 2007). Friedman et al. (2005a) found that such mothers had a higher rate of prior help seeking, but in the Austrian–Finnish study mentioned, about 30% of offenders had sought help for mental health reasons in the year before the crime, regardless of sex (Putkonen et al., 2010).

Being such a multifaceted crime, filicide has proved difficult to categorize (Pruett, 2002; Silva and Leong, 2003). Nevertheless, several classifications have been proposed, and may help the clinician. One of the most influential was by Resnick (1969), who suggested six main categories:

1. altruistic (e.g. to save the child from the 'evil world');
2. acutely psychotic;
3. unwanted child;
4. accidental;
5. spousal revenge;
6. neonaticide.

Since 1969, several others have modified this, usually keeping neonaticide as a separate group, but with otherwise different reasoning. Scott (1973), for example, considered motivation to be too subjective, overdetermined, or defensive to be helpful, and yet suggested looking at the origin of the 'impulse to kill', which led him to five categories:

1. unwanted child;
2. mercy killing;
3. aggression associated with mental pathology;
4. stimulus arising from outside the victim;
5. stimulus arising from the victim.

After research with a series of 89 women recruited over six years in a pretrial prison sample, d'Orban (1979) offered the most detailed classification, with six categories, which he ranked according to their approximate frequency within a population of maternal filicides:

1. battering mothers (36 cases);
2. mentally ill mothers (24 cases);
3. neonaticides (11 cases);
4. retaliating mothers (9 cases);
5. unwanted children (8 cases);
6. mercy killing (1 case).

Approximately a decade later Bourget and Bradford (1990) suggested:

1. pathological (altruistic or homicide–suicide);
2. accidental (battered child or other behaviour with non-lethal intent);
3. retaliating;
4. neonaticide;
5. paternal.

This classification was later modified Bourget and Gagné (2002) to

1. mentally ill;
2. fatal abuse;
3. retaliating;
4. mercy killing;
5. other/unknown filicide.

Each of these five categories was then modified with further specifications variously of suicidal intent, substance abuse and predictability.

Thus, although there is no single agreed classification of filicidal women, the categories generated by one researcher are recognizable in those generated by another. Further, Stanton and Simpson (2002) caution that sharp separation between fatal child abuse and mentally abnormal filicide is not invariably possible. Then, too, although most of these women may act alone, in some cases they act in conjunction with their male partners. In this case, the intimate partners tend to be generally violent and abusive and the women themselves may be victims and able neither to protect themselves nor their children. The dynamics are frequently those of the 'battered woman', with fear often keeping the women in abusive relationships (Walker 1979). Krischer et al. (2007), in their classification, simply stuck to the distinction of victim's age: neonaticide, infanticide, and filicide, and we will explore the first two of these in a little more depth.

Neonaticide

The killing of a newborn within the first 24 hours of her/his life is commonly assumed to be a female crime. Women are more often implicated than men but, according to 1996 and 2001 NCISH data from England and Wales, this crime is not exclusive to them (Flynn et al., 2007). A definition of neonaticide which extends the neonatal period for these purposes to 3 months has been proposed, to be consistent with biological and psychological determinants, according to the American Pediatric Association and the American College of Obstetrics and Gynecology guidance (Kaye et al., 1990), but other literature generally limits the relevant time period to 24 hours.

As the stigma of illegitimacy has decreased in Western countries, availability of contraception and abortion increased, and welfare support has become available to people without any income, so recorded figures for infanticide have probably become closer to reality, although this is probably still the most likely form of homicide to remain hidden. Even allowing for possible under-reporting, however, neonaticide is a crime of low prevalence (Marks and Kumar, 1993; Mendlowicz et al., 1998). In England and Wales, NCISH data for 1996–2001 showed that 49 (44%) of 112 children killed while under the age of 12 months were under 3 months, but just 8 (7%) were within 24 hours of birth (Flynn et al., 2007). A population-based study in the USA for the years 1985–2000 found a rate of 2.1 per 100,000 per year of newborns killed or discarded by a parent (Herman-Giddens et al., 2003). Both violence and neglect have been implicated (Bonnet, 1993; Marks and Kumar, 1993; Resnick, 1970; Putkonen et al., 2007b).

Mothers who deny or conceal their pregnancy are at risk for neonaticide and this makes prevention extremely difficult (Craig, 2004). Preparations for the birth and child care have usually been negligible or non-existent (Brezinka et al., 1994; Green and Manohar, 1990; Resnick, 1970), even, as in Finland, where they would bring economic benefits (Putkonen et al., 2007b). Further typical characteristics are the mother's low income, her separation from the father and her lack of social supports (Oberman, 1996; Sadoff, 1995). There is a subgroup of married women who commit this offence (Putkonen et al., 2007b), but they are more likely to have a psychotic illness. Haapasalo and Petäjä's (1999) found that neonaticidal mothers reported significantly fewer problems and were less likely to seek help prior to the killing than mothers who killed even slightly older children. While many studies emphasize the youth of neonaticidal mothers, estimates of their mean age are, in fact, 21–26 years (Haapasalo and Petäjä, 1999; Mendlowicz et al., 1998; Oberman, 1996; Resnick, 1970; Spinelli, 2001; Putkonen et al., 2007b). Of all suspected neonaticides in Finland between 1980 and 2000, two-thirds of the women had been pregnant before and nearly a third (28%) had previously concealed a pregnancy (Putkonen et al., 2007b).

Motivation for killing one's newborn baby may simply be the elimination of an unwanted child (Resnick, 1970; Sadoff, 1995; Putkonen et al., 2007b). Fear of rejection may also play a role (Pitt and Bale, 1995; Putkonen et al., 2007b), but the mother's apparent disconnection from her pregnancy has led to consideration of dissociative disorders as well as personality disorder. A systematic study, using a valid screening instrument, the Dissociative Experiences Scale, confirmed a high incidence of pregnancy denial and dissociative symptoms as characteristic of neonaticides, including dissociative psychosis (Spinelli, 2001). These psychotic symptoms and amnesia were brief, however. Perpetrators who have a psychotic illness, as noted, form a small, particularly unusual group of older mothers (Putkonen et al., 2007b).

Infanticide

Infanticide is the killing of a child during her/his first year of life. It has been seen as a crime embedded in and responsive to the societies in which it occurs (Spinelli, 2003), differing in some of its characteristics according to whether it occurs, for example, in a European welfare state or in starvation levels of poverty in a developing country. In ancient cultures, for example in the Babylonian and Chaldean civilizations of 4000–2000 BC, infant sacrifice almost certainly occurred; ancient Greece and Rome justified infanticide on grounds of population control, eugenics and illegitimacy (Spinelli, 2003). Some countries still harbour such practices. According to the popular press they particularly affect female infants and are already creating a population imbalance.

In North America and some other Western countries, infanticide was so common in the seventeenth century that punishments became increasingly severe (Oberman, 1996; Spinelli, 2004); the stigma of illegitimacy and poverty were powerful motives. Legal developments in England and Wales are considered in chapter 2, tracing legislation from the 1624 Act to Prevent the Murthering of Bastard Children, through the long period in which such killing was a capital offence, to the Infanticide Acts of 1922 and 1938 (there is similar legislation in Northern Ireland, but no such legislation in Scotland, see chapter 4). This legislation was more or less replicated in adjusted models in at least 22 nations (Oberman, 1996). In England and Wales, it applies only when the victim is under 12 months old, even though, as noted, women who are sufficiently unwell to qualify may have taken the lives of their other children too. In the USA, however, American medical experts have disagreed on the issue of post-partum mental disorders and their association with infanticide, and there are no statutes which specifically govern infanticide (Kaye et al., 1990; Macfarlane, 2003). Oberman (1996) described the dialectical moral outrage there and the three basic societal positions toward women who kill their children: denial (the most common), punishment and prevention. Spinelli's (2003) classification of infanticide into five categories of neonaticide: assisted/coerced, neglect-related, abuse-related and mental illness-related killings has much in common with d'Orban's classification of the wider concept of filicide.

Longer term outcome for women after having killed another person

Women rarely kill, so it is very unusual to find any study of long-term outcome for such women. A records study of 132 Finnish women who had undergone forensic psychiatric examination after homicide (84) or attempted homicide (48) is an exception (Putkonen et al., 2001a, 2003). In Finland, there is an over 90% clear-up rate for homicide, and at the time of the study almost all of those apprehended were psychiatrically examined. Over half of these women had killed an intimate partner, about a quarter a friend or acquaintance and 17 of them (14%) their own child. Follow-up was until death or the census date in May 1999, which ever came sooner, so could have been for up to 17 years; the mean was 7 years for those who died and 11 years for the survivors. According to the National Register of Deaths, 22 of the women had died within the period, only eight of whom had certainly died from 'natural causes' (Putkonen et al., 2001b). Using standardized mortality ratios as an indicator of risk, it was apparent that these women had a 200-fold elevation in the risk of unnatural death, rising to 400-fold for suicide specifically. Although some caution should be exercised in respect of the actual figures, as they are not based on large numbers, it is nevertheless apparent that these women form a very vulnerable group.

The other main concern in this Finnish series was about re-offending (Putkonen et al., 2003). Nearly a quarter of these 132 women committed a further offence after the homicide and within the follow-up period. Four of them committed a further homicide, and for 15% overall the offence was violent, all of which is rather similar to re-offending among comparable men in Finland. Eleven of the women who re-offended did so either while institutionized or before conviction on the first offence; 80% of the other re-offenders did so within 2 years of their release from the holding institution (hospital or prison). Factors associated with recidivism were a diagnosis of personality disorder, prior criminality, substance misuse and young age. This echoed Eronen's (1995) findings.

Generally Growing Out of Crime?

Delinquent girls grown up

Growing up is different for girls and boys, emotionally and functionally. A Finnish study from the 1990s, using self-report, written essays and interviews as material found four features of girls which appeared to restrict them along any path to delinquency: (1) the perception of her body as a woman's; (2) her sexual reputation; (3) interdependency in relationships; (4) the idea of normal womanhood as antipathetic to that of a person who commits crimes (Honkatukia 1998). 'Bad girl femininity' was a despised form of femininity. This is reflected in the difference we have already noted between girls and boys in criminal pathways, and factors affecting these (Moffitt et al., 2001). While such a population based study may give the most unbiased perspective on personal pathways through adolescence, there is invariably a problem that the groups of interest to professionals in criminal justice or health systems are small. Outcome studies of groups defined by their mental ill health and/or delinquency may, thus add useful additional information.

Lewis et al. (1991) completed a small follow-up study of 21 female delinquents, and also found that early organic difficulties were not predictive of adult criminality for them. This study, however, also suggested high mortality, as did a later review (Pajer, 1998). Such girls tend to be suicidal, addicted to alcohol and other drugs, and unable to acquire education, work training or sustain jobs. Furthermore, most become enmeshed in violent relationships. A substantial Norwegian study followed up 459 girls and 437 boys, with a mean age of 14.9 years at first admission to the study, until they reached a mean age of 39.5 years, using research interviews and records data (Kjelsberg and Dahl, 1999). For the girls, four factors contributed significantly and independently to criminality. These were behaviour or personality disorder, comorbid substance misuse disorder, experience of verbal abuse at home and disciplinary problems in school. In this respect, only the comorbid psychoactive substance misuse disorders constituted a unique risk factor for adult criminality for the girls. We have already mentioned the study of Miller et al. (2010), which found a discernible but small group of girls whose early onset of delinquency persisted beyond adolescence. As we do meet women in clinical practice who have had a very early onset of offending which has persisted through their life course, we are inclined to believe that Dunedin birth cohort only differs in this respect (Moffitt et al., 2001) because the number of such women is so small that identification of such a group is marginal.

Lewis and colleagues (1991) went on to express the view that incarcerating female delinquents may contribute to their ongoing violent dysfunctional life styles. In 1997, the Howard League for Penal Reform concluded that the punitive ethos of prison is unsuitable for dealing with damaged children and recommended that all girls under 18 be moved out of the prison system. Although there has been a slight reduction in both numbers and length of custodial sentences given to 10–17-year-old girls in England and Wales, and to 18–20-year-old women (Howard League, 2006), there is still a long way to go in establishing more effective ways of dealing with young female offenders in terms of prevention of recidivism, mental health problems and, often not adequately considered, their potentially adverse impact on future generations.

Older women and desistance from crime

Statistics on re-offending among women and girls in England and Wales, referring to the late 1990s, tended to follow the patterns indicated by the Moffitt–Caspi research just described – women desisted from offending at an earlier stage than men (Home Office, 2004a; Harper et al., 2005). There are indicators, however, that, with the increase in women's involvement with the criminal justice system, so recidivism patterns are also increasing and changing. The situation is currently quite complicated. In 2008, female offenders did still have a lower re-offending rate than men, but their 16% increase in re-offending from the previous year was higher than the increase among men (4%) and, among those who actually re-offended, women did so at a much higher rate than the men (Ministry of Justice, 2010b). All this raises powerful arguments that the current system must become more attuned to the needs of women (e.g. Corston, 2007).

WOMEN, MENTAL DISORDER AND OFFENDING

Three questions reverberate around links between mental disorder and offending among women:

- Are girls/women who offend more or less likely to suffer from a relevant mental disorder than their male peers?
- Are any differences associated with mental health problems mainly attributable to different, perhaps changing attitudes to the reporting of crime by people with mental disorder, and/or easier detection of their crime, than attitudes to or detection of crime by their healthier peers?
- When girls/women do suffer from a relevant disorder, or commit an offence, is that disorder or that offending precisely similar to that of their male peers, or are there distinctive female characteristics to the disorder, to the offending or to the way in which the two are linked?

The main disorders which have been implicated in female offender populations are developmental disorders, personality disorders, substance misuse, psychosis and depression.

Conduct Disorder, Attention Deficit Hyperactivity Disorder (ADHD) and Other Developmental Disorders Among Girls

ADHD and conduct disorder in childhood and adolescence have been associated with an increased risk of later criminality, and substance abuse later on, but the prevalence of these disorders is dissimilar in girls and boys (e.g. Babinski et al., 1999; Barkley et al., 2004). Girls are less likely to have ADHD or conduct disorder, although they are more likely to have depressive disorders than boys. There is, however, some evidence that the relative impact on offending or its consequences may differ according to gender. Fazel(s) et al. (2008) completed a systematic review and meta-analysis of all 25 then published surveys of adolescents in juvenile detention or correctional facilities, which, between them, accounted for 2,972 girls and 13,778 boys. The average rate of ADHD was 18.5% (range 9–28%) among the girls, compared with just 11.7% (4–19%) among the boys, although girls and boys were more similar with respect to conduct disorder (53% [32–73%]:53% [41–65%] respectively). Both girls and boys had a similarly low rate of psychosis (about 3%), but the girls were disproportionately affected by major depression (29% [22–36%]:10.6% [7–14%] respectively). Among 15–21 year olds undergoing court-ordered forensic psychiatric assessments in Sweden, gender patterns appeared similar, although numbers of girls and young women were too small for statistical analysis; the higher prevalence of childhood developmental disorders and depression but lower prevalence of psychosis and substance misuse disorders were the features that best distinguished them either from adults undergoing similar examination and, psychosis excepted, from general psychiatric inpatients of the same age (Fazel (M) et al., 2008).

When Gaub and Carlson (1997) reviewed the field, they found a number of sex differences in the presentation of ADHD had been reported: girls displayed greater intellectual impairment, lower levels of hyperactivity and lower rates of other externalizing behaviour than their male peers. Subsequently, evidence has been presented that when distractibility and hyperactivity is present among girls with ADHD, these features may be more predictive of alcohol and/or illicit drug misuse as well as poor academic achievement and poor peer relationships than they are among boys (Elkins et al., 2007; Sihvola et al., 2011). Faraone et al. (2000) studied two groups of girls, 140 patients with ADHD and 122 comparison participants without ADHD, and found that familial transmission of ADHD generalizes to families of ADHD girls. Their data suggest that familial risk factors cannot account for either sex differences in prevalence or the clinical variability of DSM-IV subtypes. There is also research highlighting different patterns of anomalous frontal lobe development among girls and boys with ADHD (Mahone et al., 2011). More work is needed to determine if true sex differences in features of ADHD exist and whether they have implications for treating the disorder differently in girls and boys.

Personality Disorder

The cluster B personality disorders (see chapter 16) generally, and antisocial/dissocial personality disorder and borderline personality disorder in particular, have the strongest link with offending for women as well as for men. In his review of the prevalence of antisocial personality disorder, Moran (1999) observed that in all 14 community based studies published at that time, from a range of European countries, the USA, Canada, New Zealand, Hong Kong and Taiwan, the lifetime prevalence of antisocial personality disorder was lower among women than men, although the New Zealand and Taiwan differences were not significant. By contrast, although borderline personality disorder is often viewed as a disorder of women, according to a substantial interview study of over 34,000 people in the USA, the prevalence of borderline personality disorder was similar by gender (Grant et al., 2008). This last study suggested, however, that women may suffer more disability in relation to borderline personality disorder, so the prevailing perception of sex distribution may arise because of differential presentation to services. Certainly, among women as among men, personality disorder is a risk factor for offending, although differences in prevalence of personality disorder among female and male offenders vary to some extent according to the method of assessment. In a national prison survey across England and Wales, using interview and a clinical consensus diagnostic approach, Gunn et al. (1991) found similar rates of personality disorder among female as among male sentenced prisoners, while Maden et al. (1995) found rather higher rates among women than men while on remand in prison awaiting trial or sentence. Also in a national England and Wales survey, but using the Structured Clinical Interview for DSM-IV (SCID-II), Singleton et al. (1998a) rated just under one-third of the women as having antisocial personality disorder, but about two-thirds of the men, while rates of borderline personality disorder were similar (about 20%). In Finland, among homicide offenders, rates of antisocial personality disorder were only slightly lower among women (22%) than among men (31%) (Putkonen et al., 2011a). In secure hospitals in the UK, a significantly higher proportion of the women than the men have a personality disorder, with borderline personality disorder predominating among the women (e.g. Butwell et al., 2000; Jamieson et al., 2000; Coid et al., 2000), but this probably reflects selection bias. Clinicians tend to feel more confident about treating women than men when the diagnosis is one of personality disorder. Unusually for this field, there has, in fact, been much more research into the effectiveness of both pharmacological and psychological treatments of these disorders among women than men (see chapter 16).

Application of the concept of psychopathy to women

The Psychopathy Checklist-Revised (PCL-R; Hare, 2003) combines ratings of a historically chaotic lifestyle with ratings indicative of currently impaired affective empathy. It is often used as a tool for predicting the likelihood of recidivism as well as an adjunct to personality description. It has been described in more detail elsewhere in this book (chapter 16). Here we consider the extent to which it offers a useful construct for women. Studies among female offenders have increasingly shown that, while it may have relevance in the assessment of their risk of violence, there are special features differentiating women from men in this regard (e.g. Logan and Weizmann-Henelius, 2012; Nicholls et al., 2005; Dolan and Völlm, 2009; Kreis and Cooke, 2011). In particular, as might be expected from the generally later onset of offending, already described, the antisocial items of the PCL-R may not be as relevant to women as to men (e.g. Forouzan and Cooke, 2005; Verona and Vitale, 2006). Likewise, the items of glibness and grandiose sense of self-worth have been found muted or distorted in women compared with men (Forouzan and Cooke, 2005), while poor behaviour controls have been noted as more common in 'psychopathic women' (Strand and Belfrage, 2005). The term 'psychopathy' carries a good deal of stigma and we urge caution in its use to designate vulnerable if antisocial women as variously 'glib, grandiose, cunning and manipulative, sensation seeking, impulsive and irresponsible, promiscuous, criminally versatile and parasitic pathological liars with shallow affect, lack of remorse or guilt and failing to take responsibility for their action', all of which words or phrases are categories within the construct. As Meier (1990) illustrates, for clinicians, the terminology is most useful for indicating when it is essential to pay attention to the counter-transference in the clinical relationship.

In the USA and Canada the proportion of female offenders acquiring a score of 30 or more on the PCL-R is between 9% and 31% across studies (Salekin et al., 1997; Vitale et al., 2002; Warren et al., 2003); in Finland the estimate is about 11% (Weizmann-Henelius et al., 2004). A Finnish study of homicide offenders reported a prevalence 9% using the cut-off of 30, or 22% with a cut-off of 25 (Weizmann-Henelius et al., 2010a,b). Even higher prevalence figures have been reported using the lower threshold among female offenders (e.g. Grann, 2000; Jackson et al., 2002; Warren et al., 2003), although not in clinical settings (Nicholls et al., 2005; Vitale et al., 2002).

Salekin et al. (1997) found that the factor structure of the PCL-R differed between women and men. In a sample of 103 female jail detainees, they found a two-factor model broadly resembling Hare's (1991) original description, but with different items loading on the factors than in men. In women 'poor behavioural control' and 'impulsivity' loaded on both factors, but 'many short term marital relationships' did not load on either. Thus for women factor 1 was best characterized by lack of empathy, proneness to boredom and sensation seeking, while factor 2 characterized early behavioural problems, adult antisocial behaviour and promiscuity. Another contrast with male studies was a positive correlation between anxiety and psychopathy scores, particularly on factor 2. Further studies found factor 1, but not factor 2, to predict general recidivism in female detainees and prisoners (Salekin et al., 1998; Richards et al., 2003). Grann (2000), however, found the items 'callous/lack of empathy' more elevated among men, while 'promiscuous sexual behaviour' was more recorded among women. He expressed the concern, however, that these results might only indicate gender bias arising from the PCL-R itself, the interview, or the material recorded in the official records. Debate continues about whether 2- or 3-factor models best describe a subgroup of female offenders (Cooke and Michie, 1997; Jackson et al., 2002; Warren et al., 2003; Strand and Belfrage, 2005; Dolan and Völlm, 2009; Schaap et al., 2009). A number of studies have emphasized emotional instability (Kreiss and Cooke, 2011), using the clinical assessment tool the Comprehensive Assessment of Psychopathic Personality (CAPP; Kreis et al., 2012), and impulsivity (Kreiss and Cooke, 2011; Komarovskaya et al., 2007) as the most prominent traits among 'prototypical psychopathic women', whether or not directly linked to recidivism. This raises the question as to whether the construct of psychopathy has anything to offer here which is different from a diagnosis of borderline personality disorder. Indeed, Hicks et al. (2010), with female prisoners, described a 'secondary psychopathy' which seemed more-or-less indistinguishable from an externalizing variant of borderline personality disorder.

Research findings with respect to antecedents of and comorbidities with so-called psychopathy in women also carry echoes of borderline personality disorder. Weizmann-Henelius et al. (2010a,b) found that the impact of adverse childhood experiences, death of a parent, parental psychiatric problems, and sexual abuse on both PCL interpersonal/affective and lifestyle factor scores was stronger among women than men, although parental alcohol abuse had a lesser impact on the antisocial factor scores in women than in men. Verona et al. (2006) found that, among a sample of female prisoners, a history of childhood physical and sexual abuse was associated with the social deviance factor, the current lifestyle and antisocial factors, but not with the prior interpersonal/affective factor.

Insofar as finding comorbidity with personality disorders is clinically meaningful, women have been found to have more than double the male inmate prevalence rates on seven of the 13 categorical personality disorder types measured (borderline, dependent, depressive, histrionic, obsessive–compulsive, schizotypal, and self-defeating) (Coolidge et al. 2011). Others have suggested that such differences in supposed personality disorder comorbidity explain some of the gender differences found in the manifestation of psychopathy (Logan and Weizmann-Henelius, 2012). On balance, exploration of the use of the PCL-R with women seems to have offered academic interest but no practical or clinical advantage for the assessment, understanding or management of female offenders, whereas recognition of the presence of a cluster B personality disorder is likely to be helpful if it leads to appropriate treatment.

Substance Misuse and Offending Among Women

One of the many problems posed by personality disorder among women, as among men, is the elevated rate of substance misuse compared with the general population, although, of course, substance misuse may be a stand alone problem, or indeed complicate other disorders too. Alcohol and drug misuse is mainly dealt with in chapter 18, but we will make brief reference to particularly female problems here. Alcohol use is among the strongest risk factors for violence among women (e.g. Boles and Miotto, 2003; Martin and Bryant, 2001), the latter finding that it was three times as likely that intoxication was associated with violence

among women as among men. Illicit drug use is more likely than alcohol misuse to be associated with acquisitive crime among women and men alike.

Alcohol and drug dependent women with a criminal record seem to represent two different populations. According to Modestin and Rigoni (2000), drug dependent women tend to have more criminal convictions (excluding drugs offences) than their alcohol dependent peers, and to be younger, more likely to be unemployed and of low socio-economic status, having started offending earlier and come into contact with treatment facilities earlier. Differences between women and men who abuse drugs have been studied in Sweden since 1969, where women have consistently made up about one-quarter of illicit drug users (Byqvist, 2006). As a group they are consistently younger than the men, despite a general increase in average age of users. Drug using women are less likely to generate illegal income, although they tend to finance their habit by illegal means. They are best characterized as a marginalized group without homes, work, or social contacts outside the drug taking community (Byqvist, 2006).

There is some evidence that even among substance misusers women offend less than men (Byqvist, 1999), but substance misuse is a particularly prominent problem for women in prison. Fazel et al. (2006) conducted a systematic review of the prevalence of substance misuse and dependence among prisoners on reception into custody. They found 13 studies with, collectively, data on 3,270 women and 4,293 men. Prevalence of alcohol abuse or dependence was similar (W: 10–24%, M: 18–30%) but of illicit drug abuse or dependence rather higher among the women (W: 30–60%, M: 10–48%).

Psychosis and Offending Among Women

The lifetime risk of schizophrenia, the psychotic disorder most strongly associated with violence and other crime, is similar between women and men (Jablensky, 2003), but, except in certain familial cases, even with onset in young adulthood, women tend to develop the disorder rather later than men; in addition they have a second, much later peak of incidence (Häfner et al., 1998). It has been argued that this may offer some relative protection for women from some of the worst social consequences of the disease (Häfner et al., 2003). We have already noted that, nevertheless, psychosis seems to account for proportionately more violence among women than men, at least in Sweden (Fazel and Grann, 2006). Although perhaps in part mediated by substance misuse comorbidity (Fazel et al., 2009), the extent to which there is an independent association between psychosis and substance misuse, the extent to which the psychosis may be consequent on the substance misuse or the extent to which the substance misuse may be seen as a complication of the psychosis is rarely clear. It has long been noted that, while women generally are less likely to be implicated in violent behaviour than men, in the context of admission to hospital with psychosis, the prevalence of violence is similar or even higher for women (e.g. UK: Fottrell, 1980; USA: Tardiff, 1983; Switzerland: Aberhalden et al., 2007), with an exceptionally elevated rate within forensic mental health services (Rutter et al., 2004). At least in forensic mental health samples, violence is even more likely to post-date the onset of psychosis among women than men (Jones et al., 2009).

It is difficult to be sure whether women with psychosis who become offenders differ in their psychotic presentation from their male peers, or, indeed, their female peers who do not offend, but various suggestions emerge from the literature. Women in secure mental health services in England appear, in contrast to those with psychosis outside such services, to have been younger at age of onset of their psychosis than the men, and more likely to have been victims of childhood sexual abuse (Heads et al., 1997). Swanson et al. (2002), with a US sample of people with schizophrenia and other psychosis, found that for men there was a direct relationship between illness and victimisation, but for women such association was mediated by illness characteristics and social circumstances, suggesting, perhaps, a wider range of routes for intervention among such women. Female offender-patients with psychosis, as women without, seem to be catching up with men in terms of comorbid substance misuse (MacMahon et al., 2003). There is little information on details of symptom presentation, but a suggestion that, while they may be as likely as men to respond to passivity delusions, they may be less prone to responding to threatening delusions (Teasdale et al., 2006).

Within psychotic groups, as outside them, women tend to desist from crime sooner than men do (Lindqvist and Allebeck, 1990; Wesseley et al., 1994), and, in spite of their inpatient difficulties with violence, they are more assured of community discharge than the men (Jamieson and Taylor, 2002) and more likely to do better than the men after discharge, at least in terms of re-offending (Jamieson and Taylor, 2004; Soyka et al., 2007).

Depression and Offending Among Women

Psychotic depression may be particularly dangerous for women. In their 10-year study (1955–1964) of all attempted and completed homicides throughout what was then West Germany, Häfner and Böker (1973/82) found that men outnumbered women in a sex distribution which was less striking than for crime overall (3.5:1) except among those suffering from affective psychosis. They noted its similar distribution in the general population, but that for completed homicides depressed women outnumbered depressed men by 6:1. The rare

daughter-perpetrated parricide is generally associated with depression (Bourget et al., 2007).

In the UK a more mixed picture has been reported but, again, depression most affects the proportionate contribution of women and men to homicide. In National Confidential Inquiry into Suicide and Homicide (NCISH) data on 1,594 homicides recorded in England and Wales between 1996 and 2000, for every one woman in the cohort without mental disorder, there were ten men (NCISH, 2001). Having schizophrenia reduced the male: female ratio to 8:1, but a major affective illness reduced it to 3:1. The smaller Scottish cohort (227 homicides, 196 with psychiatric reports) was more similar to the German national study (Scottish overall ratio of men: women 10:1; male:female ratio among those with depressive illness was 1:10). In a Finnish 8-year homicide cohort, 83 of whom were women, the relative gender impact of serious depression was similar (age-adjusted odds ratios W1.8:M1.6) (Eronen et al., 1996a).

Depressive and suicidal tendencies have been linked to both non-violent as well as violent offending among women (Loucks and Zamble, 1999). Fazel et al. (2010) compared the risk of violent crime of individuals with bipolar disorder with the general population and found that women with bipolar disorder had a higher risk of violent crime than men with bipolar disorder (4.1 vs. 1.9). As with schizophrenic psychoses, the relationships were complicated by substance abuse.

Filicide is perhaps the crime most associated with women's depression. Bourget et al. (2007) found, in their review, that up to 70% of filicidal mothers were depressed or psychotic and more than half (55%) completed suicide after killing their child(ren). Reference has already been made to a study of complete national Austrian and Finnish cohorts in which it was found that although a third of filicidal parents were depressed, regardless of sex, the suicide rates were higher among the men (Putkonen et al., 2010). A study of 10 cases of maternal infanticides found that an irritable, severely depressed mood with crying spells, insomnia, fatigue, anxiety, suicidal ideation, or even psychotic thoughts were common elements in presentation (Kauppi et al., 2008), most of these mothers having been seen at home by a healthcare official; the killing occurring when the mother, against her wishes, was left alone with the baby. Psychotic depression was not, however, found to be typical of neonaticide offenders in a Finnish series (Putkonen et al., 2007b).

SERVICES FOR WOMEN

Women in Prison

Women are generally held in separate prisons from men; where not, they are housed in separate wings. We have already noted that they form a tiny minority of prisoners. Table 20.1 sets out the picture in a bit more detail.

515

Table 20.1   Proportions of women in prisons in different countries with year of information[1]

USA[2]	8.6% (2004)	New Zealand	6.1% (2005)
Spain	7.9% (2006)	Finland	6.3% (2006)
Australia	6.8% (2005)	Argentina	5.3% (2002)
Sweden	5.2% (2005)	Germany	5.0% (2005)
UK	5.7% (2006)	Canada[3]	5.0% (2004)
China[4]	4.6% (2003)	Scotland	4.8% (2006)
Japan	5.9% (2005)	France	3.7% (2005)
Russian Federation	3.3% (2005)	Republic of Ireland	2.3% (2006)

[1]Adapted from: Walmsley, 2006.
[2]12.3% of local jail inmates, 6.9% of state and federal prisoners.
[3]only adult prisoners.
[4]only convicted prisoners.

Proportions will change slightly over time, for example in England and Wales there had been a steady increase in the female prison population between 1999 and 2004, but between 2005 and 2009 it decreased, to about 5% (Ministry of Justice, 2010b). The minority status of women here means that there are fewer prisons for them and, in smaller countries, often only one with certain specialist facilities, so that women are more likely than men to be held at a long distance from their home communities. This can be a particularly serious problem for women who have been the principal or sole carer for their children.

The demographics of female prisoners in relation to men may differ between countries. In England and Wales, they are generally rather similar to those of men, although in the Office of National Statistics survey for England and Wales in 1997 (Singleton et al., 1998), a higher proportion of sentenced women were aged 30 and over compared with other prisoner groups.

In the USA, women make up a rather larger proportion of the incarcerated population. In a nationally representative survey of US jail inmates, 11.6% were women. Their mean age was 33.4 years (95% CI = 33.0–33.9), which was nearly 2 years older than the mean age of male inmates (31.7 years; 95% CI = 31.4–32.1) (Binswanger et al., 2010). Just over half of the women (52%) had been married compared with little more than a third of the men (38%), but women were about half as likely to have been in employment and slightly more of them had been homeless before the arrest (17%:12%). This picture of a higher marriage rate but greater educational, economic and general social disadvantage among the women was similar to that found in a slightly earlier US survey of 536 men and 704 women leaving jail between 1997 and 2004 (Freudenberg et al., 2008).

Another major difference between women and men in prison is that the women appear more likely to have mental health problems. According to figures for England and Wales (Singleton et al., 1998a), about twice the proportion of women had previously been in treatment for mental disorder (W:40%; M:20%). Post-traumatic stress disorder rates were reported in this study; about twice as many pretrial women as men met criteria for this (9%:5%), but only a slightly higher proportion of sentenced women (5%:3%). An earlier, more clinically oriented national survey in England and Wales (Maden et al., 1994a,b; 1995) found that rates for most mental disorders studied were around twice as high among women as men, with 57% of women having at least one clinical diagnosis of mental disorder compared with 38% of the men. Correlates of such disorder were similarly elevated among the women, for example a third of the women had a declared history of self-harm compared with just 17% of the men, and over a quarter of the women were taking psychotropic medication in prison compared with only 8% of the men.

Other research has also suggested that incarcerated woman are more likely to have had traumatic experiences than their male peers but at least as likely to have substance dependence and, in some but not all correctional populations, antisocial personality disorder (Lewis, 2006; Fazel and Baillargeon, 2011). Teplin et al. (1996) compared disorder rates of women in US jails to those of women in the wider community, finding that rates of schizophreniform psychoses were similar, but substance abuse/dependency and antisocial personality disorder rates were significantly higher in prison and comorbidity was common. In the Binswanger et al. (2010) jail survey mentioned above, there were several significant sex differences in psychiatric diagnoses, including depressive disorder (W 35.5%: M 17.4%), bipolar disorder (W 20.7%: M 8.7%), psychosis (W 6.0%: M 4.4%), post-traumatic stress disorder (W 11.3%: M 4.4%), personality disorder (W 8.7%: M 4.7%), drug dependence (W 45.7%: M 34.5%) alcohol dependence (W 18.9: M 23.3%) and any psychiatric disorder (W 43.6%: M 21.6%); all except the sex difference in psychotic disorders remained significant after controlling for demographic and socioeconomic factors. Although there were sex differences in drug and alcohol dependence, these differences did not mediate the relationship between sex and the other medical or psychiatric disorders examined. Elsewhere, figures also indicate high psychiatric morbidity among women in prison. In Australia, Hurley and Dunne (1991) found that more than half of women prisoners had a current psychiatric disorder, most commonly adjustment, personality or substance use disorders. A later Australian study showed that the women in prison had higher rates of psychiatric morbidity than men – 61%:39% (Butler et al., 2005). A study of German prisoners found no sex differences in total prevalence of mental disorders or illicit drug-related disorders, but a lower rate of alcohol-related disorders among the women than the men in prison (W 26.5%: M 46.7%) and higher rates of affective (W 12.2%: M 5.5%) and neurotic, stress-related and somatoform disorders (W 32.7%: M 12.3%) (Watzke et al., 2006).

Overall, however, the international picture is of more similarity than difference between mental disorder rates among women and men in prison, the main difference lying in the lower rates of personality disorder among women (Fazel and Danesh, 2002). In Fazel's more recent review of surveys across Western countries (Fazel and Baillargeon, 2011) the similarity of psychosis rates among female and male prisoners was confirmed, together with a substantially lower rate of antisocial personality disorder and a rather higher rate of drug misuse or dependence and of post-traumatic disorders, but more similar rates of other mental disorders, including depression.

An additional, special issue for women in prison is the fate of their children. Corston (2007) estimated that about two-thirds of women in prison in England and Wales were living with their children before they came into prison, and around 18,000 children are separated from their mothers by imprisonment each year. It is likely that these figures represent a minimum estimate, because it is recognized that women in prison tend to be avoidant of declaring their children, because they fear that arrangements they have made for their care will be disrupted and the children possibly removed permanently. Moreover, some women are pregnant when they are imprisoned. Figures for this are even harder to obtain than estimates of live children; women are not obliged to declare a pregnancy, and it is presumed that many do not. Caddle and Crisp (1997) estimated that about 100 women in prison in England and Wales were then pregnant, and the number of places in mother and baby units in prisons there more or less fits with that. Some women who are pregnant on reception to prison will have left before delivery, although such are the home circumstances of these women, many of whom did not choose to be pregnant, that this is not necessarily a good thing for the health of baby or mother (Edge, 2006). Nevertheless, among women who deliver in prison, the risk of premature delivery or a low birth weight baby is high (Knight and Plugge, 2005).

Prison treatment programmes

Resources are scarce in prison so, aside from essential medication for major mental disorders, 'treatment' is generally only offered to sentenced prisoners, and, increasingly, only to those serving longer sentences. So-called treatment programmes are generally targeted at reducing harm in the context of specific problems and, where so, are referred to in more detail in the relevant chapters, including personality disorder (16), addictions (18), sex offending (10) and violence (9). Generally drawing on a mix of cognitive behavioural principles and knowledge of criminogenic factors, many of these programmes were first developed and evaluated in the Canadian correctional system. At least as delivered in England and Wales, they tend to follow a rigid programmatic design, and delivery is audited using a variety of methods, including video-monitoring to ensure strict adherence to the sessional material. Report after report, at least for England and Wales, emphasizes the different needs of women in prison from those of men, and the risk that, because the service is tuned to the majority, the needs of these women will not be met. Corston (2007), for example, approached the issue in terms of the Equality Act 2006. She was explicit about not arguing for a different sentencing framework in this context, nor for never sending women to prison, but insisted that 'equal outcomes require different approaches' with respect to treatment within the system. She argued for the formation of an inter-departmental government ministerial group to ensure formation of an appropriate strategy. There is now a considerable body of research to support this.

So, what is remediable for women? In line with some of the earlier points on theories on female offending, after reviewing the literature on criminogenic needs, Gelsthorpe (1999) concluded that the substantial sex differences in offending behaviour were related to differences in opportunity, upbringing and societal expectations. Among these, Sorbello et al. (2002) particularly highlighted the educational and employment disadvantages of women, which were factors in their involvement in the drug trade and prostitution, if only to support their children; education and work programmes might ameliorate here. Hamlin and Lewis (2000) found that one in eight women in prison in England and Wales had literacy difficulties, and that, although about three-fifths of sentenced women attended some sort of educational or vocational course, there was still much unmet need. Only one-third of women found work on release and, among the unmet needs was training in job seeking skills, such as application and interviewing techniques. Martin and Hesselbrock (2001) developed a classification of women in prison, which we will describe in a little detail, because it provides a good illustration of the diversity of problems faced by these women and the staff who try to help them. These authors suggested four main types of incarcerated women.

1. *The spirited*: most often involved in drug crimes, often dependent on cocaine and/or alcohol; had experienced comparatively little childhood trauma, but have the highest rates of physical abuse from a partner; have no greater than average mental illness rates; have strong family supports.

2. *The inured:* the oldest group; mainly property offenders; opiate abusers; average rates of childhood trauma (for prisoners); lowest rates of current physical abuse but high rates of sexual abuse; lowest rates of illness; highest rates of adult arrests.

3. *The troubled:* involved with violent and public order offences, with low rates of adult arrest; highest rate of traumatic childhood experiences; highest rates of mental disorder (antisocial personality disorder, post-traumatic stress disorder, depression) but least likely to be substance abusers; few social or family supports, lowest family support.

4. *The volatile:* the youngest group; mainly public order, property and violent offences; harmful home environments; relatively high rates of mental illness (depression and post-traumatic stress disorder) and most likely to be alcohol dependent; highest rates of sexual abuse experiences; fewest social supports.

It is hardly surprising in the face of such diversity that there has been so much concern that prisons have not been meeting the needs of such women. One explanation offered is that prison programmes for women have centred on problem reduction and harm avoidance rather than skill and capability enhancement, and that a more holistic approach with gender specific components is called for (e.g. Andrews and Bonta, 1998). Extending this, McGuire (2002) has shown an emerging consensus for a multi-modal approach to interventions in all parts of the criminal justice system, while Partridge (2004) has described its application to case management in community services. Harper and Chitty (2005) provided an excellent overview of the state of the evidence for programme outcomes for women up to that date, cautioning that although the criminogenic needs literature may be robust, evaluation of programmes informed by it has a long way to go. Outcome measures are still almost entirely confined to re-offending, an important measure but hardly reflecting the holistic ideology. The best research designs had weakly matched comparison groups, and they identified no randomized controlled trials. In their later, rapid evidence assessment, Lart et al. (2008) noted the growing literature which then included three meta-analyses and 16 primary studies. They too expressed concerns about the quality of studies, noting only one randomized trial and that, in other studies, not only was matching of comparison groups weak, but also women in the comparison groups were often receiving some other kind of intervention. Richie's (2009) summary of what a model prison programme for women should include suggests a four point strategy:

1. comprehensive programmes so that work to meet multiple needs can be brought together in one place;

2. community development and linkages to incorporate policy-level work, community organization and social change strategies;

3. empowerment and consciousness raising approaches to develop a sense of hope, orientation towards the future and a willingness to take responsibility;

4. community mentoring, care and consistency to help learning from successful role models.

Given that substance misuse is such an important issue in the criminality of women, some more gender-specific prison-based substance misuse treatment programmes have been evaluated. Van Voorhis et al. (2010) found that unresolved substance misuse among women in correctional settings is among the needs most strongly associated with recidivism, and concluded that shifting such high risk women from a punitive model to a rehabilitative one would make good sense for them and for society. In an evaluation study of a prison-based substance misuse programme in the USA, 473 women and 1,842 men were recruited as treatment and control participants in a multi-centre study (Pelissier et al., 2003). They found that, despite the greater number of life problems among women than men, women had lower 3-year recidivism rates and rates of post-release drug use than did men. For both women and men, however, those completing treatment had longer survival times than their untreated peers, and the authors speculated that, while this programme might have met the needs of women better than those of men, the women might simply have been less likely to relapse, irrespective of the treatment. In a study of 98 federally sentenced female offenders in Canada, Dowden and Blanchette (2002) reported a significant reduction in general recidivism for treated substance abusers.

In 1998, Welle et al. reported three main approaches to drug treatment for women offenders in the USA:

1. treatment of drug use as a way of preventing relapse and recidivism;

2. treatment of drug use and criminality as separate issues;

3. treatment of traumatic states, viewed as triggering, complicating, and protracting drug use and criminality.

In group 1, gender-specific approaches provided a separate and safe therapeutic environment for women, helping them to construct their own drug histories and to identify and thus cope with their own specific needs in this respect. The approach created a recovery-oriented programme culture that valued women, and identified triggers of relapse, yielding taught strategies to cope with drug craving as well as the emotions that surface during recovery. Positive role modelling was central. Approaches dealing with criminal activity (group 2) were divided into a range of drug treatment interventions, and a cognitive approach to alter 'criminal thinking' patterns. Victim experiences were approached with programmes in group 3; although there is no agreement across programmes about whether such experiences should be central treatment or a secondary area, it was clear that talking about such trauma did illuminate important aspects of drug use and criminality. In addition, a matter which sometimes needed specific attention was that here, as in England and Wales, many women committed crimes to support their intimate partner's drug use financially as well as their own, and these male co-defendants sometimes pressured the women not to participate in treatment.

Mother and baby units

For over 100 years, mothers have been allowed to have their babies with them in prison in the UK, but not until the early 1980s were there any formal arrangements made. Since then, women who give birth in prison and anyone else with a child of under 18 months may be eligible to be placed in a mother and baby unit (MBU) and keep her child with her. There are eight mother and baby units for England and Wales within prisons or secure training centres, with a combined capacity for over 100 children. Each candidate for admission is assessed by a multidisciplinary team, and the decision made by an admission board according to the best interest of the child (Google: Prison Service Order (PSO), 4801). A mother and baby unit liaison officer is available at every women's prison to advice and help women with their applications. A number of other European countries offer similar arrangements, again emphasizing the best interests of the child. An international survey of women's prisons, however, found different ideas about how the imprisoned mother should be treated, varying from an arrangement that allows the mother and child to stay together all day, to a system whereby the child goes to an outside nursery by day so that the mother can work (Germany); this may also improve appropriate stimulation for the child (11 million, 2008). The most child-centred system was in Frondenberg, in Germany, where 16 mothers live with their children in self-contained flats until the children reach the age of 6, and the prison staff do not wear uniforms.

Maternal morbidity in the mother and baby units is high. Birmingham et al. (2006) surveyed mothers in these units in England and Wales and found that nearly two-thirds had a mental disorder of some kind, more or less equally divided into one of three groups – alcohol or other drug misuse in the year prior to imprisonment, personality disorder, or neurotic illness, mainly depression. No one had a functional psychotic disorder. The characteristics that distinguished MBU residents from the rest of the female prison population were more stable backgrounds, but more frequent drug offences. Evaluation for the units appeared to select out women with psychosis, major child care problems and other social difficulties.

Very little is known about what happens to women and their children after they move on from a prison MBU, although Catan (1988, 1989) studied babies who spent 4 months or longer on such units and found that the infants had begun to decline in their cognitive and locomotor abilities towards the end of this period. The concern was that they were insufficiently stimulated. A later study of attachment relationships in children of incarcerated mothers highlighted a need for special support for families affected by maternal imprisonment, to promote stable, continuous placements for children (Poehlmann, 2005). An Australian review of studies of parenting programmes for prisoners found that these have the potential to improve the parenting skills, knowledge and confidence of incarcerated parents (Newman et al., 2011). A particular concern otherwise is that the prison system may only be consolidating cycles of disadvantage.

Specialist Forensic Mental Health Services for Women

Policy matters

It is government policy in England and Wales that mental health services, including forensic mental health services should be gender specific (Department of Health, 1999d,h, 2002, 2003). This is partly because of the expressed preferences of the women concerned, partly because of perceived risks to them, and partly because of special treatment needs. Separate services should reduce immediate risk of harm from abusive or predatory men, but reliance on segregation by sex alone for safeguarding the women needing these services will not be sufficient. Mezey et al. (2005) interviewed 31 female patients and 58 male and female staff in single-sex forensic mental health units, where about half of the women have an unequivocal psychotic illness. Although none of the women reported a sexual assault, being threatened, bullied or violently assaulted by other women was not uncommon, and a number of women said that after the experience they would prefer to be on mixed wards. Among staff, not all considered that the segregation had been helpful, while some observed that it was useful to protect the male patients from the women, some of whom they regarded as sexually provocative and intrusive. The women and the staff alike recognized the need for additional measures. Both groups thought that more trained and fewer agency staff would help, and the women wanted better staff visibility. Staff were more concerned with improving the layout of the unit, but also creating more trusting relationships with the women so that the women could always voice their concerns and know that they would be taken seriously. Over an issue as important as personal safety, there should be an imperative to commission research on the impact of a major service change such as this, but good outcome studies are still awaited on this as on so much other change in the format of service delivery.

The specialist hospital services and the women using them

There have been a number of studies comparing women with men in high (e.g. Butwell et al., 2000; Jamieson et al., 2000) and medium (e.g. Coid et al., 2000) specialist secure hospital services in England and Wales. Women make up a slightly larger proportion of the resident population than in prisons, but still they are in the minority. Up to 20% of patients in most medium security units are women. After a sustained effort to reduce their presence in high security, there is now a single 50-bedded high security hospital unit for England, at Rampton hospital. Divided into four wards, it is entirely self-contained within the campus. Such reduction was attained in part by creating a new tier of service 'women's enhanced medium secure services' (WEMSS). The three units – in north-west London, the east midlands and the north-west of England, are similar to any other medium security hospital service in terms of their perimeter and procedural security, but have enhanced relational security and provide staff who are especially skilled in behavioural treatment techniques, and particularly dialectical behaviour therapy (DBT) for its special role in helping women who self-harm (Linehan et al., 1991, 2006). These forms of security are discussed in more detail in chapter 24. The recent history of women's secure mental health service development in England and Wales has been described by Parry-Crooke and Stafford (2009) and Sarkar and di Lustro (2011). In Scotland too an evidence-based case has been made for reform (Thomson et al., 2001). As hospital units, English and Welsh medium security units have a great deal more flexibility than prisons in terms of treatment models adopted to underpin the therapeutic milieu of the services. Applications described included an attachment model (Barber et al., 2006) and a trauma-based model (Mason, 2006). They seem theoretically promising, but have not been formally evaluated.

The most common diagnosis for women in secure hospital services is, as for men, of a psychotic illness, although more women have affective disorders or affective qualities in their illnesses; a much higher proportion of women have a diagnosis of at least one personality disorder, most commonly borderline personality disorder. The offending component of the reasons for admission to secure hospital conditions also differs from that of men; the largest offender subgroup is of women who have been convicted of arson – about 40% – sex offending is not an issue, and an important minority of women have never been convicted of an offence, but their violent behaviour – generally to themselves as well as to others – has been of such an order that it cannot be contained outside specialist secure conditions (Butwell et al., 2000; Coid et al., 2001; Jamieson et al., 2000). Women remain vulnerable within secure hospitals, which seem less protective for them in some respects than they are for men. In a study of completed suicide among

high security hospital patients, rates were 40 times higher among women during the inpatient period compared with seven times higher among the men than would be expected in the general population, while post-departure the rates were 45 times and 23 times higher respectively (Jones et al., 2011). In other respects, however, there are indications that outcomes are better for such women. For high security hospital patients it has been found that all the surviving women may expect to return to community living, whereas this is not true for the men (Jamieson and Taylor, 2002) and, after allowing for type of disorder, type of index offence, age at discharge and type of discharge (directly to the community or not) and length of time in the community, women were three times less likely to re-offend than the men (Jamieson and Taylor, 2004); none of the women were multiple re-offenders. The difference was less striking for women leaving medium security, for whom the unadjusted risk of re-offending was about half that of the men, but, after entering factors including previous offending and self-harm, this difference was much reduced (Maden et al., 2006).

Specific treatment issues for women in mental healthcare settings

There is not much research into sex specific treatment issues, even for offenders with schizophrenia (Taylor and Bragado-Jimenez, 2009). Antipsychotic medication is generally regarded as the mainstay of treatment for psychosis, and for reduction or prevention of both violence (Steinert et al., 2000; Swanson et al., 2000) and victimization (Hiday et al., 2002) in that context. There is good reason for more gender specificity in antipsychotic medication research, as women tend to have higher serum neuroleptic levels than men, and higher risk of some side-effects, such as hyperprolactinaemia (Rädler and Naber, 2007). Information about medication effects which are specific to women with psychosis is, however, difficult to find because trials either exclude women or they form only a minority subsample, and their data are rarely analysed separately. Two earlier systematic reviews, one of efficacy of second generation antipsychotics (Davis et al., 2003) and one of their role in relapse prevention (Leucht et al., 2003) do not mention women at all. A naturalistic, but prospective cohort study in Finland with 847 female and 1,383 male patients with schizophrenia and schizoaffective disorder, followed over 7 years after discharge from hospital, showed no overall differences between the sexes in incidence of rehospitalization (Tiihonen et al., 2006), but specified that haloperidol appeared less helpful in this respect for women.

The influence of female sex hormones on the course of psychosis has received some consideration. Women appear to be more vulnerable to psychotic breakdown when post-partum and after the menopause (Häfner et al., 1998, 2003) and there have been observations that the psychotic symptoms of schizophrenia vary in the course of the menstrual cycle (Hallonquist et al., 1993; Riecher-Rössler et al., 1994), with improvement during higher oestradiol levels in mid-cycle. A Cochrane review found four small random contolled trials of adjunctive treatment with oestrogen, with or without progesterone, which, collectively, showed no benefit (Chua et al., 2005), although a subsequent trial proved more promising (Kulkarni et al., 2008).

Psychological treatments for women with psychosis have received a bit more research attention. Cognitive behavioural therapy (CBT) has become popular in treatment of people with schizophrenia in the UK (see chapter 14), but its evaluation among people with psychosis who have been violent is largely anecdotal. Anger has been successfully treated with CBT in this context (Renwick et al., 1997) and a single-blinded randomized controlled trial of CBT compared with social activity therapy showed that some women (14%) had significant improvements in their delusions and violent behaviour (Haddock et al., 2009). Insofar as differences between men and women in overall response to CBT have been considered (6/7 studies reviewed by Gould et al., 2001), there is no suggestion of a sex difference. In practice, CBT for psychosis tends to be focused on beliefs about illness and improving treatment engagement. Ritsher et al. (1997) surveyed 107 women and 59 men in rehabilitation, and found women more likely than men to want to talk about 'normal concerns' rather than illness; normal concerns tended to be about personal relationships as well as general and reproductive healthcare.

Treatment of borderline personality disorder, by contrast, has been much better evaluated in women than in men, whether the main treatment is pharmacological or psychological (see chapter 16).

CONCLUSIONS

Offending and incarceration rates among women have been subject to some fluctuations through the latter years of the twentieth century and the beginnings of the twenty-first, but women remain a small minority of those who present to the criminal justice system. Around 13–17% of criminal convictions are against women. They form an even smaller proportion of prisoners, but perhaps as high a proportion as 10–20% in specialist forensic mental health services. There is some difference between female and male prisoners in rates of formally designated mental disorder, but any further differences in such disorder rates in mental health services probably reflect selection bias. There is a general consensus, however, that the health and social problems of women present a different order of challenge to those of men both in criminal justice and mental health services. This is partly because of the nature and extent of their difficulties but also because, until their index contact with the criminal justice or health system, they may well

have had sole responsibility for one or more children. Some of their own personal difficulties may arise from specifically gender related physiological issues, such as hormonal cycles, some from gender related psychological issues, such as the tendency to turn distress and rage onto themselves, and some from indirectly gender related issues in their exceptional vulnerability if reared in highly disadvantaged or abusive families. Accordingly, there have been calls for special strategies for treatment of women in both health and criminal justice services, and dedicated services for them have begun to emerge. There is as yet, however, very little research evidence that any particular service framework or specific treatment is superior to any other. Given the fairly small populations of such women at any one site, perhaps only co-operation between researchers at various sites – internationally as well as nationally – offers the prospect of significant progress.

In addition to the direct needs of the women, it is important to think also of the needs that arise for others as a result of their difficulties, and in particular, where the women have children, the needs of those children. Ideally, work on this would take place in partnership with the women, but there may anyway be tasks to be done for immediate protection of the child's health and safety, for the longer term protection of disadvantage and morbidity in the child(ren) and, indirectly, for promoting the woman's wellbeing as a mother for reducing the likelihood that she will harm or even kill her child(ren).

Brookman and Maguire (2004) offered preventive strategies against homicide, which include

- educational programmes/campaigns to prepare parents better for the stresses of childcare, and to emphasize the particular fragility of young babies, for example if shaken;
- expansion of home visit programmes and midwife and health visitor support, both before and after childbirth;
- counselling and respite services for those families identified as suffering undue stresses/pressures and where the mother may be regarded as potentially 'at risk' of harming herself or her baby or other children;
- multi-agency co-operation and responses once a 'high-risk' family has been identified, to prevent further risk of abuse/neglect;
- more attention to the creation of a social climate which is protective of infants and children.

Psychosis and/or severe depression after childbirth needs specialist treatment, and we note again that in England and Wales, there is evidence that there have been no fatalities – of mother or child – when mother and baby had been admitted to a specialist mother and baby unit (Oates, 2003).

Of course, not all women are mothers, and anyway we do not want to suggest that mothers should only be defined by their children. Since personality and substance use disorders are major problems for offending women, it is clear that improved care of those suffering from substance abuse disorders is needed, including ease of access to services, as well as enlightened treatment programmes for women with personality disorder. In addition, girls as well as boys who are identified at home or at school as having behavioural problems and/or using psychoactive substances should have early access to adequate assessment and treatment. Accurate early intervention is likely to make a difference (Kjelsberg and Dahl, 1999; Harrington and Bailey, 2003, 2004; see also chapters 16 and 19).

21

Older people and the criminal justice system

Edited by
Pamela J Taylor

Written by
Seena Fazel

Older people may be involved with the criminal justice system (CJS) in a variety of ways. Before moving to the main focus of this chapter – the older person as an offender – it is worth brief consideration of some of their other roles in the CJS, and the extent to which there is a pertinent evidence base which has a bearing on these. Brank (2007) reviewed the literature on older people as eyewitnesses, jurors and parties to a case and whether age *per se* restricts access to the courts. As she points out, eyewitnesses of any age are not renowned for the accuracy of their identifications, but older people, although regarded as more honest (e.g. Allison et al., 2006), have generally been found to be less accurate as witnesses (e.g. Brimacombe et al., 2003), although there are exceptions to this (e.g. Neuschatz et al., 2005). There has been little research with older jurors, even in terms of demographics, beyond review of the potential strengths and limitations. Age limits vary across the UK and Ireland: England and Wales are 18–69 (http://www.hmcourts-service.gov.uk); Northern Ireland 18–70 (http://www.courtsni.gov.uk); Scotland 18–65 (http://www.adviceguide.org.uk/scotland/law_s/law_legal_system_s/law_taking_legal_action_s/jury_service_scotland.htm. Ireland has no upper age limit (http://www.courts.ie/courts.ie/library3.nsf/PageCurrentWebLookUPTopNav/Jury9020Service).

In the USA, rather than set upper age limits for jury service, some states allow older people (e.g. aged 70 in Florida) to be excused on request. The same spirit largely applies to lawyers; while in England and Wales judges must retire at 70 (http://www.judicialappointments.gov.uk), this does not apply to higher court judges in the USA, nor to prosecuting or defending attorneys, who have been 'productive well into their 80s' (Adams, 2000). There appears to be no research into this productivity.

The perceptions and realities of older victims of crime are covered in chapter 28.

Increasing interest has been directed towards 'older offenders' since the late 1990s, but how are they defined? Crime tends to be committed by younger people, and some have regarded 45, or even 40, as elderly for offenders

(Aday, 2003). This chapter is mostly about people of 60 and over – eligible for special services within the UK's national health services, among women starting to draw their state pensions, although men do not do so until 65, and age limits are rising. Demographic trends show rising numbers of people in these age groups in Western countries, and also larger numbers of older men accumulating in jails and prisons. A steady stream of articles in the media has highlighted this issue, some in the UK describing 'senile delinquency' (Frean, 1999), an 'elderly crime wave' and, in certain other countries, the term 'grandpa jails' has been used.

HOW MANY OLDER OFFENDERS?

In England and Wales, there were 2,174 indictable offences by those aged over 60 in 2003 (Home Office, 2005). This represents 0.7% of all indictable offences – a proportion that has not changed much since 1993 (Fazel and Jacoby, 2002). The absolute number of offences has also remained at a similar level, but official statistics may not represent the true picture of antisocial behaviour in older people, particularly if the police disproportionately drop charges or caution them. Age-related data from the Home Office do not support this. The Crown Prosecution Service has guidance on prosecution of older people on its website (http://www.cps.gov.uk). Nevertheless, it is worth noting that, in one of the few community based studies of older offenders, Needham-Bennett et al. (1996) found that of 367 consecutive arrests of people aged 60 or over, less than 10% were prosecuted. Nearly two-thirds of the arrests had been for shoplifting, mostly groceries of small value. Police referred the arrestees to their primary care physician or to the police doctor more often than to any other agency. Of the 50 arrestees who had a research interview, nearly one-third were identified as psychiatric cases.

Although neither the numbers nor the proportion of crimes committed by older persons appear to have increased since the late 1990s, the number of sentenced

Table 21.1   The rise in population of men aged 60 and over in prison establishments in England and Wales from 1989 to 1999 expressed as a percentage of imprisoned males of all ages (Home Office 2000 – Cm 4805. HMSO, London). For 2000 onwards the proportion is for sentenced prisoners only

Year	1992	1993	1994	1995	1996	1997	1998	1999	2000	2001	2002	2003	2004	2005	2006	2007
Percentage of all ages	1.3	1.4	1.5	1.6	1.7	1.8	1.8	2.2	2.2	2.3	2.4	2.3	2.3	2.4	2.6	2.9

prisoners aged 60 and above in England and Wales more than doubled between the years 1992 to 2002 (from 454 to 1,508) (Home Office, 2000c). This partly reflected overall increases in the prison population in England and Wales, which rose from 37,000 to 57,000 in the same period, but the proportion of prisoners of 60 or over doubled over this time – to 2.4% (see table 21.1). The trend has continued. In March 2008, there were 2,242 prisoners of 60 or over in England and Wales (2.9% of all male prisoners), including 454 of 70 and over.

A similar trend has been observed in America, where the number of prisoners aged 55 and over increased from 48,800 in 1999 to 71,900 in 2004 (Beck, 2000; Harrison and Beck, 2005). In Canada, growth in the population of older offenders in prison has been more than 10 times the growth of the population of younger offenders (Uzoaba, 1998).

The number of receptions of elderly men to prisons in England and Wales has also increased, but not as fast as the residential numbers. In 1998, there were 661 prison receptions of those aged over 59, compared to 339 in 1993 (Fazel and Jacoby, 2000). Criminologists call this 'punitive bifurcation', whereby those in prison are staying in for longer sentences, while the admission rates are growing less quickly. Few older people entering prison are likely to be first time offenders; Taylor and Parrott (1988), for example, in a series of 63 pretrial remand receptions to one prison in 1979/1980 found that over 80% of those of 55 or over had previously been convicted. There were only 20 sentenced women of 60 or over in prison in England and Wales in 2004, which represented just 0.6% of the female sentenced population. Between 1997 and 2003, the sentenced population of women over 50 increased from 60 to 172; these women, like the men, were serving longer sentences (HM Inspectorate for Prisons, 2004).

In Canada, sentenced prisoners over the age of 50 fall into one of three main groups: those who were incarcerated young and grew old in prison (10%); those recalled, whether or not after a new offence (17%); and those admitted late in life (73%) (Uzoaba, 1998). The pattern in the USA looks slightly different, but was as follows for those aged 55 and over: 13% incarcerated young and who aged in prison; 46% career criminal recidivists; 41% first time offenders incarcerated for the first time (Steffensmeier and Motivans, 2000). Among serious offender patients in England and Wales, that is people convicted of a criminal offence and then placed under hospital orders with restrictions on discharge, 282 (6.5%) of the total of over 4,000 in the year 2002 were aged 60 or over; 282 of them were in hospital and 105 conditionally discharged at this time (O'Sullivan and Chesterman, 2007). Age at the index offence ranged from 20 to 75 years, but just 37 of them had committed this offence when aged 60 or over. Mechanisms by which people become first time offenders in older age are far from clear. It is unlikely that there is any single explanation but, where disorders of mental health such as depression or dementia, which are particularly likely to be new problems for people in this age group, are relevant, it may be either that they precipitate or drive offending or, in some cases, make it hard for a previously 'successful' criminal to remain 'effective'.

WHAT SORT OF CRIME?

2003 was chosen as a year to study prisoners in England and Wales in more depth. Table 21.2a shows the offence categories for convictions for people of 60 and over in that year. Among the women, by far the largest proportion of crime was acquisitive (theft and handling: 46%; fraud and forgery: 28%). Physical contact crimes of any kind were unusual. Among the men, by contrast, sexual offences were the largest single offence category with 22% of all convictions in that age group, just over the number for theft and handling. Under 14% of convictions were for violence against the person. Separately, figures produced for England and Wales by the National Confidential Inquiry into Suicide and Homicide (2006) showed that although most homicides are committed by younger people, in the period April 1999 to December 2003, 104 (4%) were committed by people of 55 or over including 11 by people 75 or over. Among the 60 people who were aged 59 and over, two-thirds of the homicides had killed his/her spouse, compared with about one-third in the younger groups. This higher risk to spouses, relative to younger homicide offenders, was also found in a Chicago sample, where it was shown that the older homicide was more likely to follow through with suicide (Fazel et al., 2007a). At any age, however, interpersonal violence which results in a criminal conviction is itself unusual. Among the elderly with dementia, non-criminalized aggression and interpersonal violence are recognized as common problems which require management (e.g. Talerico et al., 2002).

There has been considerable attention given to sex offending among older people, not least because, as table 21.2b shows, among men, the proportion of all offences which are sex offences increases steadily by age group, from young to old. In prisons in England and Wales, about half of the elderly sentenced male prisoners are sexual offenders – a proportion that has been increasing since the early 1990s. In 1993, 43% of the sentenced male prison population in England and Wales of 60 or over were sexual offenders; by 1998 this had risen to 49%, and by 2004 to 57%. Large numbers of incarcerated elderly sexual offenders are also found in other Western countries. In Canada, for example, half of the over 59-year-old male sentenced prison population are sexual offenders (Uzoaba, 1998). In the USA, Lewis et al. (2006) showed that, sexual offending or not, sexually transmitted diseases are common among older offenders. This is important, as clinicians may wrongly assume lower sexual activity and thus miss risk of this kind among older people.

ASSOCIATIONS BETWEEN PSYCHIATRIC DISORDER AND OFFENDING IN OLDER AGE

To date, no population-based studies of crime in older persons have been conducted. Overall, information on associations between crime and mental disorder in this age group is limited, and most surveys are from selected samples at various stages in the criminal justice system. Some of these provide information for the development and planning of forensic psychiatric and prison healthcare services. Studies examining the pattern of psychiatric morbidity in older offenders referred for assessment and treatment (Heinik et al., 1994; Rosner et al., 1991; Barak et al., 1995), and whether this is different from younger offenders, are particularly useful in this regard. The largest study of this type was of psychiatric diagnoses in 203 older criminals referred for inpatient assessment prior to sentencing in Sweden, comparing them to younger referrals (Fazel and Grann, 2002). Among those offenders aged 60 or over, the proportion with any psychotic illness was about the same as among the younger men (31%), but with less schizophrenia (7%:12%) and more affective psychosis (7%:4%) recorded among the older forensic psychiatric referrals than among the younger ones. Personality disorder was less likely to have been diagnosed in the older group (20%: 32%); dementia was more likely (7%:0.3%), as were cerebral lesions (5%:2%), but non-toxic organic psychoses were similarly distributed between older and younger referrals (3.8%:3.4%). There were no other significant differences between older and younger referrals in diagnostic distribution. Further details may be found in Fazel and Grann (2002).

In England and Wales, in 1988–1994, an investigation of referral patterns to secure hospitals found the referral rate to be surprisingly low considering the degree of psychiatric morbidity in older offenders. In seven of the then 14 health regions there, only 2% of all admissions were of individuals age 60 or over. There was no increase in the number of older men being admitted over the study period (Coid et al., 2002). Similarly the proportion of referrals of people of 65 or over to a large medium secure facility in London between 1990 and 2002 remained steady at 1.4% (Tomar et al., 2005).

Table 21.2a Indictable offences in England and Wales in 2003 by those aged 60 and over (Home Office 2005, IOS 263–05)

Offence category	Men	Women
	N (%)	N (%)
Violence against the person	257 (13.6%)	29 (10.4%)
Sexual offences	409 (21.6%)	1 (0.4%)
Burglary	23 (1.2%)	0 (0.0%)
Robbery	7 (0.4%)	1 (0.4%)
Theft and handling stolen goods	402 (21.2%)	129 (46.1%)
Fraud and forgery	245 (12.9%)	78 (27.9%)
Criminal damage	42 (2.2%)	6 (2.1%)
Drug offences	124 (6.5%)	12 (4.3%)
Other indictable offences	309 (16.3%)	17 (6.1%)
Indictable motoring offences	76 (4.0%)	7 (2.5%)
Total	1,894 (100.0%)	280 (100.0%)

Table 21.2b Proportion of sentenced men imprisoned in England and Wales in 2004 for sexual offences as percentage of all sentenced prisoners for respective age group (Home Office 2005, IOS 263–05)

All ages	21 to 24	25 to 29	30 to 39	40 to 49	50 to 59	60+
9.9%	3.5%	4.0%	8.4%	18.0%	34.2%	57.4%

525

Psychiatric Morbidity Among Older Prisoners

Fazel et al. (2001a) studied 2003 sentenced male prisoners aged 60 or over who agreed to a semi-structured interview (Fazel et al., 2001a). At the time, they represented nearly one-fifth of such men in England and Wales. One in three had a potentially treatable mental illness and nearly a third had a diagnosis of personality disorder. The details are shown in table 21.3. Allowing for substance misuse diagnoses too, over half (53%, CI 46–60%) of the sample had a psychiatric diagnosis (mental illness or personality disorder). This is a higher level of mental *illness* than that found in surveys of adult prisoners more generally, which typically find that one in seven prisoners have a potentially treatable mental illness (Fazel and Danesh, 2002). The 5% with psychotic illness is, however, broadly consistent with the calculation of 4% found in the systematic review of adult prisoners of all ages (Fazel and Danesh, 2002); it is also consistent with figures in an earlier study in one large English pretrial prison sample (Taylor and Parrott, 1988). Perhaps the difference in time frame is relevant, but one would expect that the most sick prisoners would have been filtered out by the time of sentencing, and so the proportion of psychosis among sentenced prisoners to be much lower.

In the study of 203 older men in prison, it was apparent that depression constituted the largest single diagnostic group, with 30% of them so diagnosed. This

Table 21.3 Psychiatric diagnoses among sentenced male prisoners aged 60 and over in England and Wales (n = 203)

Diagnoses	No. (%) of prisoners
Psychoses:	
Depressive	9 (4)
Other	1 (1)
Total	10 (5)
Neuroses:	
Depressive	51 (25)
Hypochondriasis	1 (1)
Total	52 (26)
Organic disorders:	
Dementia	2 (1)
DSM-IV personality disorder:	
Antisocial personality disorder	17 (8)
Any personality disorder	61 (30)
Current substance abuse/dependence	10 (5)
Total psychiatric morbidity*	108 (53)

*Total is less than the sum of individual disorders because some prisoners had more than one disorder.
(Adapted with permission from Fazel S, Hope T, O'Donnell l, and Jacoby R (2001a) Hidden psychiatric morbidity in elderly prisoners. *British Journal of Psychiatry* 179: 535–9.)

was a higher prevalence than among younger male prisoners, which is typically around 10% (Fazel and Danesh, 2002). This prevalence of depression among older men is also higher than that a large community study of men of similar age which used the Geriatric Mental State interview, which found 6% had a depressive illness (Saunders et al., 1993). Nevertheless, among older prisoners, factors associated with depression were similar to those identified among their community resident peers (Copeland et al., 1999). Thus, depression was about twice as likely among prisoners with a past psychiatric history or poor physical health. The standardized mortality ratio for suicide in male prisoners aged 60 or over is five times that of men in the general population of similar ages, a proportionate excess similar to younger age groups (Fazel et al., 2005).

Although there has been much less research with older women in prison, there is one North American case record study which compared women and men over the age of 55. The women and the men had similar rates of mental illness (women: 17%; men: 16%) (Regan et al., 2002).

Alcohol and Substance Abuse

Alcohol abuse and dependence is a particular problem in older prisoners. In a UK study of remand prisoners, Taylor and Parrott (1988) reported a steady increase with age in the proportions of prisoners experiencing alcohol withdrawal symptoms. Such symptoms were observed in one-third of prisoners over 65. A large US study reported that 71% of inmates over 55 years in Iowa reported a substance misuse problem compared with over 90% in younger age groups, but that, compared with younger prisoners, the older ones were more likely to abuse alcohol only (Arndt et al., 2002).

OLDER SEX OFFENDERS

There have been a number of studies of older sex offenders with a particular emphasis on recidivism rates. These appear to be lower than among younger sex offenders discharged from criminal justice and secure hospital settings in the USA (Barbaree et al., 2003; Hanson, 2002; Langan et al., 2003). One explanation advanced for this is lower sexual arousal in older men (Barbaree et al., 2003), another is increased self-control with age (Hanson, 2002), but cohort effects may also be relevant. A major problem with many of these studies is that they do not allow for time at risk, and survival in the community in any sense may be curtailed for the older men. Type of offensive behaviour may also be relevant. One Canadian study investigated differences in recidivism rates after release from prison or secure hospitals (without accounting for time at risk), by comparing rapists, incest offenders, and extra-familial child molesters (Hanson, 2002). This suggested that recidivism rates were negatively correlated to age in rapists, but less so in other types of sexual offenders. A study of all sex offenders released from Swedish prisons also explored age-related factors, and found that the rate of recidivism at 9 years post-release was 6.7% in the over 55 year olds compared with 43% in those aged under 25. Having a stranger victim was the strongest risk factor in the over 55s, but appeared not to be associated with recidivism in the under 25s (Fazel et al., 2006).

In older prisoners incarcerated for sexual offences, similar prevalence rates of mental illness have been found compared with other older male inmates. Elderly sex offenders, however, had increased schizoid, obsessive compulsive, and avoidant personality traits in one study, supporting the view that sex offending in the elderly may be more associated with personality factors than with mental illness or organic brain disease (Fazel et al., 2002a). In addition, gross impairments to frontal lobe function were not found compared with other offenders (Fazel et al., 2007a).

SERVICE AND TREATMENT IMPLICATIONS

If, as described above, 5% of older prisoners have a psychotic illness, then, using 2004 figures, at any one time about 70–80 of sentenced male prisoners aged 60 or over in England and Wales would be psychotic, almost all with a depressive psychosis. Most clinicians and prison staff would agree that these men should be transferred to a hospital – whether secure or not – for treatment. In addition, according to similar calculations, around 400 older inmates there would be suffering from a major but non-psychotic clinical depression. It may be that most of these could be treated appropriately within the prison setting, but there must be substantial improvements in prison healthcare for this to happen. In a study of such older men, only 14% of all depressed prisoners (n=60) reported being treated with anti-depressants, although three-quarters of this sample were being prescribed medication and being seen by prison doctors for their physical health needs (Fazel et al., 2004). Similar problems with likely under-treatment of psychiatric illness have been found in the USA, where, in one study (Koenig et al., 1995), 13 of 16 older prisoners with active psychiatric disorders received no treatment.

Nevertheless, this population poses particular challenges for prison health services. Older depressed men may not come to the attention of prison medical staff as they sit quietly in their cells, not causing any problems for prison officers and not posing a security risk. A number of possible service improvements may assist. First, ways of improving the identification of depression in older inmates should be considered. This may include raising the general awareness among all prison staff of the increased risk of depression in the older prisoner. Prison officers should be encouraged to refer older prisoners for psychiatric assessment if they appear withdrawn or isolated – not only more obviously depressed. Among clinical staff working in prisons, a similar increased awareness is essential; the commissioning of prison health services from the mainstream National Health Service should improve the situation. A screening questionnaire for depression at prison reception for those aged 59 and above may also be helpful. The 15-item version of the Geriatric Depression Scale would be well suited to the prison environment as it is simple to administer, designed for community samples, and only takes a few minutes to complete (Sheikh and Yesavage, 1986). Prisoners could be identified at reception, by referral from the wings by prison officers, or when seen for physical problems.

Such educational interventions, though, are not sufficient – even in the wider community. The Hampshire Depression Project, a randomized control trial of an educational intervention for the detection and treatment of depression in primary care in the UK, found that an educational programme based on clinical practice guidelines did not improve the recognition or outcome of depression in a community setting (Thompson et al., 2000). Regular review of prisoners' medical records, with a view to aligning medication régimes with identified illnesses, would be a simple but effective intervention (Fazel et al., 2004). Then, too, structural changes to the delivery of healthcare in prisons elsewhere have been shown to improve outcomes. An impressive initiative to improve the medical care of all inmates in the state of Texas, for example, was a form of managed care – a general term for the activity of organizing doctors, hospitals and other providers into groups in order to improve the quality and cost-effectiveness of healthcare. Part of the model was that two Texas medical schools assumed responsibility for the delivery of medical care for prisoners. This included direct university involvement in primary ambulatory care clinics in each prison, prison hospitals on regional level, and a prison hospital on an academic medical campus. Psychiatric services available were group and individual psychotherapy, psychopharmacology and crisis-intervention counselling. A key part of the success of this initiative, it was argued, was the integration of prison health services with an academic medical school and its affiliated hospitals. Other areas that were highlighted included the use of standard disease-management guidelines, a common formulary, specific training for doctors, use of chronic care clinics, and technologies such as telemedicine and electronic medical records (Raimer and Stobo, 2004).

Although, as yet, rates of dementia among prisoners remain low, the chronicity of other mental health conditions and the extent of physical ill-health among some has led to concerns about the potential for a growing need for the equivalent of prison nursing home care (Kerbs, 2000a,b) and even terminal care (Yampolskaya and Winston, 2003). Such needs may not be confined to prisons. When older people need secure hospital care, there are few staff in specialist hospital secure services who are trained to care for the full range of health and social needs.

A structural change that has been considered is the development of specialist services for older offenders. In the UK, a number of authors have considered the development of supraregional medium secure units, which may be able to focus their treatment régimes more appropriately to older offenders and provide a safer setting. In particular, the admission of older individuals with dementia to standard medium or low secure units would be problematic as the medical and allied healthcare staff there would have had little training and experience in dealing with such patients. The problem, though, is that supraregional units are likely be quite far away from the family and friends of these patients, and to the community settings to where they will eventually be transferred.

The case for separate prison wings appears to be stronger. In the USA, by 1998, at least 12 states had set up separate facilities for older prisoners, perhaps in part in response to stated preferences for being away from the noise and aggression of younger inmates (Aday, 2003). In the UK, there are a few, including one in the north-east (HMP Frankland), one in the north-west (HMP Wymott), one in the south-west (HMP Kingston) and east (HMP Norwich). Older prisoners differ from their younger peers in the extent of their physical health problems and disabilities (Fazel et al., 2001b) and their psychosocial needs as well as their psychiatric problems. HM Inspectorate of Prisons (2004) noted, after interviewing 442 male and 47 female prisoners, that high rates of victimization from younger inmates are a concern. The physical condition and structure of the prison – designed for young, active people – can be difficult for older, frailer inmates, and particularly for those with limited mobility. A range of measures to improve the physical environment of prison was suggested in this report. These include housing such prisoners on lower landings, under separate régimes, and improving training for prison staff. Improvements more specifically for older women prisoners were identified in a study by Wahidin (2003).

There are various arguments for and against age-segregated facilities. In favour is the likelihood of less victimization and the feeling of more safety, the relative ease of organization of separate régimes, and several US studies reporting that older prisoners want age-segregated facilities. Against this view is that segregation may lead to neglect of this group of inmates; specialist facilities are

likely to be further away from their home if they have one; and possible problems with a lack of social stimulation and participation in prison activities (Howse, 2003). From a wider prison perspective, specialist units tend to be more expensive, despite cost savings on security and incident management; one US estimate is that costs for a prisoner of 60 or over are at least three times those for younger prisoners (McDonald, 1995). Older prisoners may, however, provide a stabilizing influence for younger prisoners (Rubenstein, 1984).

A qualitative study with older people in a high security hospital, and the staff looking after them, brought out some of these tensions too. Most were not resident on what had been envisaged as a specialist unit for them; it had become a unit for 'vulnerable patients', which they said, with some justice, translated in practice as sex offenders (Yorston and Taylor, 2009). If asked, older prisoners might take the same view; 'the majority' of the vulnerable prisoners in HMP Wymott, for example, are sex offenders (Fry and Howe, 2005). Both staff and patients in the high security hospital nevertheless considered that a major issue in management was that these older offender patients had little in common with either their younger offender patient peers or with people of similar age in other institutional settings. It was considered that, as a generally articulate group, these patients could play a large part in determining their most satisfactory placement; this could be true of older prisoners too.

Sentencing policy for the elderly perhaps needs further consideration. According to Gallagher (2001), the Director of Corrections in Canada noted that 50% of older prisoners remain incarcerated beyond their full parole eligibility; some prisoners are undoubtedly reluctant to leave what has become their most familiar community and, for some, suitable alternatives have proved hard to find. Does incarceration at this age create exceptional dependency? Much debate has been generated over the policies of successive UK governments, and the problems of incarcerating persons who pose little risk to the public. This problem is exemplified in the case for individuals who develop dementia whilst in custody (Fazel et al., 2002b). Recidivism research in a variety of criminal justice and mental health settings has shown low rates of re-offending for older criminals (Hanson, 2002; Bonta et al., 1998), and yet few are first time offenders. How useful for older offenders are those factors generally accepted as useful in predicting re-offending in younger ones? What are the main mechanisms for first time offending in later life? These, with the dependency question, are perhaps three current research priorities for this group.

22
Dangerousness

Edited by
Pamela J Taylor

Written by
Nicola S. Gray
John Gunn
David V James
John Monahan
Robert J Snowden
Pamela J Taylor
Julian Walker
Lisa J Warren

1st edition authors: **John Gunn and John Monahan**

INTRODUCTION

The title of this chapter has given us pause. The government commissioned report which laid the foundations for modern forensic psychiatry in the UK [(Home Office, Department of Health and Social Security (Butler), 1975] used the term 'dangerousness', but it is now rarely used in clinical practice. After a man was convicted of high profile homicides which had occurred shortly after his departure from a hospital, a later government intervention in England and Wales brought the concept of 'Dangerous and Severe Personality Disorder' into being (Home Office, 1999), although this terminology has since been confined to history (see chapter 16). The conjunction of words was generally not welcomed by clinicians, and may have been a factor in the UK in consolidating a preference for use of the term 'risk', generally here shorthand for a concept of risk of a seriously adverse event. 'Risk' is sometimes, though, a term used so unthinkingly by clinicians that the question 'risk of what?' invokes puzzlement, so we have retained the title word of dangerousness to emphasize that our concern here is with risk of serious harm to others.

Clinicians are expected to be able to calculate risk of serious harm by people with mental disorder, and to take appropriate actions accordingly, in clinical practice, and sometimes for the courts or in other parts of the criminal justice system. This has long been so, but progressively more has been expected of them after highly publicized individual cases. In the UK, it has commonly been the rare cases of stranger homicide by a person with psychosis, in the USA

an important landmark was *Tarasoff,* although the latter illustrates one of the most important issues of all – that recognition of threat or risk, and even its systematic assessment is not enough. Resultant, appropriately informed management strategies are essential.

In order to assess and manage risk as accurately and effectively as possible, clinicians need reliable and valid tools to help them with the task, a good understanding of the strengths and limitations of those tools, the training to use them appropriately, a clear understanding of the nature of the task they are being asked to perform at any given time and an appropriate modesty about their abilities in this regard. Considerable weight may be put on an 'expert's' opinion on risk in court. This, coupled with its centrality in decisions about compulsory detention in and discharge from hospital in the UK, the USA and many other countries too, means that clinicians' judgments of risk may have a very powerful effect on the rights of the individual, but also, potentially, on his or her safety and that of others in the community. Risk assessment is, therefore, a very serious business, and so we take a very critical perspective of the tasks, tools and processes.

The range of risk assessment aids available indicates, in part, that there is no perfect solution for the task, but in part also that there are different tasks to be done. Answers to questions about which instruments to use follow partly from clarity about what is to be done – is it primarily risk assessment alone or is it one in which the clinician expects to be active in risk reduction (Skeem and Monahan, 2011)? This chapter cannot cover all of the potentially useful aids available. It is mainly about the theory and practice of the assessment of risk of serious harm to others and of explicit threats of harm. These tasks overlap, but also have some differences. More detailed descriptions of three of the risk assessment and management aids which are most commonly used in clinical practice in English speaking countries are provided as illustrative of first the actuarial tool, which bases more-or-less fixed predictions on static historical factors, secondly, structured clinical/professional judgment, which offers a more dynamic approach including guidance on change in risk over time, and third, a computer aided rapid assessment. Readers should be aware of parallel instruments more commonly used in the criminal justice system which, in the UK include the brief actuarial Offender Group Reconviction Scale (OGRS, Howard et al., 2009), the structured professional judgment scales such as the Level of Service Inventory – Revised (LSI-R, Andrews and Bonta, 1995) or the Assessment Case Management and Evaluation System (ACE, Gibbs, 1999; Raynor et al., 2000), and the tools which are more specific to particular behaviours, such as the sex offender risk assessment instruments (see chapter 10).

THEORETICAL ISSUES

Some Concerns and Needs

Concern about use of the word 'dangerousness' is partly because it is so widely used, has more than one application and is not value free. If typed into a search engine it yields hundreds of thousands of web references. It is a term applied both to a property which threatens human beings and which is ascribed to them. Scott (1977) warned that clinicians with powers to detain people in hospital have to be particularly careful of the concept:

dangerousness is a term which raises anxiety and is therefore particularly open to abuse, especially to over-response of a punitive, restrictive or dissociative nature.

Douglas and Wildavsky (1983) provide a further warning:

Can we know the risks we face, now or in the future? No, we cannot; but yes we must act as if we do.

Adams (1995) elaborates:

Some act knowing that their knowledge is partial and conditional. Others, of strong belief and conviction, manage to conjure certainty out of ignorance. Yet others, those advocating a scientific approach to risk, act as if uncertainty is a temporary condition that can be overcome by dint of more research. They divert attention away from the question of how to act in the face of uncertainty by focusing their energies on the impossible task of removing uncertainty.

Such warnings recur. Taleb (2007) takes human blindness about randomness as the central theme in his book *The Black Swan*. He is particularly scathing of the use of historical data for predicting events of large impact. Clinicians are generally aware that a single catastrophic event is neither a good predictor – criminal homicide, for example, is rarely a recidivist event – nor readily predicted. They generally seek patterns in behaviour, but these help most with prediction of similar behaviours. Taleb, again, urges caution in making predictions solely or even principally on past behaviour patterns:

You derive solely from past data a few conclusions ... with projections for the next thousand, even five thousand days. On the thousand and first ... a big change takes place that is completely unprepared for by the past (p.41).

Taleb, however, is not only concerned with some of the perceptual errors and plethora of unforeseeable events inherent in prediction failures, but also in the mathematical ignorance and statistical fallacies that bedevil interpretations of risk. In England, the miscarriage of justice in *Clark* shows the seriousness of the consequences when an expert is unaware of his difficulties in this regard and the Court, in turn, unable to perceive them. The statistical fallacy which appeared, at the least, to have substantially influenced the outcome of the trial led to the Royal Statistical Society (2002) recommending that statistical evidence should be presented in court only by appropriately qualified statistical experts, as would be the case for any other form of expert evidence. The Royal Statistical Society went on to develop a series of guidelines, the first perhaps more pertinent to forensic scientists in practice, but the principles are important for all expert witnesses (Aitkin et al., 2010).

Gigerenzer and Gaissmaier (2008; see also Gigerenzer and Muir Gray, 2011) also take up the theme of statistical illiteracy in the clinical professions, politicians and public alike, and focus especially on the nature of risk communication. They take examples from the treatment and prevention of ill health, but the underpinning concepts are the same. They call for better education in statistics for everyone, and:

... teaching statistical literacy as the art of solving real-world problems rather than applying formulas to toy problems about coins and dice.

They particularly ask for more transparency in the way in which probabilities, or risks, are presented. They advocate use of mortality rates rather than survival rates and, perhaps of most relevance here, frequency statements rather than event probabilities, natural frequencies rather than conditional probabilities and absolute rather than relative risks. They illustrate this point with population based statistics about cancer risks, but one small example from forensic psychiatric service development will serve here. In the early days of medium security hospital unit development in England, one of us visited a new regional unit. The local newspaper response to its recent expansion was blazoned in the headline 'Danger Patients Double'. How frightening – but, in fact, the unit had expanded its population from five patients to ten!

Actuarial and Clinical Risk Assessment: Principles and Comparisons

The three main components of so-called dangerousness (National Research Council, 1989) lead neatly into concepts of risk as understood by forensic mental health clinicians:

1. the nature of the projected harm;
2. 'risk factors' – the qualities that influence the chances of that harm happening in reality; and
3. 'risk level' – the probability that the harm will actually occur.

So, what is risk? There is a generally accepted position of distinguishing between 'objective risk' and 'perceived risk' (Royal Society for the Prevention of Accidents, 1992). The former is construed as 'real' and measurable, obeying laws of statistical theory and is the matter for experts. The mathematics is, however, about probability, not certainty. The tension between 'objective risk' and 'perceived risk' is reflected in clinical practice in the actuarial versus clinical judgment debate. It is arguable that, in some respects, there is little to choose between the approaches, with both potentially using similar information from which to build conclusions, including clinical variables, dynamic variables, protective factors and contextual information. The perceived advantages of the clinical approach include the interactive nature of data collection, in part deliberately open and unstructured so as to avoid imposing preconceived ideas onto the person being assessed, and in part structured in similar ways to the more formal assessment tools, and that it is always individualized. The main criticism of this approach is that the judgment itself may be subjective and opaque, and, possibly, just one clinician's perception. Clinicians generally have great respect for the actuarial approach but also two main concerns – that it may be unduly based on static, unchangeable factors and that it lacks specificity to the individual case.

Advocates of actuarial and clinical methods in prediction of risk of harm, despite the growing science, seem unfortunately to have been characterized as much by their fervor as by their science. Meehl (1954) made it his life's work to advocate for actuarial methods, which he and his co-workers generally referred to as 'mechanical prediction methods'. The aims of a review and meta-analysis with Grove (Grove and Meehl, 1996) were forcefully stated:

The purposes of this article are (a) to reinforce the empirical generalization of actuarial over clinical prediction with fresh meta-analytic evidence; (b) to reply to common objections to actuarial methods; (c) to provide an explanation for why actuarial prediction works better than clinical prediction; (d) to offer some explanations for why practitioners continue to resist actuarial prediction in the

face of overwhelming evidence to the contrary; and (e) to conclude with policy recommendations, some of which include correcting for unethical behavior on the part of many clinicians.

and

We conclude that this literature is almost 100% consistent ... with results obtained by Meehl in 1954. Forty years of research has not altered the conclusion .... It has only strengthened that conclusion (Grove and Meehl, 1996).

This more polemical article, countering clinicians' fears and objections to their position, drew on their cited meta-analysis of 136 studies identified through systematic review of health and behavioural literature, but long preceded publication of that meta-analysis (Grove et al., 2000). Actual findings were

On average, mechanical-prediction techniques were about 10% more accurate than clinical predictions. Depending on the specific analysis, mechanical prediction substantially outperformed clinical prediction in 33%–47% of studies examined. Although clinical predictions were often as accurate as mechanical predictions, in only a few studies (6%–16%) were they substantially more accurate.

Studies focusing on violence as an outcome after a prediction of violence raise more doubts, although also hint at possible explanations for confusion. Buchanan and Leese (2001) conducted a systematic review of *prospective* studies published between 1970 and 2000 which compared clinical and actuarial risk assessment. They identified 23 studies, in just 21 of which the sensitivity, specificity and positive predictive power had been or could be calculated. The studies covered mixed diagnoses with no particular diagnosis dominating, despite the title of the paper which implied focus on personality disorder. Actuarial tools were shown to perform rather better than clinical judgment alone, but overall sensitivity using actuarial tools was hardly better than chance, and specificity only slightly better than that. They then considered positive predictive power, allowing for study heterogeneity and assuming a generous base rate of 9.5% of violence; positive predictive power was only 0.17 (0.14–0.19). If applied to indicate grounds for detention, this would indicate a need to detain six people in order to prevent one act of violence while still failing to prevent others. Had they chosen to calculate for the sort of very serious offences about which we are most concerned, which have a much lower base rate, the predictive power would have been much lower still. Szmukler (2001, 2003) carries forward arguments about the ethics of this. Buchanan's (2008) later publication is more optimistic about the field as are the more recent analyses by McDermott et al. (2011) and Yang et al. (2010).

Lidz and colleagues published a series of reports comparing actuarial assessment with clinical judgment based on the same US emergency room data. In the first (1993), they expressed their findings in terms of clinical judgment being a better predictor of future violence than chance among men, but not women, even after controlling for the static or historical factors of age, race, sex *and* violence. Later, after more complex statistical analyses, they found an advantage for actuarial assessment over clinical judgment (Gardner et al., 1996a,b). Why was this? It is not clear, but experiments from the domain of cognitive psychology show that humans find it difficult to cope with multiple variables and track the influence of them, instead focusing on the variables that they *believe* to be important. Plesk and Greenhalgh (2001) led a series of articles on the application of complexity science to healthcare. This model allows for the multiplicity of interacting and self-regulating systems within the body and behaviour of any individual, and between the person and his or her wider environment, and that each system is dynamic and fluid. A small change in any one part of this web of interacting systems, they say, may lead to much larger change in another. Adams (1995), a geographer whose main interest in risk assessment related to road safety, took up the interactive theme:

> *Human behaviour will always be unpredictable; it will always be responsive to human behaviour, including yours.*

So, is this all just to counsel despair? No, it is rather to encourage the transparency that Gigerenzer and Gaissmaier (2008) call for, and, with it, accurate knowledge about the observation and measurement aids that have been created to help identify and scale risk in clinical practice, and to recognize their limitations as well as their strengths. In clinical situations it is also to foster relevant interventions informed by formal risk assessments as well as more traditional clinical assessments and to ensure frequent re-evaluation of all the circumstances, for detection of positive and/or negative change. There must be constant mindfulness in a clinical situation that relief of distress and improvement in symptoms and signs of disorder is important in itself, but may also reduce the risk of harm, while failure to bring relief will almost certainly sustain or even worsen the risk. As Maden so wisely says in his guide to managing the risk of harm by a person who has active symptoms of mental illness:

> *The most risky decision is to deny treatment or to turn a patient away (Maden, 2007, p.159).*

In the clinical situation, therefore, risk assessment should be part of the wider assessment which informs management and treatment. In 1993, the National Health Service Executive (NHSE) offered a useful template from a management perspective, which remains valid. *Identification* of the possibility of risk is a necessary precursor to its assessment. *Analysis* is a precursor to risk control, and this comes in a number of forms. The first is not much more than a wish: risk elimination. Almost all activity in practice is designed to reduce risk of harm, to avoid it or to lower its cost. Clinicians generally believe that they are mainly concerned

with *risk reduction,* and perhaps the third category of *reducing seriousness of harm*. It may be that on occasion, though, they are avoidant of risk; some inquiries after homicide suggest diagnostic manipulation may be a factor in not accepting patients who are recognized as difficult and potentially harmful (e.g. Ritchie et al., 1994; Spokes, 1988; Taylor and Gunn, 2008). From a clinician or organizational perspective, though, the resultant decisions, having categorized the risks, are to accept them or to transfer them, with the organization additionally having to take decisions about funding risk. The final, and crucial point in the NHSE model is that once risk is acknowledged and accepted, the task is far from over. Rather, this should set in train a *continuous cycle of reassessment and analysis, with adjustments to management strategies thus informed.*

Assessment, done well, gives a good picture of the here and now and, when that is distressing or threatening, supports plans for improving it. It is then necessary to check whether those plans are working, whether any previously unseen strengths or protective factors are emerging or whether any other adverse factors have surfaced, and keep adjusting the response accordingly. A Swiss risk assessment instrument, which is perhaps less well known internationally than those which we will discuss in more detail, explicitly has two forms for the different phases of the process. The risk-needs level of the Forensic Operationalized Therapy/Risk Evaluation System (FOTRES) is completed once at the onset of any new contact with an offender-patient, but the FOTRES risk management level is scored repeatedly – on each occasion when the current risk of re-offending needs to be re-assessed (Rossegger et al., 2011). If more than one offence/risk is at issue, risk for each must be assessed separately.

Actuarial risk assessment

The term 'actuarial' simply refers to the way in which information is put together. Using such an approach, the risk decision is made through a set of formulae, or mathematical expressions, and thus may be implemented by a computer after input of accurate data. Mossman (1994, 1995, 2009) provides excellent, if complex, reviews of these. Application of actuarial risk assessment does require making a link between group data and the individual under assessment. It is a widely used approach, for example in calculating insurance premiums, but it sits uneasily in the criminal court, with its standards of 'beyond reasonable doubt' and when the consequences of such an assessment may be deprivation of liberty. It is thus important to know something about the statistical strengths and limitations of such risk assessment.

At first sight, the limitations are considerable. Hart et al. (2007) present their mathematical construction on the difficulties. They apply the 95% confidence interval, as a commonly applied indicator of the range within which an event or finding can be expected in 95% of cases. Their observation is that the chances of such confidence diminish with reduction in sample size, and become negligible when applied to a sample of one – the individual. Mossman and Selike (2007) immediately challenged the use of standard confidence intervals in such circumstances, partly because they should only be applied to estimated population proportions based on random samples. An additional issue is that, while actuarial assessments may draw on data which describe the proportions of groups with certain characteristics who will have a particular outcome, the prediction required is binary – this person under examination will or will not re-offend, or this person will or will not fail to take necessary medication. Statisticians continue to debate the best way forward. Cooke and Michie (2010) suggested that it lies in prediction intervals, but Scurich and John (2011) say neither will do, and calculation of 'credibility intervals' within a Bayesian approach is what is required. Here, the population for reference data is evaluated according to a binary outcome for each individual, each outcome treated as a mutually exclusive and independent event and all members of the population as independent; the prediction for any new individual can then be calculated according to the fit of the individual to this prior calculation, modified by the number of successes and failures. The larger the number of prior observations required in order to observe the postulated outcome, the lower the probability of that outcome for the individual under assessment, and the smaller the number, the higher the likelihood. Oleson (2010) shows the application of various statistical models along these lines with useful effect for the individual case (albeit in a cochlear implant trial rather than among offenders with mental disorder).

We have written as though the two main approaches to risk assessment may be mutually exclusive, but that is mainly because researchers have tended to investigate only one at a time, or to compare them in a spirit that they expect one to be so superior that the other would be superfluous. It is unfortunate that there is little research on combined approaches, because that is what so often happens in practice. Van den Brink et al. (2010) evaluated the risk assessment and management of 83 offender-patients in community care and found that, for this small series, dynamic risk factors had an incremental predictive value over static factors, and the clinical judgment added further predictive power. This does, however, have parallels with the structured clinical judgment approach described more fully below.

RISK ASSESSMENT AND STRUCTURED JUDGMENT TOOLS

Since 1990, there have been considerable strides in development of aids to risk and threat assessment in clinical practice. There is a better grasp of the importance but limitations of immutable, historical factors, such as previous offending, and the utility of more dynamic factors. There is recognition that while there is a place for lengthy and detailed assessments, most practitioners – clinical or otherwise – have little time available for each individual case, and brief, more clinician-friendly assessments are needed. Hartvig et al. (2006) describe development of a brief assessment based on the HCR-20 (see below). The COVR, described in some detail below, is also especially helpful in this context. There is acknowledgement too that it is vital to have the people who are or have been under assessment – the patients – more directly involved in the process, as well as others who are close to them socially (Robert, 2006; Royal College of Psychiatrists, 2008). There has probably been insufficient attention to systematic description and qualitative study (Litwack, 2002), which still has a role in informing theory and management of unusual cases. This kind of research approach is, however, most difficult where perhaps most needed, because of the increased risk it carries of identifying individual cases. Nevertheless, it has been usefully applied, for example in learning more about protective factors. Haggard et al. (2001) detailed a small group of men who had a large number of the factors which would put them in a high risk group for re-offending, but who, in fact, did well. Use of computer simulations may prove to be a useful innovative approach. In a preliminary trial of use of video material about social interactions likely to be difficult or provocative for people in a group who had Asperger's syndrome or psychosis, patients were asked to describe at key points what they would do in particular situations known to have triggered aggression or physical violence in the past; staff were also asked how the patients would react (Wijk et al., 2009). Both patients and staff found the process realistic, engaging and relevant. A full trial is now needed.

There is a plethora of tools to aid risk assessment which have been subject to research evaluation, and more that have not. Higgins et al. (2005) surveyed 66 randomly selected mental health trusts throughout England and found that, although about half were using risk assessment forms, at this time a content analysis indicated wide variation between them. This may be problematic for clinicians who want to embrace the principle of clear communication about risk.

Actuarial assessments of risk have been developed by testing which of a large number of possible variables best 'predict' the future outcome of interest, here harm to others. The word 'predict' is put in quotation marks here because, very often, studies identifying risk factors have measured factors at time 1 in relation to factors at time 2, but were not designed as prediction studies and, in some cases, data were not even collected prospectively. To date there are three main classes of study used to generate risk assessment tools. One is reliant on a main effects analysis

– essentially the analysis of a single, large data set. The Violence Risk Appraisal Guide (VRAG), described more fully below, is a good example of this. Another depends on systematic literature review and meta-analysis, so that the main effects from the literature form the basis of the scale. The 20-item Historical, Clinical and Risk Management Scale (HCR-20) is an example of this, although, strictly, it should be described as an aid to structured professional or clinical judgment rather than an actuarial risk assessment tool. Both the VRAG and the HCR-20 incorporate a version of the psychopathy checklist (PCL). Some use the revised version – the PCL-R (Hare, 2003) – as a risk assessment tool in its own right (e.g. Gendreau et al., 2002; Grann et al., 1999; Hare et al., 2000). While this should

be noted, in this text, the PCL-R is treated primarily as a measure of an important personality trait and dealt with in chapter 16. The third approach is based on interaction effects analysis which, like the main effects analytical approach, uses a single data set, but makes allowance in the analysis for interactions between risk factors and sets up a hierarchy of questions, with choice of later questions determined by answers to the earlier ones. The main example here is the Classification of Violence Risk (COVR), the third of the tools which we describe in more detail below.

Tables 22.1 and 22.2 summarize the main factors included in some risk assessment aids for clinical or criminal practice.

Table 22.1 Violence risk factors

Category	Subcategory	Factor	1. COVR	2. HCR-20	3. LSI-R[1]	4. Steinert[2]	5. VRAG
Dispositional	Demographic	Age	✓			✓	
		Gender	✓			✓	
		Race	✓				
		Social class	✓				
	Personality	Personality style	✓				
		Anger	✓				✓
		Impulsiveness	✓	✓			✓
		Personality disorder	✓	✓		✓	
		Psychopathy	✓	✓		✓	✓
	Cognitive	IQ	✓			✓	
		Neurological impairment	✓			✓	
Historical	Family history	Child rearing	✓		✓		
		Child abuse	✓				✓
		Family deviance/violence	✓		✓	✓	✓
	Work history	Employment	✓	✓	✓		✓
		Job perceptions	✓				
	Education		✓		✓		
	Mental health history	Prior hospitalization	✓			✓	
		Treatment compliance	✓	✓			
		Previous inpatient violence				✓	
	Crime and violence	Arrests	✓	✓	✓	✓	✓
		Incarcerations	✓	✓	✓		
		Self-reported violence	✓	✓			✓
		Violence to self	✓			✓	
		Previous violence		✓	✓	✓	✓
		Young/age at first violent incident		✓	✓		
	Other	Early maladjustment		✓			
		Relationship instability		✓			
		Prior supervision failure		✓	✓		
Contextual	Social support	Living arrangements	✓		✓	✓ (over-crowded)	
		Activities of daily living/leisure	✓		✓		
		Perceived support	✓	✓			
		Social networks (criminal/supportive)	✓	✓	✓		
		Relationship (marital)			✓		

Table 22.1 *(continued)*

Category	Subcategory	Factor	1. COVR	2. HCR-20	3. LSI-R[1]	4. Steinert[2]	5. VRAG
	Other	Perceived stress	✓	✓			
		Means for violence	✓				
		Destabilizers		✓			
		Financial problems			✓		
		Staff attitudes/experience				✓	
		Legal status					✓
Clinical	Axis I diagnosis		✓	✓	✓	✓	✓
		Hallucinations	✓	✓	✓	✓	✓
		Thought disorder				✓	
		Symptom severity	✓	✓	✓	✓	
		Violent fantasies	✓				✓
	Social functioning		✓			✓	✓
	Substance abuse	Alcohol	✓	✓	✓	✓	✓
		Other drugs	✓	✓	✓	✓	
	Other	Unresponsive to treatment		✓			
		Insight		✓		✓	
		Negative attitudes		✓	✓	✓ (hostility)	
		Emotional problems			✓	✓	
		Plans lack feasibility		✓			
		Loss of conscience					✓

[1] Andrews and Bonta, 1995; Austin et al., 2003. Main use in criminal justice services
[2] Steinert 2002, designed for inpatients

Table 22.2 List of factors comprising three key risk prediction tools (PCL-R, HCR-20, VRAG)

PCL-R (Hare, 2003)	HCR-20 (V2) (Webster et al., 1997)	VRAG (Harris et al., 1993)
(1) Glibness/superficial charm	H1 Previous violence	1. PCL-SV score
(1) Grandiose sense of self-worth	H2 Young age at first violent incident	2. Elementary school maladjustment
(1) Pathological lying	H3 Relationship instability	3. DSM-III diagnosis of personality disorder
(1) Conning/manipulative	H4 Employment problems	4. Age at index offence
(1) Lack of remorse or guilt	H5 Substance misuse problems	5. Lived with both parents to age 16
(1) Shallow affect	H6 Major mental illness	6. Failure on prior conditional release
(1) Callous/lack of sympathy	H7 PCL-SV score	7. Non-violent offence score
(1) Failure to accept responsibility	R3 Lack of personal support	
(2) Need for stimulation/proneness to boredom	H8 Early maladjustment	8. Marital status
(2) Parasitic lifestyle	H9 Personality disorder	9. DSM-III diagnosis of schizophrenia
(2) Poor behavioural controls	H10 Prior supervision failure	10. Victim injury (index offence)
(2) Early behavioural problems	C1 Lack of insight	11. History of alcohol misuse
(2) Lack of realistic long-term goals	C2 Negative attitudes	12. Female victim (index offence)
(2) Impulsivity	C3 Active symptoms of major mental illness	
(2) Irresponsibility	C4 Impulsivity	
(2) Juvenile delinquency	C5 Unresponsive to treatment	
(2) Revocation of conditional release	R1 Plans lack feasibility	
Promiscuous sexual behaviour	R2 Exposure to destabilizers	
Many short-term marital relationships	R4 Non-compliance with remediation attempts	
Criminal versatility	R5 Stress	

Factor 1=affective; Factor 2=lifestyle; H=historical; C=clinical; R=risk.

The Violence Risk Assessment Guide (VRAG)

What is the VRAG?

The VRAG (Harris et al., 1993; Quinsey et al., 1998, 2006) is designed to predict violence (broadly defined) and is probably the most widely tested and researched actuarial instrument. It was devised in Canada, using a construction sample of 618 serious male offenders with mental disorder. The dependent variable (outcome) was made up of charges or convictions for a violent offence (or a behaviour that would have led to such a charge had it not been for a return to maximum security). Forty-two dependent variables were initially tested, and 42 items encoded as possible predictors, with the 12 most significantly related to a violent outcome chosen to construct the VRAG (see table 22.2). The items are combined using a weighting procedure based on the contribution of the individual item to the prediction of violence in the construction sample (Harris et al., 1993; Quinsey et al., 1998). Factors were regarded as 'protective' if their presence lowered the risk score (e.g. a past diagnosis of schizophrenia). The final VRAG score may range from −26 to +38. The authors propose that this score can then be used to allocate the person under assessment into a 'risk bin', which, in turn, may be used to make a specific prediction about the likelihood of violence over a set time period, the original authors say 7–10 years.

Does the VRAG work?

The effectiveness of prediction aids is generally now tested according to signal detection theory, using receiver operating characteristics/curves (ROCs). This method was chosen by researchers as it does not need arbitrary thresholds to decide on 'dangerous or not' and is immune to base rates, whereas other measures such as 'correct predictions', sensitivity or odds ratios are influenced by base rates, prohibiting comparisons. Using signal theory, it is theoretically as possible to compare an instrument's performance on rare events, such as murder, as on more common ones, such as any violence, and comparisons may be made across instruments, places and times.

The ROC is, essentially, a graph plotting sensitivity of the instrument against its specificity. Sensitivity is the extent to which the tool can capture all true cases – here the cases of correct prediction of violence – and specificity is the extent to which it only captures true cases – here indicated by the rate of false alarms or incorrect predictions of violence. The result is expressed in terms of the 'area under the curve' (AUC). A random outcome will result in a straight diagonal between the axes, and the resulting AUC will be 0.5; anything less than this means that the test is performing less well than chance, and anything higher that it has a better performance than chance. The perfect tool – which does not exist – would have 100% true positives and

no false positives, and thus 'the curve' would be a straight line up the vertical axis; the AUC would be 1.0. In practice, an AUC of 0.56 is seen as a small, but useful effect size, 0.64 as a medium effect and 0.71 as a large effect (Rice and Harris, 2005b).

The initial study of the VRAG (Harris et al., 1993), and other follow-ups of this study group, showed that, in these terms, the VRAG is a good predictor of violence (AUC=0.76). Whilst this is encouraging, one expects good risk prediction in a construction sample, as the weights of the various factors have been optimized so as to give the best fit to this sample. Part of this fit will be based on sound reproducible factors that predict violence, but part of this fit will be due to statistical noise that will be different in other samples, even if the samples are based on the same population. Thus, some shrinkage in the instrument's predictive ability must be expected when it is applied to new test samples (Wiggins, 1973). It is important to see how well the instrument performs in samples with different characteristics.

There are many reports of the potential of the VRAG to be a significant predictor of violent recidivism among people released from a forensic setting in North America (Barbaree et al., 2001; Douglas et al., 2005; Glover et al., 2002; Harris et al., 2002; Harris et al., 1993; Harris et al., 2003; Rice and Harris, 1995a, 1997b), although some independent researchers have not had such success in similar North American populations (Kroner and Mills, 2001; Loza et al., 2002). Harris et al. (2004) were the first to evaluate the use of the VRAG with women. The AUC did not differ significantly between the women (0.73) and the men (0.71). Outside North America, several studies from Scandinavia (Grann et al., 2000; Grann and Wedin, 2002; Tengström, 2001) and elsewhere in mainland Europe (Pham et al., 2005; Urabaniok et al., 2006; Kroner et al., 2007) are all in agreement that the VRAG is a good predictor of violence in the community, with a range of AUCs from 0.68 to 0.73. Snowden et al. (2007) have performed what is, to date, the largest study of the VRAG in the UK. They scored the VRAG on over 500 patients released from medium secure units, based on information at the time of discharge; the patients were then followed up for 2–5 years. Official criminal records were obtained from the Home Office Offenders' Index. The AUC proved to be 0.77 for prediction of violent offending. Another UK study, in a smaller sample, over a shorter period, found a respectable if smaller AUC (0.66) (Doyle and Dolan, 2006b).

As a series of studies from North America and Europe are generally in agreement about the predictive ability of the VRAG, with an AUC of around 0.75, it seems likely that the VRAG will produce similar results in similar cultures. This also suggests that the factors which predict violence do not differ much between these cultures. Further research would be warranted in very different cultures.

Many offenders have intellectual disabilities (ID). In the UK, Gray et al. (2007) compared the performance of the VRAG between patients with a clinical diagnosis reflecting ID and patients who had no such diagnosis; in both groups the AUC was 0.74 over 5 years, similar to the finding of Quinsey et al. (2004) in North America. In different fields again, the VRAG has also been shown to be effective among male perpetrators of domestic violence and among sex offenders (Barbaree et al., 2001; Hilton et al., 2001). Finally, evaluation of the VRAG has been extended to patients who have not offended (Harris et al., 2004). They used a slightly modified version of the VRAG in order to re-examine the data from the large-scale study of over 1000 people just discharged from a psychiatric inpatient stay in the USA, known as the MacArthur Violence Risk Assessment Study (Monahan et al., 2001, and see also below). These patients were evaluated by interview and collateral informants every 10 weeks for 1 year. The AUC for the VRAG was 0.72, representing a large effect size.

The VRAG was designed for a follow-up period of 7 years, but for most purposes this is far too long. Thus, it is important to know if the VRAG loses its power for shorter periods. Two studies suggest not. Snowden et al. (2007) found that the VRAG had a larger AUC (0.86) over a 6-month follow-up than over a 5-year follow-up (0.76). Doyle et al. (2002) examined inpatient violence over 3 months and found AUCs of 0.71 for any violent act and of 0.64 for the most serious violent acts.

Summarizing the evidence on the VRAG

The most notable thing about the studies just described is their consistency in indicating that the VRAG is a statistically good predictor of violence, and, in turn, that the factors which indicate its likelihood are similar across many settings.

The Historical Clinical and Risk Management Scale (HCR-20)

What is the HCR-20?

The HCR-20 is a structured clinical judgment instrument, which is so named as it contains historical, clinical and risk management items (Webster et al., 1997). It was developed from a systematic review and meta-analysis of the empirical literature concerning factors that relate to violence, and was modified to its present form after clinical trials. Twenty variables (see table 22.2) are coded on a 3-point scale: 'absent', 'somewhat present', or 'definitely present'. The historical factors are, by definition, 'static', or immutable – such as history of offending; the clinical and risk management factors are dynamic, and thus potentially changeable factors. The HCR-20 does not contain any 'thresholds' for making risk decisions, as it is a clinical aid, rather than an absolute predictor. In the process of providing the evidence for rating each HCR-20 item, a risk formulation is generated for the individual under assessment, and, thus, an appropriately informed risk management/treatment plan can follow. Key risk factors can, though, be extracted and clearly communicated to everyone with a need to know, whether other clinicians or people working in other agencies, such as probation officers or, when an individual is subject to public protection procedures, to the police.

Does the HCR-20 work?

The first full report of the utility of HCR-20 was with a sample of just under 200 patients followed into the community for an average of around 2 years (Douglas and Webster, 1999). The AUC for prediction of any violence was 0.76; for violent crime it was 0.80. Since this initial study there have been many validations of the HCR-20 as an aid to prediction of violent acts – in North America (Douglas and Ogloff, 2003a,b; Douglas et al., 2005; Fujii et al., 2005; Kroner and Mills, 2001; McNiel et al., 2003; Nicholls et al., 2004) and throughout Europe (Belfrage et al., 2000; Dahle, 2006; de Vogel and de Ruiter, 2004, 2005, 2006; Dernevik et al., 2002; Dolan and Khawaja, 2004; Doyle and Dolan, 2006b; Gray et al., 2003, 2004, 2007; Grevatt et al., 2004; Pham et al., 2000, 2005; Strand et al., 1999). Nearly all these studies are in agreement that the HCR-20 is a useful instrument, returning AUCs with a range of 0.60–0.82. It is impossible for us to cover each of this large number of studies in any detail. For further information, the reader is referred to a useful website which keeps track of reports in this area (http://kdouglas.wordpress.com/hcr-20). Here, we elaborate on a few of the key findings. A new revision of the HCR-2 is due in 2013.

There has been on-going debate about the role of clinical variables in the prediction of violence (e.g. Doyle and Dolan, 2006b). The meta-analysis done by Bonta et al. (1998) suggests that clinical variables are not great predictors of violence, particularly when other factors, such as drug or alcohol abuse, are taken into consideration. This result, like the finding from the VRAG construction sample, is puzzling in view of the findings from population based and household studies on the relationships between psychosis and violence. It is the sort of finding that makes clinicians concerned about the weight they should place on such studies for the specific groups of people with whom they work. An issue here is that many studies treat dynamic factors as if they are static factors, when, in fact, pathways and interactions are important – for example psychosis may be a factor in progression to substance misuse.

The clinical (C) subscale of the HCR-20 is rated on current clinical state; these factors are also important when considering the 'R' or risk management subscale. Gray et al. (2003) examined the usefulness of the C scale in a prospective study of inpatient violence in medium secure units in the UK. They rated patients on the HCR-20 at time of admission and then charted the patients' behaviour for the first 3 months in the unit. In line with many other studies, the total HCR-20 score predicted group membership well (AUC for violence=0.81). The C scale was, in itself, also a good predictor of actual physical violence (AUC=0.79), indicating that the current clinical presentation is likely to be important in making a risk assessment in this situation. Gray et al. (2004) then followed patients who had been discharged from UK medium secure units. Risk assessments were pseudo-prospective in that the HCR-20 was coded using only information that was available to clinicians at the time of discharge; the average follow-up period was 6 years, with a minimum of 2 years. Under these circumstances the HCR-20 was only a moderate predictor of reconvictions (AUC=0.61) and, crucially, the C scale had no positive predictive value. It is perhaps unsurprising, however, when the focus is specifically on re-convictions, rather than violence more generally, that actuarial tools which rate the past in terms of the exact target outcome (e.g. re-convictions, using the OGRS, Copas and Marshall, 1998) offers a better prediction prospect. There are many biases in whether, after a violent incident, an individual is processed through the criminal justice system or not, one of which is having a previous record, so risk assessment tools like the OGRS may be somewhat circular. Nevertheless, this pattern of results has been replicated in a sample of over 1000 mentally disordered offenders followed for even longer (Gray et al., 2007). Furthermore, indications that the C scale is most predictive of violence *in the short term* have been found elsewhere (Doyle and Dolan, 2006b; Grevatt et al., 2004; McNiel et al., 2003; Dolan and Khawaja, 2004; Douglas et al., 1999). In this respect, only the findings of Strand et al. (1999) differ.

It is important to reflect on the finding that clinical variables coded at admission to a secure hospital unit appear to predict short-term violence (Gray et al., 2003) but not violence over the longer term after discharge from the unit (Gray et al., 2004). If a scale is *dynamic*, then, by definition, an individual's score on this scale is likely to change over time. Measures on a dynamic scale will need repetition at intervals, which are likely to differ in length according to pattern of illness or nature of a critical clinical symptom. Then, too, if the C scale is coded at discharge, as it perhaps should be as part of standard practice, a low score would be expected at this point – otherwise a decision to discharge would be unlikely. This should not, however, be taken as an indication that the clinical state will necessarily remain stable; factors in the clinical state which are pertinent to violence could well recur. In fact, it is arguable that a high C scale score on entry to a hospital

unit, coupled with a low C scale score on discharge, should particularly alert the clinician to a need for regular re-rating on this scale. While maintenance of a low band on the C scale should not lead to complacency, it could support other indicators of continued wellbeing and safety, while a shift to a higher category should alert the clinicians to a need for more radical re-assessment and perhaps a change in management.

Reports on the examination of the validity of HCR-20 in a variety of specific subgroups have begun to emerge. Nicholls et al. (2004), for example, followed up 95 women for an average of 2 years after discharge to the community (range 1–3 years). They found that the HCR-20 was as effective in predicting community violent crime for women as it is for men (AUC=0.75 for men; 0.80 for women). de Vogel and de Ruiter (2005), however, examined both inpatient violence and violent recidivism and found much lower AUCs for women than for men. One report of the HCR-20 being used among women in a US high security prison found that, in common with the psychopathy checklist (PCL-R) among women, its only predictive value was for minor crime (Warren [J.I.] et al., 2005). It was no better than chance for prediction of violent crime generally, and worse than chance for homicide. The HCR-20, however, was designed for use with clinical samples, so this finding with prisoners may better reflect a problem with its use with prisoners than any failure with women.

Studies of the VRAG cited schizophrenia as a protective factor against violence, but most patients in forensic mental health (FMH) services in the UK, and many other countries too, have a schizophrenic illness. Large et al. (2011), thus, singled out people with schizophrenia as a group for evaluating prediction of risk of various violent acts based on a hypothetical instrument for risk categorization. They drew this up according to guidelines on sensitivity and specificity suggested by Mossman (2009) and from their review of the literature. It resulted in substantial over-classification of violence risk. How does the more systematically evaluated HCR-20 perform? Gray et al. (2011) obtained the criminal records of complete cohorts of men from four independent sector medium security hospital units at various times during the 1990s and early 2000s. The HCR-20 was rated from the complete clinical records of the men by researchers blind to the main outcome, which was at least one criminal conviction for violence in the 2 years after discharge. Five diagnostic groups were of sufficient size for separate analysis (more than 100 in each) in the total cohort of 890 men – schizophrenia, mood disorders, personality disorder, intellectual disability and substance misuse disorders. Overall the violent recidivism rate was 19%, with the men with personality disorder most likely to be in the recidivist group, and the men with schizophrenia or intellectual disability least likely. The HCR-20, used more here as an actuarial tool than as a structured aid to clinical judgment, significantly predicted recidivist group membership for all diagnostic groups, but with strongest effect for schizophrenia and intellectual disability and weak effects for personality disorder.

As noted, the last study, in common with many of the others just described, used the HCR-20 as an actuarial instrument, by rating each item on a 0–2 scale, then adding up the scores. The HCR-20, however, was designed to guide clinical judgment rather than to be used as an actuarial tool. Two studies which compared these different uses of the HCR-20 report that its correct use outperforms its use as an actuarial tool (de Vogel and de Ruiter, 2005; Douglas et al., 2003). The HCR-20 may thus be useful as an actuarial instrument, but it has added value as an aid to clinical judgment.

Summarizing the evidence on the HCR-20

The research base for the HCR-20 is unrivalled by that for any other instrument relevant to assessment of risk of harm to others in clinical samples. Its performance so far suggests a widespread utility, with some data specifically underscoring the importance of using it as it was designed – as an aid to clinical judgment rather than as an actuarial tool.

Using Risk Assessment and Structured Clinical Judgment Aids in Forensic Psychiatric Practice

The research evidence base for the reliability of the VRAG and the HCR-20 goes beyond their original construction samples, and they have a well-established capacity for showing whether a person belongs to a low, medium or high risk group. Their use in practice has several advantages:

- ensuring that all information relevant to violence and other antisocial behaviour is considered;
- transparency in method and recording of the assessment;
- greater clarity, therefore, in communicating about these issues – for the person under assessment as well as clinicians and others seeking to help that person. This is particularly important, as poor communication within and between clinical disciplines and other agencies has often been highlighted as a key failure when there has been a major, possibly preventable tragedy, such as a homicide by a person who was in contact with psychiatric services in the months before that homicide.

If these instruments are to be used effectively, those using them need appropriate training in their use, together with regular refresher sessions to check that rating remains reliable. For clinicians, this is similar to many other aspects of their work, maintained at a high level by continuing professional education/development, reflective practice and appraisal. On occasion, credentials with respect to risk assessment may be requested in court. It is as important to be transparent about these as about the process of the assessment and, as part of that to be able to set out the limits of the risk assessment process as well as its benefits. Just as there is no place in court for insisting that the diagnostic manuals offer more to diagnosis than an aid to reliability, so the same must be clear for risk assessment aids. Thus, in these circumstances, specific scale scores are to be as much avoided in the courtroom as in clinical practice.

There is technically no reason why the risk assessment aids discussed so far should not be used outside FMH services, and indeed they have been, but they are time consuming and require training for use. Arguments that such risk assessments take too long to complete would be foolish when working with offender-patients, as the collection of data from the patient, from relatives and others who know the patient well as well as from all records is what takes the time, and this all has to be done anyway. It is recognized, however, that there are circumstances, such as presentation of an unknown patient to an emergency room and/or an acute admission to general psychiatric services and/or when advice is sought at a police station about a person with suspected mental disorder, that rapid judgments must be taken, often based on partial information. There has now considerable progress in developing aids for clinicians in these circumstances too, (e.g. Hartvig et al., 2006; Monahan et al., 2006; Webster et al., 2006). We will consider the second of these in more detail, not least because it is also an example of a structured, systematic approach thought to reflect *in vivo* clinical judgment – through interactive analysis.

The Classification of Violence Risk (COVR)

In the USA, the potential for imposition of tort liability for negligence on mental health professionals who fail to anticipate and avert a patient's violence to others has become commonplace. Violence risk assessment is widely assumed by policy makers and the public to be a core skill of the mental health professions. 'Dangerousness to others' remains a dominant standard for formal admission to hospital (inpatient commitment) and for community orders (outpatient commitment). The Classification of Violence Risk (COVR©) (Monahan et al., 2005a) was developed with the goal of offering clinicians in *general* mental health services an actuarial aid to their predictive decision-making.

The COVR is an interactive software program designed to estimate the risk that an acute psychiatric patient will be violent to others over the next several months after discharge into the community. Using a laptop or desktop computer, the COVR guides the evaluator through a brief review of the clinical record and a 10-minute interview with the patient. After the requested information has been entered, the COVR generates a report that contains a statistically valid estimate of the patient's violence risk, including the 95% confidence interval for that estimate, and a list of the risk factors that the COVR took into account to produce the estimate. The tool is simple and quick to use, and does not require the extensive training recommended for the other tools discussed. Its development, however, required extensive, theoretically driven data collection, and complex statistics. This has been done in three stages. First, information was collected in a substantial research project – the MacArthur development study; secondly, the use of the resulting tool was validated in an independent sample by the same research team; and thirdly, validation has been undertaken by other researchers in other countries.

The MacArthur Development Study

In the MacArthur Violence Risk Assessment Study (Monahan et al., 2001) 1,136 patients in acute psychiatric facilities were assessed on 106 potential risk factors for violent behaviour. Criteria for inclusion in the study were: (a) civil admission; (b) age between 18 and 40 years; (c) English speaking; (d) being of Caucasian, African American, or Hispanic ethnicity; and (e) a medical record diagnosis of schizophrenia, schizophreniform disorder, schizoaffective disorder, depression, dysthymia, mania, brief reactive psychosis, delusional disorder, alcohol or other drug abuse or dependence, or a personality disorder. The risk factors measured in the research fell into four general domains, the relatively fixed dispositional factors and historical factors and the potentially more changeable contextual and clinical factors (see also table 22.1).

For the risk factor analyses, patients were followed for 20 weeks in the community after discharge from the hospital. Measures of violence to others included official police and hospital records, patient self-report, and the report of the collateral informant (most often, a family member) who knew the patient best in the community. The criterion measure of violence to others consisted of any one or more of four acts: (1) any battery with physical injury; (2) the use of a weapon; (3) threats made with a weapon in hand; or (4) sexual assault.

Development of the actuarial risk assessment instrument then relied on classification tree methodology (Breiman et al., 1984). Classification trees focus on interactions, rather than on main effects. This approach allows many different combinations of risk factors to classify a person as high or low risk, here of being violent. Based on a sequence established by the classification tree, the first question asked of the data set concerns all individuals being assessed. The programme chooses the next question, depending on the answer to the previous one, with this process continuing until each individual is classified by the tree into a final 'risk class'. Using only those risk factors commonly available in hospital records or through routine assessment in clinical practice, this approach made it possible to place all patients into one of five classes of risk of violence during the first 20 weeks following discharge into the community. The expected prevalence of violence of these five risk classes was 1%, 8%, 26%, 56%, and 76%, respectively.

The statistical approach underlying classification

The study employed Chi-squared Automatic Iteration Detector (CHAID) software (SPSS, 1993) to assess the statistical significance of the bivariate association between each of the 106 eligible risk factors measured in the hospital and the dichotomous outcome measure of violence in the community after discharge. In order to be chosen as a risk factor at each step, a variable had to have the most statistically significant value of chi-square, with $p < 0.05$ significance as a minimum necessary condition for risk factor selection. Once a risk factor was selected, the sample was partitioned according to the values of that risk factor (e.g. high or low anger scores). This selection procedure was repeated for each of the resulting groups, thus further partitioning the sample. The goal of this partitioning process was to identify groups of individuals who shared the same risk factors and who also shared the same values on the outcome measure of violence.

Next, the recursive partitioning approach was extended in an iterative fashion. That is, all participants not classified into groups designated as either 'high risk' (defined as *at least* twice the sample's base rate for violence) or 'low risk' (defined as *at most* half the sample's base rate for violence) in the first iteration of CHAID were pooled together and reanalysed in a second iteration of CHAID. This iterative process continued until it was not possible to classify any additional groups of participants as either high or low risk (with no group allowed to contain fewer than 50 individuals). The resulting model was termed an iterative classification tree, or ICT. The output of the ICT model consisted of a series of end-nodes, each of which corresponded to a specific group of individuals with an estimated prevalence of violence.

Finally, in order to minimize overfitting the data (i.e. capitalizing on chance) and to bring to bear a wider range of influential risk factors in assessing risk of violence, the authors estimated several different ICT models to obtain multiple risk assessments for each participant. Multiple ICT models, each of which contained a different set of risk factors, were combined to produce risk assessments that were much more accurate than any single model taken alone. This approach showed considerable accuracy, producing an area under the ROC of 0.88.

The National Institute of Mental Health Validation Study

The successful construction of an actuarial model does not necessarily mean that the instrument will perform well when applied to new samples of individuals. As a rule, models constructed using procedures that rely on associations between variables in a particular sample are apt to lose predictive power when applied to new samples (Efron, 1983). This 'shrinkage' is due to capitalization on chance associations in the original construction sample. Thus, it is essential to validate models prospectively on new samples to ensure that adequate levels of predictive power are maintained. Therefore, a prospective validation of the multiple ICT model of violence risk assessment was conducted (Monahan et al., 2005b). In this research, violence risk assessment software incorporating the multiple ICT procedures was administered to independent samples of acute inpatients (n=157), who were classified as at high or low violence risk, and then followed up prospectively as discharged patients.

In practice, COVR software was used to screen patients at two sites: Worcester, MA (a site in the development study) and Philadelphia, PA (a new site, not included in the development study). The selection criteria for this validation study were slightly broader than those used in the MacArthur development study; the lower age limit of 18 was retained but the upper limit extended to 60 years. There was no limitation on racial or ethnic background and there was no exclusion at all by diagnosis. Expanding the eligible sample in this fashion allowed for both comparison of the validation results with the original sample on which the software had been developed and testing of the validity of the software in assessing violence risk for a broader group of patients.

Laptop computers loaded with the COVR software were available at each facility. After informed consent had been given, chart and demographic information was entered, followed by patient screening with the software. Where patient self-report information did not appear in the chart, this was included in data entry for the study and where patient responses were inconsistent with anything in the record, probe questions were asked to clarify these answers. The software was administered by research interviewers, most often psychology graduate students. The average length of time taken to complete data collection and entry from the chart and the patient was 10 minutes.

Following the original MacArthur analysis strategy, patients were assigned to one of three risk categories: (1) high-risk (equivalent to risk classes 4 and 5, the highest two risk classes in Banks et al., 2004), with an expected rate of violence of 63.6%; (2) average-risk category (equivalent to risk classes 2 and 3, the intermediate risk classes in Banks et al., 2004), with an expected rate of violence of 15.6%; or (3) low-risk (equivalent to risk class 1, the lowest risk class in Banks et al., 2004), with an expected rate of violence of 1.2%. After the administration of the COVR was complete, the site co-ordinator examined the risk classification to determine if the examinee was eligible for the community follow-up study. The patients' hospital clinicians were blind to the risk classification.

All of the high-risk individuals and a random sample of the low-risk individuals were selected for follow-up. Given limitations on resources, the need to maintain an adequate sample size in the groups that were followed, and because the primary aim of the study was to validate the high- and low-risk designations, the group of patients assessed as falling within the intermediate category were not followed up in the community. Patients who had been selected for follow-up were recontacted in the community and interviewed at 10 weeks and 20 weeks after the date of discharge.

Using the strict operational definition of violence from the original study, results indicated that 9% of the individuals classified by the COVR at hospital baseline as at low risk of violence were actually violent in the community within 20 weeks after discharge, compared to 35% of the individuals classified as at high risk of violence. When all individuals were blindly reclassified using the slightly more inclusive operational definition of violence which also used information about violence that occurred in a hospital or jail in that follow-up period, the rate of violence observed in the low-risk group remained at 9%, but the rate of violence observed in the high-risk group rose to 49%.

The validation study thus found the expected shrinkage in discriminative ability of the tool, but nevertheless, supported its predictive abilities. The proportion of people in the low-risk group who were actually violent (9%) was higher than the 1.2% of the original MacArthur study and the proportion in the high risk group lower (49%) than in that developmental study (63.6%). Although it is likely that this difference in figures represents the natural shrinkage referred to, it could reflect a difference in the base rate of violence between the samples.

Validation of the COVR outside the USA

The COVR software was constructed and first independently validated with samples of general psychiatric inpatients in acute civil facilities in the USA (McDermott et al., 2011). The next steps included evaluating its predictive value for similar people in other countries, for offender-patient samples and for people in the criminal justice system, perhaps without such marked mental disorder. In the UK, Snowden et al. (2009) reported a 6-month prospective study of 52 patients at four medium-security forensic psychiatric hospital units. Both the COVR and the VRAG were administered. The authors concluded:

both [instruments] have good – and approximately equal – risk prediction ability (p.1,525).

They go on to note that:

Depending on the amount of collateral material, the COVR takes 15 minutes [to administer] compared with three hours for the VRAG. Thus, for some uses, such as for screening large samples, the COVR may have distinct practical and financial advantages over the VRAG (Snowden et al., 2009, p.1525; cf. Doyle et al., 2010).

More recently, Sturup et al. (2011) studied violent behaviour in the community among general psychiatric patients (n=331) 20 weeks after they had been discharged from facilities in Stockholm. The COVR had been completed with the patients at the time of discharge. The authors reported:

The base rate of violent behaviour was 5.7% and a ROC-analysis showed that the AUC for COVR was 0.77. Since there were few patients in the high risk groups, the 95% confidence interval for the proportion of violent patients was wide. The base rate of violent behaviour is relatively low in Sweden and prediction is therefore difficult. The predictive validity of COVR software is comparable to other risk assessment tools (p.161).

From evidence of predictive value of the COVR to its use in clinical practice

It is important to keep in mind that COVR software is useful in informing, but not replacing, clinical decision-making on risk of violence. The authors recommend a two-stage violence risk assessment procedure in which first the COVR is administered, then the results of that are reviewed by a clinician in the context of additional relevant information gathered from clinical interviews, significant others, and/or available records. The actuarial risk score produced by the COVR would stand, but supplementary information might affect clinical predictive accuracy, probably for the better, but not invariably so. Certainly, data obtained in addition to those collected by the COVR may properly impact violence risk assessment and should not be ignored. A low-risk patient who makes a convincing threat to harm another person in the future, for example, might be dealt with more cautiously than his or her COVR score would suggest. Careful audit of clinicians' revisions would be an important part both of reflective practice and future research – indeed this principle would be applied with advantage to use in practice of indications from any actuarial or structured risk assessment aid. Questions to be considered in addition to notes on outcome would include (1) *how often* on reviewing actuarial risk estimates clinicians feel it necessary to revise those estimates; (2) when they do feel it necessary to revise them, *why* they do so; (3) by *how much* do they revise them.

Judgment about the degree of risk posed by a patient is merely the beginning of the process of risk management,

and risk management is not the only reason for more structured approaches to treatment. For a patient judged to present a lower risk of violence to others, there may be reasons, nonetheless, to keep him or her hospitalized, including risk to the patient himself or herself, need for further diagnostic assessment or treatment trials, and extended discharge planning. Conversely, even higher risk patients may reasonably warrant hospital discharge, for example when appropriate plans have been put in place to manage that risk in the community, and the gains to the patient and others from discharge justify any risk taken (Monahan et al., 2005b).

THREAT ASSESSMENT AND MANAGEMENT

Most clinical risk assessment is driven by concern on the part of the clinician raised by the actions of the patient or by aspects of mental disorders which have been linked in some way with violence or other harm. In some cases, however, the presenting or presented individual is explicitly threatening to do serious harm. This creates an additional dimension for the assessment process, and calls for an awareness of the state of the evidence on likely outcomes.

The making of threats is a ubiquitous and often mundane element of human interaction. A single, empty threat uttered in a moment of irritation or anger is rarely of much importance. Threats become of concern when they evoke distress, when they are warnings, when they are uttered repeatedly and indiscriminately regardless of impact, and when they are a component of a course of conduct aimed at gaining an outcome through intimidation. Threats may be made directly to the putative victim, or to a third party, the most obvious concern for clinicians being that during an assessment or treatment session the patient may make a threat to kill someone – perhaps someone s/he knows, perhaps a public figure. Threats to commit criminal acts, particularly those involving violence, are classified as criminal offences in most jurisdictions. Threats may be made as a form of emotional expression (affective) or issued as calculated means towards an end (instrumental) (Meloy, 2006), but whatever the motive behind them, threats are warnings of possible harm. The form of harm which tends to preoccupy assessors is physical injury or death, but other less visible forms of harm may be as destructive – induction of fear and distress – and still others a nuisance and expensive – embarrassment, inconvenience and the waste of resources. Mental health professionals are often confronted by patients issuing threats, and the making of threats is not an infrequent reason for referral to FMH services. A central issue in threat assessment is the presence and relevance of various forms of mental disorder but, whereas threat to oneself in the form of declarations of suicidal intent has been subject to systematic outcome studies, there is a limited evidence base on outcomes of threats to others.

According to the British Crime Survey (Hough, 1990), in the 12 months prior to data collection, 1.7% of adults had received at least one threat that had frightened them. A very similar figure (1.6%) has been established in the USA (Bureau of Justice Statistics, 2006) and in a number of other countries too (van Kesteran et al., 2000). How often are such threats actually followed by the threatened violence? An earlier consensus in the US literature, which more recent studies are beginning to overturn, suggested that threats were largely irrelevant, or even protective (e.g. Dietz et al., 1991a; Calhoun, 1998; Quinsey et al., 2006):

Threats are not that big a deal. That's right, you read it correctly (Meloy, 2000, p.161).

This rather counter-intuitive position was largely based on idiosyncratic interpretation of studies of threats and their outcome in particular groups or environments, and does not necessarily translate into other populations. Circumscribed groups have included workers in the workplace (Cole et al., 1997) or families in the home (Felson and Messner, 2000, although see also threats and stalking paragraph, below). Warren et al. (2008) identified a cohort of all those convicted of threats to kill over a 2-year period in the Australian state of Victoria, obtaining their criminal records for review 10 years later to determine any subsequent convictions. Of 613 individuals, 44% had been convicted of at least one violent offence, including 19 cases of homicide (3%). The subsequent conviction rate was significantly higher in those when threats to kill had previously been the major or sole charge. More than 40% of the threateners had had prior contact with the mental health system, and those with mental disorders were significantly more likely to have subsequent convictions for violence (58%). At 10 years, 4.5% of the sample had died by suicide. Rates of both homicide (3/100) and suicide (4/100) were similar to those described earlier by MacDonald (1968), and much higher than figures for the general population. A predictive model for actual physical violence following conviction for threats was derived from this sample. The combination of mental disorder, younger age at first conviction, substance abuse and the *absence* of other previous criminal convictions had good predictive value (AUC 0.77). In a later study of people who had threatened specifically to kill another person and who were attending a purpose-designed clinic within FMH services, the 1-year rate of violent acts was 20%, including one homicide and two suicides (Warren et al., 2011). Here prior violence was a risk factor, together with untreated mental disorder, substance misuse and limited education.

Threats to Public Figures

Celebrities

Dietz et al. (1991b) examined the characteristics of 1800 threatening and otherwise inappropriate letters sent by 214 people to 22 Hollywood celebrities, taken from the files of a Los Angeles-based security firm. A sample of those who subsequently attempted to approach the celebrity was compared to a sample of people who confined their activities to writing. The authors examined the hypothesis that threats increased the risk of approach behaviour, and therefore the risk of potential violence. The authors defined a threat as 'any offer to do harm, however implausible'. About one-fifth of those who had written to a celebrity had issued a threat, when so, usually more than once. Most were conditional, usually a demand for personal attention. The threats were also analysed for presence of a plan, means, and opportunity. Four per cent of the writers threatened to kill the celebrity. None of these variables had any significant association with making or not making an approach to the celebrity.

Mohandie et al. (2006) examined a non-random sample of people who had engaged in stalking-type behaviours against celebrities. The rate of violence was extremely low (2%). This figure may have been influenced by the high levels of security surrounding most celebrities. Four out of the five who attacked had previously threatened; 17% of those who directly threatened subsequently attacked.

US presidents

Early research on attacks and assassinations of public figures in the USA focused on the small number of presidential assassins (Clarke, 1982, 1990), people who had stopped at threatening the president (Rothstein, 1964, Megargee, 1986), or those who had visited the White House and behaved in a peculiar manner or insisted on seeing the president (Hoffman, 1943; Sebastiani and Foy, 1965; Shore et al., 1985). Most in the latter two groups were unmarried, unemployed men in their mid-30s with a diagnosis of schizophrenia and a history of compulsory psychiatric admission. Rothstein (1964, 1966, 1971) went so far as to propose the existence of a 'presidential assassination syndrome' based on such studies, but Megargee (1986), in a psychometric study comparing 45 people who had threatened presidents with 45 who had not, found that the only characteristic that the threateners appeared to share was a fixation on the presidency. Freedman (1971) observed that, according to these studies, no one who had threatened the president had ever gone on to attack him:

No 'syndrome' of potential presidential assassins can be based on writers of threatening letters... Indeed, as far as we know, the threat may be inversely rather than directly related to the act.

Members of the US Congress

Dietz et al. (1991a) conducted the first systematic study of threatening and otherwise inappropriate letters to members of the US Congress. Of 86 people identified, 20 had threatened assassination. Using a random stratified sampling method, they compared the letters of the 43 people who made an approach to the 43 who did not, finding that fewer of the approachers (33%) made a threat than those who did not approach (84%). So, although some of the people who threatened did make an approach, it was this sort of information that led to the idea that threats might be 'protective' against actual harm.

Scalora et al. (2002a) worked with the US Capitol Police, responsible for the security of the US Congress, and thereby were able to study 4,387 reported cases held in an electronic database which had involved threats and other problematic contact between 1993 and 1999. The most prevalent threatening contact was by letters or faxes (39%). Telephone harassment and threats were also common (27%). One-third made a direct or veiled threat; again, this was very significantly less likely to have occurred among those who had made an approach to the Congress member concerned than those who had not. Nevertheless they noted:

Threats cannot be ignored, as 21% of the approaches were preceded by threatening statements and 42% of the violent approaches involved prior threatening statements (Scalora et al., 2002a, p.3).

Scalora and his colleagues (2002b) then compared a random sample of 104 people who approached compared with 212 who had not, all from the Capitol Police database. A logistic regression, which produced a model comprising four variables, correctly classified 82.5% of the overall sample. People who approached Congress members were more likely to have had prior contact with other federal agencies, to have identified themselves during the contact, to have engaged in multiple methods of contact, and to have used less threatening language during their contacts. By contrast, 44% of whose who had approached had engaged in contact behaviour before the approach, and, among these, most were mentally ill, had contacted other targets, and used threatening, demanding and incoherent language (Meloy et al., 2004).

The US judiciary

Calhoun (1998) studied 3,096 inappropriate communications to federal judicial officials between 1980 and 1993 which had been documented by the Analytical Support Unit of the US Marshals' Office. An 'inappropriate communication' was defined as 'any contact or approach to a federal judicial official – written, telephonic, verbal, through an informant, or by some activity – that is unwarranted, ominous, threatening, weird, bizarre, or untoward'. Sixty-six per cent of cases involved writing letters or telephoning. Other cases involved 'suspicious activity' – acts or gestures that the victim found threatening. In over 90% of the cases for whom an outcome could be determined, there was no evidence of any attempt to carry out the threat, and the person making the threat was never heard from again

('specious threat'). In 118 cases (4%), court officials had been assaulted, and two federal judges were assassinated ('violent threat'). In the remaining 4% of cases, the assailant tried to carry out his/her threat, but was 'unsuccessful' in harming anyone ('enhanced threat'). Although most threats were communicated by telephone or writing, only 1% of these had a violent outcome. Some other suspicious *activity* may increase grounds for concern; in 40% of cases this had occurred when there had been a violent outcome and in 18% when the individual had at least tried to harm. Calhoun (1998) suggested categorizing those who threaten into 'hunters' or 'howlers'. All but about 4% of howlers are content only to rant and rave against an injustice that they think they have suffered, whereas hunters often do not explicitly threaten with words, but rather approach their target from an early stage ('suspicious activity') and most of these go on to an aggressive or violent outcome. In one important way, those who threaten the judiciary differ from those who target celebrities or politicians. They are rarely, if ever, total strangers but, rather, angry people known to their putative victims through a court appearance.

The Exceptional Case Study (ECS)

The ECS (Fein et al., 1995; Fein and Vossekuil, 1998, 1999), conducted by a psychologist and a senior agent for the US Secret Service, was the largest study undertaken of the assassination and attempted assassination of public figures. The aim was to identify indications of factors associated with progression to attack to inform useful interception on the pathway to attack. Their prime focus was on individuals who, between 1949 and 1996, had assassinated, near-lethally assaulted or otherwise attacked anyone under the protection of the Secret Service, including presidential figures at home and visiting heads of state, but they added other major officials and office holders, celebrities and chief executives of major companies to have sufficient numbers for analysis. They identified 83 cases involving 74 incidents; 46% had been attacks or assassinations and 54% 'near-lethal approaches', in which the person had been apprehended with a weapon in the vicinity of the putative victim. Attackers had typically planned over many months, often practising with their chosen weapon and reconnoitring the attack site. The ECS concluded that threats were of little predictive value (Fein and Vossekuil, 1999).

This conclusion arose from their observation that none of the 43 assassins or attackers had communicated a direct threat to their victim before the attack, and less than 10% of the entire sample had made any direct threat at all. Their resultant advice – that a focus on threats was therefore not productive – was, however, belied by their finding that two-thirds of their sample had a history of 'indirect, or conditional threats about, or to, the 'target', and so there were warnings that could have resulted in some attempts at preventive intervention, had there been a system to detect and evaluate them.

They were similarly dismissive about the role of mental illness:

> *...from an operational perspective, a focus on mental illness may not be useful in preventing assassination ...*

but said also:

> *No attacker or near-lethal approacher has ever been a model of emotional well-being. Almost all had psychological problems. However, relatively few suffered from mental illnesses that caused their attack behaviours (Fein and Vossekuil, 1999, p.331).*

In fact, 61% of their cases had had previous contact with a mental health professional and 43% had a history of delusional ideas, and it may have been the researchers' own belief systems that led to denial that focus on mental illness could be helpful. They believed that severe, untreated mental illness must disable a person's problem solving abilities, thus preventing them from mounting an attack, and

> *even for those attackers that were mentally ill, in almost every case an attack was a means to achieve some end, such as calling attention to a perceived problem (Fein and Vossekull, 1998, p.183).*

The emerging UK literature on threats towards prominent people

There is now an emerging UK literature on threats and attacks on prominent people, arising from the work of the Fixated Research Group (http://www.fixatedthreat.com). This concerns non-terrorist incidents involving 'the fixated', that is those people with a pathological pre-occupation with a person or cause which they then pursue to an irrational degree (Mullen et al., 2009; and see chapter 15). The group, led by one of us (James), carried out a survey of such attacks on elected politicians in the UK and Western Europe covering the period 1990–2004 (James et al., 2007 for Fixated Research Group). There were 23 episodes over the 14 years, spread across eight countries, 19 of which involved national politicians and two the mass shooting of local politicians. The remaining two cases were attacks on mayors of major cities (Vienna and Paris). In the two mass shootings, a total of 22 people were killed and 34 injured. In the remaining 21 cases, three attacks resulted in deaths, two being of the politicians attacked and one of a third party who intervened. Three attacks resulted in serious injury – paraplegia, a severed carotid artery, and a serious knife wound to the abdomen. Twelve of the 22 known attackers had a mental disorder. Attacks resulting in death or serious injury were significantly associated with a history of mental disorder and the presence of delusions (for further discussion of the relationship of pathological beliefs to violence, see chapters 14 and 15). These two factors were also associated with previous warning behaviours which occurred in nearly half of the cases (10/23), and included threatening and/or chaotic deluded letters to the politicians concerned, posters, newspaper advertisements, attempted law suits against the government, leafleting the public and telling friends of their intention to attack. In some cases, these behaviours had gone on for years. A similar picture was found in a subsequent study of 14 non-terrorist attackers of public figures in Germany between 1968 and 2004 (Hoffman et al., 2011).

A further study examined 23 attacks on the life or safety of the British monarch or a member of their immediate family between 1778 and 1994 (James et al., 2008). At least eight of these attackers warned prior to the attacks; given the gaps in the records, it is probable that some others also gave notice of their intent to attack the royal. In addition, the Fixated Research Group (2006) studied a random selection of inappropriate approaches to members of the British Royal family, recorded in the 2,332 files held by Royalty Protection Police (James et al., 2010a). As in the US studies, it was found that those who included threats in their letters were less likely to go on to engage in inappropriate approaches than those who did not. Among those who had made inappropriate approaches, however, the subgroup who had also made threats were more likely to attempt to breach security cordons (James et al., 2009), and such behaviours were significantly related to motivation, especially the pursuit of idiosyncratic quests for 'justice'. This points to the importance of inter-relationships between threat and approach behaviours, underlying motivation and psychopathology – subsequently explored by the Fixated Research Group in relation to proxies for violence (James et al., 2010a), persistence (James et al., 2010b) and approach and escalation (James et al., 2010c). Comparison with original data from a number of US studies illustrates that very similar associations apply to US samples (Meloy et al., 2011).

Threats and Stalking

Threat is implicit in many of the behaviours that constitute stalking, such as following, repeatedly approaching and subjecting to surveillance, but explicit threats are also common. In studies of stalking victims, 30–40% report having been explicitly threatened (Pathé and Mullen, 1997; Hall, 1998; Mullen et al., 1999). The figure is higher (over 60%) where the study refers to stalkers referred for forensic evaluation (Mullen et al., 1999; Harmon et al., 1998; Meloy and Gothard, 1995). Here, violence is associated with previous threats (Meloy et al., 2001; Rosenfeld and Harmon, 2002). False positive rates in terms of subsequent violence (i.e. a threat not followed by violence) range from 41 to 75%; false negative rates (the absence of a threat preceding violence) range from 13 to 23% (Meloy,

545

2002). Mullen and colleagues (1999) found that the frequency of stalkers making threats and the likelihood of their carrying out their threats varied according to stalker motivational type (see also chapter 15). The most likely to threaten their victim are the resentful (87%) and the rejected (74%), but the groups most likely to act violently on their threats are the rejected and the predatory. The victims most likely to be threatened are ex-intimates (Mullen et al., 2000; Meloy and Gothard, 1995), who are also the people most likely to be assaulted (Meloy et al., 2001; Farnham et al., 2000; Purcell et al., 2002; Pathé and Mullen, 1997). Standard instruments for the assessment of violence risk (e.g. HCR-20) are unreliable in stalking situations, and in consequence, the Stalking Risk Profile was developed, a structured professional judgment tool which takes account of underlying motivation (MacKenzie et al., 2009). This is also structured for use in the assessment of risk in those who repeatedly threaten public figures.

Mental Illness, Psychological Dysfunction and Threats

The order of frequency of relationship between mental illness and threats may, then, depend in part on the particular group under study. A US study of people threatening presidents (Logan et al., 1984) found that virtually all had had prior psychiatric care, usually in an inpatient setting. On the other hand, the group of people who are perhaps most likely to issue threats is ex-intimate stalkers, and, as a group, they have a low rate of mental illness (MacKenzie et al., 2010).

Mental illness was over-represented (over 40%) in a general population sample of those convicted of threats to kill (Warren et al., 2008), and even higher proportions have been found in other samples, including one of 102 people sent for court-ordered evaluations (58%) after threatening someone (Barnes et al., 2001). In the latter sample, there were also high rates of personality disorder and substance abuse. In a study of 69 people who threatened to plant bombs, just one-fifth were known to suffer from mental disorder (Häkännen, 2006), but mental illness was present in at least 83% of those who had threatened or made inappropriate communications or approaches to members of the Royal Family (James et al., 2010c), a situation which is hardly new. In *Sketches of Bethlem* (A Constant Observer, 1823) the author wrote of

> a class of lunatic visitors who were... so assiduous and troublesome in their visits to Buckingham House and in their endeavours to gain admission there (pp.164–5).

The Intelligencer, a newspaper in Washington DC, in its edition of 21 April 1835 noted what we take to be a similar tendency, despite the possible *double entendre* in the statement:

> It is a notorious fact that this city, being the centre of government, is liable to be visited by more than its proportion of insane persons (quoted by Hoffman, 1943, p.571).

The interacting roles of mental illness and warning behaviours in attacks on public figures were perhaps definitively stated by Dietz and Martell (2010), bringing resolution to the contradictory views discussed above:

> Every instance of an attack on a public figure by a lone stranger for which adequate information has been made publically available has been the work of a mentally disordered person who issued one or more pre-attack signals in the form of inappropriate letters, visits or statements...

People with mental illness, like their illness-free peers, commonly make threats, so how seriously should they be taken? Vaddadi and colleagues (1997) examined 101 family members of mentally disordered people, and found that 46% had been threatened by their sick relative. McNeil and Binder (1989) reviewed 253 files of psychiatric admissions to test the relationship between pre-admission threats and ward-based violence. They found that patients who uttered threats in the 2 weeks before admission were significantly more likely to be both physically and verbally assaultive in their first 3 days in hospital.

Psychological studies with people who threaten are underway. They focus especially on the nature and extent of communication skills, problem-solving skills, intelligence, discrepancies between verbal and performance abilities, anger expression and capacity for attachment and attachment style. The working hypothesis is that people with impaired skills for communicating complex emotions may be more ready to resort to threats than those who have higher level skills (Warren et al., 2012).

Threat Assessment and Management

Evaluation of threat must contribute to its management. Such approaches may involve both police and mental health responses, depending on individual case details. The following account concentrates on mental health responses.

Threat assessment is currently limited by the paucity of outcome research and a lack of prospective studies of people who threaten and of their management. In these circumstances, it is necessary to combine clinical experience and basic epidemiological knowledge about this group with studies of risk assessment and management in other areas. Generally relevant actuarial risk assessment and structured professional judgment tools have been described above, although in some circumstances, such as domestic threat and stalking, more specific instruments are preferable, such as the Spousal Assault Risk Assessment Guide (Kropp et al., 1999) and the Stalking Risk Profile (MacKenzie et al., 2009). Given that relevant issues concern psychological and social factors, as well as mental disorder, a 'problem behaviours' approach has also been advocated (Warren [LJ] et al., 2005). In this approach, not only are individual factors, such as mental illness, substance abuse, age and gender and the relationship with the person threatened considered, but also qualities in the relationship with the person being threatened, including possible jealousy and/or evidence of desperation, the stated motivation, plausibility of the threat and evidence of preparation. The various elements of the assessment are combined to formulate a risk reduction plan. This may include treatment for a relevant mental disorder, and also interventions known to reduce the risk of violence in any population (McGuire, 2003; Mullen, 2006). A functional analysis model is used to determine the factors which initiate and maintain the problem behaviour, which in turn facilitates the employment of cognitive behavioural interventions to challenge any cognitive distortions which may predispose to the threats, resolution of skill deficits and modification of inappropriate social and interpersonal interactions (MacKenzie and James, 2011).

Threat assessment and public figures

Threat assessment and management units have been set up in a number of jurisdictions to evaluate the threat to politicians and royalty from individuals who engage in threatening or inappropriate behaviours or communications.

US strategies in threat assessment, pioneered by the Secret Service, reflect the findings of the ECS and concentrate on interrupting the 'pathway to violence'. Three principles of threat assessment are delineated (Fein and Vossekuil, 1998; Borum et al., 1999):

- targeted violence is the result of a potentially understandable process of thinking and behaviour, so the task is to understand it;
- violence emerges from an interaction between the potential attacker, past stressful events, current situation and the target, so the task is to find those links;
- target-related factors must be investigated, in terms of familiarity on the part of the person threatening with the target's lifestyle patterns and the target's physical vulnerability.

Assessment involves a detailed analysis of the history, mental state, motives and capabilities of the person making the threats. Phillips (2006) proposed a typology of presidential attackers, based loosely on the stalking typology of Mullen and colleagues (2000, and chapter 12).

A common feature in threat assessment and management units, given the prevalence of mental disorder in those raising concern for public figures, is joint working between mental health professionals and law enforcement agencies. This may be in the form of liaison arrangements, as with the US Secret Service (Coggins and Pynchon, 1998), or joint units, as with the Capitol Police (Scalora et al., 2002a) or the Swedish Security Police. In the UK, a new joint police–mental health unit was established in 2006 by the Home Office and Department of Health, known as the Fixated Threat Assessment Centre (FTAC) (http://www.fixatedthreatassessmentcentre.com). Referrals are jointly investigated by police case-workers and forensic community psychiatric nurses, with supervision by forensic psychiatrists and psychologists. Mental health and police data are gathered, a structured risk assessment is undertaken using the public figure section of the Stalking Risk Profile (MacKenzie et al., 2009), and a management plan is formulated to reduce risk. This may involve referral to local psychiatric services for hospital admission, compulsory if necessary, or recourse to prosecution. Cases are followed up in a structured manner, and, where mental disorder is an issue, joint work with local psychiatric services is standard. Of the first 100 people assessed by the FTAC, 93 were taken on by psychiatric services; 53 had to be detained in hospital under mental health legislation. FTAC interventions reduced concern to low levels in 80% of cases (James et al., 2010d).

Threat assessment and management: conclusions

Threats that evoke anxiety or fear must be assessed and managed. Serious violence is commonly preceded by threats, even if most threats are not followed by violence. Threats may themselves be psychologically harmful to the victim. They may be considered as akin to promises; not all are kept, which can engender a false sense of security in clinicians, but many are (Mullen, 1997). Among people with mental illness, threats to others should be taken with at least the same seriousness as threats to self; further, threats are not only associated with violence to others, but also to self. Reduction of risk of harm may be achieved by treatment of mental disorder when this is relevant, but may also require specific psychological interventions to improve an individual's social skills and self-esteem. Legal sanctions may be appropriate, especially if clinical interventions are not indicated or are, in themselves, insufficient.

COMMUNICATING ABOUT RISK

A risk management plan is only as good as the time and effort put into communicating its findings to others (Department of Health, 2007).

There is widespread acknowledgement that when serious violence by someone with a mental disorder occurs, there have often been problems with communication, whether between staff in the clinical team, between teams, between clinicians and other agencies or, perhaps more crucially, between patients, their families and clinicians. Despite this, there is little research on

547

communication about risk. There is a good deal of face validity in the notion that risk assessment is best done as a clinical team or even as an inter-agency exercise, but there has been little testing of how people work at such tasks under such conditions, and none on the quality of the outcomes. What happens if members of the team bring conflicting evidence to the discussion, or hold different views on its interpretation? How are such differences resolved? Is there an optimal way of reaching a final formulation? Research into the ways in which intelligent people deal with their differences in groups is not encouraging, suggesting polarization with debate (Myers and Lamm, 1976). It would be important to know more about this in a clinical or multi-agency setting.

A useful exception to the dearth of research with clinicians at the clinical coalface has been about the nature of language in communicating risk decisions. Monahan et al. (2002) studied the effects on 324 forensic and 466 general psychologists of two qualities in describing unwanted behaviour. More vivid language and presentation of the material in a frequency format was characterized by the sort of expression:

Of every 100 patients similar to Mr. Jones, 20 will ...

while a probability format would be

Patients similar to Mr. Jones have a 20% chance of ...

The frequency format drew the forensic but not the general clinical psychologists towards more conservative management – 'get a second opinion' or 'do not discharge now' (see Scurich and John, 2012). Heilbrun and colleagues (2004) asked 500 clinical psychologists, randomly selected from the American Psychological Associations' database, to rate six approaches to communicating risk on a Likert scale. The preferred style of communication involved identifying factors likely to increase risk of violence in the individual under assessment and specifying interventions to reduce this risk.

If clinicians are to practise risk assessment and management in ways which engage the service user on the one hand and non-clinical personnel, such as the police, on the other, then questions must be asked about how such involvement will affect outcome. Could patients become much more reticent if they saw clinicians as being too close to the police or other law enforcement personnel? The Royal College of Psychiatrists (2008) calls for protocols for sharing information between agencies. Clinicians and others are committed to making this work, but there must be transparency here too about how. Could the widespread use of standard tools forewarn more competent service users, or their lawyers, about how to obtain more 'desirable' rather than more accurate 'results' on risk assessment? – or at least avoid the acquisition of findings that they might perceive as more 'damaging' as they would mitigate against release? To what extent would it

be helpful to develop investigative measures that rely less on direct questions or simple observations and more on less consciously accessible or controllable material. An example of this in psychometric testing could lie in using paradigms to determine choice of material when under competing modes of presentation, or comparative duration of attention-neutral, violently charged or sexually charged material (e.g. Gray et al., 2005). More use of more formal assessments of interpersonal relationships may also be of value in determining when relationships are coming under potentially dangerous pressure. These might draw on Operational Psychodynamic Diagnostics (OPD) for evaluating the wider picture (Cierpka et al., 2007; see also chapter 16), or tools like the working alliance inventory (Horvath and Greenberg, 1989), or ratings of expressed emotion (e.g. Moore et al., 2002; see also chapter 16), to test qualities in relationships between clinicians and patients, and how they change, over time.

RISK ASSESSMENT AND MANAGEMENT: BRINGING IT ALL TOGETHER

They are all guessing; if they knew for certain, they would not be dealing with risk (Adams, 1995).

Once it is acknowledged that prediction of future violence cannot produce any certainties and that, in any case the main clinical task is to improve the safety of patients, their families and the wider community, it is easier to move forward, and it is necessary to do so. The Department of Health in England (2007) rightly puts most emphasis on management:

Positive risk management as part of a carefully constructed pan is a required competence for all mental health practitioners (p.9).

The Scottish Risk Management Authority (RMA), a public body which was created by the Criminal Justice (Scotland) Act 2003, has provided a list of criteria and competencies for risk assessors in this field (see also chapter 4). They are struggling to find enough people who qualify at this level, but nevertheless it is worth considering their counsel of as near perfection as may be possible within this field. A risk assessor should have, as basic, membership of a professional body where applicable, be of good standing within his/her professional community or field, have qualifications and experience, and commitment to maintaining and improving clinical standards. More specific requirements are then to evidence competencies as accredited risk assessors, including knowledge of the criminal justice system, of risk assessment tools, of risk formulation and report writing, of information management and communication skills, of multi-agency working and of the process of the Risk Management Authority *per se.* Again, though, a key issue is risk management – knowledge of current best practice in immediate interventions and in management over the longer term.

For the English Department of Health document, positive risk management is defined as any risk-related decision which –

- conforms to relevant guidelines;
- is based on the best information available;
- is documented; and
- the relevant people are informed (p.8).

The document, further, endorses the use of a range of risk assessment tools, while observing:

> They are an *aid to clinical decision making not a substitute for it (p.8, their emphasis).*

and noting that best practice dictates that

> Risk management should be conducted in a spirit of collaboration and based on a relationship between the service user and their carers that is as trusting as possible ... [it] must be built on a recognition of the service user's strengths and should emphasize recovery (p.11).

There is a growing consensus, endorsed by the Royal College of Psychiatrists (2008), that clinicians must constantly remind themselves that, for people with a mental disorder, prevention of harm is likely to be more achievable than its prediction, and so much more important. In 2000, Munro and Rumgay analysed the findings of all 40 of the independent inquiries up to that date of a homicide by someone who had been in contact with mental health services in England and Wales at some time before the homicide. The inquiry teams, with all the time, effort and advantage of hindsight that they brought to the process concluded that in only one-quarter of the cases that the homicide could have been predicted. They also concluded, however, that about two-thirds of them could have been prevented if adequate treatment had been delivered.

As far as possible, clinicians should base all their practice, including the practice of risk assessment, on research evidence and be systematic and transparent in the assessment and assiduous in documenting this, together with resultant management plans which, in turn, must be followed through and subject to cycles of re-evaluation. The primary goals, which are almost invariably fully compatible with reduction in risk of harm are relief of distress and improvement in mental state for the presenting patient – and those with whom s/he comes in contact. For people with an abnormal mental state who may pose a risk to others, Maden's (2007) 10 principles are useful:

- violence is your business;
- there is no alternative to risk management;
- good violence risk management is good for patients;
- hope for the best, but plan for the worst;
- prediction is impossible but prevention can be easy;
- not all violent acts are equal;
- standardized assessments help clinicians but do not replace them;
- aspire to the best but give what you can afford (never tailor the recommendation to fit what is available);
- write it down;
- when in doubt, treat.

CONCLUSIONS

Assessment of risk of harm to others is never an end in itself. Structured risk assessment aids have an important role for the clinician, whenever risk assessment is required or indicated. The more commonly used named aids have, as described, an established reliability and validity profile, but there is a gap in their evaluation (Todd et al., in preparation). If they are to be applied widely in clinical practice, then it is essential to know that they really make a difference in reducing violence among the people to whom they are applied. Controlled trials of the instruments we have discussed in detail here have not yet been done. Two open follow-up studies of management informed by the HCR-20 yield opposite results. Among 39 men with 'dangerous and severe personality disorder' in an English high security hospital, Daffern et al. (2009) compared rates of aggression at baseline and then in two subsequent periods after use of the HCR-20 and the Dynamic Appraisal of Situational Aggression (DASA; Ogloff and Daffern, 2006) to inform management. Rates of aggressive incidents were not affected between time 1 and time 3. Belfrage et al. (2004) studied the application of the HCR-20 in a high security prison sample of 47 men with a violent criminal history. Again, management was informed by the scores. On reassessment not less then 3 months and not more than 24 months later there was a significant reduction in violent incidents, but no change in HCR-20 scores. The only controlled study we know of in the field is of a substantial Swiss sample (Abderhalden et al., 2008), evaluated using the Brøset Violence Checklist (BVC: Almvik and Woods, 1998). Over 2,000 patients from 14 inpatient hospital wards (of 86 approached) were included, patients from nine of the wards randomly allocated and the remainder according to preference. There was a significant reduction in any incident, in actual physical attacks and in coercive measures in the wards using the BVC, with the effect most marked in the 'preference wards'. So, there is some evidence that a risk assessment aid is doing what we hope, helping clinicians to reduce the rate of violent incidents, but this is an important area for further research.

It is advisable for clinicians, forensic clinicians especially, to have had recognized training in the use of at least one of the evidence based risk assessment aids. Where it is possible to generate scores, these may be useful for research, but it is best not to rely on such numbers in clinical or inter-agency communications – explicitly so in the case of the HCR-20. In general, risk assessment for clinicians is the first step in that part of the management and/or treatment which deals with the safety of a person with mental disorder who might be violent. Mossman (2009) also raises another important issue, that individual risk assessment, however important it may be for a particular person and his or her contacts, should not replace public health measures:

We know that behaviors and conditions, such as smoking and obesity, are clearly associated with poorer health.

Though medicine responds to diseases ... that are linked to smoking and obesity and makes efforts to monitor and detect them, the optimal approach is to adopt a 'population strategy of prevention' ... rather then try to detect who will die prematurely.

Preventing violence is not really different.... A society sincerely concerned about reducing violence will seek broad measures that address known risks for violence among persons both with and without mental health problems.

We agree, while emphasizing that the individual and public health approaches are not mutually exclusive.

23

Principles of treatment for the mentally disordered offender

Edited by
Pamela J Taylor

Written by
Peter F Buckley
Gill McGauley
Jen Clarke
Estelle Moore
Elena Carmen Nichita
Paul Rogers
Pamela J Taylor

1st edition authors: Fred Browne, Gisli Gudjonsson, John Gunn, Gary Rix, Leslie Sohn and Pamela J Taylor

No single approach, no matter whether it is predominantly 'organic and constitutional', or predominantly 'psychodynamic', can be ubiquitously and at all times successful (Cox, 1978).

But even the most apparently 'insane' violence has a rational meaning to the person who commits it … and even the most apparently rational, self-interested, selfish or 'evil' violence is caused by motives that are utterly irrational and ultimately self-destructive … Violent behaviour, whether it is labelled 'bad' or 'mad', is psychologically meaningful (Gilligan, 1992).

Forensic mental health services are most commonly described in terms of their security, and indeed this may be the characteristic that most distinguishes them from their generic counterparts. The quality that most distinguishes them from their penal counterparts, however, is the delivery of a wide range of treatments, tailored for the individual patient. Treatment is more than safe and humane management or containment. It is an intervention which may be expected to have a direct effect on improving health. Where mental disorder can be shown to have a causative role in violent or antisocial behaviour, successful treatment delivers not only health, but also safety.

Even after adopting this definition of treatment, it is sometimes hard to know, in practice, what to include under its banner. Specific treatments will generally be of limited benefit unless good general care is in place. Legislators follow a pattern which the layman would readily recognize, setting medication or surgical interventions apart from other treatments, here in terms of consent procedures. Within UK mental health legislation, however, such activities as nursing, care, habilitation and rehabilitation are included in a broad category of treatment if given under medical supervision, albeit not requiring the formal consent of the patient (e.g. S145, MHA 1983); 'psychological interventions' are specified too in the more recent legislation for England and Wales (MHA, 2007), but, again, within this broader category. For people with disorders of mental health, there is no doubt that the environment in which treatment is to take place may itself be therapeutic (e.g. Lees et al., 1999) or counter-therapeutic (e.g. Goffman, 1961; Wing and Brown, 1970). Wing (1990) went on to emphasize that environments which impair mental health are not confined to physical institutions, but may occur in community settings too. With respect to 'counter-therapy', people with a more psychodynamic perspective on personal growth and change would emphasize the risk of development and reinforcement of pathology in an institution which replicates some or all of the experiences of deprivation and/or abuse commonly present in the childhood of people resident in the services. So, because of its potentially powerful effects for good or ill, we consider the therapeutic milieu here as well as well as more specific treatments. An important feature of effective treatment within a forensic mental health framework is effective multidisciplinary/multiprofessional working both in creating and maintaining a safe therapeutic milieu and delivering specific treatments.

CREATING A THERAPEUTIC ENVIRONMENT WITHIN A SECURE SETTING

Creation and maintenance of a therapeutic milieu is a responsibility for every member of the clinical team, regardless of professional discipline; however, in an inpatient unit, nursing staff have an especially important role in this. 'Forensic nursing' is a young discipline compared with other branches of nursing. Unlike forensic psychiatry within the framework of psychiatry, it is not recognized as a separate specialism within mental health nursing. Since the 1990s, however, nurses working with offender-patients have attempted to establish their distinct specialist qualities (Robinson and Kettles, 2000). Discussion about this has followed a similar pattern to that which preceded it, and which continues, in forensic psychiatry. Do forensic nurses really have or require a body of knowledge, theory and skills that can be distinguished from that of colleagues in general adult mental health nursing? Or, are they merely extending application of pertinent skills, such as risk assessment and risk management? Is a 'forensic nurse' defined only by the place in which s/he works, such as a secure hospital unit? After all, a person with, say, schizophrenia, and accused of an offence, could be in an acute mental health unit one week, in a remand prison the next and in a medium secure hospital unit the week after that, but this person's clinical presentation, needs, and risks may not have changed at all during this time.

Balancing Care and Control

There is no healthcare setting without some tension between care and control; effective treatment and containment of infections, for example, or treatments which involve immunosuppression, must often impose some behavioural limits on the primary sufferer and their contacts alike. In general, however, there is an expectation that people who choose to present to health services will retain their autonomy by entering into a partnership with the clinicians to decide on the nature, extent and duration of their care and treatment. Society has particular expectations of forensic mental health services for protecting the public, and staff in such settings are acutely aware of the need for accurate assessment and management of the day-to-day risks of a patient harming others, so security and containment measures have to be implemented alongside care and treatment. Patients too, perhaps especially security hospital patients, generally expect and want such measures. As one young man in a high security hospital personality disorder unit once asked 'How would you feel sleeping in the same place as 23 other psychopaths if the staff weren't in control?'

An ongoing 'care versus control' debate (e.g. Kitchiner, 1999; Whyte, 1997) therefore remains important for ensuring that the principles for practice remain fresh. High levels of skill, explicit standards and constant monitoring are essential to ensuring that the relationship between care and control remains appropriate to the task (Rae, 1993). Rae notes that there is no place for denial of risk, but nor should a security culture ever allow care and sensitivity to be seen as signs of weakness. Others have also raised concerns that secure hospital environments may become brutal for both staff and patients (Mason and Mercer, 1998; Whittington and Balsalmo, 1998).

Part of the difficulty in creating a safe but therapeutic milieu for people at risk of seriously harming others in the context of mental disorder is that, while in some respects care and control are antithetical, in other respects they are very closely related. It is this entanglement that may sometimes lead to difficulties. A simple example is illustrative: each morning patients get up early to make themselves tea; they have been doing this safely for months, perhaps years. In order to do so, however, they have to handle a dangerous weapon – boiling water – and have access to an area filled with potential risks – the kitchen; a nurse has to be present to supervise; a manger inspecting the unit considers this is far too dangerous and requires a more restrictive policy; or, perhaps, an incident occurs – a distressed patient flings a mug of hot coffee across the kitchen, or one whose fascination with fire was thought to be coming under control places some paper towels under the lit grill – here, surely, is hard evidence that allowing patients access to the kitchen is dangerous? In the immediate aftermath of such incidents, even patients may demand restrictions on kitchen access, and this may be appropriate in the short term; a problem arises if this is then necessarily adopted across the unit indefinitely, with no patient ever again during their residence there able to choose freely when to have a hot drink, or to decide how it is made, or to co-operate with others in making it; rather they must all queue for a lukewarm brew only when there are plenty of nurses around.

Transparency about what is being done and why, regular review of practice within the framework of explicit policy and involvement of patients both in policy reviews and in day-to-day safety of the environment are all essential. Engagement of patients in this process too may be therapeutic; on the one hand they tend to feel more committed to honouring rules which either they have had some part in setting, or they can better understand for having discussed them, and on the other they have the opportunity to model themselves on staff. This approach operates in its fullest form in a 'true' therapeutic community (see chapter 16), and security is no bar to its successful use; it has been well established in prison settings such as Grendon (Gunn et al., 1978) and hospital settings such as Broadmoor (Newrith et al., 2006). Resources, however, will, to a large degree, determine care options. With little resource, there is little clinical time available, and procedural controls have to be more prominent in managing potential risks. Indeed, inadequate funding, resulting in too few or too inexperienced personnel, may even preclude adequate assessment of each case, another factor in blanket security measures being applied, with too little consideration of individual need. Thus, while nurses are on the front line of determining resolution of the care versus control equation, the matter is a concern for the whole service – beyond even the clinical team to the health board, trust or other providing organization. A major task for nurses when exercising professional accountability for decision-making is to consider *and record* how a range of external factors, such as bed occupancy or funding, influences their day-to-day decisions and quality of care; a connecting task for service managers is to have an accurate understanding of how resources, or lack of them, affect culture and climate in any unit.

Nursing Roles: Facilitators and Barriers to Creating a Therapeutic Environment

Proximity to patients, breadth of role and professional identity

Being at the forefront of combining delivery of a safe environment with more specific interventions, nurses in secure hospital settings generally have a much wider range of tasks in their day-to-day work than any other of the professions. In an ordinary working day, the forensic nurse may be assessing a new admission, monitoring the physical environments, searching a patient for potential weapons or drugs, administering medication, ensuring all physical health needs are met, carrying out 1:1 observations and supervision, managing seclusion or supporting patients in other crises, escorting a patient to court, escorting a patient on a home visit, or escorting another on a rehabilitation visit to the wider community. None of these activities is passive; the nurse is continually monitoring mental state and behaviour, assessing and reassessing risks of each assigned patient, while integrating that information with knowledge of the patient and mix of staff at any one time. Many, but not all, take on more specific psychological therapies with individuals or groups. Perhaps because of this breadth of work, nurses may struggle more than the other disciplines with their sense of professional identity. They perceive a risk on the one hand of merely following 'the medical model', or on the other of simply replacing it with 'the psychological/ psychotherapy model'. One way through such dilemmas is to develop certain treatments with particular nursing perspectives. The development of cognitive behavioural nursing therapy (CBNT) from the more generic CBT is an example of this (Newell and Gournay, 1994), albeit here specifically for anxiety in outpatients. Rogers (1997) reported on the successful implementation of a CBNT service in one medium security hospital. CBNT is now quite widely available as a resource in secure hospitals and has been extended into prison healthcare centres too (e.g. Kitchiner, 1999, 2000). The fact that the CBT is nurse delivered has many benefits, if, for example, the nurse is working on the ward where the patient resides, ensuring that coaching, enhanced support and motivational models can be general-

ized through other members of staff too. If not ward based, the nurse will have had experience of working on the wards, ensuring that s/he fully understands the strengths and weaknesses of using CBT in inpatient settings, for example knowing what tenets of the therapy can be supported by nurse colleagues and what cannot.

Nursing observations

In inpatient facilities, the observation of patients is one of the most important duties to them. Good observation has two main components: knowing what to observe and having the ability to communicate the observations effectively. The task of observing has recently been scrutinized by the Standing Nursing Midwifery Advisory Committee (Department of Health, 1999i) and the National Institute for Clinical Excellence (NICE, 1999g). Both resultant sets of guidelines emphasize the importance of engaging positively with the patient so that the process of observation is as therapeutic as possible. The latter requires every NHS Trust to have a policy on special observations which must include

- who may instigate observation;
- who may increase or decrease observation levels;
- who must review the level of observation;
- when reviews must take place;
- how patient perspectives will be taken into account;
- a process ensuring full clinical team review whenever observations above a general level are used for more than one week.

Every patient must have his/her observation level defined on admission, after preliminary observation and consultation between at least a qualified nurse and the patient's psychiatrist (or responsible clinician (RC)/responsible medical officer (RMO) for a detained patient). At some point the whole multidisciplinary team should review this. Decisions to change the level of observations should generally only be taken in consultation between nursing and medical staff. The decision to reduce observation levels must follow a joint risk assessment. An increase in observation levels may be made by nursing staff alone if the patient is judged to show increased risk of harm to self or others, but this decision should be followed as soon as possible by a multidisciplinary review. Each decision must be noted in the patient's records, with reasons for it.

Four levels of observation are recognized.

1. *General observation.* This is the minimum acceptable level for all inpatients. The patient's location should be known to staff, but it is not necessary that s/he is kept within sight at all times. At least once per shift, a nurse should set aside a dedicated time to assess the patient's mental state and engage with him/her, to ensure both development of a caring and therapeutic relationship and regular re-evaluation of the patient's mood, behaviours and risks, always completing a written record.

2. *Intermittent observation.* This is one step above general observations, including all aspect of those, but, in addition, the patient's whereabouts must be checked every 15–30 minutes, with exact times specified in the notes. This level is for patients who are potentially, but not immediately, at risk of suicide/self harm or disturbed/violent behaviour. Patients who have previously been on a higher level of observation but who are recovering will require intermittent observation as a 'step down'.

3. *Within eyesight observation* is required when the patient might attempt to harm him/herself or others at any time. The patient must be visible at all times. Other specific safeguards may be added, for example removal of anything that could become a weapon. It may be necessary to search the patient and his/her belongings. The ability to do this in a way which is not only sensitive and proportionate to the actual risks, but which the patient may find helpful, is an important skill.

4. *Within arm's length observation.* This observation level is used for patients who are at the highest risk of harming themselves or others and who need to be observed in close proximity. On rare occasions, as described for Carly, below, more than one member of staff may be necessary. Issues of privacy, dignity and consideration of gender in allocating staff remain important, but the overriding duty here is to preserve safety.

One issue that may arise while caring for patients at high levels of observation is the need to observe the patient on occasions when s/he is attending to basic bodily functions or personal hygiene. The team should discuss these matters carefully and clear decisions should be made about whether, for example, the patient is observed bathing or using the lavatory. The latter may also arise when there is a need to monitor drug use particularly closely. While most of us would be uncomfortable with such observations, there may be additional reasons to be exceptionally circumspect with the very patients who most need such attention. A substantial proportion of them have suffered physical or sexual abuse at some stage in their lives; some have complained that having staff 'intrude' on such intimate acts feels like a replication of such abuse. Decisions about such observations should also be clearly recorded, with explicit mention made of every possible situation when it may be necessary to make observation continuous, or, indeed, if it may be briefly suspended for a specific purpose.

Nurse:patient dynamics and dealing with unintended transferences

Perhaps the greatest challenge for forensic mental health nurses is the complexity of working in intense, volatile environments in the absence of a coherent theoretical framework to inform their practice. Existing nursing models have failed to deal with the impact of the nature and intensity of the long-term contacts to which nurses are exposed in secure environments. Offender-patients are not admitted to secure services voluntarily, and are rarely enthusiastic about engaging in therapeutic activities. They commonly have deeply disturbed backgrounds, in which neither caring nor authority figures – in the family or in professional services – have left them feeling cherished or safe. Welldon (1997) describes a resultant tendency to having poor impulse control, and being suspicious and filled with loathing towards people in authority, but having, alongside this, a desperate need to be cared for and understood. This ambivalence is transmitted to all staff, but perhaps most acute with nurses. Nurses frequently describe feeling confused, frustrated and at a loss when trying to develop 'a trusting therapeutic relationship' with patients (Motz, 2001). Then, as well as having to carry the patient's projected state in day-to-day current reality, the nurse is responsible for caring, supporting and reassuring patients on the one hand while, on the other, having to get involved in restraining them or giving medication forcibly if the need arises, and often refusing at least some of the patient's requests for various freedoms, including leave. They seem forced to re-enact in the here and now the conflicting strategies of the patient's original caregivers. While other disciplines may also experience such tensions, it is nurses, with the greatest amount of face to face contact, who have to confront such difficulties most directly and consistently. In an attempt to reduce their own resultant psychological distress, forensic mental health nurses may then engage in defensive practices, such as rigid boundary setting or rationing the amount of time they spend with patients. This may further replicate patients' past experiences of abuse and neglect and apparently confirm the validity of anti-authority beliefs. While boundary setting is essential in providing safety and consistency for offender-patients, it must be properly thought through and understood. It can be extremely difficult to retain the Rogerian ideal of warm positive regard and accurate empathy (Rogers, 1961) when feeling frightened, vulnerable and unsupported.

The sort of difficulties just described may, then, be regarded as more-or-less general to most staff/patient relationships, but perhaps at their most testing between nurses and patients. Other difficulties may be more specific to the individual case as uninvited transferences occur. Development of transference in a therapeutic relationship – essentially the patient acting in that relationship in the here and now as if towards a significant other person in an earlier relationship – may be actively fostered in psychodynamic approaches to psychotherapy (see below), in which case the therapist is not only prepared for this to occur, but ready to use the experience therapeutically. When transference has not been sought, however, it may not immediately be recognized, and/or those who have not been psychodynamically trained may struggle to cope with it. A case example may help to illustrate such difficulties:

Carly first came to the attention of social services when she was 14 months old, severely malnourished and lying in an excrement covered cot. Taken into care, she spent the next 9 years in various foster homes as repeated attempts to return her to her family broke down. At the age of 12, she reported that her foster father had been sexually abusing her for the previous 3 years. She spent the next 3 years in children's homes and secure children's units. She often ran away, and started frequent self-harm – mainly cutting herself, but also misusing alcohol and other drugs. This escalated to include overdoses, tying ligatures round her neck and setting fires. Her first contact with mental health services was at 18; by the age of 19 she was resident in a medium security unit.

On the unit, Carly was described as sexually provocative to male staff and male patients; she was transferred to conditions of high security after attempting to strangle a female member of staff. There, she developed an eating disorder, her self-harming behaviour became increasingly life threatening and she was often violent towards staff. She regularly complained of 'hearing voices' of a derogatory nature and experienced severe mood swings. After prescription of clozapine she improved sufficiently to engage with a dialectical behaviour therapy (DBT) programme. With her mood more stable, her voices no longer troublesome and her impulsivity and self-destructiveness largely under control, she returned to medium security on a rehabilitative pathway.

At first she appeared to settle well, actively engaging in a DBT programme on the unit, and embracing the opportunities of being in a less restrictive environment and having access to community facilities. Carly was also keen to re-establish contact with her family, but numerous attempts to arrange this failed, and each failure was associated with a self-harm incident. She wanted to maintain contact with some high security hospital staff, but that was refused.

Carly had been allocated a male primary nurse. It appeared that he had developed a positive therapeutic relationship, with Carly keen to engage in individual sessions. Other members of the nursing team, though, observed that Carly was dressing seductively and acting flirtatiously in his presence. Her self-harm resumed when he was going off duty or due to go on leave. These other nurses became critical of his interventions; they accused him of being 'too soft' and suggested that he should be more confrontational and set limits around her behaviour. During a supervision session the primary nurse described feeling 'out of his depth' and asked that someone else should take over. He was moved to another ward and replaced with a senior female nurse. Over the next 8 weeks Carly deteriorated, to a point that she needed 1:1 nursing observations for her own safety, increased to 2:1 observations when she voiced thoughts of taking a nurse hostage. She was returned to high security after secreting a lighter and setting a fire in her room.

What could be learned from this case, where efforts to provide good care and evidence based treatment had gone so badly wrong? Carly had been 'word perfect' when describing her understanding of mindfulness, as described by Linehan (1993) including distress tolerance, emotion dysregulation and interpersonal effectiveness. The apparent safety of this highly structured way of working with her was not in itself wrong but, alone, it could not encompass the transference issues and the practical tasks to be dealt with. First, perhaps because of Carly's desperation to leave the high security hospital, her attachment to the staff and fellow patients there had been underestimated; her repeated requests to visit them, or have them visit her, were refused on grounds of policy at both hospitals. The time she had spent in the high security hospital, however, had been the longest period of her life she had spent in any one place, and possibly the first where she had come to feel safe. Another rupture of her attachments just when she had achieved a sense of safety, without her having any sense of control over what was happening as 'the authorities know better', was, in effect, a replication of her adverse childhood experiences; it could only set her up to resume her pathological coping mechanisms.

Carly's most positive early relationship had been with the foster father who had abused her; she described him as mostly being 'attentive' and making her feel 'special and loved'. At some stage in her recovery process, the appropriately supervised allocation of a male primary nurse would have been a good plan, but, at the vulnerable moment of the severing of the high security hospital attachments, Carly had responded in the only way she knew and had unconsciously sexualized her relationship with the male nurse (Evans and Clarke, 2000). Staff in the medium security unit replicated yet one more time the authoritarian removal of a relationship that had almost worked for her; return of extreme emotional dysregulation in such circumstances is not uncommon (Adshead, 2004). The correct strategy would have been to support and supervise the male nurse to work through the transference with her, and perhaps also to have allowed her more autonomy in her choices of high security hospital contacts at least for an interim period. Aiyegbusi (2004) has noted that traditional nursing models, which do not consider relationship patterns and attachments in this way, are not robust enough either to prevent relapse or to treat it effectively when it occurs. Nevertheless, at least in the UK, surveys carried out as background to the Standing Nursing Midwifery Advisory Committee Report on Inpatient Care (DoH, 1999i) and the UK Central Council for Nursing, Midwifery and Health Visiting Report on the Prevention and Management of Violence (UKCC, 2001), show that there is still far too little supervisory provision.

Provision of time for nurses to extend their roles beyond reflective practice into appropriate supervision of their therapeutic endeavours is an extra demand on already stretched budgets and yet if, as in this case, the cost of not funding this is a patient's return for a second period of high security hospital care, setting aside for a moment the personal tragedy, where is any real economy? Nor is the problem solely financial; in some areas of the UK, and doubtless many other countries too, people with the appropriate psychodynamic training and experience to provide such supervision are not available, even for ready money. In this particular case, it was agreed that the nursing team would implement a psychodynamic 'nursing core team approach', this being nurse led albeit within the multidisciplinary team structure. It incorporates attachment theory (Bowlby, 1988) to develop a containing, consistent relationship within which it is safe, over repeated interactions, to challenge previous expectations and beliefs around disturbed attachment patterns. The building of a secure base with the nursing team is a vital step towards facilitating engagement in other therapeutic work with other disciplines (Barber et al., 2006). In this case, on Carly's return for a second attempt to continue treatment in medium security, the core nursing team was allocated to work alongside the primary nurse, to reduce the intensity of damaging re-enactments and, in particular, to support a male member of staff in the primary therapeutic role to work through the traumas of previously damaging relationships with male carers.

Therapeutic strategies for reducing violence by patients or their relatives

Although our main focus is on people who are resident in specialist forensic mental health services, it is worth noting that concern about violence by patients or their relatives is a concern for healthcare staff more generally, throughout the world (e.g. Joint Programme on Workplace Violence, WHO, 2000). Aside from any injuries that may result, it is a substantial source of stress and cost (di Martino, 2003; see also chapter 28). For England and Wales, the Health and Safety Executive (http://www.hse.gov.uk/index.htm) promotes guidance and periodic re-evaluation of the situation, major concerns about worsening violence rates having been expressed in a National Audit Office (2003) report, and professional concerns that there has been no improvement since then (BMA, 2008). Staff working in mental health services are second only to staff in accident and emergency settings with respect to risk of being verbally abused, threatened or actually assaulted, although separate figures are not given for forensic mental health services.

Prevention, management and treatment strategies change little in principle over the years; translating strategy into practical plans poses more of a challenge. Taylor and Schanda (1999) provide one overview of the issues involved, drawing on Hinde's (1993) model of contextual social levels, each of which will need attention, with additional allowance for interaction between the levels:

- individual behaviour;
- short-term interactions between individuals;
- relationships involving a series of interactions over time between individuals who know each other, such that each interaction is affected by previous ones and, often, by the expectation of future ones;
- groups – separate consideration of patient and staff related factors will be needed here;
- wider society.

Individual patients' issues are mainly considered within the developmental and specific disorder chapters. Here we focus on staff characteristics and staff–patient interactions, while acknowledging that patient–patient interactions may be critical, and require monitoring by staff, and that the wider social network can never be ignored. This may be because of its impact on the patient's capacities, as in Carly's case, or because relatives or others close to the patient may actually perpetrate violence on him/her – generally then part of a longer pattern – or on staff. Although relatives and others may have a high propensity for violence, the history of which may not be as accessible to staff as the patient's history, risk of relatives' aggression may also be reduced by the basic strategies of recognizing that they are themselves in a stressful situation just by virtue of having a relative in hospital. Additional stresses of keeping them waiting, searching them without explanation or courtesy, or expecting them to travel long distances at inconvenient times without offering appropriate support may all add to their burden and/or provide flashpoints.

The physical environment undoubtedly has a role to play in facilitating or stressing interpersonal work (see also chapter 24). Poor environments not only reduce satisfaction but also increase fear and maintain isolation. The Department of Health (2002a) offered robust observations in its *Mental Health Policy Implementation Guide: Adult Acute Inpatient Care Provision*:

> *Poor standards of design, lack of space and access to basic amenities and comforts in much of our current inpatient provision have contributed to and reinforced service users' negative experiences of inpatient care as unsafe, uncomfortable and untherapeutic.*

In considering the physical environment, it is worth thinking too that it is, in the words of the Royal College of Psychiatrists' (1998) report, 'Not just Bricks and Mortar'. As noted earlier, it includes the facilities that support activities of daily living. Hunter and Love (1996) conducted an extensive analysis of violent incidents in a California hospital in order to inform procedures that would reduce the frequency and seriousness of violence there. These focused on mealtimes, peak times for assault as in so many residential settings. A number of changes were implemented, including a change in eating utensils, playing music recommended by the music therapists as calming, increasing the amount of space available, improving the social skills of those serving the meals, and offering selective opportunities for progressing through the dining areas according to ability to take responsibility for behaviour. Unlike so many other such programmes, they did evaluate outcome, but on a naturalistic basis, and observing that they did not have the luxury either of insulating the changes from other changes happening in the institution simultaneously, or teasing out the relative effectiveness of components of the change. It is possible that the introduction of the plastic cutlery offered no advantage, as the patients no longer attacked with cutlery anyway, and there was a 40% reduction in violent incidents in the year after the change compared with the year before, together with a reduction in nursing costs. Trends in violence over a longer period were, however, less convincing. It is important to conduct evaluation of such changes, as confidence in, belief in or consensus about change is not enough. Palmstierna and Wistedt (1995) found a trend towards increased violence rates on a psychiatric intensive care unit after patient numbers had been halved. The change had been informed by a finding that patients with schizophrenia, although not others, were significantly more likely to be violent when patient numbers on the ward rose (Palmstierna et al., 1991). The failure to reduce violence frequency after reducing crowding was not, however, necessarily evidence that this had not been a useful intervention, but rather that it may be necessary to note and adjust for unexpected effects too. Here, Palmstierna and Wistedt speculated that the greater capacity for privacy which followed the changes had a countervailing effect.

Watt and colleagues studied the effectiveness of pre-admission nursing assessment for a hospital medium security unit in terms of ensuring a good starting base for treatment (Watt et al., 2003a,b). After each assessment, the nurse was asked to list the physical and social environmental needs of the patient, allowing for patient mix, staff/patient ratios and any other special environmental consideration. Patient mix, it was suggested, should explicitly include gender distribution, and religious, political, cultural and ethnicity issues. The nurse was then asked to draft a plan to meet these needs. This partly follows from observational research that wards with good leadership, structured staff roles and predictable routines have less violence than wards which do not (e.g. Katz and Kirkland, 1990).

We have already explored the importance of some staff factors in violence generation and prevention. One of the most difficult areas lies in actual demonstration that enhanced training makes a difference. Carmel and Hunter (1990) examined the effect of specific training in violence management, comparing nine wards in a Californian hospital where more than 60% of the staff had completed such training with 18 wards where proportions of trained staff were much lower. Injury rate, but not violent incident rate, was lower on wards with a higher proportion of trained staff. In a small, but randomized study of two forms of violence management training compared with no such training, the trained staff groups had a similar advantage over the untrained group in lowering assault rate (Phillips and Rudestam, 1995). Preventive interventions may, however,

be perceived as aversive, and have the opposite effect from that intended. When Whittington and Wykes asked staff (1994) about the precursors of 100 violent incidents, they found that over half had been preceded by some staff action to prevent harm or absconding. Lancee et al. (1995) engaged consenting patients in a 24-hour role play with nurse actors employing a range of interactional styles, including belittlement, platitudes, generic responses, solutions without options, explanation of rules without possible courses of action, expressions of concern without options and expressions of concern with options. For all diagnostic groups, belittlement generated significantly more anger than other styles and affective involvement with options significantly less. Patients with schizophrenia were unable to differentiate between styles other than these. The finding of a relationship between staff styles and anger would fit with a finding by Smoot and Gonzales (1995) that, when two units were compared – one in which a training programme to increase staff empathy for patient needs had been introduced and one in which it had not – the empathy training unit had a decrease in staff turnover, less sick leave, fewer seclusion or restraint episodes and lower expenditure. The potential importance of attention to empathic relating between staff and patients has been increasingly recognized from another perspective, a growing literature on 'expressed emotion' (EE) between staff and patients (Berry et al., 2010). There is a strong suggestion that it is a variable trait, which is as likely to follow from the patient's state as to influence it (Moore et al., 1992), although high EE and rejection by staff does appear to have an adverse effect on the progress of people with schizophrenia at least (Ball et al., 1992; Oliver and Kuipers, 1996; Heresco-Levy et al., 1999; Van Humbeeck et al., 2001; Levy et al., 2005). More specifically among patients in forensic mental health services, patient irritability, argumentativeness and violence rather than symptoms were associated with high staff EE ratings (Moore et al., 2002).

Seclusion and restraint

Even when prevention strategies fail and a violent incident occurs, it can often be managed within the main body of the unit, or by buffering the patient from the general stresses of being with the other patients and supporting him or her to remain in his or her own room until the crisis has passed. Additional medication may help (see below) but, occasionally, seclusion or restraint may be required. These are procedures primarily implemented to safeguard people at a time of acute crisis (see chapter 24), the question here is whether seclusion can ever be therapeutic. In 1813 Tuke wrote:

In the construction of asylums, cure and comfort ought to be as much considered as security, and I have no hesitation in declaring that a system which, by limiting the power of the attendant, obliges him not to neglect his duty, and makes his interest to obtain the good opinion of those under his care, provides more effectively for the safety of the keeper, as well as for the patient, than all the apparatus of chains, darkness and anodynes.

Tuke was proposing an alternative to mechanical restraint, through the interpersonal relationship between the patient and the attendant. Nearly 200 years later, it is discouraging that the evidence base for choosing the most therapeutic way of managing a patient in the kind of crisis that also threatens others remains unclear. A Cochrane review (Salias and Fenton, 2001) concluded:

In the absence of any controlled trials in those with serious mental illness, no recommendation can be made about the effectiveness, benefit or harmfulness of seclusion or restraint. In view of data from non-randomized studies, use should be minimized for ethical reasons.

The then UKCC (United Kingdom Central Council for Nursing, Midwifery and Health Visiting, now the NMC: the Nursing and Midwifery Council) commissioned a literature review, and similarly found:

no high quality studies that evaluated either the use of restraint or of seclusion in those with mental illness (UKCC, 2002).

After 3 further years, in England, the National Institute for Clinical Excellence could do no better (NICE, 2005):

In the absence of any controlled trials in those with serious mental illness, no recommendation can be made about the effectiveness, benefit or harmfulness of seclusion or restraint.

Although the reduction in stimulation achievable by seclusion might have a short term therapeutic advantage for certain patient groups, in practice, there is no evidence to deviate from the position set out in chapter 24 – that seclusion *per se* is for containment only, needs close monitoring if it must occur, and efforts must be made to continue reducing its use.

OCCUPATIONAL, SPEECH AND LANGUAGE, CREATIVE AND ARTS THERAPIES IN SECURE SETTINGS

People with long-standing mental disorder may become so preoccupied with their symptoms and distress that they lose the ability to look after themselves; if disorder strikes at a particularly young age they may never have adequately acquired the kind of activities that sustain independent living or keep boredom at bay. Occupational therapy has a crucial role to play at all stages of treatment of offender-patients. It is it important to assess at the earliest possible stage of admission to any forensic mental health service what will be needed to facilitate (re)habilitation, and to develop a treatment plan accordingly. In addition, it has been well recorded that there are dangers in failing to ensure that people can function with an appropriate

measure of independence and have opportunities for activities which may offer some diversion from distress even during the most acute phase of illness (Special Hospitals Service Authority, 1993).

Another basic prerequisite to treatment is that people should have enough language ability to be able to communicate their problems adequately. This becomes even more critical if psychotherapy is to be an essential part of treatment. Most forensic mental health services have occupational therapists as essential members of the clinical team, helping to ensure the treatment milieu as well as offering specific therapeutic initiatives, but few have speech and language therapists. Those of us who have experienced the value of this expertise, especially in facilitating the treatment of personality disorder, would advocate their presence (see France and Kramer, 2001).

Creative therapies include art, drama, dance-movement and music therapies, creative therapists generally having a first degree in a related arts subject followed by postgraduate clinical training to diploma or masters level. Arts therapists are particularly valued for patients who cannot access 'talking therapies'. These therapies tend to focus on aspects of self expression and interpersonal relatedness (Smeijsters and Cleven 2006). The rationale is that they enhance communication, imagination and interpersonal transactions – in essence, the behaviours and cognitions involved in mentalization (see below). Although some arts therapists may have had CBT training, they have traditionally been linked to psychodynamic models of understanding. There are, however, very few randomized controlled trials (RCTs) of the effectiveness of arts therapies in the treatment of mentally disordered offenders. Two Cochrane reviews, albeit not specific to offender-patients, conclude that the lack of studies prevents any conclusions about positive or negative effects of arts therapies in the treatment of schizophrenia (Ruddy and Dent-Brown, 2007; Ruddy and Milnes, 2009); one is more promising (Mössler et al., 2011). There is less evidence for their use in the treatment of personality disorder, although the reduction in anger levels after treating some young men with personality disorder (Reiss et al., 1998) suggests that trials of such interventions would be worthwhile.

PHARMACOLOGICAL TREATMENTS

Use of medication for people in forensic mental health services may be for the primary illness. Where this is driving any violence, the treatment for the illness will also be the treatment for the violence. As far as possible, disorder specific treatments are described in the disorder chapters. Matters are rarely that simple, however. Although people may present with a mental disorder for the very first time after having committed an offence, most people with both mental health and behavioural difficulties commonly present to services with violence or other offending after treatment has failed in some way. There may be a variety of reasons for this, not necessarily mutually exclusive, which have to be disentangled. Symptoms of the illness may provide a barrier to taking medication. In a delusional state, for example, the medication may be construed as poisonous or contaminated in some way, or in a severely depressed state as pointless. The medication may leave the individual incompletely treated. A common example is that medications for schizophrenia often deal with the so-called positive symptoms, but not the negative ones, and make such patients particularly vulnerable to taking supplements – licit or illicit – so that judgment about treatment fails. Furthermore, drugs may have idiosyncratic effects, or may interact and so adequate doses of an essential medication in some circumstances may prove to be inadequate in others. An example of the latter affecting many patients who have been in secure hospital settings, where smoking may be banned, is the interaction between clozapine and nicotine, described more fully below. Most medication used for any mental illness has unpleasant or unwanted side-effects, and busy clinicians may not spend sufficient time working out subtle adjustments with the patient such that, at worst, the patient sees the concern and care that attend any prescription, encouraging discussion of difficulties or treatment lapses, and, at best, enjoys minimal side-effects too. Then, too, the illnesses of some patients prove truly medication resistant. It is rare even for people with a personality disorder to have no interest at all in feeling and functioning better; the challenge in some cases is for clinicians to harness that interest, and to remember also that it is a common human trait to be 'delinquent' about treatment unless very ill or closely supervised. Most of us with concerns about how patients 'fail to comply' with treatment have a few pills left over from a course of antibiotics or have defied an instruction from some clinician when we think we know better about our own individual situation. Effective treatment using medication requires much more clinical skill than writing a prescription.

Pharmacological management of chronic, recurring violence *per se* also has to be considered from time to time, and much of this section will be devoted to that, although as many of the medications on which we rely for such intervention are from antipsychotic groups, so there is necessarily some overlap in accounts. It is important to be aware that subtle changes in advice occur with regularity, and it is useful, for this and any other treatment matter, to keep checking sources such as the Cochrane Library of systematic literature reviews (www.thecochranelibrary.com), which deals exclusively with randomized controlled trials (RCTs), and the Database of Abstracts of Reviews of Effects (DARE, http://www.crd.york.ac.uk/cms2web), which goes beyond these in its scope. DARE may also be accessed through Cochrane. Although RCTs are widely accepted as the gold standard for evaluating the effectiveness of a treatment, it is commonly a problem in forensic mental health services that patients fall well outside the average range of people able to take part in such trials, and so resulting guidance is likely to have its limitations. Such guidance is nevertheless increasingly available at national levels, and it is important to be aware of it. For England, for example, the National Institute for Health and Clinical (now Care) Excellence (NICE), funded by the National Health Service, but 'an independent organization responsible for providing national guidance on promoting good health and preventing and treating ill health', includes all levels of evidence in its reviews and guidance, including professional consensus (http://www.nice.org.uk). NICE covers all clinical practice and interventions, not just psychiatry. Specifically for schizophrenia, in the USA, the schizophrenia Patient Outcomes Research Team (PORT) publishes regular reviews and guidance on evidenced based treatment for this condition (e.g. Dixon et al., 2010). Professional bodies also provide regularly updated guidance, for the UK, for example the Royal College of Psychiatrists (www.rcpsych.ac.uk) is a source of *Council Reports* on a variety of matters, collating research evidence and professional consensus and generally including service user advice. In the USA the American Psychiatric Association, in a similar way, provides *Practice Guidelines*, and also *Task Force Reports* from time to time (http://www.psych.org).

Violence in the Context of Mental Disorder

The prevalence of violence in the context of specific mental disorders and current understanding of the nature of disorder–violence relationships are considered in other chapters (12–18), but, in brief, psychotic illnesses, especially schizophrenia, personality disorders and certain substance misuse disorders have been most strongly linked, while intellectual disabilities and some specific brain abnormalities may also play a role. There has been concern that acceptance of such links and a medical role in treatment of violent acts by individuals with mental illness may add to the stigma already perceived to be associated with mental disorder (Torrey, 1994), but this is not a reason for treatment avoidance. There is a view that violence occurs mainly when affected individuals are non-compliant with their medications, and thus actively psychotic, and/or when they are abusing drugs and/or alcohol (Torrey, 1994; Steadman et al., 1998), but it is not uncommon to see true medication resistance among people resident in forensic mental health services. Nevertheless, there is an undoubted problem when people with mental disorders abuse alcohol or other drugs. In the McArthur risk assessment study, comparison of 1,136 discharged patients with mental disorders with 519 controls living in the same neighbourhoods found no significant difference in the rate of violence by patients who did not abuse drugs or alcohol and their matched controls who, similarly, did not do so (Steadman et al., 1998). Abuse of drugs or alcohol significantly raised the rate of violence in both groups, but more in the group with a major mental illness. In an independent US study, Swanson et al. (1998) confirmed links between substance use and medication non-compliance and serious violence in a treated community sample of people with schizophrenia. In common with most other studies of alcohol or other drug use among people with mental disorders, however, these studies described neither reasons for the use of these substances nor the timing of abuse onset in relation to the mental disorder. There is evidence that for people with psychosis specifically, different treatment strategies are likely to be necessary for people with relatively pure forms of illness and those who are ill and also misuse drugs and alcohol (see also chapter 14); other comorbidities are also common both in schizophrenia generally (Buckley et al., 2009) and among offender-patients with schizophrenia specifically, although among the latter, the extent of association with personality disorder depends in part on the measures used (chapter 14).

Medication for Violence?

A wide variety of medications has been recommended for treating aggression, whether or not such drugs are those of choice for the primary disorder. In all instances, from both medico-legal and clinical perspectives, it is important to acknowledge and appreciate that no medication is specifically indicated for treating aggression or violence, since these are not drug specific domains. It is preferable to think in terms of some more-or-less disorder specific medications being better than others for lowering the risk of violence within the disorder groups for which they are evidenced as being clinically effective.

Medications for which there is evidence of value in containing aggression in the context of mental disorder include first generation/typical/older and second generation/atypical/generally newer antipsychotics, benzodiazepines, beta-blockers, mood stabilizers and selective serotonin reuptake inhibitors (SSRIs) (Brieden et al., 2002). The term first generation antipsychotic (FGA) is a collective for several classes of drugs: the *phenothiazines*, such as chlorpromazine, thioridazine or perphenazine; the *butyropherones*, such as haloperidol; the *phenylbutylpiperidines*, such as pimozide; the *thioxanthenes*, such as flupenthixol; and the *substituted benzamides*, such as sulpiride. Second generation antipsychotics (SGAs) include amisulpiride, aripiprazole, clozapine, olanzapine, quetiapine, risperidone and ziprasidone. Probably, for treatment for schizophrenia, the weight of evidence favours the SGAs (Lieberman et al., 2003; Duggan et al., 2005; Davis et al., 2003), although the US National Institute of Mental Health Clinical Antipsychotic Trials of Intervention Effectiveness (CATIE) provides a dissenting voice in finding the two broad groups of antipsychotic more-or-less equivalent (Lieberman, 2005). Concerns have been expressed, though, that this study has insufficient power for substantive conclusions (Kraemer et al., 2009). There is no

specific association between anxiety disorders and violence (Swanson et al., 1990), but heightened anxiety in the context of other mental disorders may be a trigger for violence. Benzodiazepines, for example diazepam, are sedative and very effective anxiety reducing drugs (e.g. Dubrovsky, 1990; Perry et al., 1990), but there is a risk of tolerance, and therefore dependence, so, when they are used, gradual tapering after stabilization is recommended (Fricchione, 2004). Beta-blockers act primarily on the physical manifestations of anxiety. They do not carry addictive potential and thus may be used in preference to benzodiazepines, but, although they have been shown to be more effective than placebo in treating anxiety (e.g. Peet and Ali, 1986), they are not therapeutically superior to benzodiazepines (Hallstrom et al., 1981). Anticonvulsant medications (e.g. Muller-Oerlinghausen et al., 2000) and lithium (e.g. Takahashi et al., 1975) have been found to have mood stabilizing properties in bipolar disorders. Finally, SSRIs make up a class of drugs which act by preventing the reuptake of the neurotransmitter serotonin and have been shown to be as effective as other classes of antidepressant in relieving depression (e.g. Geddes et al., 2006; Qaseem et al., 2008).

Once decisions about links between violence and the primary disorder have been taken in any particular case, other factors for assessment before deciding on the appropriate medication will be whether the problem with violence is acute, with potentially very serious and immediate harm to the patient and/or others, or whether it is a more chronic problem, perhaps related to other behavioural traits. A considerable difficulty in interpreting the literature on effectiveness of one medication or another in reducing violence is that violence is not treated homogeneously (see also chapter 9). It is unlikely, for example, that repeated violence accompanying acute agitation and distress has much in common with the planned, instrumental violence of an occasional homicidal assault. There may also come a point when the frequency of violence is so extreme that unique solutions are required. A woman, for example, known to one of us, for whom a variety of basic management, medication and psychosocial interventions had little impact, had over 800 violent incidents over a 4-year inpatient stay, many resulting in serious injuries to herself or others, does not seem very similar to a man who has thumped staff and patients several times in a dinner queue during the first month of his inpatient admission. Then, too, some studies use surrogate measures for violence. This is not surprising as, even among people with a propensity for violence, many will be violent too infrequently to be confident that any treatment is having an effect if the main concern, actual physical violence, is the only outcome measure. Unfortunately, measures such as hostility, for all their face value, do not necessarily correlate with actual violent acts (Gunn and Gristwood, 1975). It follows too that, where researchers have stuck to measurement of actual violent acts, there will be a bias towards selection of those that tend to be highly visible and repeated in an inpatient setting, and the review which follows tends to reflect that. This may be a problem for generalizing any findings, not only for the reasons just given, but also because there is evidence that risk factors for violence differ considerably between inpatient and outpatient conditions (Tardiff et al., 1997). Within these constraints, however, there is growing evidence that some medications may be particularly helpful in reducing violence.

Acute agitation and violence

According to the Expert Consensus Guideline for the treatment of behavioural emergencies (Allen et al., 2003), second generation antipsychotics (SGA) are now preferred for treating agitation in the context of a primary psychotic illness, but benzodiazepines are preferred for other conditions, or where the diagnosis may not be clear. Table 23.1 shows the preferred medications if oral administration is an option. If it is impossible to persuade an agitated psychotic patient to take medication by mouth, or the clinical situation is rapidly deteriorating, a rapidly acting, intramuscular preparation of an antipsychotic (typical or atypical), a benzodiazepine, or the combination of the two may be necessary (see table 23.2). Three SGAs are currently available in a form which may be injected (see also

below), and one of these would be considered to be first line treatment of acute psychotic agitation if parenteral administration is necessary, not least because transition to maintenance treatment with an appropriate oral antipsychotic is easier. First generation antipsychotics (FGA) are, however, still used with good results (Battaglia et al., 1997), alone or in combination with benzodiazepines. Risk of extrapyramidal signs (EPS), especially acute dystonia or akathisia, may limit use of FGAs. Although some SGAs can produce akathisia, they are less likely to do so than FGAs. The adverse metabolic effects, which are more pronounced with SGAs than FGAs, are not an immediate consideration in a crisis. Thus, the clinician has a good range of options (see table 23.3). The important issues are to gain control over aggressive behaviour and to initiate treatment with minimal adverse effects. At first, the extent to which the choice of the medication in the acute management will carry over to the stabilization phase is often not clear, and need not be a major consideration, although the variety of forms in which some of the medications are available enhances opportunities for continuity between the acute intervention and stabilization. Whether such continuity is ultimately more efficacious has not been adequately researched to date.

Table 23.1   Choice of oral medication for acute agitation and threatened violence

Provisional diagnosis	First line	Second line
No clear diagnosis	Benzodiazepines (BDZ) alone	BDZ + haloperidol Risperidone alone BDZ + risperidone Halolperidol alone Olanzapine alone
Organic cause	–	Haloperidol alone Risperidone alone
Stimulant intoxication	BDZ alone	BDZ + haloperidol Olanzapine alone Risperidone alone Haloperidol alone BDZ + risperidone
Alcohol intoxication	–	BDZ alone
Schizophrenia	Olanzapine alone Haloperidol alone Risperidone + BDZ Haloperidol + BDZ	Quetiapine alone Haloperidol alone Ziprasidone alone Olanzapine + BDZ Ziprasidone + BDZ Divalproex alone
Mania	Olanzapine alone Divalproex + antipsychotic Risperidone + BDZ Haloperidol + BDZ Risperidone alone	Olanzapine + BDZ Quetiapine alone BDZ alone Haloperidol alone Ziprasidone + BDZ
Psychotic depression	–	Olanzapine alone
Personality disorder	–	BDZ alone Olanzapine alone Risperidone alone Quetiapine alone

Information drawn from: Expert Consensus Guideline Series. (2005) Treatment of behavioral emergencies. *Journal of Psychiatric Practice,* **11**:5–108, but these guidelines do not include all currently available antipsychotics.

Table 23.2 Choice of parenteral medication for acute agitation and threatened violence

Provisional diagnosis	First line	Second line
No clear diagnosis	Benzodiazepine (BDZ) alone	BDZ + haloperidol Risperidone alone Haloperidol alone Olanzapine alone BDZ + risperidone
Organic cause	Haloperidol alone	Haloperidol alone Risperidone alone
Stimulation: intoxication	BDZ alone	BDZ + haloperidol Olanzapine alone Risperidone alone Haloperidol alone BDZ + risperidone
Alcohol intoxication	–	BDZ alone
Schizophrenia	Olanzapine alone Haloperidol + BDZ Ziprasidone alone Ziprasidone + BDZ	Haloperidol alone Olanzapine + BZD (this combination is not recommended in the package insert)
Mania	Olanzapine alone Haloperidol + BDZ	Ziprazidone alone Ziprasidone + BDZ BDZ alone Olanzapine + BDZ Haloperidol alone
Psychotic depression	Olanzapine alone	Ziprazidone alone Haloperidol + BZD Haloperidol alone Ziprasidone + BDZ
Personality disorder	BZD alone	Haloperidol + BDZ Olanzapine alone

Drawn from: Expert Consensus Guideline Series. (2005) Treatment of behavioral emergencies. *Journal of Psychiatric Practice,* **11**:5–108, but these guidelines do not include all currently available antipsychotics.

Table 23.3 Available formulations of second generation antipsychotic medications

Agent	Oral	Oral soluble	Oral liquid	Short-acting IM	Long-acting IM
Clozapine	+	+	–	–	–
Risperidone	+	+	+	–	+
Olanzapine	+	+	–	+	+
Quetiapine	+ (1)	–	–	–	–
Ziprasidone	+	–	–	+	–
Aripiprazole	+	–	–	+	–
Paliperidone	+ (2)	–	–	–	(3)
Asenapine	–	+	+	–	–
Iloperidone	+	–	–	–	–

(1) Available in extended release preparation.
(2) Developed as an extended release preparation.
(3) In clinical trial development.
Drawn from: Expert Consensus Guideline Series. (2005) Treatment of behavioral emergencies. *Journal of Psychiatric Practice,* **11**:5–108, but these guidelines do not include all currently available antipsychotics.

Persistent aggression and violence

There are studies confirming the effectiveness of some antipsychotic medications in reducing aggression and violence in the context of psychosis, with clozapine, olanzapine and haloperidol each having been shown to be effective under RCT conditions. Clozapine probably has the greatest effect (Krakowski et al., 2006), although there is no clear consensus among physicians regarding the treatment of aggression (Buckley et al., 2003). Most clinical information on treating aggression has been collected for atypical antipsychotics, particularly clozapine. According to Expert Consensus Guidelines (Expert Consensus Panel for Optimizing Pharmacologic Treatment of Psychotic Disorders, 2003) the first line in treating persistent aggression is an SGA; if this is not effective, or not effective enough, even though there is incontrovertible evidence that the patient has actually been taking it during the period of observation, then the next step is to try a typical antipsychotic, alone or in combination with a benzodiazepine or a mood stabilizer (table 23.4). It is important, however, to appreciate that these guidelines are now several years old and many of the newly available SGAs were unavailable when they were developed. The subsequent CATIE study has little to add, finding an overall medication effect, with medication adherence except among patients with a history of childhood conduct disorder, and no particular advantage for any specific drug (Swanson et al., 2008); a possible group advantage for perphenazine over quetiapine is probably not going to help guide the clinician in an individual case. The findings, however, have to be taken in context of the fact that specific drug groups were sometimes quite small and attrition over time variable between them. Before considering action possible in the event of non-compliance, each relevant medication will be reviewed in a little more detail.

Atypical/second generation antipsychotics (SGA)
Clozapine

Clozapine is one of the best studied antipsychotic medications for the treatment of aggression as a problem which overlaps with various psychiatric illnesses. Soon after the approval of clozapine for use in the USA, Wilson (1992) observed that not only were patients with chronic, treatment resistant schizophrenia likely to get symptom relief from it but also that involuntary movements were less likely than with typical neuroleptics. They also improved significantly in social abilities. Volavka (1999) conducted a retrospective analysis of the effects of clozapine on hostility and aggression in 331 patients with schizophrenia. At baseline, nearly one-third of them (31.4%) had been physically violent, but after an average of 47 weeks of treatment with clozapine only four were still violent. The reduction in violence could neither be explained by sedation nor

antipsychotic effects. It was striking that patients who had comorbid substance misuse disorders were just as likely to show improvement in psychopathology, social behaviours and reduced violence as those who had 'pure' schizophrenia. In a 12-week double blind RCT of clozapine, olanzapine and haloperidol, Krakowski et al. (2006) found a hierarchy of effect on interpersonal violence indicators as measured by the Modified Overt Aggression Scale (MOAS), with clozapine being superior to olanzapine which was, in turn, superior to haloperidol; there was no difference between the medications in antipsychotic effect. This fits with findings from the Volavka group (Volavka et al., 1993, 2002, 2004). Furthermore, related characteristics including aggression and hostility also responded best to clozapine (Citrome et al., 2001).

Kraus and Sheitman (2005) examined changes in the number of violent episodes and the need for seclusion and restraint during 3 months before and after a group of five persistently violent patients received clozapine. There was a marked decrease in violent episodes and the use of seclusion and restraint after clozapine. In an earlier study, number of hours in seclusion or restraints was reduced after the first month and more than halved after 6 months of treatment with clozapine (Buckley et al., 1995), consistent with still earlier findings (Mallya et al., 1992; Ebrahim et al., 1994). An independent group of US researchers (Chengappa et al., 2002) reported similar results in a large sample of state hospital patients with schizophrenia or schizoaffective disorder. Furthermore, there is evidence that clozapine reduces the cost of services in such circumstances (Buckley, 1999; Glazer and Dickson, 1998). Improvement in social function on the one hand and reduction in violence on the other led to reduction in recidivism and re-arrest rate among people with psychosis (Frankle et al., 2001) even when criminal histories had been well established. In this last study, among 165 patients with 1,126 arrests between them (mean number of arrests 6.8), the 65 patients who had taken clozapine had significantly lower arrest rates from the 100 patients who did not, although there were also differences related to sex and time of onset of illness. Spivak

Table 23.4 Selecting first and second line drug treatments for persistent violence

Problem	First line	Second line	Other second line
Persistent violence and aggression	Clozapine Risperidone	Olanzapine Long-acting injectable atypical	Quetiapine Ziprasidone Aripiprazole Long-acting depot conventional or atypical
Adjuvant treatment for persistent aggression		Valproate Lithium	Carbamazepine Beta-blocker BDZ Gabapentin ECT Lamotrigine Topiramate

Drawn from: Expert Consensus Guideline Series. (2005) Treatment of behavioral emergencies. *Journal of Psychiatric Practice*, **11**:5–108, but these guidelines do not include all currently available antipsychotics.

and his team (1997) found that both impulsiveness and aggressiveness decreased after clozapine prescription, but their sample was small. A later study, however, endorsed such findings (Spivak et al., 2003), albeit here in relation to suicidal impulsivity and aggression; again, the change was independent of changes in symptoms of mental disorder. In Israel, Rabinowitz et al. (1996) also showed a reduction in serious aggression after clozapine, as did Hector (1998) in Canada and Dalal et al. (1999) in a high security hospital sample in the UK. Swinton and Haddock (2000), in a case control study of long-stay violent patients in a high security hospital because of their propensity for violence and perceived risk to the public, found that after clozapine they were significantly more likely to attain discharge than their peers under conventional antipsychotic prescription.

Although clozapine is not approved by the FDA for use in children and adolescents, an open-label study (Kranzler et al., 2005) was conducted to evaluate its effectiveness on aggressive behaviour by treatment-refractory adolescents (age range 8.5–18) with schizophrenia. As in a small, earlier study (Chalasani, 2001), Kranzler's group enjoyed a statistically significant decrease in frequency of administration of emergency oral medications, of emergency parenteral medications and seclusion episodes during weeks 12 to 24 of clozapine treatment compared with their baseline condition.

Clozapine is only available for oral consumption, but there is an oral rapid disintegrating form for reducing treatment compliance difficulties. There is no injectable form, rapidly acting or otherwise. It is unlikely that there ever will be because of the risks of bone marrow suppression, consequent agranulocytosis and loss of the ability to respond effectively to infection. At higher doses, seizures may be an additional potential side effect. In either case, it is important to be able to clear the body quickly of the drug, and any long-acting variant would be too risky. Longer term treatment with clozapine therefore demands high levels of treatment compliance, not least because of the risk of rebound psychosis and acute recurrence of violence (Special Hospitals' Treatment Resistant Schizophrenia Group, 1996).

Risperidone

Although the evidence is more compelling for clozapine, there are studies supporting the use of risperidone for reducing aggressive behaviour. In contrast to clozapine, information on the use of risperidone and the other SGAs comes only from studies of patients with a wider range of diagnoses, albeit including schizophrenia. It is therefore hard to distil this literature to give clear guidance, but there are a few studies which are more specific to aggression in psychosis. A US study of 74 patients in a state psychiatric hospital (Chengappa et al., 2000) showed a reduction in use of seclusion and restraints and violent behaviour after risperidone. A Hungarian study showed that risperidone as

well as olanzapine were superior to haloperidol in reducing hostile and aggressive behaviours over 6 months of treatment (Bitter et al., 2005). Three other studies however (Citrome et al., 2001; Buckley et al., 1997; Beck et al., 1997) found risperidone and typical antipsychotics equally efficacious in treating the aggression and agitation.

Aggressive young people may also benefit, although studies to date have been with very small numbers. Schreier (1998) evaluated risperidone in 11 children and adolescents (5.5–16 years), alone or in combination with mood stabilizers; it apparently helped their mood disorders and aggressive behaviours. In the USA, Federal Drugs Agency (FDA) approval has been obtained for its use in autistic disorders. Risperidone is indicated for the treatment of both the internally and externally directed irritability and aggression which may sometimes be associated with them in children and adolescents. Several studies, worldwide, have subsequently showed improvement in the disruptive and aggressive behaviours by children with autistic spectrum disorders (Pandina et al., 2007; Troost et al., 2005; Nagaraj et al., 2006; McDougle et al., 2005).

Risperidone is available in all preparation types: regular tablets, rapid disintegrating tablets, liquid and long-acting intramuscular (IM) injections, making the transition from acute treatment to maintenance treatment easier.

Olanzapine

In the treatment of psychotic symptoms olanzapine has a well known place among the atypical antipsychotics (Lieberman et al., 2003), being effective for both positive and negative symptoms, but with a special advantage over FGAs for negative symptoms (Lindenmayer et al., 2007). In the treatment of aggression related to psychotic states there is some dissenting evidence on its place; one study found it to be superior to haloperidol in reducing the number and severity of aggressive incidents (Krakowski et al., 2006), but another did not (Citrome et al., 2001). Gerra et al. (2006) studied olanzapine to see whether it has an effect on addictive behaviours. Although it did not reduce them, nor the risk of relapse in opiate dependent individuals, it was observed that it was useful in reducing hostility and aggression in this group of individuals during substitution maintenance treatment. In children with severe conduct disorder, it has been found to have a specific role in reducing the risk of affective-impulsive but not controlled-predatory violence (Masi et al., 2006).

Since development of an injectable form, olanzapine has seen some use in emergency departments, as a treatment for agitation. It has been shown to be effective in this context for agitation in acute mania (Meehan et al., 2001), schizophrenia and dementia, in these cases producing no more sedation than patients treated with haloperidol or lorazepam, and bringing a sense of calm rather than nonspecific sedation (Battaglia et al., 2003; Wright et al., 2001). Olanzapine has now become available in a long-acting injectable formulation.

The range of formulations of olanzapine makes this an additional SGA which is useful for facilitating transition between acute intervention and maintenance treatment.

Quetiapine

Quetiapine is another drug which appears to have an advantage over haloperidol in alleviating agitation and hostility during an acute exacerbation of psychosis (Chengappa et al., 2003), doing so at doses of 150–750 mg, independently of general or specific improvements in psychosis, as rated on the Brief Psychiatric Rating Scale (BPRS) or of sedation. Arango and Bernado (2005), by contrast, compared quetiapine with placebo for patients with schizophrenia and found improvements in hostility, as rated on the BPRS, to be highly correlated with improvements in positive symptoms, although there was no consistent relationship between sedation and hostility. Buckley and colleagues (2007), in a large sample, found that, after 3 weeks of treatment, quetiapine was an effective and appropriate treatment for agitation and aggression associated with bipolar mania, either alone or in combination with valproic acid or lithium. As yet, it has not been shown to be effective for aggression associated with dementia, even though it may be helpful for dementia related psychosis, without either worsening parkinsonism or precipitating other extrapyramidal symptoms (Kurlan, 2007; Tariot et al., 2006).

Quetiapine is available in immediate and sustained release oral tablets, but there is, to date, no intramuscular preparation of this drug.

Ziprasidone

The first atypical antipsychotic to be available in an injectable form was ziprasidone. It has a rapid onset of action. There is a considerable body of evidence of its effectiveness in treating schizophrenia, schizo-affective or bipolar disorders but the focus here, as in the other sections, is on its value with respect to modifying violent behaviour. Brook et al. (2000) found that with intramuscular (IM) delivery it was significantly more effective in reducing the symptoms of acute psychosis and agitation and was better tolerated than IM haloperidol; movement disorders in particular were less likely. The first US study showed that the effect on agitation was dose dependent, a 10 mg dose being more efficient than a 2 mg dose (Lesam et al., 2001). It was well tolerated, without reports of acute dystonia or behavioural disinhibition, and there was only one report of akathisia. Further studies were concordant (Mendelowitz, 2004; Zimbroff et al., 2005), and added that, although side-effects could be troublesome – insomnia, headache, and dizziness in fixed-dose trials and insomnia and hypertension in flexible-dose trials – changes in the QTc were minimal and comparable with the ones seen after administration of haloperidol IM (the QTc is an indicator on an electrocardiogram of potentially risky changes in conduction of impulses through heart

muscle). In under 18 year olds, IM ziprasidone was similar in effect to olanzapine in reducing aggression (Khan and Mican, 2006), and there were no major side-effects. Three case reports documented an immediate calming effect for adolescents (Hazaray et al., 2004). At the other end of life, IM ziprasidone was effective for agitation as well as psychotic symptoms in elderly patients (Barak et al., 2006), again with no major side effects. Current advice in the event of acute agitation is for initiation of treatment for psychosis with an intramuscular form, but changing quickly to oral capsules. These are the only available forms of ziprasidone; there is no long-acting preparation.

Aripiprazole

There is worldwide consensus that aripiprazole is effective against positive and negative symptoms of schizophrenia or schizo-affective disorder, and is safe and well-tolerated (Kane et al., 2002; Swainston et al., 2004; Sullivan et al., 2007). It may have an advantage over typical and atypical antipsychotics other than clozapine in medication resistant schizophrenia (Kane et al., 2007). Its effectiveness in agitation with mania (Zimbroff et al., 2007) or other psychosis (Tran-Johnson et al., 2007) has been demonstrated when used in injectable form. In the latter study, 50 centres collaborated, yielding 357 patient participants. The Positive and Negative Syndrome Scale-Excited Component score was reduced after 45 minutes, compared with 105 minutes for haloperidol.

There is an intramuscular form of aripirazole for use in acute crises. A long-acting injectable formulation is under development.

Typical/first generation antipsychotics (FGA)

For many years the so-called typical or FGA antipsychotic drugs represented the only specific pharmacological treatments for psychosis, with or without violence. High doses were sometimes used to contain violence (Hirsch and Barnes, 1994), but the results were modest, and the evidence base for this practice poor. Furthermore, the higher the dose the worse was the side-effect profile, particularly with respect to extrapyramidal signs. While patients themselves may not always be particularly aware of tardive dyskinesia, they are very distressed by the physical rigidity of parkinsonian symptoms and signs, so, in addition to potential damage to health, this may be a factor in failures to comply with treatment. Akathisia may be an additional side-effect of concern because it may exacerbate agitation, even being mislabelled as escalating aggression, leading to a vicious cycle of higher doses of medication and worsening akathisia, leading to even higher doses, and so on.

Haloperidol was the most prescribed of the FGAs for violence, not least because it has a low side-effect profile relative to most other FGAs. As a general rule, high potency and mid potency antipsychotics were preferred because of their lower rate of anticholinergic side-effects.

Benzodiazepines

Benzodiazepines have a calming effect, and may be used alone or in combination with an antipsychotic for acute agitation (Salzman et al., 1991; Gillies et al., 2010). They are generally available for oral or parenteral administration. Some of them (e.g. flunitrazepam) have been shown to be as effective as haloperidol in containing aggression (Dorevitch et al., 1999), but the combination of 2 mg lorazepam with 5 mg haloperidol has been found to be better than lorazepam alone in this respect (Bieniek et al., 1988). Another study found midazolam rapidly sedating and calming when compared with droperidol and ziprasidone (Martel et al., 2005). Benzodiazepines with a rapid onset of action, such as lorazepam, are preferable, but their continued use is not recommended because of pharmacological tolerance and the risk of dependence. Although they do not have the side-effects of the antipsychotic medications, they can produce respiratory depression, excessive sedation, or paradoxical disinhibition at high doses. Special care is needed when using benzodiazepines with patients who have intellectual disability, traumatic brain injury, or other organic impairments.

Mood stabilizers

Anti-convulsants and lithium make up this group. In a systematic literature review of RCTs, it has been shown that, as a group, they have a significant advantage over placebo for the treatment of impulsive aggression, but with only 10 eligible studies, of various drugs, yielding 347 participants in trials with minimum bias, there seems more to be learned here (Jones et al., 2011). Study methods are heterogeneous, but there are indications that lithium and some anti-convulsants are more effective in this regard than some other anti-convulsants. Other work focuses on hostility rather than impulsive aggression or repeated violence.

Lithium has a long history in treatment of aggression among people with intellectual disability (e.g. Worrall et al., 1975; Dale, 1980; Spreat et al., 1989; Thibaut and Colonna, 1992), PD (e.g. Sheard, 1975, 1976) and even, in two cases, substantial brain injury (Bellus et al., 1996), adding support to the findings of Glenn et al. (1989). There is evidence of effectiveness and safety among children with conduct disorder too. Campbell et al. (1995) compared lithium with placebo in 50 children, finding it superior to placebo for treatment-refractory severe aggression and explosiveness; Malone and colleagues (2000) studied a larger sample, but found that use of lithium was associated with adverse effects in such groups, so, should only be used for short-term treatment.

Among the anti-convulsants, divalproex sodium may be useful as an adjunctive agent in reducing hostility in the first week of treatment with risperidone or olanzapine among patients in an acute episode of schizophrenia. In their RCT, Citrome et al. (2004) found a significant reduction in the hostility scores among patients given the combination. Hollander et al. (2001) and Frankenberg and Zanarini (2002) also found some advantage for people with borderline personality disorder, although these patients had not been recruited for treatment of aggression (see also chapter 16). Gobbi et al. (2006) advocated further investigation of valproate or topiramate in RCTs after finding that, alone or in combination with neuroleptics, they reduced aggression scale scores as well as number of psychotic episodes among patients with psychosis. A factor in the difficulties in treating aggression in the context of developmental disability is that sedative medications may have a paradoxical effect and worsen any agitation, but topiramate may be promising here too (Janowsky et al., 2003). After a case report by Yassa and Dupont (1983) that carbamazepine freed a previously untreatable patient with schizophrenia from aggressive behaviour, two RCTs have confirmed the efficacy of carbamazepine/oxcarbazepine in the context of psychosis (Mattes, 2005; Stanford et al., 2005); the Stanford study also showed that carbamazepine was slightly slower than phenytoin or valproate in achieving the reduction in aggression.

Non-Compliance with Medications

Failure to take medication as prescribed occurs for a variety of reasons, singly or in combination. These include poor insight into the need for medication (Buckley et al., 2007), simple difficulty in remembering and/or ability to lead a sufficiently organized lifestyle to take medicines appropriately and avoidance of unpleasant side-effects. Weight gain in particular is thought to affect adherence to anti-psychotics, especially among the SGAs (Meltzer and Fleischacker, 2001; Mackin et al., 2007) (see also below). There is some evidence too that people with psychosis and comorbid personality disorder and/or substance misuse disorders (Wilk et al., 2006) may particularly struggle with compliance, but there has been little inquiry into the nature of relationships between illness, medication compliance, personality factors and use of illicit drugs.

It is difficult to help patients who cannot or will not take their medication appropriately. A standard technique to protect against abrupt withdrawal is to persuade the patient to take depot preparations of medication where an appropriate one is available, but this may be counterproductive if the patient is particularly averse to injections or particularly susceptible to side-effects from such preparations. Where it is important to know whether a person is taking his/her medication, and even how much of it, it is useful to monitor blood levels. This cannot be done for all drugs, while for others it may only be possible to confirm that metabolites are present but not whether effective therapeutic levels have been reached, but for a few, including lithium and anti-convulsants, levels can and should be monitored regularly, not only as confirmation that the patient is receiving an effective dose, but also that that dose is not exceeded, with risks of toxicity. Knowledge that such monitoring may be done may in itself help compliance, although there is a risk that patients will only take their medication on the day of testing, with a concomitant risk of swinging blood levels, so blood testing is an adjunct to and not a substitute for astute clinical assessment.

Patient and family education, compliance and/or side-effect monitoring may each help, as may more complex interventions, including family therapy, and 'adherence therapy'. Interventions have variously been offered by psychiatrists, others in the clinical team and pharmacists, but with generally inconsistent or disappointing findings and, where there is any success with the more complex interventions, little clarity as to whether it is through improved medication compliance or the intervention itself. Haynes et al. (2008) updated their earlier Cochrane systematic review of RCTs of any intervention designed to improve treatment adherence, for any medical condition, including mental disorders other than substance addictions. They required an 80% follow-up rate for study inclusion. For both short-term (4/10) and long-term (36/83) treatments fewer than half of the interventions had had any effect on adherence; in just 25 of those in the case of long-term treatments had there been a positive effect on at least one clinical outcome. They observed that the adherence strategies tended to be unduly complex and, although not explicit in the summary, this certainly applied to the mental health interventions as just described. Perhaps at the least such a review will help those mental health practitioners who think that in failing to adhere to medication their patients are somehow uniquely awkward!

If such therapeutic efforts are not immediately bearing fruit, an option for people who may pose a risk of harm to themselves or others may be involuntary outpatient commitment. There are various community treatment provisions in England and Wales, although generally a reluctance to specify the taking of a particular medication in this context (see also chapter 24). 'Mandated community treatment' has been most thoroughly studied in the USA. An early study of this approach by Swanson and colleagues (2000) showed promise in terms of long-term stability of patients under such provisions, and an overview by Hiday (2003) noted that one of the positive effects was the decreased risk of such patients becoming victims of violence themselves. In the USA, 'leverage' is also used – benefits, including disability income or housing, have been made dependent on treatment attendance. Although also applied in the UK, its use is less frequent than in the USA (Burns et al., 2011). Such approaches require ethical debate as well as evidence of effectiveness, given the range of people taken into the programmes (Swanson et al., 2006).

Robbins et al. (2006) interviewed 200 outpatients, however, and found that those for whom housing had been used as leverage were much *more* likely than others to believe that this is effective in helping people to stay well. A more recent study of what in New York they prefer to call 'assisted outpatient treatment', under 'Kendra's Law' (see also chapter 24) has added further confirmation of the benefits of this level of coercion (Swartz et al., 2009). Here, a strategy of voluntary signed agreements to take medication was also tried, but mandated arrangements had the advantage. It may be, however, that the benefits lie as much in binding the clinicians into the treatment of potentially reluctant and rejecting patients as tying the patients into services.

PHYSICAL HEALTHCARE

A healthy diet and exercise are important for reducing the risk of chronic disease and increasing general wellbeing, and most developed countries have begun to acknowledge and adopt strategies in line with World Health Organization recommendations (WHO, 2004b). The risk of compounding poor diet and lack of exercise with smoking is particularly high among people with severe mental illness (McCreadie, 2003), while increasing use of atypical antipsychotics has added a higher risk of metabolic syndrome and type 2 diabetes (Holt, 2004; Bushe and Leonard, 2004; Zhang et al., 2004). Offender populations also tend to suffer from poor diet and poor general health (Eves and Gesch, 2003), and weigh further against their chances of health through smoking, alcohol and other drug misuse, as do people in forensic mental health services. The fact that they are confined there means that the service providers have a role in seeking to improve this situation, by building physical health monitoring and promotion into any treatment plan.

Six main areas of physical healthcare intervention are relevant here: dietary interventions, obesity treatments, exercise therapy, smoking cessation treatments, dental education and education about health and medication. The last area has already been dealt with, above, so the following discussion is confined to the first five areas.

Systematic reviews of healthy eating programmes for the general population have suggested mixed benefits, with the later review yielding rather more encouraging effects than the earlier one (e.g. Ammerman, 2002). Very little such evaluative work has been done with institutionalized populations; a systematic review of school based studies was not very encouraging (Kristjansson et al., 2009). The only study specifically with people with severe mental illness was community based, and showed health benefits from offering free fruit and vegetables to people with schizophrenia, but the new eating pattern and its benefits were not sustained once the free fruit was no longer available (McCreadie, 2005). There is no reason in principle why people in psychiatric treatment should not also have a trial

567

of medication to aid weight loss (Cormac et al., 2004), but it is important to keep checking national guidance here. Sibutramine, for example, was withdrawn in January 2010 because of attendant increased risk of heart attacks or strokes, as was orlistat (NICE, 2006).

Fish oil consumption has been advocated as a dietary supplement for people with depression or schizophrenia (Peet, 2004), but it remains unclear whether there are substantial enough benefits to sustain prescription in practice, as trial results are inconsistent (Hallahan and Garland, 2005; Irving et al., 2011).

The importance of physical activity to general health is regularly publicized, and periods of moderately stressful exercise most days of the week formally recommended (e.g. American College of Sports Medicine, 2000; Chief Medical Officers, 2011). Evidence is growing that schemes to promote such activity have a modest effect for people generally (Foster et al., 2005), and a Cochrane review is underway to find out about the relationship between exercise and mental health. There is some evidence of its effectiveness with some conditions familiar to forensic mental health clinicians, including alcohol abuse (e.g. Donaghy et al., 1991, 1997), depression (Babyak et al., 2000) and schizophrenia (Faulkner and Spark, 1999); there is no evidence on effectiveness of exercise programmes against re-offending (Home Office, 1999).

Cessation of smoking in secure mental health settings has been a source of considerable debate. For England and Wales, for example, the Health Act 2006 prohibited smoking in all enclosed public places and workplaces, and from July 2008 mental health units were included in this; sleeping and communal areas have been made smoke-free, but staff have been ambivalent about a complete ban of smoking in long-stay units at least, perceiving it as having a benefits in relieving stress and boredom, facilitating social contacts and reducing risk of aggression (Jochelson, 2006); in addition, in a secure setting, staff may be concerned about even further encroachment on human rights to autonomy, already heavily compromised and denying patients even the right to a legal, if unhealthy pleasure. Shetty et al. (2010) completed a retrospective study of patients in a 60-bedded medium secure hospital unit for 3 months before and 12 months after a smoking ban. The 50 smokers got through a mean of 21 cigarettes per day (range 5–50); most objected to the policy change and three threatened violence to staff if it were implemented. About half used nicotine replacements, and other supports were offered. There was no change in rates of aggression or use of emergency medication. The main problem was that just over 40% of the patients had been on clozapine, and there was a significant increase in clozapine blood levels in this group, with four needing a change in dose. During an inpatient stay, such fluctuations would be manageable, but the risks of fluctuating levels at a time in transition to the community and a return to smoking would have to be taken into account in an overall management strategy. Cormac et al. (2010) did a similar but larger study in a high security hospital; 298 patients were included, 73% of whom had been smokers before the ban. Again, much support of the various kinds described below had been offered to the patients, and the Cormac group also found no evidence of increase in incidents after the ban. Of added interest here was that over half of the patients had expected their mental health to be adversely affected by the ban and about 27% thought that their physical health would be adversely affected; after the ban, 39% and 25% thought their mental or physical health, respectively, actually had improved.

There is little doubt about the physical health benefits that would accrue from a smoking ban, as smoking is the most extensively documented cause of disease ever investigated in medical research (WHO, 2006) and at least twice as many psychiatric patients as people in the general population are regular smokers (Kelly and McCreadie, 2000). There is good RCT evidence of effective smoking cessation treatments and clinics for the general population (West et al., 2000); there is less evidence more specifically with psychiatric groups (Addington et al., 1998) or prison groups (Richmond et al., 2006), but what there is is positive. Controlled clinical trials of nicotine replacement therapy show that it increases the chance of smoking cessation (Anonymous, 1999), and this would not be contraindicated for people in psychiatric treatment. Buprenorphine is also effective, but would be contraindicated with some psychiatric conditions (Anonymous, 2000). NICE (2008b) guidance is that everyone should be advised to stop smoking, and support services provided, with supporting details.

Dental Health Education

Psychiatric patients tend also to have worse dental hygiene than the general population (Lewis et al., 2002; Cormac and Jenkins, 1999), as do prisoners (Heidari et al., 2007), and patients in forensic mental health services will require access to a dental service for remedial work and advice. Although the importance of adherence to oral hygiene régimes in those already suffering from periodontal disease has been demonstrated (Renz et al., 2007), and a review of RCTs of psychological approaches to improving oral hygiene behaviour confirmed their effectiveness in the general population (Niederman, 2007), improvements seem to be temporary, and long-term behaviours were little changed. It is unlikely that forensic mental health service patients will be any better in this respect, so ongoing monitoring by staff is likely to be necessary.

PSYCHOLOGICAL TREATMENTS

Something of a paradox exists at the heart of any notion of evidence-based practice: acknowledgement of the need for systematic examination of treatment inherently conveys uncertainty about its value or usefulness (Frank, 2004). As just seen, it is there for many aspects of physical treatments, but it often seems that this sense of uncertainty affects psychological treatments more. Shortcomings in the evidence base for the psychotherapies generally are real, but nowhere is the complexity and atypical nature of case material presented by patients more apparent than in a secure hospital setting (Davies et al., 2007). Nevertheless, clinical trials indicate that cognitive behavioural therapy (CBT) is an effective treatment for a range of mental illnesses and substance misuse disorders (Roth and Fonagy, 1996; Enright, 1997; Butler et al., 2006), most of which are as pertinent to people with those disorders who offend as to those who do not. There is also emerging evidence of the potential of CBT for the treatment of personality disorders (e.g. Abramovich, 2006; Beck et al., 2007, and see chapter 16). Here, the 'leading' cognitively based psychological therapies – CBT itself, dialectical behaviour therapy (DBT) and mentalization based therapy (MBT) – have been described as 'promising', albeit inconclusive, in terms of their cost-effectiveness (Brazier et al., 2006) and as having 'elements of respectability' (e.g. Bateman and Tyrer, 2004c; chapter 16). Accredited prison-based programmes are based on cognitive behavioural formulations of offending, and many have demonstrated positive impacts on their key target: a reduction in rates of recidivism and/or lapses into offence-related behaviour (Lipton et al., 2002; Hollin and Palmer, 2006).

What Is Cognitive Behavioural Therapy (CBT)?

The origins of CBT lie in classical learning theory, with its focus on observable behaviours, and in the assumption that irrational thinking processes are influential and maintained through reinforcement. The main aim of the cognitive behavioural therapies is therefore to encourage the patient to attend to the relationship between their thoughts and behaviour and the impact of both on themselves and others. A primary objective is to elicit and challenge dysfunctional core beliefs, using an array of techniques including monitoring, de-catastrophizing/normalizing, identification and challenge of (dysfunctional) thoughts, undermining negative assumptions, and promoting adaptive strategies for coping. The sharing of information about the problem/illness is another core component of the intervention.

The therapist–patient relationship in CBT is collaborative, with a clear emphasis on identified problems. Patients are encouraged to monitor their thinking and behaviour, and perhaps to keep a diary or make notes in order to gain insight into patterns of cognition and action. The focus in sessions is related to the emotions and thoughts experienced in a range of situations, and the personal meanings that the patient has attached to these. It will be important to establish how the past may unhelpfully affect the person

in the present. Once a pattern is identified, the patient is empowered to modify styles of thinking. CBT shares with other psychotherapies the fundamental principle that thinking, feeling and actions are responses to the meaning of events as much as to the events themselves (Frank, 1986).

Three generations of cognitive therapies (CTs): e.g. Beck's CBT; rational emotive behaviour therapy, (REBT; Ellis, 1962); mindfulness-based CT (Segal et al., 2004); cognitive analytic therapy (CAT; Pollock et al., 2006); acceptance and commitment therapy (ACT; Thompson, 2007) all have a wide application because they are time-limited, comparatively well evaluated, easily learnt by therapists from a range of training backgrounds, and generally accessible to patients (Davidson, 2000). The goals of intervention with CBT are clear, and the patient's motivation is strongly reinforced by support and suggestion from the therapist (Roth and Fonagy, 1996). Dobson (2001) has articulated three fundamental propositions that all CBTs share: (i) that cognitive activity affects behaviour; (ii) that it can be monitored and altered; and (iii) behavioural change may be effected through cognitive change. Whilst it has been shown to be the case that people are helped by a range of these techniques this does not mean that CBT is simple or simplistic. Problems are rarely as straightforward as they seem at first (Guilbert, 2006). The histories of offender-patients are typically replete with intervention failure (Taylor, 1997). For those with personality disorder in particular, interventions, particularly unmonitored/unsupervised interventions, may contribute to adverse iatrogenic outcomes (Jones, 2007).

CBT in Forensic Hospital Settings

Given the typical complexity of the personal histories and problems of many offender patients, phased treatments in forensic settings are likely to be indicated, organized within the CBT model, in conjunction with medication as required, and depending on the severity of the problem(s), with the broad goal of generating greater flexibility of response in interpersonal situations.

Drawing on Christine Padesky's innovations within CBT, Chrząstowski (2006) proposes the following stages which underpin a range of its applications: (1) identification of the old system of beliefs; (2) construction of a new system of beliefs; (3) strengthening of the new system; and (4) the prevention of relapse. The cognitive behavioural model, as advanced by the major theorist–clinicians (including Beck, Young, Padesky and Linehan), thus assists in providing a framework for identifying the cognitive schemas (long-standing beliefs) implicated in the maintenance of disorder together with a range of techniques to alleviate distress. Cognitive therapy, with its foundation in information processing theory, attends to schemas that develop as a means of organizing (childhood) experience, giving rise to concepts of self and others. In personality disorder, maladaptive schemas are hypervalent and thus evoked across many situations, underpinning behaviour that is maladaptive in new situations (Davidson, 2000). Schemas that relate to self-identity are likely to be resistant to change.

Although the core principles of CT for personality disorder are simple and intuitively appealing, leading to a conceptualization of personality disorder as an exaggerated pattern of behaviour that has promoted individual survival in the past, change takes time, and if (serious) offending has been one of the outcomes of behavioural strategy 'mis-application', it is likely that a much greater intensity of treatment will be required. With regard to 'dose', Lipsey (1995) observes that delivery of more than two contacts per week, amounting to more than 100 hours of treatment, is likely to be more effective for the most challenging (high risk) offenders than lower 'doses'.

Absence of progress may be dealt with through re-conceptualization of case material, and attention to ruptures in the therapeutic alliance (Leahy, 2003; J. Beck, 2005; A. Beck et al., 2007). An important mechanism of action in CBT strategies is, therefore, the provision of a framework within which unhealthy actions are identified and described, and the rationale for alternative responses is shared with the patient. The joint understanding achieved in the articulation of a 'formulation' of the offender-patient's problems *and* strengths is critical planning within the wider context of their pathway of care within and across services. Based on a synthesis of criminological and mental health targets for intervention (Howells et al., 2004), a clinical–forensic formulation is presented in outline in figure 23.1.

Cognitive behavioural treatments are inherently empowering given their focus on specific psychological and practical skills. They enable patients to tackle their problems by harnessing their own resources. Improvements are therefore attributable to the patient's efforts, in collaboration with their therapists.

Stages of Engagement with Therapy

A potential benefit of secure hospital provision is that it provides some asylum for the offender-patient from the pressures of life in the community, in the words of one patient, a 'shield' (Cox, 1978, p.273), within which former patterns of relating/defence can be safely examined and possibly relinquished. When detention is a given, the clinical task becomes how to make this time optimally productive. Receptivity to intervention typically varies over the duration of an admission. Symptoms generally dominate the clinical picture at the outset of an admission to a forensic mental health service. Once these improve, personality disturbance, diagnosable for the majority, tends to become more apparent. The challenge of remaining hopeful despite likely treatment barriers, including suicide related behaviours, self-mutilation, sabotage, withholding/reluctance to disclose and antisocial tendencies, tends then to become more prominent (Stone, 2006). In trying to establish a reasonable baseline within the forensic setting, from which progress or its absence can be measured, it is important to be able to distinguish core pathological personality traits from reactions to detention/custody (Singer, 2005). It is to be anticipated that detention will have a somewhat

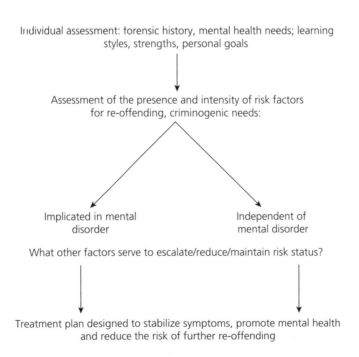

Figure 23.1   An outline of clinical–forensic formulation objectives.

different initial impact on some personality traits than on others; problems with 'authority', for example, and antisocial reactions to it, are particularly likely to be elicited in a hierarchical institution.

Broadly speaking, the main task for the early months, or even years, of treatment is stabilization, the middle phase of treatment brings remediation, while the end phase includes rehearsal of skills and consolidation as preparations for leaving. Residents of therapeutic communities have described a similar 'progressive' and sequential therapeutic process, opening with a more observational style of participation, through active engagement in high impact activity, towards a period of detachment from the intensity of therapy as preparation for leaving the facility (Genders and Player, 1995). Critical features of change in therapeutic environments for offender-patients are likely to include a realization of 'self' and the need for therapy, coupled with a willingness to ask for and receive help (Miller et al., 2006).

At one extreme of the spectrum, there are patients who remain resolutely 'unwilling' and therefore difficult to engage for many years. Whilst avoidance (of change or reality) is one maintaining factor, and evidence for its treatability by CBT techniques in *non*-forensic populations is promising (Emmelkamp et al., 2006), the added impact of the forensic setting and its dialectics (mad–bad; treatable–untreatable; compliant–resistant) can contribute to chronicity for this subgroup. Remaining alert to critical periods in the care pathway, for example a change of ward or team or ethos, and small shifts in therapeutic opportunity (windows of insight), can assist here, but much depends on the sensitivity of the therapeutic environment and multi-modal formulation of case material.

Compartmentalization of needs, linked to strategies for meeting them, is a necessary aspect of clinical work with forensic patients with complex life histories, often invaded by trauma and experiences of abuse (Quayle and Moore, 2006). Research with clinical populations highlights links between abuse in childhood *and* adulthood and a range of psychiatric disorders, but particularly, in a forensic context, schizophrenia (e.g. Read et al., 2003; chapter 11), personality disorder (e.g. Paris et al., 1994; chapter 13) and with harm to self and others (e.g. Widom and Maxfield, 2001). The implications are far-reaching for forensic services with regard to the need for accurate formulation and comprehensive treatment planning that can anticipate disturbances of attachment, and the role of trauma in the development of psychopathology (Allen, 2001; Allen and Fonagy, 2006; chapter 28).

The Dual Focus on Mental Health Restoration *and* Offending Behaviour

The tradition in penal systems for grouping offenders by their actions/convictions is also influential in forensic hospital settings. While some dangerous or unwanted behaviours may follow directly from the illness, not all do so, and it is important to have the capacity to assess, and where appropriate, meet 'criminogenic needs' as well as health needs. The treatment of a mentally disordered offender-patient may thus be enriched by drawing on risk/reconviction reduction literature as well as mental health restoration literature (Rice and Harris, 1997b). This literature, often known as the 'what works' literature, is under constant evolution and evaluation, enhanced by the process of accreditation in the prison service (e.g. Lipton et al., 2000; McGuire, 1995; 2008; see also chapters 9, 10). The clinical problems frequently encountered in high security, including aggression, institutional management challenges and life skills deficits are also those associated with the highest risk of future violence, and it is appropriate that they constitute treatment targets for many offender-patients. Table 23.5 shows how the multiplicity of CBT-based interventions, drawing from both health and criminal justice system sources, might come together in a programme for serious offenders, bearing in mind also, the typically three phase framework for treatment delivery.

There is evidence that offenders respond better to multi-modal and participatory programmes (Miller et al., 2006). Interventions within hospital settings, however, are 'nested', with the ward-based milieu providing a therapeutic setting in or from which individual sessions, analytically/arts therapy-oriented groups and cognitive behavioural groups may be offered in a concurrent timetable of therapies.

Table 23.5 Outline of applications of CBT-based intervention in forensic mental health services

Stage of admission	Mental health needs	Offence-related needs and risk reduction interventions
Engagement enhancement	Understanding mental illness/personality disorder Cognitive enhancement/remediation skills training	Motivational interviewing Thinking skills (e.g. ETS; R&R)
Intensive treatment	CBT for psychosis/PD (schema therapy) DBT for PD/self-harm Substance misuse Anger management (mentalization-based therapy)	Sex offending Violent offending Perpetration of homicide Arson/fire-setting
Consolidation	Relapse prevention plans Coping with stigma/discrimination Preparing to leave	Maintenance of change and non-offending identity (e.g. leading a 'good life')

Indeed, in low security settings, for less serious, but often recidivist offenders, the time scale available may make such contemporaneous work a necessity (Davies et al., 2010). The breadth of material covered within one treatment package necessarily presents problems with determining the specificity and evaluation of its components; the findings of complex treatments are inevitably as difficult to interpret as the disturbance is to treat (Campbell et al., 2000). Despite the difficulties, cognitive behavioural interventions that target symptom reduction, introduce skills for managing interpersonal difficulties and improve general functioning, have been associated with positive changes for outpatients with personality disorder over the longer term (Wilberg et al., 1998). Forensic inpatients in CBT for maladaptive coping and social skills have demonstrated definable improvements over time, evidenced, for example, in a reduction in oppositional behaviours (Timmerman and Emmelkamp, 2005).

Treatment Modality: Individual Sessions and/or Group-work

Individual sessions with a psychotherapist using CBT, or another model, is an analogue of the secure base in attachment that can assist in making meaning of problems, and exploring thoughts, feelings, hopes, wishes, and dreams (Tobias et al., 2006). Patients often express a preference for 1:1 meetings over group-work (e.g. Ryan et al., 2002), but a need for both, one potentiating the value of the other, may be indicated. Since offender-patient populations are characterized by heterogeneity, much clinical time is absorbed in describing differences, and the unique story of each patient. It is, however, in the awareness of similarity and common experiences – such as thinking styles, emotion processing, the experience of shame – that therapies may serve to unite otherwise alienated individuals; the strength of group-work lies here. The task of a skilled facilitating team is to intensify the emotional experience of the members of the group commensurate with their capacity to bear them (Cohen, 1997). The voice of patients, increasingly heard within forensic services (Sainsbury et al., 2004; Ryan et al., 2002; Carey et al., 2007), underscores a preference for clearly defined and well explained treatments *and* flexibility about therapeutic model; rigid adherence to a model has been experienced as *un*helpful (National Institute of Mental Health in England, 2003).

The origins of group therapy lie in the response of clinicians during and after the Second World War to overwhelming numbers of referrals to psychiatry, and echoes of this type of pressure can be found in the primarily educational targets of rehabilitation programmes for large numbers of prisoners in the penal system today. As just indicated, however, the role of psychotherapeutic groups goes far beyond any simple calculation of processing more

people. It is difficult to encompass the diversity of the theoretical orientations within group therapy which can range from the analytical – unstructured, patient-led or interpretive – to training, when groups are highly structured, facilitator-led and didactic. Any of this work may constitute group therapy by virtue of the number of patients and staff involved, but the rationale and mechanisms of action are different.

Yalom (1995) made a substantial contribution to our access to therapeutic forces in action in therapy groups, whether the task is to learn skills for coping with mental illness, to reflect on the impact of a homicide, or both. The presence of others influences how and what we learn (Kellett et al., 2006). If resistance to being in a group can be recognized, contemplated and overcome (Cohen, 1997), an 'adaptive spiral' of interpersonal learning can be set in motion, within which group members try out new behaviours as they integrate their emotional experiences with cognitive understanding. For groups that are cognitive behavioural (e.g. task-focused, time-limited) in orientation, group process factors are used to optimize clinical outcomes; the group is more than the sum of its individual members (Beiling et al., 2006). Participation in a group requires flexibility and the ability to keep the mind 'on line' in the face of emotional challenge (Tobias et al., 2006). Group therapy offers guided practice in exploring the minds of others, and observation of how others are affected by interpersonal interactions. Meta-analysis of the effectiveness of CBT groups with adult offenders highlights positive outcomes, including improved interpersonal functioning, enhanced self-esteem and anger management, and reductions in anxiety and disciplinary actions (e.g. Morgan and Flora, 2002). If group and individual therapies for a given problem are similarly effective, group interventions might be considered the 'treatment of choice' on the grounds of *cost*-effectiveness (Marziali and Monroe-Blum, 1995). Complexity of presentation and breadth of need, however, caution against any such generalization for offenders with mental disorder.

The demands required of people in group psychotherapy include attention, respect for others and adherence to group rules or contracts. Not all patients can initially sustain these, but such skills can and do develop over time, often as illness becomes less prominent. The difficulties of entering group-work have been well articulated. They include holding uncomfortable anticipatory images of the group situation and possible events therein; some patients describe aversive previous experiences. In addition, there may be lack of psychological mindedness, emotional dysregulation and contagion from the anxiety of others, collective feelings of resistance and lack of knowledge or acceptance of the group targets (Nichols, 1976). Solutions might involve: extended pre-group preparation, assessment and orientation to group-work (Shine, 2007), motivational warm-ups and analysis of 'readiness for treatment' (Day et al., 2007) and, if the group has commenced, work with the destructive forces to resolve conflict (Dub, 1997).

Listening to feedback from patients who drop out is also a valuable source of information. Chiesa and colleagues (2000) described patient accounts of factors contributing to early termination of treatment, which included feeling misunderstood or vulnerable in sessions, feeling insufficiently heard by therapists, feeling too great an expectation was placed upon them, lack of privacy inherent in the treatment process, inflexible delivery of interventions, and lack of information about what to expect in the therapy. A similar set of de-motivators was identified by inmates undertaking group-work in prison: lack of action points, rigidity of time structure and staff appearing uninterested were amongst their concerns (Cooper and Hopper, 2004).

Applications of CBT in Forensic Settings and Their Effectiveness

Mental health restoration

1. Early stages: psycho-education

Provision of information about diagnosis, services, and treatments at the outset of an extended admission is, at best, helpful to recipients, and at worst 'neutral' in impact as a 'low contact, high volume' type of intervention (Brown et al., 2006). When suitably timed, so that it is not too early, when patients may still be 'mindblown' about their whereabouts and/or the aftermath of a tragedy, and not too late, when they have worked out for themselves what others think about them as an offender, forensic mental health patients highly endorse the experience of sharing information about diagnosis and its impacts (Vallentine et al., 2010). The orientation of patients to therapy through education about diagnosis (D'Silva and Duggan, 2002), learning about treatment models, the process of change, and gaining some skills in group-work, can all contribute to towards inculcating a state of readiness for further therapy (Shine, 2007).

2. Early stages: cognitive remediation

Cognitive and neuropsychological impairments associated with major mental illness underpin responses to treatment and rehabilitation. Cognitive 'deficits' (general impairments in processes such as perception, memory and attention) may be assessed and distinguished from more temporary responses to illness, such as depression, demoralization and low motivation. Vulnerability to schizophrenia has a pervasive impact on cognitive and social functioning, with a range of aetiological pathways (Spaulding et al., 1994). Deficits which relate to social cognition, defined as the 'ability to act wisely in social interactions', may place constraints on social and vocational recovery for patients; hence the development of 'cognitive enhancement' therapies to meet these needs (Hogarty

and Flesher, 1999). Such intervention encourages behaviour appropriate to unrehearsed social contexts, including awareness of responses to others and their impacts. A personally relevant understanding of illness is sought, requiring active participation in the forming and maintaining of treatment plans.

Other cognitive remediation interventions help patients to develop concentration and memory skills through practice and rehearsal, with the impact of improving outcome more generally (Wykes et al., 1999). Hodel and West (2003) demonstrated the positive impact of goal-directed 'action training' with offender-patients, this being a twice-weekly 20-session programme to help with cognitive deficits identified by staff involved in their treatment. Patients reported feeling less aggressive after the course, and a shift in this direction was endorsed by staff who knew them well.

3. 'Active treatment': CBT for psychosis

A substantial proportion of patients in forensic mental health services have persistent symptoms despite antipsychotic medication and its associated benefits during the acute phase of illness. Cognitive behavioural techniques have been developed with the purpose of promoting: explanations of the onset and maintenance of symptoms, the detection of stressors, and skills for coping with a diagnosis of schizophrenia. The notion of a continuum from normal to abnormal underlies CBT models of psychopathology, which facilitates the exploration (and challenge) of cognitive biases (Kingdon and Turkington, 2005). A bias can be said to be present when a person notices, pays attention to, or remembers some types of information better than others, and is problematic when coupled with anxiety or distress.

For patients with psychosis, CBT has been used to interrupt vicious cycles between thoughts (interpretations of events), responses to events (behaviour) and feelings (emotions), particularly for people hearing voices, in individual and group-based sessions (Wykes et al., 1999). The evidence base according to RCTs, however, is modest, and not for want of effort. Jones et al. (2010), in updating their earlier systematic review, found 30 papers describing 19 trials. CBT with standard care did not reduce risk of relapse or readmission compared with standard care alone, although, for those admitted to hospital, it did reduce risk of staying there. Just two RCTs showed medium term reduction in psychotic symptoms; this improvement was not sustained after a year. Nor was there a difference between CBT and supportive psychotherapy. Furthermore, these studies of CBT explicitly excluded people who might bear any resemblance to offender-patients, and none considered adverse effects of treatment (see also chapter 14). One study, however, suggests that CBT in these circumstances holds promise (Haddock et al., 2004), but the effectiveness of individual CBT for patients with psychosis and comorbidities, in particular substance misuse diagnoses, has yet to be established robustly (Barrowclough et al., 1996). However, CBT is recommended in England as an intervention for psychosis (NICE, 2009). Preliminary findings from at least one clinical trial indicate benefits of *group* CBT for reducing feelings of hopelessness or low self-esteem for those with persistent positive symptoms (Barrowclough et al., 2006; Saksa et al., 2009). Early data from a UK trial of CBT for psychosis in a forensic setting, where the criminogenic needs linked to psychosis are complex (e.g. coping with homicide), indicates other promising outcomes, including greater disclosure of troubling symptoms (Williams et al., 2007); a US naturalistic study echoes this (Garrett and Lerman, 2007).

Early observations on the type of recovery from an experience such as psychosis highlight the uniqueness of each person's recovery style. Nevertheless, two broad types have been identified: 'sealing over' (the less said about the experience the better) and the 'integrative', where there is motivation to place the experience within a coherent perspective (McGlashan et al., 1976). Laithwaite and Gumley (2007) studied accounts of recovery from psychosis generated by patients in a high security forensic mental health setting, and found similar types of reflection on the experience of psychosis. Some patients provided rich, contextualized descriptions, others said little; most talked about the importance after the illness of re-defining themselves in the context of their relationships with friends and family. Qualitative research of this kind helps our understanding of the process of recovery from psychosis, which involves much more than a reduction in symptoms, is life-long, and will include features such as hope, identity definition, making sense/meaning of illness, and taking responsibility for relapse management (Andresen et al., 2003; Forchuk et al., 2003). Cognitive behavioural interventions (e.g. Williams, 2004) have the potential to generate hope and confidence in dealing with illness, but dealing with the impact of detention and offence-specific issues will form an extra part of the recovery process in any forensic setting. The 'recovery model' as a service ethos mitigates against negative counter-transferential biases that may occur in any mental health service, and promotes attendance to patient preferences and choices (Roberts and Wolfson, 2004).

4. 'Active treatment': CBT for personality disorder

In their meta-analysis of psychodynamic and cognitive behavioural treatments for personality disorder, Liechsenring and Leibling (2003) found that the CBT was generally of much shorter duration (weeks rather than years). This may account for the smaller overall effect size for CBT compared with the psychodynamic interventions in this review. The key adaptations in CT for personality disorder are the emphasis on core beliefs, as opposed to dysfunctional thoughts, and the techniques articulated for maintaining a collaborative alliance (Beck et al., 2007). A 'socratic' stance is implicit in the process of guided questioning which assists patients to become more aware of the

way in which they tend to interpret events; thought records promote alternative, potentially less dysfunctional ways of thinking. For cluster B disorders (including borderline and antisocial personality disorders), the most common in forensic mental health services, the treatment usually involves crisis management, self-help instruction, self-monitoring of skills and schema-based formulation in 1:1 sessions. Reduced rates of suicidal acts and lowered depression have been observed after patients have attended as few as three CT sessions (Davidson and Tyrer, 1996). This team went on to run a multi-centre study of CBT for people repeatedly harming themselves. Although this larger study also showed that CBT had an impact, there were variations with therapist competence and by diagnosis. Patients with borderline personality disorders did *less* well (Tyrer et al., 2004). (See chapter 16 for an extended review of trials.)

The application of the cognitive model and the concept of schemas is central to many of the programmes developed for groups of offenders within the prison service (see chapters 9 and 10 and below), where the purpose is to describe and account for cycles of offending behaviour and, ultimately, reduce re-offending, with some success (e.g. Friendship et al., 2002). As Bjorgvinsson and Hart (2006) observed, CT encourages its participants to 'stop and think'. In order to help make automatic thought processes more explicit, the therapist may ask: 'what went through your mind before that happened?', and particularly for offenders, attention is drawn to the actions preceding an offence that have been dismissed by them in perpetrator mode as 'seemingly irrelevant'.

5. 'Active treatment': DBT for self-harm and/or emotion dysregulation and problems with impulse control

Dialectical behaviour therapy (DBT) is a manualized therapy which integrates: behavioural techniques (functional analysis), cognition (skills training), support/validation of the person's efforts to make sense of his/her experiences (empathy, and direction in the management of the impact of trauma), and Eastern practices of mindfulness (Linehan, 1993). Originally developed for use with women with borderline personality disorder who presented with chronic suicide related behaviours, applications have proliferated. This is possibly because DBT combines principles of change with acceptance, helpful where problems are enduring, and skills training, which may foster optimism and a sense of practical purpose and direction for its treatment *providers*. The total package integrates individual psychotherapy with concurrent group-based skills training, access to skills generalization, and regular team-based consultation for therapists (Linehan, 1993; Swales et al., 2000).

A Dutch RCT of DBT for women with personality disorder (Verheul et al., 2003) replicated the early findings of the impact of DBT on the frequency and severity of suicide attempts (Linehan et al., 1991, 1994). Bateman and Tyrer (2004c) concluded that the benefits of DBT are greatest with regard to reducing self-harm, with general improvements even in forensic mental health settings (Low et al., 2001; Trupin et al., 2002; see also chapter 16). It has been argued that DBT is particularly well suited to the treatment of violent aggression and poor impulse control (Evershed et al., 2003) and, as such, also provides a framework for working with emotionally *in*sensitive antisocial presentations (Berzins and Trestman, 2004).

DBT for male offenders involves weekly group *and* individual sessions, targeting problem-solving, contingency management, cognitive modification, exposure procedures and skills training. Adaptations are likely to be necessary for use by detained patients, who cannot 'self-soothe' by, for example, going for a walk 'away from it all' (Evershed et al., 2003). Keeping offender-patients/inmates in treatment may well be difficult, perhaps especially if they are told that they will be 'expelled' for antisocial behaviour. In a survey of DBT in American facilities for juvenile offenders, DBT training for staff, designed to provide them with alternatives to restrictive punishment of self and other-directed aggressive behaviour, did result in a reduction of punitive actions in a 10-month DBT programme, but only for those staff who had received the full DBT training. In this setting, staff who had been partially trained in DBT made *greater* use of room confinement for rule infringements (Berzins and Trestman, 2004). As the authors comment, the latter would constitute non-adherence to the DBT model.

Reducing concurrent behavioural problems

Lapses in anger control and misuse of substances both pose challenges for the management of offender-patients, and the prevalence of substance misuse in the population is particularly high (D'Silva and Ferriter, 2003). Most patients will therefore need interventions to assist with anger, generally nearer the beginning of the treatment process, and substance misuse, perhaps later on as the prospect of lessening security appears. There is, though, a difficulty in acquiring good evidence or effectiveness. Prohibition of the use of illegal substances and aggression in secure institutions is essential, but how can patients be adequately exposed to the provoking factors to test their success in treatment? What surrogates for actual violence or abuse of substances would be good enough for these purposes?

CBT in the management of anger

CBT-based treatments provide a framework for making sense of the chronic anger experienced by many offender patients and with strategies to monitor their levels of arousal, and cope with irritation without resorting to aggression. Early promise (Beck and Fernandez, 1998) has been endorsed by 20 years of research which has produced a coherent picture and robust evidence base. Vecchio and O'Leary (2004) report 'moderate to large' effect sizes for adults treated for anger problems, concluding that CBT is the treatment of choice for problems with anger *expression,* such as outbursts of rage. CT is more effective for the *suppression* of anger.

Anger as an emotion should be distinguished from hostility, which is a persistent attitude or trait, and from violence, which is an action with intent to harm, and from the more catch-all concept of aggression. Such distinctions underpin the various interventions available across a range of services (Vecchio and O'Leary, 2004). In England and Wales, HM Prison service offers the CALM programme (Controlling Anger and Learning to Manage it), a 24-session programme, originally designed in Canada for men who had offended because of anger or loss of emotional control (Winogron et al., 1996). Dowden and Serin (2001) describe an anger management programme for violent offenders which, in a matched comparison outcome study, yielded significant reductions in violent *and* non-violent recidivism. This only occurred, however, for those assessed as being in the high-risk group for re-offending, who endorsed increased insight into anger, knowledge of anger management skills and enhanced self-competence on completing the programme.

What works with one population may not, however, work with another (Jones and Hollin, 2004). For anger management, this is particularly likely to be the case if anger resonates with the person's sense of identity (Deffenbacher et al., 2002); an offender-patient who relies on the expression of anger as a primary mode of communication is unlikely to seek to change this. Novaco's (1975, 1997) adaptation of Meichenbaum's (1975) stress inoculation training takes into account the likelihood that therapists will encounter resistance to treatment in patients who are chronically angry. An adaptation with a focus on cognitive preparation for therapy, enhanced understanding of the cognitive and physiological aspects of anger, skills acquisition, and the opportunity to apply new skills, are recommended as part of the intervention package. In contrast to the CALM programme, interventions in high/medium security hospitals have involved only small numbers of participants (Renwick et al., 1997; McMurran et al., 2001; Quayle and Moore, 1998). In the main, findings are comparable: individual and group interventions generate reductions in anger-driven behaviours after the intervention, but the 'dose' required should be determined by risk status. Jones and Hollin (2004) describe a 36-week programme involving skills training in a group and 1:1 meetings for patients with personality disorder, resident in a high security hospital. These patients reported a decrease in the frequency and intensity of their anger which was maintained for at least 4 weeks after the intervention. In keeping with the longer duration of intervention for such patients, length of follow-up should also be extended. Booster sessions and/or other forms of review of the application of skills learnt are likely to be required.

575

CBT for substance misuse

In a recent review of what works within substance misuse treatments for offenders, McMurran (2007b) reported that evidence on effectiveness is most persuasive for CBT (and concept-based therapeutic communities). The development of motivational interviewing techniques (Miller and Rollnick, 2002) and the application of the stages of change model (Prochaska and Di Clemente, 1984) have enhanced cognitive behavioural interventions for substance misusers, by providing patients and therapists with a more tailored formulation of the ambivalence about change that so often characterizes patient presentation here, and some strategies for responding to it. The need for specific treatment for substance misuse, given its links to offending and other risks, is well articulated, for people with mental disorder and substance misuse together, after 25 RCTs there is little evidence to support one approach over another on a variety of measures, including relapse of severe mental illness, violence to others, patient satisfaction with substance misuse services, and their social functioning and employment (Cleary et al., 2010) of former users. For non-offenders, interventions to supplement routine treatment, in which more healthy alternatives to substance misuse are explicitly promoted (e.g. the Norwegian 'Better Life Program', Grawe et al., 2007), have been associated with improvements in global functioning and reductions in substance misuse for patients with dual disorders.

The earliest accredited programmes for substance misuse in the UK were targeted at medium risk offenders in the community (Addressing Substance Related Offending, ASRO, McMurran and Priestley, 2004), and have been adapted for prison inmates (P-ASRO). In their review of community treatments (including ASRO), Hollin and colleagues (2004) highlight the problem of non-attendance and refusal to engage. Although only 29% of those who were referred completed treatment, completers were significantly less likely to be re-convicted. A preliminary replication of this with a small offender-patient sample found some significant improvements in attitudes about future substance misuse after completion of group-work in a high security hospital; urine screening evidence of ongoing use in the hospital was associated with drop-out (Morris and Moore, 2007).

Risk reduction: CBT-based interventions for offending

1. Foundation work through skills training

Cognitive skills programmes, such as Reasoning and Rehabilitation (R&R, Porporino and Fabiano, 2000a) and Enhanced Thinking Skills (ETS, Clark, 2000a) were first introduced into prisons in the early 1990s, just prior to the first publications on evaluation of illness/deficit-based CBT in mental health services. Over the next decade, thinking skills courses were running in most prison establishments in England and Wales (Clarke et al., 2004). The hypothesis underpinning cognitive skills training in the prison system is that cognitive skills deficits, including poor reasoning, problem-solving and self-control, explain offending behaviour, and that acquisition of such skills will improve with training. Comparative evaluation of R&R and ETS suggests that both are effective (Blud and Travers, 2001), with re-conviction rates for treated offenders up to 14% lower than for those who have not undertaken the training (Friendship et al., 2002).

An advantage of such cognitive skills programmes is that they are perceived as worthwhile by most of the adult men who graduate from the course; after the course, they cite enjoying such benefits as improved behaviour, self-confidence, literacy and interpersonal skills (Clarke et al., 2004). The expectation of lower re-offending rates for programme participants compared with their matched counterparts has been realized in many settings, with community and institutional populations, low and high-risk offenders (Tong and Farrington, 2006). Similarly, short-term benefits of ETS courses are emerging as important for offender-patients, who endorse some reductions in 'criminal thinking style' post-training (Tapp et al., 2007). The longer term impacts of such courses are not yet known. It may be cautiously concluded that they have an important role within the rehabilitation pathway, whether the participant is an offender and/or has mental health problems. Adaptations have been made to R&R for mentally disordered offenders specifically, such that the cognitive skills deficits underlying communication skills (attention, memory and information processing) are targeted (Young and Ross 2007); research on the effectiveness of these revisions is underway.

2. Offence-specific targets: fire-setting

There is currently no accredited programme for arsonists offered within HM Prison or probation services (Palmer et al., 2007); they make up a relatively neglected subgroup of offenders in this respect (Taylor et al., 2002b). Interventions with young fire-setters have tended to be educational, aimed at diverting those at risk into more productive actions, and often including the presentation of information about the dangers of fire from fire safety professionals. Historically, individual CBT-based interventions for fire-setters with mental disorder have more often been undertaken in hospitals than elsewhere (Smith and Short, 1995).

Formulation within a CBT framework of the function(s) served by fire-setting may help patients to attend to events, feelings and cognitions that precede and arise as a consequence of the offence (Jackson et al., 1987; Clare et al., 1992) and to develop alternative strategies for coping with complex emotions. Following their 40-session CBT group for convicted arsonists, Taylor and colleagues observed a reduction in fire interest and improvements in coping skills, both of which were key targets of the intervention.

Swaffer and colleagues (2001) described the complex needs of arsonists in high security forensic mental health services, and discuss the benefits of their multi-modular intervention, including sessions on dangerousness, skills development, insight and awareness, and relapse prevention, with a focus on practical strategies to break offence cycles. Groups for fire-setters are in place in all three English high security hospitals, the duration typically exceeding 24 sessions.

3. Offence-specific targets: violence

Reduction in violence and enhancement of safety for all is one of the most important functions of forensic mental health services, but systematic literature reviews on the prevention of violence have not, to date, delivered strong support for the value of any specific cognitive treatment for offender-patients in this respect, including CBT (see also chapter 9). Leitner and colleagues (2006) argue that this is because research has been ill-equipped to address the complexity of relationships here: the risk assessment literature focuses on long-term individual characteristics but the intervention literature on short-term symptom control. A cognitive behavioural approach can bridge this gap to an extent, through delineating antecedents to violence. Where offending behaviour has emerged during development, use of concepts of the self and others in relation to attachment representations which may trigger violent responses under certain circumstances may be useful. Thus, different offences committed by the same individual, for example a sexual offence and a non-sexual violent offence, may be approached systematically as separate areas of need arising from separate developmental processes (Timmerman and Emmelkamp, 2005 a,b).

Historically, the focus on reducing violence lay in anger control but, more recently, attempts have been to link treatment to a more complex conceptual model, thus widening the scope and targets of intervention for violent offenders (Howells et al., 1997). In planning treatment, it is useful to consider clinical hypotheses to explain the unwanted behaviour: that hostile schemas contribute to violent behaviour, by distorting expectancies in ambiguous/conflict-prone situations; that aggressive beliefs elicit and sustain violence; that impulsivity and arousal prevent inhibition of aggressive reactions to perceived stress. Most CBT-based interventions for violence thus aim to enable participants to describe to an/other(s) the chain of events that led to their offending, including their thoughts, feelings, attitudes, motives, and actions; next they are encouraged to explore alternative responses to any similar situation in the future. The Life Minus Violence (LMV) programme, designed for high risk offenders, comprises a minimum of 125 sessions over nine modules including: motivation, managing stress, how I got here, emotion regulation, information processing, consequences of violence, empathy-related problems, interpersonal skills and relapse prevention (Ireland, 2007).

In their extensive review of programmes designed to reduce re-offending, Harper and Chitty (2004) note the rapid expansion of interventions that are specifically tailored to deal with violence in a domestic context, or the wider community, such as the 'Think First' probation programme, or *Aggression Replacement Training*. Since many have only quasi- or non-experimental evaluation studies to support their application, interpretation of findings is difficult. In relation to violent offending in particular, the 'what works?' literature highlights the need to target intervention by risk status. Higher than expected attrition rates are seriously problematic, because those referred who start but do not complete interventions seem to be at highest risk of re-offending. People with a history of violent offending who are coerced into treatment do not demonstrate changes, especially in short-term cognitive interventions (Lambert et al., 2007), so improvements in selection for treatment are as important as efforts to retain people in the programmes.

Treatment developments are more positive for patients whose offence is formulated as being driven by a failure of anger management. *Aggression Control Training* (including anger awareness, social skills, moral reasoning and self-regulation techniques) appears to be particularly beneficial (Hornsveld, 2005). The Canadian *Violence Risk Program* (VRP), used in conjunction with the *Violence Risk Scale*, which is a collaborative risk assessment process, incorporates 'cognitive-behavioural approaches and social learning principles within a relapse-prevention framework' to reinforce small, incremental improvements in behaviour (Wong et al., 2007). This group has shown that the VRP helps to reduce the frequency and intensity of violent acts in institutions, and can enable the reintegration of previously segregated prisoners into more mainstream settings (Wong et al., 2005).

4. Offence-specific targets: sexual offending

There are few sex offenders who manage to cross the threshold into forensic mental health services, so expending resource on specific interventions for them may seem disproportionate (Timmerman and Emmelkamp, 2005), but this is often a somewhat circular situation, with admission inappropriate if treatment is not available, but treatment not provided in the absence of the clientele. In high security hospital studies in Germany (Dudeck et al., 2007) and England (Clarke et al., 2011) sexual offenders were found to be more likely than other patients to meet criteria for narcissistic personality disorder and to have been abused themselves as children. The needs of sex offenders with psychosis in medium security hospital settings (Crassati and Hodes, 1992), however, are likely to be different again, but a clinical–forensic formulation process (see also figure 23.1) can highlight and allow response to such differences by accommodating both the clinical and the criminogenic factors.

The work of William Marshall and colleagues (e.g. 2006) has contributed substantially to enhancing a cognitive behavioural understanding of sex offending. Their research has shown that sex offenders tend to have low self-esteem, social skills deficits, problems with intimacy, cognitive distortions, deviant sexual arousal and interests, which all serve to maintain and escalate the risk of recidivism. Consequently, a main aim of CBT-based programmes is to enhance resilience. Other common features of those programmes that have been formally evaluated include their focus on empirically based risk factors for re-offending and individual need and analysis of offending. Intervention is usually offered in groups, conferring several benefits, but most particularly the facilitation of constructive dialogue between offenders about the realities of their actions. A serious issue is that, to engage at all, potential participants have to feel reassured that confidentiality can be retained in the group. This may well be disproportionately difficult among sex offenders; it must be acknowledged that this is a particularly sensitive area. Furthermore, when programmes are delivered in prison, at least in England and Wales, the sessions are videoed. This is for audit of programme adherence, to ensure that it does not deviate from the manual, but this may also discourage people from open engagement so long as they perceive a risk that 'the authorities' can review their most vulnerable therapeutic moments.

Nevertheless, anecdotally, sex offender patients as a group tend not to drop out of treatment, they do their CBT 'homework' and participate in exercises designed to promote perspective-taking (Van Nieuwenhuizen, 2005). In this Dutch study, the sexually violent male forensic patients who followed the treatment programme reported that they had gained insight into their own problems, even after 16 sessions. Feedback from sex offender treatment programme (SOTP) graduates in medium security prisons suggested that over three-quarters of them rated the SOTP 'very helpful' (Beech et al., 1998). This could be interpreted as encouraging, given that those who regard treatment positively are more likely to internalize its messages. Wakeling and colleagues (2005) interviewed 46 SOTP attendees, who listed self-development gains and awareness of others as positive outcomes and, despite mixed feelings about being in a group with other sex offenders, acknowledged the value of their peers' presence – in 'realizing you are not alone'. In a high security hospital sample of sex offenders who had completed group-work treatment, Clarke et al. (2011) reported that every patient interviewed (N=17) recommended the intervention to other sex offenders, despite having experienced group-work as personally demanding and often emotionally draining: 'I got an awful lot out of it, but I can see why people didn't want to be there: it was a daunting task.'

HM prison service is the largest 'treater' of sex offenders in the UK, so the special confidentiality issues for the programmes there, and their acceptability to offenders, are important. The SOTP (Falshaw et al., 2003) has been subject to various analyses over time (e.g. Sex Offender Treatment Working Group, 1990; Wood et al., 2000; Hanson et al., 2002; Lösel and Shmucker, 2005; Hansen et al., 2009; see also chapter 10). Caution permeates interpretation of the findings in view of the nature of the offences and the fact that 'failure' of intervention may not be observed in treatment but many years later on; static risk factors appear to account for much of the variance in recidivism over the longer term (Hanson et al., 2004). A 2004 Cochrane review of nine RCTs of psychological treatments for sex offenders found 'no effect' of treatment (Kenworthy et al., 2004), but has been withdrawn pending update, and the other reviews are more positive. Use of the SOTP model with offender-patients, however, some of whom are referred to hospital services following failure to engage with or de-selection from a prison-based SOTP may be more problematic. It has been suggested that specific additional intervention to alleviate the effects of early trauma may improve psychosocial wellbeing and function, as well as criminal prognosis (Dudeck et al., 2007). The integration of 'creative' therapeutic modules with the programme may assist in achieving this (Smeijsters and Cleven, 2006).

For an extended discussion of sex offender treatment, see chapter 10, which also incorporates use of medication to help contain sexual drive, useful in some cases to facilitate establishment of psychological treatments and/or to support the individual until progress can be made in these other treatments.

The Process of Consolidation

Preparation is required for leaving any closed institution or long-term treatment. This need is probably most widely met through 'relapse prevention', a term that arises in both clinical and primary offender literatures. More often than not, this work is a component of skills training programmes. Relapse prevention, further to recovery from an acute episode of psychosis, involves learning to identify early warning signs of illness and taking steps to intervene quickly if these emerge. An offender may follow the same principles: learning to self-monitor for 'high risk' situations and take action to prevent a lapse into re-offending. The 'relapse prevention' module/component of programmes usually draws together the accumulation of tasks and experiences, insights or 'learning points' from the course/group, a key CBT technique in preparing to generalize the skills gained from the therapy. Leaving the institution will be likely to raise anxieties about change and the future (Adshead et al., 2005), and this can be used to stimulate review of the adaptations over time to the experience of detention (Zamble and Porporino, 1990). Patients with dependent or avoidant personality traits may find this phase the most challenging.

In forensic hospital settings, it is rarely enough simply to state that change has happened; patients are generally aware that change must be demonstrated over time – in the consistency of their actions. If self-focused responses to detention, such as desiring release from guilt/responsibility, quick-fix solutions or emphasizing personal loss dominate over other-centred responses, such as acknowledgement of the impacts of offending on others, acceptance of culpability and consideration of others' feelings and experiences, then progression to lower levels of security will be less quickly realized. Groups designed to foster reflection may assist here.

Stigma and Discrimination

Forensic psychiatry patients report that recovery needs are less about remission of symptoms than their management, and/or overcoming the effects of detention, including loss or disruption in relationships and social role (Corrigan, 2004; Wahl, 1999). Stigma has been defined as a sign of 'disgrace or discredit, which sets a person apart from others' (Byrne, 2000). The experience of the stigma of mental illness (shame, blame, secrecy, exclusion, stereotyping) is a powerful negative attribute in all social relations. Offender-patients have the extra 'disgrace' of their dangerous or antisocial behaviour. How best to address this in treatment for offender-patients has yet to be determined (Penn and Wykes, 2003), but the very small literature on the value of CBT in enhancing self-esteem for those with long-term mental health problems (Knight et al., 2006) suggests that this would merit inclusion in therapeutic programmes for offender-patients (Williams et al., 2011), and evaluation in that context.

How Much Real Difference Is There Between CBT-Based Treatments in Forensic Mental Health Services and General Adult Psychiatric Services?

Most people who become patients in forensic mental health services have previously been patients in generic mental health services, so it could be argued that real differences are slight. A feature which may distinguish offender-patients is that motivation for change cannot be assumed (McMurran, 2002), and many of the adaptations of CBT for forensic mental health services relate to this issue. These adaptations include extension of the engagement process, attendance to the alliance, and the duration and intensity of treatment. The general complexity of the presentation of patients to forensic mental health services, and their particular likelihood of having suffered severe disadvantage or abuse in childhood are other features. Themes which seem to be common to interventions which are more likely to 'work' for most offender-patients are those that encourage

powerful attachment relationships, communicate compassion, warmth and intimacy, use metaphor in place of direct confrontation, instil hope and reduce isolation (Bateman and Fonagy, 2000).

CBT interventions sit well within a need-based/skills-based (Roberts, 1995) organization of treatments within and across forensic services (Gudjonsson and Young, 2007). There is much to be gained from the integration of models which overlap between the clinical and criminal justice interface (Howells et al., 2004). There is evidence that it is possible for patients with serious mental health problems to develop meaningful relationships, to become more aware of the nature of their own and others' mental states, to learn to self-monitor, be soothed when distressed, and not act violently or otherwise offensively on impulse. If this is true for some, the challenge is open to adapt and research interventions for all.

ATTACHMENT AND PSYCHODYNAMIC PSYCHOTHERAPIES

The Role of Psychodynamic Psychotherapy

Psychodynamic psychotherapy can provide understanding of the meaning of an offender-patient's criminal acts, not only to the patient but also to the treating team and containing service (Cordess and Williams, 1996). Psychodynamic or psychoanalytic psychotherapy is an umbrella term for a range of treatments which vary in both how they are delivered – in an individual or group setting – and in their duration. The therapy may be a stand alone intervention or a component of a wider treatment strategy; it may also be an element in some therapeutic community programmes (Jones, 1952; Main, 1983; Cullen, 1994). In forensic mental health services, an additional role for a psychodynamic psychotherapist lies in supportive work with other clinicians and/or the clinical team as a unit, particularly assisting with recognition and management of potentially risky or toxic elements developing in clinical relationships with patients.

Irrespective of these variations, psychodynamic psychotherapies share a common aim of helping the patient understand his/her own mind and how s/he may be inadvertently (unconsciously) contributing towards his/her difficulties. Symptoms may be reduced and lasting change made possible by increasing the person's knowledge of his/her conscious and unconscious thoughts, feelings and actions. Psychoanalysts and psychotherapists have treated offenders since the origins of the discipline (Bowlby, 1944; Bromberg, 1951; Freud, 1916), but formal recognition of a specialty of forensic psychotherapy in England and Wales, like so much else in forensic mental health service development, followed the Butler Report (Home Office, DHSS, 1975); in other countries where forensic psychotherapy occurs, its recognition has followed a similar time scale (Welldon, 1994).

The contribution of psychodynamic psychotherapy to the management and treatment of offender-patients has been described as covering four main areas (see box 23.1; McGauley and Humphrey, 2003). Although these areas apply across a range of forensic services, the nature of the setting will influence the balance of the components. Psychodynamic psychotherapists working in high and medium security hospitals, for example, tend to be more heavily involved in assessment and supervision work while those working in lower security may undertake more direct treatment, not least because patients in lower security may be more available for psychodynamic treatment. Thus, as will be evident from its various roles, psychodynamic psychotherapy is not only a type of treatment but also a framework for thinking about the complexities and dynamics that arise within and between individual staff, teams and institutions treating offender-patients and those patients.

The effectiveness of forensic psychotherapy is often questioned, but empirical evidence is now as rigorously sought for this treatment as for any other. One of the underlying tensions is between what is seen as the highly structured and transparent techniques of the cognitive behavioural family of therapies and the apparently less structured, free associative and perhaps more private work of the psychodynamic treatments (Duggan, 2006). Delivery of psychodynamic psychotherapy in secure environments certainly requires adaptation of techniques and delivery, and only a proportion of offender-patients are able to use it, but even then there is often an important role for psychodynamic work in contributing to assessment. One of the most important variations, which has to be explicit with the patient, is that conventional expectations about clinical confidentiality may not apply to psychotherapy any more than to any other part of the clinical process.

Agreement over what may and may not remain in the sessions has to be reached at the outset between patient, therapist and clinical team. This depends in part on the task; when the work is confined to assessment or advice/ supervision then it would be expected that all information would be shared with the clinical team. When the task is primarily therapeutic, setting the limits to confidentiality is more difficult. Clearly any explicit threats to anyone's safety have to be shared immediately with others in the clinical team, and the patient must recognize this, but what should be shared and what remain confidential from the details of the sessions? The patient must be able to share potentially frightening material from his/her inner life; if this is recorded verbatim in the record it may easily be taken out of the context of the therapeutic process, and be damaging to patient and process alike. Ultimately, if therapy cannot proceed, this could have the potential to reduce safety for everyone. A partial solution may be that the therapist may keep their own process notes as an aide memoire, but note each session in the multidisciplinary record, and, at agreed intervals, contribute to clinical discussions about the patient and place a summary report in the main clinical record. In England and Wales at least, it is usual for patients to have full access to their own records (with specified third party information only sometimes explicitly excluded), so the patient may at any time see exactly what is on record from the sessions. Indeed, some patients find that it is a useful adjunct to the work to see an account of it 'in print'. It is certainly unacceptable for nothing at all to appear in the main clinical record. Furthermore, when therapy is occurring in an inpatient setting, it is often helpful to have discussions with others in the clinical team to agree on how to deal with material that emerges outside the sessions. It is common, even for patients in forensic mental health services who have the ability to use dynamic psychotherapy to take material out of the sessions to present to other clinicians, and thus important that those clinicians know how to handle such a circumstance.

Psychodynamic Psychotherapy with Offender-Patients

General principles

The concept of the unconscious mind is fundamental to psychodynamic thinking and practice. Consideration of unconscious mental processes contributes an additional dimension to understanding both the mind and the criminal acts of the offender as well as the impact that their complicated psychopathology has on those managing him/ her. Furthermore, there are special difficulties inherent in achieving and perceiving real, generalizable change within the protected environment of an inpatient or other institutional setting, or the coercive framework of some

---

Box 23.1 The role of forensic psychotherapy (adapted from McGauley and Humphrey, 2003)

- Direct clinical work: assessment or treatment of individuals or groups, or as an element within a therapeutic community; contributions to clinical meetings, Care Programme Approach (CPA) meetings, case conferences, team meetings and reviews.
- Supervisory work: of other professionals or of trainees who are undertaking the direct clinical work.
- Facilitation of reflective practice: helping staff to reflect on their interactions with offender-patients; aiding professionals' understanding of the psychodynamic processes in the team.
- Institutional consultation or 'institutional supervision': psychodynamically informed consultation to the institution or service from a psychodynamically trained clinician who is independent of that institution.

form of community treatment order, licence or penalty (Blumenthal, 2010).

A key assumption, described by Sohn (in Gunn and Taylor, 1st edition, chapter 17), which is central to psychotherapy with offenders, is that many assaults or abuses of others are expressions in action of a mental state which, if not remembered and understood, will repeat itself in further similar actions. As Blumenthal notes, the focus of psychodynamic psychotherapy with non-forensic patients is on the patient's psychic reality but in working with offenders, the focus is at first on the actuality of their offences. From a psychodynamic perspective, the offence has a meaning to the offender beyond the obvious harm or lawbreaking. The task is to elicit this meaning. Even those criminal acts which are planned in full conscious awareness, will have some less conscious elements (Cordess and Williams, 1996). In a forensic psychotherapeutic context, the offence is considered to have the equivalent status or role to that of a symptom. With respect to evaluating ongoing risk, psychodynamic psychotherapy may shed light on the offender's currently unconscious view of his/her past offences and the extent to which such views still preoccupy his/her mind, as illustrated in the following narratives. The narrative examples are provided to help to clarify common clinical situations. All the quotations used here, except where otherwise stated, are taken from Adult Attachment Interviews (AAI), conducted under research conditions by a trained interviewer talking with compulsorily detained offender-patients with personality disorder. The AAI is a semi-structured interview that accesses the interviewee's unconscious feelings and attitudes towards attachment-related experiences (George et al., 1985, 1996).

In addition, psychodynamic work can be used to assess the extent of the offender's capacity to own an appropriate sense of agency and responsibility, and consequently a sense of guilt for their actions, as well as an accurate empathic response towards their victims (McGauley, 1997).

AAI fragment: I find it very hard to feel guilt. Yeah I don't, I don't feel it, any. ... I don't know if I should. That's the main point that I have to figure out.

Psychodynamic psychotherapy also stresses the importance of early development in influencing adult relationships and interpersonal interactions. Genetic factors, the early environment and the interaction between them contribute to shaping personality. These repeated interactions lead to the development of internal representations of ourselves and others, often referred to as self- and object-relations. These representations act as templates directing interpersonal interactions in adulthood. A key concept in psychoanalytic theory is that these internal representations may diverge, to a greater or lesser extent, from the real external person on whom the representation is based. Those individuals who have had the good fortune of a robust genetic inheritance, coupled with a loving and secure upbringing, may still have

internalized parental representations that are experienced as critical of the individual.

Among offender-patients, most will have suffered deprived and abusive childhoods in the context of dysfunctional families or care systems. One of the legacies of such early experiences is the development of self and other representations which fail to guide the person towards establishing mature and beneficent adult interpersonal relationships. In such circumstances, internal representations of early attachment figures are commonly cruel or rejecting, while the self is represented as worthless (see also chapter 28). This self-devaluation may be a defensive redirection of anger initially felt towards an attachment figure (Bretherton and Munholland, 1999).

AAI fragment: *Are there any aspects of your early experiences that you think might have had a negative effect on the way you turned out?*

Dunno, me being bad, I'm just a bad person, ain't I? That's why I'm here. That's what I think and I think other people think it as well.

What kind of effect do you think these experiences have had on you?

Well, um… I'm just… no better than an animal now really, aren't I…

Alternatively, to assuage the pain of reality, parental representations may be idealized.

AAI fragment (re mother): Even now she don't love me, she's never shown no interest in me, she's never loved me. (Later in the interview) Yeah, she comes up to see me nearly every week, I phone her nearly every night… it's like we're more friends than a mother and daughter now, do you know what I mean, the other day she turned round to me and said 'whatever happens, I'm behind you and I'm with you.'

Offender-patients are like any others in bringing aspects of their previous experiences and relationships and their internal representations of themselves and others into their adult relationships; the differences lie in the nature of those experiences. Psychodynamic psychotherapy, whether provided individually or in a group, provides the patient with a new relationship – a professional one – and a designated time, creating a resource for remembering and understanding past and present mental states. The first task for patient and therapist is to recognize that these earlier relationships and experiences and their transformed internal representations or objects are often not consciously remembered, but nevertheless they are repeated in current relationships. The consistency and continuity of forensic psychotherapy allow these processes to become visible, in particular through aspects of the patient's internal world and its objects being transferred onto and perceived by the patient as belonging to the therapist. A characteristic of working with offenders is that aspects of the offence are also present in the transference. It is these transference processes which allow the therapist and, ultimately, the patient to access and understand how their current interpersonal relationships are driven by previous, early ones. This will include understanding offending behaviour in these terms. It has to be acknowledged, however, that not all offender-patients develop such abilities.

Psychodynamic psychotherapy and psychosis

One of the difficulties of psychodynamic work is that past mental states do not re-occur in the transference as exact likenesses of their previous form; this is especially true of patients with psychosis. Sohn noted that it is incumbent on the therapist to recognize similarities between the current material and its meaning and the previous underlying mental states (Gunn and Taylor, 1st edition, chapter 17). A fuller understanding of the patient's mental state and its expression in offensive acts can then be constructed with the patient. Unfortunately, most patients with psychotic illnesses cannot make personal use of such understanding and, by extension, psychodynamic psychotherapy. Psychosis acts as an antagonist to any attempt the non-psychotic part of the patient's mind makes to bring aspects of mental experience together as meaningful thoughts. Nevertheless, psychoanalytical thinking may contribute substantially to understanding the psychotic state in a particular individual.

So, there is no convincing evidence for treating schizophrenia or other psychotic illnesses with psychodynamic psychotherapy. Taking this to mean that psychodynamic work is redundant with respect to psychotic patients, however, especially those detained in secure settings, would be to take an unduly narrow view (McGauley, 2002). For these patients, gaining an understanding of psychotic thinking and the nature of the particular psychotic symptoms (Hinshelwood, 2004) and of the meaning of the offending act (Welldon and van Velsen, 1997) is invaluable in teasing out the relationship between violence and psychosis (Sohn, 1995).

Bion's (1967) distinction between psychotic and non-psychotic parts of the personality, which co-exist but function differently with respect to how the mind copes with psychic pain, is particularly relevant to offender-patients. As Lucas (1999) explains, if the individual can tolerate frustration and pain, then learning from experience is possible through bringing thinking to bear on the situation. The psychotic part of the mind cannot learn from experience, psychic pain and frustration cannot be tolerated and are expelled by projective processes, then experienced as hallucinatory phenomena. Bion pointed out that once these affects have been evacuated all that remains in the psychotic mind is 'logical' thinking, albeit a rather concrete logic.

Vignette: *A young man with schizophrenia, detained as a result of a serious and unprovoked assault on a member of his family, began to throw cups of cold water at various nurses. Psychodynamic work revealed that this odd behaviour occurred at times when the patient might be expected to feel angry; although the patient showed no such affect. Instead the patient projectively evacuated these feelings and believed them to be emanating from the nurse. The patient then 'logically' helped to cool down the nurses' anger.*

Although this young man's mental processing resulted in little harm, Sohn (1999) has described how such projective processes, arising in response to psychic pain, may contribute towards serious unprovoked violence. Sohn sees the links in the mind of the attacker between attacker and victim, explaining how, in some unprovoked assaults, the victim fits the need of the attacker's fantasy at that time. He gives the following example:

A patient lived in a delusional world populated by famous people who were his friends and where the sun always shone. Occasionally clouds (of depression) intruded into his fantasy world. At these moments the man would cure himself by going out into the cloudy external world and attacking somebody to make himself feel better.

One of the difficulties for psychotic patients is that the moment when thoughts or feelings come together to yield understanding is felt as intolerable by the psychotic aspects of the mind, making a destructive attack almost inevitable. This is the process that limits the use most psychotic patients can make of long-term psychodynamic work, but other essential aspects of it may still be of benefit, such as the monitoring and management of risk.

After the psychosis has been treated, it is possible that some psychotic patients may benefit more directly from psychodynamic insights. Once the patient is free of hallucinations and delusions, and ready to progress to lower security, the clinical team is delighted. The patient, however, not only now faces the commonplace anxieties that attend any major change, but s/he has lost the certainty provided by his/her delusional world, where s/he 'knows all' and is special. This may return the patient to psychic pain similar to that which set in motion the whole process leading to the offence. The patient's mental state may, therefore, deteriorate, and the voices return to psychotically allay anxiety. The patient may become hostile towards the clinical team who tried to 'rob' him/her of his/her psychotic omnipotence and peace of mind. The patient may minimize his/her symptoms, worried that revealing their existence will delay progress. Finally, the clinical team become unsettled too, feeling dismayed at the patient's deterioration and, at some level, may either blame the patient or see him/her as 'thankless'. In these circumstances, short-term psychodynamic work with the patient and close liaison with the team may help all parties to understand and negotiate the deterioration, safeguard the transfer and create a small but useful element of insight for the patient.

Most offender-patients do not remain incarcerated for ever. With partial recovery, and progression down the security gradient, they may well be able to make more use of psychodynamic work. Berke (1995) describes how the Arbours Community uses psychodynamic understanding of psychotic phenomena, coupled with the therapeutic milieu, both to contain 'mad projections' and to reduce psychotic breakdown in individuals prone to violence. For those few people with psychosis who cannot progress, there may be another role for psychodynamic psychotherapy – to 'hold' the patient (Cox, 1986), helping him/her to manage aspects of his/her disturbed internal world rather than acting them out.

The NICE (2010) guideline on treatment of schizophrenia recommends that psychodynamic principles may help professionals understand the experience of service users and their interpersonal relationships. When a patient is detained for several years, this includes helping staff understand their own relationships with that person (Van Velsen, 2010; see also below).

Offender-patients with personality disorder: The role of psychodynamic psychotherapy

Offender-patients have often been regarded as too atypical or too ill or disturbed to benefit from psychological interventions. Current evidence for treating offenders with personality disorder has been informed mainly by research and practice with people who have such disorder but who have not offended. Nevertheless, the growing evidence has been subject to a number of rigorous reviews (e.g. Bateman et al., 2005; Duggan, 2007; Warren et al., 2003; see also chapter 16). Although studies are few, with small numbers, psychodynamic psychotherapy has been shown to be at least as effective on some parameters, and perhaps better on some, as cognitively based treatment or residence in a therapeutic community (Leichsenring et al., 2003; Bateman and Tyrer, 2004c). A systematic review and meta-analysis by Salekin (2002) is particularly useful because it focuses on treatment of 'psychopathy' specifically, and, after reviewing 42 treatment studies, Salekin notes that there is little scientific basis for concluding that psychopathy is untreatable. He suggested that some traits attributed to 'psychopathy' such as lying, lack of empathy and interpersonal dysfunctional relationships may, in fact, be amenable to treatment.

Therapeutic community (TC) or TC derived treatment régimes are also considered in chapter 16, but, in brief, Lees et al. (1999) completed a systematic literature review on the effectiveness of TCs in treating people with personality disorder – and others – in secure and non-secure clinical and non-clinical settings. Broadly the review found TCs to be beneficial, although interpretation of the results was difficult due to the heterogeneous nature of the participants, the control conditions and the outcome measures. Specific effects in particular patient groups remain unclear. This review incorporated early studies of Grendon Prison (Gunn et al., 1978); subsequent studies (e.g. Marshall, 1997) have shown that completion of at least 18 months of therapeutic work at Grendon is associated with less re-offending overall than among waiting list men in the shorter (Shine, 2000) but not longer term (Taylor, 2000). There may, however, be an advantage even in the longer term for more serious offenders and those under life sentences. A naturalistic study of the former TC-derived unit for young men with personality disorder at Broadmoor hospital was not in the Lees et al. review, but also showed promise for the treatment – for men with high as well as low psychopathy-checklist scores (Reiss et al., 1996, 2000).

Challenges and recent developments in treatment

Offender-patients with personality disorder, with their often comorbid mental illnesses, their often highly disturbed upbringing and their propensity to act violently present many therapeutic challenges. When asked about who brought him up one such patient replied:

AAI fragment: The state. I was in nineteen different establishments between the ages of four and fifteen. Ten months was the longest time I spent anywhere. That place was closed down for cruelty after I left.

Such early experiences may lead to internal representations characterized by low self-worth and esteem. Such individuals find it difficult to engage in most treatments, not just psychological ones. If they do engage, the therapeutic alliance is vulnerable to ruptures when either the patient sabotages therapy and provokes the therapist into terminating treatment or the therapist withdraws when in contact with affects such as hatred and rage and an internal world populated by harsh and cruel representations. We have already seen that there is scope within the cognitive behavioural approach to treatment to watch for such ruptures, and repair them, and psychodynamic psychotherapy too provides both a framework for understanding these psychological reactions (Skogstad, 2006) and a treatment modality which encompasses repair by working closely with the attendant affective states. Sarkar and Adshead (2006) describe one such framework that conceptualizes personality disorder, in part, as a disorganization of the capacity for affect regulation, mediated by early attachment experiences. Again, earlier relationships and experiences, particularly affect laden ones, are often not remembered but are repeated in current relationships.

AAI fragment from an offender-patient with antisocial personality disorder. *What do you think the people involved thought of your actions?*

I don't know I can't read minds. I don't know, I don't think about it I don't worry about it. I only think, the only time I think about the offence really is when you lot talk to me about it. Apart from that it doesn't really cross my mind. I'm not too worried about the trial.

Sometimes, however, mental states and the actions flowing from them are remembered, but neither recognized nor understood. The psychotherapeutic task is then to help the patient achieve the necessary recognition and understanding to be able to process this mental material.

583

AAI fragment from an offender-patient with borderline personality disorder: I used to go to bed and try and rip up sheets because I was so angry but I didn't know what I was angry about.

(Later in the interview) Um ... I didn't have ... my own feelings I had her (patient's mother) feelings and colours if she liked different colours I'd like the same colours, I didn't have my own mind.

The two quotations just cited allow for discussion of the concept of mentalization, its relationship to both personality disorder and violence and the development of mentalization based treatment (MBT) as a promising, psychodynamically derived intervention for those with borderline and possibly antisocial personality disorders. Although these interviewees may not have been aware of it, both remarks contain insight. It is not so much that the first patient cannot 'read minds' but in all likelihood has a diminished capacity to mentalize and may be unable to envision the mental states of others, or may do so inaccurately. Mentalization refers to the ability to interpret the actions of oneself and others as meaningful on the basis of intentional mental states and of an understanding of the feelings, beliefs, thoughts and intentions of oneself and others (Baron-Cohen et al., 2000). The second quotation points towards the aetiology of this deficit, namely that the capacity to mentalize develops through a process of having experienced oneself in the mind of another during childhood, in the context of a secure attachment relationship (Fonagy et al., 1997).

Since 2000, Bateman and Fonagy have developed the theoretical and research base for MBT, so that it is now a manualized treatment that may be delivered by generic mental health professionals (Bateman and Fonagy, 2006b). Capacity for mentalization has been shown to be diminished in imprisoned offenders with personality disorder (Levinson and Fonagy, 2004). They suggested a developmental model of violence in which some forms of violence occur when mentalization fails. They propose that severe early trauma, in the context of impaired attachment experiences, enfeebles the development of mentalization. In adulthood, when emotionally aroused, non-mentalizing cognitive processes predominate. The individual is then more prone to experience their own mental state and those of others in physical and bodily modes, predisposing the person towards committing violent acts. Such acts may occur as either a response to misperceptions of the external world, or to evacuate intolerable mental affects or bodily sensations.

AAI fragment: When I was doing it, actually doing the fire I was happy because I was like burning the bed, the bedroom where my dad abused me... instead of like talking about it I just wanted to wipe it all away just wanted to wipe that house off the earth, I thought I'd be able to cope without that house being there. I was just thinking about all the bad things that happened in the house, I was thinking that they are all going up in smoke as well and I tried to get rid of them, I wanted to force them out of my head.

Although other psychodynamically derived manualized therapies, such as transference-focused psychotherapy (Clarkin et al., 2001) and integrated therapies, such as CAT (Ryle et al., 2000) have shown promising results in the treatment of borderline personality disorder, MBT is mentioned here specifically as its evidence base is supported by an RCT and a meta-analysis (Bateman and Fonagy, 1999, 2001, 2008, 2009; Fonagy and Bateman, 2006). It offers a theoretical basis, supported by empirical evidence, that some forms of violence occur when mentalization fails (Fonagy, 2003) and it has shown early promise in treating people with antisocial personality disorder (Bateman and Fonagy, 2003).

Staff, Services and Psychodynamics

All staff working with offender-patients are on the receiving end of dysfunctional processes, whether these emanate from the patient's psychosis or personality disturbance. The fragmented nature of the internal world of the patients, and the psychological mechanisms such as projection and splitting, they rely on to manage psychic pain and unpalatable affective states mean that internal states of mind are often chaotically externalized. In forensic mental health settings particularly, these processes evoke both conscious and unconscious reactions in staff, teams and the institution (Menzies, 1959), which, if unattended to, decrease the effectiveness of the particular therapeutic task, whether containment or treatment.

Work with offender-patients exposes professionals to a range of risks which must be assessed and managed continually. Psychodynamic psychotherapists should be part of, or work closely with, the teams managing these patients so that those clinicians involved in day-to-day management and/or in major decisions about care and containment gain as full a picture as possible of any patient's mental function and its effect on staff. The aim is to integrate psychodynamic work into all patient care and thus support and enhance it.

Psychodynamically informed reflective practice may help staff have greater awareness of an individual's capacity to harm others. Staff need a support matrix. If they feel psychologically 'held' they are more likely to be able to contain and work therapeutically with the people in their care (Cox, 1986). More specifically, psychodynamic thinking can make sense of the bizarre manifestations of a psychotic illness, and staff can help patients more with these (Jackson, 1995). In a delusional transference, the clinician no longer 'reminds' the patient of a cruel parent but 'is' that parent. This is not only disturbing for both patient and clinician, but also brings the double risk of attack on the staff member and breakdown in the patient's relationship with the treating team.

Staff must be able to withstand a multiplicity of strong emotional reactions if they are to maintain a therapeutic relationship with offender-patients. Poor, even counter-therapeutic relationships may take the form of the intense, unstable and affectively suffused relationships characteristic of borderline states, or the derogation of those offering help and attempts to deceive them, which staff managing people with personality disorders may find so provocative and castrating. At these moments, a psychodynamic view of the case may be helpful in offering a framework for conceptualizing the negative therapeutic reaction and the counter-intuitive observation that the patient is sabotaging therapy, irrespective of its modality, just at the moment it is felt to be helpful or heralding change.

At times, staff may over-identify with aspects of the internal world of their patients, perhaps as harsh parent, perhaps as victim. Either way, such identifications can lead to an increased risk of boundary violations. Many professionals would concur that the understanding that psychodynamic work can bring to such situations may lessen the likelihood of such violations.

Institutional supervision allows staff to make links between the psychopathologies of the people in the institution and particular aspects of how the institution functions. This is especially important when the forensic setting holds patients with the kind of perverse psychopathology that may induce the institution to react with collusion, cynicism or violence. Institutional supervision can also explore the nature of its social defence system. This brings us back to the tensions between the caring and custodial/control functions of the institution described by Hinshelwood (1993). In forensic mental health services, the particular anxieties are fear of destruction or corruption. The psychological defence may take the form of staff 'forgetting' the patient's offences, and/or unconsciously adopting an attitude of 'pseudo caring'. The message communicated is that the patient is no problem as s/he is so quiet. The alternative, in an attempt to control their own fears about the violence of their patients, is that staff unconsciously adopt an over-tough, controlling stance. The consequences of either culture dominating the institution have been described in several inquiry reports.

NICE guidance (NCCMH, 2003a, 2009a, 2010b) on treatment for personality disorder endorses a psychodynamic psychotherapeutic support role for staff, while a sister documents (NIHME, 2003a,b) commend its role in a training framework for staff. Psychodynamic principles may enhance the ability of staff to maintain boundaries, minimize any negative impact of working with people with personality disorder, use supervision and reflective practice, contribute to dynamic risk and needs assessment and bear hostility and aggression without retaliation.

Few practitioners work psychodynamically with offender-patients. As a scarce resource, those who are trained to do so should be deployed prudently. In summary, this means that with respect to psychosis, psychodynamic psychotherapy is generally best used to help make psychotic thinking and communications understandable while for personality disorder its contribution encompasses assessment, treatment, supervision, reflective practice and training for the workforce. A final AAI fragment illustrates how a manifest attempt to get help is discordant with the perpetrator's diminished capacity to mentalize and to think of his victim as human, removing any inhibition to further violence. A developmental perspective on violence would propose that normal developmental processes have failed for this man (Fonagy, 2003). For many offender-patients psychological help, irrespective of its modality, is too little and arrives too late. This patient is almost certainly correct that his best chance for having a normal life would have been achieved by turning back his developmental clock and giving him treatment much, much earlier, but it may be possible to build on his recognition that he had deviated from normal development and wishes otherwise.

AAI fragment: I got up and started stamping on his head and um another guy come up and dragged me off him... I rang an ambulance 'cause I thought he'd, he was dead. I went back into the kitchen where he was and I kicked him in the ribs to see if he was dead or not.

(Asked later in the interview what he would wish for if granted three wishes):

... I'd wish that I could have a normal life, normal job, normal girlfriend and I wish I could turn the clock back and start afresh.

CONCLUSIONS

Our principles, then, start with the position that most people whose severe mental disorder was a factor in offending will be able to change, at least to a useful degree, providing they receive appropriate treatment. The change must be in health certainly, but also in ownership of behaviour. Murray Cox taught the desired pathway in simple language:

I didn't do it.
I might have done it, but they made me do it.
I did it, but I was helpless in the circumstances.
I did it.
I did it and I don't want to do it again.

Many patients will feel or be alienated from services, clinicians and authority figures, and many will be almost as traumatized by their crimes as their victims, so it is often necessary to engage in a substantial period of work to achieve a stable baseline of engagement in the treatment process. Most patients will have a complex mix of problems so that a single treatment is unlikely to suffice. Most, even of those with personality disorder, are likely to benefit from medication for specific symptoms, and indeed this may be an essential enabler to prepare the way for psychological treatments. Most will need some sort of psychotherapeutic help, and everyone will need to engage or re-engage with educational or occupational activities to help (re)normalize his/her social life. Treatment is likely to be needed for the long term, and so even experienced, highly trained therapeutic staff may well need strategic support and supervision in order to be able to sustain this. From time to time, things will go wrong and clinical teams and their parent institutions, and even the wider public need to maintain awareness of this; a 100 per cent success rate is not achievable under any circumstances. That said, treatments must be evidence based as far as possible, and treating staff have a duty to keep up-to-date with the literature *and* practice consensus and to be able to demonstrate at all times that they have been working with probity. It is often observed, and probably true, that the fundamental philosophy behind the treatment process differs between general adult and forensic psychiatric practice, and, if so it is essential to be aware of this in any effort to return patients to 'mainstream' services. Adult general psychiatry in England and Wales, and perhaps elsewhere, has become a largely crisis intervention service, whereas forensic psychiatry, while working with patients towards recovery, tends to emphasize *maintenance* of 'good enough' health. Addictions services generally work to an ideal of controlled use of problem substances, forensic psychiatry would generally aim for abstaining. If the consequence of mental state deterioration, however induced, may be a serious violent offence, then crisis intervention may occasionally be necessary, but it is not a sufficient model for good practice. Conditions which can assist the patient towards attaining healthy independence, the therapeutic ideal (Jamieson et al., 2006), are likely to include long-term, constant access to experienced treatment review and a range of treatments and treatment conditions which are acceptable to the patient. The next two chapters consider frameworks for treatment in more depth.

24

Forensic mental health services in the United Kingdom and Ireland

Edited by
Pamela J Taylor

Written by
Jackie Craissati
Pamela J Taylor
Commentaries:
Lindsay Thomson (Scotland)
Fred Browne (Northern Ireland)
Harry Kennedy and
Damian Mohan (Republic of Ireland)

1st edition authors: **John Basson, Adrian Grounds, John Gunn, Pete Snowden and Pamela J Taylor**

The UK and Ireland have a long record of providing specialist secure mental health services in health service hospitals, and a more recent one of specialist community services for offender-patients. This chapter is about the development and provision of such services, so mainly about the framework for delivering specialist assessments and treatments rather than those tasks themselves.

The practice of secure hospitalization for offender-patients dates from the mid-nineteenth century. The earlier hospitals – the high security hospitals – were free standing institutions. Each was a considerable distance from other hospitals and sited nowhere near prisons. Nevertheless, they must have seemed prison-like to those who were required to live there, partly because of the physical security that they provided, but partly also because until as recently as the late 1980s the male nursing staff wore uniforms which were indistinguishable from prison officer uniforms, and most were members of the Prison Officers' Association.

The year 1975 proved to be a watershed for services, with the publication of the report of the Butler Committee (Home Office, Department of Health and Social Security, 1975). Strictly this applied to England and Wales, but it eventually influenced service development in the other parts of the UK, in Ireland and, through teaching and research exchanges, in some other countries too. A new tier of medium security hospital services was developed, foren-

sic psychiatry specialist training was established in the UK and Ireland and an academic base took a tenuous hold.

Since the 1990s, in England and Wales, these specialist services have expanded, and further specialist tiers have been added. A better numerical balance of health service availability according to their security level has been achieved, but, although placement in such services is invariably publicly funded and all the services are embedded in the mores of the National Health Service (NHS), still tensions remain over the extent to which patients can enjoy fully integrated health service provision, once seen as the ideal over a parallel system (Gunn, 1976). Since the 1990s, the high security hospitals have been drawn more fully into mainstream health services to the extent that, like all other mental health services, they are run by mental health trusts rather than central government. At the same time, they have stayed geographically separate. A lapse in security, which allowed a man to leave one of these hospitals without permission, led to a review of security led by the then Director General of the prison service (Tilt et al., 2000). Notwithstanding the evidence on the extreme rarity of such occurrences (e.g. Moore, 2000), and the different security issues posed by people with mental disorder compared with those without, large sums of money were spent on enhancing the physical security of two of the hospitals, making them appear more prison-like, although, ironically, not at the hospital where 10 of the 12 escapes had occurred. There are elements of forensic psychiatric service provision which are inescapably political. Buchanan (2002) illustrated the almost annual catalogue of government department guidance for England and Wales which emerged in the 1990s, with up to three documents in some years. This may sometimes bring funding advantages, but may also threaten good management and an appropriately therapeutic climate (Kaye, 2001). Forensic mental health clinicians, however, understand the importance of public protection, and, as an essential part of this, become familiar with effective working with people in the criminal justice system (CJS), both informally and within formal structures such as Multi-Agency Protection Panel Arrangements (MAPPAs) (see below and chapter 25). They also develop good working relationships with other relevant agencies, including the voluntary/third/independent sector and many clinicians also work closely and well with government officials and bodies.

The model vision of a fully integrated pathway between levels of secure hospital service and mainstream psychiatric services has remained elusive for many patients, and specialist forensic mental health community services, once unusual, started to become a major development in the 1990s. While forensic psychiatry and the other smaller specialties in psychiatry relate well, and have even developed joint specialty training schemes, such as forensic psychotherapy or child and adolescent forensic psychiatry, tensions remain between forensic and general adult psychiatry (Turner and Salter, 2008; O'Grady, 2008). In part, the sibling rivalry is about resources, in part the rather different approaches to major mental illness. At least as perceived by forensic psychiatrists, their general adult peers operate a predominantly crisis intervention model, whereas the forensic drive is to maintain mental health once restored or improved. Intervention at crisis point is too late when serious harm to others may be associated with deteriorating mental state. Potential tensions through generally working to a different model from most addictions services must also be recognized. When hazardous use of substances and/or dependency on drugs or alcohol constitute the primary target for treatment, substance misuse specialists generally regard controlled use as the optimal goal, whereas forensic psychiatrists will usually require abstinence. Again, the background difference lies in the potential seriousness of the consequences of relapse. If a patient fails to keep an appointment or two, s/he cannot simply be discharged, but rather has to be found, and reassessed, and more vigorously supported in maintaining future treatment commitments. It is important that we learn to work with these differences, and that they do not divide clinicians such that they cannot work co-operatively to provide the best treatment for patients. The safety, treatment and rehabilitation of patients will be optimal through appropriate co-operation; without it, patients will fall through service cracks with a higher risk of harming self and/or others. Services and safety will also be improved by listening directly to patients and their families about the need for earlier assessment and appropriate intervention and for trusting relationships that facilitate disclosure and co-operative treatment and habilitation (Robert C, 2006; Welsh Assembly Government, 2009).

Integrated treatment has taken on an extended meaning too in the growing convergence of health and criminal justice systems in providing treatment, both in England and Wales (Rutherford, 2010) and in the USA (Morrissey et al., 2009). While there has always been a measure of joint, or cross-over, working, the high and possibly growing numbers of people with mental disorder in prisons, and indeed elsewhere in the CJS, has been associated with considerable growth and innovation in this area. For England and Wales, the Bradley Report (Bradley, 2009) has made this an imperative at every stage of contact between a person with mental disorder and the criminal justice system. Rutherford's 2010 consultation document considers six areas of convergence in some detail. One desirable one lies in criminal justice liaison with mental health, to divert people with mental disorder out of the CJS altogether, where appropriate. A second useful but underused provision for convergence is the formal link between probation and health services through the Mental Health Treatment Requirement (MHTR), bringing community treatment within the structured framework of a community penalty for convicted individuals. As long ago as 1907, the Probation Act of that year highlighted an offender's mental condition as a reason for making him or her subject to probation. The NHS came into being in 1948, and The Criminal Justice Act 1948 provided for the first formalization of the combination of probation and treatment. This has been available ever since, in its current form under the Criminal Justice Act 2003, so it is surprising that these orders are still regarded as so alien, with less than 1% of community or suspended prison sentences attracting an MHTR (Solomon and Silvestri, 2008).

A third area of health and criminal justice convergence is more problematic – that of imprisonment for public protection (IPP), which captured a disproportionate number of prisoners with mental disorder, as yet providing them with too few treatment options (Rutherford et al., 2008; and see chapter 25). Mental health courts have been considered, but Rutherford (2010) argues that, in England and Wales, they would add little that cannot be achieved within the existing court structure. The remaining two convergences, like the IPP, have the potential to facilitate diversion of a person with mental disorder out of the health service. One of these is the hospital and limitation direction (hybrid order), which allows a judge to order both imprisonment and hospital treatment; hitherto unpopular with clinicians, its use could grow with pressure on beds and because of the extension of its application since November 2008 to all mental disorders. The other was the dangerous and severe personality disorder (DSPD) pilot programme, now being wound down and the funds allegedly diverted into provision of more widespread 'psychologically informed planned environments' (see also chapter 16).

Undoubted benefits of such convergence, at least in theory, include opportunities for more timely treatment for disorder, a more truly comprehensive approach to meeting the complex needs of people who are unwell but also offend, and enhancement of public safety and confidence. There are disadvantages too, including increase in the stigmatic burden such people have to bear, undue blurring of professional roles, and the ethical challenge of just how much information should be shared between systems. There is also the question of how health service personnel should deal with orders which, if breached, would generally lead to imprisonment.

CYCLES IN FEAR AND STIGMATIZATION: A BRIEF HISTORY OF SECURE MENTAL HEALTH SERVICES

Fear and intolerance of people who have a mental illness has a long history, partly because of a perception, which goes back at least into ancient Greece, that violence as well as 'wandering about' is characteristic of mental disorder (Rosen, 1968, p.98). In biblical times, hostility to a man possessed of an 'unclean spirit', who could not be held and who harmed himself, was so great that the public wanted rid of Jesus Christ for healing him as much as they wanted rid of the man himself (Mark 5:2–17). Appignanesi (2008), however, focusing exclusively on treatment of women, gives an account of the treatment of Mary Lamb which shows just how enlightened management of a serious offender with mental disorder could be towards the end of the eighteenth century in England, given a supportive family and a little money. Mary Lamb killed her mother while in a psychotic state; her subsequent management combined the more common situation of home care under the watchful eye of her brother with occasional confinement in an asylum if her mental state deteriorated. Specific treatments may have improved over time, but it would be hard to say with honesty that we have reached a point of bettering the pathway of care that she had. Accepting Appignanesi's account, later treatment of women, whether or not in such a terrible situation, deteriorated and was, at times, frankly shocking. Porter (1987a,b, 2002) is one of the best authorities on how attitudes and services have changed through the centuries, although there are also some interesting older texts (Ackernecht, 1959; Lewis, 1955; Leigh, 1961; Parry-Jones, 1971; Jones, 1972; Bynum et al., 1985, 1988).

Allderidge (1979) gives one of the best, brief overviews of historical developments, suggesting that few ideas currently prevalent in psychiatry are new. She writes that, in Britain, at least as early as the fifteenth century there was some hospital provision for 'the insane'. The Priory of St Mary of Bethlehem, Bishopsgate, was founded by Simon Fitzmary in 1247; by 1403, six insane men were included amongst other sick people – perhaps in the equivalent of the first general hospital psychiatric unit – and the Priory

soon specialized in insanity. Patients were kept there largely at the behest of friends or relatives, but brutality, including beating a mad person, appears to have been condoned. Public callousness was evident too, in that almshouses prohibited admission of the insane. The longevity of serious mental illness seems to have been understood, according to Allderidge's citation from William Gregory's fifteenth century chronicle:

> ... Bedlam. And yn that place ben founde many men that ben fallyn owte of hyr wytte ... and sum ben restoryde unto hyr wytte and helthe a-gayne. And sum ben abyding there yn for every, for they ben falle soo moche owte of hem selfe that hyt ys uncurerabylle unto man.

By the seventeenth century, the new Bethlem itself was limiting length of admission to 12 months. Patients were either cured, or discharged as incurable at that point – so there is nothing new in debates about length of stay and treatability. In another familiar move, the 'private sector' was brought in to help the insane; indeed, from the late seventeenth century until the reforming Acts and public asylum building programme of the late eighteenth and nineteenth centuries, private 'mad houses' constituted the main provision outside the home for people who were floridly ill. These asylums were built in every county. Once established, they were considered to need inspection, so lunacy commissioners were established to do so – by various other names over the years, another familiar type of body.

What might be taken as an early phase of modern *forensic* psychiatry also has modern overtones. In the eighteenth century, there was no special provision for 'criminal lunatics', who were scattered throughout prisons and workhouses. A few were in the Bethlem Royal Hospital. The attempted assassination of George III by James Hadfield stimulated the introduction of the Act for the safe custody of insane persons charged with offences (Criminal Lunatics Act 1800). Such people, whether unfit to plead or not guilty by reason of insanity, were to be kept in 'safe custody' in some suitable place. As there was no suitable place, Hadfield was sent to Bethlem, but escaped in 1802. He was recaptured, sent to Newgate prison, but not readmitted to Bethlem until 1816 (Allderidge, 1974). Bethlem was about to be rebuilt. The government provided its governors with the capital and revenue to include a state criminal lunatic asylum in its development. This was, no doubt, an attractive offer to the governors of a private foundation. The new Bethlem opened at St George's Fields in 1815 with two wings set aside for 'criminal lunatics', with beds for 45 men and 15 women, but absolutely no contact between the criminal patients and those in the main hospital. Any movement from the wards required the Home Secretary's permission; they quickly filled and became overcrowded. The wings were enlarged, but could never keep pace with demand. In 1857, 40 of the 'better class of criminal patients' were transferred to an ordinary ward of the hospital which had had a security upgrade, but the government was forced to make better provision and so a new, separate, secure hospital was built in Windsor Forest at Broadmoor, to house 500 patients. During 1863 and 1864 all the 'criminal lunatics' were transferred to the new hospital. The old criminal lunatic wings at Bethlem were then torn down, with the Treasury paying for their demolition (Alldderidge, 1974). Thus, in a now familiar pattern, the first security units for offenders with mental disorder led to the progressive rejection of criminal patients from mainstream psychiatry.

The range of facilities, concepts and laws inherited from this chequered history should perhaps have ensured that, by now, there would be facilities to match the needs of almost any patient, but 'treatability', a concept most recently introduced in the Mental Health Act 1983, was perhaps misused (see also chapters 3 and 16). New 'gaps in service provision' are constantly being identified. The government commissioned reports of the 1970s (Department of Health and Social Security, 1974 [Glancy]; Home Office, Department of Health and Social Security, 1975 [Butler]) focused on the absence of intermediate provision between high security and open conditions. More recently, the Home Office and the Department of Health worked together to try and get more widespread acceptance of a need for treatment on the part of offenders with personality disorder (National Institute for Mental Health in England (NIMHE) 2002); subsequent developments for this group, still far from enough, are dealt with more fully in chapter 16. Other apparently new needs keep emerging.

Process in service development has tended to follow a familiar pattern in the UK. Individual cases or crises from time to time trigger political angst and action; the 'Dangerous and Severe Personality Disorder' programme, currently being phased out, is one example, following the case of Michael Stone (Francis et al., 2000). Periodically, government engages all interested parties in a more considered review of service need and development (e.g. Department of Health, Home Office, 1992, for England; Welsh Assembly Government, 2009, for Wales), and substantial, sustained change occurs over a period of time.

SPECIALIST FORENSIC MENTAL HEALTH SERVICES: PHILOSOPHIES AND A THEORETICAL MODEL

Specialist forensic mental health services have four overarching tasks:

- Assessment, on request, of people who it is thought may have a combination of any mental disorder and behaviour which might put others at risk, and, depending on the outcome of the assessment, one of more of the following:
  - delivering safety – for each patient, for other patients and staff while they are hospitalized, and for others in the wider community;

- treatment of major mental disorders which have proved resistant to treatment in other settings;
- facilitation of optimal integration or reintegration into wider society.

Figure 24.1 presents pathways which may result from this approach, with referral variously coming from anywhere in the criminal justice system or from elsewhere in the health service. If the latter, referrals are generally from secondary, specialist psychiatric services, but not invariably so. Since health services in prisons are now largely provided by NHS in-reach teams (see chapter 25), it may seem a bit anomalous to refer to prison referrals, but as so many referrals are of prisoners, prison as a source of referral has been retained in the figure. Referrals may result only in reports – most usually for the court, but sometimes for another health service, concerned about capacity to continue managing a difficult and potentially dangerous case. More commonly, advice and support are sought and given on reducing the risk in a particular situation and re-establishing safety and security. Quite commonly, a process of consultation and liaison is sufficient, although it is advisable for the parties to maintain dialogue over a period of time to ensure that this has been achieved. Sometimes, admission to the specialist health services is required – sometimes with full transfer of the care, treatment and management of the patient, but sometimes with an understanding that the person has simply been transferred for further assessment and/or a brief period of stabilisation. So, again, movement in both directions between health and criminal justice systems will be likely. Where admission is required, this may be straight to any level of security, even to specialist community services, and flexibility of movement in either direction between them is then essential. The concept of risk stratification is useful here (Kennedy, 2002). Generally, movement is in a stepwise fashion from one tier of security to the immediate next level, and, where the Ministry of Justice is involved through restricted hospital orders (see also chapter 3), this is the kind of movement which is encouraged, even expected. Nevertheless, jumping across the tiers – even straight from high security to the community – is theoretically possible and still occasionally occurs.

The main tasks of forensic mental health services are achieved through a mixture of principle and evidence based practice. Principle does not require evidence, but rather includes both human decency and formal rights, as set out in the European Convention on Human Rights (q.v.) and incorporated into national human rights legislation and, in turn, more directly applicable legislation, such as mental health law. Principles largely dictate the framework for the services, while evidence underpins – or should underpin – the nature of what happens for people within that framework – the treatment. The Department of Health and Home Office 1992 Review delivered a set of principles which, strictly, apply only to services in England, but they

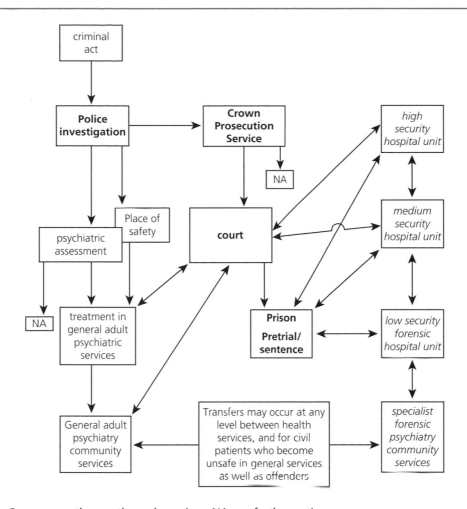

Figure 24.1   Common pathways through services. NA: no further action.

are so general that they are potentially of wider value. These principles are about

- quality of care with proper attention to individual needs;
- community rather than institutional care where possible;
- conditions of security being no greater than justified by the danger presented – to self or others;
- maximizing the chances of sustaining an independent life in the longer term;
- providing proximity to home and family if these exist.

The first four principles embody the medical ethic of maximizing autonomy and, in fact, anticipated the Human Rights Act 1998. An emphasis on proportionality is in the Act and in these principles – that, insofar as it becomes necessary to breach autonomy, that breach should never go further than necessary.

The concept of helping to sustain an independent life now has evidence as a valid, testable approach. Jamieson et al. (2006) investigated the concerns of a range of professional staff involved in the discharge of high security hospital patients, using a grounded theory approach.

Twenty professionals were recruited from discharging and receiving hospitals and from bodies charged with providing independent advice, and engaged in in-depth interviews. A theory emerged from analysis of the transcripts, incorporating a pathological dependence/independence to healthy independence continuum, with patients generally making a graduated progression along it. Sometimes, however, changes might be more sudden and substantial, in either direction, for example, moving directly from a secure hospital to the community, or, in the other direction, re-offending or relapsing and being recalled to hospital. As the theory developed, the core concern about the pathologies of dependence and independence was resolved through actions on the part of professionals actively facilitating progress towards healthy independence. Characteristics of the patient could enhance or block this, as could factors in the external environment. The active professional strategies were found to be 'paving the way' and 'testing out'. 'Paving the way' begins on admission to a security hospital, intensifies during residency, and lessens after discharge. It includes factors that prepare the patients for their post-discharge path. 'Testing out' overlaps in time with 'paving the way', but the former happens

591

to a greater extent outside. Achieving independence, or partial independence, was said to be a good outcome. Bad outcomes, such as re-offending, are 'terminators' of independence. Best outcome was community living, without recurrence of offending, and with only those supports of a patient's choice.

THE NATURE OF HOSPITAL SECURITY

Security in a clinical setting is made up of four main elements. Three of these – the physical security offered by the nature of the perimeter and internal design of the building, the procedural security of routine staff checks and the relational security which comes from the quality of the professional relationship with the patient – are the elements which enable the fourth, most important element of all, which will provide for change and sustained enhancement of safety – treatment. The latter is mainly dealt with in chapter 23; here we consider the broad mechanics of the enabling environment. Where more detail is required, the Royal College of Psychiatrists has worked together with the Department of Health in England to develop a set of security standards for medium security services, covering both public and independent sector providers (Health Offender Partnerships, 2007), and continues to review and develop guidance in this field. The College's Centre for Quality Improvement has developed a *Quality Network for Forensic Mental Health Services*, which such services are encouraged to join. Set up in 2006, among the services it offers members are national 'benchmarking', review – producing reports of such work to 'highlight areas of achievement and areas for improvement' – and facilitation of information-sharing about best practice (http://www.rcpsych.ac.uk/QNFMHS).

Physical Security

In specialist forensic mental health services, physical security refers to the nature of the perimeter walls or fence and the internal building design. For high security, there must be at least one high and distinct perimeter wall or fence which is entirely separate from the main hospital buildings. The presumption is that no one, under any circumstance, will leave the secure estate except through the front door of the establishment. This long standing high security hospital principle was endorsed by the then National Patient Safety Agency (2009) in England, albeit here referring specifically to transferred prisoners, and extended to medium security unit patients. Although said to be similar to category B prison security, the main difference in physical security from the highest security level for a prison (category A) is that the structure is not designed to prevent determined, professional 'rescues'. Security cameras may be used.

Medium security is moving ever closer to this model, although the original principle here was that the main perimeter security should be provided by the building itself, with high fences only around exercise areas. Common ground for high and medium security is that, for staff and visitors alike, entry and exit are allowed only through an 'airlock', with independent locking systems for the external and internal doors, and dedicated staff controlling the point of exit and entry. The perimeter security of a low security establishment may be no more than the envelope of the building itself and a locked door.

Other aspects of physical security rest in internal building design. Remarkably little has been written about this, even though the development of a whole new tier of secure services provided a great opportunity to plan, provide and evaluate design features. It has been regarded for some time as good practice for clinical staff to take part in such planning, but increasingly it is recognized that it is important to have input too from the patients who use or have used the services. Attractiveness of an environment is a highly subjective concept, but it may be accepted that poor physical facilities may be provocative (Watson, 1996). A widely accepted principle is that there should be good sight lines throughout the unit, while allowing appropriate privacy. Another is that patients themselves must feel safe; as part of that process, in the UK, each patient would have their own, single occupancy room, and most units would allow patients to lock their room door against all comers other than staff. There has been some research on the amount of space needed. Dietz and Rada (1982), for example, referred to the concept of 'body buffer zones', which may need to be greater than average when people are mentally unwell. More space without sufficient staff to maintain adequate observations may, however, be counter-productive (Palmstierna and Wistedt, 1995).

As in any other psychiatric unit, the most vulnerable person is often the patient him/herself, and probably the single most important physical environment feature in any psychiatric unit in the last 10–15 years has been the removal of fixed curtain and clothes rails. Inpatient suicides, in England and Wales, which were almost all by hanging, have decreased at a greater rate than in the general population, and this thought to be largely attributable to this simple design point (National Confidential Inquiry, 2010). Introduction of collapsible curtain rails was required by the Department of Health by the 1 April 2002; there have been no deaths by hanging from rails since 2003 (National Confidential Inquiry, 2009). Staff must, however, be constantly vigilant for alternative ligature points, and for other specific design features which may create dangers. In California, Hunter and Love (1996), for example, described the value of examining patterns of violent incidents over a period of time. Here, they identified environmental qualities at mealtimes as a key flashpoint, adjustment of circumstances accordingly, and then re-evaluation of incident type and rates to check for impact of the changes. Such environmental risks may be unit and/or time specific.

Earlier literature considered other building features which would enhance safety, including unbreakable glass in windows, windows which open only a little, heating, ventilation and electrical systems which are appropriately shielded, and with water and power circuits that can be isolated easily; good internal emergency communication systems are vital (Williams, 1976). This applies to emergency call systems, but is also important if a patient ever has to be secluded. A building which only allows shouted exchanges through a thick Perspex window is hardly conducive to facilitating a new therapeutic dialogue with a distressed individual. New building encourages creativity, different problems have to be faced when older buildings are being developed, as, for example, in the high security hospital estates in the 1980s and 1990s. These hospitals were ageing institutions, for the most part retaining with open plan wards. Hinton (1998) described the process of standard setting, inspection, change and audit that was put in place to deal with these buildings; many of his recommendations have been incorporated into the Health Offender Partnerships guidance cited above.

Procedural Security

Generally, procedural security is equated with those formal checks for factors thought to be associated with risk of harm by patients, which are undertaken by secure unit staff at specified intervals, perhaps daily, perhaps more frequently. Fire is the most dangerous thing that can happen in a secure building, and it is surprising that the Health Offenders Partnership (2007) does not refer to it specifically, nor, until 'quality principle' number 71 of 91 on safety and security does it refer to a general need to have emergency planning systems in place, with a requirement for a 'desktop exercise' at least once a year and 'ideally, there should be a live exercise involving one or other of the emergency services at least once every two years'. Fire posing any serious threat is rare, but it does occur, as various national news reports of 16 October 2008 confirmed: 'blaze ravages hospital buildings'. A medium secure unit, Camlet Lodge, was destroyed; fortunately the staff responded effectively and no one was injured.

Each forensic mental health unit should have a comprehensive set of policies designed to maintain safety from unsafe patient behaviours, and to safeguard those patients, and these policies must be subject to regular review. The Health Offender Partnerships (2007) document is a good source for the range of these issues, and each unit will need to take account of them, of guidance in the Codes of Practice to the mental health legislation (e.g. Department of Health, 2008a) and of local issues. At the most basic are a range of policies on observations of the state of the unit and its perimeter, inside and out, and of patients, including search policies for the patients and their rooms. Related to this may be policies on possessions and prohibited items, monies and certainly on substances of abuse. Illicit drugs have traditionally received most attention, but policies will also reflect concerns about alcohol use and smoking; reasons for the latter are three-fold. Smoking is a fire hazard as well as an irritant for non-smokers and, simply, unhealthy. As concern grows about obesity and metabolic syndrome (see also chapter 23), there may even be wider ranging policies about healthy lifestyle. Relatives and friends may be a potential source of breach of rules about prohibited or restricted items; procedural controls of visits limit such risks and also provide important information to supplement learning about the family and social dynamics. Other sources of contact may need monitoring from time to time, including phone calls and letters. Units restrict, often prohibit, access to the internet, with concerns variously including access to pornography, out of control purchases or even threatening behaviours. More specific concerns about the safety of each patient him- or herself are reflected in anti-bullying and suicide prevention policies. Particular within-unit concerns arise with respect to seclusion and restraint and to escape or absconding; more specialist concerns include child visiting and sexual/romantic relationships.

Seclusion and physical restraint

Soloff (1984) gives a history of the use of seclusion and restraint. He noted that the Greeks advocated its minimal use, but that its origins mainly lie in the religious persecution of the Middle Ages, when theories of demonic possession were favoured to account for madness. Instrumental restraint became so much the rule that by the late eighteenth century even the King of England, George III, was chained, beaten and treated with other indignities. By the early nineteenth century, however, attitudes were shifting. According to Hunter and MacAlpine (1963), Connolly expressed the matter succinctly:

> *Restraint and neglect are synonymous. They are substitute for the thousand attentions needed by the disturbed patient.*

Seclusion is still used as an aid to safeguarding others, even in specialist forensic mental healthcare. Other forms of physical restraint, such as straps, body belts and restraint garments are almost never used in the UK and, where so, almost exclusively for patients with a particular combination of repeated, serious self-harming behaviours which have not responded to other interventions (Gordon et al., 1999). Physical restraint in the sense of being held by a number of staff, generally nursing staff specially trained in control and restraint techniques, is quite commonly used in an acute behavioural crisis when an individual poses a significant threat to self or others. In this respect, Lion and Soloff's (1984) advice holds good; there is little research to advance knowledge in this field, and certainly their warning on the importance of avoiding injury or infliction of pain and of avoiding humiliation of the patient remains sound, with the important caveat:

The staff restraining the patient today will be seeking a therapeutic alliance tomorrow.

The practice of physical restraint came under particular scrutiny after the death of David Bennett (Blofeld et al., 2004). David Bennett had a lengthy history of treatment refractory schizophrenia and was a long-standing patient of a specialist medium security mental health unit. He was on atypical antipsychotic medication, but one evening, in his distress, attacked first a fellow patient and then a nurse. He was restrained and held prone on the floor for about 25 minutes, when staff realized that not only had he stopped struggling, but he was not moving at all. Attempts to resuscitate him failed. Although rare, this death under restraint was not unique, and efforts to understand the mechanism and improve practice have followed. Common ground seemed to be that the person under restraint had been in a highly excited state, taking illicit or prescribed drugs and held for a prolonged period in the prone position. Explanatory hypotheses include 'positional asphyxia', which initially increases the tendency to struggle. Other explanations lie in a build up of a number of toxic substances, including catecholamines, lactic acid, creatine phosphokinase and even potassium, leaking from damaged muscle tissue; these may together, or singly, cause cardiac dysrhythmias, maybe leading to cardiac arrest (Ball, 2005). David Bennett's death led to a substantial review of evidence about the management of violence, and a National Institute of Clinical Excellence (2005) guideline. This is wide ranging, with a good deal of emphasis on prediction and prevention of violence, and, where that fails, de-escalation. With respect to restraint, it notes that the evidence base on the dangers of positional restraint is weak. The key guidance is to keep such restraint as brief as possible and have one person designated to be responsible for protecting and supporting the patient's head and neck at all times, and monitoring vital signs.

Seclusion can be defined as the containment of a patient alone in a room or other enclosed area from which that patient has no means of egress (Royal College of Psychiatrists, 1982). A later definition (Royal College of Psychiatrists, 1990a) incorporated a requirement for supervision and a clear statement that it is for the protection of the patient or others from serious harm. Procedural guidance for England and Wales is set out in the respective Codes of Practice to the Mental Health Act 1983 (Department of Health, 2008a; Welsh Assembly Government, 2008a). They have both, essentially, adopted the later College definition, but the English Code adds a further qualification:

Its sole aim is to contain severely disturbed behaviour which is likely to cause harm to others.

People who are harming themselves or frankly suicidal are considered to need more support than can be provided by seclusion, even when closely supervised.

As would be expected, each Code (chapter 15 in the English Code and 19 in the Welsh Code) is similar in its guidance, especially on review procedures. The need for seclusion should be reviewed by two nurses after 2 hours and a doctor or suitably qualified clinician after 4 hours. In the event of continuing seclusion, further reviews should take place after every next 2 and 4 hours. If seclusion continues for more than 8 hours consecutively, or for more than 12 hours intermittently over a period of 48 hours, an independent review should take place by the responsible medical officer, with a team of nurses and other healthcare professionals who were not directly involved in the care of the patient at the time of the incident which led to the seclusion. A good record of events and the seclusion is important. The Codes contain a mix of other advice and rules, with the English version being particularly detailed. Of particular pertinence to people resident in forensic mental health services, in that many suffer seriously disturbed behaviour over long periods of time, is the question of finding out in advance of any incident what personal preferences would be in the event of ever needing some form of restraint.

The little research about management of inpatient behavioural emergencies is on patient preferences, suggests that nothing can be taken for granted, and that asking patients about it would indeed be good practice. An older US study (Sheline and Nelson, 1993) suggested that just over half of patients would prefer to be medicated, but about one-quarter preferred seclusion and ten of the 100 patients in the series said they would rather be physically restrained. In the Netherlands, just over 100 people who had experience of emergency measures were asked to fill out a questionnaire about preference and good and bad experiences of seclusion, of which 90 had experienced at least one episode, and enforced medication, of which 46 had (Veltkamp et al., 2008). Preferences were more-or-less equally divided, as were negative and positive experiences, albeit with some gender difference; men were more likely to prefer seclusion. Rest, security and being able to sleep were positive aspects of seclusion, feeling alone and locked in were among the more negative. People who had understood why the measure was used were generally more positive about it, underscoring the importance of explanations and reassurance in such extreme circumstances. Procedures do provide a safeguard for patients and staff alike, but the two most important issues are adequate therapeutic contact with the secluded patient and, as soon as possible, achieving the objective of ending the seclusion safely.

There are no controlled studies of the effects of non-pharmacological treatments for the containment of very disturbed and potentially dangerous behaviour (Muralidharan and Fenton, 2006), so procedures here are founded more-or-less on consensus. Furthermore, as medication is often given in conjunction with seclusion, it is hard to disentangle effects of interventions. Earlier reviews (e.g. Angold, 1989) were driven back to summarizing data on frequency of use, or on the perceptions of those involved, and little has changed. Within security settings, older literature suggested a disturbing effect on other patients. Mattson and Sacks (1978) noted that others become uncomfortable when one of their group is in seclusion, even if they are relieved to have him/her out of the way. The Boynton Report on Rampton Hospital (Department of Health and Social Security, 1980) suggested that, back then, seclusion increased a patient's status, possibly escalating seclusion rates; at that time, about 9% of female patients were secluded on any one day. An impression that patients calm quickly after seclusion is not matched by data in clinical observational studies, locked isolation time variously being recorded as a mean of 4.3 hours (Thompson, 1986), 1.8 hours (Soloff and Turner, 1981) and 15.7 hours (Binder, 1979).

If seclusion is anything other than a means of emergency containment, it is probably the reduction in general stimulation coupled with limited but individualized attention which is beneficial for some patients. When secluded, however, patients are usually deprived of everything except clothes and bedding, and, for these, especially nondescript, toughened articles may be provided. The walls are bare, lighting is generally under staff control and the only means of external distraction is staff observation and evaluation. This is close to sensory deprivation, which is well documented as having adverse effects. It is likely that some of the so-called prison psychoses, documented around the turn of the last century (Nitsche and Williams, 1913), were secondary to the sensory deprivation of solitary confinement, and Grassian (1983) documented the onset of similar, apparently environmentally dependent disorders in a latter day American prison. No one any longer expects seclusion to be therapeutic for the mentally normal, or even for people with neurotic or personality disorders. Insofar as there may be a small positive effect for people with schizophrenia, with a possible reduction in hallucinatory experiences (Harris, 1959), improvement in body image and boundary (Reitman and Cleveland, 1964), and lowered symptoms for those who prefer withdrawal as a coping strategy (Mehl and Cromwell, 1969), such advantages might be achieved with reduction of sensory input way short of the harshness of locked away isolation.

So, although seclusion may still be used appropriately as a means of containing very dangerous behaviour towards others, there is slight evidence of net effectiveness, and no theory as to how it might work in any positive way; it is a fairly crude method of temporarily isolating people, under conditions which must be as supportive as possible to the secluded individual and strictly monitored under the procedural guidance of the mental health legislative codes of practice. Efforts must continue to reduce its use, although reduction will require wide co-operation and a wide range of measures, not only including enhanced clinical skills and interventions to reduce need, but also staff training and adequate fiscal and policy support (Gaskin et al., 2007).

Escape and absconding

Behaviour outside a secure unit has to be considered in part because, even quite early on in their unit career, it is not uncommon for patients to have to attend other hospitals for treatments for their physical health and/or court and/or have compassionate leave to a sick or dying relative; later there will be a question of trial leaves from the unit, in preparation for moving to lower security or community living. This is a particularly important area, since there is a great deal of confusion in the scientific literature (Muir-Cochrane and Mosel, 2008) as well as the public mind (Exworthy and Wilson, 2010) about definitions of absconding; escape from within the secure perimeter, absconding from a closely escorted early outing and failure to return on time from a planned rehabilitation trip each have very different implications from the others. Moore (2000) points out, too, that absconding from secure institutions should be studied as a different phenomenon of different import from absconding from psychiatric units more generally. Most of this unwanted activity rests in leave failures, but even so, episodes are extremely rare and, correspondingly, difficult to predict (Moore and Hammond, 2000). The latter advocate particular concern about younger patients with personality disorder who are oppositional to their detention, especially if they are under shorter term assessment orders, but emphasize that even within these groups, absconding is rare, and when it occurs, adverse events even more so.

The fact that an event is rare renders it difficult to measure the impact of any changes to improve clinical effectiveness, but does not absolve staff from trying to do so. Serious offending while on unauthorized leave from a secure unit is among the most unusual of events, but it has occurred (e.g. Robinson et al., 2006). Individual inquiries such as this one vary sufficiently in their structure and style that reliance on any one may be unwise. Maden (2006) reviewed 100 inquiries after a homicide when an individual with mental illness (specifically) had previously been in contact with any psychiatric services, from across England and Wales between November 1995 and December 2002. Among the most consistent recommendations were on the need to develop a shared way of formulating, describing *and communicating* risk, with a need to incorporate structured clinical assessments of violence risk. Implicit in such recommendations is that not only the first risk assessment of a particular patient requires time and more than one individual's perceptions of the situation, but so also do subsequent assessments as his or her situation changes (see also chapter 22).

Child visiting

Best practice guidance for adult medium secure services (Health Offender Partnerships, 2007) includes a short section on safeguarding children and child visiting policies.

It is correct, as far as it goes, but institutionalising. It follows Health Service Circular 1999/222 and Local Authority Circular (99)32 (see Department of Health, 1999g), requiring policies to be in place and visiting facilities which are separate from the residential areas of the unit but within the secure perimeter. Staff who oversee the visits must have completed a special training in supervising such visits. Outcomes are to be 'no incidents involving child visiting' and 'no complaints about facilities'. Focus on the physical safety of children in this context is vital but, it is arguable, not enough.

The missing element is procedure which would safeguard the patients' children, and/or other visiting children, in any wider sense. This, however, is another area in which very little is known. It is not even known how many secure hospital residents have children. There is likely to be a tendency in such circumstances for patients to under-report here, partly, one suspects, because not routinely asked, partly because some will decline to answer even if they are. In prison, it has been estimated that at least 20% of women will not disclose that they have children (Howard League for Penal Reform, 1993). A study of a consecutive series of women admitted to one medium security hospital unit suggests that about two-thirds of women in secure hospitals will have at least one child (Taylor et al., submitted); the proportion of men in the same situation is even less clear, but probably not very different, at least among those with a personality disorder. The children are likely to have needs with respect to understanding their situation, and, whether or not they visit the parent who has been designated sick and dangerous, to be supported in coping with their feelings about it. Tobin, a guardian *ad litem* and independent social worker, described some of the difficulties in a high security hospital, where of 10 children who had been born to 12 women, only eight had visited the hospital; one child had been told her mother was dead (Tobin and Taylor, 1999). In a much earlier document, the Department of Health (1990g) asserted:

> Both parents are important even if none is no longer in the family home. Any sense of continuity no matter how tenuous is to be nurtured.

There is no evidence base on which to base policy. For the longer term health of children with parents in secure hospitals, and for the wellbeing of those parents, this should be changed.

Patients' romantic and sexual relationships

No specific guidance is given on procedures for safely managing romantic relationships in the *Best Practice* guidance (Health Offender Partnerships, 2007). This is remarkable given that most patients in specialist secure mental health units are of an age at which they would otherwise have their peak interest in sexual activity and reproducing. Furthermore, people not uncommonly become patients in a secure hospital at least in part because of difficulties in intimate relationships, which have become dangerous. Again, there is little research in the field, and it is partly for that reason that this issue is considered only within procedural security rather than under relational security where, it is arguable, it might be expected.

Patients have some rights in the matter of relationships, and entering a contract of marriage while resident in a secure hospital is not unknown (Fitzgerald and Harbour, 1999). In a small study, seven women and 18 men who were resident in a high security hospital were interviewed about their relationships (Hales et al., 2006). Two of the women and four men had been married or in long-term relationships prior to this hospitalization; none of these relationships survived the secure hospitalization. Half of these patients, however, developed a new relationship while in the hospital. Generally, it was the caring qualities in the relationships which were appreciated, but sexual activity was reported, albeit short of full sexual intercourse. The high security hospitals developed policies on relationships, to assist staff to support and safeguard patients in hetero- and same sex relationships (Taylor and Swan, 1999); have medium secure units routinely developed such policies too? Risk assessment and management of physical and emotional health and safety in the circumstances are essential, but, given the poor early relationship experiences and models which many such patients have had, from time to time it is likely to be appropriate to be more proactive in support, and in making therapy available, including couples therapy (Taylor and Swan, 1999).

Relational Security

The nature and quality of the therapeutic alliance is at the heart of relational security. The professional knowledge and skill of clinical staff, coupled with detailed knowledge of the history of each individual patient and accurate empathy, are brought together, shared within the clinical team and used to develop the individual's management, care and treatment plan. The highest levels of this form of security are dependent on adequate staff numbers, satisfactory staff training *and ongoing peer review of practice and/or supervision*. Staff numbers alone are certainly not sufficient (e.g. James et al., 1990). Relational security is the form which is least trusted by hospital managers and political masters, partly because it is more difficult to understand than walls, doors and locks, but partly also because there is a not inaccurate perception that it is most corruptible. Over time, staff may be vulnerable to developing potentially counter-therapeutic relationships with one or more particular patients (Moore et al., 2002). This sort of vulnerability is similar to degrees of malignant alienation which may occur in relation to people who repeatedly attempt suicide or serious self-harming behaviours (Watts and Morgan, 1994), a development perhaps more familiar in routine clinical practice than similar patterns in response to outwardly directed aggression. Both forms of countertransference may be prevented, or recognized and managed safely, through reflective practice. Regular access to a psychodynamically trained psychotherapist is important for specialist forensic mental health unit staff, to facilitate this reflection, with respect both to individual cases and to the dynamics of the institution (McGauley and Humphreys, 2003; see also chapter 23). For a consistent, structured approach, the interpersonal axis of the Operational Psychodynamic Diagnostics (OPD) approach (Task Force OPD, 2006; Cierpka et al., 2007) is a useful and practical aid to recognition of qualities in the therapeutic relationship which will, on the one hand, assist with recognition of adverse developments in a therapeutic relationship, which might otherwise be ignored, and on the other hand with further understanding of the individual being assessed.

After consultation with a range of interested groups, including the Ministry of Justice, the Royal College of Psychiatrists and patients and their carers and/or advocates, the Department of Health (2010) has now published a useful guide to relational security: *See Think Act*. This emphasizes the importance of recognizing that every member of staff who has regular contact with patients, including for example domestic staff, must be included in considerations of this type of security. The suggested framework for planning and monitoring secure relationships is then by quadrant in the patient's world, namely the patient's relationships:

- with staff;
- with other patients;
- with the outside world; and
- with his/her 'inside world'.

One of the most important aspects of the patient–staff relationship in this context is the setting of boundaries; the other is the creation of the kind of environment which facilitates engagement with treatment. We have included an extended discussion of patient–clinician boundaries in chapter 27. Treatment engagement was not only a feature of chapter 23, but also, because it may be so very difficult when working with people who have a personality disorder, it has also been considered in some depth in chapter 16. The Department of Health document suggests that patient–patient relationships are considered in term of patient mix and patient dynamic, outside relationships in terms of the patient's initiatives in connecting out beyond the unit and of the impact of his/her visitors while the 'inside world' is here construed as a mix of the patient's inner life and the immediate physical environment.

The Royal College of Psychiatrists (2011a) has responded with its own advice on standards within the framework of the Quality Network for Forensic Mental Health Services. In a deliberate attempt to eschew detailed, complicated process, the advice is framed around each secure hospital working within its own framework for delivering appropriate training and time for reflection on the issues. In

England and Wales, each unit must include some basic training within the induction programme containing as a minimum material as set out in the *See Think Act* document. Staff should update annually on this aspect of their training, there should be regular meetings which create the time and space for staff to reflect on such issues, contact with anyone external to the unit should be regularly risk assessed, and there should be a mechanism for monitoring the relational security policies and processes against recognised standards. Those in the *See Think Act* document provide a useful starting point (see table 24.1).

Concepts of High, Medium and Low Security in Health Services

In the UK, high, medium and low security specialist forensic hospital services have been developed to supplement general, open inpatient services, and are, or should be, distinct from psychiatric intensive care units (PICUs), which are intended for the short-term management of crises among people, generally with a mental illness, who are being treated within general psychiatric services. The concept of a high security hospital is fairly straightforward: each type of security is used to the full, with the exception that the physical security arrangements are not sufficient to prevent rescue by a highly skilled criminal team and do not include individual reinforced concrete cells. Medium security is necessarily defined in relation to the high security hospital standard at one extreme, and, in turn, low security and full freedom of movement in the community at the other. There should be little to choose between the specialist inpatient environments in terms of relational security. Medium security will be most differentiated from low but specialist security by its physical and procedural policies. In competent hands, specialist community treatment also provides good relational security for people who have been well matched to the service. Collins and Davies (2005) have offered a useful method of assessing security needs, the Security Needs Assessment Profile (SNAP), while others prefer to rely on the Health of the Nation Outcome Scale for secure services (HoNOS-secure, Dickens et al., 2007) and others use the Historical Clinical Risk 20-item scale (HCR-20, Douglas and Webster, 1999; see also chapter 22) as their standard. In Sweden (Belfrage and Douglas, 2002) and Ireland (Pillay et al., 2008) the HCR-20 has been shown to discriminate between patients at different levels of security, and, in the Swedish study, also to change over time with treatment. Cohen and Eastman (2000) have also developed a set of security standards embodied in the Admission Criteria to Secure Services Schedule (ACSeSS).

Service Structures and Planning

Principles cited earlier, about quality of care, individual needs and conditions of security being no greater then

Table 24.1   We know we are getting it right when:

Patient–team treatment engagement and boundaries	Patient–patient mix and dynamic
We have a ward purpose, philosophy and core values that patients and staff can understand. Patients and staff understand what maintaining clear boundaries means and why it is so important. We know which boundaries are non-negotiable and which we can make individual and team judgments about. We are confident in upholding the boundaries with challenging patients. Patients describe staff as being consistent and respectful. We look out for one another and feel confident to speak up if we think that a colleague has been compromised. We set a good example and are positive role models. There is a high level of engagement on our wards and patients take part in therapy and social activities. Patients describe having hope and belief in recovery. Patients describe being clear about what they need to do to make progress. We talk to patients about how they feel and plan change together We look for opportunities to reinforce therapy in everything we do with patients. Uptake of supervision is high, staff report that it is of value to them and we engage in reflective practice.	We know what our patient mix is, and understand what the limits are and when to act. We now how to respond if the patient mix needs addressing. We know how patients feel about the other patients around them. We promote tolerance and deal robustly with discrimination, bullying and harassment. We feel confident to engage with this patient group and can maintain control. We are vigilant to the possibility of collusion between patients and can detect plans to subvert security. Levels of patient violence are low. Staff turnover and sickness absence levels are low. We (patients and staff) communicate with one another about how the ward feels.
The patient's inside world	**Patients and the outside world**
We know the histories of our patients. We understand that it isn't our role to judge—but we don't ignore risk either. We can make the connection between the history of a patient and the likely responses to possible triggers. We recognize the relapse factors for each of our patients and are vigilant to the fact that patients may conceal a deterioration in their mental well-being. We recognize the effect that key anniversaries/events may have on some of our patients. We know how our patients are feeling day to day and care plans are up to date to reflect this. We involve patients in planning their care. We talk as a team during the shift and at handover. Our patients describe feeling connected and feel accountable for their care. We feel the environment enables us to engage with patients, and our patients connect positively with one another. There is a discipline and pride on our ward that is reflected in a tidy and well-cared-for environment.	We continually assess the risks of patients and care plans reflect this. There is a management plan for all escorted leaves of absence. Patients understand there are consequences to absconding. We know what our responsibilities are and how to respond if something goes wrong. Visitors feel safe in our service but are aware of the rules and the consequences of subverting them. We understand the risks some visitors might pose to patients and are vigilant about how the visit is affecting the patient before, during and after the visit. We understand the potential for some visitors to undermine the treatment plans and recovery of patients and take the appropriate action to address this.

Guidance extracted from the Department of Health (2010) *SEE THINK ACT* guide to relational security

justified by risk, have translated into ever improving fit with the pyramid planning model which dictates that the most physically secure and intensive health service provision makes up a small apex of high security hospital beds, on a wider layer of the more numerous medium security beds, and a broader and still growing layer of low security beds, which may extend into specialist hostel places. Community services, whether through liaison or direct clinical contact, may, in time, constitute the true, solid, and broadest base. These last two layers should be a shared enterprise with general adult mental health services. Translated into numbers, this reflects an overall increase in the number of specialist secure hospital beds in England and Wales, but a substantial shift even from service provision of the 1980s and 1990s in terms of proportion at each level of security. In 1958, and again in 1973, high security hospital populations in England reached a peak of between 2,300 and 2,400 occupied beds, but then there were no specialist medium security places. By the time of the Department of Health and Home Office (1992) review, the medium security unit building programme was well established, but still there were about 1,700 occupied high security hospital beds and only about 600 specialist medium security beds, with a number of research reports arguing that many high security hospital residents were being detained at an inappropriately high level of security (e.g. Maden et al., 1993). By July 2007, there were 800 high security hospital beds available (excluding the DSPD units), but only about 650 of them occupied, and around 3,700 medium security hospital beds for England and Wales (total population c. 54 million) (Rutherford and Duggan, 2007).

Another shift during this period, in England and Wales, has been in the extent of provision by the independent healthcare sector. The 1992 Department of Health and

Home Office report estimated, on evidence from notification of detained patients, that 127 beds, of a total of 2,800 for psychiatric treatment, were provided in the independent sector. While this was probably an underestimate, as noted in the report itself, the independent sector then certainly provided for a minority of offender-patients needing specialist inpatient security. Since 2007, the independent sector has provided around half of the specialist medium security beds for England and Wales. It is worth stressing again, however, that all such residency is publicly funded, and subject to the same standards and inspections as public sector provision. Estimates of people currently receiving specialist forensic mental health community services are not available.

High security hospital services are provided at national level, all in the public sector, and there are just three such hospitals for England and Wales, Ashworth in the north-west of England, Broadmoor in the south and Rampton in the East Midlands. Medium and lower security services are provided at a more local level, for population sizes of between 1.5 and 3.5 million, depending in part on density of population. They are often referred to as regional, although a criticism of the independent sector component of bed provision is that it is generally geographically dislocated from the home communities of the patients, and none attempts community rehabilitation.

Women form a minority of people needing secure mental health services – about 10–12% at any one time. A series of documents from the Department of Health in England has called for separate, dedicated services for women (Department of Health, 1999h, 2002c, 2003b), and now most units provide separate residential accommodation for them. Accommodation for women in high security hospitals has almost been phased out, with just one small unit remaining at one of them – Rampton hospital (see also chapter 20). Although this is broadly a welcome development, it does mean that those few women who need high security are almost invariably held at long distances from their home communities. Some compensation has been offered in the development of so-called women's enhanced medium security services, available in three centres (West London, Leicestershire/East Midlands, and the North West).

The separation of women's services from those for men is largely founded in the preferences of the women. There has always been concern too that men in specialist forensic mental health services may be predatory towards women. This would be a particularly dreadful problem in such settings because so many of the women have been abused, most commonly by men, through childhood and adolescence and so would be exceptionally vulnerable to further male abuse or bullying. In fact, some of these women are probably vulnerable to other, more aggressive women too (Mezey et al., 2005), so, whatever the nature of their accommodation, it is important that staff are highly trained, vigilant and skilled in relational security. There is little evidence for specific treatment needs for women who need secure hospital accommodation (Taylor and Bragado-Jimenez, 2009), but this observation has to be qualified by the fact that there is too little research specific to women. Treatment models which have been suggested as particularly useful for women's units are trauma based model (Mason, 2006) or attachment theory based (Barber et al., 2006) (see chapter 20 for more details).

Other 'super specialist' services include those for people with intellectual disability and developmental disorders (see also chapter 13), including personality disorder (see also chapter 16), and young people (see chapter 19). A tiny national high security service for people who are deaf is provided at Rampton hospital. Occasionally other pockets of expertise emerge as a need is recognized – for example for offender-patients of 65 and over (Yorston and Taylor, 2009) at one of the independent sector hospitals (see also chapter 21).

Admissions to specialist hospital security units

In England and Wales, about 40–50% of people referred for a high (Jamieson et al., 2000) or a medium (Meltzer et al., 2004a,b) security bed are actually admitted to one. The Grounds/Meltzer group went on to show the poverty of match between need and service delivery; about one-fifth of those judged to need medium security were not actually admitted, while about a quarter of those actually admitted were considered to need lower security. Grounds et al. (2004) investigated decision-making on admission to medium security units through semi-structured interview with a purposive sample of lead clinicians from 36 (of 37) medium security units in operation at the time, and subjected the narrative to qualitative analysis. They identified four basic conditions for admission – that the patient is mentally ill, has committed a serious harmful act linked with the illness, needs conditions of security and can be treated in a medium secure unit. The main factors influencing the final decision when there were competing demands on resource were staff relationships within the unit at the time of referral, relationships with the referrers, availability of clear exit routes to avoid prolonged stays and maintain turnover and the availability of alternative facilities. Very sick people in prison or the community/low security would be given preference over those in high security who had recovered sufficiently for their security to be downgraded. Lack of a clear pathway out of medium security was a major factor in the tendency to reject people with personality disorder. In our experience, it is almost impossible to establish a true referral rate to specialist security services (Jamieson et al., 2000), and very little research has been done on outcomes after the decision made, but within those limitations, there is some evidence that refusal to admit decisions are appropriate.

In a high security hospital series, 85% of those refused admission remained outside high security during the following 24 months, without incident (Berry et al., 2003). In a medium security series, where a bed was not offered, advice was given on treatment which resulted in successful management of 'the majority' of these cases outside medium security.

The occasional descriptive study of high security hospital patients in England and Wales prior to the 1970s was transformed by the setting up of the special hospitals case register, which covered all admissions from 1 January 1972 until 31 December 2000, continuing for a short while after that with data from just two of the hospitals. The strength of the register was that it combined records data from all residents with data collected at interview with almost all of them within 6 months of their admission, the interviews having been conducted by specially trained research register case workers. Through this period, men greatly outnumbered women, in a ratio of about 4:1, falling slightly over the later years (Butwell et al., 2000); men now have exclusive occupancy of two of the high security hospitals, and all but a 50-bedded unit for women at the third. The largest, and growing, group of residents was of men with mental illness, generally schizophrenia. About two-thirds of men were detained under the Mental Health Act (MHA) 1983 category of mental illness, about 25% under the category of personality disorder and the rest with varying degrees of mental impairment. Women tended to be equally likely to be classified as having mental illness or personality disorder. Almost all patients were and are detained under the criminal provisions of the MHA. Ethnic minorities were over-represented with respect to the general population, but not in relation to other treated psychosis samples (Walsh et al., 2002). A 1983 residential cohort study of patients, studied from their full clinical records, gave more detail of offending characteristics and diagnosis (Taylor et al., 1998). Nearly 90% of the men and about two-thirds of the women had been convicted of a criminal offence, with most of the people under civil detention having been seriously or persistently violent in another hospital setting. The extent of comorbidity between psychosis and personality disorder was apparent – 25% of those with psychosis had a comorbid personality disorder, using a strict ICD-10 criterion of evidence of childhood or adolescent conduct and/or emotional disorder co-terminous with a personality disorder that preceded onset of psychosis. Given such comorbid personality disorder, an additional substance misuse diagnosis was also more likely. It should be noted that others, using a dimensional approach to diagnosing personality disorder, have suggested much higher comorbidity rates (Blackburn et al., 2003).

A plethora of descriptive studies of patients in medium security units have been published since the early days of interim units. Snowden (1985, 1986) reviewed the earlier studies. Since then there has been a mix of research local to a particular unit (e.g. Hardwick et al., 2003: Birmingham; Mohan et al., 1997: North West Thames; Rickets et al., 2001: Trent; Shaw et al., 2001: the North West, which included patients from the region in high security hospitals). Lelliott et al. (2001) studied patients in medium security defined by their usual residence in an inner London health authority, about half of whom were in an NHS unit and half in an independent sector unit. The only substantial difference between these two groups was that those in the independent sector were more likely to have been referred by other psychiatric units and less likely to have been referred from the criminal justice system. Coid et al. (2001a) studied over 2,600 patients who had been admitted to one of seven secure units over a period of 7 years (1988–1994) – two covering inner London, three areas with more mixed population distribution but still with heavy urban density (West Midlands, Merseyside and North Western) and two in more rural areas (South West England and East Anglia). Main differences lay in the more urban areas taking more people from the criminal justice system and the more rural areas having greater flexibility in the range of services offered. Contrary to usual expectations of specialist medium security services two regions seemed to be operating a crisis model (NW Thames and Merseyside), but, for the rest, the largest groups were admitted after violent offending behaviour. Two of the units took no sex offenders at all at that time, none accepted many. One unit (East Anglia) had a third of patients with personality disorder which was then generally unusual in such units. Such details tend to change over time, however, in the light of demand, skills development and prevailing government pressures for particular services. Specific personality disorder services have been developed in some units since that study; Ricketts et al. (2001), in the Trent region, showed how the proportion of more serious offenders had increased over the years, and length of stay decreased, in response to demand.

Capacity planning

The capacity and organization of specialist secure mental health services are kept under regular multi-agency review, generally sponsored by one or more government offices. Needs change over time, and the units must remain fit for purpose in terms of delivering the best improvements possible in both mental health and safety. In spite of the good intentions that foster them, they constitute a major constraint on civil liberties and they are expensive.

One important route to capacity planning lies in analysis of service use, particularly in use over time. Jamieson et al. (2000) and Butwell et al. (2000), for example, examined trends in admissions and discharges to the English high security hospitals over a 10-year period (1986–1995), and considered residency patterns over the same period. An overall 16% reduction in admissions was neither spread equally across regions in England and Wales nor across types of people needing the service. Admissions of women, civil cases, people detained under the categories of psychopathic disorder or mental impairment and people coming directly from court fell. There was an increase in admissions of people whose management had broken down in institutions elsewhere, whether in prison or hospital. There was also a rise in discharges and, therefore, an accompanying reduction in bed occupancy over this period. Bed use is not, however, the same as need for beds. Bed use, rather, tends to reflect the nature and effectiveness of gate keeping, here in relation to explicit policy. There was reason to hope that, in this case, policy was building on research findings which highlighted numbers of people resident in high security hospitals without apparently needing to be there (Maden et al., 1993), but this would have principally affected the need to change discharge policy rather than admission policy. In the absence of certain services, there is commonly a perception that there is no point in referring, which may, in turn, translate into a perception that there is no demand or need. Furthermore, most specialist assessment and treatment centres deliver a range of services, including outside assessments and consultation–liaison work, but the tendency is to measure them in terms of the numbers of inpatient beds they deliver rather than their full range of activity.

Epidemiological research is the mainstay for indicators of unmet need, for example showing how many people there are in prison who have a mental disorder. It has been apparent over time (e.g. Gunn et al., 1991; Maden et al., 1995; Singleton et al., 1998a) that the development of secure hospital services has made little impact on the numbers of people with mental disorder in the prison system or, even more specifically, people in prison with a psychotic disorder, but here too there are generally translational limitations. One person with a given illness, for example, may have very different clinical needs from another, and not all need to be in a hospital. Furthermore, studies which have adopted standard interrogative interviews about mental disorder tend to identify much higher rates of disorder than those which take a more clinical approach. Estimates of need are then further complicated by the fact that evidence provided by research data collected in one geographical area may not be applicable in another. In particular, figures may need to be adjusted for psychosocial climate and relative isolation of services. Coid et al. (2001b) devised statistical models for prediction of admission rates to secure units, allowing for the various factors which might affect them according to place and over time, but then other social factors intrude which are not so easily incorporated, like a change in sentencing policy.

The Risks Inherent in Secure Institutional Services

The term institution has almost become synonymous with a closed building and community but, in fact, sociologists use the term 'institution' in three main ways (Jones and Fowles, 1984):

1. with reference to generalized social responses, such as marriage and the family;
2. with reference to more specific social responses, for example, the police;
3. to refer to residential establishments.

A key problem with many of the patients presenting to forensic psychiatry is that they have proved incapable of coping with the first category, and society regards this as deviant, particularly when failure to cope involves violent or other criminal activity. Society is scarcely more tolerant if the deviation is exclusively one of mental disorder, and it often seeks to limit such deviance by surrounding each individual concerned with prescribed, even legally enforced institutions of the second and third kinds.

The term 'total institution' is associated with Goffman (1961), who distinguished four key features of the total institution: first, all aspects of life are conducted in the same place and under the same single authority; secondly, each phase of the member's daily activity is carried on in the immediate company of a large batch of others, all of whom are treated alike and required to do the same thing together; thirdly, all phases of the day's activities are tightly scheduled, with one activity leading at a prearranged time into the next, and the whole sequence imposed from above by a system of explicit formal rulings and a body of officials; fourthly, the various enforced activities are brought together into a single rational plan purportedly designed to fulfill the official aims of the institution. Goffman stated:

In total institutions there is a basic split between a large managed group, conveniently called inmates, and a small supervisory staff. Inmates typically live in the institution and have restricted contact with the world outside the walls; staff often operate on an 8-hour day and are socially integrated into the outside world.

Goffman's approach in *Asylums* (Goffman, 1961) was ethnographic, and his work was important in articulating the experience and dynamics of the social world of the institution, although the account is a selective and partial one. He spent a year at St. Elizabeth's Hospital, Washington DC, which housed about 7,000 patients at the time, functioning almost as a small town. He made observations of patients, noting for example their degree of social withdrawal, of institutional ceremonies, such as the annual Christmas play, and noted the power structures and, in particular, the need for patients to submit and obey. He was not able to tease out which elements of behaviour were due to mental abnormality and which due to the social structure. His book has been taken as a condemnation of hospital life, which it was not, nor can his experiences of St Elizabeth's necessarily be extrapolated to all other mental hospitals of whatever size, and however funded, but it is worth considering his conclusions:

Mental hospitals are not found in our society because supervisors, psychiatrists, and attendants want jobs, mental hospitals are found because there is a market for them. If all the mental hospitals in a given region were emptied and closed down today, tomorrow, relatives, police and judges would raise a clamour for new ones, and these true clients of the mental hospital would demand an institution to satisfy their needs.

Is it an accident that the growth of forensic psychiatry's new secure units occurred at a time when the number of open beds available in psychiatric services was being reduced?

Foucault's (1967) *Histoire de la Folie* (translated as *Madness and Civilisation)* was written as a history of 'unreason'. Unreason was a concept used from the middle ages until the nineteenth century, and has a wider meaning than 'madness'. One of the things that Foucault claimed was that the asylum was concerned with the inculcation of fear and the imposition of moral judgments. Seen by Jones and Fowles (1984) as more of an image maker than a historian, Foucault's recognition of the fundamental importance of authority and power relations in institutions was, nevertheless, an important contribution. Goffman argued that, although psychiatrists and nurses try to treat behaviour as symptomatic of pathology just like physical symptoms and thus morally neutral, such a position is impossible to sustain. In every other setting, aberrant behaviour is criticized and/or punished – social order depends on it – so such mechanisms also creep into hospital life, and into psychiatric treatment.

Barton (1959) considered that long-stay patients suffered from at least two diseases, the one which triggered their admission and a secondary one: 'institutional neurosis'. He claimed that such a neurosis also occurred in prisoner of war camps, other prisons, orphanages, and tuberculosis sanatoria (consider Thomas Mann's novel *The Magic Mountain*, 1924). The clinical characteristics of this 'disorder' were apathy, lack of initiative and individuality, loss of interest, submissiveness, inability to plan for the future. Wing (1962) gave further credence to the concept when he studied male patients in two mental hospitals. He found a progressive increase with length of stay in the proportion of patients who appeared apathetic about life outside hospital. In the later 'three hospital study' (Wing and Brown, 1970), it was shown that the severity of impairments was closely associated with the degree of environmental understimulation. This study argued for the provision of more stimulating environments in order

to avoid much of what Wing called 'institutionalism'. The major conclusion drawn by Wing and Brown was that

A substantial proportion, though by no means all, of the morbidity shown by long-stay schizophrenic patients in mental hospitals is a product of their environment.

Later, however, Wing re-emphasized that the debilitating effects are to do with levels of stimulation rather than being in hospital *per se* (Wing, 1990). Indeed, Brown et al. (1966) found no significant differences in adjustment between a sample of patients returning to the community early and a sample returning late in their illness careers.

The most visible critiques of psychiatric hospitals during the last 20 years have been official inquiries, which have often arisen from public allegations of brutality or neglect. Many have been important for two reasons: first, they have played a part in achieving reform through defining some of the basic determinants of good practice; and secondly, they have enabled a better understanding of the complex reasons why institutions intended to provide care can allow neglect and inhumanity. It should not be forgotten, however, that

Yesterday's 'scandals' of the institution have already been replaced by today's 'scandals' of the community (Rose, 1986).

Martin (1984) highlighted factors from such reports including geographical isolation of the hospitals and intellectual/professional isolation within them; patients lacking support from people outside; failures to take remedial action locally, despite internal knowledge of unsatisfactory standards; failures of leadership/management; severe shortages of staff and resources; inadequacies of training; personal failings; and 'corruption of care', which occurs when

the primary aims of care – the cure or alleviation of suffering – have become subordinate to what are essentially secondary aims such as the creation and preservation of order, quiet and cleanliness.

In his general conclusions, Martin noted that failures of care result from complex chains of interconnected events, and inquiries have often had to pay more attention to the context in which care is provided than the individuals involved. The power of a group of workers is of central importance in setting standards. It may be exercised to maintain professional standards in the face of pressures, but it may also operate so as to subvert therapeutic aims, and isolate and discredit justifiable criticism. Beardshaw (1981) set out many of the group pressures which make staff stand together on, or at least keep silent about, poor standards or frank malpractice. There is the fear of not being believed, there is the strong loyalty to the peer group, there is the ignorance/uncertainty that a complaint is justified, there is lack of confidence that, even if proved, the complaint will lead to improvement, and fear that it may lead to reprisals from colleagues. Accessible channels for complaint are, therefore, important, using both internal complaints procedures and, on occasions, independent external scrutiny.

The needs and training of staff are fundamental when considering preventive and corrective remedies. Martin noted:

In the last analysis, there is no more effective remedy than staff development.

Menzies (1960) attempted a psychodynamic understanding of the problems faced by nursing staff at a London teaching hospital. The high level of known distress and anxiety among nurses frequently led to withdrawal, with one-third of trainees leaving before completing their training, and to high rates of sickness. The anxiety seemed to be precipitated by constant reminders of death, illness and disability, which trigger primitive, universal fears. Defences to this anxiety develop, she suggested, as follows: splitting in the nurse–patient relationship so that no one relationship becomes very important, depersonalization and denial of the significance of the individual, detachment and denial of feelings, ritual performance of tasks, social redistribution of responsibility and irresponsibility, 'delegation' of responsibility to superiors and avoidance of change. Hinshelwood (1993) built on these ideas (see also chapter 23). The psychodynamic approach to the health of the community in which therapy should take place has been substantial, and in many ways the therapeutic community is the antithesis of the failing institution. Haigh (1999) would suggest five universal cultural qualities: the cultures of belonging, safety, openness, involvement through living, and learning and empowerment. Blumenthal et al. (2011) evaluated psychoanalytically oriented input to the recovery process of a previously failing forensic mental health institution.

Legal rights also require some emphasis (Gostin, 1985; Hoggett, 1985). Bean (1985) notes, clinicians are inevitably 'more interested in welfare than legal norms' and tension between therapeutic aims and legal restraints protecting patients' fundamental liberties is as unavoidable as it is necessary (Grounds, 1986). Rose (1985, 1986) has drawn attention to the limitations of 'rights-based strategies', particularly their inability to deliver the social resources and services they promise. Nevertheless, there have been cases in which, for example, alleged breaches of the European Convention of Human Rights have been upheld against the UK, resulting in new safeguards concerning standards of care and reviews of detention (*A and others; X*).

A culture of inquiry

High security hospitals, worldwide, have paid the price of their former isolation, and become the focus from time to time of media exposure followed by independent and generally public inquiry (e.g., Hucker et al., 1986: Canada; Mason et al., 1988: New Zealand; Blom, 1980: Norway). Although such inquiry within or outside psychiatry is far from unique to high security hospitals, they will provide the examples here. In the UK, in May 1979, Yorkshire Television made a film about Rampton special hospital called 'The Secret Hospital', which contained serious allegations of ill-treatment of patients by staff. An enquiry was established which reported a year later (Department of Health and Social Security (Boynton), 1980), making 205 recommendations, including the setting-up of a body to inspect and monitor all institutions holding detained patients, a reduction in the number of patients at Rampton, properly designed individual treatment programmes for each patient, and management by a hospital management team consisting of a medical director, a chief nursing officer and an administrator. The *Lancet* (1980) considered that an important opportunity had been missed – to close the hospital altogether – and that the recommendations were probably too bland to be effective. It was suggested, based on American experience, that the only really effective way of improving such a hospital, if it were to continue to function, would be to provide them with academic linkages (Knesper, 1978). This would have not only the effect of creating immediate external links, but also recruiting high calibre staff for the future.

Soon after the Rampton scandal, its sister hospital in Berkshire, Broadmoor, came under scrutiny when, on 6 July 1984, a patient was found dead in his room. The Ritchie (1985) inquiry followed, with recommendations that more staff were needed in the special care unit, proper training in control and restraint should be given, that heavy sedatives should be specifically prescribed by doctors, rather than in advance and leaving actual amounts given to the discretion of nursing staff, and that heavily sedated patients should be constantly observed. Soon after, a wide-ranging independent evaluation of Broadmoor hospital was made (National Health Service Health Advisory Service, DHSS, Social Services Inspectorate, 1988). The report was very critical, noting that the hospital had:

surface characteristics of a penal institution: high external walls, barred windows, uniformed staff, security practices and keys worn openly everywhere.

and

Credible leadership is not obvious. Organizational philosophy and style are not shared. Most management activity is conducted at too high a level.

Even the Mental Health Act Commission came under fire for listing too many minor matters as

...this can distract attention and impact from the major issues.

603

This all led to a major management reorganization in 1989, which both reduced the distance between management figures and the hospitals and resulted in employment of professionally trained health service managers to work in conjunction with clinicians. A special health authority was created to manage the three high security hospitals, the so-called Special Hospitals' Service Authority (SHSA), to replace direct Department of Health management. Among its early actions was the commissioning of two further inquiries into deaths at Broadmoor hospital (SHSA, 1989, 1993), the last incorporating a review of the other two. There were concerns about possible racism, about whether more distressed and potentially violent patients had enough to do, as they had such limited access to occupational therapy, and also about the lack of research into methods of resolution of sudden and extreme violent outbursts in extremely unwell men, already on substantial doses of medication, and whose metabolic systems were commonly challenged.

Problems with their roots in old methods of working emerged, again by media exposure, at the third hospital, Ashworth, soon after the new SHSA took over (Blom-Cooper et al., 1992), again calling for closure, but nevertheless listing 90 recommendations for change. These too were reflective of a need to change the tired practices of a total institution, into which it seemed brutality had also intruded. This ensured further changes to management, including moves towards much more local management structures, which progressed well at two of the hospitals, but exposed Ashworth to further lapses. In spite of regular scrutiny from a range of internal bodies and wholly external ones, and a single in-depth review which recognized considerable advances as well as some remaining tensions (NHS Health Advisory Service, 1995), a former patient reported that a child had been allowed to visit resident patients on the personality disorder unit, with concerns about whether the child was being groomed for abuse. An independent inquiry into that personality disorder unit followed (Fallon et al., 1999). It called for the closure of the hospital, while providing a more modest 58 recommendations for change. Although alleging that 'the principal villain of the piece at Ashworth was the system', it went on to criticize in the strongest terms almost everyone who had been involved with the hospital in any professional capacity, from the Minister of Health on down. The very traumatized staff at the hospital certainly needed the psychotherapeutic support supplied from the Portman Clinic (Blumenthal et al., 2011), although some were so stigmatized by the process, albeit subsequently largely vindicated, that they were not allowed even to access this.

There is a real risk of review processes developing a perverse culture, even of becoming institutionalized themselves. Independence of inquiry after something has gone wrong, and independent periodic reviews whether or not anyone has recognized any problems, are valuable tools in bringing out the best in institutions and preventing or stopping poor practice. Concerns about the way in which the Fallon inquiry had developed (e.g. Maden, 1999) were not so different from the growing concerns over some individual homicide inquiries of the time (Thorold and Trotter, 1996; see also chapter 28), and the absence of any national standard for such work. Finally, the NHS National Patient Safety Agency (2008) provided guidance and tools for model investigations, relying particularly on root cause analysis (http://www.nrls.npsa.nhs.uk/ this website is still operative although the NPSA is not).

Outcomes for People Discharged From Secure Inpatient Services

Most studies of people who have been discharged from specialist security hospitals have serious limitations. These arise mainly out of a mix of political pressures on the one hand – to focus on non-clinical outcomes – and fiscal considerations on the other – long-term follow-up interview studies of any group are time consuming and therefore costly. Study of mentally disordered offenders rarely attracts major funding bodies. People in secure hospitals have, by definition, at least one of a range of major mental disorders, but change in mental state is not conspicuous as an outcome measure. Generally, focus is on re-offending, sometimes on mortality, and almost invariably on negative outcomes. Two exceptions stand out – the study conducted by Acres (1975) for the Butler Committee and the study of restriction order patients by Steels et al. (1998) which examined indicators of social adjustment, such as developing new intimate relationships, or becoming employed. There is an additional special problem in that many of the serious offenders with mental disorder who reach high security are unusual. This means that there are many different pathways of importance through the discharge process, but describing them may leave patients and staff vulnerable to identification. In one study of high security hospital discharges (Buchanan, 1998; Buchanan et al., 2004), an ethics committee judged much of the data collected to be unusable on these grounds. Patterns of re-offending were explored, however, with a finding of no significant association between the index offence and the nature of subsequent offences (Buchanan et al., 2003).

Another cluster of limitations lies in lack of information about the nature of treatment. At best, there is information about length of stay in the institution. Some effects may be inferred, for example the extreme unlikelihood since the turn of the millennium that patients in an English high security hospital will have access to alcohol or illicit drugs (Kendrick et al., 2002). Equally, it may safely be assumed that the likelihood is high of certain people being in a particular treatment programme after a particular date when it was instituted – for example the eclectic model for treating personality disorder in Broadmoor high security hospital (Taylor, 2006; Newrith et al., 2006), but even then there are rarely details of an individual's personal experience. Most studies simply treat the security hospitals or units as a 'black box'. Then, too, there seems to be confusion as to whether readmission to a psychiatric hospital is an indicator of poor outcome, because it implies relapse, or of improved outcome, because it implies that a previously poorly compliant patient is now responsive to clinical need.

A further major group of limitations lies in differences in social context, whether between countries studied, or over time. The length of residency, at least in high security, and the length of follow-up necessary when measuring outcomes such as serious violence, with its low base-rate, is likely to limit the extent to which it is possible to extrapolate from outcome studies of 10, 20 or more years ago to current practice. As social attitudes, behaviour, policies, availability of mind altering substances, law, availability of other specialist services and treatments change, so it is likely that a group of people who entered a security hospital in one decade will be very different from those who enter in other. It is unusual for studies to take account of this.

An enhanced technique for capturing data from a range of available records on patients after discharge from high security hospitals enabled information on outcome over 12 years to be established for all but three of the 1984 English high security hospital discharge cohort of 204 people (Jamieson and Taylor, 2002a), a much higher 'capture' rate than any previous study. Furthermore, the sample included all civil cases as well as offenders. Seventeen per cent of these people never returned to ordinary community life; older men with schizophrenia were particularly likely to fail in this respect (Jamieson and Taylor, 2002b); offending history proved irrelevant. Community living was not a necessary precursor to re-offending; 14% of the sample had re-offended while still resident in an institution. That said, median time to first reconviction was under 2 years. Nearly 40% of these patients re-offended, with a quarter of the whole group committing a further serious offence (Jamieson and Taylor, 2004). All 10 of the multiple re-offenders were men. These figures are not very different from general re-offending rate for the period, but rather higher than other UK based studies in a comparable period (e.g. Buchanan, 1998), although the difference is likely to have been accounted for by completeness of data collection in our study rather than real difference in re-offending. The findings on re-offending were more comparable with the earlier studies of Acres (1975) and Tennant and Way (1984). Good news was that, with completeness of tracing, it was established that about a quarter of the discharged patients, who, in the absence of 'events' such as re-offending or death would in other studies probably have been recorded as 'missing cases', were resident in the community without attracting attention 12 years after their discharge from a high security hospital.

A comparison between a high security hospital discharge cohort of 1984 and one of 1996, both governed by the same legislation, confirmed differences in admission characteristics and outcome (Jamieson and Taylor, 2005). The discharge cohorts were similar in size, but the later one included fewer people with personality disorder and more prison transferees rather than primary hospital disposals from court. A major difference for the cohorts was in availability of medium secure services, rare in 1984. Nevertheless, length of stay in high security was similar. The principal impact of the advent of medium security hospital services for these patients was to lengthen the overall time they were resident in some form of medium security. There was no overall difference in mortality between the samples. Re-offending rates among people with psychosis were similar in the two cohorts. Re-offending rates for those detained under the legal category of psychopathic disorder were lower in the second cohort. Perhaps, given the smaller numbers of people in this category in the later cohort, this was an indication of improved selection for treatment.

So far, there are no follow-up studies of comparable length for medium security, but the study of Davies et al. (2007) was close, with all 595 first admissions to a single medium secure unit (Trent (English East Midlands) since it opened 20 years previously region) followed for a mean of just over 9 years; 10% had died, a third of them by suicide. Almost half of all discharges had been re-convicted, and almost two-fifths readmitted at some point. In this study every effort was made to measure all violent behaviour, not just that which had led to a conviction; over a quarter of patients had been violent within 2 years of discharge and over 40% within 5. Another single unit study, drawing on an inner London population, found a 24% re-conviction rate just over 6.5 years after the discharge of 234 patients between 1980 and 1884 (Maden et al., 1999). Readmission rates, however, were high at 75%. Coid et al. (2007a) studied discharges from seven regional forensic mental health services, as described above, yielding 1,344 cases who had been admitted between 1989 and 1993 and spent at least some time in the community before 31 December 1998. The mean length of follow-up was 6.2 years. Just over 12% of the men and 6% of the women were convicted of grave offences within that period. Longer inpatient stay and restrictions on discharge were protective factors; in a separate study of the same cohort, however, it was shown that about 40% of discharges were supervised within specialist forensic services and 60% in general services – with no difference between them in type of case or outcome (Coid et al., 2007b). This is in marked contrast to findings in New Zealand, where there was a significant advantage for being supervised and cared for within specialist forensic mental health services (Simpson et al., 2006). In a complete national study of all 959 patients discharged from medium secure units in England and Wales in the year 1 April 1997–31 March 1998, 15% had been re-convicted after

2 years, just 6% of violent offences (Maden et al., 2004). Patients were followed for 12 months, with re-offending data rechecked at 24 months.

Specialist Secure Forensic Mental Health Inpatient Provision: A Summary

A variety of specialist secure inpatient services has been established across England and Wales, according to sound principles, and monitoring is generally good according to agreed standards, but on the basis of limited research evidence and with few truly satisfactory outcome studies. Undoubtedly the services are filling a niche, but accurate research evaluation is now urgently needed on how they affect the course and prognosis of the range of mental disorders and of the social correlates of these disorders. The model, described above (Jamieson et al., 2006), of working from pathological dependence to healthy independence for understanding clinical progress through the system may provide a template for this further research.

SPECIALIST COMMUNITY SERVICES WITHIN AN NHS FRAMEWORK

The Context of Specialist Community Forensic Mental Health Services

Current community treatment with offenders in England and Wales must be rooted in three separate but overlapping approaches: public protection, evidence-based practice and an end to the exclusion from health services of people with personality disorder.

Clinicians have always been mindful of risks of harm, and the importance of harm prevention. Risk assessment and management, and psychiatry as a force for control, were the most consistent themes in one multi-authored, multidisciplinary book on the care of the mentally disordered offender in the community (Buchanan, 2002). The public protection agenda has led to the development of local Multi-Agency Public Protection Panels (MAPPPs, Sections 67 and 68 of the Criminal Justice and Court Services Act 2000), which have responsibility for the monitoring and management of registered sex offenders (Home Office, 1997), violent and potentially dangerous offenders. Guidance has been updated to promote standardization of Multi-Agency Public Protection Arrangements (MAPPA) such that the various agencies – including health – have a 'duty to co-operate' (see also chapter 25). The Criminal Justice Act 2003 added further provisions for dangerous offenders, which included the availability of indeterminate sentences for public protection for sexual and violent offenders considered to pose a high risk to the public, and the provision for extended

sentences for such offenders, served on licence with the possibility of return to prison. These developments have implications for forensic mental health services in terms of the expectation that expertise will be available to assist the Court in determination of risk and treatability in complex cases and, potentially, to provide treatment while the offender is on licence. The most up-to-date guidance on MAPPA is available on the Ministry of Justice website (http://www.gov.uk).

Both the Department of Health and the National Probation Service embrace an evidence-based practice agenda with respect to community management and treatment. This rests on the premise that decision-making should be based on the explicit and conscientious use of the most up-to-date, valid and reliable research findings. A good deal of work has been undertaken to establish the effectiveness of interventions used here, and there are clear principles established for them (Bateman and Tyrer, 2004a,b,c; Craissati et al., 2002). Hollin et al. (2004) have, however, found an issue for particular concern in community programmes; treatment attrition with this group is associated with a greatly increased recidivism risk.

The third agenda was set by the Department of Health (for England), initially in their guidance paper: *Personality Disorder: No longer a diagnosis of exclusion* (NIMHE, 2002). As the title suggests, this sets the scene for encouraging mental health services to cater for personality disordered individuals within existing services, and has resulted in funding for a range of community pilot schemes within general and forensic mental health services. These developments complemented the work of the Dangerous and Severe Personality Disorder (DSPD) programmes, and should benefit from the DSPD programmes being phased out in favour of using the funds to create 'psychologically informed planned environments' (PIPEs) at every level of service needed by offenders with personality disorder (Department of Health, Ministry of Justice, 2011; see also chapter 16).

Community Management Structures

Mental health and criminal justice services are driven by apparently disparate motives: attaining mental health and public protection, respectively. Health services respond with a focus on treatment of mental disorder, with the risk that where offending behaviour is not solely attributable to treatable mental disorder, needs which are relevant to prevention of further offending may not be met, or even adequately considered. If offending behaviour does not change, public confidence is undermined. Conversely, the criminal justice system, where it has a focus on rehabilitation as well as punishment, concentrates on those who pose greatest risk of re-offending, focusing on criminogenic need, whilst psychological wellbeing remains peripheral, and yet even those serious offenders who do not reach criteria for a formal diagnosis of mental disorder often have psychological problems. The emphasis on programme delivery in the criminal justice system, perhaps especially for offenders with personality disorder, comes at a cost: high attrition rates (Chaffin, 1992; Craissati and Beech, 2001), paradoxical effects on risk (Clark, 2000b; Seto and Barbaree, 1999), or a rise in anxieties, leading to impasse. The health and criminal justice system frameworks for delivery, however, have more in common than not. Mental health services in England, for example, have, since 1991, relied on the Care Programme Approach (CPA) (Department of Health, 1990b, 1995), a progressively revised system which requires health and social services to co-operate in delivering treatment within a four point model of assessment of need, assessment informed plan, care co-ordination and regular review of the plan, all done in conjunction with the patient and his/her lay carer; although often incorporating assessment and management of risk from the outset, this was specified as an important component by the close of the decade (Department of Health, 1999e). Northern Ireland, Scotland and Wales follow similar approaches. For the offender without designated mental disorder, the probation service adopts a similar four point approach, but primarily with respect to risk of harm to others, and more emphasis on actual or putative victims; this commonly, however, incorporates assessment and management of offender needs, since instabilities and poverty in various aspects of life may be criminogenic.

Broadly speaking, offenders with personality disorder have such disparate needs, and raise such anxieties, that they have inevitably drawn the services into a greater level of communication and co-operation with each other. It is rare that a single agency would have sole knowledge of such an offender. The probation service, for example, might refer an individual to health services for help with depressive episodes or anger management; health service staff might feel able to provide such specific treatment but would ask the Local Authority to assist with housing, or the community drug service to tackle the problem of crack cocaine use. With a structure of parallel models of health and criminal justice system care, each presenting problem can be matched to its corresponding agency/professional/intervention. The advantage of parallel services is that each agency or practitioner can hold to a clear service specification, with criteria for entry designed to match fairly narrow bands of competence and resource availability within that service; each agency or practitioner can then take full responsibility for those competencies and for the service provided. The disadvantages, however, are substantial. They include the excessive burden of responsibility which is placed on a professional or agency once an individual offender is accepted into the service and, of perhaps greatest concern, the fragmentation of care which often

mirrors the fragmentation apparent in the offender's own mental state and behaviour.

An integrative management structure would rely on the core components of a model, in which assessment, treatment and management must collectively deal with the three problem domains: mental health need, offending behaviour and social functioning (Dowsett and Craissati, 2007). These domains may be considered at the individual psychological level – where mental health might represent core schema, their relationship to the individual's offending behaviour (perhaps domestic violence), and the way in which personality difficulties lead to marked interpersonal problems, particularly in the realms of intimacy. The domains can also be thought of in terms of therapeutic need: how medication and individual psychotherapy could be complemented by offence-focused cognitive group therapy, which in turn could work with some of the difficult interpersonal issues which are being highlighted in a probation hostel environment. Essentially, this structure implies that a formulation for any individual offender with personality disorder must integrate risk and offending behaviour management with an understanding of the offender's psychological functioning and his/her interpersonal strategies for managing the world around him/her. The integrative model also allows for practical needs to be met through support and medication, monitoring and supervision, and access to the usual structures of daily life, employment and housing. It should be clear that it is most unlikely that any one agency could appropriately and adequately meet need in all three areas.

Autonomous or parallel structures do allow for maximum flexibility in development of local service solutions, contracting in agencies as required. Integrated models intuitively appear to hold the solution for the fragmentation found in parallel services, but also, inevitably, have a significant impact on the autonomy of each member of the partnership, which is restricted as a result of multi-agency collaboration. This loss of control needs to be weighed against possibly the single most important advantage for professionals of an integrated model of care with this group of individuals: risk-sharing. For a few offenders, care and supervision may only be possible at all where no single agency is burdened with sole responsibility for an individual's behaviour.

Models for Community Provision for Offender-Patients

Consultation and support

Consultation services have been slow to develop in forensic mental health services, and it is arguable that this has been a missed opportunity. The process of consultation liaison or support circumvents many of the arguments put forward against individuals or organizations refraining from involvement with high risk individuals, and/or those with a personality disorder. The consultation model is based on the premise that the practitioner doing the consulting and his/her agency retain management responsibility for the individual discussed and for conveying accurate information to the consultant; the practitioner also retains responsibility for deciding whether or not to follow any advice given. The consultant has responsibility for providing sound professional advice on the basis of the information provided; as far as possible the advice would be evidence based, but, where not, founded in professional consensus. The consultant must also know and be transparent about the limits of his/her competence and expertise.

Little has been written about consultation within the forensic mental health sphere, and the evidence for its efficacy seems to be anecdotal. Where support and consultation services have been developed, they have tended to focus on provision to the probation service (see also chapter 25), where a large number of managed cases have mental health and/or personality difficulties, or to social services, often in relation to complex child protection concerns. It is arguable that clinical staff could also play a role in supporting and advising local MAPPPs rather than only accepting referrals for assessment, which is a much more resource-intensive process.

There has been some published work on forensic mental health consultation to probation hostels. Nadkarni et al. (2000) described 1 year's psychiatric input to probation approved premises: 12 (8%) residents of a total of 149 were referred, most of them complaining of depression and/or concerns about self-harm; most referrals satisfied criteria for at least one substance use disorder; one resident was suffering from an acute psychotic episode. The authors note the minimal resources required for development of such a partnership, and outline the benefits for both the agencies and the service users. They ask whether a screening tool might enhance identification of the full range of mental health problems experienced by probation hostel residents. A subsequent study of the mental health needs of the residents of all the Inner London probation hostels involved examination of the files of 209 residents and interviews with 143 of them (Cameron et al., 2000). The results confirmed that most residents had committed offences of interpersonal violence and posed at least a moderate future risk of offending; two-thirds were found to have mental health difficulties, most commonly depression with an associated risk of self harm; 15% had a history of having been admitted to a psychiatric hospital. Considerable unmet need was identified; staff at a number of the hostels had found it very difficult to access appropriate mental health services for their residents.

In south-east London, the forensic mental health service has provided consultation and support to the local probation hostels for a number of years (Blumenthal et al., 2009). For 2 years (1999–2001) one particular hostel was designated as 'specialist', and a part time psychology led forensic mental health team worked in partnership with the London Probation Service to provide an enhanced régime of support and management for high risk personality disordered offenders. This evaluation demonstrated that, within a framework of specialist provision, it was possible to manage a large number of sexual and violent offenders (76% of residents), a quarter of whom scored 25 or more on the Psychopathy Checklist-Revised (PCL-R; Hare, 2003). High levels of anxiety and alcohol misuse were self-reported by the residents, a large number of whom met the criteria for a clinical case on the Brief Symptom Inventory (Derogatis, 1993). Behaviour was monitored during the residents' stay at the hostel; one-third of them were involved in violence towards others during this period, half of whom were using drugs at the time. One quarter of the residents were arrested during their stay, but only four arrests related to acts of aggression, all fairly minor. Two-thirds of residents moved on from the hostel in mutually agreed ways ('successes'); PCL-R score of 25 or over significantly predicted 'failure' if this were defined as premature discharge, as did a resident 'telling lies' during his/her stay. Interpretation of these findings is, however, not entirely straightforward, as premature discharge in this context may have been as much to do with unresolved counter-transference reactions on the part of the staff as the direct result of resident behaviour. It is interesting that these failures had more written about them in their files, over a shorter period of time, than did the successes.

Over time, the London Probation Area has gained confidence in the placement of higher risk individuals in approved hostel premises, and residents with mental disorder are admitted to any of their premises. It is clear that some probation services manage mentally disordered offenders with competence, but officers do feel quite isolated in this task, and frustrated by difficulties in negotiating with remote, occasionally hostile, mental health service providers. Currently the south-east London consultation project provides its service to three hostels. It comprises psychological consultation in relation to residents with complex needs, with access to specialist psychological therapy if appropriate; forensic community psychiatric nursing support, including brief screening of mental state and help in accessing appropriate mental health services; and access to specialist advice from forensic occupational therapy with regard to daily living skills and specialist work placements. A similar model in north London found that their consultation and support services to approved premises was able to influence outcomes, with a 30% reduction in recalls to prison during the first year of the pilot project (S. Chan, personal communication).

Offence/behaviour specific interventions and services

Offence specific interventions have been developed and driven mainly through criminal justice agencies, and informed by the 'what works' literature (Craissati et al., 2002; McGuire, 1995; see also chapter 23). In brief, there is some limited evidence that cognitive behavioural approaches targeting criminogenic risk variables are effective in reducing recidivism, as long as offenders are able to complete treatment (Hollin et al., 2004).

There has been little uniformity in the contribution from mental health services to community interventions for offenders. Some cater only for offenders with severe mental illness. Depending on the competencies of the multidisciplinary team members, this may include provision for specialist psychological treatments. Other services, however, have focused on behaviour specific provision, that is, interventions which target offending behaviour, whether it has resulted in a conviction or not. These have tended to be for men and to fall into two main areas: violence (domestic and/or general violence) and sexual offending.

The literature on the provision of treatment to violent men, particularly those who engage in domestic violence, is large, but inconsistent (Bowen et al., 2005). Treatment models have overlapping components, and tend to be either focused on a pro-feminist psychoeducational group model (Scourfield and Dobash, 1999) or a more standard cognitive behavioural model; they can be focused on domestic violence or on generalized violence and anger control (such as Aggression Replacement Training, Goldstein et al., 2004). Treatment effects are generally found to be small but significant, as long as the violent men complete the programme. Within health services, interventions are varied, but angry or violent men do present to secondary mental health services, so there is a need. It is likely that such referrals have somewhat different characteristics from referrals to accredited programmes within the prison and probation services, and may therefore have different treatment needs, including more psychodynamic understanding and interventions which take account of high levels of interpersonal dependency (Bowen et al., 2005). Dowsett and Craissati in their 2007 book, for example, describe forensic psychology outpatient services for violent men which are based on extended assessments, the use of personality questionnaires, formulation letters shared with the men, and access to 1-day skills-based anger management workshops. Most of the men referred had experienced considerable childhood adversity, and had a long history of violence towards others, previous convictions, and borderline and antisocial personality traits with associated substance misuse. It was very difficult to predict which of them would be sufficiently motivated to take up the offer of treatment, and attrition

rates remained high, although the use of a response slip to trigger an appointment greatly reduced the number of missed sessions. As yet, there are no data available for this group on effectiveness of treatment. McMurran and colleagues (McMurran, 2001; McMurran et al., 2001) have also developed psychological interventions for 'angry aggression' and 'alcohol-related aggression' within a mental health framework, which have a small but encouraging evidence base.

Most health service staff, including those in forensic mental health services, are anxious about their role with sex offenders. There have always, however, been specialist health service projects, scattered rather thinly, and usually run in partnership with the probation service. These projects were broadly based on the standard components of sex offender treatment (Beckett et al., 1994) but, since the roll out of accredited programmes, and the development of probation expertise in the community in the late 1990s, most of these forensic mental health–probation partnerships have been dissolved. There may, however, still be a role for health services to play, perhaps in supporting the probation service, or in running parallel services for those who do not meet accredited programme criteria. Craissati et al. (2005) examined the characteristics of 240 sex offenders being managed by probation in the community over a 6-month period, and found that 37% of the sample met criteria for a personality disorder and 40% had marked traits, not necessarily reaching diagnostic criteria, from two or more clusters of personality disorder. As might be expected, levels of anxiety and dysthymia were high; 21% had a history of contact with mental health services and 10% had previously self-harmed. Although few scored 25 or over on the PCL-R, just over a quarter approached this, and might be expected to present with some challenging behaviours. The probation service were managing and treating most of these offenders, with some high risk referrals to the *Challenge Project* (see below), and a residual 18% who were not referred to any programme; this latter group were either in absolute denial, or, more commonly, were kept back from treatment on the basis of 'mental health problems' or 'learning difficulties'.

The *Challenge Project*, a community assessment and treatment programme for sex offenders in south-east London, is a partnership between the local forensic mental health and probation services. It offers a range of treatment programmes, including group work (and relapse prevention), individual cognitive behavioural treatment, and individual supportive work. With the emergence of accredited programmes, the *Challenge Project* shifted its working emphasis to sex offenders with a mental disorder – usually those with marked personality difficulties – who had previously failed to engage successfully in mainstream treatment provision.

One important aspect of managing risk in the community is determining the likelihood with which an offender, here a sex offender, will comply with treatment expectations, particularly regarding regular attendance and completion of the programme. As noted, treatment attrition is associated with significantly raised sexual recidivism risk (Marques, 1999). An examination of the child molesters in the treatment programme highlighted a number of predictive models, which were examined in relation to attrition and non-compliance (Craissati and Beech, 2001). It was found that

- having two or more childhood difficulties *and* never having cohabited correctly classified 87% of poor attenders;
- *not* having been sexually victimized as a child *and not* having had two or more childhood difficulties correctly classified 78% of compliers;
- childhood difficulties *and* contact with adult mental health services correctly classified 83% of non-compliers.

Thus, difficulties in ensuring that child molesters completed a community treatment programme could be predicted by key developmental and psychological variables, rather than offence-related variables. Initially, an examination of treatment effects for the *Challenge Project* programme yielded disappointing results. It seemed as though offenders treated within the *Challenge Project* failed slightly more often than those not treated at all (17% versus 10%), failure here meaning sexual, violent or general recidivism or recall to prison. When, however, the sample was controlled for risk level (low/medium versus high/very high), only 14% of high risk treated offenders exhibited 'sexually risky behaviours' compared with 19% of similar untreated offenders; 'sexually risky behaviours' were not only arrests or convictions for alleged sexual offending but also behaviours which appeared to be triggers or precursors of sexual offending. When the sample was controlled for risk level and whether or not the offenders had been abused in childhood (that is, the most psychologically disturbed group), the *Challenge Project* group clearly performed better than the untreated comparison group. Only 18% of treated high risk victimized offenders exhibited 'sexually risky behaviours' compared with 33% of similar untreated offenders. Outcome data for the *Challenge Project* are still under review, but these findings suggest that there is a positive role for forensic mental health services to play in treating high risk sex offenders with personality disorder, as long as there is the active support of criminal justice system agencies.

Other specialist sex offender projects have tended to focus on children and adolescents, for example the Young Abusers Project (NSPCC, London NW5 2TX; and G-MAP, Manchester, http://www.g-map.org). Both of these have mental health as one component. Assessment and individual work are otherwise inconsistently available. Other offence types, notably stalking behaviours or arson, have produced some potentially useful developments (see also chapter 15 for stalking; chapter 11 for arson), but numbers treated remain fairly small and services have not been widely rolled out.

Diagnosis specific interventions – personality disorder

Mental health services have rarely taken the lead in the development of treatment services for individuals with personality disorder, and provision for them has been patchy, although there has been some specialist therapeutic community provision. People with personality disorder are perceived as particularly challenging to services, and it is true that interpersonal and social difficulties are intrinsic to the diagnosis, and impulsive, aggressive and antisocial behaviours are commonly encountered, particularly among those with Cluster B diagnoses (including antisocial and borderline personality disorders). In addition, doubts remain about the evidence base for any treatment, although the number of studies evaluating effectiveness is increasing (see chapter 16). The guidance paper *Personality disorder: no longer a diagnosis of exclusion* (NIMHE, 2002), however, was followed with central government money to develop specialist services for offenders with personality disorder. Some of the resulting pilot projects have community elements which reflect traditional models of step-down care and multidisciplinary case management and follow-up. It is worth examining two of the pilots in more detail, as they reflect an attempt to provide stand-alone specialist community provision.

- *The Forensic Intensive Psychological Treatment Service* (FIPTS) in south London has medium security provision, a community team and a specialist hostel for offenders with personality disorder. As with many of the pilots, the community team emphasizes generic psychological competencies amongst the forensic mental health practitioners rather than an exclusive reliance on traditional professional roles. The key feature of the community team intervention is focus on the *Violence Reduction Program* (VRP, Wong and Gordon, 2013), which is run on an intensive daily basis for outpatients and embedded within a case management framework. The VRP is a North American cognitive behavioural programme which targets a wide range of criminogenic factors associated with risk of violence, and which is closely allied to the Violence Risk Scale (Lewis et al., 2013), a static and dynamic risk prediction scale for this group of offenders. Integral to the programme is a measure of readiness to engage in treatment, and the capacity to measure change in risk levels as a result of treatment.
- *The Douglass House Project* is a partnership between forensic mental health services in south-east. London and *Turning Point,* a voluntary sector care provider.

Provision is made up of specialist hostel accommodation and a community contact team and is for offenders with personality disorder who already have a history of community failure and are likely to fall into the gap between mental health, criminal justice and social care agencies. The primary aim is to provide a residential environment which gives emotional as well as physical containment, replicated in the community contact team for those offenders who do not reside within the project, for whatever reason. The staff role is pivotal in providing consistent, nurturing but boundaried responses to the residents, modeling pro-social functioning, containing emotional turmoil and interpersonal stress and promoting capacity for reflection and self-awareness. The rationale for the project integrates attachment theory and cognitive behavioural models of social problem solving to inform assessment and intervention. Access to a meaningful, structured day – in partnership with a specialist work project – is integral to the service, as is access to a range of specialist psychological interventions for sexual and/or violent offending, and psychiatric support.

Specialist Forensic Mental Health Community Services: A Summary

A worthy goal when forensic mental health services were established in the UK after 1975 was that people who had been resident in specialist hospital security units would be rehabilitated through mainstream adult general psychiatry in the NHS, and thus specialist forensic mental health services would hardly be needed. The NHS has been emphasized because, although the independent healthcare sector makes extensive inpatient provision, it does not generally take on the longer term community rehabilitation work. Such integration of forensic and other mental health services for patients has been only partially achieved, so, gradually, most forensic mental health units have developed a community service to continue working with exceptionally difficult cases. This, however, is not their only function. Criminal justice agencies – most notably probation – have traditionally managed with some success a large number of offenders with mental disorder, particularly those with personality difficulties, but they have had to do so largely without specialist health service input. Forensic mental health services have a growing role to play here within the current political and policy framework. Examples of how this may be done have been considered. It would be a mistake to assume reliance on traditional models of community treatment and management, team structures and professional roles would be sufficient. It is exceptionally important in this field to ensure full engagement and retention of offenders in programmes, as starting treatment but failing to complete may yield worse outcomes than no treatment at all. The growing expectation that forensic mental health services will participate in developing services for offenders with personality disorder will necessitate acquisition of new competencies for many of the clinicians. Specialist mental health projects of this kind are resource intensive; it is unlikely that they will be sufficiently widely available to meet all needs. In addition, therefore, such specialist providers will need to develop the skills to provide training, support, and consultancy to those agencies – probation and MAPPPs particularly – where there is already some experience and expertise in the management of offenders with complex needs, but the more specifically medical and psychological skills are lacking.

HEALTH SERVICE BASED FORENSIC PSYCHIATRY SERVICE PROVISION IN SCOTLAND

Service Organization and Policy Framework

All legislative and policy decisions relating to health for Scotland's 5.2 million people are the responsibility of the Scottish Parliament and the Scottish Government (McManus and Thomson, 2005). Health services are organized by 14 health boards within defined geographical areas, 11 of which provide some form of forensic mental healthcare. They are also managed on a divisional basis, with psychiatry commonly found in the primary care and community division. The exception to this is the State Hospital, the high security psychiatric hospital for Scotland and Northern Ireland, which is managed by a special health board – the State Hospitals' Board for Scotland.

The Forensic Mental Health Services Managed Care Network was established by the Scottish Executive in 2003, to oversee the development and organization of forensic mental health services in Scotland (Scottish Executive, 2002). It has no purchasing power or managerial control, but exists to promote and co-ordinate standards of practice, as well as their development. It has produced several reports on topics such as learning disability, women, levels of security and personality disorder (http://www.forensicnetwork.scot.nhs.uk/).

Government policy in this field was set out in *Health, Social Work and Related Services for Mentally Disordered Offenders in Scotland* (Scottish Office, 1998a). Mentally disordered offenders are defined as those who are:

considered to suffer from a mental disorder as defined in mental health legislation, whether or not they are, or may be, managed under its provisions and come to the attention of the criminal justice system.

The policy established guiding principles for the care and treatment of mentally disordered offenders, which are very similar to those for England and Wales, including the use, as far as possible, of care in community rather than in institutional settings; conditions of no greater security than is justified by the degree of danger they present to themselves or to others; and facilities as near as possible to their own homes or families.

Mental Health (Care and Treatment) (Scotland) Act 2003

The Mental Health (Care and Treatment) (Scotland) Act 2003, implemented in October 2005, explicitly sets the framework for the practice of forensic psychiatry. This is covered at more length in chapter 4, but here it is worth restating the principles for service provision. These are

- participation of the patient in the process;
- respect for carers, including consideration of their views and needs;
- the use of informal care wherever possible;
- use of the least restrictive alternative;
- the need to provide the maximum benefit to the patient;
- non-discrimination against a mentally disordered person;
- respect for diversity regardless of a patients' abilities, background and characteristics;
- reciprocity in terms of service provision for those subject to the Act;
- the welfare of any child with a mental disorder being considered paramount;
- equality.

Hospital Treatment

The high security psychiatric hospital

The State Hospital is located in rural Lanarkshire, midway between Glasgow and Edinburgh, and opened in 1948. It provided a specialist secure psychiatric service, combining high and medium secure care, for all of Scotland and Northern Ireland until the opening of medium secure units in the south-east of Scotland (The Orchard Clinic) in 2001, Northern Ireland (The Shannon Clinic) in 2005 and the west of Scotland in 2008. The State Hospital now provides a high security environment throughout, with major perimeter security. With the current development of three further medium secure units in Scotland and the introduction of appeals against level of security in May 2006, its role has become ever more strictly limited to people unequivocally requiring high security.

It is for people who require conditions of special hospital security because of their 'dangerous, violent or criminal propensities'. Following research on the security needs of its patients (Thomson et al., 1997), it has been entirely rebuilt on its existing site, but with 140 rather than its previous 250 beds, becoming fully operational in July 2011. There are specific services for people with learning disability. Patients have access to therapeutic, educational, occupational and recreational services (Thomson, 2000). All patients are compulsorily detained under the Mental Health (Care and Treatment) (Scotland) Act 2003 or the Criminal Procedure (Scotland) Act 1995; 60% of them also subject to a restriction order. Consultant psychiatrists have autonomy in admission decisions.

One analysis of referrals to the State Hospital found that admitted patients were more likely to have displayed dangerous behaviour secondary to psychosis (Pimm et al., 2004). There were 41 admissions and 36 discharges during the year 2004–2005. Approximately one-fifth of transferred patients are readmitted (Duncan et al., 2002). The State Hospital population has been studied extensively (Thomson et al., 1997). The average age of the patients was 34.6 years (range 17–67 years); 88% were men; 70% had a diagnosis of schizophrenia, 13% of learning disability and 5% a primary diagnosis of antisocial personality disorder (ASPD). A comorbid diagnosis of ASPD was found in 27% of patients, 48% had a history of heavy or abusive use of alcohol and 47% had used illegal drugs on at least one occasion. A fifth of patients were transferred from prison and a third came from local psychiatric hospitals following incidents of violence, menace, self-harm, absconding, fire raising or sexually inappropriate behaviour. The remainder were admitted from court. Most patients (83%) had a history of criminal convictions prior to the index offence. Physical health problems were present in more than half the patients and adverse childhood events were reported in almost three-quarters. At the time of the original survey more than half the patients were said not to require high security, and there was little evidence that such facilities were required for women at all (Thomson et al., 2001), hence the rebuilding and reorganization.

Outcome measures, as in England and Wales, have focused on re-offending, showing that in this respect the State Hospital compares favourably with the Scottish prison service. Over an average follow-up period of 11.5 years, 31% of patients discharged from the State Hospital were found to have been convicted of any offence, and 19% of a violent offence, two-thirds of these offences occurring within the first 2 years of discharge. In the Scottish prison service, 60% of prisoners are re-convicted within 2 years. Follow-up over an 8–10-year period just of the original study cohort with schizophrenia ($n = 169$) showed that 75% leave high security, but only just under half (46%) reach the community within that time. Three-quarters were involved in a violent incident during the follow up period; for one-quarter the violent incident resulted in the victim needing hospital treatment. Fifteen per cent were re-convicted, 5% overall of a violent offence. One-third had an episode of self harm during the follow-up period, although completed suicide was rare (Ramsay et al., 2001). Leaving high security was associated with a history of drug abuse, broken by the admission, whereas remaining in the State Hospital was associated with an index offence leading to admission together with ongoing positive symptoms of psychosis and violent incidents. Reaching the community was associated with a history of alcohol and drug dependence, better social function and better contact with friends and/or relatives while in high security, whereas ongoing positive symptoms and inappropriate sexual behaviour were associated with continued hospital care. Only 11 of the cohort sustained an intimate relationship and two had paid employment. A comparison of patients with schizophrenia drawn from high security hospitals throughout the UK found that national cohorts were similar in offence histories but that Scottish patients with psychosis were more likely to have comorbid substance misuse diagnoses and/or a personality disorder and less likely to come from ethnic minorities (Taylor et al., 2008). Recognition of the extensive problem of substance abuse within the Scottish forensic mental health population has led to major developments in management (Steele et al., 2003; MacIntyre et al., 2004; Ritchie et al., 2004).

A comparison of patients with schizophrenia in the State Hospital with those placed elsewhere in Scotland found that male patients of younger age at first psychiatric hospital admission, poorer educational attainment, and a history of alcohol or drug abuse in a close relative were more likely to be admitted to high security. High security patients also had more lifetime symptoms of schizophrenia/psychotic symptoms, had more admissions to psychiatric hospital for longer periods, more police contacts and greater use of benzodiazepines prior to State Hospital admission (Millar et al., 2000). Doody et al. (2000) explored factors which distinguished State Hospital patients with intellectual disability.

Specialist forensic medium security psychiatric services

The Orchard Clinic, the first medium secure unit in Scotland, opened in Edinburgh in January 2001, with 50 inpatient beds mainly for Lothian, Borders and Forth Valley Health Board areas, although it will take out of area transfers. It is a purpose built facility with one acute and two rehabilitation wards for people with major mental illness, but not those with a primary diagnosis of learning disability, traumatic brain injury or personality disorder (Nelson, 2003). Patients are generally over the age of 18, detained under mental health or criminal procedure legislation and must present a risk to others or themselves because of their mental illness such that medium secure care is the most appropriate and least restrictive treatment setting. It is expected that length of stay will not exceed 2 years. Non-offender patients who present major behavioural problems, chiefly risk to others, may occasionally be admitted. The Rowenbank Clinic is a medium security unit of 74 beds, for the west of Scotland and for the national medium security learning disability unit. A further, 30-bedded unit is due to open in Perth in 2013.

Specialist low security psychiatric services

There are six low security units led by forensic psychiatrists in Scotland, together providing 173 beds. These vary from adapted wards to purpose built units. In addition, some parts of the country (e.g. Fife or Highlands) make use of intensive psychiatric care units for offenders with mental disorder, although it is recognized that this is not ideal.

Independent sector facilities

Unlike the rest of the UK, Scotland has few private forensic psychiatric facilities. The Churchill Clinic in Ayr opened in May 2004, with 12 low security and 12 intensive psychiatric care beds for patients with mental illness. There is also a low secure unit for patients with learning disability in Dundee.

Specialist forensic community psychiatric services

The development of community forensic mental health teams in Scotland has been *ad hoc*. They vary considerably in different parts of the country. Glasgow has the Douglas Inch Clinic, Forth Valley has a community forensic mental health team and Perth has a day hospital for mentally disordered offenders, truly providing specialist facilities, but many other services survive purely with general adult psychiatrists and access to a community psychiatric nurse. There are, however, some serious offenders with a moderate to high risk of future violence who do require ongoing forensic services. Forensic mental health services are also provided to the prison service, the courts and the police, both separately from and in conjunction with MAPPA.

The Future of Forensic Psychiatry in Scotland

Scottish forensic psychiatry is continuing its process of major change, starting from the 2003 Mental Health Act, the building of a new high security hospital, development of medium security hospital units and proposals for other new services and establishment of a School of Forensic Mental Health in 2007. In all this, it is essential that strong ties with general psychiatric services are maintained, both to ensure rehabilitation of patients and safeguard ease of access to forensic services.

HEALTH SERVICE BASED FORENSIC PSYCHIATRY SERVICE PROVISION IN NORTHERN IRELAND

Northern Ireland is a small geographical area, approximately 80 miles across, with a population of around 1.7 million. It is a separate jurisdiction within the UK, with, since 2010, a devolved legislature, the Northern Ireland Assembly, and separate organizational structures for its Criminal Justice System and its Health and Personal Social Services.

Development of Forensic Mental Health Services

The development of specialist forensic mental health services in Northern Ireland has followed a protracted course. During the late 1970s, in parallel to similar developments in the rest of the UK, plans were drawn up to build a medium security hospital unit at Purdysburn Hospital (subsequently known as Knockbracken Healthcare Park), which occupies a 275 acre (110 hectares) parkland site on the outskirts of Belfast. Little practical progress was made, however, partly for financial reasons, and partly for political ones – not least that during the last 3–4 decades of the twentieth century 'the troubles' had a powerful influence on most forms of secure provision in Northern Ireland. Health service–employed psychiatrists continued to provide services for offenders with mental disorder by visiting the prisons, mostly on a sessional basis. Some people who had been charged with or convicted of an offence who were ill, most commonly with schizophrenia, were transferred to the psychiatric hospital for the area where they lived, generally to a locked ward there. A few men with major mental illness or severe mental impairment and considered to pose an imminent risk of harm to others were transferred to a high security hospital outside Northern Ireland, usually the State Hospital in Scotland, and similar women to Rampton, in England, to be returned when considered safe to do so. Numbers of patients from Northern Ireland needing high security in any one year, however, rarely exceed single figures. There is currently no framework of inter-related mental health legislation that allows the transfer of patients from Northern Ireland to conditions of high security in the Republic of Ireland.

In 1984, the Department of Health and Social Services published *Mental Health – the Way Forward* after a Review Committee visited existing services and consulted with statutory and voluntary bodies and other interested parties. This document acknowledged the economic constraints of that period, and proposed that, instead of building a new, purpose designed medium secure hospital unit, the six psychiatric intensive care units in the province should be upgraded to become so-called 'high intensive nursing care units'. Notwithstanding the prevailing philosophy in the rest of the UK – that prisoners with mental illness should, as far as possible, be transferred to hospital – the report also endorsed maintenance of the status quo with respect to treatment in prison:

the treating of mentally ill prisoners should as far as possible be undertaken by the Prison Medical Service (para 6.27, p.61).

In retrospect, it seems likely that, in Northern Ireland, the policies of that era were influenced by the ongoing civil disturbance that had seen a number of violent incidents in hospitals specifically and, in the early 1980s, the hunger strikes and prison escapes that drew the attention of the world to the Northern Ireland prisons. It seems likely that government, the public and even mental health service providers viewed prison transfers to hospital with some fear and concern. In addition, there was no 'product champion', to drive forward a specialist development with energy and enthusiasm.

Significant progress was made in 1988. A new prison – Maghaberry Prison – was opened some 20 miles outside Belfast, and an inter-agency psychiatric team was formed, based in the prison healthcare centre and led by the first consultant psychiatrist appointed to a specialist post in forensic psychiatry. In 1994, a joint Northern Ireland Office and Department of Health and Social Services working party recommended the development of a medium secure hospital unit for Northern Ireland within the health service. This recommendation was incorporated into the Department of Health and Social Services Regional Plan for 1997–2002 which stated:

by 2002 a Medium Secure Unit should be established in Northern Ireland and comprehensive arrangements should be in place so that, where appropriate, people with mental illness can be diverted from the Criminal Justice System.

Funding was granted in 2000 and the 34-bed Shannon Clinic was opened in 2005, on the site originally identified (Knockbracken Healthcare Park). In contrast to the situation in many other parts of the UK, there was no interim specialist secure service to prepare the way in Northern Ireland, thus the opening of this unit represented a bold step forward, and the culmination of an intensive process that included agreeing principles and values for the service and the design of the building, then elaborating policies and procedures and recruiting and training staff.

Other developments in forensic services followed, including a new inpatient learning disability unit in 2006 (Sixmile, at Muckamore Abbey Hospital) and four community forensic mental health teams. The latter were created to provide services across Northern Ireland, giving priority to patients discharged from the Shannon Clinic and founded in a four-tier model, ranging from one-off consultations (tier 1) to taking full responsibility for the care of the individual (tier 4). A community forensic learning disability service is also under development.

At present there are no forensic services run by the independent healthcare sector in Northern Ireland, although individual patients may be referred to such services in other parts of the UK if all available specialist beds within Northern Ireland are occupied, or if there is some special reason to do so, such as a need to separate the individual from his/her family or victims. The voluntary sector continues to provide services to forensic patients, such as day services and accommodation, and/or independent advocacy services.

The first major review of forensic mental health services in Northern Ireland was completed in 2007 as part of the Bamford Review (see chapter 25). A Regional Forensic Advisory Group was established in 2005 to help co-ordinate policy and service implementation, while the work of the Bamford Review was ongoing. A subgroup of the Mental Health and Learning Disability Taskforce has subsequently taken a lead in developments. This subgroup is reviewing some of the gaps and shortcomings in service provision, such as low secure services and provision for women. As Northern Ireland is a small jurisdiction, it has proved straightforward to make the most of these different streams of work starting in a sequence which might have been more awkward elsewhere.

Practical Aspects of Working in Forensic Mental Health Services in Northern Ireland

Practitioners who work in forensic mental health services in Northern Ireland share many of the challenges faced by forensic practitioners working elsewhere. In practice it seems that no attempt at a precise definition and no sophisticated organizational structure will ever establish a clear cut-off between a forensic and a non-forensic patient; the reality is that if services are to operate in a co-ordinated manner, service providers must develop co-operative working relationships with each other and they must share an ethos of working in partnership for the benefit of the patient and his or her carers.

As elsewhere, the organization of forensic services in Northern Ireland must try to accommodate apparently opposing forces such as centralization and localization; risk aversion and risk appetite; innovative, experimental services and standardized, evidence-based approaches. We may espouse explicit values and principles to guide the development of our services but implementing these values and principles into day-to-day and moment-to-moment practice can be much more difficult. We may struggle to comprehend and respond appropriately to the range of emotional reactions aroused in us by patients who are also offenders and by perpetrators who are also victims. We may feel gratified that we can provide services for mentally disordered offenders, yet the patients under our care are only a few from the many. We must recognize that our best efforts

at providing treatment do little, if anything, to address underlying causes and/or to interrupt the routes whereby people become mentally disordered offenders. In addition, the highly emotive nature of our work makes it difficult to promote and foster the public understanding and appreciation required to ensure that our services receive ongoing support and priority.

Certain difficulties that are inherent to working in forensic mental health services may be aggravated or increased in a small jurisdiction, for example difficulties are often encountered in training and recruiting the range of staff required. It can also be more difficult to provide services to meet the special needs of some groups of patients, such as women, because their numbers are so small. There can be fewer opportunities to develop more specialized services because of the smaller numbers of patients in each category. Smaller clinical services may also lack sufficient critical mass to form a local academic base or to support stand-alone research projects. Membership of research networks or organizations such as the Forensic Psychiatry Research Society (http://www.fprs.org/) can help overcome isolation and can foster opportunities for collaboration. Similarly, small services are at risk of lagging behind in implementing the latest advances in clinical practice; they may become complacent or more susceptible to the vagaries of idiosyncratic individual practitioners. Therefore it is particularly important to maintain strong connections with bodies such as the Royal College of Psychiatrists' Quality Improvement Network to help ensure that services remain supported and that their practice generally sits securely within the mainstream. Smaller services may also be more vulnerable to attacks on their funding sources or adverse political, managerial or public influence.

Clinicians working in a small jurisdiction such as Northern Ireland face the additional challenge of developing and maintaining their awareness of services and legislation in neighbouring jurisdictions so that they can appreciate the implications of transferring patients back and forth for treatment. As illustrated in chapter 4, the mental health legislation is different from other jurisdictions in the UK; different criteria for detention mean that, under some circumstances, some patients may be liable to detention in one jurisdiction and not in another; this can become a difficulty particularly when the diagnosis is revised. Clinicians who transfer patients from Northern Ireland to the State Hospital in Scotland for treatment in conditions of high security should know, for example, that the patients may be able to appeal against detention in conditions of excessive security under the provisions of the Mental Health (Care and Treatment) (Scotland) Act 2003, even though no such provision currently exists in Northern Ireland's mental health legislation.

Although working in a small jurisdiction such as Northern Ireland poses its particular difficulties, none of these is insurmountable and, as indicated, there are compensations and advantages too. It is beneficial to have an awareness of different legislative frameworks and organizational structures and to consider the merits and demerits of the different models. It is probably easier to meet and form co-operative working relationships between the wide range of individuals in the many organizations that interface with forensic psychiatric services and this may greatly add to the richness of clinical experience, provide opportunities to develop new combinations or types of services and promote a stronger sense of the place of forensic mental health services within society. It is also probably easier to provide continuity of clinical care for patients through a range of settings than it is in larger countries with varying administrative boundaries, which have not always been co-terminous.

With all these influences at play the scene should be set for the further advancement of forensic mental health services in Northern Ireland, continuing on the one hand to differentiate services so that their staff become more adept and expert at their specialized functions and, on the other, to integrate them within the broader range of services. Forensic mental health services continue to require development that is based on understanding the needs of all the relevant parties, but particularly the patients and their often ambivalent attitudes to the 'treat' we offer in our treatments.

HEALTH SERVICE BASED FORENSIC PSYCHIATRY SERVICE PROVISION IN IRELAND

The Central Mental Hospital – the oldest secure hospital in Europe

The National Forensic Mental Health Service is based at the Central Mental Hospital, Dundrum, Dublin. It provides high, medium and low security on one campus, with community out-reach and prison in-reach services for the Republic of Ireland, with a population of 4.4 million. The Central Mental Hospital opened in 1850, established by an 1845 Act of the London Parliament. It is the only forensic mental health facility in the State. Following independence in 1922, there was a hiatus while legislators and the courts dealt with other issues. Pressure for change came from cases in the European Court of Human Rights (*Croke*), criticisms by the Council of Europe Committee for the Prevention of Torture, new, progressive Government policies (Department of Health and Children, 2001, 2006) and a series of blueprints for reform of the health service generally (e.g. Hanley Report, 2003). Relevant new legislation was implemented in 2006 – the Mental Health Act 2001 and the Criminal Law (Insanity) Act 2006 (Kennedy, 2007).

New Services in Ireland

Pathways Organization

Between 2000 and 2005, the National Forensic Mental Health Services underwent a process of reinvention and reform, with a substantial investment in human resources. Nurse-led therapeutic environments and multidisciplinary mental healthcare were particularly emphasized. Reform was planned by means of a series of reviews of the service as it was then (O'Neill et al., 2003) and its place in the Irish mental health services (O'Neill et al., 2002; Wright et al., 2008), taking account of the population as a whole (O'Neill et al., 2005), including the prison population (Linehan et al., 2002; Linehan et al., 2005; Duffy et al., 2006; Wright et al., 2006; Curtin et al., 2009). These surveys led to a revision of the service, first emphasizing need and provision beyond the hospital walls, with rapid development of prison in-reach and court liaison services led by psychiatrists and specialist nurse practitioners. The latter developed initially for remand prisoners, and was then extended to sentenced prisoners. Support and advice for community mental health teams has developed into a substantial workload. This continues to raise debate about the boundaries between general and forensic mental health services, a problem being lack of low secure and longer term secure beds generally. This discourse has led to the development of a series of structured professional judgment instruments for allocating patients to the appropriate level of therapeutic security (Kennedy et al., 2010).

The Central Mental Hospital has been reorganized into a transparent recovery pathway (Pillay et al., 2008). This also represents a system for the stratification of patients to appropriate levels of therapeutic security according to their current needs. The recovery route runs from high secure admission and intensive care units to medium secure units and on to low secure and pre-discharge units, where a forensic rehabilitation and recovery team takes the pre-discharge patient seamlessly through conditional discharge to highly supported community residences and, finally, independent living.

Prison in-reach and court liaison

The main remand prison for the State receives about 70% of all remand committals. People in this group have a high rate of psychosis and other psychiatric morbidity on reception (Curtin et al., 2009). A disproportionate number of severely mentally ill people accumulate on remand compared with other jurisdictions (Linehan et al., 2005). A successful model of screening followed by diversion from custody is now in operation for those charged with minor offences who are found to have major mental illnesses (O'Neill, 2006). This has allowed the Central Mental Hospital to focus on admitting only those in need of higher levels of therapeutic security.

Admission to Forensic Mental Health Service criteria

The publication and validation of a structured professional judgment instrument (Kennedy et al., 2010) for the assessment of need for therapeutic security and the prioritization of those on waiting lists is intended to make communication clearer, whether this is in court, with community mental health teams, prisons, funding and commissioning agencies or the patients themselves. Criteria were first summarized as part of a description of the components of therapeutic security and systems for providing secure mental health services integrated into psychiatric services more generally (Kennedy, 2001, 2002, 2007). The factors identified as determining the appropriate level of therapeutic security include seriousness of violence, seriousness of suicidal behaviour, immediacy of risks of violence and suicide, specialist forensic need, propensity for absconding, need to prevent access to various forms of contraband or weapons, victim sensitivity and public confidence issues, complex risk of violence, institutional behaviour and legal processes. The urgency of admission, once placed on a waiting list, depends on different factors, some specific to the location of the patient at the time of referral, others to life threatening mental health factors and suicide prevention, human rights issues, such as the need to minimize use of seclusion or restraint, systemic factors, such as catchment area, resource and commissioning issues, and legal urgency.

Pillars of care

Treatment of patients in the Central Mental Hospital is systematized into five 'pillars', overseen by a programme planning committee. These five pillars are: (i) physical health; (ii) mental health; (iii) drugs and alcohol; (iv) problem behaviours; (v) social, occupational and family relationships (Kennedy et al., 2010). Each of these is delivered by a combination of group work in validated treatment programmes and individual work with appropriate therapists. Each pillar is organized broadly to deliver a preliminary short course, suitable for those in admission or intensive care units who may still be symptomatic due to mental illness or who may have only a short stay in the hospital. This is followed, for rather longer stay patients in the medium security wards, by a 'full' treatment programme, typically consisting of about 20 sessions, and, finally, a 'top-up' or continuing support phase which may continue after discharge.

The treatments in each domain or pillar may have to be organized into meaningful sequences. This may be as basic as doing literacy work before diary keeping is possible, or improving self-awareness and self-monitoring through metacognitive training and enhanced thinking skills, dialectic behaviour therapy or some of its component modules before going on to anger management and healthy relationship programmes. The organization and planning of these 'pillars' into coherent sequences, according to assessments of need, has been systematized into a written integrated care pathway (Gill et al., 2010). This provides a means of auditing the delivery of timely assessments and interventions.

The therapeutic working day

Treatments are often demanding and must be paced, to accommodate individual learning styles. A planned therapeutic working day is important as a means of ensuring time for the other components of a balanced and fulfilling life. Work or equivalent occupation, sport, leisure and self-expression, contact and communication with friends and relatives all need time. The prevention of negative symptoms or institutionalization requires access to leave and activities outside the hospital at the earliest opportunity. The hospital model of combining high, medium and low security on one campus ensures that there are no administrative or legal delays to early access to leave and other de-institutionalizing activities.

Discharge criteria

The preparation of a structured professional judgment instrument for the triage of those referred for admission led to similar style instruments for assessing readiness for movement to lower security, including moves to the community. When discharge occurs, it may be subject to conditions or may be absolute (Kennedy et al., 2010; Kennedy, 2002). The factors relevant to decisions to move from higher to lower levels of therapeutic security, or to progress from no leave outside the secure perimeter through accompanied leave to unaccompanied leave divide into programme completion items and recovery items.

Programme completion items derive from the five pillars of care described above. These can be rated according to a set of criteria derived from the theories underpinning modern treatments including the cycle of change (Procheska and DiClementi, 1983), recovery (Andresen et al., 2010), Maslow's hierarchy (1943) and staff assessment of engagement. Recovery items include: (i) stability; (ii) insight; (iii) rapport and working alliance; (iv) leave; and (v) dynamic risk.

A multidisciplinary rehabilitation and recovery team takes over the care of pre-discharge patients who had been detained under the Criminal Law (Insanity) Act 2006 for 2 or more years at the Central Mental Hospital. This team continues the care, treatment and supervision of released forensic patients.

Future Developments in Ireland

The organization and governance of a therapeutically effective, recovery-oriented service for mentally disordered offenders is a constant process of renewal and reform as secure institutions are inherently vulnerable to stigma, financial neglect and a tendency towards a culture of custody and stasis rather than recovery. In part this stasis arises from a reluctance to take therapeutic risks. The managers and political custodians of secure mental health services must be aware of the limits of risk management and the necessity to take controlled risks. These problems are particularly likely in small populations where there may be limited access to influences from services in other jurisdictions. The best means of maintaining a therapeutic ethos is through constant development. This should be humane and aspirational in purpose, but scientific and rigorous in its processes. An international perspective has proved essential to developments in Ireland. One challenge is to ensure that all disciplines at all levels of seniority and experience are exposed to outside influences and maintain a clinically scientific ethos after qualification. This may now be taken for granted among medical specialists, but is often neglected in other disciplines. The Quality Network for secure services, co-ordinated by the UK Royal College of Psychiatrists, is useful, as are international academic bodies such as the International Association of Forensic Mental Health Services, with multidisciplinary membership.

25
Offenders and alleged offenders with mental disorder in non-medical settings

Edited by
Pamela J Taylor

Written by
Julian Corner and Sarah Anderson

Ian Lankshear and Annette Lankshear

Jane Senior and Jenny Shaw

Pamela J Taylor

With commentaries for Scotland by Lindsay Thomson, Northern Ireland by Fred Browne and Republic of Ireland by Enda Dooley

1st edition authors: **Maureen Barry, Paul d'Orbán, Enda Dooley, Gisli Gudjonsson, John Gunn, David Hall, Stephen Stanley and Pamela J Taylor**

Forensic psychiatry is not only founded in good multidisciplinary practice but also in sound multi-agency work. The advantages of this lie in the wealth of expertise and range of perspective that can be brought to bear on improving individual and public health and safety. Tensions lie in the fact that the different agencies hold expressly different primary loyalties. Furthermore while the usual contacts in these circumstances – lawyers, police, prison staff, probation officers and voluntary workers – variously have their own personal, professional and/or organizational standards, not all have professional bodies and structures in the same sense as doctors do. The scope for misunderstanding is considerable. In England and Wales, since the introduction under the Criminal Justice and Courts Act 2000 (consolidated in the Criminal Justice Act 2003) of Multi-Agency Public Protection Arrangements (MAPPA) for the assessment and management of sexual and violent offenders, it has never been more important to understand each other's aims, strengths and limitations. Worldwide, there is increasing recognition of the mental ill-health burden borne by a high and probably rising proportion of people presenting to any criminal justice system, creating an imperative for new ways of coping with need. In the USA, for example, Morrissey et al. (2009) are among those calling for new models of collaboration between criminal justice and mental health systems; they recommend a system of mental health courts. In England and Wales, government reports or government commissioned reports (e.g. Cabinet Office, 2007; Rennie and Roberts, 2008; HM Inspectorate

of Prisons, 2007; Corston, 2007; Bradley, 2009) similarly ask for the various agencies to work together. This is founded in a vision of seizing the resultant opportunity to save lives, improve health and cut crime by responding to mental health needs of offenders appropriately and at the earliest possible opportunity. The Department of Health consultation which led to the Rennie and Roberts (2008) report endorsed the vision that offenders and their families should receive standards of care equivalent to those in the wider community 'which are well resourced and their effectiveness measured'.

WORKING WITH THE POLICE

In most cases, the police are the first point of contact with the criminal justice system and there is an early opportunity through police intervention and liaison to engage services and potentially avoid future problems. I was surprised to discover that the police stage is currently the least developed in the offender pathway in terms of engagement with health and social services ... (Bradley, 2009, p.34).

The organization and delivery of policing, like other public services, is under a near constant process of review and reform. The current position for England and Wales is set out mainly in the Police Act 1996, which consolidated several other pieces of legislation, including the Police Act 1964, parts of the Police and Criminal Evidence Act 1984 and the Police and Magistrates' Courts

619

Act 1994. Scotland and Northern Ireland have separate legislation. For England and Wales, again, the Police Act 1997 amended elements of the 1996 Act, making provision for some additional bodies, including the National Criminal Intelligence Service and the Police Information Technology Organization (PITO), among the duties of the latter being to oversee criminal records and enhanced criminal records certificates. The Police and Justice Act 2006 established a National Policing Improvement Agency (NPIA), replacing the PITO, made several provisions on new powers, including the powers and duties of community support officers, and amended the Computer Misuse Act 1990, to make provision about the forfeiture of indecent images of children.

The Home Office is ultimately responsible for policing in England and Wales (the Scottish Executive in Scotland). The Home Office website (http://www.homeoffice.gov.uk) publishes regularly updated information on the organization of the 43 police forces in England and Wales and the numbers of people employed within them. These numbers vary over time, with 2011 figures showing some reduction, but there are of the order of 230,000–240,000 fulltime equivalent employees at any one time, about 60% of whom are police officers. At the time of writing, the principal influence of the Home Office is through the National Policing Board, chaired by the Home Secretary. Each force, however, is run by a local independent police authority. This is made up of local councillors and other local community members, who hold its chief constable to account, and also ensure commitment and input to policing from the community it serves. An important development in this context has been neighbourhood policing, and the creation of Safer Neighbourhood Teams and Crime and Disorder Reduction Partnerships (CDRPs) in which the police link with local authorities and other support agencies, including health. Bradley (2009) notes that this framework should provide a good basis for improved individual and public safety.

Several bodies have improvement or monitoring roles for the police, including the NPIA, supported by the Home Office and police-led, Her Majesty's Inspectorate of Constabulary (HMIC) (http://www.hmic.gov.uk), a government funded but independent body, and the Independent Police Complaints Commission (IPCC) (http://www.ipcc.gov.uk). In addition, the police have their own professional bodies: the Association of Chief Police Officers (ACPO), the Police Federation and special interest groups such as the National Black Police Association and the British Association of Women Police.

The police have a wide range of roles, covering traffic and other social controls, keeping the peace, prevention and detection of crime and the arrest and processing of suspects of crime, providing the Crown Prosecution Service with evidence for prosecution and presenting cases in court. They have a custody role during early phases of investigation and detention to await appearance in court, and may have to provide a 'place of safety' pending examination by mental health professionals within the provisions of the Mental Health Acts (MHA) 1983, amended 2007. Whether a person is perceived to be at risk because of possible mental disorder, victim of crime, or alleged perpetrator of crime, a prospective patient's first contact with non-medical systems is, thus, commonly with the police. In one category alone – that of people detained in police stations as places of safety under section 136 of the MHA 1983 – such contacts amounted to 11,500 people in 1 year (2005–2006; Docking et al., 2008).

Police-Led Collaboration

People with health difficulties are very vulnerable in police custody; a small but important number die there from their disorders (e.g. Docking and Menin, 2007). Clinical services are generally commissioned by the police force, with most healthcare overseen by a 'forensic medical examiner', often, but not invariably contracted from a local general practice. Some police custody suites also employ a community psychiatric nurse, and/or other mental health professionals, whether through direct commissioning or in partnership with the local primary care trust (PCT). They may also call in specialists on a case-by-case basis to determine health needs, supporting people in custody, but where necessary and possible, transferring them to a hospital.

In England and Wales, section 136 of the MHA 1983 allows a police constable to take someone s/he regards as having a mental disorder and in need of protection, or who is likely to harm others, from a public place to a place of safety for a period up to 72 hours, for assessment by a doctor and a social worker. The MHA 2007 has changed little in this respect, except to broaden the concept of mental disorder, but it does allow for the possibility of transferring the person between 'places of safety' to optimize conditions for him/her. The codes of practice to this legislation, though, make it clear that routine use of police custody in this regard is to be deplored, and it is to everyone's advantage to have clear, agreed local policies about good procedure in such cases. The Sainsbury Centre for Mental Health (2008) called for police to have better training in mental health issues, for health services to be more available to them and for joint commissioning of services. The Royal College of Psychiatrists (2011b), in a report endorsed by the Association of Chief Police Officers as well as a number of other relevant bodies, has set out guidance on good practice in this area.

There is little research in the field. The Royal College of Psychiatrists (2011b) conducted a systematic review of the literature and identified only 28 relevant articles, almost all of them published before 1997, most London based and all of them descriptive. Two commissioned publications, one by the IPCC (Docking et al., 2008) and the other by the London Development Centre (Bather, 2006), give useful information, the first national, and the latter London focused. One study from outside London suggested that the police are, in fact, familiar with and good at recognising severe mental abnormality (Sims and Symonds, 1975); they found that over half (57%) of 252 people referred by police over 12 months in Birmingham had a psychotic illness and all but 46 were admitted to hospital. The Royal College of Psychiatrists' review states that, overall, published studies suggest that the hospital admission rate arising from section 136 detention is over 80%. A fairly consistent finding is that most people assessed under section 136 had previously been patients in mental health services, often under an MHA order (e.g. Dunn and Fahy, 1990; Pipe et al., 1991; Turner et al., 1992). There is concern that, at least in London, people from African/British Caribbean groups are over-represented (Rogers and Faulkner, 1987; Dunn and Fahy, 1990; Turner et al., 1992; Simmons and Hoar, 2001; Bather, 2006).

Szmukler et al. (1981) found that, in London, patients admitted to hospital after section 136 detention were less likely to continue in treatment than other patients. It may be that resistance to helping these patients on the part of psychiatric staff is a factor in their premature discharge. Dunn and Fahy (1987) studied police perception of the problem in a 23% sample of London police stations. In over half of these stations police thought that mental hospitals provided inadequate support for their dealings with such cases, and over 70% thought medical and social work responses inadequate. The Royal College of Psychiatrists (2011) report seeks to guide towards a better situation, advising that there should be sufficient hospital places to meet local need, with defined standards and a dedicated staff 24 hours a day, adequate numbers of appropriately trained staff, appropriate means of transport and support during transport, and systems for monitoring standards and outcome. Some police stations, however, are trialing custody units with a community psychiatric nurse on permanent standby.

People detained under section 136 are an important group because of their exceptional vulnerability, but generally cases require general psychiatry services rather than specialist forensic psychiatry services. Nevertheless, in more difficult cases, it may be useful for the two specialisms to liaise. Other situations may arise when a person has been arrested on a serious charge and the police are concerned about his/her immediate health and safety and/or his/her fitness to be interviewed.

Police interviews as evidence

The use of confession as evidence of wrong-doing is as old as recorded history, as is coercion and even torture to extract confessions. This is puzzling, because an admission of guilt under such circumstances would seem intrinsically unreliable, but it is now widely recognized that there may also be far more subtle influences on the nature of confessions. In civilian life, it is the police who are at the forefront of taking evidence of crime, including the taking of confessions and it is of paramount importance, therefore, that the police make it clear to a suspect that s/he is being interviewed as a suspect, that they (the police) are skilled in appropriate interview techniques, record those interviews, and have the ability to recognise vulnerabilities in an individual which make false confession more likely. They must also know how to institute appropriate procedures to protect both the rights of that individual and safeguard the justice process. If this is not done, defendants may challenge police evidence on the grounds that a confession statement was incorrectly obtained. Assessment by a psychiatrist or psychologist may be requested in assessing an individual's fitness to be interviewed under these circumstances.

A case which substantially influenced interviewing practice in England is the *Confait* case. Three youths, one of them with intellectual disability, were convicted, on their own confession, of killing Maxwell Confait. Two years later the convictions were quashed and the Home Secretary set up a judicial inquiry (Fisher, 1977). Fisher concluded that the confession statements were unreliable because the police had questioned the men in breach of the Judges' Rules on police interviews, in use since 1912, but as revised in 1964. Then, these constituted a code of practice which did not have the force of law, but police were expected to follow it, with disciplinary or civil liabilities if not. There were two breaches in *Confait*: first that two of the interviewees were under 17, but interviewed without an independent adult being present, and second that the intellectually disabled man was 'prompted' by the interviewing officers.

Matters of police interrogation were among the things referred to in the Royal Commission on Criminal Procedure (1981). One important effect of this Commission was the Police and Criminal Evidence Act (PACE) 1984. This was implemented in 1986, giving force of law to the Judges' Rules. It remains the law in England and Wales, now supplemented by eight Codes of Practice: A, on stop and search; B, on entry and search of premises; C, on detention and questioning of non-terrorist suspects; D, on identification parades; E, on audio-recording interviews; F, on video-recording (this is not a statutory mode of recording, but if chosen, rules must be followed); G, with amendments to A necessary in light of S110 of the Serious Organized Crime and Police Act 2005; H, requirements for the detention, treatment and questioning of terrorism suspects. Since 2005, Wales has had its own codes. All these codes and other information and updates on implementation of PACE may be downloaded from the Home Office website (www.homeoffice.gov.uk/police/powers/pace-codes). Suspects who are detained by police must be informed of their legal rights, a process which includes a caution which must be given on arrest:

You do not have to say anything. But it may harm your defence if you do not mention when questioned something which you later rely on in Court. Anything you do say may be given in evidence.

Anyone who is thought to have a mental illness or an intellectual disability must have an 'appropriate adult' with him/her during any interview, as must a person under the age of 18; an appropriate adult may be a relative, but others are also eligible, including psychiatrists. The role of the appropriate adult is to give advice, support communication and ensure that the interview is conducted properly. In any case in which the defendant is incoherent, other than through drunkenness alone, the custody officer must summon a doctor. Code C sets out the full guidance for England.

If a doctor is involved in this procedure, the tasks are to make sure that the accused is fit to be interviewed at all and, if so, that the interview is carried out appropriately given the mental state of the accused. Advice may be given as to how mental abnormalities, such as delusions, thought disorder or amnesia, could make the interview unreliable. One feature which a frightened or abnormal suspect may exhibit is suggestibility, with the effect of agreeing too readily with leading questions. If this is an issue before, during or after an interview, a separate psychological opinion should be sought. Gudjonsson (1984a) has developed a scale of interrogative suggestibility which can improve objectivity in distinguishing between false confessors and deniers (Gudjonsson, 1984b; and see also chapter 6).

The prevalence of false confessions is not certainly known. The problem has been reported in many countries, usually from the perspective of case series. Gudjonsson and colleagues have advanced knowledge of prevalence considerably, and of risk factors for the occurrence of false confessions. In one survey of over 24,500 high school students from across seven European countries, they found 2,726 who had been interrogated by police; nearly 14% (375) reported having made false confessions to the police (Gudjonsson et al., 2009). Factors associated with falsely confessing were a history of substance abuse, of having been attacked or bullied and/or, for the boys only, of sexual abuse. A study of over 10,000 Icelandic college students showed that previous contact with the police may also be a factor; of those arrested just once, 3% reported making a false confession, but of those with more than one arrest, 12% reported false confessing (Gudjonsson et al., 2006). Among Icelandic prison inmates too, first estimates from self-report were about 12% (Sigurdsson and Gudjonsson, 2001), but later estimates suggested higher rates (Gudjonsson et al., 2008). The best estimate from North America is from a survey of over 600 police officers who reported their own estimates from experience, which yielded a lower figure of just under 5% (Kassin et al., 2007).

There is much reason to hypothesise that people with mental disorders would be particularly vulnerable to false confession – faulty perceptions, impaired judgment, anxiety, impulsivity, suggestibility, depression related guilt and poor self-control or ability to tolerate uncertainty are among the characteristics of many disorders which might logically be expected to distort the process. Despite this, there is little research on the nature and extent of the vulnerabilities of people with mental disorder. Gudjonsson et al. (2006), in the Icelandic student study, found that depression was significantly associated with making a false confession. Redlich et al. (2010) interviewed 1,249 offenders with mental illness across six sites in the USA, from California to New York, and asked them about their false confession and also their false guilty plea experiences. Over 80% of them had a schizophrenia spectrum disorder, bipolar disorder or major depression. Over a fifth (274, 22%) claimed to have made a false confession at some time, and over a third (453, 36.5%) a false guilty plea, albeit with considerable variation between sites (9–28%, 27–41% respectively). Eighty per cent of those reporting a false confession said that they had made one at least two or three times. These figures, therefore, tend to confirm that people with major mental illness are, indeed, more vulnerable to this problem.

Kassin, Gudjonsson, Redlich and others together provide a valuable overview from both North American and European perspectives on the nature and risks of what they term 'police-induced confessions' (Kassin et al., 2010). Examples of applications informed by this work are given in chapter 6.

Psychiatrist-Led Collaboration

Sometimes it is the psychiatrist, or other clinician, who needs to ask for police help with a particular individual. The guiding principles for the psychiatrist in such circumstances lie in the Declaration of Geneva (see Appendix 4) and requirements for confidentiality in the doctor – patient relationship, and when these may or should be breached. For England and Wales there is common and statute law which has to be considered too. The statute framework lies in the Human Rights Act 1998 and the Data Protection Act 1998, but there is much other legislation which covers specific issues ranging from the Abortion Act 1967 and its subsequent amendments and regulations, through public health legislation to more recent terrorist legislation. Exceptionally, the interests of people other than the presenting patient have to over-ride the interests of the patient him- or herself. The Crime and Disorder Act 1998 gives professional clinicians and/or the relevant healthcare organization some authority, and therefore protection, in this respect. Failure to take action in respect of continuing suspected offences would be bad psychiatric practice. Not the least of the functions of psychiatry is to prevent a person who already has the burden of mental disorder from harming him/herself further through harming others.

The doctor–patient relationship requires, however, that any reporting to the police of serious, imminent threat or actual harm is done with the utmost sensitivity and concern for the continuing welfare of the patient. It should only be done after consultation with the patient, unless the patient is genuinely unreachable. If the patient has friends or family members that s/he trusts, it is generally best to consult them too, providing the patient consents. During the course of discussion, the purpose of the report to the police should be made clear. Every step should be scrupulously documented in writing in the patient's clinical record. As with all crisis management in any psychiatric specialty, the aim is to bring about sufficient change in the balance of relationships between the patient, the environment and his/her potential victims that safety is restored. One possible outcome of police involvement is that allegations of dangerous behaviour can be thoroughly investigated and documented in ways beyond the skills or resource of psychiatry. Another is that, if the evidence supports concerns or allegations about dangerousness, legal steps may be taken to change the status of the potential victims where these are few and known, perhaps through legal injunction to bar the patient from access. The status of the patient may be changed in some way; if for example, a case is proven against him/her in court s/he may be bound into a treatment or supervision contract, or be detained in hospital. For those patients who retain some control over their behaviour, confirmation from the police and the court that they must accept some responsibility for it may be a catalyst for improvement in therapy.

All citizens have responsibilities to assist the police with relevant information when it is reasonable to suspect that a crime may have been committed. Patients, however, may disclose to a doctor that they have committed an offence and expect him or her to honour this confidence. Whether this is possible depends on a variety of subtle factors. Honouring such confidence is not in itself a criminal offence (Finch, 1984), whereas obstructing police enquiries could be. In court, the doctor may be forced to disclose information. It is worth noting that hearsay from a patient does not constitute evidence. It is not the same as a sworn statement made within the Judges' Rules. The Royal College of Psychiatrists (2010) has issued guidance on this.

The first step for the doctor after a patient's disclosure of offending is to assess the likely truth of the statement in the context of the patient's clinical state. Patients may occasionally lie to gain attention or defend against a sense of inadequacy; perhaps more commonly, their account may be unconscious fantasy or even a delusional memory. Debate with a colleague or peer group about whether the disclosure should be further shared may be the best first step in making

a decision on how to proceed. The debate should examine not only the likely truthfulness of the disclosure, but also its relevance to the current problem, and its potential for being repeated. Medical defence organizations are always prepared to offer further support or advice for doctors in such circumstances. Other formal responsibilities include informing the local police and the Home Office (or other appropriate government department) when a patient on a restriction order under the MHA 1983, life licence or parole fails to report as agreed, or 'gives cause for concern'. In addition to the Royal College of Psychiatrists' guidance on confidentiality, already mentioned, it is worth being familiar with MAPPA 2012 (multi-agency public protection arrangements), available on the Ministry of Justice website (http://www.justice.gov.uk/offenders/multi-agency-public-protection-arrangements).

If a case is reported to the police, contact should be made with the most senior police officer available, the continuing interest of the psychiatrist made clear to that police officer and, where possible, the clinician involvement maintained. At first, the police may be highly sceptical and require some corroborative evidence that it is worth spending resources to pursue the case further. It is important for the psychiatrist to assist the patient to obtain a legal adviser if s/he does not already have one, and to liaise with that legal adviser during the period in which the police are making enquiries. If the patient should be remanded in custody, one or more visits to the patient during that period are valuable in helping the patient to understand that s/he has not been abandoned, and in gathering further information for reports that may be required. A couple of case examples may be useful.

Case 25.1

Mr A had already been convicted of several offences of arson, and had previously been under a restricted hospital order. After a long period of stability, he was free of all orders, but continuing with voluntary support and supervision. His situation, however, changed substantially when his girlfriend left him. Soon after this, he destroyed five separate properties by fire within a day or two, although harming no one. Two days later, at a routine outpatient appointment, he told a junior psychiatrist about this. The consultant was contacted immediately, and came to see the patient. After discussion, the patient agreed that the police had to be informed. This was done in his presence in the hospital consulting room. The police later interviewed him, and charged him with arson. He was seen regularly during the remand period. He was found guilty on five counts of arson, but sentence was set aside in favour of a new hospital order with restrictions. Back within this framework, he started to make good progress again.

Case 25.2

Mr B, with several criminal convictions for serious violence, sought help for his aggression, but also bragged about it. On one occasion, unusually, he came drunk to his outpatient appointment. He suddenly threatened to kill his doctor. He stood up, apparently to do so, but displaced his aggression on to a nurse who had just arrived to assist, knocking him to the ground and injuring him. Mr B then turned his attention to the wall, beating it so savagely that he broke two carpal bones in his hand before accepting sufficient medication to calm him. He was admitted to hospital for 48 hours. The nurse considered that assault charges should be pressed. Mr B's consultant psychiatrist considered that it did not seem to be against his long-term interests to be interviewed by the police about his behaviour. The consultant then discussed this with Mr B, explaining the decision to invite the police to interview him, and that charges might follow. At the same time, Mr B was reassured that he would receive all support through the court proceedings.

The police were initially reluctant to pursue the matter, but after a written report from the psychiatrist, did so. Mr B was given both the report to the police and the subsequent report to the court to read for himself. At the magistrates' court, he was convicted of actual bodily harm. A small fine was imposed and a compensation order made. The patient expressed relief: 'I know where I am this time', and during further treatment began to express interest in whether the nurse was receiving the compensation instalments, and, then, whether he had recovered. This was the first indication of concern that he had ever shown for one of his victims.

Any hospital will benefit from its staff having discussions with the police from time to time about a range of issues. These may include the level and management of violence in the hospital, policies on theft and policies on absconding patients. There should be no hesitation about this on the part of the hospital authorities and the medical profession. The police are uniquely well-placed to advise on many aspects of crime and violence prevention. In exceptional circumstances, they may provide emergency assistance within the hospital if requested to do so. Furthermore, it is now expected under MAPPA arrangements that any healthcare organization responsible for assessing and treating people will have a memorandum of co-operation agreed so that a framework for safe and appropriate management of individual cases is already in place.

Social Worker-Led Collaboration

Another point of contact between police and psychiatrist lies in case conferences called by social services departments to review the progress of children at risk and other victims of domestic violence. The doctors who attend these conferences are frequently general practitioners, but they may be psychiatrists treating either the potential victim or the potential aggressor. There is a good deal of sensitivity about, indeed resistance to, the transfer of information about the behaviour of a patient/client between professionals in different disciplines in such case conferences,

but, even though there is a real risk of information being mishandled on occasion, the need for everybody to be fully informed in such a dangerous area is paramount. The Royal College of Psychiatrists' (2010) guidance on confidentiality provides a useful framework for good practice here.

Contractual Work With the Police

There are no psychiatrists who work for the police in a full time capacity, but contractual work may be undertaken. The possibility of being contracted to provide services for custody units has already been mentioned. From time to time, police ask for assistance in detecting crime, although where this happens in any substantial way this is more likely to be offered by psychologists. David Canter has led this field in the UK, from a background of architectural psychology (e.g. Canter and Youngs, 2008, 2009). Gisli Gudjonsson, a clinical psychologist and formerly a policeman, has done pioneering work with the police on police interviewing (e.g. Gudjonsson 1993, 2000; Gudjonsson et al., 2008). Other work with police has included support during sieges and training.

Sieges

The psychiatrist's role in police run sieges is very limited. The police are fully responsible for the conduct of the operation, and any negotiation with hostage takers is done by specially trained police officers. Psychiatrists may be asked for an evaluation of the state of mind of the hostage taker(s), and must generally come to a view on very limited information. They may be allowed to listen to conversations between the police negotiator and the hostage taker, and, at most, give questions to the negotiator which may help elucidate this. On the few occasions when a siege involves a hostage taker with undoubted mental illness or otherwise compromised mental state, in the UK at least, the hostage taker is generally acting alone and in a domestic setting. Such sieges are often over quickly and rarely last longer than 48 hours; it is unusual for direct involvement of a psychiatrist at the scene. At first sight paradoxically, those sieges for which psychiatrists have been called to attend generally involve several individuals, commonly with political motives, who, at least at the start of the episode are in a state of normal mental health. Problems with which the psychiatrist may be able to help arise because these situations tend to be enduring, in which case the mental health of the hostage takers, hostages and even police negotiators may be compromised as the pressure builds. The hostages, as generally least prepared for the situation, are most vulnerable to development of symptoms, and indeed some may have had physical or mental health problems before capture. Guidance is always to recommend seeking to negotiate sick hostages out of the stronghold as a matter of priority, never to send in anyone to treat them within the stronghold, and very rarely to supply any medication. Once in the stronghold, the use of any such medication is out of clinical control, and even delivering standard, regular prescription medications could lead to dangerous misuse. Stress, both from the inherent anxiety of the situation, but also from lack of sleep may affect any participant in the process; within the stronghold, uncertain nutrition may result in health problems for either hostages or hostage takers. There has been very little research in this field, so most advice must be offered on a pragmatic basis. Attempts to use speech samples to measure changing stress responses have not proved successful (Gunn and Gudjonsson, 1988).

Training

Psychiatrists may be asked to assist with police training. The most commonly needed assistance in this regard is in the recognition and management of mental disorders and intellectual disabilities during interview and custody. Occasionally more specialist training has been required – for example to police negotiators in training. In this latter case, each course included a half day with a psychiatrist who discussed the medical problems arising at a siege, and their implications for negotiation.

Psychiatrist to the Police Officer

Police officers may be referred as patients, by their internal medical services or through ordinary National Health Service arrangements. There are special points to be considered. First there is the 'macho' image which a predominantly male and 'tough' profession gives itself. This means that it is especially courageous for a policeman to seek psychiatric help; many who need it fail to seek it, and those who do may put their job in jeopardy because of the attitudes of their colleagues. To many in the police force, psychiatric distress or disorder equates with weakness and unreliability, yet police work is acknowledged as being stressful (Ainsworth and Pease, 1987). Officers may be overworked, and often have to deal with psychologically disturbing events. They are sometimes attacked, injured, captured, or see a colleague die and, as a result, are at risk of developing post-traumatic stress disorders. Untreated, these disorders may lead to inefficiency, time off work for somatic symptoms and/or, on occasions, to strange, damaging and even criminal behaviour. Senior officers may expect reports about police-patients. Whether it is right to provide such reports should be discussed with the patient; the nature of the referral, and thus the 'clinical contract' with the referrer and with the patient, will determine the correct response in most cases. Difficult psychiatric decisions may include advising an officer to change his/her work, either within the police force, or away from it. Usually, however, (and senior staff may need to be educated to this fact) a responsible, effective police officer can generally be

restored to health and work, even if he/she requires sick leave and treatment for an affective illness or anxiety state. The more crippling psychiatric disorders such as schizophrenia, severe personality disorder and dementia are not compatible with police work.

PEOPLE WITH MENTAL DISORDER IN PRISON

The transformation of prisoners into patients has never done more than relieve jails of the obviously disordered. They have always had to cope with the residual problem of the prisoner whose degree of disorder, though marked enough to interfere with discipline and communication, is not sufficient to satisfy the psychiatric criteria of the day (Walker and McCabe, 1973).

A much later statement of purpose from HM Prison Service for England and Wales calls for prisoners to be looked after with humanity within the over-arching requirement for them to be kept in custody. One reason given for this is so that they may lead law-abiding and useful lives, both in custody and after release. The prison service acknowledges that the delivery of high quality healthcare services, especially mental healthcare, has an important role in this, placing special emphasis on continuity of care and safe management through 'vulnerability points', for example at times of arrival into or departure from prison (Ministry of Justice, 2006).

Delivery of prison healthcare is far from standard internationally. Dressing and Salize (2009) highlight the differences across 24 of the countries in the European Union. The frameworks within which such services are delivered differ to an extent even between the constituent countries of the UK. Although, technically, England and Wales now share an offender management service, even there, some of the documents we will cite have been redrafted for Wales, to try and reflect any unique conditions in demand for, or availability of, services. In some respects, this is one of the many 'parochial areas' in forensic psychiatry, and yet the tensions between managing prisons and delivering healthcare constitute common ground across the world. The section focuses on England and Wales, and sometimes just England, with examples of development through evidence, lobbying, debate and evolving policies; this differs from the USA, where change tends to follow from litigation, and class action litigation in particular (Metzner, 2009). Background data, however, have been drawn from anywhere in the world where these issues have been studied, and we suspect that the cycles of debate and change in England and Wales will be at least recognizable elsewhere.

Although our focus has to be healthcare in prisons, and there is insufficient space to explore in depth the wider qualities of prisons and concepts of imprisonment, it is important for healthcare staff working in prisons to have some grasp of these issues, and vital for anyone commissioning or setting up services. Two criminology-led books provide useful reviews and sources of information on these more general aspects. One, *The Effects of Imprisonment* (Liebling and Maruna, 2005), highlights just how little is known about the impact of such confinement. As places of mere punishment, it is arguable that prisons perform well; they are effective in depriving people of liberty and most of the opportunities that are generally seen as essential to the human condition including autonomy, sense of personal security, sexual choices, work, and therefore, to a large extent, sense of identity other than that imposed by the institution. As places of reform, they do not have a good record, with recidivism rates after imprisonment high; in England and Wales 47–55% of adults leaving custody re-offend within 12 months according to police national computer figures (Ministry of Justice, 2009). The negative side-effects of imprisonment on health are much less clear. For sure the association between poor health, disease and imprisonment is strong, but research sequencing the relationships is not. Qualitative work with offenders suggests that the risks must be high, but good longitudinal quantitative work is rare (Walker et al., in press). The second multi-authored book, conceived by criminologists, is the *Handbook on Prisons*. This covers a wider range of material, and is a useful introduction to the world of prisons for anyone who may work there (Jewkes, 2007). Not to be confused with this, *The Prisons Handbook* is an annual guide to each of the prisons in England and Wales, and also a source of advice, new reports, regulations and articles on contemporary issues (www.prisonshandbook.co.uk).

A Brief History of Healthcare and Its Limitations for People With Mental Disorder in Prison

The physical and mental healthcare needs of prisoners have been an important consideration since the early development of the penal system in England. One of the first critics of the prison environment and its effect on health was the social reformer, John Howard. He had himself been imprisoned in France, in 1756, and after his return to England, and his appointment in 1773 as High Sheriff of Bedford, he inspected Bedford Gaol. He highlighted neglect and lack of interest by jailers, and a sense of moral decay and idleness pervading the prison. He then toured other English jails and gave evidence to the House of Commons, which resulted in the Act for Preserving the Health of Prisoners in Gaol 1774, obliging local justices to appoint a resident medical officer to each jail (Sim, 1990) 'to improve the sanitary state of prisons and ... the health of the prisoners'. In 1775, he started a tour of prisons in France, Belgium, Holland, Italy, Germany, Spain, Portugal, Denmark, Sweden, Russia, Switzerland, Malta, Asia Minor and Turkey, and soon instituted a second tour of English prisons to test

implementation of the Gaol Acts. His resultant books are, *The State of Prisons in England and Wales, With an Account of Some Foreign Prisons*, first published in 1777 and *An Account of the Principal Lazarettos in Europe*, 1787. Both are still available in facsimile. Among his many concerns was an unsuitable population mix within the prisons, contributing to an unhealthy atmosphere whereby the most experienced offenders were housed with children, petty thieves and the mentally disordered, the latter often unintentionally providing a source of amusement for other prisoners. In spite of his legislative success, however, healthcare standards in prisons have often remained subject to widespread criticism. The rest of this brief historical account will focus on healthcare in prisons; for those interested in a wider history of prisons in England and Wales, Edwards and Hurley (2002) provide an introduction and sources on behalf of the Prison Headquarters Library.

During the nineteenth century, concerns about the appropriateness of prison as a suitable environment for the mentally ill took the form of attempts to remove some of the most obviously mentally disordered to hospitals, first to a separate wing for criminal lunatics at the Bethlem Royal Hospital in London, and then to Broadmoor, which was built specially (see also chapter 24). These initiatives did not herald an end to the detention of people with mental disorder in prison, however, as, simultaneously, special provision was being created within the prison system for those who were not to be transferred to hospital. Thus, in 1864, the group of mentally disordered prisoners at Dartmoor Prison was transferred to Millbank Penitentiary in London and, in 1897, Parkhurst Prison was designated to house prisoners assessed as 'unfit for ordinary penal discipline because of some mental instability other than insanity' (cited in Gunn, 1985). In 1895, the Report of the Gladstone Committee recommended that all prison medical officers should have experience in the subject of lunacy, thus acknowledging the likelihood of mental disorder remaining a significant problem in prisons (Prisons Committee, 1895).

Throughout the nineteenth century, prison régimes developed a focus on the restoration of the 'moral fortitude' of offenders. These took the form of introducing vocational instruction to aid prisoners to gain honest employment on release, religious instruction to encourage repentance before God, and the operation of silent régimes to prevent offenders morally corrupting each other through association. Prison medical officers contributed to these moralistic régimes with a range of crude techniques, including the sanctioning of cold baths, electric shocks, strait-jackets and dietary restrictions as punishments to effect control over refractory prisoners and those suspected of feigning mental illness. Medical interventions became part of the very fabric of prison life, whereby:

Prison doctors not only were caught up in, but also contributed to the debates about the philosophy and practice of punishment. The disciplinary strategies which lay at the heart of penalty were legitimized by the interventions which Medical Officers made (Sim, 1990).

As the twentieth century unfolded, prison medical officers expanded their role and influence beyond the prison itself, most notably with the provision of psychiatric reports to courts, leading to an acceptance of the practice of prisoners being remanded into custody for a period of medical observation. Alongside reports to courts, prison medical officers also published papers in scientific journals about criminality and mental disorder. In the 1920s and 1930s the medical officer of Birmingham Prison, Hamblin-Smith, emphasized both the importance of multi-agency work and recommended the establishment of treatment units within prisons, although his subsequent trial of work there led him to conclude:

There are the strongest objections to combining the ideas of punishment and medical treatment: the subject is certain to look upon the treatment as part of the punishment (Hamblin-Smith, 1934).

In 1939, the visiting psychotherapist to Wormwood Scrubs, Hubert, and a prison medical officer, East, extended this experiment there to include, but also go beyond, psychoanalytic methods. This led them to recommend the establishment of a special penal institution with a psychiatric emphasis to ascertain the value of psychological treatment in the 'prevention and cure' of crime (East and Hubert, 1939). It was not until 1962 that these recommendations were fulfilled with the opening of Grendon Underwood therapeutic community prison. This and other therapeutic communities within and outside prisons are considered in more detail in chapter 16.

When the National Health Service (NHS) was established in the UK in 1948, prison-based healthcare remained separate, answerable to the Home Office. From primary care to inpatient psychiatric treatment, almost all of it was delivered 'in-house'. Doctors were directly employed to the post of prison medical officer, with their own hierarchy and pay scales, and the few other healthcare staff were almost all nurses, or prison officers who had had some training in healthcare skills. In the latter part of the twentieth century, the Prison Medical Service, by then renamed the Prison Health Service, was often criticized publicly. This was variously for the numbers of suicides in prisons, allegedly inappropriate use of psychotropic medication as a disciplinary aid for refractory prisoners and poor standards of care overall (e.g. Scraton and Gordon, 1984; Ralli, 1994) and for being 'invisible' and lacking any external accountability. This was considered to be due largely to its separation from the mainstream NHS (Smith, 1984). The British Medical Association (BMA), in a brief report of 2001, weighed in:

the prison medical service has been in an acute crisis for some time.

This paper criticised shortage of resources, lack of appropriately qualified staff, interference from prison governors in clinical decision-making, professional isolation and a lack of training opportunities for doctors and other healthcare staff in prisons (BMA, 2001).

Criticism of healthcare standards in prisons also came from Her Majesty's Inspectorate of Prisons (HMIP) (1996). This is an independent body which reports, now directly to the Ministry of Justice, on all aspects of prison life in England and Wales (see also below). Two studies distilled findings from inspections of the extent and quality of healthcare across a number of prisons, appraising quality and scope against a set of quality of care standards drawn up by the inspectorate (Reed and Lyne, 1997, 2000). The 1997 study focused on 19 prisons and reported wide variation in healthcare quality across the sites, with core problems common to a number of prisons. None of the prisons had at this stage conducted the required health needs assessment exercise; in nine of the 19 establishments, primary care services were being provided by inadequately trained doctors; none of the prisons provided a full multi-disciplinary mental health team. The main recommendation was that the provision of healthcare be disaggregated from the custodial mechanisms of the prison and taken over by the Department of Health.

The 2000 study focused specifically on the quality of 13 prison inpatient care units for the mentally ill. Most were criticized for their unsatisfactory physical environment; levels of cleanliness and physical layouts were considered unacceptable, hampering effective observation. With regard to staffing, no unit was overseen by a doctor who had completed specialist psychiatric training and under a quarter of the nursing staff or healthcare officers had had any mental health training. Doctors and nurses constituted the whole of the mental health team in most of the prisons, with little input from allied disciplines. Impoverished régimes were common, with prisoners unlocked, on average, for only 3.5 hours a day with long, unbroken periods of confinement at night. Time out of cell offered limited therapeutic, purposeful or diversional activities. Further concerns were expressed about the use of seclusion, high use of which appeared to correlate closely to periods of restricted staff availability. When transfer to NHS facilities was agreed, waits for suitable placements were protracted (Reed and Lyne, 2000).

In 2006, a process of transfer of responsibility of healthcare delivery from Home Office to Department of Health was completed. In 2007, the chief inspector further reviewed mental healthcare in prisons. Whilst acknowledging that its quality and extent had improved since the instigation of the formal partnership between the NHS and HM Prison Service in 1999, it also noted continuing gaps in provision, with unmet need, poorly developed models of primary mental healthcare, and failures to recognize mental health needs, or to consider adequately the specific needs of women or black and minority ethnic (BME) prisoners. It was also realistic about mainstream healthcare failures:

When mental health in-reach teams rode to the rescue of embattled prison staff they found a scale of need which they had neither foreseen nor planned for. Four out of five mental health in-reach teams felt that they were unable to respond adequately to the range of need.

....[in prison] need will always remain greater than the capacity, unless mental health and community services outside prison are improved and people appropriately directed to them: before, instead of and after custody (HMIP, 2007).

In the same year, the Royal College of Psychiatrists (2007a) issued guidance for psychiatrists on delivering psychiatric services in adult prisons.

Current Prison Healthcare Policy for England and Wales

In 1997, the Health Advisory Committee for the Prison Service took up the concept of equivalence of healthcare for people while they were in prison. For people with mental disorders, this meant that there was an expectation that, in prisons as in the community, most mental ill-health could be dealt with at primary care level and that specialist mental healthcare should be provided by multidisciplinary teams, using the Care Programme Approach (CPA) (Department of Health, 1999e,f) as a mechanism through which to plan, deliver and co-ordinate care between prison and community.

A formal shift in policy direction to achieve this equivalence of treatment between prisons and the NHS was heralded in 1999 with the publication of *The Future Organization of Prison Healthcare* (HM Prison Service/National Health Service Executive, 1999). The document was the report of a joint working group from these organizations after deliberations on the issues raised by *Patient or Prisoner?* (HMIP, 1996). The problems associated with providing healthcare in prison settings were revisited:

[healthcare in prisons] is often reactive rather than proactive, over-medicalized and only exceptionally based on systematic health needs assessment... [with an] over reliance on healthcare beds within prisons and a medicalized model of care (HM Prison Service/National Health Service Executive 1999).

The group embraced a public health agenda, acknowledging that good healthcare and health promotion in prisons should help individuals to function to their maximum potential on release and, as others before them, that this might assist in reducing offending, and also longer term morbidity in a high risk sector of the general public. If this resulted in medium- to long-term reductions in demand on the NHS, then it would be cost effective too. It was accepted that the prison service and the NHS needed to adopt 'a more collaborative and co-ordinated approach' to providing healthcare in prisons, supported by a formal duty of partnership. This fell short of the recommendations of earlier reports which overwhelmingly supported the adoption of prison healthcare services wholly within the NHS, but it was argued that, at least this pragmatic approach to managing change would retain the expertise of both parties in what would be a complex work programme. In 2002, it was announced that budgetary responsibility for healthcare in public sector prisons would be transferred from the prison service to the Department of Health, with full commissioning responsibility for prison-based services to be devolved to primary care trusts in stages; this process was completed by April 2006. Prisoners have wide ranging health needs, so physicians, venereologists, gynaecologists, opticians, dentists and a host of others may hold clinics in prisons. Our main concern here, however, is with mental health services.

A separate line of documents set out the more specific developmental needs for mental healthcare: *Changing the Outlook* (Department of Health/HM Prison Service, 2001) which charged prison-based services with the need to develop in line with wider NHS policy and the *National Service Framework for Mental Health* (Department of Health, 1999i). The need for improved identification of mental disorder at reception and the adoption of a community-care service model was noted, the latter encouraging mental health outreach work on the residential wings of prisons rather than heavy reliance on medically orientated inpatient care. Improved health promotion in prisons, improved staff training and peer support schemes were also emphasized. The importance of a long-term, comprehensive approach with most individuals was underscored in the guidelines published as the *Offender Mental Healthcare Pathway* (Department of Health/NIMHE, 2005). These guidelines provided recommended interventions and key objectives at each stage of an offender's contact with the criminal justice system, based on reviews of the available literature and innovative clinical practice. The stated aim was to provide 'end to end management of offenders' mental health needs', in line with the objectives of the National Offender Management Service (NOMS) which has integrated the prison and probation systems (Home Office, 2004b). All this undoubted good intent would be more likely to be effective if prison budgets were not subject to year on year cuts while the resident population continues to expand. So, what is the extent of mental ill health among prisoners?

Prevalence of Mental Disorder in Prisons

Fazel and Danesh (2002) conducted a systematic review of interview studies of the prevalence of major psychiatric disorders among people in prison in western countries and published between January 1966 and January 2001. They identified 62 studies from 12 countries across Europe, North America and Australasia which, between them, included 18,530 (81%) men and 4,260 women. Overall, remarkably similar proportions of pretrial and sentenced prisoners had a psychotic illness (279/7,193, 4% male detainees and 309/8,854, 3% sentenced men; 86/2,160, 4% female detainees and 33/804, 4% sentenced women). Higher proportions of prisoners had a major depressive illness, but again similar among pretrial and sentenced people (men: 312/3,635, 9%; 431/3,996, 11% respectively; women: 212/1,269, 11%; 138/1,229, 12%). The other major category considered was personality disorder, examined in 28 of the studies; the proportions of prisoners suffering such disorders were much higher again, but once more there was little difference by prisoner type (men: 1709/3,717, 46%; 3,404/7,080, 48%; women: 348/1,713, 20%; 283/1,334, 21%). For psychosis and depression, the findings were remarkably similar between countries. Extrapolated onto actual prison populations, these figures would mean that there must be over 12,000 prisoners in England and Wales alone with serious mental illness. In the USA, a conservative estimate would be of over a quarter of a million.

Sirdifield et al. (2009) reported an update of their own previous systematic review, conducted at the same time as that of Fazel and Danesh, which they say includes 18 new studies, although in fact some appear to be new but based on data already included in the earlier work and one focuses on homicide offenders, some of whom were prisoners, but some of whom almost certainly were not. They found similar estimates of prevalence of mental illness and that prevalence of personality disorder was more variable. Also, where Fazel and Danesh had chosen not to consider substance misuse disorders in their review on the basis that these are likely to differ substantially in the base populations between countries, Sirdifield et al. did so, and drew out substantial comorbidity rates of 40–90%. Fazel and Seewald (2012) updated the earlier review, now including 33,588 prisoners worldwide and confirming similar rates of mental disorder.

Singleton et al. (1998b), for the Office of National Statistics (ONS), surveyed all 131 prisons in England and Wales in operation at the time of the survey. Overall, 3,142 prisoners were interviewed, an 88% participation rate of those selected. In a two-phase design, all prisoners were interviewed by lay interviewers using the Clinical Interview Schedule-Revised (CIS-R) to identify neurotic disorder, the AUDIT questionnaire problem drinking, the SCID-II screening instrument for personality disorder and a tool, developed during their previous private household studies, to elicit drug dependence and self-harm ideation. One in five participants was interviewed by a clinician using the Schedules for Neuropsychiatry (SCAN) and the full SCID-II to detect psychosis and personality disorder respectively. Data from the SCAN interviews were used to identify factors in the lay interviews that were indicative of psychosis to allow a calculation of 'probable psychosis' across the whole sample. Overall, the survey indicated that nine out of every ten prisoners had at least one of five disorder categories: neurosis, psychosis, personality disorder,

alcohol abuse or drug dependence (Singleton et al., 1998). Of additional interest here is that all types of prisoners returned high rates of symptoms such as sleep problems and worry. Rates of neurotic disorders were high. In common with findings from general household studies, these were higher among women prisoners than their male peers, and, here, for both men and women, rates for remand prisoners were higher than those for the sentenced population. Seventeen per cent of male remand prisoners and 21% of female remand prisoners were diagnosed with a current neurotic depressive episode; 11% of both male and female remand prisoners were experiencing generalised anxiety disorder. Twelve per cent of male remand and 23% of female remand prisoners reported having experienced suicidal thoughts in the past week.

This survey also reported high rates of substance abuse among prisoners, with over 85% of respondents reporting smoking, hazardous drinking or drug dependence in the year before imprisonment. There were correspondingly high rates of substance abuse co-existing with other types of mental disorder. For those assessed as hazardous drinkers, the proportions with two or more other mental disorders ranged from 59% of male sentenced to 87% of female remand prisoners. Over 75% of all prisoners who were drug dependent had two or more other mental disorders.

In an earlier, representative national survey of sentenced (Gunn et al., 1991a,b) and pretrial prisoners (Maden et al., 1995; Brooke et al., 1996) across England and Wales, service needs were assessed in addition to diagnoses. Conclusions were that most treatment needs could be met within prisons, with about 10% of sentenced male prisoners likely to require this level of service input, as would about twice the proportion of the women; a further 5% of men and 7% of women were estimated to need therapeutic community involvement. Three per cent of the men (more of the older than the younger ones) and only a slightly lower proportion of the women were considered to require transfer to an NHS hospital, including most (88%) with psychosis. About 5% of the men (9% of women) were thought to need further assessment. Proportions needing transfer were higher for the pretrial prisoners. Nine per cent of the remand men, for example, were thought to need transfer to the NHS, 18% prison-based healthcare, 14% treatment in a therapeutic community and, reflecting high rates of substance misuse, 15% motivational interviewing.

A wholly independent study by Birmingham et al. (1996), of adult pretrial men in one English prison, yielded rather similar findings of need. Three per cent required immediate transfer to a psychiatric hospital, including 70% of those with psychosis. A further 20% of the total sample was judged to require outpatient referral to psychiatric services whilst in prison and 6% required assessment and management as an inpatient in the prison healthcare centre.

One of us (Senior, 2005) undertook a study in a large English local prison for adult men to establish, from their clinical presentation, the service level needs of those with any type of mental health problem. For most of those with needs for treatment for mental illness, this could be done within prison at a level of service analogous to primary care (55%); a further 35% were thought to require intervention from services analogous to community mental health services and the remaining 10% were considered to require more intensive input. This last might be achievable in a prison mental health unit, but some would require transfer to an NHS hospital under mental health legislation. These figures, however, take no account of the substantial need for help with substance dependence and/or hazardous use of substances; if all these received appropriate treatment, then two-thirds of the population of the prison would require intervention from specialist substance misuse services.

An important problem in interpreting much of the prevalence work, and even some of the needs work, rests in its cross-sectional nature. Aside from some separation between pretrial and sentenced prisoners, it is not clear *when* it is best to assess people from the perspective of need. Clearly an initial screen for life-threatening conditions, including suicidal ideation, is essential, but the very few studies that have taken a longitudinal perspective suggest that there is a tendency for pretrial prisoners to stabilize and even improve (Harding and Zimmerman, 1989; Andersen et al., 2000; Taylor et al., 2010), although one US study found that anxiety increased (Oleski, 1977) and one Swiss study found that non-substance related insomnia is likely to be chronic (Elger, 2004). Men serving long-term sentences seem to adjust (e.g. Bolton et al., 1976; Sapsford, 1978). These few studies, however, constitute about the sum of longitudinal work with prisoners in ordinary locations. A few more examine change over time, but usually according to specific aspects of imprisonment, such as overcrowding or isolation (Walker et al., in press).

There is a paucity of evidence, too, regarding the efficacy and suitability of different treatment modalities when offered within prison, except possibly with regard to treatment of personality disorder in therapeutic community conditions (see chapter 16). Brooker et al. (2003) undertook a review of the effectiveness literature on routine mental health interventions for prisoners. They identified just six studies which detailed the results of prison-based treatment for people with psychotic disorders. No studies were found of treatment for prisoners with neurotic or stress-related disorders, despite such people constituting such a large group in prisons.

There are undoubted difficulties in conducting randomised controlled trials (RCTs) of treatment in prisons. These include concern about the reality of un-coerced consent to participation as well as possibly impaired capacity in the event of more serious disorder. Resources are so very scarce in prison, that it is understandably not high on the list of priorities of prison staff to be supporting such work, nevertheless, some of us have completed a successful pilot of an RCT; it can be done, but it is so much harder than in routine clinical practice. A number of recommendations for future research priorities in prisons have been made to help overcome the difficulties (Rennie et al., 2009). These include the development of prison specific measures for routine use by staff there, the identification of a range of potential models of prison mental health service delivery and exploration of the relationship between different models of service delivery and prisoner outcome and the systematic evaluation of mental health services in prisons using standardized outcome measures.

Mental Health Services in Prisons

Assessing health needs on reception into custody

The traditional time for identification of mental disorder in a prisoner is on reception into prison. The reception area is busy, and a lot of tasks have to be completed with each person under great pressure of both time and numbers. Most prisoners arrive in prison in the early evening, following a court appearance earlier that day. The timing and environment of reception is not satisfactory for any comprehensive assessment of health needs. Nevertheless, health screening is essential. The first week of custody is especially risky in terms of suicide (Shaw et al., 2004). In England and Wales, screening is usually now done by primary care nursing staff (who may or may not have specific mental health training), using a structured, validated instrument which was developed partly in response to research which demonstrated that reception screening was poor at identifying mental illness (Birmingham et al., 2000). This requires yes/no answers to a small number of questions as being indicative of requiring further assessment for possible mental illness. For women, a history of self-harm and previous prescription of psychotropic medication were found to be good indicators of serious mental illness; for men, a history of psychiatric treatment and a charge of homicide were also significant indicators (Parsons et al., 2001; Gavin et al., 2003; Carson et al., 2003). Screening at reception after transfer from another prison is usually more superficial; prisoners' medical records are supposed to be transferred with them, but are often delayed in the system, so continuity of care is therefore heavily reliant upon the diligence of healthcare staff.

Even with structured screening, evidence suggests that many of those in need of further assessment and possible intervention for mental health problems are still not being recognized. As part of their thematic review on mental health, HMIP compared the proportion of people identified as having a potential problem at reception with indication of mental health problems on a self-rating scale, the General Health Questionnaire 12 (GHQ12) (Goldberg, 1992). Just 17% of a sample of 237 prisoners disclosed a psychiatric history at reception, but of the 220 (93%) of them who completed the GHQ, 50% scored levels that indicated primary or secondary mental health needs (HMIP, 2007). It is difficult to know what to make of these findings, however.

They are probably not measuring equivalent problems. In a study employing multiple measures of mental state among prisoners, some of us found that a standard research interview of mental state revealed less 'caseness' than a standard self-rating schedule, although all of the interview cases were subsumed in the self-rated group (Taylor et al., 2010). Self-rating scales seem more likely to pick up general levels of distress which are important to the individual but not the same as mental disorder.

A further issue is that the majority of prisoners in most western countries are likely to have been abusing alcohol, illicit drugs or both. Both toxicity and withdrawal affect mental state. Where either is suspected on reception, then a further mental state screening must be done when these acute problems have passed. Some prisons have a 3-week detoxification programme, albeit providing little more than chemical support for the detox. It would make sense to repeat the health screen at the end of this period.

Meeting the mental health needs of prisoners at primary care level

Primary care should be the foundation stone of healthcare provision in prison, as in the wider community (Department of Health/HM Prison Service, 2001). Roles incorporate identification and management of sub-clinical problems, including stress-related problems, treatment of common mental health problems, and both gate-keeping and facilitation of referral to specialist mental health services when clinically indicated. In spite of this, in England and Wales at least, there is evidence that primary care services in prisons are not yet operating effectively in this role. Pearce et al. (2004), in a national study of doctors working in prisons, found that, although 58% of respondents dealt with mentally ill prisoners, only one-third reported having had accredited training or a recognized qualification in psychiatry. Despite the multiplicity of health problems presented by prisoners, most could be treated within primary care (Senior, 2005), providing that its delivery is further developed in prison.

Primary care provision is still variable across the prison estate; some establishments are served by locum/temporary doctors but at others, local general practitioners undertake the work. Prisoners have higher consultation rates than members of the wider community, partly due to a lack of access to methods of self help and simple remedies, and partly due to higher rates of illness (Williamson, 2006; Marshall et al., 2001). In England and Wales, equivalence with primary care mental health services outside prisons would include improved health promotion, access to self-help literature, incorporation of good practice guidelines, for example National Institute of Clinical Excellence (NICE) guidelines for the treatment of common problems, including depression, anxiety and self-harm (e.g. NICE, 2004, 2009, 2011, and updates). It would also entail continuity of care between prison and community-based services. The Sainsbury Centre for Mental Health (2006) completed a scoping exercise in this area. The Royal College of General Practitioners and the Royal Pharmaceutical Society (2011) have published a useful guide to prescribing medications for prisoners for pain, epilepsy and a range of psychiatric conditions, which takes account of the higher than average misuse of medication in such a setting, not simply by the individual for whom it is prescribed taking too much or too little, but the potential that 'in possession' medication creates for trading and for bullying. Nevertheless, they note that every prison should have a policy with regard to medication generally, and in possession medication specifically, the latter, at best, providing an important form of autonomy for those prisoners whose risk assessment in this regard suggests that they would be able to cope responsibly and safely.

Community care interventions in prison – mental health in-reach services

Effort to replicate in prisons the wider shift away from inpatient-centred treatment towards community-based services means a reduction in beds in the prison healthcare centre, or hospital wing, in favour of development of ordinary location, wing-based services, using a community mental health team model. Realignment of services also means development of day-care services. Prison mental health 'in-reach' teams are expected to provide improved planning of treatment throughout imprisonment and into the post discharge phase, adopting the Care Programme Approach (CPA). It was assumed that, in England and Wales, teams could thus cover about 5,000 prisoners at any one time. Prisoners with severe and enduring mental illness were to be the early focus of intervention, with a longer term intention to extend the benefits to anyone with mental health problems, regardless of severity.

Evidence is emerging, however, that in-reach teams frequently struggle to achieve even the early goals (Sainsbury Centre for Mental Health, 2006). Overall, whilst 80% of prisons now have operational in-reach teams, usually nurse-led, only 19% of those teams considered that they could actually meet prisoner need (HMIP, 2007). More specifically, a study was carried out for the English Department of Health, using standardised research diagnostic tools to examine in-reach contact (Shaw et al., 2009). This found that, of prisoners assessed as being in a current episode of a major mental illness (schizophrenia, other functional psychotic illness or major depressive disorder), only 35% were subsequently assessed by in-reach mental health professionals within their first month in custody; prisoners with psychotic illness were more likely to be accepted into in-reach caseloads than those with major depression. Past contact with mental health services significantly increased the likelihood of receiving treatment. In the study prisons, examination of the cases accepted for in-reach care revealed that, on average, slightly under a third of them had a severe and enduring mental illness; the remainder had a diagnosis of personality disorder, were substance abusers, had mild to moderate mental health problems or undetermined needs or were considered to be at risk of self-harm. So, evidence is that, although prison in-reach services have been established in most prisons, and multidisciplinary involvement has improved, there is still much to be achieved to meet the new service ideals.

Inpatient care and transfer under mental health legislation

With changes in the locus of provision of psychiatric treatment more generally, it had begun to appear that dedicated prison hospital beds were over-provided. In 1997/98, there were 29 such beds per 1,000 prisoner years compared with about 4.5 psychiatric beds per 1,000 of the general population in England and Wales (Marshall et al., 2001). Although, logically, the use of inpatient facilities should be limited to prisoners who need 24-hour nursing observation and care, this order of prison bed availability, allied with low tolerance of disturbed behaviour on ordinary prison wings, resulted in a lower admission threshold than in the wider community. Prison hospital régimes have nevertheless been criticized as offering a paucity of purposeful activity or therapeutic engagement (Reed and Lyne, 2000). They also suffer from a lack of clear purpose, partly given the mix of physical and mental health problems there. There must be a question as to whether prison hospital beds for mental illness should ever be more than transiently occupied. If a person really requires 24-hour nursing for more than a day or two, s/he should be in a proper health service facility. In the UK, prison beds, whether or not designated for treatment of mental illness, do not constitute hospital beds within the meaning of the Mental Health Act 1983, a position unchanged by the 2007 Act. Thus, among their limitations is that, except in a bona fide emergency, treatment cannot be enforced, however necessary to the individual's wellbeing or to the safety of others.

Under current mental health legislation in England and Wales, the Secretary of State for Justice may direct the transfer to hospital of a prisoner, whether pretrial or sentenced (see chapter 3 for details). Despite a rise in the number of prisoners with mental disorder being transferred to hospital, there have been difficulties with the process over many years, especially in delays (e.g. Blaauw et al., 2000; Earthrowl et al., 2003; Isherwood and Parrott, 2002). Mackay and Machin (2000) found that a decision on transfer took 50 or more days in a fifth of cases, perhaps a deterioration since Robertson et al. (1994) found an average delay between being accepted for an NHS bed and admission of 5–6 weeks. Someone identified in the wider

community with mental health problems at this level could expect to be admitted almost immediately, so this hardly reflects the much sought after equivalence for prisoners.

Delays may be due to a number of factors, most commonly shortage of health service psychiatric beds (e.g. Home Office and Department of Health and Social Security, 1975; Isherwood and Parrott, 2002). Amongst the non-completed transfers reported by Mackay and Machin (2000), over 44% were due to lack of suitable bed availability. Other factors delaying transfer include disagreements over the required level of security (Mackay and Machin, 2000), disputes over the catchment area of local hospitals (Robertson et al., 1994), reluctance of hospitals to admit prisoner-patients (Blaauw et al., 2000), and disagreements over severity of illness (Dell et al., 1993). Studies of individual differences reveal longer waiting times for prisoners requiring high security placements (Isherwood and Parrott, 2002) or diagnosed with personality disorder (Rutherford and Taylor, 2004). Worse even than delays, transfers have been rejected outright for diverse reasons, including the prisoner's perceived dangerousness (Coid, 1988), longer duration of illness, multiple handicaps and need for long-term care (Hargreaves, 1997), disputes between prison and hospital (Robertson et al., 1994) and psychiatrists' refusal to assess certain prisoners or their 'blacklisting' by hospitals (Dell et al., 1993).

One obvious effect of such delays is a reliance on prisons to care for and manage people with the most serious mental disorders, a situation which may result in adverse events such as suicide and self-harm amongst waiting prisoners (Brooke et al., 1996; Rutherford and Taylor, 2004) and/or location in 'stripped cell conditions' (Coid et al., 2003). The Department of Health undertook a 2-year programme of work to reduce these delays, ending in April 2007, supported by its then procedural guidelines on resolving problems as they arose throughout the transfer process. Emphasis was given to early identification of need for hospital treatment, with the premise that no delays in accessing suitable treatment should be because the person needing the service was in prison. A national evaluation of the impact of this found considerable improvements in transfer arrangements, with the lowest ever recorded transfer times, but that still more is required (Offender Health Research Network, 2008), in part likely to follow only from more radical change, including review of NHS bed occupancy and increased use of diversion at police custody or early court hearing stages. Nevertheless, resultant guidance is for a 14-day transfer window (Department of Health, 2011).

Suicide and Self-Harm Among Prisoners

Suicide is the single most common cause of death in custodial settings. This is of concern in itself, but it has a special resonance here because such institutions are responsible for the health and safety of their residents. Given that jails and prisons worldwide tend disproportionately to accumulate those people who would be at higher risk of suicide were they to be in the wider community – younger men, people with mental disorder and/or substance misuse disorders, people with heavy burdens of stress and people often with limited resilience – it is hardly surprising that the risk of suicide and other self-harm is so high. Special problems attend the management of suicide and self-harm in prison, however, because the resources in such institutions are always stretched and the most consistently available staff are correctional officers, often with little experience of such difficulties and no specific training in their management until they take up post. The problem of suicide in prisons is so widespread that the World Health Organization (WHO) regularly updates advice on suicide prevention in prisons, most recently in 2007 (World Health Organization, International Association for Prevention of Suicide, 2007). Acknowledging that the specifics of prevention strategies will differ in response to local resources and inmate needs, these bodies argue that certain elements form a common ground for best practice:

- a training programme (including refreshers) for correctional staff and care givers to help them recognize suicidal inmates and respond appropriately;
- attention to the general prison environment, including levels of activity, safety, culture and staff–prisoner relationships;
- minimizing bullying;
- systematic screening of prisoners on arrival and throughout their stay;
- a mechanism to maintain communication between staff about high risk inmates;
- written procedures on minimal requirements for support; on routine visual checks and continuous observations for acutely suicidal inmates and on use of restraints as a last resort;
- appropriate treatment for any mental disorder;
- development of sufficient internal resources or links to external community-based mental health services to ensure further specialist evaluation where appropriate;
- a strategy for debriefing when a suicide occurs, to identify ways of improving detection, monitoring and management (and, we would add, supporting staff and other prisoners in such circumstances).

More specific to England and Wales, an important landmark in the process of improving practice in respect of suicide and suicide risk in prisons was the thematic review of the Chief Inspector of Prisons *Suicide is Everyone's Concern* (HMIP, 1999). The terms of reference are themselves instructive:

To offer informed advice to the Prison service to enable it to maintain, in every establishment, the best possible practice in order to assist and support:

- *prisoners who may be at risk of self-harm and suicide*

- *the next of kin of prisoners who appear to have committed suicide*
- *staff and prisoners affected by the above.*

The Royal College of Psychiatrists (2002) provided a formal response in the form of a Council Report, with 26 recommendations. All these documents have much in common, but each has important details to add. The Chief Inspector's document was addressed principally to government ministers and the director general of the prison service, but also coroners. It expressed particular concerns about the 'full impact' of death in custody, and that effective contingency plans should be available in all institutions and that these should include consideration of the needs of relatives for early information and sensitive contact. A self-inflicted death will inevitably result in a coroner's inquest in England and Wales, and both prison staff and relatives have to be prepared for that. The College document was particularly for psychiatrists, and, in addition to already familiar themes on prevention and on management of the aftermath, called for every psychiatrist to have experience in prisons during training so as to understand fully the limitations of psychiatric treatment in prisons; it also emphasized the importance of keeping vulnerable people out of prison. At about the same time, the Department of Health published the wider *National Suicide Prevention Strategy for England*, which outlined ways to achieve a reduction of at least 20% in the overall death rate from suicide by 2010, inclusive of prison populations (Department of Health, 2002b, updated 2012). These papers propose improved assessment, care planning and risk management, improved health screening on reception into prison to detect mental disorder, substance abuse and vulnerability to suicide/self harm. It also called for the development of peer support schemes.

Figures for suicide rates in prisons vary from country to country, but in almost all they are higher in prisons, age for age and sex for sex, than in the general population. A study in England and Wales in 1996 found the prisoner rate to be 102/100,000; this compared to the general population rate, matched for age and sex, of 13.6/100,000 (Sattar, 2001). It is difficult to keep up-to-date on prevalence figures; Fazel and Benning (2009), for example, highlighted an increase in rates among women in England and Wales, but had had to curtail their study at 2004. Brooker et al. (2010) have shown continuing downward trends in self-inflicted deaths, although not self-harm, finally reducing among women in prison and high security prisoners as well as male prisoners generally. The Prisons and Probation Ombudsman for England and Wales publishes figures for all fatalities annually, together with individual inquiry reports into every death in prison, young offenders' institutions, immigrant removal centres and approved probation hostels (http://www.ppo.gov.uk). Perhaps reflecting an improvement in preventive strategies, since 2000 there has been a fall in self-inflicted deaths in custody, sustained since 2008 (Independent Advisory Panel on Deaths in Custody, 2011).

The ONS England and Wales prison survey found that 7% of male and 16% of female sentenced prisoners reported attempting suicide in the year before interview (Singleton et al., 1998). These figures were much higher in the remand population (15% and 27% respectively); 7% of the sentenced men and 10% of the sentenced women reported at least one act of actual self-harm during their current prison term. Nearly a third of all completed suicides occur within 1 week of initial reception into custody, indicating the need for emphasis on effective assessment, support and prevention at the earliest stages of custody (Shaw et al., 2003). People seem especially vulnerable at times of change, and another period of peak risk is in the first month after leaving custody (Pratt et al., 2006).

The ONS survey identified eight factors which distinguished those who had attempted suicide in the year before the study and those who had not (Singleton et al., 1998b); these were: age (suicide attempters younger), ethnicity (more attempters white), diagnosis (25–50% psychosis compared with 5% non-psychotic prisoners; more with severe neurotic disorder), being on psychotropic medication (attempters 2–3 times more likely), having been a psychiatric inpatient (attempting men up to three times and attempting women up to six times more likely), social support (attempters had lower levels), and adverse life events (attempters more likely to have experienced recent or lifetime violence or other abuse). Criminological theories of suicide highlight differences between suicide attempters and non-attempters in prison according to their experiences of custody rather than inherent personal differences. Suicide attempters were more likely to perceive themselves as 'worse off' than their peers in custody in terms of their opportunities for work, education or recreation. They generally tended to spend longer in their cell and found it harder to cope with imprisonment or relieve their boredom (Liebling, 1993, 1995, 1998). Another relevant factor is that the experience of the suicide of a peer, perhaps even in the same cell, is traumatic (Hales et al., 2003; Hales, 2009).

Fazel et al. (2008) brought these issues together in a systematic review of all published studies of prisoners who had died by suicide and been compared with total or randomly selected populations of prisoners who had not. They identified 34 studies covering 4,780 cases of suicide, and remarkably consistent findings. Among demographic variables, being male or white nearly doubled the risk of suicide; being married increased it. Prison-related factors were being on remand or being a life-sentenced prisoner, either quadrupling the risk; single cell occupancy increased it nine-fold. Clinical factors included having a history of alcohol use, or of attempted suicide or a current psychiatric diagnosis, but by far the most important risk factor was recent suicidal ideation, which raised the risk 15-fold.

Being able to ask about suicidal thoughts in a way that encourages confidences about them is a vital attribute in any member of staff working with prisoners.

Suicide and self-harm assessment and management in prisons in England and Wales currently follow the Assessment, Care in Custody and Teamwork (ACCT) system. This was introduced to improve multidisciplinary care for prisoners through promoting more proactive identification of at-risk prisoners. ACCT then focused on ensuring detailed needs assessments and care plans were undertaken, based on principles similar to the Care Programme Approach; introduction of a case-manager to co-ordinate care delivery and the sharing of risk-pertinent information; encouraging staff to engage actively with prisoners to promote their safety, rather than relying solely on observation; and ensuring the active engagement of the individual prisoner with the care process.

The prison service in England and Wales has encouraged peer support or 'buddy' schemes for some years, such as the *Insiders' Scheme,* for which selected prisoner volunteers are trained to support new receptions. Much the most important and widespread scheme with respect to suicide prevention is the *Listeners' Scheme,* whereby, since 1991, prisoners have been selected, trained and supported by the Samaritans (http://www.samaritans.org). Listeners work in the same way as any other Samaritan volunteers, listening to their fellow prisoners about distress or suicidal thoughts, in complete confidence. (Other prisoner peer support schemes generally do not enjoy confidentiality criterion.) A study of the scheme confirms generally positive staff and prisoner attitudes towards it; while possibly under-accessed, use patterns are similar to those in the wider community (Jaffe, 2012).

Other Special Issues Among Prisoners

Prisons are disproportionately occupied by adult men charged with or convicted of acquisitive crimes or crimes of violence. We would hesitate to say that prisons are designed for them, but special issues in prisoner management arise when people fall outside these demographic and criminological norms. Separate institutions or separate wings in prisons are provided for the larger minorities in this context – women, and offenders aged 15–17 and, to date, between 18 and 20. Such provision is provided in part to safeguard such people, who are potentially more vulnerable in a mainstream prison setting, and in part because such groups do have their own special needs. Provision for sex offenders may also be provided separately on the same kind of basis – for protection, since many are vulnerable to attack, but also because they have their own particular treatment needs. Separate prisons, custodial units or prison régimes which have some clinical resonance are dealt with in the relevant chapters (children and adolescents, chapter 19; people with intellectual difficulties, chapter 13; personality disorders, chapter 16; sexual offenders, chapter 10; women, chapter 20 and older offenders, chapter 27). Some of the specifics of work with people who are using substances to harmful levels are covered in chapter 18.

HM Inspectorate of Prisons (HMIP) is an independent body which, in England and Wales, provides:

independent scrutiny of the conditions for and treatment of prisoners and other detainees, promoting the concept of 'healthy prisons' in which staff work effectively to support prisoners and detainees to reduce reoffending or achieve other agreed outcomes.

Its tasks include both fully announced and unannounced inspections of individual prisons, youth offender institutions, immigration centres and, in conjunction with HM Inspectorate of Constabulary, of prisoners held in police cells. All reports are published, and provide a mine of information about the present state of prisons in England and Wales. In addition, HMIP conducts regular thematic reviews, which collate information, including research information where available, on specific issues which are important to the safety and rehabilitation of prisoners. These, together, provide far wider coverage of special issues for prisoners than is possible here, and we recommend viewing the website (http://www.justice.gov.uk/Publications/inspectorate-reports/hmi-prisons/thematic-research-prisons/thematic-reports-and-research.htm).

The remaining issues which we will consider more fully here are the management of overseas prisoners, issues around treatment of suspected or actual terrorists or other political prisoners and people on life terms of imprisonment, but first one which cuts across all these, the matter of black and minority ethnic (BME) status.

Black and minority ethnic (BME) issues in prison

Concern about BME prisoners was raised to a new level by the tragedy of Zahid Mubarek in 2000. Mr Mubarek was a 20-year-old, non-violent man, of Asian-British family, serving a short prison sentence, the first time he had ever been in prison. For 6 weeks he had to share a cell with another young man, Robert Stewart, who had a violent history, was bragging about committing the first murder of the millennium, openly expressing racist views and who also appeared to have an abnormal mental state. For this 6-week period, Mr Mubarek seemed to handle the situation remarkably well, until the night Stewart made a brutal attack on him, and he died of his injuries. The initial presumption was that this was a racist crime. Perhaps it was, but at least it was mediated by the more conventionally pathological aspects of Stewart's mental state. It was also 'typical' in one important sense of prison homicides in England and Wales. Between 1990 and 2001, there had been 26 homicides in a prison population growing from about 45,000 to about 65,000, nearly half of them occurring in a shared cell, and all but one of them being the killing of one cell mate by another. Mr Mubarek's case was particularly shocking because of the racist issues uncovered in the system. A first question was why a young man like Zahid Mubarek should have received a prison sentence at all for a relatively minor offence; his offending career had lasted for about 10 months, during which he had accumulated 11 offences, mainly of breaking into cars and in the context of having developed a drug problem and struggling to keep clinic appointments. As the public inquiry into the case remarked, however: 'the Inquiry's terms of reference … were not wide enough to include sentencing policy' (Keith, 2006). The public inquiry was the third inquiry into the killing, the prison service having conducted its own, and the Commission for Racial Equality also having completed one. The Home Office initially resisted the public inquiry. Mr Mubarek's parents had to battle through the Courts to get it established. It transpired in the course of the inquiry that there was no requirement on prisons at that time to publish race equality policies or schemes, so one recommendation had to be basic: the Home Office should promote legislation to add each prison to the list of bodies required to publish policies according to the Race Relations Act 1976. For the rest, though, the matters raised seemed more general. The inquiry acknowledged, for example, the problem of under-resourcing, but also noted that the tragedy had happened in what was then a 'failing prison', and that tragedies such as this are disproportionately likely to happen where management is weak and communications poor. The mental health issues were also highlighted most strongly, calling for more training for prison staff in recognizing mental health problems; while not downplaying the importance of treating psychosis, there was also emphasis that many non-psychotic disorders also need specialist treatment. Another key recommendation was that anyone strongly suspected of having a mental disorder should have a personal prison officer who would become fully aware of his/her background and who would make a particular effort to get to know him/her and his/her fluctuations in mental state.

The Chief Inspector of Prisons keeps BME interests under regular review. The 2005 thematic review (HMIP, 2005) acknowledged that the four tests for a 'healthy prison': safety, respect, purposeful activity and resettlement were not invariably met, with some Asian prisoners in particular reporting than they felt unsafe. Bullying was perceived to remain a problem. This report was wide-ranging, and made the important observation that the oft proposed solution of recruiting more staff from black and minority ethnic groups, while helpful, was not enough in itself, and that some of the staff also felt that they were not treated equally. Perhaps the most important observation for our concerns here was

By and large healthcare providers did not recognize or provide for the specific needs of those communities in relation to either their mental or physical health.

In 2009, the material was updated with particular reference to BME women (HMIP, 2009). Elsewhere, we have noted that it is unusual for trials of psychotropic medication to report clearly and separately on specific effects for women or for people from non-white ethnic groups (chapter 23); possible differences in effectiveness of more psychotherapeutic interventions and, indeed of the so-called treatment programmes for prisoners, have similarly not been evaluated by these demographic differences. This is undoubtedly an area for high quality research initiatives.

Management of overseas prisoners

There are three distinct but equally important issues concerning overseas prisoners – first, liaison with other countries and international bodies to share knowledge and concerns and, in so doing, agreement on guidance for raising standards in prisons and their management generally; secondly, provision of support for British Citizens held in prisons outside the UK; and thirdly, appropriate treatment of foreign nationals held in UK prisons.

In the UK, the welfare of prisoners internationally has long been a key concern for the International Centre for Prison Studies. The Centre has made an important contribution to generation, dissemination and application of knowledge in the field throughout the world, albeit perhaps with a stronger focus on human rights rather than healthcare issues *per se* (http://www.prisonstudies.org).

The World Health Organization (WHO), as would be expected, focuses specifically on health in prisons (www.euro.who.int/prisons). The WHO Health in Prisons Project (HIPP) was set up in 1995 in recognition of widespread gaps between public health services and prison healthcare, and to support member states in closing these gaps through national and international effort. As ever in the history of prisons, the problem of communicable disease was probably the main driving force, with the advent of HIV/AIDS, but there is a substantial mental health component to the programme. The WHO 2007 Trenčín statement, for example, calls on member countries to recognize that prisons alone cannot meet the mental health needs which are so common in prisons, but rather that community health services must take responsibility for delivery of treatment as needed and governments, through legal policy and process, should facilitate this.

Notwithstanding the range of challenges presented by the prison system in England and Wales, becoming a prisoner overseas creates additional special problems, not least the extra sense of isolation and probable lack of knowledge about rights and how to access services. In many cases, however, where prisons are even less resourced than they are in the UK, the most basic access to healthcare may not be available. In addition to government monitoring and appropriate support where possible, through British embassy and consulate staff, an independent sector organization, called Prisoners Abroad, provides support to people while they are held in overseas prisons, regardless of their stage in the criminal justice process, and also to such people on their return to the UK and to their families. For further information, see http://www.prisonersabroad.org.uk.

Numbers of foreign nationals in prison in England and Wales are not insubstantial. In April 2006, there were about 10,000 individuals from 172 different countries, accounting for 13% of the prison population at the time (HM Inspectorate of Prisons, 2006). This 2006 thematic review found that healthcare needs were rated by such prisoners as being fourth in the hierarchy of importance to them, after language, immigration and family contact. Some issues, like substance misuse, were not as prominent as among British nationals, but distress rates were high, particularly among the women, and communication difficulties sometimes a barrier to accessing help. There was particular concern about managing potentially suicidal prisoners unless there is good enough assistance with communication.

Life terms of imprisonment

Life imprisonment is the mandatory sentence in the UK for murder committed by a person of 21 years or over. It is also the maximum sentence for a range of other serious offences including manslaughter, rape and arson. In addition, with the Criminal Justice Act 2003, the indefinite sentences of 'imprisonment for public protection' (IPP) became available for individuals convicted of offences which do not carry a life sentence as such, but who are considered to pose a serious threat of harm to the public; for young offenders, similar principles apply, but the new sentence was referred to as 'detention for public protection' (DPP). For simplicity, we will use the term IPP to include the DPP, as, in practice, there is little difference in their operation. The effect of both is the same as that of a life sentence to the extent that the sentence is, effectively, in two parts. There is the period of punishment, known commonly as the tariff, which is fixed by the trial judge, although sometimes adjusted up or down at appeal; the offender cannot be released from prison before completing this period. There is then the indefinite component. In order to secure release from this the individual has to be able to show that his/her risk towards others has become low. 'Lifers' and people under IPP sentences are in a different category from other prisoners, partly because the psychology of an indeterminate sentence is different from that of fixed term sentences and partly because special administrative and other procedures are set up to deal with them (see chapter 2). Both groups are likely to include a disproportionately high number of people with mental disorder or dysfunction. Although the Legal Aid, Sentencing and Punishment of Offenders Act 2012 abolished the imposition of IPPs and DPPs from May 2012, it did nothing for those already sentenced this way.

Before the abolition of capital punishment, there were very few lifers. The Gowers Report (Royal Commission on Capital Punishment, 1953) made brief reference to the prevailing view that the lifer should be encouraged to make a fresh start by his own unaided efforts. Between 1957 – the year of the Homicide Act – and 1964 – the last year before abolition of capital punishment – the population of lifers had risen from 122 to 365. Ten years later numbers had nearly doubled, and by 1984 there were nearly 2,000 lifers in England and Wales. Numbers had been rising considerably even before the introduction of IPP when this part of the Criminal Justice Act 2003 was implemented on 1 April 2005. By 31 March 2008, there were 4,170 prisoners serving IPPs out of a total of 10,911 serving an indeterminate sentence (HM Prison Service, 2008). By June 2009, a total of 12,520 prisoners were serving indefinite sentences, including 474 women and seventy 15–17 year olds (Ministry of Justice, 2009). A factor in the continuing rise in these numbers is the difficulty such prisoners have in accessing programmes in prison, and, therefore, in being able to show that they have changed sufficiently for release on licence once their tariff is complete. By July 2008, for example, of 4,619 prisoners serving IPP sentences, just 31 had been released (Rutherford et al., 2008).

Lifers and psychiatric disorder

Older studies in the UK and elsewhere in Europe (e.g. Sapsford, 1983; Taylor 1986 in England and Wales; Heather, 1977 in Scotland; Rasch, 1981 in Germany) all showed high rates of all forms of mental disorder among lifers. Rutherford et al. (2008) examined information on prisoners from previously unpublished government reports, including data from the Offender Assessment System (OASys), a risk assessment tool which incorporates some evaluation of needs, and interviewed staff and prisoners in three prisons. There appeared to be a hierarchy across prisoner groups, with IPP prisoners generally more likely to manifest psychiatric problems than lifers, who, in turn, were more likely to do so than people in the general prison population. With respect to psychiatric treatment, for example, 18% of IPP prisoners, 17% of lifers and 9% of general population prisoners had such a history; this pattern held for receiving treatment in prison, and, more specifically, for being on medication. Differences were more striking with respect to needing clinical assessment for personality disorder: 66% for IPPs, 41% for lifers and 34% for general population prisoners. In terms of 'criminogenic need' assessment, more than half of the IPP prisoners had an 'emotional wellbeing' need compared with 40% of lifers and 30% of the general prison population. The report highlights the barriers to meeting these needs, in a mixture of reluctance on the part of the prisoners to seek help, difficulties in accessing adequate services if they do try, and under-resourcing of health services and difficulties fitting healthcare to prison

management needs, which might include sudden transfer of prisoners. Failure to meet mental health needs in these circumstances is not only a problem in itself, but also it commonly means that prisoners with such unmet needs are unable to access the mainstream prison programmes, and their chances of a successful parole or licence application are thus reduced.

Remarkably little is known about the mental health over time of people under indefinite prison sentences. Coker and Martin (1985) studied two cohorts of male lifers released in England and Wales between 1960–64 and 1970–74. Overall, recidivism rates were low, most were in stable accommodation and just over 60% found employment. They found a small subgroup of men, however, who were stuck in a chaotic lifestyle, with at least six changes of accommodation during the 5 years of follow-up, higher recidivism rates and stories strongly suggestive of mental disorder in many cases. Work with long-term and indefinite prisoners is difficult to interpret. The more polemical (e.g. Cohen and Taylor, 1972), theoretically argued and qualitative work (e.g. Jewkes, 2005) raises expectations of finding extensive psychological damage as a result of uncertainty about release and length of confinement, but the little existing empirical work suggests otherwise (Bolton et al., 1976; Richards, 1978; Sapsford, 1978). This dissonance may show the importance of going beyond the individually rich and colourful data from small-scale qualitative research, but the empirical studies were conducted a long time ago, when lifers were relatively unusual in the prison system, and perhaps attract more care and attention. Furthermore, 'absence of detectable psychological deterioration' has its limitations as a positive statement of health.

Other Extreme Circumstances in Prison

Life or IPP sentences yield only one category of extreme stress which may attend imprisonment in special circumstances. It is impossible to provide an exhaustive list, but since the Anti-Terrorism, Crime and Security Act 2001, people detained under these provisions have been added to the cluster of those who may have to stay in prison under uncertainty about release, here often without charge. The impact of such detention on eight such people caused sufficient concern that first a small group of psychiatrists issued a public statement about it (http://news.bbc.co.uk/1/hi/uk/3739926.stm), followed by a Royal College of Psychiatrists' statement, which extended such consideration to asylum seekers awaiting tribunal decisions or deportation, people transferred to secure hospitals just before the end of their sentence and some of those transferred to the so-called dangerous and severe personality disorder (DSPD) programmes (Royal College of Psychiatrists, 2005). The essential points are that the College and its psychiatrists are committed to providing services for such people, but that these are unlikely to neutralize the impact of such circumstances; a particular concern was that many such individuals would be exceptionally vulnerable with respect to their mental health in the light of a common earlier experience of extremely traumatic events.

People in such positions, with little conventional negotiating option or autonomy left to them, may resort to a variety of self-destructive actions as the one way left to them of exerting some power in the situation. Hunger strikes have been one such form of behaviour, particularly associated with political activists under detention. In the UK, suffragettes and Irish Republican Army (IRA) prisoners have been notable examples. The dilemma is about how to provide the most appropriate medical care in the circumstances, and particularly when, if at all, to enforce nutrition. Fessler (2003) systematically reviewed the literature on ethics and legal codes pertaining to hunger strikers as well as psychological state during voluntary and involuntary starvation. Although the literature was too heterogeneous for statistical analysis, Fessler found evidence that starvation changes psychological function in a way that is likely to impair competence. This is a factor behind guidance on the assessment of hunger strikers, which should be repeated daily in order, as far as possible, to build a relationship with the individual and understand fully his/her wishes with respect to likely changing circumstances, and an advance directive on management if *in extremis*. The British Medical Association is clear that no patient who is refusing food, capable of making a rational judgment in this respect and is aware of the consequences of refusing food should be force fed, and British courts have tended to endorse this position (see *Medical Ethics Today*, first published by the *BMJ* publishing group in 1993, and regularly updated since). Brockman (1999) gives a more specifically psychiatric perspective. The World Medical Association keeps its guidance under constant review, the most recent agreed in 2006. This guides the physician through a variety of such situations, from having first contact with an individual after s/he has already lost competence to dealing with the physician's own conscience in respect of allowing an otherwise healthy individual to die. At the heart of an ethical decision-making process is independence of the clinician from the detaining authority and primary concern for the fasting individual.

Healthcare Needs and Services in Prisons: Some Conclusions

Difficulties in delivering healthcare in prisons almost anywhere are systemic, longstanding and complex and not easily amenable to a 'quick fix'. This is problematic because it is also the case that, wherever the mental health of prisoners has been investigated, there are higher prevalence rates of all types of mental disorder in prison populations compared with the general community. In the UK at least, the main emphasis since the 1990s has been on the provision of community-care type interventions to prisoners with severe and enduring mental illness through the development of prison in-reach teams, but these teams are struggling to cope with the sheer weight of need in prisons. In addition, the in-reach model tends to be insufficiently multidisciplinary. Health services which are truly based in the wider community seem to have little real sense of ownership of their clientele once they are in prison, and specialist forensic mental health services tend to be overwhelmed with demand, as pathways between services are often hard to find. Most prisoners stay in prison for short periods, and lack of appropriate service attachments, perhaps especially to substance misuse services, may contribute to their early recidivism as well as their deteriorating health.

WORKING WITH THE PROBATION SERVICE

Introduction to the Probation Service in England and Wales

In May 2007, after a period of political turmoil, the Ministry of Justice was created within the UK Government, bringing the former Department of Constitutional Affairs, the Employment Tribunal Service and the National Offender Management Service (NOMS) under the aegis of one cabinet minister. The new department sits alongside the Home Office, which retains responsibility for immigration, security and asylum, the police service, crime prevention and community safety policies. It is intended that this change will create greater coherence in criminal justice processes and the handling of offenders while maintaining close coordination between the Ministry of Justice and the Home Office over matters relating to crime policy and public protection. Elsewhere in the UK, the Scottish Parliament and the Northern Ireland Assembly retain the relevant devolved responsibilities.

Organization and Management of the Probation Service in England and Wales

The Probation Service in England and Wales has a 100-year history of co-ordinating assessments to assist courts in deciding on the most appropriate and effective sentencing option related to the offence and the offender before them, and of supervising offenders once sentence has been passed. Current management arrangements, under the Offender Management Act 2007, provide for 35 Probation Trusts across England and Wales, which receive funding from NOMS, to which they are accountable for their performance. This nevertheless cemented a commissioner/service provider split and make the chief executives employees of the local trust rather than the Ministry of Justice or NOMS.

This also involved some amalgamations of the previous 'area boards' into the new trusts, notably the amalgamation of the four Welsh areas into a single Wales Probation Trust (the others are Suffolk with Norfolk; Staffordshire with the West Midlands; Surrey with Sussex and Durham with Teeside). Nevertheless, coterminosity with police areas has been more or less retained.

The provisions of the 2007 Act are based on Lord Carter's *Correctional Services Review* (Carter, 2003) and the Government's response to it (Home Office, 2004b). The first of two main change themes relates to the need for a seamless end-to-end offender management process from the original assessment at the point of conviction and sentence, and through the sentence itself (including both custodial and community elements) so as to reduce the likelihood of re-offending and the risk of harm to the public. The second and, for many, more contentious theme is that provision should be made to involve a wider range of providers in the supervision of offenders in the community, as has already happened in custodial sentence management, through private sector involvement.

The National Offender Management Service (NOMS) was established in order to facilitate the involvement of a wider range of providers, and to develop a separation between commissioning and delivery of services. This commissioning network of ten directors of offender management (DOM), one for each of the nine regional government office areas and one for Wales, was originally established in late 2004 for all offender related services and has evolved in line with the changing legislative background. With the implementation of the Offender Management Act 2007, the Prison and Probation Service came under a single organizational leadership within the context of NOMS with effect from 1 April 2008. This gave practical effect to an assumption within Lord Carter's report, which confirmed the directors of offender management as directly responsible for commissioning and for holding to account all aspects of offender management within their region. This separation of commissioning and provision, now well-established in the health sector, was untested in the area of offender management in the community. A basic requirement of this structure was the introduction of the *Offender Management Model*, whereby a single offender manager (employed by the local area probation service, and normally a probation officer for higher risk and more complex cases) is responsible for the assessment of the offender, sentence planning, sentence enforcement and the co-ordination of a series of 'interventions' as required by the Court or indicated by the assessment or sentence plan. In due course, it will be expected that the sentence plan will include more responsibility for decisions about the nature of the régime to be adopted in custody and the type and location of institution in which any custodial element of the sentence is served. It should be noted that when the Criminal Justice Act 2003 is fully implemented

(still not achieved in 2011 because of its resource implications) *all* offenders sentenced to custody in England and Wales will be subject to post-release supervision in the community as part of the sentence. This provision does not currently apply to adults aged over 21 who are serving prison sentences of 12 months or under.

The separation of offender management and interventions was also reinforced by the Offender Management Act 2007 which, in its final form, states that the commissioning side of the probation service's work, referred to as the 'core' or court work, will remain with the probation service for at least 3 years and this protection will only be changed by further parliamentary instrument. 'Interventions' are those activities with which an offender engages as part of the sentence requirement, and which can be sequenced within the sentence plan. These include unpaid work (formerly called community service), accredited programmes (usually based on cognitive behavioural approaches), residence in approved premises (formerly called probation hostels) and elements of the custodial régime where there is a sentence of imprisonment. It is envisaged that these interventions may, wholly or in part, be subject to market testing by the director of offender management (commissioner), or to sub-contracting by the probation service on a best value assessment basis. Under the Offender Management Act, the newly constituted probation trusts will be provided with flexibilities, under their contract with the director of offender management, which are intended to provide opportunities parallel to this in health trusts.

The probation trusts will continue to operate under service level agreements with the director of offender management, but will also be encouraged to act as local commissioners, devoting an increasing percentage of their revenue to contracts with other local private, voluntary and community organizations which will contribute to the implementation of the sentence plan in each individual case. The directors of offender management are also responsible for co-ordinating a regional plan, the aim of which is to create synergy in the provision of public services (such as education and health) to ensure that these also meet the needs of offenders and victims and contribute to crime reduction. The seven pathways for these regional *reducing re-offending action plans* are

1. accommodation;
2. employment, training and education;
3. substance misuse;
4. physical and mental health;
5. finance, benefit and debt;
6. children and families;
7. attitudes, behaviour and thinking.

All of these pathways have a direct impact on the interface between mental health services and offender supervision in the community and health professionals can expect to be involved in the development of action plans for each of them, with a particular emphasis on 1, 3, 4 and 7.

The Work of the Probation Service

The focus of probation work is the assessment of offenders for court and the supervision of both community-based court orders and the community element that succeeds custodial sentences (often referred to as licence or parole). Within England and Wales, at any one point in time, the probation service is dealing with some 250,000 established cases. It prepares approximately the same number of court reports annually. As the prison population burgeons, fundamental questions are being asked about the focus of probation resources. The increase in the prison population is a consequence both of greater use of custodial sentences generally since 2000 and of sentences of indefinite detention for public protection since the Criminal Justice Act 2003 (see above). Between 1998 and 2008, the proportion of custodial sentences increased from 23% to 43% of all disposals for offences that carry the option of imprisonment (immediate and suspended custody) (Ministry of Justice, 2010). Up to this time the number of indeterminate sentences also continued to rise, for example between June 2008 and June 2009 alone there was rise of 10% in the numbers, from 11,380 to 12,520; although fortunately this period saw a decrease for young offenders and 15–17 year olds, so the increase affected adult men and women only (Ministry of Justice, 2010). As noted above, the Legal Aid, Sentencing and Punishment of Offenders Act 2012 has now stopped the flow of IPPs and DPPs.

A continuing concern for policy-makers in managing the still increasing prison population is to prioritize the targeting of resources to ensure a reduction in crime and greater protection of the public, but the increasing interest in, and influence of, the media on policy review and direction pose a continual challenge to this balance. We observe again, that the criminal justice system in England and Wales imprisons more offenders per 100,000 of population than any other Western European country except Spain (Aebi and Delgrande, 2011). The National Audit Office (2010) has just highlighted the cost and futility of short prison sentences for the 60,000 or so adults receiving them each year in England and Wales; such people are more likely than others to remain on a recidivist path, on average having more convictions than others at the point of sentence; 60% of them are likely to re-offend within 12 months. While media pressure on the criminal justice system is in the direction of an increasingly punitive system, there is also now pressure to be more constructive (e.g. Bradley, 2009).

Court Diversion Schemes – Their Role and Governance

Diversion is a concept applied to the identification of people with mental disorder who find themselves in the criminal justice system, followed by their direction out of it into appropriate health services, especially as an alternative to imprisonment. It may occur at any stage of the criminal justice process, from arrest onwards. There is a paucity of information about the prevalence of mental disorder among people in the wider criminal justice system; most research into this has focused on prisons. While it may be that severe mental disorder leaves people more vulnerable to pretrial imprisonment if magistrates or judges are concerned that the individual may be too chaotic to keep subsequent court dates, it is likely that the prevalence of mental disorder among alleged and actual offenders in the community is not so very different from that among prisoners. Mair and May (1997) recruited a national sample of just over 1,200 people on probation in 1994 in England and Wales, representing slightly under two-thirds of those approached. Almost half said that they had mental health problems, with 30% asserting that these were severe enough to limit the work they could do. Other studies have highlighted the vulnerability to suicide among those on community sentences, with one study finding a seven-fold increase in risk compared with the general community (Pritchard et al., 1997) and another almost twice the risk of that among prisoners (Satter, 2001). A much more recent pilot prevalence study of offenders under probation supervision in Lincolnshire, a mainly rural English county, suggested that over a quarter of those sampled had a mental illness at the time of research assessment, nearly half had a personality disorder and a higher proportion still had alcohol and/or illicit drug problems. Substance misuse disorders were well recognized by probation staff, but mental illness was generally not (Brooker et al., 2011).

In the USA, court-based diversion schemes have developed in many states. Growth of specific mental health courts has been rapid, from one pioneer court in 1997 to nearly 100 across the USA by 2004 (Steadman et al., 2005). There is a distinction to be made between mental health courts and drug courts, the latter having a more specific role with hazardous and dependent drug users (National Association of Drug Court Professionals, 1997), but with similar goals of decreasing jail or prison time and increasing exposure to treatment. Drug courts have been quite extensively evaluated. Belenko (2001) completed a critical review of 37 published and unpublished studies to that date, and found that nearly half of the clientele completed the programmes, with more limited evidence, albeit including three randomized controlled trials (RCTs), that not only was there was less recidivism in the drug court groups, but also that costs tended to be lower than with standard treatment. A number of studies of mental health courts as far afield as Florida (Boothroyd et al., 2003), Washington State (Trupin and Richards, 2003; Herinckx et al., 2005), California (Cosden et al., 2005), and Tennessee, Pennsylvania, Oregan and Connecticut (Steadman and Naples, 2005) have all been broadly positive about outcomes, measured prospectively over varying periods. Advantages have included less time spent in jail and more time engaged with psychiatric services. Actual improvements in mental health were reported in the California study, which followed participants over 2 years, and employed assertive community treatment with diversion compared with 'treatment as usual', which was traditional court proceedings and *ad hoc* access to psychiatric services. Other studies were not so positive about treatment and outcome with respect to re-offending varied from 'without increasing public safety risk' (Steadman and Naples, 2005) to substantial reductions in offending (Herinckx et al., 2005). One study found only small effects in service take up (Broner et al., 2004). This last was much the largest, covering eight programmes across the USA, including New York, and included 971 diverted participants and 995 similar offenders, who were not diverted. Attrition was quite high, with the nearly 2,000 interviewees at baseline reduced to 1,300 after 12 months. Although there were some between site differences, measures of actual change in the individuals, including symptoms of mental disorder, substance use, quality of life or recidivism, indicated neither advantage nor disadvantage for either treatment condition. The truth is that people with mental disorder who present to the courts are a diverse group, some with a more complex mix of problems than others. In an ideal research world, much more refinement in selecting groups for comparison might yield more practically useful results. Research pressures, however, are always to deliver within a tight time frame, and the length of time it would take to recruit large enough homogeneous groups of interest for comparison is never available; furthermore, the nature of the populations from which these samples are recruited tends to preclude RCTs, the studies generally being described as of 'quasi-experimental non-equivalent comparison group design'. Whilst better than nothing, and reassuring in that the diverted groups certainly performed no worse than the conventionally treated, these cannot be the last word on the effectiveness of such programmes.

In the UK, too, diversion schemes have been developing, but here are variously police-based (see also above) or court-based, although not centred in separate, specialist courts (Parsonage et al., 2009). In the absence of a clear national framework, these have developed in a piecemeal fashion. A substantial number of courts across England and Wales have access to a community mental health nurse, whose management and funding differs between countries, dependent on local negotiation. The role of the nurse will differ according to his/her position in the mental health trust and their ease of access to psychiatric records, and to diaries for further assessment appointments. Important ethical issues arise, similar to those discussed with respect to court reports in chapter 6. The defendant must understand the role and affiliations of the nurse in this context, and that s/he may not be entering into a traditional nurse–patient relationship in which, as a patient, the person's interests are generally paramount. The nurse has a responsibility to ensure that this is understood. The nurse must also have complete clarity between him/herself and the mental health trust about the extent to which material from the clinical record may be disclosed to colleagues in the criminal justice system, and about any particular circumstances which may affect this. Others in the clinical service must ensure that they are fully aware of these issues too.

Arrest referral schemes linked to substance misuse treatment are promising, and dependent users may be most helped, but evaluations are inconclusive (e.g. Kennedy et al., 2012). This facility may nevertheless be useful for people with needs in relation to mental health problems. Many defendants will not, however, divulge a drug or mental health problem at this stage for fear of how the information may be used. As noted above, efforts to divert people into more appropriate services at this stage should increase following the Bradley review (2009), although methods of implementation are likely to differ between England and Wales.

The Pre-Sentence Report

The Criminal Justice Act 2003 introduced the Sentencing Guidelines Council in England and Wales, which provides advice to sentencers, with the aim of working towards consistency in sentencing and awareness of the cost implications of sentences. The guidance encourages magistrates and judges when deciding on the components of a sentence to have in mind:

i. the goal of the sentence (e.g. punishment, reduction of crime rehabilitation, public protection, reparation);
ii. the risk of the offender committing further offences; and
iii. the ability of the offender to comply with the requirements.

When the court seeks a report, a preliminary indication of the view on the seriousness of the offence and the purpose of sentence in the particular case will generally be given, and then the probation officer is expected, if asked, to undertake a focused assessment of the offender, his/her background, current social circumstances and the factors contributing to the offence and to make a sentencing proposal. In addition, the officer is required to include a risk assessment, not only of the likelihood of re-offending, but also of the degree of immediate potential physical or sexual harm to specific individuals or the public.

Reports for adult offenders (over 18 years) are prepared by the Probation Service and those for people under that age by Youth Offending Teams (YOTs). The assessment tools used to support this process are the Offender Assessment System (OASys) for adults and *ASSET*/Asset for young offenders, which provide a structure for the identification of factors that may have contributed to the offending behaviour and the likelihood of re-offending. On the basis of this assessment a proposal is made taking into account the viability and appropriateness of particular sentences.

The psychiatric report

Frequently, defence representatives will seek a psychiatric assessment as part of their preparation for representing a defendant. In these cases the report is the property of the defendant and will only be submitted to the court if the defence lawyer deems it is in his/her best interests to do so. If the report provides information that is likely to lead the court to consider a more serious sentence it may thus be withheld, even on occasions when it might be in the public interest to make the contents known.

At a later stage, the Court itself may seek a medical view as a result of information that might be provided either by the Crown Prosecution Service (CPS), in a pre-sentence report, or as a result of judicial observation in court. These reports are commissioned on behalf of the court and, on completion, will be the property of that institution. Systems for commissioning these reports vary. In some areas these may have to be ordered by the court itself, whilst in other areas the authority to instigate reports has been delegated to probation service staff. Alternatively, in courts with access to a community mental health nurse, part of their role may involve making arrangements for the assessment to be conducted.

There are practical and ethical issues around how and whether the pre-sentence and medical assessments should inform each other or be shared prior to the court appearance (see also chapter 6). In many areas, the practice is for the report-writers to discuss the contents and particularly the proposals to ensure that they are complementary, but practice varies and differences in the quality of reports and the level of co-ordination achieved are evident between those reports prepared by forensic/specialist medical practitioners and those prepared by general psychiatrists. Timing is also an issue, as there is substantial pressure on courts to ensure speed of process. This in itself may create tension as the court puts pressure on mental health services to deal quickly with court-referred clients who, therefore, may be seen to have speedier access to assessment and help than voluntary patients trying to access services routinely.

Community Orders

The Criminal Justice Act 2003 replaced the previous range of community sentences in England and Wales (probation, community rehabilitation order, community service/community punishment, and combination orders) with a single community order. The community order may, however, have any combination of 12 specific requirements depend-

ent on the seriousness of the offence, the needs of the offender, the purpose of sentencing and the risk of harm to the public. The 12 options are

- supervision
- unpaid work
- attendance at an accredited programme
- drug rehabilitation
- alcohol treatment
- mental health treatment
- residence
- specified activity
- prohibited activity
- exclusion from certain areas (often with electronic tagging)
- curfew
- attendance at an attendance centre.

Unlike the other requirements, the mental health and the drug rehabilitation elements oblige the court to ensure the offender's consent. The offender, probation officer and the mental health professional are, in effect, entering into a legal contract, but the sanction for breach falls on the offender. Very specific expectations may be set out in relation to the management, review and enforcement of the drug rehabilitation requirement, but little is stipulated in relation to the mental health treatment requirement. In the event of failure to comply, the probation officer must return the offender to court. The most common outcome in this event is that the offender is imprisoned.

Take-up of the mental health treatment requirement has been slow, and one of the main barriers to it may be the time it takes to get a psychiatric report. There is also some reluctance on the part of professional clinicians because of their concern over the consequences of breach (Khanom et al., 2009). Missed appointments are widely held to constitute a breach of the mental health treatment requirement, but non-compliance with specific elements of treatment rarely so.

Inter-Agency Information Sharing

There is no reference material available to guide criminal justice personnel on information sharing. Medical practitioners have their professional codes as one form of guidance. For psychiatrists who are members of the Royal College of Psychiatrists, the central governing body of the College regularly updates guidance on information sharing. The most recent guide takes account of inter-agency working as, for example, through MAPPA (Royal College of Psychiatrists, 2010). It is expected, however, that such requirements will be managed through local negotiation of protocols. These must specify the means by which information is exchanged to ensure the effective accountability of the offender to the court, without compromising patient consent and confidentiality. The findings of Her Majesty's

Inspectorate of Probation (HM Inspectorate of Probation, 1993) remain relevant in highlighting the variable extent to which effective communication takes place to enable aspects of joint supervision, under such arrangements as a community penalty with a mental health treatment requirement, to be brought together in a coherent whole. Clark and colleagues (2002) provide further evidence of the continuing tension between treatment and punishment, suggesting that more effective communication can make joint supervision arrangements more effective both for the patient/offender and for the justice system. Both of these publications cite examples of poor decisions in that they were made by one practitioner without any reference to the other in the partnership, this in spite of the fact that they having a direct bearing on the outcome and the efficacy of the order.

The clear lesson, reinforced by numerous enquiries, is that agreement at the outset on the roles and purposes of each party to any supervision arrangement – here probation officer and psychiatrist or psychologist – and the extent of involvement by each in the decision-making of the other, can help to provide a more coherent service for the patient. For medical practitioners, the core of the dilemma is to define the point at which their duty of care towards an individual is superseded by a wider responsibility for public safety. For his/her part, the probation officer/offender manager requires a clear indication of the patient's diagnosis, prognosis and treatment, together with regular feedback about his/her level of co-operation and compliance. All three partners in the order benefit from discussion about the implications of any breakdown in co-operation, given that this normally leads to action in the court for breach of its order.

Enforcement/compliance

Throughout the first decade of the twenty-first century, the Probation Service in England and Wales has moved towards the management of more serious offenders and to being 'a law enforcement agency', this last phrase first being used about the Service by a Home Office Minister (Paul Boateng) in 2001. He seemed to take the view that the primary focus should therefore be on challenging and changing offending behaviour rather than dealing directly with social welfare issues. One consequence of this is that the criminal justice system should be making ever greater efforts to divert offenders whose welfare and treatment needs exceed any immediate and serious threat they may pose to public safety – into community services other than the Probation Service.

The probation role in community supervision is now to act on assessments of risk and *criminogenic* need, with a view to implementing programmes to change the offending behaviour, ironically often based on cognitive behavioural treatments. The aim is to reduce re-offending and risk of harm whilst simultaneously holding the offender to account both for his/her conduct and co-operation with rehabilitative and reparational work. The implementation of court-ordered supervision is governed by *offender management standards*, which require explicit integration of the work with offenders before, during and after custody. These standards set out clear criteria for the enforcement of orders with some limited scope for discretion in individual cases. There is a fine balance to be struck between these tight standards and a patient's engagement with treatment.

Whether an individual should receive punishment for refusing or discontinuing treatment must depend on the risk posed and the extent to which the person is deemed to be responsible for his/her actions. Elements of court-ordered supervision are generally specified as part of the sentence, but the requirement for psychiatric treatment is the single exception. Here, it is left to the clinical judgment of the practitioner to identify and review details of the treatment needed. This must be undertaken, however, within the context of the offender's accountability for their actions and compliance with the court's expectations.

Community mental health services are primarily geared to deal with patients voluntarily seeking help and the management of those whose behaviour has brought them formally into the purview of the criminal justice system frequently gives rise to professional dilemmas. The balance between individual accountability for behaviour and the need for treatment in order to resolve problems that may be beyond the individual's control is a fine one, and studies undertaken into community mental health teams and their engagement with statutory orders offer evidence of the unease felt by many practitioners (e.g. Vaughan et al., 2000).

The long-running discussion around mental health legislative reform (see chapter 3) throws the tension between voluntary and compulsory treatment régimes into sharp relief. The inter-play between public protection and individual human rights is the stuff of heated debate and frequent litigation. The approach of helping agencies, which here include police and probation services, must be to ensure that health needs are met, as far as possible, through easy access to attractive services and voluntary arrangements. This should make it a rarity to need to rely on a court order to enable necessary treatment to which a patient could not otherwise gain access. Studies of mental health problems among prisoners provide ample evidence (see above) of how much is still to be achieved in this regard, as people continue to slip through the treatment net. One method used to facilitate the communication and mutual understanding between mental health and probation staff, is to have 'surgery' times when psychiatrists are available in probation offices for staff to discuss specific cases. Bowden (1978) described such a model, and one of us (PJT) ran such a 'surgery' for many years in the form of weekly hour-long seminars at a central London probation office. Such support arrangements can facilitate the preliminary exploration of treatment options and also identify access routes to the care programme approach for specific cases, whether or not a formal legal requirement exists. A further option is to have probation staff seconded on a liaison basis to multi-agency community forensic teams. There are complex issues of governance, accountability, finance and casework responsibility to be resolved through the development of protocols, but the potential benefits are substantial. Reports of work of this kind in Wessex in the 1990s were encouraging (Badger et al., 1999).

The Role of Inter-Agency Strategic Bodies

Drug Action Teams (DATs), or their counterparts in Wales, Scotland and Northern Ireland, have been created to balance the availability of services to all in need with a means of facilitating services ordered as part of a court sentence. No such statutory arrangement exists to establish inter-agency structures in respect of mentally disordered offenders and it is left to local initiative and practice to develop such co-ordination. A particularly frequently encountered dilemma for probation officers in the assessment and supervision of offenders is that of dual diagnosis or multiple comorbidities. They find it difficult, if not impossible to mobilize mental health services to work coherently with such problems. In areas where services have adopted joint appointments, or developed protocols between substance misuse and mental health service providers, communication and liaison has resulted in a better service for all patients, not only offender-patients.

Assessment of Risk

Risk assessment is a key responsibility of anyone undertaking evaluations for the courts or for the purposes of supervision. This is dealt with more extensively elsewhere (chapter 22), but in brief, the main areas of concern are risk of offending, risk to self, and the risk of harm to the public. It is the last of these that forms the priority for the probation and prison services and risk assessment has to take account of both the likelihood of a dangerous act being repeated and its probable impact. The probation service relies on the OASys assessment mechanism, and its secondary tools, which have been specifically designed for domestic violence and for sexual offences, as a framework for identification of those cases where there is such a risk of harm that multi-agency planning is needed. Within the MAPPA, covered in detail below, there is some separation in considering risks posed while someone is in custody and those which are anticipated on his/her return to the community. The need for such separation has been evidenced in mental health services (Tardiff et al., 1997).

Multi-Agency Public Protection Arrangements (MAPPA)

The Criminal Justice and Court Services Act 2000 (amended by Criminal Justice Act 2003) provided a statutory basis for shared assessment and management of the following offenders whose behaviour is considered to pose a significant risk of harm to the public:

> category 1: registered sex offenders
> category 2: violent and other sex offenders
> category 3: other offenders considered to pose a risk of serious harm to the public

The Act created a statutory authority comprising police, prison and probation services which is required to establish a Strategic Management Board for MAPPA for each police force area. Other agencies have a statutory duty to co-operate with the arrangements, including local authorities and health trusts or boards (Ministry of Justice, 2012a). Evaluation of MAPPA has confirmed their consistency and effectiveness (Maguire et al., 2001; Kemshall et al., 2005), Guidance is updated regularly (https://www.justice.gov.uk/government/organisations/ministry-of-justice).

Developing local MAPPA systems

Agreement must be reached within each mental health trust in England and Wales about how the interface between mental health services and MAPPA will be managed. It is vital that all mental health agencies which provide any services to people who are also offenders or who pose a threat to others should engage with the MAPPA processes at this level. It is also essential that the service providers themselves engage, as appropriate, at an individual level. Consideration should always be given to referral into the system of any person thought to pose a serious threat to others, regardless of whether s/he is already under any formal supervision or not. This should ensure co-ordinated planning for his/her support and surveillance. Numerous high profile tragedies have shown up the fault lines in communication between the various agencies engaging with aspects of a patient's situation, many resulting in full independent and even public inquiries (see chapter 28). Further, the assessment and management of risk should remain a continuous process, irrespective of whether legal or court orders remain in force. Agencies also, however, need to balance those priorities dictated by rigid definitions of core statutory responsibilities and those by assessment of how much more can be achieved by pro-active engagement and treatment.

Wider public disclosure

A further controversial subject to be considered in joint planning for case management of serious offenders in the community is that of public disclosure. There is heated, ongoing debate about the extent to which local communities should have information about offenders who live in their midst and who may pose a significant risk either to specific individuals, a class of individuals, or to the wider community. Sustained local and national media campaigns continue to push for a replication of US legislation, popularly known as 'Megan's law'. This was a federal amendment to earlier legislation, the Jacob Wetterling Crimes Against Children and Sexually Violent Offender Act 1994, also named for a child victim. The 1994 Act required all states to develop registries of the addresses of sexual offenders living in the community, and Megan's 1996 amendment required all of them to allow public access, albeit giving discretion as to how and how much. Pressure for 'Sarah's law' in the UK began to grow following the high profile murder of Sarah Payne in 2000. Early in 2010, the Home Secretary announced that, following a limited pilot evaluation of such a public information scheme, it would be rolled out nationally through 2010 and 2011. In fact, Pawson's (2002) systematic review, hampered as it was by the varied enactments at US state level, concluded that the only outcome study (Schram and Milloy, 1995) which had demonstrated a non-significant reduction in recidivist behaviour and faster apprehension after re-offending in this context, had significant design flaws. All but one of the subsequent US studies have also failed to show evidence of reduction in recidivism of sex offenders or improved safety of children following these laws (see also Welchans, 2005; Zevitz, 2006). The one study that did find show some change was substantial, of over 8,000 released sex offenders in Washington State before and after passage of the statutes (Washington State Institute for Public Policy, 2005). Overall, felony recidivism was unchanged, but after the 1996 amendments, there was a 20% reduction in violent felony recidivism and a 70% reduction in sexual felony recidivism, albeit both from a low base rate. The document further stresses that this does not imply cause and effect, as other relevant changes also happened in the period, including more severe sentencing, which would have specifically removed these more serious offenders from the sampling frame. Inaccuracies on the registers are common (e.g. Levenson and Cotter, 2005). Levenson et al. (2007) studied the effect on the sex offenders themselves, and on their families; on the positive side, a majority of the 239 interviewed said that they were more motivated to prevent re-offending, but on the negative, a majority also said that the stresses imposed made recovery more difficult and 16% reported that partners or other family members had been threatened.

The MAPPA system has so far sought to deal with this issue by ensuring the presence of lay advisors on the strategic management boards to monitor and question policy development. Each Board is also required to develop a protocol dealing with disclosure of information to identified community representatives or groups (such as school headteachers) under the authority of a senior officer in either the police or probation services. This requires careful handling, especially where mental health is a factor in the risk. Further complexities are afforded by the requirements of the Sex Offenders Act 1997 for the registration and monitoring of all convicted offenders who are required to register with the police for a prescribed period of time after conviction or release from custody. The police undertake monitoring visits and share information via the MAPPA system to partner agencies. Assessments are made as to how information about treatment and diagnosis should be handled in any disclosure process, taking into account its effect on both the patient and the community. The risks of heightening community tension, increasing the vulnerability of individuals (both perpetrators and victims) and of discouraging co-operation with treatment, support or surveillance have to be carefully weighed. The *Review of the Protection of Children from Sex Offenders* (Home Office, 2007) made proposals for the piloting of wider reactive disclosure arrangements which are under implementation. Individuals may now, for example, instigate a police check on prospective partners if they have vulnerable children and there are restrictions on placing child sex offenders 'in approved premises immediately adjacent to schools and nurseries'; in addition, public access to sex offender registers has been piloted.

The Victim's Perspective

The Criminal Justice and Court Services Act 2000 gave a statutory responsibility to probation staff to consult and notify victims about the release arrangements for offenders serving a custodial sentence of 12 months or more for a violent or sexual offence (section 69). Many measures and pronouncements from government spokespersons have spelt out the need for the criminal justice system to give greater consideration to the needs and wishes of the victim, and the Domestic Violence, Crime and Victim's Act 2004 extended such rights for victims to those of people who are detained by the Court under mental health legislation. The concern of many victims is to ensure that their experience is acknowledged; and recent steps such as the use of victim impact statements in court proceedings have facilitated this. With respect to more serious crimes, however, many have valid concerns about the offender returning to live close by, and every effort would be made to respect this. In order to maintain appropriate confidentiality between the parties, the probation officer working with the offender would always be independent of the officer working with the victim (Rawsthorne, 1998; see also chapter 28).

Working With the Probation Service: Some Conclusions

The substantial association between offending and mental disorders means that there must be a shared commitment between mental health services and criminal justice agencies of all kinds, but the most natural relationship in many ways is with the probation service in promoting rehabilitation, personal and wider community safety. Structures to support joint working are becoming ever more formal, both with respect to inter-agency working, as within the MAPPA structure, and at an individual level, as, for example, in running a community sentence with a mental health treatment requirement. In parallel with this preventive engagement comes an argument for preventative detention and enforced treatment or containment as evidenced in the efforts of several Home Secretaries to launch programmes for those who are deemed not amenable to conventional treatments – including the now defunct dangerous and severe personality disorder (DSPD) initiatives (see also chapter 16). The future must lie with greater engagement in partnerships in the early stages of assessment of mental health problems and, where possible, diversion and the implementation of programmes of intervention that simultaneously meet health and criminogenic needs, while monitoring the offender during the time s/he is being re-integrated into the community.

WORKING WITH VOLUNTARY AGENCIES

The National Council for Voluntary Organizations (NCVO) recognizes a range of self-governing charitable or non-profit-making organizations, of various sizes and organizational types, which explicitly work within a structure which is independent of government and yet may, from time to time, work alongside government agencies. Voluntary sector organizations (VSOs), sometimes also known as third sector organizations, rely heavily on volunteers, are for public benefit, and variously deliver services, advocate or lobby on behalf of their named interest group, facilitate co-operation locally, nationally and internationally, as relevant, and/or raise funds for their activities. The relationship between voluntary organizations and mentally disordered offenders (MDOs) is complex. On the one hand, the voluntary sector's classic role of working horizontally across systems and social policy areas lends itself well to working with a group of people who have to interact both with the criminal justice and mental health systems; on the other, VSOs are often driven by an ethos that privileges the individual over the 'system', and they have difficulty with categorizations that the system seeks to impose. 'MDO' is a construct that may be viewed as stemming much more from the needs and priorities of the statutory system than from those of the individuals it describes, although here, it seems ironic that this shorthand was introduced by our voluntary sector authors, not having been much favoured elsewhere in this book.

Many VSOs are created out of a desire to work with the most excluded members of society. Their members therefore have difficulty in engaging with a construct such as 'MDO' that is exclusive and fails to recognize equally high levels of need among people who do not fit within its parameters. VSOs certainly work with offenders who have mental disorder, but many will interpret their remit much more widely as working with people who have been arrested or imprisoned and who are not coping. The concept of 'coping' is crucial here: it describes a person's mental and emotional vulnerability as s/he attempts to engage with the system. It does not rest on any particular diagnosis, or the person having committed any particular offence, it simply describes an unmet need that calls for a response.

Almost as important is the difficulty for VSOs in working with two systems, the mental health and criminal justice systems, both of which can be highly coercive. VSOs are often accountable at some level to the users of their services, many of whom will view both systems with extreme suspicion. A key dilemma is, therefore, whether VSOs can work within these systems without being seen to work for them or to be too closely enmeshed with them. An increasing trend in England and Wales for the voluntary sector to provide public services presents considerable challenges for VSOs wanting to work with mentally disordered offenders if 'the system' is not perceived by the users of their services as working in their interests.

A further problem for the voluntary sector in working with mentally disordered offenders is the highly reductive and stigmatic nature of the label 'MDO'. Although it is not a label that we favour or use much in this book, it is quite widely used in practice, arising from legislation and is used by many organizations within the criminal justice system, including the Ministry or Justice and the Crown Prosecution Service. In almost all cases, VSOs will wish to advocate positively for their service users and will prefer to use person-centred language, such as 'people with mental health problems who have offended'. Even this language can present ethical dilemmas by suggesting a distinct category of people. Most VSOs will prefer to emphasize complexity and diversity in their users' needs and will stress highly individual histories of exclusion and vulnerability rather than adopt a more convenient shorthand.

These ideological and ethical dilemmas make the criminal justice system very tricky ground for some mental health charities, but, nevertheless, examples of imaginative and needs-led practice have emerged. This section examines the background to these before surveying the types of practice currently available and then drawing together some of the common principles underpinning these.

Background to Voluntary Agency Work With Offenders With Mental Disorder

Voluntary sector organizations have a long history of working within both the mental health and the criminal justice systems, and also with people who are so marginalized that they have contact with both but are barely in either – people who are homeless (Jones, 1992; Bonner et al., 2008, 2009). As for any other VSO, they fulfil at least three broad functions: advocacy for the individual, provision of services for the individual, and lobbying for the class of people they particularly serve. This last function also often means that some engage in or commission research, so that, where appropriate, their arguments are as strongly evidence-based as possible.

Mental health charities such as *Rethink*, *Mind*, *Together* and the *Richmond Fellowship* have become important national providers of services to the NHS. They are now competitors for substantial shares of the mental health 'market' but they also continue to work collaboratively, through forums like the Mental Health Alliance, to advocate independently for the rights of the individual within the system. Others, such as the *Centre for Mental Health* (formerly the *Sainsbury Centre*), have taken research, analysis and efforts to influence government policy as their main roles.

Criminal justice charities are more diverse in terms of scale, role and funding, but some national organizations have emerged, such as *Nacro*, *Catch 22*, the *Prison Reform Trust* and *Victim Support*, and international ones, such as the *Howard League for Penal Reform*. In addition, the criminal justice system is more obviously populated by a proliferation of much smaller VSOs that focus on niche interests, such as prisoners' families and community safety. More recently, VSOs that have been working in other areas have been attracted into the criminal justice system, most notably housing associations, drugs charities and education, training and employment charities.

For a long time, VSOs in both the mental health and criminal justice sectors have recognized that there is significant overlap between their areas of work, but the response was largely limited to campaigning and occasional pilot activity. This has begun to shift since the 1990s, as VSOs have started to recognize that offenders with mental disorder may become particular casualties of 'silo' delivery. VSOs have sought to extend and diversify their business base by developing innovative and distinctive expertise and specialisms. Many of the VSOs, such as the *Centre for Mental Health*, *Together* and *Rethink*, that have traditionally been concerned with mental health, have become increasingly focused on people with mental health problems within the criminal justice system, and have developed specific work streams accordingly.

Offenders with mental health problems are an obvious client group for the voluntary sector, because so many are known to be inadequately engaged with statutory organizations. Several reports and surveys have identified high levels of unmet need among them, not forgetting also physical ill health (e.g. Bridgwood and Malbon, 1994) and the special difficulties of young people (Harrington et al., 2005; see also chapter 19, and other subgroups, such as women [see chapter 20]). A survey of mental disorder among prisoners by the ONS (Singleton et al., 1998b) found that up to 11% of those with an identifiable mental disorder had turned down treatment or help when offered it in the year before imprisonment and up to 14% had turned it down in the year since coming into prison. By contrast, up to 10% had requested help but not received it in the year before imprisonment and up to 21% had not received requested help in the year since coming into prison.

Where voluntary sector organizations have responded, they have attempted to work with the individual to achieve improved access to support and treatment within the system, rather than to replace the system. They have positioned themselves at referral points in the criminal justice system, such as police stations, courts and prisons, and have assumed assessment, advocacy and advice roles. Most innovatively, they have crossed organizational boundaries to work with the multiple needs of mentally disordered offenders, following models established by organizations such as *Elmore* (http://www.elmoreteam.org.uk) and *Revolving Doors* in London (http://www.revolving-doors.org.uk).

The Need for the Voluntary Sector

Need for the voluntary sector to work with mentally disordered offenders, thus, most commonly emerges through failures in engagement between them and statutory services. Ways in which such breakdown may occur in non-medical settings can be broadly summarized in the following ways (O'Shea et al., 2003).

1. Most mental health professionals have little experience of the criminal justice system while people in the criminal justice system rarely have much mental health expertise. Each system therefore relies on the other to support this client group, but a truly joint approach is unusual in practice. This is often because neither system is willing or able to prioritize the resources needed, each seeing the problems as the responsibility of the other.

2. Offenders, or alleged offenders, with mental disorder are often subject to the 'inverse care law', which dictates that the greater the individual's needs, the less care they are likely to receive (Tudor Hart, 1971). Their problems are commonly multiple and inter-related, so they may become labelled as beyond help. Such complexity often requires carefully co-ordinated support from a large number of agencies, and breakdown may occur because there is no one responsible for such co-ordination, which is in itself resource intensive.

3. Many (alleged) offenders have serious mental health problems which are not seen as crossing a critical threshold, so they are not prioritized for help. This is where the categorical approach to diagnosis taken by most psychiatrists, even encouraged by the courts' taking an interest in how the person's condition fits with definitions in one or other of the diagnostic manuals, is so unhelpful. Furthermore, few psychiatrists see treatment of substance misuse as central to their work, and yet it is probably the single greatest health need among offenders, and complicates many other conditions.

4. Entry into the criminal justice system is characterized by its unpredictability, which can further disrupt the coherence and continuity of a care plan; it means that assessment of need often has to be undertaken under pressure in an unsuitable environment. There are so many points in the system when a vulnerable offender may be lost to services.

5. (Alleged) offenders themselves are often resistant to support, often because they have had extremely poor experiences of authority and institutions, but sometimes because they are afraid of the perceived stigma with respect to other prisoners of being seen as a 'nutter'. They may therefore fail to disclose problems.

The role of the voluntary sector should not be understood solely as meeting real or perceived shortcomings in statutory provision. Its unique contribution is increasingly being understood as much more than just filling a gap (HM Treasury, 2002). Its independence and track record of innovation and flexible expertise allow it to work differently and offer things that statutory services may not be in a position to offer.

Voluntary Sector Responses

The national picture of voluntary sector services designed specifically for offenders with mental disorder is still patchy, and they are often precariously funded. Perhaps because the needs of such people are so varied, and the pattern of services in each locality so different, it would be extremely difficult to make a well-defined funding stream available to relevant VSOs. They are often, therefore, reliant on piecing together multiple funding courses, some national government support and some charitable subsidy. There is a well-established practice of consulting VSOs in some courts and communities, but service provision is not always possible. There are, however, pockets of good practice across the UK, which reflect a diversity of approach in operation of VSOs. In their respective independent reviews of vulnerable groups within the criminal justice system, both Corston (2007) for women offenders and Bradley (2009) for offenders with mental health problems and/or intellectual disabilities, have acknowledged the vital role that the voluntary sector has to play in provision of holistic support to these people at all stages in the criminal justice system. We will now outline some examples of good practice.

Community-based schemes

Organizations such as *Revolving Doors Agency* have developed schemes that can respond to the needs of mentally disordered offenders in the community. Their aim is to offer a continuity of approach and care between the various episodes in the criminal justice system. Revolving Doors accept referrals from police stations, courts and prisons, and offer support from one stage to the next, staying with some clients well beyond their involvement in the criminal justice system. They offer a combination of emotional and practical support, using a 'link working' approach to help the client to overcome the barriers between him or her and the services that could help improve his/her health and stop offending. Few of the clients of this link worker service were found to be receiving appropriate services, such as primary care, benefits, treatment for addictions and/or supported housing on referral to the schemes, and nearly half required support across 6–10 sectors within a 3-month period (O'Shea et al., 2003). The link worker model helps its clients navigate their way through the system and develop the skills for engaging with services constructively. The teams also work to co-ordinate services within a local area for offenders with complex needs.

In addition, VSOs have been instrumental in the development of women's community centres – for female offenders and other vulnerable women, many of whom have past and/or current experiences of trauma and of poor mental health. The centres, such as *Anawim* and *Calderdale*, provide safe, women-only environments which focus on strengths and building self-esteem, and act as 'one-stop-shops' into a range of other support services. Many also deliver community sentences or intensive alternatives to custody in a women-only setting. The national roll out of these centres was recommended by Corston (2007) in her review of women in the criminal justice system.

Court support

Responsibility for the assessment and care of people with mental health problems passing through the courts sits between the courts, health services and probation service. In many areas, the probation service provides an assessment and diversion service but, in others, there is a failure to provide any service because of multi-agency deadlock. In some areas, VSOs such as *Together* have secured funding to place mental health practitioners in courts, where they are delegated responsibility for tasks such as the initial assessment of people who may require diversion into the health system. They often also perform a liaison and advocacy role, to ensure that needs such as housing and strengthening relationships with families, friends and employers are met. These services too are inconsistently available and, even where they are, are often not resourced to work with all appropriate clients.

Prison-based support

The main expansion in voluntary sector work with mentally disordered offenders has been in prison. Most prisons now host a range of VSOs, such as *Nacro, SOVA, Apex Trust* and *Citizens Advice*, which work to support the resettlement process. Although few of these explicitly focus on work with offenders with mental disorder, inevitably, they act for many people who have such difficulties, as prevalence of mental health problems among prisoners is so high. Most obviously in prisons, VSOs assist with housing problems, substance misuse, education and training. VSOs such as the *Rehabilitation of Addicted Prisoners Trust* (RAPT) are major providers of the Counselling Assessment Referral Advice and Throughcare (CARAT) service, available in all English and Welsh prisons, as well as offering community-based interventions as part of the drug interventions programme.

Some VSOs, such as the *Prisoners Advice and Care Trust* (PACT) and the *Southside Partnership* more specifically focus on work with mental and emotional problems as well as practical matters. *PACT*, for instance, has pioneered work at the point of entry into prison, when mental and emotional difficulties are likely to be at their most acute. 'First night' services provide emotional support and attempt to deal with some of the most pressing problems facing people at this point, in the hope that this will also have the advantage of reducing anxiety levels and risk of self-harm and suicide. One key challenge of this work is to gain the immediate trust of prisoners, who may still be in a state of shock at being in prison. They may be distrustful of offers of help, having been round the system many times, they may be detoxing from alcohol and/or drugs, or they may simply want to avoid all contact with anyone until they leave prison again. For women in particular, 'first night' services may involve securing the wellbeing of their children; this may be particularly problematic as often they are unwilling to disclose that they have children, either because they are fearful of their being taken into care, or because they are reluctant for their families to know that they are in prison. Other services, such as *Together Women*, have staff or volunteers who go into prisons both to provide emotional support and to link women with community-based services, including women's centres.

Peer support

Prisoners are increasingly recognized as a resource for each other. *St Giles Trust* has developed a now renowned peer-led model for the provision of housing support within prisons and 'through the gate' practical support to prisoners on release. Other organizations train prisoners to provide interpersonal support. The best known and tried example of this is the *Samaritans'* development of the 'listeners' scheme (see also above).

Helplines

Several voluntary sector organizations, most obviously *Nacro* and the *Prison Reform Trust*, offer a national telephone advice service both for prisoners and their families, while national mental health charities such as *MIND* and *Rethink* offer similar services for people with mental health problems. The *Howard League for Penal Reform* has a programme funded to assist people aged 21 or under in prison or a secure children's home, through the provision of free legal advice and representation on a range of issues which might affect them while in custody. While for the most part these services are not specifically for (alleged) offenders with mental disorder, they do deal with many of the concerns about mental illness and the criminal justice system. A particular advantage of voluntary sector run helplines in such circumstances is that they may be able to offer confidential advice about where to access help with mental illness when prisoners or their families are fearful of disclosing a problem. The *Samaritans* also offer emotional support helplines in some prisons.

Arts and creative work

Many organizations, such as the *Creative and Supportive Trust* (CAST) and *Clean Break*, use arts and creative work to offer a safe, alternative means of working with some of the most vulnerable offenders. The *Arts Alliance* is a coalition of arts organizations working within the criminal justice system, aiming to promote arts in the criminal justice sector and broker relationships between public bodies and voluntary organizations. Arts-based interventions have the goal of increasing self-esteem and self-confidence. As well as developing creative skills, some organizations also use arts-based approaches as innovative ways of improving basic life or employment skills, for example *Safe Ground* has a drama-based parenting programme.

Principles of Engagement

Workers in most voluntary organizations understand that their unique contribution lies in two key objectives, first, creation of a positive relationship with the mentally disordered offender, which may lead to other positive relationships, and secondly, provision of practical support across institutional boundaries.

Creating a positive relationship with alleged and convicted offenders who have mental disorder

It is common for people with mental health problems who are in the criminal justice system to have experienced serious difficulties in their previous relationships, as children and as adults, both with family and with professionals. Many will have experienced the loss of a parent through death, parental separation, imprisonment and/or hospitalization; physical, emotional and/or sexual abuse; and/or being taken into care; and/or being excluded from school. Their adult situations of being imprisoned, hospitalized, rejected by services, or having their own children taken into care are, in some respects, a repetition of those earlier experiences. Often services designed to help have been experienced as coercive, unduly interventionist and/or punitive. This makes it difficult for such people to distinguish care from punishment, and is no foundation for the trusting relationships which could facilitate change. VSOs can sometimes break though such barriers.

Persistence

Voluntary sector organizations try at all times to take a non-punitive approach, staying with their client even when s/he infringes the ground rules of the service. This may make all the difference to ultimate engagement. In an attempt to reject a service before it rejects them, people in such situations will often act in ways they believe will terminate that relationship; at least this gives them some sense of control. Some may be abusive, some simply not turn up for appointments. With many statutory services, this behaviour often produces the intended result, with services withdrawing support. When VSO workers persist, they send a clear message to their clients that they are not going to abandon them suddenly, and this can form the basis for progress.

Choice

VSOs nevertheless offer their clients the choice of whether or not to engage. The choice simply to talk to someone, in the knowledge that this does not have to carry a treatment implication, may prove to be a vital first step towards accessing appropriate services. The individual may then be able to start thinking through what s/he wants for him/herself, and learn that s/he really may have some choices. Even within a coerced treatment framework, there is generally still scope for choice about individual treatments or activities if the individual knows how to express his/her wishes in this respect. Support in mainstream services is often predicated on a condition of readiness for change, for example a dependent drinker having already given up alcohol or an offender making a full acknowledgement of fault. VSOs may offer their clients the opportunity to demonstrate a wish for change even when they don't feel ready to take all the necessary steps.

Assertive engagement

Many offenders with mental disorder have a complex mix of problems, such as homelessness, drug misuse and institutionalization, each of which alone would challenge any person's ability to engage with statutory services, but collectively form a substantial barrier. Such a mix tends to lead to missed appointments and moves of residence at short notice, which disrupts relationships with key workers. VSOs are often able to meet clients where they are most comfortable, at their home or hostel, in a café, on the street, or, if necessary, in prison or court.

Role-modelling

Many mentally disordered offenders express their frustration with their circumstances and with services by acting out against the services that they need. The voluntary sector can help clients to model more productive behaviours, perhaps by accompanying them to a housing department or GP surgery, and demonstrating appropriate behaviour and successful, non-destructive strategies for interaction and problem-solving. Peer support from ex-offenders who have reformed their lives can provide an inspirational role model for someone who shares some of the adverse, earlier experiences but has not yet found a successful way of getting beyond them.

Engagement without assessment

VSOs are able to work with clients before a full and formal assessment has been made. With some statutory organizations, many people have to wait a long time just for assessment. This often proves to be a gate-keeping measure, not least because it can increase the risk of that person walking away from the services, sometimes with hostility. Conversely, statutory services may put so much resource into assessment that clients find themselves being assessed again and again without actually reaching the treatment or practical support sought. VSOs are not generally bound by rigid procedures, so they are able to start responding immediately to urgent need while also assessing the longer term requirements.

Provision of practical support across institutional boundaries

For many offenders with mental disorder, entering the criminal justice system multiplies their range of needs; being imprisoned can add homelessness, debt, and family breakdown to an existing list of, say, mental illness, hazardous drinking, illiteracy and unemployment. For many, the shortfalls in service responses only re-enact the fractures and chaos in their past. Structure and coherence seem to be required above all. Helping the person to complete a small but important task, such as ensuring that a pet is temporarily rehomed, may provide a first achievement along a road of enabling him/her to have some influence on his/her world. VSOs may be uniquely well placed to do this.

Navigation

A number of reports have concluded that people with complex needs require a new form of professional to help them navigate the system (Keene, 2001; Rankin and Regan, 2004). A complex response is likely to be counterproductive. Many offenders, with or without mental health problems, have considerable difficulty in filling out application forms and understanding the different rules of each system. A 'service navigator' or 'link worker' is able to work with an individual across organizational boundaries, and, from the worker's knowledge of the systems, so the individual can find a gateway into the various forms of help s/he needs.

Co-ordination

VSOs may play a vital role in bringing together a range of organizations, each of which alone might be unwilling to take responsibility.

Advocacy

Independent advocacy is a role whereby a support worker can represent the wishes of his/her client to the system. This is a difficult role, which requires continuing opportunities for reflective practice as it is easy for the worker to slip into a position of representing what s/he thinks the client needs.

Working With the Voluntary Sector: Some Conclusions

Prospects for the future of voluntary sector work with offenders who have mental disorder are uncertain. On the one hand, there is an unprecedented level of interest in their pathways into prison, and a desire at every level to reduce their numbers there. There is also a renewed push to transfer public service provision into the voluntary and independent sectors, this may threaten many of the voluntary sector's advantages of independence and flexible working. Movement towards 'payment by results' as a funding mechanism means that funding will become dependent on outcomes rather than outputs. This may increase the chance that flexible approaches will flourish. There is, however, concern that such mechanisms may ask the voluntary sector to shoulder an untenable level of financial risk.

A great deal will hinge on the evidence base for the voluntary sector approach, and whether commissioners, social investors and primary contractors – who may be able to shoulder the financial burden – are persuaded that a flexible social care model can be applied effectively within a criminal justice setting. The voluntary sector has rarely been able to evidence its success in working with mentally disordered offenders, due both to a lack of funding for research and the small caseloads of many of the organizations involved. A voluntary organization which might help

here – a charity dedicated to funding research in the field – does not exist at all. People with heart disease, or cancer, or AIDS, or a host of other physical health problems can count on such charitable funding, and the implicit public support that goes with it. This is yet another area in which people with mental disorder who come into conflict with the law are socially excluded.

SERVICE PROVISION FOR OFFENDERS WITH MENTAL DISORDER IN SCOTLAND

Pathways to Services

Mentally disordered offenders in Scotland may be diverted from the criminal justice system to mental health services at any stage of the criminal justice process. They may also be returned unless a final disposal is made solely to psychiatric services (see figure 25.1). The criminal justice process can proceed in tandem with an individual's assessment and treatment, or at a later stage. The policy guiding the interactions between these services is established (Scottish Office, 1998a; see also McManus and Thomson, 2005).

In Scotland, convicted offenders with a primary diagnosis of personality disorder who receive a custodial disposal are sent to prison or to a young offenders' institution (YOI), and not to psychiatric hospital. Offenders with personality disorder were included within the remit of the MacLean Committee (Scottish Executive, 2000) which reported on sentencing disposals for, and the future management and treatment of, serious sexual and violent offenders who may present a continuing danger to the public. Its recommendations were largely enacted in the Criminal Justice (Scotland) Act 2003 and came into effect in 2006. These included the:

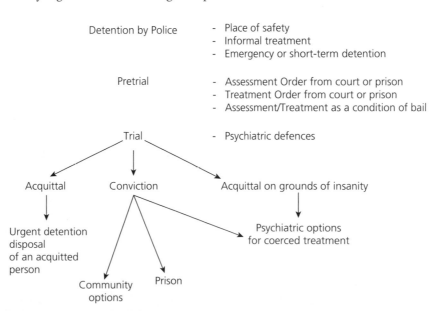

Figure 25.1 Criminal Justice and Mental Health Systems: Diversion in Scotland.

- creation of the risk management authority (RMA) which has responsibility for setting standards, guidelines and guidance on risk assessment and risk management, training and accreditation, and policy and research;
- introduction of a risk assessment order (RAO), a 90- to 180-day period of assessment to allow preparation of a risk assessment report to assist the court in determining risk to the public at large; an RAO may be applied by the Court to an offender convicted of a serious violent or sexual offence, or an offence that endangers life;
- introduction of an order for lifelong restriction imposed on the basis of risk if the court believes, on a balance of probabilities, that

> the nature of, or the circumstances of the commission of, the offence of which the convicted person has been found guilty either in themselves or as part of a pattern of behaviour are such as to demonstrate that there is a likelihood that he, if at liberty, will seriously endanger the lives, or physical or psychological wellbeing, of members of the public at large.

The emphasis in the legislation arising from the MacLean Committee report is on seriousness of the offence and future risk presented, rather than on a specific diagnosis such as 'psychopathy' or severe personality disorder (see chapter 4 for more details on the law).

Police

Place of safety

The Mental Health (Care and Treatment) (Scotland) Act 2003 allows an individual to be removed by police from a public place to a place of safety for the purpose of a medical examination (see also chapter 4). In Scotland, a place of safety is usually a psychiatric hospital or an accident and emergency department.

Psychiatric services to police stations

Psychiatric services to police stations vary across Scotland. In some areas psychiatrists will attend, often following an initial assessment by a forensic medical examiner (FME), but in others the FME must decide whether admission to hospital or further psychiatric follow-up is required. The following issues must be considered.

1. *Fitness to remain in custody:* As in England and Wales, major physical or mental illness with immediate and serious risk to health and safety may require transfer to hospital.
2. *Assessment and treatment needs:* An individual may be fit to remain in custody but require further assessment and/or treatment of a mental disorder. Medical advice can be given to the police on medication or on observation regarding risk of self-harm whilst in custody, to the

patient, to the court or prosecutors (procurators fiscal). Inpatient psychiatric care may be arranged on a voluntary basis or be under emergency or short-term orders of the Mental Health (Care and Treatment) (Scotland) Act 2003.

3. *Fitness to be interviewed:* A police officer must consider, prior to any interview, whether an individual is fit for this. Medical or legal criteria regarding fitness for interview do not currently exist. Factors to be considered include the detainee's ability to understand the police caution after it has been fully explained; his/her orientation in time, place and person and ability to recognize the key persons present during the police interview.
4. *Need for an appropriate adult:* The role of the appropriate adult is similar to that in England and Wales, but their use and organization are different. Appropriate adults may be used for a victim, witness, suspect or accused person, to provide support and assist communication between that individual and the police. Scottish Office (1998b) guidance encouraged establishment of appropriate adult schemes throughout Scotland, but these schemes have no statutory basis, unlike their counterparts in England and Wales. There are 16 appropriate adult schemes for the whole of Scotland (Thomson et al., 2004). It is for the court to decide whether the absence of an appropriate adult at interview brings the admissibility of the statements made by the interviewee into question. This has occurred on two occasions to date (*Milligan; HMA*).

In Scotland, appropriate adults are required to understand mental disorder, have experience and/or training in dealing with people with mental disorders, be able to communicate with such people, and understand that, whilst their professional qualifications and experience may be relevant to their appointment as an appropriate adult, they are not acting in their professional role. Appropriate adults may not be police officers, employees of the police force, relatives, friends or current or former carers of the interviewee, or someone in a long-term professional relationship with him/her. An appropriate adult may also be required in court or in a range of other circumstances, such as fingerprinting or identification parades.

Court

Diversion and psychiatric disposals

In most areas of Scotland a psychiatric service is provided to the courts, most commonly in the form of responding to requests for psychiatric reports. In some areas there are formal court liaison schemes, for example at Glasgow Sheriff Court (White et al., 2002). Different legal options are available to courts for diversion of people with mental disorder to mental health services at varying stages of the criminal justice process (see chapter 4). On minor charges only, procurators fiscal may decide, in part because of the presence of a mental disorder, that it is not in the public interest to proceed with a case. It is a procurator's fiscal duty to bring the known presence of a mental disorder in an accused person to the attention of the court. A new order for urgent detention of an acquitted person for up to 6 hours for the purpose of a medical assessment came into force in October 2005.

Drug courts

Drug courts have been established in Scotland (McIvor et al., 2003), with the aim of decreasing drug abuse and associated offending by offering treatment-based disposals within a deferred sentence framework, under drug treatment and testing orders or probation orders with a condition of drug treatment. The court deals with adults with a recognized pattern of drug misuse and related offending. Potential candidates on minor charges are identified by the prosecution service from police reports. The custody court may refer suitable cases to the drug court if the accused pleads guilty. The case is adjourned for 4 weeks for a social inquiry report, a drug action plan and results of drug testing. Cases are reviewed monthly and can be breached if the person is non-compliant.

Prison

The average daily prison population in Scotland is over 8,000. The prevalence of psychiatric disorders found there is shown in table 25.1. In prison, prevalence of psychosis is probably lower than in England and Wales, but otherwise rates of disorder are similar. The Scottish Prison Service (2002) aims to provide psychiatric services within prison equivalent to those available to people in the community.

On reception, all prisoners have a physical and mental health assessment. A detailed risk and needs assessment comes later for longer stay prisoners; problematic prisoners are referred to risk management groups. All closed prisons have visiting psychiatrists, and some have mental health teams. Legislation for transferring prisoners to psychiatric hospital is used about 70 times a year. Scottish prisoners do not have even the proposed 14-day transfer wait faced by their counterparts in England and Wales (McKenzie and, Sales, 2008), but numbers for transfer are very small. Of 22 people in this study, documentation had been completed for 16 in 3 days or less, and all but one of the remainder within the week of referral; actual transfer to hospital generally then happened within 3 further days (Fraser et al., 2007). Aside from overall population size difference, factors which may explain the relative ease of transfer in Scotland include:

- the lower rate of imprisonment compared with England and Wales (152:156 per 100,000);
- the lower prevalence of psychosis in Scottish prisons (psychosis is the illness most likely to result in transfer);
- the higher rate of psychiatric bed provision in Scotland than England and Wales (55:30 per 100,000; Information and Statistics Division (Scotland), 2009; Department of Health, 2009);
- a stronger tradition of local mental health and prison service co-operation in Scotland, with personal contacts promoting ease of transfer.

There are no mental health beds in Scottish prisons. There are some specific initiatives for prisoners with mental health problems, for example the day programme at HM Prison Perth, or the Open Doors Programme in HMP Barlinnie (Bartlett et al., 2001). The key to success with all such programmes is information sharing and a multidisciplinary approach. Other programmes exist for problems such as alcohol abuse, violent behaviour or sexual offending. Drug abuse is a particularly serious problem among prisoners in Scotland, so drug free areas, mandatory drug testing and maintenance prescribing are well established.

Table 25.1 Prison studies of psychiatric morbidity in Scotland

Authors	Study cohort	Measures	Results
Cooke (1994)	247 male remand and convicted prisoners	SADS-L	7.3% major psychological disorders[1] 32% neurotic disorder[1] 38% alcohol dependence[2] 20.6% drug abuse/dependence[2]
Davidson et al. (1995)	389 male remand prisoners	CIS	2.3% psychosis[1] 24.8% neurotic disorder[1] 22% alcohol abuse/dependence[2] 73% drug abuse/dependence[2]
Bartlett et al. (2000)	119 male receptions in one week to HMP Barlinnie	CIS-R SCAN	5% psychosis[1] 30% depression/anxiety disorder[1] 79% drug abuse[2]

[1]Point prevalence. [2]Lifetime diagnosis. [3]Present in past year

Suicide rates in Scottish prisons have fallen to fewer than five deaths per year (Bird, 2008). *Act to Care* is the suicide risk management strategy of the Scottish Prison Service. All prisoners are assessed on reception into prison for risk of self-harm but staff can complete an *Act* form at any time. This is a system that triggers a decision-making and review process. A prisoner's risk of self-harm is assessed as high, medium or low. Decisions are taken about his/her needs, location in prison and involvement with activities. The *Act* system allows for a degree of flexibility, for example not all high risk prisoners are placed in anti-ligature cells, but each is assessed by a nurse, doctor (if required) and hall (wing) manager. A case conference is called within 24 hours of *Act* form completion, and then up to a maximum of every 72 hours. Through-care arrangements are made if required following an individual's removal from the *Act*. In addition, *listeners'* schemes exist in some prisons (see p.661).

Through-care, linking care within prison to care in the community, is mainly organized by social workers, but health staff contribute for those prisoners with recognized health needs. The care programme approach should be used for those with major mental disorders.

Criminal Justice Social Work

The criminal justice social work service in Scotland is the equivalent to the probation service elsewhere. Although integrated into social work departments since 1968, it is directly funded by the Scottish Government. Its main aims are to tackle criminal behaviour and decrease risk of re-offending, to supervise offenders in the community, and to assist prisoners in re-settling in the community after release from custody. Prisoners on parole or life licence are managed in the community by criminal justice social workers.

In Scotland, the Management of Offenders etc. (Scotland) Act 2005 established Community Justice Authorities and multi-agency public protection arrangements (MAPPA). Under these, the police, local authorities and the Scottish prison service must establish joint arrangements to assess and manage the risk posed by sexual and violent offenders. This includes the NHS when the sexual or violent offenders also have mental disorder. The principles and aims of MAPPA in Scotland are precisely the same as in England and Wales, although there has been gradual incorporation of different groups – registered sex offenders from April 2007; mentally disordered offenders on restriction orders since April 2008. Management of MAPPA cases at levels 2 and 3 is reviewed at MAPPA meetings. Risk assessment and management is central to their work. The NHS in Scotland has taken a proactive role in MAPPA through an information sharing concordat, the establishment of a forensic network MAPPA health group and by training through the School of Forensic Mental Health.

SERVICE PROVISION FOR OFFENDERS WITH MENTAL DISORDER IN NORTHERN IRELAND

Strategic Context

In April 2010, policing and justice functions were devolved from the Westminster Government to the Northern Ireland Assembly, with the creation of a new government department, The Department of Justice (DOJ). This had been preceded by a period of intense activity reviewing services in the field.

In October 2002, the Minister for Health, Social Services and Public Safety in Northern Ireland established an independent review of the effectiveness of policy and service provision for people with mental health problems and/or intellectual disability and of the Mental Health (Northern Ireland) Order 1986. This comprehensive review has produced a number of reports on policy, services and legislation under one overarching title: The Bamford Review of Mental Health and Learning Disability (Northern Ireland) (2007, http://www.dhsspsni.gov.uk). It included the first major review in Northern Ireland of forensic mental health and learning disability services (Bamford 2006; also available in full from the website). This observed that

> people in need of forensic services are some of the most marginalized, stigmatized, vulnerable and poorly understood individuals in Northern Ireland and the services to meet their needs are some of the least developed.

Existing services were examined, together with the needs of individuals in police stations, on bail, attending court, in prison or on probation and detailed recommendations for service development then made. The forensic report supported the principles-based approach that permeated the whole of the Bamford Review. In particular, it advocated that the Department of Health, Special Services and Public Safety should provide services at key points in the criminal justice system to identify and assess people suffering, or thought to be suffering, from mental disorder. It proposed that these individuals should have access to services that are equivalent to those available in the rest of our society. Furthermore, it recommended co-operative planning between criminal justice agencies and health and personal social services, to ensure co-ordinated service delivery. It also considered the assessment and management of risk of recidivism or further harm to others, with resulting recommendations which included the establishment of a regional inter-agency network.

Following public consultation, and against a backdrop of re-organization of health and social services, the Northern Ireland Executive developed an action plan in 2009, subsuming plans for the development of forensic services within the overall framework to be taken forward by the *Health and Social Care Mental Health and Learning Disability Taskforce*. A *Bamford Monitoring Group*, led by the *Patient and Client Council*, was also established to help ensure change in frontline services. In March 2010, the Criminal Justice Inspection Northern Ireland published *Not a Marginal Issue*, a report on Mental Health and the Criminal Justice System in Northern Ireland. This report recognized the importance of making appropriate provision for mentally disordered offenders, making a series of recommendations. These included formation of a joint Health and Criminal Justice Board to bring together all organizations relevant to developing strategy.

When policing and justice functions were devolved from Westminster to the Northern Ireland Assembly in April 2010, the Northern Ireland Department of Justice (DOJ) was established. The DOJ has five agencies – the Northern Ireland Prison Service, the Northern Ireland Courts and Tribunals Service, the Compensation Agency, the Forensic Science Agency and the Youth Justice Agency. The DOJ also sponsors a number of non-departmental bodies affiliated with policing and justice.

The Service Pathway

Police

Place of safety

Article 130 of the Mental Health (Northern Ireland) Order 1986 provides powers for a police constable to remove a person who appears to be suffering from mental disorder and to be in immediate need of care or control from a public place to a place of safety. The constable must think that such removal would be in the interests of the person or would protect the public.

Police station liaison scheme

A screening, assessment and referral service for mentally disordered offenders in police stations was first implemented in Northern Ireland in 1998. The Belfast scheme was based on a model of diversion at the point of arrest, and shared some features with community psychiatric nurse liaison schemes to police services. A review of this service considered that it had played an important role in developing and facilitating liaison between psychiatric services and the criminal justice system and promoted better understanding of the relationship between mental disorder and crime (McGilloway and Donnelly, 2004).

Fitness to be interviewed

Guidance on the assessment of fitness to be interviewed is contained in Annexe G of Code C of the Police and Criminal Evidence (Northern Ireland) Order 1989 (Codes of Practice) (Number 3) Order 2007 (see also chapter 4).

Appropriate adult scheme

The Police and Criminal Evidence (NI) Order 1989 states that when a police officer has any suspicion that a person due to be interviewed as witness, victim or suspect may have a mental disorder, s/he must contact an 'appropriate adult'. The Bamford Review identified several problems with the old scheme. Since June 2009, *MindWise*, an independent mental health charity, has been contracted to deliver the NI Appropriate Adult Scheme.

Police Ombudsman

The Police Ombudsman is responsible for independent and impartial investigation of police complaints. The Office of the Police Ombudsman is a non-departmental public body administrated by the Department of Justice.

Bail

There are no specific services in Northern Ireland for those on bail who suffer from mental health problems. The Bamford Review recommended research on the feasibility of reducing the number of mentally disordered people in prison by providing a broader range of bail facilities.

Courts

There are no courts specifically for people with mental health or substance misuse problems. Healthcare services for prisoners include a scheme which provides liaison with the Laganside Court Complex in Belfast.

Psychiatric reports for the courts are requested by the defence, the prosecution or the court; there is no statutory scheme to provide routine psychiatric reports.

Prisons

In April 2008, responsibility for prison healthcare in Northern Ireland was transferred to the health service, specifically to the South Eastern Health and Social Care Trust. A Partnership Board has been established with representatives of the prison service, the Trust and the Regional Health and Social Care Board. This Board is responsible for monitoring the quality and level of health services and for developing and agreeing prison healthcare policy and standards. Clinical governance committees were also established.

As prison healthcare is provided by a health and social care trust, it falls under the aegis of the Regulation and Quality Improvement Authority (RQIA), the independent body responsible for monitoring and inspecting the availability and quality of health and social care services and encouraging improvements in them. The RQIA has taken over the responsibilities of the Mental Health Commission, including 'remedying any deficiency in care or treatment'.

Independent Monitoring Board (IMB)

Members of the Independent Monitoring Board (formally the Board of Visitors) act as independent observers of all aspects of prison régime and, as such, have free access at all times to the prison to which they are appointed. Their work is voluntary and unpaid. Their function includes satisfying themselves that the facilities available allow prisoners to make purposeful use of their time and that provision for their healthcare is acceptable.

Prisoner Ombudsman

The Prisoner Ombudsman is independent of the Northern Ireland Prison Service (NIPS). Her remit includes investigation of complaints from prisoners or visitors to prison, and deaths in prison.

Prison healthcare

Despite the plethora of organizations that have been established in Northern Ireland to provide safeguards, unsatisfactory gaps in mental health services for prisoners remain. In particular there is no high security hospital in Northern Ireland, so the few people who require this cannot be transferred out of the jurisdiction until the courts have disposed of their cases, and must then go to Scotland. The Bamford Review highlighted the fact that prisoners suffering from mental illness or severe mental impairment may thus be unable to access the treatment and care they require for several years.

Parole Commissioners for Northern Ireland

The Parole Commissioners deal with the release and recall of life sentence prisoners, prisoners sentenced to indeterminate or extended custodial sentences and also the recall of people who received determinate sentences.

The Probation Board for Northern Ireland (PNBI)

The functions of the PBNI include conducting risk assessments, providing pre-sentence reports to courts, supervising offenders in the community and in prison, assisting offenders towards the prevention of crime and providing reports for Parole Commissioners. The PBNI also provides programmes for offenders subject to community supervision, to enable work on offending behaviour which may reduce risk of re-offending and protect the public.

Public Protection Arrangements

Since 2001, there has been a system in Northern Ireland for assessing and managing the risk posed by sex offenders. Originally this was known as the Multi-Agency Sex Offender Risk Assessment and Management (MASRAM) arrangement. In 2008, the process was broadened to include violent offenders and it became known as the Public Protection

Arrangements Northern Ireland (PPANI). The provisions include placing statutory obligations on police, probation and social services to work in partnership on the assessment and management of risk posed by offenders and potentially dangerous persons (PDPs) in the community.

The Voluntary Sector

The Bamford Review recognized the increasing importance of the voluntary sector and advocated its inclusion in co-ordinated service delivery.

OFFENDERS AND ALLEGED OFFENDERS WITH MENTAL DISORDER IN NON-MEDICAL SETTINGS IN IRELAND

As in other jurisdictions, during the first decade of the twenty-first century, there has been a greater political and operational emphasis on dealing with the difficulties associated with people with mental health problems coming into contact with criminal justice agencies. The key tasks are seen as meeting the needs of this group in the least restrictive conditions, while maintaining public safety.

Working with the Police

Ireland has a single national police service (An Garda Síochána) of about 14,500 officers, under the day to day operational management of a central government appointed commissioner. The Minister for Justice, Equality, and Law Reform is responsible to government for the performance of the Garda Síochána. In addition to their crime prevention and enforcement roles the Garda have a role under the Mental Health Act 2001. Under its section 12, when a person is suspected of suffering from a mental disorder and possibly posing a risk to self or others, s/he may be taken into custody for a medical examination. In 2009, a joint report of the Mental Health Commission and Garda Síochána made recommendations aimed at streamlining the interface between the police and mental health agencies and enhancing their liaison. These included implementation of national primary care and mental health strategies, development of national emergency statutory social work services to be available at all times, improved Garda training in mental health issues, development of court diversion services and exploration of the feasibility of development of jointly staffed crisis intervention teams.

With increasing recognition of the potential vulnerability of suspects with mental disorder who may be questioned by the Garda, regulations on safeguards to be applied in custody have been amended to recommend that a 'responsible adult' should attend police interviews with persons suffering from mental disorder.

Clinicians Working in Prison

Research in the Irish Prison system (Linehan et al., 2005; Duffy et al., 2006; Wright et al., 2006; Curtin et al., 2009), as in other jurisdictions, has confirmed an excess of many mental disorders among both male and female prisoners compared with the general population. Consequent recommendations for services mirror those arising from a number of strategic service reviews: integration of community and forensic mental health services together with ongoing collaboration with drug treatment services (Department of Justice, Equality and Law Reform, 2001; Mental Health Commission, 2006; Department of Health and Children, 2006). Development of these recommendations – that custodial healthcare, including mental healthcare, should come within the direct remit of the Department of Health and Children rather than the Department of Justice, Equality, and Law Reform – has not yet progressed to the same extent as in England and Wales, with formal transfer of responsibility, but it is moving in that direction. Completion of this development would require a confluence of political will between the relevant government departments.

Despite resource limitations, there has been substantial progress in organization of health services in prison. The introduction of professionally qualified nurses across the prison estate has helped to promote an ethos of equivalence with community services. Focus is on seeking to minimize chronic health deficits and prevent further damage in a disadvantaged group. Given long standing difficulties in accessing inpatient beds in the only mental health unit available to prisoners (Central Mental Hospital, Dundrum), greater emphasis has been placed on improving access to mental health assessment and treatment in prison through better in-reach services. This has been helped by development of an electronic prison healthcare record, the Prison Medical Record System (PMRS), intended to be comprehensive, covering primary care and specialist interventions while in prison.

Notwithstanding the 65% increase in the Irish prison population between 1998 and 2009, reaching a record of 4,258 in March 2010, together with an increase in annual turnover (Irish Prison Service, 2009) the number of self-inflicted deaths among prisoners has remained static at 4–5 per year. This is attributed to a combination of improved drug treatment services to prisoners, regular telephone access to families, access to in-cell television, and improvements in access and organization of prison-based mental health services.

A particular concern in Ireland has been the rapid increase in the ethnic and racial diversity of the prison population since the 1990s. Before then, the population was almost exclusively Irish, but by 2004 over 20% of prison committals were non-nationals, coming from over a hundred countries. This has led to a variety of special issues including need for language interpreters, difficulties in tracing previous healthcare records, and in co-ordinating healthcare provision between prison and home community.

Working With the Probation Service

In Ireland the probation service functions as an agency of the Department of Justice, Equality, and Law Reform (which also oversees police, prison, immigration, and crime prevention). Its role is to assess and manage offenders in the community or in prison or other places of detention on behalf of the Court and/or the prison service.

Court Diversion and Psychiatric Disposal

With increasing recognition of the disproportionate numbers of people with mental disorder who find themselves before a court and their need to be directed to more appropriate services, there has been development of a more formal Prison Mental Health In-reach and Court Liaison Service (PICLS) in the Dublin area, where most need arises (O'Neill, 2006; McInerney and O'Neill, 2008). This development has been successful in achieving the goal of ensuring that people whose primary need is for mental health services do not enter the criminal justice system and that, if this occurs, they are diverted back to the community mental health services as soon as possible. The success of this initiative in the Dublin area will facilitate extension to other committal prisons around the country.

Drug courts

In Ireland, as elsewhere, there is major overlap between low-grade acquisitive criminality and serious drug misuse. Following the US experience of Drug Courts, where non-violent drug addicted offenders may receive a therapeutic disposal in lieu of a prison sentence, a pilot Drug Court was set up in Dublin in 2001, and established in 2006. Offenders are referred to the Court by a probation officer. While evaluation of the pilot scheme indicated promise (Courts Service, 2002) in terms of completion rates, desistance from drugs and reduced re-offending, numbers were small and later completion rates were lower, threatening continuation of the Court; however, it has been extended (*Irish Times*, 25.09.2011).

26
Ethics in forensic psychiatry

Written by
John Gunn
Pamela J Taylor

Say what you will about the Ten Commandments, you must always come back to the pleasant fact that there are only ten of them (Mencken, 1916).

CODES AND PRINCIPLES

Ethics is a branch of philosophy. It is the study of how moral ideas develop, how they interact, how they relate to other aspects of human learning and how they may be applied in practice. Medical ethics should be a systematic study of how moral principles can be applied to the practice of medicine. This chapter reflects the bias of this book and focuses on medical ethics, but many of the issues considered have relevance for other professions as well. Medicine is a highly value laden subject. The very definitions of disease and the attending on sick people are based on moral assumptions. These moral assumptions have changed with time, and will change further in the future, keeping within the broader ethical framework of the society in which they are placed, and they have to be tested within the peer group of other doctors.

Morality so pervades psychiatry that every chapter in a psychiatric textbook will embrace moral issues either implicitly or explicitly. Questions about the suitability of retaining and treating people with mental disorder in prison are, for example, in large part moral ones. Scientific information about the efficacy of treatment in prison will influence the argument, but such scientific knowledge is unlikely ever to override completely the moral debate. This chapter on ethics is a chapter more for raising questions than for providing answers.

Discourse on ethics frequently starts with the Greeks and the Hippocratic Oath (see appendix 4), or with Hammurabi and the Babylonians. Musto (1991) takes the reader from Greece and Rome to the religions of the middle ages, up to the French Revolution, and into nineteenth-century Britain. This is appropriate as the modern medical profession did not really begin until the nineteenth century in spite of its apparently long history. In 1803, Thomas Percival published his famous *Medical Ethics*. It is even now of interest and resonant with some modern values, but it also illustrates our point that ethics are related to time and culture and some elements are subject to change. Percival says, for example:

> The law justifies the beating of a lunatic in such manner as the circumstances may require. But a physician, who attends an asylum for insanity is under an obligation of honour as well as of humanity, to secure to the unhappy sufferers, committed to his charge, all the tenderness and indulgence compatible with the steady and effectual government. And the strait waistcoat, with other improvements in modern practice, now precludes the necessity of coercion by corporal punishment.

Percival also noted:

> It is a complaint made by coroners, magistrates, and judges, that medical gentlemen are often reluctant in the performance of the offices, required from them as citizens qualified by professional knowledge to aid the execution of public justice. These offices, it must be confessed, are generally painful, always inconvenient, and occasionally an interruption to business of a nature not to be easily appreciated or compensated.

He went on to suggest that

> as they [these offices] *admit of no substitution, they are to be regarded as appropriate debts to the community.*

Fewer doctors are, these days, reluctant to go to court and few of them would regard themselves as paying a debt to the community when they do so. In almost 200 years, the balance of duty to the community has altered, so that now a modern Percival might be urging the doctor to attend less to the attractions of court work and more to the treatment needs of patients.

Percival's book influenced the first code of ethics of the American Medical Association, drafted in 1847 (Musto, 1991). Much has happened since then, the ill-conceived eugenics movement which was so widespread internationally at the beginning of the twentieth century, and most particularly the Second World War with its gross violations of medical ethics by Hitler's Nazis (see also chapter 27). The early stages of 'racial purification' involved the compulsory sterilization and killing of psychiatric patients, before proceeding to the killing of Jews. Torrey and Yolken

(2010) describe this extraordinary phase of 'trying to eradicate' schizophrenia, and its paradoxical consequences, but people with other mental disorders and/or intellectual disability were also under threat. A range of 'this must never happen again' responses occurred after that war, including the development of the United Nations, the formation of the Council of Europe with its Convention of Human Rights (see appendix 1) and a range of written medical codes. Perhaps such extraordinary 'eradication' attempts have not been repeated, but van Voren (2010) notes other subsequent use of psychiatry for political purposes, citing, among others, the concerns about the Soviet Union in the 1970s and 1980s and some current concerns about China. The most important codes for psychiatrists are the World Medical Association *Declaration of Geneva* (1948, amended 1984, 1994, 2005 and 2006), and its associated International Code of Medical Ethics (1949, amended 1968, 1983, and 2006), the World Psychiatric Association *Declaration of Hawaii* (1977, revised 1983) superseded by the *Declaration of Madrid* (1996 amended in 1999, 2002 and 2005). The sadistic 'experiments' of the Nazi doctors, which were not in the least bit scientific, were dealt with in Nuremberg, at the trials, and also in the 1947 *Nuremberg Code* of ethics for medical research. This was subsequently followed by the World Medical Association *Declaration of Helsinki* (1964, revised 1975, 1983, 1989, 1996, 2000, 2004 and 2008). This was insufficient for the American Psychiatric Association which published *The Principles of Medical Ethics with Annotations Especially Applicable to Psychiatry* in 1973. These too have been revised from time to time. The international codes are listed in full with, as far as possible, weblinks, in appendix 4.

A glance at this list of codes, with all their revision dates may suggest that ethics change quite frequently. Moral opinions do change with time and circumstances, for example when, if ever, abortions should be carried out, but it is not the case that the fundamentals of medical practice change very much and there may be a tendency to over codify. Do the Americans really need separate codes from those applicable to the rest of the world? They contribute to the international documents anyway. In May 2005 the American Academy of Psychiatry and the Law (AAPL) adopted its latest version of *Ethics Guidelines for the Practice of Forensic Psychiatry*. In 2008 in Seattle the annual meeting of the American Academy staged a debate about the applicability of these guidelines to countries outside the USA, a form of which was later published (Grounds et al., 2010). This is of interest, however, not only for the question of whether some countries might hold themselves apart from others, but also whether forensic psychiatrists might also seek separate status in this respect from their general peers. Opinion is divided, and, here, not by country. One of the debaters in that conference (JG) stands by his opinion that if the World Psychiatric Association code (*The Madrid Declaration*) is followed then forensic psychiatry probably does not need any additional codes; this perspective is echoed by Myers:

> *I also find the concept specious that there is a different moral universe in which the forensic psychiatrist dwells. I believe that psychiatrists who practise forensic psychiatry are bound by the same moral obligations as any other psychiatrist, including practising competently, being honest, respecting others, maintaining confidentiality to the extent possible.*

What is the purpose of a written code? When the authors qualified in medicine one of us had to stand in a group and swear to obey the Hippocratic Oath, the other was given the option of signing the Geneva declaration, this in spite of public perceptions many doctors do not take an oath or sign anything when they qualify in Britain. Does this matter? When Karl Brandt went on trial as the leader of a group of doctors who tortured Jews and others in the name of some sort of perverted medical science, he said that no one takes any notice of the Hippocratic oath even when it is hanging on his wall (Burleigh, 1994). That was certainly true for him, is it true for others? Is medical practice ethical because of the codes or would most of us who join the profession keep to those principles anyway?

Most doctors would be hard-pressed to recite the details of any of the medical codes, including the Hippocratic Oath and the Declaration of Geneva, yet most are aware that their daily working life is governed by the fundamental precept *primum non nocere* (first, do no harm) often expressed as 'non-maleficence', which roughly means 'given an existing problem, it may be better not to do a particular thing, or even to do nothing, than to risk causing more harm than good.' This recognizes that no intervention of any power is without unwanted as well as wanted effects.

It could be argued, although such an argument may be unpopular, that the additional codification, which seems to be occurring with an ever greater frequency, is bureaucratic and unnecessary for the discerning psychiatrist who understands the basic principles of, say, The Madrid Declaration. It is sometimes suggested that physicians are at sea when significant ethical dilemmas arise and either that they hanker after written rules or that they need them. Maybe therefore these written rules save some situations but the physician who does not understand in his or her bones the force and significance of not doing harm to any person/patient is unlikely to be changed into a first rate doctor by the publication of a code of ethics or detailed practice guidelines.

A complication is that as the world becomes more legalistic and more bureaucratic, legal rules have developed to regulate the conduct of all professions such that clients can sue members of those professions. There is therefore specific case law which can be regarded as equivalent to an ethical code and which can only be disregarded with the risk of a lawsuit, perhaps an expensive one. The main driver for this in Europe is the European Convention on Human Rights and its court (see appendix 1 and chapter 2). The Human Rights Act 2000 introduced into the United Kingdom most of the rights and freedoms given by the European Convention.

TEACHING AND LEARNING ETHICS

Whilst the introduction of sanctions against unethical practitioners is one way to control the behaviour of doctors, and thus safeguard patients, another is to provide them with better and more detailed education. Not all British medical education includes courses on ethics and philosophy as basic subjects. In 1980, the General Medical Council (GMC) recommended that ethics should be taught to all medical students. Belfast was one of the first medical schools to follow this guidance, setting up a 3-week fourth year course, compulsory for all medical students. The topics included autonomy, consent, telling the truth, confidentiality, allocation of resources, limitation of treatment, resuscitation, euthanasia, defining death, autonomy for adults as well as the rather special issues it raises with children, management of the intellectually handicapped, child abuse, research ethics, prenatal fetal diagnosis, impaired autonomy and paternalism (Irwin et al., 1988). The authors found that the students had a number of problems, including difficulty in appraising critically opposing moral points of view and an inadequate foundation in general ethical theory, which proved a barrier to grasping ethical ideas.

Philosophical discussions are unusual in medical schools, and hardly central to modern psychiatry, and yet ethics cannot really be learned without them. Rosner, who taught forensic psychiatry in New York for many years, provided a lecture course which gave the budding forensic psychiatrist an overview of different approaches to ethical thinking (Grounds et al., 2010). He taught that every clinician should ask him or herself what makes a particular decision 'right' within the agreed framework of their profession. His view is that this important step is forgotten when 'ethics' are invoked. Rosner's approach is to get his students to understand some of the philosophy behind ethics and to think for themselves. This is an unusual approach when most teachers are focusing on case law and the codebook. Ethical codes may exist without justification. For ethical relativists, a professional code is right because members of the profession say that it is, while for subjectivists (emotivists), an ethical statement captures the emotion attached to the acts and so 'x' is good or bad because it feels so. Neither of these positions, Rosner suggests, is very satisfying. Justification adds a more cognitive component into the making or adoption of an ethical code. Rosner argues that there are six main ways of justifying here.

1. *Divine command.* According to this view, popular among Christian, Muslim and Jewish believers, something is right because God commanded it. The justification for the Ten Commandments, for example, is that God commanded obedience to them.

2. *Natural law.* This idea is attributed to St Thomas Aquinas; it holds that God endowed us with the rational capacity to derive ethical rules from observations of the empirical facts of the world we live in. For natural law ethicists, there is a necessary connection between reason and what is right. Such an ethical code is not arbitrary, and must benefit the persons who subscribe to it.

3. *Tradition.* Traditionalists believe that an ethical code is right because people who adhere to it have always regarded it as right. The Hippocratic Oath is right because Western doctors have accepted it for over 2000 years. Traditional ethics fixes ethics forever, preventing the growth and development of ethical standards for human conduct.

4. *Utilitarianism (Consequentialism).* In this moral view an ethical code is right because compliance with it produces the greatest good for the greatest number of people. For consequentialist ethicists, there is a necessary connection between goodness and rightness, and the ends justify the means.

5. *Deontology.* Deontological ethics are dutiful ethics governed by absolute rules – the opposite of utilitarianism. Kant was their most famous exponent. He believed that we are governed by reason which leads to imperatives. If I am thirsty I must drink; this is contingently or hypothetically right because it leads to a desired outcome. Other things (imperatives) are absolute and unconditional duties because they are right in themselves and society depends on them. Kant called these categorical imperatives. He argued that it is wrong to steal because society would break down if we were allowed to steal; therefore honesty is a duty with no exceptions. Morality does not come from wanting to be honest, it comes from resisting temptation to be dishonest. Goodness is in the struggle. This rigid approach cannot be entirely sustained, however. Kant believed, for example, that there are no exceptions to the rule against lying – not even to save someone's life. As Rosner asks of this approach, 'What do you do in occupied Holland if you are hiding Ann Frank and her family when the Nazis knock on the door and ask if you know where they are?' Kant would say, 'Tell the truth'.

6. *Feminist ethics.* Twentieth-century feminists argue that there are sufficient female–male differences for a separate feminist ethic to be required. Men, they suggest, are interested in abstract and impersonal principles (note deontology above) while women are interested in caring and personal relationships.

Not being deontological or Kantian in outlook, we take the view that medical ethics are largely a matter of consensus around the maxim of not being harmful while endeavouring to do good. In working with offender-patients, however, the potential difficulties are immediately apparent. For an offender-patient, what is the harm to be avoided? Being locked up because of a chance that something bad might happen otherwise when there is also a chance it may not? How does the clinician balance his/her duty to the patient with his/her duty to the wider public? Laws and codes have to be studied as they give good contemporary limits and guidance; the Hippocratic maxim should remain at the centre of considerations, but ethics need frequent discussion and they should have a more prominent place in basic training and in continuing professional development. A few examples of contemporary ethical questions may illustrate this.

SOME CONTEMPORARY QUESTIONS

Balance of Interests

It is not uncommon for the needs of one person to conflict with those of another. To what extent does the doctor have responsibilities to others besides his or her patient? When ill-health gives rise to conflict, doctors are sometimes expected to be the means of arbitration. If, for example, a person presents with one of a list of specific infections, the doctor not only has a duty to the patient to provide treatment, but also, in many countries, has a legal obligation to society to take steps to prevent the individual from spreading the disease. Absolute confidentiality can no longer apply, and the doctor must notify the relevant authorities of the patient's disorder, whether the patient wishes so or not. Psychiatrists also have a special role in medicine with their powers for compulsory detention. Where an individual is thought to be at risk of acting dangerously the psychiatrist may, even without the patient's consent, have a duty to warn relevant people or authorities. In these circumstances the patient has a right to know what confidences are being broken and why.

Each psychiatrist comes to the role of arbiter with at least three interacting identities: as an individual, as a member of society, and as an agent of someone. S/he may represent the patient directly, or indirectly through the patient's legal representative. S/he may be a representative of society, which is not synonymous with the state but, in practice, it is commonly the state that purports to represent society. In England this occurs through bureaucracies such as the Crown Prosecution Service, the Ministry of Justice or the Department of Health. Less commonly, the psychiatrist acts for the police, or for a pressure group. The demands of these different agencies may conflict. The psychiatrist will not feel entirely free of obligations to other agencies, even when s/he is expressly acting for one of them.

The most influential factor in attempting to balance the needs of a patient and the needs of society must be knowledge. This will include factual knowledge of the nature and course of mental disorder, of the kinds of risks it may entail, and, in forensic psychiatry, knowledge of criminology and of the law. Detailed, accurate knowledge of the patient and his or her circumstances is also essential, as presentation of disorder, its outcome and risks may be subject to individual variation. Ignorance, where knowledge is available, is unethical.

Sometimes, however, the body of knowledge is poor, and this may lead to arbitrary behaviour by psychiatrists. The position of many psychiatrists on the assessment and treatment of personality disorder is perhaps reflective of this problem. Personality disorder is a condition for which knowledge is growing, but still limited, and interpretation of the consensus commonly pessimistic. Such issues, and ways of overcoming problems of engagement with people with disorders of personality are dealt with more fully in chapter 16.

It is worth highlighting a qualitative evaluation of narratives on the concerns of psychiatrists in general and forensic mental health services about working with people who have a personality disorder. This evaluation revealed a core concern of 'echoing the pathology', in which the complex pathologies of these disorders tend to be reflected in the behaviours and attitudes of professionals (Jones, 2010). Barriers to resolving this concern included lack of knowledge about the treatments and the skills needed to deliver them effectively. Others have confirmed that factors facilitating treatment include provision of appropriate training (Miller et al., 1996; Krawitz, 2004; Commons et al., 2008), supervision and reflective practice (Moore, 2011). The treatment of such patients under compulsion is unusual and unpopular; however, their voluntary treatment continues to form a tiny part of the average psychiatrist's work. Prisons, by contrast, which have to take in those sent there, have large numbers of people with personality disorder when measured clinically (Gunn et al., 1991); few, however, are treated, and recidivism rates are high.

Is prison the right place for people with a recognized mental disorder? What happens to the few patients who do go to the small number of personality disorder secure units being developed in the National Health Service? We need research that will identify the changes that occur in those patients and the factors that brought the changes about. It can be argued that failure to study the needs and progress of individuals with such disorders is, in itself, unethical. This, however, takes us into broader social ethics. The search for hypothetical particles (the Higgs boson particle) and dark matter commands vastly more funding than medical research. Within clinical research, we have no reason to believe that the relative proportions of funds available for research per annum per life lost varies much between countries or has changed much over time since Reiss and Roth's (1993) analysis: for cancer $794, for AIDS $697, for cardiovascular diseases $441, but for violence just $31.

Confidentiality

Appropriate confidentiality is essential to psychiatric treatment. The UK General Medical Council (GMC) (2009) guidance on this expresses the principles very well:

Confidentiality is central to trust between doctors and patients. Without assurances about confidentiality, patients may be reluctant to seek medical attention or to give doctors the information they need in order to provide good care. But appropriate information sharing is essential to the efficient provision of safe, effective care, both for the individual patient and for the wider community of patients.

The Council's 'guidance' amounts to a set of rules that have to be followed:

Confidentiality is an important duty, but it is not absolute. You can disclose personal information if: (a) it is required by law; (b) the patient consents – either implicitly for the sake of their own care or expressly for other purposes; (c) it is justified in the public interest.When disclosing information about a patient, you must:

a. *use anonymised or coded information if practicable and if it will serve the purpose;*
    i. *be satisfied that the patient:*
    ii. *has ready access to information that explains that their personal information might be disclosed for the sake of their own care, or for local clinical audit, and that they can object, and*
b. *has not objected;*
c. *get the patient's express consent if identifiable information is to be disclosed for purposes other than their care or local clinical audit, unless the disclosure is required by law or can be justified in the public interest;*
d. *keep disclosures to the minimum necessary; and*
e. *keep up to date with, and observe, all relevant legal requirements, including the common law and data protection legislation.*

In the UK, the duty of confidentiality of doctor to patient is enshrined in common law, but various, apparently competing statutes affect this, including the Human Rights Act 1998, the Data Protection Act 1998 and the Freedom of Information Act 2000. No patient in the UK has an absolute legal right to medical confidentiality, as exists in some states of America under the Privilege Statutes (Group for the Advancement of Psychiatry, 1960). The GMC sets out a number of exemptions, for example when a breach of confidentiality may be thought to be in the patient's own interest, although this may need to be fully justified

subsequently, or the doctor may have an overarching social obligation in the case of a highly dangerous condition, such as a duty to report the name of a patient with epilepsy to a driving authority. It is even possible under GMC guidelines to widen the notion of 'public interest' so that if a doctor is confident that his/her patient has committed a serious crime, then s/he may be allowed to help the police to arrest this patient.

A good book for amplifying this section on medical confidentiality is the one edited by Cordess (2001). This includes contributions from psychoanalysts, lawyers, general psychiatrists, a child psychiatrist, forensic psychotherapists and others. It arose from conference debates on confidentiality. Cordess was clearly dismayed by the trend towards expecting doctors to disclose more and more about their patients. He gives an example of where the expectation of disclosing illegal sexual behaviour was, in effect, required by GMC guidelines but, in reality, was in the interests of nobody, not the patient, nor the alleged previous victim, nor the public. The contrast between the absolute confidentiality allowed for lawyers' transactions and the relative confidentiality for psychiatrists' transactions is stark and increasing. It is also of interest that priests, who do not have legal immunity for material heard in the confessional, do not feel obliged to betray confidences and rarely come into conflict with the law about this.

Before we follow a trail of envy of lawyers' privilege with respect to confidentiality, we should reflect on how it is that there is such a contrast between lawyers and doctors here. Would doctors and patients really be better off with a rule of absolute confidentiality? The reason that lawyers are able to work with absolute confidentiality is that they generally have brief relationships with their clients and do not see themselves as involved in wider issues beyond their 'instructions'. A profession which has acquired wider responsibilities beyond the consulting room, into the patient's future, and into the public arena accepts that a balance has to be struck between total secrecy and wider health concerns. Psychotherapists in particular will need to negotiate an understanding with the patient and others about what may and what may not be held in confidence within the sessions. Retention of the possibility of confidentiality in most aspects of psychotherapeutic work is so important, and yet increasingly challenged by those outside the clinical team, that we repeat here a short section from p.607.

The patient must be able to share potentially frightening material from his/her inner life; if this is recorded verbatim in the record it may easily be taken out of the context of the therapeutic process, and be damaging to patient and process alike. If the therapy cannot then proceed, this would have the potential of reducing safety for everyone. A partial solution may be that the therapist may keep his/her own process notes as an aide memoire, but note each session in the multidisciplinary record, and, at agreed intervals, contribute to clinical discussions about the patient and place a summary report in the main clinical record.

Medical records, their accessibility and ownership, are a continuing area of confusion. It is generally in the interests of patients that full and accurate records are kept, but while the ownership of the record falls to the employing authority, ownership of the data within it is less clear. Modern psychiatric care is multi-professional, and forensic psychiatric care is generally multi-agency at least at some stages of treatment. The effective involvement of others requires sharing of information. Not all colleagues, whether or not employed by health authorities, subscribe to professional bodies with disciplinary powers, such as the GMC, nor do they necessarily share the same ethical principles. Social workers have found difficulties with the requirement in some parts of England in that clients' records may be subject to local government scrutiny. Any attempt to provide a patient with suitable treatment and facilities may thus endanger confidentiality. Does this make some disclosures to social workers unethical? Can safeguards against important breaches of security be devised? In all cases the patient should know what is likely to happen to information given to the doctor. In fact, such dilemmas may hardly exist if the patient is fully involved in the process at every step and disclosure of information is kept to the minimum necessary for purpose. Senior and colleagues (2011) have conducted preliminary research on data sharing protocols. They sent questionnaires on multi-agency information sharing to patients and staff in one English health region. Consent from the patients was not hard to obtain; most of them assumed data were shared anyway. On this basis it was possible to set up a pilot database which was explicitly independent of any one service. Each patient had readily given consent to inclusion of his/her data as considered essential by the professionals.

Patients may request reports about their health for an employer, an employment agency, the Department of Work and Pensions, an insurance company or a housing authority. It is recommended that such material be marked 'in confidence' and exclusively for the attention of the person or body to whom it is addressed. Such marking, however, is not legally binding, and the patient must be aware that this is true, even in circumstances in which the information is apparently being given for his or her benefit. Privileged information passed to other people is out of the patient's and the doctor's control. Information should not be passed to a third party without the express (usually written) permission of the patient or informant. It is essential to recognize here that consent of the patient with respect to a particular report cannot be taken to imply consent of others referred to in the report. In our experience this issue particularly arises with respect to relevant family history. It may, for example, seem important,

as part of building the case that the person being reported upon has schizophrenia, to note that his/her mother and grandfather had schizophrenia. If, however, those people have not given their consent to that information being made public, it should not be included in the report. If consent is not possible in these circumstances, the reporting clinician may be able to refer more generally to a family history of illness which would add weight to the diagnosis of schizophrenia.

Unless required in law, clinical case notes, which include data from a variety of sources, should not be handed over in their entirety, unless permission has been gained from every contributing source. Where this has not been possible, the name of each informant may be given to the third party for consultation. In the UK, if patients are under such legal restraints as a restriction order (see chapter 3), they lose most of their rights to confidentiality as civil servants and others require full information about such patients from the responsible doctor or clinician and the social worker/supervisor. Others, such as employers, landlords, future spouses/companions, may all have a right to know something of a patient's history. When a patient refuses permission even for limited data transfer, then this fact and its consequences has to be made clear to all parties concerned. A patient's general rights to confidentiality do not override a potential victim's rights to be forewarned. Indeed, in England and Wales, the Domestic Violence, Crime and Victims Act 2004 extended to restricted patients the statutory requirement (under the Criminal Justice and Court Services Act 2000) to notify victims of an index offence about review dates and consult them about release arrangements.

All these matters are discussed more fully in the Royal College of Psychiatrists' (2010) *Good Psychiatric Practice* guidance on confidentiality and information sharing. The first appendix of this document covers all current law relating to confidentiality. This guidance embraces the GMC principles, given above, and adds:

Individuals or their legal representatives, and individuals with parental responsibility for children, who have not yet attained capacity, have a right to control the access and disclosure of their own health information or that of the person for whom they have responsibility through the giving or withholding of consent.

For any non-consented disclosure of confidential information, healthcare professionals must have regard to the necessity, proportionality and risks attendant on the disclosure, as well as to the complex set of diverse values operating in any particular situation.

Individuals or their legal representatives, and individuals with parental responsibility for children, who have not yet attained capacity, have a right to access in a timely manner their own health information or that of the person for whom they have responsibility.

In law, a 'child' is defined as a person under the age of legal majority (18 in the UK), but it is a common convention, which is followed by the Royal College of Psychiatrists, that those of 12 years and under are referred to as 'children' and those aged 13 years and above, but not yet the age of legal majority, as 'young people'.

It is central to the development of therapeutic relationships that children and young people should be able to trust the professionals treating them in order to engage with treatment and to disclose information which is necessary for their treatment. The basic duty of a health professional to maintain patient confidentiality ... also applies when patients are children and young people. However, for children and young people, these ethical principles must be balanced against other ethical principles: (1) the importance of protection of children and young people, as vulnerable members of society still in the process of development, from harm ...; (2) the rights of families rather than individuals, in particular recognizing the importance of parental figures, family life and relationships to children and young people.

Ethical conflicts are particularly acute when concerns arise about risks to children and young people and there may be conflict between the needs of the child or young person and their desire for confidentiality or between their needs and those of key adults, including parents. In mental health settings, there are often additional difficulties such as conflict or difficult relationships between children or young people and parents or health professionals. In such situations, the issue of sharing information and keeping secrets can become the focus of conflict and struggles for power and control. The resolution of such conflicts requires working in a respectful manner with all individuals involved, including the children and young people themselves.

The Duty to Warn

A person who explicitly threatens a named individual or individuals poses a somewhat different set of problems from the person who is non-specifically risky. It is essential to understand something of the dynamic between the person threatening and the person under threat. More commonly than not, the person under threat may need to be engaged in protecting him- or herself in addition to the steps being taken to reduce the risk from the threatener. Sometimes the person under threat may be way outside the threatener's social circle; this problem is dealt with in the section on threat assessment and management in chapter 22. Formulation of an effective plan for protecting a named potential victim is, however, far from straightforward, and raises yet further questions about disclosure.

This area came to particular prominence in the USA with a far reaching legal decision in the state of California in *Tarasoff*.

In brief, a student at the University of California, Prosenjit Poddar, was in psychotherapy, when he revealed that he intended to kill a fellow student, Tatiana Tarasoff, a person with whom he had entertained ideas of a relationship, but who had made it plain to him that she wanted no intimacy with him. The therapist informed the police of this threat. The police interviewed Mr Poddar and decided to take no action. Subsequently, he left treatment and, sometime after that, killed Ms Tarasoff. Her family sued the university for damages, lost the suit initially, but won it on appeal on the grounds that therapists have a duty to warn potential victims. This was modified in a further special appeal that therapists have a duty to protect potential victims. This could be done by warning the potential victim, talking to the police, or admitting the patient to hospital. A more extensive account of this case is provided by Dyer (1988) and Bruckner and Firestone (2000).

Appelbaum et al. (1989) discussed the impact that this Californian case has had on the rest of the USA, including new laws in other states, the large amounts of compensation being awarded in a few cases, and the general anxiety among psychiatrists. Yet this case did not herald the end of psychotherapy for offenders as some had feared. Gradually practitioners have come to see the ruling as not only protecting potential victims but also the patient under treatment. The failure to adequately warn Ms Tarasoff was directly harmful to *both* patient and victim. This is a particularly good principle to bear in mind when treating such conditions as pathological jealousy. Further problems which have to be managed in this context include the fact that the patient's therapist cannot also become the victim's therapist or protector, but may have to assume a brief role in ensuring that the potential victim has access to appropriate support and advice.

Nevertheless, each case has to be judged on its merits. Langton and Torpy (1988) wrote of a 23-year-old man with sadistic sexual fantasies who asked for psychiatric help. He said he had embarked on attempted sexual assaults on several women, but he also indulged in homosexual sadomasochism and his genitals and nipples were pierced with metal rings and bars. He had a collection of knives. His masturbatory fantasy was to imagine following a woman, attacking her with a knife and then forcing her back to his bedsit where he would tie her up, stab her to death and masturbate beside her body. He insisted on strict confidentiality. Compulsory admission was considered, but rejected on the grounds that he would then refuse to co-operate with treatment. Reporting to the police was considered, but rejected on the grounds that he would not talk to them, further how could they protect a potential victim when none had been identified. Instead, he was seen regularly for outpatient psychotherapy. Antilibidinal drugs were tried without success. After 14 months he removed his genital piercings, became more self-confident, disposed of his weapons and his books on sadism, found work and stopped attending therapy sessions. At 20 months, he sought further treatment because he was in a difficult homosexual relationship. Did the therapists take the right decisions? Opinions will divide. The one weakness in this story is the lack of mention of peer group discussion, a procedure which is always illuminating, often reassuring and, it is argued here, essential.

What to Tell the Patient

The patient may know less about his/her own case than do their advisers. This may be justifiable if the patient's mental capacity will not allow full disclosure or comprehension, but such a situation should not be routine or arise without deliberation. In the UK, impairment of mental capacity is generally regarded as task specific – people who may not be able to decide about the principle that they should be in hospital may nevertheless be able to take other decisions about specific treatments, or about whether to participate in research, or about whether to marry. It is unusual for people to be so incapacitated that they should not have access to their medical records if they wish to do so. In Britain, the Data Protection Act 1998 (DPA) gives citizens the right of access, subject to certain exemptions, to information about themselves. This Act has to be read in conjunction with the Access to Medical Reports Act 1988 (AMR). The DPA gives us the right to access and control structured information kept about us; the AMR gives access to unstructured information and some rights in respect of medical reports which have been requested by third parties. This means that a patient (or his/her representative) may inspect his/her medical record. Partial exclusions from the declared file may be made if the information is 'likely to cause serious harm to the physical or mental health of the patient or any other individual', or if it is 'relating to or provided by an individual other than the patient, who could be identified from that information'. These partial exclusions may be made without telling the patient they have been made, although they may be subject to formal legal scrutiny if, for example, they are to be used as part of a case for continuing detention in hospital and submitted to a Mental Health Review Tribunal hearing. The patient may have incorrect information corrected, and his/her refutation of any other recorded material documented. All this means that it is always good practice to write in the clinical record not only accurately, but with the expectation that the patient will read it. Any third party information which may not be disclosed must be clearly separated and marked as such. When patient A has had altercation with patient B, patient B's name should be removed from any copies of the records given to patient A.

Sergeant (1986) reviewed a consecutive sample of 100 of his own case notes and found that 90% of the records contained sensitive items about the patients themselves, their friends or relatives, including unintelligible notes, alarming comments or insulting comments. Problems of this kind ought to be remediable with improved practice. Comments about the feelings of relatives, for example fear, will remain pertinent and sensitive. In no fewer than 18 cases, Sergeant believed that access to the full record could have provoked a serious reaction, such as a suicide attempt or violent outburst. Many interviewees had given the data in strict confidence; they might be less frank in future. Atkinson (1989) pointed out that some patients with schizophrenia have hitherto not been told their diagnosis (although their relatives may have been) on the grounds that it might harm them, yet there is no research to support this hypothesis. Soskis (1978) found that a sample of patients with schizophrenia knew little about their diagnosis and almost nothing about the benefits of drug treatment, but were extremely well-informed about the risks and side-effects of such treatment. The converse was true for medical patients.

Parrott et al. (1988) have taken up the issue of patient access to records specifically for the patient in a forensic psychiatry service and found it surprisingly problem-free. Legally, all reports submitted to a court are 'public' documents, so a patient could have access from that source if s/he insisted. In practice, if reports have been commissioned by the patient's solicitor, the patient will usually be given access anyway up. A more serious worry is the extent to which sensitive information could be made really public. In Britain, reports are generally handled with the sensitivity of some of the information therein in mind, and judges and magistrates can often be persuaded that all or part of the report should not be read out in open court.

We believe it is good practice in nearly all cases to let the patient see all reports about him/her and, whenever possible, they should also be discussed with the patient by the writer of that report. Possible exceptions to this rule include paranoid patients and those with severe mental handicap, but even patients from these groups should not routinely be excluded from such practice. This process can be more than informative, it can also be therapeutic. An important problem arises, however, if the patient holds copies of his/her reports. Most patients, perhaps particularly while resident in hospital or prison, may not have the facilities, or perhaps the skills, to protect their own documents. They may all too easily breach their own confidentiality by accident. Clinicians may discourage patients from holding their own copies on this basis, and may also have to be vigilant on a patient's behalf because solicitors will often provide the patient with substantial quantities of sensitive documents anyway. One solution during inpatient treatment is to provide a locked filing cabinet where patients may keep their own selected records, with near-immediate access through staff only.

665

Working With the Patient's Lawyer

Both doctors and lawyers take instructions from their patients/clients, but each may see their responsibilities differently. The doctor should and usually does put most of the emphasis on his or her relationship with a patient in terms of the patient's best interest, and negotiating the best outcome for the patient with that patient. Lawyers are expected to take the client's instructions unless they have good reason to believe that they are dishonest. Sometimes lawyers discount the complications which arise from lack of capacity. Indeed, some lawyers maintain that instructions must be taken unamended irrespective of the patient's capacity. This may lead to some medico-legal conflict and on occasions unfortunate results for the patient. An example of how this may arise, with one non-essential fact changed in order to protect the offender's identity:

A woman developed grandiose and destructive religious ideas. She was charged in connection with serious harm to a woman she had been trying to help according to her religious tenets. When giving her history, she pointed out that it says in the Bible (*St Matthew's Gospel* 5.3): *'If thy right hand offend thee, cut it off'*. It had, and it was verified that she nearly did. The reporting psychiatrist suggested that she was developing schizophrenia, and arranged for a bed in an open psychiatric hospital should the Court agree to a hospital order. The patient's lawyer chose to suppress the psychiatric report, because the woman herself wanted to run a religious defence and go free. In the event she was found guilty. The judge considered her dangerous and passed a sentence of imprisonment, unaware of the psychiatric background. The woman quickly became overtly psychotic and threatening in prison, was transferred to a maximum security hospital and remained there for more than 10 years.

This example demonstrates a range of the potential difficulties in doctor–lawyer–patient relations. It is a further example of how the reporting clinician may have little influence on what information actually goes before the Court, although here it is in the direction of too little rather than too much. The patient wished to expound on her motives and be exonerated of guilty intent. She neither believed she was insane nor wished to be labelled so. The doctor, too, doubted the guilty intent, but argued probable mental disorder and tried to secure appropriate care. The lawyer chose to exercise selective control on the information available to the court because that is what his client asked him to do. Treatment priorities were totally disregarded. In a future such case in England, it might be tempting to submit the psychiatric report to the court anyway following the *Edgell* decision (see also McHale, 1991).

The Psychiatrist as Agent of Society

Actions breaching confidentiality to protect the public may be partly justified on the grounds that they are also in the best interests of the patient. It is of no value to a patient to harm someone else. On the other hand, society's use of the psychiatrist can be more blatant and less therapeutic in the courts and the penal system. Psychiatry can, for example, be discredited in order to secure a conviction, only to be restored to credibility for the sake of imposing a punitive sentence or transferring a patient to hospital at the point of release from prison or continuing to detain an indefinitely detained individual whose discharge or release to the community is already under consideration. In the European Union, at present, the death penalty has been outlawed, so there is no question of doctors being involved in death penalty cases. In spite of the World Psychiatric Association position on the participation of doctors in capital cases, in some countries worldwide, including some states of the USA, doctors may be under pressure to 'act for society' in this respect (se also below).

There are especially complicated problems for doctors working in institutions which are established by the State expressly to control the behaviour of individuals. In the UK, much overt pressure has been overcome by distancing management of health services from the criminal justice system and/or direct government control. High security hospitals were taken out of direct Department of Health control in 1990, when they were transferred into management by the Special Hospitals' Service Authority; however, independence was far from complete (Kaye, 2001) and clinical views were hardly taken into account when huge expenditure on enhancing physical security was authorized after a report commissioned from, essentially, the prison service (Exworthy and Gunn, 2003). After years of criticism of healthcare in prisons in the UK (see Smith, 1984) and, finally, recommendations from HM Inspector of Prisons (1996) that the NHS should assume responsibility for the health of prisoners, the NHS did finally take over commissioning of health services for prisoners in England and Wales between 2003 and 2006. During this process, the principle of equivalence was established – that prisoners should be entitled to expect the same standard of healthcare as that provided in the community, and have similar access to NHS beds (Health Advisory Committee for the Prison Service, 1997). So far so good, but the prevalence of mental disorder is high among prisoners, no part of the prison service is recognized as a hospital under mental health legislation and people do not invariably get the transfers to hospital care that they need in spite of, or perhaps because of, time targets aimed at reducing transfer delays (see also chapter 24). There is an ever-present ethical threat that legislation may one day be adjusted to designate some areas in prisons as recognized hospitals. In the meantime, Earthrowl et al. (2003) have suggested that case law may allow treatment to be provided in prison in other than strict emergency situations for the incompetent-to-decide prisoner when it is in his/her interests, while noting that this has ethical implications. Other more specific issues relating to the medical needs versus the medicalization of needs among prisoners – such as matters pertaining to hunger strikers, or alleged terrorists, are dealt with in chapter 25.

Working With the Police

As with other areas of conflict over medical work, working with the police necessitates a clear understanding of psychiatric objectives and a deliberate decision on each occasion, balancing the needs of the patient, or potential patient, the needs of other people, and the needs of the police service itself. There is not much dilemma, for example, in the use of medical knowledge to assist the police in releasing a person taken hostage, provided the police make every effort also to arrest the hostage taker unharmed. Before the suicide bomber became a terrorist weapon, psychiatrists were sometimes called upon to assist in sieges initiated by terrorists. Most of the work in England was carried out by a specialist unit in the Metropolitan Police, and the special ethical questions that this raised are considered in an anonymous paper (Psychiatrist, 1993).

It is probably not the business of doctors to act as moral advisers to the police in their own dilemma of balancing risk to the hostage taker against risk to hostage. Some areas of police work are, however, more problematic. An especially onerous responsibility arises when a doctor is called to a police station to decide whether an individual is fit to be detained or fit to be interviewed. A mistake here may be a factor in precipitating, for example, a death by suicide in custody, or a false confession. As with other ethical dilemmas, it is not only wise judgment between the needs of the individual and the needs of the community which is required, but also a high degree of psychiatric knowledge and skill (see also chapter 24). Ochberg and Gunn (1980) drew attention to five important issues in this type of multiprofessional working, which can probably be generalized beyond strictly medical–police co-operation. They are the nature and strength of professional identity, health ethics, transfer of information, peer review, and ethics.

1. Psychiatrists should never lose their distinctive role; they are not policemen, prison officers, social workers, nurses or anyone else at all. For a psychiatrist, the tenets of psychiatry must come first. Nevertheless, effective inter-agency discussion is essential.

2. The World Health Organization (WHO) distinguishes medical ethics, the ethics of person-to-person relationships, from health ethics, defined as the accountability of governments to their populations in regard to health matters (WHO, 1975). Unfortunately, the concept of health ethics is left vague as 'the attainment by all peoples of the highest possible level of health'. It probably means that any member state of the United Nations has the responsibility to see that the services it provides, and these services include the police service and the prison service, should be compatible with high levels of health for all citizens. It would, therefore, be unethical in WHO terms for police or prison department policies to endanger the health of citizens, but also unethical for doctors not to remain vigilant to this possibility and, if concerned, they should have a means of registering this and should not collude with anything which would endanger health.

3. The best source of information on this topic is the online *Journal of Health Ethics* (www.ojhe.org) in which CM Klugman (vol. 4, no.1) sets out some principles of health ethics. There are also articles on withholding and withdrawing life support, disaster ethics and healthcare personnel, and ethical considerations for conducting cancer medical studies.

4. Transfer of information is dealt with in more general terms above.

5. Peer review has been stressed repeatedly as an important safeguard against unethical practice, and we do so again here.

6. We have already also made the point that education in ethics should be fundamental to all medical education, and ensconced in continuing professional development. Throughout a medical career, new issues will inevitably present from time to time, and, to an extent, ethical principles change too.

The Right to Treatment

It is the professional duty of a physician to ameliorate disease and relieve suffering. Duties are often the counterweight to rights and vice versa. In respect of treatment, however, there is no legal 'right' as such. The nearest to a legal statement concerning a possible right to treatment (and it is not actually a law) is article 25 (1) of the United Nations Universal Declaration of Human Rights:

> *Everyone has the right to a standard of living adequate for the health and well-being of himself and of his family, including food, clothing, housing, medical care and necessary social services, and the right to security in the event of unemployment, sickness, disability, widowhood, old age or other lack of livelihood in circumstances beyond his control.* http://www.un.org/en/documents/udhr/

In the discussions leading to the early twenty-first century British mental health acts, the Royal College of Psychiatrists argued that a patient should have treatment as of right if they are admitted to hospital under compulsion – the reciprocity principle. This concept was accepted within the law in Scotland and is explicitly included in the Mental Health (Care and Treatment) (Scotland) Act 2003 (see chapter 4), but not in the 2007 mental health legislation for England and Wales. The European Court of Human Rights has defined a number of legal obligations on detaining authorities (see chapter 3), but not the right to treatment as such. Nevertheless we believe it ought to be accepted as a moral and professional obligation that detained patients have optimal treatment available to them as of right; we would argue that there is a similar duty towards those individuals who are detained in criminal justice institutions, since they are no longer free to access treatment for themselves.

In the USA, these matters have been argued, to some extent, in their civil courts and the best exposition of the issue was given by Judge Bazelon (1969), outside of court, when he said:

> Ideally, we should be able to ensure that each involuntarily committed patient receives the best and most appropriate treatment. But if psychiatrists cannot agree what this might be in the individual case, it is nevertheless essential to ensure that the patient confined for treatment receives some form of therapy that a respectable sector of the psychiatric profession regards as appropriate.

Note that, as elsewhere, the peer group is the reference point.

If it were fully accepted that anybody who is diagnosed with a mental disorder using agreed criteria (say an international classification) should have the right to treatment for it if they so wish, and treatment is defined in terms of appropriate medicines, nursing, psychological treatments *and* community support, then this doctrine would have a profound impact on national and international psychiatry. Medical attitudes would have to change, new resources would have to be found, prisons would have to change, and many more prisoners would have to be moved out of prison into health facilities. It is the attitudinal change which is perhaps the toughest. Laws and moral values ultimately depend upon peer group reference. If, as often seems the case, doctors are as hostile to troublesome and offensive patients as everyone else, then such patients will always get a raw deal.

Consent to Treatment

A patient's 'right' which has had far more attention than the right to treatment is the right not to have treatment. The first and fundamental point that is now widely agreed and incorporated into the law in most countries is that, when patients embark upon treatment, they should either know and understand what they are letting themselves in for, and agree to it, that is they should give real and informed consent, or, if for some reason that is not possible, they should have their interests safeguarded by others, through laws and agreed procedures. These issues and the law in England and Wales covering consent to treatment are set out in chapter 3.

Research in Forensic Psychiatry

Many people are suspicious of the very word 'research', imagining that there can be no prospect of personal benefit

to research participants but a real risk of harm to them. Almost by definition, people who come to forensic psychiatric services have mental disorders which are difficult to treat or have already proved refractory to medication and sometimes other treatments too. For many, their best hope lies in high quality research, but rarely are the positive aspects of research emphasized. Although it is proper in most current research with offenders and offender-patients to advise them that there may be no personal advantage to them in participating, in fact, as research participants, they will almost certainly receive more attention than they would otherwise, which they may enjoy and from which they may benefit. They may also get a sense of satisfaction in being able to do something for others. Many have said so. Treatment must be based on sound knowledge derived from research, and clinical styles and methods may be improved by the importing of research methods of inquiry and scepticism. For these treatment reasons, research is inherently ethical unless the research procedures can be shown to be flawed. A set of principles for biomedical research was enunciated by the World Medical Association in 1964 (the Declaration of Helsinki), amended in 1964, and revised in 1975, 1983, 1989, 1996, 2000, 2004 and 2008 (see appendix 4). The frequency of updating gives a clue to the difficulties and the rate of change in this area. Although not designed specifically for psychiatric patients, these documents do form a useful basis for all research with patients. Emanuel et al. (2000) produced a didactic set of proposals for the ethical basis of clinical research. They proposed seven requirements to ensure that research is 'ethical': (1) value; (2) scientific validity; (3) fair subject selection; (4) favourable risk–benefit ratio; (5) independent review; (6) informed consent; and (7) respect for the people enrolled.

Research ethics committees, which try to put such guidance into practice, are now common in most Western countries. They function as gatekeepers allowing approved, that is morally approved projects, to pass while rejecting others. The best ethics committees require evidence of scientific rigour, which is important, as a project which cannot have a useful scientific outcome is morally dubious. Herein, however, a problem may sometimes arise as ethics committees vary in composition and skills, and have been known to set in motion extended complex inquiries about the science of a study for which evidence of external scientific peer review had already been provided. Ethics committees also apply varying moral criteria (Lock, 1990), but are themselves rarely if ever subject to scrutiny. In the UK, it is now usual for ethics committee members to have some training in the work, but, not least because forensic mental health research forms a small part of their work, few people associated with research governance understand this field; very few of them have visited, for example, prisons or secure hospitals and they are apt to believe that research on people who have lost their freedom is inherently unacceptable.

Research with prisoners and compulsorily detained patients developed a bad name, because there was a phase, mainly in the USA, when such people were bribed to undertake dangerous research, so that, for example, the study of induced dependency on opiates was encouraged by offers of earlier release. Such practices have been stopped, can be easily prevented, and should not now be used as a reason to prevent studies in secure institutions. Most prisoners and detained patients are able to give real consent if given the opportunity to do so, and all studies with offenders report a refusal rate. Some prison interview studies report a low refusal rate, because, as mentioned above, many prisoners actually enjoy talking to outside researchers, they queue up and those who are not included may even demand to know why they are not in the sample!

Rarely has a 'right to research participation' been contemplated, or the morality of not doing research, or of denying the possibility of research participation, although a review by Eichelman et al. (1984) is an exception to this, and these issues are coming to greater prominence in the UK. We have already referred to the potentially ethical problem of under-funding in this area, but there are substantial bureaucratic barriers too, and these were tackled robustly in a report by the Academy of Medical Sciences (2011) when the government asked the Academy to review the regulation of health research involving human participants. The academy argued that the UK's regulation and governance framework around health research should be underpinned by the following four principles:

1. To safeguard the wellbeing of research participants.
2. To facilitate high-quality health research to the public benefit.
3. To be proportionate, efficient and co-ordinated.
4. To maintain and build confidence in the conduct and value of health research through independence, transparency, accountability and consistency.

While stopping short of arguing for a right to be included in research, in addition to presenting the case for a more streamlined governance pathway, which they describe in some detail, they call for a cultural change in the NHS, to embed health research as a core function. This, they suggest, requires widespread communication to promote public and patient engagement. They also recommend that research be formally and irreversibly embedded into NHS leadership, through appropriate metrics and incentives, for training in the NHS workforce to ensure that it can support research and ensure that each Trust has an executive director with specific responsibilities to promote health research.

Some of these recommendations are being implemented, although it remains to be seen whether the number of approval bodies really will reduce. The burden of each requiring their own, often different sets of papers about each research project in order to be able to approve it, really is, as

the Academy puts it, stifling health research in the UK. For forensic mental health research, research promotion and facilitation need to spread to the criminal justice system too. Some parts are reasonably content to accept health service approvals for health research; others, such as the prisons, require them and whenever more than one prison area is involved require completion of their own application papers too. The Offender Health Research Network provides a 'toolkit' on line to help researchers through this tricky pathway (http://www.ohrn.nhs.uk/toolkit).

Although we have emphasized here research with adults in the UK, similar issues pertain to work with younger offenders, and in others countries (Lana et al., 2012). An issue which is of considerable importance, over and above the needs of the prospective participants, is that the bureaucracy must not stifle development of good and responsible relationships with the institutions – open or closed – where the research data collection will take place. Hospitals, the probation service, prisons and other such bodies have a responsibility to deliver services safely and well according to their own policies and procedures, and researchers must respect that, learning enough about the host organization to be able to function appropriately there. They must also be willing to spend time explaining to the staff who will be giving their time to support the research, what it may achieve and why their input is therefore worthwhile. It is important, where possible, to identify a person within the organization who will act as the key link person and as 'research champion and facilitator' for the particular study. We ourselves have been particularly grateful for that in a prison context, where another, special ethical issue may arise – should the researcher carry keys? There is a school of thought that this is wholly inappropriate – on the research side because it may imply too close a relationship with the prison system, and on the prison side because researchers may not be trusted. Where prisons will contemplate this, and include researchers in basic security training, we have found it safe, enabling much more effective use of researcher time while placing less burden on the already over-stretched prison staff.

An important difficulty, which has been only partly resolved to date, lies in the crucial issue of communication between researcher and prospective participant. Ethics committees in England and Wales demand a research participant information sheet in a question and answer format that in the briefest form runs to about three pages of typescript; there is no evidence of its utility. Early research showed a tendency for information in such sheets to be written as if it is to be presented in a medical journal, rather than in a writing style more accessible to the public, such as a local newspaper (Morrow, 1980), and it is well recognized that a higher than average proportion of offenders struggle with literacy. We develop and provide such forms; they are useful as an aide memoire for the researcher and as a record of what has been discussed, but we have always taken care to talk with the prospective research participants about what is being proposed. Davidson et al. (2011) confined their study to men with personality disorder, but their evidence that, when trying to come to a decision about research, people prefer to talk about the issues, rather than read papers or an electronic presentation, is unlikely to be confined to this group. The safety and confidentiality of information is a matter for all research, and there is always potential for a limit to confidentiality if participants give information which indicates that they may be about to do some to harm themselves or to others. The difficulties of offender populations make it more likely that such matters may arise. The consent process must take account of this, and the limits to confidentiality should always be explicit. For example, if an individual indicates a plan to escape, this must be reported to the security authorities. If a person of 17 or under discloses that s/he has been a victim of abuse, that fact must, in law, be reported to social services, or, within closed institutions, to a designated person. For persons under 16, the parent or guardian must also have an opportunity to consider the research. Among young offenders, where family relationships may be less than ideal, this may create a further ethical dilemma.

Competence to consent is, of course, central to a discussion on research. The mentally incapacitated patient may not be able to provide consent in the same degree as the fully competent patient, although many frankly psychotic patients *are* capable of discussing their consent in meaningful terms. People with hallucinations and/or delusions have volunteered for research while understanding that they were being invited to act as 'guinea pigs', and have initiated sophisticated debate about that and other relevant matters including the effective duration of their consent if they were to give it, while others have made it clear that they want nothing to do with the research. This last, of course, poses a difficult scientific problem because those who drop out, for whatever reason, may be those who would benefit most from the research findings. How can paranoid patients be excluded from a study of the needs or treatment of people with psychosis? Will not that invalidate the results? Edlund et al. (1985) explored some of the biases and other adverse consequences of 'fail-safe' mechanisms with respect to research participation when dealing people whose competence may be impaired. Treatment can, ultimately, only be tested adequately with those for whom it is intended. While severely disabled patients should never be disadvantaged by being submitted to unsound or damaging research, neither should they be deprived of taking part in research into their condition. Where there is doubt about competence to consent to relevant proposed research, but the prospective patient-participant appears to have no objection, permission to proceed with the research should be sought through consultation with relatives, close friends, patient advocates or nurses and doctors caring for (as opposed to researching into) the patient. Proxy consent has no legal standing, but the process of checking with one or more of the people who know the patient well and care about him/her will act as an additional safeguard of the patient's interests. Ethics committees should assist in determining the appropriate level of consent, and soundings about 'consent' from the patient should continue after the initial apparent agreement to the research. Furthermore, even with an incompetent patient, it is not difficult to discern whether the research procedure itself, whether interview or procedure, is causing distress or harm. If it does, it should be modified, postponed or abandoned.

A particular concern about research with offenders, whether on remand or being considered for parole, is that such a person could give information to a researcher which could be damaging to his/her case if fed into the system; an offender might, for example, reveal hitherto undetected offences. Scrupulous attention does, therefore, have to be given to safeguarding all information about which undertakings on confidentiality were made. It is sometimes feared that courts could demand a researcher's confidential record. This is most unlikely, if only because reported information would be hearsay and most other information of no direct relevance to the particular offence. Such demands have never happened in Britain. In England and Wales, some years ago, the then Director of Public Prosecutions confirmed in an answer to a query about one of our research projects with pretrial prisoners that he would not take such a step. Another fear is of a subpoena-happy defence lawyer who believes that confidential research records could help his client, but we have never encountered this either. The few solicitors who have enquired about such information have always respected their client's privacy when matters are explained.

The Psychiatrist in Court

Weinstock (1988) surveyed 102 members of the psychiatry and behavioural section of the American Academy of Forensic Sciences and found that the work most often quoted as giving rise to ethical problems was testifying in court. The principal concerns were being a 'hired-gun', withholding part of the truth to endorse a particular legal position, or giving sworn testimony without adequate knowledge.

One point sometimes made in the USA (e.g. Sadoff, 1988) is that it is unwise for a treating psychiatrist to testify about his/her patient, even though lawyers and judges may believe that such testimony is the most effective because this is the clinician who knows the patient best. The argument is that the treating doctor is bound to be biased in favour of his/her patient. We would argue, on the contrary, that in an adversarial system this is no disadvantage and any bias is well understood. In Europe, practice in this respect is so varied that there is no true position (Taylor et al., 2012). The general view in Britain is that the most satisfactory recommendations to courts are likely to come from the service provider, since s/he knows best the likely fit between the prospective patient and his/her services. Furthermore, British law requires that there is evidence of a doctor who is willing to treat in a specified hospital before a hospital order can be made. Evidence from a treating or potentially treating clinician is straightforward when the reporting clinician is doing so as an NHS employee, as there is no financial gain from the transaction, and an offer of treatment is also evidence of willingness to take responsibility for the recommendation. The private/independent healthcare sector also, however, has a prominent role in the delivery of forensic mental health services. Cynics might argue that there would be gain there from recommending inpatient treatment, but, as affiliations are transparent, and the case presented has to be taken as a whole, this does not seem a very great danger in the UK.

An important issue in the writing of reports is the power of the negative comment. It is much easier to persuade a court that someone is dangerous, or bad, or in need of long-term incarceration than any of the opposites. One reason is that societal bias against the mentally abnormal offender is generally negative (Hill, 1982), and negative comments are likely to be flowing with the general attitudinal current. Negative comments may be necessary, providing they are medical, founded in evidence and do not amount merely to moral judgments. The prognosis of a particular illness may appear poor, for example, or the risk of re-offending high, but the evidence, and the limits of evidence, for such conclusions should be transparent. A factual but balanced picture is required, so that the individual's strengths are recorded as well as his/her disorders and dysfunctions and set in the context of whatever management and/or treatment is available and appropriate. A negative comment in a negative background (e.g. this man is an untreatable psychopath) is unlikely to be challenged and is tantamount to fixing for the accused a long prison sentence – not the business of psychiatry. A value free description of the same clinical evidence might refer to core emotional and empathic dysfunctions.

While many clinicians who are UK-based express confidence in the adversarial system, because, at best, it allows both sides of a particular story to be aired openly, and for the Court to make a judgment accordingly, the reality is that legal 'side taking' may sometimes be powerful, and clinicians become vulnerable to the requirements and pressures which are so different to those prevalent in their more familiar clinical environment. We are concerned here with the kind of differences raised by Aubert (1963b) and quoted at the beginning of chapter 6.

All it would take is for the clinician to be a little unsure of him- or herself, being anxious to please, and one or more of the layers to have a slightly bullying or contemptuous manner on the one hand or an infinitely flattering manner on the other, and the unwary clinician may be steered along a pathway not originally intended. Then, it is too late to back down; it would look foolish, or incompetent. The ethical position is to know the limits of one's own expertise and of the profession as a whole. We will explore some cases where devastating and unjust consequences appeared to follow from some failings across the medico-legal divide, and guidance which has followed to try and prevent repetition of such difficulties.

HEURISTIC CASES

1. **Sally Clark** gave birth to a boy, Christopher, in September 1996. He was found dead in his basket at 11 weeks. A post-mortem examination was carried out by a Home Office pathologist, Dr Alan Williams who gave evidence that he found bruises on the body and a small split and slight bruise in the frenulum. He considered that these findings were consistent with minor harm caused during the resuscitation attempts. He also found evidence of infection in the lungs and as a result he concluded that the cause of death was a lower respiratory tract infection. The case was treated as a case of Sudden Unexpected Infant Death Syndrome (SUIDS or 'Cot Death') and death was certified as 'natural causes' (http://www.sallyclark.org.uk/lockyer.html).

Mrs Clark and her husband decided that the best bereavement therapy was another baby. So, Harry was born in November 1997. He was three weeks premature but was a healthy baby. Eight weeks later he too suddenly collapsed and died. Again Dr Williams carried out a post-mortem examination. This time he found injuries, which he considered to be indicative of non-accidental injury, consistent with episodes of shaking on several occasions over several days. He concluded, therefore, that shaking was the likely cause of death.

Sally Clark was arrested in 1998 and tried for the murder of both sons. Her third son was born in 1999, the year of her trial, and survived.

Dr Williams told the court that he had found that Harry had a swollen spinal cord, leading him to the conclusion that he had been shaken to death. However, there were no tears to the brain, no intra-retinal haemorrhages, no subdural haemorrhages in the spine and no para-spinal injuries.

One of the most controversial aspects of the prosecution case was the statistical evidence presented by Professor Sir Roy Meadow, an ex-president of the Royal College of Paediatrics and Child Health. He quoted from the latest Confidential Enquiry into Sudden Death in Infancy (CESDI, 1996) reporting a two-year study into the *Sudden Unexpected Death in Infancy* (SUDI) and he noted that 1 in 8543 reflected the risk of there being a single SUID within a family like the Clarks. He was then asked about the probability of two such deaths within such a family. He gave the astonishing reply that to calculate that you have to multiply 8543 by 8543 which gives an approximate chance of 1 in 73 million. He went on to say:

In England, Wales and Scotland there are about say 700 000 live births a year, so it is saying by chance that happening will occur about once every hundred years.

Under cross-examination he added:

It's the chance of backing that long odds outsider at the Grand National, you know; let's say it's a 80 to 1 chance, you backed the winner last year, then the next year there's another horse at 80 to 1 and it is still 80 to 1 and you back it again and it wins. Now here we're in a situation that, you know, to get to these odds of 73 million you've got to back that 1 in 80 chance four years running, so yes, you might be very, very lucky because each time it's just been a 1 in 80 chance and you know, you've happened to have won it, but the chance of it happening four years running we all know is extraordinarily unlikely. So it's the same with these deaths. You have to say two unlikely events have happened and together it's very, very, very unlikely.' (Clark 2)

Professor Berry, for the defence, was one of the four editors of the CESDI study. He made the point that simply squaring the figure was an illegitimate over simplification. The report made clear that the figures did not

take account of possible familial incidence of factors other than those included in the table.

It ended with the warning:

When a second SIDS[1] death occurs in the same family, in addition to careful search for inherited disorder, there must always be a very thorough investigation of the circumstances.

Further, the trial judge tried to divert the jury away from reliance on this statistical evidence. He said:

I should, I think, members of the jury just sound a word of caution about the statistics. However compelling you may find them to be, we do not convict people in these courts on statistics. It would be a terrible day if that were so. If there is one SIDS death in a family, it does not mean that there cannot be another one in the same family.

Sally Clark was convicted in November 1999. She appealed unsuccessfully in October 2000 arguing that the pathological evidence that Harry died of shaking was too flimsy, *Clark 1.* In the trial Dr Williams had said that haemorrhages at the back of the eyes were evidence of shaking: Professor Luthert (for the defence) thought these were artefactual or possibly due to asphyxia. Yet after the trial the Crown Prosecution Service acknowledged that Dr Williams had identified two other baby deaths from natural causes when there had been haemorrhages in the orbit and on the surface of the back of the eye, and also an adult case with the same findings.

It is worth dealing with the second appeal at some length. One of the best ways of learning about ethics is to consider cases which raise

serious ethical issues, and we are quoting at length from this one, because we think discussion about the medical expert roles in this case ought to form part of the teaching of basic courtroom ethics.

The second appeal was allowed because yet further fresh evidence had emerged. Documents were discovered amongst the records of the hospital where Harry died. The judgment said:

During the course of the post-mortem examination swabs and samples from Harry's faeces, stomach tissue and fluid, blood, lung tissue, bronchus, throat and cerebrospinal fluid ('CSF') were taken by Dr Williams and he submitted these for testing on 27 January 1998, the day of the post-mortem examination. Staphylococcus aureus (SA) was isolated in Harry's stomach tissue and fluid, lungs, bronchus, throat and CSF.

Professor Morris, from Morecambe Bay Hospitals NHS Trust was called to give evidence at this second appeal. He explained that

SA is commonly found in the upper airways of infants aged two or three months, but it does not normally occur in the trachea, bronchus and lungs. Finding Staph aureus in the lungs is, therefore, significant. ... Of greater significance was the finding of Staph aureus in the CSF. Since the fluid is normally sterile, the finding of Staph aureus in pure growth was he considered highly significant.

He noted that the cerebrospinal fluid (CSF) also contained 80 nucleated cells per microlitre and a raised protein level, both signs of inflammation. Professor Morris concluded that

Overwhelming staphylococcal infection is the most likely cause of death.

He thought that the evidence was sufficiently strong that no other diagnosis could be sustained.

Dr Klein, a Consultant in Paediatric Infectious Diseases and Immunology disagreed but he said that the data

did not fit with anything I have ever seen.

The decision of the Court was that

It follows as the Crown acknowledged, that since there was evidence that was not before the jury that might have caused the jury to reach a different verdict on the count in respect of Harry; the verdict on that count has in our judgment to be viewed as unsafe and must be quashed... the conclusion that the verdict in respect of Harry's death is unsafe necessarily leads to a conclusion that the verdict in respect of Christopher's death is also unsafe and it too must be quashed.

The judgment went on

The microbiological results were undoubtedly known to Dr Williams. He had taken the samples and submitted them for testing by the hospital's laboratory. ... However Dr Williams made no reference to these results nor even to having submitted these samples for examination in any of the three statements he made for the trial. ... In respect of Harry, Dr Williams in his evidence available pre-trial said: 'There is no evidence of acute

---

[1] To illustrate the horror of acronyms SUIDS and SIDS mean the same thing.

infection. There is no evidence that this child died as a result of natural disease.' In order to reach that conclusion, it is clear on his own evidence that Dr Williams had had to consider the unusual test results and reach conclusions as to why they could safely be discounted. There is no reference to his consideration of these matters nor of the reasoning by which he discounted the potential significance of these matters in his evidence pre-trial... It is clear, however, that the jury were interested in these matters and it shows a commendable awareness on their part that they asked a question that certainly provided an opportunity for these matters to be revealed even if it did not directly require the revealing of the information. ... 'Are there blood tests for Harry?'... Mr Spencer for the Crown provided the jury with this explanation: 'As I understand it, the answer is that there was no blood sample taken for chemical analysis at the Hospital in the case of Harry as there was for Christopher. There was a blood sample taken at post-mortem which was simply for screening for the presence of drugs and it's been pointed out to me in the medical notes that there was a blood sample taken at the hospital for culture, in other words to see if there was any bacteria in that sample. That is as I understand it, but Dr Williams will be able to confirm'.

In correspondence Dr Williams said:

It is not my practice to refer to additional results in my post-mortem unless they are relevant to the cause of death, as the specimens were referred to another consultant.

The judges said.

We find that explanation wholly unacceptable. If it does correctly state Dr Williams' practice, then on the evidence available to us his practice is completely out of line with the practice accepted by other pathologists to be the standard. ... It is tantamount to saying 'If I can discount it, nobody else need consider it'.

The judges then said of the statistical evidence:

It is unfortunate that the trial did not feature any consideration as to whether the statistical evidence should be admitted in evidence and particularly, whether its proper use would be likely to offer the jury any real assistance. Inherent in the evidence were dangers. The jury were required to return separate verdicts on the two counts but the 1 in 73 million figure encouraged consideration of the two counts together as a package. If the jury concluded that one or other death was not a SIDS case (whether from natural causes or from unnatural causes), then the chance that the other child's death was a SIDS case was 1 in 8543 and the 1 in 73 million figure was wholly irrelevant. In any event, juries know from their own experience that cot deaths are rare. ... Putting the evidence of 1 in 73 million before the jury with its related statistic that it was the equivalent of a single occurrence of two such deaths in the same family once in a century was tantamount to saying that without consideration of the rest of the evidence one could be just

about sure that this was a case of murder. If the figure of 1 in 73 million accurately reflected the chance of two cot deaths in the same family, then the whole of the CONI (Care of Next Infant) scheme was effectively wasted effort. ... Quite what impact all this evidence will have had on the jury will never be known but we rather suspect that with the graphic reference by Professor Meadow to the chances of backing long odds winners of the Grand National year after year it may have had a major effect on their thinking notwithstanding the efforts of the trial judge to down play it. ... It seems likely that if this matter had been fully argued before us we would, in all probability, have considered that the statistical evidence provided a quite distinct basis upon which the appeal had to be allowed.' The appeal was allowed and both convictions were quashed (Clark 2).

In October 2001 the Royal Statistical Society issued a press release, expressing its concern at the misuse of statistics in the courts (http://www.sallyclark.org.uk/RSS.html). They analysed the flawed statistics used by Professor Meadow and said:

The well-publicized figure of 1 in 73 million thus has no statistical basis. Its use cannot reasonably be justified as a 'ballpark' figure because the error involved is likely to be very large, and in one particular direction. The true frequency of families with two cases of SIDS (sudden infant death syndrome) may be very much less incriminating than the figure presented to the jury at trial. Aside from its invalidity, figures such as the 1 in 73 million are very easily misinterpreted. Some press reports at the time stated that this was the chance that the deaths of Sally Clark's two children were accidental. Society does not tolerate doctors making serious clinical errors because it is widely understood that such errors could mean the difference between life and death. The case of R v. Sally Clark is one example of a medical expert witness making a serious statistical error, one which may have had a profound effect on the outcome of the case. Although many scientists have some familiarity with statistical methods, statistics remains a specialized area. The Society urges the Courts to ensure that statistical evidence is presented only by appropriately qualified statistical experts, as would be the case for any other form of expert evidence.

Consideration of these themes on the ethics of the nature of evidence giving in court cannot be considered as complete without considering a series of similar cases following Sally Clark's.

2. **Angela Cannings** was charged, in April 2002, with the murder of three of her children who had died in infancy; the charge in respect of one child was dropped but she was tried for the murder of two others, Jason and Matthew. The first specialist witness called by the Crown was Professor Meadow. Again, he was particularly concerned by the extreme rarity of a third infant death in the same family. He said:

The fact that a previous child had died in the family is relevant because that combination of circumstances, that sort of story is one that is very typical of a child who has died as a result of smothering. So my medical diagnosis there would be probable smothering.

Although the charge against Mrs Cannings in respect of her baby Gemma, who also died in infancy, was dropped some of the details of that death were allowed into the trial as 'background'. In her summing up Mrs Justice Hallett said:

You have not heard about Gemma's death to justify the kind of approach referred to by Mr Mansfield; the Lady Bracknell approach. This is not a case whereby you could say 'to lose one baby is misfortune, two carelessness, three murder'. As you will appreciate, members of the jury, that is just inappropriate – totally.

No direct evidence of physical assault on the babies was forthcoming but, nevertheless, the jury convicted Mrs Cannings on both counts. After conviction Mrs Justice Hallett had to pass two mandatory life sentences. She said:

There was no medical evidence before the court that suggested there was anything wrong with you when you killed your children... I have no doubt that for a woman like you have committed these terrible acts of suffocating babies there must have been something seriously wrong with you. All the evidence indicates you wanted the children and, apart from these terrible incidents, you cherished them... As you know I have no alternative but to impose sentences of life in prison on you. This in my judgment is a classic kind of injustice that can be caused by mandatory sentencing. It's not my decision when you will be released, but I intend to make it known in my remarks that, in my own view, you will never be a threat to anyone in the future.' (Cannings)

In December 2003 the Court of Appeal (Criminal Division) quashed the two convictions of murder against Angela Cannings. They gave a very detailed and erudite discussion of the issues raised at the trial. Important points included the results of a study of 6373 families who had lost a child by a cot death (SIDS) which concluded:

The occurrence of a second unexpected infant death within a family is not a rare event and is usually from natural causes.

After reviewing some of the other defence evidence, the Court of Appeal concluded:

What is abundantly clear is that in our present state of knowledge, it does not necessarily follow that three sudden unexplained infant deaths in the same family leads to the inexorable conclusion that they must have resulted from the deliberate infliction of harm. There is acceptable evidence that even three infant deaths in the same family may be natural, and may indeed all properly be described as SIDS.

After more discussion about the remaining medical disagreements in the trial, a slight note of frustration emerged when they acknowledged the difficulties of understanding the deliberations of the jury which does not, in English law, provide a set of reasons for its decision. They quoted from Sir Robin Auld's Review of the Criminal Courts of England and Wales, 2001.

... The time has come for the trial judge in each case to give the jury a series of written factual questions, tailored to the law as he knows it to be and to the issues in evidence in the case. The answers to these questions should logically lead only to a verdict of guilty and not guilty.' (http://www.criminal-courts-review.org.uk)

The judges further acknowledged the difficulty of deciding cases where doctors are in dispute. and science cannot give definite answers. but concluded:

Justice may not be done in a small number of cases where in truth a mother has deliberately killed her baby without leaving any identifiable evidence of the crime. That is an undesirable result, which however avoids a worse one. If murder cannot be proved, the conviction cannot be safe. In a criminal case, it is simply not enough to be able to establish even a high probability of guilt. Unless we are sure of guilt the dreadful possibility always remains that a mother, already brutally scarred by the unexplained death or deaths of her babies, may find herself in prison for life for killing them when she should not be there at all. In our community, and in any civilized community, that is abhorrent.

A good account of the ordeal suffered by Mrs Cannings, the long-term damage it has done to her, her perspective on the trial and on the appeal are in the book she wrote after her release together with a journalist (Cannings and Lloyd Davies, 2006).

3. **Trupti Patel** was tried, June 2003, for the murder of three of her children. Her second child, a boy, died unexpectedly at the age of two months, in December 1997. Eighteen months later, another son died, aged just 15 days. Autopsies yielded no explanations for the deaths, but a daughter who died at the age of 22 days in June 2001 was found to have four broken ribs. Prof Meadow gave his usual evidence about cot deaths not recurring in families, but this time the defence called a genetics expert, Professor Michael Patton, who testified that several cot deaths in the same family could be caused by an undiscovered genetic defect, and that the chances of experiencing more than one cot death could be as high as one in twenty. The court also heard evidence that Patel's maternal grandmother lost five children in infancy, but that her remaining seven children were alive and well. In summing up Mr Justice Jack said:

It is not enough to say that an event is rare so it is unlikely to be the cause of something. One has to look at the likelihood of the other possible cause, or other possible causes. That is the danger with what may be happening here in saying that three SIDS (sudden infant death syndrome) deaths in a family would be very unusual, therefore the deaths are unnatural. How rare would three asphyxiations be, particularly where, as is the case here, the mother loved her children and was immediately distraught and regretful? We simply do not know. We have not had any evidence about that. It is hardly common is it? That is obvious. That is the competing cause of the deaths and nobody has evaluated its likelihood.

Mrs Patel was acquitted, by the jury, on all three counts. (http://en.wikipedia.org/wiki/Trupti_Patel)

Aftermath

In June 2005 Dr Alan Williams was found guilty of serious professional misconduct by the General Medical Council (see *Williams*). A panel found that he had been incompetent in doing the post-mortem examination on Christopher Clark. He was also found to have been incompetent in performing the post-mortem examination on Harry Clark and to have failed in his duty as an expert witness. The chairman of the panel said:

Whatever your own views, even if reasonable, you had a responsibility as an experienced forensic pathologist to consider whether test results might need to be openly discussed, before being discounted, in order to prevent any risk of a miscarriage of justice.

The panel found no evidence of general incompetence and so, although he was banned for 3 years from Home Office pathology work or coroners' cases, he was allowed to continue working as a consultant histopathologist (Dyer, 2005a).

The following month, in July 2005, Professor Roy Meadow was also found guilty of serious professional misconduct by the General Medical Council. A panel told him that he had acted beyond the limits of his expertise and abused his position as a doctor in giving erroneous and misleading statistical evidence at Mrs Clark's trial. The panel accepted that he had not intended to mislead but was

an eminent paediatrician whose reputation was renowned throughout the world.

The panel considered that his eminence and authority, which gave the misleading evidence such great weight, carried with it an exceptional responsibility to take meticulous care in a case of this grave nature. They concluded that his errors, compounded by

repetition over a considerable period of time, were so fundamental and so serious it is the panel's view that a period of suspension would be inadequate, not in the public interest and would fail to maintain public confidence in the profession.

The chairman of the fitness to practice panel told him that he had undermined public confidence in doctors who play a pivotal role in the criminal justice system as expert witnesses.

The Administrative Court, however, in the person of Mr Justice Collins, sitting alone, put him back on the register. The judge ruled that the GMC's punishment of Professor Meadow was 'unduly harsh'. He warned that such disciplinary treatment could cause other doctors to become reluctant to appear in child abuse cases, citing an exodus of willing experts since the ruling. He said:

He made one mistake[2], which was to misunderstand and misinterpret the statistics. It was a mistake, as the panel accepted, that was easily and widely made. It may be proper to have criticized him for not disclosing his lack of expertise, but that does not justify a finding of serious professional misconduct.

After he heard about his reinstatement Professor Meadow said:

Children can only be protected from abuse if those who suspect abuse are able to give their honest opinion without fear of retribution. This is an important decision for paediatricians and all doctors, nurses, teachers and other professionals who may have to express difficult and sometimes unpopular opinions in the course of giving evidence in court. They should be able to do so without the fear of prosecution by the General Medical Council or other professional regulators.' (Meadow 1) (Freeman, 2006).

The GMC appealed against the reinstatement, but it was upheld by the Court of Appeal in October 2006. In an 82-page judgment Lord Justice Auld said that Professor Meadow was undoubtedly guilty of 'some' professional misconduct:

He relied initially on statistical figures of uncertain source and scientific value.

But:

I could not contemplate erasure as an appropriate penalty for his uncharacteristic honest errors in this difficult case.' (Meadow 2)

After the birth of her first child, Sally Clark's father reported that she had suffered from depression and had dealt with that with occasional binge drinking. That was treated as not relevant at her trial. She had little opportunity to grieve the death of her children. After she was acquitted and returned to her husband and surviving son, she was unable to recover from the psychological effects of the miscarriage of justice, which tend to be very persistent (see also chapter 28). In November 2007, while her son was at school, she was found dead at home, with alcohol in her blood, at the age of 42. During her time in prison, her father's view was unequivocal:

Sally is where she is because of bad medicine, bad statistics, and because the will to win prevailed. The jury, doubtless confused by medical contradictions, fell back on sound bites to reach a majority verdict 10–2. (http://www.sallyclark.org.uk/)

---

[2] I This is clearly wrong; the judge did not note that the General Medical Council had said that Professor Meadow's errors were compounded by repetition.

Comment

There is much to learn from this series of events. The issues concern law, clinical medicine, medical ethics, general social morality, and even psychiatry. Psychiatry does not play a prominent role in the stories, but that is part of their educational value.

There are a number of substantial legal issues which haunt this narrative. The first was expressed forcefully by Mrs Justice Hallett when she sentenced Angela Cannings. Politicians have persistently ignored advice from both lawyers and doctors about the injustice of the inflexible mandatory sentence for murder. This seems to be, paradoxically, in response to pressure from the tabloid press – paradoxically because, uncharacteristically in these cases, the press has largely been on the side of the defendants rather than rooting for ever more severe punishment. Another issue is almost entirely unspoken although the masterly judgment given at Mrs Cannings' appeal referred to Sir Robin Auld's view that the time has come to try and find out the reasoning of the jury when making their judgment. Few question the appropriateness of a jury trial in complex cases turning on disputed expert evidence (but see Jenkins, below). The easier but important legal problem in these cases was the failure of the courts in the first instance to balance the evidence appropriately. The Royal Statistical Society is correct. Professor Meadow's ludicrous statistics should have at least been challenged by someone who knew something about statistics. Does the reader feel inclined, as we do, to question the wisdom of giving experts largely unfettered rights when expressing their opinions in court? The judge in the case did urge caution about the use of such statistics, but did not or was not able to ensure that the expertise was examined appropriately. Are there some forms of expression which should perhaps be denied to the expert? Could an 'honest mistake' become an unacceptably biased opinion when dramatic analogy is introduced? Research on expert witness credibility is a little disturbing, as far as it goes. Brodsky et al. (2010) have drawn from literature on credibility factors from a range of sources to develop a witness credibility scale. Tested only with undergraduates so far, they found that a four-factor structure best explained credibility – knowledge was one of them. The other three were 'likeability', 'trustworthiness' and 'confidence', all highly subjective ratings. This also brings us to the issue of jury research. Again, there is little, and findings are mixed, perhaps because of the differing nature of evidence, but also because very often researchers use undergraduate students as 'mock jurors'. *Behavioral Sciences and the Law* has published a useful themed issue (2011, issue 3) on these matters, and unpacks the relative value of the different research strategies. Jury processing styles as well as witness characteristics are each likely to influence outcome. Other than that, we are largely dependent on a journalist's accounts of the process (Grove, 1998; Malcolm, 1990).

The clinical issues in these cases appear to be primarily the concern of paediatricians and pathologists, not psychiatrists or other mental health clinicians, although they do raise questions about factitious disorder by proxy and maternal homicide. However there are wider ethical issues for any clinical expert. How do we give expert evidence with due confidence when the evidence is truly scientifically defensible, but with due diffidence and modesty where it is not? How do we retain our commitment to cautious statement and modesty if harassed in open court to be more certain? How do we express complicated, technical details in lay language which can be understood by lay people without distorting the science we are trying to represent? May a wish to do good of one kind carry serious risks of harm of another? To tell the jury that the odds against the defendant having murdered her second child, simply because she has had two infant deaths, is 1 to 73 million, just like the odds of backing four outside winners in the Grand National in successive years, is, as the Court of Appeal noted, is a certainly. It would have tantamount to telling the jurors that it is a certainty. It and ultimately he didn't but it would have done Meadow and Mrs Clark much less damage if it had been tackled immediately. The problem is that courts are still, to some extent, awestruck by 'experts' with lots of letters after their name and impressive CVs. It may also be that in this case Meadow, who once gave wise advice on expert evidence (e.g. Mitchels and Meadow, 1989; Meadow and Mitchels, 1989), who cared about the safety of children and was highly regarded, allowed his campaign against the killing of infants to overwhelm his objectivity. He became well known because of his papers on Munchausen by proxy and later by observing in his textbook something that became known as 'Meadow's law' which states that: '*one sudden infant death is a tragedy, two is suspicious and three is murder, unless proven otherwise.*' This is a piece of logical nonsense which is quite inappropriate even to think about when giving evidence in a court of law in which somebody's liberty is at stake. The first rule of medicine '*primum non nocere*' seems to have taken a back seat. Courts are not the place for zeal or campaigning. It is particularly important that expert witnesses do not become hired guns and that they do not see themselves as working primarily for the prosecution or for the defence but are equally capable of giving objective evidence and opinion on both sides of the adversarial divide. In the cases described here there were serious miscarriages of justice which led to immense suffering in a number of families, including the surviving children of the mothers accused. We must never tire of reminding ourselves of our duty to do no harm and to remember that not all of our development over time is necessarily for the better. This is why some structure in continuing professional development is so essential, within a peer group who are honest and constructive.

These cases raise general social and political issues too. These are perhaps been most cogently expressed in an article in *The Times* by Simon Jenkins (2003) – the medical expert is criticized but viewed within the context of a system which is failing around him:

The courts of justice are the same as tried the Salem witches. They summon juries to pass public judgment on these wretched women, calling in aid a witch-finder general, the hawkish Professor Sir Roy Meadow. He has no time for classic jurisprudence. To him a mother is guilty unless 'proven otherwise'. Two cot deaths are suspicious and three are murder. To hell with any genetic propensity to multiple deaths. This is tabloid justice... The system is rotten. In British trials experts are paid not to help the court with impartial evidence, as is customary in most other countries. They are paid to lend a veneer of objectivity to one side in the argument. The hope is that 12 good citizens, the jury, can dig out the truth from this melange of professional bias and emotion. It is theatre, not justice... (In Mrs Patel's case)... (t)he prosecution case relied on the extraordinary thesis that Mrs Patel was having one child after another to satisfy a craving for murder. It told the jury to ignore her remorse since it was 'an intention to kill that came to Mrs Patel in one moment and left her the next'. I know such lawyers claim to be only role-playing, to be putting a case, however implausible, before the mercy of the jury. Perhaps Sir Roy is no more than playing a role too. Perhaps the whole system is a game of seeing how much public money can be spent on putting women in jail, which Britain does more than any country in Europe. If so, the system is inhuman and ludicrously inappropriate. The adversarial system, the distortion of evidence, the onus to prove innocence and the hyping of juries are all medieval and barbaric... Cot deaths should clearly be handled by an examining magistrate in chambers, as in Scandinavia and elsewhere.

The issues for psychiatry are various and profound. Mrs Justice Hallett asked the central question which psychiatry finds so difficult to deal with. She was in effect saying that the woman she had to sentence was to be pitied and helped rather than condemned. Whatever else had happened she had lost her babies, a terrible tragedy for a mother, and, if she had been guilty of killing, then no one had stopped to ask the fundamental question as to why this happened. If any of these women had killed her babies, particularly when they were weeks old, a severe mental abnormality would be highly likely and probably eminently treatable.

Where were the psychiatrists in these cases? Were they never called, even though these women had been accused of murder? If called, how should a psychiatrist deal with the invitation to give evidence, particularly at the trial phase of a murder hearing if the accused denies the charge and the evidence against the accused rests almost entirely on a flawed statistical inference. First and foremost, psychiatrists and other clinicians surely have a role in improving the mental health of defendants, whatever the charges against them, and whatever the quality of the evidence in the criminal case. The health of the central character in the drama, the defendant, must always be a medical concern, whoever employs the physician or psychiatrist. It is perfectly possible to fulfil all of the doctor's court duties fully without abandoning concern for the defendant's health and welfare. Things would be a lot safer and easier in this respect if there were much more discussion and exchange of information between the defence and the prosecution in serious cases. Even if the defendant does not suffer from a mental disorder, there may still be a role for the psychiatrist. Any involvement with the criminal justice system as an accused person is stressful for most people. In cases of death or serious injury within the family, and even when the accused really is the perpetrator, this stress is exceptionally high. When a child has just died, his or her mother is likely to be profoundly affected by that; when the child, or one of her children, is under a year old, then her physiological state is likely to be compromised too (see also chapter 20). To be more specific, in cases of cot death paediatricians and psychiatrists should work closely together. Finally, if any doctor is speaking the truth, the whole truth, and nothing but the truth he or she will draw the attention of the court to gaps in knowledge, to the uncertainty of the opinion to be given, to the possibility of entirely different hypotheses to his or her own.

THE DEATH PENALTY

Arguments against the death penalty *per se* have been made elsewhere (e.g. Gunn, 2009), and by many authors. It is not a big issue for doctors practising in the European Union (EU) as it is one of the conditions of membership of the EU that capital punishment shall not take place in any member country. Capital punishment is still practised, however, in many other countries with China, Iran and the USA heading the list for numbers executed. The Third World Congress on Prison Healthcare, in Bristol in 1988 (Trafford, 1990), stated that the Congress:

opposes any and all participation by health professionals in any action which could be interpreted as cooperating with the execution of the death penalty.

This was ratified by the World Psychiatric Association in 1989 and remains the international ethical position.

Outside Europe, this principle is frequently broken. Some doctors simply don't see the point, how else would the United States and China be able to medicalize their execution processes in the way they do? Who inserts the needle if the execution is by lethal injection? If it is an execution ancillary, who teaches them how to do it? Who advises on lethal doses? Who certifies death when it is all over? If doctors stood back from executions according to international ethical code, then countries keen on judicial killings would have to devise other methods, methods they have given up usually because of squeamishness which did not exist in the past. The Chinese describe their new system of travelling execution vans in some provinces in which lethal injections are administered as 'more humane', and they always have a doctor in attendance.

Any doctor working in or thinking of working in a prison in an American state which still has the death penalty must read the important review *Breach of Trust: Physician Participation in Executions in the United States* written by a consortium of bodies opposed to the death penalty (http://www.hrw.org/reports/1994/usdp/index.htm). They recommended, among other things, that the laws and regulations of all death penalty states should incorporate American Medical Association (AMA) guidelines on physician participation. In particular, laws mandating physician presence and pronouncement of death should be changed specifically to exclude physician participation.

A much more difficult issue is raised, in part, by the context of the US system retaining people, including sick people, on death row for many years. The AMA and the APA are clear that it is ethically prohibited for a psychiatrist to restore mental health for the purpose of restoring competence to be executed, but what should the physician do in respect of mental illness which is causing great suffering to the individual, or putting the individual at increased risk of harming others? We part company with Weinstock et al. (2010), when they appear to be arguing that competence to be executed assessments can be ethical. The safest approach must be to follow AMA and APA guidance to eschew all involvement, but their contemplation of the problem of 'double effect and unintended consequences' and potentially conflicting duties is important, at its most acute for death row cases, but not confined to them.

Writing in the *American Medical News* (an AMA online newsletter) O'Reilly reported that a survey conducted in the *Journal of Medical Licensure and Discipline* by Ty Alper, Associate Director of the University of California, Berkeley School of Law's Death Penalty Clinic, found that only seven death-penalty states incorporated the American Medical Association's (AMA's) ethics code. Alper is reported as saying:

> There is this perception that many people, including judges, have that because of the AMA ethical code, doctors can't participate and won't participate in executions when the reality – and we've learned this through the legal cases that have been brought – is that doctors do participate and are willing to participate.

> The AMA guidelines are just that – guidelines – and not enforceable in most circumstances (http://www.ama-assn.org/amednews/2010/02/22/prsb0222.htm).

On the other hand, laws in Illinois and Kentucky specifically bar doctors from the execution chamber and the AMA has revoked one physician's membership 'for participation in execution by lethal injection', according to Black and Sade (2007). They said:

> all participants...regulating the medical profession – federal and state government, licensing authorities, professional societies, and individual physicians – should consider the specific role of physicians in society, which is preventing and healing illness and relieving suffering. The core requirement for that role is trust in the profession, which is advanced and preserved by ethical principles. Any form of participation causing death by lethal injection is unethical because it violates the physician's role, thereby undermining trust.

So, codes and guidelines have a limited role in preserving the ethical integrity of the medical profession. As we move into chapter 27, it may seem that the struggle to keep ethical standards raised high is hopeless but there are other tools available such as leadership, better and more focused recruitment, systems of identifying unethical practice earlier and perhaps most important, more and better continuing education and development, including ethical education and development.

27
Deviant and sick medical staff

Edited and written by

John Gunn

With contributions from **Rob Hale, Tony Maden and Pamela J Taylor**

Whatever houses I may visit, I will come for the benefit of the sick, remaining free of all intentional injustice, of all mischief and in particular of sexual relations with both female and male persons, be they free or slaves.
Hippocrates 4–500 BC

Most of us have had the experience of being treated by an effective caring doctor and most others have fantasies that the vast majority of the medical profession are like Dr Lydgate in Middlemarch (Eliot, 1871). We also know that this idealization is flawed and that the power of medicine can be used for ill as well as good. A great travesty of medical knowledge occurred in the early part of the twentieth century when medicine in its scientific mode started to turn its back on the individual and indulge in science-fiction type activities such as eugenics and euthanasia. The ideas for eugenics came from Britain and the United States and were taken up with alacrity by Sweden and Germany. The Nazi party in Germany, after it had seized power, turned these ideas into racial cleansing by large-scale extermination. Mass murder is not impossible without medical skills but it is made a lot easier with them and doctors designed gas chambers and selected individuals, at first the intellectually disabled and the mentally ill, as unfit to live because they were a burden on society and might reproduce their own deficiencies.

All sorts of explanations have been given as to why this might have happened but perhaps Burleigh (1994), the Cardiff historian, gives the simplest:

People go into medicine for all sorts of reasons utterly unconnected with a vocation to do good. They are no more or less 'idealistic' than people who become businessmen, chemists, engineers, historians, journalists or lawyers. If these men and women had hoped for socio economic advancement, then the depression and changes in the health system under Weimar led many of them to radical politics and a visceral hatred of the Republic. Roughly 45% of doctors were members of the Nazi party, and many more doctors belonged to the SS than comparable professionals, with the sole exception of lawyers. Their medical education tended to treat ethics as an obligatory side line, somehow unconnected with the more important scientific side of their training. This was what Brandt meant when at his trial he said: 'one may hang a copy of the oath of Hippocrates in one's office but nobody pays any attention to it.' In any case, even the Hippocratic oath was subject to creeping reinterpretation, with medical historians redefining ethics away from concern with the individual in favour of the health of the biological collective.

Focusing on psychiatry, there are, perhaps, eight ways in which psychiatric power can be abused (Gunn, 2006):

1. 'social purification';
2. people who are mentally normal treated as mad;
3. psychiatric techniques used for oppression;
4. the punishment of mentally disordered people;
5. general maltreatment;
6. excessive/inappropriate use of treatments;
7. cruel and dangerous experiments;
8. not treating mental disorder.

The Nazi system was the most extreme example of 'social purification' using medical techniques. It was of course a political system concerned with an extremely distorted view of public health, but nevertheless individual doctors collaborated in significant numbers. There is little to suggest that they had to do this in fear of their lives although as Burleigh indicates to do so was probably thought to be a good career move! The so-called 'doctors trial' *Brandt* at Nuremberg in 1946/7 lists 15 major medical crimes including euthanasia (most would call this murder), high-altitude experiments, freezing experiments, malaria experiments, mustard gas experiments, seawater experiments, epidemic jaundice experiments, poison experiments, and incendiary experiments. Pictures of 23 of the 27 medical and administrative defendants can be found on Wikipedia (http://en.wikipedia.org/wiki/Doctors%27_Trial).

THE MEDICAL POWER BALANCE

The individual consults a doctor for help, sometimes for advice, usually because of symptoms, dysfunction or distress. In these situations a social hierarchy is established and the client/patient has some degree of vulnerability. It is almost impossible to equalize the doctor/patient relationship. Relationship imbalances can be exploited. Rarely the patient exploits the situation, e.g. by providing incorrect information or manufacturing signs and symptoms (see chapter 17) or even sexually. The doctor can exploit the situation financially and/or sexually and act out neurotic or psychotic behaviour in ways not available in other settings. Nevertheless it is remarkable that exploitation of any kind is unusual.

In any doctor/patient relationship the two individuals develop feelings for one another, some positive, some negative. It can be argued that the relationship that develops between the doctor and the patient is not only inevitable but should be used in the treatment. The psychoanalytic perspective is that feelings are related to relationships that the patient has experienced in the past; the feelings about those previous relationships are 'transferred' into the present doctor/patient setting. The analysts argue that these feelings need to be recognized, understood and explained, 'interpreted', or else they will interfere with the treatment. These feelings are two-way and the therapist needs to understand his/her feelings and have them interpreted, or at least discussed by his/her supervisor. Professionals undertaking any of the psychotherapies should have a supervisor. For the forensic psychiatrist negative feelings towards the patient or client are of special importance. Some offender patients give rise to feelings of disgust, revulsion, fear and anger in most onlookers because of the behaviour they undertake. The psychiatrist, although used to encountering serious antisocial behaviour, is not immune from these feelings. S/he needs to recognize the feelings, learn techniques of separating feelings about the behaviour from feelings concerning the perpetrator of the behaviour and discuss difficulties in these areas with his/her supervisor. The analysts are probably right, some of the more extreme negative feelings aroused in the practitioner are related to previous experiences in the practitioner's past or to other pathology. The feelings which patients develop for their doctors are often called the 'transference' in line with the theory just outlined and the feelings which doctors develop for their patients the 'countertransference'. We will return to this below.

To reiterate, the power ratio in a medical consultation plus the intimacy and indeed the privacy which is an integral part of it can be misused so that patients can be mistreated and used in a variety of ways; sometimes they are. Furthermore, it is not only patients who are abused at times but also other staff who come within the purview of a senior doctor's influence. For example, medical students have usually seen or experienced bullying during their training. Silver and Glicken (1990) conducted a survey of abuse, as seen by the students, in one American medical school. Almost half of the students studied said they had been abused sometime whilst at medical school. Many of them indicated that the most serious episode of abuse affected them for a month or more. One student described how he was examining a fellow student's eye when he discovered a painful corneal abrasion and decided to stop the examination. His teacher said to go on as this gave an opportunity to learn how to force the patient to co-operate even if they are in pain. Another reported being hit on the knuckles with an instrument for holding a forceps improperly during stitching. This happened repeatedly and the student now says s/he has a scar on the back of his/her hand. A disgruntled student commented, 'As far as I am concerned it's been three years of constant abuse and humiliation'. There is no reason to suppose that this kind of behaviour is confined to US medical schools. Remedies for this problem were suggested by the students and included specific education about bullying for medical teachers, a grievance committee to which students could turn in confidence and a disciplinary process for persistent offenders.

These accounts give a clue as to the way in which patients may be abused, for example the report that one teacher thought it a good idea to force medical examinations on reluctant patients in pain. A matter which is rarely discussed among doctors is the habituation they may require for tolerating other people's pain and misery so that they come to regard the patient more as a 'subject' or even object rather than as a person with specific sensitivities.

BOUNDARIES AND OFFENCES

Ordinary social discourse is limited by boundaries. We respect one another's social space, for example we knock on doors to seek permission for entry, we understand there are limits to the discussions we can have with friends, colleagues, and relatives. We say things to our intimates that we do not say to strangers. There are social conventions about touching others such as handshakes, kisses, congratulatory hugs and the like. If we make significant errors with these boundaries social sanctions may follow. The medical encounter has a unique set of boundaries which have to be carefully constructed and monitored. There are occasions when it is appropriate for a stranger to a doctor to undress in front of that doctor and there are occasions when it is certainly not appropriate for that to happen. Much more subtle boundary changes and rules apply when psychotherapy is undertaken. The treatment is largely private, covers intimacies, and is sometimes difficult to distinguish from other intimate social encounters which have an entirely different purpose and rules structure.

Any psychiatrist of experience will, for example, have encountered his or her own sexual feelings towards patients and will certainly have been aware on occasions of sexual feelings from a patient. This may be the development of transference during the course of psychotherapy. It is to be distinguished from the development of similar feelings in social encounters and it has to be acknowledged, discussed and supervised. Yet it is possible for some practitioners to simply exploit the different rules pertaining in the medical office. A visit to the General Medical Council (GMC) website will show that there are many sexual offences committed by doctors within their practice which have little or nothing to do with transference but are blatant examples of the misuse of medical opportunities and power. Some of the assaults are on staff working within a medical office or practice. The GMC website (www.gmc-uk.org) is very informative, giving the range of misconduct which doctors are reported for; matters ranging from dishonesty, hostile and neglectful behaviour towards patients, drunkenness, assaults, drug offences, misuse of prescriptions and inappropriate sexual activity. In 2003, 23 cases alleging sexual assault or indecency were heard, some 6% of the total cases. The 2009 statistics indicated that the allegation most commonly resulting in erasure (the GMC's severest sanction) was 'improper relationship with a patient', 15 cases and 'indecent behaviour' added another seven cases.

Some of these miscreants suffer from psychiatric disorders, including sexual disorders. In the 1970s, Denis Hill, then a prominent member of the GMC, introduced a health screening system so that those doctors in trouble, who had health problems, could be diverted to a health committee and provided with appropriate support and treatment until they were fit to return to practice. As the twentieth century came to a close and general public punitiveness increased, this system was abolished. Doctors can still be referred as a condition of suspension of practice to psychiatric and other medical help, but they no longer bypass the general disciplinary processes.

In 1986 Gartrell et al. published the results of a survey of US psychiatrists: 7% of the male and 3% of the female respondents said that they had had sexual relations with a patient; 40% of these offending psychiatrists sought help with their problem. In most cases the sexual relationship began during treatment or within 6 months of termination. A small minority of these cases resulted in a long-term relationship or marriage. The majority of the offenders acknowledged that they engaged in sexual contact with patients for their own sexual or emotional gratification. They also believed that patients with whom they were involved had predominantly positive feelings about the sexual contact yet the majority of the psychiatrists in the survey who had been sexually involved with their own therapists rated the experience as exploitative and harmful. The authors concluded that:

Completing an accredited psychiatric residency clearly does not protect against subsequent sexual contact with patients.

They recommended that residency training programmes include specific training on sexual abuse by psychiatrists. They believe that offenders should be encouraged to seek professional consultation and that patients should be assisted with the negative consequences of involvement with their therapists. The study underlines the need for close supervision of psychotherapy.

These problems are, of course, not confined to medical practitioners; others such as nurses and psychologists also have codes forbidding sexual contact with patients, but they too have a significant number of transgressors. A review (Pope, 1990) of the research into therapist–patient involvement showed that between 85 and 96% of the reported activity was a male therapist with a female patient. The one published study (American) across three disciplines suggested there is a no difference between psychiatrists, psychologists, and social workers in respect of their sexual misconduct. Usually the patients are younger than the therapists and in a significant minority of cases the patient is a minor under the age of consent (Bajt and Pope, 1989). There is no study which has found support for the premise that therapists who undergo personal therapy are less likely to become sexually involved with their patients. Indeed, Gartrell and her colleagues (1986) found that offender psychiatrists were more likely to be male, to have completed an accredited residency and to have undergone personal psychotherapy or psychoanalysis. Patient characteristics do not seem to be predictive of which patients will become victims.

Pope and Vetter (1991) conducted a US national survey of 1,320 psychologists who were randomly selected from the membership directory of the American Psychological Association; they found that half the respondents reported assessing or treating at least one patient who had been sexually intimate with a prior therapist. A total of 958 sexual intimacy cases were reported. Most cases involved female patients and most involved intimacies prior to termination. Harm occurred in at least 80% of the instances in which therapists engaged in sex with a patient after termination. However, respondents reported that in about 4% of the 1,000 cases in which the issue of sexual intimacies arose, the allegations were false (http://www.kspope.com/sexiss/sex2.php). Pope classified the 958 patients who had engaged in sexual intimacies with a therapist as follows:

5% were minors at the time of the intimacies;
3% married the therapist;
32% experienced incest or other child sex abuse;
10% of patients had experienced rape prior to intimacies with therapist;
11% required hospitalization at least partially as a result of the intimacies;
14% attempted suicide;

1% committed suicide;

17% achieved complete recovery from any harmful effects of intimacies;

20% were seen pro bono or for a reduced fee;

12% filed a formal complaint.

Most writers are adamant that sexual contact between therapist and patient is both exploitation and highly damaging to the patient and therefore should never be contemplated, not even long after the treatment has ended. Applebaum and Jorgenson (1991) suggested that this is too extreme and they proposed that a 12-month period from the end of the treatment, with absolutely no contact between the parties, should elapse before sexual contact should be contemplated. However the arguments against this are strong, for example Herman et al. (1987) argued that:

Patients enter therapy in need of help and care. By virtue of this fact, they voluntarily submit themselves to an unequal relationship in which their therapists have superior knowledge and power. [...] Neither transference nor the real inequality in the power relationship ends with the termination of therapy. In our opinion, the notion that exceptions to the rule of abstinence can be allowed in the name of love or marriage reveals either a naive romanticism or an insufficient understanding of the nature of the therapeutic relationship or both. Similarly, pragmatic efforts to define a post-termination waiting period, after which sexual relations might be permissible, disregard both the continued inequality of the roles of the therapist and former patient and the timelessness of unconscious processes, including transference.

Pope (1990) quotes Cummings and Sobell's (1985) finding that American courts have ruled that the emotional transference of psychotherapy is still extant even though the treatment has concluded. Pope noted that the prevalence of sexual misconduct by therapists is declining, at least in the USA. This is a tentative observation and the reasons for this (if it is true) are not entirely clear, but he suggested that significant factors are new legislation and tough decisions by the courts (even granting large damages when the sexual encounter of psychotherapy went on to marriage[1] – see Boodman (1989)).

---

[1] In 1989, a District of Columbia Court awarded $1 million in damages in a divorce case to Frederica Lehrman Carmichael, who said her husband – a psychologist whom she met when she consulted him for problems in her second marriage – committed malpractice by having sex with her while she was a patient. The judge found that although the psychologist married her in 1983, he continued to treat her until 1986, thereby committing malpractice. The judge wrote that the woman, an heiress to the Giant Food fortune, saw her psychologist-husband as a 'savior from all of the things that were haunting her life,' while he regarded her as the answer to his pressing financial problems.

ABUSE IN INSTITUTIONS

The patient/staff power ratio is even bigger within an institution. Patients are often totally subservient, having to follow a detailed set of rules; they are rarely able to come and go as they please and they frequently don't have mentors or others who are independent of the institution to turn to if they are feeling exploited. Such arrangements have a high risk of staff abusing patients and constant vigilance by senior staff and by outside independent organizations is essential. In many ways general maltreatment is the root of other types of psychiatric abuse. It encompasses inhumane conditions, a lack of respect for patients, and taking advantage of their vulnerability.

In 1965, a letter was written to *The Times* in London, complaining about the treatment of geriatric patients in some institutions. One of the correspondents, Barbara Robb (1967), wrote a book *Sans Everything*; a book which was castigated at the time as containing wild and irresponsible allegations. In fact, she quoted evidence from six nurses about quite appalling abuse by other nurses. Patients were neglected, left in dirty clothes, hit if they transgressed any rules, were left without food at times and generally mocked. One nurse reported, 'The thrice-daily doses of medicine are a major source of amusement to the charge nurses. Many, many times have I seen Largactil, etc, poured from a large bottle into a patient's tea with absolutely no pretence at measurement.' The book was about elderly patients trapped in subservient and degrading circumstances in mental hospitals and eventually the book was vindicated, at least in part, by other more official damning reports which followed: they were well described by Martin (1984) in his book *Hospitals in Trouble*.

The types of abuse that have been recorded include violence and bullying, the misuse of treatments and the withholding of freedoms and privileges as punishments. It is tempting and easy to use excess sedation or antipsychotic tranquillization to calm a patient or to force them to do something the patient objects to. One blatant misuse of a therapeutic agent in England was the application of unmodified ECT (i.e. without anaesthetic or muscle relaxant) 'in an emergency' to stun and thus quieten fractious aggressive patients; a procedure used infrequently but unashamedly in one hospital in the 1970s, but discontinued when it was brought to light.

Sexual misconduct also occurs in residential settings; the abuse of children has been mentioned in chapter 10. At an international meeting in Prato, Italy Maden reported significant misconduct between staff and patients on a secure hospital unit designed for the treatment of men suffering from personality disorders. Female nurses and psychology assistants were in a number of incidents seduced into sexual activity with one or two of the male patients, sexual activity which was at first hidden from senior staff. To the uninitiated such breaches of regulations in a secure institution seem almost incomprehensible or are explained simply in terms of bad men taking advantage of naive or needy women. This superficial construction will probably suffice in order to tighten regulations and increase senior staff vigilance but it will not suffice for training professionals.

However, transference and countertransference probably have a large role in such activities. It is therefore worth attending to the views of an experienced forensic psychotherapist, who has a special interest in the psychodynamics and the therapeutic processes which occur in secure institutions, Rob Hale.

Any interaction between two people involves the meeting of two minds and their effect on one another. We are considering the interaction between a professional and a patient in a clinical setting – in this case a secure hospital.

The patient, and the therapist bring to the encounter their histories, i.e. life experiences stored in both conscious and unconscious memories, expectations, fears and fantasies. Yet, as professionals, we may be reluctant to accept that this is so. We can hide ourselves behind a professional role and deny that we are emotionally affected by our patients. Our patients will either collude by accepting that apparently detached role or they may challenge it. We fondly assume that our emotional reactions are opaque to our patients (and to our colleagues), and are none of their business. Whilst this may be superficially true and allow us to work comfortably, it is important to examine the obverse.

The feeling state generated in a patient in a clinical encounter is made up firstly of the expectations s/he has of the professional and which are based on previous life experience. Thus his or her prediction is that all professionals are say, authoritarian or uninterested or untrustworthy because this was how s/he experienced important figures, particularly parents, in the past. Equally his or her own experiences may have been positive leading to an optimistic expectation. This is the 'internal working model'. Secondly, and more immediately, the feeling state is influenced by the patient's actual experience of the professional over the period of the clinical interaction. The internal working model and the current perception combine to form the transference that is, what the patient feels for the professional.

The reciprocal is the countertransference. This however can usefully be divided into two component parts – the true countertransference and what has been designated 'the affective response of the therapist/professional' (King, 1978). True countertransference is determined by our own prejudices and experiences. It comes largely from our own unconscious. A simplistic example would be 'my father missed no opportunity to belittle me and he wore glasses

and had a moustache. The patient in front of me happens to have a moustache and glasses and I find myself being defensive towards him because I feel he's constantly trying to undermine me as a professional.' In this instance the professional experiences emotions which relate to his own past and bear no relationship to the patient in front of him; this is the true countertransference.

If by contrast I (the professional) had quite a good relationship with my father but every time I see this patient I experience the same feeling of irritation and of being undermined, it is because this patient has made me do so at this particular point in time. The need to attack and undermine authority, which exists largely in the unconscious part of the patient's mind, has been projected into my mind and I have accepted the projection. The feelings I experience have been created by the patient's past as opposed to mine. Strangely neither the patient nor I are aware of the process. The same process may exist with feelings of say sadness, anxiety or anger.

The mode of communication may be verbal or non-verbal – gestures, intonation, glances, silences. However it is more likely that the patient will DO something which provokes a response in the professional. This is acting out, a term first described by Freud for emotions which cannot be experienced or expressed in the therapeutic setting, but which find expression in actions (usually destructive) outside the therapeutic space. The term has since been broadened to a propensity to action rather than verbal communication; but it is important to retrieve the original meaning that acting out is the symbolic representation of an unconscious memory in which the emotions are experienced by others. The original trauma, which was experienced passively by the patient in very early childhood, is now reversed and visited on those around them. (It is their very unconsciousness that makes these memories so powerful.) The provocation to acting out is a current situation which mirrors the original traumatic scenario of say, humiliation or abandonment; the patient, however, does not recognize the impending psychic danger but finds him/herself doing something, but not knowing why or having only a superficial explanation for the actions; the blame and responsibility is placed on others.

As the actions of our patients provoke emotions in us as professionals we often find ourselves doing things in response. We may defend ourselves against physical attack – not unreasonably; but we may do something which we recognize, on reflection, as retributive and an over-reaction. This is the essence of what is termed 'acting out in the countertransference'. How much of this response comes from what the patient has projected into us, and how much comes from our own unconscious is the central work of the therapeutic endeavour.

683

Our emotional responses to our patients then, give us important information about the psychic structure and content of their inner world; they also are the means whereby we may be able to give the patient a 'new' experience of relationships – the 'corrective experience'. For the most part when we encounter a relatively less disturbed patient suffering say from neurotic depression or a physical illness which is deemed to be 'not the patient's fault' it is our sympathy and concern that the patient evokes; we do our utmost to help the patient and we feel good about what we have done.

In the forensic setting our experience can be very different and is well described by Hinshelwood in his 1999 paper 'The Difficult Patient'. Here he examines our responses firstly to the psychotic patient and secondly to the patient with severe personality disorder.

The psychotic patient challenges us because his or her logic is incomprehensible, or at least we are unable to understand or empathize with his/her communication. We can observe the distress but we cannot share the perceptions or distortions of the outside world. We regard the patient's plight with perplexity and our concern and curiosity are largely at an intellectual level. The patient does not stimulate or challenge us at a deeper emotional level. In this sense they remain 'outside us'.

Compare this to our reaction to the patient with a severe personality disorder. With him or her we are immediately drawn into concern which all too rapidly is destroyed by the experience of being tricked, seduced, conned, coerced, pressurized, blackmailed and ultimately discarded in favour of another. Small wonder that we hate these patients and react in a way that can make us ashamed of what we have done. Some patients have an uncanny capacity to exploit and corrupt us.

Where the psychopathology is primarily in the area of perverse sexuality we find ourselves in turns intrigued, seduced, revolted and morally corrupted. Such patients present us with our greatest therapeutic challenge because despite the fact that we are aware of their lifelong experience of rejection and moral censure we find ourselves reacting in an identical way, which we know will only confirm their previous view of the world and prevent any therapeutic process. In our negative reaction to such patients we can all too easily overlook the fact that their acting out is the only means they have of communicating their own distress and confusion about the present and more particularly the past. Acting out is a form of recovered memory although the patient and also the professional do not recognize it as such. It is through the true nature of the professional's emotional reaction to the acting out (the 'affective response') that we may have access to the patient's unconscious processes which drive his or her behaviour and determine his or her affective state.

To be able to confront, tolerate, understand and contain the patient's distress and more importantly his or her destructiveness in a non-retributive way is the challenge both to us as professionals and the institutions within which we work, charged as they are with the care of such pathological individuals. It is our job not to fall foul of the patient's propensity to bring out the worst in us, both for our own (and our institution's) survival. More importantly we need to stay sane and healthy for our patients so that they can learn for the first time that relationships do not have to be exploitative or parasitic, that they will not destroy us, but that, notwithstanding their attempts to get us to behave otherwise, we can think about them and the meaning of their actions and projections and we can regard them with respect and deserving of our care. In so doing, eventually, we may confound the severely personality disordered patient's internal predictions and end up trusting and even liking them – experiences they have never had of themselves.

How, then does an institution and the professionals working within it stay healthy, sane and able to be a therapeutic community in the broadest sense? For an institution the starting point must be the physical environment, the presence of staff in sufficient numbers and the routines and rules, which give predictability and containment. The institution must be able to examine itself regularly within a structured forum with a commitment to the process from the most senior person downwards. There may be a need for some stratification so that the responsibilities and external pressures on senior managers can be explored separately from the roles and responsibilities of, say, ward managers. This consultative process is best carried out by someone who is external to the institution.

SEXUAL ASSAULT

Between July 2004 and July 2005, three independent reports on four miscreant doctors. The Matthews (2004) report concerned Dr Richard Neale, a gynaecologist, who was struck from the canadian medical register. He remained on the British register. It is of interest in that it illustrates the ways in which things can go wrong within the NHS but is less relevant to our concerns here than the other reports.

Clifford Ayling

Dr Clifford Ayling was convicted of 13 indecent assaults on 10 women patients and jailed for 4 years in December 2000. He qualified in 1963 then worked in a number of hospitals in and around London until 1974 when he was employed as a part-time clinical assistant in obstetrics and gynaecology in Kent. From 1981 he moved to general practice. The complaints which led to

Dr Ayling's convictions for sexual assault related to inappropriate touching or examination of women's breasts or sexual organs. Dr Ayling was a single-handed general practitioner. In the report's recommendations Pauffley (2004) noted that there are no organizations within the NHS with specific responsibility for sexualized behaviour amongst healthcare professionals. The report recommended that accredited training should be provided for all Patient Advice and Liaison Service (PALS) officers in this potential aspect of their work and that the same training should also be given to complaints staff. The report recommended that copies of any written records regarding such complaints should be placed on the practitioner's personnel file. A further recommendation was that primary care trusts (PCTs) should develop specific support programmes for single-handed practitioners. The report was vague on chaperone policy except to say that any patient should be able to ask for and get a health professional as a chaperone if he or she wishes; this should not be left to friends and relatives.

Kerr and Haslam

The Kerr/Haslam (Pleming) report is in two volumes (Secretary of State for Health, 2005). It encompasses 36 chapters and 811 pages before the appendices are reached. It concerns the flagrant sexual misconduct of two psychiatrists towards their patients over many years. For example, a patient described how when she consulted Kerr he exposed himself to her saying 'this is what you need'. The public inquiry into Kerr and Haslam described how these psychiatrists got away for decades with indecently assaulting and seducing patients, an enormous systems failure. The first complaint against Kerr was in 1965 – by a woman patient who reported being told that sex would cure her. By the 1980s there had been nearly 30 separate complaints about him but none was taken sufficiently seriously to prompt a full investigation. When a senior nurse raised the alarm after learning a patient had had an affair with Kerr, she was demoted.

The accounts the inquiry heard from patients were strikingly similar. Allegations were of unscheduled domiciliary visits, or appointments being arranged for the end of clinics when there would be few nursing staff around. Kerr would then expose himself and 'invite' patients to perform sexual acts (often of masturbation or oral sex) upon him, sometimes suggesting that this was part of their treatment. A number of patients also alleged that full sexual intercourse took place. A number of women described his ability to make them comply with his wishes, leaving them confused and guilty about their own actions and afraid to complain in forthright terms.

Haslam treated well-educated female patients referred for depression by making them feel special with flattering remarks, and taking them to trysts for sexual intercourse as part of their treatment. One patient realized that she was not so special when seeing a blonde-haired woman waiting for the next appointment. Haslam made a reference to 'one blonde in, one brunette out'. The patient subsequently made contact with the blonde woman who confirmed that Haslam was 'propositioning her', flattering her and suggesting they have an affair. Another of his 'treatments' was a full body massage in the absence of a chaperone. The Inquiry heard evidence on how on occasions this was carried out in isolated parts of the hospital or out of hours.

The main concern of the inquiry was that these activities went on for years; complaints were made to various individuals including general practitioners and nurses but nothing was done. Even during the inquiry potential witnesses had 'forgotten' having received complaints. The analysis in the report is about why this should be the case and how such persistent behaviour could be stopped in the future.

The inquiry concluded that medical appointment procedures were not rigorous enough, there was no procedure for supporting patients, consultants had undue power and unclear accountability. Consultants were loyal to one another and there was a tolerance of sexualized behaviour; there was disbelief that doctors might abuse their patients. There was a predominantly male hierarchy of doctors and a predominantly female nursing cohort, there was no multidisciplinary working. Patients feared retribution, punishment and/or withdrawal of treatment. There was a rigid interpretation, or even misinterpretation, of the legal position pertaining to the requirement for patient confidentiality – such that it overrode patient safety.

The inquiry pointed out that the sexual abuse of vulnerable adult patients may be far more prevalent than generally realized or accepted, but at the same time recognized that the abuse of patients is, and should be treated as, very unusual and that allegations of sexual abuse, of whatever kind, are not all genuine, indeed that allegations of sexual abuse are easy to make, and difficult to refute.

Both doctors were removed from the medical register and stripped of their membership in the Royal College of Psychiatrists. The recommendations of the report were focused on education and training, and the promotion of an obligation to speak out. Staff at all levels should be trained in the identification and preservation of proper boundaries, and the harm caused by boundary transgressions, commencing at undergraduate level through all the relevant professions. The message must be reinforced in induction training and in continuous professional development. The message must be supported by clear and enforceable codes of conduct by NHS Trusts and by the regulatory bodies. There must be clear boundaries, clear sanctions, and no tolerance of the abuse of patients.

Many things have changed since the end of the twentieth century when these things happened and the

Pleming recommendations have largely been implemented. However education in boundary issues remains insufficient because education in all psychotherapy concepts and practices is still very thin. Prevention of this kind of misconduct is extremely difficult. Education is currently our best hope but core research into the origins of such aberrant behaviour is sorely needed.

Before moving on to even more destructive behaviour we should perhaps note that even in sexual offending we are dealing with power systems and throughout the problem is an imbalance of power. The problem for the female patient, and it's nearly always females who are subject to sexual abuse by doctors and nurses, is that they are doubly weakened in the patient role because they are not only subject to medical power but also to masculine power.

CLINICIDE AND CASK

Robert Forrest (1995), a forensic toxicologist, coined the term 'caregiver associated serial killings' (CASK) to describe the unnatural deaths of multiple patients in the course of clinical treatment. Kaplan (2007) used the narrower term 'clinicide' to refer to murders by doctors.

Medicine deals with matters of life and death. Medical science includes knowledge of how to prolong life and how to shorten life. Doctors and nurses are well placed, in terms of their skills to prematurely end life, and therefore strict taboos against such action have developed. Medical practice is based on trust and patients, as a rule, see doctors and nurses as caring and practically incapable of deliberately harming them. There is then a great sense of shock when doctors and nurses break the taboo and cause deliberate harm.

There are many examples of the abuse of medical knowledge to kill rather than comfort or heal, but the most notorious and extensive has been mentioned above – the story of the progression of eugenics to euthanasia and then racial murder in the 1930s in Germany. There is insufficient space to deal with this here, but psychiatrists should be aware of the extensive role played by psychiatrists in the story, helping the authorities to set up the gas chambers in mental hospitals initially and then selecting patients for euthanasia (see, for example, Torry and Yolken, 2010). Doctors were active in designing gas chambers including the later purpose-built camps for killing Jews and gypsies, advising on the appropriate toxic gases, and in the earlier stages providing false death certificates to make relatives believe that their murdered relatives had died of natural causes. Good accounts are given by Dicks (1972) and Burleigh (1994).

Yorker (2006), in a literature search, identified 45 health professionals in 14 countries, since 1970 who were convicted of serial murder and 45 other cases who were also investigated for probably harming patients. At least 2,113 patients died suspiciously while in the care of a convicted healthcare provider. It turned out that nurses are more likely to kill their patients than doctors; it was also true that more cases occurred in the USA then in any other country but the combined totals of Dr Shipman and Nurse Allitt give England an unwanted distinction in this matter.

Kaplan (2009) has produced a comprehensive account of what he calls 'disturbing cases of doctors who kill'. His chapter on genocidal doctors is particularly harrowing. He argues that 'doctors as a group are highly susceptible to carrying out appalling acts on behalf of the state... In the course of their training they are desensitized by dissecting corpses, attending post-mortems and dealing with death as routine, daily events. In the process, they learn to develop a 'medical self' with a professional demeanour that shows no sign of their underlying feelings... Of all the professions, doctors have the most protracted gestation. They develop great expertise in a very narrow field while experiencing little of the real world. Much of this is done in a hierarchical environment where their elite status as doctors is continually acknowledged.' He deals with Marat, partly trained in England, Eugene Fisc, who was responsible for the genocide of the Herero people in German South-West Africa, Drs Behaeddin Sakir and Mehmett Nazim who were pivotal in the Turkish genocide of Armenians, and the psychiatrist Karadzic in Bosnia as well as the large number of Nazi doctors and psychiatrists. He is convinced that 'doctors, regardless of prestige, ability, or qualification or training, are amongst the most willing accomplices of state abuse... The basis for medical involvement in political abuse goes deep into the psychology of medicine and the personality of the practitioner. At its heart is an extreme grandiosity, a belief that 'treating' (in reality, extirpating) the illness affecting the nation is merely an extension of the ancient and honoured role of treating the sick patient'. He quotes one of the Turkish doctors involved in the Armenian tragedy, who committed suicide, as saying:

Even though I am a physician, I cannot ignore my nationhood. Armenian traitors... were dangerous microbes. Isn't it the duty of a doctor to destroy microbes? My Turkishness prevailed over my medical calling.

Beverley Allitt

Beverley Allitt was convicted of four murders, three attempted murders and six assaults at the Grantham and Kesteven Hospital, Lincolnshire in 1993 (Clothier et al., 1994). Her methods included suffocation, the injection of potassium chloride, the injection of air and the injection of insulin. Ramsland (2007), a forensic psychologist who writes about serial murder among healthcare workers, and Manners (1995), a *Daily Express* journalist, have produced useful synopses of her case.

Allitt had previously shown symptoms of factitious disorder (see chapter 17), and the psychiatrists who saw her in prison described her as suffering from Munchausen syndrome by proxy (factitious disorder by proxy). As a child, she wore bandages and casts over wounds that she would use for attention but not allow to be examined. One of four children, she seemed happy for a while, but became overweight as an adolescent. She had a healthy appendix removed but the scar failed to heal because she kept plucking at it. She also injured herself with a hammer and glass. She went on to train as a nurse and was suspected of odd behaviour, such as smearing faeces on walls in a nursing home where she trained. Her absentee level was also exceptionally high, the result of a string of illnesses. A boyfriend at that time said later that she was aggressive, manipulative and deceptive, claiming false pregnancy as well as rape, before the end of the relationship. Kelleher and Kelleher (1998) described her as suffering from a volatile temperament, becoming aggressive at times and complaining of a series of physical ailments that sent her into a hospital. For example, she complained of gallbladder pain, headaches, urinary infections, uncontrolled vomiting, blurred vision, minor injuries, appendicitis, back trouble, and ulcers.

Despite her history of poor attendance and successive failure at nursing examinations, Beverley Allitt was given a temporary 6-month contract at the chronically understaffed Grantham and Kesteven Hospital in Lincolnshire in 1991. She was 22 years old, had done only 2 years of training and wasn't a fully qualified children's nurse. When she started, there were only two trained nurses on the dayshift and one for nights.

Allitt's trial, which lasted nearly 2 months, was delayed because of her ill health, and she attended only 16 days due to illness. She had lost six stones and weighed only 97 lb. She denied four charges of murder, 11 of attempted murder, and 11 alternative charges of grievous bodily harm. No defence of insanity or even diminished responsibility was raised; the prosecution called Roy Meadow (see chapter 26) to say that she suffered from both Munchausen's syndrome and Munchausen's syndrome by proxy (see chapter 17). He told the jury that Beverley Allitt was an extreme case of a condition in which mothers killed their own children and it was very rare to find someone who suffered from both types of Munchausen's syndrome. He further said that her abnormal personality was incurable. On 23 May 1993, she was convicted of four counts of murder and nine counts of attempted murder and was given 13 life sentences with a tariff of 30 years. In prison she began to injure herself again, by stabbing herself with paper clips and pouring boiling water on her hand. She was admitted to a high security hospital under the Mental Health Act.

The Clothier report (*op cit*) set up to investigate the tragedies emphasized that the events described were extraordinary and unprecedented. It criticized failures of management and communications in the hospital, but it refuted any suggestion that Allitt could easily have been detected or stopped. Manners (1995) noted the opening remarks of Sir Cecil Clothier at his press conference in February 1994:

The dreadful lesson we have learned is that no matter how numerous and skilful staff in the hospital may be, a malevolent, cunning and deranged person can nevertheless continue to commit his or her crimes.

The report concluded that the main failure was collective. It described a general lack in the qualities of leadership, energy and drive in all those most closely associated with the management of the ward. The specialist children's nurse staffing was below the standard recommended by the region at the time, and also well below the higher professional standard for two qualified paediatric nurses to be available. The report criticized the hospital's 'sloppy' appointments procedures in recruiting Beverly Allitt, noting in particular that her serious record of ill-health was not investigated. The two consultants in charge failed to grasp that the 'cascade of collapses' in the medical conditions of patients was due to a 'malevolent cause'. The Grantham coroner refused requests by a consultant for a specialized post-mortem examination on the first victim and thus thwarted a line of inquiry that 'could have brought to a halt the whole train of events'. Other post-mortem examinations overlooked vital murder clues. The nursing management was criticized for dilatory and ineffective action' when suspicions of murder were aroused. When firm evidence was produced that one child had been injected with a poisonous dose of insulin, it took 18 days for the police to be called, during which time another baby girl died. Yet the report also conceded that in the other two other cases of serial killings by nurses known at that time, cases in the US and Canada, the behaviour took even longer to be detected.

The report made 12 recommendations, eight of them related to tougher screening procedures for potential staff; the first that all those seeking entry to the nursing profession should provide a sickness record, because the inquiry agreed with a suggestion from the Association of NHS Occupational Physicians that

excessive absence through sickness, excessive use of counselling or medical facilities, or self-harming behaviour such as attempted suicide, self-laceration or eating disorder are better guides than psychological testing'. In similar vein the inquiry recommended that 'no candidate for the nursing profession in whom there is evidence of major personality disorder should be employed in the profession.

The inquiry was at pains to avoid singling out individuals for blame saying:

Whenever some great disaster befalls the human race, the instinctive reaction of most people is to seek its cause and try to prevent a recurrence. But behind this civilized response lies a darker motivation as old as time – the urge to lay blame. The ancient notion of a scapegoat, to bear the guilt for disastrous happenings and thus relieve feelings of rage and frustration, is still with us... those whom we have criticized were subjected by chance to a test more severe than any which most of us encounter in a lifetime: so we have not striven to find fault merely to satisfy a popular urge to see the suffering in others is the proper response to one's own.

Nevertheless, the two consultants, the clinical services manager and the ward sister were all sacked after the inquiry was concluded.

In 2008 an ITV documentary called *Lady Killers* was made by Martina Cole and later became available on YouTube. There are interviews with the police officers who dealt with the case, with a 'forensic profiler', a forensic psychiatrist and one of the paediatricians. The documentary is concerned at the end to discredit any suggestion that Beverley Allitt is a psychiatric case. The forensic psychiatrist in the programme, said that the diagnosis of Munchausen by proxy has been discredited partly because of its unreliability and partly because it focuses too much on the perpetrator and not enough on the victim! Martina Cole, the presenter said:

It was a sign of those times to try and explain psychotic behaviour by labelling someone with a fancy medical term, almost to excuse their behaviour and then sending them off to rehabilitation; but the fact of the matter is, a murderer is a murderer, serial or otherwise, and no label should detract from the crime that they have committed.'

One of the paediatricians involved, Dr Nanayakkara, said:

It is in my judgment very wrong and misleading for anybody to label Beverley Allitt as belonging to either Munchausen syndrome or Munchhausen syndrome by proxy because I believe that Beverley Allitt was [a] cunning, calculating, deceptive, cold-blooded murderer.

This level of negative public distortion is entirely understandable given the immense damage that had been done to the community. The level of sadistic destructiveness is incomprehensible to most people and leaves them with a sense of bewilderment which develops into anger and the need for revenge. This, however, is counter-productive, is probably the basis of the strange anomalies in the British legal system whereby matters of responsibility are rarely discussed, and do not lead to effective prevention. The professional negativity expressed is perhaps an extreme example of an all too common attitude towards mentally disordered offenders within the medical (including psychiatric) profession. This is counter-productive and we refer the reader to the Rob Hale insertion above.

Harold Shipman

Harold Frederick Shipman (known to his family as Fred) has been described as the most prolific serial killer in modern history. He killed many of his patients during his work as a GP in Greater Manchester, at least 215 (probably 250) people using large doses of diamorphine by injection. The killings went undetected for many years, and at his trial he was convicted of 15 specimen charges. He was convicted in 2000 and sentenced to 15 consecutive life sentences; he subsequently committed suicide in Wakefield Prison in 2004.

In an analysis of Shipman's clinical practice, the Chief Medical Officer, Liam Donaldson, who had commissioned a report from Baker (Department of Health, 2001), said in the foreword 'Everything points to the fact that a doctor with the sinister and macabre motivation of Harold Shipman is a once in a lifetime occurrence'. As already noted this conclusion is somewhat flawed. The same year that the report was published Kinnell (2000) published a paper in the BMJ outlining a long list of doctors who had killed from the nineteenth century onwards; they murdered members of their families, strangers and patients. Camp (1982) produced a book called *One Hundred Years of Medical Murder*. A much more comprehensive and useful book was published in 2007 by Katherine Ramsland. It deals with doctors, female nurses, male nurses, and even healthcare managers who become serial killers. There is a suggestion that worldwide such activities are increasing even though they may be levelling out in the United States of America. Ramsland deals in some detail with some of the factors that may facilitate murder in healthcarers such as the public disbelief that it will happen, the easy availability of toxins, the itinerant nature of some nurses, etc. She has a list of recommendations to reduce the risk of these homicides occurring. She makes the remarkably simple and sensible suggestion that perpetrators who have been caught should be interviewed extensively and asked for advice on prevention. She notes how recruitment procedures become lax, especially in times of nursing shortages and urges that no one should ever be employed unless they have been thoroughly screened; and potential employers should be told of previous suspicious behaviour. The screening should, she believes, include a psychiatric evaluation.

In his inquiry Baker (*op. cit.*) discovered that Shipman had a high proportion of older women among his victims, many of the deaths occurred at home and a high proportion occurred in the afternoon; Shipman was present at death or had seen the patient shortly before death in a high number of cases and the associations between clinical history and certified cause of death (heart problems, strokes, or old age) were often weak. Baker's recommendations were concerned with monitoring performance in general practice, death rates, death certification procedures, general practice records, and the use of controlled drugs. Very simple monitoring of the demographics of death in any health service, including a general practice, would identify an outlier service fairly quickly and with more detailed further investigation might save lives.

The extensive public inquiry under the chairmanship of a High Court judge concluded (Smith, 2002–5 [http://www.official-documents.gov.uk/document/cm58/5854/5854.pdf]):

> *I am satisfied that Shipman killed more than 200 patients over a period of 23 years. After some possible early experimentation, his usual method of killing was to give an intravenous injection of a lethal dose of diamorphine, which led to death within a few minutes. With a few victims, mainly patients who were terminally ill, he sometimes gave an intramuscular injection, which would take effect and result in death within the hour. There is a suspicion that he sometimes gave large doses of sedatives, such as Largactil, to elderly patients with reduced respiratory function, so as to induce deep prolonged sleep and to make the patient vulnerable to death by bronchopneumonia.*

Smith was exercised to discover the motivation for the killings and enlisted the aid of a number of 'experts' to this end including the two senior authors of this book, but none of us was able to draw any significant conclusions because of the paucity of information about Shipman's thinking, and his unwillingness to be interviewed during the course of the inquiry, indeed his unwillingness to be interviewed by the police pretrial.

The likeliest diagnosis was the generalization which psychiatrists fall back on all too frequently, 'personality disorder'. If the term personality disorder is to be used then one useful adjective to apply to it would be the term used by Fromm (1973), 'necropholous', indicating an extreme variant of a narcissistic personality disorder in which the individual is fascinated by the process of dying and many of the trappings surrounding death. Some such people go on to obtain erotic satisfaction from corpses but there is no evidence at all that Shipman did this. Kernberg (1970, 1984) has a more appropriate label in this case 'malignant narcissism'. He says there are five features which make up this syndrome, marked narcissistic traits, antisocial behaviour (not amounting to antisocial personality disorder), a paranoid orientation, a capacity for loyalty, and a concern for others. This almost exactly describes Shipman. It doesn't explain however his 'addiction to killing' (he may well have fitted the criteria used by Gresswell and Hollin, 1997; chapter 9). Many commentators, including the journalist Carol Peters (2005), have commented on the awful experience he had as a teenager of watching his beloved mother die slowly from cancer, needing constant injections of morphine, and perhaps seeing her die on the end of a needle. Other journalists, Whittle and Richie (2000), took a series of expert opinions and concluded that the Shipman case is at odds with the usual run of serial killings, in that he was much older than the typical profile of serial killers and that superficially at least he managed to have a normal life with a wife and children as well as working with colleagues who while not liking him much did not find him alarming. They point out that his killings were not particularly violent and they were not random. They end up concluding as before that he suffered from a 'personality disorder', which Singleton et al. (1998a) tell us is suffered by 78% of the male prison population, not much value added there. Whittle and Richie (2000) quote Coid, a forensic psychiatrist, as concluding that:

> *Shipman was driven by a compulsive urge to kill... it is likely that what killing did for Shipman was to provide him with an intense feeling of exhilaration, pleasurable excitement, probably with a profound sense of satisfaction and achievement.*

Coid believed that Shipman's desire to kill may go back into childhood and that becoming a doctor simply made it easier. An interesting comment was made by the forensic toxicologist Forrest when he said that the choice of morphine was an intrinsic part of Shipman's urge to kill: '*you wouldn't use it for bodies that are going to be buried – it's been found in the tissues of mummies thousands of years old.*' Does this suggest a high level of risk taking, for Shipman would have known that some of his dead patients would indeed be buried, even although he always urged the relatives to have a cremation?

In all these speculations no one seems to have considered that he may have had a chronic grief reaction to his mother's death and that the constant rehearsal of that terrible event prevented him from destroying himself for many years (Gunn, 2010). When he was injecting himself with pethidine, he was described as seriously depressed. His mood lifted with antidepressant drugs. Was Smith correct in suggesting that whatever was causing the 'addiction' then remained with him throughout his life? He was never described as a happy individual but grumpy and aloof, withdrawn at times. Whilst in hospital he was described as a suicide risk. There is, however, no evidence that he ever attempted suicide, but finally he killed himself in prison by self-strangulation with a sheet. Was the forging of the will an exceptional behaviour for him as Smith suggests? He had earlier forged many prescriptions and, further, sought to engage his general practitioner partners in his fraudulent activity. Does the apparent recklessness of the forging of the will speak of personality characteristics, perhaps a narcissistic need be recognized for his cleverness in so many undetected killings? Or, does it better reflect an understanding that he had come to the end, a cry for help? Did he secretly expect the morphine poisoning to be revealed at an earlier stage? How far can his apparently phobic avoidance of dealing with the loss of his mother be implicated in his later career? When he was arrested for drug abuse early in his career was there an opportunity for reparative psycho-therapy at that point? We will never know.

Soothilll and Wilson (2005) urge us to examine the social framework surrounding these killings. The Baker report also encourages us to take this position, in spite of what the Chief Medical Officer said at the beginning of it. Many, but not all, of Shipman's victims were older women, his record-keeping was poor, he practised largely alone (even when he theoretically had partners) he was known to flout the rules concerning the prescribing of controlled drugs. Dr Shipman was seen by his patients as a good and caring man.

COMMENTARY

Why should medicine be so prone to such monstrous lapses? Perhaps it isn't: perhaps as some people say it's not whether doctors and nurses become sex offenders and murderers, perhaps it's that some sex offenders and some murderers become doctors and nurses. This is a bit sim-plistic but it is an acknowledgement of the universality of destructiveness, violence, and sadism in human beings and the universality of the abuse of power.

It is not just medicine that is perverted for destructive ends. One story from the 1930s may illustrate. Doctors helped design the gas chambers for the Nazi regime but they didn't develop the Zyklon B gas which was eventually used in the Holocaust; that needed expertise in chemistry. Germany had the services of a skilled chemist called Fritz Haber. He developed mustard gas from chlorine in the First World War. His wife pleaded with him not to do this but he wouldn't listen to her, so she shot herself. After the war he won the 1918 Nobel Prize in chemistry for inventing a process to produce ammonia from nitrogen, a vital means of improving agricultural fertility. The following year he was charged as an international war criminal for further-ing the campaign of chemical warfare. He also invented Zyklon A gas but this needed further development to make the efficient Zyklon B – a development which he couldn't carry out because he had to flee to England as he was a jew (Kean, 2010)!

There are several themes which run throughout the cases given above. The first, and perhaps the most impor-tant, is that medicine, unlike other branches of science, has a very strong ethic or code to protect its use for beneficial purposes, and in particular to benefit individual people. Following that there is a theme that selecting individuals to become nurses and doctors is critically important and in the cases described proved to be flawed, hence the preoc-cupation in most of the reports with improving selection processes and trying to weed out those with abnormal tendencies. The third theme is that medical institutions are not very good at spotting when abuse of patients is begin-ning. This leads to further recommendations for improving processes to do that, so that further abuse can be prevented

earlier. Prevention in another sense is also a theme and so some emphasis is given in some reports to improving edu-cation of those who will undertake psychotherapy.

As with many educational processes, we really don't know what matters in training and background under-standing. Fundamental personality problems are not improved simply by education. This is one of the flaws in the otherwise commendable prison approach of virtu-ally insisting that sex offenders in prison undertake sex offender treatment programmes. Is the situation better for those of us who believe we do not have such fundamental problems? We simply don't know. In the absence of infor-mation we have to rely on intuition and face validity. We should perhaps also assume that current levels of educa-tion concerning patient/doctor relationships are too few and superficial. Efforts are made within the world of psy-chotherapy to remedy this but it is clear from the examples in this chapter it is not just psychotherapy that endangers patients.

The obvious matter to focus on at an early stage in training is the question of boundary violations. Dale et al. (1999) suggest that there are eight practical areas to be covered as preliminary. These are role, time, place and space, gifts, clothing, language, self-disclosure and physi-cal contact. Clarification of role should be discussed and recorded in the notes; a number of writers and reports suggest that sessions that last longer than the scheduled time or which are placed outside normal working hours are risky; gifts are difficult to generalize about but, as a rule, they should be discouraged; the names used for therapist and patient should be carefully thought about; self-disclo-sure by the therapist is intrusive and almost always a risk to the patient; handshakes and the like may be appropriate but hugging is often dangerously close to sexualized touch-ing. The Royal College of Psychiatrists (2007b) *Report 146* amplifies this list by pointing out that treatment should not take place in a practitioner's home, indeed should not generally take place outside the workplace and wherever possible psychiatrists should avoid a dual role such as being the responsible clinician as well as the therapist. It is thus clear that hard and fast rules are difficult to make but these are the areas of discussion that should inform the beginner and should be raised in supervision.

Pope et al. (2006) have written a useful book *What Therapists Don't Talk About and Why* which is now in its second edition as a guide in the training of psychothera-pists. They tried to question the myths, taboos and secrets, those topics which are uncomfortable to talk about, so that difficult and dangerous material can be made explicit. One of the important myths they tried to expose is that 'good' therapists never have sexual feelings about patients, don't become sexually aroused during therapy session sessions, don't vicariously enjoy the (sometimes) guilty pleasures of their patients' sexual experiences and don't have sexual fan-tasies or dreams about their patients. They suggest working in groups which encourage honesty, self-examination and risk-taking with respect for participants including everyone's right to privacy within the group. Support from senior members for younger or less experienced members is crucial. It may however be more appropriate in many therapeutic settings for individual supervision to be the norm.

The Clothier report put much emphasis on screening out individuals with fairly obvious psychopathology. Denman (2010) suggested that it is not only the highly psychopathological individual who is of concern but also the therapist who persuades him- or herself that sexual contact can be part of the treatment, and she quoted Simon (1999) who described an escalation from minor boundary infringements to overt sexual misconduct.

Denman (2010) suggested that

given the universal nature of sexual drives, it should be hardly surprising that among the many pairs of individuals who meet regularly to talk about intimate matters, some will end up having sex.

Indeed there have been debates from time to time as to whether sexual contact with patients and ex-patients should be allowed. In the early days of psychoanalytic treatments it was not always frowned upon. In a letter to Sigmund Freud in 1905, Carl Jung said 'Miss Sabina Spielrein, a medical student, suffers from hysteria...

In the course of her treatment the patient had the bad luck to fall in love with me. She continues to rave blatantly to her mother about this love and her secret spiteful glee scaring her mother is not the least of her motives. Therefore the mother would like, if needed, to have her referred to another doctor, with which I naturally, concur.

She remained however Jung's patient and at one point was admitted to hospital. After discharge she continued to see Jung as an outpatient until 1909. Looking back in her diary she said:

We came to know each other, we became fond of each other without noticing it was happening; it was too late for flight; several times we sat 'in tender embrace'. Yes, it was a great deal!

As contraception was also mentioned that was not much doubt this was a consummated affair. Jung himself notes that he is happy at last to have hopes of loving a person who isn't smothered in the 'banality of habit'. He felt 'calmer and freer' after their meetings (Appignanesi, 2008). We know now that such encounters are almost always harmful and are therefore prohibited by the medical duty of doing no harm.

A longish list of therapist risk factors is given by Norris et al. (2003) including life crises, transitions (e.g. changing jobs), illness, loneliness, idealization (e.g. of celebrity patients), shame, envy, denial about problematic issues and 'true love'. Once again it is clear that the really central issue here is transference, especially countertransference. This

paper also makes clear that not all boundary issues are sexual. The authors of the paper quoted a psychiatrist who saw a woman for 10 years during which he sold her two boats, bought china, glassware and a coin collection from her cheaply and finally bankrupted her. Maybe another central issue is power. It is possible that people are attracted to the healing professions to counteract their feelings of powerlessness. The behaviour mentioned here is almost always a misuse of the power differential in the healer/patient relationship.

Few of the official reports and all too little of the literature deals with the question of supervision. For every psychiatrist to be supervised for every type of treatment is clearly impossible, but everybody should have a knowledgeable colleague to turn to for support and advice if required. Psychotherapy should always be accompanied by skilled senior supervision to protect both therapist and patient and should deal with boundaries and feelings as well as the more difficult matters of interpretations (if these are used) and always, whatever the type of psychotherapy, matters of transference and countertransference.

These remedies don't go far enough, although nobody has yet devised anything better. What is required is an understanding of how perverse activities arise in individuals before or after they have joined the caring professions; we only have the beginnings of that. Is there any way in which the ethic of beneficence can be strengthened? It is notable that although most members of the public believe that doctors take an oath, few of them do. Nurses don't have an oath to take. Would universal oath taking of say the Geneva code, after appropriate seminars discussing it, improve matters?

The neglected topic in all this discussion is treatment of the miscreant practitioners. Snowden (2010) in the Royal College of Psychiatrists book on doctor/patient abuse deals briefly with 'remediation'. Few people will be interested in treating those who have killed, even although their personal needs may be the greatest. Beverley Allitt is a long-term patient in a special hospital and presumably receiving treatment for her two factitious disorders. Fred Shipman although terminally ill did not wish to have treatment and it is no surprise that those wishes were granted and that he is now dead. The two predatory sex offender doctors, Kerr and Haslam, fail to meet any of Snowden's initial criteria for treatment: insight, acceptance of the seriousness of the problem, empathy with victims, commitment to change. It is difficult to know whether these four criteria should necessarily be an absolute bar to treatment but they certainly are in the present climate. The treatments which are offered are usually cognitive behavioural treatments although some (Gabbard, 1999) offer psychodynamic treatment. Educational methods are also used in cases where it is considered that there is no underlying sexual disorder; Snowden advocates that they be tried in Britain.

691

One of the difficulties of treating doctors is their reluctance to own up to medical problems of any kind, let alone those that are embarrassing, related to mental illness, or behaviour disturbances. Added to that is the problem that many doctors use unusual channels for any help they do seek e.g. via friends or colleagues, perhaps bypassing their general practitioner – indeed many younger doctors don't even have a GP. Following the suicide of Dr Daksha Emson, which included the homicide of her daughter Freya in 2000, an inquiry (North East London Strategic Health Authority, 2003) concluded that two important factors in this tragedy were the stigma of mental illness together with the fact that Daksha was both a doctor and a patient. The inquiry made 17 recommendations including issuing an anti-discriminatory code of practice binding on NHS employers, compulsory anti-stigma training for all senior clinical staff and senior managers, the setting up of a Department of Health group to examine the matter and the development of a protocol for doctor-to-doctor consultations

The Department of Health (2008c) group noted the special problems facing doctors with psychiatric disorders, especially within-profession stigma and confidentiality. They recommended that all doctors should be registered with a GP but that every Trust should have a well-advertised confidential service provided by another trust so that any doctor can get help quickly and without embarrassment. Treating doctors should not have a social relationship with the potential patient and they should be sufficiently senior to command the respect of the potential patient. Standards and types of treatments should be identical for medical practitioners and all other patients. The report also recommended the use of confidential extramural services which are available to all doctors but are not well publicized. It lists 15 organizations with their contact details as an appendix. Part of that appendix is reproduced in this textbook even though the editors are aware that such lists become out of date quite quickly. The important thing is that anyone who has any concern for the health of the medical profession should ensure that such lists are available and publicized.

Looking back at the cases mentioned in this chapter, it is fairly clear that Haslam and Kerr did not have supervision or easy access to advice and it seems extremely unlikely that they considered consulting a psychiatrist for their own needs mainly because their insights about their problems were quite low. In such cases, as the report indicates, early recognition of the problem by others and prevention of further practice is the only practical approach. If that had been available would they have availed themselves of medical help? It seems unlikely but it is possible.

The other three clinicians who each committed homicide were all psychiatric patients at some point. However they all shared with Kerr and Haslam poor insight and a reluctance to discuss the more antisocial aspects of their problems. In the case of Daksha Emson it was clearly the psychosis, which she had had before, which drove her behaviour and which should have been picked up and thoroughly treated. It can be argued that Beverley Allitt should have been kept in long-term care for her factitious disorder and she should have been steered away from any type of hospital work. In hindsight, Fred Shipman probably had some form of depressive disorder much of his life; this was certainly the case when he was treated in hospital for his pethidine addiction. There is an argument that a patient with chronic depression who becomes an opiate addict should remain under medical surveillance on a very long-term basis. The difficulty with this argument in Shipman's case is that he almost certainly would have not co-operated even if this had been offered; his narcissism/arrogance would have intervened. Psychiatric disorder in doctors is not uncommon yet few who suffer mental health problems seek or get professional help. Provision for doctors is underdeveloped. There is a view that being ordinary citizens doctors should obtain all their medical services via standard procedures using a general practitioner. Many doctors don't even have a general practitioner! It is now becoming more broadly accepted that when doctors need psychiatric help they need help away from their immediate workplace and they need very special levels of confidentiality. In London the Deanery, which has responsibility for medical education, has acknowledged the difficulties by providing an NHS funded service called Med Net. This provides specialized treatment, usually psychotherapy, for doctors who consult it. It is focused on the Tavistock Clinic with other psychotherapists from the Maudsley Hospital. Garelick et al. (2007) have described 121 doctors who have been referred to this special service. The main presenting problems were depression, anxiety, interpersonal, self-esteem and work-related issues. However, only 9% of the doctor-patients were severe cases. About 25% were on sick leave at the time of consultation, and 42% were considered to be at risk of suicide. Males and females were equally represented and there were no significant differences in the types of presenting pathology. The service is even open to medical students.

Doctors who are homicidal or sexually abusing their patients are not likely to consult this or any other kind of service. Perhaps the best-known clinic for serious offender doctor-patients is that run by Gabbard and Lester at the Baylor College of Medicine in Houston, Texas. Their patients are usually referred after they have been identified as offenders and are under some sort of professional restraint. They have written an important text on the psychoanalytic approach to these seriously affected practitioners (Gabbard and Lester, 1995), mainly involving an understanding of the patient's boundary problems and violations. They classify their physician-patients into four groups, those who are psychotic (the smallest group), which they call psychopathic, those with paraphilias, those that they designate as having 'love sickness', and a group who exhibit 'masochistic surrender' (their term). The pathology tends to turn on abnormal narcissism.

It is possible to argue that the common thread running through these cases is poor insight. Psychiatry has a great deal to do to improve our understanding of insight problems and how best to manage them. We could do worse than build on the meaning and understanding already provided by dynamic psychotherapy. Gabbard and Lester urge us to analyse the pathology of the superego especially superego lacunae and to understand narcissistic mortification which may be a mental phenomenon close to psychosis. All of which requires us to have a working knowledge of psychodynamic theory and above all the skill to interview empathically and set out a detailed mental state. In such complex and borderline psychotic cases cognitive behaviour programmes will not be enough, they will not address the behavioural manifestations but not the heavily defended underlying psychopathology. As we indicated in the introduction, this is not a textbook of psychotherapy but the reader may be helped in cases as difficult as the ones considered here to consult the Gabbard and Lester book.

Two core aspects of psychiatric treatment are frequently neglected. These are boundaries and transference, including countertransference. Somehow these rarely get into the psychiatric syllabus and yet they play a role in all psychiatric encounters. Transference is not only something to be aware of but it can be a powerful therapeutic tool. These important issues are relevant for all mental health professionals, not just psychiatrists. Forensic psychiatrists may have a role in educating and supporting fellow practitioners in these matters, and indeed they may be called upon to treat transgressors. Thus the skills and the ethics needed for this work should have a high priority in forensic psychiatry training.

28
Victims and survivors

Edited by
Pamela J Taylor

Written by
Sharif El-Leithy
John Gunn
Felicity Hawksley
Michael Howlett
Gillian Mezey
David Reiss
Jenny Shaw
Jonathan Shepherd
Nicola Swinson
Pamela J Taylor
Jayne Zito
Felicity de Zulueta

For many years now I have attempted to find an alternative to the word 'victim'. 'Injured party'; 'wounded'; 'casualty'; 'sufferer'; 'survivor', all describe a part of the experience but as yet I have not been able to find a suitable English word to adequately describe the experience of being a victim. At a recent conference in Holland I raised the issue and was told that the Dutch also struggle with this question. The Dutch word actually means 'sacrificial victim' and thus is even stronger than the English (Waite, 2007).

No one chooses to be a victim. In cases of serious violence, sexual assault, international disasters or acts of terrorism, the emotional trauma is invasive and in addition to any physical legacy. Many victims equate victimhood with failure or weakness, and would rather be described as 'survivors'. In many cases this will be a more accurate term, and, if so, we ask their indulgence where we have used the word victim.

Although trauma comes in many forms, including major natural disasters and war, there is much common ground in the consequences, so we consider briefly a range of traumatic experiences. There are also important reasons for specific consideration of people who have been victims of traumatic crimes, or acts which could result in prosecution. They are at the heart of our work.

We have placed prevention of victimisation at the centre of forensic psychiatry. Primary prevention is the ideal, and we give some consideration to how learning from victim experiences may lead to primary preventive strategies. Study of the prevalence and consequences of crime through its victims provides a different, perhaps more accurate perspective of crime than study of offenders who, by definition, are only those perpetrators who got caught.

From a perspective of offender-patient work, there are at least three reasons for therapeutic and preventive approaches.

- A history in childhood and/or adulthood of experience of serious trauma is common among people who become offenders, people who develop psychiatric symptoms and disorders, and when disorder and serious offending occur together.
- People whose behaviour is outside usually accepted social norms and people with mental disorders are particularly vulnerable to becoming victims of such trauma.
- An important, if small subgroup of people with mental disorder may seriously harm others, psychologically and/or physically, and, if untreated or inadequately treated may persist in doing so. Recognition and

treatment of trauma related aspects of the presentation may be particularly important for this group.

Services for mentally disordered offenders must take these issues into account. Appropriate treatment of trauma-related aspects of their disorders will not only increase each person's chances of (re)gaining his or her own sense of safety but also, by enhancing his/her ability to function effectively at all stages of the health and criminal justice processes, including rehabilitation, reduce the risk of secondary and tertiary victimisation.

Mental health and support services for victims of crime are scarce. Far too little is routinely provided, and yet there is considerable knowledge about the emergence of traumatic reaction states and how to alleviate them. We consider theoretical models and the evidence for intervening and, occasionally, for not intervening.

Aside from treatment considerations, forensic psychiatrists and psychologists may be asked to provide reports on people who have been victims of serious trauma for the civil or criminal courts, in the former where compensation may be an issue, in the latter where it may be essential to test links between a reported history of trauma and later criminal acts. Reports for courts and other official bodies are, however, dealt with in chapter 6.

LEARNING FROM VICTIMS AND SURVIVORS

Independent and Public Inquiries

Internationally, one of the most consistent stimulants for change in law or services for offenders with a mental disorder is individual tragedy, perhaps driven by hope that the victim did not die in vain. Generally, this follows the unusual circumstance of a person with mental disorder killing one or more persons unknown to him/her. Some examples of such landmark cases are given in chapter 14. Of particular importance here, in 1992 Jonathan Zito was killed by a man with incompletely treated psychotic illness whom he had never previously met. The resultant inquiry into this man's circumstances (Ritchie et al., 1994), together with campaigning by Jonathan Zito's widow, resulted in the establishment of two separate systems of inquiry after homicide to learn from such tragedies and try to prevent recurrences. One was the mandatory requirement for independent inquiry into each individual case when a person who had been in contact with psychiatric services had killed, and the other a more systematic approach to complete national data collection.

Individual case inquiries

A tradition was long established in the UK for discretionary inquiries into an individual case in the event of concern that services might have failed in some way, or lessons could be learned from detailed examination of the events surrounding a particular adverse outcome. In 1994, the NHS Executive made it mandatory in England and Wales that there should be an independent, perhaps public inquiry into any homicide by a person who had been in contact with psychiatric services prior to that homicide (NHS Executive HSG (94)27). At that time, there was no prescribed procedure (Thorold and Trotter, 1996; see also chapter 3). The *mandate* was cancelled in July 2010, but inquiries continue and the now demised NHS National Patient Safety Agency (NPSA) provided useful guidance for their conduct in the form of root cause analysis (NPSA, 2008).

Individual homicide inquiry reports: The effects

Reports from individual homicide inquiries are often interesting to read, and their conclusions may be convincing. Each has closely examined a unique series of events. Summary reports (Sheppard, 1996; Petch and Bradley, 1997; Reith, 1998; Munro and Rumgay, 2000; Maden, 2006) and the *National Confidential Inquiry into Homicide and Suicide* are likely to be more useful. There is evidence, however, of more attention to and better remembering of individual narratives than collated reports (Nisbett and Ross, 1980), perhaps as the former evoke emotions. The brain may process specific instances more centrally, affecting the individual reader more than do overviews, which may be dealt with more peripherally (Petty and Cacioppo, 1984). Individual cases may also generate more counterfactual alternatives to the salient features of the case than summaries of several events (Sherman and McConnell, 1995).

Homicide inquiries have several explicit purposes, but often implicit ones too. These may include consoling secondary victims, or blaming professionals (Peay, 1996). The process of conducting an individual homicide inquiry may have positive effects, but may also victimise the perpetrator, his/her family, the services involved and even the family of the victim(s) (Szmukler, 2000). The perpetrator and his/her family members may all be exposed to the media spotlight whilst their lives are investigated, in a way that generally does not occur if the perpetrator had no contact with mental health services. The resulting written report is made public, which usually means that everyone concerned has lost all rights to confidentiality around the homicide – indefinitely. Generally, negative stereotypes of anyone with mental disorder are reinforced and mental health services suffer through the process, especially in reduction of staff morale. Almost invariably outcomes are that mental health services are obliged to focus on risk, diverting staff time to procedures which assess dangerousness, patients who are not perceived as risky may get less attention and services may become increasingly coercive.

Inquiry recommendations have been made in many areas, including service planning, multidisciplinary teamwork, research, healthcare standards, mental health legislation, inpatient care, risk assessment and management, hospital discharge arrangements including application of the *Care Programme Approach* (see chapter 24), supervised discharge orders, supervision registers, inter-agency working, residential care, the practice of future inquiries and central government (Petch and Bradley, 1997), but evidence is awaited on how many of these recommendations, even when appropriate, are implemented, and with what effect. Individual inquiries may have their greatest impact in the locality where the homicide occurred and at the time of publication; they tend to have less effect nationally. They are an expensive and sometimes ineffective way of assisting the families of the victims (Reith, 1998); it is rarely possible, however, to get information on the costs of such inquiries, particularly where they result in professional defence cases. It is not clear whether they achieve their objectives or represent value for money.

Understanding some of the limitations on individual inquiries

The individual inquiry process has been criticised (Peay, 1996) in terms of its excessive subjectivity, its retrospective approach (Peay, 1999), its adversarial nature (Carson, 1996), its lack of standardised methodology and the lack of appropriate knowledge, skills or training among inquiry team members (Crichton and Sheppard, 1996). One of us (Reiss, 2001) has summarised an overall theoretical framework of the inquiry process in terms of its social psychology. Inquiries are social processes which are liable to implicit and explicit biases as a result of their constitution, structure, process and membership; these may become manifest in incorrect perceptions and misallocation of blame. Counterfactual thoughts, which express a possible but untrue past (Roese and Olson, 1995), are influenced by cognitive limitations (Kahneman and Tversky, 1982; Seelau et al., 1995) that determine which events are more likely to be changed when previous events are examined; they operate independently of the actual role of the changed event in causing the outcome. 'Upwards counterfactuals', which make reality better, underlie all such inquiries – the better outcome being that the homicide did not occur. Two types of rules may impact on their conduct: rules of availability and rules of purpose (Seelau et al., 1995).

Counterfactual rules of availability mean that people change the most accessible features of a situation, not the less accessible ones. In these terms, 'more available events' include those which have been made explicit, exceptional events, near misses, events later in a temporal chain, events earlier in a causal chain, actions (rather than inactions), and those events which are perceived as controllable (even if there was no actual control) (Kahneman and Tversky, 1982; Miller and Gunasegaram, 1990; Wells et al., 1987; Markman et al., 1995). An inquiry panel, being

dependent on the evidence presented to it, is unlikely to infer the existence of facts over and above such explicitly foreground events (Reder and Duncan, 1996), and may miss, for example, witness anticipation of being blamed if 'too much' is revealed.

The selection of counterfactuals is also likely to be partly influenced by more conscious factors (Seelau et al., 1995). The main stated aim of an inquiry is to understand how or why the homicide happened, so that events which were relevant but not considered sufficient to have determined it may be relatively ignored (N'gbala and Branscombe, 1995). Inquiries are also likely to make recommendations about factors which they consider may be influenced in the future, and to assign blame for actions where they perceive foresight and/or controllability were present (Seelau et al., 1995). Thus, availability and purpose rules may mean that findings are not based on the degree of actual influence an event had on the final outcome (Gavanski and Wells, 1989). An inquiry may therefore not alter features essential for the homicide but lead to change in factors which played no role in causing it. An inaccurate analysis of events may lead to recommendations resulting in poor future performance as well as inappropriate blame.

Inquiries may tend to assume that homicide is evidence of failure (Oyebode, 1999) even when this is not objectively the case. Unwanted outcomes are not usually viewed as unfortunate consequences of appropriate decisions. This may be perceived as interfering with ability to learn and solve problems. People tend to add new events to undo failures (Roese and Olson, 1993), which is consistent with the need to feel in control. We tend to believe that doing things leads to success, and the reason for failure is that one did not act in the necessary way to have control. Once an inquiry decides on the cause of a homicide, the event sequence is perceived to be more predictable and controllable. An inquiry may thus provide illusions of control for situations in which it was not actually present (Sherman and McConnell, 1995).

Hindsight bias is a major problem for homicide inquiries, even when the panel expresses awareness of it. The more the inquiry team perceives the outcome to be predetermined, with an understandable cause, the more likely the belief that changes in antecedent conditions and choices would have led to a different outcome (Fischoff, 1975; Hawkins and Hastie, 1990; Sherman and McConnell, 1995). The production of counterfactual changes may be supported by hindsight bias through which outcomes are seen as inevitable under the previous conditions. Both the hindsight assessment and the counterfactual inferences are, however, likely to be wrong, because not only was the outcome not as predictable as people thought (hindsight bias) but the alternative outcome based on the alteration of an antecedent was also not as likely as was believed (counterfactual-generation bias). Given a tendency to focus on decision outcomes, all these factors may lead to conclusions which turn good decisions into bad ones (Sherman and McConnell, 1995).

Even when events are, in fact, unforeseeable, we tend to believe that we should have foreseen them (Sherman and McConnell, 1995). As long as an alternative decision might have changed the poor outcome, we may believe that this was knowable and things could have been done differently. The generation of alternatives becomes a 'should have' as well as a 'could have', generating negative affect (Landman, 1993). This is one of the greatest potential barriers to the relatives and friends of the dead person(s) gleaning comfort from the process and dealing effectively with their bereavement.

Counterfactuals are not the only factors limiting an accurate perception of events; others include lack of understanding of the psychological dynamics involved (Reder and Duncan, 1996). Although there are benefits in using heuristics, developing schemas and forming categories or stereotypes to simplify a complex world and make communication easier, the world is, in fact, complex – even that world which preceded a single negative outcome. Counterfactual generation may be useful in precisely similar circumstances (Markman et al., 1993) or when an outcome is under control and therefore changeable (Roese and Olson, 1995), but needs to be used in full awareness of its limitations if, as is usual, neither situation pertains.

The UK national confidential inquiry into suicide and homicide

National confidential inquiries monitor aspects of health service organisation and practice throughout the UK, and publish regular reports. The principle is that clinicians who have been involved in the care of an inquiry case are invited to provide data in confidence to the inquiry, and, thus, information which is as accurate as possible. They are asked to provide such data in a systematic way, such that independent and blind experts in the field may review those data in themselves and in the context of similar cases and over time. More founded in research principles than individual case inquiries, these inquiries have many advantages in terms of reliability and validity, but are still subject to an important bias in that inquiry is confined to examination of care in cases with an adverse outcome. They also have an advantage in terms of relative cost. *The homicide inquiry*, for example, collects data on all homicides nationally, at an annual cost (in 2010) of around £320,000. Costs of individual inquiries are generally not made public, but each commonly exceeds that; 12 years earlier, for example, the estimate for the cost of the *Luke Warm Luke* inquiry (Scotland, 1998) was over £750,000, excluding any subsequent legal actions.

There are three such inquiries: the Confidential Enquiry into Maternal and Child Health (CEMACH), which became the Centre for Maternal and Child Enquiries (CMACE) but is under further review, which examines maternal, perinatal and infant deaths; the National Confidential Enquiry into Patient Outcome and Death (NCEPOD), which examines deaths and near misses in surgical, physician and primary care practice, and the National Confidential Inquiry into Suicide and Homicide by People with Mental Illness (NCISH), which examines all unexpected deaths of people who had been in prior contact with psychiatric services. We consider only the latter here, more-or-less exclusively in its homicide aspect.

The homicide inquiry

The aim of the homicide inquiry is data collection on everyone convicted of homicide, and detailed clinical data on those who had had prior contact with psychiatric services. It investigates the number and proportion of

- homicide perpetrators with a history of mental illness;
- perpetrators with symptoms of mental illness at the time of the offence;
- perpetrators with a history of contact with mental health services, at any time and in the 12 months before the homicide; and
- the clinical circumstances and antecedents of homicides by those under mental healthcare;
- the rate of key clinical problems (e.g. treatment refusal, loss of contact with services, substance misuse);
- changes in these statistics over time.

Homicide inquiry data collection

Started on a small scale by the Royal College of Psychiatrists, the inquiry became a research tool on its move to Manchester University in April 1996; since then, consecutive homicide cases have been identified and systematic data collection made in five stages:

1. on all homicides, from the Home Office Homicide Index, which includes details of the perpetrator, victim and method used;
2. on previous offences, from Greater Manchester Police;
3. from psychiatric reports, when prepared, from the Crown Court;
4. evidence of mental health service contact; this comes from response to submission of name and date of birth of each perpetrator to the services in his/her district of residence and adjacent districts; these individuals become 'inquiry cases';
5. clinical and service use data on inquiry cases, from former clinical teams, via a questionnaire sent to the consultant psychiatrist.

Psychiatric reports for the Court provide information on the perpetrator's mental state and any alcohol or drug use at the time of the homicide. Up to 2007, one or more such reports were obtained in about half the cases. Despite a consistent approach to data collection, numbers of reports obtained have fallen because, since *Reid*, it is no longer mandatory for the Court to seek psychiatric reports on homicide cases.

The inquiry case questionnaire asks details of: demographics; clinical history; inpatient/community care received; final contact with services; events leading to the homicide and respondents' views on prevention.

Findings from the homicide inquiry

General population homicides

The inquiry was notified of 2,670 homicides in England and Wales between April 1999 and December 2003, 1,350 (51%) for murder and 1,309 (49%) manslaughter; 106 (4%) were guilty of manslaughter by reason of diminished responsibility (NCISH, 2006). Young males formed the largest group both of perpetrators and victims. Perpetrators of homicides against a stranger were less likely to have had a lifetime history of mental illness, mental illness symptoms at the time of the offence or contact with services. Trends indicate a rise in homicides in the general population from 1973–2003, and a rise in stranger homicides, both in number and as a proportion of all homicides. People with mental illness did not contribute to these rises.

Inquiry cases

In total, 249 people (9%) convicted of homicide between April 1999 and December 2003 had been in some contact with MH services in the 12 months before the offence. This equates to 52 per year during the study period. There has been no consistent change in this figure over time. In most of these cases (74%) the responsible service was a general adult psychiatry service; the remaining cases were under alcohol and drug services (14%), child and adolescent (2%), forensic psychiatry (4%) or other (6%) services.

The commonest diagnosis was schizophrenia (74, 30%) but fewer than half (111, 45%) had severe mental illness. Over half of the people with mental illness also had at least one secondary diagnosis, commonly drug dependence, personality disorder, alcohol dependence or affective disorder. Rates of alcohol and drug misuse were generally high (85%). Seventy-five (31%) of the inquiry cases had had a previous compulsory admission.

A history of interpersonal violence had been documented in the clinical record in 103 cases (46%); a further 41 had previous convictions for violence, not documented in the notes; eight homicides were committed by patients who had previously been on a restricted hospital order because of a violent offence. There was also a high rate of documented recent violence.

Risk assessment

Mental health clinicians had seen 71 (29%) of the inquiry cases a week before the homicide, a further 71 (29%) within 1–4 weeks and the rest within 1–12 months. At final contact, 57% of the 249 cases had had an abnormal mental state – distress, depression, hostility or increased alcohol and/or drug use. Despite this, immediate risk was judged to be low or absent in 88% of cases.

Use of enhanced Care Programme Approach (CPA) to manage risk

Enhanced CPA is for people with complex needs and a risk of losing contact with services. It involves at least two agencies, generally health and social services. Only 27% (67) of homicide perpetrators in recent contact with services were under enhanced CPA. This may need closer attention in the future, since many in each group generally considered to be likely to have such needs were not in receipt of enhanced CPA, including one-third of those with schizophrenia, three-quarters with personality disorder, one-third previously detained under the Mental Health Act (MHA) 1983 and nearly half of those with a history of violence; one-third of those with severe mental illness *and* a history of violence *and* MHA detention were not under enhanced CPA. Even among those who were being cared for under such provisions, however, there was substantial non-adherence to treatment, including medication (23, 40%) or disengagement from services (23, 40%) at the time of the offence.

Findings which specifically pertain to the victims of homicide

Notwithstanding the driving forces behind the inquiry being concern for homicide victims, with a main goal of contributing to prevention of future tragedy, most focus has been on the perpetrators rather than victims of homicide. Less information is available on the victims, but a new study within the inquiry has begun (Shaw and Roscoe, 2010). Data are being examined for the years 2003–2005, with first analyses done with data on over 150 psychiatric patients who were killed in England and Wales in that period. Most were men and about three-quarters had had at least some personal contact with their killer before the fatal attack. Some had been in contact with psychiatric services in the 12 months before the homicide, suggesting an important potential opportunity for prevention. Preliminary analyses suggest first that victims who were themselves in contact with mental health services were at higher risk of being killed by a perpetrator who had also been in such contact, but, second, that clinicians had not generally considered the possibility that the person who died had been at risk of becoming a homicide victim. This is yet another reason why clinicians should be more alert to relationships between patients, whether or not of a romantic kind, and whether there are likely to be risks specific to such relationships and/or needs for support.

A systematic inquiry is thus proving to be one of the most useful initiatives to have emerged from individual tragedy. Realisation that the primary victim is not the only one to suffer from service failures is spurring new and useful lines of research within the database. Already, a need for improvements in use of widely available systems of care has been clearly highlighted. Recognition of the potential value of enhanced CPA and of its thorough application when chosen as appropriate are both evident and possible.

Learning from Workplace Violence and Bullying

It may be useful for professionals in clinical practice and allied services with a need for improved understanding of the effects of being a victim to consider a type which is much closer to the experience of many of them than most of the forms considered here – workplace violence. Workplaces vary, and workplace violence does not have an internationally accepted definition, although the International Labour Office (ILO, 2004) has developed the following:

Any action, incident or behaviour that departs from reasonable conduct in which a person is assaulted, threatened, harmed, injured in the course of, or as a direct result of, his or her work:

- *internal workplace violence is that which takes place between workers, including managers and supervisors;*
- *external workplace violence is that which takes place between workers and any other person present at the workplace.*

In the UK, the risk of being a victim of violence at work is low; 1.7% of working adults experienced external workplace violence according to the British Crime Survey (BCS) for 2002/3 (Upson, 2004). This translated to about 376,000 workers experiencing at least one assault at work, lower than the peak of 551,000 in 1997, and following a downward trend to an overall risk of assault of 0.7% and of threats of 0.8% in 2004/5 (Home Office, 2005a).

No occupations are immune but, in the UK, those most at risk are in the protective service occupations; 8.8% of police officers, for example, experienced assaults and a further 1.2% threats according to the 2004/5 BCS (Home Office, 2005a); managers and proprietors in agriculture and services followed (4.6% total), next were transport drivers (2.7% total), then personal service occupations, with health and social welfare associate professionals in this last group (2.5% total risk; 1.1% assault and 1.4% threat).

Nature of occupation is only one risk factor for workplace violence; the environment is also relevant. There may be higher risk, for example, if working alone, interacting with the public, working with things of high value (including drugs for medical purposes), interacting with distressed or violence prone people. Some occupational groups, like police officers and some clinicians and social workers, are exposed to a combination of these risky situations (Chappell and di Martino, 2006). Perpetrators of workplace violence, as determined by the 2002/03 BCS (Upson, 2004), are usually male (80% of assaults; 77% of threats); most physical assaults involved 16 to 39 year olds

(30%, 16–24; 41%, 25–39). Victims report that in almost a third of incidents the offender was under the influence of alcohol (31%); they noted use of illicit drugs in about a fifth (21%). In most incidents the perpetrators of the violence were not previously known to the victim (61%).

Most acts of internal workplace aggression take the form of emotional abuse or bullying (Keashley and Harvey, 2004). Such behaviours may include abusive supervision, social undermining (include threat to the victim's professional status or personal standing), bullying, mobbing, isolation, overwork or harassment occurring in a continuing relationship between the victim and the perpetrator (Raynor, 2005; Rayner and Hoel, 1997). Although verbal abuse and perhaps micromanagement are the stereotypical behaviours of the bullying manager and most easily identifiable, victims of bullying are actually more likely to be undermined by acts of omission, such as exclusion from regular communications or invitations to meetings (Rayner and Cooper, 2006). Perception is the key to understanding bullying (Painter, 1991). In UK surveys, 10–20% of employees have reported being bullied in the last 6 months, usually by a superior (80%), with the rest being peer bullying (e.g. Hoel et al., 2004; Lewis, 1999; Quine, 1999; Raynor, 2000; UNISON, 1997).

Factors which contribute to violent behaviour at work are mostly similar to those in other forms of interpersonal violence, encompassing personal factors, and social and environmental factors, including peer influence, management culture and style, and media factors (McDonald and Brown, 1997). Hoad (1996), examining individual risk factors, found that the most common were harbouring a grievance, frustration and irritation from being required to wait, low self-esteem, racial or sexual prejudice, perception of threat from other staff, physical discomfort, and psychological instability. Victim factors include appearance, health, age and experience, gender, personality and temperament, attitudes and expectations (Chappell and di Martino, 2006).

Consequences of violence at work include mental and physical ill-health. The 2002/3 BCS (Upson, 2004) found that nearly half (42%) of assaults at work resulted in physical injury, albeit mostly minor. Only 3% overall reported worrying about being assaulted at work by a member of the public, but this varied with occupation, being higher in health and social welfare practitioners. Over a third of youth workers, for example, said that they were fairly/very worried about assaults at work. Few workers reported that such worry had much impact on their health (<3%), but 22% of workers who had face-to-face contact with members of the public thought that it was fairly/very likely that they would be threatened at work in the next year and 10% of them said they had received no training in how to deal with violence or threats.

Although physical violence may have adverse effects on psychological health, emotional consequences of bullying may be worse (Mayhew et al., 2004). One Finnish study of municipal employees who had been bullied found that 40% of them had stress symptoms (Vartia, 1994). Other adverse effects include anxiety, depression, psychosomatic symptoms, aggression, mistrust, cognitive effects, loneliness, impaired interpersonal functioning and post-traumatic stress disorder (PTSD) (di Martino et al., 2002), potentially leading into a cycle of workplace aggression (di Martino, 2002). Costs include lost working time and security and reparative measures, in some cases encompassing legal costs, compensation and retraining (Chappell and di Martino, 2006).

Statutory measures and common-law precedents which apply to workplace violence include criminal law (e.g. dealing with violent crime or harassment), employment injury schemes (e.g. compensation for work-related injury), occupational health and safety regulations and specific legislation (Chapell and di Martino, 2006). The UK Health and Safety at Work Act 1974 legally obliges employers to ensure, so far as reasonably practicable, their employees' health, safety and welfare at work, including their freedom from workplace violence. In addition, the Management of Health and Safety at Work Regulations 1992 require employers to do structured assessments of risks employees are exposed to at work. Many countries have introduced special legislation for those in higher-risk occupations, and against special types of violence, for example sexual harassment, air rage, or against lone workers. Laws and regulations may be supported by collective agreements, at national, regional, or industry-sector level, which can allow more flexible responses.

One useful model for minimising workplace violence outlines three main areas for intervention:

- primary prevention – approaches for preventing violence before it takes place, largely focused on organisational issues;
- secondary prevention – more immediate responses to actual violence, such as emergency services, medical treatment and psychological support;
- tertiary prevention – focus on long-term care in the aftermath of violence, e.g. rehabilitation and reintegration, to reduce long-term disability (Rogers and Chappell, 2003; Chappel and di Martino, 2006).

Victim-Centred Measures of Harm: Household Crime Surveys and Accident and Emergency Records

Estimating the amount of violence in a community

Policy makers, a broad range of criminal justice, community safety and victim organisations, the media and the public all have an interest in trends in interpersonal violence. The two main violent crime measures – annual crime surveys and police data – have, however, shown conflicting trends (Dodd et al., 2004; Clegg et al., 2005). They measure different things. Household crime surveys are designed to measure citizens' experience of crime, while police data better reflect police activity, and vary with levels of surveillance or targeting, numbers of police, and changes in recording practices. Our focus is on the UK, but the same two data sources are used to measure violence in most Western countries. The International Crime Victims Survey (ICVS) (van Kesteran and van Dijk, 2010), founded in the Netherlands, brings together the British Crime Survey, similar surveys from several other European countries, Canada, Australia and New Zealand and the USA's National Crime Victimization Survey (NCVS). An additional objective measure – injury data from emergency departments – is now recognized as having important potential for accurate local violence prevention schemes (Shepherd, 2001a; Warburton and Shepherd, 2004; Sivarajasingam et al., 2002).

Police recording of violence

A major problem with police records is their incompleteness. International and national crime surveys in Sweden, the UK and the USA all demonstrate low police recording rates (Farrington et al., 1994), and biases in police recording are only partly understood. Variation in decisions to report violence to the police are among them, depending partly on circumstances and location of the incident; one study found that seven of every eight assaults which resulted in hospital treatment but which had occurred inside premises licensed to sell alcohol did not appear in police records (Shepherd et al., 1989). The ability to identify an offender and whether the act is thought of as a crime, which in turn may depend on the age and sex of the injured person, are further factors influencing reporting (Sutherland et al., 2002; Shepherd et al., 1989). Injuries to older women, for example, are much more likely to reach police records than injuries to young men (Sutherland et al., 2002). Willingness to have one's own conduct investigated (Cretney et al., 1994) and fear of reprisals are deterrents to reporting (Mayhew et al., 1989). Once a violent crime has been reported, next steps by the police will depend not only on the incident, but also on local and national police policies. Hence, even when reported, an offending act will not necessarily become an official statistic.

Homicide possibly excepted, it is not even safe to assume that the most serious violence will be detected or recorded by police. A data matching study in Atlanta, USA, for example, showed that 13% of shootings which led to emergency department treatment did not appear in city-wide police records (Kellerman et al., 2001), while a study of violence in Bristol, UK, found no significant correlation between injury severity and outcome in the criminal justice system (Shepherd et al., 1989); another UK study, in Cardiff and Swansea (Sutherland et al. 2002), showed that 75–80% of assaults resulting in hospital treatment do not appear in police records. The British Crime Survey (BCS) reports that three-quarters of 'moderately serious' violent offences do not appear in police records (Mirrlees-Black, 2001). Police recording of violent victimization is thus likely to yield a considerable underestimate of it.

Household crime surveys

The British Crime Survey, like most victimisation surveys, including the NCVS in the USA, is based on visits to representative households by interviewers who ask residents about their experiences of crime in the previous 12 months, regardless of police involvement (Mirrlees-Black, 2001). The BCS violence categories include acquaintance, domestic and stranger violence, and mugging, but not youth violence. Even here, in confidential research, it is difficult to represent the population adequately, and victimisation rates for responders and non-responders may differ. Some responders cannot be found and others refuse to be interviewed; the BCS is large by the standards of most surveys, but its estimates are imprecise, in particular for rarer offences such as serious violence. Crime surveys generally undercount crime where victim and offender know each other; responders may not think of these offences as 'real crimes', or may be reticent with interviewers; other accuracy lowering factors include forgetting, fabrication of offences, failure to realise that an incident meets the terms of the questions, remembering the incident but not that it fell within the reference period, or the converse (Sparks et al., 1977). The BCS has, however, been consistent in its violence recording since implemented in 1982, and decreases in violence since 2000, according to the BCS, parallel those in emergency department data.

Hospital emergency department data

Both systems of collecting official crime statistics thus depend, to varying degrees, on subjective factors. Public health interest in violence is reflected in national developments of systematic electronic recording of injuries presenting to hospital emergency departments, for example in Australia (Basic Routine Injury Surveillance System), Canada (Canadian Hospitals Injury Reporting and Prevention Programme (CHIRPP)), and the USA. These systems were and are not designed to complement police or national crime survey statistics, nor to be violence prevention aids (Lloyd and Graitcer, 1989; Harrison and Tyson, 1993; Mackenzie and Pless, 1999; World Health Organization, 2004c), but they may nevertheless contribute to crime prevention through collating information about those many offences which result in emergency department treatment but no report to police (Warburton and Shepherd, 2004). Identification of trends in violent crime has been facilitated by study over years of several hundred thousand assaults identified in trauma service recording systems (Sivarajasingam et al., 2002). Reliability and validity have been established in part by setting these data alongside measures of unemployment, deprivation and indicators of economic activity (Matthews et al., 2006). High rates of assault injury are associated with low economic activity reflected in house prices and youth unemployment rates, for example. These validation studies have also identified previously unrecognised correlations, for example between the size of the ethnic minority population and violence, suggesting that trauma services may offer a new opportunity to develop an early warning system for racist tension and violence (Matthews et al., 2006).

Data from emergency departments may provide a more objective measure of serious violence rates than crime reporting, as they do not depend on perception or recall that an offence has been committed but on the presence of injury needing treatment. The information is objective, and recorded soon after injury, when the event is fresh in the minds of the injured and those who accompany them. In the UK, all current emergency department recording software packages categorise injury as accident or assault, making data entry easy and reliable (Sivarajasingam et al., 2002), sensitive and specific (Sivarajasingam and Shepherd, 2001). At 14 Canadian hospitals for which emergency room data were available on injuries (the CHIRPP study), the median injury capture was 88% (range 24–100%; Mackenzie and Pless, 1999). Such data are not, however, without their limitations as indicators of community violence. There is a relative absence of minor injury data, and some specific injuries may be concealed, such as sexual violence or injuries to children; more serious injury data may be lost where access to an emergency department is limited (Lyons et al., 1995). Also, emergency department violence data generally lack completeness in terms of location of the incident, details of the perpetrator, or the relationship between the injured and the perpetrator.

Since the main responsibility of health professionals is the effective and efficient care of patients, processes for data collection and sharing need to be compatible with and sustainable in busy everyday practice. It has been established that this is best done by emergency department reception staff on first arrival of assault patients and those who accompany them (Goodwin and Shepherd, 2000), with leadership from senior emergency and trauma service clinicians, to ensure sound establishment and maintenance of the processes. Then, for prevention, effective working relationships must be forged with local authorities and the police so that data are used to best effect. In the UK, a core violence dataset has been agreed with the Home Office: six questions about precise location of the violence – e.g. which street, which licensed premises; the weapon used – e.g. fist, feet, glass, bottle, knife, firearm; number of assailants; whether the incident was reported to the police and, if not, whether the patient would like hospital staff to report on their behalf (Goodwin and Shepherd, 2000). Once the data have been collected,

NHS information technology staff anonymise them and then regularly share resultant reports with local authorities and the police. Combined with police intelligence, particular locations where violence is concentrated may be identified, as may frequency of use of, for example, particular weapons, which can then be the subject of prevention initiatives (Shepherd, 2005a). Overall, the triangulation of national violence measurements which emergency department data provide, demonstrates that BCS measures are an accurate reflection of trends. Up to and including 2011, trend lines for these two data sources follow each other precisely (consistently downwards since 2000) whereas trends derived from police data do not. Since the adoption of the new Crime Recording Standard by police forces across England and Wales, in the period up to 2007, trends derived from this source also parallel trends derived from the other two sources, but at a lower level, reflecting the continuing and consistently comparatively low levels of police ascertainment of violence (http://www.vrg.cf.ac.uk/nvit/NVIT_2012.pdf).

Apparent differences in victimisation rates according to the different systems

According to the British Crime Survey, violence in England and Wales fell by 36% between 1995 and 2004 (Dodd et al., 2004) while, over more or less the same period (1996–2004), violent offences recorded by the police in England and Wales almost doubled (Clegg et al., 2005). Similarly in the USA, an increase in rate of convictions for violent offences has occurred while violence rates have fallen (Farrington et al., 1994). Even after allowing for the limitations of BCS and similar survey data just described, such records probably provide a more accurate indication of the community burden of violent crime than official police figures. Factors which explain increases in police recorded violence include increased police numbers and/or activity; in England and Wales, for example, numbers rose to 138,000 in 2004 from 127,000 in 1997, when there was also an increase in the proportion of violent crimes reported, from 35% in 1999 to 41% in 2002/3. Police targets also change, for example recording of alcohol-related violence increased after 2000; between 1999 and 2002/3 a requirement for the police to record common assault and harassment as violent crimes contributed to the apparent increase in violent crime from 36% to 53% over that period (Home Office, 2005b). Also, in 2002, National Crime Recording Standards (NCRS) were introduced to promote recording consistency and to allow a more victim-led approach. Recording of alleged as well as proven offences led to an estimated inflation of 23% in recorded violent crime in 2002/3 alone (Home Office, 2005b).

National assault injury surveillance in England and Wales, from a representative sample of major emergency departments, has shown a 12% fall in violence nationally, from an estimated 351,000 assault-related attendances in 2000 to 309,000 in 2004 (Sivarajasingam et al., 2009, 2013),

after 5 years when no significant trends were identified (Sivarajasingam et al., 2002). This is smaller than the BCS indication of reduction in violent victimisation, but in the same direction, affecting mainly males and females aged 0–17 years, women of 18–30 years and women of 51 years and over (Sivarajasingam et al., 2009). Increased rates of violence-related harm were detected exclusively among 11–17-year-old females, 1995–2000 (Home Office, 2005b). A Danish study suggests that the small overlap – here just 23% – between victims known to the police and victims treated in hospital is a finding that crosses national boundaries (Faergemann, 2006).

Alcohol and violence from a victim perspective

The effects of alcohol on human aggression have been a focus of intense research interest (see chapter 18), but its effects on becoming a victim less so. Borges et al. (2004), in an innovative, case-crossover study, used usual alcohol consumption during the 12 months prior to assessment as the control value and found that the relative risk of injury in the hour after alcohol consumption was over four times that when there had been no drinking (RR 4.33, CI 3.55–5.27). Findings were supported by analyses of blood alcohol levels on admission to the emergency department. Violence-related risk of injuries also varied with presence of alcohol dependence and usual frequency of drunkenness. The authors concluded that, although each episode of alcohol consumption resulted in increased short-term risk of injury, especially violence-related injury, people with the lowest usual involvement with alcohol were at higher risk than those who generally drank more heavily.

The acute effects of alcohol on aggression are moderated by individual differences and contextual factors (Giancola et al., 2003). Alcohol plays an important role in the intergenerational transmission of family violence (Giancola et al., 2003). Violence typology has prompted research on problem drinking in the context of intimate partner violence perpetration and victimisation. In a controlled study, problem drinking was found to predict violence victimisation as well as violence perpetration for both men and women (White and Chen, 2002), but partner drinking increased the risk of becoming a victim of violence for women only.

Studies drawing a link between alcohol consumption, drug abuse and violence more generally are legion (see chapter 18), but some do find alcohol in the victim as well (Gerson, 1978; Collins, 1982). In an explanatory model developed by Markowitz (2000a), violence is a 'utility function' of alcohol, rather than a choice in the traditional sense. When violence is expected, then the person maximises utility and chooses the level of alcohol consumption, but if violence is not expected then the level of alcohol consumption is chosen without regard to potential effects on violence or victimisation.

Public health solutions to prevention of victimisation

Pencheon et al. (2006) noted renewed interest in public health in the last two decades of the twentieth century. They attributed this in part to realisation that continued investment in individual clinical care brings diminishing returns for the community, but partly to recognition that some problems tackled so successfully by public health actions in the nineteenth century and the first half of the twentieth century had not disappeared, violence among them. Factors motivating health professionals, especially trauma surgeons, to involve public health specialists in violence prevention include the enormous morbidity and mortality arising from it, and a sense of injustice if nothing is done to prevent treated victims from re-entering a cycle of harm (Shepherd, 2001a; Warburton and Shepherd, 2004, 2006; Krug et al., 2002).

The US Public Health Service (Institute of Medicine, 1988) has listed 10 core activities of public health:

1. preventing epidemics;
2. protecting the environment, work places, food and water;
3. promoting healthy behaviour;
4. monitoring the health status of the population;
5. mobilising community action;
6. responding to disasters;
7. assuring the quality, accessibility and accountability of medical care;
8. reaching out and linking higher risk and hard to reach people with needed services;
9. researching to develop new insights and innovative solutions; and
10. leading the development of sound health policy and planning.

Public health, like the rest of medicine, requires sound evidence, clear objectives and effective communication. A public health approach to prevention thus involves altering risk in populations. It may produce small benefits for each individual, but the effects for the population may be substantial. An example here is the adoption of toughened plastic glasses and bottles in bars, which may have little effect on the life of one particular drinker in a pub or nightclub, but reduces glass-related injuries by tens of thousands across the population as a whole (Warburton and Shepherd, 2000; see also below).

The World Health Organization Report on Violence and Health (WHO, 2002) demonstrated that it is essential for investment in prevention strategies to cross service sectors and government department boundaries. Leadership from the health sector is vital, given the morbidity and mortality from violence, and its underestimation in criminal justice records. The WHO definition of violence is 'the intentional use of physical force or power, threatened or actual, against oneself, another person, or against a group or community,

that either results in or has a high likelihood of resulting in injury, death, psychological harm, maldevelopment, or deprivation'. The WHO further divides violence into three subtypes: self-directed violence, interpersonal violence and collective violence. Its report suggests strategies for targeting both the root causes of violence and its situational determinants:

1. increase the capacity for collecting data on violence;
2. research violence – its causes, consequences and prevention;
3. promote the primary prevention of violence;
4. promote gender and social equality and equity;
5. strengthen care and support services for victims;
6. bring it all together in national action plans.

In contrast to criminal justice approaches, which depend on definitions of violence according to complex classifications of crime, a public health approach focuses on straightforward concepts of physical and psychological injury. This can bring simplicity and clarity to prevention, in spite of the fact that an ecological model of violence acknowledges that no single factor can explain why some people or groups are at higher risk of interpersonal violence and others relatively protected from it (see chapter 19).

In some countries, epidemiological findings from emergency room data, as described above, have prompted legislative change, for example the Crime and Disorder Act 1998 in England and Wales which imposes responsibility on health services, local government and the police to work together to audit and prevent crime (Warburton and Shepherd, 2006). Primary care data also have potential for both guiding national understanding and leading injury prevention planning (Wanless, 2004). A clause of the Police Reform Act 2002 brought primary care trusts and local health boards (in Scotland and in Wales) formally into these local partnerships, thus enabling communities to use local information for more effective prevention. Disclosure of injury data to city authorities, the police, and local media, for example, may enhance prevention by drawing attention and crime prevention resources to the locations of violence (Warburton and Shepherd, 2004). Local police task forces may thus, for example, gain evidence to target violence hotspot licensed premises and/or oppose drinks/entertainment license applications by the alcohol industry (Warburton and Shepherd, 2004). Late night transport arrangements, changes in the routes of police patrols, transfer of police resources away from safe city suburbs to city centres, relocation of fast food outlets in city centres and the pedestrianisation of entertainment areas may also be indicated. One evaluation showed that the effectiveness of such prevention work was significantly enhanced when emergency physicians, within a local crime prevention partnership, confronted nightclub management with injury images advised them that injuries in their premises were being audited in the local trauma service and that audit results would be published (Warburton and Shepherd, 2004).

Implementation of these pioneering measures in Cardiff has been followed by an overall decrease of 35% in numbers of assault patients seeking emergency treatment (2000–2005) compared with 18% elsewhere in England and Wales over the same period. Furthermore, according to Home Office data, by 2005 Cardiff was experiencing lower levels of 'all violence' and robbery than all but four of the 55 other towns and cities in England and Wales with a population of greater than 100,000 (Cambridge, Colchester, Southend and York; Gibbs and Haldenby, 2006). In its Home Office 'family' of 15 socioeconomically similar cities it has been the safest city from violence or robbery for 3 years (2003–2006). These findings show that having data is an important first step, but the way in which they are shared with key local agencies is also critical. Closed circuit television (CCTV), gradually included in such planning since 1990, undoubtedly has its part to play too. Its installation has been associated with increased police detection of violence (+11%) and decreased rates of emergency department treatment for injuries (–3%) in cities which have adopted it, while cities which had not showed no change in such rates over the same period (Sivarajasingam et al., 2003).

This is familiar territory for public health specialists. In his classic epidemiological study which paved the way for the construction of London sewers to prevent cholera outbreaks, John Snow – an anaesthetist – painstakingly mapped cholera hotspots in Victorian London (Centres for Disease Control, 2004). Similar skills are now being deployed to identify and eliminate violence hotspots (Warburton and Shepherd, 2006). More could be achieved if such prevention measures were employed rigorously to the supply of alcohol. An inverse relationship has been found between alcohol prices and hospital treatment for injuries sustained in violence – lower beer prices are associated with higher chances of trauma service treatment (Matthews et al., 2006).

Combining patient care with practical prevention

A care pathway for the management of people injured in violence has been developed which combines treatment with prevention at every level of care and evaluated in a series of randomised controlled trials (see figure 28.1) (Shepherd, 2005b).

Traditionally, the management of trauma patients has focused on physical injuries to the exclusion of most other outcomes. The care pathway described here was designed also to target a range of risk factors, including the precise locations in which injury was sustained, the weapons used and alcohol misuse. It takes account of the mental health outcomes of violence – anxiety, depression and PTSD and possible consequent need for mental health interventions (Shepherd, 2005b). In this pathway, primary prevention is exemplified by the partnerships just described and removal of glass as an important weapon, secondary prevention is exemplified by brief alcohol misuse interventions

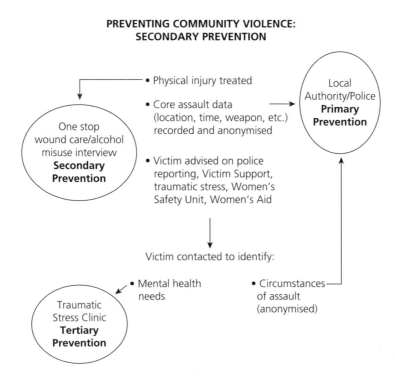

PREVENTING COMMUNITY VIOLENCE: SECONDARY PREVENTION

Figure 28.1   Care pathway for assault patients attending trauma services.

(motivational interviews) in the trauma clinic and magistrate courts, and tertiary prevention is exemplified by providing cognitive behavioural therapy (CBT) to prevent PTSD (Shepherd, 2005b).

Primary prevention: Preventing glass injury

Trauma surgery research in the 1980s first formally identified bar glasses and bottles as weapons (Hocking, 1989; Shepherd et al., 1990a,b). Three-quarters of resulting injuries were on the face and likely to result in long-term scarring (Shepherd et al., 1990a). Laboratory research then concluded that glasses which were tempered in the manufacturing process were much more resistant to breakage and, when they did break, they disintegrated into harmless, cuboid pieces with blunt edges rather than the sharp edges of non-toughened glass (Shepherd et al., 1993). A community randomised controlled trial (RCT) of glass types was then carried out with 57 public houses in the West Midlands and South Wales. The results underscored the importance of evaluating even those interventions which seem so well-founded in theory (Warburton and Shepherd, 2000). To everyone's surprise, the injury rate was 60% higher in the intervention group – in those licensed premises which had been restocked with toughened glass. In further laboratory testing of the glassware used, an error in the glass tempering process was found. Finally this was remedied (Anonymous, 1997) and a manufacturing standard recommended. Successive British Crime Surveys have demonstrated that, in the year before the switch, 13% of injuries as a result of violence between strangers involved the use of glasses or bottles as weapons and that in the year after the switch this had reduced to 4%, which equates with an annual reduction of such injuries of 81,000 (95% CI: 47,000–115,000) (Mirrlees-Black, 2001). Use of alternative materials – particularly plastic materials – may reduce the risks even further (Coomaraswamy and Shepherd, 2003), important since reductions in glass injury have not been maintained.

Secondary prevention of victimisation: Reducing alcohol misuse

Substantial reductions in road traffic injury as a result of drink drive legislation and law enforcement prompts optimism that changing alcohol consumption behaviour may achieve other reductions in harm (Shepherd, 2001b). A practical way of achieving this has emerged from research on brief motivational interviews designed to link alcohol misuse with risky behaviour in the minds of drinkers and, based on this, to prompt them to decide to reduce alcohol intake. This is a way of capitalising on 'teachable moments' represented, for example, by an alcohol misuse-related admission to hospital or the aftermath of an alcohol-related injury (Gentilello et al., 1999). Several meta-analyses of brief interventions have shown them to be '...as effective as more expensive

specialist treatment' in a range of healthcare settings, including trauma services and in doubling the chance of modifying consumption after 6–12 months (Effective Healthcare Research Team, 1993; Mattick and Jarvis, 1994).

Trauma clinics provide an excellent opportunity for delivering these brief interventions (Smith et al., 2003), since trauma clinic nurses can be trained to administer them concurrently with standard wound care (removing sutures, for example). An RCT of this approach in maxillofacial clinics, which patients usually attend 5–7 days after their injury and when they are sober, has demonstrated effectiveness. One year later, for males aged 15–35 who had consumed seven units of alcohol or more in the 6 hours prior to their facial injury, the brief intervention converted one in five at-risk patients to safe drinking levels *in addition* to those who had reduced alcohol consumption as a direct result of the injury (Smith et al., 2003). The results of an RCT of a similar intervention delivered to offenders who had caused injury, immediately following sentencing in magistrates' courts, also demonstrated a significant reduction in injury sustained in the first year after the intervention, although it had no significant effect on violence, other offending or alcohol misuse or consumption (Watt et al., 2008). In sum, this evidence suggests that reducing alcohol misuse reduces the risk of injury more than the propensity to be violent.

A more obvious public health approach to reduction of victimisation through alcohol misuse lies in the economics literature (see also chapter 18). Several studies have found an inverse relationship between alcohol consumption and alcohol prices. Using the National Family Violence Survey in the USA, Markowitz and Grossman (1998, 2000) studied the effects of state excise beer taxes on child abuse, and on the price of alcohol on spousal abuse and physical assault by teenagers (Markowitz, 2000a). In another study Markowitz (2000b), using aggregate international data, found that violence rates were associated with alcohol prices. Cook and Moore (1993) conducted a time series analysis of the effects of alcohol prices on crime rates in the USA, showing a causation pathway from the price of alcohol to alcohol consumption and from alcohol consumption to acts of violence resulting in violent injury.

Tertiary prevention: Preventing post-traumatic stress disorder

Any traumatic event, including violence, may precipitate an acute psychological response characterised by intense emotional arousal and recurring thoughts and images which are distressing (Bisson and Shepherd, 1995). Such responses are normal and, for most people, they will naturally diminish over time (Rothbaum and Foa, 1993). Some people who have experienced trauma, however, will go on to develop major, life disrupting mental health problems, most notably post-traumatic stress disorder (PTSD), but also, sometimes, depression or other conditions. Once

PTSD has become chronic, it is likely to become a life-long disabling condition (MacFarlane, 1998) so, where possible, prevention is essential.

The risk of developing PTSD may differ according to the nature of the trauma, with being a victim of criminal assault probably among the highest risk precipitants. After physical injury generally, its prevalence has been estimated as occurring in about 30% of cases (Bisson and Shepherd, 1995), rather lower than the 47% estimated by Rothbaum with respect to sexual assaults against women (see also below). Long-term psychological responses are more pronounced after violence than after accidents. In a study of patients with jaw fractures, for example, although levels of anxiety and depression were similar after 1 week, by 3 months levels had reduced only in the accident group (Shepherd et al., 1990c).

Attempts have been made to prevent PTSD and other psychiatric disorders by providing psychological interventions shortly after major traumatic events. Evaluation of such attempts has shown that prevention is far from straightforward. National clinical guidelines for England offer the best evidence-based pathway for the time being (NICE, 2005a; see also Foa et al., 2002 in the USA). A first, and most fundamental point is that PTSD tends to be under-recognised in both primary and secondary care, so sensitive, routine assessment for psychological distress or dysfunction in people with a known history of exposure to trauma is important. For those seeking emergency treatment for injury, this may be the only point of contact with services, and so the only opportunity to make relevant links for them. Nevertheless, routine screening of all individuals who present with traumatic injuries is considered unnecessary except in high risk groups, such as asylum seekers or those involved in major disasters or terrorist attacks (Brewin et al., 2008).

Early interventions with a view to prevention of PTSD are considered further below (p.754 *et seq.*) but, in brief, for those with mild symptoms in the first month, a period of 'watchful waiting' is recommended as spontaneous recovery is likely. Single session 'debriefing' in the immediate aftermath of an incident is no longer recommended for *individuals*, and may even impede natural recovery (Rose et al., 2003). Immediate intervention is, however, recommended when individuals are suffering severe psychological symptoms in the early aftermath, which may include a brief version of standard psychological therapies (e.g. Bisson et al., 2004).

Learning from Victims and Preventing Harm: Conclusions

What does all this mean for mental health and criminal justice practitioners? First, it means that a proportion, perhaps a substantial proportion of injuries sustained in violence can be prevented through proper attention to its victims. Secondly, health professionals may contribute effectively to this prevention by ensuring that injury data are collected and shared appropriately with other agencies. Thirdly, it shows that health and other agencies, including local government and the police, can work effectively together to improve local community safety. This is all in addition to work on individual cases as in the now statutory, crime reduction and community safety partnerships (Multi-Agency Protection Panels, see also chapter 25). The same lessons as those learned in multidisciplinary teams apply: joint approaches work well in the context of active, frank debate and where there is mutual trust and commitment to the task in hand – here prevention rather than cure.

Prevention in terms of the narrow confines of medical specialisation is now often considered to be the purview of public health but this attitude should change. All specialists with long-term appointments are authoritative citizens in the towns and cities in which they live. Legislation and guidance such as the European Directive on Human Rights, the Human Rights Act 1998, data protection legislation and crime prevention legislation all encourage and make provision for such collaboration. Regulatory bodies already encourage and expect prompt collaboration with the police and other agencies responsible for the prevention of domestic violence and child protection. The UK General Medical Council has recently published guidelines on the reporting of gun shot wounds by emergency physicians (Shepherd, 2004; see also chapter 25).

The development of effective, brief mental health interventions, whether to reduce alcohol consumption or to prevent post-traumatic anxiety, depression and/or other stress disorders, means that mental health professionals should develop strong links with trauma services so that care pathways, like the one described here, can be fully instituted.

VOLUNTARY AND NON-STATUTORY BODIES INSPIRED BY VICTIMS

Nowhere is the perception of the psychosocial needs of the victim as an unfortunate but largely unwelcome reality more apparent than in the results of fund-raising efforts by victims' voluntary sector organisations. Public generosity may surge in the immediate aftermath of a disaster, but the chronic, less overtly spectacular needs of victims of crime or chronic abuse are a different matter. *Victim Support* still struggles, and is considerably larger than all the other single-issue organisations in the field. It is as yet unclear whether the UK government's proposals for England and Wales, Getting It Right for Victims, if implemented, will only damage this system of provision, as these organisations fear, or may enhance the sort of local collaboration just described (https://www.official-documents.gov.uk/document/cm82/8288/8288.pdf). The *Zito Trust* survived for 15 years to complete its self-ordained tasks, but this was largely due to central government funding.

Victims and Forensic Mental Health Services

Defining and describing the role of voluntary/non-statutory/third-sector organisations working with victims and survivors within forensic mental health services is complicated by the fact that so many people are both surviving victims and offenders. Then, too, any third-sector organisation working with victims in this field must develop a good understanding of the role played by the police, criminal courts, prisons, the law, health and social services, probation and other victim support organisations – few of them with a unique perspective on working with offenders who have mental disorder. A particularly useful aspect of forensic mental health services in these terms, however, is the understanding of the variety of people who are or have been victims and their needs. Perusal of just one of the specialist forensic mental health journals, *Criminal Behaviour and Mental Health,* finds coverage of deliberate self-harm in prisons, later criminality among people referred to psychiatric services as children, 'crack, cocaine, crime and women', the health risks of prison tattooing, and the pathways into antisocial behaviour among men with personality disorder. Forensic mental health services grapple with complexities other professional disciplines are reluctant to take on, or which are not seen as the concern of generic mental health services.

Another feature unique to forensic mental health services is the stark reality that, in the main, the primary patients will only come into contact with them after at least one terrible act has already happened, and the criminal justice process has determined that hospitalisation is appropriate. The perpetrator thus becomes a patient in a secure setting of some kind, and, as such, s/he is likely to receive some of the best and most expensive services on offer, but is also subject to close supervision in the community. Victims and survivors are the necessary, though unwilling, component parts that complete the jigsaw.

The Voluntary Sector

Where does the voluntary sector fit into these arrangements? Some organisations primarily provide services for people with mental illness and/or for serving and former prisoners (see chapter 25). A handful are primarily for victims. Many of the mainstream organisations are household names (e.g. *Rethink*: http://www.rethink.org; *Mind*: www.mind.org.uk), with more substantial funding streams to match. They derive much of their income from providing residential and other services throughout the country for a range of vulnerable people who come to them through health and/or social services. They have regional offices and local community facilities and also offer advocacy, representation and advice; they publish and disseminate a range of relevant material, and they have the resources and capacity to engage in sophisticated political lobbying. Other organisations provide an invaluable if more limited service to smaller groups, but they barely generate adequate funds.

Few of these organisations, however, would describe themselves as 'forensic mental health charities'. Few work explicitly, or even at all, with offenders with mental disorder or their victims, although a handful provide residential services to people considered difficult to place in mainstream NHS facilities. A good example is *St Martin of Tours* (www.stmartinoftours.org.uk), a housing association in London which describes itself as 'one of the few voluntary sector organisations [providing] services for people with forensic histories in London'; *Revolving Doors* (http://www.revolving-doors.co.uk) is another, and has been working to improve the lives of 'those who are caught up in a damaging cycle of crisis, crime and mental illness' for over 10 years. *The Zito Trust* was perhaps the only organisation which set out to work exclusively for victims of offenders with mental disorder, an obvious niche within the overall framework of forensic mental health services. It is worth examining the background to the Trust's development, to see how it evolved and had to diversify, what influence it had, what perception other agencies and individuals have of it, and, without it, how the future appears for victims and survivors of certain crimes.

The Zito Trust

The Zito Trust was founded as a direct consequence of personal tragedy. A number of other organizations have the same provenance, and are sometimes loosely described as single issue focus groups (other examples are *Roadpeace*: http://www.roadpeace.org; *Brake*: http://www.brake.org.uk and *Disaster Action*: http://www.disasteraction.org.uk). Jayne Zito set up *The Zito Trust* in 1994, in response to the traumatic loss of her husband Jonathan Zito in 1992. He had been killed in a random attack at a tube station in London by a man with a long history of violence and contact with mental health services, but who had been failed by the system responsible for his care, in and out of hospital; the Ritchie report (Ritchie et al., 1994) revealed a catalogue of errors and missed opportunities.

Other victim-inspired 'incidents' also revealed gaps in service, ranging from the case of Ben Silcock, who, when mentally ill, climbed into the lions' den at London Zoo, to the killing of a healthcare professional, Georgina Robinson, in Torbay (Blom-Cooper et al., 1995). They focused a spotlight on the ineffectiveness of health and other agencies in a number of areas. Closure of the old asylums realised considerable capital revenue, but little of this was spent on developing the community infrastructure needed to support patients or staff into the new systems. Still today evidence remains of widespread budget deficits, service cuts and 'ear-marked' funds being syphoned off to deal with pressures elswhere in the NHS (*Rethink*, 2006).

The Zito Trust started with the aim of providing support and advice to *anyone* with difficulties because of the absence or breakdown of services – both patient-perpetrators of violence and their victims. It made use of the findings from the more than 400 independent inquiries into homicide published during 1994–2010, to push for reforms in three discrete areas: implementation of community treatment orders, provision of NHS services for people with personality disorder(s) and enhanced rights for victims of mentally disordered offenders. Until 2007, mental health law reform was a major, unresolved issue (see chapter 3).

After 1994, UK governments responded to the concerns of victims in an unprecedented way (Home Office, 2002, 2003a). The Victims' Charter now has statutory force and there is a code of practice specifically for victims of crime (Office for Criminal Justice Reform 2005; see also below). Victims are able to make personal statements to a judge in Court, and, in cases of murder or manslaughter, a project is being piloted which allows victims to deliver impact statements, themselves or through a representative, after conviction but before sentencing (Home Office, 2005c). Far from being a necessary but inconvenient part of the criminal justice process, victims (and witnesses) have been given a meaningful voice and a central part to play in the development of policy and law (Criminal Justice System, 2004). Members of the second Victims Advisory Panel, set up by the Home Office in 2006, are victims of crimes such as burglary, antisocial behaviour, hate crime, and include survivors of victims of serious violent crime. The panel examines ways in which victims and witnesses are treated, particularly by the criminal justice system, and recommendations are made directly to Ministers. One of us (Jayne Zito) was a member of the inaugural panel for three years, thereby influencing policy development.

Victims of Mentally Disordered Offenders

Many of the concerns raised by *The Zito Trust* are highlighted in the following case summaries, which illustrate why there had to be change:

Mrs A's 80-year-old mother was killed by a man well known to MH services. He had followed her home from a supermarket and forced his way into her home, where he stabbed her over thirty times. Mrs A was well supported by a police liaison officer, but not contacted by anyone from health or social services about the independent inquiry into the homicide which was established following the judicial process. She had to locate the relevant official herself in order to get an invitation to give evidence to the inquiry. She was not subsequently told about the press conference when the inquiry report was published.

Mrs B's son was pushed under a train and killed by a man in treatment for schizophrenia at the time, although he had stopped taking his medication prior to the attack. Mrs B was not given any information about any of the processes which followed her son's death, including information about the inquest and court case. She was not offered any counselling. Two years later an independent homicide inquiry was set up; Mrs B was invited to attend, but not given any information about what the process would involve. After the inquiry she received a letter from the health authority responsible for the care of the man who had killed her son. This offered her money to cover funeral expenses, but no explanation of her legal rights or suggestion to seek professional legal advice.

Ms C's father was killed by a woman, Ms X, who had been reported to various agencies for her threats against the family over a period of two years. After Ms X's conviction, the judge sent her to a medium secure hospital unit under an indefinitely restricted hospital order of the MHA 1983. Ms C remained a potential victim, so felt uncertain and nervous about attending the inquiry to give evidence. She was not offered any practical advice or support in this matter. She was not even told in the letter giving her the date and venue of the inquiry whether it would be held in private or in public, or in the presence or absence of the offender. When Ms X appealed to be discharged from her order by a mental health review tribunal, Ms C was told she could not make formal representation to the tribunal, nor attend the hearing, and was not entitled to know the outcome, even though she was worried about her safety.

Ms D witnessed the death of her mother outside the family home. The perpetrator had recently been receiving treatment for mental illness. Ms D's trauma was exacerbated by the process which unfolded: no contact from the responsible health authority or mental health trust, no offer of counselling or other support, and no information concerning the perpetrator, on the grounds of patient confidentiality.

Some of the key principles which arose from these case summaries are

- absence of a structure in which the victim of a serious crime was automatically engaged, with appropriate support, in the legal processes which must follow, which places additional, unacceptable burdens on that victim;
- this may reflect a widespread assumption that victims do not need or want such involvement, or even information or advice; it may merely reflect thoughtlessness;
- many victims who, in fact, do want all this, are thus forced to engage with complex and often unsympathetic bureaucratic processes and agencies even to get information, which increases their suffering;
- ideals of client/patient confidentiality have been used by all agencies to restrict the flow of information to victims, carers and other agencies.

While at least some of these issues have been covered by government statements on victim rights and/or the legislation described below, others are largely untouched by such changes, for example:

- there is no routine offer of referral for professional, NHS specialist services following a tragedy;
- there is no nationally established system of advocacy to represent the needs of victims;
- there is, generally, little understanding of the vulnerability and isolation experienced by the victim.

Voluntary Bodies: The Future

There is still much to be done, but development of voluntary organisations in response to personal experience is often constrained by their size. They do not generally have the infrastructure and resources to plan far ahead. An important issue is that it may be inherent in having been victimised that many people who have been through major trauma are constrained by its health consequences from promoting their own cause (for details of health effects, see below). If the people who need such organisations are commonly unable to promote them, it is difficult to catch the eye of the wider public, but not impossible as *The Zito Trust's* work has demonstrated. Diversifying to link work between fields of victimisation may be useful (National Audit Office, 2006), for example with survivors of larger scale disasters such as the Ladbroke Grove and Marchioness-Bowbelle shipping tragedy in the Thames (Health and Safety Commission, 2000; Clarke, 2001). From time to time, too, success may be underscored by noticing that the stated aims of such an organisation have been achieved, and realising the ultimately difficult task of winding it up. *The Zito Trust* achieved this too. It closed in 2009, with its specific goals met, perhaps thereby also creating new opportunities for areas in the field which are as yet under-served. As noted above, outcome of 2012 UK government consultations is awaited.

THE GROWING CENTRALITY OF VICTIMS OF SERIOUS CRIME IN THE CRIMINAL JUSTICE SYSTEM

Law and Statutory Framework

The publication of the Victim's Charter in 1990 (Home Office, 1990) heralded a drive to give victims of crime a greater voice in criminal justice proceedings. Before this, the victim's role was acknowledged only indirectly, for example by the judiciary in sentencing decisions or by the Parole Board when setting licence conditions relating to victim protection. Furthermore, although efforts to inform and support such victims had been growing, they were generally undertaken by voluntary sector groups. The Charter established the centrality of victims' rights, and criminal justice agency obligations to them. Its replacement, the Victim's Code (Criminal Justice System, 2006), may be seen as even greater direct recognition within the criminal justice system, evidenced by new arrangements for victims' advocates at both trial and pre-release stages of

criminal justice, and subsequent further guidance (Ministry of Justice, 2010a). The underlying principles of reparation focus on ensuring that victims understand their role in the overall processes by which offenders were brought to justice.

During the 1990s, the probation service worked with victims and their families on a discretionary basis, focusing on those victims of serious sexual or violent crime where the offender had been sentenced to four or more years of imprisonment. In some probation areas, considerable expertise was developed (e.g. Rawsthorne, 1998), but, in others, no service to victims was offered at all. These arrangements were formalised with the introduction of the Criminal Justice and Court Services Act 2000. Probation boards thereby acquired a statutory duty to provide information to victims at key stages of the offender's sentence and consult with the victims about conditions relating to the victim or his/her family to be attached to the offender's release. The duty is cast in terms of the probation service's responsibility to offer the service. Victims may, if they wish, opt not to be contacted further.

The duty, when first implemented in April 2001, applied to victims of sexual or violent offences where the offender had received a prison sentence of 12 months or more, but did not include offenders with mental disorder who were subject to the MHA 1983. This duty was extended to such patients subject to restrictions by the Domestic Violence, Crime and Victims Act 2004. The Mental Health Act 2007 brought in similar arrangements for victims of unrestricted patients.

Principles and Purpose of Victim Contact Work

The probation service's work with victims commences after the offender is sentenced; engagement with victims prior to that is undertaken by Witness Care Units or police family liaison officers. Every probation area will have a dedicated Victim Contact or Liaison Unit. Contact with victims is undertaken by Victim Liaison Officers (VLOs), who are specially trained to undertake this sensitive work (Ministry of Justice, 2010). The VLO will provide the victim with general information about the sentence the offender has been given and offer the opportunity to receive information at 'key stages' during the period in custody or, in the case of restricted patients, during their hospital stay. This will include information about the timing of reviews, temporary release from custody and decisions about release on licence. It is important to recognise that victims will receive a 'base level' of information relevant to their protection and security; they will not be given detailed information, for example about the offender's progress in custody or hospital, medical treatment or exact location of release. The VLO consults with victims to ensure that they have the opportunity to express their views about release conditions, which could include restrictions on contact with victims and their families or the offender's exclusion from specified locations.

Victim contact work is undertaken separately from offender work, to ensure confidentiality of victim information and an appropriate separation from issues relating to the management of the offender, but VLOs do work closely both with the Offender Managers (OMs), responsible for the case management of offenders throughout their sentence, and the clinicians responsible for treating those with mental disorder. The process of proposing conditions relating to the offender's release requires engagement between the VLO and the OM/clinician to ensure that conditions agreed are proportionate and afford the victim sufficient protection. An effective flow of information from the victim to those responsible for the supervision and/or treatment of offenders is also vital to ensure that the offender's risk is managed appropriately and any interventions are appropriately targeted and delivered. The VLO may attend multiagency public protection arrangements (MAPPA; see also chapter 25) for offenders or patients subject to these, to ensure that relevant victim information is considered and informs risk management.

In many instances, victim information will offer unique insights which are invaluable in challenging the offender's behaviour and holding him/her to account for his/her actions, and more accurate information about behavioural or environmental triggers to violence or offence details. Bentley (2006) not only argues strongly for a change in emphasis in clinicians' engagement with victims, but also stresses the need for justifiable decision-making where clinicians decide not to seek their input through victim liaison officers. As well as being vital to protection of the specific victim, victim contact work makes a key contribution to public protection and wider community safety.

Operation of the Victim Contact Scheme with Offenders with Mental Disorder

Initial contact with victims

Responsibility for contact with the victim(s) of an unrestricted patient rests with the hospital where s/he is being treated. For the victims of restricted patients or prisoners, responsibility for contact rests with the Probation Trust in the area where the victim lives, rather than where the offender is sentenced or being treated. Victim contact units (VCUs) established in each area administer the victim contact scheme. They receive notification of cases from witness care units attached to courts for those sentenced to imprisonment: for mentally disordered offenders, information will come via the Ministry of Justice Mental Health Unit or, for those transferred from prison, directly from the clinical team in the hospital of residence. The qualifying criteria for victim contact for such cases are:

- the offender has been convicted of a sexual or violent offence (as defined in section 35 of the Domestic Violence, Crime and Victims Act 2004);
- and made subject of a hospital order *with* a restriction order; or
- the person was unfit to plead but found to have done the act; or charged and found not guilty by reason of insanity in respect of a relevant offence *and* made subject to a restricted hospital order;
- individuals convicted of a sexual or violent offence who are made the subject of a hospital direction and limitation direction;
- those sentenced to 12 months or more imprisonment for a sexual or violent offence and transferred from prison under a transfer direction and restriction direction.

Following notification of a case, the VLO will contact the victim and ascertain if s/he wishes to have ongoing contact; those who do not are not contacted again, but retain the right to rejoin the scheme. The VLO will provide the victim with general information about the mental health system and detention review processes and more specific information at certain key stages of the patient's stay in hospital, for example when home leave is being considered, if s/he should abscond or when a First-tier Tribunal (Mental Health) hearing is scheduled. The victim will be encouraged to share his/her concerns about the patient's potential risk to the victim/victim's family and to make his/her preferences known on any conditions around the patient's release. The VLO will be the primary conduit for information flowing between the care team and the victim, and vice versa, throughout the patient's hospital stay. It is for clinical teams and the VLO to decide on appropriate levels of ongoing communication and information sharing in each case.

Contact while the patient is in hospital

Where a victim receives a visit from the VLO, a report will be prepared and forwarded to the responsible clinician (RC). All such reports will be marked 'Confidential – not to be shared with the patient' and must be kept in the third party section of the patient's file, to which the patient should have no access. The patient's file must be flagged so that the VLO can be alerted to all key stages at which the victim should be consulted, including town or home leave. Victim contact details must be readily accessible to nursing staff for use, according to a pre-considered and documented plan, if an offender absconds, but must be stored securely. In the event of a patient absconding, the police and the VLO must be advised immediately.

Contact during preparation for discharge

Early planning of discharge is essential, so that the victim has adequate opportunity to make representations in the light of information about the possibility and timing of release, possibly including a submission to a First-tier Tribunal (Mental Health). The clinical team and the VLO should reconsider any risk of harm and how best to support the victim throughout the release processes. The care team may invite the VLO to meetings to consider risk management and discharge arrangements. This will include consideration of conditions of discharge relevant to the victim, such as no contact or geographical exclusions, or options for undertaking joint restorative work with the victim prior to the patient's discharge.

Particular care needs to be taken in cases of intra-familial violence, especially if the patient is to be rehabilitated in the victim's home. It must be clearly established that the victim has freely agreed to the resettlement plan, and not been under duress by the patient, or even professionals on his/her behalf.

First-tier tribunals (mental health)

Since 1 July 2005, the Domestic Violence, Crime and Victims Act 2004 has given victims of paragraph 3 (see above) offenders with mental disorder the right to make representations to the First-Tier Tribunal (Mental Health). The tribunal notifies the VLO of hearing dates, and of the outcome. It is presumed that any victim representation will be disclosed to the patient, unless the tribunal has ruled that disclosure would adversely affect the health or welfare of that patient or others. If the victim makes application for non-disclosure which is not accepted, then s/he should be advised and invited to consider alternative options for presenting his/her views. Victims may apply to the tribunal to attend the oral hearing to give evidence; VLOs will support victims through the application and tribunal processes.

Discharge and aftercare in the community

The care team must ensure that the patient's care plan documentation includes all relevant victim information including full details of any restrictions or exclusion zones and details of the action required in the event of breach of conditions. Links should be maintained between the care team and the VLO, who will report promptly any concerns about breaches of conditions which relate to victims. Advice is given to victims to notify the police immediately if they have any fears of immediate danger to themselves or their families.

Effective practice issues

Among a number of important practice issues for working correctly and effectively with victims of offenders with mental disorder, the first relates to the timing of initial victim contact. This should never occur prior to trial or, where there has been a finding of unfitness to plead prior to the establishment of the facts. The most difficult issue rests

in finding the appropriate balance between embedding consideration of victims' needs throughout the patient's care while retaining appropriate boundaries in information sharing.

Victim information must not be disclosed to the patient unless the victim so wishes and has given explicit consent. Improper disclosure could have an impact on the victim's safety. The potential for conflict of interests is considerable when gathering information from victims to inform treatment or risk assessment of the offender, and this work should not override victims' needs. The VLO will assist, by advising the treatment team, and in some circumstances, may attend meetings between this team and the victim. Responsibility for patient confidentiality rests with the responsible clinician. Although the principle is generally that only 'base level' information is disclosed to the victim, this concept becomes artificial when, as is more common than not, the victim is or was part of that patient's close social circle. Where possible, the overriding principles of proportionality must govern decision-making, as is illustrated in case law cited by Bentley (2006).

The Rights of Victims of Crime in England and Wales: Conclusions

Since 1990, victims of crime have had growing rights for their voices to be heard and to influence certain aspects of offender management, including the management of offenders with mental disorder. While these rights are primarily intended to endorse their central role in a crime which affected their lives and to improve their subsequent safety, there is likely to be a wider impact on public safety more generally if processes are working well. This, as so much else in this field, requires VLOs, clinicians and care teams to find ways of sharing information and working together appropriately.

REACTIONS TO TRAUMA AND FORMS OF POST-TRAUMATIC DISORDER

The Nature of Trauma

The Greek word 'trauma' is applied to distressing events, from minor adversity and loss to major life-threatening events and disasters. For the purpose of making a diagnosis of post-traumatic stress disorder (PTSD), however, the definition of 'trauma' has been formalised as an event or situation 'of an exceptionally threatening or catastrophic nature, which is likely to cause pervasive distress in almost anyone' (ICD-10, WHO, 1992); in the American classification, the stressor is specified as 'an event or events that involved actual or threatened death or serious injury or a threat to the physical integrity of self or others', resulting in a response of 'intense fear, helplessness or horror' (or disorganised/agitated behaviour in children) (DSM-IV, APA,

1994). Green (1990) proposed two main stressor dimensions common to all extreme events: *threat* to one's own life or bodily integrity and *loss*, as in exposure to the violent/ sudden loss of or serious harm to a loved one, learning of exposure to a noxious agent or killing/seriously harming another. Psychological threat is also important (e.g., Pathé and Mullen, 1997; chapter 15).

Epidemiological studies indicate that 60–89% of individuals will be exposed to serious trauma in their lifetime (Kessler et al., 1995, 1999; Breslau et al., 1998). Risk factors for such exposure include poverty and low education (Ullman and Siefel, 1994, Breslau et al., 1995), male sex (Breslau et al., 1998), younger age (Ullman and Siegel, 1994; Norris, 1992), a personal or family history of psychiatric disorder (Breslau et al., 1991; Ullman and Siegel, 1994) and/or substance misuse (Breslau et al., 1991). According to US epidemiological studies, most commonly reported traumas are witnessing someone being badly injured or killed, involvement in a flood, fire or natural disaster or being in a life-threatening accident (Kessler et al., 1995). The traumas which are most likely to give rise to PTSD are exposure or participation in combat for men and rape and sexual molestation for women (Kessler et al., 1995).

Post-Traumatic Stress Disorder

The most recognisable and specific of the more lasting difficulties which may follow major trauma is PTSD. The symptoms typically include re-experiencing of the trauma in the form of vivid memories, nightmares and flashbacks, in which the individual feels or acts as if the trauma is happening again. Strenuous efforts to avoid the activities, places and people that arouse such recollections follow, together with emotional numbing and detachment. Chronic physiological over-arousal with disturbances in sleep and concentration tend to accompany these, together with irritability and anger problems and a heightened startle reaction.

In nearly two-thirds of cases, PTSD is complicated by comorbid psychiatric conditions, especially major depression and/or alcohol or illicit drug misuse (Kessler et al., 1997; Mueser et al., 1998; Reynolds et al., 2005). Substance misuse commonly arises through trying to 'block out' the more distressing symptoms of PTSD, and especially the increased arousal (Chilcoat and Breslau, 1998a,b; McFarlane, 1998). Although perhaps underexplored in clinical practice (Jacobson et al., 1987), when given the opportunity, psychiatric patients generally tend to report high rates of having been abused in childhood (Jacobson and Richardson, 1987) and of current violent victimisation (Walsh et al., 2003) with PTSD (e.g. Spitzer et al., 2001; Gray et al., 2003; Papanastassiou et al., 2004). Psychosis specifically has been linked to trauma, with or without PTSD (Helzer et al., 1987; Davidson et al., 1991; Mueser et al., 1998;

Kessler et al., 1995; Shore et al., 1989; see also chapter 11). High rates of PTSD have been reported among offenders, with or without personality disorder (Spitzer et al., 2001), with mental illness (Gray et al., 2003; Papanastassiou et al., 2004), and when young (Steiner et al., 1997; Fondacaro et al., 1999; Gibson et al., 1999).

For most people who develop PTSD, symptoms arise within 6 months of the trauma, but delayed onset forms occur (Andrews et al., 2007). At least half of the people who develop PTSD recover spontaneously within a year, but up to half do not, even after many years (Davidson et al., 1991; Kessler et al., 1995; Breslau et al., 1998; Kilpatrick et al., 1987). Failure to recover within 9 months of the trauma suggests that further spontaneous improvement is unlikely (Norris and Kaniasty, 1994), so treatment is vital here.

Complex PTSD

Standard definitions of PTSD may not adequately describe the range of difficulties experienced by victims of protracted traumas, such as childhood abuse, domestic violence or torture (Schnurr et al., 2002). A complex form of PTSD has been recognised among victims of prolonged and repeated traumas which manifest with more pervasive problems, including personality changes (Herman, 1992). These may include emotional dysregulation, self-harm, somatic and dissociative symptoms, interpersonal problems and altered perceptions of the self and the perpetrator (Herman, 1992, 1997; Roth et al., 1997; van der Kolk, 2005). Often shame, rather than fear, is the predominant emotion, and/or a sense of hopelessness or despair.

Epidemiology of PTSD

Only about one in four people who are exposed to a traumatic event will develop PTSD. In US studies, the lifetime prevalence of PTSD has been estimated as 1–9% (Davidson et al., 1991, $n = 2,985$, North Carolina, 1.3%; Kessler et al., 1995, US representative national household survey (rnhs), $n = 5,877$, 7.8%; Kessler et al., 2005a, rnhs, $n = 9,282$, 6.8%; Breslau et al., 1998, $n = 2,181$, Detroit 9.2%). European figures are also within this range (Frans et al., 2005, Swedish questionnaire survey, $n = 1,824$, lifetime prevalence 5.6%; Perkonigg et al., 2000, German representative community survey, 1% men, 2.2% women). In Australia a 12-month national prevalence study ($n = 10,641$) yielded a figure of 1.33%, towards the lower end of the range. For comparison, Kessler's 12-month prevalence was 3.5% (Kessler et al., 2005b).

Figures for more specific groups show differences. Men appear to be at greater risk than women of experiencing any type of trauma except for sexual assault and molestation, but at lower risk than women of developing PTSD (e.g. Breslau et al., 1997; Kessler et al., 1995; Perkonigg et al., 2000).

Risk Factors for Developing PTSD

As it is clear that not everyone who is exposed to trauma develops PTSD, there has been considerable interest in risk factors for the disorder. A meta-analysis of 14 factors included studies of 28 military and 49 civilian samples, of sizes between 25 and 4,127. Factors such as sex, race and age at trauma were inconsistently predictive, while personal or family psychiatric history or history of child abuse were more consistently predictive but of small effect (Brewin et al., 2000a). The nature of the trauma and peri-traumatic factors had a consistent and somewhat larger effect. A later meta-analysis (Ozer et al., 2003) of seven predictors across 68 studies, only just over half of which had been included in its predecessor, came to a similar conclusion. Family history, prior trauma and prior adjustment had the smallest effect sizes and trauma factors larger ones, with peri-traumatic dissociation being the largest ($r = 0.35$).

Incident-Related Forms of PTSD of Importance in Forensic Psychiatry

PTSD after head injury

A radical shift of perspective on the relationship between head injury and PTSD has become necessary. For some time, the prevailing view was that head injury was somehow protective (Mayou et al., 1993; McMillan, 1996; Sbordone and Liter, 1995), in that the victim may not remember the trauma itself. In a series of case studies, however, more extensive data from returning war veterans has forced more research. Bryant et al. (2000) evaluated 96 patients 6 months after a severe traumatic brain injury and found that over a quarter (26, 27%) had PTSD. Only five patients reported intrusive memories of the incident, but 25 had heightened emotional reactivity and nightmares. Turnbull et al. (2001) had a low return rate to their survey of over 300 brain injured patients, but found that amnesia for the event offered some protection only against intrusive memories of the event; intrusive psychiatric distress occurred regardless. Creamer et al. (2005) studied 307 consecutive admissions to a trauma centre in Australia. Just over 10% of the patients developed PTSD within 12 months of the incident. There was no significant relationship between recall of the incident and development of PTSD. Large studies of soldiers returning from combat in Iraq (Hoge et al., 2008) and Afghanistan (Schneiderman et al., 2008) show highest rates of PTSD among those who not only had head injuries but who actually lost consciousness. Debate remains over the extent to which severity of the injury may mediate its effects on PTSD, and the extent to which location of the main area of injury is more important. Koenigs et al. (2007) found a lower incidence of PTSD among soldiers who had suffered damage to one of two areas of the brain: the ventro-medial prefrontal cortex and/or the anterior temporal lobe and amygdala. Taber and Hurley (2009) provide a useful overview.

Families and close associates of homicide victims

It is not only the person who dies who is the victim of a homicide. The act also creates secondary victims in the family and friends of that person, and perhaps the wider community too. Homicide differs from other crimes because of its irreversibility, and because of the stigma and social taboo surrounding it, which affect all those who were close to the primary victim (Raphael, 1997). These differences result in qualitatively and quantitatively different responses from those to other crime victims and from normal bereavement responses (Mezey et al., 2002). A diagnosis of 'traumatic grief' has been proposed to incorporate the two core components of trauma and loss (Horowitz, 1997; Prigerson et al., 1997, 1999). Other effects may be physical ill-health, cognitive impairments, psychological disorders, including PTSD, depression, phobic avoidance, and impaired work and social function (Rynearson, 1984; Murray-Parkes, 1993; Mezey et al., 2002). Being a woman and/or a parent increases the risk of such disorder (Murphy et al., 1999).

Most support for such victims of homicide in the UK is still provided by the voluntary sector, spearheaded by individuals who are themselves survivors of such experience (Brown et al., 1990; Rock, 1998). Such groups are greatly valued by those who use them, but there has been little evaluation of their effectiveness and concerns are sometimes raised as to whether membership of such groups leads to some individuals becoming effectively 'frozen' in their identity as victims (Rock, 1998). Government initiatives, as described above, to give the victim a more central place in the justice process, include pilot projects in a number of British Crown Courts, in which victims are given the opportunity to address the Court directly, or through an advocate (DCA, 2005). Again, there has been no evaluation of the impact of these schemes.

Domestic violence

The current UK definition of domestic violence is 'any incident of threatening behaviour, violence or abuse (psychological, physical, sexual, financial or emotional) between adults who are, or have been in an intimate relationship' (Home Office, 2005d). It is the most likely of all forms of violence to go undetected, with empirical data supporting the view that the family may be the most dangerous place in society (Stanko, 1990). Part of the problem is the ambivalence in most societies to 'interfere' in the home, while there have been periods in UK history, and there are some places still, where mutilation of a child is seen as an advantage in soliciting money; child harming may still be seen as a route to care and attention in so-called

Munchausen by proxy behaviours (see chapter 9). Martin's 1978 book on violence in the family provides a full and useful historical perspective. Dale et al. (1986) also provided a useful introduction.

Most cases are of abuse of a woman by her male partner, but domestic violence may involve other family members, same-sex partners and the abuse of men by women partners. There is growing acceptance that domestic violence is an important social and public health issue (BMA, 1998). Worldwide, it affects 10–69% of the population over a lifetime; the 12-month prevalence is 3–52% (WHO, 2002). In the UK, about 21% of women and 10% of men will suffer domestic violence in their lifetime, and 10% and 2%, respectively, in any one year (Walby and Allen, 2004). Higher rates of domestic violence often reflect gender inequalities in society (WHO, 2002), but also poverty, poor education (in perpetrator and victim), alcohol and other drug misuse (perpetrator and victim) and previous victim experiences (Levinson, 1989; Coid et al., 2001; WHO, 2002).

Domestic violence is associated with a range of adverse social and health outcomes (BMA, 1998; Walby and Allen, 2004). Battered woman syndrome (BWS) was first described in the 1970s (Walker, 1979), but was then largely displaced by PTSD, as this become recognised as a discrete psychiatric diagnosis (American Psychiatric Association, 1980). The battered woman syndrome consists of emotional, cognitive and behavioural deficits that are induced in the victim as a consequence of being subjected to severe, repeated abuse by an intimate partner over a prolonged period. Two of the core components of the so-called battered woman syndrome are learned helplessness (Walker, 1979) and traumatic bonding/attachment to the perpetrator (Dutton and Painter, 1981). Both make it extremely difficult for victims to separate physically and/or emotionally from their abusive partners. If they do leave, victims not only take on the burden of providing for themselves, and perhaps their children, but also of trying to remain hidden from their partner. Rather than reducing the risk of violence, leaving home may escalate violence and threats, including stalking (Campbell, 2003; and see chapter 15).

Victims of domestic violence are at greater risk of mental health problems, compared with women who have not been abused. A meta-analysis found such victims had significantly increased rates of depression and suicidal thoughts, PTSD or substance misuse than in the general population (Golding, 1999). There is a 'dose response' relationship between severity of abuse and severity of psychiatric symptoms, which may persist even after the immediate threat of abuse has been removed (Walker, 1979). This must be taken into account when assessing and managing risk.

Between 40% and 70% of female victims of homicide are killed by a current or former spouse or partner, compared with 4–8% of male victims of homicide (WHO,

2002). Predictors of domestic homicide include: frequency of violent assaults; presence/severity of injuries; alcohol intoxication or substance misuse in the perpetrator, and for women in the victim; explicit threats to kill; sexual violence; suicidal ideation on the part of the victim and easy access to a weapon (Browne, 1987). Among 220 cases of women killed by their partners Campbell et al. (2003) found that the man's unemployment, abuse during pregnancy, threats of harm to any child and threatened or actual separation were all significant exacerbating factors. Morbid jealousy in the perpetrator and stalking behaviours are also more common in lethal than non-lethal cases of domestic violence.

Given the prevalence, risks and public health concerns associated with domestic abuse, the Department of Health (DH) has recommended that all women receiving healthcare should be asked about domestic abuse (DoH, 2005b) as women are unlikely to disclose it unless directly questioned (Walby and Allen, 2004). Risk assessment must be carried out whenever domestic violence is suspected and communicated to the victim, to allow her/him to make informed and safe choices.

Rape victims

The Sexual Offences Act 2003 defines rape as non-consensual penile penetration of the mouth, vagina or anus. The defendant must demonstrate that his belief that the complainant was consenting was reasonable. Some individuals may be judged incapable of giving free consent – because of disability, unconsciousness or incapacitation through alcohol or other drugs, being in fear of harm or under threat. The 2001 British Crime Survey found that 24% of women and 5% of men had been subjected to some form of sexual assault at least once in their lifetime (Kershaw et al., 2001). Women were similarly more likely (5%) than men (3%) to have reported rape or less serious sexual assault (0.9% and 1.5%, respectively).

Only about one in seven women raped report it to the police; many victims of rape or sexual assault never tell anyone about it (Walby and Allen, 2004.) Fear is the commonest reason for not reporting rape, including fear of reprisal, of public identification, of having to give evidence in Court and of being failed by the legal system (Campbell et al., 2001). The effect of reporting on long-term psychological adjustment is unclear, and may be contradictory. For some, the experience of giving evidence in court may be empowering, but for others the court appearance, which often involves public humiliation and personalised attacks on their credibility or morality, is a form of secondary traumatisation (Lees, 1996). The verdict appears to be of less importance in influencing psychological state and recovery than whether the victim feels well treated (Temkin, 1999). Adequate preparation for court may help to minimise the stress of giving evidence. In the UK, such support is often provided by voluntary, charitable organisations, such as *Victim Support*.

About one-third of women who report rape develop long-term psychosocial problems, which tend to be more severe and chronic than after non-sexual violence (Resnick et al., 1993). Rape trauma syndrome was first described in the 1970s (Burgess and Holmstrom, 1974), but never formalised or validated as a psychiatric diagnosis. Nevertheless, it may be helpful in understanding some of the apparent paradoxes in the observed behaviour of victims of serious sexual assault, including the tendency to acquiesce rather than fight back when attacked, the submissive stance taken by many during the act and the gratitude sometimes expressed towards their attacker, when freed.

Most rape victims initially exhibit symptoms of PTSD, for example re-experiencing the trauma, avoidance and hyperarousal, in the weeks following the assault, which spontaneously resolve in many cases (Kilpatrick et al., 1979). For some, however, the condition may persist for many years, if left untreated (Kilpatrick et al., 1989). The risk of this is highest when the rape was completed rape, and/or the victim was injured and/or thought she would die (Resnick et al., 1993); other predictors of chronicity include prior psychological or social problems, previous victimization, particularly childhood abuse, past psychiatric illness, drug or alcohol misuse and/or lack of a supportive network (Ellis et al., 1981; Atkeson et al., 1982; Frank and Anderson, 1987; Santiago et al., 1985). As well as being at risk of PTSD, rape victims also experience higher rates of depression, suicidal ideation, generalised and phobic anxiety, alcohol and drug dependence and sexual dysfunction as well as physical health problems than do victims of non-sexual assaults (Kilpatrick et al., 1985; Ellis et al., 1981; Atkeson et al., 1982; Santiago et al., 1985; Waigandt et al., 1990). They also feel high levels of guilt, loss of confidence and self-esteem, as well as relationship difficulties, with excessive dependence, inability to trust and sexual dysfunction. Men who have been seriously sexually assaulted have the same range of difficulties (Mezey and King, 1989; Coxell et al., 1999).

Trauma among military personnel

The earliest accounts of PTSD-type disorders were from war veterans. Debate continues, however, as to whether the military are particularly vulnerable to PTSD, given their exceptional experiences, if the resulting disorder is unique to their circumstances and/or whether it predisposes to a significantly increased risk of antisocial behaviour.

The (US) Centers for Disease Control (1988) examined the health of veterans for up to 20 years after returning from Vietnam. At the time of examination, 2% still met criteria for PTSD, about twice the rate in the general population at the time (Helzer et al., 1987). Up to 15% of the veterans had met criteria during combat or at some time in the 20 years. PTSD, however, accounted for little of the pathology. Suicide, violence to others, alcoholism, divorce and unemployment rates were all high. Hearst et al. (1986) found a significantly higher mortality rate up to 10 years after the draft among Vietnam veterans compared with those who had stayed at home. Concern was commonly expressed about a possible link between PTSD and subsequent violence in previously law-abiding people. Shaw et al. (1987) were unable to show any link between PTSD and a crime which led to imprisonment, after controlling for prior personality disorder and alcohol use. Other studies did report an association (Wilson and Zigelbaum, 1983; Solursh, 1988; McFall et al., 1991). Organic brain damage was implicated in higher levels of PTSD in a double blind study of soldiers exposed to Agent Orange (Levy, 1988).

A new generation of studies has emerged following combat in Iraq and Afghanistan, together with familiar concerns. In many countries, including the UK, mainstream media report high imprisonment rates among veterans; the Howard League's (2010) review found otherwise, but that imprisoned veterans were more likely to be in prison for violent offences. A definitive study is awaited. Assuming some real basis for these reports, it is difficult to know how much weight to place on well conducted studies of PTSD in veteran when only half to two-thirds of those selected respond. In many circumstances such participation might be seen as adequate if not good, but if the residual population is particularly likely to be made up of the hard to reach and socially excluded, then findings must be interpreted with caution. Hotopf et al. (2006), for example, in a large (10,000+) British cohort study with 56–65% return rates, reported little difference between personnel deployed into fighting zones compared with reservists, with a tendency for the reservists to show more symptoms. Elbogen et al. (2010), in the USA, in a much smaller volunteer study of 672 veterans, found a PTSD rate of 46% and alcohol misuse rate of 23%. The particular importance of the Elbogen study, however, is that they were able to make a link between hyperarousal rather than other PTSD symptoms, and each of the aggression measures employed – aggressive impulses or urges, difficulty in managing anger, and problems in controlling violence. Traumatic brain injury and alcohol misuse were related to the aggression measures, but not independently from the hyperarousal.

Perhaps for clinical purposes, the important issue is less one of the frequency of a relationship between military experience and PTSD, but more an acknowledgement that, for at least some returning veterans, psychological problems are a major difficulty and, where so, in many cases also for their families and wider communities through intoxication or antisocial actions. Friedman (2006) offers a useful clinical formulation and treatment strategy.

Responses to major accident, disaster and terrorist attack

Although we explored typology in more detail in the first edition of this book (Taylor et al., 1993), there is insufficient space to do so here. Essential issues for survivors of mass incidents are similar to those after any large-scale trauma, in that many will cope well, but some will not, and the need for help in the longer term is more likely to be related to the nature and experience of the incident than pre-existing factors (Brewin et al., 2000a; Ozer et al., 2003). One difference when many people have been involved in an incident simultaneously is that it is important to have planned in advance for triaging and meeting the likely demand, while avoiding potentially harmful interventions, such as individual debriefing (Rose et al., 2003), and being ready to offer more appropriate treatment as needed at a later stage.

Victims of torture

Survivors of torture have witnessed and/or been subjected to exceptional multiple traumas perpetrated by another human being, often over months or years and against a background of detention in inhumane conditions (Mollica et al., 1993). Their physical injuries may have resulted in chronic pain, disability and/or neurological impairment. If they have had to flee their country, they may also struggle with problems of displacement and resettlement in a host country, bringing multiple concurrent stressors that exacerbate a sense of immediate threat underlying PTSD (Grey and Young, 2008). The latter include housing, finances, family separation, the immigration process and associated threat of repatriation. Stigmatisation and the sense of loss of social role are also important. All these factors may increase the severity of PTSD.

Victims of miscarriage of justice

No criminal justice system is infallible. We have noted elsewhere that single cases have led to changes in the law on police interrogation in England and Wales (see chapters 6, 25) and protective measures for individuals who may be particularly vulnerable in these circumstances. We have noted specifically that scientifically based evidence has proved fallible, and that the 1993 Royal Commission on Criminal Justice led to the setting up of the Criminal Cases Review Commission (CCRC) for England, Wales and Northern Ireland, and a separate, similar commission in Scotland. When a wrongful conviction occurs, potential consequent damage is widespread through society. Beyond the immediate victim and his/her family, many others suffer too, including the victims of the original offence who have to cope with the fact that the person(s) who they thought had committed the crime did not in fact do so, and the real criminal may still be free, any new victims if the actual criminal went on to commit further crimes, and society itself through loss of confidence in the legal process and, probably, financial penalties incurred through the lengthy legal processes attempting to restore some justice (Cole, 2009).

There are no accurate figures on the frequency with which miscarriages of justice occur. Huff et al. (1996), in the USA, elicited a 65% response rate from law enforcement officials, prosecutors, judges and other lawyers of 353 approached. Their collective estimate was that 0.5% of cases going to court would end in a miscarriage. In a later calculation, based on Uniform Crime Reports, Huff (2004) suggested that this would mean that about 7,500 people arrested each year would be wrongly convicted. The main point is that the numbers are not trivial, and the UK is unlikely to be substantially different in this respect. Furthermore, the cases likely to come to notice are those where people have been convicted of serious crime(s), have families and/or political figures to support their cases, and access to sufficient funds to secure good legal advice. Wrongful conviction on minor charges is unjust and harmful too, but attracts little attention and its frequency is unknown.

Literature on the psychological consequences of having been a victim of miscarriage of justice is slight. Grounds (2004) has conducted one of the few systematic explorations of this, working with just 18 cases, all men and all of whom he had personally assessed in a 12-year period, conducting interviews with the men over 2 days and, independently, with family members who knew the men well. Fifteen of them had been falsely convicted of murder, and the others of serious offences. All but four had been in prison in excess of 4 years (range 9 months to 19 years); 10 had served more than 11 years. Grounds expressed surprise at the nature and extent of their disorders, and, indeed, a popular image is of the celebratory, often smiling news conference on the steps of the Court of Appeal after a successful hearing there. Grounds' expectations, however, had been more scientifically based. He writes that the men he saw had not had psychiatric problems of any note prior to their false conviction and that he had relied on literature about imprisonment which suggests that, even for people serving long sentences, there is little evidence of psychological damage as a result of imprisonment (see chapter 25). In 14 of the 18 cases, there was enduring change of personality, 12 met criteria for PTSD, 13 met criteria for depressive illness while in prison and 10 had had depressive illnesses after leaving prison. A few used alcohol or illicit drugs to cope. All are also angry men, and the expression of that anger may be one of the hardest things for the therapist. It is uncomfortable to be in the room with such anger; it is anxiety provoking when projected on to the parties perceived as responsible for the miscarriage. All of the men described by Grounds were struggling in some way to adapt after release. None had had any professional assistance with returning to the community, in spite of having lost so many years and being so traumatically separated from their families and communities – they were not, after all, offenders who would qualify for support with reintegration into society. O'Brien (2008) has written his personal account of the experience.

Grounds seeks an explanation in the idea that the experience 'disrupts the victim's assumptive world'. This does seem to be a major issue, of genuine puzzlement that a system, which they truly believed to be just, failed for so long to recognise their innocence and failed to give them the safety that they had expected. Grounds does not mention another factor, which one of us (PJT) has experienced in working with a number of such men, which is that they are constantly retraumatised in the experience of seeking justice – first in the repetition of the experience in the process of exoneration, and then in the cases which often follow against their alleged tormentors. This can include being required to listen to tapes of their original interviews by the police.

Grounds (2004) recommends a pragmatic approach to helping such people, to include early advice about the problems likely to be encountered, specific treatments as indicated for specific disorders, and long-term support.

PSYCHOLOGICAL UNDERSTANDING OF POST-TRAUMATIC STRESS DISORDER

Since the late 1980s, different models for understanding PTSD have been developed. As indicated above, PTSD, in its simple form, may be regarded as a form of anxiety disorder. The complex form usually arises from long-term interpersonal stress, often childhood abuse. It is this form that is most commonly seen in tertiary forensic mental health services. Its origin can best be understood from the perspective of attachment theory.

PTSD From an Attachment Perspective

The aetiology and transgenerational transmission of PTSD with an attachment framework

We have already noted that many events qualifying as a trigger for PTSD are, in fact, quite commonly experienced, and none are so powerful that exposure typically leads to PTSD (Kessler et al., 1999). Furthermore, overall, PTSD develops in a minority of those exposed to such trauma (15–25%; Maes et al., 2000), and NICE (2005) suggested that the most important risk factor is lack of social support. Yehuda (1997) found that only those victims of a road traffic accident whose response led to a lower than normal release of cortisol developed PTSD. This is the opposite of what would be expected if PTSD were an anxiety disorder and led her to postulate that PTSD may in fact reflect a

'biologic sensitisation disorder rather than a post traumatic stress disorder'. Wang (1997) attributed this sensitisation to changes in the attachment system observed in insecurely attached children, who show a similar lowering of the cortisol response during stressful separation. Yehuda et al. (2002) noted that not only Holocaust survivors, but also their adult offspring have low cortisol levels. She also found that Israeli soldiers whose parents were Holocaust survivors had higher rates of PTSD than their counterparts. These findings show that a vulnerability to PTSD can be transmitted down the generations. The question remained, however, as to how. Could it be through the attachment behaviour of the traumatised mother to her child as suggested by the work of van Ijzendoorn et al. (1997), which showed a 75% correspondence between a mother's attachment and that of her child? In 2005, Yehuda and her team found that the infants of mothers who suffered from PTSD following the destruction of the World Trade Center also had lower levels of cortisol, including those infants, who, at the time of their mother's traumatic experience, were still in the womb during the third trimester of pregnancy. It seems that the mother, through her maternal behaviour, can affect the DNA methylation of critical genes in her offspring (Meaney and Szyf, 2005), in this case by reducing the cortisol response to a traumatic event and thereby increasing the individual's vulnerability to PTSD. From this perspective, PTSD is not an arbitrary constellation of symptoms but rather the manifestation of a disrupted attachment system, the effects of which may be transmitted down the generations.

Such an understanding may help in both the assessment of complex PTSD and its treatment (de Zulueta, 2006a,b). It also enables one to make sense of the psychosomatic aspects of PTSD as well as the cultural variations in its presentation and thereby deal with some of the criticisms made by Summerfield (2001) and Bracken et al. (1992) in relation to the way the West imposes its models of care on communities who often have their own social approaches to loss, war and disasters.

The psychobiological substrate of attachment behaviour

Bowlby (1969, 1973, 1980, 1988) and his colleagues showed that, like all mammals, human infants are genetically predisposed to want access or proximity to an attachment figure and that their attachment behaviours are triggered by fear, the same feelings of fear and helplessness experienced when traumatised.

Since infants are totally dependent on their caregiver in early life, any threat to a child's sense of security will activate the attachment system, resulting in a characteristic sequence of behaviours described by Bowlby: protest, despair and detachment. Such reactions are not confined to humans, and research with primates has revealed similar behaviours (e.g. Harlow, 1974) together with specific neural substrates in the brain, in particular in the right limbic and para-limbic areas and that part of the supra-orbital area which is deeply connected to the autonomic nervous system and critical to the modulation of the emotional regulation involved in attachment processes (Schoure, 2000, pp.30–32). Attachment behaviour is also partly mediated by endogenous opiates, so much so that it has been described as an 'opiate addiction' (Panksepp et al., 1985, p.25). Indeed, the distress symptoms produced by separation are similar to those seen in narcotic withdrawal states. Plant opioids and endogenous opiates alleviate both physical pain and separation distress (Panksepp, 2003). Other naturally occurring substances involved include oxytocin, which, with dopamine, produces an energised feeling state, and serotonin, which is linked to levels of dominance in the hierarchy.

Psychobiological attunement and the formation of 'internal working models'

When human infants are born, they do not have the ability to regulate their arousal and emotional reactions. They cannot soothe themselves nor can they maintain psychophysiological homeostasis. It is through the development of attachment bonds that a complex process of psychobiological attunement takes place between infant and caregiver. The sensitive caregiver responds to the infant's signals through holding, caressing, feeding, smiling and giving meaning to the infant's different experiences. This normally leads to

1. the infant's early physiological and hormonal systems being regulated by his/her primary caregiver; thus, in the securely attached child, the hypothalamo-pituitary-adrenocortical (HPA) system, which is highly reactive at birth, becomes better modulated, to produce a normal response in relation to specific stressors;

2. a matching of inner states between mother and infant described by Stern as 'affect attunement' (Stern, 1985, pp.140–142).

Both of these phenomena are essential for affect modulation and the maintenance of intimate attachments in later life, which, in turn, become resilience factors in times of stress. As development takes place, infants become alert to the physical and emotional availability of their caregivers, who may be sensitive and responsive to the child's attachment needs, or unpredictable, rejecting and frightening. These repeated experiences are synthesised in the infant's mind to become what Bowlby called 'internal working models' of how the attachment figure is likely to respond to the child's attachment behaviour. The effects of these models have become the focus of research, using the *strange situation in infants* test (Ainsworth et al., 1978, Main and Hesse, 1992). These researchers found that 1 year olds responded in different ways to separation from their caregivers, depending on how secure their attachment was to that caregiver.

Reflective functioning

Studies using the Adult Attachment Interview (AAI) have shown that if the caregiver or other individual to whom the child is attached demonstrates 'reflective functioning' by giving meaning to the infant's experiences and sharing and predicting his/her behaviour, the child can internalise this capacity (Fonagy and Target, 1997). This capacity for 'mentalization' enables people to understand each other's mental states and intentions and is fundamental to their developing a sense of agency, continuity and ability to interact successfully with others. It protects children and adults from some of the deleterious effects of abuse by reducing their risk of re-enacting past traumatic experiences, and can thus be seen as a resilience factor.

Secure and Insecure Attachments

Secure attachments

A securely attached child has a mental representation of the caregiver as responsive in times of trouble. Such children feel confident, and are capable of empathy and of good attachment formation (Siegel, 2001). They do not get involved in abusive behaviours in later life (Troy and Sroufe, 1987). Their caregiver is accessible and responds appropriately to their emotional expressions, be they positive or negative.

These regulated events allow for the expansion of the child's coping capacities and account for the principle that the security of the attachment bond is the primary defence against trauma induced psychopathology (Schore, 1996).

Insecure attachments

Insecure attachments develop when infants have no mental representation of a responsive caregiver in times of need, such as when feeling fearful or helpless. These infants develop different access strategies towards their caregiver, in order to survive. Three types of insecure attachment behaviours have been recognised, using the *strange situation test* (Ainsworth et al., 1978). The percentages below relate to a 'middle class' sample.

1. *Anxious-ambivalent type* (12%), with inconsistent early caregivers, who subsequently tend to develop anxiety disorders (Sroufe, 2005).

2. *Avoidant type* (20–25%), who maintain proximity to their rejecting caregiver, but avoid eye contact and behave as if not attached; their heart rate, however, suggests separation fear. They develop conduct disorders and tend to deny the importance of attachments (Sroufe,

2005). Both avoidant and anxious ambivalent infants may become abusers and/or victims when interacting with other insecure children.

3. *Disorganised infants* (15%) show unpredictable responses to their caregiver, often freezing in trance-like states similar to adult sufferers of PTSD (Main and Hesse, 1992). The caregivers of such infants had little capacity to attune themselves to the infant and thereby induce traumatic states of enduring negative affect in the child, either by frightening him/her or by being frightened themselves. This may be observed in women who have been raped and whose children can trigger in them the traumatic memories of what they experienced at the hands of the rapist. The terrified and terrifying behaviour of such individuals leaves their infant in a state of 'fear without solution', since their source of comfort and security, represented by the attachment figure, has become the source of their terror. In addition, not least, because their caregiver cannot interactively repair the damage caused. As a result, the infant is left with little capacity to regulate his/her intense emotions, one of the most far-reaching effects of early trauma and neglect (van der Kolk, 1996a,b). Poor reflective functioning may also follow. Both may predispose to disturbed and violent behaviour later on.

Attachment and dissociation: The development of the 'traumatic attachment'

The infant's psychophysiological response to a state of 'fear without solution' in relation to their caregiver may elicit two separate responses.

1. A 'fight–flight response', mediated by the sympathetic nervous system. This blocks reflective symbolic processing with the result that traumatic experiences are stored in sensory, somatic, behavioural and affective state, and is manifest in hyperarousal (Perry et al., 1997).

2. If this 'fight and flight response' is not possible, a parasympathetic dominant states takes over, and the infant 'freezes' to conserve energy. In this state, endogenous opiates are released to produce numbing of pain, and a loss of vocalisation (Nijenhuis et al., 1998); this phenomenon may be seen under the PET scanner (Rauch et al., 1996).

In traumatic states of helplessness or 'fear without solution', both these responses may be activated, leading to an 'inward flight' or dissociation. Children or adults who have lived in fear of their caregiver will maintain their desperately needed attachment to him/her by developing an idealised attachment through dissociation from their terrifying memories of being abused (Short, 2001). This psychic survival takes place, however, at the cost of creating different representations of themselves in relation to their caregiver. This, in turn, results in a lack of self-continuity in

relation to the 'other', such as is seen in people with borderline personality disorder (Fonagy and Target, 1997; Ryle, 1997; de Zulueta, 1996). A 19-year follow-up study of infants with disorganised attachment illustrates this pathway in practice (Ogawa et al., 1997).

At a cognitive level, these children tend to take the blame for their own suffering, but retain an idealised version of their caregiver as well as feeling that they are in control, a crucial defence against their unbearable feelings of helplessness. It also gives them the hope that, one day, if they can behave better, they will get the love they yearn for. This powerful, ferociously maintained cognitive defence has been called the 'moral defence' (Fairbairn, 1952, pp.65–67). Unfortunately, it also reinforces attachment to and identification with the abusing parent. Work on the 'traumatic attachment' and its cognitive distortion is central to treating adult patients with a history of child abuse (de Zulueta, 2006c,d). Similar cognitive distortion may arise in adult onset trauma, but this is more accessible to modification, for example using CBT (Foa and Jaycox, 1999) or Eye Movement Desensitization and Reprocessing (EMDR; Shapiro, 1989a,b; and below).

The resulting sense of self

Mead's (1934) work reminds us that, if the individual possesses a sense of self, it is only in relation to other selves. He saw the self not as a structure, but as a process of interactions between organisms (p.179). This is in keeping with findings from attachment research, where the development of the self can be seen as taking place in two stages:

1. the individual self is born out of integration with the attachments to his/her caregivers, their relation to each other and to his/her siblings;

2. as the child grows up, the social context in which the child is reared begins to impinge more directly on his/her development, moulding his/her sense of identity to the community's sense of identity, language and relationships with the outer world.

In Western individualistic societies, one's sense of self tends to be based on the individual's achievements, but in Africa and in the Middle East and Far East, 'you are what others make you' (Zulu proverb). Shaming by rejection is an extremely powerful method of making people 'toe the line', both at home and in the community. So, for example, whilst it is acceptable for young people in the West to challenge their parents' views as they grow up, this may not be allowed in some traditional Muslim or African families, where parents hold an almost sacred position. These important differences must be born in mind when therapists from one culture try to work with people from another, for example when Western reared and trained people work with traumatised refugees from disaster areas across the world.

Once the self is seen as an organiser of inner and outer experiences that ensures a sense of perceived identity, then we can understand how

> *Any interruption of our personal identity is invariably experienced as a loss of the very sense of reality, undoubtedly the most disrupting and devastating emotion that any human being can feel (Guidano, 1987, p.87).*

This may mean that, even if people have been brought up to feel fairly secure and confident within the context of home, the experience of severe chronic traumatisation elsewhere, such as racism or other forms of abuse or discrimination, may lead to feelings of helplessness and/or humiliation and loss of capacity to empathise with 'the other', and thereby dehumanised. It is this that may predispose such individuals to acts of violence (de Zulueta, 2006a).

Implications of PTSD as an Attachment Disorder

Disordered sensitization

Feelings of terror and helplessness, inherent in the experience of abuse and neglect during the first 2 years of life may result in toxic chemical reactions which negatively impact on the developing brain. Over-stimulation and under-stimulation of the neuronal circuits at critical periods of brain growth variously lead to pruning or over-stimulation of the synapses, and probably also to changes in cortisol secretion, such as suppression of cortisol levels in avoidant infants (Capitanio et al., 1985, p.81; Tennes et al., 1977) and maltreated children (Hart et al., 1995; Gunnar and Donzella, 2002). These early changes in function of the hypothalamo-pituitary-adrenocortical (HPA) system in early life enabled Wang (1997, p.164) to make sense of Yehuda's findings among road traffic accident victims, outlined earlier, and to support her conclusions that

> *It may be that PTSD reflects a biologic sensitization disorder rather than a post-traumatic stress disorder (Yehuda, 1997, p.69).*

Yehuda's findings in relation to low urinary cortisol levels found in Holocaust survivors suffering from chronic PTSD were replicated in Vietnam veterans, whose urinary cortisol levels are strongly negatively correlated with the degree of emotional numbing they experience (Yehuda, 1997, pp.58–61). To make sense of these findings, Henry (1997) examined PTSD from an attachment perspective. He remarked (p.11):

> *Thus life changes lead through the psychosocial trauma they impose to the chronic paradox of a state of arousal of the fight/flight system together with an absence of emotional skills critical for socialization and attachment behaviour.*

In addition to re-experiencing the trauma and emotional numbing, Henry also noted the presence of alexithymia. Generally defined as the inability to describe emotions in words, alexithymia also refers to inability to symbolise or use fantasy to cope with disturbing feelings, leading to a tendency to act rather than think. It has been linked with an interhemispheric transfer deficit, which is more likely to occur with repeated trauma, as is common in sexual abuse (Zeitlin, 1993). This ties up with the finding that the brains of survivors of child sexual abuse show deficits in the development of their corpus callosum (Siegel, 2001, p.83), while re-experiencing the trauma and arousal seem more closely associated with dysfunctions of the locus coeruleus, amygdala and hippocampus. Henry also noted that significantly raised catecholamine/cortisol ratios have been found in PTSD; increasing degrees of alexithymia are linked to increasing separation of those two systems.

Henry further suggested that trauma may lead to functional rather than anatomical dissociation of emotional processing between hemispheres. Rauch et al. (1996) used positron emission tomography (PET) to explore this, showing that people with PTSD exposed to a traumatogenic stimulus, such as their own recorded account of their traumatic experience, had decreased blood flow in Broca's area (the speech area, generally in the left dominant hemisphere), indicating reduced activity there. Increased blood flow/activity in the right limbic and paralimbic systems and visual cortex have also been noted (Schore, 2001), which may explain the visual symptoms of PTSD, such as flashbacks. Taken together, these findings fit with clinical observations that traumatised patients often report an inability to speak when attempting to talk about their traumatic experience; some, like traumatised children, even become mute. The idea that psychological trauma can lead to a dissociation of emotional processing across the two hemispheres could explain the success of EMDR to treat PTSD (Shapiro, 1995b; see also below).

Emotional dysregulation is fundamental to PTSD

The loss of ability to regulate the intensity of feelings is the most far-reaching effect of early trauma and neglect as well as of adult PTSD (van der Kolk, 1996a,b). A tendency to self-medicate with drugs or alcohol may follow, as may violence to restore self-esteem. Inability to modulate emotions will also predispose to the reliving of past traumatic experiences. In van der Kolk's opinion, it is the victim's compulsion to repeat the trauma that lies at the heart of the traumatic origins of violence. Such re-traumatisation may produce endogenous opiate release. Pitman and colleagues (1990) described this in a group of eight Vietnam veterans suffering from PTSD, when they were exposed to a 15-minute film clip of the Vietnam War; seven of them showed a 30% reduction in pain perception, and were found to have released the equivalent of 8 mg of morphine.

This same phenomenon can also be elicited by patients suffering from childhood induced PTSD when they cut or otherwise re-traumatise themselves in search of emotional relief.

A particularly important emotion in PTSD is that of shame. It is unbearable in people who have been neglected and/or abused, because it involves a sense of self that has been made to feel invalidated and humiliated. This leads to a belief that one's needs are shameful, then self-loathing and feeling of being a social outcast, perhaps followed by dissociative reactions and/or violent acting out. Recognition of shame, and attention to its manifestations, is therefore very important when treating people suffering from PTSD.

Some grasp of likely brain damage or dysfunction in PTSD is important when working with patients. Western therapeutic approaches tend to be verbal and cognitive, so tapping into dominant cerebral hemisphere function, but affect modulation is moderated mainly through non-dominant hemisphere processes. Talking therapies on their own are thus likely to have a limited effect when affective dysregulation is the main problem. Here, non-verbal interventions are required, such as dance, cultural rituals, drama or art therapy, or approaches using bilateral hemispheric stimulation, such as EMDR, as well as sensorimotor therapy (Ogden, 2006).

The Importance of Social Support

Once it is accepted that PTSD is the manifestation of an attachment disorder, it is also clear that re-integration of its sufferers with their families and wider communities is essential for their healing. Dutra et al. (2008) examined suicide risk among chronically traumatised people, applying Young's schema questionnaire, and found that the social isolation/alienation schema, together with the sense of defectiveness/shame and failure, was most highly correlated with suicide risk.

PTSD is more likely to follow from man-made than natural disasters, due to the meaning survivors attach to the catastrophic event (Scurfield, 1985), although pre-traumatic circumstances are also important in determining whether or not PTSD develops (Andrews et al., 2000; Ozer et al., 2003). It is normal for people in fear or distress to turn to others for help and support. The sharing of experience of danger and loss as adults often brings people together, thus providing the victims with valuable support and reassurance; children may be more isolated by traumatic experiences. Outsiders often, but not always, demonstrate considerable good will and offers of help, although in individualist Western cultures this may not happen as people tend to see victims as responsible for what happened to them. Cultural characteristics are relevant both in how survivors experience the trauma and to the community response.

PTSD as an Attachment Disorder: Conclusions

The conceptualisation of PTSD as an attachment disorder has many useful applications. It provides a basis for understanding many of its characteristic symptoms and why, in so many cases, these 'melt away' as individuals feel supported and integrated into their community. It offers an infrastructure for treatment of those traumatised people who go on to suffer from PTSD, whether because of their pre-existing internal attachment vulnerability or because of the nature of the trauma and/or current continuing threat in their external environment (de Zulueta, 2006d). An attachment-based frame of reference facilitates the integration of findings from research into brain structure and function with more psychosocial evidence. Any therapeutic approach should incorporate the idea that PTSD is, essentially, a socialisation disorder so must take account of the presence or absence of support structures and, where present their nature and quality, and allow for brain dysfunction.

Recent evidence relating to the epigenetic transmission of a vulnerability to PTSD is important for prevention, since it implies that trauma-related violence may be transmitted down the generations if not treated (de Zulueta, 2006, pp. 210–33).

PTSD From a Cognitive Behavioural Perspective
Psychological processes in PTSD
Coping and adaptation

People who have been able to negotiate their early development fairly successfully develop working assumptions about the world as safe and predictable, people as benevolent or trustworthy and the self as capable. Trauma, by its nature, threatens these assumptions (Janoff-Bulman, 1992). Successful adaptation to a traumatic event involves understanding and reconciling it in relation to such previously held beliefs, commonly seen as 'coming to terms with' the event and its consequences. Horowitz (1976) suggested that the PTSD symptoms of intrusions and avoidance represent a response to extreme stress that facilitates adaptation. Hence, a victim relives and reviews their trauma as they try to reconcile the experience against pre-trauma beliefs and ideas but, to cope with becoming emotionally and cognitively overloaded, they also avoid, suppress and inhibit the memory. Over time, the person oscillates between intrusion and avoidance, with the intensity of each phase decreasing, until cognitive and emotional resolution is achieved. Inability to reconcile the event in these ways leads to persisting PTSD symptoms.

Horowitz's (1976) model helps to explain how PTSD symptoms may be part of a normal reaction and of a disorder. It highlights the centrality of personal meaning, and the potentially maladaptive role of some coping strategies, particularly avoidance. Aldwin (1999) suggested that the nature and quality of coping strategies may be more important to the development of PTSD than the nature of the trauma. Emotion-focused coping strategies, including avoiding memories, suppressing thoughts and feelings, self-isolation and wishful thinking, have been associated with persisting PTSD in diverse groups including Second World War soldiers, rape and assault victims and road accident survivors (Fairbank et al., 1991; Valentiner et al., 1996; Ehlers et al., 1998).

Associative learning

Keane et al. (1985) applied learning theory to explain most of the prominent features of PTSD. During traumatic events, people experience intense emotions, dominated by fear and physiological arousal. Through classical conditioning, this emotional reaction becomes strongly associated not only with the threatening event, but also with myriad other previously neutral stimuli, such as sights, smells and sounds present at the time. Subsequently, if the individual encounters these cues, they re-experience the traumatic memories and the same emotional reaction as during the trauma.

Normally, with repeated exposure to reminders and in the absence of actual threat, this reaction would gradually subside. Some people, however, tend to avoid such reminders, to minimise immediate distress, and this prevents natural extinction of the conditioned reaction, so maintaining PTSD. This kind of short-term relief may also lead to an increasingly constricted life, with emotional numbing, detachment and depression. The treatment implication is that the individual must be helped to eliminate avoidance and confront his/her trauma cues until the emotional reaction subsides.

Extending these ideas, Foa and colleagues (Foa et al., 1989; Foa and Jaycox, 1999) proposed that, in PTSD, traumatic events become represented in memory by a large network of erroneous associations between intrinsically harmless stimuli from the event and severe threat perceptions – so-called 'fear structures'. After an assault, for example, stimulus elements (youth, alley, alcohol smell, knife), response elements (terror, trembling, escape) and threat perceptions (danger of death, helplessness) become connected. Matching features later encountered (e.g. smelling alcohol) activate the fear structure, triggering intrusive memories of the assault alongside matching emotional and behavioural responses. These triggers become so numerous and unavoidable that they create a sense of danger everywhere. Furthermore, the intensity of the danger associations in the PTSD memory prevents their integration with other corrective information in memory (e.g. alcohol as enjoyable). The implication for treatment is that the fear structures need to be reactivated repeatedly in the absence of real threat, to weaken the associations with danger and integrate other benign memory associations.

Memory

The nature of the traumatic memories forms a distinctive feature of PTSD. Sufferers often find that their intentional recall of the trauma is fragmented, poorly organised and missing details, and they may struggle to give a coherent account of the events. Conversely, they report a high frequency of involuntarily triggered memories, experienced as vivid sensory impressions without the awareness of remembering which is characteristic of normal autobiographical memories. Often these involve an intense reliving of parts of the event in the present, with all the accompanying physical and emotional sensations. This observation has led several researchers to suggest that PTSD is the result of differences in the encoding, organisation and retrieval of trauma memories. (Ehlers and Clarke, 2000; Brewin et al., 1996).

Brewin et al. (1996) suggested that a disconnection between two parallel memory systems underlies PTSD. The first is verbally accessible memory, reflected in oral accounts and containing information the person was able to attend to consciously before, during and after the trauma. This is integrated with other autobiographical memories and may be deliberately retrieved. The second system encodes lower-level sensory and perceptual information, including emotional and body responses, as sensory impressions and vivid images. Under intense threat, and where events happen very quickly, the ability to appraise much of this information consciously is limited. Without a corresponding verbal memory, these sensory memories are hard to retrieve and communicate, and are not integrated with other personal memories to give them a temporal context. Instead, they are triggered involuntarily when situational reminders are encountered, and are experienced as current. The treatment implication is that when a survivor is able to focus deliberately on the content of flashbacks, rather than suppressing them, and verbalise them, sensory memories may be re-encoded as verbal memories. This provides him/her with temporal context, and so inhibits emotional arousal in the present (Brewin and Holmes, 2003).

Ehlers and Clarke (2000) also suggest that flashbacks arise when memories of trauma are poorly integrated into their context of time, place, and other autobiographical memories. Lacking context, they are easily triggered by matching cues, difficult to access verbally, and possess a sense of 'nowness' while lacking integration with subsequent normal memories that horrific outcomes do *not* materialise. If at worst, for example, the victim believes s/he will be killed, this memory is not integrated with the information that, in fact, s/he survived and survives. During retrieval, therefore, the memory is experienced with the same intense emotions as if the fatal prediction were true.

Appraisals and meanings

Subjective perceptions of the level of threat during trauma are as important to the development of PTSD as objective measures, including injury (Blanchard et al., 1995). In addition, in the period following trauma, victims may develop negative, highly idiosyncratic explanations about the event that may contribute to distress and portray the trauma as having wide and timeless implications rather than being discrete and time-limited (Ehlers and Clark, 2000). Appraisals can focus externally – 'the world is dangerous or unpredictable' – or internally – 'I was to blame, I attract disaster, I deserved to be victimised'.

Negative appraisals associated with the persistence of PTSD include catastrophic interpretations of one's own emotional responses – 'I am weak for feeling upset' – of the stress – 'I am going mad' – of the consequences of the event – 'my life is ruined' – and of other people's reactions – 'no one cares', 'they think I am crazy' (Dunmore et al., 2001). This final category fits with evidence that the perceived quality of social support is a strong risk factor for PTSD (Andrew et al., 2003; Clapp and Gayle Beck, 2009).

Appraisals can also be associated with dysfunctional coping or safety-seeking behaviours, for example believing the world is a dangerous place may trigger strategies of avoidance, withdrawal, over-vigilance or taking excessive precautions; believing PTSD symptoms are a sign of madness may trigger thought suppression through over-activity or substance misuse. Higher cognitive themes, or schemas, regarding safety, trust, power, esteem and intimacy may also be disrupted (McCann and Pearlman, 1990).

Emotional reactions

Fear and helplessness during trauma are central to PTSD. Among violent crime victims, early intensity of these emotions strongly predicted PTSD at 6 months (Brewin et al., 2000b); amongst victims of a terrorist attack sense of loss of bodily and emotional control most strongly predicted subsequent PTSD (Simeon et al., 2003), while amongst victims of torture, 'mental defeat', the perceived loss of all autonomy, characterised those with PTSD years later, even after controlling for severity of torture (Ehlers et al., 2000).

Clinical studies have generally identified a wider range of emotional reactions, including guilt, shame, anger, disgust, betrayal, humiliation and sadness (Freyd, 1996; Grey and Holmes, 2008). Novaco and Chemtob (2002) emphasised anger and shame as predictors of the course of PTSD, while Kubany et al. (2004) were most impressed by guilt and self-blame in groups as diverse as domestic violence victims and Vietnam combat veterans.

Dissociation

Trauma victims often experience changes in awareness of themselves and their surroundings during and after the event. Collectively referred to as dissociation, these experiences can range from transient feelings of numbness and detachment; changes in time, space and body perceptions to persistent depersonalisation, derealisation and amnesia (Putnam, 1993).

Mild, transient dissociation is not uncommon in healthy people, particularly when exposed to acute stress. Most soldiers undergoing intense survival training, for example, report dissociative reactions (Morgan et al., 2007). Up to three-quarters of adult victims report some dissociation during trauma (Marmar et al., 1998), but this persists in only a small proportion (Briere, 2006). Physical or sexual abuse in childhood, however, differs in that either is strongly associated with dissociative symptoms in adulthood (Muilder et al., 1998). Although there may be factors over and above the age of the victims here, as dissociation generally appears more likely when traumas are several, severe and/or chronic (Chu and Dill, 1990), developmental stage may be critical as just described in the attachment sections above.

Dissociation may be a form of defence, enabling the individual to separate from both the physical and psychological pain of the trauma, and subsequently from the distress of recollecting traumatic memories (Briere et al., 2005). Levels of dissociation during, and particularly after trauma are strongly predictive of the development of PTSD (Ozer et al., 2003; Briere et al., 2005), although these may be tautology here, as dissociation is also a major diagnostic feature of acute stress disorder (Bryant, 2006). Dissociation may be implicated in PTSD by interfering with both the immediate encoding and subsequent emotional processing of trauma memories. Dissociative symptoms may themselves become aversive and interfere with normal mental functions; they may become a focus for other maladaptive coping behaviours such as self-harm (Suyemoto, 1998).

Cognitive Behavioural Models of PTSD

The emotional processing model of PTSD

Drawing mostly on studies of sexual assault victims, Foa et al. (1999a) developed a general model for understanding PTSD, which integrates emotional processing with learning theory. They proposed that recovery requires particular efforts in emotional processing of the traumatic memory structures. Typically, over time, most trauma victims will encounter new, safe situations which nevertheless match features of their trauma in some way. Recovery occurs when the individual can recognise the repeated disconfirmation of danger, changes to the fear structure result and symptoms reduce. Failure to recover is when processing of the memory structures remains inadequate. This may be due to internal characteristics of the fear structures and/

or unavailability of corrective information. Avoidant coping strategies may be implicated, preventing the necessary repeated activation of the memory structure, reducing opportunities to disconfirm feared outcomes. Pre-trauma beliefs will also be relevant, for example in the extent to which they reinforce negative or positive evaluations of the world, or if overly rigid optimism was shattered by the trauma.

The treatment implications of the emotional processing model are to help people overcome their avoidance, encourage them to activate the fear structure fully, and identify and incorporate relevant corrective information about themselves and the world.

The integrated cognitive model of PTSD

Ehlers and Clark (2000) have developed a clinical model that synthesises several cognitive behavioural theories of PTSD. At its heart is the idea that PTSD symptoms persist when an individual processes a traumatic event in a way that produces an ongoing sense of serious threat. They suggest that trauma memories are poorly elaborated and contextualised with other autobiographical memories, leaving them disjointed and hard to access intentionally on the one hand, but easily triggered, and lacking a past 'time stamp' on the other. The trauma memory 'hotspots', relating to the worst parts of trauma, thereby lack crucial context and remain impervious to other information that might positively update their meaning and associated emotion. The intrusions, flashbacks and nightmares of PTSD are indicative of these poorly elaborated memories.

A variety of negative appraisals of the trauma, its consequences and implications also contribute to the sense of continuing threat. These meanings are often very personal and go beyond what most people would find distressing about the trauma. They include appraisals of the victim's own actions, the responses of others and/or the personal meaning of the symptoms. Such appraisals lead to a variety of coping behaviours intended to avoid or reduce the sense of threat, but inadvertently maintaining or exacerbating it. This occurs through preventing elaboration of the memory, for example by not discussing the event; preventing disconfirmation of negative appraisals, for example by taking excessive precautions; or by increasing symptoms, for example by suppressing thoughts. Pre-trauma beliefs and coping styles may interact with any or all elements of this model.

The treatment implications of this integrated cognitive model of PTSD are threefold: need to work on facilitating elaboration and update of the traumatic memory, to modify negative, distressing appraisals of the trauma and to disrupt those dysfunctional coping strategies which maintain symptoms.

FROM VICTIM TO SURVIVOR: HELP AND TREATMENT

Immediate Psychological Intervention for All – the Case for Caution

Through the 1980s and 1990s, the natural wish to relieve distress after major trauma stimulated development of interventions to alleviate immediate misery and prevent development of long-term psychological disorder. Often termed 'debriefing', these interventions typically involved discussing the traumatic event in detail in a single session in the immediate aftermath of the event (e.g. Mitchell, 1983). Enthusiasm for these 'quick fixes' was not, however, matched by a robust evidence base. Empirical evaluation started to raise general concerns (Raphael et al., 1995), and a view emerged that debriefing could sometimes be harmful (Kenardy, 2000). More recently, a Cochrane review found little evidence for the effectiveness of routine debriefing in preventing PTSD, and some evidence that it might be harmful, possibly interfering with natural recovery processes (Rose et al., 2003).

Such 'one-off' interventions are not now recommended as part of routine practice with individuals (NICE, 2005). It is worth remembering, however, that debriefing was not originally designed for use with individuals, but for natural social groups experiencing trauma in the course of their work – for example emergency or aid workers. In such circumstances, debriefing may still have a useful role if provided in a timely way and as part of an overall package of care (Lovell-Hawker, 2008). Further, none of this suggests that it is unhelpful to provide practical interventions, for victims, that normalise their emotional reactions, promote adaptive coping and encourage them to access support from those around them. This approach is best typified by 'psychological first aid', a modular programme developed initially for disaster survivors, but applicable across diverse settings, and which takes explicit account of the natural resilience of victims (Vernberg et al., 2008).

Evidence-Based Treatments for PTSD

There is no single treatment that is recommended as the definitive solution for victims of trauma. Interventions should be chosen on the basis of need, symptom severity and patient choice, and may include both pharmacological and psychological treatments (APA, 2004; NICE, 2005). On the pharmacological side, a number of antidepressant medications have been shown to have some effectiveness; hypnotics may be helpful to improve sleep. Two main categories of psychological approach emerge from the evidence base – cognitive behavioural treatments, which focus on memories of the traumatic event, collectively known as trauma focused cognitive behaviour therapy (TF-CBT), and eye movement desensitization and reprocessing (EMDR), an intervention which involves focus on the traumatic memories while making rapid lateralised eye movements. Other treatments, including psychodynamic and systemic psychotherapies, have been developed, but have a more limited evidence base and are not recommended for more routine practice.

For people with mild symptoms, an initial period of watchful waiting is helpful, along with information on adaptive coping strategies. A proportion of victims with acute PTSD will recover spontaneously during these first few weeks. For these with more severe initial symptoms and those for whom PTSD symptoms persist beyond 3 months, however, psychological treatment is recommended as the first line treatment of choice. Medication is an alternative where psychological treatment is unavailable, unwanted or unsafe. It is feasible to provide 4–6 session adaptations of standard TF-CBT with good results (Bisson et al., 2004; Bryant, 2006). The most effective psychological treatment, however, comprises of 12–20 sessions when there is comorbidity, or the patient has suffered multiple traumas, and this may be offered with reasonable prospect of success at any stage. More prolonged or repeated traumas, however, may need lengthier treatments still, often made up of a number of distinct phases in the process (e.g. Herman, 1992; Cloitre et al., 2002). For a subgroup, PTSD may, however, prove to be a lifelong, disabling condition, even with prolonged and/ or repeated treatment, and the best that may be achieved lies in symptom management rather than alleviation.

A systematic review and meta-analysis of outcome studies for psychological treatments of PTSD showed that, across a range of trauma groups, TF-CBT is the most effective, and as effective as the best drug treatment (van Etten and Taylor, 1998), although many studies showing effectiveness do not differentiate type of trauma (e.g. Ehlers et al., 2005). A later review of 25 RCTs similarly showed that TF-CBT offered significant clinical benefits for people with PTSD over either waiting list controls or supportive/non-directive therapies (Bisson et al., 2007); the mean effect size compared favourably with that for CBT for depression or anxiety. Most sample sizes, however, have been small, and up to 30% of people have dropped out of treatment, and not included in the analyses. TF-CBT has been found effective for specific victim groups, including rape (Foa et al., 1999a; Resick et al., 2002), childhood sexual abuse (Cloitre et al., 2002), domestic violence (Kubany et al., 2004) and displaced refugees (Neuner et al., 2004).

The high drop-out rate is of particular concern, because it suggests that TF-CBT is not well tolerated by a subgroup of people who need treatment. It is often associated with a temporary increase in symptoms, and the focus on traumatic memories may be the limiting step (Ehlers and Clarke, 2008). Special care is required to modulate the pace of treatment, ensuring that patients do not become overwhelmed.

An additional concern is that, even after trauma-focused therapies (including EMDR), about one in three patients still meet diagnostic criteria for PTSD (Bradley et al., 2005). This suggests that standard treatment protocols of 8–12 sessions may not be enough or that, for a sub-group of individuals, maintenance therapy may be an advantage.

Meta-analyses of trials of EMDR, generally of high quality and including RCTs (Bradley et al., 2005; Hertlein and Ricci, 2004; Maxfield and Hyer, 2002), have concluded that it is effective. A number of international bodies have formally recommended it as a therapy for PTSD and related post-trauma psychopathology (American Psychiatric Association, 2004; Bleich et al., 2002; Clinical Resource Efficiency Support Team, 2003; Department of Veterans' Affairs and Department of Defense, 2004; Dutch National Steering Committee, 2003; French National Institute of Health and Medical Research, 2004; National Institute for Clinical Excellence, 2005a). EMDR has also been tested as a treatment for sex offenders, in part because of their likelihood of childhood victimisation (Ricci, 2006; Ricci et al., 2006).

The explanation for the effectiveness of EMDR remains uncertain, although possibilities have been considered in the section above on attachment, and several neurobiologists have suggested mechanisms (Siegel, 2002; Stickgold, 2002; van der Kolk, 2002). Research supports involvement of working memory and the orienting response. Eye movements have been found to reduce emotional disturbance and strength of memories and increase ability to retrieve episodic memories (Andrade et al., 1997; Barrowcliff et al., 2003; Barrowcliff et al., 2004; Christman et al., 2003; Kavanagh et al., 2001; Kuiken et al., 2001–2002; Sharpley, 1996; van den Jout, 2001).

The Treatment Process

Preliminary assessment

First, it is important for the assessor and the person being assessed to be clear about the reasons for any clinical assessment. An assessment for medico-legal purposes will primarily be an information seeking task, in order to provide an opinion to assist a court or tribunal in some aspect of the justice process, and may or may not assist the assessee. Clinical assessment with the possibility of treatment in mind, however, is the foundation for the therapeutic relationship necessary for the effective delivery of that treatment. It is important, in either case, to find an appropriate time during the assessment to establish whether the person being assessed is under any continuing risk of harm. This will be particularly important in cases of domestic violence, or childhood abuse and perhaps also in some criminal cases, but there may be basic tasks to be undertaken to safeguard the individual in any circumstance. Some specific aspects of the assessment may, however, vary according to the treatment model, and useful reviews of assessment approaches have been provided by Simon (2003) and Wilson and Keane (2004).

Even assessment with the prospect of treatment poses several difficulties, not least being the distress elicited when discussing horrific experiences and the patient's understandable wish to avoid such discussions; the therapist may find him/herself wishing to avoid this too. Another problem is that the traumatic events have often occurred months or years previously, and self-report is commonly the main or only source of information. Passage of time, neurological injuries and mental state may all affect recall, but also particular distortions of recall are core elements in the psychopathology of PTSD. Pratt et al. (2006) offer guidance on assessing PTSD under a range of circumstances and suggest that structured clinical diagnostic interviews should be used where possible, with detailed questions about the traumatic events, covering frequency, duration, age at trauma, perception of threat and injury. Symptoms should similarly be assessed for their frequency, intensity and duration and examples of any disability arising from them elicited. In addition, the possibility of comorbidity should be closely examined – depression and substance misuse disorders are common, but other conditions, including psychosis, may be present. A mix of interview and questionnaires may be helpful initially, in case an individual has particular difficulty with any one form of self-expression; repetition of structured self-ratings may be helpful in monitoring progress. Keane et al. (1985) explicitly encouraged a multi-method approach to diagnostic assessment, which would also add review of clinical records and interviews with people who know the presenting patient well. One of the most useful techniques for getting beyond vague descriptions of 'trauma' or 'abuse' or 'distress' is to ask when 'X' last happened and then draw out a detailed description of the specifics of that occasion and the related cognitions, affects and actions. An account of personal strengths and qualities of social networks will be pertinent to treatment sustainability and the extent of its likely benefits.

Establishing and measuring PTSD

A number of scales and questionnaires have been developed to help the systematic investigation of PTSD, for example the Clinician Administered PTSD scale (CAPS; Blake et al., 1995). Given the likelihood of comorbidities, for research purposes, this might be best administered alongside a general psychiatric interview, such as the Structured Clinical Interview for DSM-IV (SCID; First et al., 2000), if

categorical diagnostic documentation is the goal, or the Comprehensive Psychopathological Rating Scale (CPRS; Åsberg et al., 1978) for measurement of change over time. Other scales more specific to traumatic reactions range from brief screening tools, such as the Trauma Screening Questionnaire (Brewin et al., 2002), to detailed dimensional measures, such as the Posttraumatic Diagnostic Scale (Foa et al., 1997).

Three steps are important to confirming a diagnosis of PTSD. The first is to determine that the individual has indeed been exposed to trauma of the nature or degree indicated in either or both of the main diagnostic manuals (ICD-10; DSM-IV), which may mean exploring one event, a constellation of events or a lifetime history. The second step is to identify not only the full extent of the symptoms, but also how they relate in their content to specific traumas, particularly in the re-experiencing and avoidance of symptoms. The third step is to clarify how dysfunctions and disability relate to specific symptoms, through eliciting specific examples and incidents.

Treatment assessment and formulation

Assessment for treatment includes identification of the symptoms and signs to be targeted, allows for prediction of likely outcome and, where the condition is complex, life-threatening and/or enduring, prioritisation within the treatment strategy.

Assessment for CBT thus begins by establishing the history of the patient's problems, his/her current perspective on them, and their consequences for him/her and his/her coping strategies. Sources of information include immediate verbal descriptions, guided self monitoring between sessions and observations in the sessions. Questionnaires are often used to supplement this, for example to help in quantifying important aspects such as mood, anxiety, activity and sleep. The goal is to develop an individualised formulation of the relevant triggers, negative appraisals, memory characteristics and dysfunctional coping strategies characteristic of PTSD.

Symptom triggers can be identified through analysis of specific episodes of intrusive memories or emotional reactions, looking for potentially matching cues in the environment (Grey et al., 2002). Keeping a diary of flashbacks is helpful in this respect. Probing memories of the trauma within the session should identify gaps and confusion, and underlying negative themes or appraisals (Foa and Rothbaum, 1998). Encouraging the patient to write an impact statement – here for therapeutic purposes, not the court – may be similarly helpful in bringing negative themes to awareness of patient and therapist alike (Resisk and Schnicke, 1993); the Post-traumatic Cognitions Inventory has also been used for this (Foa et al., 1999b). Dysfunctional coping strategies may be identified by enquiring or monitoring how the individual copes with his/her symptoms, and the steps s/he now takes in order to feel safe. Such formal approaches help to focus treatment more accurately.

Treatment using the family of cognitive behaviour therapies (CBT) for PTSD

Core principles

CBT relies on understanding the relationship between an individual's thoughts, feelings, actions and context. The treatment is structured, time-limited, problem-oriented, and focuses on the 'here and now'. The therapist takes an active, directive and educational role. A fundamental concept is that the therapist and patient are working together, to construct an individualised formulation of what causes and maintains the patient's problems. Treatment procedures are determined accordingly, and change is continuously measured using structured psychometric tools.

Several versions of CBT for PTSD have been developed, but the most effective appear to be those that emphasise systematic exposure to trauma memories and reminders, alongside restructuring of negative appraisals (Bisson et al., 2007), collectively known as trauma-focused CBT (TF-CBT). Specific protocols include Prolonged Exposure (PE) (Foa and Rothbaum, 1998), Cognitive Processing Therapy (CPT) (Resick and Schnike, 1993), and Trauma-Focused Cognitive Therapy (TFCT) (Ehlers et al., 2005) There is considerable overlap between the approaches, and they share techniques, but they differ in their underlying theories, and in their relative emphasis on particular techniques. Treatment protocols usually comprise 8–12 sessions of therapy, lasting 60–90 minutes per session, with between session 'homework' an integral part of treatment. More complex presentations, multiple traumas or comorbidities may require extension of these protocols, supplementary or more radically different approaches.

The therapeutic relationship

Trauma-focused CBT requires the patient to overcome his/her natural tendency to avoid thinking and talking about the trauma. A clear explanation of the rationale for treatment is essential, with examples of what it may be like. A description of the potential benefits is important, but the therapist must not be avoidant of acknowledging negative aspects, for example temporary increases in intrusions when discussing memories. The risks of treatment tend to be much less well considered in relation to psychological therapies than physical treatments, like medication (Jones et al., 2004). Failure to consider this with a patient who is struggling with trust could be particularly damaging, and a clearly balanced explanation of what is to happen, and why, will assist people to engage fully in otherwise emotionally aversive tasks.

At first the patient may view a proposal which involves ceasing to avoid the trauma as counterintuitive, or even potentially dangerous. The therapist must therefore work actively to develop a strong therapeutic alliance, confidence in the treatment itself and in his/her expertise. This may be difficult when working with survivors of interpersonal trauma, for whom trusting someone else may be particularly difficult or frightening (Riggs et al., 2006).

Basic therapy skills such as warmth, empathy, and active listening facilitate development of the therapeutic alliance. Validation of the patient's emotional responses and coping strategies as understandable in the light of events, is particularly important, as is recognition of his/her difficulties in abandoning avoidance behaviours. It is necessary to foster a sense of control over the therapeutic process, in direct contrast to the loss of control experienced during trauma. This includes true collaboration in agreeing overall goals and specific targets for treatment.

Psychoeducation

Next steps in treatment are likely to lie in information sharing about symptoms of PTSD, their prevalence and commonly associated problems, such as shame and anger. The patient is thus helped to identify his/her own reactions, and deal with his/her misconceptions of symptoms as indicative of weakness or madness. Offering alternative explanations may help, for example that intrusions represent the mind's attempts to process the trauma, or that depression relates to a life constricted by avoidance of trauma reminders.

Anxiety management and coping

Some protocols incorporate teaching strategies to help the patient cope with anxiety. Prolonged exposure, for example, has a specific breathing retraining component, informing patients about the effects of rapid and shallow breathing when anxious, and guiding them on how to slow their breathing, consciously separating breaths as a way of modifying anxiety (Jaycox et al., 2002). If dissociation is a problem, particularly if it interferes with discussing traumatic memories, grounding techniques may be taught (Kennereley, 1996) to help patients 'put the brakes on' intense arousal (Rothchild, 2000). Although some approaches, such as trauma-focused cognitive therapy, eschew them, on the basis that they prevent the individual discovering that anxiety responses are essentially harmless, such educative techniques may sometimes be essential to overcoming arousal sufficiently to allow treatment to take place at all (Rothchild, 2000).

Where dysfunctional coping is identified, this may be targeted, and the patient encouraged to drop or reverse the behaviour, for example use of alcohol to improve sleep or self-isolation. Cognitive coping strategies may be another area for work, typically using behavioural experiments to demonstrate their unforeseen effects; in the case of thought suppression, for example the patient may be helped to recognise paradoxical increases in intrusive thoughts. Alternatives are created, such as accepting and allowing thoughts (Ehlers et al., 2005).

Behaviours intended to control threat, such as constant vigilance for signs of danger, or carrying weapons, may be tackled in a similar way. Such precautions inadvertently increase preoccupation with danger without conferring significant increases in objective safety. Resetting these behaviours to pre-trauma levels, or rediscovering 'normal' precautions, may be helpful. Often this involves frank discussion of the relative benefit of the coping behaviours against the emotional cost of maintaining the disorder.

Working with traumatic memory

Construction of a detailed, coherent narrative of the trauma holds a central role in TF-CBT. This may serve several functions, including promotion of a gradual reduction in associated fear response, correction of beliefs that remembering the event will be unbearable or trigger mental catastrophe, contextualising the memory into other autobiographical knowledge and facilitating incorporation of corrective information about the event (Harvey, Bryant and Tarrier, 2003).

The commonest approach is imaginal reliving, in which the patient visualises and simultaneously describes the event, including his/her thoughts, feelings and sensory impressions. In order to maximise his/her engagement with the memory, s/he is encouraged to describe the event in the present tense and first person, and to focus on its most distressing moments. The therapist helps the patient to modulate his/her emotional reactions, and also to attend to aspects that might be salient to interpretation of events. Afterwards, time is allowed to 'cool down' and to discuss the reactions.

Typically, reliving the trauma in this way takes 45–50 minutes, and is recorded onto audiotape for subsequent daily review as homework. The process is repeated across sessions, until the emotional reaction is reduced and the memories lose their sense of 'nowness'. A number of other techniques may serve a similar function, including repeatedly writing out detailed narratives of the event (Resick and Schnike, 1993), reconstructing the event with diagrams and models, and revisiting the site of the trauma (Ehlers et al., 2005). Where there were multiple traumas, it may be helpful to construct a visual timeline of the events, placing them within the context of the individual's biography.

Exposure to reminders

Memory work is usually closely integrated with real-life exposure to trauma-related cues, to help the patient recognise that these are not inherently dangerous, and to reduce triggered re-experiencing symptoms. Typically s/he is helped to create a list of people, places and activities associated with the trauma, and to practise gradual exposure to these cues until emotional reactions subside. After a rape, for example, this might include seeing a man of similar appearance, being touched, walking though a car park at night, or reading about an assault in the news (Jaycox et al., 2002). For some, particularly interpersonal traumas, this may be exceptionally difficult (Armstadter et al., 2007). Care should be taken not to expose to situations where fear or avoidance would be reasonable.

Another technique is to help the patient to identify the stimuli that precipitate symptoms, by learning first to recognise how current triggers and their context differ from that of the trauma and then to create more adaptive intrusions while focusing on the differences between trigger and trauma (Ehlers et al., 2005). A victim of stabbing, for example, found that a feature of the trauma memory was the light glinting off the blade; this meant that similar experiences of glinting metal, such as the sun on a car, would trigger intrusions. The task became to seek out harmless glinting metal objects intentionally, shifting focus from its past (dangerous) to current (safe) meaning.

Cognitive restructuring

Cognitive restructuring involves teaching identification and evaluation of excessively negative appraisals of the trauma and its consequences, the self, the world and the future (Marks et al., 1998). Typically this involves Socratic questioning, and behavioural experiments to test out negative predictions and generate a more balanced view. Appraisals of responsibility for the trauma, for example, are tackled with questions such as 'How could you have known it was going to happen? What other options did you consider at the time? Could your actions have prevented something worse?' (Shipherd et al., 2006). A visit to the trauma site may help test out these ideas, often confirming that the patient had little chance to predict or avoid the trauma (Ehlers et al., 2005).

Similarly, appraisals about being unable to handle distress can be tested through imaginal reliving, or entering feared situations and remaining there. Feelings of having permanently changed since the trauma are tackled by encouraging the patient to return to valued activities and relationships that s/he has given up since the trauma. A series of structured modules could be introduced to work on common themes of safety, trust, power, esteem and intimacy, with each involving a review of evidence, followed by rewriting the trauma account to include the new perspectives (Resick and Schnike, 1993).

While these discussions can help to modify some appraisals, the disjointed recall of the trauma may prevent emotional change. Hotspots in the trauma narrative may be updated, for example by actively incorporating corrective information, while asking the patient to create a vivid image of the hotspot (Ehlers et al., 2005).

Treating complex PTSD

People with complex PTSD generally do not tolerate standard TF-CBT well, and may experience symptom worsening, often resulting in dropping out of treatment (Scott and Stradling, 1997). Empirically supported treatments for them generally involve stepwise or phased treatments, with more initial emphasis on self-skills training and stabilisation (Briere, 2002).

Victims of severe childhood abuse may thus be able to benefit from TF-CBT for PTSD, once they learn such skills (Levitt and Cloitre, 2005). One approach is Skills Training in Affective and Interpersonal Regulation plus Modified 'Prolonged Exposure' (STAIR-MPE), a manualised, phased treatment incorporating skills training as preparation for more subtle use of imaginal reliving (Cloitre et al., 2002). In this respect it is similar to other phased treatments, such as Dialectical Behaviour Therapy (DBT) for borderline personality disorder (Linehan, 1993) and, indeed, incorporates much of the affect regulation module of DBT. Skills taught include labelling feelings, tolerating distress and regulating emotions, alongside interpersonal skills such as assertiveness and flexible responding within relationships; the skill training includes role-play and continued self-monitoring. Application of the new skills is then supervised during the exposure phase, which includes more explicit use of coping to tolerate the process of reliving. Initial evaluation indicates that the treatment is effective in reducing both PTSD symptoms and interpersonal problems in this group, although drop out rates are high (Cloitre et al., 2002).

Another promising approach is 'imagery rescripting' therapy. This involves asking the patient to relive key abuse memories from their perspective as the abused child, then asking them to imagine entering the scene as they are now and, from this adult perspective, to confront the perpetrator and rescue and comfort the child (Smucker and Dancu, 2005). This approach appears to be helpful with feelings of shame and anger and increasing mastery of those abuse memories typically characterised by intense helplessness, and possibly better than standard verbal restructuring in changing underlying negative self-belief.

Victims of domestic violence often experience guilt and shame over issues unique to their plight, such as the effects of the violence on their children or decisions to stay in abusive relationships (Kubany and Watson, 2002); they commonly have histories of being abused as children and often, too, they have experienced multiple and prolonged traumas which have included sexual abuse, threats and stalking. All this contributes not only to PTSD severity, but also to additional problems such as deficits in assertiveness, often manifest in part by ambivalence about separating from the partner.

Kubany and Watson (2002) developed a multi-modal treatment specifically for this group, which includes units on tackling guilt-related beliefs and negative self-talk, on self-advocacy and empowerment skills, on learning ways to identify and avoid real potential perpetrators, and on ways to manage unwanted contact with (ex-)partners. The authors emphasise, though, that, if the relationship with an abusive partner is continuing, or there is overt ongoing threat, treatment for PTSD is usually contra-indicated. Here, work should be about developing safety plans and deciding on the future of the relationship.

Torture victims receive special reference in NICE guidance on PTSD. A phased model of treatment is recommended for this group (NICE, 2005a). Phase 1 involves establishing safety and stabilisation, including attending to ongoing social stressors, medical and family issues; phase 2 involves trauma-focused treatment and grief work; phase 3 focuses on community re-integration, through work, leisure and political activities. A detailed description of appropriately modified TF-CBT is provided by Grey and Young (2008).

Torture survivors, frequently distressed by their reactions and behaviour during torture, often describe a sense of mental defeat at this time and of permanent change afterwards (Ehlers et al., 2000). Treatment may involve reframing reactions under torture, both as normal responses to extreme stress and necessary for survival (Regel and Berliner, 2007). Education about the nature of torture may be helpful too, including the fact that it is designed to induce helplessness. Grief and mourning for the former self, or perceived secondary victims, may require additional work.

When a person has experienced many traumas over a long period, it may be difficult to decide on the treatment focus, so helpful first therapeutic steps may be to construct a detailed life-story, placing the traumatic experiences within it and alongside events in their wider socio-political context (Neuner et al., 2002; Grey and Young, 2008). Experiences which are most distressing and most represented in intrusive PTSD symptoms may then be processed as in standard TF-CBT. As neither patient nor therapist may be fluent in the same language, an interpreter may be needed. This does not preclude treatment, but additional protocols may then be required (d'Ardenne et al., 2007).

Treatment using eye movement desensitization and reprocessing (EMDR)

EMDR was developed by Shapiro in 1987 to treat victims of traumatic stress (Shapiro, 1989, 1995, 1996, 2002). Despite the name, eye movement is just one of several forms of stimulation which may be used. The total approach incorporates procedures derived from several psychological schools, including psychodynamic, cognitive behavioural, interpersonal, experiential, and body-centred therapies. The aim of treatment for trauma victims goes beyond reduction in anxiety, as EMDR is an information processing therapy. It can therefore deal with images, beliefs, emotions,

729

physical responses, increased awareness and interpersonal systems. A variety of different structured protocols have been developed for various pathologies, and therapeutic procedures should also be customised to the needs of the person needing treatment. During EMDR, the patient's attention is directed to both past and present experiences whilst at the same time focusing on an external stimulus. S/he is then asked to let the new material which arises become the material which is used in association with the next set of stimuli. This consecutive sequence of attending to the bilateral stimulation and the developing personal associations is repeated numerous times during a single session.

The phases of treatment using EMDR

Treatment is formally divided into eight phases which may overlap or be repeated, as required (Shapiro, 2001).

1. *Taking a history.* This must include ensuring that the person is ready for treatment and that the programme can be applied safely. During this phase the patient and therapist will together identify potential targets for EMDR processing which, in addition to the traumatic event itself, include more recent upsetting events, contemporary situations that produce emotional distress, related incidents in the past, and skills and behaviours needed for the future.

2. *Preparation.* Developing a therapeutic relationship, explaining the treatment, practising the eye movements, teaching emotional arousal reduction techniques, and addressing any fears the person may have. The therapist needs to be sure that the patient has sufficient expertise and ability to cope with emotional disturbance, and has a stable enough mental state. If supplementary skills or preparatory stabilisation is needed then the therapy now focuses on these. The patient can then employ techniques to reduce emotional disturbance as required, either during or between the sessions (it is not intended that these should be required after completion of treatment).

3. *Assessing core problems.* Detailed assessment of the trauma and cognitive framework, the nature and extent of the arousal emotions and of body sensations follow. The patient is usually asked to identify the most distressing visual image of the trauma, a negative self-belief and a preferred positive cognition. The validity of these is rated using the Validity of Cognition Scale (VOC; Shapiro, 1989b) and the Subjective Units of Disturbance Scale (SUDS; Wolpe, 1982), both of which are also used subsequently to assess progress.

4. Stages 1–3 use the bilateral stimulus, first for *desensitisation*, then

5. *installation of the new positive cognitive framework;*

6. a *body scan* to address any remaining physical sensations; and

7. working with abreaction and techniques to *resolve blocked processing.*

8. *Re-evaluation,* finally incorporates mutual examination of previous work and progress, more recent triggers of disturbance and at 'future templates' – imagined future events which may require different responses.

During phases 4–7 of the treatment, the procedures are structured so that the patient is initially instructed in a standardised way to focus on various aspects of the distressing memory. S/he is directed to concentrate on the previously identified mental picture of the trauma, the associated negative belief and the accompanying distressing emotions. The therapist then provides the bilateral stimulation – in the form of a visual stimulus, sounds which alternate between each ear, or tactile stimulation for 20–30 seconds or more, depending on the individually assessed needs. Next, the therapist asks the patient to allow his/her mind to go blank and report whatever thought, feeling, memory, image or sensation s/he experiences, before using his/her clinical judgment on how best to facilitate the next focus of attention. Usually the patient is encouraged to take as much control as possible over the association process. The procedures allow for the patient to be supported when distressed with resumption of treatment when again appropriate. This cycle is repeated many times in a single session, and as many sessions as necessary provided.

A satisfactory conclusion to the treatment is reached when the patient indicates that no psychological distress related to the targeted memory remains. The clinician then focuses attention on the previously identified preferred positive belief, or sometimes a better one if this has emerged during treatment. Focus is returned to the incident, and the bilateral stimulus applied. After a number of sets, the patient usually indicates that s/he has a higher level of confidence in the positive cognition. The therapist then explores body sensations with the patient. Any negative ones are processed with the stimulus; positive ones can be enhanced in a similar fashion. As part of closure, the therapist requests that the patient makes a note of any related material that arises outside of the sessions.

Adaptive information processing: an EMDR variant

Shapiro (1995, 2001) has outlined the adaptive information processing (AIP) model which provides an explanation for why unprocessed traumatic experiences have negative effects, including dysfunctional and antisocial behaviour. The AIP model proposes that the brain is affected by the intense emotional arousal evoked by the initial experience and is subsequently unable to process the information to a satisfactory adaptive resolution. As a result, the perceptions, cognitions, affect and bodily sensations associated with the trauma become inappropriately isolated in the memory network of the victim because they are not stored in a similar fashion to memories of non-traumatic events. Similar events, or reminders of the original event which are subsequently encountered, act as a trigger to this dysfunctionally stored material and cause the person's perspective on the present to be adversely affected by inappropriate affect and incorrect cognitions. The eight phases of EMDR (Shapiro, 1995, 2001, 2002) facilitate the retrieval of the traumatic memories in a controlled and structured context and, in this way, act as a catalyst for correct processing and, eventually, more normal storage of the memory (Siegel, 2002; Stickgold, 2002; van der Kolk, 2002).

FROM VICTIMS TO SURVIVORS: CONCLUSIONS

So, much can be done to help victims of crime but, in spite of substantial improvements both in meeting their needs and acknowledging their central role in the process of understanding and preventing crime, there remains scope for much more attention to them and to their experiences. Barriers to achieving this may partly lie in the nature of the mental health difficulties that may follow major and/or repeated trauma, which leave the primary victim – and sometimes staff in the services which should be helping him/her – with a sense of guilt or fault and, often, a sense of helplessness too, preventing appropriate action. Systems responses, like individual inquiries, contrary to their intent, may exacerbate problems unless the traumatised individuals at the heart of the inquiry have adequate support throughout, and access to treatment if they need it and, ultimately, appropriate control over their situations. The spirit of constructive truth seeking, with publication and/or other forms of wider dissemination of relevant anonymised data, shared in the development of community prevention activities or better service planning, seems a good way forward from wider public health and prevention perspectives. When substantial trauma occurs, however, there are individual treatment needs to be met too.

APPENDIX 1
The European Convention on Human Rights

Convention for the Protection of Human Rights and Fundamental Freedoms (as amended by Protocol No. 11) Rome, 4.XI.1950

The full title of the European Convention first signed in Rome in 1950 is usually abbreviated to the European Convention on Human Rights (ECHR). It is available on the Council of Europe website at http://conventions.coe.int/treaty/en/Treaties/Html/005.htm. An abbreviated version is used here, the omissions deal with matters which are not central to the practice of psychiatry. The convention has 59 articles, but those in section 1, given here are the most relevant to psychiatry and at times the most contentious. There are also 13 protocols which are later additions. The last of these is given here because of its significance.

The first thing to notice is that the European Convention is based almost entirely on the Universal Declaration of Human Rights proclaimed by the United Nations in 1948. The European Convention has thus strengthened the Universal Declaration by giving it the force of law within a treaty framework signed by all the members of the Council of Europe together with a court to enforce it. As far as the United Kingdom is concerned the human rights principles have been further strengthened by the Human Rights Act 1998 which is largely based on the European Convention and can be enforced in UK courts.

The European Convention on Human Rights

The Governments signatory hereto, being Members of the Council of Europe,

Considering the Universal Declaration of Human Rights proclaimed by the General Assembly of the United Nations on 10 December 1948;

Reaffirming their profound belief in those Fundamental Freedoms which are the foundation of justice and peace in the world and are best maintained on the one hand by an effective political democracy and on the other by a common understanding and observance of the Human Rights upon which they depend;

Being resolved, as the Governments of European countries which are like-minded and have a common heritage of political traditions, ideals, freedom and the rule of law to take the first steps for the collective enforcement of certain of the Rights stated in the Universal Declaration;

Have agreed as follows:

Section i. Rights and Freedoms

ARTICLE 2

1. Everyone's right to life shall be protected by law. No one shall be deprived of his life intentionally save in the execution of a sentence of a court following his conviction of a crime for which this penalty is provided by law.

2. Deprivation of life shall not be regarded as inflicted in contravention of this article when it results from the use of force which is no more than absolutely necessary:

   (a) in defence of any person from unlawful violence;

   (b) in order to effect a lawful arrest or to prevent escape of a person lawfully detained;

   (c) in action lawfully taken for the purpose of quelling a riot or insurrection.

ARTICLE 3

No one shall be subjected to torture or to inhuman or degrading treatment or punishment.

ARTICLE 4

1. No one shall be held in slavery or servitude.

2. No one shall be required to perform forced or compulsory labour.

3. For the purpose of this article the term forced or compulsory labour' shall not include:

   (a) any work required to be done in the ordinary course of detention imposed according to the provisions of Article 5 of this Convention or during conditional release from such detention;

   (b) any service of a military character or, in case of conscientious objectors in countries where they are recognized, service exacted instead of compulsory military service;

   (c) any service exacted in case of an emergency or calamity threatening the life or well-being of the community;

   (d) any work or service which forms part of normal civic obligations.

ARTICLE 5

1. Everyone has the right to liberty and security of person.

   No one shall be deprived of his liberty save in the following cases and in accordance with a procedure prescribed by law:

   (a) the lawful detention of a person after conviction by a competent court;

   (b) the lawful arrest or detention of a person for non-compliance with the lawful order of a court or in order to secure the fulfilment of any obligation prescribed by law;

   (c) the lawful arrest or detention of a person effected for the purpose of bringing him before the competent legal authority of reasonable suspicion of having committed and offence or when it is reasonably considered necessary to prevent his committing an offence or fleeing after having done so;

   (d) the detention of a minor by lawful order for the purpose of educational supervision or his lawful detention for the purpose of bringing him before the competent legal authority;

   (e) the lawful detention of persons for the prevention of the spreading of infectious diseases, of persons of unsound mind, alcoholics or drug addicts, or vagrants;

   (f) the lawful arrest or detention of a person to prevent his effecting an unauthorized entry into the country or of a person against whom action is being taken with a view to deportation or extradition.

2. Everyone who is arrested shall be informed promptly, in a language which he understands, of the reasons for his arrest and the charge against him.

3. Everyone arrested or detained in accordance with the provisions of paragraph 1(c) of this article shall be brought promptly before a judge or other officer authorized by law to exercise judicial power and shall be entitled to trial within a reasonable time or to release pending trial. Release may be conditioned by guarantees to appear for trial.

4. Everyone who is deprived of his liberty by arrest or detention shall be entitled to take proceedings by which the lawfulness of his detention shall be decided speedily by a court and his release ordered if the detention is not lawful.

5. Everyone who has been the victim of arrest or detention in contravention of the provisions of this article shall have an enforceable right to compensation.

ARTICLE 6

1. In the determination of his civil rights and obligations or of any criminal charge against him, everyone is entitled to a fair and public hearing within a reasonable time by an independent and impartial tribunal established by law. Judgment shall be pronounced publicly by the press and public may be excluded from all or part of the trial in the interest of morals, public order or national security in a democratic society, where the interests of juveniles or the protection of the private life of the parties so require, or the extent strictly necessary in the opinion of the court in special circumstances where publicity would prejudice the interests of justice.

2. Everyone charged with a criminal offence shall be presumed innocent until proved guilty according to law.

3. Everyone charged with a criminal offence has the following minimum rights:

   (a) to be informed promptly, in a language which he understands and in detail, of the nature and cause of the accusation against him;

   (b) to have adequate time and the facilities for the preparation of his defence;

   (c) to defend himself in person or through legal assistance of his own choosing or, if he has not sufficient means to pay for legal assistance, to be given it free when the interests of justice so require;

   (d) to examine or have examined witnesses against him and to obtain the attendance and examination of witnesses on his behalf under the same conditions as witnesses against him;

   (e) to have the free assistance of an interpreter if he cannot understand or speak the language used in court.

ARTICLE 7

1. No one shall be held guilty of any criminal offence on account of any act or omission which did not constitute a criminal offence under national or international law at the time when it was committed. Nor shall a heavier penalty be imposed than the one that was applicable at the time the criminal offence was committed.

2. This article shall not prejudice the trial and punishment of any person for any act or omission which, at the time when it was committed, was criminal according the general principles of law recognized by civilized nations.

ARTICLE 8

1. Everyone has the right to respect for his private and family life, his home and his correspondence.

2. There shall be no interference by a public authority with the exercise of this right except such as is in accordance with the law and is necessary in a democratic society in the interests of national security, public safety or the economic well-being of the country, for the prevention of disorder or crime, for the protection of health or morals, or for the protection of the rights and freedoms of others.

ARTICLE 9

1. Everyone has the right to freedom of thought, conscience and religion; this right includes freedom to change his religion or belief, and freedom, either alone or in community with others and in public or private, to manifest his religion or belief, in worship, teaching, practice and observance.

2. Freedom to manifest one's religion or beliefs shall be subject only to such limitations as are prescribed by law and are necessary in a democratic society in the interests of public safety, for the protection of public order, health or morals, or the protection of the rights and freedoms of others.

ARTICLE 10

1. Everyone has the right to freedom of expression. this right shall include freedom to hold opinions and to receive and impart information and ideas without interference by public authority and regardless of frontiers. This article shall not prevent States from requiring the licensing of broadcasting, television or cinema enterprises.

2. The exercise of these freedoms, since it carries with it duties and responsibilities, may be subject to such formalities, conditions, restrictions or penalties as are prescribed by law and are necessary in a democratic society, in the interests of national security, territorial integrity or public safety, for the prevention of disorder or crime, for the protection of health or morals, for the protection of the reputation or the rights of others, for preventing the disclosure of information received in confidence, or for maintaining the authority and impartiality of the judiciary.

ARTICLE 12

Men and women of marriageable age have the right to marry and to found a family, according to the national laws governing the exercise of this right.

ARTICLE 13

Everyone whose rights and freedoms as set forth in this Convention are violated shall have an effective remedy before a national authority notwithstanding that the violation has been committed by persons acting in an official capacity.

ARTICLE 14

The enjoyment of the rights and freedoms set forth in this Convention shall be secured without discrimination on any ground such as sex, race, colour, language, religion, political or other opinion, national or social origin, association with a national minority, property, birth or other status.

PROTOCOL NO. 13 Concerning the abolition of the death penalty in all circumstances. Vilnius, 3.V.2002

The member States of the Council of Europe signatory hereto, convinced that everyone's right to life is a basic value in a democratic society and that the abolition of the death penalty is essential for the protection of this right and for the full recognition of the inherent dignity of all human beings; wishing to strengthen the protection of the right to life; noting that Protocol No. 6 to the Convention, concerning the abolition of the death penalty, signed at Strasbourg on 28 April 1983, does not exclude the death penalty in respect of acts committed in time of war or of imminent threat of war; being resolved to take the final step in order to abolish the death penalty in all circumstances, have agreed as follows:

Article 1. Abolition of the death penalty

The death penalty shall be abolished. No one shall be condemned to such penalty or executed.

Article 2. Prohibitions of derogations

No derogation from the provisions of this Protocol shall be made under Article 15 of the Convention.

Article 3. Prohibitions of reservations

No reservation may be made under Article 57 of the Convention in respect of the provisions of this Protocol.

Article 4. Territorial application

1. Any state may, at the time of signature or when depositing its instrument of ratification, acceptance or approval, specify the territory or territories to which this Protocol shall apply.

2. Any state may at any later date, by a declaration addressed to the Secretary General of the Council of Europe, extend the application of this Protocol to any other territory specified in the declaration.

APPENDIX 2
Mental Health Act 1983
AS AMENDED BY THE MENTAL HEALTH ACT 2007

Department of Health WARNING

This text has been prepared by Department of Health officials. While every effort has been taken to ensure that it is accurate, it should not relied on as a definitive text of the Act. It has been produced solely to help people understand the effect of the Mental Health Act 2007. It is not intended for use in any other context.

Department of Health, Mental Health Programme

Editors' warning

This amended text has been consolidated, shortened and further edited for this book. A good deal of material has been omitted which is not considered central to the practice of forensic psychiatry.

John Gunn and Pamela Taylor

Editors' preliminary notes

1. The legislation is written as though it is concerned only males but females are intended to be included as well.

2. 'Medical' as a description, e.g. of practitioners, is largely expunged.

3. This text is inaccurate in places partly because of continually changing legislation and partly because of staggered dates of implementation.

4. Part five of the Act has been omitted entirely because mental health review tribunals no longer exist in England, they have been replaced by the first tier of the amalgamated Tribunal (Mental Health) www.mhrt.org.uk/. In Wales they have been replaced by the Mental Health Review Tribunal for Wales www.wikimentalhealth.co.uk/Mental_Health_Review_Tribunal_for_Wales_Rules_2008

PART I

APPLICATION OF ACT

1 Application of Act: 'mental disorder'

(1) The provisions of this Act shall have effect with respect to the reception, care and treatment of mentally disordered patients, the management of their property and other related matters.

(2) In this Act – 'mental disorder' means any disorder or disability of the mind; and 'mentally disordered' shall be construed accordingly; and other expressions shall have the meanings assigned to them in section 145 below.

(2A) But a person with learning disability shall not be considered by reason of that disability to be –

   (a) suffering from mental disorder for the purposes of the provisions mentioned in subsection (2B) below; or

   (b) requiring treatment in hospital for mental disorder for the purposes of sections 17E and 50 to 53 below, unless that disability is associated with abnormally aggressive or seriously irresponsible conduct on his part.

(2B) The provisions are –

   (a) sections 3, 7, 17A, 20 and 20A below;

   (b) sections 35 to 38, 45A, 47, 48 and 51 below; and

   (c) section 72(1) (b) and (c) and (4) below.

PART 2

COMPULSORY ADMISSION TO HOSPITAL AND GUARDIANSHIP

Procedure for hospital admission

2 Admission for assessment

(1) A patient may be admitted to a hospital and detained there for the period allowed by subsection (4) below in pursuance of an application (in this Act referred to as 'an application for admission for assessment') made in accordance with subsections (2) and (3) below.

(2) An application for admission for assessment may be made in respect of a patient on the grounds that –

    (a) he is suffering from mental disorder of a nature or degree which warrants the detention of the patient in a hospital for assessment (or for assessment followed by medical treatment) for at least a limited period; and

    (b) he ought to be so detained in the interests of his own health or safety or with a view to the protection of other persons.

(3) An application for admission for assessment shall be founded on the written recommendations in the prescribed form of two registered medical practitioners, including in each case a statement that in the opinion of the practitioner the conditions set out in subsection (2) above are complied with.

(4) Subject to the provisions of section 29(4) below, a patient admitted to hospital in pursuance of an application for admission for assessment may be detained for a period not exceeding 28 days beginning with the day on which he is admitted, but shall not be detained after the expiration of that period unless before it has expired he has become liable to be detained by virtue of a subsequent application, order or direction under the following provisions of this Act.

3 Admission for treatment

(1) A patient may be admitted to a hospital and detained there for the period allowed by the following provisions of this Act in pursuance of an application (in this Act referred to as 'an application for admission for treatment') made in accordance with this section.

(2) An application for admission for treatment may be made in respect of a patient on the grounds that –

    (a) he is suffering from mental disorder of a nature or degree which makes it appropriate for him to receive medical treatment in a hospital; and

    (c) it is necessary for the health or safety of the patient or for the protection of other persons that he should receive such treatment and it cannot be provided unless he is detained under this section; and

    (d) appropriate medical treatment is available for him.

(3) An application for admission for treatment shall be founded on the written recommendations in the prescribed form of two registered medical practitioners, including in each case a statement that in the opinion of the practitioner the conditions set out in subsection (2) above are complied with; and each such recommendation shall include –

    (a) such particulars as may be prescribed of the grounds for that opinion so far as it relates to the conditions set out in paragraphs (a) of that subsection; and

    (b) a statement of the reasons for that opinion so far as it relates to the conditions set out in paragraph (c) of that subsection, specifying whether other methods of dealing with the patient are available and, if so, why they are not appropriate.

(4) In this Act, references to appropriate medical treatment, in relation to a person suffering from mental disorder, are references to medical treatment which is appropriate in his case, taking into account the nature and degree of the mental disorder and all other circumstances of his case.

4 Admission for assessment in cases of emergency

(1) In any case of urgent necessity, an application for admission for assessment may be made in respect of a patient in accordance with the following provisions of this section, and any application so made is in this Act referred to as 'an emergency application'.

(2) An emergency application may be made either by an approved mental health professional or by the nearest relative of the patient; and every such application shall include a statement that it is of urgent necessity for the patient to be admitted and detained under section 2 above, and that compliance with the provisions of this Part of this Act relating to applications under that section would involve undesirable delay.

(3) An emergency application shall be sufficient in the first instance if founded on one of the medical recommendations required by section 2 above, given, if practicable, by a practitioner who has previous acquaintance with the patient and otherwise complying with the requirements of section 12 below so far as applicable to a single recommendation, and verifying the statement referred to in subsection (2) above.

(4) An emergency application shall cease to have effect on the expiration of a period of 72 hours from the time when the patient is admitted to the hospital unless –

    (a) the second medical recommendation required by section 2 above is given and received by the managers within that period; and

(b) that recommendation and the recommendation referred to in subsection (3) above together comply with all the requirements of section 12 below (other than the requirement as to the time of signature of the second recommendation).

(5) In relation to an emergency application, section 11 below shall have effect as if in subsection (5) of that section for the words 'the period of 14 days ending with the date of the application' there were substituted the words 'the previous 24 hours'.

5 Application in respect of patient already in hospital

(1) An application for the admission of a patient to a hospital may be made under this Part of this Act notwithstanding that the patient is already an in-patient in that hospital or, in the case of an application for admission for treatment, that the patient is for the time being liable to be detained in the hospital in pursuance of an application for admission for assessment; and where an application is so made the patient shall be treated for the purposes of this Part of this Act as if he had been admitted to the hospital at the time when that application was received by the managers.

(2) If, in the case of a patient who is an in-patient in a hospital, it appears to the registered medical practitioner or approved clinician in charge of the treatment of the patient that an application ought to be made under this Part of this Act for the admission of the patient to hospital, he may furnish to the managers a report in writing to that effect; and in any such case the patient may be detained in the hospital for a period of 72 hours from the time when the report is so furnished.

(3) The registered medical practitioner or approved clinician in charge of the treatment of a patient in a hospital may nominate one (but not more than one) person to act for him under subsection (2) above in his absence.

(3A) For the purposes of subsection (3) above –

(a) the registered medical practitioner may nominate another registered medical practitioner, or an approved clinician, on the staff of the hospital; and

(b) the approved clinician may nominate another approved clinician, or a registered medical practitioner, on the staff of the hospital.

(4) If, in the case of a patient who is receiving treatment for mental disorder as an in-patient in a hospital, it appears to a nurse of the prescribed class–

(a) that the patient is suffering from mental disorder to such a degree that it is necessary for his health or safety or for the protection of others for him to be immediately restrained from leaving the hospital; and

(b) that it is not practicable to secure the immediate attendance of a practitioner or clinician for the purpose of furnishing a report under subsection (2) above, the nurse may record that fact in writing; and in that event the patient may be detained in the hospital for a period of six hours from the time when that fact is so recorded or until the earlier arrival at the place where the patient is detained of a practitioner or clinician having power to furnish a report under that subsection.

(5) A record made under subsection (4) above shall be delivered by the nurse (or by a person authorised by the nurse in that behalf) to the managers of the hospital as soon as possible after it is made; and where a record is made under that subsection the period mentioned in subsection (2) above shall begin at the time when it is made.

(6) The reference in subsection (1) above to an in-patient does not include an in-patient who is liable to be detained in pursuance of an application under this Part of this Act or a community patient and the references in subsections (2) and (4) above do not include an in-patient who is liable to be detained in a hospital under this Part of this Act or a community patient.

(7) In subsection (4) above 'prescribed' means prescribed by an order made by the Secretary of State.

6 Effect of application for admission

(1) An application for the admission of a patient to a hospital under this Part of this Act, duly completed in accordance with the provisions of this Part of this Act, shall be sufficient authority for the applicant, or any person authorised by the applicant, to take the patient and convey him to the hospital at any time within the following period, that is to say –

(a) in the case of an application other than an emergency application, the period of 14 days beginning with the date on which the patient was last examined by a registered medical practitioner before giving a medical recommendation for the purposes of the application;

(b) in the case of an emergency application, the period of 24 hours beginning at the time when the patient was examined by the practitioner giving the medical recommendation which is referred to in section 4(3) above, or at the time when the application is made, whichever is the earlier.

(2) Where a patient is admitted within the said period to the hospital specified in such an application as is mentioned in subsection (1) above, or, being within that hospital, is treated by virtue of section 5 above as if he had been so admitted, the application shall be sufficient authority for the managers to detain the patient in the hospital in accordance with the provisions of this Act.

(3) Any application for the admission of a patient under this Part of this Act which appears to be duly made and to be founded on the necessary medical recommendations may be acted upon without further proof of the signature or qualification of the person by whom the application or any such medical recommendation is made or given or of any matter of fact or opinion stated in it.

(4) Where a patient is admitted to a hospital in pursuance of an application for admission for treatment, any previous application under this Part of this Act by virtue of which he was liable to be detained in a hospital or subject to guardianship shall cease to have effect.

Guardianship

7 Application for guardianship

(1) A patient who has attained the age of 16 years may be received into guardianship, for the period allowed by the following provisions of this Act, in pursuance of an application (in this Act referred to as 'a guardianship application') made in accordance with this section.

(2) A guardianship application may be made in respect of a patient on the grounds that –

(a) he is suffering from mental disorder of a nature or degree which warrants his reception into guardianship under this section;

(b) it is necessary in the interests of the welfare of the patient or for the protection of other persons that the patient should be so received.

(3) A guardianship application shall be founded on the written recommendations in the prescribed form of two registered medical practitioners, including in each case a statement that in the opinion of the practitioner the conditions set out in subsection (2) above are complied with; and each such recommendation shall include –

(a) such particulars as may be prescribed of the grounds for that opinion so far as it relates to the conditions set out in paragraph (a) of that subsection; and

(b) a statement of the reasons for that opinion so far as it relates to the conditions set out in paragraph (b) of that subsection.

(4) A guardianship application shall state the age of the patient or, if his exact age is not known to the applicant, shall state (if it be the fact) that the patient is believed to have attained the age of 16 years.

(5) The person named as guardian in a guardianship application may be either a local social services authority or any other person (including the applicant himself); but a guardianship application in which a person other than a local social services authority is named as guardian shall be of no effect unless it is accepted on behalf of that person by the local social services authority for the area in which he resides, and shall be accompanied by a statement in writing by that person that he is willing to act as guardian.

8 Effect of guardianship application, etc

(1) Where a guardianship application, duly made under the provisions of this Part of this Act and forwarded to the local social services authority within the period allowed by subsection (2) below is accepted by that authority, the application shall, subject to regulations made by the Secretary of State, confer on the authority or person named in the application as guardian, to the exclusion of any other person –

(a) the power to require the patient to reside at a place specified by the authority or person named as guardian;

(b) the power to require the patient to attend at places and times so specified for the purpose of medical treatment, occupation, education or training;

(c) the power to require access to the patient to be given, at any place where the patient is residing, to any registered medical practitioner, approved mental health professional or other person so specified.

(2) The period within which a guardianship application is required for the purposes of this section to be forwarded to the local social services authority is the period of 14 days beginning with the date on which the patient was last examined by a registered medical practitioner before giving a medical recommendation for the purposes of the application.

(3) A guardianship application which appears to be duly made and to be founded on the necessary medical recommendations may be acted upon without further proof of the signature or qualification of the person by whom the application or any such medical recommendation is made or given, or of any matter of fact or opinion stated in the application.

(4) If within the period of 14 days beginning with the day on which a guardianship application has been accepted by the local social services authority the application, or any medical recommendation given for the purposes of the application, is found to be in any respect incorrect or defective, the application or recommendation may, within that period and with the consent of that authority, be amended by the person by whom it was signed; and upon such amendment being made the application or recommendation shall have effect and shall be deemed to have had effect as if it had been originally made as so amended.

(5) Where a patient is received into guardianship in pursuance of a guardianship application, any previous application under this Part of this Act by virtue of which he was subject to guardianship or liable to be detained in a hospital shall cease to have effect.

9 Regulations as to guardianship

(1) Subject to the provisions of this Part of this Act, the Secretary of State may make regulations –

(a) for regulating the exercise by the guardians of patients received into guardianship under this Part of this Act of their powers as such; and

(b) for imposing on such guardians, and upon local social services authorities in the case of patients under the guardianship of persons other than local social services authorities, such duties as he considers necessary or expedient in the interests of the patients.

(2) Regulations under this section may in particular make provision for requiring the patients to be visited, on such occasions or at such intervals as may be prescribed by the regulations, on behalf of such local social services authorities as may be so prescribed,

and shall provide for the appointment, in the case of every patient subject to the guardianship of a person other than a local social services authority, of a registered medical practitioner to act as the nominated medical attendant of the patient.

General provisions as to applications and recommendations

11 General provisions as to applications

(1)   Subject to the provisions of this section, an application for admission for assessment, an application for admission for treatment and a guardianship application may be made either by the nearest relative of the patient or by an approved mental health professional; and every such application shall specify the qualification of the applicant to make the application.

(1A) No application mentioned in subsection (1) above shall be made by an approved mental health professional if the circumstances are such that there would be a potential conflict of interest for the purposes of regulations under section 12A below.

(2)   Every application for admission shall be addressed to the managers of the hospital to which admission is sought and every guardianship application shall be forwarded to the local social services authority named in the application as guardian, or, as the case may be, to the local social services authority for the area in which the person so named resides.

(3)   Before or within a reasonable time after an application for the admission of a patient for assessment is made by an approved mental health professional, that professional shall take such steps as are practicable to inform the person (if any) appearing to be the nearest relative of the patient that the application is to be or has been made and of the power of the nearest relative under section 23(2) (a) below.

(4)   An approved mental health professional may not make an application for admission for treatment or a guardianship application in respect of a patient in either of the following cases –

(a) the nearest relative of the patient has notified that professional, or the local social services authority on whose behalf the professional is acting, that he objects to the application being made; or

(b) that professional has not consulted the person (if any) appearing to be the nearest relative of the patient, but the requirement to consult that person does not apply if it appears to the professional that in the circumstances such consultation is not reasonably practicable or would involve unreasonable delay.

(5)   None of the applications mentioned in subsection (1) above shall be made by any person in respect of a patient unless that person has personally seen the patient within the period of 14 days ending with the date of the application.

(7)   Each of the applications mentioned in subsection (1) above shall be sufficient if the recommendations on which it is founded are given either as separate recommendations, each signed by a registered medical practitioner, or as a joint recommendation signed by two such practitioners.

12 General provisions as to medical recommendations

(1)   The recommendations required for the purposes of an application for the admission of a patient under this Part of this Act or a guardianship application (in this Act referred to as 'medical recommendations') shall be signed on or before the date of the application, and shall be given by practitioners who have personally examined the patient either together or separately, but where they have examined the patient separately not more than five days must have elapsed between the days on which the separate examinations took place.

(2)   Of the medical recommendations given for the purposes of any such application, one shall be given by a practitioner approved for the purposes of this section by the Secretary of State as having special experience in the diagnosis or treatment of mental disorder; and unless that practitioner has previous acquaintance with the patient, the other such recommendation shall, if practicable, be given by a registered medical practitioner who has such previous acquaintance.

(2A) A registered medical practitioner who is an approved clinician shall be treated as also approved for the purposes of this section under subsection (2) above as having special experience as mentioned there.

(3)   No medical recommendation shall be given for the purposes of an application mentioned in subsection (1) above if the circumstances are such that there would be a potential conflict of interest for the purposes of regulations under section 12A below.

12A Conflicts of interest

(1) The appropriate national authority may make regulations as to the circumstances in which there would be a potential conflict of interest such that—

(a) an approved mental health professional shall not make an application mentioned in section 11(1) above;

(b) a registered medical practitioner shall not give a recommendation for the purposes of an application mentioned in section 12(1) above.

(2) Regulations under subsection (1) above may make –

(a) provision for the prohibitions in paragraphs (a) and (b) of that subsection to be subject to specified exceptions;

(b) different provision for different cases; and

(c) transitional, consequential, incidental or supplemental provision.

(3) In subsection (1) above, 'the appropriate national authority' means –

    (a) in relation to applications in which admission is sought to a hospital in England or to guardianship applications in respect of which the area of the relevant local social services authority is in England, the Secretary of State;

    (b) in relation to applications in which admission is sought to a hospital in Wales or to guardianship applications in respect of which the area of the relevant local social services authority is in Wales, the Welsh Ministers.

(4) References in this section to the relevant local social services authority, in relation to a guardianship application, are references to the local social services authority named in the application as guardian or (as the case may be) the local social services authority for the area in which the person so named resides.

13 Duty of approved mental health professionals to make applications for admission or guardianship

(1) If a local social services authority has reason to think that an application for admission to hospital or a guardianship application may need to be made in respect of a patient within their area, they shall make arrangements for an approved mental health professional to consider the patient's case on their behalf.

(1A) If that professional is –

    (a) satisfied that such an application ought to be made in respect of the patient; and

    (b) of the opinion, having regard to any wishes expressed by relatives of the patient or any other relevant circumstances, that it is necessary or proper for the application to be made by him, he shall make the application.

(1B) Subsection (1C) below applies where –

    (a) a local social services authority makes arrangements under subsection (1) above in respect of a patient;

    (b) an application for admission for assessment is made under subsection (1A) above in respect of the patient;

    (c) while the patient is liable to be detained in pursuance of that application, the authority have reason to think that an application for admission for treatment may need to be made in respect of the patient; and

    (d) the patient is not within the area of the authority.

(1C) Where this subsection applies, subsection (1) above shall be construed as requiring the authority to make arrangements under that subsection in place of the authority mentioned there.

(2) Before making an application for the admission of a patient to hospital an approved mental health professional shall interview the patient in a suitable manner and satisfy himself that detention in a hospital is in all the circumstances of the case the most appropriate way of providing the care and medical treatment of which the patient stands in need.

(3) An application under subsection (1A) above may be made outside the area of the local social services authority on whose behalf the approved mental health professional is considering the patient's case.

(4) It shall be the duty of a local social services authority, if so required by the nearest relative of a patient residing in their area, to make arrangements under subsection (1) above for an approved mental health professional to consider the patient's case with a view to making an application for his admission to hospital; and if in any such case that professional decides not to make an application he shall inform the nearest relative of his reasons in writing.

(5) Nothing in this section shall be construed as authorising or requiring an application to be made by an approved mental health professional in contravention of the provisions of section 11(4) above or of regulations under section 12A above, or as restricting the power of a local social services authority to make arrangements with an approved mental health professional to consider a patient's case or of an approved mental health professional to make any application under this Act.

15 Rectification of applications and recommendations

(1) If within the period of 14 days beginning with the day on which a patient has been admitted to a hospital in pursuance of an application for admission for assessment or for treatment the application, or any medical recommendation given for the purposes of the application, is found to be in any respect incorrect or defective, the application or recommendation may, within that period and with the consent of the managers of the hospital, be amended by the person by whom it was signed; and upon such amendment being made the application or recommendation shall have effect and shall be deemed to have had effect as if it had been originally made as so amended.

(2) Without prejudice to subsection (1) above, if within the period mentioned in that subsection it appears to the managers of the hospital that one of the two medical recommendations on which an application for the admission of a patient is founded is insufficient to warrant the detention of the patient in pursuance of the application, they may, within that period, give notice in writing to that effect to the applicant; and where any such notice is given in respect of a medical recommendation, that recommendation shall be disregarded, but the application shall be, and shall be deemed always to have been, sufficient if –

    (a) a fresh medical recommendation complying with the relevant provisions of this Part of this Act (other than the provisions relating to the time of signature and the interval between examinations) is furnished to the managers within that period; and

    (b) that recommendation, and the other recommendation on which the application is founded, together comply with those provisions.

(3) Where the medical recommendations upon which an application for admission is founded are, taken together, insufficient to warrant the detention of the patient in pursuance of the application, a notice under subsection (2) above may be given in respect of either of those recommendations.

(4) Nothing in this section shall be construed as authorising the giving of notice in respect of an application made as an emergency application, or the detention of a patient admitted in pursuance of such an application, after the period of 72 hours referred to in section 4(4) above, unless the conditions set out in paragraphs (a) and (b) of that section are complied with or would be complied with apart from any error or defect to which this section applies.

17 Leave of absence from hospital

(1) The responsible clinician may grant to any patient who is for the time being liable to be detained in a hospital under this Part of this Act leave to be absent from the hospital subject to such conditions (if any) as that clinician considers necessary in the interests of the patient or for the protection of other persons.

(2) Leave of absence may be granted to a patient under this section either indefinitely or on specified occasions or for any specified period; and where leave is so granted for a specified period, that period may be extended by further leave granted in the absence of the patient.

(2A) But longer-term leave may not be granted to a patient unless the responsible clinician first considers whether the patient should be dealt with under section 17A instead.

(2B) For these purposes, longer-term leave is granted to a patient if –

(a) leave of absence is granted to him under this section either indefinitely or for a specified period of more than seven consecutive days; or

(b) a specified period is extended under this section such that the total period for which leave of absence will have been granted to him under this section exceeds seven consecutive days.

(3) Where it appears to the responsible clinician that it is necessary so to do in the interests of the patient or for the protection of other persons, he may, upon granting leave of absence under this section, direct that the patient remain in custody during his absence; and where leave of absence is so granted the patient may be kept in the custody of any officer on the staff of the hospital, or of any other person authorised in writing by the managers of the hospital or, if the patient is required in accordance with conditions imposed on the grant of leave of absence to reside in another hospital, of any officer on the staff of that other hospital.

(4) In any case where a patient is absent from a hospital in pursuance of leave of absence granted under this section, and it appears to the responsible clinician that it is necessary so to do in the interests of the patient's health or safety or for the protection of other persons, that clinician may, subject to subsection (5) below, by notice in writing given to the patient or to the person for the time being in charge of the patient, revoke the leave of absence and recall the patient to the hospital.

(5) A patient to whom leave of absence is granted under this section shall not be recalled under subsection (4) above after he has ceased to be liable to be detained under this Part of this Act.

(6) Subsection (7) below applies to a person who is granted leave by or by virtue of a provision –

(a) in force in Scotland, Northern Ireland, any of the Channel Islands or the Isle of Man; and

(b) corresponding to subsection (1) above.

(7) For the purpose of giving effect to a direction or condition imposed by virtue of a provision corresponding to subsection (3) above, the person may be conveyed to a place in, or kept in custody or detained at a place of safety in, England and Wales by a person authorised in that behalf by the direction or condition.

17A Community treatment orders

(1) The responsible clinician may by order in writing discharge a detained patient from hospital subject to his being liable to recall in accordance with section 17E below.

(2) A detained patient is a patient who is liable to be detained in a hospital in pursuance of an application for admission for treatment.

(3) An order under subsection (1) above is referred to in this Act as a 'community treatment order'.

(4) The responsible clinician may not make a community treatment order unless –

(a) in his opinion, the relevant criteria are met; and

(b) an approved mental health professional states in writing –

(i) that he agrees with that opinion; and

(ii) that it is appropriate to make the order.

(5) The relevant criteria are –

(a) the patient is suffering from mental disorder of a nature or degree which makes it appropriate for him to receive medical treatment;

(b) it is necessary for his health or safety or for the protection of other persons that he should receive such treatment;

(c) subject to his being liable to be recalled as mentioned in paragraph (d) below, such treatment can be provided without his continuing to be detained in a hospital;

(d) it is necessary that the responsible clinician should be able to exercise the power under section 17E (1) below to recall the patient to hospital;

(e) appropriate medical treatment is available for him.

(6) In determining whether the criterion in subsection (5)(d) above is met, the responsible clinician shall, in particular, consider, having regard to the patient's history of mental disorder and any other relevant factors, what risk there would be of a deterioration of the patient's condition if he were not detained in a hospital (as a result, for example, of his refusing or neglecting to receive the medical treatment he requires for his mental disorder).

(7) In this Act –

'community patient' means a patient in respect of whom a community treatment order is in force;

'the community treatment order', in relation to such a patient, means the community treatment order in force in respect of him; and

'the responsible hospital', in relation to such a patient, means the hospital in which he was liable to be detained immediately before the community treatment order was made, subject to section 19A below.

17B Conditions

(1) A community treatment order shall specify conditions to which the patient is to be subject while the order remains in force.

(2) But, subject to subsection (3) below, the order may specify conditions only if the responsible clinician, with the agreement of the approved mental health professional mentioned in section 17A(4)(b) above, thinks them necessary or appropriate for one or more of the following purposes –

(a) ensuring that the patient receives medical treatment;

(b) preventing risk of harm to the patient's health or safety;

(c) protecting other persons.

(3) The order shall specify –

(a) a condition that the patient make himself available for examination under section 20A below; and

(b) a condition that, if it is proposed to give a certificate under Part 4A of this Act in his case, he make himself available for examination so as to enable the certificate to be given.

(4) The responsible clinician may from time to time by order in writing vary the conditions specified in a community treatment order.

(5) He may also suspend any conditions specified in a community treatment order.

(6) If a community patient fails to comply with a condition specified in the community treatment order by virtue of subsection (2) above, that fact may be taken into account for the purposes of exercising the power of recall under section 17E (1) below.

(7) But nothing in this section restricts the exercise of that power to cases where there is such a failure.

17C Duration of community treatment order

A community treatment order shall remain in force until –

(a) the period mentioned in section 20A(1) below (as extended under any provision of this Act) expires, but this is subject to sections 21 and 22 below;

(b) the patient is discharged in pursuance of an order under section 23 below or a direction under section 72 below;

(c) the application for admission for treatment in respect of the patient otherwise ceases to have effect; or

(d) the order is revoked under section 17F below, whichever occurs first.

17D Effect of community treatment order

(1) The application for admission for treatment in respect of a patient shall not cease to have effect by virtue of his becoming a community patient.

(2) But while he remains a community patient –

(a) the authority of the managers to detain him under section 6(2) above in pursuance of that application shall be suspended; and

(b) reference (however expressed) in this or any other Act, or in any subordinate legislation (within the meaning of the Interpretation Act 1978), to patients liable to be detained, or detained, under this Act shall not include him.

(3) And section 20 below shall not apply to him while he remains a community patient.

(4) Accordingly, authority for his detention shall not expire during any period in which that authority is suspended by virtue of subsection (2)(a) above.

17E Power to recall to hospital

(1) The responsible clinician may recall a community patient to hospital if in his opinion –

    (a) the patient requires medical treatment in hospital for his mental disorder; and

    (b) there would be a risk of harm to the health or safety of the patient or to other persons if the patient were not recalled to hospital for that purpose.

(2) The responsible clinician may also recall a community patient to hospital if the patient fails to comply with a condition specified under section 17B(3) above.

(3) The hospital to which a patient is recalled need not be the responsible hospital.

(4) Nothing in this section prevents a patient from being recalled to a hospital even though he is already in the hospital at the time when the power of recall is exercised; references to recalling him shall be construed accordingly.

(5) The power of recall under subsections (1) and (2) above shall be exercisable by notice in writing to the patient.

(6) A notice under this section recalling a patient to hospital shall be sufficient authority for the managers of that hospital to detain the patient there in accordance with the provisions of this Act.

17F Powers in respect of recalled patients

(1) This section applies to a community patient who is detained in a hospital by virtue of a notice recalling him there under section 17E above.

(2) The patient may be transferred to another hospital in such circumstances and subject to such conditions as may be prescribed in regulations made by the Secretary of State (if the hospital in which the patient is detained is in England) or the Welsh Ministers (if that hospital is in Wales).

(3) If he is so transferred to another hospital, he shall be treated for the purposes of this section (and section 17E above) as if the notice under that section were a notice recalling him to that other hospital and as if he had been detained there from the time when his detention in hospital by virtue of the notice first began.

(4) The responsible clinician may by order in writing revoke the community treatment order if –

    (a) in his opinion the conditions mentioned in section 3(2) above are satisfied in respect of the patient; and

    (b) an approved mental health professional states in writing –

        (i) that he agrees with that opinion; and

        (ii) that it is appropriate to revoke the order.

(5) The responsible clinician may at any time release the patient, but not after the community treatment order has been revoked.

(6) If the patient has not been released, nor the community treatment order revoked, by the end of the period of 72 hours, he shall then be released.

(7) But a patient who is released under this section remains subject to the community treatment order.

(8) In this section –

    (a) 'the period of 72 hours' means the period of 72 hours beginning with the time when the patient's detention in hospital by virtue of the notice under section 17E above begins; and

    (b) references to being released shall be construed as references to being released from that detention (and accordingly from being recalled to hospital).

17G Effect of revoking community treatment order

(1) This section applies if a community treatment order is revoked under section 17F above in respect of a patient.

(2) Section 6(2) above shall have effect as if the patient had never been discharged from hospital by virtue of the community treatment order.

(3) The provisions of this or any other Act relating to patients liable to be detained (or detained) in pursuance of an application for admission for treatment shall apply to the patient as they did before the community treatment order was made, unless otherwise provided.

(4) If, when the order is revoked, the patient is being detained in a hospital other than the responsible hospital, the provisions of this Part of this Act shall have effect as if –

    (a) the application for admission for treatment in respect of him were an application for admission to that other hospital; and

    (b) he had been admitted to that other hospital at the time when he was originally admitted in pursuance of the application.

(5) But, in any case, section 20 below shall have effect as if the patient had been admitted to hospital in pursuance of the application for admission for treatment on the day on which the order is revoked.

18 Return and readmission of patients absent without leave

(1) Where a patient who is for the time being liable to be detained under this Part of this Act in a hospital –

    (a) absents himself from the hospital without leave granted under section 17 above; or

(b) fails to return to the hospital on any occasion on which, or at the expiration of any period for which, leave of absence was granted to him under that section, or upon being recalled under that section; or

(c) absents himself without permission from any place where he is required to reside in accordance with conditions imposed on the grant of leave of absence under that section, he may, subject to the provisions of this section, be taken into custody and returned to the hospital or place by any approved mental health professional, by any officer on the staff of the hospital, by any constable, or by any person authorised in writing by the managers of the hospital.

(2) Where the place referred to in paragraph (c) of subsection (1) above is a hospital other than the one in which the patient is for the time being liable to be detained, the references in that subsection to an officer on the staff of the hospital and the managers of the hospital shall respectively include references to an officer on the staff of the first-mentioned hospital and the managers of that hospital.

(2A) Where a community patient is at any time absent from a hospital to which he is recalled under section 17E above, he may, subject to the provisions of this section, be taken into custody and returned to the hospital by any approved mental health professional, by any officer on the staff of the hospital, by any constable, or by any person authorised in writing by the responsible clinician or the managers of the hospital.

(3) Where a patient who is for the time being subject to guardianship under this Part of this Act absents himself without the leave of the guardian from the place at which he is required by the guardian to reside, he may, subject to the provisions of this section, be taken into custody and returned to that place by any officer on the staff of a local social services authority, by any constable, or by any person authorised in writing by the guardian or a local social services authority.

(4) A patient shall not be taken into custody under this section after the later of –

(a) the end of the period of six months beginning with the first day of his absence without leave; and

(b) the end of the period for which (apart from section 21 below) he is liable to be detained or subject to guardianship or, in the case of a community patient, the community treatment order is in force.

(4A) In determining for the purposes of subsection (4)(b) above or any other provision of this Act whether a person who is or has been absent without leave is at any time liable to be detained or subject to guardianship, a report furnished under section 20 or 21B below before the first day of his absence without leave shall not be taken to have renewed the authority for his detention or guardianship unless the period of renewal began before that day.

(4B) Similarly, in determining for those purposes whether a community treatment order is at any time in force in respect of a person who is or has been absent without leave, a report furnished under section 20A or 21B below before the first day of his absence without leave shall not be taken to have extended the community treatment period unless the extension began before that day.

(5) A patient shall not be taken into custody under this section if the period for which he is liable to be detained is that specified in section 2(4), 4(4) or 5(2) or (4) above and that period has expired.

(6) In this Act 'absent without leave' means absent from any hospital or other place and liable to be taken into custody and returned under this section, and related expressions shall be construed accordingly.

(7) In relation to a patient who has yet to comply with a requirement imposed by virtue of this Act to be in a hospital or place, references in this Act to his liability to be returned to the hospital or place shall include his liability to be taken to that hospital or place; and related expressions shall be construed accordingly.

Duration of authority and discharge

20 Duration of authority

(1) Subject to the following provisions of this Part of this Act, a patient admitted to hospital in pursuance of an application for admission for treatment, and a patient placed under guardianship in pursuance of a guardianship application, may be detained in a hospital or kept under guardianship for a period not exceeding six months beginning with the day on which he was so admitted, or the day on which the guardianship application was accepted, as the case may be, but shall not be so detained or kept for any longer period unless the authority for his detention or guardianship is renewed under this section.

(2) Authority for the detention or guardianship of a patient may, unless the patient has previously been discharged under section 23 below, be renewed –

(a) from the expiration of the period referred to in subsection (1) above, for a further period of six months;

(b) from the expiration of any period of renewal under paragraph (a) above, for a further period of one year, and so on for periods of one year at a time.

(3) Within the period of two months ending on the day on which a patient who is liable to be detained in pursuance of an application for admission for treatment would cease under this section to be so liable in default of the renewal of the authority for his detention, it shall be the duty of the responsible clinician –

(a) to examine the patient; and

(b) if it appears to him that the conditions in subsection (4) below are satisfied, to furnish to the managers of the hospital where the patient is detained a report to that effect in the prescribed form;

and where such a report is furnished in respect of a patient the managers shall, unless they discharge the patient under section 23 below, cause him to be informed.

(4) The conditions referred to in subsection (3) above are that –

(a) the patient is suffering from mental disorder of a nature or degree which makes it appropriate for him to receive medical treatment in a hospital; and

(c) it is necessary for the health or safety of the patient or for the protection of other persons that he should receive such treatment and that it cannot be provided unless he continues to be detained; and

(d) appropriate medical treatment is available for him.

(5) Before furnishing a report under subsection (3) above the responsible clinician shall consult one or more other persons who have been professionally concerned with the patient's medical treatment.

(5A) But the responsible clinician may not furnish a report under subsection (3) above unless a person –

(a) who has been professionally concerned with the patient's medical treatment; but

(b) who belongs to a profession other than that to which the responsible clinician belongs, states in writing that he agrees that the conditions set out in subsection (4) above are satisfied.

(6) Within the period of two months ending with the day on which a patient who is subject to guardianship under this Part of this Act would cease under this section to be so liable in default of the renewal of the authority for his guardianship, it shall be the duty of the appropriate practitioner –

(a) to examine the patient; and

(b) if it appears to him that the conditions set out in subsection (7) below are satisfied, to furnish to the guardian and, where the guardian is a person other than a local social services authority, to the responsible local social services authority a report to that effect in the prescribed form;

and where such a report is furnished in respect of a patient, the local social services authority shall, unless they discharge the patient under section 23 below, cause him to be informed.

(7) The conditions referred to in subsection (6) above are that –

(a) the patient is suffering from mental disorder of a nature or degree which warrants his reception into guardianship; and

(b) it is necessary in the interests of the welfare of the patient or for the protection of other persons that the patient should remain under guardianship.

(8) Where a report is duly furnished under subsection (3) or (6) above, the authority for the detention or guardianship of the patient shall be thereby renewed for the period prescribed in that case by subsection (2) above.

20A Community treatment period

(1) Subject to the provisions of this Part, a community treatment order shall cease to be in force on expiry of the period of six months beginning with the day on which it was made.

(2) That period is referred to in this Act as 'the community treatment period'.

(3) The community treatment period may, unless the order has previously ceased to be in force, be extended –

(a) from its expiration for a period of six months;

(b) from the expiration of any period of extension under paragraph (a) above for a further period of one year, and so on for periods of one year at a time.

(4) Within the period of two months ending on the day on which the order would cease to be in force in default of an extension under this section, it shall be the duty of the responsible clinician –

(a) to examine the patient; and

(b) if it appears to him that the conditions set out in subsection (6) below are satisfied and if a statement under subsection (8) is made, to furnish to the managers of the responsible hospital a report to that effect in the prescribed form.

(5) Where such a report is furnished in respect of the patient, the managers shall, unless they discharge him under section 23 below, cause him to be informed.

(6) The conditions referred to in subsection (4) above are that –

(a) the patient is suffering from mental disorder of a nature or degree which makes it appropriate for him to receive medical treatment;

(b) it is necessary for his health or safety or for the protection of other persons that he should receive such treatment; &(macr;c) subject to his continuing to be liable to be recalled as mentioned in paragraph (d)below, such treatment can be provided without his being detained in a hospital;

(d) it is necessary that the responsible clinician should continue to be able to exercise the power under section 17E(1) above to recall the patient to hospital; and

(e) appropriate medical treatment is available for him.

(7)   In determining whether the criterion in subsection (6)(d) above is met, the responsible clinician shall, in particular, consider, having regard to the patient's history of mental disorder and any other relevant factors, what risk there would be of a deterioration of the patient's condition if he were to continue not to be detained in a hospital (as a result, for example, of his refusing or neglecting to receive the medical treatment he requires for his mental disorder).

(8)   The statement referred to in subsection (4) above is a statement in writing by an approved mental health professional –

   (a) that it appears to him that the conditions set out in subsection (6) above are satisfied; and

   (b) that it is appropriate to extend the community treatment period.

(9)   Before furnishing a report under subsection (4) above the responsible clinician shall consult one or more other persons who have been professionally concerned with the patient's medical treatment.

(10) Where a report is duly furnished under subsection (4) above, the community treatment period shall be thereby extended for the period prescribed in that case by subsection (3) above.

20B Effect of expiry of community treatment order

(1)   A community patient shall be deemed to be discharged absolutely from liability to recall under this Part of this Act, and the application for admission for treatment cease to have effect, on expiry of the community treatment order, if the order has not previously ceased to be in force.

(2)   For the purposes of subsection (1) above, a community treatment order expires on expiry of the community treatment period as extended under this Part of this Act, but this is subject to sections 21 and 22 below.

21 Special provisions as to patients absent without leave

(1)   Where a patient is absent without leave –

   (a) on the day on which (apart from this section) he would cease to be liable to be detained or subject to guardianship under this Part of this Act or, in the case of a community patient, the community treatment order would cease to be in force; or

   (b) within the period of one week ending with that day, he shall not cease to be so liable or subject, or the order shall not cease to be in force, until the relevant time.

(2)   For the purposes of subsection (1) above the relevant time –

   (a) where the patient is taken into custody under section 18 above, is the end of the period of one week beginning with the day on which he is returned to the hospital or place where he ought to be;

   (b) where the patient returns himself to the hospital or place where he ought to be within the period during which he can be taken into custody under section 18 above, is the end of the period of one week beginning with the day on which he so returns himself; and

   (c) otherwise, is the end of the period during which he can be taken into custody under section 18 above.

(3)   Where a patient is absent without leave on the day on which (apart from this section) the managers would be required under section 68 below to refer the patient's case to a Mental Health Review Tribunal, that requirement shall not apply unless and until –

   (a) the patient is taken into custody under section 18 above and returned to the hospital where he ought to be; or

   (b) the patient returns himself to the hospital where he ought to be within the period during which he can be taken into custody under section 18 above.

(4)   Where a community patient is absent without leave on the day on which (apart from this section) the 72-hour period mentioned in section 17F above would expire, that period shall not expire until the end of the period of 72 hours beginning with the time when –

   (a) the patient is taken into custody under section 18 above and returned to the hospital where he ought to be; or

   (b) the patient returns himself to the hospital where he ought to be within the period during which he can be taken into custody under section 18 above.

(5)   Any reference in this section, or in sections 21A to 22 below, to the time when a community treatment order would cease, or would have ceased, to be in force shall be construed as a reference to the time when it would cease, or would have ceased, to be in force by reason only of the passage of time.

21A Patients who are taken into custody or return within 28 days

(1)   This section applies where a patient who is absent without leave is taken into custody under section 18 above, or returns himself to the hospital or place where he ought to be, not later than the end of the period of 28 days beginning with the first day of his absence without leave.

(2)   Where the period for which the patient is liable to be detained or subject to guardianship is extended by section 21 above, any examination and report to be made and furnished in respect of the patient under section 20(3) or (6) above may be made and furnished within the period as so extended.

(3) Where the authority for the detention or guardianship of the patient is renewed by virtue of subsection (2) above after the day on which (apart from section 21 above) that authority would have expired, the renewal shall take effect as from that day.

(4) In the case of a community patient, where the period for which the community treatment order is in force is extended by section 21 above, any examination and report to be made and furnished in respect of the patient under section 20A(4) above may be made and furnished within the period as so extended.

(5) Where the community treatment period is extended by virtue of subsection (4) above after the day on which (apart from section 21 above) the order would have ceased to be in force, the extension shall take effect as from that day.

21B Patients who are taken into custody or return after more than 28 days

(1) This section applies where a patient who is absent without leave is taken into custody under section 18 above, or returns himself to the hospital or place where he ought to be, later than the end of the period of 28 days beginning with the first day of his absence without leave.

(2) It shall be the duty of the appropriate practitioner, within the period of one week beginning with the day on which the patient is returned or returns himself to the hospital or place where he ought to be (his 'return day') –

    (a) to examine the patient; and

    (b) if it appears to him that the relevant conditions are satisfied, to furnish to the appropriate body a report to that effect in the prescribed form;

and where such a report is furnished in respect of the patient the appropriate body shall cause him to be informed.

(3) Where the patient is liable to be detained or is a community patient (as opposed to subject to guardianship) the appropriate practitioner shall, before furnishing a report under subsection (2) above, consult –

    (a) one or more other persons who have been professionally concerned with the patient's medical treatment; and

    (b) an approved mental health professional.

(4) Where –

    (a) the patient would (apart from any renewal of the authority for his detention or guardianship on or after his return day) be liable to be detained or subject to guardianship after the end of the period of one week beginning with that day; or

    (b) in the case of a community patient, the community treatment order would (apart from any extension of the community treatment period on or after that day) be in force after the end of that period,

he shall cease to be so liable or subject, or the community treatment period shall be deemed to expire, at the end of that period unless a report is duly furnished in respect of him under subsection (2) above.

(4A) If, in the case of a community patient, the community treatment order is revoked under section 17F above during the period of one week beginning with his return day –

    (a) subsections (2) and (4) above shall not apply; and

    (b) any report already furnished in respect of him under subsection (2) above shall be of no effect.

(5) Where the patient would (apart from section 21 above) have ceased to be liable to be detained or subject to guardianship on or before the day on which a report is duly furnished in respect of him under subsection (2) above, the report shall renew the authority for his detention or guardianship for the period prescribed in that case by section 20(2) above.

(6) Where the authority for the detention or guardianship of the patient is renewed by virtue of subsection (5) above –

    (a) the renewal shall take effect as from the day on which (apart from section 21 above and that subsection) the authority would have expired; and

    (b) if (apart from this paragraph) the renewed authority would expire on or before the day on which the report is furnished, the report shall further renew the authority, as from the day on which it would expire, for the period prescribed in that case by section 20(2) above.

(6A) In the case of a community patient, where the community treatment order would (apart from section 21 above) have ceased to be in force on or before the day on which a report is duly furnished in respect of him under subsection (2) above, the report shall extend the community treatment period for the period prescribed in that case by section 20A(3) above.

(6B) Where the community treatment period is extended by virtue of subsection (6A) above –

    (a) the extension shall take effect as from the day on which (apart from section 21 above and that subsection) the order would have ceased to be in force; and

    (b) if (apart from this paragraph) the period as so extended would expire on or before the day on which the report is furnished, the report shall further extend that period, as from the day on which it would expire, for the period prescribed in that case by section 20A(3) above.

(7) Where the authority for the detention or guardianship of the patient would expire within the period of two months beginning with the day on which a report is duly furnished in respect of him under subsection (2) above, the report shall, if it so provides,

have effect also as a report duly furnished under section 20(3) or (6) above; and the reference in this subsection to authority includes any authority renewed under subsection (5) above by the report.

(7A) In the case of a community patient, where the community treatment order would (taking account of any extension under subsection (6A) above) cease to be in force within the period of two months beginning with the day on which a report is duly furnished in respect of him under subsection (2) above, the report shall, if it so provides, have effect also as a report duly furnished under section 20A(4) above.

(10) In this section –

'the appropriate body' means –

(a) in relation to a patient who is liable to be detained in a hospital, the managers of the hospital;

(b) in relation to a patient who is subject to guardianship, the responsible local social services authority;

(c) in relation to a community patient, the managers of the responsible hospital; and 'the relevant conditions' means –

(a) in relation to a patient who is liable to be detained in a hospital, the conditions set out in subsection (4) of section 20 above;

(b) in relation to a patient who is subject to guardianship, the conditions set out in subsection (7) of that section;

(c) in relation to a community patient, the conditions set out in section 20A(6) above.

22 Special provisions as to patients sentenced to imprisonment, etc

(1) If –

(a) a qualifying patient is detained in custody in pursuance of any sentence or order passed or made by a court in the United Kingdom (including an order committing or remanding him in custody); and

(b) he is so detained for a period exceeding, or for successive periods exceeding in the aggregate, six months, the relevant application shall cease to have effect on expiry of that period.

(2) A patient is a qualifying patient for the purposes of this section if –

(a) he is liable to be detained by virtue of an application for admission for treatment;

(b) he is subject to guardianship by virtue of a guardianship application; or

(c) he is a community patient.

(3) 'The relevant application', in relation to a qualifying patient, means –

(a) in the case of a patient who is subject to guardianship, the guardianship application in respect of him;

(b) in any other case, the application for admission for treatment in respect of him.

(4) The remaining subsections of this section shall apply if a qualifying patient is detained in custody as mentioned in subsection (1)(a) above but for a period not exceeding, or for successive periods not exceeding in the aggregate, six months.

(5) If apart from this subsection –

(a) the patient would have ceased to be liable to be detained or subject to guardianship by virtue of the relevant application on or before the day on which he is discharged from custody; or

(b) in the case of a community patient, the community treatment order would have ceased to be in force on or before that day, he shall not cease and shall be deemed not to have ceased to be so liable or subject, or the order shall not cease and shall be deemed not to have ceased to be in force, until the end of that day.

(6) In any case (except as provided in subsection (8) below), sections 18, 21 and 21A above shall apply in relation to the patient as if he had absented himself without leave on that day.

(7) In its application by virtue of subsection (6) above section 18 shall have effect as if –

(a) in subsection (4) for the words from 'later of' to the end there were substituted 'end of the period of 28 days beginning with the first day of his absence without leave'; and

(b) subsections (4A) and (4B) were omitted.

(8) In relation to a community patient who was not recalled to hospital under section 17E above at the time when his detention in custody began –

(a) section 18 above shall not apply; but

(b) sections 21 and 21A above shall apply as if he had absented himself without leave on the day on which he is discharged from custody and had returned himself as provided in those sections on the last day of the period of 28 days beginning with that day.

23 Discharge of patients

(1) Subject to the provisions of this section and section 25 below, a patient who is for the time being liable to be detained or subject to guardianship under this Part of this Act shall cease to be so liable or subject if an order in writing discharging him absolutely from detention or guardianship is made in accordance with this section.

(1A) Subject to the provisions of this section and section 25 below, a community patient shall cease to be liable to recall under this Part of this Act, and the application for admission for treatment cease to have effect, if an order in writing discharging him from such liability is made in accordance with this section.

(1B) An order under subsection (1) or (1A) above shall be referred to in this Act as 'an order for discharge'.

(2) An order for discharge may be made in respect of a patient –

   (a) where the patient is liable to be detained in a hospital in pursuance of an application for admission for assessment or for treatment by the responsible clinician, by the managers or by the nearest relative of the patient;

   (b) where the patient is subject to guardianship, by the, by the responsible local social services authority or by the nearest relative of the patient

   (c) where the patient is a community patient, by the responsible clinician, by the managers of the responsible hospital or by the nearest relative of the patient.

(3) Where the patient falls within subsection (3A) below, an order for his discharge may, without prejudice to subsection (2) above, be made by the Secretary of State and, if arrangements have been made in respect of the patient under a contract with a National Health Service trust, NHS foundation trust, Local Health Board, Special Health Authority or Primary Care Trust, by that National Health Service trust, NHS foundation trust, Local Health Board, Special Health Authority or Primary Care Trust.

(3A) A patient falls within this subsection if –

   (a) he is liable to be detained in a registered establishment in pursuance of an application for admission for assessment or for treatment; or

   (b) he is a community patient and the responsible hospital is a registered establishment.

(4) The powers conferred by this section on any authority, trust, board (other than an NHS foundation trust) or body of persons may be exercised subject to subsection (3) below by any three or more members of that authority, trust, board or body authorised by them in that behalf or by three or more members of a committee or sub-committee of that authority, trust, board or body which has been authorised by them in that behalf.

(5) The reference in subsection (4) above to the members of an authority, trust, board or body or the members of a committee or sub-committee of an authority, trust, board or body –

   (a) in the case of a Local Health Board, Special Health Authority or Primary Care Trust or a committee or sub-committee of a Local Health Board, Special Health Authority or Primary Care Trust, is a reference only to the chairman of the authority, trust or board and such members (of the authority, trust, board, committee or sub-committee, as the case may be) as are not also officers of the authority, trust or board, within the meaning of the National Health Service Act 2006 or the National Health Service (Wales) Act 2006; and

   (b) in the case of a National Health Service trust or a committee or sub-committee of such a trust, is a reference only to the chairman of the trust and such directors or (in the case of a committee or sub-committee) members as are not also employees of the trust.

(6) The powers conferred by this section on any NHS foundation trust may be exercised by any three or more persons authorised by the board of the trust in that behalf each of whom is neither an executive director of the board nor an employee of the trust.

24 Visiting and examination of patients

(1) For the purpose of advising as to the exercise by the nearest relative of a patient who is liable to be detained or subject to guardianship under this Part of this Act, or who is a community patient, of any power to order his discharge, any registered medical practitioner or approved clinician authorised by or on behalf of the nearest relative of the patient may, at any reasonable time, visit the patient and examine him in private.

(2) Any registered medical practitioner or approved clinician authorised for the purposes of subsection (1) above to visit and examine a patient may require the production of and inspect any records relating to the detention or treatment of the patient in any hospital or to any after-care services provided for the patient under section 117 below.

(3) Where application is made by the Secretary of State or a Local Health Board, Special Health Authority, Primary Care Trust, National Health Service trust or NHS foundation trust to exercise any power under section 23(3) above to make an order for a patient's discharge, the following persons, that is to say –

   (a) any registered medical practitioner or approved clinician authorised by the Secretary of State or, as the case may be, that Local Health Board, Special Health Authority, Primary Care Trust, National Health Service trust or NHS foundation trust; and

   (b) any other person (whether a registered medical practitioner or approved clinician or not) authorised under Part II of the Care Standards Act 2000 to inspect the establishment in question; may at any reasonable time visit the patient and interview him in private.

(4) Any person authorised for the purposes of subsection (3) above to visit a patient may require the production of and inspect any documents constituting or alleged to constitute the authority for the detention of the patient, or (as the case may be) for his liability

to recall, under this Part of this Act; and any person so authorised, who is a registered medical practitioner or approved clinician, may examine the patient in private, and may require the production of and inspect any other records relating to the treatment of the patient in the establishment or to any after-care services provided for the patient under section 117 below.

25 Restrictions on discharge by nearest relative

(1) An order for the discharge of a patient who is liable to be detained in a hospital shall not be made under section 23 above by his nearest relative except after giving not less than 72 hours' notice in writing to the managers of the hospital; and if, within 72 hours after such notice has been given, the responsible clinician furnishes to the managers a report certifying that in the opinion of that clinician the patient, if discharged, would be likely to act in a manner dangerous to other persons or to himself –

    (a) any order for the discharge of the patient made by that relative in pursuance of the notice shall be of no effect; and

    (b) no further order for the discharge of the patient shall be made by that relative during the period of six months beginning with the date of the report.

(1A) Subsection (1) above shall apply to an order for the discharge of a community patient as it applies to an order for the discharge of a patient who is liable to be detained in a hospital, but with the reference to the managers of the hospital being read as a reference to the managers of the responsible hospital.

(2) In any case where a report under subsection (1) above is furnished in respect of a patient who is liable to be detained in pursuance of an application for admission for treatment, or in respect of a community patient, the managers shall cause the nearest relative of the patient to be informed.

26 Definition of 'relative' and 'nearest relative'

(1) In this Part of this Act 'relative' means any of the following persons: –

    (a) husband or wife or civil partner;

    (b) son or daughter;

    (c) father or mother;

    (d) brother or sister;

    (e) grandparent;

    (f) grandchild;

    (g) uncle or aunt;

    (h) nephew or niece.

(2) In deducing relationships for the purposes of this section, any relationship of the half-blood shall be treated as a relationship of the whole blood, and an illegitimate person shall be treated as the legitimate child of

    (a) his mother, and

    (b) if his father has parental responsibility for him within the meaning of section 3 of the Children Act 1989, his father.

(3) In this Part of this Act, subject to the provisions of this section and to the following provisions of this Part of this Act, the 'nearest relative' means the person first described in subsection (1) above who is for the time being surviving, relatives of the whole blood being preferred to relatives of the same description of the half-blowwod and the elder or eldest of two or more relatives described in any paragraph of that subsection being preferred to the other or others of those relatives, regardless of sex.

(4) Subject to the provisions of this section and to the following provisions of this Part of this Act, where the patient ordinarily resides with or is cared for by one or more of his relatives (or, if he is for the time being an in-patient in a hospital, he last ordinarily resided with or was cared for by one or more of his relatives) his nearest relative shall be determined –

    (a) by giving preference to that relative or those relatives over the other or others; and

    (b) as between two or more such relatives, in accordance with subsection (3) above.

(5) Where the person who, under subsection (3) or (4) above, would be the nearest relative of a patient –

    (a) in the case of a patient ordinarily resident in the United Kingdom, the Channel Islands or the Isle of Man, is not so resident; or

    (b) is the husband or wife or civil partner of the patient, but is permanently separated from the patient, either by agreement or under an order of a court, or has deserted or has been deserted by the patient for a period which has not come to an end; or

    (c) is a person other than the husband, wife, civil partner, father or mother of the patient, and is for the time being under 18 years of age;

    (d) the nearest relative of the patient shall be ascertained as if that person were dead.

(6) In this section 'husband', 'wife' and 'civil partner' include a person who is living with the patient as the patient's husband or wife or as if they were civil partners, as the case may be (or, if the patient is for the time being an in-patient in a hospital, was so living until the patient was admitted), and has been or had been so living for a period of not less than six months; but a person shall not be treated by virtue of this subsection as the nearest relative of a married patient or a patient in a civil partnership unless the husband, wife or civil partner of the patient is disregarded by virtue of paragraph (b) of subsection (5) above.

(7) A person, other than a relative, with whom the patient ordinarily resides (or, if the patient is for the time being an in-patient in a hospital, last ordinarily resided before he was admitted), and with whom he has or had been ordinarily residing for a period of not less than five years, shall be treated for the purposes of this Part of this Act as if he were a relative but –

(a) shall be treated for the purposes of subsection (3) above as if mentioned last in subsection (1) above; and

(b) shall not be treated by virtue of this subsection as the nearest relative of a married patient or a patient in a civil partnership unless the husband, wife or civil partner of the patient is disregarded by virtue of paragraph (b) of subsection (5) above.

27 Children and young persons in care

Where –

(a) a patient who is a child or young person is in the care of a local authority by virtue of a care order within the meaning of the Children Act 1989; or

(b) the rights and powers of a parent of a patient who is a child or young person are vested in a local authority by virtue of section 16 of the Social Work (Scotland) Act 1968,

the authority shall be deemed to be the nearest relative of the patient in preference to any person except the patient's husband or wife or civil partner (if any).

28 Nearest relative of minor under guardianship, etc

(1) Where –

(a) a guardian has been appointed for a person who has not attained the age of eighteen years; or

(b) a residence order (as defined by section 8 of the Children Act 1989) is in force with respect to such a person, the guardian (or guardians, where there is more than one) or the person named in the residence order shall, to the exclusion of any other person, be deemed to be his nearest relative.

(2) Subsection (5) of section 26 above shall apply in relation to a person who is, or who is one of the persons, deemed to be the nearest relative of a patient by virtue of this section as it applies in relation to a person who would be the nearest relative under subsection (3) of that section.

(3) In this section 'guardian' includes a special guardian (within the meaning of the Children Act 1989), but does not include a guardian under this Part of this Act.

(4) In this section 'court' includes a court in Scotland or Northern Ireland, and 'enactment' includes an enactment of the Parliament of Northern Ireland, a Measure of the Northern Ireland Assembly and an Order in Council under Schedule 1 of the Northern Ireland Act 1974.

29 Appointment by court of acting nearest relative

(1) The county court may, upon application made in accordance with the provisions of this section in respect of a patient, by order direct that the functions of the nearest relative of the patient under this Part of this Act and sections 66 and 69 below shall, during the continuance in force of the order, be exercisable by the person specified in the order.

(1A) If the court decides to make an order on an application under subsection (1) above, the following rules have effect for the purposes of specifying a person in the order –

(a) if a person is nominated in the application to act as the patient's nearest relative and that person is, in the opinion of the court, a suitable person to act as such and is willing to do so, the court shall specify that person (or, if there are two or more such persons, such one of them as the court thinks fit);

(b) otherwise, the court shall specify such person as is, in its opinion, a suitable person to act as the patient's nearest relative and is willing to do so.

(2) An order under this section may be made on the application of –

(za) the patient;

(a) any relative of the patient;

(b) any other person with whom the patient is residing (or, if the patient is then an in-patient in a hospital, was last residing before he was admitted); or

(c) approved mental health professional.

(3) An application for an order under this section may be made upon any of the following grounds, that is to say –

(a) that the patient has no nearest relative within the meaning of this Act, or that it is not reasonably practicable to ascertain whether he has such a relative, or who that relative is;

(b) that the nearest relative of the patient is incapable of acting as such by reason of mental disorder or other illness;

(c) that the nearest relative of the patient unreasonably objects to the making of an application for admission for treatment or a guardianship application in respect of the patient;

(d) that the nearest relative of the patient has exercised without due regard to the welfare of the patient or the interests of the public his power to discharge the patient under this Part of this Act, or is likely to do so; *or*

(e) that the nearest relative of the patient is otherwise not a suitable person to act as such.

(4) If, immediately before the expiration of the period for which a patient is liable to be detained by virtue of an application for admission for assessment, an application under this section, which is an application made on the ground specified in subsection (3)(c) or (d) above, is pending in respect of the patient, that period shall be extended –

(a) in any case, until the application under this section has been finally disposed of; and

(b) if an order is made in pursuance of the application under this section, for a further period of seven days;

and for the purposes of this subsection an application under this section shall be deemed to have been finally disposed of at the expiration of the time allowed for appealing from the decision of the court or, if notice of appeal has been given within that time, when the appeal has been heard or withdrawn, and 'pending' shall be construed accordingly.

(5) An order made on the ground specified in subsection (3)(a), (b) or (e) above may specify a period for which it is to continue in force unless previously discharged under section 30 below,

(6) While an order made under this section is in force, the provisions of this Part of this Act (other than this section and section 30 below) and sections 66, 69, 132(4) and 133 below shall apply in relation to the patient as if for any reference to the nearest relative of the patient there were substituted a reference to the person having the functions of that relative and (without prejudice to section 30 below) shall so apply notwithstanding that the person who was the patient's nearest relative when the order was made is no longer his nearest relative; but this subsection shall not apply to section 66 below in the case mentioned in paragraph (h) of subsection (1) of that section.

30 Discharge and variation of orders under s 29

(1) An order made under section 29 above in respect of a patient may be discharged by the county court upon application made –

(a) in any case, by the patient or the person having the functions of the nearest relative of the patient by virtue of the order;

(b) where the order was made on the ground specified in paragraph (a) (b) or (e) of section 29(3) above, or where the person who was the nearest relative of the patient when the order was made has ceased to be his nearest relative, on the application of the nearest relative of the patient.

(1A) But, in the case of an order made on the ground specified in paragraph (e) of section 29(3) above, an application may not be made under subsection (1)(b) above by the person who was the nearest relative of the patient when the order was made except with leave of the county court.

(2) An order made under section 29 above in respect of a patient may be varied by the county court, on the application of the person having the functions of the nearest relative by virtue of the order or on the application of the patient or of an approved mental health professional, by substituting another person for the person having those functions.

(2A) If the court decides to vary an order on an application under subsection (2) above, the following rules have effect for the purposes of substituting another person –

(a) if a person is nominated in the application to act as the patient's nearest relative and that person is, in the opinion of the court, a suitable person to act as such and is willing to do so, the court shall specify that person (or, if there are two or more such persons, such one of them as the court thinks fit);

(b) otherwise, the court shall specify such person as is, in its opinion, a suitable person to act as the patient's nearest relative and is willing to do so.

(3) If the person having the functions of the nearest relative of a patient by virtue of an order under section 29 above dies –

(a) subsections (1) and (2) above shall apply as if for any reference to that person there were substituted a reference to any relative of the patient, and

(b) until the order is discharged or varied under those provisions the functions of the nearest relative under this Part of this Act and sections 66 and 69 below shall not be exercisable by any person.

(4) An order made on the ground specified in paragraph (c) or (d) of section 29(3) above shall, unless previously discharged under subsection (1) above, cease to have effect as follows –

(a) if –

(i) on the date of the order the patient was liable to be detained or subject to guardianship by virtue of a relevant application, order or direction; or

(ii) he becomes so liable or subject within the period of three months beginning with that date; or

(iii) he was a community patient on the date of the order,

it shall cease to have effect when he is discharged under section 23 above or 72 below or the relevant application, order or direction otherwise ceases to have effect (except as a result of his being transferred in pursuance of regulations under section 19 above);

(b) otherwise, it shall cease to have effect at the end of the period of three months beginning with the date of the order.

(4A) In subsection (4) above, reference to a relevant application, order or direction is to any of the following –

    (a) an application for admission for treatment;

    (b) a guardianship application;

    (c) an order or direction under Part 3 of this Act (other than under section 35, 36 or 38).

(4B) An order made on the ground specified in paragraph (a), (b) or (e) of section 29(3) above shall –

    (a) if a period was specified under section 29(5) above, cease to have effect on expiry of that period, unless previously discharged under subsection (1) above;

    (b) if no such period was specified, remain in force until it is discharged under subsection (1) above.

(5) The discharge or variation under this section of an order made under section 29 above shall not affect the validity of anything previously done in pursuance of the order.

34 Interpretation of Part II

(1) In this Part of this Act –

'the appropriate practitioner' means –

    (a) in the case of a patient who is subject to the guardianship of a person other than a local social services authority, the nominated medical attendant of the patient; and

    (b) in any other case, the responsible clinician; 'the nominated medical attendant', in relation to a patient who is subject to the guardianship of a person other than a local social services authority, means the person appointed in pursuance of regulations made under section 9(2) above to act as the medical attendant of the patient;

'registered establishment' means an establishment –

    (a) which would not, apart from subsection (2) below, be a hospital for the purposes of this Part; and

    (b) in respect of which a person is registered under Part II of the Care Standards Act 2000 as an independent hospital in which treatment or nursing (or both) are provided for persons liable to be detained under this Act;

'the responsible clinician' means –

    (a) in relation to a patient liable to be detained by virtue of an application for admission for assessment or an application for admission for treatment, or a community patient, the approved clinician with overall responsibility for the patient's case;

    (b) in relation to a patient subject to guardianship, the approved clinician authorised by the responsible local social services authority to act (either generally or in any particular case or for any particular purpose) as the responsible clinician;

(2) Except where otherwise expressly provided, this Part of this Act applies in relation to a registered establishment, as it applies in relation to a hospital, and references in this Part of this Act to a hospital, and any reference in this Act to a hospital to which this Part of this Act applies, shall be construed accordingly.

(3) In relation to a patient who is subject to guardianship in pursuance of a guardianship application, any reference in this Part of this Act to the responsible local social services authority is a reference –

    (a) where the patient is subject to the guardianship of a local social services authority, to that authority;

    (b) where the patient is subject to the guardianship of a person other than a local social services authority, to the local social services authority for the area in which that person resides.

PART III

PATIENTS CONCERNED IN CRIMINAL PROCEEDINGS OR UNDER SENTENCE

Remands to hospital

35 Remand to hospital for report on accused's mental condition

(1) Subject to the provisions of this section, the Crown Court or a magistrates' court may remand an accused person to a hospital specified by the court for a report on his mental condition.

(2) For the purposes of this section an accused person is –

    (a) in relation to the Crown Court, any person who is awaiting trial before the court for an offence punishable with imprisonment or who has been arraigned before the court for such an offence and has not yet been sentenced or otherwise dealt with for the offence on which he has been arraigned;

    (b) in relation to a magistrates' court, any person who has been convicted by the court of an offence punishable on summary conviction with imprisonment and any person charged with such an offence if the court is satisfied that he did the act or made the omission charged or he has consented to the exercise by the court of the powers conferred by this section.

(3) Subject to subsection (4) below, the powers conferred by this section may be exercised if –

    (a) the court is satisfied, on the written or oral evidence of a registered medical practitioner, that there is reason to suspect that the accused person is suffering from mental disorder; and

    (b) the court is of the opinion that it would be impracticable for a report on his mental condition to be made if he were remanded on bail;

but those powers shall not be exercised by the Crown Court in respect of a person who has been convicted before the court if the sentence for the offence of which he has been convicted is fixed by law.

(4) The court shall not remand an accused person to a hospital under this section unless satisfied, on the written or oral evidence of the approved clinician who would be responsible for making the report or of some other person representing the managers of the hospital, that arrangements have been made for his admission to that hospital and for his admission to it within the period of seven days beginning with the date of the remand; and if the court is so satisfied it may, pending his admission, give directions for his conveyance to and detention in a place of safety.

(5) Where a court has remanded an accused person under this section it may further remand him if it appears to the court, on the written or oral evidence of the approved clinician responsible for making the report, that a further remand is necessary for completing the assessment of the accused person's mental condition.

(6) The power of further remanding an accused person under this section may be exercised by the court without his being brought before the court if he is represented by an authorised person who is given an opportunity of being heard.

(7) An accused person shall not be remanded or further remanded under this section for more than 28 days at a time or for more than 12 weeks in all; and the court may at any time terminate the remand if it appears to the court that it is appropriate to do so.

(8) An accused person remanded to hospital under this section shall be entitled to obtain at his own expense an independent report on his mental condition from a registered medical practitioner or approved clinician chosen by him and to apply to the court on the basis of it for his remand to be terminated under subsection (7) above.

(9) Where an accused person is remanded under this section –

    (a) a constable or any other person directed to do so by the court shall convey the accused person to the hospital specified by the court within the period mentioned in subsection (4) above; and

    (b) the managers of the hospital shall admit him within that period and thereafter detain him in accordance with the provisions of this section.

(10) If an accused person absconds from a hospital to which he has been remanded under this section, or while being conveyed to or from that hospital, he may be arrested without warrant by any constable and shall, after being arrested, be brought as soon as practicable before the court that remanded him; and the court may thereupon terminate the remand and deal with him in any way in which it could have dealt with him if he had not been remanded under this section.

36 Remand of accused person to hospital for treatment

(1) Subject to the provisions of this section, the Crown Court may, instead of remanding an accused person in custody, remand him to a hospital specified by the court if satisfied, on the written or oral evidence of two registered medical practitioners, that

    (a) he is suffering from mental disorder of a nature or degree which makes it appropriate for him to be detained in a hospital for medical treatment; and

    (b) appropriate medical treatment is available for him.

(2) For the purposes of this section an accused person is any person who is in custody awaiting trial before the Crown Court for an offence punishable with imprisonment (other than an offence the sentence for which is fixed by law) or who at any time before sentence is in custody in the course of a trial before that court for such an offence.

(3) The court shall not remand an accused person under this section to a hospital unless it is satisfied, on the written or oral evidence of the approved clinician who would have overall responsibility for his case or of some other person representing the managers of the hospital, that arrangements have been made for his admission to that hospital and for his admission to it within the period of seven days beginning with the date of the remand; and if the court is so satisfied it may, pending his admission, give directions for his conveyance to and detention in a place of safety.

(4) Where a court has remanded an accused person under this section it may further remand him if it appears to the court, on the written or oral evidence of the responsible clinician, that a further remand is warranted.

(5) The power of further remanding an accused person under this section may be exercised by the court without his being brought before the court if he is represented by an authorised person who is given an opportunity of being heard.

(6) An accused person shall not be remanded or further remanded under this section for more than 28 days at a time or for more than 12 weeks in all; and the court may at any time terminate the remand if it appears to the court that it is appropriate to do so.

(7) An accused person remanded to hospital under this section shall be entitled to obtain at his own expense an independent report on his mental condition from a registered medical practitioner or approved clinician chosen by him and to apply to the court on the basis of it for his remand to be terminated under subsection (6) above.

(8) Subsections (9) and (10) of section 35 above shall have effect in relation to a remand under this section as they have effect in relation to a remand under that section.

Hospital and guardianship orders

37 Powers of courts to order hospital admission or guardianship

(1) Where a person is convicted before the Crown Court of an offence punishable with imprisonment other than an offence the sentence for which is fixed by law, or is convicted by a magistrates' court of an offence punishable on summary conviction with imprisonment, and the conditions mentioned in subsection (2) below are satisfied, the court may by order authorise his admission to and detention in such hospital as may be specified in the order or, as the case may be, place him under the guardianship of a local social services authority or of such other person approved by a local social services authority as may be so specified.

(1A) In the case of an offence the sentence for which would otherwise fall to be imposed –

(a) under section 51A(2) of the Firearms Act 1968,

(b) under section 110(2) or 111(2) of the Powers of Criminal Courts (Sentencing) Act 2000

(c) under any of sections 225 to 228 of the Criminal Justice Act 2003, or

(d) under section 29(4) or (6) of the Violent Crime Reduction Act 2006 (minimum sentences in certain cases of using someone to mind a weapon), nothing in those provisions shall prevent a court from making an order under subsection (1) above for the admission of the offender to a hospital.

(1B) References in subsection (1A) above to a sentence falling to be imposed under any of the provisions mentioned in that subsection are to be read in accordance with section 305(4) of the Criminal Justice Act 2003.

(2) The conditions referred to in subsection (1) above are that –

(a) the court is satisfied, on the written or oral evidence of two registered medical practitioners, that the offender is suffering from mental disorder and that either –

(i) the mental disorder from which the offender is suffering is of a nature or degree which makes it appropriate for him to be detained in a hospital for medical treatment and appropriate medical treatment is available for him; or

(ii) in the case of an offender who has attained the age of 16 years, the mental disorder is of a nature or degree which warrants his reception into guardianship under this Act; and

(b) the court is of the opinion, having regard to all the circumstances including the nature of the offence and the character and antecedents of the offender, and to the other available methods of dealing with him, that the most suitable method of disposing of the case is by means of an order under this section.

(3) Where a person is charged before a magistrates' court with any act or omission as an offence and the court would have power, on convicting him of that offence, to make an order under subsection (1) above in his case then, if the court is satisfied that the accused did the act or made the omission charged, the court may, if it thinks fit, make such an order without convicting him.

(4) An order for the admission of an offender to a hospital (in this Act referred to as 'a hospital order') shall not be made under this section unless the court is satisfied on the written or oral evidence of the approved clinician who would have overall responsibility for his case or of some other person representing the managers of the hospital that arrangements have been made for his admission to that hospital, and for his admission to it within the period of 28 days beginning with the date of the making of such an order; and the court may, pending his admission within that period, give such directions as it thinks fit for his conveyance to and detention in a place of safety.

(5) If within the said period of 28 days it appears to the Secretary of State that by reason of an emergency or other special circumstances it is not practicable for the patient to be received into the hospital specified in the order, he may give directions for the admission of the patient to such other hospital as appears to be appropriate instead of the hospital so specified; and where such directions are given –

(a) the Secretary of State shall cause the person having the custody of the patient to be informed, and

(b) the hospital order shall have effect as if the hospital specified in the directions were substituted for the hospital specified in the order.

(6) An order placing an offender under the guardianship of a local social services authority or of any other person (in this Act referred to as 'a guardianship order') shall not be made under this section unless the court is satisfied that that authority or person is willing to receive the offender into guardianship.

(8) Where an order is made under this section, the court shall not –

(a) pass sentence of imprisonment or impose a fine or make a community order (within the meaning of Part 12 of the Criminal Justice Act 2003) in respect of the offence,

(b) if the order under this section is a hospital order, make a referral order (within the meaning of the Powers of Criminal Courts (Sentencing) Act 2000) in respect of the offence, or

(c) make in respect of the offender a supervision order (within the meaning of that Act) or an order under section 150 of that Act (binding over of parent or guardian), but the court may make any other order which it has power to make apart from this section; and for the purposes of this subsection 'sentence of imprisonment' includes any sentence or order for detention.

38 Interim hospital orders

(1) Where a person is convicted before the Crown Court of an offence punishable with imprisonment (other than an offence the sentence for which is fixed by law) or is convicted by a magistrates' court of an offence punishable on summary conviction with imprisonment and the court before or by which he is convicted is satisfied, on the written or oral evidence of two registered medical practitioners –

(a) that the offender is suffering from mental disorder; and

(b) that there is reason to suppose that the mental disorder from which the offender is suffering is such that it may be appropriate for a hospital order to be made in his case, the court may, before making a hospital order or dealing with him in some other way, make an order (in this Act referred to as 'an interim hospital order') authorising his admission to such hospital as may be specified in the order and his detention there in accordance with this section.

(2) In the case of an offender who is subject to an interim hospital order the court may make a hospital order without his being brought before the court if he is represented by an authorised person who given an opportunity of being heard.

(3) At least one of the registered medical practitioners whose evidence is taken into account under subsection (1) above shall be employed at the hospital which is to be specified in the order.

(4) An interim hospital order shall not be made for the admission of an offender to a hospital unless the court is satisfied, on the written or oral evidence of the approved clinician who would have overall responsibility for his case or of some other person representing the managers of the hospital, that arrangements have been made for his admission to that hospital and for his admission to it within the period of 28 days beginning with the date of the order; and if the court is so satisfied the court may, pending his admission, give directions for his conveyance to and detention in a place of safety.

(5) An interim hospital order –

(a) shall be in force for such period, not exceeding 12 weeks, as the court may specify when making the order; but

(b) may be renewed for further periods of not more than 28 days at a time if it appears to the court, on the written or oral evidence of the responsible clinician, that the continuation of the order is warranted;

but no such order shall continue in force for more than twelve months in all and the court shall terminate the order if it makes a hospital order in respect of the offender or decides after considering the written or oral evidence of the responsible clinician, to deal with the offender in some other way.

(6) The power of renewing an interim hospital order may be exercised without the offender being brought before the court if he is represented by counsel or a solicitor and his counsel or solicitor is given an opportunity of being heard.

(7) If an offender absconds from a hospital in which he is detained in pursuance of an interim hospital order, or while being conveyed to or from such a hospital, he may be arrested without warrant by a constable and shall, after being arrested, be brought as soon as practicable before the court that made the order; and the court may thereupon terminate the order and deal with him in any way in which it could have dealt with him if no such order had been made.

39 Information as to hospitals

(1) Where a court is minded to make a hospital order or interim hospital order in respect of any person it may request –

(a) the Primary Care Trust or Local Health Board for the area in which that person resides or last resided; or

(b) the National Assembly for Wales or any other Primary Care Trust or Local Health Board that appears to the court to be appropriate,

to furnish the court with such information as that Primary Care Trust or Local Health Board or National Assembly for Wales have or can reasonably obtain with respect to the hospital or hospitals (if any) in their area or elsewhere at which arrangements could be made for the admission of that person in pursuance of the order, and that Primary Care Trust or Local Health Board National Assembly for Wales shall comply with any such request.

(1A) In relation to a person who has not attained the age of 18 years, subsection (1) above shall have effect as if the reference to the making of a hospital order included a reference to a remand under section 35 or 36 above or the making of an order under section 44 below.

(1B) Where the person concerned has not attained the age of 18 years, the information which may be requested under subsection (1) above includes, in particular, information about the availability of accommodation or facilities designed so as to be specially suitable for patients who have not attained the age of 18 years.

39A Information to facilitate guardianship orders

Where a court is minded to make a guardianship order in respect of any offender, it may request the local social services authority for the area in which the offender resides or last resided, or any other local social services authority that appears to the court to be appropriate –

(a) to inform the court whether it or any other person approved by it is willing to receive the offender into guardianship; and

(b) if so, to give such information as it reasonably can about how it or the other person could be expected to exercise in relation to the offender the powers conferred by section 40(2) below; and that authority shall comply with any such request.

40 Effect of hospital orders, guardianship orders and interim hospital orders

(1) A hospital order shall be sufficient authority –

(a) for a constable, an approved mental health professional or any other person directed to do so by the court to convey the patient to the hospital specified in the order within a period of 28 days; and

(b) for the managers of the hospital to admit him at any time within that period and thereafter detain him in accordance with the provisions of this Act.

(2) A guardianship order shall confer on the authority or person named in the order as guardian the same powers as a guardianship application made and accepted under Part II of this Act.

(3) Where an interim hospital order is made in respect of an offender –

(a) a constable or any other person directed to do so by the court shall convey the offender to the hospital specified in the order within the period mentioned in section 38(4) above; and

(b) the managers of the hospital shall admit him within that period and thereafter detain him in accordance with the provisions of section 38 above.

(4) A patient who is admitted to a hospital in pursuance of a hospital order, or placed under guardianship by a guardianship order, shall, subject to the provisions of this subsection, be treated for the purposes of the provisions of this Act mentioned in Part I of Schedule I to this Act as if he had been so admitted or placed on the date of the order in pursuance of an application for admission for treatment or a guardianship application, as the case may be, duly made under Part II of this Act, but subject to any modifications of those provisions specified in that Part of that Schedule.

(5) Where a patient is admitted to a hospital in pursuance of a hospital order, or placed under guardianship by a guardianship order, any previous application, hospital order or guardianship order by virtue of which he was liable to be detained in a hospital or subject to guardianship shall cease to have effect; but if the first-mentioned order, or the conviction on which it was made, is quashed on appeal, this subsection shall not apply and section 22 above shall have effect as if during any period for which the patient was liable to be detained or subject to guardianship under the order, he had been detained in custody as mentioned in that section.

(6) Where –

(a) a patient admitted to a hospital in pursuance of a hospital order is absent without leave;

(b) a warrant to arrest him has been issued under section 72 of the Criminal Justice Act 1967; and

(c) he is held pursuant to the warrant in any country or territory other than the United Kingdom, any of the Channel Islands and the Isle of Man, he shall be treated as having been taken into custody under section 18 above on first being so held.

Restriction orders

41 Power of higher courts to restrict discharge from hospital

(1) Where a hospital order is made in respect of an offender by the Crown Court, and it appears to the court, having regard to the nature of the offence, the antecedents of the offender and the risk of his committing further offences if set at large, that it is necessary for the protection of the public from serious harm so to do, the court may, subject to the provisions of this section, further order that the offender shall be subject to the special restrictions set out in this section and an order under this section shall be known as 'a restriction order'.

(2) A restriction order shall not be made in the case of any person unless at least one of the registered medical practitioners whose evidence is taken into account by the court under section 37(2)(a) above has given evidence orally before the court.

(3) The special restrictions applicable to a patient in respect of whom a restriction order is in force are as follows –

(a) none of the provisions of Part II of this Act relating to the duration, renewal and expiration of authority for the detention of patients shall apply, and the patient shall continue to be liable to be detained by virtue of the relevant hospital order until he is duly discharged under the said Part II or absolutely discharged under section 42, 73, 74 or 75 below;

(aa) none of the provisions of Part II of this Act relating to community treatment orders and community patients shall apply;

(b) no application shall be made to a Mental Health Review Tribunal in respect of a patient under section 66 or 69(1) below;

(c) the following powers shall be exercisable only with the consent of the Secretary of State, namely –

(i) power to grant leave of absence to the patient under section 17 above;

(ii) power to transfer the patient in pursuance of regulations under section 19 above or in pursuance of subsection (3) of that section; and

(iii) power to order the discharge of the patient under section 23 above; and if leave of absence is granted under the said section 17 power to recall the patient under that section shall vest in the Secretary of State as well as the responsible clinician; and

(d) the power of the Secretary of State to recall the patient under the said section 17 and power to take the patient into custody and return him under section 18 above may be exercised at any time; and in relation to any such patient section 40(4) above shall have effect as if it referred to Part II of Schedule 1 to this Act instead of Part I of that Schedule.

(4) A hospital order shall not cease to have effect under section 40(5) above if a restriction order in respect of the patient is in force at the material time.

(5) Where a restriction order in respect of a patient ceases to have effect while the relevant hospital order continues in force, the provisions of section 40 above and Part I of Schedule 1 to this Act shall apply to the patient as if he had been admitted to the hospital in pursuance of a hospital order (without a restriction order) made on the date on which the restriction order ceased to have effect.

(6) While a person is subject to a restriction order the responsible clinician shall at such intervals (not exceeding one year) as the Secretary of State may direct examine and report to the Secretary of State on that person; and every report shall contain such particulars as the Secretary of State may require.

42 Powers of Secretary of State in respect of patients subject to restriction orders

(1) If the Secretary of State is satisfied that in the case of any patient a restriction order is no longer required for the protection of the public from serious harm, he may direct that the patient cease to be subject to the special restrictions set out in section 41(3) above; and where the Secretary of State so directs, the restriction order shall cease to have effect, and section 41(5) above shall apply accordingly.

(2) At any time while a restriction order is in force in respect of a patient, the Secretary of State may, if he thinks fit, by warrant discharge the patient from hospital, either absolutely or subject to conditions; and where a person is absolutely discharged under this subsection, he shall thereupon cease to be liable to be detained by virtue of the relevant hospital order, and the restriction order shall cease to have effect accordingly.

(3) The Secretary of State may at any time during the continuance in force of a restriction order in respect of a patient who has been conditionally discharged under subsection (2) above by warrant recall the patient to such hospital as may be specified in the warrant.

(4) Where a patient is recalled as mentioned in subsection (3) above –

(a) if the hospital specified in the warrant is not the hospital from which the patient was conditionally discharged, the hospital order and the restriction order shall have effect as if the hospital specified in the warrant were substituted for the hospital specified in the hospital order;

(b) in any case, the patient shall be treated for the purposes of section 18 above as if he had absented himself without leave from the hospital specified in the warrant.

(5) If a restriction order in respect of a patient ceases to have effect after the patient has been conditionally discharged under this section, the patient shall, unless previously recalled under subsection (3) above, be deemed to be absolutely discharged on the date when the order ceases to have effect, and shall cease to be liable to be detained by virtue of the relevant hospital order accordingly.

(6) The Secretary of State may, if satisfied that the attendance at any place in Great Britain of a patient who is subject to a restriction order is desirable in the interests of justice or for the purposes of any public inquiry, direct him to be taken to that place; and where a patient is directed under this subsection to be taken to any place he shall, unless the Secretary of State otherwise directs, be kept in custody while being so taken, while at that place and while being taken back to the hospital in which he is liable to be detained.

43 Power of magistrates' courts to commit for restriction order

(1) If in the case of a person of or over the age of 14 years who is convicted by a magistrates' court of an offence punishable on summary conviction with imprisonment –

(a) the conditions which under section 37(1) above are required to be satisfied for the making of a hospital order are satisfied in respect of the offender; but

(b) it appears to the court, having regard to the nature of the offence, the antecedents of the offender and the risk of his committing further offences if set at large, that if a hospital order is made a restriction order should also be made,

the court may, instead of making a hospital order or dealing with him in any other manner, commit him in custody to the Crown Court to be dealt with in respect of the offence.

(2) Where an offender is committed to the Crown Court under this section, the Crown Court shall inquire into the circumstances of the case and may –

(a) if that court would have power so to do under the foregoing provisions of this Part of this Act upon the conviction of the offender before that court of such an offence as is described in section 37(1) above, make a hospital order in his case, with or without a restriction order;

(b) if the court does not make such an order, deal with the offender in any other manner in which the magistrates' court might have dealt with him.

(3) The Crown Court shall have the same power to make orders under sections 35, 36 and 38 above in the case of a person committed to the court under this section as the Crown Court has under those sections in the case of an accused person within the meaning of section 35 or 36 above or of a person convicted before that court as mentioned in section 38 above.

(4) The powers of a magistrates' court under section 3 or 3B of the Powers of Criminal Courts (Sentencing) Act 2000 (which enable such a court to commit an offender to the Crown Court where the court is of the opinion, or it appears to the court, as mentioned in the section in question) shall also be exercisable by a magistrates' court where it is of that opinion (or it so appears to it) unless a hospital order is made in the offender's case with a restriction order.

44 Committal to hospital under s 43

(1) Where an offender is committed under section 43(1) above and the magistrates' court by which he is committed is satisfied on written or oral evidence that arrangements have been made for the admission of the offender to a hospital in the event of an order being made under this section, the court may, instead of committing him in custody, by order direct him to be admitted to that hospital, specifying it, and to be detained there until the case is disposed of by the Crown Court, and may give such directions as it thinks fit for his production from the hospital to attend the Crown Court by which his case is to be dealt with.

(2) The evidence required by subsection (1) above shall be given by the approved clinician who would have overall responsibility for the offender's case or by some other person representing the managers of the hospital in question.

(3) The power to give directions under section 37(4) above, section 37(5) above and section 40(1) above shall apply in relation to an order under this section as they apply in relation to a hospital order, but as if references to the period of 28 days mentioned in section 40(1) above were omitted; and subject as aforesaid an order under this section shall, until the offender's case is disposed of by the Crown Court, have the same effect as a hospital order together with a restriction order.

45 Appeals from magistrates' courts

(1) Where on the trial of an information charging a person with an offence a magistrates' court makes a hospital order or guardianship order in respect of him without convicting him, he shall have the same right of appeal against the order as if it had been made on his conviction; and on any such appeal the Crown Court shall have the same powers as if the appeal had been against both conviction and sentence.

(2) An appeal by a child or young person with respect to whom any such order has been made, whether the appeal is against the order or against the finding upon which the order was made, may be brought by him or by his parent or guardian on his behalf.

Hospital and limitation directions

45A Power of higher courts to direct hospital admission

(1) This section applies where, in the case of a person convicted before the Crown Court of an offence the sentence for which is not fixed by law –

(a) the conditions mentioned in subsection (2) below are fulfilled; and

(b) the court considers making a hospital order in respect of him before deciding to impose a sentence of imprisonment ('the relevant sentence') in respect of the offence.

(2) The conditions referred to in subsection (1) above are that the court is satisfied, on the written or oral evidence of two registered medical practitioners –

(a) that the offender is suffering from mental disorder;

(b) that the mental disorder from which the offender is suffering is of a nature or degree which makes it appropriate for him to be detained in a hospital for medical treatment; and

(c) that appropriate medical treatment is available for him.

(3) The court may give both of the following directions, namely –

(a) a direction that, instead of being removed to and detained in a prison, the offender be removed to and detained in such hospital as may be specified in the direction (in this Act referred to as a 'hospital direction'); and

(b) a direction that the offender be subject to the special restrictions set out in section 41 above (in this Act referred to as a 'limitation direction').

(4) A hospital direction and a limitation direction shall not be given in relation to an offender unless at least one of the medical practitioners whose evidence is taken into account by the court under subsection (2) above has given evidence orally before the court.

(5) A hospital direction and a limitation direction shall not be given in relation to an offender unless the court is satisfied on the written or oral evidence of the approved clinician who would have overall responsibility for his case, or of some other person representing the managers of the hospital that arrangements have been made –

(a) for his admission to that hospital; and

(b) for his admission to it within the period of 28 days beginning with the day of the giving of such directions;

and the court may, pending his admission within that period, give such directions as it thinks fit for his conveyance to and detention in a place of safety.

(6) If within the said period of 28 days it appears to the Secretary of State that by reason of an emergency or other special circumstances it is not practicable for the patient to be received into the hospital specified in the hospital direction, he may give instructions for the admission of the patient to such other hospital as appears to be appropriate instead of the hospital so specified.

(7) Where such instructions are given –

(a) the Secretary of State shall cause the person having the custody of the patient to be informed, and

(b) the hospital direction shall have effect as if the hospital specified in the instructions were substituted for the hospital specified in the hospital direction.

(8) Section 38(1) and (5) and section 39 above shall have effect as if any reference to the making of a hospital order included a reference to the giving of a hospital direction and a limitation direction.

(9) A hospital direction and a limitation direction given in relation to an offender shall have effect not only as regards the relevant sentence but also (so far as applicable) as regards any other sentence of imprisonment imposed on the same or a previous occasion.

45B Effect of hospital and limitation directions

(1) A hospital direction and a limitation direction shall be sufficient authority –

(a) for a constable or any other person directed to do so by the court to convey the patient to the hospital specified in the hospital direction within a period of 28 days; and

(b) for the managers of the hospital to admit him at any time within that period and thereafter detain him in accordance with the provisions of this Act.

(2) With respect to any person –

(a) a hospital direction shall have effect as a transfer direction; and

(b) a limitation direction shall have effect as a restriction direction.

(3) While a person is subject to a hospital direction and a limitation direction the responsible clinician shall at such intervals (not exceeding one year) as the Secretary of State may direct examine and report to the Secretary of State on that person; and every report shall contain such particulars as the Secretary of State may require.

Transfer to hospital of prisoners, etc

47 Removal to hospital of persons serving sentences of imprisonment, etc

(1) If in the case of a person serving a sentence of imprisonment the Secretary of State is satisfied, by reports from at least two registered medical practitioners –

(a) that the said person is suffering from mental disorder; and

(b) that the mental disorder from which that person is suffering is of a nature or degree which makes it appropriate for him to be detained in a hospital for medical treatment and

(c) that appropriate medical treatment is available for him;

the Secretary of State may, if he is of the opinion having regard to the public interest and all the circumstances that it is expedient so to do, by warrant direct that that person be removed to and detained in such hospital as may be specified in the direction; and a direction under this section shall be known as 'a transfer direction'.

(2) A transfer direction shall cease to have effect at the expiration of the period of 14 days beginning with the date on which it is given unless within that period the person with respect to whom it was given has been received into the hospital specified in the direction.

(3) A transfer direction with respect to any person shall have the same effect as a hospital order made in his case.

(4) (repealed)

(5) References in this Part of this Act to a person serving a sentence of imprisonment include references –

(a) to a person detained in pursuance of any sentence or order for detention made by a court in criminal proceedings or service disciplinary proceedings (other than an order made in consequence of a finding of insanity or unfitness to stand trial or a sentence of service detention within the meaning of the Armed Forces Act 2006);

(b) to a person committed to custody under section 115(3) of the Magistrates' Courts Act 1980 (which relates to persons who fail to comply with an order to enter into recognisances to keep the peace or be of good behaviour); and

(c) to a person committed by a court to a prison or other institution to which the Prison Act 1952 applies in default of payment of any sum adjudged to be paid on his conviction.

(6) In subsection (5)(a) 'service disciplinary proceedings' means proceedings in respect of a service offence within the meaning of the Armed Forces Act 2006.

48 Removal to hospital of other prisoners

(1) If in the case of a person to whom this section applies the Secretary of State is satisfied by the same reports as are required for the purposes of section 47 above that

(a) that person is suffering from mental disorder of a nature or degree which makes it appropriate for him to be detained in hospital for medical treatment; and

(b) he is in urgent need of such treatment; and

(c) appropriate medical treatment is available for him;

the Secretary of State shall have the same power of giving a transfer direction in respect of him under that section as if he were serving a sentence of imprisonment.

(2) This section applies to the following persons, that is to say –

(a) persons detained in a prison, not being person serving a sentence of imprisonment or persons falling within the following paragraphs of this subsection;

(b) persons remanded in custody by a magistrates' court;

(c) civil prisoners, that is to say, persons committed by a court to prison for a limited term, who are not persons falling to be dealt with under section 47 above;

(d) persons detained under the Immigration Act 1971 or under section 62 of the Nationality, Immigration and Asylum Act 2002 (detention by Secretary of State).

(3) Subsections (2) and (3) of section 47 above shall apply for the purposes of this section and of any transfer direction given by virtue of this section as they apply for the purposes of that section and of any transfer direction under that section.

49 Restriction on discharge of prisoners removed to hospital

(1) Where a transfer direction is given in respect of any person, the Secretary of State, if he thinks fit, may by warrant further direct that that person shall be subject to the special restrictions set out in section 41 above; and where the Secretary of State gives a transfer direction in respect of any such person as is described in paragraph (a) or (b) of section 48(2) above, he shall also give a direction under this section applying those restrictions to him.

(2) A direction under this section shall have the same effect as a restriction order made under section 41 above and shall be known as 'a restriction direction'.

(3) While a person is subject to a restriction direction the responsible clinician shall at such intervals (not exceeding one year) as the Secretary of State may direct examine and report to the Secretary of State on that person; and every report shall contain such particulars as the Secretary of State may require.

50 Further provisions as to prisoners under sentence

(1) Where a transfer direction and a restriction direction have been given in respect of a person serving a sentence of imprisonment and before his release date the Secretary of State is notified by the responsible clinician, any other approved clinician or a Mental Health Review Tribunal that that person no longer requires treatment in hospital for mental disorder or that no effective treatment for his disorder can be given in the hospital to which he has been removed, the Secretary of State may –

(a) by warrant direct that he be remitted to any prison or other institution in which he might have been detained if he had not been removed to hospital, there to be dealt with as if he had not been so removed; or

(b) exercise any power of releasing him on licence or discharging him under supervision which could have been exercisable if he had been remitted to such a prison or institution as aforesaid,

and on his arrival in the prison or other institution or, as the case may be, his release or discharge as aforesaid, the transfer direction and the restriction direction shall cease to have effect.

(2) A restriction direction in the case of a person serving a sentence of imprisonment shall cease to have effect, if it has not previously done so, on his release date.

(3) In this section, references to a person's release date are to the day (if any) on which he would be entitled to be released (whether unconditionally or on licence) from any prison or other institution in which he might have been detained if the transfer direction had not been given; and in determining that day there shall be disregarded –

(a) any powers that would be exercisable by the Parole Board if he were detained in such a prison or other institution, and

(b) any practice of the Secretary of State in relation to the early release under discretionary powers of persons detained in such a prison or other institution.

(4) For the purposes of section 49(2) of the Prison Act 1952 (which provides for discounting from the sentences of certain prisoners periods while they are unlawfully at large) a patient who, having been transferred in pursuance of a transfer direction from any such

institution as is referred to in that section, is at large in circumstances in which he is liable to be taken into custody under any provision of this Act, shall be treated as unlawfully at large and absent from that institution.

(5) The preceding provisions of this section shall have effect as if –

(a) the reference in subsection (1) to a transfer direction and a restriction direction having been given in respect of a person serving a sentence of imprisonment included a reference to a hospital direction and a limitation direction having been given in respect of a person sentenced to imprisonment;

(b) the reference in subsection (2) to a restriction direction included a reference to a limitation direction; and

(c) references in subsections (3) and (4) to a transfer direction included references to a hospital direction.

51 Further provisions as to detained persons

(1) This section has effect where a transfer direction has been given in respect of any such person as is described in paragraph (a) of section 48(2) above and that person is in this section referred to as 'the detainee'.

(2) The transfer direction shall cease to have effect when the detainee's case is disposed of by the court having jurisdiction to try or otherwise deal with him, but without prejudice to any power of that court to make a hospital order or other order under this Part of this Act in his case.

(3) If the Secretary of State is notified by the responsible clinician, any other approved clinician or a Mental Health Review Tribunal at any time before the detainee's case is disposed of by that court –

(a) that the detainee no longer requires treatment in hospital for mental disorder; or

(b) that no effective treatment for his disorder can be given at the hospital to which he has been removed,

the Secretary of State may by warrant direct that he be remitted to any place where he might have been detained if he had not been removed to hospital, there to be dealt with as if he had not been so removed, and on his arrival at the place to which he is so remitted the transfer direction shall cease to have effect.

(4) If (no direction having been given under subsection (3) above) the court having jurisdiction to try or otherwise deal with the detainee is satisfied on the written or oral evidence of the responsible clinician –

(a) that the detainee no longer requires treatment in hospital for mental disorder; or

(b) that no effective treatment for his disorder can be given at the hospital to which he has been removed,

the court may order him to be remitted to any such place as is mentioned in subsection (3) above or, subject to section 25 of the Criminal Justice and Public Order Act 1994, released on bail and on his arrival at that place or, as the case may be, his release on bail the transfer direction shall cease to have effect.

(5) If (no direction or order having been given or made under subsection (3) or (4) above) it appears to the court having jurisdiction to try or otherwise deal with the detainee –

(a) that it is impracticable or inappropriate to bring the detainee before the court; and

(b) that the conditions set out in subsection (6) below are satisfied,

the court may make a hospital order (with or without a restriction order) in his case in his absence and, in the case of a person awaiting trial, without convicting him.

(6) A hospital order may be made in respect of a person under subsection (5) above if the court –

(a) is satisfied, on the written or oral evidence of at least two registered medical practitioners, that;

(i) the detainee is suffering from mental disorder of a nature or degree which makes it appropriate for the patient to be detained in a hospital for medical treatment; and

(ii) appropriate medical treatments is available for him; and

(b) is of the opinion, after considering any depositions or other documents required to be sent to the proper officer of the court, that it is proper to make such an order.

(7) Where a person committed to the Crown Court to be dealt with under section 43 above is admitted to a hospital in pursuance of an order under section 44 above, subsections (5) and (6) above shall apply as if he were a person subject to a transfer direction.

52 Further provisions as to persons remanded by magistrates' courts

(1) This section has effect where a transfer direction has been given in respect of any such person as is described in paragraph (b) of section 48(2) above; and that person is in this section referred to as 'the accused'.

(2) Subject to subsection (5) below, the transfer direction shall cease to have effect on the expiration of the period of remand unless the accused is sent in custody to the Crown Court for trial or to be otherwise dealt with.

(3) Subject to subsection (4) below, the power of further remanding the accused under section 128 of the Magistrates' Courts Act 1980 may be exercised by the court without his being brought before the court; and if the court further remands the accused in

custody (whether or not he is brought before the court) the period of remand shall, for the purposes of this section, be deemed not to have expired.

(4) The court shall not under subsection (3) above further remand the accused in his absence unless he has appeared before the court within the previous six months.

(5) If the magistrates' court is satisfied, on the written or oral evidence of the responsible clinician –

(a) that the accused no longer requires treatment in hospital for mental disorder; or

(b) that no effective treatment for his disorder can be given in the hospital to which he has been removed,

the court may direct that the transfer direction shall cease to have effect notwithstanding that the period of remand has not expired or that the accused is sent to the Crown Court as mentioned in subsection (2) above.

(6) If the accused is sent to the Crown Court as mentioned in subsection (2) above and the transfer direction has not ceased to have effect under subsection (5) above, section 51 above shall apply as if the transfer direction given in his case were a direction given in respect of a person falling within that section.

(7) The magistrates' court may, in the absence of the accused, send him to the Crown Court for trial under section 51 or 51A of the Crime and Disorder Act 1998 if –

(a) the court is satisfied, on the written or oral evidence of the responsible clinician, that the accused is unfit to take part in the proceedings& and

(b) the accused is represented by an authorised person.

53 Further provisions as to civil prisoners and persons detained under the Immigration Acts

(1) Subject to subsection (2) below, a transfer direction given in respect of any such person as is described in paragraph (c) or (d) of section 48(2) above shall cease to have effect on the expiration of the period during which he would, but for his removal to hospital, be liable to be detained in the place from which he was removed.

(2) Where a transfer direction and a restriction direction have been given in respect of any such person as is mentioned in subsection (1) above, then, if the Secretary of State is notified by the responsible clinician, any other approved clinician or a Mental Health Review Tribunal at any time before the expiration of the period there mentioned –

(a) that that person no longer requires treatment in hospital for mental disorder; or

(b) that no effective treatment for his disorder can be given in the hospital to which he has been removed,

the Secretary of State may by warrant direct that he be remitted to any place where he might have been detained if he had not been removed to hospital, and on his arrival at the place to which he is so remitted the transfer direction and the restriction direction shall cease to have effect

Supplemental

54 Requirements as to medical evidence

(1) The registered medical practitioner whose evidence is taken into account under section 35(3)(a) above and at least one of the registered medical practitioners whose evidence is taken into account under sections 36(1), 37(2)(a), 38(1), 45A(2) and 51(6) (a) above and whose reports are taken into account under sections 47(1) and 48(1) above shall be a practitioner approved for the purposes of section 12 above by the Secretary of State as having special experience in the diagnosis or treatment of mental disorder.

(2) For the purposes of any provision of this Part of this Act under which a court may act on the written evidence of any person, a report in writing purporting to be signed by that person may, subject to the provisions of this section, be received in evidence without proof of the following –

(a) the signature of the person; or

(b) his having the requisite qualifications or approval or authority or being of the requisite description to give the report.

(2A) But the court may require the signatory of any such report to be called to give oral evidence.

(3) Where, in pursuance of a direction of the court, any such report is tendered in evidence otherwise than by or on behalf of the person who is the subject of the report, then –

(a) if that person is represented by an authorised person, a copy of the report shall be given to that authorised person;

(b) if that person is not so represented, the substance of the report shall be disclosed to him or, where he is a child or young person, to his parent or guardian if present in court; and

(c) except where the report relates only to arrangements for his admission to a hospital, that person may require the signatory of the report to be called to give oral evidence, and evidence to rebut the evidence contained in the report may be called by or on behalf of that person.

55 Interpretation of Part III

(1) In this Part of this Act –'authorised person' means a person who, for the purposes of the Legal Services Act 2007, is an authorised person in relation to an activity which constitutes the exercise of a right of audience (within the meaning of that Act);[1]

'child' and 'young person' have the same meaning as in the Children and Young Persons Act 1933;

'civil prisoner' has the meaning given to it by section 48(2)(c) above;

'guardian', in relation to a child or young person, has the same meaning as in the Children and Young Persons Act 1933;

'place of safety', in relation to a person who is not a child or young person, means any police station, prison or remand centre, or any hospital the managers of which are willing temporarily to receive him, and in relation to a child or young person has the same meaning as in the Children and Young Persons Act 1933;

'responsible clinician', in relation to a person liable to be detained in a hospital within the meaning of Part 2 of this Act, means the approved clinician with overall responsibility for the patient's case.

(2) Any reference in this Part of this Act to an offence punishable on summary conviction with imprisonment shall be construed without regard to any prohibition or restriction imposed by or under any enactment relating to the imprisonment of young offenders.

(4) Any reference to a hospital order, a guardianship order or a restriction order in section 40(2), (4) or (5), section 41(3) to (5), or section 42 above or section 69(1) below shall be construed as including a reference to any order or direction under this Part of this Act having the same effect as the first-mentioned order; and the exceptions and modifications set out in Schedule 1 to this Act in respect of the provisions of this Act described in that Schedule accordingly include those which are consequential on the provisions of this subsection.

(5) Section 34(2) above shall apply for the purposes of this Part of this Act as it applies for the purposes of Part II of this Act.

(6) References in this Part of this Act to persons serving a sentence of imprisonment shall be construed in accordance with section 47(5) above.

(7) Section 99 of the Children and Young Persons Act 1933 (which relates to the presumption and determination of age) shall apply for the purposes of this Part of this Act as it applies for the purposes of that Act.

PART IV

CONSENT TO TREATMENT

56 Patients to whom Part 4 applies

(1) Section 57 and, so far as relevant to that section, sections 59 to 62 below apply to any patient.

(2) Subject to that and to subsection (5) below, this Part of this Act applies to a patient only if he falls within subsection (3) or (4) below.

(3) A patient falls within this subsection if he is liable to be detained under this Act but not if –

(a) he is so liable by virtue of an emergency application and the second medical recommendation referred to in section 4(4)(a) above has not been given and received;

(b) he is so liable by virtue of section 5(2) or (4) or 35 above or section 135 or 136 below or by virtue of a direction for his detention in a place of safety under section 37(4) or 45A(5) above; or

(c) he has been conditionally discharged under section 42(2) above or section 73 or 74 below and he is not recalled to hospital.

(4) A patient falls within this subsection if

(a) he is a community patient; and

(b) he is recalled to hospital under section 17E above.

(5) Section 58A and, so far as relevant to that section, sections 59 to 62 below also apply to any patient who –

(a) does not fall within subsection (3) above;

(b) is not a community patient; and

(c) has not attained the age of 18 years.

57 Treatment requiring consent and a second opinion

(1) This section applies to the following forms of medical treatment for mental disorder –

(a) any surgical operation for destroying brain tissue or for destroying the functioning of brain tissue; and

(b) such other forms of treatment as may be specified for the purposes of this section by regulations made by the Secretary of State.

---

[1] Definition of 'authorised person' inserted by paragraph 597 of Schedule 21 to the Legal Services Act 2007, but that amendment is not yet in force.

(2) Subject to section 62 below, a patient shall not be given any form of treatment to which this section applies unless he has consented to it and –

    (a) a registered medical practitioner appointed for the purposes of this Part of this Act by the Secretary of State (not being the responsible clinician (f there is one) or the person in charge of the treatment in question) and two other persons appointed for the purposes of this paragraph by the Secretary of State (not being registered medical practitioners) have certified in writing that the patient is capable of understanding the nature, purpose and likely effects of the treatment in question and has consented to it; and

    (b) the registered medical practitioner referred to in paragraph (a) above has certified in writing that it is appropriate for the treatment to be given.

(3) Before giving a certificate under subsection (2)(b) above the registered medical practitioner concerned shall consult two other persons who have been professionally concerned with the patient's medical treatment but of those persons –

    (a) one shall be a nurse and the other shall be neither a nurse nor a registered medical practitioner; and

    (b) neither shall be the responsible clinician (if there is one) or the person in charge of the treatment in question.

(4) Before making any regulations for the purpose of this section the Secretary of State shall consult such bodies as appear to him to be concerned.

58 Treatment requiring consent or a second opinion

(1) This section applies to the following forms of medical treatment for mental disorder –

    (a) such forms of treatment as may be specified for the purposes of this section by regulations made by the Secretary of State;

    (b) the administration of medicine to a patient by any means (not being a form of treatment specified under paragraph (a) above or section 57 above or section 58A(1)(b) below) at any time during a period for which he is liable to be detained as a patient to whom this Part of this Act applies if three months or more have elapsed since the first occasion in that period when medicine was administered to him by any means for his mental disorder.

(2) The Secretary of State may by order vary the length of the period mentioned in subsection (1)(b) above.

(3) Subject to section 62 below, a patient shall not be given any form of treatment to which this section applies unless –

    (a) he has consented to that treatment and either the approved clinician in charge of it or a registered medical practitioner appointed for the purposes of this Part of this Act by the Secretary of State has certified in writing that the patient is capable of understanding its nature, purpose and likely effects and has consented to it;

    (b) a registered medical practitioner appointed as aforesaid (not being the responsible clinician or the approved clinician in charge of the treatment in question) has certified in writing that the patient is not capable of understanding the nature, purpose and likely effects of that treatment or being so capable has not consented to it but that it is appropriate for the treatment to be given.

(4) Before giving a certificate under subsection (3)(b) above the registered medical practitioner concerned shall consult two other persons who have been professionally concerned with the patient's medical treatment, but of those persons –

    (a) one shall be a nurse and the other shall be neither a nurse nor a registered medical practitioner; and

    (b) neither shall be the responsible clinician or the person in charge of the treatment in question.

(5) Before making any regulations for the purposes of this section the Secretary of State shall consult such bodies as appear to him to be concerned.

58A Electro-convulsive therapy, etc.

(1) This section applies to the following forms of medical treatment for mental disorder –

    (a) electro-convulsive therapy; and

    (b) such other forms of treatment as may be specified for the purposes of this section by regulations made by the appropriate national authority.

(2) Subject to section 62 below, a patient shall be not be given any form of treatment to which this section applies unless he falls within subsection (3), (4) or (5) below.

(3) A patient falls within this subsection if –

    (a) he has attained the age of 18 years;

    (b) he has consented to the treatment in question; and

    (c) either the approved clinician in charge of it or a registered medical practitioner appointed as mentioned in section 58(3) above has certified in writing that the patient is capable of understanding the nature, purpose and likely effects of the treatment and has consented to it.

(4) A patient falls within this subsection if –

    (a) he has not attained the age of 18 years; but

(b) he has consented to the treatment in question; and

(c) a registered medical practitioner appointed as aforesaid (not being the approved clinician in charge of the treatment) has certified in writing –

(i) that the patient is capable of understanding the nature, purpose and likely effects of the treatment and has consented to it; and

(ii) that it is appropriate for the treatment to be given.

(5) A patient falls within this subsection if a registered medical practitioner appointed as aforesaid (not being the responsible clinician (if there is one) or the approved clinician in charge of the treatment in question) has certified in writing –

(a) that the patient is not capable of understanding the nature, purpose and likely effects of the treatment; but

(b) that it is appropriate for the treatment to be given; and

(c) that giving him the treatment would not conflict with –

(i) an advance decision which the registered medical practitioner concerned is satisfied is valid and applicable;

(ii) a decision made by a donee or deputy or by the Court of Protection.

(6) Before giving a certificate under subsection (5) above the registered medical practitioner concerned shall consult two other persons who have been professionally concerned with the patient's medical treatment, but of those persons –

(a) one shall be a nurse and the other shall be neither a nurse nor a registered medical practitioner; and

(b) neither shall be the responsible clinician (if there is one) or the approved clinician in charge of the treatment in question.

(7) This section shall not by itself confer sufficient authority for a patient who falls within section 56(5) above to be given a form of treatment to which this section applies if he is not capable of understanding the nature, purpose and likely effects of the treatment (and cannot therefore consent to it).

(8) Before making any regulations for the purposes of this section, the appropriate national authority shall consult such bodies as appear to it to be concerned.

(9) In this section –

(a) a reference to an advance decision is to an advance decision (within the meaning of the Mental Capacity Act 2005) made by the patient;

(b) 'valid and applicable', in relation to such a decision, means valid and applicable to the treatment in question in accordance with section 25 of that Act;

(c) a reference to a donee is to a donee of a lasting power of attorney (within the meaning of section 9 of that Act) created by the patient, where the donee is acting within the scope of his authority and in accordance with that Act; and

(d) a reference to a deputy is to a deputy appointed for the patient by the Court of Protection under section 16 of that Act, where the deputy is acting within the scope of his authority and in accordance with that Act.

(10) In this section, 'the appropriate national authority' means –

(a) in a case where the treatment in question would, if given, be given in England, the Secretary of State;

(b) in a case where the treatment in question would, if given, be given in Wales, the Welsh Ministers.

59 Plans of treatment

Any consent or certificate under section 57, 58 or 58A above may relate to a plan of treatment under which the patient is to be given (whether within a specified period or otherwise) one or more of the forms of treatment to which that section applies.

60 Withdrawal of consent

(1) Where the consent of a patient to any treatment has been given for the purposes of section 57, 58 or 58A above, the patient may, subject to section 62 below, at any time before the completion of the treatment withdraw his consent, and those sections shall then apply as if the remainder of the treatment were a separate form of treatment.

(1A) Subsection (1B) below applies where –

(a) the consent of a patient to any treatment has been given for the purposes of section 57, 58 or 58A above; but

(b) before the completion of the treatment, the patient ceases to be capable of understanding its nature, purpose and likely effects.

(1B) The patient shall, subject to section 62 below, be treated as having withdrawn his consent, and those sections shall then apply as if the remainder of the treatment were a separate form of treatment.

(1C) Subsection (1D) below applies where –

(a) a certificate has been given under section 58 or 58A above that a patient is not capable of understanding the nature, purpose and likely effects of the treatment to which the certificate applies; but

(b) before the completion of the treatment, the patient becomes capable of understanding its nature, purpose and likely effects.

(1D) The certificate shall, subject to section 62 below, cease to apply to the treatment and those sections shall then apply as if the remainder of the treatment were a separate form of treatment.

(2) Without prejudice to the application of subsections (1) to (1D) above to any treatment given under the plan of treatment to which a patient has consented, a patient who has consented to such a plan may, subject to section 62 below, at any time withdraw his consent to further treatment, or to further treatment of any description, under the plan.

61 Review of treatment

(1) Where a patient is given treatment in accordance with section 57(2), 58(3)(b) or 58A(4) or (5) above, or by virtue of section 62A below in accordance with a Part 4A certificate (within the meaning of that section), a report on the treatment and the patient's condition shall be given by the approved clinician in charge of the treatment to the Secretary of State –

   (a) on the next occasion on which the responsible clinician furnishes a report under section 20(3), 20A(4) or 21B(2) above in respect of the patient; and

   (b) at any other time if so required by the Secretary of State.

(2) In relation to a patient who is subject to a restriction order, limitation direction or restriction direction subsection (1) above shall have effect as if paragraph (a) required the report to be made –

   (a) in the case of treatment in the period of six months beginning with the date of the order or direction, at the end of that period;

   (b) in the case of treatment at any subsequent time, on the next occasion on which the responsible clinician makes a report in respect of the patient under section 41(6), 45B(3) or 49(3) above.

(3) The Secretary of State may at any time give notice directing that, subject to section 62 below, a certificate given in respect of a patient under section 57(2) or 58(3)(b) or 58A(4) or (5) above shall not apply to treatment given to him after a date specified in the notice and sections 57, 58 and 58A above shall then apply to any such treatment as if that certificate had not been given.

(3A) The notice under subsection (3) above shall be given to the approved clinician in charge of the treatment.

62 Urgent treatment

(1) Sections 57 and 58 above shall not apply to any treatment –

   (a) which is immediately necessary to save the patient's life; or

   (b) which (not being irreversible) is immediately necessary to prevent a serious deterioration of his condition; or

   (c) which (not being irreversible or hazardous) is immediately necessary to alleviate serious suffering by the patient; or

   (d) which (not being irreversible or hazardous) is immediately necessary and represents the minimum interference necessary to prevent the patient from behaving violently or being a danger to himself or to others.

(1A) Section 58A above, in so far as it relates to electro-convulsive therapy by virtue of subsection (1)(a) of that section, shall not apply to any treatment which falls within paragraph (a) or (b) of subsection (1) above.

(1B) Section 58A above, in so far as it relates to a form of treatment specified by virtue of subsection (1)(b) of that section, shall not apply to any treatment which falls within such of paragraphs (a) to (d) of subsection (1) above as may be specified in regulations under that section.

(1C) For the purposes of subsection (1B) above, the regulations –

   (a) may make different provision for different cases (and may, in particular, make different provision for different forms of treatment);

   (b) may make provision which applies subject to specified exceptions; and

   (c) may include transitional, consequential, incidental or supplemental provision.

(2) Sections 60 and 61(3) above shall not preclude the continuation of any treatment or of treatment under any plan pending compliance with section 57, 58 or 58A above if the approved clinician in charge of the treatment considers that the discontinuance of the treatment or of treatment under the plan would cause serious suffering to the patient.

(3) For the purposes of this section treatment is irreversible if it has unfavourable irreversible physical or psychological consequences and hazardous if it entails significant physical hazard.

62A Treatment on recall of community patient or revocation of order

(1) This section applies where –

   (a) a community patient is recalled to hospital under section 17E above; or

   (b) a patient is liable to be detained under this Act following the revocation of a community treatment order under section 17F above in respect of him.

(2) For the purposes of section 58(1)(b) above, the patient is to be treated as if he had remained liable to be detained since the making of the community treatment order.

(3)   But section 58 above does not apply to treatment given to the patient if –

    (a) the certificate requirement is met for the purposes of section 64C or 64E below; or

    (b) as a result of section 64B(4) or 64E(4) below, the certificate requirement would not apply (were the patient a community patient not recalled to hospital under section 17E above).

(4)   Section 58A above does not apply to treatment given to the patient if there is authority to give the treatment, and the certificate requirement is met, for the purposes of section 64C or 64E below.

(5)   In a case where this section applies, the certificate requirement is met only in so far as –

    (a) the Part 4A certificate expressly provides that it is appropriate for one or more specified forms of treatment to be given to the patient in that case (subject to such conditions as may be specified); or

    (b) a notice having been given under subsection (5) of section 64H below, treatment is authorised by virtue of subsection (8) of that section.

(6)   Subsection (5)(a) above shall not preclude the continuation of any treatment, or of treatment under any plan, pending compliance with section 58 or 58A above if the approved clinician in charge of the treatment considers that the discontinuance of the treatment, or of the treatment under the plan, would cause serious suffering to the patient.

(7)   In a case where subsection (1)(b) above applies, subsection (3) above only applies pending compliance with section 58 above.

(8)   In subsection (5) above –

'Part 4A certificate' has the meaning given in section 64H below; and

'specified', in relation to a Part 4A certificate, means specified in the certificate.

63 Treatment not requiring consent

The consent of a patient shall not be required for any medical treatment given to him for the mental disorder from which he is suffering, not being a form of treatment to which section 57, 58 or 58A above applies, if the treatment is given by or under the direction of the approved clinician in charge of the treatment.

64 Supplementary provisions for Part IV

(1)   In this Part of this Act 'the responsible clinician' means the approved clinician with overall responsibility for the case of the patient in question and 'hospital' includes a registered establishment.

(1A) References in this Part of this Act to the approved clinician in charge of a patient's treatment shall, where the treatment in question is a form of treatment to which section 57 above applies, be construed as references to the person in charge of the treatment.

(1B) References in this Part of this Act to the approved clinician in charge of a patient's treatment shall, where the treatment in question is a form of treatment to which section 58A above applies and the patient falls within section 56(5) above, be construed as references to the person in charge of the treatment.

(1C) Regulations made by virtue of section 32(2)(d) above apply for the purposes of this Part as they apply for the purposes of Part 2 of this Act.

(2)   Any certificate for the purposes of this Part of this Act shall be in such form as may be prescribed by regulations made by the Secretary of State.

(3)   For the purposes of this Part of this Act, it is appropriate for treatment to be given to a patient if the treatment is appropriate in his case, taking into account the nature and degree of the mental disorder from which he is suffering and all other circumstances of his case.

PART IVA

TREATMENT OF COMMUNITY PATIENTS NOT RECALLED TO HOSPITAL

64A Meaning of 'relevant treatment'

In this Part of this Act 'relevant treatment', in relation to a patient, means medical treatment which –

    (a) is for the mental disorder from which the patient is suffering; and

    (b) is not a form of treatment to which section 57 above applies.

64B Adult community patients

(1)   This section applies to the giving of relevant treatment to a community patient who –

    (a) is not recalled to hospital under section 17E above; and

    (b) has attained the age of 16 years.

(2) The treatment may not be given to the patient unless –

    (a) there is authority to give it to him; and

    (b) if it is section 58 type treatment or section 58A type treatment, the certificate requirement is met.

(3) But the certificate requirement does not apply if –

    (a) giving the treatment to the patient is authorised in accordance with section 64G below; or

    (b) the treatment is immediately necessary and –

        (i) the patient has capacity to consent to it and does consent to it; or

        (ii) a donee or deputy or the Court of Protection consents to the treatment on the patient's behalf.

(4) Nor does the certificate requirement apply in so far as the administration of medicine to the patient at any time during the period of one month beginning with the day on which the community treatment order is made is section 58 type treatment.

(5) The reference in subsection (4) above to the administration of medicine does not include any form of treatment specified under section 58(1)(a) above.

64C Section 64B: supplemental

(1) This section has effect for the purposes of section 64B above.

(2) There is authority to give treatment to a patient if –

    (a) he has capacity to consent to it and does consent to it;

    (b) a donee or deputy or the Court of Protection consents to it on his behalf; or

    (c) giving it to him is authorised in accordance with section 64D or 64G below.

(3) Relevant treatment is section 58 type treatment or section 58A type treatment if, at the time when it is given to the patient, section 58 or 58A (respectively) would have applied to it, had the patient remained liable to be detained at that time (rather than being a community patient).

(4) The certificate requirement is met in respect of treatment to be given to a patient if –

    (a) a registered medical practitioner appointed for the purposes of Part 4 of this Act (not being the responsible clinician or the person in charge of the treatment) has certified in writing that it is appropriate for the treatment to be given or for the treatment to be given subject to such conditions as may be specified in the certificate; and

    (b) if conditions are so specified, the conditions are satisfied.

(5) In a case where the treatment is section 58 type treatment, treatment is immediately necessary if –

    (a) it is immediately necessary to save the patient's life; or

    (b) it is immediately necessary to prevent a serious deterioration of the patient's condition and is not irreversible; or

    (c) it is immediately necessary to alleviate serious suffering by the patient and is not irreversible or hazardous; or

    (d) it is immediately necessary, represents the minimum interference necessary to prevent the patient from behaving violently or being a danger to himself or others and is not irreversible or hazardous.

(6) In a case where the treatment is section 58A type treatment by virtue of subsection (1)(a) of that section, treatment is immediately necessary if it falls within paragraph (a) or (b) of subsection (5) above.

(7) In a case where the treatment is section 58A type treatment by virtue of subsection (1)(b) of that section, treatment is immediately necessary if it falls within such of paragraphs (a) to (d) of subsection (5) above as may be specified in regulations under that section.

(8) For the purposes of subsection (7) above, the regulations –

    (a) may make different provision for different cases (and may, in particular, make different provision for different forms of treatment);

    (b) may make provision which applies subject to specified exceptions; and

    (c) may include transitional, consequential, incidental or supplemental provision.

(9) Subsection (3) of section 62 above applies for the purposes of this section as it applies for the purposes of that section.

64D Adult community patients lacking capacity

(1) A person is authorised to give relevant treatment to a patient as mentioned in section 64C(2)(c) above if the conditions in subsections (2) to (6) below are met.

(2) The first condition is that, before giving the treatment, the person takes reasonable steps to establish whether the patient lacks capacity to consent to the treatment.

(3) The second condition is that, when giving the treatment, he reasonably believes that the patient lacks capacity to consent to it.

(4) The third condition is that –

    (a) he has no reason to believe that the patient objects to being given the treatment; or

    (b) he does have reason to believe that the patient so objects, but it is not necessary to use force against the patient in order to give the treatment.

(5) The fourth condition is that –

    (a) he is the person in charge of the treatment and an approved clinician; or

    (b) the treatment is given under the direction of that clinician.

(6) The fifth condition is that giving the treatment does not conflict with –

    (a) an advance decision which he is satisfied is valid and applicable; or

    (b) a decision made by a donee or deputy or the Court of Protection.

(7) In this section –

    (a) reference to an advance decision is to an advance decision (within the meaning of the Mental Capacity Act 2005) made by the patient; and

    (b) 'valid and applicable', in relation to such a decision, means valid and applicable to the treatment in question in accordance with section 25 of that Act.

64E Child community patients

(1) This section applies to the giving of relevant treatment to a community patient who –

    (a) is not recalled to hospital under section 17E above; and

    (b) has not attained the age of 16 years.

(2) The treatment may not be given to the patient unless –

    (a) there is authority to give it to him; and

    (b) if it is section 58 type treatment or section 58A type treatment, the certificate requirement is met.

(3) But the certificate requirement does not apply if –

    (a) giving the treatment to the patient is authorised in accordance with section 64G below; or

    (b) in a case where the patient is competent to consent to the treatment and does consent to it, the treatment is immediately necessary.

(4) Nor does the certificate requirement apply in so far as the administration of medicine to the patient at any time during the period of one month beginning with the day on which the community treatment order is made is section 58 type treatment.

(5) The reference in subsection (4) above to the administration of medicine does not include any form of treatment specified under section 58(1)(a) above.

(6) For the purposes of subsection (2)(a) above, there is authority to give treatment to a patient if –

    (a) he is competent to consent to it and he does consent to it; or

    (b) giving it to him is authorised in accordance with section 64F or 64G below.

(7) Subsections (3) to (9) of section 64C above have effect for the purposes of this section as they have effect for the purposes of section 64B above.

(8) Regulations made by virtue of section 32(2)(d) above apply for the purposes of this section as they apply for the purposes of Part 2 of this Act.

64F Child community patients lacking competence

(1) A person is authorised to give relevant treatment to a patient as mentioned in section 64E(6)(b) above if the conditions in subsections (2) to (5) below are met.

(2) The first condition is that, before giving the treatment, the person takes reasonable steps to establish whether the patient is competent to consent to the treatment.

(3) The second condition is that, when giving the treatment, he reasonably believes that the patient is not competent to consent to it.

(4) The third condition is that –

    (a) he has no reason to believe that the patient objects to being given the treatment; or

    (b) he does have reason to believe that the patient so objects, but it is not necessary to use force against the patient in order to give the treatment.

(5) The fourth condition is that –

    (a) he is the person in charge of the treatment and an approved clinician; or

    (b) the treatment is given under the direction of that clinician.

64G Emergency treatment for patients lacking capacity or competence

(1) A person is also authorised to give relevant treatment to a patient as mentioned in section 64C(2)(c) or 64E(6)(b) above if the conditions in subsections (2) to (4) below are met.

(2) The first condition is that, when giving the treatment, the person reasonably believes that the patient lacks capacity to consent to it or, as the case may be, is not competent to consent to it.

(3) The second condition is that the treatment is immediately necessary.

(4) The third condition is that if it is necessary to use force against the patient in order to give the treatment –

    (a) the treatment needs to be given in order to prevent harm to the patient; and

    (b) the use of such force is a proportionate response to the likelihood of the patient's suffering harm, and to the seriousness of that harm.

(5) Subject to subsections (6) to (8) below, treatment is immediately necessary if –

    (a) it is immediately necessary to save the patient's life; or

    (b) it is immediately necessary to prevent a serious deterioration of the patient's condition and is not irreversible; or

    (c) it is immediately necessary to alleviate serious suffering by the patient and is not irreversible or hazardous; or

    (d) it is immediately necessary, represents the minimum interference necessary to prevent the patient from behaving violently or being a danger to himself or others and is not irreversible or hazardous.

(6) Where the treatment is section 58A type treatment by virtue of subsection (1)(a) of that section, treatment is immediately necessary if it falls within paragraph (a) or (b) of subsection (5) above.

(7) Where the treatment is section 58A type treatment by virtue of subsection (1)(b) of that section, treatment is immediately necessary if it falls within such of paragraphs (a) to (d) of subsection (5) above as may be specified in regulations under section 58A above.

(8) For the purposes of subsection (7) above, the regulations –

    (a) may make different provision for different cases (and may, in particular, make different provision for different forms of treatment);

    (b) may make provision which applies subject to specified exceptions; and

    (c) may include transitional, consequential, incidental or supplemental provision.

(9) Subsection (3) of section 62 above applies for the purposes of this section as it applies for the purposes of that section.

64H Certificates: supplementary provisions

(1) A certificate under section 64B(2)(b) or 64E(2)(b) above (a 'Part 4A certificate') may relate to a plan of treatment under which the patient is to be given (whether within a specified period or otherwise) one or more forms of section 58 type treatment or section 58A type treatment.

(2) A Part 4A certificate shall be in such form as may be prescribed by regulations made by the appropriate national authority.

(3) Before giving a Part 4A certificate, the registered medical practitioner concerned shall consult two other persons who have been professionally concerned with the patient's medical treatment but, of those persons –

    (a) at least one shall be a person who is not a registered medical practitioner; and

    (b) neither shall be the patient's responsible clinician or the person in charge of the treatment in question.

(4) Where a patient is given treatment in accordance with a Part 4A certificate, a report on the treatment and the patient's condition shall be given by the person in charge of the treatment to the appropriate national authority if required by that authority.

(5) The appropriate national authority may at any time give notice directing that a Part 4A certificate shall not apply to treatment given to a patient after a date specified in the notice, and the relevant section shall then apply to any such treatment as if that certificate had not been given.

(6) The relevant section is –

    (a) if the patient is not recalled to hospital in accordance with section 17E above, section 64B or 64E above;

    (b) if the patient is so recalled or is liable to be detained under this Act following revocation of the community treatment order under section 17F above –

        (i) section 58 above, in the case of section 58 type treatment;

        (ii) section 58A above, in the case of section 58A type treatment;

  (subject to section 62A(2) above).

(7) The notice under subsection (5) above shall be given to the person in charge of the treatment in question.

(8) Subsection (5) above shall not preclude the continuation of any treatment or of treatment under any plan pending compliance with the relevant section if the person in charge of the treatment considers that the discontinuance of the treatment or of treatment under the plan would cause serious suffering to the patient.

(9) In this section, 'the appropriate national authority' means –

    (a) in relation to community patients in respect of whom the responsible hospital is in England, the Secretary of State;

    (b) in relation to community patients in respect of whom the responsible hospital is in Wales, the Welsh Ministers.

64I Liability for negligence

Nothing in section 64D, 64F or 64G above excludes a person's civil liability for loss or damage, or his criminal liability, resulting from his negligence in doing anything authorised to be done by that section.

64J Factors to be considered in determining whether patient objects to treatment

(1) In assessing for the purposes of this Part whether he has reason to believe that a patient objects to treatment, a person shall consider all the circumstances so far as they are reasonably ascertainable, including the patient's behaviour, wishes, feelings, views, beliefs and values.

(2) But circumstances from the past shall be considered only so far as it is still appropriate to consider them.

64K Interpretation of Part 4A

(1) This Part of this Act is to be construed as follows.

(2) References to a patient who lacks capacity are to a patient who lacks capacity within the meaning of the Mental Capacity Act 2005.

(3) References to a patient who has capacity are to be read accordingly.

(4) References to a donee are to a donee of a lasting power of attorney (within the meaning of section 9 of the Mental Capacity Act 2005) created by the patient, where the donee is acting within the scope of his authority and in accordance with that Act.

(5) References to a deputy are to a deputy appointed for the patient by the Court of Protection under section 16 of the Mental Capacity Act 2005, where the deputy is acting within the scope of his authority and in accordance with that Act.

(6) Reference to the responsible clinician shall be construed as a reference to the responsible clinician within the meaning of Part 2 of this Act.

(7) References to a hospital include a registered establishment.

(8) Section 64(3) above applies for the purposes of this Part of this Act as it applies for the purposes of Part 4 of this Act.

PART V

MENTAL HEALTH REVIEW TRIBUNALS

78 Procedure of tribunals

(1) The Lord Chancellor may make rules with respect to the making of applications to Mental Health Review Tribunals and with respect to the proceedings of such tribunals and matters incidental to or consequential on such proceedings.

In November 2008 he changed the tribunal system for England under Statutory Instrument 2008 No. 2705 (L. 17) Tribunals And Inquiries, England And Wales and introduced new rules for the reconstituted Mental Health Review Tribunal for Wales Rules. See
www.opsi.gov.uk/si/si2008/uksi_20082705_en_1
www.mhrt.org.uk/
www.wikimentalhealth.co.uk/Mental_Health_Review_Tribunal_for_Wales_Rules_2008

PART VIII

MISCELLANEOUS FUNCTIONS OF LOCAL AUTHORITIES AND THE SECRETARY OF STATE

Approved mental health professionals

114 Approval by local social services authority

(1) A local social services authority may approve a person to act as an approved mental health professional for the purposes of this Act.

(2) But a local social services authority may not approve a registered medical practitioner to act as an approved mental health professional.

(3) Before approving a person under subsection (1) above, a local social service authority shall be satisfied that he has appropriate competence in dealing with persons who are suffering from mental disorder.

(4) The appropriate national authority may by regulations make provision in connection with the giving of approvals under subsection (1) above.

(5) The provision which may be made by regulations under subsection (4) above includes, in particular, provision as to –

(a) the period for which approvals under subsection (1) above have effect;

(b) the courses to be undertaken by persons before such approvals are to be given and during the period for which such approvals have effect;

(c) the conditions subject to which such approvals are to be given; and

(d) the factors to be taken into account in determining whether persons have appropriate competence as mentioned in subsection (3) above.

(6) Provision made by virtue of subsection (5)(b) above may relate to courses approved or provided by such person as may be specified in the regulations (as well as to courses approved under section 114A below).

(7) An approval by virtue of subsection (6) above may be in respect of a course in general or in respect of a course in relation to a particular person.

(8) The power to make regulations under subsection (4) above includes power to make different provision for different cases or areas.

(9) In this section 'the appropriate national authority' means –

(a) in relation to persons who are or wish to become approved to act as approved mental health professionals by a local social services authority whose area is in England, the Secretary of State;

(b) in relation to persons who are or wish to become approved to act as approved mental health professionals by a local social services authority whose area is in Wales, the Welsh Ministers.

(10) In this Act 'approved mental health professional' means –

(a) in relation to acting on behalf of a local social services authority whose area is in England, a person approved under subsection (1) above by any local social services authority whose area is in England, and

(b) in relation to acting on behalf of a local social services authority whose area is in Wales, a person approved under that subsection by any local social services authority whose area is in Wales.

115 Powers of entry and inspection

(1) An approved mental health professional may at all reasonable times enter and inspect any premises (other than a hospital) in which a mentally disordered patient is living, if he has reasonable cause to believe that the patient is not under proper care.

(2) The power under subsection (1) above shall be exercisable only after the professional has produced, if asked to do so, some duly authenticated document showing that he is an approved mental health professional.

Visiting patients

116 Welfare of certain hospital patients

(1) Where a patient to whom this section applies is admitted to a hospital, independent hospital or care home in England and Wales (whether for treatment for mental disorder or for any other reason) then, without prejudice to their duties in relation to the patient apart from the provisions of this section, the authority shall arrange for visits to be made to him on behalf of the authority, and shall take such other steps in relation to the patient while in the hospital, independent hospital or care home as would be expected to be taken by his parents.

(2) This section applies to –

(a) a child or young person –

(i) who is in the care of a local authority by virtue of a care order within the meaning of the Children Act 1989, or

(ii) in respect of whom the rights and powers of a parent are vested in a local authority by virtue of section 16 of the Social Work (Scotland) Act 1968;

(b) a person who is subject to the guardianship of a local social services authority under the provisions of this Act; or

(c) a person the functions of whose nearest relative under this Act are for the time being transferred to a local social services authority.

After-care

117 After-care

(1) This section applies to persons who are detained under section 3 above, or admitted to a hospital in pursuance of a hospital order made under section 37 above, or transferred to a hospital in pursuance of a hospital direction made under section 45A

above or a transfer direction made under section 47 or 48 above, and then cease to be detained and (whether or not immediately after so ceasing) leave hospital.

(2) It shall be the duty of the Primary Care Trust or Local Health Board and of the local social services authority to provide, in co-operation with relevant voluntary agencies, after-care services for any person to whom this section applies until such time as the Primary Care Trust or Local Health Board and the local social services authority are satisfied that the person concerned is no longer in need of such services; but they shall not be so satisfied in the case of a community patient while he remains such a patient.

(2B) Section 32 above shall apply for the purposes of this section as it applies for the purposes of Part II of this Act.

(3) In this section 'the Primary Care Trust or Local Health Board' means the Primary Care Trust or Local Health Board, and 'the local social services authority' means the local social services authority, for the area in which the person concerned is resident or to which he is sent on discharge by the hospital in which he was detained.

Functions of the Secretary of State

118 Code of practice

(1) The Secretary of State shall prepare, and from time to time revise, a code of practice.

(2) The code shall, in particular, specify forms of medical treatment in addition to any specified by regulations made for the purposes of section 57 above which in the opinion of the Secretary of State give rise to special concern and which should accordingly not be given by a registered medical practitioner unless the patient has consented to the treatment (or to a plan of treatment including that treatment) and a certificate in writing as to the matters mentioned in subsection (2)(a) and (b) of that section has been given by another registered medical practitioner, being a practitioner appointed for the purposes of this section by the Secretary of State.

(2A) The code shall include a statement of the principles which the Secretary of State thinks should inform decisions under this Act.

(2B) In preparing the statement of principles the Secretary of State shall, in particular, ensure that each of the following matters is addressed –

(a) respect for patients' past and present wishes and feelings,

(b) respect for diversity generally including, in particular, diversity of religion, culture and sexual orientation (within the meaning of section 35 of the Equality Act 2006),

(c) minimising restrictions on liberty,

(d) involvement of patients in planning, developing and delivering care and treatment appropriate to them,

(e) avoidance of unlawful discrimination,

(f) effectiveness of treatment,

(g) views of carers and other interested parties,

(h) patient wellbeing and safety, and

(i) public safety.

(2C) The Secretary of State shall also have regard to the desirability of ensuring –

(a) the efficient use of resources, and

(b) the equitable distribution of services.

(2D) In performing functions under this Act persons mentioned in subsection (1)(a) or (b) shall have regard to the code.

119 Practitioners approved for Part IV and s 118

(1) The Secretary of State may make such provision as he may with the approval of the Treasury determine for the payment of remuneration, allowances, pensions or gratuities to or in respect of registered medical practitioners appointed by him for the purposes of Part IV of this Act and section 118 above and to or in respect of other persons appointed for the purposes of section 57(2)(a) above.

(2) A registered medical practitioner or other person appointed by the Secretary of State for the purposes of the provisions mentioned in subsection (1) above may, for the purpose of exercising his functions under those provisions or under Part 4A of this Act, at any reasonable time –

(a) visit and interview and, in the case of a registered medical practitioner, examine in private any patient detained in a hospital or registered establishment or any community patient in a hospital or establishment of any description or (if access is granted) other place; and

(b) require the production of and inspect any records relating to the treatment of the patient there.

(3) In this section, 'establishment of any description' shall be construed in accordance with section 4(8) of the Care Standards Act 2000.

120 General protection of detained patients

(1) The Secretary of State shall keep under review the exercise of the powers and the discharge of the duties conferred or imposed by this Act so far as relating to the detention of patients or to patients liable to be detained under this Act or to community patients and shall make arrangements for persons authorised by him in that behalf –

    (a) to visit and interview in private patients detained under this Act in hospitals and registered establishments and community patients in hospitals and establishments of any description and (if access is granted) other places; and

    (b) to investigate –

        (i) any complaint made by a person in respect of a matter that occurred while he was detained under this Act in, or recalled under section 17E above to, a hospital or registered establishment and which he considers has not been satisfactorily dealt with by the managers of that hospital or registered establishment; and

        (ii) any other complaint as to the exercise of the powers or the discharge of the duties conferred or imposed by this Act in respect of a person who is or has been so detained or is or has been a community patient.

(2) The arrangements made under this section in respect of the investigation of complaints may exclude matters from investigation in specified circumstances and shall not require any person exercising functions under the arrangements to undertake or continue with any investigation where he does not consider it appropriate to do so.

(3) Where any such complaint as is mentioned in subsection (1)(b)(ii) above is made by a Member of Parliament and investigated under the arrangements made under this section the results of the investigation shall be reported to him.

(4) For the purpose of any such review as is mentioned in subsection (1) above or of carrying out his functions under arrangements made under this section any person authorised in that behalf by the Secretary of State may at any reasonable time –

    (a) visit and interview and, if he is a registered medical practitioner or approved clinician, examine in private any patient in a hospital or establishment of any description; and

    (b) require the production of and inspect any records relating to the detention or treatment of any person who is or has been detained under this Act or who is or has been a community patient.

(6) The Secretary of State may make such provision as he may with the approval of the Treasury determine for the payment of remuneration, allowances, pensions or gratuities to or in respect of persons exercising functions in relation to any such review as is mentioned in subsection (1) above or functions under arrangements made under this section.

(7) The powers and duties referred to in subsection (1) above do not include any power or duty conferred or imposed by Part VII of this Act.

(8) In this section, 'establishment of any description' has the same meaning as in section 119 above.

123 Transfers to and from special hospitals

(1) Without prejudice to any other provisions of this Act with respect to the transfer of patients, any patient who is for the time being liable to be detained under this Act (other than under section 35, 36 or 38 above) in a hospital at which high security psychiatric services are provided may, upon the directions of the Secretary of State, at any time be removed into any other hospital at which those services are provided.

(2) Without prejudice to any such provision, the Secretary of State may give directions for the transfer of any patient who is for the time being liable to be so detained into a hospital at which those services are not provided.

(3) Subsections (2) and (4) of section 19 above shall apply in relation to the transfer or removal of a patient under this section as they apply in relation to the transfer or removal of a patient from one hospital to another under that section.

PART IX

OFFENCES

126 Forgery, false statements, etc

(1) Any person who without lawful authority or excuse has in his custody or under his control any document to which this subsection applies, which is, and which he knows or believes to be, false within the meaning of Part I of the Forgery and Counterfeiting Act 1981, shall be guilty of an offence.

(2) Any person who without lawful authority or excuse makes, or has in his custody or under his control, any document so closely resembling a document to which subsection (1) above applies as to be calculated to deceive shall be guilty of an offence.

(3) The documents to which subsection (1) above applies are any documents purporting to be –

    (a) an application under Part II of this Act;

    (b) a medical or other recommendation or report under this Act; and

    (c) any other document required or authorised to be made for any of the purposes of this Act.

(4) Any person who –

    (a) wilfully makes a false entry or statement in any application, recommendation, report, record or other document required or authorised to be made for any of the purposes of this Act; or

    (b) with intent to deceive, makes use of any such entry or statement which he knows to be false,

    shall be guilty of an offence.

(5) Any person guilty of an offence under this section shall be liable –

    (a) on summary conviction, to imprisonment for a term not exceeding six months or to a fine not exceeding the statutory maximum, or to both;

    (b) on conviction on indictment, to imprisonment for a term not exceeding two years or to a fine of any amount, or to both.

127 Ill-treatment of patients

(1) It shall be an offence for any person who is an officer on the staff of or otherwise employed in, or who is one of the managers of, a hospital, independent hospital or care home –

    (a) to ill-treat or wilfully to neglect a patient for the time being receiving treatment for mental disorder as an in-patient in that hospital or home; or

    (b) to ill-treat or wilfully to neglect, on the premises of which the hospital or home forms part, a patient for the time being receiving such treatment there as an out-patient.

(2) It shall be an offence for any individual to ill-treat or wilfully to neglect a mentally disordered patient who is for the time being subject to his guardianship under this Act or otherwise in his custody or care (whether by virtue of any legal or moral obligation or otherwise).

(3) Any person guilty of an offence under this section shall be liable –

    (a) on summary conviction, to imprisonment for a term not exceeding six months or to a fine not exceeding the statutory maximum, or to both;

    (b) on conviction on indictment, to imprisonment for a term not exceeding five years or to a fine of any amount, or to both.

(4) No proceedings shall be instituted for an offence under this section except by or with the consent of the Director of Public Prosecutions.

128 Assisting patients to absent themselves without leave, etc

(1) Where any person induces or knowingly assists another person who is liable to be detained in a hospital within the meaning of Part II of this Act or is subject to guardianship under this Act or is a community patient, to absent himself without leave he shall be guilty of an offence.

(2) Where any person induces or knowingly assists another person who is in legal custody by virtue of section 137 below to escape from such custody he shall be guilty of an offence.

(3) Where any person knowingly harbours a patient who is absent without leave or is otherwise at large and liable to be retaken under this Act or gives him any assistance with intent to prevent, hinder or interfere with his being taken into custody or returned to the hospital or other place where he ought to be he shall be guilty of an offence.

(4) Any person guilty of an offence under this section shall be liable –

    (a) on summary conviction, to imprisonment for a term not exceeding six months or to a fine not exceeding the statutory maximum, or to both;

    (b) on conviction on indictment, to imprisonment for a term not exceeding two years or to a fine of any amount, or to both.

129 Obstruction

(1) Any person who without reasonable cause –

    (a) refuses to allow the inspection of any premises; or

    (b) refuses to allow the visiting, interviewing or examination of any person by a person authorised in that behalf by or under this Act or to give access to any person to a person so authorised; or

    (c) refuses to produce for the inspection of any person so authorised any document or record the production of which is duly required by him; or

    (d) otherwise obstructs any such person in the exercise of his functions,

      shall be guilty of an offence.

(2) Without prejudice to the generality of subsection (1) above, any person who insists on being present when required to withdraw by a person authorised by or under this Act to interview or examine a person in private shall be guilty of an offence.

(3) Any person guilty of an offence under this section shall be liable on summary conviction to imprisonment for a term not exceeding three months or to a fine not exceeding level 4 on the standard scale or to both.

130 Prosecutions by local authorities

A local social services authority may institute proceedings for any offence under this Part of this Act, but without prejudice to any provision of this Part of this Act requiring the consent of the Director of Public Prosecutions for the institution of such proceedings.

PART X

MISCELLANEOUS AND SUPPLEMENTARY

Miscellaneous provisions

130A Independent mental health advocates

(1) The appropriate national authority shall make such arrangements as it considers reasonable to enable persons ('independent mental health advocates') to be available to help qualifying patients.

(2) The appropriate national authority may by regulations make provision as to the appointment of persons as independent mental health advocates.

(3) The regulations may, in particular, provide –

(a) that a person may act as an independent mental health advocate only in such circumstances, or only subject to such conditions, as may be specified in the regulations;

(b) for the appointment of a person as an independent mental health advocate to be subject to approval in accordance with the regulations.

(4) In making arrangements under this section, the appropriate national authority shall have regard to the principle that any help available to a patient under the arrangements should, so far as practicable, be provided by a person who is independent of any person who is professionally concerned with the patient's medical treatment.

(5) For the purposes of subsection (4) above, a person is not to be regarded as professionally concerned with a patient's medical treatment merely because he is representing him in accordance with arrangements –

(a) under section 35 of the Mental Capacity Act 2005; or

(b) of a description specified in regulations under this section.

(6) Arrangements under this section may include provision for payments to be made to, or in relation to, persons carrying out functions in accordance with the arrangements.

(7) Regulations under this section –

(a) may make different provision for different cases;

(b) may make provision which applies subject to specified exceptions;

(c) may include transitional, consequential, incidental or supplemental provision.

130B Arrangements under section 130A

(1) The help available to a qualifying patient under arrangements under section 130A above shall include help in obtaining information about and understanding –

(a) the provisions of this Act by virtue of which he is a qualifying patient;

(b) any conditions or restrictions to which he is subject by virtue of this Act;

(c) what (if any) medical treatment is given to him or is proposed or discussed in his case;

(d) why it is given, proposed or discussed;

(e) the authority under which it is, or would be, given; and

(f) the requirements of this Act which apply, or would apply, in connection with the giving of the treatment to him.

(2) The help available under the arrangements to a qualifying patient shall also include –

(a) help in obtaining information about and understanding any rights which may be exercised under this Act by or in relation to him; and

(b) help (by way of representation or otherwise) in exercising those rights.

(3) For the purpose of providing help to a patient in accordance with the arrangements, an independent mental health advocate may –

(a) visit and interview the patient in private;

(b) visit and interview any person who is professionally concerned with his medical treatment;

(c) require the production of and inspect any records relating to his detention or treatment in any hospital or registered establishment or to any after-care services provided for him under section 117 above;

(d) require the production of and inspect any records of, or held by, a local social services authority which relate to him.

(4) But an independent mental health advocate is not entitled to the production of, or to inspect, records in reliance on subsection (3) (c) or (d) above unless –

(a) in a case where the patient has capacity or is competent to consent, he does consent; or

(b) in any other case, the production or inspection would not conflict with a decision made by a donee or deputy or the Court of Protection and the person holding the records, having regard to such matters as may be prescribed in regulations under section 130A above, considers that –

(i) the records may be relevant to the help to be provided by the advocate; and

(ii) the production or inspection is appropriate.

(5) For the purpose of providing help to a patient in accordance with the arrangements, an independent mental health advocate shall comply with any reasonable request made to him by any of the following for him to visit and interview the patient –

(a) the person (if any) appearing to the advocate to be the patient's nearest relative;

(b) the responsible clinician for the purposes of this Act;

(c) an approved mental health professional.

(6) But nothing in this Act prevents the patient from declining to be provided with help under the arrangements.

(7) In subsection (4) above –

(a) the reference to a patient who has capacity is to be read in accordance with the Mental Capacity Act 2005;

(b) the reference to a donee is to a donee of a lasting power of attorney (within the meaning of section 9 of that Act) created by the patient, where the donee is acting within the scope of his authority and in accordance with that Act;

(c) the reference to a deputy is to a deputy appointed for the patient by the Court of Protection under section 16 of that Act, where the deputy is acting within the scope of his authority and in accordance with that Act.

130C Section 130A: supplemental

(1) This section applies for the purposes of section 130A above.

(2) A patient is a qualifying patient if he is –

(a) liable to be detained under this Act (otherwise than by virtue of section 4 or 5(2) or (4) above or section 135 or 136 below);

(b) subject to guardianship under this Act; or

(c) a community patient.

(3) A patient is also a qualifying patient if –

(a) not being a qualifying patient falling within subsection (2) above, he discusses with a registered medical practitioner or approved clinician the possibility of being given a form of treatment to which section 57 above applies; or

(b) not having attained the age of 18 years and not being a qualifying patient falling within subsection (2) above, he discusses with a registered medical practitioner or approved clinician the possibility of being given a form of treatment to which section 58A above applies.

(4) Where a patient who is a qualifying patient falling within subsection (3) above is informed that the treatment concerned is proposed in his case, he remains a qualifying patient falling within that subsection until –

(a) the proposal is withdrawn; or

(b) the treatment is completed or discontinued.

(5) References to the appropriate national authority are –

(a) in relation to a qualifying patient in England, to the Secretary of State;

(b) in relation to a qualifying patient in Wales, to the Welsh Ministers.

(6) For the purposes of subsection (5) above –

(a) a qualifying patient falling within subsection (2)(a) above is to be regarded as being in the territory in which the hospital or registered establishment in which he is liable to be detained is situated;

(b) a qualifying patient falling within subsection (2)(b) above is to be regarded as being in the territory in which the area of the responsible local social services authority within the meaning of section 34(3) above is situated;

(c) a qualifying patient falling within subsection (2)(c) above is to be regarded as being in the territory in which the responsible hospital is situated;

(d) a qualifying patient falling within subsection (3) above is to be regarded as being in the territory determined in accordance with arrangements made for the purposes of this paragraph, and published, by the Secretary of State and the Welsh Ministers.

131 Informal admission of patients

(1) Nothing in this Act shall be construed as preventing a patient who requires treatment for mental disorder from being admitted to any hospital or registered establishment in pursuance of arrangements made in that behalf and without any application, order or direction rendering him liable to be detained under this Act, or from remaining in any hospital or registered establishment in pursuance of such arrangements after he has ceased to be so liable to be detained.

(2) Subsections (3) and (4) below apply in the case of a patient aged 16 or 17 years who has capacity to consent to the making of such arrangements as are mentioned in subsection (1) above.

(3) If the patient consents to the making of the arrangements, they may be made, carried out and determined on the basis of that consent even though there are one or more persons who have parental responsibility for him.

(4) If the patient does not consent to the making of the arrangements, they may not be made, carried out or determined on the basis of the consent of a person who has parental responsibility for him.

(5) In this section –

(a) the reference to a patient who has capacity is to be read in accordance with the Mental Capacity Act 2005; and

(b) 'parental responsibility' has the same meaning as in the Children Act 1989.

131A Accommodation, etc. for children

(1) This section applies in respect of any patient who has not attained the age of 18 years and who–

(a) is liable to be detained in a hospital under this Act; or

(b) is admitted to, or remains in, a hospital in pursuance of such arrangements as are mentioned in section 131(1) above.

(2) The managers of the hospital shall ensure that the patient's environment in the hospital is suitable having regard to his age (subject to his needs).

(3) For the purpose of deciding how to fulfil the duty under subsection (2) above, the managers shall consult a person who appears to them to have knowledge or experience of cases involving patients who have not attained the age of 18 years which makes him suitable to be consulted.

(4) In this section, 'hospital' includes a registered establishment.

133 Duty of managers of hospitals to inform nearest relatives of discharge

(1) Where a patient liable to be detained under this Act in a hospital or registered establishment is to be discharged otherwise than by virtue of an order for discharge made by his nearest relative, the managers of the hospital or registered establishment shall, subject to subsection (2) below, take such steps as are practicable to inform the person (if any) appearing to them to be the nearest relative of the patient; and that information shall, if practicable, be given at least seven days before the date of discharge.

(1A) The reference in subsection (1) above to a patient who is to be discharged includes a patient who is to be discharged from hospital under section 17A above.

(1B) Subsection (1) above shall also apply in a case where a community patient is discharged under section 23 or 72 above (otherwise than by virtue of an order for discharge made by his nearest relative), but with the reference in that subsection to the managers of the hospital or registered establishment being read as a reference to the managers of the responsible hospital.

(2) Subsection (1) above shall not apply if the patient or his nearest relative has requested that information about the patient's discharge should not be given under this section.

134 Correspondence of patients

(1) A postal packet addressed to any person by a patient detained in a hospital under this Act and delivered by the patient for dispatch may be withheld from the postal operator concerned –

(a) if that person has requested that communications addressed to him by the patient should be withheld; or

(b) subject to subsection (3) below, if the hospital is one at which high security psychiatric services are provided and the managers of the hospital consider that the postal packet is likely –

(i) to cause distress to the person to whom it is addressed or to any other person (not being a person on the staff of the hospital); or

(ii) to cause danger to any person;

and any request for the purposes of paragraph (a) above shall be made by a notice in writing given to the managers of the hospital, the approved clinician with overall responsibility for the patient's case or the Secretary of State.

(2) Subject to subsection (3) below, a postal packet addressed to a patient detained under this Act in a hospital at which high security psychiatric services are provided may be withheld from the patient if, in the opinion of the managers of the hospital, it is necessary to do so in the interests of the safety of the patient or for the protection of other persons.

(3)   Subsections (1)(b) and (2) above do not apply to any postal packet addressed by a patient to, or sent to a patient by or on behalf of –

(a)   any Minister of the Crown or the Scottish Ministers or Member of either House of Parliament or member of the Scottish Parliament or of the Northern Ireland Assembly;

(aa) any of the Welsh Ministers, the Counsel General to the Welsh Assembly Government or a member of the National Assembly for Wales,

(b)   any judge or officer of the Court of Protection, any of the Court of Protection Visitors or any person asked by that Court for a report under section 49 of the Mental Capacity Act 2005 concerning the patient;

(c)   the Parliamentary Commissioner for Administration, the Scottish Public Services Ombudsman, the Public Services Ombudsman for Wales, the Health Service Commissioner for England or a Local Commissioner within the meaning of Part III of the Local Government Act 1974;

(d)   a Mental Health Review Tribunal;

(e)   a Strategic Health Authority, Local Health Board, Special Health Authority or Primary Care Trust, a local social services authority, a Community Health Council, or a local probation board established under section 4 of the Criminal Justice and Court Services Act 2000;

(ea) a provider of a patient advocacy and liaison service for the assistance of patients at the hospital and their families and carers;

(eb) a provider of independent advocacy services for the patient;

(f)   the managers of the hospital in which the patient is detained;

(g)   any legally qualified person instructed by the patient to act as his legal adviser; or

(h)   the European Commission of Human Rights or the European Court of Human Rights.

(3A) In subsection (3) above –

(a) 'patient advocacy and liaison service' means a service of a description prescribed by regulations made by the Secretary of State, and

(b) 'independent advocacy services' means services provided under –

(i) arrangements under section 130A above;

(ii) arrangements under section 248 of the National Health Service Act 2006 or section 187 of the National Health Service (Wales) Act 2006; or

(iii) arrangements of a description prescribed as mentioned in paragraph (a) above.

(4)   The managers of a hospital may inspect and open any postal packet for the purposes of determining –

(a) whether it is one to which subsection (1) or (2) applies, and

(b) in the case of a postal packet to which subsection (1) or (2) above applies, whether or not it should be withheld under that subsection;

and the power to withhold a postal packet under either of those subsections includes power to withhold anything contained in it.

(5)   Where a postal packet or anything contained in it is withheld under subsection (1) or (2) above the managers of the hospital shall record that fact in writing.

(6)   Where a postal packet or anything contained in it is withheld under subsection (1)(b) or (2) above the managers of the hospital shall within seven days give notice of that fact to the patient and, in the case of a packet withheld under subsection (2) above, to the person (if known) by whom the postal packet was sent; and any such notice shall be given in writing and shall contain a statement of the effect of section 121(7) and (8) above.

(7)   The functions of the managers of a hospital under this section shall be discharged on their behalf by a person on the staff of the hospital appointed by them for that purpose and different persons may be appointed to discharge different functions.

(8)   The Secretary of State may make regulations with respect to the exercise of the powers conferred by this section.

(9)   In this section 'hospital' has the same meaning as in Part II of this Act and 'postal operator' and 'postal packet' have the same meaning as in the Postal Services Act 2000.

135 Warrant to search for and remove patients

(1)   If it appears to a justice of the peace, on information on oath laid by an approved mental health professional, that there is reasonable cause to suspect that a person believed to be suffering from mental disorder –

(a) has been, or is being, ill-treated, neglected or kept otherwise than under proper control, in any place within the jurisdiction of the justice, or

(b) being unable to care for himself, is living alone in any such place,

the justice may issue a warrant authorising any constable to enter, if need be by force, any premises specified in the warrant in which that person is believed to be, and, if thought fit, to remove him to a place of safety with a view to the making of an application in respect of him under Part II of this Act, or of other arrangements for his treatment or care.

(2)   If it appears to a justice of the peace, on information on oath laid by any constable or other person who is authorised by or under this Act or under article 8 of the Mental Health (Care and Treatment) (Scotland) Act 2003 (Consequential Provisions) Order 2005 to take a patient to any place, or to take into custody or retake a patient who is liable under this Act or under the said article 8 to be so taken or retaken –

(a) that there is reasonable cause to believe that the patient is to be found on premises within the jurisdiction of the justice; and

(b) that admission to the premises has been refused or that a refusal of such admission is apprehended,

the justice may issue a warrant authorising any constable to enter the premises, if need be by force, and remove the patient.

(3)   A patient who is removed to a place of safety in the execution of a warrant issued under this section may be detained there for a period not exceeding 72 hours.

(3A) A constable, an approved mental health professional or a person authorised by either of them for the purposes of this subsection may, before the end of the period of 72 hours mentioned in subsection (3) above, take a person detained in a place of safety under that subsection to one or more other places of safety.

(3B) A person taken to a place of safety under subsection (3A) above may be detained there for a period ending no later than the end of the period of 72 hours mentioned in subsection (3) above.

(4)   In the execution of a warrant issued under subsection (1) above, a constable shall be accompanied by an approved mental health professional and by a registered medical practitioner, and in the execution of a warrant issued under subsection (2) above a constable may be accompanied –

(a) by a registered medical practitioner;

(b) by any person authorised by or under this Act or under article 8 of the Mental Health (Care and Treatment) (Scotland) Act 2003 (Consequential Provisions) Order 2005 to take or retake the patient.

(5)   It shall not be necessary in any information or warrant under subsection (1) above to name the patient concerned.

(6)   In this section 'place of safety' means residential accommodation provided by a local social services authority under Part III of the National Assistance Act 1948, a hospital as defined by this Act, a police station, an independent hospital or care home for mentally disordered persons or any other suitable place the occupier of which is willing temporarily to receive the patient.

136 Mentally disordered persons found in public places

(1)   If a constable finds in a place to which the public have access a person who appears to him to be suffering from mental disorder and to be in immediate need of care or control, the constable may, if he thinks it necessary to do so in the interests of that person or for the protection of other persons, remove that person to a place of safety within the meaning of section 135 above.

(2)   A person removed to a place of safety under this section may be detained there for a period not exceeding 72 hours for the purpose of enabling him to be examined by a registered medical practitioner and to be interviewed by an approved mental health professional and of making any necessary arrangements for his treatment or care.

(3)   A constable, an approved mental health professional or a person authorised by either of them for the purposes of this subsection may, before the end of the period of 72 hours mentioned in subsection (2) above, take a person detained in a place of safety under that subsection to one or more other places of safety.

(4)   A person taken to a place of a safety under subsection (3) above may be detained there for a purpose mentioned in subsection (2) above for a period ending no later than the end of the period of 72 hours mentioned in that subsection.

137 Provisions as to custody, conveyance and detention

(1)   Any person required or authorised by or by virtue of this Act to be conveyed to any place or to be kept in custody or detained in a place of safety or at any place to which he is taken under section 42(6) above shall, while being so conveyed, detained or kept, as the case may be, be deemed to be in legal custody.

(2)   A constable or any other person required or authorised by or by virtue of this Act to take any person into custody, or to convey or detain any person shall, for the purposes of taking him into custody or conveying or detaining him, have all the powers, authorities, protection and privileges which a constable has within the area for which he acts as constable.

(3)   In this section 'convey' includes any other expression denoting removal from one place to another.

138 Retaking of patients escaping from custody

(1)   If any person who is in legal custody by virtue of section 137 above escapes, he may, subject to the provisions of this section, be retaken –

(a) in any case, by the person who had his custody immediately before the escape, or by any constable or approved mental health professional;

(b) if at the time of the escape he was liable to be detained in a hospital within the meaning of Part II of this Act, or subject to guardianship under this Act, or a community patient who was recalled to hospital under section 17E above, by any other person who could take him into custody under section 18 above if he had absented himself without leave.

(2) A person to whom paragraph (b) of subsection (1) above applies shall not be retaken under this section after the expiration of the period within which he could be retaken under section 18 above if he had absented himself without leave on the day of the escape unless he is subject to a restriction order under Part III of this Act or an order or direction having the same effect as such an order; and subsection (4) of the said section 18 shall apply with the necessary modifications accordingly.

(3) A person who escapes while being taken to or detained in a place of safety under section 135 or 136 above shall not be retaken under this section after the expiration of the period of 72 hours beginning with the time when he escapes or the period during which he is liable to be so detained, whichever expires first.

(4) This section, so far as it relates to the escape of a person liable to be detained in a hospital within the meaning of Part II of this Act, shall apply in relation to a person who escapes –

(a) while being taken to or from such a hospital in pursuance of regulations under section 19 above, or of any order, direction or authorisation under Part III or VI of this Act (other than under section 35, 36, 38, 53, 83 or 85) or under section 123 above; or

(b) while being taken to or detained in a place of safety in pursuance of an order under Part III of this Act (other than under section 35, 36 or 38 above) pending his admission to such a hospital,

as if he were liable to be detained in that hospital and, if he had not previously been received in that hospital, as if he had been so received.

(5) In computing for the purposes of the power to give directions under section 37(4) above and for the purposes of sections 37(5) and 40(1) above the period of 28 days mentioned in those sections, no account shall be taken of any time during which the patient is at large and liable to be retaken by virtue of this section.

(6) Section 21 above shall, with any necessary modifications, apply in relation to a patient who is at large and liable to be retaken by virtue of this section as it applies in relation to a patient who is absent without leave and references in that section to section 18 above shall be construed accordingly.

139 Protection for acts done in pursuance of this Act

(1) No person shall be liable, whether on the ground of want of jurisdiction or on any other ground, to any civil or criminal proceedings to which he would have been liable apart from this section in respect of any act purporting to be done in pursuance of this Act or any regulations or rules made under this Act, unless the act was done in bad faith or without reasonable care.

(2) No civil proceedings shall be brought against any person in any court in respect of any such act without the leave of the High Court; and no criminal proceedings shall be brought against any person in any court in respect of any such act except by or with the consent of the Director of Public Prosecutions.

(3) This section does not apply to proceedings for an offence under this Act, being proceedings which, under any other provision of this Act, can be instituted only by or with the consent of the Director of Public Prosecutions.

(4) This section does not apply to proceedings against the Secretary of State or against a Strategic Health Authority, Local Health Board, Special Health Authority or Primary Care Trust or against a National Health Service trust established under the National Health Service Act 2006 or the National Health Service (Wales) Act 2006 or NHS foundation trust.

(5) In relation to Northern Ireland the reference in this section to the Director of Public Prosecutions shall be construed as a reference to the Director of Public Prosecutions for Northern Ireland.

142A Regulations as to approvals in relation to England and Wales

The Secretary of State jointly with the Welsh Ministers may by regulations make provision as to the circumstances in which –

(a) a practitioner approved for the purposes of section 12 above, or

(b) a person approved to act as an approved clinician for the purposes of this Act,

approved in relation to England is to be treated, by virtue of his approval, as approved in relation to Wales too, and vice versa.

Supplemental

145 Interpretation

(1) In this Act, unless the context otherwise requires –

'absent without leave' has the meaning given to it by section 18 above and related expressions (including expressions relating to a patient's liability to be returned to a hospital or other place) shall be construed accordingly;

'application for admission for assessment' has the meaning given in section 2 above;

'application for admission for treatment' has the meaning given in section 3 above;

'approved clinician' means a person approved by the Secretary of State (in relation to England) or by the Welsh Ministers (in relation to Wales) to act as an approved clinician for the purposes of this Act;

'approved mental health professional' has the meaning given in section 114 above;

'care home' has the same meaning as in the Care Standards Act 2000;

'community patient' has the meaning given in section 17A above;

'community treatment order' and 'the community treatment order' have the meanings given in section 17A above;

'the community treatment period' has the meaning given in section 20A above;

'high security psychiatric services' has the same meaning as in section 4 of the National Health Service Act 2006 or section 4 of the National Health Service (Wales) Act 2006;

'hospital' means —

(a) any health service hospital within the meaning of the National Health Service Act 2006 or the National Health Service (Wales) Act 2006; and

(b) any accommodation provided by a local authority and used as a hospital by or on behalf of the Secretary of State under that Act; and

(c) any hospital as defined by section 206 of the National Health Service (Wales) Act 2006 which is vested in a Local Health Board;

and 'hospital within the meaning of Part II of this Act' has the meaning given in section 34 above;

'hospital direction' has the meaning given in section 45A(3)(a) above;

'hospital order' and 'guardianship order' have the meanings respectively given in section 37 above;

'independent hospital' has the same meaning as in the Care Standards Act 2000;

'interim hospital order' has the meaning given in section 38 above;

'limitation direction' has the meaning given in section 45A(3)(b) above;

'Local Health Board' means a Local Health Board established under section 11 of the National Health Services (Wales) Act 2006.

'local social services authority' means a council which is a local authority for the purpose of the Local Authority Social Services Act 1970;

'the managers' means —

(a) in relation to a hospital vested in the Secretary of State for the purposes of his functions under the National Health Service Act 2006, or in the Welsh Ministers for the purposes of their functions under the National Health Service (Wales) Act 2006, and in relation to any accommodation provided by a local authority and used as a hospital by or on behalf of the Secretary of State under the National Health Service Act 2006, or of the Welsh Ministers under the National Health Service (Wales) Act 2006, the Primary Care Trust, Strategic Health Authority, Local Health Board or Special Health Authority responsible for the administration of the hospital;

(bb) in relation to a hospital vested in a Primary Care Trust or a National Health Service trust, the trust;

(bc) in relation to a hospital vested in an NHS foundation trust, the trust;

(bd) in relation to a hospital vested in a Local Health Board, the Board;

(c) in relation to a registered establishment, the person or persons registered in respect of the establishment; and in this definition ' hospital' means a hospital within the meaning of Part II of this Act;

'medical treatment' includes nursing, psychological intervention and specialist mental health habilitation, rehabilitation and care (but see also subsection (4) below);

'mental disorder' has the meaning given in section 1 above (subject to sections 86(4) and 141(6B));

'nearest relative', in relation to a patient, has the meaning given in Part II of this Act;

'patient' means a person suffering or appearing to be suffering from mental disorder;

'Primary Care Trust' means a Primary Care Trust established under section 18 of the National Health Service Act 2006;

'registered establishment' has the meaning given in section 34 above;

'the responsible hospital' has the meaning given in section 17A above;

'restriction direction' has the meaning given to it by section 49 above;

'restriction order' has the meaning given to it by section 41 above;

'Special Health Authority' means a Special Health Authority established under section 28 of the National Health Service Act 2006, or section 22 of the National Health Service (Wales) Act 2006;

'Strategic Health Authority' means a Strategic Health Authority established under section 13 of the National Health Service Act 2006;

'transfer direction' has the meaning given to it by section 47 above.

(1AA) Where high security psychiatric services and other services are provided at a hospital, the part of the hospital at which high security psychiatric services are provided and the other part shall be treated as separate hospitals for the purposes of this Act.

(1AB) References in this Act to appropriate medical treatment shall be construed in accordance with section 3(4) above.

(1AC) References in this Act to an approved mental health professional shall be construed as references to an approved mental health professional acting on behalf of a local social services authority, unless the context otherwise requires.

(3) In relation to a person who is liable to be detained or subject to guardianship or a community patient by virtue of an order or direction under Part III of this Act (other than under section 35, 36 or 38), any reference in this Act to any enactment contained in Part II of this Act or in section 66 or 67 above shall be construed as a reference to that enactment as it applies to that person by virtue of Part III of this Act.

(4) Any reference in this Act to medical treatment, in relation to mental disorder, shall be construed as a reference to medical treatment the purpose of which is to alleviate, or prevent a worsening of, the disorder or one or more of its symptoms or manifestations.

APPENDIX 3
Protocol for the instruction of experts to give evidence in civil claims, from the civil justice council[1]

2. Aims of Protocol

2.1 This Protocol offers guidance to experts and to those instructing them in the interpretation of and compliance with Part 35 of the Civil Procedure Rules (CPR 35)[2] and its associated Practice Direction (PD 35)[3] and to further the objectives of the Civil Procedure Rules in general.

2.2 Experts and those who instruct them should also bear in mind para. 1.4 of the Practice Direction on Protocols which contains the following objectives, namely to:
  (a) encourage the exchange of early and full information about the expert issues involved in a prospective legal claim;
  (b) enable the parties to avoid or reduce the scope of litigation by agreeing the whole or part of an expert issue before commencement of proceedings; and
  (c) support the efficient management of proceedings where litigation cannot be avoided.

3. Application

3.2 Experts are governed by Part 35 if they are or have been instructed to give or prepare evidence for the purpose of civil proceedings in a court in England and Wales (CPR 35.2).

3.4 Courts may take into account any failure to comply with this Protocol when making orders in relation to costs, interest, time limits, the stay of proceedings and whether to order a party to pay a sum of money into court.

4. Duties of experts

4.1 Experts always owe a duty to exercise reasonable skill and care to those instructing them, and to comply with any relevant professional code of ethics. However when they are instructed to give or prepare evidence for the purpose of civil proceedings in England and Wales they have an overriding duty to help the court on matters within their expertise (CPR 35.3) This duty overrides any obligation to the person instructing or paying them. Experts must not serve the exclusive interest of those who retain them.

4.2 Experts should be aware of the overriding objective that courts deal with cases justly. This includes dealing with cases proportionately, expeditiously and fairly (CPR 1.1). Experts are under an obligation to assist the court so as to enable them to deal with cases in accordance with the overriding objective. However the overriding objective does not impose on experts any duty to act as mediators between the parties or require them to trespass on the role of the court in deciding facts.

4.3 Experts should provide opinions which are independent, regardless of the pressures of litigation. In this context, a useful test of 'independence' is that the expert would express the same opinion if given the same instructions by an opposing party. Experts should not take it upon themselves to promote the point of view of the party instructing them or engage in the role of advocates.

4.4 Experts should confine their opinions to matters which are material to the disputes between the parties and provide opinions only in relation to matters which lie within their expertise. Experts should indicate without delay where particular questions or issues fall outside their expertise.

4.5 Experts should take into account all material facts before them at the time that they give their opinion. Their reports should set out those facts and any literature or any other material on which they have relied in forming their opinions. They should indicate if an opinion is provisional, or qualified, or where they consider that further information is required or if, for any other reason, they are not satisfied that an opinion can be expressed finally and without qualification.

4.6 Experts should inform those instructing them without delay of any change in their opinions on any material matter and the reason for it.

4.7 Experts should be aware that any failure by them to comply with the Civil Procedure Rules or court orders or any excessive delay for which they are responsible may result in the parties who instructed them being penalised in costs and even, in extreme cases, being debarred from placing the experts' evidence before the court.

5. Conduct of experts instructed only to advise

5.1 Part 35 only applies where experts are instructed to give opinions which are relied on for the purposes of court proceedings. Advice which the parties do not intend to adduce in litigation is likely to be confidential; the Protocol does not apply in these circumstances[2, 3].

5.2 The same applies where, after the commencement of proceedings, experts are instructed only to advise (e.g. to comment upon a single joint expert's report) and not to give or prepare evidence for use in the proceedings.

5.3 However this Protocol does apply if experts who were formerly instructed only to advise are later instructed to give or prepare evidence for the purpose of civil proceedings.

6. The need for experts

6.2 Although the court's permission is not generally required to instruct an expert, the court's permission is required before experts can be called to give evidence or their evidence can be put in (CPR 35.4).

7. The appointment of experts

7.1 Before experts are formally instructed or the court's permission to appoint named experts is sought, the following should be established:
  (a) that they have the appropriate expertise and experience;
  (b) that they are familiar with the general duties of an expert;
  (c) that they can produce a report, deal with questions and have discussions with other experts within a reasonable time and at a cost proportionate to the matters in issue;
  (d) a description of the work required;
  (e) whether they are available to attend the trial, if attendance is required; and
  (f) there is no potential conflict of interest.

7.2 Terms of appointment should be agreed at the outset and should normally include:
  (a) the capacity in which the expert is to be appointed (e.g. party appointed expert, single joint expert or expert advisor);
  (b) the services required of the expert (e.g. provision of expert's report, answering questions in writing, attendance at meetings and attendance at court);
  (c) time for delivery of the report;
  (d) the basis of the expert's charges (either daily or hourly rates and an estimate of the time likely to be required, or a total fee for the services);
  (e) travelling expenses and disbursements;
  (f) cancellation charges;
  (g) any fees for attending court;
  (h) time for making the payment; and
  (i) whether fees are to be paid by a third party.
  (j) if a party is publicly funded, whether or not the expert's charges will be subject to assessment by a costs officer.

7.4 When necessary, arrangements should be made for dealing with questions to experts and discussions between experts, including any directions given by the court, and provision should be made for the cost of this work.

7.5 Experts should be informed regularly about deadlines for all matters concerning them. Those instructing experts should promptly send them copies of all court orders and directions which may affect the preparation of their reports or any other matters concerning their obligations.

Conditional and Contigency Fees

7.6 Payments contingent upon the nature of the expert evidence given in legal proceedings, or upon the outcome of a case, must not be offered or accepted. To do so would contravene experts' overriding duty to the court and compromise their duty of independence.

7.7 Agreement to delay payment of experts' fees until after the conclusion of cases is permissible as long as the amount of the fee does not depend on the outcome of the case.

8. Instructions

8.1 Those instructing experts should ensure that they give clear instructions, including the following: (a) basic information, such as names, addresses, telephone numbers, dates of birth and dates of incidents; (b) the nature and extent of the expertise which is called for; (c) the purpose of requesting the advice or report, a description of the matter(s) to be investigated, the principal known issues and the identity of all parties; (d) the statement(s) of case (if any), those documents which form part of standard disclosure and witness statements which are relevant to the advice or report; (e) where proceedings have not been started, whether proceedings are being contemplated and, if so, whether the expert is asked only for advice; (f) an outline programme, consistent with good case management and the expert's availability, for the completion and delivery of each stage of the expert's work; and (g) where proceedings have been started, the dates of any hearings (including any Case Management Conferences and/or Pre-Trial Reviews), the name of the court, the claim number and the track to which the claim has been allocated.

8.2 Experts who do not receive clear instructions should request clarification and may indicate that they are not prepared to act unless and until such clear instructions are received.

9. Experts' Acceptance of Instructions

9.1 Experts should confirm without delay whether or not they accept instructions. They should also inform those instructing them (whether on initial instruction or at any later stage) without delay if:

    (a) instructions are not acceptable because, for example, they require work that falls outside their expertise, impose unrealistic deadlines, or are insufficiently clear;

    (b) they consider that instructions are or have become insufficient to complete the work;

    (c) they become aware that they may not be able to fulfil any of the terms of appointment;

    (d) the instructions and/or work have, for any reason, placed them in conflict with their duties as an expert; or

    (e) they are not satisfied that they can comply with any orders that have been made.

9.2 Experts must neither express an opinion outside the scope of their field of expertise, nor accept any instructions to do so.

10. Withdrawal

10.1 Where experts' instructions remain incompatible with their duties, whether through incompleteness, a conflict between their duty to the court and their instructions, or for any other substantial and significant reason, they may consider withdrawing from the case. However, experts should not withdraw without first discussing the position fully with those who instruct them and considering carefully whether it would be more appropriate to make a written request for directions from the court. If experts do withdraw, they must give formal written notice to those instructing them.

11. Experts' right to ask court for directions

11.1 Experts may request directions from the court to assist them in carrying out their functions as experts. Experts should normally discuss such matters with those who instruct them before making any such request. Unless the court otherwise orders, any proposed request for directions should be copied to the party instructing the expert at least seven days before filing any request to the court, and to all other parties at least four days before filing it. (CPR 35.14).

11.2 Requests to the court for directions should be made by letter, containing.

    (a) the title of the claim;

    (b) the claim number of the case;

    (c) the name of the expert;

    (d) full details of why directions are sought; and

    (e) copies of any relevant documentation.

12. Power of the Court to Direct a Party to Provide Information.

12.1 If experts consider that those instructing them have not provided information which they require, they may, after discussion with those instructing them and giving notice, write to the court to seek directions (CPR 35.14).

12.2 Experts and those who instruct them should also be aware of CPR 35.9. This provides that where one party has access to information which is not readily available to the other party, the court may direct the party who has access to the information to prepare, file and copy to the other party a document recording the information. If experts require such information which has not been disclosed, they should discuss the position with those instructing them without delay, so that a request for the information can be made, and, if not forthcoming, an application can be made to the court. Unless a document appears to be essential, experts should assess the cost and time involved in the production of a document and whether its provision would be proportionate in the context of the case.

13. Contents of Experts' Reports

13.1 The content and extent of experts' reports should be governed by the scope of their instructions and general obligations, the contents of CPR 35 and PD35 and their overriding duty to the court.

13.2 In preparing reports, experts should maintain professional objectivity and impartiality at all times.

13.3 PD 35, para. 2 provides that experts' reports should be addressed to the court and gives detailed directions about the form and content of such reports. All experts and those who instruct them should ensure that they are familiar with these requirements.

13.4 Model forms of Experts' Reports are available from bodies such as the Academy of Experts or the Expert Witness Institute.

13.5 Experts' reports must contain statements that they understand their duty to the court and have complied and will continue to comply with that duty (PD35 para. 2.2(9)). They must also be verified by a statement of truth. The form of the statement of truth is as follows:

I confirm that insofar as the facts stated in my report are within my own knowledge I have made clear which they are and I believe them to be true, and that the opinions I have expressed represent my true and complete professional opinion.

This wording is mandatory and must not be modified.

Qualifications

13.6   The details of experts' qualifications to be given in reports should be commensurate with the nature and complexity of the case. It may be sufficient merely to state academic and professional qualifications. However, where highly specialized expertise is called for, experts should include the detail of particular training and/or experience that qualifies them to provide that highly specialised evidence.

Tests

13.7   Where tests of a scientific or technical nature have been carried out, experts should state:
(a) the methodology used; and
(b) by whom the tests were undertaken and under whose supervision, summarizing their respective qualifications and experience.

Reliance on the work of others

13.8   Where experts rely in their reports on literature or other material and cite the opinions of others without having verified them, they must give details of those opinions relied on. It is likely to assist the court if the qualifications of the originator(s) are also stated.

Facts

13.9   When addressing questions of fact and opinion, experts should keep the two separate and discrete.

13.10   Experts must state those facts (whether assumed or otherwise) upon which their opinions are based. They must distinguish clearly between those facts which experts know to be true and those facts which they assume.

13.11   Where there are material facts in dispute experts should express separate opinions on each hypothesis put forward. They should not express a view in favour of one or other disputed version of the facts unless, as a result of particular expertise and experience, they consider one set of facts as being improbable or less probable, in which case they may express that view, and should give reasons for holding it.

Range of opinion

13.12   If the mandatory summary of the range of opinion is based on published sources, experts should explain those sources and, where appropriate, state the qualifications of the originator(s) of the opinions from which they differ, particularly if such opinions represent a well-established school of thought.

13.13   Where there is no available source for the range of opinion, experts may need to express opinions on what they believe to be the range which other experts would arrive at if asked. In those circumstances, experts should make it clear that the range that they summarise is based on their own judgment and explain the basis of that judgment.

Conclusions

13.14   A summary of conclusions is mandatory. The summary should be at the end of the report after all the reasoning. There may be cases, however, where the benefit to the court is heightened by placing a short summary at the beginning of the report whilst giving the full conclusions at the end. For example, it can assist with the comprehension of the analysis and with the absorption of the detailed facts if the court is told at the outset of the direction in which the report's logic will flow in cases involving highly complex matters which fall outside the general knowledge of the court.

Range of report: material instructions

13.15   The mandatory statement of the substance of all material instructions should not be incomplete or otherwise tend to mislead. The imperative is transparency. The term 'instructions' includes all material which solicitors place in front of experts in order to gain advice. The omission from the statement of 'off-the-record' oral instructions is not permitted. Courts may allow cross-examination about the instructions if there are reasonable grounds to consider that the statement may be inaccurate or incomplete.

14. After receipt of experts' reports

14.1   Following the receipt of experts' reports, those instructing them should advise the experts as soon as reasonably practicable whether, and if so when, the report will be disclosed to other parties; and, if so disclosed, the date of actual disclosure.

14.2   If experts' reports are to be relied upon, and if experts are to give oral evidence, those instructing them should give the experts the opportunity to consider and comment upon other reports within their area of expertise and which deal with relevant issues at the earliest opportunity.

14.3   Those instructing experts should keep experts informed of the progress of cases, including amendments to statements of case relevant to experts' opinion.

15. Amendment of reports

15.1 It may become necessary for experts to amend their reports:
  (a) as a result of an exchange of questions and answers;
  (b) following agreements reached at meetings between experts; or
  (c) where further evidence or documentation is disclosed.

15.2 Experts should not be asked to, and should not, amend, expand or alter any parts of reports in a manner which distorts their true opinion, but may be invited to amend or expand reports to ensure accuracy, internal consistency, completeness and relevance to the issues and clarity. Although experts should generally follow the recommendations of solicitors with regard to the form of reports, they should form their own independent views as to the opinions and contents expressed in their reports and exclude any suggestions which do not accord with their views.

15.3 Where experts change their opinion following a meeting of experts, a simple signed and dated addendum or memorandum to that effect is generally sufficient. In some cases, however, the benefit to the court of having an amended report may justify the cost of making the amendment.

15.4 Where experts significantly alter their opinion, as a result of new evidence or because evidence on which they relied has become unreliable, or for any other reason, they should amend their reports to reflect that fact. Amended reports should include reasons for amendments. In such circumstances those instructing experts should inform other parties as soon as possible of any change of opinion.

15.5 When experts intend to amend their reports, they should inform those instructing them without delay and give reasons. They should provide the amended version (or an addendum or memorandum) clearly marked as such as quickly as possible.

16. Written Questions to Experts

16.1 The procedure for putting written questions to experts (CPR 35.6) is intended to facilitate the clarification of opinions and issues after experts' reports have been served. Experts have a duty to provide answers to questions properly put. Where they fail to do so, the court may impose sanctions against the party instructing the expert, and, if, there is continued non-compliance, debar a party from relying on the report. Experts should copy their answers to those instructing them.

16.2 Experts' answers to questions automatically become part of their reports. They are covered by the statement of truth and form part of the expert evidence.

16.3 Where experts believe that questions put are not properly directed to the clarification of the report, or are disproportionate, or have been asked out of time, they should discuss the questions with those instructing them and, if appropriate, those asking the questions. Attempts should be made to resolve such problems without the need for an application to the court for directions. Written requests for directions in relation to questions.

16.4 If those instructing experts do not apply to the court in respect of questions, but experts still believe that questions are improper or out of time, experts may file written requests with the court for directions to assist in carrying out their functions as experts (CPR 35.14). See Section 11 above.

17. Single Joint Experts

17.1 CPR 35 and PD35 deal extensively with the instruction and use of joint experts by the parties and the powers of the court to order their use (see CPR 35.7 and 35.8, PD35, para. 5).

17.2 The Civil Procedure Rules encourage the use of joint experts. Wherever possible a joint report should be obtained. Consideration should therefore be given by all parties to the appointment of single joint experts in all cases where a court might direct such an appointment. Single joint experts are the norm in cases allocated to the small claims track and the fast track.

17.3 Where, in the early stages of a dispute, examinations, investigations, tests, site inspections, experiments, preparation of photographs, plans or other similar preliminary expert tasks are necessary, consideration should be given to the instruction of a single joint expert, especially where such matters are not, at that stage, expected to be contentious as between the parties. The objective of such an appointment should be to agree or to narrow issues.

17.5 Experts who have previously advised a party (whether in the same case or otherwise) should only be proposed as single joint experts if other parties are given all relevant information about the previous involvement.

17.6 The appointment of a single joint expert does not prevent parties from instructing their own experts to advise (but the costs of such expert advisers may not be recoverable in the case).

Joint instructions

17.7 The parties should try to agree joint instructions to single joint experts, but, in default of agreement, each party may give instructions. In particular, all parties should try to agree what documents should be included with instructions and what assumptions single joint experts should make.

17.8 Where the parties fail to agree joint instructions, they should try to agree where the areas of disagreement lie and their instructions should make this clear. If separate instructions are given, they should be copied at the same time to the other instructing parties.

17.9   Where experts are instructed by two or more parties, the terms of appointment should, unless the court has directed otherwise, or the parties have agreed otherwise, include:

(a) a statement that all the instructing parties are jointly and severally liable to pay the experts' fees and, accordingly, that experts' invoices should be sent simultaneously to all instructing parties or their solicitors (as appropriate); and

(b) a statement as to whether any order has been made limiting the amount of experts' fees and expenses (CPR 35.8(4) (a)).

17.10   Where instructions have not been received by the expert from one or more of the instructing parties the expert should give notice (normally at least 7 days) of a deadline to all instructing parties for the receipt by the expert of such instructions. Unless the instructions are received within the deadline the expert may begin work. In the event that instructions are received after the deadline but before the signing off of the report the expert should consider whether it is practicable to comply with those instructions without adversely affecting the timetable set for delivery of the report and in such a manner as to comply with the proportionality principle. An expert who decides to issue a report without taking into account instructions received after the deadline should inform the parties who may apply to the court for directions. In either event the report must show clearly that the expert did not receive instructions within the deadline, or, as the case may be, at all.

Conduct of the single joint export

17.11   Single joint experts should keep all instructing parties informed of any material steps that they may be taking by, for example, copying all correspondence to those instructing them.

17.12   Single joint experts are Part 35 experts and so have an overriding duty to the court. They are the parties' appointed experts and therefore owe an equal duty to all parties. They should maintain independence, impartiality and transparency at all times.

17.13   Single joint experts should not attend any meeting or conference which is not a joint one, unless all the parties have agreed in writing or the court has directed that such a meeting may be held 4 and who is to pay the experts' fees for the meeting.

17.14   Single joint experts may request directions from the court – see Section 11 above.

17.15   Single joint experts should serve their reports simultaneously on all instructing parties. They should provide a single report even though they may have received *(Peet)* instructions which contain areas of conflicting fact or allegation. If conflicting instructions lead to different opinions (for example, because the instructions require experts to make different assumptions of fact), reports may need to contain more than one set of opinions on any issue. It is for the court to determine the facts.

Cross-examination

17.16   Single joint experts do not normally give oral evidence at trial but if they do, all parties may cross-examine them. In general written questions (CPR 35.6) should be put to single joint experts before requests are made for them to attend court for the purpose of cross-examination.

18. Discussions between Experts

18.1   The court has powers to direct discussions between experts for the purposes set out in the Rules (CPR 35.12). Parties may also agree that discussions take place between their experts.

18.2   Where single joint experts have been instructed but parties have, with the permission of the court, instructed their own additional Part 35 experts, there may, if the court so orders or the parties agree, be discussions between the single joint experts and the additional Part 35 experts. Such discussions should be confined to those matters within the remit of the additional Part 35 experts or as ordered by the court.

18.3   The purpose of discussions between experts should be, wherever possible, to:

(a) identify and discuss the expert issues in the proceedings;

(b) reach agreed opinions on those issues, and, if that is not possible, to narrow the issues in the case;

(c) identify those issues on which they agree and disagree and summarize their reasons for disagreement on any issue; and
     (5 Daniels v Walker [2000] 1 WLR 1382).

(d) identify what action, if any, may be taken to resolve any of the outstanding issues between the parties.

Arrangements for discussions between experts

18.4   Arrangements for discussions between experts should be proportionate to the value of cases. In small claims and fast-track cases there should not normally be meetings between experts. Where discussion is justified in such cases, telephone discussion or an exchange of letters should, in the interests of proportionality, usually suffice. In multi-track cases, discussion may be face to face, but the practicalities or the proportionality principle may require discussions to be by telephone or video conference.

18.5   The parties, their lawyers and experts should co-operate to produce the agenda for any discussion between experts, although primary responsibility for preparation of the agenda should normally lie with the parties' solicitors.

18.6   The agenda should indicate what matters have been agreed and summarise concisely those which are in issue. It is often helpful for it to include questions to be answered by the experts. If agreement cannot be reached promptly or a party is unrepresented, the court may give directions for the drawing up of the agenda. The agenda should be circulated to experts and those instructing them to allow sufficient time for the experts to prepare for the discussion.

18.7   Those instructing experts must not instruct experts to avoid reaching agreement (or to defer doing so) on any matter within the experts' competence. Experts are not permitted to accept such instructions.

18.8 The parties' lawyers may only be present at discussions between experts if all the parties agree or the court so orders. If lawyers do attend, they should not normally intervene except to answer questions put to them by the experts or to advise about the law (Hubbard).

18.9 The content of discussions between experts should not be referred to at trial unless the parties agree (CPR 35.12(4)). It is good practice for any such agreement to be in writing.

18.10 At the conclusion of any discussion between experts, a statement should be prepared setting out:
  (a) a list of issues that have been agreed, including, in each instance, the basis of agreement;
  (b) a list of issues that have not been agreed, including, in each instance, the basis of disagreement;
  (c) a list of any further issues that have arisen that were not included in the original agenda for discussion;
  (d) a record of further action, if any, to be taken or recommended, including as appropriate the holding of further discussions between experts.

18.11 The statement should be agreed and signed by all the parties to the discussion as soon as may be practicable.

18.12 Agreements between experts during discussions do not bind the parties unless the parties expressly agree to be bound by the agreement (CPR 35.12(5)). However, in view of the overriding objective, parties should give careful consideration before refusing to be bound by such an agreement and be able to explain their refusal should it become relevant to the issue of costs.

19. Attendance of Experts at Court

19.1 Experts instructed in cases have an obligation to attend court if called upon to do so and accordingly should ensure that those instructing them are always aware of their dates to be avoided and take all reasonable steps to be available.

19.2 Those instructing experts should:
  (a) ascertain the availability of experts before trial dates are fixed;
  (b) keep experts updated with timetables (including the dates and times experts are to attend) and the location of the court;
  (c) give consideration, where appropriate, to experts giving evidence via a video-link.
  (d) inform experts immediately if trial dates are vacated.

19.3 Experts should normally attend court without the need for the service of witness summonses, but on occasion they may be served to require attendance 34). The use of witness summonses does not affect the contractual or other obligations of the parties to pay experts' fees.

REFERENCES
1. http://www.justice.gov.uk/courts/procedure-rules/civil/contents/form_section_images/practice_directions/pd35_pdf_eps_prot.pdf
2. http://www.justice.gov.uk/courts/procedure-rules/civil/rules/part35
3. http://www.justice.gov.uk/courts/procedure-rules/civil/rules/pd_part35

APPENDIX 4
Ethical Codes

Oath of Hippocrates

From *Hippocratic Writings*, translated by J. Chadwick and W.N. Mann, Penguin Books, 1950.

I swear by Apollo the healer, by Aesculapius, by Hygeia (health) and all the powers of healing, and call to witness all the gods and goddesses that I may keep this Oath, and promise to the best of my ability and judgment:

I will pay the same respect to my master in the science (arts) as I do to my parents, and share my life with him and pay all my debts to him. I will regard his sons as my brothers and teach them the science, if they desire to learn it, without fee or contract. I will hand on precepts, lectures, and all other learning to my sons, to those of my master, and to those pupils duly apprenticed and sworn, and to none other.

I will use my power to help the sick to the best of my ability and judgment; I will abstain from harming or wrongdoing any man by it.

I will not give a fatal draught (drugs) to anyone if I am asked, nor will I suggest any such thing. Neither will I give a woman means to procure an abortion.

I will be chaste and religious in my life and in my practice.

I will not cut, even for the stone, but I will leave such procedures to the practitioners of that craft.

Whenever I go into a house, I will go to help the sick, and never with the intention of doing harm or injury. I will not abuse my position to indulge in sexual contacts with the bodies of women or of men, whether they be freemen or slaves.

Whatever I see or hear, professionally or privately, which ought not to be divulged, I will keep secret and tell no one.

If, therefore, I observe this Oath and do not violate it, may I prosper both in my life and in my profession, earning good repute among all men for all time. If I transgress and forswear this Oath, may my lot be otherwise.

Oath of Hippocrates (alternate translation)

I swear by Apollo the physician, and Aesculapius, and Hygeia, and Panacea and all the gods and goddesses, making them my witnesses, that I will fulfill, according to my ability and judgment, this Oath and covenant:

To hold him, who has taught me this art, as equal to my parents, and to live my life in partnership with him, and if he is in need of money to give him a share of mine, and to regard his offspring as equal to my brothers in male lineage, and to teach them this art if they desire to learn it without fee and covenant; to give a share of precepts and oral instruction and all the other learning to my sons and to the sons of him who has instructed me, and to pupils who have signed the covenant and who have taken an oath according to the medical law, but to no one else.

I will apply dietetic measures for the benefit of the sick according to my ability and judgment; I will keep them from harm and injustice.

I will neither give a deadly drug to anybody if asked for it, nor will I make a suggestion to this effect. Similarly I will not give to a woman an abortive remedy.

In purity and holiness, I will guard my life and my art.

I will not use the knife, not even on sufferers from stone, but will withdraw in favour of such men as are [skilled] in this work.

Whatever houses I may visit, I will come for the benefit of the sick, remaining free of all intentional injustice, of all mischief, and in particular of sexual relations with both male and female persons, be they free or slaves.

What I may see or hear in the course of treatment or even outside of the treatment in regard to the life of men, which on no account [ought to be] spread abroad, I will keep to myself, holding such things shameful to be spoken about.

If I fulfill this Oath and do not violate it, may it be granted to me to enjoy life and art, being honored with fame among all men for all time to come; if I transgress it and swear falsely, may the opposite of all this be my lot.

Declaration of Geneva (1948) Physician's Oath

Adopted by the 2nd General Assembly of the World Medical Association, Geneva, Switzerland, September 1948 and amended by the 22nd World Medical Assembly, Sydney, Australia, August 1968, the 35th World Medical Assembly, Venice, Italy, October 1983, the 46th WMA General Assembly, Stockholm, Sweden, September 1994.

At the time of being admitted as a member of the medical profession:

- I solemnly pledge myself to consecrate my life to the service of humanity;
- I will give to my teachers the respect and gratitude which is their due;
- I will practice my profession with conscience and dignity;
- the health of my patient will be my first consideration;
- I will respect the secrets that are confided in me, even after the patient has died;
- I will maintain by all the means in my power, the honor and the noble traditions of the medical profession;
- my colleagues will be my sisters and brothers;
- I will not permit considerations of age, disease or disability, creed, ethnic origin, gender, nationality, political affiliation, race, sexual orientation, social standing or any other factor to intervene between my duty and my patient;
- I make these promises solemnly, freely and upon my honour.

WMA International Code of Medical Ethics

Adopted by the 3rd General Assembly of the World Medical Association, London, England, October 1949 and amended by the 22nd World Medical Assembly, Sydney, Australia, August 1968 and the 35th World Medical Assembly, Venice, Italy, October 1983 and the 57th WMA General Assembly, Pilanesberg, South Africa, October 2006.

Duties of physicians in general

A physician shall:

Always exercise his/her independent professional judgment and maintain the highest standards of professional conduct.

Respect a competent patient's right to accept or refuse treatment.

Not allow his/her judgment to be influenced by personal profit or unfair discrimination.

Be dedicated to providing competent medical service in full professional and moral independence, with compassion and respect for human dignity

Deal honestly with patients and colleagues, and report to the appropriate authorities those physicians who practice unethically or incompetently or who engage in fraud or deception.

Not receive any financial benefits or other incentives solely for referring patients or prescribing specific products.

Respect the rights and preferences of patients, colleagues, and other health professionals.

Recognize his/her important role in educating the public but should use due caution in divulging discoveries or new techniques or treatment through non-professional channels.

Certify only that which he/she has personally verified.

Strive to use health care resources in the best way to benefit patients and their community.

Seek appropriate care and attention if he/she suffers from mental or physical illness.

Respect the local and national codes of ethics.

Duties of physicians to patients

A physician shall:

Always bear in mind the obligation to respect human life.

Act in the patient's best interest when providing medical care.

Owe his/her patients complete loyalty and all the scientific resources available to him/her. Whenever an examination or treatment is beyond the physician's capacity, he/she should consult with or refer to another physician who has the necessary ability.

Respect a patient's right to confidentiality. It is ethical to disclose confidential information when the patient consents to it or when there is a real and imminent threat of harm to the patient or to others and this threat can be only removed by a breach of confidentiality.

Give emergency care as a humanitarian duty unless he/she is assured that others are willing and able to give such care.

In situations when he/she is acting for a third party, ensure that the patient has full knowledge of that situation.

Not enter into a sexual relationship with his/her current patient or into any other abusive or exploitative relationship.

Duties of physicians to colleagues

A physician shall:

1. Behave towards colleagues as he/she would have them behave towards him or her.

2. Not undermine the patient-physician relationship of colleagues in order to attract patients.

3. When medically necessary, communicate with colleagues who are involved in the care of the same patient. This communication should respect patient confidentiality and be confined to necessary information.

www.wma.net/en/30publications/10policies/c8/

Madrid Declaration On Ethical Standards For Psychiatric Practice (August 2005)
Approved by the General Assembly of the World Psychiatric Association in Madrid, Spain, on August 25, 1996, and enhanced by the WPA General Assemblies in Hamburg, Germany on August 8, 1999, in Yokohama, Japan, on August 26, 2002, and in Cairo, Egypt, on September 12, 2005.

1. Psychiatry is a medical discipline concerned with the provision of the best treatment for mental disorders, with the rehabilitation of individuals suffering from mental illness and with the promotion of mental health. Psychiatrists serve patients by providing the best therapy available consistent with accepted scientific knowledge and ethical principles. Psychiatrists should devise therapeutic interventions that are least restrictive to the freedom of the patient and seek advice in areas of their work about which they do not have primary expertise. While doing so, psychiatrists should be aware of and concerned with the equitable allocation of health resources.

2. It is the duty of psychiatrists to keep abreast of scientific developments of the specialty and to convey updated knowledge to others. Psychiatrists trained in research should seek to advance the scientific frontiers of psychiatry.

3. The patient should be accepted as a partner by right in the therapeutic process. The psychiatrist-patient relationship must be based on mutual trust and respect to allow the patient to make free and informed decisions. It is the duty of psychiatrists to provide the patient with relevant information so as to empower the patient to come to a rational decision according to personal values and preferences.

4. When the patient is incapacitated and/or unable to exercise proper judgment because of a mental disorder, or gravely disabled or incompetent, the psychiatrists should consult with the family and, if appropriate, seek legal counsel, to safeguard the human dignity and the legal rights of the patient. No treatment should be provided against the patient's will, unless withholding treatment would endanger the life of the patient and/or those who surround him or her. Treatment must always be in the best interest of the patient.

5. When psychiatrists are requested to assess a person, it is their duty first to inform and advise the person being assessed about the purpose of the intervention, the use of the findings, and the possible repercussions of the assessment. This is particularly important when the psychiatrists are involved in third party situations.

6. Information obtained in the therapeutic relationship should be kept in confidence and used, only and exclusively, for the purpose of improving the mental health of the patient. Psychiatrists are prohibited from making use of such information for personal reasons, or financial or academic benefits. Breach of confidentiality may only be appropriate when serious physical or mental harm to the patient or to a third person would ensue if confidentiality were maintained; as in case of child abuse in these circumstances, psychiatrists, should whenever possible, first advise the patient about the action to be taken.

7. Research that is not conducted in accordance with the canons of science is unethical. Research activities should be approved by an appropriately constituted ethical committee. Psychiatrists should follow national and international rules for the conduct of research. Only individuals properly trained for research should undertake or direct it. Because psychiatric patients are particularly vulnerable research subjects, extra caution should be taken to safeguard their autonomy as well as their mental and physical integrity. Ethical standards should also be applied in the selection of population groups, in all types of research including epidemiological and sociological studies and in collaborative research involving other disciplines or several investigating centers.

WMA Declaration of Helsinki – Ethical Principles for Medical Research Involving Human Subjects 2008
The **Declaration of Helsinki** is the World Medical Association's (WMA's) best-known policy statement. The first version was adopted in 1964 and has been amended six times since, most recently at the General Assembly in October 2008. The current (2008) version is the only official one; all previous versions have been replaced and should not be used or cited except for historical purposes.

See www.wma.net/en/30publications/10policies/b3/

CASES Cited

Canada

Parks	R. v. Parks, (1992) 2 SCR.871 (**132**)
Starson	Starson v. Swayze, 2003 SCC 32 (2003) 1 SCR 722

Denmark

Meddelelse	Rigsadvokatans Meddelelse nr. 5/1995: Afhøringer af sigtede eller tiltalte, der er omfattet af straffelovens § 16 (**125**)

European Court of Human Rights

A	A and Others v. United Kingdom, 3455/05 (2009) ECHR 301 (**603**)
Croke	Croke v. Ireland – 33267/96 (2000) ECHR 680 (2000) (**616**)
Edwards	Paul and Audrey Edwards v. UK ECHR (Application no. 46477/99 14 March 2002 (**74**)
Keenan	Keenan v. United Kingdom, ECHR judgment 3 April 2001 (**114**)
Kudla	Kudla v. Poland, ECHR judgment 26 October 2000 (**114**)
Luberti	Luberti v. Italy, (1984) ECHR Series A No. 75 (**114**)
Renolde	Renolde v. France, ECHR judgment 16 October 2008 (**114**)
Soering	Soering v. United Kingdom, (1989) 11 EHRR 439 (**114**)
Thynne	Thynne, Wilson and Gunnel v. United Kingdom, ECHR judgment 25 October 1990 (**114**)
Winterwerp	Winterwerp v. the Netherlands. ECHR judgment 24 October 1979 (**113**, **133**)
X	X v. United Kingdom 6998/75 (1981) 4 EHRR (**114**, **603**)

South Africa

Chretian	S v Chretien 1981 1 SA 1097 (A) (**131**)
Laubscher	S v Laubscher 1988 (1) SA 163 (**131**)

UK and the Republic of Ireland

A.M.	A.M. v Kennedy (2007) IEHC 136; (2007) 4 I.R. 667 (**106**)
Alcock	Alcockv Chief Constable of Yorkshire (1992) 1 AC 310 (**52**, **53**)
Antoine	R v Antoine (2000) 2 All ER 208 (**25**)
Bailey	R v Bailey (1983) 2 All ER 503, (1983) 1 WLR 760 (**34**)
Banks	Banks v Goodfellow (1870) 5 QB 549 (**166**)
Beard	Director of Public Prosecutions v Beard (1920) AC 479 (**33**, **441**)
Betteridge	R v Betteridge (2006) EWCA Crim 400 (**47**)
Birch	R v Birch (1989) 90 Cr App R 78 (**64**)
Bolam	Bolam v Friern Hospital Management Committee (1957) 1 WLR 582, 2 All ER 118 (**60**, **168**)
Bolitho	Bolitho v City and Hackney Health Authority (1998) AC 232 (**168**)
Bournewood	R v Bournewood Community and Mental Health NHS Trust ex parte L (1998) 3 All ER 289 HL (**61**, **81**)
Bradley	Bradley (1991) 1 WLR 134 at 142 C., *Independent* 16 Nov (**42**)
Bratty	Bratty v A-G for N. Ireland (1963) AC 386; (1961) 3 All ER 523–39 (**26**)
Brennan	Brennan v H.M. Advocate (1977) JC 38 (**94**)
Brown	H.M. Advocate v Brown (1907) 5 Adam 312 (**94**)
Bryan	R v Bryan and Bryan (2006) EWCA Crim 1660 (**47**)
Burgess	Burgess R v Burgess (1991) 2 WLR 1206; (1991) 93 Cr App Rep 41 (56, 58, 308) (**26**, **290**)
Byrne	R v Byrne (1960) 2 QB 396; (1960) 3 All ER 1; 44 Cr App Rep 246 (**29**, **247**)

Cannings	Cannings (2004) 1 All ER 725, (2004) EWCA Crim 1, (2004) EWCA Crim 01, (2004) 1 WLR 2607, (2004) 2 Cr App R 7
Carraher	Carraher v H.M. Advocate (1946) JC 108 (**96**)
Chard	R v Chard (1971) 56 Cr App Rep 268 (**35**)
Clark	Clark (Sally) (2000) EWCA Crim 54, (2000) All ER (D) 1219 (**530, 671, 672, 673**)
Clarke	R v Clarke (1972) 1 All ER 219 (**34**)
Clunis	Clunis v Camden and Islington Health Authority (1998) QB 978 (**52, 58, 74, 335**)
Coonan 1	Coonan 2010 (Formerly Sutcliffe) R v (2010) EWHC 1741 (QB) (16 July 2010) (**6**)
Coonan 2	Coonan 2011 (Formerly Sutcliffe), R v (2011) EWCA Crim 5 (14 January 2011) (**6**)
Cunningham	H.M. Advocate v Cunningham (1963) JC 80 (**95**)
Davies	R v Davies (1881) 14 Cox CC 563 (**33, 35**)
Deitschmann	R v Deitschmann (2003) 1 All ER 897 (**34**)
Di Duca	R v Di Duca (1959) 43 Cr App Rep 167 (**33**)
Dingwall	H.M. Advocate v Dingwall (1867) 5 Irv. 466 (**96**)
Doyle	Doyle v. Wicklow County Council (1973) IESC 1 (**107**)
Dulieu	Dulieu v White & Sons (1901) 2 KB 669 (**51**)
Dyson	R v Dyson (1831) 7 C&P 305 (**24**)
Edwards	Edwards v UK (2001) 1 MHLR 220 (**74**)
Egdell	W v Egdell (1989) 1 All ER 1089; (1990) Ch 359 (**15, 165, 166**)
Fenton	R v Fenton (1975) 61 Cr App Rep 261 (**33, 34**)
Ferrers	R v Ferrers (1760), 19 Howell's State Trials, 886 (**147**)
Folkes	R v Folkes (2006) EWCA Crim 287 (**46**)
Fraser	Her Majesty's Advocate v Simon Fraser 1878 4 Couper 78 (88, 309) (**291, 292**)
Froggatt	Froggatt v. Chesterfield and North Derbyshire Royal Hospital NHS Trust 2002 All ER (D) 218 (**53**)
Frost	Frost v Chief Constable of South Yorkshire Police (1997) 3 WLR 1194 (**53**)
Galbraith	Galbraith v H.M. Advocate (2001) SCCR 551 (**96**)
Gittens	R v Gittens (1984) QB 698 (**34**)
Gooden	Gooden v Waterford Regional Hospital (2001) IESC 14 (**106**)
Gore	R v Gore (2007) EWCA Crim 2789 (**29**)
Hardie	R v Hardie (1984) 3 All ER 848 (**34**)
HE	HE v A hospital NHS trust (2003) 2 FLR 408 (**84**)
Heard	R v Heard (2007) EWCA Crim 125 (**33**)
Hennessy	R v Hennessy (1989) 1 WLR 287 (**26**)
HL v UK	HL v United Kingdom (2004) 40 EHRR 761, 81 BMLR 131, The Times 19th October, 17 (**61, 81**)
HMA	LB v HMA (11/4/2003) Appeal Court – Lord McCluskey, XC346/02 (**652**)
Hubbard	Hubbard v Lambeth, Southwark and Lewisham HA (2001) EWCA 1455 (**791**)
Johnson and Others	R v Johnson and Others (2006) EWCA Crim 2486 (**47**)
Johnson	R v Johnson (2007) EWCA Crim 1978 (**28**)
Kemp	R v Kemp (1956) 2 All ER 249; (1957) 1 QB 399 (57, 308) (**290**)
Kidd	H.M. Advocate v Kidd (1960) JC 61 (**95**)
Lamb	Lamb v Camden LBC (1981) QB 625 (**51**)
Lang	R v Lang (2005) EWCA Crim 2864 (**46, 47**)
Lipman	R v Lipman (1969) 3 All ER 410; (1970) 1 QB 152 (**27, 33**)
M.R.	M.R. v Byrne and Flynn (2007) IEHC 73; (2007) (**109**)
Majewski	Director of Public Prosecutions v Majewski (1976) 2 All ER 142; (1977) AC 443 (**33, 441**)
Masterman-Lister	Masterman-Lister – v. Jewell and Home Counties Dairies and – v Brutton and Company (2002) EWCA Civ 1889 (**166**)

McCann	McCann v. UK (1996) 21 EHRR 97 (**74**)
McGrady	R v McGrady (2006) EWCA Crim 1547 (**47**)
McLoughlin	McLoughlin v O'Brian (1982) 2 All ER 298; (1983) 1 AC 410 (**51**)
McNaughton	R v McNaughton (1843) 10 CI and Fin 200. West and Walk, 1977 (**27, 28, 32, 33, 34, 35, 95, 105, 106, 107, 121, 129, 130, 145, 149, 155, 163, 234, 335, 348, 352**)
Meadow 1	Meadow 1 (2006) 2 All ER 329, (2006) 89 BMLR 143, (2006) Lloyds Rep Med 233, (2006) EWHC 146 (Admin), (2006) 2 FCR 777, (2006) Fam Law 354, (2006) Lloyd's Rep Med 233, (2006) 1 FLR 1161, (2006) ACD 43, (2006) 1 WLR 1452 (**675**)
Meadow 2	Meadow 2 GMC v Sir Roy Meadow with HMAG 2007) 2 WLR 286, (2007) 1 All ER 1, (2007) QB 462, 92 BMLR 51, (2006) 92 BMLR 51, (2006) EWCA Civ 1390, (2006) 3 FCR 447, (2007) Fam Law 214, (2007) 1 QB 462, (2007) 1 FLR 1398, (2006) 44 EG 196 (**675**)
Meah	Meah v McCreamer and others (No. 2) (1986) 1 AER 943 (**51**)
Milligan	HMA v Vincent James Milligan (2003) Judgment of Sheriff A.L. Stewart Q.C., 19/3/2003, Ref. DNO 2510128 (**652**)
Multiple Claimants	Multiple Claimants v the Ministry of Defence (2003) EWHC 1134 (QB) (**104**)
Munjaz	R v Ashworth Hospital Authority ex parte Munjaz (2005) UKHL 58 (**77**)
North Glamorgan	North Glamorgan NHS Trust v Walters (2002) EWCA Civ 1792 (**53**)
Nowell	R v AWetf (1948) 1 All ER 794 (20) (**15**)
O'Driscoll	A-G v O'Driscoll (2003) JLR 390 (**106**)
Peet	Peet v Mid Kent Area Healthcare NHS Trust (2002) 1 WLR 210 (**790**)
Philip Clarke	Re Philip Clarke (1950) IR 253 (**106**)
Podola	R v Podola (1959) 3 All ER, 418; (1960) 1 QB 325 (**25, 426**)
Prior	A.G. v Prior (2001) JLR 146 (**105, 106**)
Pritchard	R v Pritchard (1836) 7 C&P 303 (**24, 106, 166**)
Quick	R v Quick and Paddison (1973) 3 All Er 347; (1973) QB 910 (59–41) (**27, 290**)
Re C	Re C (Adult: refusal of medical treatment) (1994) 1 All ER 819 (**84**)
Re F	Re F (Mental Patient: Sterilization) (1990) 2 AC 1 at 75 (**79**)
Re MB	Re MB (1997) 2 FLR 426 (**78**)
Re T	Re T (Adult: refusal of medical treatment) (1992) 4 All ER 649 (**84, 166, 167**)
Reid	R v Reid (2001), 1 Cr. App R.21, (2002)
Reid	Reid v Secretary of State for Scotland (1999) 1 All ER 481, HL (1999) 2 WLR 28 (**62, 90**)
Robson	R v Robson (2006) EWCA Crim 1414 *S* R v S (2005) EWCA Crim 3616 (**47**)
Ross	Ross v H.M. Advocate (1991) JC 210 (**95**)
Ruddle	Ruddle v Secretary of State for Scotland (1999) GWD 29 1395v (**99**)
Russell	Russell v H.M. Advocate (1946) JC 37 (**94**)
Sainsbury	R v Sainsbury (1989) 11 Cr App R (S) 533 (**164**)
Samuel	R v Samuel (2006) EWCA Crim 400 (**46**)
Savage	H.M. Advocate v Savage (1923) JC 49 (**96**)
Sharrock	R v Sharrock (2006) EWCA Crim 2296 (**47**)
Simao	Simao v A-G (2005) JLR 374 (**105**)
Singh	R v Stratford Magistrates Court (2007) EWHC 1582 (Admin) (**27**)
Sorley	Sorley v H.M. Advocate (1992) SCCR 396 (**95**)
South Australia	South Australia Asset Management Corp. v York Montague Ltd. (1997) AC 191 (1996) 3 AER 365 (**51**)
Stewart	Stewart v H.M. Advocate (No. 1) (1997) JC 183 (**94**)
Stone	Stone v South East Coast Strategic Health Authority and Ors (2006) EWHC 1668 (Admin) (**414**)
Sullivan	R v Sullivan (1983) 1 All ER 557 (**26, 27, 28**)
T. & V.	T. & V. v. the United Kingdom (1999) Human Rights Case Digest, 10, Nos 10–12, 1999, pp. 299–305(7) (**492**)

USA

References

11 million (2008) Prison mother and baby units: do they meet the best interest of the child? 11 million: London, UK http://dera.ioe. ac.uk/7418/1/force_download.php%3Ffp%3D%252Fclient_assets%252Fcp%252Fpublication%252F164%252FPrison_Mother_and_ Baby_Units.pdf (**519**)

A Constant Observer (1823) *Sketches in Bedlam.* London: Sherwood Jones. (**546**)

Abbott MW, Williams MM, and Volberg RA (2004) A prospective study of problem and regular nonproblem gamblers living in the community. *Substance Use and Misuse* **39**: 855–84. (**472**)

Abbott P (2002) Reconfiguration of the high-security hospitals: some lessons from the mental hospital retraction and reprovision programme in the United Kingdom, 1960–2000. *Journal of Forensic Psychiatry and Psychology* **13**: 107–22. (**30**)

Abderhalden C, Needham I, Dassen T, et al. (2008) Structured risk assessment and violence in acute psychiatric wards: randomised controlled trial. *British Journal of Psychiatry* **193**: 44–50. (**549**)

Abel G and Osborn CA (2003) Treatment of sexual offenders. In R Rosner (eds) *Principles and Practice of Forensic Psychiatry.* London: Arnold. (**125**)

Abel GG and Rouleau JL (1990) The nature and extent of sexual assault. In WL Marshall, DR Laws, HE Barbaree (eds) *Handbook of Sexual Assault.* New York: Plenum. (**246**)

Abel GG, Becker JV, Cunningham-Rathner J, Mittelman, MS, and Rouleau, JL. (1988) Multiple paraphilic diagnoses among sex offenders. *Bulletin of the American Academy of Psychiatry and the Law,* **16**, 153–68. (**246, 250**)

Abel GG, Becker JV, Mittelman MS, et al. (1987) Self-reported sex crimes of nonincarcerated paraphilics. *Journal of Interpersonal Violence* **2**: 3–25. (**246, 252**)

Abel GG, Huffman J, Warberg B, and Holland CL (1998) Visual reaction time and plethysmography as measures of sexual interest in child molesters. *Sexual Abuse: A Journal of Research and Treatment* **10**: 81–95. (**254**)

Aberg L and Rimmo PA (1998) Dimensions of aberrant driver behaviour. *Ergonomics* **41**: 39–56. (**278**)

Aberhalden C, Needham I, Dassen T, et al. (2007) Frequency and severity of aggressive incidents in acute psychiatric wards in Switzerland. *Clinical Practice and Epidemiology in Mental Health* **3**: 30. (**515, 549**)

Abracen J, Looman J, and Anderson D (2000) Alcohol and drug abuse in sexual and nonsexual violent offenders. *Sexual Abuse: A Journal of Research and Treatment* **12**: 263–74. (**442**)

Abram KM and Teplin LA (1991) Co-occurring disorders among mentally ill jail detainees. Implications for public policy. *American Psychologist* **46**: 1036–45. (**280**)

Abramovich E (2006) Application of CBT in an inpatient setting: case illustration of an adult male with anxiety, depression, and axis II symptoms. *Clinical Case Studies* **5**: 305–30. (**569**)

Abrams A (1983) The multiple personality: a legal defence. *American Journal of Clinical Hypnotism* **25**: 225–31. (**427**)

Abroms GM, Taintor ZC, and Lhamon WT (1966) Percept assimilation and paranoid severity. *Archives of General Psychiatry* **14**(5): 491–6. (**351**)

Academy of Medical Sciences (2005) *Calling Time. The Nation's Drinking as a Major Health Issue.* London: Academy of Medical Sciences. http://www.acmedsci.ac.uk/index.php?pid=99&puid=20 (**437**)

Academy of Medical Sciences (2008) *Brain Science, Addiction and Drugs.* London: Academy of Medical Sciences. http://www. acmedsci.ac.uk/index.php?pid=99&puid=126 (**436, 468**)

Academy of Medical Sciences (2011) *A New Pathway For the Regulation and Governance of Health Research.* London: Academy of Medical Sciences. www.acmedsci.ac.uk/p99puid209.html (**669**)

Achenbach TM and Edeibrock CS (1983) *Manual for the Child Behaviour Checklist and Revised Child Behaviour Profile.* Burlington, VT: University of Vermont. (**669**)

Ackerknecht EH (1959) *A Short History of Psychiatry.* London: Hafner Publishing. (**484**)

ACMD, *see* Advisory Council on the Misuse of Drugs.

Acres DI (ed) (1975) The after-care of special hospital patients. Appendix 3. In *The Report of the Committee on Mentally Abnormal Offenders.* Cmnd 6244. London: HMSO. (**589**)

Adams CE, Fenton MKP, Quiraishi S, and Rathbone J (2001) Systematic meta-review of depot antipsychotic drugs for people with schizophrenia. *British Journal of Psychiatry* **179**: 290–9. (**604, 605**)

Adams J (1995) *Risk.* London: University College of London. (**530, 532, 548**)

Adams Jr WE (2000) Elders in the courtroom. In MB Rothman, BD Dunlop, P Entzel (eds) *Elders, Crime and the Criminal Justice System: Myths, Perceptions and Reality in the 21st Century.* New York: Springer, pp. 87–104. (**523**)

Adams W, Kendell RE, Hare EH, and Munk-Jorgensen P (1993) Epidemiological evidence that maternal influenza contributes to the aetiology of schizophrenia. An analysis of Scottish, English, and Danish data. *British Journal of Psychiatry* **163**: 522–34. (**341**)

Adamson SJ and Sellman JD (2003) A prototype screening instrument for cannabis use disorder: The Cannabis Use Disorder Identification Test (CUDIT) in an alcohol-dependent clinical sample. *Drug and Alcohol Review* **22**: 309–15. (**457**)

Aday RH (2003) *Aging Prisoners: Crisis in American Corrections.* Westport, CT: Praeger. (**523, 528**)

Addington J, el-Guebaly N, Campbell W, et al. (1998) Smoking cessation treatment for patients with schizophrenia. *American Journal of Psychiatry* **155**: 974–5. (**568**)

Adshead G (2004) *Three Degrees of Security. Attachment and Forensic Institutions. A Matter of Security. The Application of Attachment Theory to Forensic Psychiatry and Psychotherapy.* Friedemann Pfafflin and Gwen Adshead. London: Jessica Kingsley. (**555**)

Adshead G and Bluglass K (2005) Attachment representations in mothers with abnormal illness behaviour by proxy. *British Journal of Psychiatry* **187**: 328–33. (**506**)

Adshead G and Bluglass K (2005) Attachment representations in mothers with abnormal illness behaviour by proxy. *British Journal of Psychiatry* **187**: 328–33. (**227**)

Adshead G, Charles S, and Pyszora N (2005) Moving on: a group for patients leaving a high security hospital. *Group Analysis* **38**: 380–94. (**578**)

Advisory Council on the Misuse of Drugs (2003) *Hidden Harm: Responding to the Needs of Children of Problem Drug Users.* London: Home Office. (**466**)

Advisory Council on the Misuse of Drugs (2006) *Pathways to Problems: Hazardous Use of Tobacco, Alcohol and Other Drugs by Young People in the UK and its Implications for Policy.* London: Advisory Council on the Misuse of Drugs. (**466**)

Advisory Council on the Misuse of Drugs (ACMD) (2007a) Drug Facilitated Sexual Assault. ACMD: London. http://webarchive. nationalarchives.gov.uk/+/http://www.homeoffice.gov.uk/publications/ drugs/acmd1/drug-facilitated-sexual-assault/ ACMDDFSA.pdf?view=Binary (**454**)

Advisory Council on the Misuse of Drugs (ACMD) (2007b) *Hidden Harm Three Years on: Realities, Challenges and Opportunities.* London: Home Office. (**466**)

Advisory Council on the Misuse of Drugs (ACMD) (2008) *Cannabis: Classification and Public Health.* London: Home Office. (**453**)

Aebi MF and Delgrande N (2011) Council of Europe annual penal statistics. Survey 2009. Council of Europe: Strasbourg. http://www. coe.int/t/dghl/standardsetting/cdpc/bureau%20documents/PC-CP(2011)3%20E%20-%20SPACE%20I%202009.pdf (**640**)

Agnew R (2002) Crime causation: sociological theories. In J Dressler (ed) *Encyclopaedia of Crime and Justice*, Vol. 1. New York: Macmillan, pp. 324–34. (**179**)

Aigner M, Eher R, Fruehwald S, Gutierrez-Lobos K, and Dwyer SM (2000) Brain abnormalities and violent behavior. *Journal of Psychology and Human Sexuality* **11**: 57–64. (**299**)

Ainsworth MDS, Blehar MC, Waters E, and Wall S (1978) *Patterns of Attachment: A Psychological Study of the Strange Situation.* Hillsdale, NJ: Lawrence Erlbaum Associates. (**718**)

Ainsworth MIS and Wittig, BA (1969) Attachment and the exploratory behaviour of one-year-olds in a strange situation. In BM Foss (ed), *Determinants of Infant Behaviour* Vol. 4, pp. 113–136, London: Methuen. (**396**)

Ainsworth PB and Pease K (1987) *Police Work.* Leicester, UK: British Psychological Society. (**625**)

Aitken C, Roberts P, and Jackson G (2010) *Communicating and Interpreting Statistical Evidence in the Administration of Criminal Justice 1. Fundamentals of Probability and Statistical Evidence in Criminal Proceedings.* London: Royal Statistical Society. (**530**)

Aiyegbusi A (2004) *Forensic Mental Health Nursing, Care with Security in Mind. A Matter of Security. The Application of Attachment Theory to Forensic Psychiatry and Psychotherapy.* Friedemann Pfafflin and Gwen Adshead. London: Jessica Kingsley. (**555**)

Alaerts M and Del-Favero J (2009) Searching genetic risk factors for schizophrenia and bipolar disorder: learn from the past and back to the future. *Human Mutations* **30**(8): 1139–52. (**208**)

Alcott LM (1997) *A Long Fatal Love Chase.* New York: Dell Publishing. (**373**)

Aldwin CM (1999) *Stress, Coping, and Development: An Integrated Perspective.* New York: The Guilford. (**722**)

Alexander M (1993) Should a sexual offender be allowed castration?: ethical considerations in using orchidectomy for social control. *British Medical Journal* **307**: 790–4. (**261**)

Alexander M (1999) Sexual offender treatment efficacy revisited. *Sexual Abuse: A Journal of Research and Treatment* **11**: 101–16. (**257**)

Alexy EM, Burgess AN, Baker T, and Smoyak SA (2005) Perceptions of cyberstalking among college students. *Brief Treatment and Crisis Intervention* **5**(3): 279–89. (**377**)

Alha P and Pirkola S (2006) Mielenterveyspalvelut. In U Häkkinen and P Alha (eds) *Health Service Utilization and Its Socioeconomic Determinants, Health 2000 Survey.* Publication of the National Public Health Institute, B10/2006. Helsinki: National Public Health Institute. (**501**)

Allan R, Lindsay WR, MacLeod F and Smith AHW. (2001) Treatment of women with intellectual disabilities who have been involved with the criminal justice system for reasons of aggression. *Journal of Applied Research in Intellectual Disabilities* **14**: 340–347. (**327**)

Allderidge P (1974) Criminal insanity: Bethlem to Broadmoor. *Proceedings of the Royal Society of Medicine* **67**: 897–904. (**589, 590**)

Allderidge P (1979) Hospitals, madhouses and asylums: cycles in the care of the insane. *British Journal of Psychiatry* **134**: 321–34. (**589**)

Allen J, Nicholas S, Salisbury H, and Wood M (2003) Nature of burglary, vehicle and violent crime. In C Flood-Page, J Taylor (eds) *Crime in England and Wales 2001/2002: Supplementary Volume.* Statistical Bulletin 01/03. London: Home Office, pp. 41–68. (**179**)

Allen JG (2001) *Traumatic Relationships and Serious Mental Disorders.* Chichester, UK: Wiley. (**392, 571**)

Allen JG and Fonagy P (2006) *Handbook of Mentalization-Based Treatment.* London: Wiley. (**571**)

Allen MH, Currier GW, Hughes DH, et al. (2003) Treatment of behavioral emergencies: a summary of the Expert Consensus Guidelines. *Journal of Psychiatric Practice* **9**: 16–38. (**561**)

Allison M, Brimacombe CA, Hunter MA, and Kadlec H (2006) Young and older eyewitness' use of narrative features in testimony. *Discourse Processes* **41**: 289–314. (**523**)

Almvik R and Woods P (1998) The Brøset Violence Checklist (BVC) and the prediction of inpatient violence: some preliminary results. *Perspectives in Psychiatric Care* **5**: 208–11. (**549**)

Alnaes R and Torgersen S (1997) Personality and personality disorders predict development and relapses of major depression. *Acta Psychiatrica Scandinavica* **95**: 336–42. (**398**)

Amen DG, Stubblefield M, Carmichael B, and Thirsted R (1996) Brain SPECT findings and aggressiveness. *Annals of Clinical Psychiatry* **8**: 129–37. (**302**)

American Academy of Psychiatry and the Law (2002) Practice guidelines: forensic psychiatry evaluation of defendants raising the insanity defense. *Supplement to Journal of the American Academy of Psychiatry and the Law* **30**(2): 51–60. (**120, 122**)

American Academy of Psychiatry and the Law (2005) *Ethics Guidelines for the Practice of Forensic Psychiatry.* www.aapl.org/ethics.htm (**!, 659**)

American Bar Association (1968) *Project on Minimum Standards for Criminal Justice: Pleas of Guilty (approved draft).* Chicago, IL: American Bar Association. Cited by Miller, 2003a. (**120**)

American College of Sports Medicine (ACSM) (2000) *Guidelines for Exercise Testing and Prescription,* 6th edn. Philadelphia, PA: Lea & Febiger. (**568**)

American Law Institute (1962) *Model Penal Code.* Philadelphia, PA: American Law Institute. (**121**)

American Psychiatric Association (1980) *Diagnostic and Statistical Manual of Mental Disorders*, 3rd edn. Washington, DC: American Psychiatric Association. (**10, 385, 714**)

American Psychiatric Association (1987) *Diagnostic and Statistical Manual of Mental Disorders,* 3rd edn. revised. (DSM-III-R). Washington, DC: American Psychiatric Association. (**270**)

American Psychiatric Association (1994) *Diagnostic and Statistical Manual of Mental Disorders,* 4th edn. Washington, DC: American Psychiatric Association. (**10, 17, 112, 158, 235, 271, 285, 314, 319, 346, 384, 436, 449, 469**)

American Psychiatric Association (2000) *Diagnostic and Statistical Manual of Mental Disorders,* 4th edn. Text Revised (DSM-IV-TRTM). Washington, DC: American Psychiatric Association. (**245**)

American Psychiatric Association (2001) Practice guideline for the treatment of patients with borderline Personality Disorder. *American Journal of Psychiatry* **158** (suppl.): 1–52. http://psychiatryonline.org/content.aspx?bookid=28&sectionid=1672600 (**312, 407**)

American Psychiatric Association (2005) *Guideline Watch: Practice Guideline for the Treatment of Patients with Borderline Personality Disorder.* http://psychiatryonline.org/content.aspx?bookid=28&sectionid=1682658 (**407**)

American Psychiatric Association (2013) *The Principles of Medical Ethics with Annotations Especially Applicable to Psychiatry.* Washington, DC: American Psychiatric Association. (**114, 120, 659**)

American Psychiatric Association Work Group on ASD and PTSD (2004) *Practice Guidelines for the Treatment of Patients with Acute Stress Disorder and Posttraumatic Stress Disorder.* Washington, DC: American Psychiatric Association. (**724, 725**)

Amir M (1971) *Patterns in Forcible Rape.* Chicago, IL: University of Chicago Press. (**248**)

Ammerman AS (2002) The efficacy of behavioural interventions to modify dietary fat and fruit and vegetable intake: a review of the evidence. *Preventive Medicine* **35**: 25–41. (**567**)

Ammons RB and Ammons CH (1962) The Quick Test: provisional manual. *Psychological Reports* **11**: 111–61. (**315**)

Andersen HS, Sesstoft D, Lillebæk T, et al. (2000) A longitudinal study of prisoners on remand: psychiatric prevalence, incidence and psychopathology in solitary vs non-solitary confinement. *Acta Psychiatrica Scandinavica* **102**: 19–25. (**630**)

Anderson CA and Bushman BJ (2002) Human aggression. *Annual Review of Psychology* **53**: 27–51. (**354**)

Anderson EW and Mallinson WP (1941) Psychogenic episodes in the course of major psychoses. *Journal of Mental Science* **87**: 383–96. (**434**)

Anderson EW, Trethowan WH, and Kenna JC (1959) An experimental investigation of simulation and pseudo-dementia. *Acta Psychiatrica Scandinavica* **34** (suppl. 132): 1–42. (**432**)

Anderson IM, Clark L, Elliott R, et al. (2002) 5-HT$_{2C}$ receptor activation by m-chlorophenylpiperazine detected in humans with fMRI. *Neuroreport* **13**: 1547–51. (**310**)

Anderson RA, Watson AA, and Harland WA (1981) Fire deaths in the Glasgow area. *Medicine, Science and the Law* **21**: 175–83. (**273**)

Anderson SW, Bechara A, Damasio H, Tranel D, and Damasio AR (1999) Impairment of social and moral behavior related to early damage in human prefrontal cortex. *Nature Neuroscience* **2**: 1032–7. (**199, 298**)

Andrade J, Kavanaugh D, and Baddeley A (1997) Eye-movements and visual imagery: a working memory approach to the treatment of post-traumatic stress disorder. *British Journal of Clinical Psychology* **36**: 209–33. (**725**)

Andreasen MC and Noyes R (1975) Suicide attempted by self-immolation. *American Journal of Psychiatry* **132**: 554–6. (**276**)

Andresen R, Caputi P, and Oades LG (2010) Do clinical outcome measures assess consumer-defined recovery? *Psychiatry Research* **177**: 309–17. (**617**)

Andresen R, Oades L, and Caputi P (2003) The experience of recovery from schizophrenia: towards an empirically validated stage model. *Australian and New Zealand Journal of Psychotherapy* **3**: 586–94. (**574**)

Andrew T, Hart DJ, Snieder H, et al. (2001) Are twins and singletons comparable? A study of disease-related and lifestyle characteristics in adult women. *Twin Research* **4**: 464–77. (**189**)

Andrews B, Brewin CR, and Rose S (2003) Gender, social support and PTSD in victims of violent crime. *Journal of Traumatic Stress* **16**: 421–7. (**723**)

Andrews B, Brewin CR, Philpott R, Stewart, L (2007) Delayed-onset posttraumatic stress disorder: a systematic review of the evidence. *American Journal of Psychiatry* **164**: 1319–26. (**712**)

Andrews B, Brewin CR, Rose S, and Kirk M (2000) Predicting PTSD symptoms in victims of violent crime: the role of shame, anger, and childhood abuse. *Journal of Abnormal Psychology* **109**: 69–73. (**721**)

801

Andrews D, Bonta J, Wormith J, Guzzo L, Brews A, Rettinger J and Rowe R (2011) Sources of variability in estimates of predictive validity. A specification with level of service, general risk and need. *Criminal Justice and Behavior* **38**: 413–32. (**502**)

Andrews D, Zinger I, Hoge R, et al. (1990) Does correctional treatment work? A clinically relevant and psychologically informed metaanalysis. *Criminology* **28** 369–404. (**486**)

Andrews DA and Bonta J (1995) *The Level of Service Inventory – Revised.* Toronto, ON: Multi-Health Systems. (**530, 534–5**)

Andrews DA and Bonta J (1998) *The Psychology of Criminal Conduct*, 2nd edn. Cincinnati, OH: Anderson. (**518**)

Andrews DA and Bonta JS (1994) *The Psychology of Criminal Conduct.* Cincinnati, OH: Anderson. (**530**)

Andrews DA and Bonta JS (2006) *The Psychology of Criminal Conduct*, 4th edn. Cincinnati, OH: Anderson. (**257, 518**)

Andrulonis PA, Gluech BC, Stroebel CF, and Vogel NG (1982) Borderline personality disorder subcategories. *Journal of Nervous and Mental Disease* **170**: 670–9. (**403**)

Angold A (1989) Seclusion. *British Journal of Psychiatry* **154**: 437–44. (**594**)

Annand J and Stavrakaki C (2007) Substance related disorders. In R Fletcher, E Loschen, C Stavrakaki, M First (eds) *Diagnostic Manual-Intellectual Disability (DM-ID).* Kingston, NY: NADD. (**324**)

Anonymous (1997) *Industry Switches to Toughened Glasses.* London. The Licensee. 27. (**705**)

Anton RF, Oroszi G, O'Malley S, et al. (2008) An evaluation of mu-opioid receptor (OPRM1) as a predictor of naltrexone response in the treatment of alcohol dependence: results from the combined pharmacotherapies and behavioral interventions for alcohol dependence (COMBINE) study. *Archives of General Psychiatry* **65**: 135–44. (**206**)

Anwar S, Långström N, Grann M, and Fazel S (2011) Is arson the crime most strongly associated with psychosis?–a national case-control study of arson risk in schizophrenia and other psychosis. *Schizophrenia Bulletin* **37**: 580–6. (**273, 340**)

Aos S, Phipps P, Barnoski R, and Lieb R (2001) The comparative costs and benefits of programmes to reduce crime: a review of research findings with implications for Washington State. In BC Welsh, DPFarrington, LW Sherman (eds) *Costs and Benefits of Preventing Crime.* Boulder, CO: Westview. (**182, 183**)

APA: see American Psychiatric Association.

Appelbaum PS and Jorgenson L (1991) Psychiatrist-patient sexual contact after termination: an analysis and a proposal. *American Journal of Psychiatry* **148**: 1466–73. (**682**)

Appelbaum PS, Robbins PC, and Monahan J (2000) Violence and delusions: data from the MacArthur violence risk assessment study. *American Journal of Psychiatry* **157**: 566–72. (**338, 349**)

Appelbaum PS, Robbins PC, and Vesselinov R (2004) Persistence and stability of delusions over time. *Comprehensive Psychiatry* **45**: 317–24. (**338, 349**)

Appelbaum PS, Zonana H, Bonnie R, and Roth LH (1989) Statutory approaches to limiting psychiatrists' liability for their patients' violent acts. *American Journal of Psychiatry* **146**: 321–8. (**664**)

Appignanesi L (2008) *Mad, Bad and Sad.* A History of Women and the Mind Doctors From 1800 to the Present. Virago: London. (**589, 691**)

Applebaum PS (2009) Through a glass darkly: functional neuroimaging evidence enters the courtroom. *Psychiatric Services* **60**: 21–3. (**17**)

Apsche JA and Ward Bailey SR (2005) Mode deactivation therapy: cognitive behavioral therapy for adolescents with reactive conduct disorders and/or personality disorders/traits. In MC Calder (ed) *Children and Young People Who Sexually Abuse: New Theory, Research, and Practice Developments.* United Kingdom: Russell House. (**495**)

Arango C and Bernardo M (2005) The effect of quetiapine on aggression and hostility in patients with schizophrenia. *Human Psychopharmacology* **20**: 237–41. (**565**)

Arbuthnott G (1998) Neuropharmacology. In E Johnstone, CPL Freeman, AK Zealley (eds) *Companion to Psychiatric Studies.* Edinburgh, UK: Churchill Livingstone, pp. 39–80. (**307**)

Archer J (2000) Sex differences in aggression between heterosexual partners: a metaanalytic review. *Psychological Bulletin* **126**: 651–80. (**505**)

Archer J (2002) Sex differences in physically aggressive acts between heterosexual partners: a meta-analytic review. *Aggression and Violent Behavior* **7**: 313–51. (**218**)

Arcos-Burgos M, Castellanos FX, Lopera F, et al. (2002) Attention-deficit/hyperactivity disorder (ADHD): feasibility of linkage analysis in a genetic isolate using extended and multigenerational pedigrees. *Clinical Genetics* **61**:335–43. (**193**)

Arendt H (1963) *Eichman in Jerusalem. A Report on the Banality of Evil.* New York: Penguin. (**6, 266**)

Aristotle (c BC 330, translated JAK Thomson [revised by H. Tredennick, (1976)]) *The Ethics of Aristotle.* London: Penguin Books. (**32**)

Aristotle *Ethics* – multiple editions. For a web version, see Penn State University translation with notes by JA Smith. http://www.hn.psu.edu/faculty/jmanis/aristot.htm (**369**)

Armenteros JL and Lewis JE (2006) Citalopram treatment for impulsive aggression in children and adolescents: an open pilot study. *Journal of the American Academy of Child and Psychiatry* **41**: 522–9. (**312**)

Armstadter AB, McCart MR, and Ruggiero KJ (2007) Psychosocial interventions for adults with crime-related PTSD. *Professional Psychology: Research and Practice* **38**: 640–51. (**728**)

Armstrong JL and Whitlock FA (1980) Mental illness and road traffic accidents. *Australian and New Zealand Journal of Psychiatry* **14**: 53–60. (**278**)

Arndt IO, Dorozynski L, McLellan AT, Woody GE, and O'Brien CP (1992) Controlled study of desipramine treatment of cocaine dependence in methadone treated patients. *Archives of General Psychiatry* **49**: 888–93. (**404**)

Arndt IO, McClellan AT, Dorozynsky L, Woody GE, and O'Brien CP (1994) Desipramine treatment for cocaine dependence: role of antisocial personality disorder. *Journal of Nervous and Mental Disease* **182**: 151–6. (**404**)

Arndt S, Turvey C, and Flaum M (2002) Older offenders, substance abuse, and treatment. *American Journal of Geriatric Psychiatry* **10**: 733–9. (**526**)

Arnott H and Creighton S (2006) *Parole Board Hearings. Law and Practice*. London: Legal Action Group. (**42**)

Arnott H and Creighton S (2010) *Parole Board Hearings. Law and Practice*, 2nd edn. London: Legal Action Group. (**42**)

Arscott K, Dagnan D, and Stenfert Kroese B (1998) Consent to psychological research by people with an intellectual disability. *Journal of Applied Research in Intellectual Disabilities* **11**: 77–83. (**332**)

Arscott K, Dagnan D, and Stenfert Kroese B (1999) Assessing the ability of people with a learning disability to give informed consent to treatment. *Psychological Medicine* **29**: 1367–75. (**332**)

Arseneault L, Cannon M, Murray R, et al. (2003) Childhood origins of violent behaviour in adults with schizophreniform disorder. *British Journal of Psychiatry* **183**: 520–25. (**208, 337, 342**)

Arseneault L, Cannon M, Poulton R, et al. (2002) Cannabis use in adolescence and risk for adult psychosis: longitudinal prospective study. *British Medical Journal* **325**: 1213. (**488**)

Arseneault L, Cannon M, Witton J, and Murray RM (2004) Causal association between cannabis and psychosis: examination of the evidence. *British Journal of Psychiatry* **184**: 110–7. (**208**)

Arseneault L, Moffitt TE, Caspi A, et al. (2003) Strong genetic effects on cross-situational antisocial behaviour among 5-year-old children according to mothers, teachers, examiner-observers, and twins' self-reports. *Journal of Child Psychology and Psychiatry* **44**: 832–48. (**196, 337, 342**)

Arseneault L, Moffitt TE, Caspi A, Taylor PJ, and Silva PA (2000) Mental disorders and violence in a total birth cohort: results from the Dunedin study. *Archives of General Psychiatry* **57**: 979–86. (**455**)

Åsberg M, Montgomery SA, Perris C, Schalling D, and Sedvall G (1978) The comprehensive psychopathological rating scale. *Acta Psychiatrica Scandinavica* **57** (suppl. 271): 5–27. (**294, 350, 726**)

Åsberg M, Traskman L, and Thoren P (1976) 5-HIAA in the cerebrospinal fluid: a biochemical suicide predictor? *Archives of General Psychiatry* **33**: 1193–7. (**308**)

Ash P (2003) Legal research on the web. In R Rosner (ed) *Principles and Practice of Forensic Psychiatry*. London: Arnold, pp. 811–5. (**144**)

Asher R (1951) Munchausen's Syndrome. *Lancet* **1**: 339–41. (**226, 422, 434**)

Asher R (1958) Malingering. *Transactions of the Medical Society of London* **75**: 34–44. (**432**)

Ashford M and Bailey S (2004) The youth justice system in England and Wales. In S Bailey M Dolan (eds) *Adolescent Forensic Psychiatry*. London: Arnold, pp. 409–16. (**492**)

Ashford M, Chard A, and Redhouse N (2006) *Defending Young People in the Criminal Justice System*, 3rd edn. Glasgow, UK: Legal Action Groups. (**492, 493**)

Ashton JR and Donnan S (1981) Suicide by burning as an epidemic phenomenon: an analysis of 82 deaths and inquests in England and Wales in 1978–9. *Psychological Medicine* **11**: 735–9. (**276**)

Ashworth A (2006) *Principles of Criminal Law*, 5th edn. Oxford: Oxford University Press. (**26**)

Association of Chief Police Officers (2006) *Operation Matisse: Investigating Drug Facilitated Sexual Assault*. http://www.ias.org.uk/resources/publications/alcoholalert/alert200603/al200603_p4.html (**454**)

Association of County Councils (1984) *Juvenile Courts*. Association of County Councils: London. (**480**)

Association of Directors of Social Services (1985) *Children Still in Trouble. Report of an ADSS Study Group*. Taunton, UK: Association of Directors of Social Services. (**480**)

Association of Forensic Physicians and Royal College of Psychiatrists (2006) *Substance Misuse Detainees in Police Custody: Guidelines for Clinical Management (Council Report CR132)*, 3rd edn. London: Royal College of Psychiatrists. (**448, 461**)

Astrup C (1984) Querulent paranoia: a follow-up. *Neuropsychobiology* **11**: 149–54. (**382**)

Atkeson BM, Calhoun KS, Resick PA, and Ellis EM (1982) Victims of rape: repeated assessment of depressive symptoms. *Journal of Consulting and Clinical Psychology* **50**: 96–102. (**715**)

Atkins D, Pumariega AJ, Rogers K, et al. (1999) Mental health and incarcerated youth. I: prevalence and nature of psychopathology. *Journal Child Family Studies* **8**: 193–204. (**483**)

Atkinson J (2000) *Case Studies of Female Sex Offenders in the Correctional Service of Canada*. Toronto, ON: Correction Service Canada. (**264**)

Atkinson JM (1989) To tell or not to tell the diagnosis of schizophrenia. *Journal of Medical Ethics* **15**: 21–4. (**665**)

Attwood T and Joachim R (1994) The prevention and management of seriously disruptive behavior in Australia. In N Bouras (ed) *Mental Health in Mental Retardation: Recent Advances and Practice*. Cambridge: Cambridge University Press, pp. 365–74. (**326**)

Aubert V (1963a) The structure of legal thinking. In F Castberg (ed) *Legal Essays*. Norway: Universitets-forlaget. (**14, 148**)

Aubert V (1963b) Researches in the sociology of law. *American Behavioral Scientist* **7**(4): 16–20. (**671**)

Audit Commission (1996) *Misspent Youth: Young People and Crime*. London: Audit Commission. (**478**)

Auerbach AW (1977) *The role of the therapeutic community 'Street Prison' in the rehabilitation of youthful offenders*. PhD thesis, George Washington University, USA, cited by Lees et al. 1999. (**412**)

Auerbach DB (1982) The Ganser syndrome. In CTH Friedmann, RA Faguet (eds) *Extraordinary Disorders of Human Behaviour*. New York: Plenum. (**434**)

Austin J, Coleman D, Peyton J and Johnson KD. (2003) Reliability and Validity Study of the LSI-R Risk Assessment Instrument, Final Report. National Criminal Justice reference Service, US Department of Justice: Washington, DC. https://www.ncjrs.gov/App/publications/ Abstract.aspx?id=243141 (**534–5**)

Australian Bureau of Statistics (1996) *Women's Safety, Australia, 1996*. Canberra, Australia: Commonwealth of Australia. (**374**)

Australian Bureau of Statistics (2005) *Personal Safety Survey 2005*. Canberra, Australia: Commonwealth of Australia. (**374**)

Australian Institute of Health and Welfare (2004) *Statistics on Drug Use in Australia*. Canberra, Australia: Institute of Health and Welfare. (**464**)

Ausubel DP (1961) Personality disorder is disease. *American Psychologist* **16**: 69–74. (**11**)

Averill JR (1983) Studies on anger and aggression: implications for theories of emotion. *American Psychologist* **38**: 1145–60. (**213**)

Awad AG and Voruganti LN (2008) The burden of schizophrenia on caregivers: a review. *Pharmacoeconomics* **26**: 149–62. (**355**)

Axelrod R (1984) *The Evolution of Co-operation*. New York: Basic Books. (**213**)

Babcock JC, Green CE, and Robie C (2004) Does batterers' treatment work? A meta-analytic review of domestic violence treatment. *Clinical Psychology Review* **23**: 1023–53. (**221**)

Babinski LM, Hartsough CS, and Lambert NM (1999) Childhood conduct problems, hyperactivity-impulsivity, and inattention as predictors of adult criminal activity. *Journal of Child Psychology and Psychiatry* **40**: 347–55. (**512**)

Babyak M, Blumenthal JA, Herrman S, et al. (2000) Exercise treatment for major depression, maintenance of therapeutic benefit at 10 months. *Psychosomatic Medicine* **82**: 633–8. (**568**)

Bach A (2009) *Ordinary Injustice: How America Holds Court*. New York: Metropolitan Books. (**283**)

Baddeley AD, Kopelman M, and Wilson BA (2004) *The Essential Handbook of Memory Disorders for Clinicians*. Chichester, UK: Wiley-Blackwell. (**xv**)

Badger D, Vaughan P, Woodward M, and Williams P (1999) Planning to meet the needs of offenders with mental disorders in the United Kingdom. *Psychiatric Services* **50**: 1624–7. (**644**)

Bahgwagar Z and Cowen P (2006) Neurochemical basis of aggression and impulsivity in personality disorder. In C Meux, PJ Taylor (eds) *Personality Disorders and Serious Offending Hospital Treatment Models*. London: Hodder Arnold. (**394**)

Bailey S (2002a) Treatment of delinquents'. In M Rutter E Taylor (eds) *Child and Adolescent Psychiatry: Modern Approaches*, 4th edn. Oxford: Blackwell Scientific, pp. 1019–37. (**485**)

Bailey S (2002b) Violent children: a framework for assessment. *Advances in Psychiatric Treatment* **8**: 97–106. (**487**)

Bailey S (2005) The national service framework: children come of age. *Child and Adolescent Mental Health* **10**(3): 127–30. (**484**)

Bailey S (2006) Adolescence and beyond: twelve years onwards. In J Aldgate, D Jones, W Rose, C Jeffrey (eds) *The Developing World of the Child*. London: Jessica Kingsley, pp. 208–25. (**473, 497**)

Bailey S (2007) The Relationship between risk and mental health among young offenders. In M Blyth, K Baker, E Solomon (eds) *Young People and 'Risk'*. Bristol, UK: Policy. (**486**)

Bailey S and Dolan M (2004a) Violence In S Bailey and M Dolan (eds) *Adolescent Forensic Psychiatry*. London: Arnold publishing, pp. 213–227. (**473**)

Bailey S and Dolan M (2004b) *Textbook of Adolescent Forensic Psychiatry*. London: Arnold. (**485**)

Bailey S and Tarbuck P (2006) Recent advances in the development of screening tools for mental health in young offenders. *Current Opinion in Psychiatry* **19**: 373–7. (**485**)

Bailey S, Jasper A, and Ross K (2004) In S Bailey, M Dolan (eds) *Adolescent Forensic Psychiatry*. London: Arnold Publishing, pp. 181–201. (**485**)

Bajt TR and Pope KS (1989) Therapist-patient sexual intimacy involving children and adolescents. *American Psychologist* **44**: 455. (**681**)

Bak M, Krabbendam L, Janssen I, et al. (2005) Early trauma may increase the risk for psychotic experiences by impacting on emotional responses and perception of control. *Acta Psychiatrica Scandinavica* **112**: 360–6. (**345**)

Baker AW and Duncan SP (1985) Child sexual abuse: a study of prevalence in Great Britain. *Child Abuse and Neglect* **9**: 457–67. (**250**)

Baker CD and Lorimer AR (2000) Cardiology: the development of a managed care network. *British Medical Journal* **321**: 1152–3. (**413**)

Baldry AC and Farrington DP (1996) Parenting influences on bullying and victimization. *Legal and Criminological Psychology* **3**: 237–54. (**184**)

Baldwin D and Mayers A (2003) Sexual side-effects of antidepressant and antipsychotic drugs. *Advances in Psychiatric Treatment* **9**: 202–10. (**358**)

Baldwin J (1976) The social composition of the magistracy. *British Journal of Criminology* **16**: 171–4. (**476**)

Balier C (1988) *Psychanalyse Des Complements Violents*. Paris, France: Presses Universitaires Françaises. (**136**)

Ball HN (2005) Death in restraint: lessons. *Psychiatric Bulletin* **29**: 321–3. (**594**)

Ball RA, Moore E, and Kuipers L (1992) Expressed emotion in community care staff. A comparison of patient outcome in a nine month follow-up of two hostels. *Social Psychiatry and Psychiatric Epidemiology* **27**: 35–9. (**557**)

Bamford Review of Mental Health and Learning Disability (Northern Ireland) (2006) *Forensic Services*. Belfast, UK: Department of Health, Social Services and Public Safety. www.dhsspsni.gov.uk/forensic_services_report.pdf (accessed 10.11.2011). (**654**)

Bamford Review of Mental Health and Learning Disability (Northern Ireland) (2007) *A Comprehensive Legislative Framework Report*. Department of Health, Social Services and Public Safety: Belfast. www.dhsspsni.gov.uk/legal-issue-comprehensive-framework.pdf (**103, 654**)

Bancroft J (1989) *Human Sexuality and Its Problems*. Edinburgh, UK: Churchill Livingstone. (**245, 289**)

Bancroft J (1991) The sexuality of sexual offending: the social dimension. *Criminal Behaviour and Mental Health* **1**: 181–92. (**244**)

Bancroft J (2005) The endocrinology of sexual arousal. *Journal of Endocrinology* **10**: 411–27. (**259**)

Bandura A (1969) Principles of behavior modification. Holt, New York: Rinehart and Winston. (**395**)

Bandura A (1983) Psychological mechanisms of aggression. In RG Geen, EI Donnerstein (eds) *Aggression: Theoretical and Experimental Reviews*, Vol. 1. New York: Academic Press. (**213**)

Banerjee P, Duggan C, Huband N, and Watson N (2006) Brief psycho-education for people with personality disorder – a pilot study. *Psychology and Psychotherapy; Theory, Research and Practice* **79**: 385–94. (**401**)

Banerjee S, Clancy C, and Crome IB (eds) (2002) *Co-Existing Problems of Mental Disorder and Substance Misuse (Dual Diagnosis): An Information Manual*, 2nd edn. London: Royal College of Psychiatrists. (**452, 455, 456**)

Banks S, Robbins PC, Silver E, et al. (2004) A multiple models approach to violence risk assessment among people with mental disorder. *Criminal Justice and Behaviour* **31**: 324–40. (**330, 541**)

Barak A (2005) Sexual harassment on the Internet. *Social Science Computer Review* **23**(1): 77–92. (**377**)

Barak Y, Mazeh D, Plopski I, and Baruch Y (2006) Intramuscular ziprasidone treatment of acute psychotic agitation in elderly patients with schizophrenia. *The American Journal of Geriatric Psychiatry* **14**: 629–33. (**565**)

Barak Y, Perry T, and Elizur A (1995) Elderly criminals: a study of first criminal offence in old age. *International Journal of Geriatric Psychiatry* **10**: 511–6. (**525**)

Barbaree HE, Blanchard R and Langton CM (2003) The development of sexual aggression through the life span. *Annals of the New York Academy of Sciences* 989, *Sexually Coercive Behavior*, 59–74. (**526**)

Barbaree HE, Seto MC, Langton CM, and Peacock EJ (2001) Evaluating the predictive accuracy of six risk assessment instruments for adult sex offenders. *Criminal Justice and Behavior* **28**: 490–521. (**254, 536, 537**)

Barber M, Short J, Clarke-Moore J, et al. (2006) A secure attachment model of care: meeting the needs of women with mental health problems and anti-social behaviour. *Criminal Behaviour and Mental Health* **16**: 3–10. (**520, 556, 599**)

Barber P, Brown R, and Martin D (2009) *Mental Health Law in England and Wales*. Exeter, UK: Learning Matters. (**57**)

Barbone F, Mcahon AD, Davey PG, et al. (1998) Association of road traffic accidents with benzodiazepine use. *Lancet* **352**: 1331–6. (**277, 278**)

Barboriak RN (2003) The history of correctional psychiatry. In R Rosner (ed) *Principles and Practice of Forensic Psychiatry*, 2nd edn. London: Arnold, pp. 475–83. (**124**)

Barkataki I, Kumari V, Das M, et al. (2005) A neuropsychological investigation into violence and mental illness. *Schizophrenia Research* 74: 1–13.

Barkataki I, Kumari V, Das M, et al. (2008) Neural correlates of deficient response inhibition in mentally disordered violent individuals. *Behavioral Science and the Law* **26**: 51–64. (**304, 306**)

Barkataki I, Kumari V, Das M, Taylor P, and Sharma T (2006) Volumetric structural brain abnormalities in men with schizophrenia or antisocial personality disorder. *Behavioural Brain Research* **169**: 239–47. (**299, 300, 301**)

Barker AF (1994) *Arson: A Review of the Psychiatric Literature. Maudsley Monograph No. 35.* Oxford: Oxford University Press. (**504**)

Barker M, Geraghty J, Webb B, and Kay T (1999) *The Prevention of Street Robbery*. London: Home Office Police Department. (**179**)

Barkley RA (1998) *Attention Deficit Hyperactivity Disorder: A Handbook for Diagnosis and Treatment*, 2nd edn. New York: Guilford. (**486**)

Barkley RA, Fischer M, Smallish L, and Fletcher K (2004) Young adult follow-up of hyperactive children: antisocial activities and drug use. *Journal of Child Psychology and Psychiatry* **45**: 195–211. (**512**)

Barlow J (1996) *HIV and Children – A Training Manual*. Edinburgh, UK: Children in Scotland. (**465**)

Barnard MA (1993) Violence and vulnerability: conditions of work for street-working prostitutes. *Sociology of Health and Illness* **15**: 683–705. (**464**)

Barnes MT, Gordon WC, and Hudson SM (2001) The crime of threatening to kill. *Journal of Interpersonal Violence* **16**: 312–9. (**546**)

Barnett WS (1993) Cost-benefit analysis. In LJ Schweinhart, HV Barnes, DP Weikart, (eds) *Significant Benefits: The High/Scope Perry Preschool Study Through Age 27*. Ypsilanti, Michigan: High/Scope, pp. 142–73. (**183**)

Barnicot K, Katsakou C, Marougka S, and Priebe S (2011) Treatment completion in psychotherapy for borderline personality disorder – a systematic review and meta-analysis. *Acta Psychiatrica Scandinavica* **123**: 327–38. (**408**)

Baroff GS (1996) The mentally retarded offender. In JW Jacobson, JA Mullick (eds) *Manual of Diagnosis and Professional Practice in Mental Retardation*. Washington, DC: American Psychological Association, pp. 311–21. (**332**)

Baroff GS, Gunn M, and Hayes S (2004) Legal issues. In WR Lindsay, JL Taylor, P Sturmey (eds) *Offenders with Developmental Disabilities*. Chichester, UK: Wiley, pp. 37–66. (**332**)

Baron RA (1983) Control of human aggression: an optimistic perspective. *Journal of Social and Clinical Psychology* **1**: 97–119. (**213**)

Baron-Cohen S, Leslie AM, and Frith U (1985) Does the autistic child have a 'theory of mind'? *Cognition* **21**: 37–46. (**395**)

Baron-Cohen S, Tager-Flusberg H, and Cohen DJ (2000) *Understanding Other Minds: Perspectives from Autism and Developmental Cognitive Neuroscience*. Oxford: Oxford University Press. (**584**)

Barr A (1998) *Drink: A social history*. London: Pimlico. (**440, 441**)

Barr CS, Schwandt ML, Newman TK, and Higley JD (2004) The use of adolescent nonhuman primates to model human alcohol intake: neurobiological, genetic, and psychological variables. *Annals of the New York Academy of Science* **1021**: 221–33. (**207**)

Barron L, Straus MA, and Jaffee D (1988) Legitimate violence, violent attitudes, and rape: a test of the cultural spillover theory. *Annals of the New York Academy of Sciences* **528**: 79–122. (**244**)

Barrowcliff AL and Haddock G (2006) The relationship between command hallucinations and factors of compliance: a critical review of the literature. *Journal of Forensic Psychiatry and Psychology* **17**: 266–98. (**353**)

Barrowcliff AL, Gray NS, Freeman T, and MacCulloch JJ (2004) Eye movements reduce the vividness, emotional valence and electrodermal arousal associated with negative autobiographical memories. *Journal of Forensic Psychiatry and Psychology* **15**: 325–45. (**725**)

Barrowcliff AL, Gray NS, MacCulloch SI, Freeman T, and MacCulloch JJ (2003) Horizontal rhythmical eye movements consistently diminish the arousal provoked by auditory stimuli. *British Journal of Clinical Psychology* **42**: 289–302. (**725**)

Barrowclough C and Parle M (1997) Appraisal, psychological adjustment and expressed emotion in relatives of patients suffering from schizophrenia. *British Journal of Psychiatry* **171**: 26–30. (**355**)

Barrowclough C, Haddock G, Lobban F, et al. (2006) Group cognitive-behavioural therapy for schizophrenia. Randomised controlled trial. *British Journal of Psychiatry* **189**: 527–32. (**574**)

Barrowclough C, Haddock G, Tarrier N, and Lewis S (1996) *Evaluation of Family Support and Cognitive-Behavioural Treatment Service for Schizophrenia Sufferers With Substance Misuse*. London: NHS Research and Development Grant. (**574**)

Bartholomew AA, Milte KL, and Galbally G (1978) Homosexual necrophilia. *Medicine, Science and the Law* **18**: 29–35. (**247**)

Bartlett K, Thomson LDG, and Johnstone EC (2001) *Mentally Disordered Offenders: An evaluation of the "Open Doors" Programme at HM Prison Barlinnie*. Scottish Prison Service, Occasional Paper Series, No. 2/2001. (**653**)

Bartlett P and Sandland R (2007) *Mental Health Law Policy and Practice*, 3rd edn. Oxford: Oxford University Press. (**61**)

Barton RW (1959) *Institutional Neurosis*. Bristol, UK: Wright. (**602**)

Barton WE (1987) *The History of Influence of the American Psychiatric Association*. Washington, DC: American Psychiatric Press. (**118**)

Bass C and Jones D (2011) Psychopathology of perpetrators of fabricated or induced illness in children. *British Journal of Psychiatry* **199**: 113–8. (**506**)

Bassarath L (2001) Neuroimaging studies of antisocial behaviour. *Canadian Journal of Psychiatry* **46**: 728–32. (**298**)

Bassiouni MC (1974) A survey of the major criminal justice systems in the world. In D Glaser (ed) *Handbook of Criminology*. Chicago, IL: Rand McNally College Publishing Company, pp. 527–92. (**124**)

Bateman A and Fonagy P (1999) Effectiveness of partial hospitalization in the treatment of borderline personality disorder: a randomized controlled trial. *American Journal of Psychiatry* **156**: 1563–9. (**409, 584**)

Bateman A and Fonagy P (2000) Effectiveness of psychotherapeutic treatment of personality disorder. *British Journal of Psychiatry* **177**: 138–43. (**579, 584**)

Bateman A and Fonagy P (2003) *Advances in the Treatment of Personality Disorder*. International Society for the Study of Personality Disorders Annual Conference, Munich. (**584**)

Bateman A and Fonagy P (2006a) *Mentalization-Based Treatment for Borderline Personality Disorder. A Practical Guide*. Oxford: Oxford University Press. (**393, 584**)

Bateman A and Fonagy P (2006b) The structure of mentalization based treatment. In A Bateman, P Fonagy (eds) *Mentalization-Based Treatment for Borderline Personality Disorder*. Oxford: Oxford University Press, pp. 37–59. (**584**)

Bateman A and Fonagy P (2008) 8-year follow-up of patients treated for borderline pd: mentalization-based treatment versus treatment as usual. *American Journal of Psychiatry* **165**: 631–8. (**584**)

Bateman A and Fonagy P (2009) Randomized controlled trial of outpatient-mentalization based treatment versus structured clinical management for borderline personality disorder. *American Journal of Psychiatry* **166**: 1355–64. (**409, 584**)

Bateman A and Tyrer P (2004a) Services for personality disorder: Organisation for inclusion. *Advances in Psychiatric Treatment* **10**: 425–33. (**606**)

Bateman A and Tyrer P (2004b) Drug treatment for personality disorders. *Advances in Psychiatric Treatment* **10**: 389–98. (**606**)

Bateman A, and Fonagy P (2001) Treatment of borderline personality disorder with psychoanalytically oriented partial hospitalization: an 18-month follow-up. *American Journal of Psychiatry* **158**: 36–42. (**409, 584**)

Bateman AW (2012) Treating borderline personality disorder in clinical practice. *American Journal of Psychiatry* **169**: 560–3. (**312**)

Bateman AW and Tyrer P (2004c) Psychological treatment for personality disorders. *Advances in Psychiatric Treatment* **10**: 378–88. (**569, 574, 583, 606**)

Bateman AW, Karterud S, and Van Den Bosch LMC (2005) Borderline personality disorder. In G Gabbard, JS Beck, J Holmes (eds) *Oxford Textbook of Psychotherapy*. Oxford University Press: Oxford, pp. 291–303. (**579, 583**)

Bateson G, Jackson D, Haley J, and Weakland J (1956) Toward a theory of schizophrenia. *Behavioral Science* **1**: 251–64. (**341**)

Bather P (2006) *Review of Section 136 Mental Health Act*. London: London Development Centre. (**6213**)

Bather P, Fitzpatrick R, and Rutherford M (2008) *Police and Mental Health: Briefing 36*. London: Sainsbury Centre for Mental Health. (**48**)

Battaglia J, Lindborg SR, Alaka K, Meehan K, and Wright P (2003) Calming versus sedative effects of intramuscular olanzapine in agitated patients. *The American Journal of Emergency Medicine* **21**: 192–8. (**564**)

Battaglia J, Moss S, Rush J, et al. (1997) Haloperidol, lorazepam, or both for psychotic agitation? A multicenter, prospective, double-blind, emergency department study. *The American Journal of Emergency Medicine* **15**: 335–40. (**561**)

Battaglia J, Wolff TK, Wagner-Johnson DS, et al. (1999) Structured diagnostic assessment and depot fluphenazine treatment of multiple suicide attempters in the emergency department. *International Clinical Psychopharmacology* **14**: 361–72. (**404**)

Battin SR, Hill KG, Abbott RD, Catalano RF, and Hawkins JD (1998) The contribution of gang membership to delinquency beyond delinquent friends. *Criminology* **36**: 93–115. (**177**)

Bauer CR, Shankaran S, Bada HS, et al. (2002) The maternal lifestyle study: drug exposure during pregnancy and short-term maternal outcomes. *American Journal of Obstetrics and Gynaecology* **186**: 487–95. (**464**)

Baum A and Goldner EM (1995) The relationship between stealing and eating disorders – a review. *Harvard Review of Psychiatry* **3**: 210–21. (**281, 282**)

Baumeister AA, Sevin JA, and King BH (1998) Neuroleptics. In S Reiss, MG Aman (eds) *Psychotropic Medications and Developmental Disabilities: The International Consensus Handbook*. Columbus, OH: Ohio State University, pp. 133–50. (**327**)

Bazelon DL (1969) Introduction. In DS Burris (ed) *The Right to Treatment*. New York: Springer. (**668**)

BBC (1999) Arsonists 'hit two homes an hour'. *BBC Online Network* http://news.bbc.co.uk/1/hi/uk/323736.stm (**272**)

BBC News Online (2006, February 7) BT sounds child web porn warning. http://news.bbc.co.uk/1/hi/uk/4687904.stm (**251**)

Beail N (2002) Interrogative suggestibility, memory and intellectual disability. *Journal of Applied Research in Intellectual Disabilities* **15**: 129–37. (**332**)

Bean PT (1985) Social control and social theory. In L Gostin (ed) *Secure Provision*. London: Tavistock. (**603**)

Beardshaw V (1981) *Conscientious Objectors at Work*. London: Social Audit. (**603**)

Beasley JO, Haynes AS, Beyer K, Cramer GL, Berson SB, Muirhead Y and Warren JI (2009) Patterns of prior offending by child abductors: A comparison of fatal and non-fatal outcomes. *International Journal of Psychiatry and the Law* **32**: 273–280. (**504**)

Beattie JM (1986) *Crime and the Courts in England 1660–1800*. Oxford: Clarendon. (**28**)

Beaver KM, DeLisi M, Vaughn MG, and Barnes JC (2010) Monoamine oxidase A genotype is associated with gang membership and weapon use. *Comprehensive Psychiatry* **51**: 130–4. (**199**)

Bebbington P, Jonas S, Kuipers E, et al. (2011) Childhood sexual abuse and psychosis: data from a cross-sectional national psychiatric survey in England. *The British Journal of Psychiatry*. (**345**)

Bebbington PE, Bhugra D, Brugha T, et al. (2004) Psychosis, victimization and childhood disadvantage: evidence from the 2nd british national survey of psychiatric morbidity. *The British Journal of Psychiatry* **185**: 220–6. (**344**)

Bechara A, Damasio H, and Damasio AR (2000) Emotion, decision making and the orbitofrontal cortex. *Cerebral Cortex* **10**: 295–307. (**298**)

Bechara A, Damasio H, Damasio AR, and Lee GP (1999) Direct contributions of the human amygdala and ventromedial prefrontal cortex to decision-making. *Journal of Neuroscience* **19**: 5473–81. (**298**)

Bechara A, Damasio H, Tranel D, and Damasio AR (1997) Deciding advantageously before knowing the advantageous strategy. *Science* **275**: 1293–95. (**298**)

Beck A (2000) *Prison and Jail Inmates at Midyear 1999*. Washington, DC: Bureau of Justice Statistics Bulletin. http://bjs.gov/content/pub/pdf/pjim**99**.pdf (**524**)

Beck AT (1952) Successful outpatient psychotherapy of a chronic schizophrenic with a delusion based on borrowed guilt. *Psychiatry* **15**: 305–12. (**349**)

Beck AT (1999) *Prisoners of Hate: The Cognitive Basis of Anger, Hostility and Violence*. New York: Harper Collins. (**354, 486**)

Beck AT, Freeman A, Davis DD, et al. (2007) *Cognitive Therapy of Personality Disorders*. 2nd edn. New York: Guilford. (**569, 570, 574**)

Beck AT, Ward CH, Mendelson M, Mock J, and Erbaugh, J (1961) An inventory for measuring depression. *Archives of General Psychiatry* **4**: 561–71. (**294**)

Beck JS (2005) *Cognitive Therapy for Challenging Problems. What to Do When the Basics Don't Work*. New York: Guilford. (**570**)

Beck NC, Greenfield SR, Gotham H, et al. (1997) Risperidone in the management of violent, treatment-resistant schizophrenics hospitalized in a maximum security forensic facility. *Journal of the American Academy of Psychiatry and the Law.* **25**: 461–8. (**564**)

Beck R and Fernandez E (1998) Cognitive-behavioral therapy in the treatment of anger: a meta-analysis. *Cognitive Therapy and Research* **22**: 63–74. (**215, 575**)

Beck TR (1829) *Elements of Medical Jurisprudence*. Edinburgh, UK: Longman Rees. (**430, 431**)

Becker JV (1998) The assessment of adolescent perpetrators of childhood sexual abuse. *Irish Journal of Psycholog* **19**: 68–81. (**495**)

Becker JV, Cunningham-Rathner J, and Kaplan MS (1986) Adolescent sexual offenders: demographics, criminal and sexual histories: recommendations for reducing future offenses. *Journal of Interpersonal Violence* **1**: 432–45. (**252**)

Beckett R, Beech A, Fisher D, and Fordham A (1994) *Community-based Treatment for Sex Offenders: An Evaluation of Seven Treatment Programmes*. London: HMSO. (**258, 262, 609**)

Beckson M, Bartzokis G, and Weinstock R (2003) Substance abuse and addiction. In R Rosner (ed) *Principles and Practice of Forensic Psychiatry*, 2nd edn. London: Arnold, pp. 672–84. (**124**)

Beech A, Erikson M, Friendship C, and Ditchfield J (2001) *A Six-Year Follow-Up of Men Going Through Probation-Based Sex Offender Treatment Programmes*. Research, Development and Statistics Directorate, Home Office: HMSO. (**258**)

Beech A, Fisher D, and Beckett R (1998) *STEP 3: An Evaluation of Prison Sex Offender Treatment Programme*. London: Home Office. (**578**)

Beech A, Friendship C, Erikson M, and Hanson RK (2002) The relationship between static and dynamic risk factors and reconviction in a sample of U.K. child abusers. *Sexual Abuse: A Journal of Research and Treatment* **14**: 155–67. (**255**)

Beech AR and Ward T (2004) The integration of etiology and risk in sex offenders: a theoretical model. *Aggression and Violent Behavior* **10**: 31–63. (**245**)

Beigel A, Beeren MR, and Harding TW (1984) The paradoxical impact of a commitment statute on prediction of dangerousness. *American Journal of Psychiatry* **141**: 373–7. (**133**)

Beiling PJ, McCabe RE, and Antony MM (2006) *Cognitive Behavioural Therapy in Groups*. Canada: Guilford Press. (**572**)

Belenko S (2001) Research on Drug Courts: A Critical Review 2001 update. The National Center on Addiction and substance Abuse at Columbia University. http://www.drugpolicy.org/docUploads/2001drugcourts.pdf (**640**)

Belfrage H (1994) Criminality and mortality among a cohort of former mental-patients in Sweden. *Nordic Journal of Psychiatry* **48**: 343–7. (**271, 280**)

Belfrage H (1998) A ten-year follow-up of criminality in Stockholm mental patients – new evidence for a relation between mental disorder and crime. *British Journal of Criminology* **38**: 145–55. (**280**)

Belfrage H and Douglas KS (2002) Treatment effects on forensic psychiatric patients measured with the HCR-20 violence risk assessment scheme. *International Journal of Forensic Mental Health* **1**: 25–36. (**597**)

Belfrage H, Fransson G, and Strand S (2000) Prediction of violence using the HCR-20: a prospective study in two maximum security correctional institutions. *Journal of Forensic Psychiatry* **11**: 167–75. (**537**)

Belfrage H, Fransson G, and Strand S (2004) Management of violence behaviour in correctional systems using qualified risk assessments. *Legal and Criminal Psychology* **9**: 11–22. (**549**)

Bell V, Halligan PW, and Ellis HD (2006) Diagnosing delusions: a review of inter-rater reliability. *Schizophrenia Research* **17**: 76–9. (**349**)

Bellus SB, Stewart D, Vergo JG, et al. (1996) The use of lithium in the treatment of aggressive behaviours with two brain-injured individuals in a state psychiatric hospital. *Brain Injury* **10**: 849–60. (**566**)

Benbadis SR (2005) Psychogenic non-epileptic seizures. In Wyllie E (ed) *The Treatment of Epilepsy: Principles and Practice*, 4th edn. Philadelphia, PA: Lippincott, Williams and Wilkins. (**425**)

Bender DS (2005) The therapeutic alliance in the treatment of personality disorders. *Journal of Psychiatric Practice* **11**: 73–87. (**400**)

Benn A (2002) Cognitive behaviour therapy for psychosis in conditions of high security. In D Kingdon, D Turkington (eds) *The Case Study Guide to Cognitive Behaviour Therapy of Psychosis*. Chichester, UK: Wiley. (**362**)

Bennett J (2008) The social costs of dangerousness: prison and the dangerous classes. Centre for Crime and Justice Studies: London. http://www.crimeandjustice.org.uk/publications/social-costs-dangerousness (**5**)

Bennett R (2006) Majority of parents admit to smacking children *The Times*, 20 September, p. 9. (**222**)

Bennett S, Farrington DP, and Huesmann LR (2005) Explaining gender differences in crime and violence: the importance of social cognitive skills. *Aggression and Violent Behavior* **10**: 263–88. (**216**)

Bennett T (1998) *Drugs and Crime: The Results of Research on Drug Testing and Interviewing Arrestees. Home office research study, No. 183*. London: Home Office. (**442, 443**)

Bennett T and Wright R (1984) The relationship between alcohol use and burglary. *British Journal of Addiction* **79**: 431–7. (**443**)

Bennett T, Holloway K, and Farrington D (2008) The statistical association between drug misuse and crime: a meta-analysis. *Aggression and Violent Behavior* **13**: 107–18. (**454**)

Bennie C (1998) A comparison of home detoxification and minimal intervention strategies. *Alcohol and Alcoholism* **33**: 157–63. (**445**)

Ben-Porath DB (2004) Strategies for securing commitment to treatment from individuals diagnosed with borderline personality disorder. *Journal of Contemporary Psychotherapy* **34**: 247–61. (**391, 400**)

Ben-Shakhar G (2010) The case against the use of polygraph examinations to monitor post-conviction sex offenders. *Legal and Criminological Psychology* **13**: 191–207. (**254 256**)

Benson A, Secker J, Balfe E, et al. (2003) Discourses of blame: accounting for aggression and violence on an acute mental health inpatient unit. *Social Science and Medicine* **57**: 917–26. (**356**)

Benson BA and Ivins J (1992) Anger, depression and self-concept in adults with mental retardation. *Journal of Intellectual Disability Research* **36**: 169–75. (**326**)

Bentall RP and Kaney S (1989) Content specific information processing and persecutory delusions: an investigation using the emotional Stroop test. *British Journal of Medical Psychology* **62**: 355–64. (**351**)

Bentall RP and Taylor JL (2006) Psychological processes and paranoia: implications for forensic behavioural science. *Behavioral Sciences and the Law* **24**: 277–94. (**345**)

Bentall RP, Kaney S, and Bowen-Jones K (1995) Persecutory delusions and recall of the threat-related, depression related and neutral words. *Cognitive Therapy and Research* **19**: 331–43. (**351**)

Bentall RP, Kinderman P, and Kaney S (1994) The self, attributional processes and abnormal beliefs – towards a model of persecutory delusions. *Behaviour Research and Therapy* **32**: 331–41. (**487**)

Bentley C (2006) A socially excluded group? hearing the voice of victims. *Journal of Mental Health Law* **26**: 26–43. (**710, 711**)

Bentovim A (1996) Trauma-organized systems in practice: implications for work with abused and abusing children and young people. *Clinical Child Psychology and Psychiatry* **1**: 513–24. (**259**)

Bentovim A (1998) Family systemic approach to work with young sex offenders. *Irish Journal of Psychology* **19**: 119–35. (**495**)

Bergler E (1958) *The Psychology of Gambling*. Harrison: London. (**470**)

Berke JH (1995) Psychotic interventions at arbours crisis centre. In J Ellwood (ed) *Psychosis Understanding and Treatment*. Jessica Kingsley: London, pp. 120–32. (**582**)

Berkowitz L (1989) Frustration-aggression hypothesis: examination and reformulation. *Psychological Bulletin* **106**: 59–73. (**213**)

Berlin LJ, Appleyard K, and Dodge KA (2011) Intergenerational continuity in child maltreatment: Mediating mechanisms and implications for prevention. *Child Development* **82**: 162–76. (**505**)

Berlyne N (1972) Confabulation. *British Journal of Psychiatry* **120**: 31–9. (**420**)

Berman AH, Bergman H, Palmstierna T, and Schlyter T (2005) Evaluation of the Drug Use Disorders Identification Test (DUDIT) in criminal justice and detoxification settings and in a Swedish population sample. *European Addiction Research* **11**: 22–31. (**457**)

Berrington WP, Liddell DW, and Foulds GA (1956) A re-evaluation of the fugue. *Journal of Mental Science* **102**: 281–6. (**294, 295**)

Berrueta-Clement JR, Schweinhart LJ, Barnett WS, Epstein AS, and Weikart DP (1984) *Changed Lives: The Effects of the Perry Preschool Programme on Youths Through Age 19*. Ypsilanti, MI: High/Scope. (**183**)

Berry A, Larkin E, Taylor PJ, et al. (2003) Referred to high secure care: determination of a bed/offer admission and placement after one year. *Criminal Behaviour and Mental Health* **13**: 310–20. (**600**)

Berry K, Barrowclough C, and Haddock G (2011) The role of expressed emotion in relationships between psychiatric staff and people with a diagnosis of psychosis: a review of the literature. *Schizophrenia Bulletin* **37**: 958–72. (**356, 557**)

Bertrand D and Niveau G (2006) *Médicine Santé et Prison*. Chêne-Bourg: edn.s Medicine et Hygiene. (**146**)

Berzins LG and Trestman RL (2004) The development and implementation of dialectical behavior therapy in forensic settings. *International Journal of Forensic Mental Health* **3**: 93–103. (**575**)

Bettenay C (2010) *Memory under cross-examination of children with and without intellectual disabilities.* unpublished doctoral thesis. (**162**)

Beyaert FHL (1980) The Dutch situation and some problems. *International Journal of Law and Psychiatry* **14**: 231–44. (**137**)

Bieniek SA, Ownby RL, Penalver A, and Dominguez RA (1998) A double-blind study of lorazepam versus the combination of haloperidol and lorazepam in managing agitation. *Pharmacotherapy* **18**: 57–62. (**566**)

Bierness DJ (1993) Do we really drive as we live? The role of personality factors in road crashes. *Alcohol, Drugs and Driving* **9**: 129–43. (**278**)

Bierut LJ, Dinwiddie SH, Begleiter H, et al. (1998) Familial transmission of substance dependence: alcohol, marijuana, cocaine, and habitual smoking: a report from the Collaborative Study on the Genetics of Alcoholism. *Archives of General Psychiatry* **55**: 982–8. (**201**)

Bilj RV, Ravelli A, and van Zessen G (1998) Prevalence of psychiatric disorder in the general population: results of the Netherlands mental health survey and incidence survey (NEMESIS). *Social Psychiatry and Psychiatric Epidemiology* **33**: 587–95. (**463**)

Binder RL (1979) The use of seclusion on an inpatient crisis intervention unit. *Hospital and Community Psychiatry* **30**: 266–9. (**595**)

Bingley W (1993) Surgical castration for sex offenders: no role for Mental Health Act Commission. *British Medical Journal* **307**: 1141. (**261**)

Bion WR (1967) Differentiation of the psychotic from non-psychotic personalities. *In Second Thoughts*. New York: Jason Aronson. (**582**)

Birbaumer N, Veit R, Lotze M, et al. (2005) Deficient fear conditioning in psychopathy: a functional magnetic resonance imaging study. *Archives of General Psychiatry* **62**: 799–805. (**304, 305**)

Birch CD, Kelln BRC, and Aquino EPB (2006) A review and case report of pseudologia fantastica. *Journal of Forensic Psychiatry and Psychology* **17**: 299–320. (**423**)

Bird S (2008) Changes in male suicide. I Scottish prisons: A 10-year study. *The British Journal of Psychiatry* **192**: 446–9. (**654**)

Bird SM and Hutchinson SJ (2003) Male drugs-related deaths in the fortnight after release from prison: Scotland, 1996–99. *Addiction* **98**: 185–90. (**462**)

Birmingham L, Coulson D, Mullee M, Kamal M and Gregoire A (2006) The mental health of women in prison mother and baby units. *The Journal of Forensic Psychiatry and Psychology*, **17**(3): 393–404. (**519**)

Birmingham L, Gray J, Mason D, and Grubin D (2000) Mental illness at reception into prison. *Criminal Behaviour and Mental Health* **10**: 77–87. (**630**)

Birmingham L, Mason D, and Grubin D (1996) Prevalence of mental disorder in remand prisoners: consecutive case study. *British Medical Journal* **313**: 1521–4. (**629**)

Bisson J, Ehlers A, Matthews R, et al. (2007) Systematic review and meta-analysis of psychological treatments for chronic posttraumatic stress disorder. *British Journal of Psychiatry* **190**: 97–104. (**725, 727**)

Bisson JI and Shepherd JP (1995) Psychological reactions of victims of violent crime. *British Journal of Psychiatry* **167**: 718–20. (**705, 706**)

Bisson JI, Shepherd JP, Joy D, Probert R, and Newcombe RG (2004) Early cognitive-behavioural therapy for post-traumatic stress symptoms after physical injury. *British Journal of Psychiatry* **184**: 63–9. (**706, 725**)

Bitter I, Czobor P, Dossenbach M, and Volavka J (2005) Effectiveness of clozapine, olanzapine, quetiapine, risperidone, and haloperidol monotherapy in reducing hostile and aggressive behavior in outpatients treated for schizophrenia: a prospective naturalistic study (IC-SOHO). *European Psychiatry: Journal of the Association of European Psychiatrists*. **20**: 403–8. (**564**)

Bittner E (1967) Police discretion in emergency apprehension of mentally ill persons. *Social Problems* **14**: 278–92. (**279**)

Bjerregaard B (2000) An empirical study of stalking victimization. *Violence and Victims* **15**(4): 389–406. (**374**)

Bjorgvinsson T and Hart J (2006) Cognitive behavioural therapy promotes mentalizing. In JG Allen and P Fonagy (eds) *Handbook of Mentalization-Based Treatment*. London: Wiley, pp. 157–70. (**574**)

Bjork JM, Dougherty DM, Moeller FG, and Swann AC (2000) Differential behavioral effects of plasma tryptophan depletion and loading in aggressive and nonaggressive men. *Neuropsychopharmacology* **22**: 357–69. (**309**)

Bjørkly S and Havik OE (2003) TCO symptoms as markers of violence in a sample of severely violent psychiatric inpatients. *International Journal of Forensic Mental Health* **2**: 87–97. (**350**)

Blaauw E, Roesch R, and Kerkhof A (2000) Mental disorders in European prison systems: arrangements for mentally disordered prisoners in the prison systems of 13 European countries. *International Journal of Law and Psychiatry* **23**: 649–63. (**632**)

Blaauw E, Winkel FW, Arensman E, Sheridan L, and Freeve A (2002) The toll of stalking: the relationship between features of stalking and psychopathology of victims. *Journal of Interpersonal Violence* **17**: 50–63. (**374**)

Black D (1981) The extended Munchausen's syndrome: a family case. *British Journal of Psychiatry* **138**: 446–434. (**434**)

Black L and Sade (2007) Lethal injection and physicians. State law vs medical ethics. *Journal of American Medical Assocation* **298**: 2779–81. (**678**)

Blackburn R (1974) *Personality and the Classification of Psychopathic Disorders*. SHRU Report no.10. Berks, UK: Broadmoor Hospital. (**346**)

Blackburn R (1986) Patterns of personality deviation among violent offenders: replication and extension of an empirical taxonomy. *British Journal of Criminology* **26**: 254–69. (**388**)

Blackburn R (1998) Psychopathy and personality disorder: implications of interpersonal theory. In DJ Cooke, SJ Hart, AE Forth (eds) *Psychopathy: Theory, Research and Implications for Society*. Amsterdam, Netherlands: Kluwer, pp. 269–301. (**385**)

Blackburn R and Renwick S (1996) Rating scales for measuring the interpersonal circle in forensic psychiatric patients. *Psychological Assessment* **8**: 76–84. (**389, 403**)

Blackburn R, Logan C, Donnell J, and Renwick S (2003) Personality disorders, psychopathy and other mental disorders: comorbidity among patients at English and Scottish high security hospitals. *Journal of Forensic Psychiatry and Psychology* **14**: 111–37. (**350, 397, 600**)

Blackshaw AJ, Kinderman P, Hare DJ, and Hatton C (2001) Theory of mind, causal attribution and paranoia in Asperger syndrome. *Autism* **5**: 147–63. (**487**)

Blackwood DH, Fordyce A, Walker MT, et al. (2001) Schizophrenia and affective disorders–cosegregation with a translocation at chromosome 1q42 that directly disrupts brain-expressed genes: clinical and P300 findings in a family. *The American Journal of Human Genetics* **69**: 428–33. (**209**)

Blackwood NJ, Bentall RP, Ffytche DH, et al. (2004) Persecutory delusions and the determination of self-relevance: an fMRI investigation. *Psychological Medicine* **34**: 591–6. (**313**)

Blair J and Fowler K (2008) Moral emotions and moral reasoning from the perspective of affective cognitive neuroscience: a selective review. *European Journal of Developmental Science* **2**: 303–23. (**395**)

Blair J and Frith U (2000) Neurocognitive explanations of the antisocial personality disorders. *Criminal Behaviour and Mental Health*, **10** (suppl.): 66–81. (**392**)

Blair RJ and Cipolotti L (2000) Impaired social response reversal. A case of 'acquired sociopathy'. *Brain* **123**: 1122–41. (**298**)

Blair RJR (1995) A cognitive developmental approach to morality: investigating the psychopath. *Cognition* **57**(1): 1–29. (**215, 303**)

Blair RJR (1996) Morality in the autistic child. *Journal of Autism and Developmental Disorders* **26**: 571–9. (**395**)

Blair RJR (1999a) Psycho-physiological responsiveness to the distress of others in children with autism. *Personality and Individual Differences* **26**: 477–85. (**395**)

Blair RJR (1999b) Responsiveness to distress cues in the child with psychopathic tendencies. *Personality and Individual Differences* **27**: 135–45. (**395**)

Blair RJR (2001) Neurocognitive models of aggression, the antisocial personality disorders, and psychopathy. *Journal of Neurology, Neurosurgery and Psychiatry* **71**: 727–31. (**297, 303**)

Blair RJR (2005) Applying a cognitive neuroscience perspective to the disorder of psychopathy. *Developments in Psychopathology* **17**: 865–91. (**395**)

Blair RJR (2008) The amygdala and ventromedial pre-frontal cortex: functional contributions and dysfunction in psychopathy. *Philosophical Transactions of the Royal Society* **B363**: 2557–65. (**395**)

Blair RJR, Jones L, Clark F, and Smith M (1997) The psychopathic individual: a lack of responsiveness to distress cues? *Psychophysiology* **34**: 192–8. (**395**)

Blair RJR, Mitchell D, and Blair K (2005) *The Psychopath, Emotion and Brain*. Malden, MA: Blackwell. (**395**)

Blair RJR, Sellars C, Strickland I, et al. (1995) Emotion attributions in the psychopath. *Personality and Individual Differences* **19**: 431–43. (**215**)

Blair RJR, Sellars C, Strickland I, et al. (1996) Theory of mind in the psychopath. *Journal of Forensic Psychiatry* **7**: 15–25. (**395**)

Blake DD, Weathers FW, Nagy LM, et al. (1995) The development of a clinician-administered PTSD scale. *Journal of Traumatic Stress* **8**: 75–90. (**726**)

Blake PY, Pincus JH, and Buckner C (1995) Neurologic abnormalities in murderers. *Neurology* **45**: 1641–7. (**488**)

Blanchard EB, Hickling EJ, Mitnick N, et al. (1995) The impact of severity of physical injury and perception of life threat in the development of post-traumatic stress disorder in motor vehicle accident victims. *Behaviour Research and Therapy* **33**(5): 529–34. (**723**)

Blanchard R, Christensen BK, Strong SM, et al. (2002) Retrospective self-reports of childhood accidents causing unconsciousness in phallometrically diagnosed pedophiles. *Archives of Sexual Behavior* **31**: 511–26. (**244**)

Blaszczynski AP and McConaghy N (1989) The medical model of pathological gambling: current shortcomings. *Journal of Gambling Behavior* **5**: 42–52. (**468**)

Bleich A, Kotler M, Kutz I, and Shalev A (2002) *A Position Paper of the [Israeli] National Council for Mental Health: Guidelines for the Assessment and Professional Intervention with Terror Victims in the Hospital and in the Community*. [Israeli]. Jerusalem, Israel: National Council for Mental Health. (**725**)

Bleuler E (1911) *Dementia Praecox oder Gruppe der Schizophrenien*. Leipzig-Wien: Verlag von Franz Deuticke. (**208**)

Blofeld J, Sallah D, Sashidharan S, Stone R, and Struthers J (2004) *Independent Inquiry into the Death of David Bennett*. Cambridge, UK: Norfolk, Suffolk and Cambridgeshire Strategic Health Authority. (**594**)

Blom K (1980) *Rapport om forholdene ved Reitgjerdet sykehus*. Oslo, Norway: Government Publishing Office. (**603**)

Blom-Cooper L, Brown M, Dolan R, and Murphy E (1992) *Report of the Committee of Inquiry into Complaints about Ashworth Hospital*, Vols I and II. Cmnd 2028. London : HMSO. (**604**)

Blom-Cooper L, Grounds A, Guinan P, Parker A, and Taylor M (1996) *The Case of Jason Mitchell: Report of the Independent Panel of Inquiry*. London: Duckworth. (**76**)

Blom-Cooper L, Hally H, and Murphy E (1995) *The Falling Shadow: One Patient's Mental Health Care 1978–1993*. London: Duckworth. (**76, 707**)

Blomeyer D, Treutlein J, Esser G, et al. (2008) Interaction between CRHR1 gene and stressful life events predicts adolescent heavy alcohol use. *Biological Psychiatry* **63**: 146–51. (**207**)

Bloom H and Schneider RD (2006) *Mental Disorders and the Law: A Primer for Legal and Mental Health Professionals*. Toronto, ON: Irwin Law. (**146**)

Bloor R, Crome I, Moss J, et al. (2006) *The Impact of Treatment on Female Drug-Using Sex Workers* (Research briefing 14). London : NTA. (**454**)

Blud L and Travers R (2001) Interpersonal problem-solving skills training: a comparison of RSR and ETS. *Criminal Behavior and Mental Health* **11**: 251–61. (**576**)

Bluglass R (1990) Infanticide and filicide. In R Bluglass, P Bowden (eds) *Principles and Practice of Forensic Psychiatry*. Edinburgh, UK: Churchill Livingstone. (**164**)

Blum N, St John D, Pfohl B, et al. (2008) Systems training for emotional predictability and problem solving (STEPPS) for outpatients with borderline personality disorder: a randomized controlled trial and 1-year follow-up. *American Journal of Psychiatry* **165**: 468–78. (**409**)

Blumenthal S (2010) A psychodynamic approach to working with offenders: an alternative to moral orthopaedics. In A Bartlett, G McGauley (eds) *Forensic Mental Health: Concepts Systems, and Practice* (pp. 151–62). Oxford, UK: Oxford University Press. (**581**)

Blumenthal S and Wessely S (1994) The cost of mental health review tribunals. *Psychiatric Bulletin* **18**: 274–6. (**71**)

Blumenthal S, Craissati J, and Minchin L (2009) The development of a specialist hostel for the community management of personality disordered offenders. *Criminal Behaviour and Mental Health* **19**: 43–53. (**608**)

Blumenthal S, Richards R, and Brown M (2011) Evaluation of the impact of a consultation in a secure setting. *Criminal behaviour and Mental Health*. **4**: 233–44. (**603, 604**)

Blunt LW and Stock HV (1985) Guilty but mentally ill: an alternative verdict. *Behavioral Sciences and the Law* **3**: 49–68. (**28**)

BMA: *see* British Medical Association.

Bocij P and McFarlane L (2002) Online harassment: towards a definition of cyberstalking. *Prison Service Journal* **139**: 31–8. (**377**)

Bocij P and McFarlane L (2003) Cyberstalking: the technology of hate. *Police Journal* **76**: 204–21. (**377**)

Boer DP, Hart SD, Kropp PR, and Webster CD (1997) *Manual for the Sexual Violence Risk – 20: Professional Guidelines for Assessing Risk of Sexual Violence*. The British Columbia Institute Against Family Violence: Simon Fraser University. (**255**)

Boer H and Clarke D (1999) Development and behaviour in genetic syndromes: Prader–Willi syndrome. *Journal of Applied Research in Intellectual Disabilities* **12**: 296–301. (**322**)

Boer H, Holland A, Whittington J, et al. (2002) Psychotic illness in people with Prader-Willi syndrome due to chromosome 15 maternal uniparental disomy. *Lancet* **359**: 135–6. (**322**)

Boetticher A, Kröber H-L, Müller-Isberner R, Müller-Metz R, and Wolf T (2006) Mindestanforderungen für Prognosegutachten. *Neue Zeitschrift für Strafrecht* **26**: 537–44. (**142**)

Boetticher A, Nedopil N, Bosinski HAG, and Sass H (2005) Mindestanforderungen für Schuldfähigkeitsgutachten. *Neue Zeitschrift für Strafrecht* **25**: 57–63. (**142**)

Bogenschutz MP and Nurnberg G (2004) Olanzapine versus placebo in the treatment of borderline personality disorder. *Journal of Clinical Psychiatry* **65**: 104–9. (**404**)

Bohman M (1996) Predisposition to criminality: Swedish adoption studies in retrospect. *Ciba Found Symposium* **194**: 99–109. (**188, 199, 201, 202, 203**)

Boisjoli R, Vitaro F, Lacourse E, Barker ED, and Tremblay RE (2007) Impact and clinical significance of a preventive intervention for disruptive boys. *British Journal of Psychiatry* **191**: 415–19. (**183**)

Boles SM and Miotto K (2003) Substance abuse and violence: a review of the literature. *Aggression and Violent Behavior* **8**: 155–74. (**228, 454, 514**)

Bolton N, Smith FV, Heskin KJ, and Bannister PA (1976) Psychological correlates of long-term imprisonment IV. A longitudinal analysis. *British Journal of Criminology* **16**: 38–47. (**630, 637**)

Bonhoeffer K (1904) *Allgemeine Zeitschrift Psychiatrie* **61**, 744–52. Quoted in Berlyne (1972). (**420**)

Bonkalo A (1974) Impulsive acts and confusional states during incomplete arousal from sleep: criminological and forensic implications. *Psychiatry Quarterly* **48**: 400–9. (**290, 292**)

Bonner A, Luscombe C, van den Bree M, and Taylor PJ (2008) *The Seeds of Exclusion*. London: Salvation Army. http://www.kent.ac.uk/chss/docs/TheSeedsOfExclusion-FullReport.pdf (**646**)

Bonner A, Luscombe C, van den Bree M, and Taylor PJ (2009) *The Seeds of Exclusion*. London: Salvation Army. http://www.doorwayproject.org.uk/Documents/SA%20Seeds%20of%20Exclusion%202009.pdf (**646**)

Bonnet C (1993) Adoption at birth: prevention against abandonment or neonaticide. *Child Abuse and Neglect* **17**: 501–13. (**510**)

Bonta J, Law M, and Hansen K (1998) The prediction of criminal and violent recidivism among mentally disordered offenders: a meta-analysis. *Psychological Bulletin* **123**: 123–42. (**528, 537**)

Boodman SG and Washington Post (1989) When doctors and patients become involved. *Los Angeles Times*, Article Collection 09 November. http://articles.latimes.com/1989-11-09/news/vw-1375_1_malpractice-cases (**682**)

Bools C (1996) Factitious illness by proxy. Munchausen syndrome by proxy. *British Journal of Psychiatry* **169**: 268–75. (**227, 506**)

Bools C, Neale B, and Meadow R (1994) Munchausen syndrome by proxy: a study of psychopathology. *Child Abuse and Neglect* **18**: 773–88. (**227**)

References

Boon J and Sheridan L (2001) *Stalking and Psychosexual Obsession: Psychological Perspectives for Prevention, Policing and Treatment.* UK: Wiley. (**375**)

Boor M (1982) The multiple personality epidemic. *Journal of Nervous and Mental Disease* **170**: 302–4. (**9**)

Boorse C (1975) On the distinction between disease and illness. *Philosophy and Public Affairs* **5**: 49–68. (**9, 426**)

Boorse C (1976) What a theory of mental health should be. *Journal of the Theory of Social Behaviour* **6**: 61–84. (**9**)

Boothroyd R, Porthress N, McGaha A, and Ptrila J (2003) The Broward Mental Health Court: process, outcomes and service utilization. *International Journal of Law and Psychiatry* **26**: 55–71. (**640**)

Borduin C, Henggeler S, Blaske D, and Stein R (1990) Multisystem treatment of adolescent sexual offenders. *International Journal of Offender Therapy and Comparative Criminology* **34**: 105–13. (**263**)

Borges G, Cherpitel C, and Mittleman M (2004) Risk of injury after alcohol consumption: a case-crossover study in the emergency department. *Social Science and Medicine* **58**: 1191–200. (**702**)

Borum R, Fein RA, Vossekuil B, and Berglund J (1999) Threat assessment: defining an approach for evaluating risk of targeted violence. *Behavioral Sciences and the Law* **17**: 323–37. (**547**)

Borzecki M and Wormith JS (1985) The criminalization of psychiatrically ill people: a review with a Canadian perspective. *Psychiatric Journal of the University of Ottawa* **10**: 241–7. (**280**)

Botstein D and Risch N. (2003) Discovering genotypes underlying human phenotypes: past successes from Mendelian disease, future approaches for complex disease. Nature Genetics 33: 228–37. (**192**)

Bourdon KH, Goodman R, Rae DS, Simpson G, and Koretz DS (2005) The strengths and difficulties questionnaire: US normative data and psychometric properties. *Journal of the American Academy of Child and Adolescent Psychiatry* **44**: 557–64. (**484**)

Bourgeois M (1969) Suicide par le feu à la manière de bonzes. *Annales Médico-psychologiques, Revue Psychiatrique* **127**: 116–26. (**276**)

Bourget D and Bradford JM (1990) Homicidal parents. *Canadian Journal of Psychiatry* **35**: 233–8. (**508, 509**)

Bourget D and Bradford JMW (1995) Sex offenders who claim amnesia for their alleged offence. *Bulletin of the American Academy of Psychiatry and Law* **23**: 299–307. (**294**)

Bourget D and Gagné P (2002) Maternal filicide in Quebec. *Journal of the American Academy of Psychiatry and the Law* 30: 345–51. (**509**)

Bourget D and Labelle A (1992) Homicide, infanticide, and filicide. *Psychiatric Clinics of North America* **15**: 661–73. (**508**)

Bourget D, Grace J, and Whitehurst L (2007) A review of maternal and paternal filicide. *Journal of the American Academy of Psychiatry and the Law* **35**: 74–82. (**231**)

Bournemann MAC, Mahowald MW, and Schenck CH (2006) Parasomnias. Clinical features and forensic implications. *Chest* **130**: 605–10. (**292**)

Boutros NN and Bowers MB Jr (1996) Chronic substance-induced psychotic disorders: state of the literature. *Journal of Neuropsychiatry and Clinical Neuroscience* **8**: 262–9. (**202, 203, 208**)

Bowden P (1978) A psychiatric clinic in a probation office. *British Journal of Psychiatry* **133**: 448–51. (**643**)

Bowen E, Gilchrist E, and Beech A (2005) An examination of the impact of community-based rehabilitation on the offending behaviour of male domestic violence offenders and the characteristics associated with recidivism. *Legal and Criminological Psychology* **10**: 189–209. (**609**)

Bowen P (2007) *Blackstone's Guide to The Mental Health Act 2007.* Oxford, UK: Oxford University Press. (**57, 61**)

Bowers L (2002) *Dangerous and Severe Personality Disorder: Response and Role of the Clinical Team.* London: Routledge. (**385**)

Bowers L, Nijman H, Allan T, et al. (2006) Prevention and management of aggression training and violent incidents on UK acute psychiatric wards. *Psychiatric Services* **57**: 1022–6. (**356**)

Bowlby J (1944) Forty-four juvenile thieves: their characters and home-life. *International Journal of Psychoanalysis* **25**: 19–52. (**396, 579**)

Bowlby J (1951) *Maternal Care and Mental Health.* Geneva, Switzerland: World Health Organization. (**174**)

Bowlby J (1969) *Attachment, Vol. 1, Attachment and Loss,* 2nd edn. London: Hogarth; 1982; Harmondsworth: Penguin, 1971. (**396, 717**)

Bowlby J (1973) *Separation: Anxiety and Anger, Vol. 2 Attachment and Loss.* London: Hogarth; Harmondsworth: Penguin, 1975. (**396, 717**)

Bowlby J (1980) *Loss, Sadness and Depression, Vol. 3, Attachment and Loss.* London: Hogarth; Harmondsworth: Penguin, 1981. (**396, 717**)

Bowlby J (1988) A Secure Base: Clinical Applications of Attachment Theory. London: Routledge. (**216, 556, 717**)

Boyd WH and Bolen DW (1970) The compulsive gambler and spouse in group psychotherapy. *International Journal of Group Psychotherapy* **20**: 77–90. (**471**)

Boye B, Bentsen H, Ulstein I, et al. (2001) Relatives' distress and patients' symptoms and behaviours: a prospective study of patients with schizophrenia and their relatives. *Acta Psychiatrica Scandinavica* **104**: 42–50. (**355**)

Bracken PJ, Giller JE, and Kabaganda S (1992) Helping victims of violence in Uganda. *Medicine and War* **8**: 155–63. (**717**)

Bradford J and Balmaceda R (1983) Shoplifting: is there a specific psychiatric syndrome? *Canadian Journal of Psychiatry* **28**: 248–54. (**271**)

Bradford J and Smith SM (1979) Amnesia and homicide: the Podola case and a study of thirty cases. *Bulletin of the American Academy of Psychiatry and the Law* **7**: 219–31. (P**292, 293, 294, 295**)

Bradford JMW (2001) The neurobiology, neuropharmacology, and pharmacological treatment of the paraphilias and compulsive sexual behaviour. *Canadian Journal of Psychiatry* **46**: 26–34. (**253**)

Bradford JMW and Pawlak MA (1993) Double-blind placebo crossover study of cyproterone acetate in the treatment of the paraphilias. *Archives of Sexual Behavior* **22**: 383–402. (**260**)

Bradley F, Smith M, Long J, and O'Dowd T (2002) Reported frequency of domestic violence: cross sectional survey of women attending general practice. *British Medical Journal* **324**: 271–6. (**219**)

Bradley K (2009) *The Bradley Report: Lord Bradley's Review of People with Mental Health Problems or Learning Disabilities in the Criminal Justice System*. London: Department of Health. http://www.rcpsych.ac.uk/pdf/Bradley%20Report11.pdf (**23, 316, 489, 588, 619, 620, 640, 641, 648**)

Bradley R, Greene J, Russ E, Dutra L, and Westen D (2005) A multidimensional meta-analysis of psychotherapy for PTSD. *American Journal of Psychiatry* **162**: 214–27. (**725**)

Bradley T, Tauri J, and Walters R (2006) Demythologising youth justice in Aotearoa/New Zealand. In J Muncie, B Goldson (eds) *Comparative Youth Justice*. London: Sage. (**479**)

Bragado-Jimenez MD and Taylor PJ (2012) Empathy, schizophrenia and violence: a systematic review. *Schizophrenia Research* **141**: 83–90. (**354**)

Brake (2006) What is the extent of drunk, drugged or tired driving? http://www.brake.org.uk/facts/what-is-the-extent-of-drunk-drugged-or-tired-driving.htm (**278**)

Brakel SJ, Parry J, and Weiner BA (1985) *The Mentally Disabled and the Law*, 3rd edn. Chicago, IL: American Bar Foundation. (**122**)

Bramness JG, Skurtveil S, and Mørland J (2006) Flunitrazepam: psychomotor impairment, agitation and paradoxical reactions. *Forensic Science International* **159**: 83–91. (**456**)

Brank EM (2007) Elder research; filling an important gap in psychology and law. *Behavioural Sciences and the Law* **25**: 701–16. (**523**)

Braun B (1984) Hypnosis creates multiple personality: myth or reality? *International Journal of Experimental Hypnosis* **32**: 191–7. (**426**)

Brazier J, Tumur I, Holmes M, et al. (2006) Psychological therapies including dialectical behaviour therapy for borderline personality disorder: a systematic review and preliminary economic evaluation. *Health Technology Assessment* **10**: 1–117. http://www.hta.ac.uk/fullmono/mon1035.pdf (**409, 569**)

Breiman L, Freidman J, Olshen, R, et al (1984) *Classification and Regression Trees*. Pacific Grove, CA: Wadsworth and Brooks/Cole. (**540**)

Brekke JS, Prindel C, Bae SW, and Long JD (2001) Risks for individuals with schizophrenia who are living in the community. *Psychiatric Services* **52**: 1358–66. (**334**)

Brennan PA, Mednick SA, and Hodgins S (2000) Major mental disorders and criminal violence in a Danish birth cohort. *Archives of General Psychiatry* **57**: 494–500. (**337**)

Brennan PA, Mednick SA, and Jacobsen B (1996) Assessing the role of genetics in crime using adoption cohorts. In GR Bock, JA Goode (eds) *Genetics of Criminal and Antisocial Behaviour. Ciba Foundation Symposium 194*. Chichester, UK: Wiley. (**189**)

Breslau N, Davis GC, and Andreski P (1995) Risk factors for PTSD-related traumatic events: a prospective analysis. *American Journal of Psychiatry* **152**: 529–35. (**712**)

Breslau N, Davis GC, Andreski P, and Peterson E (1991) Traumatic events and posttraumatic stress disorder in an urban population of young adults. *Archives of General Psychiatry* **48**: 216–22. (**712**)

Breslau N, Davis GC, Andreski P, Peterson EL, and Schultz LR (1997) Sex differences in posttraumatic stress disorder. *Arch Gen Psychiatry* **54**(11): 1044–8. (**712**)

Breslau N, Kessler RC, Chilcoat HD, et al. (1998) Trauma and posttraumatic stress disorder in the community: the 1996 Detroit Area Survey of Trauma. *Archieves of General Psychiatry* **55**(7): 626–32. (**712**)

Bretherton I and Munholland KA (1999) Internal working models in attachment relationships; a construct revisited. In J Cassidy, PR Shaver (eds) *Handbook of Attachment; Theory, Research and Clinical Applications*. New York: Guilford, pp. 89–111. (**581**)

Bretteville-Jenson AL and Sutton M (1996) The income-generating behaviour of injecting drug-users in Oslo. *Addiction* **91**: 63–79. (**464**)

Brett-Jones J, Garety PA, and Hemsley D (1987) Measuring delusional experiences: a method and its application. *British Journal of Clinical Psychology* **26**: 257–65. (**349**)

Brewin CR and Holmes EA (2003) Psychological theories of posttraumatic stress disorder. *Clinical Psychology Review* **23**: 339–76. (**722**)

Brewin CR, Andrews B, and Rose S (2000b) Fear, helplessness, and horror in posttraumatic stress disorder: investigating DSM-IV criterion A2 in victims of violent crime. *Journal of Traumatic Stress* **13**: 499–509. (**723**)

Brewin CR, Andrews B, and Valentine JD (2000a) Meta-analysis of risk factors for posttraumatic stress disorder in trauma-exposed adults. *Journal of Consulting and Clinical Psychology* **68**: 748–66. (**713**)

Brewin CR, Dalgleish T, and Joseph S (1996) A dual representation theory of post-traumatic stress disorder. *Psychological Review* **103**: 670–86. (**722**)

Brewin CR, Rose S, Andrews B, et al. (2002) Brief screening instrument for post-traumatic stress disorder. *British Journal of Psychiatry* **181**: 158–62. (**726**)

Brewin CR, Scragg P, Robertson M, et al. (2008) Promoting mental health following the London bombings: a screen and treat approach. *Journal of Traumatic Stress* **21**: 3–8. (**706**)

Brezinka C, Huter O, Biebl W, and Kinzl J (1994) Denial of pregnancy: obstetrical aspects. *Journal of Psychosomatic Obstetrics and Gynaecology* **15**: 1–8. (**510**)

Bridgwood A and Malbon G (1994) *Survey of the Physical Health of Prisoners 1994*. London: HMSO. (**647**)

Brieden T, Ujeyl M, and Naber D (2002) Psychopharmacological treatment of aggression in schizophrenic patients. *Pharmacopsychiatry* **35**: 83–9. (**560**)

Briere J (2002) Treating adult survivors of severe childhood abuse and neglect: further development of an integrative model. In JEB Myers, LBerliner, JBriere, CT Hendrix, T Reid, C Jenny (eds) *The APSAC Handbook on Child Maltreatment*, 2nd edn. Newbury Park, CA: Sage Publications, pp. 1–21. (**729**)

Briere J (2006) Dissociative symptoms and trauma exposure: specificity, affect dysregulation, and posttraumatic stress. *Journal of Nervous and Mental Disease* **194**: 78–82. (**723**)

Briere J, Scott C, and Weathers FW (2005) Peritraumatic and persistent dissociation in the presumed etiology of PTSD. *American Journal of Psychiatry* **162**: 2295–301. (**723**)

Briken P, Hill A, and Berner W (2003) Pharmacotherapy of paraphilias with long-acting agonists of luteinising hormone-releasing hormone: a systematic review. *Journal of Clinical Psychiatry* **64**: 890–7. (**260**)

Brimacombe CAE, Jung S, Garrioch L, and Allison M (2003) Perceptions of older adult eyewitnesses: will you believe me when I am 64? *Law and Human Behavior* **27**: 507–22. (**523**)

Brisson NJ (1983) Battering husbands: a survey of abusive men. *Victimology* **6**: 338–44. (**372**)

Bristow M (2001) The limits of responsibility. *Psychiatric Bulletin* **25**: 412–13. (**75**)

British Medical Association (1998) *Domestic Violence: A Health Care Issue?* London: British Medical Association. (**713, 714**)

British Medical Association (2001) *Prison Medicine: A Crisis Waiting to Break.* London: British Medical Association. (**627**)

British Medical Journal (BMJ) (1968) Leading article: compulsive Gambler. *British Medical Journal* **2**(5597): 69. (**468**)

British Psychological Society (2000) *Learning Disability: Definitions and Contexts.* Leicester, UK: BPS. (**314**)

British Psychological Society (2004) A Review of the Current Scientific Status and Fields of Application of Polygraphic Deception Detection. Report (26/05/04) from the BPS Working Party (www.bps.org.uk). (**256**)

Brockington IF, Oates J, George S, Turner D, Vostanis P, Sullivan M, et al. (2001) A screening questionnaire for mother–infant bonding disorders. *Archives of Women's Mental Health*, **3**: 133–40. (**223**)

Brockman B (1999) Food refusal in prisoners: a communication or a method of self-killing? The role of the psychiatrist and resulting ethical challenges. *Journal of Medical Ethics* **25**: 451–6. (**638**)

Brodsky SL, Griffin MP, and Cramer RJ (2010) The witness credibility scale: an outcome measure for expert witness research. *Behavioral Sciences and the Law* **28**: 892–907. (**676**)

Brody S (1977) *Screen Violence and Film Censorship, Home Office Research Study No. 40.* London: HMSO. (**216**)

Bromberg W (1951) A psychological study of murder. *International Journal of Psychoanalysis* **32**: 117–27. (**579**)

Bromley J and Emerson E (1995) Beliefs and emotional reactions of care staff working with people with challenging behavior. *Journal of Intellectual Disability Research* **39**: 341–52. (**326**)

Broner N, Lattimore PK, Cowell AJ, and Schlenger WE (2004) Effects of diversion on adults with co-occurring mental illness and substance use: outcomes from a national multi-site study. *Behavioral Sciences and the Law* **22**: 519–41. (**365, 641**)

Bronsich T (1992) Diagnostic procedures of personality disorders according to the criteria of present classification systems. *Verhaltenstherapie* **2**: 140–50. (**385**)

Bronsich T and Mombour W (1994) Comparison of a diagnostic checklist with a structured interview for the assessment of DSM-III and ICD-10 personality disorders. *Psychopathology* **27**: 312–20. (**385**)

Bronte A (1848) *The Tenant of Wildfell Hall*, 2nd edn. Newby, London: Thomas Cautley. (**219**)

Brook S, Lucey JV, and Gunn KP (2000) Intramuscular ziprasidone compared with intramuscular haloperidol in the treatment of acute psychosis. *Journal of Clinical Psychiatry* **61**: 933–41. (**565**)

Brookbanks W and Simpson S (eds) (2007) *Psychiatry and the Law.* Wellington, New Zealand: LexisNexis. (**146**)

Brooke D, Taylor C, Gunn J, and Maden A (1996) Point prevalence of mental disorder in unconvicted male prisoners in England and Wales. *British Medical Journal* **313**: 1524–7. (**629, 632**)

Brooker C, Flynn J, and Fox C (2010) *Trends in Self-Inflicted Deaths and Self-Harm in Prisons in England and Wales (2001–2008): In Search of a New Research Paradigm.* http://www.lincoln.ac.uk/cjmh/SIDS%20and%20Self%20harm%20pub%20Lincoln.pdf (**633**)

Brooker C, Repper J, Beverley C, and Ferriter M (2003) *Mental Health Services and Prisoners: A Review for the Department of Health.* http://webarchive.nationalarchives.gov.uk/+/www.dh.gov.uk/en/Publicationsandstatistics/Publications/PublicationsPolicyAndGuidance/DH_4084149 (**630**)

Brooker C, Sirdfield C, Blizard R, et al. (2011) An investigation into the prevalence of mental health disorder and patterns of health service access in a probation population. Lincoln: University of Lincoln. *http://www.magnacartalincoln.org/cjmh/RfPB%20Executive%20Summary.pdf* (**640**)

Brookman F (2005) *Understanding Homicide.* London: Sage. (**279**)

Brookman F and Maguire M (2004) Reducing homicide: a review of the possibilities. *Crime, Law and Social Change* **42**: 325–403. (**521**)

Brooks N (1984) Cognitive deficits after head injury. In N Brooks (ed) *Closed Head Injury: Psychological, Social and Family Consequences.* Oxford, UK: Oxford University Press. (**296**)

Brooks N, Campsie L, Symington C, Beattie A and McKinlay W (1987) The effects of severe head injury on patient and relative within seven years of injury. *Journal of Head Trauma Rehabilitation* **2**: 1–13. (**296**)

Brooks-Gordon B and Bilby C (2006) Psychological interventions for treatment of adult sex offenders. *British Medical Journal* **333**: 5–6. (**257, 416**)

Brooks-Gordon B, Bilby C, and Wells H (2006) A systematic review of psychological interventions for sexual offenders I: randomised control trials. *Journal of Forensic Psychiatry and Psychology* **17**: 442–66. (**416**)

Brooner RK, Kidorf M, King VL, and Stoller K (1998) Preliminary evidence of good treatment response in antisocial drug abusers. *Drug and Alcohol Dependence* **49**: 249–60. (**409, 444**)

Broughton N and Chesterman P (2001) Malingered psychosis. *Journal of Forensic Psychiatry* **12**: 407–22. (**431**)

Broughton R (1968) Sleep disorders: disorders of arousal? *Science* **159**: 1070–7. (**290**)

Brower MC and Price BH (2001) Neuropsychiatry of frontal lobe dysfunction in violent and criminal behaviour: a critical review. *Journal of Neurology Neurosurgery and Psychiatry* **71**: 720–6. (**212, 302**)

Brown CS, Kent TA, Bryant SG, et al. (1989) Blood platelet uptake of serotonin in episodic aggression. *Psychiatry Research* **27**: 5–12. (**307, 308, 309**)

Brown G, Bone M, Dalison B, and Wing JK (1966) *Schizophrenia and Social Care.* Oxford, UK: Oxford University Press. (**602**)

Brown GL and Goodwin FK (1984) Diagnostic, clinical and personality characteristics of aggressive men with low CSF 5-HIAA. *Clinical Neuropharmacology* **7**: S408–9. (**308**)

Brown GL, Goodwin FK, Ballenger JC, Goyer PF, and Major LF (1979) Aggression in humans correlates with cerebrospinal fluid amine metabolites. *Psychiatry Research* **1**: 131–9. (**308**)

Brown GR and Anderson B (1991) Psychiatric morbidity in adult inpatients with childhood histories of sexual and physical abuse. *American Journal of Psychiatry* **148**: 55–61. (**396**)

Brown GW, Birley JLT, and King JK (1972) Influence of family life on the course of schizophrenic disorders: a replication. *British Journal of Psychiatry* **121**: 241–58. (**341, 355**)

Brown GW, Monck EM, Carstairs GM, and Wing JK (1962) Influence of family life on the course of schizophrenia illness. *British Journal of Preventive and Social Medicine* **16**: 55–68. (**341, 355**)

Brown JS, Elliott JA, and Butler C (2006) Can large scale self-referral psycho-educational stress workshops improve the psychological health of the population? *Behavioural and Cognitive Psychotherapy* **34**: 165–77. (**573**)

Brown L, Christie R, and Morris D (1990) *Families of Murder Victims Project.* London: Victim Report. (**713**)

Brown PJ, Recupero PR, and Stout R (1995) 'PTSD substance abuse comorbidity and treatment utilization'. *Addictive Behaviors* **20**: 251–4. (**463**)

Brown S (2007) *Future Me.* London: Oberon Books. (**265**)

Browne A (1987) *When Battered Women Kill.* New York: Macmillan. (**714**)

Browne K (1995) Preventing child maltreatment through community nursing. *Journal of Advanced Nursing* **21**: 57–63. (**223**)

Browne K and Hamilton-Giachritis C (2005) The influence of violent media on children and adolescents: a public-health approach. *Lancet* **365**: 702–10. (**217**)

Browne K and Herbert M (1997) *Preventing Family Violence.* London: Wiley. (**220, 223**)

Brownell P, Berman J, and Salamone A (2000) Mental health and criminal justice. Issues among perpetrators of elder abuse. *Journal of Elder Abuse and Neglect* **11**: 81–94. (**228**)

Brownfield D and Sorenson AM (1994) Sibship size and sibling delinquency. *Deviant Behaviour* **15**: 45–61. (**177**)

Broxholme SL and Lindsay WR (2003) Development and preliminary evaluation of a questionnaire on cognitions related to sex offending for use with individuals who have mild intellectual disabilities. *Journal of Intellectual Disability Research* **47**: 472–82. (**328**)

Brüne M (2001) De Clérambault's syndrome (erotomania) in an evolutionary perspective. *Evolution and Human Behavior* **22**: 409–15. (**368**)

Brunette MF and Drake RE (1997) Gender differences in patients with schizophrenia and substance abuse. *Comprehensive Psychiatry* **38**: 109–16. (**334**)

Brunner HG, Nelen M, Breakefield XO, Ropers HH, and van Oost BA (1993) Abnormal behavior associated with a point mutation in the structural gene for monoamine oxidase A. *Science* **262**: 578–80. (**198**)

Bryant RA (2006) Cognitive behaviour therapy for acute stress disorder. In J Folette, J Ruzek (eds) *Cognitive Behavioural Therapies for Trauma.* New York: Guilford. pp. 201–27. (**723, 725**)

Bryant RA, Marosszeky JE, Crooks J, and Gurka JA (2000) Posttraumatic stress disorder after severe traumatic brain injury. *American Journal of Psychiatry* **157**: 629–31. (**713**)

Brylewski J and Duggan L (1999) Antipsychotic medication for challenging behaviour in people with learning disability. *Journal of Intellectual Disability Research* **43**: 360–71. (**327**)

Buchanan A (1998) Criminal conviction after discharge form special (high security) hospital: incidence in the first 10 years. *British Journal of Psychiatry* **172**: 472–6. (**604, 605**)

Buchanan A (1999) Independent inquiries into homicide. *British Medical Journal* **318**: 1089–90. (**75**)

Buchanan A (2002) Who does what? The relationships between generic and forensic psychiatric services. In A Buchanan (ed) *Care of the Mentally Disordered Offender in the Community.* Oxford, UK: Oxford University Press. pp. 245–63. (**587, 606**)

Buchanan A (2005) Descriptive diagnosis, personality disorder and detention. *Journal of Forensic Psychiatry and Psychology* **16**: 538–51. (**383**)

Buchanan A (2008) Risk of violence by psychiatric patients: beyond the 'actuarial versus clinical' debate. *Psychiatric Services* **59**: 184–90. (**531**)

Buchanan A and Leese M (2001) Detention of people with dangerous severe personality disorders: a systematic review. *Lancet* **358**: 1955–99. (**531**)

Buchanan A, Reed A, Wessely S, et al. (1993) Acting on delusions II. The phenomenological correlates of acting on delusions. *British Journal of Psychiatry* **163**: 77–82. (**299, 351, 361**)

Buchanan A, Reiss D, and Taylor PJ (2003) Does 'like predict like' when patients discharged from high secure hospitals re-offend? An instrument to describe serious offences. *Psychological Medicine* **33**: 549–53. (**605**)

Buchanan A, Taylor PJ, and Gunn J (2004) Criminal conviction after discharge from special (high security) hospital: the circumstances of early conviction on a serious charge. *Psychology, Crime and Law* **10**: 5–19. (**604**)

References

Buchi KF, Zone S, Langheinrich K, and Varner MW (2003) Changing prevalence of prenatal substance abuse in Utah. *Obstetrics and Gynecology* **102**: 27–30. (**464**)

Buckle A and Farrington D (1984) An observational study of shoplifting. *British Journal of Criminology* **24**: 63–73. (**271**)

Buckler JM and Green M (2004) A comparison of the early growth of twins and singletons. *Annals of Human Biology* **31**: 311–32. (**189**)

Buckley P, Bartell J, Donenwirth K, et al. (1995) Violence and schizophrenia: clozapine as a specific antiaggressive agent. *The Bulletin of the American Academy of Psychiatry and the Law* **23**: 607–11. (**563**)

Buckley PF (1999) The role of typical and atypical antipsychotic medications in the management of agitation and aggression. *Journal of Clinical Psychiatry* **60** (suppl. 10): 52–60. (**563**)

Buckley PF, Ibrahim ZY, Singer B, et al. (1997) Aggression and schizophrenia: efficacy of risperidone. *Journal of the American Academy of Psychiatry and the Law* **25**: 173–81. (**564**)

Buckley PF, Miller BJ, Lehrer DS, and Castle DJ (2009) Psychiatric comorbidities and schizophrenia. *Schizophrenia Bulletin* **35**: 383–402. (**560**)

Buckley PF, Noffsinger SGT, Smith DA, Hrouda DR, and Knoll JL (2003) Treatment of the psychotic patient who is violent. *Psychiatric Clinics in North America* **26**: 231–72. (**562**)

Buckley PF, Paulsson B, and Brecher M (2007) Treatment of agitation and aggression in bipolar mania: efficacy of quetiapine. *Journal of Affective Disorders* **100** (suppl. 1): S33–43. (**565**)

Buckner F and Firestone M (2000) Where the public peril begins: 25 years after Tarasoff. *Journal of Legal Medicine* **21**(2): 187–222. (**664**)

Budd T and Mattinson J (2000) *Stalking: Findings from the 1998 British Crime Survey*. Research Findings No. 129, Home Office Research Development and Statistics Directorate. http://www.neiladdison.pwp.blueyonder.co.uk/pdf/stalkrep.pdf (**373, 374, 375**)

Budd T, Sharp C, and Mayhew P (2005) *Offending in England and Wales: First Results from the 2003 Crime and Justice Survey*. London: Home Office. (**268**)

Bufkin JL and Luttrell VR (2005) Neuroimaging studies of aggressive and violent behavior: current findings and implications for criminology and criminal justice. *Trauma, Violence, and Abuse* **6**: 176–91. (**212**)

Bureau of Justice Statistics (2006) *Criminal Victimization in the United States: National Crime Victimization Survey*. Washington, DC: US Department of Justice. http://www.bjs.gov/index.cfm?ty=pbdetail&iid=1102, (**543**)

Burgess AW and Holmstrom LL (1974) Rape trauma syndrome. *American Journal of Psychiatry* **31**: 981–6. (**715**)

Burleigh M (1994) *Death and Deliverence*. Cambridge, UK: Cambridge University Press. (**659, 679, 686**)

Burns L, Mattick RP, Lim K, and Wallace P (2006) Methadone in pregnancy: treatment retention and neonatal outcomes. *Addiction* **102**: 264–70. (**465**)

Burns M, Bird D, Leach C, and Higgins K (2003) Anger management training: The effects of a structured programme on the self-reported anger experience of forensic inpatients with learning disability. *Journal of Psychiatric and Mental Health Nursing* **10**(5), 569–77. (**327**)

Burns T, Yeeles K, Molodynski A, et al. (2011) Pressure to adhere to treatment ('leverage') in English mental health care. *British Journal of Psychiatry* **199**: 145–50. (**567**)

Burt C (1925) *The Young Delinquent*. London: University of London Press. (**424, 481**)

Burt SA, Krueger RF, McGue M, and Iacono W (2003) Parent–child conflict and the comorbidity among childhood externalizing disorders. *Archives of General Psychiatry* **60**: 505–13. (**197**)

Burton-Bradley BG (1968) The Amok Syndrome in Papua New Guinea. *Medical Journal of Australia* **1**: 252–6. (**428**)

Bush J (1995) Teaching self-risk management to violent offenders. In McGuire (ed) *What Works: Reducing Reoffending – Guidelines from Research and Practice*. Chichester, UK: Wiley. (**213**)

Bushe C and Leonard B (2003) Association between atypical antpsychotic agents and type 2 diabetes. Review of prospective clinical data. *British Journal of Psychiatry* **184** Suppl 47: s87–93. (**567**)

Buss DM (2000) *The Dangerous Passion: Why Jealousy is as Necessary as Love and Sex*. New York: Free. (**371**)

Buss DM and Scmitt DP (1993) Sexual stratggies theory: an evolutionary perspective on human mating. *Psychological Review* **100**: 204–32. (**368**)

Butler AC, Chapman JE, Forman EM, and Beck AT (2006) The empirical status of Cognitive-Behavioural Therapy: a review of the meta-analyses. *Clinical Psychology Review* **26**: 17–31. (**569**)

Butler T, Allnutt S, Cain D, Owens D, and Muller C (2005) Mental disorder in the New South Wales prisoner population. *Australian and New Zealand Journal of Psychiatry* **39**: 407–13. (**502, 517**)

Butwell M, Jamieson E, Leese M, and Taylor PJ (2000) Trends in special (high security) hospitals. 2: residency and discharge episodes, 1986–1995. *British Journal of Psychiatry* **176**: 260–5. (**513, 520, 600, 601**)

Butzlaff RL and Hooley JM (1998) Expressed emotion and psychiatric relapse: a meta-analysis. *Archives of General Psychiatry* **55**: 547–52. (**355**)

Bynum WF, Porter R, and Shepherd M (1985) *The Anatomy of Madness Vol. 1 People and Ideas; Vol. 2 Institutions and Society*. London: Tavistock. (**589**)

Bynum WF, Porter R, and Shepherd M (1988) *The Anatomy of Madness Vol. 3 The Asylum and Its Psychiatry*. London: Tavistock. (**589**)

Byqvist S (1999) Criminality among female drug abusers. *Journal of Psychoactive Drugs* **31**: 353-62. (**513**)

Byqvist S (2006) Drug-abusing women in Sweden: marginalization, social exclusion and gender differences. *Journal of Psychoactive Drugs* **38**: 427–40. (**503**)

Byrne P (2000) Stigma of mental illness and ways of diminishing it. *Advances in Psychiatric Treatment* **6**: 65–72. (**579**)

Cabinet Office (2004) *Alcohol Harm Reduction Strategy for England*. London: Cabinet Office Strategy Unit. (**437**)

Cabinet Office (2007) *The Cabinet Office Policy Review, Building on Progress: Security, Crime and Justice*. London: The Cabinet Office. http://webarchive.nationalarchives.gov.uk/+/archive.cabinetoffice.gov.uk/policy_review (**619**)

Caddle D and Crisp D (1997) *Imprisoned Women and Mothers. Home Office Research Study 162*. London: Home Office. (**517**)

Cadoret RJ, Cain CA, and Crowe RR (1983) Evidence for gene–environment interaction in the development of adolescent antisocial behavior. *Behavioral Genetics* **13**: 301–10. (**199**)

Cadoret RJ, O'Gorman TW, Troughton E, and Heywood E (1985) Alcoholism and antisocial personality: interrelationships, genetic and environmental factors. *Archieves of General Psychiatry* **42**: 161–7. (**201**)

Cadoret RJ, Troughton E, and O'Gorman TW (1987) Genetic and environmental factors in alcohol abuse and antisocial personality. *Journal of Studies on Alcohol* **48**: 1–8. (**201**)

Cadoret RJ, Yates WR, Troughton E, Woodworth G, and Stewart MA (1995b) Adoption study demonstrating two genetic pathways to drug abuse. *Archives of General Psychiatry* **52**: 42–52. (**202, 203**)

Cadoret RJ, Yates WR, Troughton E, Woodworth G, and Stewart MA (1996) An adoption study of drug abuse/dependency in females. *Comprehensive Psychiatry* **37**: 88–94. (**202**)

Cadoret RJ, Yates WR, Troughton E, Woodworth G, and Stewart MAS (1995a) Genetic-environmental interaction in the genesis of aggressivity and conduct disorders. *Archives of General Psychiatry* **52**: 916–24. (**190**)

Caduff F (1995) Querulanz-ein verschwindendes psychopathologisches Verhaltensmuster? *Fortschritte der Neurologie-Psychiatrie* **63**: 504–10. (**382**)

Calder M, Peake A, and Rose, K (2001) *Mothers of Sexually Abused Children: A Framework for Assessment, Understanding and Support*. Lyme Regis: Russell House Publishing. (**259**)

Calhoun F (1998) *Hunters and Howlers: Threats and Violence Against Federal Judicial Officials in the United States, 1789–1993*. Washington, DC: US Department of Justice. (**543, 544**)

Calkins-Mercado C and Ogloff JRP (2007) Risk and the preventive detention of sex offenders in Australia and the United States. *International Journal of Law and Psychiatry* **30**, 49–59. (**116**)

Callaway J, Storvik M, Halonen P, et al. (2005) Seasonal variations in [3H]citalopram platelet binding between healthy controls and violent offenders in Finland. *Human Psychopharmacology* **7**: 467–72. (**307**)

Cameron A, Craissatti J, Maden A, and Scott F (2000) *Mental Health Needs Assessment of Probation Hostel Residents in London*. London: Internal document for the London Probation Area. London Probation Area. (**608**)

Camp J (1982) *One Hundred Years of Medical Murder*. London: The Bodley Head. (**688**)

Campbell C (1974) Legal thought and juristic values. *British Journal of Law and Society* **1**: 13–31. (**150**)

Campbell D (1997) *A Stranger and Afraid: The Story of Caroline Beale*. London: Macmillan. (**15**)

Campbell JC, Webster D, Koziol-McLain J, et al. (2003) Risk factors for femicide in abusive relationships: results from a multisite case control study. *American Journal of Public Health* **93**: 1089–97. (**714**)

Campbell M, Adams PB, Small AM, et al. (1995) Lithium in hospitalized aggressive children with conduct disorder: a double-blind and placebo-controlled study. *Journal of the American Academy of Child and Adolescent Psychiatry* **34**: 445–53. (**566**)

Campbell M, Fitzpatrick R, Haines A, Kinmonth AL, Sandercock P, Spiegelhalter D and Tyrer P (2000) Complex interventions to improve health. *British Medical Journal* **321**: 694–6. (**572**)

Campbell R, Wasco SM, Ahrens CE, Sefl T, and Barnes HE (2001) Preventing the 'second rape': rape survivors' experiences with community service providers. *Journal of Interpersonal Violence* **16**: 1239–59. (**714**)

Campbell WK and Sedikides C (1999) Self-threat magnifies the self-serving bias: a meta-analytic integration. *Review of General Psychology* **3**: 23–43. (**351**)

Campion D, Dumanchin C, Hannequin D, et al. (1999) Early-onset autosomal dominant Alzheimer disease: Prevalence, genetic heterogeneity, and mutation spectrum. *American Journal of Human Genetics* **65**: 664–70. (**193**)

Canning U, Millward L, Raj T, and Warm D (2004) *Drug Use Prevention Among Young People: A Review of Reviews*. London: Health Development Agency. (**492**)

Cannings A and Lloyd Davies M (2006) *Against All Odds*. London: Time Warner Books. (**674**)

Cannon TD, Kaprio J, Lonnqvist J, Huttunen M, and Koskenvuo M (1998) The genetic epidemiology of schizophrenia in a Finnish twin cohort. A population-based modeling study. *Archives of General Psychiatry* **55**: 67–74. (**208**)

Canter D and Youngs D (2009) *Investigative Psychology: Offender Profiling and the Analysis of Criminal Action*. Chichester, UK: Wiley. (**624**)

Canter DV and Ioannou M (2004) A multivariate model of stalking behaviours. *Behaviormetrika* **31**(2): 113–30. (**375**)

Canter DV and Youngs DE (2008) *Principles of Geographical Offender Profiling*. Aldershot, UK: Ashgate Publishing. (**624**)

Cantor CH (2000) Suicide in the Western world. In K Hawton, K Van Heeringen (eds) *The International Handbook of Suicide and Attempted Suicide*. Chichester, UK: Wiley, pp. 9–28. (**278**)

Capaldi DM and Patterson GR (1996) Can violent offenders be distinguished from frequent offenders? Prediction from childhood to adolescence. *Journal of Research in Crime and Delinquency* **33**: 206–31. (**17, 171**)

Capitanio JP, Weissberg M, and Reite M (1985) Biology of maternal behaviour: recent findings and publications. In M Reite, T Field (eds) *The Psychobiology of Attachment and Separation*. London: Academic Press, pp. 223–55. (**720**)

Cardno AG, Marshall EJ, Coid B, et al. (1999) Heritability estimates for psychotic disorders: the Maudsley twin psychosis series. *Archives of General Psychiatry* **56**: 162–8. (**208**)

817

Cardon LR and Palmer LJ (2003) Population stratification and spurious allelic association. *Lancet* **361**: 598–604. (**193**)

Carey TA, Mullan RJ, and Carey M (2007) Patient-led treatment: an idea whose time has come? *Clinical Psychology Forum* **117**: 9–12. (**572**)

Carlin P, Gudjonsson G, and Rutter S (2005) Persecutory delusions and attributions for real negative events: a study in forensic patients. *Journal of Forensic Psychiatry and Psychology* **16**: 139–48. (**351**)

Carmel H and Hunter M (1990) Compliance with training strategy in managing assaultive behaviour and injuries from in-patient violence. *Hospital and Community Psychiatry* **41**: 55–560. (**557**)

Carnes P (1991) Sexual addiction screening test. *Tennessee Nursing* **54**: 28–9. (**253**)

Carney M, Buttell F, and Dutton D (2007) Women who perpetrate intimate partner violence: a review of the literature with recommendations for treatment. *Aggression and Violent Behavior* **12**: 108–15. (**218**)

Carr JE and Tan EK (1976) In search of the true amok, amok as viewed within the Malay culture. *American Journal of Psychiatry* **133**: 1295–9. (**428**)

Carrillo M, Ricci LA, Coppersmith GA, and Melloni RH Jr (2009) The effect of increased serotonergic neurotransmission on aggression: a critical meta-analytical review of preclinical studies. *Psychopharmacology* **205**: 349–68. (**310**)

Carroll KM (1996) Relapse prevention as a psychosocial treatment: a review of controlled clinical trials. *Experimental and Clinical Psychology* **4**: 46–54. (**447**)

Carson D (1990a) Report to court, a role in preventing decision error. *Journal of Social Welfare Law* **12**: 151–63. (**155**)

Carson D (1990b) *Professionals and the Courts. A Handbook for Expert Witnesses.* Birmingham, UK: Venture. (**166**)

Carson D (1996) Structural problems, perspectives and solutions. In J Peay (ed) *Inquiries After Homicide.* London: Duckworth, pp. 120–46. (**696**)

Carson D, Grubin D, and Parsons S (2003) *Report on New Prison Health Reception Screening Arrangement: The Result of a Pilot Study in Ten Prisons.* Newcastle, UK: University of Newcastle. (**630**)

Carson D, Lindsay WR, O'Brien G, et al. (2010) Referrals into services for offenders with intellectual disabilities: variables predicting community or secure provision. *Criminal Behaviour and Mental Health* **20**: 39–50. (**326**)

Carter D (2003) The impact of antisocial lifestyle on health. *British Medical Journal* **326**: 834–5. (**278**)

Carter P (2003) *Managing Offenders, Reducing Crime–A New Approach.* London: Home Office. (**639**)

Carter T (2006) *Fitness to Drive.* London: Royal Society of Medicine Press. (**278**)

Cartwright R (2004) Sleepwalking violence: a sleep disorder, a legal dilemma, and a psychological challenge. *American Journal of Psychiatry* **161**: 1149–58. (**290**)

Caspi A, Langley K, Milne B, et al. (2008) A replicated molecular genetic basis for subtyping antisocial behavior in children with attention-deficit/hyperactivity disorder. *Archives of General Psychiatry* **65**: 203–10. (**199**)

Caspi A, McClay J, Moffitt TE, et al. (2002) Role of genotype in the cycle of violence in maltreated children. *Science* **297**: 851–4. (**3, 200, 394**)

Caspi A, Moffitt TE, Cannon M, et al. (2005) Moderation of the effect of adolescent-onset cannabis use on adult psychosis by a functional polymorphism in the catechol-O-methyltransferase gene: longitudinal evidence of a gene X environment interaction. *Biological Psychiatry* **57**: 1117–27. (**208**)

Caspi A, Moffitt TE, Morgan J, et al. (2004) Maternal expressed emotion predicts children's antisocial behavior problems: using monozygotic-twin differences to identify environmental effects on behavioral development. *Developmental Psychology* **40**: 149–61. (**191, 197**)

Caspi A, Taylor A, Moffitt TE, and Plomin R (2000) Neighborhood deprivation affects children's mental health: environmental risks identified in a genetic design. *Psychological Science* **11**: 338–42. (**197**)

Catan L (1988) *The Development of Young Children in HMP Mother and Baby Units.* Working Papers in Psychology Series – No. 1, Falmer, UK: University of Sussex. (**519**)

Catan L (1989) *The Development of Young Children in Prison Mother and Baby Units. Research Bulletin No 26.* London: Home Office Research and Planning Unit. (**519**)

Cecero JJ, Ball SA, Tennen H, Kranzler HR, and Rounsaville BJ (1999) Concurrent and predictive validity of antisocial personality disorder subtyping among substance users. *Journal of Nervous and Mental Disease* **187**: 478–86. (**444**)

Centers for Disease Control (1988) Health status of Vietnam veterans. *Journal of the American Medical Association* **259**: 2701–19. (**715**)

Centers for Disease Control and Prevention (2003) *Costs of Intimate Partner Violence Against Women in the United States.* Atlanta, CA: Centers for Disease Control and Prevention. (**374, 715**)

Centers for Disease Control and Prevention (CDC) (2004) 150th Anniversary of John Snow and the pump handle. *Morbidity and Mortality Weekly Report* (MMWR) **53**: 783. (**704**)

Cernkovich SA, Giordano PC, and Pugh MD (1985) Chronic offenders: the missing cases in self-report delinquency research. *Journal of Criminal Law and Criminology* **76**: 705–32. (**172**)

CESDI (1996) *The Confidential Enquiry into Stillbirths and Deaths in Infancy (CESDI) Third Annual Report 1 January-31 December 1994.* London: Department of Health. (**671**)

Chadwick J and Mann WN (1950) *Hippocratic Writings.* London: Penguin Books (**792**)

Chaffin M (1992) Factors associated with treatment completion and progress among intrafamilial sexual abusers. *Child Abuse and Neglect* **16**: 251–74. (**262, 607**)

Chalasani L, Kant R, and Chengappa KN (2001) Clozapine impact on clinical outcomes and aggression in severely ill adolescents with childhood-onset schizophrenia. *Canadian Journal of Psychiatry* **46**: 965–8. (**564**)

Chamberlain P and Reid JB (1998) Comparison of two community alternatives to incarceration for chronic juvenile offenders. *Journal of Consulting and Clinical Psychology* **6**: 624–33. (**495**)

Chan B (2010) Negative caregiving experience: a predictor of high expressed emotion among caregivers of relatives with schizophrenia. *Social Work in Mental Health* **8**: 375–97. (**355**)

Chand PK, Kumar N, and Murthy P (2010) Major self-mutilations: castration and enucleation. *German Journal of Psychiatry* **13**: 164–70. (**334**)

Chandler DW and Spicer G (2006) Integrated treatment for jail recidivists with co-occurring psychiatric and substance use disorders *Community Mental Health Journal* **42**: 405–25. (**364**)

Chandler G and McCaul M (2003) Co-occurring psychiatric disorders in women with addictions. *Obstetrics and Gynecology Clinics of North America* **30**: 469–81. (**457**)

Chandler MJ, Greenspan S, and Barenboim C (1974) Assessment and training of role-taking and referential communication skills in institutionalized, emotionally disturbed children. *Developmental Psychology* **10**: 546–53. (**394**)

Channon S (1982) The resettlement of epileptic offenders. In J Gunn, DP Farrington (eds) *Abnormal Offenders, Delinquency and the Criminal Justice System*. Chichester, UK: Wiley. (**289**)

Chao J and Nestler EJ (2004) Molecular neurobiology of drug addiction. *Annual Review of Medicine* **55**: 113–32. (**205**)

Chappell D and di Martino V (2006) *Violence at Work*, 3rd Edn. Geneva, Switzerland: International Labour Office. (**699, 700**)

Chapple B, Chant D, Nolan P, et al. (2004) Correlates of victimization amongst people with psychosis. *Social Psychiatry and Psychiatric Epidemiology* **39**: 836–40. (**3, 334**)

Charles KE and Egan V (2005) Mating effort correlates with self-reported delinquency in a normal adolescent sample. *Personality and Individual Differences* **38**: 1035–45. (**440**)

Chatham LR, Hiller ML, Rowan-Szal GA, Joe GW, and Simpson DD (1999) Gender differences at admission and follow-up in a sample of methadone maintenance clients. *Substance Use and Misuse* **34**: 1137–65. (**463, 464**)

Chen F and Greenberg J (2004) A positive aspect of caregiving: the influence of social support on caregiving gains for family members of relatives with schizophrenia. *Community Mental Health Journal* **40**: 423–35. (**355**)

Chengappa KN, Goldstein JM, Greenwood M, John V, and Levine J (2003) A post hoc analysis of the impact on hostility and agitation of quetiapine and haloperidol among patients with schizophrenia. *Clinical Therapeutics* **25**: 530–41. (**565**)

Chengappa KN, Levine J, Ulrich R, et al. (2000) Impact of risperidone on seclusion and restraint at a state psychiatric hospital. *Canadian Journal of Psychiatry* **45**: 827–32. (**564**)

Chengappa KN, Vasile J, Levine J, et al (2002) Clozapine: its impact on aggressive behavior among patients in a state psychiatric hospital. *Schizophrenia Research* **53**: 1–6. (**563**)

Cherek DR and Lane SD (1999) Effects of d,l-fenfluramine on aggressive and impulsive responding in adult males with a history of conduct disorder. *Psychopharmacology* **146**: 473–81. (**307, 309**)

Cherek DR and Lane SD (2001) Acute effects of D-fenfluramine on simultaneous measures of aggressive escape and impulsive responses of adult males with and without a history of conduct disorder. *Psychopharmacology* **157**: 221–7. (**310**)

Chermack ST and Giancola PR (1997) The relationship between alcohol and aggression: an integrated biopsychosocial conceptualization. *Clinical Psychology Review* **17**: 621–49. (**439**)

Chesney MA and Rosenman RH (1985) *Anger and Hostility in Cardiovascular and Behavioral Disorders*. Washington, DC: Hemisphere. (**215**)

Chesterman LP, Taylor PJ, Cox T, Hill M, and Lumsden J (1994) Multiple measures of cerebral state in dangerous mentally disordered inpatients. *Criminal Behaviour and Mental Health* **4**: 228–39. (**298, 299**)

Chesterman P, Terbeck S, and Vaughan F (2008) Malingered psychosis. *Journal of Forensic Psychiatry and Psychology* **19**: 275–300. (**431**)

Chief Medical Officers of the Four Home Countries (2011) Start active, stay active. Department of Health: London. https://www.gov.uk/government/uploads/system/uploads/attachment_data/file/152108/dh_128210.pdf.pdf (**568**)

Chiesa M, Drahorad C, and Longo S (2000) Early termination of treatment in personality disorder treated in a psychotherapy hospital. Quantitative and qualitative study. *British Journal of Psychiatry* **177**: 107–11. (**573**)

Chilcoat HD and Breslau N (1998a) Investigations of causal pathways between PTSD and drug use disorders. *Addictive Behaviors* **23**: 827–40. (**712**)

Chilcoat HD and Breslau N (1998b) Posttraumatic stress disorder and drug disorders: testing causal pathways. *Archives of General Psychiatry* **55**: 913–17. (**712**)

Chiswick D (1978) Insanity in bar of trial in Scotland: a state hospital study. *British Journal of Psychiatry* **132**: 598–601. (**94**)

Chiswick D (1985) Use and abuse of psychiatric testimony. *British Medical Journal* **290**: 975–7. (**94, 150**)

Chiswick D (1990) Criminal responsibility in Scotland. In R Bluglass, P Bowden (eds) *Principles and Practice of Forensic Psychiatry*. Edinburgh, UK: Churchill Livingstone, pp. 313–8. (**94**)

Chitsabesan P, Kroll L, Bailey S, et al. (2006) Mental health needs of young offenders in custody and in the community. *British Journal of Psychiatry* **188**: 534–40. (**483, 485**)

Chodoff P (1983) Paternalism versus autonomy in medicine and psychiatry. *Psychiatric Annals* **13**: 818–20. (**132**)

Choe JY, Teplin L, and Abram K (2008) Perpetration of violence, violent victimization, and severe mental illness: balancing public health concerns. *Psychiatric Services* **59**: 153–64. (**334**)

Choi-Kwon SH, Han SW, Kwon SU, et al. (2006) Fluoxetine treatment in poststroke depression, emotional incontinence, and anger proneness: a double-blind, placebo-controlled study. *Stroke* **37**: 156–61. (**310**)

819

References

Chowdari KV, Mirnics K, Semwal P, et al. (2002) Association and linkage analyses of RGS4 polymorphisms in schizophrenia. *Human Molecular Genetics* **11**(12): 1373–80. (**208**)

Christian L, Friedman D, and Thomas L (2002) *Inquests; A Practitioner's Guide*. London: Legal Action Group. (**54**)

Christianson S (1992) Emotional stress and eyewitness memory: a critical review. *Psychological Bulletin* **112**: 284–309. (**161**)

Christianson SA and Merckelbach H (2004) Crime-related amnesia as a form of deception. In PA Granhag, LA Strömwall (eds) *The Detection of Deception in Forensic Contexts*. Cambridge, UK: Cambridge University Press. (**296, 297**)

Christianson SA, Merckelbach H, and Kopelman MD (2006) Crime-related amnesia. In A Heaton-Armstrong, E Shepherd, G Gudjonsson, D Wolchover (eds) *Witness Testimony: Psychological, Investigative, and Evidential Perspectives*. Oxford, UK: Oxford University Press, pp.105–126. (**295, 296, 297**)

Christie MGA (2001) *The Criminal Law of Scotland by Sir Gerald H. Gordon*, 3rd edn. Vol 2. Edinburgh: W Green. (**94**)

Christie-Brown JRW (1983) Paraphilias: sadomasochism, fetishism, transvestism, and transexuality. *British Journal of Psychiatry* **143**: 227–31. (**246**)

Christman SD, Garvey K, Propper RE, and Phaneuf KA (2003) Bilateral eye movements enhance the retrieval of episodic memories. *Neuropsychology* **17**: 221–9. (**725**)

Christo G (2000) *Christo inventory for substance-misuse services*. http://www.drugslibrary.stir.ac.uk/documents/christo.pdf (**457**)

Christy A, Poythress NG, Boothroyd RA, Petrila J, and Mehra S (2005) Evaluating the efficiency and community safety goals of the Broward County Mental Health Court. *Behavioral Sciences and the Law* **23**: 227–43. (**364**)

Chrzastowski S (2006) Christene Padesky's approach to cognitive-behavioural therapy of personality disorders. *Psychoterapia* **1**: 39–48. (**569**)

Chu JA and Dill DL (1990) Dissociative symptoms in relation to childhood physical and sexual abuse. *American Journal of Psychiatry* **147**: 887–92. (**723**)

Chua WL, Izquierdo de Santiago A, Kulkarni J, and Mortimer A (2005) *Estrogen for schizophrenia*. Cochrane Database of Systematic Reviews 2005 Issue 4. Art.No:CD004719. DOI:10.1002/14651858.CD004719.pub2. Retrieved January 7th, 2008, from www.cochrane.org/reviews/en/ab004719.html. (**501, 521**)

Chumakov I, Blumenfeld M, Guerassimenko O, et al. (2002) Genetic and physiological data implicating the new human gene G72 and the gene for D-amino acid oxidase in schizophrenia. *Proceedings of the National Academy of Sciences of the United States of America* **99**(21): 13675–80. (**208**)

Chung T and Maisto SA (2006) Relapse to alcohol and other drug use in treated adolescents: review and reconsideration of relapse as a change point in clinical course. *Clinical Psychology Review* **26**: 149–61. (**466**)

Chung T, Maisto SA, Cornelius JR, and Martin CS (2004) Adolescents' drug and alcohol use trajectories in the year following treatment. *Journal of Studies on Alcohol* **65**: 105–14. (**466**)

Church S, Henderson M, and Barnard Mm Hart G (2001) Violence by clients towards female prostitutes in different work settings: questionnaire survey. *British Medical Journal* **322**: 524–5. (**464**)

Cicchetti D (1984) The emergence of developmental psychopathology. *Child Development* **55**: 1–7. (**484**)

Cicchetti D and Rogosch FA (2002) A developmental psychopathology perspective on adolescence. *Journal Consulting Clinical Psychology* **70**: 6–20. (**485**)

Cicchetti DV (1994) Guidelines, criteria afore valuating normed and standarized assessment instruments in psychology. *Psychological Assessment* **6**: 284–90. (**385**)

Cierpka M, Grande T, Rudolf G, et al. (2007) The operationalized psychodynamic diagnostics system: clinical relevance, reliability and validity. *Psychopathology* **40**: 209–20. (**389, 548, 597**)

Cima M, Merckelbach H, Hollnack S, and Knauer F. (2003) Characteristics of psychiatric inmates who claim amnesia. *Personality and Individual Differences* **35**: 373–80. (**293**)

Cipriani D (2009) *Children's Rights and the Minimum Age of Criminal Responsibility. A Global Perspective*. Ashgate: Farnham, Surrey. (**128**)

Citrome L, Casey DE, Daniel DG, et al. (2004) Adjunctive divalproex and hostility among patients with schizophrenia receiving olanzapine or risperidone. *Psychiatric Services* **55**: 290–4. (**566**)

Citrome L, Volavka J, Czobor P, et al. (2001) Effects of clozapine, olanzapine, risperidone, and haloperidol on hostility among patients with schizophrenia. *Psychiatric Services* **52**: 1510–4. (**563, 564**)

Civil Justice Council (2005) *Practice Direction 35, Protocol for the Instruction of Experts to give Evidence in Civil Claims*. London: Ministry of Justice (**151**)

Clapp JD and Gayle Beck J (2009) Understanding the relationship between PTSD and social support: the role of negative network orientation. *Behaviour Research and Therapy* **47**: 237–44. (**723**)

Clare AW (1986) The disease concept in psychiatry. In P Hill, R Murray, A Thorley (eds) *Essentials of Postgraduate Psychiatry*, 2nd edn. London: Grune and Stratton. (**10**)

Clare ICH and Gudjonsson GH (1993) Interrogative suggestibility, confabulation and acquiescence in people with mild learning disabilities (mental handicap): implications for reliability during police interrogations. *British Journal of Clinical Psychology* **37**: 295–301. (**332**)

Clare ICH, Murphy GH, Cox D, and Chaplin EH (1992) Assessment and treatment of fire setting: a single case investigation using a cognitive behavioural model. *Criminal Behaviour and Mental Health* **2**: 253–68. (**330, 576**)

Clare P, Bailey S, and Clark A (2000) Relationship between psychotic disorders in adolescence and criminally violent behaviour – a retrospective examination. *British Journal of Psychiatry* **177**: 275–9. (**487**)

Clark D (2000a) *Theory Manual for Enhanced Thinking Skills*. Joint Prison Probation Service Accreditation Panel. (**576**)

Clark D (2000b) The use of the hare psychopathy checklist revised to predict offending and institutional misconduct in the English prison system. *Prison Research and Development Bulletin* **9**: 10–14. (**607**)

Clark L, Roiser JP, Cools R, et al. (2005) Stop signal response inhibition is not modulated by tryptophan depletion or the serotonin transporter polymorphism in healthy volunteers: implications for the 5-HT theory of impulsivity. *Psychopharmacology* **182**: 570–8. (**309**)

Clark LA (2007) Assessment and diagnosis of personality disorder: perennial issues and an emerging reconceptualization. *Annual Review of Psychology* **58**: 227–57. (**385**)

Clark LA, Livesley JW, and Money L (1997) Personality disorder assessment: the challenge of construct validity. *Journal of Personality Disorders* **11**: 205–31. (**385**)

Clark RE, Ricketts SK, and Mchugo GJ (1999) Legal system involvement and costs for persons in treatment for severe mental illness and substance use disorders. *Psychiatric Services* **50**: 641–7. (**281**)

Clark T, Kenney-Herbert J, Baker J, and Humphreys M (2002) Psychiatric probation orders: failed provision or future panacea? *Medical Science Law* **42**: 58–63. (**643**)

Clarke A, Simmonds R, and Wydall S (2004) *Delivering Cognitive Skills Programmes in Prison: A Qualitative Study*. London: Home Office, Findings No 242. http://dera.ioe.ac.uk/11967/1/Delivering%2520cognitive%2520skills.pdf (**576**)

Clarke C, Tapp J, Lord A, and Moore E (2012) Groupwork for offender patients on sex offending in a high security hospital: investigating aspects of impact via qualitative analysis. *Journal of Sexual Aggression* **8**: 1–16. (**577, 578**)

Clarke JW (1982) *American Assassins: The Darker Side of Politics*. Princeton, NJ: Princeton University Press. (**543**)

Clarke JW (1990) *On Being Mad or Merely Angry*. Princeton, NJ: Princeton University Press. (**543**)

Clarke L and Harrison A (2001) Assessment instruments. In WJ Livesley (ed) *Handbook of Personality Disorders: Theory, Research and Practice*. New York: Guilford, pp. 277–307. (**387**)

Clarke PA, LJ (2001) Marchioness/Bowbelle: *Formal Investigation under the Merchant Shipping Act 1995*. Stationery Office: London. (**709**)

Clarke RV and Cornish DB (1985) Modelling offenders' decisions: a framework for research and policy. In M Tonry, N Morris (eds) *Crime and Justice*. Vol. 6, Chicago, IL: University of Chicago Press, pp. 147–85. (**179**)

Clarkin JF and Kendall PC (1992) Comorbidity and treatment planning: summary and future directions. *Journal of Consulting and Clinical Psychology* **60**: 904–8. (**345, 397**)

Clarkin JF, Foelsch PA, Levy KN, et al. (2001) The development of a psychodynamic treatment for patients with borderline personality disorder: a preliminary study of behavioral change. *Journal of Personality Disorders* **15**: 487–95. (**584**)

Clarkin JF, Levy KN, Lenzenweger MF, and Kernberg OF (2007) Evaluating three treatments for borderline personality disorder: a multi-wave study. *American Journal of Psychiatry* **164**: 922–8. (**409**)

Cleare AJ and Bond AJ (1997) Does central serotonergic function correlate inversely with aggression? A study using D-fenfluramine in healthy subjects. *Psychiatry Research* **69**: 89–95. (**309**)

Cleary M, Hunt GE, Matheson SL, Siegfried N, and Walter G (2010) Psychosocial interventions for people with both severe mental illness and substance misuse. *Cochrane Database of Systematic Reviews 2008*.Issue 1. Art. No.: CD001088. DOI: 10.1002/14651858. CD001088.pub2. http://onlinelibrary.wiley.com/doi/10.1002/14651858.CD001088.pub2 (**362, 448, 576**)

Cleckley H (1976) *The Mask of Sanity*, 5th edn. CV Mosby www.cassiopaea.org/cass/sanity_1.PdF. (**7, 11, 385**)

Clegg J, Hollis C, Mawhood L, and Rutter M (2005) Developmental language disorders – a follow-up in later adult life. Cognitive, language and psychosocial outcomes. *Journal of Child Psychology and Psychiatry* **46**: 128–49. (**189**)

Clegg M, Finney A, and Thorpe K (2005) *Crime in England and Wales: Quarterly Update to December 2004*. London: HMSO. (**700, 702**)

Clerget-Darpoux F, Goldin LR, and Gershon ES (1986) Clinical methods in psychiatric genetics. III. Environmental stratification may simulate a genetic effect in adoption studies. *Acta Psychiatrica Scandinavica* **74**: 305–11. (**188**)

Clifford BR and Scott J (1978) Individual and situational factors in eyewitness testimony. *Journal of Applied Psychology* **63**: 852–9. (**296**)

Clinical Resource Efficiency Support Team (CREST) (2003) *The Management of Post-Traumatic Stress Disorder in Adults*. Belfast, UK: Northern Ireland Department of Health, Social Services and Public Safety. (**725**)

Cloitre M, Koenan KC, Cohen LR, and Han H (2002) Skills training in affective and interpersonal regulation followed by exposure: a phased-based treatment for PTSD related to childhood abuse. *Journal of Consulting and Clinical Psychology* **70**: 1067–74. (**725, 729**)

Cloninger CR (1987) A systematic method for clinical description and classification of personality variants. *Archives of General Psychiatry* **44**: 573–88. (**385**)

Cloninger CR, Bohman M, and Sigvardsson S (1981) Inheritance of alcohol abuse. Cross-fostering analysis of adopted men. *Archives of General Psychiatry* **38**: 861–8. (**201, 203, 207**)

Cloninger CR, Sigvardsson S, Gilligan SB, *etal.* (1988) Genetic heterogeneity and the classification of alcoholism. *Advances in Alcohol and Substance Abuse* **7**: 3–16. (**201, 203**)

Clothier CM, MacDonald A, and Shaw D (1994) *Independent Inquiry Relating to Deaths and Injuries on the Children's Ward at Grantham and Kesteven General Hospital During the Period February to April 1991*. London: HMSO. (**686, 687**)

Coccaro EF (1992) Impulsive aggression and central serotonergic system function in humans: an example of a dimensional brain-behavior relationship. *International Clinical Psychopharmacology* **7**: 3–12. (**308, 309**)

Coccaro EF and Kavoussi RJ (1996) Neurotransmitter correlates of impulsive aggression. In DM Stoff, RB Cairns (eds) *Aggression and Violence. Genetic, Neurobiological and Biosocial Perspectives*. Mahwah, NJ: Lawrence Erlbaum Associates, pp. 67–87. (**307, 312**)

Coccaro EF and Kavoussi RJ (1997) Fluoxetine and impulsive aggressive behavior in personality-disordered subjects. *Archives of General Psychiatry*. **54**(12): 1081–8. (**242, 311, 404**)

References

Coccaro EF, Astill JL, Herbert JL, and Schut AG (1990) Fluoxetine treatment of impulsive aggression in DSM-III-R personality disorder patients. *Journal of Clinical Psychopharmacology* **10**: 373–5. (**311**)

Coccaro EF, Berman ME, Kavoussi RJ, and Hauger RL (1996b) Relationship of prolactin response to d-fenfluramine to behavioral and questionnaire assessments of aggression in personality-disordered men. *Biological Psychiatry* **40**: 57–64. (**308**)

Coccaro EF, Harvey PD, Kupsaw-Lawrence E, and Herbert JL (1991) Development of neuropharmacologically based behavioral assessments of impulsive aggressive behavior. *Journal of Neuropsychiatry and Clinical Neurosciences* **3**: S51. (**309**)

Coccaro EF, Kavoussi RJ, and Hauger RL (1995) Physiological responses to d-fenfluramine and ipsapirone challenge correlate with indices of aggression in males with personality disorder. *International Clinical Psychopharmacology* **10**: 177–9. (**308, 309**)

Coccaro EF, Kavoussi RJ, Cooper, TB, and Hauger RL (1997c) Central serotonin activity and aggression: inverse relationship with prolactin response to d-fenfluramine, but not CSF 5-HIAA concentration, in human subjects. *American Journal of Psychiatry* **154**: 1430–5. (**308**)

Coccaro EF, Kavoussi RJ, Sheline YI, Berman ME, and Csernansky JG (1997b) Impulsive aggression in personality disorder correlates with platelet 5-HT2A receptor binding. *Neuropsychopharmacology* **16**: 211–16. (**308**)

Coccaro EF, Kavoussi RJ, Sheline YI, Lish JD, and Csernansky JG (1996a) Impulsive aggression in personality disorder correlates with tritiated paroxetine binding in the platelet. *Archives of General Psychiatry* **53**: 531–6. (**308, 309**)

Coccaro EF, Kavoussi RJ, Trestman RL, et al. (1997a) Serotonin function in human subjects: intercorrelations among central 5-HT indices and aggressiveness. *Psychiatry Research* **73**: 1–14. (**307**)

Coccaro EF, Siever LJ, Klar HM, Maurer G, Cochrane K, Cooper TB, Mohs RC and Davies KL (1989) Serotonergic studies in patients with affective and personality disorders: Correlates with suicidal and impulsive aggressive behaviour. *Archives of General Psychiatry* **46**: 587–99. (**307, 308, 309**)

Cockram J, Jackson R, and Underwood R (1998) People with and intellectual disability and the criminal justice system: the family perspective. *Journal of Intellectual and Developmental Disability* **23**: 41–56. (**324**)

Coggins MH and Pynchon MR (1998) Mental health consultation to law enforcement: secret service development of a mental health liaison program. *Behavioural Sciences and the Law* **16**: 407–22. (**547**)

Cohen A and Eastman N (2000) *Assessing Forensic Mental Health Need. Policy, theory and practice*. London: Gaskell. (**597**)

Cohen CI (1980) Crime among mental patients – a critical analysis. *Psychiatric Quarterly* **52**: 100–6. (**280**)

Cohen LE and Felson M (1979) Social change and crime rate trends: a routine activity approach. *American Sociological Review* **44**: 588–608. (**179**)

Cohen MA, Rust RT, Steen S (2006) Prevention, crime control or cash? Public preferences towards criminal justice spending priorities. *Justice Quarterly* **23**:317–35 (**5**)

Cohen ML and Quinter JL (1996) The derailment of railway spine: a timely lesson for post-traumatic fibromyalgia syndrome. *Pain Reviews* **3**: 181–202. <http://www.pain-education.com/the-derailment-of-railway-spine.html> (**51**)

Cohen S (1997) Working with resistance to experiencing and expressing emotions in group therapy. *International Journal of Group Psychotherapy* **47**: 443–58. (**572**)

Cohen S and Taylor L (1972) *Psychological Survival: The Experience of Long-Term Imprisonment*. Harmondsworth, UK: Penguin Books. (**637**)

Coid B, Lewis SW, and Reveley AM (1993) A twin study of psychosis and criminality. *British Journal of Psychiatry* **162**: 87–92. (**207, 344**)

Coid J (1979) Mania à potu: a critical review of pathological intoxication. *Psychological Medicine* **9**: 709–19. (**33, 437**)

Coid J (1983) The epidemiology of abnormal homicide and murder followed by suicide. *Psychological Medicine* **13**: 855–60. (**337, 351**)

Coid J (1988) Mentally abnormal prisoners on remand: 1 Rejected or accepted by the NHS. *British Medical Journal* **296**: 1779–82. (**632**)

Coid J (1992) *DSM-III* diagnosis in criminal psychopaths: A way forward. *Criminal Behaviour and Mental Health* **2**: 904–8. (**397**)

Coid J and Kahtan N (2000) Are special hospitals needed? *Journal of Forensic Psychiatry* **11**: 17–35. (**30**)

Coid J, Fazel S, and Kahtan N (2002) Elderly patients admitted to secure forensic psychiatry services. *Journal of Forensic Psychiatry* **13**: 416–27. (**525**)

Coid J, Hickey N, and Yang M (2007b) Comparison of outcomes following after-care from forensic and adult general psychiatric services. *British Journal of Psychiatry* **190**: 509–14. (**606**)

Coid J, Hickey N, Kahtan N, Zhang T, and Yang M (2007a) Patients discharged form medium secure forensic psychiatry services: reconvictions and risk factors. *British Journal of Psychiatry* **190**: 223–9. (**605**)

Coid J, Kahtan N, Cook A, Gault S, and Jarman B (2001b) Predicting admission rates to secure forensic psychiatry services. *Psychological Medicine* **31**: 531–9. (**266, 600**)

Coid J, Kahtan N, Gault S, and Jarman B (1999) Patients with personality disorder admitted to secure forensic psychiatry services. *British Journal of Psychiatry* **175**: 528–36. (**444**)

Coid J, Kahtan N, Gault S, and Jarman B (2000) Women admitted to secure psychiatry services: I. comparison of women and men. *Journal of Forensic Psychiatry* **11**: 275–95. (**273, 340, 504, 513, 520**)

Coid J, Kahtan N, Gault S, and Jarman B (2001) Medium secure forensic psychiatry services - Comparison of seven English health regions. *British Journal of Psychiatry* **178**: 55–61. (**266, 520, 714**)

Coid J, Kahtan N, Gault S, Cook A, and Jarman B (2001a) Medium secure forensic psychiatry services. *British Journal of Psychiatry* **178**: 55–61. (**266, 520, 600**)

Coid J, Petruckevitch A, Bebbington P, et al. (2003) Psychiatric morbidity in prisoners and solitary cellular confinement. II. Special ("strip") cells. *Journal of Forensic Psychiatry and Psychology* **14**: 320–40. (**632**)

Coid J, Petruckevitch A, Feder G, et al. (2001) Relation between childhood sexual and physical abuse and risk of revictimization in women: a cross-sectional survey. *Lancet* **358**(9280): 450–4. (**714**)

Coid J, Yang M, Roberts A, et al. (2006) Violence and psychiatric morbidity in the national household population of Britain: public health implications. *British Journal of Psychiatry* **189**: 12–19. (**338**)

Coid J, Yang M, Tyrer P, Roberts A, and Ullrich S (2006) Prevalence and correlates of personality disorder in Great Britain. *British Journal of Psychiatry* **188**: 423–31. (**390**)

Coker J and Martin JP (1985) *Licensed to Live*. Oxford, UK: Basil Blackwell. (**637**)

Colby KM (1977) Appraisal of four psychological theories of paranoid phenomena. *Journal of Abnormal Psychology* **86**: 54–9. (**345, 351**)

Coldwell CM and Bender WS (2007) The effectiveness of assertive community treatment for homeless populations with severe mental illness: a meta-analysis. *American Journal of Psychiatry* **164**: 393–9. (**364**)

Cole LC, Grubb PL, Sauter SL, Swanson NG, and Lawless P (1997) Psychosocial correlates of harassment, threats and fear of violence in the workplace. *Scandinavian Journal of Work and Environmental Health* **23**: 450–7. (**543**)

Cole SA (2009) Cultural consequences of miscarriages of justice. *Behavioral Sciences and the Law* **27**: 431–49. (**716**)

Coleman E (1991) Compulsive sexual behaviour: new concepts and treatments. *Journal of Psychology and Human Sexuality* **4**: 37–52. (**246**)

Coleman J and Schofield J (2005) *Key Data on Adolescence*, 5th edn. Brighton, UK: Trust for Study of Adolescence. (**473, 483**)

Coleman K, Jansson K, Kaiza P, and Reed E (2007) Homicide, Firearms Offences and Intimate Violence 2005/06 (Supplementary Volume 1 to Crime in England and Wales 2005/2006). (**243**)

Coll GC, Kagan J, and Resnick JS (1984) Behavioural inhibition in young children. *Child Development* **55**: 1005–19. (**485**)

Collie J (1917) *Malingering and Feigned Sickness*, London: Edward Arnold. (**431**)

Collins J (ed) (1982) *Drinking and Crime: Perspectives on the Relationships between Alcohol Consumption and Criminal Behaviour*. London: Tavistock. (**702**)

Collins M and Davies S (2005) The Security Needs Assessment Profile: a multi-dimensional approach to measuring security needs. *International Journal of Forensic Mental Health* **4**: 39–52. (**597**)

Collins W (1859–60) The Woman in White. In *All the Year Round* (serialised). London: Sampson Low. (**219**)

Collinshaw S, Goodman R, Ford T, Rabe-Hesketh S, and Pickles A (2009) How far are associations between child, family and community factors and child psychopathology informant-specific and informant-general? *Journal of Child Psychology and Psychiatry* **50**: 571–80. (**483**)

Collomb H (1972) Public health and psychiatry in Africa. In *Biomedical Lectures: AFRO Technical Paper 1*. Brazzaville, Congo: World Health Organization. (**113**)

Collomb H (1979) De l'ethnopsychiatrie à la psychiatrie sociale. *Canadian Journal of Psychiatry* **24**: 459–70. (**113**)

Colom F, Vieta E, Sánchez-Moreno J, etal. (2004) Psychoeducation in bipolar patients with comorbid personality disorders. *Bipolar Disorders* **6**: 294–8. (**409**)

Comings DE, Muhleman D, Gade R, et al. (1997) Cannabinoid receptor gene (CNR1): association with i.v. drug use. *Molecular Psychiatry* **2**: 161–8. (**206**)

Commission for Healthcare Audit and Inspection (2007) Annual Report 2006/7. House of Commons, London. (**489**)

Commission on the Review of the National Policy Toward Gambling (1976) *Gambling in America*. Washington, DC: US Government Printing Office. (**467**)

Commons TAJ and Lewis A (2008) Targeted clinical education for staff attitudes towards deliberate self-harm in borderline personality disorder: random controlled trial. *Australian and New Zealand Journal of Psychiatry* **42**: 981–8. (**400**)

Compton MT, Weiss PS, West JC, and Kaslow NJ (2005) The associations between substance use disorders, and axis IV psychosocial problems. *Social Psychiatry and Psychiatric Epidemiology* **40**: 939–46. (**346**)

Conduct Problems Prevention Research Group (1999a) Initial report of the fast track prevention trial for conduct problems, I: The high-risk sample. *Journal of Consulting and Clinical Psychology* **67**: 631–47. (**184**)

Conduct Problems Prevention Research Group (1999b) Initial impact of the fast track prevention trial for conduct problems, II: classroom effect. *Journal of Consulting and Clinical Psychology* **67**: 648–57. (**184**)

Confidential Enquiry into Maternal and Child Health (CEMACH) (2007) *Saving mothers' lives: reviewing maternal deaths to make motherhood safer – 2003–2005*. London: Confidential Enquiry into Maternal and Child Health. (**466**)

Congdon MH and Abels BS (1983) *Multiple Personality: Etiology, Diagnosis and Treatment*. New York: Human Sciences. (**426**)

Conners CK (1971) Recent drug studies with children. *Journal of Learning Disability* **4**: 467–83. (**484**)

Connor M and Norman P (1996) *Predicting Health Behaviour*. Buckingham,UK: Open UNiveristy Press. (**399**)

Cook C (2000) Prevention and treatment of Wernicke–Korsakoff syndrome. *Alcohol and Alcoholism* **35**(1): 19–20. (**439**)

Cook EH and Scherer SW (2008) Copy-number variations associated with neuropsychiatric conditions. *Nature* **455**(7215): 919–23. (**209**)

Cook EH, Stein MA, Ellison T, Unis AS, and Levinthal BL (1995) Attention deficit hyperactivity disorder and whole blood serotonin levels: effects of comorbidity. *Psychiatry Research* **57**: 13–20. (**307**)

Cook P Moore MJ (1993) Economic perspectives on reducing alcohol-related violence. In SE Martin (ed) *Alcohol and Interpersonal Violence: Fostering Multidisciplinary Perspectives*. Washington: Narional Institute on Alcohol Abuse Alcoholism, National Institute of Health. (**705**)

Cooke DJ (1994) *Psychological disturbance amongst prisoners*. Scottish Prison Service, Occasional Papers, Report No. 3/1994. (**653**)

Cooke DJ and Michie C (1997) An item response theory analysis of the Hare Psychopathy Checklist-Revised. *Psychological Assessment* **9**: 3–14. (**385, 513**)

Cooke DJ and Michie C (1999) Psychopathy across cultures: North America and Scotland compared. *Journal of Abnormal Psychology* **108**: 55–68. (**385**)

References

Cooke DJ and Michie C (2010) Limitations of diagnostic precision and predictive utility in the individual case: a challenge for forensic practice. *Law and Human Behavior* **34**: 259–74. (**533**)

Cookson H (1992) Alcohol use and offence type in young offenders. *British Journal of Criminology* **32**: 352–60. (**282**)

Coolidge FL, Marle PD, van Horn SA and Segal DL (2011) Clinical syndromes, personality disorders and neurocognitive differences in male and female inmates. *Behavioral Sciences and the Law* **29**: 741–51. (**514**)

Cools R, Blackwell A, Clark L, et al. (2005) Tryptophan depletion disrupts the motivational guidance of goal-directed behavior as a function of trait impulsivity. *Neuropsychopharmacology* **30**: 1362–73. (**309**)

Coomaraswamy KS and Shepherd JP (2003) Predictors and severity of injury in assaults with bar glasses and bottles. *Injury Prevention* **9**: 81–4. (**705**)

Cooper S and Hopper D (2004) What motivates offenders to address their offending behaviour? *Forensic Update* **79**: 4–10. (**573**)

Cooper S-A, Smiley E, Morrison J, Williamson A and Allan L (2007) Mental ill-health in adults with intellectual disabilities: Prevalence and associated factors. *British Journal of Psychiatry* **190**: 27–35. (**317**)

Copas J and Marshall P (1998) The offender group reconviction scale: a statistical reconviction score for use by probation officers. *Applied Statistics* **47**: 159–71. (**538**)

Copeland J and Maxwell JC (2007) Cannabis treatment outcomes among legally coerced and non-coerced adults. *BMC Public Health* **7**: 111. (**467**)

Copeland J, Chen R, Dewey M, et al. (1999) Community-based case-control study of depression in older people. *British Journal of Psychiatry* **175**: 340–7. (**526**)

Corbett C (2003) *Car Crime*. Cullompton, Devon: Willan Publishing. (**277**)

Corbett M, Duggan C, and Larkin E (1998) Substance misuse and violence: a comparison of special hospital inpatients diagnosed with either schizophrenia or personality disorder. *Criminal Behaviour and Mental Health* **8**: 311–21. (**444**)

Cordess C (2006) The application of high-security models of care to other less secure settings. In C Newrith, C Meux, PJ Taylor, (eds) *Personality Disorder and Serious Offending. Hospital Treatment Models*. London: Hodder Arnold, pp. 258–72. (**400**)

Cordess C (ed) (2001) *Confidentiality and Mental Health*. London: Jessica Kingsley. (**662**)

Cordess C and Williams AH (1996) The Criminal Act and Acting Out. In C Cordess, M Cox (eds) *Forensic Psychotherapy, Crime, Psychodynamics and the Offender Patient*. London: Jessica Kingsley, pp. 13–21. (**579, 581**)

Cormac I and Jenkins P (1999) Understanding the importance of oral health in psychiatric patients. *Advances in Psychiatric Treatment* **5**: 53–60. (**568**)

Cormac I, Creasey S, McNeill A, et al. (2010) Impact of a total smoking ban in a high secure hospital. *The Psychiatrist* **34**: 413–7. (**568**)

Cormac I, Martin D, and Ferriter M (2004) Improving the physical health of long-stay psychiatric in-patients. *Advances in Psychiatric Treatment* **10**: 107–15. (**568**)

Cornelius JR, Clark DB, Salloum IM, Bukstein OG, and Kelly TM (2004) Interventions in suicidal alcoholics. *Alcoholism: Clinical and Experimental Research* **28**: 89S–96S. (**459**)

Cornelius JR, Soloff PH, Perel JM, and Ulrich RF (1990) Fluoxetine trial in borderline personality disorder. *Psychopharmacology Bulletin* **26**: 151–4. (**311**)

Cornell DG, Benedek EP, and Benedek BA (1987) Juvenile homicide. Prior adjustment and a proposed typology. *American Journal of Orthopsychiatry* **57**: 383–93. (**494**)

Cornish DB and Clarke RVG (1975) Residential treatment and its effects on delinquency. Home Office Research Studies 32. London: Home office. (**412**)

Correll CU, Rummel-Kluge C, Corves C, Kane JM, and Leucht S (2009) Antipsychotic combinations vs monotherapy in schizophrenia: a meta-analysis of randomised controlled trials. *Schizophrenia Bulletin* **35**: 443–57. (**360**)

Corrigan P (2004) Target-specific stigma change: a strategy for impacting mental illness stigma. *Psychiatric Rehabilitation Journal* **28**: 113–21. (**579**)

Corston J (2007) *The Corston Report*. London: Home Office. (**512, 517, 619, 648**)

Corvin A, Craddock N, and Sullivan PF (2010) Genome-wide association studies: a primer. *Psychological Medicine* **40**: 1063–77. (**194**)

Corvo K and Johnson PJ (2003) Vilification of the 'batterer': how blame shapes domestic violence policy and interventions. *Aggression and Violent Behavior* **8**: 259–81. (**447**)

Cosden M, Ellens J, Schnell J, and Yamini-Diouf Y (2005) Efficacy of a mental health court with assertive community treatment. *Behavioral Sciences and the Law* **23**: 199–214. (**364, 640**)

Costa P and McCrae R (1992a) *Revised NEO Personality Inventory (NEO PI-R) and NEO Five-Factor Inventory (NEO-FFI): professional manual*. Odessa, FL: Psychological Assessment Resources. (**385**)

Costa PT and McCrae RR (1992b) Normal personality assessment in clinical practice: the NEO personality inventory. *Psychological Assessment* **4**: 5–13. (**388**)

Costello EJ, Edeibrook C, and Costell AJ (1985) Validity of the NIMH diagnostic interview schedule for children: a comparison between psychiatric and paediatric referrals. *Journal of Abnormal Child Psychology* **13**: 579–95. (**484**)

Cotton NS (1979) The familial incidence of alcoholism. *Journal of Studies on Alcohol* **40**: 89–116. (**201**)

Coughlan AK, Rix KJB, and Neumann V (2005) Assessing decision-making and capacity in minimally-aware patients. *Medicine, Science and the Law* **45**: 249–55. (**166**)

Council of Europe Committee for the Prevention of Torture, documents and visits: Ireland. http://www.cpt.coe.int/en/states/irl.htm (**xxxi, 133, 616**)

Council of Europe, Committee of Ministers (1983) *Recommendation No. R (83) 2 of the Committee of Ministers to Member States Concerning the Legal Protection of Persons Suffering from Mental Disorder Placed as Involuntary Patients.* (**106**)

Council of Europe, Committee of Ministers (2004) *Recommendation No. Rec(2004)10 of the Committee of Ministers to Member States Concerning the Protection of the Human Rights and Dignity of Persons with Mental Disorder and its Explanatory Memorandum.* https://wcd.coe.int/ViewDoc.jsp?id=775685&Site=CM (**106, 109**)

Courtney J and Rose J (2004) The effectiveness of treatment for male sex offenders with learning disabilities: a review of the literature. *Journal of Sexual Aggression* **10**: 215–36. (**263, 328**)

Courts Service (2002) Final Evaluation of the Pilot Drug Court. Farrell Grant Sparks Consulting. http://www.justiceie/en/JELR/finalevalpilotdrug.pdf (**657**)

Cousins R, Davies ADM, Turnbull CJ, and Plafer JR (2002) Assessing care giving distress: a conceptual analysis and a brief scale. *British Journal of Clinical Psychology* **41**: 387–403. (**355**)

Couturier JL and Nicolson R (2002) A retrospective assessment of citalopram in children and adolescents with pervasive developmental disorders. *Journal of Clinical Child and Adolescent Psychopharmacology* **12**: 243–8. (**310**)

Covault J, Tennen H, Armeli S, et al. (2007) Interactive effects of the serotonin transporter 5-HTTLPR polymorphism and stressful life events on college student drinking and drug use. *Biological Psychiatry* **61**: 609–16. (**207**)

Cox M (1978) *Structuring the Therapeutic Process. Compromise with Chaos.* Oxford: Pergamon. (**551, 570**)

Cox M (1986) The 'holding function' of dynamic psychotherapy in a custodial setting: a review. *Journal of the Royal Society of Medicine* **79**: 162–64. (**583, 584**)

Cox M (1992) *Shakespeare comes to Broadmoor.* London: Jessica Kingsley. (**Preface**)

Cox M and Theilgaard A (1994) *Shakespeare as Prompter.* London: Jessica Kingsley. (**Preface**)

Coxell A, King M, Mezey G, and Gordon D (1999) Lifetime prevalence, characteristics, and associated problems of non-consensual sex in men: cross sectional survey. *British Medical Journal* **318**(7187): 846–50. (**715**)

Coyne AC, Reichman WE, and Berbig LJ (1993) The relationship. Between dementia and elder abuse. *American Journal of Psychiatry* **150**: 643–6. (**227**)

Craig AM and Kang Y (2007) Neurexin-neuroligin signaling in synapse development. *Current Opinion in Neurobiology* **17**(1): 43–52. (**209**)

Craig JS, Hatton C, Craig FB, and Bentall RP (2004) Persecutory beliefs, attributions and theory of mind: comparison of patients with paranoid delusions, Asperger's syndrome and healthy controls. *Schizophrenia Research* **69**: 29–33. (**487**)

Craig LA, Browne K, Beech A, and Stringer I (2006) Differences in personality and risk characteristics in sex, violent and general offenders. *Criminal Behaviour and Mental Health 16: 183–94.* (**388**)

Craig M (2004) Perinatal risk factors for neonaticide and infant homicide: can we identify those at risk? *Journal of the Royal Society of Medicine* **97**: 57–61. (**510**)

Craig MC, Catani M, Deeley Q, et al. (2009) Altered connections on the road to psychopathy. *Molecular Psychiatry* **14**(10): 946–53. (**302**)

Craig TJ (1982) An epidemiologic study of problems associated with violence among psychiatric inpatients. *American Journal of Psychiatry* **139**: 1262–6. (**337**)

Craissati J (1998) *Child Sexual Abusers: A Community Treatment Approach.* Hove, UK: Psychology Press. (**258**)

Craissati J (2004) *Managing High Risk Sex Offenders in the Community – A Psychological Approach.* London: Routledge. (**259**)

Craissati J and Beech A (2001) Attrition in a community treatment program for child sexual abusers. *Journal of Interpersonal Violence* **16**: 205–21. (**262, 607, 609**)

Craissati J and Hodes P (1992) Mentally ill sex offenders: the experience of a regional secure unit. *British Journal of Psychiatry* **161**: 846–9. (**577**)

Craissati J, Horne L, and Taylor R (2002) *Effective Treatment Models for Personality Disordered Offenders.* www.bulger.co.uk/prison/Personality%20Disorder%20Treatment.doc. (**606, 609**)

Craissati J, McClurg G, and Browne K (2002) The parental bonding experiences of sex offenders: a comparison between child molesters and rapists. *Child Abuse and Neglect* **26**: 909–21. (**606, 609**)

Craissati J, Webb L, and Keen S (2005) *Personality Disordered Sex Offenders.* Oxleas NHS Trust. (**606**)

Crancer A and Quiring D (1969) The mentally ill as motor vehicle operators. *American Journal of Psychiatry* **126**: 807–13. (**277**)

Creamer M, O'Donnell ML, and Pattison P (2005) Amnesia, traumatic brain injury, and posttraumatic stress disorder: a methodological inquiry. *Behaviour Research and Therapy* **43**: 1383–9. (**713**)

Crean J, Richards JB and de Wit H (2002) Effect of tryptophan depletion on impulsive behavior in men with and without a family history of alcoholism. *Behavioural Brain Research* **136**: 349–57. (**309**)

Cremona A (1986) Mad drivers: psychiatric illness and driving performance. *British Journal of Hospital Medicine* **35**: 193–5. (**278**)

Cretney A, Davis G, Clarkson C, and Shepherd JP (1994) Assaults: the relationship between seriousness, criminalization and punishment. *Criminal Law Review*: 4–20. (**700**)

Crichton J (2005) Adults with incapacity. In L Thomson, J McManus (eds) *Mental Health and Scots Law in Practice.* Edinburgh, UK: Greens. (**91**)

Crichton J and Sheppard D (1996) Psychiatric inquiries: learning the lessons. In J Peay (Ed) *Inquiries after Homicide.* London: Duckworth, pp. 65–78. (**696**)

Crichton J, Darjee R, and Chiswick D (2004) Diminished responsibility in Scotland: new case law. *Journal of Forensic Psychiatry and Psychology* **15**: 552–65. (**96**)

Crichton JHM (2000) Mental incapacity in consent to treatment: the Scottish experience. *Journal of Forensic Psychiatry* **11**: 457–64. (**91**)

Criminal Justice Inspection Northern Ireland. (2010) *Not a Marginal Issue – Mental Health and the Criminal Justice System in Northern Ireland*. http://www.cjini.org/CJNI/files/24/24d6cd45-20bb-4f81-9e34-81ea59594650.pdf (**655**)

Criminal Justice System (2004) *No Witness, No Justice: The National Victim and Witness Care Programme*. http://www.cps.gov.uk/legal/assets/uploads/files/024239%20-%20witness%20care%20project%20minimum%20requirements.pdf (**708**)

Criminal Justice System (2005) *The Code of Practice for Victims of Crime*. London: Home Office. http://www.cps.gov.uk/victims_witnesses/victims_code.pdf (**709**)

Crisp AH, Hsu LK, and Harding B (1980) The starving hoarder and voracious spender: stealing in anorexia nervosa. *Journal of Psychosomatic Research* **24**: 225–31. (**270**)

Critchley HD, Simmons A, Daly EM, et al. (2000) Prefrontal and medial temporal correlates of repetitive violence to self and others. *Biological Psychiatry* **47**: 928–34. (**301**)

Crockett LJ, Raymond Bingham C, Chopak JS, and Vicary JR (1996) Timing of first sexual intercourse: the role of social control, social learning, and problem behavior. *Journal of Youth and Adolescence* **25**: 89–111. (**450**)

Crome I, Ghodse H, Gilvarry E, and McArdle P (2004) *Young people and substance misuse*. London: Gaskell. (**465**)

Crome IB (2005) Drug abuse and the older person: a contradiction in terms? In J Pathy, J Morley, A Sinclair (eds) *Principles and practice of geriatric medicine*. Chichester, UK: Wiley, pp. 1191–204. (**467**)

Crome IB and Bloor R (2006a) Part 1: older substance misusers still deserve better services – an update. *Reviews in Clinical Gerontology* **15**: 125–33. (**467**)

Crome IB and Bloor R (2006b) Part 2: Older substance misusers still deserve better diagnosis – an update. *Reviews in Clinical Gerontology* **16**: 255–62. (**467**)

Crome IB and Bloor R (2007) Part 3: older substance misusers still deserve better treatment interventions – an update. *Reviews in Clinical Gerontology* **16**: 45–47. (**467**)

Crome IB and Day E (2002) Substance misuse. In A Elder, J Holmes (eds) *Mental Health in Primary Care* Oxford: Oxford University Press, pp. 221–40. (**452**)

Crome IB and Ghodse A-H (2007) Drug misuse in medical patients. In G Lloyd and E Guthrie (eds) *Handbook of liaison psychiatry*. Cambridge: Cambridge University Press, pp. 180–220. (**458, 461, 465**)

Crome IB and Ismail KMK (2010) Substance misuse in pregnancy. In R Powrie, M Greene, W Camann (eds) *de Swiet's Medical disorders in obstetric practice*, 5th edn. Chichester: Wiley. (**464**)

Crome IB and Kumar M (2007) Epidemiology of drug and alcohol use in young women. *Seminars in Fetal and Neonatal Medicine* **12**: 98–105. (**463**)

Crome IB, Bloor R, and Thom B (2006) Screening for illicit drug use in psychiatric hospitals: whose job is it? *Advances in Psychiatric Treatment* **12**: 375–83. (**456**)

Cross T and Saxe L (2001) Polygraph testing and sexual abuse: the lure of the magic lasso. *Child Maltreatment* **6**: 195–206. (**256**)

Crossland S, Burns M, Leach C, and Quinn P (2005) Needs assessment in forensic learning disability. *Medicine Science and the Law* **45**: 147–53. (**316**)

Crow MJ and Ridley J (1990) *Therapy with Couples*. Oxford: Basil Blackwell. (**373**)

Crown Prosecution Service (2002) *Justice For All*. Home Office: London. http://www.cps.gov.uk/publications/docs/jfawhitepaper.pdf (**708**)

Crown Prosecution Service (2006) *Disclosure Manual – Annex K. Disclosure: Experts' Evidence and Unused Material – Guidance Booklet for Experts*. UK Ministry of Justice. (**22, 23**)

Crown Prosecution Service (2011) *Prostitution and Exploitation of Prostitution*. www.cps.gov.uk/legal/p_to_r/prostitution_and_exploitation_of_prostitution/Index.html (**503**)

Cuellar AE, Snowden LM, and Ewing T (2007) Criminal records of persons served in the public mental health system. *Psychiatric Services* **58**: 114–20. (**279**)

Cuijpers P (1999) The effect of family interventions on relatives' burden: a meta-analysis. *Journal of Mental Health* **8**: 275–85. (**363**)

Cullen EC (1994) Grendon: a therapeutic prison that works. *Therapeutic Communities* **15**: 301–11. (**579**)

Cullen WD (Lord) (1996) *The Public Inquiry into the Shootings at Dunblane Primary School on 13 March 1996* Cm. 3386 TSO. www.archive.official-documents.co.uk/document/scottish/dunblane/dunblane.htm (**238**)

Cummings NA and Sobel SB (1985) Malpractice insurance: update on sex claims. *Psychotherapy* **22**: 186–8. (**682**)

Cuppleditch Land Evans W (2005) *Re-Offending of Adults: Results From the 2002 Cohort. Home Office Statistical Bulletin 25/05*. London: Home Office. (**269**)

Cure S, Chua WL, Duggan L, and Adams C (2005) Randomised controlled trials relevant to aggressive and violent people, 1955–2000: a survey. *British Journal of Psychiatry* **186**: 185–9. (**357**)

Curtin K, Monks S, Wright B, Duffy, D., Linehan, S., Kennedy, H. (2009) Psychiatric morbidity in male remanded and sentenced committals to Irish prisons. *Irish Journal of Psychological Medicine* **26**: 169–173. (**110, 616, 657**)

Cutrona CE, Cadoret RJ, Suhr JA, et al. (1994) Interpersonal variables in the prediction of alcoholism among adoptees: evidence for gene–environment interactions. *Comprehensive Psychiatry* **35**: 171–9. (**207**)

Cutter HSG, Jones WC, Maloof BA, and Kurtz NR (1979) Pain as a joint function of alcohol intake and customary reasons for drinking. *International Journal of the Addictions* **14**: 173–82. (**440**)

D'Arcy M and Gosling P (1998) *Abuse of Trust: Frank Beck and the Leicestershire Children's Homes Scandal*. London: Bowerdean. (**414**)

D'Ardenne P, Farmer E, Ruaro L, and Priebe S (2007) Not lost in translation: protocols for interpreting trauma-focused CBT. *Behavioural and Cognitive Psychotherapy* **35**: 303–16. (**729**) d'Orban PT (1971) Social and psychiatric aspects of female crime. *Medical Science and the Law* **11**: 104–16. (**498, 499, 501**)

d'Orban PT (1979) Women who kill their children. *British Journal of Psychiatry* **134**: 560–71. (**29, 164, 509**)

d'Orban PT (1983) Medicolegal aspects of the premenstrual syndrome. *British Journal of Hospital Medicine* **30**: 404–9. (**501**)

d'Orbán PT (1989) Steroid induced psychosis. *Lancet* **2**: 694.

d'Orbán PT and O'Connor A (1989) Women who kill their parents. *British Journal of Psychiatry* **154**: 27–33. (**231, 507**)

D'Silva K and Duggan C (2002) Service innovations: development of a psychoeducational programme for patients with personality disorder. *Psychiatric Bulletin* **26**: 268–71. (**401, 408, 573**)

D'Silva K and Ferriter M (2003) Substance use by the mentally disordered committing serious offences – a high-security hospital study. *Journal of Forensic Psychiatry and Psychology* **14**: 178–93. (**575**)

D'Silva K, Duggan C, and McCarthy L (2004) Does treatment really make psychopaths worse? A review of the evidence. *Journal of Personality Disorders* **18**: 163–77. (**262, 416**)

Daffern M, Howells K, Hamilton L, et al. (2009) The impact of structured risk assessments followed by management recommendations on aggression in patients with personality disorder. *Journal of Forensic Psychiatry and Psychology* **20**: 661–79. (**549**)

Dahle KP (2006) Strengths and limitations of actuarial prediction of criminal reoffence in a German prison sample: a comparative study of LSI-R, HCR-20 and PCL-R. *International Journal of Law and Psychiatry* **29**(5): 431–42. (**537**)

Dalal B, Larkin E, Leese M, and Taylor PJ (1999) Clozapine treatment of long-standing schizophrenia and serious violence: a two-year follow-up study of the first 50 patients treated with clozapine in Rampton high security hospital. *Criminal Behaviour and Mental Health* **9**: 168–78. (**564**)

Dale C, Wallis EV, and Taylor PJ (1999) Professional, contractual and volunteer relationships. In PJ Taylor, T Swan (eds) *Couples in Care and Custody*. Oxford: Butterworth Heinemann. (**690**)

Dale P, Davies M, Morrison T, and Wates J (1986) *Dangerous Families*. London: Tavistock. (**714**)

Dale PG (1980) Lithium therapy in aggressive mentally subnormal patients. *British Journal of Psychiatry,* 137, 469–74. (**566**)

Daly M and Wilson M (1988) *Homicide*. New York: Aldine de Gruyter. (**372**)

Daly M, Wilson M, and Weghorst SJ (1982) Male sexual jealousy. *Ethology and Sociobiology* **3**: 11–27. (**372**)

Damasio AR (1995) On some functions of the human prefrontal cortex. *Annals of the New York Academy of Science* **769**: 241–51. (**298**)

Damasio AR (1996) The somatic marker hypothesis and the possible functions of the prefrontal cortex. *Philosophical Transactions of the Royal Society London,* (B series) **351**: 1413–20. (**305**)

Damasio H, Grabowski T, Frank R, Galaburda AM, and Damasio AR (1994) The return of Phineas Gage: clues about the brain from the skull of a famous patient. *Science* **264**: 1102–5. (**298**)

Daniels DN, Gilula MF, and Ochberg F (1970) *Violence and the Struggle for Existence*. Boston, MA: Little, Brown. (**211**)

Darjee R (2005a) Psychiatric defences. In L Thomson, J McManus (eds) *Mental Health and Scots Law in Practice*. Edinburgh, UK: Greens. (**94**)

Darjee R (2005b) Legislation for mentally disordered offenders. In L Thomson, J McManus (eds) *Mental Health and Scots Law in Practice*. Edinburgh, UK: Greens. (**99**)

Darjee R and Crichton J (2003) Personality disorder and the law in Scotland: a historical perspective. *Journal of Forensic Psychiatry and Psychology* **14**: 394–425. (**90, 96**)

Darjee R and Crichton J (2004) New mental health legislation. *British Medical Journal* **329**: 634–5. (**90**)

Darjee R and Crichton J (2005) Reid v UK: restricted patients and the European Convention on Human Rights. *Journal of Forensic Psychiatry and Psychology* **16**: 508–22. (**99**)

Darjee R, Crichton J, and Thomson L (2000) Crime and punishment (Scotland) act 1997: a study of psychiatrists' views towards the hospital direction. *Journal of Forensic Psychiatry* **11**: 608–20. (**99**)

Darjee R, Crichton J, and Thomson L (2002) Crime and Punishment (Scotland) Act 1997: a study of sentencers' views towards the hospital direction. *Medicine Science and the Law* **42**: 76–86. (**99**)

Darjee R, McCall-Smith A, Crichton J, and Chiswick D (1999) Detention of patient with psychopathic disorder in Scotland: 'Canons Park' called into question by house of lords. *Journal of Forensic Psychiatry* **10**: 649–58. (**90**)

Darwin C (1883) *The Descent of Man*, 2nd edn. London: John Murray. (**7**)

David AS (1990) Insight and psychosis. *British Journal of Psychiatry* **156**: 798–808. (**12, 392**)

Davidson JR, Hughes D, Blazer DG, and George LK (1991) Post-traumatic stress disorder in the community: an epidemiological study. *Psychological Medicine* **21**: 713–21. (**712**)

Davidson K (2000) *Cognitive Therapy for Personality Disorder*. Oxford: Butterworth-Heinemann. (**401, 569, 570**)

Davidson K and Tyrer P (1996) Cognitive therapy for antisocial and borderline personality disorders: single case study series. *British Journal of Clinical Psychology* **35**: 413–29. (**574**)

Davidson K, Norrie J, Tyrer P, et al. (2006) The effectiveness of cognitive behaviour therapy for borderline personality disorder: results from the Borderline Personality Disorder Study of Cognitive Therapy (BOSCOT) trial. *Journal of Personality Disorders* **20**: 450–65. (**410**)

Davidson KM, Espie CJ, and Lammie C (2011) Conducting randomised controlled trials: finding better ways to explain research to people with antisocial personality disorder who have low literacy levels. *Criminal Behaviour and Mental Health* **21**: 265–78. (**670**)

Davidson M, Humphreys MS, Johnstone EC, and Cunningham Owens DG (1995) Prevalence of psychiatric morbidity among remand prisoners in Scotland. *British Journal of Psychiatry* **167**: 545–548. (**315, 653**)

Davidson M, Landerman LR, and Clary CM (2004) Improvement of anger at one week predicts the effects of sertaline and placebo in PTSD. *Journal of Psychiatric Research* **38**: 497–502. (**310**)

Davidson RJ, Putnam KM, and Larson CL (2000) Dysfunction in the neural circuitry of emotion regulation – a possible prelude to violence. *Science* **289**: 591–4. (**198, 298**)

Davies J, Howells K, and Jones L (2007) Evaluating innovative treatments in forensic mental health: a role for single case methodology? *Journal of Forensic Psychiatry and Psychology* **18**: 353–67. (**569**)

Davies J, Jones L and Howells K (2010) Evaluating individual change. Chapter 18 in *Offender Paralleling Behaviour. A Case Formulation Approach to Offender Assessment and Intervention.* Wiley: Chichester. pp. 287–302. (**572**)

Davies S, Clarke M, Hollin C, and Duggan C (2007) Long-term outcomes after discharge from medium secure care: a cause for concern. *British Journal of Psychiatry* **191**: 70–74. (**605**)

Davis J (1962) Suicide by fire. *Journal of Forensic Science* **7**: 383–7. (**276**)

Davis JE (2008) Book review, Children and sexuality: from the Greeks to the great war, ed by George Rousseau (*see below*) *Social History of Medicine* **21**: 423–5. (**249**)

Davis JM, Chen N, and Glick ID (2003) A meta-analysis of the efficacy of second-generation antipsychotics. *Archives of General Psychiatry* **60**: 553–64. (**359, 520, 560**)

Davis P, McClure RJ, Rolfe K, et al. (1998) Procedures, placement, and risks of further abuse after Munchausen syndrome by proxy, non-accidental poisoning, and non-accidental suffocation. *Archives of Diseases in Childhood* **78**: 217–21. (**506**)

Davis PJ and Gibson MG (2000) Recognition of posed and genuine facial expressions of emotion in paranoid and nonparanoid schizophrenia. *Journal of Abnormal Psychology* **109**: 445–50. (**351**)

Davison SE, Leese M, and Taylor PJ (2001) Examination of the screening properties of the personality diagnostic questionnaire 4+ (PDQ 4+) in a prison population. *Journal of Personality Disorders* **15**: 180–94. (**388**)

Day A, Howells K, Casey S, Ward T, and Birgden A (2007) Treatment readiness: and overview of Australasian work. *Issues in Forensic Psychology* **7**: 21–5. (**573**)

Day E and Crome IB (2002) Physical health problems. In T Petersen, A McBride (eds) *Working with substance users.* London: Routledge, pp. 174–188. (**452**)

Day JC, Bentall RP, Roberts C, et al. (2005) The impact of clinical variables and relationships with health professionals. *Archives of General Psychiatry* **62**: 717–24. (**356**)

Day K (1993) Crime and mental retardation: a review. In K Howells, CR Hollin (eds) *Clinical Approaches to the Mentally Disordered Offender.* Chichester, UK: Wiley. (**329**)

Day K (1997) Sex offenders with learning disability. In SG Read (ed) *Psychiatry and Learning disability.* London: Saunders, pp. 278–306. (**317**)

Dayson D (1993) The TAPS project. 12: crime, vagrancy, death and readmission of the long-term mentally Ill during their first year of local reprovision. *British Journal of Psychiatry* **162**: 40–4. (**281**)

De Clérambault G (1942) Les psychoses passionelles. In *Oeuvres Psychiatriques*, pp. 315–322. Paris: Frénésc. (**367**)

de Coster S and Heimer K (2001) The relationship between law violation and depression: an interactionist analysis. *Criminology* **39**: 799–836. (**281**)

de Graaf R, Bijl RV, Spijker J, Beekman AT, and Vollebergh WA (2003) Temporal sequencing of lifetime mood disorders in relation to comorbid anxiety and substance use disorders – findings from the Netherlands mental health survey and incidence study. *Social Psychiatry and Psychiatric Epidemiology* **38**(1): 1–11. (**463**)

De la Fuente JM and Lotstra F (1994) A trial of carbamazepine in borderline personality disorder. *European Neuropsychopharmacology* **4**: 479–86. (**404**)

De Leon G (1973) The Phoenix House therapeutic community: changes in psychopathological signs. *Archives of General Psychiatry* **28**: 131–5. (**412**)

de Oliveira-Souza R, Hare RD, Bramati IE, et al. (2008) Psychopathy as a disorder of the moral brain: fronto-temporo-limbic grey matter reductions demonstrated by voxel-based morphometry. *Neuroimage* **40**(3): 1202–13. (**300**)

de Silva P (2004) Jealousy in couple relationships. Invited Essay. *Behaviour Change* **21**: 1–13. (**373**)

de Vogel V and de Ruiter C (2004) Differences between clinicians and researchers in assessing risk of violence in forensic psychiatric patients. *Journal of Forensic Psychiatry and Psychology* **15**: 145–64. (**537**)

de Vogel V and de Ruiter C (2005) The HCR-20 in personality disordered female offenders: a comparison with a matched sample of males. *Clinical Psychology and Psychotherapy* **12**: 226–40. (**537, 538, 539**)

de Vogel V and de Ruiter C (2006) Structured professional judgment of violence risk in forensic clinical practice: a prospective study into the predictive validity of the Dutch HCR-20. *Psychology Crime and Law* **12**: 321–36. (**537**)

de Young D, Peck R, and Helander C (1997) Estimating the exposure and fatal crash rates of suspended/revoked and unlicensed drivers in California. *Accident Analysis and Prevention* **29**(1): 17–23. (**278**)

de Zulueta F (2006a) Terror breeds terrorists. *Medicine, Conflict and Survival* **22**: 13–25. (**717, 720**)

de Zulueta F (2006b) *From Pain to Violence, the Roots of Human Destructiveness,* 2nd edn. Chichester, UK: John Wiley and Sons. (**216, 717**)

de Zulueta F (2006c) The role of the traumatic attachment in the assessment and treatment of adults with a history of childhood abuse and neglect. *British Journal of Forensic Practice* **8**: 4–15. (**717**)

de Zulueta F (2006d) The treatment of psychological trauma from the perspective of attachment research. *Journal of Family Therapy* **28**: 334–51. (**719, 721**)

Dean K, Moran P, Fahy T, et al. (2007) Predictors of violent victimization amongst those with psychosis. *Acta Psychiatrica Scandinavica* **116**: 345–53. (**344**)

Deeley Q, Daly E, Surguladze S, et al. (2006) Facial emotion processing in criminal psychopathy. Preliminary functional magnetic resonance imaging study. *British Journal of Psychiatry* **189**: 533–9. (**304, 305**)

Deffenbacher JL, Dahlen ER, Lynch RS, Morris CD, and Gowensmith WW (2002) An application of Beck's cognitive therapy to general anger treatment. *Cognitive Therapy and Research* **24**: 689–97. (**575**)

Deffenbacher K (1988) Eyewitness research: the next ten years. In M Gruneberg, P Morris, R Sykes (eds) *Practical Aspects of Memory*, Vol. 1. Chichester, UK: Wiley. (**296**)

Deffenbacher KA, Bornstein BH, Penrod SD, and McGorty EK (2004) A meta-analytic review of the effects of high stress on eyewitness memory. *Law and Human Behavior* **28**: 687–706. (**161**)

DeFuentes-Merillas L, Koeter MW, Schippers GM, and van den Brink W (2004) Temporal stability of scratchcard gambling among adult scratchcard buyers two years later. *Addiction* **99**: 117–27. (**472**)

Del Ben CM, Deakin JFW, McKie S, et al. (2005) The effect of citalopram pretreatment on neuronal responses to neuropsychological tasks in normal volunteers: An fMRI study. *Neuropsychopharmacology* **30**: 1724–34. (**310**)

Del Rio MC, Gonzalez-Luque JC, and Alvarez FJ (2001) Alcohol-related problems and fitness to drive. *Alcohol and Alcoholism* **36**(3): 256–61. (**278**)

Delamonthe T (2010) Good and Bad Coroner Stories. *British Medical Journal*, 340, c1064. (**55**)

Delbrueck A (1891) *Die Pathologischen Luge and Die Psychisch Abnormen Schwindler*. Stuttgart, Germany: Karger. (**421**)

Delgado-Escueta AV, Mattson RH, King L, et al. (2002) The nature of aggression during epileptic seizures. *Epilepsy and behaviour* **3**: 550–6. (**286**)

Dell S (1984) *Murder into Manslaughter*. Maudsley Monograph No. 27. Oxford: Oxford University Press. (**30**)

Dell S, Robertson G, James K, and Grounds A (1993) Remands and psychiatric assessments in Holloway prison. I. The psychotic population. *British Journal of Psychiatry* **163**: 634–40. (**632**)

Denborough D (1996) *Beyond Prison: Gathering Dreams of Freedom*. Dulwich Centre Publications: Adelaide. (**401**)

Denman C (2010) Boundaries and boundary violations in psychotherapy. In F Subotsky, S Bewley, M Crowe (eds) *Abuse of the Doctor–Patient Relationship*. London: Royal College of Psychiatrists. (**691**)

Dennis M, Godley SH, Diamond G, et al. (2004) The Cannabis Youth Treatment (CYT) Study: main findings from two randomized trials. *Journal of Substance Abuse Treatment* **27**(3): 197–213. (**466**)

Department for Constitutional Affairs (2005) *Hearing the Relatives of Murder and Manslaughter Victims*. London: Consultation Paper HO. http://webarchive.nationalarchives.gov.uk/+/http://www.dca.gov.uk/consult/manslaughter/manslaughter.pdf (**713**)

Department for Constitutional Affairs (DCA) (2007) *Code of Practice, Mental Capacity Act 2005*. London: TSO. (**77, 78, 80, 83**)

Department of Health (1990a) *The Care of Children: Principles and Practice in Regulations and Guidance*. London: HMSO. (**596**)

Department of Health (1990b) *Caring for People. The Care Programme Approach for People with a Mental Illness Referred to Specialist Mental Health Services*. Joint Healt/Social Services Circular. C(90)23/LASSL (90) 11. London: Department of Health. (**607**)

Department of Health (1992) *Choosing with Care: The Report of the Committee of Inquiry into the Selection, Development and Management of Staff in Children's Homes (Warner Report)*. London: HMSO. (**492**)

Department of Health (1993) *Legal Powers on the Care of Mentally ill People in the Community: Report of the Internal Review*. London: Department of Health. (**74, 76**)

Department of Health (1994) *Guidance on the Discharge of Mentally Disordered People and their Continuing Care in the Community*. London: NHS Executive. (**74, 336**)

Department of Health (1995) *Building Bridges: A Guide to Arrangements for Inter-agency Working for the Care and Protection of Severely Mentally Ill People*. London: Department of Health. (**607**)

Department of Health (1997a) *Patient's Charter for Mental Health Services*. London: Department of Health. (**401**)

Department of Health (1997b) *Purchasing Effective Treatment and Care for Drug Misusers: Guidance for Health and Social Services Departments*. London: Stationery Office. (**448**)

Department of Health (1999a) *Review of the Mental Health Act 1983: Report of the Expert committee*. London (Richardson Committee): Department of Health. (**59, 60**)

Department of Health (1999b) *Review of the Mental Health Act 1983: Proposals for Consultation* Cm4480. London: TSO. (**60**)

Department of Health (1999c) *Drug Misuse and Dependence: Guidance on Clinical Management*. London: Stationery Office. (**448**)

Department of Health (1999d) *Secure Futures for Women: Making a Difference*. http://webarchive.nationalarchives.gov.uk/+/www.dh.gov.uk/en/Publicationsandstatistics/Publications/PublicationsPolicyAndGuidance/DH_4077724 (**519**)

Department of Health (1999e) *Effective Care Co-ordination In Mental Health Services: Modernising The Care Programme Approach*. London: Department of Health. http://www.cpaa.org.uk/uploads/1/2/1/3/12136843/effective_care_coordination_1999.pdf (**607, 628**)

Department of Health (1999f) *National Service Framework for Mental Health: Modern standards and service models*. London: Department of Health. http://www.nmhdu.org.uk/silo/files/nsf-for-mental-health.pdf (**628**)

Department of Health (1999g) *Mental Health Act 1983 Code of Practice: Guidance on the Visiting of Psychiatric Patients by Children*. http://westyorkscb.proceduresonline.com/pdfs/HSC%201999%2022%20.pdf (**596**)

Department of Health (1999h) *Secure Futures for Women: Making a Difference*. www.dh.gov.uk/en/Publicationsandstatistics/Publications/PublicationsPolicyAndGuidance/DH_4077724 (**519, 599**)

Department of Health (1999i) *Standing Nursing Midwifery Advisory Committee Report: Assessing Acute Concerns*. London: Department of Health. (**553, 555**)

Department of Health (2000) *An Organisation with a Memory. Report of an Expert Group on Learning from Adverse Events in the NHS.* London: TSO. (**74, 75, 76**)

Department of Health (2001) *Harold Shipman's Clinical Practice 1974–1998: A Clinical Audit Commissioned by the Chief Medical Officer.* (Baker Report) DOH: London. (**688**)

Department of Health (2002) *Safeguarding Children; A Joint Chief. Inspectors' Report on Arrangements to Safeguard Children.* London: Department of Health. http://webarchive.nationalarchives.gov.uk/+/www.dh.gov.uk/en/Publicationsandstatistics/Publications/PublicationsPolicyAndGuidance/DH_4103427 (**220**)

Department of Health (2002) *Women's Mental Health: Into the Mainstream.* http://webarchive.nationalarchives.gov.uk/+/www.dh.gov.uk/en/Consultations/Closedconsultations/DH_4075478 (**519**)

Department of Health (2002a) *Mental Health Policy Implementation Guide: Adult Acute Inpatient Care Provision.* London: Department of Health. (**556**)

Department of Health (2002b) *National Suicide Prevention Strategy for England.* London: Department of Health. http://www.nmhdu.org.uk/silo/files/national-suicide-prevention-strategy-for-england.pdf (**633**)

Department of Health (2002c) *Women's Mental Health: Into the Mainstream.* http://webarchive.nationalarchives.gov.uk/+/www.dh.gov.uk/en/Consultations/Closedconsultations/DH_4075478 (**220, 599**)

Department of Health (2003) *Mainstreaming Gender and Women's Mental Health: Implementation Guidance.* http://www.raphaelhc.org.uk/pdfs/mainstreaming_gender.pdf (**519**)

Department of Health (2003a) *Personality Disorder: No Longer a Diagnosis of Exclusion – Policy Implementation Guidance for the Development of Services for People with Personality Disorder.* London: Department of Health www.dh.gov.uk/en/Publicationsandstatistics/Publications/PublicationsPolicyAndGuidance/DH_4009546

Department of Health (2003b) *Mainstreaming Gender and Women's Mental Health.* www.dh.gov.uk/en/Publicationsandstatistics/Publications/PublicationsPolicyAndGuidance/DH_4072067 (**599**)

Department of Health (2004) *National Service Framework for Children, Young People and Maternity Services.* London: DoH. (**482**)

Department of Health (2005a) *Independent Investigation of Adverse Events in Mental Health Services.* London: Department of Health. (**74**)

Department of Health (2005b) *Responding to Domestic Abuse: A Handbook for Professionals.* Department of Health: London. http://www.domesticviolencelondon.nhs.uk/uploads/downloads/DH_4126619.pdf (**714**)

Department of Health (2007a) *Mental Health Bill. Amending the Mental Health Act 1983: Supervised Community Treatment.* Gateway reference 6420. London: Department of Health. (**76**)

Department of Health (2007b) *Best Practice in Managing Risk. Principles and Evidence for Best Practice in the Assessment and Management of Risk to Self and Others in Mental Health Services.* London: Department of Health. http://webarchive.nationalarchives.gov.uk/+/www.dh.gov.uk/prod_consum_dh/groups/dh_digitalassets/@dh/@en/documents/digitalasset/dh_076512.pdf (**547, 548**)

Department of Health (2008a) *Code of Practice Mental Health Act 1983.* Norwich, UK: The Stationery Office (TSO). http://www.lbhf.gov.uk/Images/Code%20of%20practice%201983%20rev%202008%20dh_087073[1]_tcm21-145032.pdf (**23, 48, 62, 314, 593, 594**)

Department of Health (2008b) *Refocusing the Care Programme Approach.* London: Department of Health. (**65**)

Department of Health (2008c) *Mental Health and Ill Health in Doctors.* London: Department of Health. (**692**)

Department of Health (2010) *See, Think, Act.* Department of Health: London. http://www.rcpsych.ac.uk/pdf/Relational%20Security%20Handbook.pdf (**597**)

Department of Health (2011) *Good Practice Procedure Guideline. The transfer and remission of adult prisoners under s47 and s48 of the Mental Health Act.* London: Department of Health. https://www.gov.uk/government/uploads/system/uploads/attachment_data/file/147364/dh_125768.pdf (**632**)

Department of Health (2012) *Preventing Suicide in England: A Cross-Government Outcomes Strategy to Save Lives. Assessment of Impact on Equalities.* Department of Health: London. https://www.gov.uk/government/uploads/system/uploads/attachment_data/file/137637/Preventing_suicide_equalities_impact.pdf (**633**)

Department of Health and Children (2001) *Quality and Fairness – A Health System for You.* Dublin: Department of Health and Children. www.nuigalway.ie/health_promotion/documents/strategy.pdf (**616**)

Department of Health and Children (2003) *Report of the National Task Force on Medical Staffing (Hanley Report).* Dublin: CSO. www.dohc.ie/publications/hanly_report.html (**616**)

Department of Health and Children (2006) *A Vision for Change. Report of the Expert Group on Mental Health Policy.* CSO. Dublin, Ireland. www.dohc.ie/publications/vision_for_change.html (**107, 616, 657**)

Department of Health and Department for Education and Skills (2004) *National Service Framework for Children, Young People and Maternity Services.* London: Department of Health. (**466, 482**)

Department of Health and Social Security (1974) *Revised Report of the Working Party on Security in NHS Psychiatric Hospitals* (The Glancy Report) London: HMSO. (**590, 603**)

Department of Health and Social Security (1980) (Boynton report) *Report of the Committee of Inquiry into Rampton Hospital.* London: HMSO. Cmnd 8073. (**595**)

Department of Health and Social Security (1981) *Offending by Young People: A Survey of Recent Trends,* London: DHSS. (**476**)

Department of Health and Social Security and the Welsh Office (1988) *Working together: A Guide to Arrangements for Inter-Agency Co-Operation for the Protection of Children From Abuse.* London: HMSO. (**222**)

Department of Health and Social Services (1984) Mental Health — The Way Forward. Department of Health and Social Services: Belfast. (**614**)

Department of Health and Social Services (1986) Guidelines on the Use of the Mental Health (Northern Ireland) Order 1986. http://www.gain-ni.org/flowcharts/ (**101**)

Department of Health, Department of Education and Skills (2004) *CAMHS Standard, National Service Framework for Children, Young People and Maternity Services* (NSF standard 9). London: Crown copyright. (**488**)

Department of Health, Home Office (1992) *Review of Health and Social Services for Mentally Disordered Offenders and Others Requiring Similar Services.* London: HMSO. Cm2088. (**590, 599**)

Department of Health, Ministry of Justice (2011) *Response to the Offender Personality Disorder Consultation.* London: Department of Health. (**606**)

Department of Health, Scottish Government, Welsh Assembly Government and Northern Ireland Executive (2007) *Drug Misuse and Dependence: UK Guidelines on Clinical Management.* London: NTA. (**448**)

Department of Health, Social Services and Public Safety (2000) *Strategy for Reducing Alcohol Related Harm.* Belfast, UK: Northern Ireland Executive, Department of Health, Social Services, and Public Safety. (**437**)

Department of Health, Social Services and Public Safety (2010) Promoting Good Quality Care http://www.dhsspsni.gov.uk/mhld-good-practice-guidance-2010.pdf (**101, 102**)

Department of Health/HM Prison Service (2001) *Changing the Outlook. A Strategy for Developing and Modernising Mental Health Services in Prisons.* London: Department of Health. http://www.counsellingoffenders.org.uk/ChangingTheOutlook.pdf (**628, 631**)

Department of Health/National Institute for Mental Health in England (2005) *Offender Mental Health Care Pathway.* London: Department of Health. http://www.rcpsych.ac.uk/pdf/OffenderMentalHealthCarePathway2005.pdf (**628**)

Department of Justice, Equality, and Law Reform (2001) *Report of the Group to Review the Structure and Organisation of Prison Health Care Services.* Dublin, Ireland: Department of Justice, Equality, and Law Reform. (**657**)

Department of Veterans' Affairs and Department of Defense (2004) *VA/DOD Clinical Practice Guideline for the Management of Post-Traumatic Stress.* Washington, DC: Veterans Health Administration, Department of Veterans Affairs and Health Affairs, Department of Defense, Office of Quality and Performance Publication 10Q-CPG/PTSD-04. http://www.healthquality.va.gov/ptsd/ptsd_full.pdf (**725**)

Derksen J (1995) *Personality Disorders: Clinical and Social Perspectives. Assessment and Treatment based on DSM-IV and ICD-10.* Chichester, UK: Wiley. (**400**)

Dernevik M, Grann M, and Johansson S (2002) Violent behaviour in forensic psychiatric patients: risk assessment and different risk-management levels using the HCR-20. *Psychology, Crime and Law* **8**: 93–111. (**537**)

Derntl B, Finkelmeyer A, Toygar TK, et al. (2009) Generalized deficit in all core components of empathy in schizophrenia. *Schizophrenia Research* **108**: 197–207. (**354**)

Derogatis L (1993) *The Brief Symptom Inventory.* San Antonio, Texas: Pearson Assessments, 78259–3701. (**608**)

Deutsch A (1949) *The Mentally Ill in America: A History of their Care and Treatment from Colonial Times.* New York: Columbia University Press [First published in 1937]. Cited by Prosono. (**118**)

Deutsch SI, Long KD, Rosse RB, Mastropaolo J, and Eller J (2005) Hypothesized deficiency of guanine-based purines may contribute to abnormalities of neurodevelopment, neuromodulation, and neurotransmission in Lesch–Nyhan syndrome. *Clinical Neuropharmacology* **28**: 28–37. (**322**)

DH: *see* Department of Health.

Di Forti M, Morgan M, Dazzan P, et al. (2009) High-potency cannabis and the risk of psychosis. *British Journal of Psychiatry* **195**: 488–91. (**208**)

di Martino V (2002) *Workplace Violence in the Health Sector. Country case studies: Brazil, Bulgaria, Lebanon, Portugal, South Africa, Thailand and an additional Australian study.* ILO/ICN/WHO/PSI Joint Programme on Workplace violence in the Health Sector, synthesis report, Geneva, Switzerland. (**700**)

di Martino V (2003) *Workplace violence in the Health sector.* Geneva, Switzerland: WHO. http://cdrwww.who.int/violence_injury_prevention/violence/activities/workplace/WVsynthesisreport.pdf (**556, 700**)

di Martino V, Hoel H, and Cooper C (2002) *Violence and Harassment in the Workplace.* Dublin, Ireland: European Foundation for the Improvement of Working and Living Conditions. (**700**)

Di Tella ES and Schargrodsky E (2010) *The Economics of Crime.* Chicago: University of Chicago Press. (**5**)

Dick DM, Aliev F, Krueger RF, et al. (2011) Genome-wide association study of conduct disorder symptomatology. *Molecular Psychiatry* **16**: 800–8. (**197**)

Dick DM, Li T-K, Edenberg HJ, et al. (2004) A genome-wide screen for genes influencing conduct disorder. *Molecular Psychiatry* **9**: 81–6. (**197**)

Dick HV (1972) *Licensed Mass Murder.* New York: Basic Books. (**686**)

Dickens C (1837) *Oliver Twist; or, The Parish Boy's Progress.* London: Richard Bentley. (**474**)

Dickens C (1839) *The Life and Adventures of Nicholas Nickleby.* London: Chapman and Hall. (**474**)

Dickens C (1995) *Nicholas Nickleby* (1838–9) with author's preface and notes by T.Cook. Ware: Wordsworth. (**221**)

Dickens G, Sugarman P, and Walker L (2007) HoNOS-secure: a reliable outcome measure for users of secure and forensic mental health services. *Journal of Forensic Psychiatry and Psychology* **18**: 507–14. (**597**)

References

Dickey B, Normand S-LT, Hermann RC, et al. (2003) Guideline recommendations for treatment of schizophrenia. The impact of managed care. *Archives of General Psychiatry* **60**: 340–8. (**364**)

Dickson B (2001) *The Legal System of Northern Ireland*, 4th edn. Belfast, UK: SLS Legal Publications (NI). (**87**)

Dickson SP, Wang K, Krantz I, Hakonarson H, and Goldstone DB (2010) Rare variants create synthetic genome-wide associations. *PLoS Biol* **8**(1): e1000294. (**194**)

Dietz P and Martell MA (2010) Commentary: approaching and stalking public figures – a prerequisite to attack. *Journal of American Academy of Psychiatry and the Law* **38**: 341–8. (**546**)

Dietz P, Matthews DB, Van Duyne C, Martell, DA, et al. (1991) Threatening and otherwise inappropriate letters to Hollywood celebrities. *Journal of Forensic Sciences*, **36**: 185–209. (**378, 543**)

Dietz PE (1978) Social factors in rapist behaviour. In R T Rada (eds) *Clinical Aspects of the Rapist* New York: Grune and Stratton. (**248**)

Dietz PE and Evans B (1982) Pornographic imagery and prevalence of paraphilia. *American Journal of Psychiatry* **139**: 1493–5. (**245**)

Dietz PE and Rada RT (1982) Battery incidents and batterers in a maximum security hospital. *Archives of General Psychiatry* **39**: 31–4. (**592**)

Dietz PE, Matthews, DB, Martell, DA, Stewart, TM, Hrouda, DR, and Warren, J (1991) Threatening and otherwise inappropriate letters to members of the United States Congress. *Journal of Forensic Sciences*, **36**, 1445–1468. (**378, 543**)

Dishion TJ, Patterson GR, and Kavanagh KA (1992) An experimental test of the coercion model: Linking theory, measurement and intervention. In J McCord, RE Tremblay (eds) *Preventing Antisocial Behaviour: Interventions from Birth through Adolescence*. New York: Guilford, pp. 253–82. (**182**)

Dix GE (1984) Psychological abnormality and capital sentencing. *International Journal of Law and Psychiatry* **7**: 249–67. (**114**)

Dixon A, Howie P, and Starling J (2004) Psychopathology in female offenders. *Journal of Child Psychology and Psychiatry* **45**: 1150–8. (**482**)

Dixon LB, Dickerson F, Bellack AS, et al. (2009) The 2009 schizophrenia PORT psychosocial treatment recommendations and summary statements. *Schizophrenia Bulletin* **36**: 48–70. (**358, 363, 588**)

Dobash RE and Dobash RP (1980) *Violence Against Wives: A Case Against the Patriarchy*. London: Open Books. (**372**)

Dobson F (1998) http://hansard.millbanksystems.com/commons/1998/dec/08/mental-health-services#S6CV0322P0_19981208_HOC_120 (**58**)

Dobson KS (2001) *Handbook of Cognitive Behavioural Treatments*. 2nd edn. New York: Guilford. (**569**)

Docking M and Menin S (2007) *Deaths During or Following Police Contact: Statistics for England and Wales 2006–7 (and annually since)*. London: Independent Police Complaints Commission. http://www.ipcc.gov.uk/en/Pages/reports_polcustody.aspx (**620**)

Docking M, Grace K, and Bucke T (2008) *Police Custody as a 'Place of Safety': Examining the Use of Section 136 of the Mental Health Act 1983*. London: Independent Police Complaints Commission. (**320, 621**)

Dodd T, Nicholas S, Povey D, and Walker A (2004) *Crime in England and Wales 2003/2004*. Home Office Statistical Bulletin. London: HMSO. (**700, 702**)

Dodge KA and Schwartz D (1997) Social information processing mechanisms in aggressive behavior. In DM Stoff, J Breiling, J D Maser (eds) *Handbook of Antisocial Behavior*. New York: Wiley. (**486**)

Dodge KA, Lochman JE, Harnish JD, Bates JE, and Pitt GS (1997) Reactive and proactive aggression in school children and psychiatrically impaired chronically assaultative youth. *Journal of Abnormal Psychiatry* **106**(1): 37–51. (**216**)

Doering S, Hörz S, Rentrop M, et al. (2010) Transference-focused psychotherapy v. treatment by community psychotherapists for borderline personality disorder: randomised controlled trial. *British Journal of Psychiatry* **196**: 389–95. (**410**)

Dohrenwend B, Shrout P, Link B, Martin J, and Skodal A (1986) Overview and initial results from a risk factor study of depression and schizophrenia. In JE Barrett, RM Rose (eds) *Mental Disorders in the Community*. New York: Guilford, pp. 184–215. (**340**)

Dohrenwend BP and Dohrenwend BS (1982) Perspectives on the past and future of psychiatric epidemiology. *American Journal of Public Health* **72**: 1271–9. (**390**)

Dohrenwend BP, Shrout P, Egri G, and Mendelsohn F (1980) Measure of non-specific psychological distress and other dimensions of psychopathology in the general population. *Archives of General Psychiatry* **37**: 1229–36. (**349**)

Dolan B (1997) A community-based TC: the Henderson Hospital. In E Cullen, L Jones, R Woodward (eds) *Therapeutic Communities for Offenders*. London: Wiley. (**412**)

Dolan B and Coid J (1993) *Psychopathic and Antisocial Personality Disorders: Treatment and Research Issues*. London: Gaskell. (**403**)

Dolan KA, Shearer J, and MacDonald M (2003) A randomised controlled trial of methadone maintenance treatment versus wait list control in an Australian prison system. *Drug and Alcohol Dependence* **72**: 59–65. (**467**)

Dolan M and Bishay N (1996) The effectiveness of cognitive therapy in the treatment of non psychotic morbid jealousy. *British Journal of Psychiatry* **168**: 588–93. (**373**)

Dolan M and Khawaja A (2004) The HCR-20 and post-discharge outcome in male patients discharged from medium security in the UK. *Aggressive Behavior* **30**: 469–83. (**537, 538**)

Dolan M, Anderson IM, and Deakin JF (2001) Relationship between 5-HT function and impulsivity and aggression in male offenders with personality disorders. *British Journal of Psychiatry* **178**: 352–9. (**309**)

Dolan M, Guly O, Woods P, and Fullam R (2003) Child homicide. *Medicine Science and the Law* **43**:153–69. (**509**)

Dolan M, Holloway J, Bailey S, and Kroll L (1996) The psychosocial characteristics of juvenile sexual offenders referred to an adolescent forensic service in the UK. *Medicine Science and the Law* **36**: 343–52. (**494**)

Dolan MC and Anderson IM (2003) The relationship between serotonergic function and the Psychopathy Checklist: screening version. *Journal of Psychopharmacology* **17**: 216–22. (**309**)

Dolan MC and Fullam RS (2009) Psychopathy and functional magnetic resonance imaging blood oxygenation level-dependent responses to emotional faces in violent patients with schizophrenia. *Biological Psychiatry* **66**(6): 570–77. (**305, 306**)

Dolan MC, Deakin JF, Roberts N, and Anderson IM (2002) Quantitative frontal and temporal structural MRI studies in personality-disordered offenders and control subjects. *Psychiatry Research* **116**: 133–49. (**299, 300**)

Doley R (2003a) Making sense of arson through classification. *Psychiatry, Psychology and Law* **10**: 346–52. (**274**)

Doley R (2003b) Pyromania, Fact or Fiction? *British Journal of Criminology* **43**: 797–807. (**275**)

Dollard J, Miller N, Doob L, Mowrer OH, and Sears RR (1939) *Frustration and Aggression*. New Haven, CT: Yale University Press. (**213**)

Domalanta DD, Risser WL, Roberts RE, and Risser JMH (2003) Prevalence of depression and other psychiatric disorders among incarcerated youths. *Journal of the American Academy of Child and Adolescent Psychiatry* **42**: 477–84. (**483**)

Donaghy ME (1997) *An investigation into the effects of exercise as an adjunct to the treatment and rehabilitation of the problem drinker*. PhD thesis, Medical Faculty, Glasgow University, Glasgow, UK. (**568**)

Donaghy ME, Ralston G, and Mutrie N (1991) Exercise as a therapeutic adjunct for problem drinkers. *Journal of Sports Sciences* **9**: 440. (**568**)

Donohue JJ and Levitt SD (2001) The impact of legalised abortion on crime. *Quarterly Journal of Economics* **116**: 379–420. (**5**)

Doody GA, Thomson LDG, Millar PMcC, and Johnstone EC (2000) Predictors of admission to a high security hospital for people with intellectual disability with and without schizophrenia. *Journal of Intellectual Disability Research* **44**: 130–7. (**613**)

Dooley E and Gunn J (1995) The psychological effects of disaster at sea. *British Journal of Psychiatry* **167**: 233–7. (**3**)

d'Orban PT (1989) Steroid induced psychosis. *Lancet* **ii**: 694. (**34**)

Doreleijers T (2005) 'Justicialising' juvenile offenders to a more evidence based approach. *Dutch Journal of Criminology* **47**: 38–45. (**485**)

Doren DM (2002) *Evaluating Sex Offenders: A Manual for Civil Commitments and Beyond*. London: Sage. (**254**)

Doren DM and Yates PM (2008) Effectiveness of sex offender treatment for psychopathic sexual offenders. *International Journal of Offender Therapy and Comparative Criminology* **52**: 234–45. (**262**)

Dorevitch A, Katz N, Zemishlany Z, Aizenberg D, and Weizman A (1999) Intramuscular flunitrazepam versus intramuscular haloperidol in the emergency treatment of aggressive psychotic behavior. *American Journal of Psychiatry* **156**: 142–4. (**566**)

Dougherty DM, Moeller FG, Bjork JM, and Marsh DM (1999) Plasma L-tryptophan depletion and aggression. *Advances in Experimental Medical Biology* **467**: 57–65. (**198, 309**)

Douglas J, Burgess A, Burgess A, and Ressler R (1992) *Crime Classification Manual*. New York: Lexington Books. (**274**)

Douglas KS and Ogloff JRP (2003a) The impact of confidence on the accuracy of structured professional and actuarial violence risk judgments in a sample of forensic psychiatric patients. *Law and Human Behavior* **27**(6): 573–87. (**537**)

Douglas KS and Ogloff JRP (2003b) Multiple facets of risk of violence: the impact of judgmental specificity on structured decisions about violence risk. *International Journal of Forensic Mental Health* **1**: 19–34. (**537**)

Douglas KS and Webster CD (1999) The HCR-20 violence risk assessment scheme – concurrent validity in a sample of incarcerated offenders. *Criminal Justice and Behavior* **26**(1): 3–19. (**537, 597**)

Douglas KS, Ogloff JRP, and Hart SD (2003) Evaluation of a model of violence risk assessment among forensic psychiatric patients. *Psychiatric Services*, **54**: 1372–9. (**539**)

Douglas KS, Ogloff JRP, Nicholls TL, and Grant I (1999) Assessing risk for violence among psychiatric patients: the HCR-20 violence risk assessment scheme and the Psychopathy Checklist: Screening Version. *Journal of Consulting and Clinical Psychology* **67**: 917–30. (**388, 538**)

Douglas KS, Yeomans M, and Boer DP (2005) Comparative validity analysis of multiple measures of violence risk in a sample of criminal offenders. *Criminal Justice and Behavior* **32**: 479–510. (**536, 537**)

Douglas M and Wildavsky A (1983) *Risk and Culture*. Berkeley, CA: University of California Press. (**530**)

Dowden C and Blanchette K (2002) An evaluation of the effectiveness of substance abuse programming for female offenders. *International Journal of Offender Therapy and Comparative Criminology* **46**: 220–30. (**518**)

Dowden C, and Serin R (2001) *Anger Management Programming Offenders: The Impact of Program Performance Measures*. Research Branch, Canada: Correctional Services. http://www.csc-scc.gc.ca/text/rsrch/reports/r106/r106_e.pdf (**575**)

Downs LL (2002) PMS, psychosis and culpability: sounds or misguided defense? *Journal of Forensic Sciences* **47**: 1083–9. (**501**)

Dowsett J and Craissati J (2007) *Managing Personality Disordered Offenders in the Community: A Psychological Approach*. London: Routledge. (**607, 609**)

Doyle M and Dolan M (2006a) Evaluating the validity of anger regulation problems, interpersonal style, and disturbed mental state for predicting inpatient violence. *Behavioral Sciences and the Law* **24**: 783–98. (**389**)

Doyle M and Dolan M (2006b) Predicting community violence from patients discharged from mental health services. *British Journal of Psychiatry* **189**: 520–6. (**389, 536, 537, 538**)

Doyle M, Dolan M, and McGovern J (2002) The validity of North American risk assessment tools in predicting in-patient violent behaviour in England. *Legal and Criminological Psychology* **7**: 141–54. (**537**)

Doyle M, Shaw J, Carter S, and Dolan M (2010) Investigating the validity of classification of violence risk in a UK sample. *International Journal of Forensic Mental Health* **9**: 316–23. (**542**)

Draine J, Blank A, Kottsieper P, and Solomon P (2005a) Contrasting jail diversion and in-jail services for mental illness and substance abuse: do they serve the same clients? *Behavioral Sciences and The Law* **23**: 171–81. (**365**)

Draine J, Wolff N, Jacoby JE, Hartwell S, and Duclos C (2005b) Understanding community re-entry of former prisoners with mental illness: a conceptual model to guide new research. *Behavioral Sciences and The Law* **23**: 689–707. (**365**)

Dressing H and Salize H-J (2009) Pathways to psychiatric care in European prison systems. *Behavioral Sciences and the Law* **27**: 801–10. (**625**)

Dressing H, Kuehner C, Gass P (2005) Lifetime prevalence and impact of stalking in a European population: epidemiological data from a middle-sized German city. *British Journal of Psychiatry* **187**: 168–72. (**374**)

Drgon T, Zhang P-W, Johnson C, et al. (2010) Genome wide association for addiction: replicated results and comparisons of two analytic approaches. *PLoS One* **5**(1): e8832. (**204**)

Driver and Vehicle Licensing Agency (DVLA) (2012) At a glance guide to the current medical standards of fitness to drive. DVLA: Swansea. www.dft.gov.uk/dvla/medical/ataglance.aspx (**289**)

Drury V, Birchwood M, Cochrane R, and Macmillan F (1996) Cognitive therapy and recovery from acute psychosis: a controlled trial II. Impact on recovery time. *British Journal of Psychiatry* **169**: 602–7. (**353**)

Dub FS (1997) The pivotal group member: a study of treatment-destructive resistance in group therapy. *International Journal of Group Psychotherapy* **47**: 333–53. (**573**)

Dubicka B and Harrington R (2004) Affective conduct disorder. In S Bailey, M Dolan (eds) *Adolescent Forensic Psychiatry*. London: Arnold, pp. 124–44. (**487**)

Duborg R and Hamed J (2005) Estimates of the economic and social costs of crime in England and Wales: costs of crime against individuals and households, 2003/04 in *The Economic and Social Costs of Crimes against Individuals and Households (2003/04)*. Home Office on-line report 30/05. London: Home Office. (**240, 241**)

Dubovsky SL (1990) Generalised anxiety disorder: new concepts and psychopharmacologic therapies. *Journal of Clinical Psychiatry* **51**: 3–10. (**590**)

Ducci F and Goldman D (2008) Genetic approaches to addiction: genes and alcohol. *Addiction* **103**: 1414–28. (**204, 206**)

Ducci F, Enoch M-A, Hodgkinson C, et al. (2008) Interaction between a functional MAOA locus and childhood sexual abuse predicts alcoholism and antisocial personality disorder in adult women. *Molecular Psychiatry* **13**: 334–47. (**200**)

Ducci F, Enoch M-A, Yuan Q, et al. (2009) HTR3B is associated with alcoholism with antisocial behavior and alpha EEG power – an intermediate phenotype for alcoholism and co-morbid behaviors. *Alcohol* **43**: 73–84. (**198**)

Dudeck M, Spitzer C, Stopsack M, Freyberger HJ, and Barnow S (2007) Forensic inpatient male sexual offenders: the impact of personality disorder and childhood sexual abuse. *Journal of Forensic Psychiatry and Psychology* **18**: 494–506. (**577, 578**)

Duffy DM, Linehan SA, and Kennedy HG (2006) Psychiatric morbidity in the male sentenced Irish prisons population. *Irish Journal of Psychological Medicine* **23**: 54–62. (**616, 657**)

Duggan C (2006) Dynamic psychotherapy for severe personality disorder. In C Newrith, C Meux, PJ Taylor (eds) *Personality Disorder and Serious Offending, Hospital Treatment Models*. London: Hodder Arnold, pp. 146–60. (**580**)

Duggan C (2011a) Dangerous and severe personality disorder. *British Journal of Psychiatry* **198**: 431–3. (**383**)

Duggan C (2011b) National Institute for Health and Clinical Excellence antisocial personality disorder guidance in the context of DSM-5: another example of a disconnection syndrome? *Personality and Mental Health* **5**: 122–31. (**383, 386**)

Duggan C and Gunn J (1995) Medium-term course of disaster victims. A naturalistic follow-up. *British Journal of Psychiatry* **167**: 228–32. (**3**)

Duggan C, Huband N, Smailagic N, Ferriter M, and Adams C (2007) The use of psychological treatments for people with personality disorder: a systematic review of randomized controlled trials. *Personality and Mental Health* **1**: 95–125. (**409**)

Duggan C, Huband N, Smailagic N, Ferriter M, and Adams C (2008) The use of pharmacological treatments for people with personality disorder: a systematic review of randomized controlled trials. *Personality and Mental Health* **2**: 119–70. (**404, 406, 583**)

Duggan L, Fenton M, Rathbone J, et al. (2005) Olanzapine for schizophrenia. In The Cochrane Database of Systematic Reviews. eds. Chichester, UK. Wiley. (**560**)

Duncan JM, Short A, Lewis JS, and Barrett PT (2002) Re-admissions to the State Hospital at Carstairs, 1992–1997. *Health Bulletin* **60**: 70–82. (**612**)

Dunmore EC, Clark DM, and Ehlers A (2001) A prospective investigation of the role of cognitive factors in persistent posttraumatic stress disorder (PTSD) after physical or sexual assault. *Behaviour Research and Therapy* **39**: 1063–84. (**723**)

Dunn C, Deroo L, and Rivara FP (2001) The use of brief interventions adapted from motivational interviewing across behavioral domains: a systematic review. *Addiction* **96**: 1725–42. (**459**)

Dunn J and Fahy TA (1987) Section 136 and the Police. *Bulletin of the Royal College of Psychiatrists* **11**: 224–5. (**621**)

Dunn J and Fahy TA (1990) Police admissions to a psychiatric hospital. Demographic and clinical differences between ethnic groups. *British Journal of Psychiatry* **156**: 373–8. (**621**)

Dupré E (1905) *La Mythomanie. Étude psychologique et médico-légale du mensonge et de la fabulation morbides*. Paris: Gainche. (**421**)

Dupré E (1925): La Mythomanie. In: Dupré E. (1925) *Pathologie de l'imagination et de l'émotivité*. Paris: Payot. (**421**)

Durand MA, Lelliott P, and Coyle N (2005) *The Availability of Treatment For Addictions in Medium Secure Psychiatric Inpatients Services*. (Report to the Department of Health). The Royal College of Psychiatrists' Research Unit. (**448**)

Durbin JR, Pasewark RA, and Albers D (1977) Criminality and mental-illness – study of arrest rates in a rural state. *American Journal of Psychiatry* **134**: 80–3. (**280**)

Durham J, Owen P, Bender B, et al. (1997) Alcohol consumption among pregnant and childbearing-aged women: United States, 1991 and 1995. *Morbidity and Mortality Weekly Report* **46**: 3–10. (**465**)

Durham RC, Guthire M, Morton R, et al. (2003) Tayside-Fife clinical trial of cognitive-behavioural therapy for medication-resistent psychotic symptoms. *British Journal of Psychiatry* **182**: 303–11. (**353**)

Dussich JPJ, Friday PC, Okada T, Yamagami A, and Knudten RD (2001) *Violence in Japan and America.* Monsey, NY: Criminal Justice Press. (**143**)

Dutch National Steering Committee (2003) *Guidelines for mental health care: Multidisciplinary guideline anxiety disorders.* Utrecht, The Netherlands: Quality Institute Health Care CBO/Trimbos Institute. (**725**)

Dutra L, Callahan K, Forman E, Mendelsohn M, and Herman JL (2008) Core schemas and suicidality in a chronically traumatized population. *Journal of Nervous and Mental Disease* **196**: 71–4. (**721**)

Dutton DG and Nicholls TL (2005) The gender paradigm in domestic violence research and theory: part 1. The conflict of theory and data. *Aggression and Violent Behavior* **10**: 680–714. (**218, 505**)

Dutton DG and Painter SL (1981) Traumatic bonding: the development of emotional attachments in battered women and other relationships of intermittent abuse. *Victimology* **1**: 139–55. (**714**)

Dyer AR (1988) *Ethics and Psychiatry: Toward Professional Definition*, Washington, DC: American Psychiatric Association Press. (**664**)

Dyer C (2005) Pathologist in Sally Clark case suspended from court work. *British Medical Journal* **330**: 1347. (**675**)

Earthrowl M, O'Grady J, and Birmingham L (2003) Providing treatment to prisoners with mental disorders: development of a policy: selective literature review and expert consultation exercise. *British Journal of Psychiatry* **182**: 299–302. (**632, 666**)

East WN (1927) *An Introduction to Forensic Psychiatry in the Criminal Courts* London: Churchill. (**418**)

East WN (1936) *Medical Aspects of Crime.* London: Churchill. (**250**)

East WN (1936) The relationship of alcoholism and crime to manic-depressive disorder. *British Journal of Inebriety* **33**: 167–76. (**342**)

East WN (1944) Sexual Offenders In L Radzinowicz, JWC Turner (eds) *Mental Abnormality and Crime.* London: Macmillan. (**249**)

East WN (1949) *Society and the Criminal*, London: Home OfficeHMSO. (**250**)

East WN and Hubert WH de B. (1939) *The Psychological Treatment of Crime.* London: HMSO. (**627**)

Eastman N (1996) Inquiries into homicides by psychiatric patients: systematic audit should replace mandatory inquiries. *British Medical Journal* **313**: 1069–71. (**74, 75**)

Eastman N and Campbell C (2006) Neuroscience and legal determination of criminal responsibility *Nature Reviews/Neuroscience* **7**: 311–18. (**149**)

Easton S and Piper C (2008) *Sentencing and Punishment. The Quest for Justice*, 2nd edn. Oxford: Oxford University Press. (**35**)

Eaton WW, Anthony JC, Gallow et al., (1997) Natural history of diagnostic interview schedule/*DSM-IV* major depression: The Baltimore Catchment Area follow-up. *Archives of General Psychiatry* **54**: 993–9. (**390**)

Eaves LJ, Heath AC, Neale MC, Hewitt JK, and Martin NG (1998) Sex differences and non-additivity in the effects of genes on personality. *Twin Research* **1**: 131–1. (**190**)

Eaves LJ, Krystyna A, Last P, Young A, and Martin NG (1978) Model-fitting approaches to the analysis of human behaviour. *Heredity* **41** 249–320. (**191**)

Eaves LJ, Last K, Martin NG, and Jinks JL (1977) A progressive approach to non additivity and genotype-environmental covariance in the analysis of human differences. *British Journal of Mathematical and Statistical Psychology* **30**: 1–42. (**191**)

Ebrahim GM, Gibler B, Gacono CB, and Hayes G (1994) Patient response to clozapine in a forensic psychiatric hospital. *Hospital and Community Psychiatry* **45**: 271–3. (**563**)

Ebstein RP, Novick O, Umansky R, et al. (1996) Dopamine D4 receptor (D4DR) exon III polymorphism associated with the human personality trait of Novelty Seeking. *NatureGenetetics* **12**: 78–80. (**205**)

Echeburúa E, Báez C, and Fernández-Montalvo J (1996) Comparative effectiveness of three therapeutic modalities in psychological treatment of pathological gambling: long-term outcome. *Behavioral and Cognitive Psychotherapy* **24**: 51–72. (**471**)

Economou M, Palli A, and Falloon IRH (2005) Violence, misconduct and schizophrenia: outcome after four years of optimal treatments. *Clinical Practice and Epidemiology in Mental Health* **1**: 3. http://www.ncbi.nlm.nih.gov/pmc/articles/PMC1151595/ (**364**)

Edge D (2006) *Perinatal healthcare in prison. A scoping review of policy and provision.* Manchester, UK: Offender Health Research Network. http://http://www.ohrn.nhs.uk/resource/Research/PCSysRevPerinatal.pdf (**517**)

Edlund MJ, Craig TJ, and Richardson MA (1985) Informed consent as a form of volunteer bias. *American Journal of Psychiatry* **142**: 624–7. (**670**)

Edwards A and Hurley R (2002) Prisons. Sources of information on prisoners, history and architecture. Prison Service Headquarters Library: London. (**626**)

Edwards G and Gross MM (1976) Alcohol dependence: provisional description of a clinical syndrome. *British Medical Journal* **1**: 1058–61. (**438**)

Effective Health Care Research Team (1993) Brief interventions and alcohol use. Are brief interventions effective in reducing harm associated with alcohol consumption? *Effective Health Care Bulletin* **7**: 1–13. (**705**)

Effective Interventions Unit (2002) *Using assessment data for evaluation (Evaluation Guide 7).* http://library.uniteddiversity.coop/Measuring_Progress_and_Eco_Footprinting/EvaluationGuide7.pdf (**456**)

Effective Interventions Unit (2004) *Young People With, or at Risk of Developing, Problematic Substance Misuse: A Guide to Assessment.* Edinburgh, UK: Scottish Executive. http://www.scotland.gov.uk/Resource/Doc/26350/0012827.pdf (**456, 457**)

Efron B (1983) Estimating the error rate of a prediction rule: some improvements on cross-validation. *Journal of the American Statistical Association* **78**: 316–31. (**541**)

Eggleston R (1983) *Evidence, Proof and Probability*, 2nd edn, Weidenfeld: London. **1983**

Ehlers A and Clark DM (2000) A cognitive model of post-traumatic stress disorder. *Behaviour Research and Therapy* **38**: 319–45. (**722, 723, 724**)

Ehlers A and Clark DM (2008) Post-traumatic stress disorder. The development of effective psychological treatments. *Nordic Journal of Psychiatry* **62**: 11–8. (**725**)

Ehlers A, Clark DM, Hackmann A, McManus F, and Fennell M (2005) Cognitive therapy for PTSD: development and evaluation. *Behaviour Research and Therapy* **43**: 413–31. (**725, 728**)

Ehlers A, Maercker A, and Boos A (2000) Posttraumatic stress disorder following political imprisonment: the role of mental defeat, alienation, and perceived permanent change. *Journal of Abnormal Psychology* **109**(1): 45–55. (**723, 729**)

Ehlers A, Mayou R, and Bryant B (1998) Psychological predictors of chronic posttraumatic stress disorder after motor vehicle accidents. *Journal of Abnormal Psychology* **107**: 508–19. (**722**)

Ehlers CL, Gilder DA, Slutske WS, Lind PA, and Wilhelmsen KC (2008) Externalizing disorders in American Indians: comorbidity and a genome wide linkage analysis. *American Journal of Medical Genetics B Neuropsychiatric Genetics* 147B: 690–8. (**197**)

Eichelman B, Wikler D, and Hartwig A (1984) Ethics and psychiatric research: problems and justification. *American Journal of Psychiatry* **141**: 400–5. (**669**)

Eisen M, Winograd E, and Qin J (2002) Individual differences in adults' suggestibility and memory performance. In M Eisen, JA Quas, GS Goodman (eds) *Memory and Suggestibility in the Forensic Interview*. Mahwah, NJ: Erlbaum, pp. 205–234. (**161**)

Eisenberg N (1986) *Altruistic cognition, emotion and behavior*. Hillsdale, NJ: Earlbaum. (**395**)

Eisenberger NI, Way BM, Taylor SE, Welch WT, and Lieberman MD (2007) Understanding genetic risk for aggression: clues from the brain's response to social exclusion. *Biological Psychiatry* **61**: 1100–8. (**199**)

Ekberg G (2004) The Swedish law that prohibits the purchase of sexual services. *Violence Against Women* **10**: 1187–218. (**503**)

el-Bassel N, Schilling RF, Irwin KL, et al. (1997) Sex trading and psychological distress among women recruited from the streets of Harlem. *American Journal of Public Health* **87**: 66–70. (**464**)

Elbogen EB and Johnson SC (2009) The intricate link between violence and mental disorder. *Archives of General Psychiatry* **66**: 152–61. (**338**)

Elbogen EB, van Dorn RA, Swanson JW, Swartz MS, and Monahan J (2006) Treatment engagement and violence risk in mental disorders. *British Journal of Psychiatry* **189**: 354–60. (**356**)

Elbogen EB, Wagner HR, Fuller SR, *et al.* (2010) Correlates of anger and hostility in Iraq and Afghanistan was veterans. *American Journal of Psychiatry* **167**: 1051–58. (**715**)

Eldergill A (1997) *Mental Health Review Tribunals Law and Practice*. London: Sweet and Maxwell. (**72**)

Eldridge H (2000) Patterns of sex offending and strategies for effective assessment and intervention. In C Itzin (ed) *Home Truths about Child Sexual Abuse: Influencing Policy and Practice*, London: Routledge. (**251**)

Eley TC, Lichtenstein P, and Moffitt TE (2003) A longitudinal behavioral genetic analysis of the etiology of aggressive and nonaggressive antisocial behavior. *Developmental Psychopathology* **15**: 383–402. (**196**)

Eley TC, Lichtenstein P, and Stevenson J (1999) Sex differences in the etiology of aggressive and nonaggressive antisocial behavior: results from two twin studies. *Child Development* **70**: 155–68. (**196, 501**)

Elger BS (2004) Prevalence, types and possible causes of insomnia in a Swiss remand prison. *European Journal of Epidemiology* **19**: 665–77. (**630**)

El-Guebaly N (2004) Concurrent substance-related disorders and mental illness: the North American experience. *World Psychiatry* **3**: 182–7. (**364**)

Eliott G (1871) *Middlemarch: A Study of Provincial Life*. Edinburgh and London: William Blackwood and Sons. (**679**)

Elkins IJ, McGue M, Iacono WG (2007) Prospective effects of attention-deficit/hyperactivity disorder, conduct disorder, and sex on adolescent substance use and abuse. *Archives of General Psychiatry* **64**:1145–52. (**512**)

Ellenberger HF (1970) *The Discovery of the Unconscious*. New York: Basic Books. (**426**)

Elliot C and Quinn F (2005) *Tort Law*, 5th edn. Harlow, UK: Pearson, Longman. (**51, 52**)

Elliott DS (1994) Serious violent offenders: onset, developmental course, and termination. *Criminology* **31**: 1–21. (**171, 173**)

Ellis A (1962) *Reason and Emotion in Psychotherapy*. New York: Stuart. (**569**)

Ellis BE (1991) *American Psycho*. New York: Vintage Books. (**239**)

Ellis EM, Atkeson BM, and Calhoon CS (1981) An assessment of long-term reactions to rape. *Journal of Abnormal Psychology* **90**: 263–6. (**715**)

Ellis H (1931) *Psychology of Sex: A Manual for Students*. London: William Heinemann. (**244**)

Ellis L (1988) The victimful–victimless crime distinction, and seven universal demographic correlates of victimful criminal behaviour. *Personality and Individual Differences* **3**: 525–48. (**176**)

Ellonen N, Piispa M, Peltonen K and Oranen M. (2013) Exposure to parental violence and outcomes of child psychosocial adjustment. *Violence and Victims* 28: 3-15. (**505**)

Elston RC (1998) Linkage and association. *Genetic Epidemiology* **15**: 565–76. (**192**)

Emanuel EJ, Wandler D, and Grady C (2000) What makes clinical research ethical? *Journal of American Medical Assocation* **283**: 2701–17. (**668**)

EMCDDA *see* European Monitoring Centre for Drugs and Drug Addiction.

Emlyn-Jones R (2007) Think about it till it hurts: targeting intensive services to facilitate behaviour change – two examples from the field of substance misuse. *Criminal Behaviour and Mental Health* **17**: 234–41. (**465**)

Emmelkamp PMG, Benner A, Kuipers A, et al. (2006) Comparison of brief dynamic and cognitive-behavioural therapies in avoidant personality disorder. *British Journal of Psychiatry* **189**: 60–4. (**410, 571**)

Emmins C (1986) Unfitness to plead: thoughts prompted by Glen Pearson's Case. *Criminal Law Review*: 604–18. (**24**)

English K, Jones L, Pasini-Hill D, Patrick D, and Cooley-Towell S (2000) *The Value of Polygraph Testing in Sex Offender Management*. Final research report submitted to the National Institute of Justice for grant number D97LBVX0034. Denver, CO: Colorado Division of Criminal Justice, Office of Research and Statistics. (**256**)

Ennis BJ and Hansen C (1976) Memorandum of law: competency to stand trial. *Journal of Psychiatry and Law* **4**: 491–512. (**119**)

Enoch DE and Ball HN (1991) *Uncommon Psychiatric Syndromes*, 3rd edn. London: Arnold. (**423**)

Enoch MA (2003) Pharmacogenomics of alcohol response and addiction. *American Journal of Pharmacogenomics* **3**: 217–32. (**205**)

Enoch MA, Hodgkinson CA, Yuan Q, et al. (2010) The influence of GABRA2, childhood trauma, and their interaction on alcohol, heroin, and cocaine dependence. *Biological Psychiatry* **67**: 20–7. (**207**)

Enright SJ (1997) Cognitive-behavioural therapy – clinical applications. *British Medical Journal* **314**: 1811–6. (**569**)

Erb M, Hodgins S, Freese R, Müller-Isberner R, and Jöckel D (2001) Homicide and schizophrenia: maybe treatment does have a preventive effect. *Criminal Behaviour and Mental Health* **11**: 6–26. (**337**)

Erickson SK (2005) A retrospective examination of outpatient commitment in New York. *Behavioral Sciences and the Law* **23**: 627–45. (**364**)

Erkiran M, Özünalan H, Evren C, et al. (2006) Substance abuse amplifies the risk for violence in schizophrenia spectrum disorder. *Addictive Behaviors* **31**(10): 1797–805. (**347, 454**)

Erlenmeyer-Kimling L, Adamo UH, Rock D, et al. (1997) The New York High-Risk Project. Prevalence and comorbidity of axis I disorders in offspring of schizophrenic parents at 25-year follow-up. *Archives of General Psychiatry* **54**: 1096–102. (**208**)

Eron LD, Huesmann LR, and Zelli A (1991) The role of parental variables in the learning of aggression. In DJ Pepler, KJ Rubin (eds) *The Development and Treatment of Childhood Aggression*. Hillsdale, N.J: Lawrence Erlbaum, pp. 169–88. (**171**)

Eronen M (1995) Mental disorders and homicidal behaviour in female subjects. *American Journal of Psychiatry* **152**: 1216–8. (**511**)

Eronen M, Hakola P, and Tiihonen J (1996a) Mental disorders and homicidal behavior in Finland. *Archives of General Psychiatry* **53**: 497–501. (**502, 515**)

Eronen M, Hakola P, and Tiihonen J (1996b) Factors associated with homicide recidivism in a 13-year sample of homicide offenders in Finland. *Psychiatric Services* **47**: 403–6. (**507**)

Eronen M, Tiihonen J, and Hakola P (1996c) Schizophrenia and homicidal behavior. *Schizophrenia Bulletin* **22**: 83–9. (**443, 502**)

Esquirol JED (1965) *Mental Maladies: A Treatise on Insanity*. (R. de Saussure, Trans.) Hafner: New York (Original work published in 1845). (**367, 373**)

Essock SM, Covell NH, Davis SM, et al. (2006) Effectiveness of switching antipsychotic medications. *American Journal of Psychiatry* **163**: 2090–5. (**364**)

Essock SM, Schooler MR, Stroup TS, et al. (2011) Effectiveness of switching from antipsychotic polypharmacy to monotherapy. *American Journal of Psychiatry* **168**: 702–08. (**360**)

Estroff SE (2004) Subject/subjectivities in dispute: the politics and poetics of first person narratives of schizophrenia. In R Barrett, J Jenkins (eds) *The Edge of Experience: Schizophrenia, Culture, and Subjectivity*. Cambridge: Cambridge University. Press, pp. 282–302. (**356**)

Estroff SE and Zimmer C (1994) Social networks, social support and the risk for violence among persons with severe persistent mental illness. In J Monahan, H Steadman (eds) *Violence and Mental Illness: Developments in Risk Assessment*. Chicago, IL: University of Chicago Press, pp. 259–93. (**355**)

Estroff SE, Swanson JW, Lachicotte WS, Swartz M, and Bolduc M (1998) Risk reconsidered: targets of violence in the social networks of people with serious psychiatric disorders. *Social Psychiatry and Psychiatric Epidemiology* **33** (suppl. 1): 95–101. (**355**)

Estroff SE, Zimmer CR, Lachicotte WS, and Benoit J (1994) The influence of social networks and social support on violence by persons with serious mental illness. *Hospital and Community Psychiatry* **45**: 669–79. (**355**)

European Monitoring Centre for Drugs and Drug Addiction (EMCDDA) (2007) *The State of the Drugs Problem in Europe (Annual report)*. Luxembourg: European Monitoring Centre for Drugs and Drug Addiction. http://www.emcdda.europa.eu/attachements. cfm/att_44705_EN_TDAC07001ENC.pdf (**462**)

Evans K (1983) *Advocacy at the Bar*. London: Financial Training Publications. (**148**)

Evans K, Tyrer P, Catalan J, et al. (1999) Manual-assisted cognitive-behaviour therapy (MACT): a randomized controlled trial of a brief intervention with bibliotherapy in the treatment of recurrent deliberate self-harm. *Psychological Medicine* **29**: 19–25. (**410**)

Evans N and Clarke J (2000) Addressing issues of sexuality. In C Chaloner, M Coffey (eds) *Forensic Mental Health Nursing. Current Approaches*. Oxford: Blackwell Science. (**555**)

Everington C and Fulero SM (1999) Competence to confess: measuring, understanding and suggestibility of defendants with mental retardation. *Mental Retardation* **37**: 212–20. (**332**)

Everington CT and Luckasson R (1992) *Competence Assessment for Standing Trial for Defendants with Mental Retardation*. Worthington, OH: International Diagnostic Systems. (**332**)

Evershed S, Tennant A, Boomer D, et al. (2003) Practice-based outcomes of dialectical behaviour therapy (DBT) targeting anger and violence, with male forensic patients: a pragmatic and non-contemporaneous comparison. *Criminal Behaviour and Mental Health* **13**: 198–213. (**575**)

Eves A and Gesch B (2003) Food provision and the nutritional implications of food choices made by young adult males, in a young offenders' institution. *Journal of Human Nutrition and Dietetics* **16**: 167–79. (**567**)

Expert Consensus Panel for Optimizing Pharmacologic Treatment of Psychotic Disorders (2003) The expert consensus guideline series. Optimizing pharmacologic treatment of psychotic disorders. *Journal of Clinical Psychiatry* **64**: 2–97. (**562**)

Exworthy T and Gunn J (2003) Taking another tilt at high secure hospitals. *British Journal of Psychiatry* **182**: 469–71. (**666**)

Exworthy T and Wilson S (2010) Escapes and absconding from secure units. *The Psychiatrist* **34**: 81–2. (**595**)

Eysenck HJ and Eysenck SBG (1969) *Personality Structure and Measurement*. London: Routledge & Kegan Paul. (**388**)

Eysenck HJ and Eysenck SBG (1975) *Manual of the Eysenck Personality Inventory*. London: University of London Press. (**225, 385, 388**)

Eysenck SBG and Eysenck H (1978) Impulsiveness and venturesomeness: their position in a dimensional system of personality description. *Psychological Reports* **43**: 1247–55. (**225**)

Fadhli K and Taylor PJ (submitted) Do people with psychosis who have delusions communicate about them with other people? A systematic review. (**352, 356**)

Faergemann C (2006) *Interpersonal Violence in the Odense Municipality, Denmark 1991–2002*. PhD thesis, University of Southern Denmark. (**702**)

Fahy T and Dunn J (1987) Where section 136 fails? *Police Review* **95**: 1580–1. (**48**)

Fahy T, Bermingham D, and Dunn J (1987) Police admissions to mental hospitals: a challenge to community psychiatry? *Medicine, Science and the Law* **27**: 263–8. (**48**)

Fahy TA (1988) The diagnosis of multiple personality disorder: a critical review. *British Journal of Psychiatry* **153**: 597–606. (**427**)

Fairbairn R (1952) *Psychoanalytic Study of the Personality*. London: Routledge and Kegan Paul. (**719**)

Fairbank JA, Hansen DJ, and Fitterling JM (1991) Patterns of appraisal and coping across different stressor conditions among former prisoners of war with and without posttraumatic stress disorder. *Journal of Consulting and Clinical Psychology* **59**: 274–81. (**722**)

Falconer C (2006) *A Guide to Human Rights Act 1998*, 3rd edn. London: Department for Constitutional Affairs, TSO. (**57**)

Falconer DS (1965) The inheritance of liability to certain diseases, estimated from the incidence among relatives. *Annals of Human Genetics* **29**: 51–76. (**188, 189**)

Falconer MA (1973) Reversibility by temporal lobe resection of the behavioural abnormalities of temporal lobe epilepsy. *New England Journal of Medicine* **289**: 451–5. (**285**)

Falconer MA and Taylor DC (1970) Temporal lobe epilepsy: clinical features, pathology, diagnosis and treatment. In JH Price (ed) *Modern Trends in Psychological Medicine*, Vol. 2. London: Butterworth. (**285**)

Fallon P, Bluglass R, Edwards B, and Daniels G (1999) *Report of the Committee of Inquiry into the Personality Disorder Unit at Ashworth Special Hospital*, Vols. 1 & 2. Cm 4194-1 and 4194-II. London: HMSO. (**604**)

Falshaw L, Friendship C, and Bates A (2003) *Sexual Offenders – Measuring Reconviction, Reoffending and Recidivism*. Home Office Findings No 206. London: Home Office. (**578**)

Falshaw L, Friendship C, Travers R, and Nugent F (2004) 'Searching for 'what works': HM prison service accredited cognitive skills programmes'. *The British Journal of Forensic Practice* **6**: 3–13. (**242**)

Fals-Stewart W (2003) The occurrence of partner physical aggression on days of alcohol consumption. *Journal of Consulting and Clinical Psychology* **71**: 41–52. (**442**)

Family Division (2008) *Practice Direction: Experts in Family Proceedings Relating to Children*. http://www.justice.gov.uk/courts/procedure-rules/family/practice_directions/pd_part_25a (**157**)

Famularo R, Kinscherff R, and Fenton T (1992) Parental substance abuse and the nature of child maltreatment. *Child Abuse and Neglect* **16**: 475–83. (**465**)

Fantini ML, Corona A, Clerici S, and Ferini-Stambi L (2005) Increased aggressive dream content without daytime aggressiveness in REM sleep behaviour disorder. *Neurology* **65**: 1010–15. (**291**)

Faraone SV, Biederman J, Mick E, et al. (2000) Family study of girls with attention deficit hyperactivity disorder. *American Journal of Psychiatry* **157**: 1077–83. (**512**)

Farkas AG, Colbert DL, and Erskine KJ (1995) Anonymous testing for drug abuse in an antenatal population. *Journal of Obstetrics and Gynaecology* **102**: 563–5. (**464**)

Farley M and Barkan H (1998) Prostitution, violence, and posttraumatic stress disorder. *Women and Health* **27**: 37–49. (**464**)

Farnham FR, James DV, and Cantrell P (2000) Association between violence, psychosis and relationship to victim in stalkers. *Lancet* **355**: 199. (**546**)

Farrant F (2001) *Troubled Inside: Responding to the Mental Health Needs of Children and Young People in Prison*. London: Prison Reform Trust. (**486**)

Farrell M and Marsden J (2008) Acute risk of drug-related death among newly released prisoners in England and Wales. *Addiction* **103**: 251–5. (**462**)

Farrington D, Coid J, Harnett, L, et al. (2006) *Criminal Careers and Life Success: New Findings from the Cambridge Study in Delinquent Development*. Home Office Research Findings 281. London: Home Office. (**172, 173**)

Farrington DP (1972) Delinquency begins at home. *New Society* **21**: 495–7. (**178**)

Farrington DP (1986a) Age and crime. In M Tonry, N Morris (eds) *Crime and Justice*, Vol. 7. Chicago, IL: University of Chicago Press, pp. 189–250. (**172**)

Farrington DP (1986b) Stepping stones to adult criminal careers. In D Olweus, J Block, MR Yarrow (eds) *Development of Antisocial and Prosocial Behaviour*. New York: Academic Press, pp. 359–84. (**178**)

Farrington DP (1988) Studying changes within individuals: the causes of offending. In M Rutter (ed) *Studies of Psychosocial Risk: The Power of Longitudinal Data*. Cambridge, UK: Cambridge University Press, pp. 158–83. (**172**)

Farrington DP (1989) Self-reported and official offending from adolescence to adulthood. In MW Klein (ed) *Cross-National Research in Self-Reported Crime and Delinquency*. Dordrecht, the Netherlands: Kluwer, pp. 399–423. (**172,173**)

Farrington DP (1990a) Age, period, cohort, and offending. In DM Gottfredson, RV Clarke (eds) *Policy and Theory in Criminal Justice: Contributions in Honour of Leslie T. Wilkins*. Aldershot, UK: Avebury, pp. 51–75. (**173**)

Farrington DP (1990b) Implications of criminal career research for the prevention of offending. *Journal of Adolescence* **13**: 93–113. (**179**)

Farrington DP (1991) Childhood aggression and adult violence: early precursors and later life outcomes. In DJ Pepler, KH Rubin (eds) *The Development and Treatment of Childhood Aggression*. Hillsdale, NJ: Erlbaum, pp. 5–29. (**170**)

Farrington DP (1992a) Juvenile delinquency. In JC Coleman (ed) *The School Years*, 2nd edn. London: Routledge, pp. 123–63. (**172, 174, 175, 176, 177, 178**)

Farrington DP (1992b) Criminal career research in the United Kingdom. *British Journal of Criminology* **32**: 521–36. (**173**)

Farrington DP (1992c) Explaining the beginning, progress and ending of antisocial behaviour from birth to adulthood. In J McCord (ed) *Facts, Frameworks and Forecasts: Advances in Criminological Theory*, Vol. 3. New Brunswick, NJ: Transaction, pp. 253–86. (**175, 177**)

Farrington DP (1993a) Childhood origins of teenage antisocial behaviour and adult social dysfunction. *Journal of the Royal Society of Medicine* **86**: 13–17. (**175, 176**)

Farrington DP (1993b) Understanding and preventing bullying. In M Tonry, N. Morris (eds) *Crime and Justice*, Vol. 17. Chicago, IL: University of Chicago Press, pp. 381–458. (**184**)

Farrington DP (1995) The development of offending and antisocial behaviour from childhood: key findings from the Cambridge study in delinquent development. *Journal of Child Psychology and Psychiatry* **36**: 929–64. (**317, 422**)

Farrington DP (1997) Human development and criminal careers. In M Maguire, R Morgan, R Reiner (eds) *The Oxford Handbook of Criminology*, 2nd edn. Oxford, UK: Clarendon, pp. 361–408. (**173**)

Farrington DP (1998) Predictors, causes and correlates of male youth violence. In M Tonry, MH Moore (eds) *Youth Violence*. Chicago, IL: University of Chicago Press, pp. 421–75. (**178**)

Farrington DP (2000) Psychosocial causes of offending. In MG Gelder, JJ Lopez-Ibor, and N Andreasen (eds) *New Oxford Textbook of Psychiatry*. Oxford: Oxford University Press, 2029–36. (**317**)

Farrington DP (2003a) Developmental and life-course criminology: key theoretical and empirical issues – The 2002 Sutherland award address. *Criminology* **41**: 221–55. (**179, 181**)

Farrington DP (2003b) Key results from the first 40 years of the Cambridge study in delinquent development. In TP Thornberry, MD Krohn (eds) *Taking Stock of Delinquency: An Overview of Findings from Contemporary Longitudinal Studies*. New York: Kluwer, pp. 137–83. (**171**)

Farrington DP (2005a) (ed) *Integrated Development and Life-Course Theories of Offending*. New Brunswick, NJ: Transaction. (**181**)

Farrington DP (2005b) The integrated cognitive antisocial potential (ICAP) theory. In DP Farrington (ed) *Integrated Developmental and Life-Course Theories of Offending*. New Brunswick, NJ: Transaction, pp. 73–92. (**179, 181**)

Farrington DP and Hawkins JD (1991) Predicting participation, early onset, and later persistence in officially recorded offending. *Criminal Behaviour and Mental Health* **1**: 1–33. (**179**)

Farrington DP and Loeber R (1999) Transatlantic replicability of risk factors in the development of delinquency. In P Cohen, C Slomkowski, LN Robins (eds) *Historical and Geographical Influences on Psychopathology*. Mahwah, NJ: Lawrence Erlbaum, pp. 299–329. (**172, 176**)

Farrington DP and Welsh BC (2006) A half-century of randomized experiments on crime and justice. In M Tonry (ed) *Crime and Justice*, Vol. 34. Chicago, IL: University of Chicago Press, pp. 55–132. (**181**)

Farrington DP and Welsh BC (2007) *Saving Children from a Life of Crime: Early Risk Factors and Effective Interventions*. Oxford, UK: Oxford University Press. (**181**)

Farrington DP and West DJ (1993) Criminal, penal, and life histories of chronic offenders: risk and protective factors and early identification. *Criminal Behaviour and Mental Health* **3**: 492–523. (**173**)

Farrington DP and Wikström P-OH (1994) Criminal careers in London and Stockholm: a cross-national comparative study. In EGM Weitekamp, HJ Kerner (eds) *Cross-National Longitudinal Research on Human Development and Criminal Behaviour*. Dordrecht, the Netherlands: Kluwer, pp. 65–89. (**173**)

Farrington DP, Barnes G, and Lambert S (1996a) The concentration of offending in families. *Legal and Criminological Psychology* **1**: 47–63. (**176**)

Farrington DP, Coid JW, Harnett L, et al. (2006) *Criminal Careers up to Age 50 and Life Success up to Age 48: New Findings from the Cambridge Study in Delinquent Development*. Research Study No. 299. London: Home Office. (**172, 173**)

Farrington DP, Gallagher B, Morley L, St. Ledger RJ, and West DJ (1986) Unemployment, school leaving, and crime. *British Journal of Criminology* **26**: 335–6. (**177**)

Farrington DP, Jolliffe D, Loeber R, Stouthamer-Loeber M, and Kalb LM (2001) The concentration of offenders in families, and family criminality in the prediction of boys' delinquency. *Journal of Adolescence* **24**: 579–96. (**195**)

Farrington DP, Lambert S, and West DJ (1998) Criminal careers of two generations of family members in the Cambridge study in delinquent development. *Studies on Crime and Crime Prevention* **7**: 85–106. (**172**)

Farrington DP, Langan PA, and Wikstrom P-O (1994) Changes in crime and punishment in America, England and Sweden between the 1980s and the 1990s. *Studies in Crime and Crime Prevention* **3**: 47–71. (**700, 702**)

References

Farrington DP, Loeber R, and van Kammen WB (1990) Long-term criminal outcomes of hyperactivity-impulsivity-attention deficit and conduct problems in childhood. In LN Robins, M Rutter (eds) *Straight and Devious Pathways from Childhood to Adulthood.* Cambridge, UK: Cambridge University Press, pp. 62–81. (**174**)

Farrington DP, Loeber R, Stouthamer-Loeber MS, van Kammen W, and Schmidt L (1996b) Self-reported delinquency and a combined delinquency seriousness scale based on boys, mothers and teachers: concurrent and predictive validity for African Americans and Caucasians. *Criminology* **34**: 493–517. (**172**)

Farrington DP, Loeber R, Yin Y, and Anderson S (2002) Are within-individual causes of delinquency the same as between-individual causes? *Criminal Behaviour and Mental Health 12:* 53–68. (**178**)

Fatemi SH, King DP, Reutiman TJ, et al. (2008) PDE4B polymorphisms and decreased PDE4B expression are associated with schizophrenia. *Schizophrenia Research 101:* 36–49. (**209**)

Faulkner G and Sparkes A (1999) Exercise as therapy for schizophrenia. *Journal of Sport and Exercise Psychology 21*: 52–69. (**568**)

Fava M, Vuolo RD, Wright EC, et al. (2000) Fenfluramine challenge in unipolar depression with and without anger attacks. *Psychiatry Research* **94**: 9–18. (**310**)

Fazel M, Långström N, Grann M, and Fazel S (2008) Psychopathology in adolescent and young adult criminal offenders (15–21 years) in Sweden. *Social Psychiatry and Psychiatric Epidemiology 43:* 319–24. (**512**)

Fazel S and Baillargeon J (2011) The health of prisoners. *Lancet* **377**: 956–65. (**4, 516, 517**)

Fazel S and Benning R (2009) Suicides in female prisoners in England and Wales, 1978–2004. *British Journal of Psychiatry 194:* 183–4. (**633**)

Fazel S and Danesh J (2002) Serious mental disorder in 23000 prisoners: a systematic review of 62 surveys. *Lancet* 359: 545–50. (**281, 502, 517, 526, 628**)

Fazel S and Grann M (2002) Older criminals: a descriptive study of psychiatrically examined offenders in Sweden. *International Journal of Geriatric Psychiatry* **17**: 907–13. (**525**)

Fazel S and Grann M (2006) The population impact of severe mental illness on violent crime. *American Journal of Psychiatry 163:* 1397–403. (**231, 338, 502, 507, 514**)

Fazel S and Jacoby R (2000) The elderly criminal. *International Journal of Geriatric Psychiatry* **15**: 201–2. (**524**)

Fazel S and Jacoby R (2002) Psychiatric aspects of crime and the elderly. In R Jacoby, C Oppenheimer (eds) *Psychiatry in the Elderly.* 3rd edn. Oxford, UK: Oxford University Press, pp. 919–31. (**523**)

Fazel S and Seewald K (2012) Severe mental illness in 33,588 prisoners worldwide: systematic review and meta-regression analysis. *British Journal of Psychiatry* **200**: 364–73. (**629**)

Fazel S, Bains P, and Doll H (2006) Substance abuse and dependence in prisoners: a systematic review. *Addiction 101:* 181–91. (**514**)

Fazel S, Benning R, and Danesh J (2005) Suicides in male prisoners in England and Wales, 1978–2003. *Lancet 366*: 1301–2. (**526**)

Fazel S, Bond M, Gulati G, and O'Donnell I (2007) Elderly homicide in Chicago: a research note. *Behavioural Sciences and the Law 25*: 629–39. (**525**)

Fazel S, Cartwright J, Norman-Nott A, and Hawton K (2008) Suicide in prisoners: a systematic review of risk factors. *Journal of Clinical Psychiatry 69*: 1721–31. (**634**)

Fazel S, Doll H, and Långström N (2008) Mental disorders among adolescents in juvenile detention and correctional facilities: a systematic review and metaregression analysis of 25 surveys. *Journal of the American Academy of Child and Adolescent Psychiatry 47*: 1010–19. (**482, 512**)

Fazel S, Gulati G, Linsell L, Geddes JR, and Grann M (2009) Schizophrenia and violence: systematic review and meta-analysis. *PLoS Med* **6**(8): e1000120. (**488, 502, 505, 514**)

Fazel S, Hope T, O'Donnell I, and Jacoby R (2001a) Hidden psychiatric morbidity in elderly prisoners. *British Journal of Psychiatry 179:* 535–9. (**526**)

Fazel S, Hope T, O'Donnell I, and Jacoby R (2002a) Psychiatric, demographic, and personality characteristics of elderly sex offenders. *Psychological Medicine 32:* 219–26. (**527**)

Fazel S, Hope T, O'Donnell I, and Jacoby R (2004) Unmet treatment needs of older prisoners: a primary care survey. *Age and Ageing* **33**: 396–8. (**527**)

Fazel S, Långström N, Hjern A, Grann M, and Lichtenstein P (2009a) Schizophrenia, substance abuse and violent crime. *JAMA 301:* 2016–23. (**338, 347**)

Fazel S, Långström N, Sjöstedt G, and Grann M (2006) Risk factors for criminal recidivism in older sexual offenders. *Sexual Abuse: A Journal of Research and Treatment 18:* 159–67. (**527**)

Fazel S, Lichtenstein P, Grann M, Goodwin GMl, and Långström N (2010) Bipolar disorder and violent crime. *Archives of General Psychiatry 67:* 931–8. (**337, 515**)

Fazel S, McMillan J, and O'Donnell I (2002b) Dementia in prison: ethical and legal implications. *Journal of Medical Ethics 28:* 156–9. (**528**)

Fazel S, O'Donnell I, Hope T, Gulati G, and Jacoby R (2007) Frontal lobes and older sex offenders: a preliminary investigation. *International Journal of Geriatric Psychiatry 22:* 87–9. (**527**)

Fazel S, O'Donnell I, Hope T, Piper M, and Jacoby R (2001b) Health of elderly male prisoners: worse than younger prisoners, worse than the general population. *Age and Ageing 30:* 403–7. (**528**)

Fazel S, Philipson J, Gardiner L, Merritt R, and Grann M (2009) Neurological disorders and violence: a systematic review and meta-analysis with a focus on epilepsy and traumatic brain injury. *Journal of Neurology 256:* 1591–602. (**339, 488**)

Fazel S, Sjösdedt G, Langstrom N, and Grann M (2007b) Sexual offending and the risk of severe mental illness. *Journal of Clinical Psychiatry 68:* 588–94. (**340, 525, 527**)

Fazel S, Sjöstedt G, Långström N, and Grann M (2007a) Severe mental illness and risk of sexual offending in men: a case control study based on Swedish national registers. *Journal of Clinical Psychiatry 68:* 588–96. (**253, 340**)

Fazel, S., Gulati, G., Linsell, L., Geddes, J.R., Grann, M. (2009b) Schizophrenia and violence: systematic review and meta-analysis. *PLoS Medicine,* 6: e1000120. doi:10.1371/jounal.pmed.1002120Fazel S, Lichtenstein P, Grann M, Goodwin GM, and Långström N (2010) Bipolar disorder and violent crime. *Archives of General Psychiatry 67:* 931–8. (**339**)

Federal Bureau of Investigation (2011) *Crime in the United States 2010.* www.fbi.gov/about-us/cjis/ucr/crime-in-the-u.s/2010/crime-in-the-u.s.-2010/violent-crime/murdermain (**498**)

Fedoroff JP (2009) The paraphilias. In M Gelder, JJ Lopez-Ibor, N Andreason (eds) *The New Oxford Textbook of Psychiatry,* 2nd edn. Oxford, UK: Oxford University Press. (**245, 246**)

Fedoroff JP, Fischell A, and Fedoroff B (1999) A case series of women evaluated for paraphilic sexual disorders. *Canadian Journal of Human Sexuality 8:* 127–40. (**252**)

Fein RA and Vossekuil B (1998) Preventing attacks on public officials and public figures: a secret service perspective. In JR Meloy (ed) *The Psychology of Stalking.* San Diego, CA: Academic Press. (**378, 544, 545**)

Fein RA and Vossekuil B (1999) Assassination in the United States: an operational study of recent assassins, attackers and near-lethal approachers. *Journal of Forensic Science 44*(2): 321–33. (**378, 544, 545, 547**)

Fein RA, Vossekuil B, and Holden GA (1995) Threat assessment: an approach to prevent targeted violence. NCJ 155000. Washington, DC: US Department of Justice, Office of Justice Programs, National Institute of Justice. https://www.ncjrs.gov/pdffiles/threat.pdf (**378, 544**)

Feinstein AR (1970) The pre-therapeutic classification of comorbidity in chronic disease. *Journal of Chronic Disease 23:* 455–68. (**345, 397**)

Feldman W, Feldman, E, Goodman, J et al. (1991) Is childhood sexual abuse really increasing in prevalence? *An analysis of the evidence Pediatrics* **88***:* 29–33. (**244**)

Felson RB and Messner SF (2000) The control motive in intimate partner violence. *Social Psychology Quarterly 63:* 86–94. (**543**)

Felthous A and Sass H (eds) (2007) *International Handbook on Psychopathic Disorders and the Law,* Vols. 1 & 2. Chichester, UK: Wiley. (**147, 283, 284**)

Felthous AR (1979) Competency to waive counsel: a step beyond competence to stand trial. *Journal of Psychiatry and Law* **7**(9): 471–7. (**120**)

Felthous AR (1994) The right to represent oneself incompetently: competency to waive counsel and conduct one's own defense before and after Godinez. *Mental and Physical Disability Law Reporter 18:* 105–12. (**120**)

Felthous AR (2004) Diagnostische ausschließende Kriterien für Schuldunfähigkeit wegen Geistesstörung in den USA (Diagnostic exclusionary criteria for the insanity defence in the United States) [German abstract]. *Nervenarzt 75,* Supp. 2, November, *Abstract No. 1022, p. 337, Annual Meeting of the German Psychiatric Society,* Berlin, Germany. (**121**)

Felthous AR (2010) Psychopathic disorders and criminal responsibility in the USA. *European Archives of Psychiatry and Clinical Neuroscience 260* (suppl. 2): 137–141. (**121**)

Felthous AR and Flynn L (2009) From competence to waive counsel to competence to represent oneself: the Supreme Court advances fairness in Edwards. *Mental and Physical Disability Law Reporter 33*(1): 14–17. (**120**)

Felthous AR and Sass H (2008) Introduction to this issue: international perspectives on brain imaging and the law. *Behavioral Sciences and the Law 26:* 1–6. (**283**)

Felthous AR, Kröber HL, and Sass H (2001) Forensic evaluation for civil and criminal competencies and criminal responsibility in German and Anglo-American legal systems. In H Henn, N Sartorius, H Helmchen, H Lauter (eds) *Contemporary Psychiatry,* Vol. 1, *Foundation of Psychiatry.* Berlin, Germany: Springer Verlag, pp. 287–302. (**121, 147**)

Fennell P (1986) Law and psychiatry: the legal constitution of the psychiatric system. *Journal of Law and Psychiatry 13:* 35–65. (**148**)

Fennell P (1988) Sexual suppressants and the Mental Health Act. *Criminal Law Review* 660–76. (**261**)

Fennell P (2008) Human rights, bioethics and mental disorder. *Medical Law Review 27:* 95–107. (**113**)

Fennell P (2011) *Mental Health: Law and Practice.* Bristol, UK: Jordan. (**57, 63, 66, 69**)

Fenton GW (1972) Epilepsy and automatism. *British Journal of Hospital Medicine,* 7: 57–64 (**295**)

Fenwick P (1990) Automatism: medicine and the law. *Psychological Medicine* 20 (suppl. 17): 1–27. (**295, 438**)

Fenwick P and Fenwick E (1985) *Epilepsy and the Law.* London: Royal Society of Medicine. (**26**)

Ferdinand RF, Sondeijker F, van der Ende J, et al. (2005) Cannabis use predicts future psychotic symptoms, and vice versa. *Addiction 100:* 612–18. (**488**)

Fergusson DM, Boden JM, Horwood LJ, Miller AL, and Kennedy MA (2011) MAOA, abuse exposure and antisocial behaviour: 30-year longitudinal study. *British Journal of Psychiatry 198:* 457–63. (**3**)

Fergusson DM, Horwood LJ, and Lynskey MT (1994) The childhoods of multiple problem adolescents: a 15 year longitudinal study. *Journal of Child Psychology and Psychiatry 35:* 1123–40. (**171**)

Fergusson DM, Lynskey MT, and Horwood LJ (1996) Alcohol misuse and juvenile offending in adolescence. *Addiction* **91**: 483–94. (**228, 442**)

Ferrero GL (1911) *Criminal Man.* New York: Putnam. (**285**)

Feshbach ND (1987) Affective processes and academic achievement. *Child Development 58:* 1335–47. (**394, 395**)

Fessler DMT (2003) The implications of starvation induced psychological changes for the ethical treatment of hunger strikers. *Journal of Medical Ethics 29:* 243–7. (**638**)

Fiander M, Burns T, McHugo GJ, and Drake RE (2003) Assertive community treatment across the Atlantic: comparison of model fidelity in the UK and the USA. *British Journal of Psychiatry 182:* 248–54. (**364**)

Fiebert MS and Gonzalez DM (1997) Women who initiate assaults: The reasons offered for such behaviour. *Psychological Reports* 80: 583–90. (**505**)

Fiedler K, Schmid J, and Stahl T (2002) What is the current truth about polygraph lie detection? *Basic and Applied Social Psychology* 24: 313–24. (**256**)

Finch JD (1984) *Aspects of Law Affecting the Paramedical Professions*. London: Faber and Faber. (**623**)

Fineman KR (1980) Firesetting in childhood and adolescence. *Psychiatric Clinics of North America 3:* 483–500. (**495**)

Fingarette H (1969) *Self Deception*. London: Routledge and Kegan Paul. (**419**)

Fingarette H and Hasse AF (1979) *Mental Disabilities and Criminal Responsibility*. Berkley, CA: University of California Press. (**32, 33**)

Fingerhood M (2000) Substance abuse in older people. *Journal of the American Geriatrics Society 48:* 985–95. (**448**)

Finkelhor D (1984) *Child Sexual Abuse: New Theory and Research*. New York: Free Press. (**250, 442**)

Finkelhor D (1994) The international epidemiology of child sexual abuse. *Child Abuse and Neglect 18:* 409–17. (**243**)

Finkelhor D and Jones LM (2004) *Explanations for the Decline in Child Sexual Abuse Cases*. Washington, DC: US Department of Justice. www.unh.edu/ccrc/pdf/CV58.pdf (**244**)

Finkelhor D, Hotaling G, Lewis IA, and Smith C (1990) Sexual abuse in a national survey of adult men and women: prevalence, characteristics, and risk factors. *Child Abuse and Neglect 14:* 19–28. (**252**)

First M, Spitzer R, Williams J, and Gibbon M (2000) Structured clinical interview for DSM-IV axis 1 disorders (SCID-I). In *American Psychiatric Association Handbook of Psychiatric Measures*. Washington, DC: American Psychiatric Press, pp. 49–53. (**726**)

First MB, Gibbon M, Spitzer RL, Williams JBW, and Benjamin LS (1997) *Structured Clinical Interviews for DSM-IV. Axis II Personality Disorders*. Washington, DC: American Psychiatric Press. (**387**)

Fischer G, Johnson RE, Eder H, et al. (2000) Treatment of opioid-dependent women with buprenorphine. *Addiction* 95: 239–44. (**465**)

Fischer G, Ortner R, Rohrmeister K, et al. (2006) Methadone versus buprenorphine in pregnant addicts: a double-blind, double-dummy comparison study. *Addiction* **101**: 275–81. (**465**)

Fischer M, Barkley RA, Fletcher KE, and Smallish L (1993) The adolescent outcome of hyperactive-children – predictors of psychiatric, academic, social, and emotional adjustment. *Journal of the American Academy of Child and Adolescent Psychiatry* **32**: 324–32. (**486**)

Fischhoff B (1975) Hindsight–foresight: the effects of outcome knowledge on judgment under uncertainty. *Journal of Experimental Psychology: Human Perception and Performance* **1**: 288–99. (**696**)

Fishbein DH, Dax E, Lozovsky D, and Jaffe JH (1992) Neuroendocrine response to a glucose challenge in substance users with high or low levels of aggression, impulsivity, and antisocial personality. *Neuropsychobiology* **25**: 106–14. (**308**)

Fisher BS, Cullen FT, and Turner MG (2000) The sexual victimization of college women. National Institute of Justice Publication No. NCJ 182369. Washington, DC: Department of Justice. (**377**)

Fisher H, Morgan C, Dazzan P, et al. (2009) Gender differences in the association between childhood abuse and psychosis. *The British Journal of Psychiatry* **194**: 319–25. (**345**)

Fisher RS, van Emde Boas W, Blume W, et al. (2005) Epileptic seizures and epilepsy: definitions proposed by the international league against epilepsy (ILAE) and the international bureau for epilepsy (IBE). *Epilepsia* **46**: 470–2. (**284**)

Fisher, HAP. (1977) *Report of an inquiry by the Hon. Sir Henry Fisher into the circumstances leading to the trial if three persons on charges arising out of the death of Maxwell Confait and the fire at 27 Doggett Road, London SE5*. London: House of Commons, HMSO. (**331, 621**)

Fitch WL (1992) Mental retardation and criminal responsibility. *The George Washington Law Review* **53**: 414–93. (**332**)

Fiti R, Perry D, Giraud W, and Ayres M (2008) *Motoring Offences and Breath Test Statistics England and Wales 2006*. London: Ministry of Justice. (**268**)

Fitzgerald E and Harbour A (1999) Marriages and partnerships for psyhcitric patients or prisoners: European rights and law in the UK. In PJ Taylor, T Swan (eds) *Couples in Care and Custody*. Oxford, UK: Butterworth Heinemann, pp. 23–9. (**596**)

Fitzpatrick P, Daly L, Leavy CP, and Cusack DA (2006) Drinking, drugs and driving in Ireland: more evidence for action. *Injury Prevention* **12**: 404–8. (**454**)

Flatley, J, Kershaw, C, Smith, K, Chaplin, R and Moon, D (2010) *Crime in England and Wales 2009/10* Home Office Statistical Bulletin: London. UK Statistical Authority. http://www.unodc.org/documents/southeasterneurope//Doc_5_England_Wales_Crime_Statistics_2009-10.pdf (**230, 498**)

Fleischhacker WW (2009) Second-generation antipsychotic long-acting injections: a systematic review. *British Journal of Psychiatry* **195**: s29–36. (**360**)

Fleiss JL (1981) *Statistical Methods for Rates and Proportions*, 2nd edn. New York: Wiley. (**385**)

Fleming JAE (1989) Multiple personality disorder. *British Journal of Psychiatry* **154**: 877. (**427**)

Fleminger S (2009) Head injury. In AS David, S Fleminger, MD Kopelman, S Lovestone, JDC Mellers (eds) *Lishman's Organic Psychiatry*, 4th edn. (Ch 4). Oxford, UK: Blackwell, pp. 165–279. (**296**)

Fleszar-Szumigajowa J (1969) The perpetrators of arson in forensic-psychiatric material. *Polish Medical Journal* 7: 212–19. (**275**)

Fletcher KE (2003) Childhood posttraumatic stress disorder. In EJ Mash, RA Barkley (eds) *Child Psychopathology*, 2nd edn. New York: Guilford, pp. 330–71. (**487**)

Fletcher PC, Happé F, Frith U, et al. (1995) Other minds in the brain: a functional imaging study of 'theory of mind' in story comprehension. *Cognition* **57**: 109–28. (**395**)

Flint J and MR Munafo (2008) Forum: interactions between gene and environment. *Current Opinion in Psychiatry* **21**: 315–17. (**207**)

Flores I and Calheiros JM (2002) Caracterização de uma amostra de mulheres grávidas toxicodependentes – a experiência do CAT Conde [Characteristics of a sample of drug-dependent pregnant women – the experience of CAT Conde]. *Toxicodependências* **8**: 53–62. (**463**)

Flor-Henry P (1987) Cerebral aspects of sexual deviation. In GD Wilson (ed) *Variant Sexuality: Research and Theory.* Baltimore, MD: Johns Hopkins University Press. (**244**)

Flynn PM, Craddock SG, Luckey JW, Hubbard RL, and Dunteman GH (1996) Comorbidity of antisocial personality and mood disorders among psychoactive substance-dependent treatment clients. *Journal of Personality Disorders* **10**: 56–67. (**444**)

Flynn S, Windfuhr K, and Shaw J (2009) *Filicide: a Literature Review. National Confidential inquiry into Suicide and Homicide by People with Mental Illness.* Manchester, UK: Manchester University. http://www.medicine.manchester.ac.uk/cmhr/centreforsuicideprevention/nci/reports/fili_lit_rev.pdf (**508**)

Flynn SM, Shaw JJ, and Abel K (2007) Homicide of infants: a cross-sectional study. *Journal of Clinical Psychiatry* **68**: 1501–9. (**499, 509, 510**)

Foa EB and Jaycox LH (1999) Cognitive-behaviour treatment of post-traumatic stress disorder. In D Spiegel (ed) *Psychotherapeutic Frontiers. New Principles and Practices.* Washington, DC: American Psychiatric Press, pp. 23–61. (**719, 722, 725**)

Foa EB and Rothbaum BO (1998) *Treating the Trauma of Rape: Cognitive Behavioral Therapy for PTSD.* New York: Guilford. (**726, 727**)

Foa EB, Cashman L, Jaycox L, and Perry K (1997) The validation of a self-report measure for posttraumatic stress disorder: the posttraumatic diagnostic scale. *Psychological Assessment* **9**: 445–51. (**726**)

Foa EB, Dancu CV, Hembree EA, et al. (1999a) A comparison of exposure therapy, stress inoculation training, and their combination in reducing posttraumatic stress disorder in female assault victims. *Journal of Consulting and Clinical Psychology* **67**: 194–200. (**723**)

Foa EB, Ehlers A, Clark DM, Tolin DF, and Orsillo SM (1999b) The posttraumatic cognitions inventory (PTCI): development and validation. *Psychological Assessment* **11**: 303–14. (**726**)

Foa EB, Keane TM, and Friedman MJ (2002) *Effective Treatments for PTSD: Practice Guidelines from the International Society for Traumatic Stress Studies.* New York: Guilford. (**706**)

Foa EB, Steketee G, and Rothbaum BO (1989) Behavioural/cognitive conceptualizations of post-traumatic stress disorder. *Behaviour Therapy* **20**: 155–76. (**722**)

Foley DL, Eaves LJ, Wormley B, et al.(2004) Childhood adversity, monoamine oxidase a genotype, and risk for conduct disorder. *Archives of General Psychiatry* **61**: 738–44. (**200**)

Foley SR, Browne S, Clarke M, et al. (2007) Is violence at presentation by patients with first-episode psychosis associated with duration of untreated psychosis? *Social Psychiatry and Psychiatric Epidemiology* **42**: 606–10. (**344**)

Fonagy P (2003) Towards a developmental understanding of violence. *British Journal of Psychiatry* **183**: 190–2. (**211, 215, 216, 486, 584, 585**)

Fonagy P and Bateman A (2006) Progress in the treatment of borderline personality disorder. *British Journal of Psychiatry* **188**: 1–3. (**584**)

Fonagy P and Target M (1997) Attachment and reflective function: their role in self organization. *Development and Psychopathology* **9**: 679–700. (**718, 719**)

Fonagy P, Gergely G, Jurist, EL, and Target M (2002) *Affect Regulation, Mentalisation and the Development of the Self.* London: Karnac. (**396**)

Fonagy P, Steele M, Steele H, and Target M (1995) Attachment, the reflective self, and borderline states: The predictive specificity of the adult attachment interview and pathological emotional development. In S Goldberg, R Muir and J Kerr (eds) *Attachment Theory, Social Development and clinical perspectives.* Analytic Press: New York. pp 233–78. (**396**)

Fonagy P, Target F, Steele, M, & Steele H (1997) The development of violence and crime as it relates to security of attachment. In JD Osovsky (ed) *Children in a Violent Society.* New York: Guilford. pp 150–82 (**584**)

Fondacaro KM, Holt JC, and Powell TA (1999) Psychological impact of childhood sexual abuse on male inmates: the importance of perception. *Child Abuse and Neglect* **23**: 361–9. (**712**)

Fong G, Frost D, and Stansfeld S (2001) Road rage: a psychiatric phenomenon? *Social Psychiatry and Psychiatric Epidemiology* **36**: 277–86. (**278**)

Foote CL and Goetz CF (2008) The impact of legalized abortion on crime: comment. *The Quarterly Journal of Economics* **123**: 407–23. (**5**)

Forchuk C, Jewell J, Tweedell D, and Steinnagel L (2003) Reconnecting: the client's experience of recovery from psychosis. *Perspectives in Psychiatric Care* **39**: 141–50. (**574**)

Ford CV, King BH, and Hollender MH (1988) Lies and liars: psychiatric aspects of prevarication. *American Journal of Psychiatry* **145**: 554–62. (**418**)

Forouzan E and Cooke DJ (2005) Figuring out la femme fatale: Conceptual and assessment issues concerning psychopathy in females. *Behavioral Sciences and the Law* **23**: 765–78. (**513**)

Forrest AR (1995) Nurses who systematically harm their patients. *Medical Law International* **1**(4): 114–21. (**686**)

Foster C, Hillson M, and Thorogood M (2005) Interventions for promoting physical activity. *Cochrane Database of Systematic Reviews* 2005. Issue 1, Art. No.: CD003180. http://onlinelibrary.wiley.com/o/cochrane/clsysrev/articles/CD003180.frame.html (**568**)

Fottrell E (1980) The study of violent behaviour among patients in psychiatric hospitals. *British Journal of Psychiatry* **136**: 216–21. (**515**)

Foucault M (1967) *Madness and Civilisation – A History of Insanity in the Age of Reason.* London: Tavistock. (**602**)

Fowler T, Langley K, Rice F, et al. (2009) Psychopathy trait scores in adolescents with childhood ADHD: the contribution of genotypes affecting MAOA, 5HTT and COMT activity. *Psychiatric Genetics* **19**: 312–19. (**198, 199, 202**)

Fowler T, Lifford K, Shelton K, et al. (2007a) Exploring the relationship between genetic and environmental influences on initiation and progression of substance use. *Addiction* **102**: 413–22. (**201**)

Fowler T, Shelton K, Lifford K, et al. (2007b) Genetic and environmental influences on the relationship between peer alcohol use and own alcohol use in adolescents. *Addiction* **102**: 894–903. (**207**)

Fox JA and Levin J (2012) *Extreme Killing: Understanding Serial and Mass Murder* 2nd edition. London: Sage. (**233**)

Fox JRE, Gray NS, and Lewis H (2004) Factors determining compliance with command hallucinations with violent content: the role of social rank, perceived power of the voiced and voice malevolence. *Journal of Forensic Psychiatry and Psychology* **15**: 511–31. (**353**)

France J and Kramer S (eds) (2001) *Communication and Mental Illness.* London: Jessica Kingsley. (**558**)

Francis R, Higgins J, and Cassan E (2000) *Report of the Independent Inquiry into the Care and Treatment of Michael Stone.* Kent County Council and Kent Probation Area: South East Kent Strategic Health Authority. http://www.southofengland.nhs.uk/wp-content/uploads/2012/03/Report-of-the-independent-inquiry-into-the-care-and-treatment-of-MS.pdf (**58, 75, 76, 383, 414, 590**)

Frank DA, Augustyn M, Knight WG, Pell T, and Zuckerman B (2001) Growth, development and behavior in early childhood following prenatal cocaine exposure. *Journal of the American Medical Association* **285**: 1613–25. (**341**)

Frank E and Anderson BP (1987) Psychiatric disorders in rape victims: past history and current symptomatology. *Comprehensive Psychiatry* **28**: 77–82. (**715**)

Frank JD (1986) Psychotherapy – the transformation of meanings: discussion paper. *Journal of the Royal Society of Medicine* **79**: 341–6. (**569**)

Frank JD and Frank JB (1991) *Persuasion and Healing: A Comparative Study of Psychotherapy,* 3rd edn. Baltimore, MD: John Hopkins University Press. (**407**)

Frank V (2004) Evidence-based uncertainty in mental health nursing. *Journal of Psychiatric and Mental Health Nursing* **11**: 99–105. (**569**)

Frankenburg FR and Zanarini MC (2002) Divalproex sodium treatment of women with borderline personality disorder and bipolar II disorder: a double-blind placebo-controlled pilot study. *Journal of clinical Psychiatry* **63**: 442–6. (**404, 566**)

Frankle W, Shera D, Berger-Hershkowitz H, et al. (2001) Clozapine-associated reduction in arrest rates of psychotic patients with criminal histories. *The American Journal of Psychiatry* **158**: 270–4. (**563**)

Frankle WG, Lombardo I, New AS, et al. (2005) Brain serotonin transporter distribution in subjects with impulsive aggressivity: a positron emission study with [11C] McN 5652. *American Journal of Psychiatry* **162**: 915–23. (**310**)

Franklin CA and Fearn NE (2008) Gender, race, and formal court decision-making outcomes: Chivalry/paternalism, conflict theory, or gender conflict? *Journal of Criminal Justice* **36**: 279–90. (**500**)

Franks RA and Cobb D (2006) *Mental Health (Care and Treatment) (Scotland) Act 2003.* Edinburgh, UK: Greens. (**90**)

Frans Ö, Rimmö P-A, Åberg L, and Fredrikson M (2005) Trauma exposure and post-traumatic stress disorder in the general population. *Acta Psychiatrica Scandinavica* **111**: 291–9. (**712**)

Fraser A, Thomson LDG and Graham L (2007) Time to act on behalf of mentally disordered offenders. *British Medical Journal,* 15 June. (**653**)

Frazer KA, Murray SS, Schnork NJ, and Topol EJ (2009) Human genetic variation and its contribution to complex traits. *Nature Reviews Genetics* **10**: 241–51. (**195**)

Frazzetto G, Di Lorenzo G, Carola V, et al. (2007) Early trauma and increased risk for physical aggression during adulthood: the moderating role of MAOA genotype. *PLoS One* **2**(5): e486. (**200**)

Frean A (1999) Leap in 'senile delinquency' as population ages. *Times of London,* 10 March:6. (**523**)

Freckleton I (1988) Querulent paranoia and the vexatious complainant. *International Journal of Law and Psychiatry* **11**: 127–43. (**381**)

Freedman LZ (1971) Psychopathology of assassination. In WJ Crotty (ed) *Assassination and the Political Order.* New York: Harper and Row, pp. 143–60. (**543**)

Freeman D, Garety PA, and Kuipers E (2001) Persecutory delusions: developing the understanding of belief maintenance and emotional distress. *Psychological Medicine* **31**: 1293–306. (**354**)

Freeman D, Garety PA, Kuipers E, et al. (2007) Acting on persecutory delusions: the importance of safety seeking. *Behaviour Research and Therapy* **45**: 89–99. (**354**)

Freeman S (2006) The mistake that cost Roy Meadow his reputation. *Times Online,* 17 February. (**675**)

Frei A, Völlm B, Graf M, and Dittmann V (2006) Female serial killing: review and case report. *Criminal Behaviour and Mental Health* **16**: 167–76. (**240, 507**)

French AP and Schechmeister BR (1983) The multiple personality syndrome and criminal defense. *Bulletin of the American Academy of Psychiatry and the Law* **11**: 17–25. (**343**)

French LA (2005) Mental retardation and the death penalty in the USA: the clinical and legal legacy. *Criminal Behaviour and Mental Health* **15**: 82–6. (**115, 333**)

French National Institute of Health and Medical Research (INSERM) (2004) *Psychotherapy: An Evaluation of Three Approaches.* Paris, France: French National Institute of Health and Medical Research. http://www.ncbi.nlm.nih.gov/books/NBK7123/ (**725**)

Fresán A, Apiquian R, de la Fuente-Sandoval C, et al. (2004) Premorbid adjustment and violent behavior in schizophrenic patients. *Schizophrenia Research* **69**: 143–8. (**470**)

Freud S (1905) Three essays on the theory of sexuality. In *The Complete Psychological Works of Sigmund Freud,* Vol 7, J Strachey (ed). London: Hogarth. (**482**)

Freud S (1909) Analyse der Phobie eines fünfjährigen Knaben ('Der kleine Hans') Jb. psychoanal. psycho-pathol. *Forsch* **1**: 1–109; (republished as 'Analysis of a five year old boy' in *Collected Papers.* London: Hogarth.) (**579**)

Freud S (1916) *Criminals from a Sense of Guilt. The Standard edn. of the Complete Psychological Works of Sigmund Freud.* London: Hogarth. (**232**)

Freud S (1917) Mourning and melancholia. In *Collected Papers*, Vol. 4. Trans. by J Riviere. London: Hogart. (**7,**

Freud S (1920, translated CJM Hubbach, 1922) *Beyond the Pleasure Principle*. London: International Psycho-analytical Library, Hogarth. **212**)

Freud S (1928) Dostoevski and parricide. In J Strachey (ed) *Collected Papers, 5*. New York: Basic Books. (**244**)

Freud S (1929) *Civilization and its Discontents*. London: International Psycho-analytic Library, Hogarth. (**275**)

Freudenberg N, Daniels J, Crum M, Perkins T and Richie BE (2008) Coming home from jail: The social and health consequences of community reentry for women, male adolescents, and their families and communities. *American Journal of Public Health* 98: S191–202. (**516**)

Freyd JJ (1996) *Betrayal Trauma: The Logic of Forgetting Childhood Abuse*. Cambridge, MA: Harvard University Press. (**723**)

Fricchione G (2004) Clinical practice. Generalised anxiety disorder. *New England Journal of Medicine* **351**: 675–82. (**560**)

Friedman CTH (1982) The so-called hystero-psychoses. In CTH Friedman, RA Faguet (eds) *Extraordinary Disorders of Human Behavior*. New York: Plenum. (**428**)

Friedman MJ (2006) Posttraumatic stress disorder among military returnees from Afghanistan and Iraq. *American Journal of Psychiatry* **163**: 586–93. (**715**)

Friedman SH and Resnick PJ (2011) Child murder and mental illness in parents: Implications for psychiatrists. *Journal of Clinical Psychiatry* **72**: 587–8. (**508**)

Friedman SH, Horowitz SM, and Resnick PJ (2005b) Child murder by mothers: A critical analysis of the current state of knowledge and a research agenda. *American Journal of Psychiatry* **162**:1578–87. (**508, 509**)

Friedman SH, Hrouda DR, Holden CE, et al (2005a): Filicide-suicide: Common factors in parents who kill their children and themselves. *Journal of the American Academy of Psychiatry and the Law* 33:496–504. (**508, 509**)

Friedman SH, Shelton MD, Elhaj O, et al. (2005) Gender differences in criminality: bipolar disorder with co-occurring substance abuse. *Journal of the American Academy of Psychiatry and the Law* 33: 188–95. (**508, 509**)

Friendship C, Blud L, Eriksson M, and Travers R (2002) *An Evaluation of Cognitive-Behavioural Treatment for Prisoners*. Home Office Findings, 161. London: Home Office. (**574, 576**)

Frisher M, Collins J, Millson D, Crome I, and Croft P (2004) Prevalence of comorbid psychiatric illness and substance misuse in primary care in England and Wales. *Journal Epidemiology and Community Health* **58**: 1036–41. (**338**)

Frisher M, Crome I, Macleod J, Millson D, and Croft P (2005) Substance misuse and psychiatric illness: prospective observational study using the general practice research database. *Journal of Epidemiological and Community Health* **59**: 847–50. (**488**)

Frodi A, Dernevik M, Sepa A, Philipson J and Bragesjö M (2001) Current attachment representations of incarcerated offenders varying in degree of psychopathy. *Attachment and Human Development*, **3**: 269–83. (**396**)

Fromm E (1964) *The Heart of Man. Its Genius for Good and Evil*. New York: Harper and Row. (**7**)

Fromm E (1973) *The Anatomy of Human Destructiveness*. New York: Holt, Rinehard and Winston (Penguin, 1977: Harmondsworth). (**7, 213, 686**)

Fromm-Reichmann F (1948) Notes on the development of treatment of schizophrenics by psychoanalysis and psychotherapy. *Psychiatry* **11**: 263–73. (**341**)

Fry D and Howe D (2005) Managing older prisoners at Wymott. *Prison Service Journal* **160**. (**528**)

Fu Q, Heath AC, Bucholz KK, et al. (2002) Shared genetic risk of major depression, alcohol dependence, and marijuana dependence: contribution of antisocial personality disorder in men. *Archives of General Psychiatry* **59**: 1125–32. (**203**)

Fujii DEM, Tokioka AB, Lichton AI, and Hishinuma E (2005) Ethnic differences in prediction of violence risk with the HCR-20 among psychiatric inpatients. *Psychiatric Services* **56**: 711–16. (**537**)

Fulford KWM (1989) *Moral Theory and Medical Practice*. Cambridge, UK: Cambridge University Press. (**9**)

Fullam RS, McKie S, and Dolan MC (2009) Psychopathic traits and deception: functional magnetic resonance imaging study. *British Journal of Psychiatry* **194**(3): 229–35. (**306**)

Fuller E (ed) (2008) *Drug Use, Smoking and Drinking Among Young People in England in 2007*. London: The Health and Social Care Information Centre. (**466**)

Furby L, Weinrott MR, and Blackshaw L (1989) Sex offender recidivism: a review. *Psychological Bulletin* **105**: 3–30. (**257**)

Furniss T (1991) *The Multi-professional Handbook of Child Sexual Abuse: Integrated Management, Therapy, and Legal Intervention*. London: Routledge. (**259**)

Fyer MR, Frances AJ, Sullivan T, Hurt SW and Clarkin J (1988) Co-morbidity of borderline personality disorder. *Archives of General Psychiatry* **45**: 348–52. (**397**)

Gabbard GO (1999) Psychodynamic approaches to physician sexual misconduct. In D Bloom, CC Nadelson, MT Notman (eds) *Physician Sexual Misconduct*. Washington, DC: American Psychiatric Association. (**691**)

Gabbard GO and Lester EP (1995) *Boundaries and Bounds. Violations in Psychoanalysis*. Arlington, VA: New York, Basic Books (**692**)

Gabbert F, Memon A, and Wright DB (2007) I saw it for longer than you: the relationship between perceived encoding duration and memory conformity *Acta Psychologica* **124**: 319–31. (**162**)

Gabriel SB, Schaffner SF, Nguyen H, et al. (2002) The structure of haplotype blocks in the human genome. *Science* **296**: 2225–9. (**194**)

Galahad SMS Ltd and Youth Justice Board (2004) *Substance Misuse and the Juvenile Secure Estate*. London: Youth Justice Board. (**491**)

Galanter M (1999) *Cults: Faith, Healing and Coercion*, 2nd edn. Oxford, UK: Oxford University Press. (**412**)

Galbaud du Fort G, Boothroyd LJ, Bland RC, Newman SC, and Kakuma R (2002) Spouse similarity for antisocial behaviour in the general population. *Psychological Medicine* **32**: 1407–16. (**189**)

References

Galeazzi GM, Elkins K, and Curci P (2005) The stalking of mental health professionals by patients. *Psychiatric Services* **56**(2): 137–8. (**378**)

Gallagher EM (2001) Elders in prison. Health and well-being of older inmates. *International Journal of Law and Psychiatry* **24**: 325–33. (**528**)

Galta K, Olsen SL, and Wik G (2010) Murder followed by suicide: Norwegian data and international literature. *Nordic Journal of Psychiatry* **64**(6): 397–401. (**232**)

Gambling Review Body (2001) *Report* (Budd) CM 5206. London: Stationery Office. http://www.hblb.org.uk/documents/92_GamblingReview.pdf (**467**)

Ganis G, Rosenfeld JP, Meixner J, Kievit RA and Schendan HE (2011) Lying in the scanner: Covert countermeasures disrupt deception detection by functional magnetic resonance imaging. *NeuroImage* **55**: 312–9. (**420**)

Gannon T (2010) Female arsonists. *Psychiatry: Interpersonal and Biological Processes* **73**: 173–89. (**504**)

Ganser SJM (1898, translated CE Schoser in *British Journal of Criminology*, 1965, **5**: 120–6.) Über einen Eigenartigen Hysterischen Dammerzustand. *Archiv für Psychiatrie und nervenkrankheiten* **30**: 633–40. (**434**)

Garavan H, Ross T, Murphy K, Roche R, and Stein E (2002) Dissociable executive functions in the dynamic control of behavior: inhibition, error detection, and correction. *Neuroimage* **17**: 1820–9. (**301**)

Garbarino J (2001) An ecological perspective on the effects of violence on children. *Journal of Community Psychology* **29**: 361–78. (**487**)

Garbutt JC, West SL, Carey TS, Lohr KN, and Crews FT (1999) Pharmacological treatment of alcohol dependence: a review of the evidence. *Journal of the American Medical Association* **281**: 1318–25. (**446**)

Gardner DL, Lucas PB, and Cowdry RW (1990) CSF metabolites in borderline personality disorder compared with normal controls. *Biological Psychiatry* **28**: 247–54. (**308**)

Gardner W, Lidz CW, Mulvery EP, and Shaw EC (1996a) Clinical versus actuarial predictions of violence in patients with mental illness. *Journal of Consulting and Clinical Psychology* **64**: 602–9. (**532**)

Gardner W, Lidz CW, Mulvery EP, and Shaw EC (1996b) A comparison of actuarial methods for identifying repetitively violent patients with mental illnesses. *Law and Human Behaviour* **20**: 35–48. (**532**)

Garelick AI, Gross SR, Richardson I, von der Tann M, Bland J and Hale R (2007) Which doctors and with what problems contact a specialist service for doctors? A cross sectional investigation. *BMC Medicine* **5**: 26 doi:10.1186/1741-7015-5-26. http://www.biomedcentral.com/1741-7015/5/26 (**692**)

Garety P, Fowler DG, Freeman D, et al. (2008) Cognitive-behaviour therapy and family intervention for relapse prevention and symptom reduction in psychosis: randomised controlled trial. *British Journal of Psychiatry* **192**: 412–23. (**363**)

Garety P, Kuipers E, Fowler D, Chamberlain F, and Dunn G (1994) Cognitive behavioural therapy for drug-resistant psychosis. *British Journal of Medical Psychology* **67**: 259–71. (**361**)

Garland D (1988) British criminology before 1935. *British Journal of Criminology* **28**: 1–17. (**4**)

Garmezy N and Rutter M (1983) *Stress, Coping and Development in Children.* New York: McGraw-Hill. (**484**)

Garner BA (ed) (1999) *Black's Law Dictionary*, 7th edn. St. Paul: West Group. (**120, 121**)

Garrett M and Lerman M (2007) CBT for long-term inpatients with a forensic history. *Psychiatric Services* **58**: 712–3. (**574**)

Gartrell N, Herman J, Olarte S, Feldstein M, and Localio R (1986) Psychiatrist-patient sexual contact: results of a national survey, I: prevalence. *American Journal of Psychiatry* **143**: 1126–31. (**681**)

Gaskin CJ, Elsom SJ, and Happell B (2008) Interventions for reducing the use of seclusion. *British Journal of Psychiatry* **191**: 298–303. (**595**)

Gaub M and Carlson CL (1997) Gender differences in ADHD: a meta-analysis and critical review. *Journal of the American Academy of Child and Adolescent Psychiatry* **36**: 1036–46. (**512**)

Gaudiano B (2006) Is symptomatic improvement in clinical trials of cognitive-behavioural therapy for psychosis clinically significant? *Journal of Psychiatric Practice* **12**: 11–23. (**362**)

Gaup R (1914) The Scientific Significance of the Case of Ernst Wagner in Hirsch and Shepherd (1974) qv. (**236**)

Gavanski I and Wells GL (1989) Counterfactual processing of normal and exceptional events. *Journal of Experimental Social Psychology* **25**: 314–25. (**696**)

Gavin N, Parsons S, and Grubin D (2003) Reception screening and mental health needs assessment in a male remand prison. *Psychiatric Bulletin* **27**: 251–3. (**630**)

Gayford JJ (1975) Wife battering: a preliminary survey of 100 cases. *British Medical Journal* **1**: 194–7. (**372**)

Gayford JJ (1979) Battered wives. *British Journal of Hospital Medicine* **22**: 496–503. (**372**)

Ge X, Best KM, Conger RD, and Simons RL (1996) Parenting behaviors and the occurrence and co-occurrence of adolescent depressive symptoms and conduct problems. *Developmental Psychology* **32**: 717–31. (**199**)

Gebhard PH, Gagnon JH, Pomeroy WB, and Christenson CV (1965) *Sex Offenders*. London: Heinneman. (**247, 248**)

Geddes JR, Freemantle N, Mason J, Eccles NP, and Boynton J (2006) Selective serotonin reuptake inhibitors (SSRIs) versus other antidepressants for depression Cochrane Database of Systematic Reviews 2006, Issue 3. Art. No.: CD001851. DOI: 10.1002/14651858.CD001851.pub2. The Cochrane Collaboration. http://onlinelibrary.wiley.com/doi/10.1002/14651858.CD001851.pub2/pdf (**560**)

Geddes JR, Verdoux H, Takei N, et al. (1999) Schizophrenia and complications of pregnancy and labour: an individual patient data meta-analysis. *Schizophrenia Bulletin* **25**: 413–23. (**341**)

Gee DJ and Mason JK (1990) *The Courts and the Doctor*. Oxford, UK: Oxford University Press. (**168**)

Gelder M, Gath D, and Mayou R (1989) *Oxford Textbook of Psychiatry*, 2nd edn. Oxford, UK: Oxford University Press. (**11**)

Gelernter J and HR Kranzler (2009) Genetics of alcohol dependence. *Human Genetics* **126**: 91–9. (**204, 205, 206**)

Gelernter J, Panhuysen C, Weiss R, et al. (2005) Genomewide linkage scan for cocaine dependence and related traits: significant linkages for a cocaine-related trait and cocaine-induced paranoia. *American Journal of Medical Genetics part B: Neuropsychiatric Genetics* **136**: 45–52. (**204**)

Geller JL, Fisher WH, Grudzinskas AJ, Clayfield JC, and Lawlor T (2006) Involuntary outpatient treatments 'deinstitutionalized coercion': the net-widening concerns. *International Journal of Law and Psychiatry* **29**: 551–62. (**35**)

Gelsthorpe L (1997) Feminism and criminology. In M Maguire, R Morgan and R Reiner (eds) *The Oxford Handbook of Criminology*, 2nd Edition. Oxford: Oxford University Press. pp. 511–34. (**517**)

Gelsthorpe L and Morris A (2002) Restorative youth justice. The last vestiges of welfare? In J Muncie, G Hughes, E McLaughlin (eds) *Youth Justice, Critical Readings*. London: Sage. (**478**)

Genders E and Player E (1995) *Grendon. A Study of a Therapeutic Prison*. Oxford, UK: Clarendon. (**571**)

Genders E and Player E (2010) Therapy in prison: Grendon 20 years on. *The Howard Journal* **49**: 431–50. (**412**)

Gendreau P, Goggin C, and Smith P (2002) Is the PCL-R really the 'unparalleled' measure of offender risk? A lesson in knowledge cumulation. *Criminal Justice and Behaviour* **29**: 397–426. (**534**)

General Medical Council (2004) *Confidentiality: Protecting and Providing Information*. London: General Medical. http://www.gmc-uk.org/static/documents/content/Confidentiality_0910.pdf (**662**)

Gentile SR, Asamen JK, Harmell PH, and Weathers R (2002) The stalking of psychologists by their clients. *Professional Psychology: Research and Practice* **33**: 490–4. (**378**)

Gentilello L, Rivara FP, Donovan D, Jurkovitch G, and Daramciang E (1999) Alcohol interventions in a trauma centre as a means of reducing the risk of injury recurrence. *Annals of Surgery* **230**: 473–83. (**705**)

George C, Kaplan N, and Main M (1985) *The Adult Attachment Interview*. Privileged Communication. Berkeley, CA: Department of Psychology, University of California. (**581**)

George C, Kaplan N, and Main M (1996) *The Adult Attachment Interview*, 3rd edn. Berkeley, CA: Department of Psychology, University of California. (**581**)

Gerber AJ, Kocsis JH, Milrod BL, et al. (2011) A quality-based review of randomized controlled trials of psychodynamic psychotherapy. *American Journal of Psychiatry* **168**: 19–28. (**409**)

Gerra G, Di Petta G, D'Amore A, et al. (2006) Effects of olanzapine on aggressiveness in heroin dependent patients. *Progress in Neuro-psychopharmacology and Biological Psychiatry* **30**: 1291–8. (**564**)

Gerra G, Zaimovic A, Castaldini L, et al. (2010) Relevance of perceived childhood neglect, 5-HTT gene variants and hypothalamus-pituitary-adrenal axis dysregulation to substance abuse susceptibility. *American Journal of Medical Genetics B Neuropsychiatric Genetics* **153B**: 715–22. (**207**)

Gerson L (1978) Alcohol related acts of violence; who was drinking and where the acts occurred. *Journal of Studies on Alcohol* **39**: 1294–6. (**702**)

Ghodse H (2002) *Drugs and Addictive Behaviour*. Cambridge, UK: Cambridge University Press. (**465**)

Ghodse H, Oyefeso A, and Kilpatrick B (1998) Mortality of drug addicts in the United Kingdom 1967–1993. *International Journal of Epidemiology* **27**: 473–8. (**451**)

Giancola PR (2000) Executive functioning: a conceptual framework for alcohol-related aggression. *Experimental and Clinical Psychopharmacology* **8**: 576–97. (**440**)

Giancola PR (2006) Influence of subjective intoxication, breath alcohol concentration, and expectancies on the alcohol–aggression relationship. *Alcoholism: Clinical and Experimental Research* **30**: 844–50. (**440**)

Giancola PR, White HR, Berman ME, et al. (2003) Diverse research on alcohol and aggression in humans. *Alcoholism – Clinical and Experimental Research* **27**: 198–208. (**440, 702**)

Gibbens TC and Robertson G (1983) A survey of the criminal careers of restriction order patients. *British Journal of Psychiatry* **143**: 370–5. (**316**)

Gibbens TCN (1958) Sane and insane homicide. *Journal of Criminal Law Criminology and Police Science* **49**: 110–15. (**372**)

Gibbens TCN (1983) Medicolegal aspects. In M Shepherd, OL Zangwill (eds) *Handbook of Psychiatry*, Vol. 1. *General Psychopathology*. Cambridge, UK: Cambridge University Press. (**291**)

Gibbens TCN, Palmer C, and Prince J (1971) Mental health aspects of shoplifting. *British Medical Journal* **3**: 612–15. (**295**)

Gibbens TCN, Way C, and Soothill KL (1977) Behavioural types of rape. *British Journal of Psychiatry* **130**: 32–42. (**248, 249**)

Gibbs A (1999) The assessment, case management and evaluation system. *Probation Journal* **46**: 182–6. (**530**)

Gibbs B and Haldenby A (2006) *Urban Crime Rankings*. London: Reform. (**704**)

Gibson E (1975) *Homicide in England and Wales 1967–1971*. Home Office Research Study No. 31. London: HMSO. (**232**)

Gibson LE, Holt JC, Fondacaro KM, et al. (1999) An examination of antecedent traumas and psychiatric comorbidity among male inmates with PTSD. *Journal of Traumatic Stress* **12**: 473–84. (**712**)

Giesen-Bloo J, van Dyck R, Spinhoven P, et al. (2006) Outpatient psychotherapy for borderline personality disorder: randomised trial of schema focussed therapy vs transference focussed therapy. *Archives of General Psychiatry* **63**: 649–59. (**410**)

Gigerenzer G and Gaissmaier W (2008) Helping doctors and patients make sense of human statistics. *Psychological Sciences in the Public Interest* **8**: 53–96. (**530, 532**)

Gigerenzer G and Muir Gray JA (eds) (2011) *Better Doctors, Better Patients, Better Decisions: Envisioning Health Care 2020*. Cambridge, UK: Massachusetts Institute of Technology Press. (**530**)

Gilligan J (2000) *Violence. Reflections on a National Epidemic*. New York: Putnam, pp. 9. (**551**)

References

Gil DG (1969) Physical abuse of children: findings and implications of a nationwide survey. *Pediatrics* **44**: 857–64. (**222**)

Gilbert P and Milles JNV (2000) Sensitivity to social put-down: it's relationship to perceptions of social rank, shame, social anxiety, depression, anger and self-other blame. *Personality and Individual Differences* **29**: 757–74. (**215**)

Gilburt H, Rose D, and Slade M (2008) The importance of relationships in mental health care: a qualitative study of service users' experiences of psychiatric hospital admission in the UK. *BMC Health Services Research* **8**: 92. (**356**)

Gilchrist E, Johnson R, Takriti R, Weston S, Beech A, Kebbell M. (2003) *Domestic Violence Offenders: Characteristics and offending related needs.* London: Home Office. Research findings no. 217 (**220, 442**)

Gilchrist G (2002) *Results from the Study on Psychiatric Morbidity among Female Drug Users in Glasgow.* Report to the working group on multi-mental health problems among alcohol and drug users. Glasgow, UK: Greater Glasgow NHS. (**463**)

Gilchrist G, Gruer L, and Atkinson J (2005) Comparison of drug use and psychiatric morbidity between prostitute and non-prostitute female drug users in Glasgow, Scotland. *Addictive Behaviors* **30**: 1019–23. (**464**)

Gilchrist G, Taylor A, Goldberg D, et al. (2001) Behavioural and lifestyle study of women using a drop-in centre for female street sex workers in Glasgow, Scotland: a 10 year comparative study. *Addiction Research and Theory* **9**: 43–58. (**464**)

Gill P, McKenna P, O'Neill H, Thompson J, and Timmons D (2010) Pillars and pathways: foundations of recovery in forensic mental health care. *The British Journal of Forensic Practice* **12**: 29–36. (**617**)

Gillberg C and O'Brien G (2000) *Developmental Disability and Behaviour. Clinics in Developmental Medicine*, volume 149. London: Mac Keith Press. (**320, 323**)

Gillberg C and O'Brien G (2000) *Developmental Disability and Behavioiur. Clinics in Developmental Medicine*, Vol. 149. London: MacKeith. (**320, 323**)

Gillberg C, Persson E, Grufman M and Themner U (1986) Pyschiatric disorders in mildly and severely mentally retarded urban children and adolescents: Epidemiological aspects. *British Journal of Psychiatry* **149**: 68–74. (**317**)

Gillies D, Beck A, McCloud A, Rathbone J, and Gillies D (2010) Benzodiazepines for psychosis-induced aggression or agitation. Cochrane Database of Systematic Reviews 2005, Issue 4. Art. No.: CD003079. DOI: 10.1002/14651858.CD003079.pub2. http://onlinelibrary.wiley.com/doi/10.1002/14651858.CD003079.pub2/pdf (**566**)

Gillies H (1965) Murder in the west of Scotland. *British Journal of Psychiatry* **111**: 1087–94. (**353**)

Gilligan J (1996) *Violence: Our Deadly Epidemic and Its Causes*, New York: Grosset (also published as (1997) *Violence: Reflections on a National Epidemic.* New York: Vintage Books, and as (2000) *Violence: Reflections on Our Deadliest Epidemic.* London: Jessica Kingsley) (**6, 213**)

Gimlette JD (1901) Notes on a case of amok. *Journal of Tropical Medicine and Hygiene* **4**: 195–9. (**428**)

Giovannoni JM and Gurel L (1967) Socially disruptive behavior of ex-mental patients. *Archives of General Psychiatry* **17**: 146–53. (**280**)

Giridharadas A (2008) *India's Novel Use of Brain Scans in Courts is Debated. New York Times*, 15 September. www.nytimes.com/2008/09/15/world/asia/15brainscan.html?ref=anandgiridharadas (**17**)

Glasgow DV, Osborne A, and Croxen J (2003) An assessment tool for investigating paedophile sexual interest using viewing time: an application of single case methodology. *British Journal of Learning Disabilities* **31**: 96–102. (**254**)

Glass GV (2001) Foreword. In BE Wampold (eds) *The Great Psychotherapy Debate: Models, Methods and Findings.* New Jersey: Lawrence Erlbaum and Associates. (**407**)

Glass IB (1989) Alcoholic hallucinosis: a psychiatric enigma – 1. The development of an idea. – 2. Follow-up studies. *British Journal of Addiction* **84**: 29–41; 151–64. (**439**)

Glatt MM (1982) *Alcoholism.* Sevenoaks, UK: Hodder and Stoughton. (**33**)

Glauser T, Ben-Menachem E, Bourgeois, B, et al. (2006) ILAE treatment guidelines: evidence-based analysis of antiepileptic drug efficacy and effectiveness as initial monotherapy for epileptic seizures and syndromes. *Epilepsia* **47**: 1094–120. (**289**)

Glazer WM and Dickson RA (1998) Clozapine reduces violence and persistent aggression in schizophrenia. *Journal of Clinical Psychiatry* **59**: 8–14. (**563**)

Glenn MB, Wroblewski B, Parziale J, et al. (1989) Lithium carbonate for aggressive behavior or affective instability in ten brain-injured patients. *American Journal of Physical Medicine and Rehabilitation* **68**: 221–6. (**566**)

Glover AJJ, Nicholson DE, Hemmati T, Bernfeld GA, and Quinsey VL (2002) A comparison of predictors of general and violent recividism among high risk federal offenders. *Criminal Justice and Behavior* **29**: 235–49. (**536**)

Gobbi G, Gaudreau PO, and Leblanc N (2006) Efficacy of topiramate, valproate, and their combination on aggression/agitation behavior in patients with psychosis. *Journal of Clinical Psychopharmacology* **26**: 467–73. (**566**)

Goddard HH (1922) *The Criminal Imbecile: An Analysis of Three Remarkable Murder Cases.* New York: Macmillan Co. http://babel.hathitrust.org/cgi/pt?id=wu.89034692012 accessed 26 02 2013. (**315**)

Godlaski AJ and Giancola PR (2009) Executive functioning, irritability, and alcohol-related aggression. *Psychology of Addictive Behaviors* **23**: 391–403. (**439**)

Goethals K and van Lier E (2009) Dutch training and research in forensic psychiatry in a European perspective. *Criminal Behaviour and Mental Health* **19**: 286–90. (**16**)

Goetting A (1988) When parents kill their young children: Detroit 1982–1986. *Journal of Family Violence* **3**: 339–46. (**508**)

Goff P and Dixon L (2011) Antipsychotic polypharmacy: are two ever better than one? *American Journal of Psychiatry* **168**: 667–9. (**360**)

Goffman E (1961) *Asylums. Anchor Books,* Reprinted 1968. Harmondsworth, UK: Penguin Books. (**551, 601, 602**)

Goldberg D (1992) *General Health Questionnaire (GHQ 12).* Windsor, ON: NFER-Nelson. (**630**)

Goldberg D (2005) The narrative and the bureaucratic: an analysis of an independent inquiry report into homicide. *Journal of Forensic Psychiatry and Psychology* **16**: 149–66. (**74**)

Goldberg SC, Schulz SC, Schulz PM, et al. (1986) Borderline and schizotypal personality disorders treated with low-dose thiothixene vs. placebo. *Archives of General Psychiatry* **43**: 680–6. (**404**)

Golding J (1999) Intimate partner violence as a risk factor for mental disorders: a meta analysis. *Journal of Family Violence* **14**: 99–132. (**714**)

Golding JM and Bradshaw GS (2005) Alcohol in the court room the intoxication defence. *American Journal of Forensic Psychiatry* **26**: 37–57. (**441**)

Goldman D, Oroszi G, and Ducci F (2005) The genetics of addictions: uncovering the genes. *Nature Reviews Genetics* **6**: 521–32. (**202**)

Goldman MS, Del Boca FK, and Darkes J (1999) Alcohol expectancy theory: the application of cognitive neuroscience. In KE Leonard, HT Blane (eds) *Psychological Theories of Drinking and Alcoholism,* 2nd edn. New York: Guilford, pp. 203–46. (**440**)

Goldstein A, Nensen R, Daleflod B, and Kalt M (eds) (2004) *New Perspectives on Aggression Replacement Training: Practice, Research, and Application.* Chichester, UK: John Wiley and Sons. (**609**)

Goldstein RL (2007) Criminal law: structures and procedures. In AR Felthous, H Sass (eds) *International Handbook of Psychopathic Disorders and the Law.* Chichester, UK: John Wiley and Sons, pp. 165–76. (**118**)

Golubchik P, Mozes T, Vered Y and Weizman A (2009) Platelet poor plasma serotonin level in delinquent adolescents diagnosed with conduct disorder. *Neuro-Psychopharmacology and Biological Psychiatry* **33**: 1223–225. (**307**)

Goodman M, New A, and Siever L (2004) Trauma, genes, and the neurobiology of personality disorders. *Annals of the New York Academy of Science* **1032**: 104–16. (**198**)

Goodman R (1997) The strength and difficulties questionnaire: a research note. *Journal of Child Psychology and Psychiatry* **38**: 581–6. (**484**)

Goodman R, Simonoff E, and Stevenson J (1995) The impact of child IQ, parent IQ and sibling IQ on child and behaviour deviance scores. *Journal of Child Psychology and Psychiatry* **36**: 409–25. (**316**)

Goodwin DW (1979) Alcoholism and heredity. *Archives of General Psychiatry* **36**: 57–61. (**201**)

Goodwin DW, Crane JB and Guze SB (1969) Phenomenological aspects of the alcoholic 'blackout'. *British Journal of Psychiatry* **115**: 1033–8. (**294**)

Goodwin DW, Crane JB, and Guze SB (1969) Alcoholic blackouts: a review and clinical study of 100 alcoholics. *American Journal of Psychiatry* **126**: 191–8. (**437**)

Goodwin DW, Othmer E, Halikas JA, and Freemon F (1970) Loss of short-term memory as a predictor of the alcoholic 'blackout'. *Nature* **227**: 201–2. (**437**)

Goodwin DW, Schulsinger F, Moller N, et al. (1974) Drinking problems in adopted and nonadopted sons of alcoholics. *Archives of General Psychiatry* **31**: 164–9. (**201**)

Goodwin V and Shepherd JP (2000) The development of an assault patient questionnaire to allow accident and emergency departments to contribute to Crime and Disorder Act local crime audits. *Journal of Accident and Emergency Medicine* **17**: 196–8. (**701**)

Gordon A and Wong S (2000) *Violence Reduction Program: Facilitator's Manual.* Dept of Psychology, University of Saskatchewan, Canada. www.psynergy.ca (**xl**)

Gordon H (2004) Psychiatry, the law and death on the roads. *Advances in Psychiatric Treatment* **10**: 439–45. (**278**)

Gordon H, Hindley N, Marsden A, and Shivayogi M (1999) The use of mechanical restraint in the management of psychiatric patients: is it ever appropriate? *Journal of Forensic Psychiatry and Psychology* **10**: 173–86. (**593**)

Gordon H, Kingham M, and Goodwin T (2004) Air travel by passengers with mental disorder. *Psychiatric Bulletin* **28**: 295–7. (**278**)

Gordon H, Rylance M, and Rowell G (2007) Psychotherapy, religion and drama: Murray Cox and his legacy for offender patients. *Criminal Behaviour and Mental Health* **17**: 8–14. (**Preface**)

Gordon HL, Baird AA, and End A (2004) Functional differences among those high and low on a trait measure of psychopathy. *Biological Psychiatry* **56**: 516–21. (**304, 305**)

Gordon N (1999) Episodic dyscontrol syndrome. *Developmental Medicine and Child Neurology* **41**: 786–8. (**285**)

Goring C (1913) *The English Convict.* London: HMSO. (**4**)

Gosden NP, Kramp P, Gabrielsen G, and Sestoft D (2003) Prevalence of mental disorders among 15–17-year-old male adolescent remand prisoners in Denmark. *Acta Psychiatrica Scandinavica* **107**: 102–10. (**482**)

Gosden NP, Kramp P, Gabrielsen G, Andersen TF, and Sestoft D (2005) Violence of young criminals predicts schizophrenia: a 9-year register-based follow-up of 15–19-year-old criminals. *Schizophrenia Bulletin* **31**: 759–68. (**343**)

Gosselin C and Wilson G (1980) *Sexual Variations.* London: Faber. (**245**)

Gossop M, Browne N, Stewart D, and Marsden J (2003) Alcohol use outcomes and heavy drinking at 4–5 years among a treatment sample of drug misusers. *Journal of Substance Abuse Treatment* **25**: 135–43. (**459**)

Gossop M, Powis B, Griffiths P, and Strang J (1994) Sexual behaviour and its relationship to drug-taking among prostitutes in south London. *Addiction* **89**: 961–70. (**454, 464**)

Gostin L (1983) The ideology of entitlement: the application of contemporary legal approaches to psychiatry. In P Bean (ed) *Mental Illness: Changes and Trends.* Chichester, UK: Wiley. (**149**)

Gostin L (1985) Human rights in mental health. In M Roth, R Bluglass (eds) *Psychiatry, Human Rights and the Law.* Cambridge, UK: Cambridge University Press. (**603**)

Gottesman II (1991) *Schizophrenia Genesis: The Origin of Madness.* New York: Freeman. (**208**)

Gottlieb P, Gabrielsen G, and Kramp P (1987) Psychotic homicides in copenhagen from 1959 to 1983. *Acta Psychiatrica Scandinavica* **76**: 285–92. (**507**)

Gould RA, Mueser KT, Bolton E, Mays V, and Goff D (2001) Cognitive therapy for psychosis in schizophrenia: an effect size analysis. *Schizophrenia Research* **48**: 335–42. (**521**)

Gowers SG (2004) Assessing adolescent mental health. In S Bailey, M Dolan (eds) *Textbook of Adolescent Forensic Psychiatry*. London: Arnold, pp. 3–13. (**484**)

Goyer PF, Andreason PJ, SempleWE, et al. (1994) Positron-emission tomography and personality disorders. *Neuropsychopharmacology* **10**: 21–8. (**302**)

Grafman J (1995) Structure and functions of the human prefrontal cortex. In J Grafman, KJ Holyoak, F Boller (eds). *Annals of the New York Academy of Sciences*, **769**: pp. 337–68. (**298**)

Graham J (1988) *Schools, Disruptive Behaviour and Delinquency*. London: HMSO. (**178**)

Graham K, Leonard KE, Room R, et al. (1998) Current directions in research on understanding and preventing intoxicated aggression. *Addiction* **93**: 659–76. (**447**)

Graham P and Rutter M (1968) Organic brain dysfunction and child psychiatric disorder. *British Medical Journal* **3**: 695–700. (**288**)

Granath S, Hagstedt J, Kivivuori J, Lehti L, Ganpat S, Liem M and Nieuwbeerta P (2011) Homicide in Finland, the Netherlands and Sweden. The Swedish National Council for Crime Prevention, The National Research Institute of Legal Policy, Finland and the Institute of Criminal Law and Criminology, the Netherlands. http://www.bra.se/download/18.656e38431321e85c2 4d80007748/2011_15_homicide_finland_netherlands_sweden.pdf (**507**)

Grann M (2000) The PCL-R and gender. *European Journal of Psychological Assessment* **16**: 147–9. (**513**)

Grann M and Holmberg G (1999) Follow up of forensic psychiatric legislation and clinical practice in Sweden 1988 to1995. *International Journal of Law and Psychiatry* l(22): 125–31. (**147**)

Grann M and Wedin I (2002) Risk factors for recidivism among spousal assault and spousal homicide offenders. *Psychology, Crime and the Law* **8**: 5–23. (**536**)

Grann M, Belfrage H, and Tengström A (2000) Actuarial assessment of risk for violence. Predictive validity of the VRAG and the historical part of the HCR-20. *Criminal Justice and Behaviour* **27**: 97–114. (**536**)

Grann M, Långström N, Tengström A, and Kullgren G (1999) Psychopathy (PCL-R) predicts violent recidivism among criminal offenders with personality disorders in Sweden. *Law and Human Behaviour* **23**: 205–18. (**534**)

Grant BF, Chou SP, Goldstein RB, et al. (2008) Prevalence, correlates, disability, and comorbidity of CDM-IV borderline personality disorder: results from the wave 2 national epidemiologic survey on alcohol and related conditions. *Journal of Clinical Psychiatry* **69**: 533–45. (**512**)

Grant JE, Kim SW, and Hartman BK (2008) A double-blind, placebo-controlled study of the opiate antagonist naltrexone in the treatment of pathological gambling urges. *Journal of Clinical Psychiatry* **69**: 783–9. (**472**)

Grant JE, Kim SW, and Potenza MN (2003) Advances in the pharmacological treatment of pathological gambling. *Journal of Gambling Studies* **19**: 85–104. (**442**)

Grant LD, Coscine DV, Grossman SP, and Freeman DX (1973) Muricide after serotonin depleting lesions of the midbrain raphe nuclei. *Pharmacology Biochemistry and Behaviour* **1**: 77–80. (**307**)

Grassian S (1983) Psychopathological effects of solitary confinement. *American Journal of Psychiatry* **140**: 1450–4. (**595**)

Gratz KL and Gunderson JG (2006) Preliminary data on an acceptance-based emotion regulation group intervention for deliberate self-harm among women with borderline personality disorder. *Behavior Therapy* **37**: 25–35. (**410**)

Grawe RW, Hagen R, Espeland B, and Mueser KT (2007) The better life program: effects of group skills training for persons with severe mental illness and substance use disorders. *Journal of Mental Health* **16**: 625–34. (**576**)

Gray J and Bentovim A (1996) Illness induction syndrome: a series of 41 children from 37 families identified at The Great Ormond Street Hospital for Children. NHS Trust. *Child Abuse and Neglect* **20**: 655–73. (**227, 506**)

Gray JA (1982) *The Neuropsychology of Anxiety*. Orlando, FL: Academic Press. (**307**)

Gray MJ, Pumphrey JE, and Lombardo TW (2003) Relationship between dispositional versus trauma-specific attributions and PTSD symptomatology. *Journal of Anxiety Disorders* **17**: 289–303. (**712**)

Gray N, MacCulloch M, Smith J, Morris M, and Snowden RJ (2003) Violence viewed by psychopathic murderers. *Nature* **423**: 497–8. (**387**)

Gray NS, Brown AS, MacCulloch MJ, Smith J, and Snowden RJ (2005) An implicit test of the associations between children and sex in pedophiles. *Journal of Abnormal Psychology* **114**: 304–8. (**548**)

Gray NS, Fitzgerald S, Taylor J, MacCulloch M, and Snowden R (2007) Predicting future reconviction in offenders with intellectual disabilities: the predictive efficacy of the VRAG, PCL-SV and the HCR-20. Psychological Assessment 19: 474–79. (**330, 537**)

Gray NS, Hill C, McGleish A, et al. (2003) Prediction of violence and self-harm in mentally disordered offenders: a prospective study of the efficacy of HCR-20, PCL-R and psychiatric symptomology. *Journal of Consulting and Clinical Psychology* **71**: 443–51. (**537, 538**)

Gray NS, Snowden RJ, MacCulloch S, et al. (2004) Relative efficacy of criminological, clinical and personality measures of future risk of offending in mentally disordered offenders: a comparative study of HCR-20, PCL:SV and OGRS. *Journal of Consulting and Clinical Psychology* **72**: 523–30. (**537, 538**)

Gray NS, Taylor J, and Snowden RJ (2011) Predicting violence using structured professional judgment in patients with different mental and behavioral disorders. *Psychiatric Research* **187**: 248–53. (**538**)

Gray SE, Shone MA, and Liddle PF (2000) *Canadian Mental Health Law and Policy*. Toronto, ON: Butterworth. (**146**)

Greaves GB (1980) Multiple personality 165 years after Mary Reynolds. *Journal of Nervous and Mental Diseases* **168**: 577–96. (**426, 427**)

Green B, Young R, and Kavanagh D (2005) Cannabis use and misuse prevalence among people with psychosis. *British Journal of Psychiatry* **187**: 306–13. (**488**)

Green BL (1990) Terminology and generic stressor dimensions. *Journal of Applied Social Psychology* **20**: 1632–42. (**712**)

Green C, Garety PA, Freeman D, et al. (2006) Content and affect in persecutory delusions. *British Journal of Clinical Psychology* **45**: 561–77. (**354**)

Green CM and Manohar SV (1990) Neonaticide and hysterical denial of pregnancy. *British Journal of Psychiatry* **156**: 121–3. (**510**)

Green JG, McLaughlin KA, Berglund PA, et al. (2010) Childhood adversities and adult psychiatric disorders in the National Comorbidity Survey Replication I: associations with first onset of DSM-IV disorders. *Archives of General Psychiatry* **67**: 113–23. (**345**)

Green TM (1997) Police as frontline mental health workers – the decision to arrest or refer to mental health agencies. *International Journal of Law and Psychiatry* **20**: 469–86. (**279**)

Greenberg AS and Coleman M (1976) Depressed 5-hydroxylase levels associated with hyperactive and aggressive behaviour. *Archives of General Psychiatry* **21**: 493–509. (**307**)

Greenberg D and Felthous AR (2007) The insanity defense and psychopathic disorders in the United States and Australia. In AR Felthous, H Sass (eds) *International Handbook on Psychopathic Disorders and the Law.* Chichester, UK: John Wiley and Sons, pp. 255–74. (**121**)

Greenberg JJ, Greenley R, and Benedict P (1994) Contributions of persons with serious mental illness to their families. *Hospital and Community Psychiatry* **4**: 475–9. (**355**)

Greenfeld LA and Snell TL (2000) *Women Offenders.* Washington, DC: Bureau of Justice Statistics, US Department of Justice Office of Justice Programs. http://www.bjs.gov/content/pub/pdf/wo.pdf (**510**)

Greeven PGJ (2002) *Treatment Outcome in Personality Disordered Forensic Patients: an Empirical Study.* Deventer, the Netherlands: Gouda Quint. (**138**)

Gregoire TK and Burke AC (2004) The relationship of legal coercion to readiness to change among adults with alcohol and other drug problems. *Journal of Substance Abuse Treatment* **26**: 35–41. (**445**)

Grella CE (2003) Effects of gender and diagnosis on addiction history, treatment utilization, and psychosocial functioning among a dually-diagnosed sample in drug treatment. *Journal of Psychoactive Drugs* **35**: 69–79. (**464**)

Gresswell DM and Hollin CR (1997) Addictions and multiple murder: a behavioural perspective. In JE Hodge, M McMurran, CR Hollin (eds) *Addicted to Crime.* Chichester, UK: Wiley. (**239, 689**)

Gretton HM, McBride M, Hare RD, O'Shaughnessy R, and Kumka G (2001) Psychopathy and recidivism in adolescent sex offenders. *Criminal Justice and Behaviour* **28**: 427–49. (**252**)

Grevatt M, Thomas-Peter B, and Hughes G (2004) Violence, mental disorder and risk assessment: can structured clinical assessments predict the short-term risk of inpatient violence? *Journal of Forensic Psychiatry and Psychology* **15**: 278–92. (**537, 538**)

Grey N and Holmes E (2008) "Hotspots" in trauma memories in the treatment of post-traumatic stress disorder: a replication. *Memory* 16: 788–96. (**723**)

Grey N and Young K (2008) Cognitive behaviour therapy with refugees and asylum seekers experiencing traumatic stress symptoms. *Behavioural and Cognitive Psychotherapy* 36: 3–19. (**716, 729**)

Grey N, Young K, and Holmes E (2002) Cognitive restructuring within reliving: a treatment for peri-traumatic emotional "hotspots" in posttraumatic stress disorder. *Behavioural and Cognitive Psychotherapy* 30: 37–56. (**726**)

Grice DE, Brady KT, Dustan LR, and Malcolm R (1995) Sexual and physical assault history and posttraumatic stress disorder in substance-dependent individuals. *American Journal of Addictions* **4**: 297–305. (**464**)

Griew E (1988) The future of diminished responsibility. *Criminal Law Review* 75–87. (**30**)

Griffiths D and Lunsky Y (2003) Sociosexual knowledge and attitudes assessment tool (SSKAAT-R). Woodale, IL: Stoeltinf. (**328**)

Griffiths SDM, Quinsey VL, and Hingsburger D (1989) *Changing Inappropriate Sexual Behaviour: A Community-Based Approach for Persons with Developmental Disabilities.* Brooks: Baltimore. (**328**)

Grisso T (1997) The competence of adolescents as trial defendants. *Psychology, Public Policy and Law* **3**: 3–32. (**61, 493**)

Grisso T (2000) What we know about youths' capacities as trial defendants. In T Grisso, RG Schwartz (eds) *Youth on Trial.* Chicago, IL: University of Chicago Press, pp. 139–71. (**493**)

Grisso T and Zimring FE (2004) *Double Jeopardy: Adolescent Offenders with Mental Disorders.* Chicago, IL: University of Chicago Press. (**483**)

Grisso T, Applebaum PS, and Hill-Fotouhi C (1997) The MacCAT-T: a clinical tool to assess patients' capacities to make treatment decisions. *Psychiatric Services* **48**: 1415–19. (**61**)

Grisso T, Vincent G, and Seagrave D (2005) *Mental Health Screening and Assessment in Juvenile Justice.* New York: Guilford. (**484**)

Grøndahl P, Værøy H and Dahl AA (2009) A study of amnesia in homicide cases and forensic psychiatric experts' examination of such claims. *International Journal of Law and Psychiatry* **32**:281–7. (**293**)

Groth AN and Birnbaum J (1979) *Men who Rape: The Psychology of the Offender.* New York: Plenum. (**248, 249**)

Groth AN and Burgess AW (1980) Male rape: offenders and victims. *American Journal of Psychiatry* **137**: 806–10. (**249**)

Groth AN, Burgess AW, and Holstrom LL (1977) Rape, power, anger, and sexuality. *American Journal of Psychiatry* **134**: 1239–43. (**249**)

Grounds A (1986) Psychiatry and patients' rights. *British Journal of Hospital Medicine* **36**: 147–8. (**603**)

Grounds A (2004) Psychological consequences of wrongful conviction and imprisonment. *Canadian Journal of Criminology and Criminal Justice* **46**: 165–82. (**716, 717**)

Grounds A (2004a) Forensic psychiatry and political controversy. *Journal of the American Academy of Psychiatry and the Law* **32**: 192–6. (**235**)

Grounds A, Gelsthorpe A, HOwes M, et al. (2004) Access to medium secure psychiatric care in England and Wales. 2: a qualitative study of admission decision-making. *Journal of Forensic Psychiatry and Psychology* **15**: 32–49. (**599**)

Grounds A, Gunn J, Myers WC, Rosner R, and Busch KG (2010) Contemplating common ground in the professional ethics of forensic psychiatry. *Criminal Behaviour and Mental Health* **20**: 307–22. (**659, 660**)

Grounds AT (2000) The psychiatrist in court. In MG Gelder, JJ López-Ibor Jr, Nancy Andreason (eds) *New Oxford Textbook of Psychiatry*, Vol 2. Oxford, UK: Oxford University Press. (**155, 168**)

Group for the Advancement of Psychiatry (1960) *Confidentiality and Privileged Communications in the Practise of Psychiatry Report 45*. New York: Group for the Advancement of Psychiatry. (**662**)

Grove T (1998) *The Juryman's Tale*. London: Bloomsbury. (**676**)

Grove WM and Meehl PE (1996) Comparative efficiency of informal (subjective, impressionistic) and formal (mechanical, algorithmic) prediction procedures: the clinical-statistical controversy. *Psychology, Public Policy, and Law* **2**: 293–323. (**531**)

Grove WM, Zald DH, Lebow BS, Snitz BE, and Nelson C (2000) Clinical versus mechanical prediction: a meta-analysis. *Psychological Assessment* **12**: 19–30. (**531**)

Grubin D (1991a) Unfit to plead in England and Wales 1976–1988: a survey. *British Journal of Psychiatry* **158**: 540–8. (**24**)

Grubin D (1991b) Regaining fitness: patients found unfit to plead who return for trial. *Journal of Forensic Psychiatry* **2**: 139–84. (**24**)

Grubin D (1991c) Unfit to plead, unfit for discharge. *Criminal Behaviour and Mental Health* **1**: 282–94. (**24**)

Grubin D (1992) Cross-cultural influences on sex offending. *Annual Review of Sex Research* **3**: 201–17. (**245**)

Grubin D (1998) *Sex Offending Against Children: Understanding the Risk*. Police Research Series Paper 99. Home Office: Research, Development and Statistics Directorate. www.homeoffice.gov.uk/rds/prgpdfs/fprs99.pdf (**243, 244, 252**)

Grubin D (2004) The risk assessment of sex offenders. In H Kemshall, G McIvor (eds) *Managing Sex Offender Risk*. London: Jessica Kingsley. (**254**)

Grubin D (2006) Communicating risk to the courts. In MR Kebbell, GM Davies (eds) *Practical Psychology for Forensic Investigations and Prosecutions*. Chichester, UK: Wiley. (**254, 255**)

Grubin D (2008) The case for polygraph testing of sex offenders. *Legal and Criminological Psychology* **13**(2): 177–89. (**254, 255, 256**)

Grubin D (2008a) Medical models and interventions in sexual deviance. In DR Laws, WT O'Donohue (eds) *Sexual Deviance: Theory, Assessment, and Treatment*, 2nd edn. New York: Guilford. (**252, 254, 259, 260**)

Grubin D (2008b) *Validation of Risk Matrix 2000 for Use in Scotland*. Paisley, UK: Scottish Risk Management Authority. http://www.rmascotland.gov.uk (**254**)

Grubin D and Madsen L (2005) Lie detection and the polygraph: a historical review. *British Journal of Forensic Psychiatry and Psychology* **16**: 357–69. (**256**)

Grubin D and Mason D (1997) Medical models of sexual deviance. In DR Laws, W O'Donohue (eds) *Sexual Deviance: Theory, Assessment, and Treatment*. London: Guilford. (**252**)

Grubin D, Madsen L, Parsons S, Sosnowski D, and Warberg B (2004) A prospective study of the impact of polygraphy on high risk behaviours in adult sex offenders. *Sexual Abuse: A Journal of Research and Treatment* **16**: 209–22. (**254, 255**)

Grubin DH and Gunn J (1990) *The Imprisoned Rapist and Rape*. London: Department of Forensic Psychiatry, Institute of Psychiatry. (**248, 249**)

Gudden H (1905) Die Physiologische und Pathologische Schlaftrunkenheit. *Archiv für Psychiatrie und Nervenkrankheiten* **40**: 989–1015. (**290**)

Gudjonsson G, Hayes G, and Rowlands P (2000) Fitness to be interviewed and psychological vulnerability: the views of doctors, lawyers and police officers. *Journal of Forensic Psychiatry* **11**: 75–92. (**624**)

Gudjonsson GH (1984a) A new scale of interrogative suggestibility. *Personality and Individual Differences* **5**: 803–14. (**622**)

Gudjonsson GH (1984b) Interrogative suggestibility: comparison between 'false confessors' and 'false deniers' in criminal trials. *Medicine, Science and the Law* **24**: 56–60. (**622**)

Gudjonsson GH (1986) The relationship between interrogative suggestibility and acquiescence: empirical findings and theoretical implications. *Personality and Individual Differences* **7**: 195–9. (**162**)

Gudjonsson GH (1987) The significance of depression in the mechanism of 'compulsive' shoplifting. *Medicine Science and the Law* **27**: 171–6. (**271**)

Gudjonsson GH (1988) Causes of compulsive shoplifting. *British Journal of Hospital Medicine* **40**: 169. (**271**)

Gudjonsson GH (1988a) Interrogative suggestibility: its relationship with assertiveness, social-evaluative anxiety, state anxiety and method of coping. *British Journal of Clinical Psychology* **27**: 159–66. (**161, 162**)

Gudjonsson GH (1989) Compliance in an interrogation situation: a new scale. *Personality and Individual Differences* **10**: 535–40. (**162**)

Gudjonsson GH (1990) Self-deception and other-deception in forensic assessment. *Personality and Individual Differences* **11**: 219–25. (**162**)

Gudjonsson GH (1992) *The Psychology of Interrogations, Confessions and Testimony*. Chichester, UK: Wiley. (**331**)

Gudjonsson GH (1993) Confession evidence, psychological vulnerability and expert testimony. *Journal of Community and Applied Social Psychology* **3**: 117–29. (**624**)

Gudjonsson GH (1997) *Gudjonsson Suggestibility Scales*. Hove, Sussex: Psychology Press. (**332**)

Gudjonsson GH (2003a) Psychology brings justice: the science of forensic psychology. *Criminal Behaviour and Mental Health* **13**: 159–67. (**159, 161, 162**)

Gudjonsson GH (2003b) *The Psychology of Interrogations and Confessions: A Handbook*. Chichester, UK: Wiley. (**159, 162**)

Gudjonsson GH (2007) *Suggestibility Scales*. London: Psychology Press. (**159, 161, 162**)

Gudjonsson GH and Clark NK (1986) Suggestibility in police interrogation: a social psychological model. *Social Behaviour* **1**: 83–104. (**161**)

Gudjonsson GH and Gunn J (1982) The competence and reliability of a witness in the criminal court: a case report. *British Journal of Psychiatry* **141**: 624–7. (**160**)

Gudjonsson GH and MacKeith J (1988) Retracted confessions: legal, psychological, and psychiatric aspects. *Medicine, Science and the Law* **28**: 187–94. (**160, 161**)

Gudjonsson GH and MacKeith JAC (1983) A specific recognition deficit in a case of homicide. *Medicine, Science and the Law* **23**: 37–40. (**296**)

Gudjónsson GH and Pétursson H (2007) Homicide in the Nordic countries. *Acta Psychiatrica Scandinavica* **82**: 49–54. (**338**)

Gudjonsson GH and Taylor PJ (1985) Cognitive deficit in a case of retrograde amnesia. *British Journal of Psychiatry* **147**: 715–18. (**296**)

Gudjonsson GH and Young S (2007) The role and scope of forensic clinical psychology in secure unit provisions: a proposed service model for psychological therapies. *Journal of Forensic Psychiatry and Psychology* **18**: 534–56. (**579**)

Gudjonsson GH, Hannesdottir K, and Petursson H (1999) The relationship between amnesia and crime: the role of personality. *Personality and Individual Differences* **26**: 505–10. (**295**)

Gudjonsson GH, Petursson HSkulason S, and Sigurdardottir H (1989) Psychiatric evidence: a study of psychological issues. *Acta Psychiatrica Scandinavica* **80**: 165–9. (**293**)

Gudjonsson GH, Sigurdsson JF, and Sigfusdottir ID (2009) Interrogation and false confession among adolescents in seven European countries. What backgrounds and psychological variables best discriminate between false confessors and non-false confessors? *Psychology, Crime and Law* **15**: 711–28. (**622**)

Gudjonsson GH, Sigurdsson JF, Asgeirdottir BB, and Sigfusdottir ID (2006) Custodial interrogation, false confession, and individual differences: a national study among Icelandic youth. *Personality and Individual Differences* **41**: 49–59. (**622**)

Gudjonsson GH, Sigurdsson JF, Einarsson E, Bragason OO, and Newton AK (2008) Interrogative suggestibility, compliance and false confessions among prison inmates and their relationship with attention deficit hyperactivity disorder (ADHD) symptoms. *Psychological Medicine* **38**: 1037–44. (**622**)

Gudmundsson G (1966) Epilepsy in Iceland. *Acta Neurologica Scandinavica* **43** (suppl. 25): 1–124. (**286**)

Guidano VF (1987) *Complexity of the Self: A Developmental Approach to Psychopathology and Therapy*. New York: Guilford. (**720**)

Guilbert P (2006) Challenging some myths about CBT. *British Association for the Behavioural and Cognitive Therapies Magazine* **34**: 3–5. (**569**)

Guilleminault C, Moscovitch A, Yuen K, and Poyares D (2002) A typical sexual behaviour during sleep. *Psychosomatic Medicine* **64**: 328–36. (**291**)

Gunderson JG (1996) The borderline patient's intolerance of aloneness: insecure attachments and therapist availability. *American Journal of Psychiatry* **153**: 752–8. (**392**)

Gunderson JG, Frank AF, Ronningstam EF, et al. (1989) Early discontinuance of borderline patients from psychotherapy. *Journal of Nervous and Mental Disease* **177**: 38–42. (**408**)

Gunn J (1968) Compulsive gambler. *British Medical Journal* **2** (suppl. 599): 240. (**448**)

Gunn J (1973) *Violence in Human Society*. Newton Abbot, UK: David and Charles. (**211, 214**)

Gunn J (1976) Management of the mentally disordered offender: integrated or parallel. *Proceedings of the Royal Society of Medicine* **70**: 877–80. (**587**)

Gunn J (1977) *Epileptics in Prison*. London: Academic Press. (**284, 285, 286, 287, 289, 488**)

Gunn J (1978) Epileptic homicide: a case report. *British Journal of Psychiatry* **132**: 510–13. (**287**)

Gunn J (1981) Medico-legal aspects of epilepsy. In EH Reynolds, M Trimble (eds) *Epilepsy and Psychiatry*. Edinburgh, UK: Churchill Livingstone. (**285**)

Gunn J (1985) Psychiatry and the prison medical service. In L Gostin (ed) *Secure Provision*. London: Tavistock. (**626**)

Gunn J (1986) Education and forensic psychiatry. *Canadian Journal of Psychiatry* **31**: 273–9. (**1**)

Gunn J (1991a) The trials of psychiatry: insanity in the twentieth century. In K Herbst, J Gunn (eds) *The Mentally Disordered Offender*. Oxford, UK: Butterworth-Heinemann. (**7**)

Gunn J (1991b) Human violence. A biological perspective. *Criminal Behaviour and Mental Health* **1**: 34–54. (**211, 214**)

Gunn J (1991c) Epilepsy and the law. In DB Smith, DM Treiman, MR Trimble (eds) *Advances in Neurology*, Vol. 55. *Neurobehavioral Problems in Epilepsy*. New York: Raven. (**285**)

Gunn J (2006) Abuse of psychiatry. *Criminal Behaviour and Mental Health* **16**: 77–86. (**689**)

Gunn J (2007) The death penalty: a psychiatrist's view from Europe (Ch. 23, vol. 2, pp. 343–59). In A Felthous, JH Sass (eds) *The International Handbook of Psychopathic Disorders and the Law*. Hoboken, NJ: Wiley and Sons. (**677**)

Gunn J (2010) Dr Harold Frederick Shipman: an enigma. *Criminal Behaviour and Mental Health* **20**: 190–8. (**689**)

Gunn J and Fenton G (1971) Epilepsy, automatism and crime. *Lancet* **1**: 173–6. (**286**)

Gunn J and Gristwood J (1975) Use of the Buss-Durkee Hostility Inventory among British prisoners. *Journal of Consulting and Clinical Psychology* **43**: 590. (**560**)

Gunn J and Gudjonsson G (1988) Using the psychological stress evaluator in conditions of extreme stress. *Psychological Medicine* **18**: 235–8. (**625**)

Gunn J and Maden A (1998) *Should the English Special Hospitals be Closed?* Maudsley discussion paper no. 6. London: Institute of Psychiatry. (**30**)

Gunn J and Nedopil N (2005) European training in forensic psychiatry. *Criminal Behaviour and Mental Health* **15**: 207–13. (**16, 113**)

Gunn J and Robertson G (1976) Drawing a criminal profile. *British Journal of Criminology* **16**: 156–60. (**298**)

Gunn J and Taylor PJ (1993) *Forensic Psychiatry, Clinical Legal and Ethical Issues* (first edition). Oxford, UK: Butterworth-Heinemann. (**1**)

Gunn J, Maden A, and Swinton M (1991b) Treatment needs of prisoners with psychiatric disorders. *British Medical Journal* **303**: 338–41. (**601, 629, 661**)

Gunn J, Maden T, and Swinton M (1991a) *Mentally Disordered Prisoners*. London: Home Office. (**279, 286, 513, 629, 661**)

Gunn J, Robertson G, Dell S, and Way C (1978) *Psychiatric Aspects of Imprisonment*. London: Academic Press. (**412, 447, 552, 583**)

Gunnar MR and Donzella B (2002) Social regulation of the cortisol levels in early human development. *Psychoneurendocrinology* **27**: 199–220. (**720**)

Gunter B and McAleer JL (1990) *Children and Television*. London: Routledge. (**216, 217**)

Gustafson R (1999) Male alcohol-related aggression as a function of type of drink. *Aggressive Behavior* **25**: 401–8. (**440**)

Gutheil TG and Appelbaum PS (2000) *Clinical Handbook of Psychiatry and the Law*, 3rd edn. Baltimore, MD: Williams and Wilkins. (**122**)

Guze SB (1976) *Criminality and Psychiatric Disorders*. New York: Oxford University Press. (**415**)

Guze SB, GoodwinDW, and Crane JB (1969) Criminality and psychiatric disorders. *Archives of General Psychiatry* **20**: 583–91. (**279**)

Haapasalo J and Petäjä S (1999) Mothers who killed or attempted to kill their child: life circumstances, childhood abuse, and types of killing. *Violence and Victims* **14**: 219–39. (**510**)

Habermeyer E, Rachvoll V, Felthous AR, BukhanowskyAO, and Gleyzer R (2007) Hospitalization and civil commitment of individuals with psychopathic individuals in Germany, Russia and the United States. In AR Felthous, H Sass (eds) *International Handbook on Psychopathic Disorders and the Law*. Chichester, UK: John Wiley and Sons, pp. 34–60. (**122**)

Haberstick BC, Lessem JM, Hopfer CJ, et al. (2005) Monoamine oxidase A (MAOA) and antisocial behaviors in the presence of childhood and adolescent maltreatment. *American Journal of Medical Genetics Part B Neuropsychiatric Genetics* **135**: 59–64. (**200**)

HAC: see Health Advisory Committee for the Prison Service.

Hackett S, Telford P, and Slack K (2002) Groupwork with parents of children who sexually harm. In MC Calder (ed) *Young People who Sexually Abuse: Building the Evidence Base for your Practice*. Lyme Regis, UK: Russell House. (**495**)

Hacking I (1995) *Rewriting the Soul, Multiple Personality and the Sciences of Memory*. Princeton, NJ: Princeton University Press. (**423**)

Haddad PM, Taylor M, and Niaz OS (2009) First-generation antipsychotic long-acting injections v. oral antipsychotics in schizophrenia: systematic review of randomised controlled trials and observational studies. *British Journal of Psychiatry* **195**: s20–8. (**360**)

Haddock CK, Rindskopf D, and Shadish WR (1998) Using odds ratios as effect sizes for meta-analysis of dichotomous data: A primer on methods and issues. *Psychological Methods*, **3**: 339–53. (**412**)

Haddock G, Barrowclough C, Shaw JJ, et al. (2009) Cognitive-behavioural therapy v. social activity therapy for people with psychosis and a history of violence: randomised controlled trial. *British Journal of Psychiatry* **194**: 152–7. (**361, 362, 521**)

Haddock G, Barrowclough C, Tarrier N, et al. (2003) Cognitive-behavioural therapy and motivational intervention for schizophrenia and substance misuse: 18-month outcomes of a randomised controlled trial. *British Journal of Psychiatry* **183**: 418–26. (**459**)

Haddock G, Lowens I, Brosnan N, Barrowclough C, and Novaco RW (2004) Cognitive-behaviour therapy for inpatients with psychosis and anger problems within a low secure environment. *Behavioural and Cognitive Psychotherapy* **32**: 77–98. (**573**)

Häfner H and Böker W (1973, translated H Marshall, 1982) *Crimes of Violence by Mentally Abnormal Offenders*. Cambridge, UK: Cambridge University Press. (**337, 342, 347, 349, 354, 515**)

Häfner H, an der Heiden W, Behrens S, et al. (1998) Causes and consequences of the gender difference in age of onset of schizophrenia. *Schizophrenia Bulletin* **24**: 99–113. (**501, 514, 520**)

Häfner H, Maurer K, Löffler W, et al. (2003) Modelling the early career of schizophrenia. *Schizophrenia Bulletin* **29**: 325–40. (**501, 514, 520**)

Hagerman R (2005) The **Fragile X** mutation: intertwining with autism and neurodegeneration. *Directions in Psychiatry* **25**(1): 49–58. (**321**)

Haggard U, Gumpert CH, and Grann M (2001) Against all odds: a qualitative follow-up study of high risk violent offenders who were not reconvicted. *Journal of Interpersonal Violence* **16**: 1048–66. (**533**)

Haggard-Grann U, Hallqvist J, Langstrom N, and Moller J (2006) The role of alcohol and drugs in triggering criminal violence: a case-crossover study. *Addiction* **101**: 100–8. (**456**)

Haigh R (1999) The quintessence of a therapeutic environment. In P Campling, R Haigh (eds) *Therapeutic Communities. Past, Present and Future*. London: Jessica Kingsley. (**603**)

Häkännen H (2006) Finnish bomb threats: offence and offender characteristics. *International Journal of Police Science and Management* **8**: 1–8. (**546**)

Häkkänen-Nyholm H, Putkonen H, Lindberg N, Holi M, Rovamo T, and Weizmann-Henelius G. (2009) Gender differences in Finnish homicide offence characteristics. *Forensic Science International* **186**(1–3): 75–80. (**502, 507**)

Hales H, Davison S, Misch P, and Taylor PJ (2003) Young male prisoners in a young offenders' Institution: their contact with suicidal behaviour by others. *Journal of Adolescence* **26**: 667–85. (**634**)

Hales H, Romilly C, Davison S, and Taylor PJ (2006) Sexual attitudes, experience and relationships amongst patients in a high security hospital. *Criminal Behaviour and Mental Health* **16**: 254–63. (**596**)

Hales HJ (2009) *Proximity to suicide related behaviour among young institutionalised offenders*. PhD Thesis, University of London. (**634**)

Hall DM (1998) The victims of stalking. In J Reid Meloy (ed) *The Psychology of Stalking: Clinical and Forensic Perspectives*. San Diego, CA: Academic Press, pp. 113–37. (**374, 545**)

Hall GCN (1995) Sexual offender recidivism revisited: A meta-analysis of recent treatment studies. *Journal of Consulting and Clinical Psychology*, **63**, 802–9. (**257**)

Hall I, Clayton P, and Johnson P (2005) In T Riding, C Swann, B Swann (eds) *The Handbook of Forensic Learning Disabilities*. Oxford, UK: Radcliffe, pp. 51–72. (**330**)

Hall JA and Moore CBT (2008) Drug facilitated sexual assault – a review. *Journal of Forensic and Legal Medicine* **15**: 291–7. (**454**)

Hallahan B and Garland MR (2005) Essential fatty acids and mental health. *British Journal of Psychiatry* **186**: 275–7. (**568**)

Hallahan B, Hibbeln JR, Davis JM, and Garland MR (2007) Omega-3 fatty acid supplementation in patients with recurrent self-harm: single-centre double-blind randomised controlled trial. *British Journal of Psychiatry* **190**: 118–22. (**405**)

Halligan PW, Bass C, and Oakley DA (2003) *Malingering and Illness Deception*. Oxford, UK: Oxford University Press. (**431, 434**)

Hallonquist JD, Seeman MV, Lang M, and Rector NA (1993) Variation in symptom severity over the menstrual cycle of schizophrenics. *Biological Psychiatry* **33**: 207–9. (**501, 521**)

Hallstrom C, Treasaden I, Edwards, JG, and Lader M (1981) Diazepam, propranolol and their combination in the management of chronic anxiety. *British Journal of Psychiatry* **139**: 417–21. (**560**)

Hamblin-Smith M (1934) *Prisons and a Changing Civilisation*. London: John Lane. (**627**)

Hamlyn B and Lewis D (2000) *Women Prisoners: A Survey of Training Experiences in Custody and On Release*. Home Office research Study 208. London: Home Office. (**517**)

Hampshire S (1989) *Innocence and Experience*. London: Allen Lane Press. (**7**)

Han C, McGue MK, and Iacono WG (1999) Lifetime tobacco, alcohol and other substance use in adolescent Minnesota twins: univariate and multivariate behavioral genetic analyses. *Addiction* **94**: 981–93. (**203**)

Hannon F, Kelleher C, and Friel S (2000) *General Healthcare Study of the Irish Prison Population*. Galway, Ireland: National University of Ireland. (**463**)

Hanson K (2002) Recidivism and age: follow-up data from 4,673 offenders. *Journal of Interpersonal Violence* **17**: 1046–62. (**526, 527, 528**)

Hanson R, Gordon, A., Harris, A., Marques, J., Murphy, W., Quinsey, V. and Seto, M. (2002) First Report of the Collaborative Outcome Data Project on the Effectiveness of Psychological Treatment for Sex Offenders. *Sexual Abuse: A Journal of Research and Treatment*, 14, 169–94. (**257, 328, 416, 578**)

Hanson RK and Bussiere MT (1998) Predicting relapse: a meta-analysis of sexual offender recidivism studies. *Journal of Consulting and Clinical Psychology* **66**: 348–62. (**254, 255, 261**)

Hanson RK and Harris AJR (2001) A structured approach to evaluating change among sexual offenders. *Sexual Abuse: A Journal of Research and Treatment* **13**: 105–22. (**255**)

Hanson RK and Morton-Bourgon K (2005) Predicting relapse: a meta-analysis of sexual offender recidivism studies. *Journal of Consulting and Clinical Psychology* **27**: 6–35. (**254, 255**)

Hanson RK and Morton-Bourgon K (2007) *The Accuracy of Recidivism Risk Assessment for Sexual Offenders: A Meta-analysis*. Corrections User Report #2007-02. Ottawa, Canada: Public Safety Canada. (**254**)

Hanson RK and Thornton D (1999) *Static-99: Improving Actuarial Risk Assessments for Sex Offenders*. User report 1999-02. Ottawa, Canada: Department of the Solicitor General of Canada. (**331**)

Hanson RK and Thornton D (2000) Improving risk assessments for sex offenders: a comparison of three actuarial scales. *Law and Human Behavior* **24**: 119–36. (**254**)

Hanson RK, Bourgon G, Helmus L, and Hodgson S (2009) The principles of effective correctional treatment also apply to sexual offenders: a meta-analysis. *Criminal Justice and Behavior* **36**: 865–91. (**578**)

Hanson RK, Broom I, and Stephenson M (2004) Evaluating community sex offender treatment programs: a 12-year follow-up of 724 offenders. *Canadian Journal of Behavioural Science* **36**: 87–96. (**578**)

Hanson RK, Harris AJR, Scott T, and Helmus L (2007) *Assessing the Risk of Sexual Offenders on Community Supervision: The Dynamic supervision Project*. Canada: Public Safety and Emergency Preparedness. www.publicsafety.gc.ca (**255**)

Harcourt C and Donovan B (2005) The many faces of sex work. *Sexually Transmitted Infections* **81**: 201–6. (**503**)

Harding T (1989b) Prevention of torture and inhuman or degrading treatment: medical implications of a new European convention. *Lancet* **334**: 1191–3. (**133**)

Harding T and Zimmerman E (1989) Psychiatric symptoms, cognitive stress and vulnerability factors. A study in a remand prison. *British Journal of Psychiatry* **155**: 36–43. (**630**)

Harding TW (1989a) The application of the European convention of human rights to the field of psychiatry. *International Journal of Law and Psychiatry* **12**: 245–62. (**113, 133**)

Harding TW and Curran WJ (1979) Mental health legislation and its relationship to program development. *Harvard Journal on Legislation* **16**: 19–57. (**132**)

Hardwick E, Gray D, and Humphreys M (2003) First ever admission to medium security. *Medicine, Science and the Law* **43**: 345–9. (**600**)

Hare EH (1962) Masturbatory insanity: the history of an idea. *Journal of Mental Science* **108**: 2–25. (**245**)

Hare RD (1980) A research scale for the assessment of psychopathy in criminal populations. *Personality and Individual Differences* **3**: 35–42. (**7, 385**)

Hare RD (1998) Psychopathy, affect and behavior. In DJ Cook, A Forth, RD Hare (eds) *Psychopathy: Theory, Research, and Implications for Society*. Dortrecht, the Netherlands: Kluwer Academic Publishers, pp. 105–37. (**305**)

Hare RD (2003) *The Hare Psychopathy Checklist-Revised* (PCL-R), 2nd edition. Multi-Health Systems: Toronto, ON. (**262, 297, 331, 346, 385, 388, 415, 444, 513, 534, 535, 608**)

Hare RD and Cox D (1978) Clinical and empirical conceptions of psychopathy. In RD Hare, D Schalling (eds) *Psychopathic Behaviour: Approaches to Research*. Toronto, ON: Wiley. (**346, 397**)

Hare RD, Clark D, Grann M, and Thornton D (2000) Psychopathy and the predictive validity of the PCL-R: an international perspective. *Behavioural Sciences and the Law* **18**: 623–45. (**534**)

Hare RD, Harpur TJ, Hakistian AR, et al. (1990) The revised psychopathy checklist: reliability and factor structure. *Psychological Assessment: A Journal of Consulting and Clinical Psychology* **2**: 338–41. (**385**)

Hareli S and Weiner B (2002) Social emotions and personality inferences: a scaffold for a new direction in the study of achievement motivation. *Educational Psychologist* **37**: 183–93. (**354**)

Harenski CL, Kim SH, and Hamann S (2009) Neuroticism and psychopathy predict brain activation during moral and nonmoral emotion regulation. *Cognition Affect Behavior and Neuroscience* **9**(1): 1–15. (**306**)

Hargreaves D (1997) The transfer of severely mentally ill prisoners from HMP Wakefield: a descriptive study. *Journal of Forensic Psychiatry* **8**: 62–73. (**632**)

Harlow HF (1974) *Learning to Love,* 2nd edn. New York: Jason Aronson. (**298, 718**)

Harlow JM (1848) Passage of an iron rod through the head. *Boston Medical and Surgical Journal* **39**: 389–93. (**298**)

Harmon RB, Rosner R, and Owens H (1995) Obsessional harassment and erotomania in a criminal court population. *Journal of Forensic Sciences* **40**: 188–96. (**375**)

Harmon RB, Rosner R, and Owens H (1998) Sex and violence in a forensic population of obsessional harassers. *Psychology, Public Policy, and Law* **4**: 236–49. (**545**)

Harmon RB, Rosner R, and Wielderlight M (1985) Women and arson; a demographic study. *Journal of Forensic Science* **30**: 467–77. (**273**)

Harper DW and Voigt L (2007) Homicide followed by suicide: an integrated theoretical perspective. *Homicide Studies* **11**: 295. http://hsx.sagepub.com/cgi/content/abstract/11/4/295 (**233**)

Harper G and Chitty C (2004) *The Impact of Corrections on Re-offending: A Review of What Works?* Home Office Research Study 291. London: Home Office. http://webarchive.nationalarchives.gov.uk/20110218135832/http:/rds.homeoffice.gov.uk/rds/pdfs04/hors291.pdf (**518, 577**)

Harper G, Man L-H, Taylor S, and Niven S (2005) Factors associated with offending. In G Harper, C Chitty (eds) *The Impact of Corrections on Re-offending: A Review of 'What Works' (pp. 17–29)*, 3rd edn. Home Office Research Study 291. London: Home Office. http://webarchive.nationalarchives.gov.uk/20110218135832/http:/rds.homeoffice.gov.uk/rds/pdfs04/hors291.pdf (**511**)

Harrington R and Bailey S (2003) *The Scope for Preventing Antisocial Personality Disorder by Intervening in Adolescence.* London: NHS National Programme on Forensic Mental Health Research and Development. (**399, 522**)

Harrington R and Bailey S (2004) Prevention of antisocial personality disorder: mounting evidence on optimal timing and methods. *Criminal Behaviour and Mental Health* **14**: 75–81. (**184, 399, 485, 487, 522**)

Harrington R, Bailey S, Chitsabesan P, et al. (2005) *Mental Health Needs and Effectiveness of Provision for Young Offenders in Custody and in the Community.* London: Youth Justice Board for England and Wales. http://www.yjb.gov.uk/publications/Resources/Downloads/MentalHealthNeedsfull.pdf (**485, 647**)

Harrington RC, Kroll L, Rothwell J, et al. (2005) Psychosocial needs of boys in secure care for serious or persistent offending. *Journal of Child Psychology and Psychiatry* **46**: 859–66. (**484, 487**)

Harris A (1959) Sensory deprivation and schizophrenia. *Journal of Mental Sciences* **105**: 235–7. (**595**)

Harris AW, Large MM, Redoblado-Hodge A, et al. (2010) Clinical and cognitive associations with aggression in the first episode of psychosis. *Australian and New Zealand Journal of Psychiatry* **44**: 85–93. (**344**)

Harris GT, Rice ME, and Camilleri JA (2004) Applying a forensic actuarial assessment (the violence risk appraisal guide) to nonforensic patients. *Journal of Interpersonal Violence* **19**: 1063–74. (**536, 537**)

Harris GT, Rice ME, and Cormier CA (2002) Prospective replication of the *violence risk appraisal guide* in predicting violent recidivism among forensic patients. *Law and Human Behavior* **26**(4): 377–94. (**536**)

Harris GT, Rice ME, and Quinsey VL (1993) Violent recidivism of mentally disordered offenders: the development of a statistical prediction instrument. *Criminal Justice and Behaviour* **20**: 315–35. (**535, 536**)

Harris GT, Rice ME, Quinsey VL, et al. (2003) A multisite comparison of actuarial risk instruments for sex offenders. *Psychological Assessment* **15**: 413–25. (**536**)

Harris M (2000) Psychiatric conditions with relevance to fitness to drive. *Advances in Psychiatric Treatment* **6**: 261–9. (**278**)

Harris P (1993) The nature and extent of aggressive behavior amongst people with learning difficulties (mental handicap) in a single health district. *Journal of Intellectual Disability Research* **37**: 221–42. (**326**)

Harrison J and Tyson D (1993) Injury surveillance in Australia. *Acta Pediatrica Japan* **35**: 171–8. (**701**)

Harrison P and Beck A (2005) *Prison and Jail Inmates at Midyear 2004.* Washington, DC: Bureau of Justice Statistics Bulletin. http://proxy.baremetal.com/november.org/resources/Prisoners04.pdf (**524**)

Harrison PJ (1999) The neuropathology of schizophrenia. A critical review of the data and their interpretation. *Brain* **122**: 593–624. (**207**)

Hart HLA (1963) Preface. In C Perelman (ed) *The Idea of Justice and the Problem of Argument*. London: Routledge. (**150**)

Hart HLA (1968) *Punishment and Responsibility*. Oxford, UK: Clarendon. (**22, 34**)

Hart HLA and Honoré AM (1983) *Causation of the Law*, 2nd edn. Oxford, UK: Oxford University Press. (**149**)

Hart J, Gunnar M, and Cicchetti D (1995) Salivary cortisol in maltreated children: evidence of relations between neuroendocrine activity and social competence. *Development and Psychopathology* **7**: 11–26. (**720**)

Hart SD and Hare RD (1989) Discriminant validity of the psychopathy checklist in a forensic psychiatric population. *Psychological Assessment: A Journal of Consulting and Clinical Psychology* **1**: 211–19. (**385**)

Hart SD, Kropp PR, and Laws DR (2003) *Risk for Sexual Violence Protocol (RSVP): Structured Professional Guidelines for Assessing Risk of Sexual Violence*. Burnaby, BC: Mental Health Law and Policy Institute, Simon Fraser University. (**255**)

Hart SD, Michie C, and Cooke DJ (2007) Precision of actuarial risk assessment instruments: evaluating the 'margins of error' of group v. individual predictions of violence. *British Journal of Psychiatry* **190**: s60–5. (**532**)

Hart SD, Michie C, and Cooke DJ (2007) Precision of actuarial risk assessment instruments: evaluating the 'margins of error' of group versus individual predictions of violence. *British Journal of Psychiatry* **190** (suppl. 49): s61–6. (**256**)

Hartmann HKE and Lowenstein R (1949) Notes on the theory of aggression. In A Freud (ed) *The Psychoanalytic Study of the Child*, Vol. 3. New York: International Universities Press. (**212**)

Hartshorne H and May MA (1928) *Studies in Deceit*. New York: Macmillan. (**270, 418**)

Hartvig P, Alfarnes SA, Skjonberg M, Morger TA, and Ostberg B (2006) Brief checklists for assessing violence risk among patients discharged from acute psychiatric facilities: a preliminary study. *Nordic Journal of Psychiatry* **60**: 243–8. (**533, 539**)

Harvey AG, Bryant RA, and Tarrier N (2003) Cognitive behaviour therapy for posttraumatic stress disorder. *Clinical Psychology Review* **23**: 501–22. (**728**)

Haslam J (1817a) *Considerations on the Moral Management of Insane Persons*. London: Hunter. (**86, 418**)

Haslam J (1817b) *Medical Jurisprudences, as it Relates to Insanity According to the Law of England*. London: J Hunter. (**86, 418**)

Hauser AW and Kurland LT (1975) The epidemiology of epilepsy in Rochester, Minnesota, 1935 through 1967. *Epilepsia* **16**: 1–66. (**286**)

Havard J (1960) *The Detection of Secret Homicide*. Cambridge Studies in Criminology, Vol. 9. Cambridge, UK: Cambridge University Press. (**54**)

Hawkins JD and Herrenkohl TI (2003) Prevention in the school years. In DP Farrington and J Coid (eds) *Early Prevention of Adult Antisocial Behaviour*. Cambridge: Cambridge University Press. pp. 265–91. (**399**)

Hawkins JD, Catalano RF, Kosterman R, Abbott R, and Hill KG (1999) Preventing adolescent health risk behaviours by strengthening protection during childhood. *Archives of Pediatrics and Adolescent Medicine* **153**: 226–34. (**183**)

Hawkins JD, Smith BH, Hill KG, et al. (2003) Understanding and preventing crime and violence: findings from the Seattle social development project. In TP Thornberry, MD Krohn (eds) *Taking Stock of Delinquency: An Overview of Findings from Contemporary Longitudinal Studies*. New York: Kluwer, pp. 255–312. (**171**)

Hawkins JD, von Cleve E, and Catalano RF (1991) Reducing early childhood aggression: results of a primary prevention programme. *Journal of the American Academy of Child and Adolescent Psychiatry* **30**: 208–17. (**183**)

Hawkins SA and Hastie R (1990) Hindsight: biased judgment of past events after the outcomes are known. *Psychological Bulletin* **107**: 311–27. (**75, 696**)

Hayes SC (1996) *People with an Intellectual Disability and the Criminal Justice System: Two Rural Courts*. Research reports number 5. Sydney, NSW: Law Reform Commission. (**324**)

Hayes SC and McIlwain D (1998) *The Prevalence of Intellectual Disability in the New South Wales Prison Population: An Empirical Study*. Canberra, ACT: Criminology Research Council. (**324**)

Haynes RB, Ackloo E, Sahota N, McDonald HP, and Yao X (2008) Interventions for enhancing medication adherence. *Cochrane database of Systematic Reviews 2008*. Issue 2, Art. No.: CD000011. http://onlinelibrary.wiley.com/doi/10.1002/14651858.CD000011.pub3/pdf (**567**)

Hays JR, Roberts TK, and Solway KS (1981) *Violence and the Violent Individual*. New York: Spectrum. (**211**)

Hazaray E, Ehret J, Posey DJ, Petti TA, and McDougle CJ (2004) Intramuscular ziprasidone for acute agitation in adolescents. *Journal of Child and Adolescent Psychopharmacology* **14**: 464–70. (**565**)

Heads T, Leese M, and Taylor PJ (1997) Childhood experiences of patients with schizophrenia and a history of violence: a special hospital sample. *Criminal Behaviour and Mental Health* **7**: 117–30. (**344, 345, 515**)

Heads TC, Taylor PJ, and Leese M (1997) Childhood experiences of patients with schizophrenia and a history of violence: a special hospital sample. *Criminal Behaviour and Mental Health* **7**: 117–30. (**344, 345, 515**)

Health Advisory Committee for the Prison Service (1997) *The Provision of Mental Health Care in Prisons*. London: HM Prison Service. (**628, 666**)

Health and Safety Commission (2000) *The Ladbroke Grove Rail Inquiry Report*. London: Health and Safety Commission. http://www.pixunlimited.co.uk/pdf/news/transport/ladbrokegrove.pdf (**709**)

Health Offender Partnerships (2007) *Best Practice Guidance: Specification for Adult Medium-Secure Services*. London: Department of Health. http://webarchive.nationalarchives.gov.uk/20130107105354/http://www.dh.gov.uk/en/Publicationsandstatistics/Publications/PublicationsPolicyAndGuidance/DH_078744 (**592, 593, 595, 596**)

Healthcare Inspectorate Wales (2008) *Report of a Review in Respect of Ms A and the Provision of Mental Health Services, Following a Homicide Committed in October 2005*. Caerphilly, UK: Healthcare Inspectorate Wales. http://www.hiw.org.uk/Documents/477/cardiff%20homicide%20for%20print%20final2.pdf, (**339, 383**)

Healy W (1915) *The Individual Delinquent: A Text-Book of Diagnosis and Prognosis for All Concerned in Understanding Offenders*. Boston, MA: Little Brown. (**481**)

Healy W and Bronner A (1926) *Delinquents and Criminals, Their Making and Unmaking : Studies in Two American Cities*. New York: Macmillan. (**481**)

Healy W and Healy M (1915) *Pathological Lying, Accusation and Swindling*. London: Heinemann. (**421, 422, 423**)

Hearst H, Newman TB, and Hulley SB (1986) Delayed effects of military draft on mortality. *New England Journal of Medicine* **314**: 620–4. (**715**)

Heath AC (1995) Genetic influences on alcoholism risk: a review of adoption and twin studies. *Alcohol Health and Research World* **19**: 166–71. (**201**)

References

Heath AC, Bucholz KK, Madden PA, et al. (1997) Genetic and environmental contributions to alcohol dependence risk in a national twin sample: consistency of findings in women and men. *Psychological Medicine* **27**: 1381–96. (**201**)

Heath AC, Jardine R, and Martin NG (1989) Interactive effects of genotype and social environment on alcohol consumption in female twins. *Journal of Studies in Alcohol* **50**: 38–48. (**207**)

Heath AC, Kendler KS, Eaves LJ, and Markell D (1985) The resolution of cultural and biological inheritance: informativeness of different relationships. *Behavior Genetics* **15**: 439–65. (**189**)

Heath AC, Meyer J, Eaves LJ, and Martin NG (1991a) The inheritance of alcohol consumption patterns in a general population twin sample: I. Multidimensional scaling of quantity/frequency data. *Journal of Studies in Alcohol* **52**: 345–52. (**201**)

Heath AC, Meyer J, Jardine R, and Martin NG (1991b) The inheritance of alcohol consumption patterns in a general population twin sample: II. Determinants of consumption frequency and quantity consumed. *Journal of Studies in Alcohol* **52**: 425–33. (**201**)

Heath AC, Todorov AA, Nelson EC, et al. (2002) Gene–environment interaction effects on behavioral variation and risk of complex disorders: the example of alcoholism and other psychiatric disorders. *Twin Research* **5**: 30–7. (**191**)

Heather N (1977) Personal illness in 'lifers' and the effects of long-term indeterminate sentences. *British Journal of Criminology* **17**: 378–86. (**637**)

Heaton-Armstrong A, Shepherd E, Gudjonsson G, and Wolchover D (2006) *Witness Testimony: Psychological, Investigative, and Evidential Perspectives.* Oxford, UK: Oxford University Press. (**292**)

Hector RI (1998) The use of clozapine in the treatment of aggressive schizophrenia. *Canadian Journal of Psychiatry* **43**: 466–72. (**564**)

Hedderman C and Hough M (1994) *Does the Criminal Justice System Treat Men and Women Differently?* Home Office Research and Statistics Department. Research Findings No. 10. London: Home Office. (**450**)

Heidari E, Dickison C, Wilson R, and Fiske J (2007) Verifiable CPD paper: oral health of remand prisoners in HMP Brixton, London. *British Dental Journal* **202**(2): E1. (**568**)

Heide KM (1994) Evidence of child maltreatment among adolescent parricide offenders. *International Journal of Offender Therapy and Comparative Criminology* **38**: 151–62. (**232**)

Heil P and Simons D (2008) Multiple paraphilias. In DR Laws, WT O'Donohue (eds) *Sexual Deviance: Theory, Assessment, and Treatment,* 2nd edn. New York: Guildford. (**246**)

Heilbrun K, O'Neill ML, Stevens TN, et al. (2004) Assessing normative approaches to communicating violence risk: a national survey of psychologists. *Behavioral Sciences and the Law* **22**: 187–96. (**548**)

Heim N and Hursch CJ (1979) Castration for sex offenders: treatment or punishment? A review and critique of recent European literature. *Archives of Sexual Behavior* **8**: 281–304. (**261**)

Heinik J, Kimhi R, and Hes J (1994) Dementia and crime: a forensic psychiatry unit study in Israel. *International Journal of Geriatric Psychiatry* **9**: 491–4. (**525**)

Heller LM (1994) A comparison of fluoxetine (Prozac) and sertaline (Zoloft) in treating four target symptoms of the borderline personality disorder. http://www.biologicalunhappiness.com/study.htm (**311**)

Hellerstein D, Frosch W, and Koeningsberg HW (1987) The clinical significance of command hallucinations. *American Journal of Psychiatry* **144**: 219–21. (**353**)

Hellerstein DJ, Yanowitch P, Rosenthal J, et al. (1993) A randomized double-blind study of fluoxetine versus placebo in the treatment of dysthymia. *American Journal of Psychiatry* **150**: 1169–75. (**310**)

Helzer JE, Robins LN, and McEvoy L (1987) Post-traumatic stress disorder in the general population. Findings of the epidemiologic catchment area survey. *New England Journal of Medicine* **317**: 1630–4. (**712, 715**)

Hendriks VM (1990) Psychiatric disorders in a Dutch addict population: rates and correlates of DSM-III diagnosis. *Journal of Consulting and Clinical Psychology* **58**: 158–65. (**463**)

Henggeler SW, Halliday-Boykins CA, Cunningham PB, et al. (2006) Juvenile drug court: enhancing outcomes by integrating evidence-based treatments. *Journal of Consulting and Clinical Psychology* **74**: 42–54. (**466**)

Hennig J, Reuter M, Netter P, Burk C, and Landt O (2005) Two types of aggression are differentially related to serotonergic activity and the A779C TPH polymorphism. *Behavioral Neuroscience* **119**: 16–25. (**198**)

Hennigam KM, Rosario ML, Cook TD, Wharton JD, and Calder BJ (1982) Impact of the introduction of television on crime in the United States: empirical findings and theoretical implications. *Journal of Personality and Social Psychology* **42**: 461–77. (**217**)

Henquet C, Krabbendam L, Spauwen J, et al. (2005) Prospective cohort study of cannabis use, predisposition for psychosis, and psychotic symptoms in young people. *British Medical Journal* **330**: 11–14. (**488**)

Henriksen B, Juul-Jensen P, and Lund M (1970) The mortality of epileptics. In RDC Brackenridge (ed) *Life Assurance Medicine: Proceedings of the 10th International Conference of Life Assurance Medicine.* London: Pitman. (**286**)

Henry B, Caspi A, Moffitt TE, and Silva PA (1996) Temperamental and familial predictors of violent and non-violent criminal convictions: age 3 to age 18. *Developmental Psychology* **32**: 614–23. (**175, 176**)

Henry J (1997) Psychological and physiological responses to stress: the right hemisphere and the hypothalamic-pituitary-adrenal-axis, an inquiry into problems of human bonding. *Acta Physiologica Scandinavica* **161**: 164–9. (**720**)

Henry LA and Gudjonsson GH (2006) Individual and developmental differences in eyewitness recall and suggestibility in children with intellectual disabilities. *Applied Cognitive Psychology* **21**: 361–81. (**161**)

Henwood M (2000) *Domestic Violence: A Resource Manual for Health Care Professionals.* London: Department of Health. (**217**)

Herba CM, Hodgins S, Blackwood N, et al. (2006) The neurobiology of psychopathy: a focus on emotion processing. In H Herve, J Yuille (eds) *Psychopathy: Theory, Research and Social Implications*. Mahwah, NJ: Lawrence Erlbaum. (**297**)

Heresco-Levy U, Giltsinsky B, Lichtenstein M, and Blander D (1999) Treatment-resistant schizophrenia and staff rejection. *Schizophrenia Bulletin* **25**: 457–65. (**557**)

Herinckx H, Swart M, Ama S, Dolezal C, and King S (2005) Rearrest and linkage to mental health services among clients of the Clark County mental health court program. *Psychiatric Services* **56**: 653–857. (**640, 641**)

Herjanic B and Reich IN (1982) Development of a structured diagnostic interview for children: agreement between child and parent on individual symptoms. *Journal of Abnormal Child Psychology* **10**: 307–24. (**484**)

Herman J (1992, new edition 1997) *Trauma and Recovery: The Aftermath of Violence from Domestic Abuse to Political Terror*. New York: Basic Books. (**712, 715**)

Herman JL, Gartrell N, Olarte S, Feldstein M, and Localio R (1987) Psychiatrist-patient sexual contact: results of a national survey, ii: psychiatrists' attitudes *American Journal of Psychiatry* **144**: 164–9. (**682**)

Herman-Giddens ME, Smith JB, Mittal M, Carlson M, and Butts JD (2003) Newborns killed or left to die by a parent: a population-based study. *Journal of the American Medical Association* **289**: 1425–9. (**510**)

Hernandez-Avila CA, Burleson JA, Poling J, et al. (2000) Personality and substance use disorders as predictors of criminality. *Comprehensive Psychiatry* **41**: 276–83. (**444**)

Hertlein KM and Ricci RJ (2004) A systematic research synthesis of EMDR studies: implementation of the platinum standard. *Trauma, Violence and Abuse: A Review Journal* **5**: 285–300. (**725**)

Herzberg JL and Fenwick PB (1998) The aetiology of aggression in temporal-lobe epilepsy. *British Journal of Psychiatry* **153**: 50–5. (**298**)

Hester M and Westmarland N (2004) *Tackling Street Prostitution: Towards a Holistic Approach*. Home Office Research Study No 279. London: Home Office. (**464**)

Heston LL (1966) Psychiatric disorders in foster home-reared children of schizophrenic mothers. *British Journal of Psychiatry* **112**: 819–25. (**189**)

Heuer F and Reisberg D (2007) The memory effects of emotion, stress and trauma. In D Ross, M Toglia, R Lindsay, D Read (eds) *Handbook of Eyewitness Psychology: Vol. 1 Memory for Events*. Mahwah, NJ: Lawrence Erlbaum Associates. (**161**)

Hickey N (2012) CBT for sex offenders: too good to be true? A reply to Ho and Ross. *Criminal Behaviour and Mental Health* **22**, 11–13. (**5**)

Hicks BM, Krueger RF, Iacono WG, McGue M, and Patrick CJ (2004) Family transmission and heritability of externalizing disorders: a twin-family study. *Archives of General Psychiatry* **61**: 922–8. (**203**)

Hicks BM, Vaidyanathan U, and Patrick CJ (2010) Validating female psychopathy subtypes: Differences in personality, antisocial and violent behavior, substance abuse, trauma, and mental health. *Personality Disorders: Theory, Research, & Treatment* **1**:38–57. (**514**)

Hicks JW (2003) Legal regulation of psychiatry. In R Rosner (ed) *Principles and Practice of Forensic Psychiatry*, 2nd edn. London: Arnold, pp. 850–76. (**123**)

Hiday VA (2003) Outpatients commitments: the state of empirical research on its outcomes. *Psychology Public Policy and the Law* **9**: 8–32. (**364, 567**)

Hiday VA, Swartz MS, Swanson JW, Borum R, and Wagner HR (2002) Impact of out-patient commitments on victimization of people with severe mental illness. *American Journal of Psychiatry* **159**: 1403–11. (**520**)

Hiday VA, Swartz MS, Swanson JW, et al. (1999) Criminal victimization of persons with severe mental illness. *Psychiatric Services* **50**: 62–8. (**280**)

Hien D, Cohen LR, Caldeira NA, Floam P, and Wasserman G (2010) Depression and anger as risk factors underlying the relationship between maternal substance involvement and child abuse potential. *The International Journal: Child Abuse & Neglect* **34**: 105–13. (**505, 506**)

Higgins N, Watts D, Bindman J, Slade M, and Thornicroft G (2005) Assessing violence risk in general adult psychiatry. *Psychiatric Bulletin* **29**: 131–3. (**533**)

Higley JD, King ST Jr, Hasert MF, et al. (1996) Stability of interindividual differences in serotonin function and its relationship to severe aggression and competent social behavior in rhesus macaque females. *Neuropsychopharmacology* **14**: 67–76. (**198**)

Higuchi S, Matsushita S, Imazeki H, et al. (1994) Aldehyde dehydrogenase genotypes in Japanese alcoholics. *Lancet* **343**: 741–2. (**207**)

Hilberman E and Manson M (1977) Sixty battered women. *Victimology* **2**: 460–71. (**372**)

Hilgard E (1977) *Divided Consciousness: Multiple Controls in Human Thought and Action*, New York: Wiley. (**426**)

Hill BK and Bruininks RH (1984) Maladaptive behaviour of mentally retarded individuals in residential facilities. *American Journal of Mental Deficiency* **88**: 380–7. (**326**)

Hill D (1982) Public attitudes to mentally abnormal offenders. In J Gunn, DP Farrington (eds) *Abnormal Offenders, Delinquency and the Criminal Justice System*. Chichester, UK: Wiley. (**671**)

Hill EM, Stoltenberg SF, Burmeister M, Closser M, and Zucker RA (1999) Potential associations among genetic markers in the serotonergic system and the antisocial alcoholism subtype. *Experimental Clinical Psychopharmacology* **7**: 103–21. (**205**)

Hill R and Davis P (2000) 'Platonic jealousy': a conceptualisation and review of the literature on non-romantic pathological jealousy. *British Journal of Medical Psychology* **73**: 505–17. (**369**)

Hillbrand M, Alexandre JW, Young JL, and Spitz RT (1999) Parricides: characteristics of offenders and victims, legal factors, and treatment issues. *Aggression and Violent Behavior* **4**: 179–90. (**231**)

Hilton NZ, Harris GT, and Rice ME (2001) Predicting violence by serious wife assaulters. *Journal of Interpersonal Violence* **16**: 408–23. (**537**)

Hinde RA (1993) Aggression at different levels of social complexity. In PJ Taylor (ed) *Violence in Society.* London: Royal College of Physicians, pp. 31–6. (**556**)

Hinshelwood RD (1993) Locked in a role: a psychotherapist within the social defence system of a prison. *Journal of Forensic Psychiatry* **4**: 427–40. (**585**)

Hinshelwood RD (1999) The difficult patient. *British Journal of Psychiatry* **174**: 187–90. (**684**)

Hinshelwood RD (2004) *Suffering Insanity: Psychoanalytic Essays on Psychosis.* Hove, E Sussex: Brunner-Routledge. (**582**)

Hinton R (1998) The physical environment. In C Kaye, A Franey (eds) *Managing High Security Psychiatric care.* London: Jessica Kingsley, pp. 85–98. (**593**)

Hiroeh U, Appleby L, Mortensen PB, et al. (2001) Death by homicide, suicide, and other unnatural causes in people with mental illness: a population-based study. *Lancet* **358**: 2110–12. (**280**)

Hirono N, Mega MS, Dinov ID, Mishkin F, and Cummings JL (2000) Left frontotemporal hypoperfusion is associated with aggression in patients with dementia. *Archives of Neurology* **57**: 861–6. (**302**)

Hirsch S and Shepherd M (1974, translated H Marshall) *Themes and Variations in European Psychiatry: An Anthology.* Bristol, UK: Wright. (**238**)

Hirsch SR and Barnes TRE (1994) Clinical use of high-dose neuroleptics. *British Journal of Psychiatry* **164**, 94–6. (**565**)

Hirschi T (1969) *Causes of Delinquency.* Berkeley: University of California Press. (**317**)

Hirschi T and Hindelang MJ (1977) Intelligence and delinquency: a revisionist view. *American Sociological Review* **42**: 571–87. (**316**)

Hite S (1981) *The Hite Report on Male Sexuality.* New York: Alfred Kopf. (**291**)

HM Chief Inspector of Prisons for England and Wales (1996) *Patient or Prisoner? A New Strategy for Health Care in Prisons.* London: Home Office. (**627, 628**)

HM Chief Inspector of Prisons for England and Wales (1999) *Suicide is Everyone's Concern.* http://www.justice.gov.uk/downloads/publications/inspectorate-reports/hmipris/thematic-reports-and-research-publications/suicide-is-everyones-concern-1999-rps.pdf (**633**)

HM Government (2003) *Every Child Matters.* https://www.education.gov.uk/publications/eOrderingDownload/CM5860.pdf (**466, 479**)

HM Government (2005) *Every Child Matters: Change for Children – Young People and Drugs.* http://iobi.swan.ac.uk/wp-content/uploads/2012/08/ChildSelf-Strategy-2004-Every-Child-Matters.pdf (**466**)

HM Government (2006) *Working Together to Safeguard Children: A Guide to Inter-agency Working to Safeguard and Promote the Welfare of Children.* https://www.education.gov.uk/publications/standard/publicationDetail/Page1/DFE-00030-2013 (**466**)

HM Government (2008) *Drugs: Protecting Families and Communities.* http://webarchive.nationalarchives.gov.uk/20100413151441/http://drugs.homeoffice.gov.uk/publication-search/drug-strategy/drug-strategy-20082835.pdf?view=Binary (**448, 466**)

HM Government (2009) *Healthy Children, Safer Communities.* London: Crown copyright. (**489**)

HM Government (2012) *Drug Strategy* http://www.homeoffice.gov.uk/drugs/drug-strategy-2010/ (**448, 466**)

HM Inspectorate of Prisons (1996) *Patient or Prisoner? A New Strategy for Health Care in Prisons.* London: Home Office. (**666**)

HM Inspectorate of Prisons (2004) *'No Problems - Old and Quiet': Older Prisoners in England and Wales.* London: HMSO. https://www.bulger.co.uk/prison/hmp-thematic-older-04.pdf (**524, 528**)

HM Inspectorate of Prisons (2005) *Parallel Worlds. A Thematic Review of Race Relations in Prisons.* http://www.justice.gov.uk/downloads/publications/inspectorate-reports/hmipris/thematic-reports-and-research-publications/parallelworlds-rps.pdf (**635**)

HM Inspectorate of Prisons (2006) *Foreign National Prisoners: A Thematic Review.* http://www.justice.gov.uk/downloads/publications/inspectorate-reports/hmipris/thematic-reports-and-research-publications/foreignnationals-rps.pdf (**636**)

HM Inspectorate of Prisons (2007) *The Mental Health of Prisoners: A Thematic Report of the Care and Support of Prisoners with Mental Health Needs.* London: HMIP. http://www.justice.gov.uk/downloads/publications/inspectorate-reports/hmipris/thematic-reports-and-research-publications/mental_health-rps.pdf (**169**)

HM Inspectorate of Prisons (2009) Race relations in prisons: responding to adult women from black and minority ethnic backgrounds. http://www.justice.gov.uk/downloads/publications/inspectorate-reports/hmipris/thematic-reports-and-research-publications/women_and_race-rps.pdf (**636**)

HM Inspectorate of Probation (1993) *Probation Orders with Requirement for Psychiatric Treatment.* London: Home Office. (**643**)

HM Prison Service (2008) *Life Sentenced Prisoners.* London: HM Prison Service. (**636**)

HM Prison Service/NHS Executive (1999) *The Future Organisation of Prison Health Care.* London: Department of Health. http://webarchive.nationalarchives.gov.uk/+/www.dh.gov.uk/en/publicationsandstatistics/publications/publicationspolicyandguidance/dh_4006944 (**628**)

HM Treasury (2002) *The Role of the Voluntary and Community Sector in Service Delivery: A Cross-cutting Review.* London: Her Majesty's Treasury. http://www.hm-treasury.gov.uk/d/CCRVolSec02.pdf (**647**)

HMIP: *see* HM Inspectorate for Prisons.

Ho B-C, Andreasen NC, Ziebell S, Pierson R, and Magnotta V (2011) Long-term antipsychotic treatment and brain volumes. *Archives of General Psychiatry* **68**: 128–37. (**360**)

Ho D and Ross C (2012) CBT for sex offenders. Too good to be true? *Criminal Behaviour and Mental Health* **22**: 1–6. (**5**)

Ho MK, Goldman D, Heinz A, et al. (2010) Breaking barriers in the genomics and pharmacogenetics of drug addiction. *Clinical Pharmacology and Therapeutics* **88**: 779–91. (**205, 206**)

Hoad C (1996) Violence at work: perspectives from research among 20 British employers. *Security Journal* (London) **4**: 64–86. (**699**)

Hoaken PNS and Stewart SH (2003) Drugs of abuse and the elicitation of human aggressive behaviour. *Addictive Behaviors* **28**: 1533–54. (**455**)

Hoare J (2009) *Drug Misuse Declared: Findings from the 2008/09 British Crime Survey.* Home Office Statistical Bulletin 12/09. London: Home Office. www.homeoffice.gov.uk/rds/pdfs09/hosb1209.pdf (**491**)

Hoare J and Flatley J (2008) *Drug Misuse Declared: Findings from the 2007/08 British Crime Survey – England and Wales.* London: Home Office. http://webarchive.nationalarchives.gov.uk/20110220105210/rds.homeoffice.gov.uk/rds/pdfs08/hosb1308.pdf (**466**)

Hobby MK (2006) Safety in the sleep laboratory. *Respiratory Clinics of North America* **12**: 101–10. (**292**)

Hocking MA (1989) Assaults in southeast London. *Journal of the Royal Society Medicine* **82**: 281–4. (**705**)

Hodel B and West A (2003) A cognitive training for mentally ill offenders with treatment-resistant schizophrenia. *Journal of Forensic Psychology and Psychiatry* **14**: 554–68. (**573**)

Hodges C-L, Paterson S, Taikato M, et al. (2006) *Comorbid Mental Health and Substance Misuse in Scotland.* Edinburgh, UK: Scottish Executive. http://www.scotland.gov.uk/Resource/Doc/127647/0030582.pdf (**467**)

Hodgins S (1992) Mental disorder, intellectual deficiency, and crime. Evidence from a birth cohort. *Archives of General Psychiatry* **49**: 476–83. (**337, 342, 507**)

Hodgins S and Muller-Isberner R (2000) *Violence, Crime and Mentally Disordered Offenders.* Chichester, UK: Wiley. (**242**)

Hodgins S and Müller-Isberner R (2004) Preventing crime by people with schizophrenic disorders: the role of psychiatric services. *British Journal of Psychiatry* **185**: 245–50. (**242, 362**)

Hodgins S, Hiscoke UL, and Freese R (2003) The antecedents of aggressive behavior among men with schizophrenia: a prospective investigation of patients in community treatment. *Behavioral Sciences and the Law* **21**: 523–46. (**350**)

Hodgins S, Mednick SA, Brennan PA, Schulsinger F, and Engberg M (1996) Mental disorder and crime: evidence form a Danish birth cohort. *Archives of General Psychiatry* **54**: 489–96. (**337**)

Hodgkinson T (1990) *Expert Evidence, Law and Practice.* London: Sweet and Maxwell. (**149**)

Hoel H, Faragher B, and Cooper CL (2004) Bullying is detrimental to health, but all bullying behaviours are not necessarily equally damaging. *British Journal of Guidance and Counselling* **32**: 367–87. (**699**)

Hoertel N, Le Strat Y, Schuster J-P and Limosin F (2011) Gender differences in firesetting: Results from the National Epidemiologic Survey on Alcohol and Related Conditions (NESARC). *Psychiatry Research* **190**: 352–8. (**504**)

Hoffman JL (1943) Psychotic visitors to government offices in the national capital. *American Journal of Psychiatry* **99**: 571–5. (**543, 548**)

Hoffman JP and Su SS (1998) Parental substance use disorder, mediating variables and adolescent drug use: a non-recursive model. *Addiction* **93**: 1351–64. (**465**)

Hoffman ML (1987) The contribution of empathy to justice and moral judgements. In N Eisenberg, J Strayer (eds) *Empathy and its Development.* Cambridge, UK: Cambridge University Press, pp. 47–80. (**394**)

Hoffmann J, Meloy JR, Guldimann A, and Ermer A (2011) Attacks on German public figures, 1968–2004: warning behaviours, potentially lethal and non-lethal acts, psychiatric status, and motivations. *Behavioural Sciences and the Law* **29**: 155–79. (**545**)

Hoffmann JM and Sheridan LP (2005) The stalking of public figures: management and intervention. *Journal of Forensic Science* **50**(6): 1459–65. (**377**)

Hogan DM (1998) Annotation: the psychological development and welfare of children of opiate and cocaine users: review and research needs. *Journal of Child Psychology and Psychiatry* **39**: 609–20. (**465**)

Hogarty GE and Flesher S (1999) Practice principles of cognitive enhancement therapy for schizophrenia. *Schizophrenia Bulletin* **25**: 693–708. (**573**)

Hoge CW, McGurk D, Thomas JL, et al. (2008) Mild traumatic brain injury in US soldiers returning from Iraq. *New England Journal of Medicine* **358**: 453–63. (**713**)

Hoge SK, Appelbaum PS, and Geller JL (1989) Involuntary treatment. *Review of Psychiatry* **8**: 432–50. (**122**)

Hoggett B (1985) Legal aspects of secure provision. In L Gostin (ed) *Secure Provision.* London: Tavistock. (**603**)

Hogue TE, Steptoe L, Taylor JL, et al. (2006) A comparison of offenders with intellectual disability across three levels of security. *Criminal Behaviour and Mental Health* **16**: 13–28. (**319, 331**)

Høigård C (1990) Criminality, sex and class. In N Bishop (ed) *Scandinavian Criminal Policy and Criminology 1985–1990.* Stockholm. Sweden: Scandinavian Council for Criminology. (**499, 500**)

Holcomb WR and Ahr PR (1988) Arrest rates among young-adult psychiatric-patients treated in inpatient and outpatient settings. *Hospital and Community Psychiatry* **39**: 52–7. (**279**)

Holden A (1974) *The St Albans Poisoner.* London: Hodder and Stoughton. (**233**)

Hole RW, Rush AJ, and Beck AT (1979) A cognitive investigation of schizophrenic delusions. *Psychiatry* **42**: 312–19. (**349**)

Holland A (1997) Forensic psychiatry and learning disability. In O Russel (ed) *Seminars in the Psychiatry of Learning Disabilities.* London: Gaskell, pp. 259–73. (**324**)

Holland AJ (2004) Criminal behaviour and developmental disability: An epidemiological perspective. In WR Lindsay, JL Taylor, and P Sturmey (eds) *Offenders with Developmental Disabilities.* Chichester:Wiley & Sons, Ltd. 2 –34. (**315**)

Holland T, Clare ICH, and Mukhopadhyay T (2002) Prevalence of criminal offending by men and women with intellectual disability and the characteristics of offenders: implications for research and service development. *Journal of Intellectual Disability Research* **46** (suppl. 1): 6–20. (**315, 325**)

References

Hollander E and Allen A (2006) Is compulsive buying a real disorder, and is it really compulsive? *American Journal of Psychiatry* **163**: 1670–2. (**253**)

Hollander E, Allen A, Lopez RP, et al. (2001) A preliminary double-blind, placebo-controlled trial of diavalproex sodium in borderline personality disorder. *Journal of Clinical Psychiatry* **62**: 199–203. (**405, 566**)

Hollander E, DeCaria CM, Finkel JN, et al. (2000) A randomized double-blind fluoxamine/placebo crossover trial in pathologic gambling. *Biological Psychiatry* **47**: 813–17. (**472**)

Hollander E, Kwon JH, Stein DJ, et al. (1996) Obsessive-compulsive and spectrum disorder: overview and quality of life issues. *Journal of Clinical Psychiatry* **57** (suppl. 8): 3–6. (**253**)

Hollander E, Stein DJ, DeCaria CM, et al. (1994) Serotonergic sensitivity in borderline personality disorder: preliminary findings. *American Journal of Psychiatry* **151**: 277–80. (**309**)

Hollander E, Swann AC, Coccaro EF, Jiang P, and Smith TB (2005) Impact of trait impulsivity and state aggression on divalproex versus placebo response in borderline personality disorder. *American Journal of Psychiatry* **162**: 621–4. (**406**)

Hollander E, Tracy KA, Swann AC, et al. (2003) Divalproex in the treatment of impulsive aggression: efficacy in cluster B personality disorders. *Neuropsychopharmacology* **28**: 1186–97. (**405**)

Hollin C, Palmer E, McGuire J, et al. (2004) *Pathfinder Programmes in the Probation Service: A Retrospective Analysis.* Home Office Online Report 66/04. London: HMSO. http://library.npia.police.uk/docs/hordsolr/rdsolr6604.pdf (**569, 573, 575**)

Hollin CR and Palmer EJ (eds) (2006) *Offending Behaviour Programmes: Development, Application, and Controversies.* Chichester, UK: Wiley. (**215, 242, 569**)

Holmes J and Landmaack C (2002) Managed clinical networks – their relevance to mental health services. *Psychiatric Bulletin* **26**: 161–3. (**413**)

Holmes R and Holmes S (1998) *Serial Murder*, 2nd edn. Thousand Oaks, CA: Sage. (**240**)

Holmes TH and Rahe RH (1967) The social readjustment rating scale. *Journal of Psychosomatic Research* **11**: 213–18. (**413**)

Holt R (2004) Diagnosis, epidemiology and pathogenesis of diabetes mellitus: an update for psychiatrists. *British Journal of Psychiatry* **184**: s55–63. (**567**)

Home Office (1960) *Report of the Committee on Children and Young Persons.* Cmnd. 1191. London (Ingleby Report): HMSO. (**475**)

Home Office (1965) *The Child, the Family and the Young Offender.* Cmnd.2742. London: HMSO. (**475**)

Home Office (1968) *Children in Trouble.* Cmnd.3601. London: HMSO. (**475**)

Home Office (1971) *Report of the Committee on Death Certification and Coroners.* Cmnd 4810. London: HMSO. (**54**)

Home Office (1980) *Criminal Statistics – England and Wales 1979*, Cmnd.8098. London: HMSO. (**273**)

Home Office (1989) *Judicial Statistics 1988.* London: HMSO. (**477**)

Home Office (1990) *Victims' Charter. Standards of Service for Victims of Crime.* London: Home Office. http://www.gm-probation.org.uk/files/victims-charter2835.pdf *see also* Criminal Justice System (2005) (**709**)

Home Office (1995) Circular 12/95 – Mentally Disordered Offenders: Inter Agency Working. (**23**)

Home Office (1997) *Statistics of Mentally Disordered Offenders in England and Wales, 1996.* Home Office Statistical Bulletin 20/97. London: Home Office. (**340**)

Home Office (1999) *Managing Dangerous People with Severe Personality Disorder: Proposals for Policy Development.* London: The Stationery Office. (**529**)

Home Office (2000) *Time for Reform: Proposals for the Modernization of our Licensing Laws.* Cm. 4696. Norwich, UK: The Stationery Office. (**441**)

Home Office (2001) *Making Punishments Work: A Review of the Sentencing Framework for England and Wales.* London: The Halliday Report. (**36**)

Home Office (2003a) *A New Deal for Victims and Witnesses.* London: Home Office. (**708**)

Home Office (2003b) *Death Certification and Investigation in England Wales and Northern Ireland – The Report of a Fundamental Review.* Cm. 5831. London: TSO. (**54**)

Home Office (2003c) *Prison statistics 2002: England and Wales.* London: HMSO. http://www.archive2.official-documents.co.uk/document/cm59/5996/5996.pdf (**524**)

Home Office (2004a) *Criminal Statistics*, England and Wales, 2003. London: Home Office. (**511**)

Home Office (2004b) *Reducing Crime – Changing Lives.* London: Home Office. (**628, 639**)

Home Office (2004d) Reforming the Coroner and Death Certification Service, Cm 6159 http://www.archive2.official-documents.co.uk/document/cm61/6159/6159.pdf (**54**)

Home Office (2005) Research Development and Statistics Directorate, Office for Criminal Justice Reform, personal communication, dated 10/8/05. (**523, 525**)

Home Office (2005a) *Supplementary Tables to Online Report 04/04: Violence at Work: Findings from the 2002/3 British Crime Survey. London.* London: Home Office. Cm6361 http://www.archive2.official-documents.co.uk/document/cm63/6361/6361.pdf [NB. Figures updated annually and now available from the Government's Health and Safety Executive website: http://www.hse.gov.uk] (**511, 699**)

Home Office (2005b) *Violence Against the Person – Long Term National Recorded Crime Trends, London.* Research Development and Statistics Directorate. London: Home Office. [for updates see the Government's Office of National Statistics website: http://www.ons.gov.uk (**702**)

Home Office (2005c) *Hearing the Relatives of Murder and Manslaughter Victims.* London: Home Office. http://webarchive. nationalarchives.gov.uk/+/http://www.dca.gov.uk/consult/manslaughter/manslaughter.pdf (**708**)

Home Office (2005d) *Domestic Violence: A National Report.* London: Home Office (**713**)

Home Office (2007) *Review of the Protection of Children from Sex Offenders.* London: Central Office of Information. http://webarchive. nationalarchives.gov.uk/20100413151441/http://www.homeoffice.gov.uk/documents/CSOR/chid-sex-offender-review-1306072835. pdf?view=Binary (**645**)

Home Office (2012) *Controlled Drugs List* http://www.homeoffice.gov.uk/publications/alcohol-drugs/drugs/drug-licences/controlled-drugs-list (**453**)

Home Office (2012) *Drug Strategy.* http://www.homeoffice.gov.uk/drugs/drug-strategy-2010/ (**448**)

Home Office (2013) *Recorded Crime Datasets.* http://www.homeoffice.gov.uk/science-research/research-statistics/crime/crime-statistics-internet/ (**442**)

Home Office and the Department of Health and Social Security (1975) *Report of the Committee on Mentally* Disordered *Offenders (The Butler Report) (*Cmnd *6244).* London: HMSO. (**5, 33, 529, 579, 632**)

Home Office, Department of Health and Social Security (1980) *Young Offenders.* Cmnd. 8045. London: HMSO. (**476**)

Honkatukia P (1998) Gender, social identity and delinquent behaviour http://www.retfaerd.org/gamle_pdf/1999/3/ Retfaerd_86_1999_3_s41_52.PDF (**511**)

Hook EB (1973) Behavioural implications of the XYY human genotype. *Science* **179**: 1139–50. (**323**)

Hopfer CJ, Crowley TJ, and Hewitt JK (2003) Review of twin and adoption studies of adolescent substance use. *Journal of the American Academy of Child and Adolescent Psychiatry* **42**: 710–19. (**202**)

Hopfer CJ, Stallings MC, Hewitt JK, and Crowley TJ (2003) Family transmission of marijuana use, abuse, and dependence. *Journal of the American Academy of Child and Adolescent Psychiatry* **42**: 834–41. (**189**)

Hoptman MJ, D'Angelo D, Catalano D, et al. (2010) Amygdalofrontal functional disconnectivity and aggression in schizophrenia. *Schizophrenia Bulletin* **36**: 1020–8. (**305, 306**)

Hoptman MJ, Volavka J, Czobor P, et al. (2006) Aggression and quantitative MRI measures of caudate in patients with chronic schizophrenia or schizoaffective disorder. *Journal of Neuropsychiatry and Clinical Neuroscience* **18**: 509–15. (**299, 300, 301**)

Hoptman MJ, Volavka J, Johnson G, et al. (2002) Frontal white matter microstructure, aggression, and impulsivity in men with schizophrenia: a preliminary study. *Biological Psychiatry* **52**: 9–14. (**301**)

Hopwood JS and Snell HK (1933) Amnesia in relation to crime. *Journal of Mental Science* **79**: 27–41. (**291, 293, 294, 295, 296**)

Horn P (2010) *Young Offenders. Juvenile Delinquency 1700–2000.* Amberley, Stroud. (**474**)

Horne JA and Reyner LA (1995) Sleep related vehicle accidents. *British Medical Journal* **310**: 565–7. (**279**)

Hornsveld RHJ (2005) Evaluation of aggression control training for violent psychiatric patients. *Psychology, Crime and Law* **11**: 403–10. (**577**)

Horowitz LM, Rosenberg SE, Baer BA, Ureno G, and Villasenor VS (1988) The inventory of interpersonal problems: psychometric properties and clinical applications. *Journal of Consulting and Clinical Psychology* **56**: 885–95. (**389**)

Horowitz MJ (1976) *Stress Response Syndromes.* New York: Aronson. (**721**)

Horowitz MJ (1997) *Stress Response Syndromes,* 3rd edn. Northvale, NJ: Aronson. (**713**)

Horvath AO and Greenberg LS (1989) Development and validation of the working alliance inventory. *Journal of Counseling Psychology* **36**: 223–33. (**548**)

Hotopf M, Hull L, Fear NT, et al. (2006) The health of UK military personnel who deployed to the 2003 Iraq war: a cohort study. *Lancet* **367**: 1731–41. (**715**)

Hough M (1990) Threats: findings from the British crime survey. *International Review of Victimology* **1**: 169–80. (**543**)

House of Commons (1946) *Report of the Care of Children Committee (Training in Child Care)* - cmd. 6922. London: HMSO (Curtis Committee). www.pathwaysvictoria.info/biogs/E000347b.htm (**475**)

House of Commons (1975) *Eleventh Report from the Expenditure Committee: Children and Young Persons Act 1969.* London: HMSO. (**476**)

House of Commons Health Committee (2003) *The Victoria Climbié Inquiry Report (*Lord Laming) Sixth Report of Session 2002–03 HC 570 TSO, London. (**222**)

Howard C and d'Orban PT (1987) Violence in sleep: medico-legal issues and two case reports. *Psychological Medicine* **17**: 915–25. (**290**)

Howard League for Penal Reform (1993) *The Voice of the Child. The Impact on Children of their Mothers' Imprisonment.* London: Howard League. (**596**)

Howard League for Penal Reform (2006) *Women and Girls in the Penal System.* London: Howard League. (**511**)

Howard League for Penal Reform (2010) Leave No Veteran Behind. The Inquiry into Former Armed Service Personnel in Prison visits the United States of America. Howard League for Penal Reform: London. http://www.howardleague.org/leave-no-veteran-behind/ (**715**)

Howard P, Francis B, Soothill K, and Humphreys L (2009) *OGRS 3: The Revised Offender Group Reconviction Scale. Research Summary 7/09OGRS.* London: Ministry of Justice. http://eprints.lancs.ac.uk/49988/1/ogrs3.pdf (**42, 530**)

Howells K (1998) 'Cognitive behavioural interventions for anger, aggression and violence'. In N Tarrier, A Wells, G Haddock (eds) *Treating Complex Cases: The Cognitive Behavioural Therapy Approach.* Chichester, UK: Wiley. (**242**)

Howells K and Hollin CR (1989) Clinical approaches to violence Wiley, Chichester to TV violence and their aggressive and violent behaviour in young adulthood 1977–1992. *Development Psychology* **39**: 201–21. (**212, 214**)

Howells K, Day A, and Thomas-Peter B (2004) Changing violent behaviour: forensic mental health and criminological models compared. *Journal of Forensic Psychiatry and Psychology* **15**: 391–456. (**570, 577, 579**)

Howells K, Watt B, Hall G, and Baldwin S (1997) Developing programmes for violent offenders. *Legal and Criminological Psychology* **2**: 117–28. (**577**)

Howes OD, McDonald C, Cannon M, et al. (2004) Pathways to schizophrenia: the impact of environmental factors. *International Journal of Neuropsychopharmacology* **7** (suppl. 1): S7–13. (**210**)

Howlin P (1997) '*Autism': Preparing for Adulthood.* London: Routledge. (**487**)

Howlin P and Udwin O (2006) 'Outcome in adult life for people with Williams syndrome – results from a survey of 239 families'. *Journal of Intellectual Disability Research* **50**(2): 151–60. (**323**)

Howse K (2003) *Growing Old in Prison: A Scoping Study on Older Prisoners.* London: Prison Reform Trust. http://www.prisonreformtrust.org.uk/uploads/documents/Growing.Old.Book_-_small.pdf (**528**)

Huang YY, Cate SP, Battistuzzi C, et al. (2004) An association between a functional polymorphism in the monoamine oxidase a gene promoter, impulsive traits and early abuse experiences. *Neuropsychopharmacology* **29**: 1498–505. (**200**)

Huband N, McMurran M, Evans C, and Duggan C (2007) Social problem – solving plus psychoeducation for adults with personality disorder: a pragmatic randomised clinical trial. *British Journal of Psychiatry* **190**: 307–13. (**407**)

Hublin C, Kaprio J, Partinen M, Heikkila K, and Koskenvuo M (1997) Prevalence and genetics of sleepwalking: a population-based twin study. *Neurology* **48**: 177–81. (**290**)

Hucker S, Arnup J, Busse EW, Gunn J, Richardson H, Smale S and Webster CD et al. (1986) *Oak Ridge: A Review and an Alternative.* Ontario Ministry of Health: Toronto. (**603**)

Hudson CG (2005) Socioeconomic status and mental illness: tests of the social causation and selection hypotheses. *American Journal of Orthopsychiatry* **75**: 3–18. (**341**)

Hudson SMT, Ward and McCormack JC. (1999) Offense pathways in sexual offenders. *Journal of Interpersonal Violence* **14**: 779–98. (**328**)

Huesmann LR, Eron LD, and Yarmel PW (1987) Intellectual functioning and aggression. *Journal of Personality and Social Psychology* **52:** 232–40. (**341**)

Huesmann LR, Moise-Titus J, Podolski CL, and Eron LD (2003) Longitudinal relations between children's exposure to TV violence and their aggressive and violent behaviour in young adulthood: 1977–1992. *Developmental Psychology* **39**: 201–21. (**217**)

Huff CR (2004) Wrongful convictions: the American experience. *Canadian Journal of Criminology and Criminal Justice* **46**: 165–82. (**716**)

Huff CR, Rattner A, and Sagarin E (1996) *Convicted but Innocent: Wrongful Convictions and Public Policy.* Thousand Oaks, CA: Sage. (**716**)

Hughes J and Cook C (1997) The efficacy of Disulfiram: a review of outcome studies. *Addiction* **92**: 381–95. (**446**)

Huizinga D and Elliott DS (1986) Reassessing the reliability and validity of self-report measures. *Journal of Quantitative Criminology* **2**: 293–327. (**171, 172**)

Huizinga D, Loeber R, and Thornberry TP (1993) Longitudinal study of delinquency, drug use, sexual activity and pregnancy among children and youth in three cities. *Public Health Reports* **108**: 90–6. (**173**)

Huizinga D, Weiher AW, Espiritu R, and Esbensen F (2003) Delinquency and crime: some highlights from the Denver youth survey. In TP Thornberry, MD Krohn (eds) *Taking Stock of Delinquency: An Overview of Findings from Contemporary Longitudinal Studies.* New York: Kluwer, pp. 47–91. (**171**)

Hull EM, Muschamp JW, and Sato S (2004) Dopoamine and serotonin: influences on male sexual behaviour. *Physiology and Behavior* **83**: 291–307. (**260**)

Hume D (1844) *Commentaries on the Law of Scotland Respecting Crimes.* Edinburgh, UK: Bell and Bradfute. (**95**)

Hummel P, ThomkeV, Oldenburger HA, and Specht F (2000) Male adolescent sex offenders against children: similarities and differences between those offenders with and those without a history of sexual abuse. *Journal of Adolescence* **23**: 317. (**494**)

Humphreys MS, Johnstone EC, Macmillan JF, and Taylor PJ (1992) Dangerous behaviour preceding first admissions for schizophrenia. *British Journal of Psychiatry* **161**: 501–5. (**343, 344**)

Hunter DJ and Kraft P (2007) Drinking from the fire hose – statistical issues in genomewide association studies. *New England Journal of Medicine* **357**: 436–9. (**195**)

Hunter ME and Love CC (1996) Total quality management and the reduction of inpatient violence and costs in a forensic psychiatric hospital. *Psychiatric Services* **47**: 751–4. (**556**)

Hunter R and MacAlpine I (1963) *Three Hundred Years of Psychiatry.* London: Oxford University Press. (**593**)

Huq SF, Garety PA, and Hemsley DR (1988) Probabalistic judgements in deluded and nondeluded subjects. *Quarterly Journal of Experimental Psychology* **40A**: 801–12. (**351**)

Hurley W and Dunne MP (1991) Psychological distress and psychiatric morbidity in women prisoners. *Australian New Zealand Journal of Psychiatry* **25**(4): 461–70. (**516**)

Hurn C, Gray NS, and Hughes I (2002) Independence of 'reaction to hypothetical contradiction' from other measures of delusional ideation. *British Journal of Clinical Psychology* **41**: 349–60. (**351**)

Husain A, Anasseril DE, and Harris PW (1983) A study of young-age and mid-life homicidal women admitted to a psychiatric hospital for pre-trial evaluation. *Canadian Journal of Psychiatry* **28**: 10913. (**507**)

Hustvedt A (2011) *Medical Muses: Hysteria in Nineteenth-Century Paris.* London: Bloomsbury. (**423**)

Hyler SE (1994) *The Personality Diagnostic Questionnaire 4*. New York: New York State Psychiatric Institute. (**388**)

Hyler SE, Skellman HD, Oldham JM, and Rosnick L (1990) Validity of the personality diagnostic questionnaire - revised: comparison with two structured interviews. *American Journal of Psychiatry* **33**: 73–7. (**388**)

Iacono T and Murray V (2003) Issues of informed consent in conducting medical research involving people with intellectual disability. *Journal of Applied Research in Intellectual Disabilities* **16**: 41–51. (**333**)

Independent Advisory Panel on Deaths in Custody (2011) *Statistical analysis of all recorded deaths of individuals detained in state custody between 1 January 2000 and 31 December 2010.* Department of Health, Ministry of Justice and Home Office: London. http://iapdeathsincustody.independent.gov.uk/wp-content/uploads/2011/10/IAP-Statistical-Analysis-of-All-Recorded-Deaths-in-State-Custody-Between-2000-and-2010.pdf (**634**)

Information and Statistics Division Scotland (2010) Bed Statistics: Available Beds by Speciality and NHS Board of Treatment. Information and Statistics Division: Scotland. http://www.isdscotland.org/Health-Topics/Hospital-Care/Beds/ (**653**)

Ingason A, Rujescu D, Cichon S, et al. (2011) Copy number variations of chromosome 16p13.1 region associated with schizophrenia. *Molecular Psychiatry*. 16, 17–25 (**209**)

Ingraham LJ and Chan TF (1996) Is there psychopathology in the coparents of schizophrenic adoptees' half-siblings? *Psychological Reports* **79**: 1296–8. (**189**)

Ingraham LJ and Kety SS (2000) Adoption studies of schizophrenia. *American Journal of Medical Genetics* **97**: 18–22. (**188, 208**)

Inquest Law editorial (2009) *Inquestlaw: Journal of the Inquest Lawyers Group.* Issue 18, December 2009. (**55**)

Institute of Alcohol Studies (2007) *Alcohol and Crime, IAS Factsheet.* St Ives: Institute of Alcohol Studies. (**281**)

Institute of Medicine (1988) *The Future of Public Health.* Washington, DC: Institute of Medicine. http://www.nap.edu/openbook.php?record_id=1091 (**703**)

International Labour Office (2004) *Workplace Violence in Services Sectors and Measures to Combat this Phenomenon, ILO Code of Practice.* Geneva, Switzerland: International Labour Office. http://www.ilo.org/safework/info/standards-and-instruments/codes/WCMS_107705/lang--en/index.htm (**699**)

International Schizophrenia Consortium (2008) Rare chromosomal deletions and duplications increase risk of schizophrenia. *Nature* **455**(7210): 237–41. (**209**)

Intrator J, Hare R, Stritzke P, et al. (1997) A brain imaging (single photon emission computerized tomography) study of semantic and affective processing in psychopaths. *Biological Psychiatry* **42**: 96–103. (**302**)

Ireland J (2009) Conducting individualised theory-driven assessments of violent offenders. Treatment approaches for violence and aggression: Essential content components. In JL Ireland, CA Ireland, and P Birch (eds) *Violent and Sexual Offenders.* Willan: Cullompton. Pp. 68–96; 153–178. (**577**)

Irish Prison Service (2009) *Annual Report 2008.* Longford, Ireland: Irish Prison Service. http://www.irishprisons.ie/images/pdf/annualreport2009.pdf (**657**)

Irving CB, Mumby-Croft R, and Joy LA Polyunsaturated fatty acid supplementation for schizophrenia. *Cochrane Database of Systematic Reviews 2006.* Issue 3. Art. No.: CD001257. pub2. http://onlinelibrary.wiley.com/o/cochrane/clsysrev/articles/CD001257/frame.html (**568**)

Irwin WG, McClelland RJ, Stout RW, and Stchedroff M (1988) Multidisciplinary teaching in a formal ethics course for clinical students. *Journal of Medical Ethics* **14**: 125–8. (**660**)

Isaacs S (1961) Obituary: Melanie Klein 1882–1960. *Journal of Child Psychology and Psychiatry* **2**: 1–4 (**482**)

Isherwood J, Adam KS, and Hornblow AR (1982) Life event stress, psychosocial factors, suicide attempt and auto-accident proclivity. *Journal of Psychosomatic Research* **26**: 371–83. (**278**)

Isherwood S and Parrott J (2002) Audit of transfers under the Mental Health Act from prison – the impact of organisational change. *Psychiatric Bulletin* **26**: 368–70. (**632**)

Ito TA, Miller N, and Pollock VE (1996) Alcohol and aggression: a meta-analysis on the moderating effects of inhibitory cures, triggering events, and self-focused attention. *Psychological Bulletin* **120**: 60–82. (**440**)

Jablensky A (2003) The epidemiological horizon. In SR Hirsch, D Weinberger (eds) *Schizophrenia.* Oxford, UK: Blackwell, pp. 203–31. (**514**)

Jackson HF, Glass C, and Hope S (1987) A functional analysis of recidivistic arson. *British Journal of Clinical Psychology* **26**: 175–85. (**330, 576**)

Jackson M (1995) Learning to think about schizoid thinking. In J Ellwood (ed) *Psychosis Understanding and Treatment.* London: Jessica Kingsley, pp. 9–22. (**584**)

Jackson RL, Rogers R, Neumann CS, et al. (2002) Psychopathy in female offenders: An investigation of its underlying dimensions. *Criminal Justice and Behavior* **29**: 692–704. (**513**)

Jacobs PA, Brunton M, Melville MM, Brittain RP, and McClement WF (1965) Aggressive behaviour, mental subnormality and the XYY male. (letter) *Nature* **208**: 1351–2. (**323**)

Jacobs W, Kennedy W, and Meyer J (1997) Juvenile delinquents: a between-group comparison study of sexual and nonsexual offenders. *Sexual Abuse: A Journal of Research and Treatment* **9**: 201–17. (**263**)

Jacobson A and Richardson B (1987) Assault experiences of 100 psychiatric inpatients – evidence of the need for routine enquiry. *American Journal of Psychiatry* **144**: 908–12. (**712**)

Jacobson A, Koehler JE, and Jones-Brown C (1987) The failure of routine assessment to detect histories of assault experienced by psychiatric patients. *Hospital and Community Psychiatry* **38**: 386–9. (**712**)

Jacobson J (2008) *No One Knows: Police Responses to Suspects with Learning Difficulties and Learning Disabilities: A Review of Policy and Practice.* London: Prison Reform Trust. (**316**)

Jacoby A, Baker GA, Steen N, Potts P, and Chadwick DW (1996) The clinical course of epilepsy and its psychosocial correlates: findings from a UK community study. *Epilepsia* **37**: 148–61. (**285**)

Jacoby A, Snape D, and Baker GA (2005) Epilepsy and social identity: the stigma of a chronic neurological disorder. *The Lancet* **4**: 171–8. (**285**)

Jacquemyn Y, Martens G, Ruyssinck G, Michiels I, and Van Overmeire B (2003) A matched cohort comparison of the outcome of twin versus singleton pregnancies in Flanders, Belgium. *Twin Research* **6**: 7–11. (**189**)

Jaded AR, Moore RA, Carroll D, et al. (1996) Assessing the quality of reports of randomised clinical trials: is blinding necessary? *Controlled Clinical Trials* **17**: 1–12. (**357**)

Jaffe M (2012) The Listener Scheme in Prisons: Final report on the Research Findings http://www.samaritans.org/sites/default/files/kcfinder/files/research/Peer%20Support%20in%20Prison%20Communities.pdf (**634**)

Jaffee SR, Caspi A, Moffitt TE, and Taylor A (2004) Physical maltreatment victim to antisocial child: evidence of an environmentally mediated process. *Journal of Abnormal Psychology* **113**: 44–55. (**197**)

Jaffee SR, Caspi A, Moffitt TE, et al. (2005) Nature X nurture: genetic vulnerabilities interact with physical maltreatment to promote conduct problems. *Development and Psychopathology* **17**: 67–84. (**200**)

Jaffee SR, Moffitt TE, Caspi A, Taylor A, and Arseneault L (2002) Influence of adult domestic violence on children's internalizing and externalizing problems: an environmentally informative twin study. *Journal of the American Academy of Child and Adolescent Psychiatry* **41**: 1095–103. (**197**)

James A (2004) Schizophrenia. In S Bailey, M Dolan (eds) *Adolescent Forerensic Psychiatry.* London: Arnold, pp. 152–63. (**487**)

James AC and Neil P (1996) Juvenile sexual offending: one-year period prevalence study within Oxfordshire. *Child Abuse and Neglect* **20**: 477–85. (**494**)

James DV, Finberg NA, Shah AK, and Priest RG (1990) An increase in violence on an acute psychiatric ward: a study of associated factors. *British Journal of Psychiatry* **156**: 846–52. (**596**)

James DV, Kerrigan T, Forfar R, Farnham F, and Preston L (2010) The fixated threat assessment centre: preventing harm and facilitating care. *Journal of Forensic Psychiatry and Psychology* **21**: 521–36. (**234, 547**)

James DV, McEwan TE, MacKenzie RD, et al. (2010b) Persistence in stalking: a comparison of associations in general forensic and public figure samples. *Journal of Forensic Psychiatry and Psychology* **21**: 283–305. (**545**)

James DV, Meloy JR, Mullen PE, et al. (2010c) Abnormal attentions towards the British Royal Family: factors associated with approach and escalation. *Journal of the American Academy of Psychiatry and the Law* **38**: 329–40. (**545, 546**)

James DV, Mullen PE, Meloy JR, et al (2007) The role of mental disorder in attacks on European politicians 1990–2004. *Acta Psychiatrica Scandinavica* **116**(5): 334–44. (**234, 545**)

James DV, Mullen PE, Pathé M (2008) Attacks on the British royal family: the role of psychotic illness. *Journal of the American Academy of Psychiatry and the Law* **36**(1): 59–67. (**377, 545**)

James DV, Mullen PE, Pathé MT (2009) Stalkers and harassers of royalty: the role of mental illness and motivation. *Psychological Medicine* **39**(9): 1479–90. (**545**)

James DV, Mullen PE, Pathé MT, et al (2009) Stalkers and harassers of royalty: the role of mental illness and motivation. *Psychological Medicine* **39**(9): 1479–90. (**235, 545**)

James DV, Mullen PE, Pathé MT, et al. (2010a) Stalkers and harassers of royalty: an exploration of proxy behaviours for violence. *Behavioural Sciences and the Law* **29**(1): 64–80. (**545**)

James H (1898) *The Turn of the Screw.* London: William Heinemann. (**Preface**)

James I (1976) A case of shoplifting in the eighteen century. *Prison Medical Journal* **17**: 28–30. (**271**)

James W (1890) *The Principles of Psychology* Vols. 1 & 2. London: Macmillan. (**426**)

Jamieson E and Taylor PJ (2002a) Follow-up of serious offender patients in the community: multiple methods of tracing. *International Journal of Research Methods* **11**: 112–24. (**605**)

Jamieson E, Butwell M, Taylor P, and Leese M (2000) Trends in special (high security) hospitals. 1. referrals and admissions, 1986–1995. *British Journal of Psychiatry* **176**: 253–9. (**266, 513, 520**)

Jamieson L and Taylor PJ (2002) Mental disorder and perceived threat to the public: people who do not return to community living. *British Journal of Psychiatry* **181**: 399–405. (**416, 515, 520, 605**)

Jamieson L and Taylor PJ (2004) A reconviction study of special (high security) hospital patients. *British Journal of Criminology* **44**: 783–802. (**520, 605**)

Jamieson L and Taylor PJ (2005) Patients leaving an English high security hospitals. Do discharge cohorts and their progress change over time? *International Journal of Forensic Mental Health* **4**: 59–75. (**138, 605**)

Jamieson L, Taylor PJ, and Gibson B (2006) From pathological dependence to healthy independent living: an emergent grounded theory of facilitating independent living. *The Grounded Theory Review* **6**: 79–107. (**365, 586, 591, 606**)

Janoff-Bulman R (1992) *Shattering Assumptions: Towards a New Psychology of Trauma.* New York: Free Press. (**721**)

Janowsky DS, Kraus JE, Barnhill J, Elamir B, and Davis JM (2003) Effects of topiramate on aggressive, self-injurious, and disruptive/destructive behaviors in the intellectually disabled: an open-label retrospective study. *Journal of Clinical Psychopharmacology* **23**: 500–4. (**586**)

Janowsky DS, Shetty M, Barnhill J, Elamir B, and Davis JM (2005) Serotonergic antidepressant effects on aggressive, self-injurious and destructive/disruptive behaviours in intellectually disabled adults: a retrospective, open-label, naturalistic trail. *International Journal of Neuropsychopharmacology* **8**: 37–48. (**310**)

Janssen J, Krabbendam L, Bak M, et al. (2004) Childhood abuse as a risk factor or psychotic experiences. *Acta Psychiatrica Scandinavica* **109**: 38–45. (**344**)

Jarvis TJ and Copeland J (1997) Child sexual abuse as a predictor of psychiatric co-morbidity and its implications for drug and alcohol treatment. *Drug and Alcohol Dependence* **49**: 61–9. (**464**)

Jaspers K (1910) Eifersuchtswahn. *Zeitschrift fur die gesamte Neurologie und Psychiatrie* **1**: 567–637. (*see also in translation*: Jaspers, 1923) (**368**)

Jaspers K (1923, translated Hoenig and Hamilton, 1963) *General Psychopathology*. Manchester: Manchester University Press. (**346, 384, 397**)

Jaycox LH, Zoellner L, and Foa EB (2002) Cognitive behaviour therapy for PTSD in rape survivors. *Journal of Consulting and Clinical Psychology* **58**: 891–906. (**727, 728**)

Jenkins J and Sainsbury P (1980) Single-car road deaths – disguised suicides? *British Medical Journal* **281**: 1041. (**278**)

Jenkins R, Smeeton N, and Shepherd M (1988) Classification of mental disorder in primary care. *Psychological Medicine* Monograph (suppl. 12). (**9**)

Jenkins S (2003) Trupti Patel and the rotten courts of Salem. *The Times*. 13 June. (**677**)

Jewkes R (2002) Intimate partner violence: causes and prevention. *Lancet* **359**: 1423–9. (**371**)

Jewkes Y (2005) Loss, liminality and the life sentence: managing identity through a disrupted lifecourse. In A Liebling, S Maruna (eds) *The Effects of Imprisonment*. Cullompton, UK: Willan. (**637**)

Jewkes Y (ed) (2007) *Handbook of Prisons*. Cullompton, UK: Willan. (**626**)

Jochelson K (2006) Smoke-free legislation and mental health units: the challenges ahead. *British Journal of Psychiatry* **189**: 479–80. (**568**)

John OP (1990) The 'Big Five' taxonomy. Dimensions of personality in the natural language and in questionnaires. In LA Pervin (ed) *Handbook of Personality Theory and Research*. New York: Guilford, pp. 66–100. (**385**)

Johnson G, Esposito L, Barratt B, et al. (2001) Haplotype tagging for the identification of common disease genes. *Nature Genetics* **29**: 233–7. (**194**)

Johnson JG, Cohen P, Smailes EM, Kasen S, and Brook JS (2002) Television viewing and aggressive behaviour during adolescence and adulthood. *Science* **295**: 2468–71. (**217**)

Johnson K, Gerada C, and Greenough A (2003) Substance misuse during pregnancy. *British Journal of Psychiatry* **183**: 187–9. (**465**)

Johnson RL and Shrier D (1987) Past sexual victimization by females of male patients in an adolescent medicine clinic population. *American Journal of Psychiatry* **144**: 650–2. (**252**)

Johnson T, Cho YI, Fendrich M, Graf I, and Kelly-Wilson L (2004) Substance abuse treatment need and treatment services utilization among youth entering the juvenile corrections system. *Journal of Substance Abuse Treatment* **26**. 117–28. (**183**)

Johnston I and Taylor PJ (2003) Mental disorder and serious violence: the victims. *Journal of Clinical Psychiatry* **64**: 819–24. (**334, 350, 355**)

Jolliffe D and Farrington DP (2004) Empathy and offending: a systematic review and meta-analysis. *Aggression and Violent Behavior* **9**: 441–76. (**354**)

Jones AW (2005) Driving under the influence of drugs in Sweden with zero concentration limits in blood for controlled substances. *Traffic Injury Prevention* **6**: 317–22. (**455**)

Jones C, Cormac I, Silveira da Mota Neto JI, and Campbell C (2010) *Cognitive Behaviour Therapy for Schizophrenia*. The Cochrane Collaboration. Chichester, UK: John Wiley and Sons. http://onlinelibrary.wiley.com/doi/10.1002/14651858.CD000524.pub2/pdf (**573**

Jones C, Cormac I, Silveira da Moto Neto JI, and Campbell C (2004) Cognitive behaviour therapy for schizophrenia. *The Cochrane Database of Systematic Reviews 2004*. Issue 4, Art. No.: CD000524. DOI: 10.1002/14651858. CD00054.pub2. http://onlinelibrary.wiley.com/o/cochrane/clsysrev/articles/CD000524/frame.html (**353, 361, 362, 573, 727**)

Jones D and Hollin CR (2004) Managing problematic anger: the development of a treatment programme for PD patients in high security. *International Journal of Forensic Mental Health* **3**: 198–210. (**575**)

Jones G and Talbot J (2010) No one knows: the bewildering passage of offenders with learning disability and learning difficulty through the criminal justice system. *Criminal Behaviour and Mental Health* **20**: 1–7. (**316**)

Jones H (1992) Revolving doors: report of the telethon inquiry into the relationship between mental health, homelessness and the criminal justice system. London: NACRO. (**412**)

Jones HE, Haug N, Silverman K, Stitzer M, and Svikis D (2001) The effectiveness of incentives in enhancing treatment attendance and drug abstinence in methadone-maintained pregnant women. *Drug and Alcohol Dependence* **61**: 297–306. (**466**)

Jones HE, Johnson RE, Jasinski DR, et al. (2005) Buprenorphine versus methadone in the treatment of pregnant opioid-dependent patients: effects on the neonatal abstinence syndrome. *Drug and Alcohol Dependence* **79**: 1–10. (**465**)

Jones I and Craddock N (2001) Candidate gene studies of bipolar disorder. *Annals of Medicine* **33**: 248–56. (**194**)

Jones JE, Hermann BP, Barry JJ, Gilliam FG, Kanner AM and Meador KJ (2003) Rates and risk factors for suicide, suicidal ideation, and suicide attempts in chronic epilepsy. *Epilepsy & Behavior* **4**: Suppl 3, 31–8. (**286**)

Jones K (1972) *A History of the Mental Health Services*. London: Routledge and Kegan Paul. (**589**)

Jones K and Fowles AJ (1984) *Ideas on Institutions*. London: Routledge and Kegan Paul. (**601, 602**)

Jones LF (2007) Iatrogenic interventions with personality disordered offenders. *Psychology, Crime and Law* **13**: 69–79. (**569**)

Jones LM, Finkelhor D, and Koplec K (2001) Why is sexual abuse declining? A survey of state child protection administrators. *Child Abuse and Neglect* **25**: 1139–58. (**244**)

Jones M (1952) *A Study of Therapeutic Communities*. London: Tavistock. (**579**)

Jones M (1968) *Social Psychiatry in Practice*. Harmondsworth, UK: Penguin. (**412**)

Jones M (1982) *The Process of Change*. London: Routledge. (**412**)

Jones PB, Barnes TRE, Davies L, et al. (2006) Randomised controlled trial of the affect on quality of life of second vs first-generation antipsychotic drugs in schizophrenia. *Archives of General Psychiatry* **63**: 1079–87. (**359**)

Jones R (2009) *Mental Health Act Manual*, 12th edn. London: Sweet and Maxwell. (**57, 62**)

Jones R (Rose) (2011) *A qualitative investigation of the main concerns that staff have about treating people with a personality disorder*. MSc Dissertation. Cardiff University. (**399, 661**)

Jones RM, Arlidge J, Gillham R, et al. (2011) Efficacy of mood stabilisers in the treatment of impulsive or repetitive aggressions: a systematic review and meta-analysis. *British Journal of Psychiatry* **198**: 93–8. (**566**)

Jones RM, Hales H, Butwell M, Ferriter M, and Taylor PJ (2011) Suicide in high security hospital patients. *Social Psychiatry and Psychiatric Epidemiology* **46**: 723–31. (**520**)

Jones RM, Hansen L, Moskvina V, Kingdon D, and Turkington S (2010) The relationship between self-esteem and psychotic symptoms in schizophrenia: a longitudinal study. *Psychosis* **2**: 218–26. (**351**)

Jones RM, van den Bree M, Ferriter M, and Taylor PJ (2009) Childhood risk factors for offending before first psychiatric admission in people with schizophrenia: a case-control study of special hospital admissions. *Behavioral Sciences and the Law* **27**: 1–15. (**515**)

Joseph N and Benefield N (2012) A joint offender personality disorder pathway strategy: an outline summary. *Criminal Behaviour and Mental Health* **22**(3): 210–7. (**69, 417**)

Joyal CC, Putkonen A, Mancini-Marïe A, et al. (2007) Violent persons with schizophrenia and comorbid disorders: a functional magnetic resonance imaging study. *Schizophrenia Research* **91**(1–3): 97–102. (**304, 306**)

Joyce PR, Mulder RT, Luty SE, et al. (2003) Borderline personality disorder in major depression: symptomatology, temperament, character, differential drug response, and 6-month outcome. *Comprehensive Psychiatry* **44**: 35–43. (**405**)

Juby H and Farrington DP (2001) Disentangling the link between disrupted families and delinquency. *British Journal of Criminology* **41**: 22–40. (**176**)

Jung CG (1903/1957) Collected Works of C.G. Jung, Vol. 1. *On Simulated Insanity*. London: Routledge and Kegan Paul. (Original work published 1903). (**431**)

Junger-Tas J and Marshall IH (1999) The self-report methodology in crime research. In M Tonry (ed) *Crime and Justice*, Vol. 25. Chicago, IL: University of Chicago Press, pp. 291–367. (**172**)

Junginger J (2006) 'Stereotypic' delusional offending. *Behavioral Sciences and the Law* **24**: 295–312. (**352**)

Junginger J, Claypoole K, Laygo R, and Crisanti A (2006) Effects of serious mental illness and substance abuse on criminal offending. *Psychiatric Services* **57**: 879–82. (**347**)

Jurik NC and Winn R (1990) Gender and homicide: a comparison of men and women who kill. *Violence and Victims* **5**: 227–42. (**507**)

Juul-Jensen P (1964) Epilepsy, a clinical and social analysis of 1020 adult patients with epileptic seizures. *Acta Neurologica Scandinavica* **40** (supp. 5): 1–148. (**286**)

Kafka MP (1994) Sertraline pharmacotherapy for paraphilias and paraphilia-related disorders: an open trial. *Annals of Clinical Psychiatry* **6**: 189–95. (**261**)

Kafka MP (1997) Hypersexual desire in males: an operational definition and clinical implications for males with paraphilias and paraphilia-related disorders. *Archives of Sexual Behavior* **25**: 505–26. (**253**)

Kafka MP (2003a) The monoamine hypothesis for the pathophysiology of paraphilic disorders: an update. *Annals of the New York Academy of Sciences* **989**: 86–94. (**244, 253, 260**)

Kafka MP (2003b) Sex offending and sexual appetite: the clinical and theoretical relevance of hypersexual desire. *International Journal of Offender Therapy and Comparative Criminology* **47**: 439–51. (**246**)

Kafka MP and Hennen J (2000) Psychostimulant augmentation during treatment with selective serotonin reuptake inhibitors in men with paraphilias and paraphilia-related disorders: a case series. *Journal of Clinical Psychiatry* **61**: 664–70. (**253**)

Kafka MP and Prentky RA (1994) Preliminary observations of DSM-III-R axis I co-morbidity in men with paraphilias and paraphilia-related disorders. *Journal of Clinical Psychiatry* **55**: 481–7. (**260**)

Kafry D (1980) Playing with matches: children and fire. In D Canter (ed) *Fires and Human Behaviour*. New York: Wiley. (**273**)

Kahneman D and Tversky A (1982) The simulation heuristic. In D Kahneman, P Slovic, A Tversky (eds) *Judgments Under Uncertainty: Heuristics and Biases*. New York: Cambridge University Press, pp. 201–8. (**696**)

Kales A, Soldatos CR, Caldwell AB, et al. (1980) Somnabulism. Clinical characteristics and personality patterns. *Archives of General Psychiatry* **37**: 1406–10. (**290, 291**)

Kaliski SZ (2006) *A Guide to Psycholegal Assessment in South Africa*. Oxford, UK: Cape Town. (**147**)

Kalmus E and Beech AR (2005) Forensic assessment of sexual interest: a review. *Aggression and Violent Behavior* **10**: 193–217. (**254**)

Kamarck TW, Haskett RF, Muldoon M, et al. (2009) Citalopram intervention for hostility: results of a randomized clinical trial. *Journal of Consulting and Clinical Psychology* **77**: 174–88. (**310**)

Kammerer TH, Singer L, and Michel D (1967) Les incendiaries. Etude criminologique et psychologique de 72 cas. *Annales Médico-Psychologique* **125**: 687–716. (**273**)

Kamphuis JH and Emmelkamp PM (2001) Traumatic distress among support-seeking female victims of stalking. *American Journal of Psychiatry* **158**(5): 795–8. (**374**)

Kane J, Honigfield G, Singer J, Mertzer H, and the Clozaril Collaborative Study Group (1988) Clozapine for the treatment-resistant schizophrenic. *Archives of General Psychiatry* **45**: 789–96. (**359**)

Kane JM, Carson WH, Saha AR, et al. (2002) Efficacy and safety of aripiprazole and haloperidol versus placebo in patients with schizophrenia and schizoaffective disorder. *Journal of Clinical Psychiatry* **63**: 763–71. (**565**)

Kane JM, Leucht S, Carpenter D, Docherty JP and The Expert Consensus Panel for Optimizing Pharmacologic Treatment of Psychotic Disorders (2003) The expert consensus guideline series. Optimizing pharmacologic treatment of psychotic disorders. *Journal of Clinical Psychiatry* **64** (suppl. 12): 5–19. (**358**)

Kane JM, Meltzer HY, Carson WH, et al; Aripiprazole Study Group (2007) Aripiprazole for treatment-resistant schizophrenia: results of a multicenter, randomized, double-blind, comparison study versus perphenazine. *Journal of Clinical Psychiatry* **68**: 213–23. (**565**)

Kang S-Y, Magura S, Laudet A, and Whitney S (1999) Adverse effect of child abuse victimization among substance-using women in treatment. *Journal of Interpersonal Violence* **14**: 657–70. (**464**)

Kant R, Smith-Seemiller L, and Zeiler D (2006) Treatment of aggression and irritability after head injury. *Brain Injury* **12**: 661–6. (**310**)

Kanzer M (1939) Amnesia: a statistical study. *American Journal of Psychiatry* **96**: 711–16. (**294**)

Kaplan R (2007) The clinicide phenomenon: an exploration of medical murder. *Australasian Psychiatry* **15**: 299–304. (**240, 686**)

Kaplan R (2009) *Medical Murder.* Crows Nest, NSW: Allen and Unwin. (**690**)

Karkowski LM, Prescott CA, and Kendler KS (2000) Multivariate assessment of factors influencing illicit substance use in twins from female-female pairs. *American Journal of Medical Genetics* **96**: 665–70. (**203**)

Kassin SM and Wrightsman LS (1985) Confession evidence. In S Kassin, L Wrightsman (eds) *The Psychology of Evidence and Trial Procedure.* London: Sage, pp. 67–84. (**161**)

Kassin SM, Drizin SA, Grisso T, et al. (2010) Police-induced confessions: risk factors and recommendations. *Law and Human Behavior* **34**: 3–38. (**622**)

Kassin SM, Leo RA, Meissner CA, et al. (2007) Police interviewing and interrogation: a self-report survey of police practices and beliefs. *Law and Human Behavior* **31**: 381–400. (**622**)

Kastelic A, Pont J, and Stöver H (2008) *Opioid Substitution Treatment in Custodial Settings: A Practical Guide.* Oldenburg, Germany: BIS-Verlag. (**467**)

Kaszniak AW, Nussbaum PD, Berren MR, and Santiago J (1988) Amnesia as a consequence of male rape: a case report. *Journal of Abnormal Psychology* **97**: 100–4. (**294**)

Kate Collins TB, Camfield PR, Camfield CS, and Lee K (2007) People with epilepsy are often perceived as violent. *Epilepsy and Behaviour* **10**: 69–76. (**285**)

Katz P and Kirkland FR (1990) Violence in social structure on mental hospital wards. *Psychiatry* **53**: 262–77. (**557**)

Katz S and Mazur MA (1979) *Understanding the Rape Victim: A Synthesis of Research.* New York: Wiley. (**249**)

Kaufman A, Divasto P, Jackson R, Voorhees D, and Christy D (1980) Male rape victims: non-institutionalised sexual assault. *American Journal of Psychiatry* **137**: 221–3. (**249**)

Kaufman J, Yang Z, Douglas-Palumberi H, et al. (2007) Genetic and environmental predictors of early alcohol use. *Biological Psychiatry* **61**: 1228–34. (**207**)

Kauhanen J, Hallikainen T, Tuomainen T-P, et al. (2000) Association between the functional polymorphism of catechol-O-methyltransferase gene and alcohol consumption among social drinkers. *Alcoholism. Clinical and Experimental Research* **24**: 135–9. (**206**)

Kavanagh DJ (1992) Recent developments in expressed emotion and schizophrenia. *British Journal of Psychiatry* **160**: 601–20. (**355**)

Kavanagh DJ, Freese S, Andrade J, and May J (2001) Effects of visuospatial tasks on desensitization to emotive memories. *British Journal of Clinical Psychology* **40**: 267–80. (**725**)

Kavoussi RJ, Liu J, and Coccaro EF (1994) An open trial of sertraline in personality disordered patients with impulsive aggression. *Journal of Clinical Psychiatry* **55**: 137–41. (**311**)

Kaye C (2001) A state of siege: the English high security hospitals. *Criminal Behaviour and Mental Health* **11**: 1–5. (**588, 666**)

Kaye NS, Borenstein NM, and Donnelly SM (1990) Families, murder, and insanity: a psychiatric review of paternal neonaticide. *Journal of Forensic Science* **35**: 133–9. (**509, 510**)

Kaye S, Darke S, and Finlay-Jones R (1998) The onset of heroin use and criminal behaviour: does order make a difference? *Drug and Alcohol Dependence* **53**: 79–86. (**452**)

Kazdin AE (1993) Treatment of conduct disorder: progress and directions in psychotherapy research. *Developmental Psychopathology* **5**: 277–310. (**486**)

Kazdin AE (2000) Adolescent development, mental disorders, and decision making of delinquent youths. In T Grisso, RG Schwartz (eds) *Youth on Trial, A Developmental Perspective on Juvenile Justice 2.* Chicago, IL: University of Chicago Press, pp. 33–65. (**483, 484, 497**)

Kean S (2010) *The Disappearing Spoon.* London: Doubleday. (**690**)

Keane TM, Zimmering RT, and Caddell JM (1985) A behavioral formulation of posttraumatic stress disorder in Vietnam veterans. *The Behavior Therapist* **8**: 9–12. (**722, 726**)

Keashley L and Harvey S (2004) Emotional abuse at work. In P Spector, S Fox (eds) *Counterproductive Work Behaviour: An Integration Of Both Actor and Recipient Perspectives on Causes and Consequences.* Washington, DC: American Psychological Association, pp. 201–36. (**699**)

Keeling JA, Beech, AR, and Rose JL (2007) The assessment of sexual offenders with an intellectual disability: The current position. *Aggression and Violent Behavior*, **12**: 229–41. (**329**).

Keene J (2001) *Clients with Complex Needs.* London: Blackwell Science. (**650**)

Keith J (2006) *Report of the Zahid Mubarek Inquiry.* London: The Stationery Office. http://www.official-documents.gov.uk/scripts/semaphore/official_documents/semaphoreserver.exe?TBSY=Zahid%20Mubarek%20Inquiry&PRINTDEPARTMENT=Zahid%20Mubarek%20Inquiry&DB=OPSI-Official_Documents&B=G1ZAHID%20MUBAREK%20INQUIRY (**635**)

Kelleher I, Harley M, Lynch F, et al. (2008) Associations between childhood trauma, bullying and psychotic symptoms among a school-based adolescent sample. *The British Journal of Psychiatry* **193**: 378–82. (**344**)

Kelleher MD and Kelleher CL (1968) *Murder Most Rare: The Female Serial Killer.* New York: Dell. (**240, 687**)

Kellermann AL, Bartolomeos K, Fuqua-Whitley D, Sampson TR, and Parramore CS (2001) Community-level fire arm injury surveillance: local data for local action. *Annals of Emergency Medicine* **38**: 423–9. (**700**)

Kellett S, Clarke S, and Matthews L (2006) Session impact and outcome in group psychoeducative CBT. *Behavioural and Cognitive Psychotherapy* **35**: 335–42. (**572**)

Kelly C and McCreadie RG (1999) Smoking habits, current symptoms and premorbid characteristics of schizophrenia patients in Nithsdale, Scotland. *American Journal of Psychiatry* **156**: 1751–7. (**568**)

Kelly R (1981) The post-traumatic syndrome. *Journal of the Royal Society of Medicine* **74**: 242–4. (**429**)

Kempe CH (1971) Pediatric implications of the battered baby syndrome. *Archives of Disease in Childhood* **46**: 28–37. (**221**)

Kempe CH, Silverman FN, Steele BS, Droegemueller W, and Silver HK (1962) The battered child syndrome. *Journal of the American Medical Association* **181**: 17–24. (**287**)

Kemppainen L, Jokelainen J, Isohanni M, Järvelin M-R, and Räsänen P (2002) Predictors of female criminality: findings from the Northern Finland 1966 birth cohort. *Journal of the American Academy of Child & Adolescent Psychiatry* **41**: 854–9. (**502**)

Kemshall JH, Mackenzie G, Wood J, Bailey R, and Yates J (2005) *Strengthening Multi-Agency Public Protection Arrangements (MAPPAs).* Home Office Development and Practice Report 45. London: Home Office. (**644**)

Kenardy J (2000) Current status of psychological debriefing. *British Medical Journal* **321**: 1032–3. (**724**)

Kendall T, Burbeck R, and Bateman A (2010) Pharmacotherapy for borderline personality disorder: NICE guideline. *British Journal of Psychiatry* **196**: 158–9. (**407**)

Kendell RE (1973) Psychiatric diagnoses: a study of how they are made. *British Journal of Psychiatry* **122**: 437–45. (**8**)

Kendell RE (2002) The distinction between personality disorder and mental illness. *British Journal of Psychiatry* **180**: 110–11. (**8, 384**)

Kendell RE and Jablensky A (2003) Distinguishing between the validity and utility of psychiatric diagnosis. *American Journal of Psychiatry* **169**: 4–12. (**112**)

Kendell RE, Cooper JE, Gourlay AJ, et al. (1971) Diagnostic criteria of American and British Psychiatrists. *Archives of General Psychiatry* **25**: 123–30. (**112**)

Kendler KS (1982) The season of birth of schizophrenic, neurotic and psychiatrically normal twins. *British Journal of Psychiatry* **141**: 186–90. (**189**)

Kendler KS (2001) Twin studies in psychiatric illness: an update. *Archives of General Psychiatry* **58**: 1005–14. (**190, 202**)

Kendler KS (2005) Psychiatric genetics: a methodologic critique. *American Journal of Psychiatry* **162**: 3–11. (**195**)

Kendler KS and Gardner CO Jr (1998) Twin studies of adult psychiatric and substance dependence disorders: are they biased by differences in the environmental experiences of monozygotic and dizygotic twins in childhood and adolescence? *Psychological Medicine* **28**: 625–33. (**189**)

Kendler KS, Gardner C, Jacobson KC, Neale MC, and Prescott CA (2005) Genetic and environmental influences on illicit drug use and tobacco use across birth cohorts. *Psychological Medicine* **35**: 1349–56. (**201**)

Kendler KS, Jacobson KC, Prescott CA, and Neale MC (2003a) Specificity of genetic and environmental risk factors for use and abuse/dependence of cannabis, cocaine, hallucinogens, sedatives, stimulants, and opiates in male twins. *American Journal of Psychiatry* **160**: 687–95. (**203**)

Kendler KS, Karkowski LM, Neale MC, and Prescott CA (2000) Illicit psychoactive substance use, heavy use, abuse, and dependence in a US population-based sample of male twins. *Archives of General Psychiatry* **57**: 261–9. (**202**)

Kendler KS, Kuo P-H, Webb BT, et al. (2006) A joint genomewide linkage analysis of symptoms of alcohol dependence and conduct disorder. *Alcoholism Clinical and Experimental Research* **30**: 1972–7. (**197**)

Kendler KS, Martin NG, Heath AC, and Eaves LJ (1995) Self-report psychiatric symptoms in twins and their nontwin relatives: are twins different? *American Journal of Medical Genetics* **60**: 588–91. (**189**)

Kendler KS, McGuire M, Gruenberg AM, et al. (1983) Dimensions of delusional experience. *American Journal of Psychiatry* **140**: 466–9. (**349**)

Kendler KS, Myers J, and Prescott CA (2007) Specificity of genetic and environmental risk factors for symptoms of cannabis, cocaine, alcohol, caffeine, and nicotine dependence. *Archives of General Psychiatry* **64**: 1313–20. (**203**)

Kendler KS, Neale MC, Kessler RC, Heath AC, and Eaves LJ (1993) A test of the equal-environment assumption in twin studies of psychiatric illness. *Behavioral Genetics* **23**: 21–7. (**189**)

Kendler KS, Neale MC, Kessler RC, Heath AC, and Eaves LJ (1994) Parental treatment and the equal environment assumption in twin studies of psychiatric illness. *Psychological Medicine* **24**: 579–90. (**189**)

Kendler KS, Prescott CA, Myers J, and Neale MC (2003b) The structure of genetic and environmental risk factors for common psychiatric and substance use disorders in men and women. *Archives of General Psychiatry* **60**: 929–37. (**204**)

Kendler KS, Prescott CA, Neale MC, and Pedersen NL (1997) Temperance board registration for alcohol abuse in a national sample of Swedish male twins, born 1902 to 1949. *Archives of General Psychiatry* **54**: 178–84. (**201**)

Kendrick C, Basson J, and Taylor PJ (2002) Substance misuse among mentally disordered offenders. *Criminal Behaviour and Mental Health* **12**: 112–24. (**605**)

Kennedy F (1946) The mind of the injured worker, its effect on disability periods. *Compensation Medicine*, **1**, 19–24 (**429**)

Kennedy H (2007) *The Annotated Mental Health Acts*. Dublin, Ireland: Blackwell. (**616, 617**)

Kennedy H (2008) A general theory of mental disorder and consolidated mental disability legislation: commentary on the mental capacity and guardianship bill 2008 *Medico-Legal Journal of Ireland* **5**: 1–58. (*109*)

Kennedy H and Grubin D (1992) Patterns of denial in sexual offenders *Psychological Medicine* **22**: 191–6. (**261**)

Kennedy HG (2001) Risk assessment is inseparable from risk management: comment on Szmuckler 2001. *Psychiatric Bulletin* **25**: 208–11. (**617**)

Kennedy HG (2002) Therapeutic uses of security: mapping forensic mental health services by stratifying risk. *Advances in Psychiatric Treatment* **8**: 433–43. http://apt.rcpsych.org/cgi/content/full/8/6/433 (**590, 617**)

Kennedy HG (2007) Therapeutic uses of security: mapping forensic mental health services by stratifying risk. In HY Bloom, CD Webster (eds) *Essential Writings in Violence Risk Assessment*. Toronto, ON: Centre for Addiction and Mental Health. (**617**)

Kennedy HG, O'Neill C, Flynn G, and Gill P (2010) *The Dundrum Toolkit. Dangerousness, Understanding, Recovery and Urgency Manual (The Dundrum Quartet) V1.0.21 (18/03/10). Four Structured Professional Judgment Instruments for Admission Triage, Urgency, Treatment Completion and Recovery Assessments*, Dublin, Ireland: Trinity College Dublin. http://hdl.handle.net/2262/39131 (**616, 617**)

Kennerley H (1996) Cognitive therapy of dissociative symptoms associated with trauma. *British Journal of Clinical Psychology* **35**: 325–40. (**727**)

Kenny A (1983) The expert in court. *Law Quarterly Review* **99**: 197–216. (**150**)

Kenworthy T, Adams CE, Brook-Gordon B, and Fenton M (2004) *Psychological Interventions for those who have Sexually Offended or are at Risk of Offending*. (Cochrane Review). *Cochrane Library*. Issue 3. Chichester, UK: John Wiley and Sons. (**578**)

Kerbs JJ (2000a) The older prisoner: social psychological and medical considerations. In MB Rothman, BD Dunlop, P Entzel (eds) *Elders, Crime and the Criminal Justice System: Myths, Perceptions and Reality in the 21st Century*. New York: Springer, pp. 207–28. (**527**)

Kerbs JJ (2000b) Arguments and strategies for the selective decarceration of older prisoners. In MB Rothman, BD Dunlop, P Entzel (eds) *Elders, Crime and the Criminal Justice System: Myths, Perceptions and Reality in the 21st Century*. New York: Springer, pp. 229–52. (**527**)

Kermani DJ and Castaneda RC (1996) Psychoactive substance use in forensic psychiatry. *American Journal of Drug and Alcohol Abuse* **2**: 1–27. (**124**)

Kernberg O (1975) *Borderline Conditions and Pathological Narcissism*. New York: Jason Aronson. (**7**)

Kernberg OF (1970) Factors in the psychoanalytic treatment of narcissistic personalities. *Journal of the American Psychoanalytic Association* **18**: 51–85. (**689**)

Kernberg OF (1984) *Severe Personality Disorders*. London: Yale University Press. (**689**)

Kershaw C, Chivite-Matthews N, Thomas C, and Aust R (2001) *The 2001 British Crime Survey: First Results England and Wales*. Home Office Statistical Bulletin18/01. London: Home Office. (**714**)

Kessler RC, Berglund P, Demler O, et al. (2005a) Lifetime prevalence and age-of-onset distributions of CSM-IV disorders in the National Comorbidity Survey Replication. *Archives of General Psychiatry* **62**: 593–602. (**712**)

Kessler RC, Chiu WT, Demler O, and Walters EE (2005b) Prevalence, severity, and comorbidity of 12-month DSM-IV disorders in the National Comorbidity Survey replication. *Archives of General Psychiatry* **62**: 617–27. (**712**)

Kessler RC, Crum RM, Warner LA, Schulenberg J, and Anthony JC (1997) Lifetime co-occurrence of DSM-III-R alcohol abuse and dependence with other psychiatric disorders in the national comorbidity study. *Archives of General Psychiatry* **54**: 313–21. (**712**)

Kessler RC, McGonagle KA, Zhao S, et al. (1994) Lifetime and 12-month prevalence of DSM-III-R psychiatric disorders in the United States. *Archives of General Psychiatry* **51**: 8–19. (**200**)

Kessler RC, McLaughlin KA, Greif Green J, et al. (2010) Childhood adversities and adult psychopathology in the WHO World Mental Health Surveys. *The British Journal of Psychiatry* **197**: 378–85. (**345**)

Kessler RC, Sonnega A, Bromet E, et al. (1999) Epidemiological risk factors for trauma and PTSD. In R Yehuda (ed) *Risk Factors for Post-Traumatic Stress Disorder*. Washington, DC: American Psychiatric Press, pp. 23–60. (**712, 717**)

Kessler RC, Sonnega A, Bromet E, Hughes M, and Nelson CB (1995) Posttraumatic stress disorder in the National Comorbidity Survey. *Archives of General Psychiatry* **52**: 1048–60. (**712**)

Khan SS and Mican LM (2006) A naturalistic evaluation of intramuscular ziprasidone versus intramuscular olanzapine for the management of acute agitation and aggression in children and adolescents. *Journal of Child and Adolescent Psychopharmacology* **16**: 671–7. (**565**)

Khanom H, Samele C, and Rutherford M (2009) *A Missed Opportunity? Community Sentences and the Mental Health Treatment Requirement*. London: Sainsbury Centre for Mental Health. http://www.centreformentalhealth.org.uk/pdfs/Missed_Opportunity.pdf> (**37, 642**)

Kiehl KA, Smith AM, Hare RD, et al. (2001) Limbic abnormalities in affective processing by criminal psychopaths as revealed by functional magnetic resonance imaging. *Biological Psychiatry* **50**: 677–84. (**304, 305**)

References

Kiehl KA, Smith AM, Mendrek A, et al. (2004) Temporal lobe abnormalities in semantic processing by criminal psychopaths as revealed by functional magnetic resonance imaging. *Psychiatry Research* **130**: 27–42. (**304, 305**)

Kiely J and Pankhurst H (1998) Violence faced by staff in a learning disability service. *Disability and Rehabilitation* **20**: 81–9. (**326**)

Kierkegaard S (1987) *Either/Or.* (Translated HV Hong, EH Hong) New Jersey: Princeton University Press. (Original work published in 1843). (**373**)

Kilpatrick D, Veronen LJ, and Resick PA (1979) Assessment of the aftermath of rape: changing patterns of fear. *Journal of Behavioural Assessment* **1**: 133–48. (**715**)

Kilpatrick DG, Saunders BE, Amick-McMullan AA, et al. (1989) Victim and crime factors associated with the development of crime-related post-traumatic stress disorder. *Behavior Therapy* **20**: 199–214. (**715**)

Kilpatrick DG, Saunders BE, Veronen LJ, Best CL, and Von JM (1987) Criminal victimization: lifetime prevalence, reporting to police and psychological impact. *Crime and Delinquency* **33**: 479–89. (**712**)

Kilpatrick DG, Veronen LJ, and Best CL (1985) *Factors Predicting Psychological Distress among Rape Victims. Trauma and Its Wake* Vol. II, C Figley (ed), 113–40. London: Routledge. (**715**)

Kim-Cohen J, Caspi A, Taylor A, et al. (2006) MAOA, maltreatment, and gene–environment interaction predicting children's mental health: new evidence and a meta-analysis. *Molecular Psychiatry* **11**: 903–13. (**200**)

King BH and Ford CV (1988) Pseudologia fantastica. *Acta Psychiatrica Scandinavica* **77**: 1–6. (**421, 423**)

King P (1978) Affective response of the analysis to the patient's communications. *International Journal of Psychoanalysis* **59**: 329–34. (**683**)

Kingdon DG and Turkington D (2005) *Cognitive Therapy of Schizophrenia.* Oxford, UK: Guilford. (**573**)

Kingham M and Gordon H (2004) Aspects of morbid jealousy. *Advances in Psychiatric Treatment* **10**: 207–15. (**368, 373**)

Kinnell HG (2000) Serial homicide by doctors: shipman in perspective. *British Medical Journal* **321**: 1594–7. (**688**)

Kinsey AC, Pomeroy WB, and Martin CE (1948) *Sexual Behavior in the Human Male.* Philadelphia, PA: Saunders. (**244, 246**)

Kinsey AC, Pomeroy WB, Martin CE, and Gebhard PH (1953) *Sexual Behavior in the Human Female.* Philadelphia, PA: Saunders. (**244, 246, 250**)

Kirkbride JB and Jones PB (2011) The prevention of schizophrenia – what can we learn from eco-epidemiology? *Schizophrenia Bulletin* **37**: 262–71. (**341**)

Kirov G, Gumus D, Chen W, et al. (2008) Comparative genome hybridization suggests a role for NRXN1 and APBA2 in schizophrenia. *Human Molecular Genetics* **17**: 458. (**209**)

Kirov G, Rujescu D, Ingason A, et al. Epub (2009) Neurexin 1 (NRXN1) deletions in schizophrenia. *Schizophrenia Bulletin* **35**(5): 851–4. (**209**)

Kisely S, Campbell LA, and Preston N (2011) Compulsory community and involuntary outpatient treatment for people with severe mental disorders. Cochrane Database of Systematic Reviews 2011, issue 2. Art. No.CD004408DOI: 10.1002/14651858.CD004408. pub3. John Wiley & Sons Ltd, Chichester. http://onlinelibrary.wiley.com/doi/10.1002/14651858.CD004408.pub3/full (**365**)

Kitchiner N (1999) Freeing the imprisoned mind. *Mental Health Care* **21**: 420–4. (**552, 553**)

Kivivuori J (2002) Trends and patterns of delinquency, 1995–2001. In J Kivivuori (ed) *Trends and Patterns of Self-reported Juvenile Delinquency in Finland.* Helsinki, Finland: Ministry of Justice. (**500**)

Kivivuori J and Salmi V Trends of self-reported juvenile delinquency in Finland 1995–2004. National Research Institute Publication no. 214 of Legal Policy Helsinki 2005. In Finnish, Helsinki, Finland: Ministry of Justice. (**500**)

Kjelsberg E and Dahl AA (1999) A long-term follow-up study of adolescent psychiatric in-patients. Part II. Predictors of delinquency. *Acta Psychiatrica Scandinavica* **99**: 237–42. (**511, 522**)

Klama J (1988) *Aggression.* Harlow, UK: Longman Scientific and Technical. (**213**)

Klein M (1932, translated Alix Strachey, 1975) *The Psycho-Analysis of Children.* London: Hogarth. (**482**)

Klimickie MR, Jenkinson J, and Wilson L (1994) A Study of recidivism among offenders with an intellectual disability. *Australian and New Zealand Journal of Developmental Disabilities (Journal of Intellectual and Developmental Disabilities)* **19**: 209–19. (**324**)

Klinteberg BA, Andersson T, Magnusson D, and Stattin H (1993) Hyperactive behaviour in childhood as related to subsequent alcohol problems and violent offending: a longitudinal study of male subjects. *Personality and Individual Differences* **15**: 381–8. (**171, 173**)

Klonsky ED, Oltmanns TF, and Turkheimer E (2002) Informant reports of personality disorder: relation to self-report, and future research directions. *Clinical Psychology: Science and Practice* **9**: 300–11. (**389**)

Knesper DL (1978) Psychiatric manpower for state mental hospitals. A continuing dilemma. *Archives of General Psychiatry* **35**: 19–24. (**603**)

Knight JR, Sherritt L, Shrier LA, Harris SK, and Chang G (2002) Validity of the CRAFFT substance abuse screening test among adolescent clinic patients. *Archives of Pediatrics and Adolescent Medicine* **156**: 607–14. (**457**)

Knight M and Plugge E (2005) The outcomes of pregnancy among inprisoned women: a systematic review. *British Journal of Obstetrics and Gynaecology* **112**: 1467–76. (**517**)

Knight MTD, Wykes T, and Hayward P (2006) Group treatment of perceived stigma and self-esteem in schizophrenia: a waiting list trial of efficacy. *Behavioural and Cognitive Psychotherapy* **34**: 305–18. (**579**)

Knight RA and Prentky RA (1989) Classifying sexual offenders: the development and corroboration of taxonomic models. In W Marsh, R Laws, H Barbaree (eds) *Handbook of Sexual Assault.* New York: Plenum. (**249**)

Knight RA and Thornton D (2007) Evaluating and improving risk assessment schemes for sexual recidivism: a long-term follow-up of convicted sexual offenders. US Department of Justice grant final report. http://www.ncjrs.gov/pdffiles1/nij/grants/217618.pdf (**255**)

Knopik VS, Jacob T, Haber JR, Swenson LP, and Howell DN (2009) Paternal alcoholism and offspring ADHD problems: a children of twins design. *Twin Research and Human Genetics* **12**: 53–62. (**204**)

Knorring A-Lv, Bohman M, Knorrring Lv, and Oreland L (1985) Platelet MAO activity as a biological marker in subgroups of alcoholism. *Acta Psychiatrica Scandinavica* **72**: 51–8. (**206**)

Knowles J (2003) *Accident Involvement of Stolen Cars in 1997 and 1998. TRL Report 577*. Crowthorne, UK: TRL. (**278**)

Knox SJ (1968) Epileptic automatism and violence. *Medicine, Science and the Law* **8**: 96–104. (**286, 295**)

Knutson B, Wolkowitz OM, Cole SW, et al. (1998) Selective alteration of personality and social behavior by serotonergic intervention. *American Journal of Psychiatry* **155**: 373–9. (**310**)

Koenig H, Johnson S, Bellard J, Denker M, and Fenlon R (1995) Depression and anxiety disorder among older inmates at a federal correctional facility. *Psychiatric Services* **46**: 399–401. (**527**)

Koenigs M, Huey ED, Raymont V, et al. (2007) Focal brain damage protects against post-traumatic stress disorder in Combat veterans. *Nature Neuroscience* **11**: 232–7 (**713**)

Koenigsberg HW, Reynolds D, Goodman M, et al. (2003) Risperidone in the treatment of schizotypal personality disorder. *Journal of Clinical Psychiatry* **64**: 628–34. (**405**)

Koh KG, Peng GK, Huak CY, and Koh BK (2006) Migration psychosis and homicide in Singapore: a five year study. *Medicine Science and the Law* **46**: 248–54. (**338**)

Kohlberg L (1981) *The Philosophy of Moral Development: Moral Stages and The Idea of Justice*. San Francisco, CA: Harper and Row. (**395**)

Kokish R, Levenson J, and Blasingame G (2005) Post-conviction sex offender polygraph examination: client-reported perceptions of utility and accuracy. *Sexual Abuse: A Journal of Research and Treatment* **17**: 211–21. (**256**)

Kokkevi A and Stefanis C (1995) Drug abuse and psychiatric comorbidity. *Comprehensive Psychiatry* **36**: 329–37. (**452**)

Kokkevi A, Stefanis N, Anastasopoulou E, and Kostogianni C (1998) Personality disorders in drug abusers: prevalence and their association with axis I disorders as predictors of treatment retention. *Addictive Behaviours* **23**: 841–53. (**444**)

Kolko D and Kazdin AE (1992) The emergence and re-occurrence of child firesetting: a one year prospective study. *Journal of Abnormal Child Psychology* **201**: 17–37. (**495**)

Kolowski SJ and Rossiter J (2000) Driving in Somerset. *Psychiatric Bulletin* **24**: 304–6. (**278**)

Kolvin I, Miller FJW, Fleeting M, and Kolvin PA (1988) Social and parenting factors affecting criminal-offence rates: findings from the Newcastle Thousand Family Study (1947–1980). *British Journal of Psychiatry* **152**: 80–90. (**175**)

Kolvin I, Miller FJW, Scott DM, Gatzanis SRM and Fleeting M (1990) *Continuities of Deprivation? The Newcastle 1000 Family Study*. Aldershot, UK: Avebury. (**171, 175, 176**)

Komarovskaya I, Loper AB and Warren J (2007) Role of impulsivity in antisocial and violent behavior and personality disorders among incarcerated women. *Criminal Justice and Behavior* **34**: 1499–515. (**513**)

Koob GF, Ahmed SH, Boutrel B, et al. (2004) Neurobiological mechanisms in the transition from drug use to drug dependence. *Neuroscience and Biobehavioral Reviews* **27**: 739–49. (**200**)

Kool S, Dekker J, Duijsens IJ, Jonghe F, and Puite B (2003) Efficacy of combined therapy and pharmacotherapy for depressed patients with or without personality disorders. *Harvard Review of Psychiatry* **11**: 133–41. (**410**)

Koons CR, Robins CJ, Tweed JL, et al. (2001) Efficacy of dialectical behavior therapy in women veterans with borderline personality disorder. *Behavior Therapy* **32**: 371–390. (**410**)

Koopmans JR and Boomsma DI (1996) Familial resemblances in alcohol use: genetic or cultural transmission? *Journal of Studies on Alcohol* **57**: 19–28. (**202**)

Kopelman MD (1987) Crime and amnesia: a review. *Behavioral Sciences and the Law*, **5**: 323–42. (**25, 292, 293, 294, 295, 296, 297, 420**)

Kopelman MD (2002a) Disorders of memory. *Brain* **125**: 2152–90. (**293, 296, 297**)

Kopelman MD (2002b) Psychogenic amnesia. In AD Baddeley, MD Kopelman, BA Wilson (eds) *Handbook of Memory Disorders* 2nd edn. Chichester, UK: John Wiley and Co. (**293, 296, 297**)

Kopelman MD (2009) Memory disorders in the law courts. Keynote presentation at the Royal Australian and New Zealand College of Psychiatrists, Section of Forensic Psychiatry conference, Melbourne, 12–14 November 2009. (**295**)

Kopelman MD, Green REA, Guinan EM, Lewis PDR, and Stanhope N (1994) The case of the amnesic intelligence officer. *Psychological Medicine* **24**: 1037–45. (**295**)

Kosky N and Thorne P (2001) Personality disorder – the rules of engagement. *International Journal of Psychiatry in Clinical Practice* **5**: 169–72. (**392**)

Kosky R and Silburn S (1984) Children who light fires: a comparison between firesetters and non-firesetters referred to a child psychiatric outpatient service. *Australian and New Zealand Journal of Psychiatry* **18**: 251–5. (**273**)

Koson DF and Dvoskin J (1982) Arson: a diagnostic study. *Bulletin of American Academy of Psychiatry and Law* **10**: 19–49. (**273, 274**)

Kownacki R and Shadish W (1999) Does alcoholics anonymous work? The results from a meta-analysis of controlled experiments. *Substance Use and Misuse* **34**:1897–916. (**447**)

KPMG (2000) *The Economic Value and Public Perceptions of Gambling in the UK* Report for Business in Sport and Leisure (cited in Orford et al. 2003). (**467**)

Kraemer HC, Glick ID, and Klein DF (2009) Clinical trials design lessons from the CATIE study. *American Journal of Psychiatry* **166**: 1222–8. (**359, 560**)

Kraepelin E (1896) *Psychiatrie Ein Lehrbuch für Studierende und Aerzte* (Reprinted by Arno Press, 1976) New York. (**421**)

873

Kraepelin E (1921, translated M Barclay) *Manic Depression Insanity and Paranoia*. Edinburgh, UK: ES Livingston (Original work published 1913). (**367**)

Krafft-Ebing R and Chaddock C (1904) *Text Book of Insanity*. Philadelphia, PA: FA Davies (Original work published 1879). (**367**)

Krafft-Ebing R von (1885, translated CG Chaddock, 1921) *Psychopathia Sexualis* 7th German edn. Philadelphia, PA: FA Davis. (**244, 246**)

Krafft-Ebing R von (1886, translated CG Chaddock, 1905) *Textbook of Insanity*. Philadelphia: FA Davis. (**421**)

Krakowski MI, Czobor P, Citrome L, Bark N, and Cooper TB (2006) A typical antipsychotic agents in the treatment of violent patients with schizophrenia and schizoaffective disorder. *Archives of General Psychiatry* **63**: 622–9. (**348**)

Kranzler H, Roofeh D, Gerbino-Rosen G, et al. (2005) Clozapine: its impact on aggressive behavior among children and adolescents with schizophrenia. *Journal of the American Academy of Child and Adolescent Psychiatry* **44**: 55–63. (**206, 564**)

Kranzler HR, Gelernter J, O'Malley S, Hernandez-Avila CA, and kaufman D (1998) Association of alcohol or other drug dependence with alleles of the mu opioid receptor gene (OPRM1). *Alcoholism. Clinical and Experimental Research* **22**: 1359–62. (**206**)

Kräupl- Taylor, F. (1979) *Psychopathology, its Causes and Symptoms*, rev. edn., Quatermaine: Sunbury-on-Thames. (**348, 422**)

Kraus JE and Sheitman BB (2005) Clozapine reduces violent behavior in heterogeneous diagnostic groups. *Journal of Neuropsychiatry and Clinical Neurosciences* **17**: 36–44. (**563**)

Krauss GL, Gondek S, Krumholtz A, Paul S, and Shen F (2000) 'The Scarlet E'. The presentation of epilepsy in the English language print media. *Neurology* **54**: 1894–8. (**285**)

Krausz M, Degkwitz P, Kühne A, and Verthein U (1998) Comorbidity of opiate dependence and mental disorders. *Addictive Behaviors* **23**: 767–83. (**463**)

Krawitz R (2004) Borderline personality disorder: attitudinal changes following training. *Australia and New Zealand Journal of Psychiatry* **38**: 554–9. (**400, 661**)

Kreek MJ, Bart G, Lilly C, LaForge KS, and Nielsen DA (2005a) Pharmacogenetics and human molecular genetics of opiate and cocaine addictions and their treatments. *Pharmacological Reviews* **57**: 1–26. (**200, 206**)

Kreek MJ, LaForge KS, and Butelman E (2002) Pharmacotherapy of addictions. *Nature Reviews. Drug Discovery* **1**: 710–26. (**206**)

Kreek MJ, Nielsen DA, and LaForge KS (2004) Genes associated with addiction: alcoholism, opiate, and cocaine addiction. *Neuromolecular Medicine* **5**: 85–108. (**205, 206**)

Kreek MJ, Nielsen DA, Butelman ER, and LaForge KS (2005b) Genetic influences on impulsivity, risk taking, stress responsivity and vulnerability to drug abuse and addiction. *Nature Neuroscience* **8**: 1450–7. (**200, 205**)

Kreis MKF and Cooke DJ (2011) Capturing the psychopathic female: a prototypicality analysis of the comprehensive psychopathic personality (CAPP) across gender. *Behavioral Sciences and the Law* **29**: 634–48. (**513**)

Kreis MKF, Cooke DJ, Michie C, Hoff HA, and Logan C (2012) The Comprehensive Assessment of Psychopathic Personality (CAPP): Content validation using prototypical analysis. *Journal of Personality Disorders,* **26**: 402–13. (**513**)

Kringlen, E. (1991) Adoption studies in functional psychosis. *European Archives of Psychiatry and Clinical Neuroscience* 240: 307–13. (**188, 208**)

Krischer MK, Stone MH, Sevecke K and Steinmeyer EM (2007) Motives for maternal filicide: Results from a study with female forensic patients. *International Journal of Law and Psychiatry* **30**: 191–200. (**508, 509**)

Krishef CH and DiNitto DM (1981) Alcohol abuse among mentally retarded individuals. *Mental Retardation* **19**: 151–5. (**324, 445**)

Kristjansson B, Petticrew M, MacDonald B, et al. (2009) School feeding for improving the physical and psychosocial health of disadvantaged students. *Cochrane Database of Systematic Reviews*. http://r4d.dfid.gov.uk/PDF/Articles/SR_SchoolFeeding.pdf (**567**)

Kroll L, Rothwell J, Bradley D, et al. (2002) Mental health needs of boys in secure care for serious or persistent offending: a prospective, longitudinal study. *Lancet* **359**: 1975–9. (**483, 484, 487**)

Kroll L, Woodham A, Rothwell J, et al. (1999) Reliability of the Salford needs assessment schedule for adolescents. *Psychological Medicine* **29**: 891–902. (**485, 490**)

Kröner C, Stadtland C, Eidt M and Nedopil N (2007) The validity of the Violence Risk Appraisal Guide (VRAG) in predicting criminal recidivism. *Criminal Behaviour and Mental Health* **17**: 89–100. (**536**)

Kroner DG and Mills JF (2001) The accuracy of five risk appraisal instruments in predicting institutional misconduct and new convictions. *Criminal Justice and Behavior* **28**: 471–89. (**536, 537**)

Kropp PR, Hart SD, and Lyon DR. (2002) Risk assessment of stalkers. *Criminal Justice and Behavior* **29**: 590–616. (**379**)

Kropp, P., Hart, S.D., Webster, C.D., Eaves, D. (1999) *Manual for the Spousal Assault Risk Assessment Guide* (3rd edn). Toronto, ON: Multi Health Systems (**546**)

Krueger RF, Hicks BM, Patrick CJ, et al (2002) Etiologic connections among substance dependence, antisocial behavior and personality: Modeling the externalizing spectrum. *Journal of Abnormal Psychology* **111**: 411–24. (**203**)

Krueger RF, Moffitt TE, Caspi A, Bleske A, and Silva PA (1998) Assortative mating for antisocial behavior: developmental and methodological implications. *Behavioral Genetics* **28**: 173–86. (**189**)

Kruesi MJ, Rapoport JL, Hamburger S, et al. (1990) Cerebrospinal fluid monoamine metabolites, aggression, and impulsivity in disruptive behavior disorders of children and adolescents. *Archives of General Psychiatry* **47**: 419–26. (**198**)

Kruesi MJP, Hibbs ED, Zahn TP, et al. (1992) A 2-year prospective follow-up study of children and adolescents with disruptive behavior disorders: prediction by cerebrospinal fluid 5-hydroxyindoleacetic acid, homovanillic acid, and autonomic measures? *Archives of General Psychiatry* **49**: 429–35. (**308**)

Krug EG, Dahlberg LL, Mercy JA, Zwi AB, and Lozano R (eds) (2002) *World Report on Violence and Health*. Geneva, Switzerland: World Health Organization. http://www.who.Int/violence_Injury_prevention/violence/world_report/en/summary_en.pdf (**217, 703**)

Kruk MR (1991) Ethology and pharmacology of hypothalamic aggression in the rat. *Neuroscience and Biobehavioral Reviews* **15**: 527–38. (**198**)

Kubany ES and Watson SB (2002) Cognitive trauma therapy with formerly battered women with PTSD (CTT-BW): conceptual bases and treatment outlines. *Cognitive and Behavioral Practice* **9**: 111–27. (**729**)

Kubany ES, Hill EE, Owens JA, and Iannce-Spencer C (2004) Cognitive trauma therapy for battered women with PTSD (CTT-BW). *Journal of Consulting and Clinical Psychology* **72**: 3–18. (**723, 725**)

Kuehn LL (1974) Looking down a gun barrel: person perception and violent crime. *Perceptual and Motor Skills* **39**: 1159–64. (**296**)

Kuehner C, Gass P, and Dressing H (2007) Increased risk of mental disorders among lifetime victims of stalking – findings from a community study. *European Psychiatry* **22**: 142–5. (**374**)

Kuiken D, Bears M, Miall D, and Smith L (2001–2002) Eye movement desensitization reprocessing facilitates attentional orienting. *Imagination, Cognition and Personality* **21**: 3–20. (**725**)

Kulkarni J, Gurvich C, Gilbert H, et al. (2008) Hormone modulation: a novel therapeutic approach for women with severe mental illness. *Australian and New Zealand Journal of Psychiatry* **42**: 83–8. (**521**)

Kullgren G, Grann M, and Holmberg G (1997) The Swedish forensic concept of severe mental disorder as related to personality disorders. *International Journal of Law and Psychiatry* **19**: 191–200. (**147**)

Kumari V, Aasen I, Taylor P, et al. (2006) Neural dysfunction and violence in schizophrenia: an fMRI investigation. *Schizophrenia Research* **84**: 144–64. (**304, 306**)

Kumari V, Das M, Taylor PJ, et al. (2009) Neural and behavioural responses to threat in men with a history of serious violence and schizophrenia or antisocial personality disorder. *Schizophrenia Research* **110**(1–3): 47–58. (**305, 306**)

Kumari V, Gudjonsson GH, Raghuvanshi S, et al. (in preparation) Childhood psychosocial deprivation and structural brain volumes in violent men with schizophrenia or antisocial personality disorder. (**344**)

Kumpfer KL and DeMarsh J (1986) Family environmental and genetic influences on children's future chemical dependence. In S Griswold-Ezekoye (ed) *Childhood and Chemical Abuse: Prevention and Intervention*. New York: Haworth, pp. 49–91. (**465**)

Kurlan R, Cummings J, Raman R, Thal L; Alzheimer's Disease Cooperative Study Group (2007) Quetiapine for agitation or psychosis in patients with dementia and parkinsonism. *Neurology* **68**: 1356–63. (**565**)

Kutash IL, Kutash SB, and Schlesinger LB (1978) *Violence*. San Francisco,CA: Jossey-Bass. (**211**)

La Fontaine JS (1987) *A Sociological Study of Cases of Child Sexual Abuse in Britain. Economic and Social Research Council Report No. G0023 2244*. London: Economic and Social Research Council. (**250**)

Laajasalo T and Häkkänen H (2005) Offence and offender characteristics among two groups of Finnish homicide offenders with schizophrenia: comparison of early- and late-start offenders. *Journal of Forensic Psychiatry and Psychology* **16**: 41–59. (**337, 343**)

Laajasalo T and Häkkänen H (2006) Excessive violence and psychotic symptomatology among homicide offenders with schizophrenia. *Criminal Behaviour and Mental Health* **16**: 242–53. (**337, 350**)

Laakso MP, Gunning-Dixon F, Vaurio O, et al. (2002) Prefrontal volumes in habitually violent subjects with antisocial personality disorder and type 2 alcoholism. *Psychiatry Research* **114**: 95–102. (**29, 300**)

Laakso MP, Vaurio O, Koivisto E, et al. (2001) Psychopathy and the posterior hippocampus. *Behavioural Brain Research* **118**: 187–93. (**299, 300**)

Lacey JH and Evans CDH (1986) The Impulsivist: a multi-impulsive personality disorder. *British Journal of Addiction* **81**: 641–9. (**273**)

Lachman H M, Fann CS, Bartzis M, et al. (2007) Genomewide suggestive linkage of opioid dependence to chromosome 14q. *Human Molecular Genetics* **16**: 1327–34. (**204**)

Lacroix I, Berrebi A, Chaumerliac C, et al. (2004) Buprenorphine in pregnant opioid-dependent women: first results of a prospective study. *Addiction* **99**: 209–14. (**465**)

Lader D, Singleton N, and Meltzer H (2000) *Psychiatric Morbidity among Young Offenders in England and Wales*. London: Office for National Statistics. (**279**)

Ladouceur R, Sylvain C, Boutin C, et al. (2001) Cognitive treatment of pathological gambling. *Journal of Nervous and Mental Disease* **189**: 774–80. (**471**)

Laing RD and Esterson A (1964) *Sanity, Madness and the Family*. London: Penguin Books. (**341**)

Laithwaite H and Gumley A (2007) Sense of self, adaptation and recovery in patients with psychosis in a forensic NHS setting. *Clinical Psychology and Psychotherapy* **14**: 302–16. (**574**)

Lambert EG, Hogan N, Bart S, and Stevenson MT (2007) An evaluation of CHANGE, a pilot prison cognitive treatment program. *Journal Articles in Support of the Null Hypothesis* **5**: 1–18. (**577**)

Lamberti JS, Weisman R, and Faden DI (2004) Forensic assertive community treatment: preventing incarceration of adults with severe mental illness. *Psychiatric Services* **55**: 1285–93. (**364**)

Lambrick F and Glaser W (2004) Sex offenders with an intellectual disability. *Sexual Abuse: A Journal of Research and Treatment* **16**: 381–92. (**263**)

Laming H (2009) The protection of children in the UK. A progress report. Norwich. TSO. (**223**)

Lancee WJ, Gallop R, and McCaye Toner B (1995) The relationship between nurses' limit-setting styles and anger in psychiatric in-patients. *Psychiatric Services* **46**: 609–13. (**557**)

Lancet (1978) Editorial: factitious hypoglycaemia. *The Lancet* **1**: 1293. (**295**)

Lancet (1980) Editorial: close rampton? *Lancet* ii: 1171–2. (**603**)

Lanctot KL, Herrmann N, Nadkarni NK, et al. (2004) Medial temporal hypoperfusion and aggression in Alzheimer disease. *Archives of Neurology* **61**: 1731–7. (**302**)

Lander ES (1996) The new genomics: global views of biology. *Science* **274**(5287): 536–9. (**194**)

Landes R (1938) *The Ojibwa Woman.* New York: Norton. (**428**)

Landheim AS, Bakken K, and Vaglum P (2003) Gender difference in the prevalence of symptom disorders and personality disorders among poly-substance abusers and pure alcoholics: substance abusers treated in two counties in Norway. *European Addiction Research* **9**: 8–17. (**463**)

Landman J (1993) *Regret: The Persistence of the Possible.* New York: Oxford University Press. (**697**)

Lane A, Kinsella A, Murphy P, et al. (1997) The anthropometric assessment of dysmorphic features in schizophrenia as an index of its developmental origins. *Psychological Medicine* **27**: 1155–64. (**341**)

Lane C, Goldstein NES, Heilbrun K et al. (2012) Obstacles to research in residential juvenile justice facilities: recommendations for researchers. *Behavioral Sciences & Law* **30**: 49–68. (**669**)

Lang E, Stockwell T, Rydon P, and Lockwood A (1995) Drinking settings and problems of intoxication. *Addiction Research* **3**: 141–9. (**440**)

Langan PA and Cunniff MA (1992) *Recidivism for Felons on Probation.* Bureau of Statistics, Special Report (NCJ-134177). Washington, DC: United States Department of Justice, Bureau of Justice Statistics. (**316**)

Langan PA and Levin DJ (2002) *Recidivism of Prisoners Released in 1994.* Bureau of Statistics, Special Report (NCJ-193427). Washington, DC: United States Department of Justice, Bureau of Justice Statistics. (**316**)

Langan PA, Schmitt EL, and Durose MR (2003) *Recidivism of sex offenders released from prison in 1994.* Washington, DC: US Department of Justice, Office of Justice Programs, Bureau of Justice Statistics. (**526**)

Langbehn DR, Cadoret RJ, Caspers K, Troughton EP, and Yucuis R (2003) Genetic and environmental risk factors for the onset of drug use and problems in adoptees. *Drug Alcohol Dependence* **69**: 151–67. (**203**)

Langlands RL, Jorm AF, Kelly CM, and Kitchener BA (2008) First aid recommendations for psychosis: using the Delphi method to gain consensus between memtnal health consumers, carers and clinicians. *Schizophrenia Bulletin* **34**: 435–43. (**352**)

Langley K, Fowler T, Ford T, et al. (2010) Adolescent outcomes for young people with attention-deficit hyperactivity disorder. *British Journal of Psychiatry* **196**: 135–40. (**397**)

Langley K, Heron J, O'Donovan M, Owen M, and Thapar A (2010) Genotype link with extreme antisocial behavior: the contribution of cognitive pathways. *Archives of General Psychiatry* **67**: 1317–23. (**199**)

Långström N, Grann M, and Lindblad F (2000) A preliminary typology of young sex offenders. *Journal of Adolescence* **23**: 319–29. (**495**)

Långström NL, Sjöstedt G, and Grann M (2004) Psychiatric disorders and recidivism in sexual offenders. *Sexual Abuse: A Journal of Research and Treatment* **16**: 139–50. (**253**)

Langton CM, Barbaree HE, Harkins L, et al. (2008) Denial and minimization among sexual offenders. *Criminal Justice and Behavior* **35**: 69–98. (**261**)

Langton J and Torpy D (1988) Confidentiality and a 'future' sadistic sex offender. *Medicine, Science and the Law* **28**: 195–9. (**664**)

Lansted LB, Garde P, and Greve V (2003) *Criminal Law, Denmark.* Denmark: DJØF Publishing. (**146**)

Lanzkron J (1963) Murder and insanity. A survey. *American Journal of Psychiatry* **119**: 754–8. (**354**)

LaPlante DA, Nelson SE, LaBrie RA, and Shaffer HJ (2008) Stability and progression of disordered gambling: lessons from longitudinal studies. *Canadian Journal of Psychiatry* **53**: 52–60. (**472**)

Lappalainen J, Long JC, Eggert M, et al. (1998) Linkage of antisocial alcoholism to the serotonin 5-HT1B receptor gene in 2 populations. *Archives of General Psychiatry* **55**: 989–94. (**198**)

Large M, Smith G, and Nielssen O (2009) The relationship between the rate of homicide by those with schizophrenia and the overall homicide rate: a systematic review and meta-analysis. *Schizophrenia Research* **112**: 123–9. (**337**)

Large MM and Nielssen O (2011) Violence in first-episode psychosis: a systematic review and meta-analysis. *Schizophrenia Research* **125**: 209–20. (**344**)

Large MM, Ryan CJ, Singh SP, Paton MB, and Nielsson OB (2011) The predictive value of risk categorization in schizophrenia. *Harvard Review of Psychiatry* **19**: 25–33. (**538**)

Lart R, Pantazis C, Pemberton S, Turner W, and Almeida C (2008) *Interventions Aimed a Reducing Re-Offending in Female Offenders: A Rapid Evidence Assessment (REA).* Ministry of Justice Research Series 8/08. Ministry of Justice: London. http://webarchive.nationalarchives.gov.uk/20110201125714/http://www.justice.gov.uk/publications/docs/intervention-reduce-female-reoffending.pdf (**518**)

Larzelere RE and Patterson GR (1990) Parental management: mediator of the effect of socioeconomic status on early delinquency. *Criminology* **28**: 301–24. (**177**)

Laucht M, Treutlein J, Schmid B, et al. (2009) Impact of psychosocial adversity on alcohol intake in young adults: moderation by the LL genotype of the serotonin transporter polymorphism. *Biological Psychiatry* **66**: 102–9. (**207**)

Laumon B, Gadegbeku B, Martin J-L, Biecheler M-B, and the Sam Group (2005) Cannabis intoxication and fatal road crashes in France: population based case-control study. *BMJ* **331**: 1371–4. (**278**)

Law Commission (1995) *Mental Incapacity.* Report 231. London: TSO. (**80**)

Law Commission (1998) *Liability for Psychiatric Illness.* Report 249 HC 525. London: TSO. (**52, 53**)

Law Commission (2006) *Murder, Manslaughter and Infanticide.* Report 304 HC 30. London: TSO. (**31**)

Law Commission (2009) *Intoxication and Criminal Liability.* Report 314 Cm 7526. London: TSO. (**34**)

Law J, Lindsay WR, Quinn K, and Smith AHW (2000) Outcome evaluation of 161 people with mild intellectual disabilities who have offending or challenging behaviour [abstract]. *Journal of Intellectual Disability Research* **44**: 360–1. (**326**)

Laws DR and Gress C (2004) Seeing things differently: the viewing time alternative to penile plethysmography. *Legal and Criminological Psychology* **9**: 183–96. (**254**)

Laws DR and O'Donohue WT (2008a) *Sexual Deviance: Theory, Assessment, and Treatment*, 2nd edn. New York: Guilford. (**245, 246**)

Laws DR and O'Donohue WT (2008b) Introduction. In DR Laws, WT O'Donohue (eds) *Sexual Deviance: Theory, Assessment, and Treatment*, 2nd edn. New York: Guildford. (**246**)

Lawson A (1987) *Adultery: An Analysis of Love and Betrayal.* New York: Basic Books. (**370**)

Lawson DC, Turic D, Langley K, et al. (2003) Association analysis of monoamine oxidase A and attention deficit hyperactivity disorder. *American Journal of Medical Genetics* **116B**: 84–9. (**199**)

Lazarus AA (1968) A case of pseudo-necrophilia treated by behaviour therapy. *Journal of Clinical Psychology* **24**: 113–5. (**248**)

Lazarus RS and Folkman S (1984) *Stress, Appraisal, and Coping.* New York: Spriger. (**355**)

Leahy RL (2003) *Overcoming Resistance in Cognitive Therapy.* Oxford, UK: Guilford. (**570**)

Leal J, Ziedonis D, and Kosten T (1994) Antisocial personality disorder as a prognostic factor for pharmacotherapy of cocaine dependence. *Drug and Alcohol Dependence* **35**: 31–5. (**405**)

Leary T (1957) *Interpersonal Diagnosis of Personality.* New York: Ronald. (**385, 389**)

LeBlanc M and Frechette M (1989) *Male Criminal Activity from Childhood through Youth.* New York: Springer-Verlag. (**171, 173**)

Lederman CS, Dakof GA, Larrea MA, and Li H (2004) Characteristics of adolescent females in juvenile detention. *International Journal of Law and Psychiatry* **27**: 321–37. (**482**)

Lee T, Chong SA, Chan YH, and Sathyadevan G (2004) Command hallucinations among Asian patients with schizophrenia. *Canadian Journal of Psychiatry* **49**: 838–42. (**353**)

Lees J, Manning N, and Rawlings B (2004) Therapeutic community research: an overview and met-analysis. In J Lees, N Manning, D Menzies, N Morant (eds) *A Culture of Inquiry: Research Evidence and the Therapeutic Community.* London: Jessica Kingsley, pp. 36–54. (**412**)

Lees J, Manning N, and Rawlings B. (1999) *Therapeutic Effectiveness. A Systematic International Review of Therapeutic Community Treatment for People with Personality Disorders and Mentally Disordered Offenders. CRD Report 17.* The University of York, NHS Centre for Reviews and Dissemination: York. http://www.york.ac.uk/inst/crd/CRD_Reports/crdreport17.pdf (**412, 551, 583**)

Lees S (1996) *Carnal knowledge: Rape on Trial.* London: Hamish Hamilton. (**714**)

Leff J and Vaughn C (1985) *Expressed Emotion in Families: Its Significance for Mental Illness.* New York: Guilford. (**341, 355**)

Legrand LN, McGue M, and Iacono WG (1999) Searching for interactive effects in the etiology of early-onset substance use. *Behavioral Genetics* **29**: 433–44. (**207**)

Leichsenring F and Liebling E (2003) The effectiveness of psychodynamic therapy and cognitive behaviour therapy in the treatment of personality disorders: a meta-analysis. *American Journal of Psychiatry* **160**: 1223–32. (**409, 574, 583**)

Leigh D (1961) *The Historical Development of British Psychiatry*, Vol. 1. Oxford, UK: Pergamon. (**589**)

Leitch A (1948) Notes on amnesia in crime for the general practitioner. *Medical Press*, **219**: 459–63. (**293, 296**)

Leitner M, Barr W, McGuire J, Jones S, and Whittington R (2006) *Systematic Review of Prevention and Intervention Strategies for Populations at High Risk of Engaging in Violent Behaviour. Final Report.* London: National Institute for Mental Health in England. (**577**)

Lelliott P, Audini B, and Duffet R (2001) Survey of patients from an inner-London health authority. *British Journal of Psychiatry* **178**: 62–6. (**600**)

LeMarquand D, Pihl RO, and Benkelfat C (1994a) Serotonin and alcohol intake, abuse, and dependence: clinical evidence. *Biological Psychiatry* **36**: 326–37. (**205**)

LeMarquand D, Pihl RO, and Benkelfat C (1994b) Serotonin and alcohol intake, abuse, and dependence: findings of animal studies. *Biological Psychiatry* **36**: 395–421. (**205**)

LeMarquand D, Tremblay RE, and Vitaro F (2001) The prevention of conduct disorder: a review of successful and unsuccessful experiments. In J Hill, B Maughan (eds) *Conduct Disorder in Childhood and Adolesence.* Cambridge, UK: Cambridge University Press, pp. 449–77. (**184**)

LeMarquand DG, Benkelfat C, Pihl RO, Palmour RM, and Young SN (1999) Behavioral disinhibition induced by tryptophan depletion in nonalcoholic young men with multigenerational family histories of paternal alcoholism. *American Journal of Psychiatry* **156**: 1771–9. (**309**)

LeMarquand DG, Pihl RO, Young SN, et al. (1999) Tryptophan depletion, executive functions, and disinhibition in aggressive, adolescent males. *Neuropsychopharmacology* **4**: 333–41. (**309**)

Leonard KE (2001) Domestic violence and alcohol: what is known and what do we need to know to encourage environmental interventions? *Journal of Substance Use* **6**: 235–47. (**442**)

Leone NF (1982) Response of borderline patients to loxapine and chlorpromazine. *Journal of Clinical Psychiatry* **43**: 148–50. (**405**)

Lepping P, Rajvinder SS, Whittington R, Lane S, and Poole R (2011) Clinical relevance of findings in trials of antipsychotics: systematic review. *British Journal of Psychiatry* **198**: 341–5. (**358**)

Lesch KP and Merschdorf U (2000) Impulsivity, aggression, and serotonin: a molecular psychobiological perspective. *Behavioural Sciences and the Law* **18**: 581–604. (**198**)

Lesem MD, Zajecka JM, Swift RH, Reeves KR, and Harrigan EP (2001) Intramuscular ziprasidone, 2 mg versus 10 mg, in the short-term management of agitated psychotic patients. *Journal of Clinical Psychiatry* **62**: 12–18. (**565**)

References

Leshner AI and Koob GF (1999) Drugs of abuse and the brain. *Proceedings of the Association of American Physicians* **111**: 99–108. (**205**)

Lesieur HR and Blume SB (1987) The South Oaks gambling screen: a new instrument for the identification of pathological gamblers. *American Journal of Psychiatry* **144**: 1184–8. (**470**)

Lesieur HR and Rosenthal RJ (1991) Pathological gambling: a review of the literature. *Journal of Gambling Studies* **7**: 5–34. (**470**)

Leslie AM (1987) Pretense and representation: The origins of 'theory of mind'. *Psychological Review* **94**: 412–26. (**394**)

Leslie AM and Frith U (1988) Autistic children's understanding of seeing, knowing and believing. *British Journal of Developmental Psychology* **6**: 315–24. (**395**)

Lester BM, El Sohly M, Wright LL, et al. (2001) The maternal lifestyle study: drug use by meconium toxicology and maternal self-report. *Pediatrics* **107**(2): 309–17. (**464**)

Lester D (1991) Murdering babies: A cross-national study. *Social Psychiatry and Psychiatric Epidemiology* **26**: 83–8. (**509**)

Lester G, Wilson B, Griffin L, and Mullen PE (2004) Unusually persistent complainants. *British Journal of Psychiatry* **184**: 352–6. (**380**)

Letourneau EU (2002) A comparison of objective measures of sexual arousal and interest: visual reaction time and penile plethysmography. *Sexual Abuse: A Journal of Research and Treatment* **13**: 207–23. (**254**)

Leucht S, Arbter D, Engel RR, Kissling W, and Davis JM (2008) How effective are 2nd-generation antipsychotic drugs? A meta-analaysis of placebo-controlled trials. *Molecular Psychiatry* **14**: 449–27. (**359**)

Leucht S, Barnes TRE, Kissling W, et al. (2003) Relapse prevention in schizophrenia with new-generation antipsychotics: a systematic review and exploratory meta-analysis of randomised, controlled trials. *American Journal of Psychiatry* **160**: 1209–22. (**358, 520**)

Leucht S, Corves C, Arbter D, et al. (2009) Second-generation versus first-generation antipsychotic drugs for schizophrenia. Lancet **373**: 31–41. (**359**)

Levenson JS and Cotter LP (2005) The effect of Megan's law on sex offender reintegration. *Journal of Contemporary Criminal Justice* **2**: 49–66. (**645**)

Levenson JS, D'Amora DA, and Hern AL (2007) Megan's Law and its impact on community re-entry for sex offenders. *Behavioral Sciences and the Law* **25**: 587–602. (**146, 645**)

Leventhal G (1977) Female criminality: is "women's lib" to blame? *Psychological reports* **41**(3 pt. 2): 1179–82. (**590**)

Levi M (2007) Organised and terrorist crimes. In M Maguire, R Morgan, R Reiner (eds) *The Oxford Handbook of Criminology,* 4th edn. Oxford, UK: Oxford University Press. (**235**)

Levinson A and Fonagy P (2004) The relationship between interpersonal awareness and offending in a prison population with psychiatric disorder. *Canadian Journal of Psychoanalysis* **12**: 225–51. (**584**)

Levinson D (1989) *Family Violence in Cross Cultural Perspective.* Thousand Oaks, CA: Sage. (**714**)

Levitt JY and Cloitre M (2005) A clinician's guide to STAIR/MPE: treatment for PTSD related to childhood abuse. *Cognitive and Behavioral Practice* **12**: 40–52. (**729**)

Levy CJ (1988) Agent orange exposure and post-traumatic stress disorder. *Journal of Nervous and Mental Disease* **176**: 242–5. (**715**)

Levy E, Shefler G, Loewenthal U, et al. (2005) Characteristics of schizophrenia residents and staff rejection in community mental health hostels. *Israel Journal of Psychiatry and Related Sciences* **42**: 23–32. (**557**)

Lewis AJ (1934) The psychopathology of insight. *British Journal of Medical Psychology* **14** 322–48. (**11, 12**)

Lewis AJ (1955) British psychiatry in the first half of the nineteenth century: Philippe Pinel and the English. *Proceedings of the Royal Society of Medicine* **48**: 581–6. (**589**)

Lewis C (2006) Treating incarcerated women: Gender matters. *Psychiatric Clinics of North America* **29**: 773–89. (**516**)

Lewis CE, Rice J, and Helzer JE (1983) Diagnostic interactions: alcoholism and antisocial personality. *Journal of Nervous and Mental Disease* **171**: 105–13. (**200**)

Lewis CF (2010) Female offenders in correctional settings. In CL Scott (ed) *Handbook of Correctional Mental Health* 2nd ed. (pp. 477–514). Washington, D.C.: American Psychiatric Publishing, Inc. (**515**)

Lewis CF and Bunce SC (2003) Filicidal mothers and the impact of psychosis on maternal filicide. *The Journal of the American Academy of Psychiatry and the Law* **31**: 459–70. (**503**)

Lewis CF, Baranoski MV, Buchanan JA, and Benedek EP (1998) Factors associated with weapon use in maternal filicide. *Journal of Forensic Sciences* **43** (3): 613–8. (**508**)

Lewis CF, Fields C, and Rainey E (2006) A study of geriatric forensic evaluees: who are the violent elderly? *Journal of the American Academy of Psychiatry and the Law* **34**: 324–32. (**525**)

Lewis D (1999) Workplace bullying: interim findings of a study in further and higher education in Wales. *International Journal of Manpower* **20**: 106–18. (**699**)

Lewis DO, Pincus JH, Bard B, et al. (1988) Neuropsychiatric, psychoeducational, and family characteristics of 14 juveniles condemned to death in the United States. *American Journal of Psychiatry* **145**: 584–9. (**283**)

Lewis DO, Pincus JH, Feldman M, Jackson L, and Bard B (1986) Psychiatric, neurological, and psychoeducational characteristics of 15 death row inmates in the United States. *Amercian Journal of Psychiatry* **143**: 838–45. (**283**)

Lewis DO, Yeager CA, Cobham-Portorreal CS, et al. (1991) A follow-up of female delinquents: maternal contributions to the perpetuation of deviance. *Journal of the American Academy of Child and Adolescent Psychiatry* **30**(2): 197–201. (**511**)

Lewis G (ed) (2004) *Why mothers die 2000-2002: Confidential Enquiry into Maternal and Child Health* – The Sixth Report. London: CEMACH. (**451**)

Lewis JW (1990) Premenstrual syndrome as a criminal defence. *Archives of sexual Behavior* **19**: 425–41. (**501**)

Lewis K, Olver ME, and Wong SCP (2013) The Violence Risk Scale. *Assessment* **20**: 150–64. (**610**)

Lewis NDG and Yarnell H (1951) *Pathological Fire-Setting. Nervous and Mental Disease Monographs*, Vol. 82. New York: Journal of Nervous and Mental Disease. (**273, 274, 275, 504**)

Lewis O (2002) Protecting the rights of people with mental disabilities: the European convention on human rights. *European Journal of Health Law* **9**: 293–320. (**113**)

Lewis S, Jagger RG, and Treasure E (2002) The oral health of psychiatric in-patients in South Wales. *Special Care in Dentistry* **21**: 182–6. (**568**)

Li CY, Mao X, and Wei L (2008) Genes and (common) pathways underlying drug addiction. *PLoS Computational Biology* **4**(1): e2. (**204**)

Lidberg L, Tuck JR, Asberg M, Scalia-Tomba GP, and Bertilsson L (1985) Homicide, suicide and CSF 5-HIAA. *Acta Psychiatrica Scandinavica* **71**: 230–6. (**308**)

Lidz C, Mulvey E, and Gardner W (1993) The accuracy of predictions of violence to others. *Journal of the American Medical Association* **269**: 1007–11. (**531**)

Lieb K, Völlm B, Rücker, Timmer A, and Stoffers JM (2010) Pharmacotherapy for borderline personality disorder: Cochrane systematic review of randomised trials. *British Journal of Psychiatry* **196**: 4–12. (**312, 404**)

Lieberman JA, Stroup TS, McEvoy JP, et al. (2005) Effectiveness of antipsychotic drugs in patients with chronic schizophrenia. *The New England Journal of Medicine* **353**: 1209–23. (**560**)

Lieberman JA, Tollefson G, Tohen M, et al. (2003) Comparative efficacy and safety of atypical and conventional antipsychotic drugs in first-episode psychosis: a randomized, double-blind trial of olanzapine versus haloperidol. *American Journal of Psychiatry* **160**: 1396–404. (**560, 564**)

Liebert RM and Sprafkin J (1988) *The Early Window*, 3rd edn. New York: Pergamon. (**216, 217**)

Liebling A (1993) *Suicide Attempts and Self-Injury in Male Prisons*. A Report Commissioned by the Home Office Research and Planning Unit for the Prison Service. London: Home Office. (**634**)

Liebling A (1995) Vulnerability and prison suicide. *British Journal of Criminology* **35**: 173–87. (**634**)

Liebling A (ed) (1998) *Deaths of Offenders the Hidden Side of Justice*. Winchester, VA: Waterside. (**634**)

Liebling A and Maruna S (2005) *The Effects of Imprisonment*. Cullomptom, UK: Willan. (**626**)

Liem M (2010) *Homicide Followed by Suicide*. Utrecht, the Netherlands: Utrecht University. (**233**)

Liem M and Koenraadt F (2008) Filicide: A comparative study of maternal versus paternal child homicide. *Criminal Behaviour and Mental Health* **18**: 166–76. (**508**)

Liem M, Postulart M, and Nieuwbeerta P (2009) Homicide-suicide in the Netherlands: an epidemiology. *Homicide Studies* **13**: 99–124. (**233**)

Lifford KJ, Harold GT, and Thapar A (2008) Parent–child relationships and ADHD symptoms: a longitudinal analysis. *Journal of Abnormal Child Psychology* **36**: 285–96. (**486**)

Lilienfeld SO and Andrews BP (1996) Development and preliminary validation of a self-report measure of psychopathic personality traits in noncriminal populations. *Journal of Personality Assessment* **66**: 488–524. (**305**)

Limson R, Goldman D, Roy A, et al. (1991) Personality and cerebrospinal fluid monoamine metabolites in alcoholics and controls. *Archives of General Psychiatry* **48**: 437–41. (**308**)

Linaker OM (2000) Dangerous female psychiatric patients: prevalences and characteristics. *Acta Psychiatrica Scandinavica* **101**: 67–72. (**504**)

Lind J, Oyefeso A, Pollard M, Baldacchino A, and Ghodse H (1999) Death rate from use of ecstasy or heroin. *Lancet* **354**(9196): 2167. (**451**)

Lindberg N, Tani P, Appelberg B, et al. (2003) Sleep among habitually violent offenders with antisocial personality disorder. *Neuropsychobiology* **47**: 198–205. (**290**)

Lindberg N, Tani P, Sailas E, et al. (2006) Sleep architecture in homicidal women with antisocial personality disorder – a preliminary study. *Psychiatry Research* **145**: 67–73. (**290**)

Lindelius R and Salum I (1975) Alcoholism and crime: a comparative study of three groups of alcoholics. *Journal of Studies in Alcohol* **36**: 1452–8. (**228**)

Linden RD, Pope HG, and Jonas JM (1986) Pathological gambling and major affective disorder: preliminary findings. *Journal of Clinical Psychiatry* **47**: 201–3. (**470**)

Lindenmayer JP, Khan A, Iskander A, Abad MT, and Parker B (2007) A randomized controlled trial of olanzapine versus haloperidol in the treatment of primary negative symptoms and neurocognitive deficits in schizophrenia. *Journal of Clinical Psychiatry* **68**: 368–79. (**564**)

Lindqvist P (1989) Violence against a person – the role of mental disorder and abuse. A study of homicides and an analysis of criminality in a cohort of patients with schizophrenia. Umea University Medical Dissertations. New Series No. 254. (**338**)

Lindqvist P (2007) Mental disorder, substance misuse and violent behaviour – the Swedish experience of caring for the triply troubled. *Criminal Behaviour and Mental Health* **17**: 242–9. (**346**)

Lindqvist P and Allebeck P (1990) Schizophrenia and crime – a longitudinal follow-up of 644 schizophrenics in Stockholm. *British Journal of Psychiatry* **157**: 345–50. (**280, 342, 515**)

Lindsay WR (2002) Research and literature on sex offenders with intellectual and developmental disabilities. *Journal of Intellectual Disability Research* **46** (suppl. 1): 74–85. (**328**)

Lindsay WR (2004) Sex offenders: conceptualization of the issues, services, treatment and management. In WR Lindsay, JL Taylor, and P Sturmey (eds), *Offenders with Developmental Disabilities* (pp. 163–85). Chichester: John Wiley and Sons. (**328**)

Lindsay WR (2007) Personality disorders. In N Bouras, G Holt (eds) *Psychiatric and Behavioural Disorders in Intellectual and Developmental Disabilities*. Cambridge, UK: Cambridge University Press, pp. 143–54. (**319**)

Lindsay WR and Smith AHW (1998) Responses to treatment for sex offenders with intellectual disability: A comparison of men with 1- and 2- year probation sentences. *Journal of Intellectual Disability Research* **42**: 346–53. (**329**)

Lindsay WR and Taylor JL (2005) A selective review of research on offenders with developmental disabilities: assessment and treatment. *Clinical Psychology and Psychotherapy* **12**: 201–14. (**317, 333**)

Lindsay WR, Allan R, MacLeod F, Smart N, and Smith AHW (2003) Long-term treatment and management of violent tendencies of men with intellectual disabilities convicted of assault. *Mental Retardation*, **41**: 47–56. (**327**)

Lindsay WR, Hogue T, Taylor JL, et al. (2006) Two studies on the prevalence and validity of personality disorder in three forensic intellectual disability samples. *Journal of Forensic Psychiatry and Psychology* **17**: 485–506. (**319, 324**)

Lindsay WR, Hogue TE, Taylor JL, et al. (2008) Risk assessment in offenders with intellectual disability: a comparison across three levels of security. *International Journal of Offender Therapy and Comparative Criminology* **52**: 90–111. (**331**)

Lindsay WR, O'Brien, G, Carson, D, et al. (2010) Pathways into services for offenders with intellectual disabilities: childhood experiences, diagnostic information and offence variables. *Criminal Justice and Behavior* **37**: 678–94. (**326**)

Lindsay WR, Olley S, Jack C, Morrison F, and Smith AHW (1998) The treatment of two stalkers with intellectual disabilities using cognitive approach. *Journal of Applied Research in Intellectual Disabilities*, **11**: 333–44. (**329**)

Lindsay WR, Smith AHW, Law J, et al. (2002) A treatment service for sex offenders with intellectual disability: characteristics of referral and evaluation. *Journal of Applied Research and Intellectual Disabilities* **15**: 166–74. (**317**)

Lindsay WR, Steele L, Smith AHW, Quinn K, and Allan R (2006) A community forensic intellectual disability service: 12-year follow up of referrals, analysis of referral patterns and assessment of harm reduction. *Legal and Criminology* **11**: 113–30. (**325, 329**)

Lindsay WR, Taylor JL, and Sturmey P (eds) (2004) *Offenders with Developmental Disabilities*. Chichester, UK: Wiley. (**315, 327, 333**)

Lindsay WR, Whitefield E, and Carson D (2007) An assessment for attitudes consistent with sexual offending for use with offenders with intellectual disabilities. *Legal and Criminological Psychiatry* **12**: 55–68. (**328, 329**)

Linehan MM (1993) *Cognitive-Behavioural Treatment of Borderline Personality Disorder*. New York: Guilford Press. (**555. 574, 729**)

Linehan MM (1997) Validation and psychotherapy. In A Bonhart and L Greenberg (eds) *Empathy Reconsidered: New Directions in Psychotherapy* (pp 353–92). Washington, DC: American Psychological Association. (**401**)

Linehan MM, Armstrong HE, Suarez A, Allmon D, and Heard HL (1991) Cognitive-behavioral treatment of chronically parasuicidal borderline patients. *Archives of General Psychiatry* **48**: 1060–4. (**410, 520, 574**)

Linehan MM, Dimeff LA, Reynolds SK, et al. (2002) Dialectical behavior therapy versus comprehensive validation therapy plus 12-step for the treatment of opioid dependent women meeting criteria for borderline personality disorder. *Drug and Alcohol Dependence* **67**: 13–26. (**410, 616**)

Linehan MM, Schmidt H, Dimeff LA, et al. (1999) Dialectical behavior therapy for patients with borderline personality disorder and drug-dependence. *American Journal on Addictions* **8**: 279–92. (**410, 444**)

Linehan MM, Tutek DA, Heard H, and Armstrong HE (1994) Interpersonal outcome of cognitive-behavioural treatment for chronically suicidal borderline patients. *American Journal of Psychiatry* **151**: 1771–6. (**574**)

Linehan S, Duffy DM, O'Neill H, O'Neill C, and Kennedy HG (2002) Irish travellers and forensic mental health. *Irish Journal of Psychological Medicine* **19**: 76–9. (**616**)

Linehan SA, Duffy DM, Wright B, Curtin K, Monks S and Kennedy HG. (2005) Psychiatric morbidity in a cross-sectional sample of male remanded prisoners. *Irish Journal of Psychological Medicine* **22**: 128–132. (**616, 657**)

Linehan, MM, Comtois, K. A., Murray, A. M., Brown, M. Z., Gallop, R. J., Heard, H. L., Korslund, K. E., Tutek, D. A., Reynolds, S. K., Lindenboim, N. (2006) Two year randomised controlled trial and follow-up of dialectical behaviour therapy vs therapy by experts for suicidal behaviours and borderline personality disorder. *Archives of General Psychiatry*, **63**: 757–766. (**410, 520**)

Lingford-Hughes AR, Welch S, and Nutt DJ (2004) Evidence-based guidelines for the pharmacological management of substance misuse, addiction and co-morbidity: recommendations from the British Association for Psychopharmacology. *Journal of Psychopharmacology* **18**: 293–335. (**439, 446, 448, 457, 458, 459**)

Linhorst DM, McCutchen TA, and Bennett L (2003) Recidivism among offenders with developmental disabilities participating in a case management programme. *Research in Developmental Disabilities* **24**: 210–30. (**316, 325**)

Link B, Castille DM, and Stuber J (2008) Stigma and coercion in the context of outpatient treatment for people with mental illnesses. *Social Science and Medicine* **67**: 409–19. (**365**)

Link BG and Stueve A (1994) Psychotic symptoms and the violent and illegal behavior of mental patients compared to community controls. In J Monahan, H Steadman (eds) *Violence and Mental Disorder*. Chicago, IL: University of Chicago Press, pp. 137–60. (**339, 349, 350**)

Link BG, Stueve A, and Phelan J (1998) Psychotic symptoms and violent behaviors: probing the component of 'threat/control-override' symptoms. *Social Psychiatry and Psychiatric Epidemiology* **33**: 555–60. (**350**)

Linnoila M, Virkkunen M, Scheinin M, et al. (1983) Low cerebrospinal fluid 5-hydroxyindole-acetic acid concentratrion differentiates impulsive from non-impulsive violent behaviour. *Life Science* **33**: 2609–14. (**308**)

Linton R (1956) *Culture and Mental Disorders*. Springfield, IL: Thomas. (**428**)

Lion J and Soloff PH (1984) Implementation of seclusion and restraint. In K Tardiff (ed) *The Psychiatric Use of Seclusion and Restraint*. Washington, DC: American Psychiatric Press. (**593**)

Lipsey M and Wilson D (1998) Effective intervention for serious juvenile offenders: a synthesis of research. In R Loeber, D Farrington (eds) *Serious and Violent Juvenile Offenders: Risk Factors and Successful Interventions*. Thousand Oaks, CA: Sage. (**263**)

Lipsey MW (1995) What do we learn from 400 research studies on the effectiveness of treatments with juvenile delinquents? In J McGuire (ed) *What works? Reducing Re-Offending*. Chichester, UK: Wiley, pp. 63–78. (**486, 570**)

Lipsey MW and Wilson DB (1993) The efficacy of psychosocial, educational, and behavioural treatment: confirmation from meta-analysis. *American Psychologist* **48**: 1181–209. (**263, 486**)

Lipton DS, Pearson FS, Cleland CM, and Yee D (2002) The effectiveness of cognitive-behavioural treatment methods on offender recidivism. In J McGuire (ed) *Offender Rehabilitation and Treatment: Effective Programmes to Reduce Re-Offending*. Chichester, UK: Wiley, pp. 75–112. (**569**)

Lipton DS, Thornton DM, McGuire J, Porporion FJ, and Hollin CR (2000) Program accreditation and correctional treatment. *Substance Misuse and Misuse* **35**: 1705–31. (**571**)

Lishman WA (1968) Brain damage in relation to psychiatric disability after head injury. *British Journal of Psychiatry* **114**: 373–410. (**296, 429**)

Lishman WA (1998) *Organic Psychiatry*, 3rd edn, (Ch. 7). Oxford: Blackwell Science. (**284, 286, 287, 288, 426, 429, 438, 439**)

Little M, Shah R, Vermeulen MJ, et al. (2005) Adverse perinatal outcomes associated with homelessness and substance use in pregnancy. *Canadian Medical Association Journal* **173**(6): 615–18. (**452**)

Litwack TR (2002) Some questions for the field of violence risk assessment and forensic mental health: or 'back to basics' revisited. *International Journal of Forensic Mental Health* **1**: 171–8. (**533**)

Livesley WJ (2001) *Handbook of Personality Disorders*. New York: Guilford. (**387, 388, 408**)

Livesley WJ (2005) Behavioral and molecular genetic contributions to a dimensional classification of personality disorder. *Journal of Personality Disorders* **19**: 131–55. (**386, 393**)

Livesley WJ (2007a) A framework for integrating dimensional and categorical classifications of personality disorder. *Journal of Personality Disorders* **21**(2): 199–224. (**386**)

Livesley WJ (2007b) The relevance of an integrated approach to the treatment of personality disordered offenders. *Psychology, Crime and Law* **13**: 27–46. (**386**)

Livesley WJ (2008) Toward a genetically-informed model of borderline personality disorder. *Journal of Personality Disorders* **22**: 42–71. (**393**)

Livesley WJ (2012) Tradition versus empiricism in the current *DSM-5* proposal for revising the classification of personality disorders. *Criminal Behaviour and Mental Health* **22**: 81–90. (**386**)

Livesley WJ, Jang KL, and Vernon PA (1998) The phenotypic and genetic structure of traits delineating personality disorder. *Archives of General Psychiatry* **55**: 941–8. (**386, 393**)

Lloyd C and Walmsley R (1989) *Changes in Rape Offences and Sentencing*. Home Office Research Study, Vol. 105. London: HMSO. (**248**)

Lloyd LE and Graitcer PL (1989) The potential for using a trauma registry for injury surveillance and prevention. *American Journal of Preventive Medicine* **5**: 34–7. (**701**)

Lock S (1990) Monitoring research ethical committees. *British Medical Journal* **300**: 61–2. (**668**)

Locke TF and Newcomb M (2004) Child maltreatment, parent alcohol- and drug-related problems, polydrug problems, and parenting practices: A test of gender differences and four theoretical perspectives. *Journal of Family Psychology* **18**:120–34. (**505**)

Loeber R (1988) Behavioural precursors and accelerators of delinquency. In W Buikhuisen, SA Mednick (eds) *Explaining Criminal Behaviour*. Leiden, the Netherlands: Brill, pp. 51–67. (**173**)

Loeber R, Farrington DP, Stouthamer-Loeber M, et al. (2003) The development of male offending: key findings from 14 years of the pittsburgh youth study. In TP Thornberry, MD Krohn (eds) *Taking Stock of Delinquency: An Overview of Findings from Contemporary Longitudinal Studies*. New York: Kluwer, pp. 93–136. (**171, 397**)

Loew TH, Nickel MK, Muehlbacher M, et al. (2006) Topiramate treatment for women with borderline personality disorder: a double-blind, placebo-controlled study. *Journal of Clinical Psychopharmacology* **26**: 61–6. (**405**)

Loftus EF (1979) *Eyewitness Testimony*. Cambridge, MA: Harvard University Press. (**292**)

Loftus EF, Doyle JM, and Dysert J (2008) *Eyewitness Testimony* 4th ed. Charlottesville, VA: Lexis Law Publishing. (**292**)

Logan C (2008) Sexual deviance in females: psychopathology and theory. In DR Laws, WT O'Donohue (eds) *Sexual Deviance: Theory, Assessment, and Treatment*, 2nd edn. New York: Guilford. (**252**)

Logan C and Weizmann-Herelius G (2012) Psychopathy in women: presentation, assessment and management. In *Psychopathy and Law: A Practitioner's Guide*, H Häkkänen-Nyholm H and Nyholm J. Chichester: Wiley. (**513, 514**)

Logan WS, Reuterfors DL, Bohn MJ, and Clark CL (1984) The description and classification of Presidential threateners. *Behavioral Sciences and the Law* **2**: 151–67. (**546**)

Lombroso C (1876) *L'Uomo Delinquente*. Milan: Hoepli. Translated as *Criminal Man* by Mary Gibson and Nicole Hahn Rafter (2005), Durham and London: Duke University Press. (**4**)

London Boroughs Association (1967) *Interim Report, Working Party on the Provision for Seriously Disturbed Adolescents*. (**482**)

London M, Canitrot J, Dzialdowski A, Bates R, and Gwyn A (2003) Contact with treatment services among arrested drug users. *Psychiatric Bulletin* **27**: 214–6. (**467**)

Lopez-Moreno JA, Lopez-Jimenez A, Gorriti MA, and de Fonseca FR (2010) Functional interactions between endogenous cannabinoid and opioid systems: focus on alcohol, genetics and drug-addicted behaviors. *Current Drug Targets* **11**: 406–28. (**206**)

References

Loranger A, Janca A, and Sartorius N (1995) *The ICD-10 International Personality Disorder Examination (IPDE)*. Cambridge: Cambridge University Press. (**387**)

Loranger AW (1999a) *International Personality Disorder Examination – DSM-IV and ICD-10 modules*. Odessa, Fl: Psychological Assessment Resources. (**387**)

Loranger AW (1999b) Categorical approaches to assessment and diagnosis of personality disorders. In RC Cloninger (ed) *Personality and Psychopathology*. Washington, DC: American Psychiatric Press. (**387**)

Loranger AW (2001) *OMNI Personality Inventory – Manual*. Odessa, FL: Psychological Assessment Resources. (**388**)

Loranger AW, Sartorius N, and Janca A (eds) (1997) *Assessment and Diagnosis of Personality Disorders*. New York: Cambridge University Press. (**387**)

Loranger AW, Sartorius N, Andreoli A, et al. (1994) The international personality disorder examination: the world health organization/alcohol, drug abuse, and mental health administration international pilot study of personality disorders. *Archives of General Psychiatry* **51**: 215–24. (**387**)

Lord Chancellor's Department (1999) *Making Decisions. The Government's Proposals for Making Decisions On Behalf of Mentally Incapacitated Adults*. London: The Stationery Office. (**332**)

Lorenz K (1966) *On Aggression*. London: Methuen. (**212**)

Lösel F (1995) The efficacy of correctional treatment: a review and synthesis of meta-evaluations. In J McGuire (ed) *What Works: Reducing Reoffending: Guidelines from Research and Practice*. Chichester, UK: Wiley, pp. 57–82. (**486**)

Lösel F and Bender D (2006) Risk factors for serious and violent antisocial beaviour in children and youth. In A Hagell, JD Renuka (eds) *Children Who Commit Acts of Serious Interpersonal Violence – Messages for Best Practice*. London: Jessica Kingsley, pp. 42–72. (**497**)

Lösel F and Shmucker M (2005) The effectiveness of treatment for sexual offenders: a comprehensive meta-analysis. *Journal of Experimental Criminology* 1: 117–46. (**257, 261, 578**)

Loucks A and Zamble E (1999) Predictors of recidivism in serious female offenders. *Corrections Today* **61**: 26–32. (**515**)

Loucks N (2007) *Prisoners with Learning Difficulties and Learning Disabilities – Review of Prevalence and Associated Needs*. London: Prison Reform Trust. (**315, 316**)

Lovell-Hawker D (2008) *Debriefing aid workers and missionaries: A comprehensive manual*. 3rd ed. London: People in Aid. (**724**)

Low G, Jones D, Duggan C, Power M, and Macleod A (2001) The treatment of deliberate self-harm in borderline personality disorder using dialectical behaviour therapy: a pilot study in a high security hospital. *Behavioural and Cognitive Psychotherapy* **29**: 85–92. (**575**)

Lowney KS and Best J (1995) Stalking strangers and lovers: changing media typifications of a new crime problem. In J Best (ed) *Images of Issues: Typifying Contemporary Social Problems*. New York: Aldine De Gruyter, pp. 33–57 (**373**)

Loza W and Loza-Fanous A (1999) The fallacy of reducing rape and violent recidivism by treating anger. *International Journal of Offender Therapy and Comparative Criminology* 43: 492–502. (**215**)

Loza W, Villeneuve DB, and Loza-Fanous A (2002) Predictive validity of the violence risk appraisal guide: a tool for assessing violent offender's recidivism. *International Journal of Law and Psychiatry* **25**: 85–92. (**536**)

Lucas R (1999) Managing psychotic patients in a day hospital setting. In P Williams (ed) *Psychosis (Madness)*. London: The Institute of Psychoanalysis, pp. 65–77. (**582**)

Luczak SE, Glatt SJ, and Wall TL (2006) Meta-analyses of ALDH2 and ADH1B with alcohol dependence in Asians. *Psychological Bulletin* **132**: 607–21. (**205**)

Ludwig AM, Brandsma JM, Wilbur CB, Benfeldt F, and Jameson DG (1972) The objective study of multiple personality, or are four heads better than one? *Archives of General Psychiatry* **26**: 772–7. (**426, 427**)

Lui S, Deng W, Huang X, et al. (2009) Association of cerebral deficits with clinical symptoms in antipsychotic-naïve first-episode schizophrenia: an optimised voxel-based morphometry and resting state functional connectivity study. *American Journal of Psychiatry* **166**: 196–205. (**312**)

Lund J (1990) Mentally retarded criminal offenders in Denmark. *British Journal of Psychiatry* **156**: 726–31. (**316**)

Luntz B and Widom C (1994) Antisocial personality disorder and abused and neglected children grown up. *American Journal of Psychiatry,* **151**: 670–74. (**396**)

Lurigio A (2000) Persons with serious mental illness in the criminal justice system: background, prevalence, and principles of care. *Criminal Justice Policy Review* **11**: 312–28. (**280**)

Luty J, Nikolaou V, and Beam J (2003) Is opiate detoxification unsafe in pregnancy? *Journal of Substance Abuse Treatment* **24**: 363–7. (**465**)

Lyall I, Holland A, and Collins S (1995) Offending by adults with learning disabilities and the attitudes of staff to offending behaviour: implications for service development. *Journal of Intellectual Disability Research* **39**: 501–8. (**325**)

Lynch BE and Bradford JMW (1980) Amnesia: Its detection by psychophysiological measures. *Bulletin of the American Academy of Psychiatry and the Law* 8: 288–97. (**293, 294**)

Lynskey MT, Heath AC, Bucholz KK, et al. (2003) Escalation of drug use in early-onset cannabis users vs co-twin controls. *The Journal of American Medical Association* **289**: 427–33. (**203**)

Lynskey MT, Heath AC, Nelson EC, et al. (2002) Genetic and environmental contributions to cannabis dependence in a national young adult twin sample. *Psychological Medicine* **32**: 195–207. (**202**)

Lyons MJ, True WR, Eisen SA, et al. (1995) Differential heritability of adult and juvenile antisocial traits. *Archives of General Psychiatry* **52**: 906–15. (**196**)

Lyons RA, Lo SV, and Heaven M (1995) Injury surveillance in children-usefulness of a centralised database of accident and emergency attendances. *Injury Prevention* **1**: 173–6. (**701**)

MacCall Smith RAA and Sheldon D (1997) *Scots Criminal Law*. Haywords Heath: Tottel Publishing. (**93**)

MacDonald JM (1964) Suicide and homicide by automobile. *American Journal of Psychiatry* **121**: 366–70. (**278**)

MacDonald JM (1968) *Homicidal Threats*. Springfield, IL: Thomas. (**238, 543**)

MacDonald JM (1969) *Psychiatry and the Criminal*. Springfield, IL: Thomas. (**286**)

MacDonald M, Atherton S, Berto D, et al. (2008) *Service Provision for Detainees with Problematic Drug and Alcohol Use in Police Detention: A Comparative Study of Selected Countries in the European Union* (HEUNI Paper No. 27). Helsinki, Finland: European Institute for Crime Prevention and Control. http://www.heuni.fi/Oikeapalsta/Search/1247666646138 (**467**)

MacFarlane AC (1998) The longitudinal course of post-traumatic morbidity: the range of outcomes and their predictors. *Journal of Nervous and Mental Disorders* **176**: 30–9. (**706, 712**)

Macfarlane J (2003) Criminal defense in cases of infanticide and neonaticide. In MG Spinelli (ed) *Infanticide: Psychosocial and Legal Perspectives on Mothers who Kill*. Washington, DC: American Psychiatric Publishing, pp. 133–66. (**510**)

MacIntyre A (1988) *Whose Justice? Which Rationality?* London: Duckworth. (**370**)

MacIntyre D, MacNamara N, Irwin D, Gray C, and Darjee R (2004) Substance misuse in a high security hospital: three years of urine drug testing at the state hospital, Carstairs. *Journal of Forensic Psychiatry and Psychology* **15**: 606–19. (**613**)

Mackay C (1857) *Extraordinary Popular Delusions and the Madness of Crowds*. Republished 1980. New York: Harmony Books. (**339**)

Mackay C (1869) *Memoirs of Extraordinary Popular Delusions and the Madness of Crowds*. London: Routledge. (**7, 499**)

Mackay R (2003) The Insanity Defence – Recent Developments in Jersey and Guernsey. *Jersey and Guernsey Law Review* 185–95. (**105**)

Mackay R, Mitchell B, and Howe L (2007a) A continued upturn in unfitness to plead – more disability in relation to the trial under the 1991 Act. *Criminal Law Review* **7**: 530–45. (**25**)

Mackay R, Mitchell BJ, and Howe L (2007b) Yet more facts about the insanity defence. *Criminal Law Review* **6**: 399–411. (**28**)

Mackay RD (1995) *Mental Condition Defences in the Criminal Law*. Oxford, UK: Clarendon. (**164**)

Mackay RD (2003) On Being Insane in Jersey part 3 – the case of *Attorney-General v O'Driscoll*. *Criminal Law Review* **291**. (**106**)

Mackay RD and Gearty C (2001) On Being Insane in Jersey – the case of *Attorney-General Jason Prior*. *Criminal Law Review* July 560–3. (**105**)

Mackay RD and Machin D (2000) The operation of section 48 of the mental health act 1983. *British Journal of Criminology* **40**: 727–45. (**632**)

Mackay RD and Reuber M (2007) Epilepsy and the defence of insanity – time for change? *Criminal Law Review* Oct 782–93. (**27**)

Mackenzie G (1678) *The Laws and Customs of Scotland in Matters Criminal*. Edinburgh, UK: George Swintoun. (**96**)

MacKenzie R, James D, McEwan TE, Mullen PE, and Ogloff JRP (2010) Stalkers and intelligence: implications for treatment. *Journal of Forensic Psychiatry and Psychology* **21**(6): 852–72. (**546**)

MacKenzic RD, McEwan T, Pathé MT, et al. (2009) Melbourne: Stalk Inc. and Centre for Forensic Behavioural Science, Monash University. ISBN 9870646521008. (**546, 547**)

Mackenzie SG and Pless IB (1999) CHIRPP: Canada's principal injury surveillance program. *Injury Prevention* **5**: 208–13. (**701**)

Mackin P, Bishop D, Watkinson H, Gallagher P, and Ferrier IN (2007) Metabolic disease and cardiovascular risk in people treated with antipsychotic medication. *British Journal of Psychiatry* **191**: 23–9. (**566**)

MacMahon C, Butwell M, and Taylor PJ (2003) Changes in patterns of excessive alcohol consumption in 25 years of high security hospital admissions from England and Wales. *Criminal Behaviour and Mental Health* **13**: 17–30. (**515**)

MacMillan HL, Wathen NC, Barlow J, Fergusson DM, Leventhal JM, and Taussig HN (2009) Interventions to prevent child maltreatment and associated impairment. *Lancet* **373**: 250–66. (**399**)

Maden A (1993) *Women, Prisons and Psychiatry*. London: Butterworth Heinemann, pp. 7–10. (**415**)

Maden A (2007) Dangerous and severe personality disorder: antecedents and origins. *British Journal of Psychiatry* **190** (suppl. 49): S8–11. (**416**)

Maden A, Curle C, Meux C, Burrow S and Gunn J (1993) The treatment and security needs of patients in special hospitals. *Criminal Behaviour and Mental Health* **3**: 290–306. (**599, 601**)

Maden A, Rutter S, McClintock T, Friendship C, and Gunn J (1999) Outcome of admission to a medium secure psychiatric unit. *British Journal of Psychiatry* **175**: 313–16. (**604, 605**)

Maden A, Scott F, Burnett R, Lewis GF, and Skapinakis P (2004) Offending in psychiatric patients after discharge from medium secure units: prospective national cohort study. *British Medical Journal* **328**: 1534. (**605**)

Maden A, Skapinakis P, Lewis G, et al. (2006) Gender differences in reoffending after discharge from medium-secure units. *British Journal of Psychiatry* **189**: 168–72. (**520**)

Maden A, Swinton M, and Gunn J (1992) A survey of pre-arrest drug use in sentenced prisoners. *British Journal of Addiction* **87**: 27–33. (**282**)

Maden A, Taylor CJA, Brooke D, and Gunn J (1995) *Mental Disorder in Remand Prisoners*. London: Home Office. (**513, 516, 601, 629**)

Maden A, Williams J, Wong SCP, and Leis TA (2004) A service for dangerous severe personality disorder in a high security hospital: lessons from the Canadian regional psychiatric centre. *Journal of Forensic Psychiatry and Psychology* **15**: 375–90. (**417**)

Maden T (2006) *Review of Homicides by Patients with Severe Mental Illness*. http://www.psychminded.co.uk/news/news2006/sept06/madenreview.pdf (**79, 595, 695**)

Maden T (2007) *Treating Violence: A Guide to Risk Management in Mental Health*. Oxford, UK: Oxford University Press. (**532, 549**)

Maden T, Swinton M, and Gunn J (1994a) Criminological and psychiatric survey of women serving a prison sentence. *British Journal of Criminology* **34**: 172–91. (**501, 516**)

Maden T, Swinton M, and Gunn J (1994b) Psychiatric disorders in women serving a prison sentence. *The British journal of psychiatry* **164**: 44–54. (**501, 516**)

Madge N, Hawton K, McMahon EM, Cocoran P, Diego L, Wilde E, Fekete S, Heeringen K, Ystgaard M, and Arensman E (2011) Psychological characteristics, stressful life events and deliberate self-harm: Findings from the Child & Adolescent Self-harm in Europe (CASE) Study. *European Child and Adolescent Psychiatry* **20**: 499–508. (**502**)

Madison A (1970) *Vandalism – The Not So Senseless Crime.* New York: Seabury. (**272**)

Madrid GA, MacMurray J, Lee JW, Anderson BA and Comings DE (2001) Stress as a mediating factor in the association between the DRD2 TaqI polymorphism and alcoholism. *Alcohol* **23**: 117–22. (**207**)

Maes M, Mylle J, Delmeire L, and Altamura C (2000) Psychiatric morbidity and comorbidity following accidental man-made traumatic events: Incidence and risk factors. European Archives of Psychiatry and Clinical Neurosciences **250**: 156–62. (**717**)

Magana AB, Goldstein JM, Karno M, et al. (1986) A brief method for assessing expressed emotion in relatives of psychiatric patients. *Psychiatry Research* **17**: 203–12. (**355**)

Magaro PA (1980) *Cognition in Schizophrenia and Paranoia.* Hillsdale, NJ: Erlbaum. (**351**)

Magnavita JJ (2000) Introduction: The growth of relational therapy. *Journal of Clinical Psychology* **56**: 999–1004. (**396**)

Maguire M (2007) Crime data and statistics. In M Maguire, R Morgan, R Reiner (eds) *The Oxford Handbook of Criminology.* Oxford, UK: Oxford University Press, pp. 241–301. (**266**)

Maguire M, Kemshall H, Noaks L, and Wincup E (2001) *Risk Management of Sexual and Violent Offenders: The Work of the Public Protection Panels.* Police Research Series 139. London: Home Office. (**644**)

Maher BA (1974) Delusional thinking and perceptual disorder. *Journal of Individual Psychology* **30**: 98–113. (**351**)

Maher BA (1988) Anomalous experience and delusional thinking: the logic of explanations. In TF Oltmanns, BA Maher (eds) *Delusional Beliefs.* New York: Wiley, pp. 15–33. (**351**)

Main M and Hesse E (1992) Disorganised /disorientated infant behaviour in the strange situation, lapses in monitoring of reasoning and discourse during the parent's adult attachment interview, and dissociative states. In M Ammanati, D Stern (eds) *Attachment and Psychoanalysis.* Rome: Gius Laterza and Figli, pp. 86–140. (**718, 719**)

Main M, Kaplan N, and Cassidy J (1985) Security in infancy, childhood and adulthood: A move to the level of representation. In I Bretherton and E Waters (eds) *Growing Points in Attachment Theory and Research. Monographs of the Society for Research in Child Development* **50**: 66–104. (**396**)

Main T (1946) The hospital as a therapeutic institution. *Bulletin of the Meninger Clinic* **10**: 66–70. (**412**)

Main TF (1983) The concept of the therapeutic community: its variations and vicissitudes. In M Pines (ed) *The Evolution of Group Analysis.* London: Routledge and Kegan Paul. (**579**)

Mair G and May C (1997) *Offenders on Probation.* Home Office Research Study 167. London: Home Office. http://www.ohrn.nhs.uk/resource/Policy/OffendersonProbation.pdf (**640**)

Malamud N and Skillicorn SA (1956) The relationship between the Wernicke and the Korsakoff syndrome. *Archives of Neurology and Psychiatry* **76**: 585–96. (**439**)

Malamuth MR (1981) Rape proclivity. *Journal of Social Issues* **37**: 138–57. (**249**)

Malchiodi CA (ed) (2005) *Expressive Therapies.* New York: Guilford. (**558**)

Malcolm J (1990) *The Journalist and the Murderer.* New York: Knopf/Random House. (**660**)

Malcolm J (2011) *Iphigenia in Forest Hills: Anatomy of a Murder Trial.* New Haven, CT: Yale University Press. (**15**)

Maldonado AL, Martinez F, Osuna E, and Garcia-Ferrer R (1988) Alcohol consumption and crimes against sexual freedom. *Medicine and Law* **7**: 81–6. (**442**)

Maletzky B (1991) *Treating the Sexual Offender.* Newbury Park, CA: Sage. (**258**)

Maletzky BM (1976) The diagnosis of pathological intoxication. *Journal of Studies on Alcohol* **37**: 1215–28. (**437**)

Malinowski A (2003) 'What works' with substance users in prison? *Journal of Substance Use* **8**: 223–33. (**447**)

Mallya AR, Roos PD, and Roebuck-Colgan K (1992) Restraint, seclusion, and clozapine. *Journal of Clinical Psychiatry* **53**: 395–7. (**563**)

Malone RP, Delaney MA, Luebbert JF, Cater J, and Campbell M (2000) A double-blind placebo-controlled study of lithium in hospitalized aggressive children and adolescents with conduct disorder. *Archives of General Psychiatry* **57**: 649–54. (**566**)

Malsch M, Visscher M, and Blaauw E (2002) *Stalking Van Bekende Personen* (*Stalking of Celebrities*). Den Haag, the Netherlands: Boom. (**377**)

Mammen OK, Pilkonis PA, Chengappa KN, and Kupfer DJ (2004) Anger attacks in bipolar depression: predictors and response to citalopram added to mood stabilizers. *Journal of Clinical Psychiatry* **65**: 627–33. (**310**)

Mann A and Moran P (2000) Personality disorders: a critique of the term as a basis for action. *Journal of Forensic Psychiatry* **11**: 11–16. (**383**)

Mann JJ, McBride PA, Brown RP, et al. (1992) Relationship between central and peripheral serotonin indexes in depressed and suicidal psychiatric inpatients. *Archives of General Psychiatry* **49**: 442–6. (**307**)

Mann R (2004) Innovations in sex offender treatment. *Journal of Sexual Aggression* **10**: 141–52. (**256**)

Mann RE, Carter AJ, and Wakeling HC (2012) In defence of NOMS' view about sex offending treatment effectiveness: a reply to Ho and Ross. *Criminal Behaviour and Mental Health,* **22**: 7–10. (**5**)

Mann T (1924) *The Magic Mountain.* Berlin, Germany: S Fisher Verlag. (**602**)

Manners T (1995) *Deadlier Than the Male.* London: Pan Books. (**686, 687**)

Manuck SB, Flory JD, Feerrell RE, Mann JJ, and Muldoon MP (2000) A regulatory polymorphism of the monoamine oxidase-A gene may be associated with variability in aggression, impulsivity, and central nervous system serotonergic responsivity. *Psychiatry Research* **95**: 9–23. (**199**)

Manuck SB, Flory JD, McCaffery JM, et al. (1998) Aggression, impulsivity, and central nervous system serotonergic responsivity in a nonpatient sample. *Neuropsychopharmacology* **19**: 287–99. (**199, 309**)

Marazziti D and Conti L (1991) Aggression, hyperactivity and platelet imipramine binding. *Acta Psychiatrica Scandinavica* **84**: 209–11. (**308**)

Marenco S and Weinberger DR (2000) The neurodevelopmental hypothesis of schizophrenia: following a trail of evidence from the cradle to the grave. *Developmental Psychology* **12**: 501–27. (**341**)

Markman KD, Gavanski I, Sherman SJ, and McMullen MN (1993) The mental simulation of better and worse possible worlds. *Journal of Experimental Social Psychology* **29**: 87–109. (**697**)

Markman KD, Gavanski I, Sherman SJ, and McMullen MN (1995) The impact of perceived control in the imagination of better and worse possible worlds. *Personality and Social Psychology Bulletin* **21**: 588–95. (**696**)

Markowitz S (2000a) The price of alcohol, wife abuse and husband abuse. *Economic Journal* **67**: 279–303. (**705**)

Markowitz S (2000b) An economic analysis of alcohol, drugs and violence crime. *NBER working paper 7982*, October. Cambridge, MA: National Bureau of Economic Research. http://www.nber.org/papers/w7982 (**705**)

Markowitz S and Grossman M (1998) Alcohol regulation and domestic violence towards children. *Contemporary Economic Policy* **16**: 309–20. (**705**)

Markowitz S and Grossman M (2000) The effects of beer taxes on physical child abuse. *Journal of Health Economics* **19**(2): 271–82. (**705**)

Marks I (1991) Self-administered behavioural treatment. *Behavioural Psychotherapy* **19**: 42–6. (**407**)

Marks I, Lovell K, Noshirvani H, Livanou M, and Thrasher S (1998) Treatment of posttraumatic stress disorder by exposure and/or cognitive restructuring: a controlled study. *Archives of General Psychiatry* **55**: 317–25. (**728**)

Marks MN and Kumar R (1993) Infanticide in England and Wales. *Medicine, Science, and the Law* **33**: 329–39. (**508**)

Marks MN and Kumar R (1996) Infanticide in Scotland. *Medicine Science and the Law* **36**:299–305. (**508**)

Marlatt GA (1996) Taxonomy of high-risk situations for alcohol relapse: evolution and development of a cognitive behavioural model. *Addiction* **91** (suppl.12s1): 37–49. (**446**)

Marlatt GA and Gordon JR (eds) (1985) *Relapse Prevention*. New York: Guilford. (**446**)

Marleau JD, Millaud F, and Auclair N (2003) A comparison of parricide and attempted parricide: a study of 39 psychotic adults. *International journal of law and psychiatry* **26**(3): 269–79. (**507**)

Marmar CR, Weiss DS, and Metzler TJ (1998) Peritraumatic dissociation and post-traumatic stress disorder. In JD Bremner, CR Marmar (eds) *Trauma, Memory and Dissociation*. Washington, DC: American Psychiatric Association, pp. 229–52. (**705**)

Marottoli RA, Cooney LM, Wagner R, Doucette J, and Tinetti ME (1994) Predictors of automobile crashes and moving violations among elderly drivers. *Annals of Internal Medicine* **121**: 842–6. (**278**)

Marques J (1999) How to answer the question 'Does sex offender treatment work?' *Journal of Interpersonal Violence* **14**: 437–51. (**610**)

Marques JK, Wiederanders M, Day DM, Nelson, C and van Ommeren, A (2005) Effects of a relapse prevention program on sexual recidivism: final results from california's sex offender treatment and evaluation project (SOTEP) *Sexual Abuse: A Journal of Research and Treatment* **17**: 79–107. (**257**)

Marsden D (1978) Sociological perspectives on family violence. In JP Martin (ed) *Violence and the Family*. Chichester, UK: Wiley. (**228**)

Marsden J, Gossop M, Stewart D, et al. (1998) The maudsley addiction profile (MAP): a brief instrument for assessing treatment outcome. *Addiction* **93**: 1857–67. Also at http://www.iop.kcl.ac.uk/iopweb/blob/downloads/locator/l_346_MAP.pdf (**456**)

Marsden J, Gossop M, Stewart D, Rolfe A, and Farrell M (2000) Psychiatric symptoms among clients seeking treatment for drug dependence. Intake data from the National Treatment Outcome Research Study. *British Journal of Psychiatry* **176**: 285–9. (**451**)

Marshall P (1997) *A reconviction study of HMP Grendon therapeutic Community Report*. London: Home Office Research and Statistics Directorate, Home Office, p. 53. (**583**)

Marshall T, Simpson S, and Stevens A (2001) Use of health care services by prison inmates: comparisons with the community. *Journal of Epidemiology and Community Health* **55**: 364–5. (**631, 632**)

Marshall WL (1994) Treatment effects on denial and minimization in incarcerated sex offenders. *Behaviour Research and Therapy* **32**: 559–64. (**261**)

Marshall WL (1999) Current status of North American assessment and treatment programs for sexual offenders. *Journal of Interpersonal Violence* **14**: 221–39. (**256**)

Marshall WL and McGuire J (2003) Effect sizes in the treatment of sexual offenders. *International Journal of Offender Therapy and Comparative Criminology* **47**(6): 653–63. (**416**)

Marshall WL, Barbaree HE, and Eccles A (1991) Early onset and deviant sexuality in child molesters. *Journal of Interpersonal Violence* **6**: 323–36. (**246**)

Marshall WL, Marshall LE, Serran GA, and Fernandez YM (2006) *Treating Sexual Offenders: An Integrated Approach*. New York: Guilford Press. (**578**)

Marshall WL, Thornton D, Marshall LE, Fernandez YM, and Mann R (2001) Treatment of sexual offenders who are in categorical denial: a pilot project. *Sexual Abuse: A Journal of Research and Treatment* **13**: 205–15. (**262**)

Martel M, Sterzinger A, Miner J, Clinton J, and Biros M (2005) Management of acute undifferentiated agitation in the emergency department: a randomized double-blind trial of droperidol, ziprasidone, and midazolam. *The American Journal of Emergency Medicine* **12**: 1167–72. (**566**)

Martens WHJ (2004) Fourteen ways to disturb the treatment of psychopaths. *Journal of Forensic Psychology Practice* **4**: 51–60. (**401**)

Martin BK, Clapp L, Alfers J, and Beresford TP (2004) Adherence to court order to disulfram at 15 months: a naturalistic study. *Journal of Substance Abuse Treatment* **26**: 233–6. (**446**)

Martin C and Player E (2000) *Drug Treatment in Prison: An Evaluation of the RAPt Treatment Programme.* Winchester, UK: Waterside. (**447**)

Martin JA and Penn DL (2001) Social cognition and subclinical paranoid ideation. *British Journal of Clinical Psychology* **40**: 261–5. (**487**)

Martin JP (1978) *Violence in the Family.* Chichester, UK: Wiley. (**714**)

Martin JP (1984) *Hospitals in Trouble.* Oxford, UK: Blackwell. (**602, 682**)

Martin ME and Hesselbrock MN (2001) Women Prisoners` Mental health: vulnerabilities, risks and resilience. *Journal of Offender Rehabilitation* **34**(1): 25–44. (**517**)

Martin NG, Boomsma DI, and Machin G (1997) A twin-pronged attack on complex traits. [Review] [66 refs]. *Nature Genetics* **17**: 387–92. (**190**)

Martin NG, Eaves LJ, Kearsey MJ, and Davies P (1978) The power of the classical twin study. *Heredity* **40**: 97–116. (**190**)

Martin SE (2001) The links between alcohol, crime and the criminal justice system: explanations, evidence and interventions. *American Journal on Addictions* **10**: 136–58. (**442**)

Martin SE and Bryant K (2001) Gender differences in the association of alcohol intoxication and illicit drug abuse among persons arrested for violent and property offenses. *Journal of Substance Abuse* **13**: 563–81. (**514**)

Marziali E and Monroe-Blum H (1995) An interpersonal approach to group psychotherapy with borderline personality disorder. *Journal of Personality Disorders* **9**: 179–89. (**572**)

Marzuk PM, Tardiff K, and Hirsch CS (1992) The epidemiology of murder-suicide. *The Journal of American Medical Association* **267**: 3179–183. (**233**)

Mash EJ and Dozois DJA (2003) Child psychopathology: a developmental-systems perspective. In EJ Mash, RA Barkley (eds) *Child Psychopathology,* 2nd edn. New York: Guilford, pp. 3–71. (**485**)

Masi G, Milone A, Canepa G, et al. (2006) Olanzapine treatment in adolescents with severe conduct disorder. *European Psychiatry: Journal of the Association of European Psychiatrists* **21**: 51–7. (**564**)

Masle LM, Gorea M, and Juki V (2000) The comparison of forensic-psychiatric traits between female and male perpetrators of murder or attempted murder. *Collegium Antropologicum* **24**: 91–9. (**507**)

Maslow AH (1943) A theory of human motivation. *Psychological Review* **50**: 370–96. (**617**)

Mason F (2006) Services for women with personality disorder: focus on a trauma-based approach to treatment. In C Newrith, C Meux, PJ Taylor (eds) *Personality Disorder and Serious Offending.* London: Hodder Arnold, pp. 231–9 (**520, 599**)

Mason KH, Ryan AB, and Bennett MR (1988) *Report of the Committee of Enquiry into Proceedings in Certain Psychiatric Hospitals in Relation to Admission, Discharge or Release on Leave of Certain Classes of Patients.* (The Mason Report). Wellington, New Zealand: New Zealand Ministry of health. (**139, 603**)

Mason T and Mercer D (1998) Introduction: the silent scream. In T Mason, D Mercer (eds) *Critical Perspectives in Forensic Care Inside Out.* Hampshire, UK: Macmillan, pp. 1–8. (**552**)

Masters B (1985) *Killing for Company.* London: Cape. (**239, 247**)

Matson JL, Bamburg JW, Mayville EA, et al. (2000) Psychopharmacology and mental retardation: a 10-year review (1990–1999). *Research in Developmental Disabilities* **21**: 263–96. (**327**)

Mattes JA (2005) Oxcarbazepine in patients with impulsive aggression: a double-blind, placebo-controlled trial. *Journal of Clinical Psychopharmacology* **25**: 575–9. (**566**)

Matthews HHJ (2004) *Committee of Inquiry to Investigate how the NHS Handled Allegations about the Performance and Conduct of Richard Neale,* Cm 6315. London: Department of Health. TSO (**54, 684**)

Matthews K, Shepherd JP, and Sivarajasingam V (2006) Violence-related injury and the price of beer in England and Wales. *Applied Economics* **38**: 661–70. (**704**)

Mattick R and Jarvis T (1994) Brief or minimal interventions for 'alcoholics'? The evidence suggests otherwise. *Drug and Alcohol Review* **13**: 137–44. (**705**)

Mattson MR and Sacks MH (1978) Seclusion: uses and complications. *American Journal of Psychiatry* **135**: 1210–13. (**595**)

Maudsley H (1867) *The Physiology and Pathology* of the Mind. London: Macmillan. (**431, 481**)

Maudsley H (1885) *Responsibility in Mental Disease.* London: Keegan Paul Trench. (**384**)

Maughan B and Rutter M (2001) Antisocial children grown up. In J Hill and B Maughan (eds) *Conduct Disorders in Childhood and Adolescence.* Cambridge, UK: Cambridge University Press. pp. 507–52. (**398**)

Maughan B, Pickles A, Hagell A, Rutter M, and Yule W (1996) Reading problems and antisocial behaviour: Developmental trends in comorbidity. *The Journal of Child Psychology and Psychiatry and Allied Disciplines* **37**: 405–18. (**317**)

Mawson D (1985) Delusions of poisoning. *Medicine, Science and the Law* **25**: 279–87. (**353**)

Maxfield L and Hyer L (2002) The relationship between efficacy and methodology in studies investigating EMDR treatment of PTSD. *Journal of Clinical Psychology* **58**: 23–41. (**725**)

Maxfield MG and Widom CS (1996) The cycle of violence revisited 6 years later. *Archives of Pediatrics and Adolescent Medicine* **150**: 390–5. (**175**)

May C (2005) *The CARAT Drug Service in Prisons: Findings from the Research Database.* London: Home Office. http://www.drugscope. org.uk/OneStopCMS/Core/CrawlerResourceServer.aspx?resource=ABADE102-9AF4-4AC9-8535-E4C33FB34FA8&mode=link&guid=c460f97af5e449f189088a5545d9175c (**462**)

May M (1978) Violence in the family: an historical perspective. In JP Martin (ed) *Violence in the Family*. Chichesterm, UK: Wiley. (**219**)

May PRA (1968) *Treatment of Schizophrenia*. New York: Science House. (**358**)

May T, Edmonds M, and Hough M (1999) *Street Business: The Links between Sex and Drug Markets*. Police Research series, Paper 118. London: Home Office. http://www.popcenter.org/problems/street_prostitution/PDFs/fprs118.pdf (**464**)

Mayes R and Horwitz AV (2005) DSM-III and the revolution in classification of mental illness. *Journal of the History of Behavioral Sciences* **41**: 249–67. (**10**)

Mayhew C, Chappell D, Quinlan M, Barker M, and Sheehan M (2004) Measuring the extent of impact from occupational violence and bullying on traumatised workers. *Employee Responsibilities and Rights Journal* **16**: 117–34. (**700**)

Mayhew P, Elliot D, and Dowds L (1989) *The 1988 British Crime Survey*. Home Office Research Study No111. London: HMSO. (**700**)

Mayou R, Bryant B, and Duthie R (1993) Psychiatric consequences of road traffic accidents. *BMJ* **307**: 647–51. (**713**)

McBride CM, Emmons KM, and Lipkus MT (2003) Understanding the potential of teachable moments: the case of smoking cessation. *Health Education: Research, Theory and Practice* **18**: 156–70. (**465**)

McCabe KM, Lansing AE, Garland A, and Hough R (2002) Gender differences in psychopathology, functional impairment, and familial risk factors among adjudicated delinquents. *Journal of the American Academy of Child and Adolescent Psychiatry* **41**: 860–7. (**482**)

McCabe R, Heath C, Burns T, and Priebe S (2002) Engagement of patients with psychosis in the consultation: conversation analytic study. *British Medical Journal* **325**: 1148–51. (**352, 356**)

McCabe S and Treitel P (1984) *Juvenile Justice in the United Kingdom, Comparisons and Suggestions for Change*. London: New Approaches to Juvenile Crime. (**480**)

McCann IL, Pearlman LA (1990) *Psychological Trauma and the Adult Survivor: Theory, Therapy, and Transformation*. New York: Bruner/Mazel. (**723**)

McCann JT (1998) Subtypes of stalking (obsessional following) in adolescents. *The Journal of Adolescence* **21**: 667–75. (**376**)

McCann JT (2000) A descriptive study of child and adolescent obsessional followers. *Journal of Forensic Sciences* **45**: 195–9. (**376**)

McCann JT (2001) *Stalking in Children and Adolescents: The Primitive Bond*. Washington, DC: American Psychological Association. (**376**)

McCarthy SE, Makarov V, Kirov G, et al. (2009) Microduplications of 16p11.2 are associated with schizophrenia. *Nature Genetics* **41**(11): 1223–7. (**209**)

McClanahan SF, McClelland GM, Abram KM, and Teplin LA (1999) Pathways into prostitution among female jail detainees and their implications for mental health services. *Psychiatric Services* **50**: 1606–13. (**454**)

McClellan J, Douglas D, McCurrry C, and Storck M (1995) Clinical characteristics related to severity of sexual abuse: A study of seriously mentally ill youth. *Child Abuse and Neglect* **19**: 1245–54. (**396**)

McCloskey MS, Ben-Zeev D, Lee R, Bermann ME, and Coccaro EF (2009) Acute tryptophan depletion and self-injurious behavior in aggressive patients and healthy volunteers. *Psychopharmacology* **203**: 53–61. (**309**)

McClure RJ, Davis PM, Meadow SR, and Sibert JR (1996) Epidemiology of Munchausen syndrome by proxy, non-accidental poisoning, and non-accidental suffocation. *Archives of Disease in Childhood* **75**: 57–61. (**506**)

McConaghy N, Armstrong MS, Blaszcynski A, and Allcock C (1983) Controlled comparison of aversive therapy and imaginal desensitization in compulsive gambling. *British Journal of Psychiatry* **142**: 366–72. (**471**)

McConaghy N, Blaszczynski A, and Frankova A (1991) Comparison of imaginal desensitization with other behavioural treatments of pathological gambling. A two- to nine-year follow-up. *The British Journal of Psychiatry* **159**: 390–3. (**471**)

McCord J (1977) A comparative study of two generations of native Americans. In RF Meier (ed) *Theory in Criminology*. Beverly Hills, CA: Sage, pp. 83–92. (**176**)

McCord J (1979) Some child-rearing antecedents of criminal behaviour in adult men. *Journal of Personality and Social Psychology* **37**: 1477–86. (**174**)

McCord J (1982) A longitudinal view of the relationship between paternal absence and crime. In J Gunn, DP Farrington (eds) *Abnormal Offenders, Delinquency, and the Criminal Justice System*. Chichester, UK: Wiley, pp. 113–28. (**175**)

McCord J (1983) A forty year perspective on effects of child abuse and neglect. *Child Abuse and Neglect* **7**: 265–70. (**175**)

McCord J (1991) Family relationships, juvenile delinquency, and adult criminality. *Criminology* **29**: 397–417. (**171**)

McCord J (1997) On discipline. *Psychological Inquiry* **8**: 215–17. (**174**)

McCord J and Enslinger ME (1997) Multiple risks and comorbidity in an African-American population. *Criminal Behaviour and Mental Health* **7**: 339–52. (**345, 397**)

McCord W and McCord J (1959) *Origins of Crime: A New Evaluation of the Cambridge-Somerville*. New York: Columbia. (**317**)

McCord W and Sanchez J (1982) The Wiltwyck-Lyman project: a twenty-five year follow-up study of milieu therapy. In WNM McCord (ed) *The Psychopath and Milieu Therapy*. New York: Academic Press. (**396, 412**)

McCormick RA, Russo AM, Ramiriz LF, and Taber JI (1984) Affective disorders among pathological gamblers seeking treatment. *American Journal of Psychiatry* **141**: 215–8. (**470**)

McCrae R and Costa P (1987) Validation of the five-factor model across instruments and observers. *Journal of Personality and Social Psychology* **52**: 81–90. (**388**)

McCrae RR and Costa PT (1996) Toward a new generation of personality theories: theoretical contexts for the five-factor model. In JS Wiggins (ed) *The Five-Factor Model of Personality: Theoretical Perspectives*. New York: Guilford, pp. 51–87. (**385**)

McCreadie R (2003) Diet, smoking and cardiovascular risk in people with schizophrenia. *British Journal of Psychiatry* **183**: 534–9. (**567**)

McCreadie R (2005) Dietary improvement in people with schizophrenia – randomised controlled trial. *British Journal of Psychiatry* **187**: 346–51. (**567**)

McCutcheon JP (1998) Involuntary conduct and the criminal law: the case of the unconscious driver. *International Journal of Law and Psychiatry* **21**(3): 305–14. (**279**)

McDermott B, Dualan I, and Scott C (2011) The predictive ability of the classification of violence risk (COVR) in a forensic psychiatric hospital. *Psychiatric Services* **62**: 430–3. (**531, 541**)

McDermott R, Tingley D, Cowden J, Frazzetto G, and Johnson DDP (2009) Monoamine oxidase A gene (MAOA) predicts behavioral aggression following provocation. *Proceedings of the National Academy of Sciences USA* **106**: 2118–23. (**200**)

McDonald D and Brown M (1997) *Indicators of aggressive behaviour: Report to the Minister for Health and Family Services from and Expert Working Group*. Research and Public Policy Series No. 8. Canberra, Australia: Australian Institute of Criminology. http://www.aic.gov.au/documents/0/8/C/%7B08CD1792-8D4A-4F9A-8177-3F1C530BF2FC%7DRPP08.pdf (**699**)

McDonald DC (1995) *Managing Prison Health Care and Costs*. Washington, DC: National Institute of Justice, US Department of Justice. https://www.ncjrs.gov/pdffiles1/Digitization/152768NCJRS.pdf (**528**)

McDougall C, Perry AE, Clarbour J, Bowles R, and Worthy G (2009) Evaluation of HM Prison Service enhance thinking skills programme: Report on the outcomes from a randomised controlled trial. Retrieved 29 September, 2009 from www.justice.gov.uk/publications/docs/report-on-the-outcomes-from-a-randomised-controlled-trial1.pdf (**225**)

McDougle CJ, Scahill L, Aman MG, et al. (2005) Risperidone for the core symptom domains of autism: results from the study by the autism network of the research units on pediatric psychopharmacology. *The American Journal of Psychiatry* **162**: 1142–8. (**564**)

McEwan T, Mullen PE, and Purcell R (2007) Identifying risk factors in stalking: a review of current research. *International Journal of Law and Psychiatry* **30**: 1–9. (**379, 380**)

McFall ME, McKay PW, and Donovan DM (1991) Combat-related PTSD and psychosocial adjustment problems among substance-abusing veterans. *Journal of Nervous and Mental Disease* **179**: 33–8. (**715**)

Mcfarland BH, Faulkner LR, Bloom JD, et al. (1989) Chronic mental-illness and the criminal-justice system. *Hospital and Community Psychiatry* **40**: 718–23. (**279**)

McGauley G and Humphreys M (2003) Contribution of forensic psychotherapy to the care of forensic patients. *Advances in Psychiatric Treatment* **9**: 117–124. (**580, 597**)

McGauley GA (1997) The actor, the act and the environment: forensic psychotherapy and risk. *The International Review of Psychiatry: Special edn. On Risk Assessment and Management in Psychiatric Practice* **9**: 257–64. (**581**)

McGauley GA (2002) Forensic psychotherapy in secure settings. *Journal of Forensic Psychiatry* **13**: 9–13. (**582**)

McGillicuddy NB and Blane HT (1999) Substance use in individuals with mental retardation. *Addictive Behaviors* **24**: 869–78. (**324, 444, 445**)

McGillivary J and Moore MR (2001) Substance abuse by offenders with mild intellectual disability. *Journal of Intellectual and Developmental Disability* **26**: 279–310. (**324**)

McGilloway A, Hall RE, Lee T, and Bhui KS (2010) A systematic review of personality disorder, race and ethnicity: prevalence etiology and treatment. *BMC Psychiatry*: 10–33. www.biomedcentral.com/1471-244X/10/33 (**390**)

McGilloway S and Donnelly M (2004) Mental illness in the UK criminal justice system: a police liaison scheme for mentally disordered offenders in Belfast. *Journal of Mental Health* **13**: 263–75. (**655**)

McGinley H and Pasewark RA (1989) National survey of the frequency and success of the insanity pleas and alternate pleas. *Journal of Psychiatry and Law* **17**(2): 205–21. (**121**)

McGlashan TH (1983) The borderline syndrome: II. Is it a variant of schizophrenia or affective disorder? *Archives of General Psychiatry* **40**: 1319–23. (**346, 385, 397**)

McGlashan TH, Docherty JP, and Siris S (1976) Integrative and sealing-over recoveries from schizophrenia: distinguishing case studies. *Psychiatry* **39**: 325–338. (**574**)

McGoldrick M and Gershon R (1985) *Genograms in Family Assessment*. New York: Norton. (**396**)

McGrath RJ, Cumming G, and Burchard BL (2003) *Current Practices and Trends in Sexual Abuser Management: The Safer Society 2002 Nationwide Survey*. Brandon, VT: Safer Society Press. (**256**)

McGrath Y, Sumnall H, McVeigh J, and Bellis M (2006) *Drug Use Prevention among Young People: A Review of Reviews Evidence Briefing Update*. London: National Institute for Health and Clinical Excellence. (**492**)

McGue M, Iacono WG, and Krueger R (2006) The association of early adolescent problem behavior and adult psychopathology: a multivariate behavioral genetic perspective. *Behavior Genetics* **36**: 591–602. (**204**)

McGue M, Iacono WG, Legrand LN, and Elkins I (2001) Origins and consequences of age at first drink. II. Familial risk and heritability. *Alcoholism: Clinical and Experimental Research* **25**: 1166–73. (**202**)

McGuire J (1997) Ethical dilemmas in forensic clinical psychology. *Legal and Criminological Psychology* **2**(2): 177–192. (**235**)

McGuire J (2002) Integrating findings from research reviews. In J McGuire (ed) *Offender Rehabilitation and Treatment – Effective Programme and Policies to Reduce Reoffending*. Chichester, UK: Wiley. (**518**)

McGuire J (2003) *Offender Rehabilitation and Treatment. Effective Programmes and Policies to Reduce Reoffending*. Chichester, UK: Wiley. (**547**)

McGuire J (2008) A review of effective interventions for reducing aggression and violence. *Philosophical Transactions of the Royal Society B* **363**: 2577–9. (**571**)

McGuire J (ed) (1995) *What Works: Reducing Reoffending: Guidelines from Research and Practice*. Chichester, UK: Wiley. (**416, 571, 609**)

McGuire J and Priestley P (1995) Reviewing 'what works': past present and future. In: J McGuire (ed) *What Works: Reducing Reoffending: Guidelines from Research and Practice*. Chichester, UK: Wiley, pp. 3–34. (**486**)

McHale JV (1991) Confidentiality and the examining psychiatrist. *Psychiatric Bulletin* **15**: 160. (**666**)

McInerney C and O'Neill C (2008) Prison Psychiatric Inreach and Court Liaison Services in Ireland. *Judicial Studies Institute Journal* **2**: 147–57. (**657**)

McInerny T (2000) Dutch Law and the TBS. *Criminal Behaviour and Mental Health* **10**: 213–28. (**414**)

McIntosh J, Gannon M, McKeganey N, and MacDonald F (2003) Exposure to drugs among pre-teenage schoolchildren. *Addiction* **98**: 1615–23. (**465**)

McIvor G, Eley S, Malloch M, and Yates R (2003) *Establishing Drug Courts in Scotland: Early Experiences of the pilot Drug Courts in Glasgow and Fife*. Crime and Criminal Justice Research Programme, Research Findings 71/2003. Edinburgh, UK: Scottish Executive. http://www.scotland.gov.uk/Resource/Doc/47133/0029642.pdf (**653**)

McKee GR and Shea SJ (1998) Maternal filicide: a cross-national comparison. *Journal of Clinical Psychology* **54**: 679–87. (**508**)

McKellar P (1979) *Mindsplit*. London: Dent. (**425, 426, 427**)

McKenna BG, Smith NA, Poole SJ, et al. (2003) A survey of threats and violent behaviour by patients against registered nurses in their first year of practice. *International Journal of Mental Health Nursing* **12**: 56–63. (**378**)

McKenna P (1998) Fitness to drive: a neuro psychological perspective. *Journal of Mental Health* **7**(1): 9–18. (**278**)

McKenzie N and Sales B (2008) New procedures to cut delays in transfer of mentally ill prisoners to hospital. *Psychiatric Bulletin* **30**: 20–2. (**653**)

McLaughlin KA, Green J, Gruber MJ, et al. (2010) Childhood adversities and adult psychiatric disorders in the National Comorbidity Survey Replication II: associations with persistence of DSM-IV disorders. *Archives of General Psychiatry* **67**: 124–32. (**345**)

McMahon C, Butwell M, Taylor P. (2003) Changes in the patterns of excessive alcohol consumption in 25 years of high security hospital admissions from England and Wales. *Criminal Behaviour and Mental Health* **13**: 17–30. (**348, 443, 444, 502**)

McMain SF, Links PS, Gnam WH, et al. (2009) A randomized trial of dialectical behaviour therapy versus general psychiatric management for borderline personality disorder. *American Journal of Psychiatry* **166**: 1365–74. (**410**)

McManus J (2005) The scottish legal system. In L Thomson, J McManus (eds) *Mental Health and Scots Law in Practice*. Edinburgh, UK: Green and sons. (**87**)

McManus JJ and Thomson LDG (2005) *Mental Health and Scots Law in Practice*. Edinburgh, UK: Green and Sons. (**146, 651**)

McMillan D, Hastings R, and Coldwell J (2004) Clinical and actuarial prediction of physical violence in a forensic intellectual disability hospital: a longitudinal study. *Journal of Applied Research in Intellectual Disabilities* **17**: 255–66. (**326**)

McMillan TM (1996) Post-traumatic stress disorder following minor and severe closed head injury: 10 single cases. *Brain Injury* **10**(10): 749–58. (**713**)

McMurran M (2001) A framework for the treatment of alcohol-related aggression and violence. *Journal of Substand Use* **6**: 139–44. (**609**)

McMurran M (2002) Motivation to change: selection criteria or treatment need? In M McMurran (ed) *Motivating Offenders to Change: A Guide to Enhancing Engagement in Therapy*. Chichester, UK: Wiley, pp. 3–13. (**579**)

McMurran M (2003) Alcohol and crime. *Criminal Behaviour and Mental Health* **13**: 1–4. (**228, 282**)

McMurran M (2005) Drinking, violence, and prisoners' health. *International Journal of Prisoner Health* **1**: 25–9. (**442**)

McMurran M (2007a) The relationships between alcohol-aggression proneness, general alcohol expectancies, drinking, and alcohol-related violence in adult male prisoners. *Psychology, Crime and Law* **13**: 275–84. (**440**)

McMurran M (2007b) What works in substance misuse treatments for offenders? *Criminal Behaviour and Mental Health* **17**: 225–33. (**576**)

McMurran M (2009) Motivational interviewing with offenders: a systematic review. *Legal and Criminological Psychology* **14**: 83–100. (**446**)

McMurran M and Bellfield H (1993) Sex-related alcohol-expectancies in rapists. *Criminal Behaviour and Mental Health* **3**: 76–84. (**440, 443, 446**)

McMurran M and Cusens B (2005) Alcohol and acquisitive offending. *Addiction Research and Theory* **13**: 439–43. (**443**)

McMurran M and Gilchrist E (2008) Anger control and alcohol use: appropriate interventions for domestic violence? *Psychology, Crime and Law* **14**: 107–16. (**442**)

McMurran M and McGuire J (2005) *Social Problem Solving and Offending*. Chichester, UK: Wiley. (**215**)

McMurran M and Priestley P (2004) Addressing substance-related offending (ASRO): a structured cognitive-behavioural programme for drug users in probation and prison services. In B Reading, M Weegman (eds) *Group Psychotherapy and Addiction*. London: Whurr, pp. 194–210. (**576**)

McMurran M and Theodosi E (2007) Is treatment non-completion associated with increased reconviction over no treatment? *Psychology, Crime and Law* **13**: 333–43. (**408**)

McMurran M, Charlesworth P, Duggan C, and McCarthy L (2001) Controlling angry aggression: a pilot group intervention for personality disordered offenders. *Behavioural and Cognitive Psychotherapy* **29**: 473–85. (**575, 609**)

McMurran M, Huband N, and Overton E (2010) Non-completion of personality disorder treatments: a systematic review of correlates, consequences, and interventions. *Clinical Psychology Review* **30**: 277–87. (**408**)

McMurray L (1970) Emotional stress and driving performance: the effects of divorce. *Behavioural Research in Highway Safety* **1**: 100–14. (**278**)

McNeil DE and Binder RL (1989) Relationship between preadmission threats and later violent behaviour by acute psychiatric inpatients. *Hospital and Community Psychiatry* **40**: 605–8. (**546**)

McNiel DE and Binder RL (1994) The relationship between acute psychiatric symptoms, diagnosis, and short-term risk of violence. *Hospital and Community Psychiatry* 45: 133–7. (**546**)

McNiel DE, Gregory AL, Lam JN, Binder RL, and Sullivan GR (2003) Utility of decision support tools for assessing acute risk of violence. *Journal of Consulting and Clinical Psychology* **71**: 945–53. (**537, 538**)

McSherry B (1994) Premenstrual syndrome and criminal responsibility. *Psychiatry, Psychology and Law* **1**: 139–51. (**501**)

McSweeney T, Turnbull P, and Hough M (2008) *The Treatment and Supervision of Drug-Dependent Offenders: A Review of the Literature Prepared for the UK Drug Policy Commission,* London: UKDPC. http://www.ukdpc.org.uk/publication/treatment-supervision-drug-offenders/ (**460**)

Mead GH (1934) *Mind, Self and Society from the Standpoint of a Social Behaviourist.* Chicago, IL: University of Chicago Press. (**719**)

Meadow R (1977) Munchausen syndrome by proxy: the hinterland of child abuse. *Lancet* **ii**: 343–5. (**226, 434**)

Meadow R (1982) Munchausen syndrome by proxy. *Archives of Disease in Childhood* **57**: 92–8. (**434**)

Meadow R (1989) Munchausen syndrome by proxy. *British Medical Journal* **299**: 248–50. (**434**)

Meadow R (1995) What is, and what is not, 'Munchausen syndrome by proxy'? *Archives of Disease in Childhood* **72**: 534–8. (**226**)

Meadow R (1998) Munchausen syndrome by proxy abuse perpetrated by men. *Archives of Disease in Childhood* **78**: 210–16. (**227**)

Meadow R and Mitchels B (1969) Medical reports. *British Medical Journal* **299**: 616–17. (**676**)

Meaney MJ and Szyf M (2005) Environmental programming of stress responses through DNA methylation: Life at the interface between a dynamic environment and a fixed genome. *Dialogues of Clinical Neuroscience* 7(2): 103–23. (**717**)

Measuring the Costs and Benefits of Crime and Justice (1994) http://www.smartpolicinginitiative.com/sites/all/files/Measuring%20the%20Costs %20and%20Benefits%20of%20Crime%20and%20Justice.pdf (**5**)

Mechanic D (1962) The concept of illness behavior. *Journal of Chronic Diseases* **15**: 189–94. (**423**)

Mechanic D (1986) The concept of illness behaviour: culture, situation and personal predisposition. *Psychological Medicine* **16**: 1–7. (**423**)

Mechanic MD, Resick PA, and Griffin MG (1998) A comparison of normal forgetting, psychopathology, and information-processing models of reported amnesia for recent sexual trauma. *Journal of Consulting and Clinical Psychology* **66**: 948–57. (**296**)

Medlicott RW (1968) Fifty thieves. *New Zealand Medical Journal* **67**: 183–8. (**270**)

Mednick SA, Gabrielli WF, and Hutchings B (1984) Genetic influences in criminal convictions: evidence from an adoption cohort. *Science* **224**: 891–4. (**190**)

Meehan K, Zhang F, David S, et al. (2001) A double-blind, randomized comparison of the efficacy and safety of intramuscular injections of olanzapine, lorazepam, or placebo in treating acutely agitated patients diagnosed with bipolar mania. *Journal of Clinical Psychopharmacology* **21**: 389–97. (**564**)

Meehl P (1954) *Clinical Versus Statistical Prediction. A Theoretical Analysis and a Review of the Evidence.* Minneapolis, MN: University of Minnesota Press. (**531**)

Megargee E (1986) A psychometric study of incarcerated Presidential threateners. *Criminal Justice and Behavior* **13**: 243–60. (**543**)

Mehl M and Cromwell R (1969) The effects of brie sensory deprivation and sensory stimulation on the cognitive functioning of schizophrenics. *Journal of Nervous and Mental Disease* **148**: 586–96. (**595**)

Meichenbaum D (1977) *Cognitive-Behavior Modification.* New York: Plenum. (**446**)

Meichenbaum DH (1975) *Stress Inoculation Training.* New York: Pergamon. (**327, 575**)

Meicr G (1990) Psychopathic disorders: beyond counter-transference. *Current Opinion in Psychiatry* **3**: 766–9. (**513**)

Mellsop G, Varghese F, Joshua S, and Hicks A (1982) The reliability of Axis II of DSM-III. *American Journal of Psychiatry* **139**: 1360–1. (**385**)

Melnick G, De Leon G, Thomas G, Kressel D, and Wexler HK (2001) Treatment process in prison therapeutic communities: motivation, participation and outcome. *American Journal of Drug and Alcohol Abuse* **27**: 633–50. (**467**)

Meloy JR (2000) *Violence Risk and Threat Assessment: A Practical Guide for Mental Health and Criminal Justice Professionals.* San Diego: Specialized Training Services. (**543**)

Meloy JR (2002) *Stalking and violence.* In J Boon, L Sheridan (eds) *Stalking and Psycho-Sexual Obsession.* London: Wiley, pp. 105–24. (**546**)

Meloy JR (2006) Empirical basis and forensic application of affective and predatory violence. *Australian and New Zealand Journal of Psychiatry* **40**: 539–47. (**542**)

Meloy JR and Gothard S (1995) Demographic and clinical comparison of obsessional followers and offenders with mental disorders. *American Journal of Psychiatry* **152**(2): 258–63. (**545, 546**)

Meloy JR, Davis B, and Lovette J (2001) Risk factors for violence among stalkers. *Journal of Threat Assessment* **1**: 3–16. (**379, 545, 546**)

Meloy JR, Hempel AG, Gray BT, et al. (2004) A comparative analysis of North American adolescent and adult mass murderers. *Behavioral Sciences and the Law* **22**: 291–309. (**238, 544**)

Meloy JR, James DV, Farnham FR, et al. (2004) A research review of public figure threats, approaches, attacks, and assassinations in the United States. *Journal of Forensic Sciences* **49**(5): 1086–93. (**238, 544**)

Meloy JR, James DV, Mullen PE, et al. (2011) Factors associated with escalation and problematic approaches toward public figures. *Journal of Forensic Sciences* **56**(S1): 28–35. (**545**)

Meloy JR, Sheridan L, and Hoffman J (2008) *Stalking, Threatening and Attacking Public Figures.* New York: Oxford University Press. (**378**)

Meltzer D, Tom BDM, Brugha T, et al. (2004a) Access to medium secure psychiatric care in England and Wales. 1: a national survey of admission assessments. *Journal of Forensic Psychiatry and Psychology* **15**: 7–31. (**599**)

Meltzer D, Tom BDM, Brugha T, et al. (2004b) Access to medium secure psychiatric care in England and Wales. 3: the clinical needs of assessed patients. *Journal of Forensic Psychiatry and Psychology* **15**: 50–65. (**599**)

Meltzer HY and Fleischhacker WW (2001) Weight gain: a growing problem in schizophrenia management. *Journal of Clinical Psychiatry* **62**: 1–43. (**566**)

Meltzer HY, Perline R, Tricou BJ, Lowy M, and Robertson A (1984) Effect of 5-hydroxytryptophan on serum cortisol levels in major affective disorders. II. Relation to suicide, psychosis, and depressive symptoms. *Archives of General Psychiatry* **41**: 379–87. (**308**)

Melville H (1851) *Moby Dick: The Whale.* London: Richard Bentley. (**xxvi**)

Melville H (1853) *Bartleby, the Scrivner, a Story of Wall Street.* New York: *Putnam's Magazine.* (**xxvi**)

Melville H (1924) Billy Budd, Sailor. Reprinted in *Billy Budd, Sailor and Other Stories.* Harmondsworth, UK: Penguin (1967). (**14**)

Mencken HL (1916) *A Little Book in C Major.* London: John Lane. (**658**)

Mendel G (1866) Versuche über Pflanzen-Hybriden. *Verhandlungen des naturforschenden Vereines in Brünn.* English translation: *Experiments in Plant Hybridization.* http://www.esp.org/foundations/genetics/classical/gm-65.pdf (**187**)

Mendelowitz AJ (2004) The utility of intramuscular ziprasidone in the management of acute psychotic agitation. *Annals of Clinical Psychiatry* **16**: 145–54. (**565**)

Mendelson G (1984) Follow-up studies of personal injury litigants. *International Journal of Law and Psychiatry* **7**: 179–88. (**430**)

Mendelson G (2003) Outcome related compensation: in search of a new paradigm. In PW Halligan, C Bass, David A Oakley (eds) *Malingering and Illness Deception.* Oxford, UK: Oxford University Press, pp. 220–42. (**430**)

Mendez MF (1998) Postictal violence and epilepsy. *Psychosomatics* **39**: 478–80. (**287**)

Mendlowicz MV, Rapaport MH, Mecler K, Golshan S, and Moraes TM (1998) A case-control study on the socio-demographic characteristics of 53 neonaticidal mothers. *International Journal of Law and Psychiatry* **21**: 209–19. (**510**)

Mental Health Commission (2006) *Discussion Paper Forensic Mental Health Services for Adults in Ireland.* Dublin: Mental Health Commission. http://www.mhcirl.ie/documents/publications/Discussion%20Paper%20Forensic%20Mental%20Health%20Services%20for%20Adults%20in%20Ireland%202006.pdf (**657**)

Mental Health Commission/An Garda Síochána (2009) *Report of Joint Working Group on Mental Health Services and the Police.* Dublin: Mental Health Commission. http://www.garda.ie/Documents/User/Report%20of%20Joint%20Working%20Group%20on%20Mental%20Health%20Services%20and%20the%20Police%20%202009%20(Mental%20Health%20Commisson%20An%20Garda%20Siochana).pdf (**656**)

Menzies I (1959) The functioning of social systems as a defence against anxiety: a report on the study of a nursing service in a general hospital. *Human Relations* **13**: 95–121. Republished by Menzies I *Containing Anxiety in Institutions.* London: Free Association Books. (**584**)

Menzies IEP (1960) A case study in functioning of social systems as a defence against anxiety. *Human Relations* **13**: 95–121. (**603**)

Merikangas J (2004) Commentary: alcoholic blackout – does it remove mens rea? *Journal of the American Academy of Psychiatry and the Law* **32**: 375–7. (**439**)

Merikangas KR and Weissman MN (1986) Epidemiology of DSM-III Axis-II personality disorders. In AJ Frances, RE Hales (eds) *American Psychiatric Association Annual Review,* vol 5. Washington, DC: American Psychiatric Press, pp. 258–78 (**390**)

Merikangas KR, Stolar M, Stevens DE, et al. (1998) Familial transmission of substance use disorders. *Archives of General Psychiatry* **55**: 973–9. (**201**)

Merryman JH and Pérez-Perdomo R (2007) *The Civil Law Tradition,* 3rd edn. Stanford, CA: Stanford University Press. (**19**)

Messina N, Farabee D, and Rawson R (2003) Treatment responsivity of cocaine-dependent patients with antisocial personality disorder to cognitive-behavioral and contingency management interventions. *Journal of Consulting and Clinical Psychology* **71**: 320–9. (**410**)

Meth JM (1974) Exotic psychiatric syndromes. In S Arieti (ed) *American Handbook of Psychiatry.* New York: Basic Books. (**428**)

Metzner JL (2009) Monitoring a correctional mental health care system: the role of the mental health expert. *Behavioral Sciences and the Law* **27**: 727–41. (**625**)

Meux C and Taylor P (2006) Setting for the treatment of personality disorder. In C Newrith, C Meux, PJ Taylor (eds) *Personality Disorder and Serious Offending. Hospital Treatment Models,* Ch. 17. London: Hodder Arnold, pp. 205–14. (**401**)

Meyer JH, Wilons AA, Rusjan P, et al. (2008) Serotonin$_{2A}$ receptor binding potential in people with aggressive and violent behaviour. *Journal of Psychiatry and Neuroscience* **33**: 499–508. (**310**)

Meyer JM, Rutter M, Silberg JL, et al. (2000) Familial aggregation for conduct disorder symptomatology: the role of genes, marital discord and family adaptability. *Psychological Medicine* **30**: 759–74. (**196**)

Meyer-Lindenberg A, Buckholtz JW, kolocharra B, et al. (2006) Neural mechanisms of genetic risk for impulsivity and violence in humans. *Proceedings of the National Academy of Science USA* **103**: 6269–74. (**199**)

Mezey G, Evans C, and Hobdell K (2002) Families of homicide victims: psychiatric responses and help-seeking. *Psychology and Psychotherapy: Theory, Research and Practice* **75**: 65–75. (**713**)

Mezey G, Hassell Y, and Bartlett A (2005) Safety of women in mixed-sex and single-sex medium secure units: staff and patient perceptions. *British Journal of Psychiatry* **187**: 579–82. (**519, 599**)

Mezey GC and King MB (1989) The effects of sexual assault on men: a survey of 22 victims. *Psychological Medicine* **19**: 205–9. (**715**)

Miczek KA, Covington HE 3rd, Nikulina EM Jr, and Hammer RP (2004) Aggression and defeat: persistent effects on cocaine self-administration and gene expression in peptidergic and aminergic mesocorticolimbic circuits. *Neuroscience and Biobehavioral Reviews* **27**: 787–802. (**206**)

References

Middleton D, Elliott IA, Mandeville-Norden R, and Beech AR (2006) An investigation into the application of the ward and siegert pathways model of child sexual abuse with Internet offenders. *Psychology, Crime and Law* **12**: 589–603. (**251**)

Midgley M (1984) *Wickedness*. London: Routledge and Kegan Paul. (**6**)

Mikesell RH, Lusterman DD, and McDaniel SH (eds) (1995) *Integrating Family Therapy: Handbook of Family Psychology and Systems Theory*. Washington, DC: American Psychological Association. (**396**)

Miles DR and Carey G (1997) Genetic and environmental architecture of human aggression. *Journal of Personality and Social Psychology* **72**: 207–17. (**188, 195, 196**)

Miles DR, van den Bree MB, and Pickens RW (2002) Sex differences in shared genetic and environmental influences between conduct disorder symptoms and marijuana use in adolescents. *American Journal of Medical Genetics* **114**: 159–68. (**202, 203, 501**)

Milgram S (1963) Behavioural studies of obedience. *Journal of Abnormal and Social Psychology* **67**: 371–8. (**215**)

Milgram S (1974) *Obedience to Authority. An Experimental View*. New York: Harper & Row. (**6, 215**)

Millar JK, Wilson-Annan JC, Anderson S, et al. (2000) Disruption of two novel genes by a translocation co-segregating with schizophrenia. *Human Molecular Genetics* **9**(9): 1415–23. (**209**)

Millar PMcC, Johnstone EC, Lang F, and Thomson LDG (2000) Difference between patients with schizophrenia within and without the high security psychiatric hospital. *Acta Psychiatrica Scandinavica* **102**: 12–18. (**613**)

Miller DT and Gunasegaram S (1990) Temporal order and the perceived mutability of events: implications for blame assignment. *Journal of Personality and Social Psychology* **59**: 1111–18. (**696**)

Miller EK and Cohen JD (2001) An integrative theory of prefrontal cortex function. *Annual Reviews in Neuroscience* **24**: 167–202. (**298**)

Miller FJW, Court SD, Walton WS, and Knox EG (1960) *Growing up in Newcastle upon Tyne*. Oxford, UK: Oxford University Press. (**288**)

Miller H (1961) Accident neurosis. *British Medical Journal* **1**: 919–22; 992–8. (**429**)

Miller H (1966) Mental after-effects of head injury. *Proceedings of Royal Society of Medicine* **59**: 257–61. (**429**)

Miller H and Cartlidge N (1972) Simulation and malingering after injuries to the brain and spinal cord. *Lancet* **i**: 580–5. (**431**)

Miller RD (2003a) Criminal competence. In R Rosner (ed) *Principles and Practice of Forensic Psychiatry*, 2nd edn. London: Arnold, pp. 186–232. (**120, 124**)

Miller RD (2003b) Criminal responsibility. In R Rosner (ed) *Principles and Practice of Forensic Psychiatry*, 2nd edn. London: Arnold, pp. 213–32. (**121**)

Miller S and Davenport N (1996) Increasing staff knowledge of and improving attitudes towards patients with borderline personality disorder. *Psychiatric Services* **47**: 533–5. (**400**)

Miller S, Malone PS, and Dodge KA (2010) Developmental trajectories of boys' and girls' delinquency: Sex differences and links to later adolescent outcomes. *Journal of Abnormal Child Psychology* **38**: 1021–32. (**501, 511**)

Miller S, Sees C, and Brown J (2006) Key aspects of psychological change in residents of a prison therapeutic community: a focus group approach. *The Howard Journal* **45**: 116–28. (**571**)

Miller WR (1985) Motivational interviewing: a review with special emphasis on alcoholism. *Psychological Bulletin* **98**: 84–107. (**446**)

Miller WR (1992) The effectiveness of treatment for substance abuse. *Journal of Substance Abuse Treatment* **9**: 93–102. (**446**)

Miller WR (1995) *Motivational Enhancement Therapy with Drug Abusers*. www.motivationalinterview.org/clinical/METDrugAbuse.PDF. (**261**)

Miller WR and Rollnick S (2002) *Motivational Interviewing: Preparing People for Change*, 2nd edn. New York: Guilford. (**446**)

Miller WR and Sanchez VC (1993) Motivating young adults for treatment and lifestyle change. In G Howard (ed) *Issues in Alcohol Use and Misuse in Young Adults*. Notre Dame, Paris: University of Notre Dame Press. (**459**)

Millon T (1996) *Disorders of Personality: DSM IV and Beyond*, 2nd edn. New York: Wiley. (**384**)

Millon T (1999) *Personality Guided Therapy*. Chichester, UK: Wiley. (**400**)

Millon T and Grossman S (2007) *Overcoming Resistant Personality Disorders: A Personalized Psychotherapy Approach*. New York: Wiley. (**388**)

Millon T, Davies R, ad Millon C (2009) *Millon Clinical Multiaxial Inventory Manual*, 3rd edn. MCMI-III™ Pearson Assessments: San Antonio, TX. http://psychcorp.pearsonassessments.com/HAIWEB/Cultures/en-us/Productdetail.htm?Pid=PAg505 (**388**)

Mills JF and Kroner DG (2003) Anger as a predictor of institutional misconduct and recidivism in a sample of violent offenders. *Journal of Interpersonal Violence* **18**(3): 282–94. (**215**)

Milton J (2000) A postal survey of the assessment procedure for personality disorder in forensic settings. *British Journal of Psychiatry* **24**: 254–57. (**389**)

Milton J, Amin S, Singh SP, et al. (2001) Aggressive incidents in first-episode psychosis. *British Journal of Psychiatry* **178**: 433–40. (**344**)

Milton J, McCartney M, Duggan C, et al. (2005) Beauty in the eye of the beholder? How high security hospital psychopathically-disordered patients rate their own interpersonal behaviour. *Journal of Forensic Psychiatry and Psychology* **16**: 552–65. (**389**)

Ministry of Education (1955) *Report of the Committee on Maladjusted Children* (Underwood Report). London: HMSO. (**482**)

Ministry of Justice (2006) *Continuity of Healthcare for Prisoners*. Prison Order Number 3050. London: Ministry of Justice. http://www.justice.gov.uk/downloads/guidance/prison-probation-and-rehabilitation/psipso/PSO_3050_continuity_of_healthcare_for_prisoners.doc (**625**)

Ministry of Justice (2008) *Mental Capacity Act 2005: Deprivation of Liberty Safeguards – Code of Practice*. http://webarchive.nationalarchives.gov.uk/20130107105354/http:/www.dh.gov.uk/en/Publicationsandstatistics/Publications/PublicationsPolicyAndGuidance/DH_085476 (**81, 82**)

Ministry of Justice (2009) *Population in Custody monthly tables June 2009 England and Wales*. http://www.justice.gov.uk/downloads/statistics/mojstats/population-custody/population-in-custody-06-2009.pdf (**626, 637**)

Ministry of Justice (2010) *Sentencing Statistics, England and Wales 2009*. London: Ministry of Justice. https://www.gov.uk/government/uploads/system/uploads/attachment_data/file/162991/sentencing-stats2009.pdf.pdf www.justice.gov.uk/publications/ (**268, 640**)

Ministry of Justice (2010a) *Implementation of the victim liaison service specification*. www.justice.gov.uk/downloads/guidance/prison-probation-and-rehabilitation/probation-instructions/pi_03_2010_implementation_of_the_victim_liaison_service_specification.doc (**709**)

Ministry of Justice (2010b) *Statistics on Women and the Criminal Justice System*. http://www.justice.gov.uk/downloads/statistics/mojstats/statistics-women-cjs-2010.pdf (**498, 500, 502, 503, 511, 516**)

Ministry of Justice (2011) *Criminal Statistics, England and Wales 2009*. UK Statistics Authority. (**606**)

Ministry of Justice (2012) *Report on the Implementation of Law Commission Proposals*. HC 1900. London: TSO. (**34**)

Ministry of Justice (2012a) *MAPPA Guidance 2009*. London: Ministry of Justice. www.justice.gov.uk. http://www.justice.gov.uk/downloads/offenders/mappa/mappa-guidance-2012-part1.pdf (**644**)

Ministry of Justice (Sweden) (2010) *Inquiry on Evaluation of the Ban on Purchase of Sexual Services*. Stockholm, Sweden: Ministry of Justice. English summary SOU 2010:49. http://www.sweden.gov.se/content/1/c6/14/92/31/96b1e019.pdf (**503**)

Ministry of Justice, Home Office (2007) *Murder, Manslaughter and Infanticide: Proposals for Reform of the Law*. London: Ministry of Justice. (**31**)

Minozzi S, Amato L, Vecchi S, et al. (*2011*) Oral naltrexone maintenance treatment for opioid dependence. *Cochrane Database of Systematic Reviews* 2011, Issue 4. Art. No. CD001333. DOI: 10.1002/14651858.CD001333.pub4. *The Cochrane Library*, 1, Art. No. CD001333. DOI: 10.1002/14651858.CD001333.pub2. http://onlinelibrary.wiley.com/doi/10.1002/14651858.CD001333.pub4/pdf (**463**)

Mirrlees-Black C (2001) *Confidence in the Criminal Justice System: Findings from the 2000 British Crime Survey*. Home Office Research Findings No. 137. London: Home Office. (**701, 705**)

Mitchell RE and Hodson CA (1983) Coping with domestic violence: social support and psychological health among battered women. *American Journal of Community Psychology* **11**: 629–54. (**724**)

Mitchels B and Meadow R (1989) About courts. *BMJ* **299**: 671–4. (**476**)

Mitsis EM, Halperin JM, and Newcorn JH (2000) Serotonin and aggression in children. *Current Psychiatry Reports* **2**: 95–101. (**198**)

Modai I, Apter A, Meltzer M, et al. (1989) Serotonin uptake by platelets of suicidal and aggressive adolescent psychiatric inpatients. *Neuropsychobiology* **21**: 9–13. (**308**)

Modan B, Nissekorn I, and Lewkowski (1970) Comparative epidemiological aspects of suicide and attempted suicide in Israel. *American Journal of Epidemiology* **91**: 383–91. (**276**)

Modestin J and Ammann R (1996) Mental disorder and criminality: Male schizophrenia. *Schizophrenia Bulletin* **22**: 69–82. (**280**)

Modestin J and Rigoni H (2000) Criminality in female inpatients with substance use disorders. *European Addiction Research* **6**(3): 148–53. (**514**)

Modestin J and Wuermle O (2005) Criminality in men with major mental disorder with and without comorbid substance abuse. *Psychiatry and Clinical Neurosciences* **59**: 25–9. (**347**)

Modestin J, Hug A, and Ammann R (1997) Criminal behavior in males with affective disorders. *Journal of Affective Disorders* **42**: 29–38. (**278, 281**)

Moffatt GK (2002) *A Violent Heart: Understanding Aggressive Individuals*. London: Praeger. (**278**)

Moffitt TE (1984) *Genetic influences of parental psychiatric illnesses on violent and recidivistic criminal behavior*. PhD thesis, Los Angeles, CA: University of Southern California. (**189**)

Moffitt TE (1993) Adolescence-limited and life-course-persistent antisocial-behavior – a developmental taxonomy. *Psychological Review* **100**: 674–701. (**196, 342**)

Moffitt TE (1993a) The neuropsychology of conduct disorder. *Development and Psychopathology* **5**: 135–51. (**215, 268, 501**)

Moffitt TE (2003) Life-course persistent and adolescence-limited antisocial behavior: a 10-year research review and a research agenda. In: *Anonymous*. New York: Guilford, pp. 49–75. (**173**)

Moffitt TE (2005a) Genetic and environmental influences on antisocial behaviors: Evidence from behavioral-genetic research. In: *Anonymous*. New York: Academic Press. (**188, 189, 190, 192, 196**)

Moffitt TE (2005b) The new look of behavioral genetics in developmental psychopathology: gene–environment interplay in antisocial behaviors. *Psychological Bulletin* **131**: 533–54. (**190, 192**)

Moffitt TE and Silva PA (1988) Neuropsychological deficit and self-reported delinquency in an unselected birth cohort. *Journal of the American Academy of Child and Adolescent Psychiatry* **27**: 233–40. (**174**)

Moffitt TE, Brammer GL, Caspi A, et al. (1998) Whole blood-serotonin relates to violence in an epidemiological study. *Biological Psychiatry* **43**: 446–57. (**307**)

Moffitt TE, Caspi A, and Rutter M (2005) Strategy for investigating interactions between measured genes and measured environments. *Archives of General Psychiatry* **62**: 473–81. (**191, 192**)

Moffitt TE, Caspi A, Rutter M, and Silva PA (2001) *Sex Differences in Antisocial Behaviour*. Cambridge, UK: Cambridge University Press. (**171, 173, 218, 337, 342, 499, 500, 501, 502, 505, 511**)

Moghaddam B (2003) Bringing order to the glutamate chaos in schizophrenia. *Neuron* **40**: 881–4. (**207**)

Mohan D, Murray K, Taylor R, and Steed P (1997) Developments in the use of regional secure unit beds over a 12-year period. *Journal of Forensic Psychiatry* **8**: 321–35. (**600**)

Mohandie K, Meloy JR, McGowan M, and Williams J (2006) The RECON typology of stalking: reliability and validity based upon a large sample of North American stalkers. *Journal of Forensic Sciences* **51**(1): 147–55. (**375, 379, 380, 543**)

References

Mohr JW, Turner RE, and Jerry MB (1964) *Pedophilia and Exhibitionism*. Toronto: University of Toronto Press. (**247**)

Mojtabai R (2006) Psychotic-like experiences and interpersonal violence in the general population. *Social Psychiatry and Psychiatric Epidemiology* **41**: 183–90. (**339, 340, 349**)

Mollica RF, Donelan K, Tor S, et al. (1993) The effect of trauma and confinement on functional health and mental health status of cambodians living in Thailand-Cambodia border camps. *Journal of the American Medical Association* **270**: 581–6. (**716**)

Molnar G, Keitner L, and Harwood BT (1984) A comparison of partner and solo arsonists. *Journal of Forensic Science*, **29**: 574–83 (**273, 274**)

Monahan J and Steadman H (1983) Crime and mental disorder: an epidemiological approach. In N Morris, M Tonry (eds) *Crime and Justice: An Annual Review of Research*, Vol 3. Chicago, IL: Chicago University Press, pp. 145–89. (**335**)

Monahan J, Heilbrun K, Silver E, et al. (2002) Communicating violence risk: frequency formats, vivid outcomes, and forensic settings. *International Journal of Forensic Mental Health* **1**: 121–6. (**548**)

Monahan J, Steadman H, Appelbaum P, et al. (2005a) *The Classification of Violence Risk*. Lutz, FL: Psychological Assessment Resources. (**539**)

Monahan J, Steadman H, Robbins P, et al. (2005b) An actuarial model of violence risk assessment for persons with mental disorders. *Psychiatric Services* **56**: 810–15. (**540, 542**)

Monahan J, Steadman HJ, Appelbaum PS, et al. (2006) The classification of violence risk. *Behavioral Sciences and the Law* **24**: 721–30. (**539**)

Monahan J, Steadman HJ, Silver E, et al. (2001) *Rethinking Risk Assessment: The Macarthur Study of Mental Disorder and Violence*. New York: Oxford University Press. (**338, 349, 353, 354, 537, 540**)

Money J and Lamacz M (1989) *Vandalized Lovemaps: Paraphilic Outcome of Seven Cases in Pediatric Sexology*. Amherst, NY: Prometheus Books. (**246**)

Money J and Werlwas J (1976) *Folie à deux* in the parents of psychosocial dwarfs: two cases. *Bulletin of the American Academy of Psychiatry and the Law* **4**: 351–62. (**226**)

Montandon C and Harding TW (1984) The reliability of dangerousness assessments: a decision-making exercise. *British Journal of Psychiatry* **144**: 149–55. (**113**)

Montgomery SA, Roy D, and Montgomery DB (1983) The prevention of recurrent suicidal acts. *British Journal of Clinical Pharmacology* **15**: 183–5. (**405**)

Moore E (2000) A descriptive analysis of incidents of absconding and escape from the English high-security hospitals, 1989–1994. *Journal of Forensic Psychiatry* **11**: 344–58. (**587, 595**)

Moore E (2012) Patients with personality disorder: the impact on staff and the need for supervision. *Advances in Psychiatric Treatment* **18**: 14–55. (**400, 661**)

Moore E and Gudjonsson GH (2002) Blame attribution in relation to index offence on admission to secure hospital services. *Psychology, Crime and Law* **8**: 131–43. (**391**)

Moore E and Hammond S (2000) When statistical models fail: problems in the prediction of escape and absconding from high-security hospitals. *Journal of Forensic Psychiatry* **11**: 359–71. (**587, 595**)

Moore E and Kuipers E (1999) The measurement of expressed emotion in relationships between staff and service users: the use of short speech samples. *British Journal of Clinical Psychology* **38**: 345–56. (**355**)

Moore E and Kuipers L (1992) Behavioural correlates of expressed emotion in staff-patient interactions. *Social Psychiatry and Psychiatric Epidemiology* **27**: 298–303. (**356**)

Moore E, Ball RA, and Kuipers L (1992) Expressed emotion in staff working with the long-term adult mentally ill. *British Journal of Psychiatry* **161**: 802–8. (**356, 357**)

Moore E, Kuipers L, and Ball RA (1992) Staff-patient relationships in the care of the long term adult mentally ill: a content analysis of expressed emotion interviews. *Social Psychiatry and Psychiatric Epidemiology* **27**: 28–34. (**557**)

Moore E, Yates M, Mallindine C, et al. (2002) Expressed emotion in relationships between staff and patients in forensic services: changes in relationship status at 12 month follow-up. *Legal and Criminological Psychology* **7**: 203–18. (**357, 548, 557, 596**)

Moore M (1984) *Law and Psychiatry*. Cambridge, UK: Cambridge University Press. (**150**)

Moore THM, Zammit S, Lingford-Hughes A, et al. (2007) Cannabis use and risks of psychotic or affective mental health outcomes: a systematic review. *The Lancet* **370**: 319–28. (**208**)

Mora G (1967) History of psychiatry. In AM Freedman, HI Kaplan (eds) *Comprehensive Textbook of Psychiatry*. Baltimore, MD: Williams and Wilkins, pp. 2–34. (**122**)

Moran E (1968) Compulsive Gambler. *British Medical Journal* **2**(5599): 239–40. (**468**)

Moran E (1970) Pathological gambling. *British Journal of Hospital Medicine* **3**: 59–70. (**469, 470**)

Moran P (1999) *Antisocial Personality Disorder: An Epidemiological Perspective*. London: Gaskell. (**390, 402, 512**)

Moran P, Walsh E, Tyrer P, et al. (2003) Impact of comorbid personality disorder on violence in psychosis: report from the UK700 study. *British Journal of Psychiatry* **182**: 129–34. (**346, 397**)

Morash M and Rucker L (1989) An exploratory study of the connection of mother's age at childbearing to her children's delinquency in four data sets. *Crime and Delinquency* **35**: 45–93. (**175**)

Morey L, Waugh M, and Blashfield R (1985) MMPI Scales for DSM-III personality disorders: their derivation and correlates. *Journal of Personality Assessment* **49**: 245–52. (**388**)

Morey LC (1991) *Personality Assessment Inventory - Professional Manual*. Lutz, FL: Psychological Assessment Resources. (**388**)

Morgan C and Fisher H (2007) Environmental factors in schizophrenia: childhood trauma – a critical review. *Schizophrenia Bulletin* **33**: 3–10. (**344**)

Morgan CA, Southwick SM, Hazlett MG, and Steffian G (2007) Symptoms of dissociation in healthy military populations. In E Vermetten, MJ Dorahy, D Spiegel (eds) *Traumatic Dissociation: Neurobiology and Treatment*. Washington, DC: American Psychiatric Press. (**572**)

Morgan RD and Flora DB (2002) Group psychotherapy with incarcerated offenders: a research synthesis. *Group Dynamics: Theory, Research and Practice* **6**: 203–18. (**723**)

Morris CH (2007) Civil law: structure and procedures. In AR Felthous, H Sass (eds) *International Handbook of Psychopathic Disorders and the Law*, Vol. II, *Laws and Policies*. Chichester, UK: Wiley, pp. 9–19. (**117**)

Morris M (2004) *Dangerous and Severe – Process, Programme and Person. Grendon's Work*. London: Jessica Kingsley. (**412**)

Morrison AP, Frame L, and Larkin W (2003) Relationships between trauma and psychosis: a review and integration. *British Journal of Clinical Psychology* **42**: 331–53. (**51**)

Morrison D and Gilbert P (2001) Social rank, shame and anger in primary and secondary psychopaths. *Journal of Forensic Psychiatry* **12**: 330–56. (**215**)

Morrissey C, Hogue T, Mooney P, et al. (2005) Applicability, reliability and validity of the Psychopathy Checklist – revised in offenders with intellectual disabilities: some initial findings. *International Journal of Forensic Mental Health* **4**: 207–20. (**331**)

Morrissey C, Hogue T, Mooney P, et al. (2007a) Predictive validity of the PCL-R in offenders with intellectual disabilities in a high secure setting: institutional aggression. *Journal of Forensic Psychology and Psychiatry* **18**: 1–15. (**331**)

Morrissey C, Mooney P, Hogue T, Lindsay WR, and Taylor JL (2007b) Predictive validity of psychopathy in offenders with intellectual disabilities in a high security hospital: treatment progress. *Journal of Intellectual and Developmental Disabilities* **32**: 125–33. (**331**)

Morrissey JP, Fagan JA, and Cocozza JJ (2009) New models of collaboration between criminal justice and mental health systems. *American Journal of Psychiatry* **166**: 1211–14. (**588, 619**)

Morrow GR (1980) How readable are subject consent forms? *Journal of the American Medical Association* **244**: 56–8. (**669**)

Moss HB, Yao JK, and Panzak GL (1990) Serotonergic responsivity and behavioral dimensions in antisocial personality disorder with substance abuse. *Biological Psychiatry* **28**: 325–38. (**309**)

Mössler K, Chen X, Heldal TO, and Gold C (2011) Music therapy for people with schizophrenia and schizophrenia-like disorders. *Cochrane Database of Systematic Reviews* 2011, Issue 12. Art. No.: CD004025. DOI: 10.1002/14651858.CD004025.pub3. http://onlinelibrary.wiley.com/o/cochrane/clsysrev/articles/CD004025/frame.html (**558**)

Mossman D (1994) Assessing predictions of violence: being accurate about accuracy. *Journal of Consulting and Clinical Psychology* **62**: 783–99. (**532**)

Mossman D (1995) Dangerous decisions: an essay on the mathematics of clinical violence prediction and involuntary hospitalization. *University of Chicago Law School Roundtable* **2**: 95–138. (**532**)

Mossman D (2009) The imperfection of protection through detection and intervention. Lessons from three decades of research on the psychiatric assessment of violence risk. *Journal of Legal Medicine* **30**: 109–40. (**532, 558, 550**)

Mossman D and Selike T (2007) Avoiding errors about 'margins of error'. *British Journal of Psychiatry* **191**: 561–2. (**533**)

Mostert MP (2001) Facilitated communication since 1995: a review of published studies. *Journal of Autism and Developmental Disorders* **31**: 287–313. (**333**)

Motz A (2001) *The Psychology of Female Violence. Crimes against the Body*. Hove, UK: Brunner-Routledge. (**499, 554**)

Mount F (1984) The flourishing art of lying. *The Times*, 30 April. (**432**)

Mountenay J (1998) *Children of Drug Using Parents* (Highlight no. 163). London: National Children's Bureau. (**465**)

Mowatt RR (1966) *Morbid Jealousy and Murder*. London: Tavistock. (**342, 353**)

Moyer KE (1981) Biological substrates of aggression and implications for control. In PF Brain, D Benton (eds) *The Biology of Aggression*. Alphen aan der Rija: Sijthoff and Noordhoff. (**212**)

Mrazek PJ and Haggerty RJ (eds) (1994) *Reducing Risks for Mental Disorders: Frontiers for Preventive Intervention Research*. Washington, DC: Institute of Medicine, National Academy Press. (**341**)

Mueser KT, Drake RE, and Wallach MA (1998) Dual diagnosis: a review of etiological theories. *Addictive Behaviors* **23**: 717–34. (**347**)

Mueser KT, Goodman LB, Trumbetta SL, et al. (1998) Trauma and posttraumatic stress disorder in severe mental illness. *Journal of Consulting and Clinical Psychology* **66**: 493–9. (**712**)

Mueser KT, Noordsy DL, Drake RE, and Fox L (2003) Involuntary and coercive treatments. In KT Mueser, DL Noordsy, RE Drake, L Fox (eds) *Integrated Treatment for Dual Disorders*, Ch. 17. New York: Guilford, pp. 249–66. (**448**)

Mueser KT, Sengupta A, Schooler NR, et al. (2001) Family treatment and medication dosage reduction in schizophrenia: effects on patient social functioning, family attitudes and burden. *Journal of Consulting and Clinical Psychology* **69**: 3–12. (**363**)

Mugavin M (2008) Maternal filicide theoretical framework. *Journal of Forensic Nursing* **4**: 68–79. (**508**)

Muijen M (1997) Inquiries: who needs them? *Psychiatric Bulletin* **21**: 132–3. (**75, 76**)

Muir-Cochrane E and Mosel KA (2008) Absconding: a review of the literature 1996–2008. *International Journal of Mental Health Nursing* **17**: 370–8. (**595**)

Mulder RT (2002) Personality pathology and treatment outcome in major depression: A review. *American Journal of Psychiatry* **159**: 359–371. (**398**)

Mulder RT and Joyce PR (1997) Temperament and the structure of personality disorder symptoms. *Psychological Medicine* **27**: 1315– 25. (**386**)

Mulder RT, Beautrais AL, Joyce PR, and Fergusson DM (1998) Relationship between dissociation, childhood sexual abuse, childhood physical abuse, and mental illness in a general population sample. *American Journal of Psychiatry* **155**: 806–11. (**723**)

Mullen P, Whyte S, and McIvor R (2010) *On Stalking.* Psychiatrists' Support Service. Information Guide for Psychiatrists 11. London: Royal College of Psychiatrists. http://www.rcpsych.ac.uk/pdf/11%20on%20stalkiing_final%20proof%20(2).pdf (**378**).

Mullen PE (1991) Jealousy: the pathology of passion. *British Journal of Psychiatry* **158**: 593–601. (**370**)

Mullen PE (1995) The clinical management of jealousy. *Directions in Psychiatry* **15**: Lesson 20. (**373**)

Mullen PE (1997) Assessing risk of interpersonal violence in the mentally ill. *Advances in Psychiatric Treatment* **3**: 166–73. (**547**)

Mullen PE (1999) Dangerous people with severe personality disorder. British proposals for managing them are glaringly wrong – and unethical. *British Medical Journal* **319**: 1146–7. (**68**)

Mullen PE (2002) Moral principles don't signify. *Philosophy, Psychiatry and Psychology* **9**: 19–21. (**7, 281**)

Mullen PE (2004) The autogenic (self-generated) massacre. *Behavioral Sciences and the Law* **22**: 311–23. (**238**)

Mullen PE (2006) Schizophrenia and violence: from correlations to preventive strategies. *Advances in Psychiatric Treatment* **12**: 239–48. (**547**)

Mullen PE (2008) The crimes and pathologies of passion: love, jealousy and the pursuit of justice. In K Soothill, M Dolan, P Rogers (eds) *Handbook on Forensic Mental Health.* London: Willan. (**367, 368**)

Mullen PE and Lester G (2006) Vexatious litigants and unusually persistent complainers and petitioners: from querulous paranoia to querulous behaviour. *Behavioral Sciences and the Law* **24**: 333–49. (**381**)

Mullen PE and Maack LH (1985) Jealousy, pathological jealousy, and aggression. In DP Farrington, J Gunn (eds) *Aggression and Dangerousness.* Chichester, UK: Wiley, pp. 103–26. (**349, 372**)

Mullen PE and Martin JL (1994) Jealousy: a community study. *British Journal of Psychiatry* **164**: 35–43. (**369, 370, 371**)

Mullen PE and Ogloff JRP (2009) Assessing and managing the risks of violence towards others. In M Gelder, J Lopez-Ibor, N Andreasen, J Geddes (eds) *New Oxford Textbook of Psychiatry,* 2nd edn. Oxford, UK: Oxford University Press, pp. 1991–2002. (**368**)

Mullen PE, Burgess P, Wallace C, et al. (2000) Community care and criminal offending in schizophrenia. *Lancet* **355**: 614–17.

Mullen PE, James DV, Meloy JR, et al. (2009) The fixated and the pursuit of public figures. *Journal of Forensic Psychiatry and Psychology* **20**: 33–47. (**235, 377, 545**)

Mullen PE, MacKenzie R, Ogloff JRP, et al. (2006) Assessing and managing the risks in the stalking situation. *Journal of the American Academy of Psychiatry and the Law* **34**: 439–50. (**379**)

Mullen PE, Pathé M, and Purcell R (2000) *Stalkers and Their Victims.* Cambridge, UK: Cambridge University Press. (**546, 547**)

Mullen PE, Pathé M, and Purcell R (2008) *Stalkers and Their Victims,* 2nd edn. Cambridge, UK: Cambridge University Press. (**367, 373, 375, 376, 380**)

Mullen PE, Pathé M, Purcell R, and Stuart GW (1999): Study of stalkers. *American Journal of Psychiatry,* **156**(8), 1244-9. (**375, 545, 546**)

Mullen PE, Romans-Clarkson SE, Walton VA, and Herbison GP (1988) Impact of sexual and physical abuse on women's mental health. *Lancet* **i**: 841–5. (**250**)

Müller JL, Gänssbauer S, Sommer M, et al. (2008) Grey matter changes in right superior temporal gyrus in criminal psychopaths. Evidence from voxel-based morphometry. *Psychiatry Research* **163**(3): 213–22. (**300, 301**)

Müller JL, Sommer M, Wagner V, et al. (2003) Abnormalities in emotion processing within cortical and subcortical regions in criminal psychopaths: evidence from a functional magnetic resonance imaging study using pictures with emotional content. *Biological Psychiatry* **54**: 152–62. (**304, 306**)

Muller-Oerlinghausen B, Retzon A, Henn FA, Giedke H, and Walden J (2000) Valproate as an adjunct to neuroleptic medication for the treatment of acute episodes of mania: a prospective, randomised, double-blind, placebo-controlled, multicentre study. European Valproate Mania Study Group. *Journal of Clinical Psychopharmacology* **20**: 195–203. (**560**)

Muncie J (2009) *Youth Crime,* 3rd edn. London: Sage. (**474, 477, 478, 479**)

Muncie J and Goldson B (2006) England and Wales: the new correctionalism. In J Muncie, B Goldson (eds) *Comparative Youth Justice.* London: Sage. (**479**)

Munkner R, Haastrup S, Joergensen T, and Kramp P (2003a) The temporal relationship between schizophrenia and crime. *Social Psychiatry and Psychiatric Epidemiology* **38**: 347–53. (**343**)

Munkner R, Haastrup S, Jørgensen T, Andreasen AH, and Kramp P (2003b) Taking cognizance of mental illness in schizophrenics and its association with crime and substance-related diagnoses. *Acta Psychiatrica Scandinavica* **107**: 111–17. (**343**)

Munro E (2004a) Improving safety in medicine: a systems approach. *British Journal of Psychiatry* **185**: 3–4. (**74**)

Munro E (2004b) Mental health tragedies: investigating beyond human error. *Journal of Forensic Psychiatry and Psychology* **15**: 475–93. (**74**)

Munro E and Rumgay J (2000) Role of risk assessment in reducing homicides by people with mental illness. *British Journal of Psychiatry* **176**: 116–20. (**549, 695**)

Muralidharan S and Fenton M Containment strategies for people with serious mental illness. *Cochrane Database of Systematic Reviews* 2006.Issue 3, Art No.: CD002084. DOI: 10.1002/14651858.CD002084.pub2. http://mrw.interscience.wiley.com/cochrane/clsysrev/articles/CD002084/frame.html (**594**)

Murayama M, Matsushita S, Muramatsu T, and Higuchi S (1998) Clinical characteristics and disease course of alcoholics with inactive aldehyde dehydrogenase-2. *Alcoholism: Clinical and Experimental Research* **22**: 524–7. (**205**)

Murphy GH and Clare ICH (1996) Analysis of motivation in people with mild learning disabilities (mental handicap) who set fires. *Psychology, Crime and Law* **2**: 153–64. (**329, 330**)

Murphy GH and Mason J (1999) People with developmental disabilities who offend. In N Bouras (ed) *Psychiatric and Behaviour Disorders in Developmental Disabilities and Mental Retardation*. Cambridge, UK: Cambridge University Press, pp. 226–45. (**325**)

Murphy GH, Estien D, and Clare ICH (1996) Services for people with mild intellectual disabilities and challenging behaviour: service user views. *Journal of Applied Research in Intellectual Disabilities* **9**: 256–83. (**326**)

Murphy KC, Jones LA, and Owen MJ (1999) High rates of schizophrenia in adults with velo-cardio-facial syndrome. *Archives of General Psychiatry* **56**: 940–5. (**195, 209, 210**)

Murphy R and Roe S (2008) *Drug misuse declared: Findings from the 2006/07 British Crime Survey – England and Wales*. London: Home Office. http://webarchive.nationalarchives.gov.uk/20110220105210/rds.homeoffice.gov.uk/rds/pdfs07/hosb1807.pdf (**451**)

Murphy SA, Braun T, Tillery L, et al. (1999) PTSD among bereaved parents following the violent deaths of their 12- to 28-year-old children: a longitudinal prospective analysis. *Journal of Traumatic Stress* **12**: 273–91. (**713**)

Murray R, Jones PB, Susser E, van Os J, and Cannon M (eds) (2003) *The Epidemiology of Schizophrenia*. Cambridge, UK: Cambridge University Press. (**207**)

Murray-Parkes C (1993) Psychiatric problems following bereavement by homicide. *British Journal of Psychiatry* **162**: 49–54. (**713**)

Musto DF (1991) A historical perspective. In S Bloch, P Chodoff (eds) *Psychiatric Ethics*, 2nd edn. Oxford, UK: Oxford University Press. (**658**)

Myers DG and Lamm (1976) The group polarization phenomenon. *Psychological Bulletin* **83**: 602–27. (**548**)

Myers W and Scott K (1998) Psychotic and conduct disorder symptoms in juvenile murderers. *Journal of Homicide Studies* **2**: 160–75. (**494**)

Myers WC, Burket RC, and Harris HE (1995) Adolescent psychopathy in relation to delinquent behaviours, conduct disorder, and personality disorder. *Journal of Forensic Sciences* **40**: 436–40. (**494**)

Myin-Germys I, Nicolson NA, and Deledpaul PAEG (2001) The context of delusional experience in the daily life of patients with schizophrenia. *Psychological Medicine* **31**: 489–98. (**349**)

Myslobodsky M (1997) *The Mythomanias: The Nature of Deception and Self-Deception*. Mahway, NJ: L. Erlbaum Associates. (**421, 434**)

N'gbala A and Branscombe NR (1995) Mental simulation and causal attribution: when simulating an event does not affect fault assignment. *Journal of Experimental Social Psychology* **31**: 139–62. (**696**)

Nace EP, Birkmayer F, Sullivan MA, et al. (2007) Socially sanctioned coercion mechanisms for addiction treatment. *American Journal on Addictions* **16**(1): 15–23. (**467**)

Nadkarni R, Chipchase B, and Fraser K (2000) Partnership with probation hostels: a step forward in community forensic psychiatry. *Psychiatric Bulletin* **24**: 222–4. (**457, 608**)

Nagaraj R, Singhi P, and Malhi P (2006) Risperidone in children with autism: randomized, placebo-controlled, double-blind study. *Journal of Child Neurology* **21**: 450–5. (**564**)

Nagin DS and Tremblay RE (2001) Parental and early childhood predictors of persistent physical aggression in boys from Kindergarten to High School. *Archives of General Psychiatry* **58**: 389–94. (**216**)

Nagin DS, Pogarsky G, and Farrington DP (1997) Adolescent mothers and the criminal behaviour of their children. *Law and Society Review* **31**: 137–62. (**175**)

Nair MS and Weinstock R (2007) Psychopathy, diminished capacity and responsibility. In AR Felthous, H Sass (eds) *International Handbook on Psychopathic Disorders and the Law*, Vol. 2, *Laws and Policies*. Chichester, UK: Wiley, pp. 275–301. (**121**)

Nakano S, Asada T, Yamashita F, et al. (2006) Relationship between antisocial behavior and regional cerebral blood flow in frontotemporal dementia. *Neuroimage* **32**: 301–6. (**303**)

Nance WE and Corey LA (1976) Genetic models for the analysis of data from the families of identical twins. *Genetics* **83**: 811–26. (**191**)

Napley D (1983) *The Technique of Persuasion*, 3rd edn. London: Sweet and Maxwell, p. 827. (**148**)

Nathan P and Ward T (2002) Female sex offenders: clinical and demographic features. *Journal of Sexual Aggression* **8**: 5–21. (**252**)

National Association of Drug Court Professionals (NADCP) (1997) *Defining Drug Courts: The Key Components*. Washington, DC: Office of Justice Programs, US Department of Justice. (**640**)

National Audit Office (2003) *A Safer Place to Work: Protecting NHS Hospital and Ambulance Staff from Violence and Aggression*. London: The Stationery Office. http://www.nao.org.uk/report/a-safer-place-to-work-protecting-nhs-hospital-and-ambulance-staff-from-violence-and-aggression/ (**556**)

National Audit Office (2006) *Review of the Experiences of United Kingdom Nationals Affected by the Indian Ocean Tsunami*. London: National Audit Office. http://www.nao.org.uk/wp-content/uploads/2006/11/Review_Tsunami_Experiences.pdf (**709**)

National Audit Office (2010) *Managing Offenders on Short Custodial Sentences*. *http://*www.nao.org.uk/publications/0910/short_custodial_sentences.aspx (**5, 640**)

National Collaborating Centre for Mental Health (NCCMH) (2009a) *Post-Traumatic Stress Disorder: The Management of PTSD in Adults and Children in Primary and Secondary Care*. London: National Institute of Clinical Excellence. (**310**)

National Collaborating Centre for Mental Health and Clinical Excellence (2009b) Borderline personality disorder. The NICE Guideline on treatment and management. NICE Clinical Practice Guideline 78., Commissioned by the National Institute for Health and Clinical Excellence, published by The British Psychological Society and The Royal College of Psychiatrists. http://www.nice.org.uk/nicemedia/live/12125/43045/43045.pdf (**585**)

References

National Commission on the Causes and Prevention of Violence (1969) *Final Report to Establish Justice, to Ensure Domestic Tranquility.* Washington, DC: Government Printing Office. (**216**)

National Confidential Inquiry (2006) *Avoidable Deaths. Five Year Report of the National Confidential Inquiry into Suicide and Homicide by People with Mental Illness.* Manchester: The University of Manchester. http://www.bbmh.manchester.ac.uk/cmhr/centreforsuicideprevention/nci/reports/avoidable_deaths_full_report_december_2006.pdf (**698**)

National Confidential Inquiry into Suicide and Homicide by People with Mental Illness (1999) *Safer services.* London: Department of Health. http://www.medicine.manchester.ac.uk/cmhr/centreforsuicideprevention/nci/reports/safer_services_full_report.pdf (**74, 448, 451**)

National Confidential Inquiry into Suicide and Homicide by People with Mental Illness (2001) *Safety first (Five-year report).* London: Department of Health. http://webarchive.nationalarchives.gov.uk/+/www.dh.gov.uk/en/Publicationsandstatistics/Publications/PublicationsPolicyAndGuidance/DH_4006679 (**448, 451, 452**)

National Confidential Inquiry into Suicide and Homicide by People with Mental Illness (2006) *Avoidable deaths (Five-year report).* Manchester, UK: University of Manchester. http://webarchive.nationalarchives.gov.uk/+/www.dh.gov.uk/en/Publicationsandstatistics/Publications/PublicationsPolicyAndGuidance/DH_4006679 (**448, 451, 452**)

National Confidential Inquiry into Suicide and Homicide by People with Mental Illness (2009) *Annual Report England and Wales.* http://www.bbmh.manchester.ac.uk/cmhr/centreforsuicideprevention/nci/reports/annual_report_2009.pdf (**592**)

National Confidential Inquiry into Suicide and Homicide by People with Mental Illness (2010) *Annual Report England and Wales.* http://www.bbmh.manchester.ac.uk/cmhr/centreforsuicideprevention/nci/reports/annual_report_2010.pdf (**338, 507, 592**)

National Development Team (2005) *Raising the Profile of Adults with Learning Disabilities 'Stuck' in the Secure Care System.* http://www.ndt.org.uk/projectsN/secure.html (**316**)

National Health Service Executive (1993) *Risk Management in the NHS.* London: NHS Management Executive. (**532**)

National Health Service Health Advisory Service (1995) *With Care in Mind Secure.* London: Department of Health. (**604**)

National Health Service Health Advisory Service/DHSS Social Services Inspectorate (1988) *Report on Services Provided by Broadmoor Hospital.* London: *DHSS.* (**603**)

National Health Service Information Centre (2011a) *In-Patients Formally Detained in Hospitals under the Mental Health Act 1983 and Patients Subject to Supervised Community Treatment.* Annual figures, England 2010/11. London: Health and Social Care Information Centre. (**58**)

National Health Service Information Centre (2011b) *Fifth Report from Mental Health Minimum Dataset Returns 2011.* London: Health and Social Care Information Centre. (**58**)

National Institute for Clinical Excellence (NICE) (2005) *The short-term management of disturbed/violent behaviour in in-patient psychiatric settings and emergency departments. Clinical Guideline 25.* London: NICE. www.nice.org.uk/nicemedia/pdf/cg025niceguideline.pdf (**594**)

National Institute for Clinical Excellence (NICE) (2005a) *Post-traumatic stress disorder (PTSD): The treatment of PTSD in adults and children.* CG26. London: National Institute for Clinical Excellence. http://guidance.nice.org.uk/CG26/NICEGuidance/pdf/English (**706, 725, 729**)

National Institute for Clinical Excellence (NICE); *see also* National Collaborating Centre for Mental Health and National Institute for Health and Clinical Excellence.

National Institute for Health and Clinical Excellence (2001) *The Clinical Cost and Effectiveness of Sibutramine, Withdrawn.* http://guidance.nice.org.uk/TA31 (**568**)

National Institute for Health and Clinical Excellence (2004) *Self-Harm: The Short-Term Physical and Psychological Management and Secondary Prevention of Self-Harm in Primary and Secondary Care.* NICE clinical guideline 16. London: NICE. http://guidance.nice.org.uk/CG16 (**631**)

National Institute for Health and Clinical Excellence (2005) *Violence. The Short-Term Management of Disturbed/Violent Behaviour in In-Patient Psychiatric Settings and Emergency Departments.* Royal College of Nursing: London. http://www.nice.org.uk/nicemedia/live/10964/29719/29719.pdf (**553, 558**)

National Institute for Health and Clinical Excellence (2006) Obesity. Guidance on the prevention, identification, assessment and management of overweight and obesity in adults and children. London: NICE. http://www.nice.org.uk/nicemedia/live/11000/30365/30365.pdf (**568**)

National Institute for Health and Clinical Excellence (2007a) *Psychosocial Interventions in Drug Misuse* (Clinical Guideline CG51). London: NICE. http://www.nice.org.uk/nicemedia/live/11812/35973/35973.pdf (**448, 457, 467**)

National Institute for Health and Clinical Excellence (2007b) *Methadone and Buprenorphine for the Management of Opioid Dependence* (NICE technology appraisal guidance 114). London: NICE. http://www.nice.org.uk/nicemedia/live/11606/33833/33833.pdf (**457, 467**)

National Institute for Health and Clinical Excellence (2007c) *Naltrexone for the Management of Opioid Dependence* (NICE technology appraisal guidance 115). London: NICE. http://www.nice.org.uk/nicemedia/live/11604/33812/33812.pdf (**456, 457, 467**)

National Institute for Health and Clinical Excellence (2008a) *Drug Misuse: Opioid Detoxification.* London: NICE. (**448, 456, 457,467**)

National Institute for Health and Clinical Excellence (2008b) *Smoking Cessation Services* NICE public health guidance 10. http://www.nice.org.uk/nicemedia/live/11925/39596/39596.pdf (**568**)

National Institute for Health and Clinical Excellence (2009) *Depression in Adults. The Treatment and Management of Depression in Adults.* NICE clinical guideline 90 http://www.nice.org.uk/nicemedia/live/12329/45888/45888.pdf (**631**)

National Institute for Health and Clinical Excellence (2009a) *Antisocial Personality Disorder: Treatment, Management and Prevention*. National Clinical Guideline Number 77. http://www.nice.org.uk/CG77 (see alsoNational Collaborating Centre for Mental Health.) (**407, 409, 417**)

National Institute for Health and Clinical Excellence (2009b) *Borderline Personality Disorder (BPD): Treatment and Management*. NICE clinical guideline 78. Leicester, UK: British Psychological Society (**407, 409, 417**)

National Institute for Health and Clinical Excellence (2010) *Schizophrenia. Core Interventions in the Treatment and Management of Schizophrenia in Adults in Primary and Secondary Care*. NICE Clinical Guideline 82. London: National Institute for Clinical Excellence. *see* National Collaborating Centre for Mental Health. (**583, 585**)

National Institute for Health and Clinical Excellence (2011) *Generalised Anxiety and Panic disorder (with or without Agoraphobia) in Adults. Management in Primary, Secondary and Community Care*. NICE clinical guideline 113. London: NICE. http://guidance.nice.org.uk/CG113/NICEGuidance/pdf/English (**631**)

National Institute for Mental Health in England (2003a) *Personality Disorder: No Longer a Diagnosis for Exclusion*. London: Department of Health. http://www.personalitydisorder.org.uk/assets/resources/56.pdf (**13, 383, 415, 590, 610**)

National Institute for Mental Health in England (NIMHE) (2003b) *Personality Disorder Capabilities Framework. Breaking the Cycle of Rejection*, London: Department of Health. http://www.spn.org.uk/fileadmin/spn/user/*.pdf/Papers/personalitydisorders.pdf (**585**)

National Institute on Alcohol Abuse and Alcoholism (2000) Alcohol, the brain, and behavior. *Alcohol, Research, and Health* **24**: 12–15. (**437**)

National Institute on Drug Abuse (NIDA) (1996) *National Pregnancy Health Survey*. Rockville, MD: National Institute of Health. (**464**)

National Patient Safety Agency (2008) *Root Cause Analysis Investigation Tools. www.nrls.npsa.nhs.uk/resources/?entryid45=59847* (**604, 695**)

National Patient Safety Agency (2009) *Never events. Framework 2009/10*. http://www.nrls.npsa.nhs.uk/resources/?entryid45=59859 (**76, 592**)

National Research Council (1989) *Improving Risk Communication*. Washington, DC: National Academy Press. (**256**)

National Research Council (2003) *The Polygraph and Lie Detection*. Committee to Review the Scientific Evidence on the Polygraph. Washington, DC: The National Academic Press. (**256**)

National Treatment Agency for Substance Misuse (NTA) (2001–2008) *Integrated Drug Treatment System in prisons (IDTS):* Overview. http://www.nta.nhs.uk/areas/criminal_justice/integrated_drug_treatment_system_in_prisons(IDTS).aspx (**462**)

National Treatment Agency for Substance Misuse (NTA) (2006a) *Care Planning Practice Guide*. http://www.nta.nhs.uk/uploads/nta_care_planning_practice_guide_2006_cpg1.pdf (**457**)

National Treatment Agency for Substance Misuse (NTA) (2006b) *Models of Care for Treatment of Adult Drug Misusers: Update 2006*. London: NTA. http://www.nta.nhs.uk/uploads/nta_modelsofcare_update_2006_moc3.pdf (**460**)

NCCMH: *see* National Collaborating Centre for Mental Health.

NCISH: *see* National Confidential Inquiry into Suicide and Homicide

Neale MC and Cardon LR (1992) *Methodology for Genetic Studies of Twins and Families*. Dordrecht, the Netherlands: Kluwer Academic Publishers. (**189, 190, 191**)

Nedopil N (2007) *Forensische Psychiatrie*, 3rd edn. Stuttgart, Germany: Thieme. (**146, 285**)Nedopil N, Gunn J, and Thompson L (2012) *Criminal Behaviour and Mental Health* **22**: 238–46. (**1**)

Needham-Bennett H, Parrott J, and MacDonald AJD (1996) Psychiatric disorder and policing the elderly offender. *Criminal Behaviour and Mental Health* **6**: 241–52. (**523**)

Nelson D (2003) Service innovations: the Orchard clinic: Scotland's first medium secure unit. *Psychiatric Bulletin* **27**: 105–7. (**613**)

Nelson G, Aubry T, and Lafrance A (2007) A review of the literature on the effectiveness of housing and support, assertive community treatment, and intensive case management interventions for persona with mental illness who have been homeless. *American Journal of Orthopsychiatry* **77**: 350–61. (**364**)

Nelson RJ and Chiavegatto S (2001) Molecular basis of aggression. *Trends in Neurosciences* **24**: 713–9. (**198**)

Nelson RJ and Trainor BC (2007) Neural mechanisms of aggression. *Nature* **8**: 536–46. (**306**)

Nelson S (2001) *Beyond Trauma: The Mental Health Care Needs of Women Who Survived Childhood Sexual Abuse*. Edinburgh, UK: Edinburgh Association for Mental Health. (**464**)

Nestler EJ (2001) Molecular basis of long-term plasticity underlying addiction. *Nature Reviews Neurosciences* **2**: 119–28.

Nestler EJ (2005) Is there a common molecular pathway for addiction? *Nature Neuroscience* **8**: 1445–9. (**200**)

Nestor PG (2002) Mental disorder and violence: personality dimensions and clinical features. *American Journal of Psychiatry* **159**: 1973–8. (**228, 346**)

Nestor PG, Kimble M, Berman I, and Haycock J (2002) Psychosis, psychopathy and homicide: a preliminary neuropsychological inquiry. *American Journal of Psychiatry* **159**: 138–40. (**346**)

Neuger J, Wistedt B, Aberg-Wistedt A, and Stain-Malmgren R (2002) Effect of citalopram treatment on relationship between platelet serotonin functions and the Karolinska scales or personality in panic patients. *Journal of Clinical Pharmacology* **22**: 400–5. (**310**)

Neumann CS, Hare RD, and Newman JP (2007) The super-ordinate nature of the Psychopathy Checklist-Revised. *Journal of Personality Disorders* **21**: 102–17. (**385**)

Neuner F, Schauer M, Klaschik C, Karunakara U, and Elbert T (2004) A comparison of narrative exposure therapy, supportive counselling and psychoeducation for treating posttraumatic stress disorder in an African refugee settlement. *Journal of Consulting and Clinical Psychology* **72**: 579–87. (**725**)

Neuner F, Schauer M, Roth WT, and Elbert T (2002) A narrative exposure treatment as intervention in a refugee camp: a case report. *Behavioural and Cognitive Psychotherapy* **30**: 205–10. (**729**)

Neuschatz JS, Preston EL, Burkett AA, Toglia MP, and Lampinen JM (2005) The effects of post-identification feedback and age on retrospective eyewitness memory. *Applied Cognitive Psychology* **19**: 435–53. (**523**)

New AS, Gelernter J, Yovell Y, et al. (1998) Tryptophan hydroxylase genotype is associated with impulsive-aggression measures: a preliminary study. *American Journal of Medical Genetics* **81**: 13–7. (**198**)

New AS, Hazlett EA, Buchsbaum MS, et al. (2002) Blunted prefrontal cortical 18-fluorodeoxyglucose positron emission tomography response to meta-chlorophenylpiperazine in impulsive aggression. *Archives of General Psychiatry* **59**: 621–9. (**310**)

New AS, Trestman RF. Mitropoulou V, et al. (2004) Low prolactin response to fenfluramine in impulsive aggression. *Journal of Psychiatric Research* **38**: 223–30. (**209, 310**)

Newell R and Gournay K (1994) British nurses in behavioural psychotherapy: a 20-year follow-up. *Journal of Advanced Nursing* **20**: 53–60. (**553**)

Newiss G and Fairbrother L (2004) Child abduction: understanding police recorded crime statistics. Findings 225. London: Home Office. http://steve-parker.org/urandom/2007/jun/r225.pdf (**504**)

Newman C, Fowler C, and Cashin A (2011) The development of a parenting program for incarcerated mothers in Australia: A review of prison-based parenting programs. *Contemporary Nurse* **39**: 2–11. (**519**)

Newrith C, Mex C, and Taylor PJ (eds) (2006) *Personality Disorder and Serious Offending. Hospital Treatment Models*, pp. 216–30. London: Hodder Arnold. (**552**)

Newrith C, Taylor PJ, and McInerny T (2006) Woodstock: a hospital based eclectic approach to the treatment of personality disorder. In C Newrith, C Meux, PJ Taylor (eds) *Personality Disorder and Serious Offending: Hospital Treatment Methods*. London: Hodder Arnold. (**402, 605**)

Newson J and Newson E (1989) *The Extent of Parental Physical Punishment in the UK*. London: Approach. (**174**)

Newson J, Newson E, and Adams M (1993) The social origins of delinquency. *Criminal Behaviour and Mental Health* **3**: 19–29. (**176**)

Ng Ying Kin NMK, Paris J, Schwatz G, Zweig-Frank H, Steiger H, and Nair NPV (2005) Impaired platelet [3H]paroxetine binding in female patients with borderline personality disorder. *Psychopharmacology* **182**: 447–51. (**308**)

NHS: *see* National Health Service.

NICE: *see* National Institute for Clinical Excellence or National Institute for Health and Clinical Excellence or National Collaborating Centre for Mental Health.

Nicholas S, Kershaw C and Walker A (2007) *Crime in England and Wales 2006/07* 4th edn. Home Office Statistical Bulletin http://www.homeoffice.gov.uk/rds/pdfs07/hosb1107.pdf (**219, 243, 244, 269**)

Nicholls TL, Ogloff JRP, and Douglas KS (2004) Assessing risk for violence among male and female civil psychiatric patients: the HCR-20, PC: SV, and VSC. *Behavioral Sciences and the Law* **22**: 127–58. (**537, 538**)

Nicholls TL, Ogloff JRP, Brink J, and Spidel A (2005) Psychopathy in women: a review of its clinical usefulness fro assessing risk for aggression and criminality. *Behavioral Sciences and the Law* **23**: 779–802. (**513**)

Nichols K (1976) Preparation for membership in a group. *Bulletin of the British Psychological Society* **29**: 353–9. (**572**)

Nickel MK, Muechlbacher M, Nickel C, et al. (2006) Aripiprazole in the treatment of patients with borderline personality disorder: a double-blind, placebocontrolled study. *American Journal of Psychiatry* **163**: 833–8. (**405**)

Nickel MK, Nickel C, Kaplan P, et al. (2005) Treatment of aggression with topiramate in male borderline patients: a double-blind, placebo-controlled study. *Biological Psychiatry* **57**: 495–9. (**405**)

Nickel MK, Nickel C, Mitterlehner FO, et al. (2004) Topiramate treatment of aggression in female borderline personality disorder patients: a doubleblind, placebo-controlled study. *Journal of Clinical Psychiatry* **65**: 1515–19. (**405**)

Niederman R (2007) Psychological approaches may improve oral hygiene behaviour. *Evidence Based Dentistry* **8**: 39–40. (**568**)

Nielsen DA, Ji F, Ho A, et al. (2008) Genotype patterns that contribute to increased risk for or protection from developing heroin addiction. *Molecular Psychiatry* **13**: 417–28. (**204**)

Nielssen, OB, Westmore, BD, Large, MMB and Hayes, RA (2007) Homicide during psychotic illness in New South Wales between 1993 and 2002. *Medical Journal of Australia*, **186**: 301–304. (**337**)

Nietzche F (1886) *Beyond Good and Evil* (trans. W Kaufman) Roman House (1968): New York. (**418**)

Nijenhuis ERS, Vanderlinden J, and Spinhoven P (1998) Animal defensive models as a model for trauma-induced dissociative reactions. *Journal of Traumatic Stress* **11**: 243–60. (**719**)

Nilsson KW, Sjoberg RL, Damberg M, et al. (2005) Role of the serotonin transporter gene and family function in adolescent alcohol consumption. *Alcoholism Clinical and Experimental Research* **29**: 564–70. (**207**)

Nilsson KW, Sjoberg RL, Damberg M, et al. (2006) Role of monoamine oxidase A genotype and psychosocial factors in male adolescent criminal activity. *Biological Psychiatry* **59**: 121–7. (**200, 207**)

NIMHE: *see* National Institute of Mental Health in England.

Nisbett RE and Ross L (1980) *Human Inference: Strategies and Shortcomings of Social Judgment*. Englewood Cliffs, NJ: Prentice-Hall. (**695**)

Nitsche P and Williams K (1993) *The History of Prison Psychosis*. Nervous and Mental Disease Monograph Series No 13. New York: Journal of Nervous and Mental Disease. (**595**)

Niveau G and Marten J (2007) Psychiatric commitment: over 50 years of case law from the European court of human rights. *European Psychiatry* **22**: 59–67. (**113**)

Nocon JJ (2006) Letter: Buprenorphine in pregnancy – the advantages. *Addiction* **101**: 608–9. (**465**)

Nordström MA and Kullgren G (2003) Do violent offenders with schizophrenia who attack family members differ from those with other victims? *International Journal of Forensic Mental Health* **2**: 195–200. (**350, 355**)

Nordström MA, Dahlgren L, and Kullgren G (2006) Victim relations and factors triggering homicides committed by offenders with schizophrenia. *Journal of Forensic Psychiatry and Psychology* **17**: 192–203. (**350, 354**)

Norris DM, Gutheil TG, and Strasburger LH (2003) This couldn't happen to me: boundary problems and sexual misconduct in the psychotherapy relationship. *Psychiatric Services* **54**: 517–22. (**691**)

Norris FH (1992) Epidemiology of trauma: frequency and impact of different potentially traumatic events on different demographic groups. *Journal of Consulting and Clinical Psychology* **60**(3): 409–18. (**712**)

Norris FH and Kaniasty K (1994) Psychological distress following criminal victimization in the general population: cross-sectional, longitudinal, and prospective analyses. *Journal of Consulting and Clinical Psychology* **62**: 111–23. (**712**)

Norris J (1988) *Serial Killers: The Growing Menace.* New York: Doubleday. (**239**)

Norström T (1998) Effects on criminal violence of different beverage types and private and public drinking. *Addiction* **93**: 689–99. (**228**)

North East London Strategic Health Authority. (2003) *Report of an Independent Inquiry into the care and treatment of Daksha Emson M.B.B.S., MRCPsych, MSc. and her daughter Freya.* North East London Strategic Health Authority: London. www.simplypsychiatry.co.uk/sitebuildercontent/sitebuilderfiles/deinquiryreport.pdf (**502, 692**)

Northern Ireland Executive (2007) *The Bamford Review Of Mental Health and Learning Disability (Northern Ireland). A Comprehensive Legislative Framework.* Belfast, UK: NI Executive. (**615, 654, 655, 656**)

Northrop FSC (1960) The comparative philosophy of comparative law. *Cornell Law Quarterly* **45**: 617–58. (**370**)

Northumbria University (2012) The Rickter Scale© Process. http://www.scalingnewweightsinvet.eu/wp-content/themes/thunderbolt/docs/Unique-features-of-the-RickterScale_v30.pdf (**457**)

Norton K (1992) Personality disordered individuals: the Henderson hospital MODEL of treatment. *Criminal Behaviour and Mental Health* **2**: 180–91. (**401**)

Novaco R (1975) *Anger Control: The Development and Evaluation of an Experimental Treatment.* Lexington, MA: DC Health. (**327,575**)

Novaco R. (1994) Anger as a risk factor for violence. In: *Violence and Mental Disorder. Developments in Risk Assessment.* J Monahan and HJ Steadman (Eds) Chicago University Press: Chicago. pp. 21–59. (**215, 326, 354**)

Novaco RW (1986) *Anger as a clinical and social problem.* In RJ Blanchard, DC Blanchard (eds) *Advances in the study of aggression.* New York: Academic Press. (**215**)

Novaco RW (2003) *The Novaco Anger Scale and Provocation Inventory Manual (NAS-PI).* Los Angeles, CA: Western Psychological Services. (**326**)

Novaco RW and Chemtob CM (2002) Anger and combat-related posttraumatic stress disorder. *Journal of Traumatic Stress* **15**: 123–32. (**723**)

Novaco RW and Taylor JL (2004) Assessment of anger and aggression in male offenders with developmental disabilities. *Psychological Assessment* **16**: 42–50. (**317, 326**)

Novaco RW and Taylor JL (2006) Anger. In A Carr, M McNulty (eds) *Handbook of Adult Clinical Psychology: An Evidence Based Practice Approach.* London: Routledge, pp. 978–1009. (**327**)

Novaco RW and Welsh WN (1989) Anger disturbances: cognitive mediation and clinical prescriptions. In K Howells, CR Hollin (eds) *Clinical Approaches to Violence.* Chichester, UK: Wiley. (**215**)

Novaco, RW (1997) Remediating anger and aggression with violent offenders. *Legal and Criminological Psychology,* **2**, 77–88. (**215, 575**)

NPSA: *see* National Health Service National Patient Safety Agency.

NTA: *see* National Treatment Agency.

Nuevo R, Chatterji S, Verdes E, et al. (2010/2012) The continuum of psychotic symptoms in the general population: a cross-national study. *Schizophrenia Bulletin* **38**: 475–85. (**339**)

Nunes E and Levin F (2004) Treatment of depression in patients with alcohol or other drug dependence: a meta-analysis. *Journal of the American Medical Association* **291**: 1887–96. (**459**)

Nunes KL, Hanson RK, Firestone P, et al. (2007) Denial predicts recidivism for some sexual offenders. *Sexual Abuse: A Journal of Research and Treatment* **19**: 91–105. (**261**)

Nyhan WL (1976) Behavior in the Lesch–Nyhan syndrome. *Journal of Autism and Childhood Schizophrenia* **6**: 235–52. (**210, 322**)

O'Brien CP (2003) Research advances in the understanding and treatment of addiction. *American Journal on Addictions* **12** (suppl. 2): S36–47. (**200**)

O'Brien G (1996) The psychiatric management of adult autism. *Advances in Psychiatric Treatment* **2**: 177. (**487**)

O'Brien G (2002a) Psychopharmacological interventions. In GO'Brien (ed) *Behavioural Phenotypes in Clinical Practice: Clinics in Developmental Medicine,* vol. 157. London: MacKeith. (**318**)

O'Brien G (2002b) Dual diagnosis in offenders with intellectual disability: setting research priorities: a review of research findings concerning psychiatric disorder (excluding personality disorder) among offenders with intellectual disability. *Journal of Intellectual Disability Research* **46** (suppl. 1): 21–33. (**318**)

O'Brien G (2004) *A Road Map for Care in 21st Century Asylums? Essays About Low Secure Hospital Care for People with Learning Disabilities.* London: Premium, pp. 56–61. (**325**)

O'Brien G (2008) No one knows: identifying and supporting prisoners with learning difficulties and learning disabilities: the views of prison staff. *Advances in Mental Health and Learning Disabilities* **2**: 50–3. (**316**)

O'Brien G and Bell G (2004) Learning disability autism and offending behaviour. In S Bailley, M Dolan (eds) *Adolescent Forensic Psychiatry*. London: Arnold, pp. 144–51. (**318, 325**)

O'Brien G and Pearson J (2005) 'Defining behavioural phenotypes: exploring genotype/phenotype interrelationships' In D Riva, U Bellugi, MB Denckla (eds) *Neurodevelopmental Disorders: Cognitive/Behavioural Phenotypes*. Milan, Italy: Marianai Foundation Paediatric Neurology, pp. 9–18. (**320**)

O'Brien G and Yule W (eds) (1995) *Behavioural Phenotypes. Clinics in Developmental Medicine*. London: MacKeuth, p. 211. (**319, 320**)

O'Brien G, Taylor JL, Lindsay WR, et al. (2010) A multi-centre study of adults with learning disabilities referred to services for antisocial or offending behaviour: Demographic, individual, offending and service characteristics. *Journal of Learning Disabilities and Offending Behaviour* **1**: 5–15. (**326**)

O'Brien M (2008) *The Death of Justice: Guilty Until Proven Innocent*. Aberystwyth, Ceredigion: Y Loflia. (**717**)

O'Brien M, Mortimer L, Singleton N, and Meltzer H (2001) *Psychiatric Morbidity among Women Prisoners in England and Wales*. London: Office for National Statistics. (**279**)

O'Callaghan D and Print B (1994) Adolescent sexual abusers research assessment and treatment of male abusers. In T Morrison, M Erooga, RC Beckett (eds) *Sexual Offending Against Children*. London: Routledge, pp. 146–77. (**495**)

O'Connell BA (1960) Amnesia and homicide. *British Journal of Delinquency* **10**: 262–76. (**25, 293, 294, 295, 296**)

O'Connor A (1987) Female sex offenders. *British Journal of Psychiatry* **150**: 615–20. (**250**)

O'Connor TG, Deater-Deckard K, Fulker D, Rutter M, and Plomin R (1998) Genotype-environment correlations in late childhood and early adolescence: antisocial behavioral problems and coercive parenting. *Developmental Psychology* **34**: 970–81. (**199**)

O'Daly OG, Frangou S, Chitnis X, and Shergill SS (2007) Brain structural changes in schizophrenia patients with persistent delusions. *Psychiatry Research Neuroimaging* **156**: 15–21. (**312**)

O'Donnell J, Hawkins JD, Catalano RF, Abbott RD, and Day LE (1995) Preventing school failure, drug use, and delinquency among low-income children: long-term intervention in elementary schools. *American Journal of Orthopsychiatry* **65**: 87–100. (**183**)

O'Donovan MC and Owen MJ (1999) Candidate-gene association studies of schizophrenia. *American Journal of Human Genetics* **65**: 587–92. (**194**)

O'Donovan MC, Craddock N, Norton N, et al. (2008) Identification of loci associated with schizophrenia by genome-wide association and follow-up. *Nature Genetics* **40**: 1053–5. (**209**)

O'Donovan MC, Williams NM, and Owen MJ (2003) Recent advances in the genetics of schizophrenia. *Human Molecular Genetics* **12** Spec No 2: R125–33. (**194**)

O'Farrell TJ, Fals-Stewart W, Murphy M, and Murphy CM (2003) Partner violence before and after individually based alcoholism treatment for male alcoholic patients. *Journal of Consulting and Clinical Psychology* **71**: 91–102. (**442**)

O'Grady J (2001) Commentary on 'substance misuse and violence: the scope and limitations of forensic psychiatry's role'. *Advances in Psychiatric Treatment* **7**: 196–7. (**448**)

O'Grady J (2008) Time to talk. Commentary on forensic psychiatry and general psychiatry. *Psychiatric Bulletin* **32**: 6–7. (**588**)

O'Keane V, Moloney E, O'Neill H, et al. (1992) Blunted prolactin responses to d-fenfluramine in sociopathy. Evidence for subsensitivity of central serotonergic function. *British Journal of Psychiatry* **160**: 643–6. (**309**)

O'Neill C (2006) Liaison between criminal justice and psychiatric systems: diversion schemes. *Irish Journal of Psychological Medicine* **23**: 87–8. (**110, 617, 657**)

O'Neill C, Heffernan P, Goggins R, et al. (2003) Long-stay forensic psychiatric inpatients in the Republic of Ireland: aggregated needs assessment. *Irish Journal of Psychological Medicine* **20**: 119–25. (**616**)

O'Neill C, Kelly A, Sinclair H, and Kennedy H (2005) Deprivation: different implications for forensic psychiatric need in urban and rural areas. *Social Psychiatry and Psychiatric Epidemiology* **40**: 551–6. (**616**)

O'Neill C, Sinclair H, Kelly A, and Kennedy HG (2002) Interaction of forensic and general psychiatric services in Ireland: learning the lessons or repeating the mistakes? *Irish Journal of Psychological Medicine* **19**: 48–54. (**616**)

O'Shea N, Moran I, and Bergin S (2003) *Snakes and Ladders: Mental Health and Criminal Justice*. London: Revolving Doors Agency. http://www.revolving-doors.org.uk/documents/snakes-and-ladders/ (**647, 648**)

O'Sullivan PJC and Chesterman LP (2007) Older patients subject to restriction orders in England and Wales: a cross-sectional survey. *Journal of Forensic Psychiatry and Psychology* **18**: 204–20. (**524**)

Oades RD, Slusarek M, Velling S, and Bondy B (2002) Serotonin platelet-transporter measures in childhood attention-deficit/hyperactivity disorder (ADHD): clinical versus experimental measures of impulsivity. *World Journal of Biological Psychiatry* **3**: 96–100. (**308**)

Oates K (2007) Juvenile sex offenders. *Child Abuse and Neglect* **31**: 681–2. (**252**)

Oates M (2003) Suicide: the leading cause of maternal deaths. *British Journal of Psychiatry* **183**: 279–81. (**308, 501, 521**)

Oberman M (1996) Mothers who kill: coming to terms with modern American infanticide. *American Criminal Law Review* **34**: 1–110. (**500, 510**)

Oberman M (2003) A brief history of infanticide and the law. In MG Spinelli (ed) *Infanticide. Psychosocial and Legal Perspectives on Mothers Who Kill*. Washington, DC: American Psychiatric Publishing Inc. pp. 3–18. (**508**)

Ochberg FM and Gunn J (1980) The psychiatrist and the policeman. *Psychiatric Annals*, **10** (5), 31–45. (**667**)

Odegard J (1968) Interaksjonen mellom partnerne ved de patologiske sjalusireaksjoner, *Nordisk Psykiatrisk Tidsskrift* **22**: 314–19. (**369**)

Odgers CL, Burnette ML, Chauhan P, et al. (2005) Misdiagnosing the problem: mental health profiles of incarcerated juveniles. *Canadian Child and Adolescent Psychiatry Review* **14**: 26–9. (**483**)

Odgers CL, Moffitt TE, Broadbent JM, Dickson N, Hancox RJ, Harrington H, Poulton R, Sears MR, Thomson WM and Caspi A (2008) Female and male antisocial trajectories: From childhood origins to adult outcomes. *Development and Psychopathology* **20**: 673–716. (**501**)

Offender Health Research Network (OHRN) (2008) *An Evaluation of the Department of Health's 'Procedure for the Transfer of Prisoners to and from Hospital Under Sections 47 and 48 of the Mental Health Act 1983' Initiative.* Manchester, UK: OHRN. www.ohrn.nhs.uk/resource/Research/OHRNTransfers.pdf (**632**)

Office for Criminal Justice Reform (2005) *The Code of Practice for Victims and Witnesses.* London: OCJR. (**708**)

Official Statistics of Finland (2011) Available from Ministry of Justice of Finland website, in Finnish. http://www.om.fi (**503**)

Offord DR and Bennett KJ (2002) Prevention. In M Rutter and E Taylor (eds) *Child and Adolescent Psychiatry* (4th ed.) (pp. 881–99). Oxford, UK: Blackwell Science. pp 881-899. (**399**)

Ogata SN, Silk KR, Goodrich S, Lohr NE, Westen D, and Hill EM (1990) Childhood sexual and physical abuse in adult patients with borderline personality disorder. *American Journal of Psychiatry* **147**: 1008–13. (**396**)

Ogawa JR, Sroufe LA, Weinfield NS, Carlson EA, and Egeland B. (1997) Development of the fragmented self: longitudinal study of dissociative symptomatology in a non clinical sample. *Development and Psychopathology* **9**: 855–79. (**719**)

Ogilvie E (2000) Cyberstalking. *Trends and Issues in Crime and Criminal Justice* **166**: 1–6. (**377**)

Ogloff JRP and Daffern M (2006) The dynamic appraisal of situational aggression: an instrument to assess risk for imminent aggression in psychiatric inpatients. *Behavioral Sciences and the Law* **24**: 799–813. (**549**)

Ohayon MM, Caulet M, and Priest RG (1997) Violent behaviour during sleep. *Journal of Clinical Psychiatry* **58**: 369–76. (**290**)

Ohberg A, Penttila A, and Lonngvist J (1997) Driver suicides. *British Journal of Psychiatry* **171**: 468–72. (**278**)

Okah FA, Cai J, and Hoff GL (2005) Term-gestation low birth weight and health-compromising behaviours during pregnancy. *Obstetrics and Gynaecology* **105**: 543–50. (**452**)

O'Keeffe M et al. (2007) https://www.warwickshire.gov.uk/Web/corporate/wccweb.nsf/Links/6EA919F805F3B54180257885002E4C6B/$file/Full+Report_UK+Study+of+Abuse+and+Neglect+of+Older+People+v2.pdf (**228**)

Olds DL, Eckenrode J, Henderson CR, et al. (1997) Long-term effects of home visitation on maternal life course and child abuse and neglect: fifteen-year follow-up of a randomized trial. *Journal of the American Medical Association* **278**: 637–43. (**182**)

Olds DL, Henderson CR, Chamberlin R, and Tatelbaum R (1986) Preventing child abuse and neglect: a randomized trial of nurse home visitation. *Pediatrics* **78**: 65–78. (**182**)

Olds DL, Henderson CR, Cole R, et al. (1998) Long-term effects of nurse home visitation on children's criminal and antisocial behaviour: 15-year follow-up of a randomized controlled trial. *Journal of the American Medical Association* **280**: 1238–44. (**182, 399**)

Oleski MS (1977) The effect of indefinite pretrial incarceration on the anxiety level of an urban jail population. *Journal of Clinical Psychology* **33**: 1006–8. (**630**)

Oleson JJ (2010) Bayesian credible intervals for binomial proportions in a single patient trial. *Statistical Methods in Medical Research* **19**: 559–74. (**533**)

Oliveira MM, Conti C, Saconato H, and Fernandes do Prado G. Pharmacological treatment for Kleine–Levin syndrome. *Cochrane Database Systematic Review* 2009 Apr **15**(2):CD006685. doi: 10.1002/14651858.CD006685.pub2 (**290**)

Oliver C, Demetriades L, and Hall S (2002) Effects of environmental events on smiling and laughing behaviour in Angelman syndrome. *American Journal on Mental Retardation* **107**(3): 194–200, 233–4. (**321**)

Oliver N and Kuipers E (1996) Stress and its relationship to expressed emotion in community mental health workers. *International Journal of Social Psychiaty* **42**: 150–9. (**557**)

Oliver PC, Crawford MJ, Rao B, Reece B, and Tyrer P (2007) Modified Overt Aggression Scale (MOAS) for people with intellectual disability and aggressive challenging behaviour: a reliability study. *Journal of Applied Research in Intellectual Disabilities* **20**: 368–72. (**321**)

Oliver T and Smith R (1993) *Lambs to the Slaughter.* London: Time Warner. (**414**)

Oltmanns TF (1988) Approaches to definition and study of delusions. In TF Oltmanns, BA Maher (eds) *Delusional Beliefs.* New York: Wiley. (**348**)

Olweus D (1994) Bullying at school: basic facts and effects of a school based intervention programme. *Journal of Child Psychology and Psychiatry* **35**: 1171–90. (**184, 399**)

Omerov M, Edman G, and Wistedt B (2004) Violence and threats of violence within psychiatric care – comparison of staff and patient experiences of the same incident. *Nordic Journal of Psychiatry* **58**: 363–9. (**337**)

Oosterbaan DB, van Balkom AJLM, Spinhoven PH, van Oppen P, and van Dyck X (2001) Cognitive therapy versus moclobemide in social phobia: a controlled study. *Clinical Psychology and Psychotherapy* **8**: 263–73. (**405, 411**)

OPD Task Force (ed) (2001) *Operationalized Psychodynamic Diagnostics. Foundations and Manual.* Seattle, WA: Hogrefe and Huber. (**389**)

OPD Task Force (ed) (2008) *Operationalized Psychodynamic Diagnosis. OPD-2. Manual of Diagnosis and Treatment Planning.* Göttingen, Germany: Hogrefe and Huber. (**387, 389**)

Opie I and Opie P (1983) *The Oxford Book of Narrative Verse.* Oxford, UK: Oxford University Press. (**Preface**)

Oquendo MA and Mann JJ (2000) The biology of impulsivity and suicidality. *Psychiatric Clinics of North America* **23**: 11–25. (**307**)

Orford J (1985) *Excessive Appetites: A psychological view of addictions.* Chichester, UK: Wiley. (**468**)

Orford J, Sproston K, Erens B, White C, and Mitchell L (2003) *Gambling and Problem Gambling in Britain.* Hove, UK: Brunner-Routledge. (**470**)

Ormerod D (2005) *Smith and Hogan: Criminal Law,* 11th edn. Oxford, UK: Oxford University Press. (**277**)

Ormerod D (2008) *Smith and Hogan, Criminal Law,* 12th edn. Oxford, UK: Oxford University Press. (**26, 32**)

Oroszi G, Anton RF, O'Malley S, et al. (2009) OPRM1 Asn40Asp predicts response to naltrexone treatment: a haplotype-based approach. *Alcoholism. Clinical and Experimental Research* 33: 383–93. (**206**)

Ortman J (1981) Psykisk Afvigelse og kriminel adfaerd. *Under En Søgelse Af 11533 Maend Født.* I, 1953. I det metropolitane omrde københavn. Forksningsrapport 17. Copenhagen, Denmark: Justitminsteriet. (**337**)

Ortmann J (1980) The treatment of sexual offenders: castration and anti-hormone therapy. *International Journal of Law and Psychiatry* 3: 443–51. (**260, 261**)

Orvaschel H, Pulg-Antich J, and Chambers W (1982) Retrospective assessment of pre-pubertal major depression with the Kiddie-SADS-E. *Journal of the American Academy of Child Psychiatry* 21: 695–707. (**484**)

Osborn SG (1980) Moving home, leaving London, and delinquent trends. *British Journal of Criminology* 20: 54–61. (**179**)

Oslin DW, Berrettini W, Kranzler HR, et al. (2003) A functional polymorphism of the mu-opioid receptor gene is associated with naltrexone response in alcohol-dependent patients. *Neuropsychopharmacology* 28: 1546–52. (**206**)

Otterström E (1946) Delinquency and children from bad homes. A study of their prognosis from the social point of view. *Acta Pediat* 22, (suppl. 5). (**501**)

Ottman R (1994) Epidemiologic analysis of gene–environment interaction in twins. *Genetic Epidemiology* 11: 75–86. (**191**)

Otto RK, Poythress NG, Nicholson RA, et al. (1998) Psychometric properties of the MacArthur competence assessment tool – criminal adjudication. *Psychological Assessment* 10: 435–43. (**322**)

Oudiette D, Constantinescu I, Leclair-Visonneau L, Vidailhet M, Schwartz S, et al. (2011) Evidence for the re-enactment of a recently learned behavior during sleepwalking. *PLoS ONE* 6(3): e18056. doi:10.1371/journal.pone.0018056 (**291**)

Overall JE and Gorham DR (1962) The brief Psychiatric rating scale. *Psychological Reports* 10: 799–812. (**350**)

Overpeck MD, Brenner RA, Trumble AC, Trifiletti LB, and Berendes HW (1998) Risk factors for infant homicide in the United States. *The New England Journal of Medicine* 339: 1211–16. (**508**)

Oyebode F (1999) Invited commentary: anatomy of risk. *Psychiatric Bulletin* 23: 652–6. (**696**)

Oyserman D and Martois HR (1990) Possible selves and delinquency. *Journal of Personality and Social Psychology* 59: 112–15. (**473**)

Ozer EJ, Best SR, Lipsey TL, and Weiss DS (2003) Predictors of posttraumatic stress disorder and symptoms in adults: a meta-analysis. *Psychological Bulletin* 129: 52–73. (**713, 715, 721, 723**)

Padfield N (2007) *Who to Release?* Cullompton, UK: Willan. (**42**)

Painter K (1991) Violence and vulnerability in the workplace: psychosocial and legal implications. In MJ Davidson, J Earnshaw (eds) *Vulnerable Workers: Psychosocial and Legal Issues.* New York: Wiley, pp. 159–201. (**699**)

Pajer KA (1998) What happens to "bad" girls? A review of the adult outcomes of antisocial adolescent girls. *Am J Psychiatry* 155(7): 862–70. (**511**)

Palladino CL, Singh VJ, Campbell J, Flynn H, and Gold K (2011) Homicide and suicide during the perinatal period: Findings from the National Violent Death Reporting System. *Obstetrics and Gynecology* 118: 1056–63. (**501**)

Palmer EJ, Caulfield LS, and Hollin CR (2007) Interventions with arsonists and young fire-setters: a survey of the national picture in England and Wales. *Legal and Criminological Psychology* 12: 101–16. (**576**)

Palmer I (2007) Terrorism, suicide bombing, fear and mental health. *International Review of Psychiatry* 19(3): 289–96. (**235**)

Palmour RM (1983) Genetic models for the study of aggressive behavior. *Progress in Neuro-psychopharmacolical and Biological Psychiatry* 7: 513–7. (**210, 322**)

Palmsteirna T and Wistedt B (1995) Changes in the pattern of aggressive behaviour among inpatients with changed ward organisation. *Acta Psychiatrica Scandinavica* 91: 32–5. (**557, 592**)

Palmstierna T, Huitfeldt B, and Wistedt B (1991) The relationship of crowding and aggressive behavior on a psychiatric intensive care unit. *Hospital and Community Psychiatry* 42: 1237–40. (**557**)

Pandina GJ, Bossie CA, Youssef E, Zhu Y, and Dunbar F (2007) Risperidone improves behavioral symptoms in children with autism in a randomized, double-blind, placebo-controlled trial. *Journal of Autism and Developmental Disorders* 37: 367–73. (**564**)

Panksepp J (2003) Feeling the pain of social loss. *Science* 302: 237–8. (**718**)

Panksepp J, Siviy SM, and Normansell LA (1985) Brain opioids and social emotions. In M Reite, T Field (eds) *The Psychobiology of Attachment and Separation.* London: Academic Press, pp. 3–49. (**718**)

Papanastassiou M, Waldron G, Boyle J, and Chesterman LP (2004) Post-traumatic stress disorder in mentally ill perpetrators of homicide. *Journal of Forensic Psychiatry and Psychology* 15: 66–75. (**712**)

Papolos DF, Faedda GL, Veit S, et al. (1996) Bipolar spectrum disorders in patients diagnosed with velo-cardio-facial syndrome: does a hemizygous deletion of chromosome 22q11 result in bipolar affective disorder? *The American Journal of Psychiatry* 153(12): 1541–7. (**209**)

Parhar KK, Wormith JS, Derkzen DM, and Beauregard AM (2008) Offender coercion in treatment: a meta-analysis of effectiveness. *Criminal Justice and Behavior* 35: 1109–35. (**445**)

Paris J and Zweig-Frank H (2001) A 27-year follow-up of patients with perosnality disorder. *Comprehensive Psychiatry* 42: 482–7. (**402**)

Paris J, Zweig-Frank H, and Guzder J (1994) Psychological risk factors for borderline personality disorder in female patients. *Comprehensive Psychiatry* 35: 301–5. (**571**)

Parker H and Bottomley T (1966) *Crack Cocaine and Drugs – Crime Careers.* London: Home Office. (**453**)

Parker H, Casburn M, and Turnbull D (1981) *Receiving Juvenile Justice.* Oxford, UK: Blackwell. (**477**)

Parker N (1988) *Malingering. Lecture Given to Anglo-Australian Bicentennial Meeting on Forensic Psychiatry* (unpublished). (**432**)

Parnas J (1985) Mates of schizophrenic mothers. A study of assortative mating from the American-Danish high risk project. *British Journal of Psychiatry* **146**: 490–7. (**189**)

Parrott J, Strathdee G, and Brown P (1988) Patient access to psychiatric records: the patient's *view. Journal of the Royal Society of Medicine* **81**: 520–2. (**665**)

Parry-Crooke G and Stafford P (2009) *My Life in Safe hands? Summary Report of an Evaluation of Women's Medium Secure Services.* London: London Metropolitan University. http://www.londonmet.ac.uk/fms/MRSite/acad/dass/CSER/Summary%20report%20 of%20an%20evaluation%20of%20women's%20medium%20secure%20services%202009.pdf (**520**)

Parry-Jones WL (1971) *The Trade in Lunacy: A Study of Private Madness in England in the Eighteenth and Nineteenth Centuries.* London: Routledge and Kegan Paul. (**589**)

Parsey RV, Oquendo MA, Simpson NR, et al. (2002) Effects of sex, age, and aggressive traits in man on brain serotonin 5-HT1A receptor binding potential measured by PET using [C-11]WAY-100635. *Brain Research* **954**: 173–82. (**310**)

Parsonage M, Khanom H, Rutherford M, Sidhu M, and Smith C (2009) *Diversion. A Better Way for Criminal Justice and Mental Health.* London: Sainsbury Centre for Mental Health. http://www.centreformentalhealth.org.uk/pdfs/Diversion.pdf (**641**)

Parsons S, Walker L, and Grubin D (2001) Prevalence of mental disorder in female remand prisons. *Journal of Forensic Psychiatry* **12**: 194–202. (**630**)

Parsons T (1951) *The Social System.* New York: Free Press of Glencoe. (**9, 423**)

Partridge S (2004) *Examining Case Management Models for Community Sentences* Home Office Online Report 17/04. London: Home Office.http://collection.europarchive.org/tna/20080205132101/homeoffice.gov.uk/rds/pdfs04/rdsolr1704.pdf (**518**)

Parwatikar SD, Holcomb WR, and Meninger KA (1985) The detection of malingered amnesia in accused murderers. *Bulletin of the American Academy of Psychiatry and the Law* **13**:97–103. (**293, 294, 295**)

Pascual JC, Soler J, Puigdemont D, et al. (2008) Ziprasidone in the treatment of borderline personality disorder: a double-blind, randomised placebo-controlled randomized study. *Journal of Clinical Psychiatry* **69**: 603–8. (**405**)

Patch PC and Arrigo BA (1999) Police officer attitudes and use of discretion in situations involving the mentally ill – the need to narrow the focus. *International Journal of Law and Psychiatry* **22**: 23–35. (**279**)

Pathé M (2002) *Surviving Stalking.* Cambridge, UK: Cambridge University Press. (**379, 380**)

Pathé M and Mullen PE (1997) The impact of stalkers on their victims. *British Journal of Psychiatry* **170**: 12–17. (**374, 380, 545, 546, 712**)

Patrick CJ (2006) Getting to the heart of psychopathy. In H Herve, J Yuille (eds) *Psychopathy: Theory, Research and Social Implications.* Mahwah, NJ: Lawrence Erlbaum. (**297**)

Patrick H (2006) *Mental Health, Incapacity and the Law in Scotland.* Edinburgh, UK: Tottel. (**90**)

Patrick M, Hobson RP, Castle P, Howard R, and Maughan B (1994) Personality disorder and the mental representation of early social experience. *Developmental Psychopathology* **6**: 375–88. (**396**)

Patterson GR (1979) A performance theory for coercive family interaction. In R Cairns (ed) *Social Interaction: Methods, Analysis and Illustration.* Hillsdale, IN: Erlbaum. (**213**)

Patterson GR (1982) *Coercive Family Process.* Eugene, Oregon: Castalia. (**181, 183, 495**)

Patterson GR (1995) Coercion as a basis for early age of onset for arrest. In J McCord (ed) *Coercion and Punishment in Long-Term Perspectives.* Cambridge, UK: Cambridge University Press, pp. 81–105. (**175**)

Patterson GR, Reid JB, and Dishion TJ (1992) *Antisocial Boys.* Eugene, Oregon: Castalia. (**182**)

Pauffley J (2004) *Committeee of Inquiry Independent Investigation into how the NHS Handled Allegations about the Conduct of Clifford Ayling.* Cm 6298. London: TSO. (**685**)

Pavlov IP (1927) *Conditioned reflexes: an investigation of the physiological activity of the cerebral cortex.* Oxford/New York: Oxford University Press. http://books.google.de/books?id=cknrYDqAClkC&printsec=frontcover&hl=de&source=gbs_ge_summary_r&cad =0#v=onepage&q&f=false (**395**)

Pawson R (2002) *Does Megan's Law Work? A Theory-Driven Systematic Review.* ESRC UK Centre for Evidence Based Policy and Practice. http://ec2-79-125-112-176.eu-west-1.compute.amazonaws.com/sspp/departments/politicaleconomy/research/cep/pubs/papers/ assets/wp8.pdf (**645**)

Pearce S, Gray A, and Marks L (2004) *Training Needs Analysis to Identify Primary Care Skills and Prison Specific Competences for Doctors.* Final Report to the Prison Health Group. London: Department of Health. http://www.dur.ac.uk/resources/public.health/ publications/PdtnaReportComposite-1.pdf (**631**)

Pearse J, Gudjonsson GH, Clare ICH, and Rutter S (1998) Police Interviewing and Psychological Vulnerabilities: Predicting the Likelihood of a Confession. *Journal of Community and Applied Social Psychology* **8**: 1–21. (**161**)

Peay J (1989) *Tribunals on Trial.* Oxford, UK: Clarendon. (**71**)

Peay J (1996) Introduction. In J Peay (ed) *Inquiries After Homicide.* London: Duckworth, pp. 1–8. (**695, 696**)

Peay J (1999) Thinking horses, not zebras. In D Webb, R Harris (eds) *Mentally Disordered Offenders: Managing People Nobody Owns.* London: Routledge, pp. 141–155. (**696**)

Peay J (2007) Mentally disordered offenders, mental health, and crime. In M Maguire, R Morgan, R Reiner (eds) *The Oxford Handbook of Criminology.* Oxford, UK: Oxford University Press, pp. 496–527. (**279**)

Peay J (2011) *Mental Health and Crime* (Contemporary Issues in Public Policy*).* Abingdon, VA: Routledge. (**279**)

Peet M (2004) International variations in the outcome of Schizophrenia and prevalence of depression in relation to National Dietary Practices: an ecological analysis. *British Journal of Psychiatry* **184**: 404–8. (**568**)

Peet M and Ali S (1986) Propranolol and atenolol in the treatment of anxiety. *International Clinical Psychopharmacology* **1**: 314–9. (**560**)

Pelissier BM, Camp SD, Gaes GG, Saylor WG, and Rhodes W (2003) Gender differences in outcomes from prison-based residential treatment. *Journal of Substance Abuse Treatment* **24**(2): 149–60. (**518**)

Pence E and Paymar M (1993) *Education Groups for Men who Batter*. New York: Springer. (**220**)

Pencheon D, Guest C, Melzer D, and Muir Gray JA (2006) *Oxford Handbook of Public Health Practice*. Oxford, UK: Oxford University Press, pp. xxxi–xxxiii. (**703**)

Penk WE, Flannery RB, and Irvin E (2000) Characteristics of substance abusing persons with schizophrenia: the paradox of the dually diagnosed. *Journal of Addictive Diseases* **19**: 23–30. (**454**)

Penn DL and Wykes T (2003) Stigma, discrimination and mental illness. *Journal of Mental Health* **12**: 203–8. (**579**)

Percival T (1803) *Medical Ethics or a Code of Institutes and Precepts adapted to the Professional Conduct of Physicians and Surgeons*. Manchester, UK: S. Russell (reprinted, 1985, Birmingham, AL: Classics of Medicine Library). (**658**)

Perelman C (1963) *The Idea of Justice and the Problem of Argument*. London: Routledge. (**150**)

Perkins D, Moore E and Dudley A (2007) The development of a centralised groupwork service in high security. *Mental Health Review Journal* **12**: 16–20. (**401**)

Perkins E (2003) Decision Making in Mental Health Review Tribunals Policy Studies Institute (**71**)

Perkonigg A, Kessler RC, Storz S, and Wittchen H-U (2000) Traumatic events and post-traumatic stress disorder in the community: prevalence, risk factors and comorbidity. *Acta Psychiatrica Scandinavica* **101**: 46–59. (**712**)

Perlin ML (1996) 'Dignity was the first to leave': Godinez v. Moran, Colin Ferguson, and the trial of mentally disabled criminal defendants. *Behavioral Sciences and the Law* **14**: 61–81. (**120**)

Perry A, Coulton S, Glanville J, et al. Interventions for drug-using offenders in the courts, secure establishments and the community. *Cochrane Database of Systematic Reviews* 2006.Issue 3, Art. No.: CD005193. DOI: 10.1002/14651858.CD005193.pub2. http://onlinelibrary.wiley.com/doi/10.1002/14651858.CD005193.pub2/pdf (**460**)

Perry BD, Arvinte A, Marcellus J, and Pollard RA (1997) Syncope, bradycardia, cataplexy and paralysis: sensitization of an opioid-mediated dissociative response following childhood trauma. *Journal of the American Academy of Child and Adolescent Psychiatry*. (**719**)

Perry PJ, Garvey M, and Noyes R (1990) Benzodiazepine treatment of generalised anxiety disorder. In R Noyes, M Roth, G Burrows (eds) *Handbook of Anxiety*, Vol. 4. Amsterdam, the Netherlands: Elsevier, pp. 111–24. (**560**)

Petch E and Bradley C (1997) Learning the lessons from homicide inquiries: adding insult to injury. *Journal of Forensic Psychiatry* **8**: 161–84. (**76, 695, 696**)

Peters C (2005) *Harold Shipman, Mind Set on Murder*. London: Carlton. (**689**)

Peters ER, Joseph SA, and Garety PA (1999) Measurement of delusional ideation in the normal population: introducing the PDS (Peters et al. Delusional Inventory). *Schizophrenia Bulletin* **25**: 553–76. (**349**)

Peters SD, Wyatt GE, and Finkelhor D (1986) In D Finkelhor (ed) *Sourcebook on child sexual abuse*. Beverly Hills, CA: Sage. (**243**)

Petty RE and Cacioppo JT (1984) The effects of involvement on responses to argument quantity and quality: central and peripheral routes to persuasion. *Journal of Personality and Social Psychology* **46**: 69–81. (**695**)

Petursson H and Gudjonsson GH (1981) Psychiatric aspects of homicide. *Acta Psychiatrica Scandinavica* **64**: 363–72. (**294, 337**)

Pfohl B, Coryell W, Zimmerman M, and Stangl D (1986) *DSM-III* personality disorders: Diagnostic overlap and internal consistency of individual *DSM-III* criteria. *Comprehensive Psychiatry* **27**: 21–34. (**397**)

Pham TH, Claix A, and Remy S (2000) Assessment of the historical clinical and risk-20 (HCR-20) items in a Belgian forensic sample. *European Psychiatry* **15**: 82–3. (**537**)

Pham TH, Ducro C, Marghem B, and Reveillere C (2005) Prediction of recidivism among prison inmates and forensic patients in Belgium. *Annales Medico-Psychologiques* **163**(10): 842–5. (**536**)

Pharoah F, Mari M, Rathbone J, and Wong W (2010) Family intervention for schizophrenia. *Cochrane Database of Systematic Reviews* 2010.Issue 12, Art. No.: CD000088. DOI: 10.1002/14651858.CD000088.pub3. Chichester, UK: Wiley. http://www.ncbi.nlm.nih.gov/pubmed/21154340 (**363**)

Phelan JC and Link BG (1998) The growing belief that people with mental illnesses are violent: the role of dangerousness criterion for civil commitment. *Social Psychiatry and Psychiatric Epidemiology* **33**: s7–12. (**132**)

Phelan JC, Sinkewicz M, Castille DM, Huz S, and Link BG (2010) Effectiveness and outcomes of assisted outpatient treatment in New York state. *Psychiatric Services* **61**: 137–43. (**365**)

Philips SL, Heads TC, Taylor PJ, and Hill M (1999) Sexual offending and antisocial sexual behaviour among patients with schizophrenia. *Journal of Clinical Psychiatry* **60**: 170–5. (**340**)

Philipsen A, Richter H, Schmahl C, et al. (2004b) Clonidine in acute aversive inner tension and self-injurious behavior in female patients with borderline personality disorder. *Journal of Clinical Psychiatry* **65**: 1414–9. (**405**)

Philipsen A, Schmahl C, and Lieb K (2004a) Naloxone in the treatment of acute dissociative states in female patients with borderline personality disorder. *Pharmacopsychiatry* **37**: 196–9. (**405**)

Phillips C and Brown D (1998) *Entry into the criminal justice system: a survey of police arrests and their outcomes*. Home Office Research Study 185. London: Home Office. (**23**)

Phillips D (1977) Motor vehicle fatalities increase just after publicised suicide stories. *Science* **196**: 1464–5. (**277**)

Phillips D and Rudestan KE (1995) Effect of nonviolent self-defense training on male psychiatric staff members' aggression and fear. *Psychiatric Services* **46**: 164–8. (**557**)

Phillips ML, Drevets WC, Rauch SL, and Lane R (2003) Neurobiology of emotion perception I: the neural basis of normal emotion perception. *Biological Psychiatry* **54**: 504–14. (**298**)

Phillips RTM (2006) Assessing presidential stalkers and assassins. *Journal of the American Academy of Psychiatry and the Law* **34**: 154–64. (**378, 547**)

Pichini S, Puig C, Zuccaro P, et al. (2005) Assessment of exposure to opiates and cocaine during pregnancy in a Mediterranean city: preliminary results of the 'Meconium Project'. *Forensic Science International* **153**: 59–65. (**464**)

Pickard BS, Thomson PA, Christoforou A, et al. (2007) The PDE4B gene confers sex-specific protection against schizophrenia. *Psychiatric Genetics* **17**(3): 129–33. (**209**)

Pihl RO and Hoaken PNS (1997) Clinical correlates and predictors of violence in patients with substance use disorders. *Psychiatric Annals* **27**: 735–40. (**440**)

Pihl RO, Assaad JM, and Hoaken PNS (2003) The alcohol-aggression relationship and differential sensitivity to alcohol. *Aggressive Behavior* **29**: 302–15. (**440**)

Pihl RO, Young SN, Harden P, et al. (1995) Acute effect of altered tryptophan levels and alcohol on aggression in normal human males. *Psychopharmacology* **119**: 353–60. (**309**)

Pike A, Reiss D, Hetherington EM, and Plomin R (1996) Using MZ differences in the search for nonshared environmental effects. *Journal of Child Psychology and Psychiatry* **37**: 695–704. (**191**)

Pilgrim J and Mann A (1990) The use of ICD-10 version of the standardized assessment of personality to determine the prevalence of personality disorder in psychiatric in-patients. *Psychological Medicine* **20**: 9085–992. (**389**)

Pilgrim J, Mellors JD, Boothby H, and Mann A (1993) Inter-rater and temporal reliability of the standardized assessment of personality and the influence of informant characteristics. *Psychological Medicine* **23**: 779–86. (**389**)

Pillay SM, Oliver B, Butler L, and Kennedy HG (2008) Risk stratification and the care pathway. *Irish Journal of Psychological Medicine* **25**: 123–127. (**597, 616**)

Pillemer K and Suitor JJ (1992) Violence and violent feelings: what causes them among family caregivers? *Journal of Gerontology* **47**: S165–72. (**227**)

Pilling S, Bebbington P, Kuipers E, et al. (2002) Psychological treatments in schizophrenia: I meta-analysis of family intervention and cognitive behaviour therapy. *Psychological Medicine* **32**: 763–82. (**363**)

Pillmann F, Ullrich S, Draba S, Sannemuller U, and Marneros A (2000) Acute effects of alcohol and chronic alcohol addiction as a determinant of violent crime. *Nervenartz* **71**: 715–21. (**439**)

Pilowsky I (1969) Abnormal illness behaviour. *British Journal of Medical Psychology* **42**: 347–51. (**423**)

Pilowsky I (1985) Malingerophobia. *Medical Journal of Australia* **143**: 571–2. (**435**)

Pimm J, Stewart ME, Lawrie SM, and Thomson LDG (2004) Detecting the dangerous, violent or criminal patient: an analysis of referrals to maximum security psychiatric care. *Medicine, Science and the Law* **44**: 19–26. (**612**)

Pinals DA (ed) (2007) *Stalking: Psychiatric Perspectives and Practical Applications*. New York: Oxford University Press. (**375**)

Pinel P (1801) *A Treatise on Insanity* (translated by DD Dacies) (1806). London: Cadell and Davies. Obtainable: http://books.google.com. (**384**)

Pines AM (1992) *Romantic Jealousy: Understanding and Conquering the Shadow of Love*. New York: St Martins. (**373**)

Pinheiro PS (2006) World report on violence against children. United Nations Secretary-General's Study on Violence Against Children: Geneva. http://www.unviolencestudy.org/ (**508**)

Pipe R, Bhat A, Matthews B, and Hampstead J (1991) Section 136 and African/Afro-Caribbean minorities. *International Journal of Social Psychiatry* **37**: 14–23. (**48, 621**)

Piquero AR (2000) Frequency, specialization, and violence in offending careers. *Journal of Research in Crime and Delinquency* **37**: 392–418. (**170**)

Piquero AR, Farrington DP, and Blumstein A (2007) *Key Issues in Criminal Career Research: New Analyses of the Cambridge Study in Delinquent Development*. Cambridge, UK: Cambridge University Press. (**173**)

Piquero AR, Farrington DP, Welsh BC, Tremblay RE, and Jennings WG (2009) Effects of early family/parent training programmes on antisocial behaviour and delinquency. *Journal of Experimental Criminology* **5**: 83–120. (**183**)

Pirie PL, Lando H, Curry SJ, McBride CM, and Grothaus LC (2000) Tobacco, alcohol, and caffeine use and cessation in early pregnancy. *American Journal of Preventative Medicine* **18**: 54–61. (**465**)

Pitman RK, van der Kolk BA, Scott PO, and Greenberg MS (1990) Naloxone-reversible analgesic response to combat-related stimuli in post-traumatic stress disorder. *Archives of General Psychiatry* **47**: 541–4. (**720**)

Pitschel-Walz G, Leucht S, Bauml J, Kissling W, and Engel IRR (2001) The effect of family interventions on relapse and rehospitalization in schizophrenia – a meta-analysis. *Schizophrenia Bulletin* **27**: 73–92. (**363**)

Pitt SE and Bale EM (1995) Neonaticide, infanticide, and filicide: a review of the literature. *The Bulletin of the American Academy of Psychiatry and the Law* **23**: 375–386. (**510**)

Plakun E (1994) Principles in the psychotherapy of self-destructive borderline patients. *Journal of Psychotherapy Practice and Research* **3**: 138–48. (**400, 401**)

Plant G and Taylor PJ (2012) Recognition of problem drinking among young adult prisoners. *Behavioral Sciences and the Law* **30**: 140–53. (**282, 492**)

Plaud JJ, Plaud DM, Kolstoe PD, and Orvedal MS (2000) Behavioral treatment of sexually offending behavior. *Mental Health Aspects in Developmental Disabilities*, **3**: 54–61. (**328**)

Plesk P and Greenhalgh T (2001) The challenge of complexity in health care. *British Medical Journal* **323**: 625–8. (**532**)

Pliszka SR, Rogeness GA, Renner P, and Sherman J (1988) Plasma neurochemistry in juvenile offenders. *Journal of the American Academy of Child Psychiatry* **27**: 588–94. (**307**)

Plomin R, DeFries JC, McClearn GE, and McGuffin P (2005) *Behavioral Genetics: a primer,* 4th edn. New York: Worth and W.H. Freeman. (**190**)

Plotnikoff J and Woolfson R (2007) *The 'Go-Between': Evaluation of Intermediary Pathfinder Projects.* Research Summary. London: Ministry of Justice. (**160**)

Plotzker RE, Metzger DS, and Holmes WC (2007) Childhood sexual and physical abuse histories, PTSD, depression, and HIV risk outcomes in women injection drug users: a potential mediating pathway. *American Journal on Addictions* **16**: 431–8. (**464**)

Poehlmann J (2005) Representations of attachment relationships in children of incarcerated mothers. *Child Development* **76**(3): 679–96. (**519**)

Polaschek D and Gannon T (2004) The implicit theories of rapists: what convicted offenders tell us. *Sexual Abuse: A Journal of Research and Treatment* **16**: 299–314. (**258**)

Pollak O (1950) *The criminality of women.* New York: University of Pennsylvania Press. (**500, 501**)

Pollock F and Maitland FW (1968) *The History of English Law*, Vol. 1, 2nd edn. Cambridge, UK: Cambridge University Press. (**19**)

Pollock PH, Stowell-Smith M, and Gopfert M (2006) *Cognitive Analytic Therapy for Offenders: A New Approach to Forensic Psychotherapy.* Oxford, UK: Guilford. (**569**)

Pond DA and Bidwell BH (1960) A survey of epilepsy in fourteen general practices, II. Social and psychological aspects. *Epilepsia* **1**: 285–99. (**285**)

Pope KS (1990) Therapist–patient sexual involvement: a review of the research. *Clinical Psychology Review* **10**: 477–90. (**681, 682**)

Pope KS (2006) *What Therapists Don't Talk About and Why,* 2nd edn. Washington, DC: American psychological Association. (**690**)

Pope KS and Vetter VA (1991) Prior therapist–patient sexual involvement among patients seen by psychologists. *Psychotherapy* **28**: 429–38. (**681**)

Popova S, Lange S, Bekmuradov D et al. (2011) Fetal alcohol spectrum disorder prevalence estimates in correctional systems: a systematic literature review. *Canadian Journal of Public Health* **102**: 336–40. (**465**)

Porporino FJ and Fabiano EA (2000) *Theory Manual for Reasoning and Rehabilitation Revised.* Ottawa, Canada: T3 Associates. (**576**)

Porter R (1987a) *A social history of madness.* London: Wiedenfeld and Nicolson. (**589**)

Porter R (1987b) *Mind-forg'd Manacles. A History of Madness in England from the Restoration to the Regency.* First published by the Athlone Press, published in 1990 Harmondsworth, UK: Penguin books. (**589**)

Porter R (2002) *Madness: A brief history.* Oxford, UK: Oxford University Press. (**589**)

Potoczniak MJ, Mourot JT, Crosbie-Burnett M, and Potoczniak D J (2003) Legal and psychological perspectives on same-sex domestic violence: a multisystemic approach. *Journal of Family Psychology* **17**: 252–59. (**219**)

Povey D, Coleman K, Kaiza P, and Roe S (2009) *Homicides, Firearm Offences and Intimate Violence 2007/08.* (Supplementary Vol. 2 to *Crime in England and Wales 2007/08*, 3rd edn). Home Office Statistical Bulletin 02/09. London: Home Office. (**28**)

Powell BJ, Campbell JL, Landon JF, et al. (1995) A doubleblind, placebo-controlled study of nortriptyline and bromocriptine in male alcoholics subtyped by comorbid psychiatric disorders. *Alcoholism: Clinical and Experimental Research* **19**: 462–8. (**406**)

Powell GE, Gudjonsson GH, and Mullen P (1983) Application of the guilty-knowledge technique in a case of pseudologia fantastica. *Personality and Individual Differences* **4**: 141–6. (**422**)

Power MJ, Alderson MR, Phillipson CM, Shoenberg E, and Morris JN (1967) Delinquent schools? *New Society* **10**: 542–3. (**178**)

Pratt D, Piper M, Appleby L, Webb R, and Shaw J. (2006) Suicide in recently released prisoners: a population-based cohort study. *Lancet* **368**(9530): 119–23. (**462, 634**)

Pratt EM, Brief DJ, and Keane TM (2006) Recent advances in psychological assessment of adults with posttraumatic stress disorder. In J Folette, J Ruzek (eds) *Cognitive behavioural therapies for trauma.* New York: Guilford, pp. 34–61. (**726**)

Pratt TC, Cullen FT, Blevins KR, Daigle L, and Unnever JD (2002) The relationship of attention deficit hyperactivity disorder to crime and delinquency: a meta-analysis. *International Journal of Police Science and Management* **4**: 344–60. (**173**)

Prebble J (1966) *Glencoe – The Story of the Massacre.* London: Secker and Warburg. (**229**)

Prejean H (1993) *Dead Man Walking: An Eyewitness Account of the Death Penalty in the United States.* London: Random House. (**3**)

Prentky RA (1997) Arousal reduction in sexual offenders: a review of antiandrogen interventions. *Sexual Abuse: A Journal of Research and Treatment* **9**: 335–47. (**260**)

Prescott CA, Caldwell CB, Carey G, et al. (2005) The Washington university twin study of alcoholism. *American Journal of Medical Genetics Part B: Neuropsychiatric Genetics* **134**: 48–55. (**201**)

Pressman MR (2007) Disorders of arousal from sleep and violent behaviour: the role of physical contact and proximity. *Sleep* **30**: 1039–47. (**290, 291, 292**)

Prichard J (1837) *Treatise on Insanity and Other Disorders Affecting the Mind.* Carey and Hart: Philadelphia http://books.google.co.uk/books?id=0PIRAAAAYAAJ&printsec=frontcover&source=gbs_ge_summary_r&cad=0#v=onepage&q&f=false (**384**)

Prigerson HG, Shear MK, Frank E, et al. (1997) Traumatic grief: a case of loss-induced trauma. *American Journal of Psychiatry* **154**: 1003–9. (**713**)

Prigerson HG, Shear MK, Jacobs SC, et al. (1999) Consensus criteria for traumatic grief. A preliminary empirical test. *British Journal of Psychiatry* **174**: 67–73. (**713**)

Prime J, White M, Liriano S, and Patel K (2001) *Criminal careers of those born between 1953 and 1978.* Home Office Statistical Bulletin 4/01. London: Home Office. (**172, 268**)

Prince M (1906) *The Dissociation of Personality.* London: Longmans Green. (**426, 427**)

Prins H (1990) Mental abnormality and criminality – an uncertain relationship. *Medicine Science and the Law* **30**: 247–58. (**279**)

Prins H, Tennent G, and Trick K (1985) Motives for arson (fire raising). *Medicine, Science and the Law* **25**: 275–8. (**273**)

Print B and O'Callaghan D (1999) Working with young men who have sexually abused others. In M Erooga, H Masson (eds) *Children and Young People who Sexually Abuse Others.* London: Routledge, pp. 124–45. (**495**)

Prisons Committee (Gladstone) (1895) *Report from the Departmental Committee on Prisons.* Report Cmnd 7702. London: HMSO. Full text accessible on the House of Commons Parliamentary Papers website: http://parlipapers.chadwyck.co.uk/home.do (**626**)

Pritchard C, Cox M, and Dawson A (1997) Suicide and 'violent' death in a six-year cohort of male probationers compared with pattern of mortality in the general population: evidence of accumulative socio-psychiatric vulnerability. *Journal of the Royal Society for the Promotion of Health* **117**: 180–5. (**640**)

Pritchard JK (2001) Are rare variants responsible for susceptibility to complex diseases? *Amercian Journal of Human Genetics* **69**: 124–37. (**194**)

Prochaska JO and DiClemente CC (1983) Stages and processes of self-change of smoking: towards an integrative model of change. *Journal of Consulting and Clinical Psychology* **51**: 350–95. (**617**)

Prochaska JO and DiClemente CC (1984) *The transtheoretical approach: Crossing the traditional boundaries of therapy.* Malabar, FL: Kreiger. (**576**)

Project MATCH Research Group (1997) Project MATCH secondary a priori hypotheses. *Addiction* **92**: 1671–98. (**446**)

Project MATCH Research Group (1998) Matching alcohol treatments to client heterogeneity: project MATCH – treatment main effects and matching effects on drinking during treatment. *Journal of Studies on Alcohol* **59**: 631–9. (**447, 459**)

Prom-Wormley EC, Eaves LJ, Foley DL, et al. (2009) Monoamine oxidase A and childhood adversity as risk factors for conduct disorder in females. *Psychological Medicine* **39**: 579–90. (**199**)

Prosono M (2003) History of forensic psychiatry. In R Rosner (ed) *Principles and Practice of Forensic Psychiatry*, 2nd edn. London: Arnold, pp. 14–30. (**118, 142, 143**)

Proudnikov D, Kroslak T, Sipe JC, et al. (2010) Association of polymorphisms of the cannabinoid receptor (CNR1) and fatty acid amide hydrolase (FAAH) genes with heroin addiction: impact of long repeats of CNR1. *Pharmacogenomics Journal* **10**: 232–42. (**206**)

Prout TH and Strohmer DC (1991) *Emotional Problem Scale.* Lutz, FL: Psychological Assessment Resources. (**331**)

Prudhomme C (1941) Epilepsy and suicide. *Journal of Nervous and Mental Disease* **94**: 722–31. (**285**)

Psychiatric GWAS Consortium Coordinating Committee (2009) Genomewide association studies: history, rationale, and prospects for psychiatric disorders. *American Journal of Psychiatry* **166**: 540–56. (**194**)

Puente S and Cohen D (2003) Jealousy and the meaning (or non meaning) of violence. *Personality and Social Psychology Bulletin* **29**: 449–60. (**369**)

Pulkkinen L and Pitkanen T (1993) Continuities in aggressive behaviour from childhood to adulthood. *Aggressive Behaviour* **19**: 249–63. (**171**)

Pulver AE, Nestadt G, Goldberg R, et al. (1994) Psychotic illness in patients diagnosed with velo-cardio-facial syndrome and their relatives. *Journal of Nervous and Mental Disease* **182**(8): 476–8. (**209**)

Purcell R, Moller B, Flower T, and Mullen PE (2009) A study of stalking among juveniles. *British Journal of Psychiatry* **194**: 451–5. (**376**)

Purcell R, Pathé M, and Mullen PE (2002) The prevalence and nature of stalking in the Australian community. *Australian and New Zealand Journal of Psychiatry* **36**: 114–20. (**374, 375, 380, 546**)

Purcell R, Pathé M, and Mullen PE (2004) When do repeated intrusions become stalking? *Journal of Forensic Psychiatry and Psychology* **15**(4): 571–83. (**374, 375, 379**)

Purcell R, Pathé M, and Mullen PE (2005) The association between stalking victimization and psychiatric morbidity in a random community sample. *British Journal of Psychiatry* **187**: 416–20. (**378, 380**)

Purcell S (2002) Variance components models for gene–environment interaction in twin analysis. *Twin Research* **5**: 554–71. (**190, 191**)

Purcell S and Koenen KC (2005) Environmental mediation and the twin design. *Behavioral Genetics* **35**: 491–8. (**191**)

Purcell SM, Wray NR, Stone JL, et al. (2009) Common polygenic variation contributes to risk of schizophrenia and bipolar disorder. *Nature* **460**(7256): 748–52. (**209**)

Putkonen A, Kotilainen I, Joyal CC, and Tiihonen J (2004) Comorbid personality disorders and substance use disorders of mentally ill homicide offenders: a structured clinical study on dual and triple diagnosis. *Schizophrenia Bulletin* **30**: 59–72. (**346, 397**)

Putkonen H, Amon S, Almiron MP, et al. (2009b) Filicide in Austria and Finland - a register-based study on all filicide cases in Austria and Finland 1995–2005. *BMC Psychiatry* **9**: 74. http://www.biomedcentral.com/1471-244X/9/74 (accessed 21.03.2013). (**508**)

Putkonen H, Amon S, Eronen M, et al. (2010) Child murder and gender differences – a nationwide register-based study of filicide offenders in two European countries. *Journal of Forensic Psychiatry and Psychology* **21**: 637–48. (**508, 509, 515**)

Putkonen H, Amon S, Eronen M, et al. (2011) Gender differences in filicide offense characteristics – a comprehensive register-based study of child murder in two European countries. *Child Abuse and Neglect* **35**: 319–28. (**508**)

Putkonen H, Collander J, Honkasalo M-L, and Lönnqvist J (2001a) Personality disorders and psychoses form two distinct subgroups of homicide among female offenders. *Journal of Forensic Psychiatry* **12**: 300–12. (**507, 510**)

Putkonen H, Collander J, Weizmann-Henelius G, and Eronen M (2007a) Legal outcomes of all suspected neonaticides in Finland 1980–2000. *International Journal of Law and Psychiatry* **30**: 248–54. (**509**)

References

Putkonen H, Collander J, Weizmann-Henelius G, and Eronen M (2007b) Neonaticide may be more preventable and heterogeneous than previously thought- neonaticides in Finland 1980–2000. *International Journal of Law and Psychiatry* **30**: 248–54. (**510, 515**)

Putkonen H, Komulainen EJ, Virkkunen M, and Lönnqvist J (2001b) Female homicide offenders have greatly increased mortality from unnatural deaths. *Forensic Science International* **119**: 221–4. (**511**)

Putkonen H, Komulainen EJ, Virkkunen M, Eronen M, and Lönnqvist J (2003) Risk of repeat offending among violent female offenders with psychotic and personality disorders. *The American Journal of Psychiatry* **160**: 1–5. (**511**)

Putkonen H, Weizmann-Henelius G, Lindberg N, Eronen M, and Häkkänen H (2009a) Differences between homicide and filicide offenders; results of a nationwide register-based case-control study. *BMC Psychiatry* **9**: 27. http://www.biomedcentral.com/content/pdf/1471-244X-9-27.pdf (**508, 509**)

Putkonen H, Weizmann-Henelius G, Lindberg N, Rovamo T, and Häkkänen H (2008) Changes over time in homicides by women: a register-based study comparing female offenders from 1982 to 1992 and 1993 to 2005. *Criminal Behaviour and Mental Health* **18**: 268–78. (**507**)

Putkonen H, Weizmann-Henelius G, Lindberg N, Rovamo T, and Häkkänen-Nyholm H (2011a) Gender differences in homicide offenders' criminal career, substance abuse and mental health care. A nationwide register-based study of Finnish homicide offenders 1995–2004. *Criminal Behaviour and Mental Health* **21**: 51–62. (**502, 503, 507, 513**)

Putnam FW (1993) Dissociative phenomena. In D Spiegel (ed) *Dissociative Disorders: A Clinical Review*. Lutherville, MD: Sidran, pp. 1–16. (**723**)

Putniņš AL (2003) Substance use and the prediction of young offender recidivism. *Drug and Alcohol Review* **22**: 401–8. (**456**)

Pyszora NM, Barker AF, and Kopelman MD (2003) Amnesia for criminal offences: a study of life sentence prisoners. *Journal of Forensic Psychiatry and Psychology* **14**: 475–90. (**292, 293, 294, 296, 297**)

Pyszora NM, Barker AF, and Kopelman MD (2003) Amnesia for criminal offences: a study of life sentence prisoners. *Journal of Forensic Psychiatry and Psychology* **14**: 475–90. (**425, 492, 493, 494, 496, 497**)

Pyszora NM, Fahy T, and Kopelman MD (in preparation) Amnesia for violent offences, 1: an interview study investigating characteristics and putative factors underlying memory loss. (**293, 294, 295, 425**)

Qaseem A, Snow V, Denberg TD, Forclea MA, and Owens DK (2008) Using second-generation antidepressants to treat depressive disorders: A clinical practice guideline from the American College of Physicians. *Annals of Internal Medicine* **149**: 725–33. (**560**)

Quale E (2008) Online sex offending. In DR Laws, WT O'Donohue (eds) *Sexual Deviance: Theory, Assessment, and Treatment*, 2nd edn. New York: Guilford Press. (**251**)

Qualye M and Moore E (1998) Evaluating the impact of structured groupwork with men in a high security hospital. *Criminal Behaviour and Mental Health* **8**: 77–92. (**575**)

Quayle M and Moore E (2006) Maladaptive learning: cognitive-behavioural treatment and beyond, Ch. 11. In C Newrith, C Meux, PJ Taylor (eds) *Personality Disorder and Serious Offending. Hospital Treatment Models*. London: Hodder Arnold, pp. 134–45. (**571**)

Quigley BM, Corbett AB, and Tedeschi JT (2002) Desired image of power. Alcohol expectancies, and alcohol-related aggression. *Psychology of Addictive Behaviors* **16**: 318–24. (**446**)

Quine L (1999) Workplace bullying in an NHS Trust. *British Medical Journal* **318**: 228–32. (**699**)

Quinsey VL (1984) Sexual aggression: studies of offenders against women. In D Weisstub (ed) *Law and Mental Health: International Perspectives*, Vol. 1. New York: Pergamon. (**248**)

Quinsey VL (2004) Risk assessment and management in community settings. In WR Lindsay, JL Taylor, P Sturmey (eds) *Offenders with developmental disabilities*. Chichester, UK: Wiley, pp. 131–42. (**331**)

Quinsey VL, Book A, and Skilling TA (2004) A follow-up study of deinstitutionalized men with intellectual disabilities and histories of antisocial behaviour. *Journal of Applied Research in Intellectual Disabilities* **17**: 243–53. (**330, 537**)

Quinsey VL, Harris GT, Rice ME, and Cormier CA (1998) *Violent Offenders: Appraising and Managing Risk*. Washington, DC: American Psychological Association. (**319, 330, 536, 543**)

Quinsey VL, Harris GT, Rice ME, and Cormier CA (2006) *Violent Offenders: Appraising and Managing Risk*, 2nd edn. Washington, DC: American Psychological Association. (**536**)

Rabiner EA, Messa C, Sargent PA, et al. (2002) A database of [(11)] WAY-100635 binding to 5-HT(1A) receptors in normal male volunteers: Normative data and relationship to methodological, demographic, physiological, and behavioral variables. *Neuroimage* **15**: 620–32. (**310**)

Rabinowitz J, Avnon M, and Rosenberg V (1996) Effect of clozapine on physical and verbal aggression. *Schizophrenia Research* **22**: 249–55. (**564**)

Rabkin JG (1979) Criminal behavior of discharged mental-patients – critical-appraisal of the research. *Psychological Bulletin* **86**: 1–27. (**280**)

Rachman S and Wilson GT (1980) *The Effects of Psychological Therapy*, 2nd edn. New York: Pergamon. (**407**)

Rada RT (1981) Plasma androgens and the sex offender. *Bulletin of the American Academy of Psychiatry and Law* **8**: 456–64. (**244**)

Rädler TJ and Naber D (2007) Sex-specific differences in schizophrenia. *MMW Fortschr Med* **149**: 32–4. (Abstract only in English – main article available in German). (**520**)

Rae MA (1993) Freedom to Care: Achieving Change in Culture and Nursing Practice in a Mental Health Service. Liverpool, UK: Ashworth Hospital Graphics Department. (**552**)

Raesaenen P, Hirvenoj A, Hakko H, and Vaeisaenen E (1994) Cognitive functioning ability of arsonists. *Journal of Forensic Psychiatry* **5**: 615–20. (**329**)

Raimer B and Stobo J (2004) Health care delivery in the Texas prison system: the role of academic medicine. *The Journal of the American Medical Association* **292**: 485–9. (**527**)

Raine A (1991) The schizotypal personality questionnaire (SPQ): a measure of schizotypal personality based on DSM-III-R criteria. *Schizophrenia Bulletin* **17**: 555–64. (**388**)

Raine A, Buchsbaum M, and LaCasse L (1997) Brain abnormalities in murderers indicated by positron emission tomography. *Biological Psychiatry* **42**: 495–508. (**303**)

Raine A, Buchsbaum MS, Stanley J, et al. (1994) Selective reductions in prefrontal glucose metabolism in murderers. *Biological Psychiatry* **36**: 365–73. (**302**)

Raine A, Ishikawa SS, Arce E, et al. (2004) Hippocampal structural asymmetry in unsuccessful psychopaths. *Biological Psychiatry* **55**: 185–91. (**299, 301**)

Raine A, Lencz T, Bihrle S, LaCasse L, and Colletti P (2000) Reduced prefrontal grey matter volume and reduced autonomic activity in antisocial personality disorder. *Archives of General Psychiatry* **57**: 119–27. (**299, 301**)

Raine A, Lencz T, Taylor K, et al. (2003) Corpus callosum abnormalities in psychopathic antisocial individuals. *Archives of General Psychiatry* **60**: 1134–42. (**299, 300**)

Raine A, Meloy JR, Bihrle S, et al. (1998a) Reduced prefrontal and increased subcortical brain functioning assessed using positron emission tomography in predatory and affective murderers. *Behavioural Science and the Law* **16**: 319–32. (**297, 302, 303**)

Raine A, Moffitt TE, Caspi A, et al. (2005) Neurocognitive impairments in boys on the life-course-persistent antisocial path. *Journal of Abnormal Psychology* **114**: 38–49. (**174**)

Raine A, Stoddard J, Bihrle S and Buchsbaum M (1998b) Prefrontal glucose deficits in murderers lacking psychosocial deprivation. *Neuropsychiatry Neuropsychology and Behavioural Neurology* **11**: 1–7. (**302, 303**)

Raistrick D (2001) Alcohol withdrawal and detoxification. In N Heather, T Peters, T Stockwell (eds) *International handbook of alcohol dependence and problems*. Chichester, UK: Wiley, pp. 523–39. (**438**)

Raitt F and Zeedyk S (2000) *The Implicit Relation of Psychology and the Law: Women and Syndrome Evidence*. London: Routledge. (**149**)

Ralli R (1994) Health care in prisons. In E Player, M Jenkins (eds) *Prisons after Woolf: Reform through Riot*. London: Routledge. (**627**)

Ramirez LF (1988) Plasma cortisol and depression in pathological gamblers. *British Journal of Psychiatry* **153**: 684–6. (**470**)

Ramos-Arroyo MA, Ulbright TM, Yu PL, and Christian JC (1988) Twin study: relationship between birth weight, zygosity, placentation, and pathologic placental changes. *Acta Geneticae Medicae et Gemellologiae* (*Roma*) **37**: 229–38. (**189**)

Ramsay L, Gray C, and White T (2001) A review of suicide within the State Hospital, Carstairs 1972–1996. *Medicine, Science and the Law* **41**: 97–101. (**613**)

Ramsland K (2007) *Inside the Minds of Healthcare Serial Killers*. Westport, CT: Praeger. (**686, 688**)

Rankin J and Regan S (2004) *Meeting Complex Needs: The Future of Social Care*. London: IPPR. (**650**)

Raphael B (1997) The Interaction of Trauma and Grief. In D Black, M Newman, J Harris Hendriks, G Mezey (eds) *Psychological Trauma - A Developmental Approach*. London: Gaskell, pp. 31–43. (**713**)

Raphael B, Meldrum L, and McFarlane AC. (1995) Does debriefing after psychological trauma work? *BMJ* **310**: 1479–80. (**724**)

Rapoport JL, Addington AM, Frangou S, and Psych MR (2005) The neurodevelopmental model of schizophrenia: update 2005. *Molecular Psychiatry* **10**: 434–49. (**210**)

Räsänen P, Hakko H, and Jarvelin MR (1999) Early onset drunk driving, violent criminality and mental disorders. *Lancet* **354**: 1788. (**278**)

Räsänen P, Tiihonen J, Isohanni M, et al. (1998) Schizophrenia, alcohol abuse and violent behaviour: a 26-year follow-up study of an unselected birth cohort. *Schizophrenia Bulletin* **24**: 437–41. (**443**)

Rasch W (1981) The effects of indeterminate detention: a study of men sentenced to life imprisonment. *International Journal of Law and Psychiatry* **4**: 417–31. (**637**)

Rasetti R, Mattay VS, Wiedholz LM, et al. (2009) Evidence that altered amygdale activity in schizophrenia is related to clinical state and not genetic risk. *American Journal of Psychiatry* **166**: 216–25. (**312**)

Raspe RE (1786) *The Surprising Adventures of Baron Munchausen*. FJH Darton (ed) 1930. London: Navarre Society. (**434**)

Ratcliffe S (1999) Long term outcomes in children of sex chromosome abnormalities. *Archives of Disease in Childhood* **80**: 192–5. (**323**)

Rauch SL, van der Kolk BA, Fisler RE, et al. (1996) A symptom provocation study of post-traumatic stress disorder using positron emission tomography and script driven imagery. *Archives of General Psychiatry* **53**: 380–7. (**719, 720**)

Rawsthorne MO (1998) The probation service and victims of crime. *Criminal Behaviour and Mental Health* **8**: 178–83. (**645, 709**)

Ray I (1838) *A Treatise on the Medical Jurisprudence of Insanity* (Ch. XV Simulated Insanity) Reprinted (1962) Cambridge, MA: Harvard University Press. (**118, 418, 432**)

Rayburn WF and Bogenschutz MP (2004) Pharmacotherapy for pregnant women with addictions. *American Journal of Obstetrics and Gynaecology* **191**: 1885–97. (**457**)

Rayner C (2000) *Bullying at work. Workplace Bullying Survey of Unison Police Support Staff Members*. London: UNISON. http://www.unison.org.uk/acrobat/11088.pdf (**699**)

Rayner C (2005) Reforming abusive organizations. In V Bowie, B Fisher, CL Cooper (eds) *Countering workplace violence*. Devon, UK: Willan. (**699**)

Rayner C and Cooper CL (2006) Workplace Bulling. In EK Kelloway, J Barling, JJ Hurrell Jr (eds) *Handbook of Workplace Violence*. London: Sage, pp. 121–46. (**699**)

Rayner C and Hoel H (1997) A summary review of literature relating to workplace bullying. *Journal of Community and Applied Social Psychology* **7**: 181–91. (**699**)

Raynor P, Kynch J, Roberts C, and Merrington S (2000) *Risk and Need Assessment in Probation Services: An Evaluation.* Home Office Research Study 211. London: Home Office. http://library.npia.police.uk/docs/hors/hors211.pdf (**530**)

Read J, Agar K, Argyle N, and Aderhold V (2003) Sexual and physical abuse during childhood and adulthood as predictors of hallucinations, delusions and thought disorder. *Psychology and Psychotherapy: Theory, Research and Practice* **76**: 1–22. (**571**)

Read J, van Os J, Morrison AP, and Ross CA (2005) Childhood trauma, psychosis and schizophrenia: a literature review with theoretical and clinical implications. *Acta Psychiatrica Scandinavica* **112**: 330–50. (**341, 344**)

Read PP (1981, May 17) Inside the mind of the ripper. *The London Observer.* (**6**)

Reagu S and Taylor PJ (2012) Practical legal concerns, the England and Wales Context. Ch. 17. In J Simpson (ed) *Neuroimaging in Forensic Psychiatry: From the Clinic to the Courtroom.* Oxford, UK: Wiley-Blackwell. (**17, 149**)

Reagu S, Jones, R, Kumari V, and Taylor PJ (in press) Angry affect and violence in the context of a psychotic illness: A systematic review and meta-analysis of the literature. *Schizophrenia Research* http://www.schres-journal.com/article/S0920-9964(13)00062-5/abstract (**354**)

Reason J and Lucas D (1984) Absent-mindedness in shops: its incidence, correlates and consequences. *British Journal of Clinical Psychology* **23** (Pt 2): 121–31. (**271**)

Reason J, Manstead A, Stradling S, Baxter J, and Campbell K (1990) Errors and violations on the road: A real distinction? *Ergonomics* **33**: 1315–32. (**278**)

Reder P and Duncan S (1996) Reflections on child abuse inquiries. In J Peay (ed) *Inquiries after Homicide.* London: Duckworth, pp. 79–100. (**74, 696, 697**)

Redlich AD, Summers A, and Hoover S (2010) Self-reported false confessions and false guilty pleas among offenders with mental illness. *Law and Human Behavior* **34**(1): 79–90. (**622**)

Redon R, Ishikawa S, Fitch KR, et al. (2006) Global variation in copy number in the human genome. *Nature* **444**(7118): 444–54. (**200, 209**)

Reed J and Lyne M (1997) The quality of health care in prison: results of a year's programme of semi structured inspections. *British Medical Journal* **315**: 1420–4. (**627**)

Reed J and Lyne M (2000) Inpatient care of mentally ill people in prison: results of a year's programme of semi structured inspections. *British Medical Journal* **320**: 1031–4. (**627, 632**)

Rees A and Rivett M (2005) Let a hundred flowers bloom, let a hundred schools of thought contend: towards a variety in programmes for perpetrators of domestic violence. *Probation Journal* **52**: 277–88. (**220**)

Reeves R and Rosner R (2003) Education and training in forensic psychiatry. In R Rosner (ed) *Principles and Practice of Forensic Psychiatry.* London: Arnold, pp. 52–55. (**143**)

Reeves R, Rosner R, Bourget D, and Gunn J (2007) Training and education for mental health professionals. In AR Felthous, H Sass (eds) *International Handbook on Psychopathic Disorders and the Law,* Vol. 2). Chichester, UK: Wiley, pp. 505–17. (**143**)

Regan J, Alderson A, and Regan W (2002) Psychiatric disorders in aging prisoners. *Clinical Gerontologist* **26**: 117–124. (**526**)

Regehr C and Glancy G (2011) When social workers are stalked: Risks, strategies, and legal protections. *Clinical Social Work Journal* **39**: 232–42. (**378**)

Regel S and Berliner P (2007) Current perspectives on assessment and therapy with survivors of torture: the use of a cognitive behavioural approach. *European Journal of Psychotherapy and Counselling* **9**: 289–99. (**729**)

Regier DA, Farmer ME, Rae DS, et al. (1990) Comorbidity of mental disorders with alcohol and other drug abuse. Results from the Epidemiologic Catchment Area (ECA) Study. *Journal of the American Medical Association* **264**: 2511–18. (**200, 3477, 452**)

Regier DA, Narrow WE, Kuhl EA, and Kupfer DJ (2009) The conceptual development of DSN-V. *American Journal of Psychiatry* **166**: 645–51. (**10**)

Reich JH and Green AI (1991) Effect of personality disorder on outcome of treatment. *Journal of Nervous and Mental Disease* **179**: 74–82. (**398**)

Reicher-Rössler A, Häfner H, Dütsch-Strobel A, et al. (1994) Further evidence for a specific role of estradiol in schizophrenia. *Biological Psychiatry* **36**: 492–5. (**501, 521**)

Reid AH (1972) Psychosis in adult mental defectives. *British Journal of Psychiatry* **120**: 205–18. (**317**)

Reid WH (2003) Terrorism and forensic psychiatry. *Journal of the American Academy of Psychiatry and the Law* **31**: 285–8. (**235**)

Reilly JG, McTavish SFB, and Young AH (1997) Rapid depletion of plasma tryptophan: a review of studies and experimental methodology. *Journal of Psychopharmacology* **11**: 381–92. (**307**)

Reinisch JM (1990) *The Kinsey Institute New Report on Sex: What You Must Know to be Sexually Literate.* New York: St Martin's. (**291**)

Reiss AJ and Farrington DP (1991) Advancing knowledge about co-offending: results from a prospective longitudinal survey of London males. *Journal of Criminal Law and Criminology* **82**: 360–95. (**177**)

Reiss AJ and Roth JA. (1993) *Understanding and preventing violence.* Volume I. National Academy Press: Washington: DC. (**337, 662**)

Reiss D (2001) Counterfactuals and inquiries after homicide. *Journal of Forensic Psychiatry* **12**: 169–81. (**75, 696**)

Reiss D, Grubin D, and Meux C (1996) Young 'psychopaths' in special hospital: treatment and outcome. *British Journal of Psychiatry* **168**: 99–104. (**398, 583**)

Reiss D, Meux C, and Grubin D (2000) The effect of psychopathy on outcome in high security hospital patients. *Journal of the American Academy of Psychiatry and the Law* **28**: 309–14. (**583**)

Reiss D, Quayel M, Brett T, and Meux C (1998) Dramatherapy for mentally disordered offenders: changes in levels of anger. *Criminal Behaviour and Mental Health* **8**: 139–53. (**558**)

Reist C, Nakamura K, Sagart E, Sokolski KN, and Fujimoto KA (2003) Impulsive aggressive behavior: open-label treatment with citalopram. *Journal of Clinical Psychiatry* **64**: 81–5. (**311**)

Reith M (1998) *Community Care Tragedies: A Practice Guide to Mental Health Inquiries.* Birmingham, UK: Venture. (**695, 696**)

Reitman B and Cleveland S (1964) Changes in body image following sensory deprivation in schizophrenia and control groups. *Journal of Abnormal and Social Psychology* **68**: 168–76. (**595**)

Remington G and Kapur S (2010) Antipsychotic dosing: how much but also how often? *Schizophrenia Bulletin* **36**: 900–3. (**360**)

Renaud P, Rouleau JL, Granger L, Barsetti I, and Bouchard S (2002) Measuring sexual preferences in virtual reality: a pilot study. *CyberPsychology and Behavior* **5**: 1–9. (**254**)

Rennie C and Roberts A (2008) *Improving Health, Supporting Justice: A Consultation Paper.* London: Department of Health. http://www. revolving-doors.org.uk/documents/improving-health-supporting-justice-consultation-responses/ (**619**)

Rennie C, Senior J, and Shaw J (2009) The future of offender health: evidencing mainstream health services throughout the offender pathway. *Criminal Behaviour and Mental Health* **19**: 1–8. (**630**)

Renwick SJ, Black L, Ramm M, and Novaco RW (1997) Anger treatment with forensic hospital patients. *Legal and Criminological Psychology* **2**: 103–116. (**521, 575**)

Renz A, Ide M, Newton T, Robinson P, and Smith D Psychological interventions to improve adherence to oral hygiene instructions in adults with periodontal diseases: *Cochrane Database of Systematic Reviews* 2007.Issue 2, Art. No.: CD005097. http://onlinelibrary. wiley.com/o/cochrane/clsysrev/articles/CD005097/frame.html (**568**)

Repo E and Virkunnen M (1997) Young arsonists, history of conduct disorder, psychiatric diagnosis, and criminal recidivism. *Journal of Forensic Psychiatry* **8**: 311–20. (**495**)

Resick PA and Schnicke MK (1993) *Cognitive Processing Therapy for Rape Victims.* Newbury Park, CA: Sage. (**727, 728**)

Resick PA, Nishith P, Weaver TL, Astin MC, and Fueur CA (2002) A comparison of cognitive-processing therapy with prolonged exposure and a waiting condition for the treatment of chronic posttraumatic stress disorder in female rape victims. *Journal of Consulting and Clinical Psychology* **70**: 867–79. (**725**)

Resnick HS, Kilpatrick DG, Dansky BS, Saunders BE, and Best CL (1993) Prevalence of civilian trauma and posttraumatic stress disorder in a representative national sample of women. *Journal of Consulting and Clinical Psychology* **61**: 984–91. (**715**)

Resnick PJ (1969) Child murder by parents: a psychiatric review of filicide. *The American Journal of Psychiatry* **126**: 325–34. (**508, 509**)

Resnick PJ (1970) Murder of the newborn: a psychiatric review of neonaticide. *The American Journal of Psychiatry* **126**: 1414–20. (**570**)

Rethink (2006) *A Cut Too Far : Six Months On : A Follow-Up Report into Budget Cuts Affecting Mental Health Services.* London: Rethink: www.rethink.org. (**708**)

Reuter J, Raedler T, Rose M, et al. (2005) Pathological gambling is linked to reduced activation of the mesolismbic reward system. *Nature Neuroscience* **8**: 147–8. (**436, 472**)

Reuter P and Stevens A (2007) *An Analysis of UK Drug Policy: A Monograph Prepared for the UK Drug Policy Commission.* London: UKDPC. (**467**)

Rey JM and Tennant CC (2002) Cannabis and mental health – more evidence establishes clear link between use of cannabis and psychiatric illness. Cannabis and mental health - more evidence establishes clear link between use of cannabis and psychiatric illness. *British Medical Journal* **325**: 1183–4. (**488**)

Reynolds M, Mezey G, Chapman M, et al. (2005) Co-morbid post-traumatic stress disorder in a substance misusing clinical population. *Drug and Alcohol Dependence* **77**: 251–8. (**712**)

Rhee SH and Waldman ID (2002) Genetic and environmental influences on antisocial behavior: a meta-analysis of twin and adoption studies. *Psychological Bulletin* **128**: 490–529. (**195, 196**)

Ricci RJ (2006) Trauma resolution using eye movement desensitization and reprocessing with an incestuous sex offender: an instrumental case study. *Clinical Case Studies* **5**: 248–65. (**725**)

Ricci RJ, Clayton CA, and Shapiro F (2006) Some effects of EMDR on previously abused child molesters: theoretical reviews and preliminary findings. *Journal of Forensic Psychiatry and Psychology* **17**: 538–62. (**725, 727**)

Rice DP, Kelman S, Miller LS, and Dunmeyer S (1990) *The Economic Costs of Alcohol and Drug Abuse and Mental Illness.* San Francisco, CA: Office of Financing and Coverage Policy of the Alcohol, Drug Abuse, and Mental Health Administration. (**200**)

Rice ME and Chaplin TC (1979) Social skills training for hospitalised male arsonists. *Journal of Behaviour Therapy and Experimental Psychiatry* **10**: 105–8. (**330**)

Rice ME and Harris GT (1991) Firesetters admitted to a maximum security psychiatric institution. *Journal of Interpersonal Violence* **6**: 461–75. (**275**)

Rice ME and Harris GT (1995a) Psychopathy, schizophrenia, alcohol abuse and violent recidivism. *International Journal of Law and Psychiatry* **18**: 333–42. (**443, 444**)

Rice ME and Harris GT (1995b) Violent recidivism: assessing predictive validity. *Journal of Consulting and Clinical Psychology* **63**: 737–48. (**536**)

Rice ME and Harris GT (1997a) Cross-validation and extension of the violence risk appraisal guide for child molesters and rapists. *Law and Human Behavior* **21**: 231–41. (**536**)

Rice ME and Harris GT (1997b) The treatment of mentally disordered offenders. *Psychology, Public Policy and Law* **3**: 126–83. (**571**)

Rice ME and Harris GT (2003) The size and sign of treatment effects in sex offender therapy. *Annals of the New York Academy of Sciences* **989**: 428–40. (**257, 262**)

References

Rice ME and Harris GT (2005) Comparing effect sizes in follow-up studies: ROC area. Cohen's *d*. and *r*. *Law and Human Behavior* **29**: 615. (**536**)

Rich J (1956) Types of stealing. *Lancet* **270**: 496–8. (**270**)

Richards B (1978) The experience of long-term imprisonment. *British Journal of Criminology* **18**: 162–9. (**637**)

Richards HJ, Casey JO, and Lucente SW (2003) Psychopathy and treatment response in incarcerated female substance users. *Criminal Justice and Behavior* **30**: 251–76. (**513**)

Richardson A and Budd T (2003) Young adults, alcohol, crime and disorder. *Criminal Behaviour and Mental Health* **13**: 5–17. (**440**)

Richardson DS and Hammock GS (2007) Social context of human aggression: are we paying too much attention to gender? *Aggression and Violent Behavior* **12**: 417–26. (**218**)

Richardson G, Kelly TP, Bhate R, and Graham F (1997) Group differences in abuser and abuse characteristics in a British sample of sexually abusive adolescents. *Sexual Abuse: A Journal of Research and Treatment* **9**: 239–57. (**252**)

Richmond RL, Butler T, Belcher JM, et al. (2006) Promoting smoking cessation among prisoners: feasibility of a multi-component intervention. *Australia and New Zealand Journal of Public Health* **30**: 474–8. (**568**)

Rickards L, Fox K, Roberts C, Fletcher L, and Goddard E (2004) *Living in Britain: General Household Survey 2002.* London: HMSO. (**437**)

Ricketts D, Carnell H, Davies S, Kaul A, and Duggan C (2001) First admissions to a regional secure unit over a 16-year period: changes in demographic and service characteristics. *Journal of Forensic Psychiatry* **12**: 78–89. (**600**)

Ridley AM and Clifford B (2004) The effects of anxious mood induction on suggestibility to misleading post-event information. *Applied Cognitive Psychology* **18**: 233–4. (**161**)

Ridley AM and Clifford B (2006) Suggestibility and state anxiety: how the two concepts relate in a source identification paradigm. *Memory* **14**: 37–45. (**161**)

Ridley AM, Clifford B, and Keogh E (2002) The effects of state anxiety on the suggestibility and accuracy of child eyewitnesses. *Applied Cognitive Psychology* **16**: 547–58. (**161**)

Riggins-Caspers KM, Cadoret RJ, Knutson JF, and Langbehn D (2003) Biology–environment interaction and evocative biology–environment correlation: contributions of harsh discipline and parental psychopathology to problem adolescent behaviors. *Behavioral Genetics* **33**: 205–20. (**200**)

Riggs DS, Cahill SP, and Foa EB (2006) Prolonged exposure treatment for posttraumatic stress disorder. In J Folette, J Ruzek (eds) *Cognitive behavioural therapies for trauma.* New York: Guilford, pp. 65–95. (**727**)

Righthand S and Welch C (2001) *Juveniles who have Sexually Offended: A Review of the Professional Literature.* Washington, DC: US Department of Justice, Office of Juvenile Justice and Delinquency Prevention. www.ncjrs.org/html/ojjdp/report_juvsex_offend/contents.htm. (**263**)

Righthand S, Prentky R, Knight R, et al. (2005) Factor structure and validation of the juvenile sex offender assessment protocol (J-SOAP). *Sexual Abuse: A Journal of Research and Treatment* **17**: 13–30. (**254**)

Rimmer JH, Braddock D, and Marks B (1995) Health characteristics and behaviors of adults with mental retardation residing in three living arrangements. *Research in Developmental Disabilities* **16**: 489–99. (**324**)

Rinne T, van den Brink W, Wouters L, and van Dyck R (2002) SSRI treatment of borderline personality disorder: a randomized, placebo–controlled clinical trial for female patients with borderline personality disorder. *American Journal of Psychiatry* **159**: 2048–54. (**311, 312, 406**)

Rinne T, Westenberg HG, den Boer JA, and van den Brink W (2000) Serotonergic blunting to meta-chlorophenylpiperazine (m-CPP) highly correlates with sustained childhood abuse in impulsive and autoaggressive female borderline patients. *Biological Psychiatry* **47**: 548–56. (**309**)

Risk Management Authority (2006) *Standards and Guidelines for Risk Assessment.* Paisley, UK: Risk Management Authority. (**89**)

Risk Management Authority (2007a) *Standards and Guidelines. Risk Management of Offenders Subject to an Order for Lifelong Restriction.* Paisley, UK: Risk Management Authority. (**89**)

Risk Management Authority (2007b) *Risk Assessment Tools Evaluation Directory. RATED Version 2.* Paisley, UK: Risk Management Authority. (**89**)

Risk Management Authority (2007c) *Review of Current Arrangements for Risk Assessment and Management for Restricted Patients.* Paisley, UK: Risk Management Authority. (**89**)

Ritchie G, Billcliff N, McMahon J, and Thomson LDG (2004) The detection and treatment of substance abuse in offenders with major mental illness: an intervention study. *Medicine, Science and the Law* **44**: 317–26. (**613**)

Ritchie J, Dick D and Lingham R. (1994) *The report of the inquiry into the care and treatment of Christopher Clunis.* TSO: London. (**75, 76, 335, 532, 695, 707**)

Ritchie S (1985) Report to the Secretary of State for Social Services concerning the Death of Mr Michael Martin at Broadmoor Hospital on 6th July 1984. (private circulation). (**603**)

Ritsher JE, Coursey RD, and Farrell EW (1997) A survey on issues in the lives of women with severe mental illness. *Psychiatric Services* **48**: 1273–82. (**521**)

Rivett M (2006) Treatment for perpetrators of domestic violence: controversy in policy and practice. *Criminal Behaviour and Mental Health* **16**(4): 205–10. (**221**)

Rivett MJ and Kelly S (2006) From awareness to practice: children, domestic violence and child welfare. *Child Abuse Review* **15**: 224–42. (**220**)

Rix KJB (1994) A psychiatric study of adult arsonists. *Medicine Science and the Law* **34**: 21–34. (**273**)

Rix KJB (1999a) Expert evidence and the courts. 1. The history of expert evidence. *Advances in Psychiatric Treatment* **5**: 71–7. (**148, 168**)

Rix KJB (1999b) Expert evidence and the courts. 2. Proposals for reform, the expert witness bodies and 'the model report'. *Advances in Psychiatric Treatment* **5**: 154–60. (**155, 158**)

Rix KJB (1999c) Capable of managing and administering property and affairs: old case, new law. *Journal of Forensic Psychiatry* **10**: 437–44. (**166**)

Rix KJB (2000a) The new civil procedure rules. 1. The process of dispute resolution and litigation. *Advances in Psychiatric Treatment* **6**: 219–25. (**158, 168**)

Rix KJB (2000b) The new Civil procedure rules. 2. Part 35 provisions and their implications. *Advances in Psychiatric Treatment* **6**: 219–25. (**158, 168**)

Rix KJB (2006a) England's first expert witness. *The Expert and Dispute Resolver* **11**(2): 16–18. (**148**)

Rix KJB (2006b) Psychiatry and the law: uneasy bedfellows. *Medico-Legal Journal* **74**: 148–59. (**148, 149**)

Rix KJB (2006c) Assessing mental capacity in elderly people. *Solicitors' Journal* **150**(41): 1370–1. (**166**)

Rix KJB (2008a) The psychiatrist as expert witness. Part 1: General principles and civil cases. *Advances in Psychiatric Treatment* **14**: 37–41. (**152, 168**)

Rix KJB (2008b) The psychiatrist as expert witness. Part 2: Criminal cases and the Royal College of Psychiatrists' guidance. *Advances in Psychiatric Treatment* **14**: 109–14. (**152, 153, 158, 168**)

Rix KJB and Clarkson AD (1994) Depersonalisation and intent. *Journal of Forensic Psychiatry* **5**: 409–19. (**162**)

Rix KJB, Thorn S, and Neville W (1997) Medical evidence concerning the suitability to succeed to the tenancy of a farm: 'the case of Toad of Toad Hall'. *Journal of Clinical Forensic Medicine* **4**: 25–32. (**152**)

Robb B (1967) *Sans Everything: A Case to Answer*. London: Nelson. (**682**)

Robbins PC, Petrila J, LeMelle S, and Monahan J (2006) The use of housing as leverage to increase adherence to psychiatric treatment in the community. *Administration and Policy in Mental Health and Mental Health Services Research* **33**: 226–36. (**365, 567**)

Robert C (2006) Managing risk: from the inside looking out. *Criminal Behaviour and Mental Health* **16**(3): 142–45. (**533, 588**)

Roberts C (1995) Effective practice and service delivery. In: J McGuire (ed) *What Works: Reducing Reoffending. Guidelines from Research and Practice*. Chichester, UK: John Wiley and Sons, pp. 221–36. (**579**)

Roberts G and Wolfson P (2004) The rediscovery of recovery: open to all. *Advances in Psychiatric Treatment* **10**: 37–49. (**574**)

Robertson G (1988) Arrest patterns among mentally disordered offenders. *British Journal of Psychiatry* **153**: 313–6. (**280, 340**)

Robertson G, Dell S, James K, and Grounds A (1994) Psychotic men remanded in custody to Brixton Prison. *British Journal of Psychiatry* **164**: 55–61. (**632**)

Robertson G, Pearson R, and Gibb R (1996) The entry of mentally disordered people to the criminal justice system. *British Journal of Psychiatry* **169**: 172–80. (**23, 280**)

Robins L and Rutter M (1990) *Straight and Devious Pathways from Childhood to Adulthood*. Cambridge: Cambridge University Press. (**398**)

Robins LN, West PJ, and Herjanic BL (1975) Arrests and delinquency in two generations: a study of black urban families and their children. *Journal of Child Psychology and Psychiatry* **16**: 125–40. (**176**)

Robinson A (2003) *Cardiff Women's Safety Unit: Final Evaluation*. Cardiff, UK: Cardiff University. (**220**)

Robinson D and Kettles A (2000) Overview and contemporary issues in the role of the forensic nurse in the UK. In: D Robinson, A Kettles (eds) *Forensic Nursing and Multidisciplinary care of the Mentally Disordered Offender*. London: Jessica Kingsley, pp. 26–38. (**552**)

Robinson R, Fenwick J, and Wood S (2006) *Report of the independent inquiry into the care and treatment of John Barrett*. London: NHS. http://www.psychminded.co.uk/news/news2006/nov06/Johnbarrett.pdf (**76, 595**)

Rock P (1998) *After Homicide: Practical and Political Responses to Bereavement*. Oxford, UK: Clarendon. (**713**)

Roe S and Man L (2006) *Drug Misuse Declared: Findings from the 2005/6 British Crime Survey – England and Wales*. London: Home Office. http://webarchive.nationalarchives.gov.uk/20110218135832/http://rds.homeoffice.gov.uk/rds/pdfs06/hosb1506.pdf (**464**)

Roe S, Coleman K, and Kaiza P (2010) Violent and sexual crime. In A. Walker, J. Flatley, C. Kershaw, D. Moon (eds) *Crime in England and Wales 2008/09 Volume 1 Findings from the British Crime Survey and police recorded crimeHome Office Statistical Bulletin 11/09*. London: Home Office. (**240**)

Roese NJ and Olson JM (1993) The structure of counterfactual thought. *Personality and Social Psychology Bulletin* **19**: 312–19. (**696**)

Roese NJ and Olson JM (1995) Outcome, controllability and counterfactual thinking. *Personality and Social Psychology Bulletin* **21**: 620–28. (**696, 697**)

Rofman ES, Askinazi C, and Fant E (1980) The prediction f dangerous behavior in emergency civil commitment. *American Journal of Psychiatry* **137**: 1061–4. (**349**)

Rogers A and Faulkner A (1987) *A Place of Safety*. London: MIND. (**621**)

Rogers CR (1961) *On Becoming a Person*. Boston, MA: Houghton Mifflinn Company. (**10, 554**)

Rogers K and Chappell D (2003) *Preventing and Responding to Violence at Work*. Geneva: ILO. (**700**)

Rogers P (1997) A behaviour nurse therapy service in forensic mental health. *Mental Health Practice* **1**: 22–6. (**553**)

Rogers P, Watt A, Gray NS, MacCulloch M, and Gournay K (2002) Content of command hallucinations predicts self-harm but not violence in a medium secure hospital. *Journal of Forensic Psychiatry* **13**: 245–56. (**353**)

Rogers R (2001) *Handbook of Diagnostic and Structured Interviewing*. New York: Guilford. (**388**)

Rogers R, Nussbaum D, and Gillis R (1988) Command hallucinations and criminality: a clinical quandary. *Bulletin of the American Academy of Psychiatry and the Law* **16**: 251–8. (**353**)

Rogers RD, Blackshaw AJ, Middleton HC, et al. (1999) Tryptophan depletion impairs stimulus–reward learning while methylphenidate disrupts attentional control in healthy young adults: implications for the monoaminergic basis of impulsive behaviour. *Psychopharmacology* **146**: 482–91. (**309**)

Rollnick S, Miller WR, and Butler CC (2008) *Motivational Interviewing In Healthcare*. London: The Guilford. (**408, 459**)

Ron MA (1977) Brain damage in chronic alcoholism: a neuropathological, neuroradiological and psychological review. *Psychological Medicine* **7**: 103–12. (**33**)

Ron MA (1983) The alcoholic brain: CT scan and psychological findings. *Psychological Medicine, Monograph, Suppl* **3**: 1–33. (**33, 438**)

Room R and Rossow I (2001) The share of violence attributable to drinking. *Journal of Substance Use* **6**: 218–28. (**442**)

Rooth FG (1971) Indecent exposure and exhibitionism. *British Journal of Hospital Medicine* **5**: 521–34. (**247**)

Rooth FG (1973) Exhibitionism, sexual violence and paedophilia. *British Journal of Psychiatry* **122**: 705–10. (**247**)

Rose J and West C (1999) Assessment of anger in people with intellectual disabilities. *Journal of Applied Research in Intellectual Disabilities* **12**: 211–24. (**326**)

Rose J, Jenkins R, O'Connor C, Jones C, and Felce D (2002) A group treatment for men with intellectual disabilities who sexually offend or abuse. *Journal of Applied Research in Intellectual Disabilities* **15**: 138–50. (**328, 329**)

Rose J, West C, and Clifford D (2000) Group interventions for anger in people with intellectual disabilities. *Research in Developmental Disabilities* **21**: 171–81. (**327**)

Rose N (1985) Unreasonable rights: mental illness and the limits of law. *Journal of Law and Society* **12**: 199–219. (**603**)

Rose N (1986) Laws, rights and psychiatry. In P Miller and N Rose (eds) *The Power of Psychiatry*. Cambridge, UK: Polity. (**150, 603**)

Rose RJ, Dick DM, Viken RJ, and Kaprio J (2001) Gene–environment interaction in patterns of adolescent drinking: regional residency moderates longitudinal influences on alcohol use. *Alcoholism: Clinical and Experimental Research* **25**: 637–43. (**202**)

Rose RJ, Dick DM, Viken RJ, Pulkkinen L, and Kaprio J (2004) Genetic and environmental effects on conduct disorder and alcohol dependence symptoms and their covariation at age 14. *Alcoholism. Clinical and Experimental Research* **28**: 1541–8. (**204**)

Rose S, Bisson J, and Wessely S (2003) A systematic review of brief psychological interventions ('debriefing') for the treatment of immediate trauma related symptoms and the prevention of post–traumatic stress disorder. In R Orner, U Schnyder (eds) *Reconstructing Early Intervention After Trauma*. Oxford, UK: OUP. (**706, 715, 724**)

Rosen G (1968) *Madness in Society*. Chicago, IL: University of Chicago Press. (**589**)

Rosen I (1996) The general psychoanalytical theory of perversion. In I Rosen (ed) *Sexual Deviation*, 3rd edn. Oxford, UK: Oxford University Press. (**245, 259**)

Rosenbaum M (1979) Difficulties in taking care of business: women addicts as mothers. *American Journal of Drug and Alcohol Abuse* **6**: 431–6. (**465**)

Rosenberg D (1987) Web of deceit: a literature review of Munchausen syndrome by proxy. *Child Abuse and Neglect* **11**: 547–63. (**226, 506**)

Rosenfeld B and Harmon R (2002) Factors associated with violence in stalking and obsessional harassment cases. *Criminal Justice and Behavior* **29**: 671–91. (**380, 545**)

Rosenfeld B and Lewis C (2005) Assessing violence risk in stalking cases: a regression tree approach. *Law and Human Behavior* **29**(3): 343–57. (**379, 380**)

Rosenfield I (1988) *The Invention of Memory*. New York: Basic Books. (**420**)

Rosenhan DL (1973) On being sane in insane places. *Science* **179**: 250–8. (**432**)

Rösler A and Witztum E (2000) Pharmacotherapy of paraphilias in the next millennium. *Behavioral Sciences and the Law* **18**: 43–56. (**125, 260**)

Rosman JP and Resnick PJ (1989) Sexual attraction to corpses: a psychiatric review of necrophilia. *Bulletin of the American Academy of Psychiatry and the Law* **17**: 153–63. (**247**)

Rosner R (ed) (2003) *Principles and Practice of Forensic Psychiatry*, 2nd edn. London: Arnold. (**147**)

Rosner R, Wiederlight M, Harmon R, and Cahn D (1991) Geriatric offenders examined at a forensic psychiatry clinic. *Journal of Forensic Science* **36**: 1722–31. (**525**)

Ross K, Freeman D, Dunn G, and Garety P (2011) A randomised experimental investigation of reasoning training for people with delusions. *Schizophrenia Bulletin* **37**: 324–33. (**362**)

Ross R, Fabiano E, and Ross R (1986) *Reasoning and Rehabillitation: A Handbook for Teaching Cognitive Skills*. Ottowa, Canada: The Cognitive Centre. (**213**)

Rossegger A, Laubacher A, Moskvitin K, et al. (2010) Risk assessment instruments in repeat offending: the usefulness of the FOTRES. *International Journal of Offender Therapy and Comparative Criminology* **55**: 716–31. (**532**)

Rossow I (2001) Alcohol and homicide: a cross-cultural comparison of the relationship in 14 European countries. *Addiction* **96** (Suppl. 1): S77–S92. (**442**)

Roth A and Fonagy P (1996) *What Works for Whom? A Critical Review of Psychotherapy Research*. London: The Guilford. (**569**)

Roth S, Newman E, Pelcovitz D, van der Kolk B, and Mandel F (1997) Complex PTSD in victims exposed to sexual and physical abuse: results from the DSM–IV field trial for posttraumatic stress disorder. *Journal of Traumatic Stress* **10**: 539–55. (**712**)

Rothbaum O and Foa EB (1993) Subtypes of PTSD and duration of symptoms. In JRT Davidson, EB Foa (eds) *Post-traumatic Stress Disorder: DSM-IV and Beyond*. Washington, DC: APA. (**705**)

Rothenberg M (1975) Effect of television violence on children and youth *Journal of American Medical Association* **234**: 1043–6. (**216**)

Rothschild B (2000) *The Body Remembers: The Psychophysiology of Trauma and Trauma Treatment.* New York: WW Norton. (**727**)

Rothstein DA (1964) Presidential assassination syndrome. *Archives of General Psychiatry* **11**: 245–54. (**543**)

Rothstein DA (1966) Presidential assassination syndrome II: application to Lee Harvey Oswald. *Archives of General Psychiatry* **15**: 260–66. (**543**)

Rothstein DA (1971) Presidential assassination syndrome: a psychiatric study of the threat, the deed, and the message. In WJ Crotty (ed) *Assassination and the political* order. New York: Harper and Row, pp. 161–222. (**543**)

Rounsaville BJ (1978) Theories in marital violence: evidence from a study of battered women. *Victimology* **3**: 11–21. (**372**)

Rounsaville BJ, Kranzler HR, Ball S, et al. (1998) Personality disorders in substance abusers: relation to substance abuse. *Journal of Nervous and Mental Disease* **186**: 87–95. (**444**)

Rousseau G (ed) (2007) *Children and Sexuality: From the Greeks to the Great War.* Basingstoke, Hampshire: Palgrave Macmillan. (**249**)

Rowe DC and Farrington DP (1997) The familial transmission of criminal convictions. *Criminology* **35**: 177–201. (**195**)

Rowlands MW (1988) Psychiatric and legal aspects of persistant litigation. *British Journal of Psychiatry* **153**: 317–23. (**381**)

Rowntree A (with Moore E and Taylor PJ) (2011) Confiding about delusions. BSc dissertation, Cardiff University. (**355**)

Roy A, Adinoff B, and Linnoila M (1988) Acting out hostility in normal volunteers: negative correlation with levels of 5HIAA in cerebrospinal fluid. *Psychiatry Research* **24**: 187–94. (**308**)

Roy A, Adinoff B, Roehrich L, et al. (1988) Pathological gambling. *Archives of General Psychiatry* **45**: 369–73. (**470**)

Royal College of General Practitioners and Royal Pharmaceutical Society (2011) *Safer Prescribing in Prisons.* Nottingham, UK: Nottinghamshire Healthcare. http://www.emcdda.europa.eu/attachements.cfm/att_146300_EN_UK51_Safer_Prescribing_in_Prison%20(2011).pdf (**631**)

Royal College of Physicians (2001) *Alcohol – can the NHS afford it?* London: Royal College of Physicians. http://www.alcohollearningcentre.org.uk/_library/alcoholNHS_afford_it.pdf (**437**)

Royal College of Psychiatrists (1982) Locking up patients by themselves. *Bulletin of the Royal College of Psychiatrists* **6**: 199–200. (**594**)

Royal College of Psychiatrists (1990) The seclusion of psychiatric patients. *Psychiatric Bulletin* **17**: 754–6. (**594**)

Royal College of Psychiatrists (1998) *Not Just Bricks and Mortar.* Council Report CR62. (**556**)

Royal College of Psychiatrists (2000) *Drugs: Dilemmas and Choices.* London: Gaskell. (**454**)

Royal College of Psychiatrists (2002) *Suicide in Prisons.* Council Report 99. London: Royal College of Psychiatrists. http://www.rcpsych.ac.uk/files/pdfversion/cr99.pdff (**633**)

Royal College of Psychiatrists (2005) *Statement by the Royal College of Psychiatrists in Respect of the Psychiatric Problems of Detainees Held Under the 2001 Anti-Terrorism Crime and Security Act.* (**235, 637**)

Royal College of Psychiatrists (2006) *Consensus Statement on High-dose Antipsychotic Medication.* Council Report CR138. London: Royal College of Psychiatrists. http://www.rcpsych.ac.uk/files/pdfversion/CR138.pdf (**360**)

Royal College of Psychiatrists (2007a) *Prison Psychiatry: Adult Prisons in England and Wales.* Council Report CR144. London: Royal College of Psychiatrists. http://www.rcpsych.ac.uk/files/pdfversion/cr141.pdf (**628**)

Royal College of Psychiatrists (2007b) *Vulnerable Patients, Safe Doctors: Good Practice in Our Clinical Relationships.* Council Report CR146. London: Royal College of Psychiatrists. http://www.rcpsych.ac.uk/files/pdfversion/cr146x.pdf (**690**)

Royal College of Psychiatrists (2008) *Rethinking Risk to Others in Mental Health Services: Final Report of a Scoping Group* (College Report CR150). London: Royal College of Psychiatrists. http://www.rcpsych.ac.uk/files/pdfversion/cr150.pdf (**533, 548, 549**)

Royal College of Psychiatrists (2010a) *Good Psychiatric Practice: Confidentiality and Information Sharing,* 2nd edn. CR160. London: Royal College of Psychiatrists. http://www.rcpsych.ac.uk/publications/collegereports/cr/cr160.aspx (**1, 624, 663**)

Royal College of Psychiatrists (2010b) *Specialists in Forensic Psychiatry. A Competency Based Curriculum for Specialist Training Psychiatry.* http://www.rcpsych.ac.uk/pdf/1Rehab_feb09-final.pdf (**2, 16**)

Royal College of Psychiatrists (2011a) *Standards for Relational Security* B. Hillier (ed). London: Royal College of Psychiatrists. www.rcpsych.ac.uk/pdf/Standards%20for%20Relational%20Security1.pdf (**597**)

Royal College of Psychiatrists (2011b) *Standards on the use of section 136 of the Mental Health Act 1983 (England and Wales).* London: Royal College of Psychiatrists. http://www.rcpsych.ac.uk/files/pdfversion/CR159x.pdf (**620**)

Royal Commission (1957) *Report of the Royal Commission on the Law Relating to Mental Illness and Mental Deficiency 1954–1957.* Cmd. 169. London: HMSO (Percy Commission). (**58, 87**)

Royal Commission on Capital Punishment (1953) *Report 1949–1953.* Cmnd. 8932. London: HMSO. (**636**)

Royal Commission on Criminal Justice (1993) *Report (Runciman Report).* Cmnd 2263. London: HMSO. (**159**)

Royal Commission on Criminal Procedure (1981) *Report.* Cmnd 8092. London: HMSO. (**621**)

Royal Commission on Gambling (1978) *Final Report of the Royal Commission on Gambling (Rothschild).* Cmnd.7200. London: HMSO. (**467**)

Royal Commission on Lunacy and Mental Disorder (1926) *Report (Macmillan Commission).* Cmd. 2700. London: HMSO. (**87**)

Royal Commission on Tribunals of Inquiry (1966) *Salmon Report* Cmnd 3121. London: HMSO. (**75n**)

Royal Pharmaceutical Society of Great Britain (2007) *Pharmaceutical care of detainees in police custody.* http://fflm.ac.uk/upload/documents/1176896970.pdf (**461**)

Royal Society for the Prevention of Accidents (1992) *Risk: Analysis, perception and Management.* London: Royal Society. (**531**)

Royal Statistical Society (2002) *Letter from the President to the Lord Chancellor Regarding the Use of Statistical Evidence in Court Cases.* http://www.rss.org.uk/uploadedfiles/userfiles/files/Letter-RSS-President-Lord-Chancellor-Sally-Clark-case.pdf (**17, 530**)

Rubenstein D (1984) The elderly in prison: a review of the literature. In ES Newman, DJ Newman, ML Gerwirtz (eds) *Elderly Criminals.* Cambridge MA: Oelgeschlager, pp. 153–68. (**528**)

Rubey RN, Johnson MR, Emmanuel, N, et al. (1996) Fluoxetine in the treatment of anger: An open clinical trial. *Journal of Clinical Psychiatry* **7**:398–401 (**310**)

Rubia K, Lee F, and Cleare AJ, et al. (2005) Tryptophan depletion reduces right inferior prefrontal activation during response inhibition in fast, event-related fMRI. *Psychopharmacology* **179**: 791–803. (**309, 310**)

Ruchkin V, Koposov R, and Vermerien R (2003) Psychopathology and age at onset of conduct problems in juvenile delinquents. *Journal of Clinical Psychology* **64***:* 920. (**482**)

Rudden M, Gilmore M, and Frances A (1982) Delusions: when to confront the facts of life. *American Journal of Psychiatry* **139**: 929–32. (**349**)

Rudden M, Sweeney J, and Allen F (1990) Diagnosis and clinical course of erotmanic and other delusional patients. *American Journal of Psychiatry* **147**: 625–8. (**368**)

Ruddy R and Milnes D (2009) Art therapy for schizophrenia or schizophrenia-like illnesses. *Cochrane Database of Systematic Reviews* 2005. Issue 4 Art. No.: CD003728. DOI: 10.1002/14651858.CD003728.pub2. http://onlinelibrary.wiley.com/o/cochrane/clsysrev/articles/CD003728/frame.html (**558**)

Ruddy RA and Dent-Brown K (2008) Drama therapy for schizophrenia or schizophrenia-like illnesses. *Cochrane Database of Systematic Reviews* 2007. Issue 1. Art. No.: CD005378. DOI: 10.1002/14651858.CD005378.pub2. http://onlinelibrary.wiley.com/o/cochrane/clsysrev/articles/CD005378/frame.html (**558**)

Rudrick A (1999) Relation between command hallucinations and dangerous behaviour. *Journal of the American Academy of Psychiatry and the Law* **27**: 253–7. (**353**)

Rush E and La Nauze A (2006) *Corporate Paedophilia: Sexualization of Children in Australia.* The Australia Institute: Discussion Paper No. 90 (www.tai.org.au/documents/dp_fulltext/DP90.pdf). (**244**)

Russell WR and Nathan PW (1946) Traumatic amnesia. *Brain* **69**: 280–300. (**296**)

Russo J and Wallcraft J (2011) Resisting variables-service users/survivor perspectives on researching coercion. In TW Kalkert, J Mezzich, J Monahan (eds) *Coercive Treatment in Psychiatry: Clinical Legal and Ethical Aspects.* New York: Wiley-Blackwell, pp. 213–35. (**356**)

Rutherford H and Taylor PJ (2004) The transfer of women offenders with mental disorder from prison to hospital. *Journal of Forensic Psychiatry and Psychology* **15**: 108–23. (**632**)

Rutherford M (2010) *Blurring the Boundaries. The Convergence of Mental Health and Criminal Justice Policy, Legislation, Systems and Practice.* London: Sainsbury Centre for Mental Health. http://www.centreformentalhealth.org.uk/pdfs/blurring_the_boundaries.pdf (**22, 225, 588**)

Rutherford M and Duggan S (2007) *Forensic Mental Health Services. Facts and Figures on Current Provision.* London: Sainsbury Centre for Mental Health. http://www.centreformentalhealth.org.uk/pdfs/scmh_forensic_factfile_2007.pdf (**599**)

Rutherford M, Keil J, Bruton L, et al. (2008) *In the Dark. The Mental Health Implications of Imprisonment for Public Protection.* London: Sainsbury Centre for Mental Health. http://www.centreformentalhealth.org.uk/pdfs/In_the_dark.pdf (**540, 541, 599, 637**)

Rutter M (1967) A children's behaviour questionnaire for completion by teachers: preliminary findings. *Journal of Child Psychology and Psychiatry and Allied Disciplines* **8**: 1–11. (**484**)

Rutter M (2002) Nature, nurture, and development: from evangelism through science toward policy and practice. *Child Development* **73**: 1–21. (**189**)

Rutter M and Silberg J (2002) Gene–environment interplay in relation to emotional and behavioral disturbance. *Annual Review of Psychology* **53**: 463–90. (**190, 191**)

Rutter M and Smith DJ (1995) *Psychosocial Disorders in Young People.* Chichester, UK: John Wiley. (**473**)

Rutter M, Giller H, and Hagell A (1998) *Antisocial Behavior by Young People.* Cambridge, UK: Cambridge University Press. (**482**)

Rutter M, Maughan B, Mortimore P, Ouston J, and Smith A (1979) *Fifteen Thousand Hours: Secondary Schools and their Effects on Children.* London: Open Books. (**178**)

Rutter S, Gudjonsson G, and Rabe-Hesketh S (2004) Violent incidents in a medium secure unit: the characteristics of persistent perpetrators of violence. *Journal of Forensic Psychiatry and Psychology* **15**: 293–302. (**515**)

Ryan G, Miyoshi TJ, Metzner JL, Krugman RD, and Fryer GE (1996) Trends in a national sample of sexually abusive youths. *Journal of the American Academy of Child and Adolescent Psychiatry* **35**: 17–25. (**252**)

Ryan S, Moore E, Taylor PJ, et al. (2002) The voice of detainees in a high security setting on services for people with personality disorder. *Criminal Behaviour and Mental Health* **12**: 254–68. (**401, 572**)

Ryba NL, Cooper VG, and Zapf PA (2003) Juvenile competence to stand trial evaluations: a survey of current practices and test usage among psychologists. *Professional Psychology: Research in Practice* **34**: 499–507. (**332**)

Ryle A (1993) *Cognitive Analytic Therapy: Active Participation in Change. A new integration in brief psychotherapy.* London: Churchill Livingstone. (**330**)

Ryle A (1997) *Cognitive Analytic Therapy and Borderline Personality Disorder: The Model and the Method.* Chichester, UK: Wiley. (**719**)

Ryle A and Golynkina K (2000) Effectiveness of time-limited cognitive analytic therapy of borderline personality disorder: factors associated with outcome. *British Journal of Medical Psychology* **73**: 197–210. (**584**)

Rynearson EK (1984) Bereavement after homicide: a descriptive study. *American Journal of Psychiatry* **141**: 1452–4. (**713**)

Sacks MH, Carpenter WT, and Strauss JS (1974) Recovery from delusions. *Archives of General Psychiatry* **30**: 117–20. (**349**)

Sacks S, Sacks JY, McKendrick K, Banks S, and Stommel J (2004) Modified TC for MICA offenders: crime outcomes. *Behavioral Sciences and the Law* **22**: 477–501. (**412**)

Sadoff RL (1988) Ethical issues in forensic psychiatry. *Psychiatric Annals* **18**: 320–3. (**670**)

Sadoff RL (1995) Mothers who kill their children. *Psychiatric Annals* **25**: 601–5. (**510**)

Safran JD and Muran JC (2000) *Negotiating the Therapeutic Alliance: A Relational Treatment Guide.* New York: Guilford. (**408**)

Sagami A, Kayama M, and Senoo E (2004) The relationship between postpartum depression and abusive parenting behavior of Japanese mothers: a survey of mothers with a child less than one year old. *Bull Menninger Clin* **68**(2): 174–87. (**506**)

Sagarin E (1976) Prison homosexuality and its effect on post-prison sexual behaviour. *Psychiatry* **39**: 245–57. (**249**)

Sahota K and Chesterman P (1998) Sexual offending in the context of mental illness. *Journal of Forensic Psychiatry* **9**: 267–80. (**253, 262**)

Saini A (2009) The brain police: judging murder with an MRI http://www.wired.co.uk/magazine/archiv/2009/06/features/guilty?page=all (**421**)

Sainsbury Centre for Mental Health (2006) *Policy Paper 5: London's Prison Mental Health Services: A Review.* www.centreformentalhealth.org.uk/pdfs/policy5_prison_mental_health_services.pdf (**631**).

Sainsbury Centre for Mental Health (2008a) *In the Dark. The Mental Health Implications of Imprisonment for Public Protection.* London: Sainsbury Centre for Mental Health. http://www.centreformentalhealth.org.uk/pdfs/In_the_dark.pdf (**115**)

Sainsbury Centre for Mental Health (2008b) *The Police and Mental Health.* Briefing paper 36. London: Sainsbury Centre for Mental Health. http://www.centreformentalhealth.org.uk/pdfs/briefing36_police_and_mental_health.pdf (**620**)

Sainsbury, L, Krishnan, G and Evans, C (2004) Motivating factors for male forensic patients with personality disorder. *Criminal Behaviour and Mental Health,* **14**: 29-38. (**391, 400, 572**)

Sakagami M and Pan X (2007) Functional role of the ventrolateral prefrontal cortex in decision making. *Current Opinion in Neurobiology* **17**: 228–33. (**298**)

Sakagami M, Pan X, and Uttl B (2006) Behavioral inhibition and prefrontal cortex in decision-making. *Neural Networks* **19**: 1255–65. (**298**)

Sakai JT, Young SE, Stallings MC, et al. (2006) Case-control and within-family tests for an association between conduct disorder and 5HTTLPR. *American Journal of Medical Genetics B Neuropsychiatric Genetics* **141B**: 825–32. (**198**)

Sale I (2008) Anatomy of a mass murder: psychological profile of Martin Bryant and the Port Arthur Massacre. In RN Kocsis (eds) *Serial Murder and the Psychology of Violent Crimes.* Totowa, NJ: Humana. (**238**)

Saleh FM and Berlin FS (2003) Sexual deviancy: diagnostic and neurobiological considerations. *Journal of Child Sexual Abuse* **12**: 53–76. (**260**)

Salekin RT (2002) Psychopathy and therapeutic pessimism. Clinical lore or clinical reality? *Clinical Psychological Review* **22**: 79–112. (**583**)

Salekin RT, Rogers R, and Sewell KW (1997) Construct validity of psychopathy in a female offender sample: a multitrait-multimethod evaluation. *Journal of Abnormal Psychology* **106**(4): 576–85. (**513**)

Salekin RT, Rogers R, Ustad KL, and Sewell KW (1998) Psychopathy and recidivism among female inmates. *Law Hum Behav* **22**: 109–28. (**513**)

Salias E and Fenton M. Seclusion and restraint for people with serious mental illnesses. (Cochrane Review). *The Cochrane Database of Systematic Reviews* (2000) Issue 1. Art. No.: CD001163. DOI: 10.1002/14651858.CD001163. http://onlinelibrary.wiley.com/doi/10.1002/14651858.CD001163/pdf (**558**)

Salize HJ and Dressing H (2005a) Coercion, involuntary treatment and quality of mental health care: is there any link? *Current Opinion in Psychiatry* **18**: 576–84. (**113**)

Salize HJ and Dressing H (eds) (2005b) *Placement and Treatment of Mentally Disordered Offenders: Legislation and Practice in the* [Old] *European Union.* Lengerich, Germany: Pabst Science. (**113, 146**)

Salkovskis PM (1991) The importance of behaviour in the maintenance of anxiety and panic: a cognitive account. *Behavioural Psychotherapy* **34**: 453–8. (**351**)

Salmi V, Lehti M, Siren R, Kivivuori J, and Aaltonen M (2009) *Perheväkivalta Suomessa* [Domestic violence in Finland] (Verkkokatsauksia 12/2009). Helsinki, Finland: The National Research Institute of Legal Policy. (**505**)

Salomon RM, Mazure CM, Delgado PL, Mendia P, and Charney DS (1994) Serotonin function in aggression: the effect of acute plasma tryptophan depletion in aggressive patients. *Biological Psychiatry* **35**: 570–2. (**309**)

Salter AC (1988) *Treating Child Sex Offenders and Victims: A Practical Guide.* Thousand Oaks, CA: Sage. (**261**)

Salzer MS, Schwenk E, and Brusilovskiy E (2010) Certified peer specialist roles and activities: results from a national survey. *Psychiatric Services* **61**: 520–3. (**363**)

Salzman C, Solomon D, Miyawaki E, et al. (1991) Parenteral lorazepam versus parenteral haloperidol for the control of psychotic disruptive behavior. *Journal of Clinical Psychiatry* **52**: 177–80. (**566**)

Salzman C, Wolfson AN, Schatzberg A, et al. (1995) Effect of fluoxetine on anger in symptomatic volunteers with borderline personality disorder. *Journal of Clinical Psychopharmacology* **15**: 23–9. (**406**)

Sampson O (1976) Treatment practices in British Child Guidance Clinics: an historical review. *Educational Review* **29**(1): 13–29. (**482**)

Sampson RJ, Raudenbush SW, and Earls F (1997) Neighbourhoods and violent crime: a multilevel study of collective efficacy. *Science* **277**: 918–24. (**178**)

Samuels A (1986) Non-crown prosecutions by non-police agencies and by private individuals. *Criminal Law Review* 33–44. (**50**)

Samuels J, Eaton WW, Bienvenu OJ III, et al.(2002) Prevalence and correlates of personality disorders in a community sample. *British Journal of Psychiatry* **180**: 536–42. (**389, 390**)

Sanday PR (1981) The socio-cultural context of rape: a cross-cultural study. *Journal of Social Issues* **37**: 5–27. (**244, 249**)

Sandberg AA, Koepf GF, Ishihara T, and Hauschka TS (1961) An XYY human male. *Lancet ii*: 588–9. (**323**)

Sandberg DA, McNiel DE, and Binder RL (2002) Stalking, threatening, and harassing behaviour by psychiatric patients toward clinicians. *Journal of the American Academy of Psychiatry and Law*, **30**, 221–9. (**378**)

Sanders A and Young R (2000) *Criminal Justice*, 2nd edn. London: Butterworths. (**331**)

Sanders MR, Markie-Dadds C, Tully LA, and Bor W (2000) The Triple-P positive parenting programme: a comparison of enhanced, standard and self-directed behavioural family intervention for parents of children with early onset conduct problems. *Journal of Consulting and Clinical Psychology* **68**: 624–40. (**182**)

Sanders WB (1970) *Juvenile Offenders for a Thousand Years*. Durham, NC: University of North Carolina Press. (**474**)

Santiago JM, McCall-Perez F, Gorcey M, and Beigel A (1985) Long-term psychological effects of rape in 35 rape victims. *American Journal of Psychiatry* **142**: 1338–40. (**715**)

Sapsford RJ (1978) Life-sentence prisoners: psychological changes during sentence. *British Journal of Criminology* **18**: 128–45. (**630, 637**)

Sapsford RJ (1983) *Life Sentenced Prisoners – Reaction, Response and Change*. Milton Keynes, UK: Open University Press. (**637**)

Saradjian J and Hanks H (1996) *Women Who Sexually Abuse Their Children: From Research to Practice*. Chichester, UK: Wiley. (**252, 264**)

Sarkar J and Adshead G (2006) Personality disorders as disorganization of attachment and affect regulation. *Advances in Psychiatric Treatment* **12**: 297–305. (**583**)

Sarkar J and di Lustro M (2011) Evolution of secure services for women in England. *Advances in Psychiatric Treatment* **17**: 323–31. (**520**)

Sartin RM, Hansen DJ, and Huss MT (2006) Domestic violence treatment response and recidivism: a review and implications for the study of family violence. *Aggression and Violent Behavior* **11**: 425–40. (**219**)

Saska JR, Cohen SJ, Srihari V, and Woods SW (2009) Cognitive behaviour therapy for early psychosis: a comprehensive review of individual vs group treatment studies. *International Journal of Group Psychotherapy* **59**: 357–83. (**574**)

Sattar G (2001) *Rates and Causes of Death Among Prisoners and Offenders Under Community Supervision*. Home Office Research Study 231. London: Home Office. (**633, 640**)

Saunders JB, Aasland OG, Babor TF, De la Fuente JR, and Grant M (1993) Development of the Alcohol Use Disorders Identification Test (AUDIT): WHO Collaborative Project on Early Detection of Persons with Harmful Alcohol Consumption – II. *Addiction* **88**: 791–804. (**438, 457**)

Saunders P, Copeland J, Dewey M, et al. (1993) The prevalence of dementia, depression and neurosis in later life: the Liverpool -MRC–ALPHA study. *International Journal of Epidemiology* **22**: 838–47. (**526**)

Sbordone RJ and Liter JC (1995) Mild traumatic brain injury does not produce port-traumatic stress disorder. *Brain Injury* **9**: 405–12. (**713**)

Scadding JG (1967) Diagnosis: the clinician and the computer. *Lancet ii*: 877–82. (**10**)

Scadding JG (1990) The semantic problems of psychiatry. *Psychological Medicine* **20**: 243 8. (**9, 10**)

Scalora M, Baumgartner J, and Plank G (2003) The relationship of mental illness to targeted contact behavior toward state government agencies and officials. *Behavioral Sciences and the Law* **21**: 239–49. (**378**)

Scalora M, Baumgartner J, Zimmerman W, et al. (2002a) An epidemiological assessment of problematic contacts to members of Congress. *Journal of Forensic Sciences* **47**: 1–5. (**377, 378, 544, 547**)

Scalora M, Baumgartner J, Zimmerman W, et al. (2002b) Risk factors for approach behavior toward the U.S. Congress. *Journal of Threat Assessment* **2**: 35–55. (**377, 378, 544, 547**)

Scarlett JA, Mako ME, Rubenstein AH, et al. (1977) Factitious hypoglycaemia. *New England Journal of Medicine* **297**: 1029–32. (**295**)

Schaap G, Lammers S, and de Vogel V (2009) Risk assessment in female psychiatric patients: A quasi-prospective study into the validity of the HCR-20 and the PCL-R. *Journal of Forensic Psychiatry and Psychology* **20**: 354–65. (**513**)

Schacter DL (1986) Amnesia and crime: how much do we really know? *American Psychologist* **41**: 286–95. (**295, 296, 439**)

Schalling D, Asberg M, Edmann G, and Levander SE (1984) Impulsivity, non conformity and sensation seeking as related to biological markers for vulnerability. *Clinical Neuropharmacology* **7** (Suppl 1): 747–57. (**308**)

Schanda, H., Knecht, G., Schreinzer, D., Stompe, T., Ortwein-Swoboda, G., Waldhoer, T. (2004) Homicide and major mental disorders: a 25-year study. *Acta Psychiatrica Scandinavica* **110**: 98–107. (**337, 502, 507**)

Schellenberg EG, Wasylenki D, Webster C D, et al. (1992) A review of arrests among psychiatric-patients. *International Journal of Law and Psychiatry* **15**: 251–64. (**280**)

Schenck CH and Mahowald MW (2005) REM sleep parasomnias. *Neurologic Clinics* **23**: 1107–26. (**291**)

Schenck CH, Amulf I, and Mahowald MW (2007) Sleep and sex: what can go wrong? A review of the literature on sleep related disorders and abnormal sexual behaviors and experiences. *Sleep* **30**: 683–702. (**291**)

Schenck CH, Bundlie SR, Ettinger MG, and Mahowald MW (1986) Chronic behavioural disorders of human REM sleep: a new category of parasomnia. *Sleep* **9**: 293–308. (**291**)

Schenck CH, Bundlie SR, Patterson AL, and Mahowald MW (1987) Rapid eye-movement sleep behavior disorder. *Journal of American Medical Association* **257**: 1786–9. (**291**)

Schenck CH, Hurwitz TD, and Mahowald MW (1993) REM sleep behaviour disorder: a report on a series of 96 consecutive cases and a review of the literature. *Journal of Sleep Research* 2: 224–31. (**291**)

Scher MS, Richardson GA, and Day NL (2000) Effects of prenatal cocaine/crack and other drug exposure on electroencephalographic sleep studies at birth and one year. *American Academy of Pediatrics* 105: 39–48. (**464**)

Scher MS, Richardson GA, Robles N, et al. (1998) Effects of prenatal substance exposure: altered maturation of visual evoked potentials. *Paediatric Neurology* 18: 236–43. (**464**)

Schipkowensky N (1968) Affective disorders: cyclophrenia and murder. In AVS de Reuck, R Porter (eds) *The Mentally Abnormal Offender*. London: CIBA, Churchill.

Schipkowensky N (1973) Epidemiological aspects of homicide. In S Arieti (ed) *World Biennial of Psychiatry and Psychotherapy* 2. New York: Basic Books, pp. 192–215. (**337**)

Schmidt CW Jr, Shaffer JW, Zlotowitz HI, and Fisher RS (1977) Suicide by vehicular crash. *American Journal of Psychiatry* 134(2): 175–8. (**278**)

Schmidt G (1943) Die Verbrechen in der Schlaftrunkenheit. *Zeitschrift für die Gesamte Neurologie und Psychiatrie* 176: 208–54. (**290**)

Schmidt LG, Samochowiec J, Finckh U, et al. (2002) Association of a CB1 cannabinoid receptor gene (CNR1) polymorphism with severe alcohol dependence. *Drug and Alcohol Dependence* 65: 221–4. (**206**)

Schneider F, Habel U, Kessler C, et al. (2000) Functional imaging of conditioned aversive emotional responses in antisocial personality disorder. *Neuropsychobiology* 42: 192–201. (**303, 304**)

Schneider K (1959) *Clinical Psychopathology* (trans. MW Hamilton, EW Anderson) New York: Grune and Stratton. (**422**)

Schneider RD, Bloom H, and Heerema M (2007) *Mental Health Courts: Decriminalizing the Mentally Ill.* Toronto, Canada: Irwin Law. (**146**)

Schneiderman AI, Braver ER, and Kang HK (2008) Understanding sequelae of injury mechanisms and mild traumatic brain injury incurred during the conflicts in Iraq and Afghanistan: persistent postconcussive symptoms and posttraumatic stress disorder. *American Journal of Epidemiology* 167: 1446–52. (**713**)

Schnurr PP, Friedman MJ, and Bernardy NC (2002) Research on posttraumatic stress disorder: epidemiology, pathophysiology, and assessment. *Journal of Clinical Psychology* 58: 877–89. (**718**)

Schoenbaum G, Roesch MR, and Stalnaker TA (2006) Orbitofrontal cortex, decision-making and drug addiction. *Trends in Neuroscience* 29: 116–24. (**298**)

Schoenberg MR, Dorr DA, and Morgan CD (2003) The ability of the Millon Clinical Multiaxial Inventory- 3rd edn. (MCMI-III) to detect malingering. *Psychological Assessment* 15: 198–204. (**388**)

Schore AN (1996) Experience dependent maturation of a regulatory system in the orbital pre-frontal cortex and the origin of developmental psychopathology. *Development and Psychopathology* 8: 59–87. (**718**)

Schore AN (2000) Attachment and the regulation of the right brain. *Attachment and Human Development* 2: 23–47. (**718**)

Schore AN (2001) The effects of early relational trauma on right brain development, affect regulation, and infant mental health. *Infant Mental Health Journal* 22: 201–269. (**719, 720**)

Schork NJ and Schork CM (1998) Issues and strategies in the genetic analysis of alcoholism and related addictive behaviors. *Alcohol* 16: 71–83. (**187**)

Schork NJ, Murray SS, Frazer KA, and Topol EJ (2009) Common vs. rare allele hypotheses for complex diseases. *Current Opinion in Genetics and Development* 19: 212–9. (**194, 195**)

Schory TJ, Piecznski N, Nair S, and El-Mallakh RS (2003) Barometric pressure, emergency psychiatric visits and violent acts. *Canadian Journal of Psychiatry* 48: 624–7. (**354**)

Schotte CKW (2002) Assessment of borderline personality disorder: considering a diagnostic strategy. *Acta Neuropsychiatrica* 14: 55–9. (**391, 392**)

Schram DD and Milloy CD (1995) *Community Notification: A Study of Offender Characteristics and Recidivism*. Olympia, WA: Washington State Institute for Public Policy. (**645**)

Schreier HA (1998) Risperidone for young children with mood disorders and aggressive behavior. *Journal of Child and Adolescent Psychopharmacology* 8: 49–59. (**564**)

Schreier HA and Libow JA (1993) *Hurting for Love*. New York: Guilford. (**506**)

Schreier HA and Libow JA (1993) Munchausen syndrome by proxy: Diagnosis and prevalence. *American Journal of Orthopsychiatry* 63: 318–21. (**227**)

Schulz SC, Zanarini MC, Bateman A, Bohus M, Detke HC, Trsaskoma Q, Tanaka Y, Lin D, Deberdt W, and Corya S (2008) Olanzapine for the treatment of borderline personality disorder: Variable dose 12-week randomised double-blind placebo-controlled study. *British Journal of Psychiatry* 193: 485–92. (**404**)

Schwartz HI, Mack DM, and Zeman PM (2003) Hospitalization: voluntary and involuntary. In R Rosner (ed) *Principles and Practice of Forensic Psychiatry*, 2nd edn. London: Arnold, pp. 107–15. (**122, 123**)

Schweinhart LJ and Weikart DP (1980) *Young Children Grow Up: The Effects of the Perry Preschool Programme on Youths Through Age 15*. Ypsilanti, MI: High/Scope. (**183**)

Schweinhart LJ, Barnes HV, and Weikart DP (1993) *Significant Benefits: The High/Scope Perry Preschool Study Through Age 27*. Ypsilanti, MI: High/Scope. (**174, 183**)

Schweinhart LJ, Montie J, Zongping X, et al. (2005) *Lifetime Effects: The High/Scope Perry Preschool Study Through Age 40*. Ypsilanti, MI: High/Scope. (**174, 183**)

Schweitzer NJ and Saks MJ (2011) Neuroimaging evidence and the insanity defence. *Behavioral Sciences and the Law* **29**: 592–607. (**17**)

Scodel A (1964) Inspirational group therapy. *American Journal of Psychotherapy* **18**:115–25. (**471**)

Scotland, Baroness, Kelly H, and Devaux M (1998) *The Report of the Luke Warm Luke Mental Health Inquiry,* Vols 1 and 2. London: Lambeth, Southwark and Lewisham Health Authority. (**75, 697**)

Scott D (1978) The problems of malicious fire-raising. *British Journal of Hospital Medicine* **19**: 259–63. (**273, 275**)

Scott F, Whyte S, Burnette R, Hawley C, and Maden T (2004) A national survey of substance misuse and treatment outcome in psychiatric inpatients in medium security. *Journal of Forensic Psychiatry and Psychology* **15**: 595–605. (**448**)

Scott H, Johnson S, Menezes P, et al. (1998) Substance misuse and the risk of aggression and offending among the severely mentally ill. *British Journal of Psychiatry* **172**: 345–50. (**454**)

Scott J, Chant D, Andrews G, and McGrath J (2006) Psychotic-like experiences in the general community: the correlates of CIDI psychosis screen items in an Australian sample. *Psychological Medicine* **36**: 231–8. (**339**)

Scott J, Chant D, Andrews G, Martin G, and McGrath J (2007) Association between trauma exposure and delusional experiences in a large community-based sample. *British Journal of Psychiatry* **190**: 339–43. (**344**)

Scott MJ and Stradling SG (1997) Client compliance with exposure treatments for posttraumatic stress disorder. *Journal of Traumatic Stress* **10**: 523–6. (**729**)

Scott PD (1973) Parents who kill their children. *Medicine, Science and the Law* **13**(2): 120–6. (**509**)

Scott PD (1977) Assessing dangerousness in criminals. *British Journal of Psychiatry* **131**: 127–42. (**530**)

Scott Peck M (1983) *The People of the Lie.* New York: Simon and Schuster. (**7**)

Scott S (2004) Helping children with aggression and conduct problems: best practices for intervention. *Child and Adolescent Mental Health* **9**: 92. (**486**)

Scott S, Knapp M, Henderson J, and Maughan B (2001) Financial cost of social exclusion: Follow-up study of antisocial children into adulthood. *British Medical Journal* **323**: 1– 5. (**398**)

Scott S, Spender Q, Doolan M, Jacobs B, and Aspland H (2001) Multicentre controlled trial of parenting groups for child antisocial behaviour in clinical practice. *British Medical Journal* **323**: 194–6. (**182**)

Scottish Executive (2000) *Report of the Committee on Serious Violent and Sexual Offenders.* (The McLean Committee Report) Scottish Executive: Edinburgh. http://content.iriss.org.uk/throughcare/files/pdf/longterm/lt4_risk2.pdf (**89, 99, 611, 651**)

Scottish Executive (2001) *Review of the Mental Health (Scotland) Act 1994* Edinburgh, Scotland: SE/2001/56. (**59**)

Scottish Executive (2001a) *New Directions. Report on the Review of the Mental Health (Scotland) Act 1984* (Milan Committee) SE/2001/56 Edinburgh, Scotland: Scottish Executive. (**89**)

Scottish Executive (2002) *The Right Place, The Right Time: Improving the Patient Journey for Those Who Need Secure Mental Health Care.* Edinburgh, Scotland: Scottish Executive. http://www.forensicnetwork.scot.nhs.uk/documents/The%20Right%20Place%20The%20 Right%20Time.pdf (**611**)

Scottish Executive (2002, 2007) *Plan for Action on Alcohol Problems.* Edinburgh, Scotland: Scottish Executive. http://www.sehd.scot. nhs.uk/mels/HDL2002_17.pdf Update 2007: http://www.scotland.gov.uk/Resource/Doc/166474/0045367.pdf (**437**)

Scottish Executive (2005a) *Mental Health (Care and Treatment) (Scotland) Act 2003 Code of Practice.* Edinburgh, Scotland: Scottish Executive. (**90**)

Scottish Executive (2005b) *Memorandum of Procedure on Restricted Patients.* Edinburgh, Scotland: Scottish Executive. (**99**)

Scottish Law Commission (2004) *Report on Insanity and Diminished Responsibility.* Edinburgh, Scotland: The Stationery Office. (**94**)

Scottish Office (1998a) *Health and Social Work and Related Services for Mentally Disordered Offenders in Scotland.* Edinburgh, Scotland: LTS08903. (**611, 651**)

Scottish Office (1998b) *Interviewing People who are Mentally Disordered: "Appropriate Adult" Schemes.* Edinburgh, Scotland: Home Department and HM Inspectorate of Constabulary. http://www.sehd.scot.nhs.uk/mels/HDL2006_56.pdf (**651**)

Scottish Office (1998c) *Acute Services Review Report.* Edinburgh, Scotland: Stationary Office. (**413**)

Scottish Prison Service (2002) *Positive Mental Health.* Edinburgh, Scotland. (**653**)

Scourfield J and Dobash R (1999) Programs for violent men: recent developments in the UK. *Howard Journal* **38**: 128–43. (**609**)

Scourfield J, Van den Bree M, Martin N, and McGuffin P (2004) Conduct problems in children and adolescents: a twin study. *Archives of General Psychiatry* **61**: 489–96. (**196**)

Scragg P and Shah A (1994) Prevalence of Asperger's Syndrome in a secure hospital. *British Journal of Psychiatry* **165**: 679–82. (**395**)

Scraton P and Gordon P (1984) *Causes for Concern: Questions of Law and Justice.* Harmondsworth, UK: Penguin Books. (**627**)

Scullin MH and CeCi SJ (2001) A suggestibility scale for children. *Personality and Individual Differences* **30**: 843–56. (**161**)

Scurfield R (1985) Post trauma stress assessment and treatment: overview and formulations. In C Figley (ed) *Trauma and Its Wake.* New York: Brunner/Mazel, pp. 219–56. (**721**)

Scurich N and John RS (2011) A Bayesian approach to the group versus individual prediction controversy in actuarial risk assessment. *Law and Human Behavior* **35**: 83–91. (**533**)

Scurich N and John RS (2012) Prescriptive approaches to communicating the risk of violence in actuarial risk assessment. *Psychology, Public Policy, and Law* **18**: 50–78. (**548**)

Sebastiani JA and Foy JL (1965) Psychotic visitors to the White House. *American Journal of Psychiatry* **122**: 679–86. (**543**)

Secker J, Benson A, Balfe E, et al. (2004) Understanding the social context of violent and aggressive incidents on an inpatient unit. *Journal of Psychiatric and Mental Health Nursing* **11**: 172–8. (**356**)

Secretary of State for Health (2005) *The Kerr/Haslam Inquiry (2 volumes)*. London: Department of Health. Cm 6640 (The Pleming Report). http://www.official-documents.gov.uk/document/cm66/6640/6640.pdf (**685**)

Seelau EP, Seelau SM, Wells GL, and Windschitl PD (1995) Counterfactual constraints. In NJ Roese, JM Olson (eds) *What Might Have Been: The Social Psychology of Counterfactual Thinking*. Mahwah, NJ: Lawrence Erlbaum Associates, pp. 57–79. (**696**)

Segal S (1989) Civil commitment standards and patient mix in England/Wales, Italy and the United States. *American Journal of Psychiatry* **146**: 187–93. (**133**)

Segal ZV, Williams JMG, and Teasdale JD (2004) Mindfulness-based cognitive therapy: theoretical rationale and empirical status,. In SC Hayes, VM Follette, MM Linehan (eds) *Mindfulness and Acceptance: Expanding the Cognitive-Behavioural Tradition*. New York: Guilford, pp. 45–65. (**569**)

Séguin M, Lesage A, Chawky N, et al. (2006) Suicide cases in New Brunswick from April 2002 to May 2003: the importance of better recognizing substance and mood disorder comorbidity. *Canadian Journal of Psychiatry* **51**(9): 581–6. (**452**)

Seidenwurm D, Pounds TR, Globus A, and Valk PE (1997) Abnormal temporal lobe metabolism in violent subjects: correlation of imaging and neuropsychiatric findings. *American Journal of Neuroradiology* **18**: 625–31. (**291**)

Seivewright N and Iqbal MZ (2002) Prescribing to drug misusers in practice – often effective, but rarely straightforward. *Addiction Biology* **7**: 269–77. (**462**)

Sellers CL, Sullivan CJ, Veysey BM, and Shane JM (2005) Responding to persons with mental illness: police perspectives on specialized and traditional practices. *Behavioral Sciences and the Law* **23**: 647–57. (**365**)

Selman RL (1976) Social-cognitive understanding: a guide to educational and clinical practice. In T Lickona (ed) *Moral Development and Behavior*. New York: Holt, Rinehart and Winston, pp. 299–316. (**394**)

Selzer ML and Payne CE (1962) Automobile accidents, suicide and unconscious motivation. *American Journal of Psychiatry* **119**: 237–40. (**278**)

Semple DM, McIntosh AM, and Lawrie SM (2005) Cannabis as a risk factor for psychosis: systematic review. *Journal of Psychopharmacology* **19**: 187–94. (**488**)

Senior J (2005) *The development of prison mental health services based on a community mental health model*. Unpublished PhD Thesis, University of Manchester. (**629, 631**)

Senior J, McDonnell S, Lennox C, Yao L, and Zhang N (2011) *The Development of a Pilot Electronic Multi-agency Information Sharing System for Offenders with Mental Illness*. Report to the NIHR SDO Programme and University of Manchester: Manchester, available from the first author. (**663**)

Sentencing Commission Working Group (2008) *Report*. London: The Gage Report. (**36**)

Serban G and Siegel S (1984) Response of borderline and schizotypal patients to small doses of thiothixene and haloperidol. *American Journal of Psychiatry* **141**: 1455–8. (**406**)

Sereny G (1972) *The Case of Mary Bell*. London: Eyre Methuen. Updated version 1995. London: Pimlico. (**499**)

Sereny G (1998) *Cries Unheard: Why Children Kill: The Story of Mary Bell*. London: Macmillan. (**499**)

Sergeant H (1986) Should psychiatric patients be granted access to their hospital records? *The Lancet* **2**: 1322–5. (**665**)

Seto MC and Barbaree HE (1995) The role of alcohol in sexual aggression. *Clinical Psychology Review* **15**: 545–66. (**442, 443**)

Seto MC and Barbaree HE (1999) Psychopathy, treatment behavior, and sex offender recidivism. *Journal of Interpersonal Violence* **14**: 1235–48. (**607**)

Seto MC and Eke AW (2005) The criminal histories and later offending of child pornography offenders. *Sexual Abuse: A Journal of Research and Treatment* **17**: 201–10. (**251**)

Seto MC, Cantor JM, and Blanchard R (2006) Child pornography offences are a valid diagnostic indicator of pedophilia. *Journal of Abnormal Psychology* **115**: 610–15. (**251**)

Sewell RA, Ranganathan M, and D'Souza DC (2009) Cannabinoids and psychosis. *International Review of Psychiatry* **21**: 152–62. (**455**)

Sex Offender Treatment Working Group (1990) *The Management and Treatment of Sex Offenders*. Ottawa, Canada: Solicitor General. (**578**)

Shaffer HJ and Hall MN (2002) The natural history of gambling and drinking problems among casino employees. *Journal of Social Psychology* **142**: 405–24. (**472**)

Shapiro F (1989a) Eye movement desensitization: a new treatment for post-traumatic stress disorder [see comments]. *Journal of Behaviour Therapy and Experimental Psychiatry* **20**: 211–7. (**719, 729**)

Shapiro F (1989b) Efficacy of the eye movement desensitization procedure in the treatment of traumatic memories. *Journal of Traumatic Stress Studies* **2**: 199–223. (**719, 729, 730**)

Shapiro F (1995) *EMDR: Basic Principles, Protocols, and Procedures*. New York: Guilford. (**720, 729, 730**)

Shapiro F (1996) Eye movement desensitization and reprocessing (EMDR): evaluation of controlled PTSD research. *Journal of Behaviour Therapy and Experimental Psychiatry* **27**: 209–18. (**729**)

Shapiro F (2001) *Eye Movement Desensitization and Reprocessing: Basic Principles, Protocols and Procedures*, 2nd edn. New York: Guilford. (**730, 731**)

Shapiro F (2002) Paradigms, processing and personality development. In F Shapiro (ed) *EMDR as an Integrative Psychotherapy Approach: Experts of Diverse Orientation Explore the Paradigm Prism*. Washington, DC: American Psychological Association Press, pp. 3–26. (**729, 731**)

Shapiro MB (1961) A method of measuring psychological changes specific to the individual psychiatric patient. *British Journal of Medical Psychology* **34**: 151–5. (**349**)

Sharpley CF, Montgomery IM, and Scalzo LA (1996) Comparative efficacy of EMDR and alternative procedures in reducing the vividness of mental images. *Scandinavian Journal of Behaviour Therapy* **25**: 37–42. (**725**)

Sharrock R and Cresswell M (1989) Pseudologia fantastica: a case study of a man charged with murder. *Medicine Science and the Law* **29**: 323–8. (**422**)

Shaw CR and McKay HD (1969) *Juvenile Delinquency and Urban Areas,* rev edn. Chicago, IL: University of Chicago Press. (**178**)

Shaw DM, Churchill CM, Noyes R, and Loeffer Holz PL (1987) Criminal behaviour and post-traumatic stress disorder in Vietnam veterans. *Comprehensive Psychiatry* **28**: 403–11. (**715**)

Shaw J and Roscoe A (2010) *Victims of Homicide in England and Wales: A Preliminary Report, Presented to the Steering Group of the National Confidential Inquiry into Suicide and Homicide.* http://www.bbmh.manchester.ac.uk/cmhr/ (**698**)

Shaw J, Amos T, Flynn S, et al. (2004) Mental illness in people who kill strangers: longitudinal study and national clinical survey. *British Medical Journal* **328**: 734–7. (**354**)

Shaw J, Appleby L, AmosT, et al. (1999) Mental disorder and clinical care in people convicted of homicide: national clinical survey. *British Medical Journal* **318**: 1240–4. (**231**)

Shaw J, Appleby L, and Baker D (2003) *Safer Prisons A National Study of Prison Suicides 1999–2000 by the National Confidential Inquiry into Suicides and Homicides by People with Mental Illness.* London: Department of Health. http://webarchive.nationalarchives. gov.uk/20130107105354/http://www.dh.gov.uk/prod_consum_dh/groups/dh_digitalassets/@dh/@en/documents/digitalasset/ dh_4034301.pdf (**634**)

Shaw J, Baker D, Hunt IM, Moloney A, and Appleby L (2004) Suicide by prisoners. National clinical survey. *British Journal of Psychiatry* **184**: 263–7. (**462, 630**)

Shaw J, Davies J, and Morely H (2001) An assessment of the security, dependency and treatment needs of all patients in secure services in a UK health region. *Journal of Forensic Psychiatry* **12**: 610–37. (**600**)

Shaw J, Hunt IM, Flynn S, et al. (2006) The role of alcohol and drugs in homicides in England and Wales. *Addiction* **101**(8): 1117–24. (**451**)

Shaw J, Senior J, et al. (2009) A national evaluation of prison mental health in-reach services. Manchester, UK: Offender Health Research Network. http://www.ohrn.nhs.uk/resource/Research/Inreach.pdf (**631**)

Sheard MH (1975) Lithium in the treatment of aggression. *Journal of Nervous and Mental Disease* **160**: 108–18. (**566**)

Sheard MH, Marini JL, Bridges CI, and Wagner E (1976) The effect of lithium on impulsive aggressive behaviour in man. *American Journal of Psychiatry* **133**: 1409–13. (**566**)

Shedler J and Westen D (2004a) Dimensions of personality pathology: An alternative to the five-factor model. *American Journal of Psychiatry* **161**: 1743–54. (**386**)

Shedler J and Westen D (2004b) Refining personality disorder diagnosis: Integrating science and practice. *American Journal of Psychiatry* 161: 1350–65. (**387**)

Shedler J, Beck A, Fonagy P, et al. (2010) Personality disorders in DSM-5. *American Journal of Psychiatry* **167**: 1026–8. (**384, 385**)

Sheline Y and Nelson T (1993) Patient choice: deciding between psychotropic medication and physical restraints in an emergency. *Bulletin of the American Academy of Psychiatry and the Law* **21**: 321–9. (**594**)

Shelton D (2001) Emotional disorders in young offenders. *Journal of Nurse Scholarship* **33**: 263. (**483**)

Shelton KH, Harold GT, Fowler TA, et al. (2008) Parent–child relations, conduct problems and cigarette use in adolescence: examining the role of genetic and environmental factors on patterns of behavior. *Journal of Youth and Adolescence* **37**: 1216–28. (**192, 200**)

Shepherd JP (2001a) Emergency medicine and police collaboration to prevent community violence. *Annals of Emergency Medicine* **38**: 420–7. (**700, 703**)

Shepherd JP (2001b) Criminal deterrence as a public health strategy. *Lancet* **358**: 1717–22. (**705**)

Shepherd JP (2004) NHS reporting of firearms injuries. *Firearms Consultative Committee 12th Annual Report.* HC1082:17–21. London: The Stationery Office. (**706**)

Shepherd JP (2005a) *The Contributions of Accident and Emergency Departments to Community Violence Prevention.* Cardiff, UK: Cardiff University. (**702**)

Shepherd JP (2005b) Victims in the National Health Service: combining treatment with violence prevention. *Criminal Behaviour and Mental Health* **15**: 75–82. (**704, 705**)

Shepherd JP (2007) *Effective NHS Contributions to Violence Prevention. The Cardiff Model.* http://www.alcohollearningcentre.org.uk/_ library/Cardiff_Model_–_violence_prevention1.pdf (**179**)

Shepherd JP, Huggett RH, and Kidner G (1993) Impact resistance of bar glasses. *Journal of Trauma* **35**: 935–8. (**705**)

Shepherd JP, Price M, and Shenfine P (1990a) Glass abuse and urban licensed premises. *Journal of the Royal Society of Medicine* **83**: 276–7. (**705**)

Shepherd JP, Qureshi R, and Preston MS (1990c) Psychological distress after assaults and accidents. *British Medical Journal* **301**: 849–50. (**706**)

Shepherd JP, Scully C, and Shapland M (1989) Recording of violent offences by the police: an accident and emergency perspective. *Medical Science Law* **29**: 251–7. (**700**)

Shepherd JP, Shapland M, Pearce NX, and Scully C (1990b) Pattern, severity and aetiology of injuries in victims of assault. *Journal of the Royal Society of Medicine* **83**: 75–9. (**705**)

Sheppard D (1996) *Learning the Lessons,* 2nd edn. London: Zito Trust. (**76, 695**)

Sheridan L and Blaauw E (2002) Stalker typologies and intervention strategies. *Polizei und Wissenschaft* (Special Issue on Stalking), **4**: 15–25. (**379**)

Sheridan L and Boon J (2002) Stalker typologies: implications for law enforcement. In J Boon, L Sheridan (eds) *Stalking and Psychosexual Obsession: Psychological Perspectives for Prevention, Policing and Treatment.* Chichester, UK: Wiley, pp. 63–82. (**375**)

Sheridan LP and Grant T (2007) Is cyberstalking different? *Psychology Crime and Law* **13**: 627–44. (**377**)

Sherman SJ and McConnell AR (1995) Dysfunctional implications of counterfactual thinking: when alternatives to reality fail us. In NJ Roese, JM Olson (eds) *What Might Have Been: The Social Psychology of Counterfactual Thinking.* Mahwah, NJ: Lawrence Erlbaum Associates, pp. 199–231. (**695, 696, 697**)

Sherwood RA, Keating J, Kavvadia V, Greenough A, and Peters TJ (1999) Substance misuse in early pregnancy and relationship to fetal outcome. *Neonatology* **158**(6): 488–92. (**464**)

Shetty A, Alex R, and Bloye D (2010) The experience of a smoke-free policy in a medium secure hospital. *The Psychiatrist* **34**: 287–9. (**568**)

Shi J, Levinson DF, Duan J, et al. (2009) Common variants on chromosome 6p22.1 are associated with schizophrenia. *Nature* **460**(7256): 753–7. (**209**)

Shiekh J and Yesavage J (1986) Geriatric depression scale: recent findings in the development of a shorter version. In J Brink (ed) *Clinical Gerontology: A Guide to Assessment and Treatment.* New York: Howarth, pp. 165–73. See also http://www.healthcare.uiowa.edu/igec/tools/depression/GDS.pdf (**527**)

Shifman S, Bronstein M, Sternfeld M, et al. (2002) A highly significant association between a COMT haplotype and schizophrenia. *American Journal of Human Genetics* **71**: 1296–302. (**208**)

Shine J (2000) *HMP Grendon, A Compilation of Grendon Research.* UK: Leyhill. (**583**)

Shine J (2007) Orientating patients to therapy. *Issues in Forensic Psychology* **7**: 48–54. (**572, 573**)

Shipherd JC, Street AE, and Resick PA (2006) Cognitive therapy for posttraumatic stress disorder. In J Folette, J Ruzek (eds) *Cognitive Behavioural Therapies for Trauma.* New York: Guilford, pp. 96–116. (**728**)

Shore D, Filson CR, Davis TS, et al. (1985) White House cases: psychiatric patients and the secret service. *American Journal of Psychiatry* **142**: 308–12. (**543**)

Shore JH, Vollmer WM, and Tatum EL (1989) Community patterns of posttraumatic stress disorders. *Journal of Nervous and Mental Disease* **177**: 681–5. (**712**)

Shprintzen RJ, Goldberg R, Golding-Kushner KJ, and Marion RW (1992) Late-onset psychosis in the velo-cardio-facial syndrome. *American Journal of Medical Genetics* **42**(1): 141–2. (**209**)

SHSA: *see* Special Hospitals Service Authority.

Siegel DJ (2001) Toward an interpersonal neurobiology of the developing mind: attachment relationships, 'mindsight', and neural integration. *Infant Mental Health Journal* **22**: 67–94. (**718, 720**)

Siegel DJ (2002) The developing mind and the resolution of trauma: some ideas about information processing and an interpersonal neurobiology of psychotherapy. In F Shapiro (ed) *EMDR as an Integrative Psychotherapy Approach: Experts of Diverse Orientations Explore the Paradigm Prism.* Washington, DC: American Psychological Association Press, pp. 85–122. (**725, 731**)

Siever LJ, Amin F, Coccaro EF, et al. (1993) CSF homovanillic acid in schizotypal personality disorder. *American Journal of Psychiatry* **150**: 149–51. (**309**)

Sigafoos J, Elkins J, Kerr M, and Attwood T (1994) A survey of aggressive behaviour among a population of persons with intellectual disability in Queensland. *Journal of Intellectual Disability Research* **38**: 369–81. (**326**)

Sigurdsson IF and GIdjonsson GH (2001) False confessions: the relative importance of psychological, criminological and substance abuse variables. *Psychology, Crime and Law* **7**: 275–89. (**622**)

Sigvardsson S, Bohman M, and Cloninger CR (1996) Replication of the Stockholm Adoption Study of alcoholism. Confirmatory cross-fostering analysis. *Archives of General Psychiatry* **53**: 681–7. (**207**)

Sihvola E, Rose RJ, Dick DM, Korhonen T, Pulkkinen L, Raevuori A, Marttunen M, and Kaprio J (2011) Prospective relationships of ADHD symptoms with developing substance use in a population-derived sample *Psychological Medicine* **41**: 2615–23. (**512**)

Sillaber I, Rammes G, Zimmermann S, et al. (2002) Enhanced and delayed stress-induced alcohol drinking in mice lacking functional CRH1 receptors. *Science* **296**: 931–3. (**206**)

Silva H, Jerez S, Paredes A, et al. (1997) [Fluoxetine in the treatment of borderline personality disorder]. [Spanish]. *Actas Luso-Espanolas de Neurologia, Psiquiatria y Ciencias Afines* **25**: 391–5. (**311**)

Silva JA and Leong GB (2003) Letter to the Editor. *Journal of the American Academy of Psychiatry and the Law* **31**: 143–4. (**509**)

Silva JA, Ferrari MM, Leong GB, and Penny G (1998) The dangerousness of persons with delusional jealousy. *Journal of the American Academy of Psychiatry and the Law* **26**: 607–23. (**372**)

Silver E (2000) Race, neighborhood disadvantage and violence among persons with mental disorders: the importance of contextual measurement. *Law and Human Behavior* **24**: 449–56. (**357**)

Silver E and Teasdale B (2005) Mental disorder and violence: an examination of stressful life events and impaired social support. *Social Problems* **52**: 62–78. (**357**)

Silver E, Mulvey E, and Swanson F (2002) Neighborhood structural characteristics and mental disorder: Faris and Durham revisited. *Social Science and Medicine* **55**: 1457–70. (**357**)

Silver HK and Glicken A.D (1990) Medical Student Abuse. *JAMA* **263**: 527–32. (**680**)

Silverman J and Wilson D (2002) *Innocence Betrayed, Paedophilia, the Media and Society.* Cambridge, UK: Polity. (**250, 264**)

Silverstone T (1988) The influence of psychiatric disease and its treatment in driving performance. *International Clinical Psychopharmacology* **3** (suppl. 1): 59–66. (**278**)

References

Sim J (1990) *Medical Power in Prisons. The Prison Medical Service in England 1774–1989.* Milton Keynes, UK: Open University Press. (**415, 626, 627**)

Simeon D, Greenberg J, Knutelska M, Schmeidler J, and Hollander E (2003) Peritraumatic reactions associated with the World Trade Center disaster. *American Journal of Psychiatry* **160**: 1702–5. (**723**)

Simeon D, Stanley B, France A, et al. (1992) Self-mutilation in personality disorders: psychological and biological correlates. *American Journal of Psychiatry* **149**: 221–6. (**308**)

Simmons P and Hoar A (2001) Section 136 use in the London Borough of Haringey. *Medicine, Science and the Law* **41**: 342–8. (**48, 621**)

Simon RI (1999) Therapist-patient sex: from boundary violations to sexual misconduct. *Psychiatric Clinics of North America* **22**: 31–47. (**691**)

Simon RI (2003) *Posttraumatic Stress Disorder in Litigation: Guidelines for Forensic Assessment,* 2nd edn. Washington, DC: American Psychiatric Publishing. (**726**)

Simpson AIF, Jones RM, Evans C, and McKenna B (2006) Outcome of patients rehabilitated through a New Zealand forensic psychiatry service: a 7.5 year retrospective study. *Behavioral Sciences and the Law* **24**: 833–43. (**139, 606**)

Simpson AIF, McKenna B, Moskowitz A, Skipworth J, and Barry-Walsh J (2004) Homicide and Mental Illness in New Zealand, 1970–2000. *British Journal of Psychiatry* **185**: 394–8. (**338**)

Simpson EB, Yen S, Costello E, et al. (2004) Combined dialectical behavior therapy and fl uoxetine in the treatment of borderline personality disorder. *Journal of Clinical Psychiatry* **65**: 379–85. (**311, 312, 408**)

Sims ACP and Symonds RL (1975) Psychiatric referrals from the police. *British Journal of Psychiatry* **127**: 171–8. (**621**)

Sinclair HC and Frieze IH (2000) Initial courtship behaviour and stalking: how should we draw the line. *Violence and Victims* **15**: 23–40. (**376**)

Sinclair HC and Frieze IH (2005) When courtship persistence becomes intrusive pursuit. *Sex Roles* **52**: 839–52. (**376**)

Singer I (1966) *The Nature of Love. Vol. 1. Plato to Luther.* New York: Random House. (**370**)

Singer I (1987) *The Nature of Love. Vol. 2. Courtly and Romantic.* Chicago, IL: University of Chicago Press. (**370**)

Singer JA (2005) *Personality and Psychotherapy: Treating the Whole Person.* New York: Guilford. (**570**)

Singleton N, Bumpstead R, O'Brien M, Lee A, and Meltzer H (2001) *Psychiatric Morbidity Among Adults Living in Private Households.* London: Stationery Office. (**390**)

Singleton N, Bumpstead R, O'Brien M, Lee A, and Meltzer H (2003) Psychiatric morbidity among adults living in private households, 2000. *International Review of Psychiatry* **15**: 65–73. (**463**)

Singleton N, Farrell M, and Meltzer H (1999) *Substance Misuse Among Prisoners in England and Wales.* London: Office for National Statistics. (**438, 443**)

Singleton N, Meltzer H, Gatward R, Coid J, and Deasy D (1998a) *Psychiatric Morbidity Among Prisoners in England and Wales.* London: The Stationery Office. (**242, 315, 394, 398, 415, 513, 516, 601, 689**)

Singleton N, Meltzer H, Gatward R, Coid J, and Deasy D (1998b) *Survey of Psychiatric Morbidity Among Prisoners in England and Wales.* London: Department of Health. (**629, 634, 647**)

Sinnott-Armstrong W, Roskies A, Brown T, and Murphy E (2008) Brian images as legal evidence. *Episteme* **5**: 359–73. (**17**)

Sirdifield C, Gojkovic D, Brooker C, and Ferriter M (2009) A systematic review of research on the epidemiology of mental health disorders in prison populations: a summary of findings. *Journal of Forensic Psychiatry and Psychology* **30**: s78–101. (**629**)

Sisk CL (2006) New insights into the neurobiology of sexual maturation. *Sexual and Relationship Therapy* **21**: 5–14. (**246**)

Sisk CL and Zehr JL (2005) Pubertal hormones organize the adolescent brain and behaviour. *Frontiers in Neuroendcrinology* **26**: 163–74. (**246**)

Sivarajasingam V and Shepherd JP (2001) Trends in community violence in England and Wales 1995–1998: an accident and emergency perspective. *Emergency Medicine Journal* **18**: 105–9. (**701**)

Sivarajasingam V, Morgan P, Matthews K, Shepherd JP, and Walker R (2009) Trends in violence in England and Wales 2000–2004: an accident and emergency perspective. *Injury* **40**: 820–5. (**702**)

Sivarajasingam V, Shepherd JP, and Matthews K (2003) Effect of urban closed circuit television on assault injury and violence detection. *Injury Prevention* **9**: 312–16. (**704**)

Sivarajasingam V, Shepherd JP, Matthews K, and Jones S (2002) Trends in violence in England and Wales 1995–2000: an accident and emergency perspective. *Journal of Public Health Medicine* **24**: 219–26. (**700, 701, 702**)

Sivarajasingam V, Wells JP, Moore S, Page N, Morgan P, Matthews K, and Shepherd JP (2013) *Violence in England and Wales in 2012. An Accident and Emergency Perspective.* (figures updated annually) Cardiff: Violence and Society Research Group. http://www.vrg.cf.ac.uk/nvit/NVIT_2012.pdf (**702**)

Sizemore CC (1989) *Mind of My Own: The Women Who Was Known As 'Eve' Tells the Story of Her Triumph over Multiple Personality Disorder.* New York: William Morrow and Co. (**426**)

Sizemore CC and Pittillo E (1977) *I'm Eve.* New York: Doubleday. (**426**)

Sjoberg RL, Ducci F, Barr CS, et al. (2008) A non-additive interaction of a functional MAO-A VNTR and testosterone predicts antisocial behavior. *Neuropsychopharmacology* **33**: 425–30. (**199**)

Sjöbring H (1973) Personality structure and development, a model and its application. *Acta Psychiatric Scandnavica supplement* **244**: 1–204. (**285**)

Skeem J and Monahan J (2011) Current directions in violence risk assessment. *Current Directions in Psychological Science* **20**: 38–42. (**529**)

Skeem JL, Schubert C Odgers C, et al. (2006) Psychiatric symptoms and community violence among high-risk patients: a test of the relationship at the weekly level. *Journal of Consulting and Clinical Psychology* **74**: 967–79. (**350**)

Skene L, Wilkinson D, Kahane G, and Savulescu J (2009) Neuroimaging and the withdrawal of life-sustaining treatment from patients in vegetative state. *Medical Law Review* **17**: 245–61. (**17**)

Skinner BF (1974) *About Behaviorism.* New York: Knopf. (**395**)

Skipworth J, Brinded P, Chaplow D, and Frampton C (2006) Insanity acquittee outcomes in New Zealand. *Australian and New Zealand Journal of Psychiatry* **40**(11–12): 1003–9. (**130**)

Skogstad W (2006) Action and thought: in-patient treatment of severe personality disorders within a psychotherapeutic milieu. In C Newrith, C Meux, PJ Taylor (eds) *Personality Disorder and Serious Offending, Hospital Treatment Models,* London: Hodder Arnold, pp. 161–9. (**583**)

Skuse D, Bentovim A, Hodges J, et al. (1998) Risk factors for development of sexually abusive behaviour in: sexually victimised adolescent boys. cross sectional study. *British Medical Journal* **317**: 175–9. (**494**)

Skyrme T (1983) *The Changing Image of the Magistracy.* London: Macmillan. (**22**)

Slapper G and Kelly D (2006) *The English Legal System,* 8th edn. Abingdon, VA: Routledge-Cavendish. (**52**)

Slaughter B, Fann JR, and Ehde D (2003) Traumatic brain injury in a county jail population: prevalence, neuropsychological functioning and psychiatric disorders. *Brain Injury* **17**: 731–41. (**488**)

Slomkowski C, Cohen P, and Brook J (1997) Sibling relationships of adolescents with antisocial and comorbid mental disorders: An epidemiological investigation. *Criminal Behaviour and Mental Health* **7**: 353–68. (**397**)

Slovenko R (1973) *Psychiatry and Law.* Boston, MA: Little, Brown and Company, p. 202. (**122**)

Slovenko R (1995) *Psychiatry and Criminal Culpability.* New York: Wiley. (**122**)

Slutske WS (2001) The genetics of antisocial behavior. *Current Psychiatry Reports* **3**: 158–62. (**190**)

Slutske WS, Heath AC, Dinwiddie SH, et al. (1998) Common genetic risk factors for conduct disorder and alcohol dependence. *Journal of Abnormal Psychology* **107**: 363–74. (**203**)

Slutske WS, Jackson KM, and Sher KJ (2003) The natural history of problem gambling from age 18 to 29. *Journal of Abnormal Psychology* **112**: 263–74. (**472**)

Slutsker L, Smith R, Higginson G, and Fleming D (1993) Recognizing illicit drug use by pregnant women: reports from Oregon birth attendants. *American Journal of Public Health* **83**: 61–4. (**464**)

Smeijsters H and Cleven G (2006) The treatment of aggression using arts therapies in forensic psychiatry: results of a qualitative inquiry. *The Arts in Psychotherapy* **33**: 37–58. (**558, 578**)

Smith A and Taylor PJ (199) Social and sexual functioning in schizophrenia men who commit serious sex offences against women. *Criminal Behaviour and Mental Health* **9**: 156–67. (**249, 262**)

Smith AD and Taylor PJ. (1999) Serious sex offending against women by men with schizophrenia. *British Journal of Psychiatry* **174**: 233–7. (**340**)

Smith AJ, Hodgson RJ, Bridgeman K, and Shepherd JP (2003) A randomised controlled trial of a brief intervention after alcohol-related facial injury. *Addiction* **98**: 43–52. (**705**)

Smith CA and Stern SB (1997) Delinquency and antisocial behaviour: a review of family processes and intervention research. *Social Service Review* **71**: 382–420. (**174**)

Smith CA and Thornberry TP (1995) The relationship between childhood maltreatment and adolescent involvement in delinquency. *Criminology* **33**: 451–81. (**175**)

Smith DA and Buckley PF (2006) Pharmacotherapy of delusional disorders in the context of offending and the potential for compulsory treatments. *Behavioral Sciences and the Law* **24**: 351–67. (**359**)

Smith FM and Marshall LA (2007) Barriers to effective drug addiction treatment for women involved in street-level prostitution: a qualitative investigation. *Criminal Behaviour and Mental Health* **17**: 163–70. (**464, 503**)

Smith J (2002–2005) The Shipman Report. http://www.shipman-inquiry.org.uk/reports.asp (**54**)

Smith J and Short J (1995) Mentally disordered fire-setters. *British Journal of Hospital Medicine* **53**: 136–40. (**576**)

Smith JC and Weisstub DM (1983) *The Western Idea of Law.* London: Butterworth. (**370**)

Smith K, Flatley J, Coleman K, et al. (2010) *Homicides, Firearm Offences and Intimate Violence 2008/09.* London: Home Office Statistical Bulletin. (**221**)

Smith LA, Gates S, and Foxcroft (2006) Therapeutic communities for substance related disorder. *Cochrane Database of Systematic Reviews* 2006. Issue 1, Art. No.: CD005338. DOI: 10.1002/14651858.CD005338.pub2.tr. http://onlinelibrary.wiley.com/o/cochrane/clsysrev/articles/CD005338/pdf_fs.html (**412**)

Smith PK and Sharp S (1994) *School Bullying: Insights and Perspectives.* London: Routledge. (**184**)

Smith R (1981) *Trial by Medicine.* Edinburgh, Scotland: University Press. (**28**)

Smith R (1984) *Prison Health Care.* London: British Medical Association. (**627, 666**)

Smith S, Branford D, Collacott RA, Cooper SA, and McGrother C (1996) Prevalence and cluster typology of maladaptive behaviours in a geographically defined population of adults with learning disabilities. *British Journal of Psychiatry* **169**: 219–27. (**326**)

Smith SE, Pihl RO, Young SN, and Ervin FR (1986) Elevation and reduction of plasma tryptophan and their effects on aggression and perceptual sensitivity in normal males. *Aggressive Behavior* **12**: 393–407. (**309**)

Smith SM and Hanson R (1974) 134 battered children: a medical and psychological study. *British Medical Journal* **3**: 666–70. (**222**)

References

Smith SS and Newman JP (1990) Alcohol and drug abuse-dependence disorders in psychopathic and non-psychopathic criminal offenders. *Journal of Abnormal Psychology* **99**: 430–9. (**444**)

Smoot SL and Gonzales JL (1995) Cost-effective communication skills training for state hospital employees. *Psychiatric Services* **46**: 819–22. (**557**)

Smucker MR and Dancu C (2005) *Cognitive-Behavioural Treatment for Adult Survivors of Childhood Trauma: Imagery Rescripting and Reprocessing*. Lanham, MD: Rowman and Littlefield. (**729**)

Sneed JR, Balestri M, and Belfi BJ (2003) The use of dialectical behavior therapy strategies in the emergency room. *Psychotherapy: Theory Research, Practice, Training* **40**: 265–77. (**390**)

Snowden PR (1985) A survey of the regional secure unit programme. *British Journal of Psychiatry* **147**: 499–507. (**600**)

Snowden PR (1986) Forensic psychiatry services and regional secure units in England and Wales: an overview. *Criminal Law Review*: 790–799. (**600**)

Snowden PR (2010) Dealing with offending doctors: sanctions and remediation. In F Subotsky, S Bewley, M Crowe (eds) *Abuse of the Doctor-Patient Relationship*. London: Royal College of Psychiatrists. (**691**)

Snowden RJ, Gray NS, Taylkor J, and Fitzgerald S (2009) Assessing risk of future violence among forensic psychiatric inpatients with the Classification of Violence Risk (COVR). *Psychiatric Services* **60**: 1522–6. (**541, 542**)

Snowden RJ, Gray NS, Taylor J, and McCulloch M (2007) Actuarial prediction of violent recidivism in mentally disordered offenders. *Psychological Medicine* **37**: 1539–49. (**536, 537**)

Snowdon J, Solomons R, and Druce H (1978) Feigned bereavement: twelve cases. *British Journal of Psychiatry* **133**: 15–9. (**422**)

Snyder HN (2011) Arrest in the United States, 1980–2009. Washington, DC: US Department of Justice. http://bjs.gov/content/pub/pdf/aus8009.pdf (**503**)

Snyder HN and Sickmund M (2006) Juvenile Offenders and Victims. Washington, DC: Office of Juvenile Justice and delinquency Prevention. http://www.eric.ed.gov/ERICWebPortal/search/detailmini.jsp?_nfpb=true&_&ERICExtSearch_SearchValue_0=ED495786&ERICExtSearch_SearchType_0=no&accno=ED495786 (**503**)

Snyder J and Patterson GR (1995) Individual differences in social aggression: A test of a reinforcement model of socialization in the natural environment. *Behavior Therapy* **26**: 371–91. (**317**)

Soderstrom H, Blennow K, Sjodin A-K, and Forsman A (2003) New evidence for an association between the CSF HVA:5-HIAA ratio and psychopathic traits. *Journal of Neurology. Neurosurgery and Psychiatry* **74**:918–21. (**308**)

Soderstrom H, Hultin L, Tullberg M, et al. (2002) Reduced frontotemporal perfusion in psychopathic personality. *Psychiatry Research* **114**: 81–94. (**303, 308**)

Soderstrom H, Tullberg M, Wikkelsö M, Ekholm S, and Forsman A (2000) Reduced regional cerebral blood flow in non-psychotic violent offenders. *Psychiatry Research: Neuroimaging* **98**: 29–41. (**303**)

Soeteman DI, Verheul R, Delimon J, Meerman AMM, van den Eijnden E, Rossum BV, Ziegler U, Thunnissen M, Busschbach JJV, and Kim JJ (2010) Cost-effectiveness of psychotherapy for cluster B personality disorders. *British Journal of Psychiatry* **196**: 396–403. (**417**)

Sofair AN and Kaldjian LC (2000) Eugenic sterilization and a qualified nazi analogy: the United States and Germany, 1930–1945. *Annals of Internal Medicine* **132**: 312–9. (**115, 333**)

Sohn L (1995) Unprovoked assaults-making sense of apparently random violence. *International Journal of Psychoanalysis* **76**: 565–75. (**582**)

Sohn L (1999) Psychosis and violence. In P Williams (ed) *Psychosis (Madness)*. London: The Institute of Psychoanalysis, pp. 13–26. (**582**)

Soler J, Pascual JC, Campins J, et al. (2005) Doubleblind, placebo-controlled study of dialectical behavior therapy plus olanzapine for borderline personality disorder. *American Journal of Psychiatry* **162**: 1221 24. (**406**)

Soloff PH (1981) Pharmacotherapy of borderline disorders. *Comprehensive Psychiatry* **22**: 535–43. (**403**)

Soloff PH (1998) Algorithms for pharmacological treatment of personality dimensions: symptom-specific treatments for cognitive-perceptual, affective, and impulsive-behavioral dysregulation. *Bulletin of the Menninger Clinic* **62**: 195–214. (**312**)

Soloff PH and Turner SM (1981) Patterns of seclusion: a prospective study. *Journal of Nervous and Mental Disease* **169**: 37–44. (**595**)

Soloff PH, Cornelius J, Georger A, et al. (1993) Efficacy of phenelzine and haloperidol in borderline personality disorder. *Archives of General Psychiatry* **50**: 377–85. (**406**)

Soloff PH, George A, Nathan RS, et al. (1989) Amitriptyline versus haloperidol in borderlines: final outcomes and predictors of response. *Journal of Clinical Psychopharmacology* **9**: 238–46. (**406**)

Soloff PH, Kelly TM, Strotmeyer SJ, Malone KM, and Mann JJ (2003) Impulsivity, gender, and response to fenfluramine challenge in borderline personality disorder. *Psychiatry Research* **119**: 11–24. (**309**)

Soloff, PH (1984) Historical notes on seclusion and restraint. In: Tardiff, K. ed., *The Psychiatric Uses of Seclusion and Restraint*. American Psychiatric Press: Washington, DC. pp. 1–9. (**593**)

Solomon E and Silvestri A (2008) *Community Sentences Digest*. London: London Centre for Criminal Justice Studies, King's College. (**588**)

Solursh L (1988) Combat addiction: post-traumatic stress disorder re-explored. *Psychiatric Journal of the University of Ottawa* **13**: 17–20. (**715**)

Somander LK and Rammer LM. Intra- and extrafamilial child homicide in Sweden 1971–1980. *Child Abuse Negl* **1991**(15): 45–55. (**508**)

Soothill K and Wilson D (2005) Theorising the puzzle that is Harold Shipman. *Journal of Forensic Psychiatry and Psychology* **16**(4): 658–98. (**690**)

Soothill K, Ackerley E, and Francis B (2004) The criminal careers of arsonists *Medicine Science and the Law* **44:** 27–40. (**273**)

Soothill KL and Pope PJ (1973) Arson: a twenty-year cohort study. *Medicine, Science and the Law* **13**: 127–38. (**274**)

Soothill KL, Adserballe H, Bernham J, et al. (1983) Psychiatric reports requested by the courts in six countries. *Medicine, Science and the Law* **23**: 231–41. (**113**)

Soothill KL, Harding TW, Asderballe H, et al. (1981) Compulsory admissions to mental hospital in six countries. *International Journal of Law and Psychiatry* **4**: 327–44. (**113**)

Soothill KL, Jack A, and Gibbens TCN (1976) Rape: a 22-year cohort study. *Medicine, Science and the Law* **16**: 62–9. (**249**)

Soothill KL, Jack A, and Gibbens TCN (1980) Rape acquittals. *Modern Law Review* **43**: 159–72. (**248**)

Sorbello L, Eccleston L, Ward T, and Jones R (2002) Treatment needs of female offenders: a review. *Australian Psychologist* **37**: 198–205. (**517**)

Sorgi P, Ratey J, Knoedler DW, Markert RJ, and Reichman M (1991) Rating aggression in the clinical setting a retrospective adaptation of the overt aggression scale: preliminary results. *Journal of Neoropsychiatry* **3**: 552–6. (**326**)

Soskis DA (1978) Schizophrenic and medical inpatients as informed drug consumers. *Archives of General Psychiatry* **35**: 645–7. (**665**)

Soyka M, Graz C, Bottlender R, Dirschedl P, and Schoech H (2007) Clinical correlates of later violence and criminal offences in schizophrenia. *Schizophrenia Research* **94**: 89–98. (**515**)

Soyka M, Morhart-Klute V, and Schoech H (2004) Delinquency and criminal offenses in former schizophrenic inpatients 7–12 years following discharge. *European Archives of Psychiatry and Clinical Neuroscience* **254**: 289–94. (**280**)

Sparks R, Genn H, and Dodd D (1977) *Surveying Victims*. London: Wiley. (**701**)

Spataro J, Mullen P, Burgess P, Wells D, and Moss, A (2004) Impact of child sexual abuse on mental health: prospective study in males and females. *British Journal of Psychiatry* **184**: 416–21. (**344**)

Spaulding WD, Sullivan M, Weiler M, et al. (1994) Changing cognitive functioning in rehabilitation of schizophrenia. *Acta Psychiatrica Scandinavica* **90**: 116–24. (**573**)

Spauwen J, Krabbendam L, Lieb R, Wittchen H-U, and van Os J (2006) Impact of psychological trauma on the development of psychotic symtpoms; relationship with psychosis proneness. *British Journal of Psychiatry* **188**: 527–33. (**345**)

Special Hospitals' Service Authority (1989) *Report of the Inquiry into the circumstances leading to the death in Broadmoor hospital of Mr Joseph Watts on 23rd August 1988*. London: Special Hospitals' Service Authority. (**604**)

Special Hospitals' Service Authority (1993) *Report of the Committee of Inquiry into the death in Broadmoor hospital of Orville Blackwood and a review of the Deaths of two other Afro-Caribbean Patients. 'Big, Black and Dangerous'*. London: Special Hospitals' Service Authority. (**558**)

Special Hospitals' Treatment Resistant Schizophrenia Group (1996) Schizophrenia, violence, clozapine and risperidone: a review. *British Journal of Psychiatry* **169** (Suppl. 31): 31–40. (**564**)

Spence SA (2005) Prefrontal white matter, the tissue of lies? Invited commentary. *British Journal of Psychiatry* **187**. 326–7. (**421**)

Spence SA (2008a) Can pharmacology help enhance human morality. *British Journal of Psychiatry* **193**: 179–80. (**6**)

Spence SA (2008b) Playing devil's advocate: the case against fMRI lie detection. *Legal and Criminological Psychology* **13**: 11–25 (**313**)

Spence SA, Brooks DJ, Hirsch SR, et al. (1997) A PET study of voluntary movement in schizophrenic patients experiencing passivity phenomena (delusions of alien control). *Brain* **120**: 1997–2011. (**313**)

Spence SA, Hunter MD, Farrow TFD, et al. (2004) A cognitive neurobiological account of deception: evidence from functional neuroimaging *The Royal Society* Published online 26 November. (**421**)

Spence SA, Kaylor-Hughes CJ, Brook ML, Lankappa ST, and Wilkinson ID (2008) 'Munchausen's syndrome by proxy' or a 'miscarriage of justice'? an initial application of functional neuroimaging to the question of guilt versus innocence. *European Psychiatry* **23**: 309–14. (**421**)

Sperry L (2003) *Handbook of Diagnosis and Treatment of DSM-IV-TR Personality Disorders*. London: Routledge. (**384**)

Spidel A, Lecomte T, Greaves C, Sahlstrom K, and Yuille JC (2010) Early psychosis and aggression: predictors and prevalence of violent behaviour amongst individuals with early onset psychosis. *International Journal of Law and Psychiatry* **33**: 171–6. (**344**)

Spiegel D (1984) Multiple personality as a post-traumatic stress disorder. *Psychiatric Clinics of North America* **7**: 101–10. (**426**)

Spielberger CD (1996) *State-Trait Anger Expression Inventory Professional Manual*. Florida: Psychological Assessment Resources. (**326**)

Spielberger CD, Gorsuch RL, Lushene PR, Vagg PR, and Jacobs AG (1983) *Manual for the State-Trait* Anxiety Inventory (Form Y). Palo Alto: Consulting Psychologists. (**161**)

Spinelli (2004) Maternal infanticide associated with mental illness: prevention and the promise of saved lives. *American Journal of Psychiatry* **161**:, 1548–57. (**501, 510**)

Spinelli M (ed) (2003) *Infanticide: Psychosocial and Legal Perspectives on Mothers Who Kill*. Arlington, VA: American Psychiatric Publishing. (**510**)

Spinelli MG (2001) A systematic investigation of 16 cases of neonaticide. *American Journal of Psychiatry* **158**: 811–3. (**510**)

Spitzberg BH and Cupach WR (2001) Paradoxes of pursuit: toward a relational model of stalking-related phenomena. In JA Davis (ed) *Stalking Crimes and Victim Protection: Prevention, Intervention, Threat Assessment and Case Management*. Boca Raton, FL: CRC, pp. 97–136. (**374**)

Spitzberg BH and Cupach WR (2007) The state of the art of stalking: taking stock of the emerging literature. *Aggression and Violent Behavior* **12**: 64–86. (**376**)

Spitzberg BH and Hoobler G (2002) Cyberstalking and the technologies of interpersonal terrorism. *New Media and Society* **4**(1): 71–92. (**377**)

Spitzer C, Dudeck M, Liss H, et al. (2001) Post-traumatic stress disorder in forensic inpatients. *Journal of Forensic Psychiatry* **12**: 63–77. (**712**)

References

Spitzer RL (1975) On pseudoscience in science, logic in remission and psychiatric diagnosis: a critique of Rosenhan's 'on being sane in insane places'. *Journal of Abnormal Psychology* **84**: 442–52. (**432**)

Spivak B, Mester R, Wittenberg N, Maman Z, and Weizman A (1997) Reduction of aggressiveness and impulsiveness during clozapine treatment in chronic neuroleptic-resistant schizophrenic patients. *Clinical Neuropharmacology* **20**: 442–6. (**564**)

Spivak B, Shabash E, Sheitman B, Weizman A, and Mester R (2003) The effects of clozapine versus haloperidol on measures of impulsive aggression and suicidality in chronic schizophrenia patients: an open, nonrandomized, 6-month study. *Journal of Clinical Psychiatry* **64**: 755–60. (**564**)

Spokes J (1988) *The Aftercare of Miss Sharon Campbell*. Cm440. London: HMSO. (**532**)

Spores JC (1988) *Running Amok, an Historical Enquiry*. Athens, Ohio: S.E. Asia Series No. 82, Ohio University. (**428**)

Spreat S, Behar D, Reneski B, and Miazzo P (1989) Lithium carbonate for aggression in mentally retarded persons. *Comprehensive Psychiatry* **30**: 505–11. (**566**)

Sprince A (2003) Malingering and the law: a 3rd way? In PW Halligan, C Bass, DA Oakley (eds) *Malingering and Illness Deception*. Oxford, UK: Oxford University Press, pp. 232–42. (**431**)

Springer T, Lohr NE, Buchtel HA, and Silk KR (1996) A preliminary report of short-term cognitive-behavioral group therapy for inpatients with personality disorders. *Journal of Psychotherapy Practice and Research* **5**: 57–71. (**411**)

SPSS Inc (1993) *SPSS for Windows CHAID (Release 6.0)*. Chicago, IL: SPSS. (**540**)

Spunt B, Brownstein HH, Crimmins SH, and Langley S (1996) Drugs and homicide by women. *Subst Use Misuse* **31**: 825–45. (**507**)

Sroufe AL (2005) Attachment and development: a prospective longitudinal study from birth to adulthood. *Attachment and Human Development* **7**: 349–67. (**718**)

Stadler C, Schmeck K, Nowraty I, Muller WE, and Poustka F (2004) Platelet 5-HT uptake in boys with conduct disorder. *Neuropsychobiology* **50**: 244–51. (**308**)

Stallings MC, Cherny SS, Young SE, et al. (1997) The familial aggregation of depressive symptoms, antisocial behavior, and alcohol abuse. *American Journal of Medical Genetics* **74**: 183–91. (**189**)

Stallings MC, Corley RP, Dennehey B, et al. (2005) A genome-wide search for quantitative trait Loci that influence antisocial drug dependence in adolescence. *Archives of General Psychiatry* **62**: 1042–51. (**197**)

Stallwitz A and Stöver H (2007) The impact of substitution treatment in prisons – A literature review. *International Journal of Drug Policy* **18**: 464–74. (**462**)

Stanford MS, Helfritz LE, Conklin SM, et al. (2005) A comparison of anticonvulsants in the treatment of impulsive aggression. *Experimental and Clinical Psychopharmacology* **13**: 72–7. (**566**)

Stanhope V and Solomon P (2007) Bridging the gap: using microsociological theory to understand how expressed emotion predicts clinical outcomes. *Psychiatric Quarterly* **78**: 117–28. (**355**)

Stanko E (1990) *Everyday Violence*. London: Pandora. (**713**)

Stanko E, Crisp D, Hale C, and Lucraft H (1998) *Counting the Costs: Estimating the Impact of Domestic Violence in the London Borough of Hackney*. Swindon, UK: Crime Concern. (**240**)

Stanko EA (2001) The day to count: reflections on a methodology to raise awareness about the impact of domestic violence in the UK. *Criminal Justice* **1**(2): 215–26. (**219**)

Stanton J and Simpson A (2001) Murder misdiagnosed as SIDS: a perpetrator's perspective. *Archives of Disease in Childhood* **85**: 454–9. (**506, 508**)

Stanton J and Simpson A (2002) Filicide: a review. *International Journal of Law Psychiatry* **25**(1): 1–14. (**508, 509**)

Stattin H and Klackenberg-Larsson I (1993) Early language and intelligence development and their relationship to future criminal behaviour. *Journal of Abnormal Psychology* **102**: 369–78. (**174**)

Stattin H and Magnusson D (1991) Stability and change in criminal behaviour up to age 30. *British Journal of Criminology* **31**: 327–46. (**173**)

Stavrakaki C (2002) Substance-related disorders in persons with a developmental disability. In DM Griffiths, C Stavrakaki, J Summers (eds) *Dual Diagnosis: An introduction to the Mental Health Needs of Persons with Developmental Disabilities*. New York: NADD. (**324**)

Steadman H, Mulvey E, Monahan J, Robbins P, Appelbaum P, Grisso T, Roth L and Silver E (1998) Violence by people discharged from acute psychiatric inpatient facilities and by others in the same neighborhoods. *Archives of General Psychiatry*, 55, 393–401. (**228, 355, 559**)

Steadman HJ and Naples M (2005) Assessing the effectiveness of jail diversion programs for persons with serious mental illness and co-occurring substance use disorders. *Behavioral Sciences and the Law* **23**: 163–70. (**365, 640, 641**)

Steadman HJ, Redlich A, Callahan L, Robbins PC, and Vesselinov R (2011) Effect of mental health courts on arrests and jail days. *Archives of General Psychiatry* **68**: 167–72. (**364**)

Steadman HJ, Redlich AD, Griffin P, Petrila J, and Monahan J (2005) From referral to disposition: case processing in seven mental health courts. *Behavioral Sciences and the Law* **23**: 215–26. (**640**)

Stearns PN (1989) *Jealousy: The Evolution of an Emotion in American History*. New York: New York University Press. (**370**)

Steel J, Thornicroft G, Birmingham L, et al. (2007) Prison mental health inreach services. *British Journal of Psychiatry* **190**: 373–4. (**462**)

Steele J, Darjee R, and Thomson LDG (2003) Substance dependence in schizophrenia in patients with dangerous, violent or criminal propensities: a comparison of comorbid and non-comorbid patients in a high security setting. *Journal of Forensic Psychiatry and Psychology* **14**: 569–84. (**613**)

Steels M, Roney G, Larkin E, et al. (1998) Discharged from hospital: a comparison of the fates of psychopaths and the mentally ill. *Criminal Behaviour and Mental Health* 8: 39–55. (**604**)

Steen C (2005) Cognitive-behavioural treatment under the relapse prevention umbrella. In MC Calder (ed) *Children and Young People Who Sexually Abuse: New Theory, Research and Practice Developments.* Lyme Regis, UK: Russell House, pp. 217–30. (**495**)

Stefansson H, Ophoff RA, Steinberg S, et al. (2009) Common variants conferring risk of schizophrenia. *Nature* 460(7256): 744–7. (**209**)

Stefansson H, Rujescu D, Cichon S, et al. (2008) Large recurrent microdeletions associated with schizophrenia. *Nature* 455(7210): 232–6. (**209**)

Stefansson H, Sigurdsson E, Steinthorsdottir V, et a.l (2002) Neuroregulin 1 and susceptibility to schizophrenia. *American Journal of Human Genetics* 71: 877–92. (**209**)

Steffensmeier D (1980) Assessing the impact of the women's movement on sex-based differences in the handling of adult criminal defendants. *Crime and Delinquency* 23(3): 344–56. (**500**)

Steffensmeier D and Motivans M (2000) Sentencing the older offender: is there an age bias? In MB Rothman, BD Dunlop, P Entzel (eds) *Elders, Crime and the Criminal Justice System: Myths, Perceptions and Reality in the 21st Century.* New York: Springer. pp 185–206. (**524**)

Stein DJ, Newman TK, Savitz J, and Ramesar R (2006) Warriors versus worriers: the role of COMT gene variants. *CNS Spectrums* 11(10): 745–8. (**199**)

Stein G (1993) Drug treatments of the personality disorders. In P Tyrer, G Stein (eds) *Personality Disorder Reviewed.* London: Gaskell, pp. 262–304. (**403**)

Steiner H, Garcia IG, and Matthews Z (1997) Posttraumatic stress disorder in incarcerated juvenile delinquents. *Journal of American Academy of Child and Adolescent Psychiatry* 36: 357–65. (**712**)

Steiner M, Ravindran AV, LeMelledo J-M, et al.(2008) Olanzepine plus dialectical behaviour therapy for women with high irritability who meet criteria for borderline personality disorder: a double-blind, placebo-controlled pilot study. *Journal of Clinical Psychiatry* 69: 999–1005. (**406**)

Steinert T (2002) Prediction of inpatient violence. *Acta Psychiatrica Scandinavica* 106: 133 41. (**534, 535**)

Steinert T, Sippach T, and Gebhardt RP (2000) How common is violence in schizophrenia despite neuroleptic treatment? *Pharmacopsychiatry* 33: 98–102. (**520**)

Steinert T, Wiebe C, and Gebhardt RP, (1999) Aggressive behavior against self and others among first-admission patients with schizophrenia. *Psychiatric Services* 50: 85–90. (**344**)

Stengel E (1941) On the aetiology of the fugue state. *Journal of Mental Science* 87: 572–99. (**294, 424, 427**)

Stern D (1985) *The Interpersonal World of the Infant.* New York: Basic Books. (**718**)

Stern DA, Fromm MG, and Sacksteder JL (1986) From coercion to collaboration: two weeks in the life of a therapeutic community. *Psychiatry* 49: 18–32. (**401**)

Stern GM (1976) From chaos to responsibility. *American Journal of Psychiatry* 133: 300 1. (**51**)

Stevenson H, Castillo E, and Sefarbi R (1990) Treatment of denial in adolescent sex offenders and their families. *Journal of Offender Counselling Services and Rehabilitation* 14: 37–50. (**263**)

Stevenson RL (1886) *Strange Case of Dr Jekyll and Mr Hyde.* London: Longmans, Green and Co. (**426, 427**)

Stewart D, Gossop M, Marsden J, and Rolfe A (2000) Drug misuse and acquisitive crime among clients recruited to the national treatment outcome research study (NTORS). *Criminal Behaviour and Mental Health* 10: 10–20. (**459**)

Stickgold R (2002) EMDR: a putative neurobiological mechanism of action. *Journal of Clinical Psychology* 58: 61–75. (**725, 731**)

Stirling J and the Committee on Child Abuse and Neglect (2007) Beyond Munchausen syndrome by proxy: Identification and treatment of child abuse in a medical setting. *Pediatrics* 119: 1026–30. (**507**)

Stoff D, Pollock L, Vitiello B, Behar D, and Bridger WH (1987) Reduction of ^{3}-H-Imipramine binding sites on platelets of conduct disordered children. *Neuropsychopharmacology* 1: 55–62. (**308**)

Stokes T, Shaw EJ, Juarez-Garcia A, Camosso-Stefinovic J, and Baker R (2004) *Clinical Guidelines and Evidence Review for the Epilepsies: diagnosis and management in adults and children in primary and secondary care.* London: Royal College of General Practitioners. (**288**)

Stompe T, Ortwein-Swoboda G, and Schanda H (2004) Schizophrenia, delusional symptoms, and violence: the threat/control-override concept re-examined. *Schizophrenia Bulletin* 30: 31–44. (**350**)

Stompe T, Strnad A, Ritter K, et al. (2006) Family and social inlcuences on offending in men with schizophrenia. *Australian and New Zealand Journal of Psychiatry* 40: 554–60. (**355***)

Stone AA (1976) *Mental Health and Law: A System in Transition.* New York: Jason Aronson, pp. 199–217. (**119**)

Stone AA (1982) Psychiatric abuse and legal reform. *International Journal of Law and Psychiatry* 5: 9–27. (**150**)

Stone MH (1990) *The fate of borderline patients.* New York: Guilford. (**398, 402**)

Stone MH (1993) Long-term outcome in personality disorders. *British Journal of Psychiatry* 162: 299–313. (**391**)

Stone MH (2003) Borderline patients at the border of treatability: at the intersection of borderline, narcissistic and antisocial personalities. *Journal of Psychiatric Practice* 9: 279–90. (**392**)

Stone MH (2006) Management of borderline personality disorder: a review of psychotherapeutic approaches. *World Psychiatry (WPA)* 5: 15–20. (**570**)

Stone MH (2006a) *Personality-Disordered Patients: Treatable and Untreatable.* Washington, DC: American Psychiatric Publishing. (**398**)

Stoolmiller M (1999) Implications of the restricted range of family environments for estimates of heritability and nonshared environment in behavior-genetic adoption studies. *Psychological Bulletin* **125**: 392–409. (**188**)

Strachan T and Read AP (1999) *Human Molecular Genetics 2*. New York: John Wiley and Sons. (**192**)

Strand S and Belfrage H (2005) Gender differences in psychopathy in a Swedish offender sample. *Behavioral Sciences and the Law* **23**: 837–50. (**513**)

Strand S, Belfrage H, Fransson G, and Levander S (1999) Clinical and risk management factors in risk prediction of mentally disordered offenders – more important than historical data? A retrospective study of 40 mentally disordered offenders assessed with the HCR-20 violence risk assessment scheme. *Legal and Criminological Psychology* **4**: 67–76. (**537, 538**)

Straub RE, Jiang Y, MacLean CJ, et al. (2002) Genetic variation in the 6p22. 3 gene DTNBP1, the human ortholog of the mouse dysbindin gene, is associated with schizophrenia. *American Journal of Human Genetics* **71**: 337–48. (**208**)

Straus MA (2009) Why the overwhelming evidence on partner physical violence by women has not been perceived and is often denied. *Journal of Aggression, Maltreatment and Trauma* **18**: 552–71. (**218**)

Strauss JS (1969) Hallucinations and delusions as points on continua function. *Archives of General Psychiatry* **21**: 581–6. (**349**)

Stravynski, A, Belisle, M, Marcouiller, M, et al. (1994) The treatment of avoidant personality disorder by social skills training in the clinic or in real-life settings. *Canadian Journal of Psychiatry* **39**: 377–83. (**411**)

Stromberg CD and Stone AA (1983) A model state law on civil commitment of the mentally ill. *Harvard Journal on Legislation* **20**: 275–396. (**133**)

Strous RD, Bark N, Parsia SS, Volavka J, and Lachman HM (1997) Analysis of a functional catechol-O-methyltransferase gene polymorphism in schizophrenia: evidence for association with aggressive and antisocial behavior. *Psychiatry Resesarch* **69**: 71–7. (**199**)

Strous RD, Nolan KA, Lapidus R, et al. (2003) Aggressive behavior in schizophrenia is associated with the low enzyme activity COMT polymorphism: a replication study. *American Journal of Medical Genetics B Neuropsychiatric Genetics* **120B**: 29–34. (**199**)

Sturmey P and Gaubatz M (2002) *Clinical and Counselling Psychology: A Case Study Approach*. Boston, MA: Allyn and Bacon. (**332**)

Sturmey P, Reyer H, Lee R, and Robek A (2003) *Substance Related Disorders in Persons with Mental Retardation*. New York: Kingston. (**324**)

Sturmey P, Taylor JL, and Lindsay WR (2004) Research and development. In WR Lindsay, JL Taylor, P Sturmey (eds) *Offenders with Developmental Disabilities*. Chichester, UK: John Wiley, pp. 327–50. (**315, 316, 332, 333**)

Sturup GK (1968a) Treatment of sexual offenders in Herstedvester Denmark: the rapists. *Acta Psychiatrica Scandinavia* **44**: 5–63. (**261**)

Sturup GK (1968b) *Treating the 'Untreatable'*. Baltimore, MD: The Johns Hopkins. (**261**)

Sturup J, Kristiansson M, and Lindqvist P (2011) Violent behaviour by general psychiatric patients in Sweden – validation of Classification of Risk (COVR) software. *Psychiatry Research* **188**: 161–5. (**542**)

Subhan Z (1984) Benzodiazepines and memory. *Psychiatry in Practice* **3**: 15–20. (**33**)

Sukhodolsky DG and Ruchkin V (2006) Evidence based psychosocial treatments in the juvenile justice system. *Child and Adolescent Clinics of North America* **15**: 501–16. (**486**)

Sullivan G, Bienroth M, Jones M, et al. (2007) Practical prescribing with aripiprazole in schizophrenia: consensus recommendations of a UK multidisciplinary panel. *Current Medical Research and Opinion* **23**: 1733–44. (**565**)

Sullivan HS (1953) *The Interpersonal Theory of Psychiatry*. New York: Norton. (**389**)

Sullivan J and Beech AR (2004) Assessing internet sex offenders. In MC Calder (ed) *Child Sexual Abuse and the Internet: Tackling the New Frontier*. Trowbridge, UK: Cromwell. (**251**)

Sullivan MA, Birkmayer F, Boyarsky BK, et al. (2008) Uses of coercion in addiction treatment: clinical aspects. *American Journal on Addictions* **17**: 36–47. (**445, 467**)

Sullivan PF, Kendler KS, and Neale MC (2003) Schizophrenia as a complex trait: evidence from a meta-analysis of twin studies. *Archives of General Psychiatry* **60**: 1187–92. (**208**)

Sullivan PF, Lin D, Tzeng JY, et al. (2008) Genomewide association for schizophrenia in the CATIE study: results of stage 1. *Molecular Psychiatry* **13**: 570–84. (**208**)

Summerfield D (2001) The invention of post-traumatic stress disorder and the social usefulness of a psychiatric category. *British Medical Journal* **322**: 95–8. (**717**)

Sung H, Belenko S, and Feng L (2001) Treatment compliance in the trajectory of treatment progress among offenders. *Journal of Substance Abuse Treatment* **20**: 153–62. (**401**)

Sutherland I, Sivarajasingam V, and Shepherd JP (2002) Recording of community violence by medical and police services. *Injury Prevention* **8**: 246–7. (**700, 701**)

Suyemoto K (1998) The functions of self mutilation. *Clinical Psychology Review* **18**: 531–54. (**723**)

Svartberg M, Stiles TC, and Seltzer MH (2004) Randomized, controlled trial of the effectiveness of short term dynamic psychotherapy and cognitive therapy for cluster C personality disorders. *American Journal of Psychiatry* **161**: 810–7. (**411**)

Swaffer T, Haggett M, and Oxley T (2001) Mentally disordered firesetters: a structured intervention programme. *Clinical Psychology and Psychotherapy* **8**: 468–75. (**577**)

Swainston Harrison T, and Perry CM (2004) Aripiprazole: a review of its use in schizophrenia and schizoaffective disorder. *Drugs* **64**: 1715–36. (**565**)

Swales M, Heard HL, and Williams JGM (2000) Linehan's dialectical behaviour therapy (DBT) for borderline personality disorder: overview and adaptation. *Journal of Mental Health* **9**: 7–23. (**574**)

Swanson JW, Borum R, Swartz M, and Monahan J (1996) Psychotic symptoms and disorders and the risk of violent behaviour in the community. *Criminal Behaviour and Mental Health* **6**: 309–29. (**340, 349, 350**)

Swanson JW, Estroff SE, Swartz M, et al. (1997) Violence and severe mental disorder in clinical and community populations: the effects of psychotic symptoms, comorbidity, and lack of treatment. *Psychiatry* **60**: 1–22. (**355**)

Swanson JW, Holzer CE III, Ganju VK, and Jono RT (1990) Violence and psychiatric disorder in the community: evidence from the epidemiologic catchment area surveys. *Hospital and Community Psychiatry* **41**: 761–70. (**228, 336, 338, 339, 347, 454, 560**)

Swanson JW, Swartz MS, Borum R, et al. (2000) Involuntary out-patient commitment and reduction of violent behaviour in persons with severe mental illness. *The British Journal of Psychiatry* **176**: 324–31. (**520, 567**)

Swanson JW, Swartz MS, Essock SM, et al. (2002) The social-environmental context of violent behavior in persons treated for severe mental illness. *American Journal of Public Health* **92**: 1523–31. (**345, 357, 515**)

Swanson JW, Swartz MS, Van Dorn RA, et al. (2006a) A national study of violent behavior in persons with schizophrenia. *Archives of General Psychiatry* **63**: 490–9. (**281, 350**)

Swanson JW, Swartz MS, Van Dorn RA, et al. on behalf of the CATIE investigators (2008) Comparison of antipsychotic medication effects on reducing violence in people with schizophrenia. *British Journal of Psychiatry* **193**: 37–43. (**563**)

Swanson JW, van Dorn RA, Monahan J, and Swartz MS (2006b) Violence and leveraged community treatments for persons with mental disorders. *American Journal of Psychiatry* **163**: 1404–11. (**365, 567**)

Swartz MS, Swanson JW, and Hanson MJ (2003) Does fear of coercion keep people away from mental health treatment? Evidence from a survey of persons with schizophrenia and mental health professionals. *Behavioral Sciences and the Law* **21**: 459–72. (**365**)

Swartz MS, Swanson JW, Hiday VA, et al. (1998) Violence and severe mental illness: the effects of substance abuse and nonadherence to medication. *The American Journal of Psychiatry* **155**: 226–31. (**454, 560**)

Swartz MS, Swanson JW, Steadman HJ, Robbins PC, and Monahan J (2009) *New York State Assisted Outpatient Treatment Program Evaluation.* Durham, NC: Duke University School of Medicine. http://www.omh.ny.gov/omhweb/resources/publications/aot_program_evaluation/report.pdf (**336, 364, 567**)

Swartz MS, Wilder CM, Swanson JW, et al. (2010) Assessing outcomes for consumers in New York's assisted outpatient treatment program. *Psychiatric Services* **61**: 976–81. (**336**)

Sweeney DF (1990) Alcoholic blackouts: legal implications. *Journal of Substance Misuse* **7**: 155–9. (**138**)

Swinton M and Haddock A (2000) Clozapine in special hospital: a retrospective case-control study. *Journal of Forensic Psychiatry and Psychology* **11**: 587–96. (**564**)

Sylvain C, Ladouceur R, and Boisvert JM (1997) Cognitive and behavioural treatment of pathological gambling: a controlled study. *Journal of Clinical and Consulting Psychology* **65**: 727–32. (**471**)

Szasz T (1962) *The Myth of Mental Illness.* New York: Harper and Row. (**9, 11**)

Szmukler G (2000) Homicide inquiries. What sense do they make? *Psychiatric Bulletin* **24**: 6–10. (**75, 75, 695**)

Szmukler G (2001) Violence risk prediction in practice. *British Journal of Psychiatry* **178**: 84–5. (**531**)

Szmukler G (2003) Risk assessment: 'numbers' and 'values'. *Psychiatric Bulletin* **27**: 205–7. (**531**)

Szmukler G and Holloway F (1998) Mental health legislation is now a harmful anachronism. *Psychiatric Bulletin* **22**: 662–5. (**60**)

Szmukler G, Bird AS, and Button EJ (1981) Compulsory admissions in a London Borough: 1. Social and clinical features and a follow-up. *Psychological Medicine* **11**: 617–36. (**621**)

Tabachnick N, Litman RE, and Osman M (1966) Comparative psychiatric study of accidental and suicidal death. *Archives of General Psychiatry* **14**: 60–8. (**278**)

Taber JI, McCormick RA, and Ramirez LF (1987a) The prevalence and impact of major life stressors among pathological gamblers. *International Journal of Addictions* **22**: 71–9. (**470**)

Taber JI, McCormick RA, Russo AM, Adkins BJ, and Ramirez LF (1987b) Follow-up of pathological gamblers after treatment. *American Journal of Psychiatry* **144**: 757–61. (**470**)

Taber KH and Hurley RA (2009) PTSD and combat-related injuries: functional neuroanatomy. *Journal of Neuropsychiatry and Clinical Neurosciences* **21**: iv–4. (**713**)

Taggart L, McLaughlin D, Quinn B, and Milligan V (2006) An exploration of substance misuse in people with intellectual disabilities. *Journal of Intellectual Disability Research* **50**: 588–97. (**324**)

Takahashi R, Sakuma A, Itoh K, and Kurihara (1975) Comparison of efficacy of lithium carbonate and chlorpromazine in mania: a report of collaborative study group on treatment of mania in Japan. *Archives of General Psychiatry* **32**: 1310–18. (**560**)

Taleb NN (2007) *The Black Swan.* London: Penguin Books. (**530**)

Talerico KA, Evans LK, and Strumpf NE (2002) Mental health correlates of aggression in nursing home residents with dementia. *Gerontologist* **42**: 169–77. (**525**)

Tammimaki AE and Mannisto PT (2010) Are genetic variants of COMT associated with addiction? *Pharmacogenetics and Genomics* **20**: 717–41. (**206**)

Tanay E (1969) Psychiatric study of homicide. *American Journal of Psychiatry* **125**: 1252–8. (**292**)

Tancredi LR and Brodie JD (2007) The brain and behaviour: limitations in the use of functional magnetic resonance imaging. *American Journal of Law and Medicine* **33**: 271–94. (**284**)

Tantam D, Monaghan L, Nicholson H, and Stirling J (1989) Autistic children's ability to interpret faces: a research note. *Journal of Child Psychology and Psychiatry* **30**: 623–30. (**395**)

Tapp J, Fellowes E, Wallis N, Blud L, and Moore E (2009) An evaluation of the enhanced thinking skills (ETS) programme with mentally disordered offenders in high security hospital. *Legal and Criminological Psychology* **14**: 201–12. (**576**)

Tapper C (2007) *Cross and Tapper on Evidence,* 11th edn. Oxford, UK: OUP. (**149, 157**)

Tardiff K (1983) A survey of assault by chronic patients in a state hospital system. In JR Lyon, WH Reid (eds) *Assaults within psychiatric facilities*. New York: Grune and Stratton, pp. 3–19. (**515**)

Tardiff K and Sweillam A (1980) Assault, suicide and mental illness. *Archives of General Psychiatry* **37**: 164–9. (**347, 443**)

Tardiff K, Marzuk PM, Leon AC, and Portera L (1997) A prospective study of violence by psychiatric patients after hospital discharge. *Psychiatric Services* **48**: 678–81. (**355, 561, 644**)

Tariot PN, Schneider L, Katz IR, et al. (2006) Quetiapine treatment of psychosis associated with dementia: a double-blind, randomized, placebo-controlled clinical trial. *American Journal of Geriatric Psychiatry* **14**: 767–76. (**565**)

Tarsh MJ (1986) On serious violence during sleepwalking (letter). *British Journal of Psychiatry* **148**: 476. (**291**)

Tarsh MJ and Royston C (1985) A follow-up study of accident neurosis. *British Journal of Psychiatry* **146**: 178–25. (**430**)

Task Force OPD (eds) (English translation ed. M von der Tann) *Operationalised Psychodynamic Diagnosis OPD-2. The Manual for Diagnosis and Treatment Planning*. Bern, Switzerland: Huber. (**597**)

Tavares C and Thomas G (2009) *Crime and Criminal Justice, Statistics in focus*. Eurostat 36/2009, Luxembourg: Office for Official Publications of the European Communities. (**230**)

Taylor CA, Guterman NB, Lee SJ, and Rathouz PJ (2009) Intimate partner violence, maternal stress, nativity, and risk for maternal maltreatment of young children. *American Journal of Public Health* **99**: 175–83. (**505, 506**)

Taylor DC (1969) Differential rates of cerebral maturation between sexes and between hemispheres. *Lancet* **2**: 140–2. (**501**)

Taylor DC (1969a) Some psychiatric aspects of epilepsy. In RN Herrington (ed) *Current Problems in Neuropsychiatry*. British Journal of Psychiatry Special Publication No. 4, London: Royal Medico-Psychological Association. (**285**)

Taylor DC (1969b) Sexual behavior and temporal lobe epilepsy. *Archives of Neurology* **27**: 510–6. (**285**)

Taylor JL (2002) A review of the assessment and treatment of anger and aggression in offenders with intellectual disability. *Journal of Intellectual Disability Research* **46** (Suppl. 1): 57–73. (**326, 327**)

Taylor JL and Lindsay WR (2007) Developments in the treatment and management of offenders with intellectual disabilities. *Issues in Forensic Psychology* **6**: 23–31. (**333**)

Taylor JL and Novaco RW (2005) *Anger Treatment for People with Developmental Disabilities: A Theory, Evidence and Manual Based Approach*. Chichester, UK: Wiley. (**327**)

Taylor JL, Hatton C, Dixon L, and Douglas C (2004a) Screening for psychiatric symptoms: PAS-ADD Checklist norms for adults with intellectual disabilities. *Journal of Intellectual Disability Research* **48**: 37–41. (**317**)

Taylor JL, Lindsay WR, Hogue TE, et al. (2010) Use of the HCR-20 in offenders with intellectual disability. *Submitted for publication*. (**331**)

Taylor JL, Novaco RW, Gillmer BT, and Robertson A (2004c) Treatment of anger and aggression. In WR Lindsay, JL Taylor, P Sturmey (eds) *Offenders with Developmental Disability*. Chichester, UK: John Wiley, pp. 201–20. (**327**)

Taylor JL, Novaco RW, Gillmer BT, and Thorne I (2002) Cognitive-behavioural treatment of anger intensity among offenders with intellectual disabilities. *Journal of Applied Research in Intellectual Disabilities* **15**: 151–65. (**328**)

Taylor JL, Novaco RW, Gillmer BT, Robertson A, and Thorne I (2005) Individual cognitive-behavioural anger treatment for people with mild-borderline intellectual disabilities and histories of aggression: a controlled trial. *British Journal of Clinical Psychology* **44**: 367–82. (**328**)

Taylor JL, Novaco RW, Guinan C, and Street N (2004c) Development of an imaginal provocation test to evaluate treatment for anger problems in people with intellectual disabilities. *Clinical Psychology and Psychotherapy* **11**: 233–46. (**328**)

Taylor JL, Robertson A, Thorne I, Belshaw T, and Watson A (2006) Responses of female fire-setters with mild and borderline intellectual disabilities to a group-based intervention. *Journal of Applied Research in Intellectual Disabilities* **19**: 179–90. (**330**)

Taylor JL, Thorne I, and Slavkin ML (2004d) Treatment of fire setting behaviour. In WR Lindsay, JL Taylor, P Sturmey (eds) *Offenders with Developmental Disabilities*. Chichester, UK: John Wiley, pp. 221–40. (**330**)

Taylor JL, Thorne I, Robertson A, and Avery G (2002b) Evaluation of a group intervention for convicted arsonists with mild and borderline intellectual disabilities. *Criminal Behaviour and Mental Health* **12**: 282–93. (**329, 330, 576**)

Taylor LJ (1989) *The Hillsborough Stadium Disaster*. Interim Report. London: Home Office. Cm 765. (**52**)

Taylor LJ (1990) *The Hillsborough Stadium Disaster*. Final Report. London: Home Office. Cm 962. (**52**)

Taylor M and Quayle E (2006) The Internet and abuse images of children: search, precriminal situations and opportunity. In R Wortley, S Smallbone (eds) *Situational Prevention of Child Sexual Abuse*. New York: Criminal Justice / Willan Publishing. (**251**)

Taylor PJ (1982) Schizophrenia and violence. In J Gunn and DP Farrington (eds) *Abnormal Offenders, Delinquency and the Criminal Justice System*. Chichester, UK: Wiley, pp. 269–84. (**335**)

Taylor PJ (1985a) Epilepsy and insanity. In P Fenwick, E Fenwick (eds) *Epilepsy and the Law*. London: Royal Society of Medicine. (**27**)

Taylor PJ (1985b) Motives for offending among violent and psychotic men. *British Journal of Psychiatry* **147**: 491–8. (**297, 341, 349, 353, 354**)

Taylor PJ (1986) Psychiatric disorder in London's life-sentenced prisoners. *British Journal of Criminology* **26**: 63–78. (**251, 637**)

Taylor PJ (1987) Social implications of psychosis. *British Medical Bulletin* **43**: 718–40. (**342**)

Taylor PJ (1993a) Schizophrenia and crime: distinctive patterns in association. In S Hodgins (ed) *Crime and Mental Disorder*. Newbury Park, CA: Sage Publications. (**347**)

Taylor PJ (1993b) *Violence in Society*. London: Royal College of Physicians. (**347**)

Taylor PJ (1997) Damage, disease and danger. *Criminal Behaviour and Mental Health* **7**: 19–48. (**504, 569**)

Taylor PJ (1999) Disorders of volition: forensic aspects. In C Williams, A Sims (eds) *Disorders of Volition and Action in Psychiatry*. Leeds, UK: Leeds University. pp. 66–84. (**350**)

Taylor PJ (2006a) Delusional disorder and delusions: is there a risk of violence in social interactions about the core symptom? *Behavioral Sciences and the Law* **24**: 313–32. (**353**)

Taylor PJ (2006b) Treatment of serious offenders with personality disorder: effect, effectiveness and individuality (Ch. 30). In C Newrith, C Meux, PJ Taylor (eds) *Personality Disorder and Serious Offending. Hospital Treatment Models*. London: Hodder Arnold, pp. 314–36. (**390, 605**)

Taylor PJ and Bragado Jimenez MD (2009) Women, psychosis and violence. *International Journal of Law and Psychiatry* **32**: 56–64. (**498, 505, 520, 599**)

Taylor PJ and Gunn J (1984) Violence and psychosis. I. risk of violence among psychotic men. *British Medical Journal* **288**: 1945–9. (**230, 342, 438**)

Taylor PJ and Gunn J (1999) Homicides by people with mental illness myth and reality. *British Journal of Psychiatry* **174**: 9–14. (**59, 230, 338**)

Taylor PJ and Gunn J. (2008) Diagnosis, medical models and formulations. In K. Soothill, M. P Rogers and M Dolan. (Eds) Handbook on Forensic Mental Health. Willan: Cullompton. (**7, 283, 339, 532**)

Taylor PJ and Gunn JC (1984) Violence and psychosis. *British Medical Journal* **288**: 1945–9; **289**: 9–12. (**232**)

Taylor PJ and Hodgins S (1994) Violence and psychosis: critical timings. *Criminal Behaviour and Mental Health*, **4**: 266–289. (**208, 344**)

Taylor PJ and Kopelman MD (1984) Amnesia for criminal offences. *Psychological Medicine* **14**: 581–8. (**25, 293, 294, 295, 296, 425**)

Taylor PJ and Parrott J (1988) Elderly offenders: a study of age-related factors among custodially remanded prisoners. *British Journal of Psychiatry* **152**: 340–6. (**524, 526**)

Taylor PJ and Schanda H (1999) Violence against others by psychiatric hospital inpatients with psychosis. In S Hodgins (ed) *Violence Among the Mentally Ill*. Dordrecht, the Netherlands: Kluwer Academic Publications. pp. 251–75. (**556**)

Taylor PJ and Swan T (1999) *Couples in Care and Custody*. Oxford, UK: Butterworth Heinemann. (**596, 598**)

Taylor PJ, Amos T, Dunn E, et al. (2009) *Factors mediating the effect of prison environment on the mental health of male pre-trial prisoners*. Report to the National Rand Programme on Forensic Mental Health. (*See also* Taylor et al. 2010) (**438**)

Taylor PJ, Chilvers C, Doyle M, et al. (2009) Meeting the challenge of research while treating mentally disordered offenders: the future of the clinical researcher. *International Journal of Forensic Mental Health* **8**: 2–8. (**143**)

Taylor PJ, Garety P, Buchanan A, et al. (1994) Delusions and violence. In J Monahan, Steadman HJ (eds) *Violence and Mental Disorder: Developments in Risk Assessment*. Chicago, IL: University of Chicago Press, pp. 161–82. (**12, 349, 350, 352**)

Taylor PJ, Goldberg E, Leese M, Butwell M, and Reed A (1999) Limits to the value of mental health review tribunals for offender patients. *British Journal of Psychiatry* **174**: 164–9. (**71. 165**)

Taylor PJ, Graf M, Schanda H et al. (2012) The treating psychiatrist as expert in the courts: is it necessary or possible to separate the roles of physician and expert. *Criminal Behaviour and Mental Health* **22**(4): 271–92. (**152, 671**)

Taylor PJ, Gunn J, and Mezey G (1993) Victims and survivors. In J Gunn, PJ Taylor (eds) *Forensic Psychiatry. Clinical, Legal and Ethical Issues*, 1st edn. Oxford, UK: Butterworth Heinemann. (**716**)

Taylor PJ, Hill J, Bhagwagar Z, Darjee R, and Thomson LDG (2008) Presentations of psychosis with violence: variations in different jurisdictions. *Behavioral Sciences and the Law* **26**: 585–602. (**350, 613**)

Taylor PJ, Jones R, Lougher M, et al. (submitted) Mental disorder, offending and motherhood. (**596**)

Taylor PJ, Leese M, Williams D, Butwell M, Daly R, Larkin E. (1998) Mental disorder and violence – a special (high security) hospital study. *British Journal of Psychiatry* **172**: 218–226. (**297, 343, 346, 350, 397, 444, 600**)

Taylor PJ, Mahendra B, and Gunn J (1983) Erotomania in males. *Psychological Medicine* **13**: 645–50. (**368**)

Taylor PJ, Walker J, Dunn E, et al. (2010) Improving mental state in early imprisonment. *Criminal Behaviour and Mental Health* **20**: 215–31. (**630, 631**)

Taylor R (2000) *A Seven Year Reconviction Study of HMP Grendon Therapeutic Community*. London: Home Office Research, Development and Statistics Directorate. (**583**)

Taylor RL and Weisz AE (1970) American presidential assassination. In DN Daniels, MF Gilula, FM Ochberg (eds) *Violence and the Struggle for Existence*. Boston, MA: Little, Brown. (**234**)

Taylor W and Martin M (1944) Multiple personality. *Journal of Abnormal Social Psychology* **39**: 281–300. (**426. 427**)

Teasdale B, Silver E, and Monahan J (2006) Gender, threat/control-override delusions and violence. *Law and Human Behavior* **30**: 649–58. (**350, 515**)

Temkin J (1999) Reporting rape in London: a qualitative study. *Journal of Criminal Justice* **38**(1): 17–41. (**714**)

Temkin O (1945) *The Falling Sickness*. Baltimore, MD: Johns Hopkins. (**284**)

Temple J (2010) *Time for Training*. http://www.mee.nhs.uk/PDF/14274%20Bookmark%20Web%20Version.pdf (**16**)

Tengström A (2001) Long-term predictive validity of historical factors in two risk assessment instruments in a group of violent offenders with schizophrenia. *Nordic Journal of Psychiatry* **55**(4): 243–9. (**536**)

Tengström A, Hodgins S, Grann M, Långström N, and Kullgren, G (2004) Schizophrenia and criminal offending. *Criminal Justice and Behavior* **31**: 367–91. (**346**)

Tennant A and Howells K (eds) (2010) *Using Time Not Doing Time: Practitioner Perspectives on Personality Disorder and Risk*. Chichester, UK: Wiley Blackwell. (**401**)

Tennent G and Way C (1984) The English special hospital – a 12–17 year follow-up study. A comparison of violent and non-violent offenders. *Medicine, Science and the law* **24**: 81–91. (**605**)

Tennent TG, McQuaid A, Loughnane T, and Hands AJ (1971) Female arsonists. *British Journal of Psychiatry* **119**: 497–502. (**504**)

Tennes K, Downy K, and Vernadakis A (1977) Urinary cortisol excretion rates and anxiety in normal one year old infants. *Psychosomatic Medicine* **39**: 178–87. (**720**)

Teoh JI (1972) The changing psychopathology of amok. *Psychiatry* **35**: 345–50. (**428**)

Teplin LA and Pruett NS (1992) Police as streetcorner psychiatrist – managing the mentally-ill. *International Journal of Law and Psychiatry* **15**: 139–56. (**279**)

Teplin LA, Abram KM, and McClelland GM (1996) Prevalence of psychiatric disorders among incarcerated women, I: Pretrial jail detainees. *Archives of General Psychiatry* **53**: 505–12. (**516**)

Teplin LA, Abram KM, McClelland GM, Dulcan MK, and Mericle AA (2002) Psychiatric disorders in youth in juvenile detention. *Archives of General Psychiatry* **59**: 1133–43. (**482. 483, 484, 485**)

Teplin LA, McClelland GM, Abram KM, and Weiner DA (2005) Crime victimization in adults with severe mental illness: comparison with the National Crime Victimization Survey. *Archives of General Psychiatry* **62**: 911–21. (**3, 334**)

Terman L (1911) *The Measurement of Intelligence*. Boston, MA: Houghton Mifflin. (**315**)

Tether P and Harrison L (1986) Data note 3, alcohol related fires and drownings. *British Journal of Addiction* **81**: 425–31. (**273**)

Thapar A, Langley K, Fowler T, et al. (2005) Catechol o-methyltransferase gene variant and birth weight predict early-onset antisocial behavior in children with attention-deficit/hyperactivity disorder. *Archives of General Psychiatry* **62**: 1275–8. (**199, 200**)

The Information Centre for Health and Social Care (2009) Adult psychiatric morbidity in England. http://www.ic.nhs.uk/pubs/psychiatricmorbidity07 (**315**)

The Times (1968) Compulsive Gambler to Have Brain Operation. *The Times*, 2 April. (**468**)

Theriot MT and Segal SP (2005) Involvement with the criminal justice system among new clients at outpatient mental health agencies. *Psychiatric Services* **56**: 179–85. (**279**)

Thewisson V, Myin-Germys I, Bentall RP, et al. (2005) Hearing impairment and psychosis revisited. *Schizophrenia Research* **76**: 99–103. (**351**)

Thibaut F and Colonna L (1992) Lithium and aggression in adults. *L'Encéphale* **18**: 193–8. (**566**)

Thibaut F, de la Barra F, Gorden H et al. (2010) The World Federation of Biological Psychiatry guidelines for the biological treatment of the paraphilias. *The World Journal of Biological Psychiatry* **11**: 604–55. (**259, 261**)

Thielgaard A (1984) A psychological study of the personalities of Xyy and XXY men. *Acta Psychiatrica Scandinavica Supplementum* 315 **69**. (**323**)

Thigpen C and Cleckley HA (1957) *The Three Faces of Eve*. New York: McGraw Hill. (**426**)

Thomas A and Chess S (1984) Genesis and evolution of behavioral disorders: from infancy to early adult life. *American Journal of Psychiatry* **141**: 1–9. (**393**)

Thomas A, Chess S, and Birch HG (1968) *Temperament and Behavior Disorders in Children.* New York: New York University Press. (**486**)

Thomas A, Chess S, and Birch HG (1970) The origin of personality. *Scientific American*: 102–9. (**393**)

Thomas A, Chess S, Birch HG, Herzig ME, and Korn S (1963) *Behavioural Individuality in Early Childhood*. New York: New York University Press. (**393**)

Thomas D (1979) *Principles of Sentencing*, 2nd edn. London: Heinemann. (**35**)

Thomas D (2008) *Sentencing Referencer,* rev edn. Andover, Hampshire: Sweet and Maxwell:. (**35**)

Thomas JB (1985) Psychologists, psychiatrists and special educational needs in Britain since 1944. *The Exceptional Child* **32**: 69–80. (**482**)

Thompson C, Kimmoth A, Stevens L, et al. (2000) Effect of a clinical practice guideline and practice based education on detection and outcome on depression in primary care: Hampshire depression project randomised controlled trial. *Lancet* **355**: 185–91. (**527**)

Thompson M (2007) ACT: a new acronym you need to know about. *Clinical Psychology Forum* **172**: 19–22. (**569**)

Thompson P (1986) The use of seclusion in hospitals in the Newcastle area. *British Journal of Psychiatry* **149**: 471–4. (**595**)

Thompson RS, Rivara FP, Thompson DC, et al. (2000) Identification and management of domestic violence: a randomized trial. *American Journal of Preventive Medicine* **19**: 253–63. (**220**)

Thomson AD and Pratt OE (1992) Interaction of nutrients and alcohol: Absorption, transport, utilization and metabolism. In *Nutrition and Alcohol*, RR Watson and B Watzl (eds) pp. 75–99. Boca Raton, FL: CRC Press. (**439**)

Thomson LD, Bogue JP, Humphreys MS, and Johnstone EC (2001) A survey of female patients in high security psychiatric care in Scotland. *Criminal Behavior and Mental Health* **11**(2): 86–93. (**520, 612**)

Thomson LDG (2000) Management of schizophrenia in conditions of high security. *Advances in Psychiatric Treatment* **6**: 252–60. (**612**)

Thomson LDG (2005a) Civil Mental Health Legislation. In L Thomson, J McManus (eds) *Mental Health and Scots Law in Practice*. Edinburgh, Scotland: Greens. (**90**)

Thomson LDG (2005b) The Mental Health (Care and Treatment) (Scotland) Act 2003: Civil Legislation. *Psychiatric Bulletin* **29**: 381–4. (**101**)

Thomson LDG (2005c) The mental health (care and treatment) (Scotland) act 2003: a step forward or a step into the dark? *Scottish Legal Action Group Journal* **336**: 212–6. (**101**)

Thomson LDG, Bogue JP, Humphries MS, and Johnstone EC (2001) A survey of female patients in high security psychiatric care in Scotland, *Criminal Behaviour and Mental Health* **11**: 86–93. (**520, 612**)

Thomson LDG, Bogue JP, Humphries MS, et al. (1997) The state hospital survey: a description of psychiatric patients in conditions of special security in Scotland. *Journal of Forensic Psychiatry* **8**: 263–84. (**612**)

Thomson LDG, Galt V, and Darjee R (2004) *An Evaluation of Appropriate Adult Schemes in Scotland*. Scotland: Scottish Executive Research Findings No. 78. http://www.scotland.gov.uk/Resource/Doc/26800/0029546.pdf (**651**)

Thornberry TP and Farnworth M (1982) Social correlates of criminal involvement: further evidence on the relationship between social status and criminal behaviour. *American Sociological Review* **47**: 505–18. (**177**)

Thornberry TP, Lizotte AJ, Krohn MD, Farnworth M, and Jang SJ (1994) Delinquent peers, beliefs and delinquent behaviour: a longitudinal test of interactional theory. *Criminology* **32**: 47–83. (**177**)

Thornberry TP, Lizotte AJ, Krohn MD, Smith CA, and Porter PK (2003) Causes and consequences of delinquency: findings from the Rochester youth development study. In TP Thornberry, MD Krohn (eds) *Taking Stock of Delinquency: An Overview of Findings from Contemporary Longitudinal Studies.* New York: Kluwer/Plenum, pp. 11–46. (**171**)

Thornburgh D and Lin HS (2002) *Youth, Pornography, and the Internet.* Washington DC: National Academies Press. (**245**)

Thorndike EL (1931) *Human Learning.* New York: Appleton-Century-Crofts. (**395**)

Thornhill R and Palmer CT (2000) *A Natural History of Rape: Biological Bases of Sexual Coercion.* Cambridge, MA: MIT Press. (**245**)

Thornton D (2002) Constructing and testing a framework for dynamic risk assessment. *Sexual Abuse: A Journal of Research and Treatment* **14**: 139–54. (**245, 255**)

Thornton D, Mann R, Webster S, et al. (2003) Distinguishing and combining risks for sexual and violent recidivism. *Annals of the New York Academy of Sciences* **989**: 225–35. (**254**)

Thorold O and Trotter J (1996) Inquiries into homicide: a legal perspective. In J Peay (ed) *Inquiries after Homicide.* London: Duckworth. pp. 39–49. (**604, 695**)

Tienari P, Wynne LC, Moring J, et al. (2000) Finnish adoptive family study: sample selection and adoptee DSM-III-R diagnoses. *Acta Psychiatrica Scandinavica* **101**: 433–43. (**208**)

Tienari P, Wynne LC, Sorri A, et al. (2004) Genotype–environment interaction in schizophrenia-spectrum disorder. Long-term follow-up study of Finnish adoptees. *British Journal of Psychiatry* **184**: 216–22. (**210**)

Tierney DW and McCabe MP (2002) Motivation for behavior change among sex offenders: a review of the literature. *Clinical Psychology Review* **22**: 113–29. (**262**)

Tiet QQ and Mausbach B (2007) Treatments for patients with dual diagnosis: a review. *Alcoholism: Clinical and Experimental Research* **31**: 513–36. (**460**)

Tiihonen J and Swartz MS (2000) Pharmacological intervention for preventing violence among the mentally ill with secondary alcohol- and drug-use disorders. In S Hodgins (ed) *Violence among the Mentally Ill.* The Netherlands: Kluwer Academic Publishers. (**347**)

Tiihonen J, Hallikainen T, Lachman H, et al. (1999) Association between the functional variant of the catechol-O-methyltransferase (COMT) gene and type 1 alcoholism. *Molecular Psychiatry* **4**: 286–9. (**206**)

Tiihonen J, Isohanni M, Rasanen P, Koiranen M, and Moring J (1997) Specific major mental disorders and criminality: a 26-year prospective study of the 1966 Northern Finland birth cohort. *American Journal of Psychiatry* **154**: 840–5. (**280, 337**)

Tiihonen J, Wahlbeck K, Lönnqvist J, et al. (2006) Effectiveness of antipsychotic treatments in a nationwide cohort of patients in community care after first hospitalization due to schizophrenia and schizoaffective disorder: observation follow-up study. *British Medical Journal* **333**: 224–30. (**359, 520**)

Tikkanen R, Holi M, Lindberg N, and Virkkunen M (2007) Tri dimensional personality questionnaire data on alcoholic violent offenders: specific connections to severe impulsive cluster B personality disorders and violent criminality. *BMC Psychiatry* **7**: 36. (**444**)

Tillmann WA and Hobbs GE (1949) The accident-prone automobile driver. *American Journal of Psychiatry* **106**: 321–31. (**278**)

Tilt R, Perry B, Martin C, Maguire N, and Preston M (2000) *Report of the Review of Security at the High Security Hospitals.* London: Department of Health. (**587**)

Timmerman IGH and Emmelkamp PMG (2005a) The effects of cognitive-behavioural treatment for forensic in-patients. *International Journal of Offender Therapy and Comparative Criminology* **49**: 590–606. (**577**)

Timmerman IGH and Emmelkamp PMG (2005b) An integrated cognitive behavioural approach to the aetiology and treatment of violence. *Clinical Psychology and Psychotherapy* **12**: 167–76. (**577**)

Tjaden P and Thoennes N (1998) *Stalking in America: Findings from the National Violence against Women Survey.* Washington, DC: National Institute of Justice and Centers for Disease Control and Prevention. https://www.ncjrs.gov/pdffiles/169592.pdf (**374**)

Tobias G, Haslam-Hopwood G, Allen JG, Stein A, and Bleiberg E (2006) Enhancing mentalizing through psycho-education (Ch. 13). In JG Allen, P Fonagy (eds) *Handbook of Mentalization-Based Treatment.* London: John Wiley and Sons, pp. 249–67. (**572**)

Tobin L and Taylor PJ (1999) Pregnancy and early parenting from care or custody. In PJ Taylor, T Swan (eds) *Couples in Care and Custody.* Oxford, UK: Butterworth Heinemann, pp.102– 19. (**596**)

Todd AJ, Monahan J, and Taylor PJ. (2011) Risk assessment and reducing future violence: a systematic review (in preparation). (**549**)

Toft B and Reynolds S (2005) Learning from Disasters 3rd ed. Basingstoke, UK: Palgrave Macmillan. (**76**)

Tolstoy, L (1873–1877) *Anna Karenina.* (**1**)

Tomar R, Treasaden I, and Shah A (2005) Is there a case for a specialist forensic psychiatry service for the elderly? *International Journal of Geriatric Psychiatry* **20**: 51–6. (**525**)

Toneatto T and Ladouceur R (2003) Treatment of pathological gambling: a critical review of the literature. *Psychology of Addictive Behaviors* **17**: 284–92. (**471**)

Tong LSJ and Farrington DP (2006) How effective is the RnR programme in reducing re-offending? A meta-analysis of evaluations in four countries. *Psychology, Crime and Law* **12**: 3–24. (**576**)

Tonkonogy JM (1991) Violence and temporal lobe lesion: head CT and MRI data. *Journal of Neuropsychiatry and Clinical Neuroscience* **3**: 189–96. (**298**)

Toone B (2000) The psychoses of epilepsy. *Journal of Neurology Neurosurgery and Psychiatry* **69**: 1–3. (**285**)

Topp D (1973) Fire as a symbol and as a weapon of death. *Medicine, Science and the Law* **13**: 79–86. (**276**)

Torgersten S, Kringlen E, and Cramer V (2001) The prevalence of personality disorders in a community sample. *Archives of General Psychiatry* **58**: 590–6. (**389**)

Torrey EF (1994) Violent behavior by individuals with serious mental illness. *Hospital and Community Psychiatry* **45**: 653–62. (**559**)

Torrey EF (1995) Jails and prisons – America's new mental hospitals. *American Journal of Public Health* **85**: 1611–3. (**279, 281**)

Torrey EF and Yolken RH (2010) Psychiatric genocide: nazi attempts to eradicate schizophrenia. *Schizophrenia Bulletin* **36**: 26–32. (**658, 685**)

Torvik A, Lindboe CF, and Rogde S (1982) Brain lesions in alcoholics. *Journal of the Neurological Sciences* **56**:233–48. (**439**)

Towl G (2003) *Psychology in Prisons*. Oxford, UK: BPS Blackwell. (**242**)

Tracy PE and Kempf-Leonard K (1996) *Continuity and Discontinuity in Criminal Careers*. New York: Plenum. (**172**)

Trafford PA (1990) Ethical problems of prison doctors. *British Medical Journal* **301**: 342. (**677**)

Trajanovic N, Mangan M, and Shapiro CM (2006) Sexual behavior in sleep: an internet survey. *Sleep* **29** (Abstract supplement 0793): A270. (**291**)

Tran-Johnson TK, Sack DA, Marcus RN, et al. (2007) Efficacy and safety of intramuscular aripiprazole in patients with acute agitation: a randomized, double-blind, placebo-controlled trial. *Journal of Clinical Psychiatry* **68**: 111–9. (**565**)

Traskman-Bendz L, Asberg M, and Schalling D (1986) Serotoninergic function and suicidal behaviour in personality disorders. In JJ Mann, M Stanley (ed) *Psychobiology of Suicide*. New York: Annals of the New York Academy of Sciences, pp. 168–73. (**308**)

Treiman DM (1986) Epilepsy and violence: medical and legal issues. *Epilepsia* **27** (Suppl. 2): S77–S103. (**286**)

Treiman DM and Delgado-Escueta AV (1983) Violence and epilepsy: a critical review. In TA Pedley and BS Meldrum (eds) *Recent Advances in Epilepsy*, vol. 1. London: Churchill-Livingstone. (**286**)

Tremblay RE, Nagin DS, SéguinJR, et al. (2004) Physical aggression during early childhood: trajectories and predictors. *Pediatrics* **114**: e43–e50. (**216**)

Tremblay RE, Pagani-Kurtz L, Masse LC, Vitaro F, and Pihl RO (1995) A bimodal preventive intervention for disruptive kindergarten boys: Its impact through mid-adolescence. *Journal of Consulting and Clinical Psychology* **63**: 560–8. (**183**)

Tremblay RE, Vitaro F, Nagin D, Pagani L, and Seguin JR (2003) The montreal longitudinal and experimental study: rediscovering the power of descriptions. In TP Thornberry, MD Krohn (eds) *Taking Stock of Delinquency: An Overview of Findings from Contemporary Longitudinal Studies*. New York: Kluwer/Plenum, pp. 205–54. (**172**)

Trent JW (1994) *Inventing the Feeble Mind: A History of Mental Retardation in the United States*. Berkeley: University of California Press. (**315**)

Trestman RL (2007) Research with prisoners. In OJ Thienhaus, M Piasecki (eds) *Correctional Psychiatry, Practice Guidelines and Strategies*. Kingston, NJ: Civic Research Institute. (**144**)

Treutlein J, Cichon S, Ridinger M, et al. (2009) Genome-wide association study of alcohol dependence. *Archives of General Psychiatry* **66**: 773–84. (**204**)

Tritt K, Nickel C, Lahmann K, et al. (2005) Lamotrigine treatment of aggression in female borderline-patients: a randomized, double-blind, placebo-controlled study. *Journal of Psychopharmacology* **19**(3): 287–91. (**406**)

Trollope A (1869) *Phineas Finn. St Paul's Magazine*. London: Virtue and Co. (**229**)

Trollope A (1869a) *He Knew He Was Right*. London: Smith and French. (**219**)

Troost PW, Lahuis BE, Steenhuis MP, et al. (2005) Long-term effects of risperidone in children with autism spectrum disorders: a placebo discontinuation study. *Journal of the American Academy of Child and Adolescent Psychiatry* **44**: 1137–44. (**564**)

Trotter T (1804, reprinted 1988) *An Essay Medical, Philosophical and Chemical on Drunkenness and Its Effects on the Human Body*. London: Routledge. (**441**)

Troy M and Sroufe LA (1987) Victimization among preschoolers: role of attachment relationship history. *Journal of American Academy of Child and Adolescent Psychiatry* **26**:166–72. (**718**)

Trupin E and Richards H (2003) Seattle's mental health courts: early indicators of effectiveness. *International Journal of law and Psychiatry* **26**: 33–53. (**640**)

Trupin EW, Stewart DG, Beach B, and Boesky L (2002) Effectiveness of dialectical behaviour therapy program for incarcerated female juvenile offenders. *Child and Adolescent Mental Health* **7**: 121–7. (**575**)

Tsuang MT, Boor M, and Fleming JA (1985) Psychiatric aspects of traffic accidents. *American Journal of Psychiatry* **142**(5): 538–46. (**278**)

Tsuang MT, Lyons MJ, Eisen SA, et al. (1996) Genetic influences on DSM-III-R drug abuse and dependence: a study of 3,372 twin pairs. *American Journal of Medical Genetics* **67**: 473–7. (**202**)

Tsuang MT, Lyons MJ, Meyer JM, et al. (1998) Co-occurrence of abuse of different drugs in men: the role of drug- specific and shared vulnerabilities [see comments]. *Archives of General Psychiatry* **55**: 967–72. (**202, 203**)

Ttofi MM and Farrington DP (2009) What works in preventing bullying? Efective elements of anti-bullying programmes. *Journal of Aggression, Conflict and Peace Research* **1**: 13–23. (**184**)

Tucker DE and Brakel SJ (2003) Sexually violent predator laws. In R Rosner (ed) *Principles and Practice of Forensic Psychiatry*, 2nd edn. London: Arnold, pp. 717–23. (**123, 124**)

Tucker P (2009) Substance misuse and early psychosis. *Australas Psychiatry* **17**: 291–4. (**455**)

Tudor Hart J (1971) The inverse care law. *The Lancet* **297**: 405–12. (**647**)

Tuke D Hack (1892) *A Dictionary of Psychological Medicine*. London: Churchill:. (**431**)

Tuke S, (1813) Description of the Retreat, an institution near York, for insane persons of the Society of Friends. Alexander: York. Available as an ebook: http://books.google.co.uk/books?id=SwEIAAAAQAAJ&printsec=frontcover&source=gbs_ge_summary_r&cad=0#v=onepage&q&f=false (**557, 558**)

Tunbridge RJ, Keigan M, and James FJ (2001) *The Incidence of Drugs and Alcohol in Road Accident Fatalities: TRL Report 495.* Crowthorne, Berkshire: TRL. (**278**)

Turiel E (1983) The D*evelopment of Social Knowledge: Morality and Convention.* Cambridge, UK: Cambridge University Press. (**395**)

Turk J (1992) Fragile X syndrome: on the way to a behavioural phenotype. *British Journal of Psychiatry* **160**: 24–35. (**321**)

Turkheimer E, Haley A, Waldron M, D'Onofrio B, and Gottesman II (2003) Socioeconomic status modifies heritability of IQ in young children. *Psychological Science* **14**: 623–8. (**191**)

Turnbull SJ, Campbell EA, and Swann IJ (2001) Post-traumatic stress disorder symptoms following a head injury: does amnesia for the event influence the development of symptoms? *Brain Injury* **15**: 775–85. (**713**)

Turner RM (2000) Naturalistic evaluation of dialectical behavior therapy-oriented treatment for borderline personality disorder. *Cognitive and Behavioral Practice* **7**: 413–9. (**411**)

Turner T and Salter M (2008) Forensic psychiatry: re-examining the relationship. *Psychiatric Bulletin* **32**: 2–6. (**588**)

Turner T, Ness MN, and Imison CT (1992) Mentally disordered persons found in public places. *Psychological Medicine* **22**: 765–74. (**48, 621**)

Turrell SC (2000) A descriptive analysis of same-sex relationship diverse sample. *Journal of Family Violence* **15**: 281–93. (**219**)

Tuten M and Jones HE (2003) A partner's drug-using status impacts women's drug treatment outcome. *Drug and Alcohol Dependence* **70**: 327–30. (**466**)

Tutt N (1981) A decade of policy. *British Journal of Criminology* **21**: 246–56. (**476**)

Twitchell GR, Hanna GL, Cook EH, et al. (1998) Overt behavior problems and serotonergic function in middle childhood among male and female offspring of alcoholic fathers. *Alcoholism: Clinical and Experimental Research* **22**: 1340–8. (**307**)

Tyndale RF, Droll KP, and Sellers EM (1997) Genetically deficient CYP2D6 metabolism provides protection against oral opiate dependence. *Pharmacogenetics* **7**: 375–9. (**205**)

Tyner EA and Fremouw WJ (2008) The relation of methamphetamine use and violence. A critical review. *Aggression and Violent Behavior* **13**: 285–97. (**455**)

Tyrer F, McGrother CW, Thorp CF, et al. (2006) Physical aggression towards others in adults with learning disabilities: prevalence and associated factors. *Journal of Intellectual Disability Research* **50**: 295–304. (**318**)

Tyrer P (1998) Feedback for the personality disordered. *Journal of Forensic Psychiatry* **9**: 1–4. (**401**)

Tyrer P (2000) The personality assessment schedule (PAS). In P Tyrer (ed) *Personality Disorders – Diagnosis, Management and Course.* Oxford, UK: Butterworth Heinemann. (**387**)

Tyrer P (2000a) Improving the assessment of personality disorders. *Criminal Behaviour and Mental Health,* **10** (suppl.): 51–56. (**390**)

Tyrer P (2000b) *Personality Disorders: Diagnosis, Management and Course,* 2nd edn. Oxford, UK: Butterworth-Heinemann. (**391**)

Tyrer P and Alexander J (1979) Classification of personality disorder. *British Journal of Psychiatry* **135**: 163–7. (**385**)

Tyrer P and Cicchetti D (2000) Personality assessment schedule. In P Tyrer (ed) *Personality Disorders: Diagnosis, Management and Course.* Oxford, UK: Butterworth-Heinemann, pp. 51–71. (**346, 387**)

Tyrer P and Johnson T (1996) Establishing the severity of personality disorder. *American Journal of Psychiatry* **135**: 168–74. (**391**)

Tyrer P and Simmonds S (2003) Treatment models for those with severe mental illness and comorbid personality disorder. *British Journal of Psychiatry* **44**: S15–8. (**364**)

Tyrer P and Stein G (1993) *Personality Disorder Reviewed.* Gaskell: Bideford. (**397**)

Tyrer P, Coombs N, Ibrahimi F, et al. (2007) Critical developments in the assessment of personality disorder. *British Journal of Psychiatry* (Suppl. 49): s51–59. (**488**)

Tyrer P, Tom B, Byford S, et al. (2004) Differential effects of manual assisted cognitive behaviour therapy in the treatment of recurrent deliberate self-harm and personality disturbance: the POPMACT study. *Journal of Personality Disorders* **18**: 102–16. (**411, 574**)

Tyrer S (2007) personal communication. (**488**)

Uchida H, Suzuki T, Takeuchi H, Arenovich T, and Mamo DC (2011) Low does vs standard dose of antipsychotics for relapse prevention in schizophrenia: mata-analysis. *Schizophrenia Bulletin* **37**: 788–99. (**360**)

Uhl GR, Drgon T, Johnson C, et al. (2008) Molecular genetics of addiction and related heritable phenotypes: genome-wide association approaches identify 'connectivity constellation' and drug target genes with pleiotropic effects. *Annals of the New York Academy of Sciences* **1141**: 318–81. (**204**)

Uhl GR, Liu QR, Walther D, Hess J, and Naiman D (2001) Polysubstance abuse-vulnerability genes: genome scans for association, using 1,004 subjects and 1,494 single-nucleotide polymorphisms. *American Journal of Human Genetics* **69**: 1290–300. (**204**)

UK Drug Policy Commission (UKDPC) (2008) *Reducing Drug Use, Reducing Reoffending: Are Programmes for Problem Drug-using Offenders in the UK Supported by the Evidence?* London: UKDPC. http://www.ukdpc.org.uk/wp-content/uploads/Policy%20report%20-%20Reducing%20drug%20use,%20reducing%20reoffending.pdf (**451, 460, 461, 463, 467**)

UKATT: *see* United Kingdom Alcohol Treatment Trial.

UKCC: *see* United Kingdom Central Council for Nursing, Midwifery & Health Visiting.

Ullman SE and Siegel JM (1994) Predictors of exposure to traumatic events and posttraumatic stress sequelae. *Journal of Community Psychology* **22**: 328–38. (**712**)

Ulm R, Volpicelli J, and Volpicelli L (1995) Opiates and alcohol self-administration to animals. *Journal of Clinical Psychiatry* **56**: 5–14. (**446**)

Underwood B and Moore B (1982) Perspective-taking and altruism. *Psychological Bulletin* **91**: 143–73. (**395**)

Ungvari G (1993) Successful treatment of litiginous paranoia with pimozide. *Canadian Journal of Psychiatry* **38**: 4–8. (**382**)

Unis AS, Cook EH, Vincent JG, et al. (1997) Platelet serotonin measures in adolescents with conduct disorder. *Biological Psychiatry* **42**: 553–9. (**307**)

UNISON (1997) *UNISON Members Experience of Bullying at Work.* London: UNISON. (**699**)

United Kingdom Alcohol Treatment Trial Research Team (2005a) Effectiveness of treatment for alcohol problems: findings of the randomised UK alcohol treatment trial (UKATT). *British Medical Journal* **331**: 541. (**459**)

United Kingdom Alcohol Treatment Trial Research Team (2005b) Cost effectiveness of treatment for alcohol problems: findings of the randomised UK alcohol treatment trial (UKATT). *British Medical Journal* **331**: 544. (**459**)

United Kingdom Central Council for Nursing, Midwifery and Health Visiting (2001) *Prevention and Management of Violence in Mental Health Care.* London: UKCC. (**555, 558**)

United Nations Economic and Social Council (1988) *Report of the Sessional Working Group on the Question of Persons Detained on the Grounds of Mental Ill Health* (Chairman Mrs C. Palley). Strasbourg, France: Commission on Human Rights E/CN4/Sub.2/1988/22. (**133**)

Upson A (2004) *Violence at Work: Findings from the 2002/3 British Crime Survey, Home Office Online Report 04/04.* London. http://www.hse.gov.uk/violence/bcsviolence0203.pdf (**699**)

Urabaniok F, Noll T, Grunewald S, Steinbach J, and Endrass J (2006) Prediction of violent and sexual offences: a replication study of the VRAG in Switzerland. *Journal of Forensic Psychiatry and Psychology* **17**: 23–31. (**536**)

US Public Health Service (1972) *Surgeon General's Scientific Advisory Committee on Television and Social Behavior: Television and Growing Up. The Impact of Televised Violence: Report to the Surgeon General.* Washington, DC: Government Printing Office. (**216**)

Ustinov P (1977) *Dear Me.* London: Little Brown and Company. (**334**)

Uzoaba J (1998) *Managing Older Offenders: Where Do We Stand?* Ottawa, Canada: Correctional Service of Canada. (**524, 525**)

Vaddadi KS, Soosai E, Gilleard CJ, and Allard S (1997) Mental illness, physical abuse and burden of care of relatives: a study of acute psychiatric admissions patients. *Acta Psychiatrica Scandinavia* **95**: 313–7. (**355, 546**)

Vaillant G (1987) A developmental view of old and new perspectives of personality disorders. *Journal of Personality Disorders* **1**: 146–58. (**384**)

Vaillant GE (1995) *The Natural History of Alcoholism Revisited.* Cambridge, UK: Harvard University Press. (**447**)

Valentiner DP, Foa EB, Riggs DS, and Gershuny BS (1996) Coping strategies and posttraumatic stress disorder in female victims of sexual and nonsexual assault. *Journal of Abnormal Psychology* **105**: 455–8. (**722**)

Vallentine V, Tapp J, Dudley A, Wilson C, and Moore E (2010) Psycho educational groupwork for detained offender patients: understanding mental illness. *Journal of Forensic Psychiatry and Psychology* **21**: 393–406. (**573**)

van Beijsterveldt CE, Bartels M, Hudziak JJ, and Boomsma DI (2003) Causes of stability of aggression from early childhood to adolescence: a longitudinal genetic analysis in Dutch twins. *Behavioral Genetics* **33**: 591–605. (**196**)

van den Bosch LMC, Koeter MWJ, Stijnen T, Verheul R, and van den Brink W (2005) Sustained efficacy of dialectical behaviour therapy for borderline personality disorder. *Behaviour Research and Therapy* **43**: 1231–41. (**411**)

van den Bosch LMC, Verheul R, Schippers GM, and van den Brink W (2002) Dialectical behavior therapy of borderline patients with and without substance use problems: Implementation and long-term effects. *Addictive Behaviors* **27**: 911–23. (**411**)

van den Bree MB (2005) Combining research approaches to advance our understanding of drug addiction. *Current Psychiatry Reports* **7**: 125–32. (**201, 204**)

van den Bree MB and Owen MJ (2003) The future of psychiatric genetics. *Annals of Medicine* **35**: 122–34. (**187, 190, 194**)

van den Bree MB and Pickworth WB (2005) Risk factors predicting changes in marijuana involvement in teenagers. *Archives of General Psychiatry* **62**: 311–9. (**210**)

van den Bree MB, Johnson EO, Neale MC, and Pickens RW (1998) Genetic and environmental influences on drug use and abuse/dependence in male and female twins. *Drug and Alcohol Dependence* **52**: 231–41. (**200**)

van den Bree MB, Johnson EO, Neale MC, et al. (1998) Genetic analysis of diagnostic systems of alcoholism in males. *Biological Psychiatry* **43**: 139–45. (**202**)

van den Bree MB, Svikis DS, and Pickens RW (1998) Genetic influences in antisocial personality and drug use disorders. *Drug and Alcohol Dependence* **49**: 177–87. (**200**)

van den Brink RHS, Hooijschuur A, van Os TWDP, Savenije W, and Wiersma D (2010) Routine violence risk assessment in community forensic mental healthcare. *Behavioral Sciences and the Law* **28**: 396–410. (**533**)

van den Jout M, Muris P, Salemink E, and Kindt M (2001) Autobiographical memories become less vivid and emotional after eye movements. *British Journal of Clinical Psychology* **40**: 121–30. (**725**)

van den Oord EJ, Koot HM, Boomsma DI, Verhulst FC, and Orlebeke J.F (1995) A twin-singleton comparison of problem behaviour in 2-3-year-olds. *Journal of Child Psychology and Psychiatry* **36**: 449–58. (**189**)

van der Kolk BA (1996a) Trauma and Memory. In BA van der Kolk, AC McFarlane, L Weisaeth (eds) *Traumatic Stress: The Effects of Overwhelming Experience on Mind, Body and Society.* New York: Guilford, pp. 279–302. (**719, 720**)

van der Kolk BA (1996b) The body keeps the score: approaches to the psychobiology of post-traumatic stress disorder. In BA van der Kolk, AC McFarlane L Weisaeth L (eds) *Traumatic Stress: The Effects of Overwhelming Experience on Mind, Body, and Society.* New York: Guilford, pp. 214–41. (**719, 720**)

van der Kolk BA (2002) Beyond the talking cure: somatic experience and subcortical imprints in the treatment of trauma. In F Shapiro (ed) *EMDR as an Integrative Psychotherapy Approach: Experts of Diverse Orientations Explore the Paradigm Prism.* Washington, DC: American Psychological Association Press. (**725, 731**) van der Kolk BA (2005) Developmental trauma disorder. Towards a rational diagnosis for children with complex histories. *Psychiatric Annals* **35**: 401–8. (**712**)

van Etten ML and Taylor S (1998) Comparative efficacy of treatments for post-traumatic stress disorder: a meta-analysis. *Clinical Psychology and Psychotherapy* **5**:126–45. (**725**)

van Humbeeck G, van Audenhove C, Pieters G, et al. (2001) Expressed emotion in staff-patient relationships: the professionals' and residents' perspective. *Social Psychiatry and Psychiatric Epidemiology* **36**: 486–92. (**557**)

van Ijzendoorn MH, Bakermans-Kranenberg MJ (1997) Intergenerational transmission of attachment: a move to the contextual level. In L Atkinson, KJ Zucker (eds) *Attachment and Psychopathology*. London: Guilford. pp. 135–170. (**396, 717**)

van Kesteren JN and van Dijk (2010) Key victimological findings from the international crime victims survey. In GS Shoham, P K Nepper, M Kett (eds) *International Handbook of Victimology*. Boca Raton, FL: Taylor and Francis. pp. 151–80. (**700**)

van Kesteren JN, Mayhew P, and Nieuwbeerta P (2000) *Criminal victimization in seventeen industrialised countries: key findings from the 2000 international crime victims survey*. The Hague, the Netherlands: Netherlands Ministry of Justice. (**543**)

van Loon FGH (1927) Amok and latah. *Journal of Abnormal Social Psychology* **21**: 434–44. (**428**)

van Marle HJC (2002) The Dutch Entrustment Act (TBS): its principles and innovations. *International Journal of Forensic Mental Health* **1**: 83–92. (**414**)

van Nieuwenhuizen C (2005) A treatment programme for sexually violent forensic psychiatric inpatients: development and first results. *Psychology, Crime and Law* **11**: 467–77. (**578**)

van Oorsouw K, Merckelbach H, Ravelli D, Nijman H, and Mekking-Pompen I (2004) *Alcoholic blackout for criminally relevant behaviour*. *Journal of the American Academy of Psychiatry Law* **32** (4): 364–70. (**438**)

van Os J, Hanssen M, Bijl RV, and Ravelli A (2000) Strauss (1969) revisited: a psychosis continuum in the general population? *Schizophrenia Research* **45**: 11–20. (**339**)

van Velsen C (2010) Psychotherapeutic understanding and approach to psychosis in mentally disordered offenders. In A Bartlett, GA McGauley (eds) *Forensic Mental Health: Concepts, Systems, and Practice*. Oxford, UK: Oxford University Press. (**583**)

van Voorhis P, Wright EM, Salisbury E, and Bauman A (2010) Women's risk factors and their contributions to existing risk/needs assessment. The current status of a gender-responsive supplement. *Criminal Justice and Behavior* **37**: 261–88 (**518**)

van Voren R (2010) Political abuse of psychiatry – an historical overview. *Schizophrenia Bulletin* **36**: 33–5. (**659**)

Vanamo T, Kauppi A, Kärkölä K, Merikanto J, and Räsänen E (2001) Intra-familial child homicide in Finland 1970–1994: incidence, causes of death and demographic characteristics. *Forensic Sci Int* **117**: 199–204. (**508**)

Vandello JA and Cohen D (2003) Male honour and female fidelity: implicit cultural scripts that perpetuate domestic violence. *Journal of Personality and Social Psychology* **22**: 997–1010. (**371**)

Vandenbergh DJ, Rodriguez LA, Miller IT, Uhl GR, and Lachman HM (1997) High-activity catechol-O-methyltransferase allele is more prevalent in polysubstance abusers. *American Journal of Medical Genetics* **74**: 439–42. (**206**)

Vandersall TA and Wiener JM (1970) Children who set fires. *Archives of General Psychiatry* **22**. 63–71. (**276**)

van-Velzen CJ and Emmelkamp PM (1996) The assessment of personality disorders: implications for cognitive and behaviour therapy. *Behaviour, Research and Therapy* **34**: 655–68. (**392**)

Vanyukov MM, Maher BS, Devlin B, et al. (2007) The MAOA promoter polymorphism, disruptive behavior disorders, and early onset substance use disorder: gene–environment interaction. *Psychiatric Genetics* **17**: 323–32. (**200**)

Vård och stöd till psykiskt störda lagövertädare (2006) SOU 2006:91. Stockholm, Sweden: Swedish Government Official Reports [English summary, p. 27]. (**137**)

Vartia M (1994) 'Bullying at workplaces' in Research on violence, threats and bullying as health risks among health care personnel, *Proceedings from the Workshop for Nordic Researchers*, Reykjavik, 14–16 Aug: 29. (**700**)

Vaughan P, Pullen N, and Kelly M (2000) Services for mentally disordered offenders in community psychiatric teams. *Journal of Forensic Psychiatry* **11**: 571–86. (**643**)

Vecchio TD and O'Leary KD (2004) Effectiveness of anger treatments for specific anger problems: a meta-analytic review. *Clinical Psychology Review* **24**: 15–34. (**575**)

Veit R, Flor H, Erb M, et al. (2002) Brain circuits involved in emotional learning in antisocial behavior and social phobia in humans. *Neuroscience Letters* **328**: 233–6. (**304, 305**)

Velez ML, Montoya ID, Jansson LM, et al. (2006) Exposure to violence among substance-dependent pregnant women and their children. *Journal of Substance Abuse Treatment* **30**(1): 31–8. (**452**)

Veltkamp E, Nijman H, Stolker J, et al. (2008) Patients' preference for seclusion or forced medication in acute psychiatric emergency in the Netherlands. *Psychiatric Services* **59**: 209–11. (**594**)

Ventress M, Rix KJB, and Kent JH (2008) Keeping PACE: fitness to be interviewed by the police. *Advances in Psychiatric Treatment* **14**: 369–81. (**160**)

Verdoux H and van Os J (2002) Psychotic symptoms in non-clinical populations and the continuum of psychosis. *Schizophrenia Research* **54**: 59–65. (**339**)

Verheul R, van den Bosch LM, Koeter MW, et al. (2003) Dialectical behaviour therapy for women with borderline personality disorder: 12-month, randomised clinical trial in the Netherlands. *British Journal of Psychiatry* **182**: 135–40. (**411, 574**)

Verheul R, van den Brink W, and Geerlings P (1999) A three-pathway psychobiological model of craving for alcohol. *Alcohol and Alcoholism* **34**: 197–222. (**446**)

Verheul R, van den Brink W, and Hartgers C (1995) Prevalence of personality disorders among alcoholics and drug addicts: an overview. *European Addiction Research* **1**: 166–77. (**443, 444, 446**)

Verkes RJ, Van der Mast RC, Hengeveld MW, et al. (1998) Reduction by paroxetine of suicidal behavior in patients with repeated suicide attempts but not major depression. *American Journal of Psychiatry* **155**(4): 543–7. (**310, 406**)

Verma S, Poon LY, Subramaniam M, Chong SA, (2005) Aggression in Asian patients with first-episode psychosis. *International Journal of Social Psychiatry* **51**: 365–71. (**344**)

Vermeiren R (2003) Psychopathology and delinquency in adolescents: a descriptive and developmental perspective. *Clinical Psychology Review* **23**: 277–318. (**482, 484**)

Vermeiren R, Schwab-Stone M, Deboutte D, Leckman PE, and Ruchkin V (2003) Violence exposure and substance use in adolescents: findings from three countries. *Pediatrics* 3: 535–40. (**483**)

Vermerien R, Schwab-Stone M, Ruchkin V, De Clippele A, and Deboutte D (2002) Predicting recidivism in delinquent adolescents from psychological and psychiatric assessment. *Comprehensive Psychiatry* **43**(2): 142–9. (**483**)

Vernberg EM, Steinberg AM, Jacobs AK, et al. (2008) Innovations in disaster mental health: psychological first aid. *Professional Psychology: Research and Practice* **39**: 381–8. (**724**)

Verona E and Vitale JE (2006) Psychopathy in women: Assessment, manifestations, and etiology. In CJ Patrick (ed) *Handbook of Psychopathy.* New York: Guilford. pp. 415–36. (**513**)

Verona E, Hicks BM, and Patrick CJ (2006) Psychopathy and suicidal behavior in female offenders: mediating influences of temperament and abuse history. *Journal of Consulting and Clinical Psychology* **73**: 1065–73. (**513, 514**)

Vevera J, Hubbard A, Vesalý A, and Papežová H (2005) Violent behaviour in schizophrenia. *British Journal of Psychiatry* **187**: 426–30. (**347**)

Victor M and Adams RD (1953) The effect of alcohol on the nervous system. In M Victor, RD Adams (eds) *The Metabolic and Toxic Diseases of the Nervous System: Research Publications of the Association for Research in Nervous and Mental Disease,* vol. 32 (Ch. 28). Baltimore, MD: Williams and Wilkins, pp. 511–4. (**438, 439**)

Victor M, Adams RD, and Collins GH (1971) *The Wernicke-Korsakoff Syndrome.* Oxford, UK: Blackwell Scientific. (**439**)

Viding E, Blair RJ, Moffitt TE, and Plomin R (2005) Evidence for substantial genetic risk for psychopathy in 7-year-olds. *Journal of Child Psychology and Psychiatry* **46**: 592–7. (**196**)

Vinnars B, Barber JP, Norén K, Gallop R, and Weinryb RM (2005) Manualized supportive-expressive psychotherapy versus nonmanualized community-delivered psychodynamic therapy for patients with personality disorders: bridging efficacy and effectiveness. *American Journal of Psychiatry* **162**: 1933–40. (**411**)

Virkkunen M (1974) Observation on violence in schizophrenia: on arson committed by schizophrenics. *Acta Psychiatrica Scandinavica* **50**: 145–60. (**347**)

Virkkunen M and Linnoila M (1993) Brain serotonin, type II alcoholism and impulsive violence. *Journal of Studies on Alcohol Supplement* **11**: 163–9. (**206**)

Virkkunen M, De Jong J, and Bartko J (1989) Relationship of psychosocial variables to recidivism in violent offenders and impulsive fire setters: a follow-up study. *Archives of General Psychiatry* **46**: 600–3. (**308**)

Virkkunen M, Eggert M, Rawlings R, and Linnoila M (1996) A prospective follow-up study of alcoholic violent offenders and fire setters. *Archives of General Psychiatry* **53**: 523–9. (**308**)

Virkkunen M, Goldman D, Nielsen DA, and Linnoila M (1995) Low brain serotonin turnover rate (low CSF 5-HIAA) and impulsive violence. *Journal of Psychiatry Neuroscience* **20**: 271–5. (**198**)

Virkkunen M, Nuutila A, Goodwin FK, and Linnoila M (1987) Cerebrospinal fluid monoamine metabolite levels in male arsonists. *Archives of General Psychiatry* **44**: 247. (**308**)

Virkkunen M, Rawlings R, Tokola R, et al. (1994) CSF biochemistries, glucose metabolism, and diurnal activity rhythms in alcoholic, violent offenders, fire setters, and healthy volunteers. *Archives of Psychiatry* **51**: 20–7. (**308**)

Vitale JE, Smith SS, Brinkley CA, and Newman JP (2002) The reliability and validity of the Psychopathy Checklist–Revised in a sample of female offenders. *Criminal Justice and Behavior* **29**: 202–31. (**513**)

Vizard E (2006) Sexually abusive behaviour by children and adolescents. *Child and Adolescent Mental Health* **11**: 2–8. (**495**)

Vizard E, Wynick S, Hawkes C, Woods J, and Jenkins J (1996) Juvenile sexual offenders. *British Journal of Psychiatry* **168**: 259–62. (**495**)

Volavka J (1999) The effects of clozapine on aggression and substance abuse in schizophrenic patients. *Journal of Clinical Psychiatry* **60** (Suppl. 12): 43–6. (**563**)

Volavka J and Citrome L (2011) Pathways to aggression in schizophrenia affect results of treatment *Schizophrenia Bulletin* **37**: 921–9. (**348**)

Volavka J, Czobor P, Nolan K, et al. (2004) Overt aggression and psychotic symptoms in patients with schizophrenia treated with clozapine, olanzapine, risperidone, or haloperidol. *Journal of Clinical Psychopharmacology* **24**: 225–8. (**563**)

Volavka J, Czobor P, Sheitman B, et al. (2002) Clozapine, olanzapine, risperidone, and haloperidol in the treatment of patients with chronic schizophrenia and schizoaffective disorder. *American Journal of Psychiatry* **159**: 255–62. (**563**)

Volavka J, Laska E, Baker S, et al. (1997) History of violent behaviour and schizophrenia in different cultures. *British Journal of Psychiatry* **171**: 9–14. (**343, 344**)

Volavka J, Zito J, Vitral J, and Czobor P (1993) Clozapine effects on hostility and aggression in schizophrenia. *Journal of Clinical Psychopharmacology* **13**: 287–9. (**563**)

Volberg RA and Steadman HJ (1988) Refining prevalence estimates of pathological gambling. *American Journal of Psychiatry* **145**: 502–5. (**470**)

Volkow ND and Tancredi L (1987) Neural substrates of violent behaviour. A preliminary study with positron emission tomography. *British Journal of Psychiatry* **151**: 668–73. (**302**)

Volkow ND, Tancredi LR, Grant C, et al. (1995) Brain glucose metabolism in violent psychiatric patients: a preliminary study. *Psychiatry Research: Neuroimaging* **61**: 243–53. (**302**)

Völlm B, Richardson P, McKie S, et al. (2006) Serotonergic modulation of neuronal responses to behavioural inhibition and reinforcing stimuli: an fMRI study in healthy volunteers. *European Journal of Neuroscience* **23**: 552–60. (**310**)

Völlm B, Richardson P, McKie S, et al. (2010): Neuronal correlates and serotonergic modulation of behavioural inhibition and reward in healthy and antisocial individuals. *Journal of Psychiatric Research* **44**:123–31. (**310**)

Völlm B, Richardson P, Stirling J, et al. (2004) Neurobiological substrates of antisocial and borderline personality disorder: preliminary results of a functional fMRI study. *Criminal Behaviour and Mental Health* **14**: 39–54. (**304, 305**)

Vreeland RG and Lowin BM (1980) Psychological aspects of firesetting. In D Canter (ed) *Fires and Human Behaviour*. New York: Wiley. (**495**)

Vreugdenhil C, Doreleijers TAH, Vermeiren R, Wouters LFJM, and van den Brink W (2004) Psychiatric disorders in a representative sample of incarcerated boys in the Netherlands. *Journal of the American Academy of Child and Adolescent Psychiatry* **43**: 97–104. (**482, 483, 484**)

Vrij A (2008) *Detecting Lies and Deceit*, 2nd edn. Chichester, UK: Wiley. (**421**)

Wadsworth MEJ (1979) *Roots of Delinquency: Infancy, Adolescence and Crime*. London: Martin Robertson. (**175, 176, 177**)

Wadsworth MEJ (1991) *The Imprint of Time*. Oxford: Clarendon. (**172**)

Wahidin A (2003) Doing hard time. Older women in prison. *Prison Service Journal* **145**: 25–9. (**528**)

Wahl OF (1999) Mental health consumers' experience of stigma. *Schizophrenia Bulletin* **25**: 467–78. (**579**)

Wahlberg KE, Wynne LC, Hakko H, et al. (2004) Interaction of genetic risk and adoptive parent communication deviance: longitudinal prediction of adoptee psychiatric disorders. *Psychological Medicine* **34**: 1531–41. (**210**)

Wahlberg KE, Wynne LC, Oja H, et al. (1997) Gene–environment interaction in vulnerability to schizophrenia: findings from the finnish adoptive family study of schizophrenia. *American Journal of Psychiatry* **154**: 355–62. (**210**)

Waigandt A, Wallace DL, Phelps L, and Miller DA (1990) The impact of sexual assault on physical health status. *Journal of Traumatic Stress* **3**: 93–101. (**715**)

Waite T (2007) Foreword to HP Simpson. *Justice for William*. Hook, UK: Waterside, pp. 7–8. http://www.watersidepress.co.uk/acatalog/JFW_prelims.pdf (**694**)

Wakeling HC, Webster SD, and Mann RE (2005) Sexual Offenders' treatment experience: a qualitative and quantitative investigation. *Journal of Sexual Aggression* **11**: 171–86. (**578**)

Walby S and Allen J (2004) *Domestic Violence, Sexual Assault and Stalking: Findings from the British Crime Survey*. Home Office Research Study 276. London: Home Office. http://webarchive.nationalarchives.gov.uk/20110218135832/rds.homeoffice.gov.uk/rds/pdfs04/hors276.pdf (**714**)

Walderhaug E, Lunde H, Nordvik JE, et al. (2002) Lowering of serotonin by rapid tryptophan depletion increases impulsiveness in normal individuals. *Psychopharmacology* **164**: 385–91. (**309**)

Waldinger RJ and Gunderson JG (1984) Completed psychotherapies with borderline patients. *American Journal of Psychotherapy* **38**: 190–202. (**408**)

Walker A, Flatley J, Kershaw C, and Moon D (2009) *Crime in England and Wales 2008/09 Volume 1 Findings from the British Crime Survey and Police Recorded Crime*. London: Home Office. (**282**)

Walker A, Kershaw C, and Nicholas S (2006) *Crime in England and Wales 2005/06*. London: Home Office. (**266**)

Walker DM (1980) *The Oxford Companion to Law*. Oxford, UK: Clarendon. (**19**)

Walker J and Bright J (2009a) Self-esteem and violence: a systematic review and cognitive model. *Journal of Forensic Psychiatry and Psychology* **20**: 1–32. (**215, 241, 242**)

Walker J and Bright J (2009b) Cognitive therapy for violence: reaching the parts that anger management doesn't reach. *Journal of Forensic Psychiatry and Psychology* **20**: 174–201. (**215, 241, 242**)

Walker J, Illingworth C, Canning A, Garner E, Woolley J, Taylor PJ, and Amos T (in press) Changes in mental state associated with prison environments: A systematic review. *Acta Psychiatrica Scandinavica*. (**630**)

Walker JS and Gudjonsson GH (2006) The Maudsley violence questionnaire: relationship to personality and self-reported offending *Personality and Individual Differences* **40**: 795–806. (**218**)

Walker LE (1979) *The Battered Woman*. New York: Harpers and Row. (**509, 714**)

Walker LE (1989) *Terrifying Love: Why Battered Women Kill and How Society Responds*. New York: Harper and Row. (**499**)

Walker N (1968) *Crime and Insanity in England*, vol. 1: The Historical Perspective. Edinburgh, Scotland: Edinburgh University Press. (**24, 28, 29, 32, 118, 148, 290, 335**)

Walker N (1985) *Sentencing, Theory, Law and Practice*. London: Butterworths. (**22, 118**)

Walker N and McCabe S (1973) *Crime and Insanity in England (Vol. 2)*. Edinburgh, Scotland: Edinburgh University Press. (**342, 625**)

Wallace C, Mullen P, Burgess P, et al. (1998) Serious criminal offending and mental disorder – Case linkage study. *British Journal of Psychiatry* **172**: 477–84. (**280, 337**)

Wallace C, Mullen PE, and Burgess P (2004) Criminal offending in schizophrenia over a 25-year period marked by deinstitutionalization and increasing prevalence of comorbid substance use disorders. *The American Journal of Psychiatry* **161**: 716–27. (**337, 338, 347, 507**)

Wallace JF and Newman JP (2004) A theory-based treatment model for psychopathy. *Cognitive and Behavioral Practice* **11**: 178–89. (**416**)

Waller JA (1965) Chronic medical conditions and traffic safety. *New England Journal of Medicine* **273**: 1413–20. (**277**)

Waller T and Rumball D (2004) *Treating Drinkers and Drug Users in the Community.* Oxford, UK: Blackwell. (**452**)

Wallis JD (2007) Orbitofrontal cortex and its contribution to decision-making. *Annual Reviews of Neuroscience* **30**: 31–56. (**298**)

Walmsley R (2006) World Female Imprisonment List. International Centre for Prison Studies: London. http://www.amnistia-internacional.pt/files/WFIL%202nd%20edition[1].pdf (**516**)

Walsh B (2001) Economic costs and benefits of early developmental prevention. In *Child Delinquents* R Loeber and D Farrington (eds), pp. 339–58. Thousand Oaks, CA: Sage. (**398**)

Walsh E, Leese M, Taylor P, et al. (2002) Psychosis in high-security and general psychiatric services: report from the UK700 and Special Hospitals' Treatment-Resistant Schizophrenia groups. *British Journal of Psychiatry* **180**: 351–7. (**600**)

Walsh E, Moran P, Scott C, et al. (2003) Prevalence of violent victimization in severe mental illness. *British Journal of Psychiatry* **183**: 233–8. (**3, 334, 712**)

Walsh T, McClellan JM, McCarthy SE, et al. (2008) Rare structural variants disrupt multiple genes in neurodevelopmental pathways in schizophrenia. *Science (New York, N.Y.)* **320**(5875): 539–43. (**209**)

Walshe K and Higgins J (2002) The use and impact of inquiries in the NHS. *British Medical Journal* **325**: 895–900. (**74, 75**)

Walters GD (2002) The heritability of alcohol abuse and dependence: a meta-analysis of behavior genetic research. *American Journal of Drug and Alcohol Abuse* **28**: 557–84. (**201**)

Wampold BE (2001) *The Great Psychotherapy Debate: Models, Methods And Findings.* Mahwah, NJ: Lawrence Erlbaum. (**407**)

Wang S (1997) Traumatic stress and attachment. *Acta Physiologica Scandinavica* **161**: 164–9. (**717, 720**)

Wanless D (2004) *Securing good health for the whole population.* London: HMSO. http://webarchive.nationalarchives.gov.uk/+/http:/www.hm-treasury.gov.uk/consult_wanless04_final.htm (**703**)

Warburton AL and Shepherd JP (2000) Effectiveness of toughened glassware in terms of reducing injury in bars: a randomised controlled trial. *Injury Prevention* **6**: 36–40. (**703, 705**)

Warburton AL and Shepherd JP (2004) Development, utilization and important of accident and emergency derived assault data in violence management. *Emergency Medicine Journal* **21**: 473–7. (**700, 701, 703, 704**)

Warburton AL and Shepherd JP (2006) Tackling alcohol related violence in city centres: effect of emergency medicine and police intervention. *Emergency Medicine Journal* **23**: 12–7. (**703, 704**)

Ward AD (2003) *Adult Incapacity.* Edinburgh, Scotland: W. Green. (**91**)

Ward DE (2002) Explaining evil behaviour: using Kant and M. Scott Peck to solve the puzzle of understanding the moral psychology of evil people. *Philosophy, Psychiatry and Psychology* **9**:1–12. (**7**)

Ward T and Beech AR (2008) An integrated theory of sexual offending. In DR Laws, WT O'Donohue (eds) *Sexual Deviance: Theory, Assessment, and Treatment*, 2nd edn. New York: Guildford. (**245**)

Ward T and Hudson SM (1998) A model of the relapse process in sexual offenders. *Journal of Interpersonal Violence* **13**: 700–25. (**442**)

Ward T and Keenan T (1999) Child molesters' implicit theories. *Journal of Interpersonal Violence* **14**: 821–38. (**258**)

Ward T, Polaschek D, and Beech AR (2006) *Theories of Sexual Offending.* Chichester, UK: Wiley. (**245**)

Wardle C (1991) Twentieth-century influences on the development in Britain of services for child and adolescent psychiatry. *British Journal of Psychiatry* **159**: 53–68. (**481**)

Warner L (2005) *Acute Care in Crisis* from *Beyond the Water Towers.* London: Sainsbury Centre for Mental Health. (**58**)

Warren F and Dolan B (1996) Treating the 'untreatable': therapeutic communities for personality disorders. *Therapeutic Communities: The International Journal for Therapeutic and Supportive Organizations* **17**: 205–16. (**401**)

Warren F, McGauley G, Norton K, et al. (2003) *Review of Treatments for Severe Personality Disorder*, Home Office: London, 30/03. http://www.floridatac.org/files/document/rdsolr3003.pdf (**583**)

Warren JI, Burnette M, South SC, et al. (2002) Personality disorders and violence among female prison inmates. *Journal of the American Academy of Psychiatry and Law* **30**(4): 502–9. (**503**)

Warren JI, Burnette ML, South SC, et al. (2003) Psychopathy in women: structural modeling and comorbidity. *International Journal of Law and Psychiatry* **26**: 223–42. (**513**)

Warren JI, South SC, Burnette ML, et al. (2005) Understanding the risk factors for violence and criminality in women: the concurrent validity of the PCL-R and HCR- 20. *International Journal of Law and Psychiatry* **28**: 269–89. (**538**)

Warren LJ, MacKenzie R, Mullen PE, and Ogloff JRP (2005) The problem behavior model: the development of a stalkers clinic and a threateners clinic. *Behavioral Sciences and the Law* **23**: 387–97. (**139, 547**)

Warren LJ, Mullen PE, and Ogloff JRP (2011) A clinical study of those who utter threats to kill. *Behavioral Sciences and the Law* **29**: 141–54. (**543**)

Warren LJ, Mullen PE, and Ogloff JRP (2012) The psychological basis of threatening behaviour. *Psychiatry, Psychology and Law.* online DOI: 10.1080/13218719.2012.674716 (**546**)

Warren LJ, Mullen PE, Thomas SD, Ogloff JR, and Burgess PM (2008) Threats to kill: a follow-up study. *Psychological Medicine* **38**: 599–605. (**543**)

Warren W (1952) In-patient treatment of adolescents with psychological illness. *Lancet* **1**: 147–50. (**481**)

Warren W (1971) You can never plan the future by the past. The development of child and adolescent psychiatry in England and Wales. *Journal of Child Psychology and Psychiatry* **11**: 241–57. (**482**)

Washington State Institute for Public Policy (2005) *Sex Offender Sentencing in Washington State: Did Community Notification Influence Recidivism?* Olympia, WA: Washington State Institute for Public Policy. www.wsipp.wa.gov. (**645**)

Wasserman DR and Leventhal JM (1993) Maltreatment of children born to cocaine dependent mothers. *American Journal of Diseases of Children* **147**: 1324–8. (**465**)

Wasserman GA, McReynolds LS, Lucas CP, Fisher P, and Santos L (2002) The Voice DISC-IV with incarcerated male youths: prevalence of disorder. *Journal of the American Academy of Child and Adolescent Psychiatry* **41**: 314–21. (**482, 483**)

Waterhouse R (2000) *Lost in Care, Report of the Tribunal of Inquiry into the Abuse of Children in Care in the Former County Council Areas of Gwynedd and Clwyd since 1974.* London: Dept of Health, TSO. (**221**)

Watson BE (1996) Can institution-induced anger prolong hospitalisation for patients who repress anger? *Psychiatric Services* **47**: 363–4. (**592**)

Watt A, Topping-Morris B, Rogers P, Doyle M, and Mason T (2003b) Pre-admission nursing assessment in forensic mental health (1991–2000): Part 2 – comparison of traditional assessment with the items contained within the HCR-20 structured risk assessment. *International Journal of Nursing Studies* **40**: 657–62. (**557**)

Watt A, Topping-Morris B., Mason T, and Rogers P (2003a) Pre-admission nursing assessment in forensic mental health (1991–2000): Part 1 – a preliminary analysis of practice and cost. *International Journal of Nursing Studies* **40**: 645–55. (**557**)

Watt K, Shepherd JP, and Newcombe RG (2008) Drunk and dangerous: a randomised controlled trial of alcohol brief intervention for violent offenders. *Journal of Experimental Criminology* **4**: 1–9. (**705**)

Watts D and Morgan HG (1994) 'Malignant alienation'. *British Journal of Psychiatry* **164**, 11–15. (**596**)

Watzke S, Ullrich S, and Marneros A (2006) Gender- and violence-related prevalence of mental disorders in prisoners. *European Archives of Psychiatry and Clinical Neuroscience* **256**: 414–21. (**517**)

Weaver T, Madden P, Charles V, et al. (2003) Comorbidity of substance misuse and mental illness in community mental health and substance misuse services. *British Journal of Psychiatry* **183**: 304–13. (**451, 452**)

Webb RT, Pickles AR, Appleby L, Mortensen PB, and Abel KM (2007) Death by unnatural causes during childhood and early adulthood in offspring of psychiatric inpatients. *Archives of General Psychiatry* **64**: 345–52. (**508**)

Webster B (2006) Wardens target disabled-badge cheats. *The Times,* 17 June: 19. (**278**)

Webster CD, Douglas KS, Eaves D, and Hart SD (1997) *The HCR-20 Scheme: Assessing Risk for Violence, Version 2.* Burnaby, Canada: Mental Health, Law, and Policy Institute, Simon Fraser University. (**42, 331, 388, 535, 537**)

Webster CD, Nicholls TL, Martin M-L, Desmarais MA, and Brink J (2006) Short-term assessment of risk and treatability (START): the case for a new structured professional judgment scheme. *Behavioural Sciences and the Law* **24**: 747–66. (**539**)

Webster-Stratton C (1998) Preventing conduct problems in Head Start children: strengthening parenting competencies. *Journal of Consulting and Clinical Psychology* **66**: 715–30. (**182**)

Webster-Stratton C and Hammond M (1997) Treating children with early-onset conduct problems: a comparison of child and parent training interventions. *Journal of Consulting and Clinical Psychology* **65**: 93–109. (**182**)

Wechsler D (1999) *Wechsler Adult Intelligence Scale UK,* 3rd edn. London: Psychological Corporation. (**314**)

Weder N, Yang BZ, Douglas-Palumberi H, et al. (2009) MAOA genotype, maltreatment, and aggressive behavior: the changing impact of genotype at varying levels of trauma. *Biological Psychiatry* **65**: 417–24. (**200**)

Weereratne A, Exworthy T, and Flynn C (2003*) Report of the Independent Inquiry into the Care and Treatment of H.* Taunton, UK: South West Peninsula Health Authority. (**75**)

Weiger WA and Bear DM (1988) An approach to the neurology of aggression. *Journal of Psychiatric Research* **22**: 85–98. (**298**)

Weinberg I, Gunderson JG, Hennen J, and Cutter CJ (2006) Manual assisted cognitive treatment for deliberate self-harm in borderline personality disorder patient. *Journal of Personality Disorders* **20**: 482–92. (**411**)

Weinberger DR (1995) From neuropathology to neurodevelopment. *Lancet* **346**: 552–7. (**207**)

Weinberger LE, Sreenivasan S, Garrick T, and Osran H (2005) The impact of surgical castration on sexual recidivism risk among sexually violent predatory offenders. *Journal of American Academy of Psychiatry and Law* **33**: 16–36. (**261**)

Weiner BA (1985) The insanity defense: historical development and present state. *Behavioral Sciences and the Law* **3**: 3–36. (**28**)

Weinrott MR, Riggan M, and Frothingham S (1997) Reducing deviant arousal in juvenile sex offenders using vicarious sensitization. *Journal of Interpersonal Violence* **12**: 704–28. (**263**)

Weinryb RM, Gustavsson JP, Åsberg M, and Rössel RJ (1992) Stability over time of character assessment using a psychodynamic instrument and personality inventories. *Acta Psychiatrica Scandinavica* **86**: 179–84. (**385**)

Weinstock R (1988) Confidentiality and the new duty to protect: the therapist's dilemma. *Hospital and Community Psychiatry* **39**: 607–9. (**670**)

Weinstock R, Leong GB, and Silva JA (2010) Competence to be executed: an ethical analysis post Panetti. *Behavioral Sciences and the Law* **28**: 690–706. (**678**)

Weizmann-Henelius G, Grönroos M, Putkonen H, et al. (2010a) Psychopathy and gender differences in childhood psychosocial characteristics in homicide offenders – a nationwide register-based study. *Journal of Forensic Psychiatry and Psychology* **21**: 801–14. (**514**)

Weizmann-Henelius G, Grönroos M, Putronen H et al. (2012) Gender specific risk factors for intimate partner homicide – a nationwide register based study. *Journal of Interpersonal Violence* **37**: 1519–39. (**507**)

Weizmann-Henelius G, Putkonen H, Grönroos M, et al. (2010b) Examination of psychopathy in female homicide offenders – confirmatory factor analysis of the PCL-R. *International Journal of Law and Psychiatry* **33**: 177–83. (**514**)

Weizmann-Henelius G, Putkonen H, Naukkarinen H, and Eronen M (2009) Intoxication and violent women. *Archives of Womens Mental Health* **12**: 15–25. (**505, 507**)

References

Weizmann-Henelius G, Viemerö V, and Eronen M (2003) The violent female perpetrator and her victim. *Forensic Sci Int* **133**(3): 197–203. (**507**)

Weizmann-Henelius G, Viemerö V, and Eronen M (2004) Psychopathy in violent female offenders in Finland. *Psychopathology* **37**(5): 213–21. (**513**)

Welchans S (2005) Megan's Law: evaluations of sex offender registries. *Criminal Justice Policy Review* **16**: 123–40. (**645**)

Welldon E (1994) Forensic psychotherapy. In P Clarkson, M Pokorny (eds) *The Handbook of Psychotherapy*. London: Routledge, pp. 470–93. (**579**)

Welldon E (1997) The Practical approach. In E Weldon, C Van Velson (eds) *A Practical Guide to Forensic Psychotherapy*. London: Jessica Kingsley. (**554**)

Welldon EV (1991) Psychology and psychopathology in women – a psychoanalytic perspective. *British Journal of Psychiatry,* **158** (Suppl.): 85–92. (**499**)

Welldon EV and Van Velsen C (1997) General introduction. In E Weldon, C Van Velson (eds) *A Practical Guide to Forensic Psychotherapy.*, London: Jessica Kingsley, pp. 1–13. (**582**)

Welle D, Falkin GP, and Jainchill N (1998) Current approaches to drug treatment for women offenders. Project WORTH. Women's options for recovery, treatment, and health. *Journal of Substance Abuse Treatment* **15**(2): 151–63. (**518**)

Wells GL, Taylor BR, and Turtle JW (1987) The undoing of scenarios. *Journal of Personality and Social Psychology* **53**: 421–30. (**696**)

Wells LE and Rankin JH (1991) Families and delinquency: a meta-analysis of the impact of broken homes. *Social Problems* **38**: 71–93. (**175**)

Wells-Parker E, Bangert-Drowns R, McMillen R, and Williams M (1995) Final results from a meta-analysis of remedial interventions with drink/drive offenders. *Addiction* **90**: 907–26. (**447**)

Welsh Assembly Government (2008a) *Mental Health Act 1983: Code of Practice for Wales.* London: TSO (The Stationery Office). (**594**)

Welsh Assembly Government (2008b) *Working Together to Reduce Harm. The Substance Misuse Strategy for Wales 2008-2018.* http://www.drugscope.org.uk/Resources/Drugscope/Documents/PDF/Good%20Practice/welshstrategy.pdf (**437**)

Welsh Assembly Government (Llywodraeth Cynulliod) (2009) *Review of Secure Mental Health Services.* http://www.rcpsych.ac.uk/pdf/reviewofsecurementalhealthserviceswalesap2009.pdf (**588, 590**)

Werner EE and Smith RS (2001) *Journeys from Childhood to Midlife.* Ithaca. New York: Cornell University Press. (**172**)

Wessely S (1998) The Camberwell study of crime and schizophrenia. *Social Psychiatry and Psychiatric Epidemiology* **33**: S24–8. (**280**)

Wessely S (2003) Malingering: historical perspectives. In PW Halligan, C Bass, DA Oakley *Malingering and Illness Deception*. Oxford, UK: Oxford University Press, pp 243–51. (**430**)

Wessely S, Buchanan A, Reed A, et al. (1993) Acting on delusions. I. Prevalence. *British Journal of Psychiatry* **163**: 69–76. (**12**)

Wessely SC, Castle D, Douglas AJ, and Taylor PJ (1994) The criminal careers of incident cases of schizophrenia. *Psychological Medicine* **24**: 483–502. (**342, 515**)

West DJ (1968) A note on murders in Manhattan. *Medicine, Science and the Law* **8**: 249–55. (**372**)

West DJ and Farrington DP (1973) *Who Becomes Delinquent?* London: Heinemann. (**175, 177, 316**)

West DJ and Farrington DP (1977) *The Delinquent Way of Life.* London: Heinemann. (**176, 177, 178**)

West R, McNeill A, and Raw M (2000) Smoking cessation guidelines for health professionals: an update. *Thora* **55**: 987–99. (**568**)

West SG, Friedman SH, and Kim KD (2011) Women accused of sex offenses: a gender-based comparison. *Behavioral Sciences and the Law* **29**: 728–40. (**504**)

West SG, Friedman SH, and Resnick PJ (2009) Fathers who kill their children. *Journal of Forensic Sciences* **54**: 463–8. (**508, 509**)

West, DJ and Walk, A (1977) *Daniel McNaughton, His Trial and the Aftermath*, London: Gaskell Books. (**28, 335**)

Westemeyer J, Kemp K, and Nugent S (1996) Substance disorder among persons with mental retardation: a comparative study. *American Journal on Addiction* **5**: 23–31. (**324**)

Westen D (1997) Divergences between clinical and research methods for assessing personality disorders: Implications for research and the evolution of Axis II. *American Journal of Psychiatry* **154**: 895–903. (**387**)

Westen D and Arkowitz-Westen L (1998) Limitations of axis 11 in diagnosing personality pathology in clinical practice. *American Journal of Psychiatry* **155**: 1767–71. (**385**)

Westen D and Muderrisoglu S (2006) Clinical assessment of pathological personality traits. *American Journal of Psychiatry* **163**: 1285–7. (**387**)

Westen D and Shendler J (1999) Revising and assessing Axis II, Part I: developing a clinically and empirically valid assessment method. *American Journal of Psychiatry* **156**: 258–72. (**387**)

Westermeyer J (1973) On the epidemicity of amok violence. *Archives of General Psychiatry* **28**: 873–6. (**428**)

Westermeyer J (1982) Amok. In CTH Friedmann, RA Fauget (eds) *Extraordinary Disorders of Human Behavior.* New York: Plenum. (**428**)

Weston WA (1996) Pseudologia fantastica and pathological lying: a forensic issue. In LB Schlesinger (ed) *Explorations Criminal Psychopathology: Clinical Syndromes With Forensic Implications.* Springfield, IL: Charles C. Thomas Publisher, pp. 98–115. (**423**)

Weston WR (ed.) (1987) *Probation Officers' Manual.* London: Butterworth. (**73**)

Wexler BE, Zhu H, Bell MD, et al. (2009) Neuropsychological near normality and brain structure abnormality in schizophrenia. *American Journal of Pshciatry* **166**: 189–95. (**312**)

Wexler H (1997) Therapeutic communities in American prisons. In E Cullen, L Jones, R Woodward (eds) *Therapeutic Communities for Offenders.* New York: Wiley. (**412**)

Wexler HK (1995) The success of therapeutic communities for substance abusers in American prisons. *Journal of Psychoactive Drugs* **27**: 57–66. (**447**)

Wexler HK and De Leon G (1997) The therapeutic community: multivariate prediction of retention. *American Journal of Drug and Alcohol Abuse* **4**: 145–51. (**447**)

Wexler HK, De Leon G, Thomas G, Kressel D, and Peters J (1999) The Amity prison TC evaluation. *Criminal Justice and Behaviour* **26**: 147–67. (**412**)

Wheatley M (1998) The prevalence and relevance of substance use in detained schizophrenic patients. *Journal of Forensic Psychiatry* **9**: 114–29. (**454**)

Wheeler JR, Holland AJ, Bambrick M, et al. (2009) Community services and people with intellectual disabilities who engage in anti-social or offending behaviour: referral rates, characteristics, and care pathways. *Journal of Forensic Psychiatry and Psychology* **20**: 717–40. (**326**)

Whitaker DJ, Haileyesus T, Swahn M, and Saltzman LS (2007) Differences in frequency of violence and reported injury between relationships with reciprocal and nonreciprocal intimate partner violence. *American Journal of Public Health* 97:941–7. (**505**)

White DR and Chen PH (2002) Problem drinking and intimate partner violence. *Journal of Studies on Alcohol* **63**: 205–14. (**702**)

White GL and Mullen PE (1989) *Jealousy: Theory Research and Clinical Strategies.* New York: Guilford, p. 395. (**369, 373**)

White JL, Moffitt TE, Caspi A, et al. (1994) Measuring impulsivity and examining its relationship to delinquency. *Journal of Abnormal Psychology* **103**: 192–205. (**173**)

White R and Wilner P (2005) Suggestibility and salience in people with intellectual disabilities: An experimental critique of the Gudjonsson Suggestibility Scale. *Journal of Forensic Psychiatry & Psychology* **16**: 638–50. (**161**)

White S (1991) Insanity defences and magistrates courts. *Criminal Law Review*: 501–9. (**22**)

White T, Ramsay L, and Morrison R (2002) Audit of the forensic psychiatry liaison service to Glasgow Sheriff Court 1994 to 1998. *Medicine Science and the Law* **42**: 64–70. (**651**)

Whitehead AN (1925) *Science and the Modern World.* New York: Macmillan. (Reprinted 1967. New York: Free Press) (**111**)

Whitehead T (2000) *Mary Ann Cotton: Dead But Not Forgotten.* Durham, NC: Tony Whitehead. (**240**)

Whitehorn JC and Betz B (1954) A study of psychotherapeutic relationships between physicians and schizophrenic patients. *American Journal of Psychiatry* **111**: 321–31. (**408**)

Whitehorn JC and Betz BJ (1960) Further studies of the doctor as a crucial variable in the outcome of treatment with schizophrenic patients. *American Journal of Psychiatry* **117**: 215–23. (**408**)

Whitehurst RN (1971) Violently jealous husband. *Sexual Behaviour* **1**: 32–47. (**372**)

Whitely JS (1980) The henderson hospital. *International Journal of Therapeutic Communities* **1**: 38–58. (**412**)

Whitfield JB, Zhu G, Madden PA, et al. (2004) The genetics of alcohol intake and of alcohol dependence. *Alcoholism: Clinical and Experimental Research* **28**: 1153–60. (**201**)

Whitlock A (1990) Mental disorder and dangerous driving. In R Bluglass, P Bowden (eds) *Principles and Practice of Forensic Psychiatry.* London: Churchill Livingstone, pp. 835–9. (**278**)

Whitlock FA (1963) *Criminal Responsibility and Mental Illness.* London: Butterworth. (**32**)

Whitman S, Coleman T, Berg B, King L, and Desai B (1980) Epidemiological insights into the socioeconomic correlates of epilepsy. In BP Herman (ed) *A Multidisciplinary Handbook of Epilepsy.* Springfield, IL: Thomas. (**284, 286**)

Whitman S, Coleman TE, Patmon C, et al. (1984) Epilepsy in prison: elevated prevalence and no relationship to violence. *Neurology* **34**: 775–82. (**286**)

Whittington R and Balsalmo D (1998) Violence: fear and power. In T Mason, D Mercer (eds) *Critical Perspectives in Forensic Care Inside Out* Hampshire, UK: Macmillan, pp. 64–84. (**552**)

Whittington R and Wykes T (1994) A observational study of associations between nurse behaviour and violence in psychiatric hospitals. *Journal of Psychiatric and Mental Health Nursing* **1**:85–92. (**557**)

Whittle B and Ritchie J (2000) *Harold Shipman, Prescriptions for Murder.* London: Little, Brown Book Group. (**240, 689**)

WHO: *see* World Health Organisation.

Whyte L (1997) Forensic nursing: A review of concepts and definitions. *Nursing Standard* 11: 46–7. (**552**)

Whyte S, Petch E, Penny C, and Reiss D (2008) Who stalks? A description of patients at a high security hospital with a history of stalking. *Criminal Behaviour and Mental Health* **18**: 27–38. (**378**)

Widiger TA and Samuel DB (2005) Diagnostic categories or dimensions: a question for DSM-V. *Journal of Abnormal Psychology* **114**: 494–504. (**388**)

Widom CS (1978) Toward an understanding of female criminality. *Prog Exp Pers Res* **8**: 245–308. (**499, 500, 502**)

Widom CS (1989) The cycle of violence. *Science* **244**: 160–6. (**2, 200, 344**)

Widom CS and Maxfield MG (2001) *An update on the 'Cycle of Violence'.* Washington, DC: US Department of Justice. https://www.ncjrs.gov/pdffiles1/nij/184894.pdf (**3, 200, 344, 571**)

Wiggins JS (1973) *Personality and Prediction: Principles of Personality Assessment.* Reading, MA: Addison-Wesl. (**536**)

Wijk L, Edelbring S, Svensson A-K, et al. (2009) A pilot for a computer-based simulation system for risk estimation and treatment of mentally disordered offenders. *Informatics for Health and Social Care* **34**: 106–15. (**533**)

Wijkman M, Bijleveld C, and Hendriks J (2011) Female sex offenders: Specialists, generalists and once only offenders. *Journal of Sexual Aggression* **17**: 34–45. (**504, 505**)

Wikström P-O H (1985) *Everyday Violence in Contemporary Sweden.* Stockholm, Sweden: National Council for Crime Prevention. (**179**)

Wikström P-O H (1990) Age and crime in a Stockholm cohort. *Journal of Quantitative Criminology* **6**: 61–84. (**171**)

Wilcox DE (1985) The relationship of mental illness to homicide *American Journal of Forensic Psychiatry* **6**: 3–15. (**308**)

References

Wilcox HC, Conner KR, and Caine ED (2004) Association of alcohol and drug use disorders and completed suicide: an empirical review of cohort studies. *Drug and Alcohol Dependence* **76S**: S11–19. (**451**)

Wilens TE, Biederman J, Kiely K, Bredin E, and Spencer TJ (1995) Pilot study of behavioral and emotional disturbances in the high-risk children of parents with opioid dependence. *Journal of the American Academy of Child and Adolescent Psychiatry* **34**: 779–85. (**465**)

Wiles NJ, Zammit S, Bebbington P, et al. (2006) Self-reported psychotic symptoms in the general population. Results from the longitudinal study of the British National Psychiatric Morbidity. *The British Journal of Psychiatry* **188**: 519–26. (**339**)

Wilk J, Marcus SC, West J, et al. (2006) Substance abuse and the management of medication nonadherence in schizophrenia. *Journal of Nervous and Mental Disease* **194**: 454–7. (**566**)

Wilkins AJ (1985) Attempted infanticide. *British Journal of Psychiatry* **146**: 206–8. (**29**)

Wilkins R (1993) Delusions in children and teenagers admitted to Bethlam Royal Hospital in the 19th Century. *British Journal of Psychiatry* **162**: 487–92. (**349**)

Willberg T, Karterud S, Urnes O, Pederson G, and Friis S (1998) Outcomes of poorly functioning patients with personality disorders in a day treatment program. *Psychiatric Services* **49**: 1462–7. (**572**)

Williams A (1976) The design of security units, engineering considerations. *Hospital Engineering* 6–14. (**593**)

Williams A, Moore E, Adshead G, McDowell A, and Tapp J (2011) Including the excluded: high security hospital user perspectives on stigma, discrimination and recovery. *British Journal of Forensic Practice* **3**(3): 197–204. (**579**)

Williams E (2004) *Interventions for Schizophrenia.* Oxford: Speechmark. (**574**)

Williams E (2007) CBT for Psychosis Programme: Clinical Trial. Poster, Annual Broadmoor Psychological Services Conference, Berkshire, UK. (**574**)

Williams E and Barlow R (1998) *Anger Control Training.* Oxon, UK: Winslow. (**215**)

Williams LM, Gatt JM, Kuan SA, et al. (2009) A polymorphism of the MAOA gene is associated with emotional brain markers and personality traits on an antisocial index. *Neuropsychopharmacology* **34**: 1797–809. (**199**)

Williams NM, Green EK, Macgregor S, et al. (2006) Variation at the DAOA/G30 locus influences susceptibility to major mood episodes but not psychosis in schizophrenia and bipolar disorder. *Archives of General Psychiatry* **63**: 366–73. (**209**)

Williams NM, Preece A, Spurlock G, et al. (2004) Support for RGS4 as a susceptibility gene for schizophrenia. *Biological Psychiatry* **55**: 192–195. (**209**)

Williams T (1947) A *Streetcar Named Desire.* New York: New Directions. (**18**)

Williams T (1997) Personality Disorder as a Challenge to the Criminal Justice System. In H van Marle (ed) *Forensic Focus 5 – Challenges in Forensic Psychotherapy.* London: Jessica Kingsley. (**384**)

Williams WH, Cordan G, Mewse AJ TonksJ, and Burgess CNW (2010a) Self-reported traumatic brain injury in male young offenders: a risk factor for re-offending, poor mental health and violence? *Neuropsychological Rehabilitation: An International Journal* **20**: 801–12. (**488**)

Williams WH, Mewse AJ, TonksJ, et al. (2010b) Traumatic brain injury in a prison population: prevalence and risk for re-offending. *Brain Injury* **24**: 1184–8. (**488**)

Williamson M (2006) *Improving the Health and Social Outcomes of People Recently Released from Prisons in the UK: A Perspective from Primary Care.* http://www.centreformentalhealth.org.uk/pdfs/scmh_health_care_after_prison.pdf (**631**)

Williamson RJ, Sham P, and Ball D (2003a) Binge drinking trends in a UK community-based sample. *Journal of Substance Use* **8**: 234–7. (**440**)

Williamson S, Jacobson L, Skeoch C, Azzim G, and Anderson R (2003b) Prevalence of maternal drug misuse by meconium analysis. *Archives of Disease in Childhood* **88**: A17–A21. (**464**)

Willmot P and Gordon N (eds) (2011) *Working Positively with Personality Disorder in Secure Settings: A Practitioner's Perspective.* Chichester, UK: Wiley-Blackwell. (**401**)

Willner P, Brace N, and Phillips J (2005) Assessment of anger coping skills in individuals with intellectual disabilities. *Journal of Intellectual Disability Research* **49**(Pt 5): 329–39. (**327**)

Willner P, Jones J, Tams R, and Green G (2002) A randomised controlled trial of the efficacy of a cognitive-behavioural anger management group for clients with learning disabilities. *Journal of Applied Research in Intellectual Disabilities* **15**: 224–35. (**327**)

Wilmanns K (1940) Über Morde in Prodromalstadium der Schizophrenic. *Zeit Neurologie* **170**: 583–662. (**353**)

Wilson G, Rupp C, and Wilson WW (1950) Amnesia. *American Journal of Psychiatry* **106**: 481–5. (**295**)

Wilson JP and Keane TM (2004) *Assessing Psychological Trauma and PTSD,* 2nd edn. New York: Guilford. (**726**)

Wilson JP and Ziegelbaum SD (1983) The Vietnam veterans on trial: the relation of post-traumatic stress disorder to criminal behavior. *Behavioral Sciences and the Law* **1**: 69–83. (**715**)

Wilson P (1973) *Children Who Kill.* London: Michael Joseph. (**233**)

Wilson WH (1992) Clinical review of clozapine treatment in a state hospital. *Hospital and Community Psychiatry* **43**: 700–3. (**563**)

Windham AM, Rosenberg L, Fuddy L, et al. (2004) Risk of mother-reported child abuse in the first 3 years of life. *Child Abuse and Neglect* **28**(6): 645–67. (**505, 506**)

Windle M (1999) Psychopathy and antisocial personality disorder among alcoholic inpatients. *Journal of Studies on Alcohol* **60**: 330–6. (**444**)

Winerip M (1999) Bedlam on the Streets. *NY Times Magazine,* May 23: 42–9, 56, 65–6. (**336**)

Wing JK (1962) Institutionalism in mental hospitals. *British Journal of Social and Clinical Psychology* **1**: 38–51. (**602**)

Wing JK (1978) *Reasoning About Madness.* Oxford, UK: Oxford University Press. (**10**)

Wing JK (1990) The functions of asylum. *British Journal of Psychiatry* **157**: 822–7. (**551**)

Wing JK and Brown GW (1970) *Institutionalization and Schizophrenia*. Cambridge, UK: Cambridge University Press. (**551, 602**)

Winick BJ (2003) Outpatient commitment: a therapeutic jurisprudence analysis. *Psychology, Public Policy, and Law* **9**: 107–44. (**365**)

Winogron W, Van Dieten M, and Gauzas L (1996) *Controlling Anger and Learning to Manage It (CALM)*. Toronto, Canada: Multi-Health Systems. http://www.mhs.com/product.aspx?gr=saf&id=overview&prod=calm (**575**)

Winokur G (1977) Delusional disorder (paranoia). *Comprehensive Psychiatry* **18**: 511–21. (**382**)

Winston A, Laikin M, Pollack J, et al. (1994) Short-term psychotherapy of personality disorders. *American Journal of Psychiatry* **151**: 190–4. (**411**)

Winters KC, Stinchfield RD, Botzet A, and Anderson N (2002) A prospective study of youth gambling behaviours. *Psychology of Addictive Behaviors* **16**: 3–9. (**472**)

Wish JR, McCombs K, and Edmonson B (1980) *The Socio-Sexual Knowledge and Attitude Test*. Chicago: Stoelting. (**328**)

Witte AV, Flöel A, Stein P, et al. (2009) Aggression is related to frontal serotonin-1 A receptor distribution as revealed by PET in healthy subjects. *Human Brain Mapping* **30**: 2558–70. (**310**)

Wolak J, Finkelhor D, and Mitchell KJ (2005) *Child Pornography Possessors Arrested in Internet-related Crimes: Findings from the National Juvenile Online Victimization Study*. Virginia: The National Center for Missing and Exploited Children. (**251**)

Wolf Y and Frankel O (2007) Terrorism: toward an overarched account and prevention with a special reference to pendulum interplay between both parties. *Aggression and Violent Behavior* **12**: 259–79. (**235**)

Wolff K, Farrell M, Marsden J, et al. (1999a) A review of biological indicators of illicit drug use, practical considerations and clinical usefulness. *Addiction* **94**:1279–98. (**456**)

Wolff K, Welch S, and Strang J (1999b) Specific laboratory investigations for assessments and management of drug problems. *Advances in Psychiatric Treatment* **5**: 180–91. (**456**)

Wolff S (1985) Non-deliquent disturbances of conduct. In M Rutter and L Hersov (eds) *Child and Adolescent Psychiatry – Modern Approaches*. Oxford, UK: Blackwell. (**270**)

Wolff S and McCall Smith RAA (2000) Child homicide and the law: implications of the judgements of the European Court of Human Rights in the case of the children who killed James Bulger. *Child Psychology and Psychiatry Review* **5**: 133–8. (**234**)

Wolfgang ME (1958a) *Patterns of Criminal Homicide*. Philadelphia, PA: University of Pennsylvania Press. (**232, 372**)

Wolfgang ME (1958b) An analysis of homicide-suicide. *Journal of Clinical and Experimental Psychopathology* **19**: 208–18. (**232**)

Wolfgang ME, Thornberry TP, and Figlio RM (1987) *From Boy to Man, from Delinquency to Crime*. Chicago, IL: University of Chicago Press. (**173**)

Wolpe J (1982) *The Practice of Behaviour Therapy*. New York: Pergamon. (**730**)

Wong MT, Fenwick P, Fenton G, et al. (1997a) Repetitive and non-repetitive violent offending behaviour in male patients in a maximum security mental hospital--clinical and neuroimaging findings. *Medicine, Science and the Law* **37**: 150–60. (**299**)

Wong MT, Fenwick PB, Lumsden J, et al. (1997b) Positron emission tomography in male violent offenders with schizophrenia. *Psychiatry Research* **68**: 111–23. (**303**)

Wong MT, Lumsden J, Fenton GW, and Fenwick PB (1994) Electroencephalography, computed tomography and violence ratings of male patients in a maximum-security mental hospital. *Acta Psychiatrica Scandanavica* **90**: 97–101. (**298**)

Wong S and Gordon A (2013) The Violence Reduction Programme: A treatment programme for violence-prone forensic clients *Psychology, Crime and Law* http://dx.doi.org/10.1080/1068316X.2013.758981 *also* http://www.psynergy.ca/uploads/VRP_description_paper-2013.pdf (**610**)

Wong S, Gordon A. and Gu D (2007) Assessment and treatment of violence–prone forensic clients: an integrated approach. *British Journal of Psychiatry*, **190** (suppl 49): s66–74. (**416, 577**)

Wong S, Van der Veen S, Leis T, et al. (2005) Reintegrating seriously ill and personality disordered offenders from a super-maximum security institution into the general offender population. *Journal of Offender Therapy and Comparative Criminology* **49**: 362–75. (**577**)

Wood M and Ogloff JRP (2006) Victoria's Serious Sex Offenders Monitoring Act: Implications for the accuracy of sex offender risk assessment. *Psychiatry, Psychology and the Law* **13**: 182–98. (**116**)

Wood RL and Liossi C (2006) The ecological validity of executive tests in a severely brain injured sample. *Archives of Clinical Neuropsychology* **21**: 429–37. (**212**)

Wood RM, Grossman LS and Fichtner CG (2000) Psychological assessment, treatment and outcome with sex offenders. *Behavioral Sciences and the Law,* **18**: 23–42. (**125, 587**)

Woody GE, McLellan T, Luborsky L, and O'Brian CP (1985) Sociopathy and psychotherapy outcome. *Archives of General Psychiatry* **42**: 1081–6. (**407**)

Woolfenden SR, Williams K, and Peat J (2003) Family and parenting interventions in children and adolescents with conduct disorder and delinquency aged 10–17 (Cochrane Review). *The Cochrane Library* 2003. Issue 3. Oxford, UK. (**486**)

World Health Organization (1975) *Health Aspects of Avoidable Maltreatment of Prisoners and Detainees. Evidence presented to the Fifth United Nations Congress on the Prevention of Crime and Treatment of Offenders*. Geneva: World Health Organization. (**667**)

World Health Organization (1977) *Forensic Psychiatry. Report of a Working Group, Sienna 1975*. Copenhagen, Denmark: World Health Organization. (**113**)

World Health Organization (1992a) *ICD-10 Classification of Mental and Behavioural Disorders: Clinical Description and Diagnostic Guidelines*. Geneva: World Health Organization. (**17, 112, 207, 262, 285, 314, 319, 384, 397, 436, 449, 469, 711, 714**)

World Health Organization (1992b) *Schedules for Clinical Assessment in Neuropsychiatry*. Geneva: World Health Organization. (**443**)

World Health Organization (1993) *The Classification of Mental and Behavioural Disorders, ICD-10*. Diagnostic Criteria for Research Geneva: World Health Organization. (**17, 245**)

World Health Organization (2001) *The World Health Report 2001 – Mental Health: New Understanding, New Hope*. Geneva: World Health Organization. (**133**)

World Health Organization (2002) *Workplace Violence in the Health Sector*. Geneva: World Health Organization. http://www.who.int/violence_injury_prevention/violence/interpersonal/en/WVguidelinesEN.pdf (**556**)

World Health Organization (2002a) *Reducing Risks, Promoting Healthy Life*. Geneva: World Health Organization. http://www.who.int/whr/2002/en/whr02_en.pdf (**437**)

World Health Organization (2002b) *World Report on Violence and Health*. Geneva: World Health Organization. http://whqlibdoc.who.int/publications/2002/9241545615_eng.pdf (**437**)

World Health Organization (2004a) *Alcohol and Mental Health*. Copenhagen, Denmark: WHO Regional Office for Europe. Global Status Report on Alcohol WHO, Geneva, Switzerland http://www.who.int/substance_abuse/publications/global_status_report_2004_overview.pdf (**437**)

World Health Organization (2004b) *Global Strategy on Diet, Physical Activity and Health*. Geneva: World Health Organization. http://whqlibdoc.who.int/publications/2010/9789241599979_eng.pdf (**567**)

World Health Organization (2004c) *Preventing Violence: A Guide to Implementing the Recommendations of the World Report on Violence and Health*. Geneva: World Health Organization. http://whqlibdoc.who.int/publications/2004/9241592079.pdf (**701**)

World Health Organization (2006) *Tobacco: Deadly in Any Form or Disguise*. Geneva: World Health Organization. http://www.who.int/tobacco/communications/events/wntd/2006/Tfi_Rapport.pdf (**568**)

World Health Organization Expert Committee on Mental Health (1975) *Organization of Mental Health Services in Developing Countries: Technical Report Series 564*. Geneva: World Health Organization. (**113**)

World Health Organization Health in Prisons Project and Pompidou Group (2001a) *Prisons, Drugs and Society: A Consensus Statement on Principles, Policies and Practice*. Berne, Switzerland http://www.euro.who.int/__data/assets/pdf_file/0003/99012/E81559.pdf (**467**)

World Health Organization, International Association for Prevention of Suicide (2007) *Preventing Suicide in Jails and Prisons*. http://www.who.int/mental_health/prevention/suicide/resource_jails_prisons.pdf (**633**)

World Medical Association (2006) WMA Declaration of Malta on Hunger Strikers http://www.wma.net/en/30publications/10policies/h31/index.html (**638**)

World Psychiatric Association (1989) *Declaration on the Paticipation of Psychiatrists in the Death Penalty*. http://www.wpanet.org/detail.php?section_id=5&content_id=25 (**114**)

Worling JR (2004) The estimate of risk of adolescent sexual offense recidivism (erasor): preliminary psychometric data. *Sexual Abuse: A Journal of Research and Treatment* **16**: 235–54. (**255**)

Worling JR and Curwen T (2000) Adolescent sexual offender recidivism: success of specialized treatment and implications for risk prediction. *Child Abuse and Neglect* **24**: 965–82. (**252**)

Worrall EP, Moody JP, and Naylor GJ (1975) Lithium in non-manic depressives: antiaggressive effect and red blood cell lithium values. *British Journal of Psychiatry* **136**: 464–8. (**566**)

Wright B, Duffy D, Curtin K, et al. (2006) Psychiatric morbidity among women prisoners newly committed and amongst remanded and sentenced women in the Irish prison system. *Irish Journal of Psychological Medicine* **23**: 47–53. www.ijpm.org/content/pdf/311/woman.pdf (accessed 15.11.2011). (**616, 657**)

Wright B, O'Neill C, and Kennedy HG (2008) Admissions to a national forensic hospital 1997–2003. *Irish Journal of Psychological Medicine* **25**: 17–23.http://www.drugsandalcohol.ie/6821/# (**616, 657**)

Wright J, Pickard N, Whitfield A, and Hakin N (2000) A population-based study of the prevalence, clinical characteristics and effect of ethnicity in epilepsy. *Seizure* **9**: 309–13. (**286**)

Wright JA, Burgess AG, Burgess AW, et al. (1996) A typology of interpersonal stalking. *Journal of Interpersonal Violence* **11**: 487–502. (**375**)

Wright P, Birkett M, David SR, et al. (2001) Double-blind, placebo-controlled comparison of intramuscular olanzapine and intramuscular haloperidol in the treatment of acute agitation in schizophrenia. *The American Journal of Psychiatry* **158**: 1149–51. (**564**)

Wright R and West DJ (1981) Rape: a comparison of group offences and lone assaults. *Medicine, Science and the Law* **21**: 25–30. (**442**)

Wright S, Gournay K, Glorney E, et al. (2002) Mental illness, substance abuse, demographics and offending: dual diagnosis in the suburbs. *Journal of Forensic Psychiatry* **13**: 35–52. (**281**)

Wu SS, Ma CX, Carter RL, et al. (2004) Risk factors for infant maltreatment: a population-based study. *Child Abuse & Neglect* **28**(12): 1253–64. (**505**)

Wykes T, Huddy V, Cellard C, McGurk SR, and CZobor P (2011) A meta-analysis of cognitive remediation for schizophrenia: methodology and effect sizes. *American Journal of Psychiatry* **168**: 472–85. (**363**)

Wykes T, Parr A-M, and Landau S (1999) Group treatment of auditory hallucinations. *British Journal of Psychiatry* **175**: 180–5. (**573**)

Wykes T, Reeder C, Corner J, Williams C, and Everitt B (1999) The effects of neurocognitive remediation on executive processing in patients with schizophrenia. *Schizophrenia Bulletin* **25**: 291–307. (**573**)

Wykes T, Steel C, Everitt B, and Tarrier N (2008) Cognitive behaviour therapy for schizophrenia effect sizes, clinical models and methodological rigor. *Schizophrenia Bulletin* **34**: 523–37. (**362**)

Wynne LC, Ryckoff IM, Day J, and Hirsch SI (1958) Pseudomutuality in the family relations of schizophrenics. *Psychiatry* **21**: 205–20. (**341**)

Yalom ID (1995) *Theory and Practice of Group Psychotherapy*, 4th edn. New York: Basic Books. (**572**)

Yampolskaya S and Winston N (2003) Hospice care in prison: general principles and outcomes. *American Journal of Hospice and Palliative care* **20**: 290–6. (**528**)

Yang M, Wong SCP, and Coid J (2010) The efficacy of violence prediction: a meta-analytic comparison of nine risk assessment tools. *Psychological Bulletin* **136**: 740–67. (**531**)

Yang Y, Raine A, Lencz T, et al. (2005) Volume reduction in prefrontal grey matter in unsuccessful criminal psychopaths. *Biological Psychiatry* **57**: 1103–8. (**299, 301**)

Yang Y, Raine A, Narr KL, Colletti P, and Toga AW (2009) Localization of deformations within the amygdala in individuals with psychopathy. *Archives of General Psychiatry* **66**(9): 986–94. (**300**)

Yap PM (1969) The culture bound reactive syndromes. In W Candill, T-y Lin (eds) *Mental Health Research in Asia and the Pacific*. Honolulu, HI: East-West Center Press. (**428**)

Yarnell H (1940) Firesetting in children. *American Journal of Orthopsychiatry* **10**: 272–86. (**276**)

Yassa R and Dupont D (1983) Carbamazepine in the treatment of aggressive behaviour in schizophrenic patients: a case report. *Canadian Journal of Psychiatry* **28**: 566–8. (**566**)

Yehuda R (1997) Sensitization of the hypothalamic–pituitary axis in posttraumatic stress disorder. In R Yehuda, AC McFarlane (eds) *Psychobiology of Post-traumatic Stress Disorder*. New York: New York Academy of Science. (**717, 720**)

Yehuda R, Engel SM, Brand S, et al. (2005) Transgenerational effects of posttraumatic stress disorder in babies of mothers exposed to the World Trade Center attacks during pregnancy. *Journal of Clinical Endocrinology and Metabolism* **90**: 4115–8. (**717**)

Yehuda R, Hallingan SL, and Bierer LM (2002) Cortisol levels in adult offspring of Holocaust survivors: relation to PTSD symptom severity in the parent and the child. *Psychoneuroendocrinology* **27**: 171–80. (**717**)

Yellowlees D (1878) Homicide by a somnambulist. *Journal of Mental Sciences* **24**: 451–8. (**290, 291**)

Yokely J and Boettner S (2002) Forensic foster care for young people who sexually abuse: lessons from treatment. In MC Calder (ed) *Young People Who Sexually Abuse. Building the Evidence Base for Your Practice*. Lyme Regis, UK: Russell House, pp. 309–32. (**495**)

Yorker BC, Kizer W, Lampe P, et al. (2006) Serial murder by healthcare professionals. *Journal of Forensic Science* **51**: 1362–71. (**686**)

Yorston G and Taylor PJ (2009) Older patients in an English high security hospital: a qualitative study of the experiences and attitudes of patients aged 60 and over and their care staff in Broadmoor Hospital. *Journal of Forensic Psychiatry and Psychology* **20**: 255–67. (**528, 599**)

Yoshikawa K and Taylor PJ (2003) New forensic mental health law in Japan. *Criminal Behaviour and Mental Health* **13**: 225–8. (**132, 336**)

Yoshikawa K, Taylor PJ, Yamagami A, et al. (2007) Violent recidivism among mentally disordered offenders in Japan. *Criminal Behaviour and Mental Health* **17**: 137–51. (**143**)

Young JE (1994) *Cognitive Therapy for Personality Disorders: A Schema-Focused Approach*. Sarasota, FL: Professional Resource Press. (**721**)

Young JE, Klosko J, and Weishaar ME (2000) *Schema Therapy: A Practitioner's Guide*. New York: Guilford. (**721**)

Young M, Read J, Barker-Collo S, and Harrison R (2001) Evaluating and overcoming barriers to taking abuse histories. *Professional Psychology: Research and Practice* **32**: 407–14. (**348**)

Young S and Toone B (2000) Attention deficit hyperactivity disorder in adults: Clinical issues. A report from the first NHS clinic in the UK. *Counselling Psychology Quarterly* **13**: 313–9. (**397**)

Young S, Toone B, and Tyson C (2003) Comorbidity and psychosocial profile of adults with attention deficit hyperactivity disorder. *Personality and Individual Differences* **35**: 743–55. (**397**)

Young SE, Stallings MC, Corley RP, Krauter KS, and Hewitt JK (2000) Genetic and environmental influences on behavioral disinhibition. *American Journal of Medical Genetics* **96**: 684–95. (**203**)

Young SJ and Ross RR (2007) *RandR2 for Youths and Adults with Mental Health Problems: A Prosocial Competence Training Program*. Ottawa, Canada: Cognitive Centre of Canada. (**576**)

Yourstone J, Lindholm T, Grann M, and Svenson O (2008) Evidence of gender bias in legal insanity evaluations: a case vignette study of clinicians, judges and students. *Nordic Journal of Psychiatry* **62**: 273–8. (**500**)

Yudovsky, SC, Silver, JM, Jackson, W, Endicott, J, and Williams, D (1986) The Overt Aggression Scale for objective rating of verbal and physical aggression. *American Journal of Psychiatry* **143**: 35-9. (**xxxv**)

Yuille JC and Cutshall JL (1986) A case study of eye-witness memory of a crime. *Journal of Applied Psychology* **71**: 291–301. (**296**)

Yung AR and McGorry PD (2007) Prediction of psychosis: setting the stage. *British Journal of Psychiatry* **191**: s1–s8. (**341**)

Zadok PL, Krawchuk SA, and Voas RB (2000) Alcohol-related relative risk of driver fatalities and driver involvement in fatal crashes in relation to driver age and gender: an update using 1996 data. *Journal of Studies on Alcohol* **61**: 387–95. (**443**)

Zajac R (2009) Investigative interviewing in the courtroom: child witnesses under cross examination. In R Bull, T Valentine, T Williamson (eds) *Handbook of Psychology of Investigative Interviewing: Current Developments and Future Directions*. Chichester, UK: Wiley, pp. 161–80. (**162**)

Zajac R and Hayne H (2003) I don't think that's what really happened: the effect of cross examination on the accuracy of children's reports. *Journal of Experimental Psychology: Applied* **9**: 187–95. (**162**)

Zajac R and Hayne H (2006) The negative effect of cross-examination style on children's accuracy: older children are not immune. *Applied Cognitive Psychology* **20**: 179–89. (**162**)

Zajac R, Gross J, and Hayne H (2003) Asked and answered: questioning children in the courtroom. *Psychiatry, Psychology and Law* **10**: 199–210. (**162**)

Zamble E and Porporino F (1990) Coping, imprisonment and rehabilitation: some data and their implications. *Criminal Justice and Behaviour* **17**: 53–70. (**578**)

Zammit S, Allebeck P, Andreasson S, et al. (2002) Self-reported cannabis use as a risk factor for schizophrenia: further analysis of the 1969 Swedish conscript cohort. *British Medical Journal* **325**: 1199–201. (**488**)

Zanarini MC and Frankenburg FR (2001) Olanzapine treatment of female borderline personality disorder patients: a double-blind, placebo–controlled pilot study. *Journal of Clinical Psychiatry* **62**(11): 849–54. (**406**)

Zanarini MC and Frankenburg FR (2003) Omega–3 fatty acid treatment of women with borderline personality disorder: a double–blind, placebo-controlled pilot study. *American Journal of Psychiatry* **160**(1): 167–9. (**406**)

Zanarini MC, Frankenburg FR, and Parachini EA (2004) A preliminary, randomized trial of fluoxetine, olanzapine, and the olanzapine–fluoxetine combination in women with borderline personality disorder. *Journal of Clinical Psychiatry* **65**(7): 903–7. (**311, 406**)

Zanarini MC, Frankenburg FR, Reich DB, and Fitzmaurice G (2010) Time to attainment of recovery from borderline personality disorder and stability of recovery: a 10–year prospective follow–up study. *American Journal of Psychiatry* **167**: 663–7. (**402**)

Zanarini MC, Schulz SC, Detke HC, Tanaka Y, Zhao F, Lin D, Deberdt W, Kryzhanovskaya L, and Corya S (2011) A dose comparison of olanzepine for the treatment of borderline personality disorder: A 12-week randomized, double-blind, placebo-controlled study. *Journal of Clinical Psychiatry* **72**: 1353–62. (**404**)

Zapf PA, Boccaccini MT, and Brodsky SL (2003) Assessment of competency for execution: professional guidelines and an evaluation checklist. *Behavioural Sciences and the Law* **21**: 103–20. (**114**)

Zeitlin SD, McNally RJ, and Cassidy KC (1993) Alexithymia in victims of sexual assault: an effect of repeated traumatization. *American Journal of Psychiatry* **150**: 661–3. (**720**)

Zeki S and Goodenough OR (eds) (2004) Law and the brain. Themed issue of *Philosophical Transactions of the Royal Society B* **359**: 1659–809. (**283**)

Zevitz RG (2006) Sex offender community notification: its role in recidivism and offender reintegration. *Criminal Justice Studies* **19**: 193–208. (**645**)

Zhang L, Welte JW, and Wieczorek WW (2002) The role of aggression–related alcohol expectancies in explaining the link between alcohol and violent behavior. *Substance Use and Misuse* **37**: 457–71. (**440**)

Zhang PW, Ishiguro H, Ohtsuki T, et al. (2004) Human cannabinoid receptor 1: 5' exons, candidate regulatory regions, polymorphisms, haplotypes and association with polysubstance abuse. *Molecular Psychiatry* **9**: 916–31. (**206**)

Zhang ZJ, Yao ZJ, Liu W, Fang Q, and Reynolds GP (2004) Effects of antipsychotics on fat deposition and changes in leptin and insulin levels: magnetic resonance imaging study of previously untreated people with schizophrenia. *British Journal of Psychiatry* **184**: 58–62. (**567**)

Zhao H (2000) Family-based association studies. *Statistical Methods in Medical Research* **9**: 563–87. (**193**)

Zhou J, Wang X, Li L, Cao X, Xu L, Sun Y (2006) Plasma serotonin levels in young violent offenders: Aggressive responding and personality correlates. *Progress in Neuro-Psychopharmacology and Biological Psychiatry* **30**: 1435–41. (**307**)

Zilboorg G (1941) *A History of Medical Psychology*. New York: W.W. Norton and Company. (**118, 122**)

Zilger E and Glick M (1988) Is paranoid schizophrenia really camoflaged depression? *American Psychologist* **43**: 284–90. (**345**)

Zillman D (1979) *Hostility and Aggression*. Hillsdale, IN: Erlbaum. (**213, 214**)

Zimbardo PG, Anderson SM, and Kabat LG (1981) Induced hearing deficit generates experimental paranoia. *Science* **212**: 1529–31. (**6, 351**)

Zimbroff DL, Allen MH, Battaglia J, et al. (2005) Best clinical practice with ziprasidone IM: update after 2 years of experience. *CNS Spectrums* **10**: 1–15. (**565**)

Zimbroff DL, Marcus RN, Manos G, et al. (2007) Management of acute agitation in patients with bipolar disorder: efficacy and safety of intramuscular aripiprazole. *Journal of Clinical Psychopharmacology* **2**: 171–6. (**565**)

Zimmerman G, Favrod J, Trieu VH, and Pomini V (2005) The effect of cognitive behavioral treatment on the positive symptoms of schizophrenia spectrum disorders: a meta-analysis. *Schizophrenia Research* **77**: 1–9. (**362**)

Zimmerman M (1994) Diagnosing personality disorders: a review of issues and research methods. *Archives of General Psychiatry* **51**: 225–45. (**385, 388**)

Zona MA, Palarea RE, and Lane J (1998) Psychiatric diagnosis and the offender-victim typology of stalking. In J Reid Meloy (ed) *The Psychology of Stalking: Clinical and Forensic Perspectives*. San Diego, CA: Academic Press, pp. 70–84. (**375**)

Zona MA, Sharma KK, and Lane J (1993) A comparative study of erotomanic and obsessional subjects in a forensic sample. *Journal of Forensic Sciences* **38**: 894–903. (**375**)

Zulueta: *see* de Zulueta.

Zuo L, Kranzler HR, Luo X, Cpvaut J, and Gelernter J (2007) CNR1 variation modulates risk for drug and alcohol dependence. *Biological Psychiatry* **62**: 616–26. (**206**)

Zygmunt A, Olfson M, Boyer CA, and Mechanic D (2002) Interventions to improve medication adherence in schizophrenia. *American Journal of Psychiatry* **159**: 1653–1 (**356**)

Index